S0-AKM-475

A History of the American People

NORMAN A. GRAEBNER
University of Virginia

GILBERT C. FITE
University of Oklahoma

PHILIP L. WHITE
University of Texas

HAROLD K. FAYE, MAP DESIGNER

SAM HOLMES, PICTURE CONSULTANT

A HISTORY OF THE *American People*

McGraw-Hill Book Company

NEW YORK ST. LOUIS SAN FRANCISCO DÜSSELDORF
LONDON MEXICO PANAMA SYDNEY TORONTO

A HISTORY OF THE AMERICAN PEOPLE

Library of Congress Catalog Card Number 70-118778

23874

1 2 3 4 5 6 7 8 9 0 V H V H 7 9 8 7 6 5 4 3 2 1 0

This book was set in Garamond by Ruttle, Shaw & Wetherill, Inc., and printed on permanent paper and bound by Von Hoffmann Press, Inc. The designer was Betty Binns. The editors were James Mirrielees, Cheryl Kupper, and Susan Davis. John F. Harte supervised the production.

THE COLOR INSERTS WERE PRINTED BY THE LEHIGH PRESS.

Preface

No person can fully share with others his impressions, his understanding, or his appreciation of the past. Individuals, invariably unique in their psychic makeup and belonging to different generations, regions, races, religions, classes, and political parties, all perceive the past in some distinctive manner. No one can alter the facts of history, but those concerned with the human record, historians among them, ignore some facts, exaggerate the importance of others, and, without necessarily intending to do so, often interpret the past more in accordance with their own preconceptions than in the interest of historical balance. The authors of this text are as susceptible to these prejudices as all mortals, but, like all conscientious historians we have tried to be as objective as possible while still fulfilling the historian's obligation to reveal the meaning of words and events and their relevance to the present. Where conflicts of interpretation still rage, we have attempted to do justice to each side. But we have not hesitated to exhibit preferences in the choice of interpretations when the evidence, in our judgment, warrants such selections.

Traditionally, textbook writing has emphasized narrative, the construction of an accurate and significant story of what actually occurred. More recently, the search for analysis and greater understanding and insight into human affairs has become an explicit, rather than a largely implicit, aim of the historian, and we have followed this trend. For that reason, this text is less narrowly narrative and more explicitly analytical than most. We have, furthermore, endeavored to distinguish our text in matters of synthesis, organization, and subject matter. Specialized historical works flow from the nation's presses in an ever-increasing flood—some of them clearly significant, others more significant than clear, still others neither. To keep pace with this outpouring and to incorporate significant new findings into a coherent presentation is a monumental, perhaps an almost impossible, undertaking. Still we hope that we have succeeded better than many in keeping our material historiographically fresh, our chapters digestible in length and internally consistent, and our titles and headings meaningfully descriptive.

Like other contemporary historians, we have attempted to place American history in international perspective Not only have we recognized the effects of conditions elsewhere in the world upon the history of the American people, but we have also attempted to compare American institutions at certain moments in history with those abroad in order to help the reader see what it means and has meant to live in the United States. We have, moreover, sought to write of the poor and oppressed as well as the more affluent in American society. Those millions who have lived in America without ever becoming members of the nation's dominant middle class have played an unquestionably vital role in our past. But until relatively recent times, historians have tended not only to write *of* the rich and powerful but to assume that essentially they wrote *for* such people. Even in the late 1960s when concern for the lives of the poor and oppressed clearly existed, historians found it difficult to uncover adequate sources of information except in secondhand accounts written by people who were themselves neither poor nor oppressed. Yet within the limits imposed by these circumstances, we have attempted to write a history of and for all the American people, not merely that minority which has been supposed to have "made history."

We have, in the preparation of this book, resorted to lavish illustration, especially with the unprecedented device of the picture essays, in the conviction that carefully selected illustrations may well be worth many thousands of words. These portfolios document in depth subjects that we suggest but cannot take time to explore as well as central topics that we explicitly discuss. Extended pictorial documents such as these, in this age of visual stimulation, should not only excite the student's interest but should actually enable him or her to participate, intellectually and emotionally, in each of the experiences being presented. We also believe that full color conveys a much more arresting message than simple black-and-white reproduction, and we have used it where appropriate. All the graphic elements here, two- and four-color maps and charts, the picture portfolios, the full-color sections, have been carefully coordinated to dramatize, and indeed to bring to life, the supremely significant and exciting experience of the American people.

Above all, this history of the United States has been designed to teach. Historical processes are always complex, and those who choose to examine the record for guidance must recognize the crucial forces, principles, and tendencies within each episode if their study is to serve any useful purpose. In the words of the Frenchman Jean Jaurès, those who seek the lessons of history must take from the altars of the past "the fire—not the ashes." And so we have sought to bring what is relevant in history to a generation of Americans that must face the imminent and critical problems of racial injustice, tension, and insurrection; poverty and discontent; crowded cities and violence; and foreign involvements and war that can no longer be shielded from critical and incisive public debate by phrases and slogans which traditionally expressed the ideals, not the realities, of American life. For too long Americans in high places, themselves often oblivious to the conditions blighting the lives of millions, repeated shibboleths that came easy to American though without suffering any strain or guilt and without creating any mental disturbance among those who listened. But no longer can American spokesmen speak of freedom and justice in American society as if those ideals existed for all. Demands for the nation to conform to its ideals have become too insistent and widespread to be ignored. Any meaningful response to the challenges of today and tomorrow requires understanding as well as good intent. History cannot supply the answers for the country's emotional and economic ills, but it can encourage and assist in the diagnosis, suggest the magnitude of the tasks ahead, and, by interspersing hope with caution, better assure success for the continuing processes of change.

Historical writing is too dependent on the limits of human knowledge to achieve perfection. These volumes, despite the time, patience, and care that have gone into them, cannot emerge without error. Aided by the suggestions of our readers as well as by our own continued examination of the past, however, we intend to improve each successive edition. Whatever the errors—and for these we take full responsibility—they have been rendered less numerous by the assistance we have received from scholars who have read either sections or all of this book; we have profited greatly from the critical reviews of James M. Banner, Jr., J. Leonard Bates, Donald E. Fehrenbacher, Jack P. Greene, Sheldon Hackney, Winthrop Jordon, Thomas A. Krueger, Walter LaFeber, James M. McPherson, Gerald D. Nash, Roderick Nash, James T. Patterson, Earl E. Thorpe, Richard Wade, and Bernard Weisberger. We are also grateful to Donald J. Berthrong, John S. Ezell, Russell D. Buhite, David W. Levy, Robert Shalhope, R. Alton Lee, J. Carroll Moody, David E. Conrad, Duane M. Leach, Thomas H. Buckley, and John R. Ferrell for their incisive and helpful editorial assistance. We express our deep appreciation to Cheryl Kupper, Basic Book Editor, and to Susan Davis, Editing Supervisor, for their imaginative and constructive suggestions.

Norman A. Graebner
Gilbert C. Fite
Philip L. White

Contents

PREFACE, V

1

THE DAWN OF A NEW ERA, 1

Europe before 1500, 2 *The Exploration Voyages,* 8 *The American Indians,* 14 *Spain's American Empire,* 15 *Spain's Competitors,* 16 *Europe after the Discoveries,* 17 *Imperial Rivalry,* 21 *Conclusion,* 24 *Suggested Readings,* 24

2

COMPETITION FOR COLONIES, 42

England at the Time of Colonization, 43 *Virginia,* 45 *New England,* 47 *Maryland,* 57 *British West Indies,* 58 *New Netherland,* 58 *Restoration England,* 1660–1689, 59 *New English Colonies,* 1660–1689, 60 *Carolina and Georgia,* 61 *New France,* 64 *Conclusion,* 65 *Suggested Readings,* 65

3

ECONOMIC AND CULTURAL DEVELOPMENT, 67

The Southern Economy, 68 *New England and the Middle Colonies,* 73 *Religion in Colonial America,* 83 *Racial and Ethnic Variety,* 86 *The American Social Pattern,* 87 *Education, Arts, and Science,* 89 *Conclusion,* 101 *Suggested Readings,* 102

4

IMPERIAL VERSUS PROVINCIAL AUTHORITY, 104

Seventeenth-century Crises, 105 *Eighteenth-century Developments,* 107 *Contest for a Continent,* 112 *Wartime Grievances,* 116 *Postwar Regulatory Problems,* 118 *Taxation,* 120 *A Tempest over Tea,* 128 *Conclusion,* 130 *Suggested Readings,* 131

5

FIGHTING FOR INDEPENDENCE, 133

Lexington and Concord, 134 *The Second Continental Congress,* 135 *Escalating Warfare,* 136 *Severing the Tie,* 138 *British Failure to Subdue the North,* 147 *From Revolution to World War,* 150 *Congressional Conduct of the War,* 151 *Britain Failure in the South,* 153 *Peace and Freedom,* 158 *Conclusion,* 159 *Suggested Readings,* 159

6

ADJUSTMENTS TO INDEPENDENCE, 161

From Provinces to "Sovereign" States, 162 *The Confederation of American States,* 166 *Congress and the West,* 169 *Postwar Economic Changes,* 172 *Social Change,* 176 *Conclusion,* 195 *Suggested Readings,* 196

7

FROM CONFEDERATION TO NATION, 197

Inadequacies of the Confederation, 198 *Nationalist Reform Efforts,* 201 *Toward a Constitutional Convention,* 203 *The Grand Convention,* 204 *Strengthening Federal Authority,* 212 *Separation of Powers,* 215 *The Quest for Popular Approval,* 217 *Conclusion,* 220 *Suggested Readings,* 221

8

THE FEDERALISTS IN POWER, 222

New Beginnings, 223 *Hamilton's Financial Program,* 225 *Western Problems,* 231 *Controversy over Neutrality,* 234 *Jay's Treaty,* 237 *Conclusion,* 240 *Suggested Readings,* 240

9

THE REVOLUTION OF 1800, 242

The Emergence of Political Parties, 243 *Limited War and a Constitutional Crisis,* 246 *The Revolution of* 1800, 250 *Jefferson and the Judiciary,* 253 *Jefferson and the West,* 255 *Reelection and the Burr "Conspiracy,* 258 *Freedom of the Seas,* 259 *Conclusion,* 273 *Suggested Readings,* 273

10

MR. MADISON'S WAR, 275

James Madison, 276 *More Controversy over Commerce,* 277 *The United States Declares War,* 280 *A Mere Matter of Marching,* 284 *Resisting British Invasions,* 289 *Peace without Victory,* 297 *Conclusion,* 298 *Suggested Readings,* 299

11

CONSENSUS AND CONFLICT, 1815–1828, 300

The Demise of the Federalist Party, 301 *Postwar Republican Nationalism,* 302 *New Republican Leadership,* 304 *Westward Migration and the Panic of* 1819, 321 *John Marshall: Nationalist, Conservative,* 323 *States and Localities,* 325 *The Missouri Compromise,* 327 *The Diplomacy of John Quincy Adams,* 330 *Latin American Independence and the Monroe Doctrine,* 333 *The Election of* 1824, 335 *The Adams Presidency,* 338 *The Jacksonian Triumph,* 340 *Conclusion,* 342 *Suggested Readings,* 343

12

JACKSONIAN DEMOCRACY, 345

The New Administration, 346 *Webster and Hayne,* 347 *Van Buren and Jackson,* 349 *Indian Removal,* 350 *The Tariff and Nullification,* 356 *The Bank War,* 360 *Death of the Bank,* 362 *Politics and the Election of* 1836, 370 *The Van Buren Presidency,* 372 *Banking Reform,* 373 *The Taney Court,* 374 *Log Cabins and Hard Cider,* 375 *Conclusion,* 377 *Suggested Readings,* 378

13

THE EMERGENCE OF A NATIONAL ECONOMY, 1820–1860, 380

Population Trends, 381 *Land Policies and Westward Settlement,* 381 *Agriculture in the North,* 382 *Northern Transportation and Communication,* 384 *Shipping and Overseas Trade,* 388 *Industry and the Rise of the Factory System,* 399 *The Tariff,* 401 *The Industrial Workers,* 401 *The South and Its People,* 404 *The Cotton Kingdom,* 406 *Slavery,* 408 *Yeoman Farming,* 417

Southern Transportation, Commerce, and Manufacturing, 418 *The Character and Attitudes of the South,* 421 *Urbanization North and South,* 421 *Prosperity, Depression, and Living Standards,* 423 *Conclusion,* 424 *Suggested Readings,* 425

14

THE MIND AND CULTURE OF AMERICA, 1815-1860, 427

The American Character, 428 *Education,* 429 *Newspapers, Magazines, and Lyceums,* 432 *Science and Invention,* 432 *Literature in the Young Republic,* 450 *The Fine Arts,* 453 *Religion,* 454 *Social and Humanitarian Reform,* 457 *Abolitionism and the Defense of Slavery,* 459 *Conclusion,* 469 *Suggested Readings,* 469

15

THE PARTIES AND SECTIONALISM, 471

Whigs and Democrats, 472 *The Whigs in Power,* 474 *Webster's Diplomacy,* 476 *Party Politics and Slavery,* 477 *Ties of Union,* 480 *Texas,* 482 *Politics and the Texas Question,* 484 *The Election of* 1844, 485 *Polk and the Democratic Party,* 488 *Domestic Policies,* 489 *Conclusion,* 490 *Suggested Readings,* 491

16

THE CONTINENTAL EMPIRE, 493

Penetration of the Great West, 494 *Oregon,* 495 *California,* 496 *The Oregon Settlement,* 498 *The Mormons and the Great Basin,* 501 *War with Mexico,* 502 *Military Action in Mexico,* 505 *The Treaty of Guadalupe Hidalgo,* 507 *Conclusion,* 518 *Suggested Readings,* 519

17

THE IMPENDING CRISIS, 521

The Wilmot Proviso, 522 *The Election of* 1848, 524 *The Compromise of* 1850, 525 *The Election of* 1852, 527 *The Persistent Issue of Slavery,* 529 *The Kansas-Nebraska Bill,* 530 *Reaction to the Kansas-Nebraska Act,* 532 *Bleeding Kansas,* 533 *The Election of* 1856, 535 *The Dred Scott Decision and Its Political Consequences,* 536 *Lincoln and Douglas,* 537 *The Vincible South,* 539 *The Republican Triumph,* 542 *The Secession Crisis,* 550 *Conclusion,* 552 *Suggested Readings,* 553

18

THE CIVIL WAR, 556

The Fort Sumter Crisis, 557 *Preparations for War in the North,* 558 *The South Faces War,* 560 *The Opening Campaigns,* 560 *The War in Virginia:* 1862, 562 *The War Congress,* 566 *Wartime*

Measures of Government, 567 *Emancipation,* 569 *Gettysburg, Vicksburg, and Chattanooga,* 571 *Grant in Command,* 574 *Seward's Diplomacy,* 576 *Problems of the Confederacy,* 578 *Behind the Northern Lines,* 580 *Wartime Politics in the North,* 583 *The War's End,* 584 *Conclusion,* 584 *Suggested Readings,* 595

19
POSTWAR RECONSTRUCTION, 599

The Defeated South, 600 *Presidential Reconstruction,* 601 *Triumph of the Radicals,* 604 *Congressional Reconstruction,* 607 *Reconstruction in the South,* 609 *The Election of* 1868, 612 *The Grant Regime,* 621 *Foreign Affairs,* 623 *The Liberal Republicans,* 624 *More Corruption,* 626 *The End of Reconstruction,* 626 *The Election of* 1876, 628 *Conclusion,* 636 *Suggested Readings,* 636

20
POLITICS, POLICIES, AND PERSONALITIES, 1877–1892, 639

Party Politics, 640 *The Hayes Administration,* 642 *Garfield and Arthur,* 644 *The Democratic Cleveland,* 646 *The Election of* 1888, 655 *Harrison and the Republicans,* 656 *The Freedman and Civil Rights,* 658 *Conclusion,* 660 *Suggested Readings,* 660

21
INDUSTRIAL EXPANSION AND THE AGE OF BIG BUSINESS, 662

Reasons for Industrial Growth, 663 *Transportation and Communication,* 665 *Major Industries,* 669 *Location of American Manufacturing,* 672 *Consumer Distribution,* 675 *Monopoly,* 675 *Beginning of Government Regulation,* 678 *Conclusion,* 680 *Suggested Readings,* 688

22
LABOR, IMMIGRATION, AND URBANIZATION, 690

The Economic Position of Wage Earners, 691 *Organized Labor,* 692 *Government and Labor,* 703 *Immigration,* 704 *Urban America,* 708 *The Pull of the City,* 709 *Problems of Urbanization,* 710 *Corruption and Reform in City Government,* 720 *Urban Life,* 737 *Conclusion,* 738 *Suggested Readings,* 739

23
THE LAST FRONTIER, 1865–1900, 740

Reasons for Rapid Settlement, 741 *The Mining Frontiers,* 741 *Western Ranching,* 744 *The Western Agricultural Frontier,* 747 *Retreat of the Indians,* 760 *End of the Frontier,* 764 *Conclusion,* 766 *Suggested Readings,* 766

24

AGRICULTURE, FARM POLICIES, AND THE AGRARIAN REVOLT, 1865–1896, 768

Trends in American Farming, 769 *Sectional Development,* 772 *Farm Problems,* 773 *Farm Revolt: The Grange,* 775 *The Greenback Movement,* 776 *The Farmers' Alliance and the Populists,* 777 *Cleveland's Second Administration,* 784 *The Campaign of* 1896, 786 *Conclusion,* 789 *Suggested Readings,* 789

25

AMERICAN CULTURAL LIFE, 791

The Intellectual Challenge, 792 *Religion and the Church,* 794 *The Social Gospel,* 796 *Religious Fundamentalism,* 797 *American Education,* 798 *Negro Education,* 808 *Natural Sciences,* 825 *Literary Currents,* 825 *Fine Arts and Architecture,* 828 *Popular Culture,* 830 *Newspapers, Magazines, Libraries, and the Chautauqua,* 832 *Conclusion,* 833 *Suggested Readings,* 833

26

THE NEW AMERICAN EMPIRE, 835

Pacific Markets and Coaling Stations, 836 *Samoa and Hawaii,* 838 *The Spanish-American War,* 840 *The War in the Caribbean,* 844 *Annexation of the Philippines,* 845 *War in the Philippines,* 848 *The Open Door for China,* 849 *Conclusion,* 853 *Suggested Readings,* 853

27

THEODORE ROOSEVELT AND PROGRESSIVISM, 855

The Meaning of Progressivism, 856 *Reform in the States and Cities,* 858 *The Negro and Progressivism,* 868 *Theodore Roosevelt: National Progressive Leader,* 870 *Roosevelt's Policies and Programs,* 872 *Roosevelt and the Workingmen,* 874 *Roosevelt's Second Term,* 874 *Roosevelt's Foreign Policy: Latin America,* 885 *Roosevelt's Foreign Policy: The Far East,* 890 *Conclusion,* 891 *Suggested Readings,* 892

28

HIGH TIDE OF REFORM: TAFT AND WILSON, 894

The Problems and Policies of Taft, 895 *Foreign Affairs under Taft,* 899 *The Progressive Revolt,* 1910–1912, 902 *The Election of* 1912, 903 *Wilson and His Rise to Power,* 906 *Changing America,* 907 *The New Freedom in Action,* 913 *Conclusion,* 917 *Suggested Readings,* 918

29
AMERICA AND THE GREAT WAR, 920

Wilson's New Diplomacy, 921 *Pressures on American Neutrality,* 923 *The Submarine Issue,* 924 *The Failure of Mediation,* 927 *Mobilization for War,* 939 *Economic Change,* 942 *The Quest for National Unity,* 943 *Wilson's Peace Program,* 945 *Japan's Wartime Challenge,* 947 *The European Armistice,* 948 *Wilson at Versailles,* 950 *The Great Debate,* 953 *The Great Red Scare,* 958 *Conclusion,* 959 *Suggested Readings,* 960

30
POLITICS AND SOCIETY IN THE 1920S, 963

The Election of 1920, 964 *Domestic Issues under Harding,* 966 *Scandal in High Places,* 969 *"A Puritan in Babylon,"* 970 *Progressivism and the Campaign of* 1924, 971 *More Normalcy,* 973 *The Presidential Election of* 1928, 974 *American Society in the* 1920*s,* 975 *The Negro and Normalcy,* 976 *Prohibition,* 984 *Manners and Morals,* 985 *Literary Currents,* 987 *Religion and Education,* 988 *Conclusion,* 991 *Suggested Readings,* 992

31
THE REPUBLICAN SEARCH FOR PEACE: THE 1920S, 1009

Isolationism and Internationalism, 1010 *Latin America,* 1013 *The Challenge of Europe,* 1014 *The Washington Treaties,* 1016 *The Kellogg-Briand Peace Pact,* 1018 *The Hoover Years,* 1020 *Conclusion,* 1023 *Suggested Readings,* 1024

32
PROSPERITY, HOOVER, AND THE GREAT DEPRESSION, 1026

Trends in Business and Industry, 1027 *Wage Earners in Prosperity,* 1035 *Agriculture and Farm Problems,* 1037 *Hoover as President,* 1040 *The Great Crash,* 1042 *The Depression Begins,* 1048 *The Administration Program,* 1049 *The Election of* 1932, 1052 *Conclusion,* 1054 *Suggested Readings,* 1055

33
FRANKLIN D. ROOSEVELT AND THE NEW DEAL, 1056

Roosevelt Takes Command, 1057 *Banking Reform and Abandonment of the Gold Standard,* 1058 *Early Relief Efforts,* 1059 *Help for Farmers,* 1060 *The National Industrial Recovery Act,* 1062 *The Second New Deal,* 1065 *Labor and the New Deal,* 1066

Social Security, 1067 *Utility Regulation, Conservation and Public Power,* 1068 *Reelection in* 1936, 1070 *The Court Fight,* 1071 *Recession and Fiscal Policies,* 1072 *Life in the Depression,* 1073 *Minority Groups in the New Deal,* 1085 *Conclusion,* 1087 *Suggested Readings,* 1088

34
THE CHALLENGE OF GLOBAL POLITICS: THE 1930S, 1090

Challenge of the Dictators, 1091 *Isolationism at High Tide,* 1092 *War in the Far East,* 1096 *German Expansionism,* 1097 *The Decline of American Neutrality,* 1100 *From Aid to Full Commitment,* 1103 *Crisis in the Pacific,* 1104 *Conclusion,* 1108 *Suggested Readings,* 1108

35
VICTORY OVER THE AXIS, 1111

A Strategy for Europe, 1112 *Turn of the Tide,* 1113 *The Mediterranean Campaign,* 1114 *Planning for Germany,* 1117 *Victory in Europe,* 1118 *The War in the Pacific,* 1120 *Victory on the Home Front,* 1126 *Science and Technology in Wartime,* 1130 *Nationalism and Civil Rights,* 1131 *Blacks in Wartime,* 1132 *Politics in Wartime,* 1145 *Life on the Home Front,* 1146 *Conclusion,* 1147 *Suggested Readings,* 1148

36
THE COLD WAR IN EUROPE AND ASIA, 1150

Wartime Rift in the Alliance, 1151 *Divided Europe,* 1152 *The United Nations,* 1154 *Potsdam to London,* 1156 *The Problem of Means,* 1158 *From Alliance to Containment,* 1159 *The Changing Far East,* 1164 *The Chinese Debacle,* 1166 *China and the Great Debate,* 1167 *The Korean War,* 1169 *Conclusion,* 1174 *Suggested Readings,* 1175

37
PROBLEMS AND PROGRESS UNDER TRUMAN, 1178

Harry S. Truman, 1179 *Demobilization,* 1179 *Reconversion, Economy,* 1180 *Postwar Politics,* 1184 *The Eightieth Congress,* 1185 *The Election of* 1948, 1187 *The Fair Deal,* 1190 *Communism: National Danger or "Red Herring"?,* 1192 *Conclusion,* 1193 *Suggested Readings,* 1194

38
EISENHOWER AND MODERN REPUBLICANISM, 1195

The Election of 1952, 1196 *Eisenhower the President,* 1198 *The First Eisenhower Administration,* 1199 *Communism and Internal Security,* 1203 *The Election of* 1956, 1204 *Eisenhower's Second Term,* 1206 *Agriculture and Labor in the Second Term,* 1212 *Social Welfare, Education,* 1213 *Trade and Aid,* 1214 *Economic Growth,* 1215 *Conclusion,* 1221 *Suggested Readings,* 1221

39
THE COURSE OF CONTAINMENT, 1953–1965, 1223

Eisenhower, Dulles, and Liberation, 1224 *China,* 1225 *The New Look,* 1226 *Korea and Indochina,* 1228 *Crisis in the Middle East,* 1231 *The Changing Cold War,* 1234 *Kennedy and the Eisenhower Legacies,* 1236 *Kennedy and Europe,* 1239 *Lyndon Johnson and Vietnam,* 1242 *Conclusion,* 1243 *Suggested Readings,* 1243

40
AMERICAN SOCIETY AFTER MIDCENTURY, 1246

Urbanization, 1247 *Affluence and Poverty,* 1251 *Blacks and Civil Rights,* 1254 *Education and Religion,* 1258 *Science and Technology,* 1260 *The Arts, Literature, and Mass Culture,* 1261 *Alienation,* 1264 *Conclusion,* 1283 *Suggested Readings,* 1284

41
KENNEDY AND JOHNSON, 1286

The Kennedy-Nixon Contest, 1287 *The New Frontier,* 1289 *Lyndon Johnson as President,* 1299 *The Election of* 1964, 1300 *The Great Society,* 1302 *The Warren Court,* 1303 *The Troubled Nation,* 1305 *The Price of Vietnam,* 1308 *Presidential Nominating Politics:* 1968, 1310 *The Student Rebellion,* 1312 *The Paris Talks,* 1324 *An End and a Beginning,* 1325 *From Johnson to Nixon,* 1326 *Conclusion,* 1328 *Suggested Readings,* 1330

APPENDIX, 1333

INDEX, 1357

1

The Dawn of a New Era

NOT SINCE THE EMPIRE OF ROME has a nation exerted an influence upon mankind equal to that of the United States. Through government programs, as well as through private investment and trade, the colossal American economy reaches into every region of the globe. Each year the American pattern of living evokes wider emulation among other nations, often despite outraged local opposition. To many students of government abroad as well as at home the enduring American constitutional system, extending as it does remarkable freedom both to individual citizens and to constituent states, remains a source of great admiration. Unprecedented technological and military capacity has encouraged the burgeoning American effort to inaugurate a new era of peace and security—a Pax Americana—in the world at large. The outcome of the effort, controversial at home as well as resented and resisted abroad, remains in doubt, yet the twentieth century seems destined clearly to be remembered as one of American preeminence.

Because the American Leviathan is as unique in character as it is awesome in power, it behooves the world at large as well as Americans themselves to study its historical development closely so that they might better understand it. Why, for example, have its people so often appeared to foreigners to be both crudely materialistic and sadly deficient in the creation and the appreciation of the higher forms of art? Why is physical violence so much more prevalent in the United States than it is in England or France? Why, in the abundance of its wealth and competence, has the United States not yet abolished unemployment, malnutrition, preventable illness, illiteracy, and its rural and urban slums? Why, despite its dedication to human equality, has the nation failed to eliminate prejudice against its racial and ethnic minorities, or indeed against the poor in general? To gain some comprehension of the nation's peculiar modes of thought and behavior is perhaps no less important a reason for examining its history than the desire to understand how it rose to its present heights of power.

Whatever its faults or virtues, American society is largely the product of interaction between its European heritage and the American environment. Some years ago Americans generally preferred to magnify the differences between themselves and Europeans and to attribute American distinctiveness to factors peculiar to the American experience, particularly those of the frontier. Recently, as Africa and Asia have risen to more prominent positions in world affairs, Americans have begun to acknowledge that their society does derive largely from the traditions of Western civilization. Not just in the ancestry of most of its people but also in language and religion, in social traditions, in ways of making a living, even in its pattern of government, American society reveals its European foundations. It is appropriate, therefore, that a history of the United States begin with some observations on the evolution of the enduring civilization of which it was and is a part.

Europe before 1500

By 1500, Europe was ceasing to be medieval and was becoming modern. The European economy was well along in the transition from subsistence farming to commercial capitalism, to a stage of economic development dominated by merchants and traders rather than by landowners, as in the past, or by manufacturers, as in the future. Interregional commerce had declined sharply during the slow disintegration of the Roman Empire under the pressure of "barbarian" invasions. Under the chaotic conditions then prevailing, the typical economic unit had come to be the manor, a rural village centered around the fortified home of a nobleman. There peasants, organized in a communal system, farmed the land to which they were legally bound as serfs. They met their traditional obligations to the manor lord through services, such as a certain number of days of labor yearly, and with agricultural commodities, perhaps livestock or a fixed quantity of grain. In return they received protection and the opportunity to secure a living free from the threat of dispossession.

The resurgence of long-distance trade and the growth of commercial capitalism followed the termination of the invasions. New governments established law and order, thus permitting goods to be transported with greater safety. Improvements in ship construction occurred, and extensive travel diffused the knowledge of opportunities for interregional trade.

Desire for trade with Asia increased sharply in the aftermath of the Crusades. Followers of the seventh-century Arabian prophet Mohammed, while extending their Moslem faith eastward to India and westward across north Africa into Spain, had established firm control of the eastern Mediterranean. The major exception was the eastern remnant of the Roman

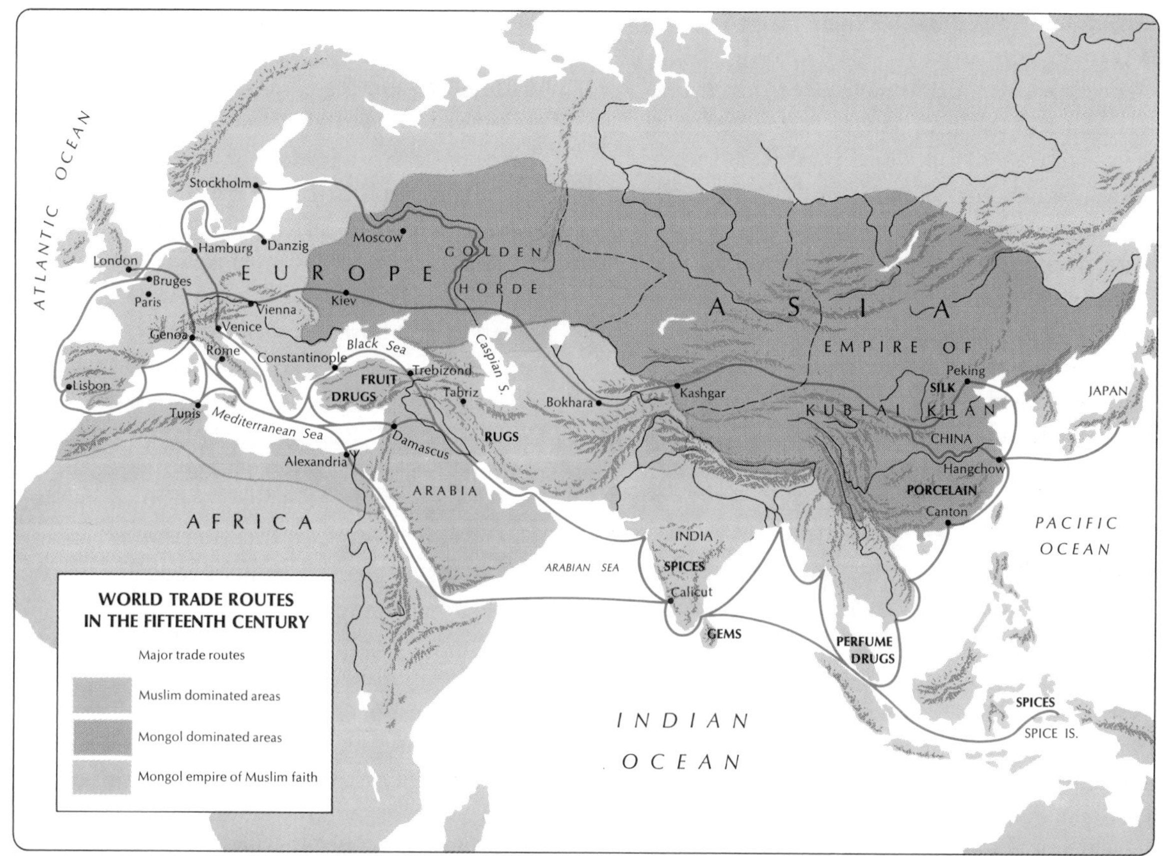

Empire, Byzantium, centered in modern Turkey. For nearly two centuries after 1096, repeated waves of Christian zealots, at times accompanied by freebooting opportunists, tried to wrest the Christian "Holy Lands" around Jerusalem from the Arabs. The Crusades failed in the end to achieve their mission, but they did impart to Europeans a taste for Asian luxuries—spices, silks, perfumes, and drugs, among others.

For Western Europeans, however, these goods were extremely expensive. Produced in southeast Asia, China, and India, they came westward chiefly in ships which brought them either to the head of the Red Sea or of the Persian Gulf. Caravans then carried the cargoes to the shores of the Mediterranean where Italian vessels picked them up and distributed them to European markets. A land route of less importance traversed China to bring silks in particular to Constantinople. On all of these routes the cargoes had to be reloaded repeatedly, a process which was often damaging and always expensive. Innumerable petty governments along the routes exacted taxes for passage. These expenses, plus the profits of numerous middlemen—for the most part, Arabs and Italians—greatly increased the price of Asian luxuries for Western Europeans, limiting the amount which they could buy and causing a serious drain on their limited supply of gold.

An idea for reducing the cost of Asian products occurred in time to many Europeans. One source of inspiration was a remarkable travel book in which the Italian Marco Polo described his twenty-year stay in China from 1275 to 1295. He made it clear that the price of Chinese goods was much lower in China than in Italy. He also reported that an unexplored ocean lapped the eastern edge of China, as was the case with the western edge of Europe. To informed people who had known theoretically for centuries that the world was round, this information hinted at the prospect of direct trade by sea between western Europe and the Orient. By eliminating both the costly land transportation and the middlemen, such a method would indeed lower the price of Asian goods in Western Europe. Merchants who could import in this way could undersell the Italians and probably replace them as distributors of Asian items for most of Europe.

To understand why there was no effort to find such a route for nearly two centuries requires reference to other aspects of European society. Religion, as the Crusades illustrate, was a paramount interest of most medieval Europeans, nearly all Roman Catholic or Eastern Orthodox Christians. The only non-Christians of note were a dispersed minority of Jews and the Moslems who retained a foothold in Spain. Education and scholarship scarcely existed outside the Church. Intellectual efforts tended to center upon salvation of the soul and to emphasize deduction from Biblical passages. The accepted authority in interpreting the untranslated Latin Bible, except among the Eastern Orthodox, was the Roman Catholic Church. The Pope, head of a hierarchic organization extending into almost every community, wielded great power, enough at times to humble kings.

Widening horizons opened by the revival of trade, by the Crusades, and by such works as Marco Polo's gradually effected a change in attitude. Europe began to experience a renaissance (rebirth). Greatly increased knowledge of pagan Greece and Rome inspired a large part of the Renaissance and brought much slavish imitation of those great societies. Under this influence, literature and art began to manifest less religious symbolism and more admiration for Greece and Rome, but they also reflected more of real human life. Thought began to be directed less exclusively toward salvation and more toward securing, by observation and experiment, information which would be useful in a material sense.

By 1500 Europeans had made many technological advances of great significance. Weapons using gunpowder (a Chinese invention) had outmoded the bow and arrow. Arabic numbers were replacing Roman numerals. Printing supplanted the laborious hand-copying of books. Techniques for making iron improved. Navigational devices, including the compass, cross-staff, astrolabe (to calculate latitude), and the mechanical clock, made it possible to determine positions at sea more accurately. The art of map making also advanced. The Portuguese caravel, a ship of deeper construction which could ride high waves better than long ships of shallow draft, provided a superior vessel for ocean sailing.

Class structure also changed greatly with the rise of commercial capitalism. When Europeans engaged largely in unspecialized labor to secure a living for their own families or their relatively isolated communities, there were three classes: the clergy, the landowning nobility, and the landworking peasants. With the growth of

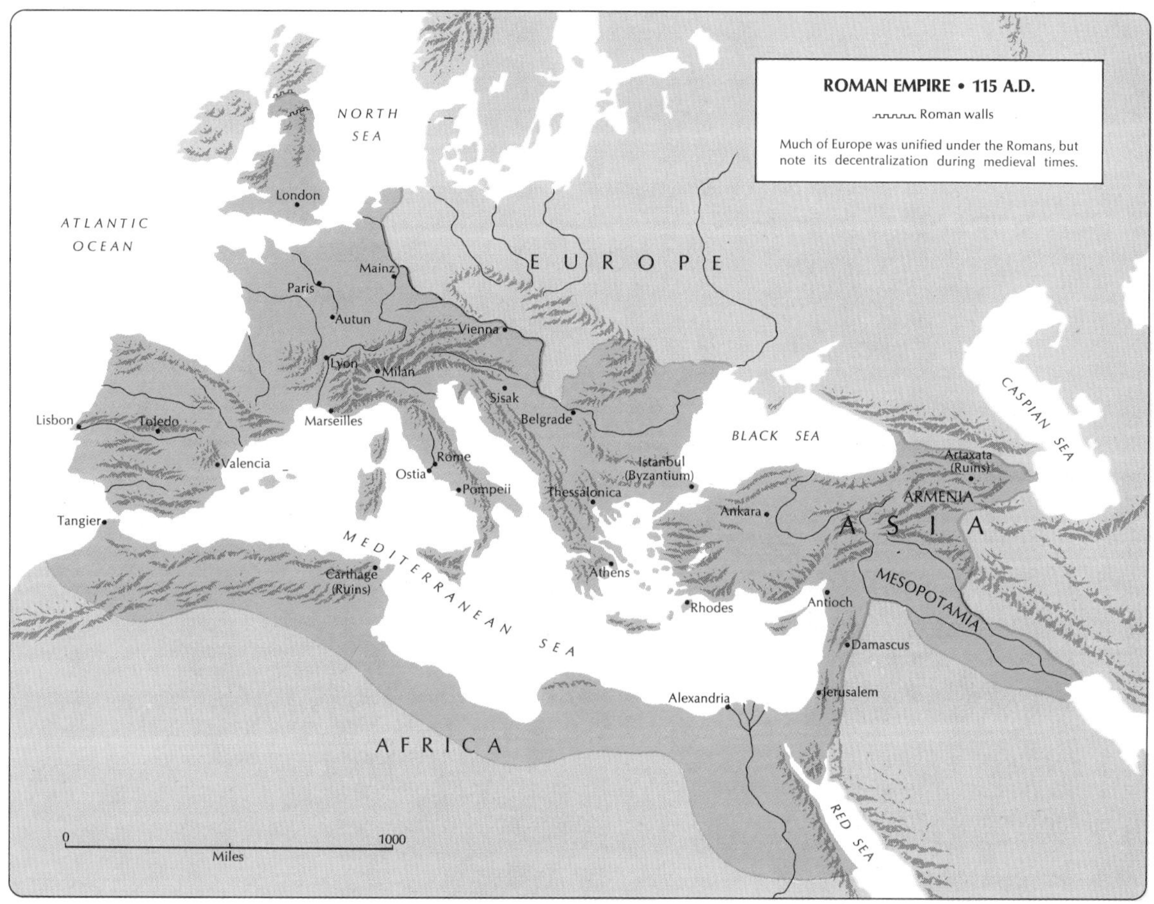

commerce there developed a bourgeois or "middle" class between the nobility and peasants. Settling at transportation centers which grew into urban communities, some of these middle-class people acted as merchants, exchanging the commodities of one region or one producer for those of another. Others in the new order worked as artisans or craftsmen in specialized production of articles for exchange. As the wealth and the numbers of the middle class increased, its leaders began to compete actively with the nobility for influence and power.

Politically, Europe had also altered sharply by 1500. Theoretically the Holy Roman Empire had established political unity comparable to the religious unity of the Catholic Church. In fact, however, power was largely decentralized. Local manor lords constituted local government. Authority superior to the manor depended on the feudal relationship of the lord to a higher member of the nobility or a king. These relationships were subject to frequent changes as a consequence of intrigue, warfare, marriages, and deaths. For these reasons, as well as because of communication problems, medieval govern-

PRENATIONAL EUROPE • 1360

Portugal and England are already unified while most of the rest of Europe, including France and Spain, remains divided among feudal states.

ment above the local level was characteristically unstable and usually weak.

By 1500 unified national monarchies of considerable power and stability had emerged. The new middle class wanted strong national governments to provide the peace and security required for its commerce. It desired other advantages which would accrue from national unity: internal free trade—no local taxes on the movement of goods—and discriminatory policies against outsiders. As commerce with foreigners increased, the middle class became

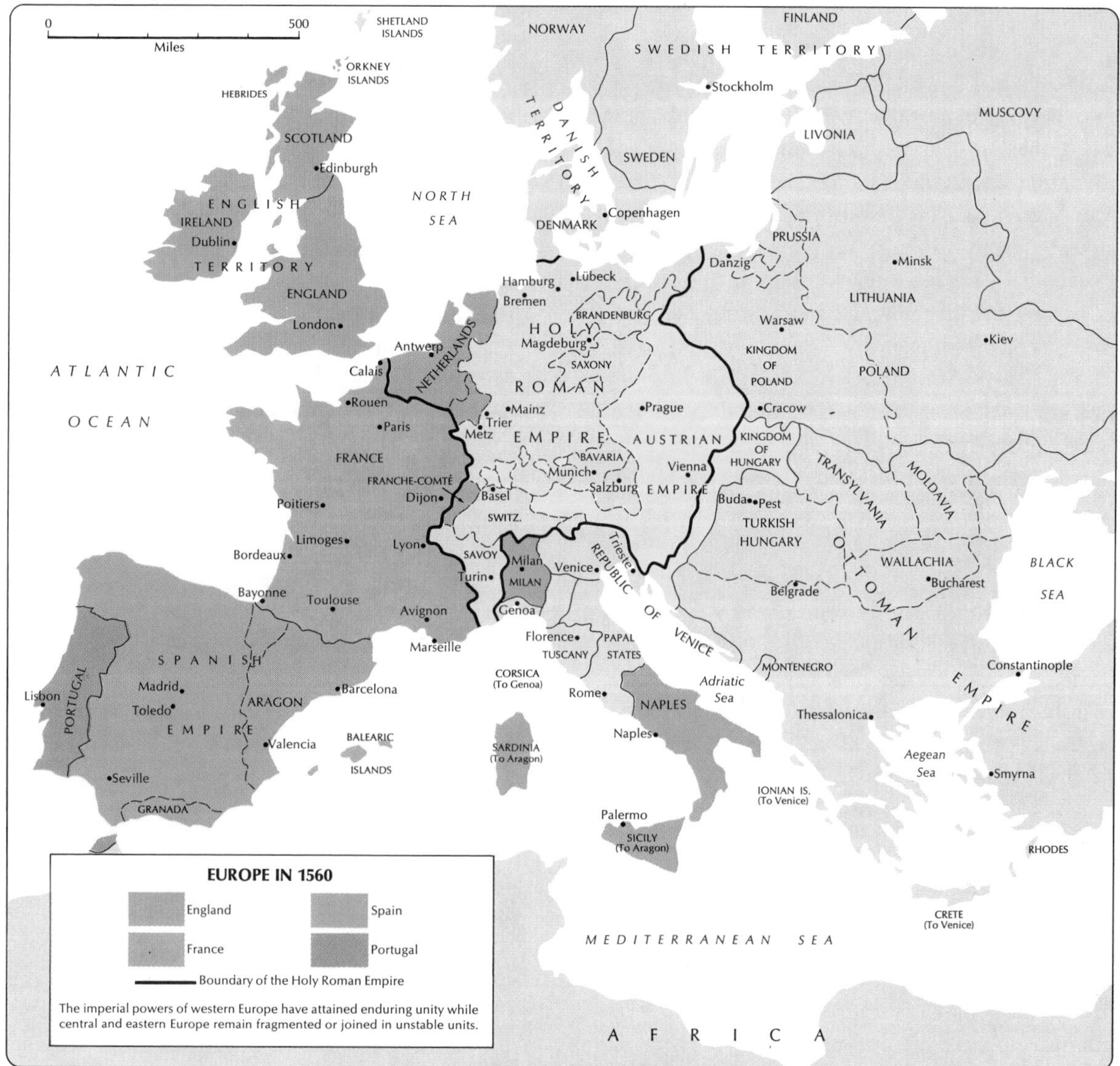

EUROPE IN 1560

The imperial powers of western Europe have attained enduring unity while central and eastern Europe remain fragmented or joined in unstable units.

more conscious of its own "national" identity and of the role of the crowned head of state as the servant of its "national" interests. For such reasons middle-class Europeans generally supported their kings in their successful efforts to transform chaotic feudal holdings into integrated nations. The major national monarchies which had achieved stability by 1500, however, were confined to the western periphery of Europe—Portugal, Spain, England, and France. These governments financed epochal exploration ventures in search of national gain.

Voyages of exploration were not entirely new to Europeans in the fifteenth century. The dynamic Norsemen six centuries earlier had been great marine explorers. After capturing Iceland from the Irish, they made it a base for westward voyages later in the ninth century. Discovering Greenland, they established another colony there which survived almost to the time of Columbus. In 986, Bjarni Herjolfsson, trying to reach Greenland from Iceland, missed his target and sighted—but did not choose to land on—what was probably the coast of Labrador. Leif Eriksson explored the region a year later and even wintered on Newfoundland, calling the country "Vinland." Thorfinn Karlesefni attempted to found a colony in Labrador but gave up within a short time because of the hostility of the Indians, whom he called "screechers." Yet so primitive were communications and scholarship that even in the fifteenth century Southern European map makers knew nothing of the Norse discoveries. Among contemporaries of Columbus only Northern Europeans, and probably not very many of them, knew that Greenland and Newfoundland existed.

By the fifteenth century, exploration had become far more systematic. National governments, supported by mercantile wealth, financed expeditions designed to serve a national interest. Commanding superior ships and armed with some knowledge of navigation, men set out on specific missions. The success which many achieved in securing advantages for their nations inspired widespread emulation.

Portugal, smallest of western Europe's new nations, pioneered in systematic exploration. A younger member of the Portuguese royal family, Prince Henry the Navigator (1394–1460), fostered expeditions which sailed farther and farther southward along the African coast. Their objectives were many, but that of greatest importance was to find a water route around Africa to Asia. Success would enable the Portuguese to undersell the Italians in the distribution of Asian goods in Western Europe.

The outcome of these voyages was spectacular. The Portuguese not only developed a lucrative trade with Africa in ivory, gold, pepper, and slaves but found a water route to Asia as well. Bartholomew Diaz, on a voyage which began in 1486, rounded the southern tip of Africa, which he designated the Cape of Good Hope, before frightened sailors forced him to turn back. For some years King John II, the successor to Prince Henry as sponsor of exploration, declined to follow through, but finally, after Columbus had traversed the Atlantic for Spain, Portugal sent out Vasco da Gama to complete what Diaz had begun. Da Gama reached India in 1498 and returned with spices and jewels priced far below those secured from the Italians. Soon the Portuguese had set up bases in India and become the principal purveyors of Asian luxuries in Europe.

Spanish exploration began with Christopher Columbus. Born to an artisan family in the Italian commercial center of Genoa, Columbus became an experienced coastal pilot and map maker. His voyages, many in the service of Portugal, had taken him not only around the Mediterranean but also north and south from Portugal in the Atlantic. In time Columbus became obsessed with the idea of reaching Asia by sailing west across the Atlantic. There was

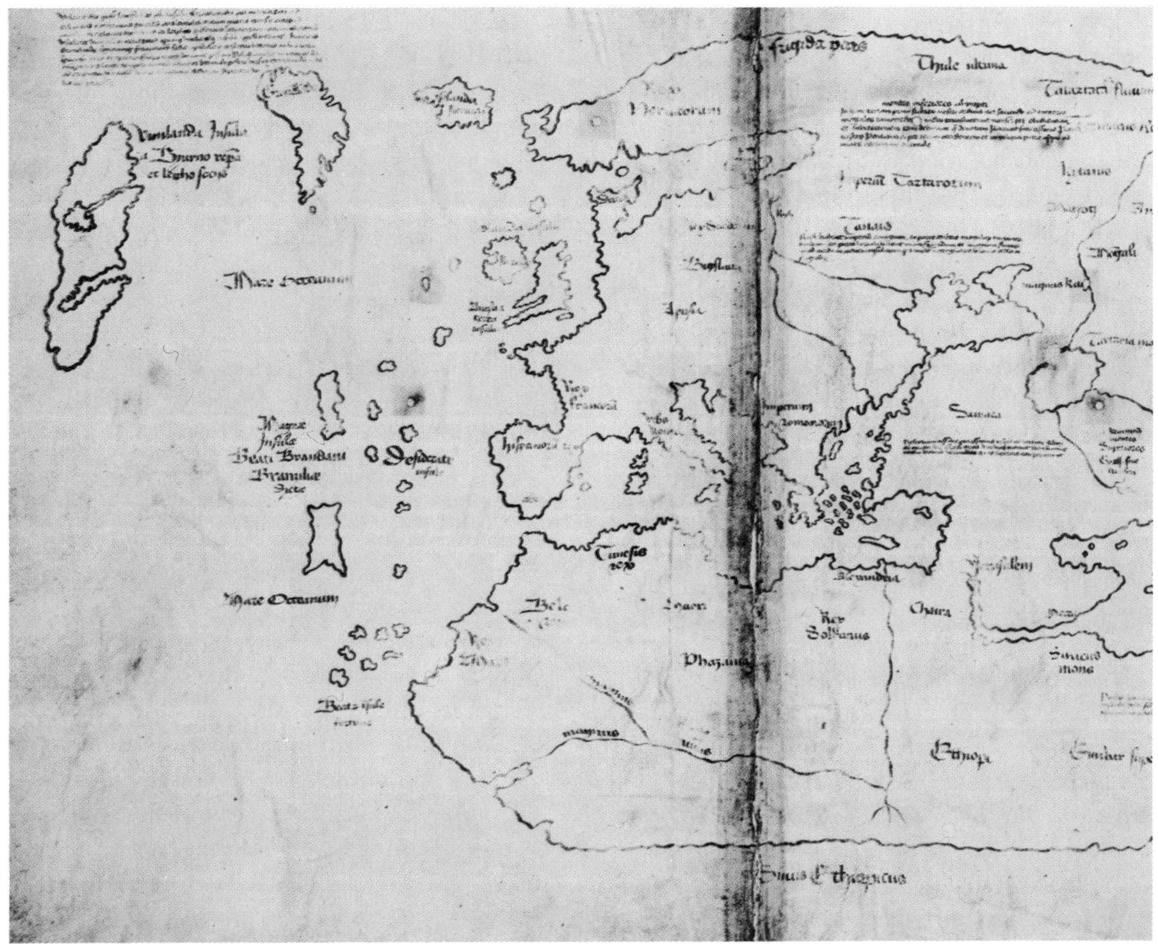

nothing theoretically novel in this. What was unique in Columbus was his determination to do it and his conviction, based on a gross miscalculation of the earth's size, that fewer than three thousand miles of ocean separated western Europe from eastern Asia.

In the early 1480s, even before Diaz reached the tip of Africa, Columbus began to seek financial backing for his expedition. He did so at first in Portugal. Portugal had then the most firmly established national government; that government had traditionally financed exploration voyages as no other had; Columbus himself had seen years of service on Portuguese vessels. The Portuguese, however, declined. They knew from experience in colonizing the Azores the difficulty of bucking the Atlantic's westerly winds. Their advisers also had more realistic notions than did Columbus as to the size of the earth. In any case, Columbus, apparently deep in debt, abandoned Portugal for Spain in 1485.

In Spain, Columbus haggled interminably with vacillating authorities. His brother Bartholomew journeyed to both England and France but received little encouragement. Meanwhile Columbus continued to press his case in Spain. There in 1492, Ferdinand of Aragon and his wife, Isabella of Castille, who had been struggling jointly to unify Spain, at last captured Granada, the only remaining stronghold of the Moors (Moslems) in the country. Pressing still further for unity, they expelled in the same year those Jews who refused to become converts to Christianity. Having thus assured Spanish unity in religion as well as in territory, Ferdinand and Isabella could turn to new ventures. Despite his own misgivings, Ferdinand acceded to Isabella's desire to give Columbus the financial support he needed.

Recalled by the Spanish rulers while on the way to press his case in France, Columbus drove a hard bargain. He and his private backers put up only one-eighth of the capital while Ferdinand and Isabella provided all the rest. Yet Columbus was to become hereditary admiral of the "Islands and Continent in the ocean" which he might "discover and subdue." He was also to receive a percentage of the new wealth secured by trade or otherwise.

With three ships (the *Nina,* the *Pinta,* and the *Santa Maria*) and about ninety men, Columbus hopefully set sail on August 3, 1492. The apprehensions of his sailors led to an abortive mutinty, but the weather was fine and the small craft encountered no real dangers. Ten weeks out from Europe, on October 12, 1492, they arrived at an island which Columbus named San Salvador (later called Watling or Watlings Island, but now again San Salvador) in the Bahamas. He pushed on to Cuba and Santo Domingo. Convinced, as he would always remain, that he had found "the Indies," then a common designation for Asia, Columbus applied the misnomer "Indian" to the native population. He kidnapped a few Indians and returned with them to the acclaim of Europe.

The subsequent voyages of Columbus proved disappointing. He tried hard to find gold, forcing the natives, whom he characterized as "fit to be ordered about and made to work," to pan it in the streams of Hispaniola (Santo Domingo), but they found little. Columbus also explored the Venezuelan and Central American coast looking for the nonexistent passage which would lead to Asia, his original goal. None of the three voyages which Columbus made later (1493–1496; 1498–1500; and 1502–1504) was rewarding. Columbus himself, partly because of his harsh but inept administration, sank further and further into disesteem. He died in obscurity in 1506.

Meanwhile the kings of Portugal and Spain disputed how to divide the world between them. In 1493, Pope Alexander VI, a Spaniard, drew a globe-encircling line 100 leagues west of the Cape Verde Islands to mark the division of non-Christian lands between the two Christian kingdoms. Portuguese dissatisfaction, however, led to the Treaty of Tordesillas in 1494, which shifted the line westward another 270 leagues. This line of demarcation put Brazil, the easternmost portion of the Americas, within the Portuguese sphere, although it was not until 1500 that a Portuguese fleet en route around Africa to Asia accidentally discovered it.

Columbus had ultimately concluded that South America was a "new world" but persisted in believing that North America was Asia. Another Italian, the Florentine merchant Amerigo Vespucci, denied that what Columbus had found was Asia. He had himself sailed along the South American coast to a point south of Buenos Aires in 1501 and 1502.

He may have made earlier voyages as well, but there is still an unresolved dispute concerning the authenticity of the letters which reported them. In any case, Vespucci labeled the area a "New World" and insisted that as in the case of Africa, the way around it to Asia lay to the south. A German geographer, Martin Waldseemueller, impressed by the letters of Vespucci, suggested that the land be named "America" in honor of "Americus Vespucius," the Latin form of the Italian name. The world accepted his suggestion.

Spanish explorations after Columbus's great discovery aimed usually at one of two objectives. The first was to find a passage around or through America to Asia, which, they hoped, would enable Spain to gain a commercial advantage in the Far East such as Portugal had secured in southern Asia. The second was to find and exploit the wealth of the New World itself.

Enthusiasm for voyages seeking a westward passage through America to Asia diminished only slightly after the remarkable feat of Ferdinand Magellan. A Portuguese in Spanish service, Magellan found his way through the treacherous straits at the tip of South America which now bear his name. Then he successfully crossed the Pacific to the Philippines, where in 1521 he was killed in a clash with natives. His crew managed to sail onward, however, to complete in 1522 the first round-the-world trip. The difficulties and the distance of this voyage made it clear that Europe's trade with the Orient would not pass via the Straits of Magellan but would follow Da Gama's route around Africa or perhaps a more northerly avenue around or through America.

As their dreams of wealth from Asian commerce faded, the Spanish turned to exploiting American resources. Seeking the source of the silver and gold found among the Indians of the Caribbean, Hernando Cortes in 1519 led some five hundred men in a Cuban-based invasion of the Aztec domain in Mexico. Aided by superior weapons, by Indian enemies of the Aztecs, and by his acceptance among some Aztecs as the legendary god Quetzalcoatl, Cortes vanquished one of the most highly developed Indian civilizations. Control over extensive deposits of silver rewarded his efforts. In the 1530s the ruthless Francisco Pizarro achieved still more spectacular success at the expense of another highly developed Indian society, the Incas of Peru. During the remainder of the century, American treasure, mostly silver but some gold as well, poured into Spain. Its effect was to inflate prices, to increase Europe's purchases from Asia, to speed up Europe's economic growth, to make Spain the envy of her rivals, and to encourage other countries not only to plunder Spanish commerce, but also to undertake rival expeditions of exploration and colonization.

Spanish explorations in what is now the United States were economically unsuccessful. Ponce de Leon explored Florida in 1513 in search of an alleged fountain of youth. Panfilo de Narvaez traversed the Gulf Coast from Florida to Texas in 1528, but only Cabeza de Vaca and a few others survived the numerous misfortunes which befell the expedition. Fray Marcos and Estaban, a Negro who had been with Narvaez, journeyed into the Indian pueblo region of the Southwest in 1539. Hernando de Soto in the years 1539–1542 tramped northward from Tampa Bay in Florida and then westward through what would become the cotton belt, but he discovered nothing more rewarding than the Mississippi River. Francisco Vasquez de Coronado made a more extensive but equally unrewarding jaunt in the

ARCTIC
GREENLAND
ICELAND
NORWAY
CABOT, 1497–1498
ENGLAND
CARTIER, 1534–1535
FRANCE
NEWFOUNDLAND
NORTH
AMERICA
VERRAZANO, 1524
PORTUGAL
SPAIN
DE SOTO
1539
COLUMBUS, 1492
PONCE DE LEON
1513
CORONADO
1540–1542
Gulf of
Mexico
BAHAMAS
PACIFIC
OCEAN
AZTEC
EMPIRE
CORTEZ
1519–1522
ATLANTIC
OCEAN
BALBOA, 1513
PANAMA
PIZARRO
1531–1533
CABRAL, 1500
DIAZ, 1486–1488
SOUTH
AMERICA
MAGELLAN, 1521
INCA
EMPIRE
VESPUCCI, 1501
VIKINGS, c. A.D. 1000
MAGELLAN, 1520
Strait of
Magellan
THE WORLD AS KNOWN TO EUROPEANS
AT THE TIME OF COLUMBUS
TIERRA
DEL FUEGO
To Spain
To Portugal

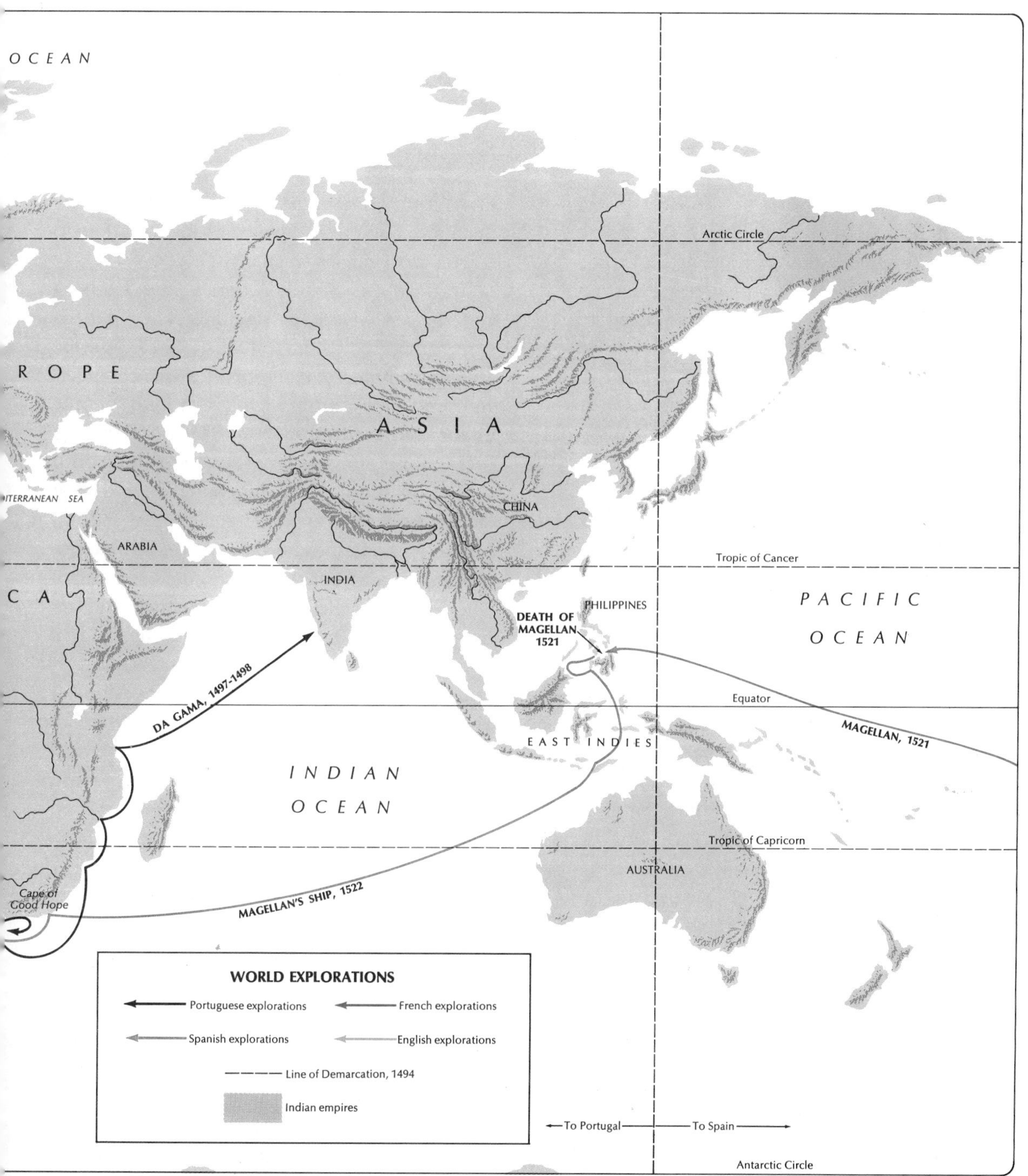
OCEAN
ROPE
ASIA
ITERRANEAN SEA
ARABIA
CHINA
INDIA
CA
PHILIPPINES
DEATH OF MAGELLAN 1521
PACIFIC OCEAN
Arctic Circle
Tropic of Cancer
Equator
DA GAMA, 1497-1498
EAST INDIES
MAGELLAN, 1521
INDIAN OCEAN
Tropic of Capricorn
AUSTRALIA
Cape of Good Hope
MAGELLAN'S SHIP, 1522
WORLD EXPLORATIONS
Portuguese explorations
French explorations
Spanish explorations
English explorations
Line of Demarcation, 1494
Indian empires
To Portugal
To Spain
Antarctic Circle

The Dawn of a New Era

path of Fray Marcos into the arid Southwest in search of the legendary Seven Cities of Cibola. They turned out to be more Indian pueblos such as Fray Marcos had seen. On the East Coast, Spanish ships sailed north to Labrador and on the West Coast as far as Oregon.

The American Indians

Spain's early clashes with the Indians began four centuries of bitter conflict. In the course of those centuries the Europeans not only fought with the "savages"; they learned from them, borrowed from them, and adjusted to them. The result of this interaction was to add leaven to the development of a distinctive American variant of European culture.

Columbus's mistake in naming the American natives "Indians" did at least fix correctly the continent of their origin. Man as a species did not evolve in America but emigrated from Asia, which was generally known in Columbus's time as "the Indies." Distinctive Indian features—straight black hair, high cheek bones, and brown skin—are similar to those of Mongolians. Archeological evidence indicates, furthermore, that Stone Age people did cross over from Asia to America in the Bering Strait or the Aleutian Island areas during the glacial period many thousand years ago. In time they scattered over both North and South America.

Tropical America from Mexico to Peru was the region in which Indian culture reached its highest levels. The Maya of Mexico in the millennium following the birth of Christ achieved a high level of political organization, built impressive pyramids, palaces, and temples, did art work which is still striking, and devised a calendar superior to that used until 1752 in the British Empire. Several centuries before Columbus, the Maya suffered conquest by the less cultured Toltec from the north, who in turn fell before another northern and still more warlike group, the Aztecs. Two centuries of Aztec predominance terminated in the Spanish conquest achieved by Hernando Cortes between 1519 and 1522.

In northern South America, the Chibcha and the Inca were outstanding. The Chibcha developed an effective calendar, carried on extensive commerce, made textiles and ceramics, and encompassed perhaps a million people under one political system. The realm of the Incas, centering in Peru but extending both north and south along the coastal region west of the Andean crest, included several million subjects in an absolute theocracy of which the ruling Inca was both high priest and sovereign. The Incas excelled in military, civil, and religious organization, in road building, and in communication. They resisted bravely but at last succumbed to the Spanish invasion of 1531 to 1533 under Francisco Pizarro. Despite the high level achieved by these Indian cultures, none of them discovered the wheel, developed written languages, domesticated animals other than dogs and llamas, or made iron tools.

Notwithstanding the gap between Indian and European cultures, the Indians afforded much of value to their conquerors. Of more lasting importance than the silver and gold which enriched Spain and indeed all Europe for roughly a century were commodities such as corn, a hybrid plant of Indian development; potatoes, another high-yield food crop which contributed significantly to the growth of European population; tobacco, a weed which has afforded gratification to millions albeit at some risk to health; and a considerable list of other commonplace but important items, including rubber, chocolate, and tomatoes.

The Indians in what is now the United States were far more primitive than those of the tropical regions. Their highest political organizations, loose confederations of tribes, were always very small. They encompassed at most a few thousand people. In all of what became the United States there were probably no more than a few million Indian inhabitants in the sixteenth century. Some of them subsisted chiefly by hunting, fishing, and food gathering, but most engaged extensively in primitive forms of agriculture as well. Corn, borrowed from the more advanced peoples to the south, was their chief crop, but they also cultivated beans, squash, and other food plants.

Although the cultural diversity was great among the Indians of North America, a number of generalizations are possible. For many tribes, warfare was the chief field of competition in which great distinction and high prestige could be won. Cowardice or failure in warfare brought disgrace and contempt. Sadistic torture of prisoners was frequent, but so was adoption into the conquering tribe. Generous sharing with visitors characterized the Indians' usual attitude toward property. Indeed, for centuries other Europeans would have occasion to confirm the early observation of Columbus that "of anything they have, if it be asked for, they . . . invite the person to accept it, and show as much lovingness as though they would give their hearts." Homes as well as other property were often communal. Trade between distant areas existed despite limited production, frequent warfare, and great problems in transportation. Corn, hides, and ornaments were the principal items of trade. Clothing came chiefly from animal hides. Tools as well as weapons were of wood and stone. Wood and hides constituted the most common building materials. Religious beliefs among the Indians required unremitting efforts to appease a number of "spirits." Disease, assisted by chronic malnutrition and warfare, kept life expectancy low. Nowhere could such people do more than delay and harass the Europeans who invaded their homelands.

Spain's American Empire

Trading with the natives rather than seizing their land for colonization by emigrants had been the original Spanish objective. In Asia and even in Africa, the Europeans had set up trading posts at which they exchanged various European items for commodities provided by the natives. In America the Spaniards found that voluntary production by the Indians, especially of gold and silver, was too limited to meet their demands. Accordingly they began to enslave Indians to increase production. As the Indians died from disease, discipline, and other causes, the Spanish began as early as the beginning of the sixteenth century to import African slaves to produce what they wanted. Thus, rather than being posts for trading with the natives, the Spanish possessions quickly took on the character of colonies, in which a small minority of Spaniards brought about the production of precious metals and various agricultural commodities by means of the enforced labor of native Indians or of imported Negro slaves.

The government of Spain's American empire, one of history's largest and most enduring, was extremely authoritarian. Fundamental power to govern lay of course with the king, advised and assisted after 1524 by a Council of the Indies which he appointed. In America viceroys appointed by the king administered vast areas, which were broken up in turn into numerous *audiencias,* many of which correspond closely to nations of the present. Officials anticipating opportunities for income bought their appointments from the king at auction after 1557. Expansion of the empire came most characteristically at the hands of self-financed *conquistadors* licensed by the government and inspired by the authorization to exploit new sources of precious metals, with a percentage for the king, or to enforce agricultural labor upon those whom they conquered. Large land grants carrying with them the right to compel labor from the unfortunate natives were a common reward for those who had access to and influence in the Spanish court.

Spain regulated the trade of its American colonies very carefully with the aim of excluding foreigners from any benefits wherever possible and maximizing returns to the home government and its supporters. For more than two centuries after 1503, Spain's American trade centered by law on the port of Seville under a regulatory agency, the *Casa de Contratacion.* Convoyed fleets set out twice yearly from Seville with supplies for the colonies and returned with sugar, dyes, and other American commodities, in addition to vast quantities of silver and gold. These treasure ships became frequent targets of Dutch and English pirates who were encouraged by their governments. Periodically Spain conferred upon one or another of the leading maritime nations the eagerly sought *asiento,* the regulated but lucrative monopoly of importing African slaves into the Spanish colonies. Spain generally permitted no foreign ships to enter her colonies, except under the *asiento,* but the lure of silver and gold brought foreign smugglers as well as pirates in great numbers to Spanish colonial waters.

Spanish religious leaders were able to preserve their monopoly far more effectively than Spanish merchants and traders. Brown-robed friars had often accompanied the original conquistadors. Indeed, in regions of what is now the southwestern United States, Catholic missionaries moved in and stayed among destitute Indians whose resources afforded no incentive for conquistadors to remain. Such zeal, encouraged by a number of deeply religious kings and reinforced after 1555 by a policy of barring all but Spanish Catholics from immigration into the colonies, assured that in Spanish America, Christian belief would be uniformly Catholic.

Spain's Competitors

Spain's success in exploration and settlement led to similar activity by its European rivals. The earliest competitor was England. In 1497, just five years after Columbus's first voyage, another of the ubiquitous Italians, John Cabot, made the first trans-Atlantic venture for the English. Cabot was a Bristol merchant who sold Asian goods purchased from the Moslem traders of the eastern Mediterranean. His aim was to make more profit by sailing straight across the Atlantic to buy directly from the Asian producers. Accordingly he persuaded Henry VII to authorize a modest venture of one ship and eighteen men. Cabot found many fish in the "Grand Banks" area off Newfoundland but no people to confirm his conviction that he had reached China. In 1498 he made a second voyage of which little is known. A decade later his son Sebastian made another voyage of which little is known, but the English by then had largely lost interest.

The French began explorations later than the English but did not become discouraged so quickly. Francis I of France in 1524 employed still another Italian, Giovanni Verrazano, to seek a passage through North America to the Pacific and China. In this quest Verrazano explored the American coastal line from North Carolina to Maine, including New York Harbor. His brother, apparently influenced by garbled Indian accounts of the Great Lakes, drew a map showing an arm of the Pacific extending to within a short distance of the Atlantic near Chesapeake Bay. For generations thereafter, Europeans encouraged by this map sought vainly to emulate in North America the feat of the Spaniard, Vasco Nuñez de Balboa, who in 1513 had struggled through 45 miles of jungle across the Isthmus of Panama to discover the Pacific Ocean.

Further French voyages, which were delayed because of problems at home, began in 1534 under Jacques Cartier. Between 1534 and 1541 Cartier made three trips up the St. Lawrence River. He dubbed the rapids above Montreal "La Chine" (China) and brought back large cargoes of what he thought to be gold and diamonds, but which proved to be "fool's gold" and quartz. The French explored no more in the sixteenth century but continued, as they had since the early years of the century, to exploit the fishing area off Newfoundland and to trade with the Indians. In time, fishermen from other parts of Western Europe joined them.

European exploration of America did not cease with Cartier, but it declined in importance as, first, plundering the Spanish and, then, colonizing became more attractive. Most of the later-sixteenth-century exploration was English. Sir Humphrey Gilbert in 1576 published an essay affirming that America was an island (because it had no Asian animals) and that therefore there must be some way around it in the north. Martin Frobisher, Gilbert himself, and John Davis in the 1570s and 1580s attempted to prove the point, though their efforts were in vain.

Europe after the Discoveries

What was the effect of the discoveries of Columbus and Da Gama upon the evolution of European society and thus upon the people who would colonize America? Walter Prescott Webb in *The Great Frontier* suggested that the effect was to inaugurate an epoch of prosperity, "the 500-year boom," which strongly influenced the basic features of modern Europe. His critics, on the other hand, have pointed out that the discoveries themselves resulted in part from the rising prosperity in Europe. Clearly, however, the nearly simultaneous discovery of the Americas, of most of Africa, and of economical routes to southern and eastern Asia added momentum to Europe's economic progress.

Development was by no means uniform in the various areas of Europe. The Atlantic countries of western Europe progressed most rapidly, but even in western Europe different national economies made different records. Portugal, although replacing Italy as the commercial center of Europe following Da Gama's voyage, was not strong enough to protect its

Asian empire from interlopers. Spain, largely because of the silver and gold produced in its American colonies, became the wealthiest nation in Europe. By spending its American wealth to buy what it wanted abroad and to meet its great military commitments, Spain did not foster the development of its own rather limited resources. It missed also the economic leadership of the Jews and the Moors whom it had expelled. The commercial areas of northern Europe (Netherlands, France, Germany, and England) benefited from American wealth in a healthier manner. Spurred by rising prices resulting essentially from Spain's expanded purchasing power, these areas increased their productive capacity, especially in woolen and linen textiles, then major items of trade. As their commercial production grew, so in a similar manner did their middle-class population, their urban centers, and their national power.

These newly risen commercial areas of Northern Europe spawned the great religious upheaval of the early sixteenth century—the Protestant Reformation. The relation between Protestantism and the rise of commercial capitalism has occasioned much dispute. Max Weber in a celebrated essay, *The Protestant Ethic and the Spirit of Capitalism,* suggested that the Protestant Reformation by imparting religious sanction to certain economic virtues, especially hard work and thrift, aided the development of capitalism. R. H. Tawney in an equally famous work, *Religion and the Rise of Capitalism,* proposed conversely that the previous development of capitalism strongly influenced the formation of Protestant views. Whichever is more nearly correct, it remains true that the Protestant Reformation was of profound importance in American history, as the vast majority of the early settlers in America were Protestants from the commercial regions of northwestern Europe.

The first of four major Protestant groups to emerge was the Lutheran. Martin Luther, a German Catholic monk, priest, and professor, touched off the reform movement in 1517 by challenging what had become a papal fund-raising device—the sale of "indulgences," or remission of punishment for a confessed sin. Unable to reform the Church from within, Luther broke completely with Catholicism. The Lutheran movement which he led affirmed that salvation came from faith, not from good works and observance of the sacraments. Interpretation of the Bible became to Lutherans a matter for the individual rather than the prerogative of the Church. Accordingly Bibles appeared in the language of the people rather than in Latin as heretofore. Lutherans also renounced the Catholic tradition of a celibate clergy and encouraged clergymen to marry. Finally, Lutherans substituted state control of religion for papal control and thereby enhanced the appeal of the movement to those who chafed under a "foreign" papacy. Lutheranism gained ascendancy in north Germany and Scandinavia. Some Lutherans emigrated from these areas to pre-Revolutionary America, but the chief importance of Lutherans for early American history lay in the example which they set for others in breaking away from Rome.

The Anabaptist movement, which was to have somewhat more influence on early American history, also had its roots in Germany. In the Peasants Revolt of 1524, militant poor people tried to end serfdom and the special privileges of nobles and clergy. Luther himself helped to suppress this revolt. In its aftermath many of the lower-class people of north Germany turned to a new religious movement. Because they insisted that baptism was mean-

ingful only to adults and not to infants, adherents of this movement were called Anabaptists, or rebaptizers. They believed in a literal application of Biblical teachings. They opposed war, tithes, oaths, a paid ministry, and social inequality. Although rigorously persecuted, Anabaptist beliefs would not die out. They came to early America not only with

Mennonites, Amish, Dunkers, and other German groups, but also with the English Baptists and Quakers.

Still more important as an influence in early America were the Calvinists. Calvinism derived from the theology of John Calvin, a Frenchman who wrote his *Institutes of the Christian Religion* in 1536 at Geneva, Switzerland. To the Calvinists, God was less a figure of love and mercy than of majestic power. Man was innately evil. Salvation came to a small minority of the elect while most, in accordance with God's "predestination," were doomed to damnation. The Bible was not just the word but the law of God, to be rigorously enforced upon a world of sinners by the elect minority assisted by the state. Control of the church, including the selection of a minister and the admission of new members, rested neither with a hierarchy nor with the state but with the local congregation of the elect. Calvinists also glorified work and thrift. The man who achieved success by working hard at his "calling" and saving his money was deemed to enjoy the favor of God. As a corollary, Calvinists tended to see extreme poverty as God's punishment for idleness and self-indulgence. Calvinism spread rapidly, especially among business people in urban centers, becoming in time the dominant theology among the Dutch (Dutch Reformed) and the Scots (Presbyterian). Calvinists were highly important minorities in France (Huguenots), in Germany (German Reformed), and in England (Puritan). Each of these groups, most notably the Puritans, brought the essentials of Calvinism to America.

Last among the major divisions of Protestantism was the Anglican – the Church of England. Its originator was Henry VIII. In order to secure a male heir to his throne Henry wanted to divorce his Spanish wife, Catherine of Aragon, who had produced only one child, Mary. As the foreign-dominated Catholic Church was not disposed to permit dissolution of his marriage and also because it controlled what many regarded as too much of England's wealth, Henry decided to nationalize it. By Parliamentary enactment he himself replaced the Pope as head of the Church in England. Advisers of Edward VI, the male heir whom Henry had finally secured by the third of his six wives, tried between 1547 and 1533 to make England rigorously Calvinist, but after Edward's early death the throne passed to his elder sister, Mary (1553–1558), who restored Catholicism with a vengeance. After her death the throne passed to the younger sister, Elizabeth, daughter of Henry's second wife. Illegitimate in the eyes of the Catholic Church, Elizabeth determined to make England Protestant once more, despite her strong personal distaste for many of the ideas and policies associated with Calvinism.

Anglicanism, as Elizabeth I established it, endured as a compromise between Calvinism and Catholicism. Control lay in the English government, but beneath the monarch the old hierarchical pattern of authority descending from bishops remained. The essential features of the ritual of worship were also retained, although English replaced Latin as the language of the service. Clergymen were permitted to marry. Faith was emphasized more than good works as a means to salvation, and the government taxed all to support its church. Many English emigrants to America were loyal supporters of this official church. Others, some Catholics but mostly Calvinists and Anabaptists, chose American exile to escape Anglican pressure to conform. Such emigrants brought with them a profound and enduring bias against a basic element in English society.

Imperial Rivalry

Religious hatreds born of the Protestant Reformation increased sharply the already-fierce rivalry among the nations of Europe. Of the four major nations in 1500 only England became Protestant. In the course of the sixteenth century, however, Catholic Portugal declined in power and a dynamic new Protestant nation emerged in the Netherlands. Upon the outcome of the struggle among these nations—Protestant England and the Dutch Republic, Catholic Portugal, Spain, and France—would depend the cultural heritage of the Americas.

At the outset, Spain was clearly the strongest of the rivals. In addition to Spain itself, the Spanish monarch held the wealthy commercial provinces of the Netherlands plus Naples and Sicily. While Cortes was conquering Mexico, Spain's ruler became Holy Roman Emperor as well and until 1556, when the two offices were separated again, could claim the loyalty of much of the area which would later become Germany.

In 1580 inheritance claims backed by a show of force enabled Spain to take over Portugal and its rich trading empire in Asia. None of Spain's rivals yet possessed significant territories other than their own homelands. Indeed, the Dutch did not gain recognition of their independence from Spain until the conclusion of a revolutionary struggle which grew out of oppression in the 1550s and dragged on until 1648.

Several factors caused Spain to lose ground in the international rivalry for power and prestige. Loss of control over the Holy Roman Empire was certainly one. Overcommitment might be considered another. Deeply dedicated to Catholicism, the Spanish expended inordinate effort, as the Protestant Reformation spread through Germany, the Netherlands, England, and elsewhere, to stamp out what they regarded as intolerably heretical belief. They carried on intermittent warfare not only with the Dutch and the English Protestants, but also with the Catholic French and the Moslem Turks, each of them major power rivals. Spain's economy, poorly endowed by nature, suffered relative neglect as warfare preoccupied the nation's ablest leaders and American treasure encouraged purchasing from foreigners. Yet, despite its declining relative position, Spain in 1600 remained master of all the Americas. As yet, no rival had secured even a firm foothold in the New World.

France spent most of the sixteenth century in the shadow of Spain. Fervent animosity between the wealthy Huguenot (Calvinist) minority and the Catholic majority occasioned much internal strife. Three times influential Huguenots tried to establish American bases from which their privateers could prey on Spanish commerce: at Rio de Janeiro in 1555; at what is now Beaufort, South Carolina, in 1562; and at St. Johns River, Florida, in 1564. Inadequately supported by their own government, each venture failed. Portugal stamped out the first. Settlers in the second gave up of their own accord; and the Spanish massacred all but 100 of the 300 settlers at St. Johns River. By the end of the century, however, France had achieved internal harmony and considerable economic progress under the able and tolerant Henry IV, a former Huguenot converted to Catholicism. In the seventeenth century, French efforts to establish American colonies to rival those of Spain would receive the full support of a powerful government and consequently would not fail.

The Dutch, long established as maritime carriers and merchants, began their climb to the status of a world power during the revolt against Spanish rule (1567 to 1648). As early converts to Calvinism they lived in dread of attempts by the Spanish to restore Catholicism. In particular they feared the methods of Inquisition which had stamped out Protestantism in Spain. They also resented oppressive taxation, the presence of Spanish military forces, and perhaps most of all the alien and authoritarian character of Spanish rule.

In their fight for independence the Dutch employed sea power, derived from their participation in fishing and commerce, both to weaken Spain and to enrich themselves. After Portugal became linked to Spain in 1580, the Dutch began taking over Portuguese trading posts in Asia. In the hope of finding a way to reach these Asian areas quickly and without skirting Spain, the Dutch dispatched the English explorer Henry Hudson on a voyage to America in 1609. Hudson explored New York Harbor and what is now the Hudson River, which flows into it. Failing to find a passage to Asia, he nevertheless did locate one of the world's finest harbors and a major avenue for penetrating the North American continent. There, in the coming "Golden Age" of Holland, would be the center of New Netherland.

Only slightly less dramatic than the progress of the Dutch in the sixteenth century was the rise of England. Henry VII had confirmed England's unity under a strong monarchy at the conclusion of the feudal Wars of the Roses in 1485. Englishmen took control of their own foreign commerce by expelling the resident Italian, Portuguese, and Hanseatic (Baltic Sea) merchants who had long controlled it. After 1550 private companies, endowed by the government with generous charters, secured sufficient capital from the sale of stock to finance expensive but rewarding commercial ventures. Such companies sought to establish trading posts in Russia (the Muscovy Company, 1553); the eastern Mediterranean (the Levant Company, 1581); and—most lucrative of all—in India (the East India Company, 1600).

English domestic production became more efficient. Coal began to replace wood as an industrial fuel. In the continuing enclosure movement ambitious landowners, some with dubious titles, dispossessed subsistence tenants and communal farmers to permit large-scale commercial production of wool for the important textile industry and of food for the growing urban populations. Some of the enormous but largely dormant wealth of the Catholic Church was converted into productive capital when Henry VIII, having confiscated the monasteries, placed the land in private hands. English military power also increased. Overcoming extreme ignorance of nautical technology by learning, even stealing, from the more proficient Spanish, the English under Henry VIII created a navy and improved greatly both the construction and the operation of their merchant ships.

From repeated conflicts with the Spanish, ebullient Englishmen drew courage to challenge Spain's presumed American monopoly. Henry VIII had defied Spain by divorcing Catherine of Aragon and making England Protestant. Elizabeth repeated the offense by restoring Protestantism after the death of Catherine's daughter, Queen Mary, and spurning politically inspired offers of matrimony from Philip II of Spain. She aided the Dutch revolt and in 1577 openly allied herself with the Dutch. Irked by continuing Spanish-supported intrigue to depose her, Elizabeth ultimately executed the Catholic claimant to her throne—Mary,

"Queen of Scots." In America, John Hawkins, an English slave trader, infuriated the Spanish by smuggling slaves into their colonies. They retaliated in 1568 in an attack off Mexico which destroyed three of Hawkins's five ships. Sir Francis Drake, a cousin and associate of Hawkins, then plundered Spanish settlements from Central America southward around the continent and north to California. A secret investor in Drake's enterprise, Elizabeth met Spanish demands that he be punished by conferring knighthood upon him. She encouraged other piratical expeditions as well.

From exploration and plunder England's objectives broadened late in the sixteenth century to include colonization. Inspiration and advice directed toward such efforts flowed from the pens of the two Richard Hakluyts, cousins of the same name, neither of whom ever crossed the Atlantic. The elder, a lawyer, wrote advice on how to establish a colony. The younger, a clergyman and scholar, wrote promotional tracts setting forth arguments designed to persuade the Queen and men of influence at court that colonizing ventures would certainly bring great economic benefit to England.

Even before the appearance of the younger Richard Hakluyt's "Divers Voyages" in 1582, Sir Humphrey Gilbert had begun colonizing efforts. Encouraged by a charter from Queen Elizabeth conferring semifeudal political and economic privileges upon him in any American colony which he might found, Gilbert set out in 1578 with his half brother, Walter Raleigh, but was forced back by bad weather. Five years later Gilbert tried again, committing most of his own fortune to the venture. This time he reached Newfoundland, long frequented by European fishing vessels, but he perished in another storm before founding a colony.

Taking up where Gilbert had left off, Walter Raleigh obtained another royal charter to found a colony in a general region which he persuaded the "Virgin Queen" to name Virginia in her own honor. Notoriously frugal, Elizabeth would make no financial contribution to Raleigh's effort, despite the persuasive arguments elaborated by the younger Hakluyt in Raleigh's support. Accordingly, Raleigh had to arrange private financing for the third expedition, which planted a colony on Roanoke Island off the coast of what is now North Carolina.

The leader of the mission, John White, was a veteran of at least one earlier voyage. When White returned to England for supplies in 1588, he found all England preoccupied with preparations for war with Spain, a war which would last from 1588 to 1604. Finally managing to get passage to America in 1591, White, on his arrival, found only ruins and the cryptic word "CROATOAN," the name of a local Indian tribe, carved on a doorpost. Among those who had mysteriously vanished were his own daughter and his infant granddaughter, Virginia Dare, the first English child born in America. In this manner England's colonization efforts of the sixteenth century came ingloriously to an end.

England's war with Spain, however, was demonstrating that in the century about to open, England would renew its challenge to Spain's domination of America. What had touched off the war was Elizabeth's execution of her Catholic rival, Mary. It was that event, crowning a long series of other offenses, which prompted Philip II to attempt an invasion of England. He crowded some seventeen thousand soldiers aboard an enormous invasion fleet and sent it into the English Channel. There speedy English vessels, employing long-range bombardment instead of the traditional boarding technique of naval warfare, defeated the Spanish fleet decisively. A heavy storm completed the rout and devastation of the Spanish Armada. While Spain's naval power probably remained greater than England's for some time after 1588, the defeat of the Armada heralded the end of Spanish domination in both the old world and the new. As the sixteenth century ended, the declining power of Spain and the rising power of France, Holland, and England presaged intense rivalry among the nations of Europe for control of North America.

Conclusion

Europe's attainment of imperial predominance over much of America, Africa, and Asia beginning in the fifteenth century followed a considerable transformation of Europe itself. Commercial capitalism, as it had for several centuries, was drawing more and more people out of subsistence farming into specialized production and trade. Tightly unified national monarchies were beginning to evolve from numerous inconsequential feudal principalities. Scientific advances and material betterment were receiving more of the attention previously dedicated largely to the achievement of religious salvation. The voyages of exploration were the undertakings of new national governments in Western Europe, seeking, in the interests of their own people, to end the monopoly of the Asian trade enjoyed jointly by the Moslems of the eastern Mediterranean and the Italians.

So rewarding was the exploitation which followed successful exploration ventures that the Europeans who enjoyed the advantage of organization under vigorous national governments began to compete ruthlessly for the acquisition of colonies. Portugal, which had pioneered in exploration, became for a time the center of European wealth as a result of commercial advantages secured by sending its ships around Africa to trading posts in Asia. Spain, exploiting American silver and gold deposits which its explorers had come upon while searching for alternative approaches to Asia, became fabulously wealthy. Meanwhile the Protestant Reformation, spreading from Germany and Switzerland into the Netherlands and England, increased opposition to the predominance of Catholic Spain. By 1600, the Dutch, the English, and the French were each seeking to share in the good fortune which had rewarded the exploration voyages of the Portuguese and the Spanish.

SUGGESTED READINGS

American distinctiveness has long fascinated both domestic and foreign observers. More than a century ago the Frenchman Alexis de Tocqueville in *Democracy in America** (4 vols., 1835–1840) identified "equality of conditions" as the hallmark of American society. Frederick Jackson Turner's brief essay *The Significance of the Frontier in American History** (1893) can even now prod the imagination to ponder the influence of frontier conditions in differentiating American from European society. More recently David Potter in *People of Plenty** (1954) fixed upon wealth as America's most distinctive feature, while Louis Hartz in *The Liberal Tradition** (1955) attributed America's relative liberalism to the absence of a feudal past.

Of the many historians who have dealt with the

An Early View of America

When the French Huguenots in 1564 made their second attempt to settle on the South Atlantic Coast of what is now the United States, they brought along with them an artist, one Jacques Le Moyne de Morgues, and assigned to him the task of making maps and portraying "the dwellings of the natives and anything else in the land worthy of observation."

On the basis of his experiences in Florida—he remained for a year and three months—Le Moyne created an illustrated report which is historically important, particularly because it reflects the lives and customs of the Timucua Indians. All but one of the paintings which illustrated the report have been lost, but their content lives on, in somewhat embellished form, in the engravings of Theodore De Bry, who published them in book form, along with Le Moyne's text, in 1591. In this form the report became available to the scholars, merchants, and political leaders of Europe and thus helped to formulate the European conception of America and the Indian in the late sixteenth and seventeenth centuries.

The picture above and those on the following pages, as well as the accompanying caption data, are taken from a rare hand-colored edition of the Le Moyne–De Bry work, "Brevis narratio . . . in Florida anno MDLXIII, Frankfort, 1591," in the collection of the Service Hydrographique de La Marine in Paris. These engravings appear here by their special permission. Le Moyne himself did not do the coloring, it should be noted; the De Bry text was not published until after his death.

The expedition which included Le Moyne established Fort Caroline in June of 1564 near the mouth of the River of May — now the St. John's — not far from present-day Jacksonville, Florida. By fall troubles beset the settlement. Food became scarce. The expedition leader, René de Laudonnière, fell ill, and there were plots against his life, desertions, and an open mutiny against him. At first the Indians welcomed the group, but the French, desperately looking for a source of gold, tried to gain the

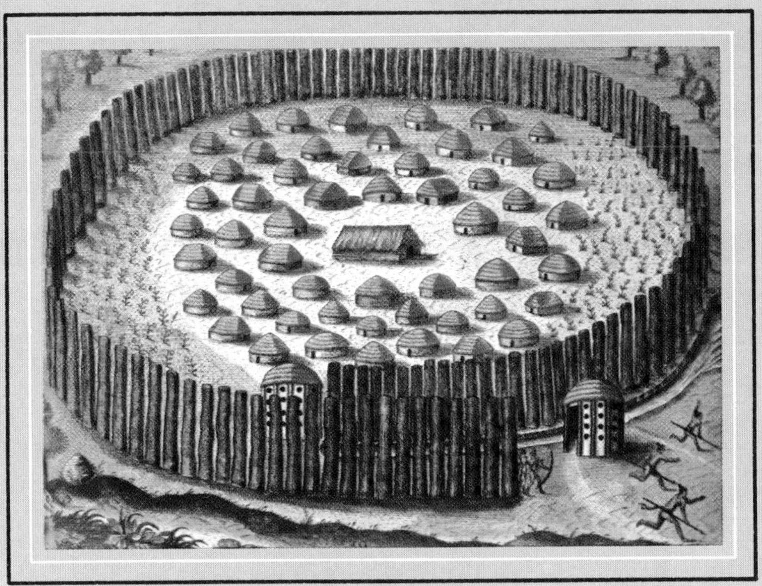

Le Moyne reported that the Indians built typical fortified villages near swift streams which were diverted through them. Two guard houses protected the entrance, and the chief's house stood at the center. According to Nicolas Le Challeux, another member of the expedition, smoldering fires under the beds discouraged the flies.

favor of rival tribes, thereby eliciting the hostility of their original friends. As the food supply dwindled to nothing, the suffering became terrible: the men ate roots and wild plants. Laudonnière, who regained command of the fort, reported that the bones of the famished men pierced their skin.

Finally help arrived from France under the leadership of Jean Ribaut, but a Spanish force, determined to dislodge the French from North America, followed close behind. Ribaut might have staved off the Spanish had not his small fleet been wrecked by a hurricane. The Spanish marched overland from St. Augustine, staged a surprise attack on Fort Caroline, and slaughtered most of its inhabitants. Only a few French escaped, among them, Le Moyne.

The ship in which he fled was blown off course and landed in England where Le Moyne remained. There he is believed to have executed his paintings. During his time in Florida, Le Moyne had ample opportunity to observe the Indians and to hear first-hand reports of their customs from other members of the expedition, but he was not present at every incident he later chose to depict. And when De Bry made his engravings from the paintings he tended to embellish and to idealize. The engravings he made from the pictures of the Indians of Virginia by the English artist John White—the originals of White's paintings are still extant and may be compared with the De Bry copies—document this tendency.

For hunting deer, the Indians disguised themselves in dressed deer skins in order not to frighten the herd and waited for them by the river at watering time. Two and a half centuries later the artist-docomentor of Western Indian life, George Catlin, depicted himself using a similar technique to get near a herd of buffalo.

The full series of the Le Moyne–De Bry pictures, in black and white, a reproduction of the only surviving color original, and the complete narratives of Le Moyne and Nicolas Le Challeux (another member of the expedition) appear in Stefan Lorant's book The New World *(Duell, Sloan and Pierce, first revised edition, 1965). That volume reproduces also the water color paintings of John White, De Bry's engravings of them, and all the known early narratives and eyewitness accounts of the first English efforts to settle in Virginia.*

Here Indians attack a crocodile with a rough log. A crocodile-watching blind appears at left. Above, they beat the animal to death. The French found the meat to be similar to veal.

.20.

17

Indian methods for healing the sick appear in the engraving at left, above. At the left, blood is drawn by mouth from an incision in the patient's head; nursing mothers consumed this blood in order to gain health and strength. The patient at right inhales the smoke of burning seeds. In the background, an Indian smokes tobacco to cure an infection. In the engraving below, "hermaphrodites," looked down upon by their tribesmen, carry out such menial tasks as caring for the contagiously ill and carrying the dead to the burial ground.

Communal storehouses constructed of stones, earth, and palm fronds (above) preserve harvests of fruit. Members of the tribe could help themselves to what they wanted, and according to Le Moyne, the Indians experienced no greed or fear of being cheated.

36

Le Moyne's picture of young men at play (left) centers on a ball game in which the object was to hit a square of reeds atop a tall pole. Other preoccupations of youth included endurance racing, bow and arrow practice, and fishing and hunting.

The body of a stag stuffed with roots and garlanded with fruits appears at the center of the spring rite (above). The chief leads prayers to the sun that the tribe's lands will be rich in such bounty during the coming year.

This tribe, led by King Outina, sought French help in a local war. The sorcerer kneels on the shield of French Lieutenant Ottigny as he divines the strength of the enemy and the site of the battle.

In typical marching formation, King Outina walks well-protected in the center, surrounded by his warriors rank upon rank. His scouts run along the periphery, ranging ahead and to the sides, while three nobles lead the group.

In a stealthy night maneuver, the attacking force sets the roofs of an enemy village on fire using arrows tipped with burning moss. The strips of bark on the men's left wrists were often used as protection against the snap of the bowstring.

Chief Outina's tribesmen routinely removed the scalp, arms, and legs of the enemy dead for trophies and shot a final arrow into the body (below). At right, French observers witness a mourning ritual. Wives of the dead beg the chief to revenge the deaths of their husbands, to care for them while they are widows, and to allow them to marry again when the mourning period ends.

.18.

The French constantly sought the gold and silver which they believed lay in the Apalatcy (Appalachian) Mountains. Le Moyne reported that one member of the expedition, La Roche Ferrière, made the long journey to the mountains and sent back gold-headed arrows, protective chest and back plates made of gold and silver, and a quantity of gold alloyed with brass. Above, the Indians collect sand from an Appalachian mountain stream and search it for grains of precious metal.

emergence of modern society in Europe, W. H. McNeill in *The Rise of the West* (1963) has the widest perspective. W. K. Ferguson's *Europe in Transition,* 1300–1520, is superbly organized. The older works of E. P. Cheyney, *The European Background of American History,* 1300–1600* (1904), and *The Dawn of a New Era** (1936), are still rewarding. Max Weber's *The Protestant Ethic and the Spirit of Capitalism** (1926) and W. P. Webb's *The Great Frontier* (1952) present interpretations of a challenging nature.

Gwyn Jones's *The Norse Atlantic Saga* (1964) provides an intelligent guide to the archeological evidence, as well as the sometimes gruesome legends of the Norse experience in America. His *History of the Vikings* (1969) puts them in their proper European context. D. W. Waters's *The Art of Navigation* (1958) affords fascinating background on the exploration voyages of the fifteenth and sixteenth centuries. J. H. Parry in *The Age of Reconnaissance* (1963) describes them fully; C. E. Nowell in *The Great Discoveries** (1954) more briefly. J. B. Brebner's *The Explorers of North America** (1933) concerns expeditions into the interior. A. L. Rowse has written vividly on *The Expansion of Elizabethan England** (1955). J. H. Parry's *The Seaborne Empire of Spain* (1966) and C. R. Boxer's *The Dutch Seaborne Empire,* 1600–1800 (1965), both treat their subjects in long-range perspective.

S. E. Morison's biography of Columbus, *Admiral of the Ocean Sea* (2 vols., 1942), is a classic. He has done a shorter work, *Christopher Columbus, Mariner** (1956). J. A. Williamson has written authoritatively on *The Cabot Voyages and Bristol Discovery* (1962). He has done a short study of *Sir Francis Drake** (1951), as has D. B. Quinn on *Raleigh and the British Empire* (1947). Garrett Mattingly's *The Armada** (1959) is as exciting as it is authoritative.

The *Indian Heritage of America* (1968) by Alvin M. Josephy, Jr., conveys readably a vast amount of fascinating information concerning Indians throughout the Americas. W. T. Hagan's *American Indians** (1961) is excellent despite its brevity. *The Indians of North America* (1961) by anthropologist H. E. Driver is very scholarly.

* indicates availability in paperback.

2

Competition for Colonies

INITIALLY EUROPEANS had regarded America chiefly as a barrier in the path to Asia. Soon, however, the area began to gain attention for its own sake. Possessed of rich resources and occupied sparsely by a people incapable of defending their territory effectively, America offered promising prospects for European exploitation. Spain quickly established control of those territories deemed most valuable. Then, early in the seventeenth century, rival European nationalities, the English, French, Dutch, and even the Swedes, began competing with Spain and each other for control of North America and the adjacent Caribbean islands.

Among the latecomers, the English enjoyed two great competitive advantages. First, their insular position, by protecting them from invasion, made a large army unnecessary and permitted them to concentrate on the development of naval power and colonies. Second, in the British colonies large numbers of European immigrants, chiefly British, developed the new continent's resources, whereas in the colonies of the other powers a small number of Europeans sought either to trade with the natives or to compel resentful Indian or African slave laborers to produce for them. By the end of the century, the English had established thriving colonies in Virginia, Maryland, New England, and the Carolinas. They had taken New Netherland from the Dutch and the important West Indian island of Jamaica from the Spanish. The English in fact held the entire coastal area north of Spanish Florida, except for modern Canada, most of which was controlled by the French.

England's delay of about a century in founding American colonies resulted chiefly from its weakness as a nation. Although England had achieved national unity even before Spain, England's population was small, its resources limited, and its wealth, naval power, and even technology were inferior to those of Spain. By 1600, however, England had made remarkable progress and was prepared to challenge Spain's pretension to exclusive possession of the Americas. Its economy produced a considerable surplus, especially of woolen textiles. It possessed shipping and enterprise sufficient to market those products in many areas abroad. Indeed, Englishmen of the time showed not just willingness but a remarkable eagerness to accept great risk in hope of great reward.

Private investors contributed much to England's imperial success. The 218 stockholders who organized the East India Company in 1600 had gained impressive profits from their early voyages. Their success in defying the Portuguese in India inspired others to compete with the Spaniards in America. But to do so they had to form private corporations. The earlier experience in Virginia had demonstrated that colonization was too expensive for a single individual. Government support was out of the question as the impecunious English government, largely dependent upon a niggardly Parliament for its income, showed no disposition to invest in colonizing.

Many Englishmen without capital were willing to commit themselves to overseas adventures in the hope of improving their circumstances. Highest on the social scale among such people were the younger sons of large land holders, left relatively poor by the systems of primogeniture and entail under which the eldest son inherited all his father's land and was forbidden by law to allow its division. Many artisans, especially those who made woolen cloth in their own homes, were also in difficulty in England during the depression from about 1620 to 1635. Still more unfortunate were farm folk who had been driven off the land.

These former farmers, accustomed to practice a primitive, subsistence agriculture on small plots or in a communal "open field" system, were victims of the enclosure movement. Their landlords, sometimes "owners" only by dint of successful assertion, wished to assemble large tracts of land in order to produce wool for the expanding woolen industry or food for the growing cities. The plight of those dispossessed was harrowing. Jobs were few. Prices had more than doubled in less than a century, as specie from America vastly augmented Europe's supply of money. Wages for agricultural laborers, fixed by justices of the peace who were leading landowners, appear to have changed little. Furthermore, the law required an unemployed person to get permission before leaving the area of his last employment. Even if he secured such authorization, he might be sent back from the new community to the old at the discretion of local authorities, lest he add to the welfare burden of local taxpayers.

Thus there were in England many poor men eager to seek better economic opportunity and capitalists willing to invest in overseas adventures, but what of government policy? American possessions, the publicist Richard

Hakluyt had argued, would assist English seamen to divert from Spain some of the "contynuall commynge of . . . [American] threasure." American colonies would also supply the timbers and naval stores, such as tar, pitch, and turpentine, necessary for the "mayneteynaunce . . . of our Navye, and . . . shippinge which is the strengthe of our Realme." English settlers in America might find gold or silver, as had the Spanish, or perhaps even the elusive northwest passage to Asia. English leaders accepted these arguments. They were also only too willing to export "idle men" who frightened householders as "sturdy beggars," burdened local government, and indeed filled the jails and "houses of correction."

To the royal officials, however, the most compelling argument for colonization was what would later be called the mercantilist theory. Thomas Mun gave it classical expression in *England's Treasure by Forraign Trade,* written in 1628 and published in 1664: "The ordinary means . . . to encrease our wealth . . . is by *forraign trade,* where in wee must ever observe this rule; to sell more to strangers yearly than wee consume of theirs in value." While this theory, especially when oversimplified, made acquisition of gold and silver rather than production the measure of a nation's wealth, it usually tended in fact to foster both. According to this argument, American colonies would give England opportunities to sell to the Indians, reduce her imports of naval materials and tropical products from foreigners, and gain revenue by selling American products in Europe. Nor did British monarchs, chronically short of income, fail to see that from such an increase in trade the royal customs revenues, as Hakluyt put it, "shall mightely be inlarged."

Religion and politics in England in the first half of the seventeenth century had an important bearing on migration to America and upon the nature of American society. Elizabeth, although ruling without much reference to Parliament from 1555 to 1603, had maintained "her subjects' love and good affections." Her successor, James I, King of Scotland since his infancy, was well meaning but offensively pedantic, "the wisest fool in Christendom," and a spendthrift. He believed implicitly in the divine right of kings, a concept widely accepted on the Continent, and in an authoritarian church as well. In fact he thought he could keep his authority in the government only as long as bishops retained similar control of the church. "No bishop," he often stated, "no king." Parliamentary leaders, many of them Puritans, resisted the attempts of James I and his like-minded son, Charles I, to impose revenue measures without consent of Parliament, and protested the refusal of Charles I to convene Parliament from 1629 to 1640. Puritans in general were indignant because Anglican Archbishop William Laud not only blocked religious reforms the Puritans wanted but insisted that they conform to unreformed Anglican practices.

The conflict which smoldered through the reign of James I (1603–1625) burst into civil war (1642–1646) under Charles I. The outcome was a Puritan, or "Roundhead," victory over the "Cavalier" forces of the King. However, the Puritans' "Commonwealth" soon disintegrated into a dictatorship headed by the military genius Oliver Cromwell. After his death, conditions deteriorated so badly that in 1660 the English people by common consent restored as King a somewhat chastened representative of the Stuart royal family, Charles II. With him returned the Elizabethan Church of England as the official, state-controlled religion.

Theoretical writing mirrored the religious and political tumult of the seventeenth century. In 1652, Thomas Hobbes in the *Leviathan* argued that the savage nature of men required them to make a "social contract" which would surrender absolute and irrevocable power to government in order to secure order. Hobbes used the idea to justify total submission to a monarch, but his identification of the people as the source of political authority had radical implications. Conservative philosophy found more visceral expression in a Cavalier's comment on Cromwell's army: "Most of the . . . officers, mean tradesmen, brewers, tailors, goldsmiths, shoemakers, and the like, a notable dunghill, if one would rake into it to find their several pedigrees: these to rebel against their masters."

Puritan opponents of the king produced classics defending their position. Among them were James Harrington's *Commonwealth of Oceana* (1656) and poet John Milton's *Areopagitica* (1644). Censorship, wrote Milton in defense of freedom of speech, tends "to the discouragement of all learning and the stop of truth, . . . by hindering . . . the discovery that might be yet further made, both in religious and civil wisdom." Harrington, believing political power tends to follow wealth, argued for a commonwealth or constitutional republic in which he assumed that dominance would lie with the gentry—untitled gentlemen of large landed estates.

Outstanding in radical thought was the work of John Lilburne, leader of the "Levellers." More Anabaptist than Calvinist in spirit, the Levellers were characterized by Cromwell as "mean fellows, alas, not a lord nor a gentlemen, nor a man of fortune . . . amongst them." What they believed, in the words of Lilburne, was that "every . . . man and woman . . . are equal and alike in power, dignity, authority and majesty, none of them having . . . any authority . . . one over . . . another. Neither can they exercise any, but merely by . . . mutual consent."

Each of these beliefs, from Hobbes through Lilburne, would be found in England's American colonies, but always in America the conservatives would be a little weaker and the radicals a little stronger than in England. The first of England's successful American colonies, however, was a business enterprise only slightly influenced by incipient religious and political quarrels.

Virginia

During the long but desultory war with Spain which followed the defeat of the Armada in 1588 the Elizabethans made little effort to found colonies. Ironically, with the restoration of peace in 1604 under pro-Spanish James I, England began to carve out an empire in the trans-Atlantic world which the Spanish regarded as exclusively their own.

Inspired apparently by the success of the East India Company and by explorers' reports, two groups of investors, one from London, the other from Plymouth and Bristol, petitioned the King in 1605 for authorization to colonize "Virginia," the name applied at that time to all prospectively English areas of America. Eager to please, the new King consented. The investors organized the London and the Plymouth Companies, respectively, the former to colonize the southern portion of the grant, and the latter the north. Just before Christmas, 1606, the London Company dispatched well over one hundred men for Virginia aboard three ships, the *Susan Constant,* the *Godspeed,* and the *Discovery.*

Arriving at Chesapeake Bay after eighteen weary weeks at sea, the newcomers quickly began to blunder. Instead of going 100 miles upstream to avoid "a low or moist place" as instructed, they founded Jamestown much nearer the sea in what proved to be a malarial swamp. Expecting to get food by trade with natives or by supply ships from home, they failed to plant enough crops. Captain John Smith claimed that, because of being five months at sea instead of the expected two, they had "both spent our victual and lost the opportunity . . . to plant." The Indians provided some food voluntarily and some otherwise, but they proved less interested in commerce than in warfare. With the natives "as fast killing without as famine and pestilence within," a phrase used to describe a later period of suffering, about half the settlers had died before a supply ship returned in midwinter.

Suffering and dying continued. In the "starving time" of 1609 and 1610 the population, which had built up to several hundred, dwindled to about sixty. The survivors were aboard ship, ready to depart, when Lord de la Warr, arriving with supplies and reinforcements, turned them back. Starvation was never again so serious. Indian relations improved, especially after 1614 when settler John Rolfe married Pocahontas, daughter of Chief Powhatan. Nevertheless mortality remained high. Only a few of those who had arrived in Virginia in the first fifteen years were still there and alive in 1622. Then, after Powhatan's death, a surprise Indian attack killed about 350 settlers, a substantial proportion of the colony. By that time, however, the settlers had found a way to make money, a discovery that settled the fate of both the colony and the natives.

How to make Virginia profitable had proved to be a difficult problem. Indian productivity was too low to make trade rewarding. Precious metals were utterly absent. The climate was not mild enough for sugar, which Spaniards grew at great profit in the Caribbean. Efforts to produce silk, wine, and other "exotic" commodities failed. Lumber and naval stores (tar, pitch, turpentine, and resin) were exported but at no great profit. Tobacco was the answer. Virginia's original tobacco was too biting to be marketable, but in 1613 John Rolfe crossed it successfully with milder West Indian varieties. By 1619 Virginia tobacco was outselling Spanish in England, and James I, who opposed smoking, was drawing solace from an import tax of 20 percent. Within a generation Virginia and her younger neighbor, Maryland, had become the world's principal sources of tobacco.

Profit eluded the London Company essentially because Virginia had no gold or silver and no prospect for rewarding trade with the Indians. Company policy, however, was also a handicap at first. The company bound its original immigrants to a seven-year contract as laborers. Largely without women, the "servants" lived an armylike existence, even existing under martial law for several years. By 1618, however, the company had begun to permit individual ownership. Servants received land grants at the end of their terms. Those who provided passage for immigrants also received a "headright" of fifty acres per person. "When our people were fed out of the common store, and laboured jointly together," a settler observed, "the most honest among them would hardly take so much true paines at their work in a week, as now for themselves they will doe in a day." After 1620 the colony appeared still healthier as the company commenced importing prospective brides for the planters.

Company reform was political as well as economic. Of surpassing importance in this respect was the creation of the Western Hemisphere's first representative legislature. In 1618 the company provided that two "Burgesses" elected freely by the inhabitants of each plantation should act with the appointed governor and his council as a general assembly "to make and ordaine . . . lawes."

The reforms, however healthy, came too late. In 1618 unhappy stockholders ousted Sir Thomas Smith, the company treasurer and an experienced executive, who was also a staunch supporter of the King. His successor, Sir Edwin Sandys, was an associate of the King's opponents in Parliament. Sandys continued Smith's reform program and added a five-year plan of his own for economic diversification. The Indian massacre of 1622, however, brought about a royal investigation in which the King showed that the company had not fulfilled its charter obligations. Accordingly, a court order annulled the charter, and Virginia became a royal province. Thereafter the King allocated land and appointed governor and council. On their investment of about £200,000, the stockholders had received no return at all. They had only begun an empire.

Royal government did not alter Virginia's new character. It is true that the Legislature did not meet from 1624 to 1629, but thereafter, from 1629 to 1640, the period in which the English Parliament itself was not permitted to convene, Virginia's burgesses did meet. In 1639, Charles I authorized annual meetings. This seemed indeed to go beyond what the original charter had promised to the settlers —that they would "enjoy all Liberties . . . as if they had been abiding . . . within . . . our Realm of England."

New England

While the London Company's workers were struggling to survive in malarial Jamestown, the Plymouth Company, which had been chartered at the same time, launched a similar enterprise in "northern Virginia." Under twenty-four-year-old Raleigh Gilbert, son of Elizabethan explorer Humphrey Gilbert, a few settlers landed in the Kennebec area of Maine. They built a ship and sent home some timber, but after enduring a Maine winter they went back to England in 1608.

Separatist Pilgrims, a small group of religious extremists who would have no truck with the Anglican Church, proved more determined. Oppressed by laws which required them to attend Anglican services and to hold no other religious meetings, Pilgrims from Scrooby in Nottinghamshire had emigrated to Leyden, in Holland, without their government's permission. There they found religious freedom but worried over the increasing worldliness of their children and the fact that, as aliens, they were excluded from craft guilds. Accordingly their leader, William Brewster, arranged with a group of London merchants to form a company which would finance their settlement in "northern Virginia." Aiming for the Hudson River in their tiny ship *Mayflower,* they landed instead in November, 1620, on Cape Cod, in the region which Captain John Smith had called "new England."

Even before the Pilgrims debarked, they had already won a place in history. First, they had received a precedent-setting commitment from James I that he would not "molest them": the government would not enforce observance of

Anglicanism upon Dissenters in America. When it became clear that they would land outside the bounds of the Virginia Company, some of the numerous non-Pilgrims aboard asserted that in consequence "none had power to command them." To meet this threat of anarchy Pilgrim leaders drew upon the religious tradition of the "covenant" to write the Mayflower Compact. Its forty-one signers agreed to "combine ourselves together into a civil Body Politick" to make "just and equal Laws . . . for the general Good of the Colony." The government which they set up later provided annual elections for governor and assistants.

Survival was less difficult at Plymouth than at Jamestown. Roughly half of the colonists died in the first winter, but the survivors, instructed by the Indians in corn culture, raised crops successfully the next year. That fall they arranged a feast of Thanksgiving with Indian guests. Trading corn to the Indians for furs, the Pilgrims made some progress toward repaying their English backers. The larger Puritan colony of Massachusetts soon overshadowed Plymouth, however, and in 1691 absorbed it. Plymouth's final gift to posterity was "Of Plymouth Plantations," a superb history written by the wise and virtuous William Bradford, longtime Governor of the colony.

Unlike the Pilgrims, the Puritans who followed them to New England were close to the mainstream of English life. They had long struggled from within to "purify" the Church of England. They wanted to eliminate "Romish" ceremonial traditions, to enforce the Sabbath observance more rigorously, to secure a better-educated clergy, to preclude the appointment of one clergyman to two or more income-yielding parishes (pluralism), and to prevent priests from residing outside their parishes (absenteeism). Above all, they wanted local congregations to have more power, the bishops less. The Calvinist background of James I gave them high hopes when he became King, but he supported the bishops fully. He assured Puritans in fact he would "make them conform" or "harry them out of the land."

Easygoing James I in fact did neither. Charles I and Archbishop Laud, however, especially in the period of "personal rule" from 1629 to 1640 when Parliament was not allowed to meet, caused thousands of Puritans to join a "Great Migration." Most went to the sugar islands of the West Indies, but enough chose Massachusetts to ensure its success.

Few still argue, as did some historians of the last generation, that the Puritans came to America to "catch fish" rather than to "praise God," but they did come organized as a business corporation. Two earlier companies, the Dorchester and the New England, founded a small settlement at Salem between 1624 and 1629, but the important firm was the Massachusetts Bay Company, chartered in 1629 to succeed the New England Company. A group of leading Puritans, largely Cambridge-educated and including theologian John Cotton and lawyer John Winthrop, bought up the controlling interest in the Massachusetts Bay Company. For reasons never satisfactorily explained, the charter omitted the usual specifications as to where stockholders should meet. Consequently, the Puritans took it with them to America and made it the constitution of an autonomous Puritan society, "a city upon a hill."

Massachusetts Puritans supplemented the company charter appreciably as their governmental system evolved. The eight Puritan "freemen" or stockholders who attended the first meeting of the company's "General Court" in 1630 reserved virtually all authority to themselves as a "Court of Assistants." Changes in

THE PURITAN HERITAGE

Of all the groups settling in the New World, none has had more pervasive influence on the American culture than the Puritans—yet no group is more difficult to understand. Science has now undercut dogmatic belief; materialism and concentration on the present moment have eclipsed concern for the spirit; moral certainty has been replaced by confusion. It is difficult to imagine what it was like to be a Puritan, but a look into one aspect of their culture—their religious art—may ease the task.

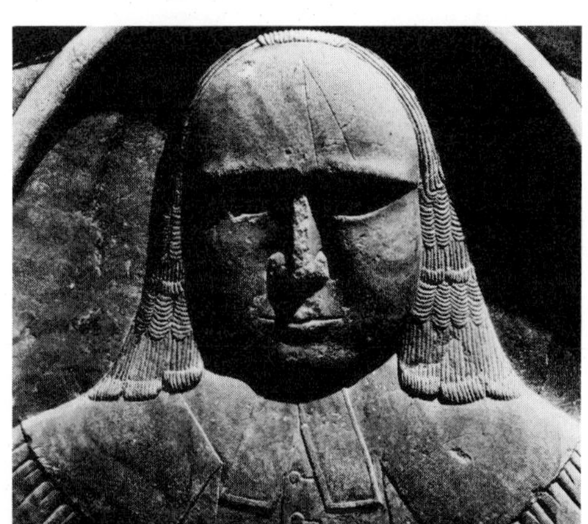

One of the most vexing problems in dealing with the religious art of the Puritans is that they have told us in no uncertain terms that they would have nothing to do with idolatry and the making of religious images. To read their literature, one would suspect that not a single religious symbol was to be found in all of New England, and yet we know that their burial grounds were filled with image-bearing gravestones. For a supposedly iconophobic people, their ready use of the traditional vocabulary of Paleo-Christian symbols is most surprising. Nevertheless, scholars who never ventured out of their dusty libraries continued to promote the idea of Puritan iconophobia well into the twentieth century.

The function of Puritan religious art in the community is still in many ways perplexing, but we can certainly get some idea of their intense preoccupation with the problems of life, death, and resurrection from even the most cursory glance at the images they created. Visual symbols made a much greater impact upon a society virtually bereft of visual materials than they would today when we are bombarded with visual data from the mass media. A picture or a relief sculpture in the seventeenth and eighteenth centuries was something rare, not an item to be quickly looked at and disposed of like the latest magazine. To understand the attraction of graven images, one must imagine a society without extensive figural art, save in the burial ground.

Religious symbols, whether visual or verbal, try to describe the nature of the unknown, and what could be more unknown than the universal mysteries of death and rebirth? That the Puritans created a symbolic art outside the confines of the institutionalized church is most interesting. Notorious organizers, the Puritans institutionalized emotional matters as few other theocentric societies in the seventeenth century ever attempted to do. For example, the profession of sainthood soon became little more than a stylized recitation of a memorized formula rather than the true story of a religious conversion. While these rigid formulas may have quelled the babbling of the merely enthusiastic, they did nothing to assuage the anguish of the religious heart.

The turn from stylized forms of profession within the framework of the church to a deeply symbolic art outside it was an obvious attempt in the face of the awful immensity of death to escape from the rigid rituals of Puritanism. But the turn toward religious art, a stylized form of expression in itself, was not something to be held against Puritanism but something appropriate to it. What began as a radical act to plumb the mysteries of

---

Among scholarly efforts which have brought new insight into the thought and feeling of the Puritans in recent years is a remarkable eight-year study of New England gravestones, Graven Images, *by Allan I. Ludwig (Wesleyan University Press, 1966). This book, which was awarded the John Addison Porter Prize at Yale University in 1964, totals nearly 500 pages of text and photographs, and is an excellent example of how systematic study of artifacts can reveal the past. A sampling of Mr. Ludwig's pictures appears here together with text and captions written especially for this volume.*

death and resurrection became, in the end, yet another stylized Puritan ritual. The most interesting feature of this progressive institutionalization of symbols is that it came from the people themselves rather than from the ministerial elite. This could never have happened in Europe. We know, for example, that as soon as monumental sculpture made its appearance in medieval France, it was taken over almost at once by the Church. Not so in New England. The symbols began and ended as wholly popular forms of expression. Hence we can say that the patterns of Puritan life were so strong at every level of society that what almost surely began as a protest against the arid verbalism and rationality of Puritan dogma became itself programmatic and dogmatic. The most mystical symbols, for example, are always found on the geographical periphery of urbane Puritanism, in faraway Chester, Vermont, for example, rather than in orthodox Boston.

Detail of the Susannah Jayne stone, 1776, Marblehead, Mass. The motif, derived from an English emblem book, pictures death triumphant in the sublunary world but encircled by a hooped snake, a Neo-Platonic symbol of the immortality of the soul.

Preceding page, a detail of the Rev. William Whitwell stone, 1781, Marblehead, Mass., and a fine example of eighteenth-century provincial baroque portraiture in coastal New England. That the majority of these portraits were done for ministers does not protect them from a charge of excessive vanity.

Detail of the left panel of the William Dickson stone, 1692, Cambridge, Mass., attributed to Joseph Lamson of Charlestown. This imp of death carries an arrow and an hourglass, combined symbols of death and time, a theme popular until ca. 1710.

Details of the Strong stone, 1749, South Windsor, Conn.; the Skinner stone, 1753, South Windsor; and the Wolcott marker of 1743 in the same burial ground. Although not in chronological order, the death's head is being transformed into a soul-effigy. Similar transformation took place throughout New England between ca. 1710 and ca. 1750.

Detail of the Sarah Yale stone, 1800, Meriden, Conn., showing a severe linear depiction of the soul-effigy in heaven. The economy of style is characteristic of Connecticut Valley carving influenced by the Neo-Classical style. Many such soul-effigies look like babies, perhaps reflecting the medieval tradition of picturing the soul as a naked baby, indicating its purity and freedom from sin.

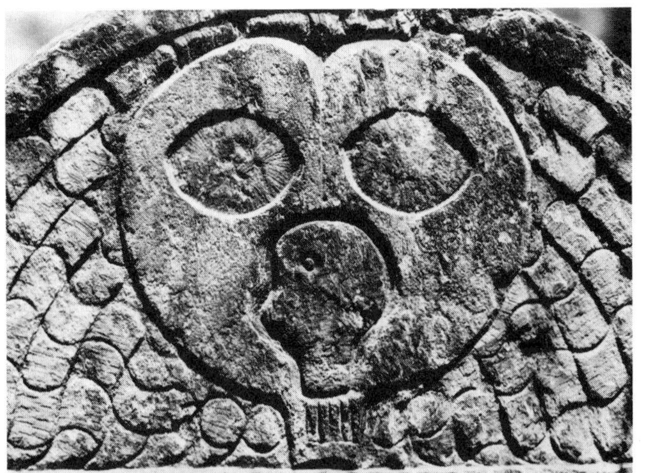

Details of the Holmes stone, 1739, Plymouth, Mass.; the Bradford stone, 1741, Kingston, Mass.; and the Washburn stone of 1743, again in Kingston. Once again the progressive transformation of the traditional death's head to the soul-effigy can be traced. In the first detail, a death's head contains a profile soul-effigy within it. In the last detail, the death's head has been fully transformed into a soul-effigy.

Following page, detail of the Samuel Green stone, 1759, Lexington, Mass. A soul-effigy in heaven appears here, the product of a long series of developments traced back to 1668 in Haverhill, Mass. It was once thought that the Green stone showed some African influence or perhaps some Celtic survival, but both hypotheses have proved false. The style was developed solely in Massachusetts.

the next few years, however, reallocated authority to the General Court, which was itself transformed from an assembly of all freemen into a representative body made up of two delegates from each town, plus the Governor, Deputy, and assistants. After 1631 only members of the government-supported church could vote. A loyalty oath, without reference to the King, bound settlers to support the government of Massachusetts. After a long struggle, town delegates in 1641 secured passage of a bill of rights called the "Body of Liberties," which went well beyond the English common law in protecting people against their government. The unicameral legislature became bicameral in 1644, when the town delegates began to sit separately from the other members. Charles I was beginning action to void the charter and transform Massachusetts into a royal province, as had been done in Virginia, when the English Civil War began.

The separation of religious from governmental functions was much sharper in Puritan New England than in England or in the Anglican colonies of the South. Although only church members had the franchise, town government was distinct from that of the local congregation, rather than merged with it as in England and the Southern colonies. Church officials could censure wrongdoers and even excommunicate them, but New England had no counterpart to the official ecclesiastical courts so powerful in the mother country. The Massachusetts Body of Liberties provided that "no church censure shall degrade or depose any man from an Civill dignitie, office or Authoritie he shall have." However, civil officials still attempted to enforce conformity to Puritan views, and town taxes still provided the minister his compensation.

Qualification for church membership was also somewhat unusual among the Calvinists of New England. English Puritans required only orthodoxy in belief and behavior. Following the lead of John Cotton, however, Massachusetts Puritans began to require in addition the narration of a "conversion experience" in which the candidate had suddenly come much closer to God and to the understanding of religious truth. This requirement reduced the proportion of the population admitted to the church and consequently the proportion permitted to vote in provincial elections as well.

New England's economy developed slowly. Until about 1640, many settlers supported themselves by selling supplies to prosperous newcomers, but the Civil War in England terminated immigration. Thereafter New Englanders began to market fish in the West Indies and southern Europe. They sold furs, timber products, meat, grain, and vegetables as well.

Education ranked high in the Puritan scale of values. Literacy was deemed absolutely essential if people were to understand and obey Biblical teachings. Accordingly, the General Court in the 1640s attempted, with less than complete success, to compel towns of fifty or more families to hire someone to teach reading and writing. Towns of 100 or more were to support a "grammar" school to prepare students for Harvard College. The General Court, aided by an endowment from John Harvard, had established the college in 1636 so that the colony might be supplied with learned ministers to guide the people in doing the will of God.

Roger Williams, another of the Cambridge-educated clergymen who emigrated to colonial America, was perhaps the most notable of many who could testify to the intensity of Puritan intolerance. Williams antagonized the orthodox majority in Massachusetts by arguing that the King had had no right to grant them Indian lands. Still more offensive to them was his assertion that government should not concern itself at all with matters of religion. Banished by the General Court, Williams in 1636 bought land from the Indians at Providence and began a new colony. "God," he would later write in a pamphlet war with his Puritan adversaries, "requireth not a uniformity of religion to be . . . enforced in any civil state; which enforced uniformity . . . is the greatest occasion of civil war, . . . persecution, . . . and . . . hypocrisy." Accordingly, when he secured a charter from Parliament in 1644 to help fend off possible aggression from Massachusetts, it provided for freedom of conscience and full separation of church and state, as well as representative government.

Other settlers exiled from Massachusetts followed Williams to Rhode Island to found other towns. Mrs. Anne Hutchinson stands out among them. While leading discussions at her home, Mrs. Hutchinson had gradually come to the Antinomian belief, heretical to most Puritans, which held that scholarly guidance and an individual's "works" mattered little with reference to salvation. What did matter was the inspiration of God's grace bestowed directly upon individuals such as herself. After her faction, including Governor Sir Henry Vane and theologian John Cotton, lost a not-entirely-fair election in 1637 to orthodox Puritans led by John Winthrop, Mrs. Hutchinson was convicted of heresy and exiled. She then helped found the town of Portsmouth in Rhode Island before moving on to New York, where in 1643 she perished at the hands of Indians.

Connecticut too was an offshoot of Massachusetts, but its founders departed voluntarily and in good religious standing. By 1636 the Reverend Thomas Hooker and others had founded several river towns in the Hartford area. In 1639 the settlers began to govern themselves under what they called "Fundamental Orders." Freemen were to elect a governor yearly, but, as in Massachusetts, a "freeman" meant a Puritan in good standing. Reflecting the spirit of the mother colony, the Fundamental Orders stated that the purpose of the "Confederation" of towns was "to mayntayne . . . the . . . purity of the gospell . . . which we now professe." It specified further that the governor must "be alwayes a member of some approved congregation." A separate colony founded at New Haven by the Reverend John Davenport in 1637 encompassed several other new towns in the area under a government with a Mosaic legal system. In 1662, however, the King's charter merged New Haven with the river towns as the colony of Connecticut, a merger which New Havenites at first regarded coldly but which in time they accepted.

New Hampshire and Maine remained in uncertain status for many years. The council for New England, a reorganized Plymouth Company which owned all ungranted lands in New England, awarded much of the area to Sir Ferdinando Gorgas and John Mason in 1622. Each tried to colonize and govern the area, but so did neighboring Massachusetts. Finally, in 1677, Massachusetts bought the claims of the Gorgas heirs and thus acquired control of Maine. New Hampshire became a separate royal province in 1679.

Like Virginia, New England had its share of Indian wars. In the Pequot War in 1637, New Englanders almost exterminated one powerful tribe. That helped preserve peace until 1675 when "King Philip's War" broke out. Indians under King Philip's leadership burned dozens of towns and killed several hundred settlers before they were defeated by several colonies linked together in the New England Confederation. Philip was killed; his wife and son were sold into West Indian slavery.

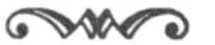

Maryland

Maryland was the last English colony begun before the English Civil War. It originated in the grateful admiration of both early Stuart monarchs, James I and Charles I, for George Calvert. A major administrator under James I, Calvert had had a hand in the Virginia Company and the Council for New England and had tried unsuccessfully to colonize Newfoundland between 1622 and 1627. After his conversion to Catholicism, a religion still tainted with disloyalty in England, he resigned his administration post in 1625, but was made a peer—Lord Baltimore—in recognition of his service. Still interested in colonization, Lord Baltimore visited Virginia in 1628. Four years later he persuaded Charles I to detach from Virginia an area north of the Potomac to be a new colony, Maryland, named officially for Queen Henrietta Maria, but actually for the Virgin Mary.

Maryland's charter, issued after the death of George Calvert to his son Cecilius, the second Lord Baltimore, granted the area to Calvert as "proprietor" rather than to a business corporation. Corporations had not only proved troublesome, especially in Massachusetts, but reflected the mistaken belief that American colonies would be profitable trading posts like those in Asia. Proprietorship correctly identified land as the major source of wealth to be found in English America. The proprietor, rather than the King, granted lands to settlers; his income came mainly from "quitrents." Another holdover from the medieval era, quitrents were a small tax (first, two shillings, and later, four shillings per hundred acres) paid in perpetuity and freeing the payer from other traditional obligations to the landlord. Maryland quitrents afforded the generally absentee Calvert family "gentlemanly" income until the American Revolution.

Economic development in Maryland proceeded rapidly. As in Virginia, tobacco sustained the economy. The example of Virginia, as well as its proximity, helped the new neighbors to minimize troublesome encounters with the nearby Indians and to avoid a "starving time."

Religious and political developments were more turbulent. George Calvert had hoped that Maryland would be a refuge for English Catholics, against whom legal discrimination was severe. Relatively few English Catholics, however, chose to migrate. Those who did constituted essentially a ruling class of large landowners, but they were always outnumbered by Protestants, even on the *Ark* which brought the first settlers in 1634. Migration from Virginia did not improve the balance. The Puritan ascendancy in England, confirmed in 1649 by the beheading of Charles I, augured poorly also. Under these circumstances the Catholic minority enacted a Toleration Act in 1649. It affirmed that those "professing to believe in Jesus Christ" should not be "discountenanced" for their religious views, prevented from exercising them, or "compelled to the . . . exercise of any other Religion." It prescribed death for those who denied the Trinity, fines or whipping for lesser heresies. As the Catholics had feared, the Protestants did gain ascendancy in the 1650s after a Catholic acting-governor had refused to acknowledge the existing Puritan government in England. The Protestants repealed the Toleration Act, but with the backing of the English government after 1656, the Calverts and the Catholic faction regained control and hastened to restore it.

British West Indies

Caribbean islands which could produce tropical products such as sugar appeared infinitely more desirable to Europe's rival imperial powers than colonies in the temperate regions of North America. Spain quickly occupied the larger islands such as Cuba and Santo Domingo, but it largely ignored the innumerable smaller ones. Long the resort of pirates preying upon Spanish commerce, these islands began in the seventeenth century to be important in addition as potential producers of sugar, tobacco, cotton, and indigo. By the time of the great Puritan emigration in the 1630s England controlled several islands, notably Barbados. This tiny island, roughly one-third the size of Rhode Island, had in the 1650s the largest population of any English colony. When Oliver Cromwell cast imperialist eyes across the Atlantic, he directed his first effort at Santo Domingo (now Haiti and the Dominican Republic). The Spanish there proved too tough, however, so he settled in 1655 for the less developed Spanish island of Jamaica. The French and the Dutch also engaged in island grabbing from the Spanish in the same period. Whatever their nationality, West Indian planters usually had their slaves produce largely for export instead of striving for self-sufficiency. The result was that the West Indies became a major market for food and lumber exporters on the continent of North America.

New Netherland

The Dutch Republic was a major world power for half a century before it gained official recognition of its independence from Spain in 1648. Aggressive Dutch Protestants had made their homeland the maritime, commercial, financial, and, in some measure, the cultural center of Europe. They had replaced the Portuguese in control of the most remunerative Asian trading posts. They were also leaders in plundering Spain's American commerce.

Dutch interest in continental North America began with Henry Hudson's voyage of 1609. No settlement followed immediately, partly because of a truce concluded with Spain the same year. When war resumed in 1621, the Dutch formed a West India Company to exploit trading and plundering prospects in America at Spain's expense. In 1624 the company set up a fur-trading post, Fort Orange, at Albany, and two years later made their well-known purchase of Manhattan Island. There New Amsterdam was founded.

Trading for furs was the principal business in New Netherland. The Hudson-Mohawk Rivers afforded the Dutch the best natural route into North America between the St. Lawrence and the Mississippi. Inhabiting that region were the five "nations" of the remarkable Iroquois Confederacy. Inveterate enemies of the Algonquin tribes of the St. Lawrence region, who were becoming allies and dependents of the French, the Iroquois quickly attached themselves to the Dutch. In time, their superior organization and skill in warfare enabled them to become middlemen in the trade between the Dutch at Albany and other Indian tribes farther west.

The acquisition of land interested other Dutchmen, particularly Kiliaen van Rensselaer, a wealthy Amsterdam merchant and company stockholder. Under the headright principle, which granted lands to those who brought immigrants, Van Rensselaer acquired enormous holdings in the Albany region. The company also gave "patroons" such as Van Rensselaer quasi-feudal powers over their tenants.

Insecurity was constant in New Netherland. In 1643 an Indian attack on Manhattan forced the Dutch to call on New England for aid. In 1655 the Dutch captured a rival Swedish settlement on the Delaware River, but still they had only a few people there adjacent to rapidly growing Maryland. To the north, New Englanders vastly outnumbered them. Settlers of New England origin were also very numerous within their colony's borders. Most serious of all threats, however, was the growing maritime power of England.

Restoration England, 1660–1689

Prosperity in England after midcentury reduced the economic pressures for migration, but it also intensified the commercial rivalry with the Dutch. Seeking to bar Dutch shipping from English commerce, Cromwell's government in 1651 passed a Navigation Act which required that imports be carried by English ships or those of the producing nation. The Anglo-Dutch naval war of 1652 to 1654 settled nothing. Charles II, "restored" to the throne in 1660 in place of his beheaded father, was no less anti-Dutch than the Puritans. He magnanimously conferred the Dutch colony of New Netherland upon his brother James, Duke of York, who sent a naval expedition to seize the colony in 1664. The second Anglo-Dutch War (1665–1667) followed. At its conclusion the Dutch ceded New Netherland to England, partly because it was incapable of self-defense, and partly because they needed to concentrate on defending their homeland from the French. The Dutch recaptured New Netherland in the last Anglo-Dutch War (1672–1674) but returned it at the war's end.

Developments in England meanwhile were transforming the nation from a French ally against the Dutch to a Dutch ally against the French. Charles II was unhappy with the requirement, fixed at his restoration, that only Anglicans could legally hold government positions. He hoped in fact to restore Catholicism to England, but he recognized the depth of public opposition. Despite assurance of French support, he refrained even from embracing Catholicism himself until almost the moment of his death. His brother and heir, James, Duke of York, was less cautious; he announced his conversion to Catholicism in 1676. Followed by exaggerated revelations of the French commitment, this act helped to provoke an outbreak of anti-Catholic, anti-French hysteria from 1678 to 1680 over the "Popish plot." Many Catholics whose only offense was their belief were executed.

In these circumstances, efforts began in Parliament to replace James in the line of succession with his Protestant daughter Mary. As she had married the Dutch ruler, William of

Orange, such a succession would both preclude the possibility of a Catholic monarch and cement an alliance with the Protestant Dutch against Catholic France. Charles II prevented Parliament from excluding his brother, who then acceded to the throne in 1685. For three years England's anti-Catholic majority tolerated a Catholic monarch. Then in 1688 the King's second wife, also Catholic, bore a son, who took precedence in the succession line over his Protestant half sister, Mary. That finished James II. A national consensus such as that which had restored Charles II in 1660 now ousted James II in favor of William and Mary. Their accession confirmed both Parliamentary supremacy and a Protestant succession. The deposed King took refuge in France where Louis XIV vowed to restore him. The ensuing War of the League of Augsburg (1689–1697), which also involved general European resistance to French expansionism, began a century of conflict between England and France for dominant status in Europe and control of North America.

New English Colonies, 1660–1689

England's conquest of New Netherland in 1664 resulted in the creation of several new colonies. For himself, the Duke of York kept as a proprietary possession the area since known as New York, which became a royal province at his accession in 1685. The "Duke's laws" which he promulgated in 1665 permitted freedom of conscience and election of local officers, but no provincial legislature. He authorized such an assembly in 1683, but after his accession he disavowed the "Charter of Liberties" which it had passed and dissolved it. On the eve of the "Glorious Revolution" which overthrew him, James II lumped New York, New Jersey, and all New England colonies into a Dominion of New England, to be governed without a representative legislature.

By gift of the Duke of York, present-day New Jersey became the possession of Sir George Carteret and Lord John Berkeley in 1664. Their "Concessions and Agreements" of 1665 permitted a representative legislature plus religious freedom and easy access to land (subject to quitrents). Quakers, including William Penn, were prominent among the bewildering succession of proprietors who bought or inherited parts of the colony. It was divided into East and West Jersey from 1676 until 1702 when the halves were rejoined to form a royal province, which shared its Governor with New York until 1738.

Pennsylvania and Delaware, the remaining colonies carved out of New Netherland, became the proprietary possessions of William Penn, a dedicated member of a new religious group, the Quakers. Chartered in 1681, Pennsylvania was apparently the repayment of a debt owed by Charles II to Penn's father, an admiral and wealthy land holder. Its charter required provincial authorities to enforce England's Navigation Acts. It also gave the King's Privy Council power to "disallow" colonial laws within five years and to hear appeals from colonial courts. Conveyance of Delaware was somewhat imprecise, but the Stuarts, both Charles II and the then Duke of York, apparently intended that Penn should have it. Penn exercised proprietary control from 1682, although Delaware had a legislature separate from Pennsylvania's after 1703.

Quaker beliefs, already represented in tolerant Rhode Island, New Jersey, and North

Carolina, were the very foundation of society in the two colonies of William Penn. The name "Quaker" originated as a derisive reference to their insistence that one should "tremble at the name of the Lord." Officially members were, and are, "Friends." George Fox, onetime shoemaker's apprentice from Nottingham, began the movement amid the religious ferment of the English Civil War in 1647. He believed that the ultimate religious authority was neither a church organization nor even the Bible but an "inner light" by which God made known the path of righteousness to each individual conscience. Associated with this concept was a dogmatic dedication to equality. One person's "inner light" was likely to be as good as another's.

Consequently, Quakers had no paid clergy. They listened respectfully to anyone, man or woman, who felt moved to speak in their ritual-free meetings. They dressed plainly, refused to observe the custom of doffing their hats in the presence of presumed social superiors, and addressed everyone, regardless of rank, as "thee" or "thou"—terms customarily reserved for people of inferior status. They were also pacifists. Deemed dangerously heretical and offensively zealous in their proselytizing, they were frequently jailed. In Massachusetts, several were executed; more suffered whipping. Yet the movement gained numerous converts in Britain and in Northern Europe as well.

Penn, a Quaker missionary jailed several times for his nonconformity, conceived his colony as a "Holy Experiment" and a refuge for Quakers and other victims of religious persecution. A representative assembly, required in fact by his charter, existed from the start. After experimenting with two "Frames of Government" in 1681 and 1682, Penn granted in 1701 a "Charter of Liberties" which abolished the appointed Council, a strongly aristocratic influence in most other colonies, in favor of a unicameral legislature. Henceforth an elected assembly and a governor appointed by the proprietor ruled Pennsylvania. The colony's legal code reduced the list of capital crimes, innumerable in England, to murder and treason. Like Roger Williams, Penn saw the Indians as entitled to compensation for their land, and he made such payment to their satisfaction. He then sold land to settlers on relatively easy terms. A quitrent was included but could not often be collected. Penn advertised his lands, with reference to religious freedom and its form of government, in pamphlets distributed widely in Britain and in Northern Europe. These circumstances, plus a prospering economy based on the sale of lumber and food, especially flour, to the West Indies, produced very rapid immigration. Prominent among the immigrants were the "Pennsylvania Dutch" (a corruption of "Deutsch," the German word for "German"), many of whom had an Anabaptist religious heritage similar in its essentials to that of the Quakers.

Carolina and Georgia

Plans for a colony between Spanish Florida and Virginia had existed before the English Civil War, but real progress began only with the Restoration. Charles II granted a proprietary charter in 1663 (which was supplemented in 1665) to eight notables, including his chief minister, the Earl of Clarendon. Most active of the proprietors in the enterprise was

Sir Anthony Ashley Cooper, later Earl of Shaftesbury. The charters authorized the proprietors to disallow provincial laws and to act as an appellate court. Religious freedom was assured, but a charter amendment in 1670 made Anglicanism the official religion.

Before the first settlers had departed from England, the proprietors promulgated the "Fundamental Constitutions," which had been drawn up by Cooper in collaboration with the political philosopher John Locke. A target of American ridicule ever since, the plan called for a hierarchy descending from the proprietors through "Landgraves," "Caciques" (Spanish for "chiefs"), and manor lords to freeholders. A few pretentious settlers tried to implement the plan, but the Assembly never endorsed it. It remained merely a plan.

The realities of settlement in time imposed another conclusion upon the proprietors of Carolina (Latin for "Charles"). Farmers from backcountry Virginia had begun settling adjacent areas of what was to become North Carolina a decade before the issuance of the charter. Limited access to ocean shipping, due to the nature of the rivers and the coastline, precluded the development of much large-scale commercial agriculture. North Carolina's settlers were typically people of little capital whose interest was subsistence farming. Among them were many New Englanders, including numerous Quakers. Disdainful Virginia planters later referred to their area as "lubberland" and to them as undesirables.

South Carolina's settlers, in contrast, included small planters squeezed out of overcrowded Barbados, cultured Protestant refugees (Huguenots) from France, and Englishmen of some capital or influence, as well as New Englanders. The splendid harbor of "Charles Towne" (settled downriver from the present site in 1670 but moved a decade later) offered every encouragement to the development of overseas commerce. Such commercial development assured from the beginning that South Carolina would be distinctly aristocratic. Official recognition that two differing societies existed came in 1712, when North Carolina received a separate government.

Present-day Georgia was part of the original Carolina grant, but fear of the Spanish in Florida (who had destroyed an infringing settlement in 1686) delayed its development for half a century. Settlement began in 1732 under the leadership of James Oglethorpe. Oglethorpe was a general who had fought against the Spanish and was eager to build a military bastion to confine them to Florida. As head of a Parliamentary investigating group, Oglethorpe had also become aware of the large numbers of noncriminal debtors languishing in English jails. He hoped to give such unfortunates a new start and establish his military bastion as well by settling them as farmers and militiamen in Georgia. The Crown accordingly conferred the land upon him and nineteen others as proprietary trustees until 1753.

Oglethorpe and his colleagues planned meticulously for the development of Georgia, but they planned more with reference to the needs of England and their conception of a good society than to opportunities in Georgia. Appalled at the volume of England's purchases of foreign silk, they fixed detailed requirements designed to develop silk production in Georgia. As in Virginia more than a century before, these plans failed. Competitive production of silk required labor which was both skilled and cheap. In Georgia, as elsewhere in America, it was neither. Considerations which seemed plausible in England had led the proprietors to exclude slaves, to limit land grants

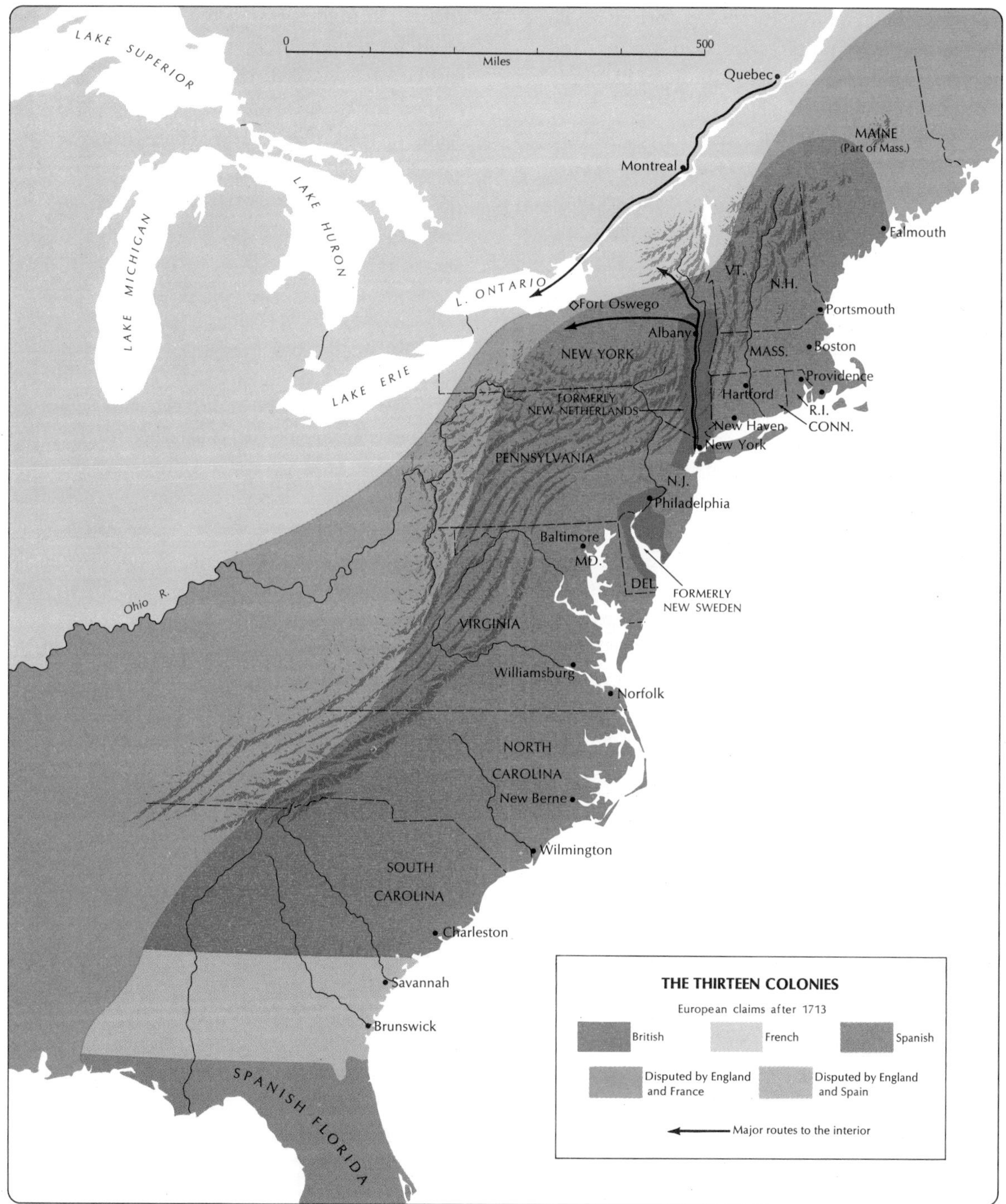

Competition for Colonies

to a maximum of 500 acres, to forbid resale of the fifty-acre plots awarded the poor, and to ban rum. The settlers, although carefully screened in England, chafed under such restrictions. They wanted particularly the opportunity to get rich, as had many South Carolinians, by cultivating rice on large plantations with Negro labor. While Georgia did afford a refuge for selected indigents and for religious refugees, chiefly German, its settlers stubbornly resisted the pattern of life prescribed for them. By 1752 when the royal government took over the province from the trustees, most of the early restrictions had been lifted and Georgia was rapidly becoming indistinguishable from South Carolina.

New France

French fishermen had begun exploiting the Grand Banks area off Newfoundland shortly after 1500. To reduce the amount of salt required to preserve their catch, they began drying fish on Cape Breton Island and the Gaspé peninsula and while waiting for their fish to dry, they traded with the Indians. Thus began the fur trade which became the economic foundation of New France. Its basis was the Indian demand for such European wares as cloth, metal pots, guns, knives, and liquor, combined with Indian ability to supply furs, chiefly beaver, which was used in making a kind of hat long in vogue among European gentlemen.

Successful colonization by the French, as with the English, began only in the seventeenth century. In 1608, while the English were floundering at Jamestown, Samuel de Champlain, who had made several earlier expeditions, founded Quebec. Two years later the French began another settlement at Port Royal (now Annapolis Royal, Nova Scotia). Like the first English colonies, these ventures of trading companies failed to return a profit.

Part of the explanation for the difficulties of French trading companies was the hostility of the Iroquois. Starting in 1609, Champlain had helped the Hurons of the St. Lawrence area to push the aggressive Iroquois farther southward. But the Iroquois struck back. Like pirates of the Spanish Main, they plundered "fur fleets" coming down the St. Lawrence waterway. In the 1640s, they drove the Hurons out of the St. Lawrence Valley and diverted much of the fur trade to their Dutch friends at Albany. In the 1660s, however, the French government took over the colony from the private investors, and its army, Europe's finest, curbed Iroquois aggressions.

Population and agricultural settlement in New France developed very slowly. By the end of the seventeenth century there were probably thirty or forty settlers in the English continental colonies for every one in New France. The reasons for the disparity were varied. The government excluded Protestants. Catholic missionaries at times discouraged immigration because they thought most immigrants were an unfortunate influence on their Indian converts. The French felt no great compulsion to leave their homeland. Much has been made of the authoritarian political structure of New France and of its essentially feudal land system as deterrents to immigration, but these differed little from conditions in France.

Despite the population advantage enjoyed by the English in America, the French cause was by no means hopeless. In Europe, for one thing, the population advantage was theirs:

they outnumbered the English more than two to one. In America most Indian tribes were on their side. So was geography. With no such Appalachian barrier as blocked the English path to the interior, the French (Marquette and Joliet) were on the Mississippi by 1673. By 1682, La Salle had followed the river to the Gulf of Mexico and claimed Louisiana in the name of Louis XIV. Thus, while the English had more people in America, the French had more land. To keep it they had in France a formidable army backed by the resources of a numerous, productive people under an aggressive, authoritarian government.

Conclusion

Ruthless as was the rivalry among the nations of early modern Europe, it was inevitable that competition for colonies would follow Spain's successful exploitation of America's resources, especially its gold and silver. By the end of the sixteenth century, the Dutch, English, and French were each strong enough to pose a challenge to Spain's monopoly. The Dutch carved out New Netherland, extending from New York to Delaware, but lost it to the English in the Anglo-Dutch Wars. The English established Virginia as an economic venture which ultimately repaid the nation, although not the original investors, by production of tobacco. Religious dissidents, chiefly Puritan, established several colonies, in New England, where they hoped to enjoy autonomy. The willingness of the British to risk the dangers of emigration for the opportunity to acquire land and improve their status made possible the creation of several other continental colonies as well. By 1700, what is now the eastern seaboard of the United States from South Carolina to Maine was firmly in British hands. France meanwhile had occupied the St. Lawrence and Mississippi Valleys and, despite the paucity of French colonists, posed a military threat to the British provinces, of which the settlers there would long remain acutely conscious.

SUGGESTED READINGS

England's seventeenth-century turmoil, which had so much influence on American history, receives a penetrating scrutiny in Christopher Hill's *The Century of Revolution*, 1603–1714 (1961). Mildred Campbell characterizes *The English Yeoman* (1942); and Lawrence F. Stone, *The Crisis of the Aristocracy*, 1558–1641 (1965). Wallace Notestein, in *The English People on the Eve of Colonization** (1954), depicts the stable features of English society. William Haller's *Rise of Puritanism** (1938) is authoritative; Alan Simpson's *Puritanism in Old and New England** (1955) is shorter and simpler.

W. F. Craven's *The Southern Colonies in the Seventeenth Century* (1949) covers its subject superbly. R. L. Morton's two volumes on *Colonial Virginia* (1960) read so easily one forgets their length. Philip Barbour has studied a leading figure in *The Three Worlds of Captain John Smith* (1964). Neither Maryland nor North Carolina has fared as well in historical literature as Virginia, but South Carolina is the subject of a fine political study by M. E. Sirmans, *Colonial South Carolina* (1966).

New England's early history has attracted innumerable scholars. On Plymouth, George Langdon's *Pilgrim Colony* (1966) provides a modern supplement to William Bradford's classic *Of Plymouth Plantations*, edited by Samuel Eliot Morison in 1952. The harsh view of Puritanism in such older works as J. T. Adams's *The Founding of New England** (1921) and V. L. Parrington's *Main Currents in American Thought: The Colonial Mind** (1927) is offset by the sympathetic consideration in several more recent works: Perry Miller's *Orthodoxy in Massachusetts** (1933), *The New England Mind: The 17th Century** (1939), and *Errand into the Wilderness** (1956); Edmund S. Morgan's *Visible Saints** (1963) and *The Puritan Dilemma** (1958), a biography of John Winthrop; Norman Pettit's *The Heart Prepared* (1966); Larzer Ziff's *The Career of John Cotton* (1962). Morgan's *Visible Saints* is the easiest of these to follow and modifies Miller's conclusions significantly. George L. Haskins's *Law and Authority in Early Massachusetts* (1960) is a superb study with a broader focus than its title suggests. Bernard Bailyn's *The New England Merchants in the Seventeenth Century* (1955) traces the development of New England's export economy. D. B. Rutman's *Winthrop's Boston* (1965) is an excellent study of the growth of that town, and Sumner C. Powell in *Puritan Village* (1963) describes the founding of a smaller town and its English background. Connecticut's early years may be seen in Robert C. Black III's *The Younger John Winthrop* (1966). Edmund S. Morgan's *Roger Williams: The Church and the State* (1967) is the most recent of several studies of Rhode Island's founder.

Really good books on the Middle Colonies are rare. William Penn still lacks a worthy biography. Among the best works on the colonial history of Pennsylvania are those of F. B. Tolles: *James Logan* (1957), which deals with a close associate of Penn's; *Quakers and the Atlantic Community* (1960), which supplements R. M. Jones's *The Quakers in the American Colonies** (1911); and *Meetinghouse and Countinghouse** (1948), which focuses on Philadelphia's Quaker merchants. The state of New Jersey has sponsored a series of short historical works which includes excellent volumes by R. P. McCormick, *New Jersey from Colony to State, 1609–1789* (1964); W. F. Craven's *New Jersey and the English Colonization of North America* (1964); and John Pomfret's *The New Jersey Proprietors and Their Lands, 1664–1776* (1964). New York's landed aristocracy may be perceived in S. G. Nissenson's *The Patroon's Domain* (1937) and L. H. Leder's *Robert Livingston* (1961).

French colonizing efforts take a major place in the magnificent multivolume work of Francis Parkman produced between 1851 and 1892, superbly abridged in one volume, *The Parkman Reader* (1955), by S. E. Morison. G. M. Wrong's *The Rise and Fall of New France* (2 vols., 1928) is more modern in tone. Gustave Lanctot's three-volume work, *A History of Canada* (1965), presents the story of New France in French-Canadian perspective.

* indicates availability in paperback.

3

Economic and Cultural Development

OVER TWO MILLION people of European and African ancestry inhabited Britain's original continental colonies by 1770. Immigration accounted for much of the population growth, but an incredibly high rate of natural increase was a still more important cause. Both reflected a continuing high level of prosperity.

American prosperity had solid foundations, especially in the abundance of land. In Europe most people had access to only small plots of land; the growth of population aggravated already-overcrowded conditions. In America most free persons could gain access to more land than they could possibly use. Producing beyond their own subsistence needs, Americans naturally exchanged their surplus for imported commodities.

Each of four colonial regions developed distinctive export economies. Virginia and Maryland, the "Tobacco Coast," became the principal suppliers of the world market for tobacco. On plantations similar to those of the Tobacco Coast, the Lower South (the two Carolinas and Georgia) produced rice and indigo for overseas sale. New England, while its farms produced little exportable surplus except timber products, earned income overseas with its fish, some manufactured items, and the sale of shipping services. The Middle, or "Bread," Colonies (New York, New Jersey, Pennsylvania, and Delaware) developed an extensive commerce based on surplus wheat and other products of family-size farms.

Gradually the transplanted Europeans who

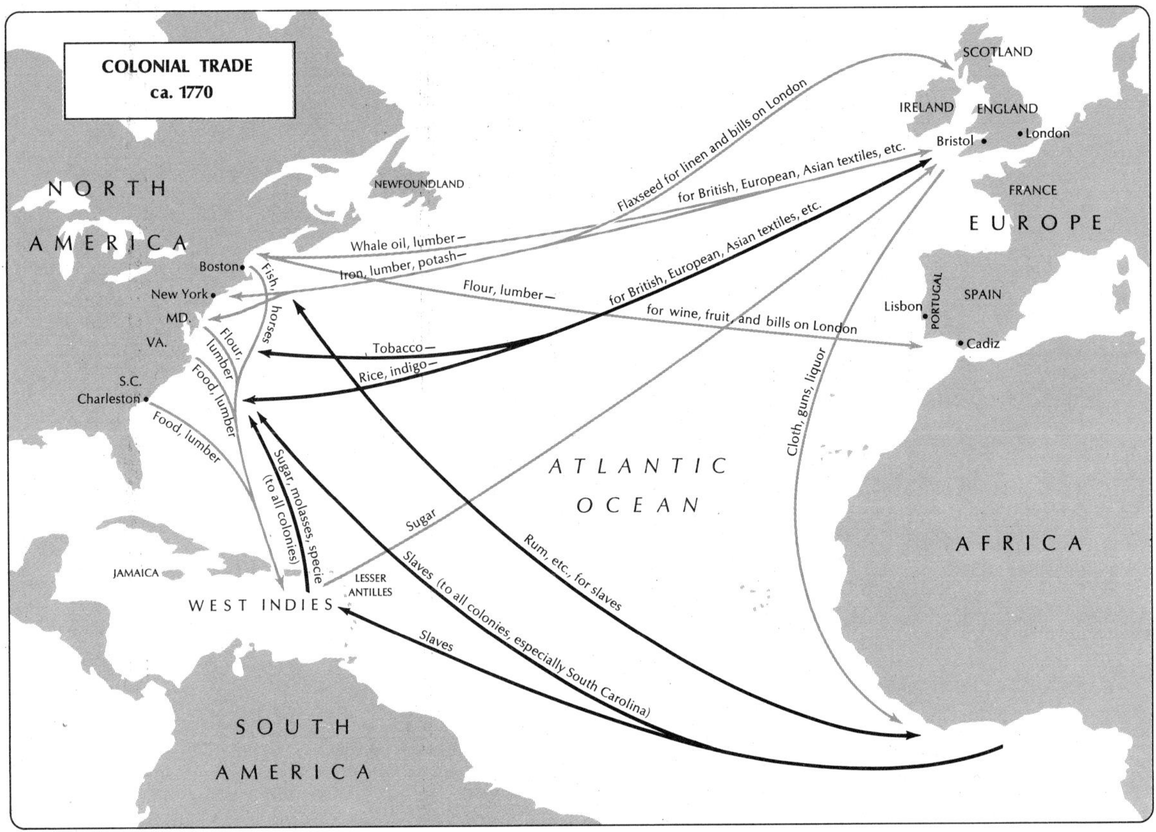

were struggling to build new communities in the American wilderness began to lose their old world identification and to adopt new patterns of living and a new self-conception. The American environment—with its hostile Indians as well as its abundance of land and timber—forced some adjustments and permitted others. The absence of nobles among the immigrants allowed men and women of middle- and lower-class backgrounds to build in America a new social order—one differing quite sharply from that of the stable agricultural regions of Europe, where aristocratic traditions carried over from feudalism still prevailed. In time Europeans began to see characteristics and interests common to these British colonial subjects and to lump them together as "Americans." The colonists, however, continued for the most part to think of themselves as British subjects of particular provinces. Only in the Revolutionary period did they begin to sense the unity attributed them by Europeans.

The Southern Economy

Below the Mason-Dixon line which separates Pennsylvania from Maryland, a longer growing season permitted cultivation of crops which could not be grown commercially in the North or in Britain. A wide coastal plain abounding in natural waterways provided Southerners with both favorable conditions for tillage and inexpensive avenues of transportation. Thus Southern settlers could expect to market their large crops cheaply and without competition from producers in Britain itself or in the Northern colonies. Accordingly, those Southern settlers who could afford to do so invested heavily both in land and in bound laborers to produce a staple agricultural commodity for export. The plantation became a characteristic feature of the Southern economy.

Tobacco, produced largely in the Chesapeake Bay area, was the most important plantation crop and by far the most important of all American exports throughout the colonial period. The European market for tobacco had grown rapidly, despite much intense opposition to the Indian habit of smoking. In the 1630s Britain was importing as much as 3 million pounds of American tobacco yearly; by the 1670s roughly 14 million pounds; by the 1770s about 100 million pounds. Such a production record was possible only because the Caribbean region had largely abandoned tobacco at an early date in order to concentrate on growing sugar, a product even more in demand.

Securing land was the first step in becoming a tobacco planter. Throughout much of the seventeenth century, men of wealth could claim 50 acres for each immigrant whose passage they had paid. By exploiting this "headright" law, often corruptly, many men built up extensive holdings. Purchasing from the government or even from speculators was also relatively easy. "Every person," a traveler claimed in 1759, "may with ease procure a small plantation, can ship his tobacco at his own door, and live independently." He exaggerated, of course, but many immigrants were able to save enough as laborers or tenants to purchase land. By 1760 thousands of such small farmers were competing with the great planters in raising tobacco for export.

Whatever the extent of his land holdings, a tobacco planter remained a "one-hogshead man," able to produce only one or two hogsheads of cured tobacco yearly, unless he could secure bound laborers. Most free persons simply would not long remain agricultural laborers when they could so easily become landowners. Recognizing the labor problem at a very early date, the London Company sent over poor orphan children to be bound to planters as apprentices. From this practice there evolved the tradition of indentured servitude, or contract labor. Shippers transported poor Englishmen to the tobacco coast and sold them to planters. The planters' payment compensated the shipper for affording passage; the indentured servant then worked for the planter, usually for about four years, to repay him. The system financed immigration, alleviated the labor shortage, and afforded immigrants both assurance of a livelihood on their arrival and training for making a living in America. "Freedom dues" fixed by local custom, sometimes including land, helped the immigrant to get started on his own. By 1666, three of every four Virginians had been or was then an indentured servant.

Not all indentured servants came voluntarily. Some were kidnap victims (though not as many as claimed to be); some twenty thousand were convicts, including major offenders as well as those jailed merely for debt. "Transportation" and fourteen years of indentured servitude was long an alternative to execution for those convicted of capital crimes in England. Oddly, some such convicts "did chuse to be hanged ere they would go thither, and were."

Indentured servants were chiefly English, until about 1660. Thereafter prosperity plus government concern over depopulation brought a decline in English emigration. Families from northern Ireland, Scotland, and Germany, however, took up the slack. Upon their arrival, families of "redemptioners" or "free willers" usually sold one or more members of the family into servitude to pay for the passage of all. In the eighteenth century, Pennsylvania replaced the Tobacco Coast as the chief market for indentured servants. Tobacco planters by then had come to prefer another bound labor system.

A passing Dutch warship, John Rolfe wrote in 1619, "sold us twenty negars." This arrival, it is worth noting, preceded that of the Pilgrims at Plymouth by one year. Considered as indentured servants rather than slaves, some of these Negroes acquired freedom, property, and even the right to vote. Gradually, however, the white population began to impose slave status upon imported Negroes. By the 1660s Virginia laws had declared that imported Negro laborers and the offspring of all slavewomen would be slaves for life.

No known evidence explains clearly why Virginia made Negroes slaves rather than indentured servants. Part of the explanation is probably historical. Slavery had long existed among West African Negroes as it had in some parts of Europe until about the time of Columbus, chiefly to provide domestic servants, however, rather than workers for commercial enterprise. After the discovery of America, a great market for slaves developed in the mines and the plantations of the Spanish and Portuguese colonies. Capitalizing upon this new market, coastal tribes in West Africa began to capture and sell greatly increased numbers of their inland neighbors in order to enlarge their own purchases of European goods, chiefly textiles, weapons, and liquor. Thus, by the time the first blacks arrived in Virginia, a century of precedent existed elsewhere in the Americas for fixing slave status upon those Negroes offered for sale as workers.

Prejudice and economic interest also contributed to fixing slave status upon Virginia Negroes. As the name "Negro" suggests ("negro" is Spanish for "black"), what impressed Europeans most about the West Africans was the darkness of their skin. Whatever the psychological explanation, this difference in color created for many Europeans an initial prejudice against Negroes and with it a desire for a social system which would hold them permanently apart as an inferior caste. Slave status served that purpose. Slave status was also economically advantageous to the purchaser. Not only did slaves serve for life rather than only a few years, but their progeny were similarly bound, not free as was the case with the offspring of indentured servants.

Despite the economic advantages they offered, Negro slaves did not become a major factor in the development of the Tobacco Coast until the eighteenth century. For most of the seventeenth century, the Dutch had been the principal purveyors of slaves, and British mercantilist principles discouraged purchasing from them. Late in the century, the British replaced the Dutch as the world's leading slave sellers, but until the end of the century the trade was monopolized legally by the somewhat complacent Royal Africa Company. The opening of the slave trade to free competition at the end of the century greatly increased the supply and reduced the price. By 1750 four of every ten Virginians were black. In Maryland, the proportion was roughly three in ten.

Historians have established relatively few

points concerning slavery in the eighteenth century. Contrary to a legend of some popularity in the South, merchants in the northern colonies played a relatively small role in the slave trade. They found it difficult to compete with English merchants in supplying what the West Africans wanted in exchange. Slave mortality was high, not only on the notorious "middle passage" across the Atlantic, but also in the "seasoning" period after arrival. No study of this subject exists for the Tobacco Coast, but in Barbados, where admittedly work was harder, food less plentiful, and the climate less healthy, nearly half of the new slaves died within three years. To the planters there it seemed that slaves would "revenge the slightest mistreatment by dying." Most slave owners in Virginia held only a few, although many large planters owned over one hundred. Accustomed to agricultural work at home, Africans took to tobacco culture more readily than did the few enslaved Indians. Many of them, reflecting a high level of artisan skills in Africa, became skilled craft workers whose services the master rented out.

British regulation was an important factor in the development of the Tobacco Coast. From 1660 one of Britain's famous Navigation Acts required that tobacco, as an "enumerated" commodity, be sent only to British ports. Initially American production was expected only to supply the British market, but by the eve of the Revolution, Britain was re-exporting 60 to 70 percent of its tobacco imports from America, sometimes over 90 percent. Thus, while Americans produced the world's supply of tobacco, it was the British who sold it to foreign markets.

Debt was a major problem for nearly all tobacco planters. "Debts had become hereditary . . . for many generations," wrote planter Thomas Jefferson, "so that the planters were a species of property annexed to certain mercantile houses in London." Probably not even the planters themselves understood clearly why this was so, but overproduction was certainly one cause. By oversupplying the world market, Chesapeake planters repeatedly depressed the price of their product. Neither crop-destroying riots nor restrictive legislation, both of which the British condemned, could solve the problem. Planters often overestimated their income from tobacco sales and ordered European goods on the same mistaken calculations. To make payments on the resulting debts, they had to ship still more tobacco, thus further depressing the price.

Diversification followed naturally from the poor prospects in tobacco culture. George Washington, a particularly acute businessman, turned to speculating in Western lands and to making cloth. Robert Carter, another wealthy planter, leased most of his lands to tenants, whom he required to grow wheat for export. He also invested in various manufacturing endeavors. Despite such efforts, however, tobacco still made up 75 percent of the value of the Tobacco Coast exports as late as 1775.

In the Lower South, the first settlers hoped to establish plantations, but they had trouble finding suitable crops. While they were experimenting, an export economy based on deer hides, cattle, naval stores, and lumber developed. Deer hides, secured in trade with the Indians, were used extensively in Europe for clothing and long remained an important export. Frontier "crackers" (so called from the noise of the whips they used) drove cattle from the wild lands of the interior to seaboard slaughterhouses which prepared meat for export. Lumbering, often a sideline industry for those who were clearing land for agriculture, enjoyed a vast market, although competition from frontier settlers in every colonial region kept prices low. On the eve of the Revolution, lumber products ranked behind only tobacco, wheat flour, rice, and fish in export value.

Naval stores (tar, pitch, turpentine, and resin) became significant exports from the Carolinas after Britain began to subsidize their production during the War of the Spanish Succession (1702–1713). Britain did so in order to be sure of a supply of materials indispensable for ship construction. Production had declined considerably, however, before the Revolution.

Rice became the export staple of the Lower South within a few years after the introduction of superior seed from Madagascar in 1695. Parliament normally taxed rice imports into Britain heavily in order to favor domestic grain growers; but rice was also enumerated; i.e., it could be exported only to British ports so that British rather than American merchants could derive the major profit from selling it to foreign consumers, chiefly in Northern Europe. After 1730 Americans could sell rice directly to Southern Europe, but roughly 60 percent of the crop still went via Britain to Northern Europe. Because rice production required heavy investment in labor and machinery, only very wealthy individuals could become rice planters. Unlike tobacco planters, colonial rice producers did not oversupply the market and thus continued to enjoy ample returns throughout the eighteenth century.

After 1748 indigo joined rice as a major plantation product in the Lower South. When properly processed, the indigo plant produced a blue-violet dye which was widely used in the British textile industry and by farm families which produced their own cloth. The Lower South could usually secure two crops of indigo yearly, as opposed to four or more in the Caribbean area, but preoccupation with sugar in the British West Indies pushed out indigo as it had tobacco. When war with France (War of the Austrian Succession, 1740–1748) interrupted the supply from the French islands, Britain began to subsidize production in her continental colonies. Instructed by Eliza Lucas who had emigrated from the West Indies, Carolina planters produced indigo profitably from 1748 until the Revolution.

Unlike the Tobacco Coast, which had no port city and was indeed an exclusively rural society, the Lower South developed a true metropolis, the city of Charleston. Large ships could not reach individual plantations as they did along Chesapeake Bay, but came to Charleston as a point of transhipment. Merchants in Charleston, as in other colonial ports, often acted as agents for British merchants, selling imported items, chiefly textiles and slaves, and buying rice, indigo, or other commodities for export. Their compensation for such services was a commission, usually about 5 percent, on both sales and purchases.

"Negro men," as merchant Henry Laurens frequently reminded his British correspondents, were "the most certain Article" for Charleston's market. Indigo planters, Laurens observed in 1755, had secured "such large Sums" for their crops that they were "all mad for more Negroes." At that time Charleston imported about 2,000 slaves annually; in 1773 the figure had soared to nearly 8,000, and blacks outnumbered whites in the province by about six to four. In Georgia, where the trustees had barred slavery until 1749, Negroes by 1770 were roughly half of the population. In North Carolina, where problems of navigation impeded the growth of the plantation system in many areas, only about 35 percent of the people were black.

Similar to old England in climate, New England could not produce the highly valued semitropical products which sustained the plantation system in the South. Likewise, graingrowing on family farms, the basis of a prosperous economy in the Middle Colonies, failed in New England to produce sufficient surplus for export. Rugged terrain, rocky soil, blights, or "blasts" which often reduced wheat yield, a scarcity of navigable waterways—all contributed to deny New England an agricultural staple. Instead New Englanders sold fish, timber products, shipping and commercial services, and even some manufactured products. In so doing they were laying the foundation for a modern industrial economy.

Still, most New Englanders made at least part of their living from the soil. Unlike the settlers in other sections, they got title to their land, except in New Hampshire, by grants from a representative legislature, rather than from an appointed royal or proprietary governor. In the seventeenth century, groups of settlers, often church congregations, received town grants, which they settled in a communal pattern. Houses clustered around a village "common," and each family worked strips of land in communal fields. This system helped sustain a sense of community and aided development of churches, schools, and militia, but it also involved irksome restrictions on individuals and wasted time coming and going to the fields. In the eighteenth century, when Indian dangers no longer helped to sustain it, the communal system of settlement yielded to integral family farms. Private speculation in land certainly occurred extensively in the eighteenth century, especially in New Hampshire under Governor Benning Wentworth, but rural New England remained remarkable for its "pleasing uniformity of decent competence." It was a society in which extreme wealth was as rare as dire poverty.

Rural New Englanders, like settlers elsewhere in the backcountry, were obliged from childhood, as one frontiersman put it, "to practice twenty different employments, with equal dexterity" in order to make a living. To gain cash income the farmer might sell some of his agricultural surplus locally, but he needed also to become a wintertime lumberman, a tavernkeeper, teamster, carpenter—whatever his own talents and the needs and opportunities of his community suggested. Conversely the lawyer, doctor, miller, blacksmith—virtually all craft and professional people—had to "moonlight" as farmers or in some other work in order to support their families. Only in the cities was it feasible to specialize in one kind of endeavor.

New England farms were usually similar in many respects. They were small, generally under 100 acres, and only partly cleared. Corn, a high-yield crop with low labor requirements, was the chief staple for food, but farmers grew a variety of other cereals and vegetables as well—although no potatoes until late in the eighteenth century. In an age when everyone thought alcohol essential to health and strength, an apple orchard enabled the family to substitute homemade hard cider for "storeboughten" rum. A few sheep and a patch of flax provided the raw materials for homemade "linsey-woolsey" clothing. A few cattle kept the family in milk, butter, and cheese. Hogs, generally turned loose to "get their living in the woods," provided most of the meat. Methods were about the same as those of medieval or even Biblical times. Oxen rather than horses were the usual beasts of burden; horses were much faster, but too expensive. Indentured servants and slaves were very few, but young men and boys provided some farm labor while saving money to get married and start farms of their own. Productivity per acre was scandalously low by European standards, but output per man and the general standard of living were undoubtedly higher.

Frontier opportunities lured many New Englanders. Probably the major reason was that uncleared land sold for about one-eighth or even one-tenth the cost of land on established farms. Settlers could achieve handsome rewards by investing some capital and several years of labor in clearing wilderness land for sale. Even "squatters" who lacked capital with which to buy land could sell "betterments" which they had made in land to which they had no title. While clearing land, frontier settlers could also make potash, essentially lye, by boiling the ashes of the trees which they burned. Potash was in great demand for "scouring" or cleaning raw wool in the British textile industry, so much so that it was often the only product of rural New England which did not have to be bartered for other commodities but commanded a cash price. In 1770 American exports of potash, produced chiefly on the northern frontier, were roughly equal in value to those of meat and exceeded by about three times those of the famous New England rum. Lumbering also afforded particularly remunerative employment in frontier areas where the forests were yet untouched. Finally, productivity per acre on freshly cleared land was likely to be about double what it was in older areas. Because of such opportunities, westward migration often lured the most enterprising inhabitants of older rural communities.

Fishing, on the other hand, sustained seaboard New England and paid for most of the region's imports. In 1770 the exports of New England's fishing industry exceeded the combined value of the rice and indigo produced on the plantations of the Lower South. Only tobacco and wheat flour were more valuable American exports. Dried cod and other fish caught in the Grand Banks area off Newfoundland were New England's major export staple, but whale oil (for lamps) and whale fins (for corsets) brought additional income. Far from being enumerated, New England fish were excluded from the British market at the behest of British fishermen. Consequently New Englanders had to market their fish in Southern Europe or in the West Indies where sugar planters generally preferred to import food for their slaves rather than grow it themselves.

From fishing, New Englanders moved easily into commerce and manufacturing. In marketing their fish they found a demand for shipping services and consequently began to operate "tramp" merchant vessels, carrying cargo wherever anyone was willing to pay them to take it. Owners of tramp ships also sent out speculative cargoes of their own. Often they could be persuaded even to sell their ships as they could be easily and cheaply replaced at home. Residing at the edge of the forest which afforded an abundant supply of raw materials for ship building, New Englanders became not only traders and carriers but important manufacturers of ships. By the time of the Revolution, American ships constituted nearly one-third of the British merchant marine.

Rum manufacturing was a New England enterprise which grew directly out of the marketing of fish in the West Indies. Molasses, the

The Resources of the New World

Europeans saw the seemingly endless bounty of nature as the most important economic quality of the New World, and extracting commodities from the land and the sea became the chief industry of the colonies. The illustration above, from Carolus Allard's Orbis Habitabilis, *published in Amsterdam in* 1690, *symbolizes the richness of both the fishing and fur trapping trades. The cold and relatively shallow waters which ran along the North Atlantic coast abounded in cod, herring, mackerel, and other food. For this reason, fish and fishing became a mainstay of commerce in New England. In the fur trade, New York had the advantage of possessing the Hudson and Mohawk River waterways leading to inland sources, a geographical accident that made New York the largest exporter of furs in the colonies.*

Above: Rare Book Division, New York Public Library

Tobacco dominated the economies of Virginia and Maryland, two colonies that were the leading tobacco suppliers to the world. Above, a crude system of weights and levers compresses tobacco for shipment by hogshead. Below, hogsheads are transported from an inland plantation in a double canoe. The tobacco label at right represents one of many brands packaged by London companies and, like most brands, boasts of using only the Virginia product. As in other pictorial representations, the inspectors examining the tobacco are about to be served some liquid refreshment by a slave. At the time of the American Revolution, the Colonies exported more than 100,000,000 *pounds of tobacco a year.*

Below and right: Arents Collection, New York Public Library

Kositzky's Best Virginia LONDON.

By 1720, *about three years after William Burgis painted his famous view of New York (of which the picture at left is a detail), the city's population was around* 7,000, *the third largest in America, ranking behind Boston with* 12,000 *and Philadelphia with* 10,000. *The view looks across the East River from Brooklyn Heights. From the pier in the foreground, Long Island farmers ship their produce and cattle by ferry to Manhattan. Several ships in the harbor fire salutes, perhaps, it has been suggested, in honor of the king's birthday. Across the river, several shipyards give evidence of the city's dependence on trade for its livelihood. Although British policies discouraged manufacturing in the colonies, the colonies inevitably began to process some of their own rich supply of raw materials. The illustration at top right depicts an eighteenth-century sawmill near Lake George, N.Y. Below is a crude woodcut advertisement of an iron manufacturer which appeared in the* New York Gazette *or* Weekly Post Boy *in* 1764. *Shipbuilding created a demand for both lumber and iron products, since these materials were essential for ship gear. At bottom, a Paul Revere illustration, which appeared in* 1774 *in the* Royal American Magazine, *shows the method of refining saltpetre, a product which became particularly important to the colonists several years later when, as revolutionists, they needed the material for making gunpowder.*

Far left: Courtesy of the New-York Historical Society, New York City
Left and above: New York Public Library, Rare Books Division
Top: Library of Congress

The colonial economy depended heavily upon both slaves and indentured servants for labor. At right are typical newspaper advertisements offering rewards for runaways and announcing the sale of a newly arrived group of slaves. Because such advertisements announcing runaway slaves or servants ran regularly, printers retained the cuts for recurrent use. Below is a plate which was used for this purpose.

Twenty Dollars Reward.

RAN away from the ſubſcribers, living at New Rochelle, on Sunday evening, the 9th inſtant; two indented GERMAN SERVANTS: John Jacob Wittmer, belonging to Mr. Liſpenard, about five feet five inches high, well ſet, has a remarkable large head, ſhort neck and broad face; halts as he walks, his right leg being much ſhorter than the left; had on, or took with him when he went off, a blue broad cloth coat, with braſs buttons, ſhort white waiſtcoat, with red embroidered flowers; corduroy breeches; light coloured worſted ſtockings; new ſhoes, and new round hat, with a band and buckle. Mr. Williams's ſervant is a tall ſlim fellow, five feet eleven inches high; ſomewhat freckled; long hair, tyed behind; had on a mixed blue and white coat; black breeches; and took with him a pair of clouded overalls, red, blue and white, which he may probably wear. Whoever apprehends the above ſervants, and will bring them to their maſters, at this place, ſhall receive the above reward, or ten dollars for either of them, with an allowance for all reaſonable charges.

LEONARD LISPENARD, jun.
DANIEL WILLIAMS.

New Rochelle, October 13, 1785. 33-6

TO BE SOLD on board the Ship *Bance-Yland*, on tueſday the 6th of *May* next, at *Aſhley-Ferry*; a choice cargo of about 250 fine healthy

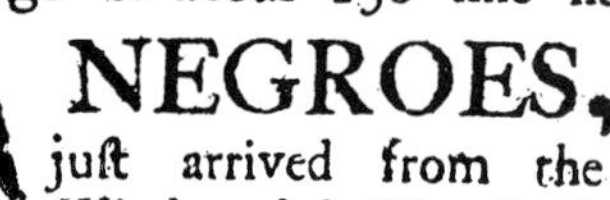

NEGROES,

juſt arrived from the Windward & Rice Coaſt. —The utmoſt care has already been taken, and ſhall be continued, to keep them free from the leaſt danger of being infected with the SMALL-POX, no boat having been on board, and all other communication with people from *Charles-Town* prevented.

Auſtin, Laurens, & Appleby.

N. B. Full one Half of the above Negroes have had the SMALL-POX in their own Country.

Above: Library of Congress
Left and top: Courtesy of the New-York Historical Society

raw material for rum, was itself a by-product of sugar refining, the major business in the West Indies. British sugar producers made their molasses into rum and sold it widely in Britain and in America. The French government, however, responded to the pleas of French brandy producers by banning the exportation of rum from its sugar islands to France. Consequently the French islands, major producers of sugar, found themselves with vast amounts of molasses for which there was relatively little demand. New Englanders, supplying fish to the sugar planters, chose often to invest their income in cheap French molasses. Some of it they sold in the colonies as molasses. Much of it they made into rum. New England rum was of very low quality, but it was also very low in price. Some went into New England ventures in the slave trade. Most remained on this side of the Atlantic, where employers used it as a liquor ration for their workers, fur traders bought it for resale to the Indians, and tavern keepers found it the most popular alcoholic beverage of the poor.

To curb New England rum production, British West Indian interests in 1733 persuaded Parliament to enact the famous Molasses Act. It imposed a tax of 6 pence per gallon, almost 100 percent of the current price, on imports of foreign molasses into the American colonies. Purportedly the act was to induce Americans to buy British rather than foreign molasses, but in fact the British sugar islands already turned most of their molasses into rum. The real purpose was to compel Americans to buy British West Indian rum rather than make their own from foreign molasses. Had it been enforced, the act would have sharply increased the price of both molasses and rum consumed in the colonies. Bribery and intimidation, however, prevented its enforcement. Americans did import Jamaican rum, chiefly for wealthier drinkers, but they also continued to make their own from foreign molasses.

Competition in commerce turned many New England merchants from import-export ventures to manufacturing. They agreed with Henry Laurens of Charleston who complained in 1755 that there were in all the colonies "too many Tradeing Men . . . in proportion to the business of the Country." Some turned to making rum or building ships. The Browns of Providence began to manufacture expensive candles from the spermaceti found in whale heads. Capitalists in Lynn, Massachusetts, began to "put out" leather to piece-rate workers who made shoes in their own homes. Cloth makers sometimes employed spinners and weavers on the same basis; sometimes they brought them together in factories, where their work could be supervised. In such ventures as well as in lumbering and making potash, New Englanders were in the vanguard of American economic development.

Manufacturing, however, faced many obstacles in the American colonies. British policy was one. Britain wanted America to concentrate on producing what Britain needed or could sell to the rest of the world, chiefly extractive industry products with low profit margins. From income derived in this way Britain expected Americans to buy relatively high-priced manufactured goods—Asian and Continental European as well as British in origin—from merchants in Britain. Accordingly Parliament enacted measures (the Woolens Act, 1699; the Hat Act, 1732; the Finished Iron Products Law, 1750) designed to restrict colonial manufacturing. Governors also received royal instructions to veto legislative measures intended to foster manufacturing. None of these measures was rigidly enforced, partly because conditions in America tended in any case to discourage extensive growth in manufacturing. Money was very scarce, either for investment or for consumer spending. Imported commodities commanded higher prestige. High transportation expenses enabled local artisans to undersell distant producers, even those who turned out a product at much lower cost. Furthermore, labor was expensive, hard to keep, and usually deficient in skill.

In the Middle, or "Bread," Colonies rural life was largely as it was in New England, except for the commercial production of wheat. Terrain, climate, and soil were all more favorable to agriculture in the coastal areas from New York to Delaware than in New England. Rich farmlands lay adjacent to excellent natural waterways, affording cheap transportation. Accordingly, farmers in this region produced wheat for export. Millers, although not all as ingenious as Oliver Evans whose Pennsylvania mills were almost entirely automated, added to the grain's value by transforming it into flour. Only in occasional years of crop failure in Britain, however, would Parliament allow Americans to market their wheat and flour in the mother country. The major markets for American producers were the West Indies and Southern Europe.

Some slaves and indentured servants were used to produce wheat, but the plantation found no more place in the Middle Colonies than in New England. Pennsylvania's Quakers, it is true, became more and more outspoken in condemnation of slavery on moral grounds, but economic considerations were probably more important in confining slavery to a small role in the area. There was a relatively low demand for American wheat in Britain and other European markets, and the labor requirements for its cultivation were not year-round but concentrated in only the spring and fall. Thus, large investment in bound laborers would have been uneconomic.

Large land holdings, too, were rare in the settled areas of the Middle Colonies, except for the Hudson Valley of New York. There much of the best land was in the possession of a few major landlords determined to hold their estates for their heirs in perpetuity, despite the hostility of their tenants who were burdened with various semifeudal obligations. Even as late as 1772, a royal governor of New York endorsed such land holdings as tending "to create subordination and counterpoise, in some measure, the general levelling spirit." By then, however, most new land grants were going to speculators whose aim was not to establish perpetual, tenant-operated estates but to accumulate quick profits from sales to ordinary settlers.

Scarcity of money was as much a problem in the Middle Colonies as it was in all the others. The Americans did earn some gold and silver in trade with the West Indies, but they almost invariably sent it off to England immediately to pay debts or to import manufactured goods. Hence they needed something else to serve as a medium of exchange. Most colonies used commodities for money, but only Virginia and Maryland did so with much success. In those colonies, receipts for tobacco deposited at government warehouses served very well. Massachusetts in the 1690s began to buy war supplies by issuing "bills of credit," or promises to pay later from future tax revenues. Other colonies did this in later wars. In peacetime, several provinces turned to "land banks," which created paper money to be lent to landowners who gave mortgages on their property as security. In the Middle Colonies, such paper money was relatively stable in value. In Rhode

Island, however, deliberate inflation led to a Parliamentary ban (1751) on both land banks and legal tender bills of credit throughout New England.

Religion in Colonial America

Religion in colonial America was highly distinctive by European standards. Of the three hierarchical forms of Christianity which dominated Western Europe—Catholicism, Lutheranism, and Anglicanism—only Anglicanism was a major force in the American colonies. Even the Anglicans, however, were only about as numerous in eighteenth-century America as Congregationalists and Presbyterians, both of whom practiced a representative system of church government. Quakers and Baptists, the remaining religious groups of considerable importance in pre-Revolutionary America, were so individualistic and egalitarian as to condone almost no religious authority at all. Thus hierarchical religions had far less importance in America than in Europe as a whole.

Equally remarkable by European standards was the absence of government support for religion in several colonies. In Rhode Island the dominant Baptists and Quakers enforced separation of church and state, as did the Quakers in Pennsylvania and Delaware. New York and New Jersey included so many religious groups that none was ever strong enough to endow itself with the support of the provincial government, although the Anglican Church did have official standing in a few localities. Only in Maryland and the remaining Southern colonies did the Church of England (Anglican) enjoy government support as it did at home. Congregationalists, it is true, held a near monopoly of religion in New England, except for Rhode Island, and required payment of taxes to support their faith. Anglicans and Baptists had gained considerable strength in Congregational New England, however, by the time of the Revolution and had even won the right to have their tax payments for the support of religion diverted to their own churches.

Anglicanism itself was different in America. An episcopal or bishop-governed church in England, the Anglican Church in America functioned until after the Revolution without a bishop. Furthermore, parish priests in England received lifetime appointments from a government-controlled hierarchy, usually on the nomination of major local land holders. In America, the vestrymen of individual parishes hired and fired parish priests at will. In England, church offices were often sinecures conferred on a political patronage basis, and the appointees were in some instances flagrantly immoral. Despite some criticism of "fox-hunting parsons" in the South, neither evil was so widespread in the colonies. In England the privilege of holding civil or military office and of attending either of the two universities was reserved to Anglicans, but Dissenters (non-Anglican Protestants) in America not only held office but were also permitted to found colleges of their own faith.

Anglicanism, despite the hostility of Dissenters, did strengthen its position as the eighteenth century progressed. Its Society for the Propagation of the Gospel, chartered in 1701, founded charity schools and did missionary work among Indians and Calvinists. Anglicans established a "mission" at Harvard's doorstep about 1760 and built a pretentious residence, which fearful Congregationalists expected would become "the Bishop's Palace." Anglicans helped found King's College (later Columbia) in New York in 1754 and in 1749 the Philadelphia institution which would become the University of Pennsylvania. Closely linked to British authority, Northern Anglican clergymen in particular inculcated "the great Principles of Loyalty and Submission to Government" and denounced "republican mobbish principles" and "servile compliance" to popular will.

Calvinism was much stronger in America than in all but a few areas of Europe. Its followers comprised not only Puritans and Presbyterians, the two leading denominations on the eve of the Revolution, but also Dutch Reformed, German Reformed, and French Huguenots. Furthermore Baptists in increasing numbers were embracing Calvinism's concept of predestination, while Anglicans were adopting Calvinist practices of congregational control.

Calvinism's reputation, especially that of its New England Puritan or Congregationalist adherents, has been attacked for many years on several grounds. New England Puritans persecuted Baptists and Quakers for their beliefs. They executed twenty "witches" in Salem, Massachusetts, in 1692. Their insistence upon the depraved nature of man and the predestination of most for damnation has also incurred criticism. Yet there was much to admire in Calvinism as it was practiced in New England. Its glorification of work and thrift helped New Englanders maintain an outstanding place in American business leadership for generations. Puritan zeal for education aided New England to attain enduring intellectual eminence. Also despite the difficulty of reconciling Calvinist concepts of predestination with social equality and representative government, it is apparent that New England was a spearhead of progress in these matters as well.

Quakers, originally members of a radical lower-class denomination, became increasingly prosperous, and in some respects conservative, in the eighteenth century. In Pennsylvania successful merchants rather than struggling artisans or farmers seemed to typify the movement. Instead of zealously seeking converts, Quakers tended to expel those who were insufficiently orthodox. Nonetheless, it was the Quaker commitment to human equality which produced the only significant opposition to slavery.

Baptists, while tending to adopt the theology of middle-class Calvinists, remained chiefly a lower-class denomination. Charles Woodmason, a profoundly biased Anglican clergyman, denounced backcountry Baptist preachers as "ignorant wretches, who cannot write" and compared a Baptist communion service to "a Gang of frantic Lunatics broke out of Bedlam."

Religious revivals, which subsequently became a permanent part of American culture, swept the colonies in a "Great Awakening" during the generation preceding the Revolution. Leaders of the Awakening sought by emotional exhortation to enable individuals to experience "conversion," a sense of mystic communion with God accompanied by new dedication to Christian values. Theodorus Frelinghuysen, a German-born minister of the Dutch Reformed Church, began the movement with prayer meetings in New Jersey during the 1720s. William Tennent, a Presbyterian immigrant who had studied at the University of Edinburgh in Scotland, inspired and trained many future revivalists of distinction, including his son Gilbert. He founded the "Log College" at Neshaminy, Pennsylvania, for that purpose in 1736. George Whitefield, an associate of

John Wesley in the English revivalist movement—which would ultimately split off from the Anglican to become the Methodist Church—made many trips to America and preached with great success under the auspices of every major denomination.

In New England the leading revivalist was Jonathan Edwards. His narrative of the "Conversion of Many Hundred Souls" reported his success as a revivalist. Later he published a distinguished essay on "Freedom of the Will," which contrasted sharply with the spirit of his famous "hell fire" sermon, "Sinners in the Hands of an Angry God."

In the South, the Presbyterians, Methodists, and Baptists all played major roles in the revival. Presbyterian Samuel Davies, later president of Princeton, enjoyed great success in Virginia between 1748 and 1758. Methodist Devereux Jarratt and Baptists Shubal Stearns and Daniel Marshall were "reviving" portions of the South on the eve of the Revolution.

The effect of the Great Awakening on American society is difficult to establish. Clearly it inspired the founding of several notable institutions of higher learning to train more ministers: Presbyterian Princeton (1746), Baptist Brown (1764), Dutch Reformed Rutgers (1766), and Congregationalist Dartmouth (1769). Yet the Awakening was at the same time anti-intellectual, for it exalted mystic enthusiasm, even that of the uneducated, as a path to religious understanding superior to the legalistic scholarship of erudite ministers. The Awakening was also highly divisive. Many "settled ministers," enjoying tax support as the official religious leaders in their communities, resented the disruption of their complacency by uneducated but enthusiastic itinerants. Religious freedom became an issue in New England when Congregational authorities jailed revivalists for unauthorized preaching or for refusing to pay taxes to support an "unconverted" minister. Anglican leaders created similar problems in Virgina.

The least tangible but perhaps most important of all the effects of the Awakening was its erosion of ancient traditions of social deference on the part of the poor toward those of superior wealth and power. Newly converted "saints" of lower-class background, the principal product of the Awakening, seem to have found in their conversion new confidence to challenge the traditional prerogatives of their social superiors who remained unconverted. It is significant that Baptists and Methodists, denominations favored by the lower classes, began at the time of the Awakening the rise in membership which, in little more than a generation, would make them the most numerous American religious groups.

At the other extreme from the revivalist movement was an intellectual school of thought called "Deism" to which, in fact, the revival was in some measure a reaction. Intellectuals influenced by physicist Isaac Newton, philosopher John Locke, and others in the late seventeenth century had come to believe that there were "natural laws" not only in astronomy, physics, and other physical sciences, but in fields such as religion and government as well. These individuals believed that through exercise of his reason man could discover the natural laws of religion as well as of science. Deism, the "natural" religion which resulted, postulated an omnipotent God who required virtuous living and allocated rewards and punishments accordingly after death. Deists rejected divine revelations, even the divinity of Christ, along with Biblical astronomy. While the doctrines of Deism and natural law were losing popularity in Europe on the eve of the

Revolution, their acceptance by American Revolutionary leaders is strikingly evident in the best-known passages of the Declaration of Independence.

Racial and Ethnic Variety

Racial and ethnic variety as well as religious diversity characterized American life from the earliest times. All three of humanity's major racial divisions, yellow and black and white, resided uneasily together in England's continental American colonies. Relations between whites and Indians (a branch of the yellow race despite their designation as "redmen") were understandably turbulent as the advancing white settlement encroached more and more upon the territories of native inhabitants whose culture was in most instances warlike. Even as late as the Revolution, few colonies were entirely secure from Indian attack.

Negroes, nearly all bound to perpetual labor as slaves, understandably harbored their own grievances against white society. Rigid discipline and constant surveillance minimized opportunities for planned uprisings, yet they occurred. In 1739 twenty whites and about twice as many blacks lost their lives in a slave insurrection in South Carolina. New York City experienced one uprising in 1712 and in anticipation of another in 1741 began a frenzy of executions (twenty-nine blacks and four suspected whites) reminiscent of the witchcraft trials of Salem. Only when the coerced confessions began to implicate people of "known credit, fortune and reputation" did the orgy end. Fear of such interracial violence was a constant feature of life in areas of large Negro population as well as on the Indian frontier.

Racial prejudice was prevalent but by no means universal. Although Indians were looked down upon, an Indian-white marriage bore much less stigma in white society than one between a white and a black. The glorification of the "noble savage" by European intellectuals may have helped to elevate Indian status, but probably their record in warfare and the relatively slight difference in physical features were more important. Most white people, including such intellectuals as Franklin and Jefferson, believed Negroes to be inherently inferior in intelligence. A few Quakers such as Anthony Benezet, who had actually taught Negro children, knew better, as did the distinguished Virginia planter William Byrd, who affirmed as a commonplace that "very bright talents may be lodged under a very dark skin." For both Indians and Negroes, however, discrimination was more rigorous than in the West Indies or in the colonies of Spain.

A diversity of European ethnic groups also distinguished American society. Here, wrote the French observer Crèvecoeur, "the poor of Europe have by some means met together" and "individuals of all nations are melted into a new [breed] of men." Intermarriage among French, Dutch, German, Irish, and other European immigrants had indeed occurred extensively, especially in the Middle Colonies. But it was also true that isolated ethnic islands remained—Dutchmen in New York's Hudson Valley, Germans and Scotch-Irish in Pennsylvania, Highland Scots in North Carolina, for example. Except in New England, where English descent was almost universal, most colonial Americans were thus likely to have neighbors or neighboring communities whose ethnic background differed from their own. Germans and Scotch-Irish were the largest of the European minority groups. Probably neither provided as much as 10 percent of the colonial population by the 1770s, however, while Negroes accounted for approximately 20 percent and the English comprised roughly 60 percent.

The American Social Pattern

To many Europeans what seemed most remarkable about colonial America was the opportunity which it afforded to middle- and lower-class people to better their station in life. For Europe's rural poor, struggling for survival usually with insecure tenure on land inadequate to meet a family's subsistence needs, the remarkable ease with which one could gain access to an ample expanse of highly productive land was a powerful incentive for emigrating to America. In sharp contrast to the situation in most areas of Europe, only about 20 percent of the white men in the Colonies in the period of the Revolution did not own land. And a large proportion of the landless individuals were young men who would become land holders before they died.

For the urban poor of Europe and indeed for those from rural areas as well, America's high wage scale was also a lure. Crèvecoeur's claim that an American workman could get "four or five times more than he can get in Europe" was exaggerated. However, the general scarcity of labor, attributable to rapid economic development as well as to the ability of so many people to exercise their preference for the security of farming, kept the wage level in America appreciably higher than in Europe. Because provisions were cheap and "the price of labour very high," wrote one immigrant, "people who are temperate and laborious have every chance of bettering their circumstances."

Poverty of course existed. Black people, who made up one-fifth of the population and over 90 percent of whom were in slavery, apparently lived in extreme deprivation, although we really know relatively little as to how their living standard compared to that of the poor in Europe. Indentured servants probably knew little luxury, although again the actual circumstances of their lives are only slightly known. In the Southern backcountry, "poor whites" made their appearance early. A traveler in the Carolinas noted Irish immigrants living on "what in England is given to the Hogs and Dogs." In Virginia during the Revolution, a Frenchman observed "miserable huts . . . inhabited by whites, whose wan looks and ragged garments bespeak poverty." The Northern colonies too had poor inhabitants, rural squatters and urban laborers, although apparently fewer relatively than the South.

Middle-class immigrants could also better their circumstances in America. Even the richest men in colonial America, it is true, were hardly more than well-to-do by European standards, but many had risen far. Virginia's "great families" of the eighteenth century sprang mostly from "ambitious younger sons of middle-class families." The "most opulent families" in New York's mercantile and landed aristocracy, avowed a contemporary, "have risen from the lower Rank of People." Fully one-third of the rich merchants who comprised the New York chamber of commerce at the time of the Revolution were self-made men. The wealthy Manigaults of South Carolina stemmed from a Huguenot refugee who began as a tavernkeeper. Thomas Hancock of Boston, who bequeathed one of America's largest fortunes to his nephew John, launched his career by selling books.

Ancestry, except in the case of Negroes, clearly had less to do with status in America than it did in Europe. In the absence of nobles and monarchs, royal governors, who were sometimes from noble English families, stood at the apex of colonial society, surrounded by wealthy landowners and merchants. The governors, however, usually returned to England within a few years; they did not found American families. In some provinces a few great families continued to be prominent for generations, but in comparison with Britain, status seemed to adjust quickly to either the acquisition or the loss of wealth.

Deference to those of higher station was a central requirement in a traditional etiquette of class relations. Governors were abjectly humble in addressing correspondence to the King or even to the nobles who were his major ministers. Leading American landowners or merchants were ostentatiously polite in addressing governors. They in turn expected artisans, shopkeepers, and farmers to be appropriately servile in the presence of "gentlemen" like themselves. Even the "middling sort" felt themselves entitled to "proper" respect from the very poor, especially from apprentices, indentured servants, and slaves. In comparison with Europe, however, this "Great Law of Subordination," as historian Carl Bridenbaugh called it, was suffering a decline in the colonies, a fact attested to by the grumbling of European gentlemen who found themselves addressed as equals by ordinary Americans whom they encountered in their travels. New Englanders in particular were frequently criticized for what many outsiders called their "levelling" tendencies.

The status of women was not quite the same in America as in England. On the one hand, no English women were either slaves or indentured servants compelled by the lash to do gang labor in the fields. Nor did English women have such a variety of tasks as the frontier housewife, whose family had largely to make everything it used—or do without. On the other hand, the laws of the Northern provinces generally afforded the wife a greater measure of protection against her husband's "discipline" than in Britain. She had somewhat greater rights, too, as an owner of property. Divorce, virtually unattainable in Britain or in the other colonies, was possible in New England but little used. Among the poor, "elopement" with a third party was a common means of terminating an unhappy marriage, although American practice in this respect apparently differed little from that of the English. Prostitution was less prominent in American than in English cities, but the same earthy, pre-Victorian attitude toward sex prevailed in America as in England. Illegitimate children were very common. Slave owners generally did not allow their slaves to marry, with the result that the very concept of legitimacy had little bearing on the lives of most Negroes.

The influence of frontier conditions upon early American society remains a matter of historical dispute. Frederick Jackson Turner, in a famous essay of 1893, argued that the "perennial rebirth" of civilization in the wilderness helped develop American democracy, equality, individualism, and nationalism. Other historians have questioned these points, stressing the leadership of urban dwellers, and identifying less salutary influences of the frontier. William Byrd, one of the first gentlemen of Virginia, thought the easy subsistence afforded in the backcountry South tended to "discharge the men from the necessity of killing themselves with work" but allowed them to keep "many sabbaths" every week. With reference to law and order on the frontier, Byrd mentioned that a backcountry magistrate who had ordered a drunk put into the stocks "was for his intemperate zeal carried thither himself, and narrowly escaped being whipped into the bargain." There were many frontier "squatters," of whom Pennsylvania's Scotch-Irish were only the most notorious, who disregarded land titles quite often in the self-righteous conviction that it was "against the laws of God and Nature, that so much land should be idle while so many Christians wanted it to labour on."

Education, Arts, and Science

Educational practices in the American colonies were generally much like those in England. Primary responsibility for educating children lay, as it did in England, with the family. Hence parents taught their offspring as much as they were able, often not very much. Middle-class parents might send their children to private schools or perhaps hire private tutors, as did the very rich. To train children for the professions as well as in various artisan crafts, parents arranged to apprentice them at about age fourteen to serve and learn from an established "master," usually for a period of seven years. Religious denominations maintained charity schools for the children of the poor. These traditions worked best in areas where both population and cash incomes were relatively high. In the colonial South, where the population was widely scattered and cash incomes were low, they served very badly. For slaves the traditional practices did almost nothing; very few Southern planters made any efforts to teach their slaves to read and write.

Only in New England did government take a significant role in education. New England's early Puritan leaders included a remarkably high proportion of Cambridge-educated scholars fully convinced of the value of education. In addition to founding a college-preparatory Latin School in 1635 and Harvard College in 1636, both essentially private institutions, Puritan leaders in 1642 enacted a law requiring all parents to see that their children could read well enough to understand religious principles and capital laws. In 1647 Massachusetts enacted a statute which required each town of fifty families to operate an elementary school and each town of 100 families to maintain a grammar or secondary school in which youth might be "fitted for the university." Precisely how well the towns met these obligations remains a matter of dispute, but they did fix an unprecedented public duty. Tuition payments by parents long continued to pay part of the costs even for elementary education, however, and attending school was not compulsory. Illiteracy was rare among New England men but perhaps as high as 40 percent among the women. Elsewhere it was still more common.

Pressure for curriculum reform at the secondary level was strong in the generation preceding the Revolution. Under attack was the old preoccupation with Latin and Greek, which were useful chiefly in preparing for ministerial careers. The curriculum preferred by the reformers featured subjects which would help students to earn a secular living.

Among the arts, painting was the first in which Americans attained recognition abroad. Benjamin West of Pennsylvania, aided by

Philadelphia merchants to study in Europe, won great acclaim in London, even from George III, despite West's undisguised sympathy for the American Revolution. Boston's John Singleton Copley, unlike West, did many of his best paintings in America before he settled in England in 1774. Both painted chiefly portraits and historical subjects. Each was outstanding at that time for his realism. Most painters who worked in the colonies were immigrants trained in Europe. Those who patronized them wanted principally portraits, sometimes with extravagant costumes and backgrounds to suggest high status, but often, especially in New England, with a realistic emphasis on individuality, including indications of one's profession or trade. Religious and mythological subjects, despite their popularity in Europe, found almost no market in colonial America.

Music in the classical tradition had little place in colonial life. Wealthy gentlemen in a few large cities organized chamber music societies in the generation preceding the Revolution, but most of the musicians were European immigrants and the works they performed were those of European composers.

Religious music encountered opposition among Calvinists, who considered it to be an emotional distraction from the intellectual pursuit of religious understanding. Thus Puritan New England tolerated no religious music except unaccompanied psalm singing. Even hymns, which began to gain popularity during the Great Awakening, aroused much protest. Among Anglicans and many of the German sects, religious music found ready acceptance, but it remained essentially European.

Folk or popular music suited the taste of most Americans. The songs themselves were usually traditional European tunes, although American variations in the words were frequent. Before the Revolution urban Americans were enjoying ballad operas, forerunners of modern musical comedies, particularly *The Beggar's Opera,* a London production of 1728 which employed many old folk tunes in a bawdy satire of English life.

Theater encountered great opposition from the Puritans in Northern urban centers while the rural character of society made it uneconomic among the more tolerant Anglicans of the South. Like their English antecedents who had stamped out theater in England during the Civil War, Northern Puritans tried to bar performances by the few traveling theatrical companies which began coming out from England more frequently after 1750. By devious means such as billing their plays as "Moral Dialogues" and calling their theaters "schoolhouses," the thespians slowly gained acceptance in the major cities, especially Philadelphia, which had become quite cosmopolitan by the 1760s. Shakespeare's dramas and eighteenth-century English comedies predominated. No American dramatist of consequence had yet appeared.

Creative writing also suffered from Puritan disapproval. Despite the examples of eighteenth-century English novelists, no colonial American wrote a novel. Particularly dogmatic Puritans disapproved even of reading novels, although poetry met their favor. Indeed, New England Puritans suffered what Moses Coit Tyler called a "lust of versification." Most of these versifiers, Tyler concluded, "it was a charity to call amateurs in the art of poetry." Particularly memorable are Michael Wigglesworth's "Day of Doom," a "grim, pathetic, horrible" rendition of the "hideous dogmas" of the Puritan creed, according to Tyler, as

Early Architecture in America

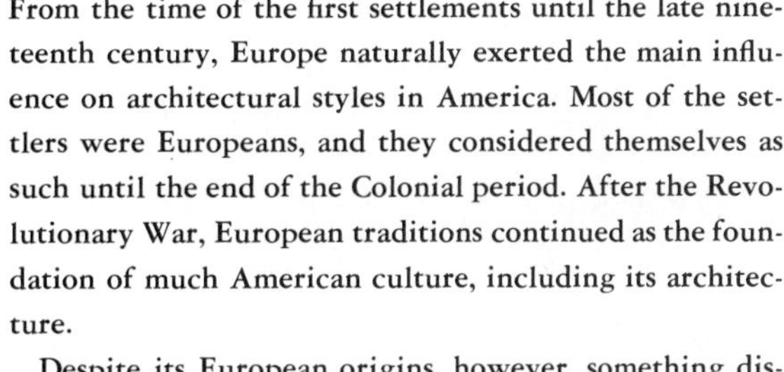

From the time of the first settlements until the late nineteenth century, Europe naturally exerted the main influence on architectural styles in America. Most of the settlers were Europeans, and they considered themselves as such until the end of the Colonial period. After the Revolutionary War, European traditions continued as the foundation of much American culture, including its architecture.

Despite its European origins, however, something distinctive and characteristic did emerge in the development of architecture in America. In selecting from the range of traditional European architectural styles, Americans stressed certain elements. They altered the European forms as they adapted them to American environments and to American building materials. To the interested observer, American architectural developments can yield insights into the history of the national culture as a whole.

The kitchen of the Bryant-Cushing House in Norwell, Mass. (left), for example, incorporates English design and methods, but at the same time mirrors the austerity and simplicity of New England Puritan life of the seventeenth century. Other American architectural developments have reflected the flourishing of the Southern plantation economy, the desire for elegance which supplanted austerity as New England prospered, and the attempt of the American founding fathers to fashion the nation on the classic models of ancient Greek democracy and the Roman republic.

The sampling of American architectural history on the pages which follow was selected with assistance of Denys Peter Myers of the Historic American Buildings Survey, a

division of the National Parks Service which, since 1933, has documented over 13,000 historic buildings and has done much to encourage their preservation. With a few noted exceptions, the photographs here are from the Survey collection on file at the Library of Congress.

Among the early traditions in American building were simplicity and the use of building materials which came easiest to hand. The New England of the Puritans made simplicity a virtue in itself, but this tendency was reinforced by the hard facts of what was still very close to frontier living: skilled workmen were in relatively short supply and money was required for elaborate building.

The McIntire Garrison House in York, Me. (left, above), probably built about 1707, accurately represents New England style during the first one hundred years of the settlement. The overhanging second story was an English mode. Like most New England houses of the period, the abundant forests of the area provided the wood for its construction. The use of brick in New England did not become widespread until later in the eighteenth-century.

Log cabins did not predominate in early American settlements, but some appeared in the Delaware River Valley built by Swedes who had similar dwellings in their home country. The example at left, below, is near Darby, Pa.

The traditions of simplicity and use of native materials are exemplified in the Kaufman House and barns near Oley, Pa., built between 1727 and 1762 (far right, below), the finest-known example of a Pennsylvania-German farm group in the Oley Valley. Pennsylvanians often built with stone because of its easy availability.

Early colonial building in the backwoods and at the mountain frontiers of the South included buildings as simple as those prevalent in the North, but the buildings which stand today and characterize the time and place are the manor houses of the great plantations. Built on enormous tracts of land granted by the Stuart monarchs, these manor houses had a grandeur not generally achieved in the North until much later. The early manor houses, grand though they were, did share a relative absence of ornamentation and a feeling of austerity. Bacon's Castle in Surry County, Va., built before 1676 (right, above), has the clustered chimney flues typical of Jacobean architecture, as does Stratford Hall in Westmoreland County (far right, above), which has also the typically Jacobean central hall with wings forming an H-plan. Abundance of clay in Virginia fostered brick as a building material, as did the great wealth of the planters who imported workmen especially to build their houses.

By the middle of the eighteenth century, most parts of settled America were ready for new and more elegant forms. Ascetic Puritan strictures had lost their hold, and in the North and South prosperous planters, merchants, sea captains, and traders looked to England where designers like Sir Christopher Wren, James Gibbs, and Robert Adams had in the late seventeenth and in the eighteenth centuries fostered and refined Renaissance influences in English architecture. Characteristic of their work were balanced façades and classical decorative devices, spacious interiors, and fine stairways. With the rise of this style, called "Georgian" after the contemporaneous line of English kings, brick came increasingly into use in New England, but craftsmen there also used wood to duplicate the effect created in stone in English Georgian buildings.

By no means the most elegant doorway of the period, but typical in its style, is that of the manse built in 1742 by the Reverend Ebenezer Gay in Suffield, Conn. (left). Classical pilasters support a broken scroll pediment, while wood, cut to look like stone, provides a frame for the door. The Chase-Lloyd House (right, above) was built in Annapolis, Md., between 1769–1771. The façade has the characteristic symmetrical organization in three parts with a central pavilion. The third-floor window echoes the arch of the Palladian doorway.

Following the Revolutionary War, the Georgian styles of the period developed into what came to be called Federal style, which had as one of its distinguishing characteristics an even greater preoccupation with ornament. The Nightingale Brown House, built in Providence, R. I., in 1792 (right, below), with its ornate "widow's walk," Palladian window, and decorative porch with balustrade provides a fine example of the Federal style.

The Georgian style had an equal impact on the South. Typical of the many Georgian mansions built before the Revolution is Westover, the Byrd mansion (below), built between 1730 and 1734 in Charles County, Va. Symmetrically placed outbuildings were commonly associated with many Southern houses. (In the case of Westover, these originally stood free of the main house.) The high-hipped roof also appeared frequently in Southern mansions of the period. Note the similarity of the doorway, with its broken scroll pediment, to the humbler version of the same design employed by the Reverend Ebenezer Gay on the preceding page.

The fortunes which enabled the building of such great Southern mansions rested on a foundation of slave labor. The design of slave quarters, usually humble, varied from plantation to plantation. An early nineteenth-century slave dormitory at Keswick in Powhatan County, Va., appears at left; its interior had a central circular chimney containing several fireplaces, and slaves slept in a circle around the chimney with their feet toward the fires.

Although Georgian design concepts persisted in the Federal style after the Revolution, the first great break with the Georgian manner came in the 1790s. As America sought a pattern for its government, a general interest in the old Roman republic stirred. In the planning of Washington, leaders like Thomas Jefferson sought a monumental Roman style. An upsurge of interest in the ancient Greek style of building followed shortly upon this passion for Roman things.

The American Greek Revival began, according to most architectural historians, in 1798, with the building of Benjamin Latrobe's Bank of Pennsylvania; by the 1820s, it dominated. According to Talbot Hamlin, the Greek Revival was "in the widest sense a popular movement deeply emotional, and despite its classic guise, deeply romantic."

Starting in the middle-Atlantic seaboard region, the Revival spread to all quarters of the nation. An inseparable part of the mythology of the antebellum South, it spawned great plantation houses like Milford, the Governor Manning plantation in the Pinewood vicinity of South Carolina (above). Careful and elegant detail characterizes the portico of the 1850 Robert A. Grinnan House in New Orleans, (right).

Smithsonian Institution

The Greek Revival, predictably, greatly affected buildings of a public character, such as the Second Bank of the United States (left, above), built in Philadelphia between 1818 and 1824 from a design by William Strickland. Pride in handsome appearance extended also to many of the factory buildings of the young republic, such as the Crown and Eagle Mills (left, below) begun in the 1820s. This mill is partly supported by an arch over the Mumford River in North Uxbridge, Mass. Here, as in the Wiscasset, Me., County Court House some vestiges of late Federal style still persist. That the North fell equally under the influence of the Greek Revival is evidenced by the Congregational Church at Cornwall, Conn. (far right, above); the William F. Keuhneman House in Racine, Wisc. (far right, below); and the interior of the Campbell-Whittlesey House in Rochester, N.Y. (right).

Landmark Society of Western New York, Inc.

well as some works of Anne Bradstreet and Edward Taylor.

Theological disputation, history, and private diaries or journals were forms of literature which enjoyed general approval. Rhode Island's founder, Roger Williams, engaged Quaker and Puritan alike in pamphlet warfare equally remarkable for its ideas and its scurrility. In the eighteenth century, New England ministers such as John Wise (*Churches Quarrel Espoused,* 1710; *Vindication of the Government of the New England Churches,* 1717) and particularly Jonathan Mayhew (*A Discourse concerning Unlimited Submission,* 1750) gave a somewhat more political cast to their disputatious essays. Jonathan Edwards, on the other hand, became more abstractly philosophical in his famous *Freedom of the Will* (1754).

History became less theological and more political. Cotton Mather's *Ecclesiastical History of New England* (1702) was in the spirit of the seventeenth century. Virginia's Robert Beverly, on the other hand, wrote *The History and Present State of Virginia* (1705) to refute the aspersions of English authors upon his province, and William Byrd sought to amuse his fellow aristocrats with an account of the peculiar mores of the backcountry in his *History of the Dividing Line* (1738). William Smith and Thomas Hutchinson wrote accounts of political history in their respective provinces (New York and Massachusetts) after mid-century; but no one except William Douglass in *A Summary, Historical and Political, of the British Settlements in North America* (1752) sought to lump all the colonies together. Even Douglass's work had a New England focus.

Late in the colonial period, three men wrote personal narratives of distinction. The saintly Quaker John Woolman forecast in his *Journal* (1774) that "when our minds are thoroughly divested of all prejudice in relation to difference of colour, . . . I believe it will appear that a heavy account lies against us as a Civil Society for oppressions committed against people who did not injure us." In an entirely different spirit, the "irrepressibly indignant" Charles Woodmason, an Anglican parson, recorded his contemptuous but fascinating views of life in the backcountry of the Carolinas. Finally, the all-round genius Benjamin Franklin produced the first classic of American literature, his *Autobiography.*

Architecture in America followed English fashions, although both castles and cathedrals were conspicuously absent. In the seventeenth century, colonists of English background built homes which, like those of rural England at the time, were quite medieval in structure—steep-roofed, gabled, often with an overhanging second story. They looked quite different, however, because Americans used wood (clapboard and shingles) for walls and roof, while the English, less abundantly supplied with forests, usually made exterior walls of plaster and roofs of thatch (straw). In the eighteenth century both Britain and America adopted the English, or Georgian, variant of Renaissance style which featured classical symmetry, columns, and pediments. Before the Revolution, frontier dwellers were beginning to rely largely on primitive log cabins (notched logs) or more substantial blockhouses (squared timbers), neither of which had much place in Europe. Plain, multipurpose "meeting houses" served for religious assemblies in the seventeenth century, but before the 1750s Americans had begun building steepled Georgian churches patterned after London's St. Martin-in-the-Fields (1721).

Science attracted gentlemen amateurs in

America as it did in Europe. Harvard still accepted Ptolemaic or earth-centered astronomy as late as 1670, and Yale even longer, but Boston merchant Thomas Brattle made observations of Halley's comet which the great Isaac Newton cited in his *Principia Mathematica.* Harvard professor John Winthrop IV carried out astonomical work respected in Europe. The Reverend Cotton Mather helped persuade fearful Bostonians to try immunization during the smallpox epidemic of 1721 and wrote an unpublished treatise on medicine. James Logan of Philadelphia and his protégé, John Bartram, were the most successful of many amateur American botanists who tried to inform curious Europeans about America's vegetation. Connecticut's Jared Eliot, in his *Essays on Field Husbandry* (1748–1759), tried to communicate to American gentlemen some of the enthusiasm for agricultural improvement then so common among the English. European interest in the "noble savage" stirred New York's Cadwallader Colden to make an anthropological inquiry into *History of the Five* [*Iroquois*] *Indian Nations* (1727). The ubiquitous Benjamin Franklin gained great renown for his *Experiments and Observations on Electricity* (1751).

Conclusion

Economic development in the American colonies proceeded rapidly within the mercantilist framework fixed by British policy. Abundant land enabled American families to work larger plots than could most Europeans and thus to enjoy a higher standard of living. A chronic labor shortage not only raised wages above European standards but led to the importation of impoverished Europeans as indentured servants and later of thousands of African Negroes as slaves. Plantation agriculture—large-scale production for the European market—developed from Maryland southward where the climate permitted production of crops which could not be grown commercially in Northern Europe. North of Maryland, farmers produced crops identical to those of Northern Europe and consequently had to look elsewhere for a market, turning chiefly to the West Indian sugar plantations and to Southern Europe. New Englanders, not well endowed for commercial farming, sold fish from the nearby Grand Banks region to the same markets. Northerners in particular made some progress in manufacturing such products as lumber, flour, iron, and ships, but America as a whole imported most of its manufactured goods and paid for them with exports of less valuable raw or processed materials. The result was deep indebtedness to Britain.

Distinctive social patterns emerged as American society grew. Calvinist and Anabaptist religious views, confined largely to bourgeois or lower-class minorities in Europe, dominated the Northern colonies and strongly influenced the Anglican South. A Great Awakening of religious fervor strengthened the evangelical denominations still more in the generation preceding the Revolution. Racial variety and racial strife were prominent as whites wrested land from the Indians and labor from Negro slaves. Both lower- and middle-class immigrants usually improved their social as well as their economic status after settling in America. Traditions of social deference encountered more resistance than in Europe, and no hereditary nobility developed. The family retained its basic responsibility for education, as in

Europe, but New England began to provide public support for schooling as well. The bourgeois character of American society impeded progress in the arts and sciences, although two American painters did win great acclaim in London.

SUGGESTED READINGS

Colonial economic history is a relatively neglected field. There are indeed the remarkable volumes published by the Carnegie Institution in the last generation, notably L. C. Gray's *History of Agriculture in the Southern United States to* 1860 (2 vols., 1933), but they are generally too formidable for all but the most determined undergraduates. Much more manageable are such works as W. T. Baxter's *The House of Hancock* (1945), which explains how "bookkeeping barter" enabled merchants to do business without money; J. B. Hedges's *The Browns of Providence Plantations* (1952); G. M. Waller's *Samuel Vetch, Colonial Enterpriser* (1960); Bernard Bailyn's *The New England Merchants in the Seventeenth Century* (1955); and Virginia Harrington's *The New York Merchant on the Eve of the Revolution* (1935).

Carl L. Bridenbaugh provides insight into the lives of *The Colonial Craftsmen* (1950). *Tobacco Coast* (1953) by A. P. Middleton is an excellent regional study with a maritime slant. Louis Morton in *Robert Carter of Nomini Hall* (1941) and A. C. Land in *The Dulanys of Maryland* (1955) convey vivid impressions of the "first families" in Virginia and Maryland respectively, including their economic activities. W. B. Weeden's *Economic and Social History of New England* (2 vols., 1897) remains rewarding despite its age. R. M. Tryon's *Household Manufacture in the United States,* 1640–1860 (1917) barely introduces a still-neglected, important topic. H. A. Innis's *The Cod Fisheries* (1940) is superb on the maritime activity which sustained so much of New England's commerce.

Among books which deal generally with colonial American culture, D. J. Boorstin's *The Americans: The Colonial Experience** (1958) and Max Savelle's *Seeds of Liberty** (1948) are outstanding. L. B. Wright's *The Cultural Life of the American Colonies** (1957) focuses on thought and the arts. Michael Kraus's *The Atlantic Civilization* (1949) puts American culture in a European setting.

Several excellent volumes distinguish the scanty literature on the arts in colonial America. Hugh Morrison relates American to European architecture superbly in *Early American Architecture* (1952). Alan Gowan's *Images of American Living* (1964) has interesting suggestions concerning the history of furniture as well as architecture. J. T. Flexner in *First Flowers of Our Wilderness* (1947) and *The Light of Distant Skies* (1954) finds American distinctiveness reflected in American painting. Jules Prown has provided a perceptive biography, as well as reproductions of most of the works of *John Singleton Copley* (2 vols., 1966). V. L. Parrington reviews colonial literature brilliantly, albeit with great partisanship, in *The Colonial Mind** (vol. I of *Main Currents in American Thought,* 1927). Julian Mates has written interestingly of *The American Musical Stage before* 1800 (1962), and Irving Lowens affords a more general discussion of *Music and Musicians in Early America* (1964).

S. E. Mead's *The Lively Experiment* (1963) is a good introduction to American religious history. Perry Miller's examination of the thought of *Jonathan Edwards* (1949) supplements Ola Winslow's biography (1940). W. G. McLoughlin's *Isaac Backus** (1967) is an excellent biography of a major Baptist leader. S. C. Henry is competent on the great *George Whitefield* (1957). L. J. Trinterud's *The Forming of an American Tradition* (1949) is excellent on Presbyterianism. Alan Heimert views the Awakening very favorably in his controversial *Religion and the American Mind* (1966). W. M. Gewehr's *The Great Awakening in Virginia* (1930) is still the best of several regional studies. M. L. Starkey's *The Devil in Massachusetts* (1949) deals popularly but reliably with the uproar over witches.

On education, Bernard Bailyn's *Education in the Forming of American Society* (1960) conceives its subject as the means by which culture is transmitted across generations and surveys the relevant literature. P. T. Monroe's *The Founding of the American*

Public School System (1940) is outstanding. On secondary education Robert Middlekauf's *Ancients and Axioms* (1963) is authoritative. S. E. Morison's *Three Centuries of Harvard* (3 vols., 1936) stands out among college histories.

Negro history has traditionally attracted chiefly those historians interested in the nineteenth century, but some notable works with an earlier focus have appeared. On African history, J. D. Fage, *Introduction to the History of West Africa* (1959) is short and to the point. J. Pope-Hennessey's *Sins of the Fathers* (1967) recounts the horrors of the slave trade. W. D. Jordan's *White over Black** (1968) studies the development of Anglo-American attitudes toward Negroes with fascinating detail and profound insight. D. B. Davis's *The Problem of Slavery in Western Culture* (1966) supplements Jordan usefully on many points. J. H. Bennett, Jr., in *Bondsmen and Bishops* (1958) affords unique insight into the life of slaves on a West Indian sugar plantation. L. J. Greene reports well on *The Negro in Colonial New England** (1942). Herbert Aptheker wrote with some exaggeration of *American Negro Slave Revolts** (1943). Edgar McManus has written *A History of Negro Slavery in New York* (1966).

European immigration of the colonial period has also received relatively little attention. However, A. E. Smith's *Colonists in Bondage* (1947) is superb on indentured servitude as a means of immigration. There are also excellent studies of particular ethnic groups such as J. G. Leyburn's *The Scotch-Irish* (1962); I. C. C. Graham's *Colonists from Scotland* (1956); and F. Klees's *The Pennsylvania Dutch* (1950).

Middle-class democracy prevailed before the Revolution, according to Robert E. Brown in *Middle Class Democracy and the Revolution in Massachusetts* (1955) and (with his wife, B. Katherine Brown) *Virginia, 1705–1786: Democracy or Aristocracy?* (1964). J. T. Main sees the situation somewhat differently in *The Social Structure of Revolutionary America* (1965), as does C. S. Synor in *Gentlemen Freeholders* (1952) (called *American Revolutionaries in the Making* in paperback). L. W. Labaree relates class to ideology with great insight in *Conservatism in Early America* (1948).

Frontier, city, and town have also intrigued colonial historians. V. W. Crane deals expertly with *The Southern Frontier** (1929); Douglas Leach with *The New England Frontier* (1966). Alden Vaughan praises Puritan conduct relative to the Indians in *The New England Frontier* (1965). Carl L. Bridenbaugh's *Cities in the Wilderness* (1938) and *Cities in Revolt* (1955) study all aspects of colonial urban life. Ola Winslow's *Meetinghouse Hill* (1952) deals with New England towns in general. Charles Grant's *Democracy in the Connecticut Frontier Town of Kent* (1961) studies one in particular.

Several contemporaries left outstanding observations of colonial life. Crèvecoeur's *Letters from an American Farmer** is a classic inquiry into American character. *Gentleman's Progress* (edited by C. L. Bridenbaugh, 1948) records the views of a Scottish traveler. German immigrant Gottlieb Mittelberger described his *Journey to Pennsylvania* (edited by Oscar Handlin and John Clive, 1960). L. B. Wright and M. Tinling edited *The Secret Diary of William Byrd* (1941) with its observations on Virginia and North Carolina. R. J. Hooker edited *The Journal of Charles Woodmason* (1953), which has indignant descriptions of life in the Carolina backcountry.

* indicates availability in paperback.

4

Imperial versus Provincial Authority

AUTHORITARIAN GOVERNMENT was on the rise in Europe during most of the colonial period of American history. It was exemplified by the absolute monarchy of France, where no representative legislature met between 1614 and 1789. In Britain the trend was moving the other way. Yet prior to the Revolution, Britain's King was still the empire's chief executive and Parliament normally did as he wished. In contrast to this pattern, two American colonies elected their own executives; and in all the others, by 1760, the representative assemblies were in some respects stronger than the governors appointed from Britain. As the governors were the principal enforcers of imperial policies, the growth of legislative power also increased colonial autonomy.

Britain's leaders had long ignored the growing "independency" of the American colonies, but in the 1750s imperial authorities began to take a harder line. First they tried to compel the representative legislatures to accept royal instructions addressed to the governors as absolutely binding. They had some success, but it was hard to keep even the governors themselves from ignoring instructions as they had long done when provincial circumstances made such a course expedient. At length Parliament, prompted by the pressure of debts from the Seven Years' War and claiming unlimited authority over the colonies, attempted to levy new taxes, first to help meet defense costs and later to pay the salaries of provincial officials previously dependent for their income on the will of colonial legislatures. Added to the resentment over Britain's western land policies, favoritism to the Anglican Church, and more stringent enforcement of commercial restrictions, these policies by 1774 had pushed Americans to the brink of rebellion.

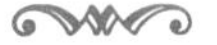

Seventeenth-century Crises

Nathaniel Bacon's dramatic rebellion against Virginia's Governor Sir William Berkeley illustrates the character of the political system which originally prevailed in the royal provinces. Berkeley was a reactionary, whose views stand starkly revealed in his famous observation: "I thank God, *there are no free schools* [in Virginia] nor printing . . . ; for *learning* has brought disobedience, and heresy, and sects into the world, and *printing* has divulged them. . . . God keep us from both!" In 1676, Berkeley, as was his right, had permitted no legislative election for fourteen years. Overproduction of tobacco had depressed prices and incomes. The government had reinstituted a poll tax, a fixed sum for each man, which compelled "the poorer sort . . . [to] pay as deeply to the publick as he that had 20,000 acres." To Nathaniel Bacon, a young, Cambridge-educated immigrant whose high status had gained him appointment to the Governor's Council, it appeared that "all power and sway is got into the hands of the rich, who . . . , having the common people in their debt, have always curbed and oppressed them." He saw little hope of improvement, as appeals had to be directed "to the very persons our complaints do accuse."

What sparked the rebellion, however, was Berkeley's refusal to authorize offensive action against the Indians. Warfare resulting essentially from white encroachment had taken the lives of about 300 Virginians and had led to a popular clamor for an attack which would "spare none" of the natives. Defying Berkeley, Bacon made himself "General by Consent of the People" and set out after Indians. A newly elected legislature, denounced by a Berkeleyite as consisting of men "lately crept out of the condition of servants," provided for increased popular participation in local government. Then Bacon contracted dysentery and died. Berkeley regained power even before the arrival of a relief expedition from England. He undid most of the reforms, executed a number of Bacon's followers, and confiscated their property. He would, a contemporary charged, have "hanged half the country" had Charles II not recalled him in 1677.

Far more important than Bacon's brief rebellion was the Glorious Revolution in England (see Chapter 2) and the revolutions in three American provinces which accompanied it. Both Charles II, who ruled from 1660 to 1685, and James II, who ruled from 1685 to 1688, hoped not only to increase royal power at home but also to consolidate a number of colonies into large administrative units to be governed without a representative assembly by a Crown-appointed governor and council. Such a pattern would correspond more closely to the presumably more efficient imperial systems of the French and Spanish. Like their relatives in England, however, the American colonists were determined to resist such absolutist efforts and, in particular, to reserve the power of taxation to their representative assemblies.

Preventing the forceful imposition of Catholicism was another goal as important to the

King's American subjects as it was to those in England itself. Evidence that the Catholics were persecuting Protestants in France, following the revocation in 1685 of the tolerant Edict of Nantes, provided powerful reinforcement to feelings already very strong. Aware that France had offered to help restore Catholicism to Britain, many Americans feared that appointees of James II, an avowed Catholic, would collaborate with French authorities in Canada to impose Catholicism upon them. Consequently when the Glorious Revolution sent James II fleeing to France for support, frightened colonials in Massachusetts, New York, and Maryland overthrew their existing governments to assure not only representative government but also their Protestant faith.

Massachusetts had most to lose from the policies of James II. During the Puritan Civil War, Massachusetts had made itself virtually independent of British authority and had assumed control of New Hampshire and Maine as well. According to Edward Randolph, a royal investigator, the people not only ignored commercial regulations but insisted that "legislative power . . . abides in them solely." Consequently, in 1684 Charles II revoked the Massachusetts charter, and James II in 1686 threw the colony along with the rest of New England into the Dominion of New England, a new administrative unit to which he later added New York and New Jersey. Sir Edmund Andros, appointed by James II as first Governor of the Dominion, was to rule with the aid of an appointed council but without an elected assembly. He had done so for three years when news of the Glorious Revolution inspired the populace to overthrow and arrest him. Under the new monarchs, William and Mary, Massachusetts received a new charter in 1691. It provided for an elected assembly and allowed the assembly a role in selecting the governor's council. Royal appointment, however, replaced election of the governor. Property ownership replaced church membership as the major qualification for voting. Massachusetts officially incorporated Plymouth and Maine, but failed to regain New Hampshire, which Britain had made a separate province in 1679.

New York, taken from the Dutch in 1664, had no legislature until 1683. Its proprietor, the Duke of York, had reluctantly established one then but quickly abolished it upon becoming James II in 1685. When the Glorious Revolution deprived him of the throne, shortly after he had put New York and New Jersey into the Dominion of New England, a popular convention elected Jacob Leisler, a German-born militia captain, as commander in chief. Exaggerating the dangers both of subversion and invasion, Leisler ruled rigorously until a governor appointed by William and Mary arrived. However, Leisler's insistence on seeing evidence that the new Governor was the agent of William and Mary rather than of James II occasioned a delay, which allowed his numerous enemies to "gratifye the malice of their party" by persuading the inebriate Governor to rush him and his son-in-law to the gallows for "treason." William and Mary did restore a legislature in New York, but provincial politics remained embittered for years by the conflict between Leislerians and their aristocratic opponents, who had always disdained Leisler and his followers as "men of meane birth sordid Education and desperate Fortunes."

Maryland, where a Catholic minority ruled a Protestant majority twenty times its size, was overdue for revolution. In fact, unsuccessful insurrections had occurred in 1659, 1676, and

1681. Protestants deeply resented what they referred to as the Catholic proprietor's "partiality . . . towards those of the Popish Religion." There were grievances on other points as well. Unfortunately for the proprietors in England, their messenger carrying the authorization to proclaim William and Mary King and Queen died en route. Without the authorization the proprietor's agents declined to make the proclamation and thus enhanced the credibility of rumors about Catholic plotting. John Coode, a Protestant agitator, led the forcible overthrow of the proprietary authorities and summoned a popular convention to institute a new government. William and Mary later declined to restore the Calvert family to political control in Maryland but did confirm their land titles. Following the conversion of Benedict Calvert to Anglicanism, however, George I returned Maryland to proprietary rule in 1715. Meanwhile the Church of England had gained official status there in 1702.

England's Glorious Revolution, defended successfully against French efforts to undo it in the War of the League of Augsburg (1689–1697), was of enormous importance for American as well as British history. For the empire as a whole it made both Protestantism and limited monarchy secure. Parliament had demonstrated by selecting William and Mary that it would choose England's rulers. It also made clear by statutory enactment that without its consent the King could not raise taxes, make or suspend laws, create new seats in the House of Commons, or refuse to call elections within a fixed time. To the Americans it appeared that these same principles should govern the relations between their appointed governors and the elected assemblies. In America, however, such principles tended not only to strengthen the representative legislatures in dealing with appointed governors but also to help free the Americans from British control, for in the colonies it was chiefly the governors upon whom the authorities in London depended to enforce colonial policies.

Eighteenth-century Developments

Despite the Glorious Revolution's restrictions upon his power, the English monarch continued to dominate imperial administration during the century which preceded the American Revolution. He commanded the armed forces, conducted diplomacy, and appointed not only all civil, military, and judicial officers but also the bishops who ruled the Anglican Church. In Parliament, as in the empire as a whole, there was still a general expectation supported by Anglican doctrine that people would normally accede to the wishes of the King. Opposition smacked of disloyalty. On the other hand, the beheading of Charles I and the expulsion of James II suggested strongly that the monarch had better exercise his powers with discretion.

Parliament's two houses, the House of Lords and the House of Commons, were by no means equal in strength. The hereditary nobles and the Anglican bishops who composed the House of Lords had lost even the power to amend money bills; they had to accept or reject those which the House of Commons passed. However, many of the great nobles who sat in the House of Lords received appointments as major ministers (administrative officers) of the Crown, and in that capacity they were among the political managers who controlled the House of Commons and ran the empire.

So great were the powers of the House of Commons that "management" or control of the House was the chief responsibility of the King's major ministers. Only the Commons could impose the new taxes required to meet rising expenditure needs, an especially critical function in wartime. The Commons had also gained the right to specify how tax funds should be expended. Thus, to get both the needed revenue and the authority to spend it, the King had to have majority support in the House of Commons.

Until the American Revolution, the King's ministers had always won him the support he needed in the House of Commons. The general custom of deference to the King's wishes explains this in part, but there were other factors of importance. While each county chose two members of Parliament under a rather wide suffrage, more than three-quarters of the members represented special borough constituencies. Boroughs were infinitely varied, but most were so constituted that great families of the nobility, those which normally provided the King's ministers, could control the elections, as indeed they did. Members of Parliament who desired royal appointments for themselves, for relatives, or for friends were also loath to offend the King by opposing his ministers. Lastly, both George I and George II chose particularly able managers who avoided crises and allowed great autonomy not only to the colonies but also to the counties at home.

In imperial administration it was the task of the King's ministers to see that the colonies brought benefit to Britain. "Every Act of Dependent Provincial Governments," wrote a colonial official in restating one of the axioms of empire, "ought . . . to Terminate in the Advantage of the Mother State, unto whom it owes its being, and Protection." It was with this goal in mind that Britain regulated colonial commerce, encouraged production of needed commodities, and discouraged the growth of American manufacturing. To design appropriate policies the government relied, more at some times than at others, upon the Board of Trade, an advisory agency including representatives of the business community. To enforce policies thus established was the responsibility of various administrative agencies, and in particular of the colonial governors.

Colonial governors administered colonies which came in three varieties: corporate, proprietary, and royal. In the corporate, or self-governing, colonies the people elected their own governors, and their laws were not subject to "disallowance" by the King's Privy Council. After 1691 only Connecticut and Rhode Island enjoyed government in this pattern. Proprietary families appointed governors in Maryland after 1715, and in Pennsylvania and Delaware; but by 1752 what would now be called nationalization had transformed all the others—each of them private ventures at the outset—into royal provinces.

Royal commissions appointing governors and "instructions" issued in the King's name theoretically fixed the constitutional systems of the eight royal provinces. In each case they required the governor to summon an "assembly of freeholders," meaning landowners, which alone could impose taxes. The governor, however, was to hold and to spend the revenue raised. The governor could not only summon the assembly when he chose, but could also adjourn it to a specified time, postpone it for an indefinite period, or dissolve it and call a new election at his pleasure. In addition, he possessed an absolute veto, one which could not be overridden. His instructions required him to use it against all measures in conflict with the laws of England which impaired the royal prerogative, restricted the sale of slaves or the dumping of convicts, aided the growth of manufacturing, or, in certain instances, omitted a "suspending clause" making them effective only after approval by the King's Privy Council. In addition, the royal governor had to send all new colonial laws to England for possible disallowance by the Privy Council.

Still other powers of the governor were important. He commanded the colonial militia, granted lands, appointed and dismissed judges, sheriffs, and justices of the peace. Theoretically he could appoint to vacant parishes ministers licensed by the Bishop of London.

On paper the powers of the royal governors seemed more than adequate to enforce imperial policy, but in practice the elected assemblies made it increasingly difficult. Governors found it harder and harder to manage their assemblies as effectively as the King's ministers managed the House of Commons. Governors of course lacked the prestige of royal birth and usually even that of noble status. They were also ordinarily outsiders and as such subject to some colonial resentment. The people whom they sought to govern included a high proportion of militant dissenters not imbued with the Anglican doctrine of nonresistance. Protestant Dissenters tended instead to believe that political authority should be representative, as it was in their churches, rather than appointive. Certainly more free adult males could qualify to vote in the colonies than in England, probably at least 50 to 75 percent, although the proportion actually voting was usually rather low. Colonial assemblies, furthermore, consisted largely if not entirely of county representatives, and thus were not dominated by members from special constituencies controlled by great families, as was the case in England.

Aided by factors such as these, colonial assemblies became more and more assertive. New York's relatively new Assembly demanded in 1711, for example, that the appointed Council, which was the upper house of the legislature, must accept or reject the Assembly's money bills without amendment, putting the Council in a position analogous to that of the House of Lords in England. When the Council pointed out that the Governor's commission placed no such restriction upon its powers, the Assembly retorted that it had "the inherent Right . . . to dispose of the Money, of the Freemen of the Colony" because it was based upon the "free Choice and Election of the People; who ought not to be divested of their Property (nor justly can) without their Consent." The Assembly prevailed—as, sooner or later, did those of the other provinces when they chose to press the point.

Their exclusive right to initiate tax measures was the basic weapon with which the assemblies won more powers. Britain expected the governors to persuade their assemblies to authorize collection of certain taxes for a number of years, if not in perpetuity, and to allow the governor to hold the money, spend it, and secure an audit. In practice, however, the assemblies often limited the duration of their tax measures to only one year, thus assuring frequent legislative sessions and a strong bargaining position. Taking advantage of the governors' revenue needs, especially in wartime, the assemblies in time took control of the power to authorize expenditures and to make the audit, as had the House of Commons in England. Unlike the House of Commons, however, the American assemblies, rather than leave tax funds in the custody of the executive, by 1760 had also taken physical possession of the revenues raised.

Making the colonial treasurer an agent of the assembly rather than a subordinate of the governor was only one of several ways in which the assemblies surpassed the House of Commons in gaining control of administration. They sometimes named commissioners to administer public works projects, named militia officers, and instructed agents or lobbyists employed to look after the colony's interests in London. At times they also used their control over the salaries of provincial officers to influence decisions, although by 1760 many such officials were deriving their income from official fees or from the British Treasury.

Assembly spokesmen always denied any intention to "wrest the Government . . . out of his Majesty's hands," but administrative officers of the Crown thought otherwise. "If they shall be allowed to go on without some remedy to put a stop to them," one official observed in 1727, "a resolve of the House of Representatives [assembly] will in time be look't on as of more force than his Majesty's positive Command, or even perhaps of an Act of Parliament if it be not accompanied with sufficient force to put it in Execution."

Two courses of action were open to the British to combat the assertiveness of the assemblies. One, urged by a governor in 1713, was that Parliament "settle" a revenue, meaning impose a tax upon the province, so that the governors thereafter would not have to depend upon the assembly for revenue. The Board of Trade endorsed the recommendation, but Parliament, respecting tradition, declined to honor it. Rumors of another approach reached the colonies in 1745. According to a veteran legislator, "A bill is prepared to be brought in this parlement . . . Commanding all Governors Councel Assemblys . . . to . . . adhere to all . . . Instructions . . . as they shall git transmited . . . from the King and his privee Councel." "If such Act Doe pas in a Law," he continued, it "stricks Emediately at the Liberty, of the Subject and Establish arbetrary pour . . . in America." He concluded correctly, however, that Parliament would probably "not Doe things so rash; for in the preparing Slavery to us would give a presedent and hand it against themselves." By choosing neither to tax the provincials, so that governors would no longer be dependent upon their assemblies, nor to order compliance with royal instructions, Parliament allowed the assemblies to go on increasing their authority. Each successful encroachment brought a greater degree of independence from British control.

Executive control of the judiciary remained much greater in the colonies than it was in Britain. The assemblies were successful in taking from the governors the power to create courts, but the more important power of removing judges from office remained with the governors to be exercised at their discretion. British judges had gained permanent, or "good behavior," tenure at the beginning of the eighteenth century, thus ending the threat of executive interference.

Civil rights in the colonies differed little from those in England. Only male property owners could vote, but even they were generally barred if they were Catholic, Jewish, or Negro (either free or slave). Indentured servitude and slavery were monumental restrictions of civil liberties in the colonies which did not exist in England. Freedom to criticize the government, in the colonies as in Britain, meant only the absence of prior restraint and did not preclude subsequent punishment if the words employed did, in the opinion of the judge, foster "an ill opinion of the government." The famous case of John Peter Zenger in 1736 did not really alter the law in this respect, but it did make clear how Americans would apply the law.

John Peter Zenger was a New York newspaper publisher who printed caustic criticisms of Governor William Cosby written by former Chief Justice Lewis Morris. Cosby was a generally unpopular governor who had removed Morris from office for rendering a decision which reduced the Governor's income. Under English law the function of the jury in Zenger's case was merely to determine whether or not Zenger had published the material in question. Zenger's lawyers, James Alexander and Andrew Hamilton, persuaded the jury, however, that making *truthful* accusations against an oppressive government was a right essential to protecting liberty and property. Accepting this argument, the jury acquitted Zenger. Thus it appeared that Americans would not punish those who criticized unpopular officials, but, as Alexander himself affirmed, "to infuse into the minds of the people an ill opinion of a just administration, is a crime that deserves no mercy." Provincial assemblies continued to see themselves as "just" and so construed "parliamentary privilege" as to allow them to punish their own critics. In Britain the House of Commons continued into the 1770s to punish those who merely reported its debates.

Local government in the colonies generally followed English patterns. In rural areas outside New England, counties were the administrative units. Appointed sheriffs were the chief law-enforcement officers, but justices of the peace, also appointed, were still more important. Together the justices were in effect a county legislature empowered to impose taxes as well as to make expenditures and pass other laws. In an administrative capacity they supervised local officers such as overseers of the poor. As judges they enforced both civil and criminal law. Governors nominally appointed sheriffs and justices of the peace, but in doing so they followed the recommendations of the local elite, as presented by one or both of the county's representatives in the assembly.

Towns rather than counties were the important units of local government in New England. Annual town meetings representing nearly all the men of the community chose the town's officers and passed local laws. The town was also the unit represented in the legislature, although with a more restricted suffrage.

Cities enjoyed only those powers which the provincial government saw fit to bestow upon them. "New York City's" charter of 1731, issued by the Governor but "confirmed" and later modified by the jealous Assembly, provided for an elected council. However, the mayor and other officers were to be appointed by the governor. Philadelphia's charter gave the city so few privileges that its citizens created a host of voluntary organizations to meet the city's needs. Boston retained its "town meeting" government rather than seek such a charter.

In the realm of political theory, John Locke's second treatise, *Of Civil Government* (1690), enjoyed high esteem on both sides of the Atlantic. Locke's basic proposition, paraphrased in the Declaration of Independence, was that officials who tried to exert "absolute power over the lives liberties and estates of the people . . . forfeit the power the people have put into their hands." In such circumstances, he continued, the people "have a right" to "provide for their own safety and security," especially the preservation of their property, under a new system of government, "such as they shall think fit."

More widely read and quoted than Locke were the popularizers John Trenchard and William Gordon, whose *Independent Whig* and *Cato's Letters* appeared in London between 1719 and 1723. Like other "Real Whigs" and "Commonwealthmen," they helped to preserve, especially among Dissenters, the thought inherited from Civil War radicals such as John Lilburne's Levellers. Although no Whig and Tory parties in the modern sense then existed, self-styled "Real Whigs" were prone to brand as "Tories" those who upheld royal prerogatives against Parliamentary encroachment. In this sense the American Revolutionaries would call themselves "Whigs" and the Loyalists who opposed them "Tories."

Contest for a Continent

While the colonial assemblies bickered endlessly with their governors, France and Britain contested for dominant status in Europe and for control of North America. Under James II, Britain had been friendly to France, but, after expelling him in the Glorious Revolution, the nation chose as its new monarchs William and Mary of the Netherlands, leaders of the League of Augsburg, a coalition of nations designed to resist the aggressions of Louis XIV of France. The War of the League of Augsburg (1689-1697) was inconclusive both in Europe and America. Seaborne New Englanders did capture Port Royal in Nova Scotia, but failed to take Quebec. The peace terms of 1697 restored Port Royal to France.

Five years later the rivals were at it again in the War of the Spanish Succession (1702–1713). Britain's major objective was to prevent the union of France and Spain which became a threat when an heir to the throne of France became ruler of Spain. New Englanders again seized Port Royal and once more failed to take Quebec. South Carolinians plundered Spanish colonial commerce and destroyed several Gulf Coast missions but failed to capture the fort at St. Augustine, Florida. In Europe the victories of the Duke of Marlborough enabled the British to achieve their basic war aim and to gain firm title to Nova Scotia (also called Acadia), Newfoundland, and Hudson Bay. From Spain, Britain gained the *asiento,* the privilege of selling a fixed number of slaves in the Spanish colonies yearly, plus the right to send one merchant ship to trade there each year.

During the generation of peace which followed 1713, France prepared assiduously for the next round in America. To guard her St. Lawrence lifeline to Canada, she built an imposing fortress at Louisbourg on Cape Breton Island. She also founded New Orleans in 1718 and extended her string of outposts (including St. Louis and Detroit) along the Mississippi and Ohio and in the area of the Great Lakes.

War began again in 1739 when a British-American force attempted to seize Cartagena in modern Colombia. This "War of Jenkins' Ear," so called because it began after Spanish authorities severed the ear of a British smuggler, merged in the 1740s into the larger European contest, the War of the Austrian Succession. This time Britain fought to prevent France and Prussia from dismembering Austria in the wake of a succession crisis. Intrepid New Englanders seized Louisbourg, but the European fighting was indecisive. Consequently the peace terms of 1748 restored all conquests, including Louisbourg.

Six years later the great imperial contest culminated in the Great War for the Empire (also called the Seven Years' War and the French and Indian War). In 1753 France had begun constructing a line of forts southward from Lake Erie across western Pennsylvania. Virginia's Governor Robert Dinwiddie first sent a youthful surveyor, George Washington, to warn off the French from territory claimed by his colony, and when that failed Dinwiddie tried to beat the French to the strategic site of modern Pittsburgh. The Virginians did get there first and began fortification, but the French drove them off and completed what they called Fort Duquesne. Meanwhile George Washington, commanding a group of Virginians, surprised and defeated a small French contingent near what is now Uniontown, Pennsylvania. Washington surrendered soon after to a superior French force, but his actions had begun, however ingloriously, a major world war, upon which the fate of the continent depended and from which would arise one of history's most significant revolutions.

Meanwhile an important intercolonial conference, summoned by the British Board of Trade, took place at Albany in 1754. Its purpose was to devise some effective means to improve relations with the Indians. The task was formidable, however, for while the French were principally fur traders whose activities actually aided the Indians to secure a better life, the English were mostly settlers who aimed to drive the Indians farther and farther west. Pennsylvania's Benjamin Franklin, seeking intercolonial unity, suggested the creation both of an intercolonial legislature with taxing powers and of a president-general appointed by the King. Authorities from the various provinces, denounced by Franklin for "their weak noodles," declined, however, even to consider his plan of union. On the other hand, the conference did make some progress with the Iroquois, traditionally anti-French, by giving them thirty wagonloads of gifts.

For three years the Great War went badly for the British. General Braddock, sent over from Britain to recapture the site of Pittsburgh, blundered into a disastrous ambush. Montcalm, the brilliant leader of the French, seized the New York frontier outposts of Oswego on Lake Ontario and Fort William Henry, not far from Albany. Indian raids terrorized the settlers on the frontier, especially those who lived in western Pennsylvania.

William Pitt, confident that only he could save the empire, took over leadership in Britain in 1757. He did reverse the tide. Concentrating Britain's military effort in America and India, he provided chiefly financial support to Frederick the Great of Prussia to keep up the fighting on the European continent. In 1758, British successes on the frontier induced the French to abandon all their forts in Pennsylvania; the great fortress of Louisbourg also fell. In 1759 General James Wolfe, still in his early thirties, conceived and implemented a daring battle plan which forced Montcalm to accept a crucial contest at Quebec. Though both generals died, the British forces triumphed. By the end of 1760, New France was in British hands. The terms of peace concluded at Paris in 1763 transferred all France's continental American possessions east of the Mississippi as well as much of India to the British. To compensate her ally for losing Florida to Britain, France gave to Spain the title to the trans-Mississippi region known as Louisiana.

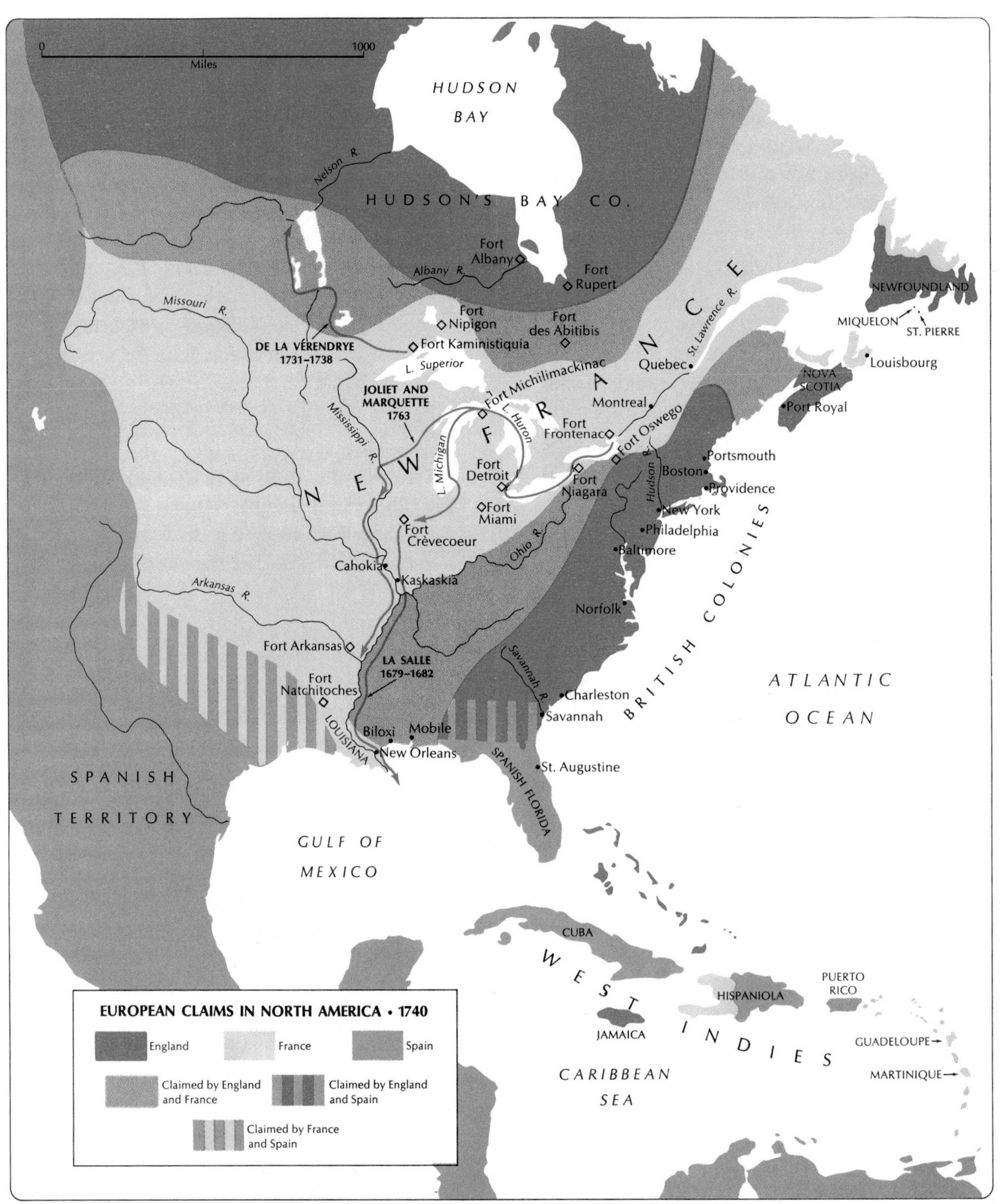

0
1000
Miles
HUDSON
BAY
Nelson R.
HUDSON'S BAY CO.
Fort Albany
Albany R.
Fort Rupert
Missouri R.
Fort Nipigon
Fort des Abitibis
DE LA VÉRENDRYE
1731–1738
Fort Kaministiquia
L. Superior
NEWFOUNDLAND
MIQUELON
ST. PIERRE
Louisbourg
St. Lawrence R.
Quebec
NOVA SCOTIA
Port Royal
JOLIET AND MARQUETTE
1763
Fort Michilimackinac
L. Huron
Montreal
Fort Frontenac
Fort Oswego
NEW FRANCE
Mississippi R.
L. Michigan
Fort Detroit
Fort Niagara
Hudson R.
Portsmouth
Boston
Providence
New York
Philadelphia
Baltimore
Fort Miami
Fort Crèvecoeur
Ohio R.
Cahokia
Kaskaskia
Arkansas R.
Norfolk
BRITISH COLONIES
Fort Arkansas
LA SALLE
1679–1682
Savannah R.
Fort Natchitoches
Charleston
Savannah
ATLANTIC
OCEAN
LOUISIANA
Biloxi
Mobile
New Orleans
SPANISH FLORIDA
St. Augustine
SPANISH
TERRITORY
GULF OF
MEXICO
CUBA
WEST INDIES
HISPANIOLA
PUERTO RICO
JAMAICA
GUADELOUPE
MARTINIQUE
CARIBBEAN
SEA
EUROPEAN CLAIMS IN NORTH AMERICA • 1740
England
France
Spain
Claimed by England and France
Claimed by England and Spain
Claimed by France and Spain

EUROPEAN CLAIMS IN NORTH AMERICA • 1763
England
France
Spain
Disputed
Proclamation Line, 1763
Boundary by proclamation, 1763
Boundary of Quebec Act, 1774
0
1000
Miles
HUDSON BAY
HUDSON'S BAY CO.
QUEBEC
SPANISH TERRITORY
INDIAN RESERVATION
BRITISH COLONIES
ATLANTIC OCEAN
GULF OF MEXICO
MEXICO
CARIBBEAN SEA
WEST INDIES
NEWFOUNDLAND
NOVA SCOTIA
GEORGIA
WEST FLORIDA
EAST FLORIDA
LOUISIANA
CUBA
HISPANIOLA
JAMAICA
GUADELOUPE
MARTINIQUE
MIQUELON (Fr.)
ST. PIERRE (Fr.)
Nelson R.
Albany R.
Missouri R.
Mississippi R.
Arkansas R.
Rio Grande
Ohio R.
Savannah R.
Hudson R.
St. Lawrence R.
L. Superior
L. Michigan
L. Huron
L. Erie
Ontario
Fort Albany
Fort Rupert
Fort Nipigon
Fort des Abitibis
Fort Kaministiquia
Fort Michilimackinac
Quebec
Montreal
Fort Frontenac
Fort William Henry
Albany
Fort Oswego
Fort Niagara
Fort Detroit
Fort Miami
Fort Duquesne (Fort Pitt)
Fort Crèvecoeur
Cahokia
Kaskaskia
Fort Arkansas
Fort Natchitoches
Biloxi
Mobile
New Orleans
Louisbourg
Port Royal
Portsmouth
Boston
Providence
New York
Philadelphia
Baltimore
Norfolk
Charleston
Savannah
St. Augustine

How to restore the American provinces to what was presumed to be proper "dependence" had begun to concern the Board of Trade even before the climactic imperial war began. Instructions to a new governor of New York in 1753, drafted by the Board but signed by the King, charged that "in open violation of our said commission and instructions," the Assembly had taken over "the disposal of public money, the nomination of all officers of government, the direction of the militia . . . which by our said commission and instructions we have thought fit to reserve to our governor only." Accordingly the King required the Governor to inform the Assembly of "our high displeasure" and to "enjoin them for the future to pay to our said commission and instructions due obedience." Specifically the King wanted the Governor to secure, "without limitation" by the Assembly on how he might spend it, a "permanent revenue" adequate to meet normal expenditures of the province. Soon after his arrival, however, the Governor committed suicide, and the Assembly, even while expressing its "Abhorrence of . . . groundless Imputations of Disloyalty," continued to make annual rather than permanent provision for the support of the government.

During the war Britain had seen fit to avoid contention with the colonies, not only over such matters as obedience to royal instructions but also over contributions to the war's cost. Rather than antagonize the assemblies by heavy financial demands, Pitt arranged for the British government to feed and arm the provincial forces, and he promised compensation to the provinces even for such costs as clothing and pay for their own military forces. The policy preserved harmony and aided the buildup of the empire's forces, but it also helped to saddle the British taxpayers with a gigantic debt while Americans remained relatively debt-free.

Trade with the enemy, on the other hand, offended Pitt's sense of patriotism. At the expense of much colonial ill will, he tried mightily to suppress trade-as-usual between the American continental colonies and the French West Indian sugar islands. Such trade was important to the Americans both to provide a market for their produce and to secure cheap molasses (see Chapter 3) and sugar. Consequently they connived to continue it through such means as fraudulent flag-of-truce vessels purportedly exchanging prisoners. When Pitt used naval patrols to stop the traffic, a typical merchant wrote "Dam them all," for he found his "Sugar Trad is Entirely Ruined."

Boston's famous quarrel with "writs of assistance" had its inception in the same situation. General writs of assistance, good for the period of a king's reign, were virtual hunting licenses authorizing customs officers to enter any premises during daylight in search of evidence of illegal importation. Officers were not impeded by any restriction such as was later written into the Fourth Amendment to the Constitution: that official searchers, in order to gain entry, must describe in particular "the persons or things to be seized." When the death of George II in 1760 necessitated the issuance of new writs, Boston merchants retained James Otis, an attorney who had been disappointed in his desire for major appointive office, to challenge their legality. The court rejected both the argument, later accepted by the King's attorney general, that no Parliamentary statute authorized the issuance of such writs in the colonies and the contention that such "instruments of slavery" violated the British Constitution, equated by Otis with "natural Equity." Although Otis lost his case in the courts, he won it in the minds of Boston's radicals, including numerous merchants.

Anglican zeal also began in the course of the war to dismay American Dissenters. The chief source of their concern was a new Archbishop of Canterbury, Thomas Secker, who assumed that position in 1758. Responding to the plea of a Massachusetts cleric who found Harvard "poysoning the Fountain of Education," the Archbishop arranged that the Society for the Propagation of the Gospel establish a "mission" at its doorstep. Congregationalists did not disappoint his expectation that it would "raise a great clamor." Secker also sought to impede Congregationalist missionary work among the Indians and at the end of the war urged his American supporters: "We must try our utmost for [American] bishops." The King's ministers chose not to stir up that particular hornet's nest, however, so that Americans were left chiefly with suspicious apprehensions.

British determination to reestablish the binding character of royal instructions, which they had temporarily abandoned at the beginning of the war, reappeared as early as 1759. A high official had informed him, wrote Benjamin Franklin from London in that year, that the government would attempt to secure what Franklin called "absolute Subjection to . . . Instructions." "The King in Council," Franklin quoted his informant as saying, "is *the Legislator* of the Colonies; . . . his Majesty's Instructions . . . are the *Law of the Land*."

Virginia's Two-Penny Act of 1758 afforded an opportunity to test the new policy. To alleviate the hardship following a drought which had cut tobacco production and tripled its price, the Legislature provided in the Two-Penny Act that during the next year all obligations fixed in tobacco could be paid at the rate of 2 pence per pound of tobacco, roughly the previous price, rather than at the much higher current price or in tobacco itself. Thus, in effect, the Two-Penny Act repealed an earlier law requiring Anglican parsons to be paid a fixed amount of tobacco to be secured by taxation in each community. The Governor's instructions required him to veto repeal measures lacking a "suspending clause" which made them effective only after approval by the Privy Council. In order to serve its purpose, however, the Two-Penny Act had to take effect at once, not a year or so later when the dilatory Privy Council might get around to considering it. Accordingly the Governor ignored his instructions and approved the Two-Penny law despite the omission of a suspending clause. A year later, after the law had served its purpose, the Privy Council disallowed it, censured the Governor for approving it, and threatened to recall him if he did not observe his instructions "punctually" thereafter. There the affair might have ended with no great animosity, had it not been for a few avaricious parsons.

Seeking to triple their income for 1758, several parsons brought suit alleging that, because it conflicted with the King's instructions, the Two-Penny Act was void from the outset rather than only from the time of disallowance. Had the courts upheld this argument, royal instructions would henceforth have bound Virginians tightly. However, the Privy Council, doubling as the empire's top appellate court, declined to hear an appeal from a decision adverse to the parson by a Virginia court. Only in one instance did a parson win his case in a local court. In that case, a hitherto obscure young lawyer named Patrick Henry exclaimed that a King who voided acts beneficial to the people "degenerated into a Tyrant, and forfeits all right to his subjects' obedience." Moved by Henry's oratory the jury awarded the parson not the £288 which he had sought but only 1 penny. In a pamphlet war on the subject, legislative leader Richard Bland argued that to accept "royal Instructions" as law to be obeyed "without Reserve" would "strip us of all the rights . . . of British Subjects, and . . . put us under . . . despotic Power."

George III, acceding to the throne in 1760, found the idea of a tough new imperial policy to his liking. Obstinate and unimaginative, the young monarch, aged 22, was also deeply conscientious and determined to make more of his constitutional powers than had his immediate predecessors, George I and George II. He ousted the popular William Pitt and altered his policies; he hounded John Wilkes into exile to silence his radical criticism. To manage the empire's affairs he relied often upon his own favorites, sometimes men of limited ability and brief political experience. He himself became chief among the nation's "borough-mongering" politicians. Though he acted within the unwritten British Constitution as most of his subjects then conceived it, his determination to reduce the colonies to "absolute obedience," says British historian J. H. Plumb, "made his presence on the throne . . . a national disaster."

Postwar Regulatory Problems

Britain's empire in 1763 rivaled that of ancient Rome in grandeur; yet, like the Romans, the British were not always able to manage the fractious "barbarians" on the imperial frontiers. The American Indians, always resentful of intruding British settlers, were not so ready as their French allies to surrender the Ohio Valley to the enemy. Goaded also by the policies of Britain's commander, Jeffrey Amherst, who discontinued gifts to the Indians as unworthy "purchasing [of] good behavior," Indian forces led by an Ottawa chieftain named Pontiac began their own offensive in 1763. Despite Amherst's contemptuous conviction that no fort commanded by a British officer could be endangered by "such a wretched enemy," Pontiac's Indians captured one after another until only Forts Pitt (Pittsburgh), Detroit, and Niagara survived. Indian enthusiasm soon waned, however, especially after they lost an engagement at Bushy Run in southwestern Pennsylvania. By the end of 1765 negotiations which committed the British to resume gift-giving had restored peace.

Even before learning of Pontiac's rebellion, British authorities in London had determined to station an army of some eight thousand men in the American West. Why they wished to do so remains uncertain. Ostensibly the object was to protect the settlers from the Indians, and vice versa. Historians have thought it odd, however, that this force was vastly greater than that deemed necessary before the war to protect the colonists against both the Indians and the French. Another object of the move, in the words of a British official, was "to retain the Inhabitants of Our ancient Province in a State of Constitutional Dependence," suggesting that Britain wanted the troops available for use in enforcing British policies to which Americans objected. Whatever the rationale for the action, the British subsequently cited the protective function of the troops as one justification for imposing unprecedented Parliamentary taxation upon the colonies.

Slowing the advance of Western settlement, whether or not the troops were there to help achieve it, was an important objective of the British. The usual haphazard migration into Indian country in violation of agreements, rather than after careful negotiation of new treaties, was sure to bring warfare with its heavy costs and disruption of the Indian trade. Furthermore British mercantilists were eager, as they saw it, to keep the settlers "within the reach of the . . . commerce of this kingdom." Those who settled beyond the Appalachians, the British believed, would be forced by transportation expenses to "ingage in the . . . manufacture of those articles . . . which they ought to take from the mother country."

To achieve the desired restriction of Western settlement Britain issued the famous Proclamation of 1763. Enlarging upon a wartime policy of 1761, the proclamation banned settlement and land grants beyond the crest of the Appalachians for an indefinite time and ordered those already settled in that area "forthwith to remove themselves." However, the British were never able to enforce the proclamation as effectively as had Pontiac in the summer before it appeared. Between 1768 and 1770 the empire's Indian agents, Sir William Johnson in the north and John Stuart in the south, negotiated agreements allowing the extension of settlement farther into Indian country.

Restrictions of colonial economic activity following the war evoked resentment and resistance, just as they had during the war. After only a brief respite, the British navy resumed its antismuggling patrol of colonial ports. Customs officers, apparently pressed to produce revenue to help meet Britain's postwar debt crisis, announced in 1764 that they would no longer accept bribes (usually a penny or less per gallon) on the importation of foreign molasses but would collect the steep legal duty of 6 pence per gallon. Vehement protests led Parliament in 1764 to reduce the tax to 3 pence. Two years later Lord Rockingham's ministry lowered it to just 1 penny but applied it to imports from British as well as foreign islands. Molasses traders and distillers thereafter had little economic basis for complaint.

Antismuggling regulations contained in the Sugar Act of 1764 also stirred resentment among American merchants. The law (also called the American Act and the Revenue Act of 1764) banned export to any European port outside Great Britain of iron, lumber, hides and skins, whale fins, potash, and pearlash—all significant items in the colonial export trade. The effect of the law, as with the enumeration of tobacco and other products much earlier, was to reduce the risk of scarcity in Britain and to assure that British, rather than American, merchants would profit from any sale of those commodities to Europeans. The law also imposed taxes (see pages 120 to 126) upon a number of commodities commonly imported into the colonies. The standard penalty for violation of these laws was the confiscation of both ship and cargo, with the resulting income to be divided equally among the arresting officer, the colonial governor, and the British government. If naval personnel made the arrest at sea, they split the income evenly with the British government. To tighten these enforcement procedures, the Sugar Act required the accused to prove full compliance with the detailed provisions of the law. It also immunized the accuser from assessment of either damages or court costs if the accused were found innocent.

Despite this obvious encouragement to indiscriminate prosecution, these provisions proved ineffective. Intimidation, bribery, and anti-British juries seem to have diminished the enthusiasm of customs officers for prosecution. In New England between 1765 and 1767, there were only six seizures and one conviction.

Controversy over enforcement of commercial regulations became more intense after 1767 when "Champagne Charlie" Townshend, then Britain's chief financial officer, instituted drastic reforms. Townshend's program included Parliamentary authorization for the hated writs of assistance, juryless vice-admiralty courts with jurisdiction over cases involving alleged evasion of customs duties, and creation of an American Board of Customs Commissioners at Boston.

Still so underpaid that "without bribery and corruption, they must starve," agents of the new customs board sought both income and official favor by seizing the sloop *Liberty* belonging to John Hancock, a wealthy Boston merchant who was a leader of the opposition to British policy. At Hancock's trial in a vice-admiralty court, his attorney, John Adams, not only demonstrated the weakness of the prosecution's case but pointed out that in Britain Hancock would have been entitled to a trial by jury. "Is there not in this . . . ," Adams demanded, "a Brand of Infamy, of Degradation, and Disgrace, fixed upon every American? Is he not degraded below the rank of Englishman?" The customs men were less zealous thereafter, but in 1770 the unwelcome troops whom they had requested for their protection fired on a Boston mob, killing a free Negro, Crispus Attucks, and four others in what Americans then branded "the Boston Massacre."

Confrontations of a similar nature occurred in other provinces as well. Henry Laurens of Charleston experienced troubles much like those of Hancock. In rural Maryland, a new and apparently desperate customs officer tried to seize several freight wagons on merely technical violations, but a mob tarred his clothes, rode him on a rail, dragged him through a mudhole, and compelled him to promise never to attempt such a seizure again.

The regulation of paper money also stirred resentment. Virginia, a latecomer to such experimentation, made unsound issues during the war with the result that British creditors complained of being paid in depreciated money. Instead of regulating the issuance of paper money so that its value would remain constant, a misguided Parliament required in the Currency Act of 1764 that the colonies retire all outstanding issues of legal tender paper money and make no more. The effect was to reduce the supply of money and further aggravate a postwar recession. Even more annoying to many Americans was Britain's insistence that their laws for the issuance of paper money which was not legal tender must include a suspending clause, making them effective only after approval by the Privy Council.

Taxation

Resentful as Americans were over royal instructions and Parliament's economic restrictions and enforcement measures, taxation was the issue which brought their relations with Britain to a crisis. At the conclusion of the war Britain faced a national debt which was double

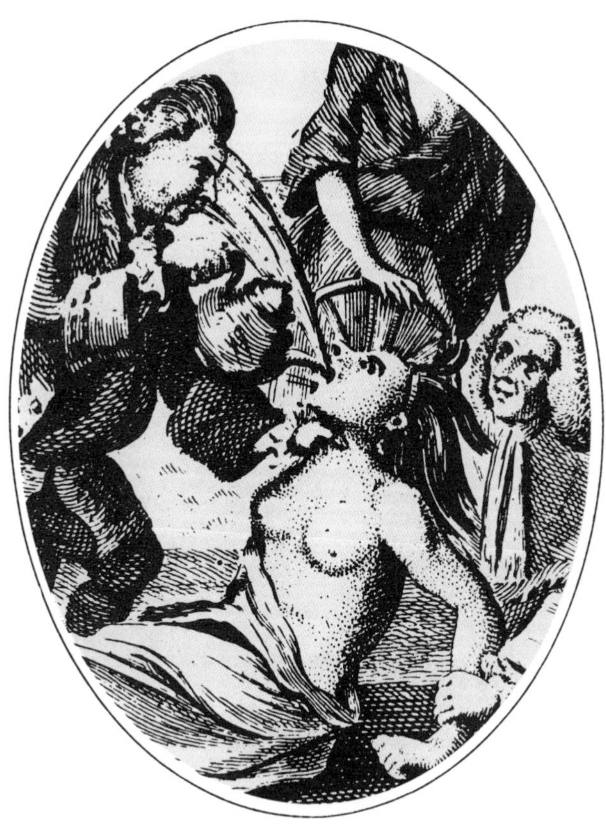

Sympathy for the Colonies

From the time of the Stamp Act and its repeal (1755–1756), popular controversy in Great Britain over the "American question" raged fiercely in the coffeehouses and clubs, in the press, and on the floor of Parliament. Notably enough, sympathy for the colonial cause ran high, an attitude also shared in France and Holland. The minority leader in the House of Lords occasionally referred to the Continental Army as "our army"; in Commons, Charles Fox wore a costume of blue and buff, the Continental colors, when speaking in the colonies' behalf. These political emotions found strident voice in one of the most popular communications media of the day: the political print. Englishmen thronged to the print shops in such numbers that one newspaper complained, "the shops collect the idle and profligate, by means of which the foot passengers are driven into the horse-road and lose their handkerchiefs."

Above, the detail from an engraving in *London Magazine*, 1774, shortly after the closing of the Boston port in retaliation for the Boston Tea Party, shows Lord North forcing a stream of scalding tea down America's throat which she as quickly regurgitates. America appears, as she frequently does in these cartoons, as a robust Indian maiden. Behind her, and out of the picture, Britannia turns away in tears.

The pro-British drawing above, "The Parricide—A Sketch of Modern Patriotism, 1 May 1776," pictures a direct reversal. Here the warlike Indian maiden America prepares to stab the fainting Britannia. The fox at right rear represents Charles Fox. "The Curious Zebra" at right embodies the colonies. Lord North tugs optimistically on his halter while the three British commissioners behind him express fainter hopes of a treaty. At the zebra's other end, Washington plans to take him for his own menagerie. In the vicious cartoon at top, George III and an Indian chief dine on the body and bones of a colonist captured at Detroit.

All pictures in this portfolio: Library of Congress

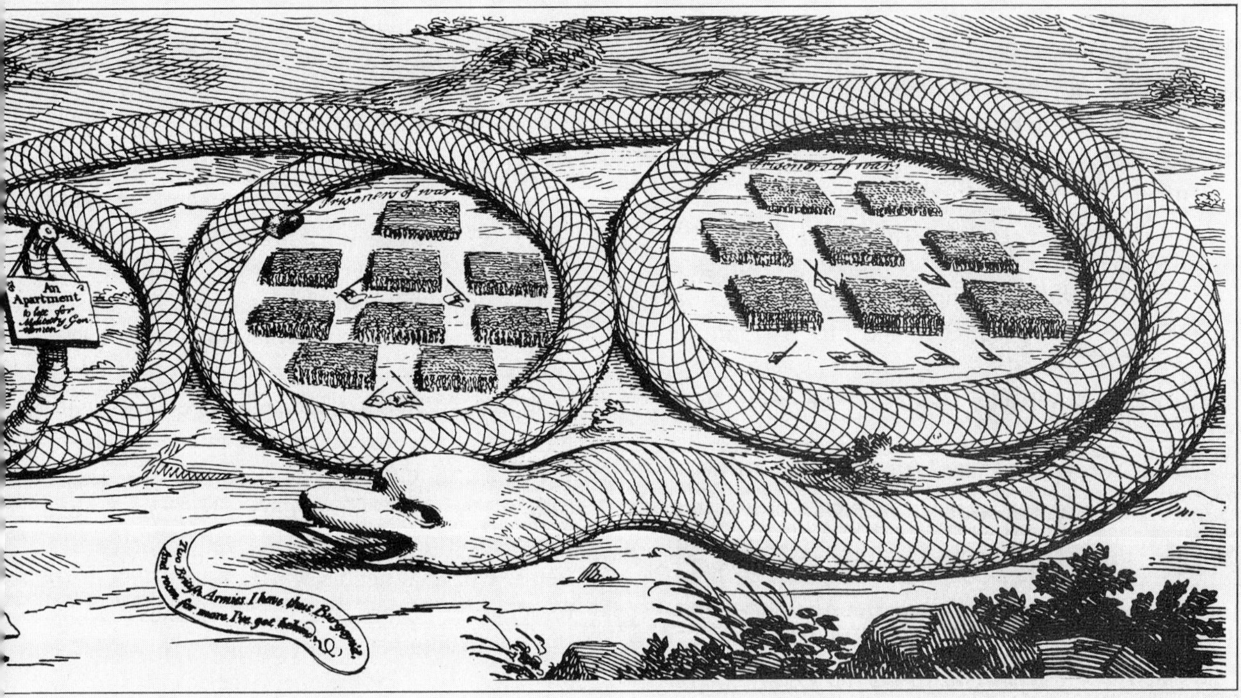

Above, a rattlesnake, an early symbol of the colonies and one used on flags before the stars and stripes, arranges itself in three coils: one encloses the troops of Burgoyne, one those of Cornwallis, while the last boasts a sign, "Apartment to Let." At the right, "Miss Mud Island" straddles a cannon firing at four British vessels. The fort at Mud Island eventually fell, but the British lost two warships. Howe sailed up the Delaware and his troops disembarked but failed to engage Washington. The piece at left, "Bunker's Hill or America's Head-Dress," satirizes not only ladies' coiffures of the time but also the British conduct of the war, as do both other British cartoons.

its prewar size. Riotous resistance greeted its new domestic taxes. In the colonies, by contrast, the provincial governments had relatively insignificant debts and the tax burdens imposed were very modest. Nearly everyone in Parliament except William Pitt assumed that that body had every right to tax the colonists for revenue as it did many of the King's domestic subjects who had no representation in its chamber. They also assumed that it would be fair to do so.

Most Americans thought otherwise. They naturally wanted to avoid increased taxes, and many of them shared the fear of Boston's Sam Adams that a body in which Americans had no representation might be tempted to impose "new taxations upon us" without limit. Most agreed as well with the Virginia Legislature that "it is essential to British Liberty that Laws imposing taxes on the People ought not to be made without the Consent of Representatives chosen by themselves." To colonial legislators generally it was crystal clear that their powers derived from their exclusive right to initiate revenue measures upon which the British governors depended to sustain necessary programs. Few felt any disposition to allow Parliament to deprive them of the basis of their power. Many agreed with William Pitt that submission to imperial trade regulations was "the price that America pays . . . for her protection." That price, estimated at £2 million yearly in 1766, seemed to many to justify economically the colonies' continued exemption from Parliamentary taxation for revenue.

Nevertheless, Parliament's Sugar Act of 1764, in addition to its regulatory and enforcement provisions, imposed colonial import taxes designed to raise revenue "for defraying the expenses of defending, protecting, and securing" the colonies. Molasses, sugar, textiles, and wines were among the items taxed. All the colonies protested. Consumption of the taxed items declined; incentive for smuggling increased. The trickle of revenue, roughly £20 thousand yearly, made little impression on Britain's national debt of £130 million.

To supplement the meager revenue of the Sugar Act, the King's chief financial officer, George Grenville, determined to impose a stamp tax. Such taxes, long employed in Britain, legally required that stamps purchased from the government be fixed on various items offered for sale. Grenville's plan was to tax newspapers, legal documents, and several other items. Colonial agents whom he consulted offered mild objections, but Parliament nonetheless enacted the law in 1765 by a large majority. To appease the Americans, the law provided that its revenue, expected to run about £100,000 yearly, would be "appropriated to the Defense of the Colonies and . . . never be drawn out of them" to England.

Much to the surprise even of colonial officials, resistance to the Stamp Act vastly exceeded that evoked by the Sugar Act of 1764. Virginia's young firebrand, Patrick Henry, newly elected to the Legislature, went so far as to insinuate that George III might meet the fate of Caesar and of Charles I. Widely publicized resolutions drafted by Henry, some of them approved by the Virginia Legislature, asserted, among other radical doctrines, that anyone upholding Parliament's presumed authority to tax Virginians "shall be deemed an Enemy to this his Majesty's Colony." In all the provinces mobs intimidated officials who showed any disposition to enforce the law. Lieutenant-Governor Thomas Hutchinson of

Massachusetts, who privately disapproved of the law, saw his splendid mansion go up in smoke. His more fortunate counterpart in New York, Cadwallader Colden, lost only his coach, burned with his effigy on top. Merchants organized an effective nonimportation movement against Britain. Delegates from nine provinces met in a Stamp Act Congress which declared, "That as the Profits of the Trade of these Colonies ultimately center in *Great Britain,* to pay for the Manufactures which they are obliged to take from thence, they eventually contribute very largely to all Supplies granted there to the Crown." Because Americans were not and could not conveniently be represented in Parliament, the Congress concluded, "no Taxes ever have been, or can be Constitutionally imposed on them, but by their respective Legislature[s]."

Pressed by British merchants whom the nonimportation movement was hurting, Parliament in 1766 repealed the Stamp Act without having carried it into effect in any of the continental colonies. Over the objections of William Pitt, who had endorsed the American position, Parliament enacted at the same time a Declaratory Act affirming its "full power . . . to bind the colonies . . . in all cases whatsoever."

Repeal of the Stamp Act assuaged Americans, but Britain's tax troubles brought renewed contention in 1767. Nearly desperate for revenue, a new ministry headed by Charles Townshend persuaded Parliament to impose taxes on lead, glass, paint, and tea imported into America. Such "external," or import, duties, Townshend believed, would be less offensive to Americans than "internal," or excise, taxes such as the Stamp Act. Unlike Grenville, Townshend intended to use the revenue for "support of the civil government" in the colonies, in order to reduce the dependence that the governors had upon the popular assemblies.

Accompanied by the authorization of writs of assistance and the creation of the American Board of Customs Commissioners mentioned above, the Townshend Duties of 1767 again provoked organized resistance. In a "Circular Letter," Massachusetts legislators urged that all the colonies "harmonize with each other" in opposing such taxes. They also defied a demand from London to rescind the letter, and when the Governor prevented formal convening of the Legislature, they arranged for town meetings to choose representatives to an extralegal convention. The convention did not attempt to take over the government; it merely protested the arrival of the British troops requested by the customs officers. When Virginia's Governor dissolved the Legislature, its members met informally to institute another nonimportation movement. In New York, mobs clashed twice with British troops, as Parliament suspended the Legislature for refusing to provide for the troops in accordance with the directive it had received from Parliament.

Again Britain ended the crisis by concessions. The meager revenue from the Townshend Duties was not worth the trouble and the economic damage of another nonimportation agreement. Consequently on March 5, 1770, the day of the Boston Massacre, Parliament repealed all of the Townshend Duties except the tax on tea. The tea tax remained, at the insistence of Lord North, the head of still another new British ministry, in order to uphold the "supremacy of Parliament." American patriots continued their boycott of British tea and increased their smuggling of tea from Holland.

Despite the bitter quarrels with Britain during the 1760s, the task of uniting Americans of different classes and from jealous provinces was monumental. To an English traveler at the end of the preceding decade, it had seemed that differences "of character, of manners, of religion, of [economic] interest" were so great among Americans that "were they left to themselves, there would soon be a civil war from one end of the continent to the other; while the Indians and Negroes would, with better reason, impatiently watch the opportunity to exterminate them altogether." In 1771, several North Carolinians lost their lives in a battle pitting forces of the Governor against backcountry "Regulators," whose major grievance was the exploitative corruption of local officials appointed by the Governor. In South Carolina the absence of local law-enforcement agencies in the backcountry forced vigilante groups to take up arms against organized bandits. Virginians bickered over religious freedom for revivalists. Pennsylvania frontiersmen beset by Indians demanded a militant policy which was resisted by the Quaker majority, while bitter factionalism split the legislative leaders. Tenant farmers in New York's Hudson Valley rose up against their landlords during the Stamp Act crisis. Violence occurred also in border quarrels involving New York, New Hampshire, Connecticut, Pennsylvania, and Virginia. Only in New England was there a degree of coherence which transcended provincial borders. Even there, differences existed between cautious gentlemen and the radical mob, as well as between a few well-placed Tories and the Whig majority. That such a disparate and contentious people did in the 1770s achieve a measure of unity was in large measure the consequence of Lord North's policies on tea.

All was not entirely quiet even before Lord North's tea policy of 1773 ended the lull following the repeal of the other Townshend Duties. South Carolina outraged the King's ministers by appropriating money to help pay the considerable debts of John Wilkes, the most virulent of the King's domestic critics. By special instruction, Britain tried to restore the Governor's lost control over expenditures, but Assembly resistance brought instead a total cessation of legislation in 1771. When Crown officers in Massachusetts announced in 1772 that they would thereafter receive their pay from the British rather than from the provincial treasury, Boston's town meeting under the leadership of Sam Adams created a Committee of Correspondence to publicize complaints against Britain. In Rhode Island a mob led by a prominent merchant burned the British custom ship *Gaspee* after it ran aground. When the British sent a commission to investigate, Virginians took offense at the intervention in local law enforcement and urged that committees of correspondence link all the colonies together in resistance.

Thus it was a still-simmering controversy which Lord North brought to a boil in 1773. One of his aims was to aid the East India Company, still the empire's agent in India. Its principal source of income was the sale of tea, which bore an import tax of 12 pence a pound on importation into Britain. Because of that high tax many Englishmen drank smuggled Dutch tea or else did without, just as the Americans were doing because of Parliament's refusal to end the Townshend Duty tax of 3 pence a pound on tea imported into the colonies. Lord North's Tea Act of 1773 provided that, for all tea reexported from Britain to the colonies, the company would receive a refund of the 12-penny British import tax. The law reduced the price of British tea in the colonies so that, despite the Townshend Duty tax, the East India Company agents could still undersell smuggled Dutch tea. Lord North intended thus to help the company sell surplus tea at a profit and, in effect, to bribe the Americans to end their boycott and thus accept the principle of Parliamentary taxation. Had he been willing to forego the second point, he could have achieved the first and maintained the same revenue pattern by ending the Townshend Duty tax and making the refund on the British tax only 9 instead of 12 pence.

American resistance to Lord North's cheap tea was surprisingly uniform. New York and Philadelphia sent it back. Charleston locked it in a warehouse. The resistance was caused not only by the Townshend Duty tax but also by favoritism in the selection of agents to monopolize sale of the bargain tea. In Boston the consignees included two sons of Loyalist Thomas Hutchinson, who had by then become Governor.

What would happen to Boston's tea depended on the outcome of a battle of wits and will between Hutchinson and the radical forces led by Sam Adams. To forestall the patriot mob, Hutchinson had customs men board the tea ship before it reached dockside. They officially "entered" the ship and fixed the obligation to pay the tax. Hutchinson then allowed the ship to dock and to be seized by the patriot mob whose wish was to return the ship to England. Backed by British warships, Hutchinson refused to allow it to leave. On December 17 the tea would become liable to seizure and public sale for nonpayment of duties. On December 16, when Hutchinson again refused to allow the ship to return to England, Adams's men unloaded its tea into Boston Harbor.

Boston's Tea Party evoked what Franklin called "great Wrath" in Britain. American sympathizers dwindled. Parliament retaliated with laws which Bostonians called the "Intolerable Acts." The Boston Port Act of 1774 closed the port by naval blockade until payment was made for both the tea and the tax. A Quartering Act authorized the army to billet troops in privately owned buildings and to secure certain supplies from the colony. The Administration of Justice Act permitted British officers accused of crimes in Massachusetts to remove their trials to Britain to escape provincial prejudice. The Massachusetts Government Act authorized the King to appoint members of the Governor's Council to serve indefinitely; it banned town meetings except for annual elections and made other changes designed to "take the executive power from the democratic part of the government." Finally, the Quebec Act, having nothing to do with the Tea Party, aroused many Americans by permitting no representative assembly in the former French province, by granting the Catholic Church a favored position, by recognizing French laws which had no provision for jury trials in civil cases, and by attaching to Quebec all the frontier territory north of the Ohio River.

Summoned by New York and Philadelphia, the Continental Congress met in Philadelphia to consider how to help the beleaguered Bostonians. Delegations representing the anti-British faction in every colony except Georgia attended. With 1 vote for each delegation, the

Congress defeated by 1 vote a plan of reconciliation drafted by Joseph Galloway of Pennsylvania. Instead it endorsed the defiant Suffolk Resolves (named for Boston's county), which Galloway branded a "complete declaration of war." After defining the American constitutional position in the words of John Adams, the Congress urged each colony to create an "Association" binding its people as in a covenant neither to export to Britain nor to import or consume British goods. It urged local committees to expose violators as "enemies of American liberty." South Carolina forced a grudging exemption of rice from the ban on exports, and Virginia won a year's delay for growers of tobacco. Before agreeing to adjourn, the members of the Congress determined that they would meet again in May, 1775. As the members departed in October, 1774, Charles Thomson, secretary of the Congress, wrote Benjamin Franklin in London, "We are on the brink of a precipice." Before Franklin had received the letter, George III had concluded: "Blows must decide."

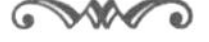

Conclusion

Between the Glorious Revolution and the end of the Great War for the Empire each of Britain's continental American colonies made great strides toward both representative government and provincial autonomy in internal affairs. The measure of their success was the power of their elected assemblies vis-à-vis the appointed governor (elected only in Rhode Island and Connecticut) upon whom the British depended principally to exercise control. According to their commissions and instructions, the governors possessed great power, but the assemblies—by virtue of exclusive control over the initiation of revenue measures—had made the governors subservient to them in many respects. In fact, in some ways they enjoyed greater power over the governors than Parliament held over the King and, quite contrary to the British experience, assemblies quite successfully resisted "management" by the governor and his agents. Even before the Great War for the Empire, authorities in Britain had recognized the extent to which the mother country had lost control of the provinces and had determined to do something about it. The war, while it delayed implementation of their ideas, demonstrated still more clearly the dimensions of the British dilemma: they could neither compel the Americans to pay what they considered a fair share of the war's costs nor prevent them until the very end of the war from carrying on trade with the enemy.

Britain tried essentially two tactics to restore its control over the colonies. First was the demand, reinforced by royal disallowance of important colonial laws, that governors and their legislatures carry out literally the King's instructions, most of them unchanged for generations and highly authoritarian in tone. That effort, dangerous in its implications for representative government in Britain itself, was largely a failure. More nearly in accord with British constitutional conceptions was the assertion that Parliament possessed unlimited authority to bind the colonies and hence could not only legislate for them, as it had done at times in the past, but could also impose taxes upon them. Recognizing that Parliamentary taxation would eviscerate their assemblies, thus negating both their representative government and their autonomy, Americans resisted by every means at hand, even boycotts and mob violence. Their tactics brought repeal of all the taxes except those of the Sugar Act and a tea tax. When Parliament in the Tea Act arranged to combat an American boycott of British tea by subsidizing the sale of the taxed tea at bargain prices, Bostonians dumped a cargo in the harbor rather than allow a stubborn governor to have it offered for sale. On this issue the revolutionary die was cast.

SUGGESTED READINGS

Bacon's Rebellion receives very favorable treatment in T. J. Wertenbaker's *Torchbearer of the Revolution* (1940), while W. E. Washburn's *The Governor and the Rebel** (1957) defends Governor Berkeley. *The Glorious Revolution in America** (1964), a selection of documents with introductory essays by M. G. Hall, L. H. Leder, and M. G. Kamen, is the best introduction to that important subject.

Britain's government provided the political model followed by the Colonies, as well as the imperial regulations which brought on the Revolution. G. O. Trevelyan's *American Revolution* (4 vols., 1909–1912), now abridged in one volume by R. B. Morris (1964), popularized a "Whig" interpretation of the period sympathetic to British and American defenders of more representative government and hostile to George III and the "Tory" supporters of royal prerogatives. L. B. Namier in *England in the Age of the American Revolution* (1930) and *The Structure of Politics at the Accession of George III* (rev. ed., 1957) convinced his generation that no Whig-Tory division of consequence existed but that numerous contending factions preoccupied with petty matters dominated the House of Commons and that George III accepted the same Whiggish principles as did nearly all his subjects. Robert Walcott in *English Politics in the Early Eighteenth Century* (1956) found Namier's major conclusion applicable to his period as well. However, J. H. Plumb in *The Origins of Political Stability: England, 1675–1725* (1967) and Geoffrey Holmes in *British Politics in the Age of Anne* (1967) both insist that Whig-Tory conflict was the focus of politics at the beginning of the century. Less argumentative are Basil Williams's *The Whig Supremacy* (rev. ed., 1962); J. B. Owen's *The Rise of the Pelhams* (1957); A. S. Foord's *His Majesty's Opposition, 1714–1830* (1964); and H. C. Mansfield, Jr.'s *Statesmanship and Party Government* (1965), a study of opposing views on the issue of the desirability for party government.

On British politics in the Revolutionary era Ian Christie's brief *Crisis of Empire* (1966) synthesizes recent scholarship effectively. More specialized works of value include John Brooke's *The Chatham Administration* (1956) and (with Namier) *Charles Townshend* (1964); Bernard Donoghue's *British Politics and the American Revolution: The Path of War, 1773–1775* (1964); B. D. Bargar's *Lord Dartmouth and the American Revolution* (1965); F. B. Wickwire's *British Subministers and Colonial America, 1763–1783* (1966); D. M. Clark's *The Rise of the British Treasury* (1960); John Shy's *Toward Lexington: The Role of the British Army in the Coming of the American Revolution* (1965); J. M. Sosin's *Whitehall and the Wilderness* (1961) and *Agents and Merchants* (1965); M. G. Kamen's *A Rope of Sand: Colonial Agents, British Politics, and the American Revolution* (1968).

On British administration as a whole, the last volume of C. M. Andrews's *The Colonial Period of American History* (4 vols., 1934–1938) is a standard source. O. M. Dickerson's *The Navigation Acts and the American Revolution* (1952) found that Americans objected more to the means of enforcement than to the Navigation Acts themselves. T. C. Barrow's *Trade and Empire: The British Customs Service in Colonial America, 1660–1775* (1967) found that the service was ineffective and that measures to improve it were significant contributions to the Revolution. S. N. Katz's *Newcastle's New York* (1968) shows the interlocking of British and provincial politics. Good studies of provincial administrators include L. Dodson's *Alexander Spotswood* (1932); J. A. Schutz's *Thomas Pownall* (1951) and *William Shirley* (1961); W. W. Abbot's *The Royal Governors of Georgia* (1959). J. H. Smith's *Appeals of the Privy Council from the American Plantations* (1950) sheds light on another form of imperial control.

To see colonial government in American perspective, J. P. Greene's *The Quest for Power: The Lower Houses of Assembly in the Southern Royal Colonies* (1963) is invaluable. It largely supersedes L. W. Labaree's long standard *Royal Government in America* (1930). L. W. Levy's *Legacy of Suppression* (altered to *Freedom of Speech and Press** in paperback, 1960) drastically changes old ideas concerning the evolution of freedom of expression. L. H. Leder's *Liberty and Authority* (1968) attempts to qualify Levy's dire conclusions. M. P. Clarke's *Parliamentary Privilege in the American Colonies* (1943) illustrates the use and abuse of that great legislative power.

Ideological issues upon which the British and American majorities differed stand forth in varying perspectives in such works as Bernard Bailyn's *Ideological Origins of the American Revolution* (1966) and *The Origin of American Politics* (1968); J. R. Pole's *Political Representation in England and the Origins of the American Republic* (1966); and Clinton Rossiter's *Seedtime of the Republic* (1953) (partially reprinted in paperback as *American Colonies on the Eve of Independence**). The views of British radicals more or less sympathetic to the Americans may be examined in Caroline Robbins's *The Eighteenth Century Commonwealthman* (1959); Ian Christie's *Wilkes, Wyvill and Reform* (1962); George Rudé's *Wilkes and Liberty* (1962); L. S. Sutherland's *The City of London and Opposition to Government, 1768–1774* (1959). D. L. Jacobson in the *English Libertarian Heritage** (1965) has edited the writings of Trenchard and Gordon, which were so influential in the Colonies.

Max Savelle's *Origins of American Diplomacy* (1968) shows the background of the colonial wars. Howard Peckham's *The Colonial Wars, 1689–1762** (1964) affords brief treatment of their military aspect. J. H. McCallum (ed.), *The Seven Years War** (1968), condenses Parkman's volumes on that conflict. Volumes VI, VII, and VIII of L. H. Gipson's monumental series on *The British Empire before the American Revolution* (14 vols., 1936–1968) are less formidable in dealing with the war than the bulk of the series as a whole might possibly lead one to suspect.

To see the American Revolution from outside one should consult R. R. Palmer's *The Age of the Democratic Revolution* (1959); Crane Brinton's *The Anatomy of Revolution** (rev. ed., 1952); Hannah Arendt's *On Revolution** (1963); and R. W. Van Alstyne's *Empire and Independence** (1965). Imperial perspective characterizes L. H. Gipson's *The Coming of the Revolution** (1954); C. M. Andrews's *The Colonial Background of the American Revolution** (1931); C. H. Van Tyne's *Causes of the War of Independence* (1922); and Esmond Wright's *Fabric of Freedom** (1961). More American in tone are Merrill Jensen's massive synthesis, *The Founding of a Nation* (1968); E. S. Morgan's brief *Birth of the Republic** (1953); B. Knollenberg's *Origin of the American Revolution** (1961); C. L. Bridenbaugh's *Mitre and Sceptre* (1962); A. M. Baldwin's *The New England Clergy and the American Revolution* (1928); Carl Ubbelohde's *Vice-admiralty Courts and the American Revolution* (1960); B. W. Labaree's *The Boston Tea Party** (1964); and A. M. Schlesinger, Sr.'s *Prelude to Independence* (1958). Schlesinger emphasizes class division among Americans in *The Colonial Merchants and the American Revolution* (1918). Herbert Aptheker's *The American Revolution** (1960) is a Marxist synthesis.

Biographical studies of value include John C. Miller's *Sam Adams* (1936); Gilbert Chinard's *Honest John Adams* (1933) and *Thomas Jefferson* (1929); Carl Van Doren's massive *Benjamin Franklin* (1938); V. W. Crane's shorter *Benjamin Franklin and a Rising People** (1959); Dumas Malone's *Jefferson: The Virginian* (1948); J. T. Flexner's *George Washington: The Forge of Experience* (1965); and Robert Meade's *Patrick Henry* (1957).

* indicates availability in paperback.

5

Fighting for Independence

FORCED BY BRITISH intransigence to choose between total submission and violent resistance, most Americans chose to fight. Fighting began when British regulars, en route to seize provincial war supplies at Concord, attempted to disarm local militiamen who had assembled at Lexington—not to resist, but to offer symbolic protest. Reacting to the bloodshed, American volunteers poured forth; the Second Continental Congress transformed them into a Revolutionary army, to be commanded by a Virginia militiaman, George Washington.

Initially, Americans fought only to compel Britain to acknowledge limits to the power of Parliament over American affairs. Their objective, the Americans often affirmed, was "restitution of our former rights and privileges"—preeminently, the right to be taxed for revenue only by the vote of their own representative legislatures. A year of fighting, however, helped persuade the majority in the resistance movement that it would be better to seek full freedom from Britain and to "institute a new government" based on republican rather than on monarchical principles.

On July 4, 1776, the Continental Congress announced its intention to the world in the Declaration of Independence. Dedication to the goal of independence sustained the Revolutionaries through eight years of ravaging warfare, years in which the British sought first to subdue the North and then, after that hope was shattered by Burgoyne's surrender at Saratoga, to restore their authority at least in the South. The surrender of Cornwallis at Yorktown ended that illusion. French assistance to the Americans in money and diplomacy, as well as in ships and men, was invaluable in attaining victory; but in negotiating the peace, the Americans found British ideas as to the new nation's territorial extent more generous than those of France. Capitalizing on Britain's desire to avoid making the United States a dependency of France, American negotiators succeeded in fixing the new nation's western border at the Mississippi and in shifting the Canadian border northward from the Ohio River to its present line.

Lexington and Concord

Through 1774 and into 1775 both Britain and Massachusetts pushed preparations for war. General Thomas Gage, British commander in chief in America, had rashly informed the King that with four regiments he could enforce the law in Massachusetts. Gage followed a conciliatory route on the whole, but in September he ordered the seizure and destruction of artillery pieces collected by the provincial militia forces on the outskirts of Boston. Militiamen flocked to the scene but offered no resistance. In their turn, American militiamen seized war materiel in a British fort at Portsmouth without opposition. The Massachusetts Assembly, in open defiance of Gage, now transformed itself into a Revolutionary "Provincial Congress" in which role it proceeded to organize a Committee of Safety under John Hancock. Special militia forces called "Minute Men" trained conspicuously for speedy action.

General Gage was in a most awkward position. As early as September, 1774, he raised to twenty thousand his estimate of the number of troops required to enforce British authority. The people, he explained, "are not held in high estimation by the Troops, yet they are numerous, worked up to a Fury, and not the Boston Rabble but the Freeholders and the Farmers of the Country." Pending reinforcements, he urged suspension of the coercive laws. In Britain, authorities remained convinced that New Englanders would back down in the face of force and that the "better sort," especially in the Middle and Southern Colonies, would lend decisive support to the British position. They rejected Gage's appeal for more troops. George III, insisting that "Great Britain cannot retract," rebuffed as well the suggestion for suspending the coercive laws. Urged on by the King, Lord Dartmouth, Secretary of State for the Colonies, instructed Gage to "arrest and imprison the principal actors . . . in the provincial Congress," even though such a step might, as Dartmouth recognized, constitute a "signal for hostilities."

Dartmouth's instructions, hedged with injunctions that Gage use his own discretion, reached the general on April 14, 1775. Exercising his discretion, Gage made no effort whatever to seize the insurgent leaders. Instead he waited until the Provincial Congress in session at Concord had adjourned and then, on April 18, dispatched a force of some seven hundred men on a night march to seize war materiel stored there.

Gage's expedition did not catch the Americans off guard. Boston silversmith Paul Revere, acting for the local Committee of Safety, carried word to John Hancock and Samuel Adams at Lexington. A British patrol captured Revere before he reached Concord, but a companion,

Dr. Samuel Prescott, got through with the warning to remove the supplies. When the British force reached Lexington at dawn, Captain John Parker and about seventy Minute Men awaited them on the common, intending only to emphasize the gravity of the situation. Major John Pitcairn, commanding an advance force of the British troops, ordered his men to surround and disarm them. Parker had instructed his men to withdraw when firing started. Who began it, whether British or American, no one knows. Pitcairn's troops, however, rushing on out of control, killed eight and wounded ten militiamen. One regular was wounded. The engagement, concluded a recent historian, approximating contemporary American estimates usually considered exaggerated, was "less a battle . . . than an hysterical massacre at the hands of badly disciplined British soldiers."

The British forces moved on to Concord and began destroying what few supplies remained. A clash there killed two Americans and three English regulars before the troops began their return to Boston. On the return march, militiamen firing from every kind of concealment killed about seventy and wounded about two and a half times that number while suffering only ninety-five casualties themselves. Next day Lord Percy, commander of the 1,200 troops dispatched to assist what remained of the original force of 700, prophesied in revision of an earlier opinion that the "insurrection here" would not "turn out so despicable as it is perhaps imagined at home."

News of the events at Lexington and Concord flew quickly in all directions. Its most immediate and most significant result was the convergence of thousands of New England militiamen on Harvard Yard at Cambridge. Within a day or two, some twenty thousand outraged Americans had assembled to put a stop to the assorted atrocities of which most believed the British guilty. At Boston, Gage's force of about four thousand became a dangerously isolated garrison. The nucleus of an American army had sprung into existence.

Western New Englanders also responded quickly to the news of Lexington. Ethan Allen and Benedict Arnold, rival rather than joint commanders, captured a precious stock of artillery from the pathetic garrison of the moldering Fort Ticonderoga. They took Crown Point as well on May 12, thus ensuring that the Champlain route to Canada would be securely in rebel hands.

The Second Continental Congress

Delegates to the Second Continental Congress convened at Philadelphia just three weeks after Lexington. To replace Peyton Randolph of Virginia, who withdrew from the presidency, the delegates named John Hancock. A few weeks later General Gage singled out John Hancock and Samuel Adams as the two exceptions in a proclamation of amnesty to repentant rebels. The Congress "adopted" the army besieging Gage at Boston, arranged to raise additional troops, issued $2 million in bills of credit to pay military costs, and made George Washington of Virginia commander in chief. In addition, Congress created a post office system and assumed control over Indian affairs.

Moderates, led by John Dickinson of Pennsylvania, were still in control however. They squelched the efforts of more radical delegates, including Benjamin Franklin and John Adams, to endorse establishment of independent governments and to open American ports to foreign ships, close British customs offices, and establish an intercolonial confederation. Instead, congressional moderates dispatched the so-called "Olive Branch Petition" to the King. In very general terms of Dickinson's choice, the petitioning majority expressed its desire for reconciliation and, as "faithful subjects," beseeched the King "to procure us relief."

Despite the suppliant tone of Dickinson's petition, even the moderates were determined to keep up forceful resistance until the British abandoned their contention that no limits whatever restricted Parliament's power to bind the Colonies. Congress rejected almost with contempt the not-very-conciliatory proposal Lord North had pushed through Parliament in February, which promised only to exempt from British taxation all colonies which made financial provisions for their own defense and civil government satisfactory to Parliament. In a "Declaration of the causes and necessities of taking up arms," Congress made clear American determination. Drafted by Dickinson and Thomas Jefferson, the declaration boiled with indignation at Parliament's "intemperate rage for unlimited domination" and at its presumption in undertaking to "give and grant our money without our consent." The document concluded with a powerful affirmation: "In our own native land, in defence of the freedom that is our birthright, . . . for the protection of our property, . . . against violence actually offered, we have taken up arms. We shall lay them down when hostilities shall cease on the part of the aggressors, and all danger of their being renewed shall be removed, and not before."

Escalating Warfare

While Congress was in session from May 10 to August 2, military leaders also took important actions. At Boston, General Gage, although reinforced by 1,100 troops and three major generals—William Howe, John Burgoyne, and Henry Clinton—was still too weak to carry the war to the Americans. But he hoped to reduce the vulnerability of his position in Boston by seizing commanding heights at Dorchester across an arm of the harbor to the south and on Charlestown peninsula to the north. Learning of his intention, the Americans moved out during the night of June 16 onto the Charlestown peninsula to occupy Bunker Hill and lower Breed's Hill, a point still closer to Boston. Gage determined to make a frontal assault on the Americans, dug in on Breed's Hill and already under British naval fire. Three times Howe led the English regulars against the American positions. His losses were appalling, but on the third try the Americans ran out of ammunition and, after some hand-to-hand combat, retreated in good order, having suffered only moderate losses. Howe's casualties were 226 killed and 828 wounded—in all, nearly half of his attacking force. As Clinton observed, "Another such [victory] would have ruined us." Had Gage followed Clinton's suggestion to land troops behind the Americans at the bottlenecked base of the peninsula known as Charlestown Neck, the result might have been significantly different.

Success on Charlestown peninsula had relieved the British of danger from that quarter, but Dorchester Heights to the south of Boston remained unoccupied. Gage left them so, as, after Gage's recall, did his successor, General Howe. In the winter of 1775–1776, General Washington, having assumed command and received authorization from Congress to bombard Boston, sent Henry Knox for Ticonderoga's cannon. On the night of March 4, 1776, American working parties, assisted by a heavy fog, began to move their newly arrived artillery onto the heights. When Howe discovered the danger in the morning, he determined to attack before his position became utterly untenable; but heavy rains delayed his move and gave him time to reconsider. Under tacit truce with General Washington, he left Boston for Halifax with all his troops and over one thousand Tories.

Meanwhile a campaign for Canada had begun. Congress in 1774 had invited Canadians to join in rebellion against Britain, but no resistance movement of significance materialized. Sir Guy Carleton, commanding the British forces in Canada, was equally hopeful of raising Loyalist forces among French Canadians and equally disappointed. Most French Canadians remained aloof. British strategists, however, agreed that the Hudson-Champlain waterway afforded, as Burgoyne put it, "precisely the route that an army ought to take" in order, with a naval blockade, to isolate and subdue intransigent New England. Even before the evacuation of Boston, Lord George Germain, successor to Dartmouth as Secretary of State for the Colonies, had approved Howe's plan to occupy New York in force, link up with another major British force from Canada on the Hudson-Champlain waterway, and invade New England from the west.

Americans, unencumbered by the necessity of transporting men and supplies across 3,000 miles of ocean, beat the British to the punch. Already in possession of Ticonderoga and Crown Point, Americans in the summer of 1775 launched an invasion designed to conquer Canada itself. In charge was a former British officer, Richard Montgomery. Held up by a stubborn garrison at St. John's for eight weeks, Montgomery finally took Montreal in November, although General Carleton escaped. Montgomery and Benedict Arnold, who with great hardship had brought another force through the Maine wilderness, jointly attacked Quebec on New Year's Eve, with disastrous results. Montgomery was killed, Arnold badly wounded, and over a third of their force was captured. Smallpox and the expiration of enlistments completed the ruin of the invading force amid the rigors of the Canadian winter. Reinforcements arrived for both sides in the spring, but their relative numbers made it clear that the invading force of 1776 would move south, not north.

Military actions in the Southern colonies were more favorable to the Americans. Late in 1775, Virginia's Governor Dunmore began recruiting a Loyalist force at Norfolk, including a Negro regiment secured by promising freedom to slaves who would desert their masters to serve. Aroused Virginia and North Carolina planters defeated Dunmore and forced him out to sea. He returned to burn part of Norfolk, a job which the rebels completed so that potential British invaders could not use it as a base.

Encouraged by reports of great Loyalist strength in the Carolinas, British strategists in 1775 determined to launch a winter offensive to restore royal authority there. Logistic problems and adverse weather, however, delayed the force proceeding from Britain. Loyalist forces, chiefly Highland Scot immigrants, marched toward the coast but suffered a devastating defeat at Moore's Creek Bridge near Wilmington on February 27, 1776. Eschewing a landing effort in North Carolina, the British expedition proceeded to Charleston, hoping to secure at least a foothold. A hastily constructed palmetto log fort, however, absorbed the day-long British naval bombardment in late June with relative impunity. According to previous commitment, the expedition then sailed off to New York, where it was to assist in a major landing effort under the command of Sir William Howe.

Severing the Tie

Increasing numbers of Americans during the winter of 1775–1776 became convinced that complete independence from Britain was desirable. British actions helped them toward that conclusion. In March, 1775, the New England Restraining Act barred New Englanders from the Grand Banks fisheries, upon which their economy depended heavily, and confined their trade to the British Isles and the West Indies. Parliament applied similar restrictions to most of the other colonies in April. George III refused to consider the "Olive Branch Petition" from the Continental Congress and, in a royal proclamation of August 23, not only declared the Colonies in "avowed rebellion" but required all loyal subjects to assist in efforts "to bring the traitors to justice." In a speech to Parliament on October 26, the King asserted that the "promoters of this desperate conspiracy" were waging "rebellious war" with the aim of "establishing an independent empire." In the Prohibitory Act of December, 1775, Parliament barred all trade with the rebellious Colonies and ordered their ships confiscated. With news of the Prohibitory Act came rumors that the British had arranged to hire foreign mercenaries, professional soldiers with an awesome reputation for ruthless plunder. In fact, Britain concluded treaties for 18,000 troops from German principalities in January, 1776, after negotiations for 20,000 Russians fell through.

Common Sense, an anonymously published pamphlet written by immigrant Thomas Paine, electrified Philadelphia in January, about a month before Americans learned of the Prohibitory Act and the employment of mercenaries. The son of a Quaker corset maker, Paine had come to Pennsylvania with recommendations from Benjamin Franklin, after experiencing both economic and marital failure in England. Dubbing George III "the royal brute of Britain," Paine ridiculed the very concept of hereditary monarchy and of a royal family sprung from "a French bastard [William the Conqueror] . . . with an armed banditti." It would be absurd, he argued, for a continent—North America—to be "perpetually governed by an island." "England," he warned, "consults the good of *this* country no farther than it answers her *own* purpose." Appealing to what would later be called isolationist sentiment, he reminded Americans that while dependent upon Britain they could never "steer clear of European contention, but would always be involved in European wars." Furthermore only by declaring their independence, he concluded, could Americans secure foreign aid in their struggle against Britain.

Congress, reconvening at Philadelphia in September of 1775 after a six weeks' recess, began to take tentative steps toward independence. Before the end of 1775, it had created a naval establishment under Com-

Documents of Revolution

Library of Congress

The cartoon above, published in 1768, warns that England's inept administration is cutting off her own colonies and she will soon be a hopeless cripple. Taxes and interference with colonial self-government were the major problems. Sugar and stamp acts, import-export quotas and duties, and other levies drove the American colonies to a common bitter resentment of King George's government.

Benjamin Franklin probably designed this tragic cartoon for London's *Political Register,* a monthly journal. The Latin banner, "Give a little something to Bellisarius," alludes to a brilliant general of the Roman Empire who was reduced to begging in his old age. Further explanation reads: "The colonies being severed from [Great Britain] she is seen lifting her eyes and mangled stumps to heaven; her shield, which she is unable to wield, lies useless at her side; her lance has pierced New England; the laurel branch has fallen from the hand of Pennsylvania; the English oak has lost its head, and stands a bare trunk." The moral: "The ordaining of laws in favor of *one* part of the nation, to the prejudice and oppression of *another,* is certainly the most erroneous and mistaken policy.... The whole state is weakened, and perhaps ruined forever!"

In 1764, new taxes were levied in the form of a Sugar Act. James Otis of Massachusetts wrote an eloquent pamphlet on the rights of the colonies (following page, left, above). Though the pamphlet was aimed at maintaining relations with England, a basic American principle was asserted here. "[No legislature can] take from any man part of his property without his consent. . . . No parts of His Majesty's dominions can be taxed without their consent; every part has a right to be represented. . . ."

The following year, England passed a Stamp Act requiring that tax stamps be attached to every newspaper page, all official documents, wills, deeds, marriage, birth, and death certificates, every legal paper of any kind. As the starting date approached, newspapers announced their own deaths. Throughout the thirteen colonies, resentment and retaliation grew. Protest groups, the Sons and Daughters of Liberty formed to harass government officials and to boycott merchants who supported England (following spread, right). Women refused to buy imported cloth and other goods. The handwritten warning on the next pages appeared the day the first shipment of tax stamps arrived in New York. Those who sold stamps were burned in effigy and, in some cases, were tarred and feathered.

2062

THE

RIGHTS

OF THE

British Colonies

Asserted and proved.

By James Otis, *Esq*;

Thursday, *October* 31, 1765. THE NUMB. 1195.

PENNSYLVANIA JOURNAL;

AND

WEEKLY ADVERTISER.

EXPIRING: In Hopes of a Resurrection to LIFE again.

hat either —
nes use of Stampt
take Care of
Person, & Effects.
Vox Populi;
We

WILLIAM JACKSON,

an *IMPORTER*; at the

BRAZEN HEAD,

North Side of the TOWN-HOUSE,

and *Opposite the Town-Pump, i*

Corn-hill, BOSTON.

It is desired that the SONS and DAUGHTERS of *LIBERTY*, would not buy any one thing of him, for in so doing they will bring Disgrace upon *themselves*, and their *Posterity*, for *ever* and *ever*, AMEN.

Liberty and Property vindicated, and the St--pm-n *burnt.*

A

DISCOURSE

OCCASIONALLY MADE

On burning the *Effige* of the

ST--PM-N.

IN

NEW-LONDON,

IN THE COLONY OF

CONNECTICUT.

Center and near left: Courtesy of the New-York Historical Society, New York City
Far left, above and below: New York Public Library, Rare Book Division
Top: Massachusetts Historical Society
Above: American Antiquarian Society

New York Public Library, Picture Collection

The colonies formed militia, Committees of Correspondence, undercover governments, and harassment groups. The British used troops to maintain civil order, to protect shipments from England, and to search for and seize arms. A number of serious incidents occurred, including the Boston Massacre in March 1770: troops fired into an unruly mob, killing five.

These pictures, as Harold Murdock has pointed out in *The Nineteenth of April* (Houghton-Mifflin, 1923), show another incident which has become glorified as the Battle of Lexington; it was not, in fact, a battle at all. On April 19, 1775, British troops marching to Concord encountered a group of colonial militiamen on the common at Lexington. The colonials were ordered to lay down their arms and disperse. As they did so a musket went off on one side or the other; the British reacted by firing into the group, killing eight. The picture above was made just after the incident by a Connecticut Minuteman, Amos Doolittle. It shows accurately that the colonials dispersed and did not fire back.

Art and patriotism, however, soon began to alter history. An 1830 drawing (right, above) shows six Minutemen firing back while two others reload. In 1855, only a few men disperse while many more return fire (right, center). The 1886 painting (right, below) is completely fictitious. Here resolute

Minutemen stand firm and fight a battle that never occurred.

The British continued to Concord where they did find a battle:

By the rude bridge that arched the flood,
Their flag to April's breeze unfurled,
Here once the embattled farmers stood,
And fired the shot heard round the world.

Right, above and below: Lexington Historical Society
Right, center: Library of Congress

One of those lured from the American cause was Major General Benedict Arnold who made secret plans to surrender West Point to the British. Although discovered, he escaped to live out his life in England. The 1780 effigy procession in Philadelphia, shown below, reviled the traitor. In the wagon, a two-faced Arnold sits with a mask in one hand; in the other, a letter from Beelzebub tells him to hang himself now that his plot has failed. Behind him, a black-robed devil shakes a purse of gold in Arnold's ear and prepares to drive him to hell with a pitchfork. A lantern at the front shows a double gallows, the traitor's reward.

News of the war traveled slowly by word of mouth and by hand-carried letter, but once received, it appeared in newspapers and in broadisdes (right). Cornwallis's retreat after his last major battle became known in Philadelphia fifteen days later. The war had ended eight days before word reached Connecticut.

The Metropolitan Museum of Art, Bequest of Charles Allen Munn, 1924

Cornwallis Retreating!

PHILADELPHIA, April 7, 1781.

Extract of a Letter from Major-General *Greene*, dated CAMP, at *Buffelo Creek*, *March* 23, 1781.

"ON the 16th Inſtant I wrote your Excellency, giving an Account of an Action which happened at Guilford Court-Houſe the Day before. I was then perſuaded that notwithſtanding we were obliged to give up the Ground, we had reaped the Advantage of the Action. Circumſtances ſince confirm me in Opinion that the Enemy were too much gauled to improve their Succeſs. We lay at the Iron-Works three Days, preparing ourſelves for another Action, and expecting the Enemy to advance: But of a ſudden they took their Departure, leaving behind them evident Marks of Diſtreſs. All our wounded at Guilford, which had fallen into their Hands, and 70 of their own, too bad to move, were left at New-Garden. Moſt of their Officers ſuffered-- Lord Cornwallis had his Horſe ſhot under him--- Col. Steward, of the Guards was killed, General O Hara and Cols. Tarlton and Webſter, wounded. Only three Field-Officers eſcaped, if Reports, which ſeem to be authentic, can be relied on.

Our Army are in good Spirits, notwithſtanding our Sufferings, and are advancing towards the Enemy; they are retreating to Croſs-Creek.

In South-Carolina, Generals Sumpter and Marian have gained ſeveral little Advantages. In one the Enemy loſt 60 Men, who had under their Care a large Quantity of Stores, which were taken, but by an unfortunate Miſtake were afterwards re taken.

Publiſhed by Order,

CHARLES THOMSON, Secretary.

Printed at N. WILLIS's Office.

New York Public Library, Emmet Collection

Glorious Intelligence!

NORWICH, OCTOBER 26, 1781.

Friday Evening, Six o'Clock.

By a Gentleman this Moment from New-London we are favoured with the following Hand-Bill.

NEWPORT, OCTOBER 25.

YESTERDAY afternoon arrived in this harbour, Capt. Lovat, of the ſchooner Adventure, from York-River, in Cheſapeake-Bay, (which he left the 20th inſt.) and brought us the [illegible] news of the ſurrender of Lord Cornwallis and [illegible] army priſoners [illegible] to the allied army under the command of our illuſtrious General, and the French [illegible] under the comm[illegible] of his Excellency the Count de Graſſe.

A ceſſation of [illegible] took place on Thurſday the 18th inſt. in conſequence of propoſals from Lord Cornwallis for a capitulation.---His Lordſhip propoſed a ceſſation of twenty-four hours, but two only were granted by his Excellency Gen. Waſhington. The articles were compleated the ſame day, and the next day the allied army took poſſeſſion of York-Town.

By this glorious conqueſt Nine Thouſand of the enemy, including ſeamen, fell into our hands, with an immenſe quantity of warlike ſtores, a forty gun ſhip, a frigate, an armed veſſel, and about One Hundred Sail of Tranſports.

NORWICH:
PRINTED BY JOHN TRUMBULL.

John Carter Brown Library, Brown University

modore Esek Hopkins, appointed a committee to sound out "friends" abroad, and welcomed a French agent bearing informal assurances of assistance. In March, 1776, Congress voted to send Silas Deane to Europe to purchase war supplies and agreed to open American ports to all but British ships so that war materiels could be landed. Privateering against the British was authorized at the same time. In May, France decided to provide assistance in the guise of sales from the fictitious Hortalez Company, conducted by a remarkable secret agent, the playwright Caron de Beaumarchais.

Efforts to postpone a declaration of independence came chiefly from the Middle Colonies, especially Pennsylvania. Under Dickinson's leadership, Pennsylvania had continued to observe meticulously the constitutional contention that the colony, although immune from the authority of Parliament, was subject to the King. To overcome the reluctance of such moderates as Dickinson to renounce loyalty to the King, Congress, inspired by Samuel and John Adams, resolved on May 15 that royal authority of every kind "should be totally suppressed." Organized militants in Philadelphia gave every indication that they intended to create a rival government for the province unless the moderates capitulated.

Virginia pushed the question to a showdown. On May 15 Virginia's Revolutionary Legislature had instructed its congressional delegation to introduce a resolution endorsing independence, foreign alliances and the preparation of a plan for intercolonial confederation. As introduced by Richard Henry Lee on June 7, the resolution included the declaration, "That these United Colonies are, and of right ought to be, free and independent states." Dickinson secured a three-week delay, during which a committee headed by Thomas Jefferson of Virginia and including Franklin, John Adams, Robert R. Livingston, and Roger Sherman was to draft a declaration. Other committees were to consider confederation of the Colonies and foreign alliances.

Congress returned to the question of independence on July 2. Dickinson again sought delay; but when the decisive vote took place, he and two other Pennsylvania moderates stayed away, and one other joined the militants. Consequently, by a 3-to-2 margin, Pennsylvania cast its vote for independence. All the other delegations also endorsed independence—except for that of New York, which declined to vote on the ground that it had not received instructions from its government.

Jefferson's draft declaration of independence, however, was not yet in a form satisfactory to Congress. For two days the delegates cut and polished the declaration. They struck out a somewhat strained passage blaming the King for the existence of slavery but made no other changes of importance. Then on July 4, Congress unanimously approved the declaration. On July 8 the crowd which heard the first public reading built a bonfire in celebration and cast into it the King's coat of arms, which had rested symbolically over the door to the statehouse in which Congress met.

What the declaration said was nothing new to the many Americans who had resisted British authorities for so long. Rather it represented a consensus in support of the Whiggish doctrines which had been best expressed by John Locke almost a century before. Jefferson merely condensed the popular ideas to two sentences and changed the list of natural rights from "life, liberty, and property" to the somewhat less specific "life, liberty, and the pursuit of happiness." Because Americans had so long emphasized their loyalty to the King, the major thrust of the declaration was to justify breaking that final tie by attributing to George III oppressive acts "which may define a tyrant . . . unfit to be the ruler of a free people." In addition, however, the declaration made clear to the British people the determination of Americans to resist the efforts of "their legislature to extend an unwarrantable jurisdiction over us."

British Failure to Subdue the North

Prospects for American independence were not good in July, 1776. While Congress was voting to fight for independence on July 2, Sir William Howe was landing on Staten Island with an army of 34,000 men, backed by enormous naval and supply forces. Washington had a growing but only half-trained army of some 20,000 to oppose him. In Canada, General Carleton, also enjoying overwhelming superiority, permitted the remnant of the American invading force to escape to Ticonderoga but prepared to move south to join Howe and thus isolate New England. Beset by personal and provincial jealousies and plagued, too, by both Tory and Indian supporters of the Crown, a rudimentary American national government prepared to stave off invasion by a nation four times its size in population, which had proved itself in the Seven Years' War the greatest of the world powers.

But for Benedict Arnold, disaster might well have overtaken the Americans in 1776. Recovered from the leg wound he had received at Quebec, Arnold spent the summer frantically building warships to contest the British advance over Lake Champlain. Because of the greatly superior mobility of waterborne forces, Carleton had to take time to do the same, and not until October was he sufficiently confident of superiority to proceed. Carleton did destroy Arnold's fleet in battles at Valcour Island and Split Rock but decided that the imminence of winter precluded further offensive effort and accordingly withdrew to Canada. Had Carleton been as successful as Howe, the British strategy for the isolation of New England might well have worked in 1776.

Sir William Howe could perhaps have quashed the Revolution in 1776 without assistance from Carleton. The Americans, anticipating that New York would be the British target after the evacuation of Boston, rashly committed themselves to defend the virtually indefensible city. A wiser course would have been to burn it, as General Nathaniel Greene ultimately suggested, so that the British would have to rebuild it in order to make it the base of future operations. Instead, Washington placed troops not only on Manhattan Island but also at Brooklyn Heights on Long Island. He would not repeat Gage's mistake at Boston in failing to occupy the commanding Dorchester Heights. But neither was Howe disposed to repeat the mistake of Bunker Hill. He flanked the entrenched American positions at Brooklyn Heights and captured two major generals with a large body of troops. Washington himself led a relief force across the East River onto the tiny pocket of Long Island remaining in American hands; fortunately Howe, despite the urging of subordinates, declined to press his advantage. The warships under his brother, Admiral Lord Richard Howe, appeared indeed to be capable of preventing Washington's escape, but, under cover of a rainy night and a foggy morning, New England fishermen ferried the American troops back to Manhattan

Island, a move out of a tight trap into a looser one.

Howe again proved dilatory, and once more Washington and the American cause escaped disaster. After some skirmishing at Harlem Heights, Washington at last got his men onto the mainland, except for a garrison of about three thousand at Fort Washington near the upper end of Manhattan. While Washington watched in anguish from Fort Lee across the Hudson River in New Jersey, Howe forced the surrender of the entire garrison. Howe's subordinate, Lord Cornwallis, then pursued Washington across New Jersey to the Delaware River. But instead of pushing on in the hope of destroying Washington's dwindling and demoralized army, the British in mid-December chose to observe the conventional European practice of giving up winter offensives.

Washington could not afford to be conventional. He needed a victory to revive American morale. "These," wrote Thomas Paine, in the first of his *Crisis* pamphlets, "are the times that try men's souls. The summer soldier and the sunshine patriot will, in this crisis, shrink from the service of their country; but he that stands it *now,* deserves the love and thanks of man and woman." New Jersey and Pennsylvania militiamen came forth. Beaten army units from the Canadian and the New York disasters responded to Washington's call. Crossing the ice-filled Delaware on Christmas Day, Washington surprised a garrison of German mercenaries —Hessians—at Trenton on December 26 and captured over nine hundred men.

Somewhat overconfident because of his victory, Washington remained in Trenton and soon found himself confronted by a superior force under Cornwallis. Slipping southward around Cornwallis's camp during the night of January 2, 1777, Washington marched north to Princeton where he defeated a small British force before moving on to the mountains of Morristown. There the terrain made his position unassailable while the location enabled him to threaten British communications across New Jersey. Cornwallis accordingly drew back to New Brunswick. Washington's daring and unconventional campaign had freed most of New Jersey from British occupation. But it had done more. As a British observer wrote: "A few days ago they had given up the cause for lost, . . . now they are all liberty mad again. . . . They have recovered their panic and it will not be an easy matter to throw them into that confusion again."

One reason for the apparent lack of aggressiveness on the part of the British in 1776 was their belief that a mere show of force might end the rebellion. In that expectation, the Howe brothers were authorized to deal with the Americans, but only to the extent of accepting submission and issuing pardons. Britain offered no concessions and, in fact, insisted that Rhode Island and Connecticut become royal provinces. A congressional committee composed of Franklin, John Adams, and Edward Rutledge did meet with Admiral Howe on Staten Island during the battle for New York, but only to make it clear that Congress meant what it had said in the Declaration of Independence.

In the campaign of 1777, Britain compounded its errors of the previous year. The rakish General John Burgoyne, who had returned to England during the winter to lobby for his own advancement, replaced the abler General Sir Guy Carleton in command of the British army in Canada. Howe abandoned his earlier plan to move up the Hudson, join the Canadian army, and then turn in overwhelming force against New England. Instead he planned to leave New England to Burgoyne, while he pacified the purportedly Tory-ridden province of Pennsylvania. Lord George Germain, Britain's chief war minister, approved the change. He did urge Howe to finish off Pennsylvania quickly so that he could cooperate with Burgoyne, but the word did not reach Howe until mid-August, when his army was at sea en route to Philadelphia.

Dilatory as always, Howe did not get his army of 15,000 on board ships and under sail until July. Finding the Delaware Bay approach to Philadelphia defended, as he had anticipated, Howe moved around into the broader Chesapeake Bay, the back door to Philadelphia. Washington gave battle at Brandywine Creek, well west of Philadelphia, but Cornwallis flanked the Americans as he had on Long Island and Washington was fortunate to get away. Howe marched into Philadelphia without further fighting, but in October Washington launched another attack against the main body of Howe's troops at Germantown, just north of Philadelphia. His plan, "too intricate for inexperienced officers and imperfectly disciplined troops," was nevertheless close to success when confusion among the Americans sent them into retreat. Howe wintered comfortably with his mistress and his liquor in Philadelphia, while the Americans endured a more Spartan existence at Valley Forge.

Burgoyne meanwhile had lost an army. When he set off southward from Canada into the wilderness in June, Burgoyne's entourage included not only British, German, Canadian, and Indian fighting men, nearly 8,000 in all, but over 100 pieces of artillery, inordinate quantities of baggage, including an extensive wardrobe for the general, and some numbers of women and even children. Another force of nearly 2,000, mostly Indians and Tories, was moving eastward through the Mohawk Valley under Colonel Barry St. Leger to meet Burgoyne in Albany. New York militiamen under Nicholas Herkimer mauled a party of St. Leger's force which had ambushed them at Oriskany. Then Benedict Arnold, marching to relieve the American garrison at Fort Stanwix, sent ahead a half-wit Tory captive and several Indians bearing awesome tales of what impended. St. Leger's Indians departed, leaving him little choice but to do the same, which he did on August 22.

Burgoyne toiled on through the wilderness. He took undermanned Fort Ticonderoga on July 5 by getting his artillery atop the commanding Mount Defiance, but the garrison escaped. General Philip Schuyler slowed his progress by felling trees and diverting streams. Now seriously short of draft animals and provisions, Burgoyne sent off a 700-man foraging party to seize supplies at Bennington, Vermont. New England militiamen, however, aroused by the murder of Jane McCrea by Burgoyne's Indians, had come forth in great numbers under General John Stark. They killed or captured virtually all of the foraging party and much of the relief party sent after it. Burgoyne had lost a portion of his army and gained no supplies, but he pushed on.

After Bennington, Burgoyne had only two hopes. One was to crush the opposing American forces in a major battle. His own dwindling supplies and the rapidly increasing numbers of Americans in arms against him dictated speedy action if he chose that course. His other hope was that General Sir Henry Clinton, whom Howe had left with a considerable army at New York, might rescue him. On September 19 Burgoyne attacked the American army, now commanded by Horatio Gates, a onetime major in the British army who had resigned and emigrated to Virginia in 1772 because his inferior social standing precluded further advancement in the British army. The battle at Freeman's Farm near Saratoga was inconclusive, but Burgoyne's casualties were 600, compared with only 300 for the Americans. Learning that Clinton was on the move, Burgoyne decided to wait, in the hope that Gates would divert much of his force to meet Clinton. Gates declined to do so.

Three weeks later, his men on half rations, Burgoyne dismissed suggestions that he retreat and took the offensive again. In the battle of Bemis Heights (or the second battle of Freeman's Farm) on October 7, during which Benedict Arnold again distinguished himself for valor, Burgoyne lost another 700 men, more than four times the American loss. By October 12, Burgoyne's 5,000 survivors were surrounded by a force several times as large. He surrendered under terms—never honored—which called for the return of his men to England. Clinton, his relief expedition both too little and too late, returned to New York.

After Saratoga, Britain virtually abandoned hope of conquering the North. The South, considered more important, more dependent economically, and more loyal, seemed a better target. British strategists also considered that the scattered population and the high proportion of Negroes would make the South an easier mark than the North had proved. In the North the new strategy would consist of naval blockade and coastal raids.

From Revolution to World War

France, relegated to inferior status at the hands of Britain in the Seven Years' War, had recognized almost from that war's conclusion the prospect that American resentments might present an opportunity to humble Britain and enhance its own relative status. During the 1760s, French Foreign Minister Choiseul hopefully magnified reports from private agents of American discontent. His successor, Vergennes, had begun as early as March, 1776, even before Congress decided to seek help abroad, to implement the Beaumarchais plan for supplying the Americans. "It is our duty," Vergennes wrote, "to seize every possible opportunity to reduce the power and the greatness of England." Vast quantities of French war supplies passed inland from Portsmouth, New Hampshire, to the army which confronted Burgoyne and from various other ports to Washington's men. American privateers also enjoyed bases in French ports.

Burgoyne's surrender at Saratoga gave Vergennes the evidence, for which he had been hoping, that the Americans might succeed. He quickly entered into negotiations with Benjamin Franklin, only recently arrived in Paris, and two other agents of Congress, Arthur Lee, former London agent of Massachusetts with whom Beaumarchais had begun negotiations, and Silas Deane, who had been working with Beaumarchais to forward supplies. From the negotiations emerged a Treaty of Amity and Commerce and a military alliance. The former was of little importance until after the Revolution, but the alliance was of great immediate significance. Its stated purpose was to secure American independence; it bound each party to make peace only with the other's consent. France renounced any claim to continental territory east of the Mississippi and received American endorsement for efforts to capture British West Indian sugar islands. From June, 1778, Britain was again at war with its ancient and most formidable foe.

Spain found the American Revolution convenient to its purposes as well. Although they contributed money to the American cause from 1776, the Spanish would neither make an alliance nor even recognize American independence. Spanish leaders had what proved to be well-founded apprehensions both for the security of their trans-Mississippi territories and over the dangerous example of republican revolution being given their own colonies. Gibraltar, however, was a major concern to Spain. When Britain declined to yield it in return for Spanish neutrality, Spain in April, 1779, concluded an alliance with France at Aranjeuz, pledging a joint invasion of England and no peace until Gibraltar was won. A great French-Spanish fleet put to sea for the invasion in the summer, but its bungling commanders seemed no more anxious to attempt a landing than were the British to attack at sea. Some anxious moments in England followed, however, before the effort was abandoned.

Vergennes assiduously sought to maintain Britain's isolation. In previous world wars of the eighteenth century, Britain had always enjoyed the advantage of a continental ally. To preclude that possibility in the War of the American Revolution, France arranged in 1779 to terminate an incipient war between her Austrian ally and Prussia. With French support, the Netherlands resisted British pressure to curtail shipment of war supplies to the allies, and in consequence, Britain declared war on the Netherlands at the end of 1780. Again with Vergennes's encouragement, neutral nations set about forming in 1780 a League of Armed Neutrality, intended to compel Britain to permit neutrals to trade freely with its enemies. While the League members were never firmly united, the very existence of the League reminded Britain of still another danger in the isolation which her superpower status and Vergennes's diplomacy had forced upon her. Without an ally, Britain from the end of 1780 was fighting a naval war with France, Spain, and the Netherlands while struggling also to suppress the American Revolution and to avoid serious offense to a hostile League of Armed Neutrality which encompassed much of the rest of Europe.

Congressional Conduct of the War

Administrative supervision of the American war effort came from the Continental Congress. Even after the adoption of the Articles of Confederation in 1781 (see Chapter 6), Congress remained only an assembly of delegates chosen, instructed, and paid by state governments. Each state delegation cast one vote. Lacking any authority to tax, to regulate commerce, or even to enforce its will, the Congress relied heavily on private individuals plus state and local officers to do its work.

Negotiations with Britain and with other nations were a major concern of Congress. While France and the "United States" were working out their two treaties in the aftermath of Saratoga, Lord North belatedly introduced peace proposals in Parliament on February 17, 1778. Parliament gave its approval in March, and a commission headed by the Earl of Carlisle arrived in Philadelphia on June 6 to treat with Congress. The timing was unfortunate. Congress had ratified the French treaties unanimously on May 4, and General Sir Henry Clinton (successor to Howe, who had resigned) was preparing to evacuate the rebel capital after less than a year of occupation. To the commission's pledges, which included exemption from revenue taxation, Congress replied that its demands were independence and the withdrawal of British troops. After futile attempts to bribe several congressmen and then to appeal over their heads to the people, the Carlisle commissioners had to return home empty handed.

In 1779 questions of foreign policy involved Congress in a controversy concerning the identity of diplomatic representatives. Franklin had been a superb and relatively noncontroversial choice for the mission to France, proving to be a wily negotiator as well as a Parisian celebrity. But his two colleagues, Arthur Lee and Silas Deane, split Congress into bitterly contending factions. Deane was pro-French and favored very modest demands against Britain, but his dubious business activities, including wartime speculations in London, involved him at the very least in a conflict of interests. Lee, while neither corrupted nor duped, was an outspoken Francophobe and an aggressive expansionist whose presence in Paris offended the French. Efforts by Lee and his supporters to dump Deane touched off a prolonged battle in Congress. In order to end the wrangling, Congress at last replaced both Lee and Deane. John Jay, a Deane supporter, became Minister to Spain and John Adams, a Lee man, peace commissioner. Both Jay and Adams, along with Franklin, would serve the new nation superbly in concluding peace.

Military appointments also occasioned bickering in Congress, but, as in the diplomatic field, the major decisions were sound. Washington, perhaps more outstanding in character than in military skills, continued to retain the confidence which Congress had originally vested in him. After Saratoga, General Thomas Conway, Dr. Benjamin Rush, and others touted Gates as a replacement for Washington, but the "Conway Cabal," or conspiracy against Washington, was apparently little more than the muted mutterings of a minority of dissidents. Appointment of the able Nathaniel Greene as Quartermaster General solved the supply problems, which had been acute at Valley Forge in the winter of 1776–1777. Failure to gratify individual ambitions for promotion frequently evoked resentment, however, notably in the case of Benedict Arnold. His unsuccessful effort to betray West Point to the British in 1780 was, at least in part, the result of Congress's failure to take what he regarded as sufficient notice of his distinguished record.

Financing the Revolution was another crucial responsibility of Congress. In the first five years (1775–1780) of the Revolutionary struggle, Congress financed the war as colonial governments had financed wars in the past—by issuing paper money. In that period "Continental" paper money provided about 81 percent of the national revenue. Borrowing from individual Americans by using "Loan Office Certificates" for security provided 11 percent, while the states supplied about 3 percent and foreign loans 4 percent. Unlike the old colonial governments, however, Congress could not tax to redeem its paper money. The states, which were supposed to redeem it on a prorated basis, declined to do so, with the result that the Continental currency ultimately depreciated greatly in value. By 1779 its value was so slight that Congress decided to issue no more. It redeemed $120 million at one-fortieth of face value in 1780, but another $71 million became worthless. In effect this depreciation in value was simply a disguised form of taxation, one which sustained the Revolution in its most critical stages.

The collapse of the paper money produced an acute financial crisis. After a winter of deprivation at Morristown in 1779–1780, two Connecticut regiments from Washington's army demonstrated their discontent on May 25, demanding full rations and settlement of the five months' back pay owed them. In January, 1781, the Pennsylvania troops who had curbed their Connecticut comrades the previous spring marched off to negotiate with Pennsylvania's government for better treatment. New Jersey troops also mutinied. By a combination of concessions, persuasion, and a few executions, the mutinies were put down, but it was obvious that the embryonic nation desperately needed a new financial basis.

To solve the problem, Congress turned early in 1781 to Robert Morris, a Philadelphia merchant with long experience in Congress. As head of a new Department of Finance which lasted until 1784, Morris did achieve minor miracles. He was unable to get the states to authorize Congress to impose an import tax, as he and other nationalists had hoped to do, nor did he pay the army on schedule until the end of the war in 1783. But he did use the army pay situation to help induce the states to respond more favorably to congressional "requisitions" and in fact secured some $2 million in that manner. He raised $4 million in new loans from abroad, mostly from France, and pared expenditures to the approximate level of income. He improved the efficiency of supply operations for the army and at Philadelphia in 1781 set up, largely with government capital, the first commercial bank in American history, the Bank of North America. He used the bank effectively to stretch the government's resources. When Morris quit in 1784, the government was solvent. Suspicion that Morris had used his office to benefit his own business interests and those of his friends was widespread, but—at least with reference to his own fortune—it was apparently without foundation.

War costs, including state expenditures, from 1775 through 1783 amounted to about $163 million. Of this the states expended about half, roughly $78 million, although the United States in 1790 assumed $18 million of this figure. Paper money paid a little over one-fourth, or $46 million; domestic borrowing a little less than one-fifth, $18 million; and foreign loans still less, $10.5 million.

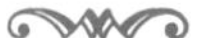

Britain's Failure in the South

British strategy after Saratoga was to maintain a naval blockade and carry out coastal raids in the North while making a major effort to subdue the South. Even in the North the plan did not work out well. Sir Henry Clinton chose to abandon Philadelphia, believing that to maintain occupation forces there would leave him too weak for effective raiding against New England. Washington attacked his rear guard at Monmouth as he moved across New Jersey, but neither side desired a major engagement and Clinton moved on to New York without further incident. A French fleet under Admiral d'Estaing arrived off New York in July, 1778, and—in conjunction with Washington's army—might have made things difficult for Clinton, but the harbor entrance proved too shallow for the larger French ships. A severe storm disrupted French-American plans to attack the British garrison at Newport, Rhode Island, and after some unpleasantness with the local populace at Boston, D'Estaing sailed off to the West Indies. Clinton withdrew Newport's garrison to assist in his attack on Charleston in 1779, with the result that a large French army under General Rochambeau debarked in Rhode Island without opposition in 1780. Consequently Clinton's New York–based raiders never moved out any farther than the lower Hudson Valley and Connecticut.

While French land and sea forces helped to frustrate Clinton's plans for extensive coastal raiding in the North, the Americans alone attempted to cope with British raiders on the frontier. Tories and Indians in 1778 committed massacres in the Wyoming Valley of Pennsylvania and at Cherry Valley in New York. General John Sullivan, dispatched by Washington, drove them back and devastated much of the Iroquois country, although he did not push on to their base at Fort Niagara. From Detroit, Colonel Henry ("Hair-buyer") Hamilton, widely believed to have paid bounties for American scalps, had fostered raids on Ohio Valley settlements. Militiaman George Rogers Clark, with authorization from Virginia's government, captured not only the British frontier outposts of Kaskaskia and Vincennes in 1779 but even Hamilton himself. Detroit remained in British hands, however, and at the end of the war the British were still strong on the northwestern frontier.

Even the war at sea produced embarrassments to Britain in the years after Saratoga. The minuscule American navy was no real threat, but in isolated engagements John Paul Jones and John Barry spectacularly bested British seamen. Naval vessels also captured nearly two hundred British merchant ships, while privateersmen caught several times as many. Britain, too, had to divert some of her blockade vessels to strengthen her defenses against the sizable naval might of France and Spain.

In the South, Britain initially enjoyed more success. Following D'Estaing's departure from Northern waters in the fall of 1778, Clinton sent off a force from New York which easily captured Savannah on December 29. With the subsequent fall of Augusta, royal government returned to Georgia. General Benjamin Lincoln, even with the support of D'Estaing's fleet, failed to recapture Georgia and in 1780 surrendered his entire army of over five thousand men at Charleston to a superior attacking force commanded by Clinton himself. Clinton wrote hopefully of recovering everything north to the Hudson River unless "a superior fleet shews itself, in which case I despair of ever seeing peace restored to this miserable country."

The immediately ensuing events made Clinton's hope seem reasonable. Congress sent Horatio Gates, hero of Saratoga, to repel the British, but at Camden, South Carolina, Gates suffered a shattering defeat on August 16, 1780, at the hands of Lord Charles Cornwallis. South Carolina irregulars also suffered at the hands of Banastre Tarleton. But rallying frontier riflemen surrounded a Tory detachment of about one thousand men at Kings Mountain on October 7 and killed or captured the entire force. Nathaniel Greene, Washington's choice to replace Gates, arrived to take command. His subordinate, Daniel Morgan, by effectively faking the usual flight of militiamen, killed or captured most of Tarleton's attacking force at Cowpens near Kings Mountain early in 1781. Greene advanced into North Carolina from Virginia. At Guilford Courthouse on March 15, he met the first of a series of technical defeats which nevertheless undid the British in the Carolinas. Too weak after his victory over Greene to renew the contest, Cornwallis moved out of the hostile interior toward the relative safety of the coast and thence northward to Virginia. Greene moved south to experience three more technical defeats, which—in conjunction with the guerrilla efforts of such men as Francis Marion, Thomas Sumter, Andrew Pickens, and Elijah Clark—had by the end of summer so weakened the invaders as to confine them to narrow enclaves at Charleston and Savannah.

In Virginia, Cornwallis was about to encounter the superior fleet which Clinton had dreaded. To conquer the Lower South, Cornwallis believed he had first to subdue Virginia, from which supplies and reinforcements came. Benedict Arnold, now in Britain's service, was already raiding widely over Virginia on Clinton's orders but with a relatively small body of troops. The arrival of Cornwallis and reinforcements built up the British army in Virginia to over 7,000. Opposing them was a small body of regular American army men, "Continentals," and growing numbers of those whom Cornwallis contemptuously dismissed as "peasantry," all under command of "the boy," the twenty-four-year-old Marquis de Lafayette, a French volunteer who had become a trusted subordinate of Washington. Lafayette could offer no resistance as Cornwallis moved to Yorktown near the mouth of Chesapeake Bay and began building a fortified base for his contemplated campaign. Clinton, characteristically indecisive, disapproved Cornwallis's plan, but—anticipating that Lord Germain was about to oust him in favor of Cornwallis—he did nothing to impede his rivalrous subordinate.

Responding to repeated American pleas, France in the meantime had sent off to the West Indies a large fleet under Admiral de Grasse. His instructions were "to detach a portion" of his fleet "to cooperate in any undertaking which may be projected by the French and American generals." Expectations were that the need to protect French and Spanish possessions and commerce in the Caribbean would severely limit the number of ships which De Grasse could spare. The British were sure that it would be only twelve or fifteen of his twenty-eight warships. Accordingly they employed several of their ships in convoying merchant fleets to England; one carried the British naval commander, Admiral Rodney, home to England for treatment of gout. His subordinate, Admiral Sir Samuel Hood, had only fourteen ships when he sailed north to meet Admiral Thomas Graves at New York, there to await the anticipated arrival of the French fleet. Since Graves proved to have just five serviceable warships, the combined British fleet numbered only nineteen. Still unknown to the British was the fact that De Grasse was bringing north his entire fleet of twenty-eight ships. In addition, a French squadron of some strength lay at Newport.

Washington had wished to aim the great French-American attack against Clinton at New York, but Rochambeau considered trapping Cornwallis to be a less difficult undertaking. De Grasse also preferred to make Cornwallis the target, and Washington acquiesced. De Grasse arrived at the Chesapeake on August 30, putting ashore some three thousand French troops to help Lafayette prevent Cornwallis's escape. On September 5, Graves and Hood arrived with their combined fleets

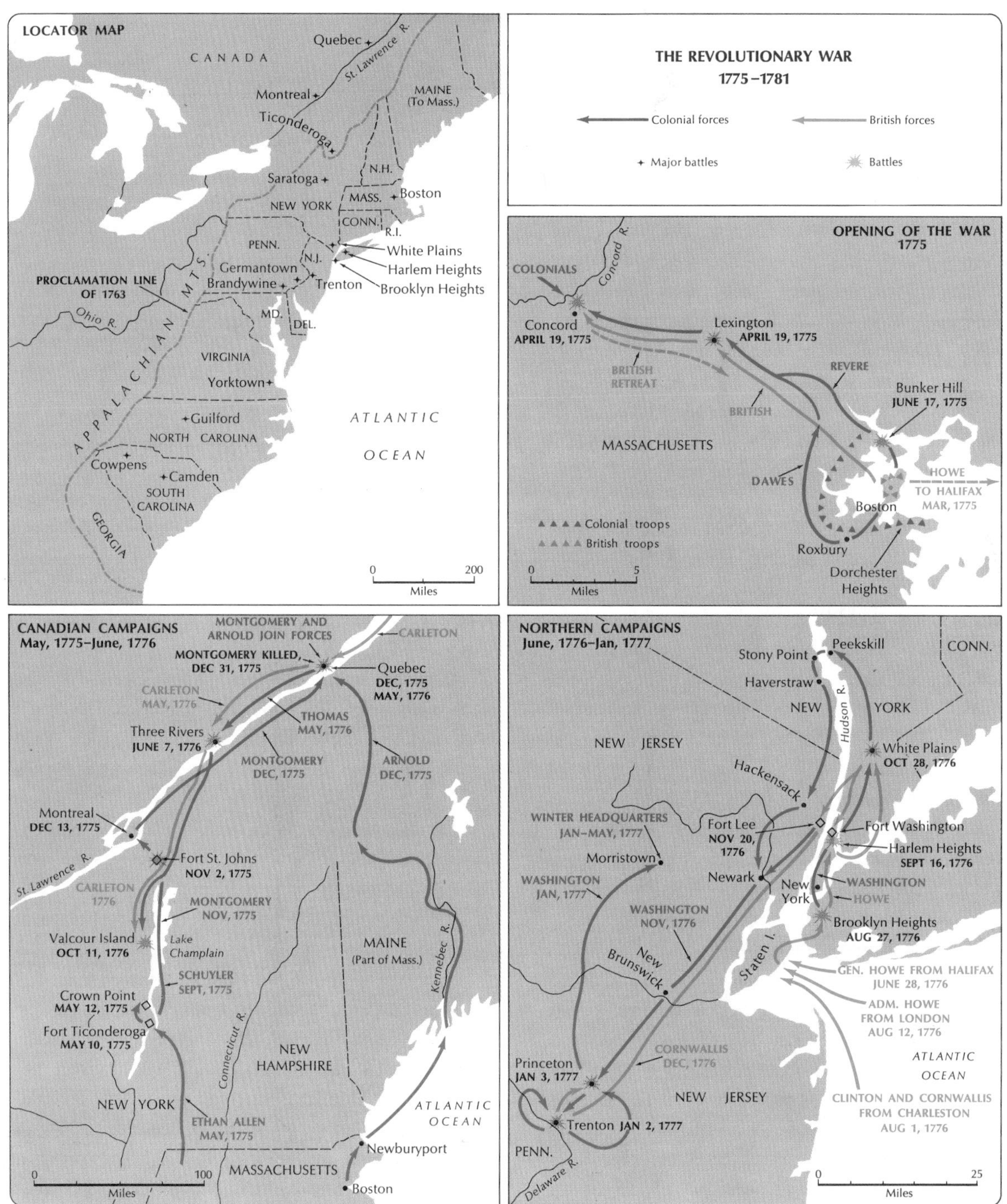
LOCATOR MAP
CANADA
Quebec
St. Lawrence R.
Montreal
MAINE (To Mass.)
Ticonderoga
N.H.
Saratoga
MASS.
Boston
NEW YORK
CONN.
R.I.
PENN.
N.J.
White Plains
Harlem Heights
Germantown
Brandywine
Trenton
Brooklyn Heights
PROCLAMATION LINE OF 1763
Ohio R.
APPALACHIAN MTS.
MD.
DEL.
VIRGINIA
Yorktown
Guilford
NORTH CAROLINA
Cowpens
Camden
SOUTH CAROLINA
GEORGIA
ATLANTIC OCEAN
0 200 Miles
THE REVOLUTIONARY WAR 1775–1781
Colonial forces
British forces
Major battles
Battles
OPENING OF THE WAR 1775
COLONIALS
Concord R.
Concord APRIL 19, 1775
Lexington APRIL 19, 1775
BRITISH RETREAT
BRITISH
REVERE
Bunker Hill JUNE 17, 1775
MASSACHUSETTS
DAWES
HOWE TO HALIFAX MAR, 1775
Boston
Roxbury
Dorchester Heights
Colonial troops
British troops
0 5 Miles
CANADIAN CAMPAIGNS May, 1775–June, 1776
MONTGOMERY AND ARNOLD JOIN FORCES
CARLETON
MONTGOMERY KILLED, DEC 31, 1775
Quebec DEC, 1775 MAY, 1776
CARLETON MAY, 1776
THOMAS MAY, 1776
Three Rivers JUNE 7, 1776
MONTGOMERY DEC, 1775
ARNOLD DEC, 1775
Montreal DEC 13, 1775
Fort St. Johns NOV 2, 1775
St. Lawrence R.
CARLETON 1776
MONTGOMERY NOV, 1775
Valcour Island OCT 11, 1776
Lake Champlain
SCHUYLER SEPT, 1775
Crown Point MAY 12, 1775
Fort Ticonderoga MAY 10, 1775
MAINE (Part of Mass.)
Kennebec R.
Connecticut R.
NEW HAMPSHIRE
NEW YORK
ETHAN ALLEN MAY, 1775
ATLANTIC OCEAN
Newburyport
MASSACHUSETTS
Boston
0 100 Miles
NORTHERN CAMPAIGNS June, 1776–Jan, 1777
Stony Point
Peekskill
CONN.
Haverstraw
NEW YORK
Hudson R.
NEW JERSEY
White Plains OCT 28, 1776
Hackensack
WINTER HEADQUARTERS JAN–MAY, 1777
Fort Lee NOV 20, 1776
Fort Washington
Harlem Heights SEPT 16, 1776
Morristown
WASHINGTON JAN, 1777
Newark
New York
WASHINGTON
HOWE
WASHINGTON NOV, 1776
Brooklyn Heights AUG 27, 1776
New Brunswick
Staten I.
GEN. HOWE FROM HALIFAX JUNE 28, 1776
ADM. HOWE FROM LONDON AUG 12, 1776
CORNWALLIS DEC, 1776
Princeton JAN 3, 1777
ATLANTIC OCEAN
NEW JERSEY
CLINTON AND CORNWALLIS FROM CHARLESTON AUG 1, 1776
Trenton JAN 2, 1777
PENN.
Delaware R.
0 25 Miles

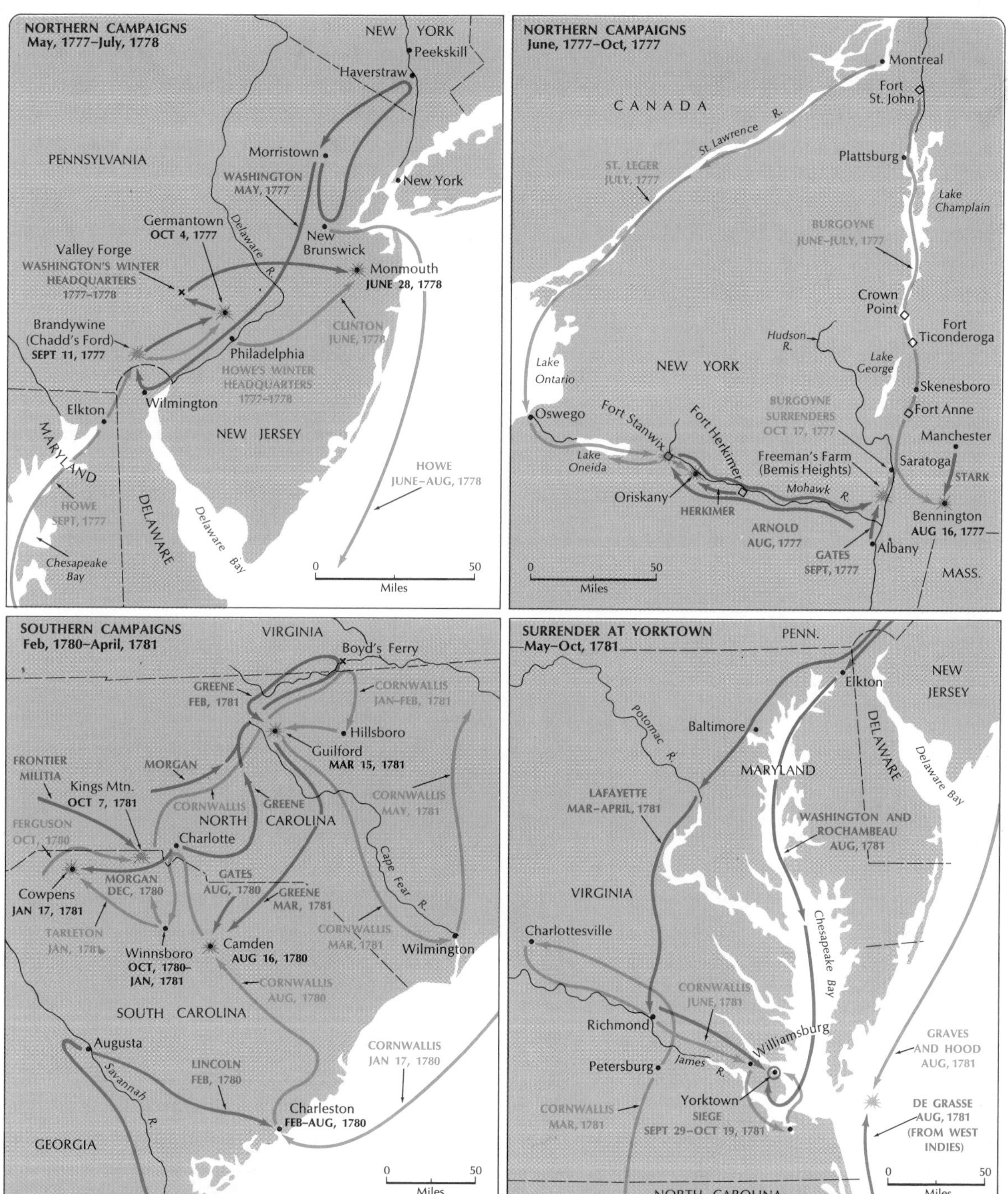
NORTHERN CAMPAIGNS
May, 1777–July, 1778
NEW YORK
Peekskill
Haverstraw
PENNSYLVANIA
Morristown
New York
WASHINGTON
MAY, 1777
Germantown
OCT 4, 1777
Delaware R.
New Brunswick
Valley Forge
WASHINGTON'S WINTER HEADQUARTERS
1777–1778
Monmouth
JUNE 28, 1778
Brandywine
(Chadd's Ford)
SEPT 11, 1777
CLINTON
JUNE, 1778
Philadelphia
HOWE'S WINTER HEADQUARTERS
1777–1778
Wilmington
Elkton
NEW JERSEY
MARYLAND
HOWE
SEPT, 1777
DELAWARE
Delaware Bay
HOWE
JUNE–AUG, 1778
Chesapeake Bay
0 50
Miles
NORTHERN CAMPAIGNS
June, 1777–Oct, 1777
Montreal
CANADA
Fort St. John
St. Lawrence R.
Plattsburg
ST. LEGER
JULY, 1777
Lake Champlain
BURGOYNE
JUNE–JULY, 1777
Crown Point
Fort Ticonderoga
Hudson R.
Lake George
Lake Ontario
NEW YORK
Skenesboro
Fort Anne
Oswego
Fort Stanwix
Fort Herkimer
BURGOYNE SURRENDERS
OCT 17, 1777
Manchester
Saratoga
Freeman's Farm
(Bemis Heights)
Lake Oneida
Mohawk R.
STARK
Oriskany
HERKIMER
Bennington
AUG 16, 1777
ARNOLD
AUG, 1777
Albany
GATES
SEPT, 1777
MASS.
0 50
Miles
SOUTHERN CAMPAIGNS
Feb, 1780–April, 1781
VIRGINIA
Boyd's Ferry
GREENE
FEB, 1781
CORNWALLIS
JAN–FEB, 1781
Hillsboro
Guilford
MAR 15, 1781
FRONTIER MILITIA
MORGAN
Kings Mtn.
OCT 7, 1781
CORNWALLIS
MAY, 1781
CORNWALLIS
GREENE
NORTH CAROLINA
FERGUSON
OCT, 1780
Charlotte
Cape Fear R.
Cowpens
JAN 17, 1781
MORGAN
DEC, 1780
GATES
AUG, 1780
GREENE
MAR, 1781
CORNWALLIS
MAR, 1781
TARLETON
JAN, 1781
Winnsboro
OCT, 1780–
JAN, 1781
Camden
AUG 16, 1780
Wilmington
CORNWALLIS
AUG, 1780
SOUTH CAROLINA
Augusta
CORNWALLIS
JAN 17, 1780
LINCOLN
FEB, 1780
Savannah R.
Charleston
FEB–AUG, 1780
GEORGIA
0 50
Miles
SURRENDER AT YORKTOWN
May–Oct, 1781
PENN.
NEW JERSEY
Elkton
Baltimore
Potomac R.
DELAWARE
MARYLAND
Delaware Bay
LAFAYETTE
MAR–APRIL, 1781
WASHINGTON AND ROCHAMBEAU
AUG, 1781
VIRGINIA
Chesapeake Bay
Charlottesville
CORNWALLIS
JUNE, 1781
Richmond
Williamsburg
GRAVES AND HOOD
AUG, 1781
Petersburg
James R.
Yorktown
SIEGE
SEPT 29–OCT 19, 1781
CORNWALLIS
MAR, 1781
DE GRASSE
AUG, 1781
(FROM WEST INDIES)
NORTH CAROLINA
0 50
Miles

Fighting for Independence

under the command of Graves. Despite their astonishment at being so badly outnumbered, they gave battle. The British fleet under Admiral Graves emerged more badly damaged than the French and consequently returned, after some delay, to New York for repairs. During the battle, eight French warships from Rhode Island had slipped into the bay with a ten-ship convoy of siege guns and supplies. Since the combined French fleets were greatly superior to anything Britain could quickly throw into the Chesapeake, Cornwallis could not hope to escape by sea.

By land, Cornwallis's situation was rapidly becoming equally hopeless. Washington and Rochambeau had faked the attack on New York which Clinton had long anticipated and were well on the way to Virginia before Clinton realized their aim. By September 24, Cornwallis with an army of 8,000 faced French and American forces of more than twice that number. On October 18, after enough resistance to demonstrate its futility, he surrendered. In the South as in the North, Britain's effort to subdue the Colonies had ended with the loss of an entire army.

Peace and Freedom

After Yorktown, Britain abandoned all hope of suppressing the American Revolution. Early in 1782, Parliament acknowledged the situation and authorized peace negotiations. Lord North, so long the agent of royal intransigence, at last resigned, as he had often sought to do in the past, and was replaced by Lord Rockingham, remembered in America as the conciliatory minister who had repealed the Stamp Act. Rockingham died in the midst of the negotiations and was succeeded by the Earl of Shelburne, another reform-minded conciliator, who envisioned unrestricted trade between America and Britain as a boon to both.

To capitalize on the conciliatory spirit of Britain's new leaders, the American representatives felt compelled to violate instructions from Congress requiring them to consult the French at every step. "We can depend upon the French," John Jay observed, "only to see that we are separated from England, but it is not in their interest that we should become a great and formidable people, and therefore they will not help us to become so." Even Shelburne noted that Vergennes's agent seemed "rather jealous than partial to America." Learning that Vergennes had arranged secret talks with the British, Jay persuaded his colleagues, Franklin and Adams, to do the same. Vergennes was somewhat taken aback to discover that the British and Americans had agreed upon peace terms without consulting him, but he found the fact convenient in persuading a reluctant Spain to abandon the war without gaining Gibraltar. When the British offered Spain the Mediterranean island of Minorca, together with both West Florida, which the Spanish had captured, and East Florida, which they had not, Spain agreed to forget Gibraltar and conclude peace. It became official on January 20, 1783, although the conclusion of formalities continued into 1784.

For the United States, the terms of the Peace of Paris were generous. The thirteen former Colonies gained explicit recognition of their independence. Britain corrected the presumption of the Quebec Act and agreed to fix the northern border approximately where it still remains, except in the Maine wilderness where ambiguous provisions had to be adjusted later.

In the West, where Spain and France had hoped to confine their ally east of the Appalachians, Britain yielded all it had; the Mississippi became the border with Spain. In the South, the surrender of West Florida to Spain fixed the border on an east-west line, the 31st parallel, through Alabama and Mississippi just slightly north of the northern border of the present state of Florida. East Florida retained what is still its border with Georgia. Tenacious bargaining by John Adams gained for Americans the "right" to fish in the Grand Banks and the "liberty" to dry fish on unsettled adjacent shores. On the troublesome issue of debts owed by Americans to British subjects, it was agreed that the United States should impose "no lawful Impediment" to their recovery. The negotiators pledged Congress also to "recommend" to the states restoration of confiscated Loyalist property. George III choked at the word "independence" when he announced the terms in Parliament, but he consoled himself with the thought that "knavery seems to be so much the striking feature of its [America's] inhabitants that it may not in the end be an evil that they become Aliens to this Kingdom."

Conclusion

Britain's dogmatic insistence upon the right of Parliament to bind Americans in any way it chose invited violence. It began at Lexington under circumstances which convinced many Americans of the barbarity of the King's troops. Initially, Americans fought only to compel restitution of what they regarded as "our former just and unalienable Rights and Privileges," but various considerations, and particularly British intransigence, led them in 1776 to declare their independence and to solicit French assistance in attaining it.

Successive British plans for crushing colonial resistance failed. The British did capture New York in 1776, but they proved unable to destroy Washington's army or—thanks to Washington's timely victory at Trenton—to demoralize the resistance forces. Their plan to isolate and subdue New England failed with the surrender of Burgoyne's Canadian-based army at Saratoga in the fall of 1777. A campaign to regain the South, complicated by French naval and military cooperation with the Americans, ended when a similar disaster overtook Cornwallis at Yorktown in 1781. Capitalizing on the desires of a new British ministry to avoid driving the Americans into complete dependence on France, astute American diplomats then gained at Paris in 1783 more generous territorial limits for an independent "United States" than the French or the Spanish had desired.

SUGGESTED READINGS

Military histories of the Revolution abound. H. H. Peckham's *The War for Independence** (1958) is concise and reliable. It attributes less to French assistance than does W. M. Wallace's *Appeal to Arms** (1951). John R. Alden in *The American Revolution** (1954), extensively altered in *A History of the American Revolution* (1969), puts military events in their political context. Eric Robson's *The American Revolution** (1955) presents a British scholar's provocative analysis of factors affecting the outcome. Another British scholar, Piers Mackesy, defends the much-criticized Lord Germain and emphasizes naval aspects of *The War for America* (1964). Defense of Germain is also the hallmark of *The American Secre-*

tary (1963) by G. S. Brown, an American. John C. Miller's *Triumph of Freedom** (1948) is a fast-moving narrative, as is Lynn Montross's *Rag, Tag, and Bobtail* (1952). A. B. Tourtellot in *Lexington and Concord** (1959) recounts those battles vividly. In *Rebels and Redcoats** (1957), G. F. Scheer and H. F. Rankin weave contemporary accounts into a flowing narrative H. S. Commager and R. B. Morris (eds.) in *The Spirit of Seventy-six* (2 vols., 1958), present contemporary accounts in a topical arrangement.

Excellent studies of a more restricted nature are also abundant. John R. Alden gives a full account of *The South in the Revolution* (1957). G. A. Billias has edited appraisals of several of *George Washington's Generals* (1964). North Callahan appraises *Daniel Morgan* (1961); Theodore Thayer, *Nathanael Greene* (1960). W. B. Willcox makes a psychological inquiry into the failure of Sir Henry Clinton in *Portrait of a General* (1964). D. S. Freeman's seven volumes on Washington are difficult; J. T. Flexner's first two volumes, *George Washington: The Forge of Experience* (1965) and *George Washington in the American Revolution* (1968), are much more enjoyable.

The battle of Saratoga is the focal point of S. D. Patterson's *Horatio Gates* (1941). S. E. Morison's biography *John Paul Jones** (1961) is as reliable as it is readable. M. F. Tracy's *Prelude to Yorktown* (1963) concerns the war in the South. H. A. Larrabee's *Decision at the Chesapeake* (1964) stresses the epochal importance of the naval battle of Yorktown. Paul H. Smith in *Loyalists and Redcoats* (1964) recounts Britain's failure to secure maximum support from their potential fifth column. Gustave Lanctot's *Canada and the American Revolution* (1967), though largely Canadian in its viewpoint, is an excellent example of international history.

The Continental Congress (1941) by E. C. Burnett is a scholarly record of that often slighted legislative body. Lynn Montross's *Reluctant Rebels* (1950) is a reliable popularization of the same subject. E. J. Ferguson's *Power of the Purse* (1961) is a superb analysis of the nation's financial problems viewed in the context of the conflict between nationalism and states' rights sentiment. C. L. VerSteeg in *Robert Morris* (1954) makes clear the remarkable achievement of the nation's first finance minister. On the most famous of the enactments of the Continental Congress, Carl L. Becker's *The Declaration of Independence* (1922) is a classic. David Hawke's *A Transaction of Free Men* (1964) traverses the same ground with a little less ideological and more political emphasis. A. O. Aldridge's *Man of Reason* (1959) is the best study of Thomas Paine available. S. F. Bemis's *Diplomacy of the American Revolution** (1935) remains unchallenged in essentials, although R. B. Morris's *The Peacemakers* (1965) greatly embellishes the story. E. S. Corwin's *French Policy and the American Alliance of* 1778 (1916) is an admirable monograph modified slightly by Alexander de Conde's *Entangling Alliance* (1958). G. Stourzh in *Benjamin Franklin and American Foreign Policy* (1954) supplements both V. W. Crane's *Benjamin Franklin and a Rising People** (1954) and Carl Van Doren's biography in recounting Franklin's long and varied diplomatic career.

* indicates availability in paperback.

6

Adjustments to Independence

INDEPENDENCE AFFORDED Americans the opportunity to recast their institutions in accordance with their own values. "To institute new government," stated the Declaration of Independence, was the right of any people who had deposed their old government for attempting to deny them their "natural" liberties. In the years following 1775, Americans did indeed institute new governments—state and federal—in patterns more acceptable to them than those provided by the British Empire. They agreed wholeheartedly that ultimate or sovereign power lay in the hands of the people and that their governments, as servants of the people, should possess only those powers enumerated in written constitutions. Most Americans agreed as well that power should be divided between state and federal governments and among legislative, executive, and judicial branches of government. Fixing precise rules for allocating power, however, occasioned serious disagreement.

Economic and social changes sharpened the contrast between independent America and the British colonial societies of the past. Once freed from Britain's mercantilist restrictions, American trade took new directions. Americans sought also to foster manufacturing, to reestablish viable monetary systems, and to promote the rapid development of wilderness land. America's exclusion from Britain's mercantilist system, however, coupled with the general loss of confidence in paper money caused considerable disruption of the economy, even temporary hardship. Slavery, the compulsory support of religion, and property qualifications on the right to vote were among the targets of reform efforts which enjoyed varying degrees of success. The people also gave clear evidence that their provincial loyalties, while still very strong, had suffered in competition with their new American identity and pride.

From Provinces to "Sovereign" States

Deeply committed to the rule of law, American Revolutionary leaders acted quickly to establish a legal foundation for the political power they had seized from Britain. "Mobs will never do to govern states or command armies," John Adams had warned, and most Americans agreed with him. Even before the decision for independence, Congress advised several colonies to form new governments for the duration of the "present dispute between Great Britain and the colonies." New Hampshire and South Carolina did so early in 1776. In less than two years after the Declaration of Independence, ten states had framed new governments. By 1780 all had done so, except Rhode Island and Connecticut, whose colonial charters served as constitutions well into the nineteenth century.

No state followed the British pattern of allowing its constitution to consist only of popular traditions. In each state the constitution was a set of written rules. This difference, however, was not new. Each colony, whether by royal charter, by the governor's commission and instructions, or otherwise, had known some written instrument which set forth its superior, or constitutional, law. The Revolution changed only the source and the character of the written constitutions under which Americans lived.

Virginia, first of the colonies to decide officially upon full separation from Britain, was also first to adopt a constitution. Framed by a convention which also acted as a legislature, the constitution reflected much satisfaction with the traditional government except as it related to British authority and to civil rights. Its major institutional innovation was to authorize annual election of the governor by joint ballot in the bicameral legislature. Though shorn of the veto and all power over the convening of the legislature except to call it to meet earlier than scheduled, the governor retained general executive authority and, with some reservations, held the power to make appointments both in the judiciary and in local government. The upper house of the legislature, previously an appointed council, now became popularly elected as the lower house had always been. The right to vote, applicable only in the choice of legislators, remained confined to owners of property.

Virginia's great constitutional innovation—one which evoked much comment in Europe as well as in America—was a declaration of rights. Its principal author was George Mason, wealthy planter, slaveholder, and land speculator. Adopted several weeks before the Continental Congress proclaimed the "United States" independent, the Virginia Declaration of Rights made many of the same affirmations which were to be included in the Declaration of Independence. At a time when most of Europe, including Britain, based political authority largely on royal will, Virginia proclaimed that power derived from the people and that magistrates were merely "their trustees and servants, and at all times amenable to them." Among the rights which individuals ought to enjoy, Virginians listed—in addition to those made famous in the Declaration of Independence—the rights of those accused of criminal acts "to be confronted with the accusers" and to be free from compulsory self-incrimination. The declaration also protected citizens against general or nonspecific warrants for search and seizure. It asserted, too, that people should enjoy freedom of speech, that "all men are equally entitled to the free exercise of religion," and that those possessed of a "permanent common interest with . . . the community" should be allowed to vote.

By far the most radical of the new state constitutions was that adopted by Pennsylvania during the summer of 1776. Because the moderates, who dominated Pennsylvania's Assembly, favored additional time for efforts to achieve reconciliation with Britain, congressional advocates of independence had virtually invited Pennsylvanians who shared their sentiments to overthrow the moderate government. Urging a government based on "the authority of the people," in contrast to the existing government which still acted in the King's name, the "independents" called a constitutional convention. Only those who would take an oath pledging support to a government based on the will of the people were permitted to vote for convention delegates.

Pennsylvania's new constitution, as it emerged from the convention, profoundly shocked "gentlemen" like John Adams, who, as a congressional advocate of independence, had had much to do with bringing it about. Adams declared that "in two years" the Pennsylvanians would "be glad to petition the crown of Britain for reconciliation in order to be delivered from the tyranny of their Constitution." The most radical provision, contravening the traditional requirement of property ownership for voting, was the extension of the right to vote to all men over twenty-one who had at least one year's residence and had paid taxes. In addition the executive, a twelve-man council chosen by ordinary voters, wielded little authority. The judges, instead of having good behavior, or permanent, tenure to assure their independence, were to serve fixed terms of seven years, thus subjecting them in time to removal for unpopular decisions. These provisions, concentrating power in the state's traditionally unicameral legislature and providing few checks and balances, appeared absurdly radical to gentlemen who had read Montesquieu's *Spirit of the Laws* (1748), William Blackstone's *Commentaries on the Laws of England* (1765–1769), and other popular writings on political philosophy. According to these highly regarded authorities, only a "mixed" government with independent power sources for "aristocratical" and "democratical" interests could hope to escape tyranny.

Several other features of the Pennsylvania constitution of 1776 were still too radical for widespread acceptance. The establishment of free schools and the elimination of imprisonment for debt were goals which would not be attained in that generation. There were no property qualifications fixed for holding office, and the religious qualifications were so vague as to send one zealous radical into opposition moaning: "[F]arewell Christianity when Turks, Jews, infidels, and what is worse Deists and Atheists are to make laws for our State." Included in the original draft of the constitution, but omitted from the approved document, was the still-radical affirmation that "an enormous Proportion of Property vested in a few Individuals is dangerous to the Rights, and destructive to the Common Happiness, of mankind; and therefore every free State hath a Right by its Laws to discourage the possession of such Property." Behind the Pennsylvania constitution was an organized minority of radicals below the rank of "gentleman." Their chief organizer was probably James Cannon, a college instructor in mathematics. What they wanted was a government highly responsive to majority opinion—without the checks of an independent executive and judiciary upon the will of the people's representatives. Their constitution went a long way to make it so. This had been the direction of political evolution in the British Empire, including the colonies, and would ultimately result in the modern British system. In the United States it would continue for some time to represent the characteristic aspiration of radicals. For the most part, however, as one observer noted in 1776, "the poorer commonalty, having hitherto had little or no hand in government, seem to think it does not belong to them to have any." Largely for this reason and its converse, that "the rich, having been used to govern, seem to think it is their right," Pennsylvania's radical constitution of 1776 survived only until 1790.

European political philosophers had long affirmed that people who had overthrown an oppressive government might, through the formation of a new "social contract," institute a new government. No one had indicated at all clearly, however, how it should be done. In most of the new American states, Revolutionary legislatures presumed to act for the people in drafting new constitutions. Only six bothered to ask specific authorization from the people to do so. None, until Massachusetts did so in 1778, offered the people an opportunity to ratify the state constitution before it went into effect. For such presumptions there were understandable explanations. Parliament had always altered the British Constitution at will. Furthermore, the Revolutionary legislatures did represent the people, at least the property-owning patriots, and the exigencies of wartime warranted some concessions to expediency.

In Massachusetts, however, the people were determined to take a more direct role in the reformulation of their social contract. In 1776, when the Legislature asked authority from the people, acting through their town meetings, to write a constitution, most responded favorably. Concord, however, resolved testily: "A Constitution alterable by the Supreme Legislature is no Security at all to the Subject against . . . Encroachment" by the government upon his "Rights and Privileges." And when the towns came to consider the Legislature's draft constitution in 1778, they rejected it overwhelmingly, partly because of dissatisfaction with various provisions, but also because it was the Legislature's product.

Legislators were content to go along with a provisional government operating more or less under the old colonial charter, but "Constitutionalists" in western Massachusetts demanded that the Legislature "call a special convention of Delegates from each Town . . . , for the purpose of forming a Bill of rights and a Constitution." Claiming that without a constitution there was no proper "Foundation" for the administration of justice, they closed the courts, thereby preventing legal action to collect debts. In 1779 the Legislature put the question to the towns. They indicated by a more than 2-to-1 majority their desire for a constitution and for a special convention to write it.

Whom would the convention represent? "The only moral foundation of government," John Adams observed, "is the consent of the people," but he confessed perplexity as to how far to "carry the principle." In the end, Massachusetts scrapped traditional property qualifications and allowed all freemen over twenty-one to vote for convention delegates and on ratification of the constitution. Paradoxically, the constitution drafted by the convention and approved by the adult freemen of the towns in 1780 reimposed a property qualification of £60 on voting for legislators. Thus Massachusetts deemed all adult freemen entitled to a voice in fixing the form of the government under which they would live but considered only men of property fit to choose those who would operate it. Such conservative features evoked much opposition and even required some juggling of the returns to support a decision that ratification had been secured. Nevertheless, in its constitutional difficulties between 1776 and 1780, Massachusetts, at the insistence of its people, had worked out a method by which people could indeed secure a form of government reflecting their wishes and endow it with their explicit consent. Nationalists intent upon instituting a new government for all the American people would ultimately profit from the example.

Separation of governmental powers appealed strongly to the people of Massachusetts. The assumption behind the idea was essentially that minority interests, particularly the wealthy, deserved an opportunity to block acts of potentially unreasonable legislative majorities. Advocates of legislative supremacy, on the other hand, believed that the legislative majority should have its way, except in reference to rights reserved to individuals or powers denied to government in general. They thought the legislature could be trusted to be reasonable. Massachusetts' constitution of 1780, drafted by the erudite John Adams, empowered the people rather than the legislature to choose the governor and endowed him with a veto power. A two-thirds vote in each house, however, could override the veto. Judges did not serve fixed terms but enjoyed permanent, or good behavior, tenure. The lower house of the legislature represented towns, while the upper chamber represented special districts of much greater size, to which seats were to be allocated in proportion to taxes paid. To assure representation of the wealthy in the upper house, its membership was limited to those who owned land worth £300 or personal property worth £600.

Common to all the new state constitutions were a number of fundamental concepts. Among these were the assumptions that government derived its authority from the people and that its function was to serve their interests. Equally universal was the assumption that governmental powers were limited: that individuals possessed fundamental rights which governments must respect. Short terms of office reflected the determination to keep government highly responsive to popular will. South Carolina gave members of its lower legislative chamber terms of two years, but elsewhere such terms were one year, except for Connecticut and Rhode Island, where the term was only six months. For the aristocratic upper houses, terms were generally longer, as much as five years in Maryland. Governors served terms of three years in New York and Delaware, two years in South Carolina, but only one year everywhere else. Local government, as in the past, enjoyed only a limited autonomy. Major local officials, especially in the cities, were generally not elected, but held office as state appointees.

Much of the early disagreement among Americans focused on the relative merits of separation of powers as opposed to legislative supremacy. Legislative supremacy, the perennial thrust of the colonial years, was at first more popular than separation of powers. Although no other state went as far as Pennsylvania, eight states authorized their legislatures to select governors; nine denied the governor a veto; and the same number gave the legislature a share of the appointive power. Yet the new constitutions revealed considerable respect for separation of powers. Eight states gave judges tenure during good behavior; three others gave them very long terms. All the states except Pennsylvania had governors who enjoyed some independence and also bicameral legislatures, in which the upper house was designed to represent the wealthy or the "aristocratical" element.

Special privileges for those who owned property aroused further debate. Several states—notably South Carolina, New Jersey, Maryland, and Massachusetts—fixed property qualifications so high as to exclude all but the wealthy from holding major offices. Other states imposed no such restrictions at all. Landholding qualifications for voting remained in force in nine states, often at a higher level for the upper than for the lower house of the legislature. Only New Hampshire, North Carolina, and Georgia followed Pennsylvania's example by substituting payment of taxes for land ownership as a prerequisite for voting. In North Carolina and Georgia, a compulsory poll tax theoretically qualified all free adult males to vote. Few as they were, these breaches in the wall of suffrage restriction, according to one leading authority on the subject, "were the most important in the entire history of American suffrage reform." They were, of course, in keeping with the basic ideology of the Revolution, which recognized all the people, not merely the owners of property, as the source of political authority.

The Confederation of American States

During the Revolution, unity of the American states was essential to the attainment of independence. "We must indeed all hang together," Benjamin Franklin is reported to have said, "or most assuredly we shall all hang separately." The Continental Congress, an assembly of delegates from the Revolutionary organizations in each colony, assumed the task of providing that unity in pursuit of independence. Its authority for several years derived not from a constitution, nor even from a treaty, but from widely recognized necessity. As early as 1775, however, a few farsighted patriots directed their endeavors toward perpetuating the Union of the states.

Fixing the basis for Union proved much more troublesome than writing constitutions for the states themselves. All the states had regularized their own constitutions by 1780, but there was still no agreement on a permanent Union among them. A year before the Declaration of Independence, Franklin had proposed in the Continental Congress. "Articles of Confederation and Perpetual Union," patterned after the plan which he had submitted to the Albany Conference twenty-one years before. Not until a year later, however, did Congress begin preparation of such a plan. Prompted by the same Virginia resolution which had cleared the way for independence, Congress established a committee to consider the matter.

A tentative plan of Union, largely the work of John Dickinson, emerged from the committee on July 12, 1776, after a month of "warm disputes." These disputes resumed in Congress itself and continued into the fall of 1777 before the "Articles of Confederation" gained congressional approval. The Articles would not become effective, however, until endorsed as well by all the states. Unanimous approval by them proved still more difficult to secure.

Western land claims provided the most divisive issue before the states. Six states which had no claims to Western lands (Maryland, Delaware, Pennsylvania, New Jersey, New Hampshire, and Rhode Island) had tried to win authority for Congress to fix western borders for those states which had extensive and often overlapping territorial claims, according to their original charters. The seven landed states blocked this action, but Maryland refused to ratify the Articles of Confederation until the landed states made a satisfactory concession. Deadlock prevailed from 1777 until 1781, while the Continental Congress continued to operate without a formal constitutional foundation.

Virginia was the chief target of the states without Western land claims. Largest of the states by far, Virginia then included what is now West Virginia and Kentucky and claimed all the area north from the Ohio River to Canada as well. Speculators from Maryland and Pennsylvania, who either had or desired an interest in Western lands, were convinced that their aspirations would suffer in competition with rivals from Virginia if that state kept control of all the land it claimed. Consequently, they lobbied assiduously for common or national control of the West so that speculators from all states would be treated impartially. Early in 1781, while Cornwallis's campaign in the South was still proceeding well, Virginia decided for "the good of the country" to cede to the United States the lands which it claimed north of the Ohio River. The cession had to be renegotiated at some length between 1781 and 1784, but Maryland, prodded by French agents who were eager at that time to foster American unity, accepted the initial act as sufficient to warrant her ratification. The Articles of Confederation became the Constitution of the United States on March 2, 1781.

Endorsement of the Articles of Confederation by all the states gave a legal foundation to the basic pattern of government which had been evolving informally. In that pattern Congress was the only federal agency of government. There was neither a Chief Executive nor a national system of courts. Congress itself represented state governments rather than people. The governments of the states chose from two to seven delegates, instructed them, and paid them. However many delegates it sent to Congress or whatever its population, each state had only one vote. Whereas the Congress could support the Army, conduct foreign relations, borrow money, and make "requisitions" against the states, it could neither tax, nor regulate foreign or domestic commerce, nor enforce its will by any means other than the Army. Limited as were its powers, the Congress could increase them only by amendment of the Articles, a procedure requiring the unanimous consent of all the states.

During the war the obvious necessity for cooperation enabled Congress to get things done, but as the war drew slowly toward its successful conclusion, the cooperative spirit faded. Attendance at congressional sessions fell off. Some states failed for a time even to name delegates. The morale of those who attended and attempted to conduct business sagged badly. The Congress, moaned one delegate, was "responsible for everything, and unable to

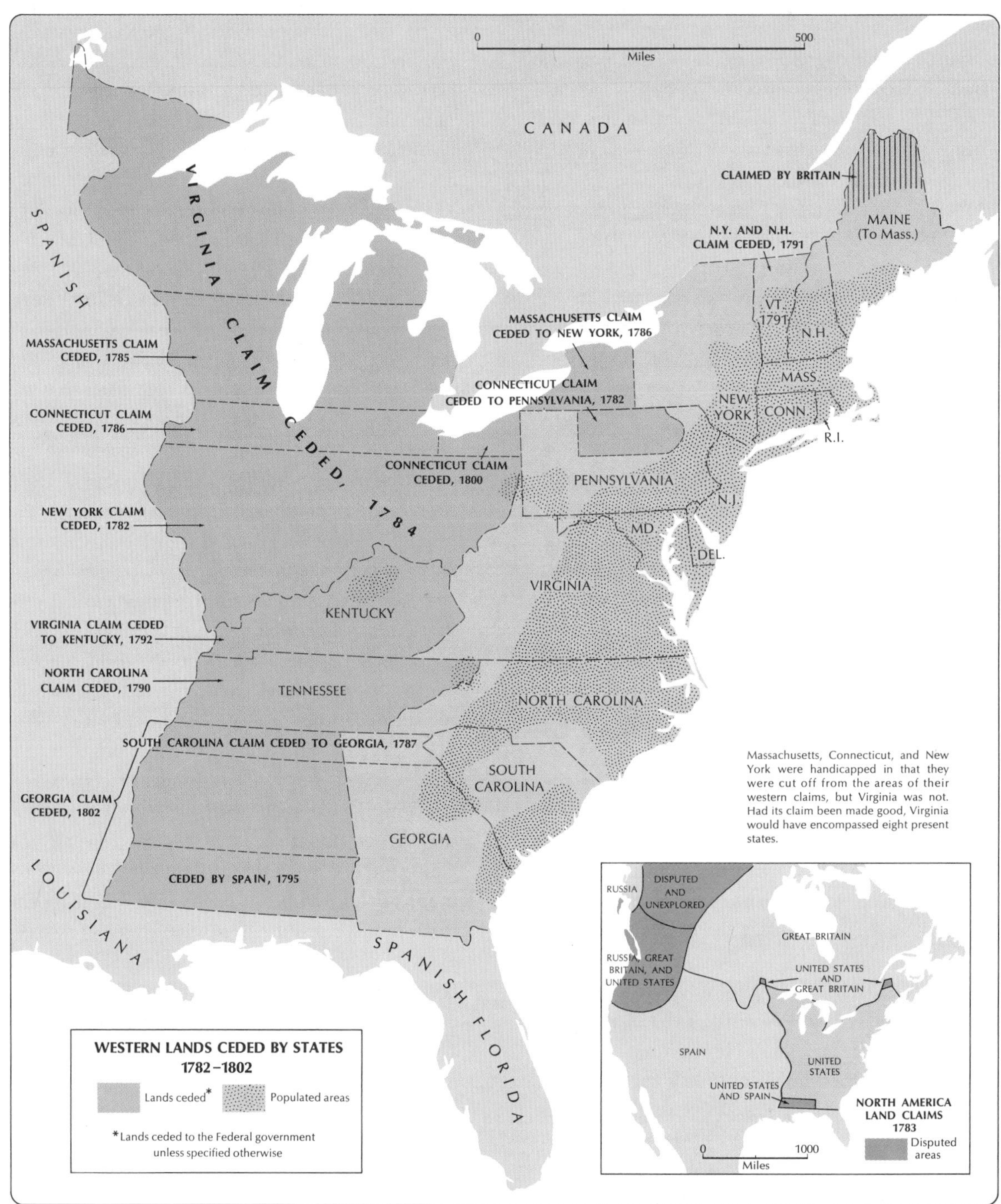

0
500
Miles
CANADA
CLAIMED BY BRITAIN
MAINE
(To Mass.)
N.Y. AND N.H.
CLAIM CEDED, 1791
VT.
1791
N.H.
MASS.
NEW
YORK
CONN.
R.I.
SPANISH
VIRGINIA CLAIM CEDED, 1784
MASSACHUSETTS CLAIM
CEDED, 1785
MASSACHUSETTS CLAIM
CEDED TO NEW YORK, 1786
CONNECTICUT CLAIM
CEDED TO PENNSYLVANIA, 1782
CONNECTICUT CLAIM
CEDED, 1786
CONNECTICUT CLAIM
CEDED, 1800
PENNSYLVANIA
N.J.
NEW YORK CLAIM
CEDED, 1782
MD.
DEL.
VIRGINIA
KENTUCKY
VIRGINIA CLAIM CEDED
TO KENTUCKY, 1792
NORTH CAROLINA
CLAIM CEDED, 1790
TENNESSEE
NORTH CAROLINA
SOUTH CAROLINA CLAIM CEDED TO GEORGIA, 1787
SOUTH
CAROLINA
GEORGIA CLAIM
CEDED, 1802
GEORGIA
CEDED BY SPAIN, 1795
LOUISIANA
SPANISH FLORIDA
Massachusetts, Connecticut, and New York were handicapped in that they were cut off from the areas of their western claims, but Virginia was not. Had its claim been made good, Virginia would have encompassed eight present states.
WESTERN LANDS CEDED BY STATES
1782–1802
Lands ceded*
Populated areas
*Lands ceded to the Federal government unless specified otherwise
RUSSIA
DISPUTED
AND
UNEXPLORED
GREAT BRITAIN
RUSSIA, GREAT
BRITAIN, AND
UNITED STATES
UNITED STATES
AND
GREAT BRITAIN
SPAIN
UNITED
STATES
UNITED STATES
AND SPAIN
0
1000
Miles
NORTH AMERICA
LAND CLAIMS
1783
Disputed
areas

do anything." Without any "visible head," the government of the United States lacked strong executive leadership and, as one patriot observed, could impart to Europeans "no very favourable opinion of our stability, wisdom, or Union." To even consider the peace treaty conferring independence, the Congress required two months to secure a quorum.

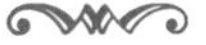

Congress and the West

Despite its general weaknesses, Congress achieved spectacular success in fixing guidelines for Western development. Definite policies for land distribution and government were necessary because of the steady westward advance of population. Settlers had been moving across the Appalachians in considerable numbers even before the Revolution, especially into Kentucky and Tennessee. Daniel Boone had cut his "Wilderness Road" in 1775, opening the Kentucky lands of speculator Richard Henderson to settlers from Virginia. Henderson's settlement at Boonesborough soon had a neighbor, Harrodsburg, established by James Harrod of Pennsylvania. By 1790, Kentucky had more than seventy thousand people and was clamoring for separation from Virginia as a new state.

Tennessee developed somewhat less rapidly. Richard Henderson had brought about the settlement of Nashville, first as a self-governing community and then (after 1782) as part of North Carolina. When North Carolina ceded the area of Tennessee to the United States in 1784, settlers in the Watauga area (northeastern Tennessee) formed the prospective state of Franklin under the leadership of John Sevier and sought admission to the Union. North Carolina revoked its cession in 1787, however, and continued to assert authority over the area of Tennessee until 1790 when the final cession occurred. Tennessee by then had some thirty-five thousand inhabitants.

How would Congress deal with Western problems? As early as 1779, Congress had resolved that lands which might be ceded to it by the states "shall be . . . formed into distinct Republican states, which shall become members of the federal union, and have the same rights of sovereignty, freedom and independence, as the other states." Such a moral commitment, however, did not solve the problem of securing the cession of Western lands by several reluctant states or providing for the settlement and early government of lands which had been ceded.

All the states which had claims to the area north of the Ohio River (Massachusetts, New York, Connecticut, and Virginia) had ceded their claims to the United States by 1786, although Connecticut kept title to the northeastern section, or the "Western Reserve," of the future state of Ohio until 1800. South of the Ohio River, however, the record was less impressive. Virginia retained title to the area of Kentucky until it became a state in 1792. North Carolina, as just noted, did not finally surrender the Tennessee area until 1790. South Carolina ceded its narrow strip across the top of modern Alabama and Mississippi, but Georgia, claiming all the rest of Alabama and Mississippi except for the Spanish portions along the Gulf Coast, refused to surrender its title until 1802. Thus, only the area north of the Ohio River, plus South Carolina's tiny cession, became subject to the control of the United States in the Confederation period after 1781.

Policies designed to develop the national

domain appeared in a number of land ordinances passed by Congress. First of these was the Ordinance of 1784, drafted largely by Thomas Jefferson. Its major effect was to recommit the Congress to the principle that new states would be formed from the area and admitted to Congress "on an equal footing" with the others. Jefferson had hoped to extend the vote at once to "free males of full age," to ban slavery, and to divide the area into ten states, for which he suggested such fanciful Latin names as Dolypotamia and Metropotamia, but Congress struck out all three provisions. The ordinance authorized home rule, or self-government for the territories, even at the very earliest stages of settlement, but Congress provided that the Ordinance as a whole should become effective only after each state had ceded its Western territories. Before that condition was met new ordinances had replaced that of 1784.

Among them was the Ordinance of 1785, a measure framed with an eye on revenue from the sale of newly ceded western lands. It applied to all such lands whose titles had been purchased from the Indians and required that the areas be surveyed in township lots 6 miles square, with each township subdivided into thirty-six lots or "sections" of 640 acres each. Half the townships were to be sold as townships; the others in lots of 640 acres. Sales were to be conducted by auction but without credit and at prices no less than $1 per acre. These terms discriminated against small farmers, who were not likely to have $640 and could rarely farm even 100 acres. The terms were much more suitable to speculators, from whom Congress hoped to secure substantial income quickly. Congress defeated a proposal to reserve one lot in each township to provide a subsidy for the religion favored by the township's majority, but it did reserve one section of land on which public schools could be constructed.

Not until 1787, on the eve of its extinction, did the Congress provide in any detail for the government of its Western territories. It acted under the prodding of speculators who saw to it that the provisions of the law were framed "for the accommodation of . . . [absentee] purchasers" as well as "inhabitants." In place of the self-government which Jefferson had envisioned for the settlers, the Northwest Ordinance of 1787 provided that, until the population reached 5,000, the government should consist of a governor, secretary, and judges, all appointed by Congress. When the population reached 5,000, the people could elect an assembly, but the governor appointed by Congress was to exercise an absolute veto. The people could also send a voteless delegate to Congress. Only when the population had reached 60,000 could the people of the area qualify for self-government and all other privileges of statehood. Because Easterners looked with horror on the prospect of a Confederacy nearly dominated by Western "depravity," the number of new states to be carved out of the Northwest Territory was fixed at from three to five, instead of the ten which Jefferson had suggested. Jefferson's proposed ban on slavery, however, was included, along with other guarantees of civil liberties. The law also fixed upon the prospective new states certain obligations. They had, for example, to allow duty-free use of their navigable waterways by citizens of other states forever.

Speculation ran rampant in the Northwest from the beginning. Behind the Northwest Ordinance itself lay the lobbying efforts of a group of New Englanders organized as the Ohio Company, with the Reverend Manasseh

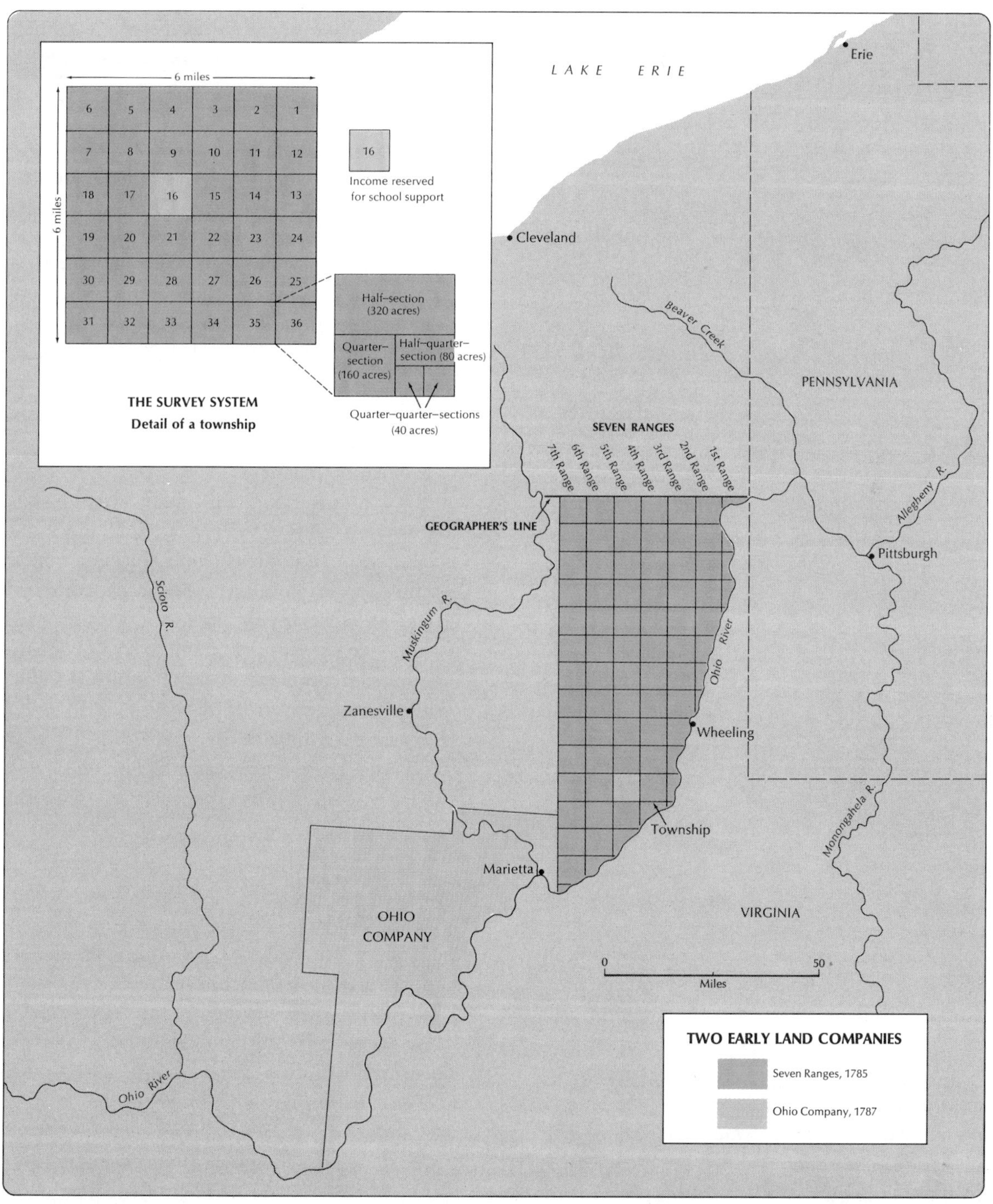
LAKE ERIE
Erie
Cleveland
6 miles
6 miles
6
5
4
3
2
1
7
8
9
10
11
12
18
17
16
15
14
13
19
20
21
22
23
24
30
29
28
27
26
25
31
32
33
34
35
36
16
Income reserved for school support
Half–section (320 acres)
Quarter–section (160 acres)
Half–quarter–section (80 acres)
Quarter–quarter–sections (40 acres)
THE SURVEY SYSTEM
Detail of a township
Beaver Creek
PENNSYLVANIA
SEVEN RANGES
7th Range
6th Range
5th Range
4th Range
3rd Range
2nd Range
1st Range
GEOGRAPHER'S LINE
Allegheny R.
Pittsburgh
Scioto R.
Muskingum R.
Ohio River
Zanesville
Wheeling
Township
Monongahela R.
Marietta
OHIO COMPANY
VIRGINIA
0
50
Miles
TWO EARLY LAND COMPANIES
Seven Ranges, 1785
Ohio Company, 1787
Ohio River

Cutler as their chief spokesman. By 1788 Cutler and his associates had purchased a large acreage and had founded Marietta, Ohio, the first legal settlement in the Northwest Territory. An unsavory aspect of the transaction was the inclusion by Congress of an option for the Scioto Company, organized by Treasury official William Duer and apparently including some members of Congress, to purchase 5 million acres. Poet Joel Barlow, an overenthusiastic agent of the Scioto Company in Paris, "sold" some of this not-yet-purchased land to Frenchmen, several hundred of whom then emigrated to the United States. The Scioto Company never exercised its option to buy and, in fact, within a few years became bankrupt. The French immigrants suffered greatly, but ultimately Congress donated to them land such as they thought they had bought before they left France. Another speculator, John Cleves Symmes of New Jersey, bought and settled land which included the site of Cincinnati, although he was never able to purchase the entire million acres for which he originally contracted.

Few laws in all American history have had such fundamental significance as the land ordinances of the 1780s. At a time when few interests bound the American states together, the ordinances expressed a national consensus concerning a common property and its development. The land allocation system, fixed with the emphasis upon raising revenue quickly, benefited speculators rather than ordinary settlers, but future changes would in some measure redress the balance. Meanwhile, as Jefferson noted, the poor would continue to use the land "in spite of everybody." Envisioning a society of independent, landowning farmers, the laws made no provision for such hallmarks of aristocracy as primogeniture, entail, quitrents, or feudal dues. They assumed instead that ordinary people would purchase land and would owe no obligation whatever to its purveyor once their payments had been made. Repudiating colonial subjugation such as Britain had sought to fix upon her colonies forever, the laws spelled out how, with temporary safeguards to the interests of absentee speculators, frontier territories across the continent would "become members of the federal union" on an "equal footing" with the original states. Finally, the Northwest Ordinance of 1787 was the first act of the government of the United States looking toward the extinction of the institution of slavery.

Postwar Economic Changes

Congress under the Articles of Confederation lacked power to effect many changes of consequence relating to economic matters; yet merely by waging a successful war for independence the Congress had profoundly altered the course of American economic development. Independence enabled Americans, at least in theory, to send their exports wherever they wished. No longer must they send their major products as enumerated commodities to Britain. Independence freed Americans as well to import directly from continental Europe and Asia, rather than having to buy goods from those areas only through middlemen in Britain. American ports could be opened to ships of every nation. Americans were now free as well to issue paper money as they saw fit to foster the development of their economy.

American independence produced, in addition, fundamental changes in land ownership.

Either Congress (for ceded Western lands) or state governments (for lands not ceded) took over the titles to public lands from the British Crown or British proprietary families. If the American governments initially followed policies rather more favorable to speculators than to settlers, it is also true that they, more than the British, attempted to foster the rapid extension of settlement, partly as a means to increase government revenue by speedy sales. Public lands became in fact a source of great public wealth, which governments used to reward Revolutionary soldiers and ultimately to subsidize schools and other desirable enterprises of considerable variety and importance.

State governments, despite their general inclination to favor speculators, ended relics of feudalism and pursued other policies inimical to aristocratic land holdings. New York ended the rights of its semifeudal manor lords to representation in its Legislature and to control of local government. All states sooner or later abolished quitrents, a now-pointless relic of feudal land tenure. Clearly more important than any of these legal changes in the relative decline of large-scale land holdings—the hallmark of aristocracy—was the competition among speculators to whom the states sold land very cheaply to resell it quickly. Prices one-fifth to one-twentieth of those prevailing in older areas operated powerfully not only to lure settlers to frontier regions but also to diffuse land ownership still more widely.

The resale of lands confiscated from Tories also contributed to the decline of the aristocracy. In every state, wealthy supporters of the Crown had held enormous landed estates, which the Revolutionary governments seized and sold to patriots. In New York, fifty-nine Tories suffered losses averaging over forty thousand acres each. It was often patriot speculators rather than small farmers who bought these confiscated lands, but such owners usually sought a speculative profit by retailing small parcels to settlers rather than creating large, tenant-operated estates to be held by their descendents forever.

Freedom from British mercantile restrictions encouraged American industry as well as commerce. Gentlemen formed private societies to promote manufacturing and to subsidize individual enterprises. Artisans and other producers beseeched state governments to impose high taxes on imports of items which they manufactured, so that they might enjoy a competitive advantage. Such tariff measures appeared desirable also to combat America's unfavorable balance of trade and reduce the drain of specie from the country. Impressed by these arguments and attracted by the lure of additional revenue, many Northern states passed tariff measures and thus, in contrast to Britain's prewar policy, encouraged the development of new iron, textile, sugar-refining, and other manufacturing enterprises. States which lacked important manufactures, however, chose usually to allow such goods to be imported from abroad without heavy taxation. By so doing, they undermined the tariff protection available to American producers in other states.

Independence was advantageous for American economic growth, but it carried a high price in the short run because Britain now excluded Americans from the many benefits they had previously enjoyed under the British mercantilist system. Each of the major economic regions of America suffered to some extent from Britain's postwar economic policies, but it was New England which suffered most. New England's economy had depended heavily upon the export of fish to the British

West Indies. Britain refused to reopen this market after the Revolution, with the result that New England exports of cod in the late 1780s were 43 percent less than they had been before the war. Maritime New England suffered, in addition, from the exclusion of American ships from British West Indian ports, from reduced British purchases of American vessels, from discriminatory duties on American whale oil imported into Britain, and from the ban in the British West Indies on the importation of American meat and dairy products. Frequent suspensions of these regulations by authorities in the British West Indies, as well as outright smuggling, brought some relief.

For the Middle Atlantic region the problem of readjustment was less acute. The staple exports of wheat and flour continued to find a West Indian market, although their importation was limited legally to British ships. Britain reduced from prewar levels its importation of iron, also produced in the Middle Atlantic region, but domestic American consumption apparently increased sufficiently to keep the furnaces in operation.

Southern economic problems also flowed from British postwar policy. About thirty thousand slaves reportedly disappeared from Virginia and twenty-five thousand from South Carolina during the war, taken by the British in many instances as a form of confiscation. Even without the benefit of the prewar enumeration policy, Britain managed largely to retain its role as processor and distributor of American tobacco, but a domestic consumption tax in Britain itself somewhat reduced the market. France arranged to do its purchasing of tobacco through a national monopoly, and this development, in conjunction with British action, tended to reduce the world price and consequently the producers' income. Indigo planters, deprived of their prewar British subsidy, found they could not compete with West Indian producers.

Americans themselves greatly aggravated their economic difficulties in 1784 by importing vast quantities of goods from Britain on credit. Hampered by the shortage of acceptable money, as well as by the British restrictions on their export trade, American merchants experienced great difficulty, first in selling the imported items, and then in making enough export shipments to pay for them. To reduce their interest costs on debts to British firms, many American merchants, unable to find commodities acceptable to Britain, arranged to send gold and silver instead. This practice aggravated the already-serious shortage of money.

Scarcity of money became in fact the most serious manifestation of a severe postwar depression. One root of the difficulty lay in the depreciation of continental paper money during the war, when it had served in effect as a form of soak-the-rich taxation. Hurt by the depreciation of paper money, many men of wealth subsequently opposed additional issues. Unfortunately, by 1784 gold and silver, which had been derived chiefly from British and French army expenditures and foreign loans, were no longer flowing into the economy rapidly enough to offset the rate at which they were being exported. As the money supply dwindled, prices, already depressed by the export problems, fell still further. Between 1784 and 1788, wholesale commodity prices in Philadelphia and Charleston declined by about 25 percent. In such circumstances farmers found it difficult to meet fixed mortgage payments, to buy imported commodities, or even to pay their taxes.

Pressures for the issuance of paper money grew accordingly. Farmers in particular sought the issuance of land bank notes, or money created by the state on the security of land mortgages. Seven states acceded to such pressures in 1785 and 1786. Some, notably South Carolina and New York, repeated the generally favorable experience of the years before the Revolution. Rhode Island and North Carolina, however, horrified creditors, first, by making their paper money legal tender, the offer of which legally discharged a debt even if the payment was refused; and second, by making inadequate provision for redemption so that the value of the currency diminished rapidly. Three states, Connecticut, Virginia, and Delaware, issued no paper money but experienced no serious unrest. Connecticut appeased its debtor citizens by lowering taxes and enacting a "stay law" allowing debtors more time to meet their obligations. In Maryland, the Senate defeated a paper money bill passed by the lower house, and violent resistance developed to the collection of debts and taxes. In New Hampshire a mob besieged the Legislature in a vain effort to secure paper money legislation; in Massachusetts violence was both more overt and more consequential.

Violence broke out in Massachusetts in the wake of seemingly honorable but unfortunate decisions by the Legislature. Frightened by the doings of paper money supporters in neighboring Rhode Island, the legislators refused to authorize any more paper money. In contrast to the Continental Congress, Massachusetts legislators determined to redeem the wartime paper money at the value which it had had when issued, even though the currency had in fact depreciated greatly. This decision more than doubled the state debt. The legislators also resolved to repay the state debt quickly, rather than inconvenience creditors and disgrace the government by delaying settlement. For much of the revenue to repay its debt, the state relied upon a poll tax—a fixed sum charged against all males over sixteen. To encourage payment of both taxes and private debts, the state law provided, as was usual in other areas as well, that the property of delinquents might be seized and sold to make good their obligations. They might even be jailed if their estates proved insufficient to meet their obligations.

Poor people in rural Massachusetts unquestionably suffered under these policies. Property seized and sold to pay debts brought far less than its value in normal times. Seizures sometimes deprived men of the means of their livelihood. Men with dependent families went to jail for inability to pay relatively small amounts. Towns hit by depression were often unwilling to pay the expenses of a delegate to the State Legislature and thus went unrepresented while the Legislature, in which wealthy communities were somewhat overrepresented, ignored petitions for paper money and stay laws. Denied relief and facing continued oppression both by seizure of their property and by incarceration for debt, the poor took matters into their own hands. By mob action they prevented the meeting or forced the adjournment of the courts, which were the instruments of their oppression. When insurgents under a former Revolutionary captain, Daniel Shays, attempted to seize arms from an arsenal at Springfield, militia forces killed four men and put the rest to flight with artillery fire. Singularly lacking in the desire to kill, the insurgents scattered before any show of force. Governor James Bowdoin's militia, supported financially by Boston merchants, eliminated all resistance before the winter of

1786–1787 had ended. Despite the wrath of such onetime radicals as Samuel Adams, who felt that "the man who dares rebel against the laws of a republic ought to suffer death," all the Shaysites condemned to death ultimately gained pardons, including Daniel Shays himself. The legislative session of 1787, while it still held out against paper money and stay laws, lowered the tax burden and exempted both household goods and tools of one's trade from seizure and sale for debt. A general improvement in economic conditions during the next few years helped also to alleviate discontent.

Social Change

Social changes of fundamental importance accompanied the American Revolution, just as they have other major revolutions in world history. Perhaps the most important change, although one difficult to characterize clearly, was the awakening of the "inferior sort," who then rose to challenge the traditional dominance of society by a landed and mercantile elite. Pennsylvania's radical constitution and Shays' Rebellion were merely two examples of the new activism inspired among previously deferential classes by the rhetoric of liberty and representative government.

Symbolizing and contributing to the change was the exodus from American society of 60,000 to perhaps 100,000 Loyalists, a greater number in relation to population than fled the later revolution in France. Between 30,000 and 50,000 American Loyalists, as they called themselves, or Tories, as the Revolutionaries called them, fought in the British army during the war. Guerilla warfare and privateering against American and allied commerce attracted many others. Many who fought in support of the British were opportunists of no deep political convictions, men whose "loyalty" changed with the fortunes of war in their own communities. Far more important, however, were those from every walk of life who were Tory because of conservative convictions, men more afraid of the Revolution's conception of representative government than of Britain's traditions of monarchical and aristocratic authority. Such conservatives were very few in New England, but somewhat more numerous in the South, especially in the backcountry, where dislike of the dominant Eastern planters was widespread and recent immigrants were many. In the Middle Atlantic region, Tories were still more numerous, accounting for perhaps as much as half the activist population in New York. The departure of the Loyalists for Canada, for Britain itself, or for the British West Indies at the conclusion of the Revolution made it easier for the Revolutionary Whigs to continue implementing their ideas.

Slavery was a standing affront to the ideology of the Revolution, and consequently it came under strong attack at the conclusion of the war. In the North, slavery served no important economic function and was unnecessary as a means of assuring white supremacy because Negroes were relatively few. New York, although smaller in total population than either Pennsylvania or Massachusetts, had by far the largest Negro population of any Northern state (21,000 in 1780); but even in New York the proportion of Negroes in the population was only about one in ten. Therefore the consideration uppermost in the minds of most Northern Revolutionary leaders with reference

Art in America: 1660–1860

Painting in America began as early as the 1600s, as far as we know from the earliest-dated painting so far located, but, presumably, pictures were painted even earlier. These early paintings of the seventeenth century were portraits, works of art with utilitarian purposes, albeit the utility was psychological rather than overtly practical. The tradition of portraiture which already existed in Great Britain reinforced this emphasis, and, indeed, portraiture remained the principal art form in the American colonies until the time of the Revolution and even afterward.

By the end of the first decade of the eighteenth century, professional portraitists from both Britain and the continent began to supercede the early artisan painters and brought at least a measure of professional competence to the art. The styles of painting naturally reflected those practiced in Europe, although at first at least, a certain lag occurred in the arrival of successive aesthetic approaches to portraiture. Only in the 1740s did the colonies begin to produce native-born

---

The portrait above of Alice Mason by an unknown artist, was painted in New England in the second half of the seventeenth century. The flat, patterned, decorative style of Elizabethan portraiture of almost 100 years earlier typifies most early New England portraiture, which was created by talented but anonymous and relatively untrained artisans.

Above: Artist unknown, Alice Mason, 1670, *oil. Adams National Historic Site.*

Asher B. Durand (1796–1886)
Kindred Spirits, 1849, *oil on canvas*
New York Public Library

As a tribute to Thomas Cole after his death, fellow landscape painter Asher B. Durand painted him in his favorite Catskills, communing with their mutual friend and interpreter of nature William Cullen Bryant.

artists who could compete successfully with their European-born-and-trained colleagues. Thus the earliest professionals who arrived usually remained as "big fish in a small pond," while those Europeans who arrived during and after the mid-eighteenth century tended to draw what patronage they could and depart. By the 1760s America had begun to produce master portraitists, especially in the person of John Singleton Copley, who could certainly rival any European visitors and could actually compete on an international level.

During the same decade, aspiring American artists began to reverse the trend and migrate to Europe, primarily to London, for their artistic education. Some, like Copley and Benjamin West, remained abroad. Others, like Charles Willson Peale, learned their craft and returned to America to become the leading painters at home. Still others, like Gilbert Stuart, became highly successful in Europe but returned to America after practicing abroad for a number of years.

Even into the early years of the nineteenth century, portraiture reigned supreme. But by the 1820s there had grown up in America a patron class with time, money, and interest enough to become collectors and to give encouragement to American painters who wished to go beyond the limits of portrait painting. Fortunately, in the domains of landscape and still-life painting, artists such as Thomas Cole, Asher B. Durand, and Raphaelle Peale were able to meet this challenge successfully, and in landscape painting particularly, a school of painters responded to the romantic interpretation of nature already being defined by the poet William Cullen Bryant among others. The glorification of the American landscape continued well into the mid-nineteenth century, but nature could stand for the handiwork of God, too, as embodied in the complex allegories of Thomas Cole. American artists' attempts at interpreting the Old Masters' themes, however, found little response in their native land, despite the acknowledged talents of such painters as Washington Allston and John Vanderlyn; even the interpretation of American historical events could find little patronage although John Trumbull was widely acclaimed and eventually patronized by the national government.

In the mid-1840s, American art had visibly begun to outgrow the dependence upon English cultural forms that had lasted despite two wars with the mother country. Patronage shifted from a few wealthy individuals to the growing middle class which demanded artistic forms easily understood and easy to respond to. Thus, by 1850 genre painting, the depiction of everyday scenes, dominated American art, and William Sidney Mount had become the most revered of American artists. His interpretation of distinctly American scenes and subjects further insured his success for this was a particularly nationalistic period in America's cultural development. Indeed, the art of midcentury can be characterized as democratic, nationalistic, and optimistic in its outlook.

The selection, text, and captions in this and succeeding fine-arts sections are by William Gerdts. Formerly curator of the Norfolk Museum of Arts and Sciences, Curator of Painting and Sculpture at the Newark Museum, and Associate Professor and Gallery Director at Johns Hopkins University, Mr. Gerdts currently lectures at Johns Hopkins, serves as vice-president of a New York City art gallery.

Eastman Johnson, a later genre painter who studied in Düsseldorf, grafted upon the American genre scene the detailed, anecdotal, and sentimental style of that art center. Düsseldorf, in fact, superseded London in the mid-nineteenth century as a training center for American artists.

Eastman Johnson (1824–1906), Old Kentucky Home, Life in the South, 1859, *oil on canvas. Courtesy of the New-York Historical Society, New York City.*

When professional portrait painters began to arrive in the Colonies, they came not only from Great Britain, but, as in the case of Justus Englehardt Kühn, from the Continent as well. In his interpretation of Eleanor Darnall (right), Kühn projects her into a fantasy world of elegant nobility far removed from her actual surroundings. Kühn probably drew upon some engraving source for his background, costume, and pose, and this is certainly the case in the portrait by a New York limner (below, left), for which the engraving has been located (below, right). Such painters naturally tended to simplify their engraving source in order to handle the complex problems of composition and modelling, and, of course, the color interpretation was original. Although such a practice may suggest plagiarism today, it was an honored basis for Colonial portraiture practiced even by such outstanding professionals as John Smibert and John Singleton Copley.

Artist unknown, John Van Cortlandt, *ca.* 1731, *oil on canvas. The Brooklyn Museum, Dick S. Ramsay Fund.*

G. Kneller, Engraving by I. Smith, The Lord Buckhurst and Lady Mary Sackvil His Sister, *mezzotint. Courtesy of the Waldron Phoenix Belknap, Jr. Research Library of American Painting at the Henry Francis du Pont Winterthur Museum.*

Justus Engelhardt Kuhn (unknown–1717), Eleanor Darnall, *cs. 1710, oil on canvas. From the Collections of the Maryland Historical Society.*

John Smibert (1688–1751), Francis Brinley, *1731, oil on canvas. The Metropolitan Museum of Art, Rogers Fund, 1962.*

With the arrival of John Smibert in New England, first in Newport, R.I., and then in Boston, the Colonies gained a portraitist of considerable power and reputation. Smibert was called upon to portray many of the leading citizens of Massachusetts in his baroque style using massive form and strong characterization; the Portrait of Francis Brinley *(above) gains further interest from its background which depicts one of the earliest painted views of Boston.*

John Singleton Copley (1738–1815), Paul Revere, 1765–1770, *oil on canvas. Courtesy of the Museum of Fine Arts, Boston. Gift of Joseph W., William B., and Edward H. R. Revere.*

The tradition of incisive realistic portraiture founded by Smibert in Boston reached its culmination just before the Revolution in the portraiture of native-born John Singleton Copley. Copley's subjects included leading merchants, statesmen, ministers, and fellow-artists such as Paul Revere, here shown in an informal, working portrait, as were several other Copley subjects, perhaps in deference to the Puritan glorification of work.

Benjamin West (1738–1820)
Penn's Treaty with the Indians, *ca.* 1771, *oil on canvas*
Courtesy of the Pennsylvania Academy of the Fine Arts

Many of the painters of the late Colonial period and of the early Republic accepted the need to paint portraits for a livelihood but hankered after subjects in the grand tradition: classical, religious, or historical events. Benjamin West was one of these. He left America in 1760 *and settled permanently in London where he achieved great success as one of the leading history painters of his day. A stout defender of the American Revolution, West remained faithful to his Colonial background in two other ways: he taught dozens of younger American aspirants, and he often depicted scenes from Colonial history such as* Penn's Treaty with the Indians *(above). John Trumbull, one of West's pupils, undertook one series of subjects that West, as history painter to George III of England, could not, namely, the history of the American Revolution (right, above). Many years later Trumbull enlarged four of these spirited late-eighteenth-century scenes to decorate the rotunda of the Capitol building. Thomas Sully of Philadelphia, America's leading portraitist of the early nineteenth century, made occasional forays into the field of historical painting, here joining the scores of other professional artists memorializing the first American President (right, below).*

Thomas Sully (1783–1872), The Passage of the Delaware, 1819, *oil on canvas. Courtesy of the Museum of Fine Arts, Boston, Gift of the Museum Owners.*

John Trumbull (1756–1843), Battle of Bunker's Hill, 1786, *oil on canvas. Yale University Art Gallery.*

Gilbert Stuart (1755–1828), General Henry Knox. *Courtesy of the Museum of Fine Arts, Boston. On Deposit by the City of Boston.*

Charles Willson Peale (1741–1827), Family Group, 1773, *oil on canvas. Courtesy of the New-York Historical Society, New York City.*

When Copley left the Colonies, the mantle for realistic portraiture fell upon the Philadelphian, Charles Willson Peale, who added, in some of his finest paintings, an emphasis upon sympathetic family interrelationships (above). The realistic portrait style of the Federal period was soon superseded, however, by the vivid, bravura brushwork and color of Gilbert Stuart (left). Stuart, a pupil of Benjamin West, had great success in London and Dublin before returning to America in 1792 *and practicing in New York City, Philadelphia, and Washington, and finally settling in Boston in* 1805. *Peale, meanwhile, had fathered "America's first family" of artists. His sons, Rembrandt, Rubens, Titian, and Raphaelle Peale became noted painters, the first an important portraitist, and the last, the finest still-life painter in America in the early nineteenth century (right).*

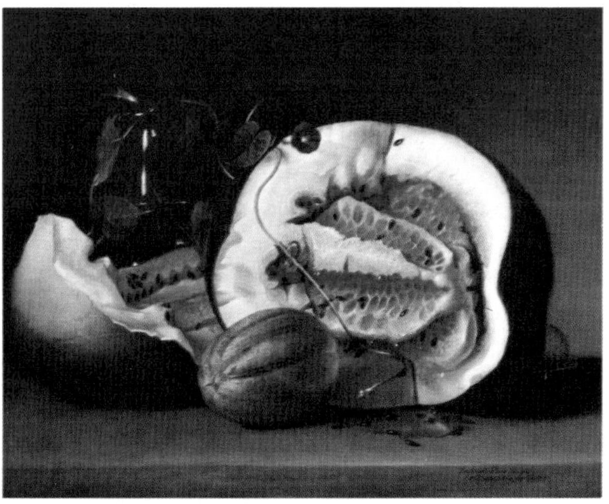

Raphaelle Peale (1774–1825), Melons and Morning Glories, 1813, *oil on canvas. Courtesy of National Collection of Fine Arts, Smithsonian Institution. Gift of Paul Mellon.*

Thomas Cole's fame, in his own time, lay in his allegorical series of paintings. These series depended upon the contrasts of two, three, four, or five separate canvases in which the artist stated his two major themes: the transience of civilization against the permanence of nature and the insignificance of man against the greatness of nature. Cole's allegories were popular here because they related to the New World itself.

Above: Thomas Cole (1801–1848), The Departure. *Courtesy of the Corcoran Gallery of Art.*
Below: Thomas Cole, The Return. *Courtesy of the Corcoran Gallery of Art.*

The 1820s witnessed the rise of interest in the depiction of nature and of man's relationship to it. Thomas Cole was our first great landscapist. In his interpretation of the Oxbow of the Connecticut River (right, above), he concentrates on the unusual aspects of nature, contrasting its stormy and serene elements. The belief in, and love of, the American landscape continued well into the middle of the nineteenth century in Jasper Cropsey's Autumn on the Hudson River *where rich, blazing color and beneficent light illuminates the scene in an almost visionary manner (right, below). Although painted in England, this work typifies what has been termed the "Hudson River" school of painting.*

Jasper Francis Cropsey (1823–1900), Autumn on the Hudson River, 1906. *National Gallery of Art, Washington, D. C. Gift of the Avalon Foundation.*

Thomas Cole (1801–1848), The Oxbow (the Connecticut River near Northampton), 1846, *oil on canvas. The Metropolitan Museum of Art. Gift of Mrs. Russell Sage,* 1908.

John Vanderlyn and Washington Allston, on the other hand, both trained in the study of the Old Masters. Represented here by classical and religious subjects, respectively, both were admired by connoisseurs in America but neglected by the general public. Vanderlyn's study of and relationship to French Neo-Classicism and Allston's kinship with Titian and the sixteenth-century Venetians brought both artists much recognition in Europe, but their painting was too foreign for the American public.

John Vanderlyn (1775–1852), Ariadne Asleep on the Island of Naxos, 1814, *oil on canvas. Courtesy of the Pennsylvania Academy of the Fine Arts.*

Washington Allston (1779–1843), Elijah Being Fed by the Ravens, 1818, *oil on canvas. Courtesy of the Museum of Fine Arts, Boston. Gift of Mrs. Samuel and Miss Alice Hooper.*

Above: George Caleb Bingham (1811–1879)
Fur Traders Descending the Missouri, *ca.* 1845, *oil on canvas*
The Metropolitan Museum of Art, Morris K. Jessup Fund, 1933

Below: William Sidney Mount (1807–1868)
Farmers Nooning
Suffolk Museum and Carriage House, Stony Brook, Long Island
Melville Collection

William Sidney Mount specialized in depicting scenes of farm and country life on his native Long Island (right). His clearly understandable and humorous genre paintings won him great success, independent as they were of European study or subject. His works, and their western equivalent, the river life scenes (above) of the St. Louis artist George Caleb Bingham, were further popularized through the engraving medium which enabled prints after the paintings of these artists to be hung in thousands of homes.

Opulent color and a sense of wealth, abundance, and optimism — nowhere more fully depicted than in the still-life painting of the day — characterized American painting at midcentury. This is particularly true of the work of Severin Roesen, one of the many refugees from the European revolutions of 1848, who fled the persecution of the Old World for the abundance of the New. Indeed, American painting of the period came to picture a vision of a new Eden, of man's second chance on earth as the American Adam. The fullest expression of this "Adamic vision" appears in the tropical landscapes of Frederic Church, where uncorrupted man lives in peace and serenity with the richness and fullness of nature. Thus, in Church's paintings, man and nature coexist in total rapport, contrasting with the earlier, dark and dramatic allegories of Church's teacher, Thomas Cole.

Above: Severin Roesen (unknown–1871), Still Life: Flowers, *oil on canvas. The Metropolitan Museum of Art, Charles Allen Munn Bequest; Fosburgh Fund, Inc., Gift; Mr. and Mrs. J. William Middendorf II, Gift; and Henry G. Keasbey Bequest, 1967.*

Below: Frederick E. Church (1826–1900), View of Cotopaxi, 1857, *oil on canvas. The Art Institute of Chicago.*

to slavery was its contradiction of the moral foundation of the Revolution — the concept that all men are equally entitled to liberty.

Still, elimination of slavery in the North came gradually. The prospective state of Vermont barred slavery in its constitution of 1777. Many Massachusetts towns from 1776 onward freed slaves and assumed the burden of caring for those incapable of self-sufficiency. In other Massachusetts towns, Negro slaves sued their masters successfully for freedom. Finally in 1783, in the case of Quock Walker, the state Chief Justice affirmed for his court that slavery was "inconsistent with our . . . constitution," whose first article began: "All men are born free." Pennsylvania in 1780 was the first state to provide by law for gradual abolition. New York failed to enact a gradual abolition law in 1785 only because of disagreement over whether or not free Negroes should be entitled to vote. By that time all Northern states except New York and New Jersey had acted to end slavery. The laggards did so ultimately in 1799 and 1804.

Equality, however, did not keep pace with freedom in the North. The assumption of Negro inferiority was virtually universal, and from it sprang laws not only against Negro voting but also against miscegenation and Negro immigration. Custom confined Negroes largely to menial jobs and to segregation in churches and schools.

In the Southern states, where one in every three or four people was a Negro and slavery was basic to both the economy and the social system, human rights won still less recognition. Southern libertarians, such as Patrick Henry, recognized the clear conflict between their principles and the ownership of slaves. Many freed their slaves under the provisions of state laws designed to encourage manumission, but others, including Henry, were "drawn along by the general Inconvenience of living without them." In the Lower South, where plantation agriculture was comparatively more prosperous and slaves relatively more numerous than in Virginia, manumission was less popular. All of the Southern states except Georgia had prohibited or severely restricted the importation of slaves by 1786, but revulsion against the institution of slavery was perhaps less important in accounting for this development than fear for the maintenance of white supremacy and concern over the balance of payments abroad. Even before the Revolution, most Southern colonies had sought to restrict the importation of Negroes, but on behalf of British slave sellers the Privy Council had consistently voided colonial laws designed to achieve that end.

Religious customs also altered in the aftermath of the Revolution. Belief in freedom of religious opinion as a "natural" or God-given right was coming to be generally accepted. State-enforced religious conformity, based to some extent on the assumption that God would reward or punish whole societies according to the extent to which its members observed His will, was losing ground.

Two states illustrated the conflict between the old and new ideas in religion. Massachusetts, over much opposition, held to the old tradition; by far the most controversial feature of the state's constitution in 1780 was the article dealing with religion. The constitution expressly assumed that happiness and good order in society "depend upon piety, religion and morality" and that "these cannot be generally diffused . . . but by . . . public worship . . . and . . . public instruction." It authorized the Legislature, therefore, to require towns to provide "at their own expense, . . . for the support of public protestant teachers of piety, religion and morality." Compulsory attendance "upon the instructions of the public teachers," with provisions for exceptions based on conscience and convenience, was to be authorized at the Legislature's discretion. The constitution did guarantee to towns the right to "elect" their public teachers or ministers and to contract with them on the matter of support. As had been true before the Revolution, individuals could earmark their religious support payments for their own sect or denomination, if they actually attended its "instructions."

Virginia, by way of contrast, was in the vanguard of the new movement for religious freedom. Thomas Jefferson drafted a "Statute of Religious Liberty" during the Revolution, but it was not enacted until 1785. Its preamble castigated the "impious presumption" by which "fallible and uninspired men, have assumed dominion over the faith of others." Compelling a man to make payments "for the propagation of opinions which he disbelieves," the statute affirmed, "is sinful and tyrannical." The law then provided specifically that "no man shall be compelled to frequent or support any religious worship . . . nor . . . suffer on account of his religious opinions." Rather, "all men shall be free to profess" their beliefs and "the same shall in no wise diminish, enlarge or affect their civil capacities." In this new spirit, reinforced by patriotic sentiment, the Church of England lost its "establishment," or government support, in all the Southern states. Legal qualifications designed to exclude Catholics from voting and holding office declined almost to the vanishing point.

Drastic reorganization of the Church of England was necessary to permit its continuance in America after the Revolution. A group of Anglican (Church of England) clergymen from Connecticut dispatched the Reverend Samuel Seabury to England in 1783 to seek consecration as a bishop and thus to become administrative head of the Church in America in place of the Bishop of London who had previously exercised that authority. The English bishops refused to consecrate Seabury when he would not swear allegiance to the British Crown, but he secured consecration from dissident bishops in Scotland. Parliament later acceded in 1787 to the consecration of two other American bishops. Thus they provided the three necessary for the consecration of added bishops and granted the separate existence of the American Episcopal Church.

Reorganization after American independence was less troublesome for other religious groups. The handful of priests who served America's 24,000 Catholics received authorization from Rome to elect one of their number as bishop. The choice fell upon Father John Carroll, a Jesuit, who was consecrated Bishop of Baltimore in 1790 at ceremonies which took place in London. American followers of the English evangelist John Wesley organized the Methodist Episcopal Church in 1784 under the leadership of Francis Asbury, even though Wesley himself remained nominally a member of the Church of England for several more years. One of the modifications from Anglican practice enabled Asbury, in effect, to designate himself a bishop. Congregationalists, Baptists, and Quakers placed so much authority in local congregations or individual members that they needed no reorganization to establish American control. Presbyterians, organized in a representative system of church government, likewise needed no change, although they did become markedly less deferential to Scottish Presbyterian authorities than they had been.

A sense of nationalism also became apparent among artists, poets, musicians, and intellectuals in general. John Trumbull of Connecticut, studying in the London studio of Benjamin West, whose historical paintings had so glorified the history of Britain, began there in the early 1780s a series of paintings celebrating the American struggle against British rule. "The greatest motive I . . . have for engaging in . . . painting," he wrote, "has been the wish of commemorating the great events of our country's revolution." In 1778 William Billings, onetime Boston tanner, put patriotic words to "Chester," a piece of sacred music which he had composed earlier; and it became, if not the Marseillaise of the American Revolution, at least a popular war song. A few years later Billings's book, *Continental Harmony,* included a work titled "Be Glad then America." Another John Trumbull of Connecticut, a lawyer related to the painter, achieved great popularity in 1782 with *M'Fingal,* an epic poem satirizing the British and their Tory supporters. Noah Webster, later to achieve immortality through his dictionary, began urging the reform of British spelling with the object of establishing "a *national language.*" "As an independent people," he argued, "our reputation abroad demands that in all things we should be federal; be *national;* for if we do not respect *ourselves,* we may be assured that *other nations* will not respect us."

Historical writing, largely provincial in its focus before the Revolution, now began to reflect a national spirit. Foremost among the nationalist historians was David Ramsay, a South Carolina doctor. In his perceptive *History of the American Revolution,* published in 1789, Ramsay noted the growth of American nationalist feeling. Before 1775, he wrote,

> Americans knew but little of one another. . . . Trade and business had brought the inhabitants of their seaports acquainted with each other, but the bulk of the people in the interior country were unacquainted with their fellow citizens [in other regions]. A continental army, and Congress composed of men from all the States, by freely mixing together, were assimilated into one mass. Individuals . . . disseminated principles of union among them. Local prejudices abated. By frequent collision asperities were worn off, and a foundation was laid for the establishment of a nation.

Still the United States in the mid-1780s was merely a loose confederation of nearly sovereign states, not yet a nation.

Conclusion

During the Revolution and the early postwar years the American people altered their society profoundly. They based their state governments upon the will of the people and, through provisions for frequent elections with a relatively wide suffrage and reasonably fair apportionment of legislative seats, arranged to keep them representative. They encountered major difficulty in reaching agreement on the amount of authority to be delegated to a federal union of states, and only after bitter argument and long delay could they form the constitutional basis of a confederation with even minimum authority. Economically, independence brought not only great opportunities for the future but also severe temporary hardship, chiefly the result of America's exclusion from the British mercantilist system and the wartime loss of confidence in paper money. Putting the Revolutionary ideology into practice helped to undermine old traditions of deference, to begin the elimination of slavery in the North, and to extend religious freedom. In making such adjustments, Americans rendered their society still more distinctive in comparison with Europe as a whole.

What happened to the political institutions of the states in the period of the Revolution is the subject of *Rebels and Democrats** (1955) by E. P. Douglass. His book largely supersedes the longer descriptive work by Allan Nevins, *The American States during and after the American Revolution* (1924). Chilton Williamson's *American Suffrage* (1960) is authoritative on state actions to extend the right to vote. For developments in Virginia, see Dumas Malone's *Jefferson: The Virginian** (1948); Irving Brant's *James Madison: The Nationalist* (1948). For Pennsylvania, see David Hawke's *In the Midst of a Revolution* (1961) and K. L. Brunhouse's *The Counter-revolution in Pennsylvania* (1942). On Massachusetts, the most authoritative discussion is the introduction by Oscar and Mary Handlin (eds.) to *The Popular Sources of Political Authority* (1966), an edition of the documents relating to the convention. *Massachusetts: Colony to Commonwealth** (1961) is a shorter selection edited by Robert J. Taylor. M. L. Starkey's *A Little Rebellion* (1955) is a good account of Shays' Rebellion. R. P. McCormick's *Experiment in Independence: New Jersey in the Critical Period* (1950) and E. W. Spaulding's *New York in the Critical Period* (1932) are also good state studies.

Conflict has raged bitterly among historians over interpretation of the Confederation period as a whole. One side, looking back to John Fiske's *The Critical Period of American History* (1888), sees American unity, political stability, and economic development each in jeopardy until rescued by the adoption of the Constitution. Another side, best exemplified in Merrill Jensen's *The New Nation** (1950), stresses the successes of the Confederation and condemns those who wished to change it as antidemocratic. C. P. Nettels in *The Emergence of a National Economy* (1962) depicts an economy much less robust than that which Jensen describes. E. J. Ferguson's *The Power of the Purse* (1961) is sympathetic to the nationalists who sought to strengthen American unity. J. T. Main, a student of Jensen's, clarifies the attitudes of Confederation supporters in *The Anti-federalists** (1961) and chronicles the transition of *The Upper House in Revolutionary America* (1967) from aristocratic to democratic. R. B. Morris in *The American Revolution Reconsidered* (1967) attempts to reach a balanced judgment and in so doing echoes in some measure B. F. Wright's *Consensus and Continuity* (1958), which dwelt on what united Americans rather than divided them.

On the West, J. M. Sosin's *The Revolutionary Frontier** (1967) is the obvious beginning point. W. H. Masterson's biography of *William Blount* (1954) and T. P. Abernethy's *From Frontier to Plantation in Tennessee* (1932) illuminate the early history of the state. B. W. Bond's *The Civilization of the Old Northwest* (1934) is excellent. R. M. Robbins in *Our Landed Heritage* (1942) affords long-range perspective on federal land policy.

Social and cultural change in the Revolutionary era is another topic on which historians have not yet reached a clear consensus. J. F. Jameson in *The American Revolution Considered as a Social Movement* (1926) scratched the surface provocatively. E. B. Greene's *The Revolutionary Generation* (1943) is more descriptive than analytical. C. W. Van Tyne's *The Loyalists in the American Revolution* (1902) has never been surpassed overall, although W. H. Nelson's *The American Tory* (1961) is an interesting essay. R. R. Palmer in *The Age of the Democratic Revolution* (1959) compares American and French treatment of those who stood by the old regime. R. B. Nye's *The Cultural Life of the New Nation** (1960) affords a general treatment beginning in 1776. J. T. Flexner's *American Painting: The Light of Distant Skies* (1954) is superb. V. L. Parrington's *Main Currents in American Thought** (1929) shows the change in American writing. P. C. Nagel's *One Nation Indivisible* (1964) discusses attitudes toward American unity.

Several recent works illuminate the history of slavery in the Revolutionary era. A Zilversmit's *The First Emancipation* (1967) attributes the ending of slavery in the North to ideological considerations. E. J. McManus's *A History of Negro Slavery in New York* (1966) follows the subject to its conclusion. L. F. Litwack's *North of Slavery* (1961) describes the sorry treatment of free Negroes in the North after 1790.

* indicates availability in paperback.

7

From Confederation to Nation

WEAKNESSES IN the Confederation government became more apparent at the end of the Revolutionary conflict. During the war popular determination to resist British domination had created voluntary enforcement agents for congressional policies in every community. With peace and independence secured, people began to think again of more narrowly personal interests and to fear for both their individual liberties and the rights of their own state governments. The Confederation's financial crisis deepened as the states ignored requisitions and Congress lacked power to impose taxes to repay its war debt. Merchants and artisans demanded help in meeting foreign competition, but because the Confederation was without any power whatever to regulate foreign or domestic commerce, they were forced to look to the states for assistance in establishing favorable terms of trade.

Persuaded that representative government and freedom for ordinary people were secure only in small states, many Americans regarded the prospective disintegration of the Confederation complacently. Nationalists, however, were determined to weld all the American states together into a powerful and prestigious nation. Failing in repeated efforts to strengthen the Confederation, they at last determined to replace it entirely with a new federal union. In the spirit of the Revolution, they were equally determined that the new government would represent the people as a whole, that it would reserve important powers to the component states, and that it would afford safeguards to assure the people that they need not fear oppression. By brilliant tactical leadership they brought about a constitutional convention, drafted a satisfactory instrument for a strong federal government, and persuaded popular conventions in the states to give it their endorsement.

Inadequacies of the Confederation

Successful as it had been in winning independence from Britain, the Confederation was unsatisfactory in many ways. It was particularly defective for peacetime diplomacy. Unable to regulate commerce or to enforce its will upon individuals or states on any matter, the Confederation could neither promise reciprocal concessions nor threaten commercial retaliation. In England, John Adams could only fume in frustration as the British continued to occupy forts on American territory, fixed commercial policies harmful to American interests, declined to send a diplomatic representative to the United States, and inquired condescendingly whether he represented one nation or thirteen.

British occupation of forts on territory officially ceded to the United States in the Treaty of Paris (1783) was the most inflammatory diplomatic difficulty confronting the Confederation. Britain had promised to evacuate "with all convenient speed" a number of posts strung along the northern frontier from Lake Superior to Lake Champlain. However, for reasons never clearly established, perhaps chiefly to preserve peace with the Indians, Britain determined not only to retain these forts but even to recapture any which the Americans might seize. As moral justification for this treaty violation, Britain alleged that the Americans were not keeping their treaty obligations regarding confiscation of Loyalist property and the debts owed by Americans to British subjects. The Confederation could not compel the states to alter their confiscation policies, nor could it force individuals to pay their debts. Neither could Congress itself assume the obligations, as it lacked the means to make the payments.

Foreign encouragement of separatist tendencies in Western regions constituted another problem which the Confederation Congress was ill-equipped to handle. Vermont, still operating in the 1780s as an unaffiliated state on land claimed by New York, depended heavily upon Canada's St. Lawrence River as its major avenue of commerce. When Levi Allen, Tory brother of Ticonderoga's cocaptor, Ethan Allen, sought a commercial treaty with Britain on behalf of Vermont, a Privy Council committee recommended that Vermont and other frontier areas be encouraged to maintain their independence and "to form Treaties of Commerce and Friendship with Great Britain." Britain made some commercial concessions to Vermonters but had made no treaty when the Allens lost control to a faction more disposed to join the other American states.

In the Ohio-Mississippi Valley, Spain more than Britain was the fomenter of separatist sentiment. Because commercial transportation was confined so largely to natural waterways, most of the American West depended upon Spanish-held New Orleans at the mouth of the Mississippi River for its access not only to foreign but even to American markets. Spain, fearing for the security of her sparsely settled territory from Louisiana eastward into Florida,

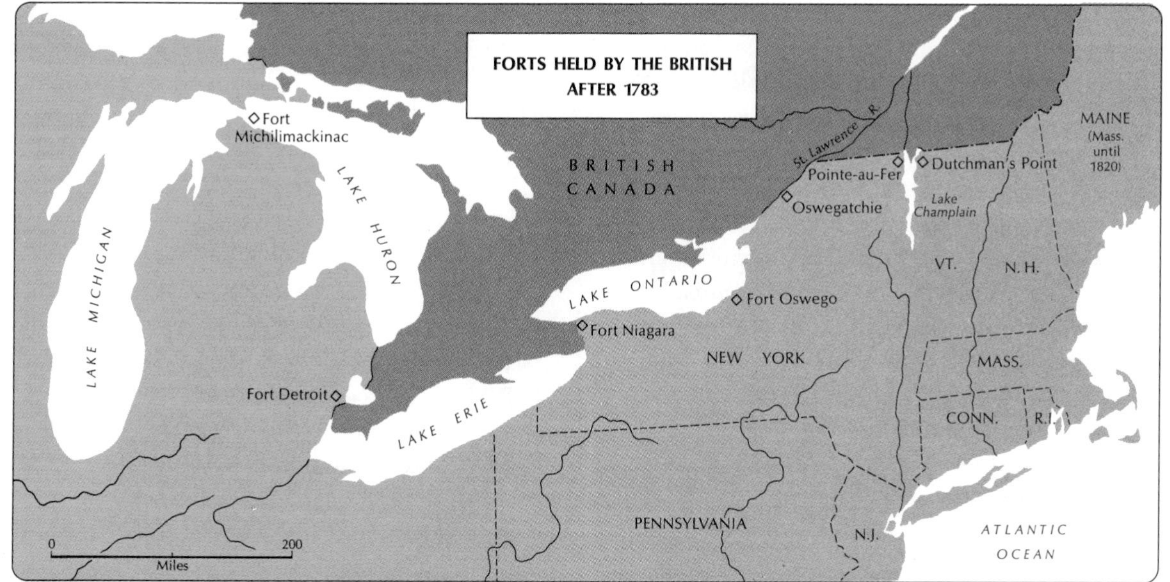

hoped to slow the westward movement of Americans or at least induce Westerners to set up independent, and consequently relatively weak, governments.

In pursuit of this policy, Spain closed the Mississippi to Americans at the end of the war. Through its Minister, Diego de Gardoqui, Spain suggested to American Secretary of State John Jay in 1784 that if the United States would give up its claim, derived from the peace treaty with Britain, to use the river, Spain would make commercial concessions in her domestic market to the United States and renounce her not-very-serious claim to the area northward from its Gulf coast settlements to the Tennessee River. Jay was willing, as was the commercially depressed North in general, but the South considered surrendering the claim to Mississippi navigation too high a price to pay for a commercial treaty. Because the five Southern states had just enough votes to bar the 9-vote majority necessary to ratify a treaty, none was concluded. Resentment in the South and West, however, continued to sustain separatist feeling.

Fostering prosperity was another function in which the performance of the Confederation government was inadequate. Although laissez faire ideas were not unknown in America even before the publication of Adam Smith's attack upon mercantilism in *The Wealth of Nations* (1776), such ideas were still new and radical in the 1780s. Most people who engaged in commerce, including seaboard farmers and urban artisans as well as merchants, were still mercantilists. As such they expected and desired a government which, like Britain's, would actively aid the accumulation of wealth by private individuals. They wished the government to impose regulations and to pay subsidies which would aid them to achieve an excess of exports over imports, thus leading to a net inflow of gold and silver from which the economy as a whole would benefit. Lacking any power over foreign or domestic commerce as well as any authority to tax, the Confederation could do virtually nothing to fulfill these mercantilistic expectations. The state governments attempted to do what was expected of them, but their small size and lack of unity on foreign trade policies were serious handicaps, especially in dealing with Great Britain, an economic colossus which still held a commanding share of American trade. Import taxes imposed by one state, for example, often succeeded less in reducing purchases of the imported items than in diverting their importation to a neighboring state. Accordingly, many seaboard farmers, as well as most urban artisans and merchants, clamored for a stronger central government.

Depressed conditions in commerce undoubtedly increased the dissatisfaction of businessmen. The causes for the postwar depression, once blamed in part at least upon the inadequacies of the Confederation, were really multiple (see Chapter 6); economic conditions probably would have been much the same for some time even under a stronger national government. It was true also that business conditions had begun to improve before a new government replaced the Confederation. Freed from British restrictions, Americans began after the war to develop new trading relations with Asia, especially China, as well as with continental Europe. Enterprising merchants, aided by cooperative local officials, found ways to circumvent British restrictions upon the West Indian trade. American producers recovered from the disruptions of wartime; and in some states reliable paper money helped to alleviate the scarcity of specie. Yet American merchants, still wedded to mercantilist ideas and forced to compete with foreigners who had the assistance of strong mercantilist governments, understandably demanded a government which could render similar advantages to them. The depression, whatever its causes and despite considerable recovery in the late 1780s, only intensified this desire.

Shays' Rebellion in 1786 and 1787 and other developments attributable in part to the depression helped also to build sentiment favorable to a stronger federal government. Although few reasonable people really feared a "federal Shays," men of wealth recognized the desirability of a federal government which could act quickly and decisively in such a crisis. Many also viewed with favor the prospect of a central government which might bar the inflationary paper money issues and the stay laws which some states had passed at the insistence of clamoring debtors. Exploiting such sentiments, nationalists viewed the occasion of Shays' Rebellion as a moment "very favorable . . . for increasing the dignity and energy of [the federal] government." One even expressed the fear that "the Insurgents will be conquered too soon."

Such rational and self-interested bases for dissatisfaction with the Confederation may have counted for less than the emotions of an emerging nationalism. American gentlemen engaging in overseas trade and those who read newspapers full of foreign "intelligence" were acutely aware that Europeans expected America to become, not a unified and powerful nation, but a geographic expression—an area full of insignificant, "petty," and anarchic states. For the Revolutionary elite, the American identification arising out of the struggle with Britain had not only replaced their British loyalty but had weakened their earlier self-conception as provincials as well. Consequently there was great demand for an *American* government worthy of respect. Washington's reaction to Shays' Rebellion affords an illustration. "I am mortified beyond expression," he wrote, "that . . . we [Americans] should by our conduct verify the predictions of our transatlantic foes and render ourselves ridiculous and contemptible in the eyes of all Europe." To his former aide, Alexander Hamilton, there was also "something . . . contemptible in the prospect of a number of petty states, with the appearance only of union, jarring, jealous and perverse, . . . weak and insignificant in the eyes of other nations." For such men, incipient national pride was among the most profound reasons for dissatisfaction with the weak Confederation.

Nationalist Reform Efforts

Repaying the money which it had borrowed to support the war was the only function of importance, except for the administration of Western lands, which Congress retained after the conclusion of peace. Accordingly, nationalists tried to make the most of it. They tried to increase the Confederation debt by taking over those incurred by states in support of the war and to use this repayment obligation as justification for amending the Articles of Confederation to confer a limited power of taxation upon the federal government. With that precedent established, nationalists hoped to expand federal powers and transform the weak Confederation into a truly national government.

Much of the opposition to the nationalist program came from individuals rather more parochial in outlook and more democratic in conviction than the nationalists. Subsistence farmers in the backcountry could expect little from a stronger national government, other than increased taxes. They neither knew nor cared how Americans were regarded in Europe. Many people of the "middling sort" shared the conviction of the aristocratic Gouverneur Morris that "the great and wealthy . . . will necessarily compose the legislative body" of the federal government. But, unlike Morris, they desired consequently to minimize federal power and retain maximum authority in the state legislatures, in which men of their own class could better afford to serve. Many shared the belief widespread in Europe that only in small states could liberty and representative government flourish and that governments of large states tended inevitably toward tyranny.

Nationalist efforts to confer a limited taxing power upon the Confederation began in 1781, even before Yorktown, and continued into 1786. "Requisitions" to the states had proved inadequate either to redeem the Confederation's Continental paper money or to meet the general revenue needs of the government. Many states found it extremely difficult to secure the specie (gold and silver) with which to meet their requisitions. Most were reluctant to part with what little specie they had, especially to pay requisitions in full when it was clear that some other states would not do so. States in which there were few creditors of the federal government were especially reluctant to part with specie, since they could be sure it was not coming back but would wind up in other states. Those states which had made great war expenditures of their own naturally felt that some priority was due their own creditors. It soon became clear that, unless Congress gained some taxing authority, the function of repaying its war debts would have to be transferred to the states. Superintendent of Finance Robert Morris, an early leader of the nationalist movement, asserted in 1781 that the "political existence of America" depended on adoption of a plan to allow Congress to collect an "impost," or duty, of 5 percent on all imports. The income from such a tax, in fact, would have paid only the interest on the federal debt, but Morris had plans for additional federal taxes if the impost won approval.

Reaction to the impost plan was generally favorable, but it foundered on that provision of the Articles of Confederation which specified that amendments would become effective only when "confirmed by the legislatures of every state." By midyear, 1782, only one state had not approved the plan. Gripped by antinationalist radicals, who saw in the impost "the Chains Rivotted" and a "Yoke of Tyranny" poised, tiny Rhode Island refused its assent. A congressional delegation began a journey to Rhode Island to reason with the legislators there but abandoned the trip upon learning that Virginia had repealed its endorsement.

Realizing that the case for American unity would weaken still more with the end of the war, Morris and his coterie of nationalists made another strong effort to gain taxing authority while peace negotiations were in progress during 1783. Morris himself thought that, even without amending the Articles of Confederation, Congress could impose taxes on the ground that authority to spend implied power to collect revenue. Capitalizing on discontent within the army, especially among officers to whom Congress could not make good its compensation commitments, the Morris group encouraged the issuance of ominous pronouncements from Washington's camp at Newburgh, New York. Washington himself, however, squelched his more aggressive subordinates, including General Gates, so that the "terror of a mutinying Army" lost some of its effectiveness as a pressure tactic. Suspected always of self-interested economic motives as well as indifference to public opinion, Morris resigned in 1784 in the hope that "the People will . . . more easily believe when they hear Truth from some other Quarter."

Federal taxing authority seemed close to realization again in 1786. Except for New York, all the states had then approved it in one form or another. Under the leadership of Governor George Clinton, New York finally agreed to allow the federal government to tax imports at 5 percent, but only under conditions which included state control of collections. Congress considered New York's conditions unacceptable. Pennsylvania, at the other extreme, held out for conferring a far wider range of taxing authority upon the federal government. Thus, even though all of the states desired some form of taxing authority for the federal government, it gained none because it could not secure the required unanimity in support of one specific proposal.

Truly ruinous conditions in Confederation finance, attributable to the absence of taxing power, seemed to presage disintegration of the federal Union. Total Confederation income in 1785 and 1786 amounted to less than one-third of the interest charges on its debts. Congress managed to pay the interest on debts due in Holland but defaulted completely on its obligations to France. State governments more and more met the interest payments on federal securities held by their own citizens. The general expectation was that ultimately all war costs, those incurred by state governments as well as by Congress, would be lumped together and apportioned by an agreed-upon formula among the states for payment.

Holders of federal securities strongly preferred payment by the federal government rather than by the states. This reflected the fact that those who had been both willing and able to back the Revolutionary cause with money were generally American nationalists. But there were economic considerations as well. Whereas Congress was committed to pay its obligations at face value in specie, the states, in many instances, preferred to redeem securities at their depreciated market value—rarely as much as half of face value—and in paper money, or at least something less valuable than specie. Many speculators purchased securities at their depreciated market value in the hope that they would ultimately be redeemed at a higher rate. Such men constituted a pressure group which favored the creation of a stronger federal government with taxing powers, but the scarcity of surviving evidence makes it impossible to determine which speculators invested most in federal securities in the 1780s or how extensive was their influence upon political developments.

Toward a Constitutional Convention

By appealing to considerations of commerce rather than of finance, the nationalists were ultimately able to secure a convention to reconsider the nature of the American Union. Demands for such a convention had been frequent from 1780 onward, as nationalists felt more and more poignantly the weaknesses of the Confederation. The leadership in arranging a convention came initially from the South. Commissioners from Virginia and Maryland met at Alexandria, Virginia, in March, 1785, to consider mutual problems relating to the navigation of Chesapeake Bay and the Potomac River. After moving from Alexandria to the spacious grounds of Washington's estate, Mount Vernon, the conferees not only agreed on joint administration of the Potomac but urged upon their respective legislatures steps such as uniform commercial regulations and currency, which were at least suggestive of economic union. This discussion led Virginia and Maryland leaders to suggest the inclusion of Pennsylvania and Delaware in a plan for building a canal to link the Chesapeake region to the Ohio River. Prompted by James Madison, a youthful legislator who had previously served in Congress, Virginia then invited all the states to a convention at Annapolis, Maryland, to consider commercial matters of common interest.

Madison's Annapolis convention, meeting in September, 1786, failed in its stated purpose but achieved a larger one. Four states, including the host state of Maryland, sent no representatives. Delegates from four other states arrived only after the convention had concluded. Thus only New York, New Jersey, Pennsylvania, Delaware, and Virginia were actually represented at Annapolis. Their twelve delegates thought it useless to consider commercial problems in view of the limited attendance, but instead approved an appeal drafted by New York's Alexander Hamilton for a new convention to meet in Philadelphia on May 14, 1787. Hamilton's resolution asserted that unspecified "defects in the System of the Federal Government" had placed the United States in a "critical" situation "calling for an exertion of the united Virtues and Wisdom of all the Members of the Confederacy." The appeal urged all states to send "Commissioners" to Philadelphia "to take into Consideration the situation of the United States" and "to devise such further provisions as shall appear to them necessary to render the constitution of the Federal Government adequate to the exigencies of the Union."

Hamilton's appeal for a convention to meet at Philadelphia proved popular in nearly every state. Congress had declined in 1786 to submit to the states the elaborate plans for strengthening the federal government which had been worked out under the leadership of Charles Pinckney of South Carolina. Its refusal resulted, however, not from disinclination to increase federal power but from despair over what might follow after the rejection of the plans for want of unanimity. Early in 1787, Congress cautiously endorsed the proposed Philadelphia convention "for the sole and express purpose of revising the Articles of Confederation and reporting [suggested changes] to Congress and the several legislatures" for their consideration. Five states had already named delegates. Except for Rhode Island, the others did so subsequently. In view of the requirement of unanimous consent to amend the Articles of Confederation, even Rhode Island's aloofness was disheartening.

In the winter which intervened between the Annapolis and the Philadelphia conventions Shays' Rebellion ran its pitiful course in Massachusetts. Historians have long attributed to it a kind of catalytic effect in consolidating support, especially among conservative men of property, for a stronger federal government. The affair did strengthen the desire in some quarters for a federal government strong enough to quell debtor insurrections quickly and to ban stay laws and inflationary issues of state paper money. But Shays' Rebellion also humiliated American nationalists such as Washington and deepened the conviction of mercantilists that a strong federal government should be established to help restore prosperity by applying mercantilist tactics.

The Grand Convention

Fifty-five men participated in the Convention which John Adams called "the greatest single effort of national deliberation that the world has ever seen." Preeminent among them was the former commander in chief, George Washington, whose popularity was so great as almost to assure public acceptance of the work of the Convention. As presiding officer, however, Washington took little part in the debates. Benjamin Franklin, the first American to achieve high distinction in the world at large, was also present, but he was too aged to do more than encourage harmony and compromise. Intellectual leadership in the deliberations fell largely to younger men, notably James Madison, who had done so much to secure a convention, and James Wilson, a Scottish immigrant who practiced law in Pennsylvania and would later sit on the Supreme Court. Gouverneur Morris, an aristocrat blessed with literary skill as well as an incisive mind, would also make significant contributions. Alexander Hamilton, the brilliant young New Yorker who shared with Madison major responsibility for the calling of the Constitutional Convention, held such extreme views on national power and executive authority that he was largely without influence in the deliberations. At the other extreme, Luther Martin, the garrulous, bibulous, but brilliant attorney general of Maryland, argued interminably in defense of states' rights. Notable absentees were John

Adams and Thomas Jefferson, both abroad on diplomatic missions, as well as Samuel Adams and Patrick Henry, then devotees of states' rights. Massachusetts's delegation did not include Adams, while Henry, selected by Virginia, "smelt a rat" and declined to attend.

Several characteristics of the Convention delegates as a group stand out. The members were relatively young: the average age was forty-two. But their level of experience was high. Nearly three-fourths had served in Congress, and most had worked in state government as well. Over half were lawyers. A substantial number had lived abroad or at least in a state other than that which they represented. Few lived in the backcountry. Most were from seaboard areas and enjoyed comfortable incomes. A handful, including Washington, were men of great wealth, with investments primarily in land. The most significant fact concerning the delegates, however, was that all but four were nationalists.

Enthusiasm, if measured by attendance, was not commensurate with the importance of the task. Scheduled to begin May 14, 1787, at the Pennsylvania State House, the Convention did not secure a quorum until May 25. Rhode Island never sent a delegation, and New Hampshire's spokesmen did not arrive until late in July, by which time two of New York's three members had gone home in disgust.

That agreement was possible on a number of important questions was evident at the outset. No one opposed the selection of Washington as presiding officer. Not every one agreed with Madison that the Convention would "decide for ever the fate of Republican Government," but all felt great respect for the seriousness of the undertaking. No one objected seriously to the suggestion that sessions be secret so that the members could express themselves openly, change positions with less embarrassment, and enjoy freedom from outside pressure. "Leaks" were, in fact, remarkably few during the four-month convention, a reflection perhaps of the importance the delegates assigned to the privacy of their discussions. While the early arrivals were waiting for the laggards, Gouverneur Morris suggested that the states with large populations "should unite in refusing to the small states an equal vote," but the Virginians feared correctly that such an effort would produce "fatal altercations between the large and small States." Accordingly, the delegates agreed readily that each state, regardless of its size, should have one vote.

Disagreement came quickly enough. The "Virginia Plan," worked out in advance by James Madison and introduced by Governor Edmund Randolph on behalf of the Virginia delegation, was too strongly nationalistic for many delegates. A prefatory resolution, suggested by Gouverneur Morris, stated that no mere "treaty" among the states would be sufficient but "that a national government" with a "supreme Legislative, Executive, and Judiciary" should be established. Although many delegates objected to these ideas, only Connecticut voted against the resolution. The Virginia Plan itself assumed that the Articles of Confederation, "the treaty," would be abandoned for a completely new constitution. Under the new constitution, there would be a bicameral legislature whose lower house would be elected directly by the people with representation apportioned among the states according to population. Its upper house was to be chosen by the lower house from candidates nominated by state legislatures, but again the number of representatives from each state would vary with population. The legislature would choose a chief executive. Power to veto legislative enactments absolutely, such as colonial governors had possessed, was to repose not in the executive alone but in a Council of Revision which included a number of judges as well as the chief executive. The Virginians provided also for a federal court system, including a supreme court. Madison wished to endow the federal government also with power to veto any act of a state legislature and to use force against a recalcitrant state. As he conceived it, the Virginia Plan would provide "a due supremacy of the national authority" and yet "not exclude the local authorities whenever they can be subordinately useful."

Opposed to the Virginia Plan were both the antinationalist minority and the representatives of smaller states. The antinationalists, who wished to retain the essential features of the Confederation, tilting the power balance in favor of the states, were so few as to be almost impotent. They included John Lansing and Robert Yates, who outvoted Alexander Hamilton to control New York's three-man delegation, and Maryland's Luther Martin. The more significant opposition came from delegates of small states, who insisted upon equal representation for all states. Delaware, New Jersey, and New York opposed representation proportional to population even in the lower house. Maryland and Connecticut joined them in the small-state effort to eliminate this principle from the higher chamber, but the proposition carried by a vote of 6 to 5.

Spokesmen for the small states and the antinationalists did not give up. The early discussions and votes had occurred in the committee of the whole, a parliamentary device to permit free discussion and nonbinding votes. Before the Convention proper took up the Virginia Plan as amended by the committee of the whole, William Paterson of New Jersey asked, and was granted leave, to present a "federal" plan, known ever since as the "New Jersey Plan," reflecting the views of the minority.

Mere modification of the Articles of Confederation was the gist of the New Jersey Plan. Significantly, however, the modifications all tended to strengthen the federal government, giving it limited power not only to tax and to regulate commerce but even to coerce states. Acts of Congress and treaties were to be "supreme law," and there was to be a supreme court of rather narrowly limited jurisdiction. Overcoming their own fears of executive tyranny, the minority which opposed the Virginia Plan suggested cautiously that Congress choose an executive whose powers would not include the veto. The United States under the New Jersey Plan would remain, however, a confederation of limited powers representing not people but strong state governments, each with an equal voice.

Opposition to the New Jersey Plan was vehement. Madison and James Wilson led the nationalist attack, while Alexander Hamilton chose the occasion to express his extreme nationalist views. Among them was the suggestion that the federal government should appoint state governors who would exercise an absolute veto over their legislatures. When the delegates in committee of the whole were asked on June 19 to choose between the Virginia and New Jersey Plans, the vote was 7 to 3 (New York, New Jersey, and Delaware) in favor of the nationalist, with Maryland's delegates evenly divided.

From June 19 to July 2, the Convention debated final approval of those provisions of the Virginia Plan relating to representation in the legislature. The proposal that the lower house should be elected by the people and the upper house by state legislatures won easy ac-

New York Public Library, Rare Book Room

The Making of the Constitution

Eleven years after the Declaration of Independence, most men felt the Articles of Confederation insufficient to meet America's needs, especially for the development of trade and the economy. An amending convention was called in Philadelphia in May of 1887 *(following page). George Washington presided; fifty-five state leaders were delegates. Opposition quickly arose over central issues: states' rights versus strong central government; rural agricultural interests versus urban business interests.*

After four months of debate and hard-won compromise, the result was not amendment of the Articles but a new document: the Constitution of the United States. It established three branches of government, their method of selection and their powers; it permitted national taxation; and it provided the framework for America's future growth. Nine of the thirteen states had to ratify the Constitution before it could become effective.

In these contemporary cartoons, ratification appears as the raising of pillars for a federal edifice. Although New Hampshire was the crucial ninth state to ratify, populous Virginia and New York were also essential. After great debate, Virginia came tenth and exerted an irresistible pull on New York, which feared the economic consequences of remaining outside the Union. Agricultural North Carolina and Rhode Island, which had boycotted the convention, lagged behind. North Carolina ratified in 1789. *Rhode Island's foundation was good; ratification in* 1790 *restored its shattered column.*

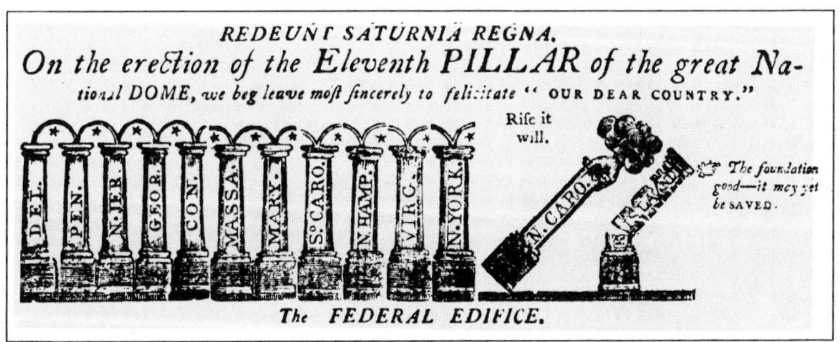

Courtesy of the New-York Historical Society, New York City

Top, left: New York Public Library, Prints Collection

Center: Detail from Signing the Constitution, *by T. P. Rossiter, Independence National Historical Park Collection*

Others: New York Public Library, Picture Collection

Those in favor of a strong national government included James Madison (above, right) and Alexander Hamilton (above, left), who together had succeeded in calling the amending convention. Benjamin Franklin (far left, center) served as an elderly advisor. James Wilson (far left, above) led nationalist debate along with Madison, Aristocratic Gouveneur Morris (far left), representing Eastern financial and commercial interests, felt governments should naturally be in the hands of "the great and wealthy."

Antifederalists at the convention largely represented important minority interests. George Mason (above) feared the loss of individual rights and later voted against ratification in Virginia. William Paterson (above, left) proposed the "New Jersey Plan" for confederation amendments. Oliver Ellsworth (above, right) of Connecticut and John Dickinson of Delaware (right) fought for equal representation of small states in the national legislature. Luther Martin (above, far right), Attorney General of Maryland, opposed a federal court system.

Above, left: Culver Pictures, Inc.
Above, center: New York Public Library, Prints Collection
Others: New York Public Library, Picture Collection

ceptance. But whether the vote of each state in the legislative chambers should be equal or in proportion to population was another matter. After much acrimonious debate, a vote of 6 to 4, on June 29, determined that representation in the lower house would be in proportion to population. Still more bitter debate followed until July 2, when the proposal to give the states equal representation in the upper chamber lost on a tie vote, 5 to 5. John Dickinson, onetime opponent of independence and draftsman of the Articles of Confederation, gave cogent expression to the determination of the small states. On behalf of Delaware, Dickinson observed that the small states were "friends to a good national government; but we would sooner submit to a foreign power than . . . be deprived of an equality of suffrage in both branches of the legislature, and thereby thrown under the domination of the larger states."

To prevent what appeared to be an imminent breakup of the Convention, moderate nationalists determined to make a concession to the small state delegates. Over the opposition of Madison and Wilson, the Convention agreed to refer the dispute to a compromise committee, which it then packed with small state and moderate delegates. The committee recommended representation proportional to population in the lower house, but an equal vote for each state in the upper house. It was subsequently agreed that members of the upper chamber should have their votes counted individually, rather than having them collectively cast one vote for their state as was done in the Continental Congress and in the Convention. The Convention approved the compromise on July 16, by a 5 to 4 vote, with Pennsylvania, Virginia, South Carolina, and Georgia in opposition, Massachusetts evenly split, and New York absent. Although first suggested by Dickinson, the provisions resolving the controversy between the small and the large states subsequently acquired the designation "Connecticut Compromise," apparently because Connecticut delegates, including Oliver Ellsworth, who "preferred doing half the good we could, rather than do nothing at all," were especially prominent among its supporters.

Disagreement over slavery arose out of the decision to apportion seats in the House of Representatives according to population. Delegates from Georgia and South Carolina thought slaves should be counted as people in the apportionment procedure. Seven other delegations thought they should not. Congress, however, was to have the power to apportion "direct taxes" among the states in relation to population, the best index of wealth available. In this instance, delegates from the major slave states thought slaves should not be counted. The solution, carried over from an agreement in the Confederation Congress in 1783, was to count three-fifths of the slaves for purposes of both representation and taxation. Population figures would come from a federal census to be taken every ten years.

Strengthening Federal Authority

Once they had gained assurance of equal representation for each state in one chamber of the legislature, delegates from the small states became much more amenable to nationalist suggestions for strengthening the new Union. In relative harmony, the delegates proceeded to remedy each of the four major deficiencies of the Confederation, giving the government power to tax, to regulate commerce, to secure amendment without unanimous consent, and to enforce federal policies. In endowing the new government with so much more power, they agreed also on the wisdom of providing safeguards against oppression by dividing authority among distinct legislative, executive, and judicial branches of government in accordance with the theory of separation of powers. It was assumed as well that the new government would possess no powers at all other than those which they put down in writing.

The authority to tax, so long sought by the Confederation, the Convention bestowed readily upon the new Congress which it created. The delegates required that measures of taxation originate in the House of Representatives, to which the people would elect members directly, but they imposed no barrier to the amendment of tax measures by the Senate, which would represent state governments. They required, in addition, that taxes be "uniform throughout the United States" and that they be imposed in order to pay debts, to provide for the common defense or the "general welfare." Southerners, their economy heavily dependent upon exports, insisted that export taxes should be barred. Four states objected, but the measure carried, partly because such taxes would in any case have violated mercantilist principles by tending to reduce sales abroad. Ambitious planters from the Lower South, anxious to increase their labor supply, secured in addition a provision limiting to $10 each the tax which might be imposed upon importation of slaves. Except for the provision concerning the apportionment of "direct taxes," no other restriction limited the power of Congress to "lay and collect taxes."

Congress also received power to regulate commerce "with foreign nations, and among the several States, and with the Indian tribes." Authority to regulate commerce wholly within any state remained, by implication, with the government of the state. Additional restrictions on the federal government's authority over commerce arose out of conflicting sectional interests. Northern mercantilists were eager for federal "Navigation Acts" which would favor American over foreign ships, both in coastal and in overseas trade. Southerners, major exporters but not ship owners, wished foreign ships to be admitted without discrimination so that the South could benefit from greater competition among ship owners. Despairing of a total ban on navigation acts, Southerners sought instead the requirement of a two-thirds vote in each house of Congress to enact such measures, a provision which would have given them what amounted to a veto power. Another important compromise occurred, however, as Southerners abandoned their efforts to restrict navigation acts in exchange for Northern agreements not to ban the importation of slaves prior to 1808 or to tax imported slaves more than $10 each. The earlier Northern agreement to prohibit export taxes may have helped put Southerners in a conciliatory frame of mind, although this did not enter the discussions at the time of the decision on navigation acts. The provisions concerning slavery, supplemented by a rigid requirement for the return of fugitive slaves from one state to another, offended the "religious and political prejudices" of many Northern delegates, but to Southerners they were important enough, as one delegate put it, to determine "whether the southern states shall or shall not be parties of the Union."

Amendment of the Constitution, impossible in practice under the Articles of Confederation, became possible, though not easy, under the provisions of the new document. Congress could propose an amendment by a two-thirds vote in each house. Alternatively (under an option never yet employed), Congress could call a special constitutional convention if so requested by the legislatures of two-thirds of the states. However proposed, amendments would become effective only when approved by three-fourths of the states, either in special ratifying conventions or through their legislatures, whichever Congress specified. Exempted from the amendment provisions—deemed to be inviolate—were those assuring an equal vote to all states in the Senate and barring interference with the importation of slaves before 1808. Thus minority interests fixed the price of union for the majority.

How to enforce federal authority, almost impossible under the Confederation, was another crucial question for the Convention. Madison's proposal in the Virginia Plan—that Congress be authorized to veto state laws in conflict with the "Articles of Union" and to employ force against recalcitrant states—won little support. Ultimately, the delegates awarded some measure of enforcement authority to each of the three branches of the proposed federal government. To Congress, the delegates awarded power "to make all laws necessary and proper for carrying into execution the foregoing [enumerated] powers, and all other powers vested by this Constitution in the government of the United States, or in any department or office thereof." In addition, Congress could "provide for calling forth the militia [state military forces] to execute the laws of the Union, suppress insurrections and repel invasions."

To the Presidency, an office created with an eye to securing, among other objectives, a more effective execution of the laws than had been forthcoming from congressional committees, the delegates awarded sweeping, although less specific, enforcement authority. "Executive power" belonged to the President, but it was not defined. The Constitution obligated the President to "preserve, protect, and defend the Constitution" and to "take care that the laws be faithfully executed," without specifying or restricting what means he might employ. The President could make recommendations to Congress on any matter whatever; he also held supreme command of the Armed Forces which Congress might provide, including the militia of the states when called into federal service.

In a new federal judiciary the delegates reposed additional enforcement power. Anti-nationalist Luther Martin, seeking to avert the creation of a federal court system, proposed a provision binding state courts to void any provisions of state laws or constitutions which conflicted with the federal Constitution, federal laws, or treaties. While binding state judges to give priority to federal over state law, Martin's proposal, included in the constitutional provision known as the "supreme law clause," left to the state courts the crucial decision as to whether or not there was conflict between the two. Elsewhere, however, the Constitution provided for a United States Supreme Court and such inferior federal courts as Congress "may from time to time . . . establish." Furthermore, the Constitution defined the federal judicial power as extending "to all cases . . . arising under this Constitution," the laws, and treaties of the United States. Some nationalist delegates construed these words as granting to federal courts the power to review the decisions of state courts whenever they involved interpretations of a federal law, a treaty, or the Constitution itself. This opinion, however, was far from universal.

With these changes the Convention had provided for an extremely powerful government. Its Congress could enact laws bearing directly upon individuals. A Supreme Court could interpret their meaning with finality, and a chief executive to whose command Congress could commit the militia forces of the states was obligated to enforce them.

New restrictions upon the states, as well as increased authority for the federal government, altered the federal-state balance of power. States could not make treaties, coin money, issue paper money in the form of bills of credit, or make anything legal tender except gold and silver. The restrictions about money had some bearing on the recent efforts of some states to assist debtors by inflationary measures. Stay laws enacted for the benefit of debtors in several states were the target of another provision requiring that no state should pass any law "impairing the obligation of contracts." In addition, a state could not, without consent of Congress, make war, build a military establishment in peacetime, conclude agreements with other states or foreign governments, tax shipping, or impose duties on imports or exports, "except what may be absolutely necessary for executing its inspection laws."

Separation of Powers

The doctrine of separation of powers, although still controversial in detail, held the confidence of the Convention to a greater degree than did legislative supremacy. Among the earliest votes of the Convention was one to the effect that the new government should be not only national, meaning stronger than the Confederation, but also that it should include legislative, executive, and judicial branches rather than only a legislature as was the case under the Confederation.

Distrust of a simple legislative majority, reflected chiefly in the creation of an independent President and judiciary, dictated also that the legislature, which the delegates continued to designate as "Congress," should be divided into two houses, as had been the rule in all the Colonies except Pennsylvania. The House of Representatives, its members apportioned among the states in proportion to population and popularly elected every two years, appeared to the Convention as the "democratical" branch essential to give fair representation to the people. The Constitution neither fixed nor barred property qualifications or other restrictions on the right to vote, except to say that in each state the legal qualifications for the electorate should be the same as those required to vote for "the most numerous branch of the State Legislature." The Senate, its members chosen as each state legislature determined and for six-year terms, appeared to the delegates as analogous to the governors' councils of colonial days or to the British House of Lords as the agent of the "aristocracy," but in fact it represented the states. Like the bodies upon which it was patterned, the Senate was to share in certain executive functions from which the lower chamber was excluded, specifically, confirmation of major executive appointments and the rendering of "advice and consent" in the conclusion of treaties.

Despite the disfavor with which most delegates viewed legislative supremacy, Congress received most of the essential powers with which the Convention endowed the new government. Among them in addition to its enforcement authority, power to tax, to regulate foreign and interstate commerce, and to initiate constitutional amendments were authority to provide for the armed forces and to declare war. Furthermore, Congress alone could authorize the expenditure of public funds. Every congressional measure was subject to veto by the President, but contrary to the rule which had prevailed in the Colonies, the veto was not absolute but could be overridden by a two-thirds vote in each of the two houses.

What should be the power and role of the President, or Chief Executive? To be truly independent of Congress, James Wilson suggested, he should owe his election to the people. But the majority felt strongly that the people would be utterly unqualified to judge the merits of candidates from states other than their own. Selection by Congress, as proposed in the original Virginia Plan, would invite intrigues which were generally undesirable and would almost certainly limit the President's independence. Ultimately the delegates settled the question, perceived by one member as the "most difficult of all on which we have had to decide," by authorizing each state legislature to provide for the selection of presidential electors equal in number to the total of the state's representatives and senators. The electors were to vote for two individuals, at least one of whom must be from another state. The candidate receiving a majority vote was to become President, and the second ranking man, Vice President. If no candidate received a majority, the House of Representatives, with one vote for each state's congressional delegation, was to make the choice from among the top five candidates. The delegates assumed that, after Washington had retired from the office to which he would be a virtually unanimous choice, the large states would control what would amount to nominations under the electoral college system and that normally no one would receive a majority in the electoral college. Consequently, the selection from among the five leading contenders would be made in the House of Representatives, with all the states entitled to just one vote. Thus the method of selecting a President represented yet another compromise between the large and small states.

Like the royal governors and the British monarch, the President under the new Constitution would bear the immediate responsibility for executing laws. "The executive power," states the first sentence in the Constitution dealing with the Presidency, "shall be vested in a President of the United States of America." Congress and the Supreme Court, as indicated previously, each held some enforcement authority, but by implication each had to rely upon the President to carry out its decisions, if they required administrative action or if they should be resisted.

As chief administrative officer, the President received additional authority of a more specific nature. With the consent of the Senate, he could appoint all major "officers of the United States." He could "require the opinion, in writing, of the principal officer in each of the executive departments." The delegates also charged the President, in the pattern of his earlier counterparts, to advise the Congress on what they called the "state of the Union," to make recommendations "as he shall judge necessary and expedient," and to call special sessions of Congress "on extraordinary occasions." Unlike the colonial governors, the President lacked not only the absolute veto but also control over legislative sessions. The Constitution required Congress to convene yearly on a day fixed by law and to terminate its session at a time fixed by mutual consent of the two houses. Again in the pattern of the British monarchy, the President received the power to pardon, to command the Armed Forces, and, with the advice and consent of the Senate and the approval of two-thirds of its members, to make treaties with foreign powers. His four-year term of office was long enough to frighten those accustomed to annual elections, but it afforded the people an opportunity, unprecedented among major nations, to remove a Chief Executive whose conduct did not meet their approval.

The provisions for a United States Supreme Court and such inferior courts as Congress might wish to create also bowed in the direction of separation of powers. The Constitution by no means stated explicitly that the Supreme Court could invalidate acts of Congress, but leading nationalists, such as Madison, assumed that the judges would void any law "violating a Constitution established by the people themselves." In contrast to the fixed terms of judges in some of the states, federal judges were to enjoy the independence afforded by good behavior tenure after appointment by the President and confirmation by the Senate.

Policy for the Western territories came under the scrutiny of the Convention at about the same time that the Confederation Congress enacted the Northwest Ordinance of 1787. Gouverneur Morris, spokesman for Eastern men of commerce, stated that he wished to fix the "rule of representation" in such a manner as "to secure to the Atlantic States a prevalence in the National Councils." More in keeping with the spirit of the Northwest Ordinance, James Wilson insisted that "the majority of the people, wherever found, ought in all questions to govern the minority." He justified this sentiment pragmatically by affirming that the majority "not only have the right [to govern the minority], but will avail itself of it whether we will or no." The Convention chose not to fix policy on this point, but left it to Congress by providing only that "New States may be admitted by the Congress into this Union."

The Quest for Popular Approval

How could the delegates put the new Constitution into effect? The Confederation Congress, in sanctioning the Convention, had referred to its purpose as that of "revising the Articles of Confederation." Disregarding the requirement of unanimous consent for amendment of the Articles, the Convention delegates provided that, when approved by conventions in nine states, their Constitution would become effective within the ratifying states. Ratification by the state legislatures was unacceptable to the nationalists because, as Madison put it, approval by the legislatures would give the document the aspect of a treaty, whereas endorsement by popular conventions would make it truly "a *Constitution.*" At New York the moribund Confederation Congress bestirred itself to consider the document produced so secretly at Philadelphia. After unrecorded, but apparently bitter debate over the merits of the work, Congress decided without opposition on September 28 to transmit the proposed Constitution to the states "in conformity to the resolves of the Convention"—but without any indication of approval.

In several states ratification came easily. Conventions in Delaware on December 7, New Jersey on December 18, and Georgia on January 2, 1788, approved the Constitution without dissent. Delaware and New Jersey were dependent economically upon larger neighbors. Georgia, still small in population, wanted help against the Indians on its frontier. Connecticut, dependent as was New Jersey upon neighbors for much of its commerce, endorsed the Constitution on January 9 by a 3-to-1 margin (128–40). Maryland, strong but squeezed between two much larger states, defeated the opponents of ratification on April 26 by 63 to 11. South Carolina, despite some inconsistent misgivings over the limited protection afforded both civil liberties and the slave trade, approved it on May 21 (149–73).

In crucially important Pennsylvania, one of the largest and most prosperous states, ratification came quickly but not without a struggle. To prevent the Legislature from summoning a ratifying convention, opponents of the Constitution deliberately stayed away from the legislative chamber so that, for lack of a quorum, the majority favorable to a convention could not act. To secure a quorum, advocates of the Constitution seized two opponents, just enough to secure a quorum, and, while compelling their attendance, proceeded to set the election of convention delegates at a date too early to permit the opposition to organize effectively and publicize its views. Pennsylvania's convention gave a quick endorsement on December 12 by a vote of 46 to 23, but the tactics employed embittered the opposition.

Massachusetts, another critical state, proceeded more deliberately to a narrower victory for the nationalists. Both Samuel Adams and John Hancock, as well as numerous Shaysite delegates to the state convention, were skeptical. Solid support among the artisans of Boston, plus hints of high federal office for John Hancock, helped to persuade enough of the doubters, including both Adams and Hancock, to produce on February 6, 1788, a decision favoring the new Constitution.

By June, 1788, eight states had endorsed the Constitution, and conclusive deliberations were about to begin in New Hampshire, Virginia, and New York. New Hampshire's towns had sent to the state convention in February a strong majority of delegates with instructions to reject the Constitution. Proponents of ratification secured an adjournment until June, however, and by that time had exercised persuasion which, together with their agreement to recommend twelve amendments, gained acceptance of the Constitution on June 21 by a vote of 57 to 47.

Government under the new Constitution could have begun after New Hampshire's actions, but it appeared essential to include both Virginia and New York. Virginia, largest of the states in both area and population, had pushed the nationalist cause with great vigor at the deliberations in Philadelphia, but in the state as a whole, antinationalist sentiments found both popular support and able advocates. Patrick Henry, George Mason, and Richard Henry Lee, in particular, expended great effort opposing acceptance of the document, which they regarded as dangerously insufficient in provisions to protect the liberties of the people. Virginia supporters of the Constitution included the venerated Washington, James Madison, Edmund Randolph (despite early waverings which led him to withhold his signature from the document at Philadelphia), and a young Richmond lawyer, John Marshall, who would ultimately amplify the Constitution greatly as Chief Justice of the United States Supreme Court. To blunt Henry's demand for the addition of a bill of rights *before* ratification, Madison ultimately pledged to

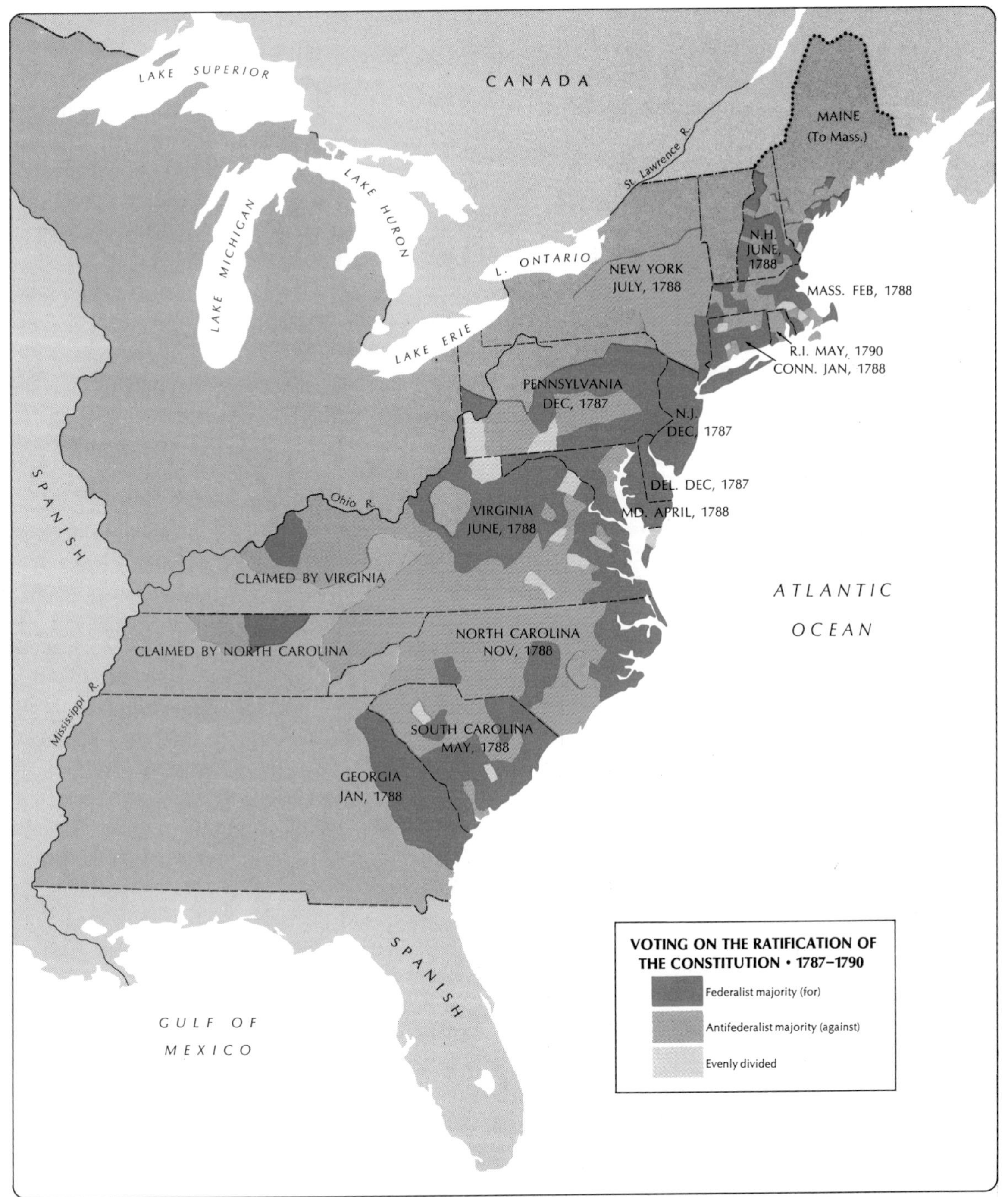
LAKE SUPERIOR
CANADA
MAINE
(To Mass.)
St. Lawrence R.
LAKE HURON
LAKE MICHIGAN
L. ONTARIO
NEW YORK
JULY, 1788
N.H.
JUNE,
1788
MASS. FEB, 1788
LAKE ERIE
R.I. MAY, 1790
CONN. JAN, 1788
PENNSYLVANIA
DEC, 1787
N.J.
DEC, 1787
SPANISH
DEL. DEC, 1787
Ohio R.
VIRGINIA
JUNE, 1788
MD. APRIL, 1788
CLAIMED BY VIRGINIA
ATLANTIC
OCEAN
NORTH CAROLINA
NOV, 1788
CLAIMED BY NORTH CAROLINA
Mississippi R.
SOUTH CAROLINA
MAY, 1788
GEORGIA
JAN, 1788
SPANISH
GULF OF
MEXICO
VOTING ON THE RATIFICATION OF THE CONSTITUTION • 1787–1790
Federalist majority (for)
Antifederalist majority (against)
Evenly divided

work for such amendments *after* ratification, "not because they are necessary [under a government possessing only delegated powers], but because they can produce no possible danger, and may gratify some gentlemen's wishes." Whether or not because of this concession, Madison's forces won approval of the Constitution on June 25, by an 89 to 79 majority.

In New York, as in New Hampshire, prospects for approval at first appeared dim. New York City was solidly favorable, but followers of Governor George Clinton, representing suspicious upstate farmers fearful of the new Constitution and its backers, held a majority of the convention seats. Some of them wavered, however, in face of evidence that the new government would take effect with or without New York's participation. A vote to approve the document only if it were amended in several ways, chiefly to protect civil liberties, lost 31 to 29. Ratification finally carried on July 26, 1788, by a vote of 30 to 27.

Historians have long attributed New York's ratification to the persuasive efforts of Alexander Hamilton and John Jay in the convention and to *The Federalist,* a series of newspaper essays written by Hamilton, Jay, and James Madison, but the evidence indicates that neither the essays nor the oratory persuaded the skeptics. What brought a sufficient number of the opponents to change sides was the desire to be part of the new American nation which was taking shape, the fear that New York City would join even without the rest of the state, and the expectation that amendments protecting civil liberties would be added after the new Constitution had gone into effect.

Advocates of the Constitution had also helped their cause somewhat by calling themselves "Federalists," a term with popular connotations, instead of "nationalists," which frightened those concerned for states' rights. Opponents of ratification, less skilled in public relations, became known as "Antifederalists."

Flat rejection of the Constitution occurred in only two states. North Carolina voted no by more than a 2-to-1 margin (184 to 84) in July, 1788, but when the new federal Congress in 1789 proposed amendments which ultimately became the "Bill of Rights," North Carolina held a second convention, which voted 194 to 77 to join the Union. Rhode Island remained adamant. It had sent no delegates to the Convention, and it refused to call a ratifying convention, staging instead a popular referendum, in which the advocates of ratification refused to participate. In 1790 a ratifying convention at last brought the reluctant Rhode Islanders into the Union by the narrow margin of 34 to 32.

Conclusion

Nationalists, who had become increasingly discontented with the Confederation after the conclusion of peace, eventually had their way. After failing in repeated efforts to strengthen the Articles of Confederation, the critics ultimately secured in 1787 a Constitutional Convention dominated by men determined to create a stronger national government. Reflecting a growing sentiment for the separation of powers rather than weak central government as the surest safeguard against oppression, the Convention proposed to replace the supreme legislature of the Confederation with a government consisting of distinct legislative, executive, and judicial branches. Fear of excessive restriction upon the freedom of individuals and state governments evoked much opposition to this plan, especially among backcountry farmers; but the general desire among the people to establish the foundations of a powerful nation, plus the nationalists' agreement to add a bill of rights, ultimately brought the states to accept the new Constitution. Thus a mere confederation of nearly sovereign states at last became a nation.

SUGGESTED READINGS

Until the twentieth century, amateur historians generally as nationalist as John Fiske (see previous chapter) wrote of the Constitutional Convention chiefly to glorify its members and its product. Something of that spirit survives in the works of twentieth-century professionals such as Charles Warren, *The Making of the Constitution* (1926), and Clinton Rossiter, *1787: The Grand Convention* (1966). More objective, factual records of what occurred have appeared also, notably Max Farrand's *The Framing of the Constitution** (1913) and Carl Van Doren's *The Great Rehearsal** (1948). Overshadowing these works for most of the century was the hostile interpretation of the Convention which arose in the progressive era. Reacting against Supreme Court decisions which made the Constitution a bar to effective regulation of business, J. Allen Smith argued that *The Spirit of American Government** (1907) as embodied in the Constitution was one of opposition to majority rule. Charles A. Beard, experimenting with the newly imported economic interpretation of history, suggested in *An Economic Interpretation of the Constitution** (1913) that economic motives had guided the Founding Fathers in writing a Constitution to serve their individual and class interests. Despite the inadequacy of the evidence sustaining Beard's conclusion it gained a wide following until overthrown by the combined efforts of R. E. Brown in *Charles A. Beard and the Constitution* (1956), Forrest McDonald's *We the People* (1958), and especially E. J. Ferguson's *The Power of the Purse* (1961). See also Gordon Wood's *Creation of the American Republic* (1969).

Somewhat incidentally the progressive attack upon the Constitution produced an upsurge of interest in its contemporary opponents, the Antifederalists. J. T. Main portrays them sympathetically in *The Antifederalists** (1961), as does R. A. Rutland in the *Ordeal of the Constitution* (1966). C. M. Kenyon, who had called them "Men of Little Faith" (*William and Mary Quarterly*, 1955, pp. 3–43), softened her indictment somewhat in introducing a selection of documents, *The Antifederalists** (1966). Morton Borden has edited what he calls the *Antifederalist Papers* (1965), and A. T. Mason has introduced with judicious comment selected papers on *The States Rights Debate: Antifederalism and the Constitution** (1964). Linda G. Depauw, studying the New York ratifying convention in *The Eleventh Pillar* (1966), shows high appreciation for Antifederalist efforts.

The Bill of Rights, the Antifederalists' price for approval of the Constitution, is the subject of two significant studies: R. A. Rutland's *The Birth of the Bill of Rights** (1955) and Irving Brant's *The Bill of Rights* (1965). Brant considers subsequent interpretations, as well as the history of the adoption of the amendments.

Biographical studies are particularly good sources on the Constitutional Convention. Best is Irving Brant's *James Madison: Father of the Constitution* (1950). Others of value include Charles P. Smith's *James Wilson* (1956); Clinton Rossiter's *Alexander Hamilton and the Constitution* (1964); R. A. Rutland's *George Mason* (1961). For a collective portrait, see Rossiter's *1787: The Grand Convention* (1966) or Nathan Schachner's *The Founding Fathers* (1954).

The Federalist papers, essays by Madison, Hamilton, and Jay in support of ratification, are available in innumerable editions, most notably that of J. E. Cooke. Max Farrand has edited the *Records of the Federal Convention of* 1787 (4 vols., 1937). Jonathan Elliot has compiled a five-volume record of *The Debates . . . on the Adoption of the Federal Constitution* (1896). W. U. Solberg has compiled a wide-ranging selection of documents with a valuable introduction in *The Federal Convention and the Formation of the Union** (1958). W. B. Gwyn's *The Meaning of Separation of Powers* (1965) examines the history of that idea in the seventeenth and eighteenth centuries.

* indicates availability in paperback.

8

The Federalists in Power

FEDERALIST LEADERS, having gained popular endorsement of the new United States Constitution, won as well the opportunity to inaugurate the new government which it prescribed. George Washington was everyone's first choice for President; his fellow Federalists secured overwhelming majorities in the first Congress. Together they acted quickly and competently to create the federal edifice for which the people had given their mandate.

Nearly every Federalist objective, however, antagonized some portion of the population. Federalists construed the Constitution broadly to increase federal authority, thus alarming those who feared for states' rights. They repaid the national and state debts in such a manner as to enrich speculators concentrated in a few Northern cities, thus alienating both Southern planters and Northern farmers. They imposed unpopular internal, or excise, taxes and used the Army to crush resistance to their collection. In foreign policy, they infuriated radical republicans who were pro-French by concluding a treaty which seemed almost to ally the United States with Britain against the French. Consequently, long before Washington left office the new nation had become deeply and indeed dangerously divided.

Would the federal government work any better under the Constitution than it had under the Articles of Confederation? There was some reason to doubt that it would. Both individually and in private groups, Americans had long demonstrated a great capacity to evade or to resist governmental policies inimical to their interests. Their new state governments had operated generally with the necessary support and observance of law, but it was not at all clear that the new federal government would be deemed worthy of respect or that it would have the capacity to enforce obedience to its policies by assertive individuals, groups, and especially the zealously autonomous states.

Returns from the first election under the Constitution in 1788 were encouraging. Federalists swept everything. Washington became President without opposition. Only two Antifederalists, both from Virginia, won Senate seats. In the House of Representatives, Federalists outnumbered the opposition 7 to 1. Rhode Island and North Carolina, it is true, had not participated, but there were already indications that each would soon terminate its resistance.

Less encouraging was the tardiness of congressmen in reporting for work. March 4, 1789, was the day fixed for the opening of Congress, but not until April 6 was there a quorum in both houses. Another three weeks elapsed before Washington could receive official certification from Congress of his election and complete the journey from Virginia to the temporary capital at New York. At last on April 30, federal officials staged the first presidential inauguration amid ceremony reminiscent of that with which the King began sessions of the British Parliament.

Ceremony and official titles indeed produced the first significant division in Federalist ranks. What underlay these seemingly trivial disputes was the desire of some to endow the President and other high federal officials with an aura of authority and dignity such as that which surrounded Britain's monarch and nobility. A majority of senators thought that the President should be addressed by some such designation as "His Elective Majesty"; they themselves would have liked to be called "Honorable." Such individuals approved the very formal receptions ("levees"), which President Washington initiated, and encouraged the public celebration of his birthday just as the King's birthday had been observed before the Revolution. Other Federalists and most Antifederalists regarded such practices as aristocratic and unbecoming to republican society. Reflecting this democratic spirit, the House of Representatives barred the conferring of the titles desired by the Senate. It became customary instead to address the Chief Executive simply as "Mr. President" and to introduce him with equal simplicity as "The President of the United States."

Eager to consolidate public support behind the new national government, Federalists under the leadership of Representative James Madison gave high priority to a bill of rights, which so many had urged in the ratifying debates. "If we can make the Constitution better in the opinion of those who are opposed to it without . . . abridging its usefulness in the judgment of those who are attached to it,"

Madison believed, "we act the part of wise and liberal men to make such alteration." On September 25, 1789, Congress approved twelve prospective amendments incorporating many of the eighty substantive changes included in the 210 amendments recommended by the ratifying conventions. Ten amendments received the endorsement of three-fourths of the states and became part of the Constitution in 1791. As Madison and other Federalists then construed the amendments, they in no way diminished the powers intended to be granted to the United States. Rather they provided only reassurance that individual liberties would be respected and that "powers not delegated to the United States . . . , nor prohibited . . . to the states, are reserved to the States respectively, or to the people."

Still seeking to reassure states' rightists without unduly weakening the federal government, the Federalist Congress, in the Judiciary Act of 1789, created a federal court system which bore all the aspects of compromise. On the one hand, it left to state courts original jurisdiction in many cases involving enforcement of federal law. This actual increase in the jurisdiction of state courts was highly gratifying to those who had feared that the state tribunals would be entirely supplanted by the new federal courts. On the other hand, as authorized by the Constitution, Congress created thirteen federal district courts and three circuit courts in addition to the Supreme Court established by the Constitution. Federal district courts were to have exclusive jurisdiction over certain types of cases, for example, those dealing with import regulations. Circuit courts, consisting of two Supreme Court justices sitting with one district judge, were to have some original jurisdiction and in addition to hear appeals from district courts. The key provision of the law, however, was that section authorizing the Supreme Court to hear appeals from the decisions of *state* as well as inferior federal courts whenever the case involved interpretation of the United States Constitution, federal laws, or treaties. This afforded reassurance to the nationalists that state courts would not block enforcement of federal law.

The division of power among three federal branches and between the nation and the states proved troublesome at the outset of Washington's administration. In providing that the President should make treaties "by and with the advice and consent of the Senate," the Constitutional Convention apparently intended that the Senate should participate in preparing the documents, much as members of the colonial councils had shared executive responsibility with the provincial governors before the Revolution. Washington had other ideas. In August, 1789, while framing instructions relating to a treaty with the southern Indians, the President appeared in the Senate chamber, occupied the presiding officer's chair, and with Vice President Adams as his reading clerk set forth several treaty provisions for which he desired Senate approval. After reading each question, the Vice President inquired of the assembled Senators: "Do you advise and consent?" When Senator Robert Morris tried to refer the questions to a committee, the President lost his temper. The Senate had its way, however, although it did agree to report within three days. But thereafter the President, when it suited him, afforded the Senate no opportunity at all to offer advice in the preparation of treaties. His policy became a precedent, which in effect eliminated the Executive's obligation to seek the *advice* of the Senate in negotiating treaties.

The Senate's role became only that of expressing or denying consent, for which the Constitution requires a two-thirds vote.

Still more troublesome was the division of responsibility between the legislative and executive branches on questions of revenue. Except for the crisis years under Robert Morris, the Confederation Congress had never been willing to entrust so crucial a function as management of the Treasury to a single executive but had always insisted upon an executive board which Congress itself supervised very closely. Only with great reluctance did Congress in 1789 accede to the arguments of James Madison that in the interest of efficiency a Treasury Department should be created and should be headed by a single executive.

Slighting the theory of separation of powers, Congress included in the law the provision that the Secretary of the Treasury should report to Congress and respond to congressional inquiries directly rather than through the President. Fearing acutely the influence of the Treasury Secretary upon the exercise of its power to initiate revenue measures, the House of Representatives insisted that the Secretary was not to report in person, but only to prepare reports for its consideration. Behind these seemingly excessive fears lay the knowledge that in Britain it was the head of the Treasury who was emerging as the nation's chief executive or Prime Minister. Ambitious Alexander Hamilton, fist Secretary of the Treasury, was also well aware of this development.

Hamilton's Financial Program

Federalist economic policies, largely but not entirely Hamilton's, had profound significance not only for the nation's economic future, but also for the development of an organized political opposition. One of the most controversial Federalist triumphs in the formulation of national economic policy concerned the payment of Revolutionary debts, both state and federal. When the new government assumed power in 1789, the United States owed nearly $12 million to foreign sources, chiefly Dutch and French, and $44 million to its own citizens. Under the Confederation, the Congress had proved incapable of meeting even the interest obligations on these sums, and state governments had to take up the burden, even though they already possessed debts of some $25 million. Under the Constitution, however, the states could no longer tax imports while the federal government had an almost unlimited authority to tax.

Obviously, Congress would inaugurate some changes relative to the repayment of the Revolutionary debt. James Madison had been wrestling with the debt problem as head of a congressional committee in the First Congress, but when Hamilton took control of the newly created Treasury Department, Madison was only too willing to dump the problem in the lap of his former collaborator. Conforming to a request from Congress, Hamilton in January, 1790, submitted a detailed "Report on Public Credit," setting forth his recommendations for dealing with the debts.

Hamilton's plan had three principal objectives. Foremost among them was the elevation of the power and prestige of the federal government over that of the states. Hamilton sought to serve that objective by demonstrating that the federal government could and would repay the entire Revolutionary war debt, both state and federal, at full face value. Another of

Hamilton's objectives was to make federal securities a major investment opportunity for the wealthy, in the expectation that "moneyed men" who made such investments would help to maintain a powerful national government in order to protect their capital. His third intention was to alleviate the chronic money shortage by greatly increasing the value of federal securities, which might then serve, at least among the wealthy, as a form of money which would not depreciate.

Hamilton's proposal to redeem all federal securities at full face value rather than at the depreciated market rate aroused extensive controversy in Congress. Antifederalists and other Hamiltonian opponents had little objection to paying the foreign debt ($12 million) at full face value in order to bolster American prestige, but they wished to pay the domestic debt ($44 million) at something nearer the market value. By reducing the amount of the debt, payment at market value would also lower the tax burden necessary to repay it and avoid paying windfall profits to speculators. Speculative purchases had indeed concentrated nearly all of the federal debt in the hands of a tiny minority of rich men whom Hamilton's policy would afford an enormous profit. As one critic expressed it, Hamilton's policy would "make noblemen and nabobs of a few New York gentlemen, at the expense of all the farmers in the United States." Since four-fifths of the federal debt belonged to people in the North, Southerners were particularly hostile to Hamilton's plan.

Under these circumstances Madison, as a Virginia congressman, had little choice but to oppose Hamilton. He demanded that some part of the payment at full face value go to the original holders of the securities. His aim purportedly was to see that justice was done to the "hardy veterans" who had been forced by economic need to sell the securities issued to them in payment for military service to "unconscionable speculators" at a fraction of their face value. To slight the veterans, Madison argued, would be "radically immoral." Most Federalist congressmen, however, agreed with Hamilton. Madison's measure, which would have been very difficult to administer, lost 36 to 13. Congress then accepted Hamilton's "funding" program, which allowed holders of federal securities to redeem them at face value for new ones bearing a somewhat lower rate of interest.

Even more controversial was Hamilton's plan for the "assumption" of most of the state debts by the federal government, again at full face value rather than at the market price. The effects would be to enhance still further the relative prestige of the federal government and to detach more of the "moneyed men" from financial dependence upon state governments. Hamilton argued that all those who had lent money to finance the Revolution, whether they had lent to the federal or to the state governments, should be repaid on equal terms. Madison objected, declaring that since 1783 some states had repaid far more of their debt than others. Conspicuous in this category were the Southern states, except South Carolina. Thus another sectional split occurred. The South, except for South Carolina, backed Madison in proposing that the debts be assumed as they had existed in 1783. But the North, on the whole, backed Hamilton in favoring "assumption" as of 1790, when the total state debt was scarcely half of what it had been at the earlier date. A clearing of accounts between the state and federal governments went on simultaneously, in the expectation that the federal government ultimately would compensate each state for expenses above its fair share of the war's cost and would in return receive compensation from those states whose actual expenses had been less than their fair share. States' rights advocates preferred this alternative, and they strongly suspected that if the United States assumed the state debts in 1790, the final clearing with the states would never be completed.

Bitter sectional division deadlocked the Congress for half a year. Utterly irrelevant diatribes on the slavery question lent heat to the dispute. Virginia's Antifederalist Senator Richard Henry Lee declared that he would prefer to dissolve the Union rather than submit, as he put it, to the rule of an "insolent northern majority." Meanwhile, Northern speculators, betting on Hamilton, went south to buy up depreciated state securities from those who believed the measure would be defeated. After North Carolina joined the Union, its Antifederalist congressmen changed the balance in the House of Representatives, making it 31 to 29 against assumption, but negotiations for a compromise which would pass the measure were in progress.

What has been called "the compromise of 1790" had something for everybody. Virginians wanted the national capital located permanently on the Potomac; they desired assurance that the clearing of state accounts would be pushed to a conclusion; and they hoped to see the relaxation of rigorous accounting standards which had limited the acceptance of Virginia's claims. They achieved each objective. States with small debts or none wanted a compensating federal handout; they received it. Certainly the most famous and, to Hamilton, the most painful of these political bargains was the transfer of the capital from his own state of New York, first to Philadelphia for ten years, and then to a site on the Potomac which President Washington would choose. Secretary of State Jefferson, recently returned from a long sojourn abroad, had a hand in completing the arrangements whereby the debts would be assumed and the capital moved. He later claimed that Hamilton had duped him, but the evidence indicates that Jefferson, consulting closely with Madison, almost certainly knew what he was doing. So did Hamilton.

Hamilton attached great importance to the establishment of a central bank, to be patterned after the privately controlled Bank of England. The capital which stockholders invested in such a bank, both in specie and in government securities, would provide backing sufficient by rule of thumb for the issuance of two or three times as much in paper money. In addition to pumping more money into the economy, the bank, as Hamilton planned it, would also serve the government as a depository of public funds, a lender, and a convenient agency for the collection of taxes and the transfer of funds from one area to another. Somewhat more controversial was the role of the bank as a regulatory agency. By returning paper money of lesser banks for redemption in specie or government securities, Hamilton's bank would be capable of embarrassing, or even breaking, banks which issued paper money in amounts much more than the customary three times their hard money reserve.

Hamilton's "Report on a National Bank" in December, 1790, quickly created a sectional division, from which there emerged a constitutional precedent of major importance. Southerners on the whole preferred state-chartered banks, if any, and found no clause in the Constitution authorizing the federal government to charter business corporations of any kind. In the House of Representatives,

19 of 20 votes opposing passage of the bank bill came from Southerners, while 36 of 39 in favor were cast by Northerners. The constitutional objections which Madison and others had raised caused Washington, in considering whether nor not to approve the measure, to ask for written opinions not only from Hamilton and Attorney General Randolph but from Secretary of State Jefferson as well.

The crux of the matter was the interpretation to be given the paragraph in the Constitution concluding the enumeration of congressional powers. It declares that Congress shall have power "to make all Laws which shall be necessary and proper for carrying into Execution the foregoing Powers." Jefferson argued that this should be construed literally, that a federally chartered bank was not at all necessary to execute any specifically granted power, and was therefore unconstitutional. Hamilton urged to the contrary that "*necessary* often means no more than needful, . . . useful, or conducive to" and that because a bank had a "natural relation" to tax collection, trade regulation, and defense, it was constitutional. Neither line of argument persuaded Washington, but because the matter was of more consequence to Hamilton's Treasury Department than to Jefferson's Department of State, he signed the bill.

Despite the political controversy which surrounded its inception, Hamilton's Bank was very successful. In chartering the Bank for twenty years, Congress had pledged itself to create no rival institutions. Accordingly the Bank enjoyed a highly privileged, in some respects a monopolistic, status. Private investors, mostly Northerners, purchased its stock—except for the 20 percent reserved to the government—and controlled the Bank's management by naming twenty of its twenty-five directors. The stockholders received handsome returns on their investment, but it was true also that the Bank served the government well, so well that Jefferson, despite his original argument that the Bank was unconstitutional, continued it without protest when he became President in 1801.

States also involved themselves in matters of money and banking, in spite of the general inclination of conservatives to distrust state governments. In 1780 there had been no banks at all in the United States, but by 1794 individual states had chartered eighteen banks and empowered them to issue paper money. By 1800 there would be thirty-two such banks. England, less in need of paper money because of its more adequate supplies of gold and silver, had only four banks in 1794.

The development of manufacturing appeared to Federalist leaders as a major means by which the United States might reduce its specie-draining imports and foster the more rapid accumulation of wealth. Instructed by the House of Representatives to devise a plan for the promotion of manufacturing which would help the United States become "independent of other nations for essential . . . supplies," Hamilton presented his famous "Report on Manufactures" in December, 1790. To encourage investment in manufacturing, Hamilton urged high import taxes (protective tariffs) on manufactured goods, government subsidies, special patent rights for inventors of labor-saving machinery, and tax-free importation of raw materials. Numerous manufacturing concerns already existed, particularly in iron, shoes, and textiles. More were founded under the stimulus both of Hamilton's report and of new state and local societies, which were formed with patriotic enthusiasm to push the United States toward economic independence.

Numerous handicaps, however, doomed many existing enterprises and impeded the industrial movement in general. Among these were the lack of experienced management and labor; the scarcity of capital and labor; and perhaps above all, the existence of profitable alternative activities. Particularly after 1793 when warfare became general in Europe, commerce and shipping attracted much liquid capital. Land remained an attractive investment as farm products and lumber rose. Hamilton's "Report on Manufactures" helped to establish a goal and identify the means to attain it, but the 1790s saw little permanent progress in the development of manufacturing.

Federalist measures of taxation achieved several important objectives. They provided, in the first instance, sufficient revenue to demonstrate that the government could cope with the vastly increased debt which Hamilton's policies had thrust upon it. United States securities in fact became a highly regarded investment both at home and abroad. Tariff protection afforded some encouragement to American producers although the taxes were quite low and did not evoke the great development in manufacturing which Hamilton desired. Tax measures designed to foster American shipping were much more successful. Finally, in enforcing collection of a hated tax on whisky, the Federalists established the power of the United States to impose excise, or "internal," as well as import, or "external," taxes.

Tariffs became the government's chief source of revenue. It was significant that the first act of the new Congress, signed by President Washington on July 4, was the Tariff Act of 1789. In the absence of a Treasury Department, its chief advocate was Representative James Madison. The measure did afford some "protection" to American producers in the form of import tax rates as high as 15 percent on such items as coaches, gunpowder, paint, and glass. Madison thought the federal government was obligated to afford some protection since the states could no longer do so under the Constitution. The major thrust of the measure, however, was to bring in revenue from low taxes on the importation of items which Americans did not produce, such as coffee, tea, wine, sugar, and molasses. New England rum-making interests forced a reduction in the planned tax on molasses, their raw material, from 8 cents a gallon to 2½ cents. There occurred another North-South conflict over taxation of imports of hemp. Prospective Southern producers wanted a high tax, while Northern shipping interests, which used hemp, wanted none. The South won. Despite such political clashes over protection, however, the tariff was the basic source of federal revenue for the next two generations.

To encourage the further development of American shipping, Congress passed the Tonnage Act of 1789. Ships entering American ports were obligated to pay 50 cents per ton if they were foreign-owned and foreign-built, 30 cents if foreign-owned but American-built, and only 6 cents if both American-owned and American-built. Import taxes were also to be reduced 10 percent on all items imported on American ships. Still other provisions effectively barred foreign ships from the coastal trade. Southern agricultural exporters, considering competition from foreign shipping to be in their interest, unsuccessfully resisted these policies. During the next generation, while the American economy remained deeply committed to overseas trade and even its internal economy depended largely on coastal shipping, these provisions helped the infant nation to become a major maritime power.

Hamilton's whisky excise tax was by all odds the most controversial of the Federalist tax measures. The somewhat unexpected assumption of the state debts increased the need for government revenue above the level derived from import taxes. To avoid a further tax on commerce as well as to beat the states to a fruitful revenue source and establish the right of Congress to impose such taxes, Hamilton had urged a license tax for distillers of whisky and a tax per gallon on their product. For many Americans this tax was intolerable. Many distillers were trans-Appalachian farmers who could not sell grain in competition with Eastern farmers because of the high cost of transporting their product across the mountains. By making their grain into whisky, they reduced its volume while increasing its value, thus improving their competitive position for Eastern sales. With little cash income, such individuals deeply resented the taxes even though they might, in time, be passed on to the consumers by a general increase in price. Western farmers, mostly Antifederalists, also objected to being taxed by a strong national government to help pay rich Eastern speculators, who held the lion's share of the national and state debts which Hamilton had arranged to redeem on such generous terms. To make matters worse, until the law was amended in 1794, individuals accused of violating the act could not be tried in state courts but only in one of the relatively few federal courts, usually in a major city far from the offender's home.

Resistance smoldered for several years until it finally reached a crisis in 1794. By then, mobs were intimidating tax collectors, as they had done before the Revolution, and interfering with court proceedings. In one instance, a mob captured the Army forces protecting a Treasury official. While the "Whisky Rebellion" occurred in many backcountry areas, particularly in the South, it was in the Pittsburgh area of western Pennsylvania that resistance was most flagrant. Here the enforcement of federal authority against popular local resistance faced its first genuine test. Acting upon its constitutional authorization to "provide for calling forth the Militia [of the states] to execute the Laws of the Union," Congress in 1792 had empowered the President, "whenever the laws of the United States shall be opposed, or the execution thereof obstructed, in any state, by combinations too powerful to be suppressed by the ordinary course of judicial proceedings, or by the powers vested in the [federal] marshalls . . . to call forth the militia of such State . . . to cause the laws to be duly executed." The only restrictions upon the President's discretion were that there be certification by a federal judge that the normal law-enforcement methods were inadequate (eliminated in 1805), and that the President first issue a proclamation calling upon those in resistance to desist.

Urged on by the militant Hamilton, President Washington acted vigorously to end the Western defiance of federal authority. On August 7, 1794, he issued the required proclamation stating: "I, George Washington, President of the United States, do hereby command all persons being insurgents . . . to disperse and retire peaceably to their respective abodes." When resistance continued after September 1, the deadline he had announced, the President called for 13,000 militiamen and set out for western Pennsylvania at the head of a larger Army than he had ever been able to gather during the Revolution. The President soon returned to Philadelphia, but Hamilton stayed with the Army and sought out the ringleaders of a rapidly dissipating resistance movement.

Twenty hapless insurgents fell into Army hands and suffered the indignity of a parade down the main street of Philadelphia and some time in jail. Two received sentences of execution for treason, but the President pardoned one as a "simpleton" and the other as "insane."

Revenue from Hamilton's whisky excise was never as high as expected, and collection costs (about 15 percent) were excessive, but in a broader perspective the tax was a major success. It provided opportunity to demonstrate that the federal government indeed had the capacity, founded in public support, to collect whatever excise taxes it chose to enact. Even before the crushing of the Whisky Rebellion, Congress had subjected several other commodities to similar taxation and would continue to do so at its discretion in the future without fear of violent resistance by organized groups.

Hamilton's triumph was short-lived. By 1795 he himself had resigned. The widespread dislike of his programs, his domination of Congress, and suspicions of financial favoritism to his friends, though largely unwarranted, had limited his usefulness. Even in retirement, however, Hamilton would command the loyalty of many dedicated Federalists, including Cabinet members and congressmen.

Western Problems

Many Eastern Federalists were only slightly less reluctant than the Indians to see American settlement extend westward. Landowners and employers themselves, they feared that rapid settlement of the West would lower land values and increase the cost of labor in their section. Since Western areas were normally Antifederalist, such migration would increase the relative political strength of the Federalists' congressional opposition as well. On the other hand, Western lands north of the Ohio River were a national asset, which would produce revenue only as settlement advanced. Properly administered by the government, moreover, the public lands might supplement Hamilton's debt policies in augmenting the fortunes of the rich.

Federalist land laws reflected more concern for federal revenue than for aiding settlers to secure homesteads. The first land law in 1796 provided for the sale of large blocks of land at what might be called wholesale rates. No purchase was to include less than 640 acres (one section) or to be sold at less than $2 per acre. Family farms were then usually about 100 acres, and the going price of frontier land sold by state governments or private speculators, who had secured title from states, was generally under $2. In 1795 Georgia, because of corruption in the Legislature, had sold 30 million acres of superior land in the Yazoo area of Mississippi at about 1½ cents per acre. In addition to the other obstacles to the purchase of federal land by ordinary settlers under the 1796 law, only two offices were provided at which purchases could be made, one at Pittsburgh, the other at Cincinnati. Credit was limited to one year. When Congress altered the law in 1800, it reduced the minimum purchase to 320 acres, allowed four years to pay, and increased the number of land offices to four. These were only small steps, however, toward enabling ordinary settlers to buy land directly from the government. Congress declined to encourage rapid settlement of the West, or even to provide "preemption rights"—a provision that squatters be given a prior right to purchase land on which they had

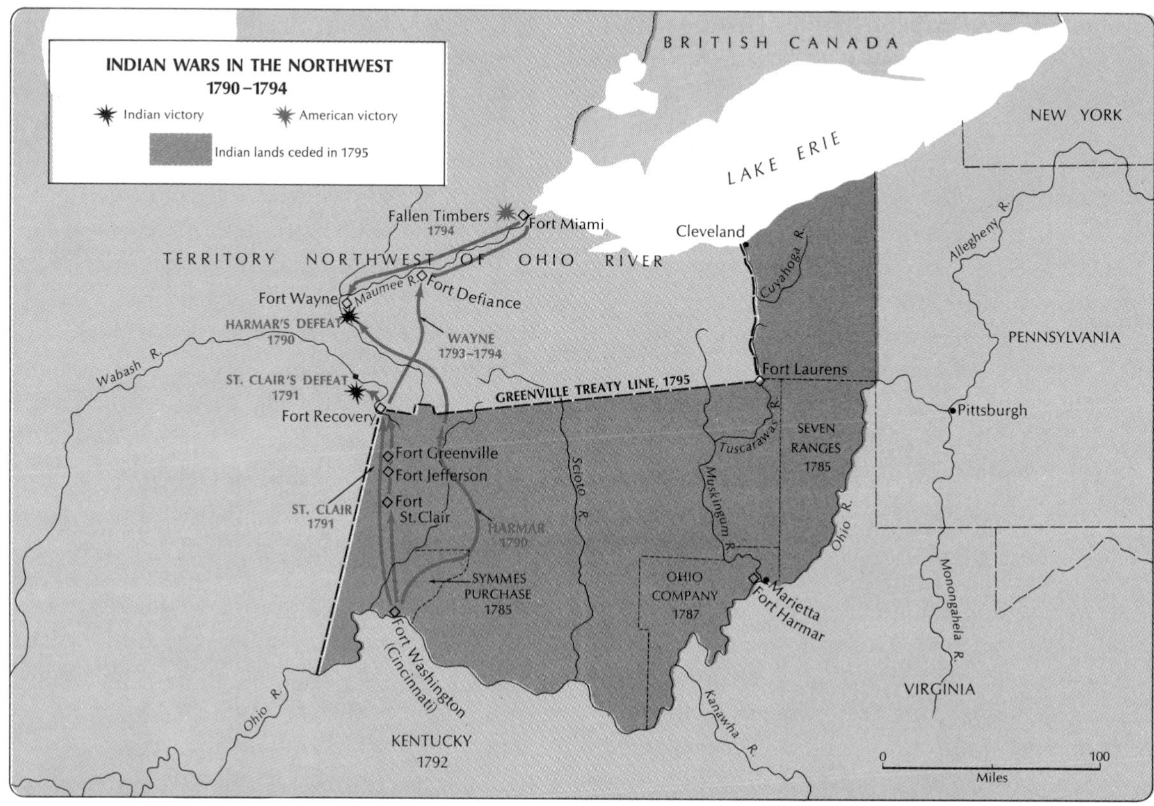

settled before the government put it up for auction to the highest bidder.

Indians were another major deterrent to the advance of settlement into the Old Northwest, the chief area actually at the disposition of the United States government. There an informal alliance of the British and the Indians constituted a perennial threat. British leaders told the Indians, in disregard of the peace treaty of 1783, that there was no British-American boundary line and seemingly invited the Indians to help them fix one well to the southeast of the Great Lakes. Britain instructed its first Minister to the United States to seek the creation of an "Indian barrier state" in the Northwest Territory, but American hostility to the idea forced him to drop it quickly. There was constant talk, however, by one British official or another of renegotiating the British-American boundary, of military adventures aimed at dismembering the Union, and of overt assistance to the Indians in resisting the encroachment of American settlement.

Federalist efforts to cope with the Indians of the Northwest met with two humiliating defeats. In 1790 President Washington sent General Josiah Harmar into northwestern Ohio to chastise Indians who had been raiding frontier settlements in areas purportedly ceded to the United States by treaties signed during the 1780s (Fort Stanwyx, 1784; Fort McIntosh, 1785). Harmar destroyed some Indian villages

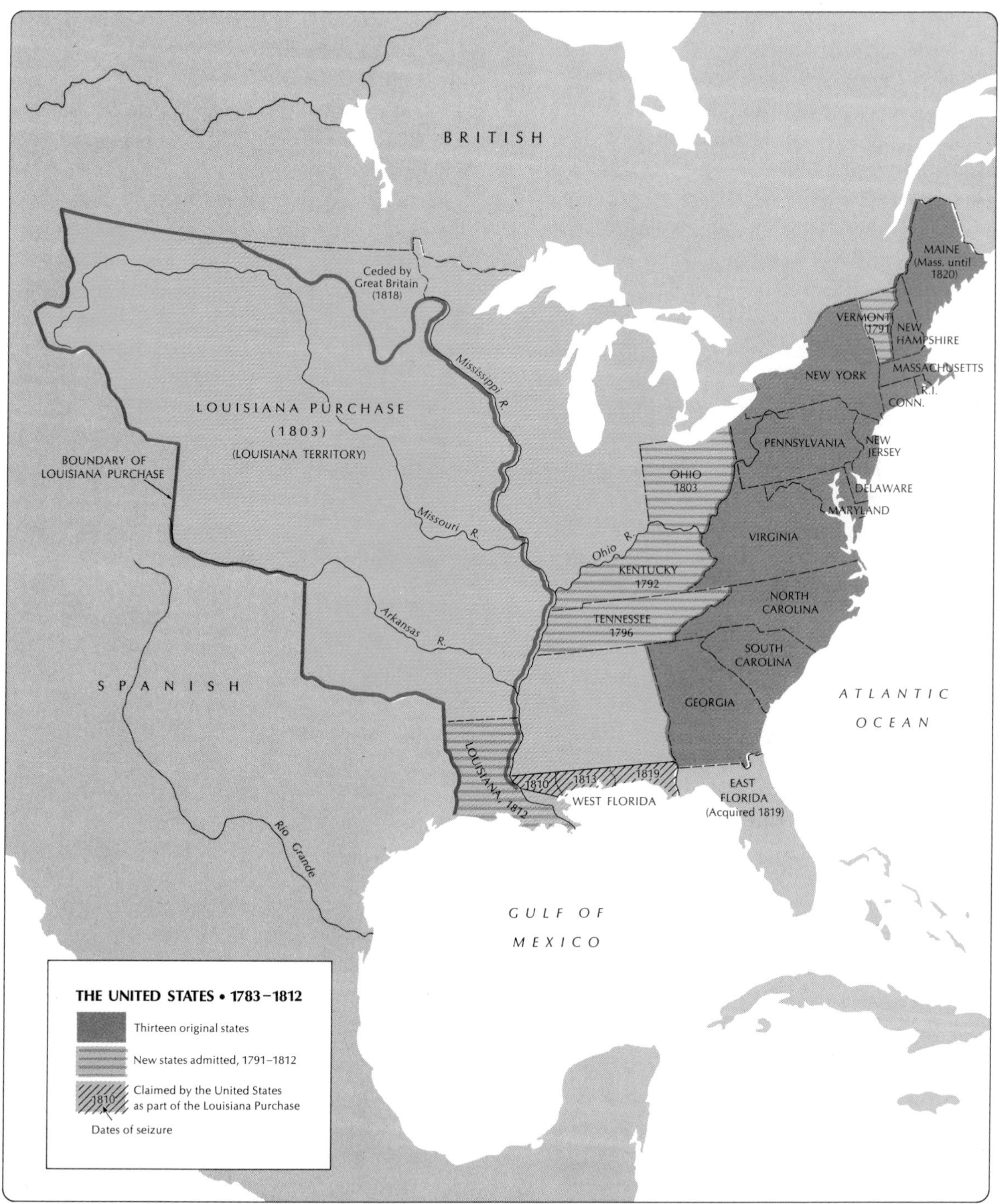
BRITISH
Ceded by Great Britain (1818)
LOUISIANA PURCHASE (1803)
(LOUISIANA TERRITORY)
BOUNDARY OF LOUISIANA PURCHASE
Mississippi R.
Missouri R.
Arkansas R.
Ohio R.
Rio Grande
SPANISH
MAINE (Mass. until 1820)
VERMONT 1791
NEW HAMPSHIRE
MASSACHUSETTS
R.I.
CONN.
NEW YORK
PENNSYLVANIA
NEW JERSEY
DELAWARE
MARYLAND
OHIO 1803
VIRGINIA
KENTUCKY 1792
NORTH CAROLINA
TENNESSEE 1796
SOUTH CAROLINA
GEORGIA
LOUISIANA 1812
1810
1813
1819
WEST FLORIDA
EAST FLORIDA (Acquired 1819)
ATLANTIC OCEAN
GULF OF MEXICO
THE UNITED STATES • 1783–1812
Thirteen original states
New states admitted, 1791–1812
Claimed by the United States as part of the Louisiana Purchase
1810
Dates of seizure

but had to retreat precipitously after he fell into an ambush near the present site of Fort Wayne. General Arthur St. Clair, territorial governor for the Northwest, repeated Harmar's humiliation in 1791 on the banks of the Wabash near the present Ohio-Indiana border. The exasperated President turned next to General Anthony Wayne, who met with greater success. In 1794 his well-trained forces devastated a band of Indians supported by Canadian militia at Fallen Timbers, almost within earshot of the British Fort Miamis on the Maumee River, not far from present-day Toledo. Wayne avoided conflict with the British regulars, who in turn disappointed Indian expectations by taking no offensive action. Wayne destroyed impressive quantities of goods belonging to British traders, however, and established Fort Wayne. At the ensuing peace conference, held at Fort Greenville in 1795, the chastened Indians agreed, in exchange for gifts and the promise of annuities, to open new territories to American settlement. The memory of Fallen Timbers helped to secure peace for many years on the northwestern frontier.

Despite all obstacles, Western settlement proceeded rapidly during the 1790s. Overriding Federalist anxieties concerning Western "barbarism" and democratic propensities, Congress admitted three new states to the Union during the decade: Vermont (1791), Kentucky (1792), and Tennessee (1796). Their combined population was only 5 percent of the national total in 1790 but had risen to 9 percent by 1800. Ohio and the western regions of New York, Pennsylvania, and Georgia were also gaining population at a very rapid rate.

Bearing out Federalist fears, several new states not only opposed the national administration but also made democratic innovations in their constitutions. Frederick Jackson Turner, historian of the frontier, undoubtedly exaggerated when he wrote that because the "wind of Democracy blew so strongly from the west," Eastern states imitatively liberalized their constitutions; yet Vermont was the first state to impose neither property-holding nor tax-paying requirements for voting. The effect was little different, however, from that in older states which made tax payment a prerequisite to voting but imposed a poll tax upon all adult males so that theoretically all adult males could vote. Baffling confusion over land titles, plus the feeling that all who were obliged to serve in the militia should be entitled to vote, persuaded Kentuckians to scrap the traditional property qualification for voting. Tennessee also opened the vote to adult males without property or tax-paying qualifications if they had six months of residence in the county. The next Western states to be admitted (Ohio, 1803; Louisiana, 1811) reverted, however, to tax payment as a qualification for voting.

Controversy over Neutrality

Problems arising from the wars of the French Revolution involved the United States in recurring diplomatic crises during Washington's second administration. The French Revolution in its initial phase (1789–1792) merely substituted limited for absolute monarchy; it accordingly met with great approval in Britain as well as in the United States. However, in its second phase (1792–1795), the French Revolution eliminated monarchy and established a republican form of government marked by extreme instability, the famous

"Reign of Terror," and territorial aggressions inspired by republican ideology as well as intense nationalism. These developments led to the rise of a reactionary spirit in Britain based on fear of republican subversion as well as French invasion. After 1793 Britain, together with much of the rest of Europe, was at war with France.

Bound to France by the "perpetual" alliance of 1778, the United States faced difficult decisions when radical French republicans engulfed Europe in war. Most Americans endorsed the republican ideology, but the Reign of Terror and a campaign against religion within France, added to the military aggressions abroad, encouraged second thoughts and altered sympathies, especially among the more aristocratic Federalists. American egalitarians, however, were likely to agree with Jefferson, who was willing to see "half the earth devastated" to insure the "liberty of the whole." The half of the earth which Jefferson was willing to see destroyed apparently did not include the United States, however, for as Secretary of State from 1790 to 1793 he favored American neutrality.

Despite a general agreement within Washington's Cabinet on a policy of neutrality, the war between Britain and France widened the differences between Jefferson and Hamilton which had begun over Hamilton's debt policies. Hamilton justified neutrality on the assumption that, although the French treaty was binding despite a change in the government of one party, it did not obligate the United States while a change in government was "in contest," or not yet final. Jefferson took the now-accepted view that the treaty bound the French and American peoples, no matter what changes had occurred in their governments, but that the United States could escape involvement because of prior violation of the treaty by France in failing to help the United States protect its territorial possessions in the Northwest against the British. Actually, the minuscule American naval and military forces made the involvement of the United States seem of little potential benefit to France, while a neutral United States, possessing a large merchant fleet, could afford France badly needed ocean transportation presumably immune from British seizure.

How to announce American neutrality was another question over which Jefferson and Hamilton differed. Jefferson thought that, by implication from its constitutional authority to declare war, Congress was the proper source for such a proclamation. Hamilton argued that as a practical matter the President should have such authority. Washington agreed with Hamilton, although he did omit the word "neutrality" from his proclamation of April 22, 1793. In addition to pledging impartial conduct toward the belligerents on the part of the government, the proclamation stated that the government would afford no protection to citizens who engaged in non-neutral acts but would rather "cause prosecutions to be instituted" against them.

Anticipating opposition, Hamilton acted quickly to defend Washington's proclamation with essays published under the pseudonyms "Pacificus" and "Americanus." In meeting the largely moral arguments of those who favored a pro-French policy, although not a declaration of war on the enemies of France, Hamilton denied that the United States had any obligation to support France. It was also doubtful, he warned, that France would win its war against the rest of the Continent. Furthermore, the woeful state of the United States Navy meant that there was no way in which the nation could make its aid effective in Europe, even if it did choose to support the French. Because the intervention of the French in the American Revolution had been designed primarily to serve French interests, Hamilton also argued that Americans owed them no debt of gratitude. Individuals might indulge the emotions of generosity, Hamilton stated, but a government could rarely, if at all, be justified in doing so. "Existing millions, and for the most part future generations," wrote Hamilton, "are concerned in the present measures of government, while the consequences of the private actions of an individual ordinarily terminate with himself." Lastly, Hamilton denied that the cause of France was the cause of liberty and warned again that any service which the United States might render to France would hardly compensate for the evils which the United States would suffer as a result. Hamilton's arguments, however, failed to slow the continuing and embarrassing assault on the President's decision.

To Madison, as to most other opponents of the administration, the proclamation appeared "a most unfortunate error." Writing to Jefferson, Madison asserted further, "It wounds the national honor, by seeming to disregard the stipulated duties to France. It wounds the popular feelings by a seeming indifference to the cause of liberty. And it seems to violate the . . . Constitution by making the Executive Magistrate the organ . . . of the nation in relation to war and peace." Urged on by Jefferson, Madison soon published articles under the name "Helvidius," seeking to refute Hamilton's arguments in support of the President's action. The publication of the opposing points of view made it evident that in the long run the issue would be resolved by appealing directly to the people.

Widespread sympathy for France meanwhile encouraged that nation's exuberant young Minister, Edmond Charles Genêt, to take actions which threatened, as Washington put it, to involve the United States in "war abroad and . . . anarchy at home." Calling himself "Citizen" Genêt, the new Minister arrived in Charleston, South Carolina, shortly before the issuance of Washington's proclamation. He began at once to equip French privateers to operate from American ports against British shipping and set up French prize courts to dispose of captured British vessels. He took steps as well to organize Americans into military units to march against Spanish Florida and Louisiana. While Genêt had little success in the latter effort, he ultimately sent out twelve privateers which captured some eighty British ships. Belatedly, the administration secured his promise to cease such actions, which did indeed threaten to involve the United States in war with Britain, but the widespread popular sympathy for France encouraged Genêt to break his word, notably in the case of the *Little Sarah.*

The *Little Sarah* was a captured British merchant vessel which Genêt transformed into the privateer, *Petite Democrate,* in violation of his promise. Hamilton wanted to use force to prevent the *Petite Democrate* from sailing, but Jefferson, always a staunch friend of republican France, persuaded the President to rely on verbal orders only. When Genêt sent his ship to sea in defiance of these orders and proceeded, in effect, to take the general question over the head of the President to the American people, his popular support diminished greatly. Pro-British Federalists exploited the situation fully, and Jefferson, concluding that Genêt was "a wreck which could not but sink all who would cling to it," tried to distinguish between the cause of France and the conduct of its offensive Minister. The administration requested his recall and secured congressional enactment of a tough neutrality law in 1794 barring exactly those practices in which he had engaged. In France there was no difficulty over Genêt's recall, for his faction (the Girondins) had lost control. The new government in fact ordered his arrest. Rather than return to an uncertain fate, Genêt remained in the United States and became in time the son-in-law of New York's Republican Governor, George Clinton.

Jay's Treaty

War with Britain still seemed imminent at the end of 1793, despite the elimination of Genêt. Britain had no desire, while engaged in a crucial conflict with France, to take on another belligerent, even one so inconsequential in strength as the United States. As usual in major European wars, however, Britain's "big navy" status threw her into controversies with any neutral nation which engaged heavily in commerce and shipping. The United States, despite its very recent emergence from colonial status, was already a major maritime power. Its ship owners and merchants were eagerly exploiting new business opportunities which war conditions in France had opened to them. Britain, pursuing economic warfare against France and also seeking to curtail America's expanding role in world trade, attempted systematically to combat the growing American participation in French commerce.

How to reconcile the determination of neutral Americans to trade with France and that of Britain to cut off its enemy's trade was the core of the British-American dispute. Americans had jumped at the opportunity when France at the outset of the war had opened to neutral ships the trade between the French West Indies and France—a commerce from which foreigners had formerly been excluded. The United States had treaty commitments, as well as self-interest, binding it to support the right of neutrals to carry noncontraband goods, including those belonging to a belligerent, to any port which was not blockaded. On the other hand, a British Order in Council of June, 1793, proclaimed all France under blockade and authorized seizure of all neutral ships carrying cargoes to France. Another order in November extended the authorization of seizure to apply to all neutral ships carrying cargoes to or from the French West Indies. In justification, Britain cited its "Rule of 1756," to the effect that trade not open in time of peace could not be opened in time of war. Britain made no announcement of its new West Indian policy until December, by which time its warships had already taken positions calculated to secure a maximum haul of American vessels. With such surprise tactics the British bagged some two hundred and fifty ships, although about half were subsequently released. Revocation of the order applying to the West Indies in January, 1794, did not greatly mollify American resentment, even among Federalists.

Most Americans were eager to punish Britain. Even before news of the West Indian seizures, Madison had introduced in Congress commercial proposals which, had they been enacted, would have constituted a virtual declaration of economic war on Britain. A nonimportation measure came within one vote of passage. As it was, the Federalists joined the opposition in enacting a thirty-day embargo on all commerce (later extended to sixty days) and took measures to improve both the Army and the Navy.

Ship seizures by the British were by no means the only prominent American grievance against England. Along the Canadian border the British still occupied American territory and aided the Indians to resist expulsion. Washington feared that the British Navy would soon resume impressing American seamen into service, as it had a few years earlier at the time of a war scare with Spain. American merchants were convinced, in addition, that their increased troubles with Algerian pirates in the Mediterranean region were an intended result of a British-Portuguese treaty which reduced Portuguese naval patrols. Continued commercial discrimination by the British against Americans rankled, as did Britain's refusal to pay compensation for slaves removed during the Revolution.

To avoid war, Washington decided to send Chief Justice John Jay, an Anglophilic Federalist of high prestige and extensive diplomatic experience, on a special mission to London. Jay faced several hazards in his forthcoming negotiations with the British. The South and West remembered him unfavorably as the diplomat who had attempted, a few years earlier, to sacrifice Mississippi navigation for Eastern commercial advantage. And ardent republicans, with their emotional commitment to France, would oppose any concession whatever to Britain.

Federalist sympathy for Britain, on the other hand, weakened Jay's position in London. Jay's instructions included the suggestion that he consult with representatives of other neutral nations concerning collective action to resist British interference with their trade. Britain was apparently unwilling to make any concession at all to dissuade the United States from cooperating in such an endeavor. Hamilton, however, made it clear to the British that major concessions were unnecessary. Hamilton was not only pro-British in the Anglo-French contest, but he was also determined to prevent any interruption of Anglo-American trade, the major source of the import tax revenue which underwrote the needs of the government in general and of his debt program in particular. To some extent Hamilton also appears to have thought that as Secretary of the Treasury he could properly exercise power over diplomatic and other governmental decisions far removed from the responsibilities of his own department. Whatever his rationalization, Hamilton informed the British Minister that the policy of the United States would be to "avoid entangling itself with European connexions." Later he reported still more specifically that the Cabinet had considered participation in an armed neutrality movement and decided against it. This information probably induced the British to take a tougher line in their negotiations with Jay, although Jay himself was not disposed to push the British very hard.

After negotiating from June into November, Jay sent home a draft treaty with the apologetic affirmation that "to do more was not possible." He had, of course, attained the major Federalist objective: he had preserved peace. Merely by concluding a treaty with Great Britain, he had also elevated American prestige. The British, in addition, agreed to evacuate forts which they occupied on American soil, although they had determined on that course without reference to Jay. Their fur traders were still to have unrestricted access to American territory, and no limitations had been placed upon the sale of weapons to the

Indians. The treaty made no reference to American claims relating to slaves removed by the British during the Revolution, but it was equally silent on the payment of compensation to exiled Tories. Pre-Revolutionary debts, claims arising out of British ship seizures, and the disputed northeastern boundary were referred to special commissions.

Americans gained far less than they had sought by way of commercial advantages. Britain agreed to treat Americans as favorably as any other foreigners in its home market, an improvement over previous conditions, and to admit American ships to India. In Article XII, the treaty provided for the admission of American ships into the British West Indies, but on such restrictive conditions that the Senate threw out the entire article. Britain made no concessions whatever on the touchy subjects of neutral trading rights and impressment of American seamen.

Anticipating uproarious protest from republicans, the Federalists kept the terms of Jay's treaty secret for as long as they could. After its submission to the Senate, however, its details leaked out and denunciations began in earnest. "Archtraitor" was among the milder epithets hurled at Jay. Hamilton was stoned while attempting to defend the treaty. Most of the denunciations came from radical republicans, who rightly regarded the treaty as putting the United States in a position distinctly more pro-British than pro-French. Even Federalists, however, objected to Article XII. It provided for admission into the British West Indies of American ships under 70 tons ("canoes" according to Madison), but it bound Americans in return to carry no molasses, sugar, coffee, cocoa, or cotton to any foreign port. Such a policy would have banned one of the most profitable activities of American ship owners, carrying West Indian products to Europe. In addition, it would have cut off the export of American cotton which, following the invention of Eli Whitney's cotton gin in 1793, was already beginning what would prove to be a meteoric rise in production. Rubbing salt in the wound, Article XII also would have committed the United States to permit the importation of West Indian products in British ships. Even after eliminating Article XII, the Federalists in 1795 could secure not one vote more than the two-thirds majority required for Senate approval.

Still the treaty was not law. President Washington, deeply angered by Britain's renewed seizure of American ships, deliberated from June until August before finally affixing his signature. He did so only after receiving from the British some captured correspondence of Secretary of State Randolph, which indicated that he was engaged in some manner of intrigue with the French. Subsequent research has vindicated Randolph of anything more than indiscretion, but Washington, construing the evidence in the perspective suggested by his Federalist advisers, deemed it necessary to dismiss Randolph, a longtime friend, and to sign the treaty, to clarify that the United States had not become a satellite of France.

To the House of Representatives, the treaty was still not final. Despite Washington's impolitic admonition that the Constitutional Convention had intended the House to have no role in treaty making, the House reiterated a demand to see papers relating to the treaty before it would agree to appropriate funds necessary to its implementation. Washington refused, thereby establishing a major precedent, and the House, under mounting pressure from the interested parties, fell into line with the tie-breaking vote of its Speaker on April

29, 1796. Despite the uproar over the treaty, it did avoid war with England and permitted the United States to develop for a number of years unhampered by the risk of war with the world's major sea power.

While Jay's treaty convulsed the United States in political wrangling, Thomas Pinckney of South Carolina concluded a far more satisfactory agreement with Spain in 1795. American grievances against Spain related chiefly to the southwestern frontier. Border claims overlapped, and the Spanish provided the Indians with supplies and encouragement to resist the advance of American settlement. Still more important, Spain controlled the outlet of the Mississippi, upon which much of the American West depended for access to markets for its products. Manuel de Godoy, who dominated Spain's government, wanted mutual territorial guarantees and an alliance, but Pinckney, citing American determination to avoid entanglement in European affairs, declined. Instead he secured—almost without reciprocal concessions—permission for Americans to use the Mississippi, including for at least three years the port of New Orleans. Spain also recognized the 31st parallel, the extreme American claim, as the border with Florida and pledged to restrain Indian attacks. Whether these Spanish concessions owed more to worry over a possible Anglo-American alliance or to fear of attack on Spain's possessions by American frontiersmen remains disputed. In any case Godoy ignored his obligations until 1798, when the agreement renewed danger of both an Anglo-American alliance and aggression by frontiersmen, inducing him to keep his earlier commitments.

Conclusion

As the end of Washington's second administration neared, Federalists could take some satisfaction in what they had achieved. They had established a strong federal government, stronger indeed than their opponents believed the Constitution warranted. They had gained the firm allegiance of the "moneyed men" of the commercial Northeast, although at the price of alienating agricultural interests of the South and West. Through Wayne's victory at Fallen Timbers, as well as Jay's treaty, they had greatly improved conditions for development of the Northwest. Pinckney's treaty, although not yet implemented, promised to achieve similar results in the Southwest. While preserving its neutrality between France and Britain, the fledgling United States had gained significant diplomatic and economic advantages. The Republic had, however, failed to win unrestricted access to the British West Indies and had been unable to force the British to renounce impressment and accept American conceptions of neutral rights in wartime trade. How effectively Washington's successors could cope with these problems was a matter of deep Federalist concern, as the nation prepared in 1796 for its first contested presidential election.

SUGGESTED READINGS

On the Bill of Rights see the works referred to in the previous chapter.

John C. Miller's *Federalist Era** (1960) is comprehensive, reliable, and delightful. The most important supplement to it is Leonard D. White's *The Federalists* (1948), an appreciative study of how the Federalists created and operated a new national government. Bray Hammond's *Banks and Politics** (1957) esteems Hamilton highly for his success with the first Bank of the United States. L. D. Baldwin in *Whiskey Rebels* (1939) deals competently with that challenge to the new government's authority.

Washington's diplomatic difficulties are the subject of several good studies. S. F. Bemis is outstanding on both *Jay's Treaty* (rev. ed., 1962) and *Pinckney's Treaty* (rev. ed., 1960). Alexander DeConde's *Entangling Alliance* (1958) recounts the problems arising from the "permanent" alliance with France. P. A. Varg's *Foreign Policies of the Founding Fathers* (1963) and Felix Gilbert's *To the Farewell Address** (1961) discuss Washington's policies in relation to American ideology. Louis M. Sears in *George Washington and the French Revolution* (1960) has given a year-by-year account of the American's reactions to the news from France. A. P. Whitaker is authoritative on the southwestern frontier in *The Spanish-American Frontier, 1783–1795* (1927) and *The Mississippi Question, 1795–1803* (1934). A. L. Burt considers the problems on the northern frontier in long-range perspective in *The United States, Great Britain, and British North America* (1940). J. P. Boyd in *Number 7* (1964) accuses Hamilton of acting secretly and improperly to alter American foreign policy in favor of Britain even before Jay's treaty. C. R. Ritcheson's *The Aftermath of Revolution* (1969) affords new insight into Jay's treaty.

Biographies which overlap the Washington administrations are not only numerous but also highly important source materials. Among the best are D. S. Freeman's *George Washington,* vols. VI and VII (1954, 1957), the latter written after Freeman's death by J. A. Carroll and M. W. Ashworth; Broadus Mitchell's *Alexander Hamilton* (2 vols., 1962), very favorable to Hamilton; John C. Miller's *Alexander Hamilton: Portrait in Paradox* (1959), both critical and appreciative; Dumas Malone's *Jefferson and the Rights of Man* (1951) and *Jefferson and the Ordeal of Liberty* (1962), carefully balanced and one of the major biographies of this generation; Gilbert Chinard's *Thomas Jefferson** (1929); Irving Brant's *James Madison: Father of the Constitution* (1950); Frank Monaghan's *John Jay* (1935); W. E. A. Bernhard's *Fisher Ames* (1965); and Richard W. Welch, Jr.'s *Theodore Sedgwick, Federalist* (1965).

Hamilton's famous reports are available in J. E. Cooke (ed.), *The Reports of Alexander Hamilton** (1964).

* indicates availability in paperback.

9

The Revolution of 1800

EVEN BEFORE WASHINGTON retired from office in 1797, opponents of his administration had formed the nation's first political party. Their aim was to wrest control of the government from the Federalists, whom they considered aristocrats or even monarchists. Led by James Madison and Thomas Jefferson, members of the new party called themselves "Republicans," thus allying themselves ideologically with the revolutionary republicans in France. They failed by only 3 electoral votes to elect Jefferson rather than Federalist John Adams to the Presidency in 1796. However, following the conclusion of Jay's treaty, which seemed almost to ally the United States with Britain against France, arrogant French leaders began an undeclared naval war against the United States. A wave of anti-French sentiment then subjected the French-sympathizing Republicans to calamitous defeat in the congressional elections of 1798.

Between 1798 and 1800, the political tide turned again, this time against the Federalists. Increased taxes made necessary by their military preparations evoked deep popular resentment. Virginia and Kentucky threatened to nullify the Sedition Act of 1798, under which Federalists had jailed several Republican editors who criticized their policies. Hamiltonian Federalists bitterly attacked their party's President for making peace with France (the Convention of 1800) instead of war. Added to accusations of aristocratic tendencies these burdens doomed Adams's reelection effort in 1800 and brought not only a Jefferson administration but a Congress as overwhelmingly Republican as it had been Federalist. Tarred indelibly as aristocrats, the Federalists never regained national power.

Professed Republicans, some more faithful than others to the Jeffersonian heritage, dominated the government for the next generation. Under the Jeffersonians, the object of the government's particular solicitude was no longer the wealthy Northeastern merchants whom Hamilton had so assiduously sought to please but rather the nation's farmers and planters. Yet what the farmers and planters wanted was not so much overt assistance from the federal government as maximum authority for state governments to meet the varying needs of particular communities and maximum freedom for individuals to pursue their own interests without special advantages afforded to any. Consequently, under Jeffersonian leadership the federal government did little of a positive nature to aid the party's supporters. Moderate and pragmatic, the Republicans merely diluted Federalist nationalism with states' rights and mercantilism with laissez faire. In foreign affairs, Jefferson was fortunate that Napoleon presented him with the opportunity to buy the Louisiana Territory; but he was unfortunate in that his efforts to compel warring Britain and France each to allow America to trade freely with the other not only failed but evoked dangerous domestic strife as well.

The Emergence of Political Parties

To the Founding Fathers, political parties, or "factions," as they called them, appeared too dangerous to be desirable. Like many modern Americans, they were unable to see clearly that such organizations, especially if highly competitive, can improve the functioning of democracy. Parties define the policy alternatives between which voters must choose; they identify, even if vaguely, the will of the majority; they provide a measure of discipline with which to implement majority wishes; and finally, when evenly matched, they tend to keep government reasonably honest, efficient, and responsive to popular will.

What the Founding Fathers saw instead amid the political turmoil of their time was the divisive influence of parties. Washington in his Farewell Address branded the party spirit as the "worst enemy" of popular government. To him it seemed partisanship would be likely to produce "geographic discrimination," or a sectional alignment of parties, thus threatening to disrupt the Union with separatist movements. Madison wrote in *The Federalist,* Number 10, of class division, or the "unequal distribution of property," as a more likely cause of "factions," but, like Washington, he considered their existence undesirable, even if inevitable.

When political parties began is still a matter of dispute. Some see the conflict of interests between social classes as the principal basis of political division and argue that such a cleavage existed from pre-Revolutionary times onward. According to this notion, middle-class and lower-class people formed the bulwark of the radical Whig opposition to Britain during the Revolutionary struggle, of the Antifederalist movement against ratification of the Constitution, and of the Jeffersonian Republican party which opposed Hamiltonian Federalism. Conversely, in this view, the upper classes appear to have been for the most part conservative

Whigs or even Tories during the Revolution, and Federalists thereafter.

At least two considerations contravene this theory. In the first place, it is clear that many individuals and even large groups resist such easy categorization. Urban artisans, for example, were chiefly radical Whigs during the Revolution but became Federalists at least temporarily during the ratification controversy. Furthermore, the very concept of a political party implies some measure of organization. Prior to the 1790s such political organizations as did exist never transcended the state level, unless one considers the Revolutionary patriots themselves as a party. Even within the few states in which political organizations did exist before the 1790s, they tended to be highly transitory and to involve only an elite minority.

Nationally organized political parties, most authorities agree, arose in the 1790s. Hamilton's debt, taxation, and banking programs aroused many rich Southern planters as well as ordinary farmers, who considered that they favored unduly a few wealthy merchants in Northern cities. To dedicated agrarians, whether rich planters or small farmers, Hamilton's program threatened to transform a rural American paradise into a commercialized, urban society, peopled less by self-reliant, landowning farmers than by cringing, dependent, slum-dwelling workers. Devotees of states' rights worried over Federalist tendencies to augment national power. Advocates of equal political rights deplored Federalist hostility to the ideology of the French Revolution and found in Federalist admiration for aristocratic Britain an ominous indication of the ultimate objective of the Federalist program.

Three events of 1791 presaged the appearance of an organized opposition party. Jefferson and Madison persuaded Philip Freneau, sometimes called "the poet of the Revolution," to establish the *National Gazette.* Its function was to do verbal battle with John Fenno's *Gazette of the United States,* which had castigated republicans vigorously since 1789, with the aid of both private and public subsidies arranged by Federalists. In lieu of outright subsidies, Freneau received a sinecure in Jefferson's Department of State. Until he fled Philadelphia during the yellow fever epidemic of 1793, Freneau's paper built up Jefferson as assiduously as it attacked Hamilton.

Thomas Paine's *Rights of Man* appeared also during 1791 in an American edition with an introductory endorsement by Jefferson. Paine vigorously defended the French Revolution against attacks by England's Edmund Burke in his *Reflections on the Revolution in France,* but Jefferson's endorsement, published without his knowledge, referred to Paine's work as an answer to "political heresies which have sprung up among us." Informed Americans, including the Vice President, construed this as a reference to John Adams's *Discourses on Davila,* which had recently deplored the "mistake" of the French in concentrating authority in a supreme legislature rather than creating a "balanced" government with powers divided among legislative, executive, and judicial branches.

Suspicious Federalists also interpreted a Northern tour of Jefferson and Madison in 1791 as an organizing effort, although it seems in fact to have been chiefly a "botanizing" vacation.

What Federalists had suspected in 1791 became reality in 1792. Republicans did indeed begin to organize. They did so chiefly in Congress under Madison's leadership. Although he had led the Federalist forces in the First Congress, Madison began rallying congressional opposition as Hamilton's debt program (see Chapter 8) came to the fore. Jefferson, holding office as Washington's Secretary of State, kept his opposition to Hamilton's program largely within the Cabinet until 1793 when he resigned and retired to Monticello. Despite these indications of a strong disinclination to lead, it was always Jefferson whom both Federalists and Republicans considered to be the chief of the opposition.

Washington's popularity was still so great in 1792 that the Republicans planned no campaign against his reelection, but they considered Vice President Adams, "the monarchical rubbish of our government," highly vulnerable. With John Beckley, clerk of the House of Representatives, as their liaison man, Madison and Jefferson arranged to run New York's Antifederalist Governor George Clinton against Adams. Adams won reelection with 77 electoral votes to Clinton's 50, but the Republicans drew some encouragement from their respectable showing.

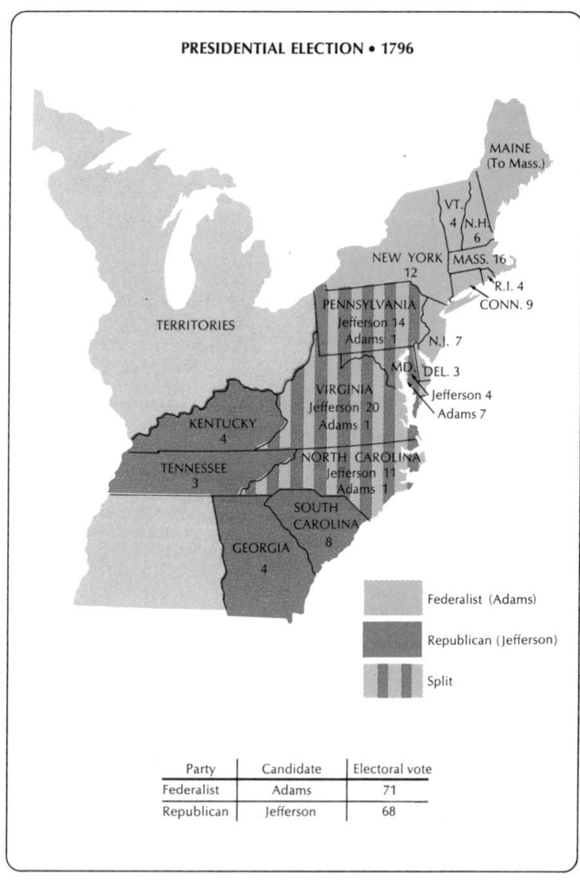

Party	Candidate	Electoral vote
Federalist	Adams	71
Republican	Jefferson	68

Party lines hardened appreciably between 1792 and 1796. Congressional Republicans kept Hamilton under fire until he resigned in 1795. By then, however, it was foreign policy rather than Hamilton's economic measures over which differences were sharpest. In particular, Jay's treaty, which ended the threat of war with Britain, deeply offended the Republican partisans of France (see Chapter 8). Even before that controversy reached its climax, Washington had stopped trying to be impartial and resolved: "I shall not . . . bring any man into any office of consequence knowingly whose political tenets are adverse to the measures which the general government are pursuing." To do otherwise, he had concluded, "would be a sort of political suicide."

When Washington announced in his Farewell Address of 1796 that he would not accept another term, Republicans eagerly put forth Thomas Jefferson as their consensus candidate to succeed him. The Federalists had little trouble agreeing on John Adams as their man. Hamilton, however, disliked Adams so strongly that he schemed to divert the votes of Southern Federalists from Adams to South Carolina's Thomas Pinckney, who—because of the popularity of his treaty with Spain—had been the party's vice presidential choice. The Constitution had invited such intrigue by failing to require separate elections for the two offices; it merely provided that electors should vote for two men and that the man with the highest electoral vote should be President while the vice presidency should go to the man who placed second. None of the candidates campaigned in the modern sense; in fact, only eight of the sixteen states provided for a popular vote in choosing electors. The rest permitted their legislatures to do the job. The outstanding campaign document was Washington's Farewell Address, which Hamilton helped him compose. With Republican admiration for France in mind, Washington cautioned against "passionate attachments" in foreign policy as well as against partisan division along sectional lines.

Sectional division such as Washington had feared was clearly evident in the results of the election of 1796. Adams, with 71 electoral votes to Jefferson's 68, had won every vote north of Pennsylvania plus a scattering largely in the upper South. Jefferson had won the two new Western states (Kentucky and Tennessee) and nearly all of the South, but nothing in the North save Pennsylvania. New England Federalists, with some knowledge of Hamilton's scheme to throw the election to Pinckney, cut the South Carolinian so severely that he received only 59 votes, thus allowing Jefferson to become Vice President. Southern Republicans, on the other hand, cut New York's Aaron Burr, the Republican vice presidential choice, so severely that he ran 20 votes behind Jefferson.

Limited War and a Constitutional Crisis

John Adams, like Washington, had secured a major place in American history before he became President. He was an outstanding leader of the Revolutionary movement, both in Massachusetts and in the Continental Congress; with Franklin and Jay, he negotiated the remarkable treaty which secured American independence. He was also the principal author of the respected Massachusetts constitution of 1780. His nonpartisan selection as Vice President under Washington, even though he considered it "the most insignificant office that ever the invention of man contrived," testified to the high esteem in which he was held.

As President, John Adams suffered from too close adherence to his own rather dogmatic political philosophy. In its simplest terms, that philosophy held that rich and poor alike, reflecting the evil nature of man, engage in a perpetual, self-interested struggle for political dominance. The function of government in general, but of the Chief Executive in particular, as Adams perceived it, was to prevent either group from gaining full power to impose its will. The fact that the Federalists controlled the Senate, the "aristocratical" branch of the government, while the Republicans dominated the House of Representatives, or "democratical" branch, throughout much of his administration probably helped confirm the President in his conclusion. What he failed to perceive (understandably, in view of the very recent emergence of political parties and their presumed impermanence) was that to be an effective leader the President must be master of his party.

Alexander Hamilton, not John Adams, was the effective leader of the Federalist party through most of Adams's administration. Not only congressional leaders, but even members of the President's Cabinet gave first loyalty to Hamilton when his views and those of the President conflicted. Adams complicated this problem by spending long periods at his home in Massachusetts, so that there was some validity to the observation of Treasury Secretary Oliver Wolcott that he and two other Cabinet members "govern this great nation."

Whether or not to make war on France was the major problem of Adams's administration. France had construed Jay's treaty—particularly America's silent acceptance of Britain's seizure of American ships carrying cargo for France—as aligning the United States with Britain in the war between the two great powers. In reprisal, French ships operating in the Caribbean and in American coastal waters captured over three hundred American merchant ships during the year preceding July, 1797. The absence of American naval power encouraged the French to expect no effective retaliation.

War with the United States, however, had no part in France's plans. The recovery of Louisiana (ceded to Spain in 1763) was one French objective. Another was to keep the United States neutral so that American merchant ships could carry cargoes to France with presumed immunity from British seizure. Another hope of the French was to see the Federalist "Anglomen" replaced by pro-French Republicans in control of the American government. War with the United States would serve none of these objectives. Still more important for France were European considerations. Although French armies had ringed the nation with satellites from Belgium to Italy, France had conquered neither the Austrian nor the British monarchies. These were high-priority targets.

Because peaceful relations between the United States and France would clearly serve the interest of both nations, Adams decided to send a mission to Paris, much as Washington had done in sending Jay to London in 1794. The three-man delegation ultimately selected included Charles C. Pinckney, brother of the Federalist vice presidential candidate of 1796; John Marshall, a Virginia Federalist; and Elbridge Gerry, a Republican friend of the President from Massachusetts. They were greeted by the French with demands that they disavow anti-French statements of the President, promise a $12 million loan, and donate $250,000 to assorted French officials before negotiations could even begin. While such demands were not entirely unprecedented, they were offensive, especially to Adams. He thought seriously of asking Congress to declare war but wisely decided to wait until the French had alienated their Republican supporters in the United States. To foster that objective Adams readily agreed to congressional demands that he make public the commissioners' report. Published with "X," "Y," and "Z" substituting for the names of the French agents, the documents evoked a great outburst of national indignation. In its wake, Congress created a Department of the Navy, authorized construction of more warships and an increase in the Army to 10,000 men. Without seeking a declaration of war, the President sent the Navy in search of French warships.

On the domestic scene, most Federalists united in a demand for repression of their Republican opponents. Some Federalists believed "a great body of domestic traitors" would abet a French invasion of the United States, as subversives had done in European areas which had fallen under French control. Should a French conquest occur, a Federalist warned, "We must receive a constitution from Paris, as the Dutch and the Swedes have been compelled to do," and submit to a puppet government headed by such an arch-Francophile as Vice President Thomas Jefferson. Such exaggerated fears afflicted only a few, but many Federalists did share Hamilton's worry that if French conquests continued, the "United States might be left alone to Contend with the Conquerors of Europe." Why Republicans in such circumstances remained sympathetic to France and opposed increased military expenditures was difficult for Federalists to comprehend.

Fear of Republican radicalism in domestic matters also concerned the Federalists. Should Republicans gain control of the federal government, their dedication to states' rights, many Federalists felt, might well jeopardize the still-precarious federal Union. The unorthodox religious views of their leaders spawned fears of atheistic, antireligious programs like those of the French republicans. Republican opposition to "aristocracy" appeared to some Federalists also to threaten traditional property rights. A Federalist's characterization of those who attended a Republican dinner succinctly expresses Federalist fears: "Here you saw an american disorganizer [states' rights advocate] and there a blundering wild Irishman, in one corner a banished Genevan [Swiss-born Republican leader Albert Gallatin] and in another a french spye [diplomat]—on one side a greasy butcher and on the other a dirty Cobler."

To help combat Republican radicalism, the Federalists in 1798 enacted four important laws. One, a Naturalization Act, extended the residence requirement for citizenship from five years to fourteen. Its objective was to prevent immigrants, for the most part prospective Republicans, from voting for several more years. An Alien Enemies Act, passed with Republican support, provided for dealing with enemy aliens in time of war. An Alien Act, limited to the remaining two years of Adams's term, authorized the President, even without a declaration of war, to deport any alien whom he judged "dangerous to the peace and safety of the United States." John Adams never employed this power, but hundreds of aliens, mostly French, left voluntarily, some primarily for business reasons. Last but most important of the new laws was the Sedition Act, a law designed to suppress Republican criticism of the Federalist administration in advance of the presidential election of 1800. It too was to be in force for only two years.

In theory, the Sedition Act actually increased freedom to criticize the government. Contrary to English tradition, the law permitted the accused to secure acquittal by proving the truth of his accusations. In addition, it required the government to show malicious intent in order to secure a conviction and authorized the jury to decide not only whether the accused had made the criticisms but also whether they constituted seditious libel. In permitting the jury rather than the judge to decide whether the words in question constituted seditious libel, Congress was following the example of the British Parliament, which had made the same provision in 1792.

In actual operation, the Sedition Act was harshly repressive. Its terms provided a fine and imprisonment for anyone who published "false, scandalous, and malicious writing" tending to bring the government "into contempt or disrepute." This has seemed to posterity a flat violation of the First Amendment to the Constitution, which states that "Congress shall make no law . . . abridging the freedom of speech, or of the press." However, it is now clear that this guarantee applied at the time, as in the English common law, only to prior restraint and not to subsequent punishment. Accordingly, Federalist prosecutors, often aided by Federalist judges, convinced Federalist juries that the words of leading Republican critics of the Adams administration did warrant punishment. Congressman Mathew Lyon of Vermont was fined and jailed for telling his constituents that the President engaged in a "continual grasp for power" and that he had an "unbounded thirst for ridiculous pomp." Editors of four of the nation's five leading Republican newspapers were convicted and punished for similar allegations.

Republicans refused to be intimidated. Their criticism continued undiminished. Considering seditious libel a matter for state rather than federal action, Kentucky's Legislature adopted a resolution drafted secretly by Vice President Jefferson affirming that each state could "judge for itself . . . the mode . . . of redress" when the "general government assumes undelegated powers." Later it specifically endorsed "nullification" as the "rightful remedy." A Virginia resolution drafted by Madison referred to the "duty" of the state to "interpose" its authority to prevent the federal government from exercising "powers not granted" in the Constitution. Virginia also asked other states to join in declaring both the Alien and the Sedition Acts unconstitutional. Most states ignored the appeal, but some affirmed in rebuttal that the nation's Supreme Court should make such determinations. Thus the nature of the federal Union as well as the question of freedom of the press became issues in the presidential contest of 1800.

Meanwhile, the naval war with France was accentuating the split between the Hamiltonian "High Federalists" and the President's more moderate following. Hamiltonians wanted a declaration of war "to enable us," as one Senator put it, "to lay our hands on traitors." Hamilton himself wanted to seize Florida and Louisiana from Spain, then an ally of France, and to cooperate with the British in liberating Latin America and capturing the Caribbean colonies of France. At Hamilton's insistence, Congress tripled the Army. President Adams persuaded ex-President Washington to accept nominal command of the Army, but he accepted only on the condition that Hamilton be made second in command and authorized to do the job until real need for Washington's services arose. Thus President Adams had to bestow effective command of an Army about to be greatly enlarged upon the chief opponent of his defensive strategy, a factional leader to whom even major Cabinet members gave higher loyalty than to the President. Adams reluctantly accepted Washington's terms, but he did not hurry to recruit men for Hamilton's Army.

Fortunately for Adams, the French were beginning to reconsider their policy. Even before the end of 1798, the expanding American Navy had largely cleared American coastal waters of French privateers and in the next two years would carry the war into the West Indies at a considerable cost to the French in warships. Vastly more serious to the French was the devastation suffered by their navy at the hands of Britain's Horatio Nelson at the Battle of the Nile in August, 1798. To Napoleon Bonaparte, coming to power in France in 1799, it seemed clear that restoration of peace with the United States was desirable so that France could use neutral American ships to combat Britain's blockade. Even before Napoleon assumed control, however, Adams had received assurances from the French government that a new American mission would be met "with the respect due to representatives of a free, independent, and powerful nation," the precise words Adams had used in fixing the only condition under which he would send another mission. To the consternation of the Hamiltonians, Adams accepted the French assurances. In 1800 a commission consisting of diplomat William Vans Murray, Chief Justice Oliver Ellsworth, and North Carolina Governor William R. Davie ended hostilities with the Treaty of Mortefontaine, also called the Convention of 1800. The treaty helped to cool domestic political hostilities as well.

The Revolution of 1800

Amid the furor over the Alien and Sedition Acts and the squabbling among Federalists over the termination of the quasi-war with France, the nation prepared for the election of 1800. The Federalists had won a victory of landslide proportions in the congressional elections of 1798 when near hysteria over the French menace gripped the nation, but thereafter the party alienated many voters. Hence, the election seemed likely to be as close as had been Adams's victory of 1796.

Hamilton's enlarged Army was proving a serious addition to the political burdens which the Federalists already bore. Many voters shared the Republican fear that its purpose was to "arm one half of the people, for the purpose of keeping the other in awe." Such fears did not diminish when the President used federal troops in Pennsylvania to arrest an ex-Federalist, John Fries, for leading a mob which liberated men who had been jailed for tax dodging. The taxes imposed to pay for the Army served also, as one contemporary observed, to "carry reason and reflection to every man's door, and particularly in the hour of election."

The Hamilton and Adams wings of the Federalist party continued to fight each other. Adams dismissed two Hamiltonians from his Cabinet: Secretary of State Timothy Pickering and Secretary of War James McHenry. Hamilton, having failed to persuade the dying Washington to oppose Adams, tried again to throw the Presidency to the party's vice presidential candidate, this time South Carolinian Charles Coatsworth Pinckney of XYZ fame, a brother of the nominee of 1796. Hamilton showed little regret when Republican Aaron Burr secured and published a copy of a pamphlet in which he had severely criticized the President.

Since each state voted at a time of its own choice, the outcome of the election long remained in doubt. Aaron Burr got the Republicans off to a good start by a brilliant organizing effort in New York City, which gave his party a majority in the state Legislature, thus transferring New York's 12 electoral votes, which Adams had won in 1796, to Jefferson's column. Adams picked up strength elsewhere, however, and in time it became clear that South Carolina's 8 votes would be decisive. Despite the candidacy of Charles Coatsworth Pinckney on the Federalist ticket, South Carolina's legislators, influenced in some measure by patronage promises held out on behalf of the Republicans by still another Pinckney, Senator Charles Pinckney, gave the state's vote and thus the election to the Republicans. Jefferson and Burr, the vice presidential choice, had 73 votes each while Adams had 65 and Pinckney 64. In the congressional elections Republicans scored an overwhelming victory, reversing the Federalist tide of 1798.

Because each of the Republican electors had voted for both Jefferson and Burr, an electoral college tie left it to the old House of Representatives elected in 1798 to choose between them. With 1 vote for each state's congressional delegation, as the Constitution requires, Jefferson on the first ballot gained 8 votes, 1 short of the necessary majority. Federalist support gave Burr 6 votes, however, while two state delegations were evenly split between Federalists and Republicans. For thirty-five ballots the Federalists held firm for Burr, while trying to exact policy commitments from Jefferson as a price for ending the stalemate. Then Delaware's only congressman, Federalist James A. Bayard, announced his intention to switch to Jefferson. In the end no Federalist voted for Jefferson, but some did abstain, with the result that Jefferson was properly chosen on the thirty-sixth ballot. Before the next election, passage of the Twelfth Amendment of the Constitution, providing separate balloting for President and Vice President, ruled out the danger that such a crisis would recur.

Thomas Jefferson, leader of a party considered, in the North at least, to be that of the "middling sort," possessed full credentials as an American aristocrat. His mother's family, the Randolphs, was one of Virginia's most distinguished. Jefferson owned thousands of acres of land and over 100 slaves. He had received a classical education from tutors and at William and Mary College. He knew several languages and was a lawyer, an inventor, and an amateur architect of distinction. He played the violin and wrote a book of intelligent commentary, *Notes on Virginia* (1785), on the economy and society of his native state. Like many other educated gentlemen of his time, he eschewed orthodox Christianity for Deism, the religion of reason. Like most Southern planters, he never allowed his perpetual burden of debts to restrict his gracious style of living.

Politically, Jefferson had much in common with the nation's farmers. In contrast to Hamilton's zeal to foster manufacturing, Jefferson wanted to foster agriculture. "Those who labour in the earth," he had written in his *Notes on Virginia,* "are the chosen people of God." He favored assistance to commerce so that surplus agricultural commodities might be sold abroad; but rather than aid manufacturing, he believed Americans should "let our workshops remain in Europe" and thus avoid the growth of cities whose mobs he considered a menace to "pure government." To serve the interest of ordinary farmers, Jefferson believed, as they did, that what was needed was not Hamiltonian mercantilism but "a wise and frugal government, which shall restrain men from injuring one another, shall leave them otherwise free to regulate their own pursuits." In particular Jefferson wished to limit the role of the federal government. He considered state governments "the most competent administrations for our domestic concerns and the surest bulwark against antirepublican tendencies."

Recognizing the problem of reconciling majority rule with minority rights, Jefferson made qualified commitments to both. On the one hand, he demanded "absolute acquiescence in the decisions of the majority, the vital principle of republics, from which there is no appeal but to force, the vital principle and immediate parent of despotism." On the other hand, he insisted that the will of the majority "to be rightful must be reasonable; that the minority possess their equal rights, which equal law must protect, and to violate would be oppression." In his list of the "essential principles of our Government," he gave first place to "Equal and exact justice to all men."

Jefferson's belief that his election effected "the revolution of 1800" has often struck historians as greatly exaggerated. They have tended to emphasize instead how little really changed. Indeed, there was none of the drastic change nor of the violence which people normally associate with revolutions. Jefferson made no effort to undo Hamilton's funding of the national debt nor the assumption by the federal government of the state debts. The Bank of the United States, which he had originally opposed as unconstitutional, Jefferson condoned as President because his Secretary of the Treasury found it useful. His federal appointees were, on the whole, slightly lower in social status than Federalist appointees had been, but the standing of "gentleman" was still nearly prerequisite to selection.

Nevertheless, a number of important changes had occurred. A rival leader had ousted the nation's Chief Executive. He did so by the novel means of an electoral process prescribed in a written Constitution rather than by violence, but the act still met some of the contemporary standards of revolution. The new leader's party had also gained firm control of the national legislature. Contemporaries recognized clearly that political power had shifted from the commercial Northeast to the rural South and West. Any consideration of secession in the next two decades would center in the Northeast, not in the South and West as it had in the Federalist era. To say that government by agents of Northern farmers and Southern planters had replaced that by representatives of a mercantile aristocracy would be an oversimplification, yet such a generalization contains elements of truth too important to overlook. Younger Federalist leaders would try to compete with the Jeffersonians in appealing to the newly awakened electorate of "middling" status, but in the nation as a whole the aristocratic image of federalism established in the 1790s would prove an insuperable handicap. The election of 1800 had turned the country from a mildly aristocratic course into one which was by contemporary standards distinctly egalitarian.

Jefferson made specific policy changes of some importance as well. His brilliant Secretary of the Treasury, Albert Gallatin, reduced by nearly one-half the considerable national debt which the Federalists had left, doing so chiefly by reducing the size of the Army. In Republican eyes, the Army was not only excessively expensive and potentially oppressive but a source of *federal* power. They preferred to rely on militia forces, which were not only part-time and hence cheaper but also in normal times under state control. Republican economies also permitted repeal of the hated whisky tax. Reluctant to offend Federalist converts to Republicanism, Jefferson resisted pressure from his supporters for wholesale removals from the federal service, but when making new appointments, he did seek to "afford Republicans a proportionate share" of federal jobs. There had been only 6 Republicans among 600 federal employees when he took office; by 1803, Republicans enjoyed a slight majority.

Social traditions which appeared aristocratic or monarchical in nature also underwent change. Instead of proceeding in stately dignity as had kings, colonial governors, and earlier Presidents to deliver formal addresses to the legislature, Jefferson sent written messages to Congress to be droned out by a clerk. The procedure ended for a century a somewhat "monarchical" custom; in addition, it enabled Jefferson to avoid calling unnecessary attention to his weakness in speaking. He also ended the very formal "levees" of the Federalist era and prescribed a much less formal code of etiquette to govern official social affairs. Privately, the

President continued to entertain lavishly, but he shocked some foreign dignitaries by receiving them in very casual attire.

Freedom to criticize federal officials broadened in the aftermath of the Sedition Act controversy but in ways which added little to Jefferson's stature. Throughout his Presidency, Jefferson clung to the Blackstone conception that freedom of the press meant only the absence of prior restraint. His objection to the Sedition Act, although he never made it public at the time, was that it was a *federal* restraint unauthorized by the Constitution. "While we deny that Congress have a right to control freedom of the press," Jefferson wrote, "we have ever asserted the right of the states, and their exclusive right to do so." Accordingly, Jefferson made no effort to extend the expiring Sedition Act and indeed pardoned those still in jail for violation of it.

Eager to conciliate the opposition, Jefferson made no effort to quell criticism for some time. By 1803, however, the attacks had become so intense that he thought it desirable to act in order to restore "credibility" to the press. He suggested privately to the Governor of Pennsylvania that "a few prosecutions of the most prominent offenders would have a wholesome effect in restoring the integrity of the presses." Prosecutions followed in the courts of several states, but only one resulted in a conviction, and that was overturned on appeal.

Three significant conclusions emerged from these controversies. New York's Legislature put into a widely copied statute the argument used by Alexander Hamilton in defense of one of Jefferson's critics: that "with good motives" a person might safely publish truth "though reflecting on government, magistracy, or individuals." The United States Supreme Court, hearing an appeal on another case, held (*United States v. Hudson,* 1812) that federal courts could not try common law (nonstatutory) crimes, such as seditious libel, but only those defined in the Constitution or in acts of Congress. Finally, the Republicans, like the Federalists before them, seem to have found that tolerating even the most offensive criticism may be less painful than trying to suppress it.

Quite contrary to their basic commitment to minimize federal functions, the Republicans increased them, or tried to, in several areas. Despite their general animosity toward the Army, the Republicans in 1803 created the United States Military Academy at West Point. Within a few years it had developed into the nation's first college of engineering, and for generations its graduates provided the nation's best-trained engineers, widely employed in private industry as well as in government service. Despite his early opposition, Jefferson in 1806 approved the appropriation of federal funds for constructing the "national road" which ultimately extended from Baltimore into Illinois. Treasury Secretary Gallatin in 1808 submitted to Congress an elaborate plan for a national network of roads and canals, but Republican orthodoxy prevailed. The impetus such a program would have given to the nation's economic growth had to await another generation.

Jefferson and the Judiciary

Federalists, ousted from both legislative and executive branches of government by the revolution of 1800, nevertheless remained firmly entrenched in the federal judiciary. Republicans, dedicated ideologically to the idea that majority will should prevail, were not pleased by the prospect that, in accordance with the theory of separation of powers, Federalist judges enjoying lifetime tenure might in some instances deny the majority what it wished. Moreover, those Republicans who were most firmly dedicated to states' rights looked upon federal courts not only as unnecessary but also as a positive threat to the power of state courts and an unwanted agency for bending the people of any state to the will of the "general" government.

Foremost among the Federalists ready to battle Republicanism from their judicial stronghold was Chief Justice John Marshall, appointed by President Adams at the very end of his term. Although Marshall had opposed the Sedition Act, he was otherwise a highly orthodox Federalist, fully determined to establish the independent power of the judiciary, to sanctify the rights of ownership, and above all to make national authority superior to that of the states. While these views by themselves assured clashes between the President and the Chief Justice, the two men, although fellow Virginians, distant cousins, and both normally quite amiable, detested each other as well.

Their first clash involved the Judiciary Act of 1801, a lame-duck measure of the Adams administration. In anticipation of a big increase in the work load of federal courts, the law provided for sixteen new federal judges. In addition it relieved the Supreme Court justices of the duty of sitting on regional circuit courts. Because the Constitution states explicitly that federal judges "shall hold their offices during good behavior," Jefferson could not replace the Federalists whom Adams had appointed to the new posts. However, the Constitution also states: "The judicial power of the United States shall be vested in one Supreme Court and in such inferior courts as the Congress may from time to time . . . establish." On the theory that what Congress could do it could also undo, the Republicans repealed the law creating the new positions and restored the provisions of the Judiciary Act of 1789 requiring Supreme Court justices to serve on regional circuit courts in addition to their other duties. Marshall tried to persuade some of the victims to challenge the Republican measure in the courts, but none chose to do so.

Meanwhile Marshall was deliberating the famous case of *Marbury v. Madison* (1803). Marbury had received one of the very last of President Adams's "midnight" appointments, that of justice of the peace in the District of Columbia. His commission had been signed, sealed, but not delivered, an oversight of the outgoing Secretary of State, John Marshall. Jefferson, who regarded such appointments as "an outrage on decency," ordered his Secretary of State, James Madison, not to deliver the commission. Marbury then asked the Supreme Court to issue an order, a "writ of mandamus," requiring Madison to do so. The Court ordered Madison to "show cause" why he should not deliver the commission, but Madison declined to do that as well.

Marshall thus found himself in an acute constitutional quandary. Section 13 of the Judiciary Act of 1789 authorized the Court to issue such orders to "any . . . persons holding office under the authority of the United States." However, the Court must ultimately rely upon the President to enforce its orders. Marshall had every reason to believe Jefferson would ignore a Supreme Court order directing him to compel Madison to do what he had already ordered Madison not to do.

Marshall's decision extricated his Court brilliantly from the dilemma. First, he scolded the administration for refusing to honor what he declared was a valid appointment and thus violating "a vested legal right." Then he concluded that his Court really lacked jurisdiction. To reach that conclusion, Marshall construed Section 13 of the Judiciary Act of 1789 as adding to the *original* (as opposed to the appellate) jurisdiction of the court. As the Constitution fixes the original jurisdiction of the court with finality, the law in question appeared "not to be warranted by the constitution." Accordingly, Marshall refused to order Madison to deliver Marbury's commission and avoided revealing the impotence of his Court to enforce such an order. To support his conclusion, Marshall's decision included a classic affirmation that, since the Constitution is the "fundamental . . . law of the nation," the courts must refuse to enforce acts of Congress which conflict with it. Although this proposition was to be important only once again before the Civil War, it assumed fundamental importance after that time.

Modern scholars make two major criticisms of Marshall's decision. First, by present standards it is improper to state a conclusion on the merits of a case over which the Court finds it has no jurisdiction. Second, it appears that the intent of Congress in enacting the law in question was not to add to the original jurisdiction of the Supreme Court but merely to provide that the Court might issue writs of mandamus on matters within its existing jurisdiction. In this view Marshall held void a valid law.

Eager to make the federal judiciary more responsible to the popular will, the Republicans in 1803 began to remove highly partisan Federalist judges by impeachment proceedings. The Constitution, while assuring federal judges tenure "during good Behaviour," also provided for their removal by impeachment proceedings for "Treason, Bribery, or other high Crimes and Misdemeanors." Normally advocates of literal construction of the Constitution, the Republicans in this instance wished to construe the language loosely, as Hamilton had in justifying the national Bank. Their first target was federal Judge John Pickering of New Hampshire. As Pickering was both an alcoholic and insane, the Republicans had little trouble getting the two-thirds vote needed in the Senate to remove him.

Next the Republicans turned to Judge Samuel Chase, the Maryland Federalist who as presiding judge had helped to jail several Republicans under the Sedition Act. Recently he had denounced the Republicans from the bench for instituting "mobocracy." The House indicted (literally impeached) Chase, but the Senate vote, despite the Republican majority of 25 to 9, fell 4 short of the 23 necessary for a conviction. Impeachment, Jefferson concluded, was "a farce which will not be tried again." The occasion thus served to reinforce the independence of the federal judiciary, but it also persuaded federal judges to restrain their partisan impulses in public. Although the Republicans never succeeded in making the federal judiciary more responsive, they did gradually achieve that result in many states by providing that judges should be elected for fixed terms rather than appointed to serve during "good behavior."

Jefferson and the West

Expansion of America's territory seemed to Jefferson and his contemporaries only a matter of time. Britain's power made northward extension of the nation's borders unlikely, but Spain's weakness marked both Florida and the vast Louisiana Territory as potential targets.

While Jefferson was winning the Presidency, however, Spain had reluctantly agreed in a secret treaty to return Louisiana to France. The actual transfer of control, delayed by Napoleon's failure to keep his part of the bargain, occurred in 1802, after Spain had secured Napoleon's promise never to sell the region. Intending to use the territory to produce food for the French sugar plantations on Santo Domingo (modern Haiti and the Dominican Republic), Napoleon planned to occupy it in force as soon as he had crushed a Negro insurrection threatening his control of Santo Domingo itself.

Jefferson's reaction to the news, despite his reputation as pro-French, was highly bellicose. He arranged to inform Napoleon indirectly that, as three-eighths of the United States depended upon New Orleans for access to markets for its produce, this country must consider the nation which possessed it "our natural and habitual enemy." "The day that France takes possession of New Orleans," he added, "we must marry ourselves to the British fleet and nation."

Informed that money would probably influence Napoleon more than threats, Jefferson arranged to send James Monroe on a mission to Paris with authorization to offer $10 million for New Orleans and Florida. Jefferson assumed that France had secured West Florida, the coastal region between modern Florida and Louisiana, but the Spanish, as the President would later discover, thought otherwise. Should Napoleon decline to sell, Monroe was to proceed to England to discuss the implementation of Jefferson's earlier threat.

Fortunately for the United States, the Negroes of Santo Domingo, aided by tropical diseases, utterly destroyed the army which Napoleon sent to subdue them. Consequently, Napoleon determined to abandon his American plans and return his attention to Europe. Thus, even before Monroe's arrival, he had suggested to the somewhat startled American Minister, Robert R. Livingston, that the United States buy all of Louisiana. Although Monroe had authorization to offer only $10 million for New Orleans and Florida, he and Livingston quickly agreed to Napoleon's price of $15 million for all Louisiana. Jefferson, too, readily accepted the price, but he worried about constitutional authorization for such a purchase. Unfounded rumors that Napoleon might change his mind persuaded him, however, that "the less we say about constitutional difficulties respecting Louisiana the better." Congress agreed and appropriated the money in 1803 without protest.

Precisely what the United States had bought remained in doubt. The United States thought that it had bought everything from the Rio Grande to the Perdido River, the present western border of Florida. Spain insisted, to the contrary, that the purchase included no coastal region other than that of what is roughly modern Louisiana. Jefferson did not choose to press the American claim aggressively, for he was convinced that in time both East Florida (modern Florida) and West Florida (coastal Alabama, Mississippi, and part of Louisiana) "cannot fail to fall into our hands."

Always interested in Western exploration and development, Jefferson had made arrangements for an exploratory expedition into the Pacific Northwest even before the Louisiana Purchase. Its commanders were Meriwether Lewis, who had been Jefferson's private secretary, and William Clark, brother of Kentucky's Revolutionary hero, George Rogers Clark. Between 1803 and 1806 Lewis and Clark journeyed up the Missouri River, across the

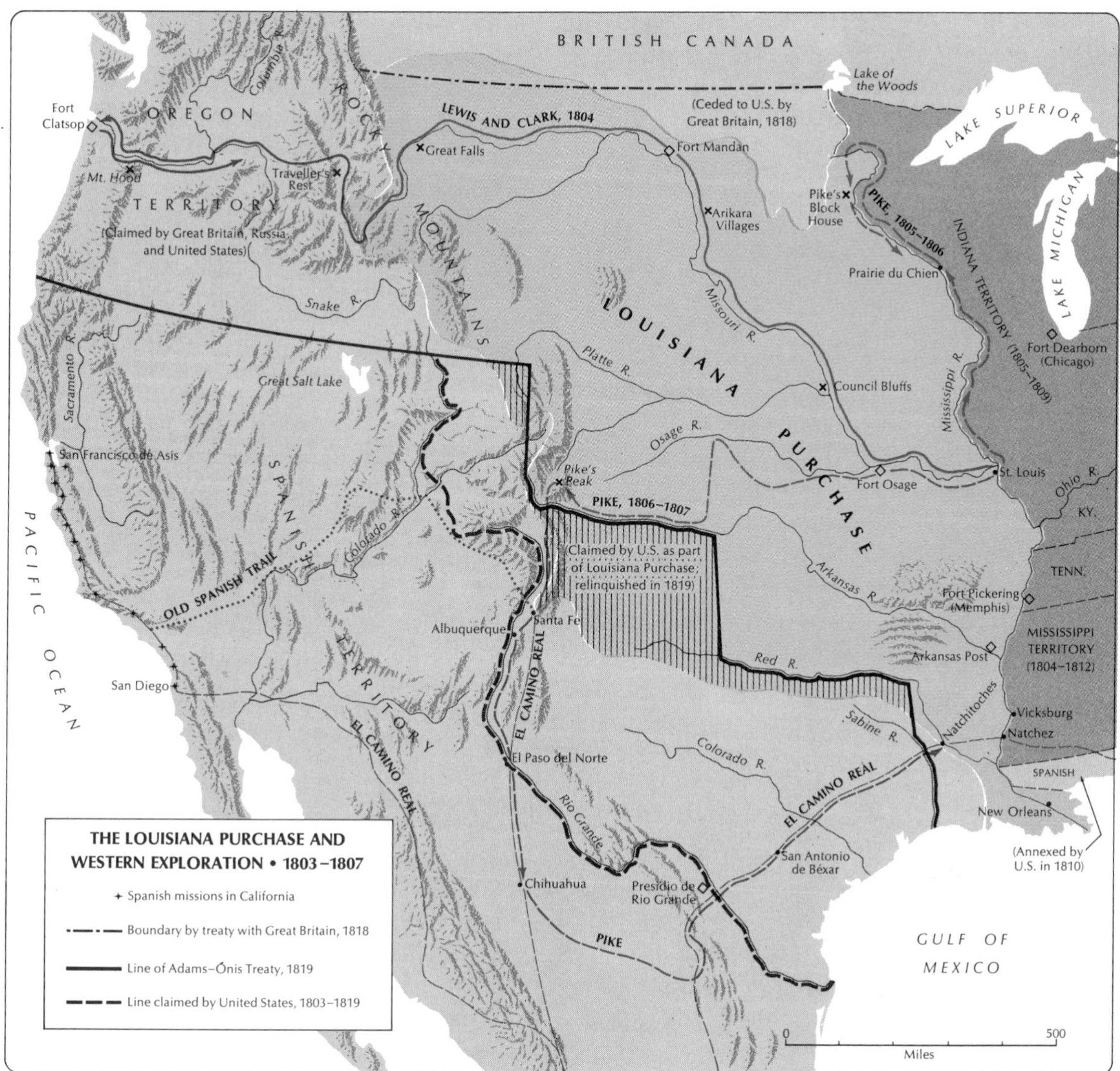

Rocky Mountains, down the Columbia River to the Pacific, and back again. Their trip strengthened the nation's claim to the northwestern territory—an area also claimed by Britain and Spain. The expedition also brought back information of interest to scholars and useful for fur traders and future settlers. For reasons which still remain mysterious, James Wilkinson, the territorial governor of Louisiana, sent Zebulon Pike to explore the source of the Mississippi in 1805–1806 and the Arkansas River in 1806–1807, but Pike's report was neither very reliable nor as useful as that of Lewis and Clark.

Western development interested the Jeffersonians as much as exploration. In admitting Ohio to the Union in 1803, Congress confirmed the promise of the Northwest Ordinance of 1785 by allocating one section (640 acres) in every township to the state to provide an endowment for education. Congress also allocated 3 percent of the revenue from the sale of federal lands in the state to be used for extending roads. The Federalists in 1800 had lowered the minimum size for federal land sales from 640 to 320 acres, reduced the down payment from one-half to one-quarter of the sale price, and allowed up to four years to pay. In the Land Law of 1804 Republicans reduced the price from $2 per acre to $1.64; the minimum purchase from 320 to only 160 acres.

Jefferson's most serious problem relating to Western development grew out of Georgia's Yazoo land fraud, a corrupt legislative deal perpetrated six years before he took office. In 1795 Georgia had "sold"—for under 2 cents apiece—30 million acres in the Yazoo area of modern Mississippi. Only one state legislator missed out on the benefits. The next Legislature, altered considerably in character, voided the sale, but not before speculators had made a number of sales to presumably innocent parties. An agreement between Georgia and the federal government in 1802, ceding the state's Western land claims to the United States, solved some of the problems, but Congressman John Randolph of Roanoke, so called to distinguish him from others in that numerous Virginia clan, blocked efforts to compensate those who had suffered when the original "sale" was voided. He continued to do so even after Marshall's Supreme Court ruled in *Fletcher v. Peck* (1810) that the constitutional provision which bars states from "impairing the Obligation of Contracts" negated Georgia's effort to undo the fraud. Congress at last approved a compensation bill in 1814 when Randolph's constituents had temporarily retired him.

Reelection and the Burr "Conspiracy"

Early portents for Jefferson's reelection were favorable. The Republicans did well in state elections after 1800 and gained in the congressional contest of 1802. The popular Louisiana Purchase of 1803 did nothing to reverse the trend. Jefferson's conciliatory attitude and moderate policies also evoked a generally favorable response. It is clear furthermore that partisan competition was bringing more of the "middling sort" to vote. Shaking off the "habit of subordination" which had long kept them from challenging their "betters," such people came forth to help repudiate federalism. To one old Federalist the explanation for the popularity of the Jeffersonians was that "The democrats [Jeffersonians] being men of inferior birth and breeding can more easily mix with the rabble. . . . They affect, with their dress and manners, to regard themselves of the Plebian order, and condescend to a familiarity of intercourse with the vulgar from which gentlemen would revolt."

Arguing that Easterners "cannot reconcile their habits, views, and interests with those of the South and West," diehard New England Federalists early in 1804 began a secessionist movement aimed at creating a "Northern Confederacy." Chief instigator of the movement was Timothy Pickering whom Adams had ousted as Secretary of State for opposing his peace policy. Hamilton refused to assist in bringing New York into the movement, but the Republican Vice President, Aaron Burr, was more cooperative. Anathema to Jeffersonians for his conduct in the contest of 1800, Burr determined to court Federalist support in a campaign for Governor of New York.

For the secessionists as for federalism in general the election of 1804 was a disaster. With Hamilton's help, the Republicans turned back Burr's effort to become Governor of New York. Jefferson, running for the Presidency against Charles C. Pinckney of South Carolina, lost only Connecticut and Delaware. His electoral margin, equaled by George Clinton in defeating his fellow New Yorker Rufus King for the vice presidency, was 162 to 14. In the new Congress, Republicans outnumbered their opponents about 5 to 1.

Burr blamed Hamilton for his defeat. Capitalizing on the growing vogue for dueling, he demanded "satisfaction" of Hamilton for alleged aspersions made during the campaign. Hamilton agreed to a duel, intending to fire without aiming to kill, but Burr did aim to kill and succeeded. Ostracized in the East as a result, Burr fled westward toward still more degradation.

Precisely what Burr intended to accomplish in the West no one has ever been able to determine. He sought $500,000 from the British for what they believed was another secessionist scheme. He plotted with General James Wilkinson, Jefferson's territorial governor of Louisiana, who was himself deeply involved in suspicious dealings with the Spanish. Whether the new political base which Burr sought was to be on American territory or Spanish, within the United States or outside it, nobody yet knows. In any case, Wilkinson betrayed him as the two were about to join forces. Burr fled southward from his Ohio River camp toward Spanish Florida, but was captured in Alabama.

At Burr's subsequent trial for treason two important constitutional developments occurred. First, Chief Justice Marshall, intent on embarrassing the President, tried to compel Jefferson to appear and testify. Jefferson refused, thereby fixing a precedent which strengthened the independence of the Presidency. Marshall did succeed, however, in frustrating the President's ambition to hang Aaron Burr. He did so by defining treason narrowly. The Constitution states that treason "shall consist only in levying war against them [the United States], or in adhering to their enemies, giving them aid and comfort." It specifies further, "No person shall be convicted of treason unless on the testimony of two witnesses to the same overt act, or on confession in open court." Reversing their usual roles in constitutional construction, Jefferson sought to have these words interpreted broadly, while Marshall became quite literal. He acquitted Burr because the government could not produce two witnesses to an overt act of treason. In doing so he altered an earlier opinion which he himself had written holding that "all those who perform any part however minute, or however remote from the scene of action, and who are actually leagued in the general conspiracy, are to be considered traitors."

Freedom of the Seas

The defense of American rights at sea troubled Jefferson throughout both his terms of office. Barbary pirates operating from the North African states of Morocco, Algiers, Tunis, and Tripoli were most bothersome in his first term. American independence had not only excluded

United States ships from the protection which Britain routinely purchased for vessels belonging to the king's subjects, but it also led Britain to encourage piracy directed at American ships in order to hinder the development of a major maritime rival. Payment of tribute to the pirates had always galled Jefferson, and in 1801 he indignantly rejected a demand from the Bashaw of Tripoli that payments be increased. In the ensuing war, American bombardment of Tripoli and assistance to an insurgent movement led to a negotiated settlement advantageous to the United States. American tribute and ransom payments for captured seamen continued until 1816 but at a relatively favorable rate compared with those paid by other powers. The nation also gained prestige.

By the time the Tripolitan War had ended, Jefferson was in still more serious trouble arising from American determination to carry on commerce with both Britain and France during the Napoleonic wars. After the collapse of his American enterprise, Napoleon turned his ambitions again to Europe and by 1805 had made himself master of much of the Continent. In the same year, however, a British fleet commanded by Horatio Nelson had crushed French naval power at the battle of Trafalgar. With Britain unable to challenge Napoleon on land and the French incapable of overcoming Britain's advantage at sea, each side, both the "tiger" and the "shark," turned increasingly to economic warfare, attempting to weaken the enemy by reducing its trade. As the chief neutral carriers, American ships fell victims in ever larger numbers to the measures of economic warfare imposed by each belligerent.

Britain's first significant act of economic war affecting the United States was a court decision of 1805 involving the American ship *Essex*. Between 1800 and 1805 the British had observed the rule fixed by their courts in the case of another American ship, the *Polly*. The *Polly* decision held that American ships carrying cargo from the French West Indies to France, a trade from which French policy had excluded them in peacetime, were not subject to seizure if they had first gone to an American port and cleared the cargo through an American customs office. Under that doctrine American ship owners had established a flourishing "reexport" trade, profitable to them and helpful to Napoleon. The *Essex* ruling jeopardized that trade by upholding seizure of such cargoes when the Americans could not prove that the shipment had been intended for the United States.

Blockade orders enforced by each belligerent added to the woes of American shipping. In 1806, Britain instituted a partial blockade of French-controlled ports; the Orders in Council of 1807 made it all-inclusive. Accordingly, American ships attempting to run the blockade were subject to seizure. Napoleon's policy, set forth in the Berlin Decrees of 1806 and the Milan Decrees of 1807, closed continental ports to British ships, a blow to Britain's export economy, and further declared Britain itself under blockade. The Milan Decrees called for seizure of any neutral ship bound to or from a British port. Although French seizures of American ships actually exceeded Britain's between 1807 and 1812, the long-range figures for the period from 1803 to 1812 show 917 British seizures to 558 for France.

British seizure of seamen from American ships, commonly called "impressment," aroused still more American indignation. Impressment alone was in fact sufficient cause for war. Behind the British policy lay a need for naval manpower which, especially before Trafalgar, was often desperate. Britain's traditional method of recruiting, dispatching "press gangs" from

A Humanist Leader

Thomas Jefferson, the nation's third president, was a leader whose capabilities, broad range of interests, and intelligence have been virtually unmatched in United States history. During his two terms as president, from 1801 to 1809, Jefferson demonstrated his talents as scholar, diplomat, legislator, natural scientist, practical economist, lawyer, political author, farmer, inventor, architect, landscape designer, university founder, educator, and advisor to the state and national governments. His inquiring mind and constant energy produced innovations that significantly shaped the development of all these areas of endeavor in America.

This watercolor portrait by Robert Field (above) shows Jefferson in his early sixties, at the time of his presidency.

Above: Courtesy of the New-York Historical Society, New York City

Before the Louisiana Purchase was completed, Jefferson persuaded Congress to appropriate $2,500 for a forty-three-man expedition headed by Capt. Meriwether Lewis (above) and William Clark (top) to explore the Missouri and Columbia Rivers and the Pacific northwest. From 1803–1806, they mapped the terrain, recorded details of Indian life, and closely observed the natural resources. Their journals were encyclopedic as the page at right proves.

The American Philosophical Society, founded in 1743 by Benjamin Franklin, was the first body to collect and investigate scientific knowledge. Jefferson supplied data, specimens, ideas, and reports, and served as Society president from 1797 to 1815.

Two Missouri bears (above) were shipped from a western expedition by Zebulon Pike. Jefferson startled Washington by keeping them on the White House lawn before he donated them to the Society. The western bird (below) was painted from specimens returned by Lewis and Clark by Charles Willson Peale, one of the most brilliant members of the Society. In the 1822 self-portrait at right, Peale reveals his own vast collection of natural history specimens: live and stuffed animals, plants, minerals, and the bones of a mastodon Peale excavated in upstate New York in 1801.

Far left, above and below: Independence National Historical Park
Left, center: Missouri Historical Society
Above and below: American Philosophical Society
Right: Pennsylvania Academy of the Fine Arts

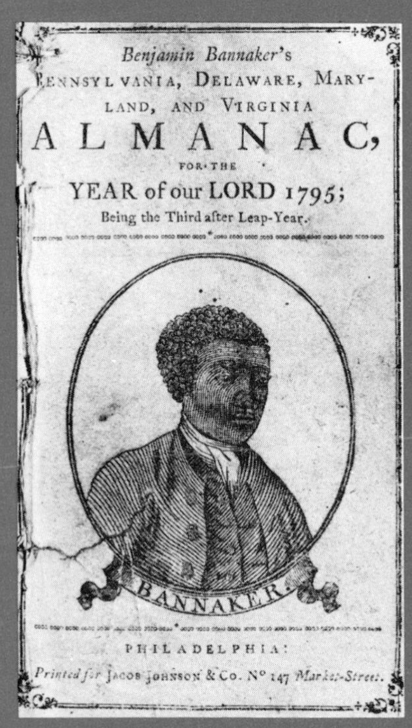

Benjamin Bannaker's
PENNSYLVANIA, DELAWARE, MARY-LAND, AND VIRGINIA
ALMANAC,
FOR THE
YEAR of our LORD 1795;
Being the Third after Leap-Year.

BANNAKER

PHILADELPHIA:
Printed for JACOB JOHNSON & Co. N° 147 Market-Street.

The son of slaves and largely self-educated, Benjamin Bannaker has been called "a black Benjamin Franklin" in tribute to his intellect and achievements. He surveyed land to lay out Washington, D.C., published highly accurate almanacs based on his own astronomical observations and calculations, and was an accomplshed engineer, naturalist, and musician. In 1791, Bannaker wrote asking Jefferson to reconcile his slaveholding with his libertarian philosophy.

Jefferson sincerely opposed slavery as an institution. He represented slaves in court, argued that children of slaves were born free, created a Virginia law forbidding further importation of slaves, and insinuated nonslavery clauses into the Northwest Ordinance. Nevertheless, he held about 150 slaves which he had inherited. He felt "to give liberty, or rather, to abandon persons whose habits have been formed in slavery is like abandoning children." Although he replied to Bannaker, "No body wishes more than I do to see such proofs as you exhibit, that nature has given to our black brethren talents equal to those of other colours of man, and that the appearance of a want of them is owing merely to the degraded condition of their existence both in Africa and America . . . ," he suspected in other writings that "the blacks . . . are inferior to the whites in the endowments both of body and mind."

Since his youth, Jefferson had eagerly investigated American Indian life and customs. He questioned travelers and traders from the West, sought out Indian visitors and local tribesmen in the East, and compiled extensive word lists of many Indian languages.

One important mission of the Lewis and Clark expedition was to establish good relations with the tribes they encountered. All chiefs received medals (right) showing President Jefferson and the hands of an Indian and white man clasped in "Peace and Friendship" under a crossed pipe and hatchet. They also received an American flag and a military uniform coat, hat, and feather.

The Osage chiefs on the opposite page were portrayed by Charles Balthazar Julien Fevret de Saint-Mémin. His technique satisfied Jefferson's passion for accuracy: first he traced the profile directly from the subject—a kind of physionotrace*—then added colors and detail in crayon.*

Left, above: Courtesy of the New-York Historical Society, New York City
Left, below: Courtesy of the American Museum of Natural History
Right, all pictures: Courtesy of the New-York Historical Society, New York City

Jefferson constantly applied his wide knowledge of science and mechanics to solving practical problems. A prolific inventor, he filled his home with devices of his own design, including a swivel chair and America's first dumb-waiter. He also designed a central heating plant. Two notable inventions are shown here. The mould-board plow (above) was easier to handle and turned a deeper furrow than those in general use. A polygraph with two pens (below) helped to ease the problem of his enormous correspondence: as he wrote with one pen, the other traced an exact copy on a second page.

Architecture was one of Jefferson's deepest interests. After traveling to France with the French architect Charles L. A. Clérisseau, Jefferson extensively remodeled and enlarged Monticello (right). Greatly influenced by the temples of antiquity, he helped to foster the Roman revival in America.

Above and below: Thomas Jefferson Memorial Foundation
Right: Bradley Smith, Photo Researchers

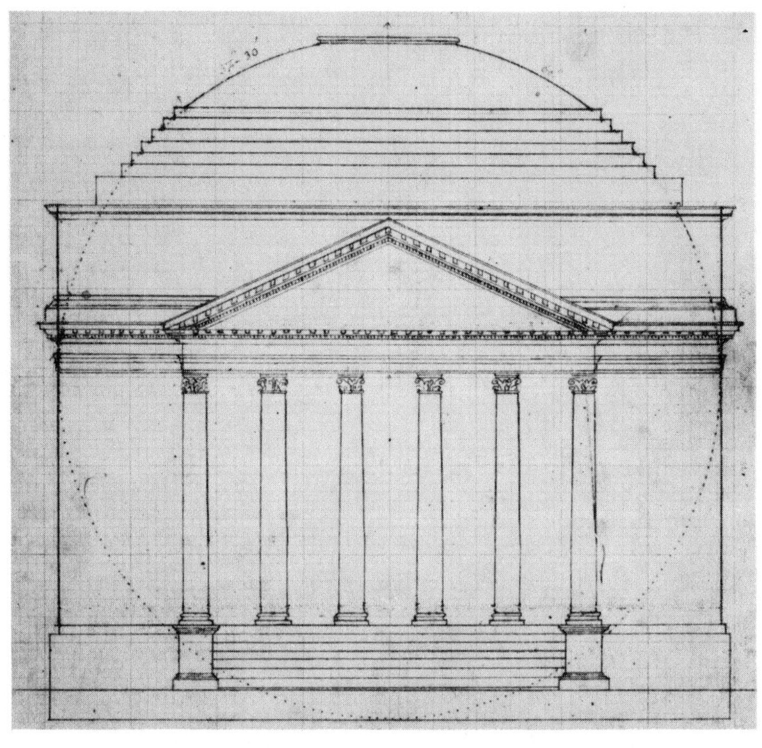

The house "Bremo" in Fluvanna County, Va. (left, below), shows the quiet elegance typical of Jefferson's influence on residential designs. Of all his architectural projects, the greatest was the building of the University of Virginia. He designed and supervised its construction during his last years. Jefferson's drawing for the library rotunda (left, above) combines the classic columns and Roman Parthenon dome he so much admired. The unusual serpentine walls (right) border the campus walks. The impressive symmetry and sweep of his campus design are evident on the next page.

Left, above: University of Virginia Library, Manuscripts Division
Left, below: Library of Congress
Right: Library of Congress
Following page: George Cserna

shorthanded vessels into port cities to shanghai a number of men sufficient to meet the need, was largely offset by the high rate of desertion, especially in American ports. Repelled by the British navy's brutal discipline, abominable food, and deplorable conditions, sailors deserted in droves to take jobs in the growing American merchant marine, in which conditions were better and the pay some three to five times higher. By 1812 about half the sailors on American ships plying foreign markets were British.

Eager to combat the rise of a rival merchant marine as well as to meet its naval manpower needs, Britain encouraged impressment from American ships at sea. Even when the sailors taken in such instances were actually British subjects, the offense to American sovereignty was great. Compounding the offense, Britain not only refused to respect naturalized American citizenship but seized many native Americans. In the decade before 1812, between 4,000 and 6,000 Americans, mostly native citizens, were impressed into the British navy.

The crowning indignity in this respect occurred in 1807. Several British deserters had enlisted for service aboard the new American warship *Chesapeake,* after the United States had rejected Britain's efforts to recover them by diplomatic means. When the *Chesapeake* put to sea, the British navy's *Leopard* demanded permission to search the ship for British deserters. Commodore James Barron of the *Chesapeake* refused, whereupon the *Leopard* fired, killing three Americans and wounding eighteen. After Barron's capitulation, the British removed four men: one British deserter; two American Negroes, who had deserted after enlisting voluntarily in the British navy; and one other American, who had "deserted" after suffering impressment.

Rather than yield to the outraged demand for war, Jefferson persuaded Congress to enact an embargo. Hastily drafted and promulgated just at the end of 1807, the embargo barred departure of American ships for any foreign port. In justification of the prohibition, Jefferson argued that "our commerce is so valuable to them [Europeans] that they will be glad to purchase it when the only price we ask is to do us justice." The embargo did hurt the British, who had taken nearly half of all American exports in 1806, but it hurt Americans too. The index of farm prices fell from a previous high of 106 in 1805 to a low of 71 in 1808. Cotton exports fell to about one-fourth of the average of the previous five years. Many Americans, particularly Federalists, regarded the consequences of the embargo as worse than impressment and ship seizures which it was designed to combat. Evasion and even defiance were common, especially in the Northeast where sympathy for Britain was strong.

Unpopular as it was in the Northeast, Jefferson's embargo did not seriously threaten the election of Secretary of State James Madison as his successor. Seizing eagerly on Washington's precedent, Jefferson declined a third term, commenting later on the enormity of his relief "on shaking off the shackles of power." Supported by Jefferson, Madison easily beat back challenges by James Monroe and George Clinton, winning 89 of the 95 votes cast in the Republican congressional caucus which served as a nominating convention. The Federalist presidential ticket of Pinckney and King, which had won only 14 electoral votes in 1804, now rose to 47, but Madison won 122. Clinton remained Vice President. The Federalists made no gains in the Senate and, despite doubling their strength in the House of Representatives, still were outnumbered there by nearly 2 to 1.

Before leaving office, Jefferson acquiesced

in the repeal of the embargo and the enactment of the Non-Intercourse Act of 1809. A compromise pleasing to neither the advocates of war nor those who merely wanted the embargo repealed, the Non-Intercourse Act banned both import and export trade with either Britain or France. However, it authorized the President to restore trade with France or Britain if either power ceased to violate American maritime rights. On its face the Non-Intercourse law seemed strong, but in fact it would afford Madison little leverage against the British.

Conclusion

Jefferson and his Republican followers significantly altered the course of the new nation's development. They created the nation's first political party, outmoding the nonpartisan political system envisaged by the Founding Fathers and leading to its replacement by an enduring two-party system. Ousting Federalist John Adams from the Presidency peacefully and in accordance with constitutional procedures, they marked a milestone in the evolution of democratic government. At the same time they managed the transfer of political power from Northeastern merchants to a coalition of Northern farmers and Southern planters, under whose guidance American society became less elitist and more egalitarian, less mercantilistic and more favorable to laissez faire, less nationalist and more disposed to exalt states' rights. European developments enabled them to double the nation's size through the Louisiana Purchase but placed them at the same time in the dilemma of trying to maintain the right of Americans to carry on commerce with each of two major belligerent powers committed to prolonged economic warfare against the other.

SUGGESTED READINGS

No consensus is yet evident among historians on the emergence of political parties. Charles A. Beard in *Economic Origins of Jeffersonian Democracy** (2d ed., 1940) saw continuity between the Antifederalists and the Jeffersonian Republicans and assumed that persisting class differences underlay such political rivalry. Alfred F. Young in *The Democratic Republicans of New York* (1967) sees essential continuity in New York from radical Whigs to Antifederalists to Republicans on the one hand and from conservative Whigs to Federalists on the other, nevertheless taking exception to Beard on many points. Noble Cunningham has studied the organization of the Republicans in *The Jeffersonian Republicans: The Formation of Party Organization** (1957). He denies the existence of the continuity asserted by Beard and Young. He insists also that party organization began in Congress under Madison's leadership and filtered down from there to the states. Other works of importance on the topic, most of them inclined toward Cunningham's view, include Paul Goodman's *The Democratic-Republicans of Massachusetts* (1964); Carl E. Prince's *New Jersey's Jeffersonian Republicans* (1967); J. E. Charles's *The Origins of the American Party System* (1956); W. N. Chambers's *Political Parties in a New Nation* (1963), largely a synthesis of earlier studies; Morton Borden's *Parties and Politics in the Early Republic** (1967), similar to Chambers's work, but shorter; M. J. Dauer's *The Adams Federalists** (1953); H. M. Tinkcom's *Republicans and Federalists in Pennsylvania* (1950); Staughton Lynd's *Antifederalism in Dutchess County* (1962); and E. P. Link's *Democratic-Republican Societies* (1942).

Many of the biographies cited in the preceding chapter are equally useful here, especially Malone's *Jefferson* and Brant's *Madison*. In addition see Raymond Walters, Jr.'s *Albert Gallatin* (1957) and

Nathan Schachner's *Aaron Burr* (1937). S. G. Kurtz's *The Presidency of John Adams* (1957) is a careful study. Page Smith's two-volume biography of *John Adams* (1962) is interesting but not very political.

Many of the diplomatic studies cited in the *Suggested Readings* after Chapter 8 are also relevant here. In addition see the two excellent monographs, Bradford Perkins's *The First Rapprochement* (1955) and Alexander DeConde's *The Quasi-war** (1966).

J. M. Smith's *Freedom's Fetters* (1956) is a full and fascinating account of the Alien and Sedition Acts, but it needs to be supplemented by Leonard Levy's *Legacy of Suppression** (1960) for long-range perspective on the evolution of the legal concept of freedom of speech. The best source on the Virginia and Kentucky Resolutions is Adrienne Koch's *Jefferson and Madison: The Great Collaboration* (1950).

Dumas Malone's great biography of Jefferson has not yet reached the presidential years. Until it does, students will have to make do with Gilbert Chinard's *Thomas Jefferson** (2d ed., 1939) or Nathan Schachner's unsympathetic study of the same title (2 vols., 1951). Several works, however, probe Jefferson's philosophy and its role in American history. Among the best of these are C. M. Wiltse's *The Jeffersonian Tradition in American Democracy** (1935); Merrill Peterson's *The Jeffersonian Image in the American Mind** (1960); Adrienne Koch's *The Philosophy of Thomas Jefferson* (1943); D. J. Boorstin's *The Lost World of Thomas Jefferson** (1948). E. T. Mudge explores the thought of a major Jeffersonian thinker in *The Social Philosophy of John Taylor of Caroline* (1939). Henry Adams was less than charitable to the erratic *John Randolph* (2d ed., 1917), although conservative Russell Kirk in *Randolph of Roanoke* (1951) found his thought congenial. Norman Risjord has recounted the political history of Randolph's following in *The Old Republicans* (1956).

For a general history of Jefferson's administrations the basic source remains the majestic work of Henry Adams, *A History of the United States of America during the Administrations of Thomas Jefferson and James Madison* (9 vols., 1889–1891). Contrary to the implication of his dreadful title, Adams wrote brilliantly, albeit with an understandable family bias against his subjects. Numerous paperback abridgements of his work are available. L. D. White in *The Jeffersonians** (1951) continues the superb administrative history begun in *The Federalists.* Alexander Balinky's *Albert Gallatin* (1958) criticizes the fiscal theories and policies of Jefferson's financial expert. Morton Borden in *The Federalism of James A. Bayard* (1955) looks at Jefferson's administration through the eyes of an opposition leader. J. S. Young's *The Washington Community,* 1800–1829 (1966) points up the increasing weakness of presidential leadership and the general confusion and insignificance of the federal government. C. P. Magrath in *Yazoo* (1966) clarifies the complexities of that issue.

Several of the works on political parties which were listed in the previous chapter remain applicable to Jefferson's administration. In addition there is the highly interesting study by D. H. Fischer, *The Revolution of American Conservatism* (1965), a study of the Federalist party after 1800, which finds Federalists very much alive and adopting Jeffersonian tactics and rhetoric. In *The Jeffersonian Republicans: Party Operations,* 1801–1809 (1963), Noble Cunningham carries on the work begun in his study of the formation of party organizations, cited above.

On Marshall's Court, the best introduction is E. S. Corwin's *John Marshall and the Constitution* (1919). From this it is quite a jump to A. J. Beveridge's four-volume appreciation, *The Life of John Marshall* (1916–1919), a classic illustration of partisan biography, or to R. K. Faulkner's *The Jurisprudence of John Marshall* (1968). Also see the weighty work of C. G. Haines, *The Role of the Supreme Court in American Government and Politics,* 1789–1835 (1944).

On the Burr incident, T. P. Abernethy in *The Burr Conspiracy* (1954) condemns the accused, while Nathan Schachner in *Aaron Burr* (1937) acquits him. J. R. Jacob's *Tarnished Warrior* (1938) provides no whitewash for General Wilkinson.

On the Louisiana Purchase the major works are E. W. Lyon's *Louisiana in French Diplomacy* (1934); George Dangerfield's *Chancellor Robert R. Livingston of New York* (1960); and Irving Brant's *James Madison: Secretary of State* (1953). W. H. Goetzmann's *Army Exploration in the American West* (1959) puts Lewis and Clark in perspective. Bernard De Voto edited *The Journals of Lewis and Clark** (1953) in one sparkling volume. General diplomatic studies of major importance are Louis N. Sear's *Jefferson and the Embargo* (1927) and Bradford Perkins's *Prologue to War** (1961), which takes up in 1805 where his *First Rapprochement* (1955) leaves off.

* indicates availability in paperback.

10

Mr. Madison's War

EUROPEAN CIVILIZATION as a whole was in great turmoil when James Madison became President of the United States. Napoleon's conquests encompassed nearly all of Europe west of Austria, and before the year 1809 had ended, Austria itself would have become yet another satellite of France. Even the Pope was Napoleon's prisoner. Only two nations offered any hope for the redemption of Europe from the conqueror's rule: Britain, supreme at sea since Trafalgar and protected by the English Channel from Napoleon's armies; and Russia, seemingly secured by its peripheral position and its vastness. To Napoleon the independence of each was an irresistible challenge.

From the very outset, Madison's administration was necessarily preoccupied with the defense of American honor and trade against offensive measures enforced by Britain and France in their economic warfare. Insults and injuries multiplied while American indignation mounted and the economy suffered. American reprisals as well as the actions of the belligerents restricted the nation's business. The country became bitterly divided over the proper American response and at last plunged into an unpopular and potentially disastrous war with Britain, a war which neither belligerent really wanted. Despite incredible mismanagement in the early stages of the war, the nation emerged at its conclusion with its territory intact, more strongly united than ever, and enjoying for the first time international recognition as a nation of consequence.

James Madison

James Madison, like his older friend and frequent collaborator, Thomas Jefferson, was a Virginia planter of aristocratic status, deeply dedicated to public service. His family was neither so prominent nor so wealthy as Jefferson's, but Madison had enjoyed a tutored education in the classics and further study, including a year of postgraduate work, at Princeton. Anglican in background, Madison disavowed sectarianism during his stay at Presbyterian Princeton where he showed great interest in theology, as well as in philosophy, science, and public law. Princeton had been a hotbed of anti-British sentiment while Madison was there, but what seems to have done most to heighten the young scholar's political concern was what he called the "hell-conceived principle of [religious] persecution" which his fellow Anglicans were then following with reference to revivalist denominations in Virginia. Together with Thomas Jefferson, he played a major part in ending that state's support of religion and establishing a greater measure of religious freedom. During the Revolution, Madison served first in the Virginia Legislature and then in the Continental Congress, taking a leading role in each.

Like his predecessors in the Presidency, James Madison had secured his place in history before becoming Chief Executive. His first great distinction came in consolidating the shaky postwar Union of the American states into an effective nation. Along with Hamilton, Madison deserves primary credit for bringing about the Constitutional Convention of 1787. No man was more influential than he in determining at that Convention what manner of government would serve best to create "a more perfect Union . . . , promote the general welfare, and secure the blessings of liberty to . . . posterity." In the struggle over ratification of the Constitution in Virginia, Madison's leadership was instrumental in defeating the opposition forces led by Patrick Henry. Madison's contributions to *The Federalist,* while not widely influential at the time, rank still among the best American writings in political science.

His great achievements did not end with ratification. In the First Congress no man did so much as did James Madison in shaping the innumerable suggestions for constitutional amendments into the ten proposals which became the Bill of Rights. Finally, it was Madison even more than the titular leader who gave the initial guidance in the formation of the Jeffersonian Republican party, the first political party in the United States.

The prospects for Madison's Presidency appeared mixed as he assumed office. In terms of experience he was supremely qualified. To his impressive earlier record he had added eight years as Secretary of State, during which time he had been a principal consultant of President Jefferson. His popular wife, Dolley, was already the leader of Washington society. At 58 he himself still possessed the capacity for hard work and rigorous thinking which had served him so well in the past. Yet Jefferson's embargo had revived the seemingly moribund Federalist opposition, and within Madison's own party extreme partisans continued to regard his moderation with distrust. Perhaps most serious of the new President's handicaps were certain of his own characteristics. Small in stature, relatively frail and shy, he lacked what one critic called "commanding talents." Because he was less forceful than his predecessor, Madison was less successful in overcoming the Republican dogma which affirmed that the President should merely execute policies fixed by Congress rather than fix them himself.

More Controversy over Commerce

What most Americans wanted when Madison took office was a policy which would compel the two major belligerents, Britain and France, to permit Americans to carry on business as usual with both. While Napoleon, under his Continental System, seized American ships which traded with Britain, the British, under their Orders in Council of 1807 (revised early in 1809), sought to seize any American ship engaging in trade with French-controlled Europe. These policies violated traditional concepts of neutral rights, impugned American sovereignty, and imposed losses not only on individual Americans but on the American economy as a whole.

How seriously belligerent restrictions on neutral trade affected American prosperity is difficult to determine. One rough indicator is the yearly value of American exports. From the beginning of the wars in Europe in 1793 until the imposition of severe commercial restrictions in 1807, the value of American exports, including reexports of French West Indian products, had increased four times. From 1807 until the American declaration of war in 1812, the highest yearly total (1810) was more than one-third below that of 1807. The declining volume in the American reexport of French West Indian products accounted for much of the reduction. American policies, such as the embargo and non-intercourse laws, also contributed.

Exports of cotton and tobacco, when unimpeded by American law, did not fall off greatly, but prices fell as supply outran effective demand. In the South and West where commercial farmers depended heavily upon such exports for their income, resentment against Britain, in particular, ran high. "The necessity . . . of resisting the British orders and forcing our way to those markets where there is a demand [for American products]," stated a Kentucky senator, "must be evident to every one."

Even more serious, perhaps, than the detriment to American economic interests was the affront to American pride. Impressment was clearly the most offensive British action in this respect, but after the *Chesapeake* incident of 1807 it became less inflammatory. Since Napoleon no longer challenged their naval supremacy, the British slacked off on impressment, but they neither renounced the practice not stopped it entirely.

Ship seizures continued to give great offense. As early as 1807, the British consul in New York observed that it was "highly grating to the Feelings of an independent Nation to perceive that . . . every Ship coming in or going out of their Harbours [is] examined vigorously in Sight of the Shore by British Squadrons stationed within their Waters." To Americans only one generation removed from the Revolution, the idea of British squadrons enforcing British regulation of American trade was entirely too reminiscent of what Congressman John C. Calhoun referred to as "the colonial state to which again that power is endeavoring to reduce us." In such circumstances, particularly as the British persistently and haughtily rejected American protests, Americans began to advocate what they envisioned as a second war for independence. The fact that such a war, as a British leader observed, would virtually ally "this favourite child of freedom . . . with the oppressor of the world" was a consequence which concerned many Federalists but relatively few Republicans. For most Republicans, it appears, immediate concern for American honor and trade obscured the potential menace of Napoleon's unbounded ambition for imperial power.

When President Madison took up his duties in 1809, Americans could trade legally with neither Britain nor France but could, under the Non-Intercourse Act, conduct commerce with neutrals. The American price for restoring free trade with Britain was the latter's renunciation of impressment and the termination of Britain's interference in American trade with French-controlled areas of Europe. Britain regarded this price as too high. The British Admiralty valued impressment as a policy which might again prove useful in an emergency to fill the crews of the royal navy. Britain's leaders did not feel that they could safely rely on the American government to return deserters. To give immunity from British seizure to American ships carrying products to France would not only benefit the French economy but also stimulate the growth of the American merchant marine as a rival to Britain's in the world carrying trade. Indeed the American merchant marine did double its size between 1802 and 1810. Finally, the British were in no great rush to secure repeal of the Non-Intercourse Act, because it operated to their benefit. France, because of its inferior naval status, could not secure American goods from neutral ports, but Britain's naval superiority enabled British merchants to conduct an extensive business with Americans at neutral sites.

Thus, far from yielding to American demands, Britain greeted the Madison administration with proposals of its own. Construing the repeal of the embargo as a sign of weakening American will and anticipating that Americans might perceive Napoleon as a threat to American as well as to European security, the British early in 1809 presented terms designed to make the United States their nonbelligerent ally against France. Specifically, the British government suggested that the United States end all restrictions on trade with Britain but retain the ban on trade with France. London went so far as to ask authorization for British ships to seize American vessels trading with France in violation of American law.

To elicit American approval of its proposals, Britain relied upon its youthful, inexperienced, and very pro-American Minister to Washington, David Erskine. In April, 1809, Erskine concluded an executive agreement with the United States, promising revocation of the British Orders in Council insofar as they restricted American trade with France in return for resumption of American trade with Britain. Madison had committed the United States to keep non-intercourse in effect against France, thus meeting Britain's terms except for that authorizing the British to enforce American law against American ships. However, apparently because the agreement put enforcement in American rather than in British hands, the Tory ministry rejected it. Before learning of their action, many Americans had dispatched ships for Britain, and the nation in general had joyfully concluded that the controversy with England had been resolved at last without resort to war.

In selecting a replacement for the now-discredited Erskine, the British compounded the indignation aroused in the United States by repudiation of the Erskine agreement. The new British Minister in Washington was Francis James ("Copenhagen") Jackson, a stiff-necked martinet, known chiefly as the messenger who had borne a British ultimatum to the Danes prior to the British navy's bombardment of Copenhagen. Even before Jackson's arrival on September 8, 1809, Madison had restored the ban on trade with Britain which had been suspended in June in accord with the Erskine agreement. When Jackson did make his appearance, he conducted himself so offensively that the government soon refused even to accept communications from him. Britain recalled him early in 1810, but he remained in the United States for almost a full year, during which time he encouraged and even subsidized Federalist attacks upon the administration. Meanwhile Britain sent no one to replace him; William Pinkney, the American Minister in London, came home convinced that Britain would yield nothing unless faced by really damaging economic sanctions.

Republicans in Congress were little more hopeful than Pinkney. In May, 1810, they enacted a law known since as Macon's Bill Number Two, immortalizing its not-very-enthusiastic sponsor, Nathaniel Macon, chairman of the House Foreign Affairs Committee. The new law meekly reopened trade with both Britain and France but promised to reward the belligerent which ended its restrictions upon American trade by reimposing non-intercourse against that nation's enemy if it failed to do the same.

Before learning of Macon's Bill, Napoleon deeply offended the United States. In his Rambouillet Decree (dated March 23, but not published until May 14) he announced his intention to confiscate all American vessels which had entered French-controlled ports during the preceding year in violation of the Non-Intercourse Act. He made a large haul of American vessels in this manner—as he had during the period of the embargo by his Bayonne Decree of 1808—although he no longer kept up his former pretense that the ships which he seized were really British rather than American.

When he learned of Macon's Bill Number Two, Napoleon, ever alert to the opportunity for self-serving duplicity, took full advantage of it. He instructed his Foreign Minister, the Duc de Cadore, to inform the Americans that his Berlin and Milan decrees would be revoked with reference to the United States, effective November 1. Though incensed by Napoleon's seizure of American vessels, Madison proclaimed on November 2 that non-intercourse would take effect against Britain at the end of three months unless she, too, repealed her obnoxious restrictions on American trade. In reality, Napoleon had no intention of abandoning his Continental System but wished only to cause Great Britain to relax its Orders in Council or to see his enemy incur increased troubles, perhaps war, with the Americans if it refused to do so. Madison may well have suspected Napoleon's insincerity, but the Cadore letter afforded a welcome opportunity to increase the pressure on Britain. "It promises us, at least," the President wrote, "an extrication from the dilemma of a mortifying peace, or war with both the great belligerents." More specifically, such a course would afford the United States the advantage of "but one contest on our hands at a time."

Meanwhile, the British economy had at last begun to experience serious dislocations. A general depression prevailed after July, 1810. It was most acute among manufacturers producing for export and may have owed as much to increasing productive capacity as to French and American interference with sales. Spurred by domestic depression, the government increased the issuance of "licenses" for trade with Napoleon's Continent. In so doing, the British were abandoning the efforts to impose scarcities on Napoleon in order to keep up sales, income, and employment in Britain itself. The government also licensed reexport of commodities secured from the Western Hemisphere, thus benefiting the British merchant marine and merchants in addition to manufacturers. To Americans the licensing system was particularly infuriating because it permitted British subjects to trade with their enemy while denying that opportunity to neutral Americans. Licensing had transformed the Orders in Council from an anti-French to an anti-American policy.

Madison's resumption of non-intercourse with Britain early in 1811 only aggravated Britain's economic difficulties. The United States had long afforded Britain its best market, buying not only more than continental Europe but as much as one-third of all British exports. Hard-pressed British manufacturers, ably organized by the Whig opposition, clamored insistently that the Tory government repeal its Orders in Council in order to permit American trade with Napoleon's Europe. If the Orders were repealed, there was good reason to hope that the United States would resume importation from Britain. Resumption of American importation would afford short-run relief to British manufacturers and reduce the incentive for Americans to develop their own manufacturing establishments and thus secure economic independence from Britain.

Throughout 1811 the Tory government refused to repeal its Orders in Council, even though such an act would have alleviated severe distress at home and might also have averted the impending war with the United States. The leaders persuaded themselves fully that the repeal of the Orders in Council would bring too much economic benefit to France and would, in addition, tend to undermine Britain's traditional dominance of the seas by giving the American merchant marine a competitive advantage. They discounted not only the likelihood of war with the United States but also the risk involved should it occur. Finally, in June, 1812, after the assassination of the Prime Minister who had conceived the Orders, the new administration yielded. Professing to believe that Napoleon's fraudulent St. Cloud decree (announced the month before but dated a year earlier) had actually ended his Continental System, the government repealed its Orders in Council on June 23, 1812. Unfortunately, the United States had lost its patience a few days before.

The United States Declares War

By 1812, a great many Americans had come to the conclusion that there must be war with Britain—if not with France as well. Indignation over the restrictions on American commerce was undoubtedly the major force contributing to the war fever, but in considering how the United States might help itself and hurt its enemy in the event of war, American attention focused on the northern and southern frontiers.

In the South, Americans had long cast covetous eyes on Spanish Florida. In the face of diplomatic resistance by the British as well as the Spanish, Jefferson had failed to validate his wishful contention that the Louisiana Purchase included West Florida, but circumstances had altered by 1810. Spain, occupied by Napoleon's forces since 1808, was in no position to resist determined American action. Britain might do so, but by 1810 the prospect of war with Britain was perhaps more likely to spur Americans on than make them pause to consider, for either East or West Florida in Spanish hands could well afford the British convenient bases for an invasion of the United States. In any event, when Americans living in the Baton Rouge area of Spanish West Florida revolted successfully in 1810, Madison quickly proclaimed West Florida (broadly defined to include the coastal regions of modern Mississippi and Alabama as well as eastern Louisiana) part of the United States. The Spanish, however, defiantly clung to their fort on Mobile Bay. With congressional encouragement, Madison sent General George Mathews, a former Governor of Georgia, to arrange a similar takeover of East Florida in 1811. Since Americans were relatively less numerous in that area, however, the military action partook far more of an aggressive invasion than of internal insurrection. Although Mathews occupied much of modern Florida, Madison, embarrassed by the general's lack of subtlety, recalled him and promised to restore Spanish control.

In the North, Americans sought territorial gain more to hurt Britain than to help themselves. "If the English do not give us the satisfaction we demand," Thomas Jefferson had stated privately at the time of the *Chesapeake* crisis of 1807, "we will take Canada." In the years that followed, more and more Americans of all sections came to realize that seizing Canada was the only way in which the relatively impotent United States could retaliate against British insults to American honor and interference with American trade.

For the frontier dwellers of the Northwest, there was an additional incentive to seize Canada. Recognizing the prospect of American invasion, British officials in Canada had long bent every effort to make sure that when war came the Indians would be on Britain's side. Their Indian agent Matthew Elliott was particularly zealous in providing the Indians with weapons and in encouraging even those who lived within the borders of the United States to resist forcefully the extension of American settlement. By 1811, British officials, fearful that Indian attacks might bring the Americans to declare war and invade Canada, had experienced a change of heart and were trying to exercise restraint, but a talented Shawnee chieftain, Tecumseh, had already begun organizing tribes both north and south of the Ohio River for offensive action.

While Tecumseh was organizing in the south, William Henry Harrison, territorial governor of Indiana, collected a large force of frontiersmen with the aim of striking first. At Tippecanoe Creek on November 7, 1811, the Indians, led in Tecumseh's absence by his brother, the Prophet, surprised Harrison, but he beat off their attack, destroyed the village which was their headquarters, and retired. No war resulted, but the incident deepened the conviction among northwestern frontiersmen that Indian attacks would plague them as long as the British remained in Canada.

At sea as well as in the Southwest and the Northwest, Americans were beginning to do more than make diplomatic representations and enforce retaliatory economic measures. When Macon's Bill Number Two reopened American trade with France, Britain had resumed an active patrol of the American coast. The royal navy not only seized vessels bound for France but began again to impress seamen from American ships. Early in 1811, the British warship *Guerrière* aroused a storm of indignation by stopping a coastal vessel just outside New York Harbor and impressing a native American. A United States Navy frigate, the *President*, put to sea with orders to protect American trade and in May, 1811, exchanged fire with the *Little Belt*, a smaller British vessel which the Americans mistook for the *Guerrière*. To the American public, the death of nine British seamen and the wounding of twenty-three others aboard the *Little Belt* avenged the loss in the *Chesapeake* incident of 1807 far more satisfactorily than the offer of compensation belatedly brought by the new British Minister.

America's more belligerent attitude became still clearer when the new Congress, elected in 1810, convened in November, 1811, for its first session. The election had brought no more than the usual turnover in Congress, but dynamic new leaders, dubbed "War Hawks" by their opponents, quickly took control. Chief among them was the new Speaker of the House of Representatives, Henry Clay of Kentucky. Youthful, vigorous, and fiercely nationalistic, Clay had argued in the Senate in 1810 for forceful resistance to "British slavery." Now he stacked the House committees, especially Foreign Affairs and Military Affairs, with fellow War Hawks, such as Peter B. Porter of western New York, John C. Calhoun and Langdon Cheves of South Carolina, and Felix Grundy of Tennessee. The Senate was less bellicose, but the President and Secretary of State James Monroe—whom Madison had chosen to replace the incompetent and politically disloyal Robert Smith—were no less determined than Clay's War Hawks, although distinctly more guarded in their public statements.

Madison's State of the Union message of November, 1811, set the tone. He accused Britain of "trampling on rights which no independent nation can relinquish" and suggested that "Congress will feel the duty of putting the United States into an armor and an attitude demanded by the crisis." Monroe's private discussions with the House Foreign Affairs Committee led one member to conclude, "The present session [of Congress] will not be closed, without an *arrangement*, or an actual *war* with Great Britain." To prepare for war Congress authorized an increase in the regular Army, which then had less than 6,000 men (although 10,000 were authorized) to a total of 35,000 officers and men. In addition, Congress provided for 50,000 state militiamen to be called into service at the President's discretion. Left unresolved was the constitutional question of whether such militia forces could serve outside the United States or merely "repel invasions." Naval expansion measures, although appealing to the opposition Federalists, roused ancient Republican prejudices and appeared futile to many in view of Britain's unsurpassable advantage. Consequently Congress defied Clay's leadership by refusing to increase the nations' naval forces. The martial spirit overcame the Republicans' traditional antipathy to taxes, but they were careful to make the revenue measures effective only upon a declaration of war.

To President Madison, intent upon preparing for war with Britain, the congressional measures appeared highly inadequate and, as such, likely to confirm the suspicion which many Federalists shared with the British that the war measures were merely a bluff, designed to secure concessions without war. Seeking to rally public opinion against Britain, Madison in March forwarded for publication by Congress the reports of a disaffected British spy which he had purchased from a French intermediary. These "Henry letters," Madison charged, showed that the British had sent their author, one Captain John Henry, into New England to work with malcontents there toward the goal of "destroying the Union and forming the eastern part thereof into a political connection with Great Britain." Unfortunately for Madison's purpose, news arrived at about the same time that French warships had destroyed several American ships carrying flour to the British armies in Spain. Consequently, many Americans were again made to feel as eager for war with France as with Britain, despite the impracticability of such a course and the difficulty of finding ways to inflict injury on France.

On April 1, 1812, Madison took another step toward war. Recent news from Britain contained no hint that the end of the Orders in Council was near. Rather it seemed, as the President expressed it, "that they prefer war with us to a repeal of their Orders in Council." In order to get American ships beyond the clutches of the British navy should hostilities begin, the President recommended that Congress enact a sixty-day embargo. He had every intention of seeking a declaration of war at the end of that period if the British had not in the meantime altered their Orders in Council to permit American trade with French-controlled ports. Congress, understanding fully the President's intention, enacted the measure quickly, on April 4, specifying, however, that it last ninety days rather than sixty.

Less than two months later the British Minister, Augustus Foster, made clear to Secretary of State Monroe where the British stood. On May 27, Foster permitted Monroe to read a dispatch from British Foreign Secretary Viscount Castlereagh, which stated explicitly that even if France should exempt the United States from the operation of her commercial restrictions, Britain would decline to do so because such a course would do "the grossest injustice to her allies as well as all other neutral nations." On June 1,1812, the President's war message went before Congress.

In his war message, the President identified five grievances against Britain. First was impressment, the continuing affront to American sovereignty by the removal of seamen, often native Americans, from American ships at sea. Second was the naval patrol off American ports which harassed commerce. Next was the improper enforcement of blockade restrictions in Europe. Trailing the list was a reference to British encouragement of Indian warfare. The heart of the message was in Madison's fourth point. In it the President called attention to Castlereagh's position. Then, with the Orders in Council as well as the licensing of British trade with Napoleon's domains in mind, he charged: "It has become, indeed, sufficiently certain that the commerce of the United States is to be sacrificed, not as interfering with the belligerent rights of Great Britain; not as supplying the wants of her enemies, which she herself supplies; but as interfering with the monopoly which she covets for her own commerce and navigation. She carries on a war against the lawful commerce of a friend that she may the better carry on a commerce with an enemy."

Congressional reaction to the President's request revealed a dangerous division in national feeling. Opposition centered strongly in the Federalist party and in the Northeastern section of the country. Not a single Federalist in either house voted in favor of war. Although nine Federalist opponents of war were Southerners, all the rest (thirty-one) were from the

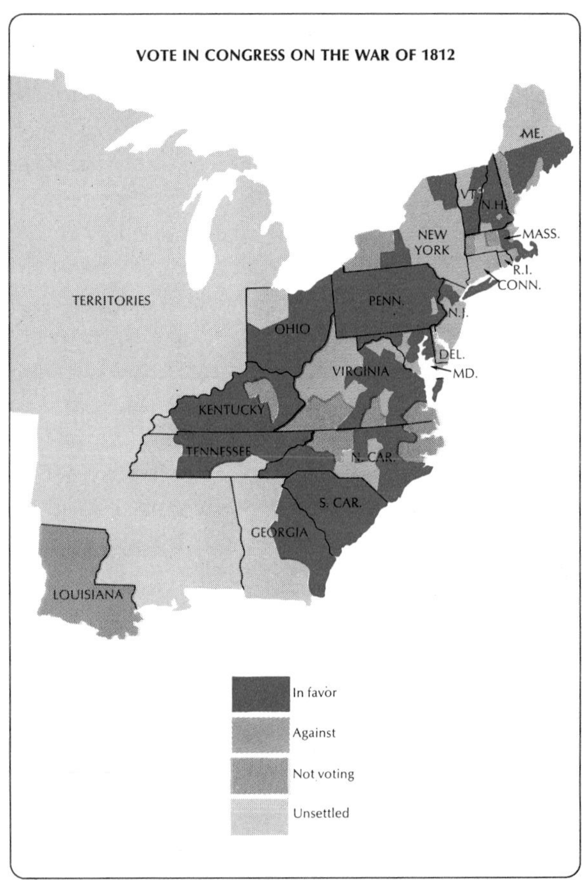

Northeast. Among Republican congressmen from that section, only the Pennsylvania delegation gave a strong vote for war. From New Jersey northward, nearly half of the Republicans, as well as all the Federalists, voted against war. On the other hand, Republicans of the South and West gave overwhelming support to the declaration.

Reasons for opposing the war were varied. Some Federalists still believed that the Republicans were puppets of France acting to aid the French dictator. Others thought that aiding Britain to overthrow Napoleon would be a wiser and more honorable course. Federalist merchants thought war would be more ruinous to their trade than were Britain's restrictive economic policies; still other Federalists believed that continued negotiation would in time bring Britain to reason. Among Republican opponents of the declaration, the most common objection was to its timing. Those who lived adjacent to Canada or in undefended seaports often preferred to prepare the nation more adequately to fight a war before beginning hostilities.

The declaration of war passed the House of Representatives 79 to 49 and the Senate 19 to 13. It became official on June 18, 1812, two days after Castlereagh announced in Parliament his government's intention to repeal the Orders in Council. Napoleon, meanwhile, with an army of 600,000 men, had begun to march on Russia, his last significant continental opponent.

A Mere Matter of Marching

To conquer Canada—and thus punish Britain or induce her to change her policies—appeared to many Americans in 1812 as "a mere matter of marching." Canada did indeed seem vulnerable. Regular army forces available for its defense numbered approximately 7,000, as opposed to 12,000 in the growing United States Army. Excluding Indians and slaves, Canada's population was only about one-sixth that of the United States. The loyalty of many of its people, notably the French Canadians and recent immigrants from the United States, was doubtful. The Indians would support the British, but their aid was at best a mixed blessing and never wholly reliable.

Severing the St. Lawrence lifeline was the

surest way to subdue Canada. Seizure of either Quebec or Montreal, both situated on the north bank of the river, would almost certainly do the job. Quebec, however, was close enough to the sea to receive easy reinforcement from Britain, and mountainous terrain separated it from population centers in the United States. Thus, Montreal, farther inland and conveniently close to the historic Champlain Valley invasion route, became the major strategic goal in American military planning. Kingston, situated at the eastern end of Lake Ontario, became a secondary target, while other invasions were slated to occur along the Niagara River and from the isolated frontier outpost of Detroit.

For the capture of Montreal, Madison relied at first on Henry Dearborn, a general whose principal qualification was seniority. The declaration of war found Dearborn in Boston concerning himself with coastal defenses and attempting to secure the assistance of New England militiamen for the march on Montreal. The Governors of both Massachusetts and Connecticut, however, refused to countenance the use of their militiamen for that purpose. On August 9, 1812, with no offensive yet under way, Dearborn agreed to an armistice suggested by the British, in the hope that news of the repeal of the Orders in Council might terminate the war. Madison did not agree. In November, Dearborn finally put his army in motion, but at the border the militia forces balked, refusing on constitutional grounds to take offensive action outside the country. Thus ended the threat to Montreal in 1812. Kingston, sharing Montreal's good fortune in being within Dearborn's command, escaped even a threat of invasion.

There was more action to the west, but no better results. General William Hull, an aging veteran of the Revolution and territorial governor of Michigan, was in charge of the force which was to invade Canada from Detroit. When Congress declared war, Hull was marching through the wilderness of northwestern Ohio toward his invasion base. Unfortunately, the British learned of the declaration of war before Hull and captured a vessel to which Hull had unwittingly committed copies of his plans as well as major supplies. By aggressive action Hull might have achieved decisive victories before the British, Canadian, and Indian forces consolidated against him. He dallied indecisively, however, worrying particularly over his long line of communications, which was indeed jeopardized both by Indians and by British naval superiority on Lake Erie. When it appeared that the brilliant British commander Isaac Brock was about to launch an attack upon Detroit with the support of a large body of Indians, Hull surrendered ignominiously without firing a shot. The British had already captured Fort Michilimackinac, the frontier fort at the head of Lake Huron, and the Indians had massacred the garrison of Fort Dearborn at the site of modern Chicago. Thus the abortive American invasion of Canada from Detroit culminated in the virtual loss of Michigan.

On the Niagara frontier incompetent leadership was also in evidence. Stephen Van Rensselaer, the first commander, was a Federalist aristocrat who owed his appointment as head of the New York militia to the desire of a Republican governor to secure a greater measure of Federalist support. He managed to commit some of his men to offensive action, but others balked at a crucial stage, with the result that the British captured many of the more aggressive Americans, including a gallant young regular Army officer with a brilliant

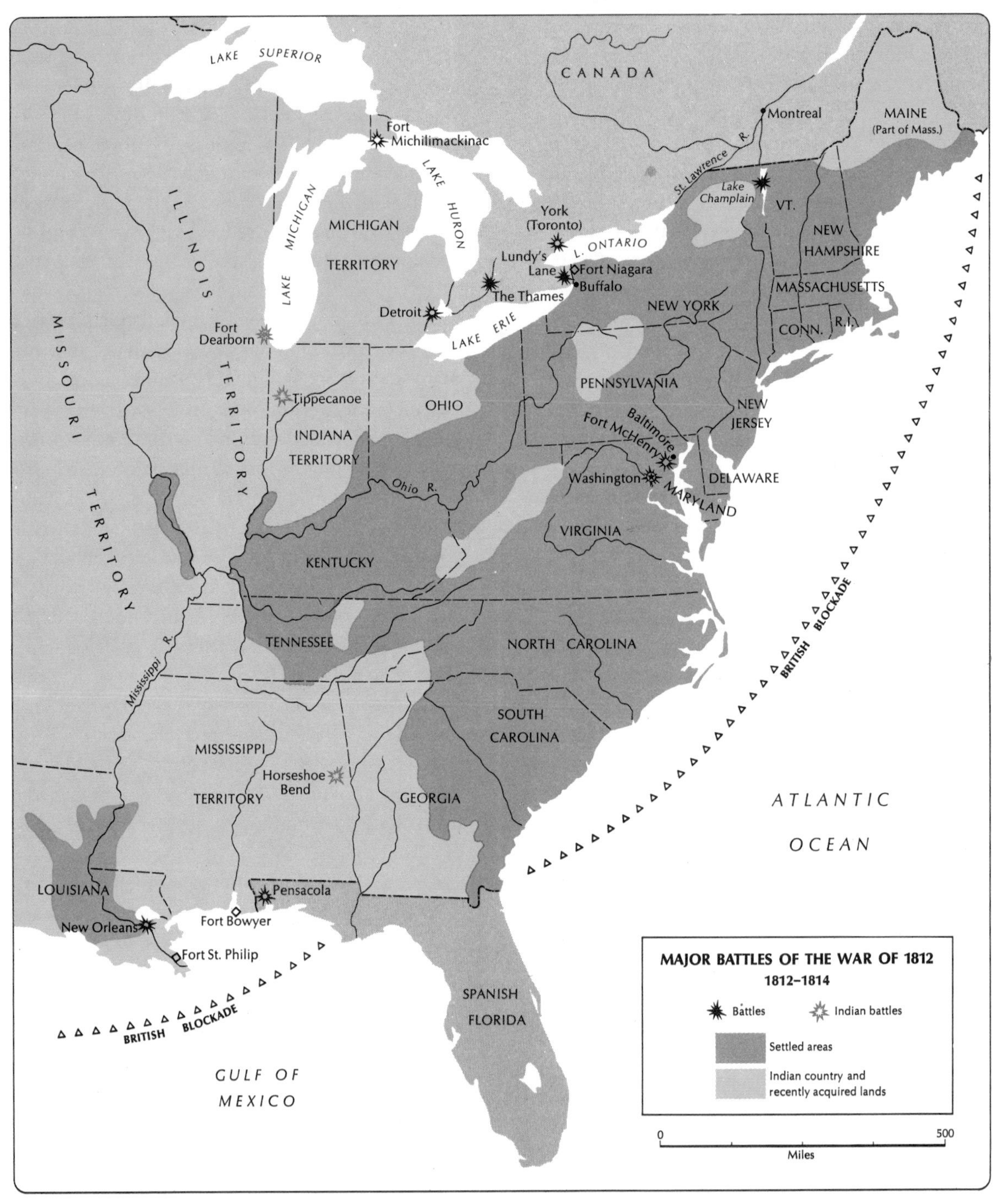
LAKE SUPERIOR
CANADA
Montreal
MAINE
(Part of Mass.)
Fort
Michilimackinac
LAKE HURON
St. Lawrence R.
Lake
Champlain
VT.
ILLINOIS
LAKE MICHIGAN
MICHIGAN
TERRITORY
York
(Toronto)
L. ONTARIO
NEW
HAMPSHIRE
Lundy's
Lane
Fort Niagara
Buffalo
The Thames
MASSACHUSETTS
MISSOURI
Detroit
LAKE ERIE
NEW YORK
Fort
Dearborn
CONN.
R.I.
TERRITORY
PENNSYLVANIA
Tippecanoe
OHIO
NEW
JERSEY
INDIANA
TERRITORY
Baltimore
Fort McHenry
Washington
DELAWARE
MARYLAND
Ohio R.
TERRITORY
VIRGINIA
KENTUCKY
TENNESSEE
NORTH CAROLINA
Mississippi R.
BRITISH BLOCKADE
SOUTH
CAROLINA
MISSISSIPPI
Horseshoe
Bend
TERRITORY
GEORGIA
ATLANTIC
OCEAN
LOUISIANA
Pensacola
New Orleans
Fort Bowyer
Fort St. Philip
SPANISH
FLORIDA
BRITISH BLOCKADE
GULF OF
MEXICO
MAJOR BATTLES OF THE WAR OF 1812
1812–1814
Battles
Indian battles
Settled areas
Indian country and
recently acquired lands
0
500
Miles

future, Winfield Scott. Van Rensselaer had the good sense to resign; but his successor, a regular Army general named Alexander Smyth, although adept at composing bombastic proclamations, proved unable to manage the logistical problem of getting his men across the river. The Niagara campaign of 1812, however, did inflict one severe loss upon the enemy. General Isaac Brock, captor of Detroit, fell dead from American rifle fire during an engagement at Queenston Heights.

American efforts to conquer Canada continued to go badly in 1813 despite some initial success. General Dearborn persuaded his superiors that campaigns in the St. Lawrence region required naval control of Lake Ontario, which in turn necessitated capture of the forts on the Canadian side of the Niagara River. A preliminary amphibious raid on York (Toronto) destroyed or captured strategic naval supplies. However, the American troops stirred up great civilian animosity by plundering and allegedly setting fire to government buildings. When Dearborn fell ill, command of the Niagara offensive fell to Winfield Scott, now back on duty after a stint as prisoner of war. Scott cleared the Canadian bank of the river, allowing several ships which had been bottled up at the navy yard at Black Rock, just above Niagara Falls, to join the American fleet on Lake Erie under Oliver Hazard Perry. Yet by the end of 1813, with the bulk of the American forces diverted to a campaign against Montreal, the British had not only reestablished themselves on the Canadian side of the river but had captured Fort Niagara on the American side and ravaged all the American settlements between the two lakes including the future metropolis of Buffalo.

Dearborn's record in the Niagara region had persuaded John Armstrong, the contentious New York Republican who had become Madison's new Secretary of War, that a change of commanders was in order. Armstrong's choice to lead the American forces to Montreal was General James Wilkinson, whose role in Aaron Burr's treason trial had established his reputation for intrigue and duplicity. Under Armstrong's goading, Wilkinson in October, 1813, advanced reluctantly down the St. Lawrence from the American base at Sackett's Harbor on Lake Ontario. Wade Hampton of South Carolina, encouraged by Armstrong to be more a rival than a subordinate of Wilkinson, was moving northwest from Plattsburgh in the Champlain region to join forces with Wilkinson for the assault on Montreal. Encountering stiff resistance, chiefly from French Canadians, Hampton pulled back. A few days later a small British force humiliated a portion of Wilkinson's army at the battle of Chrysler's Farm on November 11; whereupon he abandoned the Montreal offensive.

In the northwest, President Madison had made the popular William Henry Harrison, victor over the Indians at Tippecanoe, supreme commander. Harrison planned a fall offensive, but postponed it after a portion of his force experienced a defeat which was followed by the massacre of prisoners by Indians at Frenchtown, on the River Raisin near the Ohio-Michigan border. Still enjoying naval control on Lake Erie, the British had advanced into Ohio in the spring of 1813 and laid unsuccessful siege to Fort Meigs, not far from the site of modern Toledo.

Meanwhile, Oliver Hazard Perry, a twenty-eight-year-old naval officer, was creating a fleet with which to challenge British control of Lake Erie. Five ships of his fleet had slipped out of the Niagara River when Scott's victory in May, 1813, had given the Americans temporary

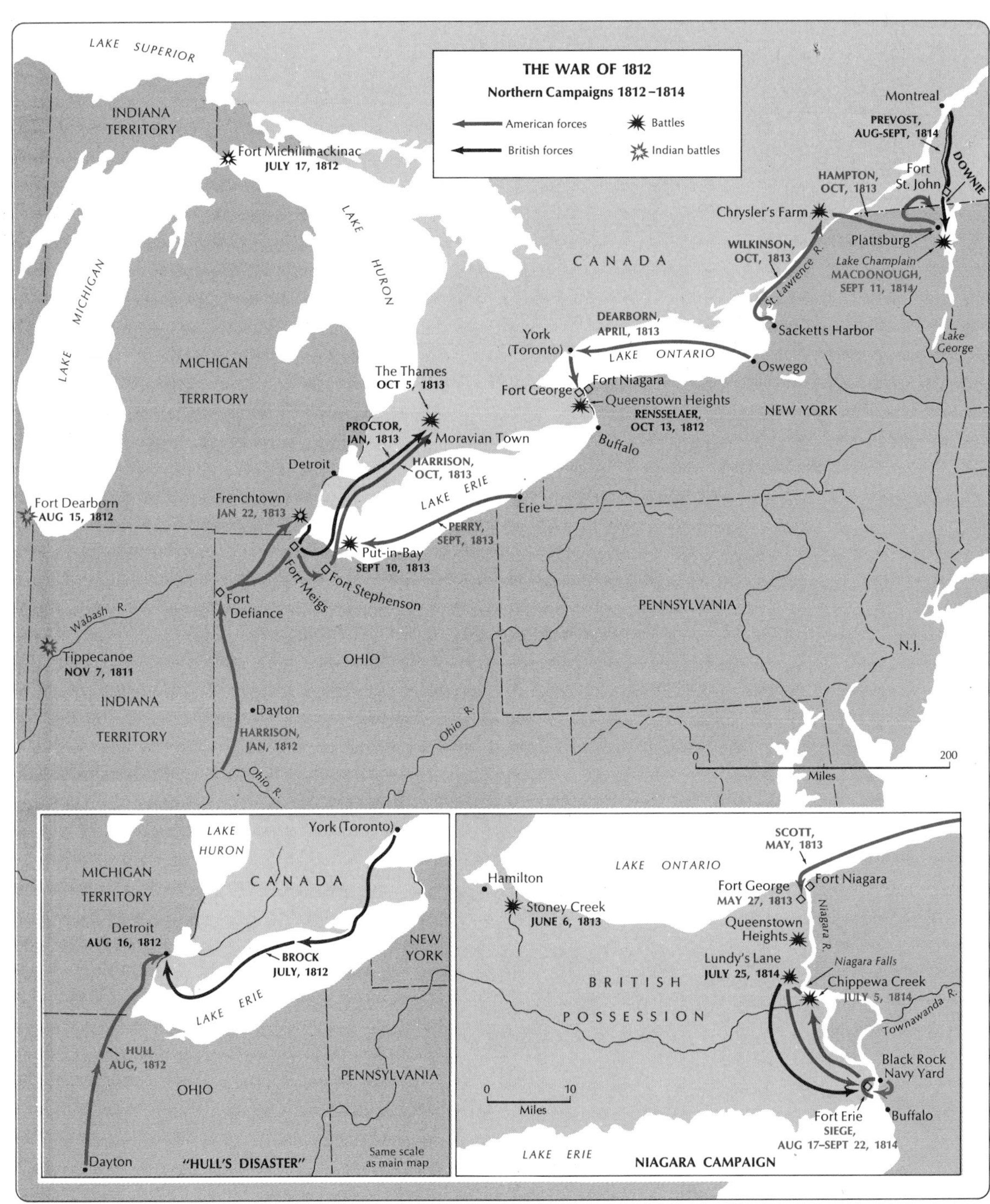
THE WAR OF 1812
Northern Campaigns 1812–1814
American forces
British forces
Battles
Indian battles
LAKE SUPERIOR
INDIANA TERRITORY
Fort Michilimackinac
JULY 17, 1812
LAKE HURON
LAKE MICHIGAN
MICHIGAN TERRITORY
CANADA
Montreal
PREVOST, AUG-SEPT, 1814
DOWNIE
Fort St. John
HAMPTON, OCT, 1813
Chrysler's Farm
Plattsburg
WILKINSON, OCT, 1813
St. Lawrence R.
Lake Champlain
MACDONOUGH, SEPT 11, 1814
Sacketts Harbor
Lake George
DEARBORN, APRIL, 1813
York (Toronto)
LAKE ONTARIO
Oswego
Fort George
Fort Niagara
Queenstown Heights
RENSSELAER, OCT 13, 1812
NEW YORK
Buffalo
The Thames
OCT 5, 1813
PROCTOR, JAN, 1813
Moravian Town
HARRISON, OCT, 1813
Detroit
LAKE ERIE
Erie
Fort Dearborn
AUG 15, 1812
Frenchtown
JAN 22, 1813
PERRY, SEPT, 1813
Put-in-Bay
SEPT 10, 1813
Fort Meigs
Fort Stephenson
Fort Defiance
PENNSYLVANIA
Wabash R.
Tippecanoe
NOV 7, 1811
OHIO
N.J.
INDIANA TERRITORY
Dayton
HARRISON, JAN, 1812
Ohio R.
0
200
Miles
LAKE HURON
York (Toronto)
MICHIGAN TERRITORY
CANADA
Detroit
AUG 16, 1812
NEW YORK
BROCK JULY, 1812
LAKE ERIE
HULL AUG, 1812
OHIO
PENNSYLVANIA
Dayton
"HULL'S DISASTER"
Same scale as main map
SCOTT, MAY, 1813
LAKE ONTARIO
Hamilton
Fort George
MAY 27, 1813
Fort Niagara
Stoney Creek
JUNE 6, 1813
Queenstown Heights
Niagara R.
Lundy's Lane
JULY 25, 1814
Niagara Falls
Chippewa Creek
JULY 5, 1814
BRITISH POSSESSION
Townawanda R.
Black Rock Navy Yard
0
10
Miles
Fort Erie
SIEGE, AUG 17–SEPT 22, 1814
Buffalo
LAKE ERIE
NIAGARA CAMPAIGN

command of both shores. Four others were under construction or undergoing alteration at Presque Isle (Erie, Pennsylvania). Hauling his guns from Pittsburgh, Perry completed his construction work in August and joined Harrison at the westen end of Lake Erie. Near Put-in-Bay, the British, commanded by a one-armed veteran of Trafalgar, Robert Barclay, moved to the attack. Outnumbered nine to six in ships, the British nevertheless enjoyed superiority in long-range guns. While the *Niagara,* one of his two largest ships, unaccountably held back, Perry in the *Lawrence* moved in close and did great damage while taking heavy punishment as well. When the *Lawrence* was virtually knocked out, Perry made his way to the *Niagara* in a rowboat. With the *Niagara,* he completed the destruction of the British fleet. "We have met the enemy," he reported, "and they are ours: two ships, two brigs, one schooner, and one sloop."

Perry's victory persuaded Henry Proctor, the British commander in the western region, to abandon Detroit and retreat up the Ontario peninsula before waterborne American forces cut him off. Tecumseh, Britain's Indian ally, opposed the decision, but he acquiesced on Proctor's assurance that they would ultimately stand and fight. Harrison, employing Perry's ships to transport part of his men across the lake, then pursued Proctor up the Thames River. Near Moraviantown, Ontario, Harrison's riflemen quickly routed Proctor's outnumbered forces in the battle of the Thames. Tecumseh's Indians, unwilling to retreat farther, bore the brunt of the fighting in which Tecumseh himself was killed.

Twenty-four months of war had accomplished little toward the conquest of Canada. As 1814 began, Montreal and the St. Lawrence were as secure as they had been at the outset of hostilities. At Niagara not only had the Americans occupied no Canadian territory, but the New York frontier had experienced destructive raids. In the west, Harrison had achieved the only conquest; at the end of 1813, he still held a small area of Canada adjacent to Detroit. Thus, after two years of offensive effort, the United States had managed only to wound the British lion slightly in the tail.

Resisting British Invasions

Napoleon's defeat permitted Britain to assume the offensive in 1814. After failing to take Moscow in the summer of 1812, Napoleon experienced disaster on his retreat during the ensuing winter. More defeats followed until the allies occupied Paris in March, 1814, and sent Napoleon into exile. Napoleon's elimination terminated Britain's needs to restrict American commerce with France and to impress seamen from American ships, root causes of the American declaration of war; but it also freed the major portion of Britain's military resources for use against the United States. The British public demanded that the government use these resources to punish the Americans for what Britains regarded as an attempted stab in the back while they fought Napoleon in Europe. "They thirst for a great revenge," wrote diplomat Albert Gallatin from London, "and the nation will not be satisfied without it."

American capacity to deny Britain her "great revenge" appeared much in doubt at the beginning of 1814. Madison's record in choosing generals and Cabinet members inspired little confidence. He had found an adequate replacement for an alcoholic Secretary of the Navy and had reluctantly substituted John Armstrong in the War Department for the incompetent William Eustis. Armstrong, a presidential aspirant concerned with enlarging his own political following, attempted to run the war behind the President's back, however, and had to be replaced before the British offensive had run its course. The militia forces upon which much of the defensive burden would necessarily fall had afforded ample evidence for doubting their ability to repulse the armies which had beaten Napoleon. Federalist New England still appeared more hostile to Madison than to Britain: New Englanders were not only supplying enemy forces but considering secession.

Financial difficulties were also approaching crisis proportions. Government borrowing was feeding inflation and privately issued paper money received in loans was coming to be regarded with extreme suspicion by government contractors. Nearly all the government's revenue derived from taxes on imports—which the British navy was about to curtail sharply. Furthermore Albert Gallatin's departure for Europe to negotiate for peace had left the Treasury in much less competent hands until A. J. Dallas took control almost at the end of the war.

Britain's war plans for 1814 had several objectives. One was to tighten the blockade of the American coast and ravage selected coastal cities. In the North, the British planned also to invade the United States to occupy the major base or bases which threatened Montreal. In the South, they would seize New Orleans and either establish an independent government in that region or return all Louisiana to Spain.

Britain's blockade was very effective. The United States, despite its great merchant marine, was not a strong naval power when the war began. Republicans had done nothing to increase the seagoing Navy beyond the sixteen ships they had inherited from the Federalists. These vessels, notably the *Constitution* under Isaac Hull and the *United States* under Stephen Decatur, did shock the British by gaining decisive victories in single-ship encounters. Such individual victories, together with raids against British whalers in the South Pacific by David Porter in the *Essex,* served chiefly, however, to give American morale a needed lift. By the summer of 1814, Britain's navy of some six hundred ships had destroyed, captured, or bottled up all the American warships except the *Constitution,* thus imposing a tight blockade upon the entire American coast. Even New England, previously exempted by reason of the British desire to encourage secessionist sentiment, now had its commerce throttled. Revenue from import taxes was reduced by more than one-half, so intensifying the financial crisis that Madison called a special session of Congress to deal with it. American privateers captured some thirteen hundred British merchant ships and even attacked towns in the British Isles, but they did not divert the British navy from its blockading function.

Ravaging coastal areas of the United States proved rewarding at first but grew increasingly costly. Raids in New England and along Chesapeake Bay brought welcome income to British commanders from the sale of plunder and encouraged still bolder ventures. Admiral Sir Alexander Cochrane and General Robert Ross together planned to attack, first, Washington, to strike a blow at American morale, and then Baltimore, to bag a fortune in merchandise.

Chain of our Union indiſſoluble !
UNITED
WE STAND;
DIVIDED—WE FALL.

The War of 1812

Before the War of 1812, American leaders attempted to stop British and French interference with United States shipping by what Thomas Jefferson hoped would be "peaceful coercion"—an embargo cutting them off from shipments of food and raw materials.

The embargo is satirized below in Alexander Anderson's classic 1813 cartoon, where the terrapin's name, "Ograbme," should be read backward. Passed in 1807, the act failed because bumper crops in Britain and new markets in South America gave the English the commodities they needed—and because there was widespread American smuggling in defiance of the law. (Anderson's terrapin has grabbed an American in the act of smuggling goods to a British ship.)

Jefferson signed a bill repealing the embargo act shortly before he left office in 1809, but the embargo was revived again in 1811. British hostilities at sea continued and, incited by the British, Indians attacked American frontiers from Canadian bases. The War Hawks, led by Henry Clay, moved into power and, with them, the country moved toward open warfare.

Above: New York State Library
Below: Prints Division, New York Public Library

Begar Mounseer Bull me no like dis new Alliance—Dere be one Yankey Man da call Mac Do-enough Take your Ships by de whole Fleet—You better try get him for I never get Do-enough made at dis rate!!!
Ay! What-What-What! Brother Jonathan taken another whole fleet on the Lakes—Must work away-work away & send some more or He'll have Canada next—
Here are more Guns for Lake service—If ever they
get there—I hear the last you sent waylaid by a sly Yankey Fox and being a Stranger he has taken
Patent Oven for Bakeing Ships
French Dough Trough—

America had only five seaworthy ships in its navy of sixteen at the start of the war, but commissioned fast, maneuverable privateers who achieved stunning successes at sea during the first year. In seven months of 1812, some five hundred British merchantmen and three frigates were reported taken by Americans. But on the Canadian front, where the War Hawks had dreamed of almost effortless victory, the war went badly. American forces capitulated without firing a shot at Detroit and mutinied against wobbly leadership at Niagara. In 1813, however, Captain Oliver Hazard Perry reversed the tide of events with a brilliant naval victory on Lake Erie, and General William Henry Harrison followed by winning at the battle of Thames River in Canada. Shown here are a contemporary American cartoon (left) and broadside celebrating (below) these naval successes.

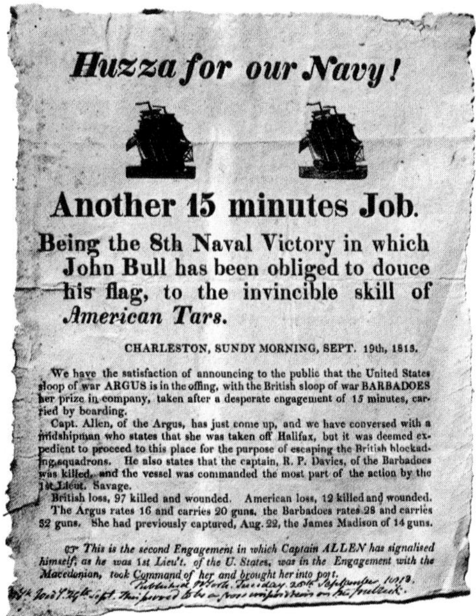

Huzza for our Navy!

Another 15 minutes Job.

Being the 8th Naval Victory in which John Bull has been obliged to douce his flag, to the invincible skill of *American Tars.*

CHARLESTON, SUNDY MORNING, SEPT. 19th, 1813.

We have the satisfaction of announcing to the public that the United States sloop of war ARGUS is in the offing, with the British sloop of war BARBADOES her prize in company, taken after a desperate engagement of 15 minutes, carried by boarding.

Capt. Allen, of the Argus, has just come up, and we have conversed with a midshipman who states that she was taken off Halifax, but it was deemed expedient to proceed to this place for the purpose of escaping the British blockading squadrons. He also states that the captain, R. P. Davies, of the Barbadoes was killed, and the vessel was commanded the most part of the action by the 1st Lieut. Savage.

British loss, 97 killed and wounded. American loss, 12 killed and wounded.

The Argus rates 16 and carries 20 guns, the Barbadoes rates 28 and carries 32 guns. She had previously captured, Aug. 22, the James Madison of 14 guns.

☞ *This is the second Engagement in which Captain ALLEN has signalised himself, as he was 1st Lieu't. of the U. States, was in the Engagement with the Macedonian, took Command of her and brought her into port.*

Left: The New-York Historical Society, New York City
Above: Prints Division, New York Public Library

Another Alexander Anderson cartoon at left shows the decapitated terrapin "Ograbme" in 1814: "To The Grave Go Sham Protectors of 'Free Trade and Sailors' Rights—And All the People Say Amen." By this time resentment against Madison and the war led Federalists in New England to consider making a separate peace with England. Another 1814 cartoon reflects Britain's interest in American commodities and pokes fun at American smugglers who were "always friendly even in the time of our Embargo." John Bull also shows his respect for American naval leaders David Porter and Oliver Perry (below).

I must have all your Flour.—All your Tobacco—All your Provisions. All your Ships.—All your Merchandize—every thing except your Porter and Perry—keep them out of my sight, I've had enough of them already.—

Pray Mr. Bull don't be too hard with us—You know we were always friendly, even in the time of our Embargo!—

Push on Jack, the yankeys are not all so Cowardly as these Fellows here. let's make the best of our time.—

Huzza boys!!! More Rum more Tobacco!—

BEST Virginia

N.E. RUM

BEST Virginia

Terms of Capitulation

Phil.a Pub.d and Sold Whole sale by Wm. Charles. Enter'd according to Act of Congress Wm. Charles Sc.

JOHNNY BULL and the ALEXANDRIANS.

Both above: Prints Division, New York Public Library

Madison picked William H. Winder, a Maryland Federalist whom the British had captured once before, to defend the capital, but Winder and his makeshift militia forces proved utterly inadequate to resist the numerically inferior British regulars. Ross captured Washington with ease and burned both the Capitol and the White House in August, 1814. At Baltimore, however, Senator Samuel Smith organized defenses far more effectively and, with the aid of the artillery in Fort McHenry, held off the British raiders. Ross himself was killed, and there were no more major raids. Baltimore attorney Francis Scott Key, observing the bombardment of his city as a prisoner on a British vessel, dashed off at its conclusion the verses which, set to the music of a popular English melody, "Anacreon in Heaven," became "The Star-Spangled Banner."

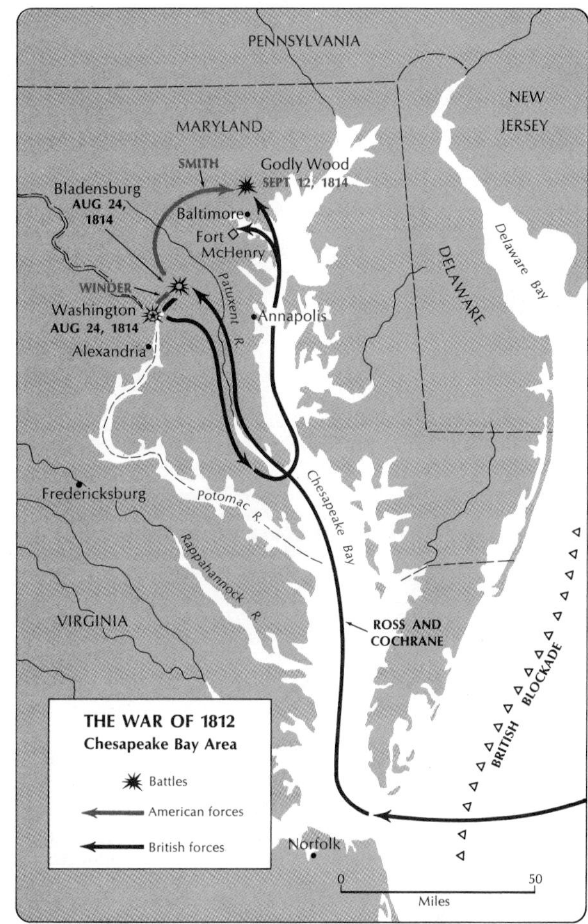

In Canada, Sir George Prevost had received orders to take either Sackett's Harbor or Plattsburgh. To assist him in the project, Britain dispatched some twelve thousand veterans of the campaigns against the French in Spain. Prevost chose to strike first at Plattsburgh, where the American General George Izard with a force of 6,000 was building fortifications. Secretary of War Armstrong, however, had meanwhile ordered Izard and the bulk of his army to the Niagara front, where severe but inconclusive fighting had recently occurred. Izard's departure left only some fifteen hundred men to hold Plattsburgh against Prevost's army of about fifteen thousand.

Prevost experienced no trouble in reaching Plattsburgh, but upon arriving he observed a fleet of four warships and ten gunboats anchored in the bay. Noted always for his caution, Prevost decided to wait for the appearance of the royal navy. On September 11, both Prevost and the newly arrived British naval force attacked. On land British regulars had little trouble with the American defenders, but the American naval commander, Lieutenant Thomas Macdonough, had so arranged his anchors that he could swing his ships around when one side was badly battered and bring fresh guns into action. By doing so successfully in mid-battle, Macdonough won a brilliant and highly important victory. His success persuaded Prevost to march his spendid army back to Canada without taking Plattsburgh.

The capture of New Orleans was by far the

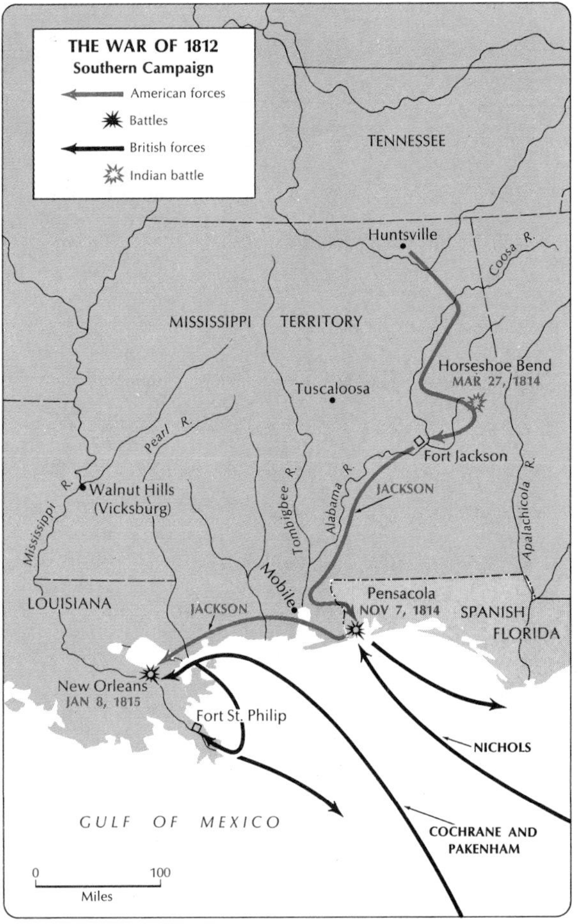

most serious of the injuries which Britain hoped to inflict upon the United States. If they succeeded at New Orleans, the British intended not only to deprive the United States of the Louisiana Territory but also to reimpose restrictions on the use of the Mississippi River as an avenue of commerce, an action which would have had detrimental effects as far to the north and east as Pittsburgh.

Fortunately, military developments prior to 1814 had strengthened the American position along the Gulf of Mexico. The government had called off an attack on Spanish Florida late in 1812, after events in the North had made it seem desirable to end the war through the assistance of neutral mediators. In 1813, however, when Britain had rejected mediation, General Wilkinson had occupied Mobile, a probable invasion site which the United States had failed to secure when it annexed the rest of Spanish West Florida in 1810. Early in 1814 Andrew Jackson, commander of the Tennessee militia, killed over five hundred Creek Indians at Horseshoe Bend on the Talapoosa River in eastern Alabama and compelled the Creeks to abandon a large portion of Georgia and a still larger segment of Alabama. Having turned back a small-scale British attempt to capture Mobile in September, Jackson, on his own initiative, invaded Spanish East Florida to drive a minor British contingent from Pensacola and to cut off the supply of weapons to the Indians through Apalachicola. These actions effectively deprived the British of Indian assistance such as Tecumseh had supplied in the North.

While Jackson concerned himself with Florida, the British were assembling a huge invasion force in the West Indies. Jackson expected the British to attack Mobile, a considerably easier target, but the British chose New Orleans, partly, it appears, because of Admiral Cochrane's desire to loot a major port. With great effort and some good fortune, the British managed to get General Sir Edward Pakenham's army of about nine thousand across shallow Lake Borgne, up an unguarded bayou, and onto one of the few expanses of solid ground amid the swamps which surround the city. The route was difficult for infantry and still more so for artillery in which the British proved fatally weak.

At dawn on January 8, 1815, the British attacked Jackson's motley force of about five thousand, which included regulars, militia,

Negroes, Indians, and pirates. The attackers moved forward across level ground raked by superior American artillery toward mud ramparts behind which Jackson had arranged four ranks of riflemen prepared to fire in turn. Before mid-morning, two thousand British bodies strewed the field, while behind the ramparts less than ten Americans lay dead. General Pakenham and several of his chief subordinates were among those killed. Five weeks later, a British diplomat arrived in New York with a tentative peace agreement which British and American representatives had signed in Belgium on Christmas Eve.

Peace Without Victory

From the outset the War of 1812 had seemed destined to end in a negotiated settlement. On learning of the American declaration of war, Britain had instructed its commanders to exercise "all possible forebearance towards the Citizens of the United States," with the hope that the United States would end the war when news of the repeal of the Orders in Council arrived. In August, 1812, Madison himself had expressed America's willingness "to accommodate all differences." His major condition for the immediate restoration of peace was that the British agree informally to end impressment. Should the British agree to do so, Madison had pledged that the United States would bar the employment of foreigners on American merchant ships. Castlereagh, however, was still of the opinion that to renounce impressment would render Great Britain incapable of securing adequate manpower for the royal navy. Accordingly, the war went on.

In the fall of 1812, the presidential election had afforded another opportunity to end the war. Madison, a noncampaigning candidate for reelection, made clear his intention to prosecute the war. Federalists, strong in the commercial areas of the Northeast and bitterly opposed to "Mr. Madison's war," named no candidate of their own but supported Mayor De Witt Clinton of New York City, a dissident Republican. Appealing chiefly to the "peace" vote, Clinton carried nearly all of the Northeast, winning a total of 89 electoral votes. Madison, carrying all the South and West in addition to Pennsylvania, Vermont, and part of Maryland, gained reelection with 128 votes. The war continued.

Russian mediation offered yet another hope for peace in 1813. Upon receiving Czar Alexander's offer, Madison dispatched Treasury Secretary Albert Gallatin and Federalist Senator James Bayard of Delaware to join John Quincy Adams, the American Minister to Russia, for talks in St. Petersburg. Suspecting that the Czar would be less than impartial on such issues as neutral rights and impressment, the British ultimately declined, but they did offer to negotiate directly.

Direct talks began at Ghent, Belgium, in August, 1814. The British, having disposed of Napoleon and wishing to punish the Americans before concluding peace, were in no hurry. They first suggested the creation of an Indian barrier state west of Ohio, the surrender of extensive territory along the Canadian border, and the extinction of the "liberty" which Americans had enjoyed since the Revolution to dry fish on British territory adjacent to the Grand Banks. After the sack of Washington, while they still anticipated capturing New Orleans, the British suggested that each nation retain the territory which it occupied at the end of hostilities.

After the Battle of Plattsburgh, however, a number of developments led Britain to soften her terms. The Duke of Wellington, when offered the opportunity to duplicate his European victories in America, replied: "That which appears to me to be wanting in America is not a general, . . . but a naval superiority on the lakes." He suggested further that "the state of military operations" warranted no territorial demands on the part of Britain. Madison also strengthened the American bargaining position by publishing the original British terms, a breach of diplomatic etiquette which served the President's purpose by producing a highly belligerent reaction from the American public. Furthermore, in the attempted reordering of Europe at the Congress of Vienna, Britain was experiencing troubles with her erstwhile allies; there were even ominous rumblings from conquered France. Because of all these circumstances, supplemented by domestic financial strain and general war-weariness, Britain's cabinet decided to end the war without concessions from the Americans and without awaiting the outcome of the planned attack upon New Orleans. Their peace commissioners found the American negotiators (Gallatin, Bayard, John Quincy Adams, Henry Clay, and Jonathan Russell) quite amenable to such a solution.

What the British and the Americans agreed to on Christmas Eve, 1814, was to stop the fighting and to restore their prewar borders. The United States, however, did keep the former Spanish territory of Mobile, which it had claimed before the war. Since neutral rights and impressment had become less urgent issues with the elimination of Napoleon, the treaty made no reference to them. It left for future commissions the troublesome questions concerning the fisheries, British navigation of the Mississippi, the northern boundary of the Louisiana Purchase, and the border between Maine and New Brunswick (uncertain since 1783).

To the American public these provisions were eminently satisfactory. Three days after the first copy reached Washington, the Senate ratified the treaty, on February 17, 1815, by a unanimous vote.

Conclusion

"Mr. Madison's War" has long puzzled historians. What apparently impelled the United States to declare war was resentment over British restriction of American commerce and the impressment of seamen from American ships. Yet it was the agricultural South and West—areas of few oceangoing ships and seamen—which favored war, while the commercial Northeast opposed it.

Several factors help to explain the apparent paradox. Most Northeasterners were Federalists, historically pro-British and prone to view all Republicans as puppets of France. They regarded living with Britain's offensive policies as a lesser evil than aiding Napoleon by making war on Britain. The people of the South and West went to war partly to gain unrestricted access to continental markets for their agricultural products and perhaps to annex adjacent territories from which their Indian enemies had received supplies and encouragement. They went to war also, however, as Republicans, traditionally anti-British and deeply concerned lest submission to British infringements of American sovereignty discredit not only the American nation but the republican principles which were the foundation of its government.

Militarily a standoff, the war nevertheless brought significant advantages to the United States. Acquisition of the future port city of Mobile was important for the economic development of what was already becoming the "cotton belt." Wartime chastisement of the Indians at the hands of Harrison and Jackson enabled frontier settlement to proceed more rapidly both in the North and in the South. Still more impressive, however, was the elevation of American prestige. To have gained a draw, whatever the reasons, with such a great power as Britain and to have crushed an invading British army so thoroughly as Jackson had at New Orleans were remarkable achievements for a fledgling nation. As the London *Times* observed, the Americans' first war with Britain made them independent; the second made them a formidable power.

SUGGESTED READINGS

Precisely why the United States declared war on Britain in 1812 still perplexes historians. Henry Adams (see *Suggested Readings* after Chapter 9) thought maritime grievances, particularly ship seizures and impressment of American seamen, were responsible. So also did A. L. Burt in *The United States, Great Britain, and British North America* (1940). Yet those offenses had their most direct effect on the commercial Northeast, which opposed the war, and had relatively little effect on the South and West, which favored it. To explain this apparent paradox J. W. Pratt expounded a tentative hypothesis in *The Expansionists of* 1812 (1925) to the effect that expansionists in the South and West wanted war because it was the only way in which they could drive out the British and Spanish upon whom their Indian enemies depended. Like Beard's hypothesis concerning the Constitutional Convention, Pratt's thesis found wide acceptance as *the* explanation of the war despite the failure of the evidence to sustain so sweeping a conclusion. In the 1960s, "national honor" became the key phrase although it tied in closely with the maritime grievances emphasized long before. Bradford Perkins's *Prologue to War** (1961) stands out among the new works, but there is much merit also in Reginald Horsman's *The Causes of the War of* 1812 (1962); R. H. Brown's *The Republic in Peril* (1964); Patrick F. T. White's *A Nation on Trial** (1965), very brief; and L. S. Kaplan's *Jefferson and France* (1967). The conflicting points of view may be seen in capsule form in Bradford Perkins (ed.), *The Causes of the War of* 1812* (1962).

Military histories of the War of 1812 are relatively few. G. Tucker wrote vividly of *Paltroons and Patriots* (1954) and *Tecumseh* (1956). F. F. Beirne's *The War of* 1812 (1949) is another good journalistic account. H. L. Coles's *The War of* 1812* (1965) is very brief but highly perceptive; it begins with a good account of the conflicting interpretations of the war's origin. J. R. Jacobs's *The Beginnings of the United States Army* (1947) shows its inadequacies. On the Canadian side, see C. P. Lucas's *The Canadian War of* 1812 (1906) or J. M. Hitsman's *The Incredible War of* 1812 (1966). A. T. Mahan's *Sea Power in Its Relation to the War of* 1812 (2 vols., 1905) is the work of a thorough scholar determined to show the advantages of great naval strength. Theodore Roosevelt's *The Naval War of* 1812 (1882) is extremely colorful.

On the peace negotiations Bradford Perkins's *Castlereagh and Adams* (1964) is still very good, although not up to the standard of his *Prologue to War.* F. L. Engelman's *The Peace of Christmas Eve* (1962) is less scholarly.

Biographies contribute to understanding of the peace negotiations as well as to other aspects of the history of the times. Outstanding among those not previously mentioned are B. Mayo's *Henry Clay* (1937); C. F. Eaton's *Henry Clay and the Art of American Politics* (1957); G. G. Van Deusen's *The Life of Henry Clay** (1937); Irving Brant's *James Madison: The President* (1956) and *James Madison: Commander-in-Chief* (1961); Marquis James's *Andrew Jackson: Border Captain* (1933); C. M. Wiltse's *John C. Calhoun: Nationalist* (1944); S. F. Bemis's *John Quincy Adams and the Foundations of American Foreign Policy* (1949).

* indicates availability in paperback.

11

Consensus and Conflict, 1815–1828

"WE ARE ALL REPUBLICANS, we are all Federalists." These words of Thomas Jefferson in 1801 suggested that what Americans agreed upon was more fundamental than the matters over which they had recently disagreed so stridently. In his first term Jefferson had done much to restore goodwill between the two political parties, but thereafter the difficulties with Britain, culminating in the War of 1812, again had poisoned the dialog of American politics. New England Federalists defied the Republican administration, sought to frustrate its war aims, and gave serious consideration to seceding from the Union. Yet within a few years after the end of the war, the Federalists allowed their national organization to die out and loudly proclaimed their dedication to Republican principles. The Republicans in power sought to ease the final hours of their expiring enemy, not only adopting much of the Federalist program but also appointing former Federalists to help administer the government. To some it appeared that an era of nonpartisan "good feelings" had at last arrived and that even the Republican party might peacefully disband as the entire nation basked contentedly in patriotic and prosperous euphoria.

Extreme Jeffersonians, however, carried on a bitter warfare against those whom they considered Federalist wolves in Republican sheep's clothing and fumed in frustration over important Supreme Court decisions rendered by that unreconstructed Federalist, Chief Justice John Marshall. When postwar prosperity yielded to depression after the Panic of 1819, political animosities became stronger still, presaging the return of partisan contention for control of the government.

The Demise of the Federalist Party

"Mr. Madison's War" had seemingly imparted new life to the Federalist party, but as if possessed by a death wish too strong to be denied, the Federalists transformed their opportunity into the occasion for their destruction. Because of their great sympathy for the British, the Federalists stopped little short of treason in their opposition to the American war effort. Not only did they refuse to allow militia forces in the states which they controlled to take part in the invasion of Canada; they also threw every impediment in the way of regular Army recruitment. Rich Federalists declined to buy government securities to help finance the war; some lent funds to Britain instead. Many New England Federalists also engaged in illegal trade with the enemy; in fact, New Englanders supplied most of the food which sustained General Prevost's army in Canada.

Federalist hostility to the war reached a climax in 1814. The Massachusetts Legislature, dominated by Federalists, proposed a convention of delegates from the New England states to consider revision of the federal Constitution. Meeting at Hartford, Connecticut, in December, 1814, official delegates of Massachusetts, Connecticut, and Rhode Island, plus representatives of local groups in Vermont and New Hampshire, debated in secret for three weeks. Early in January, 1815, after repudiating those delegates who urged secession, the Convention declared in words much like those which Madison had used in the Virginia Resolutions of 1798, that each state had a duty "to interpose its authority" to protect state sovereignty and the liberties of the people from unconstitutional acts of the federal government. In this instance the delegates had in mind a prospective draft law (which Congress in fact declined to pass). They sought authorization for the states to "assume upon themselves the defence of their territory," or, in other words, to maintain separate armies, which would be financed by the return of federal tax revenues. They urged an amendment to the Constitution which would require a two-thirds vote of Congress to admit new states, to ban commerce with a foreign nation, or to declare war. Should the federal government decline to act on these suggestions, to conclude peace, or to provide more effectively for New England's defense, another convention would meet with instructions to act "as the exigency of a crisis so momentous may require."

Ominous as these declarations seemed to the delegates who composed them, they had become ridiculous even before they could be presented to the President. Three members of a committee designated by the Massachusetts Legislature were en route to Washington for "negotiations" when news of the peace concluded at Ghent arrived at the Capitol. A few weeks earlier, Madison might well have been greatly concerned by the Convention's demands. In February, 1815, however, buoyed by the news from New Orleans as well as that from Ghent, the President laughed on learning what the Hartford Convention had wrought.

As a national political party the Federalists scarcely survived the Hartford Convention. Tarred already as advocates of aristocracy, party members now took on the additional political burdens of near disloyalty in wartime and intent to disrupt the Union. In the wave of nationalist sentiment which followed the achievement of an honorable peace with Britain and the prestigious victory over British regulars at New Orleans, the Federalists had little hope of success at the national level. They remained strong for many years in coastal areas from Maryland northward, but even with Senator Rufus King of New York, a supporter of the recent war, as their candidate for President in 1816, they carried only three states—Massachusetts, Connecticut, and Delaware. They did not try again.

Postwar Republican Nationalism

Albert Gallatin, perspicacious as always, observed in 1816 that the War of 1812 "has renewed and reinstated the national feelings which the Revolution had given." The people, he noted, "are more American; they feel and act more like a nation." Republican leaders in Congress, yielding to the Federalists their traditional parochialism and dedication to states' rights, provided ample evidence that Gallatin was right.

A peacetime national Army, so offensive to Republicans before they came to power, seemed eminently desirable to the Republicans who controlled the national government at the end of the war. Madison recommended a force of 20,000. Congress approved 10,000, about four times the number actually in service before the war.

Naval power also began to appear in a new light. Reversing their prewar position, the Republicans maintained a postwar Navy about double the strength in manpower of that which they had tolerated before the war. Hard on the conclusion of the war, the administration dispatched a naval expedition under Stephen Decatur to free American prisoners held by Barbary pirates and to induce Algiers, Tunis, and Tripoli to cease their depredations against American commerce. His victories over the Algerians enabled Decatur to achieve both goals.

Nationalism produced little change in the traditional Republican attitudes toward taxes and the national debt. Eager to avoid taxing ordinary citizens, Republicans had always opposed both direct—or property—taxes and excises—or taxes on goods produced within the country. They had preferred to finance the government through the taxation of imports, especially luxury items purchased chiefly by the rich. Wartime disruption of imports had at last forced them to impose both direct and excise taxes, but by 1820 they again had reduced revenue from these sources well below the level of the 1790s.

On the question of a national bank, lessons of economic experience combined with stronger national feeling induced some leading Republicans to change their views. In 1811, when the twenty-year charter of Hamilton's original Bank expired, Republicans in Congress had refused to renew it. Constitutional scruples such as those that Jefferson had expressed to Washington in 1791 were prominent among the reasons for allowing the Bank to expire. Freed from the regulating influence of the national Bank, state-chartered private banks, joined by a host of new ones, greatly expanded their issuance of paper money and their lending. By the autumn of 1814 banks everywhere except in New England had ceased to pay specie (gold or silver) in meeting their obligations for the excellent reason that while their obligations had grown greatly their supply of specie had declined. Confidence in their paper money declined also and, together with the wartime curtailment of imports and the high level of government spending, produced the most severe inflation of the nineteenth century. With great regional variation, prices rose as much as 50 to 90 percent.

To combat the inflationary tendencies of the state-chartered banks as well as to assist the government in managing its financial affairs generally, the Republican administration asked Congress in 1815 to re-create a national bank. Following the lead of its legislative sponsor, South Carolina's Republican War Hawk, John C. Calhoun, Congress chartered the second Bank of the United States in 1816. Kentucky's Henry Clay, who had found constitutional objections to renewing the first Bank's charter in 1811, now found none. The government provided one-fifth of the Bank's $35 million capital and named one-fifth of the Bank's directors, al-revenue from these sources well below the level of the 1790s.

Protective tariff duties for America's infant industries were still another manifestation of postwar Republican nationalism. It appeared highly desirable to the nationalists that the United States become independent of Great Britain economically as well as politically. To achieve that end, the United States, already strong in agriculture, lumbering, fishing, commerce, and shipping, needed primarily to increase its manufacturing. Accordingly, the nationalists sought to tax imports of manufactured goods severely to provide a competitive advantage to new American enterprises and thus spur their growth.

By later standards, the tariff which the Republicans enacted in 1816 was not highly protective. On cotton and woolen cloth, the duty was to be 25 percent until 1819 and 20 percent thereafter. To combat cheap Asian cloths, however, all cottons were to be taxed at a value of no less than 25 cents per yard, thus increasing the percentage of the tax on the cheaper cloth. Iron, paper, leather, and hats also received protection.

Both parties split on the tariff vote. Federalists in Congress favored it 25 to 23, while Republicans did so by about 2 to 1. Federalist opponents represented chiefly the importing merchants. Republican opponents were more likely to feel as did John Randolph that such price-raising taxes would burden in particular "poor men and slaveholders," major components of the Republican coalition. The tariff proved so popular, however, that in 1818 Congress increased the protection for iron and put off a planned reduction of the textile tariff until 1826.

Federal aid for improving transportation—"internal improvements" in the parlance of the times—was another major nationalist objective. Better inland transportation was imperative. Canals scarcely existed. With few exceptions interregional commerce, upon which the development of a truly national economy depended, was feasible only for those who had access to navigable rivers or coastal shipping. Local governments bore the basic responsibility for roads, and in most instances they were not built but "cut." As the term implies, they amounted often to little more than axe-hewn paths through the forest. Their inadequacy not only impeded commercial development but had proved in the war to be an obstacle to efficient military operations as well.

Calhoun's proposal for federal aid for internal improvements narrowly passed Congress early in 1817. It allocated for that purpose the "bonus" of $1.5 million which the national Bank was required to pay the government for its charter. Madison's last act before leaving office, however, was to veto the bill. Although he favored federal aid to improve transportation, he believed that it must await amendment of the Constitution to confer the required authority. To provide such assistance without amending the Constitution, he argued, would demand an "inadmissible latitude" in interpretation. Precedents for such action, including federal aid to the "national road" in Jefferson's administration, he dismissed as "insufficient." Thus nationalist desires for federal aid to internal improvements foundered as a consequence of Republican dedication to strict construction of the Constitution.

Postwar Republican foreign policy remained highly nationalistic, but its major achievements came several years later.

New Republican Leadership

James Monroe, a critic once charged, "hasn't got brains enough to hold his hat on." Yet in a long career which began with service in the Revolutionary Army, Monroe had been a trusted protégé of Jefferson and a close associate of Madison. In 1811, when Madison had to dump Robert Smith, his unfortunate choice as Secretary of State, he offered the post to Monroe, then Governor of Virginia. In the protracted diplomacy which ultimately concluded the War of 1812, Monroe proved himself a reasonably competent Secretary of State. In addition, he occasionally took over the War Department when incompetence there reached intolerable levels. In view of these factors it surprised no one that, as the presidential election of 1816 approached, Madison made it clear that he wished his fellow Virginian to succeed him.

Monroe's only rival for the succession was his Cabinet colleague, Treasury Secretary William H. Crawford of Georgia. Huge, handsome, affable, and ambitious, Crawford was a native Virginian who had grown up on the Georgia frontier. He had served as senator, wartime Minister to France, and Secretary of War (1815–1816) before becoming Secretary of the Treasury. In the caucus of Republican congressmen which met in March, 1816, to pick a presidential candidate, fifty-four expressed a preference for Crawford while sixty-five preferred Monroe. In the presidential election, Crawford supported Monroe against Federalist Rufus King, whom Monroe defeated by 183 electoral votes to 34. Crawford, however, made it clear that he considered his showing in the caucus to have marked him as first in line to follow Monroe.

Henry Clay was one of several party leaders strongly disposed to challenge Crawford's succession. Tall, ungainly, and unattractive in appearance, aggressive, spirited, and meddlesome in manner, Clay was, like Crawford, an émigré Virginian, a frontier dweller, a duelist, and an ebullient extrovert. Born in 1777, he won a reputation as a brilliant lawyer in Lexington, the cultural center of Kentucky, while still in his twenties. During the decade following 1800 he served in the Kentucky Legislature and the United States Senate. In 1811 he entered the House of Representatives and almost immediately gained the Speaker's chair, from which he led the War Hawks in the declaration of war against England in 1812. After serving creditably on the commission which concluded the treaty of Ghent, Clay declined Madison's

Folk Art as History

During Andrew Jackson's lifetime American folk art rose and flourished as it never had before. This creative expression of untutored painters is a self-conscious record of particular faces, scenes, and events. By describing these in great detail— one of the most common characteristics of the

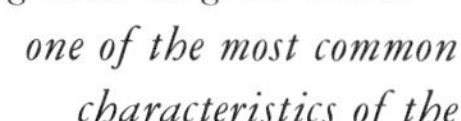

self-taught artist's work—the painter serves as the social historian of his time and place. His observations about his society make him a particularly useful critic and commentator. The examples of folk art shown here are among the most telling documents in an art that flourished from the end of the Revolution to the eve of the Civil War. During this period, the faces and manners of the rising middle class were illustrated by painters of comparable status and background. In performing a useful service that was much in demand, the self-taught painter

Terrence J. Kennedy, Political Banner, *ca.* 1840. *New York State Historical Association, Cooperstown,* N.Y.

The nineteenth-century political banner on the previous page, approximately five feet in diameter, encompasses the dominant elements of American life at midcentury. Industry, commerce, politics, and agriculture appear symbolically in this canvas by young Terence J. Kennedy of Auburn, N.Y. The eagle from the nation's seal stands zealous guard over the composite scene. The three-masted schooner and the side-wheeler sailing choppy seas at left center; the train, towpath, bridges, and canal at right center; and the anvil and bodkin in the foreground—all serve as concrete reminders of the prosperous nation's business and trade. Agrarian interests are demonstrated in the livestock, plow, and rake set around a pond fed by a waterfall. This idealization accurately reflects the inventiveness, the excitement, the prosperity that prevailed.

---

became a respected and important member of his cultural community, and his work constitutes a small mirror reflecting the appearance, possessions, and attitudes of many nineteenth-century Americans. Folk art fulfills this function admirably. Were aesthetic virtue the criterion for the works selected here, the portraits of the tire-maker as manufacturer, the sign-painter as artisan, and the pedlar as merchant would not appear; but as detailed illustrations of man's work in the new republic, they provide valuable information.

This brief glimpse of American folk art reveals only a fragment of a vast record kept in rural areas and in small towns by great numbers of naïve painters whose talents ranged from the mediocre to the sublime. Except for Lockport on Erie Canal, *a watercolor (right), all the paintings in this portfolio are oil on canvas.*

The folk paintings on the following pages are accompanied by text and captions written especially for this volume by Mary Black. Mrs. Black is co-author with Jean Lipman of American Folk Painting *(Clarkson Potter, 1967) and is Director of the Museum of American Folk Art in New York City.*

The first spadeful of dirt for the Erie Canal was turned at Rome, N.Y., in 1817; "De Witt Clinton's ditch" opened to commerce in 1825. Trade goods and agricultural products moved along the water road providing a new link between the business enterprises of the northeast and the gateway to pioneer lands.

The change in grade from Lake Erie to Albany was chiefly made up and down the water steps at Lockport. These are portrayed in the naïve and romanticized watercolor by Mary Keys, which is probably based on the print after a painting by George Catlin published in Cadwallader Colden's 1825 Canal Memoir.

Right: Mary Keys Lockport on the Erie Canal, 1832. *Munson-Williams-Proctor Institute, Utica, N.Y.*

A portrait of the New York town of Eagle Mill dramatically illustrates the change that took place in the Northeast after 1820. Rich and productive farmland surrounds the settlement to which a new mill has given its name. The factory, situated along a stream from which it receives its power, is connected to the surrounding homes, stores, and churches by a two-lane covered bridge.

Attributed to T. Wilson, Eagle Mills, N.Y., *ca.* 1845. *Abby Aldrich Rockefeller Folk Art Collection, Williamsburg, Va.*

Towns and factories lay beyond the heart of town where houses, hotels, shops, and churches testify to the work and pleasure of domestic life. Joseph Hidley was a lifelong resident of Poestenkill, N.Y., the village that became his favorite painting subject. Between 1830 and his death forty-two years later he worked as an artist and also learned taxidermy and cabinet making. In Hidley's picture of Poestenkill (left) the landscape and the people remain the same while the seasons and the vantage point change.

More often than not the craftsman lived in the heart of town. The chairmaker, David Alling of Newark, N.J., lived and worked in the attractive commercial and residential buildings seen below. Two of Alling's ladder-back chairs are set before the shop and office doors.

Left: Joseph H. Hidley, Poestenkill, N.Y., *ca.* 1855. *The Metropolitan Museum of Art, Gift of Edgar William and Bernice Chrysler Garbisch,* 1963. *Above: Artist unknown,* House and Shop of David Alling, Newark Chair Maker, 1777–1875, *ca.* 1830. *The Newark Museum, Purchase* 1939, *Thomas L. Raymond bequest.*

The three genre scenes here show the rise of industry and the increase of traffic along the nation's newly developed roads.

Often the man who became an established folk artist began life as an apprentice in sign or carriage painting. In a scene painted by an unknown artist about 1845, a painter and two assistants work on a sign that illustrates the predominant Northeastern sentiments toward support of the Union over the individual state's rights. At left, an assistant mixes oil with paint on a slab while another at the right stands ready to lay out broad areas of color. The proprietor, distinguished from the workers by his dress, is the craftsman who letters and illustrates the political sign with a portrait of the first President. Even fifty years after his death, Washington's likeness epitomized the nation's government.

Right, above, a blacksmith and his two apprentices are shown in a California shop. An impressive and instructive array of blacksmithing tools surrounds the hand-operated bellows. The owner presides over his anvil in top hat, leather apron, and shirtsleeves, while the two workers wear derbies which may provide protection against flying objects, sparks, and scraps of iron. The painter, H. M. T. Powell, worked in California in the mid-1850s after traveling there along the Sante Fe trail.

Another small businessman was the Yankee peddler (right, below). Here he displays his goods in a country kitchen already amply stocked with produce and trader's goods. Part of the traveling merchant's stock hangs along the sides of his cart outside at the farmhouse door.

Left: Artist unknown, We Go for the Union, *ca.* 1845*; and right, above: H. M. T. Powell,* Blacksmith Shop, *ca.* 1855. *Both, National Gallery of Art, Washington, D.C. Gift of Edgar William and Bernice Chrysler Garbisch. Right, below: Artist unknown,* Yankee Pedlar, *ca.* 1845. *Collection of IBM Corporation.*

Four citizens of the new republic are commemorated here in portraits that capture not only their features but also their prosperity and industry. Maxwell B. Chace (left) was a sea captain or ship owner. His vessel probably appears in the background, and the chart in his hand may indicate that New York is the ship's home port. An unidentified Indiana merchant (right) records in his ledger the artist's name, R. B. Crafft, and the approximate date of the painting, August 16, 1836. A physician in the New York town of Pine Plains, Cornelius Allerton (below) had his interest in horse-raising illustrated in the figure of a miniature saddle horse on the table beside him. William Whipper (right, below), son of a black house servant and her white employer, was apprenticed as a carpenter and joiner in his youth. The tiny gold saw on his watch chain indicates his trade and his success at the lumber trade. A free Negro, Whipper became a leader in the Abolitionist movement.

Left: Artist unknown, Sea Captain Maxwell B. Chase, *ca.* 1835. *Collection of Edgar William and Bernice Chrysler Garbisch, New York. Right, above: R. B. Crafft,* The Merchant, 1836. *Abby Aldrich Rockefeller Folk Art Collection, Williamsburg, Va. Above: Ammi Phillips,* Doctor Cornelius Allerton, *ca.* 1817. *Art Institute of Chicago. Right, below: Attributed to William Matthew Prior,* William Whipper, *ca.* 1835. *New York State Historical Association, Cooperstown, N.Y.*

Painted in southern New England only five years apart, these two family portraits illustrate the prosperity and comfort of small-town life. Although the panic of 1837 brought ruin to many families, no hint of crisis mars these insights into family life. Joseph Moore, his wife, their two children, and the orphaned children of Mrs. Moore's sister pose in their best suits and dresses against a colorful living room furnished with possessions now owned, along with the portrait, by the Boston Museum. The house at 12 Pleasant Street in Ware, Mass., appears as it did in 1839 when the artist, E. S. Field, was living with his in-laws on the same street.

Nathan Starr was a munitions maker in Middletown, Conn., where the family had manufactured arms since the end of the Revolution. The younger Starr children play at battledore and shuttlecock while their older sister watches them complacently. The wide-flung door shows the scene beyond, a view that includes the Starr factory located on the Connecticut River. The artist, Ambrose Andrews, began his career as an itinerant painter. By the 1850s he had learned to paint in academic style and exhibited at the American Art Union and the National Academy.

Left: Erastus Salisbury Field, The Family of Joseph Moore, 1839. *Courtesy of the Museum of Fine Arts, Boston, M. and M. Karolik Collection. Above: Ambrose Andrews,* The Children of Nathan Starr, 1835. *Mr. and Mrs. Nathan C. Starr, New York.*

Edward Hicks, The Residence of David Twining, 1787; *ca.* 1846. *Abby Aldrich Rockefeller Folk Art Collection, Williamsburg, Va.*

One of four versions known of the Quaker painter's boyhood home, Edward Hicks reconstructed this scene from memory. The farm appears here as it did when he first went to live with the Twinings as a child of three. No painter captured the abundance and the beauty of eastern Pennsylvania with greater skill than Hicks. The soft golden light, pink-tinged skies, and hazy distances accurately record the look of its prosperous fields. Serenity fills the air, in contrast to the excitement of the uneasy truces between the ideal and the real worlds in his Peaceable Kingdoms. *Orphaned as a child, Hicks was apprenticed to a carriage-maker when he was only thirteen, then progressed to signs. When he was twenty-one, he turned from a life that had been easy and undisciplined to become a Quaker and eventually a Quaker preacher.*

The ewe and suckling lamb, familiar from his Kingdoms *and his several versions of the* Birthplace of William Penn, *appear in all four Twining farm scenes. Although a plowman stands behind a team of horses in every farm scene but one that Hicks painted, only in this painting is the plowman black. Mary Twining Leedom and her husband are set in poses borrowed directly from the engraving that inspired Hicks's paintings of Washington crossing the Delaware.*

Twining Farm *is incisive painting. But instead of a unified composition on a single theme, here a clear staccato beat draws the eye from scene to scene. The mare with foal and cow with calf at left background are vignettes inspired by newspaper or almanac reproductions of John Anderson's woodcuts. The animals at either side, the well with a sweep handle, and an apple press for cider are typical Buck's County fixtures.*

Many of the tedious and time-consuming jobs required to maintain life in frontier communities were shared labors that became entertainment for the participants. In an art in which static scenes are the rule, the exceptions are interesting. In the painting Flax Scutching *(following spread), Linton Park depicts a lively scene in which a whole community takes part in the conversion of flax to linen thread. Armed with paddles and dressed up by western Pennsylvania standards, the group engages in scutching the flax over upright boards set into the ground. The scene is almost Flemish, but translated to American soil and placed against a background of pioneer cabins. Park was a lumberjack and his trade is reflected in the piles of logs and the neatly felled tree in the foreground.*

Linton Park, Flax Scutching Bee, *ca.* 1860. *National Gallery of Art, Washington, D.C. Gift of Edgar William and Bernice Chrysler Garbisch.*

A. Tapy, The Neigh of an Iron Horse, 1859. *Collection of Edgar William and Bernice Chrysler Garbisch, New York.*

This scene fittingly ends an era in which romanticism gave way to technology. The terrified horse gallops away from a toy-sized train as it trundles across the pastoral landscape. The streaming mane and tail of the horse repeat the arc of the railroad cars as they round a turn.

invitation to become Secretary of War and instead returned to consolidate his position in Congress. Ardently nationalist as his War Hawk record attested, Clay had always supported tariff protection and federal aid for internal improvements, which were also endorsed overwhelmingly by his constituents. Believing appointment as Secretary of State to carry with it an implicit designation as heir apparent to the Presidency (it had for Madison and Monroe), Clay in 1816 aspired openly to that position in Monroe's Cabinet.

John C. Calhoun, Clay's colleague in Congress, was still abler in sheer intellectual capacity and only slightly less ambitious. Descended from Scotch-Irish immigrants who had settled on the South Carolina frontier, Calhoun was tall, elegant, with piercing eyes and strong face, "a cast iron man." He had received a degree from Yale, and at Litchfield, Connecticut, had studied law in Tapping Reeve's law school, the first in the United States. Zealously nationalist as a congressman, Calhoun had helped to push the nation into war with Britain and during the contest supported the war effort so assiduously that one observer referred to him as "the young Hercules who carried the war on his shoulders." After the war he outdid all other nationalists in his zeal for military preparedness, reestablishment of the national Bank, internal improvements legislation, and a protective tariff.

Upon which of these contenders would Monroe bestow the top position in his Cabinet? What consolations would he afford the others? For the top spot Monroe passed up the three front-runners, choosing instead that brilliantly eccentric veteran of legislative and diplomatic wars, John Quincy Adams. Adams was supremely qualified by experience to be Secretary of State and indeed became a bulwark of the administration, but political considerations had influenced the appointment. Northerners were becoming extremely resentful not only of the "Virginia dynasty" of Presidents but also of Southern domination of the Republican party and the government. Adams was the only Northerner among the top contenders. Monroe was eager to reconcile New England to Republican rule and end partisan rivalry for all time. Choosing as his heir apparent a man who was a New Englander, a former Federalist, and the son of a Federalist President seemed likely to further these aims.

Clay and Crawford were deeply disappointed. Declining to become either Secretary of War or Minister to Britain, Clay remained Speaker of the House and used his influence to resist the administration. Crawford stayed on as Secretary of the Treasury, a "worm," John Quincy Adams wrote, "preying upon the vitals of the Administration from within its body." Calhoun, his nationalism as yet undiminished, became Secretary of War and performed with zeal. All four looked ahead to 1824 and the election of Monroe's successor.

Westward Migration and the Panic of 1819

Westward migration was another conspicuous feature of the immediate postwar years. People rushed westward for several reasons. For one thing it was safer after the war than it had been before. Horseshoe Bend and the battle of the Thames had weakened the Indians. Treaties in the wake of those victories opened vast new areas for settlement. In the South cotton prices two or three times higher than before the war also lured settlers westward to gain new land which was cheaper, more productive, and often better situated with reference to water transportation than that which was available in the older regions. North of the Ohio River the climate, by precluding cotton production, made opportunities much less spectacular, but the soil was splendid, the terrain level, and access to overseas markets much better than could be secured in the upland regions of Virginia, Maryland, and Pennsylvania. Still another factor contributing to the westward movement was the abundant supply of inflated paper money. Settlers would not have been able to buy land at such a phenomenal rate without it. With it buyers purchased land from the federal government in 1819 at a rate five times that of 1811.

So numerous were the Americans who thronged the main roads into the Appalachians, to emerge finally along the valleys of the upper Tennessee, the Cumberland, and the Kanawha, that they threatened to depopulate vast areas of Virginia and the Carolinas. North Carolina alone lost an estimated two hundred thousand people through emigration by 1816, and the exodus had only begun. Virginia soon lost even more. Planters and small farmers alike pushed across Tennessee and Kentucky into the Old Southwest. Louisiana had entered the Union in 1812; now the new migration brought statehood to Mississippi in 1817 and Alabama in 1819. But as avenues of travel the southern routes did not rival the Ohio itself. Morris Birkbeck described the westward movements of people along the National Road of Pennsylvania in 1817: "Old America seems to be breaking up, and moving westward. We are seldom out of sight, as we travel on this grand track, towards the Ohio, of family groups, behind and before us." From Pittsburgh this human stream floated down the Ohio in arks, flatboats, and scows, leaving the watercourses only with reluctance. Thousands made their way into Ohio along the Scioto and the Great Miami above Cincinnati; others penetrated the Whitewater and Wabash River Valleys of Indiana or entered the rich lowlands of Illinois opposite St. Louis. These pioneers brought Indiana into the Union in 1816; Illinois, in 1818. Culminating in 1819, the Great Migration manifested the country's speculative fever. Land prices soared with the migration until disaster struck in the Panic of 1819.

The causes of the economic disruption were external as well as internal. In 1819, facing increased competition in British and continental markets because of a general economic slowdown across Europe, American exports dropped one-fourth from the level of 1818. Cotton exports, which had been the chief support of the preceding boom, declined by one-third. British merchants, themselves hard-pressed, began to curtail credit to American importers and to increase pressure for the immediate repayment of existing debts. By 1821, American imports were less than half what they had been in 1818.

Severe deflation of a badly inflated paper currency was another aspect of the depression. Since the demise of the first Bank of the United States in 1811, state-chartered private banks had multiplied rapidly and had flooded the country with inadequately backed paper money. One of the objects which had led to the chartering of the second Bank of the United States in 1816 was the eventual resumption of specie payment throughout the nation and thus the reestablishment of public confidence in the paper money with which the nation's business was conducted.

Unfortunately, under its original leadership the second Bank bungled its job badly. Madison's choice to head the Bank was William Jones, a Philadelphia merchant who had served during the war at the Treasury and as Secretary of the Navy. As head of the Bank, Jones seemed more intent on encouraging inflation, especially in the West and South (where it was most serious but also most popular), rather than on forcing a controlled deflation. Because of the incompetence and venality of his appointees, the Bank itself was on the verge of bankruptcy when Jones resigned early in 1819.

Jones's successor, Langdon Cheves, a former congressional War Hawk from South Carolina, aimed to redeem the Bank and use it for its intended purposes. Cheves pursued both efficiency and deflation with a vengeance. By 1820 he had reduced the Bank's own currency by half and its loans by one-fourth. Cheves restored the financial health of the Bank itself but in doing so forced such a severe contraction of the currency and loans of other banks that "the people were ruined." The downturn begun by the decline of European purchasing became a major depression which lasted into the early 1820s. The Bank itself became "the monster," hated by many private bankers for its competition and its regulatory actions, hated by the people for enriching its own stockholders while impoverishing the nation through its deflationary policies. As early as 1819, public hostility toward the Bank evoked a constitutional crisis which brought the institution under the scrutiny of John Marshall's Supreme Court.

John Marshall: Nationalist, Conservative

John Marshall stands preeminent over all the men who have served as justices of the United States Supreme Court. Marshall dominated the Court as no other man has done. Not only was he seldom in the minority, but he himself wrote an unbelievably large proportion of the Court's decisions. His decisions on major cases invariably upheld the authority of the federal government against the states and of "vested" private rights against public control.

Born in a log cabin in the Virginia Piedmont in 1755, Marshall came to maturity just at the beginning of the Revolution. He served in the Continental army for several years and, as he later expressed it, became "confirmed in the habit of considering America as my country and Congress as my government." He gained a small place in history through his role in the XYZ affair and his brief tenure as Secretary of State at the end of Adams's term. His major historical achievements, however, began when Adams made him Chief Justice of the previously insignificant Supreme Court. Before the War of 1812 he had set judicial landmarks in *Marbury v. Madison* (1803), affirming the power of the Court to void acts of Congress; in the Burr treason trial (1807), defining treason; and in *Fletcher v. Peck* (1810), establishing the power of the Court to void state laws. In the postwar years Marshall rendered still more judgments of major importance.

McCulloch v. Maryland, the Bank case of 1819, was one of the most significant in Marshall's tenure. Maryland and several other states, reflecting popular animosity toward the Bank, were attempting to prevent it from operating within their borders by imposing prohibitive discriminatory taxation upon it. When the Maryland branch of the National Bank refused to pay the tax required by Maryland's discriminatory law, the state sued the Bank cashier, James McCulloch. Early in 1819 the case reached the Supreme Court on McCulloch's appeal from an adverse decision in the Maryland courts.

Marshall's decision affirmed three major points. First, he took exception to the somewhat incidental contention of Maryland's counsel that only the states were "truly sovereign." "The government of the Union," Marshall asserted, ". . . is, emphatically and truly, a government of the people." It was not from the state governments but from the popular ratifying conventions, he stated, that "the constitution derives its whole authority." Next, Marshall explicitly upheld the authority of the federal government to create the Bank. The decision hinged upon the interpretation of that portion of the Constitution which states that Congress shall have power "to make all laws which shall be necessary and proper for carrying into execution" any of the previously listed powers, such as power to tax or to regulate commerce. Marshall's interpretation of the clause was sweeping. For achieving an end or objective "within the scope of the constitution," he stated, "all means which are appropriate, which are plainly adapted to that end, which are not prohibited, but consist with the letter and spirit of the constitution, are constitutional." Finally, Marshall ruled that Maryland could not tax the Bank. The American people, as he put it, "did not design to make their government dependent on the states." The national government, he added, "though limited in its powers, is supreme within its sphere of action." Since Congress could constitutionally create a bank, no state could properly tax its operation because "the power to tax involves the power to destroy." Ohio attempted to ignore Marshall's ruling, but in *Osborn v. Bank of the United States* (1824) the Court forced Ohio into line as well.

States' rightists came into conflict with Marshall also on the question of the Supreme Court's power to hear appeals from state courts. Spencer Roane, a Virginia Antifederalist who had become an ardently orthodox Republican, was Marshall's major antagonist in this struggle. As chief justice of Virginia's top court, Roane contended that although state courts were bound by the Constitution to void state laws which conflicted with any portion of federal law, the decision of the state court should be final. Roane lost one round on that issue in *Martin v. Hunter's Lessee* (1816). With Marshall abstaining because of prior involvement in the matter, Justice Joseph Story, almost an alter ego for Marshall, had affirmed for the Supreme Court that appeals could be heard and that, contrary to the ruling of Roane's court, certain of Virginia's Tory land confiscation laws were void because of conflict with the treaty of peace which concluded the Revolution.

Roane continued to press his argument, and in *Cohens v. Virginia* (1821) it came back to the Supreme Court. Virginia had fined two brothers named Cohen for selling lottery tickets in Virginia in violation of a state law which reserved that privilege to the state itself. The Cohens claimed authorization under an act of Congress passed in 1802, but Roane's court denied that the federal law applied and, with much exaltation of state sovereignty, argued also that Virginia's decision should be final. With a liberal use of nationalist rhetoric, Marshall stated that in order for the federal government to be effective in exercising its granted powers it must have power to review the decisions of state courts whenever they involved interpretation of federal law. That indeed seemed the obvious intent behind the constitutional provision that the jurisdiction of the federal courts should extend to *all* cases arising under the Constitution, federal statutes, and treaties. Marshall's ruling that Roane had interpreted the federal law correctly (it applied only in the District of Columbia) and that the Cohens were thus properly convicted softened the blow slightly.

Gibbons v. Ogden (1824) was unique among Marshall's decisions which limited states' rights in that it was popular. The decision voided a New York State law which had granted to Robert Fulton and his backer, Robert R. Livingston, a monopoly on the operation of steamboat service between New York and New Jersey. Although Marshall shrank from denying the states any role at all in regulating interstate commerce, he did void the monopoly in question because it conflicted with an act of Congress which provided for licensing vessels engaged in coastal shipping. Marshall's ruling was well received because it gratified the numerous opponents of monopoly.

Marshall's defense of vested private rights was almost as controversial as his opposition to states' rights. In *Fletcher v. Peck* (1810) he had ruled not only that his Court could void state laws in conflict with the Constitution but also that state laws altering property rights previously conferred by the state came under the Constitution's ban on state actions "impairing the Obligation of Contracts." In the Dartmouth College case of 1819 Marshall extended the earlier ruling. The case arose out of controversy between Republicans and Federalists for control of the college, which had been established by royal charter in 1769. The Republicans, who dominated the state government, sought by state law to transform the private college run by Federalist trustees into a public institution, whose management would then be in Republican hands. Exceeding even the position taken by alumnus Daniel Webster on behalf of the trustees, Marshall held that the original charter constituted a contract which the Legislature could not alter. The effect of this ruling was to bar state legislatures from changing the terms of charters which they had bestowed, usually by separate and lenient laws, on new business corporations.

States and Localities

Despite the nationalistic atmosphere of the postwar years, the United States remained a remarkably decentralized nation. States and localities, exercising a high degree of autonomy, performed functions of enormous importance to the people. Among the matters with which they concerned themselves were economic development, education, national defense, law enforcement, public welfare, and the electoral processes.

Economic development was a matter of major concern to state and local governments. *Laissez faire,* or the idea that government should keep out of economic matters, was gaining strength, but the dominant attitude was still mercantilistic. Even at the federal level, the scarcity of legislation on economic matters reflected states' rightist opposition to *federal* action more than any objection to mercantilist principles.

At every level of economic activity, state policy was likely to be evident. States possessing unclaimed lands fixed the terms under which the land might pass into private ownership. Some states published reports for their residents on superior productive methods in home manufacturing and in agriculture. Many states established inspection systems for export products in order to maintain a good reputation—and a good price—for the state's products in foreign markets. The products traveled to market over roads which were maintained in most instances by local governments in conformity with state laws. Payments occurred normally in money issued by state-chartered banks. In addition, states might foster economic growth by issuing generous charters of incorporation to manufacturing and other business concerns, by granting tax concessions, by investing in private enterprises which needed extra capital, or even by launching state enterprises in canal or road construction, banking, or commercial production of commodities. The supreme criterion in fixing economic policy was a hard-headed calculation of the consequences.

Education, traditionally the responsibility of family, church, or the apprentice system, was becoming more a matter of public concern. New England had long required towns to provide schools at public expense, but elsewhere schools had generally lacked extensive government support. New York State, for example, began to grant aid to the towns for schools in the 1790s, but state assistance for public schools began to have real impact on education only after 1812. Even then tuition payments rather than public funds bore most of the burden, and the period of attendance for most children was brief. Nevertheless, in the postwar years local and state governments were slowly beginning to follow New England's example in assuming a major new responsibility.

To most Americans even after the War of 1812, defense appeared a joint responsibility of the national Armed Forces and the state militia. In accordance with federal law, each state maintained and trained a militia force, of which the governor was commander in chief. Though the War of 1812 had demonstrated glaring deficiencies in the militia system, it remained still unchanged after the war and figured prominently in national military planning.

Law enforcement, particularly in criminal cases, was primarily in the hands of local officials. Except in the major cities, county sheriffs confined offenders in county jails, pending trial before county judges. In colonial times such local officers had usually been appointees of the governor, and they remained so in many instances after independence. By the 1820s, however, such country law-enforcement officers were very often elected by the people whom they served. The laws which they enforced, on the other hand, were generally state laws, and by the 1820s it was becoming common practice to confine major offenders in state penitentiaries.

Welfare was primarily a responsibility of local officials who, in turn, were governed by state laws. In many areas, the major concern in administering welfare programs was to minimize the costs to the local taxpayers. Accordingly, newcomers of doubtful solvency in any town might legally be "warned out" or, if they became welfare clients, might be "transported" back to the town from which they had come. Often transportation was the major expenditure of local welfare programs. Welfare officers, sometimes called "Poor Masters," could "bind out" children of indigent families as servants; in some areas they sold the adults themselves as laborers. In the 1820s it became common to require the poor to accept virtual confinement in self-sustaining county poorhouses, often termed "workhouses," as a condition for receiving aid. Such institutions commonly housed insane people, as well as those who were incapable of self-support because they were blind, deaf and dumb, aged, or chronically ill.

Finally, states and localities were political

units of major importance. States decided who could and who could not vote. They fixed the powers and duties, more often the latter, of local governments. Their legislatures chose United States senators and, in many states until the 1820s, cast the state's electoral vote for President as well. For these reasons, as well as because of the state's major role in economic matters, state elections were the chief focus of political interest. Political parties organized far more effectively at the state than at the national level. As a new national party system began to take shape in the 1820s, it was evident that state political organizations, capable of wielding enormous influence upon the people, would retain great power.

The Missouri Compromise

What historians have often called "the era of good feelings" following the War of 1812 was really a period of transition. The Federalist party, by clinging to its aristocratic and pro-British views, had condemned itself to death, but what would result from its demise remained uncertain. Monroe, among others, sought to maintain a nonpartisan atmosphere, hoping to avoid the partisan bitterness which had been manifest during the war. The Panic of 1819 and the ensuing depression did not apparently weaken the power of the Virginia dynasty; yet, even as Monroe swept the electoral college for the second time in 1820, the seeds of political disorganization were evident. The dual impact of war and expansion had brought increased business activity and, through the laws of Congress and the decisions of the Supreme Court, had sent Jefferson's notions of a simple, agrarian society into eclipse.

But if Jefferson himself, under the pressure of economic and political necessity, had compromised with his earlier principles of minimum government, there were Americans, especially in the South, who refused to follow his lead. In Congress, John Randolph of Virginia battled the tendencies of the Madison and Monroe administrations to perpetuate a program originally designed by the Federalists. John Taylor, Virginia's noted philosopher, joined the attack, fearing that a centralized government would encourage the aristocracy which controlled it to exploit the poor. Federalism, Taylor complained to Albert Gallatin in 1823, has "changed its name and hidden itself among us." To such men, the party of Jefferson had simply been led astray. But the old Jeffersonian spirit was not dead; it still possessed the power to oppose the political tendencies of the times. After 1820 the Virginia dynasty, along with the Republican party which held it in power, would face two challenges to its leadership, one philosophic and one sectional. The sectional challenge came first.

Missouri, on the western fringe of the postwar settlement which had brought Indiana, Illinois, Alabama, and Mississippi into the Union, submitted its bid for statehood as a slave state before the end of 1819. Congress, in guaranteeing the property rights of citizens who immigrated into the Louisiana Purchase, had permitted the movement of slaves into the territories beyond the Mississippi. By 1819 several thousand Southerners had brought their slaves into the Purchase and had established cotton plantations along the rich bottom lands of the lower Missouri River as well as the west bank of the Mississippi. Approximately six thousand of the territory's sixty thousand inhabitants were slaves. Never before had Congress seriously challenged the right of any state to defend the interests of its citizens in slave property. But when the Missouri Enabling Act came before the House of Representatives late in 1819, James Tallmadge of upstate New York proposed an amendment which would prohibit the movement of additional slaves into Missouri and prepare that state for the eventual emancipation of those already there, by granting all children of slaves their freedom at the age of twenty-five. The Enabling Act, with its antislavery amendment, passed the House on a strictly sectional vote; it fell before a combination of Northern and Southern votes in the Senate.

Tallmadge had saddled Congress with perhaps the most divisive issue in its brief history. Northern congressmen had revealed both their power and their determination to block Missouri's membership in the Union as a slave state. The onetime Federalist, Rufus King of New York, who quickly assumed the leadership of the anti-Missouri movement in the Senate, argued in *Niles' Weekly Register* that Congress had the right to make all needful regulations respecting the territories of the United States and that Congress, as part of its power to admit new states, had the authority to determine the conditions under which new states would enter the Union. Among the objectives of Congress in admitting additional states, declared King, was the extension of the American principles of free government. To extend slavery beyond the Mississippi would deny freedom to a boundless region. "Such increase of the states," he warned, "whatever other interests it may promote, will be sure to add nothing to the security of the public liberties; and can hardly fail hereafter to require and produce a change in our government."

Southern Congressmen just as stoutly defended the right of slaveholders to invade the territories with their slaves and Missouri's right to enter the Union as a slave state. Senator William Pinkney of Maryland, standing firmly on the doctrine of states' rights, warned the Senate in March, 1820, that any attempt by Congress to prescribe the conditions of statehood would lead to tyranny of the federal government over the states. The decision on slavery, he maintained, was Missouri's by virtue of "its sovereign power, which, by the Constitution of the Union will belong to it when it becomes a state. . . . If it can barter away a part of its sovereignty, by anticipation, it can do so as to the whole; for where will you stop?"

Such bitter controversy focused the eyes of Congress on its young Speaker of the House, Henry Clay. Determined to end what had become a burgeoning sectional debate, Clay searched for a compromise that would bring Missouri into the Union and still preserve the sectional balance. He supported the request of Maine, then a part of Massachusetts, to be admitted to the Union as a free state and, utilizing to the full his genius for political management and persuasion, was partially successful in bringing the sections together on one measure. The Senate accepted the admission of Maine as a free state but added to the bill a provision to admit Missouri without reference to slavery. The Missouri provision having come under heavy attack in the House, Senator Jesse B. Thomas of Illinois introduced an amendment in early March which he hoped would settle the controversy. As provided in the Clay compromise, Missouri would be permitted to enter the Union without any restrictions against slavery, protecting thereby its sovereign equality with the other states. This meant that Missouri would enter the Union as a slave state and Maine as a free state. But to make the arrangement

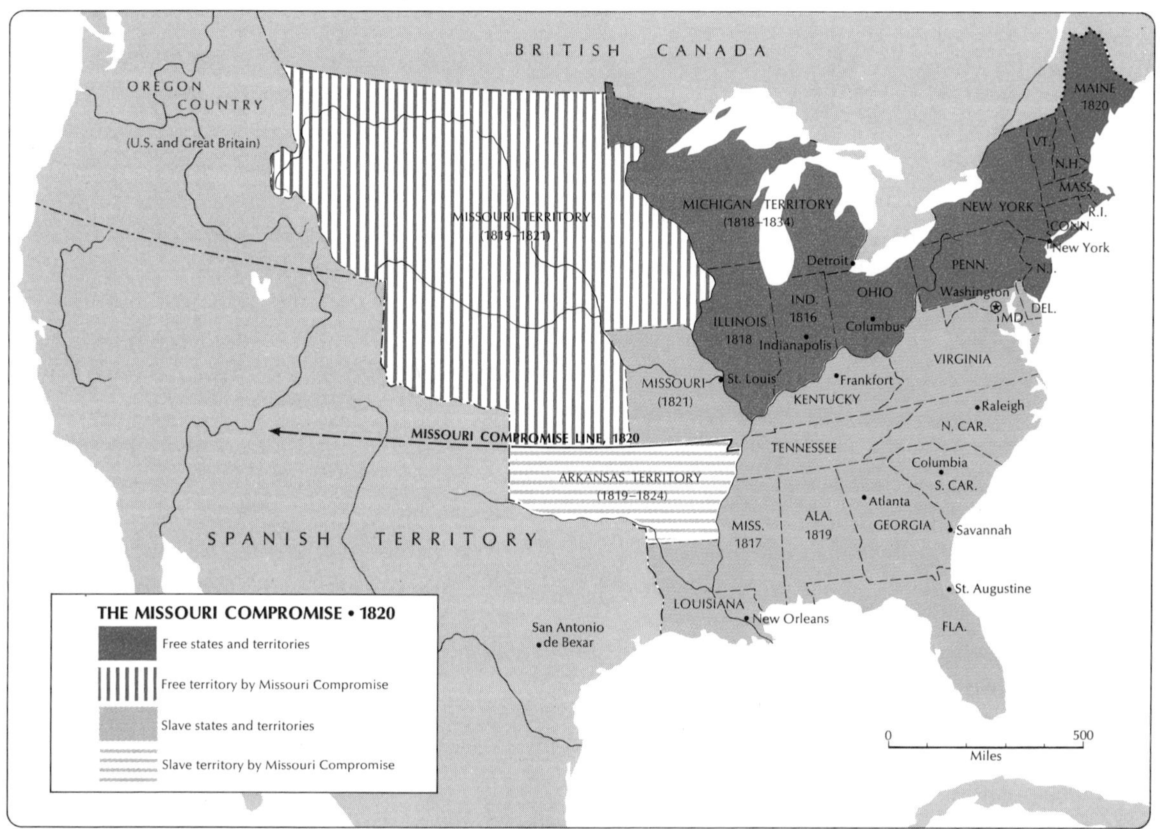

more satisfactory to those who opposed the extension of slavery, Thomas proposed that elsewhere in the Louisiana Purchase, the territory north of 36°30′, a line corresponding to the southern boundary of Missouri, would be barred to slavery forever. Clay worked tirelessly to push the Thomas compromise proposals through the House, where strong opposition existed, and the plan finally won the approval of both the House and Senate. But Missouri provoked another burst of opposition when it included a clause in its constitution which prohibited the entrance of free Negroes, this a clear violation of the constitutional right of the citizens of each state to "all Privileges and Immunities of Citizens in the several States." This time Clay pressed the Missourians to make a concession which would terminate the dispute.

In March, 1821, Congress admitted Missouri into the Union with the provision that Missouri would never exclude the citizens of any state "from the enjoyment of any of the privileges and immunities to which such citizen is entitled under the constitution of the United States." This imposition, duly accepted by Missouri, meant little, for the Missouri Legislature later restricted the movement of free Negroes into the state. For an anxious national leadership what was important in 1821 was not merely that Missouri enter the Union but that such a divisive territorial issue would not arise again. Although the nation welcomed the Missouri Compromise, the controversy had created sectional animosities over the question of slavery which no compromise could erase.

No Americans were more troubled by the Missouri issue than were the two retired Virginia Presidents, Jefferson and Madison. What disturbed them especially was the power of slavery as a political issue to divide both their party and the nation along sectional lines. Madison suspected that Senator King was concerned less with the condition of the Negro than with the state of Northern politics. He confided to Monroe in February, 1820, his fear that King's real objective was "to form a new state of parties founded on local instead of political distinctions; thereby dividing the Republicans of the North from those of the South, and making the former instrumental in giving to the opponents of both an ascendency over the whole." For Jefferson the Missouri question was "like a fire bell in the night." "I consider it at once as the knell of the Union," he warned in April, 1820. "It is hushed, indeed, for the moment. But this is a reprieve only, not a final sentence. A geographical line, coinciding with a marked principle, moral and political, once conceived and held up to the angry passions of men, will never be obliterated."

Whatever their motives in the Missouri debates, Northern spokesmen had failed to break up the Republican coalition that had placed three Virginians in the White House. The controversy had, however, seriously frayed many cords holding the old Jeffersonian alliance together. Most congressmen had refused to argue the Missouri issue on sectional grounds. Southerners still hoped to avoid the necessity of defending slavery and its expansion; the vast majority of Northerners were not yet prepared to condemn the institution, at least not in public debate. Yet the fact that a minority of Northern writers and politicians would employ the question of Missouri statehood to defy the national leadership demonstrated not only that the Republican party was no longer united politically but also that the Virginia dynasty itself was in jeopardy.

The Diplomacy of John Quincy Adams

Monroe faced challenges abroad as serious and as demanding as those at home. Fortunately for him and his administration, Congress never succeeded in undermining his constitutional prerogatives in his conduct of the country's foreign relations. In maintaining freedom of action and a remarkably high level of competence and understanding in matters of foreign policy, Monroe had the assistance of John Quincy Adams, unquestionably the most accomplished Secretary of State in the nation's history. Adams scarcely fit the stereotype of the diplomat. Approximately fifty years of age when he assumed his Cabinet duties in 1817, he was short and bald, with a belligerent demeanor and a rheumy affliction which caused his eyes to run incessantly. But, in those qualities of mind that mattered, Adams was superbly prepared for the tasks of diplomacy. His interest in the country's external relations began a quarter century earlier when he publicly defended George Washington's highly controversial foreign policies. It propelled him into long periods of service abroad, including extended stays in St. Petersburg and London, where he imbibed that realistic grasp of diplomatic limitations which kept him mindful of the difference between the essential and the ideal. For him diplomacy had one major purpose: to serve the concrete interests of the United States, as defined in geographical terms. He pointedly denied on many occasions throughout his career that a genuine foreign policy had any concern for abstract objectives. If he wished for the success of liberty and democracy in Europe and elsewhere, he made it clear that he would not and could not anchor United States policies to the achievement of such goals. For the means of enforcement, he knew, were not within his control.

As Secretary of State, Adams assumed the obligation to resolve a series of disputes with England, some of which had been left unsettled since Ghent, for he understood well that continued security for the United States hinged on good relations with that country. As early as the peace negotiations of 1782, his father, John Adams, had sought the elimination of fortifications from the Canadian-American frontier. The younger Adams, in turn, had pressed the British for such an agreement at Ghent in 1814, but again without success. Still undaunted, Adams repeated the offer in a note of March, 1816. The British government, now hoping to avoid any naval race with the United States on the Great Lakes, accepted Adams's overture. The result was the Rush-Bagot Agreement of April, 1817, which limited British and American naval armaments on the lakes to those required to enforce customs regulations. This treaty was the first reciprocal naval disarmament agreement in modern history. In removing a source of friction and expense, it admirably served the interests of both Britain and the United States.

During the following year Adams managed to achieve the long-standing desire of the United States for fishing rights off the Labrador and Newfoundland coasts. American fishermen were now permitted to catch fish and dry them on extensive sections of the northern coasts. Of equal significance was the new Secretary's effort to define the long northern boundary of the Louisiana Purchase. In the Convention of 1818, he negotiated the line from the Lake of the Woods westward along the 49th parallel to the Rocky Mountains. West of the Rockies, however, British interests were still too demanding to permit a settlement which Adams would accept. The British claimed the Columbia River as the boundary between the mountains and the Pacific. Adams, who was greatly interested in satisfying the requirement of the United States for a usable port on its Western shore, had been made aware by New England seamen that the turbulent Columbia would never fill that need. He understood also that the Strait of Juan de Fuca and Puget Sound, both north of the Columbia but south of the 49th parallel, constituted one of the world's largest and safest harbors. For these reasons, Adams would settle for no less than the extension of the boundary along 49° to the Pacific When the British negotiators proved intractable on this point, Adams agreed to a policy of joint occupation with Britain of the Oregon country west of the Rockies for a period of ten years, an arrangement which either nation could terminate on one year's notice. Thus Adams pushed the final Oregon settlement into the future when, hopefully, the diplomatic advantage might pass to the United States.

Adams's next diplomatic achievement, perhaps his greatest, came in 1819 when in the Adams-Onis Treaty he not only acquired Florida for the United States but also defined the southern boundary of the Louisiana Purchase from the Gulf of Mexico to the Pacific Ocean.

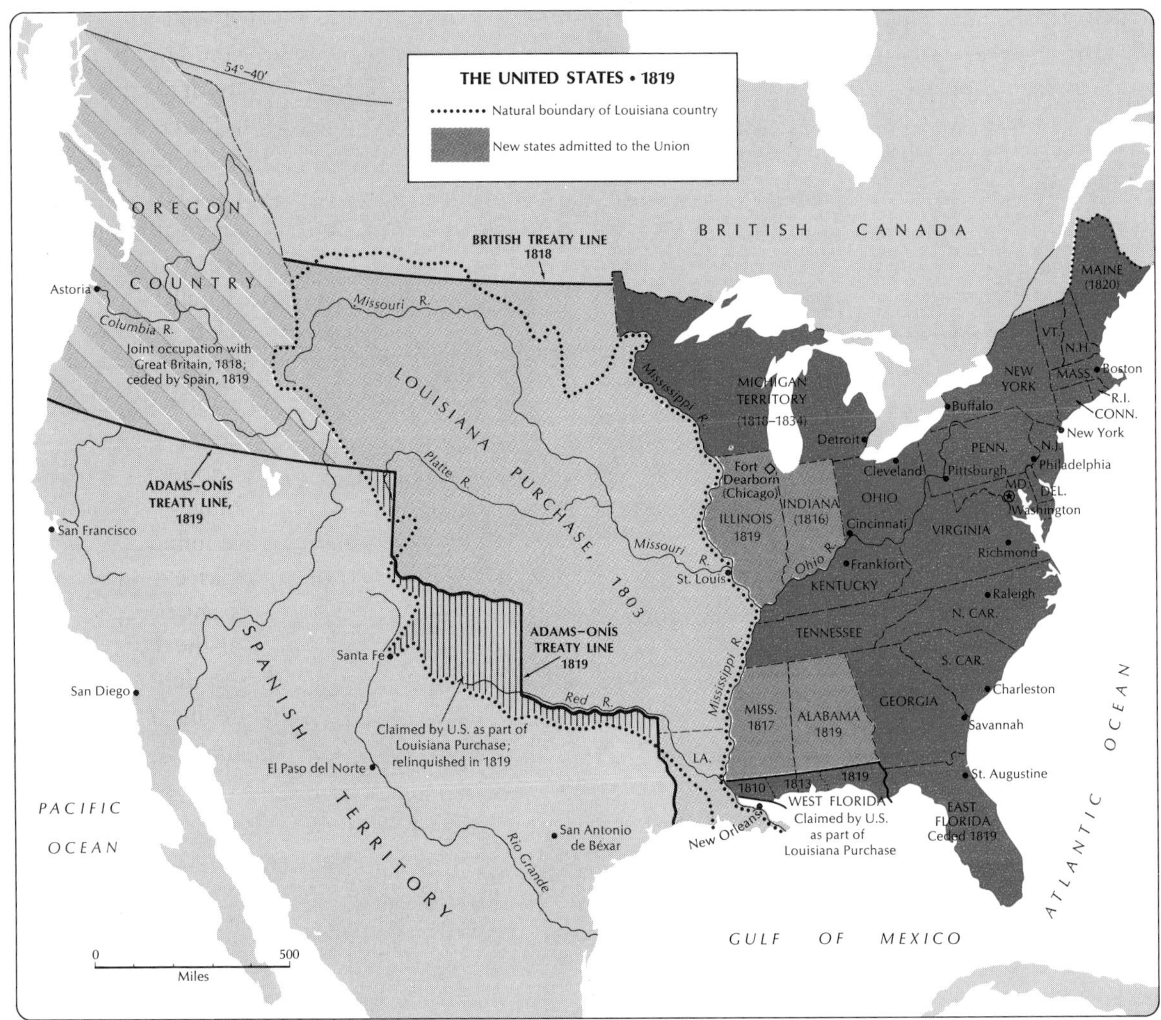

What remained of Florida in 1817 was still under Spanish rule, but the region had become a problem for the United States government simply because Spain was too plagued with political and military disorders elsewhere to maintain order in her colony. British adventurers in Florida perennially armed and incited the Florida Indians to conduct raids north of the Florida boundary. General Andrew Jackson, the hero of New Orleans, forced the Florida issue to a crisis. Carrying out his instructions to punish the Seminoles for their destruction of American lives and property, Jackson in 1818 pursued a band of Indians into Florida where he captured and executed two British agents as well as two Indian chiefs. Spain protested the action; Jackson's enemies in Congress and the Cabinet, led by Clay and Calhoun, demanded that the general be dismissed. Adams, however, defended Jackson and reminded the Cabinet that Spain had an obligation to keep order in her empire. If she could not, then she had no choice but to cede Florida to the United States. Robert Castlereagh, Britain's celebrated Foreign Minister, agreed with Adams. The Spanish weakness was so obvious that the Madrid government opened negotiations with the United States and by the Florida Treaty, signed in February, 1819, ceded Florida to the United States. At the same time the Washington government assumed the claims of United States citizens against Spain, which totaled approximately $5 million.

Adams's negotiations with the Spanish Minister then turned to the still-undefined boundary between Spanish Mexico and the southwestern United States. Spain hoped to push the line eastward and northward as far as possible; Adams, on the other hand, sought a boundary which would bring much of Texas into the United States. After weeks of proposals, counterproposals, and threats to break off negotiations, Adams achieved a transcontinental boundary that corresponded well to the historic interests and claims of the United States. The final line began at the mouth of the Sabine on the Gulf of Mexico, followed that river northward to the 32nd parallel, moved overland to the south bank of the Red River, up the Red to the 100th meridian, then north to the Arkansas, up the Arkansas into the mountains to 42°, and then along that parallel to the Pacific Ocean. This boundary left to Spain the vast region stretching from Texas to California.

Adams regarded these negotiations as the capstone of his diplomatic career. "May no disappointment embitter the hope which this event warrants us in cherishing," he wrote in his diary, "and may its future influence on the destinies of my country be as extensive and as favorable as our warmest anticipations can point! . . . The acquisition of the Floridas has long been an object of earnest desire. . . . The acknowledgement of a definite line of boundary to the South Sea forms a great epoch in our history."

Latin American Independence and the Monroe Doctrine

Adams's opportunities for action in foreign affairs stemmed not alone from Spanish weakness in Florida but also from that nation's precarious position throughout the Western Hemisphere. Napoleon's invasion of Spain in 1808 had terminated Madrid's effective control of the Spanish empire. Provisional *juntas* established by Spain's ruling classes claimed jurisdiction over Spanish America, but by 1812 their New World influence was purely nominal. Freed of Spanish commercial restrictions, the now-independent regions of Latin America opened their commerce to the world. Yankee shippers entered South American ports in large numbers. When war broke out again after 1814 between Spain and her rebellious colonies, struggling South America looked to the United States for economic, moral, and military support.

Strong pressure arose for American guardianship of Latin American independence from, among others, newspaper editor William Duane of the *Philadelphia Aurora* and Congressman Henry Clay, both of whom denounced the American government for neglecting the cause of liberty. But Monroe and Adams would not be stampeded. They recognized the preference of the people of the United States for Latin American independence, but they refused to commit the nation to a policy of involvement before the European powers had revealed their intentions or the patriots of Latin America had demonstrated their capacity to establish their independence and maintain a semblance of order. Adams doubted that the people of Latin America were capable of self-government. Nor did Adams have any interest in antagonizing Spain while the Florida issue remained unsettled. Thus the administration urged circumspection. When Monroe in March, 1818, requested a congressional appropriation to defray the expenses of a commission of inquiry to South America, Clay attached an amendment designed to force the administration to recognize the independence of the Argentine. Although Clay stepped down from the Speaker's rostrum to enter a strong plea for his measure, the House remained unconvinced and voted down the amendment, 115 to 45. Adams's policy of caution had triumphed.

Nevertheless, the Monroe administration moved irresistibly toward recognition of Latin independence. With the final ratification of the transcontinental treaty and the annexation of Florida in 1821, the administration lost its former hesitancy over possible Spanish reaction to American recognition policies. Also, before the end of 1821, Latin American patriots had finally all but destroyed Spanish influence in the hemisphere. Monroe recognized these developments in a special message to Congress on March 8, 1822. He declared that Chile, the United Provinces of the Plata (Argentina), Peru, Colombia, and Mexico were fully independent and thus could claim recognition by other nations. Congress immediately appropriated funds to meet the expense of "such missions to the independent nations on the American continent as the President might deem proper." Following formal recognition of the five new states, Latin American representatives added both numbers and variety to the Washington diplomatic corps.

Meanwhile, British trade and investments in Latin America had confirmed England's interest in the continued independence of the former Spanish empire. Although George Canning, Britain's new Foreign Minister, feared that the United States recognition of the new republics might endanger his country's economic position by inclining that region to American trade and investment, he hesitated to follow the American lead. When in 1823 an invading French army successfully restored Ferdinand VII to his full royal prerogatives in Spain, Canning suspected that France might attempt to restore the Spanish empire as well. It was possible, moreover, that France might use its influence in Spain to lay the foundation for another French empire in America. In this crisis the troubled Canning turned to Richard Rush, the American Minister in London. He suggested that Britain and the United States issue a joint declaration disavowing any territorial ambitions in Latin America but warning Europe against intervention unless that intervention should come from Spain herself. Rush, although highly flattered by this recognition of America's growing importance, insisted on referring the matter to Washington unless Britain recognized the independence of the Latin American nations immediately. This Canning refused to do. Instead, he delivered a secret warning to Paris. The French government responded in its "Polignac Memorandum" with satisfactory assurances that it had no intention of dispatching an expedition to the New World. Thus Canning, by unilateral action, had resolved the immediate challenge to British policy.

Monroe received Rush's dispatches during October, 1823. The President, who looked with favor upon the Canning proposal, sought the advice of his old friend Jefferson, in quiet retirement at Monticello. Jefferson warmly endorsed the idea. So did James Madison. But Secretary of State Adams had some convictions of his own. The Russian Minister had recently warned the Secretary that his government would not recognize Latin American independence and would support any French invasion of the former Spanish empire. Adams refused to be frightened. He doubted that France intended armed intervention in Latin America; moreover, the British navy was powerful enough to prevent it. In fact, Adams suspected that Canning's overture was aimed less at obtaining unnecessary United States support than at preventing, through the self-denying principle, future United States expansion into Texas and the Caribbean. Adams had already warned Madrid that the United States would not tolerate the transfer of Cuba, still held by Spain, to any other European power. Thus when the Cabinet met on November 7, Adams proposed that the United States stand unilaterally. "It would be more candid, as well as more dignified," said Adams, "to avow our principles explicitly to Russia and France, than to come in as a cock-boat in the wake of the British man-of-war."

Monroe, although still hesitant to take a stand against the Holy Alliance (the reactionary league of European powers headed by Russia, France, and Austria), favored a dramatic statement in behalf of the Greeks, then in revolt against Turkey. In Congress, Webster had taken up the popular Greek cause. Adams, on the other hand, argued strongly against any American meddling in the affairs of Europe, summarizing his views before the Cabinet: "The ground that I wish to take is that of earnest remonstrance against the interference of the European powers by force with South America, but to disclaim all interference on our part with Europe; to make an American cause, and adhere inflexibly to that."

This concept of two worlds Monroe embodied in his celebrated message to Congress on December 2, 1823. The so-called Monroe Doctrine declared specifically that the American continents were no longer open to European colonization and that the United States would regard any effort of the European powers to extend their government to any portion of the Western Hemisphere as a threat to its peace and safety. On the other hand, Monroe assured the nations of the Old World that the United States would not interfere with their dependencies in the New World or involve itself in matters purely European. Together Adams and Monroe had wedded American policies to the status quo in the Atlantic, a status quo which, if threatened, would have the defense of the British navy itself.

The Election of 1824

Democracy, if measured by the proportion of people exercising the franchise, grew rapidly in the United States during the first quarter of the nineteenth century. The increase in voter turnout reflected in part the relaxation of state restrictions on voting and in part the decision of voters at last to exercise legal rights long held. Of the original thirteen states, New Hampshire, Pennsylvania, New Jersey, Maryland, North Carolina, and Georgia had adopted the principle of universal manhood suffrage before the War of 1812. Still it seems clear that after 1800 the extension of voting privileges alone could not account for the increase in those actually casting ballots in state and local elections. This suggests that voter participation rested less on legal changes than on changes in habit. Eighteenth-century American society was deferential; Americans generally accepted the leadership of the landed and business elites and had no interest in contesting the established political and social order by resort to the ballot. After 1800, however, the direct appeal of the Jeffersonians to the political instincts of the masses, added to the continuing two-party rivalry between Jeffersonians and Federalists, gradually destroyed the older elitism and encouraged men both to select and then to pass judgment on their political leaders.

Monroe's second administration was free of any major political disturbances after the Missouri crisis. This pushed the illusion of party unity into the twenties. With all significant political power exercised within one broad national coalition—the Republican party—individual influence rested less on political organization than on personal magnetism or lineage. Thus the Virginian Monroe had inherited the Presidency in 1817 as Madison's natural successor. Congress had long assumed the responsibility of nominating the next President in caucus and presenting its choice to the state electors. Although it was the congressional caucus that named Monroe for a second term in 1820, so general was his acceptability that only William Plumer, Jr., of New Hampshire cast his vote for John Quincy Adams and against Monroe in the electoral college.

Despite its apparent authority in 1820, however, the caucus system was doomed. Never possessed of any genuine nominating power, it could function only as long as it represented a consensus; after 1820 the necessary consensus no longer existed. The caucus, moreover, could not satisfy the requirements of the newly enfranchised electorate, especially where the states had granted the voters rather than the legislatures the power to choose presidential electors. Distrustful of the caucus system, state legislatures, newspaper editors, and the people in mass meetings proceeded to recommend their favorites for the Presidency. The result was an open scramble for the White House in 1824.

In February, 1824, spokesmen of the old Virginia dynasty of Jefferson, Madison, and Monroe, in an effort to preserve party unity, pressed Congress for a caucus to nominate Monroe's successor. Having no promising Virginian available, the caucus, which was attended by only one-third of the Republican congressmen, turned to William H. Crawford of Georgia, Secretary of the Treasury. It was even then apparent that party leaders and editors had no intention of following the caucus's decision. As early as August, 1822, the Tennessee General Assembly had endorsed Andrew Jackson and recommended him to the American voters for their consideration. In November, 1823, a caucus of Republicans in the South Carolina Legislature had nominated John C. Calhoun, Secretary of War. Then in March, 1824, a state convention meeting at Harrisburg, Pennsylvania, denounced the congressional caucus openly and named Jackson and Calhoun for the Presidency and Vice Presidency respectively. Calhoun took the cue and removed himself from the race for the White House.

Meanwhile, in November, 1822, the Kentucky Legislature, followed by those of Missouri, Louisiana, and Ohio, had nominated Henry Clay, popular advocate of the "American System" of tariffs intended to provide both protection for American industry and funds to be used in building a national network of internal improvements. With good reason, Clay

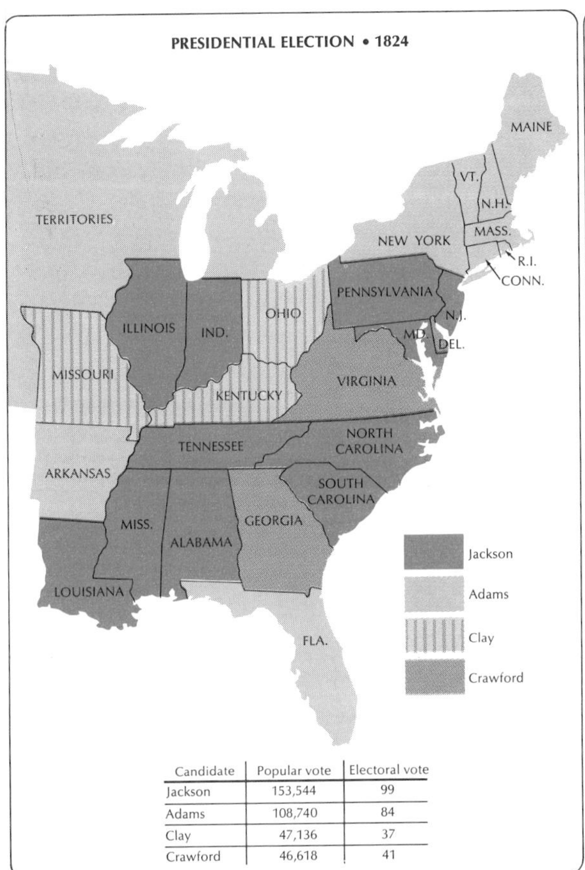

Candidate	Popular vote	Electoral vote
Jackson	153,544	99
Adams	108,740	84
Clay	47,136	37
Crawford	46,618	41

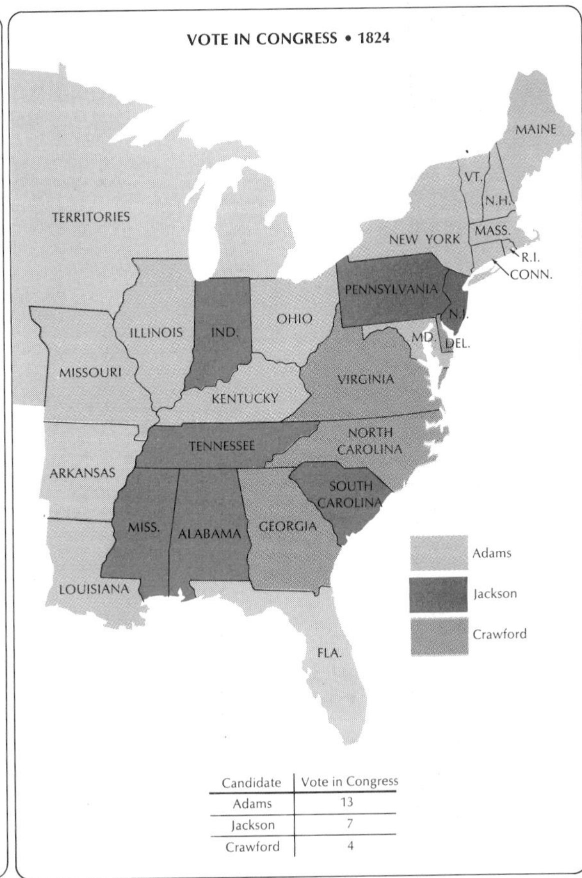

Candidate	Vote in Congress
Adams	13
Jackson	7
Crawford	4

regarded Jackson as his most dangerous opponent, noting that Jackson was the choice of many local politicians who recognized his popularity and cared little that his views on public issues were unknown.

John Quincy Adams, without party or personal following, was no less ambitious for the Presidency than Crawford, Clay, and Jackson, although he refused to campaign even when members of Congress urged him to enter the canvass actively. His national views were almost identical to those of Clay. Clay had captured the nationalist imagination with his American System; yet spokesmen of the Northeast, including powerful New York, announced their preference for Adams over his Western and Southern opponents. In the November elections Jackson, sweeping much of the West and South, gained 99 electoral votes; in the popular elections he polled 153,544 votes. Adams carried New England, as well as a majority of New York's electoral votes, to gain a total of 84, with a popular vote of 108,740. Crawford captured Georgia, Virginia, and Delaware with their total of 41 electoral votes. Clay's 37 votes came from Kentucky, Missouri, and Ohio. If Jackson had failed to obtain the required majority in the electoral college, he was still the obvious choice of the voters.

Ignoring Jackson's superior appeal to the electorate, Adams determined to make a bid for election in the House of Representatives, where each of the twenty-four states would have one vote. This was the method of election provided by the Constitution when no candidate had a majority. Adams needed six states—all of those carried by Clay and Crawford—in addition to the seven he had gained in November. Two Western or Southern states, added to his November total of eleven, would give Jackson the victory. Clay, as Speaker, was in a powerful position to control the House election, and he favored Adams over Jackson. Clay's decision to support Adams, followed by Adams's own success in lining up several key House delegations, deprived Jackson of a majority. The House, on February 9, 1825, elected Adams on the first ballot. To his own seven, Adams added Clay's three states of Missouri, Ohio, and Kentucky, as well as three states that had voted for Jackson in 1824—Louisiana, Maryland, and Illinois. The price of victory came high, for Adams, in turning to the politicians, had defied the will of the voters.

The Adams Presidency

From the day of his inauguration, Adams faced the hopeless task of prolonging an era of nonpartisan rule without strong congressional or personal support. His only hope of conciliating the many personal factions in Washington lay in the creation of a broad national program and in the careful selection of his Cabinet. With Clay and Jackson in his administration, Adams might have sustained a semblance of nonpartisan government. But Jackson would accept no appointment, and Clay could not enter the Cabinet without inviting charges of a "corrupt bargain." Clay, in supporting Adams's bid for the Presidency, had neither demanded nor received the promise of a high-level appointment. However, when Adams selected Clay for the State Department as the most experienced Western man available, he alienated the Jacksonian faction completely. Adams also failed to win the support of Calhoun and Crawford, the preeminent spokesmen of the South.

The new President, having been unable to achieve unity in his administration, turned to the task of creating an acceptable national program. To protect and enlarge the national interest in liberty and property—the twin foundations of American constitutionalism—Adams favored a strong federal government capable of directing the nation's power and resources. His concern for a program of internal improvements binding together a great continental republic, supported by moderate protection for American industry, expressed his belief in nationalism and the Federalist tradition. His earnest appeal for "laws promoting the improvement of agriculture, commerce, and manufactures, the cultivation of the mechanic and of the elegant arts, the advancement of literature, and the progress of the sciences, ornamental and profound" suggested the breadth of his vision.

Unhappily for his domestic program, the President had little support in Congress. The refusal of many senators to approve Clay's nomination as Secretary of State presaged strong opposition at the outset. Vice President Calhoun, who dominated the Senate, was never a spokesman for the administration. Webster, like Adams a former Federalist, might have served the administration well as its spokesman in the House, but Adams distrusted Webster too much to assign him that role. If the Republican party remained the nation's only organized party, it did not belong to Adams. From the beginning of Adams's administration, the forces of Jackson, Calhoun, and Crawford coalesced against the executive leadership. By 1826 this new coalition, calling itself the Democratic Republican party, captured control of the House of Representatives. Outside Congress, Adams could look only to the Northeast for effective support; elsewhere the most influential editors and politicians drifted into the opposition. Congress, under no pressure from the White House or a pro-Adams populace, was able to largely ignore the President's program. At his urging, Congress did provide about $2 million for such internal improvements as road construction and harbor improvements, a sum twice the amount spent for the purpose in all previous administrations combined. But the lawmakers disappointed the President by refusing to consider an integrated system of internal improvements for the country as a whole. The presidential term that Adams had hoped to make a great period of nation building degenerated into a time of narrow partisanship and bickering.

Adams, always conscientious in the performance of his duties, refused to ignore the troublesome problem of Indian removal. When Georgia had ceded her Western lands in 1802, the federal government had agreed to extinguish all Indian titles within that state and turn the Indian lands over to the people of Georgia. What made the fulfillment of this obligation difficult was the fact that the Cherokees and Creeks of Georgia had achieved a high state of organization and culture. Their investment in agricultural production alone was too great to make their removal easy or peaceful. But Georgians, anxious to enter the rich cotton lands of the Indians, pressed the federal government to negotiate the necessary treaties of removal.

When Adams entered the Presidency in March, 1825, he found on his desk the Treaty of Indian Springs, already approved by the Senate. Adams signed the document despite the warning of the United States Indian agent in Georgia that the treaty had been negotiated with only a small portion of the Creeks and Cherokees. Soon a delegation of Indians appeared at the White House, demanding a new treaty. A compromise Treaty of Washington, signed in January, 1826, provided that the Indians cede only their lands east of the Chattahoochee River, or about two-thirds of the territory included in the Treaty of Indian Springs. Georgia's Governor George N. Troup rejected the compromise and proclaimed his intention to have the full area claimed by the state surveyed in preparation for white settlement. Adams tried to dissuade Troup from surveying land not included in the treaty of 1826, warning him that the federal government would protect the rights of the Indians. But the Georgia Governor informed the Secretary of War that, if need be, Georgia would call out the militia to defend its interests. Although Adams recognized Indian rights, neither he nor Congress was willing to use force to protect them. Finally in November, 1827, the Creeks ceded all their Georgia lands and prepared to move. The problem of the Cherokees remained unsettled.

Despite his special aptitude for foreign affairs, Adams as President could not sustain the successes of his earlier years. In his effort to cement better commercial relations with the new nations of Latin America he faced the opposition of George Canning. Adams favored hemispheric peace and stability; Canning sought a balance of power in the New World. Whereas Adams achieved some improvement in United States relations with Argentina, Brazil, Chile, and Peru, Canning scored successes in Mexico and Colombia.

In 1826 Canning outmaneuvered Adams again at the Panama Congress. Simon Bolivar, the Venezuelan liberator, asked Britain to send a delegation to the Congress in the hope that Britain might underwrite Latin American security against future European encroachments. Canning accepted the invitation, for it presented him with an unprecedented opportunity to strengthen the balance between Europe and America. When Colombia invited the United States to send representatives to the Congress, Secretary of State Clay likewise accepted the invitation, and Adams announced that he would shortly commission ministers to attend the Congress. In his special nominating message of December 26, 1825, Adams assured the Senate that the United States policy remained one of neutrality and the avoidance of alliances with the Latin American states. The Senate approved the nominations in March, 1826, but the House balked at voting the necessary appropriations. Adams responded with a carefully argued state paper in which he demonstrated that American interests would be served by having delegates at Panama.

Such was not to be. Although the mission was ultimately funded, it was plagued by one complication after another. One commissioner resigned without leaving Washington; the other did not survive the trip. Thus no American reached the Panama Congress, which opened in June, 1826, with delegates from only four republics in attendance. The Congress accomplished little, but the British used the absence of a United States delegation to remind Latin America that Britain, not the United States, was the true friend of its independence.

The Jacksonian Triumph

No less than the presidential election of 1824, that of 1828 evolved into a contest between Adams and Jackson. The second contest, like the first, turned less on issues than on personalities. Jackson had never opposed the Clay-Adams program. His own political and social ideals were for the most part unknown, but he had somehow become identified with the aspirations of the common people. Politicians and editors across the country had rallied to his standard; so, too, had the people. Whereas Adams chose to ignore the new forces for political change, the Jacksonians embraced them eagerly.

In Martin Van Buren, Jackson acquired an accomplished political strategist. A small, balding man with muttonchop whiskers and a disarming personality, Van Buren held a commanding position in New York politics as head of the "Albany Regency," a group of orthodox Republicans with influence throughout the state. Van Buren, careful in his timing as well as in his measuring of Jackson's appeal, waited until late in 1826 to put his New York machine behind the candidacy of the Tennesseean. Equally astute politicians in other states quickly fell into line. The new Democratic coalition was a strange one. Within its ranks were men who had seldom in the past agreed on national policies but were now committed to a single movement. For this new order of politicians, Jackson's great personal popularity and his opposition to Adams were his essential assets. Not only were there more voters in the late 1820s than ever before, but also there existed among Southern planters and Northern farmers, among urban artisans, tradesmen, and members of the growing middle class everywhere enough convergence of interest to permit their inclusion within a single political movement. Still any program that would satisfy such divergent elements was elusive. In the debates of the twenties, spokesmen of the new Democratic party divided on every important issue. What gave the party some intellectual unity, however, was the vague, if traditional, preference of both the liberal-democratic elements of the North and the states' rightists and Jeffersonian philosophers of the South for less, rather than more, centralization of federal authority.

Perhaps no issue of the Adams years better illustrated the failure of the Jacksonians to agree on public policy than did the tariff. The tariff of 1824, with additional duties on wool and hemp to broaden its appeal to the North and the West, constituted a moderate increase over the tariff of 1816. Calhoun, as a spokesman for American nationalism, voted for the measure, whereas Webster did not. However Calhoun's tariff views had already entered a period of transition. He had defended earlier tariffs solely as measures of national defense, but in 1824 the country was scarcely in danger of war. Most South Carolinians, moreover, had never shared Calhoun's enthusiasm for the tariff and had never ceased to oppose it. Early in 1827, protectionists introduced a higher tariff on wool, designed to raise the tariff on imported woolens from $33\frac{1}{3}$ percent to about 50 percent of actual value. Webster, now under the influence of the rapidly expanding industrial interests of New England, drove the measure through the House, but South Carolina's states' rightists were incensed. In the Senate, Vice President Calhoun, now enlisted in the defense of Southern rights, broke a tie by casting the deciding vote against the bill. Thereafter, antitariff South Carolinians took refuge in Jackson's candidacy, for the fact that Jackson had already selected Calhoun for the vice presidency offered them some assurance that he favored tariff reduction.

When Congress met in December, 1827, the advocates of protection – having formulated their plans at a tariff convention which had met at Harrisburg, Pennsylvania, during the previous summer – doubled their efforts to commit Congress and the President to higher schedules. Adams passed the burden of conciliation to Congress. There the Jacksonians responded to the demand for tariff increases with a measure designed to gratify both farmers and manufacturers in the states of Pennsylvania, New York, Ohio, Kentucky, and Missouri where the political balance of power lay. Under the leadership of Silas Wright, a Van Buren lieutenant, they afforded firm protection for iron, hemp, raw wool, and whisky (by taxing imports of molasses from which New Englanders made rum). New England, sure to be Adams country politically, received no favors, nor did the South which was equally firm for Jackson despite its antitariff views. Manufacturers of woolen cloth, chiefly New Englanders, suffered a lowering of their protection. Yankee shipping and distilling interests found materials they imported more expensive. Southerners voted for the provisions offensive to New England, hoping to turn New Englanders against the bill as they might have done if they had not bragged too early of their cleverness. In any case a scattering of New England votes provided the victory margin. Denounced elsewhere as a "tariff of abominations," the measure nevertheless did improve Jackson's prospects in the middle states.

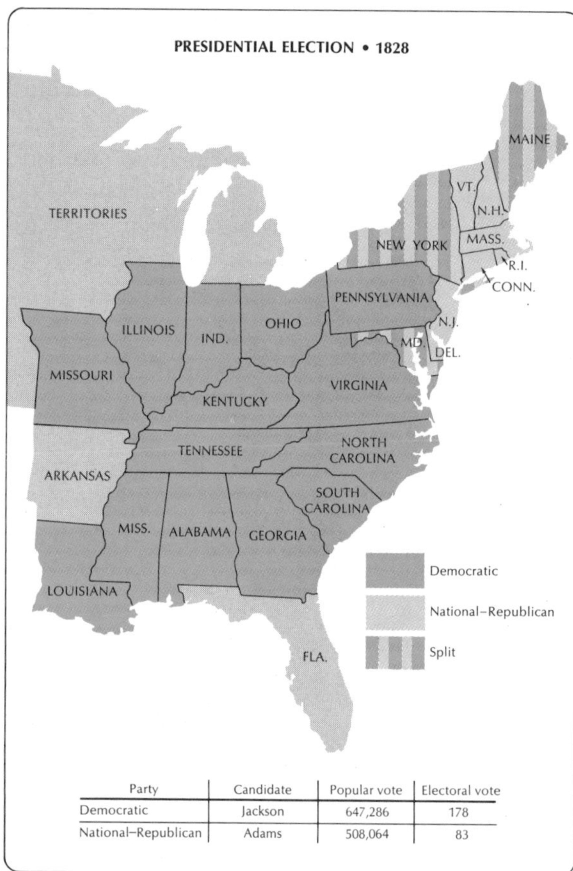

Party	Candidate	Popular vote	Electoral vote
Democratic	Jackson	647,286	178
National–Republican	Adams	508,064	83

After 1826 the Jacksonian forces in Congress determined to destroy Adams. Behind the oratory of the brilliant, if erratic, Randolph, they harassed the President and his partisans in every conceivable way. They charged the administration with extravagance and corruption. They accused Adams of attempting to perpetuate his power by building up a vast patronage, although the President actually refused to reward even his closest friends with political office. Once begun, tirades of abuse spilled over into the campaign of 1828, making it one of the most bitter in the nation's history. The press now added fuel to partisan fires. When Adams was accused of gross corruption and incompetence, his supporters replied in kind, accusing Jackson, among other things, of gross immorality in connection with his slightly irregular marriage to his beloved Rachel.

Long before November, 1828, it was clear that the Jacksonians were carrying the nation before them. Adams appeared secure only in New England; elsewhere his political strength was in doubt. With Jackson and Calhoun, as running mates, assured of victories in the South and West, Adams needed both New York and Pennsylvania if he were to be reelected. When the ballots were counted it was disclosed that Jackson had swept Pennsylvania and everything to the west and south of it, with the exception of 6 Maryland electoral votes. Jackson had captured 20 of New York's 36 votes as well. Adams had held New England, New Jersey, and Delaware. Jackson led in electoral votes, 178 to 82; in popular votes, 647,276 to 508,064.

Conclusion

While Jackson's triumph at the polls was profound, its meaning was less than clear. What notions of government and what policies had triumphed? As a national organization, the Democratic party had electioneered more for Jackson than for a program. Yet for Adams himself, defeat spelled the end of federalism. "I fell, and with me fell," he complained, ". . . the system of internal improvement by National means and National Energies. The great object of my Life therefore as applied to the Administration of the Government of the United States, has failed." In part Adams was correct. Jackson's election was indeed more than a personal triumph. In some measure it had been a triumph in principle. Many of those in both North and South who led the fight against Adams had questioned the continuing trend toward centralization. For Randolph, for Taylor, and for the old Jeffersonians, as well as for Van Buren and many of the New York Democrats, the new President represented the promise of less government.

Jackson's election marked the end of nonpartisan politics at the national level, a development encouraged by the country's democratic structure. The election neither inaugurated the rise of the common man nor brought an end to aristocracy in America, but it created for the common citizen national political machinery through which he could register his preferences and thus influence public policy. If the parties of Jackson and Clay had not displaced the political habits and personal allegiances of the past, they had laid foundations for national party structures which might encompass existing and future party organizations in the states, the cities, and even the villages. In overthrowing the nonpartisan tradition so dear to Monroe and Adams, the Jacksonians had employed new techniques of campaigning whereby politicians might bid successfully for popular support. In short, the Jacksonians, in guiding and sustaining the political revolution of the 1820s, left to the American people a vehicle for making their democracy effective.

SUGGESTED READINGS

Several good books deal with the decline of the Federalists and the nonpartisan "era of good feelings." The best overall treatment is George Dangerfield's *The Awakening of American Nationalism** (1965), which updates his earlier *Era of Good Feeling** (1952) and changes the interpretive emphasis. S. E. Morison in *The Life and Times of Harrison Gray Otis* (2 vols., 1913) affords insight into the Hartford Convention. A brief but useful account of the period from 1801 to 1829, which includes several dozen pertinent documents, is Raymond Walters, Jr.'s *The Virginia Dynasty** (1965).

On economic developments good studies are also numerous. Bray Hammond's *Banks and Politics in America** (1957) pushes its conclusions very hard but undoubtedly has revised many previous estimates. It does not entirely outmode R. C. H. Catterall's *The Second Bank of the United States* (1903). George R. Taylor's *The Transportation Revolution* (1951) is really a general economic study of outstanding quality, omitting only agriculture, which is treated in the companion volume by Paul W. Gates, *The Farmer's Age* (1960). M. N. Rothbard's *The Panic of* 1819 (1962) deserves notice. Recent preoccupation with economic growth is reflected in two perceptive works covering this period: D. C. North's *The Economic Growth of the United States, 1790–1860** (1961) and Stuart Bruchey's *Roots of American Economic Growth** (1965). No modern work has yet surpassed F. W. Taussig's *Tariff History of the United States** (8th ed., 1931).

Literature on the westward movement also abounds. F. J. Turner's *The Rise of the New West** (1906) is still well worth reading despite its age. As the title suggests, Turner presents his topic from the viewpoint of the expanding Mississippi Valley. J. D. Barnhart's *Valley of Democracy* (1953) is the work of a dedicated disciple whose concern is the Ohio River Valley. R. C. Wade with *The Urban Frontier* (1959) added a new dimension to frontier studies which traditionally have had an agrarian focus. Other works of great value on Western development include T. P. Abernethy's *The South in the New Nation* (1961); L. K. Mathew's *The Expansion of New England* (1919); L. D. Stilwell's *Migration from Vermont* (1937); R. C. Buley's *The Old Northwest* (2 vols., 1950); S. J. Buck's *Illinois in* 1818 (1917); Everett Dick's *The Dixie Frontier* (1948); and P. D. Jordan's *The National Road* (1948). In addition to the works previously cited on the Marshall Court, one might gain insight from A. C. McLaughlin's *Constitutional History of the United States* (1935); R. C. McCloskey's *The American Supreme Court** (1960), very brief; and Charles Warren's *The Supreme Court in United States History* (2 vols., 1937).

State studies of great merit are also available. In a series concerned with the role of the state in economic development, Oscar and Mary Handlin's *Commonwealth: A Study of the Role of Government in the American Economy: Massachusetts, 1776–1861* (1947) and Louis Hartz's *Economic Policy and Democratic Thought: Pennsylvania, 1776–1861* (1948) are particularly valuable. P. S. Klein's *Pennsylvania Politics, 1817–1832* (1940) is excellent.

Most of the leading figures of the 1820s have become subjects of biographies. The standard work on Monroe is W. P. Cresson's *James Monroe* (1946). S. F. Bemis has written an outstanding account of the life of John Quincy Adams. His *John Quincy Adams and the Union* (1956) contains valuable chapters on the election of 1824 and the Adams Presidency. Allan Nevins has condensed Adams's detailed and pungent memoirs into a single volume, *The Diary of John Quincy Adams, 1794–1845* (1951). Crawford's career can be followed in J. E. D. Shipp's *Giant Days; or, The Life and Times of William H. Crawford* (1909). This volume is somewhat too laudatory. The lives of the trio of Clay, Webster, and Calhoun have been commemorated in excellent biographies. The standard biography of Daniel Webster is C. M. Fuess's *Daniel Webster* (2 vols., 1930), but R. N. Current has contributed a brief biographical study of balanced judgment in his *Daniel Webster and the Rise of National Conservatism** (1955). C. M. Wiltse's *John C. Calhoun: Nationalist* (1949) remains the standard volume on Calhoun's early political career. M. L. Coit's *John C. Calhoun** (1950) is another sympathetic study. Both Gerald M. Caper's *John C. Calhoun: Opportunist* (1960) and R. N. Current's *John C. Calhoun** (1963) are useful brief accounts of Calhoun's life. Glyndon G. Van Deusen's *The Life of Henry Clay** (1937) and Clement Eaton's briefer *Henry Clay and the Art of American Politics** (1957) do credit to the career of this fascinating and popular leader. Van Buren's rising political career in the 1820s is dealt with by R. V. Remini in *Martin Van Buren and the Making of the Democratic Party* (1959). A study of Jackson's early life is Marquis James's *Andrew Jackson: The Border Captain** (1933).

Various monographic studies, many of unusually excellent quality, have covered the specific themes of the 1820s. Glover Moore in *The Missouri Controversy, 1819–1821** (1953) deals more than adequately with the Missouri Compromise. On the background of this issue see F. C. Shoemaker's *Missouri's Struggle for Statehood, 1804–1821* (1916). The best account of John Quincy Adams's diplomacy is S. F. Bemis's Pulitzer prize-winning study, *John Quincy Adams and the Foundations of American Foreign Policy* (1949). P. C. Brooks's *Diplomacy and the Borderlands: The Adams-Otis Treaty of 1819* (1931) is the standard account of that episode. The classic study of the origins of the Monroe Doctrine is Dexter Perkins's *The Monroe Doctrine, 1823–1826* (1927). Perkins has compressed this and his later works on the Monroe Doctrine into a single volume, *Hands Off: A History of the Monroe Doctrine** (1941; rev. ed., 1955). For a differing approach to the Monroe Doctrine see E. H. Tatum, Jr.'s *The United States and Europe, 1815–1823: A Study in the Background of the Monroe Doctrine* (1936). On the Latin American background see A. P. Whitaker's excellent *The United States and the Independence of Latin America, 1800–1830** (1941), as well as J. H. Powell's *Richard Rush: Republican Diplomat* (1942). Two other valuable studies are C. C. Griffin's *The United States and the Disruption of the Spanish Empire* (1937) and J. A. Logan, Jr.'s *No Transfer: An American Security Principle* (1961). Armin Rappaport has edited a useful anthology, *The Monroe Doctrine** (1964). The most recent scholarship can be found in Bradford Perkins's *Castlereagh and Adams* (1964).

Most of the biographies listed above dwell on the politics of the 1820s. But specific studies that analyze the political changes of the decade include the rewarding one by D. R. Fox, *The Decline of Aristocracy in the Politics of New York** (1919), and that by A. B. Darling, *Political Change in Massachusetts, 1824–1848* (1925). Shaw Livermore, Jr.'s *The Twilight of Federalism: The Disintegration of the Federalist Party, 1815–1830* (1962) traces another aspect of political change. J. T. Horton's *James Kent: A Study in Conservatism, 1763–1847* (1939) traces the thought of one who opposed the trends of the times. For differing views of the tariff of 1828, consult John A. Garraty's *Silas Wright* (1948) and R. V. Remini's *The Election of Andrew Jackson** (1964).

* indicates availability in paperback.

12

Jacksonian Democracy

FOR THE THRONGS who crowded into Washington on March 4, 1829, Andrew Jackson's inaugural symbolized the final triumph of democracy. So successfully had the Jacksonians characterized their assault on Adams and Clay as a contest between those who trusted and those who feared the common man, that the masses interpreted Jackson's election as a victory of their own. Twenty thousand gathered at the Capitol to see their hero take the oath of office and to listen to his inaugural address. Only when he had finished reading did they press forward to grasp the new President's hand. Before his well-wishers could surround him, Jackson retreated through the building onto a waiting horse. Thousands followed him up Pennsylvania Avenue, and with muddy boots, pushing and shoving, they pursued the disappearing figure into the White House. Friends saved the general from being trampled to death by blocking the way while he escaped through the south door. They rescued the White House and its costly furnishings by placing tubs of punch on the lawn; there, noisily but safely, gathered the masses who had come to celebrate, until they drifted away again to the farms and villages whence they had come. Conservatives who observed the antics of the crowd, were incredulous. Margaret Bayard Smith recalled, "Ladies and gentlemen only had been expected at this levee, not the people en masse. But it was the People's day, the People's President and the People would rule."

Who was this man who had captured the imagination and support of the American people? Born of Scotch-Irish immigrant parents on the western Carolina frontier in 1767, young Jackson experienced the rigors of pioneer life as well as the British invasion of the Carolina backcountry during the American Revolution. Following the war, he read law and was admitted to the North Carolina bar in 1787. The following year he moved to Nashville, Tennessee, and within a few years had become a prosperous lawyer, farmer and slave owner, politician, and judge. Appointed a major general in the state militia in 1802, Jackson rose to a stormy national prominence. His victory over the British at New Orleans in January, 1815, and his successful campaigns against the Indians made him a national hero and established his availability as a presidential candidate. Jackson—tall, erect, with lean, sharp features—was strong-willed, intolerant, and contentious. His hot temper and keen sense of personal honor drew him into numerous fights and brawls. One of his soldiers said he was "tough as hickory"; hence his nickname, "Old Hickory." Jackson was a man of action, not a clear or deep thinker. In his inaugural address, he outlined his principles, but he failed to advance any specific program to achieve his broad goals. "The Federal Constitution must be obeyed," he said simply, "state rights preserved, our national debt must be paid, direct taxes and loans avoided, and the Federal Union preserved."

The New Administration

Once ensconced in the White House, Jackson faced the necessity of welding his great following into an effective political force. Unlike Adams, Jackson was a majority President. But what was the majority will? Behind his election was no single program generally understood and accepted by party spokesmen. Instead, Jackson was trapped in a conflict of philosophies and personalities among the top men in his victorious coalition. Calhoun, representing the extreme states' rights side of the Jeffersonian tradition, had argued his case in the *South Carolina Exposition* of 1828. Calhoun had prepared this document anonymously, but its approval by the South Carolina Legislature had made it official state doctrine. Defying the "Tariff of Abominations," Calhoun had told the nation that no state need tolerate policies that enriched one section or class at the expense of another. Should the rights of a state be violated by a sectional majority in Congress, he warned, then that state, acting singly under the compact theory of government, might employ its sovereign power to nullify the law in question. Not since Jefferson's and Madison's Virginia and Kentucky Resolutions of 1798 had the states' rights position been so explicitly drawn. Thus Jackson began his administration under circumstances which presaged conflict with his own Vice President and the South Carolina nullifiers, whose agent Calhoun had secretly become.

Calhoun's elimination as a key member of the administration came quickly, but not over the question of political philosophy. Shortly before Jackson's inaugural, Senator John H. Eaton of Tennessee, already designated Secretary of War, married Mrs. Margaret O'Neale Timberlake, the daughter of a Washington tavernkeeper and widow of a Navy purser. The new Mrs. Eaton was reputedly a woman of extraordinary beauty and intelligence but also of questionable morals. For Floride Calhoun, Peggy's presence in Washington society was intolerable. In pointedly snubbing Mrs. Eaton, she set a precedent followed by a number of Cabinet wives. Jackson became incensed at this treatment of Mrs. Eaton, whose maligning he associated with that suffered in the 1828 campaign by his own wife, Rachel, now dead. When Calhoun sided with Floride, he opened a rift with Jackson that would never be healed.

Calhoun's rapid demise as a force in Jacksonian politics opened for Martin Van Buren a broad avenue to power and influence. Jackson had revealed his debt to the New Yorker by making him Secretary of State, and Van Buren was no less determined than Calhoun to control the presidential succession. Van Buren's open defense of Mrs. Eaton won him the President's gratitude and esteem, and he pressed this early advantage to the fullest. Jackson, finding his Cabinet divided and worthless, turned increasingly to a group of unofficial advisers known as the "kitchen cabinet." Prominent in this group were Van Buren and editors Amos Kendall and Isaac Hill. Van Buren's prestige and power were further enhanced when the President assigned him the management of the federal patronage. Thus, long before the first of Jackson's two terms had ended, Van Buren, "the Little Magician," had firmly established himself as heir apparent to the Presidency.

In 1829 the concept of "rotation in office" was not new. The practice of rewarding political friends with public offices had begun as early as Jefferson's Presidency. But Jackson rationalized the spoils system as an agency of democracy. Rotation in office, with appointments going generally to members of the victorious party, would not only democratize the federal service but also render it more representative of the nation's citizenry. Too many federal offices, Jackson believed, had become mere family sinecures and havens for aristocrats. To him it seemed incredible that the federal government required a specially trained bureaucracy to carry out its obligations. "The duties of all public offices are . . . so plain and simple," he said, "that men of intelligence may readily qualify themselves for their performance." Thus encouraged, hundreds of deserving Democrats besieged the White House to state their claims. To escape this pressure on his time and energy, the President sent the office seekers to Van Buren, and the Secretary filled key positions with men of his own choice—usually politicians who had served the party well. This permitted him to strengthen both the national party organization and his control of that organization. Yet Jackson and Van Buren showed restraint in the redistribution of public offices; several important areas of federal employment they scarcely touched. Under Jackson's Presidency perhaps no more than 10 percent of the public offices changed hands. Nevertheless, under Jackson and Van Buren, federal patronage became for the first time an essential element in the creation and maintenance of a democratically based political party.

Webster and Hayne

Jackson's first annual message of December, 1829, disappointed the South, for the President failed to promise tariff reform. Southern leaders now turned their eyes to the West, offering that section a freer land policy in exchange for its support on tariff reduction. It was this incipient alliance between the South and West that frightened New England protectionists and set the stage for the celebrated Webster-Hayne debate of January, 1830.

Senator Samuel A. Foot of Connecticut quite innocently opened the way for the debate when he offered the Senate, in December, 1829, a resolution designed to restrict public lands sales to those lands already offered by the government at the minimum price of $1.25 an acre. Whatever Foot's motivation, the resolution, if accepted, would have curtailed Western expansion. Meanwhile, in January, 1830, the South and West revealed their combined power by passing a special preemption act to give squatters on public lands the first option to buy the land they occupied, at the minimum government price.

Foot's resolution was especially disturbing to Senator Thomas Hart Benton of Missouri. Benton accused Foot of attempting to retard westward expansion and thus sustain a ready supply of cheap labor in the Eastern factory towns. Such bluntness was characteristic of the man. Born in North Carolina in 1782, this Missourian had moved as a young lawyer to Tennessee and then in 1815 to St. Louis. After his election to the United States Senate in 1820, he became a strong Jacksonian. In the Senate, Benton concerned himself with the interests of Western pioneers, favoring not only preemption but also "graduation." As early as 1824 he proposed that the price of unsold government land be lowered 25 cents an acre each year until it reached 25 cents; after that, whatever remained would be given to settlers.

Benton's reaction to the Foot resolution set the stage for Robert Y. Hayne of South Carolina, who now committed the South to the extremely liberal program of selling the public lands to the states in which they were located. Webster detected in this a special threat to his region, for neither free land nor tariff reduction would serve the interest of his industrialist constituents. Webster's only hope of alienating the West from the South lay in exposing the South's ideological peculiarities. Having gained the floor, Webster ignored the question of Western lands and instead pointed his attack at South Carolina and its doctrine of state sovereignty. Hayne, forced by sectional pride to reply, retreated to the theories of Calhoun, defending eventually the doctrine of nullification itself. His argument was simple and clear: ". . . though the States have surrendered certain specific powers, they have not surrendered their sovereignty."

Webster now had the opportunity for which he had been waiting—to tear down Calhoun's *South Carolina Exposition* point by point. His arguments were essentially those of John Marshall. Challenging the concept of state sovereignty, Webster described the origin of the federal government: "I hold it to be a popular Government, erected by the people, . . . and itself capable of being amended and modified, just as the people may choose it should be. It is as popular . . . as the State Governments. . . . It is not the creation of the State Governments." The people, not the states, said Webster, were sovereign. Webster rolled on, hour after hour, in what was perhaps the greatest American oration on record, his deep, rich voice and well-turned phrases sometimes amusing and always delighting the packed galleries. For those who saw and heard the "Olympian," this was an experience to remember, for never before had the Senate been so thoroughly exposed to Webster's commanding presence and intellect. No one, it was said, could be as great as Daniel Webster looked.

The clarion appeal of Webster's second reply to Hayne—"Liberty *and* Union, now and forever, one and inseparable!"—resounded across the nation as it has subsequently reverberated through American history. Van Buren found

Webster's words pleasing, for the New Englander's theories, like his own, pointed not to minority rights, as Calhoun would have preferred, but to majority rule. Nor was Webster's nationalism displeasing to Jackson. Whatever the President's views toward states' rights, he never questioned the sovereignty of the federal Union. Not long after at a Jefferson Day Dinner, in the presence of Calhoun, his Vice President, Jackson threw out a direct challenge to the champion of states' rights. "Our Federal Union," he declared in a toast which left Calhoun shaken, "—it must be preserved." The South Carolinian, his hand trembling with emotion, responded in his turn: "The Union—next to our liberty most dear. May we always remember that it can only be preserved by distributing equally the benefits and the burthens of the Union." Both men had taken their stands: Jackson for the nation and majority rule; Calhoun for constitutional and minority rights. The two would meet again.

Van Buren and Jackson

Van Buren's ultimate advantage over Calhoun lay not only in his superb relations with Jackson but even more in his genuine acceptance of the new democratic order. Whereas Calhoun looked to the checks and balances of the Constitution, placed there to protect minority rights, Van Buren accepted majority rule without qualification, with all its opportunities and dangers. The role which he assigned to himself and his party was simply that of determining and guiding the popular will toward the achievement of some national pupose. By conviction, preparation, personality, and method, Van Buren was ideally fitted for leadership in the democracy of his times. Although Calhoun's assets as a political and intellectual figure were remarkable, his philosophy of government was entirely too sectional and particularistic to attract a sizable national or party following.

In large measure, Jackson assigned Van Buren the dominant advisory role in his administration because he found the New Yorker's views to his liking. The President accepted the Secretary's faith in democracy and hoped to follow policies which conformed to the popular will. Jackson was by instinct a Jeffersonian, and, as such, he was suspicious of the centralizing tendencies of the federal government. Yet he believed strongly that the federal government must be a government dominated by the President, the only official elected by *all* the people. A conservative in things economic, he entered the White House with an abiding fear of speculation. Having been driven into bankruptcy by his own early financial extravagances, he viewed the boom of 1819, based on easy credit, and the Panic which followed, as a national expression of his own folly. As President, Jackson favored programs which he believed would reward honest labor and opposed measures that might encourage easy profits based on financial manipulation, speculation, and the use of credit. To that end he favored an economical government that would serve only the general interest. In his first annual message, he pledged the ultimate liquidation of the national debt.

Congress put the Jeffersonianism of Jackson and Van Buren to the test in April, 1830, when it passed a bill authorizing the federal government to purchase stock in a Kentucky corporation designated to build a turnpike from Maysville to Lexington. Jackson's Western advisers urged him not to veto the bill, for the West favored internal improvements. Though the

Maysville road lay within one state, it was part of a projected interstate system. But Van Buren argued against the measure, persuading the President that the time had come to terminate all federal aid to private corporations. Jackson's veto message not only denounced the Maysville road project as local in nature and therefore not eligible for federal support; it went so far as to question the constitutionality and expediency of all public programs at federal expense. The veto message, though a lasting triumph for Van Buren, began a process of alienation which gradually drove Jackson's Western advisers out of his inner circle.

Eventually the President decided to end the factionalism within his administration. In 1831 Jackson persuaded his entire Cabinet to resign, thus removing the Calhounites. The President then sent Van Buren to London as United States Minister and Eaton to Madrid, where Mrs. Eaton scored a series of new triumphs. The President built his new Cabinet around Edward Livingston of Louisiana as Secretary of State, Lewis Cass of Michigan as Secretary of War, and Roger B. Taney of Maryland as Attorney General. Meanwhile, Jackson had completely severed relations with his Vice President, and Calhoun, embittered by this turn of events, now sought revenge. His moment came in January, 1832, when, as presiding officer of the Senate, he cast the deciding vote against Van Buren's nomination to London. But when Calhoun boasted that he had finally disposed of his rival, Benton retorted, "You have broken a minister, and elected a Vice President." Van Buren, already in London for five months, returned to the United States in June to enter that year's canvass as Jackson's running mate. Calhoun resigned the vice presidency. Elected to the Senate by a compliant South Carolina Legislature, he was back in Washington in December to defend the interests of the South against any further assault from Congress or the administration.

Indian Removal

For the moment a further clash between Jackson and Calhoun appeared remote, for Jackson, in defending Georgia's rights to its Indian lands, assumed an extreme states' rights position. In 1827, the year that the Creeks ceded their Georgia lands, the highly civilized Cherokees signaled their defiance by adopting a constitution declaring themselves to be an independent, sovereign nation. A year later, when the discovery of gold in the Cherokee nation brought an influx of miners, the Georgia Legislature responded by making all whites in the Cherokee Territory subject to the laws of the state and warned that after June 1, 1830, all Cherokee laws would be considered void. After a Georgia court convicted an Indian of murder, the state, authorized by its legislature to defy a federal court order, promptly executed the Indian. Although Georgia's actions challenged federal supremacy, Jackson had no interest in defending Cherokees. Jackson did not believe, as was sometimes said, that the only good Indian was a dead Indian, but he thought that Indians had no right to stand in the way of white settlement. Georgia went on unhindered to pass laws designed to annihilate the Cherokee political structure and deprive the Indians of their lands, all in defiance of federal judicial authority. The Indians held out a few years longer, but by 1838 the great majority had moved to Indian Territory west of the Mississippi.

George Catlin painted the Plains Indians from life between 1830 and 1836, a time when much of the West was unknown and unexplored. Working in a huge area between the Mississippi and the Rocky Mountains, ranging from the northernmost United States to the Mexican Territory, he documented in pictures and words the leaders, ceremonies, and lifeways of most of the major tribes. In George Catlin and the Old Frontier, *biographer Harold McCracken has written, "It can be said with justice and justification that no other artist or writer in the field of the North American Indian and the Old West has had as long and broad an influence as George Catlin."*

George Catlin and the Indian Documents

Catlin's accomplishment grew not only from his skill and adventuresome tenacity but from his success in achieving rapport with his subjects and gaining their cooperation—a success which was the result of his real respect for the Indians and their way of life. "I love a people," he wrote, "who have always made me welcome with the best they had . . . who are honest without laws, who have no jails and no poor houses . . . who worship God without a Bible, and I believe that God loves them also . . . who are free of religious animosities . . . who have never raised a hand against me or stolen my property, where there was no law to punish either . . . and, oh! how I love a people who don't live for the love of money."

In his travels among some forty-eight tribes, Catlin did portraits of hundreds of chiefs, braves, women, and children. At Fort Pierre in South Dakota, where he painted Ha-Won-Je-Tah, The One Horn, First Chief of the Sioux (near left, below), he had to overcome objections of medicine men who feared their chief would not be able to sleep at night because he had been depicted with his eyes open. But Catlin's persuasiveness and the hitherto-unseen charm of realistic painting soon made it an honor to be painted, and his subjects sat for him in the order of their importance in the tribe. Others in this sampling include Stu-Mick-O-Sucks, The Buffalo's Back Fat, Head Chief of the Blackfeet (right), and Osceola (far left, below), whom Catlin painted after the great Seminole leader had been imprisoned.

All portraits courtesy of Smithsonian Institution

Rare Book Division, New York Public Library

While Catlin deliberately sought to record the lives of tribes which had been little touched by the white man, he was also bitterly aware of the harm the white man was doing to the Indian. From the Southeast the Choctaw, Chickasaw, Creeks, Cherokees, and Seminoles were driven west of the Mississippi into Oklahoma "territory" along a "Trail of Tears." The Sauk were driven from their villages in Illinois despite a futile war led by Black Hawk, whose portrait by Catlin is shown at right, above. The print directly above, not by Catlin, shows the Sauk being fired upon as they attempted to return to their homes. At right, below, are Catlin's two views of Wi-Jun-Jon, Pigeon's Egg Head, son of an Assiniboin chief, before and after he went to Washington to meet President Jackson. Catlin learned that after his return Wi-Jun-Jon's description of the East was so unbelievable to the tribe and his conduct so unbecoming that he was considered a liar and a disgrace and eventually was killed.

Catlin's emotions at what he saw happening are reflected in his writing about the Indian: "I have seen him set fire to his wigwam and smooth over the graves of his fathers . . . with tears of grief sliding over his cheeks, clap his hand in silence over his mouth, and take the last look over his fair hunting grounds. . . . I have seen this splendid juggernaut rolling on and beheld its sweeping desolation, and held converse with happy thousands living as yet beyond its influence, who have not yet been crushed, nor yet have dreamed of its approach. . . . I have stood amidst these unsophisticated people and contemplated with feelings of deepest regret the certain approach of this overwhelming system, which will inevitably march on and prosper, until reluctant tears have watered every rod of this fair land."

Above and below: Courtesy of Smithsonian Institution

During Jackson's Presidency, population pressures along the Mississippi Valley frontier produced dozens of treaties whereby the Indians were compelled to cede their lands and join the westward trek to designated areas across the Mississippi. The "trail of tears" proved to be costly for all these tribes in loss of life and property. The Chickasaws and Choctaws agreed to leave their tribal homes in Alabama and Mississippi and join the Creeks and Cherokees in Indian Territory. The Florida Seminoles were far less amenable. Several chiefs signed a treaty in 1832 which sent some tribesmen to the West. Chief Osceola resisted, however, and, aided by the fastness of the Everglades, chopped up and eluded the United States military forces sent against him. At the time of his capture in 1842 he had cost the nation millions of dollars. Even then, several thousand of his fellow Seminoles refused to leave the Everglades country and continued to reside there.

The effort at Indian removal produced another tragic episode in the story of Chief Black Hawk of the Sauk and Fox. Black Hawk's people resided at the confluence of the Rock River and the Mississippi. When squatters in 1831 entered the region and proceeded to tear up the Indian crops, Black Hawk retreated across the Mississippi, only to be harassed by famine and the more warlike Sioux. Driven by desperation and hunger, Black Hawk recrossed the river to his original home in Illinois. So long had the Old Northwest been free of Indian troubles that the presence of a destitute and starving band of Indians where the settlers believed they did not belong sent waves of terror across Illinois, Indiana, and even Michigan Territory. The Illinois militia converged on Black Hawk's straggling villagers, following them up the Rock River into the wilderness of southern Wisconsin. Finally catching the Indians as they attempted to escape across the Mississippi, the troops engaged in an unnecessary massacre, killing even women and children.

By the mid-thirties the most desirable lands of the Mississippi Valley had been cleared of Indian titles. The Indian tribes now resided in new "permanent" homes beyond the Mississippi, separated from the settlers by a chain of frontier posts, garrisoned by mounted troops. John Quincy Adams judged the nation's Indian policy in 1837: "We have done more harm to the Indians since our Revolution than had ever been done to them by the French and English nations before. . . . These are crying sins for which we are answerable before a higher jurisdiction."

The Tariff and Nullification

If Jackson refused to face up to Georgia on the question of Indian rights, he did not hesitate to oppose South Carolina on the issue of nullification. This time it was ostensibly the tariff that led to the clash between Jackson's nationalism and Calhoun's doctrine of state sovereignty. Jackson's second Cabinet had no more interest than the first in tariff reform. Any sharp downward revision of the high tariff of 1828 would reduce federal revenues and delay the payment of the national debt, a matter of utmost importance to Jackson. Some Southern Democrats demanded tariff reduction, but Van Buren hoped to avoid a tariff debate, fearing it would break the North-South alliance which he wished to maintain. South Carolina was impatient, however, and would tolerate no further delay. That state, traditionally one of the most prosperous states of the nation, had never fully recovered from the Panic of 1819. It was in South Caro-

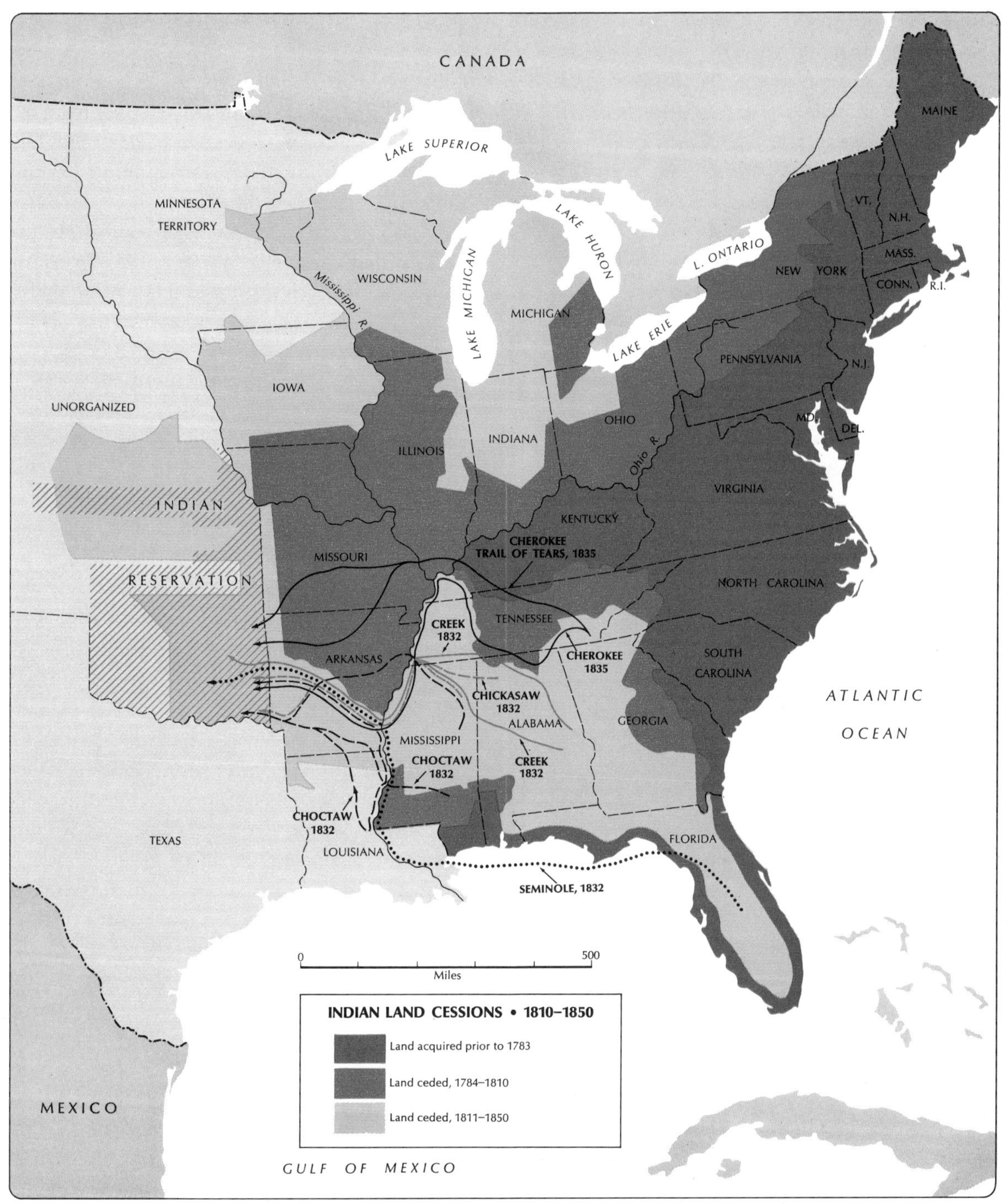
CANADA
LAKE SUPERIOR
MINNESOTA
TERRITORY
WISCONSIN
Mississippi R.
LAKE MICHIGAN
LAKE HURON
MICHIGAN
L. ONTARIO
LAKE ERIE
MAINE
VT.
N.H.
MASS.
NEW YORK
CONN.
R.I.
PENNSYLVANIA
N.J.
IOWA
UNORGANIZED
ILLINOIS
INDIANA
OHIO
MD.
DEL.
Ohio R.
VIRGINIA
INDIAN
KENTUCKY
CHEROKEE
TRAIL OF TEARS, 1835
MISSOURI
RESERVATION
NORTH CAROLINA
CREEK
1832
TENNESSEE
ARKANSAS
CHEROKEE
1835
SOUTH
CAROLINA
CHICKASAW
1832
ALABAMA
GEORGIA
ATLANTIC
OCEAN
MISSISSIPPI
CHOCTAW
1832
CREEK
1832
CHOCTAW
1832
TEXAS
LOUISIANA
FLORIDA
SEMINOLE, 1832
0
500
Miles
INDIAN LAND CESSIONS • 1810–1850
Land acquired prior to 1783
Land ceded, 1784–1810
Land ceded, 1811–1850
MEXICO
GULF OF MEXICO

lina's interest that Calhoun had deserted Clay's old assertion that the tariff served all sections and economic interests equally. By raising the price of manufactured products artificially, the tariff placed the South at an economic disadvantage in its quest for profits. By the twenties, the South generally had fallen behind the North in wealth, population, immigration, and productivity; and the fact that the South Carolina planter aristocracy had been one of the South's richest and proudest made that state's economic decline all the harder to bear. More than other states of the South, South Carolina attributed its economic problems to federal policies rather than to the causes that really mattered—soil exhaustion, inefficiency, the new competition in British markets, and, above all, the crippling competition which Eastern planters everywhere faced from the new cotton-producing regions of the Southwest.

Still, depression and tariff alone cannot explain the unreasoning fear of federal power which possessed South Carolina's tidewater aristocracy, that remarkably homogeneous and able group for which Calhoun spoke. The South Carolina tidewater was not cotton country. Its two chief crops of rice and luxury sea island cotton enjoyed good markets and never ceased to bring excellent returns. This region's concern centered on a second, more pervading, threat from the North—that of abolitionism. Only with slave labor could the planters around Charleston wrest profits from their disease-ridden swamps. The Northern attacks on slavery which followed the Missouri debates, limited as they were, exceeded what the hard-pressed South Carolinians would tolerate. Some abolitionists preached racial equality, a notion which no slave society would accept. Charleston had witnessed the effects of such doctrine in the well-planned revolt of 1822, conceived and led by Denmark Vesey, a free Negro of the city. This revolt, limited essentially to Charleston, was crushed without disaster only because some trusted Negroes revealed the plot. Nat Turner's Negro rebellion of 1831 never crossed the boundaries of Virginia, but again it sent waves of fear through the Carolina tidewater. Even as South Carolinians battled the tariff of 1827, the American Colonization Society requested federal funds to aid it in fulfilling its program of exporting to Africa those Negroes who desired to go. Congress quickly tabled the petition, but the mere existence of the request demonstrated the full vulnerability of the South to federal power. Calhoun's *South Carolina Exposition* of 1828 was responding to this Southern fear of Northern power and hostility toward slavery when it outlined a constitutional defense of Southern rights.

Clay unwittingly forced the nullification issue on South Carolina in July, 1832, when he drove a new tariff measure through Congress. This bill, passed with the aid of Southern as well as Western votes, eliminated the worst excesses of the Tariff of Abominations, but it maintained high schedules on iron and textiles and revealed a strong protariff consensus in the Congress. Even a number of representatives from South Carolina voted for the measure. For the nullifiers, however, the tariff of 1832 was a direct challenge to their state's prestige and welfare. Led by Calhoun, they carried the elections that fall and called a state convention in late November, which declared the tariff law to be "null, void, and no law, nor binding upon the State, its officers or citizens." The ordinance futher forbade federal officials to collect customs within the state after February 1, 1833, and threatened secession if the federal government chose to employ force.

Jackson met the nullification issue head on. His famous proclamation to the people of South Carolina, stern, yet kind, revealed Jackson's frontier nationalism at its best. The doctrine that a state could nullify a law of Congress that it did not like, he said, defied the letter and spirit of the Constitution and was incompatible with the existence of the Union. Jackson agreed with Calhoun that the Constitution was a compact, but he argued that the compact itself made the connections binding and ruled out the right of secession. Jackson appealed directly to the doctrines of Marshall and Webster:

> The Constitution of the United States, then, forms a *government,* not a league; and whether it be formed by compact between the States or in any other manner, its character is the same. It is a government in which all the people are represented, which operates on the people individually, not upon the States. . . . Because the Union was formed by a compact, it is said the parties of the compact may, when they feel themselves aggrieved, depart from it; but it is precisely because it is a compact that they can not. A compact is an agreement or binding obligation.

No state, declared Jackson, had the right to secede and thus destroy the nation's unity. The federal government had the authority not only to pass laws but also to enforce them.

The first effect of the President's warning was to exacerbate the crisis. The South Carolina Legislature called for volunteers to defend the state even as Jackson prepared to dispatch an army to Charleston to collect the customs. Fortunately for both sides in the quarrel, the overwhelming majority of Americans favored peace and drove the extremists into isolation. Not one state answered South Carolina's call for a national convention or supported its doctrine of nullification. Georgia, unperturbed by its massive claims to states' rights in the Indian controversy, denied that nullification could be peaceful or constitutional; an Alabama resolution declared nullification "unsound in theory and dangerous in practice." The states of the North and West condemned South Carolina's action as revolutionary. Jackson's nationalism had clearly captured the nation's sentiment.

Henry Clay, ever the great conciliator, accepted the responsibility for bringing the crisis to an end. Jackson himself had recommended tariff reform, suggesting in his December message to Congress that protection be "limited to those articles of domestic manufacture which are indispensable to our safety in time of war." Clay, working with Calhoun, now seized the issue and secured a compromise measure designed to reduce all tariffs over a ten-year period to a uniform level of 20 percent. This satisfied the nullifiers, who, after all, had centered their attack on the previous tariff. Meanwhile, Jackson asked Congress for a measure that would fully authorize him to use the land and naval forces of the United States to compel the states to comply with federal law. Late in the session Congress passed both the tariff and the "Force Bill." On March 2, 1833, as his first term approached its end, Jackson signed both measures into law. South Carolina's reassembled convention, in repealing its nullification measure, accepted the compromise tariff but threw down another meaningless challenge to Jackson by nullifying the Force Act. The nullifiers had demonstrated that a single determined state could alter national policy; they had demanded tariff reform and achieved it. Jackson, however, had demonstrated that no state could defy federal authority without facing the full might of the country's military power. This was the essential lesson which the crisis had taught, though it was clear from the nullifiers' boasts of victory that they had not learned it.

These battles of the Jackson era were merely a prelude to the final struggle which above all others illustrated the philosophical inconsistency in Jacksonian Democracy—Jackson's war on the Second Bank of the United States. This complex episode brought Jackson face to face with Clay, for it was Clay almost alone who insisted on bringing the Bank issue into partisan debate. Except for Clay, the issue might have remained dormant, at least until 1836 when the Bank's charter would expire. But Clay, having been nominated for the Presidency by the National Republican party in December, 1831, believed that he could force the issue on the Democratic party and turn it into a winning cause. The President, Clay assumed, could neither sign nor veto a measure to recharter the Bank without alienating one or more powerful factions within the Democratic party.

Two major strains in Jacksonian thought opposed the Bank—the agrarian and the democratic. The agrarians feared banks generally because of their role in speculation and the advantages which they gave to those who controlled them. Agrarians were especially opposed to the Bank of the United States because it wielded almost absolute control over the nation's credit structure. Jackson himself recalled the restraining role which the Bank had played in breaking the boom of 1819. For the urban-centered democratic radicals the issue at stake was social and economic democracy. The Bank, as a public corporation, symbolized the power and advantage of the nonproducing classes over the farmers and laborers who created wealth with their hands. The collapse of the credit and paper money system in 1819 had convinced such men as Thomas Hart Benton that the government should restrict itself to hard money, dealing only with gold and silver. In this spirit, a group of Philadelphia workingmen in 1829 blamed their hard times on the "too great extension of paper credit." Their committee reported that banking and paper money created the foundation for an artificial inequality of wealth. Such views spread rapidly through the Eastern cities, giving rise to new organizations which favored hard money and opposed national and state banking. One was the radical faction of the Democratic party in New York after 1835—the "Locofocos."

That the Bank of the United States was a powerful institution no one could have denied, least of all its able president, Nicholas Biddle. After assuming his duties in 1823, Biddle had used his Bank's authority to restrain the state banks in their extension of credit, thereby strengthening the nation's banking structure. Albert Gallatin in 1831 praised the Bank for effectively checking the "excessive issues" of the state banks and for fulfilling its obligation to produce a sound currency. Nonetheless, this regulatory power, however judiciously applied, was the Bank's undoing. Returning prosperity, feeding on a new burst of Western expansion, had created unprecedented visions of money making and a new, aggressive, entrepreneurial class. The older economic order had been built on wealth—accumulated chiefly from commerce—which its owners could invest in new enterprises. For America in the age of Jackson the older methods were too slow and limited. For the new investors, the key to success was credit, and the looser the restrictions on state banks, the greater their power to extend it. Although credit expansion could lead to inflation and eventual collapse, it could also build fortunes and develop communities. For new-breed enterprisers, claiming to be Jacksonians, the chief barrier to easy credit was the Bank of the United States, citadel of the nation's traditional, conservative business, representing established rather than speculative wealth.

Those Jacksonians who conducted the Bank war were overwhelmingly spokesmen of the new enterprise, but their phraseology was that of the agrarians and workingmen. They accused the Bank of tyranny and oppression; they identified it with special privilege and monopoly. In their praise of honest work, they identified themselves with the urban and rural lower classes, although in actual fact, as rising capitalists representing the new enterprise, they pursued wealth and economic power as much as did the Bank men. What they really opposed was the restrictive power of the older capitalists, who were centered largely in the East. This faction of Jacksonians, whatever their claims to class interest, were no more concerned with human rights than were the Bank's defenders. How they could reconcile their easy banking and credit demands with the hard money views of those for whom they claimed to speak was never clear.

Biddle, conscious of the wide support which the Bank of the United States enjoyed among conservatives generally, including such old Jeffersonians as Madison and Gallatin, received his initial shock when Jackson questioned the Bank's constitutionality in his first annual message of December, 1829. Then as pressure against the Bank slowly accumulated, Benton, in February, 1831, launched a vigorous attack on the Bank, based on class antagonism. The Bank, he said, was too powerful to be tolerated by a government of free and equal laws. "It tends," he charged, "to aggravate the inequality of fortunes, to make the rich richer, and the poor poorer; to multiply nabobs and paupers." As the Jackson press took up the cry, Biddle went to Clay and Webster for support. Still hoping to avoid a political debate over the Bank's merits, Biddle took confidence from Jackson's refusal to attack the Bank in his annual message of December, 1831. It was at this time that Clay, distrustful of Jackson and Van Buren, decided to take charge of the issue by introducing recharter petitions in both houses of Congress during January, 1832. Biddle had no choice but to support Clay's action.

The pro-Bank forces easily pushed the recharter bill through Congress, but they reckoned without the President's veto. On July 10, 1832, Jackson declared the Bank unconstitutional, unnecessary, and dangerous to liberty. Favorable Supreme Court decisions, he said, did not establish the Bank's constitutionality. Whether the Bank was *necessary* and *proper* under the enumerated powers of the federal government was a matter for Congress and the President—not the Supreme Court—to decide. Jackson found it neither necessary nor proper. The Bank conferred exclusive privileges upon a small minority of the American people in the realm of banking and finance. The benefits derived from this powerful monopoly and the rising value of its stock accrued not to the millions of Americans whose money backed the credit structure but to the stockholders, many of whom were not even Americans. The Bank, in short, was a monster, so manipulating paper money and credit as to bring artificial and ill-gotten wealth to its managers, supporters, and beneficiaries. By destroying the Bank, the President would return America to its republican ideal of simple, honest, and visible economic relationships under a frugal and limited democratic government.

Unable to carry the recharter bill over the President's veto, the Bank men took the issue into the election of 1832. Clay, nominee of what had become known as the National Republican party, campaigned mainly on the Bank question. Jackson, who received the backing of a national convention of the Democratic Republican party, was pleased to run with his friend Van Buren as the people's champion against the "monster" Bank. For the first time in American history, both leading candidates received the endorsement of popular national conventions, a practice in keeping with the growing democratic tendencies of the time. This contest would witness, as well, the broader use of new campaign techniques such as political cartoons and parades. A final novel feature of the election of 1832 was the appearance of the Anti-Mason party, the first "third" party to run a candidate in an American presidential election. After a lively campaign, Jackson swept the November election. He carried more popular votes than Clay and William Wirt (the Anti-Mason candidate) combined, and enjoyed a large majority in the electoral college—Jackson, 219; Clay, 49; and Wirt, 7. Clay's attempt to win the Presidency on the Bank issue had proved a miserable failure.

Encouraged by his resounding electoral victory, Jackson moved to kill the Bank before Biddle could organize his vast economic and political resources to push yet another recharter bill through Congress. The Bank remained the darling of the National Republican party, many leading businessmen, and much of the press. With the reduction of the national debt to the point of extinction, federal receipts, symptomatic of a booming economy, piled up in the vaults of the Bank and further extended its power to lend and thus to control the nation's money market. Jackson planned to cripple the Bank by depriving it of the government deposits, but conservative members of the Cabinet refused to support this policy. Secretary of the Treasury Louis McLane escaped the issue by securing an appointment to the State Department. William J. Duane, his successor, refused to obey orders. The exasperated Jackson then named Attorney General Taney, who shared his anti-Bank views to the Treasury. Finally in September, 1833, Jackson announced that thereafter the federal government would deposit its funds in selected state banks (named "pet banks" by Jackson's enemies).

Jackson's direct assault on the Bank provided Biddle with the excuse he needed to bring renewed pressure on Congress. Using the removal of federal funds as justification for a general contraction of the Bank's credit structure, Biddle soon produced bankruptcies and general economic decline across the nation. Petitions poured into Congress, demanding either the restoration of the deposits or the immediate recharter of the Bank. Jackson, supported by Benton and the New Yorkers, held firm. Meanwhile, Biddle overreached himself. To destroy Jackson, he had contracted credit faster than the President's decision warranted, injuring many of his own political sympathizers in the process. After Congress adjourned in 1834, the friends of the Bank forced Biddle to relax the Bank's credit. Business responded quickly, demonstrating that the Bank, in its ability to manipulate the nation's currency, had even more economic power than its enemies charged. With the expiration of its federal

Andrew Jackson: The Man and the Legend

Courtesy of the New-York Historical Society, New York City

"The most roaring, rollicking, game-cocking, horse-racing, card-playing, mischievious fellow . . . the head of rowdies hereabouts . . ." in his youth, Andrew Jackson's origins contained all the ingredients of what had not then but would later become a native American "success story." Born in the Carolina hills, defiant prisoner of the British at thirteen, Jackson studied law, and at twenty-one went adventuring in Tennessee as public prosecutor. A career as Representative and then Senator from Tennessee followed quickly—he appeared in Washington with his hair in "a queue down his back tied with an old eel skin." Then his state appointed him judge of the superior court, and he returned home temporarily. But it was as an indomitable fighter, scourge of Indians and the British, "Old Hickory," that Jackson's image acquired its ultimate rough-hewn grandeur, and it is as a romanticized, but superheroic commanding general that Asher Durand, after a work by John Vanderlyn, painted this portrait in 1828, the year Jackson became President.

Jackson's often harsh militancy did not go entirely uncriticized. During the campaign of 1828, charges and counter-charges—some substantiated, most not—flew between Jackson and Adams partisans. Below, the "coffin handbill," widely circulated during the election year, condemns Jackson for ordering the execution of six militiamen accused of mutiny in 1815. At the left, Jackson raises his sword to strike off the ears of a dissenting Congressman. The unidentified man that Jackson hangs below could well be Everyman: the caption warns that if Jackson is elected, "you will be HANGED." Popular sentiments like those expressed at the right, however, won the day.

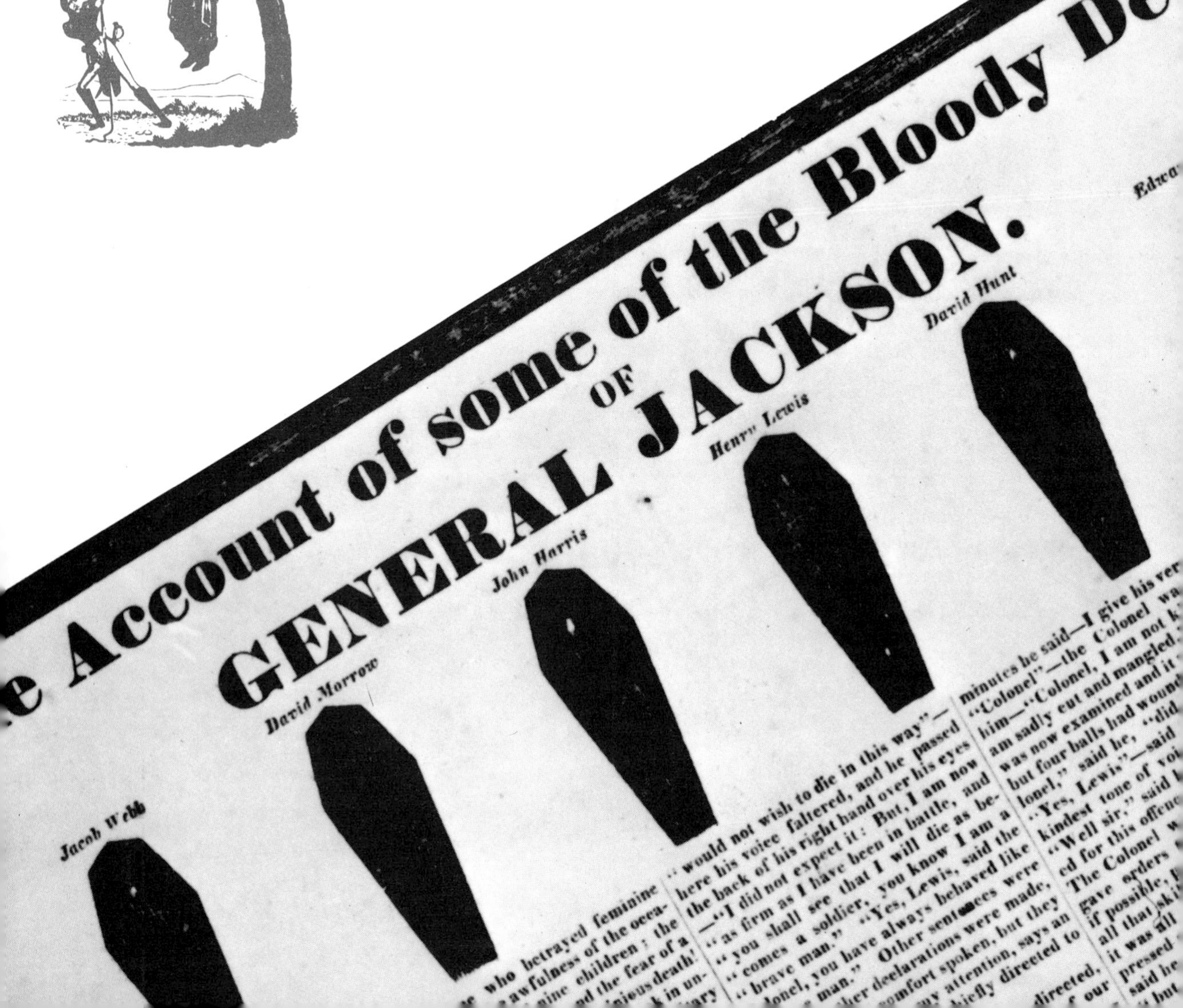

e Account of some of the Bloody De

OF

GENERAL JACKSON.

Jacob Webb

David Morrow

John Harris

Henry Lewis

David Hunt

Edwa

Jackson Forever!

he Hero of Two Wars and of Orleans

he Man of the People

HE WHO COULD NOT BARTER NOR BARGAIN FOR THE

PRESIDENCY!

, alt ugh *"A Military Chieftain,"* valued the purity of Elections and o
ors, M RE than the Office of PRESIDENT itself! Although the gre
gift of countrymen, and the highest in point of dignity of any in the w

BECAUSE

It s ould be derived from the

PEOPLE!

kades! No Reign of Terror! No Standing A
der the pay of Government, to browbeat, or

K DOWN

Representatives while in the discharg
nd vote for those who will support

CKORY

AL LAW.

All pictures: Courtesy of the New-York Historical Society, New York City

Jackson roundly defeated John Quincy Adams (left) in 1828, after gaining more popular votes but losing the 1824 election to him in the House.

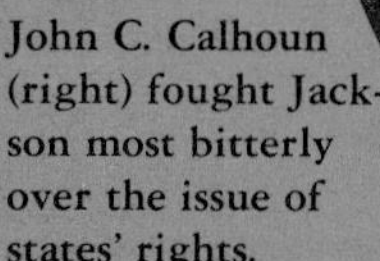

John C. Calhoun (right) fought Jackson most bitterly over the issue of states' rights.

A strong administrator, Jackson found himself surrounded by unusually capable, if not always agreeable, statesmen. The architect of Jackson's ampaign, Martin Van Buren (right) served as Secretary of State and succeeded Jackson as President. The ambitious Henry Clay (right, below) often clashed with the chief executive, as did Daniel Webster (below), who, however, joined Jackson in arguing against nullification.

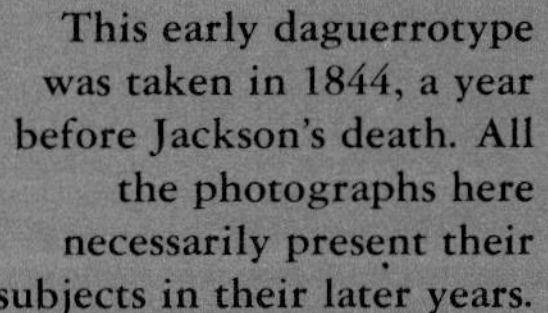

This early daguerrotype was taken in 1844, a year before Jackson's death. All the photographs here necessarily present their subjects in their later years.

Far left: George Eastman House Collection
All others: Library of Congress
Left: Courtesy of the New-York Historical Society, New York City

Personal scandals marred both Jackson's rise to political power and his presidency. Tongues wagged continuously over both his wife, Rachael, above, and Peggy Eaton. Mrs. Jackson had supposedly not been divorced when Jackson married her, a circumstance still remembered upon her death one month after his presidential election. Calhoun's wife, Floride, led the gossip about Peggy Timberlake, who married Jackson's Secretary of War, John Eaton, at the President's urging only after reputedly bearing Eaton two children. Jackson defended the Eaton's and even called a Cabinet meeting to discuss Peggy's vindication. Still, Washington remained outraged.

The satirical Robert Cruikshank drawing at the right, "The President's Levee, or All Creation Going to the White House," appeared in England in 1841. Jackson never escaped mockery in his role as "the people's President.

All pictures: Library of Congress

charter in 1836, Biddle secured a new one from the state of Pennsylvania, and the Bank continued to exist as a state bank until shattered in the Panic of 1837.

With the Bank's decline, the anti-Bank forces revealed their fundamental disagreements. The agrarians, as well as urban radicals such as New York's Locofocos, attached their continuing assault on the rich and powerful to a hard money policy. Believing bank notes to be inflationary and speculative, they demanded that the federal government reduce all circulating medium to gold and silver and require deposit banks to stop issuing and receiving notes. By driving the small notes from circulation, the hard money advocates hoped to force the banks to curtail their loans and retain their specie to meet their currency needs. But this program had no chance against the unparalleled speculation of the mid-thirties, now no longer restrained by the Bank's stabilizing influence. State banks, old and new, flooded the country with bank notes and credit. Even the deposit banks were caught up in the inflationary spiral which mounted relentlessly to its crest in 1836. Hard money men looked on aghast, while the Jacksonian enterprisers who had joined them in killing the Bank wallowed in the profits of the credit system they themselves were creating.

Henry Clay subjected the country's financial health to further hazards when he pushed a "distributing" or "deposit" bill through Congress in 1836. By January, 1835, Jackson had achieved one of the major objectives of his administration—payment of the national debt—and thereafter federal surpluses continued to mount. Clay wanted to distribute a large portion of this money to the states, where it could be used to finance internal improvements. His deposit bill, passed in 1836, was a partial triumph for his American System. Altogether, beginning early in 1837, the United States government distributed some $37 million in federal money to the state treasuries. Lavish state spending now broadened the nation's speculative base.

Alarmed by the runaway inflation, especially evident in the selling prices of federal lands, Jackson in July, 1836, issued through his Secretary of the Treasury the famous Specie Circular, specifying that henceforth all public lands be paid for in specie, or in notes redeemable in specie. Since state banks did not have specie to loan, this order greatly reduced the credit available and curtailed land sales. But Jackson's action came too late. The uncontrolled speculation, encouraged by his banking policies of the middle thirties, contributed heavily to the Panic of 1837. The American people had paid a heavy price for Jackson's destruction of the Bank of the United States.

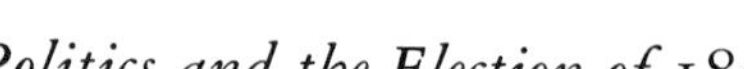

Politics and the Election of 1836

Jackson's reelection in 1832 had demonstrated the remarkable success of his party managers in building a political machine to exploit the sentiments of an egalitarian society. All the actions of the Democratic party were aimed at the voters, and none more so than the Bank veto message itself. Its language was designed to influence, not Congress, but the people—to win support outside of Congress by arousing bitter emotions against the Bank's supporters. Behind the veto message were those among Jackson's personal advisers who cared little for constitutional arguments but who recognized the essential fact that a democratic system

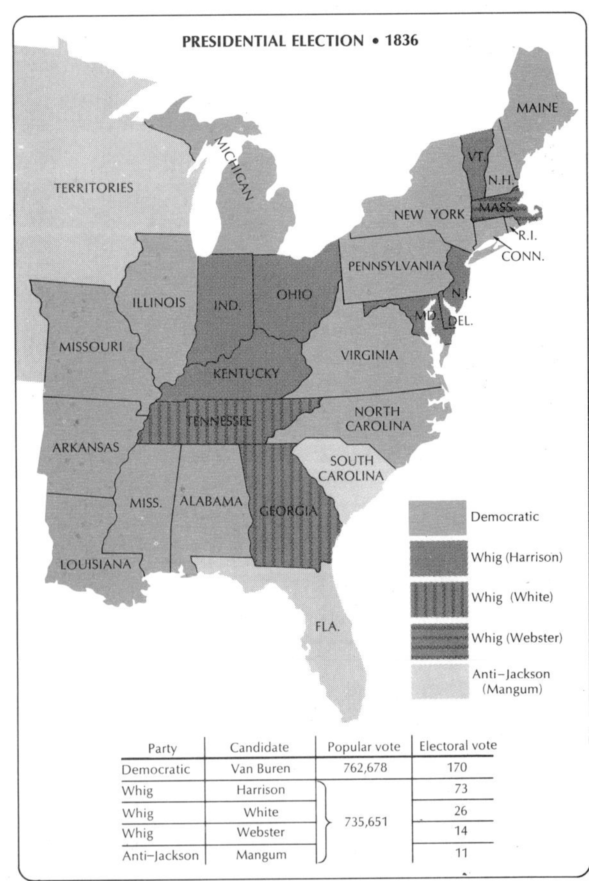

Party	Candidate	Popular vote	Electoral vote
Democratic	Van Buren	762,678	170
Whig	Harrison	735,651	73
Whig	White		26
Whig	Webster		14
Anti–Jackson	Mangum		11

placed political power in the masses, not the classes. Such key Democrats in Washington as Amos Kendall and Martin Van Buren were effective simply because they understood the necessary role of the electorate in a democratic society. Organization, not individual talent, was the key to Jacksonian politics, for it elevated the function of politics above the individual. The Jacksonians saw correctly that an organization built on specialization and interchangeability would be more effective than one based on unique, or even superb, talent. Whatever skills the party demanded could be discovered among its supporters. The loss of one individual hardly affected the party structure.

Jackson's opponents recognized the trend toward impersonality and large-scale organization in the Democratic party. In their experience it had been men, not organization, that mattered. Great men, acting as individuals, had given the Republic its early leadership and direction; superior men, Jackson's opponents believed, must continue to govern it. The Bank of the United States embodied their idea of elite leadership. Jackson's veto message disturbed them, not because the President had exceeded his authority, but because he had ignored Congress and aimed his words at the electorate. As Webster complained in his reply: "The message toils through all the commonplace topics of monopoly, the right of taxation, the suffering of the poor, the arrogance of the rich, with as much painful effort, as if one, or another, or all of them, had something to do with the constitutional questions." For men such as Webster and Biddle, Jackson, by appealing to lower-class prejudices, had broken tradition, debauched common sense, and endangered the natural social order.

Using the charge of "executive usurpation," Jackson's enemies attempted to build an alliance against him to defeat him and his party at the polls. The new Whig party, built largely around the old National Republicans, accepted Clay's American System as its creed. In 1834 it had carried a censure of Jackson through the Senate. Unable to agree on a candidate in 1836, the Whigs named three sectional favorites, hoping to split the electoral vote and deprive the Jacksonians of a majority in the electoral college, and then perhaps win the election in the House of Representatives. In the Southwest, they made a powerful bid for the conservative Democratic vote by naming Judge Hugh Lawson White, the popular Tennessee Senator and onetime Jackson supporter who had joined the Western rebellion against Jackson's Bank policies. In the North the Whigs relied chiefly on the aged General William Henry Harrison, the hero of Tippecanoe, although Webster was their man in Massachusetts. Calhoun, in the Southeast, was not a candidate, but his indifference would give little comfort to the Jacksonians.

Van Buren was the choice of the Democrats; Richard M. Johnson of Kentucky was tapped for the second spot. The successor to the mantle of the Democrats' "King Andrew" won easily in the November presidential sweepstakes, despite bitter denunciation from the Whigs. White carried Tennessee; Webster took Massachusetts, but only by a very narrow margin; Harrison revealed surprising strength, carrying seven states. But the three Whigs in aggregate received only 124 electoral votes, compared with 170 for Van Buren.

The Van Buren Presidency

Unlike his seven predecessors in the White House, Van Buren enjoyed no reputation earned in diplomacy or war. His career had been one of politics, but so uncanny was his ability to turn every opportunity into personal advancement that his friends referred to him as "the Little Magician." Emerging victorious from every conflict of Jackson's early Presidency to become Vice President in 1833, he no longer faced any opposition in 1836 as heir to the Democratic party leadership. Van Buren's popularity among party chieftains was axiomatic; such shrewdness and perspicacity would serve him well in the White House. Unwilling to create any sharp break with the Jacksonian past, Van Buren retained John Forsyth as Secretary of State; placed Joel Poinsett, another Jacksonian, in the War Department; and reserved the postmastership for Amos Kendall, the personally unimpressive but amazingly artful manager of Jackson's "kitchen cabinet."

As early as February, 1837, Thomas Hart Benton had warned the incoming President that the nation had reached the verge of financial collapse. *"You will soon feel the thunderbolt,"* he predicted. Yet Van Buren entered the White House still preferring to ignore the signs of the times. Unfortunately for the new administration, the prophets of doom had ample evidence. Bankers had extended credit far beyond the nation's specie supply. Land purchases, as well as road and canal construction, had become increasingly speculative, outstripping the needs of existent markets at home and abroad. Late in 1836 a succession of British bankruptcies forced these companies to throw their American securities on the market, thus increasing the flow of specie across the Atlantic. It required but a few major business failures in the United States during the spring of 1837 to reveal the gap between paper credits and hard money. During May, the New York banks stopped all specie payments; soon banks across the nation followed New York's example. By fall depression stalked the land. Land prices collapsed; markets evaporated.

For the next several years, the United States endured one of its worst depressions. Thousands of unemployed tramped the streets of Northern towns and cities looking in vain for work; canal and road building nearly ceased; and farm prices dropped to disastrous levels. Cotton, for example, declined from 15 to 6 cents a pound between 1836 and 1842. Not until 1843 did conditions begin to show major improvement.

Only one depressed group—the farmers—attracted much governmental attention. In his special message on the economic crisis, Van Buren in 1837 attributed the nation's distress to those speculative investments which outran its needs. What gave the American economy its ultimate security and its promise of commercial recovery, he said, were its resources and industry, especially its production of the great staple crops. This agricultural interest Van Buren would defend. To assure land to actual settlers at moderate prices and at the same time keep the agricultural communities compact, the President favored a system of "graduated" land prices. This system, first advocated by Benton in the 1820s, would permit the government to reduce the price of lands previously opened for sale but not settled because of their apparent inferiority. Van Buren believed that only by discouraging the tendency for settlers to move ahead in search of the most attractive lands could frontier outposts be transformed into prosperous and stable communities.

Van Buren's determination to defend the farmers' interests led him to support the preemption principle as well. Squatters on empty lands, he believed, should not be deprived of their improvements by speculators or men with greater resources. But he agreed that the only land policy ultimately acceptable was that of cash sales to those ready to move onto the land. Preemption laws, he feared, tended to injure public regard for federal authority, for they protected those who had broken the law in the first place by squatting on public lands. Consequently, while land policies received widespread attention, Congress enacted no major land legislation during the Van Buren administration.

Banking Reform

Behind the Panic of 1837 lay a discredited banking structure. Radicals attributed the collapse to the paper system; conservatives, among them Nicholas Biddle, blamed Jackson's refusal to recharter the national Bank. Van Buren had three choices before him. He could restore the big Bank; he could rely on an improved and regulated system of state banking; or he could accept the hard money program of separating federal fiscal policies from all banks. From the beginning of the panic, Van Buren's analysis of the crisis revealed his Jacksonian views. The overexpansion of business, he reminded the nation, had resulted from the excessive issue of bank notes and the reckless expansion of credit facilities. The resulting speculative craze had driven men from productive to unproductive pursuits, encouraging them to live luxuriously on fancied riches. The banking system, uncontrolled, had encouraged the extravagance, but the creation of a new national Bank would only raise the old menace of "a concentrated moneyed power, hostile to the spirit and threatening the permanency of our republican institutions."

Van Buren's solution to the nation's banking problem took the form of his "Independent Treasury." Having rebuked the "bloated credit system" for its devastating effect on the nation's economy, Van Buren embodied his hard money views in a plan to sever all governmental relationships with banks and hold all federal funds in subtreasuries kept under direct government control. This removal of federal funds from the business of the nation would deny those who controlled the credit structure the power to reap unearned profits from the investment of other people's money. Conservative Democrats—those who favored either a national Bank or a system of state banks—fought Van Buren's Independent Treasury plan; not until 1840 did the bill pass Congress. By thus applying the doctrine of laissez faire to the operation of the nation's banks, Van Buren forced the state legislatures to devise their own needed banking reforms. Taking as a model New York's Free Banking Act of 1838—a statute which threw open the business of banking to free competition under general restrictions—the nation moved after 1840 toward a general consensus on the banking question. State banks would continue to provide credit for a rapidly expanding economy, but henceforth state laws rather than a national Bank would impose the necessary limits on their activities.

The Taney Court

When Chief Justice John Marshall died in 1835, his personality had towered over the Supreme Court for more than a third of a century. Justice Joseph Story, who had served with Marshall for over twenty years, doubted that the Court could survive Marshall's death. Jackson soon compounded Story's fears and those of conservatives generally by naming Roger B. Taney to the chief justiceship. Born into a Federalist family of Maryland, Taney had long since deserted his Federalist heritage. His willingness as Secretary of the Treasury to execute Jackson's final assault on the Bank had made that clear. To Whig leaders, the new Chief Justice, unlike his brilliant predecessor, had neither the formal training nor a self-acquired legal reputation to fit him for the robe of justice. The Senate had once rejected Taney's appointment to the Supreme Court; only the Democratic sweep of 1836 permitted the Jacksonians to carry his confirmation against determined Whig opposition. Yet the Supreme Court under Taney lost neither its distinction nor its importance. His major decisions revealed an exceptional knowledge of the ways of law and society.

Van Buren inherited more than a new Chief Justice. Because Jackson had appointed three new justices and Van Buren was himself able to appoint two more in 1837, Democrats completely dominated the Court. Although they never rendered decisions as political partisans, their outlook toward an expanding, democratic nation steered them markedly away from the assumptions and purposes of the Marshall Court. Taney appreciated Marshall's nationalism, but he was determined to protect the states in the proper performance of their obligations. Better than Marshall, he understood the essentials of a changing America and saw that an unrestrained and federally protected commerce and industry would create serious political and legal problems, whether those problems reached the Court or not. Enough issues did reach Taney to provide material for a series of remarkable decisions.

For Taney the contract clause, which Marshall had converted into a drastic limitation on the states, required redefinition. His opportunity came early in the Charles River Bridge case of 1837. At stake was the validity of a Massachusetts law which had chartered a new corporation, the Warren Bridge Company, and granted it permission to build a bridge across the Charles River. This new bridge would compete with the Charles River Bridge, built under a charter granted fifty years before. Story, in favoring the previous charter and thus the Charles River Bridge, reverted to the doctrine of the Dartmouth College case. But Taney, speaking for the Court's majority, upheld the new Massachusetts law. In granting a state the right to "devest vested rights," Taney insisted that the states had the liberty to manage their own internal affairs: No longer would Court decisions always defend private property against state legislation. The State had duties as well as rights, said Taney, and no federal restrictions should prevent the states from performing their duties, especially those of protecting the well-being of their citizens. Conservatives feared that the Taney decision would encourage a general assault on private property. Instead, it kept the dead hand of the past from preventing the improvements required by a growing nation.

Again the Taney Court demonstrated its social and economic realism when it upheld the right of the state bank of Kentucky to issue bank notes. The Marshall case of *Craig v. Missouri* (1830) had denied that power to Missouri, on the ground that the Constitution prohibited the states from emitting bills of credit. When the Court faced the issue in *Briscoe v. The Bank of Kentucky* (1837), with Justice John McLean, a Jackson appointee, reading the decision, it reacted against the strong nationalism of the earlier Court with intent to facilitate the nation's access to paper money.

Thirdly, the Taney Court modified Marshall's noted decision which granted the federal government exclusive control of interstate commerce, even in areas where Congress had not yet acted. In 1837 the Court, in *New York v. Miln,* upheld a New York law demanding special reports from ship captains regarding all passengers entering New York Harbor. The Court argued that the state, in the interest of protecting its citizens, had the right to impose such obligations on ship captains engaged in interstate commerce. Ten years later, in the License cases (1847), Taney reaffirmed his defense of state regulation of commerce. Yet when Massachusetts and New York imposed taxes on passengers entering those states, a badly divided Court, in the Passenger cases of 1849, declared the state laws unconstitutional as an unreasonable interference with interstate commerce.

In its major decisions the Taney Court did not overturn the precedents established by Marshall. Although it tended to favor states' rights, it did not alter the basic relationship between the states and the nation. By admitting that the states could sometimes determine with greater accuracy than the federal government the needs of their own citizens, it encouraged the process by which the Supreme Court adapted constitutional law to the complexities of American life.

Log Cabins and Hard Cider

During their years of wandering through the political wilderness, the Whigs learned much from the party of Jackson. If Americans wanted democracy, they could have it with hands overflowing, for the Whigs had discovered the advantages of running popular candidates, avoiding issues—at least the divisive ones—and appealing to the emotions, not the intelligence, of the electorate. The continuing depression after 1837 gave the Whigs an initial advantage over the Jacksonians; by entertaining and amusing the masses, they could assure themselves an enthusiastic following and a large vote. In General William Henry Harrison of Ohio, the Whigs had an ideal candidate. Although born in Virginia, Harrison was a man of the frontier. As an Indian fighter he had achieved a reputation for courageous leadership at the Battle of Tippecanoe; as a general he had won additional renown for heroism in the War of 1812 in the Northwest. His political experience included the governorship of the Indiana Territory from 1801 to 1813 and membership in the House of Representatives from 1816 to 1819 and the Senate from 1825 to 1828. Yet despite all this activity Harrison possessed no firm or generally known views on political and economic questions.

Clay, the party's perennial favorite and logical candidate, confronted the Whigs with a difficult choice. The Whig nominating convention which met at Harrisburg in December, 1839, revealed the power of New York and its new Whig leadership headed by Thurlow Weed, editor of the *Albany Evening Journal.* This wire-puller extraordinary, supported by the able William H. Seward and Horace Greeley of the *New York Tribune,* convinced the Whig delegations that Clay could not carry the essential states of New York and Pennsylvania. Having scuttled Clay's nomination in the interest of party victory, the convention managers pushed through the nomination of Harrison. For the vice presidency the convention selected John Tyler of Virginia, largely to mollify Clay's friends in the South. To oppose Harrison, the Democrats at Baltimore in May, 1840, nominated Van Buren for reelection.

If the Whigs had slighted questions of national policy in 1836, they avoided such topics with a vengeance in 1840. Convinced that victory was paramount over principles, they submitted but one issue to the public—the need for a change. By avoiding the issues, Weed and his henchmen could turn Harrison's frontier background and personal qualities to special advantage. Unburdened by Clay and Webster—men who represented wealth and definite ideas—in the front ranks of the campaign, the Whigs could herald their candidate as a man of simple American virtues. Behind their slogan of "Tippecanoe and Tyler too" they began their assault on the emotions of the American people, receiving a special windfall when a *Baltimore American* editor charged that Harrison would have been content with a pension, a log cabin, and a barrel of hard cider. The Whigs accepted the challenge, claiming that they were indeed the party of hard cider and log cabins—the true representations of democracy. Although Harrison was well-to-do and lived in a large, spacious home overlooking the Ohio River, the Whigs bewildered and amused the voters with the trappings of the unsophisticated, honest, frontier life which their candidate supposedly characterized. The campaign was set to music, much of it with the frenzy and tone of a religious camp meeting.

In their denunciation of executive authority the Whigs claimed the support of Jefferson, for Jefferson had challenged Hamilton's principle of the strong President. Harrison informed an immense throng at Dayton, Ohio, that "the Augean stables of Van Burenism can be cleaned only by a Jeffersonian broom." Webster conveniently forgot his early Federalist affiliations and avowed himself a "Jefferson Democrat." Seldom given to stump oratory, Webster helped to set the tone for the campaign at Saratoga, New York, in August. He repeated the old charges, now standard for the Whigs, that the administration favored the rich and injured the poor by refusing to shield American wages with a protective tariff. Similarly the subtreasury, charged Webster, lowered wages and prices, hurting the workingmen while aiding their creditors. "While his rich neighbor . . . is made richer," said Webster, ". . . he, the honest and industrious mechanic, is crushed to earth; and yet we are told that this is a system for promoting the interests of the poor!"

For such appeals to democratic passions the Jacksonians had no answer. In victory the Whigs carried every section of the nation. They not only cut heavily into the regions of Democratic successes in 1836 but also augmented their majorities in areas where their superiority was already well established. In Connecticut, Rhode Island, Vermont, and Delaware, they carried every county. They won all but one of Massachusetts' fourteen counties. They captured normally Democratic Maine and almost doubled their vote in New Hampshire, although still failing to carry the state. They won in New York and Pennsylvania, both traditionally Democratic. They swept the Northwest, with the exception of Illinois, reducing the Democratic majority there to 1 percent. South of the Ohio, they swept the areas of Whig strength—Maryland, North Carolina, Kentucky, Tennessee, Georgia, and Louisiana. They carried Mississippi by a narrow margin for the first and only time. Harrison reduced the normal Democratic majorities in Virginia, Alabama, and Arkansas to the vanishing point. Only in Tennessee and South Carolina did the Democrats make gains over 1836. The popular vote had been relatively close, 1,275,000 to 1,129,000, but Harrison won 234 electoral votes to 60 for Van Buren.

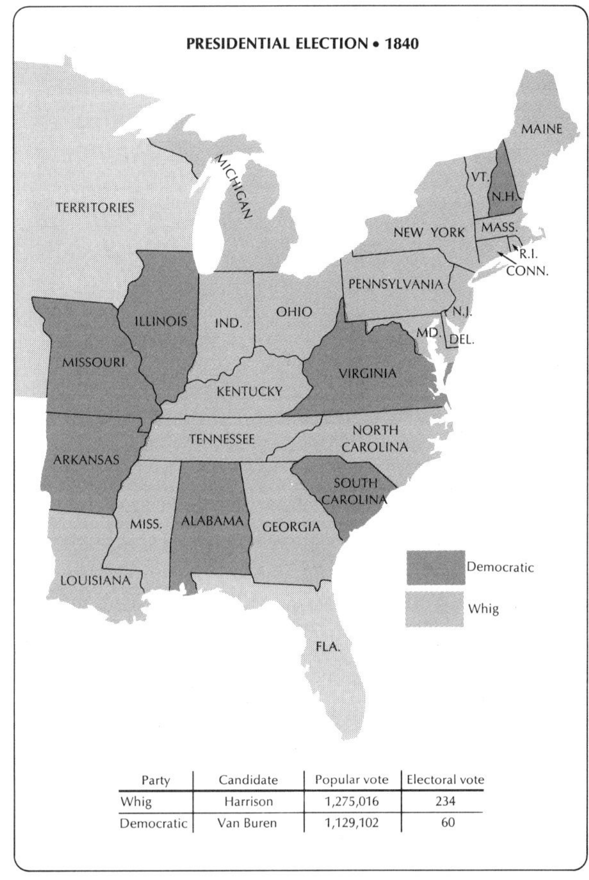

Party	Candidate	Popular vote	Electoral vote
Whig	Harrison	1,275,016	234
Democratic	Van Buren	1,129,102	60

Conclusion

Jacksonian Democracy had engaged the interest and attention of a democratic society, largely through bitter political controversy. Beyond that, did Jacksonian Democracy represent primarily a struggle for power or a broad political, social, and intellectual movement? What meaning did it convey, and whom did it reach? For the politicians, it represented an organization which had demonstrated its power to arouse and control the mass electorate. But beyond Jackson's personal image, what appealed to the thousands of voters who supported the Democratic party with such devotion? For some, undoubtedly, Jacksonianism represented the assault of the urban masses and simple farmers on the business aristocracy. For others, it signified the triumph of liberal frontier values over the conservatism of the East. Some regarded it as a victory for the American Presidency, representing the will of the people over an obstructionist Congress. Some hailed it as a victory for nationalism; others, for states' rights. Jacksonian Democracy, at best, conveyed many meanings to many people.

But did these varied concepts of Jacksonianism conform to class interests? Was Jacksonian Democracy what it claimed to be—a great crusade against privilege conducted in behalf of the poor? The very successes of the Democratic party, it would appear, required nothing less than a consistent program, clearly conceived, that served the needs of its mass constituency. Basing their appeal on emotion, the Jacksonians in the Bank war drew sharp contrasts between the virtues of equality, honesty, frugality, and hard work—which they allegedly represented—and the vices of corruption, plutocracy, privilege, inequality, and indebtedness, which they attributed to the Second National Bank. But the Jacksonian appeal, anchored to the notion of class conflict, was always divorced from action. Jacksonian policies, which included opposition to corporation charters, credit and paper money, public monopolies, and a national debt, created no more class feeling among the broad middle ranks of American society than did the programs set forth by the Whigs. The Bank's destruction demoralized the aristocrats; it eliminated the brakes on inflation; and it stimulated the new, speculative enterprise. It contributed nothing to the urban masses, the farmers, and the frontiersmen. New York's Democratic politicians and its Wall Street bankers emerged from the Bank war as the only certain victors.

SUGGESTED READINGS

Few brief periods of American history have called forth writings as vigorous, interpretive, and conflicting as has the Presidency of Andrew Jackson. Glyndon G. Van Deusen's *The Jacksonian Era, 1828–1848** (1959) contains a judicious, moderately pro-Whig survey of the Jackson years. Older, pro-Jacksonian studies are well represented by Marquis James's *Andrew Jackson: Portrait of a President** (1937) and Claude G. Bowers's *Party Battles of the Jackson Period* (1922). For the administrative history of the Jackson terms see Leonard D. White's *The Jacksonians: A Study in Administrative History** (1954).

In addition to the biographies of Clay, Webster, and Calhoun listed in the preceding bibliographical essay, several studies of excellent quality portray the careers of other important leaders in the Jackson years. Carl B. Swisher's *Roger B. Taney** (1936) traces the role of one of Jackson's Secretaries of the Treasury. W. N. Chambers in *Old Bullion Benton: Senator from the New West* (1956) and Elbert B. Smith in *Magnificent Missourian: The Life of Thomas Hart Benton* (1958) do full justice to the dramatic career of a loyal Jacksonian. Russell B. Nye in *George Bancroft: Brahmin Rebel** (1944) analyzes the life of an Eastern Jacksonian. On Van Buren's role in the Jackson administration the best available study remains that of Holmes Alexander, *The American Talleyrand* (1935).

Several foreign travelers caught the spirit of the Jackson era with amazing insight. Of these the most famous was Alexis de Tocqueville, whose *Democracy in America* (4 vols., 1835–1840) is readily available in editions of more recent years. Also enlightening, as well as entertaining, are Frances Trollope's more critical *Domestic Manners of the Americans** (1832) and Harriet Martineau's *Society in America**

(3 vols., 1834–1836). Of almost equal importance is Francis J. Grund's *Aristocracy in America** (1839). Excellent anthologies that bring colorful descriptive materials within easy access are Oscar Handlin (ed.), *This Was America* (1949); Frank Monaghan (ed.), *French Travellers in the United States, 1765–1932* (1933); Allan Nevins (ed.), *America through British Eyes* (1948); J. L. Mesick (ed.), *The English Traveler in America, 1785–1835* (1922); and W. S. Tryon (ed.), *A Mirror for Americans* (3 vols., 1952).

Indian removal presents a variety of themes, all developed in an ever-growing literature. On the Southern Indians themselves see R. S. Cotterill's *The Southern Indians* (1954) and H. T. Malone's *Cherokees of the Old South* (1956). On removal to the West the standard work is Grant Foreman's *Indian Removal: The Emigration of the Five Civilized Tribes* (1932). U. B. Phillips's *Georgia and States Rights** (1902) presents the Georgia side of the Supreme Court controversy, whereas Albert J. Beveridge in *The Life of John Marshall* (4 vols., 1916–1919) defends the Court and the Chief Justice. Nullification has been another major source of historical debate. The best exposition and defense of Calhoun's role is Charles M. Wiltse's *John C. Calhoun: Nullifier* (1949). Also useful on Southern motivation are C. S. Boucher's pro-Calhoun *The Nullification Controversy in South Carolina* (1916); Frederic Bancroft's *Calhoun and the South Carolina Nullification Movement* (1928); and C. S. Sydnor's *The Development of Southern Sectionalism** (1948). Largely superseding previous studies of nullification is W. W. Freehling's *Prelude to Civil War: The Nullification Controversy in South Carolina, 1816–1836** (1966).

Jackson, as a man of thought and action, represented a complex and changing nation. Two volumes which interpret Jackson as a symbol of the new democracy are J. W. Ward's *Andrew Jackson: Symbol for an Age** (1955) and H. C. Syrett's *Andrew Jackson: His Contribution to the American Tradition* (1953). A. M. Schlesinger, Jr., in *The Age of Jackson** (1945), interprets Jacksonian Democracy as a genuine democratic movement taking its egalitarian spirit and program, especially on the question of the Second Bank of the United States, from the urban radicals of the Northeast. Again stressing the relationship of Jacksonianism to urban America is Walter Hugins in *Jacksonian Democracy and the Working Class** (1960).

Other studies question both the democratic foundations and the wisdom of the Jacksonian movement. Thomas P. Abernethy in *From Frontier to Plantation in Tennessee* (1932) portrays Jackson as a wealthy, conservative frontier land holder. Charles G. Sellers's more recent *James L. Polk: Jacksonian, 1795–1843* (1957) presents a more balanced view of Tennessee politics. Critical of the Jacksonian leadership on bank and economic policy are W. B. Smith's *Economic Aspects of the Second Bank of the United States* (1935); Bray Hammond's *Banks and Politics in America from the Revolution to the Civil War** (1957), an especially important work; and a biography by Thomas P. Govan of the Bank's president, *Nicholas Biddle: Nationalist and Public Banker* (1959). Another important effort to explain Jacksonianism, stressing the desire of the Jackson men to return to an older, simpler America, is Marvin Meyers's *The Jacksonian Persuasion** (1957). Richard Hofstadter's essay on Jackson in his *The American Political Tradition** (1948) views the Jacksonians as ambitious, incipient capitalists. Douglas T. Miller in *Jacksonian Aristocracy: Class and Democracy in New York, 1830–1860* (1967) argues that the economic opportunities of the Jackson years and after created a greater, not a lesser, stratification of American society. Edward Pessen's *Jacksonian America: Society, Personality, and Politics** (1969) is an excellent synthesis of historical opinion on many important political and social aspects of the period.

On the Van Buren years, and especially the Panic of 1837, R. C. McGrane's *The Panic of 1837** (1924) remains the standard work. Further analysis of the nation's banking and economic structure can be found in Bray Hammond's *Banks and Politics in America from the Revolution to the Civil War** (1957) and W. B. Smith and A. H. Cole's *Fluctuations in American Business, 1790–1860* (1935). On land policy, see R. G. Wellington's *The Political and National Influence of the Public Lands, 1826–1842* (1914). On the Taney Court see C. B. Swisher's *Roger B. Taney** (1936) and A. C. McLaughlin's *A Constitutional History of the United States* (1935). The election of 1840 is described well in R. G. Gunderson's *The Log Cabin Campaign* (1957). Two satisfactory biographies of William Henry Harrison are Freeman Cleaves's *Old Tippecanoe* (1939) and J. A. Green's *William Henry Harrison* (1941).

* indicates availability in paperback.

13

The Emergence of a National Economy, 1820–1860

DESPITE PANICS and political controversies the American economy achieved remarkable growth during the early and middle years of the nineteenth century. Through the 1830s per capita income rose only about 0.6 percent annually, but thereafter it reached a growth of some 1.67 percent a year. In dollars, this meant an annual per capita rise in income from $210 to $292 yearly between 1799 and 1859. And increased income meant a constantly rising standard of living, which continued to be the envy of most foreigners. When Jenny Lind, the famous Swedish singer, arrived in the United States in 1850, she looked at the crowds and exclaimed: "How well dressed everybody is—have you no poor people in America?" There were poor people in the United States, but except for the slaves, they were better off than most of the lower economic classes in Western Europe.

Agriculture was the leading economic activity in the United States until the Civil War. Farmers were important to the economy not only because they produced an abundant food supply for a rapidly growing population, but also because they supplied most of the raw materials for the developing industries. This was especially true for the South with its large staple production of cotton and tobacco. Meat packing, flour milling, and textiles were among the manufactures which depended on agriculture for their raw materials. Although agriculture was predominant in the pre-Civil War years, the nation developed a reasonably well-balanced economy, especially in the North. Commerce, industry, mining, transportation, and services all grew swiftly and contributed to the country's substantial economic growth before 1860. Industrial advance in the North was especially rapid during the 1850s when the application of power and machinery converted handicraft complexes into productive factories.

Population Trends

In 1815 the United States was largely undeveloped economically, its rich natural resources still awaiting exploitation by farmers and businessmen. To develop this abundant natural wealth the country required a rapidly growing population which, in turn, would create unprecedented opportunities for labor, capital, and entrepreneurial skill. In 1800 the United States contained only 5.3 million people, but by 1860 it claimed more than 31 million. Of the total population in 1860, about 26.9 million were whites and 4.4 million, blacks. Most of the Negroes were slaves.

Besides the high birthrate, which added to the population, Europe dispatched an endless stream of immigrants to American shores, especially after 1840. In the peak year of immigration before the Civil War—1854—nearly 428,000 foreigners arrived. They came chiefly from Ireland, Germany, and later, the Scandinavian countries. The potato famine in Ireland in the 1840s, political difficulties, low wages, heavy taxes, and general lack of economic opportunity caused many Europeans to leave their homelands and migrate to the United States. Much of the Irish immigration remained in the growing Eastern cities, but it provided also much of the cheap labor used between 1830 and 1860 to construct the canals and railroads. Germans spread over the Middle West, some of them settling in cities such as Cincinnati, St. Louis, Chicago, and Milwaukee, while thousands more took up farming. Shortly before the Civil War, Scandinavians were migrating to Illinois, Wisconsin, and Minnesota.

Land Policies and Westward Settlement

The gradual creation of more liberal land laws encouraged the rapid westward march of settlement. The land laws of 1800 and 1804 made it easier for settlers to purchase land directly from the federal government, but these measures also encouraged speculation. In 1820 Congress abandoned the credit system, lowered the amount of land a person could buy to 80 acres, and reduced the price to $1.25 an acre. While national land laws made it increasingly easier for farmers to acquire land, some members of Congress sought additional measures to serve the interests of those willing to till the soil. The Preemption Act of 1841 was designed especially to protect actual and potential squatters against speculators who might outbid them when land was put up for sale at public auction. Thereafter those concerned most directly with national land policy began to challenge the concept that the private acquisition of public land need produce a federal revenue. They insisted rather that since the public domain belonged to the people, it should be made available to the people under the homestead principle whereby the federal government would give actual settlers 160 acres of public land. Not until 1862 did Congress incorporate this principle into law.

After 1820 settlers continued to flow into the unoccupied prairies of the great Mississippi valley. The Panic of 1819 slowed the movement for a half decade; thereafter it quickly reached flood tide until halted again by the crash of 1837. The rush of the thirties brought statehood to Michigan. Iowa entered the Union in 1846; Wisconsin, in 1848. In short, much of the Old Northwest was occupied within a single generation. Another heavy migration pushed west and south into Kentucky, Tennessee, Alabama, Mississippi, Louisiana, and even Texas. The population of Alabama, for example, increased some ten times between 1810 and 1830, as thousands of small farmers and large planters rushed into the state. Besides the attraction of land, the settlers were lured by improved roads, steamboats on the rivers, governmental control over the Indians, and the old habit of pioneering.

Agriculture in the North

General farming, which involved raising a combination of crops and livestock, prevailed throughout the Northern states during the pre-Civil War years. Corn was the dominant crop. The soil and climate in the region from Pittsburgh to Iowa were so ideally suited for corn, that a distinct "corn belt" developed in the eastern part of this region as early as the 1840s. Describing corn farming in the Scioto River Valley of Ohio in 1841, one reporter wrote: "As far as the eye can stretch in the distance nothing but corn and wheat fields are to be seen; and on some points in the Scioto Valley as high as a thousand acres of corn may be seen in adjoining fields, belonging to some eight or ten different proprietors." Indeed, from Ohio to Iowa, corn was king.

Wheat was the second most important commercial crop grown by Northern farmers before the Civil War. In the 1820s and 1830s, western New York and Pennsylvania and eastern Ohio was the leading area of American wheat production. But like corn, wheat growing moved rapidly westward to the prairies of southern Michigan, northern Indiana and Illinois, and southern Wisconsin. Northern farmers raised other crops which included oats, barley, rye, and flax. Oats was fed to livestock; barley was used in the brewing industry; and flax, in addition to providing fiber for linen production, was the source for linseed oil. Farmers also produced vegetables and fruits, both for home use and for sale.

Livestock raising was a major source of income on most Northern farms. Besides providing milk and meat for the family table, cattle, hogs, and sheep usually found ready cash markets. Livestock was driven to distant markets long before efficient transportation made it profitable to ship wheat or other bulky products over long distances. By 1815, thousands of hogs and cattle were being driven eastward to seaboard cities. An English traveler wrote in 1818 that Ohio was "filled with herds of cattle for the Philadelphia and Baltimore markets." Cincinnati and Chicago became important packing centers in the 1840s and 1850s and provided additional outlets for hogs and cattle. Dairying also became important throughout the Northern states. Commercial dairying was concentrated mostly in New England and the Middle Atlantic states, especially New York, before 1850; thereafter, the Western states, notably Wisconsin, greatly expanded their output of dairy products.

Agriculture's rapid march westward to the

Mississippi and beyond by 1860 caused the decline and readjustment of farming in the Northeast. After canals and railroads reduced the cost of transportation, farmers in New England and the Middle Atlantic states could not compete in grain and meat production with the larger and more productive farms in the West. Improved transportation brought Western flour to Boston and New York as early as the 1820s. Western farmers also had the advantage of cheap land. Consequently, farmers in the Northeast ceased trying to make a living by producing wheat, corn, hogs, and wool, and concentrated on dairying, fruit growing, vegetable farming, and other specialties. Because of their location near large cities such as Boston, New York, and Philadelphia, Northeastern farmers found good markets for their products. Here they had a distinct price advantage over farmers west of the Appalachians. But even major adjustments of production could not save many farmers in the Northeast.

The growing mechanization of farm operations was a significant reason for increased output on Northern farms. In 1800 only a few crude implements, such as plows and harrows, used power, which was provided by oxen or horses. Most farm labor was performed by hand tools not greatly different from those used by the Romans. Corn, for example, was planted, cultivated, and harvested entirely by hand. During the next half century, new and improved machines were developed for many important phases of farm production. By 1819 Jethro Wood of New Jersey had invented a successful iron plow, but this was gradually replaced by John Deere's steel plow in the late 1830s and afterwards. In 1833 Obed Hussey, and a year later Cyrus McCormick, built reapers, which within a few years greatly reduced the labor necessary for harvesting small grains. Threshing machines began to replace the flail in the 1840s; those developed by H. A. Pitt of Maine and J. I. Case of Wisconsin greatly increased the efficiency of this aspect of farm production.

Greater production resulted also from the application of science to farming. By the 1830s, agricultural reformers were urging farmers to conserve their soil, to rotate their crops, and to use fertilizer. Jesse Buel, a leading agricultural reformer in New York and editor of *The Cultivator,* wrote that "by draining, manuring, ploughing, harrowing, hoeing, and so on, we may preserve, unimpaired, the natural fertility of our soils; and that, with the aid of improved implements of husbandry and a good system of management, we may also greatly increase the profits of its culture." County and state agricultural societies also strove to promote better farming methods, and some farmers did adopt improved practices. But most Northern farmers exploited their soil without much concern for long-range productivity. Of the three factors of production—land, labor, and capital—land was the cheapest. Thus it appeared good sense to exploit the land, at least temporarily, rather than to apply expensive labor or capital in the form of fertilizer or soil-conservation practices.

The fundamental change which occurred in Northern agriculture before the Civil War was the gradual shift from self-sufficient to commercial farming. Pioneer farmers generally produced much of their own food, made some of their clothing, and manufactured such items as furniture, utensils, and soap. But as transportation improved and towns developed, farmers turned more and more to production for sale rather than for home use. By the 1850s, commercial agriculture was established and flourishing as far west as Illinois and southern Wisconsin.

Fundamental to the country's economic advance was a reasonably efficient transportation system. Early nineteenth-century political leaders were well aware of the economic importance of better transportation. Westerners were particularly insistent that roads and canals be constructed in their region. Henry Clay, for instance, was a strong advocate of federal aid to road building; and a transportation system partially financed by the national government was a crucial part of Clay's American System. By 1860 a network of roads, canals, and railroads had tied together the nation, especially the Northern section, into an economic whole. Improved transportation permitted lower freight rates, encouraged the movement of raw materials and finished products, expanded markets, and greatly stimulated general industrial growth. Traffic on the rivers, lakes, and coastal waterways increased markedly, but failed to keep pace with the railroads.

The construction of turnpikes (usually built by private corporations which charged fees to those who traveled over them) represented one of the earlier efforts to improve overland transportation. Between 1790 and the 1820s, thousands of miles of dirt and crushed-rock roads were constructed in New England, New York, Pennsylvania, and to a lesser extent, in the Southern states. The Cumberland, or National, Road was the nation's most famous turnpike. Begun in 1811 as a federal project, it ran from Cumberland, Maryland, to Wheeling, West Virginia, on the Ohio River, and by 1850 had reached Vandalia, Illinois. It proved to be the dominant overland route into the Old Northwest.

The expansion of river traffic also provided new avenues for trade and commerce. Rafts, flatboats, and barges carried people, as well as large amounts of freight, well into the nineteenth century. The development of a successful steamboat by Robert Fulton in New York in 1807 opened up a new era in river traffic. In 1811, Nicholas J. Roosevelt sent a steamboat from Pittsburgh to New Orleans, and within a few years steamboats were plying the Ohio, Mississippi, Missouri, and many lesser rivers. By 1836, some 381 steamboats operated on western rivers. Flatboats and rafts continued to be used for downstream traffic and many Ohio and Indiana settlers sent their grain down the Ohio and Mississippi Rivers to New Orleans in this manner.

But as the population spread out, neither turnpikes nor steamboats could meet the transportation needs. By 1815, a strong demand arose for the construction of canals. In New York, Governor De Witt Clinton took the lead in attempting to gain a state-financed canal which would connect Albany on the Hudson to Buffalo on Lake Erie. Such a water connection would give New York City a distinct advantage over Philadelphia and Baltimore in the competition for Western trade. In April, 1817, the New York Legislature authorized construction of the canal; eight years later, the last part of the 363-mile waterway was opened for business. Even though the canal had cost the state slightly more than $7 million, it was an immediate financial success. Almost at once western New York was infused with new economic life, and New York City benefited from commerce originating as far west as northern Ohio. Freight passed through the canal, down the Hudson River, and into the hands of enterprising New York businessmen. The construction of the canal showed, too, how a state could

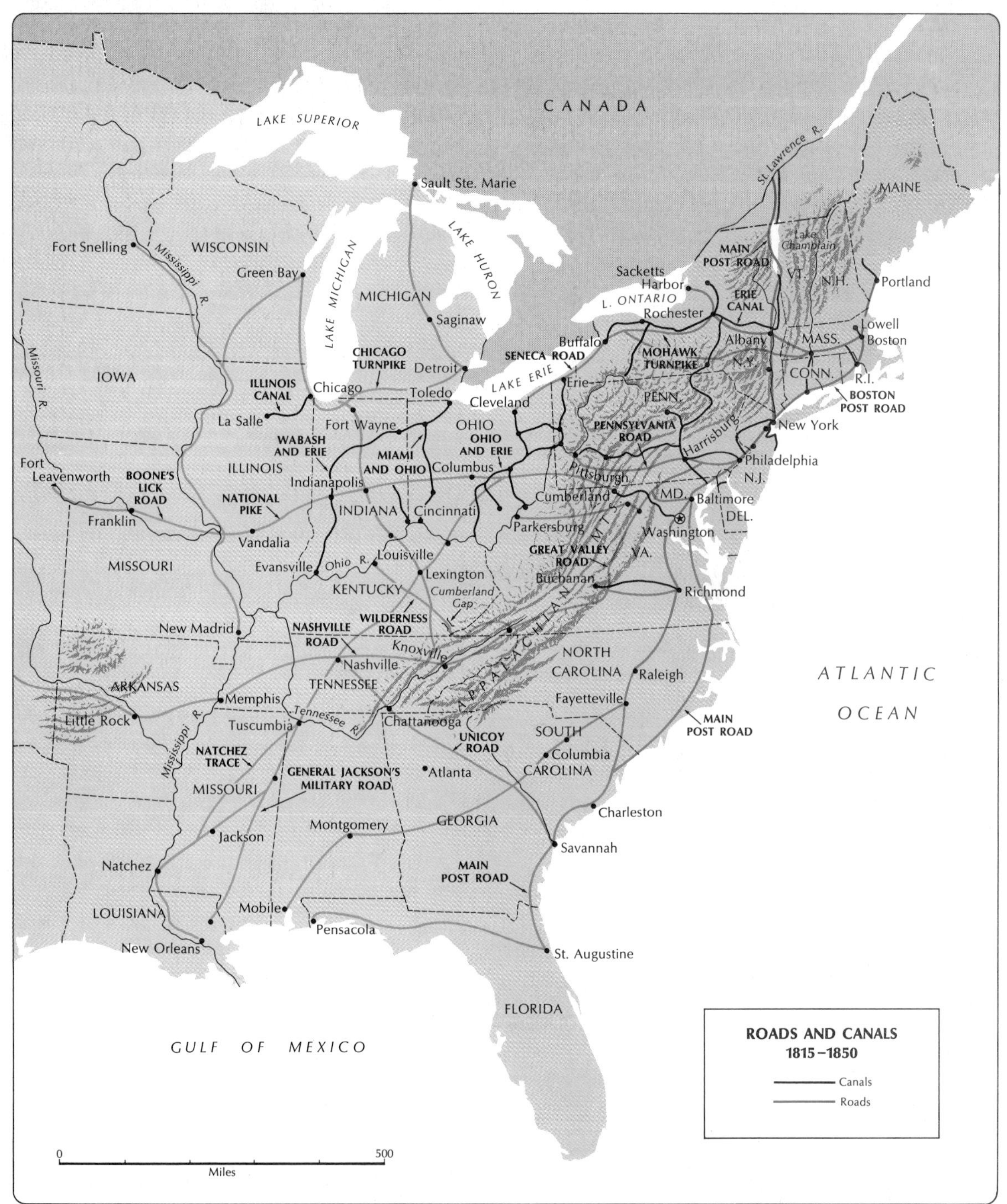

The Emergence of a National Economy, 1820–1860

contribute to general economic development by providing public credit for such an enterprise. The success of the Erie sparked a nationwide movement to construct canals.

Between 1826 and 1834 the "Pennsylvania System" connected Philadelphia and Pittsburgh at a cost of more than $10 million. Other seaboard states from New England to Virginia spent millions trying to develop successful canal systems. Western states also got into the act. Ohio built the Ohio and Erie and the Miami and Erie, both of which connected the Ohio River and Lake Erie. Most of the canals built in the 1830s were financed by the states in which they were located. But often the canals were not financially feasible; some states suffered such heavy losses in construction and operation that they were on the verge of bankruptcy. By 1840, the United States had 3,326 miles of canals, but the Canal Age had almost run its course. High construction and maintenance costs, poor management, winter losses when the canals were frozen, and the developing competition from railroads combined to bring the Canal Era to a close. Yet, while they operated—and some canals continued indefinitely—canals made a substantial contribution to the nation's economic development by reducing freight rates. Moreover, the canals, especially the Erie, reduced economic self-sufficiency and encouraged regional specialization and a more integrated economy.

In the long run, railroads answered the transportation problem most effectively. The first railroad chartered in the United States was the Baltimore and Ohio, organized in 1827 by a group of Baltimore businessmen who were interested in tapping the Western trade. Thirteen miles of track were completed by 1830. However, successful railroading had to wait on the invention of a practical steam locomotive. Following experiments with steam locomotives in England during the 1820s, the Charleston and Hamburg Railroad of South Carolina became the first railway in the United States to use a steam engine to pull a train of cars. This was in 1830. The early railroads were crude and often dangerous affairs: the rails were made of wood with a strip of iron attached, and wood-burning locomotives spit sparks, which frequently caused fires along the track and even set fire to the clothes of passengers. Harriet Martineau reported that on one railroad trip she saw a lady's shawl ignited from sparks, adding "I found that my own gown had thirteen holes in it; and in my veil, with which I saved my eyes, more than could be counted." Early cars were modeled after stagecoaches, and tied together with chains, making a train ride a jerky, rough, and generally uncomfortable experience. In addition, because of different track gauges, passengers had to make frequent changes from one train to another.

Railroading made slow progress during the 1830s, increasing from 73 to only 2,818 miles in the decade ending in 1840. Following 1840, however, track mileage expanded rapidly, especially in the 1850s. By 1860 the United States led every nation in the world, with more than 30,000 miles of operating railroads. By the late 1850s, railroads extended as far West as St. Joseph, Missouri, and strong support existed for construction of a transcontinental line. But uncompromising stands in Congress over whether the projected railroad should follow a southern or more northerly route to the Pacific Coast thwarted the building of any transcontinental railway until after the Civil War. More than two-thirds of the total railroad mileage was in the North and West, a development which tended to tie the economic interests of those regions closely together. Whereas pri-

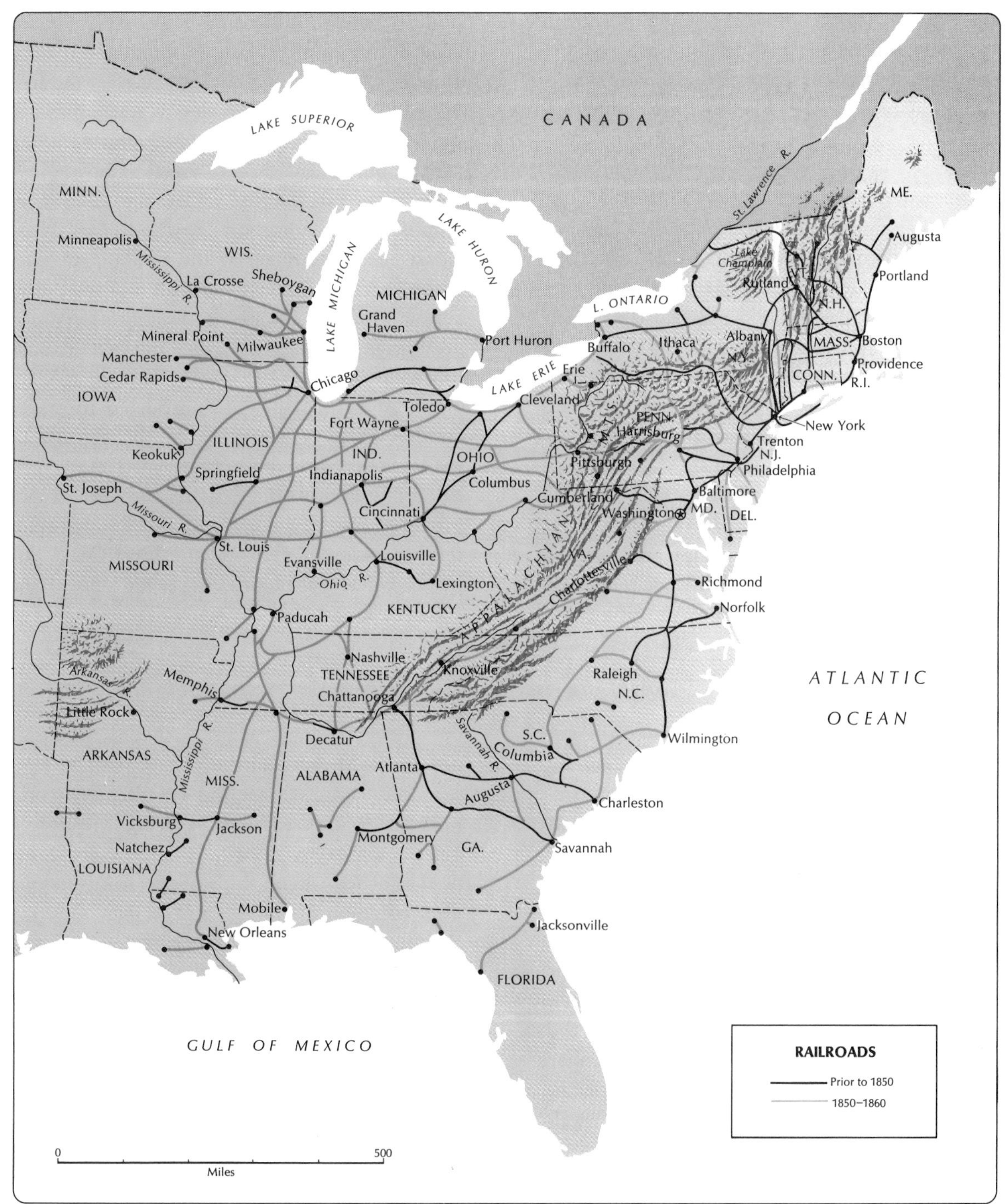
CANADA
LAKE SUPERIOR
LAKE MICHIGAN
LAKE HURON
L. ONTARIO
LAKE ERIE
St. Lawrence R.
Lake Champlain
MINN.
Minneapolis
Mississippi R.
WIS.
La Crosse
Sheboygan
MICHIGAN
Grand Haven
Mineral Point
Milwaukee
Port Huron
Manchester
Cedar Rapids
IOWA
Chicago
Toledo
Fort Wayne
Cleveland
Erie
Buffalo
Ithaca
Albany
N.Y.
Rutland
VT.
N.H.
ME.
Augusta
Portland
MASS.
Boston
Providence
CONN.
R.I.
New York
PENN.
Harrisburg
Trenton
N.J.
Philadelphia
Pittsburgh
Baltimore
MD.
DEL.
Washington
Cumberland
ILLINOIS
Keokuk
Springfield
IND.
Indianapolis
OHIO
Columbus
Cincinnati
St. Joseph
Missouri R.
St. Louis
MISSOURI
Evansville
Louisville
Ohio R.
Lexington
VA.
Charlottesville
Richmond
Norfolk
APPALACHIAN MTS.
KENTUCKY
Paducah
Nashville
TENNESSEE
Knoxville
Raleigh
N.C.
Memphis
Arkansas R.
Little Rock
ARKANSAS
Chattanooga
Decatur
Wilmington
S.C.
Columbia
Savannah R.
Atlanta
ALABAMA
MISS.
Augusta
Charleston
Vicksburg
Jackson
Natchez
LOUISIANA
Montgomery
GA.
Savannah
Mobile
New Orleans
Jacksonville
FLORIDA
ATLANTIC OCEAN
GULF OF MEXICO
RAILROADS
Prior to 1850
1850–1860
0
500
Miles

vate individuals furnished much of the capital to finance railroad building by investing in company stocks and bonds, state governments and local communities also provided much of the money for construction. The federal government also provided aid. In 1850 Congress gave 3,736,000 acres of land to the Illinois Central to help finance construction of that line between Chicago and New Orleans. This was the first of many federal land grants designed to encourage railroad building. Because of their economy, speed, and dependability, railroads by 1860 had triumphed over all other means of transportation. Railroads not only met the shipping needs of agriculture and industry far better than could roads or canals; they boosted the entire economy by creating their own demand for raw materials, labor, and financing.

Development of the telegraph and an enlarged postal system provided new means of communication, which spurred American economic growth. Samuel F. B. Morse invented a successful telegraph and obtained a patent on it in 1841. Although Morse wanted the federal government to develop a telegraph system, Congress refused to appropriate money for this purpose, and the telegraph network became a private industry. By the time telegraphic communication reached the West Coast in 1861, most of the nation had telegraph service. Likewise, extension of the postal system greatly facilitated communication. Congress gradually increased the number of post offices from only 75 in 1790 to 28,498 by 1860. At first, mail was transported by stagecoaches or river boats, but by the 1850s railroads emerged as the primary carriers of mail. The Pony Express, inaugurated in April, 1860, provided the speediest mail service between the Mississippi Valley and the West Coast, but it was a financial failure and lasted only about eighteen months.

Shipping and Overseas Trade

Overseas commerce further stimulated the expansion of the American economy, forcing, by the demands it placed on shippers, many significant changes in the character of ocean transportation. Responding to the need for scheduled sailings between the United States and England, a group of New York merchants in 1817 established the Black Ball line with four fast ships, each to make three runs per year. Through its twelve scheduled trips each year between New York and Liverpool, the line hoped to command much of the passenger and "fine freight" traffic. Eventually two additional lines—the Red Star and the Blue Swallowtail—provided additional vessels for the endeavor. By 1845 the three companies, with their fifty-two vessels, offered American businessmen and travelers three scheduled sailings per week. Meanwhile the packet lines had introduced larger, faster ships with more comfortable accommodations. During the 1820s most vessels registered only 300 to 400 tons; by the forties, sailing ships of 800 to 1,000 tons were common.

American ocean sailing reached its final and most dramatic phase with the launching of the famed clipper ships in the 1840s. These magnificent vessels, varying from 2,000 to 4,000 tons and carrying over an acre of sail, set unheard-of records for speed from the outset. Donald McKay, the noted New England shipbuilder, brought the long, narrow, high-masted clippers to their ultimate superiority with his *Surprise.* On its maiden voyage the *Surprise*

The Conquest of Distance

Beyond the eastern mountains lay the vast expanses of America and undreamed-of quantities of timber and minerals, the very resources Northern industry demanded for its rapid growth. Efficient transportation was needed to move huge loads of raw materials to the factories and then to transport finished goods to the cities of the United States and the world. After 1800, industrial demands created the major transportation networks: transportation developed to move freight first, passengers second. America grew because transportation conquered the distances.

At first, a system of toll roads and turnpikes linked the communities of the East. Eventually, a federally financed national road reached from Baltimore to Vandalia, Ill., but by then other transport was carrying most of the freight. Wagons could not move tons of materials cheaply; boats could. Although coastal waters and major rivers were used from the beginning, by 1840 they were interconnected by a great system of inland canals. Then railroads developed to span the waterless stretches of the interior; in thirty years, the railway replaced canal shipping almost entirely. It was more than a half-century before high-speed, long-haul trucking and air freight challenged the railroads.

The largest man-made link in the water system was the Erie canal. Huge quantities of goods moved on barges from New York's piers to cities across the state, to Buffalo, and on to Toledo and Detroit by way of Lake Erie. From the center of the country, raw materials—and later agricultural products—moved east on the return trip.

In addition to barges, packet boats like those pictured below traveled the canals carrying mail, small packages, and passengers. Businessmen and agents traveled West to buy materials; immigrant labor moved to build canals, railroads, and factories, to cut the timber, and to excavate minerals from the earth.

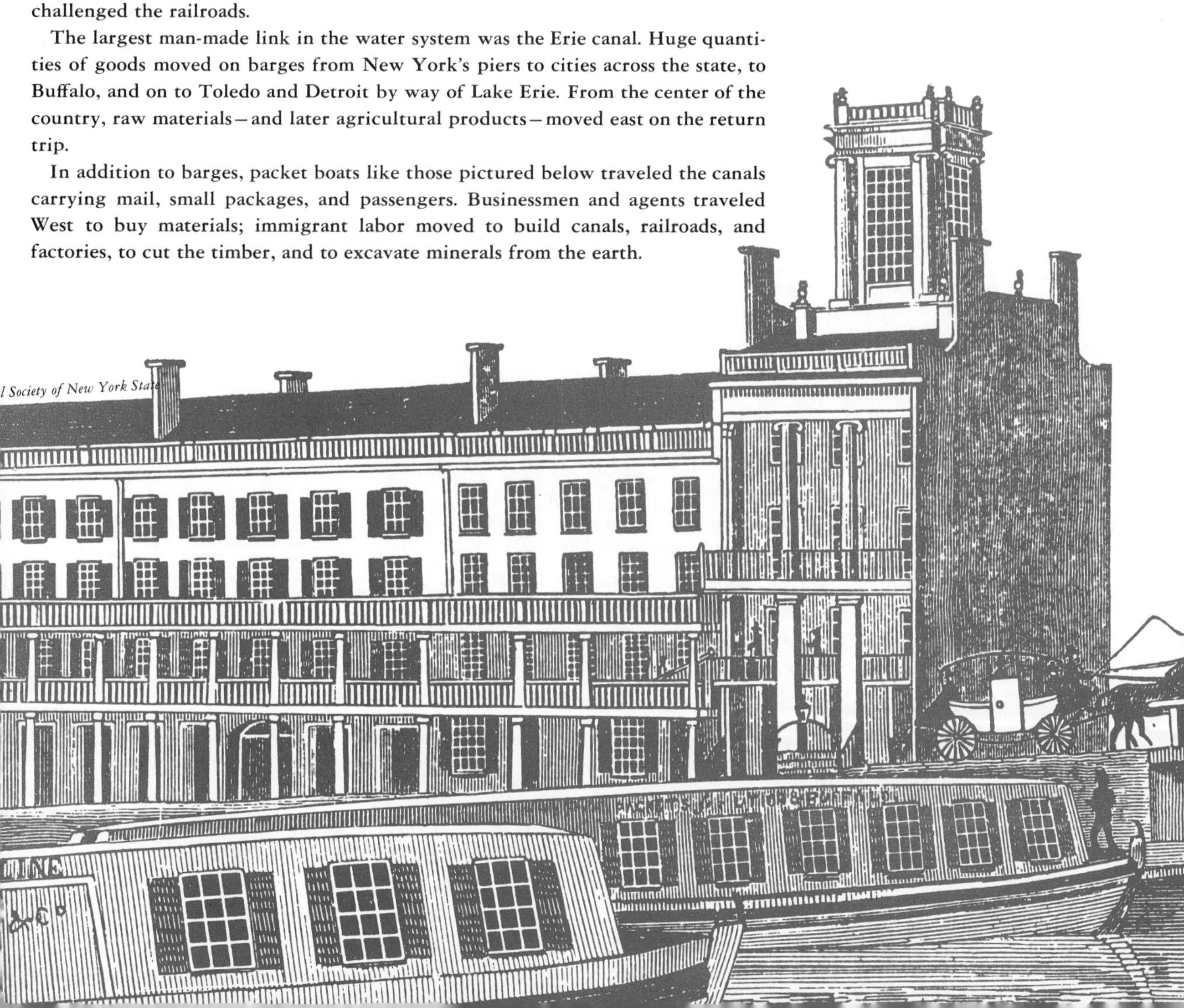

l Society of New York Sta

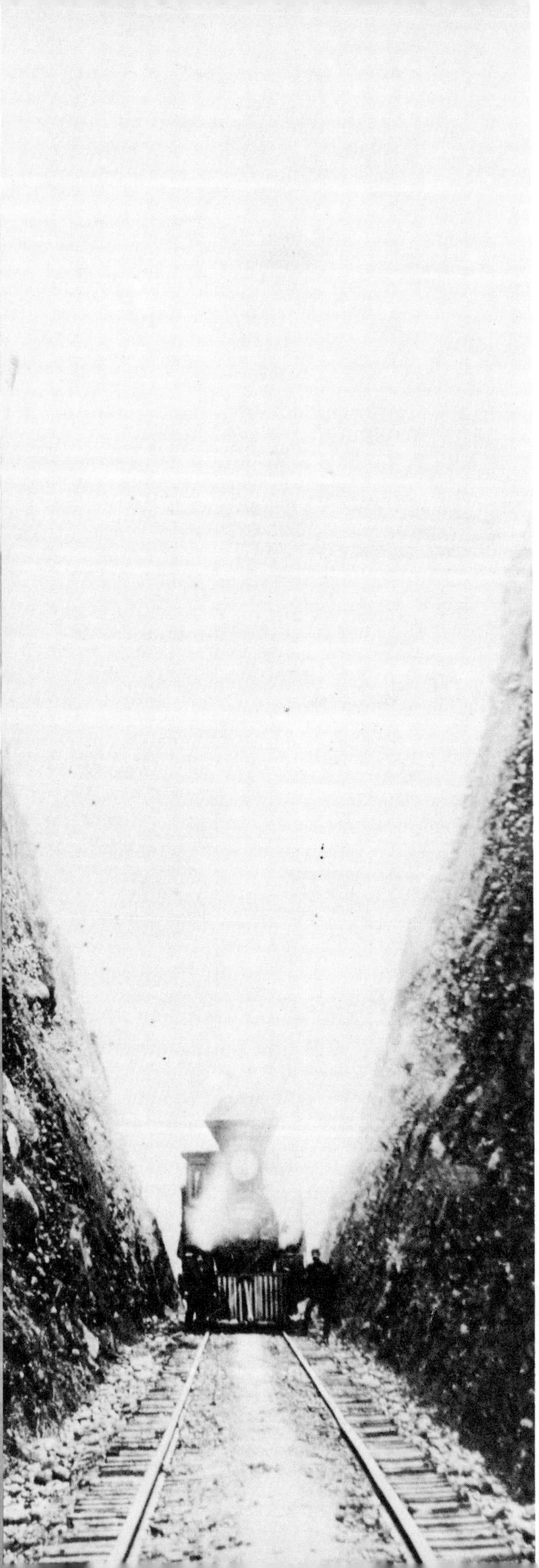

Railroads could not seriously challenge the canal traffic until they could pass over the eastern mountains. The first locomotive to cross the Alleghenies (extreme left) caused a great celebration in Pennsylvania. Nevertheless, business lost to the Erie Canal was rapidly reclaimed: the port of Philadelphia was linked to industrial Pittsburgh and to the Midwest beyond. New York met this competition by creating the New York and Erie Railroad in 1851, the first trunk line to the Midwest. Meanwhile, the Baltimore and Ohio also had completed Midwestern connections, and smaller lines formed essential feeder networks through Eastern and Midwestern states in the late 1840s and early 1850s. When the Civil War began, the need, the money, and the will were at hand for a long-discussed project—a transcontinental railroad to the Pacific.

In 1864, crews for the Central Pacific and Union Pacific began laying track east and west, every mile laid by hand. The hazards were enormous. On May 10, 1869, the rails were joined at Promontory Point, Utah. Central Pacific crews (left, center) included large numbers of Chinese laborers. Thirty-four miles east of Sacramento they carved Bloomer Cut (left) by hand and with dynamite, 63 feet deep and 800 feet long, through a solid Sierra mountain.

European immigrants, especially Irishmen, crewed for the Union Pacific. They lived on the plains in sod huts (below) like the settlers who followed them. Army units joined them in fighting off Indians.

Extreme left: Library of Congress
Left, center: The Society of California Pioneers
Left: Southern Pacific Photos by Alfred A. Hart, official Central Pacific photographer, Sacramento
Above: Library of Congress

Both above: New York Public Library, Picture Collection
Right, all pictures: Library of Congress

America had river steamboats in 1807 and added steam to an Atlantic sailing ship, the *Savannah*, in 1819. Ocean steam vessels, however, temporarily lost out to the fast United States clipper ships like the Red Jacket (top), depicted in the ice off Cape Horn in August, 1854. But steam and iron were destined to take over transportation on the high seas. In the 1850s the American Collins Line, whose ship, the *Adriatic*, is shown above, outstripped the British Cunard ships in speed and luxury, but within the decade lost their supremacy after a series of disasters at sea and financial failure.

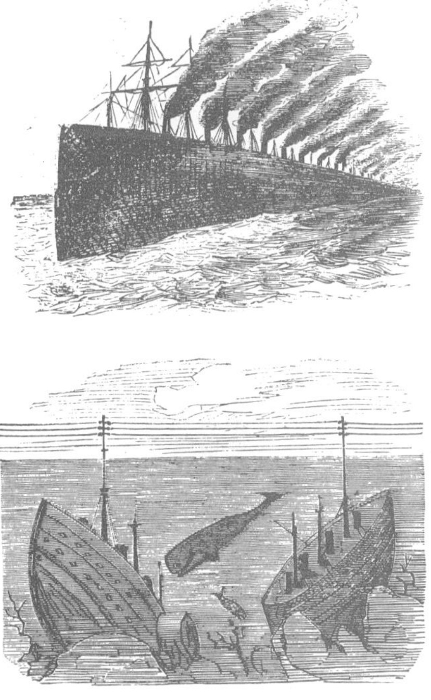

The British regained preeminence on the ocean with ships such as the *Great Western*, the *Great Britain,* the first propeller-driven ship, and the *Great Eastern* (below), the largest vessel of its time in 1858. The ships were so large and impressive that a *Harper's Weekly* cartoonist speculated facetiously about what further developments might bring (right): even when sunk, the masts of these ships would remain above water, available for a transoceanic telegraph; the great length would bring a ship's bow into port before the stern was even in sight.

Both: New York Public Library, Picture Collection

Until Samuel F. B. Morse's electric telegraph was adopted in 1844, transportation provided the only means of long distance communications; messengers and written material had to be carried from point to point. With the telegraph, electricity instantaneously flashed messages ahead to give news, to coordinate fast trains, to buy and sell, to do the nation's business. The Overland Telegraph Company completed a line from Sacramento to Midwestern terminals in 1861. The first message from California read "*May the Union Be Perpetual.*" A few years later, another line was completed with the Union and Central Pacific Railroads. At the same time, men dreamed of a trans-Atlantic telegraph, a dream realized in 1858 when the American ships *Niagara* and *Agamemnon* laid a cable to England after many unsuccessful attempts. Celebrations jammed Broadway and Union Square in New York (left). But after three weeks, the cable failed. Finally, under Cyrus W. Field's direction, the British steamship *Great Eastern* laid the first permanent cable in 1866.

Cities that served as transportation centers inevitably became the centers of commerce, industry, and population as well. Below, St. Louis is pictured in 1859, at the height of the Mississippi steamboat period.

The increased growth in the cities presented new problems: crowding, rapid population growth, large-scale immigration, and greater traffic. At bottom, New Yorkers break up a New Year's celebration of German immigrants in 1840.

The scene at the Hoboken Ferry, from an 1866 illustration (right), shows the crowded and harried situation confronting passengers as they made their way to the ferry. The pair of *Harper's* illustrations (far right and following page), present the intense contrasts to be found in the city.

Both above: Library of Congress
Both right, and following page: New York Public Library, Picture Collection

THE RICH
OF NEW YORK
YACHTING
IN THE CENTRAL PARK
AT THE UNION HOTEL SARATOGA
AT THE OPERA
IN FIFTH AVE.
AT THE SEASIDE
AT THE TOILET
IN THE PARLOR
FANCY DRESS BALL
ACADEMY OF MUSIC
SHOPPING ON BROADWAY
GREENWOOD CEMETERY

THE POOR OF NEW YORK
SEWING FOR A LIVING
DRIVEN FROM HOME
"GREAT EXPECTATIONS" A WEALTHY FAMILY.
THE OPERA
GARBAGE GATHERERS
BALL IN WATER ST.
"D'YE WANT TO BUY A DOG"
A MIDNIGHT-HAUL
FOUND DEAD IN THE STREET
"BLACK YER BOOTS"
PLEASE GIVE ME A PENNY!
POTTERSFIELD

reached California in ninety-six days, reducing by almost half the normal sailing time between New York and San Francisco. His finest ship, the *Flying Cloud,* reached California in eighty-nine days and, on its return voyage, covered 2,000 miles in one six-day period. Such speeds were not equaled by steamboats for a generation. Yet from the beginning the clipper ships were doomed. Even during the fifties the steam-power vessels began to replace them, and had taken over much of the ocean transportation by 1860.

Although relatively less important than before the War of 1812, foreign trade continued to be extremely significant in the total economy. Between 1812–1820 and 1856–1860, the average annual value of American foreign trade rose from about $186 million to $616 million, an increase of more than three times in forty years. Exports consisted almost entirely of staple agricultural products. Cotton was the country's most valuable export; between 1815 and 1860 it made up more than half the value of American shipments abroad.

Industry and the Rise of the Factory System

In creating new markets, the rapid expansion of agriculture before 1860 stimulated industry and manufacturing. The greatest industrial development occurred in the Northeast, but manufacturing expanded substantially as far west as Chicago. The growing impact of the industrial revolution can be seen in the fact that in some Northern communities manufacturing accounted for more income than farming as early as 1850. The growth of industry which accompanied its rapid agricultural expansion gave the North a well-balanced and highly productive economy.

Fortunately, the United States was in a favorable position for potential industrial development. It had abundant supplies of raw materials, such as iron ore, timber, and agricultural commodities. The many rivers provided waterpower to run the mills. Also the United States had access to Western European technology, and Americans possessed the ingenuity to develop laborsaving machines to replace hand and animal power. Furthermore, a number of prominent Americans, such as Washington and Hamilton, actively promoted manufacturing as national policy.

Manufacturing grew slowly before the War of 1812. At that time, most industrial production was in the handicraft stage, carried on in households or in small establishments which employed only a few workers. There were some larger mills producing flour, lumber, textiles, and iron, but the true factory system had not yet been introduced. The periodic European wars after 1793 tended to encourage American agriculture and commerce rather than manufacturing because both England and France needed food from the United States. However, exports and imports were severely reduced by the Embargo Act of 1807 and the Non-Intercourse Act of 1809; thus America was thrown on her own resources for manufactured goods.

Francis C. Lowell and his associates first introduced the factory system at Waltham, Massachusetts, in 1814. The Boston Manufacturing Company established by Lowell brought all phases of textile manufacturing—spinning, weaving, and dyeing—together under one management. By installing the latest machinery, including the power loom, Lowell developed the mass production of cotton cloth. Within

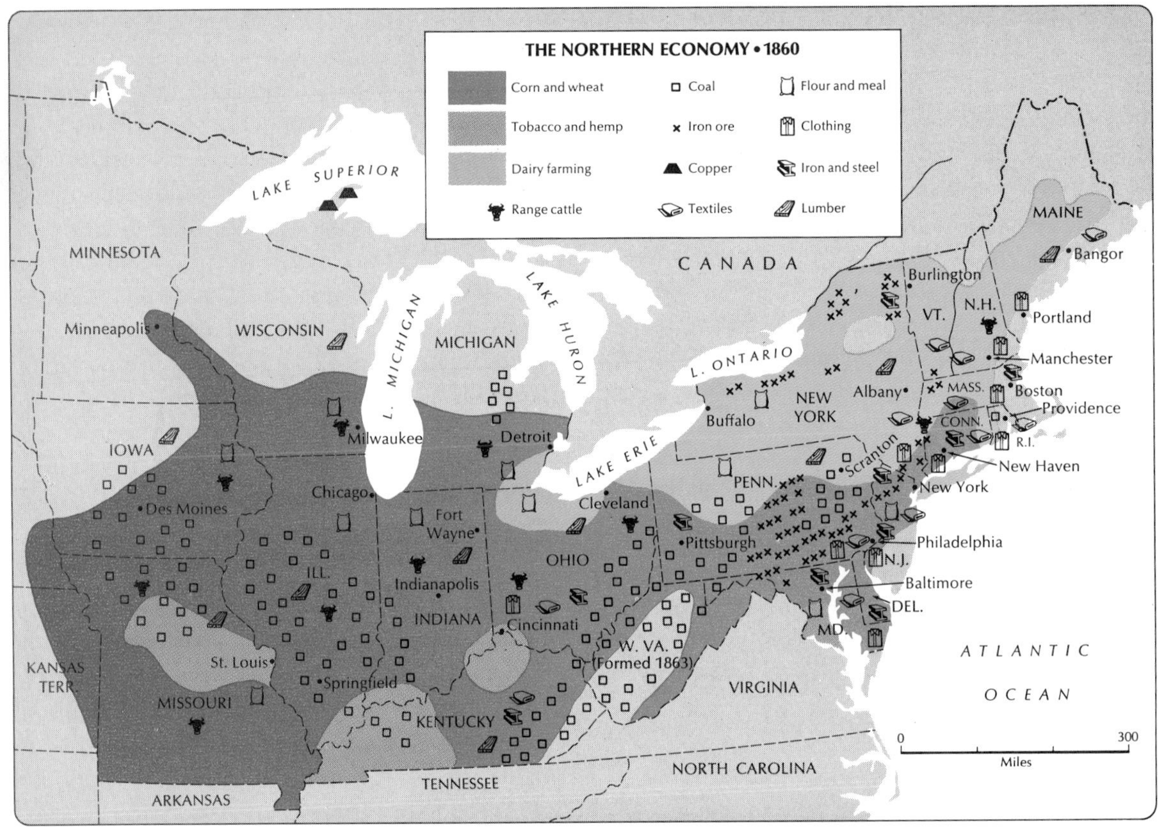

a few years enterprising businessmen established scores of textile factories; industrialists also applied factory techniques to the production of lumber, shoes, flour, men's clothing, leather, wagons and carts, and iron goods.

Each year recorded countless advances in technology and with them the introduction of new, heavier, and more basic industries. The substitution of anthracite coal for charcoal in iron manufacturing, accompanied by improved methods in the processing of pig iron, revolutionized the iron industry. By 1860 Pennsylvania, with its superb resources in coal, had become the center of iron production in the United States. Among other important technical advances in the industrial revolution was the introduction of the interchangeability of parts. This process called for the production of precision-built parts, which could then be fitted together to make the final product. Eli Whitney, a manufacturer of guns, was one of the earliest to use this method. Invention of the sewing machine by Elias Howe in 1846 and the development of such machine tools as turrets and lathes were among other significant developments which aided in the manufacturing process. By 1860, America's 140,433 manufacturing establishments were turning out products valued at nearly $2 billion. Most of this production was in New England and the Middle

Atlantic states. Income produced by manufacturing increased about ten times between 1799 and 1859. By the time of the Civil War, the United States ranked fourth and was already well on the way to becoming the world's leading industrial power. Some authorities hold that by the 1860s the United States had become second only to Great Britain as a manufacturing nation.

The expansion of American industry would not have been possible without a great increase in the market for manufactured goods. Demand was as essential as supply. Fortunately, during the pre-Civil War years, the market for industrial commodities grew rapidly because of an expanding population, rising real income per capita, and declining costs of transportation which made possible a wider distribution of products. There were also changes in the means of distributing goods. In the rural areas the general store continued to be the main form of retailing until the Civil War, but in the cities specialization developed in both the wholesale and retail trades.

The Tariff

From colonial times onward American manufacturers and their political spokesmen had demanded tariff laws to protect domestic products against cheaper imports. Tariff advocates argued that the newer, smaller, and less efficient manufacturing firms in the United States could not compete successfully with the better-established plants in Europe, especially in England. Hamilton and other Federalists had favored a protective tariff in the 1790s, but the demands became particularly strong following the War of 1812 when cheap English textiles and iron goods flooded the American market. Henry Clay was among the leading politicians who insisted that the home market must be protected for the benefit of both industry and agriculture. In response, Congress raised the tariff rates on textiles, iron bars and manufactures, and other commodities in 1816. The overall rate was about 20 percent on dutiable goods.

During the next few years protectionist sentiment grew increasingly strong in the Northeast and Northwest, and in 1824 Congress raised rates even further. Again in 1828 duties were increased. With growing opposition to protection in the South, Congress lowered tariff rates slightly in 1832; and the highly controversial "compromise of 1833" arranged to reduce duties gradually over the next nine years. The Whigs, who stood for a protective tariff, gained power in 1841. They immediately reversed the recent downward trend and raised rates in 1842. After the Democrats returned to office, they passed the Walker tariff in 1846 which provided for a general lowering of duties. In 1857 tariffs were reduced even further. It is still uncertain how important the tariff laws were to industrial development, but the tariff was probably more important as a political question than as an economic issue.

The Industrial Workers

Industrialization brought about fundamental changes in the position of American workingmen. In 1800, most workers made a living in agriculture or as skilled craftsmen who had learned their trade by the apprentice system. During the next half century, however, many of the craftsmen and the sons and daughters of thousands of American farmers took factory jobs and became part of the growing number of wage earners. Between 1820 and 1860, the number employed in manufacturing rose from about 350,000 to 1,930,000. By the latter year more than 18 percent of gainfully employed workers were in manufacturing. Employment in other segments of the nonfarm economy also increased sharply.

Industrial growth may have been hindered to some extent by the lack of skilled labor, but generally there was an adequate supply of workers. The early textile factories recruited their laborers from nearby farm communities and often employed entire families. Child labor was common, and children as young as seven or eight years old worked long hours. A company in New Jersey reported in 1828 that, of its 265 hands, 109 were men, 95 were boys and girls eight to fourteen, and 61 were women. In order to attract young, unmarried women operatives, the Boston Manufacturing Company established boardinghouses near its factories where the company provided food, shelter, and supervision.

Although factory wages were higher than in Great Britain, they were not much above subsistence levels. A factory in Paterson, New Jersey, reported in 1828 that men made $5, women $2.37, and children $1.37 weekly. By the early 1850s, male factory workers and common laborers made no more than about $6 a week in most parts of the country. The *New York Tribune* claimed in 1851 that a minimum budget for a family of five in New York was at least $10.37 a week, so it is clear why several members of the family sought some employment. Skilled craftsmen earned higher wages. In the late 1840s, carpenters received around $12 a week and some skilled ironworkers received more than $20. Workers usually labored from twelve to sixteen hours a day for these wages. Despite the fact that America was pictured as a land of opportunity, there were frequent periods of unemployment, hard times, and outright poverty.

In an effort to protect their interests, some skilled craftsmen had begun to organize as early as the 1790s. The modern labor movement in the United States did not really begin until 1827, however, with the formation of the Philadelphia Mechanics' Union of Trade Associations. Up to this time there had been no attempt to bring the individual craft unions or associations of workingmen together into a larger body, although it was clear that workers were more likely to achieve their objectives if they united on a broader basis. Nevertheless, union organization was confined mainly to skilled artisans in the cities of the Northeast; unions made practically no headway among the growing number of factory workers. In 1828, labor organized the Workingmen's Party and established the *Mechanics' Free Press*, the country's first labor paper, to promote labor's goals. During the next four years, workers were active in politics in most larger Northeastern cities.

During the period from 1827 to 1832, workers advocated a broad program of reform. Besides opposing child labor and favoring the ten-hour day, the labor groups demanded free public schools, abolition of imprisonment for debt, laws to exempt tools from seizure for debt, improved court procedures, and destruction of monopoly. Of these issues, they considered the ten-hour day and free public education to be the most important. Workers reasoned that long hours did not give them time for leisure and self-improvement, without which they would always remain little more than poorly paid slaves. Labor leaders believed that free public education was the best means by which workers could improve their position in society. Agitation by labor parties and pressure from the rising trade unions in the middle 1830s finally brought about a ten-hour day in many kinds of employment. The federal government adopted the ten-hour day for its employees in 1840.

By 1832, the labor parties, having failed to achieve their objectives by political means, began, in turn, to seek their goals through pure trade union activity. Labor formed scores of local unions in such cities as Baltimore, New York, and Philadelphia. Sometimes they struck to achieve their demands. Workers organized the National Trades Union in 1834, and when delegates from five states met two years later, membership in unions had reached an estimated 300,000. But attempts to form an effective national labor organization failed, although workers did win one important victory during this period. In 1842 the Supreme Court of Massachusetts in *Commonwealth v. Hunt* clearly asserted that workers had the legal right to organize into unions and recognized that strikes to achieve a closed shop were legal.

The progress made by organized labor in the prosperous mid-1830s came to an abrupt halt with the Panic of 1837. Under the impact of widespread unemployment, when jobless workers were literally begging for food, most of the trade unions simply disappeared. The dissolution of trade unions opened the way for all sorts of reformers and idealists to advance their solutions for labor's problems. Between the late 1830s and early 1850s, agrarianism, associationism, and cooperation all had their supporters. George Henry Evans of New York, who argued that the public land was a gift of nature and should be free for all men, formed an Agrarian League in 1840 to promote his idea. Evans envisioned the establishment of self-sufficient communities where farmers and craftsmen would labor together in peace and harmony.

Associationist reforms sought to bring people together into industrial associations called phalanxes, where they would live together and work at tasks which interested them. The Associationist movement was based on the ideas of the French writer Charles Fourier and was popularized in the United States by Albert Brisbane and Horace Greeley, editor of the *New York Tribune.* Several phalanxes were formed during the 1840s, among them Brook Farm near Boston, but they all failed within a short time because of a lack of interest among laborers. A third movement for reform among workers was the establishment of producer and consumer cooperatives. Many cooperatives were started in the 1840s, but they collapsed quickly because of inadequate capital, poor management, and the lack of a cooperative spirit among workers.

Most of the schemes advanced to help labor in the 1840s were aimed at basic changes in society which would permit workers to escape the wage system. Since none of the plans proved successful, in the 1850s workers turned back to trade union activity to strengthen their bargaining position with employers. By 1856 the cigar makers, iron molders, silversmiths, and printers had all formed national unions. Intellectuals and reformers continued to advance numerous programs of social change, but none of them had widespread appeal to workingmen. Nevertheless, the agitation by labor groups for public education, abolition of imprisonment for debt, and other reforms was highly important in the ultimate achievement of these goals.

Whereas a widely diversified economy based on agriculture, commerce, industry, and finance developed in the North before 1860, the South remained primarily agricultural. Not only did farming predominate at the expense of industrial and urban growth, but a large share of Southern wealth came from four chief staple crops—cotton, tobacco, sugar, and rice. Cotton was the South's chief money crop and the country's chief export product in the pre-Civil War years. By the 1840s, Southerners were boasting that "cotton was king." The South depended heavily on slave labor, and as time passed the Cotton Kingdom became a slave kingdom.

Population in the South fell into rather distinct social and economic classes. At the top of the scale stood the small aristocracy of large planters. In 1860 there were 2,292 planters who owned more than one hundred slaves, and 10,658 who held over fifty. However, the wealth of this small group gave them social prestige and political power far beyond their numbers. Slightly below the large planters in social and economic status were the lesser planters who had fewer slaves and farmed less land; in 1860 there were 35,616 planters who had twenty to fifty slaves. Professional men and the few business and industrial leaders were also in this general class. The idea fostered by movie producers and some novelists that most Southern whites lived on large plantations and spent their time sipping mint juleps while slaves did all of the work is entirely erroneous. Most of the people in the Old South were in the middle or lower-middle class and consisted mainly of yeoman farmers, together with skilled mechanics and tradesmen. The so-called plain people of the Old South owned very few slaves, in many cases none at all. They raised a wide variety of crops and livestock and were largely self-sufficient. Below the yeoman farmers were the poor whites, the free Negroes, and finally the slaves.

In large measure the poor whites, no less than the slaves, were an exclusive Southern phenomenon, for they could not have survived the rigors of a Northern climate. The poor whites, living generally in isolation on the least productive soils, had been largely bypassed by civilization. Some had managed to acquire small patches of land, but countless numbers existed perennially as squatters. Known variably as "crackers," "hillbillies," and "clay eaters," they spent much of their time in hunting and fishing. Some raised vegetables, planted some corn, and claimed ownership to a few head of livestock which roamed freely through the woods. Their crude huts, usually of one room, abounded with towheaded children and lean hound dogs. The men were often gaunt and emaciated, with sunken eyes, yellow skin, and poor teeth, having degenerated under the enervating assault of inadequate diets, unyielding environments, and the ravages of malaria, hookworm, and pellagra. Suffering as they did from feelings of inferiority, they often fled with their dogs at the sight of a stranger. One traveler approached the home of an unsuspecting family to be greeted at the door, he recalled, "with the barking of dogs, the squealing of pigs, and the vociferating lungs of about a dozen children who bawled out, mama, mama, here's a man."

Still lower on the social scale were the free Negroes. In 1850 some 228,000 free blacks resided in the fifteen slave states. Most were concentrated in the towns and cities of the Upper South, especially in Maryland and Virginia, although many lived in the environs of New Orleans as well. Approximately half the free Negroes were mulattoes inasmuch as masters often liberated the mulatto children of slave mothers. Many free blacks had purchased their freedom, as well as that of their wives and children, through long, hard work and savings, or had become free because of military service during the Revolutionary War. Such Southern free blacks as William T. Johnson, John Chavis, Lunsford Lane, Thomas Day, Thomy Lafon, and Jehu Jones achieved some notability. Johnson, a resident of Natchez, Mississippi, operated three barber ships, owned several hundred acres of land, loaned money, and even held title to eight slaves. Yet whatever success such men achieved was won against serious racial and legal impediments. Southern laws and customs kept most free blacks in a social, economic, and political status only slightly higher than that of the slaves. The plight of free blacks became even worse after the Nat Turner rebellion of 1831. More than ever Southerners feared that the presence of free blacks, especially the successful, would arouse further discontent and insurrection among the slaves. New laws now required free Negroes to obtain licenses to preach or to own firearms, to register with the proper courts, and to pay special taxes. They could not vote; nor could they testify in court against a white man. Increasingly they suffered from general social discrimination. By mid-century there was simply no place for the free Negro in the Southern social order.

Another quarter million free blacks lived in the North. Among those who achieved positions of respect and even distinction before 1860—as did such slaves as Phyllis Wheatley and Jupiter Hammon—were Crispus Attucks, Benjamin Banneker, Harriet Tubman, and Frederick Douglass. Still, law and custom throughout the North degraded free blacks and severely limited their political and economic activities. Despite the North's professed opposition to slavery and its rhetoric of freedom, the Northern states refused to grant Negroes the social equality accorded to other citizens. Indeed, many free state politicians, especially in the Old Northwest, sought to keep their communities white by imposing restrictions on the movement of blacks into their states. The Illinois and Indiana constitutions, adopted in 1848 and 1851 respectively, excluded blacks entirely. Throughout the North prejudice against the blacks ran deep; in many areas they received no guarantees of citizenship or personal safety. Free blacks were in constant, vigorous protest against the denial of their rights as well as against the institution of slavery itself.

At the bottom of the class structure stood the slaves. Their numbers rose rapidly to meet the demand for field hands; between 1800 and 1860 the slave population rose from 857,000 to 3,838,000. Most of the slaves were owned by a relatively small proportion of Southerners. Of the approximately 1,400,000 white families in the South in 1860, only 383,635 were owners of slaves. This meant that two-thirds to three-fourths of the families had no proprietary interest in slavery. Despite its rather sharp class distinctions, Southern society was not rigid or fixed. Many prominent Southerners who began life in humble circumstances became wealthy or achieved positions of political leadership. Andrew Jackson, Henry Clay, and Jefferson Davis all came from families of the plain people.

The South's economic development after 1800 depended heavily upon cotton. Cotton had been raised for home use during the colonial period, but it had never become as significant a commercial crop as tobacco, rice, or indigo. A series of important technical advances in the British textile industry, however, greatly increased the demand for cotton in the late eighteenth century; invention of the cotton gin made it practicable to expand production. Technological developments created an insatiable demand for cotton, producing a major shift in the Southern economy.

John Kay's perfection of the flying shuttle in England in 1733, James Hargreaves development of the spinning jenny in the 1760s, and Richard Arkwright's invention of the water frame, patented in 1769, greatly speeded up both the spinning and weaving processes. Edmund Cartwright introduced the power loom during the 1780s. With increasingly sophisticated means for processing raw cotton, England was importing about fifty-six million pounds annually by 1800, mostly from the West Indies and Brazil. Meanwhile cotton production was slowly expanding in the United States, but invention of the cotton gin by Eli Whitney in 1793 opened up the way for a tremendous growth of cotton output. A Yale graduate, Whitney was living near Savannah, Georgia, when he began his experiments on a machine to separate cotton seeds from the lint. Although the cotton gin underwent many changes, it was a relatively cheap and efficient device that could process as much cotton as the South could produce. High cotton prices in the 1790s and early 1800s caused hundreds of upland farmers in South Carolina and Georgia to begin growing cotton. In 1793, American production ranged between two and three million pounds—the equivalent of 500 to 700 bales. But between 1815 and 1859, output jumped from 209,000 to 4.5 million bales, and the United States became the world's leading cotton producer. As cotton growing became profitable, Southern farmers and planters rushed westward to find new and fertile land. By 1860, Mississippi, with a production of 1,202,207 bales, had become the nation's leading cotton state, followed by Alabama, Louisiana, and Georgia.

Although many small farmers raised some cotton to obtain a ready cash income, large-scale production on well-organized plantations became more characteristic. Developed to produce tobacco and rice during the colonial period, the plantation system was a capitalistic type of farm organization, in which slaves or indentured workers were used to produce a staple cash crop. Plantation agriculture was characterized by heavy investments in land and labor, with emphasis upon production for the commercial market. The largest cotton planters had thousands of acres of land, several hundred slaves, and could produce hundreds of bales of cotton a year. Typical of the large planters was Stephen Duncan, who lived near Natchez. In 1850 he had more than one thousand slaves and an income from cotton, after deducting expenses, of $169,354. Frederick Stanton, also of Natchez, had a slave force of 444 on his three plantations, and he produced 3,054 bales valued at $122,000 in 1858. Joseph Bond of Macon was the largest cotton producer in Georgia; in 1858, he raised 2,100 bales.

Within the so-called Cotton Kingdom there

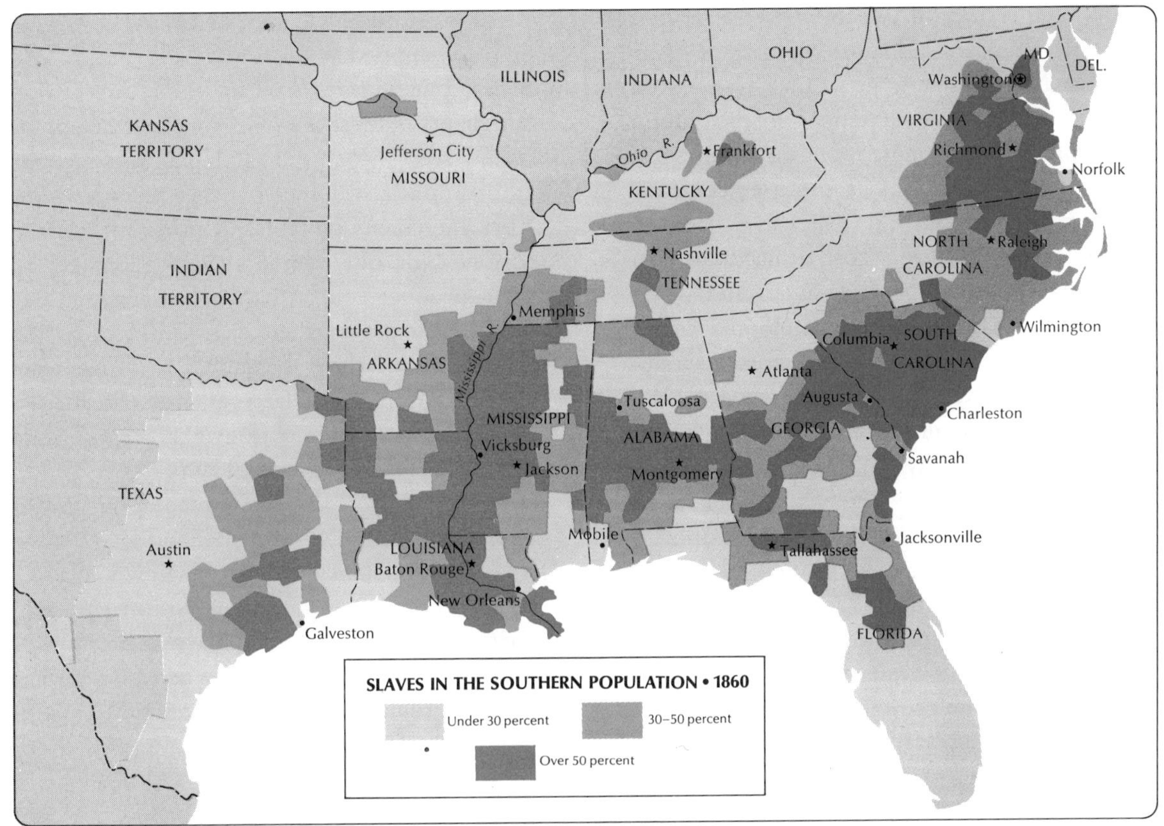

coexisted the subkingdoms of rice and sugar. These important cash crops were raised almost exclusively on large plantations and were confined to limited geographic areas. Most of the rice was grown along the coasts of South Carolina and Georgia, where the tidal flow furnished the water necessary to flood the fields. Huge estates developed, boasting thousands of acres and from 200 to 500 slaves. In 1860, one South Carolina rice plantation had more than one thousand slaves. One large planter, Thomas Allston, owned a 4,257-acre plantation on the Savannah River in Georgia; his land, slaves, and other property were valued at $527,081 upon his death in 1862. Rice production demanded a large amount of capital investment. Land, slaves, and milling machinery required such huge sums that only those with substantial financial backing could enter the business. In the 1830s and 1840s, it took anywhere from $50,000 to $100,000 even to consider beginning large-scale rice production, and in some cases much more. Obviously, rice was no crop for small farmers. Rice growing declined somewhat in the 1850s as higher cotton prices drew land and slaves into cotton farming.

The cultivation of sugarcane was limited mostly to Louisiana along the Mississippi River north of New Orleans, an area which boasted some of the largest plantations in the South. The capital requirements for sugar production ran as high or higher than those for rice growing. Land and labor were expensive. In addition, planters required costly machinery to grind the cane and process sugar, and when many of the large sugar mills adopted steam power in the 1840s, the operators accumulated further investment costs. However, the largest plantations produced as much as 1,000 tons of sugar annually and made good profits. Valcour Aime's 15,000-acre plantation, located about sixty miles above New Orleans, utilized 215 slaves to cultivate some eight hundred acres of cane. In 1852, Aime's land, slaves, buildings, and machinery were worth $701,000.

Large planters concentrated on producing a cash crop for the commercial market. Cotton growers sent their crop to dealers in New Orleans, Mobile, Augusta, or Charleston, who, in turn, shipped it on to England or to New England manufacturers. Factors or commission merchants in these and other cities arranged for credit, sold the cotton, and purchased goods and supplies ordered by the planter. New York merchants bought and sold much of the cotton. Not only did Southern planters sell their products outside the region; they also imported most of their supplies. Noting the South's peculiarities, a Natchez newspaper declared in 1842, "The large planters . . . for the most part, sell their cotton in Liverpool; buy their wines in London or Havre; their Negro clothing in Boston; their plantation implements and supplies in Cincinnati; and their groceries and fancy articles in New Orleans." Concentrating capital and labor on the production and sale of a staple crop brought in sufficient income, especially when prices were good, to render the home production even of foodstuffs undesirable.

Slavery

Even though many Americans in the late eighteenth century believed that slavery might eventually die out, the heavy demand for labor in the expanding Cotton Kingdom and among rice and sugar planters fastened the "peculiar institution" firmly on the South. Moreover, the vast majority of Americans accepted the idea of white supremacy.

Most of the work associated with raising the South's staple crops involved simple tasks, which the untrained black men, women, and children could do, though many continuously resisted. When they were not working in the fields, they cleared new land, built fences, and performed other necessary tasks. On the large plantations they worked under an overseer. While some slaves labored as field hands, others did more specialized work. Dressed in coarse clothing and barefooted much of the year, the slaves lived in cheap cabins near the master's house. They usually ate cornmeal and salt pork, supplemented by greens, vegetables, and fruits in season from their own small gardens.

The Southern states all had harsh slave codes, which were enforced with increasing rigor after the rise of abolitionism. It was lawful to mistreat and even to whip or beat slaves; and it was illegal to teach them to read or write or permit them to own property. No slave, for example, could smoke, laugh, or talk loudly in public, be out after curfew, buy liquor, or assemble in groups of more than five unless a white person

Courtesy of the New-York Historical Society, New York City

The Slave Economy

When the British journalist J. S. Buckingham toured the South in the early 1840s, he witnessed the New Orleans scene above and included it in his book *The Slaves of America.* Slaves were being sold at auction in the same rotunda with paintings, parcels of land, and other valuables. This estimation of slaves as property rather than men was later defended most staunchly by Confederate President Jefferson Davis, who maintained that abolition constituted the first step in an attack on all private property in both the North and the South.

With slaves selling for as high as $1,800, depending on the tides of the economy, the great Southern planters had enormous capital investments in slaves. A Natchez planter, Stephen Duncan, owned more than one thousand slaves, and by 1862, 2,292 planters owned more than one hundred; 10,658 held over fifty; and 35,616 held between twenty and fifty. In proportion to the total number of Southern families the percentage of slaveholders was not major—about one quarter—nevertheless they dominated the political and economic scene. This dominance was one factor in preventing the industrialization of the South, and it greatly stimulated the growth of slavery—from 857,000 in 1800 to about four million in 1860. At the outbreak of the Civil War, blacks made up more than half the Southern population.

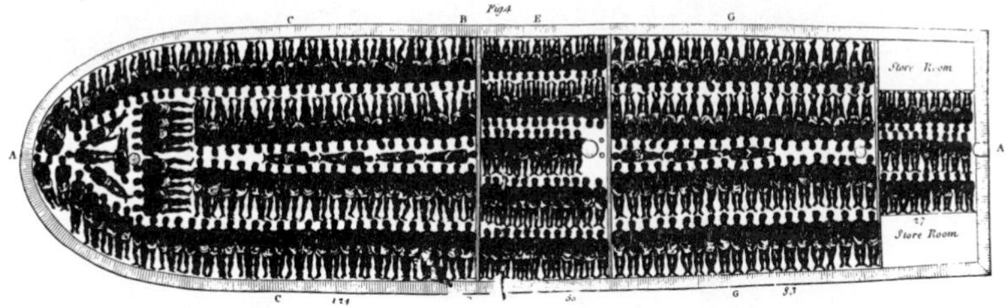

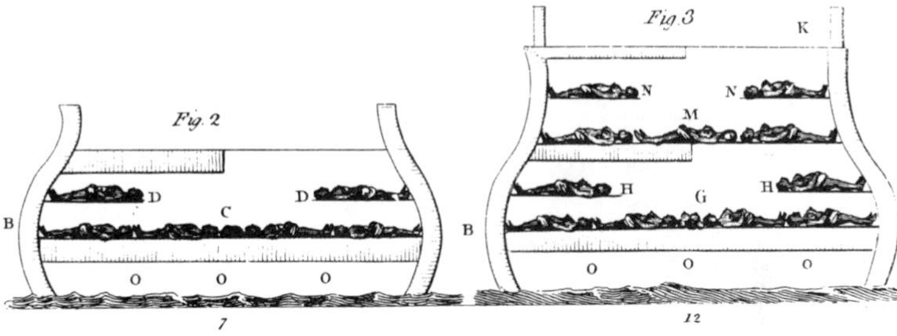

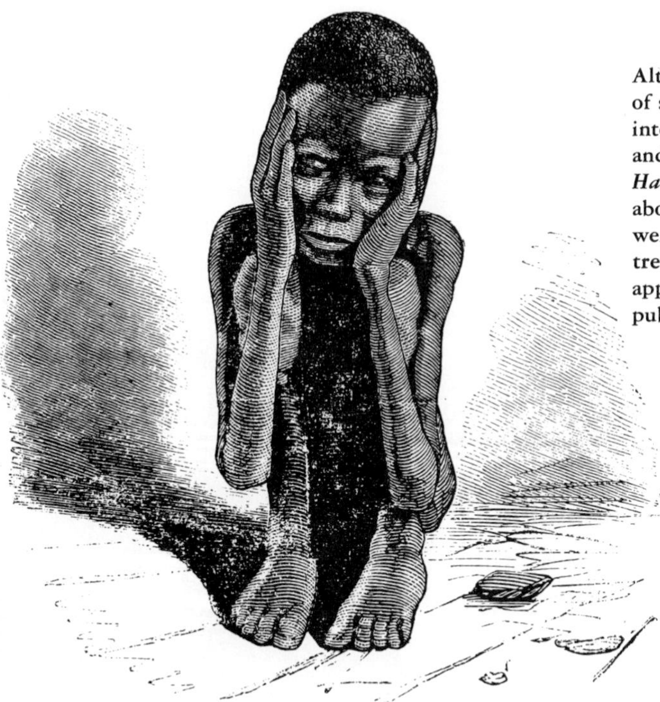

Although the Constitution forbade the importation of slaves after 1808, some 250,000 were smuggled into the country before 1860. The shipboard scene and the squatting slave boy at the left appeared in *Harper's Weekly* in 1860 after daguerreotypes made aboard the bark *Wildfire* off Key West. That slaves were considered merely cargo and that inhumane treatment was intentional become immediately apparent in the plans drawn for a slave ship and published in London in 1808 (above).

Left and above: Library of Congress
Top, all drawings: Rare Book Division, New York Public Library

The big cash crops raised for export in the South required vast amounts of hand labor. Above, Northern magazine illustrations of the period show sugar harvesting in Louisiana (left), rice cutting in South Carolina (center), and cotton being borne to the gin. At the left, cotton is prepared for the gin at Smith's plantation on Port Royal Island in South Carolina in 1862. Timothy O'Sullivan took this photograph during Union occupation of the island.

Left and above, left and right: Library of Congress
Above, center: Picture Collection, New York Public Library

While the South relied on hand labor, the North advanced not only in industrialization but in the application of machinery to agriculture. The Alexander Anderson woodcut (bottom) shows harvesting with a cradle, a method increasingly supplanted by the reaper developed by Cyrus McCormick. First demonstrated in 1831, the improved 1848 model appears at far right. By this time the Virginia-born McCormick had moved his factory to Chicago where he supplied machines for the booming farm frontier. McCormick sold a thousand reapers in 1851; by 1857 the number was twenty-three thousand. Many competitors strove to make farm machinery do more and do it better, with the result that they were frequently in court suing for patent infringements. The old hand method of threshing wheat with a flail (below) was also mechanized. At right is the J. I. Case Company's threshing machine of 1848.

Both above: Prints Division, New York Public Library
Center: Library of Congress
Right: International Harvester Company

Threshi

J. I. CASE

Having purchased of H. A. Pitts the right
manufacture Pitts' Patent Separator, and having added several imp
Tread Power Threshing Machine, with a very superior article of
years, and devoted my particular attention to improving and perfect
they manufactured east or west.

TERMS OF PAYMENT.

TREAD MACHINE.

Fifty dollars on delivery of machine (freight or warehouse charges if any;) seventy-five dollars on the first day of November; one hundred dollars on the first day of January; and sixty-five dollars on the first day of October following—all with interest.

LEVER MACHINE.

Fifty dollars on delivery of machine (freight and warehouse charges if any,) seventy-five dollars on the first day of November; ninety dollars on the first day of January; and the balance on the first day of October following—all with interest.

☞ A deduction of ten per cent. on all sums over fifty dollars paid down for either machine.

The great and increasing demand
and put in Steam Power. For the last three
Buffalo, and hope in future to be able to supply
best of mechanics. I have formerly purchased my
good castings, and sometimes poor. Having my own Furnace, I sha
against expense and loss from breakage of bad castings. I am manuf

IMPROVED WEMPL

PITT'S P

As manufactured by J. A. Pitts, of Buffalo, (al
Machines. Some of the above Machines will be geared and othe
with drum cylinder, and $325 with Iron cylinder. I will also have fo

IMPROVED TWO

with Separator; price $290 without wagon for the horse-power, and
Wheat in a day, or twice that quantity of Oats. The Lever Power M
described Machines, I will suggest the necessity of your forwarding y
you will confer a favor on him, his neighbors and myself, by inducin

CASTINGS FURNISHED FOR ALL

A. C. Sandford, Printer,

McCORMICK'S PATENT VIRGINIA REAPER

The above cut represents one of McCormick's Patent Virginia Reapers, as built for the harvest of 1848. It has been greatly improved since that time, by the addition of a seat for the driver, by a change in the position of the crank, so as to effect a direct connection between it and the sickle, (thereby very much lessening the friction and wear of the machinery, by dispensing altogether with the lever and its fixtures;) by board ribs on the reel, (which operates more ... round ones;) by a sheet of zinc on the platform, (which very much lessens the labor of raking) by an increase of the size, weight and strength of the wheels of the machine, and by improvement made on the cutting apparatus

BROWN,

OF ASHLAND, OHIO,

Having been appointed Agent for the sale of the above valuable labor-saving machine (manufactured by C. H. McCormick & Co. in Chicago, Ill.) for the Counties of Seneca, Sandusky, Huron, Richland, Ashland and Wayne, would respectfully inform the farmers of those counties, that he is prepared to furnish them with the above Reapers on very liberal terms.

The Wheat portions of the above territory will be visited ... The Agent will be ready to give any information relative to the Reaper, by addressing him at Ashland, Ashland County, Ohio.

Ashland, March, 1850.

1848

Machine Works.

PROPRIETOR.

...nd use his Patent revolving apron, in my *improved* Wemple Machine, and to ... Separator and Horse Power during the past season, I am prepared to supply all who wish to purchase a Lever or ... practical Thresher and having been engaged in manufacturing and using Threshing Machines for the last seventeen ... wants of the Western Farmer; I am now prepared to warrant my Machines the best in use. I except none ...

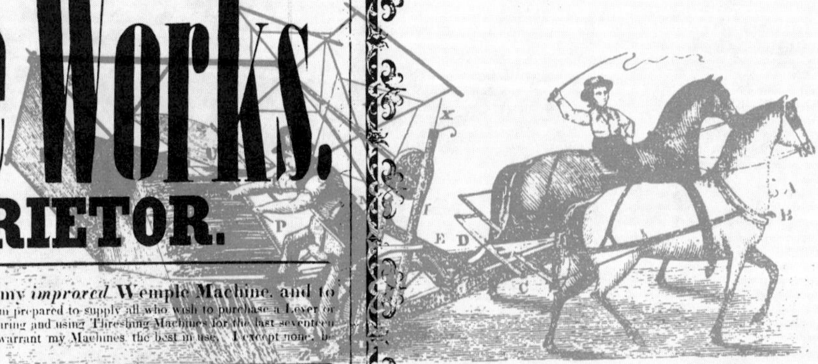

From the Wisconsin Farmer.

We have in a former number of the Farmer, noticed Mr. Case's Threshing Machine Establishment. We believe this is the largest establishment of the kind in the west. To those who are acquainted with the work of these machines, it is unnecessary to say anything in their praise. We believe these machines take the precedence of all others whenever they can be procured. We are told by those who have used them that they are the most profitable machines that can be used, both for the employer and the employed;—that one machine has cleared over $1200 during the season of threshing.

Mr. C. also keeps on hand and for sale, the most improved kinds of Lever Power. His Separators are the best in use. Mr. C. has been a practical thresher for fifteen years, and knows how to get up threshing machines just right. We would advise ...

... has induced me to enlarge my Establishment, attach an Iron Furnace ... the orders I have received for Machines; but I have now the largest and most commodious shops west of ... My lumber is all of the best quality, seasoned perfectly, and put together in a workmanlike manner by ... all kinds of castings commonly made in doing a general foundry business, consequently I have ... and see that none but the very best brands of machinery iron are used in them, thereby insuring the purchaser ...

...NE, WITH CLIMAX HORSE POWER,

...NT SEPARATOR,

...de by Marvin Hughes, of Kenosha,) with important improvements on both ... belt, so as to suit the fancies of all purchasers. My price for either of the above Machines, at the shop ...

...E TREAD POWER MACHINE,

...o-horse Tread Machine, if well attended in good grain, will thresh and clean nicely from 200 to 250 bushels ... able of threshing and cleaning, in the best manner, all that can be got to it. Should you wish either of the above ... secure one in season. If you know of any one in your vicinity who wishes to purchase a Threshing Machine ... ines before purchasing elsewhere.

...ACHINERY, AND REPAIRING DONE ON SHORT NOTICE.

Advocate Office, Racine.

Although the daguerreotype and subsequent photographic processes had been in use for twenty years before the Civil War, there is scant photographic record of the institution of slavery, little to show us how slaves lived, dressed, and looked. The group of slaves above were photographed on a Virginia plantation in 1862, shortly after the arrival of Union forces. At this period of the war, those slaves who joined up with Union armies were officially considered "contraband," or confiscated property of war.

Above: Library of Congress

was present. The letter of the law, fortunately, was generally harsher than its application. But whether the slaves were contented or miserable, they were locked in a closed system of servitude from which no escape was possible except by the will of their owner or flight, which involved great risk. The master's legal rights over the slaves were established by state law and protected by the Constitution and the courts.

The slave population tended to concentrate in staple-crop areas, where the need for labor gradually increased among the cotton, rice, and sugar planters. To meet this demand, there developed a lively internal slave trade, one of the most abusive features of the slave system, as thousands of slaves were taken from Virginia, Kentucky, and Tennessee to the Lower South. During the inflationary period following the War of 1812, healthy, serviceable hands in Alabama and Mississippi brought as much as $1,000 to $2,000. Simultaneously, many farmers in the Upper South, especially in Virginia, finding the slave system no longer profitable on their depleted soils, turned to general farming and sold their surplus slaves in the Deep South. Slave prices tended to follow those of staple crops. When cotton or sugar prices were high, the demand for labor was great, and slave prices soared upward.

The profitability of slave labor was a highly controversial question at the time, and it has provoked disagreement among later historians and economists as well. Several major facets must be considered. Its profitability for individual planters was important, but much more significant was the effect of slavery on the entire Southern economy. And the social and psychological effects of slavery on both the black and the white population demand supreme consideration. Increasing volume of research seems to indicate that slavery's influence on the overall economic development of the South was unhealthy. Because of the South's emphasis upon staple-crop agriculture—made possible largely by slave labor—manufacturing and urbanization developed much more slowly than in the North. Southerners invested a large portion of their capital in slaves, leaving relatively little money for investment in industry and transportation. Furthermore, most of the planters' money flowed out of the region to pay for food and manufactured goods from the North and Europe, as well as for the costs of marketing, insuring, and shipping their produce.

Furthermore, the presence of both a large slave class and many self-sufficient, low-income whites greatly reduced the market for goods in the South. The concentration of wealth in the hands of a few tended to keep purchasing power low, and without a heavier local demand for goods, Southerners felt little incentive to manufacture for local markets. Finally, slavery was part and parcel of a conservative economic and social system which resisted change and diversification. The planter aristocracy insisted on retaining a predominantly rural way of life. Slavery, to be sure, was not the only factor retarding more rapid economic development in the South, but it was a major influence.

Yeoman Farming

Yeoman farmers generally grew tobacco and cotton as cash crops. Some large planters also grew tobacco, one of the South's leading money crops, but more often it was raised on small family-type farms which were sometimes aided by a few slaves. Because of the large amount of labor required to produce tobacco—planting, cultivating, worming, picking, and curing—most producers had only 2 or 3 acres under cultivation, but the income per acre was relatively high compared to other crops, often reaching $50 to $60 annually. Following the American Revolution, tobacco production shifted westward from Virginia and Maryland into parts of Kentucky and Tennessee which were ideal for tobacco production. Tobacco rapidly exhausted the soil, and farmers found continued production in the older areas unprofitable. Among the South's leading cash crops—cotton, sugar, tobacco, and rice—tobacco ranked third in value in 1855. The dollar value of tobacco that year reached $17,500,000.

Corn was the South's most important crop. Almost every farmer, planter, or yeoman raised some corn, and overall it occupied more acreage and had a greater value than cotton, rice, tobacco, and sugar combined, although it was a subsistence, rather than a money, crop. Southern farmers ate corn bread, corn pone, mush, hominy, and grits, or fed it to poultry and livestock. Some corn became whisky. As late as 1850 the South produced more corn than the North, though it had lost its lead a decade later. Yeoman farmers, mainly in the Upper South, also grew wheat, as well as small amounts of oats, flax, and rye. Hemp became a major crop in Kentucky and, to a lesser extent, in Tennessee and Missouri. Border states produced Irish potatoes, grown widely for home use, and sweet potatoes, an important element in the slave diet.

Most Southern farmers, especially those in the Upper South, raised livestock. Cattle raising was a major enterprise in the border states, and by 1860 the South had 55 percent of the nation's cattle, excluding milk cows. The slave states also had more swine than any other section; horses and mules were plentiful; and farmers raised a few head of sheep. But while livestock was abundant in the South, its general quality was low. Cows produced only a small quantity of milk because of poor breeding and lack of care and feed. Most of the hogs were razorbacks, which ran wild in the woods and lived on roots and nuts.

Southern Transportation, Commerce, and Manufacturing

Southern economic growth languished not only because of that region's emphasis upon agriculture, but also because of its slow, inefficient transportation. The South had a number of navigable rivers—the James, Roanoke, Savannah, Chattanooga, Alabama, Mississippi, and Red—but as a region it lagged behind the North in the construction of roads, canals, and railroads. Much of the South was therefore isolated, and a commercial economy developed slowly in many areas. A few railroads were built in the South, but progress was slow before 1860. Charleston businessmen were among the first to advocate construction of a railroad to bring Western trade to their port. In 1828, they obtained a charter for the Charleston and Hamburg Railroad, and the first part of the road was opened for traffic in 1830. Three years later, the road was completed to Hamburg, across the river from Augusta, Georgia, a distance of 136 miles. At the time, it was the longest railway in the world. Other roads were also built to Richmond, Chattanooga, Nashville, Memphis, and New Orleans, but large regions of the South had no rail transportation even in 1860. By that time the South had a little more than

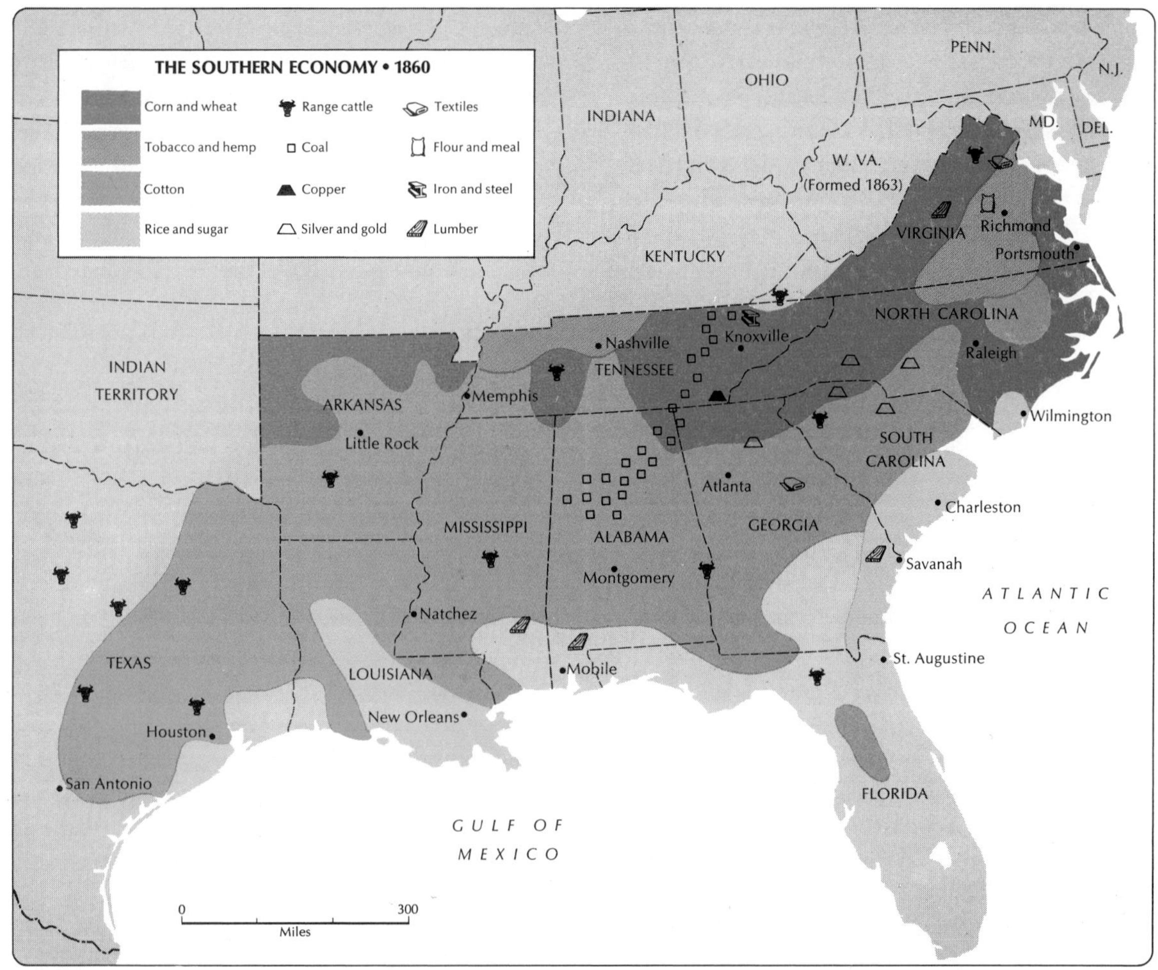

ten thousand miles of track, compared with nearly twenty thousand miles in the Northern states.

Most of the South's staple agricultural commodities which moved into national or international commerce before 1850 went by river. The Mississippi, particularly, carried cotton from Tennessee, Mississippi, and Louisiana, sugar and cotton from Louisiana, and tobacco from Tennessee and Kentucky. In the late antebellum years, railroads began to take over some of this traffic, but farmers and planters continued to rely heavily upon river transport until the Civil War. Agricultural cargoes floated down the Mississippi and its tributaries on flatboats and barges to New Orleans, where the produce was loaded on oceangoing vessels for shipment to the Northeast or to foreign ports.

Southern commerce centered around the export of staple crops and the importation of manufactured goods. Large planters sold their cotton and sugar through factors, or commission merchants, at the leading Southern ports, but small farmers usually disposed of their meager surpluses at the country store. The storekeeper commonly advanced supplies to the farmer, who expected to pay when he harvested his next crop. When the storekeeper had collected a supply of farm commodities, he forwarded the produce to urban markets. Planters and small farmers, as well as the local townsmen, bought the manufactured goods shipped in from the North or from Europe.

American foreign trade depended heavily upon Southern products. Cotton was the chief American export in the pre-Civil War years, and its sale earned much of the capital needed for general economic development. Tobacco was another important export commodity. The value of cotton exports increased from $121.5 million in the five years, 1816–1820, to $744.6 million in the period 1856–1860. In 1859–1860, Great Britain alone imported 2,344,000 bales of American cotton. Between 1821 and 1860, cotton provided 46 to 63 percent of the country's total exports. The income from cotton sales abroad provided money to pay for imported manufacturers and for part of the capital invested by foreigners in internal improvement projects. Although cotton exports produced a great deal of wealth, only a small part of it flowed back into the South. Too much of the Southern effort brought huge profits to New York and New England manufacturers, merchants, and ship owners.

Manufacturing, which would have given the South a better balanced economy, made slow progress in the pre-Civil War period. The region had some distinct advantages for industrial development, including raw materials, especially cotton, the potential for cheap labor, and waterpower. But the unfavorable circumstances outweighed the favorable factors. The competition from the cotton industry for capital and labor, an inadequate transportation system, and prejudice against manufacturing on the part of many leading Southerners all retarded industrial growth. Consequently, by 1860 the South had scarcely one-seventh of the nation's industrial establishments and turned out a mere 8 percent of the value of American manufactured products. The chief Southern manufactures comprised flour and lumber, tobacco, and textiles. Most plants were small and employed only limited amounts of capital and a few workers. William Gregg of Charleston, who established a cotton mill at Graniteville, South Carolina, in 1846, was one of the relatively few Southerners who developed successful industries in the South. The South's largest iron manufacturing works was the Tredegar Iron Works at Richmond.

Southerners bitterly resented their dependence upon the North for manufactured goods. Albert Pike told a New Orleans convention in 1855, "We rise from between sheets made in northern looms, the pillows of northern feathers, to wash in basins made in the north, dry our beards on northern towels, and dress ourselves in garments woven in northern looms; we eat from northern plates and dishes; our rooms are swept with northern brooms, our gardens dug with northern spades, and our bread kneaded in trays or dishes of northern wood or tin; and the very wood which feeds our fires is cut with northern axes, helved with hickory brought from Connecticut and New York." Believing that they were exploited by the North, Southerners urged the development of more manufacturing and the improvement of rail and river transportation, but they had achieved little progress by the outbreak of the Civil War.

The Character and Attitudes of the South

No society is entirely uniform or homogeneous, and differences in outlook, attitude, and interest existed among the social classes in the Old South. But despite the varying and conflicting socioeconomic groups, a number of factors combined to produce a rather high degree of unity. Most white Southerners lived in stable communities not disrupted by immigration. Moreover, their rural agricultural existence tended to unite them in a common view. Southerners generally looked down upon industry and finance as ranking below agriculture in worth and prestige; they clung to the idea that farming was the most honorable occupation and rural living was a superior way of life. Society in the South was basically conservative, heavily controlled by habit and tradition, and resistant to change.

The upper classes set the dominant patterns of thought and life. The great planters of the South were gracious, hospitable, intelligent, and delightful. Southerners viewed their families with pride and devotion and held a highly romantic attitude toward women. Gentlemen jealously and sometimes violently defended their personal honor and that of their ladies. They were proud of their civilization and the people who made it. Upper-class Southerners enjoyed dancing, dinners, and other social affairs in their spacious and pillared mansions, where the wives and daughters appeared in beautiful gowns and the men dressed in swallow-tailed coats. But there was a vulgar side to Southern society. Differences were often settled by brawls, fist fights, dirks, bowie knives, and pistols. "In Arkansas," wrote Henry Stanley, "to refute a statement was tantamount to giving the lie direct, and was likely to be followed by an instant appeal to the revolver or bowie." Whereas the South was unified by a rural-agricultural-conservative outlook, slavery was the dominant force which produced a strong commonality. Rich, middle class, and poor whites all shared a white skin, and nothing else solidified the heterogeneous groups in the South so much as their determination to keep the region a white man's country. Such attitudes the blacks opposed through their militant spirituals, their sermons, and their daily resistance to enslavement.

Urbanization North and South

While the South remained predominantly agricultural in the years before 1860, the rapid growth of industry and commerce produced urbanization in the North. The number of people living in communities of 2,500 or more increased much faster than the population as a whole. Between 1820 and 1860 the nation's total population rose 226 percent, whereas urban population increased 797 percent. In 1820 only two American cities had more than 100,000 people; by 1860 eight cities had reached that size and New York had passed the million mark. The major cities of the East—Boston, New York, Philadelphia, and Baltimore—remained centers of commerce rather than centers of industry.

Superficially at least, the Northeast, with its impressive urbanization, had attained economic maturity. By the fifties, its great cities changed imperceptibly year after year. Yet never before had they so completely controlled the commercial, financial, and business structure of the country. Boston, Charles Dickens observed in 1842, was a city of astonishing beauty and gaiety. Its wharves were congested and its harbor crowded. Boston's great merchants still dominated New England's society; they continued to direct much of the region's efforts seaward.

New York City was flat, straggling, and energetic—the financial emporium of the nation. Visitors were amazed by the mansions of its business aristocracy along Fourth and Fifth Avenues, the impressive hotels, A. T. Stewart's famed shopping center, Wall Street with its stock exchange and banks, and the East River with its wharves teeming with coaches, horses, wagons, baskets, and boxes, its forest of masts and flapping sails, its steam ferryboats, and its majestic ships heading out to sea. Broadway was jammed with omnibuses, coaches, phaetons, gigs, and carriages. To cross it, recalled one tourist, was "almost as much as your life was worth." New York had its share of low life. Five Points, the city's slum and vice quarter, was notorious the world over.

If urbanization made its greatest gains in the East, the Midwest was not without its urban centers, which gave leadership and direction to the region's economic evolution. To Western farmers of the forties, Jefferson's arcadian republic was no longer even a dream, for power was already shifting from the agricultural interests to bankers, speculators, merchants, promoters, and industrialists. Indeed, the farmers understood well enough that without urbanization the agricultural development of the previous decades would have been stifled. Urban centers strung out along the routes of commerce created the markets which pushed the agricultural frontier across the West.

Pittsburgh, standing at the gateway to the Ohio Valley, had once regarded that valley as her domain. By the forties, its economic aristocracy had turned from commerce to industry. The city's belching furnaces, its smoke-blackened bricks, and the din of its factories reminded the British traveler of Glasgow or Birmingham. Cincinnati, three hundred miles downstream, was the leading metropolis on the Ohio and the largest city of the West. But Cincinnati was more than a wholesale and marketing center; it was the meat-packing capital of the West—the "Empire City of Pigs." St. Louis, far to the west, was another pulsating river metropolis, a depot on the Mississippi second only to New Orleans. The commercial activity along its levee filled travelers with wonder. There, in 1847, Philip Hone, the wealthy New York merchant, counted fifty large steamboats lined up along the wharves. As far as the eye could see, he recalled, the docks were piled high with barrels of flour, bags of corn, hogsheads of tobacco, and the products of American industry soon to be lodged in the stores and warehouses of the growing city. By 1860 the population of St. Louis, like that of Cincinnati, was approaching 200,000.

New urban centers along the shores of the Great Lakes reflected even more the revolutionary changes of the 1850s. Cleveland, Detroit, Chicago, and Milwaukee were all tiny villages in 1840; a decade later all had between 15,000 and 30,000 inhabitants. Cleveland, with its easy access to Eastern markets, was beginning to bid successfully for the produce of northern Ohio. Travelers called it a handsome town, with its broad streets and tasteful houses, its spacious square and bustling wharves. Detroit's waterfront along the St. Clair River was lined with imposing wharves and warehouses. A few yards inland was spacious Jefferson Avenue with its business establishments. Milwaukee became a city almost overnight. In 1835 it had been a trading post; by 1850 its two-storied buildings were regarded as outmoded relics and were being replaced by three- and four-storied structures. The influx of population was truly astonishing. "One hundred persons, chiefly Germans, landed here yesterday," one resident wrote in 1842, "and we have a daily average of about fifty immigrants foreign and domestic."

Chicago, despite its extreme youth, was already the most promising city of the West in 1840. Its promoters boasted attractive stores, beautiful, if unpaved, streets, sidewalks, an excellent hotel, a theater, several churches, stone houses, a foundry, sawmills and flour mills, wagon and coach shops, printing establishments, brick factories, three daily newspapers, and a post office. Emigrant parties passed through almost daily, drifting onto the surrounding prairies. At harvest time in the mid-forties, wagons loaded with wheat lined up for miles along the dusty trails that led to the wharves. Chicagoans worked with a strange sense of urgency. "Every one in the place seemed in a hurry," one visitor recalled, "and a kind of restless activity prevailed which I had seen no where else in the West, except in Cincinnati." Chicago's citizens could well exude optimism, for the city's geographical position made it the natural gateway to the West. By 1860, 100,000 people resided there.

Beyond Baltimore and New Orleans urbanization in the South made only meager progress. Yet each rich agricultural district could boast at least one dominant marketing center. Charleston—a city of great charm—was the South's intellectual capital, perfumed by lavender and magnolia, freshened by sea breezes, shaded with palmettos, and dotted with spacious mansions with double verandas, beautiful churches, and a thriving, well-ordered business community. Montgomery, Alabama, and Nashville, Tennessee, were in productive farming areas; and Louisville, at the falls of the Ohio, was a strong competitor of Cincinnati. New Orleans was the South's leading port, a bustling, cosmopolitan, and prosperous city.

The movement of people to the cities brought cries of anguish from agrarians, who believed that urban life was corrupt and sinful. Writing in the *Ohio Farmer* in 1855, one reporter said: "Oh how fearful a thing is a city! How full of sin and sorrow." Another observer declared that "the farm is the natural home of man. Placed in any other condition he naturally degenerates, both physically and morally." But such warnings failed to slow the drift of farm youth into the cities.

Prosperity, Depression, and Living Standards

All aspects of the economy between 1815 and 1860 were affected by alternating periods of prosperity and depression. Although agriculture, transportation, and industry expanded greatly and conditions among many classes of workers improved, the country suffered from periods of depression and economic stagnation. The worst panics occurred in 1819, 1837, and 1857, while the most prosperous years were those immediately following the War of 1812, the middle 1820s, from 1830 to 1837, and the early 1850s. Depressions usually followed unrestricted speculation in land as well as in internal improvement enterprises.

Panic engulfed the nation in the spring of 1837 when the federal government eliminated credit purchases and demanded specie payment for land. This broke both the orgy of speculation and confidence in the circulating bank notes. Declining sales prompted foreign investors to withdraw large amounts of gold and thus create further shortages of capital and credit in the United States. The depression which followed the Panic of 1837 was long and hard. Farm prices dropped to disastrous levels, businesses went bankrupt, internal improvements projects collapsed, and thousands of laborers lost their jobs. Horace Greeley estimated that at least 200,000 were unemployed in New York City alone in January of 1838. Public soup kitchens kept the most destitute from starving.

There was a brief return of better times, especially in 1845, but it was not until after the discovery of gold in California in 1849 that the country experienced a sustained period of prosperity. Again it was land speculation, easy credit, large investments in railroads, and increased exports which stimulated the American economy. But in 1857, the bubble once more burst, following failure of the New York branch of the Ohio Life Insurance and Trust Company. Hard times were reflected in lower farm prices, a drop in land values, less railroad building, and a great deal of unemployment. Full recovery did not come until after the beginning of the Civil War.

Despite the fluctuations of the business cycle, most Americans had a better standard of living in 1860 than they had enjoyed a half-century earlier. Real income per capita, that is, income in dollars of constant purchasing power, rose about 50 percent between 1815 and 1860, most of this gain being made after 1840. Americans generally had more and better food and housing than other people of the world.

Sharp class distinctions were still based on income and living standards. A great gulf existed between the common laborer or factory worker who made his $6 a week and the rich merchant, landowner, or industrialist. For example, New York City alone had some twenty millionaires in 1845, and when John Jacob Astor died in 1848, he left an estate valued at $20 million, made largely from real estate speculation in New York. Rich New Yorkers lived in magnificent homes, rode in fine carriages, traveled abroad, and enjoyed other good things of life, while thousands of the poor existed in ground-level slums or in damp, filthy cellars. But the majority of people lived between the extremes of wealth and poverty. Most of them believed that they could improve their position almost infinitely.

Conclusion

By 1860 Americans had developed a well-balanced, productive, and expanding economy. Agriculture was the nation's principal economic activity, but commerce and manufacturing, accompanied by urbanization, made extensive gains. A varied and integrated national economy had developed, based on regional efficiency and specialization. Manufacturing, banking, and shipping were concentrated in the Northeast, and enterprising businessmen in that section provided industrial goods and services to the agricultural West and the predominantly staple-crop South. Westerners produced surpluses of grain and meat, both for domestic and foreign consumption, including foodstuffs for Southern planters and their slaves. The South's cotton crop comprised the nation's chief export and earned millions of dollars of foreign exchange—capital—needed for rapid American economic development. As Americans viewed their lengthening railroad lines, their smoking factories, their productive farms, and their rising business centers in the 1850s, it is not strange that they viewed the future with optimism and assurance.

SUGGESTED READINGS

Agriculture in the pre-Civil War Northern economy has been best covered by Paul W. Gates's *The Farmer's Age: Agriculture, 1815–1860* (1960), and Percy W. Bidwell and John I. Falconer's *History of Agriculture in the Northern United States, 1620–1860* (1925). On federal land policy consult Roy M. Robbins's *Our Landed Heritage: The Public Domain, 1776–1936** (1942) and Malcolm Rohrbough's *The Land Office Business* (1968). For the westward expansion of farm settlement and agricultural production see R. C. Buley's *The Old Northwest* (2 vols., 1950).

The best single volume on transportation is George R. Taylor's *The Transportation Revolution, 1815–1860** (1951), which also contains excellent material on industry, labor, and finance. An older and more detailed study is the *History of Transportation in the United States before* 1860 (1917) by Caroline E. MacGill and others. The history of the Erie Canal has been best told by Ronald E. Shaw in *Erie Water West: A History of the Erie Canal,* 1792–1854 (1966). The important role of canals in the country's economic growth has been ably discussed in Carter Goodrich (ed.), *Canals and American Economic Development* (1961). Louis C. Hunter's *Steamboats on the Western Rivers* (1949) is an important addition to the history of river transportation. The role of pre-Civil War railroads can be surveyed in the popular *The Story of American Railroads* (1947) by Stewart H. Holbook, but more serious students should consult specialized studies of particular lines such as *The Story of the Baltimore and Ohio Railroad, 1827–1927* (2 vols., 1928) by Edward Hungerford. One of the best railroad histories is Paul W. Gates's *The Illinois Central Railroad and Its Colonization Work* (1934). The overall impact of the railroads on the economy has been assessed in a series of discussions edited by Alfred D. Chandler, Jr., in *The Railroads: The Nation's First Big Business** (1965). Two important aspects of communication have been considered by Robert L. Thompson in *Wiring a Continent* (1947) and LeRoy R. Hafen in *The Overland Mail, 1849–1869* (1926). The westward march of urbanization is traced by Richard C. Wade in *The Urban Frontier: The Rise of Western Cities, 1790–1830* (1959).

The fullest account of industrial development before the Civil War is Volume I of V. S. Clark's *History of Manufactures in the United States* (1929). Taylor's *The Transportation Revolution, 1815–1860,* cited above, has some excellent chapters on early nineteenth-century industry. On specific industries see Caroline F. Ware's *The Early New England Cotton Manufacture* (1931) and Arthur H. Cole's *American Wool Manufacture* (2 vols., 1926). *The Rise of Cotton Mills in the South* (1921) and *William Gregg, Factory Master of the Old South* (1928), both by Broadus Mitchell, contain important material on Southern manufacturing. The development and gradual decline of home production has been discussed by Rolla M. Tryon in *Household Manufactures in the United States, 1640–1860* (1917). The best general account of technological achievements for the beginning student is John W. Oliver's *History of American Technology* (1956). Thomas C. Cochran and William Miller's *The Age of Enterprise** (1942) is an excellent survey of business development. Also of great value is Stuart Bruchey's *Roots of American Growth** (1965).

The most complete history of labor in the pre-Civil War years is Volume I of John R. Commons's *History of Labour in the United States* (1918). An excellent short account is Norman J. Ware's *The Industrial Worker, 1840–1860** (1924). See also Foster Rhea Dulles's *Labor in America** (1949) and Joseph G. Rayback's *A History of American Labor** (1959). A good study of local conditions is William A. Sullivan's *The Industrial Worker in Pennsylvania,*

1800–1840 (1955). Two studies dealing with the position of the free Negro are John Hope Franklin's *The Free Negro in North Carolina, 1790–1860* (1943) and Luther P. Jackson's *Free Negro Labor and Property Holding in Virginia, 1830–1860* (1942).

There are several good books which deal wholly or in part with pre-1860 immigration. They include Marcus Lee Hansen's *The Atlantic Migration, 1607–1860** (1940); Carl Wittke's *We Who Built America* (1939); and George H. Stephenson's *A History of American Migration, 1820–1924* (1926).

Domestic trade and commerce can be followed in Taylor's *The Transportation Revolution,* but much greater detail is provided in parts 2 and 3 of Volume I, *A History of Domestic Trade and Commerce in the United States* (2 vols., 1915) by Emory R. Johnson and associates. Lewis E. Atherton's *The Southern Country Store* (1949) and *The Pioneer Merchant in Mid-America* (1939) are excellent. On the tariff Frank W. Taussig's *The Tariff History of the United States** (8th ed., 1931) is old but still useful.

A most valuable and stimulating book which emphasizes cotton exports as a factor in America's pre-Civil War economic growth is Douglass C. North's *The Economic Growth of the United States, 1790–1860** (1961). There are several studies which deal with the role of government in the economy. Two of these are Louis Hartz's *Economic Policy and Democratic Thought: Pennsylvania, 1776–1860* (1948) and James Neal Primm's *Economic Policy in the Development of a Western State, Missouri, 1820–1860* (1954). Of first-rate importance on the role of government in financing economic growth is Nathan Miller's *The Enterprise of a Free People: Aspects of Economic Development in New York State during the Canal Period, 1792–1838* (1962). Finally, Carter Goodrich's *The Government and the Economy, 1783–1861** (1967) is excellent on this important topic.

The best survey of the history of the Old South is Clement Eaton's *The Growth of Southern Civilization, 1790–1860** (1961). The most complete treatment of Southern agriculture is Lewis C. Gray's *History of Agriculture in the Southern United States to 1860** (2 vols., 1933). Gates's *The Farmer's Age,* cited above, has several excellent chapters on agriculture in the South. A standard work on agriculture and slavery is U. B. Phillips's *Life and Labor in the Old South** (1929). There are several good state studies of pre-Civil War agriculture. These include John M. Moore's *Agriculture in Ante-bellum Mississippi* (1958) and C. O. Cathey's *Agricultural Developments in North Carolina, 1783–1860** (1956). A highly significant study of Southern society is W. R. Taylor's *Cavalier and Yankee: The Old South and American National Character* (1961).

The picture of the institution of slavery presented by Phillips in *American Negro Slavery** (1918) has been greatly modified by John Hope Franklin in *From Slavery to Freedom** (1956); Stanley M. Elkins in *Slavery: A Problem in American Institutional and Intellectual Life** (1959); and Kenneth M. Stampp in *The Peculiar Institution** (1956). On slavery in Southern cities see Richard C. Wade's *Slavery in the Cities of the South, 1820–1860** (1964). Some of the most important studies on the economics of slavery have been reprinted in Harold Woodman's *Slavery and the Southern Economy** (1966).

On cotton production see Matthew Hammond's *The Cotton Industry* (1897) and William E. Dodd's *The Cotton Kingdom* (1919). For special crops consult Joseph C. Robert's *The Story of Tobacco in America** (1949); J. Carlyle Sitterson's *Sugar Country: The Cane Sugar Industry in the South, 1759–1950* (1953); and James F. Hopkins's *A History of the Hemp Industry in Kentucky* (1951). Two excellent books which deal with the yeoman farmers are Blanche Henry Clark's *The Tennessee Yeoman, 1840–1860* (1942), and *Mississippi Farmers* (1945) by Herbert Weaver. Of great value is F. L. Owsley, *Plain Folk of the Old South* (1949). W. K. Scarborough details plantation management in *The Overseer* (1966).

* indicates availability in paperback.

14

The Mind and Culture of America, 1815–1860

JUST AS IT HAD WON its political and economic freedom from Europe, the United States moved rapidly toward gaining its cultural independence. Trends in literature, the arts, education, religion, technology, and social reform during the early nineteenth century testified to the continuing differentiation of American society. This did not mean that Americans were uninfluenced by, or divorced from, the social and intellectual currents in Europe, but they did develop ways of life and thought still more peculiarly their own than those which had existed in earlier years.

Although Americans were accused of being excessively materialistic, they by no means ignored things of the mind and the spirit. And in their cultural and intellectual life they searched for and achieved a strong individuality. During the pre-Civil War years, a widespread move took place to introduce public education at the elementary level and to make secondary school and college courses available for an increasing number of students. American education was becoming more democratic in contrast to the private and selective systems of Europe. The proliferation of denominations and the development of new religious bodies indicated a deep interest in religion, even as Puritanism continued to decline. A group of outstanding writers and artists did much to raise literature and the fine arts to high levels of competence, and they made a conscious effort to concentrate on American themes. Numerous reform movements reflected America's restless experimentalism—its discontent as well as its hope.

The American Character

Late in the eighteenth century, the Frenchman de Crèvecoeur, who spent nearly half of his life in America, had asked the question "What then is the American, this new man?" Foreigners who traveled extensively in the United States between 1815 and 1860 agreed on certain basic American characteristics and disagreed on others, but were unanimous in the belief that Americans differed markedly from their European ancestors. The combination of new political freedom, a vast and wealthy country, and the predominance of agriculture had reacted with the Old World heritage to produce a "new man."

The preeminent American trait appeared to be the habit of hard work. It took tremendous energy and labor to clear the forests, to establish farms, to build towns. This trait became so deeply imbedded in the American character that even when there was no economic necessity to toil, most Americans felt a social compulsion to perform useful labor. Far from the dishonor that it brought to the European aristocrat, in America work conferred a distinct nobility. And Americans who worked hard expected a comfortable standard of living. Indeed, European observers charged that Americans were excessively materialistic, and that, as James Buckingham wrote, they displayed "an inordinate love of gain." Yet it was easy and natural to be materialistic in a land where so many people experienced economic progress.

The great natural wealth of the United States and widespread well-being among its people inspired in most Americans a pronounced optimism and confidence in the future. They believed firmly that better things were yet to come—and within their own lifetime. Another deeply ingrained American trait, then, was the belief in progress. This spirit probably sprang from the undeniable observation that, as Charles Dickens wrote, "There is no other country on earth which in so short a time has accomplished so much." In fact, Americans were proud—even boastful—and they unabashedly scorned other political and social systems. One American with less manners than forthrightness, in speaking to the Englishwoman Frances Trollope, referred to her homeland as a contemptible little country and then "placed his feet upon the chimney-piece, considerably higher than his head, and whistled Yankee Doodle."

Americans felt a deep commitment to liberty, democracy, and equality for white men. Democratic institutions were generally considered far superior to Old World political systems, and the vast majority of people took a vital interest in the success of their form of government. As Alexander Mackay wrote, the American "feels himself to be implicated, not only in the honour and independence of his country, but also in the success of democracy." Americans believed that both their material and political interests would be best served by a democratic system. The expansion of suffrage and fuller participation by citizens in the political life of the nation in the early nineteenth century testified to this belief.

Practicality became another American hallmark. Americans had little interest in speculation or abstraction, in philosophical or theoretical inquiries. "Immediate practical results," wrote one foreign traveler, "are more attractive for the American mind, although not exclusively, than the charms of imagination." Indeed, European critics charged that Americans were indifferent to aesthetic and intellectual interests. Other American traits included hospitality, generosity, restlessness, versatility, and a special deference to women.

Americans may have been democratic, equalitarian, optimistic, self-reliant, materialistic, and individualistic. But they also possessed other, less desirable, habits, as, for example, lack of culture, race prejudice, tolerance of political corruption, easy resort to physical violence, heavy drinking, and a certain uncouthness demonstrated by tobacco chewing and indiscriminate spitting. The Englishman William Cobbett wrote that at a Harrisburg, Pennsylvania, tavern he had seen several fine, well-dressed young men who were "everything but sober. What a squalid, drooping, sickly set they looked in the morning," he added. Another writer described a man in a tavern who "took a large roll of tobacco out of his pocket, and taking an immense quid, he rolled it about in his mouth and squirted about the saliva in all directions, without paying much regard to who might come in contact with it."

Education

Early in the nineteenth century, Americans displayed an abiding faith in education as a means of lifting the nation's cultural level and guaranteeing free, democratic institutions. Thomas Jefferson had declared that the best way to prevent tyranny would be "to illuminate, as far as practicable, the minds of the people at large." He sought tax support in vain for elementary schools in Virginia but was largely responsible for founding the University of Virginia. George Washington had recommended the establishment of a national university. In 1826, New York Governor De Witt Clinton declared that the first responsibility of government was to encourage education. Demands by some of the nation's most distinguished leaders for public-supported education were backed by the clergy, publicists, and workingmen.

During the pre-Civil War period, the principle of free, tax-supported schools gradually came to be accepted throughout much of the northern United States. At the beginning of the nineteenth century, children generally obtained their education at home or in schools supported by churches and other private agencies. Some of these schools also received small amounts of public funds from local taxation. The first step toward a genuine system of public education was the establishment of free schools for pauper children. Poor people, however, resented having to declare that they were impoverished before their children could attend school tuition-free. Pauper schools were also condemned by those who believed in the principle that states and local communities should provide free education for all children. During the years after 1815, proponents and opponents fought a lively battle over tax-supported common schools. Propertied interests which balked at demands for higher taxes, people without children, and those who did not believe in universal education generally opposed free schools. One North Carolina legislator represented the sentiments of the latter group when he declared, "I hope you do not conceive it at all necessary that *everybody* should be able to read, write and cipher." This might be necessary for some professions and businesses, he added, but if a student "is to be a plain farmer, or a mechanic," such subjects "are of no manner of use, but rather a detriment." Despite such opposition, by the 1850s the principle of free public schools had won the day, at least throughout much of the North. Local taxes, some state aid, and grants of land by the federal government provided the major financial support for free public schools. In the South, tuition schools and privately financed education were more common, although during the 1840s a public school system came into existence.

Much of the educational progress made during the pre-Civil War years was attributable to Horace Mann, who became state superintendent of education in Massachusetts in 1837. He worked untiringly for better-trained teachers, improved textbooks, and modern buildings and equipment. He started the first state-supported normal school for teacher training at Lexington, Massachusetts, in 1839, and his annual reports did much to stir up the country's interest in wider educational opportunities. "In a republic," Mann wrote, "ignorance is a crime." Henry Barnard was equally effective in bringing educational reform to Connecticut and Rhode Island.

Despite increased financing, improved supervision and organization, and stronger educational leadership, the condition of most public schools was far from ideal. Funds available for buildings and equipment were insufficient, teachers were poorly trained and lowly paid, and curricula were extremely limited. Hundreds of one-room schoolhouses jammed with ungraded students were presided over by teachers who usually had no special preparation for the task and who were often not far advanced beyond their best pupils. The chief courses in grade schools were reading, writing, and arithmetic, with occasional excursions into spelling, geography, composition, and history. Teachers read the Bible regularly and everyone expected the schools to teach such principles as faith, industry, charity, and democracy. The most common textbooks were McGuffey's Readers and Noah Webster's blue-backed speller. (Webster also compiled a famous *Dictionary*, published in 1828, which was the most authoritative reference work by an American on the English language.) Beginning in 1836, William Holmes McGuffey, for a time a professor and university president in Ohio and later a professor at the University of Virginia, published his series of graded reading books which soon commanded the field. Filled with observations on piety and morality, they fitted exactly into the romantic ideals of the period.

Children who attended school at all usually stopped with the elementary grades, but some citizens demanded that the system extend upward to include secondary and college education. Private academies, chartered by the hundreds in both North and South, provided most of the secondary education in the late eighteenth and early nineteenth centuries. Their greatest development came between 1820 and 1840; by 1850, there were 6,085 academies in the United States, with a total enrollment of 263,096 students. Academies, often established by religious groups, were supported by private funds and tuition, although in some cases they did receive state aid. The academies at first existed largely to prepare students for college, but the 1830s saw a rising demand for the inclusion of more so-called practical subjects. Algebra, botany, United States history, and other new subjects were gradually introduced into the curriculum alongside Latin and Greek. Girls were permitted to attend the academies, and in some cases, special female academies were founded.

Whatever their value, academies did not meet the growing insistence on an upward extension of the public school system. Even at the height of the academy movement, many demanded public, tax-supported high schools which would educate poor and rich alike. Boston established the first high school in 1821, and others soon followed. Progress was slow, but by 1860 a reported 321 high schools were operating in the United States, more than half of them in Massachusetts, New York, and Ohio. As late as 1860 there were almost no public high schools in the South. Although the high school movement was only in its beginning stages between 1820 and 1860, it had firmly established the principle of the public secondary school and set the course for the democratization of American education which was to follow.

Before 1800, only a few well-known institutions—Harvard, Yale, William and Mary, and Princeton—which had been established by religious groups, offered the opportunity for a college education. And their primary purpose was to train ministers. Early in the nineteenth century, however, many Americans began to call for public-supported universities. Congress had granted land to the new Western states to help finance universities, and, by the time of the Civil War, the foundations of the state university system had been laid. Although several states had established universities earlier, Indiana, Michigan, and Wisconsin in the North, and Virginia, Alabama, Tennessee, and Missouri in the South all chartered universities between 1820 and 1850.

Despite the growing number of state universities, most of the colleges before the Civil War were organized and supported by religious denominations. Connecticut Wesleyan and Emory were Methodist; Oberlin, Congregationalist; Georgetown, Catholic. Some of the new colleges—Oberlin, for example—were coeducational from the beginning, but most girls who attended college before the Civil War went to special girls' schools. Mount Holyoke Seminary in Massachusetts, Elmira College in New York, and Illinois Female Academy and Rockford Seminary in Illinois were among the better-known women's colleges.

Considerable expansion and improvement took place in professional and technical education in the pre-Civil War years. The apprentice system survived, but an increasing number of doctors and lawyers began to receive formal instruction in the new schools of law and medicine. Harvard opened its law school in 1817; the University of Virginia law school opened in 1826. Baltimore started the first dental college in 1839. Established in 1824, Rensselaer Polytechnic Institute at Troy, New York, gave good instruction in applied science and technology; and after 1862, the land-grant colleges provided agricultural and mechanical education.

While education made great gains at every level, progress did not occur uniformly throughout the nation. Many poor whites in the Southern mountain regions, Western settlers, and Eastern laborers could neither read nor write. In parts of the South, a third of the white population was illiterate in 1850. Although the situation was better in the West, a resident in Illinois wrote in 1831 that "many adults, especially females, are unable to read or write, and many more, who are able to read a little, cannot readily understand what they attempt to read, and therefore take no pleasure in books and study." But many immigrants from Europe after 1840 were highy educated, and because of widespread improvement in educational opportunities scarcely 5 percent of the adult white population was illiterate in 1860.

Newspapers, Magazines, and Lyceums

Education in its broadest sense was not confined to formal schooling; people learned much of what they knew from newspapers, magazines, books, and public lectures. The American Lyceum, an important auxiliary to the classroom, was first organized at Boston in 1826 to promote learning and "the general diffusion of knowledge." While it propagandized for educational reform, it also served as a means of education in itself. The Lyceums sponsored lectures and discussions on science, literature, and other topics in hundreds of local communities. Even people in rather isolated areas had a chance to hear Horace Greeley, editor of the *New York Tribune,* Wendell Phillips, or Ralph Waldo Emerson.

Newspapers and magazines also served to diffuse knowledge and ideas among the people. In the 1830s alone, the number of newspapers increased from 800 to 1,400, and sales tripled. By the 1840s, even small towns published a weekly newspaper, and an increasing number of cities had a daily. Circulation rose rapidly after 1830 as papers became cheaper and more interesting. In 1833, Benjamin F. Day began publishing his *New York Sun* at 1 cent a copy. Imitating Day, James Gordon Bennett started the *New York Herald* in 1835. Also available for 1 cent, the *Herald* played up sensational news items, social events, and foreign coverage. Horace Greeley established the *New York Tribune* in 1841 and fought for reforms varying from abolitionism to vegetarianism. After 1848 these New York papers cooperated in their purchase of foreign news. Two significant newspapers published by Afro-Americans were *Freedom's Journal* and *The North Star.*

Magazines provided further information on many aspects of American life. The *North American Review,* founded in Boston in 1815, and *Niles' Weekly Register,* started in Baltimore in 1811, were the only magazines with national circulation. Periodicals which stressed news of economic interest were *Hunt's Merchants' Magazine* of New York and the *Commercial Review of the South and Southwest,* published in New Orleans by D. J. B. De Bow. Magazines which dealt with literature, the arts, and some contemporary social and political questions were the *North American Review, American Monthly Magazine* of Boston, the *Knickerbocker* of New York, and the *Southern Literary Messenger,* published at Richmond and edited for a time by Edgar Allan Poe. *Harper's Magazine* (1850) and *Atlantic Monthly* (1857) carried a variety of materials on cultural and political subjects. *Godey's Lady's Book* (1830) was the forerunner of modern women's magazines. Founded by Louis A. Godey and successfully edited for many years by Sarah Josepha Hale, this journal catered to every feminine interest. Mrs. Hale strongly advocated feminine health and hygiene. Among her admonitions to the ladies were directions to take up physical exercise, institute a weekly bath, and eliminate tight corsets.

Science and Invention

As might be expected, advances in science and technology were closely associated with greater educational opportunities and the broader diffusions of knowledge. During the pre-Civil War years, the United States produced a number of thoroughly creditable natural scientists

The Rise of Commercial Art

Simultaneous with the development of American literature, education, and fine art, the nineteenth century also witnessed the rise of illustrative and commercial art. Illustration became more and more important in magazines and books, and under the leadership of Nathaniel Currier (later of Currier and Ives) a flourishing market for prints to hang in the home developed. New reproduction processes permitted printing of pictures on a mass basis, and popular prints cost from six cents to a few dollars.

Meanwhile, mass production of hundreds of other products and improved transportation opened up the possibility of widespread marketing. Business seized upon the improved printing methods to advertise its products.

The pages that follow offer a sampling of commercial posters from the vast collection at the Prints and Photographs Division of the Library of Congress, selected with the assistance of Milton Kaplan, Curator of Historical Prints. Like the more familiar Currier and Ives pictures, these advertisements give some sense of what it was like to be alive in the decades before and after the Civil War.

All pictures in this portfolio: Library of Congress

While posters such as this one which promoted Moorhead's Magnetic Machine in 1848 were sometimes woodcuts, the most important medium was lithography. Invented in Munich by Aloys Senefelder in 1798, lithography appeared in America sometime between 1810 and 1820 and became increasingly popular. A turning point came in January, 1840, when Nathaniel Currier produced his hand-colored lithographs of the sinking of the steamer Lexington *and placed them on sale just three days after the disaster.*

"The tremendous success of the Lexington lithograph," Kaplan points out, "gave great impetus to this relatively new printing process. It revealed the tremendous potential of newsworthy pictures at a time when the processes now in common use for quick and accurate reproduction of drawings and photographs were mostly unknown. Commercial firms of all kinds soon realized how they could effectively make use of this new medium. To advertise their products they went to the lithographers for labels, small placards, large posters, and even barn-size pictures."

Much of the early lithography was hand-colored. Nathaniel Currier's establishment followed a factory system, with one girl assigned to each color. At the same time, however, the early lithographers experimented with mechanical means of color printing and making important improvements, particularly in the 1850s and 1860s. The prospect of impressive color, available in quantity at a reasonable price, naturally appealed to businessmen. The poster for Harrison's Handkershief Extracts (right), copyrighted in 1854, notes that it was printed in color. Historian Harry T. Peters has pointed out that printed colors are often difficult to distinguish from those done by hand, but in the 1880s hand coloring virtually disappeared.

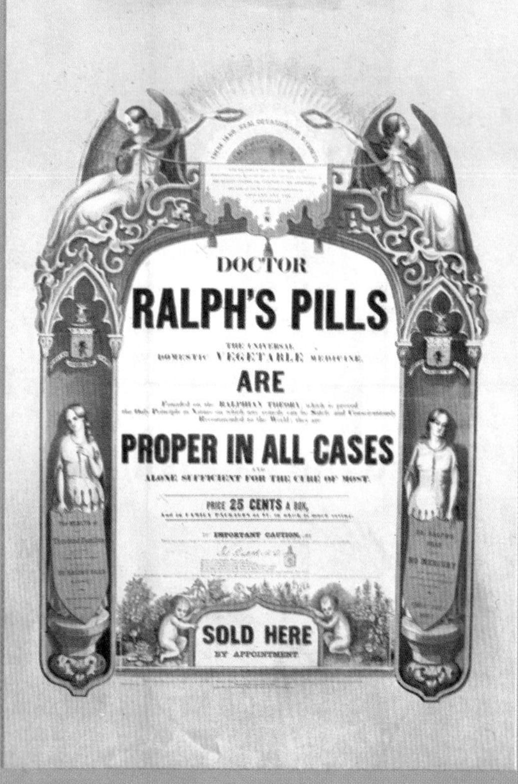

UPPER TEN
NDKERCHIEF
EXTRACTS
MOUSSELINE
MUSK
NECTAR
NEW MOWN HAY
ORANGE
ORANGE FLOWER
PATCHOULY
VIOLET
PINK
ROSE
SPRING FLOWERS
SWEET BRIER
SWEET PEA
SWEET CLOVER
TEA ROSE
VERBENA
WEST END
WHITE LILY
APOLLOS W.
Nº 10 SOUTH 7th
PHILADELPHIA
PRINTED IN COLORS BY A. BRETT Nº 6 Sth 7th St PHILa

Nineteenth-century businesses like the Lagonda Agricultural Works or Christian Stahlin's Phoenix Brewery were not averse to showing their smoking factories as well as their products. The smoke, after all, signalled their success. The Republic Fire Insurance Company poster of 1860, like some more modern insurance advertising, offers a frightening fire as an inducement, but also the reassurance of its trustees' names, among which was that of John Jacob Astor, Jr.

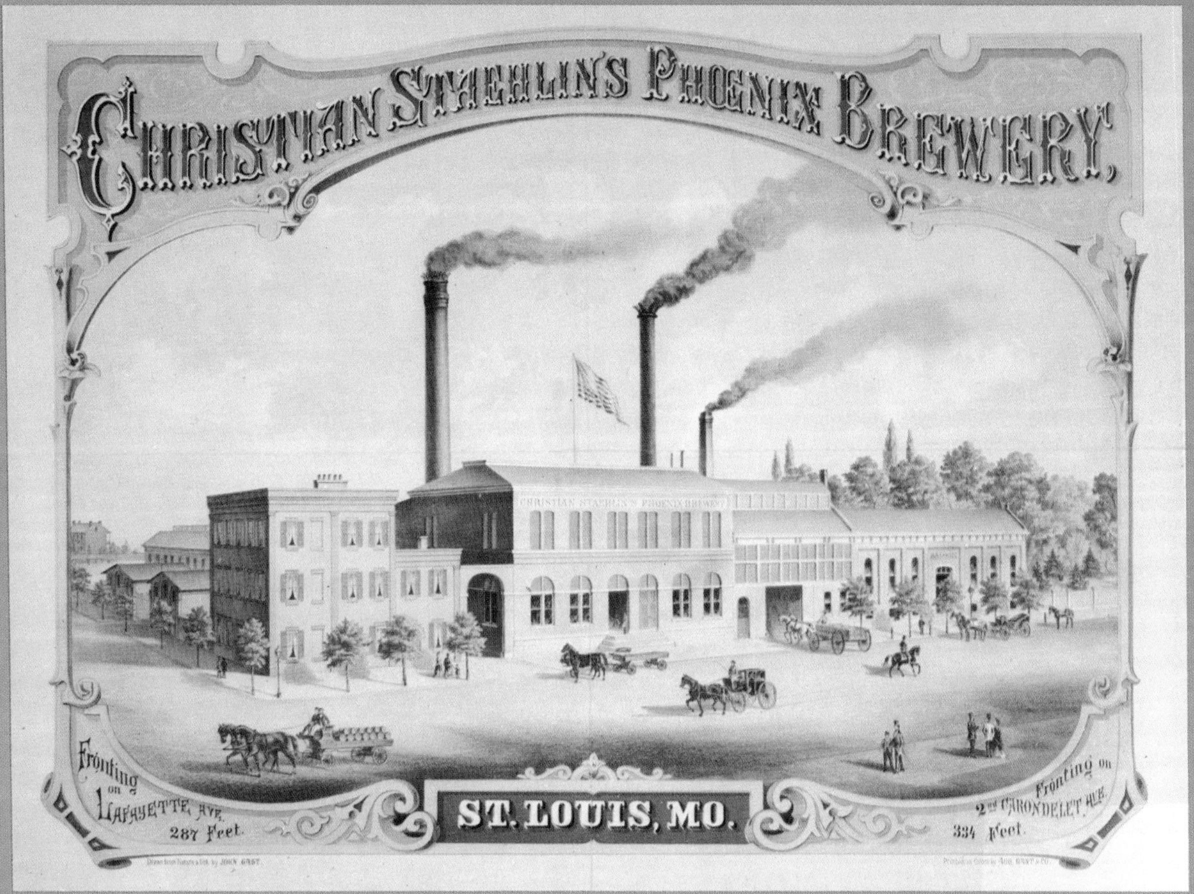

CHRISTIAN STAEHLIN'S PHOENIX BREWERY,

CHRISTIAN STAEHLIN'S PHOENIX BREWERY

Fronting on LAFAYETTE AVE. 287 Feet.

ST. LOUIS, MO.

Fronting on 2nd CARONDELET AVE. 334 Feet.

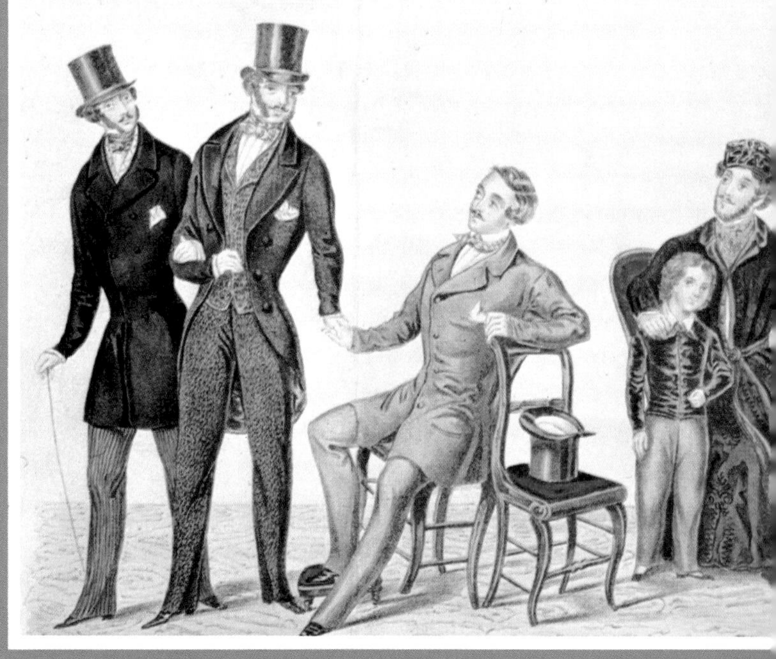

Commercial art quickly realized that it could be of obvious and immediate service to the field of fashion. The exact use to which many of the early commercial prints were put is not always clear, but one can reasonably imagine that tailors and seamstresses welcomed prints like the one at right insofar as they provided chic models to imitate and decoration for shop walls. To compare the fashions for fall and winter of 1849–1850 with the styles some twenty years later, see the following pages.

6 7 8 9 10 11 12 13

By 1872 the gentleman's swallowtail coat had declined in favor of a straighter cut, and the man appears to have had more options as to headgear, though the tophat still dominates the world of style. Women's bustles appear more pronounced, but, from floor to neck, the ladies remain thoroughly convered up and so they would continue for some time.

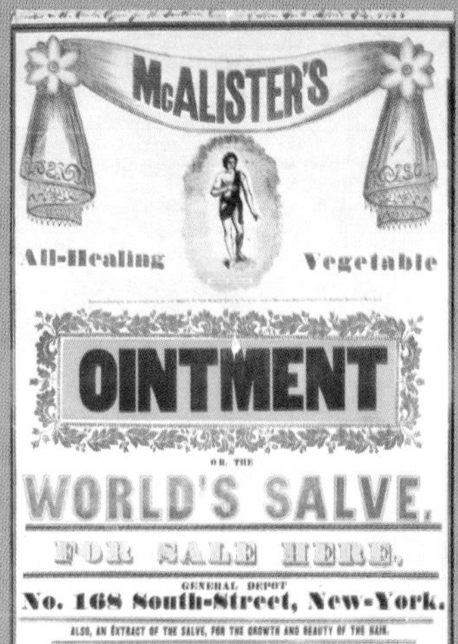

Prior to passage of the Pure Food and Drug Acts of the early 1900s, patent medicine advertising distinguished itself as a prime source for exaggerated or misleading claims. The poster for Carter's Spanish Mixture, at far right, for example, promises "permanent care for all diseases arising from an impure state of the blood or habit of the system."

Nineteenth-century poster-makers also recognized the market value of feminine beauty and references to timely matters, a phenomenon not unfamiliar today. Above right, in the advertisement for Wolcott's Instant Pain Annihilator, published in the North during the Civil War, a tiny devil, one of the sources of a headache, carries a Confederate flag. Pain arising from war worry could be banished, however, by a good draught of Wolcott's. The 1873 gargling oil poster at right makes satirical reference in its picture and text to Darwin's theory of evolution, published in 1859, which hardly enjoyed universal acceptance in the late nineteenth century.

CARTER'S
Spanish Mixture,
FOR THE REMOVAL AND PERMANENT CURE OF

ALL DISEASES
ARISING FROM AN IMPURE STATE OF THE BLOOD, OR HABIT OF THE SYSTEM.
Bennett & Beers, Druggists and General Wholesale Agents,
No. 125 MAIN STREET, RICHMOND, VA.
FOR SALE HERE.

CALLIOPE! THE WONDERFUL OPERONICON OR STEAM CAR OF THE MUSES.
AS IT APPEARS IN THE GORGEOUS STREET PAGENT OF THE GREAT
EUROPEAN ZOOLOGICAL ASSOCIATION!
BRITISH MUSEUM, ROYAL COLISEUM, GALLERY OF ART, WORLD'S CONGRESS AND GIGANTIC CIRCUS! 12 Tents! 300 Men and Horses! One Ticket Admits to All!

In the period after the Civil War, the American circus hit its full stride as a traveling purveyor of wonders, the prestige of which could sometimes be enhanced by European associations. The aquarium poster (above) is a stock lithograph which any circus could order and use. It obviously bears little relation to what a circus could actually display, but no one has ever seemed to mind exaggeration in circus posters.

STONE & MURRAY'S CIRCUS

IS COMING.

THE BEST IN THE WORLD.

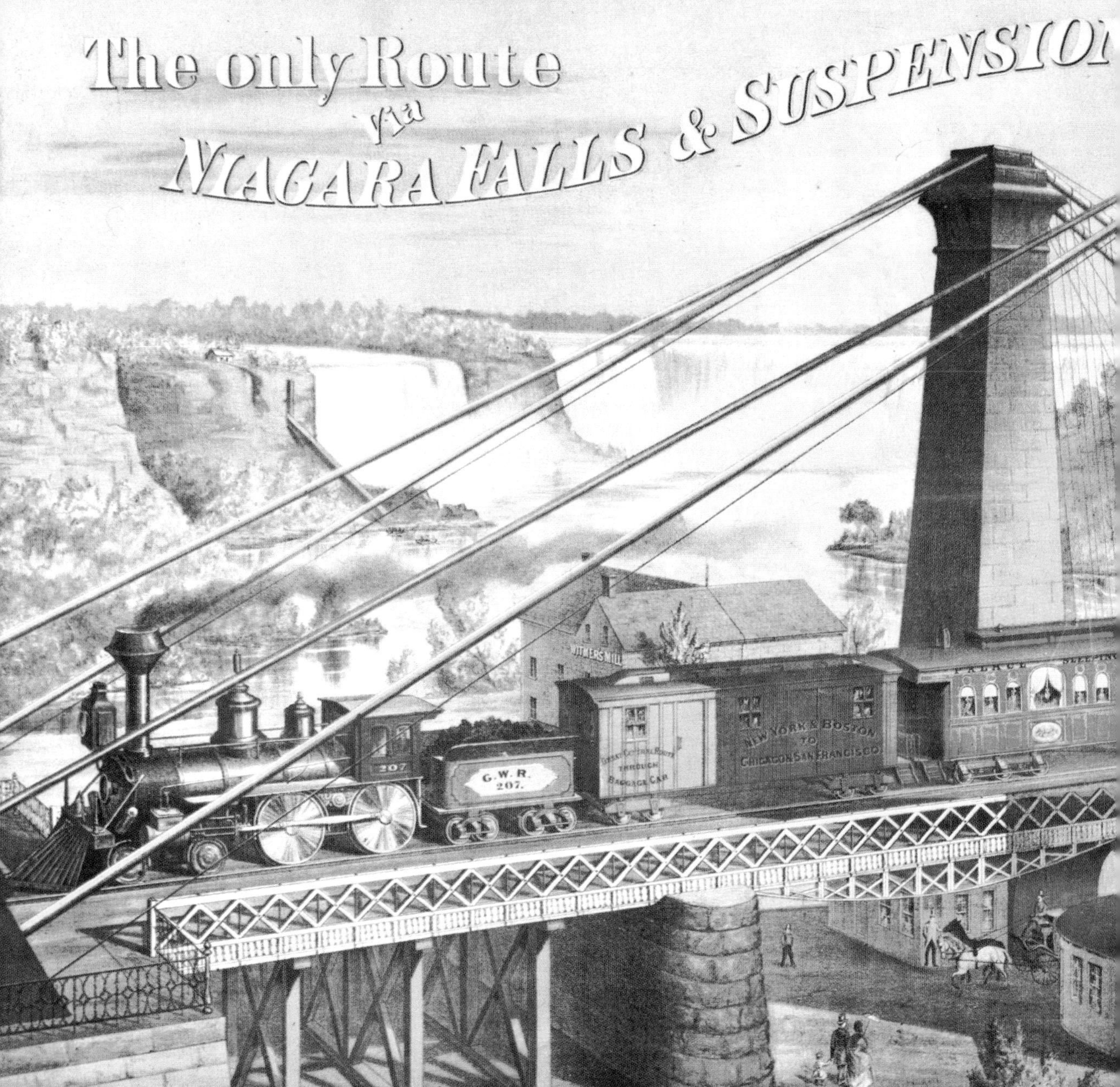

The only Route
via
NIAGARA FALLS & SUSPENSION
WITMERS MILL
207
G.W.R.
207.
NEW YORK & BOSTON
TO
CHICAGO & SAN FRANCISCO
THROUGH
BAGGAGE CAR

Railroads and steamboats became more luxurious in their decor and accommodations after the Civil War, and lithographs soon came to promote the idea of travel not just as a means of getting from place to place but as a positive pleasure. The 1876 poster at the left suggests not only the comfort of the train but the glory of Niagara Falls and the proud, sturdy suspension bridge. In the same year, millions of Americans traveled to the Centennial Exhibition in Philadelphia honoring America's one-hundredth anniversary. The stove company lithograph above is neither the first nor the last to use patriotic appeal to sell products. Here the whole world attends Uncle Sam's dinner party. The Exhibition itself appears out the window, over the world's shoulder.

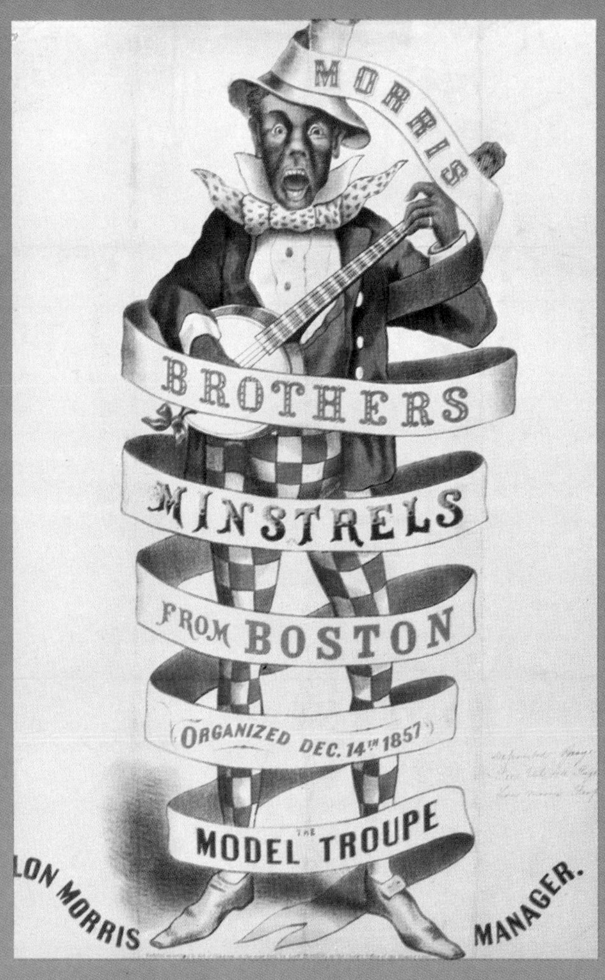

Between 1843, when the first organized troupe appeared, and the 1870s, the minstrel show became one of the most popular forms of entertainment in America. In its heydey as many as ten minstrel companies at one time played New York City alone. A typical show included songs, dances, jokes, instrumental solos, a grand hoe-down, a short musical farce, and a white-faced Mr. Intelocutor who acted as straight man for the black-faced endmen, Mr. Tambo and Mr. Bones. White performers wearing burnt cork took the Negro roles during the early period; blacks did not appear in minstrel shows until after the Civil War. Although popular, the minstrel show helped to create the unjust stereotype of the American Negro as lazy, childlike, addicted to watermelon, usually stolen, and generally not to be taken seriously.

and some inventors who gained international recognition. Asa Gray, who began teaching at Harvard in 1842, made distinguished contributions in botany; Louis Agassiz, who immigrated to the United States in 1846, did important research in both geology and zoology. Benjamin Pierce, also at Harvard, became the nation's greatest mathematician. At Yale, J. D. Dana published his *System of Mineralogy* (1837), a book which became standard in its field. Even more famous was another Yale scholar, the geologist Benjamin Silliman. Already the country's leading universities were actively engaged in basic scientific research. Joseph Henry developed important theories about electricity. J. J. Audubon, whose bird paintings became world famous, made distinguished contributions in ornithology. Significant gains also took place in medical research, especially in the field of anesthetics. In 1842, Dr. Crawford W. Long of Georgia found that ether could deaden pain; surgeons performed the first operation under ether four years later.

By the 1830s and 1840s, a new scientific spirit prevailed throughout the United States. Many people believed they saw a definite connection between democracy and science. One editor wrote in 1840, "Democracy is the cradle of science and only an unfettered mind can expand to its utmost." Scientists began to exchange ideas and cooperate in advancing scientific knowledge. Some five hundred delegates attended the first chemical convention in 1831; and in 1844, the first national scientific congress met in Washington. Senator Robert J. Walker told the participants that "the scientists could make this country the greatest and freest nation of the world." In 1848, a group of scientists formed the American Association for the Advancement of Science. Not even writers and poets could escape the growing influence of science. In his *Sonnet—To Science,* Edgar Allan Poe wrote:

> *Science! true daughter of old Time thou art!*
> *Who alterest all things with thy peering eyes.*
> *Why preyest thou upon the poet's heart?*

Already known as a practical people, Americans readily applied their scientific knowledge to everyday purposes. President Fillmore declared in 1852 that "we live in an age of progress. . . . The inventive talent of our country is excited to the highest pitch. And the numerous applications for patents for valuable improvements distinguishes this age and its people from all others." Perhaps the outstanding technological achievements after 1830 included McCormick's reaper, John Deere's plow, and other farm implements; Charles Goodyear's process of vulcanizing rubber; Elias Howe's invention of the sewing machine; Samuel Colt's revolver; David Alter's production of oil from coal; and Samuel F. B. Morse's invention of the telegraph. Americans also gained recognition for their machine tools and scientific instruments. The inventive genius of Americans was recognized at the London Exhibition in 1851, when McCormick, Colt, and Goodyear all won prizes. After using an American-built locomotive, the Pasha of Egypt exclaimed: "God is great, but those Yankees are very near perfection." Describing American technical achievements in 1854, a writer in the *London Economist* said that the United States consisted of "a whole nation of engineers, mechanics, clever workmen . . . the prospect is something wonderful for other nations to contemplate." A quick estimate of the technological advance can be gained from the patent records: between 1820 and 1860 the number of patents granted for inventions rose from 155 to 4,357.

Between 1820 and 1860, American writers produced a rich and distinctive literature. When Edward Channing, editor of the *North American Review* in Boston, and his assistant, Richard Henry Dana, read the manuscript of William Cullen Bryant's *Thanatopsis,* Dana exclaimed: "No one on this side of the Atlantic is capable of writing such verses." Such an observation was understandable in 1817, but times were rapidly changing. New York already had two outstanding literary figures, Washington Irving (1783–1859) and James Fenimore Cooper (1789–1851). It soon attracted Bryant from Massachusetts. Irving published his humorous *History of New York by Diedrich Knickerbocker* in 1809, and a decade later his noted *Sketch Book* gave readers such unforgettable characters as Rip Van Winkle and Ichabod Crane. Cooper's literary themes centered around the West, which he romanticized highly. *The Pioneers, The Last of the Mohicans,* and *The Prairie,* all published in the 1820s, won a wide reading public. Later, he wrote two more volumes in this Leatherstocking series, *The Pathfinder* (1840) and *The Deerslayer* (1841). Bryant, having moved to New York in 1825, became editor and part owner of the *Evening Post.* He had earlier published his *Poems* (1821), which included "Thanatopsis" and "To a Waterfowl." Much of Bryant's poetry dealt with nature and reflected faith in man's progress.

Despite the talent centered in New York, it was New England which dominated the literature and thought of the period. Henry Wadsworth Longfellow (1807–1882), James Russell Lowell (1819–1891), and Oliver Wendell Holmes (1809–1894) were clustered in Cambridge. Not far distant from them resided John Greenleaf Whittier (1807–1892), Nathaniel Hawthorne (1804–1864), Herman Melville (1819–1891), Ralph Waldo Emerson (1803–1882), and Henry David Thoreau (1817–1862). Longfellow settled in Cambridge to become professor of modern languages at Harvard in 1835. Within the next quarter century, he poured out a stream of poetry which placed him among the nation's top literary figures. His *Ballads and Other Poems* (1841) included "The Village Blacksmith" and "The Wreck of the Hesperus." These poems were followed by *Evangeline* (1847) and the *Song of Hiawatha* (1855). Whittier rivaled Longfellow in popularity. His sentimental poems and ballads, such as "The Old Burying Ground," "The Barefoot Boy," and later "Snow-Bound," brought him fame. Oliver Wendell Holmes, medical doctor and poet, sought to destroy the confining influences of theology. He symbolized the collapse of New England Calvinism in "The One-hoss Shay." Lowell, a poet, essayist, and editor, wrote *The Bigelow Papers* (1848), in which, with typical independence, frankness, and humor, he satirized in Yankee dialect such political issues as the proslavery faction and the Mexican War. The same year he published *The Vision of Sir Launfal.*

In his novels, Nathaniel Hawthorne described the sense of ghostly decay in Salem and his feelings of melancholia and suspense. Two of his most famous books were *The Scarlet Letter* (1850), in which he dealt with the effects of the sin of adultery on his characters, and *The House of the Seven Gables.* Herman Melville entered New England's literary circles through his close friendship with Hawthorne. Originally a New Yorker, he had gone to sea on a whaler in 1841 and returned to write his delightful sketches of life in Polynesia, *Typee* (1846) and *Omoo* (1847). His realistic tales of the sea astonished his readers. In his masterful novel *Moby Dick* (1851), he struck at the optimism and blandness of the many New England intellectuals who denied the existence of evil. Walt Whitman (1819–1892), who had lived in New York City and settled in Camden, New Jersey, following the Civil War, was the poet of individualism, democracy, and physical freedom; he wove these themes through his *Leaves of Grass,* first published in 1855.

New England may have dominated the literature of the period, but it never monopolized it. Edgar Allan Poe, whose horror tales of torture, murder, and insanity revealed his genius as well as his own instability, was born in Boston but lived out most of his life in Richmond, New York, Philadelphia, and Baltimore. William Gilmore Simms of South Carolina produced eighty-two volumes of verse, novels, criticism, and history. Writing for the popular taste in an intensely romantic fashion, Simms was widely read even though he refused to come to grips with the deep human problems with which his New England contemporaries wrestled daily. Henry Timrod and Paul Hamilton Hayne were other leading Southern writers.

Ralph Waldo Emerson's writing and thought had a universal character. Tired of the rush and discipline of urban life, he quit the ministry of his Boston church and withdrew to the freer air of Concord, Massachusetts, in 1834. Those who saw industrialism as a threat to individual freedom had two choices: they could escape in flight or they could work for reform. Emerson chose to flee. "Let the countrymen beware of cities," he warned. "A city is the paradise of trifles." But a more important reason for Emerson's retreat to Concord was his insatiable search for oneness with God. He had deserted Puritanism for Unitarianism, but even the latter's liberality could not contain him. If the Unitarians had disposed of human depravity and a vengeful God, they had failed to produce a religion of strength or passion.

Emerson, in search of a more personal religion, was attracted to the school of German Transcendentalism. Here was an order of truth that transcended all external evidence. As Fichte, the German philosopher, had written, "God becomes conscious in man, the philosopher man, the man of reason, in whom the absolute being recognizes himself. The reason gazes immediately on the eternal realities." There was something in the "involuntary soul," the "absolute being" of the German thinkers that captivated Emerson. Another stimulus for him also emanated from the Quaker notion of the "inner light," which he thought that he experienced on his strolls about Concord. To test these convictions, he embarked on a tour of Europe. One day, viewing the varieties of life in the Paris zoological garden, he suddenly became overpoweringly aware of nature as a living whole. If men could find this universal soul within themselves, they could cast off the tawdry pressures of life about them and know God. Emerson returned to Concord to contemplate his new discoveries. His break with the past was complete: God was not a person, but an impersonal force that pervaded all nature.

To achieve inner independence required time and solitude. Emerson bought a wooded lot at Walden Pond where he could devote his leisure hours to reading and contemplation. "In the woods," he wrote, "we return to reason and faith. . . . Standing on the bare ground, —my head bathed by the blithe air and uplifted into infinite space,—all mean egotism vanishes. I become a transparent eyeball; I am nothing; I see all; the currents of the Universal being circulate through me; I am part or parcel of God."

At Concord, Emerson spun out the essays that vexed some and delighted others. *Nature* (1836) expressed most of the themes on which he dwelt for the remainder of his life. He published volumes of essays in 1841 and 1844, and his *Poems* in 1847. Emerson admitted that a full experience of Transcendentalism required the sensitivity of a poet or philosopher. Not a systematic religion, it decried creeds and formal church organization, for it was above all an expression of individualism. Its converts were few but distinguished—among them, Henry David Thoreau, Bronson Alcott, William Ellery Channing, and Theodore Parker.

Occupying a room in Emerson's house at Concord was a man of small stature and roomy thoughts. To most who knew him, Henry Thoreau was a difficult man. To Emerson, he was a true disciple and friend, but nonconformist enough to keep all conversation vital and on edge. Like Emerson, Thoreau liked the out-of-doors. He cared little for the social virtues, and he found no merit in hard work or accumulation of goods. He rebuked the material forces transforming American society. "Trade," he said, "curses everything it touches." In 1845, Thoreau constructed a hut at Walden outside Concord. In *Walden* (1854), he made it clear, however, that he had sought to discover life, not to escape it. "I wanted to live deep and suck out all the marrow of life, to live so sturdily and Spartan-like as to put to rout all that was not life, to cut a broad swath and shave close to drive life into a corner, and reduce it to its lowest terms."

Other Boston intellectuals found their escape to discovery at Brook Farm. George Ripley, at one time a Boston preacher, had purchased the farm at West Roxbury, nine miles from the city. Converted to the new ideas of associationism, he decided to turn his farm into a model community. Beginning in 1841, building was added to building, member to member, until by the mid-forties Brook Farm boasted over a hundred associates. Ripley directed the work, the relaxation, and the study with singular devotion and energy. The members farmed, danced, argued, studied, and occasionally traveled to Boston for a concert or lecture. Brook Farm was a paradise for intellectuals, but it was little else. The experiment soon failed.

Much of the nation's literary taste after 1830 veered toward history. A new school of historians—William H. Prescott, John Lothrop Motley, George Bancroft, Jared Sparks, and Richard Hildreth, all New Englanders—were producing distinguished volumes. Sparks published twelve volumes of *The Life and Writings of George Washington* between 1834 and 1837 and later wrote and edited numerous other works. Bancroft's *History of the United States,* based on the author's thesis that God had directed the course of history to its culmination in the American experiment, began to appear in 1834. In 1838, Prescott published his classic narrative, *The Reign of Ferdinand and Isabella,* soon to be followed by his additional books on Spain and the Spanish Empire. Motley's volumes on the Dutch Republic, like Prescott's works on Spain, revealed extraordinary scholarship and great literary skill. These writers represented the romantic, nationalistic school of history. More objective and less influenced by romantic nationalism was Richard Hildreth. A graduate of Harvard, Hildreth published in 1849 his three-volume *History of the United States of America,* which covered the period up to 1789. In the early 1840s, young Francis Parkman was at Harvard preparing himself to write his great narrative of the history of the French in North America. A trip to Oregon in 1845 resulted in his first book, *The Oregon Trail,* published the next year; six years later appeared *The Conspiracy of Pontiac.* Parkman here revealed his unusual talents of description and narration which enlivened his whole series on France's role in North America, most of which appeared after the Civil War.

Declining publication costs and the increase in school and public libraries provided a growing opportunity for people to become familiar with the great volume of literature and history being written after 1830. The first public-supported library was established at Peterborough, New Hampshire, in 1833. Soon other communities organized libraries, and in 1849 New Hampshire passed a law permitting any town to tax for library purposes. Massachusetts passed a similar law at almost the same time. Between 1825 and 1850, about 550 libraries of all types sprang up in the United States.

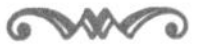

The Fine Arts

Little of the nation's wealth and energy was devoted to the fine arts in the early national period. Painters could find only a few patrons for their works. Samuel F. B. Morse traveled from city to city in an attempt to sell portraits for as little as $15. However, by 1820, wealthy merchants, cities, and even the federal government were spending more money on painting and sculpture. The principal demand in the early nineteenth century was for portraits, but the country's two greatest portrait painters, Charles Willson Peale and Gilbert Stuart, had died in 1827 and 1828, respectively. John Trumbull, another distinguished portrait painter, lived another fifteen years, but he was better known for his historical works, including the "Battle of Bunker Hill" and the "Declaration of Independence."

English artistic influences, which had dominated Peale, Stuart, and Trumbull, were declining by 1820. Artists grew disinterested in European imitation, turning instead to subjects and techniques which expressed the strength, nationalism, and independence of America. During the two decades following 1830, a new group of landscape painters chose the Hudson River region and the White Mountains as subjects to display their nationalistic pride on canvas. Together these artists became known as the Hudson River School. Thomas Doughty of Philadelphia painted the very popular "Peep at the Catskills" and "View of the Hudson," while Thomas Cole, Asher B. Durand, and John P. Kensett contributed generously to landscape paintings. The frontier regions and beyond attracted some of the period's leading painters. George Caleb Bingham's striking "Fur Traders Descending the Missouri" became a classic. George Catlin (1796–1872) painted Indian scenes as well as individual portraits, while Alfred Jacob Miller (1810–1874) made scores of sketches and watercolors of Indians, fur trappers, and other Western subjects after 1837. Albert Bierstadt (1828–1902) represented a group of painters who were attracted to spectacular scenery; his "Rocky Mountains—Lander's Peak" was among his best works (See pages 177–192 and 809–824.)

Hiram Powers (1805–1873) won international acclaim for his "Greek Slave." Otherwise American sculpture of this period was not notable. John Rogers (1829–1904) depicted everyday existence with extraordinary skill in such pieces as "Checker Players" and "Town Pump." But most of the few American sculptors who came to prominence after 1800 had usually spent long periods studying in Europe, where they were heavily influenced by neoclassicism. According to one critic, Horatio Greenough's "George Washington," which was placed in the nation's Capitol in 1841, resembled a "warrior-like Venus of the Bath." Architecture, too, was dominated by European modes, mainly the Greek style. The Bank of North America in Philadelphia, a number of state capitols, and many Southern mansions reflected the classic Greek form.

Religious and secular music expressed the sentimental character of American life in the pre-Civil War years. Lowell Mason (1792–1872), banker, writer and compiler of hymns, teacher, and president of the Handel and Haydn Society, wrote such familiar religious songs as "Nearer My God to Thee" and "My Faith Looks Up to Thee." Thomas Hastings composed hundreds of hymns and edited a large quantity of religious music which was widely adopted in Protestant church services. Revival songs were also popular.

Sentimental ballads such as those written by Henry Russell won a wide audience. Russell traveled throughout the United States, accompanied himself at the piano, and sang his own compositions, which included "A Life on the Ocean Wave" and "The Gambler's Wife." Stephen Foster (1826–1864) popularized another type of folk music and became one of the most famous songwriters in American history with such plantation melodies as "Old Folks at Home," "My Old Kentucky Home," and "Old Black Joe." These songs grew out of the folkways of the period and blackface minstrelsy. Of far greater cultural significance were the Negro spirituals which reflected the spirit and hope, as well as the trials, of slavery in the South. A well-known one is "Go Down Moses." More European musical tastes did appear; New York, Philadelphia, and some other cities had operas and symphonies, although a busy, mobile people denied them the needed public support. The United States produced no serious American composers in this period.

Religion

Americans viewed themselves, perhaps above all else, as religious people, and their religion was primarily Protestant Christianity. Deism and other forms of religious rationalism, which had been popular among such leading Americans as Jefferson, found little acceptance in the early nineteenth century, when most people preferred a warmer, more personal faith. Religion was by no means only an individual matter in America, however; it permeated almost every facet of society. Americans looked upon Christianity as the promoter and sustainer of moral rectitude and political liberty. They saw the three as inextricably bound together.

In the 1790s, it had seemed to many that there was no future for religion or the church in the new Republic. John Marshall declared that the church was "too far gone ever to be revived," and another observer had remarked that it was almost miraculous to find any young college man who belonged to a church. But the skepticism and indifference so characteristic after the Revolution gave way to religious revival after 1800. Under the influence of evangelical preaching, religious teaching in the colleges, and the leadership of some outstanding clergymen, religion experienced a notable and unexpected renewal and expansion. Moreover, when the separation of church and state became final—Massachusetts abolished taxes for church support in 1833—churches throve as never before on private contributions.

At the beginning of the nineteenth century, Congregationalism was the leading denomination in New England. Farther south, in the Middle Atlantic states, the Dutch Reformed, Episcopalians, Quakers, and Presbyterians were the dominant religious bodies. South of the Potomac, the Episcopalians held a predominant position, especially among the upper classes, but in some communities they were being overtaken by the Presbyterians. Large numbers of Catholics occupied the belt from Maryland northward to New York. Except for the Quakers, most congregations of these eastern denominations were ritualistic and formal, qualities which by and large did not fulfill the religious needs of people in the rapidly growing West. There the Methodists and Baptists came to predominate, joined later by the Disciples of Christ and other such evangelistic sects. The Methodists won thousands of converts through the efforts of such circuit-riding preachers as Peter Cartwright. Methodists and Baptists also flourished in the South.

Revivalism emerged as one highly significant development in American religious history during the second quarter of the nineteenth century. The great revivals of the early years of the century had declined in the East. But the movement soon arose in the West, and continued intermittently among the more evangelistic denominations such as the Baptists, Methodists, and western Presbyterians. Charles G. Finney, a New Englander reared in western New York and licensed to preach by the Presbyterians in 1824, was the greatest revivalist of the pre-Civil War era. Rejecting the Calvinism of his youth, Finney preached a gospel of "free and full salvation." He held numerous evangelistic meetings between 1830 and 1860, which seemed to bring remarkable results. Many ministers condemned this approach to religion, but the revivals brought new life to American Protestantism.

But some Americans preferred a more intellectual approach to their religion. In New England, Unitarians abandoned the tenets of Calvinism, rejected the Trinity and other traditional Christian beliefs, and preached the goodness of man, a loving God, religious joy, and the importance of good works. William Ellery Channing and Lyman Beecher were among the great Unitarian preachers whose influence went far beyond their pulpits. Unitarianism was especially strong among Boston's upper-class and better-educated conservatives. Universalism did not differ greatly from Unitarianism in its theology, but the acceptance of universal salvation as preached by the Universalists was confined largely to country districts of New England.

Roman Catholicism made rapid gains, especially after 1830, most of the increase resulting from German and Irish immigration. Boston, Philadelphia, New York, and Baltimore drew many Irish Catholics, and in the 1840s a large German Catholic emigration extended as far west as Missouri and Wisconsin. Most large cities supported a diocese by 1850. Two leading Irish Catholic bishops who did much to promote Catholicism were John England of Charleston and John Hughes of New York. Between 1830 and 1850 the number of Catholics rose from approximately 600,000 to 3,500,000. They did not, however, escape periodic criticism, discrimination, and charges of un-Americanism. Following a dispute over public support for Catholic schools in New York City, a strong nativist movement began in the late 1830s which led to the Know-Nothing Movement in the 1850s. The nativists demanded tight restrictions on immigration and naturalization to discourage the influx of Catholics.

The intensive interest in religion resulted also in the formation of some new religious movements. Thomas Campbell and his son Alexander, who migrated from Ireland during the first decade of the nineteenth century, wanted to proclaim the simple gospel and restore Christian unity by abandoning all creeds except the New Testament. They rejected their Presbyterian faith and for a time joined the Baptists, but in 1832 the Campbellites organized a new denomination commonly called "Christians" or "Disciples of Christ." They favored local autonomy in church government and declared that their only creed or guide was the New Testament. By 1850, they claimed more than 100,000 followers. In the early 1830s, William Miller, a New Englander with a Baptist background, began to preach the second coming of Christ. Miller attracted attention because he predicted that Christ would return on March 21, 1843. By the late 1830s, he had won thousands of supporters. As the time of Christ's return approached, some of Miller's followers sold their belongings, dressed in white robes, and went to hilltops expecting soon to be swept up into heaven. When nothing happened, Miller postponed the date. However, when Christ still did not appear, Miller and his followers gave up the idea of an immediate Second Coming; in 1846 they organized the Seventh Day Adventist Church, observing the Jewish Sabbath rather than Sunday as the day of worship.

Spiritualism attracted many people who resided in the "Burnt-over" district of western New York, a center of religious radicalism and revivalism. The Fox sisters near Palmyra in 1847 began to hear rapping and knocking noises, which purportedly were sounds from the spirit world. Although one of the sisters later admitted that the noises were nothing but a "cracking of joints" under the table, many people became convinced that it was possible to commune with the dead. Scores of books and pamphlets popularized these notions. Spiritualism fascinated many Americans, but it never evolved into an organized body of believers.

Western New York was also the home of Joseph Smith, founder of Mormonism. The son of poor parents, Smith and his family had settled near Palmyra, New York, in 1815. As a boy, Smith experienced visions, and in 1827 he said that an angel had revealed to him the location of golden plates which contained sacred writings. Smith dug up the plates and, during the next three years, translated them. This "Book of Mormon," which was printed at Palmyra in 1830, purported to be the history of settlements in America by refugees from the Tower of Babel and Jerusalem. After centuries of fighting, only Mormon, his son Moroni, and a few others remained. The records were supposedly buried by Moroni, who predicted that a prophet would finally discover them. Non-Mormons indicated that the Book of Mormon had a less miraculous origin, suggesting that it resembled other sacred and nonsacred writings known at the time, including the Old Testament. Nevertheless, an increasing number of people accepted the Book of Mormon as a spiritual guide and Smith as a prophet. Through intense missionary effort, the Church of Latter-day Saints soon won thousands of members.

During the 1830s and 1840s, Americans developed a remarkable concern for social and humanitarian reform. Spurred on by religious and democratic zeal, people believed that a new Canaan might be built here on earth. Churches and religious leaders called increasing attention to the need of temperance, better care for the insane, improved prison conditions, women's rights, education, international peace, and the abolition of slavery.

Historically, Americans had appeared to be hard drinkers, consuming large quantities of rum, hard cider, brandy, wines, and whisky. Nothing in Puritanism forbade drinking intoxicating liquors, and even the clergy drank freely. Horace Greeley wrote that during his childhood in Vermont "there was scarcely a casual gathering of two or three neighbors for an evening's social chat, without strong drink." But in the late eighteenth century, strong voices were raised against intemperance. Bishop Asbury of the Methodist Church condemned "Demon Rum"; Timothy Dwight, who became president of Yale in 1795, associated sobriety with godliness and sought to restrict student drinking. After 1800, revivalist religion inspired increasingly active support for the temperance movement. Intemperance became a sin. Opponents of liquor argued that there was a direct connection between drinking and crime and pauperism, while others complained that the social cost of caring for excessive drinkers was needlessly high. Lyman Beecher, a leader of the temperance movement in New England, admonished the clergy to refrain from drinking and to preach temperance sermons. Beecher declared that "intemperance is the sin of our land." By the 1820s, the time seemed ripe for an organized effort against liquor and the liquor traffic.

A group of temperance advocates formed the American Society for the Promotion of Temperance in 1826, and by 1834 the society claimed a million members. When the first national convention was held in 1836, the society's name was changed to the National Temperance Union. By that time a split had occurred between those who favored genuine temperance and those who insisted on total abstinence. Beginning in the late 1830s, the drive for complete prohibition tended to overshadow the less radical demand for temperance. A flood of literature appeared attacking the use of liquor. T. S. Arthur's *Ten Nights in a Bar Room* was one of the most dramatic and influential pieces of antiliquor literature. By the 1840s, prohibition forces had made great gains, and in 1851, under the leadership of Neal Dow, Maine legislators passed the first statewide prohibition law.

Care of prisoners and the abolition of imprisonment for debt also attracted the attention of reformers. Humanitarians found the dirty, overcrowded jails and the mistreatment of prisoners revolting. If criminals were to be reformed, it seemed evident that better buildings and improved administration of prisons would be absolutely necessary. The Philadelphia Society for Alleviating the Miseries of Public Prisons was one of the earliest organizations which urged better care of inmates. Besides better buildings, desired reforms included the reduction of physical punishment, the separation of the sexes, and the introduction of religious teachings in the prisons.

The old English practice of imprisonment for

debt was still widely practiced in the early nineteenth century. In 1816, for instance, New York City jails alone held some 2,000 debtors, many of whom owed less than $25. Fifteen years later, a large number of the 1,000 persons jailed in Baltimore for debt owed less than $10. People could be, and were, imprisoned for debts of only a few cents. Reformers argued that imprisonment for debt was not only inhumane, but that a debtor could not possibly pay his obligation so long as he was confined. At last, in 1821, Kentucky outlawed imprisonment for debt, and during the next forty years most states made the debtors' prison illegal.

Reformers also directed their concern at the terrible conditions which existed among the mentally ill. Prior to 1800, most insane persons were cared for by relatives who did little more than tie them up or lock them in a room. In some cases, insane persons were held in jail. In the early nineteenth century, however, reformers called for at least some degree of psychiatric treatment and state care for the mentally ill. But progress toward construction of special, tax-supported hospitals for the insane made slight headway. In 1840, most mental patients still received only private care. Dorothea Dix of Massachusetts became one of the most influential leaders in improving the care of mental patients. Miss Dix reported in 1843, after investigating conditions in her state that she had seen insane persons "in *cages, closets, cellars, stalls, pens! Chained, naked, beaten with rods, and lashed into obedience.*" She campaigned from state to state on behalf of state-supported institutions for the mentally ill. By 1860 many of the states had appropriated funds to establish mental hospitals.

While women played an important part in achieving humanitarian reform, they were interested as well in expanding their own freedoms. Many observers believed that women were shown more respect and treated better in America than anywhere else in the world, but even as late as the early nineteenth century they lived under numerous legal and social restrictions. They had no legal control over property; they could not vote; and as late as 1850, some states allowed a husband legally to beat his wife "with a reasonable instrument." For many, any woman who spoke from a public platform revealed shockingly bad manners. Frances Wright, a Scotswoman who migrated to the United States in 1818, strongly attacked the inferior position of women. She horrified most Americans by advocating not only more social and legal freedom but greater sexual freedom for women, including extramarital sex relations. Less controversial, but probably more influential, in breaking down discrimination against women were Lucretia Mott, a Philadelphia Quaker, Elizabeth Cady Stanton, and Susan B. Anthony. By the 1840s, women were appearing on public platforms to advocate a broad series of reforms, including the right to vote. Women did not, however, win that right before the Civil War.

The goal of international peace did not escape the attention of reformers. The Quakers were among the most vocal critics of war, but ministers of other denominations also roundly denounced it. Arguments against war usually were based on the teachings of Christ. As was true with most reform movements, antiwar individuals soon formed associations to promote their ideas and demands. In 1828 a group of peace advocates met in New York City and organized the American Peace Society. During the next few years, scores of books and articles advocated peace, but pacifism never won many adherents in the United States.

No reform movement in the pre-Civil War period aroused so much emotionalism as did the crusade to abolish slavery. Most Americans in the late eighteenth and early nineteenth centuries deplored slavery and hoped that somehow it might be abolished. Even some Southerners voluntarily freed their slaves. To a generation nurtured on Revolutionary principles slavery was inconsistent with liberty, incompatible with the rights of man, and contrary to Christianity. But while many Southerners opposed slavery in principle, relatively few freed their slaves because of the economic and social dilemmas which large numbers of free Negroes might create in Southern society. Slavery was an evil, but it seemed to them a necessary one.

While Southerners wrestled with their problem, Northerners moved to abolish slavery, if not necessarily discrimination. By 1804, all of the states north of the Mason-Dixon line had arranged for immediate or gradual abolition. In 1808, Congress made the foreign slave trade illegal. The freeing of slaves by law in the North and by voluntary action in the South increased the number of free Negroes, who were disliked and discriminated against in both sections. Concerned over what to do with free Negroes, the Virginia Legislature suggested in 1816 that a territory for the blacks be obtained on the coast of Africa, or elsewhere. Early in 1817, a group composed mostly of Southerners met in Washington, D.C., to form the American Colonization Society. But colonization efforts failed miserably, both as a means of removing free Negroes from the United States and as an antislavery effort. Between 1821 and 1867, only 6,000 Negroes left the United States. Most free Negroes did not wish to emigrate but wanted instead decent treatment and better economic opportunities in America. "The Colonizationists want us to go to Liberia if we will," wrote one free Negro; "if we won't go there, we may go to hell." It was soon evident that few planters would free their slaves to return to Africa; rather they would drive the free Negroes from their communities.

Meanwhile, a full-fledged abolitionist movement developed throughout the North. Ministers, editors, politicians, and others—white and black—began to raise a loud cry against what they considered a brutal evil. In 1821, Benjamin Lundy, a Quaker, established a newspaper, *The Genius of Universal Emancipation,* at Mount Pleasant, Ohio, and through its columns he demanded immediate emancipation of slaves without any compensation to the owners. By the late 1820s and early 1830s, an increasing number of Northern newspapers and magazines attacked slavery sharply.

One man who gained a particularly dominant position in the growing abolitionist campaign was William Lloyd Garrison. Born in Massachusetts in 1805, Garrison was the son of a poor sailor and a deeply religious mother. He grew up in poverty and went to work as an apprentice printer at thirteen. After serving his seven-year apprenticeship, this pious and ambitious youth quit the printing trade and associated himself with a number of reform newspapers. In 1828, he began editing the *National Philanthropist,* a temperance newspaper published in Boston. The next year, he went to Baltimore and became editor of *The Genius of Universal Emancipation,* which had been published in different places since its founding. While in Baltimore, Garrison was jailed for libel after he attacked in print a ship owner who had agreed to transport a planter's slaves to Louisiana. Bitter and indignant over his imprisonment, Garrison went to Boston, where on January 1, 1833, he began issuing his new antislavery paper, *The Liberator.*

An intense moralist, Garrison could be neither moderate nor compromising in his stand on this great social evil. He wrote that his moral indignation against slavery had reached the "acme of intensity" and that he would speak out against it regardless of the consequences. "I will be as harsh as truth and as uncompromising as justice . . . I will not retreat a single inch, and I WILL BE HEARD," he wrote in the first issue of the *Liberator.* Garrison denounced the gradual emancipation which many abolitionists favored and called for immediate freedom for the slaves. He attacked slavery as immoral and made its moral status a great national issue. He also vilified slave owners. Within a short time, a number of other effective abolitionists joined the crusade against slavery. Among them were Lewis and Arthur Tappan, New York businessmen; Theodore Weld, a partially trained minister and reformer who organized antislavery sentiment at Lane Seminary in Cincinnati and throughout the West; Wendell Phillips, a Boston lawyer and lecturer; Presbyterian minister Henry Ward Beecher; and Elijah P. Lovejoy. While Garrison continued to lead the movement in New England, Weld became the dominant abolitionist in Ohio. Frederick Douglass, an escaped slave who founded the *North Star* in 1847, became the leading Negro abolitionist. Douglass received the able and determined support of other black abolitionists such as William Wells Brown, Henry Highland Garnet, David Walker, Sojourner Truth, Harriet Tubman, and Charles Lenox Remond.

As abolitionist sentiment spread, local antislavery societies sprang up throughout the North. In December, 1833, a group of abolitionists met in Philadelphia and formed the American Antislavery Society. The abolitionist movement now shifted from individual and group criticism of slavery to a widely organized effort for national reform. During the 1830s, abolitionists published a flood of antislavery books, magazines, and newspapers, and the movement gained many adherents. Yet the extreme and uncompromising abolitionists met bitter resistance in the North. Garrison was dragged through the streets of Boston in 1835, as opponents sought to silence him; and Elijah P. Lovejoy of Alton, Illinois, was shot and killed in 1837 when he tried to defend his abolitionist press from a mob. Such incidents, however, only transformed the victims of such attacks into martyrs to the cause of abolition.

As slavery came under increasing attack, Southerners quickly came to its defense. During the 1820s, a gradual shift took place from the estimation of slavery as a necessary evil to a lively defense of it as a desirable social and economic system. James H. Hammond of South Carolina wrote: "But it [slavery] is no evil. On the contrary, I believe it to be the greatest of all the great blessings which a kind Providence has bestowed upon our glorious region." It did not require an attack by abolitionists to convince Southerners of the virtue of slavery. But abolitionism in the context of other occurrences seemed a dangerous threat to the white Southerners' institutions and to their way of life.

The Nat Turner rebellion, which occurred in southeastern Virginia in August, 1831, aroused and frightened Southerners even further.

INJURED HUMANITY;

BEING

A Representation of what the unhappy Children of Africa endure from those who call themselves

CHRISTIANS.

The husband and wife, after being sold to different purchasers, violently separated; probably never to see each other more.

When slaves are purchased by the planters, they are generally marked on the breast with a red hot iron.

A representation of a slave at work cruelly accoutred, with a Head-frame and Mouth-piece to prevent his eating—with Boots and Spurs round his legs, and half a hundred weight chained to his body to prevent his absconding.

The manner of fixing the slaves on a ladder to be flogged, which is also occasionally laid flat on the ground for severer punishment.

The Abolitionists

During the first half of the nineteenth century the cause of abolition challenged American morality. At issue was the disparity between the realities of slavery and the nation's avowed ideals—the ideals of freedom, equality, and humanity as professed by a preponderantly Christian people. This early antislavery broadside, published in New York, appeals directly to Christian conscience in its detailed descriptions of the horrifying maltreatment of blacks at the hands of slave masters.

Continuing evidence of the inhumanity and unworkability of slavery as an institution was provided by the sometimes violent protests of blacks themselves. The revolt aboard the slave ship Amistad *in 1838 (following page, above) commanded national attention and brought ex-President John Quincy Adams to the successful defense of its leaders before the United States Supreme Court. Uprisings took place as well on American soil, two of which were represented in lurid and sensational newspaper illustrations of the time (following page, center and below). The middle cut comes from a contemporary account of the Nat Turner insurrection in Virginia in 1831 which took the lives of fifty-seven whites. The bottom cut purports to represent the massacre of whites by Indians and blacks in Florida during 1835 and 1836—but it is notable that the printer has lifted several pieces from the Nat Turner woodcut to create his "illustration."*

Surrounding copy: Courtesy of the New-York Historical Society, New York City

The manner of yoking the slaves by the Mandingoes, or African slave merchants, who usually march annually in eight or ten parties, from the river Gambia to Bambarra; each party having from one hundred to one hundred and fifty slaves.

The Log-Yokes are made of the roots of trees, so heavy as to make it extremely difficult for the persons who wear them to walk, much more to escape or run away.

A front and profile view of an African's head, with the mouth-piece and necklace, the hooks round which are placed to prevent an escape when pursued in the woods, and to hinder them from laying down the head to procure rest.—At A is a flat iron which goes into the mouth, and so effectually keeps down the tongue, that nothing can be swallowed, not even the saliva, a passage for which is made through holes in the mouth-plate.

An enlarged view of the mouth-piece, which, when long worn, becomes so heated, as frequently to bring off the skin along with it.

A view of the leg-bolts or shackles, as put upon the legs of the slaves on shipboard, in the middle passage.

An enlarged view of the boots and spurs, as used at some plantations in Antigua.

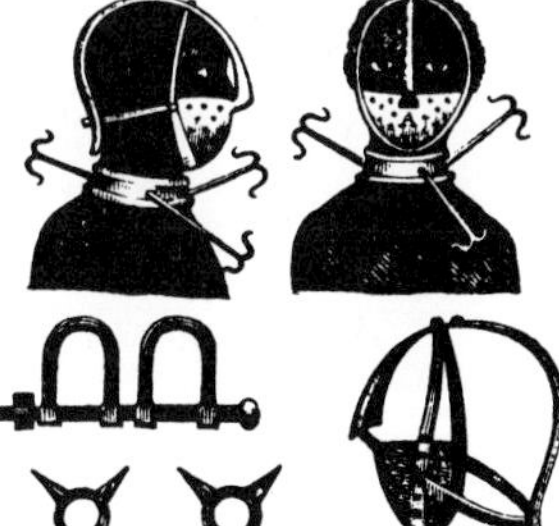

Another method in which the poor victims are placed to be flogged.

HORRID MASSACRE IN VIRGINIA.

Massacre of the Whites by the Indians and Blacks in Florida.

The American Anti-Slavery Society, formed in Philadelphia in 1833, and one of the important forces in the cause of abolition, used the popular almanac to disseminate its propaganda, and its illustrations frequently reflect the fact that abolition was by no means popular among many Northerners. The antislavery printing press of E. P. Lovejoy was set upon and destroyed by mobs three times, in New York, Ohio, and Illinois (right, above). Almanac cuts depicted the brutal punishment of a slave (right, center) and the destruction of a Northern school for black girls (right, below) among other racist activities. According to the caption for the last, "When schools have been established for colored scholars, the law makers and the mob have combined to destroy them—as at Canton, Connecticut, at Canaan, New Hampshire . . . and Zanesville and Brown County, Ohio . . ."

Above, top and center: Courtesy of the New-York Historical Society, New York City
Above: Library of Congress
Far right: Courtesy of the New-York Historical Society, New York City
Insets above, center, and below: New York Public Library

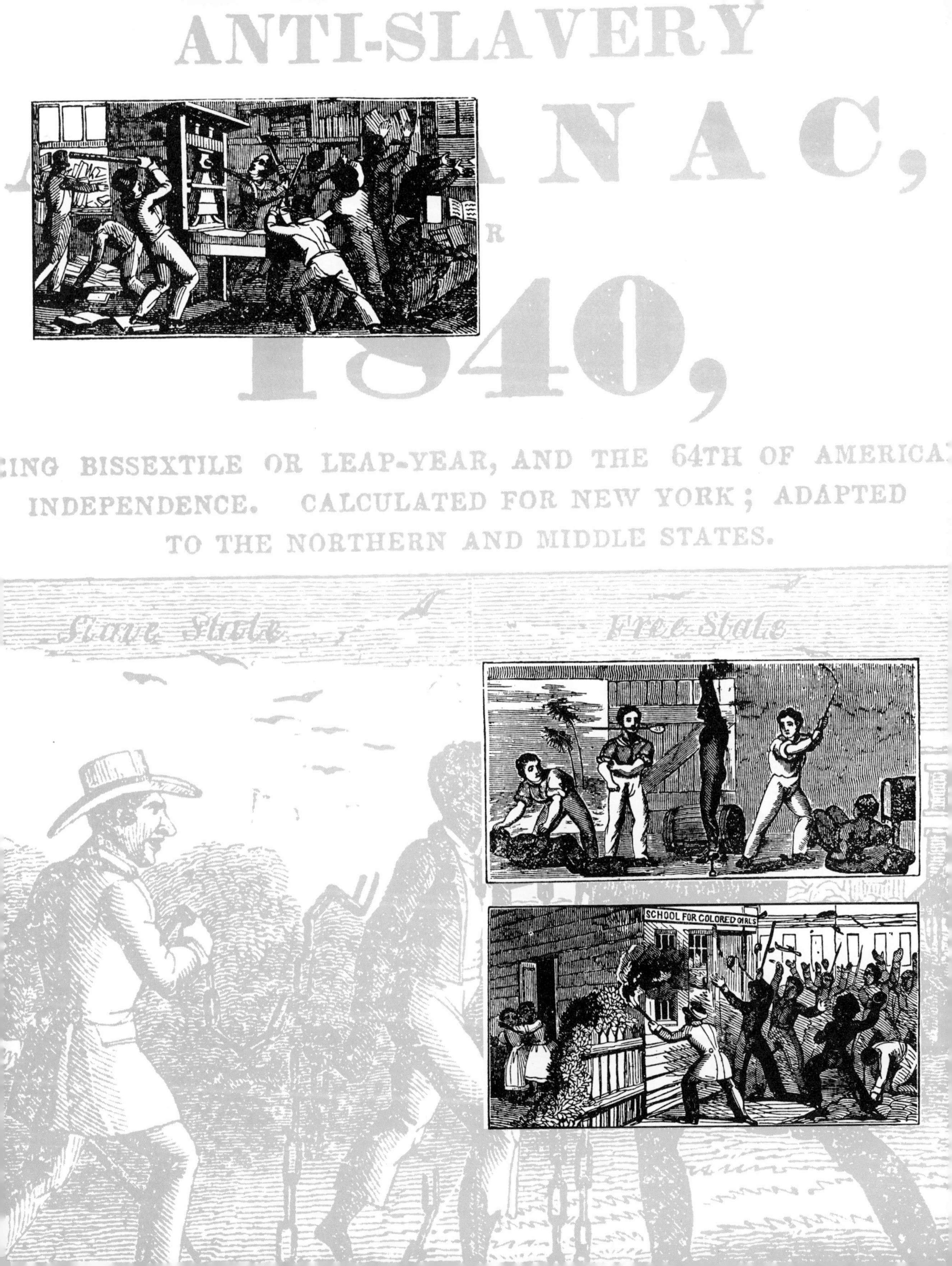

ANTI-SLAVERY

A NAC,

R

1840,

CING BISSEXTILE OR LEAP-YEAR, AND THE 64TH OF AMERICA
INDEPENDENCE. CALCULATED FOR NEW YORK; ADAPTED
TO THE NORTHERN AND MIDDLE STATES.

Slave State

Free State

SCHOOL FOR COLORED GIRLS

Library of Congress

Outstanding among Abolitionist leaders were the escaped slave, Frederick Douglas (left) founder and editor of The North Star, *and William Lloyd Garrison (left, below), editor of* The Liberator. *Garrison was uncompromising: "On this subject," he wrote, "I do not wish to think, or speak, or write, with toleration." Douglass wrote: "I base no man's right upon his color and plead no man's rights because of his color. My interest in any man is objectively in his manhood and subjectively in my own manhood."*

Among the important black Abolitionists was the Reverend Samuel Cornish (far right, above), pastor of the First Presbyterian Church of New York, who, with James Forten and John Hilton, in 1830 established an annual meeting at which blacks could consider means of improving their condition. With the pioneer black editor John Russwurm, Cornish published the newspaper Freedom's Journal. *Sojourner Truth (near right) was one of many blacks who wrote on the conditions of slaves. Henry Highland Garnett (far right, below) advised slaves, "The diabolical injustice by which your liberties are cloven down, neither God nor angels, or just men command you to suffer for a single moment."*

Library of Congress

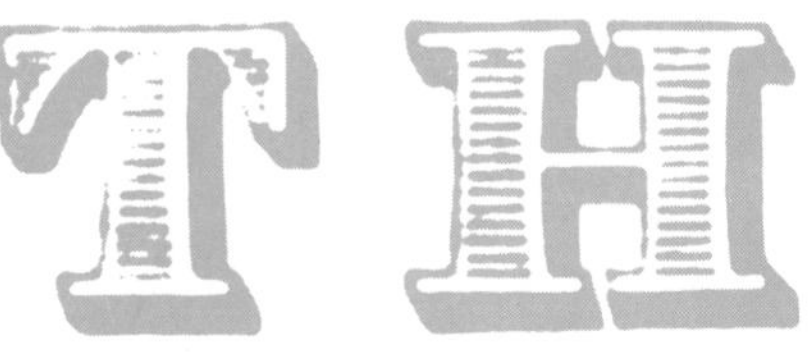

Courtesy of the New-York Historical Society, New York City

BOSTON, MASSACHUSETTS.] OUR COUNTRY IS THE WORL

Schomburg Collection, New York Public Library

Schomburg Collection,
New York Public Library

Schomburg Collection, New York Public Library

SLAVES
HORSES &
OTHER CAT-
TLE TO BE
SOLD AT
12 OC.

ERATOR.

ISAAC KNAPP, PUBLISHERS. [NO. 22.

COUNTRYMEN ARE MANKIND. [SATURDAY, MAY 28, 1831.

The Underground Railroad, described at right in a mock advertisement in the Western Citizen *in* 1844, *was not a railroad at all but a system by which opponents of slavery helped fugitive slaves escape to Canada by providing them with hiding places along the way. Harriet Tubman (far right), a Maryland slave who escaped in* 1849, *became a famous "conductor" on the railroad, helping more than* 300 *slaves to freedom during the next ten years. The drawing above shows Leon Green, a slave who escaped by hiding in a chest which was shipped to the North.*

LIBERT

NEW ARRANGEMEN

The improved and splendid Locomotives, Clarkso and Lundy, with their trains fitted up in the best style accommodation for passengers, will run their regul trips during the present season, between the borders the Patriarchal Dominion and Libertyville, Upper Canad Gentlemen and Ladies, who may wish to improve the health or circumstances, by a northern tour, are respec fully invited to give us their patronage.

SEATS FREE, *irrespective of color.*

Necessary Clothing furnished gratuitously to such have "*fallen among thieves.*"

Above: Chicago Historical Society
Right: Library of Congress

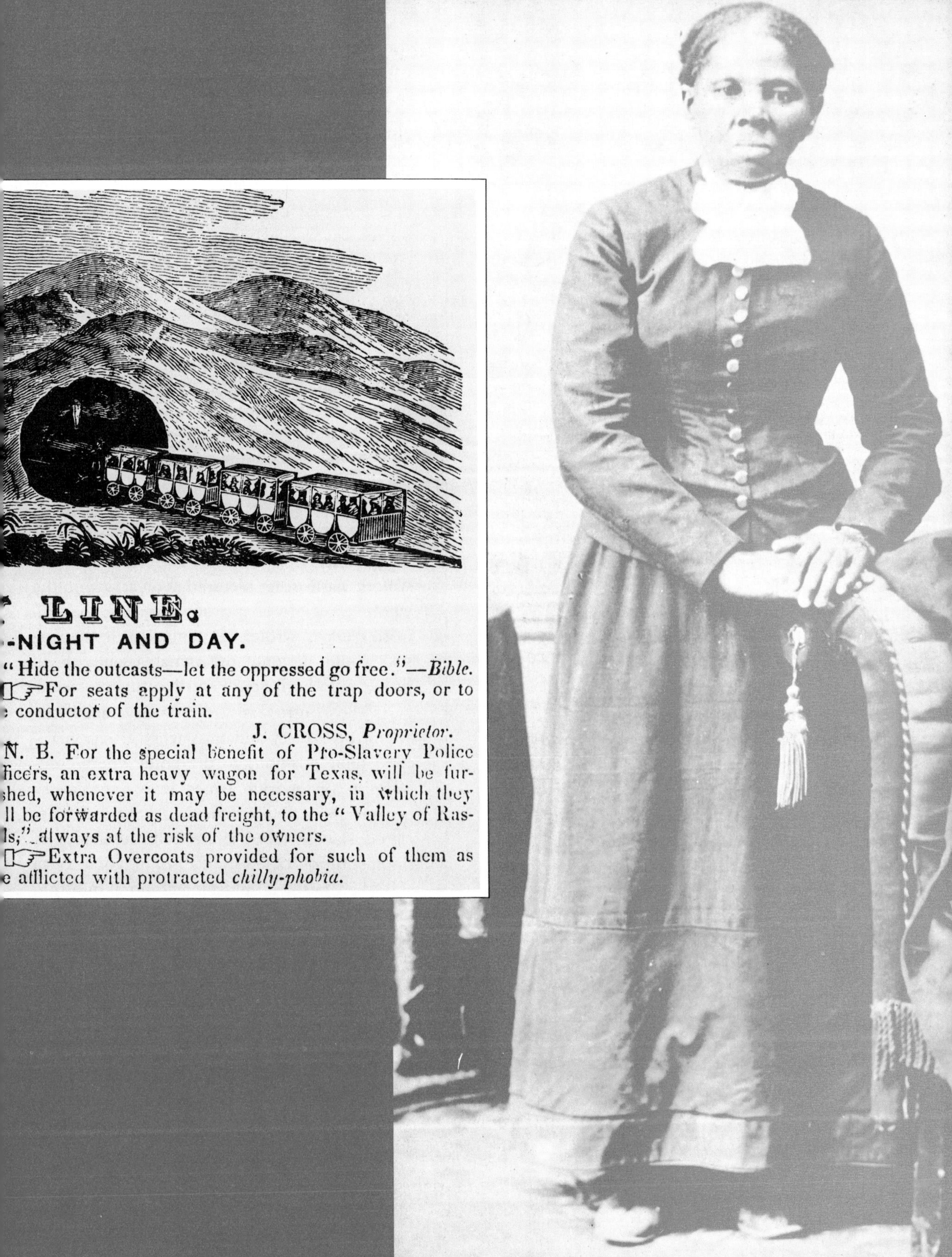
LINE.
-NIGHT AND DAY.
“Hide the outcasts—let the oppressed go free.”—*Bible.*
For seats apply at any of the trap doors, or to
conductor of the train.
J. CROSS, *Proprietor.*
N. B. For the special benefit of Pro-Slavery Police
ficers, an extra heavy wagon for Texas, will be fur-
shed, whenever it may be necessary, in which they
ll be forwarded as dead freight, to the “Valley of Ras-
ls,” always at the risk of the owners.
Extra Overcoats provided for such of them as
afflicted with protracted *chilly-phobia.*

Turner, a lay preacher, led some seventy fellow slaves in a major revolt which resulted in the death of 55 whites before he and his followers were defeated and many of them slaughtered. Fear of other slave revolts caused Southerners to harden their position in favor of maintaining slavery. During the winter of 1831–1832, the Virginia House of Delegates discussed the question of emancipation, but the defenders of slavery won by a decisive margin, partly because the abolitionists did not present what seemed a practical plan to free the slaves.

The Missouri Compromise, the activities of abolitionists, and the Nat Turner rebellion were among the major factors which prompted Southerners to justify their "peculiar institution" more vigorously and openly. As early as the previous century the South had abandoned the natural-rights theory of man and the Christian concept that every individual had equal worth in the eyes of God. Now Southerners developed a theory of society characterized by permanent class distinctions—the so-called mud-sill theory. Professor Thomas Cooper of South Carolina wrote in 1835: "We talk a great deal of nonsense about the rights of man. We say that man is born free, and equal to every other man. Nothing can be more untrue: no human being ever was, now is or ever will be born free." Chancellor William Harper of the South Carolina Supreme Court wrote that "man is born to subjection. . . . The proclivity of natural man is to be subservient." And Governor James H. Hammond of South Carolina declared that "in all social systems there must be a class to do the menial duties, to perform the drudgery of life. . . . Such a class," he continued, "you must have or you would not have that other class which leads progress, civilization, and refinement. It constitutes the very mud-sill of society and of political government."

Having rejected the liberal democratic principles of the Declaration of Independence, defenders of slavery advanced a series of arguments to vindicate their position. They declared that both history and religion supported slavery and pointed to Greek and Roman civilizations to prove their point. They quoted the Bible, especially the Apostle Paul, who advised slaves to obey their masters. Moreover, proslavery advocates claimed that slaves were better off than what they called the "wage slaves" of the North, who labored long hours under unhealthy conditions for low pay and then were discharged in their old age to shift for themselves. "White slaves," Governor Hammond called them. Slavery also was presented as a regional and national good, because the North as well as the South profited from the products of slave labor. The crusade against slavery was further pictured as an attack on the whole principle of private property. As Jefferson Davis wrote, the campaign, if successful, would be only the initial assault on all property in both South and North.

As the controversy over slavery raged, the ardent proslavery and antislavery groups hardened their positions to the point where compromise on specific issues involving slavery became increasingly difficult. Abolitionists declared slavery an absolute evil; defenders of the institution called it an absolute good. Both sides had raised a fundamental moral question—the rightness or wrongness of slavery—which would soon engulf them in a bitter quarrel, terminable only with slavery's demise. Meanwhile the blacks would protest mightily against their plight even as they contributed much to the nation with their toil, idealism, folk tales, and militant spirituals.

Conclusion

During the pre-Civil War years, most Americans were highly nationalistic—proud of their country, its institutions, and its material progress. Although they saw weaknesses in American society, they believed in their infinite correctability. Indeed, Americans demonstrated a deep concern about improving the quality of national life, as they set out to eliminate such evils as ignorance, poverty, and injustice. Education and religion were considered two of the most effective levers for raising the level of society. Expansion and improvement of public education won widespread popular support before the Civil War; and growing church membership, along with a fervid wave of revivalism, reflected an increasing devotion to religion. Although fewer Americans were seriously interested in the fine arts and literature, the United States actually showed greater national maturity as some of its painters and writers won international acclaim. The abiding concern of many people for various reforms amply demonstrated the continual American dissatisfaction with social conditions, as well as the perennial willingness of Americans to experiment in a search for a better life.

SUGGESTED READINGS

One of the best interpretations of the American character is Arthur M. Schlesinger's "What Then Is the American, This New Man," *American Historical Review,* XLVIII (January, 1943). There are also perceptive views of American society in Henry Steele Commager (ed.), *America in Perspective: The United States through Foreign Eyes** (1947). Concentrating on the 1830s and 1840s, Carl Russell Fish has discussed and analyzed American social and intellectual life in *The Rise of the Common Man* (1927), while in *Young America,* 1830–1840 (1949), Robert E. Riegel has dealt with a single decade. *The Growth of American Thought* (2d ed., 1951) by Merle Curti has excellent material on the country's intellectual trends during these years. Ralph Gabriel's *The Course of American Democratic Thought* (2d ed., 1956) is very good on this subject.

Developments in pre-Civil War education can be followed in H. G. Good's *A History of American Education* (1956), as well as in the older study by E. P. Cubberly, *Public Education in the United States* (1934 ed.). Carl Bode in *The American Lyceum: Town Meeting of the Mind* (1956) provides a good discussion of the development of the lyceum. On educational reforms, see Louise Tharp's *Until Victory: Horace Mann and Mary Peabody* (1953).

The standard survey on American religion is William Warren Sweet's *The Story of Religion in America* (1950 ed.). See also Sweet's *Religion in the Development of American Culture,* 1765–1840 (1952). Timothy L. Smith emphasizes the role of revivalism in social reform in *Revivalism and Social Reform in Mid-nineteenth Century America* (1957). C. C. Cole, Jr., also shows the connection between religion and social reform in *The Social Ideas of the Northern Evangelists,* 1826–1860 (1954). Two other excellent studies of religious manifestations are Charles A. Johnson's *The Frontier Camp Meeting* (1955), and *The Burned-over District** (1950) by Whitney R. Cross. On nativism, see Ray A. Billington's *The Protestant Crusade** (1938). For a discussion of pre-Civil War journalism, students should consult Volumes I and II of Frank L. Mott's *A History of American Magazines* (1937) and his *American Journalism: A History of Newspapers in the United States through 250 Years,* 1690–1940 (1941).

There are a number of excellent studies on American literature for the years before the Civil War.

These include Volume II of Vernon Louis Parrington's *Main Currents in American Thought** (1927), which is a classic. Also very good is Van Wyck Brooks's *The Flowering of New England, 1815–1865** (1940 ed.) and his book on *The Times of Melville and Whitman* (1947). The contributions of the nation's leading historians of the period can be examined in Michael Kraus's *The Writing of American History* (1953).

For accounts of art in American life consult Oliver W. Larkin's *Art and Life in America* (1949) and Eugene Neuhaus's *The History and Ideals of American Art* (1931). Neil Harris emphasizes art as a profession in *The Artist in American Society: The Formative Years, 1790–1860* (1966), while Lillian B. Miller shows how Americans encouraged the fine arts in *Patrons and Patriotism: The Encouragement of the Fine Arts in the United States, 1790–1860* (1966). On music see Gilbert Chase's *America's Music* (1955).

The best survey of reformism is Alice Felt Tyler's *Freedom's Ferment: Phases of American Social History to 1860** (1944). Specific reform movements are dealt with by John A. Krout in *The Origins of Prohibition* (1925); Blake McKelvey in *American Prisons: A Study in American Social History Prior to 1915* (1936); and Merle E. Curti in *The American Peace Crusade* (1929). Otelia Cromwell's *Lucretia Mott* (1958) deals with the issue of women's rights. Good biographies of other reformers include H. F. Marshall's *Dorothea Dix* (1937) and A. J. G. Perkins and Theresa Wolfson's *Frances Wright* (1939). The search by some Americans for a new social order is well covered in Arthur Bestor's *Backwoods Utopias: The Sectarian and Owenite Phases of Communitarian Socialism in America, 1663–1829* (1950).

The abolitionist campaign is most fully covered in Louis Filler's *The Crusade against Slavery** (1960) and Dwight Dumond's *Abolitionism** (1961). *The Antislavery Impulse, 1830–1844** (1933) by Gilbert H. Barnes is good, but less comprehensive. On the black abolitionists see Benjamin Quarles's, *Black Abolitionists* (1969). The biographies of abolitionist leaders add much to a better understanding of the movement. See Merton L. Dillon's *Elijah P. Lovejoy, Abolitionist Editor* (1961) and *Theodore Weld: Crusader for Freedom* (1950) by B. P. Thomas; Walter M. Merrill's *Against Wind and Tide: A Biography of William Lloyd Garrison* (1963); Gerda Lerner's, *The Grimké Sisters from South Carolina: Rebels against Slavery* (1967); and Benjamin Quarles's *Frederick Douglass** (1948) which deals with the leading Negro abolitionist. The Southern reaction to abolitionism is discussed adequately by William S. Jenkins in *Pro-slavery Thought in the Old South* (1935). Also on proslavery thought is Harvey Wish's, *George Fitzhugh: Propagandist of the Old South* (1943). Two original accounts which played a big role in the abolitionist crusade are Harriet Beecher Stowe's *Uncle Tom's Cabin** (1852) and Hinton R. Helper's *The Impending Crisis of the South** (1857).

* indicates availability in paperback.

15

The Parties and Sectionalism

IF THE TWO-PARTY TRADITION had its inception in the early struggles between Federalists and Antifederalists over ratification of the Constitution, or in the arguments between Alexander Hamilton and Thomas Jefferson over the domestic (and later the foreign) policies of the United States, it did not become a continuous, country-wide struggle for power until the 1830s. It is true that Hamilton's Federalist coalition after 1800 came under younger leadership, which contested Jeffersonian dominance with the full range of popular electioneering techniques; but that party's strength remained largely commercial and local, centering in the Northeast and Middle Atlantic states, with some pockets of support in the South. Jefferson's Republican party was thoroughly national, but after 1816 it faced no nationally organized opposition whatsoever. Jackson's initial success in 1828 left the Republican party irreparably divided. The Jacksonians, basing their power essentially on state organizations, were very strong, but the rival Adams faction, however weakened, possessed both a program—the American System—and an able, even spectacular, leadership. The intense partisanship, especially on the Bank question, which the Democratic party employed to build its phenomenal popularity, produced such disarray within its own ranks, and such determined opposition from the old National Republicans, that by 1834 the Jacksonians had driven their enemies into a second powerful coalition.

The Whig organization, like that of the Democrats, reached from the Boston waterfront to the great plantations of Louisiana. Ultimately the Whigs, in order to compete on equal terms, copied all the techniques of the Jacksonians. Each party maintained a network of partisan newspapers; each confronted the electorate at every level of political activity with a stream of candidates, orators, pamphlets, broadsides, and parades. Thousands of people converged on endless political rallies to listen for hours to speakers of national consequence—or perhaps simply to enjoy a day at the outing. It was not strange that the voters, aroused by such incessant campaigning, turned out en masse on election day. In 1840 more than twice as many Americans went to the polls as had voted for Clay and Jackson eight years earlier.

Whigs and Democrats

For the two decades of its existence as a significant political force, the Whig party challenged the Democrats in almost every state and county of the nation. More than the party of Jackson, it perpetuated both the Jeffersonian emphasis on gentility and the Hamiltonian faith in federal supremacy and power. Fundamentally the Whig party was composed of the former National Republicans—the followers of Adams and Clay. But another significant element in the Whig coalition was the Anti-Masons, centering in New York and New England, whose program of the early thirties had been hardly distinguishable from that of the National Republicans. In the South and West, where Jackson had reaped his first and greatest successes, the Whig leadership consisted largely of deserters from the Jackson cause. Often men of distinction, Whigs rebelled at the democratic radicalism represented by Jackson's war on the Bank of the United States. Henry Clay and Daniel Webster were both recognized as leaders of the party, although even Webster's New England friends granted the party's titular headship to the always popular and altogether remarkable Clay.

In Northern states, the Whig party encompassed much of the talent, wealth, and business experience of the large and growing cities. In Massachusetts, the Whigs claimed "all the decency, refinement, wealth and cultivation of the State," especially the bankers, merchants, and manufacturers for whom Webster spoke. Horace Greeley, New York City's leading Whig editor, attempted, as did other members of the Whig party, to discount any alleged philosophical differences between the Whigs and Democrats, but privately he admitted in February, 1841:

> Hitherto all the devotees of social reform of any kind, all the advocates of a higher destiny for labor, all the combatants against unjust and false social principles, in short, all the social discontent of the country had been regularly repelled from the Whig party and attracted to its opposite. This forms a heavy dead-weight against us. It strikes me that it is unwise to persist in this course, unless we are ambitious to be considered the enemies of improvement and the bulwarks of an outgrown aristocracy in the country.

Undoubtedly the Whig party in the North appealed to the leading manufacturing and commercial interests—the great men of wealth—whereas the Democratic party attracted the support of the small farmers, workingmen, and disadvantaged. But these groups were only the extremes of the political spectrum. Neither party found the support and leadership that mattered among these elements but among the great middle and lower-middle classes. It was here that the real struggle for power transpired. This required both parties to remain acutely aware of changing times and opinions. The same socioeconomic groups which provided leadership for the Whig party did so for the Democratic party as well. Democratic leaders were little less wealthy than their Whig opponents; often they were the more ambitious and avowedly materialistic enterprisers. Not even the rank and file of party supporters divided markedly along income lines. Despite some variations and contrasts in the philosophical and emotional appeals of the two parties, the great majority of the nation's voters did not base their political preferences on class interest. Conservatives who feared a mass electorate discovered that the masses had property interests of their own and that they harbored hopes and ambitions which scarcely separated them in outlook from men of wealth. Such attitudes reflected the realities of existence in a rapidly expanding nation where the opportunities for profit were legion. What the incipient capitalist demanded of the capitalist was not that the rules be changed but that they apply equally to all. It was not strange that the two parties, forced to appeal in large measure to the same socioeconomic groups, differed little in programs, techniques, and even rhetoric.

In both the North and the South, the balance of party strength was exceedingly precarious. Only in New England was one party, the Whigs, clearly dominant. In the pivotal Middle Atlantic states the combined returns from 1832 to 1852 gave the Democrats a plurality of less than 1 percent; yet New York and Pennsylvania went Whig in 1840 and again in 1848 and brought victories to the only two Whigs elected to the White House. The Northwest became a predominantly Democratic region after 1840, but the Whigs retained strongholds in the commercial centers bordering the Great Lakes and the Ohio. The South as a whole cast over three million votes in the elections of 1836, 1840, 1844, and 1848. The overall Whig majority in the four elections was 66,000 votes, or slightly more than 2 percent of the total. In the South Atlantic states, Democrats predominated. In Virginia and Georgia the Democratic party was strong in the western districts, the Whigs in the tidewater. In the Carolinas, the backcountry tended to be Whig; the tidewater, Democratic. The south central area, which furnished much of the nation's leadership, was evenly balanced. Kentucky and Tennessee were bulwarks of the Whig party, whereas the Gulf states were normally Democratic. Across the Mississippi, in Louisiana, Arkansas, and Missouri, the rich planting areas along the Mississippi, Arkansas, and Missouri Rivers were Whig; the backcountry tended to be Democratic.

The chief areas of Southern Whig strength coincided with the districts occupied by the great planters, but the ties that bound the Whig party together were urban. Here, as in the North, the core of Whig power and influence lay in the merchant class with its allies—the bankers, lawyers, and editors. If the leading planters, especially outside South Carolina, were Whig, it was not primarily because of their wealth but because of their community of interest with the merchants and their need for banking and transportation facilities. The Southern cities were not large, but they were influential and the only mercantile centers that the South possessed. Most Southern Whigs who sat in Congress were not planters; they were lawyers aligned with business interests. All the Whig issues other than internal improvements enjoyed considerable popularity in the South. For the sugar planters of Louisiana, the hemp growers of Kentucky, and the iron manufacturers of Virginia and Maryland, it was the tariff that mattered. For Southern men of wealth generally, the Whig party's opposition to Jacksonian radicalism appeared to be a source of genuine security. Southern bankers, merchants, industrialists, lawyers, and planters thus had their own party, which competed successfully in the South with the Jacksonians.

The Whigs in Power

Having swept their hero, William Henry Harrison, into the White House, the Whigs again turned to Clay as the commander of their forces in Congress who would frame a true Whig program. At last, after having been battered in Congress and at the polls for a dozen years, the followers of Clay could anticipate a rosier future. Indeed, Whig leaders interpreted Harrison's victory as a major triumph for Whig principles and assumed that the old soldier would hand over control of policy to the party's established mentors. Webster, a master of style, prepared for Harrison an inaugural address which the President-elect rejected in favor of one he had written—based on Roman history. Harrison prevailed upon Webster to take the State Department, but Clay controlled the other Cabinet posts. Having refused a Cabinet appointment for himself, Clay prepared to manage the Whig party from his seat in the Senate. Determined to present his own program to Congress as quickly as possible, he persuaded Harrison to call a special session for May, 1841.

Harrison did not live to face the Clay-controlled Congress. On April 4, 1841, a month after his inaugural, Harrison died. Thus John Tyler (1890–1862), a Virginia gentleman, became the first Vice President to move into the Presidency. A lawyer with wide political experience, having served in the House of Representatives and the Senate and as Governor of Virginia, Tyler assumed Harrison's title and duties, keeping the Cabinet intact. Clay, still hopeful of dominating the administration, presented his full-blown Whig program to Congress, only to discover that Tyler not only had a mind of his own but also that the President was not a Clay Whig at all but a believer in the Jeffersonian states' rights principles of 1798. Tyler, moreover, shared Jackson's views of executive leadership and reminded Webster that he alone would be responsible for his administration.

Clay now selected the question of a national bank as a test of strength, assuming that his control of Congress would force Tyler to submit or leave the party. Tyler had no objection to a national bank, provided that it preserved the principle of states' rights by limiting its branches to only those states which gave their consent. When Clay rammed a bank bill through Congress, Tyler vetoed it, declaring that it did not meet his requirements. Clay responded in September, 1841, with a second bill, one designed specifically to satisfy the President's constitutional scruples. This the President also vetoed. Thereafter Clay's fury, with that of his followers, knew no bounds. He asked the Cabinet to resign; everyone did except Webster. Flaming effigies of Tyler appeared across the nation; hundreds of letters threatened his assassination. Tyler himself appeared mystified by the Whig hysteria. To him, his vetoes revealed neither inconsistency nor bad faith. The Whigs had known his opposition to the American System when they nominated him. So incensed were the congressional Whigs over Tyler's apostasy that by 1842 they no longer made any effort at political reconciliation with the President. Instead, they publicly read him out of the party, indicating that Clay would be the Whig standard-bearer in 1844. Clay resigned his Senate seat in March, 1842, to devote himself to his campaign for the Presidency.

In the struggle between Tyler and Clay, the Southern Whigs, who had favored a Clay nomination in 1839, stood as a block behind the Kentuckian and his program. Only three of the fifty-five Southern Whigs in the House supported Tyler. A Southern Whig, Willie P. Mangum of North Carolina, presided at the caucus which read Tyler out of the party. None of Clay's program could have been carried through Congress during the Tyler administration without the strong support of the Southern Whigs. Even if these men were not all strong economic nationalists, they refused to quarrel over their party's program.

Having already disposed of Van Buren's Independent Treasury in August, 1841, but unable to restore a national bank, the Whigs embarked on a move to increase the tariff. The stage had been carefully prepared. In Whig minds the problem of a tariff had become associated with the matter of public lands. For a decade Clay had sponsored the movement to distribute the income from land sales among the states, for such a step could be expected to reduce federal income and make an alternative source of income—for example, an increased tariff—more attractive. The West had long advocated a general preemption law for the public domain. During 1841 both distribution and preemption bills were steered through Congress and became law. The Preemption Act granting squatters the right to purchase public land at the minimum rate of $1.25 per acre was cordially received in the West, but that same section roundly denounced distribution as a disguise for the assumption of state debts. In December, 1841, Lewis F. Linn of Missouri introduced a bill to repeal those sections of the land act which provided for the distribution of public land revenues.

Eventually, as a sop to the West, the Whigs attached the antidistribution provision to the tariff bill under consideration. Yet even with the antidistribution amendment attached, the compromise tariff of 1842 narrowly passed the Senate, 24 to 23. It declared that distribution would be suspended when the rate of duty reached 20 percent. Since tariff duties were already above that figure, no distribution of land revenue occurred under this law. The vote on the measure revealed no clear intersectional split. The Northeast was solidly behind it. Elsewhere the Whigs captured the votes they needed in Louisiana, Kentucky, and the older Northwest. John Quincy Adams, surprisingly, voted against the measure, for to him distribution was the greater issue. The tariff of 1842 was the last of the Whig legislative triumphs. George McDuffie of South Carolina opened the tariff debate again in December, 1843, by introducing a bill for tariff reduction. Whigs now upheld the tariff of 1842 with more passion than they had revealed at its original passage. Even Berrien of Georgia, who had voted against the act in 1842, opposed any revision "which must lead to nothing but instability." The Whigs managed to uphold their measure, but it was clear that the tariff issue was still not settled.

The Whig desertion of Tyler's administration in 1842 placed Secretary of State Webster in a dilemma. New England Whigs who distrusted Tyler urged him to resign. Expecting nothing of the Tyler administration, they wondered why Webster should maintain any connection with it. But Webster had gained deep satisfaction from his first administrative appointment, and he had no desire to follow in the footsteps of Clay. Tyler, for his part, had made it clear that he desired Webster to remain in the Cabinet. Many of Webster's closest business associates, moreover, opposed another Bank of the United States which concentrated so much power in the hands of one man; they had lauded Tyler's two bank vetoes. Finally, Webster had inherited the pro-British proclivities of the Federalists; the opportunity now presented him to effect an improvement in American relations with Great Britain was irresistible.

By 1842, a series of unresolved conflicts had pushed United States–British relations to the breaking point. During the Canadian rebellion of 1837, Washington had failed in its efforts to prevent the people of New York and Vermont from siding openly with the rebellion, shipping supplies, harboring refugees, and even furnishing the Canadian rebels with a small steamer, the *Caroline.* When a band of loyal Canadians in 1840 crossed the Niagara River and burned the vessel – the British government admitting its part in the affair – latent anti-British sentiment in the Northeast was fully aroused. At the same time, London antagonized the South by verbally attacking slavery and denying freedom of the seas. This conflict reached a crisis in 1842 when British officials in the West Indies refused to return blacks who had seized their slave ship, the *Creole,* and sailed her to the Bahamas. Democrats, to whom Britain had always appeared aristocratic, arbitrary, and overbearing, demanded that the Tyler administration exact satisfaction for every American grievance.

On the other hand, to Webster cordial United States relations with Britain seemed the key to both the nation's security and its economic well-being. The British government, equally disposed toward peace, dispatched Lord Ashburton to Washington in the spring of 1842 to negotiate the settlement of a lingering issue, the northeastern boundary separating Canada from the United States. Ashburton's instructions restricted him to protecting a land route from Quebec to Halifax, a strategic necessity confirmed by the War of 1812.

Webster could not negotiate a successful compromise with Ashburton until he had won approval for such an agreement from the state of Maine. This was not a simple matter, for Maine claimed almost the entire disputed area. Already the people of New Brunswick and Maine were in open conflict over the Aroostook Valley, although both sides in the so-called Aroostook War were careful to avoid bloodshed. Webster did not lack arguments favoring concession. The historian Jared Sparks had drawn from memory a red line across a map of the Northeast, ostensibly duplicating a line he had seen on a map in the French archives which Sparks assumed to have been Franklin's original of 1782. Sparks's line conceded most of the disputed area to the British. This map Webster revealed privately to the Maine commissioners, who then agreed to compromise. Freed of unreasonable domestic demands, Webster now sought a realistic settlement with Ashburton. Working through the hot Washington summer, they produced a treaty which granted the United States about 7,000 of the 12,000 square miles of disputed land. The Webster-Ashburton Treaty provided as well for the extradition of criminals from Canada to the United States and for British-American cooperation in suppressing the slave trade.

Webster next faced the task of securing public approval for his work. Using secret service funds of the State Department, he hired a persuasive journalist to secure the support of key Maine editors, men who could be troublesome if they chose to attack the treaty. In his approach to Maine and the nation, the Secretary argued that the treaty served the best interests of the United States by resolving the outstanding issues between Britain and the United States and thus avoiding war. Long before the Senate received the treaty, the nation had overwhelmingly accepted Webster's peaceful alternative. In the Senate, Benton charged that the Whig administration had sold out the interests of the South and West to those of the Northeast. But the red line map persuaded the Senate as it had the Maine commissioners: the final vote for the treaty was 39 to 9.

Party Politics and Slavery

For the vast majority of Americans in the early 1840s the federal Union appeared durable enough. A troubled minority could see that there were issues on the political horizon that would defy compromise through the American democratic process, but such issues had not as yet reached the forefront of national life. For a full generation the important questions confronting the nation had been economic—the tariff, internal improvements at federal expense, the National Bank, land policies, and distribution of the proceeds from Western land sales to the states. On such issues alone could politicians make themselves heard. The Whig party's program remained Clay's American System of tariffs for American industry and internal improvements for expanding markets. In a rapidly changing country, interests were complex and constantly shifting. Earlier tariffs had been carried by Northern and Western votes over the almost unanimous opposition of an agricultural South. But by the forties, Southern Whigs had accepted the principle of protection as the price of party unity, whereas Western Democrats had accepted Southern low-tariff arguments. Thus the tariff, by 1840, had become a party—rather than a sectional—issue, except for the Democrats of industrial New England and Pennsylvania, who joined the Whigs to create a slim majority in Congress.

Internal improvements, on the other hand, had become a sectional issue, with the North and West standing firmly against the states' rights South. On land policies the fundamental cleavage was between the settled regions of the East and Ohio Valley and the less developed regions of the West, with a divided South holding the balance of power. Jackson's successful war on the Second National Bank, the continued dominance of Jacksonians in Congress under Van Buren, Tyler's two vetoes of Bank bills, and the growing prosperity of the country relegated the National Bank issue to the realm of lost causes. On none of these great economic issues did any region stand as a bloc; in all areas there were minorities dissenting from the majorities. On some questions congressmen deserted their parties and voted the economic interests of their constituents; on others they hewed to the party line. So divided were regional and party loyalties that each new measure created its own congressional coalition.

One issue—slavery—possessed the power to alter this varied political pattern and drive men into sectional blocs. Unlike other public issues, slavery was a sectional phenomenon, moral as well as economic in nature. But not even slavery could separate national economic issues and interests along geographic lines. It might divide men, North and South, but only in their attitudes toward slavery. Politicians—at least those who led the major parties—still fought their political battles and distinguished friends from antagonists on the basis of party affiliations, disregarding the existence of slavery in the nation.

As a historic institution recognized by the Constitution and protected in the states where it existed by the principle of states' rights, slavery was by customary standards scarcely a legitimate subject for political debate at all. As an undemocratic and inhumane institution, slavery had, by the thirties, aroused a determined abolitionist movement in the North, but it was a movement largely religious in nature and one which looked to education and persuasion, not political power, as the chief elements in its crusade for human freedom. As long as slaveholders recognized no moral necessity to free their slaves and enjoyed the protection of Southern laws, there could be no clear relationship between the growth of abolitionist power in the North and the demise of slavery in the South. Slavery, unlike other evils of American society, lay outside the jurisdiction of federal action—except in the District of Columbia.

Abolitionists discovered this Achilles heel in the Southern armor as early as 1835 and flooded Congress with petitions demanding the elimination of the slave trade from the nation's capital. The constant movement through the streets of Washington of chained Negroes bound for the Southern states shocked Northern sensibilities. But for the South the presence of slaves in the capital was a matter of principle, a symbol of the national acceptance of the slave system and thus a condition to be retained in the face of abolitionist pressures.

Finally in December, 1837, Calhoun was moved to rise again to the South's defense. In an effort to commit his Democratic party to the Southern cause, he introduced a series of resolutions into the Senate which would deny Congress the right to receive petitions against slavery. His argument began with his well-known concept of the Union—that it was a compact among sovereign states. Each state enjoyed the right to determine the nature of its own institutions. It was the duty of the federal government to guarantee the security of local institutions against attack by other states or citizens. Any interference with slavery in the District of Columbia, therefore, would be an unwarranted assault on the institutions of the slaveholding states. Calhoun warned, furthermore, that resolutions designed to prevent the further extension of slavery into the territories, on the ground that the institution was immoral, denied the equality of the states and endangered the Union. By a vote largely sectional, Calhoun's resolutions were carried in the Senate. In January, 1840, the House added the so-called 21st Rule to its standing resolutions; this obligated that body to table automatically all petitions relating to slavery.

The South had won the first round in its struggle to protect its "peculiar institution," but at an enormous price. In their effort to squelch all discussion of slavery in Congress, Southern leaders had merely redoubled the determination of Northern antislavery advocates and permitted them to enlist new converts to their cause. For John Quincy Adams, now a perennial member of the House, the "gag rule" was nothing less than tyranny. He opposed it in session after session, employing every device to antagonize those who favored it. Southern extremists belabored Adams; they attempted to expel him; but they were involved in a losing cause. By 1844 the abolitionists had achieved sufficient unity among the Northern delegations to endanger Southern control of the gag issue. In December, on Adams's motion, the House rescinded the measure.

Slavery, as an issue demanding reform, entered the halls of Congress readily enough. But Garrisonian abolitionists denied the feasibility of organizing an antislavery party, believing such a move both inexpedient and unnecessary. Yet there were abolitionists, especially in the Old Northwest, who believed that political action might help remove the curse of slavery without challenging the Constitution or endangering the Union. During 1839 politically minded abolitionists organized the Liberty party and inaugurated their assault on the established party system of the nation. Following up this initiative, antislavery delegates from six states met at Albany, New York, in April, 1840, to nominate James G. Birney, a Kentucky abolitionist, for the Presidency of the United States. This first convention adjourned without creating a platform. But in 1843, when the new party named Birney again, it prepared an elaborate platform which spelled out its ambitions, if not the means whereby it intended to achieve them. Slavery, it charged, created an "impoverished and embarrassed condition" in the South, as well as a "withering and impoverishing effect" on the free states. It urged Liberty men everywhere to organize for efficient action until "despotism shall have been driven from its last entrenchment, and thanksgivings for victory in the second great struggle for Liberty and Independence shall be heard throughout the land." The platform condemned the federal government for protecting slavery and the slave trade in the District of Columbia; it demanded that federal officials no longer interfere with efforts of the free states to prevent the recapture of fugitive slaves.

Undoubtedly the antislavery politicians of the North responded to motivations primarily moral. Yet their constant references to the "slave power" suggested that their opposition to the South was partly economic and political. For too long, they charged, Southerners had dominated the federal government through their influence in the Democratic party. As a third-party movement, the Liberty party generated little numerical strength, but by the early forties it had gained the balance of power in several Northern states where the Democratic and Whig parties were almost equal in voting power. Here, as Charles Rogers, a congressman from New York, remarked in 1844, the "abolition party" had "arrived to a position where power and influence beget respect."

In Calhoun's conservative doctrines the sectional issue was joined. How could the South as a minority section defend its slave system as well as its predominantly agricultural interests? Southern fears were real. By the forties the South's population numbered scarcely two-thirds that of the North; its control of the House of Representatives was irrevocably gone. In spinning out his political philosophy of state sovereignty, Calhoun sought to protect the South against majority rule, whether the

North's political thrust should be against Southern social institutions or economic interests. Calhoun regarded the Northern urban centers as the chief threats to Southern power and influence. "To distribute power . . . in proportion to population," he warned, "would be, in fact, to give the control of government, in the end, to the cities, and to subject the rural and agricultural population to that description of population which usually congregate in them, and, ultimately, to the dregs of the population." For the moment, the South's security rested on the ability of Southern politicians to bargain successfully with Northern leaders within the two national party organizations. Already a small minority of Southerners wondered whether the everlasting struggle for Northern support was worth the effort. For them safety increasingly came to mean escape from the Union.

Ties of Union

Although the Republic was young in years, the ties that bound it together were many, varied, and strong. Tradition itself was a powerful force. Perhaps the American people, unlike the nations of Europe, lacked a cultural homogeneity, a unique language, and an ancient past. But they were nevertheless a nation. Only a few decades separated the generation of the 1840s from the common achievements that had launched the new nation and nurtured its development. Abraham Lincoln could speak with truth of the "mystic chords of memory, stretching from every battlefield and patriot grave to every living heart and hearthstone all over this broad land." Everywhere there was tangible evidence of the blessings of civil and religious liberty that had flowed from the wisdom and courage of earlier achievements. For the vast majority of Americans, the Union was the symbol of a revered past and the hope of a brilliant future.

American loyalty rested on an unshakable belief in the superiority of America's democratic institutions. Nationalism must ultimately express itself in the political state, and for a democracy this demands that the state be subject to popular control and employ its authority in the public interest. The American political system was admirably suited to foster nationalism, especially after Jefferson and Jackson had rendered assurances that the government would seek the welfare of the average citizen. Frederick von Raumer, the famed German professor and traveler, observed that America's "universal love for the republican form of government [was] a strong bond of union . . . so that neither what is peculiar nor what is general can exclusively prevail."

American nationalism was derived, secondly, from a sense of mission. This nation was the special instrument for achieving not only the material prosperity and expanding power of the American people but also the moral elevation of the entire globe. If men were really capable of self-government, declared Robert J. Breckinridge of Kentucky in 1837, then "no mortal power can estimate the height and grandeur waiting to receive us—nor compute the depth and thoroughness of that tremendous change which the influence of our spirit must operate throughout the world." What mattered was that the Republic have time to achieve its promise of greatness. "May our happy union not be torn asunder," wrote Henry Wheaton, the distinguished American diplomat, "even before we have gathered its best fruits in the successful cultivation of science and letters, under the shadow of its protecting wings; and before we have produced any works of art or genius to command the admiration and envy of posterity, and worthy of that glorious liberty, the choicest of the many blessings which Providence has showered upon us!"

For many men of business, the essence of nationalism lay not in democracy and America's mission but in the economic guarantees of the Constitution; to them, the foundations of American nationalism were material as well as emotional. The Constitution underlay the entire business structure of the nation. In that document of law and order, merchants and industrialists found the values and requirements essential to the business community. It bound the states together under one law and made possible a national market. It forced the fulfillment of contracts and protected property rights against the onslaught of radicalism. Only the national government, created by the Constitution, could promote foreign markets. It alone could negotiate favorable commercial treaties, protect American shipping and property abroad, improve harbors, maintain lighthouses, control the national currency, and secure protective tariffs. If such economic nationalism was especially congenial to Northern commercial and industrial groups, its proponents anticipated the day when all sections and classes would recognize its benefits.

Geography and national economic ties created additional material bases of American nationalism. Americans were proud of the immense extent of their country, and they sensed, too, that its physiognomy was peculiarly designed to achieve national greatness. The United States in the forties had developed a genuinely national economy based on a regional division of labor. New England and the Middle Atlantic states were devoted principally to commerce and industry. This region satisfied the demands for manufactured goods in the other areas of the nation and required the foodstuffs and raw materials of the Lake regions and the South. The Northwest was predominantly agricultural, finding its markets in both the East and the South but its source of manufactured goods and capital in the East. The South engaged chiefly in the production of staples and depended on other sections for most of its food, its markets, its capital, and its manufactures. The heavy flow of commerce along the rivers, canals, and the Great Lakes, as well as the Atlantic and Gulf Coasts, merely reflected the tendency toward a regional division of labor. This interlocking of the nation's economic interests prompted Joseph P. Bradley, a justice of the New Jersey Supreme Court, to declare that agriculture, industry, and commerce constituted "an indissoluble bond which unites and keeps *us* together as one nation, one people." Improved transportation, added the nationalists, would help to annihilate distance and strengthen the ties of Union.

Economic interdependence created a powerful bond of union. Just as the Western rivers tied together the whole Mississippi Valley and rendered disunion unthinkable, so cotton united the New England counting houses and the great Southern plantations in one community of interest. How could New England merchants criticize the labor system that produced the fibers they fed into their machines or that created lucrative markets for shoes and cotton textiles? Slave owners, who vacationed at Northern resorts, revealed themselves to be men of urbanity and established binding personal relationships with businessmen of the North. "Cotton thread holds the Union together," confided Ralph Waldo Emerson to his journal, "unites John C. Calhoun and Abbott Lawrence. Patriotism for holidays and summer evenings, with music and rockets, but cotton thread is the Union."

National churches and national political parties constituted two final forces encouraging national unity. By 1845, however, the leading churches had broken along sectional lines. When the General Convention of the Methodist Church suspended a Georgia bishop for owning slaves, the national body divided, and the Methodist Episcopal Church South came into being. In that same year, the mission societies of the Baptist Church split into Northern and Southern groupings, and the Presbyterian Church embarked on its bitter sectional struggle. Politicians proved more successful than churchmen in holding their national organizations together. Victory demanded that the parties remain united, inasmuch as a divided party was doomed at the polls. For that reason, the Whig and the Democratic parties struggled to conceal the burgeoning conflicts between North and South. The politicians' task was that of seeking out candidates and principles that would cause men to ignore sectional differences in the interest of political success. No party can face all the issues; many are self-contradictory. Victory requires a party to soften or avoid those issues that might alienate some essential element in the party coalition and to feature those with some national appeal. For that reason the parties, under devoted leadership, were the nation's strongest ties of union. The churches might divide, sectional differences might deepen, extremists might become more demanding, but as long as the two parties remained national in scope, forcing their leaders to compromise all divisive issues which confronted the nation, the Union was safe.

Texas

Texas was the first issue of the 1840s to disturb the normal functioning of political forces in the nation. American pioneers had decreed as early as the 1820s that one day Texas would force the American people into a great national decision. Moses Austin, a New Englander with business interests that carried him to Missouri, obtained a large grant of land in Texas from the Mexican government in 1821. When he died shortly thereafter, his son Stephen F. Austin assumed control of the grant and, by offers of free land, encouraged hundreds of American families to settle on his holdings. Responding to the Mexican government's liberal land policies, Americans surged into Texas in overwhelming numbers and in a decade came to dominate much of the province. By 1834 the American colony in Texas had 20,000 settlers plus 2,000 slaves. Austin opposed slavery by conviction, but the Texas frontier was so ideal for the cotton culture and yet so devoid of a good labor supply that Southern planters who entered Texas insisted on the right to bring their slaves with them. Various governments in Mexico City decreed the abolition of slavery, but they lacked the power to enforce their rulings against the opposition of Americans in Texas.

Increasingly the Texans, their ranks strengthened by an influx of colorful frontiersmen like Sam Houston and Davy Crockett of Tennessee and the Bowie brothers of Louisiana, became defiant of Mexican rule. The crisis came in 1835 when President Santa Anna proclaimed a

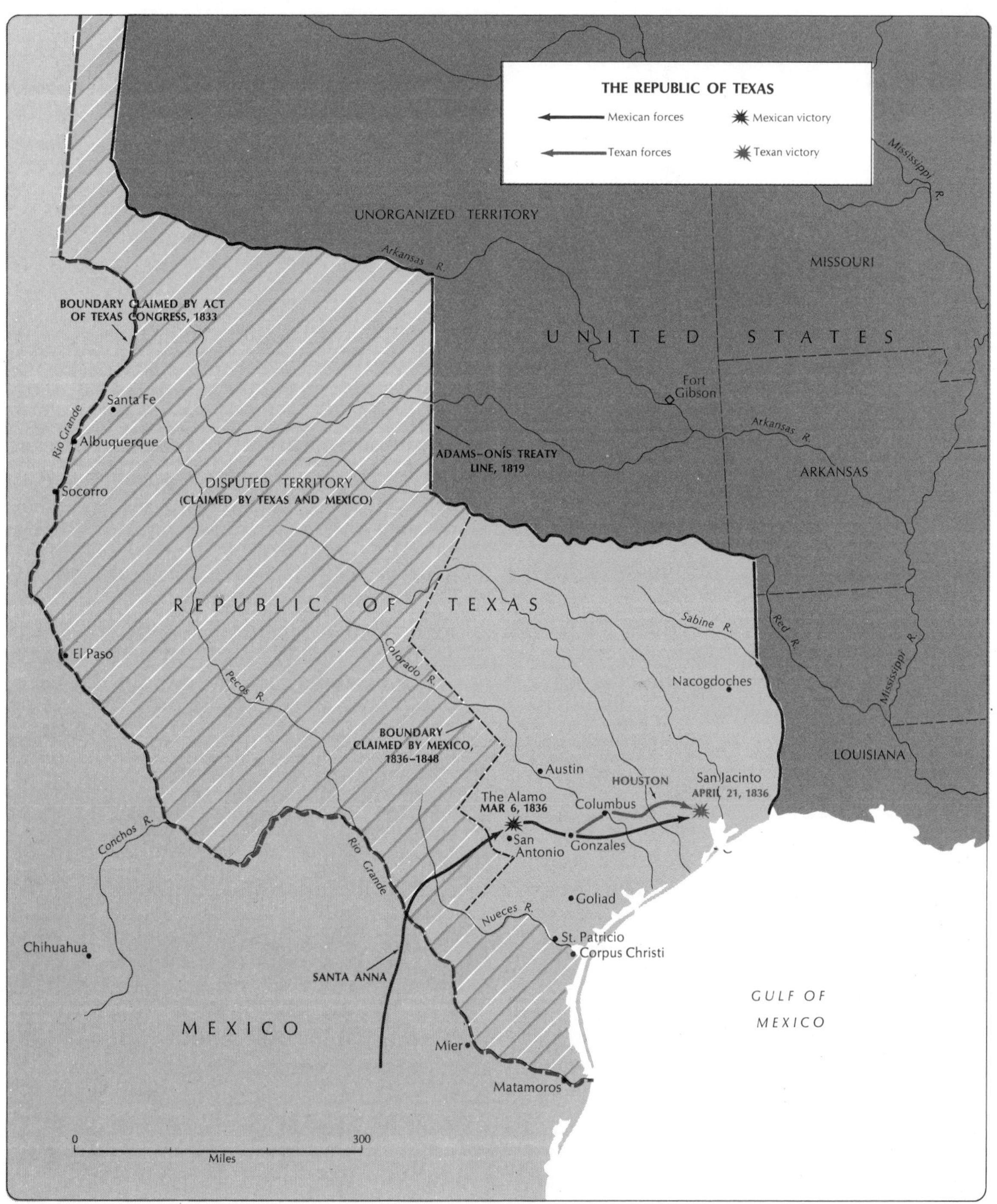
THE REPUBLIC OF TEXAS
Mexican forces
Mexican victory
Texan forces
Texan victory
UNORGANIZED TERRITORY
Arkansas R.
MISSOURI
Mississippi R.
BOUNDARY CLAIMED BY ACT OF TEXAS CONGRESS, 1833
UNITED STATES
Fort Gibson
Santa Fe
Rio Grande
Albuquerque
Arkansas R.
ADAMS-ONÍS TREATY LINE, 1819
ARKANSAS
Socorro
DISPUTED TERRITORY (CLAIMED BY TEXAS AND MEXICO)
REPUBLIC OF TEXAS
Sabine R.
Red R.
El Paso
Colorado R.
Pecos R.
Nacogdoches
Mississippi R.
BOUNDARY CLAIMED BY MEXICO, 1836–1848
LOUISIANA
Austin
HOUSTON
San Jacinto
APRIL 21, 1836
The Alamo
MAR 6, 1836
Columbus
Conchos R.
San Antonio
Gonzales
Rio Grande
Goliad
Nueces R.
St. Patricio
Corpus Christi
Chihuahua
SANTA ANNA
GULF OF MEXICO
MEXICO
Mier
Matamoros
0
300
Miles

new constitution for Mexico which terminated the former pioneer-controlled government of Texas. Thereupon the American emigrants established their own provisional government. Santa Anna now marched his army of 3,000 into Texas and closed in on San Antonio where less than 200 Texans had barricaded themselves in the Alamo, refusing to surrender. During March, 1836, Santa Anna surrounded and assaulted the Alamo and wiped out its defenders. Meanwhile the Texans persisted in their independent course, proclaiming a republic. Santa Anna, to recapture control of events in Texas, moved eastward, driving the settlers before him. Sam Houston and his Texas volunteers waited at the San Jacinto River and on April 21, fell on Santa Anna's forces, capturing the general and securing from him the promise to recognize the independence of Texas.

Never again did Mexico make a serious effort at reconquest, but the Mexican government, charging American complicity in the Texas revolution, refused to grant recognition to the new nation. Independent nevertheless, the Texans drew up a constitution and elected Sam Houston president. Would Texas maintain this independent status, seeking the recognition of other countries, or annex itself to the United States? President Jackson, fully cognizant of the Mexican charges of United States interference, hesitated to recognize the Lone Star republic, much less annex it. Finally, on March 3, 1837, the day before he left office, Jackson extended diplomatic recognition.

Politics and the Texas Question

Southern spokesmen for cotton and slavery saw in the annexation of Texas an opportunity to extend the area of both, for the Texas government had recognized the existence of slavery within that country's borders. The Missouri Compromise line barred slavery from all but a small portion of the original Louisiana Purchase, but Texas, large enough for possibly five slave states, would help to correct the balance. Southern leaders in Congress made sporadic attempts to annex Texas to the United States, but they faced the determined opposition of the antislavery forces led by John Quincy Adams. Adams's final speech against annexation took three weeks to deliver in July, 1838. It succeeded in terminating the annexation movement, thus forcing Texas to resolve her foreign and domestic problems without the benefit of United States power or leadership.

By 1842 Britain and France had recognized the Texas republic and hoped together to preserve its independence against pressures from both Mexico and the United States. Houston suggested to the two European governments that they prevail upon Mexico to grant recognition to Texas and thereby give the young nation the security necessary to sustain its independence. An independent Texas, producing cotton, sugar, and tobacco, and serving as a buffer to American expansion, conformed to British and French interests, but neither power could influence Mexican policy. No Mexican regime would have dared to recognize Texan independence. Still, during the early forties the Texas republic faced neither internal nor external crises, and many Texans no longer wished to terminate their experiment in nation building through annexation. It was the scheming of Southern politicians that dragged the Texas question after 1842 into the center of American political life.

With Webster's resignation from the State

Department in 1843, President Tyler found himself surrounded by personal friends—most of them Democratic and Southern. Clay was obviously running hard for the Whig nomination, but Tyler had not lost his political ambition and was determined to make a bid for a second term. To build the needed political influence without a party, however, required a powerful issue. Tyler found it in Texas. In October, 1843, he instructed Abel P. Upshur, his new Secretary of State, to negotiate a treaty of annexation with the Texan Minister in Washington. Before Upshur could complete this negotiation, he was killed in a naval accident; Tyler then made Calhoun Secretary of State.

Now the Texas issue moved into more powerful hands. Behind Calhoun's leadership, Southern Democrats saw the issue as an opportunity to build their own political fences. For these annexationists, Texas was a purely sectional issue—a program to expand the plantation system and increase Southern power in Congress. Andrew Jackson's celebrated letter to Aaron V. Brown in 1843 gave Southern annexationism great urgency, for, in pointing to British ambition and intrigue in Texas, the old Tennesseean raised the question of British abolitionism. For the South the destruction of slavery in Texas would constitute a special danger. Threats of such magnitude could not escape the attention of Calhoun, who, though sixty-two and approaching the end of a long, brilliant career, was still a great master of comprehension and logic.

As Secretary of State, Calhoun began to promote annexation with the sectional fervor expected of him. He opened treaty negotiations with Texas, admitting to Richard Pakenham, the British Minister in Washington, that slavery was the controlling motive in his annexationist diplomacy. "I only ask the south to stand by me," he wrote in May. "Now is the time to vindicate and save our institutions." But having cast the issue into a sectional mold, Calhoun could not carry his treaty through the Senate.

If Tyler could not control the Texas issue, neither could the Southern Democrats. A new coalition of agrarian Democrats, centering in the lower Midwest, with allies in the Southwest and the East, gradually captured the issue by nationalizing it. This group infused it with that "spiritual exaltation" known as "manifest destiny," and rode to power on its emotional impact. The leaders in this coup were such key Democratic politicians as Lewis Cass of Michigan, Stephen A. Douglas of Illinois, Edward Hannegan and Jesse Bright of Indiana, William Allen of Ohio, Robert J. Walker of Mississippi, Andrew Johnson and James K. Polk of Tennessee, James Buchanan of Pennsylvania, Daniel Dickinson and William L. Marcy of New York. These men cared nothing for the expansion of slavery. They favored annexation, Douglas said later, "upon broad national grounds, elevated far above, and totally disconnected from the question of slavery." Even before the Democratic Convention at Baltimore in May, 1844, they had pushed Calhoun aside, manipulated the Texas issue to eliminate Van Buren, and taken control of the Democratic party.

The Election of 1844

Van Buren approached the campaign of 1844 still titular head of the Democratic party and confident of another nomination. State Democratic conventions across the country generally favored him and committed more than half the convention delegates to support his candidacy.

But in the weeks before the Baltimore convention, Van Buren revealed his strong antislavery leanings by faltering on the annexation issue. When pressed by Democratic leaders, especially from the South, to set forth his views on Texas, the New Yorker announced to the press on April 27 that he regarded Texas annexation, for the moment at least, inexpedient and dangerous. This permitted opponents within the party (who had already deserted him because of their conviction that he could not carry the nation against Clay) to enlist the support of ardent Democratic expansionists.

At Baltimore the Democratic convention quickly came under the control of those party managers who were determined to deny Van Buren the nomination. Their dilemma was clear: How could they permit the committed majority to cast their votes for Van Buren and still not give him the nomination? The answer lay in the "two-thirds rule," adopted in 1832 but dispensed with in 1840. When Van Buren's opponents proposed the two-thirds rule to the delegates, the Van Buren forces knew it would prevent a Van Buren nomination and objected savagely, but despite their efforts the two-thirds rule carried. When the voting for candidates began, those pledged to Van Buren voted for him, giving him a clear majority on the first ballot. But the Van Buren nomination was doomed, for he could never command two-thirds of the votes. On the other hand, the Van Burenites could prevent the nomination of Buchanan and Cass, two leaders of the new conservative faction. Clearly a compromise candidate was required. James K. Polk of Tennessee appeared on the eighth ballot for the first time, and a stampede began during the ninth ballot, quickly giving him the unanimous vote of the convention.

James K. Polk was one of the few politicians in the nation acceptable to all factions of the Democratic party. He was a devout Jacksonian and a known devotee of Van Buren, with long experience in Congress. He had favored Texas annexation but had not engaged in any of the intrigue that overthrew the New York machine. The convention offered the vice presidency almost unanimously to Silas Wright, a close associate of Van Buren in New York who declined it. It then went to George M. Dallas, a colorless Democrat of Pennsylvania. The fact that Wright had been chosen for the vice presidency and that he was the principal author of the expansion plank in the Democratic platform indicated how completely Texas served merely as a catalyst to achieve a revolution in leadership within the Democratic party. For Wright's views on Texas coincided with those of Van Buren, and the platform itself avoided urging immediate annexation but favored instead annexation "at the earliest practicable period." The platform went on to reaffirm the party's states' rights tradition. It reminded the nation that the federal government was one of limited powers with no authority to carry out a general system of internal improvements, to establish a national bank, to interfere with slavery in the several states, or to distribute the proceeds of public lands among the states. It also called for a lower tariff.

Whig conservatives, North and South, felt threatened by the Texas issue. Annexation threatened the peace with Mexico and seemed injurious to the moderate foreign policy which they favored. Their chief concern, however, was for the Union and for the success of their party. They recalled bitterly four futile years in power that had produced little but the tariff of 1842. Now Texas was again placing the Whig program in jeopardy. Alexander M. Stephens of Georgia termed the entire annexation policy "a miserable political humbug" mounted as a ruse "to divide and distract the Whig party at the South." Clay himself summarized well the Whig stand on Texas in a letter to the *National Intelligencer* in May, 1844: "I consider the annexation of Texas, at this time, without the assent of Mexico, as a measure compromising the national character, involving us certainly in a war with Mexico, probably with other foreign powers, dangerous to the integrity of the Union, inexpedient in the present financial condition of the country, and not called for by any general expression of public opinion."

Never had the Whig party been as united as it was in 1844. The convention nominated Clay by acclamation, sure that the Kentuckian's widespread popularity would propel him into the White House. With Clay's election, they anticipated a thorough Whig regime. Their platform did not equivocate on matters of economic policy. It promised "a well-regulated currency; a tariff for revenue . . . and discriminating with special reference to the protection of the domestic labor of the country; the distribution of the proceeds of the sales of the public lands." The Whig party, having gained confidence since 1840, chose to give the American people a choice of philosophies as well as candidates.

Texas dominated the campaign. Democratic editors and politicians, convinced that Clay's reticence on the subject presented them with a winning issue across the country, quickly transformed the question of expansion into that significant expression of American nationalism known as "manifest destiny," which implied that the United States was destined by the will of Heaven to become a nation of political and territorial eminence. The doctrine attributed this inevitable growth to a homogeneous process emanating from certain unique qualities in American civilization—the energy and vigor of its people, their idealism and faith in their democratic institutions (enhanced in the forties by the dramatic achievements of the past), and their obligation to extend "the area of freedom" to their less fortunate neighbors. Formerly Americans had feared that national expansion would undermine the federal structure of the United States government; by the forties, however, the addition of many new states had convinced the expansionists—most of whom were Jacksonian states' rightists—that territorial growth would strengthen rather than weaken the position of the states in the American constitutional system. Such notions, preached by Democratic orators from every stump in the land, compelled Clay to equivocate on the Texas issue, and this helped the Democrats upset Whig calculations and wrest from them both the White House and control of Congress. The popular vote gave Polk a narrow margin: 1,337,000 to 1,299,000. The electoral vote was not so close: 170 for Polk to 105 for Clay.

So confident had the Whigs been of victory that they were disconsolate in defeat. Greeley's *New York Tribune* charged the Democrats with corruption in buying votes, especially those of the newly arrived immigrants in New York City. The editor's emphasis on New York's vote was correct. Birney's 15,000 antislavery, anti-Texas votes in New York had cut more deeply into Whig than Democratic ranks. Clay lost this key state with its 36 electoral votes by a margin of 5,000. "If the Whig party had gone into the contest as sincerely opposed to the annexation of Texas as the mass of Democrats were in favor of it," complained the abolitionist poet James Russell Lowell, "we have no doubt the result of the presidential election would have been reversed." Whigs generally agreed that their defeat did not constitute a national rejection of either Clay or his principles.

Polk's victory pointed to the immediate annexation of Texas. When Congress convened in December, 1844, the Democratic leadership brought a joint resolution of annexation before both houses. Convinced that Mexico would react violently to annexation, Senator Benton proposed negotiation with Mexico prior to annexation for the purpose of defining the boundary. By January, 1845, however, the Missourian had agreed to immediate annexation, with the question of the boundary to be left to future diplomacy. The House passed the resolution for annexation late in January; at the end of February, by a narrow vote of 27 to 25, the Senate approved an amended resolution. Tyler, anxious to proceed under the authority granted by Congress, directed the American chargé in Texas, on March 3, to invite Texas to join the Union. Polk, upon entering office the following day, upheld Tyler's action. Texas responded favorably to the American invitation and entered the Union when Congress approved its new constitution the following December.

Polk and the Democratic Party

Polk was in many respects an unlikely President. He possessed no unique qualities of mind, body, or spirit. Neither in personality nor appearance was he conspicuous. He was below average in height, with a thin face and piercing gray eyes. An uncompromising Presbyterian, he was honest and incorruptible, thoughtful and meditative, slow and measured in speech, methodical and industrious. Yet at the age of forty-nine in March, 1845, Polk was the youngest incumbent of the White House to that time. His political experience had been long and deep, giving him a knowledge of party behavior as thorough as that of any of his contemporaries. A thorough Jacksonian, a two-term Speaker of the House of Representatives, a former Governor of Tennessee, and a man well known in Democratic circles, Polk had been mentioned repeatedly as a possible vice presidential candidate in 1844. Thus his availability had been sufficiently well established to make him the logical choice of a deadlocked convention.

Polk's election to the White House was a triumph for the new Democratic leadership. Both in Congress and in the Cabinet, the expansionist element reached new heights of influence and remained the core of the Democratic organization—thus wielding major influence over national policy—until the eve of the Civil War. As a group, these men were Jacksonian in philosophy; moderate on the question of slavery; generally expansionist in outlook; devoted to the party and the Union, recognizing, as did the conservative Whig leadership, that the Union would not long survive any breakup of the two national parties along sectional lines.

If Polk entered office backed by a powerful bloc of conservative Democrats, he did not lead a united party. The Van Burenites emerged from the Baltimore convention so embittered by Van Buren's defeat that they campaigned for Polk with little enthusiasm, if at all. The conviction that they had been deprived of their command of the Democratic party by a Texas conspiracy presaged resentment toward any presidential appointees who had favored annexation. Polk, knowing the magnitude of their influence, as well as their discontent, made repeated efforts to pacify Van Buren's key followers with Cabinet posts. For one reason or another, not one member of Van Buren's New York faction was willing or able to accept the positions Polk offered.

Every major appointment to Polk's Cabinet alienated the Van Burenites. They especially resented James Buchanan and Robert J. Walker (Secretaries of State and Treasury, respectively), for these two annexationists had been among the managers of the Baltimore convention who devised the two-thirds rule to defeat Van Buren. George Bancroft, the noted Massachusetts historian and friend of Van Buren, received the Secretaryship of the Navy. But his appointment offered the New Yorkers few guarantees of future favors, and it was decidedly unpopular among the Democratic workhorses of New England.

Polk soon aggravated the humiliation suffered by Van Buren in the distribution of Cabinet offices by dismissing Francis P. Blair, Van Buren's old associate, from the administration. He closed Blair's *Washington Globe* as the party's official organ. Jackson, now approaching death at the Hermitage, fumed at Polk: "But my dear friend the movement was hasty, and as I think badly advised and I pray my god that it may not result in injury to the perfect unity of the democracy." To make matters even worse, the President invited Thomas Ritchie of Virginia to establish the *Washington Union* as the new administration paper. Ritchie's presence in the capital was extremely vexatious to Van Buren, for the editor had advocated the annexation of Texas and had eventually turned against Van Buren and fought his nomination. Thus Polk's initial appointments had completely alienated the North's most powerful Democratic machine.

Domestic Policies

On matters of domestic policy, Polk entered the White House determined to achieve tariff reduction and the reestablishment of the Independent Treasury. On the tariff issue Polk had the full support of Calhoun and the Southern Democrats. Under Calhoun's direction, Southern free-traders had reluctantly accepted the compromise tariff of 1833, only to see the duties raised in the tariff of 1842. Two years later the free-traders launched a massive assault on the Whig tariff but failed to carry their bill for tariff reduction. By 1845 Calhoun was ready to offer a bargain to the West. In November he attended the Southern and Western Commercial Convention at Memphis with a plan to save the South from its position of numerical inferiority. To the West he offered federal aid to its commerce in exchange for Western support of tariff reduction. By defining the river transportation system as a great "inland sea," Calhoun could disregard his traditional constitutional scruples about internal improvements at federal expense and could ask that Congress spend money to improve shipping on the Ohio and Mississippi Rivers. For Calhoun this was strange doctrine, but the price was not too high for a new tariff. What concerned him, he said, was not simply getting rid of obstructions for the Mississippi River improvements but removing "the only barrier that remains between the Union of the South and West."

Assured of broad Democratic backing, Polk included tariff proposals in his message of December, 1845. Submitted to Congress by Secretary of the Treasury Robert J. Walker, the new tariff bill contained ad valorem duties which were bitterly opposed by the New England industrialists. Webster, now back in the Senate, led the attack on the Walker bill. First he hoped to settle on a permanent compromise tariff with Whig endorsement, but when that failed, he settled down to defeat tariff reduction with Western votes. The West, he said, had coal and iron and sufficient capital so that when the time came, they would "see their true interest to be, to feed the northern and eastern manufacturers, as far as they may be fed, and in the mean time begin to vary their own occupation . . . and begin it they will, because they are an intelligent and active people, and cannot fail to see in what direction their true interest lies." But Webster failed to break the Democratic ranks. The vote on the Walker Tariff revealed an almost straight party alignment. The New England and Middle Atlantic states voted overwhelmingly against the measure (18 to 4), but the Jacksonians of the South and West (23 to 9) tied the vote at 27 to 27. The affirmative vote of Vice President Dallas decided the issue. Although the law created new schedules with varying rates for each category of imports, the general level of duties was cut to about 20 percent.

Webster had lost his perennial struggle to win the West to the support of the American System. The same session of Congress, again on an almost straight party vote, reestablished the Independent Treasury. After the abolishment of the earlier Independent Treasury system in 1841, the federal government had deposited its money in state banks. Now the new law divorced the government from private banking and established subtreasuries in which to deposit federal funds. It again placed the national Treasury on a specie basis. While the Walker tariff was still before Congress, the American System faced yet another test in the Rivers and Harbors bill of 1846. Overwhelmingly supported by the West, this measure passed Congress in July, 1846. Calhoun, on principles of his own, voted against the bill. President Polk vetoed the measure as requiring too large an appropriation for the nation, then at war with Mexico; an effort to carry the bill over his veto failed. Thus the summer of 1846 recorded the total collapse of the American System. Democratic opposition to the high tariff and internal improvements had been dictated essentially by Jacksonian traditions. Still the votes in Congress constituted major victories for the Southern Democrats. For Northern antislavery editors and politicians, Whig and Democrat, the fact that Calhoun again appeared victorious was sufficient proof that Polk had sold out to the slave power.

Conclusion

Such charges were false. What characterized American politics as late as 1846 was not the force of sectionalism, revolving around the issue of slavery and slavery expansion, but rather the strength and determination of the nation's two major parties to resist sectional pressures in the interest of preserving both their organizations and their philosophies of government and economics intact. The struggle for power between Whigs and Democrats was too intense and long-standing to disappear before issues that did not touch the economic well-being of most Americans. Slavery as a moral issue had entered the nation's consciousness, no longer to be submerged, but even the bitter sectional animosities which it generated scarcely touched the membership or the positions of the two major parties on the immediate political questions facing the American people.

Congressional voting on the key economic measures of the decade revealed the extent to which the parties held firm, and those Whigs and Democrats who wavered from established party positions did so not because of sectional pressure but because of regional economic self-interest. On such central issues as the National Bank, the tariff, distribution and land policy, over 90 percent of Democrats usually voted with their party; among the Whigs about 80 percent of the party membership generally followed the party line. Both parties had moderates who broke occasionally, but not one member of Congress voted consistently against the established position of his party. Most Southern Whigs were as loyal to national Whig policy as were the Whigs of New England. Even on the Texas issue party lines held firm, with the Whigs, including the Southern Whigs, almost unanimously opposed to annexation. Only on the issue of internal improvements, so universally demanded by the Western states, was there a general absence of party cohesion. Both parties split almost equally on the question of river and harbor improvement, but the divisions in both parties were as much East-West as they were North-South, with the Whigs and the Democrats of the Northeast as much opposed to Western improvements as were the spokesmen of the South. Party affiliation, not residence in a section, was still the primary determinant for individual political behavior.

SUGGESTED READINGS

The full history of party development during the age of Jackson has yet to be written. Nor is there any general consensus of opinion among historians even on what is known. In large measure the fundamental questions remain unanswered: Who were the Whigs and Democrats? Why did Americans make the political and party choices they did? Nonetheless, existing volumes reveal much that is essential. An excellent study of party strength in each section can be found in F. J. Turner's *The United States, 1830–1850: The Nation and Its Sections* (1935). Charles McCarthy's *The Antimasonic Party* (1903) remains the standard account of that political movement. The biographies of Webster and Clay emphasize the quality and purpose of the Whig party's leadership. In addition, such volumes as S. R. Gammon's *The Presidential Campaign of* 1832 (1923); E. M. Carroll's *Origins of the Whig Party* (1925); A. C. Cole's *The Whig Party in the South* (1913); and G. R. Poage's *Henry Clay and the Whig Party* (1936) relate much of that party's history. Charles G. Sellers, Jr., in "Who Were the Southern Whigs?" *American Historical Review,* LIX (January, 1954), identifies Whig leadership in the South more with the merchants and lawyers of the urban centers than with the planter aristocracy.

Lee Benson in *The Concept of Jacksonian Democracy** (1961) challenges the older view that the Whigs and Democrats can be differentiated by class and wealth. He demonstrates that the Jacksonian leadership of New York was often as aristocratic as the Whig leadership and suggests that national and religious affiliation might be the true gauge of party affiliation. Richard P. McCormick, in "Suffrage Classes and Party Alignments: A Study in Voter Behavior," *Mississippi Valley Historical Review,* XLVI (December, 1959), questions the view that the lower economic groups in American society were necessarily Jacksonian.

For the Tyler years the best study available is O. P. Chitwood's *John Tyler: Champion of the Old South* (1939). Another excellent account of Tyler's leadership can be found in R. J. Morgan's *A Whig Embattled: The Presidency under John Tyler* (1954). For Webster's diplomacy both C. M. Fuess's *Daniel Webster* (2 vols., 1930) and R. N. Current's *Daniel Webster and* *the Rise of National Conservatism** (1955) are excellent. Special monographs that contain accounts of the Webster-Ashburton negotiations are A. B. Corey's *The Crisis of* 1830–1842 *in Canadian-American Relations* (1941) and W. D. Jones's *Lord Aberdeen and the Americas* (1958). Of some value also is the older diplomatic study, J. S. Reeves's *American Diplomacy under Tyler and Polk* (1907).

Party leaders, in and out of Congress, ignored the slavery question until the late 1830s, when abolitionist groups raised the issue of slavery and the slave trade in the District of Columbia where Congress held political jurisdiction. Charles M. Wiltse in *John C. Calhoun: Nullifier* (1949) relates Calhoun's success in passing the "gag rule," whereas S. F. Bemis in *John Quincy Adams and the Union* (1956) traces the successful abolitionist efforts to rescind the tabling resolution in the House of Representatives. T. C. Smith's *The Liberty and Free Soil Parties in the Northwest* (1897) traces the efforts of antislavery leaders of the North and Northwest to introduce the slavery issue into American politics.

Several available studies analyze in detail the nature and purpose of Southern sectionalism. C. S. Sydnor's *The Development of Southern Sectionalism,* 1819–1848* (1948) is a standard work on the subject. Still rewarding is Robert R. Russel's *Economic Aspects of Southern Sectionalism,* 1840–1861 (1924). On Calhoun's important role see C. M. Wiltse's *John C. Calhoun: Sectionalist,* 1840–1850 (1951). Emphasizing the intellectual and psychological aspects of Southern sectionalism are W. S. Jenkins's excellent *Pro-slavery Thought in the Old South* (1935); C. H. Ambler's *Sectionalism in Virginia from* 1776 *to* 1861 (1910); Jesse T. Carpenter's *The South as a Conscious Minority,* 1789–1861 (1930); W. J. Cash's *The Mind of the South** (1941); Clement Eaton's *The Mind of the Old South** (1964); and J. H. Franklin's *The Militant South,* 1800–1861* (1956).

On the annexation of Texas the standard work is Justin H. Smith's *The Annexation of Texas* (1911), although much of this work has been supplemented by later studies, especially that of J. W. Schmitz, *Texas Statecraft* (1945). E. C. Barker's *The Life of Stephen F. Austin* (1929) and *Mexico and Texas* (1928) trace the migration of Americans into Texas and the resulting conflict between Mexico and Texas. Two volumes on Texan independence are W. C. Binkley's *The Texas Revolution* (1952) and Marquis James's *The Raven** (1929), a biography of Sam Houston. Another useful biography is Herbert Gambrell's *Anson Jones* (1964), a study of the last Texas president. W. R. Hogan's *The Texas Republic* (1946) is an excellent social history of the Lone Star republic. Texas' role in European diplomacy is carefully analyzed in Ephraim D. Adams's *British Interest and Activities in Texas,* 1838–1846 (1910). Elgin Williams traces American interest in Texas to land claims in *The Animating Pursuits of Speculation* (1949).

Albert K. Weinberg's *Manifest Destiny: A Study of Nationalist Expansionism in American History** (1935) has long remained the basic study of the American expansionist rationale. Another older, but still useful, book is E. D. Adams's *The Power of Ideals in American History* (1913). An excellent study of the West in literature is H. N. Smith's *Virgin Land** (1950). A recent and more critical study of American expansionism in the 1840s is Frederick Merk's *Manifest Destiny and Mission in American History** (1963). Merk's *The Monroe Doctrine and American Expansionism,* 1843–1849 (1966) reveals the extent to which American expansionism was stimulated by a contrived fear of Europe. Norman A. Graebner's *Manifest Destiny** (1968) challenges the concept that manifest destiny was a determining factor in American expansion.

The political background of the 1844 presidential election is discussed in G. G. Van Deusen's *The Jacksonian Era,* 1828–1848* (1959), as well as in two brief monographs on the presidential politics of the Tyler years, Oscar D. Lambert's *Presidential Politics in the United States,* 1841–1844 (1936) and C. N. Paul's *Rift in the Democracy** (1951). On Polk's Tennessee background see Charles G. Sellers, Jr.'s *James K. Polk: Jacksonian,* 1795–1843 (1957). Sellers's *James K. Polk: Continentalist,* 1843–1846 (1966) contains an admirable and detailed account of the election of 1844, as well as an analysis of Polk's relationship to the major issues confronting the nation in 1845 and 1846. Of great value on Polk's Presidency is Allan Nevins's one-volume *Polk: The Diary of a President** (1929), as well as C. A. McCoy's brief *Polk and the Presidency* (1960). Through a careful examination, Joel H. Silbey's *The Shrine of Party: Congressional Voting Behavior,* 1841–1852 (1967) makes clear the extent to which the parties resisted sectional pressures in the 1840s.

* indicates availability in paperback.

16

The Continental Empire

TEXAS ANNEXATION did not terminate the American impulse to expand. "The Rio Grande," predicted the *Baltimore American* in March, 1845, "has no more efficacy as a permanent barrier against the extension of Anglo-Saxon power than the Sabine possessed. The process by which Texas was acquired may be repeated over and over again." The rhetoric of manifest destiny, proclaimed so freely by Democratic politicians and editors during the debates over Texas, suggested that the United States would extend ultimately over the entire North American continent. Such was the vision described by Senator James Buchanan in March, 1844: "Providence has given to the American people a great and important mission, and that mission they were destined to fulfill—to spread the blessings of Christian liberty and laws from one end to the other of this immense continent. . . . To talk of confining the American spirit of emigration within limits was like talking of limiting the stars in their courses, or bridling the foaming torrent of Niagara." Whatever their power to arouse the American people, such words were expressions of sentiment, not of policy. Those who identified American destiny with the creation of a continental empire rarely bothered to define either the precise imperial boundaries they desired or the means whereby they intended to achieve them.

In 1845, when Texas entered the Union, much of Illinois and Wisconsin was still an unoccupied wilderness, and the westward-moving frontier was creeping across Iowa and Missouri.

To the west, the prairies rolled on for several hundred miles before they became lost in that high, level expanse known as the Great Plains. Except for the groves and patches of willow and cottonwood that marked the course of the Missouri, Platte, Arkansas, and their tributaries, the region was one continuous grassland, its thick covering of prairie grass in the east gradually thinning out into clumps of buffalo grass and sagebrush on the high, parched plains to the west. This continental grassland experienced wide extremes in temperature and rainfall, with long, cold winters followed by summers of intense heat. Over the plains roamed the great nomadic Indian tribes—the Sioux, Blackfoot, and Crow to the north; the Pawnee, Cheyenne, Arapaho, Kiowa, and Comanche to the south. The millions of buffalo that grazed the plains provided the Indians with their immediate necessities of life—food, clothing, tepees, thread, and fuel. Buffalo hunting was the major economic endeavor of the wandering tribes. Mounted on their wiry ponies—descendents of the old Spanish horses—the plains Indians were among the greatest horsemen in the world. Trappers, traders, and explorers had long regarded the region as barren and dangerous for white habitation. For American frontiersmen and pioneers of the forties, the Great Plains were an interminable barrier separating the Mississippi Valley frontier from the Rockies and the silent world beyond, which beckoned with promises of wealth and adventure.

Penetration of the Great West

St. Louis first gained distinction as the great emporium of the trans-Mississippi frontier through its control of the Rocky Mountain fur trade. From this village on the Mississippi, Lewis and Clark embarked on their expedition to the far Northwest in 1804; from there the early fur traders, such as Manuel Lisa, attempted to exploit the newly discovered beaver country in the Rockies. The reluctance of the plains Indians to trap the mountain streams, however, compelled the entrepreneur who would reap a profit from beaver skins to engage white trappers. It was William Henry Ashley who first met this challenge. He advertised for young men who desired a life of adventure and in 1823 dispatched the first group of "Mountain Men" up the Missouri. These trappers combed the Upper Yellowstone and spread southward through South Pass, a wide, gently sloping opening through the Rockies (which they discovered in 1824), to the beaver country of the Green River. Each year the Mountain Men gathered at a designated rendezvous. There they acquired fresh supplies and sent their pelts on the long journey by pack train and riverboat to St. Louis. In 1826 one of their number, Jedediah Smith, followed the Colorado River southward and westward around the Great Bend to the Mojave villages, and from there traversed the Mojave Desert into southern California. Other explorer-trappers blazed new trails: Kentuckian Sylvester Pattie, crossing the Southern deserts from the Rio Grande, reached San Diego in 1828; two years later, Tennesseean Ewing Young opened the Old Spanish Trail from Santa Fe to Los Angeles. By the forties, countless trappers, pushing out along the Arkansas, Platte, and Missouri Rivers, had pierced the successive ranges of the Rockies, crossed the deserts beyond, blazed trails through the Sierras, viewed the Bay of San Francisco, and wintered at Monterey. These men charted the routes and water holes which permitted them to cross and recross a wilderness of awesome grandeur and dimension.

Meanwhile, St. Louis had drawn the Mexican province of New Mexico into its trading empire. Santa Fe, the provincial capital, was a mere speck in a vast, enchanting world of plains and deserts broken only by a wide variety of cacti, brightly colored mesas, occasional mountains and canyons, and Indian pueblos. Yet this sleepy village of adobe huts scattered along the Rio Grande was the central market for the province's 40,000 inhabitants who looked in vain to Mexico City, 1,000 miles to the south, for manufactured goods. Even more significant, in the town resided people who had silver, gold, and furs to exchange for products of Yankee factory and mill. The vision of a profitable prairie commerce between St. Louis and Santa Fe was not lost on American traders. By the early forties, hundreds of men were involved in a traffic that carried goods valued at several hundred thousand dollars annually. The famed Santa Fe Trail had become the major highway of commerce and travel across the Southern plains.

When restless frontiersmen broke through the Rocky Mountain barrier, they entered a vast empire of mountains, deserts, and forests to which the United States had only partial title. To the Oregon country north of 42°, the United States had the old Spanish claims acquired in the Louisiana Purchase. But above the Columbia River, the United States still found itself in conflict with the expanding British Empire which pushed southward from western Canada with the Hudson's Bay Company in the vanguard. Britain's claims to the region, based on actual occupation, were strong; for as late as 1845 the Hudson's Bay Company had complete possession of the entire country north of the Columbia. British officials readily conceded all claims to Oregon south of the river. Thus the 300 miles of shaggy coast between the mouth of the Columbia and the 42nd parallel still composed the total uncontested frontage on the Pacific possessed by the United States when Polk entered the White House. And because this coast was totally devoid of harbors for ocean commerce, none of Polk's predecessors would accept the perennial British proposal for a permanent division of the Oregon country with the border at the Columbia River.

Oregon

Long before 1845, however, an enlarging American presence in Oregon was affecting the region's destiny. New England merchants had brought Oregon into the China trade as early as 1787 when they commissioned Captain Robert Gray and the *Columbia* to visit the Oregon coast in search of sea otter skins. From that moment onward, the trade grew to impressive proportions, almost solely through Boston enterprise. Looming large in Boston's success in the Pacific was the tough shipmaster William Sturgis, whose firm, Bryant & Sturgis, revived and dominated the Northwest fur trade after the War of 1812. (During that war the British had seized Astoria, John Jacob Astor's post at the mouth of the Columbia.) Until 1830, this high road of Boston commerce offered profits and excitement—rounding the Horn, bartering for furs in Oregon, trading for tea and silk in Canton. By the forties the traffic had disappeared, but through the decades it had impressed that stretch of coast from the Columbia

River to the Strait of Juan de Fuca on the minds of Yankee seamen.

During the thirties other Americans entered Oregon to transform that wilderness into a promising outpost of American civilization. Their incentives were national as well as personal. Earlier diplomats and traders had seen that only permanent American settlements would dislodge the Hudson's Bay Company from its monopoly of trade and occupation. Convinced of this, one Yankee, Hall Jackson Kelley, established a society in 1831 to encourage emigration to Oregon. His campaign, advertising the opportunities for merchants, farmers, and missionaries in that distant land, prompted Nathaniel J. Wyeth, a young adventurer, to demonstrate the feasibility of overland migration to Oregon. Wyeth's efforts opened no avenues to easy riches; but Jason Lee, a Methodist missionary who accompanied Wyeth in 1834, remained in the Willamette Valley and there established a tiny but permanent American settlement. And in 1836 the American Board of Foreign Missions, at the request of four Flathead Indians who appeared in St. Louis, sent Dr. Marcus Whitman, a Presbyterian, to the eastern Oregon country. Whitman, accompanied by his young bride, reached Oregon after a long, hard journey and immediately established missions among the Cayuse, Nez Percé, and Flathead Indians. These apparently successful missionary ventures encouraged the Catholic Church to enter the field. Father Pierre-Jean de Smet of the Catholic University in St. Louis was dispatched to the Oregon country, where in 1841 he established the mission of Sacré Coeur.

These missionaries were the vanguard. After 1842 the Midwest, awakening at last from its long depression, began to swarm. Oregon—praised by travelers, books, and pamphlets for a decade—attracted a thousand emigrants in 1843 and a similar number the following year. Arriving by riverboat at the St. Louis waterfront, the pioneers purchased equipment and supplies, headed for the staging areas to the west, and there joined the caravans for the long, arduous summer and autumn journey over the Oregon Trail. By 1845 the emigrants had sealed the fate of Oregon.

California

Beyond the Rockies south of 42°, the United States had no claims at all. Stretching from the mountains to the Pacific Coast was the Mexican province of California, still a remote and exposed wilderness after seven decades under Mexican rule. Its less than ten thousand people were almost lost in a narrow strip touching the sea. The Franciscan missions—a score of them—which nestled snugly in well-chosen valleys along the coastal ranges, thoughtfully spaced about a day's travel apart, bore evidence of better days. By the 1840s, these venerated establishments were crumbling. Stripped of their landed possessions in 1835 by the Mexican government, their priestly commissions superseded by civil authority, they had suffered an inevitable decline. The wasting away of the missions precipitated a general economic decline, for the old Spanish-American mission, no less than the medieval manor, had been the center of the provincial economy. Economically, the California of the forties was not golden. It presented a picture of desolation.

Politically, the province showed even less promise. Travelers agreed that it was drifting

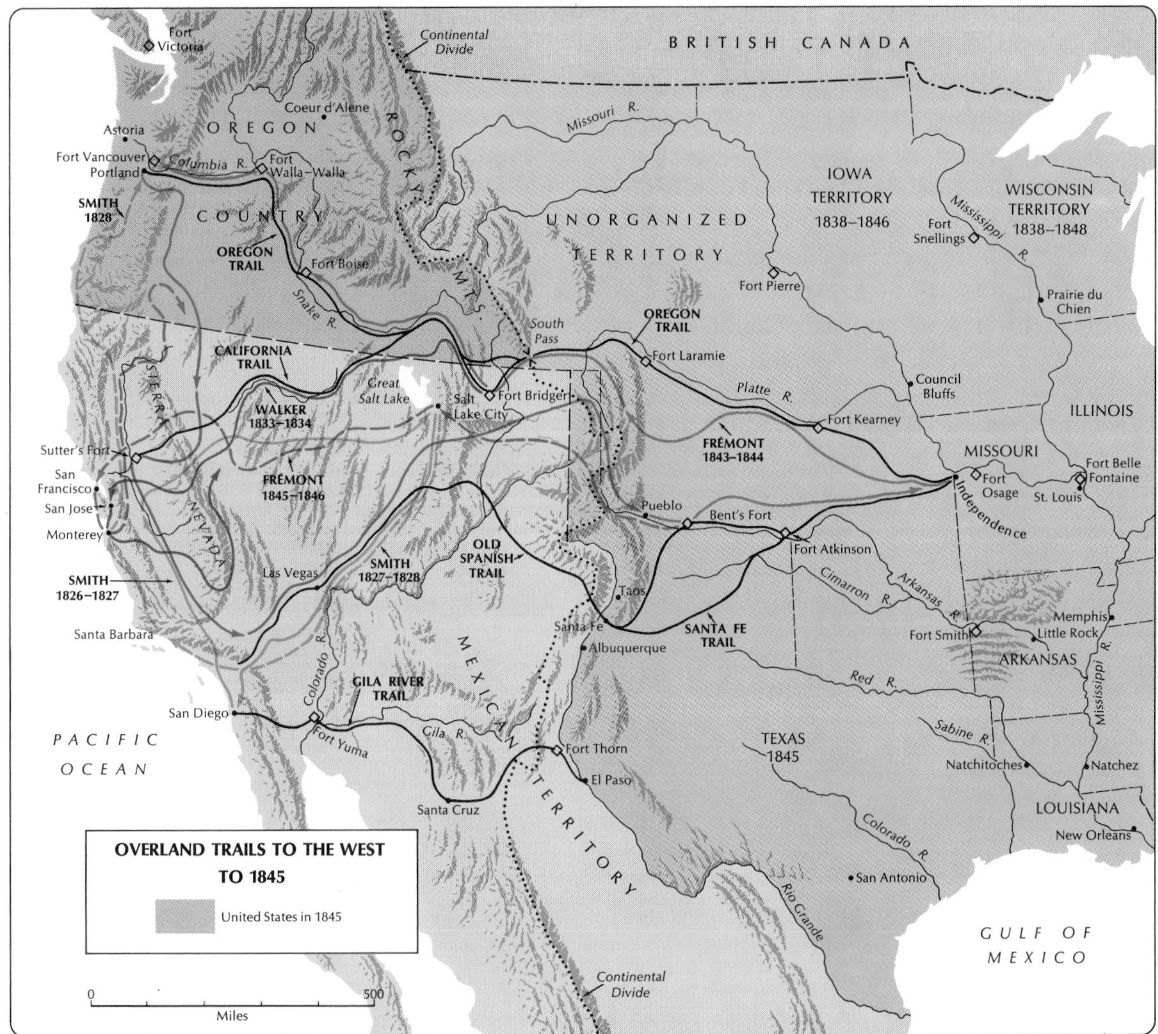

beyond the grasp of the central Mexican government. "Although I was prepared for anarchy and confusion," wrote Charles Wilkes, the noted American naval captain in 1841, "I was surprised when I found a total absence of all government in California, and even its forms and ceremonies thrown aside." San Francisco's *presidio* overlooking the Golden Gate was in ruins; two of its four walls had crumbled. Its garrison comprised one officer and one soldier. Another astute traveler suggested that California could be taken by any nation that sent one corvette and 200 men against it. The *Times* of London observed in 1845 that to conquer all California would be akin to occupying a desert island.

Yet California, like Oregon, had captured the Yankee imagination. Long before the Mexican Republic opened its ports to world shipping, Boston vessels had frequented the California coasts in search of sea otter. With the news of Mexican independence in 1822, Boston mercantile houses dispatched their ships to acquire hides in California. Bryant & Sturgis entered the hide trade with their *Sachem* in 1822. For the next twenty years, this house did a thriving business, keeping one or more ships active along the California coast at all times and maintaining a large establishment at San Diego Bay for the preparation and storage of hides. By the late thirties many Yankees originally brought to California by the hide trade had decided to remain. Thomas O. Larkin of Monterey was one of the most widely known of the American merchants then residing permanently in the tiny villages along the California coast—Yerba Buena, Monterey, Santa Barbara, Los Angeles, and San Diego. Boston's exciting commerce with California, which quickly surpassed the declining Northwest fur trade in importance, stands commemorated in Richard Henry Dana's *Two Years before the Mast* (1840), an American adventure classic.

Other Americans moved into California overland. National boundaries were meaningless in that immense wilderness west of the mountains, and hunters and trappers, pushing relentlessly onward, never hesitated in their drive toward the Pacific. By 1840, both the fur and Santa Fe trades had long since passed the zenith of their importance. But each year increasing numbers of American trappers and traders, finding their earlier profits disappearing, pushed into California, never to return. Pioneers who entered the wilderness beyond the Rockies after 1842 often chose California over Oregon, leaving the Oregon Trail and following the newly discovered routes across the Great Basin and the Sierras into northern California. From John Sutter's post on the American River they fanned out along the lower Sacramento, converting it into an Anglo-American valley. John Charles Frémont's published account of his second exploring expedition in 1844 deepened American interest in Mexican California. Lt. Frémont, an officer in the Army topographical corps and husband of Senator Benton's daughter Jesse, discovered little that was new on his first venture into the Great West; but on his second, he passed from Oregon southward through the Sierras into the Sacramento Valley, continued on to southern California, and returned through Santa Fe. His widely read account stressed those qualities of the Golden West that mattered—the disheveled state of California's government and economy under Mexican rule and the limitless commercial and agricultural possibilities which that region, under a more enterprising people, would hold for the future.

The Oregon Settlement

American pioneers who pushed into the Oregon country in 1845 finally weakened the British hold north as well as south of the Columbia. Migration to Oregon that year totaled 3,000 and doubled the population of the Willamette Valley. This simple but momentous fact revolutionized American attitudes toward this far frontier. As early as July, 1843, the settlers of the Willamette Valley met at Champoeg and there established a provisional government for the Oregon Territory. Obviously the pioneering movement, by undermining the principle of joint occupancy, was emphasizing the need for a political settlement. Western Democrats, embracing the Oregon issue, now not only demanded a final settlement with Britain but also challenged the entire British claim to Oregon. A convention of Oregon enthusiasts, meeting in Cincinnati during July, 1843, proclaimed the rights of the United States to all the territory from California to Alaska. Throughout the Midwest, the "whole of Oregon" became the popular cry. Western politicians exploited this new nationalism to solidify their position within the Democratic party. At the Baltimore convention in 1844, the party accepted these Western demands and merged the Texas and Oregon issues. Unfortunately, the Democratic claim to all of Oregon up to the Alaska line at 54°40′, while appealing politically, was untenable diplomatically.

Polk had rallied to the Democratic cry for the whole of Oregon. As President, however, whatever the avowed stand of his party, he would of necessity assume the responsibility for the further conduct of Oregon negotiations. One thing was certain—the United States would move northward from the Columbia either to the 49th parallel, the traditional American demand, or to the Alaska boundary, whether by war or diplomacy. But Polk discovered quickly that his adoption of the Democratic campaign promise of 54°40′ had destroyed his power to negotiate a reasonable settlement of the Oregon question. Accepting momentarily the long American diplomatic tradition of favoring a compromise along the 49th parallel, he offered this line to England in July, 1845. To insist on 54°40′ meant war, Benton observed; to recede from it was to abandon the platform. Polk met the danger with a halfhearted effort at negotiation, purposefully demanding more than Britain would concede.

When the Twenty-ninth Congress met in December, 1845, there was little indication that within six months the settlement of the disturbing Oregon question would be assured. Polk's message to Congress seemed to promise the extremists of his party that he would not weaken again. It no longer mattered that the American title to territory north of the Columbia was far from conclusive—and to lands above the 49th parallel, practically nonexistent. It had become, wrote John L. O'Sullivan of the *New York Morning News,* "our manifest destiny to occupy and to possess the whole of the Continent which Providence has given us." To 54°40′ proponents that seemed to settle the issue.

Yet such expansiveness was already doomed by the patent interests of American commercialism. Robert Winthrop of Massachusetts defined the objective of New England in the Oregon country. "We need ports on the Pacific," he shouted. "As to land, we have millions of acres of better land still unoccupied on this side of the mountains." William Sturgis, after three decades of intense maritime activity in the Pacific, told a Boston audience in January, 1845, that the Columbia was always dangerous for large ships and almost inaccessible for considerable periods each year. But the Strait of Juan de Fuca, he declared, was "easy of access, safe, and navigable at all seasons and in any weather." Commmercial realists who wished to secure permanent title to the magnificent Strait of Fuca pointed out that the United States could acquire all the excellent harbors in Oregon and still proffer the olive branch to England. Sturgis argued that a settlement at 49°, with the granting of Vancouver Island to Great Britain, would secure the maritime objectives of this nation and still not deny to England the navigation of the Fuca Strait, a right which, he knew, she would not relinquish peacefully.

By January, 1846, the movement for compromise in the United States had effectively challenged the hold of the extremists on American policy. The *North American Review* demanded a settlement of the Oregon question on new grounds. "We have been arguing the question for thirty years," charged the writer, "and stand precisely where we did when the discussion commenced." The debate, he declared, sounded like a "solemn mummery" in which too many ambitious politicians were preventing the vast majority from regarding the issue with perfect indifference. The writer continued: "Not one in ten thousand . . . would be immediately affected by the successful assertion of our claim to the whole of Oregon." The region was not worth the cost of the controversy. Throughout the commercial East, writers condemned the extremists for engaging in war talk to advance their political fortunes and for purposely keeping the Oregon question in a ferment to prevent its peaceful solution. Eastern merchants complained that threats of war were already hampering United States commerce over the world, for no whaler or East India merchantman would venture freely onto the high seas with a war against Britain in the offing. "This will all do famously for the valley of the Mississippi, where they have all to gain by a war and nothing to lose," grumbled Philip Hone, the noted New York merchant and diarist. "But we on the seaboard must fight all, pay all, and suffer all."

In Congress, the movement for compromise was managed by two Democratic factions: the Van Burenites, led in the Senate by John A. Dix of New York and Benton of Missouri, and the Southern wing led by Calhoun. Calhoun, supported by several other members of Congress, planned as early as February, 1846, to introduce a resolution advising the President to reopen negotiations with England for a settlement at 49°. United Whig support assured the eventual triumph of Calhoun's views in Congress. By late February, it had become obvious to the administration that a compromise on the 49th parallel would receive a two-thirds vote in the Senate. Quite contentedly, the Whigs followed the leadership of the South Carolinian. The *New York Herald* described this strange political alignment well: "The chivalry of the West goes hot and strong for 54–40 while the ardent South, and the calculating East, coalesce, for once, on this point, and quietly and temperately call for 49."

Polk could not openly accept the majority position of Congress without defying Western Democrats. But his dilemma did not prevent the British from entering the diplomatic vacuum. Increasingly after 1845, when the Hudson's Bay Company moved its main depot from Fort Vancouver to Vancouver Island, Great Britain revealed an inclination to retreat from the Columbia. Though few Americans had crossed the river, the British viewed their growing numbers to the south with dismay for they endangered the peace and threatened to disrupt the fur trade. Surrender of the Columbia was the key to the Oregon settlement. After years of hesitancy, the British government now agreed to settle the Oregon issue for an equitable distribution of ports. Lord Aberdeen, the British Foreign Minister, had established the bases of such an arrangement as early as September, 1844, when he wrote: "I believe that if the line of the 49th degree were extended only to the waters edge, and should leave us possession of all of Vancouver's Island, with the northern side of the entrance to Puget's Sound; and if all the harbors within the Sound, and to the Columbia, inclusive, were made free to both countries, . . .

this would be in reality a most advantageous settlement."

At last in the spring of 1846, Aberdeen was permitted to offer such a treaty to the United States, extending the 49th parallel to the coast, but leaving all of Vancouver Island in British hands. Polk, whose private views toward Oregon did not vary from those of the commercial Whigs, passed the responsibility to Congress. Ably supported by Whigs and Southern Democrats, he secured ratification easily. Both nations were content. Benton passed final judgment on the 49th parallel: "With that boundary comes all that we want in that quarter, namely, all the waters of Puget's Sound."

The Mormons and the Great Basin

One significant migration of the forties—that of the Mormons—did not terminate in either Oregon or California but in the region of the Great Salt Lake on the eastern fringe of the Great Basin. Unlike those who entered the Great West determined to carry American laws and institutions with them, the Mormons chose Mexican territory purposefully to escape the "oppression" of American officials and traditions.

That the Mormons would face the hostility of American society was assured by both the history and the nature of their religion. Mormonism spread rapidly from New York into the Western Reserve of Ohio and there, at Kirtland, Joseph Smith, its founder, developed the pattern of community life that came to characterize his movement. Facing economic difficulties in the wake of the Panic of 1837, the Mormons migrated to Independence, Missouri. There they aroused the animosity of the frontier settlers, who viewed them as Yankee abolitionists. Seeking a more tolerant environment, they moved back across the Mississippi in 1839 and established a settlement at Nauvoo on the Illinois bank of that river. Here Smith built a theocracy, and his tightly regulated community soon outstripped its river rivals in commerce and prosperity.

Smith faced trouble again when he announced a revelation that sanctioned polygamy, a practice in which he and other Mormon leaders were already involved. In 1843 when he ordered the destruction of a press operated by his monogamous opponents, the civil authorities arrested him and his brother Hiram for illegal destruction of property. After being once freed, the two men were arrested again on a similar charge and placed in the county jail at Carthage, where a mob surrounded the building and shot the two Mormon leaders in their cell. Brigham Young, who now assumed the leadership of the church, attempted to avenge the death of the Smiths. This brought open war with the settlers of the vicinity, forcing the Mormons to choose either to give up their unique communal and social practices or to move.

Through the years the Mormons had augmented their numbers through successful missionary activity in the Northern states as well as in England. When Brigham Young made his decision in 1846 to take his flock to the West, his resources—a hardy, determined people and an ample treasury—were sufficient to promise a successful venture. The Mormons crossed into Iowa and spent their first winter near Council Bluffs on the Missouri. Early in 1847, Young, with a small vanguard, pushed out along a route (later known as the "Mormon

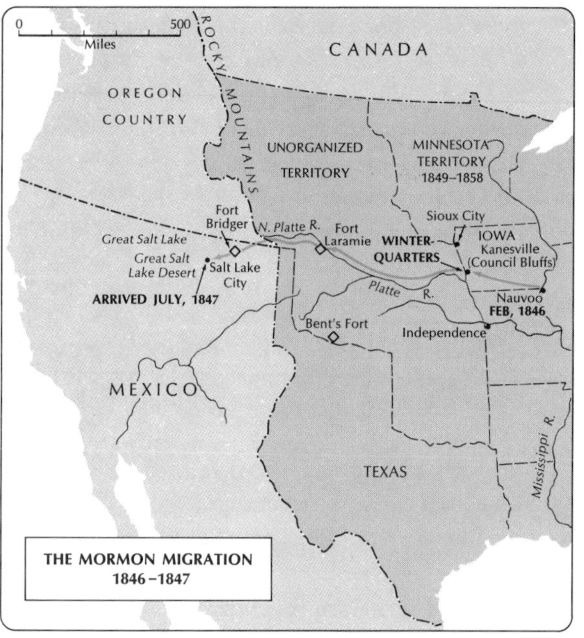

THE MORMON MIGRATION
1846–1847

Trail") which crossed the plains to the north of the Platte. In late June his party reached the basin of the Great Salt Lake. There Young established a settlement where the "Saints" at last could avoid the harassment of the "Gentiles" and gave it the descriptive title of Deseret. The Mormon migration of 1848 brought the total number of people in the new Zion to 5,000. Young's selection of this economically unpromising region satisfied certain necessary requirements of his group, especially that of escaping those community and legal pressures which warred on the practice of polygamy. Partially because the new Canaan lay in Mexican territory, but particularly because the environment was inhospitable, Young hoped that pioneers would continue to move on to Oregon or California.

The experiment might have failed without the leadership and the sense of community which Young brought to the Mormon settlement. With the power to determine all land, economic, and religious policy, Young and his associates were able to organize their people for survival. They ruled out all practices which promoted individualism at the expense of the majority. Permitting no land speculation, they put the community's limited land and water resources to maximum use by establishing small, irrigated, intensely cultivated farms. They found a ready market for their crop surplus among the migrants traveling to California; and whereas the trade added wealth to their community, their presence at the edge of the desert added immeasurably to the security of the trail.

Despite the heavy flow of outsiders through the Salt Lake settlement, Young succeeded in protecting his polygamous, theocratic society from direct interference by a monogamous, democratic nation. With the Treaty of Guadalupe Hidalgo in 1848, the United States acquired the Great Basin; two years later Congress organized Deseret as Utah Territory. Even then, Brigham Young, as the new territorial governor, was able to maintain his rigid, but shrewd and reasonable, control of both civil and spiritual affairs in the dozens of Mormon communities now scattered over the region.

War with Mexico

Polk turned to the question of California with considerable resolution during the summer and autumn of 1845, for this challenge, unlike that of Oregon, was not encumbered by politics. In California, however, American expansionism faced a dilemma only partially present in

Oregon. The United States had no legal claim to the region. The acquisition of this Mexican province required bargaining with its owner, and in 1845 the chance of negotiations with Mexico appeared slight indeed. That nation had never recognized the independence of Texas and had warned the United States repeatedly that annexation would mean war. Scarcely a month had elapsed after Polk's inauguration when Mexico severed diplomatic relations. The gesture was futile, for Mexico could not escape the power and determination of the Polk administration simply by ignoring it. Polk revealed his decision to underwrite the Texas claims, not only to recognition but also to the Rio Grande boundary, when in July he ordered General Zachary Taylor with a detachment of American troops to take up a position on the Nueces River. At the same time the Secretary of the Navy instructed Commodore J. D. Sloat, Commander of the United States fleet in the Pacific, to occupy San Francisco should Mexico declare war on the United States.

California began to worry the Polk administration in the fall of 1845. There were rumors of British designs on the Bay of San Francisco. Thomas O. Larkin, a Monterey merchant and Polk's recently appointed agent in California, informed Secretary of State Buchanan that the British and French governments were maintaining consular posts in Upper California, although neither nation had any ostensible commercial interests there. The British consul, residing on a ranch fifty miles from the coast where he could render no service to British merchants, remained in California, Larkin assured the Secretary, only to fulfill some sinister purpose. "Why they are in the Service their Governments best know and Uncle Sam will know to his cost," Larkin warned as early as July. Buchanan reported his fears to Louis McLane, United States Minister at London: "I need not say to you what a flame would be kindled throughout the Union should Great Britain obtain a cession of California from Mexico."

There was only one permanent solution to this European threat—acquisition of California. Throughout the autumn months of 1845 Polk pursued a dual program designed to acquire the province without war. Through his agent Larkin he prepared to annex the region should it, like Texas, establish its independence. Then, having been assured by informants in Mexico that the Mexican government would again accept an American commissioner, Polk in November, 1845, dispatched John Slidell of Louisiana to the Mexican capital. Through Slidell he hoped to settle the Texas boundary and purchase California directly from the regime at Mexico City. Polk authorized Slidell to offer up to $25 million for the region westward from Texas to the Pacific, including California. When Slidell was rejected by the Mexican government, Polk attempted to strengthen his diplomatic hand by dispatching General Zachary Taylor and his army to the Rio Grande, thus occupying all the territory claimed by the United States as part of Texas. By May, 1846, Polk's entire Mexican policy of acquiring California peacefully had failed. California had not achieved its independence, and Mexico had refused to sell. Moreover, when the President placed Taylor on the Rio Grande, he created a critical situation wherein a few scattered shots in a distant wilderness could involve the United States in war.

Behind the President's resort to arms lay a decade of mutual impatience and animosity. For this declining state of affairs Mexico could not escape all responsibility. Her resentment of American energy and expansionism, especially as revealed in the Texas movement for independence, was understandable. Unfortunately, this drove Mexican leaders into policies that could only produce bitter frustration and anger within the United States. Texans especially could forget neither the cruelties of Santa Anna which followed in the wake of the Alamo nor the atrocities perpetuated in the early forties by occasional Mexican raids against isolated Texas villages. American officials could not accept as reasonable the bitter Mexican reaction to Jackson's recognition of Texan independence in 1837 and the complete breakdown of satisfactory United States–Mexican relations which followed. But Mexican politicians had found it profitable politically to abuse the neighbor to the north, and by the mid-forties, especially after the American move to annex Texas, Mexican opinion against the United States was inflamed beyond control. Those who knew better, wrote Wilson Shannon, the American Minister in 1844, were not bold enough to express their opinions. Two successive Mexican governments, in 1845 and 1846, simply dared not recognize Slidell when the issues he represented were Texas and California.

Some magnanimity within the Polk administration toward Mexico might have prevented war. Mexico had broken diplomatic relations; she had not resorted to force. Time favored a return to normal diplomacy. American security, meanwhile, was not endangered. But in the balance against peace was the pressure of American public sentiment as well as a measured acquisitiveness toward California.

By May, 1846, Polk was determined to have war. His rationale for declaring it was the Mexican government's refusal to pay the claims of United States citizens against Mexico. These claims, totally legitimate, were another reflection of the chaotic state of Mexican politics. In 1839, the Mexican government had awarded American claimants a settlement of $2 million for property destroyed in Mexico. But no payment followed. Some Americans suggested during the autumn of 1845 that the United States assume the Mexican debts in exchange for California; Buchanan included such a proposal in his instructions to Slidell. Claims were no cause for war. Yet Polk, on May 9, 1846, informed his Cabinet that he intended to ask Congress for a declaration of war over claims alone. Secretary of the Navy Bancroft disapproved, preferring that the President wait until Mexico had committed some act of open hostility. That evening news arrived in Washington that, on April 25, a detachment of Mexicans had crossed the Rio Grande and fired on a company of United States dragoons. With Cabinet approval, Polk now prepared his war message, charging that Mexico had "invaded our territory and shed American blood upon the American soil." On May 13, two days after it received the President's message, Congress recognized the war and authorized Polk to accept 50,000 volunteers.

Taylor's exposed position on the Rio Grande gave the Whigs little choice but to support the President's request for volunteers, but after they had time to reconsider Polk's aggressive decisions and organize their forces for a counterattack, they turned the Mexican War into a serious political burden for the Democratic administration. Webster's apprehension rang through speech after speech: "The people . . . appear to me to demand, and with great reason, a full, distinct, and comprehensive account of the objects and purposes of this war of invasion." Several Northern legislatures, especially those of Massachusetts and Vermont, accused Polk of conducting a war of conquest designed to strengthen the "slave power" at the expense of the free states. The Whigs in Congress quite properly limited their attacks to decisions of the Polk administration; they realized that there was no slaveholders' conspiracy.

Military Action in Mexico

General Taylor took the offensive against Mexico even before Congress had approved the war resolution. Having won minor engagements at Palo Alto and Resaca de la Palma, he followed the fleeing Mexicans southward across the Rio Grande and on May 18, 1846, occupied Matamoros. Emboldened by these successes, Taylor left Matamoros in June and advanced slowly toward his major target—Monterrey, the major trading and transportation center of northeast Mexico. He followed the Rio Grande to Camargo, encamping there for six weeks while he gathered supplies. Finally in mid-August, his army of 6,000 men set out along the main road to Monterrey. As Taylor approached the city in September, his engineers reported that the city's terrain gave an overwhelming strategic advantage to the defenders. After a council of war, Taylor decided to assault the city directly, while General William Jenkins Worth with 2,000 men flanked the defenses and gained control of the Saltillo Road, thus cutting off supplies and blocking the only avenue of retreat. Worth's maneuver was a total success; several days of intense fighting gave him control of the Saltillo Road and permitted him to enter Monterrey from the west. Meanwhile Taylor, using his artillery with good effect, assaulted the city from the northeast. As the two American forces converged on the heart of the city, General Pedro Ampudia surrendered, hoping to limit the destruction. Taylor's leniency permitted the Mexican army to evacuate. In November the American invasion forces occupied Saltillo. Shortly thereafter, reinforcements reached Saltillo from San Antonio, and General Taylor prepared for a showdown with the Mexican army.

Polk was not delighted with Taylor's victories and in the pages of his diary dealt harshly with the general, accusing him of incompetence and of playing politics. Not without reason, for Whig managers were openly grooming Taylor for the party's nomination in 1848. During the autumn of 1846, Polk decided to transfer the main thrust of the American offensive to a direct assault on Mexico City through Vera Cruz. For this expedition he reluctantly selected another Whig, General Winfield Scott. To concentrate its limited resources on the Mexico City campaign, the administration ordered Taylor to establish a defense line and hold it. Convinced that Taylor's army was vulnerable, Santa Anna, having recently returned to Mexico and taken command of the Mexican army, moved northward with 20,000 men to capture or annihilate the American forces near Saltillo. During February, 1847, he struck Taylor's defenses at Buena Vista. But after one fierce day of battle, Santa Anna withdrew to San Luis Potosi. This retreat brought the north Mexican campaign to a close.

Polk's early instructions to the Pacific fleet confirmed his determination to have California in American hands at the conclusion of any war against Mexico. In May, 1846, the President ordered Colonel Stephen W. Kearny

OREGON COUNTRY
ROCKY MOUNTAINS
UNITED STATES
UNORGANIZED TERRITORY
FRÉMONT 1846
Mt. Shasta
Sacramento R.
Humboldt R.
Great Salt Lake
FRÉMONT 1845–1846
Monterey
SLOAT JULY 7, 1846
Colorado R.
Missouri R.
Mississippi R.
Fort Leavenworth
FRÉMONT 1845
SANTA FE TRAIL
Bent's Fort
Pueblo
MISSOURI
KEARNY JULY, 1846
Arkansas R.
KEARNY SEPT, 1846
Taos
Santa Fe AUG 18, 1846
Las Vegas
Los Angeles STOCKTON AUG 13, 1846
San Gabriel
KEARNY JAN 8, 1847
San Pasqual
KEARNY DEC. 6, 1846
STOCKTON JULY, 1846
San Diego
STOCKTON JULY, 1846
Gila R.
KEARNY DEC, 1846
DONIPHAN DEC, 1846
Valverde DEC 12, 1846
DISPUTED TERRITORY (CLAIMED BY TEXAS AND MEXICO)
Fort Gibson
Fort Smith
ARKANSAS
Little Rock
Red R.
Brazito DEC 25, 1846
El Paso
TEXAS
Sabine R.
LOUISIANA
Nacogdoches
Fort Jesup
Austin
New Orleans
San Jacinto
GULF OF CALIFORNIA
DONIPHAN FEB, 1847
Rio Grande R.
Sacramento FEB 22, 1847
Chihuahua
San Antonio
Goliad
Guaymas OCT 19–20, 1847
MEXICO
Nueces R.
SLOAT 1846
WOOL SEPT, 1846–FEB, 1847
TAYLOR MAR, 1846
Corpus Christi
DONIPHAN MAY, 1847
TAYLOR SEPT, 1846
Palo Alto MAY 8, 1846
SCOTT DEC, 1846
PACIFIC OCEAN
Monterrey
Matamoros
Buena Vista FEB 23, 1847
ARISTA MAY–SEPT, 1846
La Paz APRIL 13, 1847
SCOTT FEB, 1847
GULF OF MEXICO
San Lucas APRIL 13, 1847
San José MAR 30, 1847
Mazatlan NOV 11, 1847
SANTA ANNA FEB, 1847
PATTERSON JAN, 1847
Tampico
San Luis Potosí NOV 14, 1847
San Blas
SANTA ANNA MAY, 1847
SCOTT AND PATTERSON MAR–SEPT, 1847
Gulf of Campeche
Guadalajara
SCOTT OCT, 1847
Mexico City SEPT 13–14, 1847
Veracruz
SCOTT MAR 29, 1847
Manzanillo
Puebla
Cerro Gordo APRIL 17–18, 1847
SANTA ANNA MAY, 1847
SLOAT
WAR WITH MEXICO • 1846–1848
Mexican forces
Mexican victory
United States forces
United States victory
Occupied by U.S. Navy: San José
0
500
Miles

to prepare a force of frontiersmen at Fort Leavenworth for an expedition against New Mexico and California. Kearny advanced along the Santa Fe Trail and, despite warnings that the New Mexican Governor would resist an American invasion, continued to Santa Fe and occupied the village in mid-August without firing a shot. Kearny faced no resistance even when he claimed the region for the United States. Late in September, 1846, when Kearny set out for California, that province was already falling into American hands. Early in July, John Charles Frémont, on another Western exploring expedition, had supported the Bear Flag revolt at Sonoma which declared the independence of California. Several days later, on July 7, Commodore Sloat occupied Monterey, running up the American flag. Three days later, a naval force took possession of San Francisco Bay. During August, Commodore Robert F. Stockton, who had replaced Sloat, joined forces with Frémont to establish American control in Los Angeles and San Diego. Believing the region secure, both men then returned to northern California; but during September the Californians revolted and regained control of Los Angeles. Kearny, hearing of the revolt while still in the desert, fought his way into California and met Stockton at San Diego. Stockton, now reinforced, retook Los Angeles. In January, 1847, all of California was under American control.

These easy successes in Mexico and California against weakened and disorganized resistance presaged brilliant victories for Scott's expedition in central Mexico. During March, 1847, Scott's invasion forces invested the city of Vera Cruz and captured it on March 27. To avoid yellow fever in the lowlands, Scott set out immediately along the main road to Mexico City. Santa Anna, having recovered from his defeat at Buena Vista, rushed southward to meet Scott's advance at Cerro Gordo pass, and when Scott reached the pass in mid-April, he found Santa Anna in complete command of the highway. American engineers, however, discovered a route leading off to the Mexican left; over this Scott sent a division under David Twiggs. Placed under fire by direct and flanking attacks, the Mexicans retreated, Santa Anna himself narrowly escaping capture. Scott pushed on to Jalapa and on May 6 occupied Puebla. Here he prepared his final advance to Mexico City, still 75 miles to the west. Early in August, American forces entered the beautiful Valley of Mexico, flanked the Mexican defenses, and on August 20 cut up the Mexican army in two major battles—Contreras and Churubusco. At Churubusco the advancing Americans faced withering fire from the San Patricio Battalion, composed of American deserters. But Santa Anna lost a third of his effective troops in the two battles, and Mexico City lay only 3 miles away. Victories of such magnitude, deep in Mexican territory, encouraged Americans to ponder the conditions of peace.

The Treaty of Guadalupe Hidalgo

From the beginning of the war, Polk's three-pronged invasion of Mexican territory had an essentially diplomatic purpose—to gain by force what his administration had once hoped to achieve by diplomacy alone. It was Mexico's continued diplomatic resistance to Polk's wartime objectives, even in spite of American military triumphs, that compelled Washington officials to escalate the war. Had the President desired merely to guarantee the status quo antebellum, he need not have gone to the expense of a total conquest of Mexico.

During the early months of the war, the President noted repeatedly in his diary that he would accept no treaty with Mexico that did not transfer New Mexico and Upper California to the United States. Polk and his advisers viewed the ports of San Francisco and Monterey as the chief attractions in California. In June, 1846, Samuel Hooper, a Marblehead merchant, reminded the administration that a settlement at the 32nd parallel would secure Los Angeles and the Bay of San Diego. Should the United States acquire these as well as the northern ports, he continued, "it would insure a peaceful state of things through the whole country and enable [the Americans] to continue their trade as before along the whole coast." Thereafter, the administration looked to San Diego. Bancroft, Secretary of the Navy, assured Hooper that the government would accede to New England's wishes. "If Mexico makes peace this month," he wrote in June, "the Rio del Norte and the parallel of 35° may do as a boundary; after that 32° which will include San Diego." From that moment until the end of the war, the territorial aims of the Polk administration were limited to the three California ports. These war aims were in the national interest, but Polk dared not announce them publicly. The principle of territorial indemnity, under which the President hoped to acquire California, was acceptable only to those Americans who placed the responsibility for the war on Mexico. Polk did not wish to add the connotation of conquest to American military policy by revealing his war aims. To the American public, therefore, he remained silent on the subject of California as it related to the war.

Polk was so anxious to rid himself of the war that he initiated an intrigue for peace before the war had fully commenced. Informed that ex-President Santa Anna was planning to return to Mexico to resume power and that he would favor a boundary adjustment which included the Rio Grande and San Francisco Bay, Polk instructed the American commander off Vera Cruz to permit Santa Anna to pass freely into the country. The Mexican chieftain's subsequent perfidy ruined Polk's first effort at securing an immediate peace. But Webster, in a speech before the Senate in June, 1846, recommended a formal embassy to Mexico. Polk grasped at this second straw and, late in July, made formal peace overtures to the Mexican government. He saw clearly that the real crisis would occur when the Mexicans received his boundary proposals. Convinced that no administration in Mexico City could long remain in power if it ceded territory, unless it received sufficient funds to support an army, Polk followed his communication to the Mexican government with a request to Congress for $2 million to assist in overcoming the chief obstacle to peace—"the adjustment of a boundary between the two republics." The President was careful not to hint at the boundary he desired, but some members of Congress assumed logically that the President was after territory on the Pacific. The bill passed the House of Representatives but was talked to death in the Senate during the final minutes of the session. Still attempting to keep his territorial objectives secret, Polk, in his message of December, 1846, insisted that his only purpose in pursuing the war was to achieve peace.

Despite Mexico's obvious reluctance to negotiate, Polk, in his determination to escape the endless attacks in Congress and embarrassing Whig demands that he declare his war aims, grasped at the hope that the American

California State Library

Opening the West

The American West from Missouri to the Pacific was opened up and joined to the United States between the 1830s and the 1850s. It took many thousands of courageous, hardy people and an expansionist war to do the job. In the 1830s trappers and hunters pushed through Indian lands and established major trails. The 1840s saw waves of settlers in Conestoga wagons follow the same trails in search of land and business opportunities. Gold and silver discoveries brought miners and prospectors. Stage coach lines and the Pony Express kept developing communities in touch in the 1850s. The telegraph and railroads arrived in the 1860s. But the importation of Chinese laborers to work for the railroads and in the mines—such as those shown above who were part of a crew prospecting for gold in Auburn Ravine in 1852—had already laid the groundwork for the severe racial problems that emerged in the West during later decades.

John Gast's popular 1872 painting, "America's Progress," summarizes the taking of the West in a typically sanguine fashion. Progress, personified as an alabaster-breasted woman, bears a schoolbook and strings the telegraph wire as she skims the ground. That the Indians and the wild animals flee in terror before her seems to meet with total approval.

Library of Congress

OVERLAND MAIL

American Geographical Society

Library of Congress

The members of the Church of Jesus Christ of Latter-Day Saints or Mormons, formed a distinct wave of settlers. Driven out of Illinois for their religious beliefs, their communal life, and their polygamy, in 1847 they followed the Oregon trail past Fort Laramie, then turned southwest toward the Great Salt Lake in Utah. Their migration by ox-wagon and hand-cart and their subsequent prosperity in the West were firmly guided by Brigham Young (above). Young became governor of the Utah Territory before statehood. Seventeen wives survived him.

In 1848 gold was discovered at Sutter's Mill and the frantic rush to California began. By 1852 ships jammed San Francisco harbor as this three-part panoramic daguerreotype by William Shew illustrates (below). Indeed, so many ships were abandoned when even their crews deserted them for the gold fields, and so great was the demand for buildings to house expanding businesses that boats at the wharves were actually converted into stores as this possibly imaginative drawing indicates (right).

Right: Courtesy of the New-York Historical Society, New York City
Below, left, center, right: History of Photography Collection, Smithsonian Institution

EAGLE SALOON
STORESHIP
BUBB GRUB & CO
GENERAL STORE
NIANTIC HOTEL

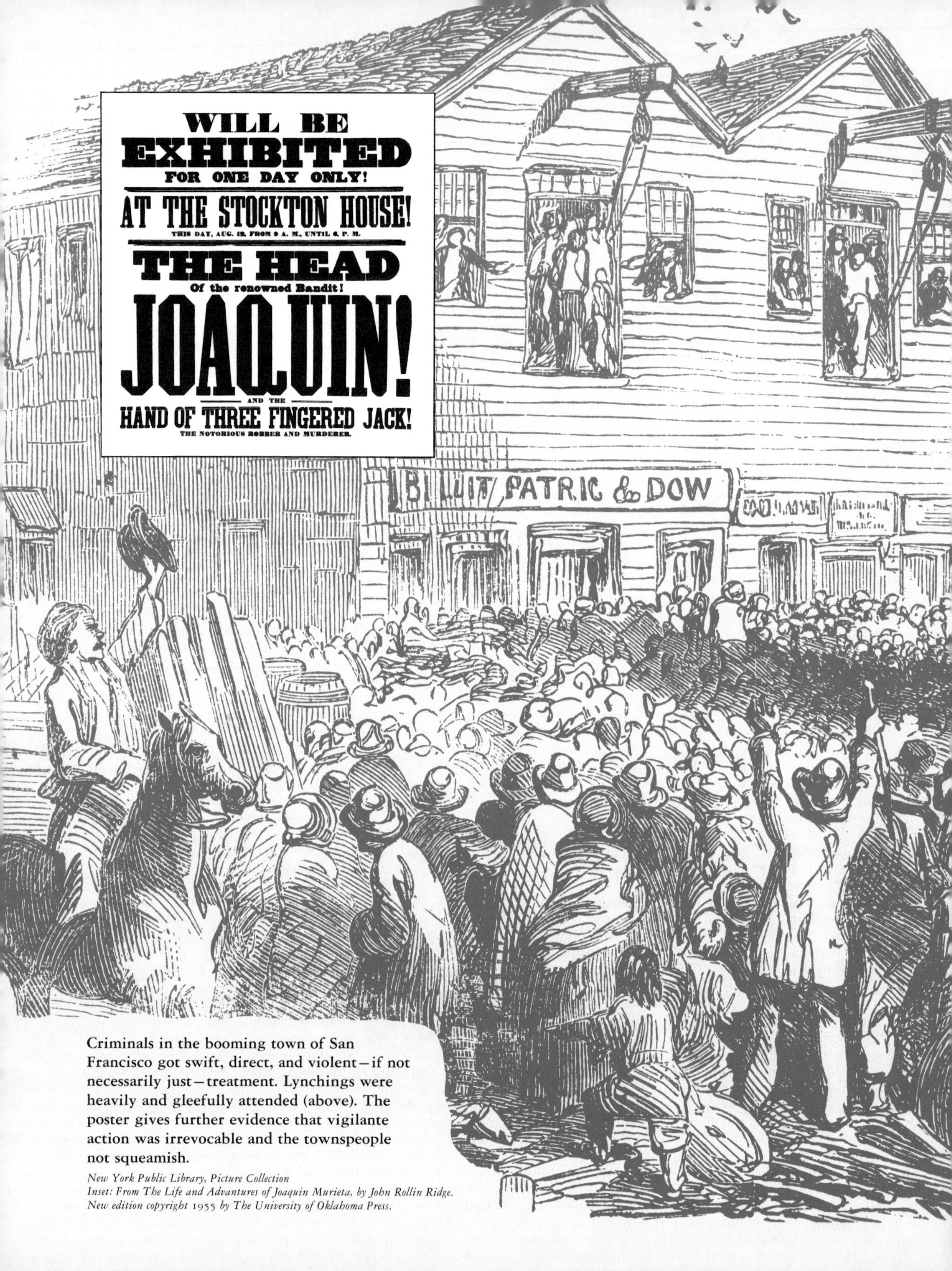

WILL BE
EXHIBITED
FOR ONE DAY ONLY!
AT THE STOCKTON HOUSE!
THIS DAY, AUG. 12, FROM 9 A. M., UNTIL 6, P. M.
THE HEAD
Of the renowned Bandit!
JOAQUIN!
AND THE
HAND OF THREE FINGERED JACK!
THE NOTORIOUS ROBBER AND MURDERER.

Criminals in the booming town of San Francisco got swift, direct, and violent—if not necessarily just—treatment. Lynchings were heavily and gleefully attended (above). The poster gives further evidence that vigilante action was irrevocable and the townspeople not squeamish.

New York Public Library, Picture Collection
Inset: From The Life and Advantures of Joaquin Murieta, by John Rollin Ridge. New edition copyright 1955 by The University of Oklahoma Press.

victories of February and March, 1847, might compel the Mexican government to admit defeat and accept his peace terms. To maintain secrecy, the President entrusted his new peace efforts to the private diplomatic mission of Nicholas P. Trist, chief clerk in the Department of State and onetime private secretary of President Jackson. Trist, departing quietly from Washington in mid-April, carried with him instructions to negotiate for no less than the entire coast of California to San Diego. Proceeding to Vera Cruz he joined Scott on the road to Puebla. Not until after the battle of Churubusco, in August, did Santa Anna agree to an armistice. He balked at Trist's terms but offered a counterproposal, which Trist forwarded to Washington for final decision. Meanwhile Santa Anna broke the armistice. Scott now made his final assault on the Mexican capital, taking Molino del Rey, after a hard battle, on September 8. Five days later his forces stormed the fortress of Chapultepec. Rather than suffer bombardment from Scott's howitzers, the officials in the capital raised the white flag. On September 17 the American Army occupied Mexico City.

Still there was no peace. Polk's initial purpose of exerting vigorous, if limited, pressure on the Mexican government—just enough to gain his precise territorial objectives—ended in miscalculation simply because no Mexican government would come forth to treat with agents of the victorious United States. By the autumn of 1847, the fear that the ephemeral nature of the Mexican governments might indefinitely prolong an expensive war convinced members of the expansionist press that the United States had no choice but to meet her "destiny" and annex the entire Mexican Republic. The *Democratic Review* observed in October: "This occupation of territory by the people, is the great movement of the age, and until every acre of the North American continent is occupied by citizens of the United States, the foundation of the future empire will not have been laid." In December, the *New York Evening Post* charged that the Mexican people did not possess the elements to exist independently alongside the United States. "Providence has so ordained it," the *Post* continued, "and it is folly not to recognize the fact. The Mexicans are *Aboriginal Indians,* and they must share the destiny of their race." During December and January, with Congress in session, Democratic orators seized control of the all-of-Mexico movement and carried this burst of expansionism to unprecedented heights of extravagance. Polk had calculated his territorial objectives too carefully to be influenced by these latest appeals to destiny. But what destroyed the all-of-Mexico movement abruptly was the work of Trist in Mexico.

When it appeared that Trist, in his armistice negotiations of August, 1847, might settle for less than his instructions demanded, Polk asked for his recall. In the letter which terminated his mission, Buchanan reminded Trist that San Diego was "for every commercial purpose of nearly equal importance to the United States with . . . San Francisco." But unknown to Washington, the elusive Mexican government made what appeared to be a serious overture to Trist and, hearing of the commissioner's recall, begged him to remain in Mexico to negotiate a settlement. Trist thereupon ignored his instructions to leave Mexico and during the month of January, 1848, negotiated the Treaty of Guadalupe Hidalgo, which was signed on February 2, 1848. In this treaty, Mexico accepted the Rio Grande as the division between Texas and Mexico and ceded all of New Mexico and California to the United States. Trist's

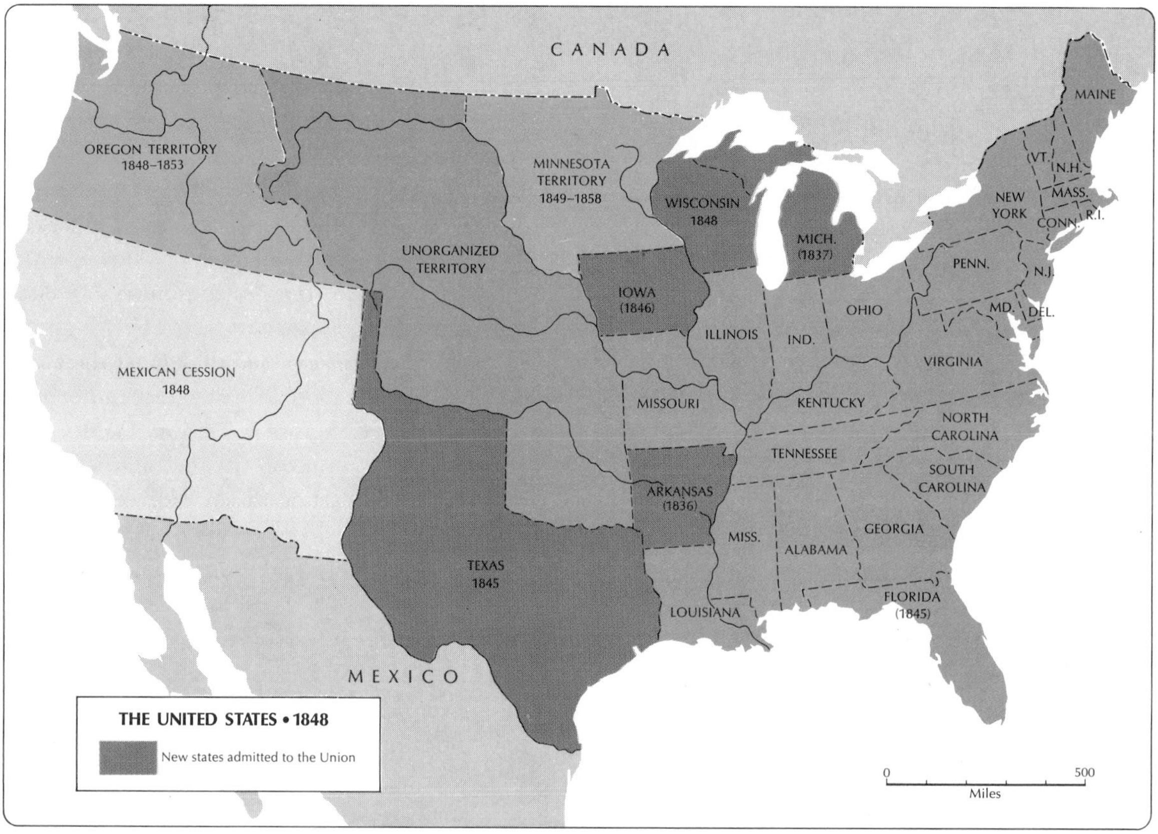

THE UNITED STATES • 1848

New states admitted to the Union

final line of demarcation across California joined the mouth of the Gila River at the Colorado River with a point on the Pacific one league south of San Diego Bay. For this Mexican Cession, the United States agreed to pay $15 million and to assume the claims of American citizens against Mexico. Polk dismissed Scott and rejected Trist, but he accepted the treaty with both hands, for it brought both the peace and the boundary settlement that he desired. Through a decade of pioneering, diplomacy, and war, an energetic, exuberant nation had carved out its continental empire. The Treaty of Guadalupe Hidalgo was merely the culmination of robust America's trek toward the setting sun.

Conclusion

So completely was the nation's responsible leadership of the forties governed, ultimately, by a sense of logic, of proportion, and of interest that its achievements proved to be both permanent and complete. For in gaining 1,300 miles of frontage on the Pacific, the United States had acquired what a full generation of seamen, merchants, and travelers had declared to be essential for the nation's future development as a Pacific power. Polk, boasting to Congress of his diplomatic achievements, pointed not to new empires of land beyond the Rockies but only to the great harbors which his administration had annexed along the distant coast.

Already in 1848 the United States was potentially the most powerful country bordering the great Pacific Ocean. This fact alone established the basis of new far-flung interests that would require the defense of diplomacy, if not war. Earlier in 1844, in the Treaty of Wanghia, the nation had secured its trading privileges in China. From the acquisition of San Francisco Bay and Puget Sound, it was but a small step to Commodore Matthew C. Perry's expedition to Tokyo Bay in 1853 to open the ports of Japan to American commerce. The immediate challenge to American power in the Pacific lay at home, however, for the nation could not make that power effective until it had linked the tiny villages of California and Oregon with the population centers of the East. Washington looked to Central America where the American interest in an isthmian canal collided with that of Britain. The Clayton-Bulwer Treaty of 1850 resolved the British-American conflict over territory, but it shelved the canal issue in the process, for both nations denied themselves the right to control or fortify unilaterally any canal which they might build.

That American sense of mission aired so fully in the debates over Texas, Oregon, California, and Mexico found another outlet in the great revolutions sweeping through Europe in 1848. The proponents of manifest destiny in Congress responded to the February Revolution in France with demands that the United States somehow guarantee its success, yet with nothing stronger or more dangerous than a congratulatory resolution. This new crusade for liberty was stimulated even further by the dramatic events in Hungary, where the Magyars under their colorful leader, Louis Kossuth, fought to cast off the yoke of Austrian Hapsburg rule. Kossuth's cause collapsed in 1849 before an invasion of Czarist troops, but the Hungarian's subsequent visit to the United States in December, 1851, turned into a triumphal procession. Yet Kossuth soon discovered, as did European revolutionaries generally, that American sentiment, whatever its appeal to democratic idealism, was no more a measure of United States policy in Europe than it had been a guide for American expansion across the continent.

SUGGESTED READINGS

Numerous books have captured the drama of exploration, trade, and settlement in the Great West beyond the Mississippi. Most notable as a survey of Anglo-American encroachment is Ray A. Billington's *The Far Western Frontier, 1830–1860** (1956). Two older, but still highly rewarding, studies of the Far West are Cardinal Goodwin's *The Trans-Mississippi West,* 1803–1853 (1922) and L. R. Hafen and C. C. Rister's *Western America* (1941). On the early trappers are three exciting works: H. M. Chittenden's *The American Fur Trade of the Far West* (3 vols., 1902); Bernard De Voto's *Across the Wide Missouri** (1947); and R. G. Cleland's *This Reckless Breed of Men: Trappers of the Southwest* (1950). G. G. Cline's *Exploring the Great Basin* (1963) is another dramatic account, as is also R. G. Athearn's more general *High Country Empire: The High Plains and the Rockies** (1960). Josiah Gregg's *Commerce of the Prairies** (1844) is the classic account of the early Santa Fe trade. Also rewarding is R. L. Duffus's *The Santa Fe Trail* (1930).

For American migration into Oregon the standard account is O. O. Winther's *The Great Northwest: A History* (1947). This is now supplemented by D. O. Johansen and C. M. Gates's *Empire of the Columbia* (1957). Also of value are R. C. Clark's *History of the*

Willamette Valley (3 vols., 1927) and the biography by Clifford M. Drury of a leading Oregon pioneer, *Marcus Whitman, M. D.: Pioneer and Martyr* (1937). Two volumes on the evolution of the Oregon Trail are Francis Parkman's classic *The Oregon Trail** (1849) and David Lavender's *Westward Vision: The Story of the Oregon Trail* (1963). A survey of early American activity in California can be found in R. G. Cleland's *From Wilderness to Empire* (1944). Biographies of two early California pioneers are James P. Zollinger's *Sutter: The Man and His Empire* (1939) and George D. Lyman's *John Marsh, Pioneer* (1930). George R. Stewart's *Ordeal by Hunger: The Story of the Donner Party* (1936) is the standard account of the tragic Donner expedition of 1846. California's early commerce can be traced in Samuel E. Morison's *Maritime History of Massachusetts, 1783–1860** (1923); Foster R. Dulles's *The Old China Trade* (1930); and Adele Ogden's *The California Sea Otter Trade, 1784–1848* (1941).

Any study of the American acquisition of Oregon and California might begin with an examination of the volumes on American expansionism by Weinberg, Merk, and Graebner cited in the preceding bibliographical essay. For the evolution of the American interest in California see R. G. Cleland's older, but still basic, *Early Sentiment for the Annexation of California, 1835–1846* (1915). Linking the far-flung activities along the distant frontier during 1846 to American expansionism is Bernard De Voto's exciting *The Year of Decision, 1846** (1943). N. A. Graebner's *Empire on the Pacific* (1955) sees American expansion to the Pacific as a search for ports. Frederick Merk's *The Oregon Question: Essays in Anglo-American Diplomacy and Politics* (1967) includes key articles published over a period of several decades. Merk's *Albert Gallatin and the Oregon Problem* (1950) is an excellent account of the Oregon negotiations of 1827. On the force of pioneering in the Oregon settlement see Melvin Jacobs's *Winning Oregon* (1938).

Several standard works relate the early history of the Mormons and their migration to Utah. W. A. Linn's *Story of the Mormons* (1902), Nels Anderson's *Desert Saints** (1942), and especially L. H. Creer's *The Founding of an Empire* (1947) are excellent accounts. For a biography of Joseph Smith see F. M. Brodie's *No Man Knows My Story* (1945). An earlier, but still useful, study of the second Mormon leader is M. R. Werner's *Brigham Young* (1925). On the economics of the Utah settlements see L. J. Arrington's outstanding *The Great Basin Kingdom: An Economic History of the Mormon People** (1958).

Justin H. Smith's *The War with Mexico* (2 vols., 1919), a highly nationalistic, but long standard, account of the Mexican War, has been challenged in most of its judgments by more recent studies. On the origins of the Mexican War the most recent book, and one which is highly critical of Polk, is Glenn W. Price's *Origins of the War with Mexico: The Polk-Stockton Intrigue* (1967). On questions of causation is the useful anthology of conflicting interpretations, R. E. Ruiz (ed.), *The Mexican War: Was It Manifest Destiny?** (1963). Three recent volumes on the Mexican War, all concerned less with causation than with the military campaigns, are A. H. Bill's *Rehearsal for Conflict* (1947); R. S. Henry's *The Story of the Mexican War* (1950); and Otis A. Singletary's brief, but judicious, *The Mexican War** (1964). Excellent biographies of the war's leading generals are Holman Hamilton's *Zachary Taylor: Soldier of the People* (1946) and C. W. Elliott's *Winfield Scott* (1937). The acquisition of California in 1848 is the special subject of Julius Klein in *The Making of the Treaty of Guadalupe Hidalgo on February 2, 1848* (1905). Pressures on the Polk administration to annex all of Mexico are delineated well in John D. P. Fuller's *The Movement for the Acquisition of All Mexico, 1846–1848* (1938).

On the growing American interest in the Far East, both before and after the Treaty of Guadalupe Hidalgo, see J. K. Fairbank's *Trade and Diplomacy on the China Coast: The Opening of the Treaty Ports, 1842–1854* (1953); Eldon Griffin's *Clippers and Consuls: American Consular and Commercial Relations with Eastern Asia, 1845–1860* (1938); F. R. Dulles's *America in the Pacific* (1932); and, on the opening of Japan, Arthur Walworth's *Black Ships off Japan: The Story of Commodore Perry's Expedition* (1946). For the Isthmian question the standard monograph is M. W. Williams's *Anglo-American Isthmian Diplomacy, 1815–1915* (1916). J. G. Gazley's *American Opinion of German Unification, 1848–1871* (1926) is excellent on the American reaction to the revolutions of 1848.

* indicates availability in paperback.

17

The Impending Crisis

CONTINENTAL EXPANSION threatened party allegiances that had held for a generation. Since the 1820s party leaders, confined by the narrow balance of regional economic interests, had built their coalitions and settled for less than they wanted. But the political climate was changing. Ambitious politicians in the Northern commercial and industrial districts were growing impatient. National policies, they charged, were out of step with progress, and progress was now measured in terms of cities, industries, and transportation facilities. These men were tired of fighting Jacksonians on matters of tariffs and internal improvements, for no group, they said, had a right to hold back the nation. Adding to their bitterness was their recurring pattern of failure. Whereas they were forced to give in on every issue, Southern Democratic opponents of governmental paternalism always seemed to have their way. The conclusion was momentous. For some Northern editors and politicians the real impediment to progress in the nation lay in a rising slave power and the national government's alleged subservience to it.

Under such circumstances a powerful minority of Americans could not view California as a legitimate national asset to be acquired by whatever means came to hand. Except for its abolitionists, even the North had accepted the annexation of Texas as a national gain. Expansion to the Pacific, however, would extend the jurisdiction of the hated slave power into a region freed by Mexican law and create additional pockets of Southern Democratic influence. On two counts—one moral and one political—Northern sectionalists determined to guarantee California's freedom in advance or prohibit its acquisition entirely. What form the sectional attack on the Polk administration's expansionist policies took would depend upon circumstances and personalities.

The Wilmot Proviso

During the brief debate of August, 1846, on the $2 million appropriation bill requested by Polk to aid him in negotiating peace with Mexico, one little-known member of Congress stumbled into immortality. While his colleagues in the House were battling the Washington heat with ice water and fans of folded newspaper, David Wilmot, a zealous member of the Van Buren wing of the Democratic party, moved to amend the administration measure by adding the proviso that "neither slavery nor involuntary servitude" should ever exist in any territory acquired from Mexico, "except for crime, whereof the party shall first be duly convicted."

The Wilmot Proviso was more than an effort to limit slavery to the South; it was an expression of political revolt. The powerful Van Buren faction had been on the verge of open rebellion against the national Democratic leadership ever since Van Buren had been deprived of the party's nomination in 1844. By opposing the expansion of slavery into California, they could not only destroy Southern dominance in the party but also embarrass Polk. Jacob Brinkerhoff of Ohio heralded the wide acceptance of the Proviso in the North "as offering unmistakable indication that the day is past when subserviency to Southern dictation is made the standard of political orthodoxy."

Southerners understood instinctively this new threat from the North. Alexander H. Stephens of Georgia recorded his anxiety in January, 1847: "The North is going to stick the Wilmot amendment to every appropriation and then all the South will vote against any measure thus clogged. Finally a tremendous struggle will take place and perhaps Polk in starting one war may find half a dozen on his hands. I tell you the prospect ahead is dark, cloudy, thick, and gloomy." Still Southern reaction to the Proviso lagged. Calhoun believed that it was a Northern issue and that the responsibility for limiting its effect on national politics lay with the North itself. His confidence in the moderate Democrats of the North was not totally misplaced, for they had not only joined the South in determining national economic policies but had also risen to the defense of the South on matters of slavery. Yet how long could they be trusted? Antislavery forces, with heavy Northern Democratic support, had carried the Wilmot Proviso through the House of Representatives. In the Senate, the bill never came up for a vote.

In February, 1847, when the administration introduced another appropriation bill to enhance its negotiating power with Mexico, Calhoun determined to base the defense of Southern rights in the territories not to the moderation of the national Democratic party but to the Constitution itself. That month he reminded the Senate that, if the North successfully excluded slavery from the territories, it would end the balance between the sections.

He issued a stern warning to the North: "The day that the balance between the two sections of the country . . . is destroyed, is a day that will not be far removed from political revolution, anarchy, civil war, and widespread disaster." Calhoun insisted that all the states had equal rights to the territories, including the right of importing slaves into them. Congress, therefore, as the agent of all the states, had no right to legislate slavery into or out of the territories. Any other conclusion, warned Calhoun, would subvert the Constitution, the rights of the states, and the Union itself. Although Calhoun's resolutions never came to a vote, Virginia's Legislature adopted his arguments in a series of resolutions, as did also Democratic conventions and mass meetings in Mississippi, Alabama, and South Carolina. Throughout the South, political extremists pledged resistance to the Proviso even if that meant such an action would eventually force the Union's dissolution.

Democratic spokesmen around Polk searched frantically for an acceptable compromise in the territories, for they were bent on national expansion. Polk and Secretary of State Buchanan favored the extension of the Missouri Compromise line to the Pacific, but Lewis Cass, leader of the administration forces in the Senate, produced the celebrated alternative of popular sovereignty in his "Nicholson letter" of December, 1847. According to Cass's plan, people of all sections would move freely into the new territories. When any new region had sufficient population to warrant a territorial legislature, that legislature would decide whether to establish or reject slavery for the region.

From the moment of its announcement, the principle of popular, or squatter, sovereignty became the official program of the moderate Democrats of the North and West. It permitted Western Democrats especially to promise their constituents new opportunities in the territories free from the competition of slave labor. This assurance lay not in any Northern legal rights but simply in the fact that Northern farmers and businessmen possessed far greater numerical strength and mobility than did the slaveholders of the South. In theory, popular sovereignty promised sectional equality in the territories; in actuality, it gave the South little chance to expand its slave system.

Southern leaders saw popular sovereignty for what it was. Although moderate Southern Democrats refused to dwell on the hopelessness of popular sovereignty as a program for the South, insisting rather that the principle of congressional nonintervention in the territories rendered the program of popular sovereignty identical with that espoused by Calhoun, diehard defenders of Southern rights viewed the Western formula as a new and dangerous challenge to sectional equality. Cass's doctrine, charged the *Charleston Mercury* in January, 1848, was merely a device to transfer political control in the territories from Northern congressional majorities to "mongrel" territorial populations consisting largely of Northerners. In mid-January, 1848, D. L. Yulee of Florida introduced a resolution in the Senate declaring that neither Congress nor a territorial legislature had the constitutional right to exclude slavery from any territory of the United States. Despite its outward appeal to the national spirit of moderation, popular sovereignty was in reality a potentially disruptive question; it was, furthermore, as dangerous to Democratic unity as the Wilmot Proviso itself.

Moderates still controlled both the Whig and Democratic parties as the country prepared for the 1848 election. Polk's Democratic party, which gathered at Baltimore in May, nominated Cass, whose residence in Michigan added to his desirability. Heavy and indolent, Cass was hardly the man to arouse enthusiasm. The platform was a bundle of platitudes condemnatory of all political efforts to meddle with the subject of slavery.

Whig leaders, called together at Philadelphia in June, were likewise prepared to pay any price for party unity and an electoral victory. Their choice was General Zachary Taylor. Before the end of 1847, Taylor had won the support of many key Whigs who recognized the minority status of their party and the desirability of nominating a popular military hero. His political views were sufficiently unknown to make him available for a party that hesitated to assume a positive stand on any but a few Whig economic issues. For Vice President, the Whigs nominated Millard Fillmore of New York, a former leader in the House of Representatives. Conservative Whigs, who controlled the convention, not only resisted all pressures to commit the party to the Wilmot Proviso; they adopted no platform at all. Yet with Taylor's nomination, the Whigs could anticipate a successful campaign. Old Zach was the man of the hour.

But the cost of Taylor's nomination came high, for the popular general was a Southerner from Louisiana and the owner of slaves. Having failed to dictate their party's platform or its candidate, the antislavery Whigs were ready to revolt. Affording the rebellion increased momentum during the summer of 1848 was the bolt of the free-soil Democrats of New York from the Democratic convention. These Van Buren Democrats had launched an organized political movement based on the Proviso when, in the autumn of 1847, they challenged the moderate Democrats for control of New York's powerful state organization. Having failed in that attempt, the New York free-soilers awaited whatever opportunities the 1848 elections might bring. When the Democratic convention nominated Cass and accepted his platform of popular sovereignty, they bolted the party, taking with them Martin Van Buren.

In mid-August such diverse antislavery elements of the North as the New York "Barnburners," New England abolitionists, "Conscience Whigs," and Liberty men gathered at Buffalo. In idealism and seriousness of purpose, no political convention in American history had ever equaled this one. The platform presented a broad program for the North—free institutions for California and New Mexico, free land for free men of the North, river and harbor improvements along the Great Lakes, tariffs for Northern industry. The delegates knew that success demanded harmony; when the committee on nominations presented the name of Van Buren, a happy pandemonium of accord broke loose. Those were days that few men present ever forgot. Despite its ephemeral nature—it was dead by 1852—the so-called Free-Soil party was an organization of major significance, for it was the first party to weld the economic aspirations of Northern industry, commerce, and agriculture to the idealism of the antislavery cause.

Taylor defeated Cass by a popular vote of

1,360,000 to 1,220,000, and his electoral majority was even more impressive. His victory, however, was scarcely reassuring for the triumphant Whigs. The Whig party had faced no issue as a national organization. In the South, Whig orators campaigned for Taylor as a slaveholder, a man whom the South could trust; in the North, they portrayed him as a proponent of the Wilmot Proviso. Thus in victory any positive decision on the slavery issue would break up that party completely. In the North, Van Buren carried not a single state, but his 291,000 votes in New York undoubtedly provided Taylor his narrow margin in that crucial state.

The Compromise of 1850

On March 4, 1849, the responsibility for resolving the thorny question of slavery in the Mexican Cession fell to President Zachary Taylor and the Whig leadership in Congress. Sectional quarrels before March had prevented every congressional effort to establish civil government in New Mexico and California. At the moment this seemed to matter little, for the Anglo-American population in the vast regions acquired by the Treaty of Guadalupe Hidalgo was still small enough to exist satisfactorily under military rule. Events in California, however, were already bringing the question of territorial government to the fore. In January, 1848, James Marshall's discovery of gold in the Sacramento Valley sparked a rush to the gold fields. Within weeks, thousands of people moved toward California—some overland by covered wagon, others by ship around Cape Horn, and still others across the jungle-ridden Isthmus of Panama. By December, 1849, California's population had reached 100,000, far more than the minimum required for statehood.

Taylor hoped to avoid a sectional conflict by disposing of the statehood issue as quickly and quietly as possible. The permanent disposal of the sectional issue, Taylor naïvely believed, required only that California and New Mexico prepare state constitutions and apply for admission to the Union as free states. By October, 1849, the Californians had framed a constitution and—without even awaiting congressional approval as required by federal statute—elected state officials as well as a congressional delegation. The President promptly recommended California's admission as a free state.

Unfortunately, the President could isolate the California issue neither from the contentiousness of Congress nor the fears of the South. There were in 1849 fifteen slave and fifteen free states, giving the South equality in the Senate. This equilibrium was believed by the South to be essential to its security. The admission of California as a free state would destroy it irretrievably. Thus when Congress reconvened in December, 1849, the Southern leadership was defiant. The parties were so splintered that caucuses meant nothing. Not until Christmas could the House elect a Speaker.

Such a crisis called for political compromise. In the waning days of January, 1850, Henry Clay presented a series of resolutions designed to settle the controversy between free and slave states. These would admit California under its free constitution; establish territorial government over the rest of the Mexican Cession without regard to slavery; redraw the Texas boundary to exclude all of New Mexico but compensate Texas by the federal assumption of her public debt; abolish the slave trade in the District of Columbia, but guarantee slavery there unless the people of Maryland and the District consented to its abolition with just compensation to the owners; pass an effective fugitive slave act; and assure the South that Congress would not interfere with the domestic slave trade. Thus did Clay seek to combine all outstanding issues into one "Omnibus bill," which would restore health to the Union and strength to the Whig party of its sponsor.

Northerners really expected little of Clay, for he was not one of them. It was the South that felt wronged by Clay's moderation, and in the Senate chamber the Southerners led the offensive against his plan. Jefferson Davis of Mississippi drew a packed gallery on February 13 when he launched the Southern attack. But the main thrust came from John C. Calhoun, so near death and so weak that his final plea for the Union had to be read by another. The Senator's reply to Clay's resolutions came on March 4, 1850. Like Davis, Calhoun saw that the real danger to the South resulted from the gradual upsetting of the old balance between the sections. Once—in the days of Washington and Jefferson—the South had felt secure in the Union. Now the North with its augmented numbers was on the verge of creating a consolidated government to pursue its own advantage. Having gained the admission of Iowa and Wisconsin, Northerners now demanded that all the new territories be carved eventually into free states. Against such aggression, the South asked for simple justice—equality in the territories, the faithful return of fugitive slaves, the end of agitation on the slavery question, and an amendment that would restore the guarantees of the Constitution. In the absence of such assurances, Calhoun concluded, the future of the Union was fraught with peril.

The North, in the person of Daniel Webster, entered the debate on March 7. But Webster, much to the chagrin of abolitionist firebrands, remonstrated with both sections to forgive and forebear in the interest of national harmony. Thanks to conciliatory attitudes like his, the crisis quickly subsided. In May a Senate committee reported out a compromise package based on Clay's resolutions. But senatorial opposition, especially among Northern Whigs, died hard, and President Taylor threw his influence solidly against the compromise. Whatever the state of public sentiment, Clay and his supporters could make little progress against such pressure. Taylor's death in July, like the death of Calhoun, removed an element of opposition. Vice President Millard Fillmore, who now entered the White House, had openly disagreed with Taylor on the compromise. His appointment of a new Cabinet revolutionized the atmosphere in Washington, and passage of the compromise was assured. When the original bill failed of passage in July, moderate Democrats, led by popular sovereignty advocate Stephen A. Douglas, promoted the legislation piecemeal, and Democratic votes quickly carried the component bills through Congress. During September, Congress completed its work on the Compromise of 1850.

In the five individual measures which formed the Compromise, Congress admitted California as a free state; it organized New Mexico as a territory under the principle of popular sovereignty, asking Texas at the same time to relinquish her western boundary claim to the Rio Grande in exchange for $10 million from the federal government; it organized Utah as a separate territory; it abolished the slave trade in the District of Columbia; and, lastly, it passed a new Fugitive Slave Act which placed federal enforcement agencies at the disposal of slaveholders. Any Negro accused of being a runaway slave lost the right of trial by jury and even the right to testify in his own behalf; a federal judge or commissioner could remand him to slavery on the presentation of merely an affidavit by any man claiming to be the owner. The law required federal marshals to uphold the act and levied heavy penalties against anyone who assisted a slave to escape. For Southerners the Fugitive Slave Act was no more than due legal recognition of their property rights and their only compensation for the admission of California as a free state. Avoiding the question of the rightness and wrongness of slavery, the Compromises of 1820 and 1850 had settled the status of that institution on every square foot of United States soil.

It became evident in the elections of 1850 that the Whig party would pay a heavy price for its role in the settlement. Webster's efforts had carried much of the North, but his refusal to condemn the Fugitive Slave law had alienated the antislavery Whigs in Massachusetts. With some Free Democratic support, these abolitionists overwhelmed the conservatives in the autumn elections. The coalition-controlled Legislature replaced Webster with antislavery Democrat Robert Rantoul and voted a six-year term to Charles Sumner. In New York, the Whig party split so badly over the Compromise issue that its only hope lay in a moderate reaction. New York replaced conservative Democrat Daniel Dickinson with another opponent of the Compromise, Hamilton Fish. Ohio sent Benjamin Wade, a bitter enemy of the Fugitive Slave Act, to the Senate, where he joined another antislavery Ohioan, Salmon P. Chase, elected two years earlier. The Compromise of 1850, in short, did irreparable harm to the Whig party of the North.

Some Southern leaders castigated the Compromise with savage fury in an attempt to prevent its acceptance in the South. Thanks in large part to Georgia's cool but decisive action, however, the diehards were frustrated. When a state convention was called for December, 1850, to consider the California bill, Georgia's newly organized Union Democrats, ably supported by Union Whigs, waged a vigorous campaign for the Compromise and were rewarded with a smashing election victory. Packed with Union delegates, the convention proceeded to adopt the famous "Georgia platform," which presented the moderate Southern position. It upheld the Compromise but warned the North that any infringement of this settlement, including modification of the Fugitive Slave Act, would terminate in disunion. State after state in the South now accepted the finality of the Compromise. Only in Mississippi and South Carolina did key leaders persist in their belief that the Compromise was a betrayal of Southern interests.

The Election of 1852

Continuance of the Compromise was the only course upon which the old Whig party could remain united. Yet it was obvious by 1852 that only to Southern Whigs was the Compromise still acceptable doctrine. So unpopular was the Compromise among Northern Whigs that no one even remotely associated with the Fugitive Slave law could win Northern support. What was for Southern Whigs the last measure of forebearance was for the North totally unacceptable. The mass of Southern Whigs nonetheless maintained their party alliance in the caucus of 1852 and even secured a campaign platform affirming the Com-

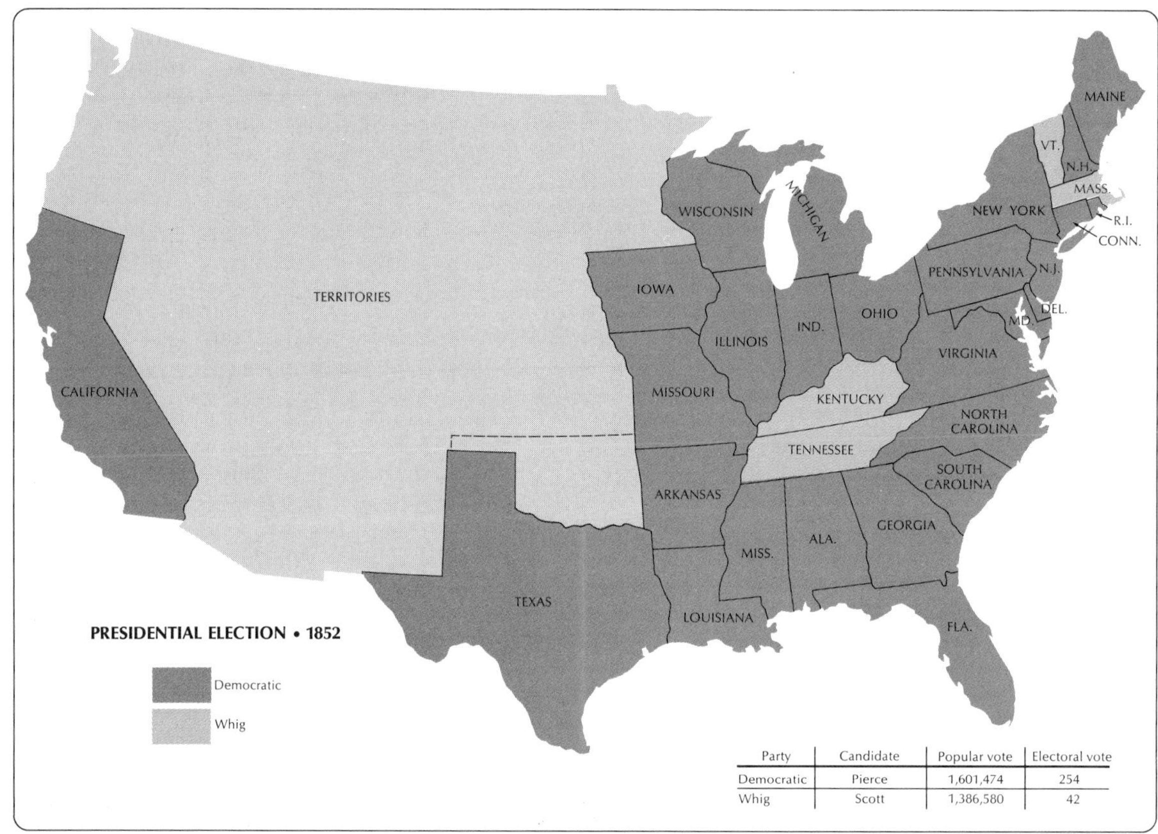

Party	Candidate	Popular vote	Electoral vote
Democratic	Pierce	1,601,474	254
Whig	Scott	1,386,580	42

promise. This formal adherence to the Compromise alienated countless Whigs, especially in the North. Widespread distrust of the Whig candidate, General Winfield Scott, among the party faithful left the Whig standard in shreds. No longer was the national Whig party capable of fulfilling the political ambitions of its adherents. Thurlow Weed admitted gravely, "There may be no political future for us."

Democratic unity and success in 1852 was not without irony. The Democratic party had borne the brunt of the extremism in both North and South in the campaign of 1848, and even after the passage of the Compromise of 1850, there was doubt that the national organization could recover its dissident elements. The split in the Southern Democracy seemed complete, but the crushing defeat of Southern extremists at the hands of the Unionists in 1851 drove them back into the Democratic fold. Both Democratic factions in the South realized finally that they required the support of Northern Democrats and that they could secure it only through party regularity. Public opinion in the South was driving all Southern factions toward an acceptance of the Compromise. On this platform, the united Democratic party of the South rejoined the national Democracy in 1852. During the debates on the Compromise, Free-Soilers had warned conservative Democrats that they must assume "decided anti-slavery ground" or they would suffer defeat at the hands of the people. But as Northern public sentiment shifted toward compromise, the vehemence of the Free-Soilers subsided. In New York, the core of the revolt of 1848, a process of fusion was well under way in 1851. In that year, a reunited Democratic organization swept most of the state offices. By the campaign of 1852, the restoration of harmony seemed complete. The Barnburners still hoped to secure a Free-Soil candidate at the national Democratic convention, but when it met in June they accepted the compromise nomination of Franklin Pierce of New Hampshire. When the Compromise plank was nailed firmly to the Democratic platform in 1852, that party became the only remaining moderating power in the nation.

Behind Pierce, the Democratic party won a landslide victory, as Scott carried only four states—Massachusetts, Vermont, Tennessee, and Kentucky. Pierce, youthful and handsome at forty-nine, a general in the Mexcian War and a lawyer, lacked the qualities of forcefulness and resiliency demanded of a successful President. Such powerful Cabinet members as Secretary of State William L. Marcy and Secretary of War Jefferson Davis dominated his administration. From conviction as well as his strong personal friendship for a number of Southern leaders, Pierce tended to accept the views of Southern Democrats on questions of sectional conflict.

The Persistent Issue of Slavery

Washington had seldom appeared more placid than during Pierce's first year in office. The new President in his inaugural praised the Compromise of 1850 as the guarantee of the country's continuing peace and prosperity. Yet those months of quiet were merely the calm before another storm. By 1854 the promise of sectional peace had evaporated. The great Compromise had not resolved the fundamental conflict in American society over the moral issue of slavery.

Abolitionist organizations in the North had never accepted the Compromise. The tiny minority of abolitionists in Congress led by Joshua R. Giddings maintained their assault on the South from their privileged position in the nation's capital. Horace Greeley's *New York Tribune* was the most influential of dozens of abolitionist-minded newspapers published from Boston to Cleveland and Chicago that belabored the South and its "peculiar institution." That the North lacked the legal and constitutional authority to touch slavery in the South the abolitionists readily agreed. Believing, however, that every fair-minded citizen must oppose the institution, they directed their appeal to the moderates in Southern society, to those who had no economic, moral, or emotional stake in the slave system.

An especially stirring abolitionist novel was Harriet Beecher Stowe's *Uncle Tom's Cabin,* published in 1852. Mrs. Stowe knew little about slavery firsthand, but as a member of a well-known and distinguished family of New England Calvinists, she had fully imbibed the doctrines of abolitionism. The pages of her book testified to her deep abhorrence of the slave system and the unhappiness and brutality it spawned. If Uncle Tom and her other characters scarcely resembled real people, their tortured existence made an indelible impression on Northern readers conditioned to believe the worst of the South. Within a year of its publication, *Uncle Tom's Cabin* had sold over three hundred thousand copies. Propaganda is more effective when it contains a considerable element of truth, and there was sufficient honesty in Mrs. Stowe's description of the evils of slavery to render the book the most influential that had yet appeared in the nation's history.

Bringing the evils of slavery home to the North most persistently was the operation of the Fugitive Slave law. Nothing could have been better designed to keep the slavery issue alive than the hunting of fugitives through the Northern streets and countrysides. The capture of a fugitive slave, even when accomplished with a minimum of disorder, served as a constant reminder of the meaning of human bondage. Many Northern abolitionists simply refused to obey the hated law. In 1851 a Unitarian minister led a Syracuse mob in the rescue of a fugitive slave named Jerry McHenry and afterward sent him on his way to Canada. That same year a Boston crowd rescued a runaway named Shadrach and arranged his escape to Canada. The legislatures of all New England, as well as those of Pennsylvania, Ohio, Indiana, Michigan, and Wisconsin, passed "personal liberty laws" which, in one form or another, forbade judges to assist Southern claimants and extended to Negroes claimed as slaves the rights of habeas corpus and trial by jury. These laws placed the burden of proof on the pursuer. In 1859 these laws drew a strong rebuke from the United States Supreme Court in the case of *Ableman v. Booth.*

Meanwhile abolitionist Whigs and Free Democrats after 1853 never relaxed their efforts to reforge the Free-Soil party. What these men needed above all was another territorial issue. Perhaps in the organization of new territories in the Louisiana Purchase north of 36°30′ some political leader might introduce the question of popular sovereignty and thus reopen the territorial debate over the slavery issue.

The Kansas-Nebraska Bill

The one issue that could revive the dangerous Free-Soil coalition Stephen A. Douglas of Illinois unwittingly supplied. The "Little Giant" was ambitious, his ultimate goal being the Presidency of the United States; and he had a program for building political fences in Illinois. His plan called for a transcontinental railroad laid westward from Chicago.

The national administration revealed its interest in such a project in 1853 when the War Department sent out engineers to survey the four feasible routes under consideration. The first was the northern route from Chicago to Puget Sound. The second was the central route from Chicago or St. Louis to San Francisco. The third and fourth routes would have tied the Far Southwest to the South through either Memphis or New Orleans. Powerful voices around Pierce favored the two southern routes because, first, they presented fewer engineering problems and, second, they traversed Texas and New Mexico, regions already organized and at least partially settled. To strengthen the claims for a southern route, Secretary of War Davis prevailed upon the President in 1853 to dispatch James Gadsden to Mexico to secure from Santa Anna, for $10 million, the Gadsden Purchase, a strip of land south of the Gila River in New Mexico lying athwart the proposed southern route. For Davis and the South the effort—though a success—was in vain. For in 1854 a congressional committee, under

Douglas's prodding, recommended a single rail link between Chicago and San Francisco.

Because of the heavy overland migration to California and the drift of settlers from Missouri and Iowa into the Nebraska Territory, Douglas decided to combine his great Western project with the organization of that territory. As chairman of the Committee on Territories, he proposed a bill in January, 1854, to organize the area without respect to slavery. Immediately a number of Southern leaders, political and ideological heirs of John C. Calhoun, combined to contest the Illinois Senator's bid for leadership. One of their number, David R. Atchison of Missouri, reminded Douglas that he needed at least four Southern votes to get his Nebraska bill out of committee. Unless slavery were permitted to enter the new territory, the votes would be withheld. Trapped between Western pressures for enactment and the need for Southern votes, Douglas offered a bill to organize the whole of unorganized Louisiana Territory, leaving the question of slavery "to the desire of the people residing therein, through their appropriate representatives." Douglas had no interest in the expansion of slavery and believed that his doctrine of popular sovereignty would exclude it from the territories. The Calhounites came to the same disturbing conclusion; with administration support they forced Douglas to offer a substitute bill creating two territories, Kansas and Nebraska, and including a specific repeal of the line of the Missouri Compromise. If the people of the new territories so voted, such a measure would make possible the introduction of slavery north of the old 36°30′ line. It was generally believed that Kansas, being adjacent to Missouri, a slave state, would vote in slavery but that Nebraska would be free.

The Kansas-Nebraska bill gave abolitionists in Congress a long-awaited opportunity. Douglas had reopened the one question on which these men could again appeal to the North on the powerful platform of the Wilmot Proviso. He had not only resurrected the question of slavery in the territories but was now applying it to regions immediately at hand—not the deserts of New Mexico a thousand miles from the frontiers of the Midwest. For years Chase, Giddings, and Sumner had awaited the issue that would permit the creation of an antislavery party capable of sweeping the North and thus controlling the nation. On January 24, 1854, Chase and his colleagues issued a document attacking the Kansas-Nebraska bill "as a gross violation of a sacred pledge; as a criminal betrayal of precious rights; as part and parcel of an atrocious plot to exclude from a vast unoccupied region immigrants from the Old World, and free laborers from our own states, and to convert it into a dreary region of despotism, inhabited by masters and slaves." The paper accused Douglas of bad faith and demagoguery in overthrowing the Compromise of 1850; it touched on very vital interests of the North and Northwest—free land, railroads, and markets. The effect was electric: indignation reached from Maine to Iowa. Throughout the North, antislavery politicians, clergymen, and editors attacked Douglas's bill with vituperation seldom witnessed in American politics.

Despite all opposition, political maneuvering forced the Kansas-Nebraska bill through Congress. Douglas later boasted: "I passed the Kansas-Nebraska Act myself. I had the authority and the power of a dictator through the whole controversy in both houses." Douglas could even chastise his enemies on the floor of the Senate. Perhaps political bargains were the decisive factors in driving the bill through the

House. In any event, the final measure corresponded closely to Douglas's original bill; it organized both Kansas and Nebraska Territories divided at the 40th parallel, permitting the people of those Territories to be "perfectly free to form and regulate their domestic institutions in their own way." Here was the principle of popular sovereignty. The Missouri Compromise line was specifically repealed.

Passage of the Kansas-Nebraska Act in May, 1854, exposed the fundamental geographic cleavage in Northern politics. Thirteen Northern congressmen who voted for the measure represented southern Ohio, Indiana, and Illinois, as well as Iowa, Pennsylvania, and New York. Twenty-six Democratic, Whig, and Free-Soil representatives from Ohio, Michigan, Wisconsin, northern Indiana and Illinois voted against it. The Lake region, represented by a combination of antislavery Whigs and Democrats again united in a great moral cause, had broken from the Jacksonian Ohio Valley.

Reaction to the Kansas-Nebraska Act

Throughout the North and Northwest, fusion meetings of Conscience Whigs and Free and Free-Soil Democrats, called to defy the Kansas-Nebraska bill, began to forge a new sectional party. Joseph Warren, editor of the *Detroit Tribune,* called a convention at Jackson, Michigan, with the following appeal: "Our proposition is that a convention be called irrespective of old party organizations, for the purpose of agreeing upon some plan of action that shall combine the whole anti-Nebraska, anti-slavery sentiment of the State, upon one ticket." In July, 1,500 enthusiasts attended a mass meeting at Jackson, adopted a free-soil platform, and gave their new party the name "Republican." This old Jeffersonian designation quickly swept the North. Antislavery politics in the mid-fifties at last carried some assurance of political success.

Southern extremists prepared to meet this new challenge to their interests, but they faced resistance everywhere. The vast majority of people residing in the South had not desired the Kansas-Nebraska Act. Many Southern editors were bitter over its introduction; it would become the rallying cry, they knew, for another antislavery agitation. But as the South felt the sting of Northern charges, editors and politicians began to appeal for Southern unity behind Douglas's measure. At issue now was the vindication of principle. If the bill itself was not significant, Northern determination was. The *Charleston Mercury* posed the key question: "Can the South stand listlessly by and see the bill repealed, when this is made the direct issue against her. . . .? There is no alternative for the South. When the North presents a sectional issue, and tenders battle upon it, she must meet it, or abide all the consequences of a victory easily won, by a remorseless and eager foe." Southern Democrats stood firmly behind Douglas. Southern Whigs, impressed by the determination of the Democrats to defend Southern equality in the territories, went over to Douglas without hesitation.

With the slow demise of the Whig organization, many Unionist Whigs embraced the incipient Know-Nothing party. This party's native American platform appealed to traditional American prejudices against foreigners, especially Catholic foreigners. The Know-Nothings opposed the election of Catholics to office and favored more stringent requirements for naturalization and citizenship. They enjoyed a brief but mushroom growth in the mid-fifties. The shock of the Kansas-Nebraska Act left thousands of ex-Whigs seeking some conservative refuge that would defend them against the radicalism of the age. Many preferred the Know-Nothing party to the Democratic party or the new Northern fusion parties. For many conservative Whigs, this promised to become the new national party to replace the old Whig organization. Between 1854 and 1856, the Know-Nothings revealed great vitality and energy, especially in New England, New York, Pennsylvania, Maryland, and the Ohio Valley—wherever the tides of Unionism ran strong.

In the fall elections of 1854, the Democratic party lost 350,000 votes and carried only two of the Northern states holding elections. In New York, the anti-Nebraska men almost swept the congressional elections. In Pennsylvania, the Whig–Know-Nothing fusionists carried the state Legislature and sent twenty-one anti-Nebraska men to Congress, losing only four seats. In Massachusetts, the Know-Nothing–Free-Soil coalition elected the Governor and gained control of the Legislature. Anti-Nebraska elements swept the elections in New Hampshire and Maine. Anti-Nebraska men captured every congressional district in Ohio and all but two in Indiana. Both states had gone Democratic in 1852 by wide margins. In Illinois, the Know-Nothings and Republicans gained control of the Legislature and elected five out of nine candidates to Congress. In Iowa, an anti-Nebraska Legislature assured the defeat of conservative Democratic Senator Augustus D. Dodge. This upsurge of Know-Nothings and Republicans almost eliminated the Whig party from national politics. The party of Clay and Webster failed because, in its desire to remain national, it refused to give full voice to the antislavery sentiments of the nation. The future lay with the anti-Nebraska parties, especially the newly organized Republicans. Kansas presented the occasion for their ultimate success.

Bleeding Kansas

Perhaps the majority of those who entered Kansas in 1854 and 1855 viewed the Territory as a typical American frontier to be exploited in the interest of profit. Among them were ordinary farmers, businessmen, and speculators, who had no interest in any sectional struggle for control of the territories. Whatever their motives in moving to Kansas, however, most Northerners in the Territory opposed slavery expansion. Some, indeed, had received assistance from antislavery emigrant societies. To offset this Northern element, pro-Southern leaders in Missouri prepared to control Kansas by flooding it with slaveholders, proslavery sympathizers, and border ruffians.

From the beginning, the Northern farmers and merchants who settled around Lawrence and Topeka comprised a clear majority of the Kansas population. To manage the political evolution of Kansas Territory in accordance with federal procedures, President Pierce dispatched Andrew H. Reeder to Kansas as territorial governor. When Reeder called a general election early in 1855, large numbers of Missourians crossed into Kansas to cast illegal votes which assured the election of a proslavery legislature and the establishment of slavery in the Territory. The free-soil elements were incensed. They sent delegates of their choosing to a constitutional convention at

Topeka and there framed a free-state constitution. The two parties and two governments began to maneuver for advantage.

In such a situation an explosion was inevitable. Whether Kansas bled or not was not as important historically as the fact that the Republican party was entering its first national campaign and desperately needed an issue. Kansas alone could keep alive the free-soil issue on which the party had been built. After violence erupted in Kansas in 1855, Northern and Republican editors had their cause, and they interpreted events in that unhappy territory to suit their own political requirements.

In May, 1856, the "sack of Lawrence" presented an episode of high excitement in the story of "Bleeding Kansas." A federal marshal, determined to arrest the free-state leaders in Lawrence, gathered a posse which attacked the village in a clear and inexcusable case of frontier outlawry. The mob destroyed Lawrence's two "free" presses, the unoccupied Free State Hotel, and damaged some shops and houses. There were two human casualties, both accidental and both Southern. Thereafter Kansas settled down to a desultory guerrilla warfare in which dozens of men were ultimately killed. The struggle was not merely over the slavery issue but over the location of county seats or the direction of internal improvements, all of which had some bearing on rising land values. But to writers seeking to inflame the Northern imagination terror was stalking the land. Throughout the North, antislavery editors called mass meetings to encourage emigration to Kansas. At a Chicago gathering in late May, over one hundred local citizens announced their intention to settle in Kansas. The assembly pledged $15,000. Similar meetings from Boston to Buffalo subscribed funds to win Kansas for freedom. Republicans portrayed the issue as a question on which hinged freedom and Northern civilization itself.

Bleeding Kansas eventually led to violence on the floor of Congress. A tense audience jammed the Senate on May 19, 1856, to hear Charles Sumner's diatribe on the "Crime against Kansas." He denounced as sacrilege and robbery the South's effort to seize Kansas and, having put the South in its place, turned to a personal vilification of his chief opponents in the Senate, the aged Andrew Pickens Butler of South Carolina and Douglas of Illinois, concluding with a lengthy tirade against the state of South Carolina. What Sumner's speech was unable to accomplish in arousing Northern sentiment on the slavery and Kansas questions Preston S. Brooks achieved shortly thereafter. This tall, amiable, and popular congressman from South Carolina, a kinsman of Butler, brooded two days over the printed speech. Then, on the morning of May 22, he entered the Senate chamber and found Sumner alone at his desk. He quickly accused Sumner of publishing a libel against his state and his relative, and with this, he proceeded to rain blows on Sumner's head with his cane. From the Northern press, pulpit, and platform, "Bully" Brooks was now attacked as a symbol of Southern depravity. The incident, declared the *New York Times,* "aroused a deeper feeling in the public heart of the North than any other event of the past ten years."

Time and issues had carried the nation far toward disruption since the Mexican War when Wilmot first introduced his Proviso. In 1846 politicians had still argued over tariffs, banks, and internal improvements. By the mid-fifties, Kansas had come to symbolize all the questions in conflict.

The Election of 1856

Less than one month after the stirring events of May, 1856—the "sack of Lawrence," Sumner's speech, and Brooks's assault—the Republican National Convention met at Philadelphia. Some delegates were old Free-Soil party leaders of 1848; others were newcomers from Whig ranks. Wilmot himself reported out the brief platform. It demanded the immediate admission of Kansas as a free state, and a federally supported railroad to the Pacific. For its candidate, the party chose John C. Frémont, a man of no political experience. Frémont was not a strong candidate, but his moderation on the slavery issue and his broad reputation as an explorer and man of action made him eminently suitable. Republicans entered the election with the conviction that victory was within their grasp.

Events elsewhere were aiding the Republican cause. As long as the nation had supported four parties—Democratic, Whig, Republican, and Know-Nothing—the Democratic party with its Jacksonian tradition and national organization was impossible to defeat. In June, the Democrats met at Cincinnati and nominated James Buchanan as a gesture of conservatism and devotion to national unity. But the Whig party had been eliminated. In New England, New York, and Ohio, most Whigs had joined the Republican party; in Maryland and Tennessee they moved into the Know-Nothing party, also known in 1856 as the American party. Elsewhere in the South, they either drifted into the Democratic ranks or acted with the Americans. In addition, the Know-Nothings were in obvious trouble. Their antiforeign, anti-Catholic bias limited their appeal except among the most conservative voters. Then their efforts to resolve internal party differences over slavery ended in confusion. When the party convention nominated Millard Fillmore and refused to repudiate its Kansas-Nebraska platform of 1855, Northern delegates withdrew, declaring that they could not support a party which so flouted Northern opinion. Most of them entered the Republican ranks. The Know-Nothing party had become sectional, its strength limited to Southern moderates who preferred the American party to the Southern Democracy.

With two parties all but eliminated in 1856, the campaign was reduced to a race between Frémont, representing a strong sectional coalition, and the Democrat Buchanan, leading the only remaining national party. When the ballots were counted in November, the Democratic party had held firm enough in the North to win. Buchanan received 174 electoral votes to 114 for Frémont. With the aid of conservative Whig votes, the Democratic party carried Pennsylvania, New Jersey, Indiana, Illinois, and California. Frémont carried all of New England, New York, and the entire Lake region, plus Iowa. Meanwhile, the last two powerful Democratic spokesmen of the Great Lakes country, Lewis Cass of Michigan and Henry Dodge of Wisconsin, lost to two Republicans. The Republican party had revealed power and energy in those areas of the North which were expanding most rapidly in wealth and population. Like the old Free-Soil party, it had aligned itself with progress and humanity. In the South the Know-Nothings carried Maryland; elsewhere the Democratic party was in control.

James Buchanan entered the White House in March, 1857, backed by a Democratic party whose continued unity rested on its ability to avoid the acceptance of any specific interpretation of popular sovereignty. Douglas claimed that the first settlers in a territory, through local or territorial governments, could exclude slavery. This would prevent, almost from the outset, the movement of slaves into a new region. Southern Democrats insisted that a territory could not make this decision until it wrote its principles into a state constitution. This would permit slaves to move freely into any of the territories. Douglas and other party leaders simply refused to face this issue during the 1856 campaign. Southern leaders knew that Buchanan favored their interpretation, but they also knew that playing with such political dynamite might blow up the party. At that moment, the Supreme Court was considering a case involving the Missouri Compromise that promised to settle forever the question of slavery in the territories. Southerners anticipated a pro-Southern decision and believed naively that the nation would accept it quietly.

In March, 1857, Chief Justice Taney read his famed decision in the case of *Dred Scott v. Sanford.* Dred Scott, born a slave in Missouri, had been taken by his owner, an army surgeon, to Illinois and then to Minnesota Territory, a territory freed of slavery by the Missouri Compromise. When Scott returned to Missouri, abolitionists persuaded him to sue for his freedom on the ground that his temporary residence in Minnesota made him free. When the Missouri Supreme Court rendered a decision against Scott, the stage was set for the highest court in the land to have its say on the matter of slavery in the territories. Speaking for the majority, Taney argued that the constitutional authority of Congress to make all needful rules and regulations for the territories did not extend to the prohibition of slavery. The Louisiana Purchase had been acquired by Congress for common use and equal benefit. Since the right of property in the form of slaves was distinctly and expressly affirmed by the Constitution, any congressional or territorial regulation which prevented anyone from holding slaves was void. Slaves were a legal form of property, and Congress had the further obligation to protect such property. Taney's argument completed the nullification of the Missouri Compromise.

For both the Republican and the Democratic parties, the Dred Scott decision was tragic. It rendered the basic plank of the Republican platform unconstitutional. At the same time it confronted Southern Democrats with their last fateful decision. They could seek the South's future security either in the legality of its principles or in the continuance of the national Democratic party. They could not do both. Democratic unity demanded that Calhoun's claims for Southern rights in the territories remain buried out of sight. But the Dred Scott decision made them the law of the land. Taney thus eased the path of Southern extremists attempting to convince the South that the future of Southern society rested on the hopeless question of slavery expansion. But the Western proponents of popular sovereignty, led by Douglas, refused to accept the principle that slavery might exist in the territories until statehood. For them, popular sovereignty was both the embodiment of frontier democracy and the only doctrine that would render the Wilmot Proviso, and thereby the Republican party, unnecessary.

Buchanan was extremely anxious to rid the nation of the divisive Kansas issue, and he thought to do so by bringing the region into the Union as a state. To this end, he dispatched Robert J. Walker to Kansas to arrange the necessary constitutional convention. When Walker arrived in Kansas, he saw that local lawlessness, rivalry, and speculation would make the functioning of popular sovereignty all but impossible. He warned Southern leaders in the territory that any Kansas constitution not submitted to the people of Kansas would be rejected by Congress. Since the Free-Soilers had by 1857 lost confidence in Kansas democracy and refused to take part in the election of delegates to the constitutional convention, the convention which met at Lecompton was completely pro-Southern. Predictably, the meeting adopted a frame of government protecting existing slave property. It gave the people of the Territory no choice but to ratify the constitution with or without the *further* introduction of slavery. Walker refused to accept either the constitution itself or the conditions of ratification.

What was to be done about Kansas was now up to the President. Under heavy Southern pressure, he repudiated Walker and committed both his administration and the Democratic party to the Lecompton constitution. The President wanted to dispose of the question promptly, and he felt that if the majority of Kansans opposed slavery, they would soon right matters there. When the Kansas convention, with administration approval, submitted the constitution for ratification, the Free-Soilers boycotted the election and permitted the constitution to pass.

Buchanan at first tried argument and patronage to break up the congressional anti-Lecompton bloc, but he finally realized that only a compromise would pass Congress. William H. English of Indiana, an administration Democrat, then proposed a House and Senate conference. The English bill would actually resubmit the constitution to the people of Kansas. If the Kansans accepted the constitution, they would receive statehood and a federal land grant. If, on resubmission, the residents rejected the constitution, the admission of Kansas as a state would be delayed until the population had reached the minimum required for a congressional seat. This move broke the ranks of the anti-Lecompton Democrats (led by Douglas of Illinois) and permitted the passage of the bill. But Kansans rejected the terms offered by Congress, thereby leaving the territorial issue alive for the politicians and keeping Kansas out of the Union.

Lincoln and Douglas

In Illinois, Abraham Lincoln prepared for the senatorial canvass of 1858, determined to drive home the wedges already splintering the Democratic party. Born in Kentucky on February 12, 1809, Lincoln had spent most of his boyhood in the wooded country of southwestern Indiana. In 1830, his family moved on to Illinois. For several years he worked as a rail-splitter, storekeeper, and postmaster in the tiny village of New Salem on the Sangamon River. In 1836 he entered the practice of law and during the following year moved to Springfield, the new capital of Illinois. During the next twenty years, he developed into one of the most successful lawyers in the state. As an old-line Whig he remained endlessly active in Illinois politics; for many years his existence was one of caucuses, conventions, and speeches. But until 1858 his efforts had won few successes—some local and state offices and one term in the United States House of Representatives. Lincoln's Whig views had failed to capture much support on the Illinois frontier, and his fundamental conservatism had dictated a marked hesitancy on the slavery question. Not until the Kansas-Nebraska Act gave that issue special significance did Lincoln seize it as a proper subject for debate. He was soon in the vanguard of Douglas's opposition in Illinois, challenging the Little Giant at every turn.

Lincoln, distinguishing clearly between slavery and its extension, took his stand on tradition and the law. As a moderate free-soiler, he attacked popular sovereignty as totally illogical. "What better moral right," he asked, "have thirty-one citizens of Nebraska to say that the thirty-second shall not have slaves than the people of the thirty-one States have to say that slavery shall not go into the thirty-second State at all?" Then Lincoln posed the core appeal of the Wilmot Proviso. "The whole nation," he said, "is interested that the best use shall be made of these Territories. We want them for homes of free white people. This they cannot be, to any considerable extent, if slavery shall be planted within them." Lincoln was no abolitionist, but like most free-soilers, he was willing to call slavery a moral wrong. His moderate condemnation of slavery, in contrast to Douglas's official attitude of unconcern for the institution, gave him support among antislavery groups where Douglas had none. Lincoln, however, accepted the principle of white supremacy. "There is a physical difference between the black and white races," he declared, "which will forever forbid the two races from living together on terms of social and political equality."

For Lincoln, seeking national recognition as a Republican leader, Douglas in 1858 was an ideal opponent, for the Illinois Democrat was the leading candidate for the Democratic presidential nomination in 1860. During the early weeks of the campaign, Lincoln pursued Douglas around Illinois to avail himself of the latter's larger crowds. Finally, in July, Lincoln challenged Douglas to a joint debate. The latter, well knowing that he had everything to lose, accepted reluctantly. Lincoln surmised that Douglas, if forced to publicly defend his views of popular sovereignty, must alienate either the voters of Illinois or his party's leaders in the South. Douglas had struggled to avoid this dilemma. He had escaped a quarrel with the South over the Kansas-Nebraska bill by terming it merely "a question of self-government." He had refused to question either the Cincinnati platform of 1856 or the Dred Scott decision. After the Lecompton debate of 1858, he continued to offer the South what he had in the past—an equal chance in the territories.

In Freeport's dusty square, on August 27, Lincoln posed the essential question haunting Douglas and the Democratic party: "Can the people of a United States territory . . . exclude Slavery from its limits prior to the formation of a state constitution?" Douglas responded with a tone of impatience: "I answer emphatically . . . that in my opinion the people of a Territory can, by lawful means, exclude slavery from their limits prior to the formation of a State Constitution . . . slavery cannot exist a day or an hour anywhere, unless it is supported by local police regulations." Thus Douglas was declaring that the people of a territory had the lawful means to introduce or exclude slavery as they saw fit. Douglas had stated his Freeport Doctrine a year earlier at Springfield and repeatedly in Congress.

Lincoln's questioning merely dramatized the hopelessness of continued Democratic unity. Douglas won the senatorial race in the Illinois Legislature later that year, but Lincoln saw the lasting significance of the debates. No longer could Douglas hold his party together. In their exchanges Lincoln and Douglas raised questions fundamental to all governmental action. How was the nation to terminate its historical involvement in the human tragedy of slavery? More than any other American of his age, Lincoln recognized this implication in the sectional conflict. Whatever the depth of the American predicament, it was obvious to him that the nation could not escape indefinitely the obligation to resolve it. In June, 1858, he reminded a Springfield audience that the conflict over slavery had not diminished. Nor would it cease, he warned, "until a *crisis* shall have been reached and passed. 'A house divided against itself cannot stand.' I believe this government cannot endure, permanently *half slave and half free.*"

Like the vast majority of Americans, Lincoln did not believe that the division would of necessity be ended with the sword. If Kansas remained free, Lincoln insisted, the entire slave structure would ultimately crumble. This doctrine permitted him to speak the language of peace and moderation and simultaneously promise the triumph of Northern principles. Whatever Lincoln's peaceful intent, however, freedom's victory still required no less than a constitutional amendment or the unconditional surrender of the slaveholders to the antislavery demands of the North. It seemed clear in the late fifties that such a capitulation would require some deep conviction among Southern planters that slavery had become a material liability. As late as 1860 that conviction was not apparent. Possessing no realistic formula for achieving the peaceful elimination of slavery in the teeth of the South's determination to maintain it, neither Lincoln nor any other antislavery politician or abolitionist of the North could present the nation with any genuine alternative but civil war to indefinite coexistence with slavery. Clearly the choices before the nation were scarcely reassuring.

The Vincible South

For the American people, the fifties were an expansive decade, whether measured by material progress at home or new dreams of empire abroad. No aspect of national life failed to respond to the great economic boom that roared along, ever upward, until 1857, when speculation and the overextension of credit again brought the nation's wealth-seekers to earth. Meanwhile, the acquisition of California in 1848 had by no means terminated the quest for new lands to annex. Cuba proved to be as enticing as it was elusive. Throughout the fifties, Democratic orators, North and South, proclaimed a crusade of annexation, denying that Spain had the right to hold the island in subjection when American destiny seemed so apparent. In October, 1854, the United States Ministers to Spain, England, and France submitted to the Pierce administration the so-called Ostend Manifesto, demanding that the United States acquire Cuba by war if not by purchase. But neither they nor the proponents of manifest destiny in Congress could discover the occasion for converting their territorial ambitions into policy. Nor were the filibustering activities of William Walker in Nicaragua between 1855 and 1857 any more productive of territorial gain. The fifties passed, despite all the claims to destiny, without any territorial gains other than the Gadsden Purchase.

Whatever their mutual hopes, interests, and ambitions—and they were legion—the North and the South in the fifties stood apart as two civilizations, increasingly distinguishable by almost every measure of human existence. Life in the North was competitive, energetic, and realistic, although European travelers also found it warm and hospitable. Here was a civilization in ferment, revealing an astonishing expansive power and mobility on every hand: crowded cities marked by opulence and poverty; mill towns, villages, and farms—all centers of an amazing productivity; pioneers and railroads building new communities in the West; river and lake steamers jammed with people on the move; German and Irish immigrants in search of new homes; popular commercial entertainment featuring P. T. Barnum and Jenny Lind. No less spectacular was the world of the intellect, subjecting every aspect of American civilization to close scrutiny. Here was a world of scholars, essayists, novelists, poets, and reformers to which no nation of Europe could offer a parallel.

Like the North, the South had its commercial and marketing centers, its villages and farms. But the uniqueness of its culture centered in its great plantations. Tradition, stability, and contentment were the hallmarks of Southern civilization—at least for the minority who enjoyed its advantages. Here was a world of magnificent mansions, of outdoor kitchens and slave quarters; of Creoles, Negroes, and mulattoes; of steamboats, cypress swamps, and crowded wharves; of cotton and tobacco; of hominy and corn pone; of gander pullings, hoedowns, and camp meetings; of gambling and dueling; of style and elegance; of poverty and repression; of violence and honor. This was a strange world, romantic and self-conscious, knowing its faults but unwilling, from fear and insecurity, to admit their existence. It was a civilization out of touch with reality. Even its future in a democratic nation was problematical, for it was not democratic.

The South did not lack its defenders who praised its elitism as the essence of its grandeur and the source of its strength. Constructing a sectional self-consciousness was an arduous task, but aggressive editors, clergymen, and politicians pursued that goal relentlessly. Their control of the Southern churches, press, and other media allowed them to build a Southern spirit. Southern writers carried the proslavery arguments of Calhoun forward to their logical conclusions. George Fitzhugh went so far as to declare in his *Sociology for the South* (1854) that slavery was preferable to all other forms of labor. "Free Society!" exclaimed one Southern editor. "We sicken of the name! What is it but a conglomeration of greasy mechanics, filthy operatives, small-fisted farmers, and moonstruck theorists? All the Northern and especially the New England states are devoid of society fitted for well bred gentlemen."

Cotton created another article of faith. Its rapid expansion in the forties and fifties gave it an appearance of strength. David Christy's *Cotton Is King* (1855) furnished the statistics and the arguments to render plausible the kingship suggested by the title. Southern confidence in the economic power of cotton underlay the aggressiveness and arrogance of Southern spokesmen as they made demands on the federal government or ran roughshod over various executive departments during the fifties. As late as 1861, Senator Hammond of South Carolina could declare: "I firmly believe that the slave-holding South is now the controlling power of the world; that no other power would face us in hostility. Cotton, rice, tobacco, and naval stores command the world. . . . The North without us would be a motherless calf, bleating about, and die of mange and starvation."

Buchanan's Presidency furthered the illusion of Southern power. Douglas's Freeport Doctrine was not reassuring, but under Buchanan, the South still determined the nature of national policy. Southern doctrines, as embodied in the Dred Scott decision, enjoyed the total acceptance of the Buchanan administration. Whatever Southern votes could not prevent in homestead, internal improvement, and railroad legislation in Congress, Buchanan could dispose of by presidential veto. Buchanan's administration was an anomaly. "Old Buck" had been nominated and elected as a member of the conservative machine that had managed the Democratic party since Polk's election in 1844. Although a Pennsylvanian, he had as President surrounded himself with Southern advisers, had accepted the Southern view of the territories, had vetoed Northern economic legislation, and had perpetuated Southern prestige in national councils far beyond existing Southern power if measured by population. Most Southerners did not care to ponder what would occur when he retired from the White House.

If abolitionism had touched the South's defenses, slaveholders generally took refuge in the fact that the attacks on their institutions came from outsiders who really knew nothing about their section. Suddenly, in 1857, a North Carolinian, Hinton Rowan Helper, dealt the South's moral and economic defenses a crushing blow. That year Helper, a non-slaveholding white who had come to detest slavery, published *The Impending Crisis of the South,* in which he sought to prove statistically that the Southern slave system had limited the South's economic growth. It was slavery, wrote Helper, that held much of the South and most of its people in poverty and backwardness. Only through the destruction of the slave system could the South enter the American race for wealth on terms equal with the North. Here was an antislavery argument from the pen of a Southerner, aimed not at the immorality of the slaveholding minority but at the economic self-interest of the majority. In 1860, only about one-fourth of all Southern white families owned slaves; the landed aristocrats who owned more than 100 slaves numbered only 3,000.

Why did the South's free population permit the planting aristocracy to commit the entire section to the defense of the slave system? Men seldom react rationally to real or imagined dangers, and the emotion-ridden Southerners of the fifties were no exception. Perhaps poorer non-slaveholding whites were too much caught up in the slave system to understand that they were its victims. If slavery hobbled their freedom, they were not conscious of it. Slavery, after all, gave status to the poor whites and even to those free farmers who were not poor. Would not an emancipated Negro, moreover, be a more formidable competitor than a slave? Many whites who regarded slavery as an obstacle to their progress had emigrated from the slave states. Most of those who doubted the morality or economic soundness of the slave culture had simply left.

Southern men of affairs—especially those in the Whig tradition—often desired nothing more than to mine coal, manufacture iron, build railroads, and spin cotton in Dixie, and they saw clearly that the achievement of such goals required both government-financed internal improvements and Northern markets. Their tragedy—and that of the nation—lay in their unwillingness to preserve their political associations with Northerners who shared their nationalism but who also identified themselves, largely as Republicans, with the cause of free soil. Though not slaveholders themselves, Southern lawyers and businessmen were often bound economically to those who held the slaves. Unwilling to break openly with their fellow Southerners on the issue of slavery and slavery extension, they demanded in vain that conservatives of the North discard the antislavery component in their program.

The general rejection of Helper's appeal by the South's free whites simply reinforced the dilemma faced by Northern antislavery reformers. The only hope for the peaceful elimination of slavery from the nation lay in the willingness of the South's business and small farming interests to join the attack on the institution. But the Southern groups that lay outside the nexus of the slave system, whatever their personal convictions, had too little in common to organize effectively against those who owned slaves and had a vested interest in retaining them. It was the failure of the nonslaveholding elements in the South to contest the leadership of the planter minority that permitted the latter to become the arbiters of the South's destiny.

Southern complacency received another rude shock in October, 1859. Backed by the moral and financial support of well-known Northern antislavery men, John Brown and a small band of men seized the federal arsenal at Harper's Ferry, hoping by this bold stroke to begin a general slave revolt and insurrection throughout the Southern countryside. Should that purpose fail, Brown hoped to conduct a guerrilla war from the hills of western Virginia. Brown was captured, tried, and sentenced by a Virginia court, and hanged a month later. But if Brown was dead, his spirit marched on. Henry Thoreau compared Brown's execution to the crucifixion of Christ, and Ralph Waldo Emerson wrote that Brown had made "the gallows as glorious as the Cross." Overnight, abolitionists established Brown as the martyr of the age.

The South was visibly shaken. John Brown's raid was an irresponsible attack from the North that no Southerner could ignore. It suddenly came home to many that Northern abolitionism, in preaching a crusade against slavery, jeopardized Southern society itself. If the North could not control its abolitionists, the South had no defense except secession.

The Republican Triumph

At Charleston in 1860, Democratic politics reached an impasse. Douglas and his supporters had tried in vain to change the Democratic convention site to another city, for Charleston was the nerve center of Southern extremism. Southern Democratic leaders had narrowed the choices confronting the convention to rule or ruin. Rather than accept Douglas and Southern inequality in the territories, they would create a Southern-rights party with a candidate and platform of its own. They were assured the support of the galleries and of the Buchanan forces who agreed with them that Douglas must be rejected.

Before the convention could reach the nominating process, it broke up over the platform. No amount of accommodation could close the gap between the Southern demand for

Steps That Led to War

The issue of Free Soil became a focal point in the political life of the 1850s, the point from which leaders North and South took the steps which led the nation into civil war.

The antislavery cartoon here shows "Slavery Being Forced Down The Throat of a Free Soiler" by leading Democrats—Stephen Douglas and

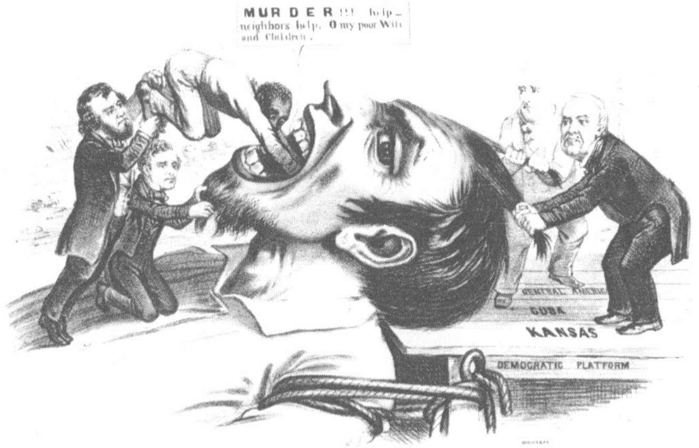

Courtesy of the New-York Historical Society, New York City

Franklin Pierce at left, James Buchanan and Lewis Cass at right. All of these politicians were Northerners themselves. In the popular call for creation of new states in the West, these Democrats sought to maintain unity with the Southern wing of the party by supporting the idea of popular sovereignty—the idea that the new territories could decide for themselves whether they wished to be free or slave states. As the cartoon shows, the idea was interpreted as proslavery by Northern Abolitionists who saw in it an issue which could be used as a rallying cry for their own political campaigns. Out of the Free Soil issue came the struggles of "Bloody Kansas," the demise of the Whigs, the split of the Democratic party, and the creation of the new Republican party. Out of it, above all, came the dynamic escalation of animosity between the North and South as each reacted and counter-reacted to the moves of the other.

"UNION IS STRENGTH."

FREE STATE

CONVENTION!

All who are favorable to union

of effort, and a permanent organization of all those who desire to make Kansas a Free State, and who wish to secure, upon the broadest platform, the co-operation of all who agree upon this point, are requested to meet in their respective districts, and appoint Delegates who shall meet in general Convention at

BIG SPRING, THIRD DISTRICT,

On Wednesday, September 5th,

For the purpose of adopting a Platform upon which all may act harmoniously who prefer Freedom to Slavery.

The nomination of a Delegate to Congress, will also come up before the General Convention.

Every District will be entitled to five Delegates for each Representative apportioned by the Governor previously to the last election.

Let no sectional or party issues distract or prevent the perfect co-operation of Free State men. Union and harmony are absolutely necessary to success. The pro-slavery party are fully and effectually organized. No jars nor minor issues divide them. And to contend against them successfully, we also must be united. Without prudence and harmony of action we are certain to fail.

Let every man then do his duty and we are certain of victory.

All Free State men, without distinction, are earnestly requested to take immediate and effective steps to insure a full and correct representation for every District in the Territory.

The Delegates to represent the First and Second Districts in the Convention, will be chosen on the occasion of the

Mass Meeting

To be held at Lawrence on August 14th. The residents of these Districts are requested to attend this meeting.

"United we stand; divided we fall."

By order of the meeting held at Lawrence, July 17, 1855.

["Kansas Free State" Print.]

Spread: Library of Congress
Insets, right and far right: Rare Book Collection, Library of Congress

The Free Soil issue took on specific identity in 1854 when Douglas pushed through Congress the bill establishing Kansas and Nebraska as territories. Almost immediately proslavery forces from Missouri and Free Soil forces backed by Northern Abolitionists moved into Kansas and commenced a fierce struggle, political and physical. Most publicized of the latter was the "sacking of Lawrence," shown here (inset above) in an illustration from *The True History of the Kansas Wars* by O. W. Merrill. A broadside of the period (inset left) carries an appeal typical of the Free Soil group. Between 1855 and 1857 Kansas had two constitutional conventions, one led by Free Soilers at Topeka and another at Lecompton controlled by the proslavery faction. This contemporary magazine illustration (spread) shows the presence of firearms and whiskey jugs at Topeka.

The election of 1860 marked the downfall of Stephen Douglas (left), the "Little Giant" who as Illinois Senator had pushed through the Compromise of 1850, put across the Kansas-Nebraska Act, and who thought that as president he could bridge the differences between Northern and Southern Democrats. When the Democratic Convention assembled in Charleston, South Carolina, in April of 1860, Southern Democratic leaders wanted a platform plank based on the Dredd Scott Decision in which the Supreme Court held that slavery was an unabridgable property right. This position, combined with 100° heat and crowded dormitory conditions resulted in short tempers, rioting on the floor, and massive walkouts by Southern delegations (right, above). The convention disbanded before nominating could begin; when it reassembled in Baltimore, Douglas got the nomination but a splinter wing of the party dominated by Southerners put up its own candidate, John C. Breckenridge of Kentucky. The Currier and Ives cartoon below depicts the divisive forces within the Democratic Party and their impending destruction by the Republicans under the leadership of Abraham Lincoln. As the alliance between Northern and Southern Democrats came to an end, the forces of secession prepared to take control of the South.

All pictures: Library of Congress

Clear the track!
Look out for the Engine, when the bell rings!
EQUAL RIGHTS
LINCOLN AND HAMLIN
ORM.
DEMOCRATIC NATIONAL NOMINATION
BRECKINRIDGE AND LANE.

full federal intervention in behalf of the almost-nonexistent slave property in the territories and the new Douglas compromise which suggested vaguely that the question of slavery extension be left to the Supreme Court. As the debates on the platform continued, the exchanges became more heated and pandemonium broke out on the floor. Convinced by the first ballot that they could not control the convention, Southerners refrained from voting.

After the platform was adopted by Northern votes, the Alabama delegation marched out of the hall, followed closely by the delegations from Mississippi, Louisiana, South Carolina, Florida, and Tennessee, plus scattered delegates from Arkansas, Missouri, Georgia, Virginia, and Delaware. The dominant proslavery leadership of the South now stood together in defiance of the North. Meanwhile, the convention maneuvered to bring the defiant Southerners back. In the interest of party harmony, the New York delegates blocked an easy Douglas nomination by insisting that he receive two-thirds of the votes of the entire convention, not merely two-thirds of those remaining. As Douglas failed repeatedly to obtain more than a bare majority of the ballots, the hopelessly deadlocked convention voted to reassemble again in Baltimore in June.

At the Front Street Theater in Baltimore, the Douglas men were firmly in control, but tension reappeared as the Southern delegations entered the convention, reiterating their sectional demands. When the balloting started and the Southerners had still not secured the withdrawal of Douglas, one Southern delegation after another left the theater and congregated at Market Hall, there to be joined by delegates from New York, Pennsylvania, Oregon, California, and Missouri. Douglas swept what was left of the convention and won the nomination. The bolters named John C. Breckinridge of Kentucky. A Southern convention which met at Richmond endorsed his nomination. The party had finally split into sectional factions. But the South had paid the greater price because it had more to lose. Whatever happened to Douglas, the North would triumph.

Republicans faced the campaign of 1860 confident and united. Much had happened in four years to increase Republican strength. Old Whig managers—Seward, Weed, and Lincoln—had modified the party's idealism and broadened its economic program to appeal to every economic interest in the North. By 1860 the Republican platform asked for tariff increases, homesteads, internal improvements, and a transcontinental railroad. Though abolitionists may have deplored the lukewarm idealism of the new leadership, they had no thought but to support the party. The major task confronting the party managers gathered at Chicago in May, 1860, was to find a presidential candidate acceptable both to the party's idealistic crusaders and to its conservative free-soilers and newcomers, who had assumed much of its control. Seward had been too long identified with the extremists; Edward Bates of Missouri, the other front-runner, was too conservative and Whiggish. Abe Lincoln, a novice in national politics who stood between the extremes, became the compromise choice.

Although Republican enthusiasm gave the 1860 campaign a guise of excitement, the near certainty that Lincoln would win made much of the campaigning seem irrelevant. Lincoln's task, and that of his party, was to convince the North that its interest in free soil was safe only in Republican hands and that popular sovereignty in Democratic hands was really no defense of Northern rights and principles at all. In his Cooper Union address of February,

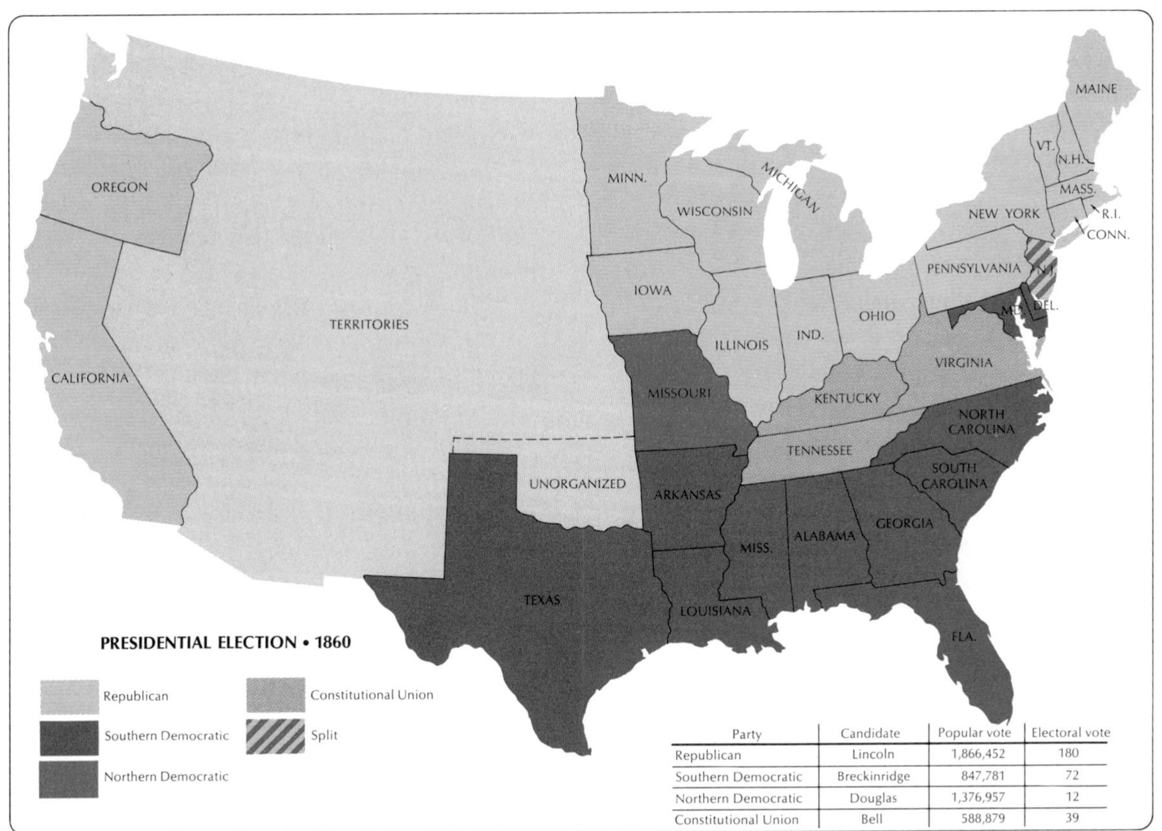

Party	Candidate	Popular vote	Electoral vote
Republican	Lincoln	1,866,452	180
Southern Democratic	Breckinridge	847,781	72
Northern Democratic	Douglas	1,376,957	12
Constitutional Union	Bell	588,879	39

1860, Lincoln had developed further his arguments in behalf of free-soilism. It was the *wrongness* of slavery, he said, that aroused the Northern opposition to its expansion. How could Douglas and the Northern Democrats really prevent slavery's expansion if they refused to call it wrong? Only those who insisted openly that slavery was immoral, Lincoln argued, possessed the determination or even the right to contain it. During the campaign, Republican editors and orators centered their condemnation of Douglas on the Cooper Union theme.

Douglas bore the burden not only of holding his Northern Democratic constituency but also of reassuring the South that it had nothing to fear from his election. In the political climate of 1860 this purpose proved impossible of achievement. In the North, Douglas could say nothing in behalf of popular sovereignty to prevent Democrats from bolting in droves to the Republican party. In the South, he battled his enemies on the issue of disunion, but few Southern Democrats were inclined any longer to support the author of the Freeport Doctrine.

Lincoln carried the entire North in November, yet he was a minority President, polling scarcely 40 percent of the popular vote. Both the Republican and Democratic parties increased their voting percentages over 1856. Lincoln increased the Republican vote by 120,000 in Pennsylvania, by 30,000 in New

Jersey, by 45,000 in Indiana, and by 76,000 in Illinois. Douglas ran a strong second to Lincoln in the popular vote (1,375,157 to 1,866,452) but carried only one state – Missouri. The Constitutional Union party, organized in 1860 to capture the conservative Unionist vote, adopted no platform on slavery. That party's wide appeal in the Unionist border states permitted its nominee, John Bell of Tennessee, to carry Virginia, Kentucky, and Tennessee. Breckinridge carried the remaining slave states. Lincoln's victory, however, did not result from the Democratic schism. Had all his opponents agreed on one candidate, he would still have pocketed all his states but California and Oregon, leaving him 21 electoral votes above a majority. Lincoln's victory resulted rather from the fact that he carried, albeit by narrow margins, those heavily populated regions of the Northeast and the Great Lakes where political and economic power had been accumulating for a decade.

The Secession Crisis

As Southerners studied the November election, they were unsure of the proper course to follow. Breckinridge's vote in the South was no evidence of overwhelming secessionist sentiment, and it is doubtful if the majority of the people in the region ever favored the breakup of the Union. Southern moderates reminded the South that Lincoln had been elected without any violation of the Constitution, and they inquired bluntly how Lincoln's Presidency could injure their section. Lincoln had obligations to the Constitution and could override the will of neither Congress nor the Supreme Court. With the support of Northern Democrats, the South could prevent the passage of a Republican program, for the Republican party had won control of neither house. Even if Republican principles held in the territories, the South could hardly lose what it never possessed. Southern Unionist editors warned that secession was less a remedy for the South's problems than were the guarantees of the Constitution.

But the Unionists were no match for their Southern opponents in exploiting crisis psychology. Such effective clichés as "Black Republicanism" and "Northern aggression," plus the threatening tone of Northern speeches and editorials, strengthened the hand of the Southern extremists. After years of expounding the doctrines of Southern rights, South Carolina fire-eaters had at last found the occasion for uniting the South in a confederacy of its own. On December 20, 1860, a convention at Charleston unanimously dissolved "the Union now subsisting between South Carolina and the other states under the name of 'the United States of America.' " Elsewhere in the South, leading politicians urged delay to give the Republican leadership a fair trial, but they were pushed aside by the excitement of the day. "The people are run mad," reported Alexander Stephens of Georgia. "They are wild with passion and frenzy, doing they know not what." By February 1, 1861, Georgia, Alabama, Mississippi, Florida, Louisiana, and Texas had left the Union. On February 4, delegates from the seceded states met at Montgomery, Alabama, and quickly organized the Confederate States of America, with Jefferson Davis of Mississippi as President and Stephens as Vice President. Even the radicals who dominated the conventions conceded the basic political truth that the secession was the work of an organized

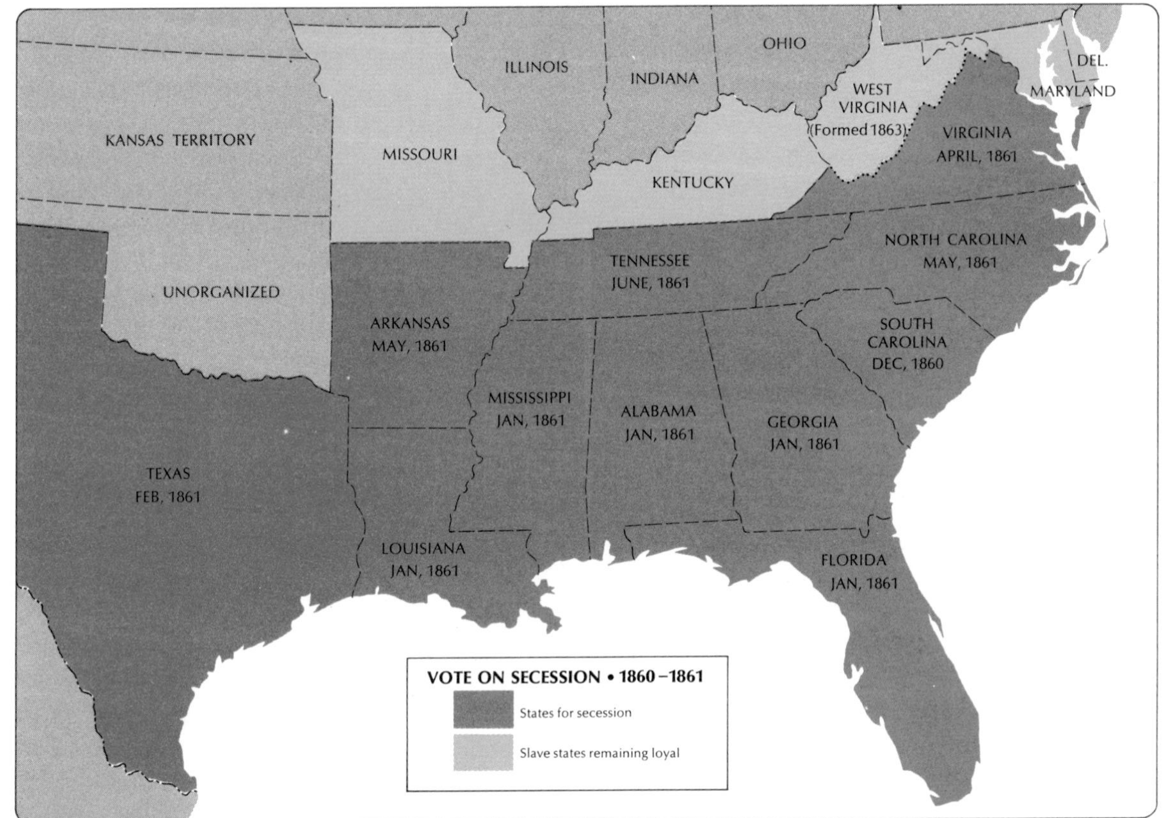

minority. This being true, their victory was never complete, for throughout the South, partisans of the Union continued to exist.

President Buchanan, in Washington, faced the secession crisis a deserted man. In his December message he denied the legality of secession. The Founding Fathers never intended to implant in the Constitution the seeds of its destruction. He had taken an oath to execute the federal laws, he declared, and no human power could absolve him from that obligation; he would continue to collect revenues and hold federal property in the seceding states. But Buchanan disclaimed all authority to use coercion. It was Congress's obligation, he said, to reestablish the proper relationship between the seceding states and the federal government. Yet he doubted that even Congress possessed the authority to use force. At the President's suggestion, Congress accepted the challenge to frame compromise measures, the Senate creating for this purpose its Committee of Thirteen under John J. Crittenden of Kentucky, and the House its Committee of Thirty-three under Thomas Corwin of Ohio. Crittenden's formula of December, 1860, became the basis of the compromise maneuvers in Congress, although his own committee refused to accept it. This plan took the form of a series of constitutional amendments which would reestablish the Missouri Compromise line of 36°30′, with slavery prohibited north of the line and protected to the south of it; deny to Congress the right to interfere with slavery in the states where it existed, as well as in the District of Columbia; protect the domestic slave trade from congressional action; compensate owners for fugitive slaves lost because of violence; and guarantee the South that no future amendments would alter the first five provisions.

While the moderates of North and South, in Congress and out, searched for a compromise, the crisis deepened. As one Southern state after another left the Union, state troops in each seized federal forts and arsenals, customhouses and post offices, naval vessels and revenue cutters, and even a United States mint. All that remained under federal control in the South by January, 1861, was Fort Sumter at Charleston, Fort Pickens at Pensacola, and Forts Taylor and Jefferson off the southern coast of Florida. Buchanan dispatched a merchant vessel, *Star of the West,* to supply Fort Sumter, but when its captain faced fire from the shore batteries in Charleston Harbor, he quickly withdrew. Thereafter, Republican leaders noted shrewdly, any opposition to a vigorous and uncompromising stand against the South could be—and certainly was—termed abject cowardice.

Searching for an adequate party response to the challenge of secession, Republican leaders gradually united on a firm stand in opposition to both disunion and compromise. In speeches and caucuses, they declared their disapproval of Southern behavior. Late in December, a large group of prominent Republicans met in Washington and agreed unanimously "that the integrity of the Union should be preserved, though it cost millions of lives." In Congress, Republican leaders organized to defeat the compromise measure, demanding that the South return to the Union before any concessions even be considered. They refused to surrender the free-soil plank of the Chicago platform. Whenever any of the Republicans wavered, observed one correspondent, "he [was] shot down in an instant by his comrades." The Republican minority moved from one anticompromise victory to another. When the final vote on the Crittenden compromise came before the Senate early on the morning of March 4, 1861, Crittenden himself moved to offer as a better solution the proposals of the peace conference which had been held in Washington during February. But Southern senators disagreed and united with the Republicans to overwhelm the substitute, 28 to 7. Then the Senate rejected the original Crittenden proposals, 20 to 19, with all the Republican votes cast on the negative side.

Conclusion

Republican leaders rejected compromise in part because it was politically dangerous, in part because it would serve no useful purpose. Free-soilism as embodied in the Chicago platform defined the Republican party's distinguishing purpose; to discard it would threaten the party with annihilation. It was a purpose, moreover, which the vast majority of Republicans took seriously. For them any compromise purchased at the sacrifice of free-soilism would be a worthless arrangement. To the Republican party, in short, the South and not the North was in error. The total responsibility for reforging the Union peacefully, therefore, lay with the secessionists.

But for the reasons which prompted their

departure the Southern states would not return, except on their own terms. They demanded guarantees which no Northern faction, least of all the Republicans, would grant them. This state of the Southern mind—and it was crucial to the events of 1861—would not lend itself to a simple or conclusive explanation. Undoubtedly Southern secessionist attitudes were an expression of fear. At stake, many believed, were both the slave system and whatever economic security the South enjoyed. For the planters, large and small, slavery represented an established labor system and a huge capital investment. To desert slavery under moral pressure, moreover, would require not only an economic adjustment but also an admission of past error. Thus national unity in 1861 rested on the North's willingness to permit the South to resolve the slavery issue in its own time and fashion. Lincoln, indeed, assured Stephens in December, 1860, that he would not interfere with slavery where it enjoyed the protection of the Constitution. Yet Lincoln added: "You think slavery is right and ought to be extended, while we think it is wrong and ought to be restricted. This, I suppose, is the rub."

Lincoln understood the crisis. The Republicans had made clear their deep dislike for slavery; this was not reassuring even if an immediate threat to slavery's existence was scarcely discernible. What magnified Southern fears—and resentments—were the antics of some Northern abolitionists. *DeBow's Review,* published in New Orleans, complained of them in 1860: "Misanthropy, hypocrisy, diseased philanthropy, envy, hatred, fanatisism, and all the worst passions of the human heart . . . continue to be the ruling characteristics of the New England Yankees." For some Southerners Clay's economic program, now the possession of a powerful Northern party, comprised a special threat to Southern agrarianism. Repeatedly in the fifties Southern leaders—and some historians in later years—pointed to the South's vulnerability to Northern economic power and policy. Still many lawyers and businessmen of the South had no interest in slavery and states' rights or any fear of tariffs and internal improvements. Economic and social tradition, however, had wedded them not only to the South's planter-dominated power structure but also to the extremists who rationalized that structure. The refusal of the Southern Unionists to defend their section against the growing power of extremism was the key to the secession movement. When a minority of extremists bound the future of Southern civilization to the elusive quest for equality in the territories (there were two slaves in Kansas in 1860), it could only split the Democratic Party and invite a Republican victory. Even then the disorganized conservatives were powerless to counter the ensuing secessionist movement. Southern hopes and fears—both tied to slavery—had been exaggerated, but they had gripped the emotions of sufficient numbers to determine the course of the South's behavior. Those who knew better had lost control.

SUGGESTED READINGS

Whatever the sectional pressures dividing the nation after 1840, they would, in large measure, endanger the Union only to the extent that they caused deterioration of the national political parties. For that reason the coming of the Civil War cannot be divorced from political history. An excellent interpretive and readable survey of the disruption of the parties, written from a moderately pro-Southern point of view, is Avery Craven's *The Coming of the Civil War** (1942; rev. ed., 1957). Craven has distilled this volume's basic themes in his *Civil War in the Making,* 1815–1860* (1959). Also his *The Repressible Conflict,* 1830–1861 (1939) remains a classic. Dwight L. Dumond reveals more sympathy toward the abolitionists in his *Anti-slavery Origins of the Civil War** (1939). Allan Nevins has covered the years from 1847 to 1861 magnificently in four volumes: *Ordeal of the Union* (2 vols., 1947) and *The Emergence of Lincoln* (2 vols., 1950). More recent is Roy F. Nichols's *The Stakes of Power,* 1845–1877 (1961). Joe H. Silbey's *The Transformation of American Politics,* 1840–1860* (1968) is an important study. A. C. Cole's *The Irrepressible Conflict,* 1850–1865 (1934) is an informative social history of the period.

Thomas J. Pressley in *Americans Interpret Their Civil War** (1954) dwells on the historic problems of Civil War causation. Two highly useful anthologies, again revealing the argument over causation, are Edwin C. Rozwenc (ed.), *Slavery as a Cause of the Civil War** (1949) and Kenneth M. Stampp (ed.), *The Causes of the Civil War** (1959).

Among the biographies of Northern leaders of the fifties are studies of two Democratic conservatives: Philip S. Klein's *President James Buchanan: A Biography* (1962) and I. D. Spencer's *The Victor and the Spoils: A Life of William L. Marcy* (1959). George Fort Milton's *The Eve of Conflict: Stephen A. Douglas and the Needless War* (1934) and Gerald M. Capers's *Stephen A. Douglas: Defender of the Union* (1959) are highly sympathetic accounts of the Illinois leader. Don E. Fehrenbacher's *Chicago Giant: A Biography of "Long John" Wentworth* (1957) traces the career of another Illinois leader. Glyndon G. Van Deusen has written the standard biographies of three leading New York Whigs: *Thurlow Weed: Wizard of the Lobby* (1947); *Horace Greeley: Nineteenth Century Crusader** (1953); and *William Henry Seward* (1967). David Donald's prizewinning *Charles Sumner and the Coming of the Civil War* (1960) is an outstanding study of the fifties.

Several Southern spokesmen of the fifties have also been portrayed in adequate biographies. U. B. Phillips's *Robert Toombs* (1913) and Rudolph von Abele's *Alexander H. Stephens* (1946) analyze the careers of two important Georgia Whigs. J. H. Parks's *John Bell of Tennessee* (1950) portrays the life of the noted Tennessee conservative. Laura A. White in *Robert Barnwell Rhett: Father of Secession* (1931) traces the career of the South Carolina extremist. On Jefferson Davis, see William E. Dodd's *Jefferson Davis* (1907); Robert McElroy's *Jefferson Davis: The Unreal and the Real* (2 vols., 1937); and the more recent, and highly laudatory, Hudson Strode's *Jefferson Davis: American Patriot* (1955).

Such specific conflicts as the Wilmot Proviso debates, the Compromise of 1850, and the Kansas-Nebraska Act have stimulated their share of excellent historical writing. The general studies previously listed, as well as the pertinent biographies, contain essential information on the country's successive sectional clashes. C. B. Going's *David Wilmot: Free-soiler* (1924) includes a full account of the authorship of the Proviso. J. A. Garraty's *Silas Wright* (1949) concludes with a discussion of the political turmoil in New York. Free-soilism in the election of 1848 receives adequate treatment in T. C. Smith's *The Liberty and Free Soil Parties in the Northwest* (1897). A useful biography of the Democratic candidate of 1848 is Frank B. Woodford's *Lewis Cass* (1950). Holman Hamilton's *Zachary Taylor: Soldier in the White House* (1951) and Brainerd Dyer's *Zachary Taylor* (1946) are excellent studies of Taylor's election and Presidency. Holman Hamilton's scholarly account of the Compromise of 1850, *Prologue to Conflict** (1964), supersedes all previous efforts to analyze the actions of Congress. A useful anthology on the Compromise can be found in Edwin C. Rozwenc (ed.), *The Compromise of* 1850* (1967). R. H. Shryock's *Georgia and the Union in* 1850 (1926) relates the political response of an important Southern state.

Good biographies of the candidates of 1852 are Roy F. Nichols's *Franklin Pierce: Young Hickory of the Granite Hills* (1931) and Charles W. Elliott's *Winfield Scott* (1937). The standard biography of Harriet Beecher Stowe is R. F. Wilson's *Crusader in Crinoline* (1941). On the Kansas-Nebraska issue, P. O. Ray's *The Repeal of the Missouri Compromise* (1909) has been superseded, in large measure, by J. C Malin's *The Nebraska Question,* 1852–1854 (1953). Roy F. Nichols has analyzed the pressures of Southern politicians on Douglas in "The Kansas-Nebraska Act: A Century of Historiography," *Mississippi Valley Historical Review,* XLIII (September, 1956).

Among the specialized accounts that trace the rise of the Republican party in the fifties are Andrew Wallace Crandall's *The Early History of the Republican Party, 1854–1856* (1930); Floyd B Streeter's *Political Parties in Michigan, 1837–1860* (1918); and Jeter A. Isely's *Horace Greeley and the Republican Party, 1853–1861* (1947). For a more general account see George H. Mayer's more recent and scholarly *The Republican Party, 1854–1964** (1964). On Know-Nothingism the standard work is Ray A. Billington's *The Protestant Crusade, 1800–1860** (1938). A more recent study of merit is W. D. Overdyke's *The Know-Nothing Party in the South* (1950).

On the issue of Bleeding Kansas, the standard account is J. C. Malin's *John Brown and the Legend of Fifty-six* (1942). Stressing again the frontier nature of the Kansas conflict is Paul W. Gates's *Fifty Million Acres: Conflicts over Kansas Land Policy, 1854–1890** (1954). The discrepancy between what occurred in Kansas and what Northern reporters and editors told their readers is revealed in the excellent article by Bernard A. Weisberger, "The Newspaper Reporter and the Kansas Imbroglio," *Mississippi Valley Historical Review*, XXXVI (March, 1950). Allan Nevins's *Frémont: Pathmaker of the West* (1939) is a brief, well-written biography. Roy F. Nichols's *The Disruption of American Democracy** (1948) is a brilliant Pulitzer prizewinning study of the Buchanan years.

Two good volumes on the Dred Scott case are Vincent C. Hopkins's *Dred Scott's Case** (1951) and C. B. Swisher's *Roger B. Taney** (1935). Robert W. Johannsen has edited the republication of the original 1860 volume of the Lincoln-Douglas debates in *The Lincoln Douglas Debates of 1858** (1965). Far more inclusive is Paul M. Angle (ed.), *Created Equal? The Complete Lincoln-Douglas Debates of 1858* (1958). Eugene H. Berwanger's *The Frontier against Slavery* (1967) traces in detail the anti-Negro prejudice of the Old Northwest and the Far West. Allan Nevins's *The Emergence of Lincoln* (2 vols., 1950) contains excellent chapters on Northern and Southern Life and thought in the late fifties. The best study of Southern society and politics in the 1850s is Avery Craven's *The Growth of Southern Nationalism, 1848–1861* (1953). On the economy of the period see G. W. Van Vleck's *The Panic of 1857* (1943). O. G. Villard's *John Brown* (1910) remains a useful study of the abolitionist crusader.

Perhaps the most judicious, yet highly sympathetic, study of Lincoln in the fifties is Don E. Fehrenbacher's *Prelude to Greatness: Lincoln in the 1850's** (1962). Lincoln's career in the Illinois Legislature is traced in Paul Simon's *Lincoln's Preparation for Greatness* (1965). On Lincoln's role in the building of the Republican party, see William Baringer's *Lincoln's Rise to Power* (1937). An excellent study of the campaign of 1860 is E. D. Fite's *The Presidential Campaign of 1860* (1911). Lincoln's role in that campaign is analyzed in R. H. Luthin's *The First Lincoln Campaign* (1944). For the South's experience in that election, see Ollinger Crenshaw's *The Slave States in the Presidential Election of 1860* (1945). A brief volume on the 1860 campaign is N. A. Graebner (ed.), *Politics and the Crisis of 1860* (1961).

Historians have subjected the secession crisis of 1860–1861 to close scrutiny. From the viewpoint of the North the two standard volumes are David M. Potter's *Lincoln and His Party in the Secession Crisis** (1942) and Kenneth M. Stampp's *And the War Came: The North and the Secession Crisis** (1950). Northern attitudes toward compromise receive incisive treatment in R. G. Gunderson's *Old Gentlemen's Convention* (1961). For the rhetoric of the crisis see the excellent symposium edited by J. Jeffery Auer, *Anti-slavery and Disunion, 1858–1861* (1963). Buchanan's dilemma is portrayed in P G. Auchampaugh's *James Buchanan and His Cabinet on the Eve of Secession* (1926). The choices confronting Northern business are analyzed in P. S. Foner's *Business and Slavery: The New York Merchants and the Irrepressible Conflict* (1941). See also Allan Nevins and M. H. Thomas (eds.), *The Diary of George Templeton Strong* (4 vols., 1952). Strong was a New York lawyer. On the South and secession is D. L. Dumond's *The Secession Movement, 1860–1861* (1931). A good companion study is U. B. Phillips's *The Course of the South to Secession** (1939). See also the following volumes of selected editorials: D. L. Dumond (ed.), *Southern Editorials on Secession* (1931); and H. C. Perkins (ed.), *Northern Editorials on Secession* (2 vols., 1942).
* indicates availability in paperback.

18

The Civil War

DURING THE CRITICAL winter of 1860–1861, President-elect Abraham Lincoln remained quietly in Springfield, Illinois, where he played host to numerous visitors and wrote occasional letters of encouragement to front-line Republicans. Lincoln agreed with the core of Republican leadership that the Republicans should avoid a split on the divisive issue of slavery in the territories. During the debate on the Crittenden compromise, Lincoln pleaded with one member of Congress to defeat it. "Prevent, as far as possible, any of our friends from demoralizing themselves and our cause by entertaining propositions for compromise of any sort on 'slavery extension,' " he wrote, "on that point hold firm as with a chain of steel." Lincoln's private views, circulated freely among Republicans in Congress, brought the majority solidly to his support.

Yet, so forceful were the demands for compromise from such powerful Republicans as William H. Seward of New York that Lincoln, to avoid alienating any faction of his party, adopted an official silence on all matters of sectional conflict. To the throngs that greeted him along his route to Washington, he spoke of the great issues engulfing the nation but refused to commit himself to any position. At Indianapolis he listed a series of questions posed by secession and concluded with the wry observation "I say I am deciding nothing, but simply giving something for you to reflect upon." Even his Republican friends were dismayed at his lack of forthrightness. Arriving in

Washington, Lincoln assured a delegation of aspiring peacemakers that the Republic's future depended not upon him but upon the nation's willingness to obey the Constitution.

The Fort Sumter Crisis

As the time for Lincoln's inauguration approached, thoughtful men wondered if he were prepared to face the grave responsibility of office. His past career held few clues. His duty, he continued to assure those who called, demanded that he employ his presidential powers to maintain the Constitution and the Union. His inaugural address on March 4, 1861, gave expression to his nationalism but suggested no specific course of action. Under no circumstances would he recognize the secession movement. "Physically speaking," he said, "we cannot separate." The ordinances of secession were "legally void" and any resistance to federal authority was "insurrectionary or revolutionary, according to the circumstances." He would execute the federal laws in all the states. "In *your* hands," he said to the South, "and not in mine, is the momentous issue of the civil war. The Government will not assail you. . . . [But] I hold that, in contemplation of universal law and the Constitution, the Union of these States is perpetual." His constitutional powers obligated him "to hold, occupy, and possess the property and places belonging to the Government, and to collect the duties and imposts." Lincoln begged the South to submit to the decision made by the election.

Lincoln's approach to the South was conciliatory and reassuring. He pledged his respect for slavery in the Southern states and agreed to enforce any workable fugitive slave law, but he rejected compromise on slavery extension and emphasized his determination to preserve the Union. Undoubtedly the new President hoped to avoid an armed conflict. Between the rival sections, a cordon of border states suspended in indecision served to muffle the friction between the extremes. By sidestepping a crisis, Lincoln might hold these states in the Union while gaining time to permit a resurgence of national sentiment in the seceded states. Reports from the South indicated that Unionist tendencies were surprisingly strong even in the Confederate administration.

One issue challenged Lincoln's policy of watchful waiting. The President had made it clear that he intended to hold Fort Sumter in Charleston Harbor, as well as the three Florida forts still in Northern hands, as symbols of the unbroken Union. Unfortunately, however, Fort Sumter quickly became a point of honor for both sections. South Carolina warned the administration that it would regard any Northern attempt to supply or strengthen the garrison as an act of aggression. While the President permitted events to drift during March, Republican Congressmen fumed. If Lincoln vacillated on this question, predicted one critic, "The South will proclaim him a Damned fool, and the North a damned Rascal." The President was not stampeded. He withheld relief until the garrison at Sumter was reduced almost to the point of starvation, and even then he duly informed the Governor of South Carolina that the ship was being sent with provisions only. Throughout the crisis he remained passive, neither withdrawing nor reinforcing the Sumter garrison. Impatient Southerners fired the first shot. On April 12, the batteries lining the mud flats and sand dunes around Charleston sent shells bursting over Fort Sumter. After thirty-four hours of constant bombardment, the Union commander, Major Robert Anderson, surrendered the Fort.

Preparations for War in the North

As the news of Fort Sumter's capitulation resounded across the nation, few failed to grasp its meaning. Emerson was among those who recalled its volcanic impact: "At the darkest moment in the history of the republic, when it looked as if the nation would be dismembered, pulverized into its original elements, the attack on Fort Sumter crystallized the North into a unit, and the hope of mankind was saved." If the South would fight for its independence, the North, resorting to arms, would make its stand for the Union. Lincoln's call on April 15 for 75,000 troops, sent the Upper South of Virginia, Arkansas, Tennessee, and North Carolina into the Confederacy. Virginia's western counties refused to bolt, however, and in 1863 entered the Union as the state of West Virginia.

What mattered in 1861 was not only the North's determination to reforge the Union but also its apparent power to do so. Of the nation's thirty-four states, twenty-three were free. Omitting the two divided states, Missouri and Kentucky, the North had a population of 20,700,000. The Confederacy had a population of only 9,100,000, of whom over 3,600,000 were blacks. But the greatest disparity in power between North and South lay in industrial productivity. The North's industries in 1860 employed 1.3 million workers; those of the South, a mere 110,000. The annual production of New York's factories alone was four times that of the entire South. In 1860, the South possessed less than a third of the nation's 31,000 miles of railroad track. The South, moreover, had few financial resources; even its banking and foreign exchange had centered in New York. The North's statistical advantage was so profound that the Confederacy in April, 1861, appeared to have no chance on the battlefield at all.

Whatever its advantages in size, wealth, and population, however, the North was totally unprepared for war. During the three preparatory months between the Sumter crisis and the assembling of Congress in July, 1861, Lincoln employed his emergency powers to inaugurate the long and tedious process of organizing the North for the coming struggle. Refusing to recognize the legality of secession, Lincoln labeled the South's action an "insurrection" but admitted that the laws of the United States were being broken on too wide a scale to be enforced by normal judicial processes. His purpose in calling for 75,000 militia, he said, was simply that of repossessing federal property and executing the laws of Congress. To meet the South's deepening resistance, however, Lincoln eventually engaged in actions that exceeded his presidential authority and, in a sense, recognized the existence of war. During April he instituted a blockade of the entire Southern coast which the Confederacy, possessing no navy, could not easily neutralize. Then, early in May, he called for additional recruits for the regular Army, exercising a power vested solely in Congress. Lincoln readily admitted that he exceeded his authority but, as he explained in his message of July 4: "These measures, whether strictly legal or not, were ventured upon, under what appeared to be a popular demand, and a public necessity; trusting . . . that Congress would readily ratify them." Congress responded, first by passing a resolution legalizing the President's decrees "as if they had been issued and done under the previous express authority and direction of the Congress of the United States," and then in late July issuing a call for 500,000 volunteers, initially for a period of up to three years, and then for the duration of the war.

Lincoln's first call for militia, suggesting a war of only three months, set off a wave of enlistments throughout the North as various communities organized military units. This expectation of a short war, along with the speed of mobilization, created massive confusion. In addition, the nucleus of the Northern military establishment was the regular Army of the United States, which numbered, in 1861, only 13,000 officers and men. When Commanding General Winfield Scott in Washington refused to scatter his forces, permitting his officers to organize and train the new volunteer units, the mobilization process became even more chaotic.

The Union debacle at Manassas during July, 1861, made it clear that the war would be neither brief nor inexpensive and that, to win, the North would require not only vastly augmented military forces but also a more efficient Army administration. By July, 1862, the demands of war forced Congress to strengthen both the militia and the regular Army. It called the militia into active service and provided for the drafting of "all able-bodied male citizens between the ages of eighteen and forty-five" into the militia. Under this law, the actual drafting was executed by the individual states.

Not until March, 1863, did Congress pass a national conscription act which declared all able-bodied male citizens between the ages of twenty and forty-five subject to military service. The conscription law provided exemptions for the physically and mentally unfit as well as for the occupants of certain federal and state offices. A draftee, moreover, could either hire a substitute or buy an exemption for $300. The scandalous operation of the conscript system resulted in a widespread quest for substitutes and payment of commutation. Under the act only 46,000 entered the Northern armies; another 118,000 bought substitutes. The law, which was basically unjust, met resistance everywhere.

As early as 1861, Northern Negroes offered their services to the Union. Nothing, it seemed, would have so completely committed the nation to granting the Negro first-class citizenship as his contribution to the Union on the field of battle. But Washington officials had no interest in challenging the racial prejudices of many Northern soldiers and refused to accept Negroes into the Union armies. Many Northerners—Lincoln among them—were convinced that the Negroes would make poor soldiers. Lincoln rejected black regiments offered by Indiana, not only, he said, because such action might turn many citizens in the border states against the North, but also because the Negro equipment would ultimately fall into the hands of the rebels. Only when Northern enthusiasm for the war began to wane in 1862 and enlistments fell off did the administration agree to the recruitment of Negro soldiers for Union armies.

The South Faces War

Southern leaders approached their war for independence convinced that they could equal the Northern effort and successfully defend their cause. To maintain a political division already established, the South could remain on the defensive, forcing the North, if it would reforge the Union, to commit greater quantities of manpower and equipment. The South also had long harbored a more intense martial spirit than had the North. Many of the best students at West Point had been Southerners, and large numbers of these men now resigned their federal posts and returned to the South to take command of Confederate forces. Well-stocked federal arsenals in the South fell into Confederate hands and gave the Southern troops, at least in the initial stage of the war, an adequate supply of excellent military equipment. The North's material advantage, if potentially overwhelming, was scarcely noticeable in 1861.

Faced with the necessity of raising an effective army, the Confederate Congress authorized the recruiting of 400,000 men for three years or the duration of the war. The fact that the legislation was confused, permitting Southerners to enter the Confederate armed forces through a variety of arrangements and for widely varying periods of time, seemed to make no difference. The rush to enlist was so overwhelming that the South faced no immediate problem in creating an adequate fighting force. In fact, the numbers of men available far exceeded the South's capacity to train and equip them.

Unfortunately for the South, this enthusiasm was short-lived. Those most devoted to Southern independence volunteered first; thereafter, soldiers entered the Confederate ranks with steadily decreasing eagerness. The reason was not hard to find. To build an effective military force, Southern officers enforced a rigid discipline which quickly dispelled any illusions that military service would be pleasant or of short duration. When one-year enlistments began to expire in the spring of 1862 and no promises of bounties or other special benefits could produce sufficient reenlistments, the Confederate Congress was compelled to impose a draft. The first law of April, 1862, subjected all able-bodied Southerners between the ages of eighteen and thirty-five to military service. In September, the upper age limit was extended to forty-five, and in February, 1864, to fifty. Exempted occupations and the privilege of hiring substitutes still kept large numbers of able-bodied Southerners out of the armed forces.

The Opening Campaigns

With their armies organized and ostensibly prepared for battle by the summer of 1861, both North and South were spoiling for a fight. Despite its lack of defenses, Washington was optimistic, for in June, General George B. McClellan, a West Point graduate, invaded western Virginia with 20,000 troops and, in a lightning campaign, cleared the region of Confederate forces. During July, however, Confederate General P. G. T. Beauregard brought a large Confederate force north to the rail junction of Manassas (Bull Run), scarcely

20 miles from Washington. Unable to resist further the Northern demands for a victory, General Irvin McDowell, the commander at Washington, sent his raw troops, followed by a mass of spectators who streamed out of the city to witness the battle, against the Confederate positions at Manassas. Through the morning hours of July 25, the Union forces advanced well against the Southern defenses. Then suddenly the tide of battle turned. Beauregard received some needed reinforcements; the Confederates counterattacked with a series of effective jabs and quickly threw the Federals into general retreat. Unable to organize any resistance along the clogged roads, the soldiers joined the flight into Washington. Beauregard's forces were too disorganized to pursue. This permitted McDowell's successor, thirty-five-year-old McClellan, to remain undisturbed in Washington until the next spring (1862) while he reorganized the capital defenses and drilled numerous raw recruits.

By contrast, nothing was quiet that winter of 1861–1862 in the West. In January, 1862, James A. Garfield's Union forces met and defeated a Confederate army near Prestonburg in eastern Kentucky. Later that month the able Union commander George H. Thomas defeated a Confederate force at Mill Springs. These victories were less than decisive, but they gave the Union control of the routes through eastern Kentucky into Tennessee. To the west were three far more important routes of transportation that penetrated deeply into Confederate territory—the Cumberland, Tennessee, and Mississippi Rivers. Two important forts, Henry and Donelson, both located near the Kentucky-Tennessee line, guarded the Tennessee and Cumberland routes, respectively. Ulysses S. Grant, with a western army, moved south along the Tennessee in February, 1862, intent upon their capture.

Grant, a West Point graduate and a veteran of the Mexican War, had only recently returned to active duty, helping to organize the Illinois volunteers under the Western command of John Charles Frémont. Personally unimpressive and completely unknown, Grant's modesty, self-assurance, and concern for detail—all demanded of a leader in the field—quickly demonstrated his remarkable generalship. Supported by a line of gunboats under Andrew Hull Foote, Grant took Fort Henry on February 6, after a minor engagement. He then transferred his small fleet to the Cumberland and ten days later, after heavy fighting, captured Fort Donelson and, with it, 12,000 Confederate prisoners of war. The Confederates under Albert Sydney Johnston now gave up their exposed position at Columbus on the Mississippi and withdrew to the area below Nashville.

Grant moved his forces southward along the Tennessee to Pittsburgh Landing near the Mississippi border, establishing his own headquarters at Savannah, 9 miles to the north. Before he could plan an advance against the new Confederate positions, however, Johnston threw his men forward against the surprised, inexperienced, and poorly organized Northern troops, centering his attack on the Union positions at Shiloh Church, 3 miles west of Pittsburgh Landing. Cut off from their units and commanders, the Union soldiers retreated in panic until stopped by Northern cavalry and guided back to the front where they were most needed. Grant himself, though injured by a fall from his horse, rushed up to the battle area and gradually by personal command turned the retreat into an advance. On that first day, the Confederates lost Johnston, their commanding general, who suffered a leg wound and bled to death. His successor,

Beauregard, recently transferred from the East, retired to Corinth. In May, General Henry W. Halleck, who had replaced Frémont as commander of the Western Department, took personal command and occupied that city. But Beauregard had withdrawn his forces secretly, keeping them intact for another campaign. Thus the first phase of the war in the West closed with Union armies holding most of Kentucky and much of Tennessee.

The War in Virginia: 1862

By the early spring of 1862, the war was a year old; and McClellan's army at Washington was three times as large as the nearest Confederate force at Manassas. Yet the Union armies in the East had not fought one major battle. While the Union commander drilled, organized, reorganized, wrote lengthy reports, assembled equipment, demanded additional troops, inspected, and held conferences with his subordinates—thereby convincing himself and others that he was leaving nothing to chance—Lincoln began to press for action by becoming his own strategist—a better one, some historians insist, than any of his generals.

Under the President's prodding, McClellan moved, but not against Manassas. Instead he placed his huge army on a flotilla and sailed it down the Potomac and Chesapeake Bay to the mouth of the James for a strike at Richmond. By May he had established his base at Fort Monroe and had assembled 112,000 troops. He took Yorktown on May 4 and, after a skirmish with Confederate troops, marched against the Confederate capital with an army which, by his own conservative estimate, had 80,000 effectives remaining. Still McClellan asked the President for additional troops. Lincoln refused, and with no reinforcements forthcoming, McClellan faced at Richmond the South's two greatest generals, Robert E Lee, now the commander of all Confederate forces, and Thomas J. ("Stonewall") Jackson. Unlike Grant, Lee had graduated from West Point with distinction. During the Mexican War, General Winfield Scott had assigned the young captain to his personal staff; thereafter, Lee had served as superintendent of West Point. Handsome, cultured, possessing a fine character and an excellent mind, Lee's reputation in 1861 was so high that he could have had the command of the Union forces in the field. But moved by a deep devotion to Virginia and her heritage, Lee had cast his lot with the South. For the defense of Richmond in 1862, Lee had 85,000 men. McClellan had perhaps 100,000, although Lee believed that he had far more.

At Richmond, Lee feared above all the reinforcement of McClellan's army. Quite cognizant of McClellan's immense caution, Lee dispatched Jackson into the Shenandoah Valley with 16,000 men to threaten Washington via Harper's Ferry. The ruse succeeded, for it brought 45,000 Union troops into the valley to oppose him. Having deprived McClellan of these possible replacements, Jackson hurried back to Richmond to join Lee in the defense of the city. McClellan began his final move against the Confederate capital on June 25, and for a week the action raged in individual battles, the most bloody on July 1 at Malvern Hill. McClellan managed his forces well, but he failed to capture Richmond.

Despite enormous effort and a vast logistical advantage the North, though striking hard at the "Heart of the Rebellion," had been unable to bring the war to a satisfactory conclusion. Republican leaders in Congress no longer trusted McClellan, doubting that he had the capacity to lead the great Army of the Potomac. McClellan moreover had made it plain that he favored a war of moderation against the South, limited to punishing the South's military forces, not its civilian population. When General John Pope, having demonstrated some military capabilities in the West, announced that he favored a vigorous prosecution of the war, Lincoln appointed him to the high command in the East and brought Halleck to Washington to take command of all the Union armies.

After brief preparations, Pope moved against the Confederate army, now under Lee and Jackson, at Manassas. In several disjointed engagements during August, 1862, the Army of the Potomac suffered a series of flank attacks from Confederate cavalry led by the dashing J. E. B. Stuart. The second battle of Manassas (Bull Run) was fought on August 29 and 30, 1862. The Union forces, now thoroughly seasoned, fought well but suffered from the lack of command organization. As the Union effort began to sputter, Lee closed in on the retreating enemy, administering heavy losses. In June, McClellan had met Lee at Richmond with 100,000 troops; by the end of August, the only Union soldiers within 100 miles of Richmond were in full retreat.

In this crisis, Lincoln sought another general and turned once more to McClellan. The young general had always been popular with the Union troops, and the knowledge that he had returned to command them prompted demonstrations of wild enthusiasm. Lincoln's orders to McClellan were verbal; it was never clear to the general what authority he had beyond the defense of the capital.

Meanwhile, in a move to free Maryland of Federal control, Lee crossed the Potomac on September 5, 1862, and occupied Frederick, Maryland. McClellan moved out to keep his forces between Lee's Army of Northern Virginia and the capital. Lee wanted to secure Harper's Ferry because it was the gateway from the Shenandoah Valley into Maryland. To take the river crossing, Lee had to divide his forces, sending Jackson with 25,000 men to capture Harper's Ferry while he proceeded to Hagerstown. Jackson met with perfect success at Harper's Ferry and took 11,000 prisoners, but Lee, already weakened and with the Potomac at his rear, decided to withdraw into Virginia. Before he could do so, McClellan on September 17 threw the Union forces against Lee's men near Sharpsburg in the war's bloodiest engagement yet—the battle of Antietam. His forces badly outnumbered, Lee quickly retreated into the Shenandoah Valley.

McClellan, still reacting slowly, crossed the Potomac late in October and by November 7 had massed his army near Warrenton. But before McClellan could make another thrust at Lee's forces, Lincoln removed him from his command and replaced him with General Ambrose E. Burnside. Burnside's tenure was brief. In mid-December he struck Lee's forces at Fredericksburg. His numerical advantage over Lee was 114,000 to 72,000, but the Confederate forces held such superior battle positions that Burnside sent wave after wave of experienced Union troops against the Confederates in vain. By nightfall, when the Union forces finally withdrew, they left behind almost 1,300 dead and 9,600 wounded, approximately twice the Confederate losses.

Fredericksburg marked the low point in Northern morale. In twenty months the North had managed to organize a magnificent army, but no general seemed capable of using it to advantage. Battles had produced casualties in abundance, but no victories. Lincoln faced an

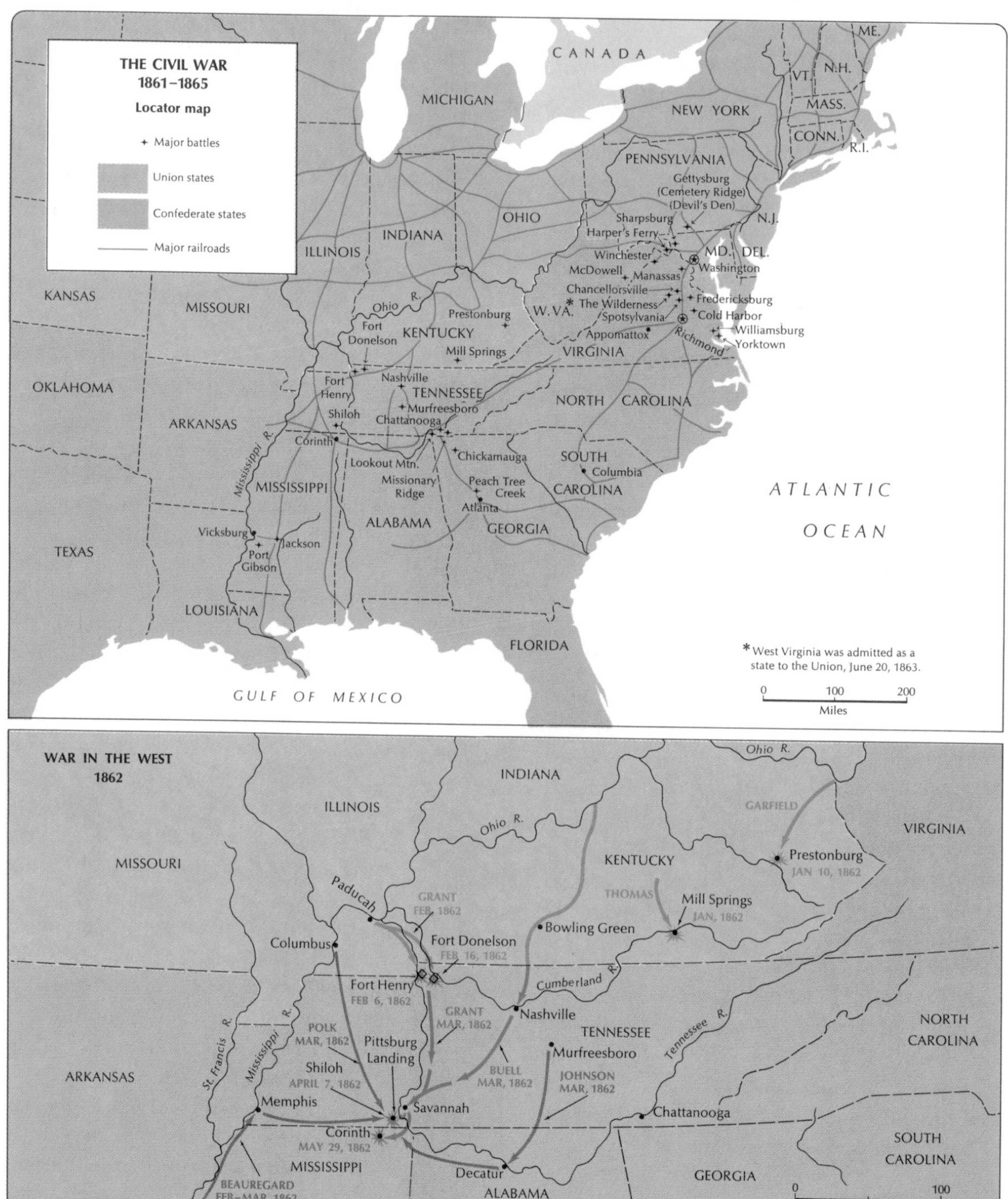
THE CIVIL WAR
1861–1865
Locator map
Major battles
Union states
Confederate states
Major railroads
CANADA
MICHIGAN
NEW YORK
ME.
VT.
N.H.
MASS.
CONN.
R.I.
PENNSYLVANIA
N.J.
MD.
DEL.
OHIO
INDIANA
ILLINOIS
KANSAS
MISSOURI
KENTUCKY
W. VA.
VIRGINIA
OKLAHOMA
ARKANSAS
TENNESSEE
NORTH CAROLINA
SOUTH CAROLINA
MISSISSIPPI
ALABAMA
GEORGIA
TEXAS
LOUISIANA
FLORIDA
GULF OF MEXICO
ATLANTIC OCEAN
Gettysburg (Cemetery Ridge) (Devil's Den)
Sharpsburg
Harper's Ferry
Winchester
McDowell
Manassas
Washington
Chancellorsville
The Wilderness
Spotsylvania
Fredericksburg
Cold Harbor
Appomattox
Richmond
Williamsburg
Yorktown
Prestonburg
Mill Springs
Ohio R.
Fort Donelson
Fort Henry
Nashville
Murfreesboro
Shiloh
Chattanooga
Corinth
Lookout Mtn.
Missionary Ridge
Chickamauga
Peach Tree Creek
Atlanta
Columbia
Mississippi R.
Vicksburg
Jackson
Port Gibson
* West Virginia was admitted as a state to the Union, June 20, 1863.
0 100 200
Miles
WAR IN THE WEST
1862
INDIANA
ILLINOIS
MISSOURI
KENTUCKY
VIRGINIA
Ohio R.
GARFIELD
Prestonburg
JAN 10, 1862
THOMAS
Mill Springs
JAN, 1862
Paducah
GRANT
FEB, 1862
Fort Donelson
FEB 16, 1862
Bowling Green
Columbus
Fort Henry
FEB 6, 1862
Cumberland R.
Nashville
GRANT
MAR, 1862
POLK
MAR, 1862
Pittsburg Landing
Shiloh
APRIL 7, 1862
TENNESSEE
Murfreesboro
BUELL
MAR, 1862
JOHNSON
MAR, 1862
Tennessee R.
NORTH CAROLINA
ARKANSAS
St. Francis R.
Mississippi R.
Memphis
Savannah
Corinth
MAY 29, 1862
Chattanooga
SOUTH CAROLINA
MISSISSIPPI
Decatur
ALABAMA
GEORGIA
BEAUREGARD
FEB–MAR, 1862
0 100
Miles

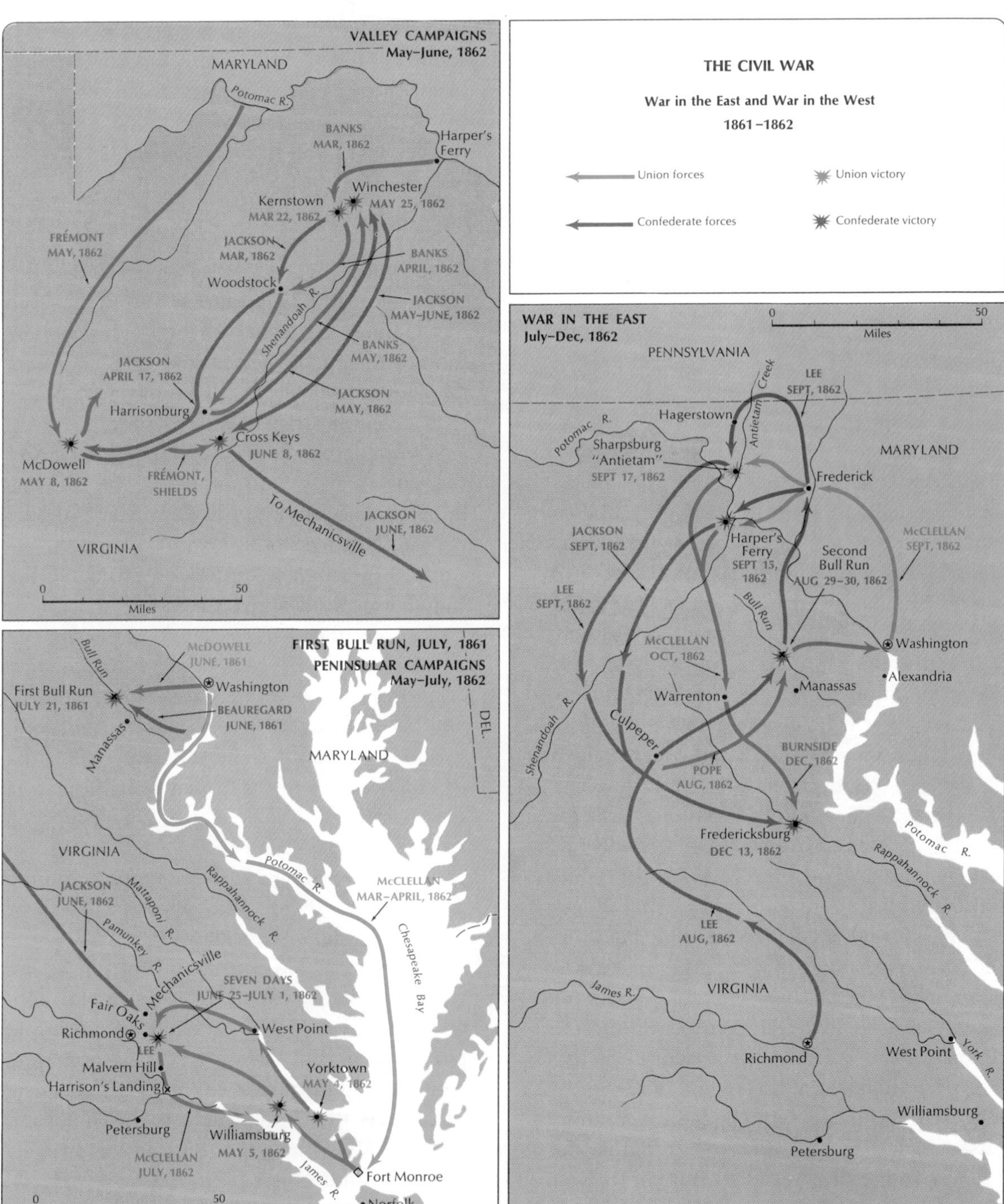
THE CIVIL WAR
War in the East and War in the West
1861–1862
Union forces
Confederate forces
Union victory
Confederate victory
VALLEY CAMPAIGNS
May–June, 1862
MARYLAND
Potomac R.
BANKS
MAR, 1862
Harper's Ferry
Winchester
MAY 25, 1862
Kernstown
MAR 22, 1862
FRÉMONT
MAY, 1862
JACKSON
MAR, 1862
BANKS
APRIL, 1862
Woodstock
Shenandoah R.
JACKSON
MAY–JUNE, 1862
BANKS
MAY, 1862
JACKSON
APRIL 17, 1862
JACKSON
MAY, 1862
Harrisonburg
Cross Keys
JUNE 8, 1862
McDowell
MAY 8, 1862
FRÉMONT,
SHIELDS
To Mechanicsville
JACKSON
JUNE, 1862
VIRGINIA
0
50
Miles
FIRST BULL RUN, JULY, 1861
PENINSULAR CAMPAIGNS
May–July, 1862
Bull Run
McDOWELL
JUNE, 1861
Washington
First Bull Run
JULY 21, 1861
BEAUREGARD
JUNE, 1861
Manassas
DEL.
MARYLAND
VIRGINIA
Potomac R.
McCLELLAN
MAR–APRIL, 1862
Chesapeake Bay
JACKSON
JUNE, 1862
Mattaponi R.
Rappahannock R.
Pamunkey R.
Mechanicsville
SEVEN DAYS
JUNE 25–JULY 1, 1862
Fair Oaks
Richmond
West Point
LEE
Malvern Hill
Yorktown
MAY 4, 1862
Harrison's Landing
Petersburg
Williamsburg
MAY 5, 1862
McCLELLAN
JULY, 1862
James R.
Fort Monroe
Norfolk
0
50
Miles
WAR IN THE EAST
July–Dec, 1862
0
50
Miles
PENNSYLVANIA
Antietam Creek
LEE
SEPT, 1862
Hagerstown
Potomac R.
Sharpsburg
"Antietam"
SEPT 17, 1862
MARYLAND
Frederick
JACKSON
SEPT, 1862
Harper's Ferry
SEPT 15, 1862
Second Bull Run
AUG 29–30, 1862
McCLELLAN
SEPT, 1862
LEE
SEPT, 1862
Bull Run
McCLELLAN
OCT, 1862
Washington
Alexandria
Manassas
Warrenton
Shenandoah R.
Culpeper
BURNSIDE
DEC, 1862
POPE
AUG, 1862
Fredericksburg
DEC 13, 1862
Potomac R.
Rappahannock R.
LEE
AUG, 1862
James R.
VIRGINIA
Richmond
West Point
York R.
Williamsburg
Petersburg

The Civil War

increasingly critical Congress; his own administration appeared to be disintegrating. The Army of the Potomac, especially its ablest officers, had no confidence in Burnside. In this new crisis, Lincoln sent for "Fighting Joe" Hooker. To Hooker's remark that the country needed a dictator, Lincoln replied, "Only those generals who gain successes can set up dictators. What I now ask of you is military success, and I will risk dictatorship."

The War Congress

Lincoln could hardly dispose of the South's challenge to the Union before he had established a working majority in Congress that approved his aims as well as his methods of conducting the war. Despite the political and military crisis of 1861 and 1862, Congress was not inclined to defer to the Executive. Democrats who had fought the Republican party throughout its brief history found it difficult, even in wartime, to accept the leadership of a Republican President. Supported by a united Republican majority, Lincoln might have ignored the Democratic opposition. But neither the pressures of war nor the requirements of party cohesion could eliminate the conflicts which separated the Republican moderates from the party's more determined antislavery elements, led by the powerful Thaddeus Stevens of Pennsylvania, Charles Sumner of Massachusetts, Zach Chandler of Michigan, and Benjamin F. Wade of Ohio.

Republican strategy toward the South evolved slowly. When the fighting began in 1861, the Republicans in Congress seemed to agree with Lincoln that the war should be fought solely to force the South back into the Union. So widespread was this sentiment that even the Republican leadership in Congress approved John J. Crittenden's resolution, passed in July by a vote of 121 to 2, that the war was "not being waged on our part . . . for any purpose of overthrowing or interfering with the right of established institutions of those States, but to defend and maintain the *supremacy* of the Constitution, and to preserve the Union." Such agreement over war aims soon evaporated. Before the end of 1861, the House balked, by a vote of 71 to 65, at reenacting the Crittenden resolution.

Wars generally have a logic of their own, and the Civil War was no exception. The South's initial military successes made it clear that only a total Northern effort would bring an acceptable peace. This realization prompted the Republican Radicals in Congress—those who spoke for the party's antislavery wing—to demand a more vigorous and intensive conduct of the war, aimed not only at the destruction of Southern military power but also at the elimination of the Southern slave system. Aware that its commitment to the Union really permitted the North no other course, they launched an increasingly vituperative assault against everyone—in Congress, the administration, and the military forces—who appeared to favor a return to the Union as it was.

Lincoln accepted the reconstruction of the Union as the one estimable goal that Northern power could achieve. This limited objective he phrased over and over again. "The sooner the national authority can be restored," he said, "the nearer the Union will be to the Union as it was. . . . My paramount object in this struggle is to save the Union." Lincoln hated slavery, but he shared the conservative conviction that it was the racial aspect of the slave question, not slavery itself, that tormented the nation. Had the slaves been indistinguishable by color from the rest of Southern society, slavery would have vanished in some previous age. Recognizing his limited power to remake Southern society or enforce the principle of equality in the South, Lincoln hesitated to touch the slave issue at all.

The early enthusiasm for the war among many Northern antislavery leaders had stemmed in part from their anticipation that it would settle the slave question forever. Charles Francis Adams had observed early in the war, "We cannot afford to go over this ground more than once. The slave question must be settled this time once for all." As the war proceeded, Northern antislavery forces became increasingly militant. The President now appeared out of step. During 1862, Radicals and abolitionists alike began to abuse Lincoln for his moderation; to condemn him for maintaining a Cabinet of conservatives who, with him, seemed to think the Union more important than emancipation; to compare him unfavorably to Buchanan for his apparent lack of firmness, resolution, and moral conviction; and to accuse him of aiding the enemy with his hesitation in the conduct of the war. To secure an immediate and vigorous pursuit of victory, Congress in December, 1861, created the Congressional Committee on the Conduct of the War. Under the leadership of Senator Wade, the committee challenged both the administration's military policies and its choice of commanders. Above all, it demanded the unlimited employment of Northern resources in punishing the South.

To punish the South and reduce its capacity to fight, the Radicals pushed through Congress a series of confiscation acts. The first measure of August, 1861, provided merely for Federal seizure of all property used for insurrectionary purposes. Thad Stevens voiced the Radical motivation clearly when he declared that if the entire South "must be laid waste, and made a desert, in order to save this Union from destruction, so let it be." In the second Confiscation Act of July, 1862, the Federal government condemned to forfeiture the property of the country's enemies—that is, those supporting the rebellion. The slaves of such Southerners, moreover, were to be liberated. It authorized the President, thirdly, to employ Negroes, even freed slaves, in the Union forces. Lincoln felt that the second Confiscation Act was too drastic and prepared a veto message explaining his disapproval, which he placed on the record. But when Congress agreed not to extend the property forfeiture beyond the life of the accused, Lincoln signed the measure. Except for its revelation of the hardening congressional attitude toward the South, the act had little immediate consequence.

Wartime Measures of Government

Congress faced the need of financing a major war with a depleted treasury. Its members assumed, in 1861, that Secretary of the Treasury Salmon P. Chase would recommend a system of wartime taxes to finance the Union war effort. Instead, he announced that the Federal government would continue Buchanan's decision to rely on deficit financing through borrowing. This announcement so completely unnerved the nation's financial circles that it produced a banking crisis and forced New York banks to suspend specie payments in December, 1861. But Chase persisted in his borrowing policies and commissioned Jay Cooke and Company as the sole agent for the sale of United States bonds. Cooke quickly disposed of the entire issue, largely to bankers and men of wealth. At the same time, Chase turned to Congress, which in July, 1862, imposed an excise tax on the manufacturers and sellers of a wide variety of civilian goods. This tax provided the government with its basic wartime income. Congress had merely to increase the rates to augment Federal revenues.

Pursuing yet another course, Congress passed a legal tender act in February, 1862, which provided for an issue of $150 million—later increased to $450 million—in United States notes, known as "greenbacks." Financing the war demonstrated forcefully the disadvantages imposed on the nation by the absence of a national banking system and a national bank note currency. Congress, pressed by Chase, established such a system in February, 1863, modifying it in June, 1864. This act provided for the creation of banks under Federal charters with a required capital of $50,000 to $200,000. These new national banks had to invest a minimum of one-third of their capital in government bonds, thereby supplying a market for Federal securities. The banks were also permitted to issue a new type of currency, national bank notes. On balance, the National Bank Act made it easier for the North to finance the war.

Placed in control of Congress by the fact of Southern secession, the Republican majority embarked on the Whig program that the powerful Jacksonian coalition had denied the country during the prewar generation. The Democratic party had terminated a long period of protectionism when it passed the Walker tariff of 1846. Another Democratic Congress pushed the tariff further downward in 1857. With the recovery of prosperity, most Northern industrialists were content with the existing tariff structure. But the iron interests of Pennsylvania, facing both continuing depression and foreign competition, demanded protection. Lincoln in 1860 had made a special bid for the Pennsylvania vote by citing his long adherence to Clay's American System. The mounting deficits of the Federal government, moreover, indicated the need for additional revenue, and in February, 1861, shortly before Buchanan left office, the Republicans passed the Morrill tariff, which, in general, returned the nation to the tariff levels of 1846. A second tariff measure, of August, 1861, was again aimed largely at raising revenue. But the act of July, 1862, granting as it did specific advantages to many items produced in the United States, was largely protective. The act of June, 1864, was designed to compensate Northern industrialists for their wartime taxes. Having through their business expansion contributed mightily to Northern power, industrialists by 1864 had achieved so favorable a position in national life that they could obtain almost any tariff level they regarded as essential. When the war ended in 1865, duties of 100 percent were common; the general average of 47 percent was double that of 1857.

For a decade, sectional jealousy had negated every congressional effort to create a transcontinental railroad. Now freed of Southern opposition, the wartime Congress passed its first transcontinental railroad bill in July, 1862. This act created two lines—the Union Pacific, charged with the task of building a railroad westward from Omaha, and the Central Pacific, instructed to build eastward from San Francisco Bay across the Sierras until the two lines met. To facilitate the construction of this vast project, the Federal government authorized not only a right-of-way and protection from the Indians, but also granted sizable gifts of public lands and issued special bonds.

Throughout the fifties, the homestead principle of free land had been heralded by Northern editors as a great boon for the whole American people. Buchanan had vetoed the Homestead bill of 1860, largely at the insistence of a disapproving South, which could anticipate no benefits from the measure. But on May 20, 1862, a determined Republican Congress passed the Homestead Act, which granted 160 acres of unoccupied public domain to homesteaders in return for the payment of nominal fees. Full title required five years of actual residence. Although praised by its champions as a reform measure, providing the laboring man a ready economic alternative when his urban conditions became intolerable, the Homestead Act's actual benefits to urban labor were limited. Not many workers had either the capital or the know-how to go West and begin farming.

During 1862, Congress also passed the Morrill Act which established the land-grant system of higher education in the United States. Behind this measure were years of agitation by Jonathan Baldwin Turner, a college professor in the Midwest who saw the need for large numbers of "industrial colleges" to meet the demands of an expanding industrial economy and suggested that they be financed in part by federal grants of land to the states. In Congress this program was advanced after 1857 by Justin S. Morrill of Vermont. Morrill's plan included land assignments to the states on the basis of population; the new colleges, he said, would emphasize a practical education for agriculture and industry. A bill to establish such a federal system passed the House in 1858 and the Senate in 1859. Buchanan vetoed it, however, partially because of constitutional scruples. Finally in July, 1862, Congress passed the measure again, and with Lincoln's signature it became law. The law granted each state 30,000 acres of public land for each of its senators and representatives in Congress. Since the grants were no more than a stimulus, individual states were expected to carry the major burden of university building themselves.

Emancipation

Whatever Lincoln's private views toward the object of the war, the logic of the times drove him inexorably toward the Radical goal of emancipation. "I claim not to have controlled events," he admitted later, "but confess plainly that events have controlled me." As the war entered its second year, the abolitionist pressures on the President were too persistent to be ignored. As President, Lincoln shouldered responsibilities that the Radicals refused to recognize. His conservatism on matters of slavery was dictated not only by his sincere constitutional scruples but also by his determination to hold the border states—Delaware, Maryland, Kentucky, and Missouri—within the Union. In accordance with his limited goal of reforging the nation, Lincoln had informed Congress in July, 1861, that he would not permit the war to "degenerate into a violent and remorseless revolutionary struggle." Only when most segments of Northern opinion seemed to support the policy did Lincoln take up the cause of the emancipation of slaves. Even then, he did so with extreme reluctance.

For Lincoln, it was always the Union that mattered. His concern for the Negro remained secondary. "My paramount object in this struggle *is* to save the Union, and is *not* either to save or to destroy slavery," he wrote in August, 1862. "If I could save the Union without freeing any slave I would do it; and if I could save it by freeing *all* the slaves, I would do it; and if I could save it by freeing some and leaving others alone I would also do that." The Union was for Lincoln preeminently a symbol of democracy—the world's last, best hope. He stressed this theme in his famed Gettysburg Address. Soldiers had given their last full measure, he declared, "that this nation, under God, shall have a new birth of freedom. . . ."

Lincoln reached his great decision in the autumn of 1862. In April, a congressional proclamation had abolished slavery in the District of Columbia. During June, a similar act had ruled slavery out of the territories. Lincoln in late summer drafted the Emancipation Proclamation, read it to his Cabinet, and awaited a decisive Union victory. In September, McClellan drove the Confederate forces from the field at Antietam. Scarcely a decisive victory, Antietam was enough for the purpose. Lincoln proclaimed that unless the rebel states returned to the Union by January, 1863, all slaves in those states, or portions of states, under arms against the Federal government would be given their freedom. On January 1, 1863, informed that none of the Southern states had complied, Lincoln declared the decree in force.

In large degree, Lincoln's proclamation was a war measure designed to bring Negroes into the Union forces. Congress had already authorized the President to enlist Negroes as soldiers. In August, 1862, the War Department instructed General Rufus Saxton, military governor of the South Carolina Sea Islands, to raise five regiments of black troops. Early in 1863 these troops engaged in a series of successful raids into Georgia and Florida. Lincoln now seemed convinced that Negro troops would assure the success of the Union cause. "The bare sight of 50,000 armed and drilled black soldiers upon the banks of the Mississippi," he wrote War Governor Andrew Johnson of Tennessee, "would end the rebellion at once."

Lincoln's judgment of emancipation as a war measure was sound. Before 1863 he had not anticipated the widespread use of black soldiers. Yet after January, 1863, the formation of Negro units was so rapid that eighteen months later Lincoln could acknowledge the presence of 150,000 black men in the Union forces. Of the Emancipation Proclamation he could say, "More than a year of trial now shows no loss by it in our foreign relations, none in our home popular sentiment, none in our white military force—no loss by it anyhow or anywhere. On the contrary, we have the men; and we could not have had them without the measure."

But as a freedom document Lincoln's proclamation was an empty gesture. It freed no slaves. The exclusion from its terms of the loyal slave states brought a gibe from the *London Spectator:* "The principle is not that a human being cannot justly own another, but that he cannot own him unless he is loyal to the United States." Only slaves dwelling in those areas in arms against the United States were declared to be free. In short, the Emancipation Proclamation freed those slaves beyond the reach of its effect and freed none under the authority of the Federal government. The North ignored the discrepancy. Thus Lincoln, despite himself, became the Great Emancipator.

As late as the spring of 1863, the Civil War in the East had produced little but military stalemate. If the North had the greater material resources and manpower, it had failed to effectively employ them. Yet it was also true that although Lee and Jackson had won a series of tactical victories, based largely on superior generalship and imagination, they had not disposed of the Northern armies. Even while they punished the Union forces in battle after battle, the enemy army grew larger, both comparatively and absolutely.

Lee had won his stunning victory at Fredericksburg in December, 1862, largely through Burnside's impatience. Despite the appalling Union casualties, Lee, with 60,000 men west of Fredericksburg, still faced a Union army far larger than his own. Hooker, with 130,000 men under his command, decided to attack, striking Lee's army from the direction of Chancellorsville while his cavalry units swept to the rear of Lee's position and cut his communications with Richmond. Lee responded by sending Jackson with 30,000 men against Hooker's right. Jackson caught General O. O. Howard's forces by complete surprise, their arms stacked and supper in preparation, and drove them back. Meanwhile Lee, with his reduced forces, awaited Hooker's assault. The attack came on May 1, 1863, and continued for five days. Unable to dislodge Lee's forces, Hooker withdrew, blaming his officers for the Union failure. One incident blurred the Confederate victory at Chancellorsville—the accidental death of Stonewall Jackson. Hooker's powerful army was still intact, and Lee, still badly outnumbered, had no interest in assaulting Hooker's forces directly. Lincoln recognized the continuing Northern advantage and instructed Hooker to harass Lee's communications, adding some critical advice, "I think *Lee's* army, and not *Richmond,* is your true objective point. If he comes toward the Upper Potomac, follow on his flank, and on the inside trace, shortening your lines, whilst he lengthens his. Fight him when the opportunity offers. If he stays where he is, fret him, and fret him."

After Chancellorsville, the maneuvering between the two opposing armies continued. Lee, somewhat contemptuous of his Northern antagonist, decided upon a bold advance into Pennsylvania. Hooker moved northward, keeping his army between Lee and the capital. But before the two forces could engage again, Lincoln replaced Hooker with General George G. Meade, a West Point graduate who had performed well as a subordinate officer in the Virginia campaigns. As Lee's advance troops approached Gettysburg on July 1, they engaged detached cavalry and infantry units of the Union army. Following this opening skirmish, Lee and Meade quickly brought their full strength into battle. The Confederates, approaching from west and northwest in ever-increasing numbers, drove the Union forces toward the southeast, where they took up a position on Cemetery Hill at the southern edge of Gettysburg. Lee took up his position along Seminary Ridge, stretching north and south one mile to the west of Cemetery Ridge.

On the second day of the battle, General Richard S. Ewell led a Confederate assault against the Union's right, failing however, to dislodge the Union forces. Meade, having held off the Confederate assaults of the second day, decided to hold his positions and await further Confederate movements. On the third day Lee, gambling on one supreme effort, ordered General George E. Pickett to pierce the Union center—an almost impossible assignment inasmuch as Pickett's men were unable to reach the Union forces on Cemetery Ridge without charging across a half mile of open ground. The final battle at Gettysburg opened with a furious cannonade between artillery units mounted on the opposing ridges. Supported by this barrage, Pickett moved his men forward into a succession of withering artillery and infantry volleys. The Confederates were cut to ribbons, and on the fourth day the battlefield was silent, for Meade refused to countercharge. Lee slowly packed up his forces and began a long, orderly retreat to Virginia.

Meanwhile Union successes in the West brought distinction to one man—General U. S. Grant. Most of the Western action between July and December, 1862, centered in Kentucky and Tennessee, where in a series of inconclusive battles the Confederate forces under General Braxton Bragg failed either to capture control of Kentucky or to hold middle Tennessee. These battles were merely the prelude to the smashing victories of the Union forces in 1863. With Halleck's transfer to Washington in July, 1862, as general-in-chief of all the land forces of the United States, Grant took command of the Union armies in the West. His primary objective was the capture of Vicksburg on the Mississippi.

Grant's assault on Vicksburg relied in part on the North's unchallenged naval supremacy. A combined Union Army-Navy operation under the command of Admiral David G. Farragut ran the forts along the lower Mississippi during April, 1862, and occupied New Orleans. In June, Farragut took a flotilla up the Mississippi but failed to capture Vicksburg, the powerful fortress which commanded a hairpin curve on the river. General William T. Sherman attempted to approach Vicksburg from the north through the swampy Yazoo Delta in December but found it hopeless. The only remaining approaches to the city were from the south and east.

In spring, 1863, Grant embarked on his most imaginative and successful maneuver of the war. Leaving his base at Memphis, he took his army to Milliken's Bend north of Vicksburg, where the Union fleet transported it across the Mississippi. Grant then marched his troops south of Vicksburg through Louisiana's marshes and swamps, while the Union craft ran the batteries at Vicksburg. By the end of April, 1863, the vessels were ready to transport Grant's army across the river into Mississippi at Bruinsburg. Grant, temporarily isolated from his source of supplies, moved rapidly. In a series of thrusts northward he defeated portions of the Confederate forces, taking Jackson, the Mississippi capital, on May 14. Five days later, having encompassed the only avenues of retreat from Vicksburg by land or water, Grant settled down to a siege of the city. For six weeks the opposing armies faced one another at distances of six hundred yards or less. By July the situation within the city had become desperate as food supplies dwindled, and the city continued to disintegrate under the endless bombardment of the Union gunboats and Grant's artillery. On July 4, John C. Pemberton surrendered his entire force of 30,000 men. No longer did the South have the military capacity to sustain losses of such magnitude. After Vicksburg the Union fleet could at last move freely on the Mississippi from its mouth to the Ohio.

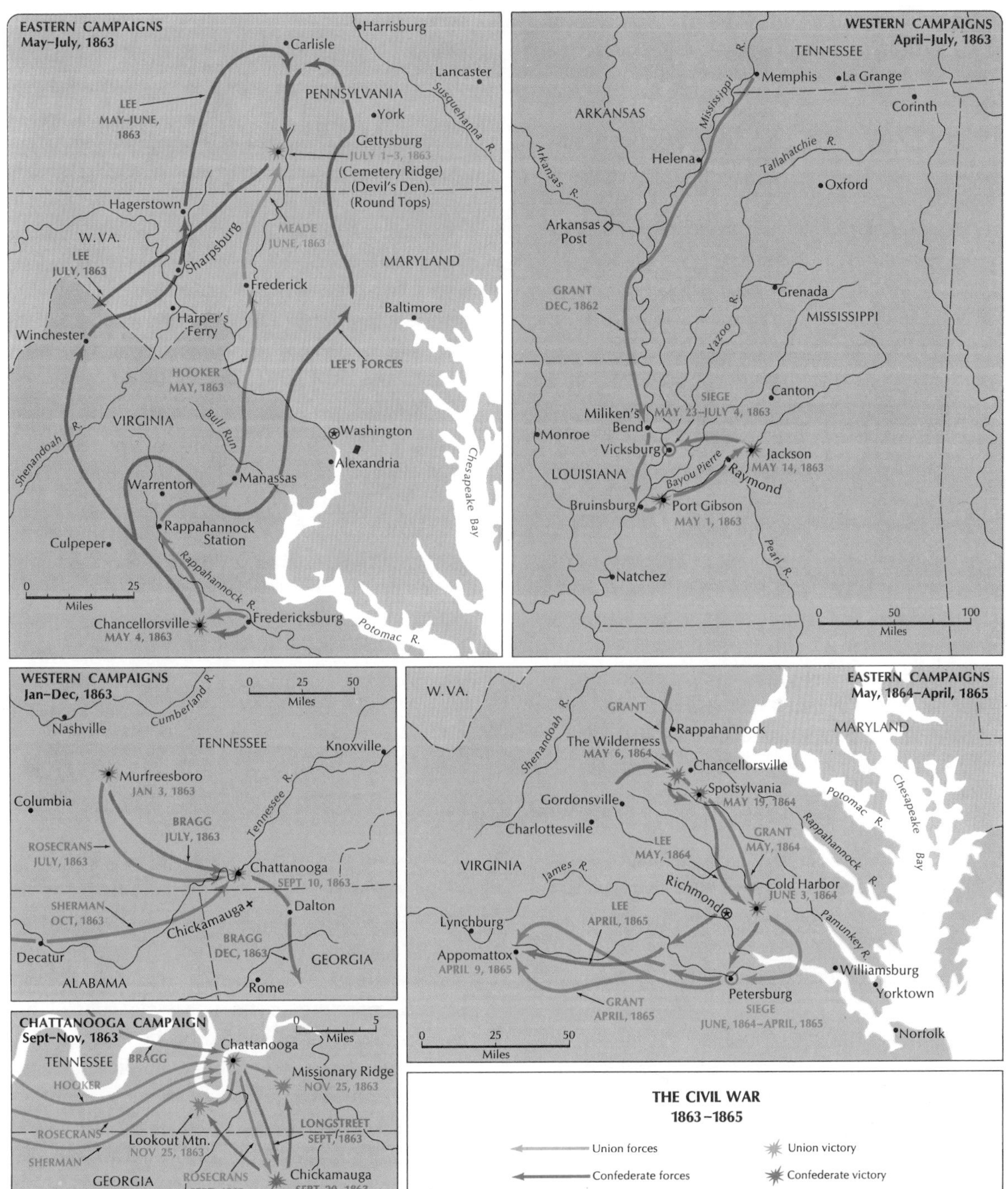

EASTERN CAMPAIGNS
May–July, 1863
Harrisburg
Carlisle
Lancaster
PENNSYLVANIA
York
Susquehanna R.
LEE
MAY–JUNE,
1863
Gettysburg
JULY 1–3, 1863
(Cemetery Ridge)
(Devil's Den)
(Round Tops)
Hagerstown
W. VA.
Sharpsburg
MEADE
JUNE, 1863
LEE
JULY, 1863
Frederick
MARYLAND
Baltimore
Harper's
Ferry
Winchester
HOOKER
MAY, 1863
LEE'S FORCES
VIRGINIA
Bull Run
Shenandoah R.
Washington
Alexandria
Chesapeake Bay
Warrenton
Manassas
Rappahannock
Station
Culpeper
Rappahannock R.
0
25
Miles
Chancellorsville
MAY 4, 1863
Fredericksburg
Potomac R.
WESTERN CAMPAIGNS
April–July, 1863
TENNESSEE
Mississippi R.
Memphis
La Grange
Corinth
ARKANSAS
Arkansas R.
Helena
Tallahatchie R.
Oxford
Arkansas
Post
GRANT
DEC, 1862
Grenada
Yazoo R.
MISSISSIPPI
SIEGE
MAY 23–JULY 4, 1863
Canton
Miliken's
Bend
Monroe
Vicksburg
Jackson
MAY 14, 1863
LOUISIANA
Bayou Pierre
Raymond
Bruinsburg
Port Gibson
MAY 1, 1863
Pearl R.
Natchez
0
50
100
Miles
WESTERN CAMPAIGNS
Jan–Dec, 1863
Cumberland R.
0
25
50
Miles
Nashville
TENNESSEE
Knoxville
Murfreesboro
JAN 3, 1863
Columbia
BRAGG
JULY, 1863
Tennessee R.
ROSECRANS
JULY, 1863
Chattanooga
SEPT 10, 1863
SHERMAN
OCT, 1863
Dalton
Chickamauga
BRAGG
DEC, 1863
Decatur
GEORGIA
ALABAMA
Rome
CHATTANOOGA CAMPAIGN
Sept–Nov, 1863
0
5
Miles
Chattanooga
TENNESSEE
BRAGG
Missionary Ridge
NOV 25, 1863
HOOKER
LONGSTREET
SEPT, 1863
ROSECRANS
Lookout Mtn.
NOV 25, 1863
SHERMAN
GEORGIA
ROSECRANS
SEPT, 1863
Chickamauga
SEPT 20, 1863
EASTERN CAMPAIGNS
May, 1864–April, 1865
W. VA.
GRANT
Rappahannock
MARYLAND
Shenandoah R.
The Wilderness
MAY 6, 1864
Chancellorsville
Spotsylvania
MAY 19, 1864
Potomac R.
Chesapeake Bay
Gordonsville
Charlottesville
GRANT
MAY, 1864
Rappahannock R.
LEE
MAY, 1864
VIRGINIA
James R.
Cold Harbor
JUNE 3, 1864
Richmond
Pamunkey R.
Lynchburg
LEE
APRIL, 1865
Appomattox
APRIL 9, 1865
Williamsburg
Yorktown
GRANT
APRIL, 1865
Petersburg
SIEGE
JUNE, 1864–APRIL, 1865
0
25
50
Miles
Norfolk
THE CIVIL WAR
1863–1865
Union forces
Confederate forces
Union victory
Confederate victory

The Civil War

Grant now shifted his chief operations away from the Mississippi toward the Confederate armies protecting Alabama and Georgia. General William S. Rosecrans, having driven off Bragg's Confederate forces in a fierce engagement at Murfreesboro, Tennessee, late in December, 1862, occupied that city. In June, 1863, after several months of preparation, Rosecrans moved toward Chattanooga, Bragg's new headquarters. During September he managed to take the city without a battle. But Lee, seeing the importance of protecting the heartland of the South, dispatched Longstreet with 11,000 men by rail to take over the defenses outside Chattanooga. There on the field of Chickamauga, Longstreet met and defeated Rosecrans in a major battle. Rosecrans drifted back into Chattanooga and prepared to make another stand in the city. The battle had been exceedingly costly to both sides, but Bragg controlled the rail lines into Chattanooga and seemed capable of rendering Rosecrans's position untenable. Confederate forces, moreover, occupied Missionary Ridge and Lookout Mountain above Chattanooga.

Grant now came to Rosecrans's support. While Union detachments opened up the Tennessee River for transportation of food, Sherman moved from Memphis as rapidly as General G. M. Dodge and his engineers could rebuild the Tennessee railroads. Grant was ready by November 23 to send his 60,000 men against Bragg's 40,000. Sherman struck the Confederate right at Missionary Ridge; Hooker's two corps advanced against the Confederate left at Lookout Mountain, carrying the height against little opposition. After two days, Bragg's forces were still concentrated on Missionary Ridge where Sherman could not dislodge them. That afternoon two divisions under George H. Thomas moved out to relieve Sherman by taking the Confederate positions at the foot of the ridge. Having achieved this, without orders but simply caught up in the spirit of battle, they swept up the ridge, dislodged the Confederate forces, and carried the crest. Bragg now retreated with what remained of his army; Tennessee had been cleared of resistance by the Confederate forces.

Grant in Command

Union victories at Gettysburg, Vicksburg, and Chattanooga during 1863 set the stage for the overwhelming Union successes that were to follow. If the Western campaigns had not shown Grant to be a great military strategist, they had proven his tenacity. Long convinced that ruthless conduct of the war would bring the Confederacy to terms, the President on March 9, 1864, presented Grant with a commission as lieutenant general and gave him command of all the Union armies. Recognizing the necessity of invading Virginia, capturing Richmond, and destroying Lee's army, the new commanding general opened his Virginia campaign in May, 1864, by pushing the Army of the Potomac across the Rapidan to the west of Fredericksburg. There in the heavily wooded and tangled "Wilderness" where he could neither plan the battle nor even control his troops, Grant met Lee's army in what quickly disintegrated into a terrible slaughter Grant lost an estimated 18,000 of his 118,000 troops. He knew, however, that he could afford such losses much more readily than Lee could the 10,000 which he left in the Wilderness. Grant, instead of retiring, continued his pursuit. The two

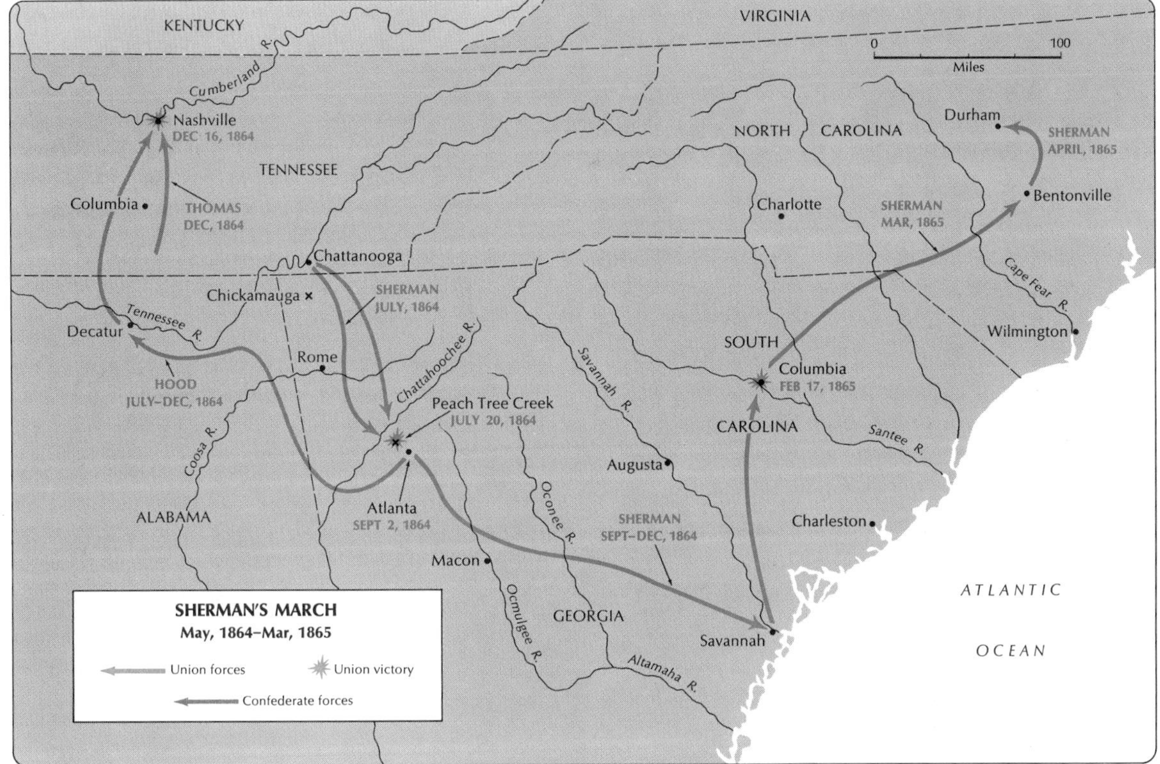

armies met again at Spotsylvania Court House in a second battle of unprecedented ferocity, then pushed on to Cold Harbor. Here Grant threw three corps against Lee's strong intrenchments, suffered 12,000 casualties, and achieved nothing. It was the greatest blunder of Grant's Virginia campaign, intensifying the demands for peace in the North and producing a feeling of regret within Grant which he carried until his death. In one month of campaigning Grant had lost 55,000 men, a number almost the equivalent of Lee's entire army. Unlike Lee, however, Grant now had access to unlimited manpower, food, and supplies. Despite Lee's heroic defense of Virginia and his tactical achievements, his Army of Northern Virginia had been proportionately more badly damaged than had Grant's.

General Grant now transferred his army across the James in a move against Richmond from the south. Between June 15 and 18 the Union forces assaulted Petersburg. Before they could move forward, Lee arrived with his army, saving Petersburg and Richmond for the moment. Grant used a month of comparative inaction to mine the Confederate position. On July 30, a mammoth explosion within the Confederate lines set off another massive assault. Never had Lee's soldiers fought as valiantly as they did on that day. At the battle's end, Lee remained in control of Petersburg and Richmond. After weeks of bloody fighting, the war in Virginia settled down to a long siege. "Hold on with a bulldog grip," Lincoln instructed his general in August, "and chew and choke as much as possible." Grant, meanwhile, directed his war of attrition aginst other Southern fronts.

At Chattanooga, Tennessee, Sherman commanded a magnificent army of 98,000 facing 53 000 Confederates under Joseph E. Johnston. Under instructions from Grant to "get into the interior of the enemy's country as far as you can, inflicting all the damage you can against their war resources," Sherman's advance through the mountains to Chattanooga had not been easy and now his lines of communication ran back over a mediocre railroad to Louisville. Johnston meanwhile engaged Sherman in a series of defensive maneuvers, avoiding a major battle as he fell back on Atlanta. Johnston was replaced by J. B. Hood, who immediately exposed his forces at Peach Tree Creek on July 20, only to take a whipping which forced his retreat to Atlanta. When Sherman's forces surrounded Atlanta and cut off the flow of supplies, Hood withdrew on September 1, and Sherman occupied the city the following day.

Sherman now did a surprising thing. He cut the railroad line to Chattanooga to protect his rear, ordered all civilians out of Atlanta, and proceeded to burn the city. On November 10, 1864, he began his famous march to the sea. Sherman's four army corps moved toward Savannah on four roads, covering a band 60 miles in width. The devastation along the route of travel was complete, including bridges, railroads, and rolling stock, as well as homes and villages. Turning northward after the capture of Savannah, Sherman invaded the Carolinas. Fortunately the city of Charleston, the center of the rebellion, was not along the route of travel. But the Union forces entered Columbia, the capital of South Carolina; before they left, the city was burned.

Grant's attention had meanwhile turned to the strategic and agriculturally rich Shenandoah Valley of Virginia. In September, 1864, he dispatched Philip Sheridan to follow Jubal A. Early's Confederate forces, recently retired from the environs of Washington, into the Shenandoah Valley and to devastate the area. Sheridan defeated the Confederates at Winchester on September 19 and then proceeded to fight his way down the valley in a series of minor engagements. Sheridan's forces scattered out across the rich valley, destroying everything—crops, livestock, buildings, railroads, and bridges. By October they had reduced one of the South's most productive farmlands to a desolate waste. At the end of 1864, although Grant had not yet disposed of Lee's army, Sherman was moving northward through the Carolinas, and Sheridan had returned from his Shenandoah venture to join Grant in a final thrust against Lee and the Confederate capital.

Seward's Diplomacy

In the vast arsenal of resources available to the North, diplomacy assumed major significance, for the country's future would be determined not only on the field of battle but also in the chancelleries of Europe. European attitudes toward the American Civil War varied from country to country, but of most general concern to Europeans was the conviction that American influence and institutions were on trial. The United States as a new world power had passed beyond the control of European diplomacy, but if the American people appeared determined to destroy their national greatness and demonstrate the failure of their political institutions, reactionary Europe could certainly cheer their efforts. Lincoln's Secretary of State, William H. Seward, undertook the necessary task of preventing European power from being thrown into the balance. To forestall European interference in this nation's affairs after the fall of Sumter, the Secretary had to deny officially that a state of war existed between North and South.

Seward became disturbed in May, 1861, when the British Queen, recognizing the existence of the Northern blockade of the South, issued a declaration of neutrality, a move duplicated by France, Spain, the Netherlands, and Brazil. This was a recognition of Southern belligerency and suggested the possibility of full diplomatic recognition of the Southern rebels. Seward hastened to warn the British and French that recognition of the Confederacy meant war with the United States.

Conscious of the importance of European goodwill to its cause, the Confederate government in November, 1861, commissioned two distinguished Southerners, James M. Mason and John Slidell, to carry the Southern quest for recognition and aid to London and Paris. At Havana they took passage for Europe on a British merchant vessel, the *Trent*. One day out, the packet was stopped by the United States warship *San Jacinto* under Captain Charles Wilkes. A search party removed the two Confederate envoys with their two secretaries and took them to Boston, where, as political prisoners, they were confined in Fort Warren. Throughout the North the exultation quickly elevated Wilkes to the stature of a hero. But when Palmerston, the British Prime Minister, received the news, he flew into a rage. "You may stand for this," he told the British cabinet, "but damned if I will!" Seward recognized the justice in the British position and gave up the case on principle. Wilkes had erred especially in removing the prisoners to the *San Jacinto* instead of taking the *Trent* into port for adjudication. Mason and Slidell, who had suspected correctly that they might serve the Confederate cause better in a Northern prison than in Europe, were sent on their way. Long before they arrived in London, the British public had lost interest in them.

During the critical months before Antietam, both England and France, convinced that the Southern cause would triumph, seriously considered intervention. Throughout the autumn of 1862, Seward exerted relentless pressure on both European governments. When the French Minister in Washington, Henri Mercier, transmitted a French offer of mediation in July, 1862, Seward warned him that "the Emperor can commit no graver error than to mix himself in our affairs." Then news of McClellan's success at Antietam produced sufficient doubt within the British and French governments to forestall any immediate decisions for involvement. In November, 1862, the British cabinet made its final decision to observe strict neutrality in the American Civil War; the French government followed the British lead.

Lincoln's Emancipation Proclamation, although designed at least partially to influence European attitudes toward the Union cause, had little influence on European sentiment and none on European action. British conservatives thought it foolhardy and anticipated a servile insurrection. British liberals, abolitionists, and workingmen lauded the Proclamation, but these groups had always favored the Union becaused it represented the cause of democracy. The diplomatic success of the North found its fundamental explanation less in economic interests and liberal sentiment than in an established diplomatic tradition. Many nations in the past had undergone internal revolution in which elements seeking power had sought to overthrow established governments. Such uprisings had succeeded and failed, but the record demonstrated that when a major nation was threatened, no external power could intervene diplomatically without running the risk of military involvement. The United States itself had recognized this danger in its decisions favoring nonintervention in the revolutions of Latin America, Greece, and Hungary.

Lincoln had no greater interest in involving the United States in Louis Napoleon's military and political intervention in Mexico. When, in 1861, Napoleon dispatched an army to Mexico and began to interfere openly in the internal affairs of that Latin American country, Seward refused to commit the United States to Mexico's defense on appeal to the Monroe Doctrine. Instead, he warned Napoleon that France could not control the political structure of Mexico because the Mexicans would not permit it. This warning, the Secretary added, was grounded on some knowledge of the political sentiments of American society.

Even when France, in 1864, established Maximilian of Austria as the Emperor of Mexico, Seward continued to avoid any open American commitment to Mexican independence. Both Lincoln and Seward recognized the need of hoarding the country's energy to preserve the Union, and they refused to dissipate American resources in involvements abroad to defend principles which they knew must succeed or fail on their own. The assumptions of the Lincoln administration proved to be accurate. Eventually Napoleon found the financial and military price of his Mexican involvement so burdensome that in 1866 he withdrew what was left of his army and permitted Maximilian to die before a Mexican firing squad.

Problems of the Confederacy

After 1862, the Confederacy struggled for independence against overwhelming odds. Southerners had overestimated the power of "King Cotton." Cotton had dominated the prewar export trade of the United States; without it, predicted the secessionists, the mills of England and France would lie idle. So confident was the South of the power of cotton to force European recognition of its interest that it instituted an embargo early in the war to force British and French intervention. Next, the South resorted to crop curtailment, producing only 1 million bales in 1862, or about one-third the crop of the previous year. In 1863, cotton production figures dipped even lower. Southerners finally resorted to destroying hundreds of thousands of bales of cotton to assure scarcity in Europe and keep cotton out of Northern hands. Too late, the South discovered that cotton was only a normal, not a miracle, weapon. Because of the heavy export of cotton in previous years, that commodity in 1861 was a glut on the British market. When Confederate policy eventually produced extensive hardship in the mill districts of England, British workingmen turned against the South for creating the shortage. Cotton had no influence whatever on the British Foreign Office. Whatever Southern hopes for European intervention still existed after Antietam were shattered by the Confederate disasters at Gettysburg and Vicksburg in July, 1863.

Southern leaders never succeeded in creating an efficient administration. President Jefferson

Davis, although completely devoted to the Confederate cause, suffered from ill health and, in any event, lacked the magnetism and vitality to sustain the Southern war effort. By 1862, many leading secessionists had begun to attack and ridicule his leadership. Eventually the entire Confederate government came under bitter criticism from the Southern press. On January 10, 1863, the *Charleston Mercury* charged that in all departments of the Confederate government "there reigned a pandemonium of imbecility, laxness, laxity, weakness and failure."

Southern weakness was economic as well as political. Despite some industrial progress in the fifties, the South could not overcome its reliance on Northern and foreign mills, factories, and shops for manufactured articles. It tried to meet the economic challenge of war by developing the art of blockade running and eventually by expanding its own industrial production. Southern editors urged the South to shift its capital to industry. But the South lacked the enterprise, skilled labor, and resources to build the productive capacity demanded by modern war. The most conspicuous industrial success of the Confederacy was the conversion of the Tredegar Iron Works at Richmond into an astonishingly productive munitions plant.

Without ordnance factories, the South in 1861 relied on large-scale imports from Europe. Still the Confederacy lost no battles because of shortages in arms and ammunition, and for this the credit must go to Josiah Gorgas, the Confederacy's chief of ordnance. Through his encouragement, the Richmond government established arsenals and foundries in key areas of Alabama, Georgia, and South Carolina, as well as a huge powder mill at Augusta. The Confederacy was far less successful, however, in obtaining adequate quantities of food and clothing. The region possessed no large textile industries, and the shoe and uniform factories eventually established never satisfied the demand. Southern railroads were always short of equipment, and the South lacked the capacity to maintain the roadbeds it had. As the war progressed, rail service suffered from broken ties, flat wheels, dilapidated cars, and powerless locomotives.

Confederate finances also reflected the South's lack of production. In four years that government raised only $25 million in liquid capital. Its accumulation each year was only twice what the Federal government spent each day. This scarcity of gold and silver forced the Confederacy to manufacture paper money in vast amounts, creating an inflation which became worse as time wore on. By 1865, the value of the Confederate dollar was equal to 1 cent in gold. The South, by destroying its cotton, had denied itself the sale of its one commodity that might have built up needed credits in Europe.

Despite its weaknesses in politics, production, transportation, and finance, the Confederacy created an army that reached 260,000 men in 1863—one of the most effective fighting forces in modern history. Through four grueling years, the Richmond government sustained a prodigious military effort and did not give up till much of the South had been systematically devastated by total war. Whatever the weaknesses in the Southern command structure and its outmoded strategies, Lee, Jackson, and others inspired their soldiers to unsurpassed feats of courage and heroism. Almost one hundred thousand Confederates died in battle, a sacrifice in relation to population greater than any European nation had ever sustained in war.

Yet Southern morale inevitably slumped as the promise of victory receded. Perhaps most people of the South had opposed the secession movement, and there was very little in the subsequent Confederate experience to convince them that the struggle for Southern independence was other than a dreadful mistake. For those who carried the war's military and civilian burden, the inefficiency of the Confederate government was unbearable. They resented laws which exempted many from military duty, especially slaveholders who had the requisite number of slaves engaged in food production. By 1864 soldiers in the South were deserting by the thousands; the whole system of supply had broken down. Southern governors, under the doctrine of states' rights, were undermining the entire Confederate war effort. Finally Lee went to Richmond to express his concern to President Davis. His impressions of the government in Richmond he recorded for his son: "I visited Congress today and they did not seem to be able to do anything except to eat peanuts and chew tobacco while my army is starving. I told them the condition my men were in and something must be done at once, but I can't get them to do anything, or they are unable to do anything. When this war began I told these people that unless every man should do his whole duty they would repent it, and now—they will repent it."

Behind the Northern Lines

Life behind the Northern lines bore little resemblance to that in the Confederacy. Northerners, no more than Southerners, could escape the emotional onslaught of the war's death and destruction, but the North, able to maintain the offensive, escaped the terrible presence of an invading enemy. One Illinois soldier, in August, 1863, reminded relatives at home of their good fortune. "I allmost sicken," he admitted, "at the thought of this war ever reaching the homes of my family and friends. I think I would be willing to . . . sacrifice my life on the soil of the Southern States to shield the soil of Illinois from the dreded tramp of an army. . . . You should be the last people to murmer at the war tax. If you could travel with the Army of the Cumberland a few days you would learn that the inhabitants of those States pay all they possess and pay it in a few hours. Women and children cry but to no avail." The North's ultimate advantage lay in the capacity of its industry, transportation, and agriculture to meet the demands of total war. Northern productivity was sufficient to supply both guns and butter. The *New York Times* reported in 1864 that the people of the North were better fed, clothed, and sheltered than ever before in the nation's history.

Northern business responded quickly to the Confederate challenge. Still, the War Department's almost limitless need for goods and equipment created totally unprecedented pressures on the nation's productive resources. Whether the government procured uniforms, munitions, or food, it soon found itself paying premium prices for second-rate merchandise. Compounding the problem and multiplying the opportunities for profiteering was the fact that the state governments controlled the raising and supplying of the volunteer forces. Through agents and members of Congress, Northern governors exerted tremendous influence in Washington, and by bidding against the War Department for supplies and equipment in both the United States and Europe, they drove prices skyward at a prodigious rate. This confusion, created by frenzied haste and conflicting procurement procedures, led to an orgy of waste, fraud, and speculation. The appointment of Edwin M. Stanton as Lincoln's second Secretary of War in early 1862 brought a modicum of order into the federal procurement system, but the problems of profiteering and corruption proved particularly intractable.

Special governmental and private agencies ministered to the health and comfort of Union troops. The United States Sanitary Commission, a civilian auxiliary to the medical bureau of the War Department, was by far the most important agency engaged in the work of sanitation and hospitalization. In addition, many private groups established military hospitals, staffed them with volunteer nurses, and effectively supplemented the efforts of the government in caring for the wounded. Their services went beyond medical care to include the supplying of books, magazines, and even financial assistance. Whether by public or private endeavor, the North reached an unprecedented degree of organization in its effort to sustain a triumphant military endeavor.

Industrialism was the foundation of the new America being forged on the anvil of war. Almost every branch of manufacturing in the North responded to wartime requirements and new protective tariffs. The cotton textile industry, deprived of its raw materials, suffered as the result of the war, but the woolen industry expanded to take its place in the New England factory towns. There was a steady increase in the output of coal, iron, and oil, the three major extractive industries; they brought additional new wealth to New England, Pennsylvania, and northern Ohio. The arms industry, which before the war could manufacture only 22,000 weapons a year, reached a capacity of 5,000 rifles per day by 1865. Every Northern city sprouted new industries, but the most spectacular advances in production came from the application of new machines and processes to industries already established.

Agricultural prosperity in the Middle West reflected not only the needs of the Union armies but also the poor harvests of Europe, from which England especially suffered in the early sixties. Between 1859 and 1862, England's importation of American grain increased fifty-fold. This continuing economic revolution on the Midwestern prairies accelerated the development of the Great Lakes country. By the sixties, Chicago had become the largest primary wheat market in the world.

From 1862 until 1865 the North's commercial and industrial leaders enjoyed an uninterrupted spree. Materialism had triumphed, bringing a new commercial and financial preeminence to New York. "Every man worships the dollar, and is down before his shrine from morning to night," wrote the famous British visitor Anthony Trollope in 1862. Secretary of the Treasury Chase in 1864 found the leading businessmen of New York more concerned over the stock market than news from the front. Exploiting the opportunities afforded by war and the economic measures of Congress, the new industrial and financial class marched unopposed to wealth and glory.

Northern labor, unorganized economically or politically, was no match for those who controlled the nation's business and governmental policies. Unsupported by congressional action, wages lagged behind prices. During the war years the average wage stood a full 43 percent above the prewar level, but the more rapid climb of prices actually reduced real wages to about two-thirds of their 1861 level. Industrialists fought the tendencies of skilled labor to organize, and the government demonstrated its open hostility by encouraging the importation of contract labor to fill the needs of business. Responding to the demands of Northern industry, Congress in 1864 created a Bureau of Immigration and authorized the importation of semi-indentured labor. Labor in general supported the war effort, but having no voice in national policy, it occasionally battled conscription, refused reenlistment, and deserted. This latent bitterness toward the maldistribution of the economic rewards erupted in a series of draft riots in New York City during July, 1863.

The Republican leadership's only unrelenting opposition centered in the lower Middle West. Douglas, before his death in 1861, warned his fellow Westerners that in war there could be no neutrals—only patriots and traitors. Much of the Ohio Valley responded to his nationalism and raised troops, but many Western Democrats never ceased to condemn the Republican administration and its wartime policies. These "Copperheads," as the Republicans called them, condemned the confiscation acts, the Emancipation Proclamation, the conscription laws, the violations of freedom of the press, and especially the "abolitionist fanaticism" to which they attributed the prolongation of the war. To the proponents of total war, such Democratic criticism was treasonable. Undoubtedly Lincoln's Democratic enemies were as partisan as those Republicans who sought to build their wartime power through special appeals to patriotism. Although Republican policies, if not the Republican party, enjoyed the overwhelming support of Northern sentiment, Lincoln could not ignore what appeared to be pro-Southern sympathies in the North, for much of the criticism directed at the war effort verged on the disloyal. Lincoln was never reluctant to use Executive power in behalf of the Union cause, but he could not harness Northern freedom of expression without challenging deeply engrained maxims of Anglo-Saxon civil liberty.

The civil liberties case of Clement L. Vallandigham was the most spectacular of the war. In May, 1863, in a speech at Mount Vernon, Ohio, this Democratic politician and outspoken critic of Lincoln's wartime efforts accused the President of avoiding compromise and needlessly prolonging the bloodshed. Vallandigham insisted that he advocated resistance only through debate and the ballot, not through acts of insurrection. Nevertheless, General Ambrose E. Burnside, then commander of the Department of the Ohio, accused him of "declaring sympathies for the enemy" and had him arrested. The military commission found Vallandigham guilty and sentenced him to close confinement for the duration of the war. Lincoln, embarrassed by the sympathetic response of many in the North to the Ohioan's appeals for liberty, escaped his dilemma by commuting Vallandigham's sentence to banishment behind the Confederate lines. Later Vallandigham escaped from the South and took up his residence in Windsor, Canada, where he continued his assault on the Republican leadership. Finally in 1864 he reentered the United States and campaigned openly for the Democratic party. The Supreme Court in February, 1864, refused to touch the Vallandigham issue. But in a similar case, that of L. P. Milligan, arrested in Indianapolis in October, 1864, the Court in the famous civil rights decision of *ex parte Milligan* of April, 1866, declared Milligan's trial by a military commission illegal, since no actual invasion had occurred and civil courts still functioned.

The actual conduct of the war enjoyed little support in Congress, the press, or the Republican party leadership. Most Republicans felt no obligations of loyalty to Lincoln. Richard Henry Dana reported from Washington, "He has no admirers, no enthusiastic supporters, none to bet on his head." This open rejection of Lincoln's leadership by members of his own party had a strong political motivation. Long-term Republican power hinged on that party's ability to exploit its wartime advantages in making further inroads among the North's Democratic constituency. To demonstrate their agreement on the fundamental objective of suppressing the "rebellion," the Republicans and the War Democrats combined early in the war to form the Union party. Yet even this maneuver failed to strengthen the Republican cause. Democratic victories in 1862, reducing the Republican majority in the House from 35 to 18, reminded the Radicals that except for the absence of Southerners they would have lost control of Congress completely. In Lincoln, the Radicals had a ready alibi and scapegoat for their failures at the polls and for the disappointments of the interminable struggle that was the war.

By 1864 the Radicals were prepared to desert the President for one of their own number. Many of them believed that there were better Republican candidates available. In this group was Secretary of the Treasury Salmon P. Chase, who regarded himself as admirably suited for the Presidency. Chase's ambition, however, was hampered by his position in the Cabinet. He could not establish his availability under the cloak of administration policy, nor could he openly announce his aspirations or attack the President. To resign his Cabinet post during the heat of war would bring accusations that he was shirking his duty. He had to be relieved, and to that end he quarreled with Lincoln and the Cabinet, but the President conceded each point. Finally in June, 1864, after Lincoln had been renominated at Baltimore, Chase again attempted to obstruct the administration and threatened to resign. This time, the President, to Chase's consternation, accepted the offer. Meanwhile during May the disaffected Radicals had met in Cleveland, heaped their customary abuse on Lincoln, and nominated John C. Frémont for the Presidency on a Radical platform.

In his fierce struggles with the Radicals, Lincoln moved with the skill of a master craftsman. Always sensitive to public trends and the demands of a restless nation, he could shift from secrecy and procrastination to firmness and decision when the occasion demanded. Often by recourse to stories and good humor he would disarm the most obstreperous callers at the White House and dismiss them later with their questions unanswered. If congressional heads would not conform to his leadership, there were powerful weapons in the presidential arsenal which he could and would employ. Behind the scenes Lincoln's agents maneuvered, lining up convention votes with executive patronage. Before any other candidate could enter the field, Lincoln had assured his own renomination. When the regular Republican convention met at Baltimore in June, Lincoln received every vote recorded. The victorious nominee then picked his own candidate for the vice presidency—Andrew Johnson, a War Democrat from Tennessee.

Lincoln's chances against the Democrats appeared less than promising. War-weariness was undermining the nation's confidence in his leadership. To capitalize on the peace sentiment, the Democrats postponed their convention until late August and then, at Chicago, nominated the popular war hero, George McClellan. The Democratic platform referred to "four years of failure to restore the Union by the experiment of war" and demanded an end to hostilities at the earliest possible moment commensurate with the restoration of the Union. McClellan, however, repudiated the peace platform and emphasized instead the need for restoring the Union. He campaigned purely as a war leader, attacking Lincoln and his administration, not for their purpose, but for their inefficiency and failure to achieve it.

Lincoln's chances brightened as the election approached. In September, Sherman entered Atlanta. The Republicans won victories in Maine and Vermont. Frémont withdrew from the race, and a last-minute Radical convention to replace Lincoln with another candidate failed to materialize. Thereafter the Radicals had no alternative but to support Lincoln.

Lincoln's election in 1864 demonstrated how inconsequential his personal popularity actually was. With the South out of the Union, he received but 52 percent of the popular vote. Powerful Democratic minorities in New York, Pennsylvania, Ohio, Indiana, and Illinois indicated that the Democratic party was far from dead, even in the North. McClellan carried only three states—Kentucky, Delaware, and New Jersey—but he had secured almost half the ballots. The campaign had demonstrated the essential fact, however, that those Northerners who believed the war unrighteous were too insignificant numerically to encourage the South or influence the North.

The War's End

The spring of 1865 saw the hopes of the South fade and collapse. Sherman was moving northward from Columbia through the Carolinas. Outside Petersburg the Confederates continued to resist. Finally on April 1, Federal troops broke the Richmond defenses and entered the ruined city. Grant trapped the remnants of Lee's ragged army at Appomattox Court House. Grant had sent to Lincoln Sheridan's telegram stating that if "the thing is pressed I think that Lee will surrender." The President replied characteristically, "Let the *thing* be pressed." It was Lincoln's final military order. Whatever Lincoln expected of the peace, he did not live to mold it. Five days after Lee's surrender, on the evening of April 14, the President attended Ford's Theater in Washington. There John Wilkes Booth entered his box and fired a bullet into his brain. Lincoln lingered through the night, then died. He had saved the Union, but the task of national reconstruction belonged to others.

Conclusion

For the victorious North the Civil War constituted the bloody divide between an older America that was agricultural, rural, humanitarian, and personalized and a new America that was industrial, urban, secular, and institutionalized. The trend toward the large-scale or-

The Documented War

The Civil War—America's grimmest, dirtiest, most bitter test—became the world's first exhaustively documented conflict. Reporters and correspondents wrote millions of words; uncountable pages of orders, plans, official papers, letters, and memoirs appeared; countless sketches, paintings, and engravings were made. But above all, there were photographs—hundreds of thousands of tintypes, daguerreotypes, and wet plate negatives recorded every facet of the struggle. For the first time an entire country truly *saw* a war.

Our primary impression of the Civil War is a visual one created by Alexander Gardner, Timothy H. O'Sullivan, and George W. Barnard, by the photographers supervised by Mathew Brady, and by hundreds of lesser known cameramen. Their images are as stark and compelling today as they were then, when the nation tore open its own flesh and bled for agonizing years.

Library of Congress

Civil War officers were often professionals, but the soldiers were ordinary men and boys who first volunteered and later were drafted from cities, farms, and plantations. For the first time families had pictures to remind them of the men at war. These photographs of Confederates (this page) and Federals (opposite) typify the many thousands sent home from training camps and the front. Usually inexpensive but durable (and therefore mailable) tintypes such as these measured about 2 × 3½ inches. Blacks, who fought valiantly for the North, encountered bitter hatred in the South. When captured, they were considered contraband, or war booty, rather than prisoners.

Above, left and right: Library of Congress
Below, far right: Library of Congress
Below right: Courtesy Chicago Historical Society

The South could never bring itself to arm Negroes, even when it desperately needed troops, but the Union Army had segregated black regiments from 1862 onward. Valiant soldiers, they comprised almost 20 percent of Federal troops by war's end.

All pictures: Library of Congress

Confederates
advancing to the capture of

All pictures: Library of Congress

Many famous illustrators covered the war for newspapers and magazines. Field artists Alfred and William Waud drew vivid sketches such as these as the basis for engravings in *Harper's Weekly.*

Clara Barton formed the Red Cross during the Civil War but field hospitals and doctors were few. An injured limb almost surely meant amputation under primitive conditions. Anaesthesia and antiseptic precautions were unknown. Infection and disease killed twice as many on both sides as died in battle.

Captured soldiers fared even worse. Conditions in North and South prison camps were horrendous, as attested to in the photograph of a Federal survivor of infamous Andersonville (following page).

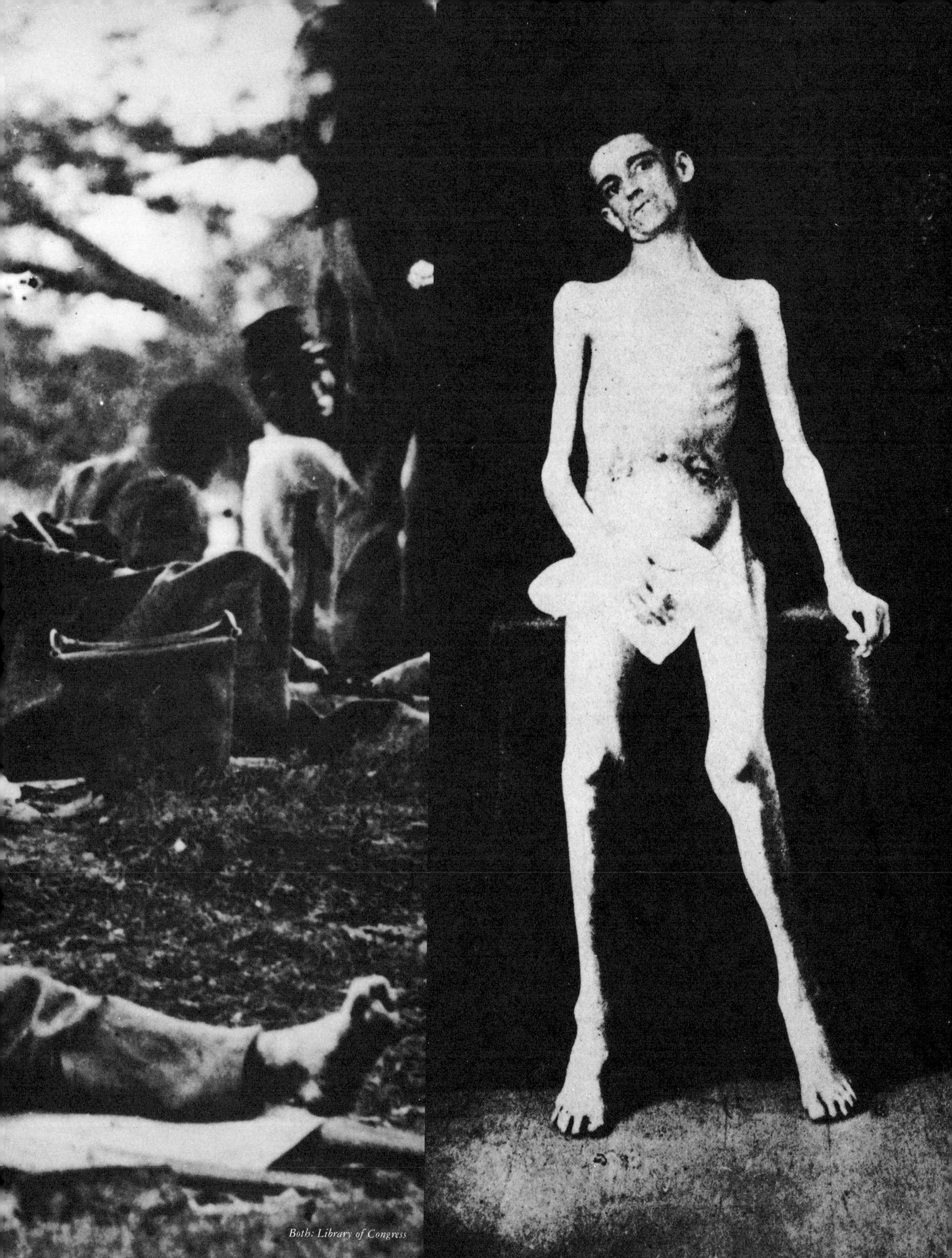

Both: Library of Congress

Library of Congress

The war was dirty, grim, grinding. New machines, new fighting techniques wreaked a physical devastation unseen before. For the first time commanders relied on reducing civilians to despair and crippling every kind of production as well as on crushing the enemy's military force. Pounding artillery, rockets, torpedoes, siege, unrelenting assault all aimed at one goal: destruction.

More men died in the Civil War than the total of all of America's other wars. The human damage was irreparable; the human attitudes remained unchanged.

Library of Congress

ganization of American life had been well under way before the war began; the need to mobilize for victory merely accelerated the process. Fundamentally what shaped the new nation was the need to create a huge army; to feed and clothe it; to supply it with munitions; to organize its sanitation, finance, and medical services; to provide it with efficient transportation; and to develop popular support to sustain it. Such a broad national effort required the coordination of efforts and acceptance of national direction. It transformed an inchoate country, once guided by individual effort without regard to public interest, into a disciplined nation, increasingly subject to national planning and control. It shifted the emphasis of human behavior from individualism to cooperation, for the interest in victory was public, not private. The nation emerged from the war a burgeoning industrial giant, pulsating with a crude energy already seeking new outlets. But the problems of peace, unlike the challenges of war, called less for engines of creation and destruction than for specific attitudes of mind, such as tolerance and understanding. And somehow for the United States in 1865, the latter attributes proved to be the more elusive. The destruction of Southern military and political resistance on the battlefield lay well within the competence of Northern power. Whether that power, once leashed, could transform Southern traditions of race and society in accordance with Northern purpose remained to be seen.

SUGGESTED READINGS

Undoubtedly the soundest one-volume study of the Civil War period is J. G. Randall and David Donald's *The Civil War and Reconstruction* (rev. ed., 1961). Two monumental histories of the Civil War, both detailed and dramatic, are Allan Nevins's *The War for the Union* (2 vols., 1959–1960), covering only the years from 1861 to 1863, and Bruce Catton's *The Centennial History of the Civil War* (3 vols., 1961–1965). A thoughtful older study is C. R. Fish's *The American Civil War* (1937). George Fort Milton's *Conflict: The American Civil War* (1941) is a useful account. Still of some value are two volumes by J. K. Hosmer in the original American Nation Series, *The Appeal to Arms,* 1861–1863 (1907) and *Outcome of the Civil War,* 1863–1865 (1907).

Lincoln has stimulated more literary effort than any other American in history; Lincoln writings now compose a library in themselves. Perhaps the best introduction to the life of Lincoln is Benjamin P. Thomas's *Abraham Lincoln: A Biography* (1952). Another full and balanced account of Lincoln's career is R. H. Luthin's *The Real Abraham Lincoln* (1960). A useful single-volume collection of Lincoln's writings is Paul M. Angle and E. S. Miers (eds.), *The Living Lincoln* (1955). The most comprehensive study of Lincoln in existence is that consisting of the six eulogistic volumes by Carl Sandburg, *Abraham Lincoln: The Prairie Years** (2 vols., 1926) and *The War Years** (4 vols., 1939). A more balanced, yet thorough, study of Lincoln is J. G. Randall's *Lincoln: The President** (4 vols., 1945–1955). (The final volume was completed by R. N. Current.) Randall's *Lincoln: The Liberal Statesman** (1947) and R. N. Current's *The Lincoln Nobody Knows** (1958) are interpretive studies of various aspects of Lincoln's career. David Potter's *Lincoln and His Party in the Secession Crisis** (1942) and R. N. Current's *Lincoln and the First Shot** (1963) discuss Lincoln's actions in the Fort Sumter crisis.

Writings on the military campaigns of the Civil War, like writings on Lincoln, have become so voluminous that the following list can suggest only the most significant. Bruce Catton's three volumes, *Mr. Lincoln's Army** (1951), *Glory Road** (1952), and *A Stillness at Appomattox** (1953), constitute a highly readable history of the Northern campaigns in the East. Catton's *This Hallowed Ground** (1956) is a vivid one-volume summary. Even more detailed and analytical, with greater emphasis on the Western campaigns, is Kenneth P. Williams's *Lincoln*

Finds a General (5 vols., 1949–1959). T. H. Williams's *Lincoln and His Generals** (1952) is briefer but more vivid. David Donald (ed.), *Why the North Won the Civil War** (1960) contains essays on the economic, political, military, and diplomatic factors in the Northern victory. From the viewpoint of the Confederacy the best military accounts are the seven classic volumes by Douglas S. Freeman: *R. E. Lee: A Biography* (4 vols., 1934–1935) and *Lee's Lieutenants* (3 vols., 1942–1944). The later campaigns have called forth their share of historical writing. Two basic studies of Gettysburg are Glenn Tucker's *High Tide at Gettysburg** (1958) and E. J. Stackpole's *They Met at Gettysburg* (1956). For the West in 1863 see Archer Jones's *Confederate Strategy from Shiloh to Vicksburg* (1961). Grant's final campaign in the East can be traced in Bruce Catton's *Grant Moves South* (1960); Bell I. Wiley's *The Road to Appomattox** (1956); and H. S. Commager (ed.), *The Defeat of the Confederacy** (1964). J. G. Barrett in *Sherman's March through the Carolinas* (1956) describes the collapse of Confederate power in the Southeast.

For the naval history of the war see Robert Carse's *Blockade: The Civil War at Sea* (1958); W. M. Robinson, Jr.'s *The Confederate Privateers* (1928); and V. C. Jones's *The Civil War at Sea* (2 vols., 1960–1962). Two special accounts of the Northern effort are R. S. West, Jr.'s *Mr. Lincoln's Navy* (1957) and J. P. Baxter's *Introduction of the Ironclad Warship* (1933). On the history of the *Alabama* see W. A. Roberts's *Semmes of the Alabama* (1938) and E. C. Boykin's *Ghost Ship of the Confederacy: The Story of the Alabama and Her Captain, Raphael Semmes* (1957). For the war in the West see R. S. Brownlee's *Gray Ghosts of the Confederacy* (1958); S. B. Oates's *Confederate Cavalry West of the River* (1961); R. H. Jones's *The Civil War in the Northwest* (1960); and R. C. Colton's *The Civil War in the Western Territories* (1959). For the border struggles in Missouri and Kansas see W. E. Parrish's *Turbulent Partnership: Missouri and the Union, 1861–1865* (1963) and Albert Castel's *A Frontier State at War: Kansas, 1861–1865* (1958). Two excellent volumes on the life of the common soldiers, North and South, are Bell I. Wiley's *The Life of Billy Yank** (1952) and *The Life of Johnny Reb** (1943). D. T. Cornish's *The Sable Arm** (1956) discusses the use of Negro troops in the war.

Biographies have been written on most of the important generals of the Civil War. On Grant's military career are L. A. Coolidge's *Ulysses S. Grant* (1917); A. L. Conger's *The Rise of U. S. Grant* (1931); J. F. C. Fuller's *The Generalship of Ulysses S. Grant* (1929); and Bruce Catton's *U. S. Grant and the American Military Tradition** (1954). W. W. Hassler, Jr., has written an excellent study of McClellan, *General George B. McClellan* (1957). Good biographies of other Union generals include Lloyd Lewis's *Sherman, Fighting Prophet* (1932); W. H. Hebert's *Fighting Joe Hooker* (1944); Richard O'Connor's *Sheridan the Inevitable* (1953); and G. G. Meade's *The Life and Letters of George Gordon Meade, Major-General, United States Army* (2 vols., 1913). For a good study of George H. Thomas, see Freeman Cleaves's *Rock of Chickamauga* (1948).

On Southern generals, in addition to Freeman's works on Lee already cited, are Clifford Dowdey's *Lee* (1965), large and beautifully written; Frank Vandiver's *Mighty Stonewall* (1957); T. H. Williams's *P. G. T. Beauregard: Napoleon in Gray** (1955); and J. H. Parks's *General Edmund Kirby Smith* (1954). Two good studies of the colorful Confederate cavalry leader are J. W. Thomason, Jr.'s *Jeb Stuart* (1930) and W. W. Blackford's *War Years with Jeb Stuart* (1945). For the career of Joseph E. Johnston, see Gilbert Govan and J. W. Livingood's *A Different Valor* (1956). In *Rebel Brass* (1956), Frank Vandiver analyzes the command structure.

Congressional attitudes toward slavery and the war were varied, creating some conflict within the dominant Republican party itself. T. H. Williams's *Lincoln and the Radicals** (1941) stresses the Radical drive for power, whereas David Donald in *Lincoln Reconsidered** (1956) cites evidence of humanitarian motivation in the Republican demands for victory and emancipation of the slaves. On the various Republican economic policies of the war years, see A. M. Davis's *The Origin of the National Banking System* (1910); W. C. Mitchell's *A History of the Greenbacks* (1903); and D. C. Barrett's *The Greenbacks and the Resumption of Specie Payments, 1862–1879* (1931). For another aspect of Radical attitudes see David Montgomery's *Beyond Equality: Labor and the Radical Republicans, 1862–1872* (1967). For a full discussion of emancipation see Benjamin Quarles's *Lincoln and the Negro* (1962) and John Hope

Franklin's *The Emancipation Proclamation** (1963).

On Civil War diplomacy, North and South, the standard works are E. D. Adams's *Great Britain and the American Civil War* (2 vols., 1925) and Frank L. Owsley's *King Cotton Diplomacy* (1931; 2d ed., 1959). Also on Confederate diplomacy are James A. B. Scherer's *Cotton as a World Power: A Study in the Economic Interpretation of History* (1916) and J. M. Callahan's *The Diplomatic History of the Southern Confederacy* (1901). European attitudes toward the American struggle can be traced in B. B. Sideman and Lillian Freedman (eds.), *Europe Looks at the Civil War** (1960); H. D. Jordan and E. J. Pratt's *Europe and the American Civil War* (1931); W. R. West's *Contemporary French Opinion on the American Civil War* (1924); and Albert A. Woldman's *Lincoln and the Russians** (1952). Philip Van Doren Stern's *When the Guns Roared* (1965) is well written but superficial and explains English inaction in terms of that nation's opposition to slavery. For studies of two important American diplomats in Europe, see Margaret A. Clapp's *Forgotten First Citizen: John Bigelow* (1947); C. F. Adams, Jr.'s *Charles Francis Adams* (1900); as well as Martin B. Duberman's *Charles Francis Adams** (1961). Jay Monaghan's *Diplomat in Carpet Slippers** (1945) is a popular account of Northern diplomacy. On United States–Canadian relations during the Civil War, see Robin W. Winks's *Canada and the United States: The Civil War Years* (1960). Dexter Perkins's *The Monroe Doctrine, 1826–1867* (1933) contains a full discussion of the Mexican problem during the Civil War.

On life behind the Confederate lines, the standard work is E. M. Coulter's *The Confederate States of America, 1861–1865* (1950). Clement Eaton's *A History of the Southern Confederacy** (1954) is another useful and balanced study. For two brief but judicious accounts see Charles P. Roland's *The Confederacy** (1960) and Frank Vandiver's *Basic History of the Confederacy** (1962). A more popular account is R. S. Henry's *The Story of the Confederacy** (1957). Among the state studies of the Confederate period are J. K. Bettersworth's *Confederate Mississippi* (1943); J. G. Barnett's *The Civil War in North Carolina* (1963); J. E. Johns's *Florida during the Civil War* (1963); and J. D. Winters's *The Civil War in Louisiana* (1963).

Dealing largely with industrial and financial problems of the Confederacy is J. C. Schwab's *The Confederate States of America, 1861–1865* (1901). R. C. Todd's *Confederate Finance* (1954) is the best book on the South's financial problems. Frank Vandiver explains the Confederate success in producing weapons in *Ploughshares into Swords: Josiah Gorgas and Confederate Ordnance** (1952). Tracing the breakdown of the Confederate railroad system are Robert C. Black in *The Railroads of the Confederacy* (1952) and A. J. Johnston with *Virginia Railroads in the Civil War* (1961). Another economic study of the South is F. B. C. Bradlee's *Blockade Running during the Civil War and the Effect of Land and Water Transportation on the Confederacy* (1925). Ella W. Lonn in *Salt as a Factor in the Confederacy* (1933) raises still another economic problem. The problems of leadership and administration are portrayed in Burton J. Hendrick's *Statesmen of the Lost Cause: Jefferson Davis and His Cabinet* (1939). R. W. Patrick in *Jefferson Davis and His Cabinet* (1944) is less critical of Davis. Still less critical is Hudson Strode in the second volume of his *Jefferson Davis* (3 vols., 1955–1964). On Confederate leaders see Rudolph von Abele's *Alexander H. Stephens* (1946); R. D. Meade's *Judah P. Benjamin, Confederate Statesman* (1943); and J. T. Durkin's *Stephen R. Mallory* (1954). W. B. Yearns's *The Confederate Congress* (1960) is an important political study. On matters of constitutionalism, see F. L. Owsley's *State Rights in the Confederacy* (1925) and C. R. Lee, Jr.'s *The Confederate Constitutions* (1963).

Life among the common people of the Confederacy is described well in Bell I. Wiley's *The Plain People of the Confederacy** (1943) and *Southern Negroes, 1861–1865** (1938). Charles W. Ramsdell's *Behind the Lines in the Southern Confederacy* (1944) is a brief but interesting account of the problems facing the Southern people during the Civil War. On problems of conscription in the South, see A. B. Moore's *Conscription and Conflict in the Confederacy* (1924). On further hardships of Southern life, see M. E. Massey's *Refugee Life in the Confederacy* (1964) and M. P. Andrews's *The Woman of the South in War Times* (1920). A. H. Bill's *The Beleaguered City: Richmond, 1861–1865* (1946) discusses life in the wartime capital. An outstanding wartime diary is R. G. H. Kean's *Inside the Con-*

federate Government (edited by Edward Younger, 1957).

Perhaps the best general study of life behind the Northern lines remains E. D. Fite's *Social and Industrial Conditions in the North during the Civil War* (1910). Wartime Washington has been described colorfully and in detail by Margaret Leech in her *Reveille in Washington, 1860–1865** (1941). Valuable studies on aspects of public life in the North include F. A. Shannon's *The Organization and Administration of the Union Army, 1861–1865* (2 vols., 1928); W. Q. Maxwell's *Lincoln's Fifth Wheel: The Political History of the United States Sanitary Commission* (1956); and R. V. Bruce's *Lincoln and the Tools of War* (1956), revealing Lincoln's interest in weapons development. Two excellent studies of Northern railroads are Thomas Weber's *The Northern Railroads in the Civil War* (1952) and G. E. Turner's *Victory Rode the Rails* (1953). Ella W. Lonn's *Desertion during the Civil War* (1928) deals with that troublesome question. On agriculture see Paul W. Gates's *Agriculture and the Civil War* (1965).

Much has been written on the social and political attitudes of the North during the Civil War. On the status of the Northern Negro see Benjamin Quarles's *The Negro in the Civil War* (1953); J. M. McPherson's *The Negro's Civil War** (1965); and V. Jacque Voegeli's *Free but Not Equal: The Midwest and the Negro during the Civil War* (1967). Two outstanding studies of Copperheadism are Wood Gray's *The Hidden War** (1942) and Frank L. Klement's *The Copperheads in the Middle West* (1960). C. F. Dunham in *The Attitude of the Northern Clergy toward the South, 1860–1865* (1942) reveals the important nature of one aspect of Northern opinion.

Lincoln's relations with Congress can be traced in Williams's *Linc ln and the Radicals** (1941) and Donald's *Lincoln Reconsidered* (1956), cited earlier. H. J. Carman and R. H. Luthin in *Lincoln and the Patronage* (1943) reveal the nature of Lincoln's political management. On Lincoln's Cabinet there are several volumes of great value: Burton J. Hendrick's *Lincoln's War Cabinet** (1946), which tends to ignore the last year of the war; David Donald (ed.), *Inside Lincoln's Cabinet: The Civil War Diaries of Salmon P. Chase* (1945); B. P. Thomas and H. M. Hyman's *Stanton: The Life and Times of Linc ln's Secretary of War* (1962); and R. S. West, Jr.'s *Gideon Welles* (1943). Allan Nevins passes judgment on the Northern leadership in his *Statesmanship of the Civil War** (1953). Also rewarding is Gamaliel Bradford's *Union Portraits* (1916). On constitutional issues see J. G. Randall's *Constitutional Problems under Lincoln** (2d ed., 1951) and D. M. Silver's *Lincoln's Supreme Court* (1956). Lincoln's success in fighting the Northern governors who sought to preserve their states' rights prerogatives during the war is analyzed by W. B. Hesseltine in *Lincoln and the War Governors* (1948). Another aspect of Lincoln's leadership can be seen in R. S. Harper's *Lincoln and the Press* (1951). LeRoy H. Fischer's *Lincoln's Gadfly: Adam Gurowski* (1964) analyzes Lincoln's troubles with this liberal Polish patriot who lived in and about Washington during the Civil War. Two enlightening studies revealing the state of national politics in 1864 are E. C. Kirkland's *Peacemakers of 1864* (1927) and W. F. Zornow's *Lincoln and the Party Divided* (1954).

*indicates availability in paperback.

19

Postwar Reconstruction

ROBERT E. LEE'S SURRENDER at Appomattox Court House in March, 1865, opened a new era in the history of the United States. Politically and morally, the nation could never return to the lost world of Lincoln's first inaugural and the Sumter crisis. Wars generally achieve more than the mere separation of the quick from the dead. Essentially they create the means whereby those who direct a country's policies can employ the force of mass destruction to achieve what they believed impossible through compromise and agreement alone. The American Civil War was no exception. John Quincy Adams had once prophesied that the major interests in conflict between the slave and the free states could best be resolved through the limitless application of Northern industrial and military might on the battlefield. Victory had come hard for the North, but it had eliminated, at least for the moment, the South's traditional influence in American national life.

But the revolution wrought by Northern arms had been moral as well as political, for the Union victories had placed the Southern slave system on the road to oblivion and now confronted the Republic with the inescapable challenge of creating a new role for the Negro in American society. Thus the Republican leadership in 1865 faced two fundamental and related questions: Under what conditions would it permit the South to reenter the Union? How could it, at the same time, translate emancipation into social, economic, and political equality for the freed slave? The national experience decreed against any permanent alienation of the South from its historic role in the nation's life. But on the question of the Negro's future in Southern society, there were no hopeful precedents. Whatever the sincerity of their moral purpose, Northern leaders would soon discover that the practical measures of refashioning the South in accordance with their image would depend less on coercion than on the continuing factors of Southern conviction, interest, and tradition.

The Defeated South

Its power of resistance destroyed, the South awaited the North's conditions of peace and contemplated the task of rebuilding its ruined economy without benefit of capital or markets. If a small minority of Southern businessmen, through war production, blockade running, or privateering, had succeeded in accumulating capital, the South generally was impoverished. Emancipation had wiped out the South's investment of more than $2 billion in slaves. Confederate securities totaling $1 billion fell worthless with the collapse of the Richmond government. Inflation, added to the economic dislocation and destruction of war, had eliminated the South's banking capital, disorganized its currency and credit structure, and undermined its commerce and industry. Union forces had systematically destroyed the South's transportation system, especially the railroads and bridges. Despair stalked the land, for the South carried the burden of defeat.

Areas that had experienced the full ravages of war lay desolate and helpless. Invading armies, whether fighting or foraging, generally manage to ruin whatever they touch, and by 1865 the Union forces had penetrated much of the South. The destruction of the countryside that separated Alexandria from Richmond, Petersburg, and Charlottesville reminded residents and travelers alike that Virginia had carried the chief burden of war. Across the Blue Ridge Mountains, General Philip Sheridan had, it seemed, fulfilled his promise to denude the Shenandoah Valley so thoroughly that " a crow could not fly over it without carrying his rations with him." Likewise the valley of the Tennessee carried the scars of invading Union soldiers. Recalled one English traveler, "The trail of war is visible throughout the valley in burnt-up gin-houses, ruined bridges, mills, and factories, of which the gable walls only are left standing, and in large tracts of once cultivated land stripped of every vestige of fencing." Ultimately no areas of the South suffered more thoroughly than those which experienced the fury of Sherman's closing campaigns through Georgia and the Carolinas. After his march from Atlanta to Savannah, the general could estimate Georgia's loss from war at $100 million, most of it wrought by deliberate waste and destruction. But this was merely a prelude to the retribution which Sherman's army exacted of South Carolina, seat of the rebellion. Carl Schurz reported in 1865 that the northward route followed by Sherman "looked for many miles like a broad black streak of ruin and desolation—the fences all gone; lonesome smoke stacks, surrounded by dark heaps of ashes and cinders, marking the spots where human habitations had stood; the fields . . . wildly overgrown by weeds, with here and there a sickly looking patch of cotton or corn cultivated by negro squatters."

Added to its physical and psychological

burdens, the South faced the necessity of integrating 4 million freedmen into its economic, political, and social structure. Although it was clear that many problems lay ahead, the blacks regarded emancipation as a time of celebration. Deserting the plantations which to them represented enslavement, many entered the cities in search of employment, educational opportunities, and a permanent status of equality and respect. But the freedmen wanted and needed far more opportunity, equality, and respect than the nation was willing to give. Thus the Negro's transition from slavery to freedom, from rural to urban life, could be neither swift nor easy. The economic and emotional forces in opposition were too powerful to be overcome. Southern whites, determined to preserve as much as possible of the South's traditional way of life, recognized the consequences of a mass invasion of the urban centers of the South. At times they resorted to violence to drive Negroes off the roads. Freedmen who reached the cities often fared little better. They crowded endlessly into urban pockets and Union "contraband camps" established specifically to sustain them through a period of relocation, overtaxing the limited facilities and food available; and countless thousands died of disease and exposure.

The sudden loss of Negro agricultural labor completed the process of disintegration in the Southern plantation system, forcing many former masters into the fields to maintain themselves and their families. Already the farms and plantations of the South revealed the decay and neglect of war, and those who turned to agricultural production in 1865 faced shortages in labor, livestock, and equipment.

Incorporating the freed blacks into Southern white society under conditions that would give the freedmen some promise of political equality, as well as economic security and social mobility, emerged in 1865 as the central challenge of Southern Reconstruction. The problem, aggravated at the outset by the issue of race, was rendered even more complex by the slave tradition, which had barred the vast majority of Southern Negroes from all educational, political, and business experience. Negro leaders attempted to close the gap between reality and promise by assuming the task of black education, beginning with the establishment of colleges for the training of teachers. They received some needed aid from missionaries representing Northern religious bodies, as well as from the Freedmen's Bureau. Established by Congress in March, 1865, the Freedmen's Bureau assigned abandoned lands to freedmen, defended them in controversies with whites, and provided food and clothing for blacks whose livelihood and security had been destroyed by emancipation. The Bureau, under the leadership of General Oliver O. Howard, was committed even before the close of the fighting to some form of governmental guardianship over the Negro. Despite its brief history and the critical opposition which it faced in both the North and the South, the Bureau secured some genuine gains for the Southern Negro.

Presidential Reconstruction

Lincoln had planned for the moment when the fighting would cease and the task of reconstruction would begin. The war would abolish slavery, but would it assure the Negro complete membership in American society? Lincoln himself was convinced that it would not. In his debates with Douglas in 1858, he had rejected the principle of black equality and pointedly assigned the superior position in national life to the white race. Lincoln desired freedom for the slaves, but beyond that he promised little. If the Negroes rejected colonization (to Lincoln the only realistic solution available), they would have no choice but to accept an inferior position in American society. The immediate problem, as Lincoln saw it, was the restoration of the Union. His program was a simple one of establishing loyal state governments in the South wherever Union forces had destroyed Confederate control. With peace, Lincoln was convinced that a moderate Republican program could induce the powerful Whig minority of the South to join the Republican party, the true heir of the Whig tradition in the North, thus reconstructing the old Whig party under the Republican banner. Lincoln suspected that most Southern Whigs had never favored the secession movement; now they seemed the best hope not only for leading the Southern states back to their former allegiance, but also for augmenting the forces of Republicanism.

Lincoln announced his practical conditions for Southern restoration in his proclamation of December 8, 1863. He offered amnesty to those who would take an oath of loyalty to the Union and would accept the acts of Congress and the proclamations of the President in regard to slavery. Lincoln specifically denied amnesty only to high-ranking military, political, and diplomatic officials of the Confederacy and to those who had relinquished their position in Congress and in the Federal service to join the Southern cause. When one-tenth of the voters of any seceding state took the oath of allegiance, that state could, upon presenting a constitution republican in form, reenter the Union. Lincoln acknowledged the sole right of the two houses of Congress to recognize the elected representatives of the restored states.

Republican Radicals in Congress denounced the President's plan. They noted correctly that it offered no guarantees of civil rights to the Southern Negroes and that it assigned to the Executive rather than to Congress the power to determine the conditions and processes of Reconstruction. Congress threw down the gauntlet to Lincoln in July, 1864, when it passed a bill introduced by Senator Benjamin F. Wade of Ohio and Representative Henry Winter Davis of Maryland which imposed more stringent requirements on the South. The Wade-Davis bill provided that Reconstruction would begin when a *majority* of the white male citizens of a Confederate state took the oath of allegiance to the United States. These voters would then elect delegates to a state constitutional convention, who must in turn take a second oath that they had never voluntarily given support to the Confederacy. The bill also increased the number of categories of Southern leaders who would be barred from voting or holding office. Lincoln killed the measure with a pocket veto and pressed forward with his own moderate program. Meanwhile Louisiana, in accordance with Lincoln's proclamation, had adopted a new constitution. Congress adjourned on March 4, 1865, however, without recognizing the new state government as constitutional.

Many Radicals—disturbed by Lincoln's course—openly professed relief at his death in April, 1865. George W. Julian reported that among his Radical friends the feeling was almost universal that Lincoln's death was a blessing to the country. Vice President Andrew Johnson's wartime condemnation of the South had convinced the Radicals that he shared their views on Reconstruction. As Wade assured the new President, "Johnson, we have faith in you. By the gods, there will be no trouble now in running the government."

But the struggle for control of federal Reconstruction policy now entered a new phase of intensity, for Johnson's notions of a proper program for the South, no less than Lincoln's, required firm Executive control. Johnson, like Lincoln, was determined to direct federal action toward the creation of a postwar political alignment that would reflect his antebellum political preferences. Those preferences, if momentarily clouded, reflected every phase of the new President's experience in politics. From his unpromising start as an illiterate tailor and local politician in Greenville, Tennessee, Johnson had climbed the rungs of Tennessee politics as a Jacksonian Democrat and a natural enemy of slaveholding Whigs. Entering the United States Senate as an outspoken Unionist, Johnson had condemned the secession movement and remained in the North until Lincoln sent him back to Tennessee as military governor. In this capacity, Johnson had called for a hard policy toward the Southern "rebels." By the spring of 1865, however, Lincoln had convinced his Vice President that a harsh policy would fail. Upon entering the White House, Johnson not only accepted Lincoln's Cabinet but also recognized the Southern state governments established under Lincoln's plan. Jacksonian that he was, Johnson preferred states' rights to centralized power in the federal government. He hoped to return the South to the control of its own destiny as quickly as possible. Never an opponent of slavery or a friend of the Negro, Johnson had no desire to use federal power in defense of black freedom. He accepted emancipation as a by-product of war, but without enthusiasm. The tensions in Southern society occasioned by emancipation, he believed, would either be resolved by the South in its own way or they would not be resolved at all. He thus limited his intentions for the South to the creation of new governments, which he hoped would rest on Democratic power. Whereas Lincoln had sought the reforging of the prewar Whig party, Johnson pursued the vision of a reborn Democratic party based on the agrarian principles of Jefferson and Jackson.

The Radicals quickly became disillusioned with Johnson when they learned that he intended neither to punish "traitors" severely nor to extend federal protection to the freedmen. Having announced that he would not call Congress into special session, Johnson proceeded to implement his own Reconstruction program through Executive action. On May 29 he issued a proclamation of amnesty for those who would take an oath of allegiance to the Union. He extended Lincoln's exclusion list, however, to include persons who had involuntarily participated in the rebellion and those whose taxable property exceeded $20,000. Thus Johnson sought to eliminate from Southern political leadership the upper-class Whigs whom Lincoln had favored. The President appointed a new Governor for North Carolina and ordered him to call a convention for the purpose of creating a new state constitution. Lincoln had recognized Virginia, Tennessee, Louisiana, and Arkansas. Johnson in June, 1865, applied the procedure established for North Carolina to the other states of the South. Before Congress met in December, 1865, all of the former Confederate states except Texas had formed constitutions and elected governments according to the Johnson plan. All except Mississippi had ratified the Thirteenth

Amendment, which became law in December, abolishing slavery officially from the land forever.

Johnson had managed to prepare the South for readmission to the Union, but he failed in his attempt to create a new agrarian utopia. The Whigs whom he opposed became the new power in Southern politics. During 1865 they won no less than eight governorships, eleven senatorships, and thirty-six seats in the House. Outside of Texas and South Carolina, Whigs captured almost nine-tenths of the congressional seats. In addition, they captured control of several Southern state legislatures and constitutional conventions. The Southern Democrats were on the defensive. Clearly Lincoln had estimated the realities of Southern politics far more accurately than had Johnson.

What undermined and eventually defeated the President's moderate program were the actions of the Southern states themselves. Under the widespread assumption that the elevation of blacks would result in the degradation of Southern white society, the racist Johnson governments resorted to the so-called Black Codes in an effort to return the South to its prewar status of economic stability and racial subjugation. These codes were designed essentially to force the Negro back to the land and hold him there with annual contracts and the denial or restriction of property rights. Some states even forbade the freedman to seek employment outside agriculture, except with special permission. Three states—Florida, Mississippi, and Texas—passed laws which established the principle of race discrimination in the use of railroads. Laws such as these illustrated the determination of the South to limit the black presence through policies of segregation. By threatening the Negro with fines and imprisonment for every deviation from the social and moral standards established by white society, the Black Codes severely limited the freedman's civil and economic rights and sometimes reduced him to a condition of peonage.

Triumph of the Radicals

When Congress met in December, 1865, its Radical leadership was determined to end the President's control of Southern Reconstruction. The Black Codes were symbolic of the South's refusal to accept the implications of emancipation. Wade revealed his loss of faith in the Johnson program when he wrote in July: "We have in truth already lost the whole moral effect of our victories over the rebellion, and the golden opportunity for humiliating and destroying the influence of the Southern aristocracy has gone forever." To make matters worse, the President not only accepted the Black Codes without a murmur, but on December 18 he rationalized them in a special message to Congress as measures designed "to confer upon freedmen the privileges which are essential to their comfort, protection, and security." The President's decision to accept white rule in the South elevated the question of the Negro's future to a central position in the struggle for power between Congress and the Executive.

Throughout the ensuing debate the Johnsonians not only supported the concept of racial inequality but also challenged the motives of those who opposed them. Many Radicals demanded a status for Negroes which most Americans would not accept. "If all whites must vote," declared Charles Sumner, "then must all blacks." Such demands for black equality, charged the conservatives, were totally unreasonable and thus must be a camouflage for a variety of Radical purposes which had no relationship to black rights at all. Giving credence to such accusations was the simple fact that the Negro vote represented political power to those who could control it. And the claim that the Radicals befriended the freedmen only to exploit them carried enough truth to be convincing. Through Negro enfranchisement, first of all, the Radicals could break the economic and political influence of the Southern leaders of the rebellion. Many Radicals such as Thad Stevens never concealed their desire to punish the "traitors." Negro suffrage, moreover, would assure the continued ascendancy of the Republican party and permit that party to complete its dual objectives of underwriting a program of civil rights for the freedmen and protecting the business interests of the North with additional tariffs, subsidies, and internal improvements. Such motivations Stevens, among others, readily admitted.

Perhaps hypocrisy abounds wherever men pursue ideals.Yet there was no doubt that the Radicals possessed their share of forthrightness and honesty. They had led the Republican party's antislavery crusade before and during the war; it was logical that their previous concern for the slaves would demand no less of them than support for a federal policy designed to guarantee the freedmen those rights which alone could perpetuate their independence. Whatever their interests, the Radical Republicans thought they had won the right to determine federal policy in the light of those interests. And it was because Johnson's program of Reconstruction threatened to deny them the moral and political fruits of victory that they prepared to challenge his leadership.

In December, 1865, the Radicals, with the support of moderates, established a Joint Committee on Reconstruction to study all Reconstruction proposals and recommend to Congress those they believed appropriate. Twelve of its fifteen members were Republican, but the moderates who dominated the committee denied that its creation was a repudiation of Johnson. Many members of Congress still hoped to avoid a clash with the President over Reconstruction and anticipated a program based on cooperation between Johnson and the Congress. Much depended upon Johnson's attitude toward the freedman, and he soon defied congressional opinion by vetoing two measures framed to extend federal protection to them. Arguing that Congress had no right to impose its will on the Southern states without their concurrence, the President vetoed the Freedmen's Bureau bill of February, 1866, through which Congress intended to extend and strengthen the wartime agency. Congress responded with a resolution that no reconstructed state could be admitted to the Union until Congress extended it recognition. While Congress debated this measure, Johnson, addressing a crowd at the White House, denounced Stevens, Sumner, and Wendell Phillips by name as traitors to the American government. Such intemperance drove congressional moderates into the arms of the Radicals and completed the break between Johnson and Congress.

By April, 1866, Congress had achieved sufficient unity to challenge the President openly. Early that month it passed a civil rights bill over his veto. This law for the first time defined citizens as all persons born in the United States, except untaxed Indians. It stated further that citizens "of every race and color" should have equal legal and property rights. Then on April 28 Congress received the long-awaited report of the Joint Committee. The report accepted the Radical view, as argued by Stevens and Sumner, that the Confederate states, by waging war against the United States, had reduced themselves to mere territories and as territories could reenter the Union only under conditions established by Congress. On June 8 the Joint Committee reminded Congress that it dared not abandon the freedmen before it had guaranteed them their rights as free men and citizens. "The whole civilized world," it warned, "would have cried out against such base ingratitude, and the bare idea is offensive to all right-thinking men."

To place the provisions of the Civil Rights Act beyond recall, the committee proposed the Fourteenth Amendment, which Congress adopted promptly. This amendment extended the guarantees of citizenship and civil rights to freedmen. Specifically, it declared that "all persons born or naturalized in the United States" and subject to its jurisdiction were citizens of both the United States and the state in which they lived. The amendment further declared that no state could deny any citizen the equal protection of the laws. Nor could any state "abridge the privileges or immunities of citizens of the United States . . . [or] deprive any person of life, liberty, or property, without due process of law." To keep the Southern states from denying freedmen the right to vote, the amendment called for reducing a state's congressional representation in the same proportion that qualified voters were denied the franchise. This seemed like an effective threat, but Congress has never enforced this provision despite the fact that eventually the Southern states kept the majority of their blacks from voting. The Fourteenth Amendment also barred from public office most high Confederates, unless approved by a two-thirds vote of Congress. Finally, it outlawed the debt incurred by the Confederacy, while guaranteeing payment of the Northern debt. Under the Fourteenth Amendment the federal government possessed the power to protect the civil rights of all people, blacks included, in the states. Only when a state had ratified the amendment could it reenter the Union. Johnson denounced the amendment as a contravention of states' rights and urged the Southern states to reject it. Ten of them did, three unanimously, and it was temporarily defeated.

This conflict over civil rights set the stage for the bitter congressional campaign of 1866. Late in August, Johnson left Washington on a speaking tour which carried him as far west as Chicago and St. Louis. However, his effort to win popular support to his cause ended in disaster. His speeches were vulgar, vindictive, and self-righteous; in violent language he denounced Congress and his enemies for subverting the government. He had fought treason in the South, he said; he was now prepared to fight it in the North. Losing control of himself, he repeatedly exchanged bitter epithets with critics in the crowds. Having driven away much of his Republican support, he found himself seeking salvation in the Democratic party, which was again upholding the principle of white rule in the South and warning against the evils of Negro equality in the North. Republican campaigning turned Johnson's affiliation with Democrats into a political liability. The Radicals accused the President of attempting to return the government to the enemies of the Union and the Negro. Those who rejected the Radical program, declared Stevens, could join the Copperheads and rebels. During the campaign, the Republicans "waved the bloody shirt" to keep alive the hatreds of the war and to identify the Democratic party with treason. The appeal to war patriotism proved its worth. The congressional elections of 1866 saw a Radical tidal wave which gave the Republicans control of every Northern state legislature, every contested governorship, and shortly two-thirds working majorities in both houses of Congress.

Congressional Reconstruction

When Congress met in December, 1866, the Radicals had the responsibility and the power to determine the future of Reconstruction. The varied experience of the Johnson program had given them time and opportunity to analyze their position and determine their objectives. To reconstruct the South on the foundation of racial equality, the Radicals had no choice but to slow the process of reunion, to force the South to discard its Black Codes, and to establish the political and legal bases of civil rights and Negro suffrage. It was this effort to secure an acceptable place in Southern life for the freedmen that comprised the core of Radical Reconstruction.

Not until two years after Appomattox did Congress launch its program of Reconstruction. It declared its basic will in the First Reconstruction Act of March, 1867, a measure affirming that "no legal State governments or adequate protection for life or property" existed in any of the eleven states of the former Confederacy except Tennessee. Passed over a presidential veto, the act thus declared all the Johnson governments illegal and announced the authority of the United States to abolish and supersede them. To establish Radical control in the region, the Reconstruction Act divided the South into five military districts, each to be placed under a military commander charged with preserving law and order. The act provided that, when a state constitutional convention, chosen under black and white suffrage but excluding Confederate leaders, had framed a constitution in conformity with the federal constitution, that constitution could be submitted to Congress for its approval. When the state received such acceptance and then adopted the Fourteenth Amendment, it would gain representation in Congress.

Still the conquest of the President was not complete, and many Radicals feared that Johnson might subvert the program through his refusal to enforce the laws. To limit the President's power over the execution of policy, Congress, in March, 1867, supported the First Reconstruction Act with two additional measures. The Tenure of Office Act forbade the President to remove civil officers approved by the Senate without first obtaining the consent of the Senate. The Command of the Army Act required the President to issue military orders only through the General of the Army, U. S. Grant. The Radicals resorted to these extraordinary invasions of Executive authority specifically to prevent Johnson from securing control of the military arm of the government and thus acquiring the means to thwart their Reconstruction program. Not satisfied with these restrictions, some members of Congress believed that the success of the Radical design demanded nothing less than Johnson's removal from office.

In February, 1868, Johnson attempted to remove Secretary of War Edwin Stanton and replace him with General U. S. Grant. The Committee on Reconstruction now had a pretext to bring an impeachment resolution before the House. This body quickly voted to bring the President to trial before the Senate. By early March the House had drawn up eleven articles, ten of which referred to the Tenure of Office Act. Article 10 accused the President of attempting through his intemperate harangues to bring the Congress into contempt and disgrace. On March 5, Chief Justice Chase organized the Senate as a court of impeachment. In a trial of two months' duration, Ben Butler led the prosecution in a vigorous and determined effort to convict Johnson. The critical vote of May 16, 1868, on the final article of impeachment, was 35 to 19, failing by one vote to achieve the necessary two-thirds majority. Having been acquitted, Johnson was permitted to complete the final months of his administration. Although he had earlier denounced every Reconstruction measure, he now abandoned his official opposition and appointed able military officers over the five military districts, permitting Radical Reconstruction to move forward uninhibited.

Simultaneously with its successful defense of the First Reconstruction Act against the encroachments of the Executive, Congress managed to sustain the program's constitutionality against an adverse decision of the Supreme Court, the case of *ex parte Milligan* in 1866. Milligan, a civilian, had been arrested during the war in Indiana for stirring up sentiment against the Union. He was sentenced by a military court to be hanged. In its decision on his appeal, the Court held that the continuance of military rule as practiced in Indiana during the war was an unconstitutional usurpation of power in an area where the civil courts were open. The fact that courts were open in the South in March, 1867, therefore, challenged the constitutionality of the First Reconstruction Act even before its passage through Congress. When *ex parte McCardle,* a case designed to put the new law to the test, actually entered the Court's schedule in 1868, Congress passed a measure over the President's veto which withdrew appellate jurisdiction from the Court in matters of habeas corpus. Congressional action in the McCardle case thus precluded the possibility of judicial interference with Radical Reconstruction.

Meanwhile the Radical program moved toward completion. By July, 1868, enough states had ratified the Fourteenth Amendment to place that constitutional guarantee of civil liberty into effect. But the amendment did not specifically include voting as a right to be protected by federal power. The Radicals had been reluctant to face the issue of Negro suffrage directly because some of the Northern states had not granted voting privileges to Negroes within their borders and had no intention of doing so. Yet the Republican need for Negro votes in the Southern states, added to the momentum of the civil rights movement itself, made it imperative that Republicans confront the issue with a constitutional provision which would guarantee Negro suffrage and, with it, an important element of Republican strength.

In December, 1868, congressional Republicans submitted a Fifteenth Amendment which declared: "The right of citizens of the United States to vote shall not be denied or abridged by the United States or by any state on account of race, color, or previous condition of servitude." Congress added enforcement measures which reenacted the Civil Rights Act of 1866 and provided penalties for violations of the Fourteenth and Fifteenth Amendments. Virginia, Mississippi, Texas, and Georgia ratified the new amendment as a condition for receiving representation in Congress. By March, 1870, the measure had been

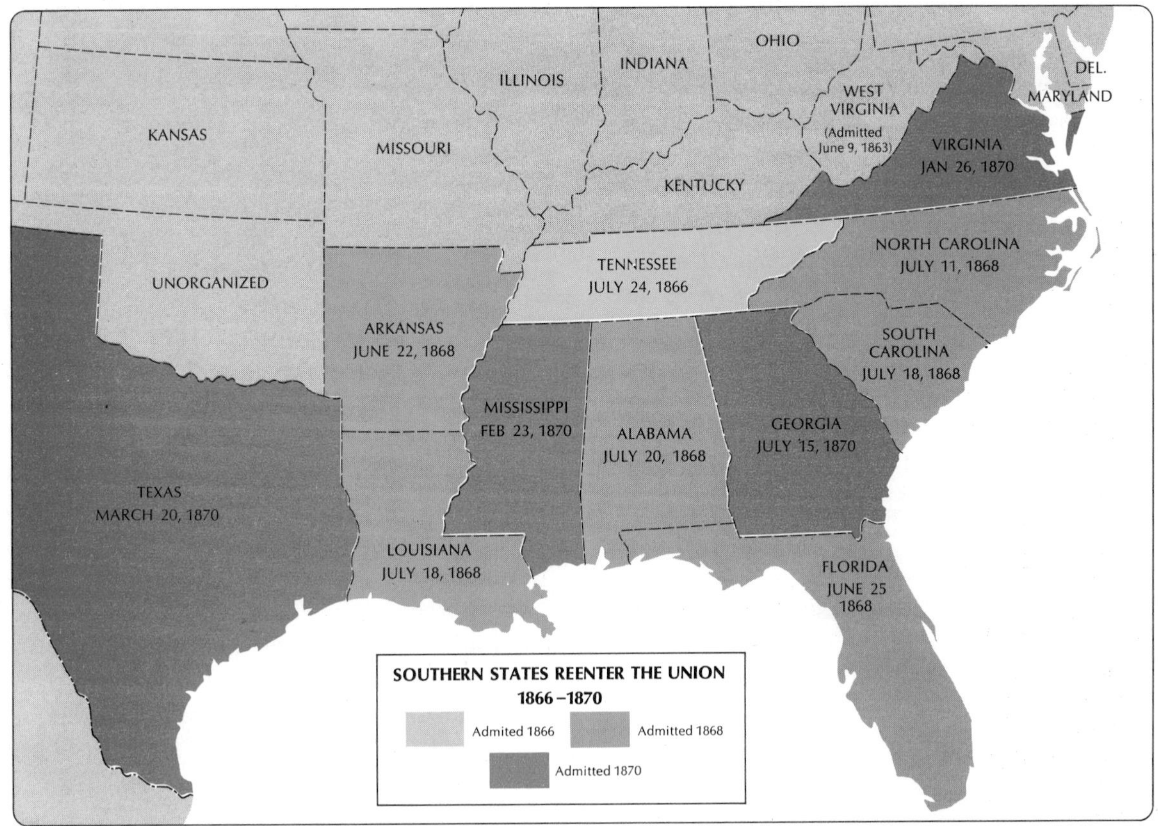

put into general effect throughout the nation. Supported by Negro suffrage, the Republican future in the South seemed assured. Southern Reconstruction now promised political rewards.

Reconstruction in the South

No Republican effort at civil reform, underwritten by Negro votes and Northern power, could have avoided the opposition and resentment of those who in 1860 had preferred disunion and war to any serious alterations in the political and social structure of the South. Three groups from the North and the South were the special objects of the bitter-enders' scorn. To them the Yankee "carpetbaggers" who invaded the South were little other than adventurers bent on plundering that section under the guise of civil reform. The "scalawags," Southern whites who aided the carpetbaggers, they viewed as traitors to the traditions and best interests of the South. The Negroes, usually ignorant and illiterate, emerged as the dupes whose votes were exploited by their white protagonists for private advantage.

Those Northerners who played a role in Reconstruction politics entered the South for a variety of reasons. Some, as Union soldiers, had been attracted by the Southern climate; others came with capital, or perhaps with no more than energy, to enter the task of rebuilding the Southern economy. Among them were travelers, missionaries, and agents of the Freedmen's Bureau. If some were opportunists, most were either genuine humanitarians or simply ordinary Northerners in search of an honest living. Carpetbaggers who entered Reconstruction governments of the South were probably motivated less by a desire to capitalize on the sudden invasion of Northern political power than by a desire to guide the South back into the Union so that the states of their adoption might regain access to Northern markets and capital.

No less than the carpetbaggers, the Southern scalawags were a complex and varied group. Among their numbers there were some opportunists in search of the advantages that temporary and unanticipated political power might bestow. Some scalawags were among the South's most distinguished citizens, but a great number of them came from the yeoman farmer class. Southern Whigs especially found an alliance with Republicans in the Reconstruction governments both natural and promising. Scalawags were the least stable element in the Southern-Radical coalition. On the one hand, they were determined, as were many carpetbaggers, to put the war-torn Southern economy on the road to recovery. If the price of restoring the South to its rightful place in the Union was the acceptance of Radical rule, the scalawags were disposed to regard the bargain as a good one. On the other hand, as Southerners, they had no genuine interest in extending civil and political rights to Negroes. The *New Orleans Times* spoke for many property-holding scalawags of that section when it declared in August, 1865, "The right to vote should be given to those only who can use it with discretion and sound judgment, and . . . it would be . . . folly to extend [our electoral privileges] at once to a class who had always been under control, and who . . . would be left to the tender mercies of party tricksters." For voters to outnumber property owners, continued the *Times,* would render property unsafe.

Every Reconstruction government rested ultimately on Negro suffrage, although Negroes themselves controlled none of them. Blacks were elected to all the state legislatures but seldom achieved high executive positions in the state governments. In South Carolina, however, blacks outnumbered whites in the Legislature; they occupied such positions as lieutenant governor, secretary of state, treasurer, speaker of the House, and associate justice of the state Supreme Court. Mississippi, Louisiana, and Florida also elected Negroes to high state offices. Altogether fourteen blacks represented the South in the United States House of Representatives; two Mississippi Negroes, H. R. Revels and Blanche Kelso Bruce, served in the United States Senate. The blacks developed some leadership within their own ranks, but in general the whites, whether carpetbaggers or scalawags, dominated Southern Reconstruction governments. In their use of power, the Negroes seldom demanded more than equal political and civil rights. In their desire to gain their ends in cooperation with the Southern whites, they made no effort to build a black party or operate outside the Radical political organization to which they felt indebted. Of course the newly enfranchised freedmen did not always use their power wisely or effectively. Without property, experience, or education, they were easily intimidated and misled by Republicans and Democrats alike. Yet within the confines of the disadvantages which they faced, their responses were generally consistent and creditable.

Radical rule began in the South with the calling of state conventions to form new constitutions for the Southern states. These conventions, dominated by the Radicals, were derided by their enemies as "black and tan" conventions. Pro-Johnson whites of the South heaped enough abuse on them to cast doubt on the quality and seriousness of the entire constitution-making process. One newspaper editor termed the South Carolina convention the "maddest, most infamous revolution in history." Actually the Southern conventions made rather modest innovations, preferring to assure the acceptability of the new governments by patterning them on the Southern constitutions of the past. Nor did the new leaders seek to impose any fundamental changes on Southern society. Delegates to several conventions proposed land laws designed to break up large estates, but all such measures failed to secure the necessary support. The new constitutions proclaimed the principle of equal rights before the law but remained vague and indefinite on questions of racial segregation in education and public conveyances; many constitutions avoided such issues completely. The new governments made no effort to disenfranchise former Confederate sympathizers or to establish restrictions on officeholding that went beyond those listed in the Fourteenth Amendment. On the other hand, they removed antebellum discriminations on regional representation, especially in Virginia, North Carolina, and South Carolina. They increased the rights of women and provided for improved systems of taxation, more equitable codes of law, and broader opportunities in education. The convention of South Carolina, the special target of Democratic abuse, produced the first genuinely democratic constitution in that state's history. It removed established restrictions on voting and officeholding which had been based not only on race but also on property qualifications. These were important changes.

Whatever their determination to rule well, the new governments could not have escaped the charges of corruption and failure brought against them by Southern whites momentarily deprived of political power. Unfortunately, too, the record of Southern Reconstruction often justified the severest accusations. The incompetence, dishonesty, and inexperience of the new officeholders produced corruption everywhere, with South Carolina and Louisiana creating the poorest records of all. Governor Henry C. Warmoth of Louisiana reputedly pocketed $100,000 one year, on a salary of $8,000. The South Carolina Legislature once paid over $200,000 for furniture not worth $18,000; it voted its speaker $1,000 to cover his losses in a horse race. Under the heading of "supplies," the Legislature voted itself perfumes, wines, whisky, watches, and carriages. Such loose expenditures sent state debts soaring. The South Carolina debt tripled between 1868 and 1871. In 1872, the total state indebtedness of the eleven former members of the Confederacy was $132 million. This increasing indebtedness was matched in most Southern states by a rapid rise in tax rates. Such a record seemed to indicate the incompetence and dishonesty of Radical rule and the ultimate failure of the Republican experiment.

Yet the full record was not quite so dismal, and the carpetbaggers, scalawags, and Negroes alone could not be blamed for all the corruption, extravagance, and vulgarity which existed.

The Radical governments faced the challenges of social disorganization and rapid economic expansion, which were exerting pressure on governmental integrity everywhere in the nation. The Whisky Ring in St. Louis and the Tweed Ring in New York stole millions during this period. Although the carpetbag Governor of Louisiana was referring to only his state when he said, "Corruption is the fashion," the statement applied to much of the country, both South and North. Moreover, many of the governments which came to power after Reconstruction were no more honest than those of the Reconstruction period. A Democratic state treasurer in Mississippi, for instance, made off with $315,612 after the return of conservative white rule.

Radical governments, whatever their weaknesses, wrote into the record a considerable body of social and economic legislation destined to stand the test of time. They established programs of compulsory education; they expanded the social services in poor relief and public works; and they created constitutions, largely on Northern models, which long survived the return of white rule to the South. As one historian of Reconstruction has written: "It is impossible to be convinced that the people who gave South Carolina so excellent a constitution, who founded good social legislation, a new system of demeanor, could at the same time in all cases be stealing, carousing, and breaking every law of decency." Perhaps the worst crime of which the Reconstruction governments could be held guilty was their violation of the American caste system.

The Election of 1868

The issues of Reconstruction which had divided the nation in 1866 dominated national politics again in the presidential election of 1868. The Republican Nominating Convention met at Chicago on May 20, several days after the failure of the impeachment proceedings against President Johnson. By a unanimous vote on the first ballot, it chose General Ulysses S. Grant as its presidential candidate and, for the vice presidency, Schuyler Colfax of Indiana. Grant served the needs of the Republican party admirably, for, as a popular war hero and the strategist of victory, he eased the Republican task of capitalizing on the lingering emotions of patriotism generated by the Civil War. Grant, moreover held no political principles or notions of executive leadership which would challenge the program of congressional Reconstruction.

Despite its general vagueness, the Republican platform contained a strong endorsement of Radical Reconstruction. On the question of Negro suffrage the Republicans hedged: "The guaranty of Congress of equal suffrage to all loyal men at the South was demanded by every consideration of public safety, of gratitude and of justice, and must be maintained; while the question of suffrage in all the loyal states properly belongs to the people of those states." A number of Northern states had refused to grant Negroes the right to vote and were thus unwilling to make the question of Negro suffrage a forthright party issue. Although the Republicans based their campaign principally on the issue of Reconstruction, they also advocated lower taxes, the encouragement of immigration, payment of the national debt, and pensions for veterans.

In an effort to challenge the Republicans on the central issue of Reconstruction, the Democratic party nominated New York's war

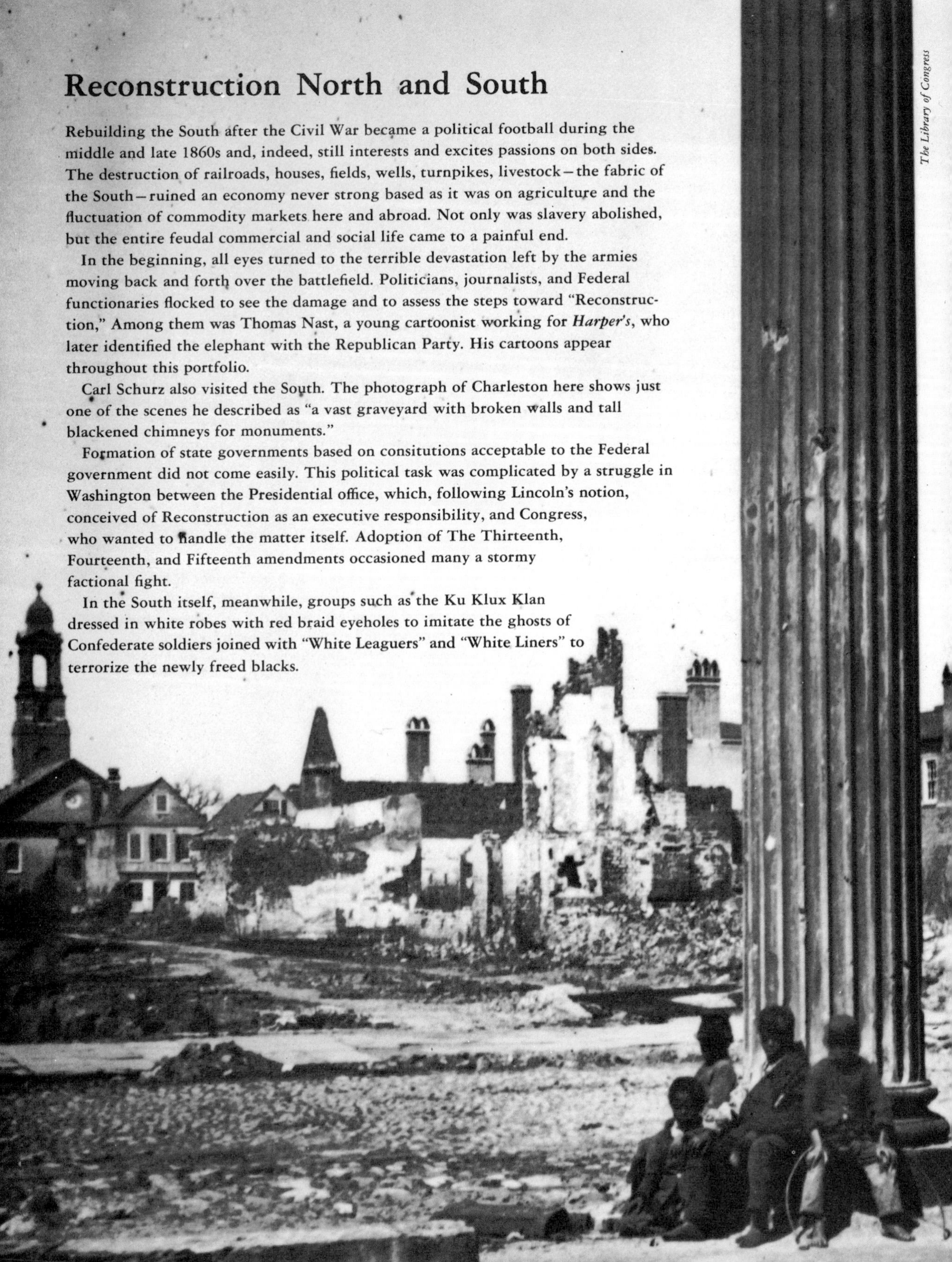

Reconstruction North and South

Rebuilding the South after the Civil War became a political football during the middle and late 1860s and, indeed, still interests and excites passions on both sides. The destruction of railroads, houses, fields, wells, turnpikes, livestock—the fabric of the South—ruined an economy never strong based as it was on agriculture and the fluctuation of commodity markets here and abroad. Not only was slavery abolished, but the entire feudal commercial and social life came to a painful end.

In the beginning, all eyes turned to the terrible devastation left by the armies moving back and forth over the battlefield. Politicians, journalists, and Federal functionaries flocked to see the damage and to assess the steps toward "Reconstruction," Among them was Thomas Nast, a young cartoonist working for *Harper's*, who later identified the elephant with the Republican Party. His cartoons appear throughout this portfolio.

Carl Schurz also visited the South. The photograph of Charleston here shows just one of the scenes he described as "a vast graveyard with broken walls and tall blackened chimneys for monuments."

Formation of state governments based on consitutions acceptable to the Federal government did not come easily. This political task was complicated by a struggle in Washington between the Presidential office, which, following Lincoln's notion, conceived of Reconstruction as an executive responsibility, and Congress, who wanted to handle the matter itself. Adoption of The Thirteenth, Fourteenth, and Fifteenth amendments occasioned many a stormy factional fight.

In the South itself, meanwhile, groups such as the Ku Klux Klan dressed in white robes with red braid eyeholes to imitate the ghosts of Confederate soldiers joined with "White Leaguers" and "White Liners" to terrorize the newly freed blacks.

The Library of Congress

Left, above: Senator Blanche Kelso Bruce of Mississippi, an escaped Virginia slave, studied at Oberlin and later owned a plantation. His Senate term ran from 1875–1881.

Left, center: Also an Oberlin graduate, John Mercer Langston, Representative from Virginia in 1890–1891, organized the law department at Howard University, sat on the Board of Health during the Grant administration, and served as Minister to Haiti under Hayes. He wrote "From the Virginia Plantation to the National Capitol" in 1894.

Left, below: Robert B. Elliott, Congressman from South Carolina, received his education at Eton and served two terms in Washington. He summed up his political philosophy in saying, "What you give to one class you must give to all."

Of the 146 members of the legislature in South Carolina, ninety were black. This legislature, shown at right, like the others in the South, tried without much success to put the war-torn economy on its feet. Representatives did make modest innovations, producing South Carolina's first democratic constitution which referred to women's suffrage and to suffrage without property ownership. Among the laws passed at this time, one made it a crime to call a man "nigger" or "yankee."

All pictures: Library of Congress

RADICAL MEMBERS

OF THE FIRST LEGISLATURE AFTER THE WAR 

President, Lieut Gov Boozer 40 Acres and a Mule.

Judas Moses. who raised the Confederate Flag on Fort Sumter!!

Jefferson Davis was to have been tried for treason by the jury shown at right, above, the first ever impanelled from both races. But Davis was released on bail, and the charges were later dropped. Meanwhile, the Reconstruction Committee met at White Sulphur Springs (right, below). To the left of General Robert E. Lee, second from left, front, sits George Peabody who started general public education in Virginia.

An allegorical lithograph of the postwar period presents a fantastic vision of hope for the spiritual reunification of the nation. Antagonists of prewar times clasp hands under the rotunda as do those in Heaven.

Spread: Library of Congress
Insets: Cook Collection, The Valentine Museum, Richmond, Virginia

2 X 6

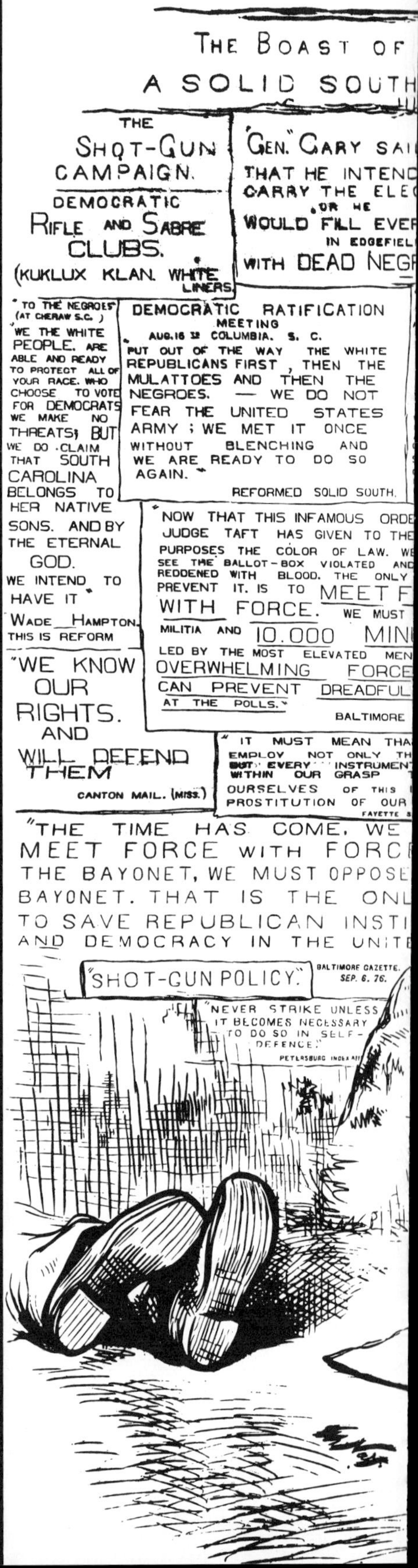

THE BOAST OF

A SOLID SOUTH

THE SHOT-GUN CAMPAIGN.

DEMOCRATIC RIFLE AND SABRE CLUBS.

(KUKLUX KLAN. WHITE LINERS.

"GEN." GARY SAI

THAT HE INTEND

CARRY THE ELEC

OR HE

WOULD FILL EVER

IN EDGEFIEL

WITH DEAD NEGR

"TO THE NEGROES" (AT CHERAW S.C.)

"WE THE WHITE PEOPLE. ARE ABLE AND READY TO PROTECT ALL OF YOUR RACE. WHO CHOOSE TO VOTE FOR DEMOCRATS WE MAKE NO THREATS; BUT WE DO CLAIM THAT SOUTH CAROLINA BELONGS TO HER NATIVE SONS. AND BY THE ETERNAL GOD. WE INTEND TO HAVE IT"

WADE HAMPTON.

THIS IS REFORM

DEMOCRATIC RATIFICATION MEETING

AUG. 16 TH COLUMBIA. S. C.

"PUT OUT OF THE WAY THE WHITE REPUBLICANS FIRST, THEN THE MULATTOES AND THEN THE NEGROES. — WE DO NOT FEAR THE UNITED STATES ARMY; WE MET IT ONCE WITHOUT BLENCHING AND WE ARE READY TO DO SO AGAIN."

REFORMED SOLID SOUTH.

"NOW THAT THIS INFAMOUS ORDE JUDGE TAFT HAS GIVEN TO THE PURPOSES THE COLOR OF LAW. WE SEE THE BALLOT-BOX VIOLATED AND REDDENED WITH BLOOD. THE ONLY PREVENT IT. IS TO MEET F WITH FORCE. WE MUST MILITIA AND 10.000 MINU LED BY THE MOST ELEVATED MEN OVERWHELMING FORCE CAN PREVENT DREADFUL AT THE POLLS."

BALTIMORE

"WE KNOW OUR RIGHTS. AND WILL DEFEND THEM"

CANTON MAIL. (MISS.)

"IT MUST MEAN THA EMPLOY NOT ONLY TH BUT EVERY INSTRUMENT WITHIN OUR GRASP OURSELVES OF THIS PROSTITUTION OF OUR

FAYETTE

"THE TIME HAS COME. WE MEET FORCE WITH FORCE THE BAYONET, WE MUST OPPOSE BAYONET. THAT IS THE ONL TO SAVE REPUBLICAN INSTI AND DEMOCRACY IN THE UNITE

"SHOT-GUN POLICY."
BALTIMORE GAZETTE. SEP. 6. 76.
"NEVER STRIKE UNLESS IT BECOMES NECESSARY TO DO SO IN SELF-DEFENCE."
PETERSBURG INDEX

Ku Klux Klan members appear in costume at far left, below. To restrain and intimidate freed Negroes and their white supporters, they fostered tarring and feathering, night-riding, and cross burning. In spite of legislation against them in 1871, the Klan reappeared in times of stress. The White League was organized to prevent Negroes from voting. Their symbol (far left, above) includes a skull; 2×6 is the size of their victim's grave.

Thomas Nast drew many pointed cartoons criticizing the White League's school-burning activities (left and below). A fierce liberal, Nast continually attacked the Klan and the White League. Nevertheless, certain nineteenth-century racial stereotypes appear in his work (see the following page).

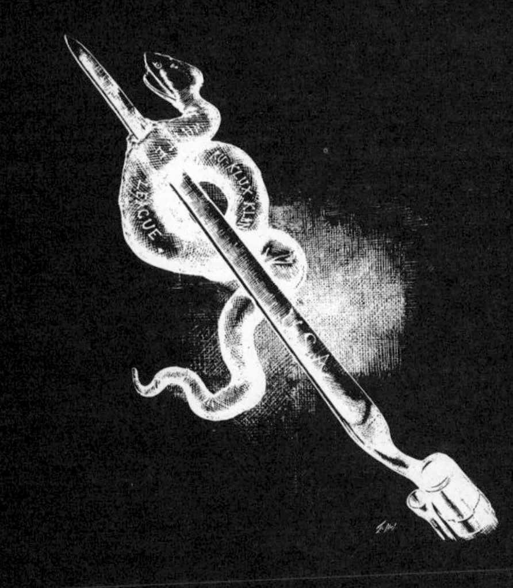

All pictures: Library of Congress

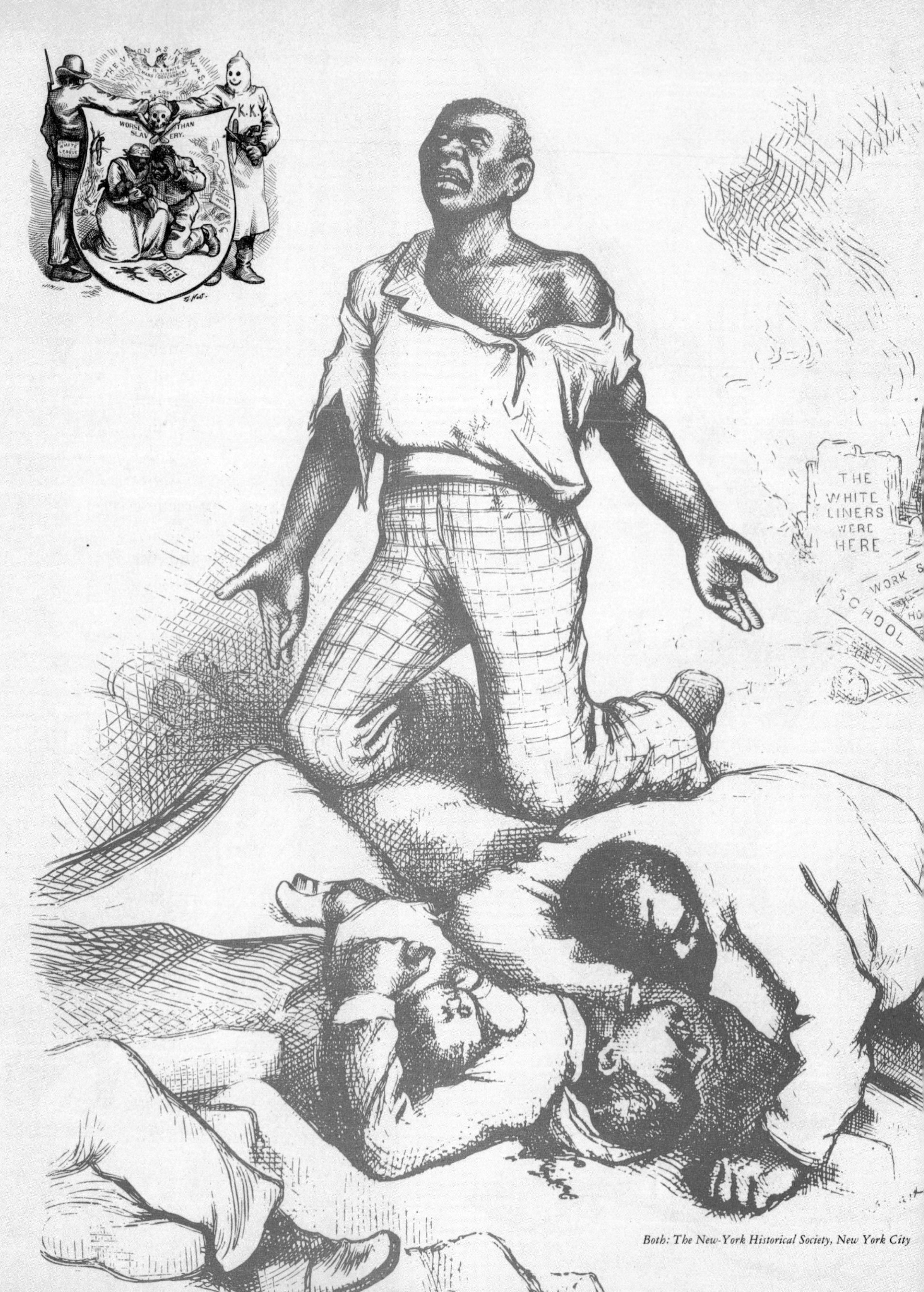

Both: The New-York Historical Society, New York City

Governor, Horatio Seymour, a persistent critic of Radical Reconstruction and Negro suffrage. The party's strongly worded anti-Reconstruction platform accused the Republican Congress of subjecting the ten Southern states "to military despotism and negro supremacy." The Republicans rallied at the Democratic attack on their favorite program. Waving the "bloody shirt," Oliver P. Morton, a leading Radical, termed Seymour's nomination a "declaration of the renewal of the rebellion." A Democratic victory, Morton warned, would return the South to the enemy and terminate the work of Reconstruction. In the South, Union League clubs organized the Negro vote for the Republicans.

Placed at a disadvantage by such Republican electioneering, the Democratic party hoped to capture the Western farm vote on the question of the currency. Much of the Republican economic program, including banking and tariff legislation, had been designed to serve the nation's expanding business interests. The grain-producing Middle West was exhibiting increasing discontent at this Republican favoritism and demanding relief from declining farm prices. Many debtors, as well as others, believed that higher prices could be brought about by inflating the currency through an expanded use of greenbacks. But Congress in the Funding Act of 1866 had adopted a deflationary program by retiring the wartime greenbacks: $10 million in the first six months and $4 million or less per month thereafter. This contraction of the currency during a time of falling prices produced a storm of protest from groups favoring inflation and forced Congress in 1868 to suspend the policy of contraction. Responding to these demands, the Democratic party in its platform advocated the "Ohio Idea," proposing that the obligations of the government be paid in greenbacks except when those obligations expressly demanded payment in gold or silver. The Republicans based their hard money appeal to the West on Unionist sentiment, reminding farmers that the redemption of government obligations, which had been contracted to preserve the Union, in anything but gold repudiated those debts. Having deftly neutralized the Democratic appeal to Western debtors, the Republican party again made Radical Reconstruction the central issue.

Grant won a solid victory and carried twenty-six states, leaving Seymour only eight. The general won about 53 percent of the popular vote. His success in the North was impressive enough, but he also carried Tennessee and five of the former Confederate states where Negro suffrage had been imposed—North Carolina, South Carolina, Florida, Alabama, and Arkansas. This Republican penetration of the South demonstrated the importance of the Negro vote to continued dominance and prompted party leaders to desert their platform declaration on Negro suffrage. When Congress met in December, 1868, the Radicals—determined to place the freedmen's right to vote beyond the power of the states—submitted the Fifteenth Amendment.

The Grant Regime

The Grant administration is well remembered for its scandal. If the nation progressed mightily during the first postwar decade in business, transportation, and agriculture, that development was not greatly aided or retarded by the corruption in the federal

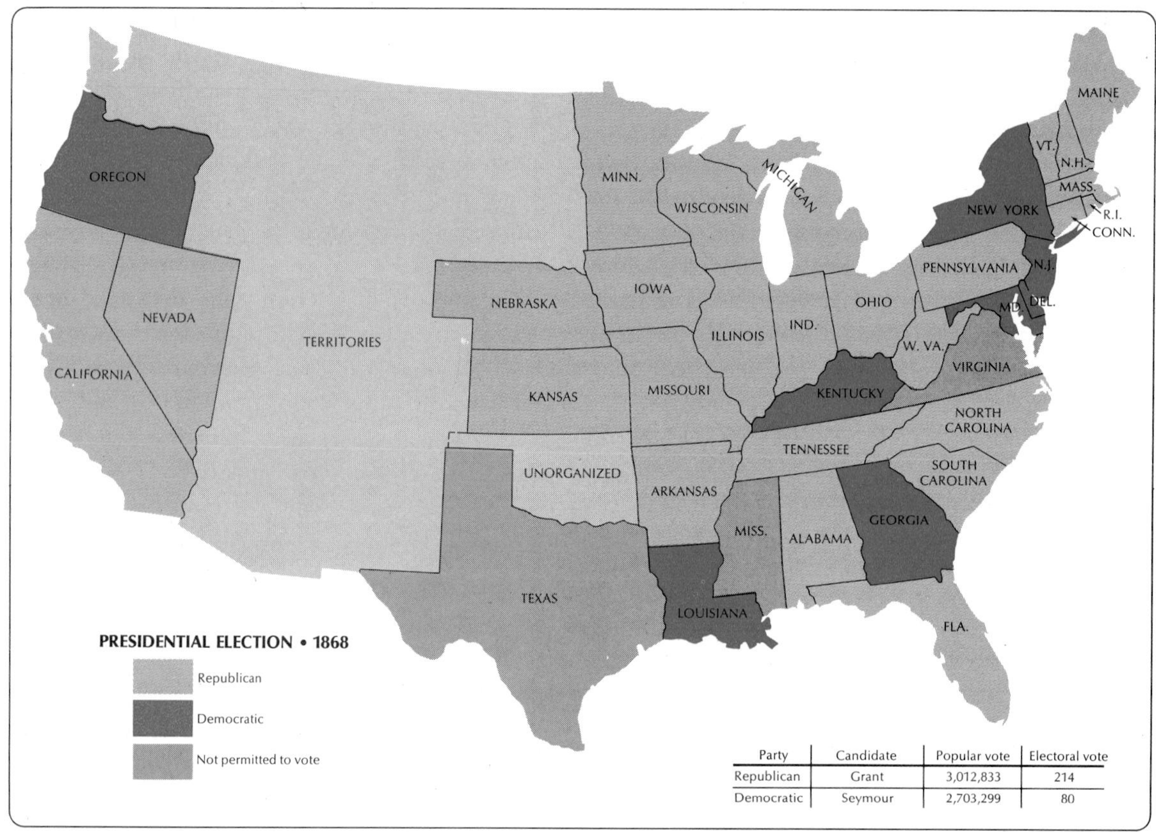

Party	Candidate	Popular vote	Electoral vote
Republican	Grant	3,012,833	214
Democratic	Seymour	2,703,299	80

government. Many of the policies that mattered had been adopted by previous Republican Congresses: the protective tariff; the national banking system; the new federal currency based on National Bank notes; subsidies for internal improvements; the Homestead law; grants of land, timber, and mineral resources to railroads and other private industries. It was a narrow program; to its critics it seemed to serve only the lords of the earth.

To sustain a course that would meet the varied needs of all the nation, the federal government required determined and dedicated national leadership. Many of the Radicals in Congress who had given direction and purpose to Republican policy, especially in the area of Southern Reconstruction, had by 1869 either died, retired, or lost office. New leaders emerged to take control of the Republican party in the days of Grant. These were, in many instances, the bosses of the powerful Republican state machines in the North, organization men for whom political office represented the opportunity for power and control, not service or reform. The spoils system was the essence of their authority; to sustain it they corrupted the federal civil service. In policy matters these "Stalwarts" were, above all, spokesmen of the status quo. Typical of their breed was Senator Roscoe Conkling of New York.

During the war years Washington had grown

accustomed to political corruption, and after Appomattox the quest for special favors continued unabated. The opportunities presented by the "Great Barbecue," comprising the nation's riches and spread by a generous government, brought a flood of wealth seekers into the Capital. Railroad builders, financiers, business agents, and promoters had profited handsomely from lucrative land grants and government contracts, special tariffs, hard money decisions, and a wide range of public expenditures. Even before Grant's Presidency, the direct relationship between expanding business and a responsive government was bordering on the scandalous. Clearly the times called for vigorous White House leadership, and Grant, popular and independent upon entering the White House, appeared eminently qualified to meet the challenge.

Yet Grant lacked the experience, knowledge, and character to protect either Congress or the White House from the politicians, adventurers, and speculators who preyed on the government. Had Grant possessed the talent to consult with and learn from others, he might still have surrounded himself with men of integrity, who could have educated him in matters of politics and civil affairs. But his inability to analyze and judge, deficiencies which he readily admitted and which made him self-conscious in the presence of superior minds, made him an easy victim for the coarser politicians who, by showing deference, could gain his ear and slowly and deliberately urge their ideas upon him until he accepted them as his own. Unable to impose high standards of honesty on the men around him, Grant permitted the White House to become the focus of governmental inefficiency and corruption.

Grant's Presidency reflected the materialism of the day. Already, during the immediate postwar years, businessmen had showered this Union hero with lavish gifts. Grant saw no need to curtail the flow of gifts after he entered the White House. Having spent years in poverty, he accepted with both hands the favors thrust upon him—without ever suspecting the price. Perhaps Grant himself remained innocent of profiteering, but he could scarcely deny reasonable requests from his wealthy hosts whose cigars he smoked and whose riches he admired. It was Grant's infatuation with wealth that made possible such episodes as the "Black Friday" gold scandal of September, 1869. Having convinced the President that he should not release gold from the federal Treasury, Jay Gould and "Diamond Jim" Fisk, two particularly unscrupulous business adventurers, set out to corner the gold market. Eventually Grant, responding to opposing advice, released enough gold to break the price, but not before countless businessmen, unable to acquire sufficient gold at a reasonable price to meet their obligations, were ruined.

Foreign Affairs

Not even in the realm of foreign affairs could Grant avoid charges of corruption. The West Indian island of Santo Domingo had won its independence from Spain in 1865, and shortly after he entered the Presidency, a group of promoters convinced Grant that the United States should annex the island. Strangely enough, the Dominican leaders themselves were so thoroughly convinced that they could best solidify their economic and political status on the island through American control that Grant's representative was able, during a visit late in 1869, to negotiate a treaty of annexation. Grant attempted to force the treaty through the Senate, only to face the determined opposition of Foreign Relations Committee Chairman Charles Sumner, who denounced the annexation as a private deal to exploit the island's riches. Although the President failed to secure ratification of this treaty, he succeeded in depriving Sumner of his chairmanship.

This episode did not prevent Secretary of State Hamilton Fish from negotiating with Britain the Treaty of Washington in 1871. Since 1869, American and British representatives had debated the question of the *Alabama* claims. United States officials insisted that England compensate this nation for the losses suffered by Union shipping at the hands of Confederate cruisers built or armed in British shipyards during the Civil War. Washington diplomats presented claims amounting to some $19 million; to this Senator Sumner added indirect losses which he thought obligated Britain to pay the United States $2 billion. Complicating the issue of claims were British-American disputes over the boundary line through the San Juan Islands in the Pacific Northwest and the matter of fishing privileges off Canada's eastern coast. The Treaty of Washington assigned the question of the *Alabama* claims to a five-man commission which awarded the United States $15 million in damages. The German Emperor arbitrated the boundary line through the San Juan Islands, upholding in general the claims of the United States. Not, however, until 1877 did a three-man commission settle the fisheries dispute. It awarded Britain $5 million for additional concessions made to American fishermen along the Canadian coast. The Treaty of Washington and the resulting settlements were important in at least two major ways: they constituted a victory for the principle of arbitration, and they gave evidence of a growing feeling of goodwill and cooperation between the two leading Atlantic powers. Certainly the treaty was one of the few distinct accomplishments of the Grant administration.

But Secretary Fish gained another success through his diplomacy when he managed to resist domestic pressures to involve the United States in the affairs of Cuba. The Cuban revolt against Spain, erupting in 1868, aroused widespread sympathy for the revolutionists in the United States, leading members of Congress to demand that the administration aid the cause of Cuban liberty by recognizing the belligerency of the insurgents. Fish convinced the President that involvement would not serve the interest of the United States. The Secretary met another crisis in 1873 when Spaniards captured the *Virginius,* a Cuban ship flying the American flag, and shot fifty-three passengers and members of the crew, some of them Americans. This time Fish obtained both an apology and an indemnity from Spain to again avert serious trouble.

The Liberal Republicans

For those who expected much of Grant, the failures of his Presidency were nothing less than appalling. Young Henry Adams became disillusioned early. "That two thousand years after Alexander the Great and Julius Caesar," he wrote in 1869, "a man like Grant should be called . . . the highest product of the most advanced evolution, made evolution ludicrous. . . . The progress of evolution from President Washington to President Grant was alone enough to upset Darwin." So thoroughly had the Republican party under Grant lost its capacity for direct and efficient performance that many of its most thoughtful leaders wondered if it had outlived its usefulness.

By 1870 many Republicans were in open revolt against the party's national leadership. Beginning in Missouri, where B. Gratz Brown led a campaign against the continuance of extreme Radical Reconstruction, the demand for reform soon spread to such key party leaders as Carl Schurz and Charles Francis Adams, as well as Republican editors like Horace Greeley of the *New York Tribune* and Edwin L. Godkin of *The Nation.* When it became clear that the Stalwarts would gain a second nomination for Grant, reform-minded Republicans met at Cincinnati on May 1, 1872, to organize the Liberal Republican party. They demanded and wrote into the new party's platform a program of tariff and civil service reform to stop the plunder of the government and called for the end of military rule in the South. No longer did the old free-soilers care to fight for the rights of the Negro. Convinced that the South possessed the power to resist Northern intentions, they concluded that principles of equality, even if embodied in law, would achieve little for the Negro. Continued Republican interference in the South, Greeley warned, would merely force the Southern Whigs into Democratic ranks and terminate abruptly all rights the Negro had won. Liberal Republicans in May, 1872, brought pressure on Congress and secured the passage of a general amnesty act pardoning all but a few hundred Confederates who had held federal offices at the time of secession.

Liberal Republican moderation on the issue of Reconstruction confronted the old abolitionists with a difficult choice. As idealists they abhorred the low state to which Grant and the Stalwarts had reduced the federal government. Most abolitionists, however, were still concerned over the welfare of the freedmen; they saw that the Liberal Republican program of sectional reconciliation would be achieved only at the price of Negro rights. Frederick Douglass, the black abolitionist, termed the Liberal Republican movement dangerous to the Negro cause and concluded that, whatever its faults, the Republican party "has within it the only element of friendship for the colored man's rights." Most old abolitionists accepted Douglass's reasoning and supported Grant's reelection campaign.

To defeat Grant, the Liberal Republicans needed the full support of the national Democratic party. But Greeley, who was selected over Charles Francis Adams as the Liberal Republican standard-bearer, only to see many of the latter's angry supporters return to regular Republican ranks, had been a lifelong critic of Democrats and during previous campaigns had waved the bloody shirt with apparent enthusiasm. Nevertheless, the Democratic party, if it would recover its lost position in national politics, had no choice but to endorse Greeley. But this action weakened the Liberal Republican coalition even further by seemingly clinching the argument of the Grant forces that the only hope for the Negro lay with the regular Republicans. Gerrit Smith summarized such sentiments well when he declared that the "anti-Slavery battle is not yet fought out—and, until it is, we shall need Grant's continued leadership." Meanwhile Grant, who had swept the Republican Convention in June, faced little organized opposition in the campaign. In victory, he lost only six states, none in the North. His majority of 700,000 popular votes was nothing less than a landslide.

More Corruption

Having been vindicated so overwhelmingly at the polls, the public officials who supported Grant now pushed corruption to the point of open scandal. Lavish congressional handouts had included land worth more than $300 million given to builders of railroads; while promoters drew exorbitant profits from collusion in the negotiation of construction and equipment contracts. Congress had granted sizable loans to the Union Pacific and the Central Pacific to encourage them to complete the first transcontinental route; thereafter these railroads battled to prevent Congress from establishing conditions of repayment. To protect its interests, the Crédit Mobilier, a construction company organized to enable several Union Pacific stockholders to profit from construction contracts, distributed blocks of stock to key members of the House and Senate. A congressional investigation instituted when this became known in the autumn of 1872 implicated such leading Republicans as Vice President Schuyler Colfax and Senator James W. Patterson of New Hampshire. A year later the same Congress that had investigated the Crédit Mobilier scandal not only voted itself a salary increase of 50 percent, from $5,000 to $7,500, but made it retroactive for two years. So great was the popular outrage, however, that Congress soon repealed the "Salary Grab Act."

No less dramatic were the new scandals within the administration itself. During the spring of 1875, Grant's third Secretary of the Treasury, Benjamin H. Bristow, uncovered the "Whisky Ring," a combination of St. Louis distillers and federal revenue agents who had defrauded the government of millions of dollars of internal revenue. But when it became apparent that this exposure involved a member of the White House staff, Grant lost all interest in the prosecution. The President's prestige, committed fully to the defense of his crony, kept the man out of prison. A second major scandal rocked the administration in 1875 with the resignation of Secretary of War W. W. Belknap. For five years Belknap had received illicit payments totaling more than $24,000 from a corrupt post trader at Ft. Sill in Indian Territory. The House brought impeachment charges against the Secretary, but when Grant accepted Belknap's resignation, the Senate, claiming that it no longer had jurisdiction, refused to proceed with the trial. By 1875 the spoils system had so undermined the civil service that Grant had abandoned the competitive system completely.

The End of Reconstruction

Had the Stalwart Republicans been able to perpetuate the country's postwar prosperity, they might have withstood the challenge of another presidential campaign. The failures of Grant's first term, well publicized by the Liberal Republicans, had not prevented the general's sweep in 1872. Throughout Grant's second term, however, factors more pervading than scandals undermined the power which the Stalwarts wielded through their dispensation of governmental favors. After 1873, Grant and his supporters faced the discontent of a depressed nation. Ambitious businessmen and promoters, caught up in the speculative spirit of the postwar years, had overextended the country's railroads as well as its agricultural, commercial, and industrial capacity. So inflated had the economy become through credit expansion that the failure in September, 1873, of Jay Cooke, the financier of the Northern Pacific Railroad, was sufficient to send the national economy tumbling into a five-year depression. Eventually mercantile failures alone totaled almost a billion dollars.

Hard on the heels of the crash came a wave of Democratic victories in the election of 1874. This election revolutionized the composition of the House of Representatives, turning a two-thirds Republican majority into a Democratic majority of seventy. In the Senate, the Republicans maintained a narrow majority. The Democrats broke the Republican hold in such states as Pennsylvania, Ohio, and Massachusetts; coalitions of Democrats and Grangers threatened Republican dominance that year in several of the prairie states.

In the South, race prejudice was undermining the entire Republican effort to reconstruct Southern society by action of the national government. Prejudice had an economic base; its easiest victories were among the low-status whites whose only claim to distinction was the color of their skin. The fact that a man was poor was less important than the fact that he was white and the poor white was especially determined that the Negro never forget the distinction of color. Oldline Whigs shared the general belief in white supremacy, but their social position and economic security reduced their fear of black equality. They accepted both Negro suffrage and the notion of legal equality between the races, partly because they believed they could control most of the Negro vote. Conservative Democrats faced the choice of competing with Whigs and Republicans for the Negro vote or resorting to demagoguery in an effort to drive the blacks out of politics and rebuild the Southern Democratic party on the votes of lower-class whites. They made the latter decision. Having marked out their avenue to power, Southern Democrats exerted whatever pressure white and black resistance demanded. Through such clandestine organizations as the Ku Klux Klan, founded at Pulaski, Tennessee, in 1866, and the Knights of the White Camelia, formed in New Orleans in 1867, they used violence and intimidation to weaken Radical control based on the Negro vote.

Neither Grant nor Congress, faced with the Southern weapons of illegal coercion, was willing to use federal power to enforce the Fourteenth and Fifteenth Amendments. From the beginning of Reconstruction the landless Negro had been a weak reed upon which to build political power and a program of civil rights in the South. Negro influence in the Reconstruction governments had never rested on the solid and enduring foundation of social and economic advancement. In its refusal to adopt a progressive land policy for the South, Congress denied the former slaves the economic independence they needed to resist political intimidation. But the causes of Republican failure in the South ran deeper. Liberal Republicans, joined by Northern businessmen interested in commercial relations with the South, had become convinced as early as 1872 that Negro rights, an elusive goal at best, held less promise for the Republican party and the nation than did a new alignment between Northern Republicans and Southern conservatives. Yankee investors and promoters with interests in the South preferred the stability that would come from conservative white rule to the instability perpetuated by faltering Reconstruction governments. Northern politicians, having become indifferent to Reconstruction, could now recall that the Civil War had been fought to maintain the Union, not to bring salvation to the Negro.

Faced with their forthcoming loss of the House when Congress would convene later in the year, the Republicans, on March 1, 1875, passed another Civil Rights Act which guaranteed equal rights to Negroes in hotels, public conveyances, amusement centers, and on juries. Through measures such as this the Republican party hoped to maintain some semblance of control over social evolution in the South. But already the Supreme Court had begun the process of curtailing federal encroachment on the traditional rights of the states. One of the most important decisions was delivered on April 14, 1873, in the *Slaughterhouse Cases.* The *Slaughterhouse Cases* grew out of legislation in Louisiana which gave monopoly privileges to a single slaughterhouse corporation in certain parishes of the state. Those who were denied business as a result of this monopoly, granted under corrupt conditions, charged that it violated the Fourteenth Amendment by denying them property without due process of law. The Supreme Court, however, decided that the Louisiana law did not violate the Fourteenth Amendment and added that Congress had not intended to expand federal power to "the entire domain of civil rights heretofore belonging exclusively to the States." In other words, fundamental civil rights remained under state protection. In *United States v. Reese* in 1876 the Court further limited the federal government's right to enforce suffrage to cases involving race and color. Thus Southern states gained the legal right to set special prerequisites, such as poll taxes, to restrict Negro suffrage. In 1883, the Supreme Court declared the Civil Rights Act of 1875 unconstitutional on grounds that the federal government had no right to protect civil rights against the actions of individuals or organizations. This decision set the stage for *Plessy v. Ferguson* in 1896, which permitted segregation on railroads if the available facilities for Negroes were equal. Three years later, the Court extended the "separate but equal" concept to schools.

The Supreme Court, upholding states' rights, had now returned to the South the essential power to govern its own race relations. The practical outcome of this situation was that the vast majority of Negroes in the South were kept economically subservient and socially segregated. Negroes had been segregated in schools from the end of the Civil War onward; beginning in 1870 in Tennessee, intermarriage had been forbidden; and Tennessee passed the first "Jim Crow" law in 1875, which separated the races on railroads and streetcars. The retreat from Radical Reconstruction had by then turned into a disorderly flight.

The Election of 1876

Encouraged by its victories in 1874 and the mounting failures of the Grant administration, the Democratic party entered the campaign of 1876 with genuine expectations of success. Beginning with Tennessee in 1869, all the states of the South except Louisiana, South Carolina, and Florida had been redeemed from the Radicals and were again under Democratic control. Democrats, like Republicans, differed on many of the economic issues before the

The Centennial Celebration

The scandals and corruption which sullied the reputation of the Grant Administration should not obscure the fact that, despite an economic recession of considerable duration, the nation grew rapidly and optimistically. Perhaps no single event better summed up the optimism of the period than America's 100th birthday party—the Centennial Celebration of 1876 held in Philadelphia. A year before this world's fair opened, the *New York Daily Graphic*, in the drawing below, depicted the entire world coming to the great exhibition. The attitude implicit in this cartoon should not be interpreted as a pure example of national egocentricity, however. The cut is a copy of one done earlier in England by George Cruikshank to herald the Crystal Palace Exhibition of 1851 in London.

Before a crowd of 100,000, President Grant opened the fair on May 10, 1876. By closing day in November, the attendance totalled 8,000,000. The ceremony included a Centennial March by the German composer Richard Wagner, commissioned for a fee of $5,000 and paid for by the Women's Centennial Committee. Bedazzled by the multiple wonders of the fair, a magazine cartoonist thought the only way to see everything in a day was to have eyes all over his head. The wonders of the fair included a statue symbolizing the Negro's emancipation from slavery, a tree composed of scythe blades, agricultural prodigies, and much, much more (following spread).

Courtesy of the New-York Historical Society, New York City

How to see everything in a day
PATENT APPLIED FOR.

Spread: Courtesy of the New-York Historical Society, New York City
All inset pictures: Library of Congress

Mon Dieu!
HOME AGAIN

The huge Corliss engine provided power for the thirteen acres of machinery in Machinery Hall and became a landmark at the fair. The cover of *Frank Leslie's Illustrated Weekly,* at right, shows the machine being started by President Grant and President Dom Pedro of Brazil. The novelist William Dean Howells called it an "athlete of steel and iron." Operated by just one man, the Corliss engine symbolized the advancing technology which spelled the death of the old era of handicrafts. Military hardware, like the Krupp cannon exhibit (above, right) stood on display about the fair-grounds, but so did more peaceful innovations, such as the demonstration kindergarten (above, left).

All pictures: Library of Congress

nation, but for their presidential candidate they agreed readily on Samuel J. Tilden, a wealthy New York lawyer who, as Governor of his state, had led an assault on Tammany Hall, the core of New York's political corruption, and had sent its head, "Boss" Tweed, to the penitentiary. For Tilden's running mate the Democrats chose Thomas A. Hendricks of Indiana. The platform called for "immediate reform" in broad areas of American political and economic life. It demanded that the Southern states "be saved from a corrupt centralism which, after inflicting upon ten States the rapacity of carpetbag tyrannies, had honeycombed the offices of the Federal Government itself with incapacity, waste and fraud." In effect, the Democrats were calling for removal of federal troops from the states where they still remained. They also attacked the protective tariff; denounced Republican financial policies, especially excessive spending; demanded that public lands be reserved for actual settlers; and called for civil service reform.

For the first time in sixteen years, Republican control of the White House was in jeopardy. The Stalwarts, who trusted no one but Grant, sought his renomination. Many Republican businessmen, however, were tired of governmental corruption and preferred new leadership. The "Halfbreeds," moderates who opposed the Stalwarts but had not bolted to the Liberal Republicans in 1872, favored the nomination of James G. Blaine, former Speaker of the House, despite the charges of corruption leveled against him. Unable to nominate Grant but bitterly opposed to Blaine, the administration forces accepted Rutherford B. Hayes as a compromise candidate for the Presidency and agreed to William A. Wheeler of New York for Vice President. Hayes's record as reform Governor of Ohio made him equally acceptable to Republican moderates and liberals. The Greenback party, responding to the discontented elements in the North, nominated New York industrialist and philanthropist Peter Cooper on a platform that demanded inflation through greater issues of paper money.

If the Democrats charged the Republicans with "wrongs" and "crimes," the Republicans retaliated in equal measure. After expressing pride in the party's history, the Republican platform warned against trusting the Democrats, "a party unworthy, recreant, and incapable." Besides, the Republicans said, the Democratic party "was the same in character and spirit as when it sympathized with treason." Republicans declared that they were "sacredly pledged" to enforce the Thirteenth, Fourteenth, and Fifteenth Amendments and protect all citizens in the enjoyment of their rights. On economic questions, the party promised to work for a return of sound money, or specie payments; to adjust the tariff, though it did not say how this would be done; and to oppose further land grants to large corporations. The public domain, Republicans declared, should be used for "free homes for the people."

In November, the initial returns gave Tilden a 250,000-vote plurality, and even Republican journals at first conceded his election. He had carried Connecticut, New York, New Jersey, and Indiana, as well as the entire South, and had 184 electoral votes. Hayes had 166. But the voting in Louisiana, South Carolina, and Florida—the three Southern states still under carpetbag and Negro rule—had been grossly irregular, permitting Republican officials there to claim Republican victories. If Hayes could get the 19 votes of these three states, he would have

185 electoral votes, or a majority of 1. There was also one disputed vote from Oregon.

The contest quickly shifted to the three Southern states where the returns were in dispute. Amidst charges and countercharges of graft, corruption, and vote stealing, both Democrats and Republicans claimed victory. Early in December the Republican electors from Louisiana, Florida, and South Carolina met in their respective capitals and cast their votes for Hayes, while Democratic electors balloted for Tilden. Both sets of returns were then transmitted to Washington, and the problem was thrown in the lap of Congress. The question now was, what votes would be counted and by whom? The Constitution simply stated that "the President of the Senate shall, in the presence of the Senate and House of Representatives, open all the Certificates and the Votes shall then be counted." But it did not specify who would do the counting. If the president of the Senate—a Republican—should make the count, he would give the disputed ballots to Hayes; if representatives of the House did the counting, Tilden would get the votes.

To deal with this delicate problem, Congress created a special electoral commission of fifteen men, made up of five from each house of Congress and five Supreme Court justices, to pass judgment on the contested election returns. Among its members were seven Republicans, seven Democrats, and one Independent. When Justice David Davis, the Independent, refused to serve, the Republicans received the fifteenth membership. The commission refused to look behind the returns and, ignoring the irregularities on both sides, gave all the contested votes to Hayes. There was much uneasiness in the country between December, 1876, and March, 1877; there was even some talk of renewed civil war, but moderate and conservative views prevailed. Hayes's election finally received official recognition on March 2, 1877, only two days before Grant was to leave office.

Hayes's victory resulted from what scholars have come to call the Compromise of 1877. Republican leadership, in winning the contested election, faced the necessity of forestalling possible violence and a Democratic filibuster in the House against the completion of the count. The best hope for a peaceful inauguration and Republican control of the next Congress, the Republicans discovered, lay with the Southern conservatives. To win their support, Hayes had only to promise certain economic benefits—federal aid for flood control, harbor improvements, and railroad subsidies—along with complete home rule, which meant giving up federal efforts to protect Negroes against political and social discrimination. Those who sought these economic objectives labored to obtain a political agreement. The nation's economic interests played a major part in winning support for the so-called Compromise of 1877.

Hayes had never favored Radical Reconstruction, and he believed, as had Lincoln, that the future of the Republic hinged on a new coalition of conservatives from both North and South. Nor did he object to the distribution of some federal largess in the South. At the same time, Southern leaders admitted that the "solid South" was not very solid and that the union of Whigs and Democrats within the Democratic party, achieved under the pressure of white-supremacy propaganda, was only a marriage of convenience. During December it became clear that many Southern Democrats would support Hayes, thus assuring an uneventful inauguration. The Compromise of 1877 gave the Republicans the Presidency, but conservative Southern whites secured dominance over the Negro, plus economic benefits such as federal aid for railroad construction. In April, 1877, the new President withdrew the remaining Union troops—now only token forces—from Louisiana, Florida, and South Carolina and thus officially terminated the era of Radical Reconstruction.

Conclusion

As a political venture Reconstruction was astonishingly successful for those who managed it. The new coalition of Republicans and Southern conservatives assured the consolidation and continued triumph of American industrial capitalism. The Republican party failed in its long effort to annex the Southern Negro vote, but this mattered little. In the North, the Republicans had employed their varied emotional and economic appeals with such effectiveness that the loss of the South to the Democrats scarcely endangered their control of Congress or the White House. Despite the Democratic resurgence in the North after 1872, the Republican party held its own in New England and the Middle States. In the teeming Great Lakes region and in the rapidly expanding West, Republican mastery was complete. Ultimately it was the party's identification with the Union that gave it the unchallengeable advantage of respectability. In many areas of the Northwest, Brand Whitlock later recalled, "it was natural to be a Republican; it was more than that, it was inevitable that one should be a Republican; it was not a matter of intellectual choice, it was a process of biological selection. The Republican party . . . was a fundamental and self-evident thing, like life, and liberty, and the pursuit of happiness, or like the flag, or the federal judiciary. . . . It was merely a synonym for patriotism, another name for the nation."

Only in their effort to bring democracy and civil rights to the South had the Republicans failed. Emancipation had neither revolutionized Southern society nor seriously altered the Negro's place in Southern life. Although Negroes voted in many parts of the South until the 1890s, their votes after 1876 were usually controlled by the conservative whites. Throughout the "black belt" of the South, upper-class whites attached the majority of Negroes to the land as tenant farmers or sharecroppers; thereafter, perennial poverty and indebtedness would keep the blacks economically immobile, socially segregated, and politically inert. From such conditions the freedmen had no escape except to federal protection, but the Supreme Court had already begun the process of limiting federal jurisdiction in civil rights cases, and the Republican party, having reaped its rewards elsewhere, had lost most of its interest in the Negro's plight. What remained to give the Negro, if not immediate comfort, at least ultimate hope, were the Fourteenth and Fifteenth Amendments—the lasting monuments to black rights erected on the ashes of Radical Reconstruction.

SUGGESTED READINGS

Were the American Civil War and the era of Reconstruction which followed a great American tragedy or the necessary price for freeing the slaves and pursuing the goal of equality? Were the Republican Radicals power-mad politicians or antislavery humanitarians? Did they fail ultimately to achieve equality of the races because the forces of reaction in the South were too powerful to be uprooted? Over questions such as these, historians have quarreled for a century. The tragic view, highly critical of both the Radical leadership in the North and the Negro-dominated Reconstruction governments in the South, found its first major expression in W. A. Dunning's *Reconstruction: Political and Economic** (1907). This general approach to Reconstruction continued to dominate such important works as Walter L. Fleming's *The Sequel of Appomattox* (1919); Claude G. Bowers's *The Tragic Era** (1929); and Robert S. Henry's *The Story of Reconstruction* (1938). That this view is still much alive is made clear by the more recent publication of E M Coulter's *The South during Reconstruction* (1947) and Hodding Carter's *The Angry Scar* (1959).

Since World War II the fundamental outlook of American historians has changed, influenced perhaps by the civil rights movement itself. Much of the newer writing on Reconstruction accepts the Radicals as sincere humanitarians; it regards the burden of Southern Reconstruction with sympathy. The first major contribution to this school of thought was W. E. B. Du Bois's *Black Reconstruction in America** (1935). Still rewarding, this study is overbalanced in favor of the Reconstruction governments. Three superb studies of Reconstruction, all moderately pro-Radical, are Kenneth M. Stampp's *The Era of Reconstruction* (1965); John Hope Franklin's *Reconstruction: After the Civil War** (1961); and Rembert W. Patrick's *The Reconstruction of the Nation** (1967). Harold M. Hyman (ed.), *New Frontiers of the American Reconstruction* (1966) is a collection of the impressive essays representing both the older and the newer schools of thought regarding Reconstruction. James G. Randall and David Donald's *The Civil War and Reconstruction* (rev. ed., 1961) is remarkably balanced in judgment.

For a description of the defeated South in 1865, see the following travel accounts: Sidney Andrews's *The South since the War* (1866); J. T. Trowbridge's *A Picture of the Desolated States* (1868; revised by Gordon Carroll as *The Desolate South,* 1956); and Robert Somer's *The Southern States since the War* (1871). W. B. Hesseltine has analyzed Lincoln's views toward the defeated South in *Lincoln's Plan of Reconstruction** (1960). Much of the historical debate over Reconstruction focuses on the purpose and program of President Johnson. Among the older pro-Johnson studies are Howard K. Beale's *The Critical Year* (1930) and George Fort Milton's *The Age of Hate: Andrew Johnson and the Radicals* (1930). Within the context of the pro-Radical school, many of the postwar studies of Johnson have been critical of him. Three examples of the new writing are E. L. McKitrick's *Andrew Johnson and Reconstruction** (1960), LaWanda and J. H. Cox's *Politics, Principle, and Prejudice,* 1865–1866 (1963); and W. R. Brock's *An American Crisis: Congress and Reconstruction** (1963).

Excellent and perceptive observations on Radical Reconstruction can be found not only in the general studies cited in the paragraphs above but also in biographies of leading congressmen and Radicals, such as the following: B. P. Thomas and H. M. Hyman's *Stanton: The Life and Times of Lincoln's Secretary of War* (1962); R. N. Current's *Old Thad Stevens* (1942); F. M. Brodie's *Thaddeus Stevens* (1959); and H. L. Trefousse's *Benjamin Franklin Wade* (1963). For a careful analysis of abolitionist attitudes toward the politicians of the Reconstruction period, see James M. McPherson's *The Struggle for Equality: Abolitionists and the Negro in the Civil War and Reconstruction** (1964). On the evolution and record of the Freedmen's Bureau, see G. R. Bentley's *A History of the Freedmen's Bureau* (1955). Joseph James in *The Framing of the Fourteenth Amendment** (1956) deals with that important piece of Radical legislation.

Reconstruction in the South has produced a large number of significant and varied studies. On the Northern invasion of the South after the war see Otto H. Olsen's *Carpetbagger's Crusade: The Life of Albion Winegar Tourgée,* (1965), an enlightening account of a representative carpetbagger. Also valuable on this theme are Martin Abbott's *The Freedmen's Bureau in South Carolina,* 1865–1872 (1967) and James E. Seften's *The United States Army and Reconstruction,* 1865–1877 (1967). On the Negro in the South during Reconstruction see V. L. Wharton's *The Negro in Mississippi,* 1865–1900* (1947); P. A. Bruce's *The Plantation Negro as a Freedman* (1889); and Otis A. Singletary's *The Negro Militia and Reconstruction** (1957). On Southern agriculture during the postwar period see F. A. Shannon's *The Farmer's Last Frontier* (1945). Edwin C. Rozwenc (ed.), *Reconstruction in the South**

(1952), is a useful anthology of conflicting views on the quality and purpose of Southern Reconstruction.

Two books which develop the issues and personalities of the 1868 campaign are C. H. Coleman's *The Election of* 1868 (1933) and Stewart Mitchell's *Horatio Seymour* (1938). W. B. Hesseltine's *Ulysses S. Grant: Politician* (1935) is a highly useful and balanced account of the Grant Presidency. Viewing Grant's leadership through the eyes of a leading Cabinet member is Allan Nevins's *Hamilton Fish: The Inner History of the Grant Administration* (1936). Matthew Josephson's *The Politicos** (1938) contains much information on the politics of the Grant years. Josephson attributes Republican motivation during Reconstruction less to humanitarianism than to a quest for permanent political and economic power. Henry Adams in *The Education of Henry Adams** (1918) includes a critical commentary on the Grant Presidency.

Dexter Perkins's *The Monroe Doctrine,* 1867–1907 (1937) remains the best reading for the Grant policies toward the Caribbean. An excellent specialized account is C. C. Tansill's *The United States and Santo Domingo,* 1798–1873 (1938). Goldwin Smith's *The Treaty of Washington,* 1871 (1941) is the best study available on the settlement with England. For the foreign-policy attitudes of a leading American editor see W. M. Armstrong's *E. L. Godkin and American Foreign Policy,* 1865–1900 (1957).

Earle D. Ross's *The Liberal Republican Movement* (1919) is old but sound. Martin B. Duberman's excellent biography *Charles Francis Adams** (1961) and G. G. Van Deusen's *Horace Greeley** (1953) analyze the campaign roles of two leading Liberal Republicans. For a perceptive discussion of one important question of 1872 see James M. McPherson's "Grant or Greeley? The Abolitionist Dilemma in the Election of 1872," *American Historical Review,* LXXI (October, 1965).

Paul H. Buck's *The Road to Reunion.* 1865–1900* (1937) analyzes superbly the forces that brought Reconstruction to an end. One factor, the Ku Klux Klan, is discussed in S. F. Horn's *The Invisible Empire* (1939). Several volumes that deal thoughtfully with the dilemma of the Negro following Reconstruction are C. Vann Woodward's *The Strange Career of Jim Crow** (1953) and *Origins of the New South,* 1877–1913* (1951); Roger Shugg's *Origins of Class Struggle in Louisiana** (1939); R. W. Logan's *The Negro in American Life and Thought** (1954); G. B. Tindall's *South Carolina Negroes,* 1877–1900* (1952); S. R. Spencer, Jr.'s *Booker T. Washington and the Negro's Place in American Life** (1955); as well as Washington's *Up from Slavery** (1901).

Paul H. Haworth's *The Hayes-Tilden Disputed Presidential Election of* 1876 (1906) is still rewarding. More recent interpretations of the election and the so-called Compromise of 1877 are Allan Nevins's *Abram S. Hewitt* (1935), the biography of a leading actor; Harry Bernard's *Rutherford B. Hayes and His America* (1954); and especially C. Vann Woodward's *Reunion and Reaction: The Compromise of* 1877 *and the End of Reconstruction** (2d ed., 1956).

*indicates availability in paperback.

20

Politics, Policies, and Personalities, 1877–1892

THE ELECTION of President Hayes established another link in the long chain of Republican political control during the post-Civil War period, a control which, except for Grover Cleveland's two nonconsecutive terms, extended to 1913. The Republicans not only dominated the Presidency; they also kept strict control of the United States Senate, where they held a majority in all but four years during the forty-four-year period after 1868. And during two of those four years, 1883–1885, the Senate was tied. In the House of Representatives, however, the two parties were about evenly divided, with the Republicans in control twenty-four of the forty-four years. The period between the Civil War and World War I can properly be called "the Republican era."

Yet, until after 1896, the Republicans were not as strong as they appeared. During the late nineteenth century, the popular vote split almost evenly, and in two presidential elections, in 1876 and 1888, the Republicans actually received a minority of the popular ballots, winning the Presidency only by carrying the states with large blocs of electoral votes. In 1880 the Republicans won with a plurality of about one-tenth of 1 percent of the popular vote. Except for a two-year period, the Republicans failed to control the Presidency, the Senate, and the House simultaneously between 1877 and 1897. Implementation of any party program was thus extremely difficult, and a legislative stalemate often resulted as Republicans and Democrats fought for control.

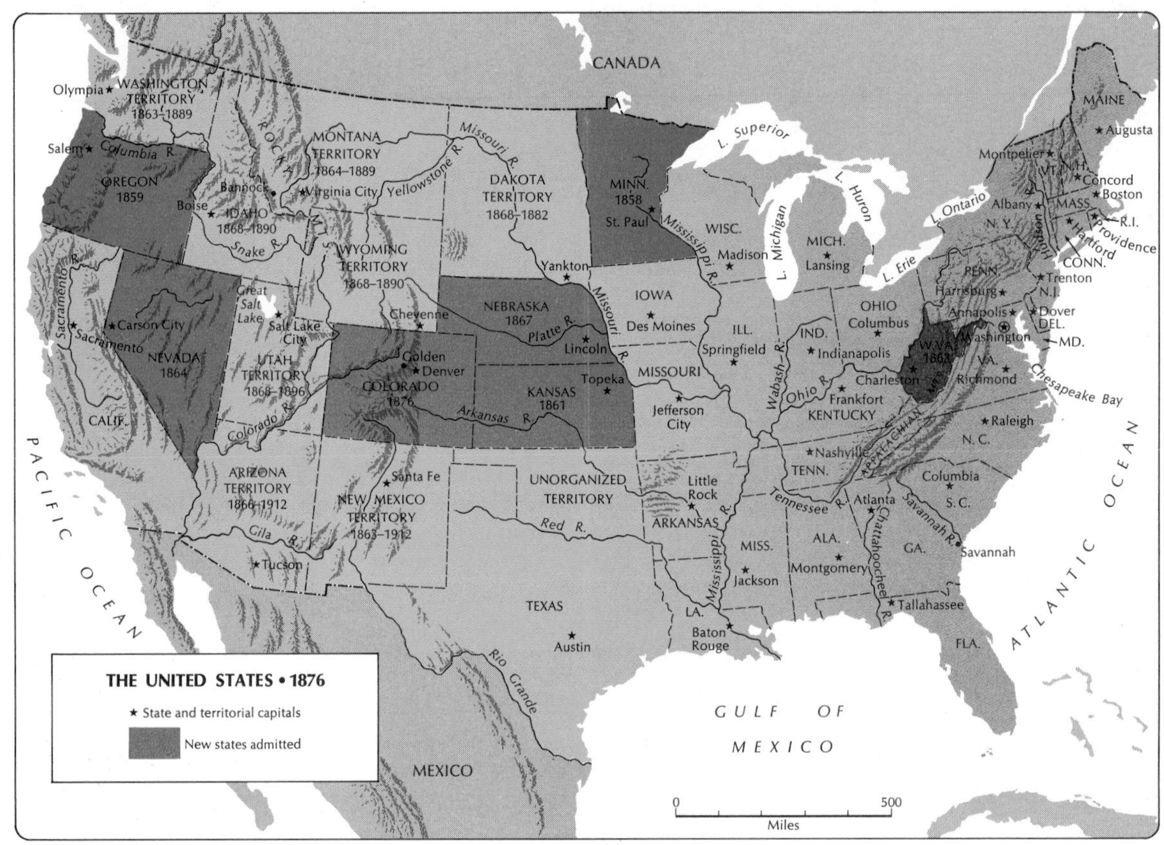

Party Politics

The last quarter of the nineteenth century has often been characterized as a dreary period politically, a time when mediocre party leaders failed to contend with the burgeoning problems facing a rapidly changing nation. Politicians seemed interested in spoils and office instead of service and principle. They appeared to ignore the great problems of industrialization, urbanization, proper disposition of the country's natural resources, labor-management relations, and other pressing questions. Lord Bryce, an Englishman writing of American life and society, wrote that "neither party has any principles, any distinctive tenets. Both have traditions. Both claim to have tendencies. Both have certainly war cries, organizations, interests enlisted in their support. But these interests are in the main the interests of getting or keeping the patronage of the government."

The majority of Republicans, as well as Democrats, were indeed most concerned with obtaining and holding office, and they spent liberally of time, effort, and money for this purpose. But the close division of political power before 1897 made it difficult for either party to enact measures in Congress which did not also have some support from members of the other major party. Strong enough to keep the Democrats from controlling the Presidency most of the time, the Republicans were not powerful enough to govern effectively by themselves. Consequently, in session after session, Congress gave more attention to politics and power than to dealing with national problems.

One of the most important political developments was the close alliance between politics and business. The Republicans generally were more successful than the Democrats in winning support from businessmen and industrialists. The Republicans supported a wide variety of programs favored by major business interests—a protective tariff for manufacturers, a liberal disposition of natural resources to railroads, and timber and mining companies, and the gold standard desired by bankers and money-lenders. Republicans also held a strong grip on the Middle Western farm vote; they won the votes of Northern veterans and some recently freed Negroes; and, once in office, they could count on the support of thousands of state and federal officeholders. They also obtained the votes of many workingmen.

Besides capitalizing on their own strength, the Republicans made every effort to identify the Democratic party with disloyalty in the South and graft and corruption in the North. The Democrats not only labored under the stigma of dishonor and disloyalty; they lacked attractive leaders. Moreover, the party was often divided on such questions as the tariff. Despite these and other handicaps, however, the Democrats appeared to have gained enough strength and unity by 1892 to control both the Presidency and Congress. Such unity, however, was superficial, and within a year a major split developed between Western Democrats and Easterners led by President Cleveland. Only in the solid South did the Democrats maintain firm and consistent control. After federal troops were finally withdrawn in 1877, all the Southern states maintained a strong Democratic majority.

Throughout the North, however, the Republican party successfully expanded and consolidated its political power at both the state and national levels by developing a program which had something for almost every major element within the party. In other words, it grew into a viable organization, gaining strength with the passing years. The state parties often allied themselves closely with business interests which provided campaign funds; and jobs distributed under the spoils system supplied energetic election workers. By organizing its sources of strength and taking advantage of Democratic divisions, the Republican party had assumed a truly dominant position by 1896, when William McKinley won the Presidency by a substantial margin.

The principal issues during the late nineteenth century were the tariff, currency and banking, civil service reform, immigration restriction, internal improvements, and government regulation of big business. The two parties differed radically over tariffs, but their other positions hardly varied at all. As Lord Bryce wrote, the two main parties "were like two bottles. Each bore a label denoting the kind of liquor it contained, but each was empty." The major battles took place among conflicting economic interests within the parties. Western Republicans, for example, demanded cheap money and inflation, while Eastern party leaders favored the gold standard. Party attitudes and actions on these questions, however, seem relatively unimportant when placed against the really vital issues that went unnoticed by self-seeking politicians.

If politicians were struggling but not quite coming to grips with the growing problems of a developing nation, the situation was by no means unique in American political history. Moreover, while these matters may seem inconsequential to twentieth-century Americans accustomed to heated debates over civil rights, federal aid to education, government spending, and foreign policy, people in the late nineteenth century considered questions such as the tariff and inflation desperately important. In campaign after campaign, they fought over these issues with an involvement and bitterness seldom seen since. If these political questions seemed unimportant to later generations, it is the times that have changed and not the capacity of people to understand better the questions that should concern them.

The Hayes Administration

Once in the White House, Rutherford B. Hayes quickly restored dignity and respectability to an office badly besmirched by the graft, corruption, and cronyism of the Grant administration. The son of an Ohio farmer, Hayes (1822–1893) attended Kenyon College and Harvard University, after which he was admitted to the Ohio bar in 1845. He joined the Republican party a decade later. Hayes performed capably if without distinction during the Civil War and was finally breveted a major general of volunteers. Elected to the House of Representatives in 1864, he served one term before returning to Ohio for two successive terms as Governor. His third gubernatorial victory in 1875 came at a time of marked Republican unpopularity, and his election earned him considerable national prestige. Honest and dignified, Hayes was neither brilliant nor magnetic; still, he was solidly capable.

Hayes assumed the Presidency under severe handicaps. Continued charges of fraud in the election of 1876 and the title "Old 8 to 7," a snide reference to the vote of the commission which made Hayes President, were sources of embarrassment. Moreover, the Republican party was sharply divided between the Stalwarts and moderates. The Stalwarts, represented by such powerful conservatives as Senator Roscoe E. Conkling of New York, opposed civil service reform and Hayes's policies toward the South. Along with other conservatives in the party, Conkling contemptuously referred to the President and his supporters as "Halfbreeds."

The first major decision confronting Hayes was the withdrawal of the remaining federal troops in the Southern states. Such an action would obviously result in complete restoration of white rule throughout the South. In April, 1877, federal garrisons withdrew from Columbia, South Carolina, and from New Orleans, Louisiana. The carpetbag Republican governments contesting for power in those states were disbanded, and the Democrats assumed control. Thus this phase of political reconstruction was at last closed.

Yet the problem of protecting the civil rights of Negroes remained unsolved. Provisions to assure federal protection to voters still existed in the Enforcement Acts of 1870 and 1872. These "Force Acts," designed to prevent intimidation of voters, directed federal marshals, deputy marshals, election supervisors, and the federal courts to protect the civil rights of Negroes. Southerners, however, wanted to eliminate all federal interference with elections, and Democrats in Congress sought to repeal or nullify the Enforcement Acts. They attached "riders" to appropriation bills denying pay to federal election supervisors and attempted in other ways to weaken national power to protect Negro voting. But President Hayes vetoed these measures. This conflict between Hayes and the Democratic Congress continued, with neither side gaining its full objectives. In 1879, the Supreme Court upheld the constitutionality of the federal election laws, but, in 1882, the outlawing of certain enforcement features rendered the laws impotent.

Once the South again fell under "Bourbon," or conservative, white rule, many Negroes lost their right to vote, especially if they tried to vote Republican. In the plantation-sharecrop areas, Negroes continued to exercise their franchise after the withdrawal of federal troops, but economic pressures usually enforced a vote for the conservative Bourbon Democratic candidates. Any attempt to vote Republican met with strong local opposition. Despite growing restrictions on Negro voting after 1877, however, the general Southern denial of the Negro franchise did not take place until the 1890s and the final repeal of the federal election statutes in 1894.

While attempting to quiet the Southern question, Hayes moved to bring at least modest reform to the civil service. The growing functions and responsibilities of the federal government were accompanied by an increasing number of administrative bureaus and agencies, which seemed to demand higher-quality and better-trained civil servants to handle the expanding public business. To meet this need, reformers such as Representative Thomas A. Jenckes of Rhode Island, George W. Curtis, and Carl Schurz began working for legislation which would provide competitive examinations for government employees. They hoped this would eliminate the evils of the spoils system and increase the efficiency of the civil service. On the other hand, politicians who benefited from the spoils system objected to reform, and by the early 1870s civil service legislation had become a major political question.

In 1871, Congress passed a law permitting the President to establish a Civil Service Advisory Board, which would prescribe rules and regulations for certain classes of government workers. The law was never effectively implemented, but Hayes believed in civil service reform and, in his first annual message, recommended that appointments be made on the basis of merit rather than political connections. The executive branch progressed in this direction, and Schurz even introduced competitive examinations in the Interior Department. Congress, however, failed to pass any general civil service legislation.

Meanwhile, following an investigation which revealed payroll padding, bribery, and smuggling, Hayes asked for the resignation of Chester A. Arthur, Collector of the Port in New York, and Alonzo B. Cornell, the Naval Officer there. Both Arthur and Cornell refused to resign. In July, 1878, when Congress was not in session, Hayes removed them. The Senate subsequently refused to approve his new appointees, but Hayes later made other, and acceptable, selections. He told E. A. Merritt, the new Collector, "Let no man be put out merely because he is a friend of Mr. Arthur, and no one put in merely because he is our friend. The good of the service should be the whole end in view." The removal of Arthur and Cornell not only reflected Hayes's effort to improve the civil service, it also settled the significant question of whether the President could make a major appointment in a state without prior approval of that state's senators.

The most important economic issue confronting Hayes was the money question. Like other Presidents in the late nineteenth century, he favored "sound money," which meant the gold standard. However, during the hard times following the Panic of 1873, the demand for inflation grew more and more audible, especially from farmers and debtors. Congress resisted this pressure and in 1875 passed the Resumption Act, which directed the Secretary of the Treasury to redeem all United States notes in coin, beginning January 1, 1879. By that time, Hayes had become President; and his Treasury Secretary, John Sherman, carried out this policy, which placed the country on a *de facto* gold standard. Angry at this action, the inflationists argued that the currency should by expanded by printing more greenbacks or by coining silver. In 1878, Congress passed the Bland-Allison Act over Hayes's veto. This measure directed that the Treasury purchase $2 to $4 million worth of silver monthly and coin it into silver dollars, a provision which did not satisfy the inflationists but merely contributed to growing differences within the Republican party.

At the same time, the country was experiencing a great deal of social and economic unrest, but Hayes appears not to have understood the underlying problems. In July, 1877, following wage reductions, the Baltimore and Ohio Railroad was struck at Martinsburg, West Virginia. The strike spread to Pittsburgh and other cities, where the strikers resorted to looting and burning which caused the loss of millions of dollars' worth of property. Hayes called out federal troops to assist in restoring order, and the strike subsequently failed. In California, Denis Kearney, a radical labor leader, demanded restrictions on Chinese immigration, attacked land monopoly, and advocated increased taxation of the wealthy. The labor and Greenback movements indicated a growing discontent with social and economic conditions, but Hayes thought only in terms of maintaining law and order and ignored the real issues at stake.

Garfield and Arthur

President Hayes gave the country a clean and somewhat more efficient government than Grant, but he provided no real leadership. Moreover, his emphasis upon civil service reform annoyed the party spoilsmen, who longed for the free-wheeling days of the Grant administration. Consequently, as the election of 1880 approached, Roscoe Conkling, John A. Logan of Illinois, and other Stalwarts sought to nominate Grant for a third term. Through thirty ballots Grant led, but the anti-Grant faction in the convention rallied behind James A. Garfield of Ohio, who finally won the nomination. To placate the Stalwarts, Republican leaders chose Chester A. Arthur as the vice presidential candidate. The Democrats nominated General Winfield Scott Hancock, a worthy veteran of both the Mexican and Civil Wars, and W. E. English of Indiana. The election of 1880 was an unexciting affair, the only major differences between the parties being the Democratic endorsement of a tariff for revenue only, while the Republicans championed protection. Both parties advocated sound money and civil service reform. Helped by returning prosperity after the long depression, Garfield squeaked by with an extremely narrow popular majority of only 7,368 votes.

A native of Ohio and a Disciples of Christ minister, Garfield had served as president of Hiram College and in the Union Army before going into politics. At the time of his election to the House of Representatives in 1863, he was a major general. Garfield's administration was short and tragic. Shot after only four months in office by Charles J. Guiteau, a disappointed office seeker, he died on September 19. This second presidential assassination in less than twenty years deeply shocked Americans who had believed that their political system had progressed beyond this kind of crime and fanaticism. Guiteau was convicted and executed for his crime within less than a year. During his brief Presidency, Garfield had occupied himself primarily with bothersome office claimants and civil service problems.

Inaugurated on September 20, 1881, President Arthur showed a reasonable understanding of the American political system when he declared: "Men may die but the fabrics of our free institutions remain unshaken." A lawyer by profession, the tall, heavily built, distinguished-appearing, new Chief Executive at least looked like a President. He had been active in the Republican party since its founding and had held a number of appointive positions before Grant named him Collector of the Port of New York in 1871. Despite his close association with the spoils system President Arthur took his duties seriously and provided a dignified and honorable administration.

The conditions surrounding Garfield's assassination, the pressure for federal appointments, and the scandals in various branches of the government service all emphasized the need for civil service reform. Reformers had little faith in Arthur, but, as it turned out, he solidly supported civil service legislation. Congress had been working on a civil service bill since 1881, under the leadership of Democratic Senator George Pendleton of Ohio. Public support and the influence of the National Civil Service Reform League, combined with Arthur's backing, finally brought about passage of the Pendleton Act on January 15, 1883. Both Republicans and Democrats supported the measure, which provided for a Civil Service Commission of three members to be appointed by the President. This Commission was to administer the law, which included competitive examinations to determine the fitness of government workers. The first order of classification placed only 13,924 positions under Civil Service, but the classified list was gradually extended by subsequent administrations.

Another lively political question in Arthur's administration was the tariff. Especially among Democrats, the demand grew louder for lower rates. Although industrialists urgently demanded high protective duties, another aspect of the question emerged in the early 1880s. Government revenues, derived largely from the tariff, far exceeded expenditures, reaching as much as $145 million by 1882 and thus drawing money out of circulation and creating a scarcity of circulating medium in the economy. Critics of the tariff argued that lower rates would not only reduce prices and the cost of living but would also lower the surpluses in the federal Treasury. A commission appointed by Congress in 1882 to study this problem recommended lowering tariff duties about 20 percent, but the definitely protectionist Tariff Act of 1883, the so-called Mongrel Tariff, left the overall duties about where they had been.

Continued surpluses in the Treasury tempted the government to more liberal expenditures. In 1882, over Arthur's veto, Congress passed an $18,743,000 rivers and harbors bill to finance public works in about five hundred different localities where, not coincidentally, federal expenditures for public improvements sometimes provided the bases for very effective local political organizations—a clear case of "pork barrel." Congress also increased veterans' pensions. By 1883, pension expenditures had risen to $66 million, compared with only $27 million in 1878. This crude type of social security went to thousands of veterans, and the Grand Army of the Republic (organization of the Union veterans) became a powerful backer of the Republican party.

The restriction of Chinese immigration also became a lively political issue during Arthur's Presidency. After 1850, thousands of Chinese had come to the United States to work in California and other Western states on the railroads, around the mining camps, and in the growing cities. Job competition and race prejudice both encouraged the rising sentiment to curb Chinese immigration. On May 6, 1882, the Chinese Exclusion Act became law. It prohibited the immigration of Chinese peasants, including skilled and unskilled workers, for a period of ten years, a restriction later extended. Congress also excluded "undesirable" immigrants such as lunatics and convicts. The law of 1882 thus established a policy of selective immigration restriction and began the gradual shift away from virtually free and unlimited movement to the United States.

The Democratic Cleveland

Despite Arthur's altogether respectable administration, little support existed for his renomination in 1884. The Republicans instead turned to James G. Blaine, perhaps the most colorful and popular Republican of his generation. Born in 1830, Blaine went to Congress in 1862, and until his death in 1893, politics was his major business. He was Speaker of the House from 1869 to 1875, then Senator from Maine. In 1881, he served briefly as Garfield's Secretary of State. A contender for the Presidency during several conventions, in 1884 this popular idol could no longer be denied the nomination, although some independents and liberals—nicknamed "Mugwumps"—complained and protested. A Stalwart, John A. Logan, became Blaine's running mate. Wallowing in self-praise and castigating the Democrats, the Republican platform called for a protective tariff, extension of civil service reform, establishment of a national bureau of labor, pensions for Union veterans, and reservation "as far as possible" of public lands for actual settlers.

The Democrats, in Chicago, united behind the nomination of Governor Grover Cleveland of New York. Born in New Jersey in 1837, Cleveland went to Buffalo as a young man, where he read law and entered practice. He served as assistant district attorney, and was elected sheriff in 1869. Chosen mayor of Buffalo in 1881, Cleveland became Governor of New York in 1882. Despite some opposition from leaders of Tammany Hall, Cleveland became the party standard-bearer on an early ballot. The ticket gained good sectional balance with the selection of Thomas Hendricks of Indiana for Vice President. The Democratic platform accused the Republicans of failure, fraud, jobbery, and other shortcomings, but,

Anti-Chinese Prejudice

The rise of anti-Chinese prejudice in the last half of the nineteenth century exemplifies the way lack of common understanding breeds fear, hatred, and violence and how a minority group may become a social scapegoat.

Sizeable numbers of Chinese immigrated to America during the early 1850s in response to the discovery of gold in California. Almost immediately Caucasian miners persecuted them, burning their tents and driving them away from many mining districts. Between 1850 and 1870 a Foreign Miner's License Tax, which was levied almost exclusively against the Chinese, raised more than $5 million, but the Chinese were excluded from the rich mining areas.

Many Chinese in California became fishermen and day-laborers in vineyards, lumbercamps, and factories and on the construction crews building the transcontinental railroad. By 1866 the Central Pacific Railroad had hired 6,000 Chinese, many of whom the railroad itself had imported from China.

But when depression struck in the early 1870s, the smouldering resentment against the Chinese flared into violence. Labor leader Dennis Kearney, head of the Workingman's Party, led a "Chinese Must Go" campaign, and riots and assaults against people and property were widespread. Legislation was passed to tax, harrass, and humiliate the Chinese, and in 1882 Congress passed an act prohibiting the entry of Chinese laborers for ten years, legislation which became even harsher in the years to follow.

During the 1870s a San Francisco firm sold this cartoon showing a symbolic Irishman and a Chinese devouring Uncle Sam.

Attitudes toward the Chinese in post-Civil War publications ranged from fascination to contempt, but the latter predominated. At the time of the Gold Rush, immigration to America from China cost only $15 – three to five times less than the cost from Europe, although later the fare rose to $50. The numbers of Chinese entering the United States increased continuously until the passage of the Exclusion Act. Between 1861 and 1870 the total was 64,301, and in the following decade it reached 123,201.

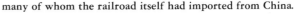

Much was made of the fact that the Chinese were not Christians, and even Bret Harte stressed it in the lyrics he wrote for the popular song, "The Heathen Chinee," a song which helped perpetuate a pejorative stereotype of the Chinese (following page). Another example of the extreme prejudice against the Chinese appears in the advertising of George Dee, manufacturer of the "Magic Washer," who used the Kearney slogan intact. It was a measure of the state of public opinion that Dee felt free to display this prejudice so openly. Thomas Nast's cartoon (following page, right, below) reflects the workingman's fear of the competition from cheap Chinese labor in the shoe industry. The Chinese manufactured shoes in more than seventy California factories, and the first time New England saw Chinese labor came when 100 Chinese strike breakers were imported by a North Adams, Mass., shoe manufacturer in the 1870s.

Library of Congress

Near right: Arnold Genthe, courtesy California Palace of the Legion of Honor
All others: Library of Congress

THE NEW
ISSUE
THE CHINESE-AMER
QUESTION

Under the leadership of Dennis Kearney (inset), the Workingman's Party helped to pass California legislation making a corporation liable to a fine of $100 to $1,000 if it hired a Chinese. The law was declared unconstitutional, but anti-Chinese riots like this one at Rock Springs, Wyoming, added to the pressure on Congress which resulted in the Exclusion Act of 1882. Commenting on exclusion, Calvin Lee wrote, "One wonders whether history would have been different if more Chinese had accepted Christianity, . . ."

like its Republican counterpart, it remained vague on major economic and political issues. The Democrats promised to "revise the tariff in a spirit of fairness to all interests," to work for "honest money," "honest civil service reform," to oppose monopoly, and to achieve equality for all citizens.

But issues made little difference in this exciting campaign of 1884. Fought mainly on a personal basis, it became undoubtedly one of the dirtiest in American history. The Democrats—joined by the Mugwumps, who had bolted the Republican party—accused Blaine of public dishonesty and tied him to the so-called Mulligan Letters. In 1869, when Blaine was Speaker of the House, he had helped to obtain a land grant for the Little Rock and Fort Smith Railroad and subsequently, along with Warren Fisher of Boston, had sold the road's nearly worthless bonds. Although Blaine denied that he had made any money out of these dealings, a series of letters kept by Fisher's bookkeeper, James Mulligan, cast doubts on Blaine's integrity. On one note, Blaine had written, "Burn this letter." Charged with using his official position for personal benefit, Blaine found his position somewhat embarrassing. As George W. Curtis, the editor of *Harper's* magazine, said, the dominant issue in the campaign was not political but moral.

Smarting under attacks of this nature, the Republicans looked for scandal in high Democratic ranks. They were not compelled to search far. In July, 1884, the *Buffalo Evening Telegraph* reported on some of bachelor Cleveland's earlier escapades with an attractive Buffalo widow, Mrs. Maria Halpin. When a child was born to Mrs. Halpin in 1874, she had named Cleveland as the father. Although no absolute proof of Cleveland's paternity existed, he had not denied the possibility and had actually made some financial arrangements for the child. The Republicans declared Cleveland a man of lax morals and unfit for the Presidency. However, while many people were initially disturbed by what they believed was a moral lapse, Cleveland's frankness and honesty in admitting the possible truth of the charge aroused widespread admiration.

In the final days of the campaign, Blaine and some of his supporters blundered badly. In New York, where the contest was very close, Blaine probably lost some Catholic votes after one of his backers, the Reverend Samuel D. Burchard, referred to the Democrats as the party of "rum, Romanism, and rebellion." Moreover, Blaine's attendance at a dinner sponsored by a number of New York millionaires, including John Astor and Jay Gould, as well as their private discussions regarding campaign funds, provided Democratic writers with exciting copy. Critics pictured "Belshazzar Blaine" living in luxury while working people starved. Tactical errors of this sort may have cost him the election.

The outcome was exceedingly close. Cleveland, who received only 23,000 more votes than Blaine, won New York's 36 electoral votes by a plurality of just 1,167, giving him a total of 219 votes in the electoral college compared to 182 for Blaine. The 25,000 ballots cast for Prohibitionist candidate John P. St. John may have hurt the New York Republicans sufficiently to give Cleveland the victory there. But on a national scale, Cleveland undeniably won on the strength of independent, Mugwump support, assisted by the general hard times and business stagnation which Democrats blamed on the Republicans. People voted for Cleveland less because of his stand on major issues than because they believed he would give the country good, honest govern-

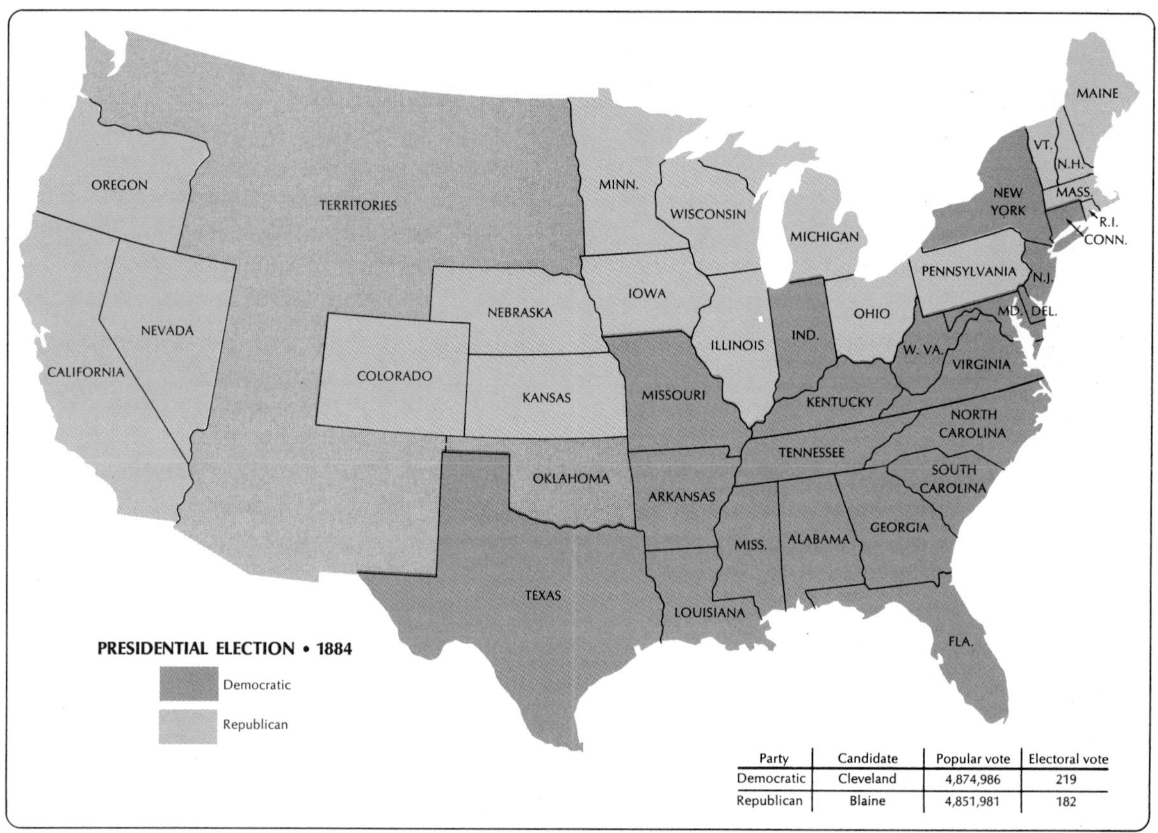

Party	Candidate	Popular vote	Electoral vote
Democratic	Cleveland	4,874,986	219
Republican	Blaine	4,851,981	182

ment. Despite the valiant image which his supporters attempted to fashion, Blaine remained for many less than trustworthy.

No political figure in American history had risen so meteorically to the Presidency as Grover Cleveland. He first attracted attention as mayor of Buffalo by successfully fighting graft and corruption in city government and working for improved sanitation and health measures. Opposition to Tammany Hall, honest and efficient administration, and general aversion to social and economic reform legislation characterized his governorship. Cleveland had conservative views regarding the role of government in social and economic affairs. In general, he held a negative concept of government, a narrow view of presidential powers. He agreed with those conservative Bourbon Democratic spokesmen of business and industry whose chief interests lay in honest and economical government. He had little knowledge of, or interest in, the needs of agriculture and labor. Hard-working, honest, independent, and above all, courageous—one supporter said he was loved "for the enemies he has made"—he lacked tact, imagination, and a personality which appealed to the masses. And he was stubborn. A short, 250-pound man with a droopy mustache, Cleveland appeared every bit as solid and uncompromising as he actually was.

With a capable and conservative Cabinet—including two Southerners, L. Q. C. Lamar of

Mississippi, Secretary of the Interior, and Augustus H. Garland of Arkansas, Attorney General—the new President faced the same problems. Of all the major legislative issues, pensions, land policies, the tariff, and money problems were still vital, lively questions. Moreover, at least two other matters demanded national attention: Indian policy and the federal regulation and control of monopolies.

Further civil service reform loomed as a major question facing the new Democratic administration. The Mugwumps, who had supported Cleveland on this issue, expected him to reduce the role of party politics in making federal appointments, and Cleveland, who had not supported civil service reform merely out of political expediency, sincerely hoped to improve current practices. He firmly believed that only qualified persons should be named to public office and that appointments should not be made, as he put it, "solely as a reward for partisan service." He told his inaugural audience that "civil service reform should be in good faith enforced." But Cleveland found that he headed a party hungry for spoils. Most Democrats agreed with the senator who viewed reform only as turning Republicans out of office and "putting honest Democrats in their places." Commenting on the pressures and conflicts over appointments, Cleveland wrote a friend: "All this time, like a nightmare, this dreadful, damnable office-seeking hangs over me." Despite his belief in the principle of administrative efficiency, most government jobs had been filled with loyal Democrats by the end of Cleveland's administration. Cleveland did advance the cause of civil service reform by extending civil service regulations to cover several thousand additional federal workers, but he was never able to resist completely the spoilsmen within his party.

Pensions for Civil War veterans also proved a nettlesome political issue. The Arrears of Pensions Act of 1879 had opened up the way for widespread graft as veterans and claims agents pressed their dishonest demands. Many of the pensioners supposed to be invalids were in perfect health. The Pension Bureau attempted to evaluate the claims fairly and justly and to weed out fraudulent claims, but a veteran turned down by the Bureau might then get his congressman or senator to introduce a special bill granting him a pension. In the middle 1880s, Congress passed hundreds of these bills, and by 1885, some 325,000 Civil War veterans were on the pension rolls. Charles Francis Adams, president of the Union Pacific Railroad and educational reformer, said: "We have seen every dead-beat, and malingerer, every bummer, bounty-jumper, and suspected deserter . . . rush to the front as the greedy claimant of public bounty."

Disgusted with what he considered a raid on the public treasury and skeptical of anything which bordered on welfare legislation, Cleveland began vetoing a substantial number of the private pension bills where he found obvious fraud. Although many Americans supported Cleveland in this stand, congressmen, individual veterans, and their official organization, the Grand Army of the Republic, loudly criticized the President's penny-pinching attitude. Moreover, Cleveland's veto of a general pension bill aroused widespread criticism.

The administration and control of Western lands also caused President Cleveland deep concern. For a time after the Civil War, the Western lands were sold and given away as though they were limitless. False entries, perjured witnesses, and dishonest surveys had, according to Land Commissioner William A. J. Sparks, enabled land monopolies "to rob the government of its lands" all over the West. This situation revolted Cleveland's sense of honesty and fair play, but an attempt at government control would certainly arouse the animosity of Westerners and their Eastern financial backers, who demanded rapid exploitation of the area's resources. Whatever Cleveland's weaknesses, however, he did not lack courage. He ordered Secretary of the Interior L. Q. C. Lamar and Commissioner Sparks to carry out a vigorous program to protect the public domain, and as a result officials required ranchers to tear down their fences enclosing government lands; the government instituted suits to recover land illegally held by railroads; and it nullified fraudulent leases. Altogether some eighty-one million acres of land were restored to federal control. Cleveland also took a more sympathetic attitude toward the rights of Indians. He tried to stop the encroachments of white settlers on Indian lands and supported the Dawes Act of 1887, which granted land to Indians on an individual basis or, as it was known, in severalty. Although this measure did not succeed in practice it seemed at the time quite progressive.

Enlargement of the Navy, begun by Arthur, continued under the Cleveland administration. Secretary Whitney reorganized the Department and let contracts for a number of small naval vessels, five cruisers, and the battleships *Texas* and *Maine*—which became famous at the time of the Spanish-American War. Other bipartisan action of the period included passage of the Interstate Commerce Act in 1887 (see Chapter 21), which was designed to curb railroad abuses.

The biggest political and economic issue faced by President Cleveland, however, was the tariff. Cleveland had once said that he really did not understand the tariff; but after much study, he gradually became convinced that tariff rates were too high and contained serious inequities. He objected to the current tariff law on two grounds. In the first place, the rates brought in too much revenue. Between 1885 and 1888, the Treasury surplus advanced from about $63 million to $132 million annually, and although the government paid off its indebtedness, excess funds remained. This contracted the currency and, as Cleveland noted, much of the nation's money was "hoarded in the Treasury" when it should have been in the hands of the people. The President declared that federal surpluses might also encourage unnecessary government expenditures and lead to "wasteful public extravagance, with all the corrupting national demoralization which follows in its train." Here again was evidence of Cleveland's opposition to what might be considered federal welfare programs. In the second place, Cleveland considered the duties to be an unjust tax upon consumers which added to the price of daily necessities, and he argued that it burdened the farmer while providing a subsidy to the manufacturer. Cleveland was no free-trader, but he objected to what he saw as unnecessarily high rates.

Cleveland became so concerned with this issue that, against the counsel of Democratic advisers, his entire annual message to Congress on December 6, 1887, was devoted to the tariff. Referring to it as a "vicious, inequitable, and illogical source of unnecessary taxation," the President called for the law to be revised at once. Early in 1888, Representative Roger Q. Mills of Texas introduced a tariff reform bill calling for lower rates on several articles and placing many items on the free list. The Mills bill passed the House on July 21, but the Republican Senate, under the leadership of protectionists such as William B. Allison and

Nelson W. Aldrich, substituted a high-tariff measure, which died in committee. Cleveland had failed to solve the economic problem, but he had stirred up a smoking political cauldron.

The Election of 1888

Despite the political uproar over the tariff, the Democrats renominated Cleveland by acclamation in 1888. The party platform condemned the Republicans for blocking tariff reform and praised Cleveland for a faithful and able administration. The Republicans, meeting at Chicago, chose Senator Benjamin Harrison of Indiana as the party standard-bearer. Levi P. Morton of New York was selected for Vice President. The main issue in the campaign was unmistakable when the Republicans announced their uncompromising support of "the American protective system" and denounced the Mills bill by name.

Besides the major issue of the tariff, the large expenditure of money also distinguished the campaign of 1888. Business and industrial interests had never before played such an open and aggressive political role in a presidential campaign. Those who benefited from protection raised large campaign funds and used every tactic to defeat Cleveland. Tariff advocates called Cleveland a "standing menace," and they pressed industrialists and businessmen for campaign contributions in an almost brutal fashion. One eager party worker wrote, "I would put the manufacturers of Pennsylvania under the fire and fry the fat out of them." James M. Swank, head of the American Iron and Steel Association, directed an unprecedented campaign on the tariff issue throughout the North, which involved an especially intense effort to win farm votes in states like Iowa and Minnesota. When all else failed, Republican advisers sought to buy votes. "Divide the floaters into blocks of five and put a trusted man with the necessary funds in charge . . . and make him responsible that none get away," wrote the Republican treasurer. Not above using money in this fashion, the Democrats simply did not have the sources of support which the Republicans could tap.

The outcome of the election was very close. Though Cleveland actually won a popular majority of more than 100,000 votes, he lost some key states, including New York and Indiana; his electoral vote was 168 compared with 233 for Harrison. The Republicans showed increased strength in all parts of the country except the South, a situation which inspired such triumphant chants as:

Down in the cornfield,
Hear the mournful sound.
All the Democrats are weeping,
Grover's in the cold, cold ground.

Shortly after the election, Cleveland wrote to a friend that "it is better to be defeated battling for an honest principle than to win by a cowardly subterfuge." In this mood, he willingly left the White House and moved to New York to practice law. His administration had been largely negative; but he had effectively defied special interests, and he had strongly supported honest and efficient practices in government. He had been content to accept the support and the policies of conservative Eastern Democrats, who controlled the party machinery and whose primary interests lay in low taxes and opposition to any government interference in the economy.

Cleveland forcefully expressed his conservatism when, vetoing an appropriation of $10,000 to provide seed for drought-stricken Texas farmers in 1887, he wrote: "I do not believe that the power and duty of the general government ought to be extended to the relief of individual suffering which is in no manner properly related to the public service or benefit. . . . The lesson should be constantly enforced that though the people support the government, the government should not support the people." As one of his biographers has said, Cleveland's ideas of liberalism and reform were "expressed in honesty, economy, and efficient governmental service." Judged on this basis rather than in terms of twentieth-century reform, which called for greatly expanded governmental powers, Cleveland was probably the strongest President in the period between Lincoln and Theodore Roosevelt.

Harrison and the Republicans

The Republicans returned to power under a mediocre leader. Benjamin Harrison (1833–1901), a prominent lawyer from Indianapolis, was the grandson of General William Henry Harrison. He had served with distinction in the Civil War, moved up in Indiana Republican politics, and in 1881, was elected to the United States Senate for one term. Personally cold and unresponsive to all but his family and very closest friends, Harrison was nonetheless sincere, earnest, and worthy. But he cast a pale shadow compared with Republican giants like Blaine, Aldrich, Sherman, or Thomas B. Reed. Moreover, he tended to be overtrusting and naïve.

For the first time since 1875, the same party controlled both houses of Congress and the Presidency and, with no occasion to shift party responsibility, the Republicans were expected to produce results by those to whom they had made lavish promises during the campaign. The Fifty-first Congress met in December, 1889, under the leadership of "Czar" Thomas B. Reed of Maine, the powerful Speaker of the House. By means of his power to give or withhold recognition of members of the House, to appoint the Rules Committee, and to refuse recognition of what he considered dilatory motions, Reed ran the House with an iron hand. He also began to count every member present in the chamber for the purpose of determining a quorum, thus preventing the large Democratic minority from blocking business by refusing to answer roll call when they were physically present. Under the leadership of Reed in the House and such powerful figures as Allison and Sherman in the Senate, the Republicans passed more important legislation than any Congress since the Civil War.

Many Republicans considered their first and most important business to be that of removing Democrats from federal office, and they did so utterly contemptuous of the civil service reforms they had promised. Thirty-two thousand of the fifty-five thousand fourth-class postmasters, for example, were replaced within eighteen months. Reformers complained, to no effect, that this action was a betrayal of the civil service principle. Harrison made some feeble attempts to resist political pressures, but he could give no real support to civil service reform. He did appoint young Theodore Roosevelt to the Civil Service Commission, but Roosevelt found himself helpless to change the situation, especially when the President refused to resist party demands. Near the end of his term Harrison placed more positions under Civil Service rules by extending the classified lists, but only after Republicans had occupied those positions.

During the campaign, the Republicans had promised liberal pensions to Civil War veterans. Declaring "God Help the Surplus," Corporal James Tanner, Commissioner of Pensions and former GAR lobbyist, insisted on the party's fulfilling its election pledges. Tanner liberalized some pension payments by administrative action, and in 1890, Congress passed the Disability Pension Act, which added many old soldiers to the pension lists. Much like the law vetoed by Cleveland in 1887, the new act gave pensions of $6 to $12 monthly to all Civil War veterans who had any physical or mental disability which required them to earn a living by manual labor, whether or not their disability was caused by military service. Payments for the widows of veterans were also liberalized. As a result of this legislation, expenditures for pensions increased from $88,842,000 in 1890 to $139,812,000 in 1895. In the long run, the total cost of pensions exceeded the expense of the Civil War itself. The Republicans had made progress in reducing the Treasury surplus, but they had accomplished this through making greater expenditures rather than by lowering tariffs or reducing taxes.

Republican leaders interpreted their victory of 1888 as a popular mandate to revise the tariff upward. In his annual message to Congress on December 3, 1889, President Harrison called for a revision of both the schedules and the administrative features of the tariff law. Representative William McKinley of Ohio, chairman of the Ways and Means Committee, introduced a measure known as "an Act to Reduce the Revenue," which raised rates on manufactured goods to the highest level in the nation's history. Average duties were boosted to nearly 40 percent of the value of the goods, and in some cases the rates were so high as to practically eliminate imports. The law repealed the duty on raw sugar, which benefited American sugar refiners more than anyone else, but then paid a subsidy of 2 cents a pound to protect the interests of domestic producers of raw sugar. Moreover, for the first time in American history, the McKinley bill included a full schedule of protective duties on farm products. The new measure, which became law in October shortly before the elections of 1890, reflected vividly the political power of those who benefited from the tariff and a markedly expanded protective system.

Meanwhile, Congress wrestled with silver legislation, a matter which continued to be of vital concern to the West and South. The unsatisfactory Bland-Allison Act of 1878, which provided for some silver coinage, had pleased no one. One thing, however, was certain: The law had not measurably inflated the currency. As hard times enveloped the West and South during the late 1880s (see Chapter 24 for a full discussion of farmers and the inflation issue), an even louder cry arose from farmers demanding that inflation be brought about by the free and unlimited coinage of silver; and when the McKinley tariff could not be passed without support from some of the inflationists, a political arrangement was made between the tariff and free-silver forces. In return for Western support of the McKinley tariff, the protectionists voted for a silver coinage bill. Here was an example of regional political bargaining between the Eastern industrial interests and the Western agriculturalists. The Sherman Silver Purchase Act, passed on July 14, 1890, provided for the government purchase of

4.5 million ounces of silver per month, with payment in Treasury notes which would be redeemable in coin, either silver or gold.

Congress also dealt with the important question of antitrust legislation in 1890. With bipartisan congressional support, the Sherman Antitrust Act became law on July 2 (see Chapter 21 for a full discussion of government regulation of business). Despite its general ineffectiveness, the Sherman Act nonetheless marked the beginning of an attempt by the federal government to curb monopoly.

Although the Harrison administration showed little concern as a whole over the worsening economic conditions and the rising discontent among Western farmers, some of its policies were popular in the West. North and South Dakota, Montana, and Washington became states in 1889; Idaho and Wyoming followed in 1890. The opening of the Oklahoma Territory in 1889 saw thousands of people rush for the coveted land; early in 1890, some eleven million acres were thrown open for settlement in the Sioux reservation of South Dakota. Defying those Westerners who favored the rapid exploitation of timber resources, Congress also passed the Forest Reserve Act of 1891, which authorized the President to withdraw timberlands for public entry.

Passage of pension, silver, tariff, and antitrust legislation marked the Fifty-first Congress as one of the most active on record. Moreover, it spent more money than any previous peacetime Congress. Outlays for public improvements, naval construction, pensions, and other functions of government increased federal spending under Harrison by about one hundred million dollars annually. Conservative critics labeled it the "billion-dollar Congress," to which Speaker Reed reputedly answered, "Isn't this a billion-dollar country?" With expenditures rising and revenues falling, due largely to changes in the tariff, the Treasury surplus declined from $85 million in 1890 to only $9.9 million in 1892. This Republican program may have been popular with party leaders, but in 1890, the people expressed their displeasure by soundly defeating Republican candidates in the midterm elections. Only 88 Republicans returned to the House of Representatives against 235 Democrats. The Senate remained Republican by 8 votes, but responsible party government ground to a halt. The tariff, more than any other issue, had brought about a major Republican defeat.

Freedmen and Civil Rights

One of the most emotional and controversial issues in the Fifty-first Congress was the attempt to pass a bill which would increase federal power over elections as a means of guaranteeing voting rights to Southern Negroes. Although relations between whites and blacks had not been intolerable in the 1880s throughout much of the South, blacks still suffered from social, economic, and political discrimination. For example, there were thirty-nine blacks in the South Carolina Legislature in 1877–1878, compared with only six in 1890–1891. The Supreme Court's decision in 1883 declaring the Civil Rights Act of 1875 unconstitutional further weakened the position of Negroes in their efforts to achieve even minimum civil rights.

In his annual message to Congress in December, 1889, President Harrison spoke out on behalf of the principle of Negro civil rights, but he failed to recommend any specific measures to reach this goal. Then in June, 1890, Representative Henry Cabot Lodge of Massachusetts introduced his Federal Elections bill. This would give national officers supervisory power over federal elections in the South under specified conditions, to protect the voting rights of Negroes. Southerners violently attacked this so-called Force Bill, charging that it would destroy states' rights and individual liberty. One Tennesseean called it "centralization run mad." Nevertheless, on July 2, the House passed the Lodge bill by a vote of 155 to 149 and was greeted by "loud applause on the Republican side."

Despite some enthusiastic Republican support, however, including that of North Carolina Negro Congressman Henry P. Cheatham, the Senate laid the measure aside to take up the tariff question. Congress again considered the matter of election laws at the next session, but neither President Harrison nor the Republican Congress pushed the measure with any determination. It was dropped from consideration early in 1891, as a result of bitter Southern opposition and the unwillingness of numerous Northern and Western Republicans to support civil rights for Southern black citizens.

The possibility of federal intervention in Southern elections angered and frightened Southerners, who did not believe that the Negro should have any effective voice in politics. Even the feeble efforts in the Fifty-first Congress to protect the rights of Negroes provoked Southerners into taking additional steps to disfranchise Negroes. In 1890, shortly after Congress considered the Lodge bill, Mississippi amended its constitution to assure that the vast majority of Negroes could not vote. Other states quickly followed Mississippi's example and enacted poll taxes, required black voters to interpret sections of the Constitution, and took other effective means to deny suffrage to Negroes. Some Southern states added Grandfather clauses to their constitutions which limited black suffrage to those whose ancestors had the right to vote in 1867. Finally what brought disfranchisement was the fear that the fusionist movement between Southern white Populists and blacks would give the latter the balance of power in Southern politics. Threatened with change, the Southern states moved quickly and effectively to resist it. Their final imposition was the white primary. Senator Ben Tillman of South Carolina said later: "We have done our level best [to disfranchise Negroes]. . . . We have scratched our heads to find out how we could eliminate the last one of them. We stuffed ballot boxes, we shot them. We are not ashamed of it." So effective was the disfranchisement that the number of registered black voters in Louisiana dropped from 130,334 in 1896 to 1,342 in 1904.

By 1901 the last Negro of the post-Reconstruction period had been removed from Congress. This situation revealed the South's determination to deny Negroes any significant participation in the region's political life. George H. White, a black representative from North Carolina, did not even run again in 1900 because he knew his cause was hopeless. When the Judiciary Committee quietly buried White's antilynching bill in January, 1900, this Negro Congressman spoke prophetically to his colleagues. "This . . . is perhaps the Negroes' temporary farewell to the American Congress," he said, "but let me say, . . . he will rise up some day and come again. These parting words are in behalf of an outraged, heart-broken, bruised and bleeding, but God-fearing people, faithful, industrious, loyal, rising people—full of potential force."

Conclusion

Both parties built viable, effective political organizations in the post-Civil War years, but the Republicans dominated the national scene most of the time. Even without distinguished leadership, the Republicans skillfully welded together support from business and industry, veterans, government workers, farmers, and even workingmen. Much of the Republican power rested on strong local and state organizations which could deliver the vote in crucial elections. Yet Republican control was tenuous. The Democratic victory of 1892 indicated how rapidly and dramatically party fortunes could change. Neither party developed a program which satisfied the needs and desires of all of its members, who often had varying regional, economic, and other conflicting interests.

By the early 1890s, the winds of political discontent were blowing within both major parties. Despite the excitement aroused by pensions, civil service, and the tariff, many Americans had come to view these as sham issues irrelevant to the nation's real problems. Leadership and policies which allied government with business and the industrial interests, at the expense of workers and farmers, appeared less and less satisfactory. While the growing concentration of industrial and financial power threatened both political and economic democracy, politicians could not or would not act to preserve egalitarian ideals. All sorts of problems unattended to—conservation of the nation's natural resources, control of excessive wealth and economic power, conditions of employment among the nation's workers, and the plight of farmers in the West and South—would eventually culminate in the political uprising of the 1890s.

SUGGESTED READINGS

There are some especially good chapters on late-nineteenth-century political history in H. Wayne Morgan (ed.), *The Gilded Age: A Reappraisal** (1963), which modify the interesting but unbalanced *The Politicos, 1865–1896** (1938) by Matthew Josephson. An important aspect of Republican policy in the South has been discussed by Vincent P. DeSantis in *Republicans Face the Southern Question: The New Departure Years, 1877–1897* (1959) and by Stanley B. Hirshson in *Farewell to the Bloody Shirt: Northern Republicans and the Southern Negro, 1877–1893* (1962). The best account of the Republican party in those years is George H. Mayer's *The Republican Party, 1854–1964** (1964), although W. E. Binkley's *American Political Parties* (1958) contains valuable chapters covering this period. For administrative history, consult Leonard D. White's *The Republican Era, 1869–1901** (1958). Two books by Russell B. Nye have contributed greatly to understanding politics in the Midwest. They are *Midwestern Progressive Politics* (1951) and *Bourbon Democracy of the Middle West, 1865–1896* (1953).

Some of the best insights into late-nineteenth-century politics can be obtained from the biographies of political leaders. Among the best are Harry Barnard's *Rutherford B. Hayes and His America* (1954); Allan Nevins's *Grover Cleveland* (1932); H. S. Merrill's *Bourbon Leader: Grover Cleveland and the Democratic Party** (1957); R. G. Caldwell's *James A. Garfield* (1931); G. F. Howe's *Chester A. Arthur* (1935); H. J. Sievers's *Benjamin Harrison* (2 vols., 1952–1959); Blair Bolles's *Tyrant from Illinois: Uncle Joe Cannon's Experiment with Personal Power* (1951); John R. Lambert's *Arthur Pue Gorman* (1953); and Leland L. Sage's *William Boyd Allison: A Study in Practical Politics* (1956).

On the New South, including its politics, it is essential to consult C. Vann Woodward's *Origins of the New South, 1877–1913** (1951). See also Albert D. Kirwan's *Revolt of the Rednecks: Mississippi Politics, 1876–1925** (1951) and the excellent *Pitchfork Ben Tillman, South Carolinian** (1944) by Francis B. Simkins. Some of the best studies on the position of the Negro include Rayford W. Logan's *The Negro in American Life and Thought: The Nadir, 1877–1901* (1954); George B. Tindall's *South Carolina Negroes, 1877–1900** (1952); C. Vann Woodward's *The Strange Career of Jim Crow** (2d ed., 1957); and Daniel D. Smith's *The Negro in Congress, 1870–1901* (1945). Growing criticism of the old parties can be traced in Chester McArthur Destler's *American Radicalism, 1865–1901** (1946).

The presidential elections have been covered in Eugene H. Roseboom's *History of Presidential Elections* (rev. ed., 1964); Herbert J. Clancy's *The Presidential Election of 1880* (1958) and George H. Knoles's *The Presidential Campaign and Election of 1892* (1942) provide accounts of two elections.

On the main political issues of the period, see Ari Hoogenboom's *Outlawing the Spoils: A History of the Civil Service Reform Movement, 1865–1883** (1961); A. B. Sageser's *The First Two Decades of the Pendleton Act* (1935); Edward Stanwood's *American Tariff Controversies in the Nineteenth Century* (2 vols., 1903); and Mary Dearing's *Veterans in Politics* (1952). The political and economic stability provided by the growing middle class has been brilliantly assessed by Robert H. Wiebe in *The Search for Order, 1877–1920* (1967).

*indicates availability in paperback.

21

Industrial Expansion and the Age of Big Business

WHILE POLITICIANS SCRAMBLED for place and power in the thirty years after Appomattox, the industrial revolution was transforming economic life in America. Between 1860 and 1894, the United States advanced from fourth to first (some authorities believe the United States ranked second as early as 1860) among the manufacturing nations of the world, and it subsequently increased its lead even further. This rise to industrial preeminence, with its many ramifications throughout all of American life and society, was the most important development between the Civil War and World War I. Business and industrial leaders, not politicians, built a truly modern America. Thousands of miles of railroads, productive mines, smoking factories, deep oil wells, and huge lumber mills all testified to the economic growth and power of a young industrial giant.

In 1859, America's 140,433 industrial establishments produced slightly less than $2 billion worth of products, but in 1914, 275,791 establishments turned out products valued in excess of $24 billion. Even beyond the Civil War agriculture had been the leading producer of wealth, but by 1890, industry had begun to replace farming as the most important sector of the economy. Domestic manufactured products not only became important in the home market, but by the 1890s they began to be of real value in the export trade. By 1912 nearly half of the nation's overseas shipments consisted of industrial products, compared with only about 15 percent in 1860. Between 1860 and 1914 industrial production rose at a rate of about 5.38 percent annually. No nation before or since has equaled the record of America in producing and distributing goods.

Reasons for Industrial Growth

What basic factors were responsible for this unprecedented industrial growth in the half century following the Civil War? First of all, the burst of industrial activity was by no means a new development but rather the acceleration and intensification of trends already in existence. The output of basic raw materials and manufactures had grown rapidly during the 1840s and 1850s. This increase in the number and size of factories makes it clear that the basis of an industrial economy had been firmly established even before the Civil War.

Economic historians disagree on the precise effect that the Civil War had on the country's industrial development. Some evidence indicates that the total industrial output was not immediately greater, as a result of war, than it would have been had peace prevailed. The war actually hurt certain industries, such as cotton textiles, because of a shortage of raw materials, and the conflict ruined most Southern industry. Nonetheless, the Civil War was important because it established a base for productive facilities and for capital formation, both of which facilitated postwar industrial expansion. Moreover, it furnished the springboard from which many businessmen jumped to successful industrial careers.

The Civil War had still further consequences. The power of the agrarian South was banished from federal councils, and national affairs came under the control of those who favored industrial development. The victorious Republican party maintained a close alliance with big business. And the government did not simply provide a favorable atmosphere for entrepreneurs; it supplied them with direct and indirect assistance. Business and banking groups benefited from tariffs, a stable national banking system, and maintenance of the *de facto* gold standard after 1878. The railroads received direct aid through grants of federal land. Liberal land policies actually permitted the industrial interests to monopolize much of the nation's natural resources, such as timber and minerals. In other words, a munificent government handed over valuable resources to private business in a most generous—almost profligate—manner.

In addition, the federal and state governments helped industry indirectly by refusing to restrict or regulate business and by restraining labor through the use of troops and court injunctions. Farm and labor demands for effective restrictions on monopoly fell on the deaf ears of a government which heard chiefly the voices of big business. Government aid and support to private enterprise were a major factor in the country's rapid industrialization.

Also of fundamental importance in America's industrial expansion was the availability of abundant quantities of natural resources. The United States was fortunate in having vast supplies of coal, iron ore, oil, copper, lead, zinc, limestone, salt, sulfur, and other minerals, as well as lumber. Although not completely self-sufficient, the nation possessed most basic resources. Coal and oil were especially important in furnishing power for manufacturing and transportation. Waterpower, particularly in the Northeast and South, provided another source of energy. During the late nineteenth century American industry shifted from animate power, furnished by men and animals, to inanimate power, furnished by engines and machines.

The basic raw material for modern industry, which required so much iron and steel, was iron ore. The traditional sources for it lay in Pennsylvania and New Jersey, but large quantities of high-grade iron ore were discovered in the Lake Superior region, the most famous productive area being the Mesabi Range in Minnesota. In 1870, only 3,831,891 tons of iron ore were mined compared with 55,526,490 in 1915.

Natural resources, without the technology to transform them into goods and commodities, have little value. It was the use of new and improved machinery and techniques of production, along with the division of labor and a better organization of men and materials, that enabled United States industrialists to assume their commanding lead in the output of manufactured products during the late nineteenth century. Standardization and interchangeability of machine parts, for example, were fundamental to mass production. These techniques were highly perfected in the late nineteenth and early twentieth centuries in such industries as farm machinery, machine tools, and automobiles. Americans may have lagged behind Europeans in pure scientific achievement, but American technicians and engineers were quicker than anyone else to apply scientific knowledge to practical purposes. The Bessemer process for manufacturing steel and the practical application of electric power were notably important technological achievements. Inventions such as the telegraph, telephone, typewriter, cash register, and the adding machine were also of inestimable value in business expansion.

The United States was fortunate in having not only adequate natural resources and technical know-how but also a sufficient supply of both common and skilled labor. Much of the labor force in manufacturing, mining, and transportation was recruited from the millions of immigrants who arrived after the Civil War; many other workers left the farms where they were no longer needed. The rapidly increasing population played a dual role in the expanding economy: it provided both a labor supply and a market for the mass-produced goods.

Industry could not have developed without capital to build factories, to buy machines, and to purchase raw materials; and here the United States again was in a fortunate position. Much of the money that had been invested in shipping and trade before the Civil War was shifted to manufacturing during and after the war. Furthermore, both personal and corporate profits were plowed back into individual businesses to purchase better machines and equipment, which in turn helped to increase the output per worker. Industrialists also borrowed large amounts of capital abroad. Unlike underdeveloped countries in the twentieth century, the United States was not starved for capital during the time it expanded industrially.

Leadership and organization in American business also played an important role. After the Civil War, the corporate structure became the most popular means of organizing large-scale businesses. The corporation had the advantages of being able to raise large amounts of capital; it was relatively permanent; and it was considered a legal person. Thus, it was an ideal instrument through which to organize and operate huge industrial, transportation, and mining enterprises.

The business leadership that emerged during these years contributed greatly to America's industrial record. Collis P. Huntington, Jay

Gould, Edward H. Harriman, William Vanderbilt, and James J. Hill were prominent railroad tycoons. John D. Rockefeller monopolized the oil industry, and Andrew Carnegie dominated steel production. Meat-packing was most highly developed by the "Big Four": Philip D. Armour, Gustavus Swift, Michael Cudahy, and Nelson Morris. John Deere and Cyrus McCormick developed large farm machine companies; in banking, Jay Cooke and, later, J. P. Morgan achieved national prominence.

To be sure, some of the nation's leading entrepreneurs were ruthless operators and sometimes outright scoundrels and thieves. Jay Gould and Jim Fisk unscrupulously manipulated the enterprises that they controlled, held public opinion in disdain, and seemed completely devoid of social responsibility. Cornelius Vanderbilt, a shrewd, vain, uncouth transportation baron who controlled the New York Central Railroad, once reputedly declared of one of his actions: "Law! What do I care about the law? Hain't I got the power?" Men of this kind were indeed "robber barons." Even they did some building, if at great economic and social cost.

On the other hand, men such as John D. Rockefeller, Andrew Carnegie, and James J. Hill may aptly be called "industrial statesmen." They were vigorous and sometimes ruthless, but they demonstrated great skill and ability in organizing facilities to produce and distribute goods. They thought in expansive, world-spanning terms, and they efficiently organized men and materials on a scale never before known. They made fabulous personal fortunes while contributing at the same time to the nation's economic welfare. Most modern Americans would not sanction many of the actions of the late-nineteenth-century business tycoons, but their results—high production and wide distribution—they have generally hailed.

Another national asset was the widespread popular desire for economic betterment. Americans believed—and still believe—deeply in progress, in the personal profit motive, and in the principle of unlimited accumulation. They believed that economic success stemmed from hard work and thrift, and these virtues they cherished with almost religious fervor. Dissatisfaction with the status quo and a belief that conditions could be improved provided the backdrop for America's general economic advance.

Transportation and Communication

A high state of industrialism would have been impossible without efficient means of transportation, and in the United States, an expanding railroad network met this need. The years from 1870 to the early twentieth century might accurately be labeled the "Railroad Age." In 1860, the United States had 30,626 miles of railroads. The New York Central, the Erie, the Pennsylvania, and the Baltimore and Ohio had blanketed the Northeast and penetrated the Midwest. The railroad system in the South was less developed, but on the eve of the Civil War, some 10,000 miles of track had been laid. Although railroad mileage expanded rapidly during the 1850s, a much greater surge of construction followed the Civil War. Between 1860 and 1890 some 135,000 miles were constructed, and by 1914 the United States boasted a rail network of 252,105 miles, more than that in all of Europe. Investment in railroads and equipment increased from $4 billion in 1876 to more than $17 billion in 1914.

The building of transcontinental railroads after 1865 accounted for the rapid expansion in total mileage. Direct rail connections between Chicago and the Pacific Coast had been widely discussed before the Civil War, but it was not until after Congress chartered the Union Pacific and Central Pacific lines in 1864 that construction got underway. The nation's first transcontinental railroad was completed on May 10, 1869, when the two lines—the Union Pacific building west from Omaha and the Central Pacific moving east from San Francisco—joined near Ogden, Utah.

Meanwhile, the Northern Pacific, which had been chartered in 1864, ran into financial difficulty and was not completed until 1883. In the Southwest, the Southern Pacific and the Atchison, Topeka and Santa Fe reached the California coast in 1881 over track either owned or leased. In 1893, James J. Hill completed his Great Northern line from St. Paul to Puget Sound. Compared with that in the West and Northeast, railroad building in the South lagged. Still, by 1890 that section had more than 50,000 miles of operating railways.

Since the transcontinentals and some of the other Western roads penetrated unsettled regions where there was little business, the railroad turned to the federal government for financial assistance or, more specifically, land grants. The first federal land grant went for the Illinois Central in 1850, and during the following decade about twenty-eight million acres of public lands went to the states to subsidize railroad building. The Union Pacific received the first direct federal land grant to a railroad in 1862. Before construction commenced, Congress liberalized the charter in 1864. Under the new arrangement, the railroad was granted ten alternate sections of land on each side of the track, or a total of 12,800 acres, for each mile constructed. Besides this, the company received a 400-foot right-of-way, plus free timber and other building materials from the public domain. Congress made even more generous land grants to the Northern Pacific.

After 1871 land grants were discontinued; but between 1850 and 1871, the federal government gave away about 175,350,000 acres of land to the railroads. Since the railroads failed to fulfill some of the construction agreements, the final total was about 131,350,000 acres. Land played an important part in financing the Western railroads. The Burlington, for example, sold land for an average of about $6 an acre in Nebraska during the 1870s, and its overall income from land approximately equaled the expense of building the line from Burlington, Iowa, to Kearney Junction, Nebraska. The sale of land by other roads also substantially helped to underwrite their costs of construction. The popular demand for railroads was so strong that the railroads were granted other kinds of assistance, too. The desire to bring a railroad through their communities prompted hundreds of cities and counties to purchase railway bonds (often mortgaging their future for many years) or to make outright contributions of property and cash. Although government land grants and public loans have received much attention, most of the capital for railroad building came from private sources. Railroad companies sold millions of dollars' worth of stocks and bonds to domestic investors, and additional millions' worth to foreigners, especially the British.

Predictably, the hurried completion of Western railroads resulted in much poor construction. Land grants were based on mileage built, and frantic efforts were made to complete a maximum number of miles as quickly as possible. As one authority has written, "It was not so much that their construction work sometimes cost 100 percent more than was warranted by expenses for labor, materials, and reasonable dividends; it was that for all this expense the nation got a very extensive but very shaky railroad system." Thousands of miles of track later had to be rebuilt, increasing total capitalization and requiring higher rates to meet interest and dividend charges.

These conditions, however, were not peculiar to the land grant railroads. Poor construction, overcapitalization, manipulation of securities, and other abuses occurred commonly in the East and South as well. Although railroading attracted some capable men who made significant contributions to the country, it also spawned more than its share of crooks and financial manipulators. Daniel Drew, Jim Fisk, and Jay Gould, for example, indulged in extremely shady business practices. In a fight over control of the Erie among these three freebooters and Commodore Vanderbilt in 1868, they issued spurious stock, bribed legislators and judges, and cavalierly flaunted the public interest. Fortunately, not all railroad leaders fitted this pattern of greed and public irresponsibility. James J. Hill built the Great Northern without benefit of land grants, except for a small one from Minnesota, and developed the country along his line. He introduced purebred cattle into the Upper Midwest, loaned money to farmers on grain stored in elevators along the Great Northern, encouraged Armour to establish a packing plant in St. Paul to provide a closer market for livestock growers, and interested himself in the conservation of natural resources. Edward H. Harriman reorganized several poorly managed roads into prosperous lines.

There were many complaints lodged against the railroads. Rebates paid to special shippers, high rates, and discriminatory charges aroused bitter criticism from farmers, small merchants, and general reformers. The powerful political influence of the railroads—gained through distribution of free passes to influential citizens, payment of retainers to lawyers, and sometimes outright bribery—also came under attack.

But even while criticisms against the railroads mounted, basic physical improvements, reduction of freight and passenger rates, and corporate reorganization and consolidation were taking place. Larger, more powerful, and faster locomotives were introduced, heavier steel rails were laid, and a standard gauge of 4 feet 8½ inches was adopted on most lines by 1886. The Westinghouse air brake, perfected in 1887; automatic couplings to connect cars; and a variety of special tank, livestock, and refrigerator cars all increased the efficiency of railroad transportation. Moreover, rates declined substantially. The drop was greatest in the East and on main lines where competition existed, but some reduction occurred on the smaller and more isolated roads as well.

The establishment of a national railroad system profoundly influenced American life. Railroads were largely responsible for the rapid settlement of the West: they advertised for immigrants, sold land to settlers on credit, and hauled people to their new homes at reduced rates. They opened up the Rocky Mountain region to large-scale mining development, established bases for future cities, and made possible the growth of industrial and agricultural specialization. The railroads were instrumental in the decline of the steamboat, which could not compete with the trains in speed and efficiency. As enormous consumers of iron and steel, railroads had a direct effect

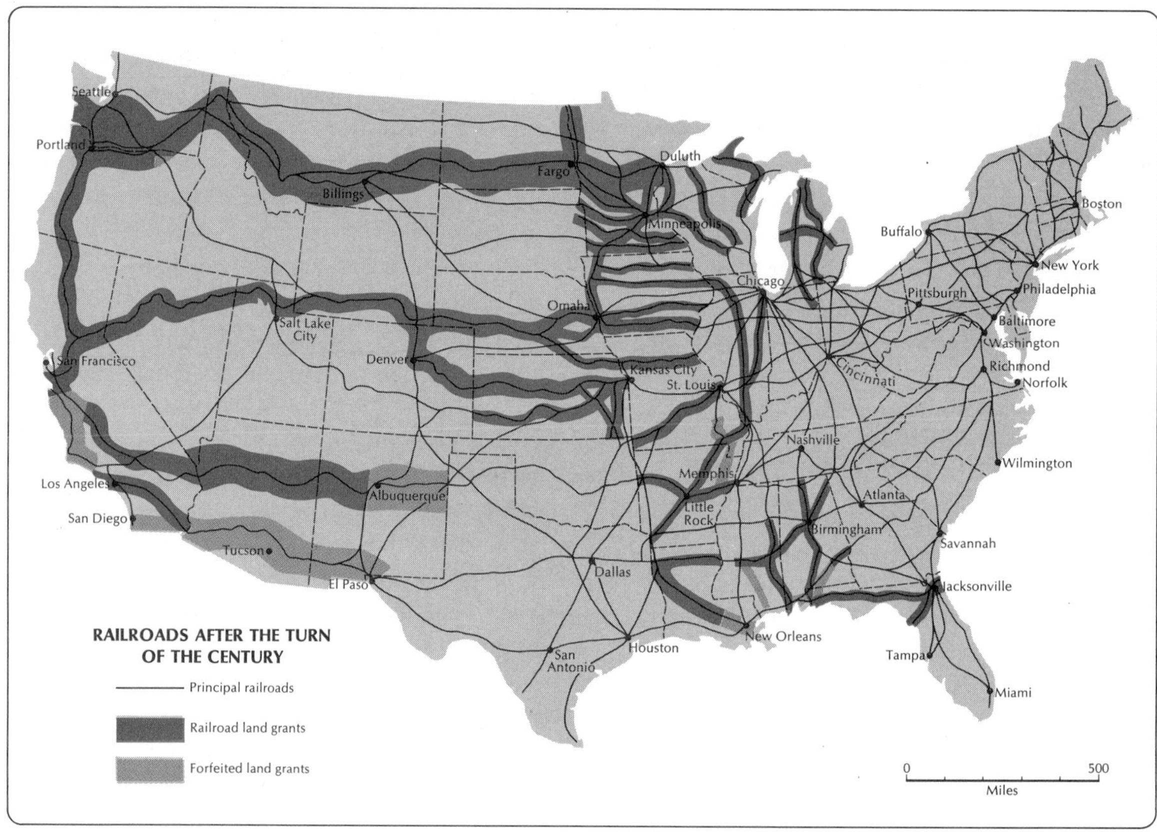

upon the welfare of those basic industries. As early as 1883, the railroads divided the country into four time zones and thus gradually eliminated the chaos created by some sixty-eight different local times. Railroads improved the speed and efficiency of the mail service; they made fortunes for some individuals; they generated warm controversies over public policy; and they gave rise to a large body of American folklore.

The railways greatly affected the overall economic development of the nation. Completion of an efficient transportation system provided American industrialists and farmers with a nationwide market and joined the various sections of the country together into an economic whole. Goods produced in Boston, for example, could now be sold easily in Chicago, St. Louis, or Denver. Southern cotton, Wisconsin lumber, or Colorado minerals could be shipped to distant factories for processing and sale. In other words, railroads provided a rather cheap, rapid, and efficient means to transport raw materials and finished products from one place to another. The American industrial revolution would otherwise have been impossible.

Other means of transportation also contributed greatly to the country's industrial growth. Pipelines became important in the movement of oil from fields to refineries in the 1870s; by 1890 there were approximately three thousand miles of trunk pipelines used in transporting petroleum. Invention of the motor car depended upon the development of a practical internal combustion engine in the 1860s. Many experiments followed this achievement, but not until the 1890s did Charles and Frank Duryea, Henry Ford, Henry Leland Olds, and other pioneers build successful automobiles. In 1904, a large caravan of automobiles arriving at the St. Louis Exposition from the East Coast signaled the new era in transportation. The most successful passenger car was Henry Ford's Model T, which he began producing on a mass basis in 1909.

American business and industry depended heavily on improvements in communication. The postal system was expanded and improved and new services were added. City delivery was begun in 1863, special delivery in 1885, and rural free delivery in 1896. The first transcontinental telegraph was completed in 1861, and Cyrus Field completed an improved trans-Atlantic cable in 1866. Following numerous experiments by different inventors, Alexander Graham Bell sent his first telephone message on March 10, 1876, to his assistant, Thomas Watson. His terse words, "Come here, Watson, I want you," began a new era in communications. The American Bell Telephone Company was chartered in 1880. Although people were at first skeptical of this revolutionary contrivance, predicting that it would never have any practical value, the number of Bell telephones increased from 50,000 to more than one million between 1880 and 1902. These developments in communications were not only helpful but absolutely essential in carrying on large-scale and complex business transactions.

Major Industries

American factories turned out a great variety of commodities, but four basic manufactures exceeded all others in number of establishments, number of wage earners, and value of products: food and kindred commodities, textiles, iron and steel, and lumber. By 1914 these four industries accounted for about 54 percent of the value of all United States manufactures. Flour milling, meat-packing, sugar refining, and processing of all kinds of canned and preserved goods were the chief food manufactures. Charles A. Pillsbury introduced new methods of milling the hard spring wheat of the Upper Midwest and developed a huge milling industry. Philip D. Armour became one of the nation's leading meat-packers. He established Armour and Company in Chicago in 1870 and was among the first to integrate the slaughtering, packing, storage, and shipping processes and to extend his operations to the manufacture of by-products—glue, oleomargarine, fertilizer, and soap. When Armour died in 1901, he left a fortune of some $50 million. Another of the nation's leading packers, Gustavus F. Swift, a Massachusetts butcher and cattle dealer who moved to Chicago in 1875, was instrumental in developing the refrigerator car, which came into general use after 1880.

Important industries also developed around canned goods, sugar, tobacco, and whisky. Starting with only a few pounds of tobacco at the close of the Civil War, James B. Duke, a poor North Carolina farm boy, and his father developed a large tobacco business. The Dukes began manufacturing cigarettes in 1881 and soon brought in machines to replace handworkers. By 1889, they produced about half the cigarettes sold in the United States. In 1890, several competing tobacco companies were organized into the American Tobacco Company under Duke's presidency.

The value of manufactured and processed food reached $4,816,700,000 in 1914, more than double the figure of 1899. Such an increase emphasized the needs of a growing urban population and the decline in self-sufficiency, even among farmers; and it proved that industrialization need not be retarded by a lack of food for nonfarm workers. In other words, resources could be rapidly shifted from agriculture to industry without placing any strain on food supplies—an extremely important factor in the nation's speedy industrialization.

Textiles ranked second to food commodities in value of products, although the industry employed more workers than any other branch of manufacturing. One of the country's oldest industries, textile manufacturing was, by 1900, a widely distributed and mammoth business—its 22,995 plants turned out $3,494,615,000 worth of products. By World War I, the United States was exporting millions of dollars in cotton manufactures.

Iron and steel, with their many semifinished and finished products, ranked third behind foodstuffs and textiles. Industrialization required a foundation of iron and steel, and the United States assumed a commanding world lead in their production during the generation after the Civil War. By 1914, more than one million workers were employed in 17,719 iron and steel establishments, whose annual output was valued at approximately $3.2 billion. Pig iron production rose from less than one million tons in 1860 to about thirty-three million in 1914; steel output increased from a mere 19,643 long tons in 1867 to thirty-seven million on the eve of World War I. The United States surpassed Great Britain in producing pig iron in the 1880s, and by 1900 American production of steel was twice that of England.

The modern industrial revolution had waited upon the discovery of a structural metal that was hard, tough, malleable, abundant, and fairly cheap—that is, steel. Tougher and less brittle than cast iron, it provided a structural material for many industrial purposes, and its production, along with the use of steampower in manufacturing and transportation, ushered in the era of modern industry.

The man most responsible for developing the American steel industry was Andrew Carnegie. Emigrating to Pennsylvania from Scotland in 1847 when he was only twelve, young Carnegie obtained his first job in a cotton mill at $1.20 a week. The next year he was employed as a messenger boy and learned to operate a telegraph key. His first piece of luck came when Thomas R. Scott of the Pennsylvania Railroad hired him as a secretary and telegrapher. When only twenty-four, Carnegie was made superintendent of the Western Division of the Pennsylvania line. Ambitious, hardworking, and daring, Carnegie began to invest small sums in various businesses but soon concentrated his investments in bridge- and ironworks.

In 1873, Carnegie organized the Edgar Thompson Steel Works, and despite the Panic of that year, moved ahead by installing the latest and most efficient equipment for making iron and steel. He organized extremely effective production and managerial teams and set out to integrate his operations by gaining control of raw materials and transportation. Henry Clay Frick had won control of a large share of the coke industry in the Connellsville area of southwest Pennsylvania, and in 1882, Carnegie purchased extensive coal deposits and numerous coke ovens from Frick, who later joined the Carnegie enterprises. Next he obtained his own supply of iron ore and then purchased railroads and freighters to ship the ore from Lake Superior to Pittsburgh. Carnegie now had his own mills, his own supply of coke and iron ore, and his own transportation.

Petroleum, one of the fastest-growing and, in the long run, one of the more important industries, provided the opportunities for the fabulous business and industrial career of John D. Rockefeller. Born in western New York in 1839, the son of a patent medicine salesman and trader, Rockefeller was fourteen when his family moved to Cleveland, Ohio. There he attended high school and took a short commercial course. Employed at the age of sixteen by a commission firm for $15 a month, Rockefeller saved a few dollars and, in 1859, formed a partnership with Maurice B. Clark. Handling meats, hay, and grain on a commission basis, Rockefeller and Clark made good profits during the Civil War as prices advanced.

The same year that Rockefeller and Clark went into business, Edwin L. Drake drilled the nation's first oil well near Titusville in western Pennsylvania. At that time, the chief product refined from crude oil was kerosene used in lamps. In 1863, Rockefeller began to make some investments in oil refining, a growing business in Cleveland; two years later, he sold his commission business and devoted his full energies to the oil industry. He formed a partnership with Samuel Andrews and, by 1869, their refineries had a daily output of 1,500 barrels. An energetic, thrifty, careful operator who watched every detail of his business, Rockefeller soon became a major figure in the oil refining industry. He formed the Standard Oil Company in 1870 and, by 1872, controlled twenty-one of Cleveland's twenty-six refineries.

Like other industrialists of the period, Rockefeller sought to integrate and control all phases of petroleum production and distribution. Rockefeller hardly needed to control all his crude supply; by controlling refining, he could indirectly influence production. Yet, in the late 1880s, Standard began investing in leases and producing wells. By 1905, about one-sixth of the crude oil required by Standard refineries came from Standard-owned wells. Through purchase and consolidation of competing properties, Rockefeller gained control of approximately 90 percent of the oil refining business by 1890. To make his operations more self-sufficient, Rockefeller manufactured his own barrels, built his own warehouses, established his own draying service, and acquired pipelines to free himself from the railroads. He manufactured hundreds of by-products: lubricants, waxes, paints, varnishes, and other petroleum derivatives. He created a distribution network to deliver products directly to consumers. Licensed dealers in most major United States cities distributed Standard Oil commodities, and Rockefeller inaugurated a tank wagon service for house-to-house delivery of kerosene. He sold large quantities of petroleum products overseas.

In a day when industrial and transportation tycoons became rich beyond most people's imagination, Rockefeller acquired a fortune which had no equal. By 1913 his wealth amounted to some $900 million, nine times that of Cornelius Vanderbilt when he died in 1877 and twice the figure for which Carnegie sold out in 1901. Such success, however, was

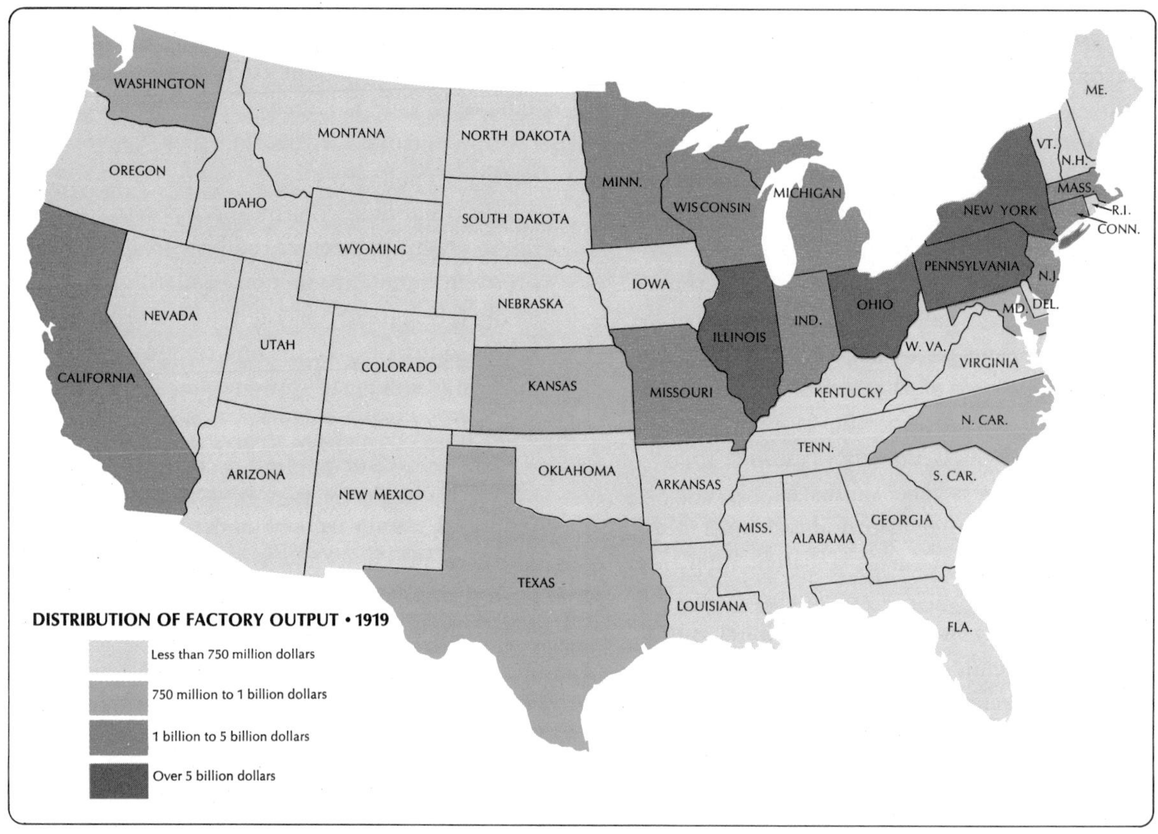

not achieved without vigorous and sometimes unfair business practices. Rockefeller, for example, cut prices temporarily to drive a difficult competitor out of business. Because of the size of his business, he could force the railroads to grant him rebates far more favorable than those granted his competitors. Standard Oil, finally, exerted strong political influence to protect its own interests. By 1890 Rockefeller had virtually monopolized the American oil industry.

Industrial advance was closely tied to the new markets generated by technological advances. Kerosene lamps and internal combustion engines became heavy users of petroleum products; the railroads increased demands for iron and steel; and meat-packing benefited from the invention of the refrigerator car. There were direct relationships, although not always clear, among improved technology, increased production, rising incomes, and expanded consumption.

Location of American Manufacturing

Although American manufactures were widely distributed geographically, the two leading regions of production were the Middle Atlantic states—New York, New Jersey, and Pennsylvania—and such North Central states as Ohio, Indiana, Illinois, Michigan, and Wisconsin.

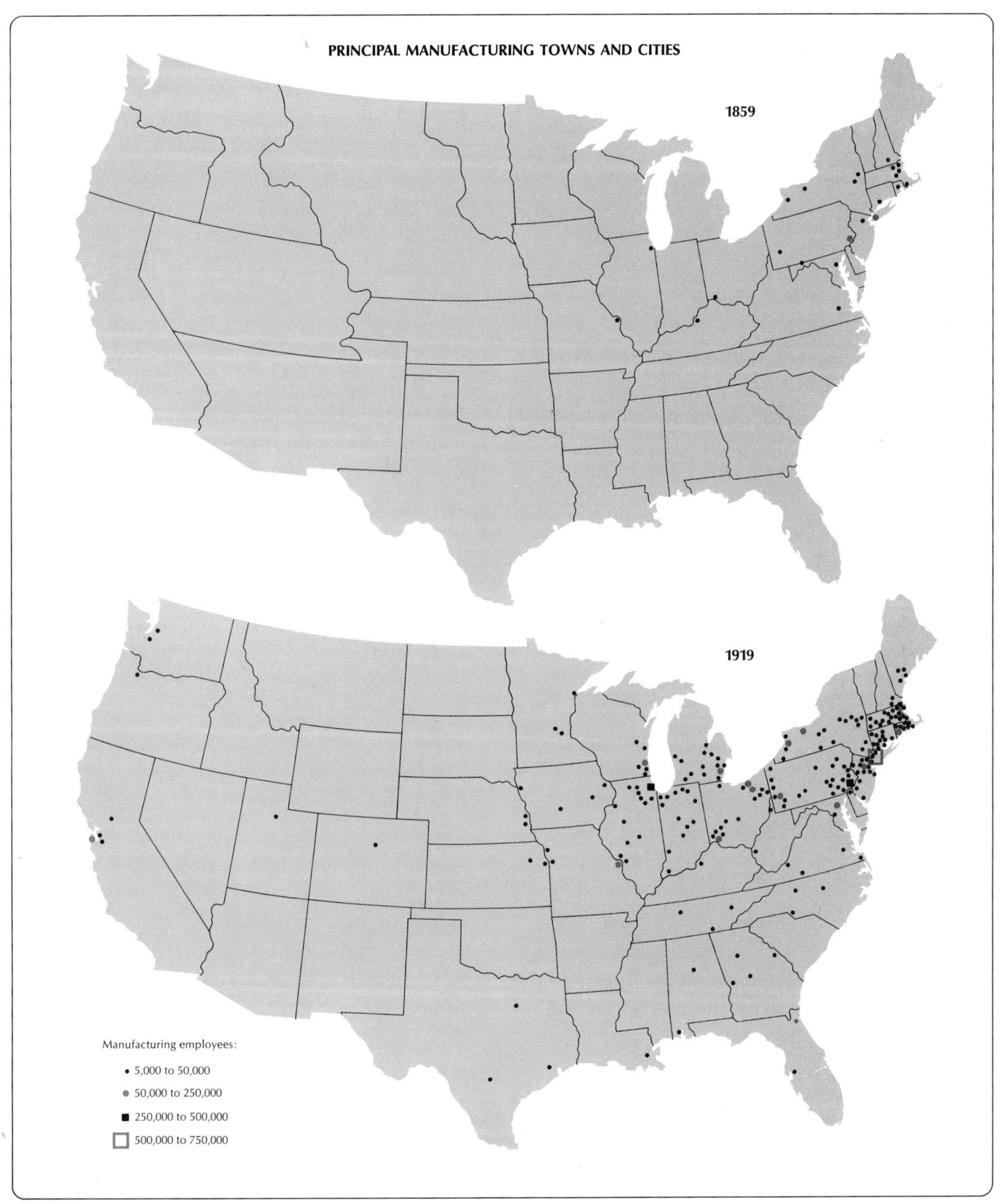
PRINCIPAL MANUFACTURING TOWNS AND CITIES
1859
1919
Manufacturing employees:
5,000 to 50,000
50,000 to 250,000
250,000 to 500,000
500,000 to 750,000

By 1914, the Middle Atlantic states produced 33 percent, and the eastern North Central states turned out 27 percent, of the value of the nation's industrial output. One of the most remarkable developments in manufacturing occurred in the upper Middle West, an area which had been chiefly agricultural at the time of the Civil War. Illinois, and Chicago in particular, became the center of the farm machine and meat-packing industries. Ohio was second only to Pennsylvania in the output of iron. New England continued to be a major industrial area, but its importance relative to other sections declined in the late nineteenth century.

The South lagged far behind the North in industrial development. The Civil War had been highly destructive of Southern manufacturing, and that troubled economic region did not make substantial industrial gains until a generation after 1865. The South lacked sufficient capital, managerial experience, and skilled labor, although the area had a favorable potential for industry. It had plentiful raw materials like cotton, coal, iron ore, petroleum, and lumber; it had a vast supply of cheap labor, needing only training and experience; abundant waterpower; a mild climate; and friendly state governments. By 1880, a number of important leaders in the South were making a conscious effort to promote manufacturing. Henry W. Grady, editor of the *Atlanta Constitution,* and D. W. Dawson of the *Charleston News and Courier* were active among those who argued that the South's economic progress depended upon industrial development. One popular slogan called for the construction of mills near the South's cotton supply.

Despite the natural advantages and the active promotion of manufacturing, however, Southern industry developed slowly until after 1880. The value of Southern manufactures was only 6.3 percent of the nation's total in 1880, compared with 9.9 percent thirty years earlier. But gradually the development of large-scale industry gained momentum. Major Southern industries included cotton textiles, iron, coal, oil, lumber, phosphates, cottonseed oil, and tobacco products. Cotton textile production became one of the South's leading industries, even outdistancing the Northern mills, especially in the output of coarser cloth. By 1909, the South was producing about 40 percent of the country's cotton goods. The South's iron and steel industry centered in the region of Birmingham, which was ideally located in relation to iron ore and coal supplies. Millions of board feet of lumber were cut annually from Southern forests.

Before 1900, most of the oil industry was concentrated in Pennsylvania, New York, Ohio, Indiana, and West Virginia, but after the great Lucas gusher at Spindletop, Texas, in 1901, the center of oil activity began to shift toward the Southwest. Oil booms in Texas, Oklahoma, and Louisiana within the next few years quickly expanded the nation's production to 265,763,000 barrels by 1914. The drilling, transportation, and refining of oil gave the South one of its leading industries. When judged in absolute terms, the South made a fair record in manufacturing before World War I, but in comparison with the Northeast and the Great Lakes states, the region, with a few exceptions, dropped further behind than it had been before the Civil War. In 1909, the sixteen Southern states produced only 12.8 percent of the value of manufactured products, although that region had 32 percent of the population.

Consumer Distribution

The mass output of manufactured commodities after the Civil War brought about important changes in distribution. Better transportation and improved means of exchange made it easier and cheaper to move goods from the factory. Consequently, the consumption of homemade articles rapidly declined, as more people purchased their canned goods, clothing, shoes, and butter at commercial retail outlets.

Although the general store remained common in rural areas, important changes in retail distribution began to appear after 1860. Following the establishment of a department store by A. T. Stewart in New York in 1861, similar stores were founded by R. H. Macy in New York, Marshall Field in Chicago, and John Wanamaker in Philadelphia. These stores sold many types of goods, with different departments specializing in certain commodities. By 1910, department store sales approximated $700 million yearly. The mail-order house, combining the functions of wholesaler and retailer, also developed during the late nineteenth century. Montgomery Ward and Company was founded in 1872, and Sears Roebuck and Company in 1886. Chain stores represented another innovation in retail distribution. The Great Atlantic and Pacific Tea Company, or the A & P, began operations in 1859 and, by 1914, had some three thousand stores throughout the United States. F. W. Woolworth's 5 and 10 cent stores, first established in 1879, became familiar to hundreds of towns and cities by the end of the century.

The advertising and promotion of brand-name goods as a means of increasing sales also developed after 1865. Many brand-name commodities were advertised on a national basis—Dr. Lyon's tooth powder, Ivory soap, Pillsbury flour, Singer sewing machines, and scores of other products. One of the biggest advertisers was the patent medicine industry, and among the most famous nostrums, which became household words in America, was Lydia Pinkham's female compound. By 1900, advertising itself had become big business; it would become a vital part of the American way of life in the twentieth century.

Monopoly

The development of large-scale business and industry was accompanied by a high degree of consolidation and, in some cases, outright monopoly. This trend, apparent by the 1880s, became increasingly pronounced later. By 1905, 11 percent of the industrial establishments controlled more than 80 percent of the capital, employed 72 percent of the workers, and produced about 79 percent of the manufactured products. As the trend toward concentration intensified, a growing demand arose among farmers, workers, small businessmen, and some intellectuals to curb this unrestricted economic power.

Combinations in transportation and industry grew rapidly after 1870 for a number of reasons. The corporate form of business organization itself was an important permissive factor. Multimillion-dollar enterprises could have been neither easily nor conveniently financed and managed by individual proprietors or partnerships. Furthermore, the technological revolution made possible and necessary much larger business units; and improved transportation permitted a single large firm to sell its products in national, and even international, markets. Panics and depressions repeatedly helped strong businesses become even stronger by purchasing weak or bankrupt competitors. Moreover, many business leaders believed that larger industries were more efficient, although this was by no means always true. Carnegie summed up this idea when he wrote in 1900: "Now, the cheapening of all these good things . . . is rendered possible only through the operation of the law, which may be stated thus: cheapness is in proportion to the scale of production." The basic economic advantages of large-scale production included a reduction of unit cost, the manufacture of by-products, and specialization in both production and management.

But the dominant reason for business and industrial combination was the desire to reduce competition and to increase profits. Considerations of business efficiency and public benefit were of secondary interest—if they were thought of at all. Many businessmen believed that excessive and destructive competition resulted from an overexpansion of productive facilities and that by coordinating and combining firms in a particular business, say refining, they could adjust output to market demand and keep prices from being forced down to unprofitable levels. Although businessmen gave lip service to the principle of competition, they sought to eliminate or reduce it in their practical business affairs.

Techniques of consolidation and monopoly differed. One of the most common comprised the integration of competing plants producing the same kind of goods into a single organization. Rockefeller had done this in the oil industry during the 1870s. Some companies also consolidated their positions by gaining control of closely related industries, as Carnegie did when he purchased coal fields, coke ovens, and transportation facilities. This "vertical integration" brought sources of raw materials, processing, and marketing together under single control.

The most elementary method for reducing competition lay in simple agreements in regard to prices, production, and service among several rival firms. In the early 1870s, businessmen turned to the pool as a more effective way of curbing competition. The railroads had already hit upon the pool as a favorite means of reducing competition, and before 1890, pools existed in the meat-packing, gunpowder, barbed wire, and other industries. However, even though pools were more strongly organized than simple agreements, they tended to break down under competitive conditions.

The trust ushered in an enforceable type of combination much more suited to the desires of businessmen who wanted to eliminate competition. The Standard Oil Trust, formed in 1879 by John D. Rockefeller, was the nation's first industrial trust. Stockholders of companies and firms assigned the voting stock of their businesses to a group of nine trustees, among whom Rockefeller was the principal figure. The stockholders received trust certificates, which drew dividends but which had no voting power. This gave the trustees complete control of all the companies which entered the agreement. After this combination, the Standard Oil Trust controlled most of the country's refining facilities, much of the pipeline network, and other related companies. The success of the Standard Oil Trust set a pattern for consolidations in cottonseed oil, linseed oil, whisky, lead, cordage, sugar, and other commodities.

The trust as a form of monopoly lasted scarcely a decade. In the late 1880s, actions were brought in state courts against several of the leading trusts on the grounds that they violated common law principles in regard to restraint of trade and monopoly and that company rights under state charters had been disregarded. After 1892, the trust as a type of business organization was abandoned, but the word "trust" continued as a common term for large-scale, monopolistic business.

With the decline of the trusts, outright mergers became more popular, but the most effective type of business consolidation was the holding company, a corporation which sought to reduce competition by purchasing control of competing firms. Between 1897 and 1902, some of the nation's most important businesses were organized under the holding company arrangement—the Standard Oil Company, reorganized under a New Jersey charter of 1899, the United States Steel Corporation, International Harvester Company, and the Northern Securities Company. By 1905, a high degree of concentration and consolidation had been achieved in oil, steel, farm machinery, sugar, and many other industries. As one poet exclaimed:

Let us corner up the sunbeams
Lying all around our path;
Get a trust on wheat and roses;
Give the poor the thorns and chaff.
Let us find our chiefest pleasure
Hoarding bounties of today,
So the poor shall have scant measure
And two prices have to pay.

We will syndicate the starlight,
And monopolize the moon,
Claim a royalty on rest days,
A proprietary noon;
For right of way through ocean's spray
We'll charge just what it's worth;
We'll drive our stakes around the lakes—
In fact, we'll own the earth.

A deep prejudice existed among the common people against the concentration of economic power, and pools, trusts, and other types of business consolidation aroused strong opposition among many citizens. But such opposition in the late nineteenth century was spasmodic, disorganized, and quite ineffective, whereas business interests were aggressive and much better united than their opponents.

Businessmen capitalized upon the American tradition which held that government restrictions or legal restraints on business were contrary to the best interests of the entrepreneur and to the economy as a whole—the doctrine of laissez faire. They argued that the nation was best served when competition operated without interference. Success was a sign of better management and greater efficiency, not a result of undesirable business practices. The destruction of some firms and monopoly control by others merely bore out the laws of natural selection and the survival of the fittest, biological concepts formulated by Charles Darwin in *The Origin of Species* in 1859. This analogy between biology and society came to be called "social Darwinism." The English philosopher Herbert Spencer developed these ideas into a systematic body of thought, which was widely accepted by such Americans as historian John Fiske and sociologist William Graham Sumner. Spencer sharply attacked government regulation and state aid of business and argued that competition should govern business relationships.

Most American businessmen did not share Spencer's rigor in denouncing state activities.

No one objected to government action favorable to his interests or legislation which promoted industrial prosperity. Spencerian philosophy, however, did provide businessmen with a scientific and sociological justification for opposing government regulation and maintaining a favorable status quo. Carnegie once said that, while competition might hurt the individual, it was best for society in general because it insured "the survival of the fittest in every department." Protestantism also buttressed, and indeed enhanced, the economic notion of laissez faire. Great wealth could be interpreted as a mark of divine favor; poverty, on the other hand, must therefore result from laziness or sin. Many business leaders emphasized the Protestant virtues of thrift, industry, and sobriety to which they laid their success.

Despite widespread economic, religious, and philosophical support for laissez faire principles, some men took strong exception to unfettered economic freedom, advocating government regulation and control of big business. In *Progress and Poverty* (1879), Henry George, a journalist and social reformer, attacked the system of holding land for speculative gain and proposed a single tax to deprive landowners of any unearned increment which accrued when social progress, rather than personal contribution, caused property values to rise. George's single-tax idea did not gain many adherents, but his book was widely read because of its lucid attack on the economic order of the day. It had a special appeal to college students. Edward Bellamy advocated nationalized industry in *Looking Backward* (1888); Henry Demarest Lloyd, in *Wealth against Commonwealth* (1894), bitterly attacked laissez faire, social Darwinism, and classical economics as existing merely to justify predatory business practices.

Beginning of Government Regulation

The antitrust movement to curb business and industrial consolidation, which developed after 1870, grew not from particular theories of political economy but from a pragmatic effort to solve definite problems and to correct specific abuses. Relatively few critics wanted to change the American system in any basic way. They hoped only to expand government control and regulation in order to protect the small and the weak against exploitation by a few economic giants. Most antitrust advocates in the late nineteenth century did not accept business consolidation as inevitable. They felt that the power of the state must be invoked to restore competitive conditions and to smash monopolies.

Midwestern farmers, as well as important elements of the business community, singled out the railroads in their first widespread and well-organized attack on big business. The farmers had been anxious to have railway lines extended to their communities, but by the early 1870s they were complaining bitterly against high and discriminatory rates and other harmful practices. The Grange, the country's most important farm organization, and other independent and antimonopoly parties then beginning to thrive in the Midwest supported demands for state regulation. Chicago business interests joined in this demand. In 1871 and 1873, laws were passed in Illinois which set freight and passenger rates and regulated the charges for storing grain in warehouses. Minnesota, Wisconsin, and Iowa, among other states, passed similar "Granger" laws. Most of these statutes attempted to establish maximum rates either by specific legislation or by action of a railroad commission.

Unfortunately, the Granger laws were not very effective. The railroads exploited every type of propaganda and political pressure to nullify the effectiveness of legislation or to get it repealed. Their highly successful campaigns had, by the late 1870s, resulted in the revocation or weakening of most restrictive measures. Meanwhile, the railroads attacked the laws in court, charging that such regulations violated the Fourteenth Amendment which says that no "state shall deprive any person of life, liberty, or property, without due process of law." Corporations were persons under the law, and railroad attorneys argued that restrictive laws denied the companies full property rights. In *Munn v. Illinois* (1877), the Supreme Court upheld an Illinois law of 1871 designed to regulate warehouse rates for grain storage. In the opinion of Justice C. J. Waite, when "one devotes his property to a use in which the public has an interest, he, in effect, grants to the public an interest in that use, and must submit to be controlled by the public for the common good."

This clear-cut judicial victory had little practical significance, however. Regulatory laws had already become impotent; furthermore, regulations imposed by one state could never be effective when most of the major railroads ran through other states as well. Moreover, in the Wabash case in 1886, the Supreme Court held that states could not control railroads engaged in interstate commerce since the Constitution granted this function to the federal government; thus, control of the railroads would await the action of Congress. Though ineffective in itself, state regulation at least paved the way for federal regulation.

Even as farm and other groups pressed for state control of railroads and other large-scale enterprise, Congress was considering federal action to curb abuses in interstate transportation. In 1874, the House of Representatives passed the McCrary bill, which called for a federal commission to regulate rates. Although this and subsequent measures failed in the Senate, some congressmen and senators continued to push the issue. A report headed by Senator Shelby B. Cullom of Illinois in 1885 declared that "no general question of governmental policy occupies at this time so prominent a place in the thought of the people as that of controlling the steady growth and extending influence of corporate power and of regulating its relations to the public."

By this time, even some of the railroads themselves favored regulation as a way to reduce cutthroat competition. After reconciling differences between the House and Senate, the Interstate Commerce Act at last became law on February 4, 1887.

This act forbade discrimination in rates among localities, provided that all rates must be "reasonable and just," made it illegal to charge more for a short haul than for a long haul, and outlawed rebates and pooling. An Interstate Commerce Commission of five members appointed by the President was to administer the law. But the law did not give the Commission power to regulate rates, and if the Commission challenged the reasonableness of a rate, it had to prove its contention in court. The federal courts at this time were in no mood to impose any genuine regulation on the railroads. In the Maximum Freight Rate case, ten years after the creation of the Commission, the Supreme Court still held that the Commission had no power to set rates. Nevertheless, the Interstate Commerce Act made a significant start toward effective regulation.

Understandably, the initial demand for government regulation of big business had focused on the railroads—the biggest business of the day and the most likely to have a direct effect upon the lives of many people. However, before legislation to bring railroads under control was secured, a broad antitrust movement had also developed in the 1880s to deal with growing monopolies in oil, steel, and other industries. Again the states and territories took the lead, and by 1890 some fourteen of them had legal prohibitions against monopolies. Although President Cleveland never gave strong support to government regulation, he expressed a popular feeling when he said in 1887 that "Corporations, which should be the carefully restrained creatures of the law and the servants of the people, are fast becoming the people's master." Both the Democrats and Republicans recommended regulation of trusts in their platforms of 1888.

In December of 1889, Senator John Sherman of Ohio introduced a trust-control measure. Sherman had not intended to make an extended argument for it because he believed that "the public facts upon which it is founded and the general necessity of some legislation were so manifest that no debate was necessary to bring those facts to the attention of the Senate." However, debate on the measure extended over several months, and the Sherman Antitrust Act was not signed by President Harrison until July 2, 1890, after a vote of 252 to 0 in the House and 52 to 1 in the Senate.

The Sherman Antitrust Act made illegal "every contract, combination in the form of trust or otherwise, or conspiracy, in restraint of trade or commerce among the several states or with foreign nations." Secondly, "every person who shall monopolize, or attempt to monopolize, or combine or conspire with any other person or persons, to monopolize, any part of the trade or commerce among the several States, or with foreign nations, shall be deemed guilty of a misdemeanor." The government could bring criminal and civil suits against violators of the act, who might be fined a maximum of $5,000 or sentenced to a year in jail, or both. Persons injured by violators of the law could sue for threefold damages.

The Sherman Antitrust Act did not deter industrial consolidation and monopoly very effectively. In fact, more mergers and a greater degree of business concentration took place after the law was passed than before. Why? In the first place, the law itself was vague. It left the definition or interpretation of monopoly or restraint of trade to the courts, which usually took the business point of view. In the E. C. Knight case of 1895, for example, the Supreme Court held that the American Sugar Refining Company had not violated the Sherman Antitrust law even though the company controlled about 98 percent of the nation's sugar refining. For more than a decade the federal government made no serious attempt to enforce the law, and it remained a dead letter on the statute books until after Theodore Roosevelt became President in 1901.

Conclusion

Between 1865 and 1900, the United States changed from a predominantly agricultural nation to the world's leading industrial power. In the process, scarcely any phase of American life went untouched. Improved communications and transportation stimulated and en-

The Triumph of Mass Production

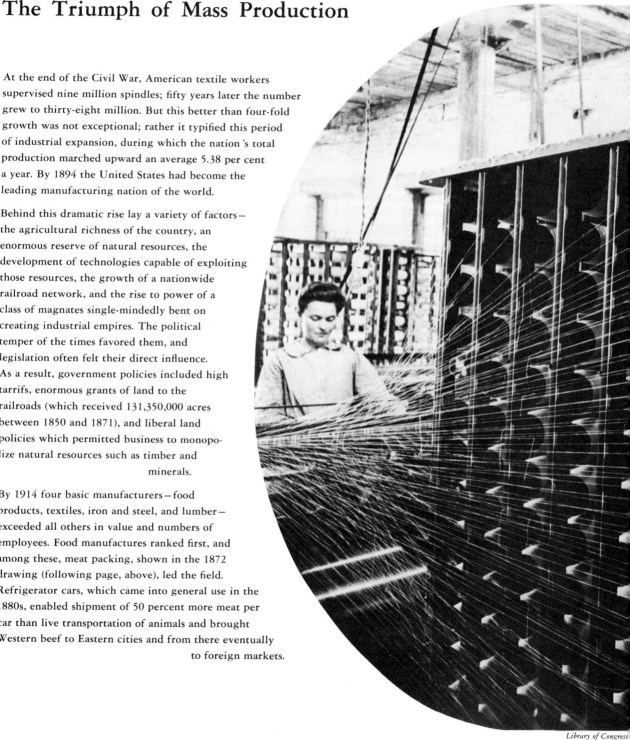

At the end of the Civil War, American textile workers supervised nine million spindles; fifty years later the number grew to thirty-eight million. But this better than four-fold growth was not exceptional; rather it typified this period of industrial expansion, during which the nation's total production marched upward an average 5.38 per cent a year. By 1894 the United States had become the leading manufacturing nation of the world.

Behind this dramatic rise lay a variety of factors—the agricultural richness of the country, an enormous reserve of natural resources, the development of technologies capable of exploiting those resources, the growth of a nationwide railroad network, and the rise to power of a class of magnates single-mindedly bent on creating industrial empires. The political temper of the times favored them, and legislation often felt their direct influence. As a result, government policies included high tarrifs, enormous grants of land to the railroads (which received 131,350,000 acres between 1850 and 1871), and liberal land policies which permitted business to monopolize natural resources such as timber and minerals.

By 1914 four basic manufacturers—food products, textiles, iron and steel, and lumber—exceeded all others in value and numbers of employees. Food manufactures ranked first, and among these, meat packing, shown in the 1872 drawing (following page, above), led the field. Refrigerator cars, which came into general use in the 1880s, enabled shipment of 50 percent more meat per car than live transportation of animals and brought Western beef to Eastern cities and from there eventually to foreign markets.

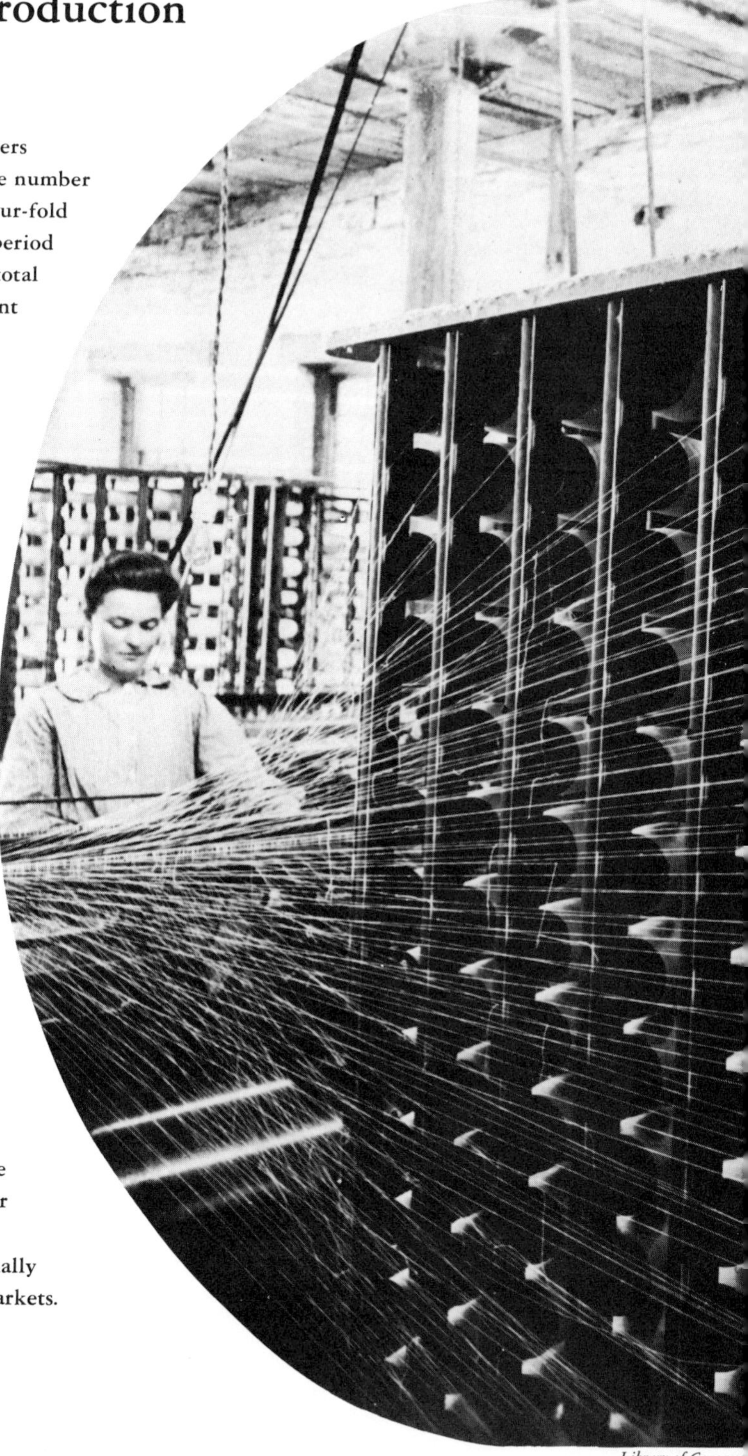

Library of Congress

Ruthless exploitation of the great virgin timber stands of the West, such as that shown in one 1869 *Harper's Weekly* illustration (left, below) had become common. The nation's original stands of virgin forest totalled some 800,000,000 acres, but by the beginning of the twentieth century, less than 200,000 remained.

Western mining for precious metals, like that at Idaho Springs, Colorado (below), also built great fortunes and swelled the nation's wealth; in twenty years the famed Comstock Lode in Virginia City, Nevada, yielded over $300,000,000 in gold and silver. The extraction and processing of oil and iron constituted an even greater source of wealth, however.

Below, left: Courtesy of the New-York Historical Society, New York City; all others: Library of Congress

Two of the greatest industrial organizers of the age were John D. Rockefeller, shown at far left with one of his attorneys, and Andrew Carnegie, above. Rockefeller's Standard Oil Company by 1890 controlled 90 percent of the nation's oil refining, and with his other interests, such as the Mesabi iron range shown below, he amassed a fortune of $900,000,000. Rockefeller founded the University of Chicago and provided some $500,000,000 for other philanthropic projects including the Rockefeller Foundation which he established in 1913.

Carnegie's success rested on the most advanced technical methods, such as the Bessemer process (left), which removed impurities from steel by forcing air through the molten metal and cut the price from $300 a ton to $35, and controlling production and transportation of raw materials. To feed his furnaces, Carnegie bought coal mines, coke ovens, leased iron mines from Rockefeller, and purchased railroads and freighters to ship the materials to his factories. In 1901 Carnegie sold his interests for some $447,000,000 and devoted the rest of his life to philanthropies including the establishment of some 2,800 libraries.

Far left, both: Brown Brothers; left: The Tamiment Institute Library; above: Library of Congress; below: The National Archives

The accumulation of great wealth resulted not only in philanthropy but personal expenditure on a lavish scale unknown before the Civil War. The Byron photo from Grace Mayer's book *Once Upon a City* (left) shows the brick and stone chateau built for Cornelius Vanderbilt II —just one in a two-mile row of millionaires' mansions on New York's Fifth Avenue in the 1890s. The private railroad car provided another convenience and status symbol for men of great wealth. The personal car of George M. Pullman (right) was built for him in 1877. The dining room appears in the foreground, the parlor, with an organ at which guests sang hymns after dinner, in the rear. The new wealth manifested itself in spectacular parties as well. The indoor "horseback dinner" (right, below) was staged in New York at Sherry's in 1903 by the "American Horse King" C. K. G. Billings.

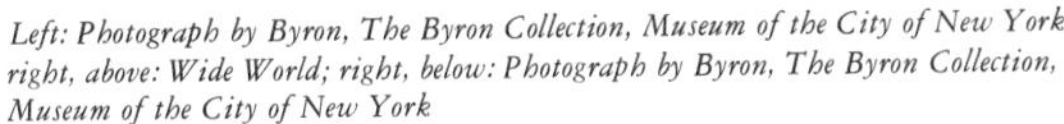

Left: Photograph by Byron, The Byron Collection, Museum of the City of New York; right, above: Wide World; right, below: Photograph by Byron, The Byron Collection, Museum of the City of New York

couraged national unity, and the mass production and distribution of consumer goods brought about greater standardization and uniformity in tastes and styles. Industrialization was accompanied by a rapid growth in urbanization, as the burgeoning industries drew both local farmers and immigrants from abroad to jobs in urban factories. This concentration of population created many problems which continued to plague the industrial centers into the twentieth century. Most importantly, America's industrial revolution effected an increase in wealth and standard of living. Plants and factories turned out an increasing amount of goods which more and more people enjoyed. Between 1859 and 1909, the annual average per capita income in dollars of constant purchasing power rose from $285 to $482, an increase of nearly 100 percent. This achievement, however, was not accomplished easily or without cost: in particular, the loss of independence and individuality. Besides this, an essentially rural people experienced agonizing adjustments as they sought to fit into an urban, industrial society. Industrialism, then, was more than factories, turbines, railroads, and mass production—it was a spirit, a way of life, which Americans had accepted.

SUGGESTED READINGS

The best general history of the late-nineteenth-century industrial economy is Edward C. Kirkland's *Industry Comes of Age: Business, Labor and Public Policy, 1860–1897** (1961). Older but still useful is Ida M. Tarbell's *The Nationalizing of Business, 1878–1898* (1936). Matthew Josephson presents a lively but extremely critical account of business leadership in *The Robber Barons: The Great American Capitalists, 1861–1901**. In *The Age of Big Business* (1919), Burton J. Hendrick provides a brief survey, while part of Thomas C. Cochran and William Miller's *The Age of Enterprise** (rev. ed., 1961) furnishes a good interpretation of the period. Samuel P. Hays traces the ways in which different groups responded to industrialism in *The Response to Industrialism, 1885–1914** (1957). The best assessment of American economic thought is Joseph Dorfman's *The Economic Mind in American Civilization, 1865–1918* (1949). For general economic trends see the excellent survey, *American Business Cycles, 1865–1897* (1959), by Rendigs Fels.

Railroads and their contribution to the nation's economic development have been studied in detail. The beginning student should start with John Moody's *Railroad Builders* (1919). Other general studies include *Railroad Leaders, 1845–1890* (1953) by Thomas C. Cochran; Edward C. Kirkland's *Men, Cities, and Transportation: A Study in New England History, 1820–1900* (1948); Julius Grodinsky's *Transcontinental Railway Strategy, 1869–1893* (1962); and John F. Stover's *The Railroads of the South, 1865–1900* (1955). Railroads also receive attention in Oscar Winther's *The Transportation Frontier: Trans-Mississippi West, 1865–1890* (1964). Ira B. Clark's *Then Came the Railroads: The Century from Steam to Diesel in the Southwest* (1958) is excellent. A highly controversial interpretation of the role of railroads can be found in Robert W. Fogel's *Railroads and American Economic Growth* (1964). Among the best studies of individual lines or systems are Richard C. Overton's *Burlington West* (1941); James B. Hedges's *Henry Villard and the Railways of the Northwest* (1930); *History of the Union Pacific* (1923) by Nelson Trottman; and the brief but interpretative account by Robert W. Fogel, *The Union Pacific Railroad: A Case Study in Premature Enterprise* (1960). Some of the best data on railroad history can be found in the biographies of railroad leaders: J. G. Pyle's *The Life of James J. Hill* (2 vols., 1917); Oscar Lewis's *The Big Four: The Story of Huntington, Stanford, Hopkins, and Crocker* (1938); Julius Grodinsky's *Jay Gould* (1957); and George Kennan's *E. H. Harriman* (2 vols., 1922).

On industrial development see Witt Bowden's *The Industrial History of the United States* (1930); V. S. Clark's *History of Manufactures in the United*

States (1929), vol. II; and the short, lively survey by Burton J. Hendrick, *The Age of Big Business* (1919). Industrial expansion in the South has been covered by Broadus Mitchell and G. S. Mitchell in *The Industrial Revolution in the South* (1930). Growth of large-scale corporate enterprise can be traced in the following business histories and biographical studies: Burton J. Hendrick's *The Life of Andrew Carnegie* (2 vols., 1932); Allan Nevins's *Study in Power: John D. Rockefeller, Industrialist and Philanthropist* (2 vols., 1953); Ralph W. and Muriel E. Hidy's *Pioneering in Big Business, 1882–1911: History of the Standard Oil Company* (1955); John C. Carroll's *Armour and His Times* (1938); William T. Hutchinson's *Cyrus Hall McCormick* (2 vols., 1930–1935); Joseph R. Smith's *The Story of Iron and Steel* (1918); and J. W. Jenkins's *James B. Duke* (1927). For a survey of technological advances see John W. Oliver's *History of American Technology* (1956), as well as studies on inventions such as Richard N. Current's *The Typewriter and the Men Who Made It* (1959) and H. C. Passer's more general *The Electric Manufacturers, 1875–1900* (1953).

There are several excellent studies on monopoly and attempts at government control of big business. Among the useful older works are John Moody's *The Truth about the Trusts* (1904); Myron W. Watkins's *Industrial Combinations and Public Policy* (1927); and Charles R. Van Hise's *Concentration and Control* (1912). Newer studies of antitrust policies are Clair Wilcox's *Public Policies toward Business* (1960); Simon H. Whitney's *Antitrust Policies: American Experience in Twenty Industries* (1955); and Hans B. Thorelli's *Federal Antitrust Policy* (1955). Gabriel Kolko argues in *Railroads and Regulation, 1877–1916* (1965) that the movement in favor of regulation was basically of a conservative character.

Edward C. Kirkland has examined the ideas of businessmen in *Dream and Thought in the Business Community, 1860–1900** (1956), while Sigmund Diamond views the public attitude toward rich business leaders in *The Reputation of the American Businessman* (1955).

*indicates availability in paperback.

22

Labor, Immigration, and Urbanization

THE INDUSTRIAL REVOLUTION meant a great deal more to American life than the building of factories and the production of goods. Among other things, it had a profound effect upon workingmen; it attracted millions of immigrants to the United States; and it contributed to the rapid growth of cities.

Between the Civil War and World War I, wage earners struggled to adjust to the factory system and to win a larger share of the fruits of industrialism. They sought to improve their position by organizing into unions in order to increase their bargaining power with employers. Workers also looked to both state and national governments for legislation favorable to labor. Although many laborers worked long hours for low wages and under rather unfavorable conditions, by the early twentieth century the position of workingmen had improved substantially.

Meanwhile, millions of immigrants streamed to America. Many of these newcomers went to Midwestern farms, but the great majority of them settled in the nation's growing industrial and commercial centers. The immigrants were city builders. With a steady flow of immigrants into American cities, and the vast internal movement of Americans from the farm to the city, the United States rapidly developed into a predominantly urban nation. By 1920 slightly more than half of the total population lived in what the Census Bureau classed as urban communities. This shift from a primarily agricultural nation to one principally industrial and urban was one of the most fundamental developments in the history of the country.

The Economic Position of Wage Earners

A marked change occurred in the employment of the nation's labor force after the Civil War. Early in the nineteenth century the great majority of workers were engaged in some phase of agriculture, but between 1860 and 1910 the total labor force in agricultural pursuits declined from 60 percent to only 31 percent. In the same period those employed in manufacturing establishments rose from 18 to 28 percent. As more and more workers came to be employed in factories, where they were dependent upon wages for their income, they lost any remaining self-sufficiency—either in terms of producing some of their own food and clothing or as independent skilled craftsmen.

Most workers admitted to themselves that they would never be self-employed, so their major objectives were better wages, shorter hours, and improved working conditions. In the late nineteenth century, hours were long, wages were low, and conditions of work were difficult when judged by modern standards. For example, in 1890 the average workweek for America's industrial workers was about 58 hours while average earnings were only 21 cents an hour. Twenty years later, the average workweek had dropped to 54.6 hours, and hourly pay had risen only to 28 cents. However, averages are deceiving, and the workweek for many factory workers was much longer, reaching 72 hours weekly in the iron and steel industry. In 1900 the average annual wage for workers in manufacturing was $435. Despite this seemingly low figure, real wages had risen about 48 percent between 1860 and 1890.

Among the basic economic changes which influenced the position of workingmen in the post-Civil War years were the development of large corporations, which employed hundreds and even thousands of workers; the increasingly interstate character of business; and the rapid mechanization of industry. The growing use of machines and the division of labor in factory production at first threatened, then finally destroyed, the historic position of many types of skilled craftsmen. Although the labor market expanded rapidly, most of the demand centered on semiskilled and unskilled wage earners to operate machinery.

The rise of huge corporate businesses also greatly changed the position of wage earners. When industry was in the hands of small individual enterprises or partnerships, there could be close relationships between workers and management. The owner of the business would be likely to be familiar with the needs and problems of his workmen through firsthand knowledge and contact. But in the case of industrial and transportation corporations such as Standard Oil or the New York Central Railroad, which employed hundreds of workers, the personal relationship between employer and employees vanished. By its very nature and organization, the corporation was impersonal. Moreover, the corporation was primarily interested in profit-making, and the personal needs of workers were given only secondary consideration. Labor was considered a commodity to be purchased at the cheapest possible price. The manager of one of New England's early textile factories expressed this situation: "I regard my workpeople just as I regard my machinery. So long as they can do my work for what I choose to pay them, I keep them, getting out of them all I can."

Although somewhat less basic, other problems also plagued wage earners in the late nineteenth century. The growing number of immigrants tended to depress wages; and the passing of the frontier about 1890, with the vanishing prospect of acquiring good farmland, either free or at cheap prices, ended any hope that factory or potential factory workers could move West. Very few workers actually ever left the factory and went to the farm, and Western lands did not provide a real safety valve for urban and industrial discontent. The main population movement, in contrast, was from farm to city. Nevertheless, the fact that there was the possibility of leaving industrial employment and seeking land may have had some effect in maintaining better working conditions and higher wage standards in America than in Europe. But more important was the fact that Western farms drew millions who, if land had not been available, would have joined the ranks of industrial labor and depressed wages below their current levels.

The problems which faced industrial wage earners in the "Age of Big Business" emphasized the need for unified action by the workers, but one of labor's major difficulties in the post-Civil War years was the lack of unity in its own ranks. No agreement could be reached among labor leaders and their followers on either basic objectives or the means of achieving them. Some leaders hoped to escape the wage system through cooperatives or some kind of general social or political reform, while others insisted that the labor movement should concentrate primarily on higher wages and shorter hours. Differences also arose over whether organized labor should attempt to aid both skilled and unskilled workers or whether it should concentrate only on improving the welfare of skilled craft workers. Unionization was also retarded because American workers were slow to give up the dream of self-employment and hesitated to accept the fact that there was little or no prospect of escape from industrial employment where they worked for someone else.

Organized Labor

Organization of the National Labor Union in 1866 was the first attempt of workers to form a genuine national union. Throughout its short existence the National Labor Union emphasized two major objectives: the eight-hour day and inflation. A leader in the National Labor Union and the strongest proponent of the eight-hour-day movement was Ira Steward, a thirty-five-year-old Boston machinist.

Beginning in 1867 the NLU devoted more and more attention to the money question. The idea of inflation was pleasing to those workers who wished to set up producer and consumer cooperatives. And forming cooperatives, many felt, would be a practical way to escape the wage system. William H. Sylvis, who became president of the NLU in 1868, declared: "We must adopt a system which will divide the *profits* of labor among those who produce them." As workers sought to establish a cooperative grocery store or foundry, they immediately ran into the problem of obtaining capital and credit. To meet this need, they proposed that the federal government inaugurate an interconvertible bond plan to provide working capital for as little as 3 percent interest. The Iron Molders Union, in which Sylvis was a prominent leader, established several cooperatively owned foundries in 1866, but these enterprises failed. In 1872 the NLU became involved in politics, and when its efforts were unsuccessful, the union collapsed and disappeared.

Of more importance was the Noble Order of the Knights of Labor. Organized in Philadelphia in 1869 by Uriah S. Stephens, the Knights was a secret organization which attempted to bring together all workers into one big union. Although most of the early membership consisted of skilled trade unionists, the union was open to unskilled, semiskilled, men, women, and anyone else who was "working for wages or who at any time worked for wages," without regard to sex, color, race, or position. Even farmers and small businessmen were welcome. Secrecy was considered essential in order to keep management from learning of the union's plans.

The major or "first principles" of the Knights of Labor included education "to create a healthy public opinion on the subject of labor"; a legislative program which would benefit workingmen; and the formation of mutual benefit societies and cooperatives. In laying down this basic program, Stephens argued that labor must organize to protect its fundamental welfare. Yet, he declared, "we mean no conflict with legitimate enterprise, no antagonism to necessary capital." The Knights were not interested in any class struggle. They really hoped to bring about a new order of society through cooperative effort. Here was another attempt by organized labor to escape what Stephens called "wage slavery."

The Knights of Labor grew very slowly because of both hard times following the Panic of 1873 and employers' strong opposition to unionization. By 1878 the Knights had only 9,287 members. The hostility of employers resulted in blacklisting trade union leaders, lockouts, and legal prosecutions. To protect their interests, workers struck back in a series of bitterly fought strikes during the late 1870s. Among the most notable labor-management disputes were those involving coal miners in Pennsylvania, cigar makers in New York, textile workers in Massachusetts, and railroad employees in many parts of the country. Perhaps the most publicized conflicts were the Great Railroad Strikes of 1877, which began in July against the Baltimore and Ohio Railroad at Martinsburg, West Virginia. After a second 10 percent wage cut, the workers refused to permit trains to move either east or west until their wages were restored. Two hundred federal troops arrived after two days, and the strike was broken, but meanwhile the strike had spread to other cities and to other railroads. In Pittsburgh, a strike against the Pennsylvania Railway created such a tense situation that both the local militia and state troops from Philadelphia were brought in to preserve order. The attempt by the soldiers to clear the tracks on July 21 resulted in a pitched battle between the troops and strikers supported by an unruly mob. When the smoke cleared, twenty-six persons were dead. An outbreak of violence, looting, and burning followed, which took more lives and destroyed railroad property valued at some $5 million before order was restored.

Labor unrest in 1877 was not confined to the East. At the very time troops were restoring law and order in Pennsylvania, radical labor activity was developing in California under the leadership of Denis Kearney. The organized agitation by workers was aimed at the Chinese, who, it was charged, worked for lower wages and took jobs from native Americans. A violent anti-Chinese demonstration began in San Francisco on July 23 and lasted for two days, during which time $100,000 worth of property was destroyed. Later in 1877, Kearney was elected president of the Workingmen's party on a platform which demanded unity among workingmen, opposition to the Chinese, and destruction of land and financial monopolies.

The first national assembly of the Knights of Labor took place about six months after the disorders in San Francisco and Pittsburgh. These events had emphasized the need for a genuine national labor organization, but the question still remained unanswered as to whether the Knights could fulfill this need. At their first national meeting early in 1878 the Knights reiterated their faith in education, cooperation, and legislation, but the Order then broadened its demands to attract wider support. The assembly urged that public lands be reserved for actual settlers and favored the establishment of a federal bureau of labor statistics, the abolition of the contract labor system, and the acceptance of the eight-hour day.

In 1879 the Knights of Labor entered a new phase of its history. Up to that time the various assemblies had clung to the first principles and had largely avoided strikes. But in that year Terence V. Powderly replaced founder Stephens as Grand Master Workman. Although Powderly advised caution in matters of strikes, the Knights became more aggressive after 1880 and turned increasingly to strikes and boycotts as means of achieving their objectives. A few of these local strikes were successful, but labor lost most of the important disputes. However, successful strikes against the Union Pacific in 1884 and Jay Gould's Wabash; Missouri, Kansas and Texas; and Missouri Pacific Railroads in February and March of 1885 brought a flood of members into the union's ranks. Hundreds of locals were formed within a few months, and between 1885 and early 1886, membership in the Knights increased from 111,395 to 729,677. But these successes gave labor a false sense of power, for the fundamental weaknesses of the Knights soon became evident. In March, 1886, another strike against Gould's southwestern railroads showed where the real economic power lay. Gould brought in strikebreakers and refused to negotiate any of the disputed points with workers. In time the employees had to give in on every issue.

Despite the prominence of strikes and boycotts in the activities of the Knights of Labor after 1880, Powderly and other leaders continued to emphasize the desirability of establishing cooperatives. Most members were reluctant to support this idea until they saw the futility of strikes. By 1885, there was a strong demand among rank-and-file members to set up productive cooperatives as well as a few cooperatively owned distribution outlets. Organized labor established scores of cooperative enterprises between 1884 and 1887, including mines and foundries. But most of the businesses were small and had a brief existence. Some labor cooperatives were forced out of business by bitter competition from private enterprise, while others failed because of inefficient management and lack of capital. Never again did American labor make cooperation a major objective.

The cooperatives' failure and the loss of important strikes were two of the most obvious reasons why membership in the Knights of Labor dropped from more than seven hundred thousand to about one hundred thousand between 1885 and 1890. But there were even

The New American and Organized Labor

Dynamic applications of technology between the Civil War and World War I enabled the United States to settle its frontiers and to become a leading industrial power. There were two major human results: a mammoth wave of immigration into the country, and the first widespread organization of working men into labor unions. Immigration and unionization inevitably affected each other.

Twenty-three million foreign-born came to America between 1860 and 1910 in a movement which reached progressively higher levels: 2.8 million in the 1870s, 5.2 million in the 1880s, 8.8 million from 1900 to 1910. Prior to 1890 a majority of the immigrants came grom Great Britain, Germany, and the Scandinavian countries, and many of them, spurred on by aggressive advertising of railroads and the states, settled on the cheap farm lands of the West. When most of the cheap and free lands were taken, the next wave of immigrants, from Middle Europe, Italy, and Russia for the most part, settled in or near the growing industrial centers. The handsome Italian family above, photographed by Lewis W. Hine as they prepared to debark at Ellis Island in New York in 1905, was a part of this wave.

George Eastman House Collection

The increasing flow of new immigrants provided the labor and much of the intellectual talent that made the United States an industrial leader among the nations of the world. But their presence in large numbers also tended to depress wages. In 1890 the average work week was 58 hours (72 hours in the iron and steel industry) and average earnings were 21 cents per hour. By 1900 the average annual wage for manufacturing workers was $435. As individuals, the workers had little chance of making themselves heard by the increasingly impersonal managements of industry which could easily dip into the pool of immigrant labor to replace the worker who asked too insistently for higher wages. In this situation, labor could find strength only in organization.

For many immigrants, such as those shown on deck in New York harbor in 1906 (following spread, left), the move to the United States proved an exhausting physical and psychological ordeal. It began in crowded steerage quarters aboard ship, and in many cases ended when the immigrant was tagged to be sent off to an inland destination. In between periods of quarantine, red tape, strange surroundings and tongues, and physical and mental tests assaulted the senses. On the following page, immigrants receive physical tests at Ellis Island (above) and undergo intelligence tests (below). At the right, an Italian family photographed by Lewis Hine searches the pier for their lost baggage.

Above: Brown Brothers; right: George Eastman House Collection; all others: Library of Congress

Left and center: The Tamiment Institute Library; above and below: Library of Congress

Leaders in the labor movement in the three decades following the Civil War interested themselves in a wide range of measures which would benefit all of labor, rather than concentrating on wage gains for workers in specific crafts and trades. William H. Sylvis (above, left), president of the National Labor Union, in 1868, believed, "We must adopt a system which will divide the profits of labor among those who produce them." Uriah S. Stephens (above, center) organized the Knights of Labor in 1869 as a secret organization in the hope of bringing about a new order of society through cooperative effort. Terrence Powderly (right) who took leadership of the Knights in 1879, stood against secrecy for the Knights, for caution in strikes, and for labor sharing the benefits of production through cooperatives. Here Powderly is introduced at the tenth annual convention of the Knights in 1886 by delegate Frank J. Farrell. Women delegates also came to the 1886 convention of the Knights (above, right). Many early unionists supported women's rights and suffrage.

In response to a 10 percent wage cut, railroad workers in 1877 staged strikes across the country which soon became violent. The cavalry charged demonstrators in Chicago, (below) and rioters burned the Lebanon Valley Bridge (far right). But the Knights declined after 1885, and for the balance of the century, workers lost most of their disputes. The 1892 strike against the Carnegie Steel Works at Homestead, Pa. (right), was among the most bitterly fought defeats.

All pictures: Courtesy of the New-York Historical Society, New York City

Above: Culver Pictures, Inc.; below: Library of Congress

The International Workers of the World led one of the most widely publicized strikes of the period before World War I in Lawrence, Mass., in 1912. Above, Massachusetts militia confront the striking Lawrence textile workers. Protesting a reduction in wages, the strikers clashed with police when management attempted to reopen the struck mills. One woman was killed, and nationwide sympathy for the strikers created such pressure on management that they got their increases. The police car below, used in the Cincinnati strike of 1910, symbolizes the violence that recurred again and again in labor disputes.

more fundamental factors which caused the gradual extinction of the Order. In the first place, the Knights lacked unity and solidarity. It had proven impossible to weld so many different kinds and classes of labor into a single effective organization. The Knights of Labor suffered most of all from a growing lack of support among the skilled workers in the trade unions, who had little faith in the prospect of organizing all workers into one big union or of ever escaping the wage system. Also, the violence associated with the Haymarket Riot in Chicago in May, 1886, hurt the Knights of Labor as well as the entire labor movement. This unfortunate incident grew out of a strike against the McCormick Harvester Works in Chicago and resulted in the death of four people.

Despite the progressive decline of the Knights of Labor after 1886, the Order had made some valuable contributions during a period when labor was struggling to find direction and purpose. It was largely due to pressure from the Knights that Congress abolished contract labor in February, 1885. The Knights also played a part in persuading Congress to establish a federal Bureau of Labor Statistics in 1884. Finally, the Noble Order stimulated general labor sentiment against monopoly and, in this sense, created at least some spirit of unity among workers.

Meanwhile, a basically different type of labor organization was emerging. The new movement was based on the idea that the best hope for workingmen lay in organizing strong, independent trade unions. In the late 1870s and early 1880s, trade unions experienced a marked revival, following their heavy losses after 1873. Leaders such as Samuel Gompers and Adolph Strasser of the Cigarmakers were among the trade union leaders who opposed the political approach of the National Labor Union and rejected the one-big-union policy of the Knights as impractical and unrealistic. Gompers and Strasser believed in a simple wage-conscious philosophy which held that trade unions should be strengthened in order to bargain effectively with employers rather than to serve as a steppingstone to self-employment. This type of wage consciousness rejected cooperatives, greenbackism, socialism, and other general reforms which were designed to replace the wage system. The main objective of this type of unionism was the increase of bargaining power for workers within the existing capitalistic framework.

In December, 1886, delegates claiming to represent more than 300,000 trade union members met in Columbus, Ohio, to form the American Federation of Labor. The preamble of the AF of L constitution declared that because of the struggle between the "oppressors and the oppressed of all countries," workers must combine for "mutual protection and benefit." Samuel Gompers was elected the first president, and from 1886 until his death in 1924, Gompers was the driving force behind the growth and development of the AF of L. It was this short, stocky, immigrant cigar maker of Dutch-Jewish ancestry who set the tone and direction of the organization.

Having abandoned any idea of escaping the wage system, the AF of L sought to increase the power of individual trade unions so they could bargain more effectively with employers. If bargaining failed, then the union would resort to strikes and boycotts as a means of exerting economic pressure on management. To improve their elusive bargaining position, the AF of L unions levied dues on their members for the purpose of building up strike funds and providing other benefits to workers. The

AF of L accepted the capitalistic system but was determined that labor should enjoy more of its benefits. The emphasis was upon immediate and practical goals such as higher wages, shorter hours, and better working conditions. This was a philosophy of opportunism. When Strasser was asked about the ultimate aims of the AF of L, he declared: "We have no ultimate ends. We are going on from day to day. We are fighting only for immediate objects." Gompers referred to the whole AF of L approach as "pure and simple unionism." Since the AF of L believed primarily in economic action, it strongly opposed any affiliation with political parties. Instead, the AF of L rewarded their friends and punished their enemies at the polls. Gompers and most AF of L leaders also opposed any alliance or affiliation with radical or revolutionary groups.

Organization of the AF of L was the real beginning of the modern labor movement, and for the next half century it was the principal representative of organized workers in the United States, although, because of internal dissension, the failure of some strikes, and the hard times which followed the Panic of 1893, membership grew slowly before 1898. In that year the Federation could claim only 265,000 members, not many more than a decade earlier. But after the return of prosperity in 1899, membership increased rapidly. By 1914 the AF of L boasted 2,021,000 members, or about 79 percent of organized labor.

Despite its apparent success, the AF of L failed to organize workers in the principal mass-production industries such as coal, oil, and steel. Furthermore, many unions which were only becoming established in the late 1880s were crushed by the bitter opposition from employers and by the depression of the 1890s. For example, in June, 1892, a strike by Amalgamated Association of Iron and Steel Workers against the Carnegie Steel Works at Homestead, Pennsylvania, failed completely. After considerable bloodshed as a result of fighting between workers and Pinkerton detectives, the Governor called out the state militia to restore order and break the strike.

Labor lost another important industrial conflict in the Pullman strike of 1894. The Pullman Company had recently cut wages; and when it refused to negotiate any of the differences with its employees, the local unions voted to strike. This developed into a lockout by the company. The American Railway Union, representing some 150,000 railroad workers and headed by Eugene V. Debs, held its annual meeting in Chicago during June and urged arbitration between the company and the Pullman workers. When Pullman declined this suggestion, the ARU voted to quit handling Pullman cars. Nothing changed in train operations except that Pullman cars were disconnected. When workers refused to handle Pullman cars they were fired, and in turn the whole crew would quit, tying up the train. By early July most Midwestern lines were affected.

The contest soon became one between the American Railway Union and the General Managers' Association which represented the railroads. The General Managers' Association brought in strikebreakers and, to keep the trains moving, succeeded in getting about 3,400 supporters of the roads deputized as federal marshals. Considerable violence and damage to property occurred in the first days of July, and this served as an excuse for the actions which finally defeated the strikers. On July 2 railroad officials obtained a federal district court injunction prohibiting any interference with the mails or the transportation of goods in interstate commerce. The next step was for President Cleveland to send in federal troops on the pretense that local and state authorities could not maintain order. These actions by the government completely crushed the strike. Governor John P. Altgeld of Illinois, a friend of labor, heatedly protested the sending of federal troops to Chicago, but the President insisted that it was necessary to keep the mails moving and to preserve law and order. In the aftermath Debs and several associates were indicted for violating the court injunction, and the ARU president was sentenced to six months in jail.

A small, but hard-core, radical labor movement existed in the United States between the Civil War and World War I, but it never achieved much of a following. Made up of Socialists, Anarchists, and Syndicalists, the radicals called for fundamental changes in the American industrial and labor system. Organized in 1877, the Socialist Labor party entered local elections in such cities as Chicago and New York and attempted to infiltrate the trade union movement. The Socialists made very little headway, however, until the 1890s when Eugene V. Debs emerged as the movement's principal leader. He proposed a program of public ownership of basic industries and transportation, abolition of the wage system, and a number of more moderate reforms. By 1901 Debs had united most of the Socialists into the Socialist Party of America. Some workers, however, considered Debs too conservative, and in June, 1905, a group of these radicals met in Chicago and organized the Industrial Workers of the World. Headed by William D. ("Big Bill") Haywood, a onetime farmer, miner, and labor organizer, the IWW advocated direct and violent action to overthrow the capitalistic system. Haywood talked freely of using the bomb and the torch. One basic IWW statement said that workers and employers had nothing in common, that "between these two classes a struggle must go on until the workers of the world organize as a class, take possession of the earth and machinery of production and abolish the wage system." The IWW set out to organize miners, migratory farm and lumber workers, immigrant textile workers, and others who had been largely ignored by the regular trade unions. But the extreme radicalism of the IWW had only a limited appeal, and the organization probably never had more than 60,000 members.

The radical labor movement never had a strong hold on American workingmen. The idea of overthrowing the capitalistic system and establishing a socialist state never gained much support among workers because it was contrary to American middle-class concepts and traditions. The Socialist attack on private property was considered to be not only bad economics but un-American. Most citizens did not believe in the inevitable struggle between the worker and employer classes postulated by Karl Marx. The fluidity of American society permitted many citizens to improve their economic and social conditions to such an extent that they had no desire to change the economic system which made this possible.

Government and Labor

Although the American Federation of Labor sought its main objectives through trade union action, labor as a whole gained substantial benefits from both state and national legislation between 1865 and World War I. During those years a sizable body of labor law was enacted to protect and improve the position of workers. Union leaders usually gave their support to labor legislation, but most of the political pressure was exerted by middle-class reformers. This was especially true during the progressive movement after 1900. Even though legislators were often slow in passing reforms desired by labor, they were less responsible for obstructing progress than were the courts.

As explained earlier, the federal government inaugurated an eight-hour day on public works in 1868, set up a Bureau of Labor Statistics in 1884, and abolished contract labor in 1885. In 1903 Congress created a Department of Commerce and Labor. A separate Department of Labor was given full Cabinet status in 1913. Congress passed a federal employer's liability law in 1908 which provided compensation for certain government employees in case of accidental injury. In 1914 a section of the Clayton Antitrust Act forbade court injunctions in labor disputes unless they were necessary "to prevent irreparable injury to property." The La Follette Seamen's Act of 1915 did much to improve the wages and working conditions of men on American merchant vessels, and the next year the Adamson Act established an eight-hour day for the nation's railroad workers. Congress also passed the Keating-Owen bill in 1916 forbidding the interstate shipment of mine products produced by children under sixteen and products from factories which hired children under fourteen. This effort to protect children failed. In 1918 the Supreme Court declared the law unconstitutional.

The states passed even more significant labor legislation. By 1916 when the Keating-Owen bill was passed, some thirty-seven states had enacted child-labor laws. Often these were tied to compulsory school attendance. A number of states also tried to limit the hours of work in certain dangerous occupations or among specific classes of workers. As early as 1874 Massachusetts passed an effective measure limiting the work of women and children in factories to ten hours daily. In 1896 Utah enacted a law which restricted work in mines to eight hours a day. Oregon passed a law regulating the hours of work for women in 1903, and this law was upheld by the Supreme Court in 1908 in the case of *Muller v. Oregon*. A New York law providing a ten-hour day for bakers had been declared unconstitutional in *Lochner v. New York* in 1905, but later the Court relaxed its position on this question. Other matters of vital interest to workers were workmen's compensation and employer's liability laws. Wisconsin passed an employer's liability law for railroad workers in 1875, and many other states enacted similar prolabor laws between 1880 and 1910. These laws were generally limited to specific occupations and actually did not go much beyond lessening the legal obstacles for workers in injury suits. Although Maryland and Montana had passed workmen's compensation statutes earlier, the New York law of 1910 set the pattern. Labor would have received more benefits from state and federal lawmakers if the courts had not declared many laws unconstitutional.

Immigration

Some of the problems of labor in the late nineteenth century were directly or indirectly associated with the quickening flow of immigration. Millions of European immigrants eagerly sought jobs in mining, manufacturing, and transportation at wages which were little above

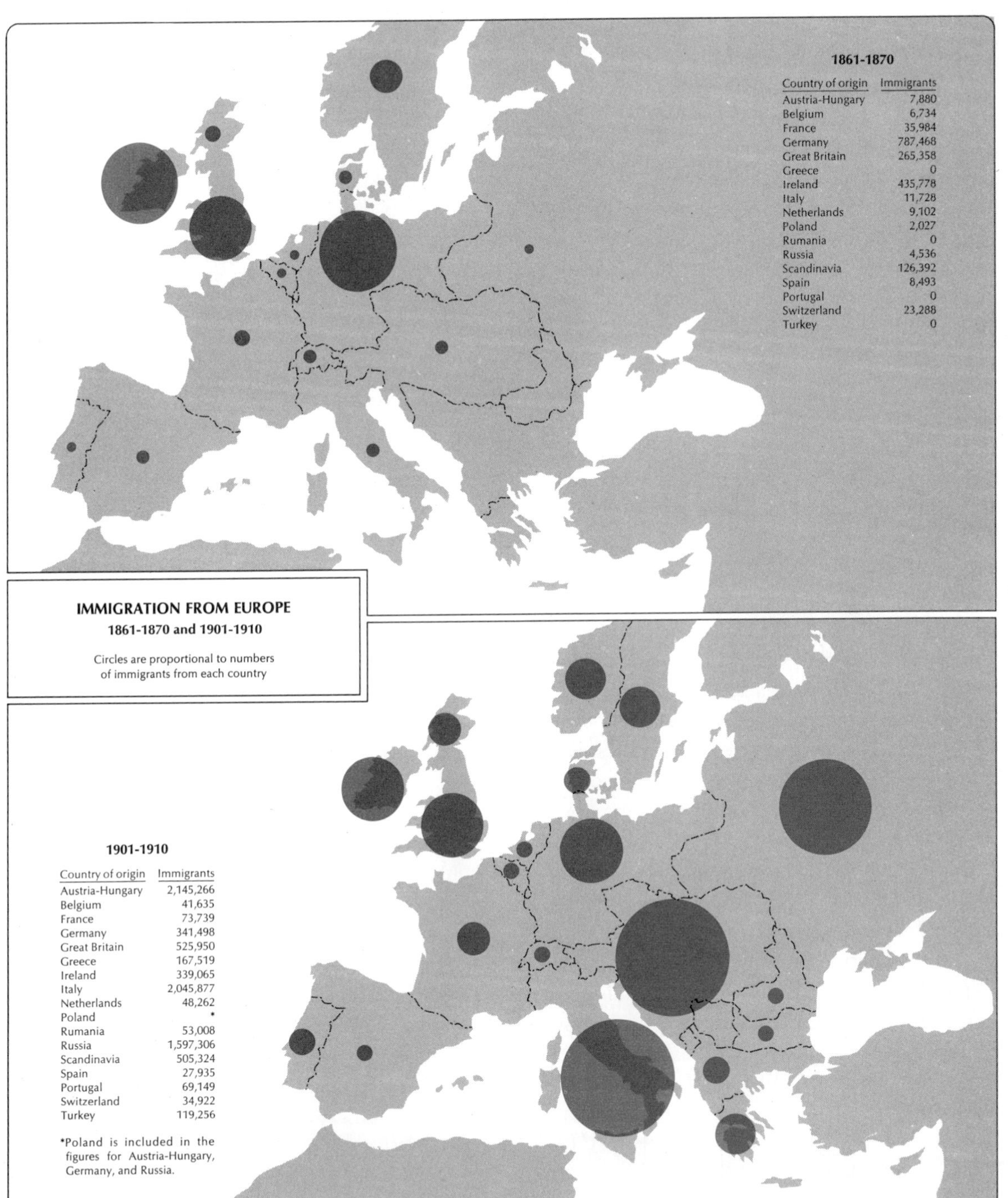

1861-1870
Country of origin Immigrants
Austria-Hungary 7,880
Belgium 6,734
France 35,984
Germany 787,468
Great Britain 265,358
Greece 0
Ireland 435,778
Italy 11,728
Netherlands 9,102
Poland 2,027
Rumania 0
Russia 4,536
Scandinavia 126,392
Spain 8,493
Portugal 0
Switzerland 23,288
Turkey 0
IMMIGRATION FROM EUROPE
1861-1870 and 1901-1910
Circles are proportional to numbers of immigrants from each country
1901-1910
Country of origin Immigrants
Austria-Hungary 2,145,266
Belgium 41,635
France 73,739
Germany 341,498
Great Britain 525,950
Greece 167,519
Ireland 339,065
Italy 2,045,877
Netherlands 48,262
Poland *
Rumania 53,008
Russia 1,597,306
Scandinavia 505,324
Spain 27,935
Portugal 69,149
Switzerland 34,922
Turkey 119,256
*Poland is included in the figures for Austria-Hungary, Germany, and Russia.

the subsistence level. It was relatively easy for employers to resist demands for wage increases so long as there was a steady influx of penniless immigrants who required immediate employment. There was almost a constant surplus of labor in the post-Civil War years, and during long periods of depression in the 1870s and 1890s unemployment and underemployment were high. But even so, wages were better in the United States than in Europe, and most immigrants were able to live better in America than they had as peasants in Europe.

In the half century between 1860 and 1910, some twenty-three million foreigners migrated to America. As had been true before the Civil War, most of them came in search of better economic opportunities. America had always been considered a land of hope and opportunity where men could gain a new start in life. But besides this, there were new forces at work in both the United States and Europe which interacted to attract ever-increasing numbers of immigrants. In the first place the United States needed much more labor to develop its farmlands and man its factories and mines than before 1860. Consequently, many agencies encouraged Europeans to migrate to America. At the same time, conditions in Europe stimulated immigration as farmers and farm laborers in England, Ireland, the Scandinavian countries, and Germany experienced frequent periods of crop failures, low prices, and hard times.

The same pattern of immigration established before the Civil War continued down to about 1890, with the main body of immigrants arriving from Northern and Western Europe. In the 1880s about 72 percent of all immigrants came from that part of Europe. Hundreds of thousands of Scandinavians settled on Midwestern farms as well as in such cities as Milwaukee, Chicago, and Cincinnati. Most immigrants from England and Ireland remained in the eastern seaboard cities. Very few immigrants settled in the South, because that section provided neither the agricultural nor the industrial opportunities which they were seeking.

By 1890 the tide of immigration from Northern and Western Europe began to decline, and the so-called old immigration, the nationals who had historically peopled America, was soon replaced by the "new immigration" from Southern and Eastern Europe. The change which took place can best be seen in the figures. Between 1881 and 1890 only 18 percent of American immigrants originated in the countries of Southeastern Europe, but in the decade from 1891 to 1900 this number reached 71 percent. The chief sources of the new immigration were the Austro-Hungarian Empire, Italy, and Russia, in that order. But thousands of Greeks, Syrians, Poles, and Orientals also arrived. Most immigrants from Eastern Europe were Catholics, but in their numbers were thousands of Jews.

These millions of new immigrants moved to the United States for about the same reasons as the Northern and Western Europeans. Basic economic changes throughout much of the Austro-Hungarian Empire and in parts of Italy had a disastrous influence upon peasants and agricultural laborers. The redistribution of land, tariff restrictions, and other economic influences left peasants in difficult circumstances. In Russia, religious and political factors, as well as hard times, encouraged emigration. Seeking to escape persecution, large numbers of Russo-German Mennonites and other pietist groups left Russia and settled in the Dakotas, Nebraska, and Kansas.

Although the new immigrants were a rural, peasant people, most of them settled in the growing industrial centers of the Northeast and Midwest rather than on farms. It was this multitude of Italians, Russians, Austrians, Croatians, Bohemians, Hungarians, and Poles which supplied the cheap labor for America's industrial revolution. By the early 1900s they had taken over most of the jobs in mines, textile mills, and certain other manufacturing industries. The new immigrants were industrial workers and city builders. Whatever their preferences, they could not have entered farming, for they lacked both the capital and the farming experience to succeed on the Western plains; and, in any event, most of the good land was already occupied when the new immigrants arrived. By the time large numbers of Southern and Eastern Europeans reached the United States, there was even a strong trend away from the farm by native Americans themselves.

Since America was a nation peopled by immigrants, the immigrant contribution had always been great. This was no less true of those who arrived in the late nineteenth century than of those who had immigrated earlier. Yet by the 1870s, a demand arose to restrict immigration. The campaign against the Chinese by Denis Kearney and his followers in the late 1870s resulted in passage of the Chinese Exclusion Act of 1882. The same year Congress also forbade the entrance of certain undesirables—convicts, lunatics, idiots, and those who might become public charges. These laws were selective and were designed to meet only specific problems; they did not reverse previous immigration policy by demanding general restriction. But a move calling for more general restriction was beginning to gain support. It was not immigration as such, but the type of immigration, which stimulated the growing demand for some form of general restrictive legislation. From time to time, there had been sporadic outbursts of nativism in American history; by the late 1880s, nativists were seeing something sinister and dangerous in the influx of Italians, Slavs, Jews, and others from Southern and Eastern Europe. The American Protective Association organized in 1887 was mainly opposed to Catholics, but it also worked to curb the influx of all foreigners. Critics of unlimited immigration argued that these new immigrants were clannish and did not become assimilated as quickly or completely as those from Northern and Western Europe. Moreover, some argued that the immigrants from Southern and Eastern Europe were racially inferior, a view which stemmed from a feeling of Nordic superiority. Others said that the new immigrants and some of the older ones were radical and unsympathetic to American middle-class traditions.

By the 1890s Congress could not ignore the demand for immigration restriction. In 1897 lawmakers passed a measure sponsored by Senator Henry Cabot Lodge of Massachusetts which required a literacy test of all immigrants. This bill was clearly aimed at Southern and Eastern Europeans, among whom illiteracy was high. President Cleveland, however, vetoed the measure. But from this time forward there was a relentless drive to obtain some type of immigration restriction. Finally, in 1917 Congress passed a law over President Wilson's veto which denied admittance to aliens over sixteen who could not read English or some other language. The head tax was also raised to $8. The law of 1917 represented a definite change in American immigration policy. It was the first major step toward strict limitation and replaced the concept of selection, which had been designed to keep out only certain specified groups like the Chinese.

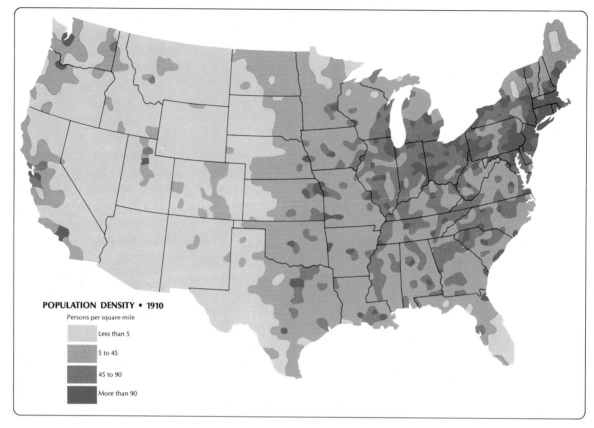

POPULATION DENSITY • 1910

Persons per square mile

Less than 5

5 to 45

45 to 90

More than 90

Urban America

In 1860 the United States was predominantly rural. Most people were engaged in agriculture, and about 80 percent of the population actually resided on farms or in small villages. Only 20 percent lived in towns and cities of 2,500 or more, the census definition of an urban area after 1880. Of all the nation's cities, New York alone had more than one million people, and only eight cities could boast more than 100,000. But the transition from a rural to a predominantly urban nation was one of the most notable developments in American history following the Civil War. This trend was all the more remarkable because of the speed with which it occurred. By 1900 urbanization, with all of its benefits, problems, and prospects for a fuller life, became the mark of a truly modern America.

The changing physical landscape reflected the shift to an urbanized society. Railroad terminals, smoking factories, skyscrapers, apartment houses, street cars, electric turbines, and department stores were all signs of an emerging urban America. A further evidence of change was the increased pace of life in the cities. Indeed, the vitality, dynamic quality, variety, and restless experimentalism in society centered in the urban communities where the only constant factor was change itself. Although many Americans expressed regret at the grow-

ing predominance of the city, those who held to rural standards and values fought a losing battle. The isolated, static, and individualistic character of rural society was no match for the excitement, opportunities, and challenge offered by the nation's growing cities.

Urbanization did not proceed uniformly throughout the nation. New England and the Middle Atlantic states contained the highest percentage of city dwellers. In Massachusetts, for example, nearly 93 percent of the people lived in cities by 1910; in New York that figure reached 79 percent. In the older Middle West the growth of cities such as Chicago, Milwaukee, Cleveland, and St. Louis indicated the importance of urbanization in that region. The three West Coast states also experienced rapid urban growth. On the other hand, urbanization developed much more slowly in the South, although by 1910, the expansion of transportation, commerce, and industry had greatly increased the population of older cities such as New Orleans and stimulated the growth of new urban centers like Birmingham. However, the South remained predominantly rural in the nineteenth and early twentieth centuries. Only somewhat more than 20 percent of the population in that region was urban by 1910.

In some regions the urban impact had a depressing effect upon the surrounding rural communities. Much of New England presented a discouraging picture of abandoned farms and sickly villages in the late nineteenth century as people forsook the countryside and rushed to the larger towns and cities. In the 1880s hundreds of townships in New England lost population. Commenting on a nearly deserted village in Vermont, one observer wrote: "The church was abandoned, the academy dismantled, the village lived on one side of the broad street, and he who owned the farm on the south lived on the other, and they were the only inhabitants." Even in Ohio and Illinois hundreds of rural townships lost population in the 1880s, even though both states made substantial gains in total population. Throughout much of the United States the rural world was contracting at the expense of the burgeoning cities.

The Pull of the City

In 1871 a Milwaukee editor wrote that sooner or later "the young man in the country . . . will be sucked into one of the great [urban] centers of life." And so it was in the late nineteenth century, as country and village boys filled the roads and highways on their way to the towns and cities. What created the irresistible pull of the cities? First of all, it is significant to note that the city had always been the nerve center of civilization. This was no less true in the United States than in ancient Greece or medieval Europe. Cities normally provided a wide variety of services; they were the cultural, religious, educational, and entertainment centers; and perhaps most important, cities provided many types of economic opportunity for restless and ambitious individuals. Undoubtedly, more people migrated from farms to towns and cities because they believed they could improve their economic position than for any other reason.

Indeed, the Rockefellers, Carnegies, Vanderbilts, and other tremendously rich Americans in the late nineteenth century made their money in city-based businesses. These successes convinced many farm youths that in the city any achievement was possible. Streams of success literature emphasized this thesis. Although very few migrants to the cities ever became millionaires, their chances of earning a larger income and enjoying a higher standard of living were better there than on the farm. Employees in urban factories averaged between $400 and $500 annually in 1900, compared with only $260 for farm workers.

The concentration of population and the accumulation of wealth in the cities made possible many social and cultural advantages not found in the more isolated rural communities. The towns and cities supported libraries, theaters, opera, music conservatories, art galleries, and other cultural and educational institutions. Probably most urbanites ignored these cultural opportunities because of disinterest or lack of money, but their availability added greatly to the city's attractiveness. An increasing number of country people considered a Saturday trip to town, the country fair, a meeting of the literary society, occasional picnics, and other rural amusements much less exciting than a dramatic production, a musical, or even a prizefight staged in the cities. Urban communities had better schools, churches, newspapers, and medical services. City living not only promised higher living standards, but greater cultural, educational, and recreational enjoyments as well. As one observer wrote: one could "shop better, . . . dress more fashionably, . . . give parties more conveniently, . . . get better concerts, and see more sights."

Problems of Urbanization

Rapid urbanization created a host of difficult problems. What blighted city life for many was the absence of adequate housing. Unable to afford individual houses or good apartments, newcomers crowded into cramped and filthy tenements, which were built in large numbers after the 1880s. Tenements were usually four to six stories high, with each floor divided into several family units consisting of two to four poorly ventilated and dimly lighted rooms. Many tenement rooms had no outside exposure whatever. One unfortunate family in New York lived as follows: "The man, his wife, and three small children shivering in one room through the roof of which the pitiless winds of winter whistled. The room was almost barren of furniture; the parents slept on the floor, the elder children in boxes, and the baby was swung in an old shawl attached to the rafters." Describing the Italian section in New York, another observer wrote: "Here the mud, dirt, and filth, the stinking humidity, the incumbrances, the disorder of the streets are beyond description." Although conditions in the tenements were well known, it was not until Jacob Riis published his book *How the Other Half Lives* in 1890 that widespread public attention was drawn to the economic, social, and political problems arising out of slum conditions.

Millions of new urbanites also suffered from a lack of such public services as running water, garbage disposal, and general sanitation. As late as the 1870s, hogs ran loose eating the refuse in the city streets. Sewage was often dumped in the closest river or lake without any precautions taken to guard the general health. Adequate water was frequently a problem, and it was not uncommon for several urban families to rely on a single outlet. The danger of fire was always present. The conges-

The completion of the Brooklyn Bridge, shown here under construction, in 1883 caused a problem typical of city growth. Because travel to and from Brooklyn became easier, more transients came into the city. Six days after the bridge opened, traffic was so heavy that the creaking of the bridge caused a panic in which twelve people were killed as they scrambled for shore. The building of the New York subways also succeeded in transporting bigger crowds to already crowded areas.

The Big City

Drawn by the promises of greater opportunities, wealth, and excitement, rural residents and immigrants from Europe poured into America's cities following the Civil War—an influx of such proportions that it rapidly changed the very quality of city living and engendered problems which still remain unsolved. The urban population, which in 1860 constituted 20 percent of the national total, had by 1900 grown to some 40 per cent.

The growth of New York City can be taken as symptomatic of the trend toward urbanization which affected other metropolitan areas of the nation. By 1860 New York was already the third largest city in the world, with a population of about 800,000, but in the dynamic development of the postwar period, bigness begat even greater bigness: by 1910 the population of greater New York stood at nearly five million.

The Brooklyn Public Library

All pictures: Library of Congress

Rapid growth caused overcrowding in housing and public facilities as this tenement cross-section and the inset 1873 scene at Bellevue Hospital (below) indicate. But New York flourished as a cultural center. Fashionable ladies in 1873 rode the Lord and Taylor department store elevator (near left). The scenes at the far left show the annual cleaning of the paintings at the National Arts Club and the opening of the Museum of Natural History at its new Central Park building in 1877.

For the poor who immigrated to New York, the crowded, impersonal city proved a difficult place to live and raise a family. The poor suffered most from sanitation problems like that shown in the 1893 Riis photograph, left, below. The indifference or outright hostility of the city led many immigrants to join organizations based on their national origin in an effort to regain some sense of community and a political voice.

The New York City families at right were photographed about 1910.

Left, above, and both right: Brown Brothers; left, below: Photograph by Jacob A. Riis, The Jacob A. Riis Collection, Museum of the City of New York

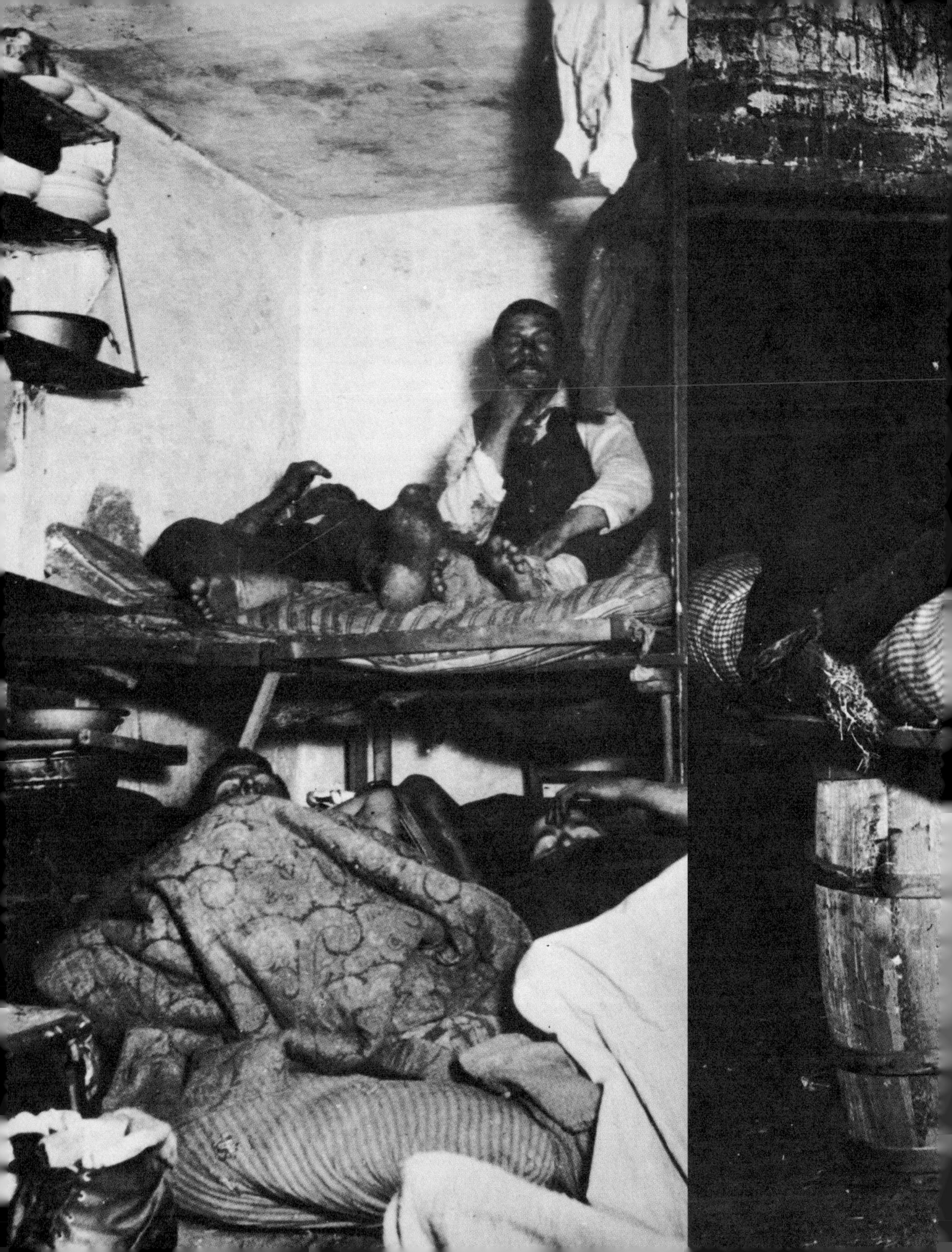

The full horror of life among the very poor in New York came to public attention via the writing and the photographs of Danish-born Jacob Riis, author in 1890 of *How The Other Half Lives.* The photograph at far left shows an airless lodging where a night's sleeping space could be bought for five cents. The man at near left had been sleeping in this cellar for four years when Riis photographed him. The two street waifs below told Riis they "didn't live nowhere." In 1900 the New York State Tenement House Commission reported that 43,000 Manhattan tenement houses, inhabited by more than a million people, failed to provide adequate light and air, perfect sanitation or "even passable home environment."

When city government could not handle the human problems that rose out of rapid urbanization, private organizations and charities tried to fill the vacuum (following page). Below, a visiting nurse crosses the housetops of the lower East Side on her rounds. Right, above, a volunteer from a Jewish women's charitable group reads to a patient. Right, below, babies were taken in at the New York City Lodging House, a temporary refuge provided for the penniless by the city government after Riis led a successful campaign against the city's practice of housing indigents in the jails.

All photographs by Jacob A. Riis, The Jacob A. Riis Collection, Museum of the City of New York

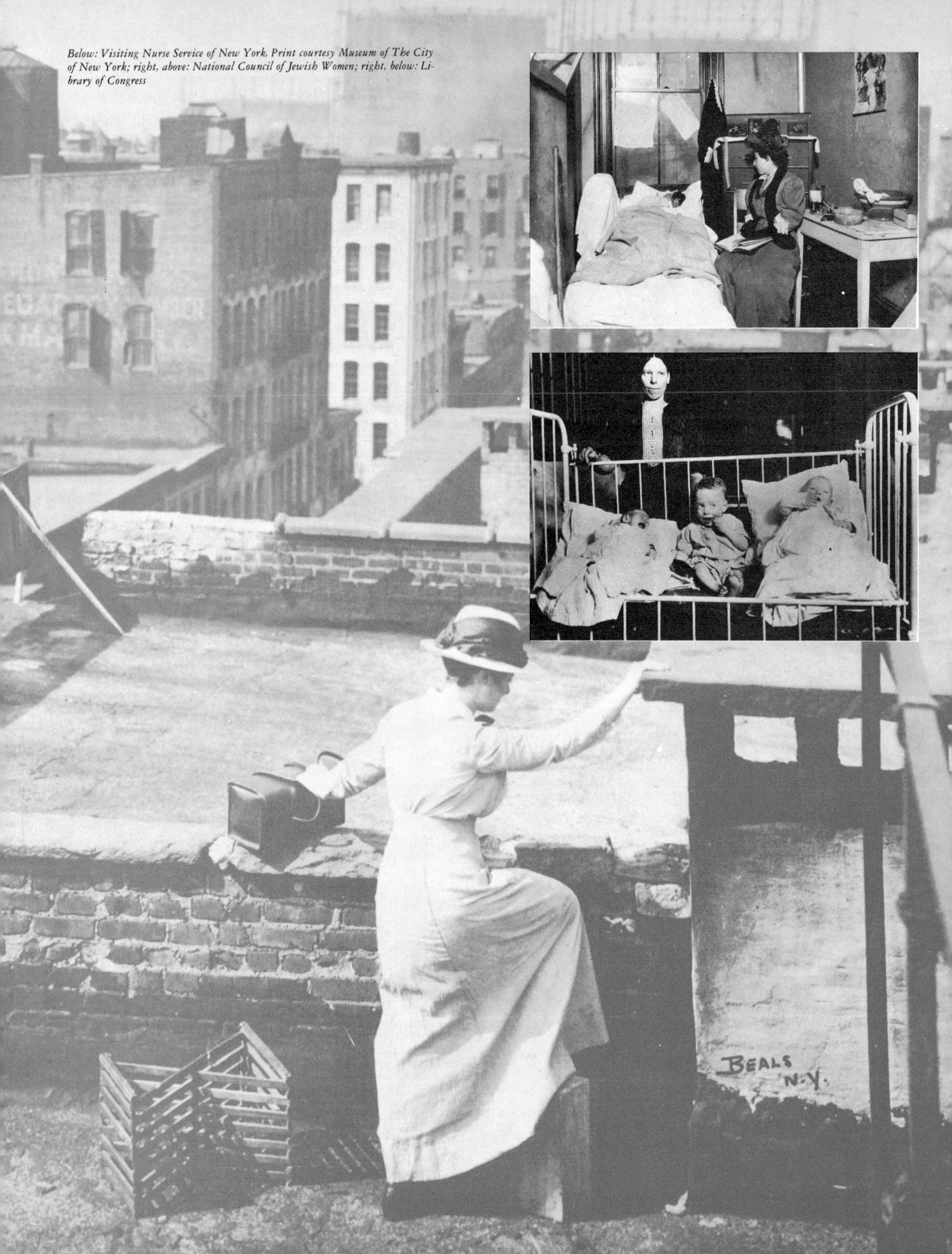

Below: Visiting Nurse Service of New York, Print courtesy Museum of The City of New York; right, above: National Council of Jewish Women; right, below: Library of Congress

tion which resulted from a heavy concentration of population also created severe problems for the traditional systems of transportation. With thousands of people going to work at about the same time, it was obvious that they could not all drive a horse and buggy or ride in horse-drawn cabs. City life demanded faster and more efficient transit. In the same way, candles and kerosene lamps were unsuited for the growing demands of urban living.

At best, these and other problems in American cities were only partially solved during the late nineteenth and early twentieth centuries. Some of the needs for housing were met by the construction of new apartments as well as additional homes in the growing suburbs. But, unfortunately, most of the urban poor were crammed into an ever-growing number of dirty and dangerous tenements. By 1900 there were some 43,000 tenements in New York City occupied by about 1.5 million people. To meet transportation needs, cities built brick and asphalt streets and instituted more efficient types of public transportation. By the turn of the century, overhead railways, cable cars, and subways were hauling the urban multitudes. The construction of central water systems, often owned and operated by the cities themselves, provided a more adequate and safer water supply. Cities met the problem of waste and sewage disposal by burning garbage and introducing filter and treatment plants. However, sewage continued to be a problem, polluting rivers, lakes, and other natural receptacles. In 1880 the *Chicago Times* reported that the city was enclosed by "solid stink."

Electric lights met the needs for urban lighting. Although artificial gas remained the basic source of city light well into the 1880s, advances in electrical technology brought a rapid shift to electric lights. First introduced in Cleveland in 1879 by a brilliant engineer, Charles F. Brush, arc lamps soon spread to other cities. But a more important advance was the incandescent lamp patented by Thomas A. Edison in 1880. Companies which built central power stations provided the increasing demands for electric power. By 1884, for example, eleven firms in Chicago were supplying that city with electric lighting. Despite the increased safety and efficiency of electric lights, however, gas lighting continued in many cities well into the twentieth century.

Crime harassed the rapidly growing cities. Most large cities had their quota of pickpockets, petty thieves, swindlers, confidence men, robbers, and even murderers. Criminals often concentrated in the slum areas where gangs of hoodlums operated untouched by the law. Prostitution flourished openly. Criminal and illegal activities sometimes continued with the tacit approval of city and police officials. In 1874 the *Chicago Tribune* charged that the feeble effort to stamp out prostitution amounted to a "co-partnership of Chicago with harlotry." Attempts to achieve better law enforcement and to reduce crime met with only meager success, although in some cities new measures such as the installation of alarm systems, the appointment of special detectives, and putting police under a merit system had improved the situation by the turn of the century.

Urban crowding affected people's actions and attitudes in many ways. Race prejudice, for example, was strong in most cities, particularly against the Negroes and Orientals, but some national groups such as the Italians and Irish also suffered from various types of discrimination. The black population remained relatively small in Northern cities before 1900, but discrimination was no less apparent. It was felt in housing, in public accommodations, and in attitudes. In Chicago, white and black citizens discussed race relations at a meeting in February, 1890. This indicated at least some recognition of the problem.

Corruption and Reform in City Government

Urbanization limited the achievement of good government. As Josiah Strong wrote: "To administer the affairs of a village of 1,000 inhabitants is a simple matter, requiring only ordinary intelligence; the government of a city of 100,000 is much more complicated; while that of a city of 1,000,000 or of 5,000,000 demands expert knowledge, ability and character of the very highest order." Unfortunately, not enough concern, knowledge, or character was present in late-nineteenth-century cities to provide honest and efficient government. Scandalous conditions involving dishonest elections, political graft and corruption, and police payoffs characterized the political life of many large cities. James Bryce, the keen English observer of the American scene, wrote in 1893: "The government of cities is one conspicuous failure of the United States."

One of the worst aspects of city government was the close and often corrupt relationship which developed between city officials and businessmen who stood to profit either from special licenses and franchises or from lax enforcement of the laws. Politicians organized and maintained political machines with the financial support of business interests, who paid politicians handsomely for street railway, electric lighting, and other public utility franchises, from which they in turn gained millions of dollars. After investigating conditions in St. Louis, "Muckraker" Lincoln Steffens wrote of Colonel Ed Butler, the city's political boss: "His business was boodling. . . . It involves, not thieves, gamblers, and common women, but influential citizens, capitalists, and great corporations. For the stock-in-trade of the boodler is the rights, privileges, franchises, and real property of the city, and his source of corruption is the top, not the bottom, of society."

Urban bosses also gained support for their political machines from newly arrived immigrants and other low-income groups who were willing to exchange their votes for such considerations as a job, a bushel of coal, a week's groceries, or some other favor. Most new immigrants who jammed into American cities were strangers to democracy; they were much more interested in gaining a livelihood than in doing their civic duty or guaranteeing efficient and uncorrupted government. The city bosses often assisted these helpless people when no one else would; but, as a result, the immigrants became easy prey for the ward boss, whose job it was to round up votes at election time.

City after city became trapped in the web of corrupt governmental administration. One of the most notorious examples of dishonest government was the Tweed Ring in New York City. Born in New York in 1823, William M. Tweed was a rough, congenial, unscrupulous fireman who rose to become president of the Board of Supervisors. Once he had gained political control in New York in 1868, Tweed set out to enrich himself and his friends. The Ring awarded city contracts at ridiculously high prices to printing, paving, and other companies in which they had an interest. The city treasurer, a member of the Ring, paid millions of dollars in fictitious bills. The Ring forced contractors

Library of Congress

Theatre: Life on the Road

Just after the Civil War two major developments occurred in the American theater. In New York, the musical spectacle was born with *The Black Crook* in 1866. Audiences ignored the inane story as they flocked to see musical numbers performed by a hundred French ballet dancers "in close-fitting flesh-colored silk 'tights,' and as little else as the law permits." Nothing like that had been seen before. The show earned more than a million dollars in sixteen months and producers of theatrical spectacles such as the Kiralfy Brothers clamored for the rights to subsidiary production. The burlesque show on one hand and American musical comedy on the other descended directly from *The Black Crook.*

Outside New York "the road" came into existence. Railroads enabled touring companies to transport productions throughout the country. The regional stock company playing a repertoire of well-worn chestnuts gave way to new casts performing just one play moving quickly from town to town. As plays became New York hits—and even if they did not—traveling casts and scenery were assembled to take the same show on the road. Contemporary farces and melodramas pleased road audiences most and the advertising promised breath-taking adventure.

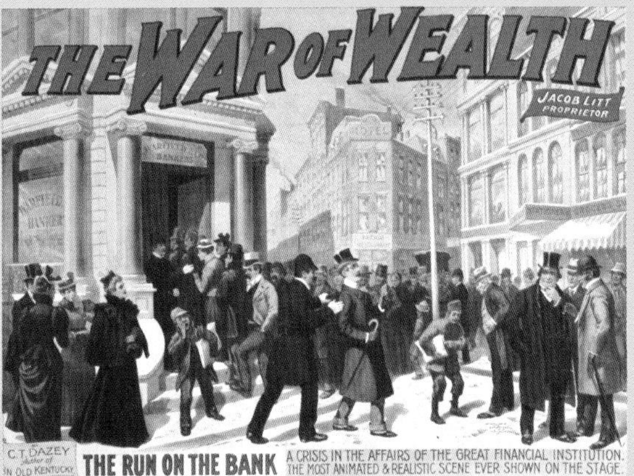

THE WAR OF WEALTH
JACOB LITT PROPRIETOR
C.T. DAZEY
IN OLD KENTUCKY
THE RUN ON THE BANK
A CRISIS IN THE AFFAIRS OF THE GREAT FINANCIAL INSTITUTION.
THE MOST ANIMATED & REALISTIC SCENE EVER SHOWN ON THE STAGE.

Library of Congress

THE COMEDY DRAMA SUCCESS
ONLY A SHOP GIRL
BY MARIE WELLESLEY STERLING
HULDA: "YOU ARE ONLY A LOW SHOP GIRL!" EVE: "AN HONEST SHOP GIRL, AS FAR ABOVE A FASHIONABLE IDLER AS HEAVEN IS ABOVE EARTH!"

Courtesy of the New-York Historical Society, New York City

Because thrilling conflict lured audiences, road show posters concentrated on climactic scenes. In the mid-1890s social and political themes began to appear as a backdrop for dashing action. *The Last Stroke* (right) ostensibly dealt with American involvement in Cuba, but it really concentrated on a last minute rescue from a firing squad and the hero's grasping an American flag to save the heroine as a cliffside balcony collapsed.

Economic problems were presented as personal conflict between rich and poor, management and labor, big business and the common man. *The War of Wealth* (top) exemplified the "financial" melodrama. In addition to "the most animated & realistic scene ever shown on the stage," it advertised a scene of devastating class discrimination: "Marcia's Contemptuous Rejection of the Junior Partner." Many plays like *Only A Shop Girl* (above) emphasized righteous vindication of the working class; everyone knew which side the audience was on.

THE LAS
"STOP! THIS MAN IS AN AMER

Library of Congress

STROKE
A STORY OF
CUBA'S FIGHT
FREED
BY
I.N. MORRIS.
JACOB L.
PROPRIE
OUS ACTION OF THE AMERICAN CONSUL
CITIZEN. IF YOU TOUCH A HAIR OF HIS HEAD, I'LL HANG EVERY MAN OF Y

Library of Congress

Library of Congress

Stereotyped situations and characters created a greatly distorted picture of the city for road audiences. The joys of being a stranger in New York (left) were supposed to tantalize the unsophisticated and lure them to the metropolis; or so the advertising said. City politics (left, below) appeared in equally simplistic terms. *The Queen of Chinatown* (right) had everything: wicked orientals, double trap doors, a rat-filled dungeon, and the Queen shot by her villainous lover as she helped a Naval lieutenant rescue his kidnapped sister from an opium den. Everyone knew that big cities were like that.

Library of Congress

THE QUEEN OF CHINATOWN

BY JOSEPH JARROW

HURLED BY HIGHBINDERS THROUGH THE RAT PIT'S DOUBLE TRAP

VIOLA ALLEN

TWELFTH NIGHT

Courtesy of the New-York Historical Society, New York City

Certain favorites ran in New York year after year and many became perennials on the road as well. "The classics" meant primarily Shakespeare, whose name did not appear on the elegant Broadway posters of the 1880s and 1890s (left) although the star's did.

Contemporary hits included *Peter Pan* (right, above), Ethyl Barrymore's first triumph, *Captain Jinks of the Horse Marines*, and *Peg O' My Heart.* William Gillette went on from playing a Union Army spy in his immensely popular *Secret Service* (right, below) to create the first Sherlock Holmes on the stage.

Library of Congress

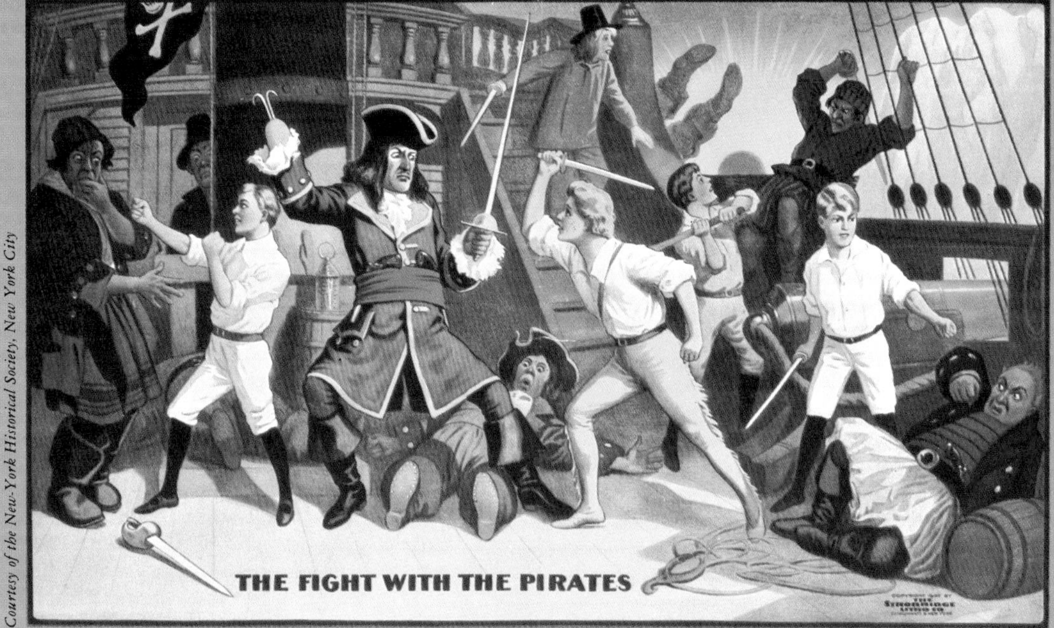

Courtesy of the New-York Historical Society, New York City

Library of Congress

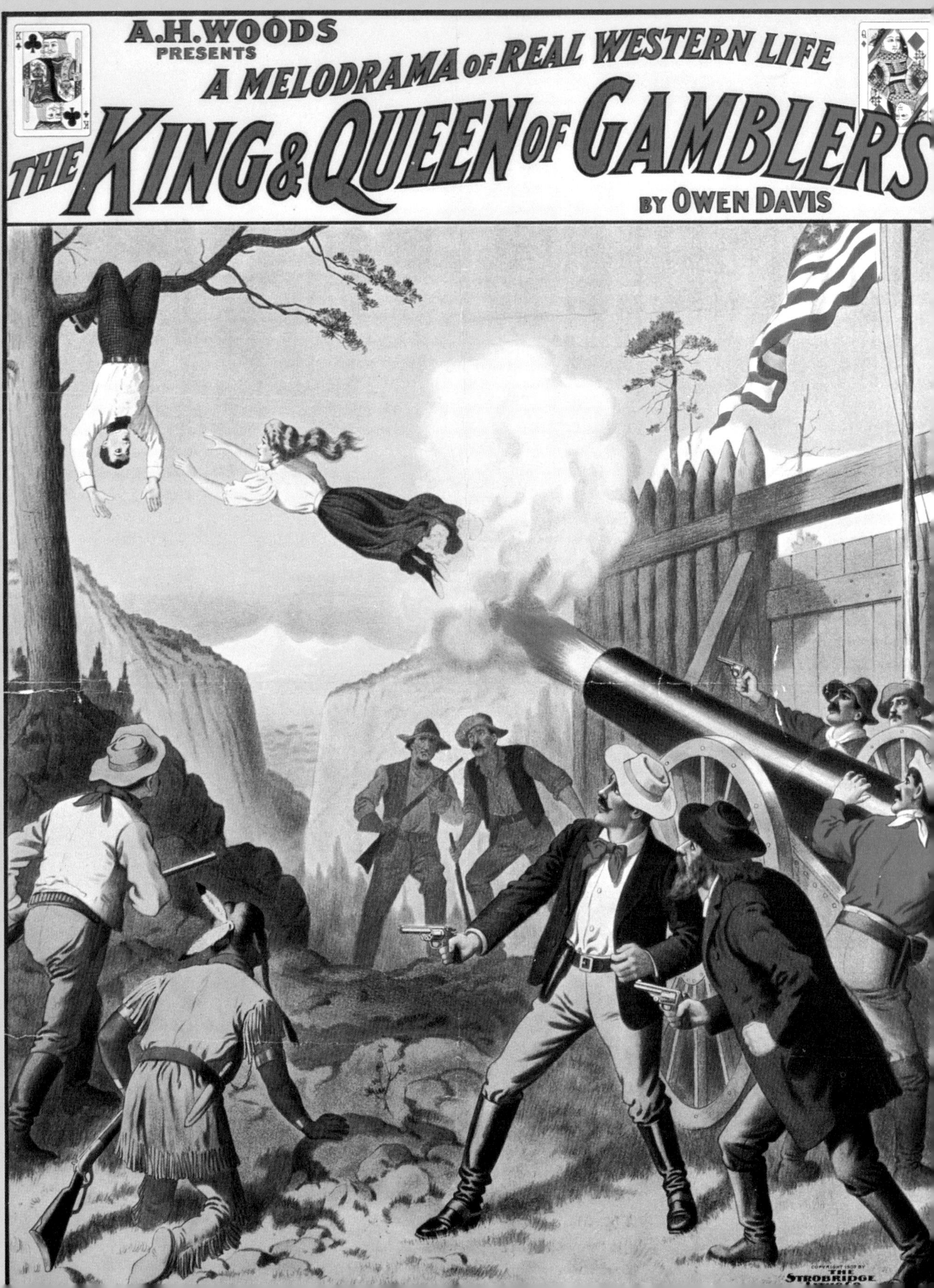

A.H. WOODS
PRESENTS
A MELODRAMA OF REAL WESTERN LIFE
THE KING & QUEEN OF GAMBLERS
BY OWEN DAVIS
THE
STROBRIDGE

Melodrama demanded the thrilling action that gave rise to outlandish plots and increasingly complex scenic effects. David Belasco pioneered absolute authenticity of detail in his New York productions. Road shows emphasized daring rescues, exotic locales, and spectacular props such as locomotives and air ships. Few thrillers could live up to the "actual scenes" their posters claimed to represent.

Library of Congress

Above: Library of Congress

Above and below: Courtesy of the New-York Historical Society, New York City

After 1890 onstage climaxes of startling reality were essential to any self-respecting melodrama. Great inventiveness and complex craftsmanship were devoted to fires, storms, earthquakes, and volcanic eruptions. Whole cities, oceans, mountain ranges were created. Although traveling companies tended to simplify the scenic effects the theater in general strove toward the visual scope and naturalistic detail that only the motion picture could achieve. By 1915 the movies did do it and soon stage melodrama became hollow thunder.

Courtesy of the New-York Historical Society, New York City

FORD'S
PRESENTING
OMPANY
THE POWER OF GOLD
E ON THE REGENT'S CANAL, LONDON.
TUALLY PORTRAYS AN EXACT SIZE CANAL-BOAT DRAWN BY LIVE HORSES; SHOWING THE WORKI
A REPRODUCTION OF EVERY-DAY ENGLISH CANAL-BOAT LIFE, EMBODYING THE PERFECTION
APHS TAKEN ON THE SPOT; AND INTRODUCING THE POSITIVE NOVELTY OF IMPORTED ANIMALS. (THIS EFFE
ICS OF THE ENTIRE PRESS, THE GREATEST SCENE EVER PRODUCED ON ANY STA

THE MOST MARVELOUS AND ONLY ATTRACTION OF ITS KIND IN THE WORLD
SINGER'S MIDGETS
3 MIDGET ELEPHANTS
30 WONDERFUL MIDGETS
20 PONIES

Courtesy of the New-York Historical Society, New York City

The fantastic, unusual, and bizarre dominated whole areas of indoor theater. American circuses grew from displays of animals and skilled riding in the 1750s to extravagant collections of daring performers, exotic creatures, and curiosities from around the world by the mid-nineteenth century. The air ship (above, right) may have been displayed in the Barrett Shows of the 1880s, but it never flew. By this time P. T. Barnum had created the American Museum and the Hippodrome arena in New York, managed specialty performers from Europe, and just merged his circus with James Bailey's. In 1907 the Ringling Brothers joined the combined circuses and "The Greatest Show On Earth" was born.

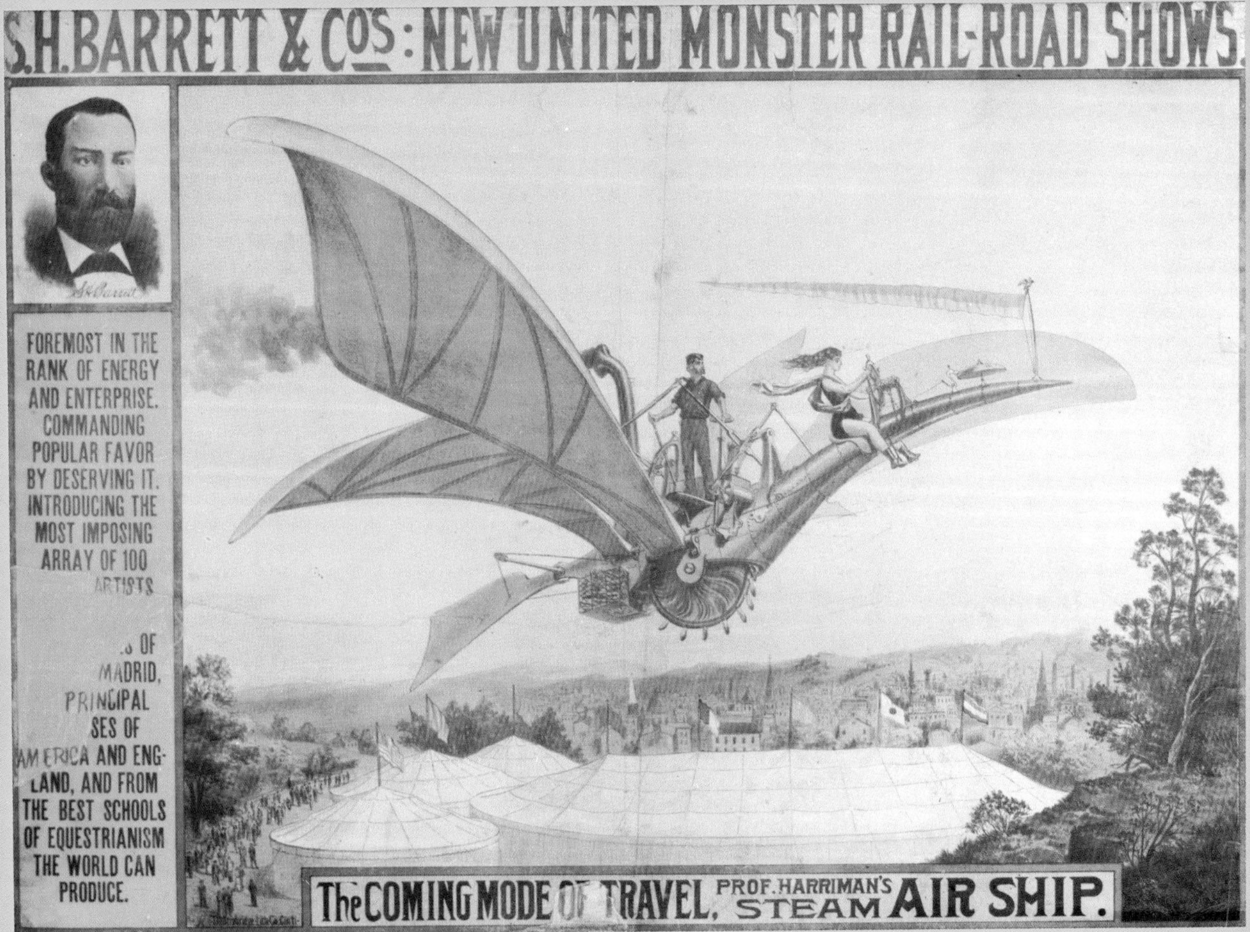

S.H.BARRETT & CO'S: NEW UNITED MONSTER RAIL-ROAD SHOWS.
FOREMOST IN THE RANK OF ENERGY AND ENTERPRISE. COMMANDING POPULAR FAVOR BY DESERVING IT. INTRODUCING THE MOST IMPOSING ARRAY OF 100 ARTISTS
MADRID,
PRINCIPAL
AMERICA AND ENGLAND, AND FROM THE BEST SCHOOLS OF EQUESTRIANISM THE WORLD CAN PRODUCE.
The COMING MODE OF TRAVEL, PROF. HARRIMAN'S STEAM AIR SHIP.

Library of Congress

KELLAR
IN HIS LATEST MYSTERY
SELF DECAPITATION

Library of Congress

Variety shows, later called vaudeville, brought a great diversity of performers onto American stages from about 1880 to the 1930s. Along with dancers, singers, jugglers, monologists, and comics, star acts such as Singer's Midgets (left, above) provided almost a whole show in themselves. They displayed trained animals, played instruments, sang and danced, performed dramatic excerpts. Such talented and unusual performances brought down the house.

Harry Kellar, a top vaudeville attraction, also had his own full-length evening magic show as later did Howard Thurston, Harry Houdini, and Harry Blackstone. In 1897 Kellar could be seen cutting off his own head to baffle audiences.

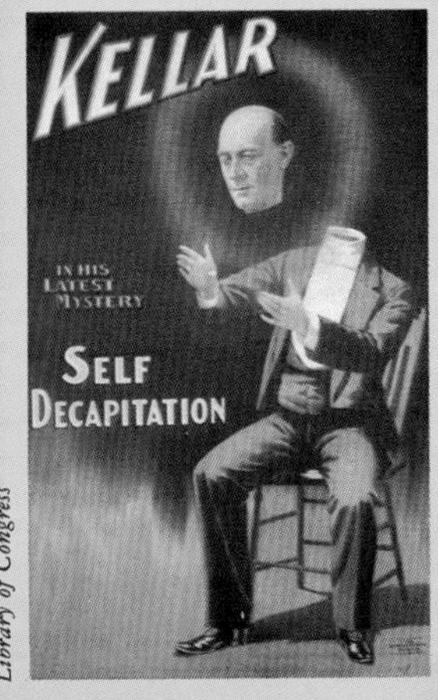

The spectacular appeal of live performers doing thrilling things extended beyond the theater. Organized sports found their great audiences among city-dwelling Americans. Professional baseball existed from its beginning in 1839 and remained an unequaled favorite from the Civil War to the late 1960s. College football gained popularity in the 1890s but professional teams did not take shape until about 1920.

Library of Congress

Horse racing and boxing, legacies of the Greeks and Romans, have always been associated with betting. Elegant tracks first appeared in resort areas close to major cities during the 1880s.

The Marquis of Queensberry boxing rules introduced gloves, a limited number of three-minute rounds and other modern standards. They were adopted for prize fights in 1889, but battles remained bloody, especially the bout in which Jack Johnson lost the heavyweight title in 1915.

Courtesy of Personality Posters, Inc., New York City

Courtesy of the New-York Historical Society, New York City

The road brought "culture" to small towns on the Chatauqua, Lyceum, Redpath, and similar program circuits. Lecturers tried to enliven "The Glories of Greece," "Washington, the Paris of America," and other topics with colored lantern slides. Lyman Howe left them all behind in 1897 with the newest innovation: pictures that moved to illustrate his talk on the Spanish-American War.

Few dreamed how completely a variety-show novelty—the movies—would remake America's theatrical scene. By 1916 road plays valiantly proclaimed that they were "Played by Living Men and Women" but they had already lost the battle. Town halls and village opera houses across the country began installing projectors, road companies disbanded, and for twenty-five cents audiences gave their hearts to shadows flickering on a screen.

Both: Courtesy of the New-York Historical Society, New York City

to pad their bills and then pocketed the excess millions. Tweed was reputedly worth $12 million in 1870. Although Tweed's power was finally broken, and he died in jail in 1877, New York was controlled periodically by bosses during the rest of the nineteenth century. The situation in many other cities was little better.

Inefficient and dishonest city government did not go unchallenged. By the 1880s and 1890s demand for change had become widespread, and reformers organized civic federations, municipal leagues, and other groups to fight for good government. Urban reformers demanded a competitive civil service and stressed the need for better governmental organization. Cities discovered that they required better charters, reduced control by state governments, new methods of administration, as well as honest elections. Some reformers determined to restructure city government to make it more efficient and responsive to the needs and wishes of a majority of the people. Many cities adopted the short ballot; others placed more power in the hands of the mayor; some replaced the old mayor-council system with the commission type of government. First introduced in Galveston, Texas, in 1901, following a devastating flood the year before, the commission plan provided for a commission, usually of some five members, which decided all major questions of policy. Other municipalities adopted the city-manager plan. This called for a manager to handle the day-to-day administration, under the general supervision of a commission or council.

Meanwhile, a few reform mayors improved their city governments and made national reputations for themselves and their cities. Hazen S. Pingree was elected mayor of Detroit in 1889. During his seven years in office he reduced the power of utility companies, exposed grafting councilmen, and convinced the city to establish a municipally owned electric light system. In 1897 Toledo citizens elected Sam M. "Golden Rule" Jones as mayor. A wealthy businessman, Jones improved the police system, reduced hours for city employees, and increased the efficiency in the public works department. Brand Whitlock followed Jones as Toledo's mayor and continued a reform program until 1913.

Urban Life

Most American cities grew haphazardly, without any particular plan or design. The streets were often narrow and crooked; building codes were poorly enforced, permitting a variety of structures to be built in the same area. Cities often retained no open spaces for recreation. The cities were dirty, unkempt, congested, and often ugly. The wide variations in architectural forms, the elevated trains, dusty streets, laundry hanging from windows, and crude advertising displays gave cities a depressing appearance. In addition, the contrast in physical appearance among different parts of most cities was astonishing. The dirty, run-down, slum areas of New York, for example, made an especially ugly picture contrasted to the palatial homes of a Vanderbilt, Jay Gould, or William Rockefeller. The elegant residences on Fifth Avenue, which in some cases had cost several million dollars, reflected conspicuous expenditures both inside and out. As transportation facilities improved, many middle-class residents moved from cities to the mushrooming suburbs.

Class lines, based mainly on income and standard of living, were sharply drawn in the urban communities. The rich not only occupied fine office buildings in the new business centers but enjoyed the theater, opera, world travel, and lavish parties. In 1897 the Bradley Martin ball in New York cost an estimated $369,200. In 1900 Andrew Carnegie's personal income approached $23 million, and the wealthy Chicago merchant Marshall Field was said to earn $700 an hour. Millions, on the other hand, worked for as little as $300 and $400 a year, and shopgirls in New York did not earn more than $5 to $6 a week. The poor had to be satisfied with cheap amusements or spend their spare time in the "workingman's club," the saloon. Most Americans, generally identified as the middle class, lived between these extremes.

The plight of the poor was serious, and it did not go unnoticed. As cities became larger and problems multiplied, social and philanthropic organizations developed to help those unfortunates who, for some reason, could not provide the necessities of life for themselves. Private agencies, church groups, and local governments organized relief programs and participated in recreational and educational work. A new approach to the problem of social services for the urban poor was the concept of settlement houses. Under this plan, social workers established refuges in the midst of the slums and there provided leadership and assistance to those overwhelmed with social problems. Some fifty settlement houses came into existence after 1890 in Northern and Western cities, the most famous being Hull House, established by Jane Addams on Chicago's South Halstead Street in 1889.

The decline of individualism, a decrease in self-sufficiency, and the growth of interdependence were directly associated with urbanization. Unlike country people, who still retained a considerable amount of independence, city residents relied on others for most of their basic needs—their jobs, their housing, their food and entertainment. At the same time, life in the city was also more impersonal. Some of the functions previously reserved to the family and home were taken over by the factory, school, and social or recreational agencies. Urbanization was thus more than a mere transfer of people from farms and villages to cities. It meant a completely new way of life. Yet it was one chosen by an increasing number of Americans in the late nineteenth century, for, although cities posed many problems, they also provided outstanding economic, social, and cultural advantages. The fundamental changes produced in America by urbanization created deep fears and anxieties among many citizens, who associated the restlessness of the 1890s with the disappearance of the frontier and the passing of a simpler way of life. Wrote one observer: "We are no longer free from the kind of social maladies that have afflicted the Old World."

Conclusion

Although workers made economic gains in the late nineteenth century, upward mobility was difficult for most laboring men, as well as for their children. Yet, they made enough economic progress so that they maintained their faith in the American system of enterprise. Moreover, the prospect of better conditions than could be found in Europe attracted millions of immigrants to the United States to partake of at least some of America's riches.

The nation's growing wealth and economic power became by the end of the 1800s concentrated in the cities, and this development in turn caused social and economic problems to emerge which would make themselves felt in urban America far into the twentieth century.

SUGGESTED READINGS

The standard histories of immigration include Carl Wittke's *We Who Built America* (1939); George H. Stephenson's *A History of American Immigration, 1820–1924* (1926); M. L. Hansen's *The Immigrant in American History** (1940); and Maldwyn A. Jones's *American Immigration** (1960). Oscar Handlin's *The Uprooted* (1951) shows the emotional and psychological impact of emigration on those who left their European homes and came to the United States. The strong feelings against foreigners and Catholicism have been excellently described by John Higham in *Strangers in the Land: Patterns of American Nativism, 1860–1925** (1955).

The most complete history of labor in this period is all of Volume II and parts of Volumes III and IV of *History of Labor in the United States* (1918) by John R. Commons and others. A short, lively survey is Samuel P. Orth's *The Armies of Labor* (1919). Henry Pelling has looked at the American labor movement from the British viewpoint in *American Labor** (1960). Parts of Foster R. Dulles's *Labor in America** (2d ed., 1961) and Joseph G. Rayback's *A History of American Labor** (1959) also have good sections.

Norman J. Ware's *The Labor Movement in the United States, 1860–1895** (1929) deals mostly with the Knights of Labor. On the American Federation of Labor, see *The AF of L in the Time of Gompers* (1957) by Philip Taft. The best biography of Gompers is Bernard Mandel's *Samuel Gompers: A Biography* (1963). For the radical labor movement see Howard H. Quint's *The Forging of American Socialism* (1953); David A. Shannon's *The Socialist Party of America** (1955); and Paul F. Brissenden's *The I. W. W.: A Study of American Syndicalism* (2d ed., 1950). Black labor has been treated in Charles H. Wesley's *Negro Labor in the United States, 1850–1925* (1927).

Conflicts between labor and management have been examined in detail in Donald L. McMurry's *The Great Burlington Strike of* 1888 (1956); Louis Adamic's *Dynamite: The Story of Class Violence in America* (rev. ed., 1934); Almont Lindsay's *The Pullman Strike** (1942); and Henry David's *History of the Haymarket Affair** (1936). The best discussions of wages up to 1890 are Clarence D. Long's *Wages and Earnings in the United States,* 1860–1890 (1960) and Paul H. Douglas's *Wages in the United States,* 1890–1926 (1930).

The best introduction to urban development in the late nineteenth and early twentieth century is *The Urbanization of America,* 1860–1915 (1963) by Blake McKelvey. This should be supplemented by the older, but still excellent, *The Rise of the City,* 1878–1898 (1933), by Arthur M. Schlesinger. There is abundant statistical data in A. F. Weber's *The Growth of Cities in the Nineteenth Century* (1899). Charles N. Glaab has included a number of useful readings on specific aspects of urbanization during this period in *The American City: A Documentary History** (1963).

Details of urban development can best be obtained in the histories of individual cities. See Bessie L. Pierce's *A History of Chicago* (3 vols., 1937–1957); Blake McKelvey's *Rochester: The Flower City,* 1855–1890 (1949); Bayrd Still's *Milwaukee* (1948); Harold C. Syrett's *The City of Brooklyn,* 1865–1898 (1944); and William G. Rose's *Cleveland: The Making of a City* (1950).

Corruption in urban political affairs has been graphically discussed by Lincoln Steffens in *The Shame of the Cities** (1904); M. R. Werner in *Tammany Hall* (1928); and S. J. Mandelbaum in *Boss Tweed's New York* (1965). Life in the city slums has been well described by Jacob Riis in *How the Other Half Lives** (1890). The development of the ghetto is covered by Gilbert Osofsky's *Harlem: The Making of a Ghetto, Negro New York,* 1890–1930 (1966) and Seth M. Scheiner's *Negro Mecca: A History of the Negro in New York City,* 1865–1920 (1965).

* indicates availability in paperback.

23

The Last Frontier, 1865 – 1900

AT THE CLOSE of the Civil War most of the vast region of plains, mountains, and deserts between Kansas City and San Francisco remained unsettled. Here was the "last frontier," more than one billion acres awaiting the miner, farmer, rancher, lumberman, and businessman. Exploitation of the West's tremendously rich natural resources had only begun in 1865; thereafter pioneer Americans settled this last frontier with breathtaking speed. Within a single generation practically all of the Great West, as it was known to contemporaries, had been occupied, and the Director of the Census wrote in 1890 that "the unsettled area had been so broken into by isolated bodies of settlement that there can hardly be said to be a frontier line." Three years later, Frederick Jackson Turner, a young University of Wisconsin historian, declared that American history could be best understood in terms of the influence of the frontier on the political and social evolution of the United States.

Western history in the late nineteenth century centers around the acquisition and development of land, minerals, lumber, water, and other resources. People rushed into the region by the thousands in the hope of gaining a share of the wealth, which seemed to be theirs for the taking. Mines, ranchlands, farmlands, and timber, as well as speculative business ventures, lured men and capital from all over the world. The story of the settlement and exploitation of the last frontier gripped the interest and imagination of Americans more firmly than almost any other aspect of their history and has left enduring traditions.

Reasons for Rapid Settlement

There were a number of important factors which contributed to the rapid settlement of the unoccupied West after 1865. The mining boom which drew thousands of Forty-niners into California was duplicated many times by the Fifty-niners and their followers in Nevada, Colorado, Idaho, Montana, and elsewhere. During and after the Civil War, men rushed to previously isolated and unsettled regions in search of gold and silver, and news of one mining strike after another advertised the West as nothing had ever done before. Development of the range cattle industry also gave wide and favorable publicity to opportunities in the West by the late 1870s.

The improvement and expansion of transportation facilities contributed greatly to rapid settlement. Not only did stage and freight companies extend their lines, but railroads penetrated almost every section of the West between the 1860s and 1890s. Completion of the first transcontinental railway between Omaha and San Francisco in 1869 was only the beginning of an entire network of transcontinentals and branch lines which spread over the Western landscape by 1900. Moreover, the federal government contributed to rapid Western settlement through generous land policies for farmers; land grants to railroads, which encouraged speedier construction; and restrictions on the movement of Indians. With few exceptions, the Indians did not block westward settlement after 1870.

Finally, the strong desire for land was perhaps the most important single factor in bringing the frontier to an end. Tens of thousands of settlers rushed westward between 1865 and 1900 and rapidly occupied the prairie-plains, the Pacific Northwest, and most of the good land in California and the Rocky Mountain region. Altogether then, the West was quickly settled as a series of separate but interdependent frontiers. Miners, cattlemen, railroad builders, and farmers hastily overran that great undeveloped region, settled it, and brought it into an integral economic, political, and social relationship with the rest of the nation.

The Mining Frontiers

Between 1858 and 1875 eager prospectors swarmed over the mountains and deserts of the American West, searching for gold and silver. A decade after the rich strikes in California, new discoveries were made in Nevada and Colorado, and in the early 1860s restless miners located additional wealth in Idaho and Montana. By the 1860s prospectors were singing:

> *"Farewell, old California, I'm going far away.*
> *Where gold is found more plenty,*
> *In larger lumps, they say."*

For years there had been rumors of gold in the Pike's Peak region of Colorado. Then in the summer of 1858 prospectors discovered gold near the present site of Denver. When word of this discovery reached eastern Kansas and Missouri, thousands of hopeful gold-seekers rushed to Colorado, only to meet failure and disappointment. Most of them returned home in the winter of 1858–1859. However, early in 1859 John S. Gregory, an experienced gold miner from Georgia, and George H. Jackson, a former California miner, found gold in paying quantities west of Denver in the vicinity of Central City. Miners also located gold along Boulder Creek. Reports of these riches brought a flood of prospectors to the region around Denver and Boulder, and by the summer of 1859 an estimated one hundred thousand people were feverishly seeking their fortunes with pan and sluice box.

At about the same time, miners were prospecting in Gold Canyon in western Nevada. They found small amounts of the precious metal, but their claim also contained large amounts of blue-gray quartz which proved to be rich in silver. Henry T. P. Comstock bluffed his way into a share of the claim, giving his name to the fabulous silver deposits known as the Comstock Lode. Reports of the discovery in June, 1859, brought the usual rush of prospectors and speculators to the new bonanza. Gold Hill and Virginia City quickly became bustling, boisterous, and flourishing mining towns. Miners and prospectors seemed forever on the move in search of new strikes. In 1860 E. D. Pierce discovered gold near Lewiston, Idaho, and within the next two years Placerville, Idaho City, and Silver City were among Idaho's major centers of mining activity. Meanwhile, big strikes were located in Montana. By 1862 Helena and Virginia City had drawn hundreds of miners. General John Pope reported in February, 1866, that "people in incredible numbers continued to throng across the great plains to the rich mining territories, undeterred by the seasons, by hardship and privations, or by the constant and relentless hostility of the Indian tribes." The last major gold rush occurred in the Black Hills of Dakota, mostly around Custer City and Deadwood. Some prospectors ranged over the Southwest in Arizona and New Mexico, but rewards for placer miners in that desolate region were meager.

It was placer mining which drew thousands of prospectors to the widely scattered diggings throughout the Far West. This type of mining required very little equipment and simple techniques. Besides a pack of supplies to meet his personal needs, about all that a miner needed was a pan and shovel. After scooping up a pan of dirt and gravel along a stream, he "washed" it by swirling water in the pan. This rinsed the lighter foreign matter away and isolated the heavier gold which sank to the bottom where it could be retrieved. Panning for gold was slow, hard work, and most prospectors did not make more than a few dollars a day. Some miners, however, were known to have received as much as $500 for a day's work, and an unusually lucky miner in Idaho earned $6,600 in one day. A report of this kind had an electrifying effect in provoking a mass stampede toward the area where such a strike had occurred.

Scores of mining camps became bustling communities of several thousand people almost overnight, but many of them were abandoned with equal speed as new strikes were reported or the surface gold played out. In most places, pan and sluice-box mining lasted only a short time, because most of the gold and silver was deeply imbedded in quartz. It required capital, machinery, and engineering skill—which individual miners did not possess—to extract gold and silver under these conditions.

Life in the mining camps was transitory, crude, rough, and sometimes dangerous. Men lived in tents, cabins, wagon boxes, and even out in the open during the initial rush. Prices of necessities were fabulously high, with flour sometimes selling for 85 cents a pound and potatoes at $27 a bushel. The camps swarmed not only with miners, but with speculators, traders, saloonkeepers, teamsters, and women of the street. Vice and violence flourished in the mining camps. Mark Twain, who as a young man worked on the Virginia City, Nevada, *Enterprise,* wrote that murder, robberies, assassinations, and knifings were the order of the day. Twain said that "to be a saloonkeeper and to kill a man was to be illustrious" in Virginia City. In a single twenty-four-hour period, one "woman was killed by a pistol shot, a man was brained with a sling shot," and another man was "disposed of permanently." The red-light district was large and well populated, and it was said that an energetic and thrifty girl could make more money than a hardworking miner.

Despite a certain amount of lawlessness, prospectors organized mining districts to register and protect claims, and miners' courts and vigilante groups maintained a degree of law and order. Miners dispatched justice quickly by whipping or hanging, thus eliminating the need of holding culprits for trial in so-called leaky jails. The economy of these communities was highly unstable and fluctuated with the success or failure of the miners to find gold or silver. More stable conditions came to prevail as large companies moved in heavy equipment to process the ore, hired labor, and provided business for merchants, professional men, and other permanent settlers. Where high-paying ore existed, such as at Virginia City, Nevada (silver), Butte, Montana (copper), or Deadwood, Dakota (gold), town life centered around the employment and income provided by the mining companies.

Social conditions became stabilized in most mining communities within a relatively short time, and circumstances such as those described by Mark Twain at Virginia City did not survive. More permanent settlers usually gained control, and within a few years these people established newspapers, schools, churches, libraries, lodges, and other institutions common in the older settled East and Middle West. For example, prospectors entered the region which became Lake City in southwestern Colorado in 1875, and hundreds of miners rushed to the area in the spring of 1876. A newspaper appeared in June, 1875, and by December a private school was in operation, soon to be followed by a public school. Twenty men formed a Masonic Lodge. The Presbyterians completed the first church in November, 1876, and a miners' library was opened in 1877. So, while Lake City had its saloons, bawdy houses, and gambling dens, what one contemporary called the "decent element" soon transplanted the culture and refinement which the residents had known elsewhere.

The widely scattered mining frontiers exerted a powerful influence on the settlement and development of the West. The mining strikes familiarized Americans with the vast region between the Missouri River and the Pacific Ocean and advertised the area's tremendous resources. People were drawn westward much faster than would otherwise have been the case. Trading posts and cities sprang into existence to provide miners with supplies. Towns such as Sacramento, Walla Walla, Salt Lake City, Denver, and Helena were among those which developed as Western supply centers. The rapid occupation of new areas created a strong demand for better and faster transportation—stage and freight lines, steamboats, and especially railroads.

Moreover, the rush of people into previously unoccupied areas hastened political organization throughout the West. Colorado, for example, became a territory in 1861, only two years after the initial gold rush, and Idaho and Montana gained separate territorial status in 1863 and 1865 respectively. The mining frontiers also had an important effect on Western agricultural development. The high prices of food in the isolated mining camps caused many emigrants to take up farming, which often proved more profitable than panning for gold. Agriculture soon became firmly established in many remote regions of the West, and farmers learned that with irrigation and proper techniques abundant supplies of agricultural produce could be raised in the semiarid and arid West. By 1870 the annual value of farm products in Colorado was nearly as great as that of gold and silver. In addition, the output of about $1.5 billion worth of gold between 1860 and 1890 permitted the United States to go on a *de facto* gold standard in 1879, and the production of about $901 million in silver helped to emphasize the money question, the most important political issue in the late nineteenth century. Finally, the Western mining industry created a class of new-rich businessmen such as George Hearst of California and William A. Clark of Montana, who made vast fortunes and reveled in conspicuous living.

Western Ranching

Development of the range cattle industry was another exciting and important event which did much to advertise the West and to bring the frontier to an end by the 1890s. Cattle raising had always been an important frontier enterprise in the United States. Herds of 1,000 head were not uncommon in Ohio in the 1830s, and the "prairie cattle kings" in Illinois and Indiana developed large operations during the 1840s and 1850s. By the 1840s ranching had also become a substantial business in Texas.

Several major factors contributed to the establishment and growth of the Western range cattle industry after 1865. Some herds had appeared early along the emigrant trails to Oregon. By the 1850s a few ranchers in Idaho, Wyoming, and Montana maintained herds of several hundred head. In 1859 Horace Greeley reported that one Wyoming resident had "quietly accumulated some fifty horses, three or four hundred neat cattle, three squaws, and any number of half-breed children." This man was reputedly worth $75,000. Thus emigrants to Oregon, as well as the Mormons, provided much of the initial breeding stock for the Western cattle business. Furthermore, the discovery of gold and silver throughout the West provided additional markets for livestock producers. Cattlemen now found that they could dispose of beef to miners, Army posts, railroad builders, and emigrants traveling West.

Perhaps most important, however, was the fact that ranchers discovered that the semiarid plains and valleys of the West provided excellent natural conditions for large-scale cattle raising. The short grama and buffalo grasses on the Great Plains were especially nutritious, and they retained most of their value even after drying up in the late summer and fall. This meant that cattle could forage on the open range the year around. Best of all from the viewpoint of the cattlemen, most of the region between the Texas Panhandle and the Canadian border was in the public domain, was largely unoccupied, and could be grazed at very little or no cost. Thus if the ranges of the central and northern plains could be stocked and markets found for increased amounts of beef, ranchers could expect good profits. Many of the cattle needed to stock these ranges came from Texas.

During the Civil War, the market for Texas cattle had been effectively severed by the Union blockade. Consequently, the number of cattle rose rapidly, and prices dropped to as little as $4 and $5 per head by 1865. At the time there was no rail transportation between Texas and the Midwest. If Texans, therefore, could drive their cattle to the nearest railroad in Missouri or Kansas, they might sell them for as much as $20 or $30 a head. Although some cattle were driven from Texas to Illinois in the 1840s, the "long drive" did not begin in a systematic way until 1866. That year some 260,000 head were driven northward, mostly to Sedalia, Missouri.

The outbreak of cattle disease known as Texas fever in Missouri, Illinois, and other places where Texas cattle had been driven or shipped brought violent reactions from farmers and livestock men. If cattle were to be taken north, it seemed necessary to establish trails farther west, so that the Texas animals would not contaminate the livestock of farmers in settled communities. The man who initially worked out such an arrangement was Joseph G. McCoy, a wealthy and prominent cattle dealer of Springfield, Illinois. McCoy visited Kansas in 1867 and decided to make the little village of Abilene on the Kansas Pacific Railroad a shipping point for Texas cattle. When this news reached Texas, cattlemen drove about 35,000 head to Abilene later that year and twice that many in 1868.

During the next few years thousands of cattle were driven north to a succession of cowtowns such as Newton, Wichita, and Dodge City in Kansas, and Kearney and North Platte in Nebraska. Stories and legends developed around the trailing of herds from Texas up the Chisholm Trail and other routes, but cattle driving was neither easy nor exciting. The life of a cowboy was dirty and hard—anything but glamorous. Sometimes the herds stampeded because of fright or thirst. Andy Adams wrote in *The Log of a Cowboy* that one herd became "as ungovernable as the waves of an ocean" because of heat and thirst. After another herd had milled around for hours, Adams recalled, it "turned back over the trail, and the utmost efforts of every man in the outfit failed to check them. We threw our ropes in their faces, and when this failed, we resorted to shooting; but in defiance of the fusillade and the smoke they walked sullenly through the line of horsemen across their front. . . . In a number of instances wild steers deliberately walked against our horses, and then for the first time a fact dawned on us that chilled the marrow in our bones,—*the herd was going blind.*" Black as well as white cowboys rode the ranges and followed the herds.

By 1880 the stage was set for a tremendous boom in the Western cattle business. The ranges had been stocked all the way from Texas to Montana. Millions of buffalo had been killed for their hides in the 1870s, reducing this source of competition for grass on the public domain. At the same time, the Indians had been brought under stricter control. Furthermore, prices for beef rose, and markets expanded rapidly both in domestic urban centers and in foreign countries. Railroad transportation had been extended into much of the Western country, which made it easier and more convenient to market cattle from widely dispersed ranges.

Speculation, large-scale operations, the use of Eastern and foreign capital, and typical Western optimism characterized the range cattle boom of the 1880s. In the early years of the decade, newspaper accounts, magazine stories, and books advertised widely the favorable prospects for ranching and gave the impression that large profits awaited almost any investor. Such optimistic writing fired people's imaginations and prompted Easterners and foreigners to invest millions of dollars in ranching operations. As one authority observed, Scottish and English "drawing rooms buzzed with the stories of this last of Bonanzas; staid old gentlemen, who scarcely knew the difference between a steer and a heifer, discussed it over their port and nuts."

By the middle 1880s both small and large ranches dotted the Western plains and valleys. The Swan Land and Cattle Company near Cheyenne, Wyoming, was typical of some of the big outfits in that area. Financed by Scottish capital, this company owned and controlled thousands of acres of land, ran an estimated 100,000 head of cattle, and was worth about $4 million in 1883. The XIT ranch in the Texas Panhandle was even more extensive. Organized by a Chicago syndicate and supported by foreign capital, the XIT ranged around 110,000 head of cattle over millions of acres, and by 1886 was valued at more than $5.5 million. Cattlemen not only bought large acreages, but, by gaining control of water holes, they were able to graze much of the surrounding public domain just as though they owned it. In some cases ranchers illegally fenced huge sections of government land.

In some Western states and territories, livestock men formed their own associations to deal with problems of brands, roundups, overcrowding of the ranges, and other matters of importance to cattlemen. The Wyoming Stockgrowers Association was the most powerful organization of this kind in the West. It performed many of the functions of a regular government in that Territory.

The Western range cattle industry reached its height between 1882 and 1886. Its very success, however, led to the decline of free-range ranching. Overexpansion of the cattle business had two closely related and unfortunate effects. The ranges became so overstocked that there was not enough grass to feed the cattle under normal conditions. Moreover, the greatly increased numbers caused a sharp and disastrous price decline. In 1884 Western cattle brought about $5.60 a hundred pounds in Chicago, but a year later the price had dropped to around $3.50. Later prices went even lower. Part of the price decline was associated with the decrease of foreign markets.

Most cattlemen did not provide winter feed and shelter for their livestock, and they suffered heavy losses during the periodic hard winters on the Plains. The great blizzard of January, 1887, following a hot, dry summer, killed thousands of cattle. Some companies lost 50, 75, and even as high as 90 percent of their herds. Low prices and hard winters caused many companies to go bankrupt. Another serious problem for the cattlemen was the penetration of dirt farmers onto the Great Plains in the late 1880s. These "sodbusters" broke up much of the former range and forced cattlemen to contract their operations. The day of the free range was for the most part gone. To meet these challenges, cattlemen adjusted and reorganized their operations. They grew hay and forage for winter feed, furnished winter protection for their cattle, fenced their own land, and leased additional acreages. Thus Western ranching existed on a more stable basis by 1900.

The range cattle industry was highly important in settling the last frontier. It was another source of favorable publicity; cattlemen were the first to use and to show the value of the semiarid Great Plains; ranching, like mining and railroads, attracted Eastern and foreign capital into the West to help in the region's economic development; and it stimulated railroad building and helped to open up the country. Finally, the ranchers' frontier created a legend about the American West that continued unabated almost a century later.

The Western Agricultural Frontier

At the end of the Civil War, the Western edge of farm settlement followed a rough line which angled southwestward from near St. Paul, Minnesota, to somewhat west of Fort Worth, Texas, and then on south to the Rio Grande. There were tongues of settlement farther west, but not many farmers had gone beyond Topeka, Kansas, or a few miles west of Omaha, Nebraska. Much of the unsettled area of southwestern and western Minnesota, northwestern Iowa, eastern Dakota, and eastern and central Nebraska and Kansas contained fertile soil and usually received enough rainfall to raise good crops. Beyond this Western prairie area, beginning at about the 98th or 99th meridian and extending to the base of the Rocky Mountains, was the Great Plains, a vast semiarid region whose farming potential was yet unknown in 1865. Farther west the Mormons had become successful farmers around Salt Lake City by the 1850s and 1860s, and there were also major agricultural communities in California and Oregon. Most of the country between Kansas City or Omaha and the Pacific Coast, however, still awaited the settler's plow, but the strong desire for land quickly drew farmers into the unoccupied Western areas. Within a generation after the Civil War, the best lands had been settled.

In 1865 a farmer could obtain public land by purchase, preemption, or under the Homestead Act of 1862. A great deal of public land was sold directly by the government, while under preemption a settler could obtain a quarter section (160 acres) of land by fulfilling certain residence and improvement requirements and then paying $1.25 an acre. The Homestead Act permitted a citizen who was twenty-one years of age, or a person who had declared his intention to become a citizen, to file an entry at a government land office on 160 acres of the public domain. The only cost was a small filing fee. The settler was required to make improvements and live on the land for five years, after which the government would grant him full ownership. If the homesteader did not want to wait five years to obtain title, he was permitted to pay $1.25 an acre after a specific time, and he would then receive his land title, known as a "final patent." Westerners had worked for years to obtain this legislation, and many people regarded free land a great victory for democracy because it would give more citizens an economic stake in society. As Governor Alvin Saunders of Nebraska said, "What a blessing this wise and humane legislation will bring to many a poor, but honest and industrious family." Although the democratic aims of the law were not entirely realized, the Homestead Act did help thousands of settlers become established farmers, especially in Minnesota, Dakota, Nebraska, and Kansas.

Other land laws included the Timber Culture Act of 1873, the Desert Land Act of 1877, and the Timber and Stone Act, passed in 1878. The only one of these measures of much interest or value to farmers was the Timber Culture Act. Under this law a person could enter an additional 160 acres of government land, and the only requirement, except a filing fee, was that the settler plant forty acres of trees on the land. This was later reduced to ten acres. The Timber Culture Act sprang from the conviction that trees grown on the Western prairies and Great Plains would reduce the winds, increase the moisture, and improve the climate for agriculture. It also permitted Western farmers to acquire larger acreages, since a settler could file on both a homestead and a timber culture claim. The Desert Land Act was designed to promote irrigation in the arid West. A person could file for 640 acres in certain Western states and territories by paying 25 cents an acre down, and after irrigating part of the land and paying an additional dollar an acre, he would be granted full title within four years by the government. Much graft and corruption centered around this law, and not many settlers were able to establish farms under its provisions. Ranchers, however, took advantage of the measure to gain control of large acreages at cheap prices. The Timber and Stone Act permitted a person in some Western states and territories to buy 160 acres of land for $2.50 an acre. The land was to be "unfit for cultivation," contain no valuable minerals, and be used largely for its timber and stone.

Many settlers were drawn westward by the prospect of obtaining land; what speeded the settlement of the West after the Civil War, however, were the railroads. People still continued to make their way westward in wagons, but railroads provided fast and comparatively cheap transportation into many remote areas. Following completion of the Union Pacific in 1869, the Santa Fe reached western Kansas in 1870, and the Northern Pacific arrived at Bismarck, Dakota, in 1873. These and other main and branch lines not only provided transportation, but they also carried on vigorous promotional campaigns and advertised the West's economic opportunities. Railroad companies hoped to attract immigrants both because they had land to sell and because they wanted to promote business along their lines. They distributed millions of pamphlets and brochures, sent agents to the East and to Europe, and did everything possible to present the Western agricultural frontier in favorable terms.

During the first decade after the Civil War, most settlers moved into the rich prairie lands of southwestern and western Minnesota, eastern Dakota, and as far west as central Nebraska and Kansas. Most pioneers were poor. Their property usually did not consist of more than one or two horses or a team of oxen, two or three milk cows, a plow, and a few household goods. They hoped to make a living and add to their equipment from the sale of crops and a few head of livestock. In Minnesota and Dakota, wheat was the major crop, while pioneers in Nebraska and Kansas generally relied on corn. Farm operations were very small; after years of effort most frontier farmers did not cultivate more than 30 or 40 acres of crops or own more than a few head of livestock. Their annual incomes often did not exceed $100 in cash.

So long as crops were good and prices favorable, Western farmers were able to extract a fair living. However, since most of them had little or no capital reserve, one or two poor years could spell disaster. In the middle 1870s, settlers all the way from Minnesota to south-central Kansas suffered terribly because of drought and grasshopper devastations. After grasshoppers had destroyed his crops, a farmer

This house of one settler disappearing into the horizon of the Great Plains, recorded in this early Geological Survey photograph emphasizes the almost unreal vastness of what was, between 1860 and 1900, the stage for a whole series of historic dramas. Here the advancing white man displaced the Plains Indians as well as the Indian's principal economic resource—the buffalo. Here for a period of not much more than twenty-five years a vast open range existed, inviting the cattle industry to expand and flourish on the free grass of government land from Texas to Montana. Here in the late 1870s a new boom developed, as farmers began a great western migration. Barbed wire, first manufactured in America in 1874, enabled the farmer to protect his crops from roving cattle—and also enabled the great cattle barons to fence, for their own use, huge areas of the public domain.

The open range closed at last, and by the 1890s the best of the frontier lands had been occupied. Settlers came from the eastern states, both northern and southern, from Germany, Russia, England, France, Switzerland, Belgium, Canada and the countries of Scandinavia. Between 1860 and 1900, 1,414,276 new farms were established in the nineteen Western states and territories, and 400,000,000 acres of farming land, most of it west of the Mississippi, were added to the total American acreage under cultivation.

Settling the Frontier

W. D. Johnson, U.S. Geological Survey

...Men volunteering for t
and subsist themselves a
paid for their services at
cents per day. A compe
also be given to any body
livered to this office.

The story of Western expansion also became the story of brutal encroachment of the white man upon the lands held by the Indian, an encroachment which the Indian resisted in many bloody battles before he succumbed. Government bounties encouraged the killing of Indians in Minnesota. According to the Museum of the American Indian, "amounts up to $100 per scalp were paid, regardless of age or sex, and friendly Indians were often raided by professional 'bounty hunters' for the reward." A section of the Minnesota General Orders of 1863 (above and below) displays one such offer and payment.

While the most effective body of public opinion supported settlement of what had been Indian land,

THE DAILY GRAPHIC

An Illustrated Evening Newspaper.

VOL. VII. NEW YORK, FRIDAY, MARCH 12, 1875. NO. 626.

STATE

J. C. Davis, Sioux Scalp,
Oscar Malmros, Postage S
J. B. Horne, Canisters,
Peter Mack, Labor in Ars
Geo. Gentlich, "
John F. Catlin, 2 copies U
Temple & Beaupre, Pow
D. M. Baldwin, Transpo

vice will have to arm, equip
own expense, and will be
ate of one dollar and fifty
of twenty-five dollars will
h scalp of a male Sioux de-

some white people protested the invasion. The front page of the New York *Daily Graphic* protests the white trespass into the Black Hills of Dakota, the site of the last major American gold rush. The caption quotes the Indian as saying, "The Black Hills are mine, and the United States have promised to protect me against the invasion. If you keep not your word with me, why should I keep mine with you? The villainy you teach me I will execute, and it shall go hard but I will better the instruction."

Indian resistance cost settler's lives, but by 1890 it was almost entirely broken. The photograph at the right shows the victims of the Battle of Wounded Knee being gathered for burial.

URER.	403	
- -	25	00
for Office,	25	00
- - -	3	12
- - -	30	00
- - -	33	75
ilitary Laws,	10	00
Lead, -	61	80
f Arms		

Far left: The New-York Historical Society, New York City; left, above and be Courtesy of the Museum of the American Indian, Heye Foundation; above: Sm sonian Institution, National Anthropological Archives, Bureau of Ethnology Collection

THE S. D. BUTCHER DOCUMENT

Solomon Devoe Butcher created one of the most important records of frontier life. Starting in 1886 and continuing, with interruptions, for some twenty years, Butcher wrote and photographed the history of Custer County, Nebraska. Butcher's pictures depict the culture of the sod house, a form of building which the settlers used in the absence of cheap, readily available wood. The sod was cut into 18 inch strips and laid like bricks, providing a home that was warm in winter and cool in summer, but hard to live in during extended periods of rain. The pictures from Butcher's collection here and on the pages that follow, are reproduced through the courtesy of the Nebraska Historical Society and with the assistance of Harry E. Chrisman, who in 1965 secured the republication of the rare *Pioneer History of Custer County,* and Purcell Publishing Co., whose *Sod Walls,* by Roger Welsch, is based largely on the Butcher collection. The Chrisman sisters in Custer County, 1886, appear below. The photograph at left shows a typical dugout which used the contour of the land to provide several of its walls. The following spread, above, shows a photograph taken by Butcher in 1904 of the new town of Comstock, Nebraska, when wood was more available and had replaced sod as the most common building material. By contrast, the 1888 farm, with corn planted up to the homesteader's front door, utilizes the older sod construction.

All pictures on these and following pages: S. D. Butcher, Nebraska State Historical Society

in western Minnesota wrote that, unless outside help came soon, he and his family faced starvation. Governor Robert W. Furnas of Nebraska told the Legislature that many Western pioneers had lost their entire year's work in 1874 and "had no means to support themselves and their families during the winter or to provide for next year's crops."

As a result of these conditions, frontier settlement stalled and even reversed itself in some Western communities. But in the late 1870s a new boom developed, and within another decade farmers had pushed onto the Great Plains and occupied central Dakota, western Kansas and Nebraska, eastern Colorado, and northwest Texas. As farmers moved to the semiarid plains west of the 99th meridian, they found new geographic conditions which demanded change and adjustment. So long as settlement had been confined to the more humid areas east of the 98th meridian, settlers found enough timber for building and wood for fuel. But when they moved to the treeless prairie-plains frontier, they had to build their houses out of sod and to burn twisted hay or dried buffalo and cow manure for fuel. Water was also a problem on the Great Plains, and wells often had to be drilled 100 or 200 feet deep. The old oaken bucket could not be used to draw water under these conditions. Consequently, farmers adopted windmills as a source of power. The need for fencing was met by the use of barbed wire, which had been introduced in the 1870s.

The sod house, barbed wire, and the windmill were tangible evidences of the changes necessary for successful settlement on the Great Plains frontier. However, they were not as important as the adjustment in farm organization and agricultural practices. Because of limited and irregular moisture, farmers found that they had to adopt drought-resisting crops; they obtained better results by summer fallowing their land, which meant leaving part of it idle each year so that it would store up moisture; they had to build up reserves of feed to use in dry periods; they needed more land than a quarter section, which was not enough in a semiarid region; and they had to organize farm operations around a combined crop-livestock enterprise. Farmers who did not make the proper adjustments were sure to fail; those who organized their farming practices to fit the geography of the area had a much better chance to succeed.

During the 1870s and 1880s farmers occupied one frontier after another in the West. Thousands of settlers went to Oregon and Washington, as well as to California. Even the arid Rocky Mountain region drew many farmers, who developed and improved irrigation practices and made some desert areas highly productive. Not all of the movement on the frontier went from east to west. In the 1880s thousands of settlers pushed into eastern Oregon and Washington from communities west of the Cascades and from California. Moreover, settlement pushed out in every direction from such centers of population as Salt Lake City, Denver, and Walla Walla, just as earlier pioneers had fanned out from Cleveland, Detroit, Chicago, and Milwaukee.

By the late 1880s there remained unsettled in the West very little good farmland which could be farmed without irrigation. One previously restricted area, however, yet remained unexploited. That was Oklahoma. The eastern part of this region had been reserved for the Five Civilized Tribes, which included the Cherokee, Choctaw, Chickasaw, Seminole, and Creek, while certain plains tribes had been settled in the western section after the Civil

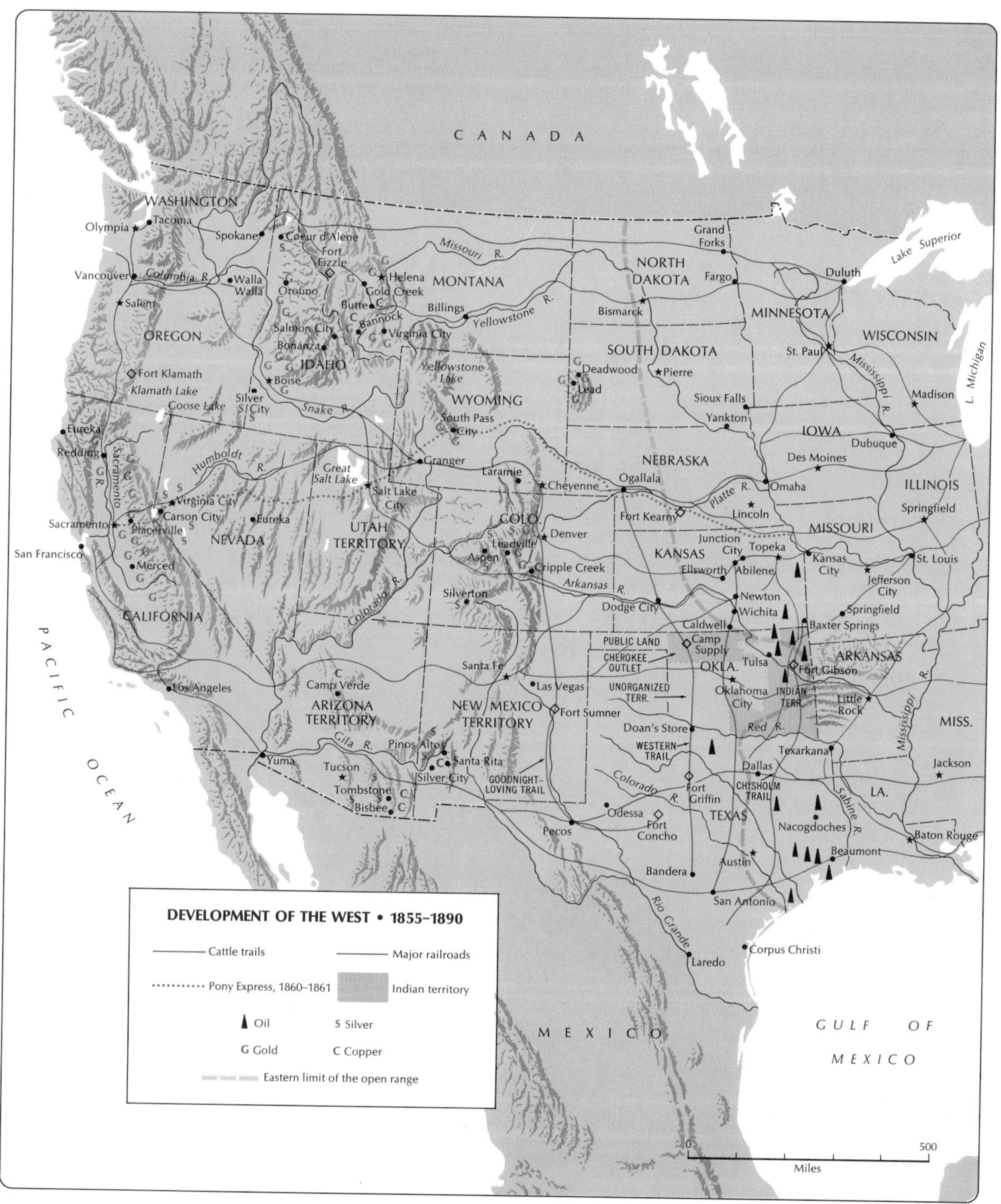

The Last Frontier, 1865–1900

War. Since very little, if any, good land remained unoccupied in Dakota, Nebraska, Kansas, and Texas, by the late 1880s strong pressure had developed to open Oklahoma to white settlement. Whites argued that the Indians did not make full use of their large holdings. Prospective settlers wanted the federal government to make the Indians take individual allotments of land and throw open the remainder of the tribal holdings for white settlement. After several years of agitation, the unassigned lands in central Oklahoma were finally opened.

Since there were more land-seekers than available quarter sections, the government adopted a new method of distribution—the land run. Prospective settlers camped near the border of the new territory, and the run began at noon on April 22, 1889. Describing the situation, one contemporary wrote: "Along the line as far as the eye could reach, with a shout and a yell the swift riders shot out, then followed the light buggies or wagons and last the lumbering prairie schooners and freighters' wagons, with here and there even a man on a bicycle and many too on foot,—above all a great cloud of dust hovering like smoke over a battlefield. It was a wild scramble, a rough and tumble contest filled with excitement and real peril." In a single day, places like Guthrie and Oklahoma City grew from virgin prairie to towns of several thousand citizens.

Between 1860 and 1900 waves of settlers established some 1,141,276 new farms in the nineteen Western states and territories. This newly settled region added greatly to the output of wheat, cattle, and other basic agricultural products and helped to make the United States one of the world's greatest exporters of farm commodities. Though many Western farmers met severe hardships on the agricultural frontier, more than any other group, they were responsible for bringing the frontier to an end.

Retreat of the Indians

Pressure from the advancing white men's frontiers finally destroyed all Indian resistance to white encroachment and forced the Indians to move into restricted areas. This was the last chapter in the long history of Indian retreat before onrushing settlers, who insisted that the federal government make Indian lands available for white settlement. However, the Western tribes did not surrender easily. Before peace was achieved on the Indian frontier in the 1890s, many bitter and costly battles had been fought between the United States Army and the Indians. Justice may not have been on the side of the whites, but they had the power to achieve their goals. At times they exerted this power with a terrible vengeance.

At the end of the Civil War there were approximately 275,000 Indians west of the Mississippi River. Among the major tribes were the Sioux, Crow, and Blackfeet in the North; the Cheyenne and Arapaho on the Central Plains; Comanche, Kiowa, and Apache in the Southwest; and the Ute, Snake, and Bannock in the Great Basin. The Five Civilized Tribes occupied what later became the eastern part of Oklahoma. Many other tribes lived in widely scattered areas elsewhere throughout the Great West.

The Treaty of Fort Laramie in 1851 had provided territorial boundaries for a number of the plains tribes, including the Sioux, Cheyenne, and Arapaho. However, the whites' desire to open eastern Kansas, Nebraska, and Dakota to settlement and the need to move the

Indians in Iowa and Missouri farther west soon brought violations of the Fort Laramie agreements. Moreover, the influx of prospectors into the Cheyenne and Arapaho lands around Pike's Peak in 1859 aroused bitter Indian hostility. The steady pressure of whites against the dwindling Indian land holdings and the destruction of the wild game caused many Indian leaders to conclude that they must rely on force to protect their lands and way of life.

During the 1860s Indians and whites met in a series of bloody conflicts. In 1862 the Sioux attacked the Minnesota frontier, destroying a great deal of property and killing more than four hundred and fifty whites before they were defeated by an army under the command of Colonel H. H. Sibley. Two years later the Cheyenne and Arapaho brought death and destruction to the Colorado frontier. Striking back fiercely at the Indians, the Colorado militia led by Colonel J. M. Chivington attacked Chief Black Kettle and about five hundred Cheyenne and Arapahoes at Sand Creek in southeastern Colorado in November, 1864. Within a few hours, between four hundred and five hundred Indians had been shot, knifed, or beaten to death. The Chivington Massacre worsened relations between whites and Indians throughout the West. Intermittent fighting continued during the next two or three years.

Some army commanders believed that the so-called Indian problem could only be solved through decisive military action. Complete submission or extermination seemed to them to be the only answer. On the other hand, many Easterners, including senators and congressmen, felt that the problems of Indian-white relations could best be solved by enticing the Indians to accept smaller areas of land and encouraging them to give up their nomadic ways. Such a policy, it was believed, would reduce friction and maintain peace by keeping the Indians away from white settlements. But how could the federal government keep the Indians who were accustomed to roaming over large areas within definite boundaries? And how could it make whites recognize that the Indians had fundamental rights to land on which pioneer farmers hoped to settle?

At a council on Medicine Lodge Creek in October, 1867, the Kiowa, Comanche, Cheyenne, and Arapaho tribes agreed to reservations on the Southern plains. The next year, by a second Treaty of Fort Laramie, the Sioux accepted a permanent reservation west of the Missouri River in Dakota. However, these treaties did not restore peace. Dissatisfied over their chiefs' ceding away millions of acres of land, angry Cheyenne and Arapaho warriors ravaged the Texas and Kansas frontiers in 1868. The Army responded vigorously to these depredations, and in November, Colonel George A. Custer defeated Chief Black Kettle and his followers on the banks of the Washita near the Texas border. The Indian raids continued, nevertheless, and it was not until June of 1875, after six or seven years of intermittent fighting, that the Indians were completely beaten in Texas. Defeated, humiliated, and broken, they were forced back to life on their reservations.

A rush of settlers into the Black Hills in 1875 and 1876 violated the Treaty of Fort Laramie and aroused the worried Sioux. Chiefs Crazy Horse and Sitting Bull began collecting arms and warriors near the Little Big Horn in Montana. When the Indian Office could not stop the prospect of another uprising, the Army was again ordered into action. In the spring of 1876, several military groups moved against the recalcitrant Sioux. At the Little

Big Horn, Colonel Custer, who had won fame as an Indian fighter against the Cheyenne and Arapaho, stumbled into a far superior Indian force, and he and his 265 men were completely wiped out.

But this victory only postponed Indian defeat. Within a few months the Sioux had surrendered to the military power of General Alfred H. Terry. The Sioux war of 1876 ended the main Indian resistance in the North, although a few sporadic outbreaks occurred in subsequent years. In the Pacific Northwest, Chief Joseph and his Nez Percé followers were forced to surrender in 1878 after nearly two years of intermittent fighting against a much superior United States armed force. Among two of the lesser-known, but highly effective, military units which helped to provide frontier defense were the Negro Ninth and Tenth Cavalry regiments.

The solution of the Indian problem had been primarily a military one. But meanwhile the Indians had been weakened by whisky, disease, and destruction of the buffalo, which had eliminated one of the Indians' essential sources of support. Forced mostly into barren and unproductive areas, the Indians had no choice but to give up their independence and accept government support.

Although most whites supported military action against the Indians, harsh army tactics pricked the consciences of many Americans, and by the late 1870s and early 1880s, the Indians' plight was receiving widespread attention. In 1881 Helen Hunt Jackson presented a highly emotional and somewhat distorted account of the relations between the federal government and the Indians in her book *A Century of Dishonor.* She attributed most of the wrongs to a lack of government planning combined with people's unconcern for Indian welfare. Other reformers and humanitarians also raised a cry against government Indian policies.

The agitation of reformers gave added support to new policies which were already being developed in Washington. In 1871 Congress had abandoned the old policy of dealing with Indian tribes through formal treaties. This step tended to break down tribal organization and authority. The Indian Office set up special courts to handle Indian cases in 1883 and thereby further reduced the power of the chiefs.

This policy of destroying tribal organization and fitting the Indians into the white man's society culminated in passage of the Dawes Act in 1887. Sometimes called the Indian Emancipation Act, this law gave the President authority to have Indian reservations surveyed and to allot land to individual Indians. The head of each family was to receive 160 acres and each minor child 40 acres. An unmarried Indian over eighteen years of age was to receive 80 acres. Indian land holders were also to become citizens of the United States. In order to keep unscrupulous whites from somehow cheating Indian owners out of their land, the Indians were prohibited from selling or alienating their holdings before twenty-five years. This provision was modified in the Burke Act of 1906, which gave the Secretary of the Interior discretionary power to lessen the time period required of Indians before they could gain title to their land. The Dawes Act did not apply to the Five Civilized Tribes in Oklahoma, who opposed the breakup of tribal authority and control. However, after 1897 they, too, were placed in the position of having to accept individual allotments by the Dawes

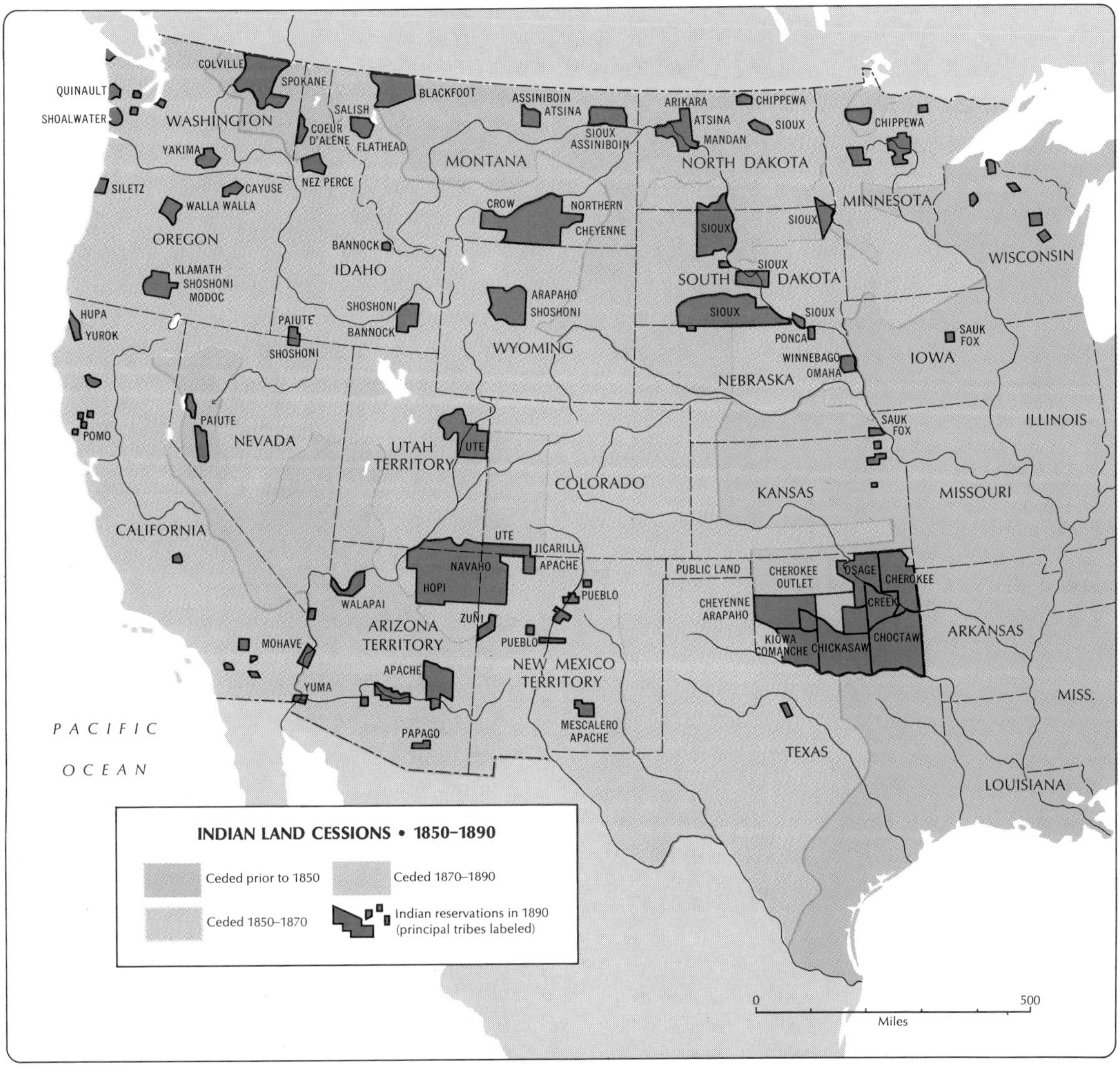

INDIAN LAND CESSIONS • 1850–1890

Ceded prior to 1850

Ceded 1850–1870

Ceded 1870–1890

Indian reservations in 1890 (principal tribes labeled)

Commission, which had been appointed five years earlier.

It soon became apparent that the attempt to make successful farmers out of the Indians and to fit them into a white-dominated economy had failed miserably. It was not possible to make a decent living on much of their land, which was poor and nonproductive. Moreover, Indian lands were in time fragmented and divided through inheritance and sale, and thousands of Indians sank into stark poverty. After subjugation they were never properly assimilated into the mainstream of America's national life. No real answer has been found to the economic and social problems of Indians even in the twentieth century.

Rapid westward migration brought the frontier to an end within a generation after 1865. Settlement of the West had a number of important influences on American life. In the first place, Westerners exerted strong pressure on Congress to provide statehood for the newly settled regions west of the Missouri River. After Nebraska became a state in 1867 and Colorado in 1876, no additional states were admitted until 1889. But then, within the next few years, some ten states were added to the Union. These included the Dakotas, Washington, and Montana in 1889; Idaho and Wyoming in 1890; and Utah in 1896, after Congress insisted that the Mormons abandon polygamy. Oklahoma achieved statehood in 1907; New Mexico and Arizona, five years later.

Admission of twelve new states after 1867 gave the West a degree of political power far out of proportion to its population. Most of the Western states did not continue to grow at the same rate as those settled earlier and, consequently, their equality in the United States Senate gave them an undue amount of political influence.

Furthermore, the exploitive nature of the economy which developed in the mining and lumber industries stimulated a high degree of labor unrest throughout the region. The Industrial Workers of the World, formed in 1905, was strongest around the mines and lumber camps and represented one of the most radical political and economic movements in United States history. The economic problems and natural hazards associated with Western farming, particularly on the Great Plains, intensified agrarian discontent, which climaxed in the Populist movement of the 1890s. Despite the purported individualism and independence of Westerners, problems connected with settlement in parts of the West encouraged the growth of governmental powers and functions. For example, in the arid and semiarid regions, people called on the federal government to aid in developing irrigation because the cost of constructing large-scale dams and ditches was more than could be successfully undertaken by individuals, or even private corporations. In 1902 Congress passed the Newlands Act, which provided federal aid for irrigation projects.

Not only did the dramatic settlement of the last frontier carry important political and economic implications for the nation, but also it encouraged the creation of a distinctive literature. Aspects of Western life became the subject matter for some of the country's most outstanding writers, including Bret Harte, Samuel Clemens (Mark Twain), Hamlin Garland, Willa Cather, and Ole Rölvaag. Bret Harte brought the mining frontier into literary prominence with his *The Luck of Roaring Camp* (1870), *The Outcasts of Poker Flat, The Idyll of Red Gulch,* and other stories. He stamped his interpretation upon the California mining region to such an extent that it came to be called "the Bret Harte country." Samuel Clemens went west from Missouri in 1861 and spent five years prospecting, writing, and lecturing in Nevada and California. *Roughing It* (1872) added both to the Western heritage and to the literary realism of the late nineteenth century. The book dealt with travel across the plains, life in Virginia City, Nevada, and unsuccessful mining ventures.

The farmers' frontier found a number of

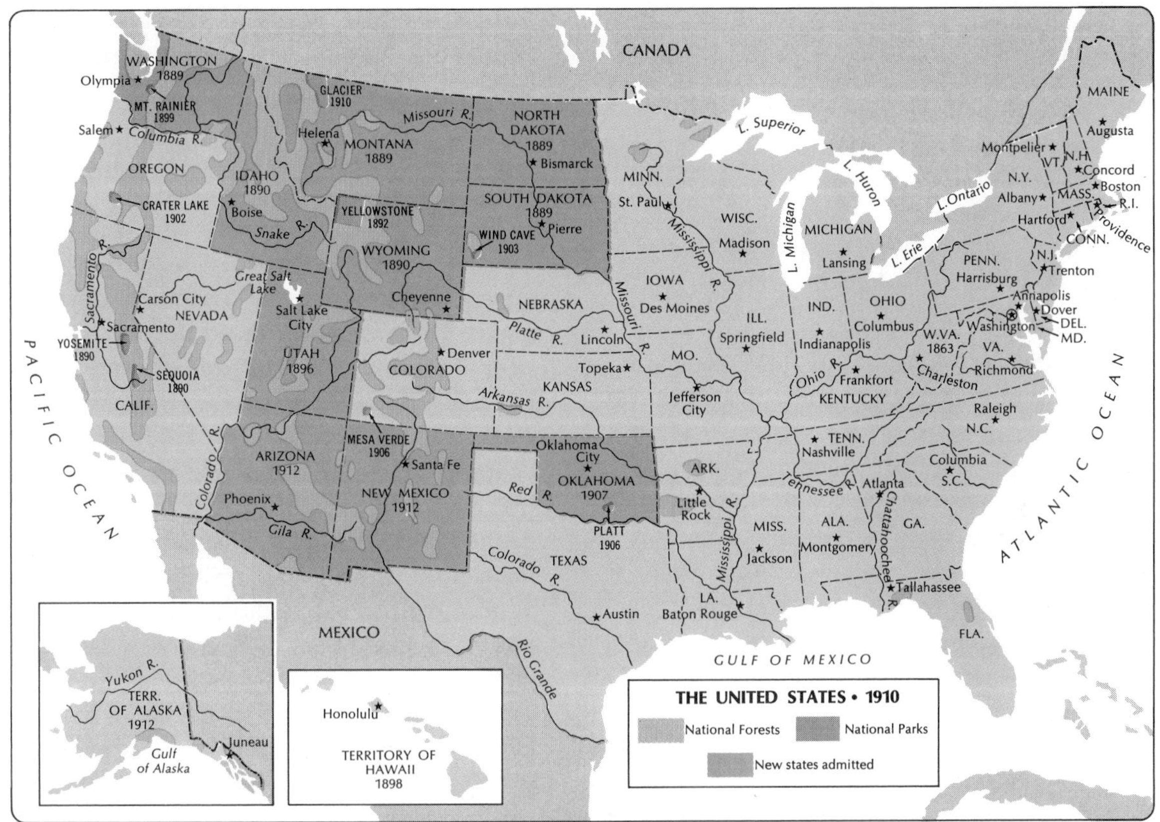

literary interpreters. These writers generally pictured Western rural life as hard, dreary, barren, and unprofitable. In *A Son of the Middle Border,* Hamlin Garland related the pioneering history of his own family which settled finally on the black prairies of Dakota. Garland recorded in most vivid terms the droughts, snowstorms, poverty, monotony, and cultural barrenness of Western farm life. He emphasized these themes in *Main-Travelled Roads.* But the most powerful novel dealing with pioneer life was Ole Rölvaag's *Giants in the Earth.* This was the story of a Norwegian family which settled in Dakota in the 1870s. Per Hansa, the story's central figure, was a symbol of thousands of pioneers during that period who struggled to build homes on the inhospitable frontier. Western pioneer life contributed something as well to the nation's music and poetry. Plaintive and sad cowboy songs, such as "Bury Me Not on the Lone Prairie" and "The Dying Cowboy," eventually became popular in all parts of the country. Farm life on the prairies and Great Plains found a musical description in "The Little Old Sod Shanty on the Claim." One verse and the chorus are:

"I am looking rather seedy now
While holding down my claim
And my victuals are not always served the best
And the prairie dog keeps barking so

That I can scarcely sleep
In my little old sod shanty in the West."

"Oh! the hinges are of leather
And the windows have no glass
While the board roof lets the howling blizzards in,
And I hear the hungry kiyote
As he sneaks up through the grass,
'Round my little old sod shanty on my claim."

In 1890 the Director of the Census wrote that, in the traditional sense, there was no longer any frontier in the United States. This was not true in the strict sense, because there was still a great deal of unsettled public land available. Indeed, more homesteads were filed after 1890 than before that date. But most of the unsettled lands were in the semi-arid or arid parts of the West and were unproductive without irrigation. So the Director was correct when he implied that most of the good land which could be dependably farmed under conditions of natural rainfall was gone.

Three years later historian Frederick Jackson Turner declared that the census statement "marks the closing of a great historic movement." He then explained that "up to our own day [1893] American history has been in a large degree the history of the colonization of the Great West. The existence of an area of free land," he continued, "its continuous recession, and the advance of American settlement westward, explain American development." Turner believed that continuous contact with the frontier over a period of nearly three centuries had deeply affected the American character. He argued that the frontier had contributed to "a composite nationality for the American people," that it had promoted democracy and stimulated independence and individualism. He also attributed such traits as materialism, practicality, and an inventive turn of mind to frontier experiences. Although other historians later challenged the so-called Turner Thesis, Turner's ideas had a marked effect upon historical writing and even on public thinking and action.

Conclusion

The central question which arises from the disappearance of the frontier is clear. Did this development produce any noticeable changes in American life? Was there any definite break in the pulse or pattern of national development around 1890? The frontier may have influenced the American character, but the people's energies were already being directed into new channels—toward business, industry, and overseas expansion. Rapid industrialization was absorbing much of the national purpose. Indeed, the idealized man was no longer a hard-handed farmer, but a middle-class worker who lived in the city and earned a comfortable salary. There continued to be a great deal of romanticism connected with the last frontier, but this was projected mostly by those who had never experienced pioneer life. The pioneering West was gone even if its traditions lived on.

SUGGESTED READINGS

The best general survey of the trans-Mississippi West is L. R. Hafen and C. C. Rister's *Western America* (1950). All of the general histories of the American West also devote a good deal of attention to that region during the period of settlement and growth after the Civil War. Ray Allen Billington's

Westward Expansion (3d ed., 1967) is the most comprehensive treatment, but other good accounts can be found in T. C. Clark's *Frontier America* (1959) and Robert E. Riegel and Robert G. Athearn's *America Moves West* (4th ed., 1964). The best interpretation of the impact of the frontier on American life and culture is Ray Allen Billington's *America's Frontier Heritage** (1966). It is basic to read Frederick Jackson Turner's "The Significance of the Frontier in American History," which first appeared in the *Report of the American Historical Association*, 1893, but has been reprinted many times elsewhere.

General studies which deal with different areas of the trans-Mississippi West include C. C. Rister's *The Southwestern Frontier, 1865–1890* (1947); W. E. Hollon's *The Southwest: Old and New** (1961); Robert G. Athearn's *High Country Empire** (1960); O. O. Winther's *The Pacific Northwest* (1947); L. J. Arrington's *Great Basin Kingdom** (1958), which considers the Mormons; Earl S. Pomeroy's *The Pacific Slope* (1965); and John Caughey's *California* (2d ed., 1953). *The Sod-house Frontier, 1854–1890* (1937) by Everett Dick is a delightful social history, mainly of the Nebraska and Kansas frontier. In *The Great Plains** (1931), W. P. Webb has discussed the problems of settling that region. Henry Nash Smith advances a bold interpretation in *Virgin Land: The American West as Symbol and Myth** (1950).

Land policies have been carefully treated by Roy M. Robbins in *Our Landed Heritage** (1942); Paul W. Gates in *Fifty Million Acres** (1954), which is a discussion of disposal of the public domain in Kansas; and E. Louise Peffer in *The Closing of the Public Domain* (1951). Excellent studies on the Western territories are Earl S. Pomeroy's *The Territories and the United States, 1865–1890* (1947) and the works of Howard Lamar: *Dakota Territory, 1861–1889** (1956) and *The Far Southwest, 1846–1912* (1966).

The best survey of Western mining is Rodman Paul's *The Mining Frontiers of the Far West, 1848–1880** (1963). Another excellent account is William S. Greever's *The Bonanza West: The Story of the Western Mining Rushes, 1848–1900* (1963). Two older but still useful works are Glenn C. Quiett's *Pay Dirt: A Panorama of American Gold Rushes* (1936) and T. A. Rickard's *A History of American Mining* (1932). See also Watson Parker's *Gold in the Black Hills* (1966) and Clark C. Spence's *British Investment and the American Mining Frontier, 1860–1901* (1958). *The Company Town in the American West* (1966) by James B. Allen includes aspects of Western economic and social history.

The Western cattle industry has been adequately treated in E. E. Dale's *The Range Cattle Industry* (1930); Ernest S. Osgood's *The Day of the Cattleman** (1929); and Louis Pelzer's *The Cattlemen's Frontier* (1936). An important phase of the cattle business has been considered by Gene M. Gressley in *Bankers and Cattlemen* (1966). In *The Cattle Kings* (1961), Lewis E. Atherton has emphasized the role of ranchers in influencing Western cultural developments. For a popular account of Western sheep raising, see C. W. Towne and E. N. Wentworth's *Shepherd's Empire* (1945). On Western agriculture see Gilbert C. Fite's *The Farmers' Frontier, 1865–1900* (1966).

On the Indians, W. T. Hagan presents an excellent brief survey in *American Indians** (1961). There are histories of many Indian tribes which deal in some way with the problems of the red man and government policy relating to him. Among the better works are *A Sioux Chronicle* (1956) by George E. Hyde; Donald J. Berthrong's *The Southern Cheyennes* (1963); A. M. Gibson's *The Kickapoos* (1963); and E. C. McReynolds's *The Seminoles* (1957). On the Indian wars see P. I. Wellman's *The Indian Wars of the West* (1954); C. M. Oehler's *The Great Sioux Uprising* (1959); E. I. Stewart's *Custer's Luck* (1955); and R. G. Athearn's *William Tecumseh Sherman and the Settlement of the West* (1956). *The Military Conquest of the Southern Plains* (1963) and *The Buffalo Soldiers: A Narrative of the Negro Cavalry in the West* (1967) by William Leckie are important contributions to the history of Indian military defeat. On government Indian policy consult E. E. Dale's *The Indians of the Southwest* (1949); Henry Fritz's *The Movement for Indian Assimilation, 1860–1890* (1963); and Loring B. Priest's *Uncle Sam's Step-children: The Reformation of the United States Indian Policy, 1865–1887* (1942).

Some of the best works on the last frontier were written by literary figures. See Mark Twain's *Roughing It** (1872); Hamlin Garland's *A Son of the Middle Border* (1917); Willa S. Cather's *O Pioneers!** (1913); and Ole E. Rölvaag's *Giants in the Earth** (1929).

*indicates availability in paperback.

24

Agriculture, Farm Policies, and the Agrarian Revolt, 1865 — 1896

FEW CHANGES during the late nineteenth century were more important than those associated with American agriculture. Farming had always been the principal means of making a living in the United States, but by 1890 this condition had changed. The census of that year showed that the value of farm products was exceeded by the value of industrial commodities, and whether or not farmers recognized the fact, agriculture for the first time had dropped to a position of secondary importance in American history. The urban-industrial aspects of American life were rapidly becoming its most characteristic and spectacular as well as its most troublesome.

Despite its relative decline in the overall economy, agriculture experienced tremendous expansion in the post-Civil War years. Between 1860 and 1910 farm acreage more than doubled, and the number of farms jumped from about two million to nearly 6.5 million. This rapid enlargement of the agricultural domain was stimulated by liberal federal land policies; encouragement by the Western states seeking more population; and enticements offered by the railroads, which had millions of acres of land for sale. As farmers scattered out over the western prairies, the Great Plains, and beyond the Rocky Mountains in the half century after 1860, they occupied more land than had their forefathers since the first landing at Jamestown in 1607.

Farm production made phenomenal gains. In 1859 the output of corn, the nation's leading grain crop, was 838 million bushels, but a half century later it reached more than 2.5 billion bushels. In that same period, wheat production jumped from 173 million to 657 million bushels, an increase of nearly 400 percent. The per capita output of wheat rose from 5.5 bushels in 1859 to 8.6 bushels in 1899. The production of cotton rose from 4.5 million to 10.6 million bales—of 500 pounds each—between 1859 and 1909, while the number of hogs, cattle, horses, and other livestock increased with equal rapidity. Thus abundant production of food and fiber assured the American people an adequate, high-protein diet, and a liberal supply of raw materials for manufacturing.

In the late nineteenth century most of American agriculture shifted to a strictly commercial basis, meaning that farmers produced crops primarily for the commercial market rather than for their own use. They sold their commodities for money and bought manufactured goods rather than striving for self-sufficiency. This involved greater specialization, and many farmers raised only one, or at most a few, cash crops such as wheat, cotton, corn, and hogs, or dairy products. American farmers had always produced some surplus for sale, but now production for the market became the chief end of farming. These changes rendered the individual farmer increasingly vulnerable to economic forces beyond his control.

The great expansion of agricultural output would not have been possible without the phenomenal improvements in farm technology which occurred after 1865. American farmers had always sought to lighten their work and increase their output with tools and machines, but most of the machinery available in 1860 was crude and inefficient. Horse and ox-drawn plows, cultivators, mowers, and reapers were in use, but the tremendous potentiality of horse-powered machinery had not yet been realized by most farmers. The Civil War stimulated the use of machinery because of the shortage of manpower on farms, but the most significant developments came later. In the years after the Civil War, improved plows, manufactured by John Deere and James Oliver, and better harrows, grain drills, cultivators, mowers, and other machines came into widespread use. But the greatest advances were made in harvesting and threshing equipment for small grain. The McCormick reaper was a great improvement over the sickle or scythe for cutting grain, but models sold before the Civil War still required men to rake the grain off the cutting bar and tie it into sheaves. The development of the self-binder, which cut and bound the grain in a single operation, was the step which greatly reduced the need for manpower in harvesting. In 1878 John F. Appleby invented a successful twine binder, which soon replaced wire for tying the grain bundles. The horse-drawn twine binder removed the last obstacle to large-scale harvesting of wheat and other small grains. Threshing machines were also improved, and by the late nineteenth century they were powered by steam engines in many areas.

The employment of more and better machines greatly increased the efficiency of farm labor. A wheat grower with the latest equipment in 1896 could produce, with the same time and effort, eighteen times more wheat

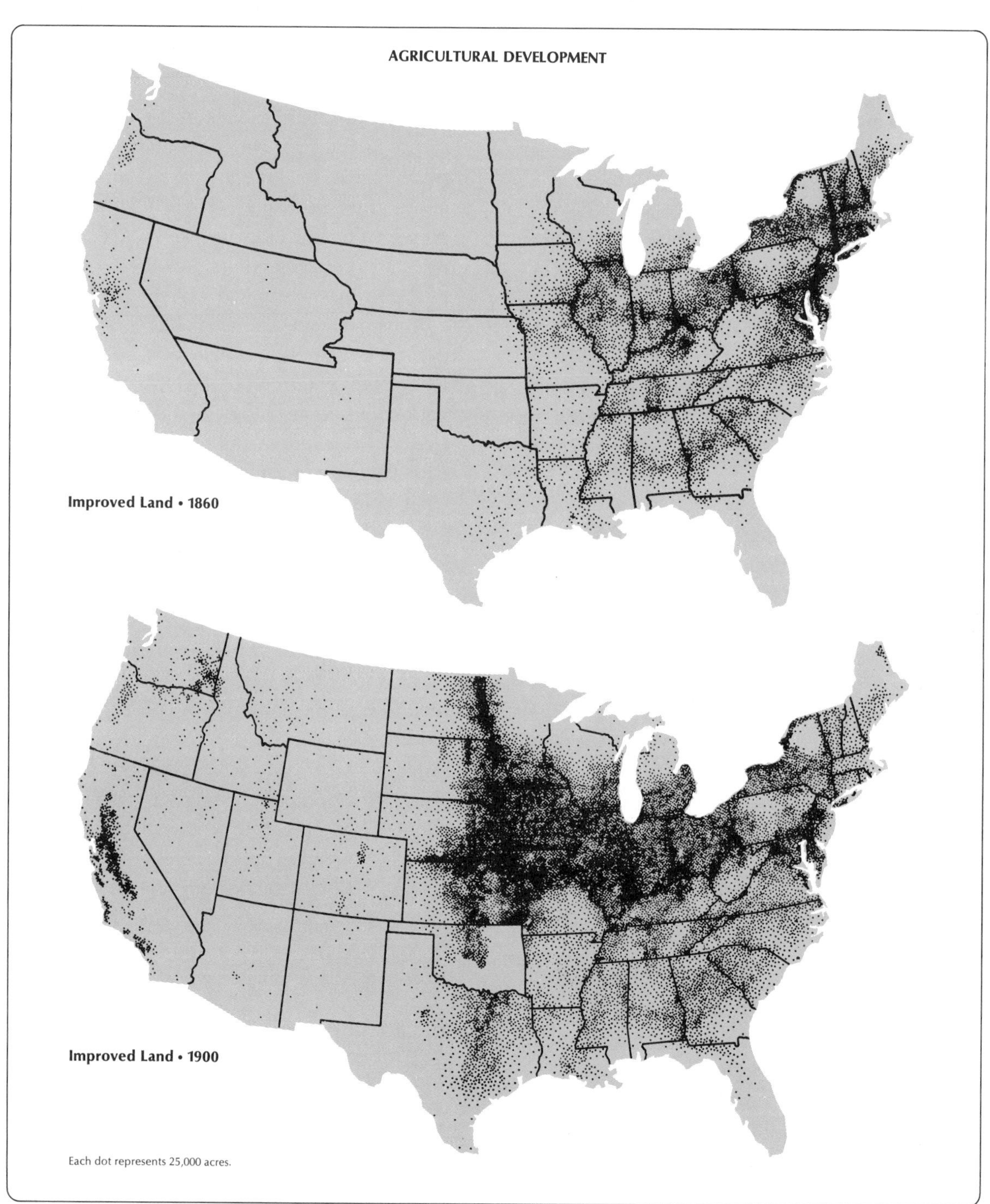
AGRICULTURAL DEVELOPMENT
Improved Land • 1860
Improved Land • 1900
Each dot represents 25,000 acres.

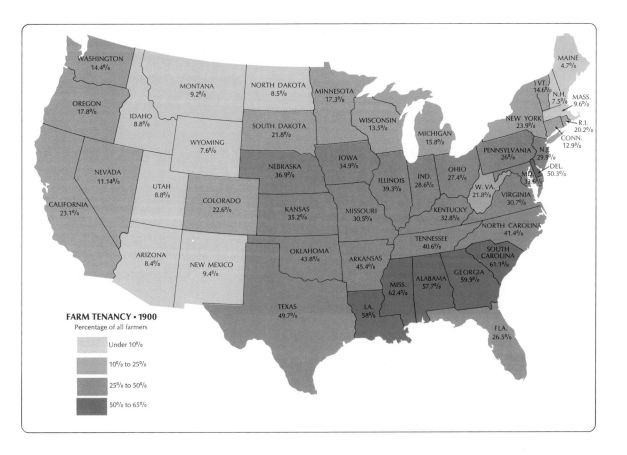

FARM TENANCY • 1900

Percentage of all farmers

Under 10%
10% to 25%
25% to 50%
50% to 65%

WASHINGTON 14.4%
OREGON 17.8%
CALIFORNIA 23.1%
NEVADA 11.14%
IDAHO 8.8%
MONTANA 9.2%
WYOMING 7.6%
UTAH 8.8%
ARIZONA 8.4%
COLORADO 22.6%
NEW MEXICO 9.4%
NORTH DAKOTA 8.5%
SOUTH DAKOTA 21.8%
NEBRASKA 36.9%
KANSAS 35.2%
OKLAHOMA 43.8%
TEXAS 49.7%
MINNESOTA 17.3%
IOWA 34.9%
MISSOURI 30.5%
ARKANSAS 45.4%
LA. 58%
WISCONSIN 13.5%
ILLINOIS 39.3%
MICHIGAN 15.8%
IND. 28.6%
OHIO 27.4%
KENTUCKY 32.8%
TENNESSEE 40.6%
MISS. 62.4%
ALABAMA 57.7%
GEORGIA 59.9%
FLA. 26.5%
SOUTH CAROLINA 61.1%
NORTH CAROLINA 41.4%
VIRGINIA 30.7%
W. VA. 21.8%
MD. 33.6%
DEL. 50.3%
PENNSYLVANIA 26%
N.J. 29.9%
NEW YORK 23.9%
CONN. 12.9%
R.I. 20.2%
MASS. 9.6%
VT. 14.6%
N.H. 7.5%
MAINE 4.7%

than his forefather did in 1830. In 1894 it required but fifteen hours to sow and harvest 40 bushels of corn, compared with thirty-nine hours in 1855. As one writer has stated: "Agricultural machinery increased the efficiency of farm work, enlarged the acreage which could be tilled, freed millions of farmers' children so they could seek employment in the cities, lightened the burden and drudgery of farm labor, helped to raise the standard of living for many farm families, assisted in supplying cheap raw materials for America's expanding industries, and helped to provide millions of dollars worth of commodities for the export market."

There were also other factors which helped to increase agricultural output. Improved plant and livestock breeds, better tillage methods, irrigation, the use of more fertilizer, and the policies of the federal government all combined to increase farmers' efficiency. The United States Department of Agriculture, created in 1862 and given full Cabinet status in 1889, distributed seeds, promoted the planting of new and improved crops, and in general sought to better farming practices. Also in 1862 Congress passed the Morrill Act, providing land grants for new agricultural and mechanical colleges. The Hatch Act of 1887 set up federal experiment stations.

The great expansion in American agricultural output was closely associated with the settlement of new lands in the Mississippi Valley, the agricultural heartland of America. In the area from Ohio to eastern Nebraska a "corn-hog belt" developed, which was one of the most productive cereal and livestock empires in the world. Although Ohio ranked first in corn production in 1849, Illinois and Iowa became the leading centers of corn growing after the Civil War. In the Western prairies and Great Plains, wheat became the principal cash crop. Just as corn production had moved westward from Ohio to Iowa, the center of wheat output shifted west from Illinois to the Dakotas and Kansas. Wheat production lent itself to large-scale operations, and mechanization reached its highest development in such great wheat-producing areas as the Red River Valley of North Dakota.

Southern agriculture suffered severely during the Civil War, and it was several years after 1865 before farming in the South recovered its prewar position. One of the greatest problems facing Southern planters and large farmers was the adjustment from slave to free labor. For a time planters attempted to employ freedmen for wages, but a shortage of cash and the lack of experienced workers caused this effort to be abandoned in favor of a tenant system. Although there was widespread discussion about distributing land to newly freed Negroes, and many freedmen hoped to obtain 40 acres and a mule, this program was never implemented. As it turned out, the freedmen remained landless and had nothing to sell except their labor. Landowners, on the other hand, were short of capital and labor, and this presented the problem of bringing landowners and landless workers together into some sort of productive and profitable arrangement. The sharecrop, or tenant, system was the result.

Sharecropping operated on a somewhat standard formula. Under this arrangement the landowner received one-third of a crop for the use of the land and the tenant or sharecropper received one-third for his labor. The remaining one-third was divided between the landlord and tenant on the basis of who provided the machinery, fertilizer, and other items necessary to produce the crop. There were very few cash tenants in the South; most worked on a share basis. Sometimes tenancy was a means to ownership, but this did not happen often. For the most part both black and white sharecroppers and tenants found themselves engulfed in a system of economic dependency, low incomes, and perpetual debt, from which they could not escape.

The position of most black farmers in the South did not improve with time. And it made little difference whether they were day laborers, tenant operators, or owners. By 1910 Mississippi, for example, recorded 164,488 of its 274,382 farmers as blacks. Of these blacks only 24,949, or some 15 percent, owned their land. The situation was not much better in Alabama or Georgia. Nevertheless, black families grew nearly 40 percent of the nation's important cotton crop. Total income for a black family was often no more than $100 to $200 a year, and that mainly in the form of store credit. Mired in poverty and unable to progress to the status of landowners, hundreds of blacks migrated to Kansas in 1879 under the leadership of a fellow black man, Benjamin

Singleton. The majority of these "Exodusters" failed to become successful farmers in Kansas, however, and most of them returned South or settled in Midwestern towns and cities.

Although cotton production was hard hit during the Civil War, it continued to be the South's leading crop in the postwar years. By the late 1870s production was exceeding the prewar high of 4.5 million bales annually, and output advanced rapidly in succeeding years. In 1909 production reached about 10.7 million bales, or more than three times what it had beem forty years before. Cotton occupied 40 percent of the improved farmland in Georgia and South Carolina by 1909, indicating the great importance of this crop to the economy of some Southern states and to the South as a whole. In 1899 cotton accounted for about 32 percent of the value of all Southern crops. Mississippi had been the nation's leading cotton state in 1860, but production shifted westward after the Civil War, and by 1889 Texas ranked first.

Other principal cash crops raised by Southern farmers were tobacco, sugar, and rice. Virginia and Maryland, which had historically been the major tobacco-producing states, lost that leadership to Kentucky and Tennessee. About 1890 the demand by the cigarette industry for bright flue-cured tobacco greatly stimulated production in North Carolina, where the soil and climate were ideally suited for this type of tobacco. Between 1859 and 1909 tobacco production more than doubled. Rice production also moved westward then, and Louisiana, Texas, and Arkansas replaced South Carolina as the center of rice output. The growing of sugarcane for commercial purposes was largely confined to Louisiana.

It was the abundant productivity of American farms that assured the nation's population an adequate supply of high-protein food at reasonable prices. Meat, eggs, milk, vegetables, and fruit, in addition to cereals, were all-important in the average diet. Moreover, farm products provided the raw materials for some of the nation's largest manufacturing establishments, notably cotton textiles, meat-packing, and flour milling. Besides this, agricultural surpluses made up the majority of American exports. In 1860, for instance, some 82 percent of the nation's total exports consisted of farm products, and fifty years later they still provided more than half of American shipments overseas. Exports of cotton, wheat, and meat were particularly important in earning the foreign exchange necessary to pay for industrial imports.

Farm Problems

Despite the heavy production of farm commodities and their immeasurable economic contribution to the nation as a whole, individual farmers were confronted with many difficult problems in the late nineteenth century. The twenty-year period which followed the early 1870s was one of gradually declining prices, which reached their lowest point in 1894. The result was increasing debt, growing tenancy, and general hard times for many farmers. Farmers were also burdened by heavy transportation charges, excessive marketing costs, and a tax system which bore heavily on rural producers. In general, income from farm labor was considerably below that from other types of enterprise. In 1900 the annual per capita income of workers on farms was only $260.

The basic problem that farmers faced, however, was their poor bargaining position compared with other major elements in the economy. Farmers were in the unenviable situation of having control over neither the prices of their own commodities nor those of the manufactured goods which they bought. For example, dealers in wheat or cotton set the price of those commodities on the basis of world conditions, total demand, and other factors. The farmer had to sell for the offered price or make no sale at all. On the other hand, when a farmer wished to buy a piece of machinery or some other manufactured commodity, he had to pay the asking price or get along without it. Any bargaining that did take place was not between equals but between sellers who controlled their prices and farmers who did not. In economic language, the terms of trade were unfavorable to farmers as they sought to exchange raw and unprocessed products for finished manufactured goods. Part of the reason for this situation was that farmers operated on an individual, competitive basis, while other groups in the economy combined to reduce or eliminate the depressing effect on prices which competition tended to create.

Under such market conditions farmers suffered from a disparity between the prices they received for their products and the price of industrial commodities which they purchased. It was the relationship between farm and nonfarm prices which was so troublesome to the farmer. In other words, if cotton brought 10 cents a pound and a plow cost $50, it would take 500 pounds to buy a plow. But if cotton dropped to 5 cents and the price of the plow remained the same, it would take 1,000 pounds, or twice as much, to buy the same implement.

Most farmers in the late nineteenth century, however, did not recognize their basic position of weakness in the economy. Moreover, they refused to admit that they suffered from surplus production. Farmers argued that they were not prosperous because of the exactions of big business, bankers, and land monopolists who squeezed the profits out of farming. Agricultural spokesmen charged that farmers suffered from high transportation charges, excessive interest rates, a deflationary monetary policy, and disposal of the public domain to railroad, timber, and mining monopolies.

Many of the farmers' complaints were directed at the railroads. Critics charged that rates were both unreasonably high and discriminatory and that service was poor. The railroads were bitterly denounced, too, for their political activities, which included granting free passes to influential citizens, lobbying, and, in some cases, outright bribery. Even though freight rates dropped substantially after 1870, farmers continued to view the railroads as a major cause of their difficulties. Farmers also condemned what they considered the excessive cost of marketing and the setting of prices by monopolistic big business. The middlemen, as one writer put it, came to symbolize "the heartless monopolies and soulless corporations." Many farmers sincerely believed that they were ruthlessly exploited by agents of the farm machine, fertilizer, cottonseed oil, beef, and other trusts.

Agricultural producers were equally, if not more, disturbed by inadequate credit facilities and high interest rates. Farmers usually needed some credit, even if they obtained free land from the government, since construction of farm buildings, fencing, a water supply, and farm machinery all cost money. And interest rates were high. Credit charges on loans secured by real estate mortgages were seldom less than 6 percent, and 8 to 10 percent was common before the turn of the century. In 1890 one farmer wrote that Nebraska had three crops: "One is a crop of corn, one a crop of freight rates, and one a crop of interest." Once a farmer had mortgaged his property, a poor crop, bad management, or low prices could bring financial stringency and foreclosure. As a result of hard times and foreclosures, the amount of tenancy increased alarmingly throughout the country, rising from 25 to 35 percent between 1880 and 1900.

Farmers also faced other pressing problems. The tax system in most farm states bore disproportionately heavily upon owners of real property. While businessmen might hide their stocks and bonds from the tax assessor, the farmer's land and livestock were always in plain sight. Moreover, agricultural producers had to combat the destructive and unreliable forces of nature. Hungry grasshoppers, sudden hailstorms, or searing drought often destroyed crops. Thus, suffering from the ravages of nature, low prices, increasing debts, and even declining social prestige, farmers became restless and discontented.

Farm Revolt: The Grange

When farmers saw that they could not solve their problems individually, they turned to joint efforts. They had observed the economic benefits which organization had brought business and, to a lesser extent, labor. Why, they asked, could not farmers improve their position by working together toward common objectives? The Patrons of Husbandry, or Grange, was the first nationwide farm organization. Formed in 1867 by Oliver H. Kelley of Minnesota, the Grange sought to advance the lot of farmers through education, cooperation, and social improvement. It was a secret organization and admitted women to full and equal membership.

At first the Grange grew slowly. However, price declines after 1871 aroused farmers to militant action against monopolies and concentrated wealth. They saw the Grange as an organization through which they might combine to bring the monopolies under control and perhaps achieve other economic goals. Also by the early 1870s the idea of producer and consumer cooperatives appealed to many farmers, who saw the need of placing agriculture in a better bargaining position with business. By 1874 the Grange boasted a total membership of 800,000.

Although the Grange was nonpolitical, individual Grangers became identified with various independent, reform, and antimonopoly parties which flourished in the Midwest during the 1870s. The main political effort of farmers in the Midwest after 1871 was directed toward legislation to regulate railway abuses, and by 1874 a number of Midwestern states had enacted so-called Granger Laws. In 1871 the Illinois lawmakers passed legislation to regulate passenger fares and freight rates on railroads and also provided state control over grain warehouses. Under pressure from some business interests as well as farmers, Minnesota, Iowa, and Wisconsin also passed laws to regulate railroads.

The political victories of farmers, however, were more apparent than real. Although the United States Supreme Court upheld the constitutionality of the Illinois statute fixing maximum warehouse charges for storing grain (*Munn v. Illinois,* 1877), on the grounds that a state could regulate private property which was clothed with a public interest, state regulation was not very effective. By 1880, most of the state regulatory laws had been repealed or weakened so that they had little restraining power over corporations. Nonetheless, the Grangers and other farm groups had demonstrated that farmers could exert great political influence if they organized and united in support of particular objectives.

Meanwhile, Grange members sought to obtain direct economic benefits by forming cooperatives as a means of reducing the cost of supplies and of marketing their products. The *Patron's Handbook* of 1874 announced that "we must dispense with the surplus of middlemen, not that we are unfriendly to them, but we do not need them. Their surplus and their exactions diminish our profits." Grangers established many consumer cooperatives in the 1870s, as well as creameries, elevators, and other kinds of producer and marketing cooperatives. These associations generally failed, however, because of inefficient management, insufficient credit, and lack of a true cooperative spirit among farmers.

Between 1874 and 1880 Grange membership dropped from about 800,000 to 150,000. This decline followed the failure of the cooperatives, the gradual return of better times, internal dissensions, the inability to win permanent political victories, and the decline of member loyalty. The Grange continued as a national farm organization, but its emphasis shifted to social and educational objectives. The influence of the Grange in the 1870s, however, was significant. It was the first genuine national farm organization in American history, and it set a political and economic pattern for successive farm groups.

The Greenback Movement

The Grange program did not really come to grips with the problem of low prices and farm debt, and during the 1870s a growing number of farmers sought a cure for their ills in currency inflation. Farmers believed in the quantity theory of money, which held that commodity prices rose and fell in relation to the volume of currency in circulation. Therefore, they argued, agricultural prices could be raised if the federal government would expand the circulation of paper currency, or greenbacks. Debtors were especially concerned with the money problem. If they incurred debts in periods of high prices such as the Civil War, they found it difficult to repay their loans when prices fell. For example, if a farmer borrowed $500 when wheat brought $1.50 a bushel and had to repay it when wheat was selling for $1, his debt had increased by 50 percent. On the other hand, farmers would benefit if they could repay their loans at a time when farm prices were higher than they were when the money was borrowed.

In 1865, there were some $433 million worth of greenbacks in circulation, but despite pressure from inflationist groups, the Grant administration followed a deflationary policy. By 1870 the amount of greenbacks had dropped to $356 million. Some currency expansion occurred following the Panic of 1873, but Grant vetoed a bill which would have raised the total to $400 million. Angered by this decision, the inflationists turned to political action. The Greenback political movement was launched at a meeting in Indianapolis in November, 1874, and two years later the Greenback party ran Peter Cooper, the elderly New York philanthropist, for President on a platform which called for greatly expanded issues of paper money.

Failing to win much popular support in 1876, the Greenbackers widened their appeal to both farmers and workers. Besides currency expansion, they advocated taxation of national bonds, a federal income tax, exclusion of Chinese immigration, restriction of working hours in industry, and abolition of child labor. On this broadened platform, the Greenback party polled about one million votes in the midterm elections of 1878 and elected at least fifteen congressmen favoring inflationary policies. In the presidential campaign of 1880, James B. Weaver of Iowa polled 308,000 votes. But with better times in the early 1880s, the movement declined. Inflation continued to be a popular issue among farmers, however, and the demand for cheap money was a unifying force among discontented agrarians.

The Farmers' Alliance and the Populists

Despite the decline of the Granger and Greenback movements, farm unrest continued unabated. Deflationary monetary policies, exactions by industrial trusts, railroad abuses, and other conditions kept farmers dissatisfied. During the 1870s numerous farmers' clubs and organizations were formed in Texas to advance agricultural interests, and in 1879 a statewide farmers' alliance was organized. At first the Texas Alliance stressed social objectives and cooperative buying and selling, but in 1886 the Alliance demanded inflation, higher taxes on land held for speculation, a law to regulate interstate commerce, and heavier taxes on railroad property. Grievances varied from community to community, but these demands reflected a general concern of farmers over land policies, transportation, and an adequate supply of currency.

The driving force behind the Texas Alliance was C. W. Macune, who set out to extend the organization throughout the entire South. In 1887 the Louisiana Farmers' Union and the Texas Alliance united to form the National Farmers' Alliance and Cooperative Union of America. The Agricultural Wheel, an Arkansas farm organization which had been organized in 1882, joined the National Farmers' Alliance in 1888. Meanwhile, Colonel L. L. Polk of North Carolina, editor of *The Progressive Farmer,* had been busy organizing farmers in his state. By 1888 most of the Southern farm organizations had united into what was commonly called the Southern Alliance. Black farmers were not admitted to the white groups, so in 1888 they established the Colored Farmers' National Alliance. By 1890 the white and black alliances may each have had as many as one million members.

At the same time discontented farmers in the North were forming additional protest groups. In 1880 Milton George of Chicago, editor of the *Western Rural,* organized the Northwestern, or Northern, Alliance. Spreading out from Illinois, the Northern Alliance recruited approximately 400,000 members by 1887, with the largest and most militant membership in Kansas where drought and low prices had stimulated seething unrest among farmers. The Northern Alliance was interested in three major areas of reform—land, transportation, and money. Insistence on strict government regulation of the railroads soon gave way to demands for government ownership, and Alliance members advocated free and unlimited coinage of silver as a means of raising prices and helping debtors. The Alliance, which demanded that public lands be distributed only to actual settlers, also favored an income tax and revised patent laws.

With strong farm groups in both the North and South, agricultural spokesmen faced the task of bringing the Northern and Southern Alliances together into a single national organization. At a meeting in St. Louis in December, 1889, efforts were made to unite the two groups. They reached agreement on some common objectives, including the free and unlimited coinage of silver, government ownership of transportation and communication, abolition of national banks, and a graduated income tax. The Southern Alliance advanced what was known as the "subtreasury plan" for the purpose of improving marketing conditions and inflating the currency. Under this scheme, a subtreasury with numerous local branches would be established. Farmers could deposit such products as cotton and wheat in these subtreasuries and receive a loan in paper money equal to 80 percent of the value of the stored commodities. It was thought that this system would permit farmers to hold their crops, rather than sell them, at times when prices were low. Moreover the loans issued against the produce would expand the currency and have a general inflationary effect. Although the Northern and Southern Alliances were unable to achieve organic unity, they did agree on a number of basic principles designed to increase farm income.

By 1890 some of the more militant Alliances in the North had concluded that they could realize their objectives through political action alone. In July, members of the state Alliance and some other reform groups, including the Knights of Labor, organized a People's party in Kansas. Independent or People's parties were also formed in Nebraska and the Dakotas. Having become convinced that farmers could expect nothing from either the Republicans or the Democrats, farmers in these states were determined to make a clean political sweep. The most bitter and vigorous campaign occurred in Kansas, where Mary Elizabeth Lease, "Sockless" Jerry Simpson, and William A. Peffer berated the economic royalists and the "bloodhounds of money." Mrs. Lease reportedly urged farmers "to raise less corn and more hell." It is doubtful if she ever really made this statement, but conservatives were thoroughly frightened by her descriptive language. Despite the lack of funds and proper political organization, farmers won some spectacular victories. Kansas elected Peffer to the United States Senate, while voters in South Dakota sent James H. Kyle to Washington. In the South protesting farmers moved to take over the Democratic party. "Pitchfork" Ben Tillman won the governorship in South Carolina, and Thomas E. Watson of Georgia went to the House of Representatives, with the backing of discontented farmers. When Congress met in 1891, at least fifty congressmen were members of, or sympathetic to, the Farmers' Alliance.

The strongest unifying force among farmers by 1890 was the demand for currency inflation. The move for cheap money had continued with varying degrees of intensity in the agricultural regions ever since the 1870s, but with increasing debt burdens and low prices, farmers pressed this demand with renewed vigor after 1888. Although there were still those who favored increasing the number of greenbacks, by 1890 free and unlimited coinage of silver was considered the best way to bring about inflation.

The Mint Act in 1792 provided for coinage of both gold and silver at a ratio of approxi-

By the turn of the century, new farm machinery was a source of family pride, and when photographs like this were taken, mother and daughter put on their best clothes for the picture. The same machinery did, however, become the source of a dilemma: it vastly increased farm production and created low prices for the farmer.

Machinery had, for example, enabled the farmer of 1896 to produce eighteen times as much wheat as the farmer of 1830 could. The products of the American farm had become the principal United States export and benefited the whole country by earning foreign exchange which helped to finance American industrial expansion.

The individual farmer, however, was in a poor bargaining position. Operating on a competitive basis, no one farmer could control prices or production. He had to accept the offered prices for his produce and pay the manufacturer's asking price for the equipment and supplies he needed.

A host of other problems also plagued the farmer—high and discriminatory freight rates, high marketing costs, inadequate availability of credit, and high interest. These seemed to farmers to be the real source of their financial insecurity, and it was these that they combined to attack through such movements as the Grange, the Greenback Party, the Farmer's Alliance, the People's Party, and the campaign for free coinage of silver.

The Farmer's Dilemma

ictures, Inc.

From 1870 on, more and more farmers thought the solution to their problems lay in increasing the amount of currency in circulation, and they supported the Greenback Party. After the election of 1884, however, the Farmers Alliance movements became the most dynamic expression of farm unrest. By 1890 the more militant Alliances were involved in political action, and many leaders believed that free silver was the way to create inflation. Some of the most intense political action came where Alliances joined with other groups to form People's Parties. In Kansas, Mary Elizabeth Lease (below) made fiery speeches calling for "money, land, and transportation," abolition of the foreclosure system, and the power to make loans directly from the government. The Kansas Populists in the 1890 election won the governorship and control of the state senate, and they believed they had won the state house of representatives. Republicans denied this claim, and at one point Populists bearing rifles seized the legislative chambers; the next day Republicans battered through the doors. Finally the Populists agreed to let the courts settle the matter, and sergeants-at-arms took control (left). The Republican-controlled court ruled in favor of the Republicans.

Left: Kansas State Historical Society
Above: Library of Congress

In 1896, Free Silver became a major party issue when the Democrats adopted it as a campaign plank and William Jennings Bryan (left) gave it eloquent expression. The Populists, who had polled more than a million votes with James B. Weaver in 1892, threw their support to Bryan. Despite his dynamism and a speaking tour of 18,000 miles, Bryan lost to William McKinley. The defeat of the Populists, along with rising prosperity, brought about their collapse and signalled the triumph of industrialism over the power of the farmer. Farmers were not so well organized again until after World War I. The idea that industrialists were "milking" the farmer did not die easily however, as shown in the cartoon below.

Left: Culver Pictures, Inc.
Above: Library of Congress

mately 16 to 1. This assumed that gold was sixteen times more valuable than silver. But after 1834 very little silver was coined, and in 1853 the minting of all silver coins except the dollar was discontinued. In 1873 Congress removed the silver dollar from the coinage list. Very little attention was paid to this law because the commercial value of enough silver to coin a dollar was worth slightly more than 100 cents in gold so people who had silver sold it commercially. During the 1870s, however, the production of silver in the American West increased greatly, and by 1877 the 371.25 grains of silver necessary to mint a dollar was worth only 90 cents in gold on the commercial market. Silver producers now wanted to mint their silver into dollars but found this was impossible because of the Coinage Act of 1873. Farmers who saw the coinage of millions of silver dollars as a means to inflate the currency teamed up with the silver miners in demanding free and unlimited coinage of silver at a ratio of 16 to 1 with gold. The law of 1873 demonetizing silver was now denounced as the "Crime of '73," and pictured as a dastardly scheme of bankers to deflate the currency, to the detriment of farmers and workers.

In July, 1877, Representative Richard P. Bland of Missouri introduced a free-silver bill, which passed the House but was drastically modified in the Senate. As mentioned in Chapter 20, the result was the Bland-Allison Act, which authorized the Treasury to coin $2 to $4 million worth of silver dollars a month. However, the Secretary of the Treasury in succeeding years bought the legal minimum; thus the law's inflationary effects were inconsequential. Even though there was some increase in the total per capita circulation of money between 1886 and 1890, the price levels declined slightly, much to the distress of Western and Southern farmers. Farmers complained that the government's monetary policy was deflationary and beneficial only to creditors and moneylenders.

Following further agitation, Congress enacted the Sherman Silver Purchase Act in 1890, but it failed to satisfy either farmers or silver miners. Under this law the Treasury was authorized to purchase 4.5 million ounces of silver per month, to be paid for with treasury notes. These notes were redeemable in either silver or gold, but the Treasury followed the policy of redeeming them only in gold. The Sherman Silver Purchase Act neither maintained the price of silver, which was of interest to silver miners, nor inflated the currency, which was of concern to agriculturalists. It was a compromise which really pleased no one.

Local and state successes in the election of 1890 convinced an increasing number of farmers that the time had come to form a national third party which would protect the interests of agriculture. Following several preliminary meetings, delegates met in Omaha in July, 1892, to nominate candidates and launch their campaign. Declaring that "we meet in the midst of a nation brought to the verge of moral, political, and material ruin," the delegates complained that "corruption dominates the ballot box, the Legislatures, the Congress, and touches even the ermine of the bench."

The platform of the People's, or Populist, party called for the free and unlimited coinage of silver, government ownership of railroads and telephone and telegraph lines, a system of postal savings banks, a graduated income tax, and an increase in the amount of circulating currency to at least $50 per capita. Additional resolutions recommended the Australian, or secret, ballot; the initiative and referendum; a single term for President; and the direct election of senators. The convention also favored a shorter workday for industrial laborers; it denounced contract labor, and expressed opposition to the use of Pinkerton detectives in breaking up strikes. James B. Weaver, a Civil War veteran, former congressman, and a tested leader of the farm movement from Iowa, was nominated for President, and James G. Field of Virginia for Vice President.

Only the spirited and energetic activity of the Populists enlivened an otherwise dull and uninspiring campaign in 1892. Although President Harrison had made many enemies, there was no practical alternative to his renomination for a second term. Whitelaw Reid was chosen as his running mate. Like the Republicans, the Democrats did not have a very appealing list of possible candidates. Most rank-and-file Democrats seemed to favor Cleveland, although there was considerable opposition to him in the West and South because of his sound money views. In the Democratic strongholds of the East, however, Cleveland had strong support, and he won the nomination on the first ballot. As a sop to discontented Westerners, Adlai E. Stevenson of Illinois was nominated for Vice President. Neither Cleveland nor Harrison took to the stump in what was probably the quietest and cleanest campaign since the Civil War.

In the final voting, Cleveland won a smashing victory with 277 electoral votes to 145 for Harrison and 22 for Weaver. Cleveland surprised even the Democrats by carrying such states as Illinois, Wisconsin, and California, though his election reflected a widespread dissatisfaction with the Harrison administration rather than general approval of Democratic promises. Weaver's popular vote of 1,040,886 was highly encouraging to the Populists. The Populist candidate carried four states and won some electoral votes in others. Based on their showing in 1892, the Populists began to plan for the midterm election of 1894 and the presidential campaign two years later. The tide of agrarian discontent still ran strong.

Cleveland's Second Administration

Discontented farmers and workers could expect little sympathy from Grover Cleveland. His economic views were similar to those held by the country's conservative business and banking leaders. Henry Clay Frick of the Carnegie Corporation wrote shortly after the election: "I am very sorry for President Harrison, but I cannot see that our interests are going to be affected one way or another by the change in administration." Cleveland appointed a conservative Cabinet which contained no one sympathetic with the plight of agriculture and labor. In his inaugural address the President promised to maintain "a sound and stable currency" and labeled free silver a dangerous "heresy."

Within a little more than two months after Cleveland took office on March 4, the Panic of 1893 rocked the nation's economy and ushered in a prolonged depression. Bankruptcies and panic selling on the New York Stock Exchange during the last days of the Harrison administration indicated a dangerous situation. On May 5 the National Cordage Company failed, and following in rapid succession scores of other businesses and industries closed their doors. Causes of the economic downturn included a withdrawal of gold by foreign countries, which threatened the gold standard, and a decline in railroad investment. Perhaps more important still was the long depression and low purchasing power in the agricultural and labor sectors of the economy.

Cleveland believed that the country's "unfortunate plight" stemmed largely from the Sherman Silver Purchase Act of 1890, which caused a drain on the Treasury's gold reserve. Financiers generally held that the United States must keep at least $100 million worth of gold in the Treasury in order to maintain the gold standard. As the federal gold supply dwindled, Cleveland urged Congress to repeal the Sherman Silver Purchase Act. Congress did this in October, 1893. However, the gold supply continued to decline, and by early 1894 it had dropped to $66 million. The Treasury now turned to selling bonds to acquire sufficient gold to replenish the reserve. One of the two issues sold in 1894 was purchased by J. P. Morgan and Company at a handsome discount. Following sharp criticism for trafficking with Wall Street bankers, the Treasury early in 1896 sold a $100 million bond issue to the general public, and the financial crisis passed.

While Cleveland had preserved the gold standard, he had aroused bitter opposition among political critics. Democrat William Jennings Bryan said that the people owed Cleveland the same gratitude that a passenger would toward "the trainman who has opened a switch and precipitated a wreck." Cleveland's monetary policy was politically disastrous; it did not help to restore confidence, nor did it improve economic conditions. The President was soon involved in another political tussle when he urged Congress to lower tariff rates. For years he had believed that high tariffs were an unfair tax on consumers and that rates should be reduced. The Wilson-Gorman tariff, passed in 1894, lowered rates slightly but not as much as Cleveland desired. The law not only failed to please the President but aroused opposition in other quarters as well. One of the most notable features of the Wilson-Gorman bill was the inclusion of an income tax, which had been demanded by Western and Southern agrarians.

While congressmen and senators argued over the money and tariff issues, hard times gripped every part of the country. The "Gay Nineties" were everything but gay. Unemployed men drifted from place to place in search of work or relief. Vagrants and tramps overflowed city centers, and in some communities many people "approached beggary." A number of people thought that the federal government should sponsor work relief projects to help jobless men. Jacob S. Coxey, a well-to-do Ohio businessman and reformer, dramatized this demand in the spring of 1894 when he led a march of unemployed men to Washington in support of his Good Roads Bill. This measure, already introduced in Congress, called for the Treasury to issue $500 million in legal tender currency which would be spent on road construction. It was believed that this bill would not only provide employment but would at the same time inflate the currency and help fight the depression. But Coxey was arrested for walking on the Capitol lawn, and Congress ignored his demands and those of other "industrial armies" which marched on Washington.

Unemployment and reduced wages for those still working produced widespread labor strife by 1894. The most spectacular conflict between management and organized labor was the Pullman strike (see pages 702–703), which had important political consequences. Cleveland's actions further alienated workers from the Democratic administration and brought the

President under increasing attack. Cleveland's antilabor attitude and his support for the gold standard when farmers wanted free silver and inflation, coupled with the general depression, spelled trouble for the Democratic party. In the midterm elections of 1894, the Republicans gained a heavy majority in the House of Representatives and nearly won control of the Senate. Moreover, the conservative position of the Supreme Court angered many people. Besides upholding the business viewpoint in several cases involving industrial monopoly, the Supreme Court in the case of *Pollock v. Farmers' Loan and Trust Company* in 1895 struck down the income tax provision included in the Wilson-Gorman tariff. On every hand it seemed to an increasing number of farmers and workers that the government was dominated by special interests that were unsympathetic to the masses of citizens.

The Campaign of 1896

As depression and hard times persisted, the issue of free and unlimited coinage of silver came to overshadow all other political issues. Support for free silver was not limited to the Populists or other so-called radicals. Large elements in both the Republican and Democratic parties also demanded monetary inflation. For years an advocate of inflation, Senator Henry Moore Teller of Colorado led a growing free-silver faction in the Republican party, and William Jennings Bryan of Nebraska was rapidly gaining leadership of Western and Southern inflationist Democrats. These and other political leaders were supported in their campaigns by the American Bimetallic Union and the National Bimetallic League. One of the most effective spokesmen for free silver was William H. Harvey, who wrote a little paperback book entitled *Coin's Financial School,* published in 1894. It sold thousands of copies and was more thoroughly read by many Americans than the Bible.

As the presidential election of 1896 approached, the money question threatened to sweep all before it. The Republican Convention met in June at St. Louis. While the party was split on the silver issue, the gold standard faction was clearly in control. Delegates sang:

Gold, gold, gold,
I love to hear it jingle.
Gold, gold, gold,
Its power is untold.

For the women they adore it,
While the men try hard to store it;
There is not a better thing in life than
Gold, gold, gold.

After the delegates voted down a Teller amendment to the platform calling for free silver, the convention adopted a plank calling for bimetallism which really meant the gold standard. Then, in a dramatic move, Senator Teller rose and, followed by twenty-two other delegates, bolted the convention. This symbol of revolt had no measurable effect on the convention. Besides standing for gold, the platform pledged allegiance to tariff protection. The Republicans then nominated William McKinley of Ohio to head the ticket and named Garret A. Hobart of New Jersey as their vice presidential candidate. McKinley had the powerful backing of Marcus A. Hanna, a wealthy Cleveland industrialist who had spent a great deal of time and money to assure his friend's nomination. Born in 1843, McKinley served four years in the Union Army, after which he read law and began practicing at Canton, Ohio. He was not brilliant or sophisticated, but he worked hard, had a friendly manner, and inspired confidence. He served in the House of Representatives most of the time between 1876 and 1891. In the latter year he was elected Governor of Ohio.

While the free-silver forces fought a losing battle within Republican ranks, they were gradually acquiring control of the Democratic party. Cleveland's devotion to the gold standard and his alignment with conservative industrial and banking interests had caused him to lose most of his earlier support in the agrarian West and South. One Westerner referred to the President as a "fossilized reminiscence," and another critic said the country needed something besides "a government of brains, belly and brass." Silver sentiment was rampant among the masses of Democrats. When the delegates assembled for their nominating convention at Chicago in July, the silver forces were clearly in control. All they needed was a fearless, articulate leader, and the silverites found their man in thirty-six-year-old William Jennings Bryan.

Bryan was born and raised in a conservative, fundamentalist Illinois home. He completed college, read law, and then settled down to practice at Jacksonville in 1883. He developed a modest business, but in 1887 moved to Lincoln, Nebraska, where opportunities seemed greater for an ambitious young attorney. Bryan had a keen interest in politics and ran successfully for the House of Representatives in 1890. During his two terms in Washington, he became widely known for his discussions of the tariff and his stand for free silver. By 1896, he had won a national following on the silver issue. A dedicated agrarian, Bryan fought entrenched privilege with all of his might.

Bryan's greatest asset as a politician was his ability as a public speaker. During the Democratic convention, when the delegates were debating the money question, he electrified the huge crowd by concluding a ringing speech in favor of free silver with the words: "You shall not press down upon the brow of labor this crown of thorns, you shall not crucify mankind on a cross of gold." While Bryan already had more support than Richard Bland of Missouri or any of the other prospective candidates, this powerful address helped to win him the nomination on the fifth ballot. Then to appeal to the conservative interests, the Democrats nominated Arthur Sewall, a wealthy Maine businessman, for Vice President. The platform demanded free and unlimited coinage of silver, a tariff for revenue only, and an income tax. It also called for stricter regulation of corporations and opposed court injunctions in labor disputes.

Bryan's nomination and the inclusion of a free-silver plank in the Democratic platform placed the Populists in a most difficult position. If they ran a Populist candidate, the free-silver vote would be split and assure McKinley's election. If, on the other hand, they supported Bryan, the Populists would probably be absorbed by the Democratic party and lose their identity as a separate party. After some heated arguments at their convention in July, the Populists finally decided to fuse with the Democrats and nominate Bryan. But to maintain some degree of party independence, they named Thomas E. Watson of Georgia as their vice presidential nominee. The gold standard Democrats refused to back Bryan and nominated John M. Palmer of Illinois and Simon B. Buckner of Kentucky for President and Vice President respectively.

McKinley had hoped to campaign primarily

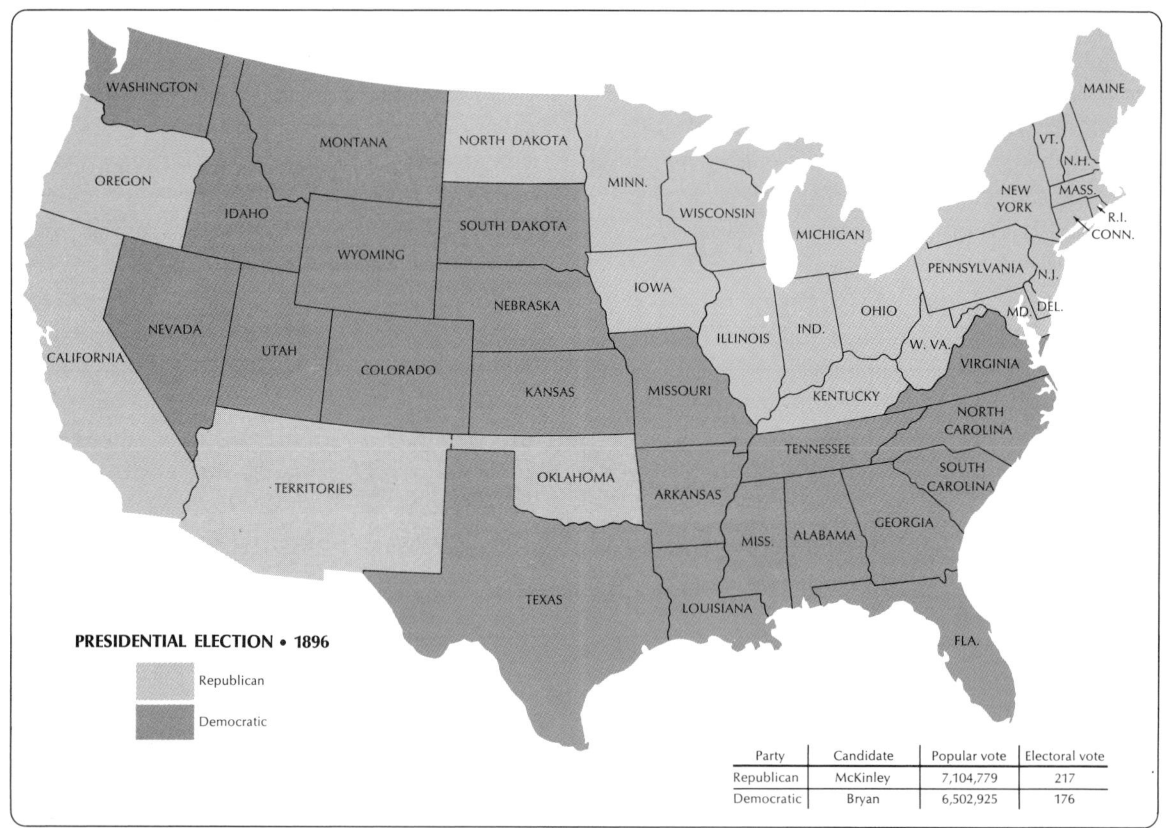

Party	Candidate	Popular vote	Electoral vote
Republican	McKinley	7,104,779	217
Democratic	Bryan	6,502,925	176

on the tariff question, but soon free silver eliminated every competing issue. Bryan carried on a whirlwind speaking tour and sharply denounced Republican economic policies, which, he declared, plundered the great mass of citizens. He argued that free silver would liberate the economy and restore prosperity. While Bryan traveled more than 18,000 miles and made some six hundred speeches, McKinley staged a front porch campaign under the guidance of Mark Hanna, a masterful political organizer. The Republicans employed hundreds of speakers and distributed tons of literature. They pictured McKinley as a solid, dependable, and capable leader, and the "Advance Agent of Prosperity." Bryan, on the other hand, was presented as an un-American radical, whose election would threaten the country's very foundations. Critics labeled him a "rattle-pated idiot," a "lunatic," an "anarchist," and a "mouthing, slobbering demagogue whose patriotism is all in his jawbone." The campaign was bitter and highly emotional. When the votes were counted on November 3, McKinley polled 7,104,779 to Bryan's 6,502,925. Bryan carried most of the South and West; McKinley won a majority in the Northeast.

A number of factors accounted for Bryan's defeat. McKinley's campaign was highly organized, and the Republicans spent a minimum of $3 million. Bryan probably spent less than

$300,000. Moreover, Bryan's free-silver arguments appealed neither to workers, who feared higher food prices, nor to the more prosperous farmers. Urban workers, as well as farmers from Iowa to Pennsylvania, tended to support McKinley. Both of these groups were actually attracted by McKinley's protective tariff arguments. Bryan, too, was hurt by feelings against the Democratic party which grew out of the depression; and he was unable to counteract the Republican resurgence which had begun in 1894. While Bryan was no doubt the strongest candidate the Democrats could have named in 1896, given the circumstances, no Democrat could have won.

The McKinley-Bryan contest was the most important political campaign between 1860 and 1912. It produced the sharpest class conflict of any election in that period. To a considerable extent, silver and gold were only symbols, one representing agriculture and the other industry and commerce. The real question of the election was which interest would control the federal government. Industrialism won, and from that point onward the power of agriculture in the councils of the nation declined rapidly.

Conclusion

McKinley's election destroyed the farm movement which had been such a potent political force during the previous quarter century. Yet, the Populists and other farm groups had made an important and lasting contribution to American political and economic life. Many of their ideas for reform, including the income tax, parcel post, postal savings, and stricter regulation of big business, were later adopted. Their discussion of the money question stimulated consideration of new banking and currency legislation, and something like the subtreasury plan was adopted to help farmers later in the New Deal. Populist support for the initiative and referendum, direct primaries, and direct election of senators was also notable.

Some writers have accused the Populists of being provincial, nativist, anti-Semitic, and irrational, and have said that they were motivated by a threatened loss of status in American society. These critics have maintained that the Populists would not accept industrialism and were trying to restore some earlier agrarian ideal. But the evidence supporting these interpretations is far from conclusive. Perhaps they are not even especially important. The real significance of the Populists lay in their identification of some specific economic abuses in both the agricultural and industrial sectors of the economy and in their effort to correct them through government action. As the Populist platform declared in 1892: "We believe that the powers of government . . . should be expanded . . . as rapidly and as far as the good sense of an intelligent people and the teachings of experience shall justify, to the end that oppression, injustice, and poverty shall eventually cease in the land." In this respect the Populists as well as other agrarian protesters were in the liberal reform tradition.

SUGGESTED READINGS

Fred Shannon's *The Farmer's Last Frontier: Agriculture, 1860–1897** (1945) is the best and most complete history of late-nineteenth-century farming. On the agricultural settlement of the trans-Missouri West see G. C. Fite's *The Farmer's Frontier, 1865–1900* (1966). Among the best regional studies of agriculture are *From Prairie to Corn Belt* (1963) by Allan G. Bogue; Hiram M. Drache's *The Day of the Bonanza: A History of Bonanza Farming in the Red River Valley of the North* (1964); Eric E. Lampard's *The Rise of the Dairy Industry in Wisconsin* (1963); *Sugar Country: The Cane Sugar Industry in the South.* 1753–1950 (1953) by J. Carlyle Sitterson; and A. M. Tang's *Economic Development in the Southern Piedmont,* 1860–1950: *Its Impact on Agriculture* (1958). There is valuable material on Southern agriculture in H. H. Donald's *The Negro Freedman* (1952); R. B. Vance's *Human Geography of the South* (1932); and A. F. Raper and I. D. Reid's *Sharecroppers All* (1941).

For the development of farm mechanization see Leo Rogin's *The Introduction of Farm Machinery in Its Relation to the Productivity of Labor in the Agriculture of the United States during the Nineteenth Century* (1931); R. M. Wik's *Steam Power on the American Farm* (1953); and the popular *Machines of Plenty* (1955) by Stewart H. Holbrook.

The best brief treatment of agriculture's basic economic problems is found in Theodore Saloutos's "The Agricultural Problem and Nineteenth Century Industrialism," *Agricultural History,* XXII (July, 1948). Farm problems and the causes of agrarian discontent are also considered by Shannon in *The Farmer's Last Frontier**, cited above; in John D. Hicks's *The Populist Revolt** (1931); and Theodore Saloutos's *Farmer Movements in the South,* 1865–1933* (1960). Earl W. Hayter deals with the problem of farmers' adjusting to industrialism in *The Troubled Farmer* (1968). Accounts of the farmers' revolt are numerous. Besides the works of Hicks and Saloutos, readers should see Solon J. Buck's *The Agrarian Crusade* (1919) and *The Granger Movement** (1913). Carl C. Taylor's *The Farmers' Movement,* 1620–1920 (1953) and Murray R. Benedicts's *Farm Policies in the United States,* 1790–1950 (1953), are two other general works which include good material on late-nineteenth-century agrarian discontent. Specialized studies which are excellent include Walter T. K. Nugent's *The Kansas Populists* (1963) and Norman Pollock's *The Populist Response to Industrial America** (1962), which contradict the stimulating but controversial interpretation found in Richard Hofstadter's *The Age of Reform** (1955). Other good local studies of populism are Robert P. Brooks's *The Agrarian Revolution in Georgia,* 1865–1912 (1914) and R. C. Martin's *The People's Party in Texas* (1933). Among the best biographies of agrarian leaders are Francis B. Simkins's *Pitchfork Ben Tillman, South Carolinian** (1944); C. Vann Woodward's *Tom Watson, Agrarian Rebel** (1938); Martin Ridge's *Ignatius Donnelly* (1962); and Robert C. Cotner's *James C. Hogg: A Biography* (1959).

On political conditions in the 1890s see H. U. Faulkner's *Politics, Reform, and Expansion** (1959). J. Rogers Hollingsworth explains the difficulties within the Democratic party in *The Whirligig of Politics* (1963). Margaret Leech's *In the Days of McKinley* (1959) and H. Wayne Morgan's *William McKinley and His America* (1963) deal adequately with the winner in 1896. The old biographies of Bryan, John C. Long's *Bryan: The Great Commoner* (1928) and Paxton Hibben's *The Peerless Leader* (1929), are not very satisfactory. Paolo E. Coletta's *William Jennings Bryan, Political Evangelist,* 1860–1908 (1964) is much better and represents the first volume of a three-volume biography. Paul W. Glad's *McKinley, Bryan, and the People** (1964) is an excellent survey of the election of 1896 and the politics which preceded it. *The Presidential Election of* 1896 (1964) by Stanley L. Jones is the most complete account of that important campaign and election. The role of the Populists in 1896 has been well analyzed by Robert F. Durden in *The Climax of Populism: The Election of* 1896* (1965). Most of the above works contain discussions of free silver, the leading political issue of the 1890s. For additional reading on silver see *Henry Moore Teller, Defender of the West* (1941) by Elmer Ellis; and D. R. Dewey's *Financial History of the United States* (rev. ed., 1936). On the money question in an earlier period consult Irwin Unger's excellent study, *The Greenback Era: A Social and Political History of American Finance,* 1865–1879 (1964); and W. T. K. Nugent's *Money and American Society,* 1865–1880 (1968).

*indicates availability in paperback.

25

American Cultural Life

IMPORTANT SOCIAL, cultural, and intellectual changes accompanied the vast economic transformation which occurred in the United States during the late nineteenth century. Developments in the natural and social sciences, literature, education, religion, and the fine arts all testified to a vibrant cultural and intellectual life. It was probably true, as foreign critics and many others charged, that Americans were excessively materialistic; but they did not live by bread alone, nor were they devoid of culture. As Lord Bryce wrote, "Manners are becoming in America more generally polished, life more orderly, equality between the sexes more complete, the refined pleasures more easily accessible than they have ever been among the masses of any people."

The intellectual and cultural changes of the late nineteenth century produced deep strains and conflicts within American society. Many people found it hard to adjust to unfamiliar ideas, changing institutional patterns, and different social standards. An increasing emphasis upon making money, the growing impersonality of urban living, greater mobility, and reputedly declining moral standards were among the factors which caused many people to believe that Americans were forsaking the ways of their forefathers, that they were somehow losing the good things in their national life. But this was generally the reaction of those who did not approve of change or the direction it took. And they are to be found in every generation.

Nothing upset the fundamental thought patterns of Americans or had such a far-reaching intellectual influence as the ideas embodied in the evolutionary hypothesis of the British scientist Charles Darwin. In *The Origin of Species,* published in 1859, Darwin wrote that species had not been created independently and were not immutable. Rather, he said, "those belonging to what are called the same genera are lineal descendants of some other generally extinct species." Such modifications had been produced by natural selection. In conclusion, Darwin stated that probably all organic beings "which have ever lived on this earth have descended from some one primordial form, into which life was first breathed." Man, according to Darwin, was not the special creation of God but the product of millions of years of evolution.

Darwinism created controversy and furor in both scientific and religious circles. Its challenge to tradition was profound. In giving scientific support to the concepts of change, emergence, and the evolutionary process, Darwinism attacked supernaturalism and absolutes in every form. Absolutes could have no place in a thought system where everything was changing in accordance with natural laws or principles. If man had evolved through natural selection from some animal form, supernaturalism with its ideas of special divine creation and intervention in the affairs of men could not be accepted. Even the means of arriving at truth must be reconsidered. To the Darwinist, truth was not something revealed by God, but something men strove to discover through reason and experimentation.

Religion especially felt the impact of Darwin's writings, but evolutionary concepts also affected law, history, education, economics, and most aspects of American intellectual life. For instance, no longer was the law or the Constitution considered as something absolute and fixed; they were seen as growing and changing continually to meet the demands of the times. Oliver Wendell Holmes, Jr., wrote in *The Common Law* (1881) that "the law embodies the story of a nation's development through many centuries and that in order to know what it is, we must know what it has been, and what it tends to become." The new view toward law was at least partly responsible for a more liberal interpretation of the Constitution where social and economic matters were involved.

In the field of history, a number of the most prominent scholars came under the influence of evolutionary thinking. James Harvey Robinson of Columbia University saw human history evolving out of the struggle between the common people and the upper classes, while Frederick Jackson Turner of the University of Wisconsin and Harvard declared that American institutions had been changed and influenced chiefly by the country's physical environment, particularly the frontier. Economic institutions, too, were coming to be viewed not as something fixed but as responses to changes created by new conditions. The idea, for instance, that government should not regulate or control business gave way before the demand to bring large-scale corporate enterprise under some degree of regulation. The new generation of economists, represented by Richard T. Ely, John Bates Clark, and Thorstein Veblen, attacked older economic ideas and emphasized that the modern economy was the result of practices and habits which had evolved over many generations. Indeed, the evolutionary concepts of change and emergence challenged almost every phase of economic thought.

This application of evolutionary principles to society as a whole became known as "social Darwinism." Herbert Spencer, the great English philosopher, declared that the concepts of biological evolution, including natural selection and survival of the fittest, applied also to social systems. According to Spencer, man was improving constantly through the emerging social processes, and eventually a new human nature and an improved social system would emerge. Among those who popularized Spencer's ideas in America were William Graham Sumner, a professor of social science at Yale, and the historian John Fiske. Sumner argued that life was a struggle for existence and that inequality was a natural state of affairs. Since he believed that society had developed gradually through evolutionary processes, Sumner denied that it could be improved by legislative or governmental action. Nothing, wrote Sumner, could be done to improve society; men could only wait for the results of natural social processes. Sumner not only expressed the concept of social Darwinism, but he played on the traditional American ideas of hard work, thrift, and virtue. His writings supplied a strong philosophic and scientific basis for an already-strong individualism in American life.

Social Darwinism provided a defense for laissez faire capitalism and a rationale for success, but an increasing number of Americans rejected the concept's negativism by the 1880s. More and more people from many walks of life held that social abuses could be eliminated and improvements made through man's conscious effort. The late nineteenth and early twentieth centuries were alive with dissenters who refused to accept depression, violent labor-management disputes, slums, the unequal distribution of wealth, child labor, and other undesirable conditions without attempting to discover correctives. Grangers, Populists, labor organizers, a growing number of church leaders, and scholars insisted that social progress would come less through evolution than through positive human, even governmental, action based on rational thought. Among the leading intellectuals who rejected social Darwinism was Lester Frank Ward, the father of sociology in the United States, who argued that social improvement depended upon education and the application of intelligence to the imperfections in modern society.

Closely associated with Darwinism in upsetting traditional thought patterns was the philosophy known as pragmatism. Among the leading pragmatists were Charles S. Pierce, a philosopher and physicist; William James, a professor of philosophy and psychology at Harvard; and John Dewey, a leading philosopher and educator who taught at several universities before settling at Columbia in 1904. In essence pragmatism taught that the truth of ideas must be tested by experience. Truth was not something absolute or final, but was evolutionary and changing. It was not something handed down by God, but something man found for himself through testing and experimentation. As James explained, "A pragmatist turns his back resolutely and once for all upon a lot of inveterate habits dear to professional philosophies. He turns away from abstraction and insufficiency, closed systems, and pretended absolutes and origins." Rejecting all forms of determinism, James attributed basic social progress to man's willingness to act on faith, to take risks, to subject beliefs to the test of experiment. Dewey carried this concept further and applied it to the group as well as to the individual. Ideas were to be judged by their results, not by some preconceived notions which had no practical or experimental basis. Reality grew out of experience. Investigation based on skepticism was the philosophical method by which men would discover what they considered to be true. James's "philosophy of practicality" appealed strongly to Americans. Always a practical people, Americans found here a philosophy which gave meaning to their individual and national experience.

James H. Tufts, a social psychologist at the University of Chicago, well summarized the changes in late-nineteenth-century thought when he wrote: "My generation has seen the passing of systems of thought which had reigned since Augustus. The conception of the world as a kingdom ruled by God, subject to his laws and their penalties, which had been undisturbed by the Protestant Reformation, has dissolved. . . . The sanctions of our inherited morality have gone. Principles and standards which had stood for nearly two thousand years are questioned." Nowhere were the new scientific and philosophic currents more sharply felt than in religion where the adherents of Christianity believed themselves totally betrayed.

Religion and the Church

Most Americans claimed adherence to the Christian faith. As Alexis de Tocqueville wrote in the 1830s, "There is no country in the whole world in which the Christian religion retains a greater influence over the souls of men than in America." The people and their leaders professed a belief in God, in the Bible as the revealed word of God, and in the Church, both Protestant and Catholic, as God's divine instrument through which Christ would speak to men. Although only some 15 to 20 percent of the people were church members in 1860, the influence of religious faith on the lives and conduct of the population was far greater than these numbers would imply.

But by the 1860s and 1870s, traditional religious thought and programs were coming under severe attack as a result of new ideas in natural science, Biblical criticism, and philosophic concepts which emphasized the role of man in the world rather than God. Probably nothing disrupted accepted religious ideas so much as did Darwin's theory of evolution, the new findings in geology, physics, and the other natural sciences. God had not created the world in six days as recorded in Genesis, said the scientists; it had evolved through eons of geologic time. Man had not been formed in the image of God; he had evolved from some unknown primordial form. Man really was no special creation at all; he was simply the highest of the animal forms. An increasing number of intellectuals considered such widely held Christian beliefs as the virgin birth of Christ and Christ's death and resurrection as myths and illogical folk tales which could not be scientifically verified. Moreover, scholars began to examine the Bible with the same critical approach that they applied to any other historical text or document. These investigations seemed to prove that the Bible had been compiled over a period of centuries and that God had not moved the hands of those who wrote Holy Writ. These and other ideas challenged the very foundation of supernaturalism, which was the basis of Christian faith—a faith which held that man was a child of God, created in His image, and that God intervened in the affairs of His faithful followers through Christ and governed them through the Church.

During the 1870s, and to a greater extent in the 1880s, a lively and sometimes highly emotional conflict emerged between science and religion. The popular controversy over evolution did not really arise until after Darwin published his book entitled *The Descent of Man* in 1871. While traditional Christianity was on the defensive, theologians and philosophers, and even some natural scientists, defended supernaturalism. In his *Systematic Theology* published in 1873, Charles Hodges upheld the infallibility of the Bible, and William G. T. Shedd supported many of the historic Christian beliefs in his book *Dogmatic Philosophy* (1888).

The controversy was both enlivened and embittered by the picturesque attacks on religion by the well-known agnostic Robert G. Ingersoll. The son of a Congregational minister, Ingersoll practiced law and fought the strict Calvinism of his father. He believed that religion fettered the human mind and that only the destruction of supernaturalism could free it from religious shackles. He did not deny the possibility of God, but he said, "I do not know . . . I do not believe." According to Ingersoll, human progress did not depend on God, but on man in league with science. His Holy Trinity was not God, Christ, and the Holy Spirit but observation, reason, and experience, the trinity of science. Relying on the power of man rather than God, Ingersoll declared: "If abuses are destroyed, man must destroy them. If slaves are freed, men must free them. If new truths are discovered, man must discover them. If the naked are clothed; if the hungry are fed; if justice is done; if labor is rewarded; if superstition is driven from the mind; . . . all must be the work of man." Ingersoll's religion was the religion of humanity. He scoffed at miracles, lectured on such topics as "The Mistakes of Moses," and angered clergy and laity alike by attacking every vestige of religious faith and practice.

But Ingersoll represented an extreme point of view. Most intellectuals did not completely reject religion. Rather, they attempted to accommodate science and religion. Many liberal clergymen and theologians accepted evolution, but instead of considering it as a destroyer of religion, they declared that it represented the working out of God's magnificent plan for mankind. Others said that there could be no genuine conflict between science and religion because they were two different aspects of life. The Bible, after all, was not supposed to be a scientific text; it was a guide to conduct and faith. An increasing number of ministers forsook religious fundamentalism with its emphasis upon personal salvation and adopted instead a liberal, humanistic kind of gospel which found no conflict with evolutionism. Henry Ward Beecher, minister to an upper-class congregation in Brooklyn, was one of the most popular clergymen and lecturers among liberal churchmen. Greatly influenced by pragmatism as well as evolution, Beecher said that he "formed a theology by practice . . . and the things that really did God's work in the hearts of men I set down as good theology." Evolution and the higher criticism affected Catholics less than Protestants inasmuch as the Vatican maintained the authority to determine truth. Still, no part of Christianity went untouched.

While natural science threatened some of the basic thought patterns of Christianity, critics attacked the programs and practices of the churches themselves. It was widely charged that the churches had failed to deal with social and economic problems and had made no effort to apply the Christian faith to practical affairs. The otherworldliness of Christians, critics said, had caused them to ignore their responsibilities for improving conditions among people here and now. The church had a duty to deal with such human problems as labor relations, poverty, war, minority rights, political corruption, and other practical matters. This was called the social gospel—as contrasted with the gospel of individual salvation, which had been the hallmark of Protestant Christianity heretofore.

Washington Gladden, a leading minister in Columbus, Ohio, was one of the most prominent clergymen to concern himself with broad social and economic issues. He was especially active in efforts to solve labor-management disputes. As head of an Ohio commission, he investigated labor conditions with the hope of improving relations between workers and their employers. Josiah Strong, secretary of the Evangelical Alliance, also emphasized social religion, and his book *Our Country,* sold hundreds of thousands of copies. In 1896, C. M. Sheldon, a Topeka, Kansas minister, wrote a book entitled *In His Steps* which eventually sold more than 20 million copies in the United States and abroad. Sheldon challenged Christians to live according to the principles of Jesus. "If the church members were all doing as Jesus would do," he wrote, "could it remain true that armies of men would walk the streets for jobs, and hundreds of them curse the church, and thousands of them find in the saloon their best friend?"

Several new organizations came into existence to promote religious teaching and social service. The Young Men's Christian Association was transplanted from England in 1851, and the Young Women's Christian Association established its first branch in New York in 1858. The YMCA and YWCA were both evangelically oriented, but they also provided social benefits for young men and women in urban communities. These included classes, study programs, reading rooms, and recreational activities. The Salvation Army, another import from Great Britain, appeared in the United States in 1880. Besides fundamentalist religious services, the Salvation Army provided low-cost rooming houses, food kitchens, employment bureaus, and other help to the down-and-out in large cities. The formation of the Woman's Christian Temperance Union in 1874 resulted from a more energetic effort of churchwomen to deal with what they considered a major social issue of the day.

As a result of their missions and social service programs, Protestants made some gains in winning supporters in the cities. They generally were less successful, however, than the Roman Catholics. By the 1880s many Catholic immigrants poured into the urban centers from Southern and Eastern Europe, where they turned naturally to the Catholic Church. Moreover, Catholic parishes were often located in the working-class districts whereas Protestant churches were more likely to be found in the middle- and upper-class neighborhoods. Parish priests gave help and comfort to the poor of all nationalities. This held Catholics in the church and won new converts. Cardinal Gibbons of Baltimore and other Catholic leaders made efforts to socialize the church and especially to serve the needs of workingmen. By the 1880s both Protestants and Catholics were demonstrating a much higher degree of social consciousness than ever before, and the social gospel was becoming widely accepted.

Religious Fundamentalism

But most churchmen still preferred fundamentalism, supernaturalism, and emphasis on personal salvation. Indeed, liberal theology and socialized religion did not greatly affect the general body of Christians. The popularity of evangelist Dwight L. Moody testified to the fact that the "old-time religion" was still very much alive. Moody and his song leader, Ira A. Sankey, toured English and American cities, where thousands responded to Moody's vivid and moving sermons and to Sankey's emotional songs. Sankey wrote numerous hymns which became dear to the heart of Protestant America, including "The Ninety and Nine." While Moody emphasized personal conversion, he did not threaten his listeners with hellfire or eternal damnation. Rather, he stressed God's compassion for man. One of his most popular sermons was "God's Love for the Sinner." Moody was not indifferent to social needs; among other things, he established a girls' school at Northampton, Massachusetts.

The strength of religious conservatism was also reflected in the establishment of numerous fundamentalist groups which broke off from major denominations. For example, the Free Methodist, Wesleyan Methodist, Nazarene, and other "holiness" groups separated from the parent Methodist Episcopal Church. These offshoots claimed that the Methodist Church had departed from the basic teachings of Methodism's founder, John Wesley. The fundamentalists stressed a literal interpretation of the Bible as God's word, the virgin birth of Christ, His death and resurrection, and the forgiveness of sin. The South was traditionally fundamentalist in religion; thus religious liberalism made less progress there than in other sections of the country.

Most of the new denominations which arose during the late nineteenth century were offshoots of the older fellowships. However, the Church of Christ, Scientist, commonly known as Christian Science, was a completely new church. It developed out of American religious soil and appealed especially to city dwellers. Christian Science was founded in 1875 by Mrs. Mary Baker Eddy, a New Englander who believed that she had been healed of a nervous disorder. Her ideas were first published in *Science and Health with Key to the Scriptures* (1875), in which she declared that sin, sickness, and evil were not real but existed only in men's minds. Mrs. Eddy established the Mother Church in Boston in 1882; by 1906 her followers numbered some 85,000. Christian Science provided relief from urban tensions and reflected the special needs and aspirations of women.

Church membership generally made striking gains in the United States after 1860. During that period, population grew about three and one-third times, while church membership increased more than seven times. Total membership rose from 4.8 million in 1860 to 21.7 million in 1890 and climbed to about 33 million in 1906. Of these communicants, 20 million were Protestant, about 12 million were Roman Catholic, and another 1 million were Jewish, Eastern Orthodox, and Mormon (Latter Day Saints). Protestantism was strongest in the South, Midwest, and West, especially among farmers and small-town people. Catholics had their greatest strength in the large cities of the Midwest and Northeast. Although Catholics were not as numerous as Protestants throughout the country as a whole, their numbers were growing more rapidly because they controlled the migrants in the booming cities. Jewish as well as Catholic congregations benefited from immigration. Although most Jews remained Orthodox, Reformed Judaism, led by Rabbi Isaac M. Wise, became increasingly popular among American middle-class Jews.

American Education

If Americans were somewhat less than fully committed to formal religion, their faith in education seemed quite beyond challenge. They accepted without question a direct connection between public education and national progress. Indeed, to many education was the best means of expanding democracy, creating more wealth, improving morals, increasing individual opportunity, and building the good society. William T. Harris, superintendent of the St. Louis school system (later United States Commissioner of Education from 1889 to 1906), wrote in 1871: "The spirit of American institutions is to be looked for in the public schools to a greater degree than anywhere else." Although there were serious inadequacies in educational administration, curriculum, financing, and state laws governing schools, great improvements in both the quantity and quality of education were made between the Civil War and the end of the nineteenth century. Except in the South, where public education did not become rooted before 1900, the country moved rapidly toward the dream of universal, public, tax-supported education. Between 1870 and 1910 the level of illiteracy dropped from 20 to 6 percent of the total population.

During the post-Civil War years students entered schools at all levels in ever-increasing numbers. Between 1870 and 1910, public school enrollment rose from 6.9 to 17.8 million. Most of this growth occurred in the first eight grades, but the number attending public high schools increased from about 80,000 to 915,000. Private schools taught thousands more. College enrollments also revealed high gains, rising from only 52,000 in 1870 to 355,000 forty years later. Compulsory school attendance, typically for children from eight to fourteen, was an important factor in the growing enrollments. By 1898 some thirty-one states and territories had laws setting minimum attendance requirements, though unfortunately, these statutes were often poorly enforced. With more children in school, expenditures for education jumped sharply. The cost of public elementary and secondary education rose from $63.4 million in 1870 to $426 million in 1910.

Important changes in curriculum occurred at all levels of education, but particularly in the high schools and colleges. In the elementary schools, McGuffey's Readers, with their emphasis upon morality, thrift, industry, and patriotism, continued to be popular as late as 1900. Overall, the main emphasis was on teaching the 3 R's, with a little grammar, geography, and history added. The high schools introduced more courses in science and the humanities,

College education, like almost everything else, boomed after the Civil War. The total number of colleges, which in 1860 *stood at* 246 *had grown to* 494 *in* 1899. *Enrollments which in* 1870 *amounted to* 52,000 *in* 1910 *swelled to* 355,000.

Brown Brothers

Campus Life

Important to this growth were both private philanthropy and the Morrill Land Grant Act under which the Federal Government gave the states 11,000,000 *acres of land* (30,000 *acres for each member in Congress) to finance the establishment of agricultural and mechanical colleges. Every state in the union established land grant institutions and thus provided for the beginning of many state universities. By the* 1920s *these institutions accounted for one-third of the college enrollment in America. The postwar period also saw the founding of a number of special colleges for women and for blacks.*

Student life of the period—the Yale class (above) practices surveying in this 1881 *photograph—had rather more formal dimensions than that found on campuses today. Student involvement in politics and social issues, where it existed at all, had little of the force that it does in the second half of the twentieth century. Students did, however, put abundant energy into athletics and they helped to create a national institution—intercollegiate football.*

For a student at the Ivy League colleges in the 1870s, such as the one taking his ease in his room at Yale (left) college meant some hard work, but it also meant some involvement with the exciting and sometimes brutal game of intercollegiate football. The first game, between Princeton and Rutgers, took place in 1869, with 25 men on each team. By the mid-1870s, Harvard, Yale, and Columbia were into it, and the game began a rapid evolution. Team size shrank to 15 and then 11, and the gridiron pattern of the field and the system of first downs were introduced.

Rough hazing of freshmen, (below, right) commonly occurred, and brutality became increasingly characteristic of football as well. By the turn of the century, free-for-alls, like the one shown below, aroused popular reaction against the game. A Chicago newspaper reported that during the 1905 season 18 college and secondary students had been killed and 159 injured. President Theodore Roosevelt called a White House conference of Ivy League representatives to rid the game of brutality. Football survived the changes. The game had ritual force on many campuses, bringing the student body and alumni to peaks of weekend excitement. At right, students at Stanford in 1910 put finishing touches on what must have been a dangerously impressive bonfire.

Left and below, center: Culver Pictures, Inc.; above: Stanford University; below: Picture Collection, New York Public Library

A few women's schools existed before the Civil War, but higher education for women did not figure importantly until the postwar years, and not until then did women's colleges offer courses comparable to those offered for men. By 1900 Vassar, Smith, Wellesley, Bryn Mawr, Radcliffe, and Barnard had all been established, and many Western and Midwestern colleges were coeducational. A formality little seen today characterized life in the women's colleges, just as it did in the men's. At left, students at Bacone College in Oklahoma in 1908 march from their dormitory; above, a Wellesley girl in 1902 prepared a chafing-dish supper in her room for some of her classmates.

Some student concern for political and social issues manifested itself in both men's and women's colleges, but student demonstrations were relatively unimpressive. At right, above, Vassar girls parade on campus for women's suffrage. Women's colleges also tended to emphasize traditional rites. At right, below. Vassar girls participate in the traditional spring daisy chain, a phenomenon which died only recently.

By 1900 women were active in a number of sports and university women led the way. The coeducational University of Nebraska became a pioneer in physical education. At right, center, the girls take the hurdles.

Left and right, below: Culver Pictures, Inc.; above: Picture Collection, New York Public Library; right above: Vassar College; right, center: University of Nebraska

Francis Benjamin Johnston, Library of Congress

A number of colleges for Negroes were established in the postwar years, although many of them, particularly Hampton Institute in Virginia and Tuskegee Institute in Alabama, put frank and heavy emphasis on vocational training. The possibly posed Francis Benjamin Johnston photographs here show a carpentry class at Hampton (left); an American history class, which had Indians as well as blacks among its students (not to mention the model), also at Hampton (following page, above); and a chemistry lab in 1902 at Tuskegee (following page, below). Other schools for blacks founded during the period include Fisk, Howard, and Atlanta universities.

Both: Francis Benjamin Johnston from Collection, The Museum of Modern Art, New York

along with some additional history and geography. These courses were designed primarily for students planning to enter college. Another major development was an increasing emphasis upon the vocational arts, including manual training as well as household and commercial subjects for non-college-bound students. In addition, college educators relaxed some of their rigid course requirements and introduced the elective system, which gave students a wider choice of subject matter.

John Dewey was the foremost educational philosopher of the period, and by the early twentieth century his ideas permeated many American schools. Dewey taught at the University of Chicago from 1894 to 1904, then moved to Columbia University. Thereafter Columbia became the fountainhead of new educational thought. Dewey looked upon education as a means of reforming society, but he believed that in achieving this end the school must approach real life situations. In other words, he discounted knowledge acquired from memorization and learning by rote and insisted that children learned by playing together, expressing themselves, making things, and participating in group activities—in short, learning by doing and experiencing.

Higher education received strong impetus from the passage of the Morrill Land Grant Act of 1862 which granted to every state 30,000 acres of public land for every senator and representative it had in Congress, to help it establish an agricultural and mechanical college. These colleges were intended to serve those, especially, who wanted practical education and who, besides, had little or no opportunity to attend such institutions as Harvard or Yale. Some states established separate agricultural colleges, while others integrated the agricultural college into the state university.

No less than the land-grant colleges, the large number of technical schools reflected a growing emphasis upon practical education. These schools met the rising educational demands of a rapidly growing industrial and technical society. The Massachusetts Institute of Technology which began operation in 1865, Lehigh University, and the Case School of Applied Science, later Case Institute, were among the leading technical institutions. Special women's colleges were also established in the post-Civil War years. Henry F. Durant, who established Wellesley, said he wanted to "found a college for the glory of God by the education and culture of women."

The demand for professional and graduate education also rose sharply in the late nineteenth century. Earlier in American history, lawyers, doctors, dentists, and even clergymen had been trained in a haphazard manner or had acquired their education through what amounted to apprenticeship. If a young man wanted to become an attorney, he read law in the office of a practicing lawyer. Harvard and the University of Virginia, among others, had established their famous law schools before the Civil War, but it was not until after 1870 that the number of law schools expanded sufficiently to meet the need. Medical education followed a similar pattern, and by 1900 the nation's medical schools were turning out in excess of 5,000 trained doctors a year. Teacher training kept pace with other professional education

Higher education benefited greatly from the distinctive leadership provided by a number of strong college and university presidents. Charles W. Eliot at Harvard, Andrew E. White of Cornell (1868–1885), William Rainey Harper at Chicago (1891–1906), James B. Angell at Michigan (1871–1909), and Daniel Coit Gilman at Johns Hopkins (1875 -1901) all made major contributions. Serving as president of Harvard from 1869 to 1909, Eliot was a skilled administrator who worked for what he called the "new education." He introduced the elective system and emphasized the need to teach natural sciences, mathematics, and modern foreign languages. At Johns Hopkins, Gilman set up the nation's first genuine graduate school.

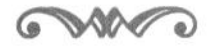

Negro Education

Once they had achieved freedom, Negroes had an insatiable appetite for learning. Viewing education as a lever to lift themselves out of dependency and poverty, they eagerly flocked to the schools established by Northerners after 1865. One of the principal aims of the Freedmen's Bureau and various religious denominations in the immediate post-Civil War South was the expansion of education for freed Negroes. Between 1865 and 1880 most of the Negroes who gained any education at all received it in schools supported by Northern charities. By 1870 the Freedmen's Bureau had spent some $5 million on Negro education; church and philanthropic groups had provided millions more. Hundreds of Northern teachers invaded the South to man the new schools.

At the same time, many Southerners demanded public, tax-supported education. Some Southern states passed laws in the 1860s and 1870s providing public schools for both whites and blacks on an integrated basis, but these laws were never satisfactorily implemented. Lack of a tradition of public education in the South, opposition from whites who did not want to pay taxes to educate blacks, and absence of a strong tax base in most Southern communities combined to retard public education for the great majority of Southern youth, but especially for blacks. Conditions became even worse for blacks when the South established a completely separate school system for them. Segregation received legal approval in the separate-but-equal doctrine promulgated by the Supreme Court in *Plessy v. Ferguson* (1896), which applied to schools as well as to transportation and other public facilities. At the turn of the century, black education seemed capable only of assuring a high level of black illiteracy. Thousands of black children had no opportunity to attend school at all, and it was rare for a black youth to attend college.

However, after 1865 a number of black colleges were established to provide black educational leadership and to prepare blacks for tasks in an industrial society. In 1868 Samuel C. Armstrong, the son of American missionaries in Hawaii, established Hampton Normal and Agricultural Institute in Virginia. The leading black educator in the post-Civil War years was Booker T. Washington, a former slave and student at Hampton, who became the first president of Tuskegee Institute in Alabama when it opened with thirty students in 1881. Other private colleges for Negroes included Fisk University in Nashville, Howard University in Washington, D. C., and Atlanta University. Three Southern states established separate publicly supported colleges under the Morrill Land Grant Act of 1862, but these institutions were usually starved for funds. Congress in 1890 supplemented the original Morrill Act with a monetary grant and now ordered the Southern states to establish colleges for blacks who had been largely neglected under the operation of the initial law.

Another prominent black educator and scientist was George Washington Carver. Born

Art in America: 1865–1905

Nineteenth-century painting in the post-Civil War period generally reflects the pessimism and melancholy which characterized the age in general. The Civil War proved the all-too-bitter truth that the dream of America as new Eden was false and that America could experience a holocaust as great as corrupt Europe had ever produced. Allied to this in the later nineteenth century was the accumulation of great collections of antiques and Old Master's paintings by the nouveau riche who were interested in achieving "instant culture" and a correspondent lessening of support for native, contemporary American art.

Sculpture first felt this impact. While the neoclassic school continued to produce its marmoreal allegories, gods, and goddesses until the end of the century and even beyond, the meaning of such works for Americans greatly diminished as the concept of the United States as a second Greek democracy proved illusory. Sculpture continued to thrive in America, however, and in one area, that of city and state military monuments, at least, the Civil War provided a great springboard for sculptural production.

The Hudson River School continued to flourish with its exploration of American scenery in meticulously rendered detail, but the most successful artists to employ this stylistic approach were painters such as Frederic Church, who applied his talent to the interpretation of the grandiose scenery of the North American West, and Albert Bierstadt, who painted unexplored South America. New currents were entering into American landscape painting, however, particularly from France, where the more personal and more lyrical interpretations of nature inspired such American artists as George Inness.

The great triumvirate of American painters of the period included Thomas Eakins, Winslow Homer, and Albert Pinkham Ryder. The first two were the

---

Hiram Powers was the first American sculptor to achieve international prominence. His sculpture of The Greek Slave, *above all, embodied the neoclassic ideals derived from a study of the art of antiquity and applied to a contemporary allegory where it had an appeal that was sentimental, religious, and moral.*

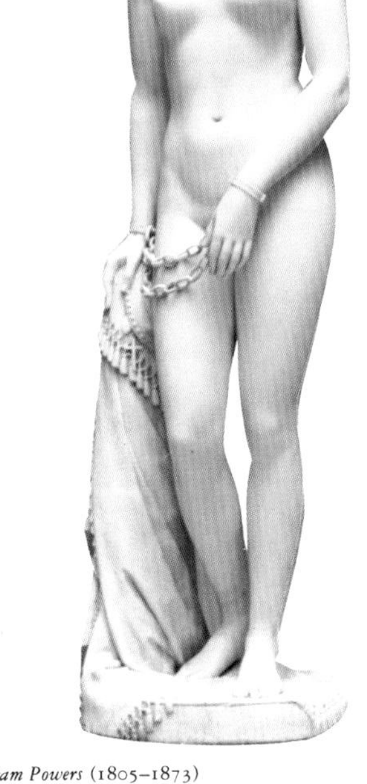

Hiram Powers (1805–1873)
The Greek Slave, 1843, *marble*
In the collection of The Corcoran Gallery of Art.

Far left: Alfred Pinkham Ryder (1847–1917)
The Race Track *or* Death on a Pale Horse, *ca.* 1910, *oil on canvas*
The Cleveland Museum of Art, the J. H. Wade Collection.

Death on a Pale Horse *is unique among the works of Albert Pinkham Ryder: his largest painting and a very personal conception relating to a friend who committed suicide after losing at a race track. Even here, however, we have the private vision, the simplified forms, the dark pallette, and the thick paint so typical of Ryder.*

greatest American realists of the century, the former applying his prodigious talents to create incisive, intimate interpretations of people and figures. This approach and his sad, monochromatic pallette justly has earned Eakins the cognomen, "the American Rembrandt." Homer was one of the greatest painters of the sea, and, while the most successful of these three artists, like Eakins, he divorced himself from contemporary society. Even more isolated from the life around him, Ryder retreated into an imaginary fantasy world, sometimes drawn from the depths of his mind, sometimes reinterpreting Biblical and literary themes, but always in a very personal way.

The greatest artists working in America during this period had little contact with American society, unlike their pre-Civil War predecessors. Other American painters divorced themselves even further from their native milieu and became expatriates, following in the footsteps of the Benjamin West and John Singleton Copley but for very different reasons. James A. M. Whistler spent his whole artistic life in Paris, London, and Venice, producing works variously influenced by the French realist Courbet, the English Pre-Raphaelites, and the newly discovered Japanese art, but ultimately, in the highly refined sensibility of his "art for art's sake" credo, creating a body of work very individual, modern, and almost abstract. John Singer Sargent became the greatest portraitist of his era, painting the likenesses of the internationally and socially prominent and affluent, first in France, then in England. French Impressionism influenced the work of both these painters, but it was Mary Cassatt who became a member of that group of French artists devoted to the study and depiction of light, color, and atmosphere. Miss Cassatt spent her entire artistic career in France, but other American artists, such as Childe Hassam, studied there and then returned to America to introduce these more colorful and happy aspects into American art at the very end of the century.

Devoted to the style and principles of such painters as Claude Monet, Childe Hassam, among other painters so influenced, introduced Impressionism to America. Indeed this approach became so popular here that a group of artists, Hassam among them, gathered together to form "The Ten," which became a sort of Impressionist academy.

Left: Childe Hassam (1859–1935)
The Stewart Mansion, New York City
Santa Barbara Museum of Art. Gift, Preston Morton Collection.

Augustus Saint-Gaudens (1848–1907), Adams Memorial, 1891, *bronze. Rock Creek Cemetery, Washington, D.C.*

The reaction to neoclassicism in sculpture took the form of heroic, bronze historical monuments. Augustus St. Gaudens was the greatest of these late-nineteenth-century sculptors. His great Civil War monuments —that of Colonel Shaw in Boston and the Farragut and Sherman statues in New York (right, above)— were not so much inspired by sculpture of antiquity as by that of the Renaissance, and this period in American sculpture is often referred to as the "Renaissance Revival." A more personal, private, almost mystical note can be sensed in St. Gaudens' memorial to Mrs. Henry Adams. But St. Gaudens was hardly the only accomplished sculptor of the period. His best-known contemporary was Daniel Chester French who rose to rapid fame with his Minute Man *(right, below). The work had a stirring, patriotic appeal, but, a close look reveals its direct derivation from the Apollo Belvedere transformed into an American subject and interpreted in the medium of bronze.*

Above: Augustus Saint-Gaudens (1848–1907)
General William Tecumseh Sherman Memorial, 1892–1903, *bronze*
Central Park, New York City.
Right: Daniel Chester French (1850–1931)
The Minute Man, 1874–1875, *bronze*
Concord, Mass.

Albert Bierstadt (1830–1902), Wolf River, Kansas. *The Detroit Institute of Arts.*

The techniques of the Hudson River School, reinformed by study at the great German art center of Düsseldorf, inspired the painting of Albert Bierstadt, the most famous interpreter of the scenery of the American West. Far from the urban centers of the East and remote from national conflict, the Adamic vision could survive, and Bierstadt's enormous canvases commanded prices not only astronomical but beyond any sums previously paid to American painters. Thomas Moran, a slightly younger painter of the West, based his style instead upon that of the English painter, James Mallord Turner, and thus brought a new sense of dashing brushwork and brilliant color to his equally large Western canvases. Going beyond Bierstadt, Moran sought romantic interpretation, beyond factual accuracy, a feeling popular enough to influence the founding of the National Parks system to protect the natural monuments he was immortalizing.

Thomas Moran (1837–1926), Grand Canyon of the Yellowstone, 1893–1901, *oil on canvas*
National Collection of Fine Arts, Smithsonian Institution. Gift of George D. Pratt.

George Inness (1825–1894)
Peace and Plenty, 1865, *oil on canvas*
The Metropolitan Museum of Art. Gift of George A. Hearn, 1894.

George Inness completely abandoned the Hudson River meticulousness of his youth and instead, after studying the art of Corot, Rousseau, and other French Barbizon painters, created more generalized yet more poetic landscapes in which topography was of distinctly minor interest. The art of Inness's middle years, from the mid-1850s to the mid-1870s was solid, massive, and dramatic (right). About the time of his move to Montclair, N.J., in 1878, his style became increasingly delicate and feathery until all details disappeared in a soft, generalized, and harmonious atmosphere, merging figures, animals, shrubbery, and trees (above). In this, Inness followed the development of his French predecessor, Corot.

George Inness (1825–1894), Trout Brook, 1891, *oil on canvas*
Collection of the Newark Museum, Purchase Members Fund, 1965.

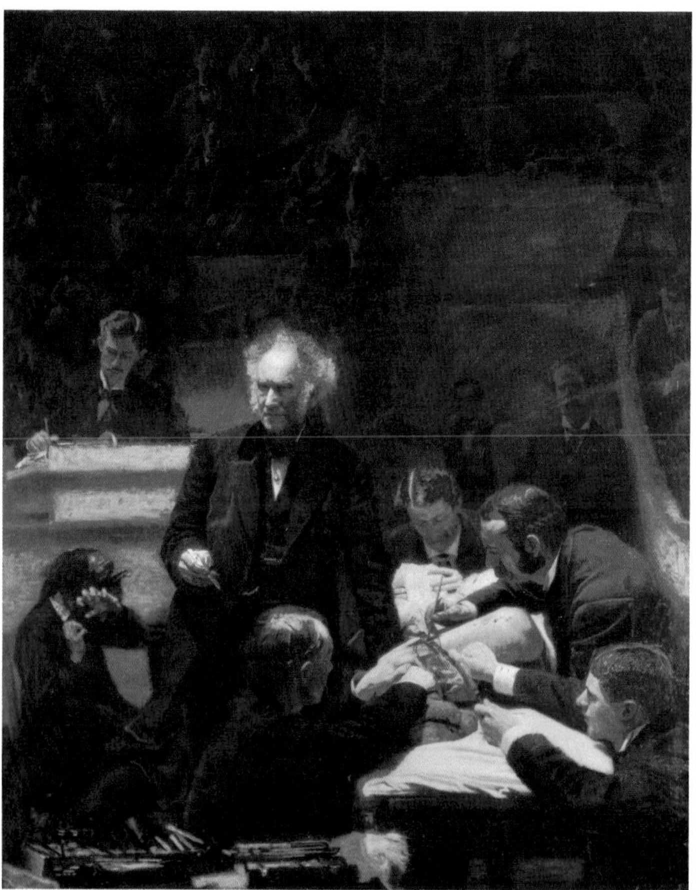

Left: Thomas Eakins (1844–1916), The Gross Clinic, 1875, *oil on canvas. Courtesy of the Jefferson Medical College of Philadelphia. Below: Thomas Eakins,* The Concert Singer—Portrait of Weda Cook, 1892, *oil on canvas. Philadelphia Museum of Art. Right: Thomas Eakins,* Salutat, 1898, *oil on canvas. Addison Gallery of American Art, Phillips Academy, Andover, Mass.*

One of the greatest realists of the nineteenth century, Thomas Eakins was the best figure painter that America produced. The academic French artist, Gerome, with whom he studied, imbued him with a sense of form and structure; and the intense, moving realism of such seventeenth-century Spanish artists as Ribera also impressed him deeply. Eakins' feeling for form and anatomy and his interest in character and individuality in portraiture were never more magnificently and graphically expressed than in his The Gross Clinic *(left), which shocked and horrified his contemporaries in its lack of sentiment and uncompromising realism.*

Most of Eakins' sitters and subjects, even in his portraits, were friends and relatives, and it is not surprising that he often endows them with a sympathetic, rather intimate melancholy (right). Eakins' pallette was dark and sombre—in his portraits as well as his figure studies. Both a painter and teacher of anatomy, Eakins could study and depict the unclothed human form most naturally in the fighting ring (far right) and the swimming hole. These vigorous and masculine paintings emphasize the solid, powerful forms of his subjects in a completely unposed, nonartificial way.

EAKINS
1898

Left: Winslow Homer (1836–1910), Long Branch, New Jersey, 1809, *oil on canvas. Courtesy of the Museum of Fine Arts, Boston, Charles Henry Hayden Fund. Below: Winslow Homer,* Northeaster, 1895, *oil on canvas. The Metropolitan Museum of Art. Gift of George A. Hearn,* 1910.

Right: Winslow Homer, Canoe in Rapids, 1897, *water color on paper. Courtesy of the Fogg Art Museum, Harvard University, Louise E. Bettens Fund. Below: Winslow Homer,* The Fox Hunt, 1893, *oil on canvas. Courtesy of the Pennsylvania Academy of the Fine Arts.*

If Eakins was America's finest realist figure painter, Winslow Homer was our greatest realistic painter of nature. Even his earlier work conveys the freshness, airiness, and naturalness of the outdoors where man and nature sympathetically join (left, above). Increasingly, however, after the early 1880s, Homer's art became more sombre and more powerful, and the human figure either more monumental and rugged in his battle against the forces of nature (above, right) or absent entirely, leaving only the interaction and conflict of a few natural elements —the irresistible force of the sea and the immovable timeless rocks of the shore (left, below). The great Fox Hunt *(right, below) is unique in its delicate outlines, flat forms, and sense of pattern. Here Japanese influences combine with a sense of the rugged battle for survival in nature. Homer was also a great watercolorist, whether applying the medium to the hunters of the Adirondacks or the richer, more colorful life of Florida and the Caribbean. Indeed, this period witnessed the birth of watercolor as an independent art form in America, and the nation was fortunate in having such great interpreters of the medium as Homer, Thomas Moran, and John Singer Sargent.*

Albert Pinkham Ryder (1847–1917), Toilers of the Sea, *before* 1884, *oil on wood. The Metropolitan Museum of Art, George A. Hearn Fund,* 1915.

John LaFarge (1835–1910), Bridle Path, Tahati, *ca.* 1890, *watercolor. Courtesy of the Fogg Art Museum, Harvard University, Bettens Fund.*

The greatest of the solitary American painters of a fantasy world, Albert Pinkham Ryder certainly qualifies as a late-nineteenth-century romantic. Among his dark, glowing paintings, almost all small, his marines are the best known (above). Their sense of quiet simplicity and interest in abstract shapes brought Ryder the praise and admiration of many contemporary artists. If Ryder was the most individual of our visionaries, a number of others, such as John LaFarge, brought a more cultured, intellectual background to their religious and allegorical scenes. At the left, LaFarge exhibits his knowledge and understanding of Renaissance painting, particularly the art of Raphael and Titian. Indeed much American painting and sculpture in the late nineteenth century acknowledges a debt to the Italian Renaissance.

American still-life painting of the late nineteenth century took on a radically different form from the bright and colorful fruit and flower painting of earlier years. William Michael Harnett, the most famous still-life specialist, always paints in a very masculine way, sometimes emphasizing trophies of the hunt (right). His deceptively realistic style seems actually to project forms into the viewer's space.

Right: William Harnett (1848–1892), After the Hunt, 1885, *oil on canvas Courtesy, California Palace of the Legion of Honor, San Francisco. Mildred Anna Williams Collection.*
Below: William Merritt Chase (1849–1916), In the Studio, *not dated, oil on canvas. The Brooklyn Museum. Gift of Mrs. C. H. De Silver in memory of her husband.*

Harnett received some of his training in Munich which had superseded Düsseldorf as the greatest German art center. For American painters, Munich stood primarily for dashing, dark, vigorous figure painting, modeled after Dutch seventeenth-century prototypes, particularly the art of Franz Hals. Frank Duveneck and William Merritt Chase (left, below) were the greatest and most influential of the Americans who brought the Munich style back to this country. Chase became the greatest art teacher of the period. His fluidly painted, scintillating views of his famous studio, filled with antiques and bric-a-brac, are among his most charming and original works.

Above: James Abbott McNeill Whistler (1834–1903)
Nocturne in Black and Gold: The Falling Rocket, *ca.* 1874
oil on panel The Detroit Institute of Arts.

Left: James Abbott McNeill Whistler (1834–1903)
The White Girl, 1861–1862, *oil on canvas*
National Gallery of Art, Washington, D.C. Harris Whittemore Collection.

Right: John Singer Sargent (1856–1916)
Madame X (Mme Gautreau), 1884, *oil on canvas*
The Metropolitan Museum of Art, Arthur H. Hearn Fund, 1916.

England and France have claimed with as much or more justification than America a number of the most important expatriate American painters of the late nineteenth century. One of these is Whistler, a most original artist who began working in the realistic manner of the Frenchman, Gustave Courbet (far left). In England, Whistler abandoned realism for his own form of Impressionism where the viewer's response to his effects became most important (near left). Whistler's interest in the formal relationships of artistic arrangements was in part inspired by his profound knowledge of Oriental art. To disclaim any interest in subject matter in his later work, Whistler often gave his paintings musical titles, such as symphony, nocturne, and so forth.

Perhaps more internationally famous than Whistler but primarily a society portraitist, John Singer Sargent worked with bravura brush work and scintillating colors. Sargent interpreted his often famous and prominent subjects with an emphasis on their positions in society and their elegant backgrounds (right), rather than on the incisive characterizations of Eakins.

Mary Cassatt (1845–1926), Caresse Enfantine, 1902, *oil on canvas. National Collection of Fine Arts, Smithsonian Institution. Gift of William T. Evans.*

Impressionism—the investigation of the phenomena of light, color, and atmosphere, often at the expense of mass and space—had a more immediate and enthusiastic reception in America than in its native France, thanks to the support and activity of Mary Cassatt, probably the most famous American woman artist. Miss Cassatt, herself an American expatriate, allied herself with the French Impressionists, but particularly Edouard Degas; like him, she never abandoned her interest in solid figure painting, a phenomenon particularly evident in her often-repeated theme of the mother and child.

in 1864, the son of slave parents, Carver received a master's degree in agriculture from Iowa State College and then settled at Tuskegee to teach and conduct research. His most famous work involved the search for industrial uses for the peanut. Despite such individual triumphs, however, discrimination, proverty, and lack of leadership held all levels of black education in the South to a minimum during the late nineteenth century.

Natural Sciences

Advances in science reflected the improvements in American education. A number of American scholars made distinctive contributions to scientific advancement in the post-Civil War years. Most of the basic research was done in the nation's leading universities, such as Harvard, Yale, and Johns Hopkins. A growing number of industries maintained chemists, physicists, and other scientists in their plants, but these men usually concentrated on applying the results of scientific research to practical purposes rather than expanding the realm of theoretical knowledge.

J. Willard Gibbs, a quiet, reserved physicist at Yale. did basic research in thermodynamics which brought him international fame. In astronomy, Simon Newcomb greatly enlarged man's knowledge of the solar system. By the 1890s the United States had the most powerful telescopes in the world available for research in astronomy. Although American scholars failed to pursue much basic research in chemistry, compared with their European counterparts, they did apply new chemical knowledge to industry and agriculture on a broad scale. Chemists were employed by steel makers, oil refineries, and other manufacturers, as well as in agricultural experimentation. American scientists also carried on extensive research in geology, zoology and plant sciences. Medical science experienced great progress as advances were made in surgical techniques and germ control. Appendectomies and similar operations, which had formerly been dangerous and often fatal, became quite routine. Dr. J. D. Bryant of New York performed one of the most famous operations of the period when he removed a malignant growth from President Cleveland's jaw in July, 1893, thereby saving the President's life. Deaths from diphtheria and tuberculosis dropped substantially as sanitation and other public health measures improved.

Literary Currents

Between 1865 and World War I American letters entered an era of major transition. The changes which took place in literature were closely associated with the industrial revolution and its effects on all phases of American life and culture. Romanticism and sentimentalism in literature declined sharply during the 1870s, to be followed by the rise of realism in the 1880s and a burst of realistic naturalism in the 1890s and early twentieth century. Yet the literary history of the period cannot be clearly categorized or placed in neat chronological divisions because of extensive overlapping. Furthermore, similar subjects prompted greatly different literary responses. Growing wealth and materialism furnished the themes embodied in the stories of Horatio Alger. But such themes had little relationship to those of William

Dean Howells in *The Rise of Silas Lapham.* There was, moreover, a wide gulf between the higher forms of literary art and the writing which appealed to the masses.

The persistence of romantic, moralistic, and sentimental writings throughout the last third of the nineteenth century reveals much about the tastes and intellectual level of the American reading public. Books with a moral, those which drew sharp contrasts between good and evil, and those with religious themes were far more widely read than novels dealing realistically with major social, economic, or political problems. Mary J. Holmes, who began her writing career in the 1850s, turned out her moralistic novels at a rate of nearly one a year well into the 1880s. Setting her stories in Virginia and Maryland, Mrs. E. D. E. N. Southworth wrote about beautiful heroines and ugly villains. In the perennial conflict between righteousness and evil, truth and goodness always prevailed over the forces of darkness. Mrs. Southworth's books enjoyed a wide reading public as late as the 1890s. Novels with religious themes sold by the millions. It is not surprising that in a period of rapid economic and social change people were attracted to books which even in fictional form provided assurance and proved the ultimate triumph of right. Elizabeth Stuart Phelps's *The Gates Ajar* (1868) and the Reverend E. P. Roe's *Barriers Burned Away* (1872) were both best sellers. However, few books of fiction compared in popularity with Lew Wallace's religious novel of 1880, *Ben Hur.*

Success through self-help had always been a popular American theme and never more so than in the 1870s and 1880s. Playing on this deeply held idea, Horatio Alger (1834–1899) wrote more than 100 books for juveniles, including *Luck and Pluck* and *Tattered Tom.* Alger's poor heroes always achieved success through hard work, courage, and virtue. Other highly popular writings were the dime novels which flowed from the publishing house of Erastus F. Beadle. These stories sold by the millions, made Beadle a millionaire, and provided enjoyment for a full generation of Americans. The dime novels were filled with daring, suspense, and violence, but they maintained high moral standards. The heroes seldom swore or drank.

Some of the best post-Civil War writing was achieved by a group of "local color" writers. These authors abandoned romanticism and presented a truthful, realistic portrayal of their subjects and regions, but they did so in a sensitive and restrained manner. Their realism was confined largely to description and dialect; they gave little attention to analysis. Samuel Clemens ("Mark Twain," 1835–1910), one of the leading local colorists, wrote *Roughing It* (1872), *The Adventures of Tom Sawyer* (1876), *Life on the Mississippi* (1883), and *Huckleberry Finn* (1885) —all exciting stories which brought him national, and even international, fame. Other local color writers included Edward Eggleston, who faithfully described aspects of mid-nineteenth-century rural life in Indiana in *The Hoosier Schoolmaster.* New England found an interpreter in Sarah Orne Jewett (1849–1909), whose *A Country Doctor* (1884) and *The Country of the Pointed Firs* (1896) were good examples of regional fiction. The South produced a number of strong local color writers. George W. Cable wrote about the Creole society in New Orleans in *The Grandissimes* (1880), and the same year Joel Chandler Harris began to record authentic Negro stories in his Uncle Remus tales.

The local color novelists served as an effective intellectual bridge between the earlier romanticism and the realism of the 1880s, best exemplified in the work of William Dean Howells (1837–1920) and Henry James (1843–

1916). Literary realism, Howells wrote, "is nothing more and nothing less than the truthful treatment of material." Henry James, the brother of the famous philosopher and psychologist William James, became disillusioned and unhappy with the lack of culture and intellectual sophistication in the United States and moved to London in 1876. From that vantage point and drawing inspiration from such European realists as Balzac, Zola, and Tolstoy, James dealt frankly and directly with problems of human relationships and what he considered the provincialism of American culture. In *The American* (1877), *Daisy Miller* (1879), and *The Portrait of a Lady* (1881), he explored the interactions of different characters with American and European cultural backgrounds.

Howells was generally considered the best American literary craftsman and man of letters in the late nineteenth century. After learning the printing and publishing business by working on his father's newspaper, he turned to writing. Howells displayed his realism in *A Modern Stance* (1882) and *The Rise of Silas Lapham* (1884). In *The Rise of Silas Lapham,* he related the events in the troubled life of an uncultured, self-made industrialist in Boston. This was the first attempt in American fiction to deal realistically with the price of self-made business success.

Fiercer and grimmer types of realism sprang out of the West from the pens of writers who viewed farm and small-town life as drab, barren, and depressing to both mind and spirit. E. W. Howe, a Kansas newspaperman, described the shallow, petty, and unhappy existence in and around Atchison, Kansas, in *The Story of a Country Town* (1884). Better known were the works of Hamlin Garland (1860–1940), whose *Main-Travelled Roads* (1891), *A Son of the Middle Border* (1917), and other writings depicted the great gulf between the romantic ideal of happy farm life and the actual misery and cultural void of rural existence in the West. In the South, Virginia's Ellen Glasgow rose to national prominence as a regional writer, although she belonged to a somewhat later period. Most of her work appeared after the turn of the century. In *The Voice of the People* (1900) and *The Battle Ground* (1902), she began to compile a social history of postwar Virginia.

The stark Western realism of Garland and Howe in portraying rural life was more than matched by a group of young naturalists and social critics who pursued urban themes. One distinguishing mark of the new naturalism of the 1890s was the frank discussion of sex, which would have been unacceptable in the 1870s and 1880s. Although not a contemporary success, Stephen Crane's *Maggie, A Girl of the Streets* (1892) exemplified the trend in realistic naturalism. Here Crane described frankly the unhappy and futile life of a prostitute without the slightest touch of sentimentality. Frank Norris, Theodore Dreiser, and Jack London (see page 858) were among other novelists who contributed to the school of naturalistic realism. By the 1890s many American writers were emphasizing social criticism, and they increasingly found their themes in the influence of industrialism on American society.

Poets in the late nineteenth century found a wide reading public. James Whitcomb Riley achieved prominence in the 1880s with such well-known poems as "When the Frost Is on the Punkin," and "The Ole Swimmin' Hole." Before Eugene Field's early death cut down a promising career, he had in the late 1880s won attention with "Little Boy Blue" and *A Little Book of Western Verse.* Sidney Lanier, a Georgian, wrote dialect poems, including "The Son of the Chattachoochee," and "Thar's More in the

Man Than Thar Is in the Land." Protesting drudgery and the exploitation of labor, Edwin Markham wrote "The Man with the Hoe" (1899), an exceptionally moving depiction of futility, and many other poems which became popular at that time.

Fine Arts and Architecture

Realism in literature paralleled a new emphasis upon realistic portrayal in painting. Though some artists continued the romantic treatment of their subjects, which had been so characteristic before the Civil War, a group of talented portrait and landscape painters raised their art to a new level of realism and excellence. Thomas Eakins (1836–1910) followed his own advice of peering deeply into American life and then portraying what he saw accurately and realistically. George Inness (1825–1894) painted some of the more powerful landscapes in the period and was especially successful in combining light, shadows, and color. Some of the more realistic and thoroughly American landscapes came from the brushes of Winslow Homer (1836–1910). Finally settling on the Maine coast, Homer painted scenes of his locality—the coast, the ocean, and fishermen. The paintings of Albert P. Ryder (1847–1914) remained largely unknown as he toiled in a tiny, cluttered New York studio, where he did his best work between 1873 and 1898. In "Toilers of the Sea" and "Death on a Pale Horse," he used heavy colors, blurred lines, and vague images. Ryder was something of a mystic, and this was reflected in his paintings. Hence the rich imagery of his work went largely unappreciated in a period when realism was in vogue. Besides painting landscapes and executing murals, John La Farge (1835–1910) made a unique artistic contribution by designing and manufacturing the best stained glass yet seen in America.

Two of the period's most significant artists were John Singer Sargent and James McNeill Whistler. Sargent (1856–1925) was an especially skilled and sensitive portrait painter, although his portraits of wealthy patrons were less realistic than those by Eakins and some of his other contemporaries. His portraits always had a luster, and his subjects reflected strength and elegance, qualities which were particularly evident in "The Wyndham Sisters." Here, with great technical skill, Sargent portrayed three beautiful, noble, and elegant ladies in soft white coloring against a dark background. While Sargent was best known by contemporaries for his portraits of prominent people, later critics held that his watercolors were his most distinctive work. Whistler (1834–1903) was one of America's most original artists. During his productive career, Whistler produced many paintings, scores of etchings, and about one-hundred-fifty lithographs. His most famous painting was "Portrait of the Artist's Mother." Whistler considered himself a realist, but in both thought and practice he was more of an impressionist.

Italian neoclassicism dominated the form and spirit of American sculpture throughout the 1870s. The popular statue "Greek Slave," done by Hiram Powers, was perhaps the best American example of this art form. After 1880, however, a number of younger American sculptors came under the influence of French naturalism. Foremost among the new generation of brilliant sculptors was Augustus Saint-Gaudens (1848–1907), who studied three years at the École des Beaux-Arts in

Paris. His early triumph was a statue of Admiral David Farragut, first shown in Paris in 1880 and then brought to New York the following year. This work gave Saint-Gaudens quick and favorable recognition. Among his other famous works were "The Seated Lincoln" in Chicago and the statue called "Grief," done for Henry Adams in memory of his wife. Almost entirely American-trained, Daniel Chester French (1850–1931) was another highly talented and sensitive sculptor who achieved prominence in the late nineteenth century. He produced many notable works, but his statue of Lincoln in the Lincoln Memorial in Washington, D.C., is probably his greatest artistic achievement. Slightly younger than French, Lorado Taft (1860–1936) was a native of Illinois who studied art in Paris and then returned to Chicago, where he did some of his best pieces. These included "The Blind" and "Solitude of the Soul." Other outstanding sculptors included George Grey Barnard, Paul Bartless, Henry Augustus Lukeman, and Gutzon Borglum. Borglum gained attention in the late 1890s and early 1900s with his Western paintings and bronzes, but he later won international fame by carving the massive monument at Mount Rushmore in South Dakota.

Like other aspects of culture in the United States, American architecture drew heavily upon European forms. Indeed, it was a hodgepodge of Roman, Italian, and Gothic styles. Those who constructed expensive mansions for wealthy businessmen generally tried to emulate French chateaus or Italian villas rather than to build anything distinctively American. The better houses were built of heavy stone and had high, steep roofs, turrets, and towers. They were decorated with conspicuous bric-a-brac and stood behind iron fences. Although these European modes continued into the twentieth century, the dominant trend among American architects after 1870 was the achievement of concepts and forms which would suit modern industrial life. There was a growing emphasis upon function and environment.

Henry Hobson Richardson (1838–1886) brought some order out of architectural confusion when he returned after 1865 from France where he had studied at the École des Beux-Arts. He introduced the French Romanesque style in Boston's Trinity Church, which was completed in 1879. He also built the Marshall Field Building in Chicago. While Richardson used heavy Romanesque forms, he moved toward less ostentation and more functional design. By the 1880s, urban centers required taller office buildings to compensate for the shortage of land. Fortunately, a shift from masonry construction to steel frames at this time, along with the improvement of elevators, opened the way for the building of skyscrapers. John A. Root and Daniel Burnham went further than others in developing bold, strong lines for office buildings.

While Richardson, Louis H. Sullivan, and a few others gradually broke from the past, it was a young iconoclast, Frank Lloyd Wright, who developed a specifically American architecture. Wright (1869–1959) studied engineering at the University of Wisconsin and then worked in the office of Sullivan and Adler in Chicago during the early 1890s. He emphasized the functional, or what he called the organic, style of construction, and in designing houses he lowered the roof to match the landscape, expanded the window space to increase natural lighting, and used more glass and other new building materials. While Wright's unusual designs were ahead of their time in the 1890s, by 1910 he was having a marked influence upon architecture. The functional style finally prevailed in America, although classical and other European forms remained dominant during the nineteenth century. Daniel Burnham and other architects who planned "White City" for the World's Columbian Exposition in Chicago in 1893 adopted the classical design.

Popular Culture

Although the nation produced a distinguished group of painters, sculptors, and architects during the late nineteenth century, there existed a big gap between the higher forms of art and popular culture. The mass of Americans found intellectual and cultural satisfaction, as well as entertainment, in lectures, road shows, spectator sports, circuses, popular music, Currier and Ives prints, and photography. Lectures by William Rainey Harper, Russell Conwell, William Jennings Bryan, or any one of scores of other speakers greatly broadened the intellectual horizons of hundreds of thousands of Americans between the Civil War and World War I. The growth of cities provided the wealth and population to support expanded theater productions, and road companies played before audiences in hundreds of isolated communities. It was a rare treat to see Edwin Booth as Hamlet, or Georgiana Drew, the mother of Lionel, John, and Ethel Barrymore, in "The Princess Royal." American drama in the postwar years generally avoided realism and relied on comic or sentimental situations. (See pages 721–726.)

To attend a circus was an unforgettable event in the lives of many postwar Americans. Gawking country boys, small-town residents, as well as their city cousins, marveled at the human freaks, the clowns, the daring acrobats, and the wild animals. P. T. Barnum and James A. Bailey developed a three-ring circus, "the greatest show on earth," which traveled widely throughout the United States after 1875. In 1883 William F. Cody dramatized the Old West and excited Eastern and European audiences alike with the unusual acts in his Buffalo Bill's Wild West Show.

Americans were also entertained by minstrel shows, vaudeville, and light musicals. Minstrel shows, performed mainly by white men who blackened their faces with burnt cork, reached their height in the 1870s and 1880s. Composed of songs, dances, skits, and witty dialogue, these performances drew crowds in both country villages and large cities. Some Negro groups were formed, adding originality and authenticity to the minstrel shows. Theaters staging vaudeville, or variety shows, were found in most major American cities by the late 1880s and soon pushed minstrel performances into the entertainment background. The introduction of motion pictures in the 1890s, first shown as a part of vaudeville, soon replaced vaudeville as the principal source of popular entertainment. Thomas A. Edison developed an improved moving picture film, which he exhibited in 1894; and two years later Thomas Armat invented a projection machine which made it possible to show motion pictures before large audiences. The first regular movie theater opened in Pittsburgh in 1905, where patrons were entertained by the first American story film, *The Great Train Robbery.* This was the beginning of what was to become a major American industry.

Americans in the late nineteenth century had a passion for popular music, most of which was sentimental, moralistic, and melodramatic.

"After the Ball," "My Mother Was a Lady," and "O Promise Me" were typical popular hits during the 1890s. But the more distinctive American contributions to music were the blues, ragtime, and jazz. Jazz grew out of the minstrel songs and Afro-American folk music with its syncopated beat. The "King of Ragtime" was Scott Joplin, a Negro who made history in 1899 with his "Maple Leaf Rag." Though classical music found a rather limited appreciation in the United States, symphony orchestras and grand opera were by no means completely absent. New York and Boston both had symphony orchestras by the 1880s; New York opened the Metropolitan Opera House in 1883.

Spectator sports found growing acceptance among urban residents who seemed increasingly less interested in their own physical exercise. Horse racing was extremely popular in the 1880s, but gambling around the racetracks alienated many of the "better element" from this sport. Prizefighting was brutal and sometimes bloody. Rules were almost nonexistent; participants hit, clawed, gouged, and wrestled until one man gave up. In 1882 John L. Sullivan won the world championship, which he held until 1892, when he was beaten by "Gentleman Jim" (James A.) Corbett. By that time skillful boxing was beginning to replace the earlier rough-and-tumble affairs. Baseball became professionalized shortly after the Civil War, and by the 1890s paid attendance at games played by professional clubs reached several million annually.

Americans were characteristically "joiners." The various fraternal orders, college clubs, farm organizations, church groups, and literary and benefit societies attracted millions of members. The Masons, Odd Fellows, Knights of Pythias, Knights of Columbus, and the Elks were among the scores of popular secret societies in the late nineteenth century. These groups offered close associations and a feeling of belonging to people who were finding life in the cities increasingly impersonal. By 1900 more than six million persons were affiliated with the multitude of secret societies.

Others joined organizations to achieve certain specific social and political reforms. Formation of the Woman's Christian Temperance Union in 1874 was an organized effort to oppose drinking and to fight the saloon. Under the leadership of Frances E. Willard, the WCTU sought to eliminate the evils of liquor through education and political pressure. The American Equal Rights Association and the National Woman Suffrage Association, led by Susan B. Anthony and Elizabeth Cady Stanton, worked diligently for woman suffrage. By 1900 several states and territories had given women the right to vote, and a national movement was well under way to achieve a constitutional amendment which would grant all qualified women the franchise. Not all of the organizations to which Americans flocked had such lofty motives as those supporting woman suffrage and temperance. During the late 1880s and early 1890s, thousands of Americans joined the nativistic, anti-Catholic American Protective Association, formed in 1887 by an Iowan, Henry F. Bowers. The APA was a descendant of the Know-Nothings of the 1850s and fitted into the tradition of intolerance and bigotry which had come to the fore from time to time in American society. Strong among rural Americans who resented the Catholic immigrants flooding American cities, the APA demanded stricter naturalization laws, opposed Catholic political candidates, and fought to abolish parochial schools.

Much of American cultural and intellectual development received its popularization in the nation's newspapers and magazines. The number of dailies increased from 971 to 2,226 between 1880 and 1900, giving urban readers and even the residents of smaller cities access to daily newspapers. There were thousands of weeklies and semiweeklies, which were read chiefly by farmers and small-town residents. After the establishment of Rural Free Delivery in 1896, some farmers bought subscriptions to a city daily.

Major trends in newspaper publishing after the Civil War included growing sensationalism, a greater use of syndicated material, a heavier reliance on the news-gathering services, wider news coverage, the use of special features, and improved efficiency in production which resulted from such technological advances as the linotype, developed in the 1880s. Furthermore, large newspapers were themselves becoming big business, more dependent upon advertising than subscriptions for their income.

Between the 1870s and 1890s new leadership arose in the American newspaper field. In 1872 two of the most famous men in journalism—Horace Greeley, founder of the *New York Tribune*, and James Gordon Bennett, who started the *New York World*—died. Among the new leaders in the newspaper world were Joseph Pulitzer, E. W. Scripps, William Randolph Hearst, and Adolph S. Ochs. Pulitzer, a Hungarian-born immigrant, bought the *St. Louis Post-Dispatch* in 1878 and the *New York World* in 1883. Hearst, heir to a mining fortune, owned the *San Francisco Examiner* and later bought the *New York Morning Journal*. While both Pulitzer and Hearst emphasized sensationalism, which gave rise to the term "yellow journalism," Adolph S. Ochs, in 1895, purchased the sickly *New York Times* and set out to win readers by developing a reputation for public concern and comprehensive news coverage. Ochs soon pushed the *Times* to unquestioned primacy among American newspapers. But papers generally maintained circulation with cartoons and special features, while press services eased the burden of news gathering.

Magazines were available for readers of almost every level and interest, and they contributed substantially to the country's general educational advance. *Harper's Magazine*, a monthly begun in 1850; the *Atlantic Monthly*, started in 1857; and *Scribner's*, which first appeared in 1871, appealed to intellectuals. These periodicals carried travel accounts, articles of historic interest, stories, and serious discussions of public questions. *Harper's Weekly*, established in 1857 and later edited by George W. Curtis, had a wider appeal because of its spicy campaign against graft and dishonesty. Thomas Nast, a clever and imaginative cartoonist, became a staff artist in 1862, and his telling cartoons, along with revealing articles, were partly responsible for destroying the Tweed Ring. E. L. Godkin founded the *Nation* in 1865. Largely a journal of opinion, its influence went far beyond its very limited and selective readership.

Ten- and fifteen-cent magazines, which were within the financial reach of a larger number of Americans, were introduced in the 1890s. Samuel S. McClure founded *McClure's* in 1893 and set the price at 15 cents. At about the same time Frank Munsey established *Munsey's* and lowered the price to 10 cents. Besides being cheap, these magazines carried more material of popular interest. They published articles on controversial current topics, short stories, and materials of social concern. The establishment of the *Ladies' Home Journal* by Cyrus Curtis in 1883 reflected the appeal being made to certain special groups.

Libraries were a further source of general educational improvement. Most large cities had public libraries supported by taxation or private philanthropy, sometimes by both. By 1900 even many smaller towns could boast the presence of one of those nine thousand public libraries in the United States. Andrew Carnegie contributed $60 million to the building of libraries in hundreds of American communities, and the "Carnegie Library" became one of the most familiar and influential institutions in many towns and cities. For people who had neither the desire nor the materials to read, public lectures played a significant educational role. The Chautauqua movement emerged from its humble beginnings in New York State in 1874 to become, during the next 50 years, a remarkably effective source of popular education and entertainment. Many prominent leaders traveled from place to place, lecturing on literature, politics, economics, travel, and other subjects. Among the more popular speakers was the Reverend Russell H. Conwell. In his famous lecture "Acres of Diamonds," which he delivered some five thousand times between 1869 and 1913, Conwell stressed the idea that opportunity lurks everywhere and that every man can and should become rich, then use his money for the benefit of others.

Conclusion

While there was widespread criticism of American social, political, and economic life during the last three decades of the nineteenth century, together with insistent demands for reform, most citizens seemed satisfied with their culture and society. They boasted of their economic gains and fully believed that American democracy was superior to any other form of government. They were proud of their advances in science, education, literature, philosophy, social science, and law. Americans considered themselves a religious people, and as many of them looked at the nation they concluded that it had been especially blessed by God. The demands for change and reform advanced principally by farm and labor groups in the 1880s and 1890s were not strong enough to overcome the nation's general satisfaction.

SUGGESTED READINGS

The Emergence of Modern America, 1865–1878 (1927) by Allan Nevins; Arthur M. Schlesinger's *The Rise of the City* (1933); and H. U. Faulkner's *The Quest for Social Justice,* 1898–1914 (1931) treat the nation's social and cultural history between the Civil War and the First World War. Dealing more specifically with intellectual history are the pertinent chapters in Ralph Gabriel's *The Course of American Democratic Thought* (2d ed., 1956); *The American Mind** (1950) by Henry Steele Commager; Vernon L. Parrington's *Main Currents in American Thought** (1930), vol. 3; and Merle Curti's *The Growth of American Thought* (3d ed., 1964). Morton G. White has also dealt with aspects of intellectual history in *Social Thought in America: The Revolt against Formalism* (1949). The impact of Darwinism can be traced in the essays edited by Stow Persons, *Evolutionary Thought in America* (1950), and Richard Hofstadter's *Social Darwinism in American Thought, 1860–1915** (1944).

On education see H. G. Good's *A History of American Education* (1956), and R. F. Butts and Lawrence A. Cremin's *A History of Education in the United States* (1953). One of the most important histories of education is Cremin's *The Transformation of the School: Progressivism in American Education, 1876–1957** (1961). On Southern education, see C. W. Dabney's *Universal Education in the South* (2 vols., 1936). Horace Mann Bond's *The Education of the Negro in the American Social Order* (1934) is an excellent account of Negro education. Higher education can best be studied in the histories of individual institutions. S. E. Morison's *Three Centuries of Harvard* (1936); Hugh Hawkins's *Pioneer: A History of Johns Hopkins University* (1960); and Merle Curti and Vernon Carstensen's *The University of Wisconsin: A History* (2 vols., 1939) are all excellent.

A rising interest in religious history has produced a number of excellent volumes which deal partially or wholly with the late nineteenth century. For an introduction to the period see the relevant sections of John T. Tracy's *American Catholicism* (1956) and Winthrop S. Hudson's *American Protestantism** (1961), as well as the pertinent parts of William W. Sweet's *The Story of Religion in America* (1950 ed.). Newer, general histories of religion in America include Edwin S. Gaustad's *A Religious History of America* (1966) and Clifton E. Olmstead's *History of Religion in the United States* (1960). On the response of churches to social problems see Henry F. May's *Protestant Churches and Industrial America** (1949); Charles H. Hopkins's *The Rise of the Social Gospel in American Protestantism, 1865–1915** (1940); A. I. Abell's *The Urban Impact of American Protestantism, 1865–1900* (1943) and *American Catholicism and Social Action** (1960); and Robert T. Handy (ed.), *The Social Gospel in America* (1966). Revivalistic faith can be studied in Stewart C. Cole's *The History of Fundamentalism* (1931); Gamaliel Bradford's *Dwight L. Moody: A Worker in Souls* (1927); and William W. Sweet's *Revivalism in America** (1944). Christian Science is viewed favorably in Lyman P. Powell's *Mary Baker Eddy* (1950). On the Negro church see Carter G. Woodson's *The History of the Negro Church* (1921) and W. E. B. Du Bois's *The Negro Church* (1903). See also R. W. Logan, *The Negro in American Life and Thought* (1954).

The history of newspapers and magazines and their role in a democracy can be followed in F. L. Mott's *American Journalism* (2d ed., 1950) and Volumes 3 and 4 of Mott's *History of American Magazines* (1938, 1957).

American literary developments in these years can best be traced in Vernon L. Parrington's *Main Currents in American Thought** (1930), vol. III, and Van Wyck Brooks's *The Confident Years, 1885–1915* (1952). Everett Carter's *Howells and the Age of Realism* (1954) considers perhaps the most important literary figure of the period, as well as some of Howells's contemporaries. Studies dealing with some of the period's other outstanding writers include Bernard De Voto's *Mark Twain's America** (1951 ed.); Thomas Beer's *Stephen Crane: A Study in American Letters* (1923); R. H. Elias's *Theodore Dreiser, Apostle of Nature* (1949); W. P. Randel's *Edward Eggleston** (1963); and Jean Holloway's *Hamlin Garland: A Biography* (1960). Of the best surveys of Southern writing are J. B. Hubbell's *The South in American Literature, 1607–1900* (1954) and Gregory Paine's *Southern Prose Writers* (1947).

Parts of the following studies contain valuable material on various phases of the fine arts, as well as architecture: Oliver W. Larkin's *Art and Life in America* (1949), especially parts 2 and 3; Samuel Isham's *The History of American Painting* (1942); Eugene Neuhaus's *The History and Ideals of American Art* (1931); Lorado Taft's *History of America's Sculpture* (1930); and James T. Flexner's *A Short History of American Painting* (1950). Lewis Mumford's *The Brown Decades: A Study of the Arts in America* (1931) deals mainly with painting and architecture. Gilbert Chase, in *America's Music* (1955), includes some excellent sections on music between the Civil War and World War I, while M. C. Hare's *Negro Musicians and Their Music* (1936) discusses the musical contributions of black Americans.

On the popular American idea of economic progress, see Irvin G. Wyllie's *The Self-made Man in America: The Myth of Rags to Riches** (1954) and John Tebbel's *From Rags to Riches: Horatio Alger and the American Dream* (1963). On the chautauqua see R. C. and Victoria Case's *We Called It Culture: The Story of Chautauqua* (1948).

*indicates availability in paperback.

26

The New American Empire

THE AMERICAN ACQUISITION of Oregon and California in the 1840s was more than an isolated gesture designed to round out the nation's continental domain. It was also part of the process of extending United States commercial and political interests ever westward toward the Orient. One of the guiding motivations of American continental expansion had been the quest for the three major harbors along the Pacific Coast—Puget Sound, San Francisco Bay, and San Diego Harbor—where large cities would emerge one day to propel American commercial, industrial, and naval power toward the great open ports of the Orient.

Through half a century Boston merchants had laid the foundations for an expanding American interest in the Orient. Their established position at Canton prompted the John Tyler administration to negotiate the Treaty of Wanghia in 1844, an agreement guaranteeing American merchants the most-favored-nation treatment in China. This principle—the foundation of all United States commercial diplomacy—assured American merchants in any foreign port conditions of trade at least as advantageous as those enjoyed by the citizens of any other nation. Under this agreement, citizens of the United States continued to gain all the commercial and extraterritorial rights in China which the British and French were wrenching by force of arms from the Chinese government. Meanwhile the invasion of the northern Pacific by New England whalers and traders had gradually transformed Hawaii into an important outpost for Boston's commercial and missionary activity. Early American-Hawaiians had scarcely anticipated the annexation of Hawaii by the United States, yet their comparative proximity to the California coast brought those islands well within the range of official American concern long before midcentury.

The increased traffic between California and China in the early fifties, added to the projection of a San Francisco–Shanghai steamship line, suddenly focused the attention of the United States government on the hermit nation of Japan. These important islands lay astride the "great circle route" from San Francisco to key ports along the north China coast. During 1854 Commodore Matthew C. Perry secured a treaty which destroyed Japanese isolation and established the foundation not only for increased American trade there but also for the legal, administrative, and economic modernization of that country. From the beginning, the American penetration of the Orient was devoid of the political and intellectual restraints that characterized this nation's relations with Europe. During the fifties William H. Seward termed the Pacific "the chief theater of events in the world's great hereafter." As Secretary of State he acquired Alaska in 1867 and began the process of pushing open new doors for American commerce in the Pacific.

Pacific Markets and Coaling Stations

China hung low on the American horizon largely because of its domestic infirmities. No event of the century so completely undermined China's power and prestige as the Taiping Rebellion which occurred between 1850 and 1864. French and British victories against the rebels helped to save the ruling Manchu dynasty. But some Americans wondered how the United States could protect its commercial interests in China against possible efforts of the great Western powers to exploit China's obvious weakness and obtain special territorial and commercial concessions. The Treaties of Tientsin, imposed on China in 1858 by these powers, opened eleven additional treaty ports, established the right of diplomatic representation in Peking, the Chinese capital, and recognized the right of missionaries to proselytize freely in China. Several Western powers, moreover, secured control of border areas which the Chinese had regarded as vassal states. Russia gained a large region south of the Amur and east of the Ussuri rivers in 1860. Between 1862 and 1867 France annexed Indochina. Britain occupied Burma, attached it to India, and imposed on China a new Indo-Chinese boundary favorable to India.

Anson Burlingame, the first American Minister to Peking (in 1861), embraced the growing American concern for China's independence. Under Burlingame the United States assumed for the first time the role of special protector of the Chinese nation. During his years in China, Burlingame devoted himself to securing pledges from the great powers to preserve what remained of China's territorial integrity. He made his chief contribution to Chinese interests, however, when, in 1867, he entered the service of the Chinese government to head its special mission to the Western world. In July, 1868, he negotiated a special treaty with Seward in Washington, whereby the United States agreed formally to respect China's territorial and administrative integrity. Burlingame continued on to London, Paris, Stockholm, Copenhagen, The Hague, Berlin, and St. Petersburg. In none of these capitals, however, could he negotiate self-abnegation treaties such as he had secured in Washington.

Korea, like Japan a hermit nation, likewise attracted Americans in search of trade. In 1871 the United States dispatched an expedition of five warships to investigate conditions in Korea and, if possible, to negotiate a commercial treaty which would open that country to foreign commerce. Greeted with cannon shot and unable to communicate with Korean authorities, the Americans leveled several Korean forts and sailed away. It was left for the Japanese to break down Korean seclusion.

Behind America's accelerating involvement in the Pacific were intellectual, social, and economic developments of the first magnitude. Throughout the Western world, expansion had become the order of the day. By the eighties Britain, France, Belgium, Holland, and even Germany had inaugurated policies of partitioning Africa and the islands of the Pacific into colonies. Much of this new imperialistic spirit and the rivalries it generated resulted from the Darwinian notion of a competitive order in which only the fittest—whether individuals or nations—could survive. Such American writers as John Fiske and Josiah Strong urged the United States government to enter the race for empire, for no other nation's power, energy, productivity, and institutions, they said, appeared to be so completely the products of natural selection. No nation seemed more fit to bring the backward and disorganized regions of the world under the protection or control of Western civilization. Fiske boasted in 1885 that the "work which the English race began when it colonized America is destined to go on until every land on the earth's surface that is not already the seat of an old civilization shall become English in its language, its religion, in its political habits and traditions, and to a predominant extent in the blood of its people." Religious groups entered this civilizing mission with enthusiasm, demanding the participation of government to carry Christianity—the religion of the West—to the "barbarian" peoples of Asia, Africa, and the Southern Seas.

Perhaps a more tangible incentive to American activity in the Pacific lay in the sometimes depressed state of the American economy. After 1865 American business had pushed the nation's industrial capacity beyond domestic demand. So speculative was most of the railroad and industrial construction that it repeatedly toppled the national economy into periodic depressions, the worst of them blanketing the years 1873–1878 and 1893–1897. Each depression stimulated business consolidation and strengthened the hand of the strongest enterprises, but it also demonstrated the need of foreign markets if the economy were ever again to perform at full capacity. To meet the challenge the nation seemed to have no choice but to reconstruct its economy or compete for foreign markets and points of strategic significance, especially in the Pacific.

Accepting in principle their obligation to secure the needs of American business abroad, the nation's leaders were careful to limit official policy to the quest for markets, not acquisitions. James G. Blaine emphasized this distinction in August, 1890. "Under the beneficent policy of protection," he said, "we have developed a volume of manufactures which, in many departments, overruns the demands of the home market. . . . Our great demand is expansion. I mean expansion of trade with countries where we can find profitable exchanges. We are not seeking annexation of territory." Blaine himself had conformed to this principle during the previous year when, as Secretary of State, he called the Pan American Conference in Washington to acquaint the Latin American representatives with the variety and quality of American production.

Yet the opportunities for easy annexations soon produced the appealing concept of "strategic bases." President Benjamin Harrison admitted to Blaine in 1891 that "as to naval stations and points of influence, we must look forward to a departure from the too conservative opinions which have been held heretofore." Such notions had been persuasively argued by Alfred T. Mahan in his *Influence of Sea Power upon History* (1890). This volume, based upon lectures delivered at the Naval War College, developed the theme that sea power—embracing commerce, naval vessels, bases, and even colonies—was essential for national greatness. England had pointed the way. To provide coaling stations was, for Mahan, the first duty of any government concerned with developing its national power. Through additional books and articles Mahan's thesis reached an ever-widening audience, and in the Harrison administration his words began to bear fruit. Harrison's Secretary of the Navy, Benjamin F. Tracy, inaugurated a naval building program between 1890 and 1893, with the construction of the new steel battleships *Maine, Oregon,* and *Olympia.* The minimum prerequisite for overseas expansion—ships—had now been created and was available for immediate use.

Samoa and Hawaii

Mahan and his devotees in government shared a broad objective that included an isthmian canal, as well as several key bases in the Pacific. Mahan foresaw future conflict in the Pacific Ocean between the Occident and the Orient. In preparation for this eventuality the United States, in Mahan's view, required not only a large navy and a canal, but also island outposts in the mid-Pacific. Many Americans, both inside and outside the government, agreed. An American agent in the Pacific had reported to the Secretary of State in December, 1886: "It is now quite certain that an interoceanic canal across the Isthmus of Panama is one of the possibilities of the not very distant future, and it needs only a glance at the map to see that when that fact is accomplished the key of maritime dominance in the Pacific, and to some extent the intercontinental commerce of the world, will be held, not alone by Hawaii, but jointly by Hawaii and Samoa."

American interest in Samoa was not new. For over half a century, American navigators had called at these important islands of the South Pacific in search of items for the China trade. The Samoan Islands possessed a major attractiveness because they commanded several important sea lanes between San Francisco and Australia. In Pago Pago, on the island of Tutuila, the Samoans had one of the world's most beautiful and capacious harbors—the possible site of a great naval base. During 1872 an American naval officer sailed into Pago Pago and there negotiated a treaty with the local chief, which granted the United States exclusive rights to a naval base in the harbor in exchange for "the friendship and protection" of the United States. Samoan leaders even suggested annexation. The United States Senate, however, rejected both the treaty and the proposal of annexation. Finally in 1878 Secretary of State William M. Evarts negotiated with a representative of the

Samoan chiefs a treaty which granted the United States a naval base at Pago Pago. But American rights in the Samoan Islands were not exclusive. Germany gained special privileges at Saluafata near Apia, while the British acquired the right to a naval base anywhere, except at Saluafata or the United States site at Pago Pago. Thus Samoa became the center of a three-nation rivalry.

In 1884 Germany, through its representatives in Apia, made clear its intention to establish a protectorate over all the Samoan Islands. In an attempt to defend American interests and secure a general agreement, Secretary of State Thomas F. Bayard invited British and German representatives to confer in Washington on the Samoan question. The conference, finally convening in 1887, settled nothing, however. Bayard could not persuade the Germans to drop their demand for a mandate over the islands; and the British, in exchange for German support in the Middle East, supported the German cause. This display of German ambition aroused Congress to action, and it appropriated special funds to strengthen the American defenses at Pago Pago. Soon the President ordered three United States naval vessels to Apia, where the Germans had their naval base. There the Americans faced three German and one British warship with decks cleared for action. A deeper crisis was averted when a sudden hurricane wrecked all the German and American ships; the British vessel managed to ride out the storm.

This tragedy cleared the air in Washington and Berlin, as well as in Samoa. Bayard now made it clear that the United States was concerned less with commercial privileges than with the independence of the Samoan Islands. Bismarck responded by calling a tripartite conference, which opened in Berlin late in April, 1889. Although all three powers agreed to respect the independence of the islands, the rivalry between the United States and Germany continued. President Grover Cleveland and his Secretary of State, Walter Q. Gresham, declined to press the matter. In November, 1898, during the Presidency of William McKinley, the United States and Germany—Britain having withdrawn its interest—negotiated a permanent division of the Samoan Islands. Although some Americans objected that this division violated Samoan sovereignty, the expansionist disciples of Captain Mahan easily carried the day.

Nor could Hawaii escape the consequences of United States expansion into the Pacific. As early as midcentury, American traders, missionaries, and seamen had gained control of Hawaii's foreign commerce and had converted the island economy to the production of sugar. This created a problem of fundamental significance, for the only lucrative outlet for Hawaiian sugar lay in the United States, where Louisiana sugar interests controlled the national market. The failure of the Senate, in 1867, to approve a commercial treaty, which might have opened the American market to Hawaiian sugar, raised the issue of annexation, for some Hawaiian planters, even at that early date, preferred markets to independence. Seward that year admitted his interest in annexation, as did a later Secretary of State, Hamilton Fish, in the 1870s, but few Americans shared their enthusiasm. During Secretary Fish's incumbency, in 1875, the government in Washington finally concluded a commercial treaty with the islands, which provided a free market for Hawaiian sugar in the United States in return for a pledge by Hawaii to maintain its integrity and independence. In the 1884 renewal, the United States secured the exclusive right to a naval base at Pearl Harbor. Hawaii's annexation awaited only the proper time and occasion.

Domestic sugar producers unwittingly propelled the question of United States–Hawaiian relations to the point of decision when, in the McKinley tariff of 1890, they had sugar placed on the free list but then gained a bounty of 2 cents per pound on the domestic product, thus enabling their own sugar to undersell the Hawaiian. This renewal of commercial discrimination exposed an underlying conflict of interest in the islands. Annexation alone would fully reopen the American market, but many of the leading Hawaiian planters opposed annexation from fear that United States contract-labor laws would eliminate from the islands the supply of cheap Oriental labor. What eventually unified the planters was the islands' growing political instability. In 1887 the foreign elite had imposed a liberal constitution on a weak Hawaiian king. Queen Liliuokalani's accession to the throne, in 1891, created a mood of uncertainty, for she had already made clear her dissatisfaction with the status quo. John L. Stevens, the annexationist United States Minister at Honolulu, advised Washington in November, 1892, that the impending crisis in the government of Hawaii would create a golden opportunity for annexation. Finally in January, 1893, the Queen announced her decision to promulgate a new constitution which would return the government of the islands to native rule. The community of foreign planters and merchants retaliated by establishing a provisional government and turning to Stevens for protection. Stevens promptly landed 150 marines from the warship *Boston,* recognized the provisional government as the *de facto* government of Hawaii, and finally went so far as to proclaim Hawaii a protectorate of the United States. The provisional government promptly offered a treaty of annexation; but before the Senate could act, Grover Cleveland entered the White House.

For Cleveland, these events in Hawaii were a serious reflection on American justice. He immediately dispatched James H. Blount, a former congressman from Georgia, to Honolulu to conduct an investigation. Blount hauled down the American flag and ordered the marines back to their ship. But if Cleveland could prevent annexation, he could not restore the Queen to power against the determined opposition of the planters. On July 4, 1894, the Americans in Hawaii established a republic, prepared either to maintain their independence or to accept annexation. Events played into their hands when in 1897 Japan dispatched a warship to Hawaii to underscore its anger at the decision of the Hawaiian government to bar some eleven hundred Japanese immigrants, in total violation of its 1896 treaty with Japan. Under pressure, the Hawaiian government relented. But in Washington the new McKinley administration reacted to the threat by quickly negotiating an annexation treaty and sending it to the Senate for approval. Queen Liliuokalani, then in Washington, pleaded with the State Department to withdraw the treaty. Though she could not prevent annexation, the Senate did: it rejected the treaty overwhelmingly. Once more the anti-imperialists had consigned annexation to the category of lost causes.

The Spanish-American War

As late as the mid-1890s, a traditional conservatism that shied away from extensive overseas commitments still governed the foreign relations of the United States. Cleveland had refused to consider the question of Samoan or Hawaiian annexation, and his successor

McKinley had failed, in 1897, to push an annexation treaty through the Senate. But suddenly in 1898 and 1899 there no longer seemed to be any limits to American commitment in the Pacific. Oddly, the immediate occasion for the headlong thrust of American power and influence into the Far East was not found in the Pacific at all; it lay in Cuba, where since 1895 the Cuban people had been in revolt against Spain. The Cuban revolutionaries well understood the American weakness for causes which could be represented as humanitarian, and the Spanish government, by employing measures of extreme repression in Cuba, had unwittingly played into their hands.

By 1896, when the Spanish general Valereano Weyler arrived in Cuba and proceeded to put into effect his ruthless campaign against civilians, the Cuban revolutionary *junta* in New York—along with the Cuban League, its counterpart with branches in a number of large American cities—had already launched a general campaign of propaganda to arouse and enlist the sympathies of the United States for Cuban independence. Unable alone to sustain a successful revolution, the Cuban leaders understood from the beginning that their success hinged on the assistance of the United States. To aggravate Spanish hostility toward the United States, the *junta* organized filibustering expeditions, which failed to influence events in Cuba but brought the anticipated Spanish complaints that the United States, by permitting such expeditions to outfit on American soil, was helping the revolution. To defend the nation from such charges, President Cleveland, both in June, 1895, and July, 1896, issued proclamations of neutrality.

What assured the ultimate success of the Cuban cause was the overwhelming support it received from the American newspaper press. Editors throughout the East and the Midwest stressed the disruptive effect of the Cuban struggle on American trade and investments. At that time Americans had some fifty million dollars invested in Cuba. William Randolph Hearst's *New York Journal* and Joseph Pulitzer's *New York World,* as well as other papers, satirized the Spanish government as a political anachronism and charged it with gross disregard for humanity in its abuse of Americans and Cubans alike. In time the press came to despise official American neutrality and to demand policies of intervention in behalf of Cuban independence. Republican editors attempted to discredit Cleveland because of his lack of enthusiasm for the Cuban revolution; some accused him of being pro-Spanish. With McKinley's election, a number of Republican newspapers, such as the *Chicago Tribune,* boasted that the incoming administration would adopt a more humane, civilized, and patriotic policy. But most Republican editors, sobered by their party's victory, now advised caution.

Between 1895 and 1897 editors and political leaders agreed generally that Cuba demanded some positive American response. It became increasingly clear, however, that short of direct military involvement the United States could not counter the continuing Spanish repression. Cleveland's policy of neutrality had not secured peace; and in his final message to Congress in December, 1896, he admitted that the perennial strife in Cuba had created pressures for war. Should the struggle degenerate into a useless destruction of life and property, he concluded, "a situation will be presented in which our obligations to the sovereignty of Spain will be superseded by higher obligations, which we can hardly hesitate to recognize and discharge." The United States could not resolve the dilemma through the purchase of Cuba, for

Spain would not sell. Nor would the recognition of Cuban belligerency or independence assure peace on the island. Influential Americans insisted that Spanish policy endangered American interests in the Caribbean, but they could suggest no solution to the Cuban question short of the infusion of American military power.

McKinley entered the White House in March, 1897, still hopeful of avoiding that choice. He had no greater desire than his predecessor to go to war. Yet he recognized the need to bring to an end the evident confusion in Cuba, and to that end he launched a diplomatic offensive against Spain. Convinced that Spain lacked the power to establish peace in Cuba, the President anchored his program to Spanish concessions. His new Minister to Madrid, Stewart L. Woodford, left Washington in the summer of 1897, armed with instructions which condemned the Spanish methods of warfare and demanded that Spain, in the interest of humanity, "put a stop to this destructive war and make proposals of settlement honorable to herself and just to her Cuban colony and to mankind." The United States, the President made clear, stood ready to assist Spain in finding such a solution. McKinley revealed the limited choice before him: Either Spain would stop the fighting in Cuba or the United States would use military force to restore the peace.

Spanish authorities in Madrid understood the demands which United States policy placed upon them. The new Liberal Ministry in Spain, which gained power in October, 1897, was determined to avoid a war which it could not win. It recalled Weyler and instructed his successor to revoke the oppressive policies. Then, in November, 1897, the Liberal regime offered autonomy to the Cubans. Neither the Liberal Ministry nor the Spanish Queen, Woodford informed McKinley, could do more without wounding Spanish pride and violating Spanish tradition. In Cuba, Spain faced an enemy it could never defeat. The only hope for Spanish policy, therefore, lay in the willingness of Cuban leaders to settle for autonomy rather than full independence.

These circumscriptions on Spanish actions determined the future of Spanish-American relations. Few in Washington or Madrid believed a settlement possible. In his message to Congress in December, 1897, McKinley asserted that Spain deserved every reasonable chance to prove the efficacy of her policies. But he warned that, if Spanish policy failed, the United States, in response to the demands of civilization and humanity, might be duty-bound to intervene with force. Woodford, like McKinley, questioned the sincerity of the Spanish proposals. But even if they were genuine, he worried that the Cuban rebels would not accept them. The Ambassador's fears were wholly justified. In January, 1898, Havana rioted in defiance of Spain's decree of autonomy. McKinley dispatched the U.S.S. *Maine* to Havana to lend moral and material support to the American consul general there in his effort to protect United States citizens and property.

Spanish officials understood well enough that the new riots in Cuba demonstrated the utter failure of their policy. But they also knew that it was American encouragement that stiffened the resistance of the Cuban insurgents to compromise. On January 17, the Queen informed Woodford that Cleveland had promised to sever all official American support for the rebels if Spain would grant autonomy. When McKinley refused to denounce the rebels, the Spanish government gave vent to its frustration by condemning the United States for permitting the establishment on its soil of revolutionary organizations which labored freely for the separation of Cuba from Spain. Spain now had no choice but to abandon Cuba completely, turn to Europe for moral and military support, or prepare for war. The Liberal Ministry, playing for time, attempted to rally Spanish sentiment behind its determination to defend what remained of Spanish policy.

During February and March, 1898, a series of incidents drove the United States and Spain toward war. The publication in the American press of a private letter written by Dupuy de Lôme, the Spanish Minister in Washington, critical of the President and raising doubts about Spain's good faith, aggravated the nation's anti-Spanish sentiment and forced the Minister's recall. Far more serious, however, was the destruction of the battleship *Maine* in Havana's harbor on February 15, with a heavy loss of life. Spanish behavior following the incident was impeccable; and officials in Washington, including the President, accepted the news with remarkable restraint. But widespread public opinion, whipped up by the press, demanded war. "Remember the Maine" became the battle cry.

Thereafter, events that brought conflict closer came in rapid succession. Congress, early in March, voted $50 million to assist the administration in strengthening the nation's defenses. On March 17, Senator Redfield Proctor of Vermont reported to Congress what he had seen on a recent tour of Cuba, describing in detail the suffering of an island people ravaged by thirty years of desultory civil war, terrorism, and Spanish reprisals. Proctor's speech, because of the Senator's known temperance on the Cuban question, had a profound effect on American opinion. Then on March 28 the naval board of inquiry appointed by McKinley to investigate the *Maine* tragedy issued its report. Without attempting to fix responsibility, the board concluded nevertheless that the battleship had been destroyed by a mine. Congressional and public opinion now reached a new level of intensity. The American Secretary of State again urged Spain to make peace with Cuba, even at the price of independence.

As the crisis mounted in April, Republican congressmen and editors warned the President that if he did not lead the country into a popular war, others would. One Cabinet member criticized the President's hesitancy: "He is making a great mistake. He is in danger of ruining himself and the Republican Party by standing in the way of the people's wishes. Congress will declare war in spite of him. He'll get run over and his party with him." At last McKinley, in the interest of preserving both party unity and executive control of foreign policy, assumed responsibility for leading the nation to war. Woodford, still hopeful of peace, had reported on April 5 that the Queen had agreed to six months' unconditional suspension of hostilities in Cuba, thus providing time for the establishment of permanent peace. Five days later Woodford assured the President that by August 1 he could obtain peace by negotiation on the basis of either autonomy or independence for Cuba. "I hope," Woodford added, "that nothing will now be done to humiliate Spain, as I am satisfied that the present Government is going . . . as fast and far as it can. With your power of action sufficiently free you will win the fight on your own lines." Still, on April 11, 1898, McKinley sent his war message to Congress. Congress debated the message for a week and then adopted four resolutions, which recognized Cuban independence, demanded a Spanish withdrawal, and authorized the President to employ the nation's military forces to achieve the American purpose. Lastly, Congress asserted, in the famed Teller Resolution, its determination to leave the Cuban people, following the island's pacification, in possession of their government. By April 21 the United States had severed relations with Spain and entered a war for Cuban independence.

The War in the Caribbean

Despite the nation's lack of military preparedness in 1898, the conflict with Spain appeared to be, as John Hay said, "A splendid little war." Spain, after a century of declining power and morale, was incapable of sustaining effective resistance on either land or sea. This weakness, thoroughly anticipated by American officials, permitted the United States to enter the war with a standing Army of only 28,000 troops. Congress quickly authorized an Army of 62,000, to be supplemented with 125,000 volunteers. In addition, the President could accept three volunteer cavalry regiments into the Armed Forces. One of these, the Rough Riders, transformed its commander, Theodore Roosevelt, into a popular war hero.

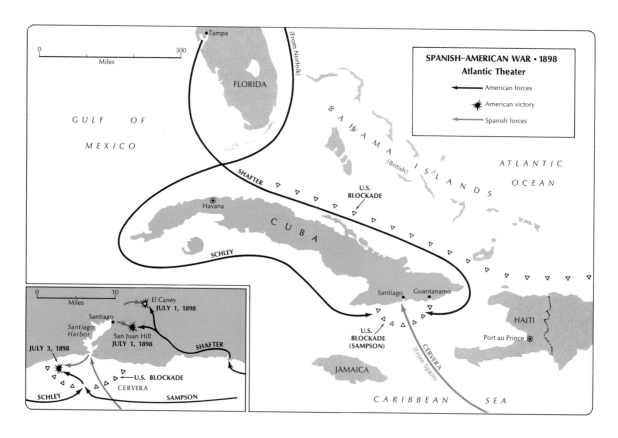

Of necessity the fighting centered in Cuba. There, in its initial phase, the United States

Atlantic fleet, under Admiral William T. Sampson and Commodore W. S. Schley, blockaded the decrepit Spanish fleet in Santiago Harbor along Cuba's southern coast. Meanwhile, United States regular and volunteer units assembled, amid indescribable confusion, at Tampa, Florida, and Chattanooga, Tennessee, in preparation for assaults against Spanish forces in Cuba and Puerto Rico. Rather than strike Havana, the commanding general of the Army, Nelson A. Miles, decided to send General William R. Shafter with an American force (which included the Rough Riders) against Santiago. The force left Tampa and managed to stage a landing on Cuban soil. It moved toward Santiago, winning battles at El Caney and San Juan Hill, yet seemed incapable of launching an attack on Santiago itself. But when the Spanish fleet steamed out of the harbor, only to be destroyed by the blockading American squadron, the garrison at Santiago capitulated. Spanish power in Cuba had collapsed in scarcely more than a month. Another American force had meanwhile occupied Puerto Rico. Unable to continue the fighting, the Spanish government, in July, asked for the terms of peace. On August 12, an armistice granted the United States control of Puerto Rico; an island in the Ladrones, later determined as Guam; and possession of Manila until the conclusion of a formal treaty.

Annexation of the Philippines

On May 1, 1898, Admiral George Dewey's United States squadron had sailed into Manila Bay and destroyed Spain's Pacific fleet at anchor. This victory did not presage an annexationist movement, for it was logical that the United States should strike Spanish power wherever it existed. Still, this sudden display of United States naval might in the distant Philippines and the possibilities which it opened for American empire building were not lost on a small but well-placed and influential body of expansionists in Washington. Even at that early date such men as Roosevelt, Mahan, Senator Henry Cabot Lodge of Massachusetts, and Senator Albert J. Beveridge of Indiana had expansion in mind. It was Roosevelt who, as Assistant Secretary of the Navy, had ordered Dewey to Manila. And on April 27, four days before Dewey's great victory, Senator Beveridge declared before a Boston audience: "In the Pacific is the true field of our earliest operations. There Spain has an island empire, the Philippine Archipelago. It is poorly defended. . . . In the Pacific the United States has a powerful squadron. The Philippines are logically our first target." It is possible that McKinley, with an eye on the Philippines, had delayed his war message so that the fast cruiser *Baltimore* could reach Dewey with a special cargo of ammunition before Congress acted in favor of war.

With Dewey's victory, the McKinley administration moved quickly to establish American control of the Philippines. Dewey himself maintained a blockade of Manila Bay and kept the German squadron under Admiral von Diederichs at a safe distance. Meanwhile a Spanish army held the city. Complicating the situation for the United States, however, was the successful Filipino insurgency which, having freed the islands of Spanish control, was already closing in on the capital. Ignoring the clouded political status of the Philippines, McKinley, on May 11, ordered General Wesley Merritt to Manila in support of Dewey. During June and July a contingent of more than 10,000 American soldiers arrived at Manila Bay. These forces, supported by Emilio Aguinaldo's insurgents, assaulted and occupied Manila on August 13. Next day American officials proclaimed Spain's capitulation.

This display of American power in the Pacific sealed the fate of Hawaii. Those who had vainly pushed Hawaiian annexation during 1897 had not allowed the issue to die. In January, 1898, Roosevelt declared in *Gunton's Magazine:* "We must take Hawaii. . . . If we do not take Hawaii ourselves we will have lost the right to dictate what shall be her fate. . . . Hawaii cannot permanently stand alone, and we have no right to expect other powers to be blind to their own interests because we are blind to ours. If Hawaii does not become American then we may as well make up our own minds to see it become European or Asiatic." On May 4, three days after the battle of Manila Bay, the annexationists brought a joint resolution for Hawaiian annexation before Congress. Two months later the measure had gone through committees onto the floor of both houses. Requiring no more than a bare majority, the measure passed the House, on June 15, by a vote of 209 to 91, with 49 abstentions. The Senate concurred, after a determined debate staged by the Democratic minority, 42 to 21. The nation's overwhelming expansionist sentiment, as reflected in Congress, centered in the Republican leadership of the Northeast and the Upper Middle West. "We need Hawaii," McKinley wrote, "as much and a good deal more than we did California. . . . It is manifest destiny."

Unlike Samoa and Hawaii (two independent island groups), the Philippines, as Spanish territory, had been of necessity off limits to prewar American imperialist ambitions. Prior to Dewey's victory there could have been absolutely no sentiment for Philippine annexation. Finley Peter Dunne's Mr. Dooley remarked that the American people "did not know whether the Philippines were islands or canned goods." Against the immediate background of the country's burgeoning interests in the Pacific, however, the reduction of Spanish power in the Philippines confronted the United States with an unanticipated dilemma. What was to be the disposition of the islands, now no longer under Spanish control? At the outset the United States had four clear choices. It could return the islands to Spain, or it could grant them independence, as it had promised Cuba. It could transfer the islands to another power, or it could retain them as possessions of the United States. That this nation was drawn relentlessly toward annexation does not mean that it had no other choices. But the decision to destroy Spanish power in Manila had been crucial, for it closed all easy avenues of retreat from a self-imposed dilemma.

Dewey's victory at Manila unleashed an expansionist drive among American editors, politicians, intellectuals, and businessmen toward the Philippines. Both Northern commercial groups and Protestant missionary societies had concluded as early as May, 1898, that the acquisition of these islands would serve the nation's interests by enlarging the American naval, mercantile, and cultural role in the western Pacific. Still, official United States policy toward the Philippines evolved slowly. Throughout May and June, 1898, expansionists in Congress and the administration argued with the President on the necessity of acquiring the Philippines. Lodge reported to Roosevelt in late May that the President seemed to be grasping the essentials of a Philippine policy. In June, Secretary of State William Day informed Lodge that perhaps the nation could not escape its destiny in the Philippines.

From this declared interest in the Philippines

the President did not retreat. His directive to the American peace commission made clear his determination to acquire at least a portion of the Philippine archipelago: "There is a very general feeling that the United States, whatever it might prefer as to the Philippines, is in a situation where it can not let go, . . . and it is my judgment that the well-considered opinion of the majority would be that duty requires we should take the archipelago." Thereafter the President faced the task of defining his precise objectives in the Philippines, a task which he entrusted to his peace commission.

McKinley, with the support of Congress, had destroyed American continental isolation by the annexation of Hawaii. But the acquisition of the Philippines threatened to extend American political and military commitments across the Pacific, where other nations possessed greater naval power than did the United States. Despite the magnitude of this distant commitment, McKinley made no effort to rationalize his decision to annex the Philippines except in terms of the nation's obligation to humanity. The President's persistent refusal to remind the American people of the price of empire became exceedingly pronounced during his tour of the Midwest in October, 1898. In speech after speech, he dwelt on the accidental nature of this country's *de facto* possession of the Philippines and its special responsibility to the Filipinos which, he insisted, flowed from that possession. For example, he declared at Cedar Rapids, Iowa: "We accepted war for humanity. We can accept no terms of peace which shall not be in the interests of humanity." Later at Boston he repeated, "Our concern was not for territory or trade or empire, but for the people whose interests and destiny, without our willing, had been put into our hands." By attaching the issue of empire to humanitarian sentiment rather than national interest, McKinley assured himself a favorable public response; but in the process he deserted those principles of statecraft which had guided the nation through its first century of independence.

From late October until December, 1898, McKinley faced a divided peace commission, then deliberating in Paris. Four members of the commission — Whitelaw Reid, editor of the *New York Tribune,* Senators Cushman K. Davis of Minnesota and William P. Frye of Maine, and former Secretary of State Day, chairman of the commission — favored the annexation of all or part of the archipelago. But Senator George Gray of Delaware, the only Democrat on the commission, was absolutely opposed. He warned McKinley that annexation would invite trouble, making necessary "a navy equal to the largest of powers," a greatly enlarged military establishment, and increased taxes. Despite such advice, McKinley instructed the commission to claim the Philippines as indemnity for the cost of the war. Late in November the commission framed its final demands on the Spanish government — the cession of Puerto Rico, Guam, and the entire Philippine archipelago to the United States in exchange for $20 million. Spain reluctantly accepted these terms in the Treaty of Paris on December 10, 1898.

In Washington the treaty faced bitter opposition both within and without the halls of Congress. In November a group of distinguished citizens, including former President Grover Cleveland and industrialist Andrew Carnegie, formed the opposition Anti-Imperialist League. Members of the League detected in the acquisition of the Philippines not only a violation of the nation's democratic and constitutional principles but also a departure from America's traditional conservatism in foreign policy. Their assertion that the United States was overextending itself in the Pacific raised issues from which there was no escape. The acquisition of distant territories would entail financial and military burdens with few rewards. The United States, wrote Carnegie, lacked not only the naval power to protect the Philippines but also the will to create it. Some antiexpansionists—for example, Carnegie—conceded the need for a coaling station in the Philippines; they denied that the United States needed more. "Must Great Britain own the whole of Spain," demanded Republican conservative Carl Schurz, "in order to hold Gibraltar?" Schurz feared that Philippine annexation so completely overcommitted the nation that it would reduce the United States to utter reliance on the British fleet. Such indebtedness to Britain would demand a price of its own. "If we do take the Philippines," Schurz concluded, "and thus entangle ourselves in the rivalries of Asiatic affairs, the future will be . . . one of wars and rumors of wars, and the time will be forever past when we could look down with condescending pity on the nations of the old world groaning under militarism and its burdens."

Stronger in argument than in organization, the anti imperialists could not stem the tide of annexationism. Business interests, which envisioned the Philippines as a steppingstone to Chinese trade, insisted on holding the islands. "With our flag floating within 500 miles of Hong Kong," said the *New York Journal of Commerce,* the United States would be in a strong position to expand its markets in the Far East. Along with the quest for wider markets, the imperialists in Congress rode the crests of a national pride, strengthened by easy military successes, and a sense of Anglo-Saxon superiority, which encouraged the acceptance of responsibility for allegedly inferior peoples. Expansionist speeches in Congress were laden with visions of profit and glory—for commerce, industry, and religion. Even William Jennings Bryan, fresh from military service, argued in Washington that the Filipinos would benefit from the American investment in money, administration, and defense. He urged his fellow Democrats to approve the treaty. If Bryan changed even one vote, his presence was invaluable for McKinley and his supporters in the Senate. For when that body, after a month of intense debate, settled down to vote, fifteen Democrats joined forty-two Republicans to carry the treaty against the twenty-seven senators who opposed it. Two senators switching to the minority side would have meant its defeat. Lodge reported to Roosevelt, "The line of opposition stood absolutely firm. . . . [It was the] hardest fight I have ever known, and probably we shall not see another in our time where there was so much at stake."

War in the Philippines

The Treaty of Paris did not automatically establish American rule in the Philippines. Aguinaldo, the leader of the insurrection, had assumed that the Philippine Islands, like Cuba, would receive their independence as a consequence of the Spanish-American War. After American forces occupied Manila in August, 1898, however, Aguinaldo was ordered to withdraw his Filipino insurgents from the city. Philippine disillusionment culminated with the announcement of the Treaty of Paris. On February 4, 1899, a clash outside Manila set off what soon evolved into a long, costly war for control of the islands. The insurrectionary government controlled almost all the islands in the archipelago and commanded an army of 20,000. The native forces, having general support among the people but lacking modern weapons, resorted to guerrilla warfare, which spread rapidly through the islands. To put down this insurgency, the United States spent millions of dollars, committed thousands of troops, and resorted to drastic antiguerrilla tactics.

Within the United States this struggle against a backward, native population divided the nation into bitter factions, for on the line were both the nation's principles and its prestige. Mark Twain attacked the American effort to hold the islands, suggesting a new American flag "with the white stripes painted black, and the stars replaced by a skull and crossbones." The *Nation* complained that American repression was "bringing disgrace upon the American name and civilization." But other Americans demanded that the United States press on to victory to fulfill its obligations to civilization. Eventually the issue evolved into one of national prestige and honor. *Harper's Weekly* agreed with McKinley that, if the United States abandoned the Philippines under pressure, "we should be an object of derision to Europe and the Orientals would consider us of no account." There were those who insisted that the protestations in the United States were encouraging the enemy and prolonging the war. Both the war and the protests continued unabated, however, until April, 1902, when the insurgents finally surrendered and recognized American rule.

The Open Door for China

As the nineteenth century neared its close, events in China drew the United States into even deeper commitments in the western Pacific. American commercial and missionary activity in China had long sustained an interest in Washington and elsewhere in that country's internal peace and stability. It became clear in 1894 that China was incapable of protecting its political and territorial integrity against external pressure, when Japan, in a brief war, easily disposed of Chinese resistance, dispossessing China by treaty of Formosa, the Pescadores, and the strategic Liaotung Peninsula. Moreover, Japan forced China to recognize the independence of Korea and grant Japanese citizens the same trading privileges in China then enjoyed by citizens of the great Western powers. Neither the United States nor Great Britain chose to interfere. But Russia, Germany, and France, at China's invitation, demanded that Japan, in the interest of peace, return the Liaotung Peninsula to China. United States Minister to China, Charles Denby, warned Peking that the price of European assistance would run high. Japan, unable to resist such combined pressure, complied with the demand. But Tokyo observed what followed with embitterment.

Unfortunately China's troubles had only begun, for Russia's ambitions toward China were at least the equal of Japan's. Having gained possession of Vladivostok and undertaken the construction of the Trans-Siberian Railway to strengthen her presence in East Asia, Russia joined Germany and France in dividing China "like a melon" into spheres of influence. During March, 1897, France gained control of the island of Hainan. In November German troops, employing the murder of two German Catholic priests as a pretext, seized

Kiaochow, a port on the Shantung Peninsula, a seizure legalized in March, 1898, as a leasehold. Not to be outdone, Russia that month forced from the Chinese government a twenty-five-year lease to the fine harbor at Port Arthur. China seemed in danger of disappearing piecemeal.

American business groups operating in China, especially the American-China Development Company and the American exporters of cotton goods, viewed these developments with grave concern. Left unopposed, the European powers would eventually wipe out the equal trading and investment privileges which Americans enjoyed in China. In January, 1898, Minister Denby reminded the McKinley administration that present trends toward exclusive economic spheres would tend to destroy American markets in China. "We should urge on China," he wrote, "the reform of all evils in her government which touch American interests, and the adoption of vigorous measures in the line of material progress." Denby believed it essential that the United States government officially denounce the actions in China of the German, Russian, and French governments. The United States, having only commercial, financial, and missionary interests in China, could, he believed, best protect those interests through a Chinese government strong and efficient enough to defend the principle of equal opportunity among foreign groups operating in China.

British interests in China were far more extensive than those of the United States, for Britain had long dominated the foreign commerce of China through the British-operated Chinese Imperial Maritime Customs Service. Unwilling to use force to maintain its free access to all Chinese ports, the British government sought the introduction of United States power into the Asian equation. For that reason, British officials urged the United States to acquire Hawaii. In March, 1898, the British government, through its Minister in Washington, approached the McKinley administration for a cooperative policy "in opposing any action of foreign powers which would tend to restrain the opening of China to the commerce of all nations." McKinley expressed sympathy with British purpose but, having been assured by Germany and Russia that they had no intention of defying the principle of open trade in China, informed the British that he saw no reason to depart from America's traditional policy of noninvolvement. That spring, moreover, the United States was facing the immediate problem of Cuba. During 1898 the British government encouraged the United States to acquire the Philippines, but it reversed its policies in China. Convinced that the Peking government was too weak to protect British interests in China, London officials acquired a lease of Weihaiwei, a port on the Shantung Peninsula opposite Port Arthur. Next, they acquired special concessions in the Yangtze River Valley and at Kowloon, opposite Hong Kong. Britain had thus retreated to the policy of leaseholds which it had at an earlier time condemned.

When Secretary of State John Hay, in September, 1899, finally issued the famous Open Door Notes, his action was largely unilateral. The occasion for the actual formulation of the notes was the visit of Alfred E. Hippisley to Washington. Hippisley, a private British citizen employed by the Chinese Maritime Customs Service, was completely devoted to Chinese interests. Hippisley saw that European and British policy in China was reducing the customs receipts of the Chinese government and, with them, any hope of building an efficient Chinese administration. His bitter opposition to the trends within China was fully shared by the McKinley administration. Thus when Hippisley, during a visit to his wife's relatives in Baltimore, renewed his acquaintance with William W. Rockhill, Hay's adviser on Far Eastern matters, he found a receptive audience. Hippisley doubted that Washington could terminate the spheres of influence in China; he hoped merely that the United States, by restating her treaty rights in China, might encourage the other powers to maintain the principle of commercial equality in the ports which they controlled. Rockhill forwarded the gist of Hippisley's memorandum to Secretary Hay. Hay instructed Rockhill to prepare notes to be sent to the European powers.

The Open Door Notes, sent originally to Russia, Great Britain, and Germany (and later to Italy, France, and Japan) requested assurances from each nation that it would not interfere with the treaty rights or special interests of other countries within its sphere of influence in China. Hay asked, moreover, that each country involved in China in no way interfere with any treaty port or vested interest; that it allow the collection of existing Chinese tariffs, irrespective of spheres of influence; and that it treat its own citizens and other nationals alike in making such assessments as harbor dues. In his note to Britain, Hay even seemed to oppose the spheres of influence already established. The replies, especially from Britain and Russia, approved in principle the commercial "Open Door"; otherwise they were evasive. Yet the Secretary chose to announce to the world in March, 1900, that his notes had brought favorable responses from all six nations. The acceptance of his proposals, Hay declared, was "final and definite." Some six months later, when China's Boxer Rebellion compelled the powers to dispatch troops to rescue their nationals from the besieged legations at Peking, the Secretary reiterated that the American purpose in China included preserving Chinese territorial and administrative integrity, as well as safeguarding for all nations "the principle of equal and impartial trade with all parts of the Chinese Empire."

Much of the American and European press took Hay's diplomatic exchanges at face value and praised the Secretary for his momentous success. Yet Hay's apparent achievements in behalf of China carried the seeds of disaster, for they, like the acquisition of the Philippines, confirmed an illusion that the United States could have its way in the Orient at little or no cost to itself. Only the more realistic observers noted that Hay's diplomacy had either committed the United States to the use of force or it had achieved nothing, for no nation would have compromised its essential interests in China merely at Hay's request. As Alfred Thayer Mahan wrote in December, 1900, the United States could not "count upon respect for the territory of China unless we are ready to throw not only our moral influence but, if necessity arise, our physical weight into the conflict, to resist an expropriation, the result of which might be to exclude our commerce and neutralize our influence." Mahan observed that both Russia and Japan, the two dominant powers in the Far East, had far greater interests in China than did the United States. But the Open Door policy, by establishing a powerful and somewhat exaggerated American concern for the commercial and territorial integrity of China, rendered any nation which might challenge Chinese will the potential enemy of the United States. Traders, missionaries, and officials shared the responsibility for creating and sustaining this strange and unprecedented spirit of paternalism toward China.

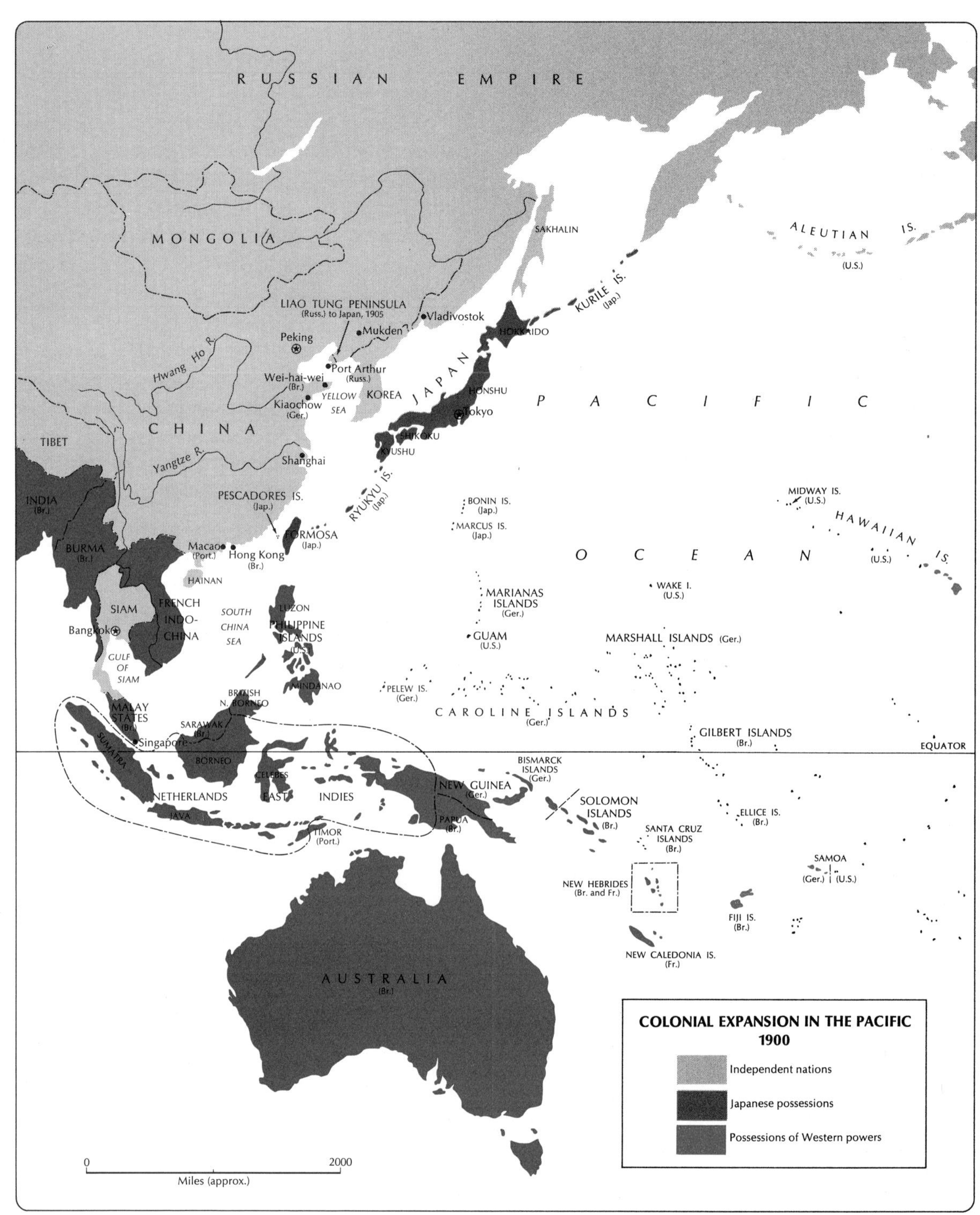
RUSSIAN EMPIRE
MONGOLIA
SAKHALIN
ALEUTIAN IS.
(U.S.)
KURILE IS.
(Jap.)
LIAO TUNG PENINSULA
(Russ.) to Japan, 1905
Vladivostok
Mukden
Peking
HOKKAIDO
Hwang Ho R.
Port Arthur
(Russ.)
Wei-hai-wei
(Br.)
YELLOW SEA
KOREA
JAPAN
HONSHU
Kiaochow
(Ger.)
Tokyo
PACIFIC
CHINA
TIBET
SHIKOKU
KYUSHU
Yangtze R.
Shanghai
INDIA
(Br.)
PESCADORES IS.
(Jap.)
RYUKYU IS.
(Jap.)
BONIN IS.
(Jap.)
MIDWAY IS.
(U.S.)
MARCUS IS.
(Jap.)
HAWAIIAN IS.
(U.S.)
BURMA
(Br.)
Macao
(Port.)
Hong Kong
(Br.)
FORMOSA
(Jap.)
OCEAN
HAINAN
MARIANAS ISLANDS
(Ger.)
WAKE I.
(U.S.)
SIAM
FRENCH INDO-CHINA
SOUTH CHINA SEA
LUZON
PHILIPPINE ISLANDS
Bangkok
GUAM
(U.S.)
MARSHALL ISLANDS (Ger.)
GULF OF SIAM
MINDANAO
PELEW IS.
(Ger.)
BRITISH N. BORNEO
CAROLINE ISLANDS
(Ger.)
MALAY STATES
(Br.)
SARAWAK
(Br.)
GILBERT ISLANDS
(Br.)
SUMATRA
Singapore
EQUATOR
BORNEO
BISMARCK ISLANDS
(Ger.)
CELEBES
NEW GUINEA
(Ger.)
NETHERLANDS EAST INDIES
SOLOMON ISLANDS
(Br.)
JAVA
PAPUA
(Br.)
ELLICE IS.
(Br.)
SANTA CRUZ ISLANDS
(Br.)
TIMOR
(Port.)
SAMOA
(Ger.) (U.S.)
NEW HEBRIDES
(Br. and Fr.)
FIJI IS.
(Br.)
NEW CALEDONIA IS.
(Fr.)
AUSTRALIA
(Br.)
COLONIAL EXPANSION IN THE PACIFIC
1900
Independent nations
Japanese possessions
Possessions of Western powers
0
2000
Miles (approx.)

Conclusion

By 1900 the United States had become a major Asiatic power, with colonies in the western Pacific some seven thousand miles from American shores. It had committed itself, at least morally and emotionally, to the commercial Open Door and the territorial integrity of China. Already American business anticipated increased markets and investment opportunities in China, especially in mining and railroads. Whatever the actual American interests in that country, official Washington would view any changes in the equilibrium of East Asia as a matter of vital concern. Thus the dramatic events of 1898 and 1899 had revolutionized the nation's attitudes toward the external world.

Editors, politicians, and businessmen looked confidently to the Far East as the new stage for American activity; at the same time they revealed no hesitancy in assigning to Washington major responsibility for the management of that region's future evolution. In January, 1900, Senator Beveridge dramatically acknowledged the new American interest in the Pacific: "The Philippines are ours forever. . . . And just beyond . . . are China's illimitable markets. We will not retreat from either. . . . The power that rules the Pacific is the power that rules the world. . . . That power will forever be the American Republic." The possible, even probable, consequence of such optimism for American foreign relations was clear only to a minority of intellectuals, who warned that no American interest in the Pacific merited carte blanche commitments. Indeed, American expansion into the Pacific triumphed with such negligible national effort that it failed completely to challenge the American people's isolationist habits of mind. It never occurred to most citizens, or even to their leaders, that these new obligations in the Pacific might one day make exorbitant demands on the American Republic.

The Spanish-American War and its aftermath not only made the United States an Asiatic power; it also produced an absolute American hegemony in the Caribbean. Acquisition of Puerto Rico and *de facto* control of Cuba gave the United States special interests in that area which it would subsequently guard jealously. Having acquired colonies and dependencies in the far Pacific as well as at its Caribbean doorstep, the United States would come to know the problems, the responsibilities, and the expense of empire. In time, the American people learned more, perhaps, than they cared to know about the world beyond their nation's continental borders; but once upon the road to world prominence, the logic of the course would not permit them to turn back. Nor did they immediately have any desire to do so. The war with Spain and subsequent expansion struck a responsive chord in America, feeding national and racial pride, promising lucrative trade, redeeming the traditional belief in the nation's mission, and incidentally redounding to the benefit of the Republican party which had been responsible for it all. The fact that the arrival of the United States as a great power—symbolized rather than caused by the "splendid little war"—had caught the imagination of most Americans in 1899 did not escape that perspicacious critic Mr. Dooley. "We're a gr-reat people," intoned his friend Mr. Hennessey. "We ar-re that," replied Finley Peter Dunne's Irish bartender. "We ar-re that. An' th' best iv it is, we know we ar-re."

Two older studies of the American penetration of the Pacific, are Foster R. Dulles's *America in the Pacific* (1932) and Tyler Dennett's *Americans in Eastern Asia* (1922). Excellent discussions of United States interest in Hawaii can be found in Sylvester K. Stevens's *American Expansion in Hawaii,* 1842–1898 (1945) and William A. Russ, Jr.'s *The Hawaiian Revolution,* 1893–1894 (1959). G. H. Ryden ably treats the Samoan question in *The Foreign Policy of the United States in Relation to Samoa* (1933). Foster R. Dulles provides a highly useful background on expansionism in his *Prelude to World Power: American Diplomatic History,* 1860–1900 (1965) and summarizes American empire building in *The Imperial Years** (1956). Walter LaFeber's *The New Empire: An Interpretation of American Expansion,* 1860–1898* (1963) emphasizes economic forces in United States expansion, as does also Charles A. Beard and G. H. Smith's *The Idea of National Interest: An Analytical Study of American Foreign Policy** (1934). Thomas J. McCormick similarly stresses economic motivation in his *China Market: America's Quest for Informal Empire* (1967). Paul A. Varg analyzes interestingly the nonexistent nature of the China market in "The Myth of the China Market, 1890–1914," *American Historical Review,* LXXIII (February, 1968). William E. Livezey has presented an excellent account of Mahan's influence in *Mahan on Sea Power* (1947).

For long the standard account of the background of the Spanish-American War was Julius W. Pratt's *Expansionists of* 1898 (1936), which stresses expansionist ideology, public opinion, and the business interests which either desired or opposed the war. E. R. May's *Imperial Democracy: The Emergence of America as a Great Power* (1961) and H. Wayne Morgan's *America's Road to Empire** (1965) are more recent and provide better balance in discussing the domestic and foreign background of the conflict between Spain and the United States. Walter Millis's *The Martial Spirit** (1931) presents a lively and generally critical account of United States policy toward Spain. J. E. Wisan's *The Cuban Crisis as Reflected in the New York Press,* 1895–1898 (1934), treats well the role of newspapers in stirring up war sentiment, as does also M. M. Wilkerson's *Public Opinion and the Spanish-American War* (1932). Wilfrid H. Callcott's *The Caribbean Policy of the United States,* 1890–1920 (1967) is also valuable for a study of the Cuban situation after 1895. Frank Freidel's *The Splendid Little War** (1962) is a short, dramatic, and pictorial history of the military and naval engagements. Robert L. Beisner's *Twelve against Empire* (1968) deals perceptively with the antiexpansionists. Henry F. Graff (ed.), *American Imperialism and the Philippine Insurrection** (1969), is an exciting and disturbing account of American behavior in the Philippine war, taken from testimony given before the Senate Committee on the Philippines in 1902.

Among the more valuable biographies which deal with late-nineteenth-century foreign affairs are C. C. Tansill's *The Foreign Policy of Thomas F. Bayard,* 1885–1897 (1940); G. R. Dulebohn's *Principles of Foreign Policy under the Cleveland Administrations* (1941); and Alice Felt Tyler's *The Foreign Policy of James G. Blaine* (1927). Although not specifically studies of foreign affairs, the following books are also valuable: Allan Nevins's *Grover Cleveland* (1934); Margaret Leech's *In the Days of McKinley* (1959); H. W. Morgan's *William McKinley and His America* (1963); and J. A. Garraty's *Henry Cabot Lodge: A Biography* (1953). Howard K. Beale's *Theodore Roosevelt and the Rise of America to World Power** (1956) is an outstanding volume.

On American policy toward China the standard account remains A. Whitney Griswold's *The Far Eastern Policy of the United States** (1938). Another excellent survey is A. L. P. Dennis's *Adventures in American Diplomacy,* 1896–1906 (1928). Two highly useful, specialized accounts are Paul A. Varg's *Open Door Diplomat: The Life of W. W. Rockhill* (1952) and C. S. Campbell, Jr.'s *Special Business Interests and the Open Door Policy* (1951). Samuel F. Bemis (ed.), *American Secretaries of State and Their Diplomacy* (1929), vol. IX, contains a study of John Hay. Foster R. Dulles has an essay on Hay in Norman A. Graebner (ed.), *An Uncertain Tradition: American Secretaries of State in the Twentieth Century** (1961). Both of these studies of Hay are favorable, as is Tyler Dennett's *John Hay: From Poetry to Politics* (1934).

*indicates availability in paperback.

27

Theodore Roosevelt and Progressivism

WILLIAM MCKINLEY'S ELECTION in 1896 seemed to assure the continuation of the status quo politics which had characterized most of American political life since the Civil War. The defeat of the free-silver movement and the demise of the Populists appeared to remove the chief disruptive forces from the American scene. There were few, if any, clear predictions of major change. McKinley signed the Dingley tariff of 1897, which raised rates to the highest point in American history up to that time; in 1900 Congress passed the Gold Standard Act. In the presidential campaign of that year, McKinley defeated Bryan by an even larger majority than he had compiled four years earlier. The election returns offered proof that the nation approved of McKinley and his policies. To both the conservative politician and the casual observer, the nation seemed an astonishing success.

But outward indications were misleading. A widespread demand for political, economic, and social change rumbled beneath the surface of an outwardly reassuring national consensus. The decade of the 1890s had been an especially restless period, when men and women examined the nation's institutions closely and too often found them wanting. With time the reform urge became so widespread at the local, state, and national levels that it produced, after 1900, that massive effort to correct the evils of American society known as the "progressive era."

The progressive movement was an extremely complex phenomenon. It was not an integrated or unified quest for reform; rather it encompassed a wide variety of objectives and interest groups. In general the progressives demanded the regulation of big business, a federal income tax, labor legislation, woman suffrage, prohibition, direct election of United States senators, the direct primary, the initiative and referendum, municipal reform, and many other political, social, and economic improvements. Individual progressives did not support all of these goals, or perhaps even a majority of them, but together their efforts constituted what was commonly called the progressive movement. There were, moreover, broad areas on which progressives generally agreed.

In the first place, progressivism embraced political reform, which to most progressives meant creation of government fully responsible to the popular will. For many progressives democracy assumed the proportions of a panacea. Believing that the problems of democratic government could be solved by more democracy, they would grant the people a more direct voice in government. To that end they favored the direct primary method of nominating candidates; the direct election of senators; the initiative and referendum; and, in some cases, the recall of judges.

Secondly, the progressive movement sought a reduction in the political power of business and industrial interests and the elimination of what they considered the unholy alliance between government and special interests. To that end reformers hoped to extend federal control over the nation's large industrial, financial, and transportation corporation. There was probably no other issue on which so many progressives agreed.

Thirdly, progressives hoped to improve the lives and increase the opportunities of the poor and underprivileged. They insisted that the government possessed both the power and the obligation to tackle such problems as slum clearance, long hours, abolition of child labor, workmen's compensation, unemployment insurance, mothers' pensions, better care of prisoners, and other social reforms. The progressives would place more responsibility on government in areas where it had earlier exerted little influence. Overall, the most notable aspect of the progressive movement was its underlying purpose of expanding the power and functions of government as a factor in American life.

Progressivism was truly a national movement. Reformers represented all sections and all classes; they existed in both major political parties, and they represented both urban and rural areas. But much of the strongest support centered in the growing cities. Many progressive leaders came from reasonably well-to-do families, had attended college, and were often young. Whereas most social classes joined in the demand for reform, the backbone of the movement was found among the great middle class, including white-collar workers and professionals such as businessmen, lawyers, and publishers. Some historians have suggested that many of the upper-middle- and middle-class, white-collar, urban professional and intellectual leaders supported progressivism to maintain their leadership and social status, which seemed threatened by great corporate tycoons, rising labor leaders, and political bosses. But the urban middle class had no monopoly on either the leadership or membership of the progressive movement. Demand for reform was also strong in rural areas. Robert M. La Follette in Wisconsin and Peter Norbeck in South Dakota were among the rural progressives who led their states into advanced programs of reform.

Although progressivism had a nature and character of its own, it grew out of the criticism and discontent so prevalent in American society in the late nineteenth century. Social critics such as Henry George, writers such as Henry D. Lloyd, and economists such as Richard T. Ely and Thorstein Veblen all had raised serious questions about American society. Moreover, the demands of the Grange, Greenbackers, and Populists, as well as some labor groups, measured the widespread discontent with political and economic conditions.

The progressive movement responded to specific conditions and abuses in American society which many citizens considered dangerous to the nation's welfare and to democratic institutions. Above all, people feared the power of the huge corporations then emerging as the dominant factor in American economic life. Not only did big business exercise overwhelming power over the entire economy, but bankers and industrialists influenced government as well. This was not a new development; but as businessmen achieved greater wealth, they turned to politics to protect their economic interests. The president of the sugar trust admitted candidly the practice and motives of large businesses in contributing campaign funds: "In the State of New York where the Democratic majority is between 40,000 and 50,000 we throw it their way. In the State of Massachusetts where the Republican majority is doubtful, they probably have the call. . . . Where there is a dominant party, where the majority is very large, that is the party that gets the contribution, because that is the party that controls the local matters."

What finally aroused millions of Americans to support reform were the dramatic revelations of a group of journalists known as the "Muckrakers." This group of able writers received their special designation when Theodore Roosevelt once referred to them as people who were always raking in the muck. The Muckrakers investigated many undesirable aspects of American life and exposed these conditions in popular writings for all to see and read. The rise of 10- and 15-cent magazines in the 1890s provided an outlet for muckraking articles, sometimes called the "literature of exposure." The Muckrakers assured that the public, once made cognizant of the corruption, would demand political and economic reform. In their writings the Muckrakers were specific in naming financiers, industrialists, and members of Congress who appeared to violate the public interest.

McClure's topped the list of the highly successful muckraking magazines. Publisher S. S. McClure hired a competent staff of writers, which included Lincoln Steffens, Ida Tarbell, and Ray Stannard Baker. He provided them time and money to investigate thoroughly any topic on which they chose to report. *McClure's* commanded national attention in October, 1902, when it published the first of a series of articles by Lincoln Steffens on corruption in city government. This was perhaps the first genuine muckraking article of the progressive era. Entitled "Tweed Days in St. Louis," the Steffens article revealed the extent to which graft and corruption were rampant in that city. In addition to articles on political dishonesty, *McClure's* published critical accounts of big business. Late in 1902 Ida Tarbell published her first article on the history of the Standard Oil Company. Ray Stannard Baker, the third of *McClure's* distinguished trio of writers, wrote on labor as well as conditions among Negroes.

Much of the writing by Muckrakers attacked industrialists, financiers, and big business in general. Thomas W. Lawson, a successful speculator, assailed stock market practices in *Frenzied Finance,* while Charles Edward Russell wrote critical articles on the beef trust. David Graham Phillips, in his *Treason of the Senate,* called the roll of the members of the United States Senate who responded favorably to business pressures in the writing of tariff schedules. In attacking railroad rebates, Ray Stannard Baker argued that big business crushed its smaller competitors through favoritism in shipping charges. Burton J. Hendrick attacked the illegal and immoral practices of life insurance companies. Muckrakers thus exposed the evils of American society on a broad front; even the churches and the press came under criticism.

Leading novelists in the early century joined the Muckrakers in placing the American economic system under sharp indictment. In *The Octopus* (1901) and *The Pit* (1903), Frank Norris sharply criticized the power of the railroads and grain speculators, respectively. Theodore Dreiser's *The Financier* and *The Titan* lashed out at greed and the lack of social responsibility among the rich. Jack London went even further in denouncing the American system. His novel *The Iron Heel* (1907) described class warfare between what he termed exploiting capitalists and the workers. Upton Sinclair's *The Jungle* was a detailed and sickening exposé of the meat-packing industry.

Reform in the States and Cities

Many of the most important reforms of the progressive period were inaugurated at the state and city level. In the states the progressives attempted to destroy the influence of powerful political bosses, personified by such figures as Matthew Quay of Pennsylvania and Thomas C. Platt of New York. Ray Stannard Baker once wrote that local government had "become a government of the Bosses, by the Bosses, and distinctly for the Bosses." The power of men such as Quay and Platt and others like them across the country was usually built on their connections with big business. The railroads, insurance companies, public utilities, industrial corporations, and banks all exerted tremendous political pressure. Progressives could break the influence of such organizations only by wresting control from the hands of the bosses. To that end they supported measures which would put government more directly in the hands of voters and would extend the states' powers of regulation and control.

Robert M. La Follette brought progressivism to Wisconsin when that state elected him to the governorship in 1900. La Follette led and pushed Wisconsin lawmakers into a broad program of progressive reform. Before he went to the United States Senate in 1906, the Wisconsin Legislature had passed a direct primary law, raised taxes on railroads and other corporations, brought the railroads under stricter control, passed a law to regulate lobbying, and inaugurated civil service in state employment. La Follette supported a state income tax which the state adopted after he left office. Moreover, while he was Governor, La Follette called

Library of Congress

The Progressive Spirit

Theodore Roosevelt's stern dictum, "Every man holds his property subject to the general right of the community to regulate it," became the slogan of the Progressives. Some worked toward conservation of the land, others vented their outrage on the evils of child labor, and still others called for direct elections or home rule for cities; but all believed that the nation could ameliorate its problems by government control over trusts, monopolies, corporations, and combines.

A great change had occurred in America: the country had developed from an agricultural community to an industrial and commercial one, and in so doing, a great many people came to work for a very few. Giant enterprises rose in a short period of time, and in this rush to supply the country with the products of new technology, the laboring man and the farmer found themselves the victims.

Before long a group of intelligent men and women arose to point out to government where its laissez-faire policy failed. Some of these writers, called "Muckrakers," cried out that it was time to prevent corporations from engulfing great tracts of public land with no concern for its potential productivity; time to stop the railroads from joining forces to squeeze the farmer; time to provide for the incompetent and infirm, to regulate the working hours of young children, to destroy conditions that produced six million illiterates, and to allow the new and scientific health information to reach everyone.

The cartoon above shows Uncle Sam viewing the situation with alarm.

Brown Brothers

Library of Congress

McClure's Magazine, led the publishers in exposing social evils at the turn of the century. Famous Muckrakers included Ray Stannard Baker, above, associate editor of *McClure's*. Upton Sinclair, right above, was best known for his novel *The Jungle.* Ida M. Tarbell, right center, wrote the two-volume *History of the Standard Oil Company.* Lincoln Steffens, bottom right, deplored the connection between businessmen and politicians in his book, *The Shame of the Cities.*

Library of Congress

Culver Pictures, Inc.

Brown Brothers

The fight against child labor became one of the most important causes of the period. In 1900, well over a million and a half children under sixteen worked in dangerous and unhealthy conditions. The National Child Labor Committee was formed in 1904, and within a few years, a remarkable photographer, Lewis W. Hine, joined the effort; his pictures appear here and on the following pages. Hine's work helped to arouse public sentiment against the employment of children, and the practice diminished (but by no means disappeared) under the pressure of public opinion and state legislation.

Both: Library of Congress

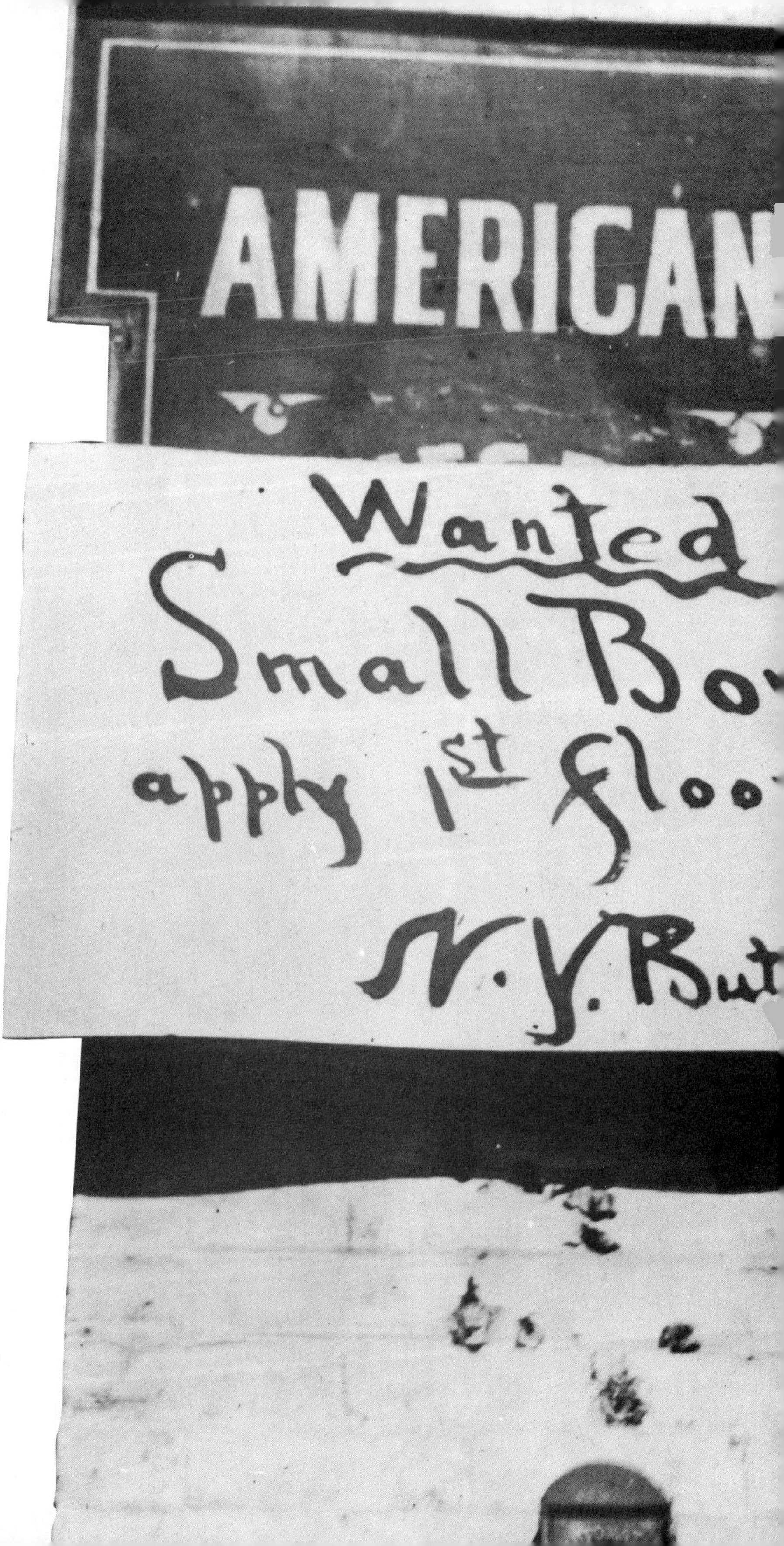

E IS A MESSENGER BOY
DURING THE DAY
MESSENGERS GO
TO ALL PARTS
OF THE CITY
E IS A GO BETWEEN
ERRAND BOYS
THESE HAUNTS
HE IS A VICTIM
HIS WORK GIVES HIM
BY PERSONAL CONTACT
AN INTIMATE
ACQUAINTANCE WITH
VICE AND CRIME
STARTS HIM DOWN HILL

Hine photographed children at work on city streets, in factories, in fields, and most tellingly, in the coal mines. His pictures appeared in publications and on exhibit panels like the one at left, which was designed to stimulate state legislation to regulate hours, wages, and conditions.

All pictures: Library of Congress

Far left, above and below, and below: Schomburg Collection, N.Y. Public Library; near left: National Urban League; right: Brown Brothers

After the Reconstruction period, the lot of the Negro remained desperate. Since the Progressives did not take a particularly strong stand in his behalf, the Negro had to fight his own battles for reform. Dr. W. E. B. DuBois, right, author of *The Souls of Black Folk*, was one of the founders, in 1909, of the National Association for the Advancement of Colored People, and he edited its magazine, *The Crisis*. Mary White Ovington, left above, and a few liberal whites supported the group. A frequent and influential writer for the magazine was James Weldon Johnson, above. Blacks also made advances in education under leaders such as Mary McCloed Bethune, left, who founded Bethune-Cookman college in 1904.

The Progressive era and Woodrow Wilson's New Freedom were scarred by lynchings and race riots. One of the worst occurred in July, 1917, in East St. Louis, Illinois. Blacks in New York protested the riot and its aftermath with a silent parade (next page), and a Negro newspaper urged President Wilson to act.

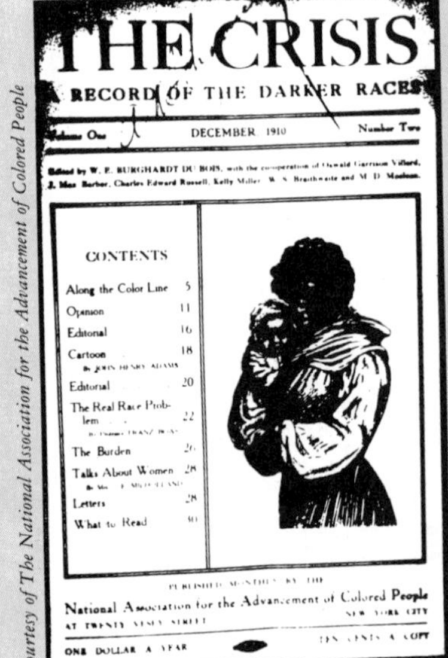

THE CRISIS

A RECORD OF THE DARKER RACES

Volume One — DECEMBER 1910 — Number Two

Edited by W. E. BURGHARDT DU BOIS, with the cooperation of Oswald Garrison Villard, J. Max Barber, Charles Edward Russell, Kelly Miller, W. S. Braithwaite and M. D. Maclean.

CONTENTS

Along the Color Line 5
Opinion 11
Editorial 16
Cartoon 18
Editorial 20
The Real Race Problem 22
The Burden 26
Talks About Women 28
Letters 28
What to Read 30

National Association for the Advancement of Colored People

NEW YORK CITY

ONE DOLLAR A YEAR

Courtesy of The National Association for the Advancement of Colored People

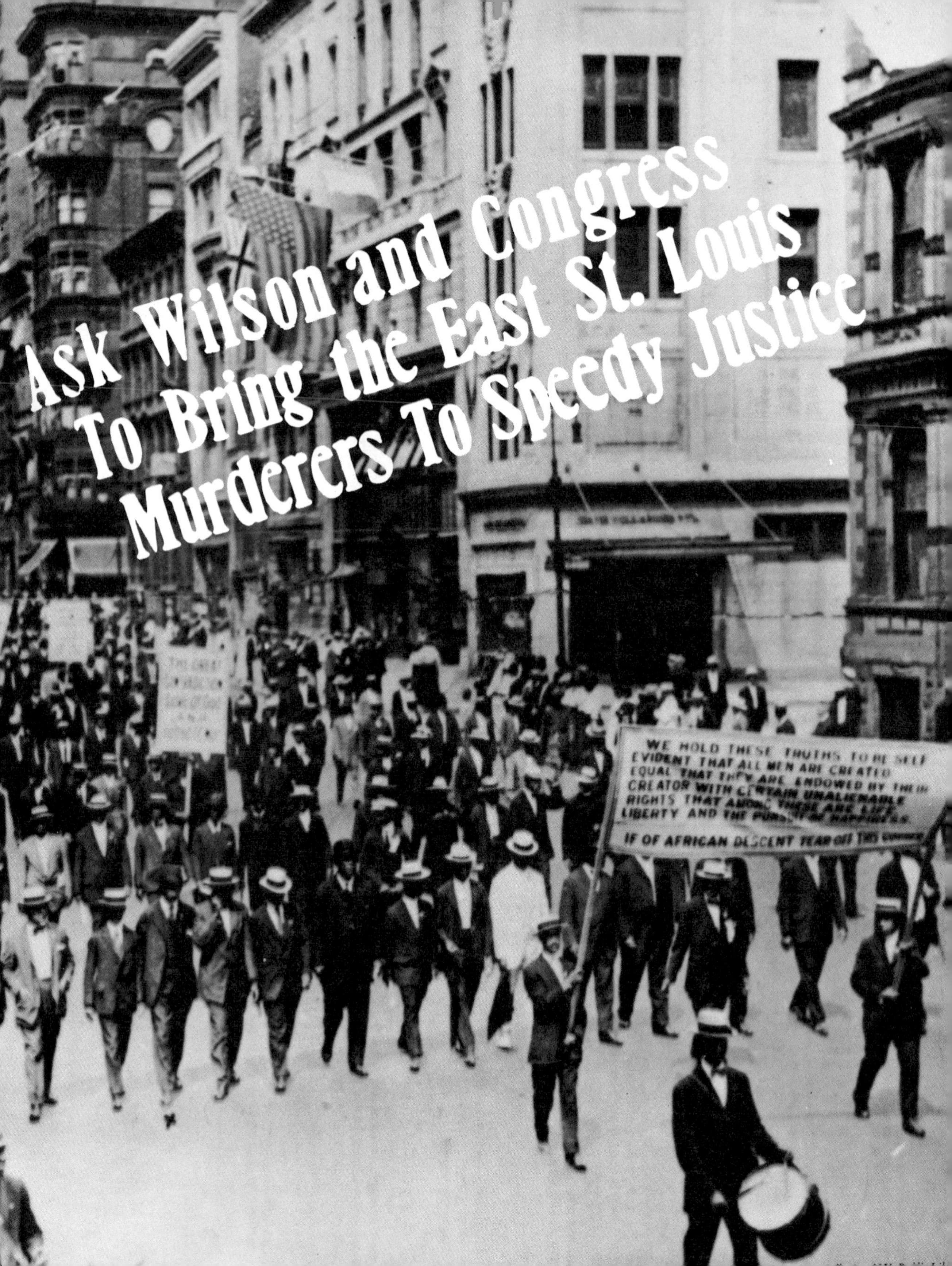
Ask Wilson and Congress
To Bring the East St. Louis
Murderers To Speedy Justice
WE HOLD THESE TRUTHS TO BE SELF
EVIDENT THAT ALL MEN ARE CREATED
EQUAL THAT THEY ARE ENDOWED BY THEIR
CREATOR WITH CERTAIN UNALIENABLE
RIGHTS THAT AMONG THESE ARE LIFE
LIBERTY AND THE PURSUIT OF HAPPINESS
IF OF AFRICAN DESCENT TEAR OFF THIS

on specialists at the University of Wisconsin to help solve problems of state government. University professors provided a kind of "brain trust" for Wisconsin progressivism and set a pattern for the broader use of intellectuals in government service.

Progressivism at the state level had already become nationwide. States throughout the country revealed a remarkable interest in reform legislation. Other Midwestern states were especially active in enacting progressive laws. The South Dakota Legislature in 1898 adopted an initiative and referendum law, and in 1907, that state's lawmakers passed a direct primary statute, legislation to prohibit free railroad passes, a measure requiring publication of campaign expenses, and one that forbade corporation contributions to campaign funds. In Iowa, Governor Albert B. Cummins fought conservative Republicans and entrenched economic interests on behalf of reform legislation. In neighboring Missouri, Joseph W. Folk be came Governor in 1904 on a platform calling for a war against special privilege.

If progressivism was strong in the Midwest, it was by no means confined to that region. On the West Coast, Governor William S. U'Ren of Oregon set an outstanding example of progressive leadership; his reforms included the initiative and referendum as well as a direct primary. California's Governor Hiram Johnson defeated a powerful political machine backed by the Southern Pacific Railroad. In the South, the election of Jeff Davis as Governor in Arkansas (1901), James K. Vardaman in Mississippi (1903), and Hoke Smith in Georgia (1906) demonstrated that Southern reformers were throwing off the yoke of conservative, Bourbon rule. Although Southern legislatures enacted measures to control large corporations, they did not favor equal political rights for Negroes. Despite their appeals to democracy, Southern progressives actually attempted to disfranchise those Negroes who had not already been denied the right to vote.

Besides passing laws designed to give voters a more direct voice in government and to regulate big business, state legislatures enacted a wide variety of social legislation. Laws to prohibit child labor or to establish maximum hours and minimum wages in certain industries, safety legislation, and accident insurance all reflected a growing concern for industrial workers. Between 1909 and 1917, nineteen states passed measures regulating the hours of work for women; others strengthened existing laws. New York passed a workmen's compensation act in 1910, and other states soon followed. This new emphasis on measures to protect workers reflected the social and economic problems growing out of a rapidly industrializing and urbanized society. In passing social legislation, the states used their police powers to protect the health, safety, and public welfare of the people. Progressives at the state level also worked for such far-reaching reforms as the direct election of senators, prohibition, and woman suffrage. All of these objectives had been achieved by 1920 with the approval of the Seventeenth, Eighteenth and Nineteenth Amendments to the Constitution.

A unique, yet important, regional reform movement was the Nonpartisan League of North Dakota. Formed by Arthur C. Townley, a bankrupt farmer and Socialist, in 1915, the Nonpartisan League went far beyond demands for control of monopoly. The League sought to establish state-owned enterprises, which, it believed, could solve the problems of credit and marketing for hard-pressed farmers. Among these were elevators and flour mills, a state bank, a program of hail insurance on farm crops, and a home building association to promote home ownership for North Dakotans. In 1919 the Legislature of North Dakota enacted much of the League program. Though the Nonpartisan League was not an integral part of the progressive movement, its demand to expand state powers to deal with pressing economic issues placed the League in the progressive tradition. Progressives everywhere looked to increased governmental powers to correct what they saw as unnecessary political, economic, and social evils in society.

There was fully as much need for political reform in the large American cities as in state governments. Josiah Strong observed in *The Challenge of the City* (1907) that in the city, "maladjustments of society create the sorest friction. . . . It is chiefly in the city that the enormous powers of organization and of centralized wealth are wielded; and it is there that these powers must feel the wholesome restraint of righteous laws and of an enlightened popular conscience." There was little evidence of enlightened consciences or righteous laws in most American cities by the late nineteenth century; after 1900 the Muckrakers—especially Lincoln Steffens with his articles in *McClure's*—dramatized the widespread graft and corruption in many of them.

What was required for urban reform appeared clear enough. Cities, first of all, needed freedom from interference by state legislatures. This objective stimulated the movement for so-called home rule, which would permit a city to determine the nature of its own government. By 1914 twelve states had granted some degree of home rule to at least certain classes of cities. Many cities adopted the commission form of government, thereby placing government in the hands of a small group of qualified men who generally headed, in addition, the key city departments of police, fire, water, and sanitation control. One of the commissioners usually acted as mayor. This plan ended the system of checks and balances, which had existed between the old council and mayor, for the commission commanded both legislative and administrative functions.

The commission system of city government brought improvements, but it lacked the executive and administrative authority to guarantee an efficient administration. From this secondary need grew the city-manager plan. Under this arrangement, the commission hired a trained administrator of city affairs and turned the executive functions of government over to him. Staunton, Virginia, first introduced the city-manager plan in 1908. The ordinance establishing this plan declared that the manager would have "entire charge and control of all the executive work of the city in its various departments." The formation of a City Managers' Association in 1914 indicated the growth of this new profession.

The Negro and Progressivism

Unfortunately, the widespread demand for increased democracy, together with social and economic reform, which characterized the progressive movement did not extend to Negroes. Some Muckrakers discussed the plight of the Negro, and friends of Negroes established centers and agencies to help them in the Northern cities, but black citizens found little more than sympathy for their particular problems. Progressivism generally did not challenge the second-class status of Negro citizenship. The Southern states persistently denied

Negroes the right to vote, and the political role of Negroes in the North was almost as insignificant. Negroes suffered from social and economic discrimination as well. One New York official said in 1900 that "it's getting so the colored people have no rights in this city." Labor leaders denied Negroes membership in unions; at times industrialists hired them as strikebreakers. State laws which segregated Southern schools faced no threat from the courts after the Supreme Court upheld the doctrine of separate-but-equal accommodations in the case of *Plessy v. Ferguson* (1896). But the black schools were in almost every case grossly inferior. They usually lacked well-trained teachers, decent physical facilities, and anything else that cost money. Whereas social segregation was almost absolute in the South, many Northerners were little more liberal in their attitude toward the Negro and his desire for equality. Northern hotels frequently denied accommodations to the prominent black leader Booker T. Washington.

Throughout the United States there was very little social intercourse between blacks and whites. President Theodore Roosevelt aroused a storm of protest when he invited Washington, then head of Tuskegee Institute, to have dinner with him on October 16, 1901. Southerners fumed at Roosevelt for what a Memphis newspaper called the "most damnable outrage ever." While President Roosevelt declared he would have Washington "to dine just as often as I please," he made no defense of black rights. Nor did he repeat the affair.

Individual progressives spoke out on behalf of Negro rights, but they had little or no influence on public policy. During Woodrow Wilson's Presidency, Negroes probably lost ground in their drive for equal treatment. Federal departments on occasion segregated black employees, and the armed services barred them from all but the lowest ranks. The Virginia-born President accepted the removal of many Negroes from federal employment without so much as a mild protest. After visiting the city of Washington in 1913, Booker T. Washington wrote: "I have never seen the colored people so discouraged and bitter as they are at the present time."

Among Negroes themselves, there was no agreement as to the means by which they could best improve their condition. Washington, spokesman for the older and more conservative black leaders, held that Negroes must develop greater economic opportunities and then work hard to advance themselves. As president of Tuskegee Institute after 1881, Washington emphasized industrial education and believed that Negroes could raise their economic status by learning trades and crafts. He did not press for intellectual leadership or social equality.

After a brief but highly popular speech in Atlanta, Georgia, in 1895, Washington emerged as the most widely accepted black philosopher of education and social action. For his race he championed self-help, thrift, hard work, acceptance of racial segregation, deemphasis of politics, and patience. By the early twentieth century, however, a group of young militant blacks broke with Washington and demanded the social, economic, educational, and political rights of full citizenship. They inaugurated a policy of fighting Jim Crowism, lynching, segregation, and every additional type of discrimination. Dr. W. E. B. Du Bois was the principal leader of this group. He voiced some of his early ideas in *The Souls of Black Folk* (1903) and later in a new militant periodical, *The Crisis,* which began publication in 1910. Especially after the terrible race riots in Springfield, Ohio, in 1904, in Atlanta, Georgia, and Brownsville, Texas, in 1906, and in Springfield, Illinois, in 1908, a minority of liberal whites gave support to black aims and objectives as expressed by Du Bois. In 1909 a group of blacks and whites founded the National Association for the Advancement of Colored People. Incorporated in 1910, the NAACP consisted primarily of intellectuals who set out to raise the Negro to *full* social, political, and economic equality. But progress was slow. The widespread terror and violence employed against Negroes illustrated the intolerance of the early years of the century. For Negroes generally the American dream of equality remained only a dream.

Still there was continuous and positive action. In 1911 Eugene K. Jones and George E. Haynes, with others, founded the National Urban League, an organization for the uplift of urban blacks. Also, to win more respect for his race and to rectify its neglect in history, Carter Godwin Woodson, in 1915, organized the Association for the Study of Negro Life and History. The next year he began publication of the *Journal of Negro History* and, later, the *Negro History Bulletin.* Dr. Woodson founded the Associated Publishers and took the lead in making "Negro History Week" a popular national celebration. Afro-Americans found satisfaction, moreover, in the distinguished inventions of such blacks as Jan Matzeliger, Elijah McCoy, John P. Parker, and Granville T. Woods, as well as in Jack Johnson's winning of the heavyweight boxing title and Matt Henson's sharing in the discovery of the North Pole in 1909.

Black ghettoes became a rather common characteristic of Northern cities in the early years of the twentieth century. Previously blacks had lived in smaller, isolated communities —perhaps one, two, or three blocks surrounded by whites—but by 1914 large numbers of blacks were concentrated in New York's Harlem, on Chicago's South Side, and in older, crowded sections of other major cities. In many urban communities residential segregation now had the sanction of local laws which specifically designated all-white and all-black blocks. But discriminatory pressures, responding to racist social theory, went far beyond the statutes. Many Negroes found it almost impossible to obtain acceptable housing. This gradual forcing of Negroes into ghettoes after 1900 resulted from increasing economic and social discrimination against blacks during the very period when Americans were demanding reform in most other areas of national life.

Theodore Roosevelt: National Progressive Leader

On September 6, 1901, Leon Czolgosz, an anarchist, approached President William McKinley at a reception in Buffalo, New York, and shot him with a concealed weapon. The nation waited sorrowfully while the President lingered for eight days and then died. Upon taking the oath of the presidential office, Theodore Roosevelt promised to "continue, absolutely unbroken, the policy of President McKinley for the peace, prosperity and the honor of our beloved country." Long before he left office in 1909, however, Roosevelt had broken with much of the post-Civil War tradition in American politics. Aware of the country's many accumulating and unanswered problems and sensitive to the burgeoning spirit of reform, Roosevelt became a vigorous exponent of progressive ideas.

Theodore Roosevelt was born of well-to-do parents in New York on October 27, 1858. Physically weak as a boy and bothered with asthma, he worked hard to build up his body and became a strong advocate of physical fitness. He enjoyed all the advantages of an upper-class youth which then included travel abroad and a Harvard education. In 1881 he won election to the New York Legislature and served three terms in Albany. Although he worked with the reform element in New York, the young Roosevelt was conservative in politics. In February, 1884, his wife died, and Roosevelt sought to assuage his grief with a turn at ranching in western North Dakota. During the next three or four years, he spent considerable time in the West, but he also devoted some attention to his writing. His first book, *The Naval War of* 1812, appeared in 1882, and later in the eighties he completed several biographies and began his better-known *The Winning of the West.* Between 1889 and 1897 he served as United States Civil Service Commissioner and president of the Police Board in New York City. Following his resignation as police commissioner in 1897, he entered McKinley's administration as Assistant Secretary of the Navy. However, at the outbreak of war with Spain in 1898, Roosevelt obtained a commission as a lieutenant colonel and helped to organize the Rough Riders.

Roosevelt's return from Cuba coincided with Boss Thomas C. Platt's search for a respectable and prestigious candidate for the governorship of New York. Roosevelt seemed to fit the requirements. He campaigned hard and emerged victorious by a narrow margin. During his governorship, Roosevelt maintained his independence, but he made little effort to break the prevailing political machine or to push for many reforms. He did achieve better civil service legislation and a law to tax corporation franchises. In addition, he made some strong administrative appointments. But even these mild inclinations toward reform displeased Boss Platt, who sought to kick Roosevelt upstairs by obtaining his nomination as the party's vice presidential candidate in 1900. Roosevelt did not want this honor; he said that he would "rather be anything, say a professor of history." After his election he thought of taking up law, but his plans were rendered irrelevant by a pistol shot.

Theodore Roosevelt was a man of wide and varied interests. He was a strong advocate of, and participant in, the strenuous life. He liked sports and sometimes held boxing bouts in the White House. He traveled widely and frequently in both the United States and abroad. He liked all kinds and classes of people and was equally at home with kings, scholars, farmers, and workers. He appreciated literature and history and wrote more books than most professional historians. He liked politics and was a skillful politician. Ambitious and competitive, Roosevelt appreciated power, but he desired to use power only for what he considered the public good. Like most other progressives, he viewed issues in a moral light and held firm views on what was good and what was evil. Overall, Roosevelt was a highly controversial and contradictory figure. Above all, he was a leader. He was exceptionally adept at welding noncooperative, and sometimes conflicting, groups into a unit for political power and action. By education, experience, and temperament, Roosevelt was exceptionally well qualified to assume the Presidency.

Roosevelt moved cautiously during his first presidential term. His initial message to Congress was filled with generalities; there was nothing in it to frighten or worry conservatives. He emphasized the trust problem but urged caution in any action taken; he said that organized labor deserved protection but declared that workers must not be permitted to abuse their power. Roosevelt was realistic enough to know that he must work with Congress and that both the House and Senate were ruled by conservatives. Power in the Senate centered around multimillionaire Nelson W. Aldrich of Rhode Island; John C. Spooner, a brilliant Wisconsin lawyer; Orville H. Platt of Connecticut, and William B. Allison of Iowa. In the House of Representatives, Joseph B. Cannon of Illinois, Speaker after 1903, was a tough and dedicated conservative who soon ran the House with an iron hand. For Roosevelt to buck this congressional power structure directly would have been foolhardy. Moreover, there were still few progressives in Congress to support detailed and carefully planned economic reform proposals.

Despite what may have seemed to be a lack of vigorous leadership in his first term, Roosevelt took a number of actions and supported programs which firmly identified him with the surging demand for reform. In February, 1902, the Attorney General revealed that the Department of Justice would commence an antitrust suit against the Northern Securities Company, a huge railroad combine. At about the same time, the President involved himself in the anthracite coal strike and demonstrated a much fairer attitude toward organized labor than that displayed by his predecessors. Also in 1902 Roosevelt appointed Oliver Wendell Holmes to the Supreme Court. Holmes turned out to be one of the greatest liberal judges ever to sit on the high bench. Conservationists were pleased when Roosevelt supported the Newlands Act in 1902, which provided federal funds for reclamation projects in the West.

Another leading issue confronting Roosevelt was the regulation and control of big business. Here his attitudes and actions placed him squarely in the progressive mold. Roosevelt's campaign against monopoly secured for him the title of "trustbuster," although Roosevelt accepted bigness in business as natural and therefore had no great interest in trustbusting. He did institute forty-two antimonopoly suits, but both of his successors, William Howard Taft and Woodrow Wilson, exceeded that number. Roosevelt earned the name "trustbuster" partly because he revived and implemented the Sherman Antitrust Act, which had been almost a dead letter on the statute books since its passage in 1890. Above all, Roosevelt brought the entire question of monopoly and corporate abuses before the country more clearly than had any previous President.

Roosevelt did not oppose all large corporations; he objected only to the abuses of corporate power. In other words, he made a distinction between good and bad big business. Mr. Dooley captured the President's sentiments with considerable accuracy when he wrote: " 'Th' trusts,' say he, 'are heejous monsthers built up by th' inlightened intherprise if th' men that have done so much to advance progress in our beloved counthry.... On wan hand I wud stamp thim undher fut; on the other hand, not so fast.' "

Roosevelt had little faith in antitrust laws based on the nineteenth-century idea of competition. Rather, he preferred to preserve the efficiency and economic benefits of large business and industry but at the same time assure the public protection against abuses through strict government regulation. He wrote in 1905 that "what is needed is not so much the effort to prevent combinations as a vigilant and effective control of the combinations formed." Roosevelt favored the creation of a federal administrative agency with power to investigate and control large corporations engaged in interstate commerce which violated or abused the public interest. His plan called for the regulation, not the destruction, of big business.

In line with these ideas, Roosevelt gave strong support to the establishment of a Bureau of Corporations, which would have power both to investigate industrial enterprises doing business in interstate commerce and to report its findings to the President for action. This Congress enacted, over strong protests, as a part of the bill which established a Department of Commerce in 1903. In obtaining the amendment which provided for the Bureau of Corporations, the President demonstrated his effective political leadership.

But Roosevelt knew that he could not convince a conservative Congress to pass a law which would effectively regulate large corporations, so he turned to the Sherman Antitrust Act as the only practical weapon at hand. A suit against the $400 million Northern Securities Company offered an ideal opportunity to test the authority of the Sherman Act to thwart the massive power of banking and railroad capital. Organized in 1901 by J. P. Morgan, Edward H. Harriman, and James J. Hill, the Northern Securities Company controlled either directly or indirectly most of the railroads west of the Mississippi, including the Great Northern, Northern Pacific, Burlington, Union Pacific, and Southern Pacific. This large holding company appeared to be in clear violation of the Sherman Antitrust Act, and Roosevelt knew that a government victory in such a case would bring plaudits from the great majority of people. In 1904, two years after accepting the suit, the Supreme Court in a 5-to-4 decision held that the Northern Securities Company was an unlawful combination in restraint of trade. Meanwhile, Roosevelt had supported additional regulatory legislation. In 1903 Congress passed the Elkins Act, which made it illegal for a railroad to deviate from its published rates.

Recent historical scholarship has shown that legislation to regulate big business received the support of important elements in the business community. Some businessmen and industrialists were tired of the cutthroat competition and saw government regulation and control as a way to restrain the activities and power of their rivals. Others viewed moderate regulation as a substitute for much stricter government control. The president of the Pennsylvania Railroad wrote to President Roosevelt in 1901: "We believe that it is better policy to assist in framing and passing a reasonable measure [government regulation] now than to have a more drastic and perhaps a seriously injurious one forced upon us by public clamor." One committee of the National Association of Manufacturers supported the Pure Food and Drug Act, while other business leaders favored the meat-inspection act. This backing of federal regulation by important segments of the business community added another dimension to progressivism and indicated how widespread the search for greater order in business had become.

Roosevelt and the Workingmen

At the same time that Roosevelt took a much firmer stand against big business than his predecessors, he also demonstrated more understanding and sympathy for the problems and conditions of workingmen. Like most progressives, Roosevelt believed that workers should receive justice and fair treatment. Although he approved of unions, Roosevelt did not give strong support to organized labor, in part because he rejected the idea of classes and feared that organized labor, like organized capital, might abuse its power. The test of Roosevelt's attitudes came in the anthracite coal strike of 1902.

For many years unrest and dissatisfaction among workers had plagued the anthracite mines of northeastern Pennsylvania. The employees had not received a pay raise between 1880 and 1900, and by the latter date their annual wage averaged only $560 a year. In 1899, John Mitchell became head of the United Mine Workers. The next year his men struck and won a 10 percent pay increase. But in May, 1902, a new crisis gripped the anthracite coal fields. This time, besides asking for more pay, Mitchell and his union demanded a shorter workday, more honest weighing of coal, and union recognition. Now the mine operators became adamant and refused any plan of arbitration or mediation. George F. Baer, head of the Philadelphia and Reading Coal and Iron Company, expressed their attitude when he said that "the rights and interests of the laboring men will be protected and cared for, not by the labor agitators, but by the Christian men to whom God in his infinite wisdom has given the control of the property interests of the country." Roosevelt had no sympathy for this "divine right of property" philosophy; he urged the warring parties to settle on some compromise. But the strike dragged on, and by September coal shortages had created extensive suffering in some communities. The operators hoped that, as in the past, federal troops would be called out to maintain order until they broke the strike. Roosevelt, who became bitter over such displays of arrogance, let it be known that he might use troops to take over the mines and produce coal. This threat finally prompted the operators to accept mediation; the strikers returned to work late in October. Roosevelt appointed the Anthracite Coal Strike Commission, which heard hundreds of witnesses over the next several months. The Commission finally awarded workers a 10 percent pay raise, some reduction in hours, and other reforms. But the workers did not win recognition of their union.

Roosevelt's Second Term

Roosevelt's dynamic leadership and action created enemies among the special interests, but the people as a whole admired and respected him. His personal popularity became clear in the campaign of 1904. No Republican could successfully contest his nomination; he was chosen unanimously as the party's standard-bearer. Unwilling to face certain defeat with another William Jennings Bryan nomination, the Democrats in 1904 sought a conservative candidate and nominated Judge Alton B. Parker of New York. But Parker was no match for the popular Roosevelt, who swept to victory with 7,628,000 votes, compared with only 5,084,000 for Parker. The Republicans also won a smashing victory in Congress.

Roosevelt's sweeping victory gave him a new feeling of confidence. During his second term, at least until 1907, he demonstrated stronger leadership and an even greater commitment to progressive reform. He now concentrated on the problem of business regulation and control. In December, 1905, he informed Congress that it was absolutely essential to give the federal government effective supervision over corporate power. In this connection, he recommended the creation of a strong administrative agency with power to prevent "unjust and unreasonable" railroad rates. It required all the political pressure and skill which the President could muster to drive an enforceable measure through Congress. Finally, in June, 1906, after weeks of bitter debate and considerable compromise Congress passed the Hepburn Act. This important law gave the Interstate Commerce Commission power to determine just and reasonable railroad rates, subject to court review. In other words, upon complaint of a shipper, the Commission could set aside the old rate and impose what it considered a reasonable one, but the carrier could always appeal this decision to the courts. The law also permitted the Commission to examine railroad records and to require uniform accounting practices. The act enlarged the ICC from five to seven members and extended its control to include express, sleeping-car, and pipeline companies. Passage of the Hepburn Act was a major step in making the railroads one of the nation's more strictly regulated industries.

Although most progressives considered railroad legislation of prime importance, they also demanded greater national regulation of certain other industries, notably food and drugs. For years Dr. Harvey W. Wiley, chief of the Bureau of Chemistry in the United States Department of Agriculture, had been campaigning for pure food and drug laws. Wiley had found that food processors preserved meat and milk with harmful chemicals and that dishonest labeling of patent medicines endangered the people's health. The Bureau of Chemistry reported in 1900 that 152 preservatives were advertised as effective means of keeping meat and fish fresh without ice. Patent medicines which contained such elements as opium, cocaine, and alcohol were widely advertised and sold. One of the most commonly used patent medicines was Lydia E. Pinkham's Vegetable Compound which, according to the advertisements, did more for the nation's ailing women than did their family physicians.

While it might seem strange that anyone would fight pure food and drug legislation, the opposition was strong. The *New York Sun* scoffed at Wiley's campaign for truthful labeling and gave him the titles of "chief janitor and policeman of people's insides." The patent medicine interests exerted effective pressure against passage of any legislation by threatening to withdraw their advertising accounts from newspapers and magazines which favored regulation. Nonetheless, those who favored controls finally prevailed. In June, 1906, after Roosevelt had asked for action, Congress passed the Pure Food and Drug Act. This law prohibited the sale in interstate commerce of any misbranded or adulterated food or drugs and provided means of enforcement and penalties for violations.

At the same time Congress considered a law to clean up the meat-packing industry. For years it had been known that much of the meat being processed came from unhealthy animals and was prepared under the most unsanitary conditions. However, like other representatives of big business, the so-called beef trust strongly opposed effective regulation. The publication early in 1906 of Upton Sinclair's muckraking novel *The Jungle* created a public stir and aroused the President. Sinclair's book dealt with the nauseating and sickening conditions surrounding Chicago's meat-packing industry. Describing the production of sausage, Sinclair wrote: "These rats were nuisances, and the packers would put poisoned bread out for them, they would die, and then rats, bread, and meat would go into the hoppers together." Despite strong opposition from the packers and their political supporters, Congress, with Roosevelt's strong backing, passed the meat-inspection law in June, 1906. This measure outlawed the sale in interstate or foreign commerce of "meat and meat products which are unsound, unhealthful, unwholesome, or otherwise unfit for human food."

Many progressives were deeply concerned about preserving the nation's rapidly dwindling supply of natural resources. Loose and sometimes corrupt administration of the land laws in the late nineteenth century had permitted corporate interests to gain control of water-power sites and mineral, forest, grazing, and farm lands and to exploit them for private gain. The growing demand for conservation took three forms. In the first place, conservationists sought to arouse the general public in support of a national conservation movement. With Roosevelt's strong backing, passed the meat-ists had an effective leader who publicized the need for conservation and organized support for specific policies. Roosevelt was greatly influenced and assisted by the knowledgeable and dedicated Gifford Pinchot, who had become chief of the Bureau of Forestry in the Department of Agriculture in 1898. Pinchot probably had more influence on the conservation movement than any other single individual. Secondly, conservationists believed that a broad survey of the country's natural resources was necessary to determine their best use on a scientific, planned basis. Finally, most conservation leaders insisted that the federal government withdraw large areas of forest, mineral, and other lands from public entry.

Conservation leaders were concerned primarily with the scientific management and efficient use of natural resources. They wanted policy making and administrative matters in the hands of qualified technicians rather than those of politicians or pressure groups. Roosevelt said in 1908: "Let us remember that the conservation of natural resources . . . is yet but part of another and greater problem . . . the problem of national efficiency, the patriotic duty of insuring the safety and continuance of the Nation."

President Roosevelt declared in his first annual message to Congress that "the forest and water problems are perhaps the most vital internal problems of the United States." As noted earlier, he gave presidential support to passage of the National Reclamation Act in 1902. This law provided that funds from the sale of public lands in the West would be used to finance irrigation projects. Roosevelt was also deeply interested in expanding the federal forest reserves. Previous Presidents had withdrawn some forty-six million acres of forest lands under a law of 1891, but Roosevelt increased this figure to about one hundred fifty million acres. He also withdrew coal, oil, and phosphate lands from public sale. Besides this, he established five new national parks and some game preserves. Near the end of his administration, Roosevelt placed many of the best waterpower sites under federal control.

Theodore Roosevelt

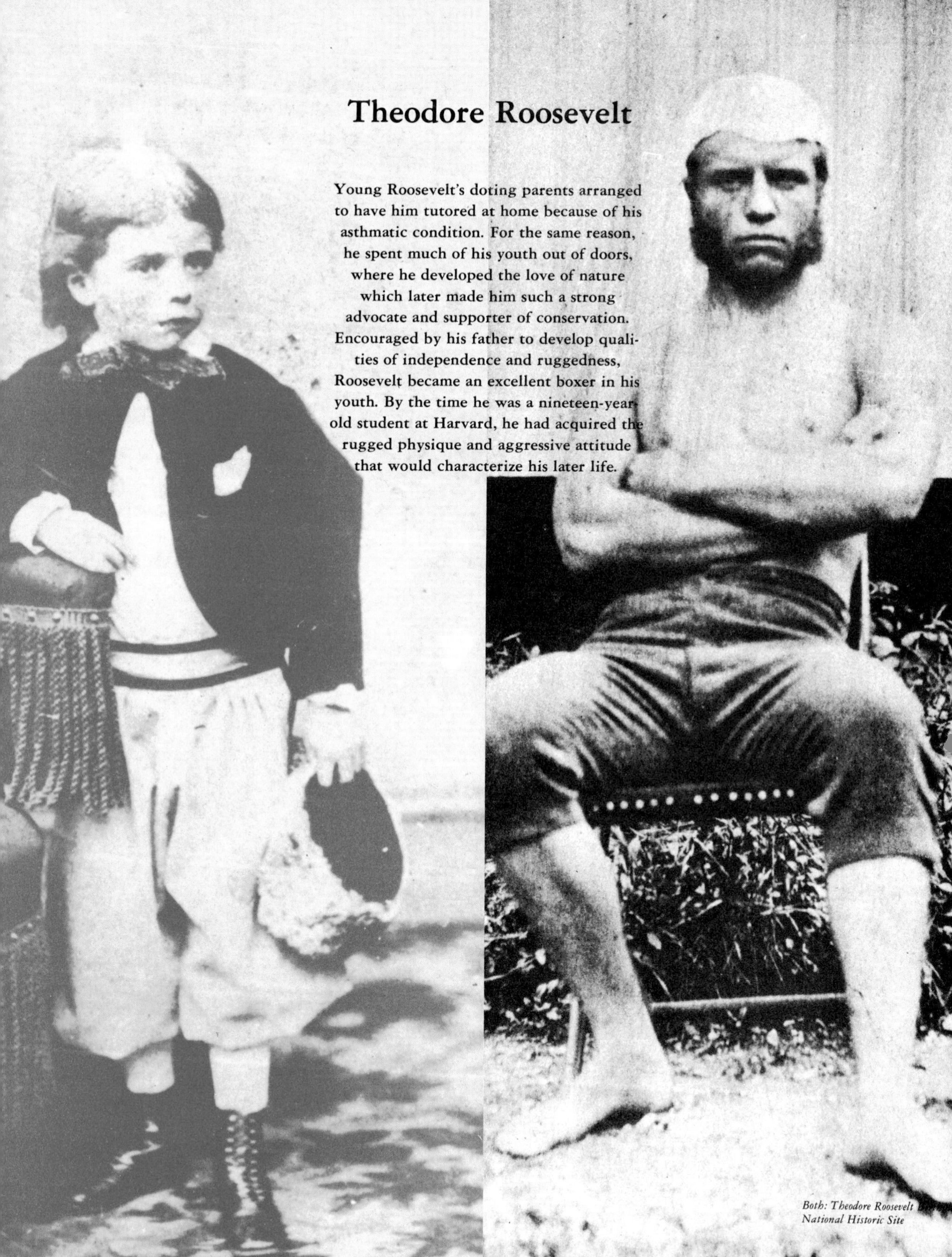

Young Roosevelt's doting parents arranged to have him tutored at home because of his asthmatic condition. For the same reason, he spent much of his youth out of doors, where he developed the love of nature which later made him such a strong advocate and supporter of conservation. Encouraged by his father to develop qualities of independence and ruggedness, Roosevelt became an excellent boxer in his youth. By the time he was a nineteen-year-old student at Harvard, he had acquired the rugged physique and aggressive attitude that would characterize his later life.

Both: Theodore Roosevelt Birthplace National Historic Site

Married to his second wife, Roosevelt took the role of doting husband and father of a growing family. One more son followed after the family group below was photographed.

Imaginary depictions of the Battle of San Juan Hill, like that at right, above, enhanced Roosevelt's image as a dashing hero. The actual "charge" appears in the photograph below.

Below: Courtesy of the American Museum of Natural History; right, above and below: Stefan Lorant Collection

An active sportsman, Roosevelt, expected his family, advisers, and associates to accompany him in his exercises. He and his family took long hikes at their Sagamore Hill estate (below), and he was a fierce rock climber in Washington's Rock Creek Park where reporters had a hard time keeping up (left). This love of the outdoors undoubtedly influenced his fight for conservation. At right, he attends the dedication of a redwood forest in California.

Left: Stefan Lorant Collection; below and right: Theodore Roosevelt Birthplace, National Historic Site

EEK
FOR PRESIDENT
BULL MOOSE
PARTY
Humpty Dumpty sat on the wall.
Humpty Dumpty had a bad fall.
All the ex-bosses
And Bully Moose men,
Can never put Humpty up again.
"MY BOY!"

As soon as his presidential term ended, Roosevelt left on an eleven-month hunting trip in Africa. When he finally returned to America, he found himself enthusiastically greeted by press and public alike, as the cartoon at far left demonstrates.

The rift between the conservatives and progressives in the Republican Party had become irreparable, and Roosevelt almost immediately jumped into the middle of the battle. Backed by the Progressives, he ran against Taft on the Bull Moose ticket and split the Republicans. The Bull Moose Party lived only briefly, however, ending with the defeat of Taft and Roosevelt by Woodrow Wilson.

Despite deep disappointment after his defeat in the 1912 election, Roosevelt continued to work and travel. The death of his son Quentin, an aviator in France, came as a serious blow, and six months later Roosevelt himself died. One of his last photographs shows him with his granddaughter.

Far left: Library of Congress; left: Stefan Lorant Collection; inset: Brown Brothers; right: Theodore Roosevelt Birthplace, National Historic Site

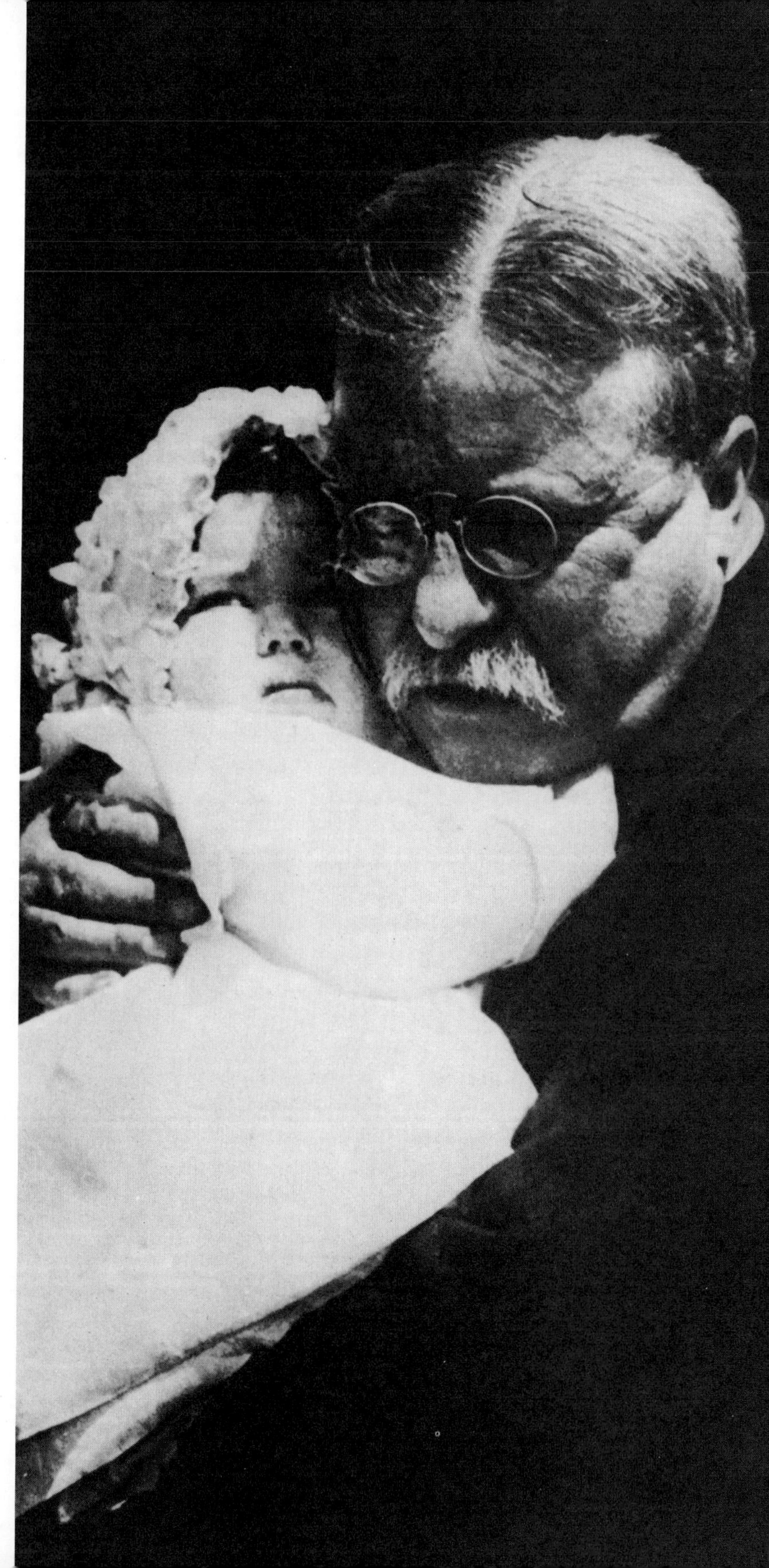

Theodore Roosevelt Birthplace, National Historic Si

Roosevelt's calling of the Governor's Conference on conservation in May, 1908, did much to publicize conservation programs and policies and led to the appointment of a National Conservation Commission later in the year. The Commission was instructed to prepare a general survey of the country's natural resources which could be used as a guide for developing additional public policies. By the end of his second administration Roosevelt faced stiff congressional opposition over his conservation program, but until he left office in 1909 he continued to achieve what he could through executive action alone.

Even the Panic of 1907 did not seem to diminish Roosevelt's popularity among the masses. The year 1907 began on a prosperous note, but by early spring the prices of commodities and securities had begun to decline. By early fall, money was tight and credit scarce. On October 22 the Knickerbocker Trust Company of New York closed its doors, and the next day panic selling struck the Stock Exchange. During the next few months bank and business failures plagued the economy. Fearing another catastrophe similar to that of the nineties, countless citizens, bankers included, demanded wholesale reform of the economy.

One direct result of the panic and financial crisis was passage of the Aldrich-Vreeland Act in 1908. This law permitted national banks to issue more currency and to relieve credit stringencies. But more important, the law provided for a Monetary Commission to study credit and monetary problems. This investigation, under the leadership of Senator Aldrich, revealed the need for major improvements in the nation's financial structure. Some of these needs were finally met in the Federal Reserve Act of 1913.

The panic of 1907 had been caused largely by excessive speculation in stocks and bonds, but Roosevelt's critics charged that his antibusiness attitude had destroyed business confidence and brought on the Panic. While the controversy raged for several months between the President and his opponents, Roosevelt became increasingly critical of big business. He declared on one occasion that the Panic had been caused by "the speculative folly and the flagrant dishonesty of a few men of great wealth." Indeed, during his last year in office, Roosevelt was much more outspoken against large, corporate enterprise than he had ever been before. He also advocated measures which most members of the business community strongly opposed. These included inheritance and federal income taxes, and the national incorporation of large firms engaged in interstate business. The country was becoming increasingly progressive by 1907 and 1908, and Roosevelt shifted with the dominant thought.

Roosevelt's Foreign Policy: Latin America

If Roosevelt's training and sympathies qualified him to lead the country along the road of domestic reform, he was equally well equipped to deal with foreign affairs. He had traveled to Europe several times and had not only observed European peoples and countries firsthand but had become personally acquainted with foreign political, diplomatic, and intellectual leaders. Probably no President since John Quincy Adams had a greater interest in, or better understanding of, European affairs. Moreover, Roosevelt had an internationalist outlook and believed that the United States should take a more active part in world affairs. Near the end of his Presidency, he wrote: "I wish that all Americans would realize . . . that we are and that we shall be involved in all great questions . . . the whole American people must become accustomed to this idea. They must be made to feel and understand these international interests."

Roosevelt understood that international influence depended in large measure on national power. To sustain the worldwide responsibilities he believed essential, Roosevelt advocated, first, a larger and more efficient Navy. As President he argued incessantly for increased naval appropriations and displayed some of the nation's sea power when, in 1907, he sent sixteen warships around the world. Secondly, Roosevelt lent support to Secretary of War Elihu Root's Army reforms. In 1901 Root established the Army War College, which provided special training for high command officers; and two years later Congress approved the Secretary's plan for an Army General Staff. Strongly nationalistic and even jingoistic at times, he believed in the superiority of Anglo-Saxon culture and reminded the British of their responsibility for order in Asia and Africa. Roosevelt did not hesitate to use force against lesser-developed peoples or countries in the Caribbean when he believed that nothing less would guarantee the American interests in the region.

The Spanish-American War had left the United States with far-flung interests in both Latin America and the Far East. Roosevelt's foreign policy in the Caribbean aimed at building and protecting a canal across Central America, stabilizing shaky governments in certain Latin American countries, discouraging intervention by any European power in the Western Hemisphere, and expanding the meaning of the Monroe Doctrine. Roosevelt was concerned especially with the achievement of political stability in the Caribbean area, where he considered the United States to have vital interests. The cornerstone of stability in the Caribbean was United States control over Cuba. After the Spanish defeat in 1898, United States military forces under General Leonard Wood ruled the island; and during the period of occupation, which ended in 1902, American authorities worked hard to improve sanitation, education, and other social conditions in Cuba. But even after the military withdrawal, American sentiment and interest called for some form of continuing control.

The Platt Amendment offered a solution to the problem of giving Cuba independence and at the same time retaining American influence and power in the island. The Platt Amendment contained eight major provisions, of which two appeared essential. The United States acquired the right to intervene in Cuba both to protect life and property and to preserve Cuban independence. Secondly, the amendment required Cuba to lease or sell to the United States land necessary for coaling or naval stations. The outcome of this stipulation was the United States acquisition of the naval base at Guantanamo. Cuban leaders strongly objected to the Platt Amendment, but they had no power to block it. Besides becoming a part of the Cuban constitution, the articles of the Platt Amendment became the subject of a formal treaty signed in May, 1903. For all practical purposes, Cuba thereby became a protectorate of the United States. Cuba also became heavily dependent upon United States markets and capital resources.

One of Roosevelt's major foreign-policy objectives in the Caribbean region was acquisition of the right to build an American-controlled canal across Central America. His concern over an interoceanic canal reflected a much older American idea which held that the United States had vital interests in that region. The immediate need for such a water route seemed clear enough. During the Spanish-American War the U.S.S. *Oregon* required ninety-eight days to sail from the West Coast around South America to join the Caribbean fleet off Cuba. Acquisition of colonies in both the Caribbean and the Pacific in 1899 stressed even further the desirability of a direct water route connecting the two oceans.

Before the United States could obtain the necessary canal rights, it required an abrogation of the old Clayton-Bulwer Treaty, signed with Great Britain in 1850. This agreement provided for joint control of any isthmian canal which either nation might build. In November, 1901, the Hay-Pauncefote Treaty ended the joint arrangement under the Clayton-Bulwer pact and thus opened the way for the United States to build and fortify its own canal. From that point onward Roosevelt played the dominant role in securing a route and beginning the construction of an isthmian canal.

Two routes, crossing either Nicaragua or Panama, were feasible. Initially, Roosevelt favored Nicaragua, as had the Walker Commission appointed by McKinley to investigate and recommend the best route. The cost of building across Panama had been made prohibitive by the demands of the New Panama Canal Company, headed by Philippe Bunau-Varilla. This Frenchman had become chief engineer of the old French company that had tried to dig a canal across Panama in the 1880s. By asking approximately $100 million dollars for the French rights and interests, Bunau-Varilla had boosted the total estimated price for digging across Panama to $60 million more than the cost of a canal through Nicaragua. But, realizing that United States construction across Nicaragua would destroy the value of his claim, Bunua-Varilla in 1902 cut the price of the French assets to $40 million and set out to persuade Congress and the President that the Panama route was the best available. In June, 1902, the Spooner Amendment substituted Panama for Nicaragua, provided that Colombia (of which Panama was a part) would approve the transaction and that the French would sell their interests for $40 million.

Without difficulty American negotiators secured the Hay-Herran Treaty with Colombia, which granted America permission to build a canal across Panama in return for a payment of $10 million outright, plus $250,000 a year in rental. But the Colombian congress rejected the treaty, chiefly because it thought the financial arrangements unsatisfactory. Rather than rely on further negotiation with the Colombian government, Roosevelt determined to move ahead unilaterally. He favored the seizure of Panamanian territory, whatever Colombian desires, but Bunau-Varilla's plotting rendered United States action unnecessary. The Frenchman arranged a so-called revolution, which took place in Panama on November 3, 1903. Aware of the approaching coup, Roosevelt had ordered United States naval vessels to be placed strategically where they could prevent Colombia from landing additional troops at Colon to put down the uprising. When Panama declared her independence from Colombia, the United States recognized the new government with indecent haste and, on November 18, signed a treaty with Panama. Bunau-Varilla represented the new republic. This treaty provided for a payment to Panama of $10 million, plus $250,000 annually, to begin after nine years, for a zone 10 miles wide. Moreover, the United States agreed to maintain the in-

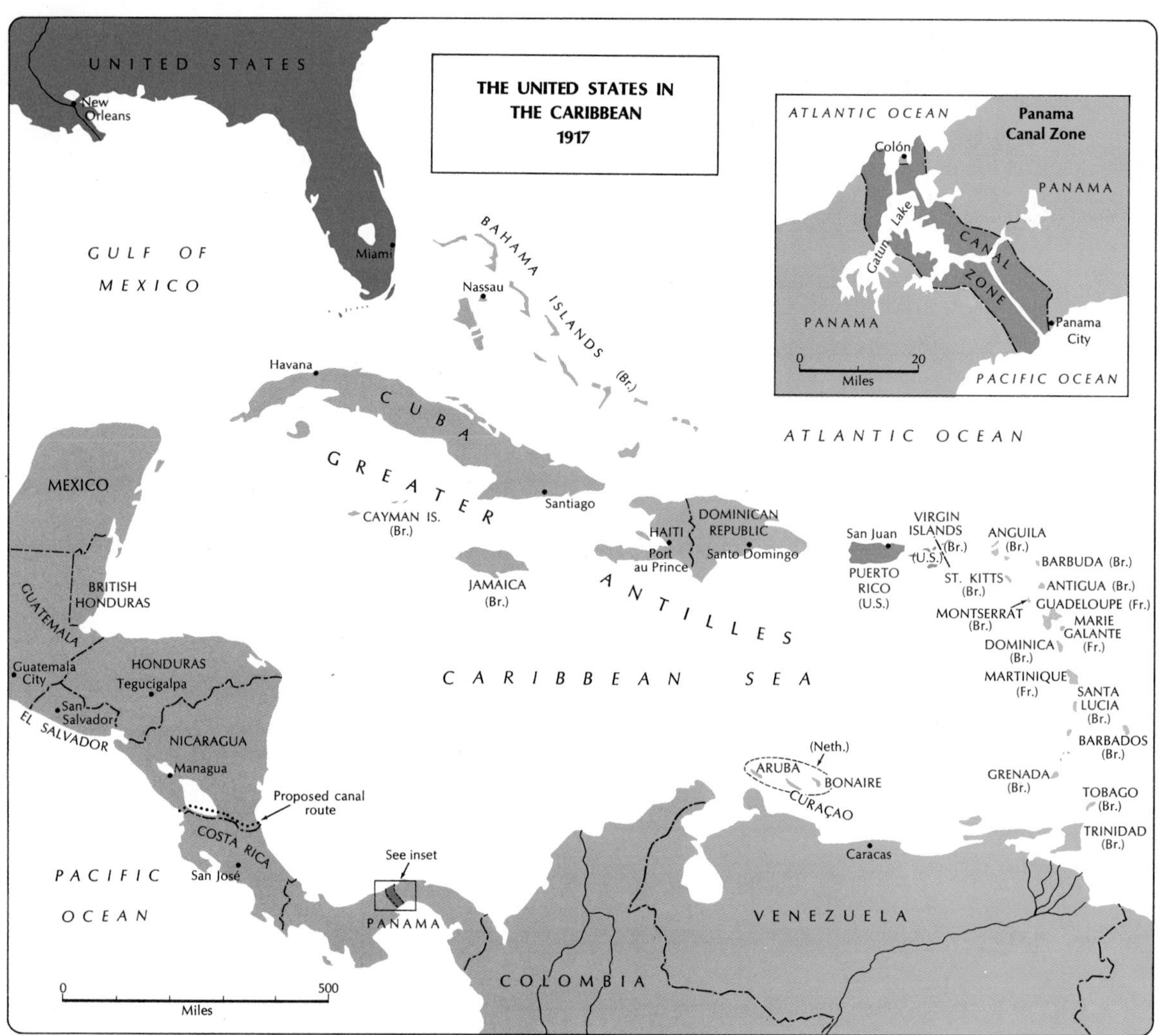

dependence of Panama, thus reducing that country, in effect, to the level of a protectorate.

Canal construction began in 1904. When the canal was opened for traffic in 1914, it had cost some $400 million. Although the Canal Zone became an anchor in the American defense perimeter in the Caribbean and it was a great boon to commerce, the methods by which Roosevelt achieved the American objectives aroused distrust and antagonism toward the United States throughout Latin America. Roosevelt never admitted that the United States had acted unethically. He believed firmly that Colombia had acted in bad faith and that the original treaty would have elevated Colombia to a position of major importance in

Latin American affairs. Convinced as well that the canal would serve the interests of the entire world, he insisted that his own actions, in securing the Canal Zone, were the correct ones.

During negotiations over the Panama Canal route, Roosevelt became involved in another diplomatic controversy, this time in Venezuela. For years the Venezuelans had contracted heavy debts to European and American creditors and had ignored demands for payment. In December, 1902, Germany and England, two of the largest creditors, decided to collect their debts by force. They blockaded five ports and fired some shots into Venezuelan harbors. The previously arrogant dictator, Cipriano Castro, now called on the United States to arbitrate the debt problem. Roosevelt, who was primarily concerned over the possibility of a German challenge to the principle of the Monroe Doctrine, urged that the Venezuelan dispute be settled by arbitration. England quickly agreed, and shortly Germany did the same. A mixed commission and the Hague Permanent Court of Arbitration finally settled the claims of the creditors. Roosevelt later said that he had forced the Germans to accept arbitration, but the President actually exaggerated his own role in the settlement. Nevertheless, Roosevelt had made it clear that the United States would not permit outside interference in the Western Hemisphere which might threaten the vital interests of the United States.

Roosevelt was extremely sensitive to the possibility of any foreign intervention in the Caribbean and Central American region, for he felt that any such interference would jeopardize American security. But only if the United States assumed the responsibility for maintaining political and economic stability in that area, he believed, could it prevent outside intervention. In May, 1904, he wrote: "If a nation shows that it knows how to act with decency in industrial and political matters, if it keeps order and pays its obligations, then it need fear no interference from the United States. Brutal wrong-doing, or an impotence which results in a general loosening of the ties of civilized society, may finally require intervention by some civilized nation, and in the Western Hemisphere the United States might act as a policeman, at least in the Caribbean region." Since then this has become known as the "Roosevelt Corollary" to the Monroe Doctrine.

Roosevelt soon had occasion to implement and test this policy in Santo Domingo. By 1903 that Caribbean nation had become virtually bankrupt and was heavily in debt to several major European powers. Foreign creditors had from time to time threatened to intervene. Roosevelt strongly opposed such a possibility and let it be known that, if any country intervened, it would be the United States. After an invitation from the Dominican president, Roosevelt did intervene early in 1905 and made an agreement whereby the United States would supervise the collection and disbursement of the country's customs receipts. Forty-five percent of the income was to be used for local government and fifty-five percent for the settlement of foreign debts. This arrangement worked satisfactorily, although the Senate refused to ratify it. In any event, the maintenance of political stability had become a basic objective of America's Caribbean and Canal diplomacy. The Roosevelt administration fulfilled this purpose in large measure by acquiring rights to the Panama Canal Zone, by maintaining a protectorate over Cuba, and by helping to guarantee order in small, unstable countries, including the colony of Puerto Rico.

Roosevelt was also vitally concerned with American interests in the Far East. He supported the Open Door policy in China, although both he and Secretary of State John Hay feared privately that the policy contained the seeds of overcommitment, and thus embarrassment, for the United States. What Roosevelt sought above all in the Far East was a balance among China, Japan, and Russia which would prevent any single combination of forces in the Orient from challenging this country's limited, but growing, interests there. At the same time that the United States attempted to develop its trade and protect the interests of China, it faced the task of guarding the Philippines. Japan, the rapidly rising power of the Far East, loomed as the long-run threat to the balance of power there, but in 1901 Russian expansion into Manchuria presented the immediate danger to peace in Asia and the territorial integrity of China. Although Roosevelt strongly opposed Russia's disrespect for the Open Door principles, he recognized that the United States did not have enough power in the Far East to change the course of events. This disturbed the President, for he was realist enough to know that successful policies required far more than bluff to underwrite them. However, he resorted with some success to diplomacy to achieve the American objective of limiting Russian influence in Manchuria through peaceful agreement.

Russian advances into Manchuria and finally into Korea came in direct conflict with Japanese interests in that area, and in 1904 war broke out between Japan and Russia. Roosevelt was pleased with the rapid-fire Japanese victories because, as he wrote his son, "for several years Russia has behaved very badly in the Far East, her attitude toward all nations, including us, but especially toward Japan, being grossly overbearing." Japan seemed to be defending the Open Door, or as Roosevelt put it, "Japan is playing our game." Roosevelt informed Germany and France that if they went to the aid of Russia, the United States would help Japan.

Roosevelt's central interest, however, lay in mediating the war. Aided by a major Japanese naval victory in May, 1905, Roosevelt managed, in August, to bring representatives of Japan and Russia to Portsmouth, New Hampshire, for a peace conference. The Japanese arrived with a strong diplomatic position. Their military forces had won the battles. They had, moreover, an unseen ally in Great Britain, with whom they had signed the Anglo-Japanese Alliance in 1902. A few days before the peace conference opened, Secretary of War Taft, on his way to the Philippines, met with Count Katsura, Premier of Japan, and agreed to what became known as the Taft-Katsura Memorandum. In this agreement, fully supported by Roosevelt, the United States approved of Japan's control over Korea, while Japan declared that she had no "aggressive designs whatever on the Philippines."

The Japanese acquired almost everything they demanded at Portsmouth, except a large cash indemnity. Russia recognized Japan's predominant interests in Korea, granted concessions to the Japanese in Liaotung, and gave Japan the southern half of Sakhalin Island. Both countries agreed to evacuate Manchuria. But Roosevelt would not support the Japanese demand for a $600 million cash payment from Russia. Consequently, despite the fact that Japan did make great gains, official and popular reactions to the treaty in Japan were extremely critical, and the Japanese held the United States responsible for their failure to receive a cash indemnity. The Treaty of Portsmouth, by greatly strengthening Japan in the Far East, was a major step toward upsetting the balance of power. By the time the treaty was signed, Roosevelt had second thoughts about his support of Japan. He had really hoped that Russia and Japan would each "have a moderative action on the other," but this now seemed unlikely. In the Root-Takahira agreement of 1908, the United States and Japan promised to maintain the status quo in the "region of the Pacific Ocean" and to respect the territorial possessions of one another in that area. This reflected again American concern for the protection of the Philippines, which lay outside the range of effective United States naval or military power.

Also during Roosevelt's administration, the United States worked out basic policies for governing the Philippines, its largest and most important colony. Most American officials, including Roosevelt, believed that before the Philippines could become self-governing or independent, they would have to remain under American tutelage for a long period. In 1901 Roosevelt appointed William Howard Taft as Governor General of the Islands, and in July of the next year Congress passed the Philippine Organic Act. This law designated the Philippines an "unorganized territory," placing it under the control of a Governor General and a commission, which had executive, legislative, and judicial powers. The commission arranged to redistribute some land to peasants—especially lands formerly held by the Catholic Church; sought to improve health and education; and inaugurated a variety of reforms.

Many Filipinos, however, wanted their freedom. When the United States permitted them an elective assembly in 1907, the Speaker of the House, Sergio Osmena, pleaded for immediate independence. Manuel Quezon was among other nationalists who resisted continued United States domination. While the Filipinos gained more self-government under Roosevelt, as well as under later Presidents (they got an independent upper house in the Jones Act of 1916), it was not until the late 1920s and early 1930s that widespread support for Philippine independence developed in the United States.

Conclusion

Theodore Roosevelt, as President of the United States, left an indelible impression on the American consciousness. His administration was one of the three or four most active and dynamic in the nation's experience before 1909. It led the nation, sometimes fumblingly, into a new course of governmental responsibility and economic reform at home and into new ventures abroad, especially in the Caribbean. Roosevelt's relations with the Far East, if unprecedented, at least revealed that he possessed a clear conviction that the means and the ends of policy must be kept in balance. What guided Roosevelt generally was his acceptance of limits to his sphere of action. Early in his administration he agreed to demand nothing of the Republican party that would endanger its unity. He often needled the Republican Old Guard; he never defied it. He accepted, in large measure, what the Republican leadership in Congress could give him, not what he might have obtained from a more liberal coalition of Republicans and Democrats.

Roosevelt's reforms were considerable. Moreover, they pointed the direction to greater reforms under future administrations. Finally, Roosevelt managed to carry his party almost unscathed through a period of intense public criticism of American business—and the Republican party, more than the Democratic, was the party of business. By voicing with considerable passion the sentiments of progressivism, Roosevelt grounded much of the nation's ire which would normally have struck the Republican party. This, in itself, was a remarkable political achievement, as well as an unheralded service to the Republican party. It revealed again the unusual deftness which Roosevelt displayed in his management of the presidential office.

SUGGESTED READINGS

George E. Mowry's *The Era of Theodore Roosevelt, 1900–1912** (1958) is the best survey of progressivism in the early twentieth century. Eric F. Goldman's *Rendezvous with Destiny: A History of Modern American Reform** (1952) interprets progressivism by considering reform thought, while *The Age of Reform: From Bryan to F. D. R.** (1955) by Richard Hofstadter finds much of the impetus for reform in what he calls "the status revolution."

Among the excellent books dealing with progressivism at the state level are George E. Mowry's *The California Progressives** (1951); R. S. Maxwell's *La Follette and the Rise of the Progressives in Wisconsin* (1956); H. L. Warner's *Progressivism in Ohio, 1897–1917* (1964); R. E. Noble's *New Jersey Progressives before Wilson* (1946); and L. G. Geiger's *Joseph W. Folk of Missouri* (1953). On some of the urban reformers see T. L. Johnson's *My Story* (1911); F. C. Howe's *Confessions of a Reformer** (1925); and Fremont Older's *My Own Story* (1925). The contributions of Brand Whitlock have been well described by J. Tager in *Intellectual as Urban Reformer* (1968). Also see *The Autobiography of William Allen White* (1946); Herbert Croly's *The Promise of American Life** (1909); Lincoln Steffens's *The Autobiography of Lincoln Steffens* (1931); and Ira Kipnis's *The American Socialist Movement, 1897–1912* (1952).

General economic and social conditions can be followed in H. U. Faulkner's *The Decline of Laissez Faire, 1897–1917* (1951) and *The Quest for Social Justice, 1898–1914* (1931). Evaluations of the role of the business community in reform can best be studied in Robert H. Wiebe's *Businessmen and Reform: A Study of the Progressive Movement* (1962) and Gabriel Kolko's *The Triumph of Conservatism: A Reinterpretation of American History, 1900–1916** (1963), which argues that business interests directed the course of events much along the lines they desired. Robert Morlan deals with the growing radicalism in some rural areas in *Political Prairie Fire: The Nonpartisan League, 1915–1922* (1951).

The Muckrakers have been interpreted by Louis Filler in *Crusaders for American Liberalism* (1939); in C. C. Regier's *The Era of the Muckrakers* (1932); and in D. M. Chalmers's *The Social and Political Ideas of the Muckrakers** (1964). Elmer Ellis has written an admirable biography of Finley Peter Dunne, the nation's wit and censor during the progressive period, entitled *Mr. Dooley's America* (1941). On specific reforms see James H. Timberlake's *Prohibition and the Progressive Movement, 1900–1920* (1963); Roy Lubove's *The Urban Community: Housing and Planning in the Progressive Era** (1967) and *The Progressives and the Slums: Tenement House Reform in New York City, 1890–1917* (1963); Aileen S. Kraditor's *The Ideas of the Woman Suffrage Movement, 1890–1920* (1965); and Allen F. Davis's *Spearheads for Reform: The Social Settlements and the Progressive Movement, 1890–1914* (1967). On the position of the Negro, see August Meier's *Negro Thought in America, 1880–1915: Racial Ideologies in the Age of Booker T. Washington** (1963); F. L. Broderick's *W. E. B. Du Bois: Negro Leader in a Time of Crisis** (1959); W. E. B. Du Bois's *Dusk of Dawn* (1940); and part of John H. Franklin's *From Slavery to Freedom** (2d ed., 1956).

For biographical studies of Theodore Roosevelt see W. H. Harbaugh's *Power and Responsibility: The Life and Times of Theodore Roosevelt** (1961), which is comprehensive but friendly in tone; Henry Pringle's *Theodore Roosevelt** (1931), which was the standard biography for many years; and the short, lively interpretation by J. M. Blum, *The Republican Roosevelt** (1954). One of the best ways to gain an understanding of Roosevelt is to read *The Letters of Theodore Roosevelt* (8 vols., 1951–1954), edited by E. E. Morison and others. Mowry has also analyzed Roosevelt's role as a progressive in *Theodore Roosevelt and the Progressive Movement** (1946).

On the question of monopoly and business concentration during the Roosevelt administration see Charles R. Van Hise's *Concentration and Control: A Solution to the Trust Problem in the United States* (1912). Pure food and drug legislation has been well covered by O. E. Anderson in *The Health of a Nation: Harvey W. Wiley and the Fight for Pure Food* (1958). Labor problems have been considered in *The Anthracite Coal Strike of 1902* (1957) by R. J. Cornell and Marc Karson's *American Labor Unions and Politics, 1900–1918* (1958). On conservation, *The Gospel of Efficiency: The Progressive Conservation Movement, 1890–1920* (1959) by S. P. Hays is excellent, as is *The Politics of Conservation, Crusades and Controversies, 1897–1913* (1962) by E. R. Richardson. One of the best accounts of the struggles over conservation policy can be found in M. N. McGeary's *Gifford Pinchot: Forester Politician* (1960).

The best account of Roosevelt's foreign policy is Howard K. Beale's *Theodore Roosevelt and the Rise of America to World Power** (1956). His policies are also dealt with in H. C. Hill's *Roosevelt and the Caribbean* (1927); W. H. Callcott's *The Caribbean Policy of the United States, 1890–1920* (1942); D. C. Miner's *The Fight for the Panama Route* (1940); Dexter Perkins's *The United States and the Caribbean* (1947); and A. L. P. Dennis's *Adventures in American Diplomacy* (1928). On the Far East see A. W. Griswold's *The Far Eastern Policy of the United States** (1938); P. J. Treat's *Diplomatic Relations between the United States and Japan, 1895–1905* (1938); *Theodore Roosevelt and the Japanese-American Crises* (1934) by T. A. Bailey; and F. R. Dulles's *America's Rise to World Power, 1898–1954** (1955).

*indicates availability in paperback.

28

High Tide of Reform: Taft and Wilson

REPUBLICAN STRENGTH AND UNITY, so evident during and after the election of 1904, continued through the presidential campaign of 1908. The highly popular Roosevelt was in full command of the party and could have won another nomination had he wanted it. But Roosevelt refused to be considered for what he assumed would be a third term, although he played a major role in naming his successor and carrying the party to victory again. Even as William Howard Taft entered the White House, however, the growing divergence between Republican progressives and conservatives forecast trouble for the Republican organization. Unfortunately, Taft lacked the flexibility and political skill to deal successfully with the intraparty conflicts. His refusal to support more advanced reform measures and his split with Roosevelt over both personal and policy matters finally produced Republican divisions which opened the way for the victory of Democrat Woodrow Wilson in 1912.

Wilson had won a reputation for strong, courageous leadership as Governor of New Jersey; and by the end of the 1912 campaign he had become committed to progressive principles. A strong, effective executive who believed in the need for continued economic and social reform, Wilson was an ideal leader to push the cause of progressivism beyond its achievements under Roosevelt and Taft. The first Wilson administration witnessed the final triumph of the progressive movement before the demands of war engulfed the waning reform.

Following his thumping victory in 1904, Roosevelt announced that "under no circumstances will I be a candidate for or accept another nomination." Although counting himself out as a candidate in 1908, Roosevelt had no intention of permitting an open convention. Several months before the Republicans met, Roosevelt made clear his preference for his Secretary of War, William Howard Taft. With Roosevelt's backing, Taft captured the convention vote on the first ballot. Having lost heavily with a conservative candidate in 1904, the Democrats nominated William Jennings Bryan for a third time. By 1908 Bryan had gone far toward reuniting the Democratic party which had been divided so deeply during the 1890s. Bryan's continued leadership was based on his party loyalty, large personal following, and dramatic airing of national issues. Although the Democratic platform was more progressive than its Republican counterpart, again the Republicans won an impressive victory. Taft's popular majority was 1.2 million; the electoral count was 321 to 162. The Republicans maintained their large majorities in the House and Senate. Despite Bryan's third defeat, the Democrats were in a stronger position than at any time since 1892, and continued Republican dominance would depend upon Taft's skill in maintaining a reasonable degree of party harmony. But it was in his role as party chief that Taft experienced his greatest failure.

William Howard Taft brought not only unquestioned ability but also a wide variety of experience to the White House. Born in 1857 at Cincinnati, he was graduated from Yale and then studied law. He held a number of judicial posts before McKinley selected him to head the Philippine Commission in 1900. The next year Taft became the first civil Governor of the islands. In 1904 Roosevelt appointed him Secretary of War. Taft and Roosevelt were close personal friends; often the President used Taft as a troubleshooter for the administration. Taft was a large, good-natured, easygoing, affectionate, modest, and tolerant man. He weighed 326 pounds in 1906, when he returned home from a trip to the Philippines, but by strenuous dieting he reduced his weight to 250 pounds within a short time. Deliberate in both thought and action, Taft preferred a calm, judicious approach to problems rather than a hasty impetuosity.

Many of Taft's troubles in the Presidency stemmed from his personality. He had little interest in the hustle and bustle of politics and once wrote his wife: "Politics, when I am in it, makes me sick." He was not aggressive and disliked many of the activities expected of a President. Taft's chief shortcoming as President, however, was his failure to respond to the country's progressive sentiment. He was basically conservative. His progressive ideas had reached their limit by 1907, before his election, and his thinking on political principles and economic reform thereafter remained largely static. Taft, in fact, seemed to become more conservative as his administration progressed. Unfortunately for Taft and his reputation as President, a large faction within the Republican party, along with many Democrats, were moving toward more advanced progressivism. Taft's weakness as President, then, centered around his basic conservatism, which was accentuated by a lack of compromise, flexibility, and political finesse.

In his inaugural address Taft pledged "the maintenance and enforcement" of the major Roosevelt reforms. Hewing close to the Republican platform, Taft called for regulation of big business and recommended "proper federal supervision and restriction" of abuses in stock and bond sales. Emphasizing the need for conservation of resources, he explained that saving the forests and improving waterways were "proper governmental functions which must involve large expenditures if properly performed." He promised reform of the banking laws to secure greater elasticity in the forms of "currency available for trade." Even a postal savings bank, he said, would "not be unwise or excessive paternalism." Taft also suggested greater protection for workingmen against industrial abuses. He devoted considerable attention to the Negro question and demanded a downward revision of the tariff. Here was a call for moderate progressivism along the lines already laid down by Roosevelt. At the close of the President's speech, Roosevelt grasped his hand and said: "God bless you, old man. It is a great state document." The two friends seemed as close as ever. A few days later, on March 23, 1909, Roosevelt sailed for an African hunting trip. By no means a Roosevelt fan, J. P. Morgan, it was reported, urged every lion to do its duty!

Never quite at home in the White House, Taft was left to implement a progressive program as leader of a party already showing signs of internal dissension. Differences between Taft and the progressive Republicans became clearly evident in the fight over tariff revision, a troublesome political question which Roosevelt had studiously avoided. But Taft was committed to modifying the Dingley law of 1897, and he intended to carry out the platform and his campaign promises. Introduced in the House by Representative Henry C. Payne, the new bill lowered tariff duties substantially. But in the Senate, the proposed lower tariff schedules were modified beyond recognition. Senator Aldrich proposed scores of amendments raising rates on such important products as lumber, iron, and textiles. Angered at the Aldrich proposals, a group of Midwestern progressives, including Senator La Follette, bitterly fought the amendments. More than tariff rates were at stake. To these insurgents Aldrich symbolized Eastern industrial and moneyed interests which were exploiting Western farmers.

The Senate fight over the tariff placed Taft in a difficult position. He could accept the views of Aldrich and the Senate majority, even though he opposed their rates; or he could support the insurgents and uphold his principles. But the President had nothing in common with the Westerners and really did not understand them. He used his influence to moderate some of the highest schedules. But when the bill came to his desk, he signed it against the wishes of the Western progressives. Later he blundered badly when he told a crowd at Winona, Minnesota, that "on the whole . . . I think the Payne bill is the best bill that the Republican Party ever passed." Taft's praise of the law in a region which had opposed the measure indicated his lack of political judgment and sagacity. Actually, the Payne-Aldrich tariff was more important politically than economically. Its main influence was to divide the Republican party. Western progressives fumed at Taft and accused him of siding with Eastern reactionaries and special interests. Already some progressives complained that Taft had sold out to Aldrich, Cannon, and the Old Guard and in the process had abandoned the Roosevelt policies.

To these progressive Republicans who were

beginning to distrust Taft, the Ballinger-Pinchot controversy seemed to be clinching evidence that the President was betraying Roosevelt and progressive principles. Several background events led up to the dispute over conservation policies in 1909. In the first place, Roosevelt and many of his friends hoped that Taft would retain James A. Garfield, son of former President Garfield and a strong conservationist, as Secretary of the Interior. Taft, however, named Richard A. Ballinger, a Seattle lawyer. Ballinger had served for a time as Land Commissioner under Roosevelt, and his appointment initially received general approval. Very shortly after he took office, however, Ballinger restored to private entry some of the Western lands which had been withdrawn the last months of the Roosevelt administration, and placed them in the public domain. A lawyer with deep respect for the law, Ballinger claimed that his predecessors had set aside these lands illegally. Taft agreed. Many ardent conservationists, however, became skeptical of Ballinger's and Taft's devotion to conservation. Gifford Pinchot, Roosevelt's good friend and chief of the Forest Service, became especially critical of Ballinger.

When charges against Ballinger were presented to Taft, he rejected the idea that his Secretary of the Interior had done anything legally or morally wrong or that he was unfriendly to conservation. Pinchot, however, continued to attack the administration and called Ballinger "the most effective opponent the conservation policies have yet had." Taft was now faced with the difficult problem of dealing with an embarrassing fight within his official family. Since the President believed that Ballinger was a loyal conservationist and had done nothing wrong, he dismissed Pinchot summarily early in 1910, ignoring warnings that the dismissal of Pinchot would alienate the Roosevelt people and thus injure the party. The Ballinger-Pinchot controversy drove a wedge between the Taft administration and Roosevelt's followers. Taft regretted this and wrote that he hoped not to create a "rupture" with Roosevelt, but Pinchot hurried to Africa and told his former chief that Taft had betrayed conservation. At home some of Roosevelt's friends already contemplated passing up Taft in 1912 and again supporting Roosevelt for President.

Despite the charges, Taft's record on conservation was in fact excellent. In some areas he even exceeded what Roosevelt had done. In 1909 he withdrew more than 3 million acres of oil land in California and Wyoming from all forms of public entry. The Withdrawal Act of 1910 gave the President specific authority to take back land from any private ownership; this provided the legal authority to do what Roosevelt had already done by executive action.

That event which best reflected the growing division in Republican ranks came early in 1910, when the insurgents challenged the power of the Speaker of the House, Joseph Cannon. Led by a young Republican from Nebraska, George W. Norris, the insurgents moved to amend the rules of the House in several important ways. They wanted to exclude the Speaker from the powerful Committee on Rules, which controlled the flow of legislation in the House; to enlarge the committee; and to make the committee elective rather than appointive by the Speaker. These proposed changes threw the House into an uproar. Cannon and his conservative backers tried every tactic and strategy to defeat the measures, but a coalition of insurgent Republicans and Democrats finally passed them after a hectic twenty-nine-hour session. This was a victory for legislative reform, but the bitter fight was to leave deep and lingering scars on the Republican party.

By 1910 it was obvious that Taft had failed as a political leader. No longer heading a united party, he now leaned openly toward the conservatives and ignored most of his progressive support. The midterm elections of 1910 merely aggravated these Republican divisions. In a number of strong Republican states the most heated campaigns occurred in the primaries, where progressives fought conservatives for control of the party machinery. These internal divisions, plus a general dissatisfaction with Taft, led to disaster for the Republicans in the fall elections. Democrats swept to victory in the House of Representatives by a margin of 226 to 161. Champ Clark of Missouri became the new Speaker of the House in 1911.

Taft's decline as President resulted less from his failures than from his inability to dramatize his achievements. Taft once complained that he lacked glamour. During his administration, progressivism continued unabated, but most people seemed to see only the President's mistakes. Nonetheless, the Taft administration instituted more suits against industrial monopolies under the Sherman Antitrust Act than "trustbuster" Roosevelt had done. Suits begun against the American Tobacco Company and Standard Oil under Roosevelt were concluded in 1911. That same year Taft began proceedings against the United States Steel Corporation. He also supported the Mann-Elkins Act of 1910, which strengthened the power of the Interstate Commerce Commission.

President Taft gave his backing to a variety of other reforms. The law establishing Postal Savings Banks, which had been advocated for many years, was finally enacted in 1910. "I am as pleased as Punch," Taft said upon signing the bill; "it is one of the great Congressional accomplishments." Establishment of a parcel post system in January, 1913, was of special moment to farmers, because thereafter they, with others, could have packages delivered with their other mail. In 1912 a Children's Bureau was set up in the Department of Commerce and Labor to deal with "matters pertaining to the welfare of children and child life among all classes of our people." One of Taft's last acts as President on March 4, 1913, was to sign a bill creating a separate Department of Labor. Congress passed the Mann Act in 1910, which made it illegal to transport women across state lines for immoral purposes. Also in 1910 Congress passed the first law enacted to require representatives to publicize their campaign expenses; the next year Congress extended this obligation to senators. An important, but little-known, measure was passed in 1911, forbidding the use of white phosphorus in the manufacture of matches. This chemical had resulted in a high incidence of disease among workers in American match factories. The Seventeenth Amendment to the Constitution, providing for the direct election of senators, was submitted to the states for ratification in 1912 and became effective the following year. New Mexico and Arizona were admitted as the forty-seventh and forty-eighth states in 1912. Taft also lent some support to the income tax amendment, the Sixteenth. This amendment became part of the Constitution in February, 1913, a few days before Taft left the White House. In the long run, the federal income tax was of tremendous economic and social importance. It provided the revenue needed to meet the cost of expanding government services and endowed the federal government with the power to equalize income.

Foreign Affairs under Taft

When Taft became President in 1909, the jingoism and expansionism of the Spanish-American War period had largely disappeared. Whereas Taft had a deep interest in American affairs abroad, he intended to avoid crises and conflicts which would require the application of American power. There were occasions during his administration when he used American troops to implement foreign policy, but he preferred legal and diplomatic processes to any show of force. His Secretary of State, Philander C. Knox, was an able lawyer who had served both McKinley and Roosevelt as Attorney General. Like Taft, Knox was strongly devoted to peace and order and opposed to adventurism in diplomacy.

Except in the Caribbean region, American external relations remained calm and peaceful during the four Taft years. Taft ignored the warning of intellectuals who cited the European balance of power as the nation's greatest historic concern. Believing rather that the United States should abstain from any political or diplomatic entanglements in Europe, Taft kept clear of the growing conflicts there which were driving the great powers toward war.

Toward Asia and Latin America, where the gains from intervention promised to outweigh the costs, Taft's policies were scarcely isolationist at all. Taft and Knox were convinced that they could stimulate American overseas trade and investment without running any risks of conflict or war. Taft defined his fundamental objectives in 1910: "We believe it to be of the utmost importance that while our foreign policy should not be turned a hair's breadth from the straight path of justice, it may well be made to include active intervention to secure for our merchandise and our capitalists opportunity for profitable investment. . . . There is nothing inconsistent in the promotion of peaceful relations, and the promotion of trade relations." In the Far East, Taft attempted to maintain and even to strengthen the Open Door policy, but he assumed he could achieve this goal by reliance on economic rather than military means. It was in the Caribbean – Central American area, a region which Taft and Knox considered vitally important to American political and economic interests, that the United States supplemented economic with military power to achieve its objectives. It was here that Taft implemented his so-called Dollar Diplomacy with positive action.

Taft, like Roosevelt before him, believed that political and economic stability in the region of the Caribbean was essential for the security of the United States. The building of the Panama Canal emphasized the strategic interests of the United States in that portion of the hemisphere. Except as a last resort, however, Taft would refrain from the use of force to achieve peace and political order in the small Latin American republics. American investments alone, he believed, would assure the stability which he sought. Furthermore, such investments would remove any threat of intervention by foreign creditors. After American bankers had made investments in any of these republics, the State Department could use its power and influence to protect the investors from revolution and possible default. If peace and order proved to be too elusive for diplomatic means alone, then the President could resort to actual armed intervention, but even then it would be limited to the support of governments friendly to American investments. Taft characterized this policy as one of "substituting dollars for bullets."

Despite outward appearances, Dollar Diplomacy did not represent simply the selfish use of a pliant State Department by United States investment bankers. In most cases government officials urged investors to make loans against their will to unsettled Latin American countries. Having succumbed to this pressure, the bankers expected, logically, that the State Department would support them by guarding their investments. Despite the general lack of formal treaty guarantees, United States capital flowed into Latin America in considerable volume during the early years of the twentieth century. In Latin America, the United States possessed the power to implement its policies, but in so doing it angered and alienated those Latin Americans who resented the resulting interference in their internal affairs.

Under the principle of Dollar Diplomacy, the Taft administration extended United States commitments in the Far East far beyond what the Roosevelt administration had regarded as acceptable. Willard Straight, the American consul general at Mukden, Manchuria, feared that Japanese encroachment following the Russo-Japanese War would undermine both the Chinese and the American interests in Manchuria unless the United States adopted a strong anti-Japanese policy. In 1908 he had recommended to Elihu Root, Roosevelt's Secretary of State, that the United States support a railroad project in Manchuria which would offer competition to the Japanese-controlled South Manchurian Railway. Root had recognized in this proposal a clear infringement on the Japanese sphere of interest and had refused to support it. Meanwhile in the State Department, Third Assistant Secretary Huntington Wilson, whose views toward Manchuria coincided with those of Straight, had converted a department circular on the Open Door into a long indictment of Japan. Root, still unwilling to embark on any anti-Japanese policy, struck out the indictment. Roosevelt and Root had no desire to give Japan a completely free hand in Manchuria, but neither did they intend to commit the United States to a crusade against Japanese expansion. Shortly before leaving the White House, Roosevelt advised his successor to avoid trouble with Japan "by preventing the occurrence of conditions that would invite war. . . ."

But in 1909 the Taft administration quickly converted the Open Door principle into an anti-Japanese weapon. As the representative of an American investment group, Straight now proposed the formation of a Chinchow-Aigun railway in Manchuria, again designed to offer direct competition to the Japanese line. For Taft this reliance on investment as a device to ease the Japanese out of Manchuria was a logical extension of Dollar Diplomacy. As he expressed it, "The nations that finance the great Chinese railroads and other enterprises will be foremost in the affairs of China, and the participation of American capital . . . will give the voice of the United States more authority in that country, which will go far toward the preservation of the administrative entity of China." Already the project for applying Dollar Diplomacy to China was at hand. In 1909, a group of French, German, and English bankers, supported by their governments, arranged a loan to aid China in the construction of the Hukuang Railway in southern China. Knox insisted that the United States was equally concerned with the development of China and demanded that New York bankers be permitted to share in the China loan.

Then in November, 1909, Secretary Knox extended this investment concept to a neutralization proposal which would place all Manchurian railroads under international control and thereby undermine Japan's growing economic interest in South Manchuria. Roosevelt warned Taft and Knox that their effort to commit the United States to a sharply anti-Japanese policy in Manchuria would either involve the nation in a policy of bluff or endanger Japan's interests so completely that it would lead to war. "The 'open door' policy in China," he wrote to Taft in December, 1910, "was an excellent thing, and will I hope be a good thing in the future, so far as it can be maintained by a general diplomatic agreement; but as has been proved by the whole history of Manchuria, alike under Russia and Japan, the 'open-door' policy, as a matter of fact, completely disappears as soon as a powerful nation determines to disregard it, and is willing to run the risk of war rather than forego its intention." The neutralization proposal had the effect of driving the Japanese and Russians into one bloc, and in 1910 the two powers signed an agreement whereby they pledged to support one another in their respective spheres of influence.

With the collapse of the neutralization scheme, Knox turned to the bankers' consortium and, in 1911, negotiated a portion of a loan for American investors. But in 1912 Japan and Russia again undermined Knox's ambitions, when they entered the consortium and immediately ruled out all loans which would interfere with their economic interests in Manchuria. Taft's application of Dollar Diplomacy to China proved to be an immediate failure and an ultimate disaster. The United States did not have the power, or even the intent, to support the investment and commercial Open Door in Manchuria against the special and greater interests of other powers. Yet Taft and his advisers had committed the nation so completely to the principle of the Open Door in China that they, in effect, had placed the United States and Japan on a collision course from which neither could withdraw.

In his last annual message to Congress on December 3, 1912, Taft summarized the nation's foreign policy: "The relations of the United States with all foreign powers remain upon a sound basis of peace, harmony, and friendship." The United States, he continued, had given support to trade, had helped to preserve stability in Latin America, and had worked for peace. "We have emerged full grown as a peer in the great concourse of nations," he concluded. "We are now in a larger relation with broader rights of our own and obligations to others than ourselves."

But Taft's administration, despite its emphasis on peaceful processes, had planted the seeds of future trouble. His policies, set in open defiance of warnings by the nation's leading intellectuals, had cast American diplomacy in a dangerous Asia-first mold. Taft rejected the idea that an enduring European balance of power had given the American people a century of almost absolute security at little or no cost to themselves. That security, some said, would not survive a British defeat at the hands of Germany in Europe's approaching war. It was in Europe, then, that the critical interests of the United States were at stake, and those interests demanded a positive American policy designed to protect the historic European balance of power. But the Taft administration, in extending United States open door commitments into Manchuria, largely in an effort to block the Japanese, had neglected the deeper, more critical challenge of Europe completely.

When Theodore Roosevelt returned from his world trip on June 18, 1910, a large and enthusiastic crowd welcomed him in New York. Republicans anxiously awaited his choice of position in the struggle between Taft and the progressives, but the former President carefully avoided any public commitments. Yet it was clear that Roosevelt returned from abroad with a decided coolness toward his successor, the result possibly of Taft's decision to dismiss some key Roosevelt appointees, the unfriendly editorials regarding Roosevelt written by the President's brother, and Taft's known antagonism toward some of Roosevelt's old friends. At first Roosevelt tried to avoid an open break with the President. Republican disunity, he knew, would only help the Democrats, and Roosevelt detested Democrats.

Roosevelt's Western speaking tour in the summer of 1910 widened the growing gulf between him and Taft. It is not clear why he made the tour, but his words had very important results. They threw Roosevelt into the national limelight and dropped the President from popular attention. Even more important was the fact that Roosevelt now gave stronger support than ever before to progressive ideas: in his numerous speeches and interviews he identified himself with the vanguard of progressivism. His views were best summarized in his noted speech entitled "The New Nationalism," delivered at Osawatomie, Kansas, late in August, 1910.

Roosevelt declared that he stood for "the square deal." He insisted that all groups must have justice but argued that "property shall be the servant and not the master of the commonwealth." The people, he said, must effectively control big business. To achieve this end, Roosevelt recommended "publicity of corporate affairs," prohibition of corporate funds for political purposes, and stricter government supervision of large enterprises engaged in interstate commerce. He also advocated both a graduated income tax and an inheritance tax. Turning to the problems of labor, Roosevelt declared that workmen's compensation and child-labor laws, as well as legislation to enforce better sanitary and safety conditions, were needed for workers. He demanded more extensive conservation measures and political reforms "to make our political representatives more quickly and sensitively responsive to the people." Roosevelt explained that he was not asking "for overcentralization; but I do ask," he said, "that we work in a spirit of broad and far-reaching nationalism when we work for what concerns our people as a whole." The interests of all the people, he said, could be effectively guarded only by the national government. Here Roosevelt merely repeated what he had read in Herbert Croly's *The Promise of American Life* (1909).

Roosevelt's discussion of public issues revealed above all his grasp of the programs and ideas current in progressive thought. Indeed, many conservatives considered him nothing less than radical. His observations on the use of private property for the welfare of all, his support for labor, his implied criticism of the courts, and his call for greatly expanded national powers all seemed dangerously leftish to conservatives.

By late 1910 many progressive Republicans had become firmly convinced that Taft must be replaced by a strong progressive candidate in 1912. The first formal step toward this end occurred in January, 1911, when a group of anti-Taft Republicans met at the home of Senator La Follette in Washington and formed the National Progressive Republican League. Officially the League's object was to promote "popular government and progressive legislation," but it soon became clear that the group's chief purpose was to push the presidential candidacy of Senator La Follette. In June, La Follette announced officially that he would seek the Republican nomination in 1912. During the succeeding months he campaigned throughout the Midwest, greeted everywhere by large crowds. La Follette was a tried and proven progressive, and it was apparent that he enjoyed wide, popular support.

But it was also apparent that many progressives who argued openly for La Follette's nomination hoped privately that Roosevelt would seek the nomination on a progressive platform. After the urging of his many friends, the former President responded to a request from eight governors on February 24, 1912, "My hat is in the ring." "I will accept the nomination for President," he wrote, "if it is tendered to me." Progressives now tumbled over one another to join the Roosevelt forces.

La Follette was bitter at this turn of events and charged Roosevelt with using him as a stalking horse to test the popularity of progressivism. In actuality, however, Roosevelt was the choice of the vast majority of Progressive Republicans. In the states where people had a chance to express themselves on convention delegates, Roosevelt men won consistently. Roosevelt's critics, however, refused to accept this view; they charged that he had destroyed party harmony in his mad quest for power. One detractor scoffed at Roosevelt in a parody on the Apostles' Creed:

> I believe in Theodore Roosevelt, maker of noise and strife, and in ambition his only creed (My Lord). He was born of the love of power and suffered under William Howard Taft, was crucified, died and buried. He descended into Africa. The third year he arose again from the jungle and ascendeth into favor and sitteth on the right hand of his party, whence he shall come to scourge the living and the dead.

Why did Roosevelt make this decision to seek the nomination when his action was almost certain to divide the party and ensure victory for the Democrats? In the first place, his friends extended enormous pressure on him. Too, he was motivated by his irritation with Taft, and it is possible that he was bored with private life. But most important, Roosevelt wanted to wield power, and the best place to wield power was in the White House. He wanted sincerely to implement his objectives. Again, this required that he be President. Roosevelt would fight to the last.

The Election of 1912

Roosevelt arrived at Chicago shortly before the Republican National Convention opened on June 18, in order to be on hand to direct his own forces in the fight for the nomination. When a reporter asked him how he felt, Roosevelt replied, "I'm feeling like a bull moose." Subsequently, the bull moose would become the symbol of the new Progressive party to be formed. A high degree of emotionalism and almost religious fervor imbued Roosevelt and his followers. On the eve of the convention, Roosevelt addressed thousands of his loyal supporters and climaxed his remarks with the stirring words, "We stand at Armageddon, and we battle for the Lord."

When the convention officially opened the next day, Republicans were hopelessly split. The Taft forces, however, were able to dominate the convention through the President's control of both the Republican National Committee and the Credentials Committee. However, when Taft's backers renominated the President on the first ballot, Roosevelt charged that Taft had stolen the nomination. Actually, Taft had used the same kind of party control to gain his renomination that Roosevelt had used in 1908 to dominate the convention and name Taft. What mattered was who wielded the power. To run with Taft, the convention chose John Sherman again as the vice presidential candidate. The platform called for a protective tariff, restrictions on monopoly, banking and currency reform, conservation of natural resources, restrictions on "undesirable immigration," economy and efficiency in government. It was a modern platform, designed to cover a broad spectrum of national opinion.

As the Republican Convention adjourned, a new party was being formed. That night in Orchestra Hall, Roosevelt told a madly cheering throng that he would accept the nomination of a new progressive party if it were offered to him. The response of those in attendance made it clear that a new party would be organized and that Roosevelt would be its candidate. In August the progressives met again in Chicago for their formal convention. Grimly serious but at the same time highly emotional, the crowd listened to Roosevelt as he gave his "Confession of Faith." He attacked the two old parties, which, he said, were "boss-ridden and privilege-controlled" and represented only the rich. The delegates cheered wildly and sang:

Thou wilt not cower in the dust,
Roosevelt, O Roosevelt!
Thy gleaming sword shall never rust,
Roosevelt, O Roosevelt!

Thus the Progressive party, or Bull Moose party, was formally launched. Without much discussion, the delegates named Roosevelt as their standard-bearer and Hiram Johnson, the progressive Governor of California, as his running mate.

In their platform the Progressives declared that the old parties had "become the tools of corrupt interests," and that the new party would "build a new and nobler commonwealth." The party pledged political reforms; legislation giving people the power to override certain court decisions; prohibition of injunctions in labor disputes; a wide variety of laws to protect workers; a strong federal administrative commission to control big business and monopoly; currency reform; conservation; and graduated federal income and inheritance taxes.

Meanwhile the optimistic Democrats watched the quarreling Republicans with deep satisfaction and enlivened hopes for victory. The leading candidates were Champ Clark of Missouri, Speaker of the House; Woodrow Wilson, Governor of New Jersey; and Representative Oscar Underwood of Alabama. When the convention opened, Clark had more delegates than Wilson. But through the astute efforts of his managers and his identification with the progressive forces, Wilson finally gained the lead. Bryan contributed to Wilson's nomination by attacking the reactionary and big business supporters of Clark. When Underwood's supporters finally bolted, Wilson received the nomination on the forty-sixth ballot.

Wilson's selection meant victory for the progressive forces within the Democratic party. The platform expressed Bryan-type progres-

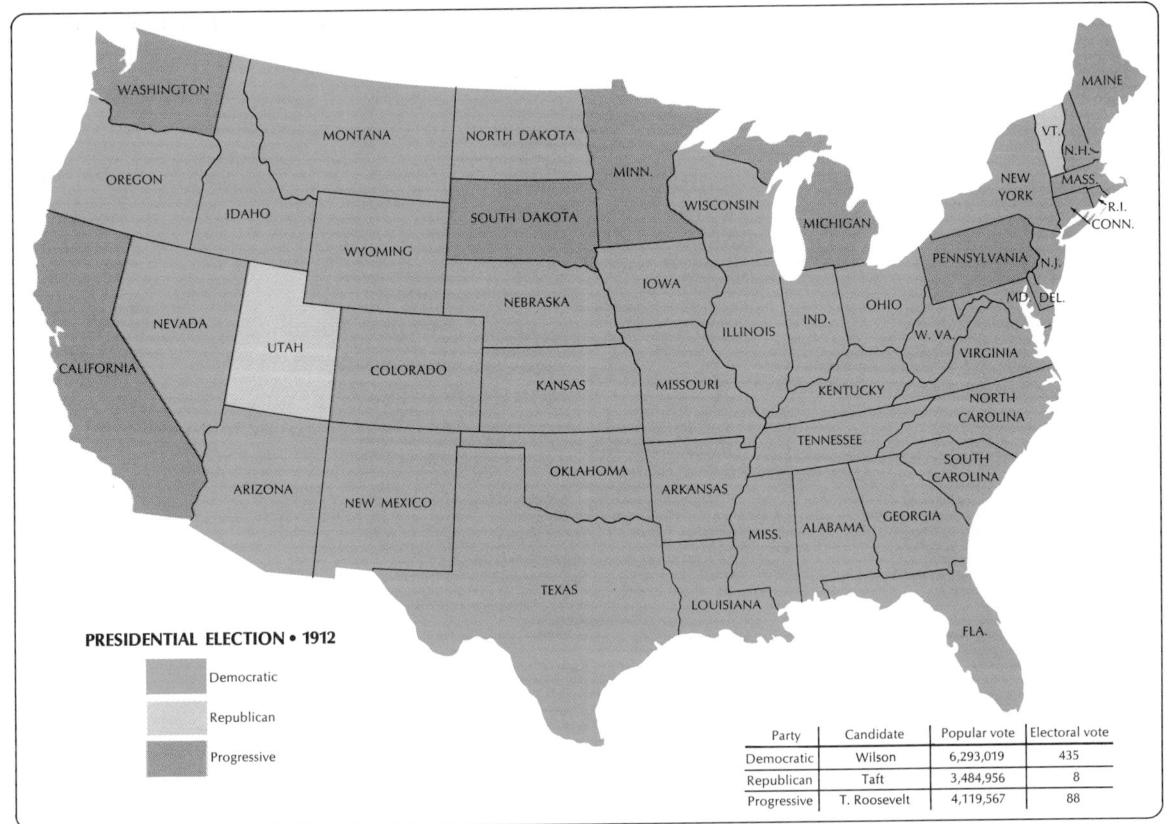

Party	Candidate	Popular vote	Electoral vote
Democratic	Wilson	6,293,019	435
Republican	Taft	3,484,956	8
Progressive	T. Roosevelt	4,119,567	88

sivism and recommended "a tariff for revenue only"; control of big business both through strengthening the Sherman Antitrust Act and through passing additional restrictive laws; an income tax; popular election of senators; a law to prohibit corporate contributions to campaign funds; new banking legislation and control of the "money trust"; additional regulation of railroads; rural credits to assist farmers; labor legislation; and conservation of natural and human resources.

Wilson and Roosevelt quickly dominated the contest of 1912. Taft conducted no real campaign, and few prominent people worked for his election. Roosevelt delivered speech after speech to explain his New Nationalism. Even after being shot and wounded by a fanatic in Milwaukee on October 14, Roosevelt told his hushed audience that he would speak "as long as there is life in my body." Wilson, meanwhile, worked hard to unite the Democrats and to popularize his New Freedom. He elevated the trust problem to major importance in his campaign, advocating strict government regulation to restore business competition.

With the Republican vote split, Wilson had only to win the normal Democratic vote to be assured of victory. In November, Wilson gained 6,293,019 votes; Roosevelt, 4,119,507; Taft, 3,484,956; and Debs, the Socialist candidate, 901,873. Wilson received a minority of the popular vote and polled fewer ballots than Bryan had received in 1908, but his electoral college majority was overwhelming. He had 435 to Roosevelt's 88. Taft carried only two states with 8 electoral votes. The three progressive candidates—Wilson, Roosevelt, and Debs—had a combined vote of more than 11 million. Not all of these 11 million voters favored progressive principles, of course, but it seems clear that a large majority of the electorate in 1912 favored continued economic, social, and political reforms.

Wilson and His Rise to Power

The new President, Thomas Woodrow Wilson, was born in Staunton, Virginia, in 1856. Of Scotch-Irish ancestry, he was the son of Joseph R. Wilson, minister of the First Presbyterian Church in Staunton. The family moved to Georgia the next year. Growing to manhood in the South, Wilson adopted Southern views on such economic questions as the tariff, and he held the traditional Southern attitude toward Negroes. He was graduated from the College of New Jersey in Princeton. Later he studied law and then earned a Ph.D. in history and political science at Johns Hopkins University. He published his dissertation, *Congressional Government,* in 1885, a study which brought Wilson unusual prominence for a young scholar. Frankly critical of the American political system of divided powers, he expressed admiration for the British system of party leadership and responsibility. In 1890 he returned to his alma mater, Princeton, where he taught and wrote until 1902 when he became president of the university.

Princeton's new president was of slender build and just short of 5 feet 11 inches tall. He had a narrow face, blue-gray eyes, and a prominent jaw which seemed to signify determination. Except among a few close friends, Wilson tended to be cold and distant. He often displayed stubbornness, for to him it was more important to cling firmly to principles than to take part in any compromise. Wilson had great confidence in his own judgment and expressed little tolerance for those who disagreed with him. At the close of an argument with him at Princeton, a faculty member said, "Well, Dr. Wilson, there are two sides to every question," to which Wilson replied sharply, "Yes, a right side and a wrong side." Wilson was deeply religious and, like his predecessors at Princeton, a loyal Presbyterian. He found difficulty in working with others, but nevertheless proved to be an effective administrator.

In 1910 the New Jersey Democrats needed a respectable candidate for governor—one who had no mark of bossism on him. Wilson appeared to be the ideal man, and because of some difficulties at Princeton, he was ready to leave the university. Campaigning on a reform program, he defeated his Republican opponent by a large majority. Until the election of 1910 Wilson had been known as a political conservative, but as Governor of New Jersey he inaugurated a progressive administration. He demonstrated strong executive leadership in pushing through a direct primary law, a corrupt practices act to reduce dishonesty in elections, legislation to regulate public utilities, and a workmen's compensation law. This program made him a national figure by 1911.

During the campaign of 1912, Wilson developed his New Freedom program. Like many other progressives, he viewed the power and influence of big business as one of the great unsolved questions facing Americans. Yet he was vague on the means required to resolve the problem of monopoly and industrial power. Eventually Wilson relied on Louis Brandeis, a brilliant and progressive lawyer from Boston, to develop his policies on trust control. Brandeis emphasized the need for legislation to control big business and enforce competition. This would guarantee industrial freedom. During the campaign of 1912 Wilson declared that American enterprise was no longer free, because "the laws of this country do not prevent the strong from crushing the weak." His answer to the problem was to prohibit monopoly by guaranteeing competition. Other aspects of Wilson's New Freedom included tariff reduction, labor legislation to protect workingmen, and political reform. Wilson opposed the protective tariff because, to him, it represented "governmental favoritism" to special groups and the reduction of competition.

Although Wilson relied on his Cabinet and other advisers, especially his good friend from Texas, Colonel Edward M. House, the new President himself was determined to head the new administration. Having expressed admiration for executive leadership and responsibility, he now had an opportunity to put his concept of government into practice at the national level. He had written in 1907 that the President "is . . . the political leader of the nation, or has it in his choice to be. The nation as a whole has chosen him, and is conscious that it has no other political spokesman. His is the only national voice in affairs. Let him once win the admiration and confidence of the country, and no other single force can withstand him, no combination of forces will easily overpower him." Later he stated that "we have grown more and more inclined to look to the President as the unifying force of our complex system, the leader of both his party and his nation." Wilson, like Roosevelt, added strength and power to the presidential office.

Changing America

Wilson's America had lost much of its rural character and was becoming a nation of cities. By 1914 the country's population had reached nearly 100 million, but less than one-third of this number lived on farms. Increasingly, the urban areas were setting the pattern of national life. The rise of the cities merely reflected the nation's growing wealth. That wealth totaled some $186 billion in 1912, or eleven times what it had been a half century before. Compared with most peoples of the world, Americans had an enviable standard of living. Average annual per capita income reached almost $500 by 1914. This higher income provided better food, clothing, and shelter, as well as more money for education, leisure, and other purposes than Americans had ever enjoyed before. Unfortunately, many people did not share the advantages of private enterprise, but there was a growing concern for this minority. Indeed, one of the essential elements in the progressive movement was the provision of greater care and better opportunities for the underprivileged.

The rapidity of social change was itself perhaps the most notable characteristic of American society; much of it flowed naturally from urbanization and the rising standards of living. President Wilson recognized this. During the campaign of 1912, he said: "The life of America is not the life that it was twenty years ago; it is not the life that it was ten years ago."

In the early years of the century Americans were more restless and mobile than in any previous generation. Symbolic of their new energy and mobility was the automobile. In 1909 President Taft rode to his inauguration in a horsedrawn carriage; four years later the horsepower which conveyed Wilson to his inauguration was under the hood of an automobile. This represented a startling and fundamental change in a period of only four years. In 1900 automobiles had been regarded either as the playthings of the rich or as objects of interest for tinkering mechanics. In 1914 Henry Ford alone produced 258,356 units of his famous Model T, and other manufacturers turned out nearly as many more cars. Ford and his cheap, mass-produced car added mobility and enrichment to the lives of many Americans.

This restlessness influenced American literature, social life, and the position of women. The hard-hitting works of such novelists as Frank Norris, Jack London, and Theodore Dreiser were beginning to replace the romantic fiction and religious novels of the previous generation. These writers attempted to come to grips realistically with the problems emanating from rapid social and economic change. Americans were also seeking new amusements and a faster social pace. In the cities, people were beginning to frequent cabarets and enjoy late evening restaurant life. Young folks, who found the waltz and the two-step far too slow for their generation, eagerly began dancing the faster fox-trot or the more acrobatic bunny hug, turkey trot, or grizzly bear. The words of an Irving Berlin song ran, "If they do that dance in heaven, Shoot me, 'hon,' tonight at seven." The new dances prompted the *New York Sun* to ask: "Are we going to the dogs by the ragtime route?" By 1914 most towns and cities also had movie theaters.

Nowhere were the new and changing moods in America better expressed than in the growing freedom and independence of women. Dress styles forsook rustling petticoats and raised the hemline above the ankle. By 1914 it was claimed that "of all the details and underraiment that belonged in a woman's wardrobe ten years ago, the only one that survives is the stocking." This was not true, but designers and manufacturers made every effort to emphasize modernity and beauty. One advertiser claimed that "Bon Ton corsets, nonrustable, make you look and feel younger." Those who considered women's hair their crowning glory were shocked and chagrined when Irene Castle, the famous dancer, set the style for bobbed hair in 1914. Women not only demanded the ballot; they marched, took jobs outside the home, and showed their independence in other ways. A few daring young ladies smoked an occasional cigarette, to the horror of most citizens. A New York policeman in 1904 told a woman in an automobile who was lighting a cigarette, "You can't do that on Fifth Avenue," and promptly arrested her.

Americans were rapidly becoming avid sports fans, mostly as spectators rather than as active participants. Boxing, baseball, and football contests drew hundreds of thousands of people annually. In 1913, some 151,000 persons watched Philadelphia defeat New York in baseball's World Series. Football crowds of 50,000 were not uncommon. Powerful Jack Johnson, a Negro, won the world heavyweight boxing title in 1910 by defeating James J. Jeffries. Moreover, urban citizens found relaxation and enjoyment in the growing number of playgrounds and parks.

But Americans were also concerned with the mind and the spirit. Free, tax-supported schools underlay the nation's educational

The Suffragettes

Until well into the twentieth century, women enjoyed only second- or third-class citizenship in most states. As pioneers and settlers of the West, women had labored alongside men to open up the country, but still they could not own property. They had campaigned ardently for the abolition of slavery, but when blacks received full citizenship—if only temporarily—women did not. In most states all a wife's possessions and earnings belonged to her husband. A woman could be divorced but could seldom sue for divorce. Her role was to keep the house, bear the children, and be respectful. For decades feminist leaders had protested these injustices.

Women's suffrage groups sprang up just after the Civil War; in 1890 they formed a national association. By then almost all women's organizations concentrated on a single goal: to get the vote. With the vote, they reasoned, would come the power to correct inequities, to create change. The suffragettes concentrated on public education. They had to convince the men who voted and governed that a great injustice existed. Public rallies, forums, speeches, discussion groups, articles, parades, pageants, demonstrations, and airship ascensions all constituted part of the effort.

Brown Brothers

Library of Congress

Library of Congress

The first International Convention of Women met in Washington in 1888. Among the leaders (below) were Elizabeth Cady Stanton (in front, right), who had organized the first woman's rights convention in 1848; Susan B. Anthony (fourth from left, front), America's most active and famous feminist and previously a temperance leader; and Frances Willard (left, standing), organizer and president of the Woman's Christian Temperance Union. Most feminists strongly opposed alcohol, and prohibition became law two years before woman suffrage.

Above, a terpsichorean pageant on the steps of the Treasury building in Washington depicted women's rights. Even tugboats bore the message.

Tamiment Institute Library

Brown Brothers

Several territories, of which Wyoming was first, had granted suffrage to women before becoming states. By 1913 twelve such states had helped force the Nineteenth Amendment through Congress. Two-thirds of the states, then had to ratify the amendment to put it into force. But many men vigorously opposed the idea. Their logic, as the storefront below indicates, led to the conclusion that women had the right to have no rights.

Brown Brothers

Women had the force of reason, justice, and morality backing their argument but the states proceeded slowly with ratification. The happy group above had just received word in 1919 that the Nineteenth Amendment had reached the half-way point with ratification by California. Then the pace increased; within a year Tennessee became the thirty-eighth state to ratify, and voting rights for women became law.

Brown Brothers

system, and by 1914 more than 19 million students attended elementary and secondary schools. Education was moving in new and important directions. Progressive educators like John Dewey of Columbia University were insisting that schools should be more child-centered and that students should have more freedom. At the same time, there were increasing demands for education in the practical arts, agriculture, and homemaking. College enrollments rose rapidly. It is both interesting and significant that Presidents Roosevelt, Taft, and Wilson all had college degrees from leading Eastern universities.

Judged by church membership, Americans appeared religious. About 40 percent of the people claimed church membership in 1914. But much of this membership was nominal and did not represent any deep or living religious faith. Biblical criticism and new developments in science continued to weaken the hold of traditional Christianity. Liberal churchmen emphasized more and more the proper role of the church in social change and insisted that the task of Christians and the church was to improve life in this world. Puritanism and fundamentalism, with their emphasis on personal salvation, however, remained strong.

American society, despite its change and flux, had not broken completely from its former moorings. People experienced conflict in attempting to hold to old values while they came under the influence of new ideas, new technology, and new social conditions. But the great majority of citizens continued to believe in the moral values of truth, justice, and loyalty; they were optimistic and had faith in progress. When Woodrow Wilson entered the White House, most Americans could look at their society and find it good.

The New Freedom in Action

In his inaugural address on March 4, 1913, Wilson outlined a specific program which, to him, called for implementation. Lower tariffs, banking and currency reform, restrictions on abuses in the industrial system, expansion of scientific services, better credit for agriculture, and conservation of natural resources were among his favorite reforms. Government, too, said Wilson, had a responsibility for safeguarding the health of the nation and protecting individual workers who could not, by themselves, obtain justice. This was not a day of triumph, the President concluded. It was a day of dedication. He summoned "all honest men, all patriotic, all forward-looking men" to his side.

Wilson's first legislative objective was tariff reduction. Both he and the Democratic party were committed to this end. As a presidential candidate, Wilson had considered tariff revision second only to monopoly control in his reform program. He felt that the protective tariff gave special advantages to certain big businesses by eliminating foreign competition. Moreover, he believed that the tariff raised the cost of living and was therefore an indirect and unjust tax on consumers. Tariff reduction, as a political issue, however, was complicated by the fact that a number of Democrats favored protection for special industries within their constituencies. Sugar producers in Louisiana, textile manufacturers in North Carolina, and wool growers in the West were among those who wanted some degree of protection. Confronted with opposition among Democrats as well as Republicans, Wilson had to exercise strong party leadership to obtain tariff revision.

In the House, Representative Oscar Underwood of Alabama prepared a tariff bill which lowered duties on many items. This passed by a large majority after the President exerted strong pressure. In the Senate, however, where the measure was under the management of Senator F. M. Simmons of North Carolina, tremendous opposition arose. Only after the President publicly denounced the numerous lobbyists who were working against tariff revision and took a strong stand on behalf of the measure did the Underwood-Simmons bill pass on October 2. It lowered ad valorem rates, on the average, about 10 percent. There were actually 958 reductions and only 86 increases. This was the first major downward revision of the tariff since the Civil War. The final measure also included the important income tax provision. This set normal income tax rates at 1 percent on incomes over $3,000 for a single person, with an additional tax (surtax) of 1 percent on net income from $20,000 to $50,000. The law graduated rates upward to a maximum of 6 percent on incomes in excess of $500,000. Referring to the lower tariff duties and the progressive income tax, the jubilant Secretary of Agriculture, David F. Houston, declared, "I did not much think we should live to see these things."

For students of the nation's economy in 1913, banking and currency reform appeared far more essential than tariff revision. The Panic of 1907 had emphasized again the weaknesses of the national banking system. By 1912 political leaders had joined businessmen, bankers, farmers, economists, and others in demanding modification of the country's banking structure and relief from what was known as the "money trust." The two major weaknesses of the banking system were the inelasticity of the currency and the concentration of credit facilities. Under the National Banking Act of 1863, there was no way provided to expand or contract credit to meet the needs of business or agriculture. For example, in rural areas farmers required credit in the spring during planting season, but the banks had no way of expanding their resources at that time to meet this special need. Furthermore, most of the credit was concentrated in the large banks of major cities such as Chicago, Boston, and New York. Progressives were especially critical of the growing concentration of money and credit in the hands of the finance capitalists such as J. P. Morgan. Thus Congress faced the challenge not only of providing for more elastic credit but also of breaking the monopoly over money and credit enjoyed by the money trust. The National Monetary Commission, commonly known as the Aldrich Commission, set up under the Aldrich-Vreeland Act of 1908, finally recommended new legislation in 1912.

After months of debate, Congress finally passed the Glass-Owen bill in December, 1913, which established the Federal Reserve System. The new law divided the country into twelve districts and set up a Federal Reserve bank in each district. All national banks were required to become members of the system; state-chartered banks were urged to join. Member banks had to subscribe at least 6 percent of their capital stock and surplus to the capital stock of the Federal Reserve bank in their district. In other words, the Federal Reserve banks were bankers' banks, owned by the individual members. The bill provided for a new type of currency known as Federal Reserve notes. These were printed by the Treasury but held in custody of the Federal Reserve banks. The law required that Federal Reserve banks must keep a 40 percent gold reserve behind all Federal Reserve notes. A seven-man

Federal Reserve Board, appointed by the President, supervised the system.

To increase the elasticity of the currency, member banks could rediscount commercial paper, such as notes and mortgages, with the Federal Reserve bank. This meant that the reserve bank loaned money to the local bank on this type of security. To expand credit locally, a banker could acquire additional money for lending by putting up his commercial paper for security at the Federal Reserve bank. With more money in hand, he could then meet the expanding needs of his customers. Expansion and contraction of credit would be regulated or controlled by what was known as the rediscount, or interest, rate. To expand credit, the Federal Reserve Board would reduce rediscount rates to bankers, who in turn could charge lower interest rates to local customers. To restrict credit, the Board could raise the discount rate, thus discouraging borrowing and possibly checking speculation and inflation. The Federal Reserve System supplied better credit facilities, a sounder currency, and greater national coordination of the country's monetary and banking systems. It also represented much greater intervention and responsibility by government in the economy, a fact which was of special importance.

Having achieved tariff and banking legislation, the new administration turned to antitrust problems. In 1912 Wilson had centered his campaign around the control of big business, and the Democratic platform had demanded laws which would make it "impossible for a private monopoly to exist in the United States." Wilson believed that competition was the best regulator of business and favored legislation which, he hoped, would guarantee competitive practices. Wilson's solution to the problem of monopoly was a revision of the Sherman Antitrust Act to spell out precisely what behavior was unlawful. Roosevelt and his followers, however, still believed that strict regulation of big business by a strong federal commission was the best approach to the question of monopoly and business concentration.

Wilson finally accepted the idea of a strong regulatory commission, and in September, 1914, Congress enacted the Federal Trade Commission Act. This law established a Commission, composed of five members appointed by the President, which was authorized to prevent unfair methods of competition. If it found a business engaged in unfair or illegal practices, the Commission could issue "cease and desist" orders to eliminate such methods of competition. Businessmen, however, could appeal the orders of the Commission to the courts. After passage of this law, Wilson lost interest in legislation designed to forbid unfair competition by statute. Nevertheless, in October, 1914, Congress passed the Clayton Antitrust Act, which did make certain business actions unlawful. Among other provisions, the law forbade price discrimination between purchasers of commodities, and it outlawed discounts or price reductions made on condition that the purchaser not buy from another supplier. Although the Clayton Act strengthened the Sherman Antitrust law, the new measure was still relatively ineffective because of qualifying statements which said that specific actions were illegal only if they *substantially* lessened competition or created monopoly. Such distinctions were not easy to demonstrate in court. Wilson also believed the measure weak; but he did not complain because the Clayton Act was no longer central to his antitrust program.

The most controversial provisions in the Clayton Antitrust Act were those designed to exempt labor and farm organizations from prosecution under the antitrust laws and to abolish injunctions in labor disputes. Samuel Gompers, president of the American Federation of Labor, officials of the Farmers' Union, and other labor and agricultural leaders pressed hard for these reforms. Gompers wrote early in 1914 that immunity from injunctions "is the paramount issue before the working people of our land." But Wilson refused to support what he regarded to be undemocratic, class legislation. A final compromise declared that "nothing contained in the anti-trust laws shall be construed to forbid the existence and operation" of farm and labor organizations and that neither these organizations nor their members should be considered "illegal combinations or conspiracies in restraint of trade under the anti-trust laws." Another section declared that court injunctions could not be granted in any dispute between employees and employers "unless necessary to prevent irreparable injury to property, or to a property right." Gompers happily declared that the anti-injunction provision was labor's Magna Carta. Actually, this section did not substantially alter labor's position under the law or under existing court interpretations. Wilson had no intention of exempting labor unions completely from court orders or injunctions while other groups in society were subject to them.

In 1913 and 1914, Wilson and the Congress had concentrated on tariff, banking, and monopoly legislation. By the latter year some of Wilson's closest advisers were urging him to give business a breathing spell, and the President made a conscious effort to prove that he was not, indeed, antibusiness. Bankers and business leaders became visitors at the White House, and Wilson appointed a number of conservatives to the Interstate Commerce Commission and the Federal Reserve Board. Wilson, it seemed, relied much more on conservatives than on the Bryan faction of his party. After the summer of 1914, the outbreak of war in Europe temporarily diverted Wilson from further reforms. Critical diplomatic questions now occupied most of his time and attention. And the country seemed to agree with Wilson's more conservative outlook. In the midterm elections of 1914, the Democratic majority in the House was cut from 73 to 25. Regular Republicans gained in key states.

If Wilson believed that he had largely completed his mission by 1914, Congress continued to enact progressive measures despite presidential indifference or opposition. One of the most important of these laws was the La Follette Seamen's Act, approved March 5, 1915. Authored and supported by Andrew Furuseth, president of the International Seamen's Union, this law was designed to assure better living and working conditions on ships under American registry. It reduced the power of captains, set minimum food standards, increased safety requirements, and made changes in the method of wage payments.

As the nation contemplated the presidential election of 1916, the political situation did not look encouraging for Wilson and his party. Greater Republican unity and strength, dissension within Democratic ranks, and the war issue all dimmed Democratic prospects. The best chance for victory seemed to lie in more advanced social reform, which might win the support of all progressives regardless of party. This need for issues which would bring wider political backing drove President Wilson further along the road of domestic reform in 1916. His appointment of Louis D. Brandeis to the Supreme Court in January, 1916, indicated a revived and extended progressivism on the part of the President.

Wilson soon gave his support to a wide variety of agricultural and labor legislation. In July, 1916, Congress, with hearty presidential blessing, passed the Federal Farm Loan Act. This new measure provided for establishing twelve federal farm land banks, one in each of the Federal Reserve districts. Each bank was to be capitalized at $750,000, with the funds being supplied at first largely by the government. Farmers did not borrow directly from the bank, but through their locally organized, cooperative, farm loan associations. Farmers could borrow up to 50 percent of the value of their land and 20 percent of the value of their improvements. Interest rates were kept relatively low, and loans could run from five to thirty years, repayable in annual installments. Farmers at last had a law which would meet their particular needs for long-term credit.

Congress that year enacted other important agricultural legislation. The United States Warehouse Act permitted the issuance of receipts by licensed warehouses against properly stored farm produce. These receipts could be used as collateral for bank loans. The Cotton Futures Act required certain federal standards for trading in cotton futures, and the Grain Standards Act established standards for grain sold in interstate commerce. Of great importance to farmers with automobiles was the Rural Post Roads Act. This law inaugurated the policy of spending federal money to match state funds in the building of so-called rural post roads. Agricultural education also received support from the Wilson administration. In 1914 Congress passed the Smith-Lever Act to assist in "giving education and practical demonstrations in agriculture and home economics to persons not attending" land-grant colleges. In 1917 Congress passed the Smith-Hughes Act, which provided federal matching funds to encourage the teaching of vocational agriculture and home economics in the secondary schools.

Congress and the President also devoted attention to the needs of labor. In August, 1916, lawmakers passed the Kern-McGillicuddy bill, which provided workmen's compensation for federal employees. The Keating-Owen child-labor bill became law a short time later. Two years after it was passed the Supreme Court declared this statute unconstitutional in the case of *Hammer v. Dagenhart,* but Congress at least had tried to eliminate this social evil. Railroad workers made great gains under Wilson. In 1916 Congress passed the Adamson Act, which set eight hours as the standard workday on all lines exceeding 100 miles. (For a more complete discussion of labor gains, see page 704.)

Conclusion

Even before Wilson's reelection in November, 1916, the progressive movement had largely run its course. The ardor of some reformers had begun to cool as they saw many progressive objectives achieved. Moreover, the attention of the President and Congress was diverted increasingly toward international problems and the threat of war. But the changes wrought between 1900 and 1917 were of fundamental importance, and they left a permanent imprint upon the nation and its people. The American people had set out to solve the problems emerging from unregulated industrialism, and, to a considerable degree, they had been able to achieve their objectives by means of the positive state.

Progressivism marked the expansion of governmental powers at both the state and national levels. It expressed itself in greater government regulation, as well as in a large increase in state and federal functions. Between 1900 and 1917 these included primarily more protection for labor, control over money and banking, protection against impure food and drugs, credit for farmers, and conservation of natural resources. It was the income tax which, in the long run, provided the money to underwrite many of the new federal programs and to permit steps toward the social welfare state. Progressives had sought to make government more responsible to the people by adopting such measures as the primary, initiative and referendum, direct election of senators, and woman suffrage. But progressives also believed that political and economic reform went hand in hand—that one without the other would solve few problems. One of the greatest failures of the reformers was their unwillingness to insist on equal rights for Negroes. Throughout the progressive era, Negroes continued to suffer from discrimination in housing and employment and in the exercise of their political rights. Only a few weak voices were raised against racial injustice.

It is true that the progressive movement did not solve all the political, economic, and social problems facing the United States, but it demonstrated how improvements could be brought about without revolution or radical change. As the observant chronicler of American life Frederick Lewis Allen wrote in *The Big Change,* the progressive movement showed "that when the ship of state was not behaving as it should, one did not need to scrap it and build another, but could, by a series of adjustments and improvements, repair it while keeping it running." In essence this was progressivism. It was also the American way of bringing about change.

SUGGESTED READINGS

The best and most complete biography of William Howard Taft is Henry Pringle's *William Howard Taft* (2 vols., 1934). On Taft's political problems see K. W. Hechler's *Insurgency: Personalities and Politics of the Taft Era* (1940). George E. Mowry's *Theodore Roosevelt and the Progressive Movement** (1946) argues that Taft's difficulties in the Presidency stemmed from his basic conservatism. Biographies which throw further light on the Taft years are Richard Lowitt's *George W. Norris: The Making of a Progressive,* 1861–1912 (1963) and T. R. Ross's *Jonathan Prentice Dolliver* (1948). The election of 1912 has been most adequately discussed by Arthur S. Link in the first volume of his multivolume biography of Woodrow Wilson, entitled *Wilson: The Road to the White House** (1947). A briefer account of the election of 1912 can be found in Link's excellent volume *Woodrow Wilson and the Progressive Era,* 1910–1917* (1954).

Besides consulting the standard texts in diplomatic history for Taft's foreign policy, see also the evaluation of Philander C. Knox in S. F. Bemis (ed.), *American Secretaries of State and Their Diplomacy* (1929), vol. IX, as well as the selection on Knox by Walter Scholes in Norman A. Graebner (ed.), *An Uncertain Tradition: American Secretaries of State in the Twentieth Century** (1961). Charles Vevier has dealt with America's China policy in *The United States and China* (1955); while *The Manchu Abdication and the Powers,* 1908–1912 (1935) contains additional information on the United States interest in the Far East. The reciprocity controversy has been discussed by C. C. Tansill in *Canadian-American Relations,* 1875–1911 (1943).

The best study of Woodrow Wilson and the fullest account of his administration is Arthur Link's yet uncompleted multivolume biography. Up to 1968, Link had published *Wilson: The Road to the White House** (1947); *Wilson: The New Freedom** (1956); *Wilson: Struggle for Neutrality,* 1914–1915

(1960); *Wilson: Confusions and Crises, 1915–1916* (1964); and *Wilson: Campaigns for Progressivism and Peace, 1916–1917* (1965). Link has provided an excellent summary of the first Wilson administration in *Woodrow Wilson and the Progressive Era, 1910–1917**, cited above. Good single-volume biographies of Wilson are H. C. F. Bell's *Woodrow Wilson and the People* (1945) and J. A. Garraty's *Woodrow Wilson* (1956), while John Blum's *Woodrow Wilson and the Politics of Morality** (1956) provides a critical interpretation of the Wilson Presidency. Other general studies include Volume I of F. L. Paxson's *American Democracy and the World War* (1936–1948), entitled *Pre-war Years, 1913–1917* (1936).

On specific major issues in Wilson's first administration, see the relevant parts of F. W. Taussig's *Tariff History of the United States** (8th ed., 1931), which deals with the Underwood-Simmons tariff. H. P. Willis' *The Federal Reserve System* (1915) and P. M. Warburg's *The Federal Reserve System* (2 vols., 1930) have covered the origin and development of the new banking system. For a discussion of the income tax see the pertinent sections in D. R. Dewey's *Financial History of the United States* (1936) and W. J. Schultz and M. R. Caine's *Financial Development of the United States* (1937). Antitrust legislation has been discussed by Charles W. Dunn in both *The Federal Anti-trust Law* (1930) and *The Federal Trade Commission: An Experiment in the Control of Business* (1932). Books dealing with labor issues in the years just before World War I include Volume III of *History of Labour in the United States* (1935) by John R. Commons and others, and Philip Taft's *The A. F. of L. in the Time of Gompers* (1957). The radical labor movement has been considered by Paul F. Brissenden in *The I. W. W.* (1920).

A great deal of information on the Wilson years can be gleaned from the writings of members of his Cabinet. Useful insights can be found in *Eight Years with Wilson's Cabinet* (2 vols., 1926) by Secretary of Agriculture D. F. Houston; W. C. Redfield's *With Congress and Cabinet* (1924); W. G. McAdoo's *Crowded Years* (1931); and *The Wilson Era: Years of Peace, 1910–1917* (1944) by Secretary of the Navy Josephus Daniels.

The social history of the period can be traced in Walter Lord's *The Good Years** (1960) and H. U. Faulkner's *The Quest for Social Justice* (1931).

* indicates availability in paperback.

29

America and the Great War

ON JUNE 28, 1914, a Serbian nationalist assassinated Archduke Franz Ferdinand, heir to the Austrian throne, at the Bosnian city of Sarajevo. That event proved to be a watershed in the history of the modern world, for it brought to an end a century of slow, but steady, progress toward liberalism and democracy and opened a new age of violence, revolution, dictatorship, and war. Assassinations were common enough in early twentieth-century Europe, but the murder of the Archduke brought into direct conflict two powerful, thoroughly armed alliances. Each alliance, convinced that it could win and that firmness alone would prevent a general war, refused to compromise under pressure. Behind Serbia stood Russia, encouraging Serbian resistance; behind Russia—France and England. Germany extended equal guarantees to Austria-Hungary.

Events of 1914 bore a significance beyond the world's immediate understanding. Yet those German and French soldiers who rushed into the battle of the Marne would touch the lives of the American people as few, at that moment, could anticipate. For Europe, in the failure of its diplomacy to avoid war, had entered upon a suicidal struggle of sufficient magnitude to place its great stabilizing traditions in jeopardy. Indeed, so enormous was the ultimate power expended, so great the death toll, so balanced the forces locked in battle, that Europe could escape from its self-imposed catastrophe only by calling upon external power. It was the outside world to which Britain and France were aligned—Australia, New Zealand, eventually and most importantly, the United States—that brought final victory to the Allies. The Great War of 1914 demonstrated that Europe's balance of power, self-contained for three centuries, had become submerged in a worldwide balance in which Europe's destiny would henceforth be determined in large measure by power that lay outside the European Continent.

Wilson's New Diplomacy

Within weeks after its outbreak, the Great War of Europe disintegrated into a massive, immobile war of attrition. It quickly became clear that the two alliance systems possessed unprecedented power to destroy but not necessarily the power to win. For the United States this condition became a matter of grave decision. No nation can avoid an existing war if those directly involved become convinced, for reasons of their own, that their victory requires major demands on those who claim to be neutral. Wartime Europe would not permit the United States the freedom to pursue its own interests unmindful of the vicissitudes of war when the traditional European system was in danger of collapse. That America's productivity would be thrown into the balance was foretold by its long tradition of trading openly and massively with Europe's belligerents in time of war. Thus the crucial question was not whether the United States would become involved in Europe's war but how it would become involved and what its role would be in the final disposition of that war. Such decisions would rest, in large measure, on the views and understanding of President Woodrow Wilson.

Wilson had entered the White House surprisingly uninformed about the intricacies of diplomacy. Neither as a scholar nor as a practicing politician had Wilson studied international affairs with the intensity and insight which he revealed in his political writings, his formulation of domestic policy, or his relations with Congress. "It would be an irony of fate," he wrote to a friend shortly before his inaugural, "if my administration had to deal chiefly with foreign affairs." As President, Wilson faced the termination of what had been, for his country, a century of security from Europe's dangers. But as he searched his mind and the past for ideas to guide the policies of the nation, which was rapidly losing its isolation, he accepted a body of thought and a set of purposes which denied the validity of almost every important element in the nation's diplomatic tradition from Washington to Cleveland.

Wilson and his first Secretary of State, William Jennings Bryan, rejected emotionally and intellectually the necessity of war. But what was unique in their preferences for peace was less their devotion to peace than the means by which they sought to achieve it. Wilson, once aroused by Europe's disaster, determined to build a peace structure on two basic notions regarding human society. The first, rooted in his Presbyterian faith, assumed a just and sovereign God and a universe based on His moral law. For Wilson the laws of righteousness applied to nations as well as to individual men. The essential task of leadership, therefore, was that of demanding high standards of conduct from people and nations and encouraging them to subordinate selfish interests to the greater interests of peace and human progress. The second of Wilson's basic postulates concerned method. The best agency for achieving moral progress, he believed, was democracy, the political embodiment of man's essential goodness and rationality. Wilson's world view, in short, looked to a moral order in which humankind, reasoning rightly and expressing its will through a worldwide democratic order, would compel aggressive, monarchical, or tyrannical rulers to avoid any unjust and irrational use of power.

It was completely fitting that Wilson's Secretary of State, the near-pacifist Bryan, negotiated during his first year a series of bilateral treaties whereby the signatories agreed not to resort to war except at the end of a twelvemonth period. It was thought that a year would be long enough for tempers to cool and for diplomats to determine the superior legal and moral position in any conflict. "The sense and substance [of these treaties]," declared Wilson in October, 1914, three months after Europe's signatories had gone to war, "is that whenever any trouble arises the light shall shine on it for a year before anything is done; and my prediction is that after the light has shone on it for a year, it will not be necessary to do anything; that after we know what happened, then we will know who was right and who was wrong." Even as the guns spoke, American diplomats amused the foreign ministers of the warring nations by suggesting that they invoke the documents they had signed.

Wilson soon discovered occasions for putting his new diplomacy into effect. Convinced that the Taft policy of supporting the Six Power Consortium in China would undermine that nation's territorial and administrative integrity and thus constitute a form of imperialism, Wilson withdrew United States support. His objection, not based on any specific knowledge of China or of American interests in the Far East, was that any monopolistic grant to a foreign financial group was undemocratic.

In Latin America, Wilson's moralism spelled intervention, not withdrawal, for the issues were different. The President, in March, 1913, announced to the press that he intended to promote the interest of the common people in the Western Hemisphere. "We can have no sympathy," he said, "with those who seek to seize the power of government to advance their own personal interests and ambitions." Under this principle he denied recognition to Victoriano Huerta of Mexico, who assumed power in 1913 following the overthrow and murder of his predecessor. To rescue the Mexican population from such a dictator, the President encouraged the sale and shipment of arms to Huerta's political enemies. In April, 1914, following the arrest of some American sailors at Tampico, United States forces occupied Vera Cruz. Ultimately Wilson's Mexican policies had the desired effect. Huerta, facing ever-stronger political and military opposition, fled to Spain, and in 1915 the United States recognized Venustiano Carranza.

With even greater confidence Wilson dispatched American marines to Haiti and Santo Domingo, two Caribbean republics, to restore order. These involvements again brought a measure of political stability to the two nations, but not because the Latin Americans accepted democracy or the legitimacy of Wilson's actions. They responded positively simply because they were powerless to challenge the will of an American President. Many educated Latin Americans, interested in law and order, lauded the President's purpose and hoped that his mission might eventually triumph. Many, however, strongly objected to the use of force and United States interference in the affairs of independent states.

Pressures on American Neutrality

In the view of most Americans, Europe's decision for war in 1914 exceeded the limits of rationality. How could Europe, the most civilized of continents, terminate a century of unprecedented material and institutional progress by engaging in such self-destruction? For weeks editors had reassured their readers that war was impossible. The *New York Times* proclaimed as late as July 28, "That war is too dreadful for imagining and because it is too dreadful it cannot happen." When at last editors accepted the reality of conflict, they still could say with the *Independent:* "Luckily we have the Atlantic between us and Europe. It is their war, not ours." Such convictions dictated an official policy of noninvolvement. Most Americans applauded the President's proclamation of neutrality, as well as his appeal that they be "impartial in thought as well as in action." The war, Wilson said simply, is one "with which we have nothing to do, whose causes cannot touch us." Remaining neutral the United States would keep herself free "to do what is honest . . . and truly serviceable for the peace of the world."

Impartiality soon proved to be an illusion. The American people might want peace, but they could not remain neutral. For the vast majority of them it mattered who won. "Hyphenated" Americans—immigrants and first-generation Americans—generally favored national policies that served the countries of their origin. Many of the nation's 12 million German-Americans and Irish-Americans openly supported the German cause. But overwhelmingly, American sentiment as a whole favored the Allies. For old-line Americans, largely of English descent, the ties of culture, tradition, and interest were too firm to be broken. Indeed, pro-British editors, from August, 1914, onward, warned the nation that German militarism and autocracy threatened the established order in Europe. With the British-dominated balance of power in danger of destruction, they asked, could the United States remain neutral and permit the war to run its normal course? *Harper's Weekly* reminded its readers that it was the guardianship of the British navy that had permitted the United States to develop internally without carrying the burden of armaments. Some observers warned, moreover, that Germany could not become a major maritime power in the Atlantic without obtaining coaling stations or colonies in the Caribbean. Thus German ambitions on the high seas seemed to constitute a threat to the Monroe Doctrine.

Washington officialdom, overwhelmingly representative of the country's Protestant, middle-class culture, was admittedly pro-British from the beginning. Robert Lansing, first counselor in the State Department, and Walter Hines Page, United States Ambassador to London, regarded German autocracy as a threat to American democracy. Wilson's trusted adviser, Colonel Edward House, warned the President in August, 1914, "German success will ultimately mean trouble for us." Wilson hoped to avoid war with the Central Powers, but he admitted that he believed a German victory would force the United States into the mold of a militaristic nation. This conviction—that the security of the United States demanded a British victory—really left no room in official thought or action for policies of genuine neutrality. Specific pressures militating against United States neutrality—the British propaganda campaign, the huge American financial investment in the Allied cause, and German submarine warfare—raised the concrete issues which drove Washington and Berlin apart. But basic to their every quarrel was the absence of any mutual interest—other than peace—that might hold the two countries together. As the war progressed, the nation's desire to avoid the conflict yielded to that of preventing a German victory.

The role of British propaganda in driving the nation to intervention is not clear. The British government mounted a massive assault on American emotions. Having cut the transAtlantic cable to Germany, the British and French governments were in a position to ensure that Americans viewed the war through Allied eyes. By commanding the news, they could expose the American people to only those aspects of the war which reflected adversely on German conduct. German actions often reduced much of the British propaganda effort to that of reporting; for the invasion of Belgium, the execution of British nurse Edith Cavell, the long-range shelling of Paris, the aerial bombardment of cities, the use of the submarine against defenseless merchant and passenger vessels all had the effect of outraging the American mind. German propaganda, on the other hand, was clumsy and largely ineffective. To be effective, propaganda, like seeds, must fall on fertile ground; the very ease with which British propaganda instilled hatred in the United States demonstrated how little that effort mattered in shaping the actual decisions of a thoroughly unneutral country.

Similarly the enormous financial commitment to Britain and France was less the cause of the ultimate American decision for war than evidence that the nation's financial and industrial leaders favored an Allied victory. The failure of neutrality came first. Had the nation's industrialists been less partisan they would have retooled for war production to satisfy British and French demands with far less enthusiasm. Conditions in the Atlantic reinforced the preferences of American industrialists and financiers, for British control of the seas made it far simpler to lend and sell to the Allies than to Germany. The partisanship of the American business community became even more pronounced when New York bankers pressed the Wilson administration for permission to finance Allied purchases in the United States. In August, 1914, the President, on Bryan's advice, had restricted private loans to the belligerents, in accordance with the official policy of neutrality. "Money," warned Bryan, "is the worst of all contrabands because it commands everything else." Still the State Department, to maintain Allied trade, permitted short-term Allied credit arrangements with American banks. And in 1915, when it became apparent that the Allies could no longer sustain their war effort—and hence their purchases in America—without additional credit, Wilson overruled Bryan and abandoned all restrictions on loans. The way was thus cleared for the public sale of Allied bond issues. By the time the United States became an active belligerent in April, 1917, American investors had contributed secured loans in excess of $2 billion to the Allies' war effort.

The Submarine Issue

Ultimately Berlin's reliance on the submarine to control British waters created the point of friction in United States–German relations that led to war. But, as in matters of production and investment, it was the absence of genuine neutrality that mattered. Had the outcome of the war been of no concern to the government and people of the United States, this nation could have eliminated the submarine issue completely by either insisting on equal access for all belligerents to American production or, to protect its interest in peace, by completely terminating its war trade. Jefferson in his embargo had once made the latter choice. But after 1914, the United States insisted upon the right to ship food and munitions to Britain. Thereby, it forced Germany to face the final alternative of losing the war on the high seas or running the risk of an American declaration of war. Wilson's demand that Germany restrict her use of the submarine was simply his attempt to bridge the gap between a desire to secure a British victory and a desire to avoid war. Fundamental to the submarine issue, therefore, was Germany's continuing need to deprive the Allied war effort of the advantage of American production and the American President's defiance of that purpose.

Germany recognized her dilemma early in the war when the United States refused to challenge the British policy of interfering with neutral commerce in the North Sea. Britain, as early as August, 1914, determined to use its naval power to impede the movement of goods into Germany and, more specifically, to control American shipping. British war vessels stopped American ships en route to Germany, as well as to neutral ports, and examined them for contraband, broadly defined. In November, the British mined the North Sea so thoroughly that no ship could proceed without specific instructions from British officials. Finally, in March, 1915, the British placed all trade with Germany under penalty of confiscation. Particularly disturbing to the German government was the willingness of the United States to accept this massive infringement on its neutral rights, for this demonstrated, as nothing else could have done, America's refusal to endanger the British war effort.

Britain's success in monopolizing the expanding industrial production of the United States compelled Germany to retaliate by the only effective means available to her. On February 4, 1915, the German government, in a dispatch to Washington, announced its intention to establish a war zone around the British Isles. The United States State Department was reminded that Britain had put a stop to even legitimate neutral commerce with Germany and that neutral nations, generally, had acquiesced. Since nations such as the United States, out of deference to British policy, refused to assert their neutral rights, Germany in defense of her own vital interests, would retaliate against British policy. German vessels could not guarantee the safety of persons or cargoes belonging to neutrals, the note warned; therefore the United States should keep its ships, goods, and citizens out of the war zone.

Wilson's response was, in a sense, an economic declaration of war against Germany. Should German vessels attack a ship carrying an American flag and destroy the lives of American citizens, he wrote Berlin, the United States would view the attack as a violation of its neutral rights and would "hold the Imperial German Government to a strict accountability." In such an event, the United States would take any steps necessary to safeguard American lives and property. The President, in short, would tolerate no German policy that impeded the flow of American goods and citizens to England. Germany's dilemma was simply that the only naval weapon available to her was, by maritime tradition, as illegal as it was effective. The submarine, a frail and basically defenseless craft, could not practice the historic rules of "visit and search" without running the risk of destruction from ramming or, in the case of armed merchantmen, from a sudden, direct hit. As a matter of self-protection, a submarine commander had no choice but to launch his torpedoes and run, thereby deserting his obligation for the safety and welfare of survivors. This unprecedented moral and legal problem posed by the submarine, rather than its effectiveness as a destroyer of commerce, determined Wilson's response to the new German policy.

German officials, seeking a tenuous balance between an effective blockade of Britain and the avoidance of trouble with the United States, agreed to respect neutral flags and operate, as far as possible, under the traditional rules of maritime warfare. Within weeks after the announcement of the blockade, however, German torpedoes sank the British liner *Falaba,* with the loss of one American crewman, and damaged the American tanker *Gulflight.* Shortly thereafter, the German Ambassador bought a newspaper advertisement in the New York press, warning Americans to avoid travel on British vessels. On May 7, a submarine sank the giant British liner *Lusitania* off the Irish coast, with the loss of almost 1,200 persons, including 128 Americans. With a large segment of the American press demanding some sort of reprisal, Wilson on May 10 asserted: "There is such a thing as a man being too proud to fight. There is such a thing as a nation being so right that it does not need to convince others by force that it is right." The State Department's note of May 13 was rather mild, reminding Berlin that Germany had again broken the rules of maritime warfare and insisting that it take immediate steps to prevent a recurrence. The Germans replied that the *Lusitania* had been carrying munitions and guns and hence was no ordinary merchant vessel.

Germany's response to the *Lusitania* note served to split Wilson's advisers. Some favored a second, more determined, warning to Berlin; others, led by Bryan, argued the legitimacy of the German position. The Secretary of State, taking seriously the official posture of American neutrality, reminded the President early in June that he had not objected to the sinkings when American citizens were not involved. It was essential, Bryan said, to keep Americans out of the war zone. When the President rejected his advice and dispatched a second, more belligerent, *Lusitania* note, Bryan resigned. To succeed him Wilson named Lansing, already known for his extreme pro-British sympathies. Wilson, like Bryan, argued the case in terms of American lives, not American commerce. But unlike Bryan, he saw himself as the special protector of international law and morality. Preferring principle to expediency—at least in his relations with Germany—he refused to keep Americans at home or to relent in his opposition to German submarine practices. For the moment he had his way. Berlin, still hopeful of avoiding a break with the United States instructed its U-boat commanders on June 6 not to sink passenger vessels, neutral or belligerent, without warning.

Twice within the next twelve months Germany and the United States went to the brink of war. After two Americans lost their lives when a German submarine torpedo sank the British liner *Arabic* in August, 1915, Germany's moderate Chancellor Theobald von Bethmann-Hollweg soothed ruffled American feelings by offering apologies, indemnities for the dead, and the assurance that submarine attacks on merchant shipping were suspended. Again, in early 1916, after the sinking of an unarmed French passenger ship, the *Sussex,* resulted in the injury of several Americans, President Wilson's stern ultimatum extorted from the Berlin government new assurances that no unresisting merchant or passenger vessel would be sunk without warning and without provisions for the safety of noncombatants. Thus the first stage of the submarine controversy ended with a self-denying German pledge exempting all belligerent or neutral merchant ships from attack by German U-boats. One momentous fact remained. Wilson had so fully committed America's honor and prestige to holding Germany to "strict accountability" for losses of American lives and property through German submarine attack that a renewal of submarine warfare by Germany must almost inevitably lead to war.

The crises of 1915–1916 convinced President Wilson that the United States had to prepare for war while continuing to work for peace. Early in 1916 he placed himself at the front of the burgeoning preparedness movement by proposing to Congress that the Army be drastically enlarged and the Navy undertake a building program which would make it second to none by 1925. He carried the fight to the American people in an extended speaking tour and, after a sharp struggle with pacifist groups and many progressives, succeeded in getting most of his preparedness program through Congress.

The Failure of Mediation

Officially Wilson might limit American relations with Germany to the defense of neutral rights. Yet he was acutely aware that the United States, with its amazing productivity, had become the key to the gigantic struggle raging in Europe. The Central Powers, led by Germany, would not accept defeat without warring on American neutral rights as a final act of desperation. During 1916, as the European armies experienced the totally unprecedented bloodbaths of Verdun and the Somme, Wilson recognized the danger to United States neutrality well enough to conclude that only the termination of the war could assure this country's continued peace. Early in 1916 he supported Colonel House's mediation plan by dispatching him to Europe. In London, House negotiated with the British Foreign Minister the House-Grey Memorandum, a document which promised that the President, at some moment regarded opportune by the British and French governments, would propose a conference to end the war. Should Germany reject reasonable terms, the United States "would probably enter the war against Germany." When, however, Wilson suggested after Germany's *Sussex* pledge that the time for a conference had arrived, London, now convinced that an Allied victory was possible, rejected the proposal outright. The British government simultaneously tightened its blockage of the Continent and its control of neutral shipping. Subsequent British censorship of United States mail and blacklisting of American firms regarded as pro-German embittered Wilson; he even considered the drastic step of prohibiting loans and reducing exports to the Allies. Still he did neither, partly because Britain was induced to make concessions, partly because the American President would not endanger the Allied war effort.

With his mind on peace in 1916, Wilson entered his campaign for reelection. Unsure of his power to avoid war and desirous of running on his domestic record, the President hoped to play down the foreign-policy issue. The Republican leadership, having broken the power of the Progressive revolt, anticipated victory behind Charles Evans Hughes, the distinguished former Governor of New York and associate justice of the United States Supreme Court. The Republicans' plan was to capitalize on Wilson's alleged failure to protect the nation's honor in his quarrels with Germany over the submarine. Wilson recognized a badly divided nation and hoped to avoid extremes by emphasizing the importance of patriotism. But the Democratic National Convention could not resist the temptation to praise Wilson for his success in keeping the nation out of war. Therefore, with some reluctance, Wilson campaigned on his record of preserving American neutrality. This proved to be an attractive issue and encouraged the Democrats to identify Hughes with the more bellicose Republicans and to accuse him of favoring war. At the same time Wilson stressed his legislative record. Appealing to peace and progressivism, Wilson won a narrow victory, holding the South and capturing the major states of the West.

Backed by the November victory, Wilson made a final peace effort on his own initiative. During December, he dispatched identical notes to all belligerent governments, requesting statements of war aims. The Allies feared and resented Wilson's action, for his new posture appeared too genuinely neutral. The effort was doomed to failure, simply because the war's toll predisposed the contestants to seek compensation that could come only with victory. None of the replies to Wilson's notes offered any promise of peace. Wilson voiced another plea for peace without victory in his noted Senate speech of January 22, 1917. "Only a peace between equals can last," he warned. Again he was rebuffed. His appeal to peace without victory was an appeal to a peace without gain; this no nation at war dared to consider.

Committed to victory by force of arms, the German high command, like the Allies, now reached a crisis of decision. Powerful spokesmen for the German army, especially Field Marshal Paul von Hindenburg, were demanding a resumption of unrestricted submarine warfare in a no-holds-barred effort to stop the flow of food and munitions into England and France. Without such a policy, he warned, he could no longer take responsibility for what might occur on the Western Front. In early 1917 the struggle behind the scenes between the cautious Bethmann-Hollweg and the impatient military chiefs came to a head. On January 8 it was decided that the U-boats would be released on February 1. The German Ambassador in Washington informed Lansing of the decision on January 31. Now every vessel afloat in English waters was subject to attack without warning. Wilson, following his *Sussex* threat, severed diplomatic ties with Germany.

With his choices disappearing before him, the President still hoped to avoid the necessity of sending men into Europe's most horrible of wars. Yet the pressures for involvement were relentless. Reports from Europe indicated that the Allies were on the verge of economic and military collapse. Meanwhile American ship captains remained in port, unwilling to enter the war zone without armaments. On February 26, the President attempted in vain to wrest authority from Congress to mount guns on merchant vessels; on February 25, the destruction of the British liner *Laconia* had demonstrated German determination to control English waters. The day before, the President had received a copy of a telegram, intercepted by

World War I: Attitudes and Reality

From 1914 until 1917, the United States felt increasing pressure to enter the war in Europe on the side of the Allies. This pressure, however, did not go unresisted; many Americans worked for peace—from the Socialists Eugene Debs and Victor Berger to the industrialist Henry Ford, who chartered the ocean liner *Oscar II* to take a group to Europe in the hope of establishing a conference for continuous mediation. Some of Ford's supporters appear on the ship's deck above.

President Wilson's own efforts to restore peace included sending Colonel Edward House abroad to sound out both the Allies and Germany. But peace efforts came to nothing. After two years of war, the combatants wanted results, not peace "without victory." Meanwhile, propaganda from England and France flooded the United States, softening the isolationism of people here. Finally, reaction to German submarine attacks on American shipping swept the nation into war.

Underwood and Underwood

The American propaganda effort, masterfully directed by George Creel, issued more than one hundred million pamphlets, posters, and newspaper editorials in its attempt to engage every segment of the American public in the war effort. At far right, socialite ladies pull a hurdy-gurdy up Fifth Avenue as they sell songs for the benefit of the troops. At near right, an artificial battleship stands in New York's Union Square to stimulate bond sales.

Left, below, the Women's Camouflage Corps practices its work on a city street. Left, a milk fund drive memorializes Lafayette. Below, a Chicago newspaper made movies of servicemen's families and sent them overseas as morale boosters although viewing conditions may have been difficult. Here the family of Eddie Brand poses for the movie camera.

Blindfolded, President Wilson picked out one of the pellets in the "gold fish bowl," thereby drafting one of the first members of the AEF (following page). Twenty-three years later Franklin D. Roosevelt reached into the same bowl for the number of a draftee in World War II. Approximately twenty-four million men between the ages of eighteen and forty-five registered for the World War I draft, of whom two million served in France.

Near left: Underwood and Underwood; far left above: The National Archives, Paul Thompson; all others: U. S. War Dept. General Staff, The National Archives

Inset and right, below: U.S. War Dept. General Staff, The National Archives; below and far right: U.S. Signal Corps, The National Archives; above: United Press International

World War I gave the world its first demonstration of the appalling destructive power of modern armaments. In four years, according to one estimate, 8,500,000 men of the Allied and Central powers died in battle, behind the lines, or from disease. Tens of thousands, like the plastic surgery cases above, left, sustained lifelong damage. Beyond the official casualties lay the starvation, homelessness, and unmeasured suffering of civilians.

The armistice brought rejoicing men home (following page). A group of the "Harlem Hell Fighters," holders of an outstanding combat record, appear at right.

Both above: United Press International; below: Brown Brothers; left: The National Archives

he National Archives, Paul Thompson

British intelligence, in which Alfred Zimmermann of the German Foreign Office proposed that Mexico enter an alliance with Germany in the event of an American declaration of war. For her efforts Mexico would receive the return of Texas, New Mexico, and California. Now as the sinkings mounted during late February and March, the American press demanded war. On April 2, the President read his war message to Congress, committing the nation both to victory and to the creation of a just and lasting peace. Congress responded quickly, the Senate adopting the war resolution on April 4 by a vote of 82 to 6; and the House two days later, 373 to 50. The United States was now at war.

Mobilization for War

America's declaration of war did little for the European Allies at first except to raise their morale. German submarines continued to destroy Allied shipping at the rate of 900,000 tons per month. Allied armies in France, unable to recover from the gigantic losses of 1916, had reached the point of despair. The U.S. Navy Department immediately assigned destroyers to antisubmarine duty in an effort to neutralize the German sea offensive. Wilson, meanwhile, pushed Congress for appropriations to create an effective war machine. General Joseph Joffre, commander of the French army in 1916, had estimated that a half million Americans would be required to assure an Allied victory. Once the United States began to mobilize, however, the War Department, under Secretary Newton D. Baker, proceeded to organize an army of 4 million men. This feat was made possible by the Selective Service Act of May 18, 1917, a statute requiring all men between the ages of twenty-one and thirty (later extended to forty-five) to register for the draft. So effective was the military mobilization that within eighteen months the United States was able to transport an American Expeditionary Force of 2 million soldiers to France.

American economic adjustment to the demands of war had begun long before April, 1917. By 1917 Allied borrowing and the sale of Allied securities had pumped $5 billion of purchasing power into the American economy, enough to produce a major boom in the steel and munitions industries. Allied purchases of wheat, meat, and sugar had produced unprecedented prosperity in American agriculture as well. For a time the unregulated American economy responded to Europe's demands with considerable success, but as early as 1915 the pressure created havoc in the competition for raw materials, for labor, and for control of the limited railroad and port facilities. Prices shot upward, causing distress among American workingmen and European buyers alike. Not until 1917, however, did the United States declaration of war give the federal government the needed incentive to organize the wartime economy.

On matters of national preparedness, federal coordination of industry had begun as early as 1915. The decision to expand the Navy led, in August, 1915, to the creation of a Committee on Industrial Preparedness concerned primarily with the future needs of the military services. The committee's chief task was that of preparing an inventory of American industries capable of producing munitions. As the pressure of Europe's war undermined the prospects of avoiding belligerency, the national leadership prepared to extend its control over the nation's life. The Military Appropriations Act of August, 1916, established a Council of National Defense with an advisory commission to plan the creation of a large military force. Although the National Defense Act of June, 1916, gave the President power to make demands on American industry in the interest of national defense, Congress's continuing assumption that the United States would not send troops abroad, its limited appropriations, and the isolationist outlook of many of its members retarded the development of an effective governmental organization for war. With the American entry in April, 1917, the War Department still found it impossible to coordinate the estimates of the various bureaus for the material required to equip an army of a million men. To meet the obvious need for coordination, the Council of National Defense in July, 1917, established the War Industries Board. Still it was not until after the appointment of Bernard Baruch to the chairmanship of the Board in the spring of 1918 that the problems of materials allocation were finally brought under control.

The War Industries Board, having no authority to make contracts, could operate only through other governmental offices as an advisory and informational agency. The Board's authority and prestige lay in the body of its accumulated knowledge and in the general recognition among officials and industrialists that the only alternative to cooperation was absolute chaos. It had the power to establish priorities and fix prices; its decisions, once established, generally determined the behavior of others. To bring general efficiency to American production, as well as to conserve raw materials and transportation, the War Industries Board introduced standardization of products and a sharp decrease in the number of styles and designs. This made it possible for countless industries to contribute to the manufacture of rifles, artillery, and other military items. The Board curtailed the production of many commodities meant primarily for civilian consumption, permitting the automobile industry, for example, to operate at only 25 percent of capacity in 1918. Controlling prices by agreement, not law, the Board enjoyed considerable success in limiting the prices of most basic raw materials. Consumer prices, however, continued to inch upward throughout the war, bringing large profits to many producers and merchandisers. Unable to limit profits, the federal government, in October, 1917, imposed a tax on those that exceeded the average of the immediate prewar years.

Europe's struggle exerted pressure on the nation's food supply as well as on its industrial resources. The export of American food rose from a yearly average of 7 million tons during the years 1912 to 1914 to over 12 million tons in 1917–1918 and over 18.6 million in 1918–1919. Competitive bidding for raw and processed foods created both wild price increases and much profiteering. To regulate the sale and shipment of food products the President asked Congress for special legislation. The Lever Act of August, 1917, established both the Food Administration and the Fuel Administration, the latter agency especially designed to govern the use of coal. To head the important Food Administration the President called on Herbert Hoover, the American mining engineer known for his brilliant success in handling Belgian relief during the early years of the war. Hoover's program as food administrator was similar to that of Baruch's for industry. Operating with a minimum of regulations and a staff of volunteers, Hoover managed to bring remarkable order to the

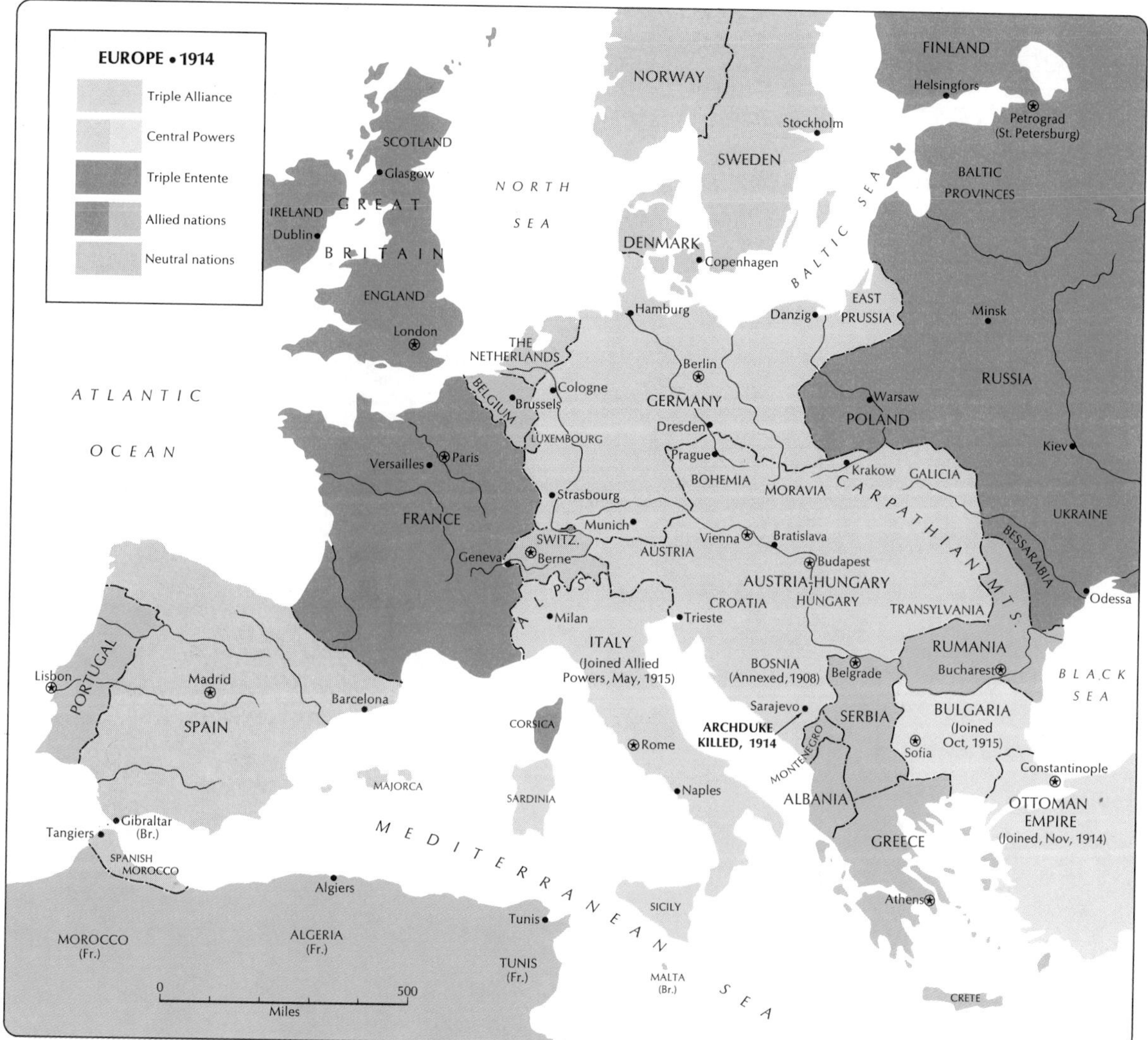

marketing and distribution of grain. He encouraged the production of hogs and wheat, two essential commodities, by establishing prices that guaranteed a profit to both farmers and processors. He opposed price controls in the retail market but asked the nation's women to practice restraint in their purchases of wheat and meat. By curtailing food consumption and the profit margins of food processors, Hoover reduced the gap between the prices paid to farmers and the prices paid by consumers. Indeed, farmers and consumers had never enjoyed a more mutually beneficial relationship than under Hoover's direction.

United States shipments of food and equipment to Europe required a tremendous fleet of merchant vessels. In September, 1916, even before the United States entered the war, the

0
500
Miles
NORWAY
SWEDEN
SCOTLAND
Glasgow
GREAT
BRITAIN
IRELAND
Dublin
ENGLAND
London
NORTH SEA
DENMARK
DEEPEST RUSSIAN PENETRATION, 1915
Hamburg
Danzig
Tannenberg
THE NETHERLANDS
See inset
ATLANTIC OCEAN
DEEPEST GERMAN PENETRATION SEPT 1914
Brussels
BELGIUM
Cologne
Berlin
GERMANY
Dresden
LUX.
ARMISTICE LINE NOV 11, 1918
Paris
Prague
Cracow
Strasbourg
Munich
AUSTRIA
Vienna
Bratislava
Berne
SWITZ.
FRANCE
Budapest
HUNGARY
ALPS
Milan
DEEPEST AUSTRIAN ADVANCE
Trieste
PORTUGAL
Lisbon
Madrid
SPAIN
ITALY
CORSICA
Rome
MONTENEGRO
MAJORCA
SARDINIA
Naples
ALBANIA
SPANISH MOROCCO
SICILY
MOROCCO (Fr.)
ALGERIA (Fr.)
TUNISIA (Fr.)
RIO DE ORO (Span.)
WORLD WAR I • 1914–1918
Central Powers
Neutral nations
Allied nations
Areas of intense submarine warfare
MEDITERRANEAN
TRIPOLITANIA (Italian)

LINE OF THE BREST–LITOVSK TREATY, 1918
Petrograd
Moscow
RUSSIA
Minsk
FRONT, OCT, 1917 (RUSSIAN REVOLUTION)
DEEPEST PENETRATION BY THE CENTRAL POWERS, 1918
Kiev
DEEPEST RUSSIAN PENETRATION, 1915
UKRAINE
Odessa
BLACK SEA
Constantinople
TURKEY
OTTOMAN EMPIRE
DARDANELLES FRONT, 1915
CRETE
CYPRUS
SEA
SYRIA
Damascus
Jerusalem
EGYPT (Br.)
Cairo
ARABIA
ARMENIA
CASPIAN SEA
TURKESTAN
PERSIA
Baghdad CAPTURE MAR 11, 1917
PERSIAN GULF
NORTH SEA
THE NETHERLANDS
ALLIED ADVANCE FALL, 1918
Ypres
Brussels
BELGIUM
Meuse R.
GERMANY
Rhine R.
FRONT JAN, 1915
Amiens
LUX.
Soissons
Seine R.
Paris
Château-Thierry
Marne R.
Verdun
St. Mihiel
ARMISTICE LINE NOV 11, 1918
GERMAN ADVANCE MARCH–JULY, 1918
DEEPEST GERMAN PENETRATION, 1914
FRANCE
Western Front
0 100
Miles
SWITZ.

shortage of tonnage under British and American control prompted Congress to establish the United States Shipping Board to direct the flow of goods across the Atlantic. With the declaration of war in April, 1917, Congress chartered the United States Emergency Fleet Corporation to oversee the construction of a "bridge of ships" to the Allies. Under the direction of Edward H. Hurley, the Emergency Fleet Corporation succeeded in producing hundreds of vessels—enough to meet the demands of war. In 1918 alone American yards launched over 2.6 million tons. The huge yard at Hog Island, near Philadelphia, demonstrated the efficacy of constructing ships by mass-production techniques, although the Hog Island yard did not deliver its first ship until December, 1918, almost a month after the end of the war.

William G. McAdoo, Secretary of the Treasury, produced another triumph for federal regulation as chairman of the United States Railroad Administration. At the outbreak of the war, the railroad industry revealed all the ills of excessive competition, especially the duplication of terminal facilities, tracks, and rolling stock—all suffering from underuse. Without the coordination of shipments among railroads or between the railroads and the shipping facilities along the Atlantic seaboard, rail traffic became so congested that it neared the point of breakdown. When, late in 1917, the Railroad Administration gained control of the nation's rail transportation, the situation seemed hopeless. By assuring the railroads a fair profit, assigning skilled engineers to the running of the trains, directing traffic by shorter routes, increasing carloads, enforcing the common use of terminals, and coordinating railroad and ocean shipping, the Railroad Administration soon got the nation's freight moving. At war's end the railroads, despite the unprecedented volume of traffic they carried, again had a surplus of 300,000 cars.

Economic Change

Ultimately the cost of the war had to be borne by the American people through loans and taxes. Britain and France created a heavy demand prior to American entrance into the war by draining their own resources and establishing credit in the United States through the sale of securities. For the United States government the cost of the involvement from April, 1917, to June, 1920, was approximately $24 billion. During this period the United States covered Allied demands on the American economy with government loans totaling about $9.5 billion. The nation met these expenditures with $10.7 billion in special wartime taxes and $23 billion in deficit spending. In August, 1919, the war debt had reached $24.5 billion. It was this growing indebtedness that exerted the wartime pressures which resulted in rising prices. To increase tax revenues the government resorted to special income, excess profits, and excise taxes. By far the most important of these was the excess profits tax which, in the year ending June 30, 1918, yielded over $2 billion. At first the government, in its borrowing, relied on bank credit. Eventually it supplemented this source with huge flotations of Liberty Bonds, of which 30 percent, totaling $7 billion, were purchased by citizens with annual incomes of $2,000 or less. Altogether, the United States financed about 34 percent of the war cost through taxes and the rest by borrowing.

Responding to the demands of war, the American economy proved itself an astonishingly productive machine. Agriculture was the exception. Despite the heavy demands placed on American agriculture by the war, poor climatic conditions held production in 1916 and 1917 below the two previous years. In 1918, with agricultural prices double what they had been before the war, agricultural production exceeded that of 1914 by only 1 percent. But in industry, mining, and transportation, annual production in the war years far outstripped that of 1914. In certain industries the expansion was phenomenal. In 1917 the 45 million long tons of steel production doubled the prewar level. Aluminum production that year was more than twice what it had been before the war.

Those responsible for the miracle of domestic production in wartime—labor, agriculture, and industry—did not share equally the rewards of prosperity. The labor picture was mixed. President Wilson's War Labor Board, established in April, 1918, represented the interests of labor in wartime industrial disputes. It ruled out strikes and lockouts in the cause of industrial production, but it also encouraged unionization by recognizing the principle of collective bargaining. Union membership responded to the opportunities created by the war. By 1919 Samuel Gompers's AF of L boasted a membership of 4.1 million as compared with 2.7 million in 1914. But labor made its wartime gains largely from full and continuous employment rather than from wage increases, for the rise in wages barely kept pace with the soaring cost of living. And if factory workers made only small gains from their increased wages, those with fixed incomes suffered a comparative depression in the midst of wartime prosperity. The nation's farmers fared much better, for wartime food demands resulted in rapidly rising prices and a gain in farm income from $4 billion in 1914 to $10 billion in 1918.

By far the greatest profits, of course, went to the giant corporations engaged in war production. The net incomes of large American corporations, as a whole, almost doubled between 1913 and 1916, reaching $7 billion in the latter year. Facing a heavy excess profits tax, corporations deflated their profit margins by paying large salaries and bonuses to their top officials. Thus the private income of business executives rose sharply. The number of those whose incomes ranged between $30,000 and $40,000 increased from 6,000 in 1914 to 15,400 in 1918. By the end of the war some 42,000 Americans had entered the millionaire class.

The Quest for National Unity

Unfortunately the mobilization of the American economy proved to be much simpler than the mobilization of the American mind. Thousands of Americans never accepted the necessity, much less the morality, of America's decision to enter the war. A powerful and vociferous minority among them, convinced that the United States had no vital interest in a German defeat, continued to attack the Wilson administration. Conscious of the need for national unity, the President, on April 14, 1917, appointed his Committee on Public Information. Under its vigorous and thoroughly dedicated chairman, George Creel, this committee assumed the task of mobilizing national sentiment in support of the war. By appealing to patriotism and anti-German sentiment among the nation's intelligentsia, Creel managed to enlist artists, actors, writers, and educators, who flooded the country with propaganda pamphlets, posters, and carefully prepared newspaper editorials. Creel unleashed on the country thousands of public speakers, who barraged movie audiences, public gatherings, schoolrooms, women's clubs, and even foreign language groups with anti-German oratory.

Wilson, in his conduct of the war, enjoyed from the beginning the nonactive support of a vast majority of Americans who, with varying degrees of enthusiasm, simply accepted the decisions of government without question. But the support which he required to silence his opposition came from a powerful minority of national leaders, among them Theodore Roosevelt, who believed that the government had the obligation to smother all wartime dissent. Some who favored repression did so from a genuine fear or hatred of German militarism, others from patriotic convictions which placed all wartime policies above the moral and intellectual right of debate. After April, 1917, leading proponents of the war recommended stern reprisals against dissenters before it was too late. Elihu Root delighted a crowd at the Union League Club in August by declaring that "there are men walking about the streets of this city tonight who ought to be taken out at sunrise tomorrow and shot for treason."

In accepting the Espionage Act of June, 1917, Congress established a policy of wartime repression that Lincoln had rejected as unnecessary during the Civil War. The law was designed to discourage, by fines up to $10,000 and imprisonment up to twenty years, any "false reports or false statements" which might interfere with the successful operation of the nation's military and naval forces or with the processes of recruitment and enlistment. The Espionage Act failed to quiet the antiwar activities of radical and pacifist groups, so Congress broadened its definition of espionage in the Sedition Act of May, 1918, to include anyone who might obstruct the sale of United States bonds or "willfully utter, print, write, or publish any disloyal, profane, scurrilous, or abusive language about the form of government of the United States, or the Constitution . . . or the flag of the United States, or the uniform of the Army or Navy, or bring the form of government . . . into contempt." The new law silenced more critics, but not all of them.

Armed with these two measures, federal officials proceeded to censor movies and the press. They ordered the motion picture industry to bury all pacifist films. Major newspapers and magazines were no challenge to the censors, for, with few exceptions, they reflected the conventional attitudes and sympathy for the war. What occupied the censors was not even occasional major newspapers such as Oswald Villard's *New York Evening Post,* which opposed national policy, but the dozens of small radical and reform presses which never ceased to condemn the war. In August, 1917, the government ordered the New York postmaster to bar the radical publication *Masses* from the mails. In November, 1917, it suppressed two Socialist papers, the *Milwaukee Leader* and the *New York Call.* Under the Trading with the Enemy Act of October, 1917, the government put restrictions on the foreign language press. Such federal pressure compelled most German language newspapers to drop their criticism and support the war.

Ultimately the nation's drive for conformity centered on individuals. Among those convicted under the Espionage and Sedition laws, the most notable were Eugene V. Debs and

Victor L. Berger, both leading spokesmen of the Socialist party. Debs, who defended the right of free speech at Canton, Ohio, in June, 1918, and then for two hours attacked capitalism and predicted the ultimate triumph of socialism, was indicted for provoking resistance to the United States government and ultimately sentenced to ten years in prison. Berger, editor of the *Milwaukee Leader,* was indicted in 1918 for his antiwar editorials, and in February, 1919, with four other Socialists, received a twenty-year prison sentence. Later he won an appeal to the United States Supreme Court and thus did not serve his sentence. But the case of Charles T. Schenck, general secretary of the Socialist party, was perhaps most noteworthy, for it presented the occasion for Justice Oliver Wendell Holmes's opinion in *Schenck v. United States,* upholding the conviction on the grounds that the defendant's words had created "a clear and present danger" to the national security.

Wartime pressures for conformity were private and local as well as public and federal. In almost every community editors and patriotic groups exerted great moral, economic, and social pressure on those who disapproved of the war or its conduct. In many regions of the United States, German-Americans suffered untold abuse because of the general assumption that they favored a German victory. To assure orthodoxy in word and thought, many patriotic societies attempted to ban everything German: operas, symphonies, sauerkraut, even the German language. Whatever the exertions of the Wilson administration and its supporters to silence the war's critics, they never succeeded in convincing a significant minority of intelligent Americans that the nation's involvement was wise or just.

Wilson's Peace Program

It was obvious even before mobilization began that the United States possessed the physical strength to bring victory to England and France, and thus right the European balance—at least temporarily. But far more important for the twentieth century than American involvement in the Great War was the nature and purpose of that involvement. Victory demanded American production and manpower, both readily available in huge quantities, but victory and stability were not synonymous. Thus the critical challenge to Wilson's wartime leadership lay in his conceptualization of America's proper role in world politics. His choices were basically two. He could, in ending a tradition of political and military isolation from Europe, introduce the United States to an established international system on that system's terms. Or he could reject that system as outmoded and incapable of protecting the interests of the United States. The President chose the second course.

After April, 1917, Wilson accepted the obligation not only to organize and direct the nation's great power toward the achievement of an Allied victory in Europe, but also to lead the world toward the establishment of a rational international order. Long before the United States entered the European conflict, the President had assigned it a totally unprecedented role in history. This nation's political, social, and moral uniqueness, he believed, had given it a transcendent mission to serve humanity. America was born, he said, that all men might be free. In his inaugural of March 4, 1913, he asked that the government "be perfected so that it might be put to the service of humanity." Europe's wartime experience rendered this American mission all the more essential. Wilson, after August, 1914, informed the nation repeatedly that Europe beckoned, not alone for material aid, but for leadership in creating a world of lasting peace and security. For him that world required, above all, the establishment of free governments everywhere. "Only free peoples," he said, "can hold their purposes and their honor steady to a common end and prefer the interests of mankind to any interest of their own." Increasingly, Wilson's postulate for world peace and stability was the principle of self-determination. It was essential, he said, "that every people should be left free to determine its own polity . . . unhindered, unthreatened, unafraid, the little along with the great and powerful." As a logical extension of this purpose, the President condemned imperialism, autocracy, aggression, and every other irrational use of force for the repression of populations. In his war message of April, 1917, Wilson insisted that the United States would enter Europe's struggle to save the world from the misuse of power. "It is a fearful thing," he admitted, "to lead this great peaceful people to war. . . . But the right is more precious than peace, and we shall fight for the things which we have always carried nearest in our hearts—for democracy, for the right of those who submit to authority to have a voice in their own governments, for the rights and liberties of small nations, for a universal dominion of right by such a concert of free peoples as shall bring peace and safety to all nations and make the world itself at last free."

After April, 1917, Wilson's crusade for humanity required a program capable of translating the nation's wartime efforts into a structure of lasting peace. Most Americans agreed with the President that Germany carried primary responsibility for the war. But for him the real trouble lay not in Germany but in the European system of diplomacy. The President required an alternative that would anchor relations among nations, not to the will of the governments, but to the will of mankind. Wilson's commitment to a world organization came slowly. The Great War, with its unprecedented horrors, had driven thoughtful Europeans and Americans alike to the realization that the prevention of another war demanded a new world order. One group of concerned Americans had organized the League to Enforce Peace in 1915. Their central problem lay in their inability to frame a system of collective security. Would its coercive powers rest upon force or world opinion? Leaders of the League to Enforce Peace generally believed that the mere accusation of aggression, following a minute examination of rival claims, would prevent the great majority of wars. Wilson, like the others, could not define the role of force and national commitment in a system of collective security, but events compelled him to accept the league idea in principle. Addressing a meeting of the League to Enforce Peace in May, 1916, he publicly endorsed American membership in a postwar international organization. Again, in his noted speech before the Senate on January 22, 1917, he reaffirmed the American commitment to membership in a league of nations.

In September, 1917, Wilson established The Inquiry, a group of experts to frame specific war aims for the United States. What exerted pressure on Wilson as well as the European Allies was the Russian Revolution of 1917. During November the Bolsheviks drove the Provisional Government from power and threatened to take Russia out of the war. Hesitant to face German negotiators alone, the Bolsheviks requested that the Western Allies enter the quest for peace by formulating a liberal peace program acceptable to Germany. Aided by a long memorandum from The Inquiry, the President now prepared his "Fourteen Points" address which he delivered to a joint session of Congress on January 8, 1918. Wilson argued for open diplomacy; self-determination for the alien peoples in the German, Austro-Hungarian, and Turkish empires; freedom of the seas; and the reduction of armaments. But, for Wilson, the fourteenth point was the one that mattered: "A general association of nations must be formed under specific covenants for . . . mutual guarantees of political independence and territorial integrity to great and small states alike." This speech elevated Wilson to a primary position among allied leaders and brought him the support of liberal sentiment throughout the world. Wilson had presented a program which at last seemed to make the burden of the war worthwhile. Unfortunately there was little possibility that Wilson's peace program would survive the end of the fighting. Whereas his Fourteen Points promised a just settlement, they solved few of the genuine conflicts in human society. His notions of justice could sustain a common hope only as long as people ignored their specific, individual preferences. Everyone favored the rights of humanity. Neither Americans nor Europeans, however, could agree on whose rights should be paramount, for no settlement could guarantee the rights of all. Wilson's phraseology raised every human political and territorial aspiration, but in practice the rights of humanity would be precisely what the spokesmen of the victorious powers chose to make them.

Wilson's peace program failed to keep Russia in the war, for the Bolsheviks not only imposed a ruthless dictatorship over the Russian people but also negotiated a peace with the Central Powers. This permitted the Germans to transfer massive forces from the Eastern to the Western Front for the 1918 offensive. The President balked at recognizing a thoroughly undemocratic regime in Russia, whereas Lansing worried less about its undemocratic nature than its militant ideology of world revolution. Perhaps an American policy which distinguished between Bolshevism and Russian liberalism could still return the Russian revolution to its initial democratic course. But if the Wilson administration denied recognition to the Bolshevik regime, it hesitated to commit the United States to the Allied effort to overthrow the Bolsheviks and restore the Eastern Front. In mid-1918 the President approved limited armed intervention in Siberia and northern Russia, but basically he believed that the question of the Russian government was an internal matter for the Russians themselves to decide. In the Bolshevik Revolution the President did not desert his principles of self-determination.

Japan's Wartime Challenge

Even before 1917 Japan issued a warning that the President's concept of a just peace would have rough sailing in the real world of power politics. The Tokyo government had recognized in the European war an unprecedented opportunity to expand, at China's expense, its imperial role in the Far East. Late in August, 1914, Japan declared war on Germany and proceeded to occupy the German-held Shantung Peninsula in north China, as well as the

German islands in the north Pacific—the Marianas, Carolines, and Marshalls. Then to strengthen their hand in China while Europe was still at war, Japanese officials confronted a weak Chinese government with their Twenty-One Demands. By stalling, the Chinese managed to eliminate the six most stringent Japanese demands, but in May, 1915, under a direct ultimatum, China agreed to the fifteen that remained. These included the recognition of Japanese rights in Shantung.

Washington watched Japan's aggression, determined to protect China but, if possible, to avoid direct involvement in the Far Eastern conflict. During March, 1915, Secretary of State Bryan, to reassure Japan, acknowledged the fact "that territorial contiguity creates special relations between Japan and these districts." In May, however, he warned Japan that the United States would recognize no treaty imposed on China which impaired American treaty rights, Chinese integrity, or the principle of the Open Door. Facing a direct conflict with the United States over China, the Tokyo government, in October, 1915, joined the European alliance fighting Germany, and by 1917 had forced from her hard-pressed European allies an acknowledgment of Japanese claims to Shantung and the German islands north of the equator. In exchange, Japan agreed to convoy Australian troops to Europe.

After April, 1917, both the United States and Japan faced the prospect of a direct and bitter diplomatic confrontation at the peace table. It appeared essential, therefore, that the two allies reach a wartime understanding on the China question. In August, 1917, the Japanese government sent a mission to the United States under Viscount Kikujiro Ishii to confer with American leaders. Ishii sought American recognition of Japan's "paramount interests" in China, and Colonel House urged Wilson to accept the Japanese request. The President, however, made it clear to Ishii that the United States desired nothing less than Japanese observance of the Open Door principle. With this Ishii agreed, but in his subsequent negotiations with Lansing he insisted that any agreement include a statement of Japan's special interests in China. Both Lansing and Ishii wanted a formal agreement; to obtain it they employed the intriguing device of incorporating both the American and the Japanese viewpoints in the same document. The Lansing-Ishii Agreement of November 2, 1917, recognized "that Japan has special interests in China, particularly in that part to which her possessions are contiguous." At the same time the two nations agreed to adhere to the principle of the Open Door, or equal opportunity for commerce and industry in China. Such conflicting phraseology could be interpreted to mean anything or nothing, as individual Japanese, Chinese, and American officials and editors might prefer.

The European Armistice

Wilson faced the central challenge to his wartime leadership in Europe. He understood, with good reason, that the European Allies did not share his liberal peace program except at the upper level of vague generality. As time went on, the President learned of the secret treaties whereby the Allied Powers had promised one another certain long-standing territorial objectives. But Wilson refused to commit the United States government to any Allied arrangements or even to acknowledge openly the existence of the secret treaties. He assumed that the war's end would find the Allies so dependent upon the United States for economic and military aid that he could impose on them his own conceptions of a proper peace. Hence Wilson guarded his independence of action by refusing to enter a formal alliance with Britain and France, officially designating the United States only as an "Associated Power" in the Western coalition.

But Wilson had anchored his intent to determine the postwar settlement not only to his wartime diplomatic independence but also to the nation's military contribution to victory. The successful organization of the economy and popular support for the war provided a strong base for the creation of effective American fighting units overseas. To command the American Expeditionary Forces in France, Wilson chose General John J. Pershing, an able and imposing officer. So rapid and successful had been the American effort to create, train, and equip an army that Pershing's units began to arrive in France before the end of 1917. This raised a sharp controversy over their final training and commitment to battle. In the interest of speed, British and French commanders wanted American forces amalgamated with their own. Pershing opposed amalgamation, explaining to the President, "We must look forward to bearing a very heavy part in this conflict before it ends, and our forces should not be dissipated for a temporary emergency. Moreover, it is unnecessary to say, when the war ends, our position will be stronger if our army acting as such shall have played a distinctive and definite part." Wilson, recognizing the diplomatic advantage that would come with demonstrable American successes, upheld Pershing's decision. The American forces were kept intact and given their own sector on the Western Front.

In March, 1918, Germany launched a desperate offensive, driving the British back in the Somme valley and the French to the Marne. During June, American forces counterattacked, pushing the Germans back across the Marne at Chateau-Thierry and clearing Belleau Wood. The Germans, on July 15, made another drive toward Paris; but three days later their effort was finished. Fresh American forces had made the difference. General Ferdinand Foch, Allied Supreme Commander, now ordered his counteroffensive. On August 8, the British broke through the Hindenburg Line, while French and American forces destroyed German resistance along the Aisne-Marne, St. Mihiel, and Argonne sectors. Then began the Allied push across France. Now as the British and French rolled over the German army along the Northern and Central Fronts, Pershing's command pushed forward along the Southern Front at Meuse-Argonne. In October, German army leaders, thoroughly demoralized, urged the German government to seek armistice terms from President Wilson. This it did to end what had been the bloodiest war in history. American battle deaths of 48,000 were small compared with the 1,300,000 French and 900,000 British killed, but Pershing and the Americans had played the decisive role in the Allied victory of 1918.

On October 12, the German government, under Prince Max of Baden, agreed to an armistice based on Wilson's Fourteen Points. To assure the Allies that he was protecting their interests, Wilson demanded the abdication of the Kaiser as a condition of peace. On October 20, Prince Max accepted the President's terms and promised sweeping political reforms based on democratic procedures. The President forwarded the German replies to Allied leaders only to discover that they anticipated a total

German collapse and therefore had no interest in an armistice based on the quite liberal Fourteen Points. Wilson thereupon threatened to repudiate any Allied program that conflicted with his views; Colonel House, meanwhile, warned the British and French governments that unless they agreed to the Fourteen Points the United States would leave the war. Thus pressured, the Allied Supreme War Council on November 4 approved a prearmistice agreement, based largely on the Fourteen Points but with two qualifications concerning freedom of the seas and damages to civilians in German-occupied territory. On November 11, German representatives signed the Armistice, bringing the long, exhaustive war to an end.

Wilson at Versailles

The moment of peacemaking for which Wilson had so assiduously prepared himself had arrived. American power and prestige seemed to tower above a stricken Europe. Unencumbered by wartime concessions, the President was confident that he could impose his conditions on Europe. The opinions of mankind which, believed Wilson, had responded to his ideals, would crush those who stood in the way. "National purposes," he proclaimed in September, 1918, "have fallen more and more into the background and the common purpose of enlightened mankind has taken their place."

Wilson, accompanied by a large American delegation, crossed the Atlantic during December, 1918, aboard the *George Washington.* Wilson's reception in Europe was tumultuous, reaffirming his impression that Europeans welcomed him as the savior, not of their interests in victory, but of mankind. When the Versailles Peace Conference opened in Paris on January 12, 1919, delegations from thirty-two nations were present. From the beginning it was clear that the issues at stake in the Conference were too complex to permit their settlement in general sessions. Of necessity, therefore, the Big Four—Wilson, Lloyd George of England, Georges Clemenceau of France, and Vittorio Orlando of Italy—took command of the Conference and conferred as a Council of Four. The newsmen who jammed Paris soon discovered to their dismay that the four leaders, despite Wilson's past condemnation of secret diplomacy, would conduct their business in secrecy.

Wilson now learned to his sorrow that Europe's interest in his leadership, after all, lay in his capacity to produce men and material for the Allied cause, not in the nobility of his vision for humanity. Europe's spokesmen could discover in the international system no substitute for power politics and all of its accouterments. Wilson's condemnation of Europe's diplomacy they either resented or ignored. Wilson came to Paris to avoid any negotiation within the framework of the secret treaties. But his efforts to eliminate them with appeals to abstract principles such as self-determination fell on deaf ears. "God gave us the Ten Commandments," was Clemenceau's cynical comment, "and we broke them. Wilson gave us the Fourteen Points. We shall see." For such sarcasm Wilson was unprepared. Professor Thomas A. Bailey described Wilson's predicament well: "With his head in a daze, and his feet tangled in a web of secret treaties, he battled his adversaries at a serious disadvantage."

Fortunately for Wilson, the independence of Eastern Europe, so prominent an objective in his Fourteen Points, flowed easily from the collapse of the Central Powers. Even before the Versailles Conference met, the peoples of Eastern and Southeastern Europe had established a new political order; the Conference had merely to recognize the change. Still this fulfillment of the principle of self-determination proved to be agonizingly difficult, for Wilson could not tidy up the map of Europe by establishing a series of new nations, each representing a national grouping. Past migration and conquests made self-determination for Europe totally impractical. Nor did the Conference hesitate to assign German territory to the new Slavic nations. Danzig, an important Baltic seaport in the German enclave of East Prussia, presented a special problem, for any Polish corridor to Danzig would not only attach a German population to Poland but also separate a body of East Prussians from the German nation. The Conference granted Poland a corridor and designated Danzig as a free city, all in defiance of the principle of self-determination. For what seemed good strategic reasons, the Conference assigned the Germans of the Sudeten region to Czechoslovakia.

Italy, in accordance with the secret Treaty of London of 1915, claimed and received the Austrian Trentino to the Brenner Pass, as well as Trieste on the Dalmatian coast below the port of Fiume. Wilson accepted these arrangements despite their defiance of the principle of self-determination. But Wilson rejected the Italian claims to Fiume, for this port constituted the new Yugoslavia's only outlet to the sea. When Wilson, on April 23, 1919, appealed directly over the heads of the Italian delegation to the people of Italy on the question of Fiume, the delegation left the Conference. Returning two weeks later, Orlando managed to reserve the issue for later negotiation between Italy and Yugoslavia. Wilson's solution of applying plebiscites to troublesome areas had the effect of avoiding rather than solving the problems inherent in the assigning of territory to specific nations. It is significant, moreover, that he never applied the doctrine of self-determination to the victors at all. The Versailles Conference did not touch the established empires of Britain, France, Belgium, Holland, or the United States. In practice, the principle of self-determination became a readily available device for punishing the losers, especially in the region of Eastern Europe. By assigning primarily German areas to the new Slavic states, the Versailles Conference served neither the Wilsonian goal of self-determination nor the cause of peace.

Germany confronted the Allies with questions equally demanding and far more divisive. France, through its spokesman Clemenceau, sought the dismemberment of Germany through the creation of one or two Rhenish republics along the west bank of the Rhine. Wilson argued, in a series of long, violent debates, that French demands ignored both the prearmistice agreement and the principle of self-determination. When Clemenceau, in exasperation, accused Wilson of being pro-German, the President prepared to abandon the Conference. Clemenceau now yielded on the question of the Rhenish republics but gained the right to a French occupation of the Rhineland and special guaranty treaties by which Britain and the United States promised to come to France's aid in the event of future unprovoked German attack. France gained as well the permanent demilitarization of the west bank of the Rhine, the limitation of the German ground forces to 100,000 men, and the complete elimination of German naval and air forces. On the matter of reparations, Wilson faced both Clemenceau and Lloyd

George, each backed by a determined public opinion that demanded payment by Germany of the entire cost of the Allied war effort. In the end Wilson agreed in principle to heavy, but undefined, reparations to be paid by Germany, and accepted a specific treaty article assigning to Germany and her allies full responsibility for the war.

Wilson accepted readily the notion that the former German colonies should not be returned to Germany, but he intended that they should be governed by small nations under an international mandate. During the war Britain and her dominions, along with Japan, had occupied the German colonies in Africa and the Pacific and demanded at Paris that their possession be recognized by treaty. Eventually Wilson recognized the right of occupation for Britain and the dominions, although he held tenaciously to the principle that these colonies came under a political mandate of the League of Nations for the protection of the native peoples. Under the new mandate system the German islands in the Pacific north of the equator passed to the control of Japan.

On the question of Shantung, Wilson was less successful. The Japanese based their case for retention of Shantung on their nation's contribution to the Allied war effort in the Pacific, on the Allied wartime guarantees, and on the rights of conquest and occupation. Wilson argued that German rights in Shantung reverted to China with the German defeat. At Wilson's insistence, V. K. Wellington Koo, the Chinese Ambassador to the United States and head of the Chinese delegation at Paris, addressed the Big Four, basing his appeal on the American principles of self-determination and the Open Door. He reminded the delegates that China had signed its wartime agreements with Japan under duress. He terminated his argument by insisting that the Chinese people had the right to govern their own territory. Koo had won a moral victory, but he did not dissuade the British and French leaders from honoring their wartime pledges to Japan. Against the three Allies, standing as one on the Shantung question, Wilson's principles had no chance. He agreed finally to a clause transferring Shantung to Japan on the latter's promise that the territory would be returned eventually to China. The Chinese delegation showed its chagrin by refusing to sign the treaty.

Wilson's record at Versailles was one of compromise. His ideal had proved ineffective when confronted by the specific political, territorial, and security interests of the Allies. But for Wilson one issue outweighed all others—the establishment of the League of Nations. This question, if resolved satisfactorily, would in time permit some evolution toward a world that conformed to his vision of a peaceful international order. The French favored a league, but one that would underwrite with force a European balance of power and thereby guarantee French security. The French plan, presented on February 3, 1919, proposed the creation of an international army and a general staff with power to make critical demands on the member states. Wilson, on the other hand, anticipated a league that would replace power politics with a universal alliance against war and the use of force. Wilson's league would rely on the leadership of the major powers and on the cooperation of all. Underlying his league would be a general harmony of interest in peace and justice, reflected in a rational world opinion.

In presenting his Covenant to the Peace Conference on February 14, the President declared that its success would depend ultimately on the "moral force of the public opinion of the world." Armed force, he admitted, "is in the background in this program, . . . and if the moral force of the world will not suffice, the physical force of the world shall. But that is the last resort." By holding the Conference together and making numerous concessions on other questions, Wilson managed to embody a League of Nations in the Treaty of Versailles. A combination of American and British ideas, the Covenant provided for an Assembly in which all nations would be represented, a Council composed of the major powers, and a Secretariat. Wilson considered Article X which guaranteed the "territorial integrity and political independence" of all members to be "the heart of the covenant."

On May 17, 1919, the victors summoned representatives of Germany to Paris to receive the treaty. They granted the Germans several days to study the terms and to propose modifications. Unable to introduce any significant changes, the Germans accepted the treaty almost as presented. They had little choice, for their refusal to sign the document would have triggered an Allied invasion of Germany. On June 28, German representatives not associated with the wartime leadership signed the treaty in the Hall of Mirrors at Versailles.

The Great Debate

Treaty in hand, Wilson returned to Washington on July 8, 1919, prepared to battle with the Senate for its approval. The President, at that crucial moment, faced a powerful partisan challenge to his leadership at home as the result, in part, of his own decisions. Against the advice of several Democratic friends, he chose, during the November, 1918, elections, to make his forthcoming negotiations in Paris hinge on a Democratic congressional victory. The election of a Republican majority, he warned the nation, would be interpreted in Europe as a repudiation of his leadership. This permitted Republican congressmen to interpret their victories in 1918 as indeed a repudiation of the President's leadership. They now possessed the power, moreover, to make their resentment effective. Wilson had fanned that resentment by failing to appoint a prominent Republican to the peace commission. Indeed, three of the men he named to join him on the commission—House, Lansing, and General Tasker H. Bliss—were associated with his administration. The fourth, Henry White, a noted diplomat, was only a nominal Republican. Despite the fact that he would face a Republican majority in the Senate, the President had made no effort to consult those Republican leaders who would determine the ultimate fate of his treaty.

During the President's absence in Paris, Republican leaders in Washington, guided by Senator Henry Cabot Lodge of Massachusetts, had worked out their strategy of opposition. Lodge's motives in challenging the President were complex. The Massachusetts Senator harbored both a deep personal dislike for Wilson and a profound distrust of his leadership. He had long been convinced, moreover, that the particular League plan proposed by Wilson would not serve the interest of the United States. Lodge's criticism—and that of his Republican colleagues—raised legitimate questions regarding the League's contemplated role. There was also in Lodge's opposition a strong element of partisanship. As Republican leader in the Senate, he saw early that Republican prospects in the 1920 presidential election

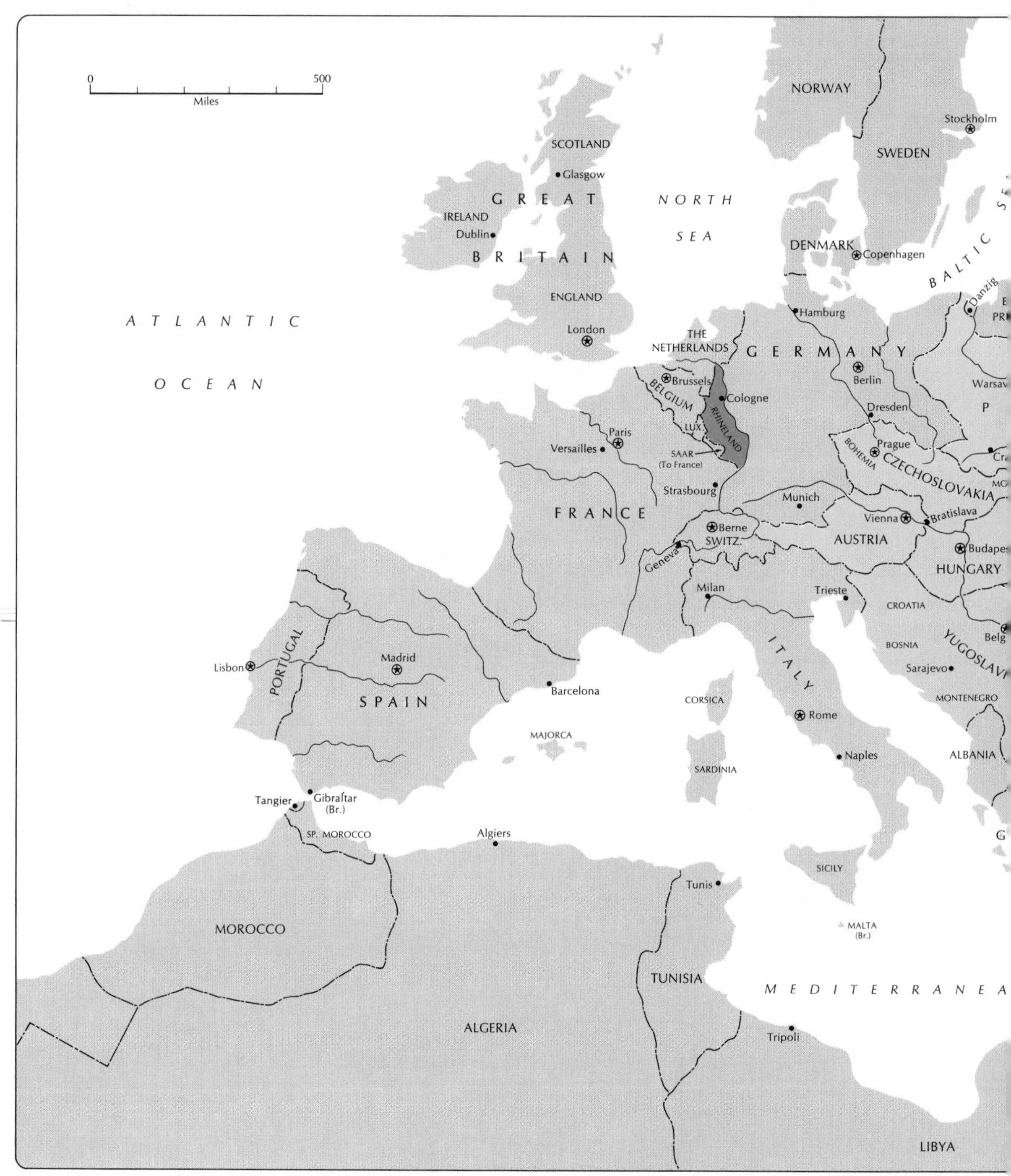
0
500
Miles
NORWAY
Stockholm
SWEDEN
SCOTLAND
Glasgow
GREAT
BRITAIN
IRELAND
Dublin
NORTH
SEA
DENMARK
Copenhagen
BALTIC
Danzig
Hamburg
ENGLAND
London
ATLANTIC
OCEAN
THE
NETHERLANDS
GERMANY
Berlin
Brussels
BELGIUM
Cologne
RHINELAND
LUX.
Paris
Versailles
SAAR
(To France)
Dresden
Prague
BOHEMIA
CZECHOSLOVAKIA
Strasbourg
Munich
FRANCE
Berne
SWITZ.
Geneva
Vienna
Bratislava
AUSTRIA
HUNGARY
Milan
Trieste
CROATIA
BOSNIA
YUGOSLAVIA
Sarajevo
MONTENEGRO
ALBANIA
ITALY
Rome
Naples
CORSICA
SARDINIA
MAJORCA
Barcelona
PORTUGAL
Lisbon
Madrid
SPAIN
Tangier
Gibraltar
(Br.)
SP. MOROCCO
Algiers
Tunis
SICILY
MALTA
(Br.)
MOROCCO
TUNISIA
MEDITERRANEA
ALGERIA
Tripoli
LIBYA

EUROPE AND THE NEAR EAST • 1920
New independent nations
Mandated to Allied powers
Allied occupation zone
Petrograd
Moscow
Minsk
Kiev
UNION OF SOVIET SOCIALIST REPUBLICS
ARAL SEA
UKRAINE
BESSARABIA
Odessa
CASPIAN SEA
TURKESTAN
Bucharest
BLACK SEA
ARMENIA
Constantinople
TURKEY
Ankara
PERSIA
SYRIA
(To France)
CYPRUS
CRETE
Beirut
IRAQ
(To Britain)
KUWAIT
PALESTINE
(To Britain)
TRANSJORDAN
(To Britain)
NEUTRAL ZONE
PERSIAN GULF
Alexandria
EGYPT
ARABIA

hinged on that party's success in handling the League issue. Lodge suspected that the Democratic party and much of the nation were united behind the President. Unless the Republican party could be organized behind one moderate program in opposition to Wilson's League and could eventually convert popular sentiment to the support of its views, the party's chances in 1920 were less than promising. In preparing the Republican position, Lodge worked in what he regarded to be the best interests of his party. As he wrote to Albert J. Beveridge in March, "My first duty is to keep the Republican Party in the Senate together." Lodge read his first warning to Wilson early in March, 1919, when he circulated the so-called Round Robin resolution among Senate Republicans. This declared, in effect, that the League of Nations, as proposed by the Peace Conference, was unacceptable to the Senate. When Lodge presented the resolution to the Senate, the chairman ruled him out of order, but Lodge proceeded nonetheless to read the names of the thirty-seven Republican signers. Clearly the President was in trouble.

To achieve a united Republican front against Wilson, Lodge required the support of Senators Hiram Johnson and William E. Borah, as well as other Republican irreconcilables who opposed any kind of League as basically un-American and contrary to the country's historic foreign policies. Lodge in the summer of 1919 suggested to Borah that a number of amendments or resolutions to the League Covenant might better defend the American interest than Wilson's League. When Borah agreed to support Lodge's strategy, Lodge prevailed upon the Republican elder statesman Elihu Root to draft a series of reservations. Among these was the principle that the United States would accept no mandate and employ no armed forces without permission of Congress. In addition, the Monroe Doctrine was to be considered "wholly outside the jurisdiction of the League of Nations." These and other reservations, Lodge insisted, were not meant to destroy the League or keep the United States out of it. They were designed to define more precisely American obligations to the League's security system. To strengthen his hand in the Senate, Lodge packed his Foreign Relations Committee with known opponents of the League.

Wilson accepted Lodge's challenge with the determination to reject any compromise. On July 10, 1919, the President presented the treaty to the Senate, making it clear that he expected prompt and unqualified approval. To reject the League, he warned, would break the heart of the world. He concluded his speech with high emotion: "The stage is set, the destiny disclosed. It has come about by no plan of our conceiving, but by the hand of God who led us into this way. We cannot turn back. We can only go forward, with lifted eyes and freshened spirit, to follow the vision."

Much of the subsequent debate on the League revolved around Article X, which stipulated that League members accepted the obligation to preserve against external aggression the territorial integrity and political independence of fellow members. Article X disturbed not only isolationists but also many Americans who believed that the United States should play an active role in world affairs. Wilson insisted repeatedly that Article X, backed by the solemn promises of the world's leading nations, would stop aggressive war absolutely. But critics other than isolationists demanded some explanation of the American commitment to collective security when it seemed clear that no nation would vindicate Article X unless the aggression threatened its own vital interests. Wilson attempted to skirt the issue by distinguishing between moral and legal obligations. The United States, in the event of aggression, had a choice. No less than other countries, it could decide when and where it would become involved in military action under Article X. Yet, critics asked, how could collective security be effective if no nation could be compelled, beyond its own interest, to support it? To be effective, said Lodge, the League would require such infringements on sovereignty that no one, not even the President, would favor it. "What will your league amount to," asked Borah, "if it does not contain powers that no one dreams of giving it?"

But Republican criticism of the League went deeper. Many saw in the League an agency for perpetuating the status quo with all of its injustices. The League appeared to be no more than a bulwark of the existing order. As Elihu Root wrote of the League: "If perpetuated, it would be an attempt to preserve for all time unchanged the distribution of power and territory made in accordance with the views and exigencies of the Allies in this present juncture of affairs. It would necessarily be futile. . . . It would not only be futile; it would be mischievous. Change and growth are the law of life, and no generation can impose its will in regard to the growth of nations and distribution of power, upon succeeding generations."

As the summer of 1919 dragged on, public sentiment ran hard toward the moderate Republican position which favored joining the League, but with reservations. Tormented by Lodge's tactics of delay, Wilson decided to carry his case to the country. Against the advice of his doctor, he left Washington on September 3, 1919, opening his speaking tour in Ohio and moving slowly through the Middle West to the Dakotas. In this region he met with only partial success, for many of his isolationist audiences there were indifferent to the League. In both the Northwest and in the great cities of California, however, he faced large and enthusiastic crowds. Finally, he turned eastward, speaking in Nevada, Utah, Wyoming, and Colorado. The President everywhere defended Article X as the guarantor of peace. Always his appeal centered on the American desire to avoid another war. Without the League, he said repeatedly, there would be no collective security; without collective security there would be no peace. At Pueblo, on September 25, Wilson reminded his audience of the graves of American soldiers in France and implored them to support his program so that Americans would never again die on foreign battlefields. That speech ended his tour. Broken by the strain of one of the greatest forensic efforts in the nation's history, the President returned to Washington. On October 2 he had a stroke, and in his final eighteen months as President, Wilson was largely incapable of managing the nation's affairs.

In November, 1919, the Republicans embarked on their final strategy to defeat Wilson's treaty. While the stricken President urged Senate Democrats to oppose any modification of the treaty, the Republican majority passed the reservations one by one. Thereafter the disposition of the treaty lay with Wilson. On November 18, he instructed the Democrats to vote against approval of the Lodge reservations. He declared that the Lodge formula did "not provide for ratification but, rather, for the nullification of the treaty." On the following day the Senate rejected the treaty with the reservations by the overwhelming vote of 55 to 39. Joining the Democrats were the irreconcilables who, in the colorful phrase of Senator

Borah, wanted the League "twenty thousand leagues under the sea." The Democratic leadership then moved for approval of the treaty as Wilson wanted it. Again the treaty failed, this time by a vote of 53 to 39, with the Republican majority voting against it as a bloc. Many Democrats, believing it preferable to enter the League with the Lodge reservations than not at all, now broke ranks. When the Senate took its final vote in March, 1920, enough Democrats voted for the Lodge reservations to produce a majority of 49 to 35, but this figure was still 7 votes short of the necessary two-thirds. Wilson's twenty-three unbending Democrats, joined by the Republican irreconcilables, had defeated the treaty. As one staunch irreconcilable observed, "We can always depend on Mr. Wilson. He never has failed us."

The Great Red Scare

Armistice negotiations had removed the danger of Germany but seemingly exposed the nation to the more insidious threat of bolshevism. By 1919 the Bolsheviks (Communists) had consolidated their power in Russia and declared ideological warfare on the non-Soviet world. Newspapers reported the horrors of Bolshevik rule and warned the American people that their institutions were not immune to subversion. What gave credence to such fears was the tendency of American radicals to praise the Bolshevik Revolution in Russia and to disseminate the doctrines of world revolution emanating from the Third International of the world Communist movement.

In a general atmosphere of unease, specific events of 1919 set off the Great Red Scare. It began in February when Mayor Ole Hanson, supported by the press, interpreted the general strike in Seattle as a Bolshevik-inspired assault on American values, rather than as a typical postwar labor-management dispute. Soon it was reported that unknown radicals had sent bombs to prominent officials. Most of the bombs never reached their destinations, but one damaged the house of Senator Thomas W. Hardwick of Georgia. Several May Day riots intensified the contagion of fear. On June 2 a series of explosions destroyed property in several cities. That day a bomb damaged Attorney General A. Mitchell Palmer's house in Washington. The Boston police strike of September, 1919, followed in November by the massive steel strike, again raised the specter of radical influence.

In Washington the reaction was determined. Senator Knute Nelson of Minnesota demanded legislation to protect the nation's citizens against the circulation of dangerous literature through the mails. John W. Summers of Washington introduced a new sedition bill in November by warning the House that it must stamp out "anarchy, sedition, disloyalty, I.W.W.ism, Bolshevism, radicalism, and un-Americanism in all their various forms." Meanwhile Attorney General Palmer moved to curb the Reds with executive power. During November, 1919, his agents rounded up hundreds of radicals, including dozens of officers and members of New York's Union of Russian Workers. During December, 1919, the Justice Department deported as radicals over two hundred aliens. One anti-Red critic recommended the slogan "SOS"—ship or shoot.

During January, 1920, Congress came close to adding its weight to Palmer's crusade. On January 10, the Senate passed a sedition law by a voice vote. But in refusing to concur, the House terminated the movement toward a new era of repression. The excesses of hysteria and arrests without cause, culminating during January, 1920, in the suspension of five Socialists from the New York Legislature, convinced responsible Americans that the witch hunt had gone too far. The *Literary Digest* reported on January 20 that the suspension of the five Socialists produced almost universal condemnation by Republican, Democratic, and Socialist newspapers alike. In Washington, Louis F. Post, Assistant Secretary of Labor, canceled hundreds of Palmer's deportation orders when it became clear that the basis of deportation was generally no more than membership in some organization labeled subversive by the Attorney General. While Palmer clamored for more drastic legislation to be passed which would punish sedition, the nation generally regained its composure during the spring of 1920.

The crusade against radicalism effectively slowed the release of wartime offenders fom state and federal prisons. With victory in November, 1918, many progressives joined the Socialists in demanding general amnesty for those held in prison because of their opposition to the war. As early as December, 1918, Secretary of War Newton D. Baker received a petition with 15,000 signatures recommending pardons for conscientious objectors. Much of the pressure for amnesty centered on the imprisoned Socialist leader Eugene V. Debs. Attorney General Palmer, in denying Debs's release, explained that he would be bitterly assailed by those who considered Debs a dangerous radical. President Wilson also refused to support amnesty for political prisoners, and Debs, along with others, remained in jail. In December, 1921, a new President, Warren G. Harding, released Debs and almost two dozen other political prisoners. Two years later, President Calvin Coolidge, following the advice of a special commission, set free the remaining wartime prisoners.

Conclusion

After April, 1917, the American people, under the leadership of Woodrow Wilson, chose to defend their interest in a stable Europe with a major military effort. That involvement reestablished, at least on the surface, the traditional order of power which had served so well the historic security interests of the United States. But if the United States had played an essential role in protecting British and French leadership in European affairs, then this country's continued involvement in the defense of those nations was necessary to maintain the European balance. At Versailles, for the first time in the nation's history, an American President had become a major arbiter of the affairs of Europe and the world. But Wilson had been unable to remake the world at Versailles. World affairs thereafter would *not* be governed by laws that transcended the policies and interests of individual nations, some of which had not even accepted the provisions of the Versailles Treaty. Yet Wilson, in his insistence that he was creating a new world order, failed to communicate the knowledge of his failure to the American people.

Having determined the nature of Europe's reconstruction with its power, the United States, in the backwash of the great debate, would suddenly withdraw that power either under the assumption that the League of Nations, once established, would indeed maintain the peace of the world or that, even if the League failed, nothing was likely to occur which would again demand a massive military response from the United States. Both assumptions would prove to be wrong.

SUGGESTED READINGS

The most comprehensive account of Wilson's foreign policy is found in Arthur S. Link's multivolume biography of Woodrow Wilson. The five published volumes carry Wilson's role up to the United States declaration of war against Germany in 1917. Link's *Wilson the Diplomatist** (1957) comprises a brief, but highly judicious, set of essays on Wilson's wartime and immediate postwar policies. Harley Notter has provided a good account of Wilson's foreign policies to 1917 in *The Origins of the Foreign Policy of Woodrow Wilson* (1937). For general studies of Wilson's Mexican policy see S. F. Bemis's *Latin American Policy of the United States** (1943); H. F. Cline's *The United States and Mexico** (1953); and J. F. Rippy's *The United States and Mexico* (rev. ed., 1931). Of special importance is Howard Quint's *An Affair of Honor: Woodrow Wilson and the Occupation of Vera Cruz* (1962). On Wilson and the Far East see Tienyi Li's *Woodrow Wilson's China Policy, 1913–1917* (1952) and R. W. Curry's *Woodrow Wilson and Far Eastern Policy, 1913–1921* (1957).

United States entry into the Great War has long been a subject of major concern among historians. Two very useful anthologies which trace the historic debate over the breakdown of American neutrality are Herbert J. Bass (ed.), *America's Entry into World War I: Submarines, Sentiment, or Security?** (1964) and Daniel M. Smith (ed.), *American Intervention, 1917: Sentiment, Self-interest, or Ideals?** (1966). Smith has analyzed the role of national interest as detected by a number of historians in his article, "National Interest and American Intervention, 1917: An Historiographical Appraisal," *The Journal of American History,* LII (June, 1965).

Revisionist studies highly critical of Wilson's role in American intervention began in the twenties and increased in intensity during the thirties. One of the first, stressing propaganda and economic factors, was C. H. Grattan's *Why We Fought* (1929). Walter Millis's *The Road to War* (1935) attributed United States entry largely to Wilson's strong bias in favor of the Allies, as did C. C. Tansill in his *America Goes to War* (1938). Similarly, both A. M. Morrissey's *The American Defense of Neutral Rights, 1914–1917* (1939) and Edwin Borchard and W. P. Lage's *Neutrality for the United States* (2d ed., 1940) are critical of Wilson's efforts at neutrality. On the other hand, Charles Seymour in his *American Neutrality, 1914–1917* (1935) defended Wilson's policies. N. D. Baker's *Why We Went to War* (1936) also attributes United States intervention to the German submarine. More recent studies of the submarine issue are Karl E. Birnbaum's *Peace Moves and U-Boat Warfare: A Study of Imperial Germany's Policy toward the United States, April 18, 1916–January 9, 1917* (1958) and S. R. Spencer, Jr.'s *Decision for War, 1917** (1953). John M. Blum in his *Woodrow Wilson and the Politics of Morality** (1956) attributes intervention to Wilson's failure to meet the submarine challenge except in legalistic terms. Although he overemphasizes the role of British propaganda, H. C. Peterson, in his *Propaganda for War* (1939), presents a superb account of the British effort to win American sympathy.

Several excellent studies of the neutrality period tend to conclude that Wilson's policies combined idealism with some realistic concern for the German threat to the Atlantic world. Ernest R. May's *The World War and American Isolation, 1914–1917* (1959) is a judicious, balanced study based on archival research conducted in both the United States and Europe. F. L. Paxson's *Pre-war Years, 1914–1917* (1936) remains a commendable account. Edward H. Buehrig's *Woodrow Wilson and the Balance of Power* (1955) is an excellent volume, which shows that Wilson was motivated more by idealistic than realistic concepts of world politics. Daniel M. Smith's *The Great Departure: The United States and World War I, 1914–1920** (1965) again sees Wilson as combining idealism and practicality. Three of Link's monumental volumes cover the years 1914 to 1917: *Wilson: The Struggle for Neutral-*

ity, 1914–1915 (1960); *Wilson: Confusions and Crises,* 1915–1916 (1964); and *Wilson: Campaigns for Progressivism and Peace,* 1916–1917 (1965). Barbara W. Tuchman's *The Zimmermann Telegram** (1958) stresses the importance of this note in pushing the United States toward war.

Several biographical studies deal with American foreign policy during the neutrality period. W. J. and M. B. Bryan's *The Memoirs of William Jennings Bryan* (1925) contains valuable insights into the thought of Wilson's first Secretary of State. D. M. Smith has analyzed carefully the role of Lansing in his *Robert Lansing and American Neutrality,* 1914–1917 (1958). On Lansing see also *War Memoirs of Robert Lansing* (1935). Norman A. Graebner (ed.), *An Uncertain Tradition: American Secretaries of State in the Twentieth Century** (1961), contains essays on Bryan and Lansing. Studies of two congressmen involved in the neutrality struggle are A. M. Arnett's *Claude Kitchen and the Wilson War Policies* (1937) and Monroe Billington's *Thomas P. Gore: The Blind Senator from Oklahoma* (1967).

On American economic mobilization see W. F. Willoughby's *Government Organization in Wartime and After* (1919); Herbert Stein's *Government Price Policy in the United States during the World War* (1939); B. M. Baruch's *American Industry in the War* (1921); Baruch's *Baruch: The Public Years* (1960); W. C. Mullendore's *History of the United States Food Administration,* 1917–1919 (1941); J. M. Clark's *The Costs of the World War to the American People* (1931); and E. L. Bogart's *Direct and Indirect Costs of the Great World War* (2d ed., 1920). John Steuben's *Labor in Wartime* (1940) and Samuel Gompers's *American Labor and the War* (1919) trace labor's role in the war effort.

On molding public opinion see George Creel's *How We Advertised America* (1920); J. R. Mock's *Censorship,* 1917 (1941); and J. R. Mock and Cedric Larson's *Words That Won the War* (1939). Herbert Hoover has included some perceptive observations in his volume of memoirs, *Years of Adventure,* 1874–1920 (1951). H. G. Peterson and G. C. Fite's *Opponents of War,* 1917–1918* (1957) reflects the wartime hysteria and traces the attacks on those who opposed the war. See also Zachariah Chafee, Jr.'s *Free Speech in the United States** (1941).

American military policy is covered thoroughly in E. M. Coffman's *The War to End All Wars: The American Military Expeience in World War I* (1968). The older study of F. L. Paxson, *America at War,* 1917–1918 (1939), is solid. E. M. Coffman provides an excellent account of the contributions of Chief of Staff Peyton C. March in *The Hilt of the Sword: The Career of Peyton C. March* (1966). On naval action see W. S. Sims and B. J. Hendrick's *The Victory at Sea* (1920) and T. G. Frothingham's naval history, *The United States in the War,* 1917–1918 (1926).

Wilson's preparations for peace have received brief but excellent treatment in Link's *Wilson the Diplomatist** (1957) and Charles Seymour's *American Diplomacy during the World War* (1934). Lawrence E. Gelfand's *The Inquiry: American Preparations for Peace,* 1917–1919 (1963) is illuminating on the evolution of Wilson's peace proposals. On Wilson's troubles at home see Seward W. Livermore's *Politics Is Adjourned** (1966) and Selig Adler's *The Isolationist Impulse** (1957). A thorough discussion of the Armistice can be found in Harry R. Rudin's *Armistice* 1918 (1944) and David F. Trask's *The United States in the Supreme War Council* (1961). On Wilson's decision to go to Paris see James D. Startt's "Wilson's Mission to Paris: The Making of a Decision," *The Historian,* XXX (August, 1968). The influence of the Russian Revolution on the development of Wilson's liberal peace program is analyzed brilliantly in George F. Kennan's *Russia Leaves the War** (1967) and N. Gordon Levin, Jr.'s *Woodrow Wilson and World Politics: America's Response to War and Revolution* (1968). On the Lansing-Ishii negotiations see Burton F. Beers's *Vain Endeavor: Robert Lansing's Attempt to End the American-Japanese Rivalry* (1962).

Much has been written on Wilson's role at the Versailles Peace Conference. Ray S. Baker has presented a detailed account of Wilson as a peacemaker in *Woodrow Wilson and World Settlement* (3 vols., 1922). Paul Birdsall's *Versailles Twenty Years After* (1941) and Thomas A. Bailey's *Woodrow Wilson and the Lost Peace** (1944) are excellent studies of the Paris Peace Conference. F. S. Marston discusses the organization of the Conference in *The Peace Conference of* 1919 (1944). Useful accounts by contemporaries are E. M. House and Charles Seymour's *What Really Happened at Paris* (1921); J. T. Shotwell's *At the Paris Peace Conference* (1937) and

B. M. Baruch's *The Making of the Reparation and Economic Sections of the Treaty* (1920). J. M. Keynes's *The Economic Consequences of the Peace* (1919) is a perceptive and critical evaluation of the work of the Peace Conference. The Shantung question at Versailles receives excellent treatment in Russell H. Fifield's *Woodrow Wilson and the Far East: The Diplomacy of the Shantung Question* (1952). Various historical views of Wilson's role in the development of the League of Nations have been combined in the useful volume edited by Ralph A. Stone, *Wilson and the League of Nations** (1967).

Among the excellent accounts of the great debate over the League of Nations in the United States are D. F. Fleming's *The United States and the League of Nations,* 1918–1920 (1932); T. A. Bailey's *Woodrow Wilson and the Great Betrayal** (1945); W. Stull Holt's *Treaties Defeated by the Senate* (1933); John A. Garraty's *Henry Cabot Lodge: A Biography* (1953); and M. C. McKenna's *Borah* (1961). The insecurity of the immediate postwar months has received excellent treatment in R. K. Murray's *The Red Scare: A Study in National Hysteria,* 1919–1920* (1955).
*indicates availability in paperback.

30

Politics and Society in the 1920*s*

THE ELECTION of President Warren G. Harding in 1920 ushered in a period of political conservatism which lasted throughout the decade. The reaction against President Wilson and his policies, the opposition to the expanding role of government which was characteristic of the progressive movement, the influence of businessmen on governmental action, and a high degree of postwar prosperity all combined to strengthen the conservative position. Harding spoke of the return to normalcy, which meant reduction of the functions of the federal government, except for special groups. Neither Harding nor Coolidge believed in strong executive leadership. One of the most significant aspects of the political history of the 1920s was the decline in the power and prestige of the Presidency, which had been so greatly enlarged by Theodore Roosevelt and Wilson. But in the postwar decade people did not demand strong presidential leadership. They were tired of reform and of great causes. They wanted to be left alone, to enjoy themselves, and to make money.

At the same time, however, rising standards of living, advances in science and improved technology, and new intellectual currents combined to produce rapid and profound social change in America. Life moved at a faster pace, and young people threw off personal restraints which they considered unacceptable. The 1920s was a time of reevaluation of popular standards and mores and a period of restlessness, confusion, and even conflict in social relations.

The Election of 1920

The election of 1920 was profoundly significant, not because of the great issues faced by the candidates, but because of those that were ignored. For the postwar campaigning constituted, above all, a national effort to break from the past without necessarily coming to grips with the present. The sudden ending of the war, followed closely by the Red Scare and the great debate over the League, created an immediate collapse of wartime emotions. Because the national leadership, headed by the President himself, was incapable of explaining American involvement in the Great War in terms which they could understand, countless citizens now considered the great crusade for democracy to have been a pointless destruction of life. By 1920 the attacks on the Democratic leadership had shattered the spell of "the war to end all war." Boies Penrose, the Republican boss of Pennsylvania, observed, "Any good Republican can be nominated for President and can defeat any Democrat." He was correct.

Beyond Republican ascendancy in 1920 lay the character of the Republican party itself. That party, about to regain the White House, had come under the command of its most conservative elements. Republican progressives had defected to the Bull Moose party to defeat Taft in 1912, but in the process they had handed over the Republican party completely to the Old Guard. When the progressives drifted back into the Republican fold after 1916, they were unable to regain any official recognition from the party managers. Many Republican liberals, such as Harold L. Ickes, refused to rejoin the Republican party on such terms and merely drifted as political mavericks through the years of Republican dominance. What mattered in 1920, therefore, were the objectives of Republican conservatives as represented by the congressional Old Guard.

The Republican Convention opened in Chicago on June 8. The front-running candidates for nomination were General Leonard Wood, a conservative nationalist and old associate of Theodore Roosevelt, and Frank O. Lowden, a distinguished businessman and governor of Illinois. From the opening speech, however, newsmen detected a strong undercurrent for a little-known senatorial backbencher named Warren G. Harding. When the balloting began, Wood and Lowden, running neck and neck, led the field by a wide margin, but neither could approach the required majority. Yet both candidates found it impossible to support the other. On the ninth ballot the Wood and Lowden forces, having demonstrated to their favorites that they could not win, bolted to Harding. The tenth ballot was a mere formality. For the vice presidency the party then named Calvin Coolidge, the Governor of Massachusetts.

Gathering at San Francisco, the Democratic party carried the full burden of Wilson's illness and declining popularity. The President, still a powerful voice in the party, refused to name a favorite in an apparent effort to secure the nomination for himself. Two members of the Cabinet, Secretary of the Treasury McAdoo and Attorney General Palmer, fought for the nomination through thirty-eight ballots until the party leaders agreed, at last, on James M. Cox, former Governor of Ohio. For the vice presidency they selected Wilson's Assistant Secretary of the Navy, Franklin D. Roosevelt.

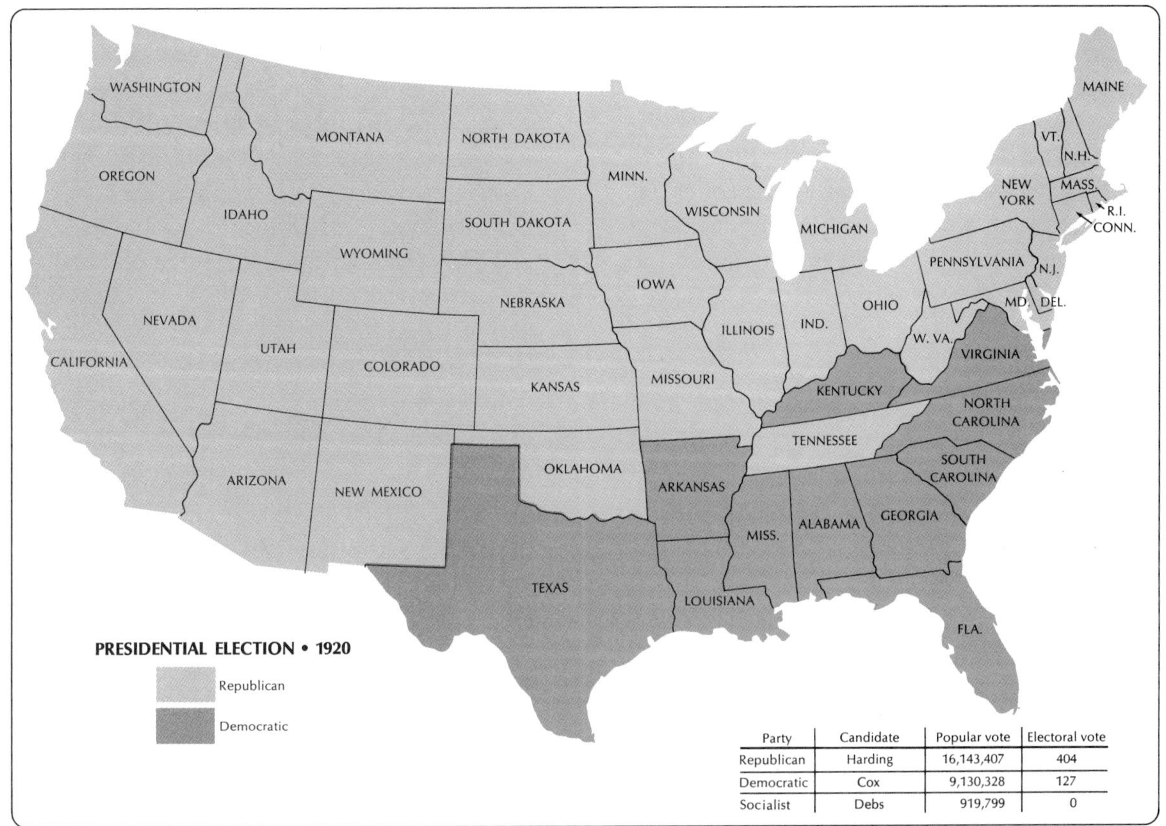

Party	Candidate	Popular vote	Electoral vote
Republican	Harding	16,143,407	404
Democratic	Cox	9,130,328	127
Socialist	Debs	919,799	0

Wilson had predicted that the 1920 presidential campaign would be a "solemn referendum" on the League of Nations issue. Although the Democratic nominees agreed to accept reservations which would not impair the Covenant, they supported League membership sufficiently to sustain the enthusiasm of the Wilsonian intellectuals in the cities. But Cox and Roosevelt faced large defections among Western farmers and isolationists generally.

Harding had set the tone of his campaign as early as May, 1920, when he declared in his uniquely florid style: "America's present need is not heroics, but healing; not nostrums, but normalcy; not revolution, but restoration; not agitation, but adjustment; not surgery, but serenity." Such speeches—described by McAdoo as "an army of pompous phrases moving over the landscape in search of an idea"—captured the national mood, for everyone desired an escape from crisis and a return to "normalcy," even if "normalcy" for the farmer had no relationship to "normalcy" for the banker. On the League issue Harding, acting on Lodge's advice, remained especially vague. By alternating an occasional commitment to *some* international organization with outright rejection of the League, he delighted all elements in his party. To neutralize Cox's appeal on the League issue, thirty-one leading Republicans, including Root, Hughes, and Taft, signed a statement which promised that Harding, if elected, would favor United States membership with reservations in the League of Nations. Harding could scarcely be called a strong candidate, yet so overwhelming was the reaction against Wilson and the war that he received over 16 million votes, representing 61 percent of the total cast, to approximately 9 million for Cox. Eugene Debs, running as the Socialist candidate from an Atlanta prison, received over 900,000 votes. Thenceforward it could make no difference politically what disposition the Republican party might make of the League issue. The American people had shown that, with the Republican leaders, they did not want the burdens of an intellectually and physically demanding foreign policy.

Domestic Issues under Harding

Harding was a friendly, easygoing politician who really had none of the qualities needed in the Presidency. His career in Ohio politics had been mediocre, and he made a poor record in the United States Senate, partly because he had never taken his duties seriously. He was a poor judge of men; he permitted friendship and political cronyism to dictate some key appointments; he knew little about economics; and he viewed the Presidency as a honor rather than a responsibility. He also had some serious shortcomings of character. For a time he engaged in extramarital love affairs and had a daughter born out of wedlock. But despite his glaring weaknesses, the American people responded warmly to this handsome, democratic, congenial man who in many ways seemed like one of them.

A number of important political and economic problems faced the new administration. Partly because of the postwar depression which began in 1920, Congress and the President found various groups demanding special legislation. Veterans wanted a bonus; businessmen demanded higher tariffs and tax reduction; labor unions were among those insisting on tighter immigration restrictions; and hard-pressed farmers were turning to Congress for legislative relief. Most of these matters were holdovers from the last days of the Wilson administration, when little could be done because of a deadlock between Congress and the President. But now, with a strong Republican Congress and a pliant Chief Executive, action on these matters was not long in coming.

With the support of both businessmen and farmers, Congress passed the Emergency Tariff Act in May, 1921. It was followed a little more than a year later by the Fordney-McCumber tariff law which raised rates to their highest point in American history up to that time. This measure increased duties on such farm commodities as wheat, wool, and sugar, and on chemical products, chinaware, textiles, and other industrial goods. The Fordney-McCumber Act expressed the growing economic nationalism of the period, but it encouraged foreign countries to increase their tariffs and almost eliminated the possibility that European nations would pay their war debts to the United States.

Another reflection of the strong postwar nationalism was the demand for immigration restriction. World War I had effectively reduced immigration, but following the Armistice large numbers of foreigners again began arriving in the United States. Many citizens opposed this new influx of immigrants because, as one writer explained it, "these newcomers were far removed in speech, customs, habits of thought,

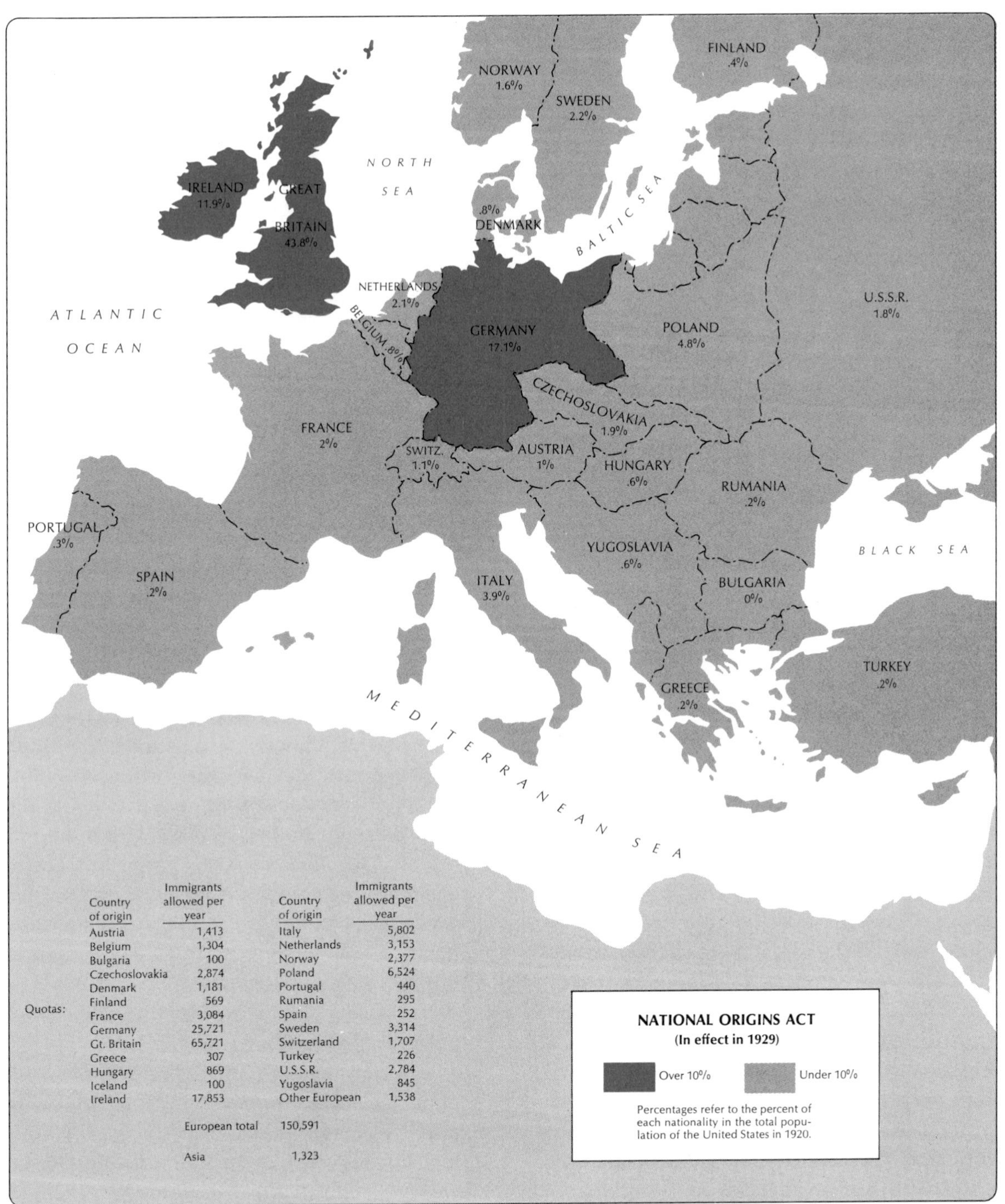

Quotas:

Country of origin	Immigrants allowed per year	Country of origin	Immigrants allowed per year
Austria	1,413	Italy	5,802
Belgium	1,304	Netherlands	3,153
Bulgaria	100	Norway	2,377
Czechoslovakia	2,874	Poland	6,524
Denmark	1,181	Portugal	440
Finland	569	Rumania	295
France	3,084	Spain	252
Germany	25,721	Sweden	3,314
Gt. Britain	65,721	Switzerland	1,707
Greece	307	Turkey	226
Hungary	869	U.S.S.R.	2,784
Iceland	100	Yugoslavia	845
Ireland	17,853	Other European	1,538
	European total	150,591	
	Asia	1,323	

and appearance from the original stock of this country." Workingmen opposed increased immigration because of its threat to United States wage scales; and businessmen and others favored restriction in the hope of barring radical political doctrines which, they said, were imported by foreigners. In 1921 Congress passed the Emergency Quota Act which provided that only 3 percent of a nationality resident in the United States in 1910 could come to America in any one year. This law was less restrictive against Southern and Eastern Europeans than many people wished. After Coolidge became President, Congress enacted a new law. Under the Immigration Act of 1924, only 2 percent of a particular nationality residing in the United States in 1890 would be admitted each year. By setting the date back to 1890 the law was much more discriminatory against Southern and Eastern Europeans, because at that time very few people from that part of Europe had settled in the United States. The 1924 law also excluded the Japanese. Beginning in 1927 immigration was to be limited to an annual quota of only 150,000. The quota given to each country was to be determined by dividing the total by the percentage of each nationality in the United States in 1920. The United States had thus adopted a plan of restrictive immigration and had abandoned its historic policy of admitting most of those who desired to enter the United States.

The Republican policy of reduced government spending and large tax cuts had Harding's enthusiastic support, and Secretary of the Treasury Andrew W. Mellon took the lead in achieving these goals. Mellon believed that lower taxes on high incomes were especially important because businessmen would then have more money to invest in job-producing enterprises. In keeping with this fiscal philosophy, Congress in 1921 repealed the excess profits tax and lowered surtaxes on large incomes from a wartime high of 65 percent to 50 percent. This was only the beginning of a series of tax reduction measures passed by Republicans in the 1920s which were helpful chiefly to those with large incomes.

There was a close connection between tax reduction and Harding's opposition to adjusted compensation for veterans. Men who had fought in World War I strongly believed that their country owed them more than the $30 a month which most of them had received while those who stayed at home earned high wages. Harding was sympathetic to the demands of servicemen, but he opposed a federal bonus, as it was generally called, because he felt that extra government expenditures would not permit lower taxes and a balanced budget. As soon as Congress convened in April, 1921, it became evident that the lawmakers were intent on passing some form of bonus legislation. Supported by the American Legion, which had been organized in 1919, Congress voted an adjustment compensation bill. Harding, however, killed it with a veto. Coolidge also opposed bonus legislation because of the cost. But after he became President, Congress passed a law over his veto in the presidential election year of 1924. The measure provided for paying military personnel $1 for each day of service in the United States during World War I and $1.25 for each day served outside the country. Many veterans were eligible for payments of $500 to $1,000.

Harding did give support to one basic administrative reform—the Budget and Accounting Act of 1921. With the growth of federal receipts and expenditures, it had become increasingly clear that the country needed an improved budgetary system. The law provided for a Director of the Budget and a Comptroller General. Both officials were appointed by the President with Senate approval, and they worked as an arm of the executive branch. The Director of the Budget evaluated requests for funds and recommended a budget to the President, who then sent it on to Congress. The Comptroller General saw to the proper accounting of expenditures. Harding chose Charles G. Dawes, an able Chicago banker, as the first budget director. Over the years, the Director of the Budget became one of the most powerful men in government because he determined how much money Congress should be asked to appropriate for each governmental agency.

Scandal in High Places

Harding's term in Washington was more plagued by petty graft and major scandal than any administration since that of Grant. Although he was honest himself, the President's loose morals did not command respect from his associates and subordinates and may even have encouraged some of them to treat law and morality lightly. The "Ohio Gang," as his followers from back home were commonly known, engaged in all kinds of corrupt activities. Some of them used their official positions and friendship with Harding to enrich themselves. Before Jess Smith, a close friend of Attorney General Harry Daugherty, shot himself in Daugherty's apartment in May, 1923, he had been engaged in such illicit activities as selling pardons, paroles, and liquor permits. When someone asked Smith if he planned to take a government job, he reportedly answered that he could make more money working for nothing! "My God, how the money rolls in," he once remarked. In the Veterans' Bureau, headed by Charles R. Forbes, officials practically gave away surplus war goods in return for financial benefits. Forbes was convicted of bribery. Another scandal involved the Alien Property Custodian's office run by Thomas R. Miller.

As if it were not enough to be betrayed by several of his lesser appointments, Harding's old friend Albert B. Fall, whom he had named Secretary of the Interior, turned out to be a crook. Fall became deeply involved in the Teapot Dome scandal, and only Harding's death before the worst became known saved the President from further embarrassment and agony. The Teapot Dome affair arose out of controversy between the East and West over federal conservation policies and from conflicts between Navy and Interior Departments over leasing of oil reserves which had been set aside earlier by Presidents Taft and Wilson. In May, 1921, control of the oil reserves was transferred from the Navy Department headed by Edwin Denby to the Interior Department where they came under Fall's administration. Less than a year later Fall leased Teapot Dome in Wyoming to Harry F. Sinclair, and subsequently the Elk Hills reserve in California to Edward M. Doheny. These agreements were made without public bids. Doheny indicated how valuable these leases were when he later testified, "We will be in bad luck if we do not get $100,000,000 profits." But Sinclair and Doheny were not the only ones to turn a profit. An investigation revealed that Fall, who resigned in 1923, had received nearly $500,000 from those who stood to gain from the oil reserves. In 1929, after a long court battle, Fall was convicted of accepting a bribe. He was fined $100,000 and sentenced to one year in jail.

Scandals in the Harding administration left a permanent mark on his Presidency, and the low level of morality reflected the degree of public indifference to the honest and efficient conduct of national affairs. As William Allen White wrote, "Harding's story is the story of his times, the story of the Prodigal Son, our democracy that turned away from the things of the spirit, got its share of the patrimony ruthlessly and went out and lived riotously and ended it by feeding among the swine." But corruption and immorality were not the worst features of the Harding administration. He did not know how to lead; he did not believe in executive leadership; and he permitted the nation to drift in those postwar years when it needed firm direction. He died on August 2, 1923, in San Francisco during a return trip from Alaska. People deeply mourned the death of this kind, generous President who had freed Eugene V. Debs from prison and supported the eight-hour day for steelworkers, but Americans had lost a friend, not a leader.

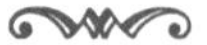

"A Puritan in Babylon"

Harding's successor, Calvin Coolidge (1872–1933), came from a diligent family in rural Vermont which had achieved modest prosperity but no distinction. He was graduated from Amherst, attended law school, and began practicing in Northampton in 1898. Coolidge held a series of minor offices in Massachusetts before being elected successively a member of the state legislature, lieutenant governor, and then governor. He came to national attention in 1919 when he received credit for ending the Boston police strike. Coolidge was a shy, taciturn puritan who believed in the traditional values of hard work, industry, thrift, and morality. A small man with a sharp face and sandy-colored hair, he looked, as one critic said, more like a money shark than a President. Coolidge had few intellectual or cultural interests; he was a poor conversationalist except when he exhibited a dry wit.

Coolidge was a dedicated economic and political conservative who was well qualified to carry on the policies associated with normalcy. In his first annual message, he told Congress that government expenditures and taxes must be reduced and that the tariff schedules should not be changed. He believed these policies would benefit business and industry, which he considered chiefly responsible for the nation's economic progress. Contrary to the position held by agrarians, Coolidge sincerely believed that what was best for industry was best for America. This accounts for his favoritism toward business and his opposition to farm relief legislation. Fearful of expanding government powers, he maintained that "there is an inescapable personal responsibility for the development of character, of industry, of thrift, and of self-control. These do not come from the government, but from the people themselves."

By the time Coolidge took office a great deal was known about malfeasance in the Harding administration. Consequently, one of the President's first tasks was to restore integrity and morality in government. He did this by gradually forcing out of office those who had discredited Harding. Besides cleaning up the administration, Coolidge gave attention to the principal measures then before Congress. These included immigration restriction, tax reduction, a bonus for veterans, and agricultural legislation. Coolidge enthusiastically supported the Immigration Act of 1924 and was equally devoted to lower taxes. The Revenue Act of 1924 reduced income taxes from 8 to 6 percent and lowered maximum surtaxes from 50 to 40 percent. This law was especially beneficial to high income groups. Coolidge's opposition to a cash bonus could not defeat an adjusted compensation measure for veterans in a Congress that soon would have to face the voters. On the agricultural question, Coolidge took a position which was unpopular among many Midwestern Republicans when he opposed any attempt by the federal government to raise farm prices.

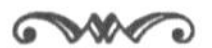

Progressivism and the Campaign of 1924

Despite the political conservatism of the Harding and Coolidge administrations, a rather strong undercurrent of progressivism existed during the 1920s. But lacking national leadership, effective organization, and attractive policies, the postwar progressives were little more than bothersome critics of the conservative Republican majority. Only in 1924 did the progressives provide some minor threat to the prevailing power structure. A good example of progressive ineffectiveness was the fight over government ownership and operation of facilities at Muscle Shoals on the Tennessee River in northern Alabama. Senator Norris and a number of other progressives favored federal operation of plants and equipment constructed at Muscle Shoals during World War I and hoped to expand the generating capacity in order to produce cheap electricity and low-cost fertilizer for farmers. Many conservatives preferred the assignment of these facilities to private enterprise and supported Henry Ford, who offered $5 million for a ninety-nine year lease of Muscle Shoals. However, Ford's proposal was rejected, and he withdrew his offer in 1924. It was important that the progressives kept the dam sites open for later development by the Tennessee Valley Authority, but this was at best a negative victory.

The vibrant progressivism of Theodore Roosevelt and Woodrow Wilson had declined as early as 1918, and postwar events weakened the reform movement even further. Liberals had become disillusioned with the government's attack on civil rights during the war and the subsequent period of the Great Red Scare; labor had been weakened by strong antiunion policies; and farmers had become unhappy over the government's wartime restrictions. By the 1920s, too, most intellectuals had lost interest in progressive causes, and the prosperity of the 1920s bred conservative attitudes. Furthermore, the progressives had no effective organization.

Much of the progressive strength centered in the agricultural Midwest, where farmers suffered from heavy debts, low prices, and inadequate incomes. By the spring of 1922 many Midwestern Republicans were becoming highly critical of the Harding administration. Progressive Republicans won some significant victories in the midterm election of 1922, althought conservatives were never in danger of losing control of Congress or the Presidency. Nevertheless, both rural and urban progressives decided that it was time to challenge the national administration. The first step toward the organization of a national progressive movement occurred in February, 1922, when representatives of agriculture and labor, some Socialists, and miscellaneous reformers met in Chicago to form the Conference for Progressive

Political Action. During the next two years these groups discussed periodically the formation of a third party. At last the progressives decided to enter the presidential race. Meeting in Cleveland on July 4, 1924, they nominated Senator La Follette for President. After lashing out at the corrupting power of private monopoly, the Progressive party platform called for public power, government ownership of railroads, effective farm relief, labor legislation which would guarantee workers the right of collective bargaining, and more liberal payments to veterans. This inclination to solve problems by expanding government powers placed the new party strictly in the progressive tradition.

While the Progressives were organizing for 1924, most Republicans were rallying behind the renomination of Calvin Coolidge, who had announced late in 1923 that he would seek a full term. When the delegates met in Cleveland on June 10, 1924, Coolidge was nominated on the first ballot. Most Republicans apparently agreed with Henry Ford, who said, "The country is perfectly safe with Coolidge. Why change?" Charles G. Dawes received the vice presidential nomination. Progressive Republicans sputtered and complained, but they could do nothing. The Republican platform expressed the prevailing conservatism and called for "rigid economy in government," tax reduction, high tariffs, and farm relief.

While the Republican Convention was brief and quiet, the Democratic gathering was long, loud, and controversial. The leading candidate appeared to be William G. McAdoo, who had been Secretary of the Treasury under President Wilson. While McAdoo had considerable support throughout the West and South, Eastern Democratic leaders favored Governor Alfred E. Smith of New York. A product of Tammany Hall, a Catholic and a "wet," Smith was a controversial figure to spokesmen of the Southern and Western Democracy. A split soon developed in the convention which was intensified when the Smith forces backed a resolution specifically denouncing the Ku Klux Klan. McAdoo's supporters attempted to defeat this move because of Klan strength in the Midwest and South where McAdoo had his greatest support. Although the resolution was narrowly defeated, the rift had become so wide that neither McAdoo nor Smith could win the nomination. As a result, the convention turned to a compromise candidate and chose John W. Davis, a handsome, conservative lawyer from West Virginia and New York. Davis was closely associated with big business. To remove this political stigma from the ticket, the convention voted Governor Charles W. Bryan of Nebraska, brother of William Jennings Bryan, the vice presidential nomination. The Democratic platform demanded lower tariffs, some form of aid for farmers, conservation, and government operation of Muscle Shoals.

Since Coolidge abstained from personal campaigning, much of the Republican effort fell to vice presidential nominee Dawes. Believing that Davis was no threat to victory, Dawes directed his campaign largely against La Follette, whom he pictured as a flaming radical. He urged people to "keep cool with Coolidge" and pictured the President as a solid, reliable leader who had restored integrity to public life and led the nation to prosperity. The main issue, Dawes said, was "whether you stand on the rock of common sense with Calvin Coolidge, or upon the sinking sands of socialism with Robert M. La Follette." The result was another sweeping Republican victory as Coolidge piled up more votes than Davis and La Follette combined. The President won 15,-

817,000 popular votes, while Davis and La Follette received 8,385,000 and 4,832,000 respectively. La Follette won more support than any other third-party candidate up to that time. He carried his home state of Wisconsin and ran ahead of Davis in eleven other Western states, but his were mostly protest votes. Judged by the outcome of the election, Coolidge was pursuing precisely those policies wanted by a majority of the people.

More Normalcy

Never in doubt about the correctness of his policies, Coolidge accepted the election of 1924 as a mandate to continue the program which Harding had begun. In his annual message to Congress, the President declared that "rigid economy in public expenditures" was the lasting remedy for economic ills. He explained that reduced taxes had been largely responsible for the country's general prosperity and that "economy reaches everywhere. It carries a blessing to everybody." Therefore, he recommended further tax cuts and argued that lower surtaxes on high incomes would actually produce more revenue by encouraging business expansion. He told Congress that operations at Muscle Shoals were "better suited to private enterprise" and urged that the properties there be sold or leased. Whereas he hoped something could be done to restore agricultural prosperity, Coolidge warned again that "the government cannot successfully insure prosperity or fix prices by legislative fiat." He insisted that prosperity came from "the natural working out of economic laws."

The dominant political issues in the second Coolidge administration were tax reduction and farm relief. Although taxes had been slashed in 1921 and again in 1924, Secretary Mellon wanted even larger cuts. He advanced the idea that lower taxes "increases the amount of capital which is put into productive enterprises, stimulates business, and makes more certain that there will be more $5,000 jobs to go around." Mellon saw a direct relationship between monetary and fiscal policy—in this case low taxes—and full employment. Responding to the demand for lower taxes in 1926, Congress reduced the highest surtax rate to 20 percent, compared with 65 percent in 1921, repealed the gift tax, and reduced estate levies. Most of these benefits went to the wealthy, although corporate taxes were to be raised 1 percent over the following two years. In 1928 Congress made additional tax reductions, including a cut in the corporate income tax.

Despite lower taxes, the federal government was able to maintain a Treasury surplus throughout the 1920s. By opposing new government programs and cutting expenditures to about $3 billion a year, the Treasury enjoyed an annual average surplus of about $1 billion from 1923 to 1929. This enabled Congress to reduce the national debt (which had jumped to some $24 billion by 1920) to around $16 billion in 1929. Praising these policies, Coolidge told Congress in 1928: "Four times we have made a drastic revision of our internal revenue system, abolishing many taxes and substantially reducing almost all others. Each time the resulting stimulation to business has so increased taxable incomes and profits that a surplus has been produced." The President exaggerated the economic benefit of his tax laws, but the obvious business boom seemed to justify his policy.

Farm relief was a much more lively political

question. By 1925 farm groups, especially those in the normally Republican Midwest, had become well organized and were pushing hard for the McNary-Haugen bill, a plan which would involve the federal government in raising farm prices. But Coolidge, in vetoing McNary-Haugen bills in 1927 and 1928, said that farmers must solve their own problems. He warned against overproduction and argued that the most government could do would be to encourage cooperative marketing. Between 1925 and 1928 Congress and the President remained at loggerheads over agricultural policy.

Despite the fact that he alienated many farmers, Coolidge's popularity remained exceedingly high. By 1928 increasing farm prosperity had even reduced discontent in the rural regions. The great majority of Americans applauded Coolidge when he told Congress in his last annual message in December, 1928: "The country can regard the present with satisfaction and anticipate the future with optimism." Three months later Coolidge left the White House amidst glowing praise from his countrymen. The President's negativism was considered a virtue, and his conservatism a blessing. The *New York Times* editorialized that Coolidge had "fitted exactly into the needs and inarticulate desires of the American people when he became president."

The Presidential Election of 1928

In August, 1927, President Coolidge announced from his vacation headquarters in the Black Hills, "I do not choose to run for president in 1928." Speculation persisted that Coolidge hoped to be drafted for another term, but in December he declared that his decision should be respected. Although Coolidge's withdrawal opened the way for other candidates, when the convention met in Kansas City in June, Herbert Hoover had a commanding lead among the delegates. He was closely identified with the exuberant prosperity of the 1920s and had won high praise from the business community for his efficient administration of the Department of Commerce. Some Midwestern farm leaders heartily disliked Hoover because of his opposition to agricultural legislation, and favored Governor Frank Lowden of Illinois, who had assisted in the fight for farm relief. Despite this opposition, the convention nominated Hoover on the first ballot. The platform called for continued tariff protection, tax reductions, government economy, farm relief without "putting the government in business," and support for prohibition.

About a month later the Democrats met in Houston. Alfred E. Smith, who had been denied the nomination four years earlier, was the leading candidate. A poor boy from New York's lower East Side, Smith had worked his way up in politics until he won the governorship in 1918. He believed in strong executive leadership, and as governor he had pushed through a number of social and administrative reforms. Smith was a Roman Catholic and he argued that prohibition should be repealed. The main opposition to Smith's candidacy came from "dry" Protestants in the South and West. They shouted, "We do not choose to vote for booze," but the delegates had their minds made up and Smith won on the first ballot. To give the ticket geographical and religious balance, the convention named Senator Joseph T. Robinson of Arkansas, a dry and a Methodist, for Vice President. Even though Smith's position on prohibition repeal was clear, the Democratic platform pledged an honest effort to enforce the Eighteenth Amendment. This contradiction between the position of the candidate and the platform did nothing to help the Democrats.

The campaign of 1928 took place in a period of booming prosperity, labor peace, almost full employment, and improved conditions among farmers. Under these circumstances it is not surprising that the Republicans emphasized the connection between their policies and good times throughout the nation. Hoover talked freely about the prospect of a chicken in every pot and two cars in every garage, and the party advertised that "prosperity didn't just happen." The Democrats sought to discount the claim that there was any relationship between prosperity and the Republican party, but their arguments fell on deaf ears.

Conditions were such in 1928 that no Democrat could have won the Presidency, but Smith had special liabilities which assured his defeat. He was a Catholic, a wet, and a Tammany Hall man. No Catholic had ever been elected President, and millions of people believed that such an event should never happen. Although Hoover expressed no religious prejudice, many of his supporters warned against electing a Catholic. "If Smith is elected will the Pope of Rome rule the United States?" asked one Missouri voter. In any event, Hoover won by a landslide. He polled 21,392,000 votes, while Smith gained only 15,016,000. Republicans had convinced a majority of the voters that victory for their party was the key to continued prosperity. Despite what appeared to be a political catastrophe for the Democrats, a close analysis of the results showed that they had done better than the returns indicated. Smith ran well in many large cities, and this was important in a country where urbanization was increasing rapidly. He also reduced the Republican majorities in some of the strongest Republican agricultural states. In other words, the overall political trend was favorable to the Democrats. But in November, 1928, discouraged Democrats could see no ray of hope. Conservative Republicanism was triumphant.

American Society in the 1920s

The 1920s have been called the "jazz age" and the "roaring twenties," terms which imply that people were primarily interested in having fun and ignoring more serious matters. It is true that many people danced the Charleston, made bathtub gin, and read sexy novels, but the picture of a whole nation going mad in pursuit of pleasure is highly distorted. The period's deeper meaning can be found in the urban-rural conflict. Rural Americans attempted to preserve their old ideals and values when these were being threatened by urban patterns of thought and action. The fight over prohibition, controversies surrounding the Ku Klux Klan, and the battle over the teaching of Darwinism illustrate some of the issues which divided rural from urban Americans.

One of the most significant developments in the 1920s was the growth of urbanization and its effect upon American life. Although cities had been growing rapidly for a century, the nation had remained predominantly rural. But in 1920 the census bureau found 51.4 percent of the people in towns and cities of 2,500 or more. By the end of the decade 56.2 percent of the population was urban. Urbanization developed so swiftly that at the end of the 1920s no more than 25 percent of Americans still resided on farms. Urban influences spread to every crossroads and village in the United States. Cities not only produced most of the wealth, but they set the patterns of action and conduct for a great majority of citizens. Music, literature, clothing styles, entertainment exemplified by the radio and movies, and mass communication all found their source in urban America, and these influences tended to standardize the thinking and actions of most people.

Most metropolitan areas had large numbers of recent immigrants. Moreover, thousands of Negroes moved to Northern cities during and after World War I. By the 1920s, most of the nation's big cities had a polyglot population of different races and nationalities, a condition which caused many white Americans to fear for the country's future stability and progress.

The 1920s were a highly nationalistic period. Most Americans believed that their institutions were clearly superior to anything found in foreign countries, and they were intolerant of any criticism of the American way of life. The demand for conformity which had been forced on citizens during World War I, and then again during the Great Red Scare, continued throughout the decade, although to a much lesser degree. Some liberal ministers lost their pulpits, teachers were fired, and writers came under attack by conservatives who demanded "100 percent Americanism," as they defined the ideal. High-tariff laws, restrictions on immigration, strong opposition to any brand of radicalism—communism, socialism, or the IWW—were all reflections of intense nationalism.

Organization and growth of the Ku Klux Klan also reflected a raucous and intolerant nationalism. Formed again in 1915 by William J. Simmons and a few followers in Georgia, the Klan proposed to "unite white male persons, native born gentile citizens . . . who owe no allegiance of any nature to any foreign government, nation, institution, sect, ruler, or people." The Klan opposed black rights and insisted on maintaining white supremacy in the South. It also attacked Jews and Catholics. In 1923 a Klan leader equated Roman Catholicism with "foreign idealism" and infidelity. The Klan denounced Jews because they supposedly had foreign financial connections. At first the Klan grew slowly, but after 1920, it experienced phenomenal expansion and by 1924 it had 4 or 5 million members.

Most of the Klan's membership came from the small towns of the South, Midwest, and Far West, where people feared the blacks, suspected the Catholics, disliked recent immigrants, and had a rigid idea of morality and acceptable conduct. These ideas appealed mainly to rural Americans, who considered cities to be the headquarters of sin and evil. In Oklahoma, Texas, Indiana, and a few other states, the Klan became a strong political force in the early 1920s, but its influence declined after 1924 because of poor leadership and lack of worthwhile objectives.

The Negro and Normalcy

The attitude of the Ku Klux Klan toward the black man was not unlike that held by a majority of Americans, both North and South. Despite the fact that thousands of blacks had fought gallantly in World War I—171 members of the black 369th Infantry were decorated by the French government—they came home to the same old economic, social, and political discrimination. And blacks resented more than ever the position of inferiority forced upon

Prejudice and Progress

The revival of the Ku Klux Klan seemed just one more symptom of the struggle between the ideas of rural America and those of the new urban and technological culture in the 1920s. The original Klan was organized in 1865 by former Confederate general Nathaniel B. Forrest. Its tactics of terror having prevailed in the South, the Klan quieted down, only to be reactivated in 1915. During the 1920s membership grew to four or five million. Now, however, the Klan operated in the North as well. Not merely against equal rights for blacks, now it came out against a host of other things: Catholics, Jews, immigrants, liquor. By 1925 the Klan was so strong it held a mass parade down Pennsylvania Avenue past the White House.

In a time of change the Klan appealed to certain native-born, rural, Protestant Americans. In its publications it proclaimed the virtues of a free press, the ballot, law enforcement, 100 percent Americanism, and the Holy Bible. Some of its Klaverns distributed baskets of food to the poor at Thanksgiving and Christmas. But in the atmosphere it created vigilantism too often replaced the process of law. From 1920 through 1925, for example, 225 lynchings took place in the United States.

New York Public Library

Above and left: Culver Pictures, Inc.; top: Schomburg Collection, New York Public Library

While government did little to advance the economic welfare or civil rights of blacks during the 1920s, the Negro himself made an increasingly important impact on the cultural scene, particularly in entertainment and the arts.

During this decade, jazz, a form developed largely by blacks, won widespread and enthusiastic acceptance. Great jazz artists of the period include Louis Armstrong, fourth from left in King Oliver's Band (center piece); Duke Ellington (above); Jelly Roll Morton, Thomas "Fats" Waller, J. P. Johnson, and W. C. Handy. On Broadway a series of musicals featured black stars like Florence Mills (right, above), Ethel Waters, Bill Robinson, and Josephine Baker.

A figure of special importance in the entertainment world was Paul Robeson, who established himself as a singer of spirituals on the concert stage where other black performers, including Marion Anderson (right) and Roland Hayes sang both classical and operatic arias. Robeson also became a leading actor in such plays as *All God's Chillun Got Wings* by Eugene O'Neill (right, below). Other important black actors in the 1920s included Charles Gilpin, Rose McClendon, and Richard Harrison.

Above: Brown Brothers; below: Culver Pictures, Inc.

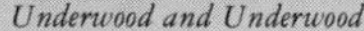

Underwood and Underwood

Schomburg Collection, New York Public Library

The 1920s also saw a flowering of black literary talent. A man who popularized black writers was Dr. Alain Locke (facing page, below, right), professor of philosophy at Howard University, critic, and essayist, who in 1925 published an anthology, *The New Negro.* Important black poets of the period were Claude McKay (facing page, below, left), author of *Harlem Shadows* and several novels, Countee Cullen (facing page, below, center), who wrote *Color* and *The Black Christ*, and Langston Hughes (above right), whose *Weary Blues* was the first of his many books. Among fiction writers were Walter White (above), author of the novels *The Fire in the Flint* and *Flight*, short-story writer Nora Zeale Hurston (right, above), and Jean Toomer, Wallace Thurman, Nella Larsen, and Jessie Fausset. The NAACP's *The Crisis* and *Opportunity*, a magazine founded for the Urban League by sociologist Charles S. Johnson, encouraged literary talent. Less well-known than the writers, a number of blacks distinguished themselves in other fields, including the historians Rayford W. Logan and Carter Woodson, sociologist E. Franklin Frazier, biologist Ernest Just, economist Abram Harris, a number of medical scientists, and many painters.

Schomburg Collection, New York Public Library

Brown Brothers

In 1925, A. Philip Randolph (left, below) organized the Brotherhood of Sleeping Car Porters and became an increasingly important labor leader and spokesman for Negro rights. When many industries having government contracts at the outbreak of World War II would not hire blacks, Randolph's call for a march on Washington forced government action. In 1960 Randolph led in forming the Negro American Labor Council to fight prejudice in organized labor.

Brown Brothers

Schomburg Collection, New York Public Library

National Association for the Advancement of Colored People

Leading groups in the struggle for black progress during the 1920s included the NAACP and the National Urban League, but a new, more colorful, and more radical group, the Universal Negro Improvement Association, also had a following. The NAACP, with more than four hundred branch offices across the nation, fought for black rights in the courts and

Brown Brothers

sought support for legislation such as the Dyer antilynching bill. The Urban League worked against discrimination in hiring practices. The UNIA, however, through its dynamic leader Marcus Garvey (above) held that blacks could prosper only by returning to Africa. The Ku Klux Klan approved Garvey's scheme and most black intellectuals denounced it, but between 1917, when it was organized, and 1923, the "Back to Africa" movement received some $10 million from its black supporters—Garvey rejected white aid. With these funds Garvey established The Black Star Line for transporting blacks to Africa and supported his African Legion which wore uniforms of green, black, and red. In 1921 the UNIA convention in New York drew 25,000 delegates and named Garvey "Provisional President General of Africa." In 1923 Garvey was sentenced to five years in prison on a charge of using the mails to defraud, and in 1927 he was deported to his native Jamaica.

them. Many had left the South during the war and migrated to the Northern cities where they obtained jobs in industry and, like the returning black veterans, were not prepared for the intolerant attitudes of Northern whites. As Negroes sought better housing, improved education, and equal accommodations in public conveyances, they ran into a wall of resistance in the North just as they had in the South.

National tensions and the revival of the Ku Klux Klan carried the bitter tradition of riots and lynchings into the postwar period. There were violent race riots in Chicago, Tulsa, and other American cities between 1919 and 1921. Earlier, Southerners had murdered thousands of blacks in the process of restoring exclusive white rule in the South. This disrespect for the life, rights, and property of black Americans often rested on false stereotypes of people of African descent. Although the nation experienced almost four thousand lynchings from 1889 to the end of the 1920s, Congress passed no antilynching legislation and no President acted vigorously against this practice.

Throughout the 1920s, the National Association for the Advancement of Colored People and the National Urban League assaulted bigotry and fought to gain greater social, economic, and educational rights for blacks. But discrimination gave way slowly, if at all. Marcus Garvey's Universal Negro Improvement Association, which emphasized race pride, had a substantial following in the early 1920s. Many blacks had been taught to despise Africa and blackness and to exalt things European. Garvey made heroic efforts to remedy this. His only solution for the "race problem" was the emigration of black Americans to Africa where they would build a great nation. His movement suffered defeat, but lived on as an inspirational symbol. No plan or organization did much to change the unequal position of blacks in American society. They continued, in general, to remain second-class citizens.

Negroes, however, did gain recognition in literature and the arts. So many able Afro-American writers and artists were active during the 1920s, and after, that the movement with which they were consciously associated became known as the Negro or Harlem Renaissance. What characterized the work of the group was great technical skill, race pride, and a certain militancy. Among the leaders were Langston Hughes, Claude McKay, Countee Cullen, James Weldon Johnson, Jessie Redmond Fauset, Walter White, Noble Sissle, Catherine Dunham, and Richard Wright. Johnson published *The Book of American Negro Poetry* in 1922; that year McKay, an immigrant from Jamaica, wrote a book of verse, *Harlem Shadows,* which expressed bitter resentment toward the treatment of blacks in America. Seven years later Countee Cullen's *Black Christ* appeared. Both Jessie Redmond Fauset's *There Is Confusion* (1924) and Walter White's *Fire in the Flint* (1924) confronted some of the problems facing Negroes in their effort to establish a place in American society. White's *Rope and Faggot: A Biography of Judge Lynch* was a well-researched study of lynching. Much of this creative effort seemed to culminate in the appearance of Richard Wright's novel, *Native Son,* in 1940.

On the stage, Paul Robeson played in Eugene O'Neill's *All God's Chillun Got Wings* (1924); in 1930 Richard B. Harrison performed in *The Green Pastures.* Negro musical revues were well attended in the 1920s; and Louis Armstrong became one of the hottest jazz artists of all time. Noble Sissle and Eubie

Blake produced the music for "Shuffle Along," one of the more popular musicals of the period. Solid achievements such as these indicated that blacks had abundant talent; what they lacked was the opportunity to demonstrate that talent on a broader front.

Prohibition

Prohibition was an issue which deeply divided Americans in the 1920s. When the Eighteenth Amendment went into effect on January 16, 1920, it represented the culmination of a long campaign to outlaw the manufacture and sale of intoxicating liquor. Maine led the way with prohibition legislation in 1851, and by 1916 some twenty-three states had gone dry. Campaigns by the Prohibition party, the Woman's Christian Temperance Union organized in 1874, and the Anti-Saloon League formed in 1893 had been highly effective in winning support for prohibition. Moreover, prohibition became a major progressive reform which gained support especially from old stock middle- and upper-class reformers. Prohibition had gained ground rapidly before World War I, and during the war people argued that grain should be used for food instead of liquor. In 1917 Congress passed the prohibition amendment by large majorities, and by 1919 enough states had ratified the amendment to make it a part of the Constitution.

Once the Constitution had prohibited the manufacture and sale of intoxicating liquor—it did not make drinking illegal—Congress had to interpret the term "intoxicating." Later in 1919 Congress passed the Volstead Act, which defined intoxicating liquor as any drink containing over one-half of 1 percent alcohol. On the evening before prohibition was to become effective, Wayne Wheeler, head of the Anti-Saloon League, said, "A new nation will be born. . . . Tonight John Barleycorn makes his last will and testament." Wheeler wished everyone "a happy dry year." But people who wanted liquor continued to obtain it illegally through the misuse of druggists' prescriptions, importation from Canada and the West Indies, local distilling, and redistillation of industrial alcohol.

Enforcement proved difficult, although in the early years of prohibition the law was quite effective throughout much of the nation. The amount of liquor consumed dropped sharply, and alcoholism and alcohol-related diseases declined very substantially. However, by 1923, enforcement was breaking down. Congress never provided sufficient money to hire the agents needed to enforce the law, and in communities which opposed prohibition little was done to abolish the liquor trade. Moreover, crime and corruption fed on the illicit liquor traffic. Al Capone, Chicago's leading racketeer in the late 1920s, controlled much of the liquor business, as well as other illegal activities, and his gang killed those who tried to infringe on his business. This aspect of the prohibition story, however, has been greatly exaggerated by popular writers. Nevertheless, by 1924 much of the mass media had become highly critical of prohibition and had begun calling for some modification to be made in the Volstead Act.

What rendered prohibition embarrassing to politicians and law-enforcement agencies alike was the refusal of many wealthy citizens to alter their drinking habits. Never had drinking been so fashionable. It was largely the rich who made crime and racketeering profitable. Presi-

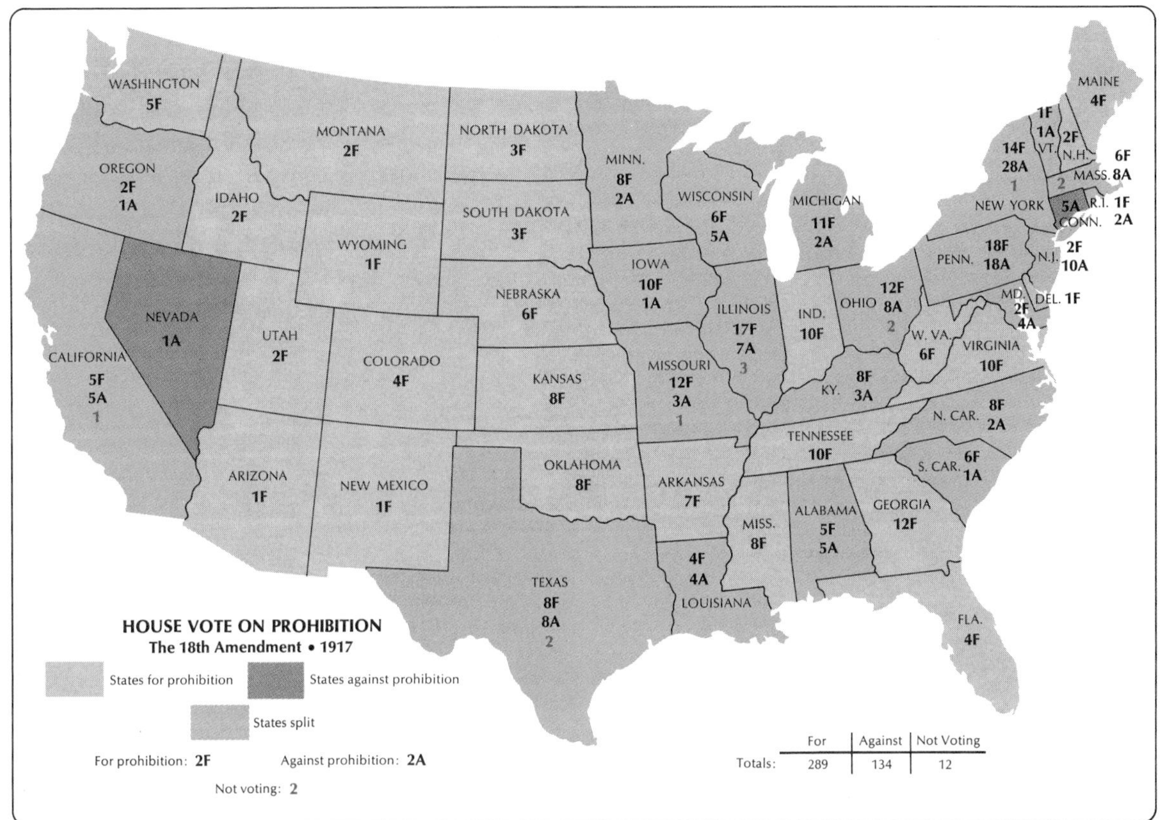

dent Hoover became so concerned about the whole problem that in 1929 he appointed a commission headed by George W. Wickersham to study that "great social and economic experiment." Reporting in 1930, the commission recommended continuing prohibition but offered few constructive suggestions on how to enforce the law. So confusing was the Wickersham report that it led one columnist to observe that "the distinguished jurists seem t' feel that if we'd let 'em have it the problem o' keeping 'em from getting it would be greatly simplified." By that time, however, it was becoming clear that an increasing number of Americans were having serious doubts about prohibition as a national social policy.

Manners and Morals

Society is always changing, but in the 1920s social change seemed to be swifter and more dramatic than in previous generations. People had more leisure and money, the automobile provided them with greater mobility, and radios and movies furnished them a new, passive form of entertainment. There was an unusual restlessness throughout the country. Youth demanded more freedom and rebelled at customary social restraints. Women sought to escape the restrictions placed on them by law and tradition and demanded full equality with men. In the nation's social life, then, the 1920s were full of unrest, social criticism, and rapid change.

No single thing had a more profound effect on American society than the automobile. "Why on earth do you need to study what's changing this country?" asked one observer. "I can tell you what's happening in just four letters: A-U-T-O!" The automobile age had started before World War I, and by 1920 the number of passenger cars registered in the United States had reached more than eight million. But this was only the beginning. By 1930 about twenty-three million automobiles were traveling on American streets and highways. Expanded use of the automobile not only gave people much more mobility, but also affected courtship, vacation travel, employment, and recreation. In large measure it was responsible for breaking down the isolation of farmers and reducing urban-rural differences. By the 1920s the automobile had become a distinct part of the American way of life.

Radio and movies broke down the older and more conservative types of entertainment which individuals and groups had once provided for themselves. Commercial broadcasting began in Pittsburgh in 1920. Seven years later millions of Americans listened regularly to music, drama, and sports. Some 40 percent of the nation's families owned radios by 1930. Movie theaters attracted crowds of anxious entertainment-seekers in towns and cities all the way from New York to San Francisco. Silent pictures had given way to sound films in most places by 1929.

The constant search for excitement and amusement reflected the deep restlessness in American society. Mah Jong, crossword puzzles, marathon dancing, and jazz music were popular for varying periods in the 1920s as people rushed from one entertainment fad to another. Spectator sports such as baseball, football, and prizefighting attracted millions of fans. Babe Ruth of the New York Yankees was baseball's idol, and in 1927 the "king of swat" hit sixty home runs to establish a record not broken until the 1960s. Harold "Red" Grange of the University of Illinois, one of the greatest football players of all time, packed spectators into the Big Ten university stadiums. Prizefighting had two of history's greatest champions in Jack Dempsey and Gene Tunney. Dempsey defeated Jess Willard in 1919 and held the heavyweight crown until 1926 when he lost to Tunney.

The music and dances of the 1920s were another expression of the national mood. The most popular dances, at least among the younger people, were the fast and acrobatic Charleston and the Black Bottom. Such songs as "The Love Nest," "Hot Lips," and "I Gotta Have You" indicated the popularity of songs stressing love and sex. The popularity of jazz, made famous by Paul Whiteman and his orchestra, was another reflection of the demand for a faster tempo in entertainment. "Jazz it up a bit" became a common expression among young people. The Negro influence on music was also seen in jazz and blues songs such as "St. Louis Blues" and "Memphis Blues."

The actions of a growing number of young people, especially young women, deeply worried and alarmed older Americans. Short, above-the-knee dresses; acrobatic dancing, such as the Charleston; necking parties; and the frank discussion of sex by the country's youth all demonstrated that they were bent on freedom. Girls shocked their parents as they brazenly smoked in public; some of them frequented speakeasy bars. The antics of young people convinced many citizens that degeneracy had displaced decency and that carnality had destroyed morality. The *Pittsburgh Observer,* a Catholic paper, complained in 1923 that "there has been a change for the worse during the past year in feminine dress, dancing, manners, and general moral standards."

It was not easy to bridge the marked and agonizing generation gap which existed between young people and their elders. Many spokesmen for the younger generation were frankly critical of the society which they had inherited from their parents, a society which most mature Americans looked upon as the best in the world. "The older generation has certainly pretty well ruined this world before passing it on to us," wrote one youthful observer in 1920. "They give us this thing, knocked to pieces, leaky, red-hot, threatening to blow up; and then they are surprised that we don't accept it with the same attitude of pretty decorous enthusiasm with which they received it, way back in the 'eighties." To be sure, only a minority of the nation's youth threw off the restrictions of the past and the standards of their parents, but the change indicated visibly that a new social day had dawned.

Literary Currents

Restlessness, a desire to break from the past, and criticism of American culture were expressed in much of the popular literature of the 1920s. F. Scott Fitzgerald shocked thousands of readers with his novel *This Side of Paradise,* published in 1920. His leading character, Amory Blaine, engaged in a variety of drinking and loving bouts which purportedly represented the actions of many young people of that time. During the next few years scores of novels were written around the themes of alcohol and sex without coming to grips with anything of much social importance except the idea of youthful revolt against the restricting puritanism of their forebears. Such titles as *Flaming Youth* and *Unforbidden Fruit,* by Warner Fabian, became best sellers; Victor Marguerite's *The Bachelor Girl* and E. M. Hull's *The Sheik* abounded with love and passion.

Works of serious social criticism were also popular in the 1920s. Sinclair Lewis pictured the mean, dull life of a small Midwest town in *Main Street* (1920). He wrote of Gopher Prairie: "It is negation canonized as the one positive virtue. It is the prohibition of happiness. It is slavery self-sought and self-defended. It is dullness made God." Two years later Lewis analyzed what he considered the petty commercialism of an American small-town businessman in *Babbitt.* Lewis's novel *Elmer Gantry* was a vitriolic attack against the clergy, whom he portrayed as carnal and dishonest. In *Winesburg, Ohio* (1919) Sherwood Anderson told a series of stories which described the frustration, shallowness, and loneliness of life in a small American community. Theodore Dreiser's *An American Tragedy* (1925) related the story of a young man who ruined his life and finally met death because of his unrestrained desire for wealth and position. Ernest Hemingway became a self-conscious member of the critical generation with his *The Sun Also Rises.* The writings of Lewis, Dreiser, Anderson, and Hemingway sold by the hundreds of thousands, yet few people agreed with their hopelessness, criticism, and rejection of American culture. They personified the writers who were cynical and defeatist about America. They were part of the so-called lost generation, many of whom spent much of their time in Paris complaining about their native land, but living off its fruits. Most Americans, on the other hand, believed theirs to be the best society man had ever created.

Perhaps the sharpest critic of white, middle-class, Protestant society was H. L. Mencken. Through the columns of the *American Mercury* Mencken attacked almost every aspect of American life. He ridiculed religion, prohibition, Christian marriage, and the popular service clubs. To him, the Bible-believing South was "the boobery," and its people "boobus Americanus." He called for more sexual freedom and living for the moment. But by 1927, his appeal to the so-called highbrows was losing its attraction, and the circulation of the *American Mercury* declined sharply.

Most popular fiction in the 1920s, however, did not follow sex themes or stress the undesirable aspects of American life and culture. The writings of Zane Grey, Harold Bell Wright, Willa Cather, Booth Tarkington, and Edna Ferber provided no break from the past and were much more widely read than the works of Fitzgerald or Lewis. Cather's *My Antonia* (1918) and *Death Comes for the Archbishop* (1927) demonstrated her power to understand the people and their problems on the frontiers of Nebraska, New Mexico, and Arizona. Ferber's *So Big* (1924), which won a Pulitzer prize, and *Cimarron* realistically caught the spirit of excitement and drama in the settlement of the Southwest. Zane Grey's Western stories sold by the millions. Of the many books written on World War I, Ernest Hemingway's *A Farewell to Arms* (1929) described the feeling and meaning of that conflict most poignantly.

The 1920s witnessed a prolific outpouring of popular books on history and philosophy, as well as serious studies in the humanities and social sciences. H. G. Wells's *Outline of History* (1921), Will Durant's popularly written *Story of Philosophy* (1926), and Hendrik Willem Van Loon's *Story of Mankind* were typical of the so-called outline books of the period. Cooperative works greatly expanded both the breadth and depth of the nation's history. The *Dictionary of American Biography,* begun in 1928, expanded to twenty-one volumes by 1944. The *Chronicles of America* series (1918) were elementary but briskly written volumes which covered the period from Columbus to about 1920. In sociology Robert S. Lynd and his wife, Helen, used the survey method to probe into the contemporary social life of Muncie, Indiana, and published their results in *Middletown: A Study in Contemporary American Culture* (1929). A great deal of information on the economy appeared in the basic two-volume study entitled *Recent Economic Changes in the United States* (1929).

Religion and Education

Although Americans considered themselves a religious people, traditional Christianity experienced some trying times in the years between World War I and the Great Depression. In the first place, the increasing emphasis upon science and the acceptance of newer theological views tended to cast doubt on some of the basic Christian beliefs. For example, one survey of five hundred ministers revealed that only forty-six of them thought it was necessary to believe in the virgin birth of Christ to be a Christian. Such ideas shook many church members and left them confused and uncertain about their faith.

Churches also came under the influence of the prevailing business philosophy of the prosperous 1920s. Indeed, some church and lay leaders pictured Jesus as a successful businessman and attempted to sell Christianity much as they would sell soap or cigarettes. The most popular nonfiction book in the middle 1920s was Bruce Barton's *The Man Nobody Knows*. Barton presented Jesus not as a man of sorrows, but as a skilled executive who "picked up twelve men from the bottom of business and forged them into an organization that conquered the world." Sermon titles also carried business themes. Ministers advertised such Sunday morning topics as "Public Worship Increases Your Efficiency." Many in the church, then, worshipped the idol of success and seemed to ignore the deeper spiritual meanings of Christianity.

A third factor which deeply affected organized religion was the competition provided by sports, the movies, and the automobile. By the 1920s millions of nominally faithful Christians were finding other things to do on Sunday. Instead of going to church they took a drive in the country, played golf, watched a baseball game, or went to a movie. While many communities tried to prohibit them, Sunday movies were shown in most cities by the late 1920s.

Despite these conditions, the number of churches and church membership grew in the postwar decade. The country had some 232,000 churches and synagogues with a total membership of 54.5 million in 1926, an increase of nearly 13 million members during the previous ten years. There were some 32 million Protestants, divided into more than 200 separate denominations; 18.6 million Catholics; and approximately 4 million of the Jewish faith. The rate of increase among Catholics was slackening off because of the drop in immigration. By 1926, some 55 percent of the American people over thirteen years of age were church members, a higher percentage than at any previous time in American history.

The trend toward liberalism and modernism in theology continued, especially in the larger denominations and those affiliated with the Federal Council of Churches. Many, though not all, of these same religious leaders also demonstrated a keen interest in the social gospel. These churchmen believed that the church was an agency to remake society here and now, and they supported programs which would establish justice, help the poor, and bring peace on earth. But fundamentalists were still strong. They held firmly to the Bible as the absolute word of God and insisted that one could not be a true Christian if he did not believe in the virgin birth, the physical resurrection of Jesus, and the second coming of Christ. Religious conservatives emphasized a visible spiritual conversion and charged that modernists gave only intellectual assent to the faith. "Billy" Sunday, the great revivalist of the day, drew huge crowds as he denounced sin.

Many fundamentalists favored and even sought laws designed to protect the thought and action of the public. The court case which challenged the Tennessee law forbidding the teaching of evolution illustrated the conflict between science and religion and between liberals and fundamentalists. In 1925, John T. Scopes was arrested for teaching evolution at Dayton, Tennessee. Clarence Darrow, a brilliant but irreligious criminal lawyer, defended the young biology teacher while William Jennings Bryan, conservative Presbyterian and elder statesman of the Democratic party, assisted the prosecution. Much of the court argument centered around the truth of the Bible and freedom to teach. The antievolutionists won the case, but Scopes was later freed on a technicality. The strain of defending his fundamentalist views in the terrible July heat contributed to Bryan's death a short time later. Despite Bryan's evident ignorance of science, religious conservatives believed that he had given an admirable defense to the true faith.

For many years, most Americans had been committed to public, tax-supported education, at least through high school. Moreover, by World War I, progressive educators had generally accepted John Dewey's ideas of the child-centered school. For a number of years fewer classical subjects such as Greek and Latin had been offered, and high schools were adding what were considered more practical courses, such as agriculture and business arithmetic. To a large extent, the trends in education in the 1920s were a continuation of changes which had been in progress for at least a generation.

Rapidly growing enrollments at all levels and greatly increased school expenditures reflected the faith of the American people in education. The total number of children in school from kindergarten through the twelfth grade rose from 23.2 million in 1920 to 28.3 million a decade later. By 1920 more than 81 percent of the nation's children between five and seventeen years of age were in school. While total enrollment advanced 21 percent in the 1920s, the number of students going to high school jumped more than 100 percent. This emphasized the increasing importance being attached to a high school education, not only as preparation for college but as training for life. The number of college students nearly doubled during the decade, reaching more than a million in 1930.

As had been true earlier, educational opportunities varied greatly in different parts of the United States and between urban and rural schools. There were still thousands of one-room, ungraded country schools where a minimum amount of learning occurred. Here teachers had often had no more than a high school education themselves, or at most one or two years of college. There was a conspicuous absence of books other than the simple texts. Some students did well, but it was more in spite of the schools than because of them. In the South, educational opportunities for blacks and many poor whites were extremely inadequate and in some cases nonexistent. The results of such limited educational facilities for blacks could be seen in the high rate of illiteracy, which was nearly four times as great among the nonwhite population as among the whites. Hundreds of thousands of black children received no preparation to attend high school or college, or to live in an increasingly technological society.

Strong emphasis was placed on science both inside and outside the universities. Although much of the commentary on science was poorly prepared and sometimes inaccurate, newspapers, magazines, and books kept people informed on the latest scientific developments. Widespread discussion of evolution made many people aware for the first time that scientists had placed man in the animal kingdom, and this realization contributed measurably to the conflict between religion and science. Psychology was among the newer and most popular branches of science, and the ideas of Sigmund Freud, the famous Austrian physician, commanded widespread attention. Indeed, many people seemed to believe that psychology was going to solve all of the problems of personality and human relationships. In other areas, Arthur H. Compton of the University of Chicago won a Nobel prize in 1927 for his contributions to X-ray research, and B. S.

Hopkins did distinguished work in chemistry at the University of Illinois. Alexis Carrell made outstanding advances in medicine. Almost every field of natural science showed progress during the 1920s, but the average citizen was interested chiefly in its practical application to his living standards. The development of plastics, rayon, and alkyd resins were only a few of the products which grew out of the new science.

Many people received much of their education from newspapers and magazines rather than in any formal classroom. Every large city had one or more daily newspapers, and most small towns published a weekly. By the 1920s the major dailies had become huge business enterprises, devoted largely to the creation of a product which would sell and attract advertisers. In order to appeal to all kinds and levels of readers, newspapers carried comic strips; special features; sentimental columns, such as advice to the lovelorn; fiction; news and editorials. Newspapers after 1920 became increasingly uniform in appearance and content, as people in all parts of the country read the same Associated Press news stories, the same syndicated columnists, and even the same comic strips. In this respect newspapers added to the growing conformity of thought and action in American life.

Two of the most notable developments in magazine publishing were the founding of *Reader's Digest* by Dewitt Wallace in 1922 and the establishment of *Time* by Henry R. Luce the following year. H. L. Mencken doubted if either venture would succeed. In his usual caustic manner, however, he admitted that a people who would elect Harding might fall for *Time*. *Reader's Digest,* he said, was "so bad it may go over." But Mencken was more clever than accurate. Both *Time* and *Reader's Digest* became huge successes because the magazines filled a need for busy people who wanted their reading condensed and digested.

Conclusion

President Harding caught the spirit of the times when he called for normalcy. To most Americans this meant maintaining things much as they had been in prewar America. In the 1920s there was a strong reaction against any further expansion of governmental powers to promote the general welfare such as that which had characterized the progressive movement. By sensing this mood and acting on it, the Republicans were easily able to win the Presidency and to control Congress by large majorities. As long as prosperity continued, the Republican administrations seemed to be acting in the national interest and they received wide popular endorsement.

At the same time, American social and cultural life underwent some basic changes. Rapid urban growth, greater mobility emphasized by growing use of the automobile, greater freedom for youth, and new intellectual currents combined to produce major innovations in American society. Although some observers charged that Americans in the postwar years were purposeless and lacked serious aims and objectives, during this period enduring contributions were made in literature, history, education, science, and the fine arts. The vast majority of Americans were proud of their country and devoted to its institutions. As they viewed their society before the stock market crash in October, 1929, all but a few critics continued to pronounce it good.

There are several excellent surveys of the 1920s. These include W. E. Lauchtenburg's *The Perils of Prosperity, 1914–1932** (1958); John D. Hicks's *Republican Ascendancy, 1921–1933** (1960); H. U. Faulkner's *From Versailles to the New Deal* (1950); and Arthur M. Schlesinger, Jr.'s *The Crisis of the Old Order, 1919–1933** (1957). F. L. Paxson's *Post-war Years, 1918–1923* (1948) is a satisfactory account of the unsettled postwar period through the Harding administration.

The best biographies of Harding are Andrew Sinclair's *The Available Man: Warren Gamaliel Harding* (1965) and Francis Russell's *The Shadow of Blooming Grove: Warren G. Harding and His Times* (1968), while the racy *Incredible Era: The Life and Times of Warren Gamaliel Harding** (1939) by S. H. Adams is less balanced but more colorful and interesting. The best study on Coolidge is D. R. McCoy's *Calvin Coolidge: The Quiet President* (1967). Biographies of other leaders prominent in the 1920s add a great deal to a better understanding of the politics of the period. These include Oscar Handlin's *Al Smith and His America** (1958); J. A. Garraty's *Henry Cabot Lodge* (1953); Alfred Lief's *Democracy's Norris* (1939); and M. C. McKenna's *Borah* (1961). On the presidential elections see Wesley Bagby's *The Road to Normalcy: The Presidential Campaign and Election of 1920* (1962); K. C. MacKay's *The Progressive Movement of 1924* (1947); R. V. Peel and T. C. Donnelly's *The 1928 Campaign* (1931); and E. A. Moore's *A Catholic Runs for President* (1956), an account of Al Smith's campaign to reach the White House.

The scandals of the Harding administration have been treated in a lively fashion by Adams in *The Incredible Era,* cited above, as well as in Volume VI of Mark Sullivan's *Our Times* (1935). On the background of Teapot Dome, see J. Leonard Bates's *The Origins of Teapot Dome* (1963); and for a full account of the episode consult Burl Noggle's *Teapot Dome: Oil and Politics in the 1920s* (1962).

American society in the 1920s has drawn an unusually large number of writers and interpreters. An excellent introduction to the period is Henry F. May's "Shifting Perspectives on the 1920's," *Mississippi Valley Historical Review,* XLIII (December, 1956). The most perceptive contemporary account is F. L. Allen's *Only Yesterday** (1931). Volume VI of Sullivan's *Our Times, The Twenties* cited above contains a wide variety of material on American life and culture, but it lacks unity and organization. P. W. Slosson's *The Great Crusade and After, 1914–1928* (1930) is a good survey of the period's cultural history. Some of the social changes which were occurring in America are shown in the study of Muncie, Indiana, published in 1929 by R. S. and H. M. Lynd in *Middletown**.

The Great Red Scare has been most fully treated by R. K. Murray in *Red Scare: A Study in National Hysteria, 1919–1920** (1955). On the Ku Klux Klan see J. M. Mecklin's *The Ku Klux Klan* (1924), and the more recent *The Ku Klux Klan in American Politics* (1962) by A. S. Rice; as well as C. C. Alexander's *The Ku Klux Klan in the Southwest** (1965). Prohibition has been dealt with by Charles Merz in *The Dry Decade* (1931) and Herbert Asbury in *The Great Illusion* (1950), but the best history of this attempted social reform is Andrew Sinclair's *Era of Excess: A Social History of the Prohibition Movement** (1962). The position of Negroes in the 1920s has been treated by J. H. Franklin in part of his *From Slavery to Freedom** (2d ed., 1956) and in the extensive work of Gunnar Myrdal, *An American Dilemma: The Negro Problem and Modern Democracy** (2 vols., 1944).

Generally critical contemporary evaluations of American culture have been summarized in *Civilization in the United States: An Inquiry by Thirty Americans* (1922), edited by Harold E. Stearns. On religion see the relevant sections in Norman Furniss's *The Fundamentalist Controversy, 1918–1931* (1954); Paul A. Carter's *The Decline and Revival of the Social Gospel, 1920–40* (1956); and *American Catholicism and Social Action** (1960) by A. I. Abell. Educational trends may be followed in Lawrence A. Cremin's *The Transformation of the School: Progressivism in American Education, 1876–1957** (1961).

Literary trends are well treated in Lloyd Morris's *Postscript to Yesterday: American Life and Thought, 1896–1946** (1947); J. Hoffman's *The Twenties** (1955); and Volume III of V. L. Parrington's *Main Currents in American Thought** (1930).

*indicates availability in paperback.

Art in America: 1905–1940

In the early twentieth century, the more progressive elements in American art took two directions. The first, in a native idiom, led toward a new and vigorous interpretation of the contemporary scene, particularly the world of urban America. The group of artists concerned with this theme were dubbed "The Ashcan School" because of their nonidealizing tendencies, or "The Eight," because the major New York group exhibition of their work in 1908 *included eight painters. Even this group, however, included only five artists devoted to depicting the contemporary urban world and its inhabitants in broad, slashing brush strokes—Robert Henri, John Sloan, George Luks, Everett Shinn, and William Glackens. Glackens would shortly abandon the dramatic approach of these early years for an American version of Renoir's Impressionism. The other members of "The Eight"—Ernest Lawson, an Impressionist landscapist, Arthur B. Davies, an idealizing dreamer, and Maurice Prendergast, who developed a very personal form of Post-Impressionism—allied themselves with the urban realists only in sympathy against the entrenched academics.*

Meanwhile, in the first two decades of the century a progress of American painters found their way to Europe, studying and absorbing the new, revolutionary movements of Cubism, Orphism, Futurism, and Abstraction—

such men as Marsden Hartley, Max Weber, Joseph Stella, Alfred Maurer, and others whose works were greeted, on their return to America, with complete incomprehensibility and hostility. Indeed, Modernism aroused the greatest aesthetic controversy of the early twentieth century when pictures in this style appeared at Alfred Stieglitz' New York Gallery, "291," at such exhibitions as the 1913 Armory Show which presented the first comprehensive survey of advanced European tendencies, and the Forum Exhibition of American Modernism of 1916.

Among those in partial retreat from Modernism, Marsden Hartley, in this crude but powerfully expressionistic treatment of the Maine landscape, for example, was among the most original as he emphasized solid massiveness in depicting mountains, trees, water, and clouds.

Marsden Hartley (1877–1943)
Mt. Katahdin, Autumn No. 1, 1939–40, *oil*
F. M. Hall Collection, University of Nebraska Art Galleries.

The isolationism which set in after World War I and affected American political life had its cultural counterpart in the arts. Many of the leading American Modernists abandoned their progressive tendencies and fell back upon a form of modified realism. Weber returned to a new exploration of his first great inspiration, Cézanne; Stella turned to a form of exotic mysticism; and Hartley painted expressionistic landscapes and figure studies in New Mexico and then Maine. Only Stuart Davis and Charles Demuth continued to explore and develop later forms of Cubism. That geometric concentration and sharpness of form, however, was applied to an interpretation of American industrialism in the work of the "Immaculate" or "Precisionist" artists, such as Charles Sheeler, who came to be called "Cubist-Realists."

The reaction against European Modernism also gave birth to the Regionalist school which advocated the denial of advanced foreign influences and a return to native American subject matter. A group of Midwestern artists, Grant Wood, John Stewart Curry, and Thomas Hart Benton, found even the Eastern cities too contaminated by foreign ideas. In the 1920s and 1930s, both realism and regionalism received new impetus, and regional schools of different degrees of conservatism and modernism developed throughout the nation. One form of realism had particular significance and attracted a large number of talented painters. "Social Realism" involved artists such as Ben Shahn, Jack Levine, and others who were concerned with the problems of war, refugees, workers, and urban ills and corruption.

During these years, the most original tendencies in American sculpture did not parallel painting, and neither urban realism nor abstraction and other forms of modernism found much of a sculptural counterpart. Rather, a stylized linearism, as personified in the work of Paul Manship and later given a powerful, expressionist interpretation by Manship's pupil, Gaston Lachaise, constituted the most striking sculptural development. The 1920s also saw a return to direct carving of wood, alabaster, and stone by such sculptors as William Zorach, John Flannagan, and José de Creeft, who made use of the unique color, texture, grain, and even shape of their basic materials.

Gaston Lachaise followed his master, Manship, in retaining an emphasis on simple, curvilinear outlines and sleek surfaces, but he endowed his gigantic figures with such a sense of voluptuousness and sensuousness that they seem almost to grow and expand before us.

Gaston Lachaise (1882–1935), Standing Woman, 1912–1927, *bronze.*

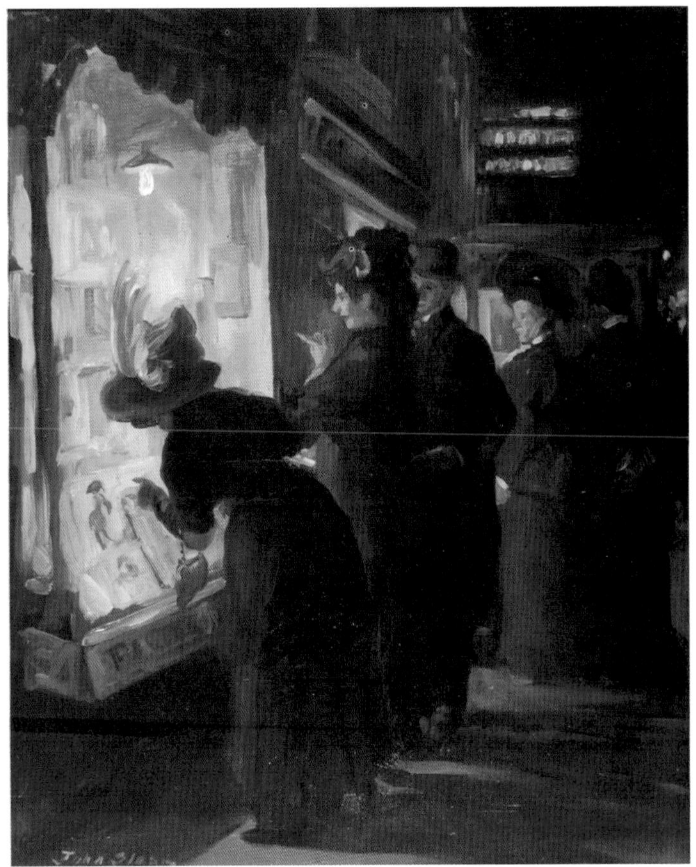

Of "The Eight," or "Ashcan School," John Sloan was the foremost painter of the urban scene itself and the life of the people in the cities. He matched these vivid scenes with an equally vivid technique.

John Sloan (1871–1951)
Shop Window, 1901, *oil*
The Newark Museum. Gift of Mrs. Felix Fuld, 1925.

Robert Henri was the leading spirit of "The Eight." Primarily a figure and portrait painter, he chose sympathetic, appealing subjects which he interpreted with vivid brush work and dramatic and rich color.

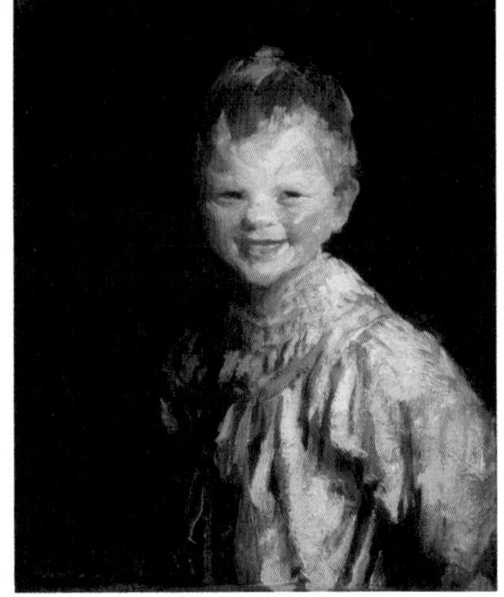

Robert Henri (1865–1929)
Laughing Child, 1907
Collection Whitney Museum of American Art, New York

Until about 1911 *or* 1912 *William Glacken's work was devoted to similar themes (right). His technique finds its ancestry in the painterly heritage of the Frenchman, Manet, and the Americans who studied in Munich—Frank Duveneck and particularly William Merritt Chase. A number of other painters did share a devotion to contemporary realism with "The Eight," however, including Jerome Myers, Glenn Coleman, and best-known and most successful of all, George Bellows. Bellows' outstanding figure painting is best seen in his powerful, expressive prize-fighting scenes with their emphasis upon action and ruggedness (below).*

William Glackens (1870–1938)
Park on the River, 1905
The Brooklyn Museum, Dick S. Ramsay Fund.

George Bellows (1882–1925), Both Members of This Club, 1909, *oil on canvas*
National Gallery of Art, Washington, D. C. Gift of Chester Dale.

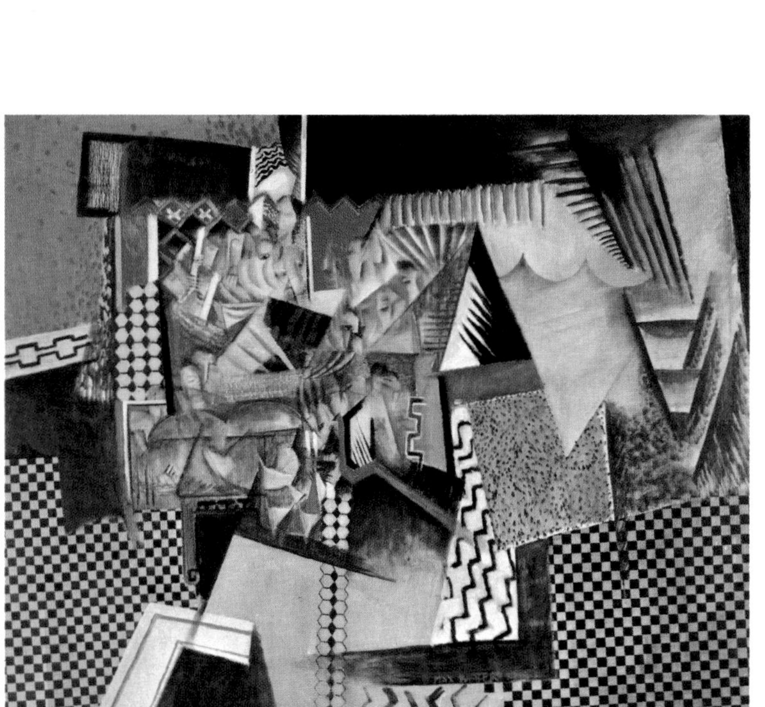

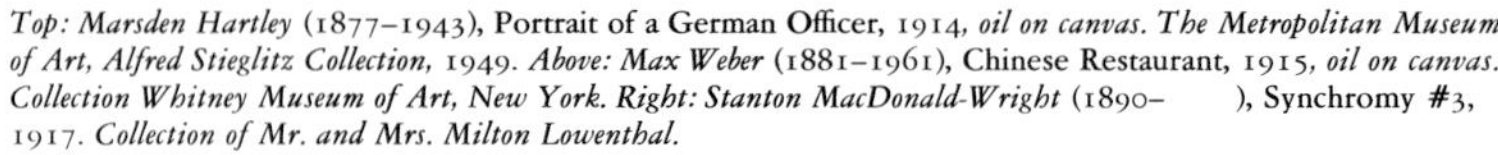

Top: Marsden Hartley (1877–1943), Portrait of a German Officer, 1914, *oil on canvas. The Metropolitan Museum of Art, Alfred Stieglitz Collection,* 1949. *Above: Max Weber* (1881–1961), Chinese Restaurant, 1915, *oil on canvas. Collection Whitney Museum of Art, New York. Right: Stanton MacDonald-Wright* (1890–), Synchromy #3, 1917. *Collection of Mr. and Mrs. Milton Lowenthal.*

While the painters of the Ashcan School pursued their realistic art at home, other artists went to Europe and studied the revolutionary Modernism of the young Picasso, Matisse, and Kandinsky. In Germany at the beginning of World War I, Marsden Hartley created vivid, semi-abstract, geometric patterns based upon military flags, banners, and insignia (left, above). Max Weber inspired first by Matisse and the Fauve movement, worked with raw color and vivid chromatic contrasts; later he turned to the flat, geometric and kaleidoscopic forms of Cubism and Futurism applied to New York subjects (left, below). Joseph Stella, was even more inspired by Italian Futurism, which found its most vivid American interpretation in the paintings Stella did of the Brooklyn Bridge (right), then considered a symbol of advanced technology. Weber and Stella brought these new movements back to America; Stanton MacDonald Wright, along with Morgan Russell, founded a movement in Paris known as Synchromism which, like the native French Orphism, consituted a coloristic, dynamic rebuttal (below) to the monochromatic, static character of Cubism although both shared an interest in near-abstraction and the use of geometric shapes.

Joseph Stella (1877–1946), The Bridge, 1922, *gouache.*
The Newark Museum. Purchase 1937, *Felix Fuld Bequest.*

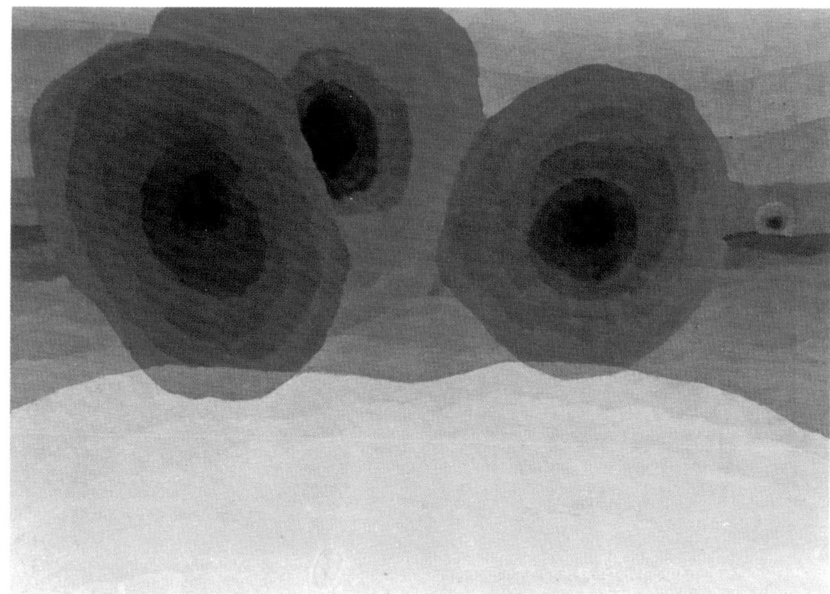

Arthur G. Dove (1880–1946), Fog Horns, 1929, *oil.*
Colorado Springs Fine Arts Center.

John Marin (1870–1953), Maine Islands, 1922, *watercolor.*
The Phillips Collection.

Hartley, Weber, Stella, and MacDonald Wright were American followers and counterparts of Europe's leading Modernists. Arthur Dove's oils, watercolors, and collages, some among the earliest American abstractions, made up a more individual contribution, evocative paintings often with loose naturalistic associations based upon the suggestiveness of shapes and sounds (left, above).

John Marin developed a very individual, shorthand calligraphy in his vivid watercolors of Maine. The fragmentation of forms (left, below) is based upon Cubism, but the sense of movement, and his recreation of structure with interior frames, is his own. While the reaction against Cubism set in in both America and Europe after 1920, Stuart Davis continued to investigate the breaking-up of forms in flat, two-dimensional patterns. His dynamic conjunctions and interweaving of color areas have often been likened to the rhythms of contemporary jazz (below).

Stuart Davis (1894–1964), Report from Rockport, 1940, *oil. Collection of Mr. and Mrs. Milton Lowenthal.*

One of the most strikingly original and distinctly American movements of the 1920s and 1930s was called "Precisionism"; its practitioners were referred to as "The Immaculates" because of their use of sharply defined, precise forms. Charles Sheeler best characterizes these artists who often devoted their talents to the depiction of the industrial landscape (right, above). Devoid of irregular shapes and outlines, these paintings omit any trace of the accidental. This emphasis upon geometric regularity is a Cubist heritage perhaps most clearly seen in the work of Charles Demuth, where the flat patterns and linear overlays never destroy the recognizability of the subject (below).

Charles Demuth (1883–1935), My Egypt, 1927, *oil on composition board. Collection, Whitney Museum of American Art, New York.*

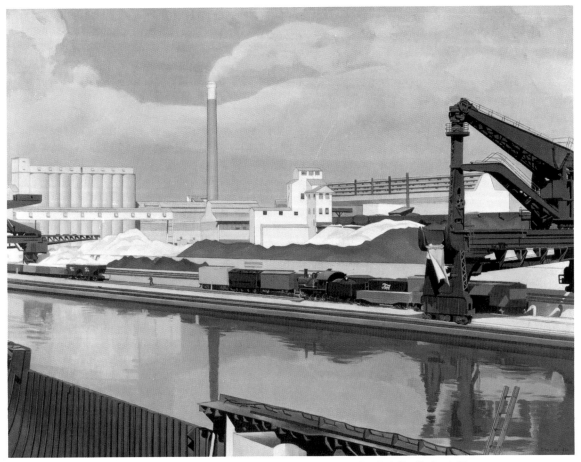

Charles Sheeler (1883–1965), American Landscape, 1930. *Collection, The Museum of Modern Art, New York, Gift of Abby Aldrich Rockefeller*

Precisionist clarity of form found its most original interpretation in the flower and leaf studies of Georgia O'Keeffe. Here the magnification of the object and the elimination of everything accidental transmits an effect on the one hand nearly abstract, and on the other, seemingly pulsating with a sense of growth and life.

Georgia O'Keeffe (1887–)
The White Flower, 1931, *oil*
Collection, The Whitney Museum of Art, New York.

Grant-Wood (1892–1942), American Gothic, 1930, *oil on beaver board. Courtesy of the Art Institute of Chicago, Friends of American Art Collection.*

The reaction to European Modernism found its highest expression in the work of those artists who depicted the world of the rural Midwest. The most original talent among these Regionalists was Grant Wood, who revived a meticulous technique to satirize the grim smugness of the people of his region (left). Charles Burchfield interpreted the Victorian heritage of America's towns in Surrealist, dream-like fashion. In these monumental watercolors, Burchfield gives an anthropomorphic character to his old buildings, with their window-eyes, door-mouths, and haunted, alive expressions (right). A more straightforward melancholy appears in the old structures and their lonely inhabitants depicted in Edward Hoppers's urban scenes (below). These paintings are quiet descendants of the urbanism of the Ashcan School, but they gain in structure and monumentality from a subtle overlay of Cubist logic and geometry.

Top: Charles E. Burchfield (1893–1967), Church Bells Ringing, Rainy Winter Night, 1917, *watercolor on paper. The Cleveland Museum of Art. Gift of Mrs. Louise M. Dunn in Memory of Henry G. Keller. Above: Edward Hopper* (1882–1967), Early Sunday Morning, 1930, *oil on canvas. Collection, Whitney Museum of American Art, New York.*

Nearly all of the advanced American Modernists of the decade between 1910–1920 *retreated to more conventional, certainly more realistic artistic styles in subsequent years. Hartley's later style has already been discussed. Among other painters, Peter Blume is probably America's best known Surrealist, creating dreamlike images in a meticulous and minute style. In "The Eternal City," his most famous canvas, he used this approach to caricature the impact of Mussolini and Fascism.*

Both Jack Levine and Ben Shahn acknowledged their involvement with the problems of the period in their art, and they are appropriately known as "Social Realists." Jack Levine often depicted gangsters and corrupt politicians in a biting, satirical manner (left, below), while Ben Shahn is perhaps best known for his much shared sympathy with the executed Sacco and Vanzetti, his artistic protest expressing outrage against social injustice (right). Both artists utilized expressionist techniques, that is, they make use of distortions of natural forms for emotional, dramatic effects: Shahn's approach is very linear; Levine concentrates upon broad, fluid masses of rich paint.

Left, above: Peter Blume (1906–), The Eternal City, 1934–1937, *oil on composition board. Collection, The Museum of Modern Art, New York. Mrs. Simon Guggenheim Fund.*
Left, below: Jack Levine (1915–), Election Night, 1954. *Collection, The Museum of Modern Art, New York. Gift of Joseph R. Hirshhorn.*
Right: Ben Shahn (1898–), The Passion of Sacco and Vanzetti, 1931–1932, *tempera on canvas. Collection, Whitney Museum of American Art, New York.*

The major innovation in American sculpture of the early twentieth century, combined a simplification of form with sharp, sleek linearism and the suggestion of movement stemming from the Art Nouveau movement and constituting a reaction to the historical monuments and generalized allegories of such artists as Saint Gaudens and French. Paul Manship was the most outstanding sculptor to take this direction. He was also one of the leading teachers of the following generation of sculptors.

Paul Manship (1885–1966)
Diana
Museum of Art, Carnegie Institute, Pittsburgh, Pa.

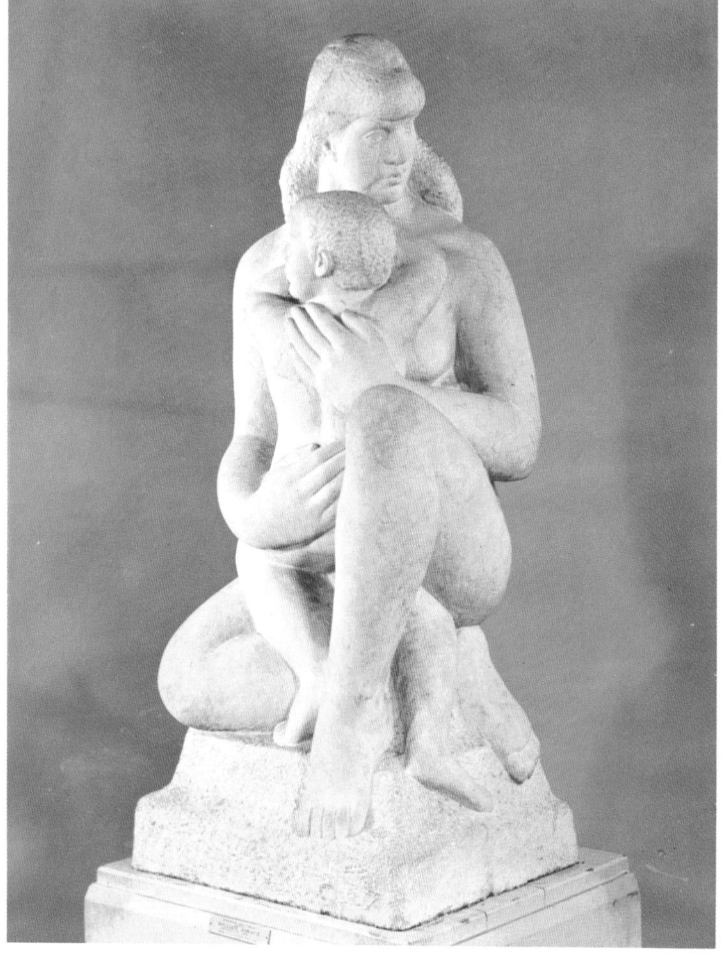

Stone carving in the mid-nineteenth century involved only the sculptor preparing the design and hired workmen executing the carving. The return to carving by artists such as William Zorach and others came about 1920. The subjects of such representational sculpture are usually quite conservative, but the artists often allowed the shape of the block to determine the final form, and they often chose special, exotic woods, marbles, or other stones to take advantage of peculiar colors, variations in the grain of the material, and other qualities intrinsic to the medium.

William Zorach (1887–1966)
Mother and Child, 1927–1930, *Spanish marble*
The Metropolitan Museum of Art, Fletcher Fund, 1952.

31

The Republican Search for Peace: The 1920s

TO A NATION recently at war, the peace of the early twenties seemed remarkably secure. At Versailles the Allies, by agreement among themselves, had assigned to Germany the sole responsibility for causing the Great War. From that reading of history emerged the welcome conclusion that postwar peace demanded little more than German adherence to the conditions imposed at Versailles. For many Americans Europe again had moved beyond the realm of national concern. Such easy assumptions, not shared by all Americans, denied at least two inescapable lessons of United States involvement. First of all, the refusal of the nation to forego the advantages of wartime trade, added to its ultimate unwillingness to accept any continental challenge to British and French security, demonstrated that the American people could not escape a major European war, especially one that ventured onto the Atlantic. Secondly, Woodrow Wilson had not reordered the international system. In the future, as in the past, the United States, if it intended to exert a long-range influence, would perform in the international arena according to the traditional rules of diplomacy. Sound American policy, therefore, would avoid both the extreme position of denying all interest in the political and military affairs of Europe and Asia and that of identifying its interests with the liberal aspirations of humanity everywhere. Instead it would recognize and protect a variety of specific national interests that had historically sustained its welfare and security.

Unfortunately the American people derived precisely the wrong conclusions from their involvement in Europe's war. Wilson's peace efforts had driven American thought toward the very extremes against which the past had warned. His crusade to transform the American role abroad in accordance with his idealistic purposes had succeeded only too well. So completely had he eliminated the concept of national interest as a guiding principle of diplomacy that only with extreme difficulty would the nation ever again agree on the goals and assumptions which should determine its policies abroad. Even those who anticipated a leadership role for the United States in postwar international affairs would embrace, not a limited, balancing performance amid the pressures of power politics, but a Wilsonian pursuit of peace and stability the world over. In theory, at least, they would oppose any changes in the status quo which resulted from the employment of force. On the other hand, Wilson's failure to translate the American war effort into a new world order led to an isolationism which insisted that the nation's policies need not venture abroad at all. Thus, despite the extent and enthusiasm of the country's commitment to the Great War, the United States emerged from that struggle unprepared emotionally or intellectually to sustain a carefully measured involvement in world politics commensurate with its interests and power.

Isolationism and Internationalism

Isolationism—a state of mind denying the existence of any American political or military interests outside this hemisphere—flowed logically from a deep postwar disillusionment with both Wilson and the war. The wartime President had promised the American people a new world order which he could not achieve; by ignoring the genuine gains that lay within the range of victory, he never adequately explained to his countrymen why their involvement had been both necessary and successful. Many preferred to judge Wilson by his own standards, and by those standards he had failed. It was not strange, therefore, that millions of Americans after 1919 concluded that the United States had gained little from its wartime experience except prohibition, the flu, American Legion parades, and the Russian colossus. The noted journalist Oswald Garrison Villard concluded that it would have been better to take the lives of the American soldiers in cold blood on Broadway. Endlessly in the twenties Americans calculated the number of hospitals, libraries, and college buildings they could have constructed with the billions consumed to fight the war. With time the disillusionment became profound.

Isolationism revolutionized the nation's attitudes toward onetime friends and foes alike. So pro-British had been the wartime crusade against Germany that Americans, on the rebound, would naturally acquire some dislike for England. If that nation was responsible for what appeared to be a needless United States involvement in the war, then Britain was indeed the true enemy of American interests. Irish-Americans shared the bitterness of American nationalists toward England and the war. Not only had British troops repressed the Irish rebellion of 1916, but Wilson, who proclaimed the principle of self-determination with such enthusiasm, had also refused at Versailles to touch the territorial interests of the Western Allies. German-American organizations such as the Steuben Society, opening again the question of national responsibility for the war, were pleased to report that Germany was no more responsible for the Great War than were France and Russia. Indeed, by the mid-twenties few Americans still thought of Germany as a European antagonist. In the eyes of many isolationists, Germany in 1925 appeared far more heroic than England. Similarly Asian minorities within the United States—Indian, Chinese, and Korean—harbored an intense resentment toward Wilson because of his failure to apply the torch of self-determination to the colonial empires of the victors in Asia and Africa. Nowhere after 1920 did the political reality of the underdeveloped continents fit the Wilsonian description. Isolationism, in rejecting an imperfect world, reflected a widespread and understandable sense of national security. As such, however, isolationism could hardly establish the foundations for a realistic approach to the task of sustaining that world which United States leadership at Versailles had helped to create.

But internationalism was as oblivious to reality as was isolationism; both were strangers to the nation's nineteenth-century traditions. Indeed, isolationism and internationalism had more in common than the debates of the twenties would suggest. Both denied that the United States had a vital interest in any particular political and military configuration outside the Western Hemisphere. Whereas isolationism limited the nation's legitimate concerns to matters at home, internationalism asserted that American interests were universal—wherever mankind might be oppressed or in danger of aggression. Neither really focused on concrete issues which touched the nation's interests clearly and specifically. Isolationism stopped short of them; internationalism soared far beyond them. Whereas isolationism denied that the United States had any postwar role to play in world affairs, internationalism insisted that the United States play an active role. No more than isolationists, however, would internationalists accept the obligation that the country employ its power to enforce those arrangements in world politics that reflected its basic interests. Every internationalist scheme of the twenties emphasized the requirement, not of specific commitments abroad, but of agreements, declarations, and institutions which would confront any aggressor with a combination of international law, signed promises, or world opinion. In practice, all the new international agencies, such as the League of Nations and the World Court, embodied the effort of the favored nations—in the twenties, the victorious democracies—to establish the means whereby they might perpetuate a status quo which served their interests without the necessity of specific commitments, adequate defenses, or the danger of conflict. Concepts of peace and peaceful change became the bulwark of the status quo, for as long as nations rejected the legitimacy of force, they denied themselves both the right and the power to alter the international order except in matters of little or no consequence.

Whatever their opposition to foreign commitments, Americans had no desire to escape the world of commerce and investment. Between 1922 and 1929 the net movement of capital out of the United States totaled some $3.6 billion. Businessmen demanded that their government sustain their privileged economic position everywhere on the globe. For a nation of worldwide business interests, peace was of the essence; therefore, it was not strange that many citizens insisted that the country accept a moral responsibility for the peace. These generally conflicting objectives established the bounds of national behavior. The Republican administrations of the twenties, in their perennial support of business interests abroad, satisfied the demands of those who believed in the principle of "America first." Their vigorous involvements in pursuit of peace delighted those who believed that the United States thereby served its own interests and those of humanity. Finally, their assurance that involvement did not constitute commitment—at least where it might be costly—pleased all Americans who accepted the apparent stability of the world's peace structure as genuine and durable. United States external policies after 1920 varied from narrow nationalism to limited internationalism, all designed to serve the nation's specific interests in trade and progress as well as its general interest in the peaceful evolution of the postwar era. It was not strange, therefore, that successive Republican administrations enjoyed a broad, popular consensus on questions of foreign policy.

Nationalism came first. Throughout the twenties American tariff policies scarcely reflected the nation's status as the world's leading creditor. That role historically had required the encouragement of international trade, even at the sacrifice of some domestic industry and agriculture. It demanded, moreover, a national willingness to accept adverse trade balances which might enable debtor nations to reduce their international financial obligations. Unfortunately for those countries which required United States markets, however, the American economy was so prosperous, efficient, and well balanced that many items of world trade faced direct competition from United States production. To accentuate the problem of international trade, the United States Congress not only adopted a series of emergency tariffs in 1921 but also, in the Fordney-McCumber tariff of 1922 (described in detail in Chapter 30), established a tariff barrier so high as to prevent almost all profitable exchange between the United States and the world market.

The same debtor complex determined the nation's attitude toward the $10 billion in Allied war debts still owed the American government. Official Washington regarded these debts less as an American contribution to the Allied war effort than as separate financial obligations to be paid in full. Nor would the United States concede that the Allied capacity to pay had any relationship to German reparations. The Coolidge administration did take a direct interest in Europe's financial troubles when it encouraged American bankers to accept the Dawes Plan in 1924, whereby they agreed to lend money to Germany to ease German reparations payments. Later, in 1929, the United States participated in formulating the Young Plan (named after American businessman Owen D. Young), which reduced German reparations from $33 to $9 billion with the hope that Germany would then fulfill her international financial obligations. Meanwhile the United States continued to press the Allies for payments on their war debts. Even after reducing the debts and lowering interest rates, the United States was unable to collect much of what was due from its European debtors. As German prosperity returned, Americans invested large sums in German industries and utilities, giving Germany the dollars necessary to make some reparation payments to France and other allies, who, in turn, then paid about $2 billion of their war debts to the United States. Thus there was a connection between reparations and war debts whether or not the United States cared to admit it.

Although Washington refused to facilitate international exchange with freer trade policies, it continued to encourage the outflow of American capital. Under the direction of its Secretary, Herbert Hoover, the Department of Commerce after 1921 enlarged its overseas operations to gigantic proportions. Supplementing the activities of United States consular offices abroad, the Department scoured foreign economies in search of investment opportunities. These the Department advertised to American investors through pamphlets and press releases. Well might an American consul complain in 1928: "As diplomatic functions today are mainly economic, this places the Department of Commerce in control of the substance of diplomacy, and leaves the Department of State with social representation only."

With its commerce and capital flowing into Europe, Asia, and Latin America, the United States of the twenties was hardly isolated from pressures on the international system. Curtis Wilbur, Secretary of the Navy, demonstrated the full extent of the nation's involvements abroad when he addressed the Connecticut Chamber of Commerce in May, 1925: "Americans have over twenty millions of tons of merchant shipping to carry the commerce of the world, worth three billion dollars. We have loans and property abroad, exclusive of government loans, of over ten billions of dollars. . . . These vast interests must be considered when we talk of defending the flag. That flag must be defended unhesitatingly and with all our power whenever attacked. . . . To defend America we must be prepared to defend its interests and our flag in every corner of the globe." United States interests abroad were not as global as Secretary Wilbur suggested. The nation's purposes did not encompass even the limited national interests embodied in the Versailles Treaty. The Secretary had expressed the sentiments of a powerful, confident, and unchallenged nation, not the guidelines of established national policy.

Latin America

Nowhere was United States involvement abroad more unrestrained in the twenties than in Latin America where its past interference, even political and military, had seldom been expensive. Interventionism was still the rule, but it was beginning to wane under a continuous moral and legal assault. Wilson, during the war years, had stressed the right of self-determination; this, in turn, created new impediments to the use of power in controlling the internal affairs of smaller nations. Although the United States still occupied several republics of Central America and the Caribbean after the Great War, Secretary of State Charles Evans Hughes insisted that the United States meant no injury to any of them and interfered only to help them solve their internal problems. Not until 1924 did United States troops evacuate Santo Domingo. With the establishment of a modicum of political order in Haiti during the twenties, the United States withdrew its marines from that country. Meanwhile this nation maintained a force of several thousand marines in Nicaragua to maintain a semblance of civil order. Its effort in 1927 to supervise elections and disarm the country resulted in a long anti-guerrilla campaign.

Increasingly, Latin Americans condemned the United States for its refusal to deal with the Caribbean states on the basis of equality.

This indignation culminated at the Pan-American Conference at Havana in 1928, when Hughes, who headed the American delegation, declared that the United States had the right to protect the lives and property of its nationals in a country whose government was ineffective. American relations had reached a crisis, for it was clear that continued United States intervention would generate physical resistance as well as further moral condemnation. Hughes now made it clear that the United States would intervene only when the security of the United States demanded it. Finally, later in 1928, J. Reuben Clark, a State Department officer, released his *Memorandum on the Monroe Doctrine.* Somewhat inaccurately, Clark insisted that past United States intervention in Latin American affairs had sought only to guarantee hemispheric "freedom, independence and territorial integrity against the imperialistic designs of Europe." But in denying that the Monroe Doctrine had ever served purely as an instrument for maintaining order, Clark's memorandum was further evidence that the United States was abandoning its interventionist policies of the past. Through his able emissary Dwight Morrow, President Coolidge in 1927 managed to resolve several perennial conflicts of interest with Mexico. And President-elect Hoover laid the foundations of the Good Neighbor policy by embarking on a goodwill tour of Latin America in late 1928. As President, Hoover not only liquidated a number of concrete disputes but also renounced completely all American pretensions to hegemony in the region of the Caribbean.

The Challenge of Europe

For the United States after 1920 only a continued concern for European affairs could protect its interest in peace or reap any permanent gains from the involvement in the Great War. The necessity for a clearly conceived policy toward Europe lay primarily in the twentieth-century power revolution within Europe itself. The Great War had demonstrated that the old balance of power which had preserved Europe's stability—and with it, this nation's security—no longer existed. The Allied victory of 1918 had created the illusion of British and French supremacy, but this supremacy was viable only when underwritten by the full power of the United States. The Versailles Treaty, of necessity, established the conditions of postwar international stability. It provided for French military preponderance on the Continent, for on that preponderance hinged the future security of Europe. Second, it recognized the new Slavic states of East Europe. In a sense, these two essential elements of the post-Versailles European order were related, for the independence of fragmented Eastern Europe would scarcely outlast the eclipse of French military dominance on the Continent.

For the moment neither of Europe's potential giants—Germany and Russia—loomed as a threat to the Versailles settlement. Germany's defeat temporarily removed any danger posed by that nation. The Germans labored under a series of military limitations designed to curtail their warmaking capacity. Still the Great War had broken neither the German military potential nor the determination of the German leadership to elevate that nation again to a major, perhaps dominant, role in European politics. Even in defeat, Germany remained potentially the most powerful and the most threatening country of Europe.

Russia emerged as an even greater problem, but one of a unique character. For what made that nation loom as a special danger to the West and its traditions was less the power which it wielded than the ideology and long-range purpose which its rhetoric conveyed. Indeed, the Great War had produced two giant crusades against the evils of tyranny and war. Western ideology, embodied in Wilson's Fourteen Points, identified peace with the triumph of democracy and self-determination, all under the aegis of the League of Nations. Simultaneously Lenin presented his program for peace, a program based on world revolution and the classless society. Lenin's agency for the achievement of his democratic world order was not the League but the Communist International. Russia's new leadership made clear its intention to align the proletarians of all countries in one global contest with international capitalism, designated by Karl Marx as the enemy of mankind's peace and welfare.

The easy and apparently successful isolation of the Soviet Union from the affairs of Europe after Versailles misled a generation of world leaders. For Russia, like Germany, possessed untold reserves of power and energy. Emerging from World War I economically, politically, and militarily weak, the new Russia embarked upon a massive program of general development intended to meet both the needs of public welfare and the requirements of national security. To the Kremlin the United States and Western Europe were the enemy. The Soviets' feeling of insecurity bordered on paranoia. Joseph Stalin, Lenin's successor, warned the Russian people in 1931 that "those who lag behind are beaten. . . . We are fifty or a hundred years behind the advanced countries. We must make good this lag in ten years. Either we do it or they crush us."

Long before the mid-twenties Germany and Russia threatened the most vulnerable, and yet the most fundamental, territorial arrangements of the Versailles Treaty. It was only the momentary eclipse of German and Russian influence in European diplomacy after 1917 that permitted the balkanization of Eastern Europe. Within the new Slavic states themselves, with the exception of Czechoslovakia, there existed no power or energy capable of maintaining the region in independence and economic stability. Russia's invasion of Poland in 1920, albeit provoked by Western behavior, illustrated that nation's contempt for the Eastern European settlement. It was Poland's successful resistance, not Western determination, that saved Eastern Europe from the Russian assault. Clearly one of the two major powers bordering the new Slavic states had not accepted their boundaries as a permanent arrangement.

Britain, France, and Germany together might have guaranteed the political and territorial integrity of Eastern Europe. But they disagreed both in their intentions toward that region and in their attitudes toward one another. France, long outclassed by Germany as a military power, could discover little reason for confidence in the Allied triumphs of 1918, for she understood that her dominance of the Continent rested on the continued support of Britain and the United States. Yet France's unrealistic demands upon Germany for reparations, followed by her occupation of the German Ruhr in 1923, antagonized not only Germany but Britain and the United States as well.

Unlike France, Great Britain viewed Germany as an essential element in the reconstruction of a prosperous and stable postwar Europe and thus favored the development of German energy and resources. Lloyd George made it clear in 1921 that England regarded

Germany as a necessary bulwark against Russia and thus had no interest in guaranteeing Germany's eastern frontiers. The Locarno Treaties of 1925, regarded by Europeans as the high point of postwar British, French, and German cordiality, reaffirmed Germany's boundaries on the west but pointedly failed to include any guarantees for the status quo in Eastern Europe. Yet British faith in Germany's acceptance of the Versailles settlement was misplaced, for German ambition, no less than that of Russia, encompassed changes in the political structure of Slavic Europe. The treaty's eastern provisions, especially those regarding Austria, Czechoslovakia, Danzig, and the Polish Corridor, created resentment and focused German attention on Eastern Europe where the minimal interests of the West, added to the internal weakness of the new Slavic states, presented long-range opportunities for challenging the territorial limitations imposed at Versailles. Still any German effort to annex Austria, curtail Czechoslovakia, or partition Poland could result only in catastrophe.

Perhaps a united and totally committed alliance of Britain, France, and the United States could still have underwritten Europe's long-term stability by guaranteeing both French military dominance—at least over Germany—and the political structure of Eastern Europe. But Britain and the United States, by their refusal to sustain the wartime alliance with France and their decision, whether purposeful or not, to cast Eastern Europe adrift, had, as early as the mid-twenties, consigned the Versailles system to eventual oblivion. For both nations this instability in the Versailles structure would eventually demand a willingness either to use force in defense of the political integrity of Eastern Europe or to accept diplomatically whatever changes appeared consonant with their fundamental interests. For the moment, however, such troublesome but inescapable decisions appeared most remote.

The Washington Treaties

Japan emerged from the Versailles Conference as one of its chief beneficiaries. Despite Wilson's opposition, her diplomats had managed to formalize the Japanese claims both to Shantung and to Germany's Pacific islands north of the equator. But Japan, no less than Germany and Russia, entered the postwar era as a dissatisfied power. Not only were Japan's designs on China still unrealized but also, as the dominant power of East Asia, she was now determined to substitute for the imperial structures of the West in Asia a Far Eastern hegemony of her own. To undermine Western influence in Southeast Asia and the western Pacific Japan possessed two significant weapons: her own expansive power, backed by an impressive navy; and the force of anticolonialism, which had been deepened and augmented by the Versailles settlement. These two drives—Japanese expansionism and Asian anticolonialism—converged in their opposition to traditional Western dominance over the peoples and resources of the Orient. Confronted with this dual challenge, the Western nations in the Pacific faced choices neither broad nor promising.

During the war, the United States Congress had embarked on an extensive naval building program designed especially to offset Japanese sea power in the Pacific. Following Germany's defeat, however, Wilson's projected naval program threatened to involve Britain, Japan, and the United States in a naval arms race which many isolationists regarded as unnecessarily dangerous and costly. On December 14, 1920, Senator Borah introduced a resolution asking the President to call a conference with England and Japan to arrange a holiday in naval armament. Borah's resolution won such widespread approval in the press and Congress that the new Harding administration could not ignore it. Even editors who defended the need of United States naval supremacy agreed overwhelmingly that a multinational agreement on naval limitation would serve the dual American interest in external security and tax reduction.

For the United States in 1921 the achievement of such conflicting objectives as tax and naval reduction, the containment of Japan, and the abrogation of the Anglo-Japanese Alliance was a sizable order. Yet at the level of paper treaties and government propaganda, Hughes gained all of these objectives at the Washington Conference. To render any forthcoming naval treaty effective, Hughes in August, 1921, sent invitations to Italy and France as well as to Britain and Japan. The three European powers accepted with enthusiasm, but Japan, suspecting correctly that the conference would be concerned primarily with the status quo in the Far East, demanded that Hughes announce the conference agenda in advance. The Tokyo government warned that it had no interest in discussing matters that pertained to Japan's postwar position in China and the Pacific. Eventually the Japanese, pressured by the worldwide desire for naval reduction, sent a powerful delegation to Washington despite Hughes's refusal to publish an agenda. To round out the conference, the State Department brought in four lesser nations with interests in the Far East, including China itself.

On Armistice Day—November 11, 1921—President Harding opened the long-awaited Washington Conference amid the high expectations of a peace-hungry world. Hughes, proclaiming in his keynote address that the only way to disarm is to disarm, astonished delegates, naval experts, and newsmen alike with his sweeping proposal to halt battleship construction and to scrap sizable tonnage already in existence. In that speech the Secretary sank more naval power than all the naval battles of history combined. He then proposed a 5-5-3 ratio in capital ships among the United States, Britain, and Japan, with ratios of 1.75 each for France and Italy. Knowing the British devotion to cruisers, Hughes omitted smaller vessels from his program. Japan refused to accept her assigned ratio of capital ships unless the United States, Britain, and France agreed not to fortify their possessions in the western Pacific—including American-owned Guam and the Philippines. Having no desire to fortify these distant islands anyway, Hughes readily agreed to the Japanese demands, and the signatories put their names to the Five Power Pact. Another agreement, the Four Power Pact, specifically terminated the Anglo-Japanese Alliance of 1902 and substituted for it a general declaration of mutual respect for the status quo in the Orient and a promise to consult in response to any danger which threatened the stability of the region. It was signed by the United States, Great Britain, France, and Japan. The last of the Washington agreements, the so-called Nine Power Pact, reaffirmed the principles of the Open Door and pledged respect by all nations in attendance for the territorial integrity of China. Almost unnoticed, the United States achieved a settlement of the Shantung question, which the Japanese had promised Wilson at Versailles. On February 4,

1922, Chinese and Japanese delegates signed a treaty which restored Shantung to China and provided for China's purchase of the Japanese-controlled railway in Shantung with funds provided by Japanese bankers under a fifteen-year loan. This settlement protected Japan's economic, but not its administrative, supremacy in the province.

Harding submitted the treaties to the Senate with the assurance that they contained "no commitment to armed force, no alliance, no written or moral obligation to join in defense." Lodge, defending the Four Power Pact, denied that the principle of consultation implied a promise to rescue any Far Eastern victim from aggression. Even while they explained that the Washington Treaties entailed no obligation or alliance, the internationalists proclaimed that the treaties would guarantee the stability of the Pacific region. It was not strange that measures which promised so much for so little won the overwhelming support of Congress. One Senator alone cast his vote against the Five Power Pact, and Senate approval for the Nine Power Pact was unanimous. But the Four Power Pact, even with a reservation attached specifically disclaiming any obligation by the United States to defend anyone, triumphed by a margin of only four votes.

These much-heralded achievements at Washington in 1922 were no more than ephemeral. The Five Power Pact terminated all competition in capital ships, but it did not limit the building of cruisers, destroyers, submarines, and a wide variety of auxiliary craft. It made Japan the dominant naval power in the western Pacific. By agreeing to the nonfortification of Guam, the United States denied itself the only base in the Pacific from which it might protect the Philippines, for the latter islands lay well outside the effective range of vessels based in Hawaii. Without naval bases, Guam and the Philippines were hostages; with bases, they were a challenge to Japan. The Four Power Pact was totally without substance, for it conveyed no more than vague promises which, Harding and the Senate agreed, the United States never intended to fulfill. It was not clear, moreover, that the abrogation of the Anglo-Japanese Alliance served any useful purpose. It simply isolated Japan diplomatically and removed any restraining influence which Britain might have exercised within the alliance. Nor did the Nine Power Pact offer China any genuine guarantees against Japanese expansionism. Secretary Hughes's subsequent negotiations with the Japanese over the cancellation of the Lansing-Ishii Agreement, which ultimately failed, made it clear that the assertive spirit of the United States–Japanese wartime agreement, not the Nine Power Pact, defined Japanese intentions toward China.

The Kellogg-Briand Peace Pact

The reliance of Americans in the 1920s on paper—on stocks and bonds at home and treaties without obligations abroad—culminated in the Kellogg-Briand Peace Pact of 1928. Eventually this effort to outlaw war won the overwhelming support of internationalists, isolationists, and pacifists—all those Americans, indeed, who placed their faith in agreements and agencies designed to focus the supposedly crippling power of international law and world opinion on any nation that dared to break the peace. Still the movement to outlaw war developed slowly. During April, 1927, on the tenth anniversary of the United States declaration of war against Germany, Aristide Briand, the French Foreign Minister, addressed a message to the American people proposing a Franco-American agreement to outlaw war between the two nations. For Salmon O. Levinson, a wealthy Chicago businessman, and other proponents of outlawry, Briand's suggestion came as a message of salvation. The French overture also attracted the attention of leading New York internationalists like President Nicholas Murray Butler of Columbia University. When Washington failed to acknowledge Briand's proposal, Butler not only rebuked the Coolidge administration in an open letter to the *New York Times* but also, on a trip to Washington, pressed his friends in the State Department for a statement on the issue. At the suggestion of State Department officials, Butler asked a group of Columbia professors, headed by historian James T. Shotwell, to frame a bilateral draft treaty on outlawry. Briand at the same time prepared his own version of an ideal agreement.

While the State Department continued to avoid the issue, a crusade to outlaw war began to sweep the country. Butler touched it off with a speaking tour which started in Denver and ended in Augusta, Georgia. Levinson returned from Europe and immediately entered the campaign. Leading Midwestern newspapers gave the issue enthusiastic coverage. Jane Addams of Hull House, Chicago, presented the President a petition with 30,000 signatures encouraging him to take the initiative. When the League of Nations Assembly convened in September, 1927, the Polish representative introduced a resolution asking the League to renounce all wars of aggression and to employ every pacific means available to settle international disputes. Briand responded by reminding the Assembly that the universal conscience of mankind constituted a perfect tribunal to prevent aggressive war. On September 27, the Assembly unanimously adopted the Polish resolution, branding wars of aggression an international crime. This League action sent Coolidge and his Secretary of State, Frank B. Kellogg, in search of some antiwar formula that would mollify both Briand and the American peace advocates.

Kellogg soon found the answer to Briand's bilateral proposal in a multilateral treaty to outlaw war. Assured of national support, Kellogg in December submitted the idea of a multilateral pact to the French government. Paris's response, though affirmative, was less than enthusiastic. French officials saw immediately that a multilateral treaty, designed to eliminate the danger of war everywhere, would expand the international commitment to the status quo so completely that it would destroy all sense of specific obligation among the major powers for the peace of the world. But the American press, oblivious to the fundamental issue raised by outlawry—that of obligation—for the most part responded to Kellogg's proposal with unbounded enthusiasm. "Oh, the miracle of it!" exclaimed Levinson. Even as Kellogg prepared to leave for Europe to sign the agreement, President Coolidge was expressing his opinion: "It holds a greater hope for peaceful relations than was ever before given to the world."

Kellogg joined Briand and dozens of other leading diplomats in Paris late in August, 1928. The occasion of the signing of the Kellogg-Briand Peace Pact was magnificent, and Briand responded to it with an appropriate speech. He reminded those who demanded sanctions that the treaty rested on the sanction of "moral forces, among which is that of public opinion." What nation, he asked, dared to oppose such forces? Though some diplomats remained skeptical of the treaty's value, sixty-four nations eventually signed the document. Officially, at least, they consigned war to oblivion. Some Americans were jubilant. Declared the *Boston Herald:* "It is a thing to rejoice over, it is superb, it is magnificent." It was, said Nicholas Murray Butler, "the longest step forward to the establishment and protection of permanent peace that history records." For Carrie Chapman Catt the world was moving unmistakably toward Biblical ploughshares and pruning hooks. For the *Christian Science Monitor* the agreement was a great moral gesture in need of some agency to make it effective; and Rabbi Stephen S. Wise of New York labeled it the wishbone rather than the backbone of peace.

In the Senate the treaty faced little opposition, and with good reason. When had a document promised so much without cost or obligation? Kellogg himself reassured the Senate Foreign Relations Committee that the pact was devoid of commitment except the commitment not to make aggressive war. His own correspondence with other nations made clear the absence of any obligation. "They knew perfectly well," he said, "that the United States would never sign a treaty imposing any obligation on itself to apply sanctions or come to the help of anybody." Some Senators, in their enthusiasm for the treaty, dismissed the question of means as nonessential. Senator Robert Wagner of New York hailed the treaty "as a great and lasting crystallization of the human will to peace, as an example of a popular treaty rather than a diplomats' alliance." Amid such oratory the Senate, on January 15, 1929, endorsed the treaty by a vote of 85 to 1. So painless was the nation's involvement in another impressive effort for peace that isolationists and internationalists alike could share the apparent triumph. The Kellogg-Briand Pact had in truth merely reinforced the mistaken American illusion that the nation could sustain the world's security through moral leadership alone, without cost or obligation.

The Hoover Years

By the late twenties Republican foreign policy had achieved such visible success that it had won the overwhelming endorsement of the American people. So thorough had been the Republican recovery of power in 1920 that the Democratic party hesitated thereafter to test American opinion on questions of external relations. Seeing that election as a triumph for isolationism, the Harding administration refused at first even to answer communications from the League of Nations. Not until 1923 did the United States government begin to recognize the League's usefulness and to send observers to its conferences. In 1924 it assigned an official delegate to the Second Opium Conference and began to engage actively in the League's humanitarian ventures. So friendly and cooperative had the United States become toward the League of Nations by 1929 that congressional isolationists complained that the nation had joined the League in all but name. But such complaints no longer found an audience. So expansive had been America's share of world trade, so reassuring the Europe of the twenties, so apparent the contributions of the League to international stability, that countless Americans viewed the Versailles peace structure with increasing satisfaction.

Herbert Hoover entered the Presidency prepared to exert restrained leadership in world affairs. He pushed cooperation with the League to the highest point of the decade, especially on such questions as the international control of narcotics, human slavery, sea and air traffic, and radio communication. Although Hoover was not one to commit the nation to the use of force, he did hope to forward the noncoercive attempts to achieve peace begun by the Washington Treaties and the Kellogg-Briand Peace Pact. It was at his suggestion that invitations to the London Naval Conference were issued by Prime Minister Ramsay MacDonald of Great Britain in October, 1929.

In January, 1930, Great Britain and the United States, along with France, Italy, and Japan, began discussions in London on the issue of naval disarmament. The two continental powers, France and Italy, soon proved to be too distrustful of one another to agree to significant naval reductions. Yet as Frank Simonds of the *Review of Reviews* understood, France was the key to the conference's success. The British and the Americans, he reported, "were always seeking formulae which would give the French the semblance of security without the reality, the French were always demanding the reality and rejecting the semblance." When neither Britain nor the United States came up with ironclad security guarantees, Italy and France refused to sign the more important articles of the treaty. Britain, the United States, and Japan signed an agreement limiting cruisers on a ratio of 10-10-6, and submarines and other auxiliaries at 10-10-7. Britain was specifically permitted an escape from these provisions in the event of a threat from France and Italy to her traditional naval supremacy in Europe. No new capital ships were to be constructed until 1936. The treaty did little to limit the world's navies. The United States would have required a major naval building program if it were even to approach the treaty's rather generous quotas.

Hoover attempted to resolve the vexing questions of war debts and reparations, but without much success. With economic crises both at home and abroad, in June, 1931, the President suggested a one-year moratorium, or standstill arrangement, on the payment of intergovernmental debts. Both debtors and creditors agreed to this. But what would happen when the time came to resume payments? In the summer of 1932 the concerned European powers met at Lausanne, Switzerland, and agreed to scale down German reparations payments to a mere $750 million, providing the United States would reduce its claims for war debts proportionately. This the Hoover administration refused to do. Thus the entire question of war debts and reparations remained open at the end of the Hoover years. Early in 1933 Adolf Hitler came to power in Germany and quickly made it clear that he had no intention of making reparations payments. Meanwhile, war debt payments to the United States all but stopped; except for Finland, no country paid its full account.

That internationalism which found its ultimate expression in the Nine Power Pact, the Kellogg-Briand Peace Pact, and the movement for naval limitation constituted the essence of United States policy under successive Republican administrations. Despite such activity, the nation was no better prepared, intellectually or emotionally, to respond to another European challenge in the late twenties than it had been in 1914. As the Depression settled down on the United States and the world, the faith which the American people had once placed in paper arrangements no longer mattered. As Lewis Einstein warned in the *North American*

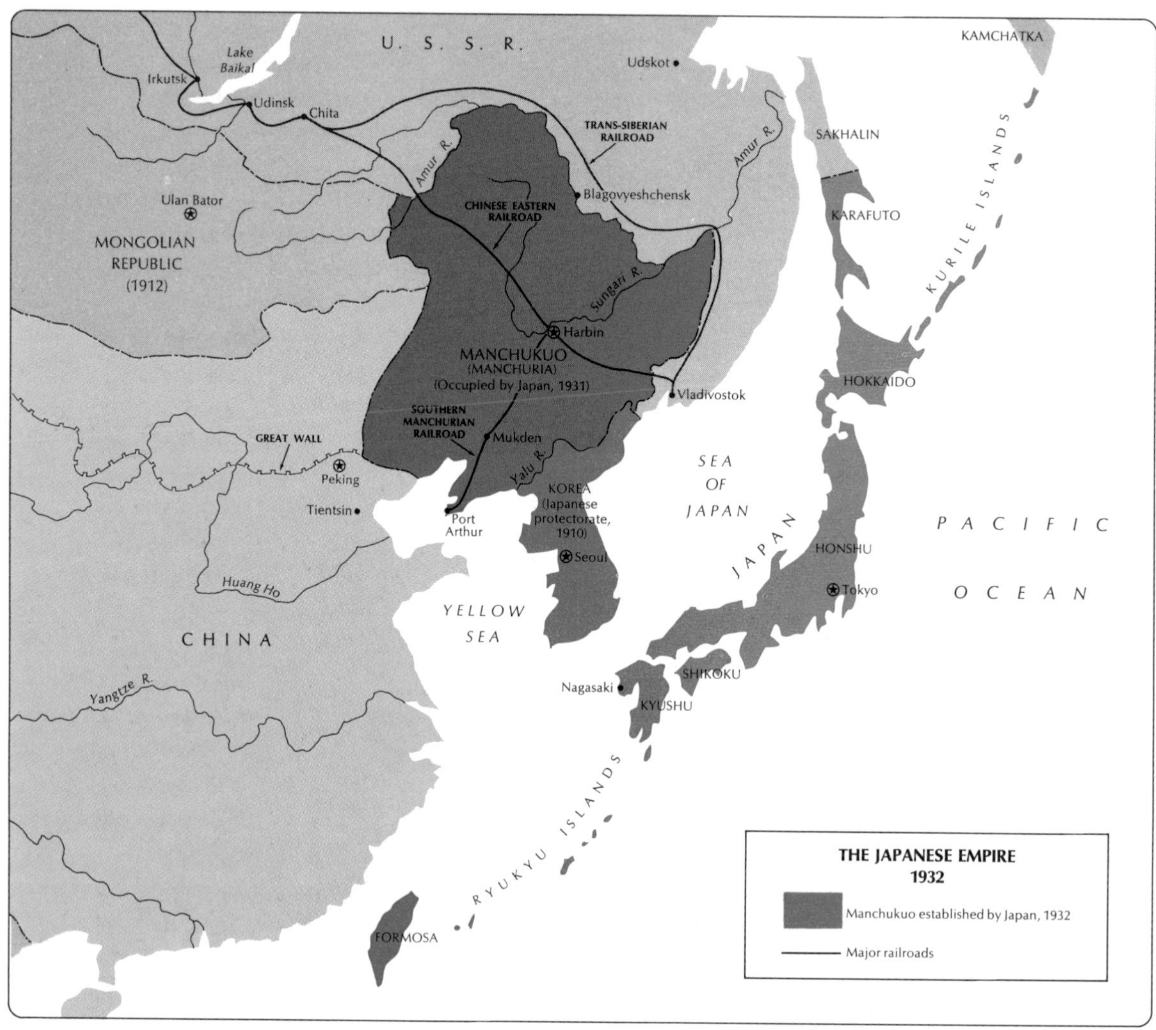

Review of September, 1931, "Beyond current platitudes of peace and good-will, beyond a predilection for forms of legal remedy which we are only ready to accept for questions of secondary interest, beyond pushing our dwindling exports on an impoverished Europe, what more has been our recent foreign policy?" There was little prospect that the Hoover administration, in a day of inward-looking nationalism promoted by hard times, could prepare the nation to meet any forceful challenge to the status quo.

Suddenly in September, 1931, an armed clash outside Mukden, Manchuria, shattered the peace of Asia and challenged all the assumptions upon which the West had erected its elaborate peace structure. Behind the struggle for Manchuria lay a network of unequal treaties which had given Japan a variety of special privileges in Manchuria, including the right to station troops along the South Manchurian Railway. Chinese nationalism and antiforeign feelings in the twenties directed much of China's energy toward the elimination of Japanese influence in Manchuria. In 1929 the Chinese nationalists attempted unsuccessfully to wrest from Russia control of the Chinese Eastern Railway in North Manchuria. Finding Japanese investments, as well as Japan's favored position in South Manchuria in jeopardy, Japanese militarists exploited the Mukden incident of September, 1931, to rationalize their determination to establish total military and political sway over Manchuria. Where would this assault on the peace treaties terminate?

This Japanese action, by its very success, exposed the gap between the ends and means of United States Far Eastern policy. Whereas this nation's objectives in the Orient, as defined in the Nine Power Pact of 1922, sought the indefinite continuation of the status quo in China, the United States had demonstrated repeatedly its disinclination to employ force in the defense of China. To avoid the necessity of either accepting diplomatically the changes wrought by Japan or of undoing the Japanese aggression with counterforce, the Hoover administration resorted to the doctrine of nonrecognition. In January, 1932, Secretary of State Henry L. Stimson informed both the Chinese and Japanese governments that the United States would recognize no territorial changes on the Asian mainland which resulted from the use of force or threats. The League of Nations, meanwhile, lacking the firm support of the great democracies, was powerless to act. Yet its mild rebuke of Japan, based on the Lytton Commission's report which in general supported the American principle of nonrecognition, was sufficient to prompt the Japanese to withdraw dramatically from the world body in 1933.

These events demonstrated that world opinion was either impotent or wrong-minded. Yet in his defense of the American action, Stimson insisted that nothing had occurred in Manchuria to challenge the applicability of either the Nine Power Pact or the Kellogg-Briand Pact. In a letter to Senator Borah, dated February 24, 1932, Stimson declared: "These two treaties represent independent but harmonious steps taken for the purpose of aligning the conscience and public opinion of the world in favor of a system of orderly development by the law of nations, including the settlement of all controversies by methods of justice and peace instead of by arbitrary force." But public opinion had failed to stop Japan. Confronted by no opposition of significance, the Japanese proceeded to reorganize Manchuria into the puppet state of Manchukuo. Clearly the United States was entering a time of decision. But any decision, whether diplomatic or military, was potentially too costly to appeal to a nation that had been led to expect too much of its foreign policies.

Conclusion

Japanese aggression did not destroy the peace system of the 1920s; it merely exposed its weaknesses. The Versailles Treaty had established a body of international relationships defining the interests, territorial and institutional, of the victorious democracies. Western diplomacy after 1919 had consisted of a massive effort to reinforce this status quo by adding one paper agreement to another. United States leadership had contributed two landmarks to that endeavor—the Nine Power Pact and the Kellogg-Briand Peace Pact. As long as all signatories of these two pacts accepted the principles embodied in them, the world would be stable indeed. The fact that some nations—notably Germany, Russia, and Japan—had made clear their rejection of fundamental elements in the Versailles structure, especially with regard to Eastern Europe and China, was not in itself a measure of diplomatic failure. No major treaty could possibly establish a worldwide political and territorial arrangement which would satisfy all peoples over a long period of time. Throughout history it was the endless minor adjustments, whether wrought by force or not, which had given a measure of longevity to prominent historic settlements. But the new diplomacy, backed by the treaties of the twenties, declared the use of force to be illegal.

Change after 1920, to be legitimate had also to be peaceful, its limitations to be prescribed by world opinion. Thus the new diplomacy of the twenties differed from tradition in two essential respects: it rejected all change not underwritten by general agreement, and it ruled out the use of force. In short, it contained no provision for the creation or the acceptance of minor shifts in the world's political and territorial structure. Thus the great democracies based their hopes for the future on the assumption that there existed a worldwide harmony of interest in peace which would hold all nations to their agreements. In a supposedly rational world, peace would always take precedence over amibition or aggression. But the Japanese had demonstrated beyond all doubt that this necessary harmony of interest in peace and peaceful change did not exist. Trapped by their own conviction that they had eliminated power politics, the democracies simply could not respond. Nor was this the end of their dilemma. Some governments with the power to make war continued to harbor objectives which exceeded the limits of peaceful change. For the democracies, after 1932, the choices were clear. Either they would accept alterations in the status quo which others had achieved by the limited exertion of force or they would fight another major war to sustain inviolate the world which they had designed at Versailles.

SUGGESTED READINGS

Among the good introductions to Republican foreign policy after 1920 are L. Ethan Ellis's *Republican Foreign Policy, 1921–1933* (1968); Selig Adler's *The Isolationist Impulse** (1957) and *The Uncertain Giant** (1965); and David F. Trask's *Victory without Peace: American Foreign Relations in the Twentieth Century** (1968). The best history of the diplomacy of the Hoover administration is Robert H. Ferrell's *American Diplomacy in the Great Depression: Hoover-Stimson Foreign Policy* (1957). United States economic foreign policy can be examined in B. H. Williams's *Economic Foreign Policy of the United States* (1929), as well as in the National Industrial Conference Board's *Trends in the Foreign Trade of the United States* (1930). On American economic interests abroad see Cleona Lewis's *America's Stake in International Investments* (1938); Herbert Feis's *The Diplomacy of the Dollar** (1950); and the important essay by William A. Williams, "The Legend of Isolationism in the 1920's," *Science & Society,* XVIII (Winter, 1954). Another valuable study of economics and foreign policy is Joseph Brandes's *Herbert Hoover and Economic Diplomacy* (1962), an analysis of the role of the Commerce Department. On the question of war debts consult H. G. Moulton and Leo Pasvolsky's *War Debts and World Prosperity* (1932).

On United States relations with international

organizations see D. F. Fleming's *The United States and World Organization, 1920–1933* (1938) and *The United States and the World Court* (1945). United States relations with Latin America receive sympathetic treatment in S. F. Bemis's *The Latin American Policy of the United States** (1943). On specific areas of Latin America are Dexter Perkins's *The United States and the Caribbean* (1947) and H. F. Cline's *The United States and Mexico** (1953). Bryce Wood's *The Making of the Good Neighbor Policy** (1961) discusses the improvement in United States–Latin American relations during the twenties, as does also Alexander DeConde's *Herbert Hoover's Latin American Policy* (1951).

One of the earliest and best accounts of the Washington Conference is R. L. Buell's *The Washington Conference* (1922). Merlo J. Pusey's *Charles Evans Hughes* (2 vols., 1951) provides an excellent description of Hughes's role at the conference. One aspect of the conference can be studied in C. L. Hoag's *Preface to Preparedness: The Washington Conference and Public Opinion* (1941). The question of postwar disarmament has received adequate treatment in B. H. Williams's *The United States and Disarmament* (1931) and Merze Tate's *The United States and Armaments* (1948). Harold and Margaret Sprout discuss naval matters thoroughly in *Toward a New Order of Sea Power: American Naval Policy and the World Scene, 1918–1922* (1940). United States naval policy receives further analysis in Raymond G. O'Connor's *Perilous Equilibrium* (1962), a study of the 1930 London Naval Conference. Far Eastern problems relating to the Washington Conference are examined in some detail in A. Whitney Griswold's *The Far Eastern Policy of the United States** (1938). The Senate's relationship to the Washington Treaties receives excellent, and at times amusing, treatment in J. C. Vinson's *The Parchment Peace: The United States Senate and the Washington Conference, 1921–1922* (1956). Also of value is Vinson's "The Annulment of the Lansing-Ishii Agreement," *Pacific Historical Review*, XXVII (February, 1958).

The outlawry of war and the Kellogg-Briand Peace Pact have attracted superb scholarship. On outlawry see John E. Stoner's *S. O. Levinson and the Pact of Paris* (1942) and J. C. Vinson's *William E. Borah and the Outlawry of War* (1957). Two excellent volumes on the Kellogg-Briand Pact are the early one by D. H. Miller, *The Peace Pact of Paris* (1928), and especially Robert H. Ferrell's *Peace in Their Time: The Origins of the Kellogg-Briand Pact* (1952). L. Ethan Ellis's *Frank B. Kellogg and American Foreign Relations, 1925–1929* (1961) is a general study of the Kellogg years but contains a brief discussion of the Pact of Paris. Kellogg, in Ellis's estimation, was far less than an outstanding Secretary of State.

On the crisis of 1931–1932 in Manchuria see S. R. Smith's *Manchurian Crisis, 1931–1932* (1948). H. L. Stimson has described his role in *The Far Eastern Crisis: Recollections and Observations* (1936), as well as in Stimson and McGeorge Bundy's *On Active Service in Peace and War* (1947). Richard N. Current has contributed two important studies of Stimson and the Manchurian crisis in *Secretary Stimson: A Study in Statecraft* (1954) and in "The Stimson Doctrine and the Hoover Doctrine," *American Historical Review*, LIX (April, 1954). Another excellent study is Armin Rappaport's *Henry L. Stimson and Japan, 1931–1933* (1963). R. H. Ferrell has contributed generally favorable studies of Kellogg and Stimson in S. F. Bemis (ed.), *The American Secretaries of State and Their Diplomacy* (1963), vol. XI. Moderately critical are the accounts of Hughes, Kellogg, and Stimson in Norman A. Graebner (ed.), *An Uncertain Tradition: American Secretaries of State in the Twentieth Century** (1961).

* indicates availability in paperback.

32

Prosperity, Hoover, and the Great Depression

EXCEPT FOR the short-lived depression of 1921 and 1922, the decade after World War I was unusually prosperous. Increased industrial efficiency, expanded production, high profits, nearly full employment, and a rising standard of living characterized those postwar years. Gross national product, or the total production of goods and services, increased from $74.2 to $104 billion between 1919 and 1929, and annual per capita income rose fom $710 to $857 in dollars of the same purchasing power. Especially between 1923 and 1929, the United States enjoyed one of its most prosperous periods in history. More production and wider distribution of goods meant better living standards for millions of Americans. They had more automobiles, more household conveniences, better housing, and more leisure than ever before. To be sure, many citizens, including those in urban slums, the uneducated and untrained, the handicapped, and tenants and sharecroppers on the farm, did not earn enough to maintain what might be considered a decent standard of living, but overall there was no place in the world where so many had so much. In accepting the presidential nomination in 1928, Herbert Hoover said: "We in America today are nearer to the final triumph over poverty than ever before in the history of any land." Indeed, no President in the twentieth century took office under what appeared to be more favorable circumstances than did Herbert Clark Hoover. The country was prosperous and enjoyed peace both at home and abroad. A stock market boom associated with his inauguration on March 4, 1929, seemed to reflect business confidence and the prospect of continued bright days ahead. Yet within six months a severe stock market panic precipitated a major depression. The optimism so prevalent before 1929 soon gave way before the realities of hard times. Hoover's popularity rapidly eroded under an avalanche of business losses, unemployment, low farm prices, and general discouragement and frustration. By 1932 the country was looking for new, more flexible leadership. The electorate repudiated both Hoover and his policies.

Trends in Business and Industry

During the 1920s there was a rapid acceleration of the major trends already established in American business and industry. These included larger units of production, technological advances, mass output of goods, increased labor efficiency, and improved management practices. One of the most important developments was the continued growth of large-scale, corporate enterprise, and the domination of leading industries by a few giants. By the end of the 1920s, for example, Ford, the Chrysler Corporation, and General Motors produced 83 percent of the automobiles; three or four meat-packers handled most of the meat which moved in interstate commerce; two companies, General Electric and Westinghouse, manufactured the bulk of the nation's electrical equipment; and three tobacco firms produced most of the tobacco products. It had become clear by the postwar decade that the antitrust laws had done little to curb the growth of concentrated wealth and monopoly.

Increased industrial efficiency and mass production were other major trends in American manufacturing. These came about from advancing technology: the use of new sources of power, chiefly electricity; better planning; scientific management; and industrial research, which resulted in the discovery of improved techniques and new products. As a result of these changes, industrial productivity rose sharply during the 1920s. In manufacturing the annual rate of growth averaged about 5.4 percent, which was about one-fifth above that of the prewar period. Because of increased efficiency, a wide variety of relatively low-cost consumer goods—automobiles, household commodities, chemical products, and others—flowed from American factories in a steady stream. The Committee on Recent Economic Changes reported in 1929 that "never before has the human race made such progress in solving the problem of production."

To a large extent the prosperity of the 1920s rested on a group of newer, expansive industries, as well as extensive construction. The most important new industry was motor vehicles. Production of automobiles, trucks, and buses not only provided an abundance of jobs and a market for numerous raw materials, but also created a whole group of related economic activities from road building to service stations. By 1929 the value of motor vehicles produced reached $5.3 billion, and the industry employed 447,000 workers, or about 5 percent of all the wage earners in manufacturing. Between 1920 and 1929 the annual sales of automobiles, trucks, and buses jumped from 2,227,000 to 5,337,000, and total registrations nearly tripled. Assembly-line production, which Henry Ford had introduced in 1914, rapidly brought the price of cars down to within the reach of most families. The output of so many automobiles created a huge demand for steel, glass, paint, leather, and other products, and their operation provided the foundation for another major industry—oil.

Henry Ford set the pattern for the expanding automobile industry. A machinist and later an engineer for the Edison Illuminating Company of Detroit, Ford invented his first car in 1896. Seven years later he founded the Ford Motor Company, and in 1908 he began selling the famous Model T. Through mass production Ford strove for greater efficiency and lower prices. As Ford stated it, "Get the prices down to the buying power." Ford did exactly that. By 1924 some models of the famed Model T could be bought for less than $300. To provide ample purchasing power for the increasing flow of commodities, he favored good wages. Ford raised wages to $5 a day in 1914 at a time when that was far higher than the going figure in manufacturing.

Other rapidly expanding industries included petroleum, radios, household appliances, chemicals, and public utilities. Discovery of the Greater Seminole field in 1926 and the Oklahoma City field two years later provided a flood of oil to meet even the most extravagant demands for motor fuel. Wax, asphalt, and other derivatives of oil also became important. The chemical industry rose to a very important position in the economy by the 1920s. Cosmetics, toilet preparations, synthetic fibers, as well as the more traditional chemical compounds, found ready markets. Radios and household appliances were in strong demand among people with rising incomes who wished to enjoy the luxury and convenience of electrically powered equipment.

From the viewpoint of stimulating the economy and creating jobs, construction was highly significant. Total expenditures on private building totaled more than $11 billion in 1926 and never fell below $7 billion in any year between 1922 and 1930. Hundreds of thousands of new private homes were needed to meet the demands of returning veterans and other families, and businessmen built thousands of new commercial establishments. Much of the private building was in the mushrooming suburbs to which millions of people migrated in the postwar years.

American foreign trade contributed further to postwar prosperity. During World War I the United States had shifted from a debtor to a creditor nation—that is, it had more investments abroad than foreigners had in this country. By 1919 America's creditor position in the private sector amounted to about $3.7 billion. During the following decade the United States became the world's leading creditor, and New York replaced London as the world's banking and financial center. This situation occurred at least partly because the United States maintained a favorable balance of trade, which means that the nation sold more goods and services overseas than it imported. In 1928, America's favorable balance reached more than $1 billion. The United States exported an increasing number of manufactured goods, especially automobiles, machinery, electrical supplies, gasoline, and other products. Despite the growing importance of manufactured commodities in American foreign trade, agricultural exports held firm during most of the 1920s.

Not all businesses were prosperous in the 1920s. Some of the older, more competitive industries such as bituminous coal, shoes, shipping, and textiles were among those which experienced difficult times. During the decade, coal production declined and hundreds of

Symptoms of Prosperity

F. Scott Fitzgerald, shown here as he celebrated Christmas with his wife and daughter in Paris in 1925, has been called "the poet-prophet of the Jazz Age" by popular historian Paul Sann. In books such as *This Side of Paradise, Tales of the Jazz Age*, and *The Great Gatsby*, Fitzgerald caught that mixture of disenchantment and restless excitement which characterized America in the 1920s. He was one of many American writers—including Ernest Hemingway, John Dos Passos, and Sherwood Anderson—who spent much of their time in Europe.

Brown Brothers

Fitzgerald and his wife threw themselves into the fast, flamboyant life of the Jazz Age. They played hard, they worked hard, and their way of life finally took a tragic toll. Zelda Fitzgerald entered a mental institution, where she perished in a fire in 1939. Fitzgerald died of a heart attack a year later, at the age of forty-four. His work reflects the 1920s, but it does more than simply record the passing scene. In his concern with the symbolically important, the timeless, the form and grace of his expression, he achieved true artistry. T. S. Eliot wrote to him of *The Great Gatsby*: "It seems to me to be the first step that American fiction has taken since Henry James. . . ."

The nation unwittingly provided the mechanism that gave the 1920s its hectic, lawless character when it passed the Eighteenth Amendment prohibiting the sale of liquor. Evangelist Billy Sunday saw Prohibition as the beginning of a golden age. "The slums will be only a memory," he said, "We will turn our prisons into factories . . . Hell will be forever for rent." But Congress had appropriated far too little money to enforce the law; it provided only 1,550 agents to police the entire American coastline and hundreds of businesses which used industrial alcohol, as well as the activities of thousands of moonshiners, bootleggers, and racketeers—those who saw Prohibition as a chance to get rich. Often accused of corruption, federal agents nevertheless confiscated more than a million gallons of illicit liquor, seven million gallons of beer, and 96,000 pieces of distilling equipment in 1925 alone. Even if the corps of agents had been larger, however, Prohibition would not necessarily have succeeded. The affluent and upwardly mobile nation, disillusioned about old ideals and standards, was apparently in the mood for a party. The hip-flask symbolized the time as the drawing by John Held, Jr., one of the best-known visual chroniclers of the time, shown on the next page, indicates.

Although liquor could be sold for medicinal purposes legally, abuse of this provision of the law was widespread, as the photographs on the next two pages testify. At top left federal agents are shown as they auctioned off liquor seized by customs men in 1921. The agents in the picture at left center are destroying beer that had been labeled as lubricating oil.

As the 1920s began, women's fashion—and public behavior—underwent changes that by previous standards could only be considered shocking. The ladies bobbed their hair, shortened their dresses, smoked in public, and laughed and danced in speakeasies throughout the nation. In Chicago, women were arrested for defying a law that banned the wearing of abbreviated bathing suits on the public beaches (above right).

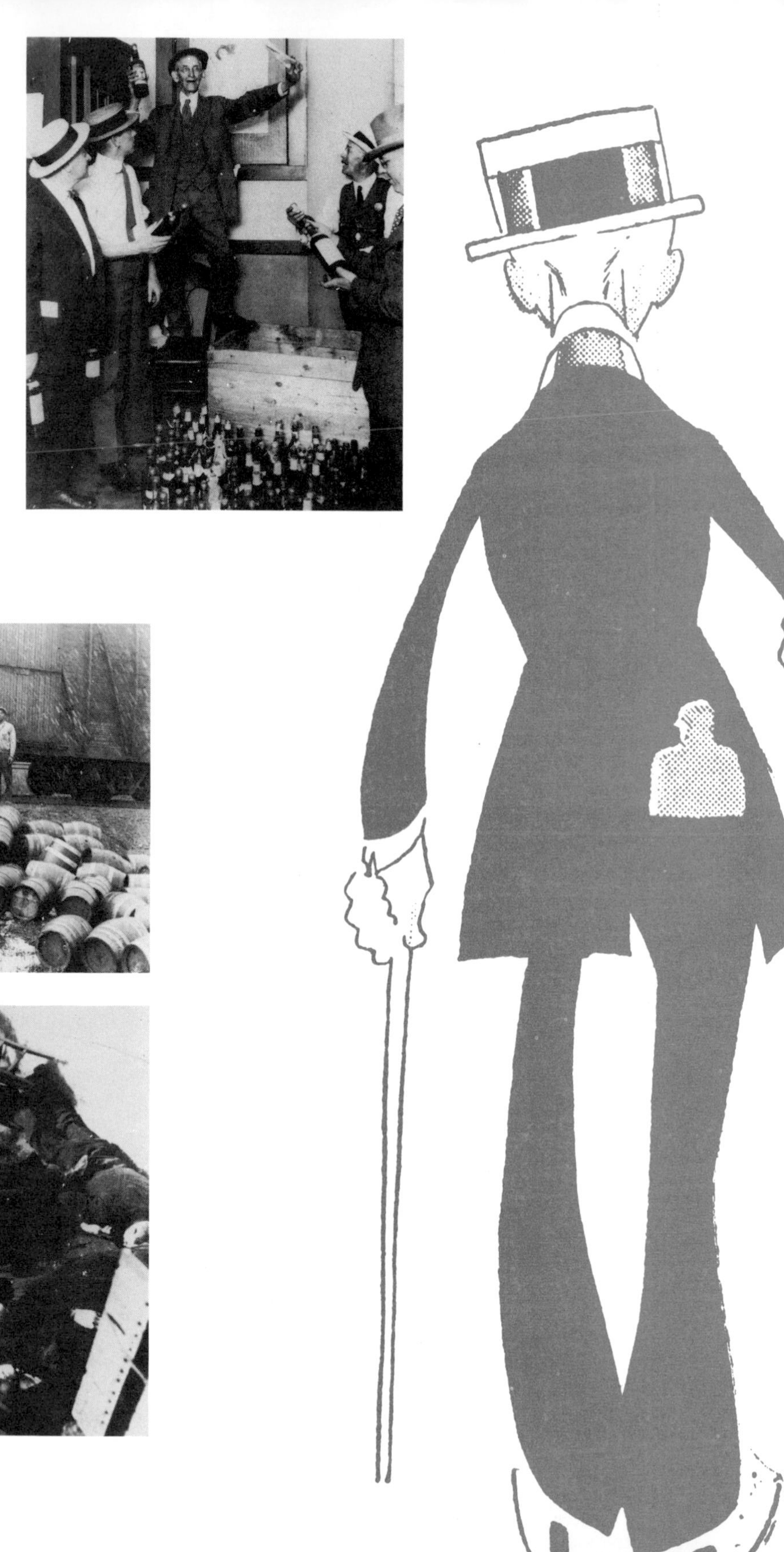

By the end of the decade, Chicago was known less for its law enforcement than for its crime. Throughout the nation racketeers made Prohibition a big business, and nowhere more successfully than in Chicago. At the height of his power there, mobster Al Capone commanded 700 henchmen and an empire that federal agents estimated to earn $105,000,000 during 1927 in proceeds from liquor, gambling, brothels, and other rackets. Rival gangs struggled for the Chicago spoils, and gangland killings became common. The most sensational was the Valentine's Day Massacre of 1929, shown below at far left. Public indignation at this dramatic demonstration of lawlessness helped to initiate a Federal investigation that sent Capone to prison for income tax evasion.

Left, above, center, and below, and above: United Press International; center: Culver Pictures, Inc.

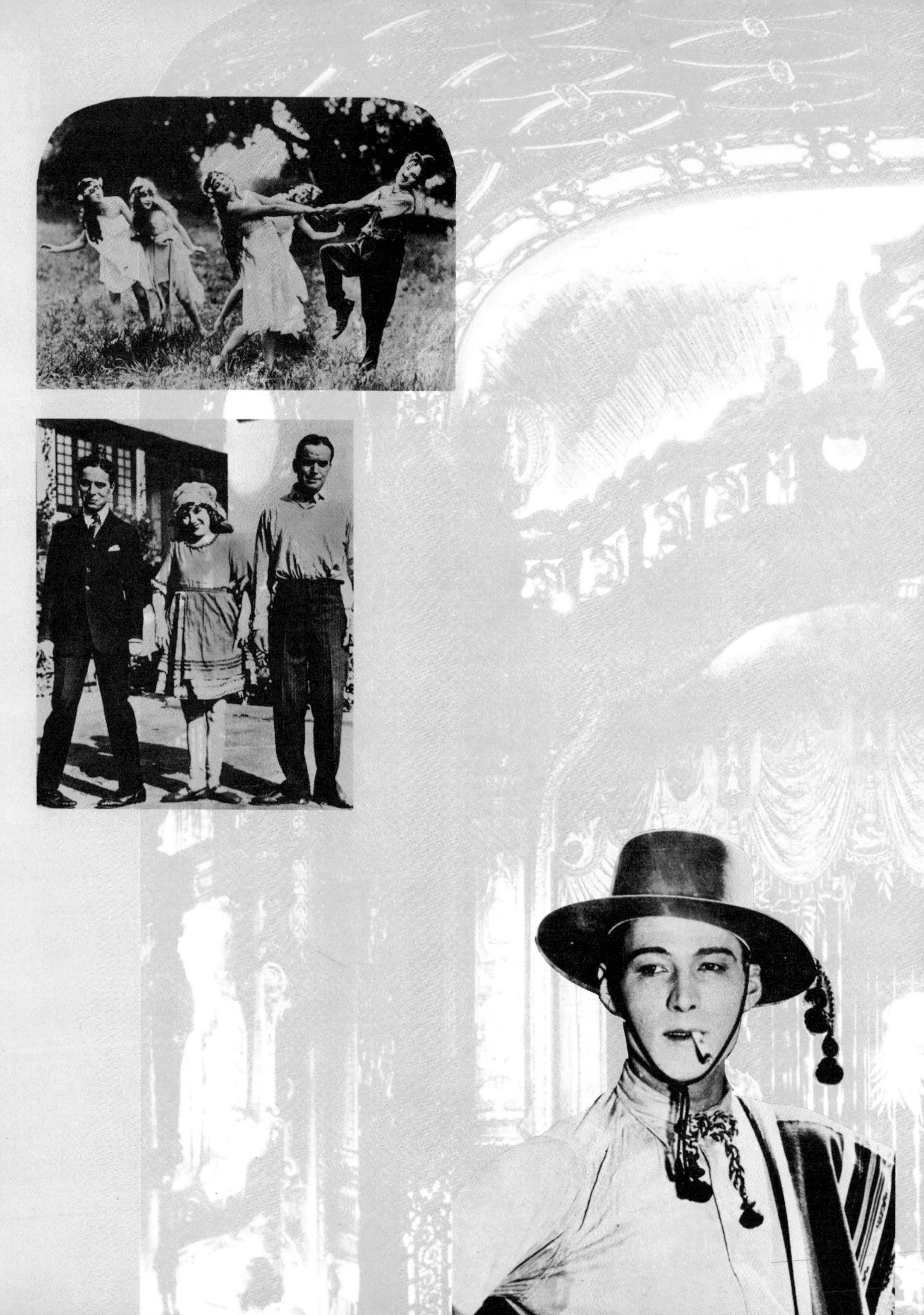

During the 1920s, movies also became big business, and mammoth production companies bought out independent theater owners to create chains of ornate movie palaces – like the Paramount theatre in Brooklyn, N.Y., shown here – that exemplified the showy affluence of the period. Average weekly theater admissions rose from forty million in 1922 to eighty million in 1929. The stars of the day included Rudolph Valentino, at left, below, who set the style for the series of Latin lovers that followed him. Charlie Chaplin (top left), Mary Pickford (left center), and Douglas Fairbanks, reigned even before 1920, and they continued to score great successes. During the 1920s Chaplin appeared in two of his greatest classics, *The Kid* in 1920 and *The Gold Rush* in 1925. Chaplin's sense of pantomime and visual humor were so effective that he chose to keep his work silent even after the advent of talking pictures. In 1927, *The Jazz Singer* with Al Jolson (below) contained only 291 spoken words, but the talkies brought an end to the careers of many stars whose voices failed to match their looks in elegance.

Left, above, center, and below: Brown Brothers; spread: From The Best Remaining Seats: The Story of the Movie Palace *by Ben M. Hall; below: The Bettmann Archive*

mines closed down. Coal mining was a highly competitive industry; but more than this, coal was forced to compete increasingly with gas and electricity as a source of power. Long before 1929 the coal industry bordered on depression. Textiles also suffered during the 1920s. Production of cotton and woolen goods remained high, but prices were weak and profits small. Increasing competition from rayon and silk also hurt the cotton and woolen industries. Cotton textile manufacturers continued to move southward at a rapid pace. They sought to move closer to their raw material and to take advantage of cheaper labor, cheaper power, and the tax benefits of Southern states.

Both ocean shipping and railroads faced difficult problems in the postwar years. At the close of World War I the United States had a large excess of merchant ships, of which some 60 percent was owned by the government. In line with the philosophy of getting the government out of business, Congress passed the Jones Act in 1920, which provided for the sale of government-owned ships on generous terms. Some vessels were sold for as little as 10 percent of what the government had paid for them. But the industry was so depressed that sales went slowly. The Jones-White Act of 1928 granted shippers increased subsidies for carrying the mail and permitted government loans to buyers. But nothing seemed to revive the industry, and by 1930 only about one-third of America's imports and exports were carried in American bottoms.

Although railroads invested billions of dollars in the 1920s to improve their operations and services, they were not prosperous. For one thing, they faced growing competition from automobiles and trucks. The Transportation Act of 1920 ended wartime government operation of the railways and then authorized the consolidation of the railroads into a limited number of large, integrated systems. In this manner Congress hoped to encourage the lines to increase their efficiency and gain a higher return on their investment. The Interstate Commerce Commission considered 6 percent a fair return, but railroad profits generally did not reach that point in the 1920s.

By the 1920s the efficiency and productivity of American industry demonstrated that most problems of production had been solved. Plants and factories, using mass-production methods, turned out an ever-increasing quantity and variety of goods. But what about distribution? It was clear that an economy based on mass production cannot function without mass consumption. Consequently, businessmen developed and improved their marketing and sales techniques to encourage consumers to buy the commodities which existed in such abundance. Installment credit, new and changing styles, and advertising were among the means employed to increase demand. President Coolidge declared in 1926 that "mass production is only possible where there is mass demand. Mass demand has been created almost entirely through the development of advertising."

Although consumer credit had been used for many years, it reached unprecedented proportions in the 1920s. People bought automobiles, radios, furniture, jewelry, clothing, and many other commodities on the installment plan. In 1927, for example, some 75 percent of the automobiles and an equal percentage of radios were purchased on credit. An abundant supply of money provided the necessary funds for a rapid expansion of purchases on time payments. More than ever before, manufacturers emphasized changes in styles and models to stimulate consumption.

Advertisers appealed to every human want and emotion in their effort to create demand for particular commodities. Certain products, it was claimed, would make people happy or healthy, give them popularity or prestige. Packard advertised that "a man is known by the car he keeps." If a woman failed in love, it was implied that she had halitosis, which could be cured by using Listerine. "Reach for a Lucky instead of a sweet," said the American Tobacco Company advertisement—and keep trim and desirable. Those who were unsuccessful in business or social intercourse were led to believe that the *Book of Etiquette* could solve their problems. Newspapers, magazines, billboards, direct mail, and the radio constantly bombarded consumers with slogans and appeals to buy this or that product. Advertising itself became big business, and by 1927 some $1.5 billion was being spent to create consumer preference.

Business and industry benefited greatly from a friendly public and a sympathetic government. It was widely held that business was the backbone of the nation and that what was good for business was good for the entire country. Businessmen occupied a high position in the public mind, and it was considered good economics to give governmental support to the wants and needs of businessmen. The *Wall Street Journal* reported that "never before, here or anywhere else, has a government been so completely fused with business." President Coolidge added his observation that "the business of America is business." In light of these views, it is not surprising that many federal policies were designed to assist business and industry. The Fordney-McCumber tariff of 1922 raised duties on a number of manufactured goods specifically to reduce the competition from foreign producers and thus permit higher prices for domestic products. Tax policies were also geared to help big business. In 1926 Congress approved the depletion allowance for certain minerals which provided a tax benefit to businessmen in those industries. This was especially helpful to the oil industry.

The Harding and Coolidge administrations practiced rigid economy and resisted expenditures for social services so that taxes could be lowered on business and still produce enough revenue to reduce the wartime debt. While Secretary of Commerce, Hoover helped business both by improving the Department's statistical services and by promoting greater foreign trade and commerce. The federal government also indirectly helped business by abandoning any serious attempts to enforce the antitrust laws. The Federal Trade Commission virtually ignored growing monopolies and made little effort to regulate or restrict business or industry in any way.

Wage Earners in Prosperity

Most wage earners benefited to at least some extent from the growing industrial prosperity of the 1920s. Jobs were plentiful, and wages more than kept up with the cost of living. The average earnings of employed wage earners (adjusted to changes in prices) increased about 24 percent between 1921 and 1928. Not all workers enjoyed the same economic progress, but overall, wage earners enjoyed a rising standard of living. Between 1921 and 1928, average hourly wages in manufacturing increased steadily from 51 to 56 cents while annual income to wage earners advanced about $200. The income of workers in trade, the service industries, transportation, and construction also rose. While wages were going up in keeping with a long trend in American industry, hours of work declined. Between 1890 and 1914 the average workweek in manufacturing had dropped from sixty to fifty-four hours; by 1926 the usual workweek was about fifty hours. Higher wages and shorter hours were possible because of the increased efficiency and productivity of labor. In manufacturing, output per worker rose more than 20 percent between 1923 and 1929.

Except for the depression years of 1921 and 1922, unemployment was not a major problem in the postwar years. Data on jobless workers are not very accurate, but all available evidence points to a low rate of unemployment. There were less than 2 million workers without jobs in 1927, and some of these were either unwilling or unable to work. Some of the unemployment which did exist resulted from technological unemployment. Although, in the long run, technical advances created additional jobs, some workers were too immobile to seek positions elsewhere and therefore experienced temporary or permanent unemployment.

Although labor generally shared in the prosperity of the 1920s, not all workers made enough to provide themselves and their families with a decent standard of living. Many low-paid employees in the service industries, personal servants, migrant workers, and especially members of minority groups such as Spanish-Americans and blacks were among those who were bypassed by the good times. In 1929 the bottom 10 percent of the nation's families received only 2 percent of the national income. This figure had not changed measurably during the previous decade. But whatever problems some workers faced in the 1920s, labor as a whole was better off than in any previous peacetime period. Wage earners bought better homes, vacationed more, traveled to work in automobiles, and spent more educating their children. Hundreds of thousands of them moved to the suburbs and joined middle-class America.

Improved labor conditions, however, did not result from the power or influence of unions. Organized labor was actually weaker at the end of the 1920s than at the beginning. Indeed, membership in unions declined from about 5 million in 1920 to around 3.6 million ten years later. Most union members were affiliated with the American Federation of Labor, and a majority of these were in the skilled crafts. Workers in the large, mass-production industries such as steel, farm machinery, textiles, and chemicals were not organized.

Whereas unions had made substantial gains during World War I, it soon became clear that American industry had accepted the organization of labor only because of government pressure and as a patriotic gesture. As soon as the war ended, industrial leaders began fighting the principle of unionization, and by 1920 employers were engaging in a full-scale campaign for the open shop, or what they called the "American plan." An Indiana industrialist declared that "we will not employ an individual in any part of the plant that does not sign an individual contract in which it is expressed that he is not and will not become a member of a labor organization while in our employ." Management also resisted unionization by discharging men who attempted to organize unions, by hiring espionage agents to gather information on labor leaders, and by employing strikebreakers. Antiunion spokesmen also damaged workers' efforts to organize by charging that some labor leaders were radical, un-American, and even Communistic.

Some businessmen fought trade unions by supporting what became known as "welfare capitalism." Workers who were treated well, ran the principle, would not be attracted by the appeals of union leaders. Practically this meant more pleasant working conditions, with drinking fountains and recreational facilities as well as group insurance, bonuses, and even stock sales to workers at reduced prices. At the same time businessmen sponsored company unions. These unions gave workers the appearance of representation and bargaining power with management; but since company unions were always financed and controlled by the company, their leaders could not speak freely and independently for the workers.

Unions also had other problems. For one thing they lacked vigorous and aggressive leadership. Samuel Gompers, president of the AF of L until his death in 1924, and his successor William Green were both conservative trade union leaders who showed little interest in organizing the great mass-production industries. Even John L. Lewis, head of the more militant United Mine Workers, voted for Coolidge in 1924. Labor leaders, in other words, made little effort to change the strong conservative attitudes which existed in regard to unions.

Agriculture and Farm Problems

Agriculture's position in the American economy continued to decline relatively in the post-World War I years. By 1930 agriculture was responsible for only about 10 percent of the national income. At the end of the 1920s, farm operators had an average annual net operating income of only $943, including both those products consumed on the farm and the rental value of farm homes. On a per capita basis this was less than $300 a year for people in agriculture, compared with an annual average income of $775 for all Americans. In the ten Southern states where cotton accounted for more than 50 percent of the farm income, yearly cash receipts from farm produce averaged only $197 per capita.

Low farm income did not stem from lack of efficiency or poor productivity. Throughout the decade American farms became larger and more efficient. In 1920 American farming was still geared to the horse and mule, but during the following decade tractors went a long way toward transforming and modernizing agricultural production. Although only 13 percent of all farms had tractors in 1930, the distribution of such equipment across the country was uneven. Tractor-drawn machinery also increased agricultural efficiency. By the middle 1920s thousands of farmers in the wheat belt were using the combined harvester-thresher which greatly reduced labor requirements for harvesting. Better plows, cultivators, drills, planters, and other machines were also a part of the general advance in mechanization. Farmers planted improved seeds, used more fertilizer, bred better livestock, and developed better management. This increased efficiency rather than an expanding acreage accounted for the fact that farmers usually produced more than they could sell at profitable prices. Economists explained the low incomes of farmers by pointing out that farmers were investing too much land, labor, and capital in agricultural production. Consequently, returns were poor.

The postwar farm depression began in the summer of 1920 and remained especially severe until 1923. Within eighteen months after June, 1920, wheat prices fell from more than

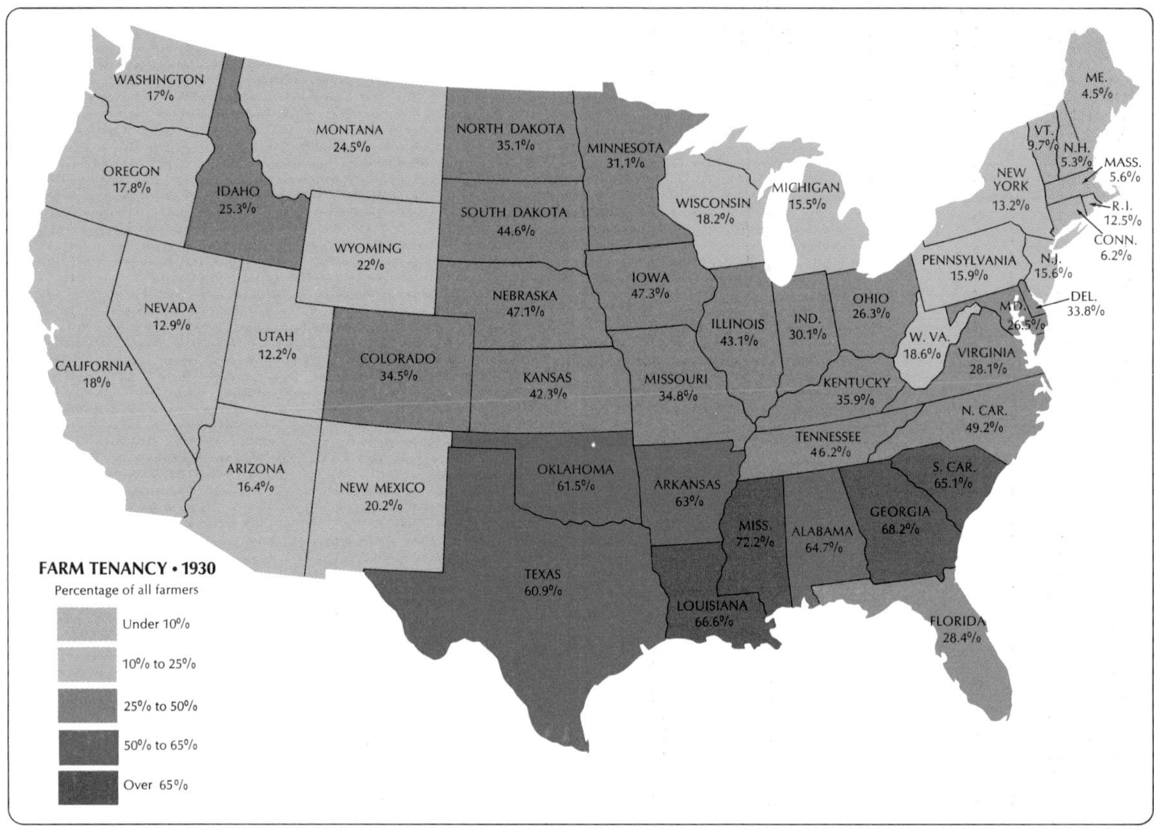

$2.50 a bushel to less than $1, and cotton dropped to as little as 13 cents a pound, after having brought 35 cents in 1919. Between 1919 and 1921 net farm income declined from $9 billion to about $3.3 billion. Farm prices went down faster and further than the prices of other commodities. By 1921 farm products had lost one-fifth of their purchasing power. The decline in prices and income resulted from continued heavy production, a lack of purchasing power in foreign countries, and a loss of some export markets to competitors such as Canada and Australia.

No domestic question plagued the Harding and Coolidge administrations more than the depression in agriculture. By 1921 friends of the farmers were proposing a variety of relief measures. Some favored outright government price-fixing for farm products, while others believed that cooperative marketing, more liberal credit, tariff protection, and regulation of the commodity and livestock exchanges would solve the problems. In 1921 a group of Western and Southern senators organized the Farm Bloc to push farm legislation through Congress. Since many farmers blamed their difficulties on middlemen and speculators, three laws were enacted to deal with marketing problems. These included the Packers and Stockyards Act (1921) and the Capper-Tincher Grain Futures Act (1922), which placed livestock and grain marketing under federal control, and the Capper-Volstead Cooperative Marketing Act of 1922, which exempted processing and marketing cooperatives from the antitrust laws. Many farm leaders also believed that tight credit was one of the farmer's chief troubles. In 1923 Congress passed the Intermediate Credits Act, which set up twelve intermediate credit banks to provide money for banks and agricultural corporations which could then make more credit available to farmers.

But none of these measures reached the heart of the farm problem—surpluses, low prices, and the disparity between the prices of farm and nonfarm commodities. In 1922 George N. Peek, president of the Moline Plow Company, and his associate Hugh Johnson developed a plan which they called "equality for agriculture." Recognizing that the problem rested in the surplus, that is, the amount produced above domestic demand and that which could be exported profitably, Peek and Johnson advocated segregating the surplus and disposing of it abroad for whatever it would bring. With the surplus removed, they believed that, behind the tariff wall, the income from a commodity sold on the domestic market would rise. Their aim was to raise prices enough to provide farmers a "fair exchange value," or parity prices, for their products. To achieve this objective, Peek proposed the establishment of a government corporation to purchase and dispose of the price-depressing surpluses.

In the spring of 1924, Senator Charles L. McNary of Oregon and Representative Gilbert N. Haugen of Iowa introduced a bill incorporating Peek's ideas. The first McNary-Haugen bill sought to raise the prices of eight basic agricultural commodities—wheat, flour, corn, cotton, wool, cattle, sheep, and swine—to a point where they would have the same purchasing power as they had between 1909 and 1914 when prices were considered fair to farmers. To raise prices, the government would establish a corporation with an appropriation of $200 million to purchase and sell abroad any market-depressing surpluses of these basic commodities. If the corporation bought products at the higher domestic price and then sold them abroad at the lower world price, it would lose money. To pay these losses, farmers were to be taxed on each bushel or pound of a commodity sold. This was known as the equalization fee. Corporation officials would calculate the losses on their foreign sales and then assess farmers of that particular crop enough to make up the deficit. But the farmer would be better off, because for that part of his production sold on the domestic market he would receive a considerably higher price; and his total income, even after paying the equalization fee, would be higher.

There were two unusual aspects of the McNary-Haugen bill. In the first place, it aimed at guaranteeing farmers prices which would give their products the purchasing power they had in the period 1909–1914. This was the concept of parity prices. Secondly, the idea of relying on an agency of the federal government to achieve this goal was a sharp break from tradition. And it was these very aspects of the proposal which aroused such bitter opposition. Businessmen, consumers who feared higher food prices, some economists, and many political leaders opposed the bill. President Coolidge was among the measure's sharpest critics. He opposed any kind of government price-fixing and argued that the plan was economically unsound.

Although Congress defeated the McNary-Haugen bill in 1924, its supporters organized, lobbied, and continued to push for enactment.

Widespread opposition in the nonfarm sector and lack of unity among the agricultural groups further handicapped the campaign for federal farm relief. But the McNary-Haugenites would not give up, and in 1927 Congress finally passed a McNary-Haugen bill. Coolidge still opposed this approach to agricultural relief, and he killed the measure with a stinging veto. After another strong campaign in Congress, lawmakers enacted a modified McNary-Haugen bill the following year. Coolidge also vetoed this measure. There was little for the advocates of farm relief to do but await whatever action President-elect Herbert Hoover might take. Nevertheless, the campaign for farm relief in the 1920s was important in the economic history of the nation. It demonstrated that many farmers in addition to economists and political leaders had come to realize that without a governmental program for crop limitation, agriculture would never achieve much prosperity. It established as well the parity-price concept, which came to be the major goal of farm groups.

Hoover as President

When Hoover became President in March, 1929, general economic conditions were excellent. Even the agricultural situation had improved so much that farm prices were about 90 percent of parity. Properly impressed with what he saw around him, Hoover declared in his inaugural address that "ours is a land rich in resources; stimulating in its glorious beauty; filled with millions of happy homes; blessed with comfort and opportunity. In no nation are the fruits of accomplishment more secure."

Hoover's elevation to the Presidency climaxed a highly successful career in business, philanthropy, and public service. Born in 1874 at West Branch, Iowa, Hoover was graduated from Stanford University with a degree in geology. Thereafter his employment in 1897 with an English mining firm took him to many parts of the world. By World War I he had made a substantial fortune. From 1914 to 1928 he devoted himself largely to public service. He served as director of Belgian relief in 1914, became head of the United States Food Administration in 1917, and then directed American postwar relief efforts in Europe. By 1920 Hoover had become a national figure with the reputation of a good administrator. As Secretary of Commerce, he held a prominent place in both the Harding and the Coolidge administrations.

Hoover's basic philosophy alone explains his actions, or lack of them, when he faced the depression in late 1929. He was a strong believer in individualism, personal initiative, individual liberty, and equality of opportunity. In his view, economic progress rested on competition, free enterprise, and minimum regulation to preserve "individual initiative" against domination by a few. Hoover strongly objected to extending government power into or over the economy because, he said, "you cannot extend the mastery of government over the daily working life of a people without at the same time making it the master of the people's souls and thoughts."

In the six months of his administration prior to the stock market crash, Hoover dealt with two principal issues—agricultural relief and the tariff. During the campaign of 1928 Hoover had promised that, if elected, he would call a special session of Congress to deal with these problems. Addressing Congress on April 16, the President outlined some of the farmers' difficulties but warned that they could not be cured by legislation or "by the Federal government alone." But, he added, "farmers and their organizations can be assisted to overcome these inequalities." Hoover believed that an effective tariff, some advice to farmers on production, and the creation of agricultural marketing cooperatives would be of help to farmers. To achieve such goals, he recommended establishment of a Federal Farm Board with power to implement his proposals. Hoover made it clear that he would not tolerate any legislation of the McNary-Haugen variety which had been before Congress from 1924 to 1928.

The widely heralded Agricultural Marketing Act, which became law on June 15, allegedly placed agriculture "on a basis of equality with other industries." It provided for a powerful Federal Farm Board, which would encourage the formation of national marketing associations for farm commodities. Congress appropriated $500 million to supply needed credit to assist the cooperatives in holding crops and marketing them in a more orderly fashion. Hoover had great faith in the orderly production and marketing of farm products as a means of improving agricultural prices and incomes. He believed that the cooperatives, should they become sufficiently strong and well organized, could influence prices in the marketplace. The new law also permitted the Federal Farm Board to set up stabilization corporations to buy farm commodities in the open market as a means of maintaining prices in periods of unusual price-depressing surpluses.

Although the Federal Farm Board was successful in encouraging the formation of agricultural marketing associations, general economic conditions created problems which the cooperatives were unable to meet. Within a few months after the new law went into effect, prices began to fall in the wake of the stock market crash. When the wheat, cotton, and other cooperatives found themselves helpless to maintain prices, the Board created stabilization corporations, which bought wheat and cotton on the open market in the hope of stopping the dangerous price decline. But large production continued even in the face of lower prices, and the Board soon found that it could not support prices without considerably more money. By the fall of 1931, after two years of operation, the Board held millions of bushels of wheat and large quantities of cotton. Altogether, it ultimately lost some $345 million on its transactions.

For Herbert Hoover the tariff was an accurate measure of the nation's economic welfare. In asking Congress to make "limited changes" in the tariff, Hoover argued that both agriculture and industry would benefit from higher import duties which would protect the domestic market. Congressman Willis C. Hawley of Oregon introduced a tariff bill, which passed the House in May, 1929. Whereas this measure raised duties on minerals, textiles, dyestuffs, and other commodities, most of the upward revisions were modest. Strong pressure for greatly increased rates developed in the Senate where representatives of high protection were firmly entrenched. Senators Reed Smoot of Utah and Joseph R. Grundy of Pennsylvania were among the most outspoken advocates of extreme protection. A coalition of Democrats and insurgent Republicans attempted to block the move for higher duties, but without success.

As finally passed after a year of bitter discussion and debate, the Hawley-Smoot bill made some 890 upward revisions in the tariff. It raised rates an average of about 7 percent over those of the Fordney-McCumber law, thus bringing duties to the highest level in American history. Congress also accepted the flexible provision insisted on by the President. This section permitted the Tariff Commission to recommend an increase or decrease of as much as 50 percent in rates to equalize the cost of production in the United States and abroad. More than 1,000 economists urged the President to veto the measure, but Hoover signed it, declaring that the higher tariff was in the national interest.

The Great Crash

Unfortunately for Hoover's popularity and his place in history, the exuberant prosperity which accompanied his election had almost run its course. But general optimism prevailed until the time of the stock market crash on October 29, 1929. A study on *Recent Economic Changes,* for example, implied that panics and depressions were a thing of the past in the United States. Political leaders, businessmen, and economists generally agreed that the future was bright. Early in October, Charles E. Mitchell, chairman of the National City Bank of New York, stated that "the industrial situation of the United States is absolutely sound." But these and other encouraging predictions proved terribly wrong. Stock prices broke sharply on September 5 and followed an erratic course during the next several weeks. On October 24, or Black Thursday, excessive selling drove prices down to disastrous levels. Conditions reached a crisis on October 29 when frantic stockholders offered 16,410,000 shares for sale at ruinous prices, and some stocks found no takers at any figure. This sudden collapse of the stock market bankrupted hundreds of thousands of stockholders, and hundreds of brokers, speculators, and financiers. While the crash affected most severely the stock market and financial community, it heralded the beginning of a long and cruel depression.

What caused the Great Depression? The stock market crash was not so much a cause of the Depression as it was a reflection of basic weaknesses in the economy. Despite favorable surface conditions, there were during the 1920s underlying defects in the American economy. Speculation and credit buying could not hide these fundamental faults. In the first place, some major industries did not experience the general prosperity which characterized most of the economy. Agriculture especially lagged behind as farmers struggled against debt and relatively low prices. Meager farm income meant that farmers lacked purchasing power to buy their share of the increasing output of goods and services. Coal, textiles, and shoes were among other industries which suffered from overexpansion and low profits. Moreover, while employment rose during the 1920s, the biggest gains were in the low-paid service trades rather than in those industries where earnings were high. There was a 50 percent gain in manufacturing output between 1920 and 1929, but the number of industrial workers remained the same.

Furthermore, the condition of American foreign trade was not as healthy as it appeared. During the postwar years, American exports were heavy, and the United States enjoyed a favorable balance of trade—that is, it sold more goods abroad than it purchased. High tariffs contributed to the favorable balance but aggravated the problem of payment. For

Crash and Aftermath

Wall St. Lays An Egg blared *Variety*, unaware that this disaster would mark the beginning of America's Great Depression. A decade of overproduction, vastly overextended credit, wild spending, and get-rich-quick psychology finally collapsed in October, 1929.

United Press International

Left: Brown Brothers; above: United Press International

Never had so many been jobless. Workers registered for unemployment relief by the millions and stood in line at soup kitchens like the one above in New York City. Those with enough money to buy a crate of apples went into curbside business (left). Nothing that might earn a little money was rejected.

Reaction ranged from despair to fury. The Bonus Expeditionary Force—thousands of angry World War I veterans—marched to Washington to demand full payment of a bonus voted them eight years before. They camped in parks and fields and harassed Congress and the city. Federal troops under Gen. Douglas MacArthur (below, left) finally burned their shacks and drove them away.

Inset, near left: Underwood and Underwood; all others: United Press International

eigners paid for large quantities of imports with dollars derived from investments by Americans in foreign securities. In some measure Americans paid for their own exports through foreign loans. This was a dangerous situation, for if United States citizens reduced or stopped their lending overseas, the country's exports would decline. After 1928, Americans did begin to curtail their loans abroad, and exports soon dropped rather sharply.

Much of the economic expansion in the 1920s resulted from heavy investments in new plants and equipment. These expenditures created demand for capital goods and provided additional jobs. But the building of more productive facilities was predicated on an expanding consumer market to buy the goods flowing out of the new factories. Although demand by consumers was generally strong before 1929, it could not equal the growing output of goods and services. Without enough earned income to purchase the production of American farms and factories, people resorted to large-scale credit buying. Any curtailment in credit would reduce consumer purchases, which in turn would discourage capital investment and create unemployment. By 1929 the American capacity to produce had outrun the capacity to consume on the basis of available income.

Unequal distribution of income was a big factor in creating economic maladjustments during the twenties. Too much of the nation's income went to upper income groups in the form of profits and dividends. In 1929 the top 10 percent of the families received 39 percent of the total income. Since people in this income bracket had little need for more consumer goods, they tended to invest their money in more productive facilities, or, in many cases, to speculate on the stock market. More investment in plant and equipment increased the country's production beyond what could be absorbed at current prices. Farmers and workers who could have consumed much more were unable to do so because of low incomes. About 42 percent of American families earned less than $1,500 a year in 1929. To create enough purchasing power to absorb the increasing production of goods and services, wages could have been raised or prices lowered. Or the government might have raised the taxes on high-income groups and spent the money on public services. Conservative political leaders, however, strongly opposed this idea. In any event, in the consumer-oriented American economy, the expenditures of consumers needed to be kept high if prosperity were to continue.

Too much buying on credit, added to heavy stock market speculation and manipulation of securities sustained a level of selling which far exceeded purchasing power from wages and salaries. Prosperity became increasingly artificial. Stock prices began to increase sharply in 1924, and the speculative mania based on a boom psychology continued until the October crash. The price of many stocks went to fantastic heights. During the summer of 1929 alone Westinghouse stock shot up from 151 to 286 and AT & T from 209 to 303. Often there was no relation whatever between company dividends and the price of stock. Speculators were interested only in capital gains. But the values were artificial, and a loss of confidence which turned buyers into sellers could, and indeed did, set off a panic.

By the fall of 1929 a variety of factors had combined to bring the "new economic era" to an end. Lack of prosperity in certain basic industries such as agriculture; an export trade which depended heavily on American loans abroad; the poor distribution of income; a bad corporate structure which permitted promoters and grafters to bleed company assets and take advantage of innocent investors; and stock speculation and manipulation all played a part in the economic conditions that brought on the tragic Depression.

The Depression Begins

Initial reaction to the stock market crash was not one of panic or discouragement. Hoover assured the nation on October 25 that "the fundamental business of the country, that is, production and distribution of commodities, is on a sound and prosperous basis." A few days later Robert P. Lamont, Secretary of Commerce, said there were "none of the underlying factors which have been associated with or have preceded the declines in business in the past." William Green, president of the American Federation of Labor, expressed the view that "within a few months we will be back to a normal state in the industrial and economic life of the nation."

But President Hoover was worried over the future of the economy. He wanted desperately to avoid an economic slump with its unemployment, farm foreclosures, and business failures. The danger was that any major drop in consumer purchasing power would cause producers to reduce output and, with a slumping market, to discharge unneeded workers. Unemployment would restrict demand for agricultural and industrial commodities even further, causing more layoffs. To prevent this vicious downward cycle from gaining any momentum Hoover accepted the need for sustaining prices, wages, employment, and investment at or near their current levels. If this could be done, the stock market crash would not turn out to be the forerunner of depression. Hoover believed that these objectives could be achieved through voluntary action.

At a series of White House meetings, Hoover urged businessmen to maintain wage rates and employment, to increase spending on new plants and equipment, and to avoid price cuts. He advised labor to avoid demands for higher wages. The President also called for expanded federal public works and requested governors to enlarge expeditures for state construction. Moreover, after Hoover recommended easier credit, the New York Federal Reserve Bank reduced the rediscount rate from 5 to 4½ percent. Explaining his actions to Congress on December 3, Hoover declared that he had instituted "systematic . . . cooperation with business" in order to sustain wages and employment and to prevent economic decline and individual hardships. Meanwhile, at Secretary Mellon's urging, Congress in December reduced both corporate and individual income taxes. Although a few critics opposed tax reduction, Hoover's forthright actions in attempting to stem an economic depression received high praise from many people. The editor of the *New York Times* wrote on December 1 that "too much praise cannot be given the President for the prompt and resolute and skillful way in which he set about reassuring the country after the financial collapse."

Despite some optimistic predictions that voluntary business-government cooperation would assure continued prosperity, it soon became evident that the country was sliding into a depression. By the spring of 1930, some 4 million people were jobless. Regardless of Hoover's urging, businessmen could not easily maintain employment and wages in the face of weakening demand. Despite frequent optimistic statements by the President, conditions went from bad to worse.

By early 1933 every aspect of the economy appeared calamitous. Farm prices had declined to disastrous levels, and net agricultural income had dropped to only one-third of what it had been in 1929. Wheat sold for more than $1 a bushel before the Depression began; in 1932 it brought as little as 25 cents. Cotton prices slumped by two-thirds. Unemployment rose with every new estimate. From 4 million in the spring of 1930 the number of jobless jumped to at least 12 million in early 1933, when approximately one-fourth of the labor force was without work. Thousands of industrial, financial, and other business firms went broke, and the Dow-Jones index of fifty leading industrial stocks fell from an average of 364 to 62 between 1929 and 1933. More than 2,000 banks, some of them large institutions, closed their doors in 1931 alone, wiping out billions in deposits. Everywhere one looked in 1932, he was faced with want, distress, and bankruptcy. Bread and soup lines lengthened as unemployment rose, and cities and counties were faced with heavy demands for relief. Men trudged the streets looking for work, but increasingly they were met with signs which read, "No Help Wanted Here."

The Administration Program

Meanwhile, the President struggled to create a program which he believed would help the country return to better times. Hoover was not callous or indifferent to the needs of suffering people. Indeed, much of his reputation rested on his earlier humanitarian and relief work in Europe. But in devising plans and programs to fight the growing Depression, he was restricted by his basic philosophy, which held that economic recovery depended on the actions of private industry and that the needy must be cared for by local or state relief agencies. The federal government, he claimed, had no business entering the field of direct relief. Yet, despite these firmly held views, Hoover attempted more to combat the Depression than had any other previous President in similar circumstances. But he did not do enough, or, as his critics charged, he did the wrong thing. Hoover failed to understand that the Depression following 1929 was not another ordinary decline in the business cycle but a period of fundamental social and economic change. His weakness lay in refusing to recognize that the federal government was the only agency with adequate resources to solve the nation's problems.

As the Depression became worse, demands grew for federal funds to finance job-creating public works, as well as for direct relief for the unemployed. Hoover favored a modest increase in federal projects to help relieve unemployment and to increase purchasing power, but he never viewed this type of government spending as a major attack on the Depression. He believed that the basic fight against hard times must come from the private sector. Nevertheless, Hoover stepped up expenditures for roads, federal buildings, and other public projects. Work began on Hoover Dam on the Colorado River in 1930, and by 1932 the federal government was spending about $500 million a year on public works.

By late 1930 the question of providing relief for needy people became a matter of pressing national concern. Private agencies and local communities, which had historically supplied help for destitute citizens, found that demands greatly exceeded their limited resources. In light of this situation, a growing number of political leaders insisted that only federal funds could provide sufficient relief. But Hoover held that reliance on the federal Treasury would break down the "sense of individual generosity" and strike "at the roots of self-government." The thing to do was "to mobilize and organize the infinite number of agencies of self-help in the community." In October, 1930, Hoover appointed Colonel Arthur Woods to head an Emergency Committee for Employment, which was to work with governors and private groups to coordinate and stimulate the nation's voluntary relief agencies. Special relief committees were set up in most large cities during the winter of 1930–1931, but they did not have enough funds to accomplish much. Even though conditions rapidly grew worse, Hoover clung to his principles. He declared in December, 1931, that "the federal government must not encroach upon nor permit local communities to abandon that precious possession of local initiative and responsibility."

Hoover believed that economic recovery depended primarily on the actions of private enterprise. To assist business, he favored an expansion of credit. In October, 1931, financial and business leaders reluctantly responded to presidential pressure and formed the National Credit Corporation to provide credit to weak banks and other businesses. But this agency proved entirely inadequate. Meanwhile, Eugene Neyer, head of the War Finance Corporation during World War I, sought to develop a federal credit agency. In December, 1931, Hoover gave the proposal token backing, and in January, 1932, Congress established the Reconstruction Finance Corporation. While it can hardly be considered an administration measure, the RFC was the most important antidepression legislation enacted during Hoover's Presidency. The new law authorized the RFC to lend up to $2 billion to banks, insurance companies, railroads, and other large businesses to stave off bankruptcy or to expand their operations. Congress assumed that the saving of a bank or insurance company would protect depositors and policyholders and that any credit which permitted business expansion would create more employment.

By the winter of 1931–1932 some 10 million Americans were unemployed. Desperation stalked the land. Children cried from cold and hunger, mothers wept, and fathers cursed their misfortunes. Entire families in some cities lived on as little as $2 and $3 a week for food, and millions in rural areas, especially the South, received no relief at all. Men pawed through garbage cans and fought over scraps of food. Such pitiful conditions brought increasing demands for federal appropriations for direct assistance. The La Follette–Costigan bill called for an appropriation of $375 million for relief, but it went down to defeat in February, 1932, as did other relief measures. Under growing pressure for federal aid, Hoover in March finally supported the congressional authorization to distribute 40 million bushels of wheat and 5 million bales of cotton held by the Federal Farm Board. Hoover insisted that the Red Cross distribute the flour and cloth made from these commodities, however, and thereby maintained his principle of not having the federal government engage in actual distribution of relief. But such limited relief failed completely to meet the burgeoning needs. Finally, in June, 1932, Hoover approved a loan from the Reconstruction Finance Corporation of up to $300 million, which could be used for direct relief. Although the amount was clearly insufficient, the federal money was a boon to hard-pressed state relief agencies. The same bill permitted the RFC to lend up to $1.5 billion to the states for self-liquidating public works.

In July, 1932, Congress provided for creation of a Home Loan Bank System to assist homeowners who were about to lose their homes. The RFC made available $125 million to supply funds for twelve new rediscount banks which could furnish additional credit to banks, savings and loan associations, and other financial institutions which held home mortgages. Congress hoped that extra credit would take the pressure off these weakened agencies and permit them to extend further credit. However, the law came too late to save many homes.

Despite some expansion of public works, creation of the RFC and the Home Loan Banks, and loans to the states for relief, Hoover's program seemed timid and inadequate to a growing number of Americans. By the winter of 1931–1932 demands had risen from many quarters for a much broader federal attack on the Depression. At the same time the public mood underwent a noticeable change. As people lost their homes and farms through foreclosure, as unemployment increased and men tramped the streets looking for work, as bread and soup lines lengthened, and as hopelessness gripped the nation, there was increasing talk of radical revolution. One Oklahoma rancher, who had lost his land and cattle by foreclosure, declared, "we have got to have a revolution here like they had in Russia," and an unemployed Detroit worker with four children said that the Soviet system was "a better system than we've got" because the Russians provided work for all. In his book *Toward Soviet America* (1932), William Z. Foster, a leading Communist, wrote that the only hope for American workers was "the revolutionary way."

Although there were relatively few genuine revolutionaries even at the depth of the Depression, radical talk and bitter criticism of the American economic system indicated the deep and widespread frustration and discontent. What so many people objected to was the fact of starvation amidst plenty. Americans were hungry while wheat surpluses filled grain elevators; they were naked while warehouses bulged with surplus cotton; they needed manufactured goods while the factories stood idle. In other words, all of the means of production were at hand—land, labor, capital, technology—but the masses were in dire want. As the famed British economist John Maynard Keynes wrote in 1932, it was "not a crisis of poverty, but a crisis of abundance." But no one seemed to know what could be done to attack economic stagnation and utilize abundance.

An increasing number of Americans believed that somehow consumer purchasing power must be expanded to create demand for farm and factory production. This could be done, they argued, with large doses of federal spending. Such suggestions greatly alarmed Hoover. He warned Congress in May, 1932, that measures to increase spending must be rejected "unless they be for undoubted emergency." "The issue before the country is the reestablishment of confidence," he declared, and the best way to speed recovery was to end delays "in balancing the budget through immediate passage of revenue measures and reduction of Government expenditures." This was the President's answer to the spenders who, he said, were terrifying the nation.

Hoover's repeated predictions that conditions would soon improve, his call for personal and national restraint, and his devotion to economy and a balanced budget could not deter the angry demands for action. During the summer of 1932 there were unusual manifestations of discontent as veterans marched on Washington and hundreds of Midwestern farmers went on strike. As the Depression steadily deepened, veterans of World War I insisted on full payment of the bonus which Congress had voted them in 1924. Under pressure from the American Legion and other spokesmen for the veterans, Congress had passed a bill over Hoover's veto in February, 1931, permitting a veteran to borrow up to 50 percent of his total bonus. But this did not satisfy the veterans, who believed that they deserved all of their bonus money. In May and June, 1932, hundreds of veterans marched on Washington to lobby for the Patman bill then before Congress. Although Patman's measure, which called for paying veterans what remained of their bonus, passed the House, it died in the Senate. After Congress adjourned in July, many veterans returned home, but several thousand stayed on. As tensions rose, conflicts occurred between veterans and the police—two veterans were shot and mortally wounded—and federal troops under General Douglas MacArthur were called out to remove the Bonus Expeditionary Force. Hoover believed that Communist agitators had made this action necessary, but critics charged that the President had acted hastily and unwisely.

Almost simultaneously, trouble erupted in the Middle West as farmers resorted to direct action to raise agricultural prices. In May militant farmers under Milo Reno organized the National Farmers' Holiday Association at Des Moines, Iowa. The farm strike began in August when farmers around Sioux City and Council Bluffs, and some near Des Moines, picketed the highways and blockaded attempts to deliver milk and livestock to market.

The Election of 1932

The continuing depression, which had produced deep social, economic, and political unrest, added up to trouble for the Republican party as the 1932 election approached. The basis of Republican strength four years earlier—business and industrial prosperity and Hoover's personal popularity—had been shattered beyond recognition. Many faithful Republicans had no hope that Hoover could be reelected, but practical politics dictated his renomination. In June a dreary and pessimistic convention in Chicago mechanically named Hoover and Curtis the party's standard-bearers.

The Republican platform praised Hoover's leadership and blamed the Democrats for prolonging the Depression by introducing dangerous and unsound legislation which unsettled the economy. Specifically, it called for emergency loans to the states for relief, continued tariff protection, banking reform, maintenance of the gold standard, and cooperative marketing for farmers. On the troublesome question of prohibition, the Republicans avoided the issue of outright repeal by proposing that people vote on a constitutional amendment which would allow the states to deal with the problem. For depression-ridden voters the platform would scarcely stir up hope or confidence.

In contrast, the Democrats met in Chicago on June 27 with high expectations. Governor Franklin D. Roosevelt of New York had

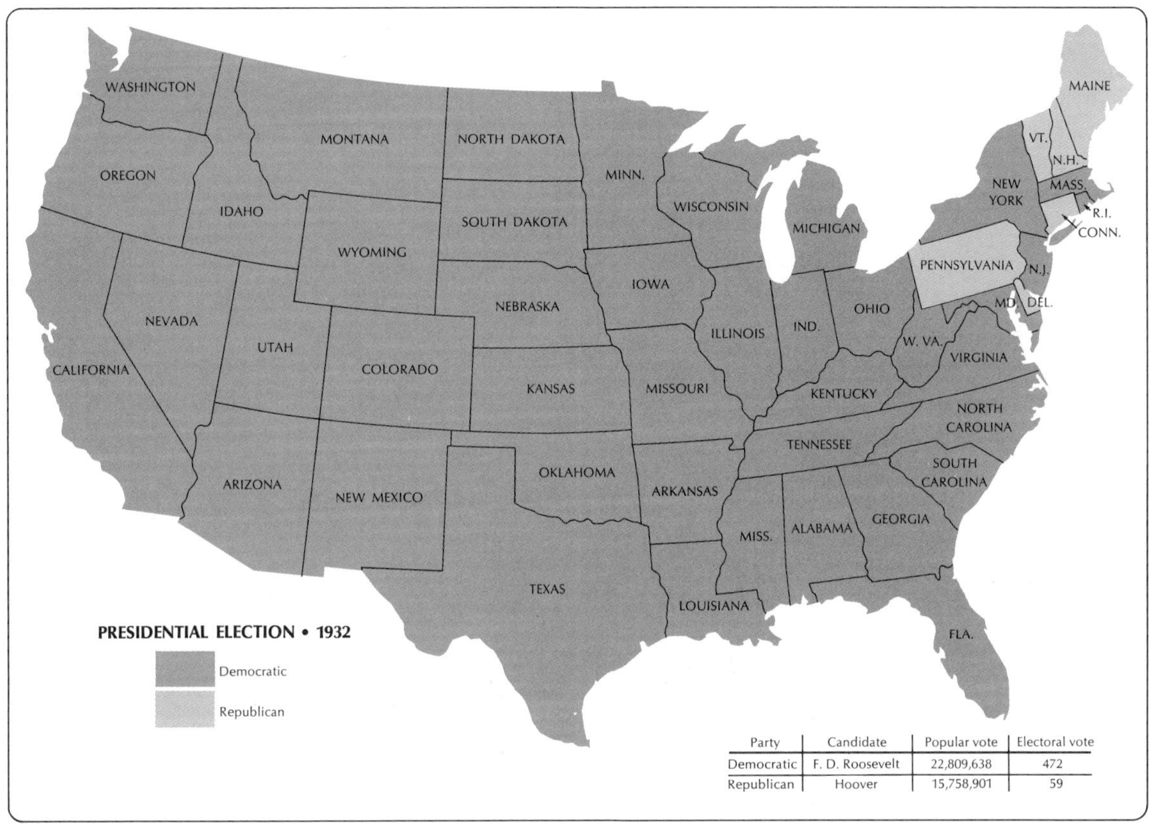

Party	Candidate	Popular vote	Electoral vote
Democratic	F. D. Roosevelt	22,809,638	472
Republican	Hoover	15,758,901	59

emerged as the leading Democratic candidate. His strongest support existed among the more progressive elements of the party in the South and West who resented the conservative, business-oriented control which John J. Raskob, national party chairman, and Alfred E. Smith had exerted over the party since 1928. Elected Governor in 1928 during a Republican landslide, Roosevelt had demonstrated unusual political talents, and he had informed himself in detail of the problems facing his state and the nation. During his governorship he supported public power, conservation, labor legislation, and a large program of unemployment relief. His political record, plus a familiar name, a successful fight against poliomyelitis contracted in 1921, and a pleasant personality placed Roosevelt in a commanding position. Roosevelt won the nomination on the fourth ballot, after California and Texas swung to his support. The convention chose John Nance Garner of Texas, Speaker of the House after the Democrats won control in 1930, as the vice presidential candidate. Shattering precedent, Roosevelt flew immediately to Chicago to deliver his acceptance speech to an excited and expectant crowd. He attacked the Republicans, declared that the Democratic party was "the bearer of liberalism and of progress," and promised relief, public works, the repeal of prohibition, aid to farmers' reform legislation, and tariff reduction. The delegates cheered madly when Roosevelt pledged "a new deal for the American people."

There was nothing to encourage the Republicans as they entered the campaign. A number of leading progressives, including Senators Norris and La Follette, deserted the party and supported Roosevelt. Senator Norris wrote an article for *Liberty* magazine entitled "Why I Am a Better Republican Than President Hoover" and speculated that if Lincoln were alive he would vote for Roosevelt. Hoover attempted to explain that Republican policies had nothing to do with causing or continuing the Depression, but the President and his party could not disassociate themselves from that responsibility.

If people failed to react favorably to Hoover, they responded warmly and enthusiastically to Roosevelt. Despite the fact that he could not stand or walk without braces on his legs, Roosevelt campaigned so vigorously that people hardly realized that he was handicapped. He traveled more than 25,000 miles and spoke to scores of audiences. His so-called brain trust, composed of advisers such as Raymond Moley and Rexford G. Tugwell of Columbia University and M. L. Wilson of Montana State College, supplied him with ideas and materials for his speeches. Roosevelt directed his campaign toward the "forgotten man." He promised farm relief, stricter regulation of business, a reduction of trade barriers, relief and public works, repeal of prohibition, and public power. He urged economy and a balanced federal budget. On these last points Hoover and Roosevelt seemed to agree.

Although Roosevelt described his objectives only in general terms, it was evident that he planned to attack the country's economic problems by expanding federal power and responsibility. Hoover may have made too sharp a distinction between his policies and the Roosevelt program, but there was a basic difference. "This campaign is more than a contest between two men. It is more than a contest between two parties," he said. "It is a contest between two philosophies of government." Hoover charged that Roosevelt's proposals "would destroy the very foundations of our American system." But people were more interested in bread and jobs than in philosophies of government; they wanted a change in Washington. Roosevelt won a resounding victory, carrying all but six states. His popular majority was 22,809,636 to only 15,758,901 for Hoover. The Democrats also swept Congress with 310 to 117 in the House of Representatives and 60 to 35, with one independent in the Senate. The Republican rout was complete.

Conclusion

The Hoover administration started under the most favorable circumstances. But Hoover had hardly become adjusted to the White House when a stock market crash signaled the beginning of a terrible depression. Hoover continued to regard the economy as basically sound; he believed that recovery depended principally upon the action of business and industrial leaders. But when it became evident that private interests could not or would not turn the economic tide, he supported a modest program of government action. The federal government did more to fight depression under Hoover than it had under any previous President. But even so, many people considered the President's programs inadequate, and strong sentiment arose for greater government action to achieve recovery. When Hoover refused, the voters elected a new leader who promised a broad attack on the Depression.

The best survey of the economy in the 1920s is George Soule's *Prosperity Decade: From War to Depression,* 1917–1929* (1947). However, the works by Hicks, Leuchtenberg, and Faulkner cited in the *Suggested Readings* at the end of Chapter 30 all contain material on economic developments. On business and industry see T. N. Carver's *The Present Economic Revolution* (1925); *America's Capacity to Produce* (1934), by E. G. Nourse and associates; and *America's Capacity to Consume* (1934) by Maurice Leven and associates. For the important automobile industry see R. C. Epstein's *The Automobile Industry* (1927) and Allan Nevins and F. E. Hill's *Ford: Expansion and Challenge,* 1915–1933 (1957). Industrial concentration has been well analyzed by A. A. Berle, Jr., and Gardiner C. Means in *The Modern Corporation and Private Property* (1933). J. W. Protho considers the business mind in *The Dollar Decade: Business Ideas in the 1920's* (1954).

The Lean Years: A History of the American Workers, 1920–1933* (1960) by Irving Bernstein is an excellent account of labor and its problems during those years. There are also good chapters in F. R. Dulles's *Labor in America: A History** (2d ed., 1961) and Joseph Rayback's *A History of American Labor** (1958). On income and the standard of living during the post-World War I years see Simon Kuznets's *National Income and Its Composition,* 1919–1938 (1941) and T. D. Eliot's *American Standards and Planes of Living* (1931).

Books dealing with farm problems include J. D. Black's *Agricultural Reform in the United States* (1929); E. R. A. Seligman's *The Economics of Farm Relief* (1929); pertinent chapters in M. R. Benedict's *Farm Policies in the United States* (1950); and Theodore Saloutos and John D. Hicks's *Twentieth Century Populism: Agricultural Discontent in the Middle West,* 1900–1939* (1951). James H. Shideler provides an excellent discussion of the approaches to farm problems in *Farm Crisis,* 1919–1923 (1957), while G. C. Fite traces the NcNary-Haugen bills in *George N. Peek and the Fight for Farm Parity* (1954).

A good biography of Herbert Hoover yet remains to be written. However, for uncritical and adulatory accounts see Eugene Lyons's *The Herbert Hoover Story* (1959) and David Hinshaw's *Herbert Hoover, American Quaker* (1950). The best account of Hoover's administration is H. G. Warren's *Herbert Hoover and the Great Depression** (1959). Richard Hofstadter's *The American Political Tradition** (1948) contains a stimulating essay on Hoover. Hoover defends his administration and explains the Depression in terms of foreign economic influences in *The Memoirs of Herbert Hoover* (1952).

There are several good general works which include valuable material on the Hoover years. These include A. M. Schlesinger, Jr.'s *The Crisis of the Old Order** (1957); Broadus Mitchell's *Depression Decade: From New Era to New Deal,* 1929–1941* (1947); and Dixon Wecter's *The Age of the Great Depression,* 1929–1941 (1948). F. L. Allen's *Since Yesterday: The Nineteen-thirties in America, September* 3, 1929–*September* 3, 1939 (1940); and Volume I of Charles A. Beard's *America in Midpassage* (1939).

On the causes of the Depression see J. K. Galbraith's *The Great Crash,* 1929* (1955) and Chapter I of Arthur B. Adams's *Our Economic Revolution* (1934). Irving Fisher's *The Stock Market Crash and After* (1930) gives the views of one of the period's leading economists. A. U. Romasco is critical of Hoover's handling of the Depression in *The Poverty of Abundance: Hoover, the Nation, the Depression** (1965), while Murray N. Rothbard criticizes government efforts to solve depression problems in *America's Great Depression* (1963).

The failure of Hoover's farm program is well covered in Saloutos and Hicks's *Agricultural Discontent in the Middle West* and Murray Benedict's *Farm Policies of the United States,* 1790–1950, both cited above. Financial and tax policies can be traced in Paul Studenski and H. E. Krooss's *Financial History of the United States* (1952). Jesse H. Jones, first head of the Reconstruction Finance Corporation, has traced the history of that agency in *Fifty Billion Dollars: My Thirteen Years with the RFC,* 1932–1945 (1951). A good brief analysis of the election of 1932 can be found in R. V. Peel and T. C. Donnelly's *The* 1932 *Campaign: An Analysis* (1935), but the best account of Roosevelt's victory in 1932 is Frank Freidel's *The Triumph,* Vol. II of his *Franklin D. Roosevelt* (1956).

*indicates availability in paperback.

33

Franklin D. Roosevelt and the New Deal

BY THE WINTER of 1932–1933 a mood of deep national crisis gripped the American people. Despair and hopelessness stalked the land. Hoover's talk of economic recovery had become increasingly absurd in the light of conditions in business, agriculture, banking, and employment. Citizens generally shared the belief that something basic was wrong in a society where millions went hungry and ill clothed in the midst of plenty. By early 1933 passive resignation gave way to demands that the national leadership tackle those problems whose solutions were beyond the capabilities of individuals or local and state governments. There was some call for radical revolution, for a complete change in the system, but the great majority of people hoped to solve their problems within the traditional American framework. They did conclude, however, that the federal government was the only agency with sufficient power and resources to meet the crisis at hand.

But what precisely could or would the new administration do to revive national confidence and to restore economic recovery? Although Roosevelt had promised a New Deal, he had not indicated the precise content of his intentions. During the next six years, however, the President, supported by Congress and the country, developed a broad program of relief, recovery, and reform. Roosevelt demonstrated that under proper leadership, democracy could work successfully in time of extreme emergency.

Roosevelt Takes Command

Franklin Delano Roosevelt (1882–1945) was extraordinarily well prepared to assume leadership in 1933. Experienced in both state and national political affairs, he possessed a flexible mind, a buoyant and optimistic spirit, a sensitivity to the needs of people, and a dedication to the American democratic tradition. Roosevelt was not restricted by tradition or hampered by a rigid economic philosophy. He was an experimenter and an innovator; he held no brief for old remedies which were unsuited to new problems. He declared in 1931 that "a new economic and social balance calls for positive leadership and definite experiments which have not hitherto been tried." "It is common sense to take a method and try it," he said later. "If it fails admit it frankly and try another. But above all try something." Roosevelt believed in greatly enhanced federal powers and insisted that the government had a responsibility to meet the needs of its citizens and to solve the problems caused by the Depression. Moreover, he favored vigorous executive leadership and promised in his inaugural address to use all of his constitutional powers to wage war against the economic emergency.

The New Deal which began to emerge in March, 1933, was largely pragmatic. It was the outcome of many ideas, with roots in the Square Deal and New Nationalism of Theodore Roosevelt, the New Freedom of Woodrow Wilson, and the trade association movement of the 1920s. But the New Deal was not entirely devoid of an underlying philosophy or plan. Although the origins of the New Deal philosophy and programs were extremely complex, the mainstream of New Deal thought was directed toward both restricting the abuses of financial and business power and advancing the welfare of farm and labor groups. Some aspects of the New Deal were damned by critics as being socialistic and un-American, but Roosevelt was no radical. He believed in a middle course of action. Basically, the New Deal sought to preserve and strengthen the capitalistic system by distributing its fruits more broadly.

In his first inaugural address, Roosevelt exuded confidence and hope. Turning the neat phrase for which he became so famous, the President said, "The only thing we have to fear is fear itself." But, he continued, the country had fallen on evil days because of the "unscrupulous money changers," and he called for a restoration of social values. He asked for a strict supervision of banking and credit, a program to put people to work, a balance between income and expenditures, and a "good neighbor policy" in world affairs. The President's talk of discipline, duty, and a recovery of "precious moral values" struck a popular mood among citizens who felt that somehow the nation had lived riotously and then fallen upon evil times. Like a thundering prophet of old, Roosevelt called for repentance. If normal processes of government failed, he would "ask the Congress for . . . broad Executive power to wage a war against the emergency. . . ."

Meanwhile, crisis had piled upon crisis. The banking collapse had become so serious by inauguration day that Roosevelt and his advisers gave its solution first priority. Between 1930 and March, 1933, some 5,504 banks had ceased operation. As banks closed, with losses to depositors running into the billions, people rushed to withdraw their funds from those which still remained open. The situation had become so critical by the fall of 1932 that in October the Governor of Nevada closed the banks of his state in order to stop withdrawals by panicky depositors. Other governors soon took similar action.

By the time Roosevelt took office most of the nation's banks had been closed by state action. Roosevelt and his advisers considered it imperative somehow to restore confidence in the banking system. Following a confusing and harried weekend, Roosevelt proclaimed a national bank holiday on Monday, March 6. He suspended all banking functions except such minor services as making change. This gave the administration time to work out legislation to place before the special session of Congress called for March 9. The bank holiday may have caused inconvenience, but people applauded Roosevelt's courage in acting. When Congress met a few days later, Roosevelt strongly urged "immediate action" on the Emergency Banking Act. Within eight hours both houses had passed the measure and it had been signed by the President. The new law permitted the Reconstruction Finance Corporation to provide additional capital for state and national banks, the Federal Reserve to issue greater quantities of notes to relieve any shortage of currency, and the Secretary of the Treasury to call in all gold coins and gold certificates. Finally, the law provided for the appointment of "conservators" to examine the conditions of closed banks and to make arrangements for their reopening. There was nothing radical about this legislation. The government acted to save the private banking system, not to nationalize the banks. "Capitalism," wrote Raymond Moley, "was saved in eight days."

Within scarcely a week many banks had reopened under a clean bill of health from conservators. Only about 5 percent of the banks were closed permanently. On March 12, in the first of his radio "fireside chats," Roosevelt assured the people that it was "safer to keep . . . money in a reopened bank than under the mattress." With confidence restored, funds began flowing back into the banking system. The crisis had ended. One of the most important aspects of the Emergency Banking Act was the removal of the United States from the gold standard. On March 10 Roosevelt issued an order forbidding the export of gold except for "legitimate and normal business requirements." Then on April 5 another execcutive order directed all persons to turn over their gold to the Federal Reserve banks by May 1. A joint resolution of Congress on June 5 completely destroyed the gold standard by outlawing clauses in public and private contracts which required payment in gold. The right of individuals to hold, export, or to demand payment in gold had been nullified.

As business continued to stagnate in the summer of 1933 and pressure mounted for effective inflationary policies, Roosevelt and his advisers, notably Professor George F. Warren of Cornell University, decided that price levels could be raised by lowering the gold content of the dollar. In practical terms this meant raising the price of gold above the current figure of $20.67 an ounce. The President on January 31, 1934, finally set the new price at $35 which devalued the dollar to 59.06 cents. A day earlier Congress had passed the Gold Reserve Act which made Federal Reserve notes redeemable in "lawful money" instead of gold. With the coinage of gold prohibited, the nation abandoned the gold standard completely. However, the President's monetary policies had no noticeable affect upon prices or recovery.

Once the banking crisis had been brought under control, Congress proceeded to inaugurate some basic reforms in the banking system. The Glass-Steagall Act was passed on June 16. It placed tighter federal controls on the national banks, separated commercial from investment banking, and permitted branch banking under specific circumstances. The law's most popular feature, however, was the provision guaranteeing bank deposits. It authorized a Federal Deposit Insurance Corporation which insured deposits in member banks up to $5,000 (later raised to $10,000).

Passage of the Emergency Banking Act was the beginning of a hectic period of New Deal history commonly referred to as the First Hundred Days. Congress and the people were in the mood to follow the President without serious question. Humorist Will Rogers declared that "if he burned down the capital we would cheer and say 'well, we at least got a fire started anyhow.'" Roosevelt took advantage of this popular psychology to push through a broad program of antidepression legislation.

Early Relief Efforts

After Roosevelt had surmounted the immediate banking crisis, the most serious problem facing the nation was that of unemployment. At least a quarter of the labor force was without work. States and local communities had nearly exhausted their relief funds; only loans from the Reconstruction Finance Corporation afforded the most meager help to hungry and ill-clothed citizens. Reports of extreme suffering flooded state and federal agencies. A Philadelphian explained that "one woman said she borrowed 50 cents from a friend and bought stale bread for 3½ cents per loaf, and that is all they had for eleven days except for one or two meals." In response to such conditions, on March 21 Roosevelt said that it was essential for recovery that Congress enact measures "aimed at unemployment relief." In specific his recommendations included "grants to states for relief work," and "a broad public-works labor-creating program."

Ten days later Congress established the Civilian Conservation Corps. The CCC was designed specifically to help young men between the ages of seventeen and twenty-five who could not find jobs. They were maintained in camps and put to work planting trees, beautifying parks, building dams, and performing other useful tasks, for which they received $30 a month. By 1942 more than two million youths had been given work on CCC projects.

Congress passed the Federal Emergency Relief Act on May 12. This law at last recognized that relief was a national problem. The lawmakers approved $500 million for grants to the states to help relieve distress among the unemployed. Roosevelt placed administration of the law in the hands of Harry L. Hopkins, who had headed relief work in New York State during Roosevelt's governorship. Hopkins quickly organized the program, and within a few days money was pouring into the states for both direct and work relief. By the summer of 1933, FERA was sponsoring a wide variety of work relief projects employing approximately one million persons; but the resources and activity of the FERA were entirely inadequate to meet relief needs as the fourth winter of the Depression approached. Consequently, President Roosevelt created the Civil Works Administration on November 9, 1933. The CWA quickly expanded the work relief program. By January, 1934, about 4,260,000 workers found employment on government projects, and in this way were sustained through the winter months. The CWA was abandoned in July, 1934, and the whole relief load fell back on the FERA.

Help for Farmers

Relief, however necessary, was no solution to unemployment. The answer to the country's basic problems was a revival of the entire economy. Much of the agrarianism in the economic thinking of the period held that the return of general prosperity depended upon improved agricultural purchasing power. Farm leaders argued that low agricultural income had helped to precipitate the Depression and that farm prices must be raised before good times could return.

Conditions among farmers were critical. Huge surpluses and poor demand for food and fiber both at home and abroad had driven prices down to disastrous levels. Wheat brought as little as 25 cents a bushel, chickens 4 cents a pound, eggs 8 cents a dozen, and hogs $2 and $3 a hundred pounds. Considering 1910–1914 as equaling 100, the prices of agricultural products had fallen to 65 by 1932. Consequently, debts became a crushing burden and thousands of farmers lost their homes through foreclosure. In this atmosphere of crisis, Congress passed the Agricultural Adjustment Act in May.

The central purpose of the AAA was the elevation of farm prices to a level which would give agricultural commodities the same purchasing power which they had enjoyed in the period 1909 to 1914. This was the principle of parity, or "equality of purchasing power," for which farmers had been striving for over a decade. To achieve this price objective, production and consumption had to be brought into balance by reducing output through production controls. Farmers who signed agreements to cut acreage were to receive benefit payments directly from the federal government. Funds for these payments were to come from a special tax paid by processors of farm commodities. Thus, farmers would not only receive higher prices as a result of reduced production but they would also receive checks from the Treasury. Growers of eight basic commodities—wheat, cotton, corn, tobacco, rice, hogs, milk, and milk products—were eligible for benefit payments in exchange for reducing production.

It became imperative to implement the AAA quickly. Crops already had been planted, and farmers had made no effort to reduce production voluntarily. The prospect of another bumper crop caused the agricultural planners sleepless nights. "Wherever we turn to deal with an agricultural commodity," said George N. Peek, Administrator of the AAA, "we have in prospect a race with the sun." But Peek and his staff slashed red tape and within a few weeks had signed 1,032,000 cotton growers to contracts designed to reduce acreage by more than 10 million acres. Since the cotton was already planted, it became necessary to plow up part of the growing crop. This brought cries of horror from many people. Cotton farmers received $178 million in benefit payments in 1933, and in addition the price of cotton advanced from about 5 to 8 cents a pound under the influence of reduced supplies. Widespread drought in the Wheat Belt in 1933 greatly reduced production and made it unnecessary to plow up growing wheat. Nonetheless, adjustment payments were given to farmers who agreed to cut their acreage in 1934 and 1935. Production control was also undertaken for tobacco and rice; and to raise hog prices, the AAA killed 6.1 million pigs and 222,000 sows in the latter part of 1933. The next year corn-hog farmers received benefit payments to reduce pig litters and corn acreage.

The AAA was an extensive experiment in national planning. Never before had the federal government developed such a comprehensive program to bring relief to a depressed sector of the economy, but there had grown up a feeling that farmers were in an unfavorable bargaining position with other economic groups and that they needed "the centralizing power of government" to improve their position. The implications of such broad federal action were not lost on contemporaries, and they produced sharp criticism. Representative Joseph Martin, Republican of Massachusetts, termed the law dictatorial and warned that "we are on the way to Moscow." Most farmers opposed acreage restriction in principle, but they were willing to cooperate, at least temporarily, in return for benefit payments.

Opponents of the AAA believed they had won a major victory against an un-American farm program when on January 6, 1936, the Agricultural Adjustment Act was placed under constitutional ban. In *United States v. Butler et al.*, the Supreme Court justices, in a 6-to-3 decision, held that processing taxes were unconstitutional and that Congress had no power to control agricultural production. Although the program was purportedly voluntary, the Court said that the power to "confer or withhold unlimited benefits is the power to coerce or destroy." Moreover, said the Court, agriculture was a local business and Congress had no constitutional power to regulate it

The Supreme Court decision in January, 1936, outlawing processing taxes and benefit payments to farmers who curtailed their acreage, left agriculture without any relief program. Congress, however, promptly passed the Soil Conservation and Domestic Allotment Act, which was aimed at accomplishing much the same purposes as the original AAA. Under the new legislation farmers were to be paid not for withdrawing land from production but for soil conservation practices. Those who substituted "soil-conserving" for "soil-depleting" crops—the principal crops in surplus such as cotton, corn, and wheat—became eligible for direct government payments. Thus the bill avoided the objections of the Supreme Court, and farmers continued to receive funds for restricting production and following sound conservation practices. Congress overcame the illegal processing taxes by providing benefit payments through direct appropriations.

The Soil Conservation and Domestic Allotment Act was replaced by the Agricultural Adjustment Act of 1938, commonly referred to as the second AAA. It retained the soil conservation features of the earlier law, but the Secretary of Agriculture received more authority to control surpluses. If acreage restriction failed to control price-depressing surpluses, the Secretary was empowered to establish marketing quotas to regulate the amount of each basic commodity which a producer could sell. If the farmer exceeded his quota or allotment, he was subject to a penalty tax. Moreover, the new law authorized the Secretary to make loans against commodities stored in government warehouses, expanding the activities of the Commodity Credit Corporation, which had been set up in 1933 for this purpose. The idea of storing surpluses in time of plenty was referred to as Secretary Wallace's "ever-normal granary" program, from Joseph's experiences in ancient Egypt. Despite efforts to restore a favorable condition between supply and demand, farm surpluses accumulated and agricultural income remained relatively low until World War II.

Benefit payments for acreage reduction and price-support legislation provided little or no help for the poorer tenants, sharecroppers, and migratory farm workers. Some method of helping these very-low-income farmers became by 1935 a pressing issue for such New Dealers as Secretary of Agriculture Henry A. Wallace and Rexford Tugwell. In April, President Roosevelt established the Resettlement Administration, which sought to retire millions of acres of submarginal land and to resettle the occupants where they could make a better living. This program ran into many obstacles, but eventually about nine million acres of submarginal land were purchased and some farmers were moved to more favorable locations. The New Deal made a further attempt to rehabilitate low-income farmers when Congress in 1937 passed the Bankhead-Jones Farm Tenancy Act. This measure authorized loans to tenants, laborers, and sharecroppers to help them buy farms. The Farm Security Administration was created in 1937 to assist the poorest class of farmers. It provided rehabilitation loans, established migratory labor camps, and set up FSA cooperative communities as a part of the program. These laws represented a distinct phase of New Deal reform. Little constructive can be said for the results of some activities of the Resettlement Administration and the FSA, but they showed a genuine concern for the welfare of neglected and downtrodden elements of the farm population.

As early as June, 1933, the Farm Credit Act abolished or reorganized some of the older farm credit agencies while at the same time creating new ones. Debt-burdened farmers received further relief in the Frazier-Lemke Farm Emergency Act of June, 1934. This law permitted a farmer who could not meet his mortgage debt and was in danger of foreclosure to appeal to a federal district court for relief. If the farmer demanded it, the court was required to let him remain on the farm for five years and to pay the creditor a rent set by the judge. This five-year moratorium for the farmer the court declared unconstitutional in May, 1935, because it denied creditors their property rights. However a revised measure passed in August met Court objections.

The National Industrial Recovery Act

If millions of jobless workers were to find regular employment, the wheels of industry had somehow to be started. On June 16, 1933, Congress passed the National Industrial Recovery Act, which incorporated the administration's program to bring about industrial recovery. It was to remain in effect for two years. Hugh S. Johnson, who had been associated with the War Industries Board in World War I, was appointed Administrator.

Many business leaders, as well as others, believed that industry's chief trouble came from excessive competition. Cutthroat competition, they argued, reduced profits, forced wage reductions, and increased unemployment. As Bernard M. Baruch explained: "Lower wages—lower costs—lower prices—and the whole vicious cycle goes on." Before 1933 a number of businessmen recommended intelligent planning which would reduce vigorous competition and bring supply into line with demand. The central question, however, was not whether there should be planning but who should do it. Eventually, the principle of government-business cooperation won the day. Johnson and Baruch both pointed to the War Industries Board as an example of successful planning and cooperation between government and business. If this could be achieved in wartime, why not during a domestic economic crisis?

The stated purpose of the law was to promote cooperation among businessmen, to eliminate unfair competition, to increase consumption of agricultural and industrial products by expanding purchasing power, to reduce unemployment, and to improve labor standards. Roosevelt explained that the measure aimed at assuring "a reasonable profit to industry and living wages for labor, with the elimination of the piratical methods and practices which have not only harassed honest business but also contributed to the ills of labor."

To achieve these elusive objectives, representatives of most major industries and government were to frame what were erroneously called "codes of fair competition." These codes included such things as minimum prices, production controls, specific credit terms, particular service standards, and many other provisions. Once a code had been drawn up and approved by the President, its provisions became legally binding on all business in that particular industry. This was industrial self-government under federal supervision.

Section 7a of the law guaranteed employees the right to organize and to bargain collectively, and it required employers to comply with minimum-wage and maximum-hour provisions in the codes. The minimum-wage figure varied in different geographic areas and in different industries, but it was 40 cents an hour in about one-half of the codes. A maximum of forty hours a week was provided in 85 percent of the codes, which covered approximately half of the employees of industries under the NRA. Some codes prohibited labor by children under sixteen. "This ancient atrocity went out in a day," Roosevelt exclaimed, "because this law permits employers to do by agreement that which none of them could do separately and live in competition." The Blue Eagle of the NRA became the symbol of industrial recovery, and the idea of spreading work and increasing payrolls was promoted by emotionalism and pageantry reminiscent of wartime.

By shortening the workweek and reducing child labor, the new NRA program extended jobs to more than two million workers in 1933. But the overall contribution of the NRA to recovery was meager at best. Dividing up available employment among more workers by reducing hours may have been temporarily beneficial, but it did not solve the problem of creating new jobs. Moreover, despite the President's plea to hold the line, prices went up as fast or faster than wages, and there was no substantial increase in purchasing power. After the initial boomlet there was no marked increase in employment or in the volume of production. Like the AAA, the NRA was basically a program of scarcity. The total effect on the economy was like giving an aspirin to a very sick man who needed an operation. While the NRA did not stimulate recovery to any extent, it did encourage such permanent reforms as minimum wages, maximum hours, the elimination of child labor, and the establishment of collective bargaining for workers as a national policy.

Opposition to the law developed immediately. Big business disliked it because of the labor provisions; lawyers thought it unconstitutional; consumers believed it responsible for higher prices; small business considered it favorable to the large corporations; and trust-busters objected to suspending the antitrust laws. Moreover, internal administrative conflicts caused further trouble, and Johnson resigned as Administrator under pressure in September, 1934. The final days of NRA before it was declared unconstitutional in May, 1935, were filled with uncertainty and division.

Title II of the NRA created a Public Works Administration. The PWA was designed to supplement other provisions of the basic law by expanding employment on public works. About half of the cost of these projects was to be furnished by PWA and the other half by states and municipalities. Besides supplying new jobs on public projects, it was thought that increased purchases of cement, lumber, steel, and other products by the government would stimulate the entire economy. This was part of the New Deal's pump-priming activities, which were designed to increase employment, expand purchasing power, and swell capital investment. The PWA was a basic part of the Administration's recovery program and was not a relief measure. Ultimately some $4 billion was spent by PWA on dams, educational buildings, and other construction.

Besides the legislation already discussed, Congress passed other important measures during the First Hundred Days. On May 18, Senator George W. Norris's dream was finally realized when Congress approved the Tennessee Valley Authority. The Securities Act of May, 1933, was followed in 1934 by a broader and more permanent measure, the Securities Exchange Act. This measure required stock exchanges to register with the Security and Exchange Commission, while brokers were required to present information about the companies whose stock they sold. The Commission sought to prevent misrepresentation in the sale of securities and, in general, tried to provide reliable information for those who wanted to invest. The law went a long way toward eliminating the worst stock market abuses and provided some protection for investors.

Despite passage of what appeared to be needed and worthy measures, by 1935 there were signs everywhere that the New Deal honeymoon was over. Businessmen were becoming not only apprehensive but outright critical. One manufacturer declared that he intended to take a year off from his business and work for Roosevelt's defeat. "So many businessmen have been so deeply engrossed in their private business that they have permitted half-wits to seize the Government," he said. Roosevelt's call for higher taxes on business in 1935, his attack on what he called "the royalists of the economic order" in his annual message of January, 1936, and the subsequent passing of an undistributed profits tax stirred up bitterness and anger among conservatives. Roosevelt accused his critics of ingratitude.

The Supreme Court, moreover, became a

major barrier to economic planning as it outlawed several New Deal measures. In 1935 the Court declared the National Recovery Act, the Frazier-Lemke Bankruptcy Act, and the Railroad Retirement Act unconstitutional; and, as mentioned earlier, in January, 1936, it struck down the Agricultural Adjustment Act. The court killed the NRA by a unanimous decision in the case of *Schechter Poultry Company v. United States.* The Schechter Poultry Company of New York had been convicted in the circuit court of violating the live poultry code. The Supreme Court held, however, that the authority granted by Congress to the President for code-making was an unconstitutional delegation of legislative power. Furthermore, the defendants, said the Court, were not engaged in interstate commerce, and therefore the law was an unconstitutional federal invasion of areas reserved for the states.

The Second New Deal

By 1935 there was a noticeable shift from an emphasis upon relief and recovery measures to concern with social and reform legislation. In what came to be known as the "Second Hundred Days" ending in August, 1935, Congress enacted a wide variety of banking, labor, social security, and other reform laws. Because the administration stressed reform and social welfare legislation, some historians have pointed to 1935 as the dividing point between the first and the second New Deals. It is easy to overemphasize the differences between the outlook and accomplishments of the New Deal before and after 1935, because most of the reform measures adopted between 1935 and 1938 had been under consideration for many years. But Congress passed so much basic social legislation after 1935 that it ushered the United States finally into the position of a welfare state. The New Deal's early relief efforts, although helpful, had by late 1934 and 1935 proved to be both insufficient and morally undesirable. After abandoning the CWA in July, 1934, the relief program in large part was nothing more than a federal dole, which Harry Hopkins called "the most degrading" kind of relief. By January, 1935, some five million families and individuals were on emergency relief rolls. After studying the problem, Roosevelt declared, on January 4, that the federal government should quit the business of relief and provide work for able but destitute workers.

Still the shift in New Deal policies came slowly. Roosevelt's message to Congress in January, 1935, proposed a limited program and promised a quiet session. He spoke of the need for personal security among the aged and unemployed, but his measures seemed to stress consolidation rather than expansion. At the same time the President could not ignore the deep and persistent problems still facing the nation.

Congress responded to the President's request for a work relief program by passing the Emergency Relief Appropriation Act in April, 1935. This law appropriated $4.88 billion for "relief, work relief, and to increase employment by providing useful projects." On May 6, the Works Progress Administration was set up with Harry Hopkins as administrator. Hopkins moved quickly, and within a few months the WPA had organized thousands of work relief projects, which included the construction of airports, schools, highways, libraries, playgrounds, and parks for general public use. WPA projects were also developed to employ musicians, artists, and other professional persons who could not find regular employment. Between 1936 and 1941, the WPA employed an average of about two million workers per month, but a high was reached in November, 1938, when 3,238,000 persons were engaged in government-financed projects. The Federal Emergency Appropriation Act also authorized the National Youth Administration. This program provided part-time work for high school and college students so they could earn enough money to continue their education.

Expenditures for direct relief and work projects were largely responsible for increased federal deficits after 1933. Between 1933 and 1940, the various national relief agencies spent approximately $15 billion, more than half of which was expended by the WPA. In return, several million people were given employment, and the nation profited from having better school buildings, parks, roads, and other physical assets. But despite these large outlays, the Depression held on stubbornly and Roosevelt's critics said he was spending the country into bankruptcy and endangering historic American freedoms. But WPA merely inaugurated a whole spectrum of new policies.

Labor and the New Deal

Following the Schechter case, the administration faced the task of salvaging some of the benefits which had been extended to labor in the NRA. On August 5, 1935, the President signed the National Labor Relations Act, commonly called the Wagner Act. This law gave workers the right to form unions and to bargain collectively "through representatives of their own choosing." The law established a National Labor Relations Board, which was empowered to investigate and issue cease-and-desist orders as a means of preventing unfair labor practices. When the measure was challenged on constitutional grounds, the Supreme Court upheld it on April 12, 1937, in the case of *National Labor Relations Board v. Jones and Laughlin Steel Corporation*.

Besides guaranteeing collective bargaining, Congress in June, 1938, passed the Fair Labor Standards Act, which provided for minimum wages and maximum hours. President Roosevelt had said earlier that "a self-supporting and self-respecting democracy can plead no justification for the existence of child labor, no economic reason for chiseling workers' wages or stretching workers' hours." The Fair Labor Standards Act set minimum wages for employees producing goods for interstate commerce at 25 cents an hour and limited the regular workweek to forty-four hours. The law prohibited children under sixteen from working in most industries, making unnecessary a constitutional amendment dealing with child labor. Many workers, however, such as those in agriculture, were exempt from provisions of the law. In any event, the New Deal had gone a long way by 1938 in providing decent wages, more leisure time, and the abolition of child labor, all of which had been among the historic aims of workingmen.

Meanwhile, a fundamental split was occurring in the ranks of organized labor. The key conflict resulted from disagreement over the best means to organize the millions of workers in the great mass-production industries such as steel, automobiles, and rubber. The American Federation of Labor, which claimed more than 80 percent of the union membership, had historically organized its members on a craft, or trade union, basis. However, by the 1920s and early 1930s, the AF of L came under increasing attack from leaders within its own ranks who wanted to organize the mass-production workers in industrial unions. John L. Lewis, president of the United Mine Workers, headed a group of aggressive labor leaders who argued that workers in a particular industry such as steel should be organized in a single large industrial union instead of on the basis of crafts and trades. In November, 1935, Lewis and other unionists formed the Committee for Industrial Organization to organize industrial unions within the framework of AF of L. President William Green denounced this action and in August, 1936, the AF of L suspended the CIO unions.

In 1936 the CIO began an aggressive campaign to organize steelworkers. Within a few months it extended its organizing efforts to workers in the automobile, glass, rubber, and other mass-production industries. By the end of 1937 the CIO claimed a total of 3.7 million members. This was approximately 300,000 more than were affiliated with the AF of L, which had been active for more than a half century. The great industries such as steel and automobiles did not succumb easily to union organization. They fought unions and collective bargaining with every weapon at their command, including strikebreakers, lockouts, discrimination in hiring, and aid from the local police. But when Ford finally recognized the United Auto Workers in June, 1941, some four years after General Motors had done so, it symbolized a victorious climax for organized labor. Overall, New Deal legislation was a major factor in strengthening labor's bargaining position and economic welfare.

Social Security

One of the most fundamental New Deal reforms was the Social Security Act approved by the President on August 5, 1935. Here the Roosevelt administration broke sharply with the past. Most citizens had accepted the idea that people should care for their own needs through individual savings in old age and in periods of unemployment. Local and state governments had historically provided some direct relief, and church and charitable organizations had also helped the needy. Some states had passed old-age pension laws, but the payments were small and varied greatly from state to state.

The increasing popularity of pie-in-the-sky panaceas prompted Roosevelt to become more concerned about suitable social security legislation. Dr. Francis E. Townsend of California won millions of supporters for his old-age pension plan, which called for paying every man and woman over sixty years of age $200 a month as long as the money was spent within thirty days. Funds were to be raised by a special sales tax. Townsend supporters formed clubs all over the United States, and by 1935 Townsend claimed that he had five million backers. Huey P. Long of Louisiana advocated a Share-Our-Wealth program, in which he recommended providing every family with the necessities of life with income derived from heavy taxes on high incomes. Father Coughlin, a Detroit priest, won millions of followers with his plan for inflation, nationalization of certain industries, and a living wage for all industrial labor.

These demands undoubtedly hastened passage of the Social Security Act of 1935. A broad and comprehensive measure, the law provided for old-age insurance, federal aid to the states for old-age pensions, unemployment insurance, aid to dependent children, and support for various public health programs. The old-age insurance provision, commonly called social security, was the only part of the law administered solely by the federal government. A federal tax on both employees and employers provided funds from which payments could be made to qualified people over sixty-five. Many workers, including agricultural and casual laborers, state employees, and domestic servants, were exempt from benefits of the original law, but later amendments extended coverage to millions of additional workers.

Title I of the law was designed to encourage an improved and more uniform system of old-age pensions among the states and to help people who were not covered by old-age insurance. The federal government promised to contribute up to $15 a month for each qualified person over sixty-five receiving a state old-age pension, providing the state plan met federal specifications. Of basic importance to labor was the law's provision for unemployment insurance. Funds were raised to make payments to unemployed workers by placing a federal tax on employer payrolls. The social security law had many defects, but it represented a tremendous advance in the role and responsibility of the federal government for the general welfare of the American people.

Utility Regulation, Conservation, and Public Power

Another New Deal reform passed in August, 1935, was the Public Utility Holding Company Act. The purpose of this law was to reduce the abuses of holding company control in the field of public utilities. With some exceptions, holding company operations were limited to "a single integrated public-utility system, and to such other businesses as are reasonably incidental, or economically necessary or appropriate to the operations of such . . . system." The law's constitutionality came under attack, but the Supreme Court upheld its provisions in 1938.

One of the most controversial legislative reforms sought by Roosevelt in 1935 was tax revision. In a special message to Congress on June 19, the President called for "progressive taxation of wealth and of income" and "a wider distribution of wealth." Specifically, Roosevelt recommended higher income and inheritance taxes and a graduated corporate income tax. What created such deep consternation among many people was the President's frank desire to use taxation as a means of checking economic power and helping small competitive business. Congress refused to give the President everything he asked for, but it did raise rates on large estates and high incomes and levied an excess profits tax on corporations.

Conservation of natural resources was another broad area of reform in which the President had been personally interested for many years. From the beginning of his administration, Roosevelt gave strong support to soil conservation and flood control. The Department of Agriculture, working through the Soil Erosion Service and later the Soil Conservation Service, carried on an aggressive program after 1933 in an attempt to reclaim millions of acres of land eroded by wind and water. The SCS encouraged better land management practices with government financial help to thousands of farms. In 1934 Congress enacted the Taylor

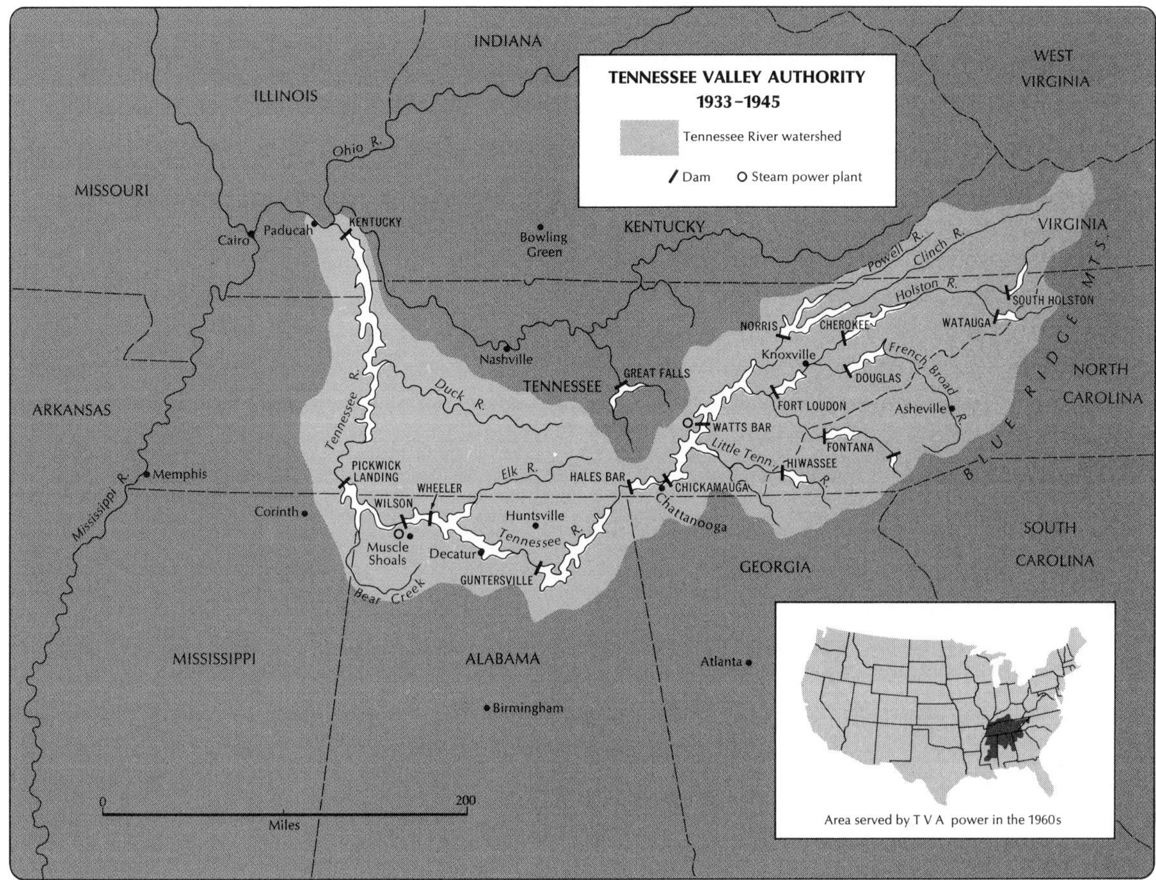

Grazing Act, which authorized the Secretary of the Interior to establish grazing districts and to institute improved land practices on ranges which had been nearly ruined by overuse.

Conservation was also one of the major objectives of the Tennessee Valley Authority, approved on May 18, 1933. For more than a decade, Senator Norris of Nebraska had been working to obtain government operation of the Muscle Shoals properties on the Tennessee River in northern Alabama. In 1928 President Coolidge vetoed a Norris bill which provided for government operation of these facilities; a similar measure fell before a Hoover veto in 1931. This, Hoover said, would "break down the initiative and enterprise of the American people." Scarcely any issue separated Hoover and Roosevelt so sharply. Hoover vigorously opposed public power projects; Roosevelt favored federal development of the nation's power resources.

Most of the controversy surrounding the history of TVA has dealt with electric power development. However, the law listed navigation, flood control, and the development of agricultural resources as the program's prime objectives. To control floods, to aid navigation, and to generate electricity, the TVA built thirty principal dams on the Tennessee and tributary rivers. Nine of the high-level dams created huge reservoirs, often referred to as "the Great Lakes of the South." River navigation became possible from Paducah, Kentucky, to Knoxville, Tennessee—a distance of some 630 miles. The production of fertilizer and the planting of trees, grass, and soil-conserving crops went a long way to curb erosion and restore soil fertility in an area where farm income was very low. Basically TVA sought an economy of abundance for an entire region.

The Tennessee Valley Authority authorized the production and sale of power, with preference being given to "states, counties, municipalities and cooperative organizations." Especially the TVA hoped to increase the use of electricity upon farms in the region. Although the private power companies fought TVA's distribution of electricity in every possible manner, this experiment in economic and social planning prevailed against all attacks. The TVA played a major part in the lowering of charges for electricity and in rebuilding the economy of the Tennessee Valley. Other federal power projects included those on the Columbia River at Bonneville, Oregon, and Grand Coulee in Washington, begun in 1933.

Reelection in 1936

As the election of 1936 approached, the President came under severe attacks from those groups who had become alienated from the New Deal and its programs. Some of the most vocal Roosevelt-haters had formed the American Liberty League in 1934 to combat what they considered to be dangerous and un-American developments in the Roosevelt administration. They now intended to block the President's renomination and reelection. Among the dominant leaders of the Liberty League were such prominent Democrats as Alfred E. Smith and Jacob J. Raskob. To these critics the New Deal was Socialistic, even Communistic, filled with "Reds and Pinks," and destroying the Constitution. But when the Democrats met in convention at Philadelphia late in June, they renominated Roosevelt and Garner on the first ballot. The Democratic platform praised the New Deal and promised more reforms along the lines already marked by the administration.

The Republican party had been so shattered by defeats in 1932 and 1934 that it approached the campaign with neither a program nor a distinguished personality to lead the party. In searching for a man to challenge Roosevelt, the Republicans finally agreed on Governor Alfred M. Landon of Kansas. Landon had withstood the earlier Democratic landslide and had given his state an efficient and moderately progressive administration. Warning that "America is in peril," the platform sharply castigated the New Deal for dishonoring American traditions and betraying its pledges to the people. The Democrats, according to official Republican doctrine, were guilty of waste and extravagance, and of fostering bureaucracy. The Republicans promised to encourage business, to help labor and agriculture, to provide relief without confusion and partisanship, and to balance the budget.

Besides the Republican opposition to Roosevelt, there existed a conglomeration of leftish critics such as Dr. Francis Townsend, the old-age pension advocate; Father Coughlin; and followers of the late Huey P. Long who had been assassinated in 1935. These forces combined in June, organized the Union party, and named Representative William Lemke of North Dakota as their man.

Landon, it was evident, had no chance to win despite his energetic campaigning and a *Literary Digest* poll which predicted a Republican victory. James A. Farley, who directed the Democratic campaign, declared that the Kansan would only carry two states. Farley was right. Roosevelt received over eleven million more votes than Landon and won all the electoral votes except those of Maine and Vermont. Congress also continued heavily Democratic. The result was a smashing personal victory for President Roosevelt, who by that time had begun to weld a variety of economic, social, and ethnic groups into an effective political organization. Farmers, workers, urbanites, recent immigrants, Jews, and millions of blacks made up a coalition which the Republicans would not challenge successfully until 1952.

The Court Fight

Roosevelt's tremendous popular victory in 1936 and the return of a strong Democratic Congress strengthened his determination to bring about some changes in the Supreme Court. Following Court decisions which outlawed several basic New Deal measures, the President became increasingly critical of the Court's conservatism. He referred to the narrow interpretation of interstate commerce in the Schechter case as reflecting a "horse-and-buggy" philosophy. In February, 1937, he presented his plan of reform. The most important part of the President's program was his request that the number of Supreme Court justices be increased from nine to a possible fifteen. A retirement feature of the plan would permit the President to appoint a new justice (up to a total of fifteen) for each one over seventy, who might or might not choose to retire at that time. Roosevelt revealed his motives, perhaps too clearly for his own political good, when he said that "modern complexities call . . . for a constant infusion of new blood in the courts." He was convinced that reactionary judges were remaining on the Court as long as physically possible—one judge was past seventy-five and had served since 1910—in order to block reform legislation.

The President's request for additional Supreme Court members raised a storm of protest. His plan was labeled a "court-packing" scheme, which would permit the Executive to run roughshod over the Constitution. Immediately a number of leading Senators, including such stalwart Democrats as Burton K. Wheeler and Joseph C. O'Mahoney, organized to defeat the proposal. Although most Republicans opposed Roosevelt's Court proposals, they were happy to follow the Democrats into the battle against the Court proposal. Joseph T. Robinson of Arkansas, the Majority Leader and a loyal party man, led the contest for the administration until July, when he died in the middle of the fight. After weeks of bitter struggle, Congress rejected Roosevelt's suggestion to enlarge the Court.

But even before Congress turned down this so-called judicial reform, the Supreme Court handed down a number of decisions upholding New Deal laws. In March and April, 1937, the Railway Labor Act, a revised Frazier-Lemke farm mortgage law, and the Wagner Act were all declared constitutional. These decisions, especially that dealing with the Wagner Act, caused many people to conclude that the President's demand to enlarge the Court was unnecessary. Somewhat facetiously, Senator James F. Byrnes of South Carolina reportedly remarked after the Wagner Act decision: "I don't know what effect the court decision will have on the President's plans, but I do know what effect the President's plans have had on the Court." As one wag declared, "A switch in time saved nine." Whether the Court took a different attitude as a result of presidential pressure, or whether New Deal legislation was drawn more carefully to avoid charges of unconstitutionality, the result favored the administration.

Recession and Fiscal Policies

While Congress wrestled with proposed Court changes, the recession which began in September of 1937 dealt the New Deal's recovery program a harsh blow. During the last quarter of 1936, it appeared that genuine prosperity was at last returning. Although there were still 8 to 10 million unemployed, nonfarm employment was picking up, and industrial output, corporate profits, and real income were all increasing. But in the first part of 1937 the economy leveled off, and by September the country slipped back into a full-fledged state of depression—although the Democrats preferred the term "recession." The economic decline between September, 1937, and June, 1938, was one of the most drastic in American history. Industrial production dropped 33 percent in that nine-month period, profits declined 78 percent, and national income 13 percent. Employment in manufacturing dropped 23 percent. What caused this sharp economic reversal?

Perhaps the substantial cut in government expenditures was the major cause of the recession. Between January and March, 1937, monthly net federal outlays declined by some $300 million. This had the effect of reducing personal incomes and the purchasing power necessary to sustain production. Furthermore, at a time when increased private investment was needed to offset reduced government spending, the Federal Reserve system increased the cost of credit. Finally, the poor outlook for profits also tended to discourage private investment.

The recession of 1937–1938 forced Roosevelt and his advisers to examine more intensively than before questions dealing with budget and fiscal policies. By early 1938 the role and function of government spending had become a vital issue. Basically, President Roosevelt believed in a balanced budget. He accepted deficit financing after 1933 only under pressure of an inescapable national emergency. Roosevelt promised repeatedly to balance the budget as soon as business and agriculture recovered. Yet he considered large-scale spending and federal loans as one means of helping to restore prosperity. In other words, Roosevelt accepted the concept of pump priming, that government spending would stimulate private investment so that deficit financing could be discontinued. But the recession of 1937 gave the pump-priming theory a rude shock. When the government, after four years of deficit financing, finally reduced its expenditures, private funds did not fill the investment gap. Why had the pump lost its prime?

By the late 1930s one group of economists maintained that the United States had reached a point of economic maturity. This meant that industrial expansion had permanently slowed down to the point where private investment could not absorb the accumulated savings. To compensate for this, they said, heavy government expenditures, another name for public investment, were necessary to keep the economy operating at a high level. The importance of government spending was emphasized by the famed British economist John Maynard Keynes in his book *The General Theory of Employment, Interest, and Money,* published in 1936. Keynes stressed the need for public spending to stimulate economic expansion when private investment was insufficient to provide full employment. There is no evidence, however, that Keynes, who visited the United States in 1934, had any direct influence on New Deal fiscal policies after 1937. Rather, some of the practical politicians who had the President's ear urged greatly enlarged federal expenditures and deficit financing. Marriner Eccles of the Federal Reserve Board and Harry Hopkins were probably more responsible than any other persons for convincing Roosevelt that the federal government needed to spend at a much higher rate. Neither of these Roosevelt advisers were sullied by economic theory; they simply saw the need for a program to stimulate business and to provide jobs.

In a special message on April 14, 1938, President Roosevelt declared that "today's purchasing power . . . is not sufficient to drive the economic system at higher speed. Responsibility of government requires us . . . to supplement the normal processes and . . . to make sure that the addition is adequate." Congress did not accept everything the President suggested but in 1938 it increased appropriations for federal relief and other purposes by some $3 billion. As Tugwell pointed out, despite some bitter opposition to large-scale deficit financing and warnings of financial disaster ahead, the resistance in Congress "melted before the attractions of public spending." The national deficit jumped from $1.4 billion in 1938 to $3.6 billion in 1939. Although most Americans, including the President, clung to the sanctity of balanced budgets, the New Deal established the pattern of using government fiscal policy—taxing, borrowing, and spending—to help direct and govern the economy. Between 1933 and 1940 the federal debt rose from $19.5 billion to nearly $43 billion as the government borrowed large sums to meet relief and other needs.

Life in the Depression

For most people during the Great Depression life was a struggle to gain the bare necessities of existence. In the mid-1930s more than 40 percent of the nation's families lived on less than $1,000 a year; millions of them earned less than $500 annually. Southern sharecroppers and migrant workers were among those receiving as little as $100 a year. Millions of jobless families received relief, but it was seldom enough to cover the cost of food, clothing, and shelter. The thing that most people remembered about the Depression of the 1930s was the scarcity of money. They had not only to watch their dollars, but to guard their nickels and pennies as well.

Shortages of money produced important changes in the daily lives of people. Car owners often ran their automobiles until the vehicles simply defied repair. Children's college educations had to be postponed because parents could not pay even modest tuition charges of less than $100 in state-supported institutions. Trips to the doctor and dentist were delayed until a major emergency forced a family to seek medical attention; at the Methodist Hospital in Mitchell, South Dakota, patients sometimes paid their bills in produce, a situation not uncommon in rural communities. Even with federal food distribution after 1933, millions of families had inadequate diets. They ate greater quantities of cheaper, starchy foods, and schoolchildren often went without lunch. It was a grim existence for millions of Americans. The only thing that made the lack of money and resulting poverty tolerable was the fact that the condition was so widespread. Poor families knew that most of their neighbors shared their hardships and insecurity.

The Depression instilled widespread restlessness and rootlessness in American life as people wandered about looking for some way to improve their condition. Hitchhikers lined the highways, and railroad boxcars were filled with men who drifted aimlessly from one place to another. Men stole or begged a few vegetables and cooked their stew in cans over open fires along the railroad tracks, areas commonly known as "the jungles." An unusually large migration took place from the Great Plains which, because of severe droughts between 1934 and 1936, became a Dust Bowl. The wind whipped up still greater economic hardship in this large area of mid-America. Thousands of farmers in Oklahoma, Kansas, west Texas, and eastern Colorado left their homes and headed toward California in old jalopies piled high with personal belongings. John Steinbeck caught the spirit and dealt with the problems of this migration in his best-seller *The Grapes of Wrath* (1939).

The Depression was extremely hard on young people. While the National Youth Administration, formed in 1935, helped hundreds of thousands of youths to continue their education, other millions did not have enough money to attend either high school or college. Even those young people who managed to achieve a high school or college education found that there was no job for them after graduation. The records show that, during the middle 1930s, more than a quarter of the young people in their late teens and early twenties had never held a regular job. The schools themselves had a difficult time. There was an abundance of teachers but not enough money to pay them. Many teachers were paid with warrants, which could only be cashed at a considerable discount. Country schoolteachers were fortunate if they received as much as $60 a month, and even college professors commonly earned less than $2,000 a year.

With the inauguration of the five-day week in many industries—to say nothing of those without work—people had more leisure time in the 1930s than ever before. People spent hours before their radios listening to sports, news, music, and drama. Among the most popular radio programs were "Amos 'n' Andy" and "The Lone Ranger," which first appeared in 1933. Movies became increasingly popular. Most pictures were aimed strictly at entertainment; very few of them sought to deal with current social problems. Walt Disney produced full-length, animated pictures, of which "Snow White and the Seven Dwarfs" (1938) was the most famous. "Gone with the Wind" (1936) and "The Good Earth" (1937) drew huge crowds. Those who enjoyed dancing or listening were treated to unusual fare by the big name bands. Benny Goodman, Guy Lombardo, Tommy Dorsey, and Count Basie were among the most popular bandleaders, and Louis Armstrong won great acclaim as an individual performer. "Swing," "boogie-woogie," and "in the groove" were expressions related to new developments in popular music. Youngsters danced the Big Apple and the Suzy-Q, both of which were fast and acrobatic.

The Depression

The depression of the 1930s affected virtually every family in the nation and caused such drastic dislocations for many that it became to millions of Americans an emotional as well as a financial depression. Between twelve and fifteen million workers—about one quarter of the labor force—were out of work by 1933, and by the middle 1930s more than 40 percent of the nation's families lived on less than $1,000 a year. Some, like the migrant workers in the Dorothea Lange photograph below, did not see much more than $100 in cash in a year. Those who had saved their money were not spared. Bank failures—5,504 of them between 1930 and 1933—wiped out the life-savings of millions.

As the months of joblessness rolled into years, thousands of workers felt an increasing sense of personal powerlessness. Self-confidence, and confidence in the traditional American values of initiative, thrift, and competition wavered. And so it happened that the nation elected to follow Franklin Delano Roosevelt, a leader who radiated self-assurance and energy and who told the people, "The only thing we have to fear is fear itself."

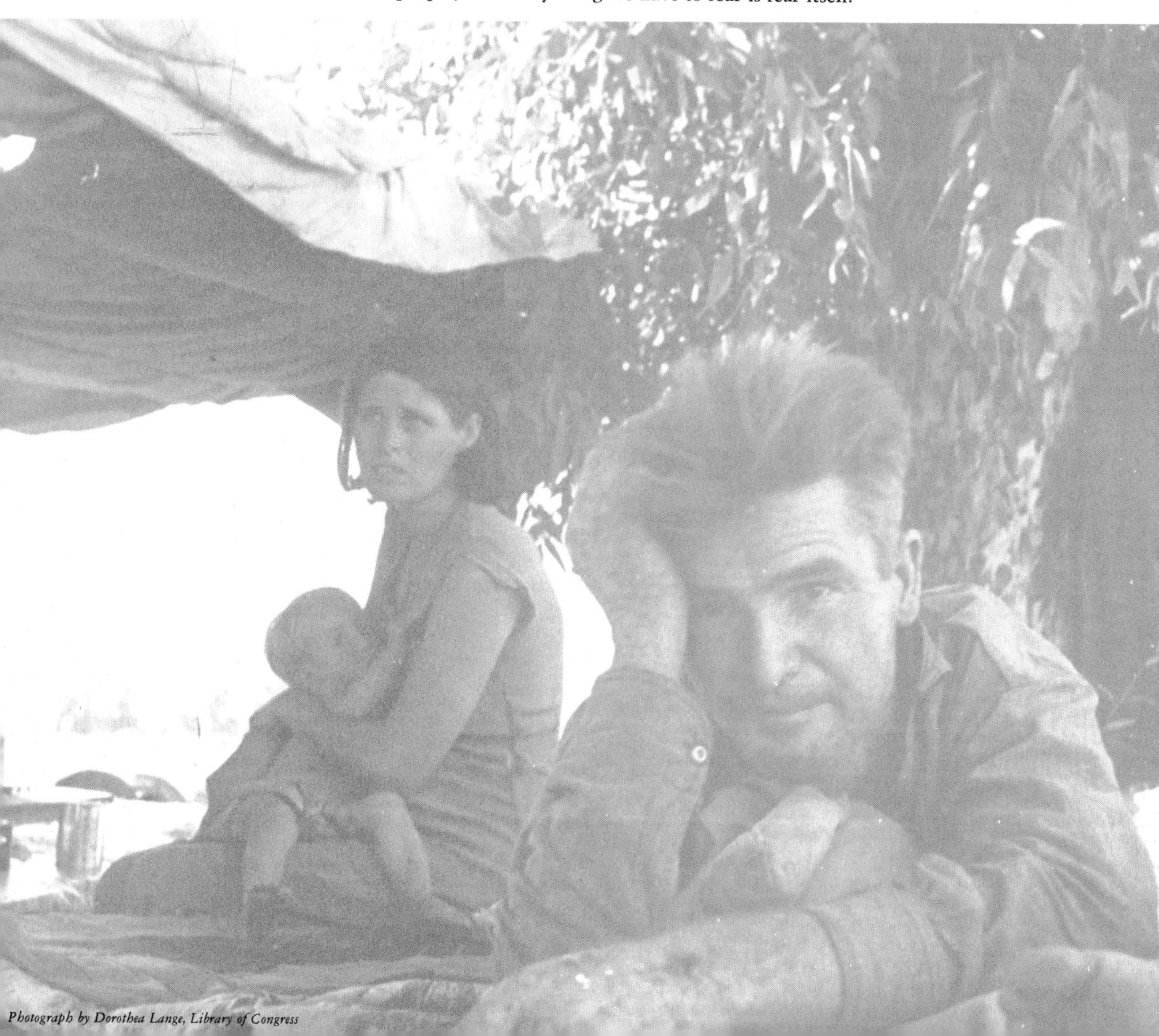

Photograph by Dorothea Lange, Library of Congress

Growing up on a great Hudson River estate in Hyde Park, New York, Roosevelt's upbringing insured the self-assurance that constantly marked his outward personality. This quality shines out in most of his photographs—missing, perhaps, in the picture of him as a boy at the wheel of his grandfather's yacht (above) but very apparent in the view of him in his riding outfit taken when he was eleven (left). Roosevelt went to the "best" schools—Groton, Harvard, and Columbia Law, ran successfully for the New York State Senate, and served as Assistant Secretary of the Navy during the Wilson administrations. In 1920 the Democrats nominated him as their candidate for Vice-President. Projecting his characteristic verve, he campaigned with the Presidential candidate, James M. Cox (right, above).

In 1921, at the age of thirty-nine, Roosevelt was stricken with infantile paralysis. Rebuilding his physical strength, forced him into relative political inactivity for seven years. He maintained his political ties, however, and received the nomination for governor of New York by acclamation at the State Democratic Convention in 1928. He won by a small margin and in the same year helped Santa Claus at the Beekman Street Hospital in New York (right, center). Two years later he was reelected by a margin of around 725,000 votes—the highest ever bestowed on a New York state candidate—and the victory helped him to secure the presidential nomination in 1932. In the final days of the campaign (right, below) he appeared with Al Smith, unsuccessful Democratic presidential candidate in 1928, at his side.

Left and above: Franklin D. Roosevelt Library; right, all pictures: United Press International

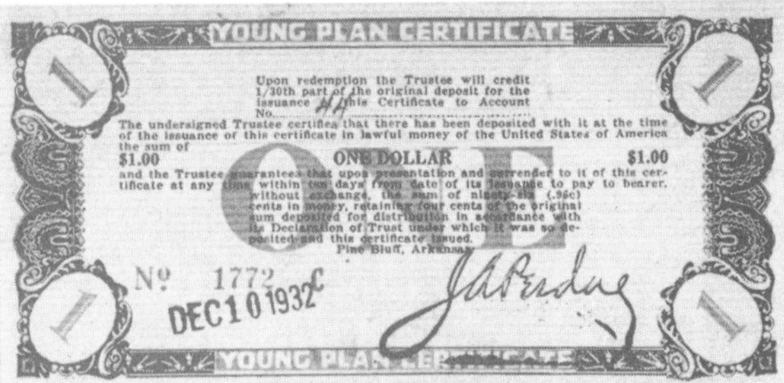

YOUNG PLAN CERTIFICATE

Upon redemption the Trustee will credit 1/30th part of the original deposit for the issuance of this Certificate to Account No. ......

The undersigned Trustee certifies that there has been deposited with it at the time of the issuance of this certificate in lawful money of the United States of America the sum of

$1.00 ONE DOLLAR $1.00

and the Trustee guarantees that upon presentation and surrender to it of this certificate at any time within ten days from date of its issuance to pay to bearer, without exchange, the sum of ninety-six (.96c) cents in money, retaining four cents of the original sum deposited for distribution in accordance with its Declaration of Trust under which it was so deposited and this certificate issued.

Pine Bluff, Arkansas

Nº 1772 C

DEC 10 1932

YOUNG PLAN CERTIFICATE

In 1933, as breadlines lengthened and banks closed, local governments and banks issued scrip money of their own, like the "Young Plan" dollar (above). By Roosevelt's inauguration on March 4, state governments had ordered most of the nation's banks closed. In his address Roosevelt promised action and immediately declared a national bank holiday for March 6. By March 9, his banking legislation was in Congress. Thus began the famous "first hundred days," during which the executive branch fed Congress an unprecedented volume of proposals for programs to restore the country's economic health.

Perhaps most unusual was the National Industrial Recovery Act. Under the NRA, businessmen were asked to set up industry-wide codes which would set minimum prices, production controls, credit terms, encourage minimum wages and maximum hours, provide for collective bargaining, and eliminate child labor. Some businessmen, however, felt the law gave too much power to labor. Some liberals thought price-setting against the consumer's interest. The Supreme Court invalidated the NRA in May, 1935, but the law established the administration's support for collective bargaining and minimum wages and maximum hours.

In another early move, Roosevelt created the Tennessee Valley Authority. The TVA would provide electric power for four and a half million people, as well as improved navigation, nitrate production, industrial power, flood and erosion control, and recreation facilities. Other New Deal power projects included dams on the Columbia River in Oregon, on the Missouri River at Fort Peck, Montana, and the Grand Coulee Dam in Washington state.

The Works Progress Administration, one of the best known of the New Deal projects, did not begin until 1935, after the government had tried other systems for putting the unemployed to work. The WPA built airports, schools, highways, libraries, playgrounds, and parks and provided work projects for writers, musicians, artists, and actors. Between 1936 and 1941, an average of 2,000,000 workers per month earned an average monthly wage of $56. One of the many murals painted under this program (far right, below) depicts the concert given by Marian Anderson at the Lincoln Memorial in Washington, D.C., after she had been denied the right to sing in Constitution Hall.

NRA
MEMBER
U.S.
WE DO OUR PART

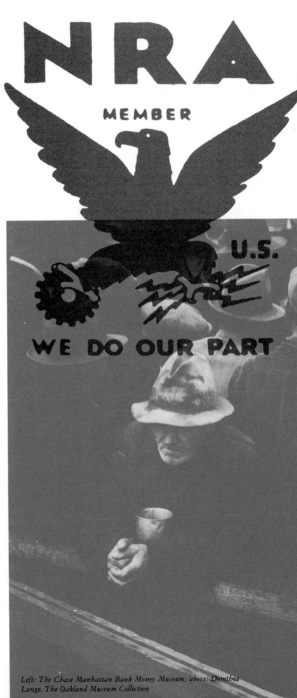

Left: The Chase Manhattan Bank Money Museum; above: Dorothea Lange, The Oakland Museum Collection

see Valley Authority

Library of Congress

The Agricultural Adjustment Act (AAA) sought to increase farmer income by paying him to decrease production, a move which also served to keep up the prices for what the farmer did produce. In 1936 the Supreme Court voided the Agricultural Adjustment Act of 1933, but Congress passed a substitute law which accomplished largely the same purposes while meeting the court's objections. In the meantime, the Roosevelt administration had turned some of its attention to helping a section of the farm population which did not receive checks for keeping land out of production—the poor tenants, sharecroppers, and migratory workers—and the farmers who held small acreages.

Designed to help the poorest farmers, the Farm Security Administration provided rehabilitation loans, camps for migrant laborers, and cooperative communities, and in many ways the agency had a useful if not notable impact. One project of the FSA, however, did leave a lasting impression—the photographic project. Under the direction of Roy Stryker, a small team of talented photographers took hundreds of thousands of pictures, creating an emotional documentary report on rural America during the Depression which conveys a human meaning that no statistics can. From the FSA collection at right, above, is Arthur Rothstein's famous dust bowl picture taken in Cimmaron County, Oklahoma. The other pictures here, by the late Dorothea Lange, show, below, a class-conscious sign in a gas station in Kern County California; right, below, two families from Missouri looking for work in California; and at far right, a migrant mother, about whom Miss Lange wrote: "She sits under a shelter on the edge of the pea fields, with no work because the crop froze. On this morning the family sold the tires from their automobile, for food."

Top: FSA Photograph by Arthur Rothstein, Library of Congress; all other pictures: FSA Photographs by Dorothea Lange, Library of Congress

Encouraged by a sympathetic Democratic administration and inspired by dynamic leadership, organized labor rose to prominence in the 1930s. The gain did not come, however, without bitter struggles, both within the labor movement and in conflicts with management. The new unions worked for gains in wages or shorter hours but particularly for the principles of the closed shop and exclusive representation in collective bargaining. Management of some of the industries, including some steel and auto companies, fought the unions with strikebreakers, lockouts, and aid from the local police. In one of the most violent strikes, at the Republic Steel Company in Chicago in 1937, police killed ten strikers and strike sympathizers. At left, police battle striking truck drivers in Minneapolis in 1937. Below, labor leader Walter Reuther comforts a fellow unionist beaten up in a struggle at the Ford Dearborn plant in 1937.

During the Roosevelt years Congress passed legislation which has benefited organized labor ever since. After the Supreme Court invalidated the NRA, important measures included the National Labor Relations Act and the Fair Labor Standards Act.

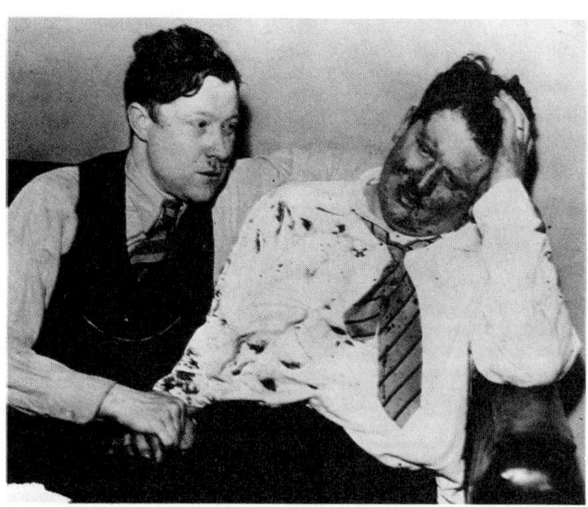

Left: The National Archives
Above: United Press International

Wide World Photos

The strain of the depression years, the years of World War II, and age itself all took their toll on Roosevelt. The photograph above was taken in 1933, shortly after his inauguration. The one below records the changes in his appearance as he campaigned for his fourth term as President in 1944. Less than six months later, on April 12, 1945, Roosevelt died of a stroke at Warm Springs, Georgia.

United Press International

Several writers attempted to deal specifically with the Depression, but most popular novelists seemed interested primarily in getting people's minds off their day-to-day troubles. In this class were Pearl Buck's *The Good Earth* (1931), a story set in China; *Gone with the Wind* by Margaret Mitchell (1936); and Kenneth Roberts's *Northwest Passage* (1937). Searching for happiness and contentment, millions of readers enjoyed such books as Walter B. Pitkin's *Life Begins at Forty* (1933), and Dale Carnegie's *How to Win Friends and Influence People* (1937). However, William Faulkner, Ellen Glasgow, and James T. Farrell all wrote powerful and relevant novels during the Depression years, and both Erskine Caldwell in *Tobacco Road* (1932) and John Steinbeck in *Grapes of Wrath* dealt meaningfully with the effect of harsh environments on people.

If people were discouraged and uncertain, they did not turn to religion for solace or direction. Both Protestant and Catholic churches added members, but growth was slow and much of the membership showed little interest. Speaking of traditional religious ideas, one young man said: "I believe these things but they don't take a large place in my life." People were more likely to listen to the radio on Sunday than to attend church. Frederick Lewis Allen concluded that "the shock of the Depression did not find the churches, by and large, able to give what people thought they needed."

Yet people continued to search for answers. Referring to social and economic reform, one youth declared in 1932: "If someone came along with a line of stuff in which I could really believe, I'd follow him pretty nearly anywhere." People wanted some brand of social salvation, but they were uncertain how to detect it or how to achieve it. The old certainties were gone. As Archibald MacLeish wrote: "We don't know—we can't say—we're wondering." Surveying college youth in 1936, *Fortune* magazine reported: "The present-day college generation is fatalistic . . . the investigator is struck by the dominant and pervasive color of a generation that will not stick its neck out. It keeps its shirt on, its pants buttoned, its chin up, and its mouth shut. . . . Security is the summum bonum of the present college generation." Yet despite rather widespread discouragement and uncertainty about the future, most Americans continued to believe that they could somehow solve their problems. A few people joined the Communist party, but plans to achieve social salvation outside the capitalistic system and by undemocratic means did not attract many adherents.

Minority Groups in the New Deal

Franklin D. Roosevelt showed greater interest in the welfare of blacks, Mexican-Americans, Indians, and other citizens who were outside the mainstream of American society than had any President up to his time. Not only did he personally sympathize with their second-class economic and social position, but Roosevelt brought numerous people into his administration who had a genuine concern about improving conditions among these groups. Harold Ickes, who had been president of the local NAACP chapter in Chicago, Rexford Tugwell, Harry Hopkins, officials in the Farm Security Administration, as well as Mrs. Roosevelt, were among the New Deal leaders who fought for the rights and welfare of underprivileged minorities.

Negroes suffered severely during the

Depression. Unemployment among blacks was about double that of whites, as white workers replaced blacks in even the lowest and most menial jobs. Blacks also frequently met discrimination in the distribution of relief. Moreover, the two central New Deal agencies designed to restore recovery, the NRA and the AAA, actually hurt rather than helped many blacks. The NRA codes did not really protect black workers because most of their jobs were not covered by wage and hour agreements. To many, NRA meant "Negroes Ruined Again." The AAA also hurt blacks throughout the rural South. As Southern landowners were paid to take land out of production, they dismissed thousands of farm tenants and sharecroppers, who often became day laborers or homeless migrants.

Some New Deal programs, however, provided new opportunities. About 200,000 black youths served in the CCC, although generally on a segregated basis, and many thousands received educational assistance through the NYA. The Resettlement Administration and the Farm Security Administration also helped many rural black families improve their position. But more important than specific programs was the fact that many blacks received responsible positions in the Roosevelt administration. For example, Robert L. Vann of Pittsburgh served as Special Assistant to the Attorney General and William H. Waite, Dean of the Howard University Law School, became Assistant Solicitor in the Department of the Interior. Some people even referred to Roosevelt's black advisers as the "Black Brains Trust."

The bonds of discrimination and segregation were not removed, though they were loosened during the New Deal years. Roosevelt was not an activist in extending Negro rights, but he did become a symbol for justice and equality. Consequently, Negroes rapidly shifted their political loyalty to Roosevelt and the Democratic party, to become an important part of the political coalition which elected Roosevelt again and again.

The Great Depression intensified the already unsatisfactory situation among America's Indian population. Designed to create independent farmers through allotments of individual land holdings, the Dawes Act of 1887 had failed miserably. In some cases Indians had sold their land; in other instances, holdings had become fragmented through inheritance. Without enough productive land, education, or job skills, thousands of Indians lived in poverty and disease. During the 1920s a number of reformers, notably John Collier, secretary of the Indian Defense Association, called for a new approach to Indian policy. Rather than trying to force Indians to adopt the ways of white men, he recommended preservation of Indian culture. In 1934 Congress passed the Wheeler-Howard Act, which provided ways to set up tribal self-government, to improve Indian economic life through loans to Indian business ventures, and to help educate Indian youth. However, this approach to Indian problems was at best only partially successful.

Migrant workers, often Mexican-Americans, constituted yet another group of underprivileged citizens who failed to make any substantial gains under the New Deal. Living always on the edge of disaster, these cotton, fruit, and vegetable pickers, who followed the harvest from one part of the country to the other, experienced difficult and often tragic times. Working for extremely low wages, living in places hardly fit for animals, and often unable to send their children to school, the migrants drifted about the country in search of enough work to maintain existence. Late in the 1930s the Farm Security Administration established migrant labor camps, which provided better housing and social facilities, but the program was completely inadequate to meet the needs of the people. Here was another group of hard-core poor which New Deal programs failed to reach.

Conclusion

Despite the large amount and variety of legislation enacted in the New Deal period, it required the impact of World War II to bring complete economic recovery to the United States. New Deal efforts to aid employment were partially successful at best. By 1939, after six years of New Deal programs, agricultural prices were still below parity; manufacturing production was slightly lower than a decade earlier; corporate profits had not reached the level of 1929; and unemployment still totaled about nine million. However, when 1939 is compared with 1932, advances could be noted in almost every aspect of economic life. Corporate profits were up; farm prices were higher; unemployment was less; and per capita income after taxes (in dollars of constant buying power) had risen from $679 in 1933 to $925 in 1939.

If the New Deal fell short of restoring full prosperity, it reestablished faith and confidence in the American system. Moreover, the reform measures were of fundamental importance. Labor benefited both from the right to bargain collectively as well as from minimum wages and maximum hours. New laws regulating banking and security sales protected bank depositors and investors. Electricity had been cheapened and introduced into millions of homes. Old age had been brightened by the prospect of social security.

Expansion of government functions and responsibilities was the most meaningful aspect of the New Deal. Although government powers had been growing for many years, they developed faster and in the direction of social welfare after 1933. The government intervened extensively in the economy to help the so-called little people in American society, especially farmers and workers. The expansion of government in business is best illustrated by TVA, but by 1941 there were some fifty New Deal corporations which could perform business functions. The growing role of all phases of government in the economy may be seen in the fact that local, state, and federal expenditures accounted for 14.5 percent of the gross national product in 1939, compared with only 3 percent a decade earlier.

By the eve of World War II Americans were living in a "mixed economy." Private enterprise continued to be the mainspring of economic activity, but government had assumed a type of partnership role in which it assumed responsibility for individual and national welfare. During the New Deal years, a majority of the electorate accepted the notion that the federal government was responsible for the general welfare and security of all Americans. Whether the trends established and enlarged during the 1930s were for good or evil, they produced fundamental and permanent modifications in American life and society.

Roosevelt's role in bringing about these changes had been crucial. His personal magnetism, his identification with millions of forgotten Americans, his skillful political leadership, and his ability to work with practical and possible alternatives were all important in achieving social and economic reform. The President was not always consistent, and he sometimes shifted his commitments in ways which were distressing to some of his supporters. But he moved within the American tradition of compromise and gradual change. Therein lay his strength—and perhaps the underlying reason for his success.

SUGGESTED READINGS

The best-balanced, but still incomplete, biography of F. D. Roosevelt is Frank Freidel's *Franklin D. Roosevelt* (1952–), three volumes of which had appeared by 1969. *The Lion and the Fox* (1956) by James M. Burns is a serious, well-researched study but rather critical of Roosevelt's leadership. E. E. Robinson is highly unfriendly to Roosevelt in *The Roosevelt Leadership* (1955). In *The Democratic Roosevelt* (1957), R. G. Tugwell has provided many unusual insights into Roosevelt's character and career. On Roosevelt's thought see D. R. Fusfeld's *The Economic Thought of Franklin D. Roosevelt and the Origins of the New Deal* (1956).

By far the most meaningful general survey of the New Deal is W. E. Leuchtenberg's *Franklin D. Roosevelt and the New Deal** (1963). The economic history of the period has been given detailed treatment by Broadus Mitchell in *Depression Decade* (1947), while Dixon Wecter has emphasized the social history of the period in *The Age of the Great Depression* (1948). In *Since Yesterday* (1940), F. L. Allen has provided an interesting but more impressionistic picture of society in the 1930s. One of the earliest and still useful surveys of the New Deal is Basil Rauch's *A History of the New Deal,* 1933–1938* (1944), which stresses the differences between the first and second New Deals. Beginning students will benefit greatly from the brief survey of Denis W. Brogan's *The Era of Franklin D. Roosevelt* (1950), and Dexter Perkins's *The New Age of Franklin D. Roosevelt,* 1932–1945* (1957). In *The Coming of the New Deal** (1958), A. M. Schlesinger, Jr., provides a detailed and stimulating account of the major issues during the first two years of the New Deal.

Many of Roosevelt's associates have written about the President and New Deal policies. Among the best accounts is that by Secretary of Labor Frances Perkins, *The Roosevelt I Knew* (1946); Raymon Moley's *After Seven Years* (1939), which is especially rich in detail on the early New Deal, as is Moley's later and more reflective *The First New Deal* (1966); and Samuel I. Rosenman's *Working with Roosevelt* (1952). The career of one controversial New Dealer has been traced by Bernard Sternsher in *Rexford Tugwell and the New Deal* (1964).

On the question of agriculture and farm relief see G. C. Fite's *George N. Peek and the Fight for Farm Parity* (1954); J. L. Shover's *Cornbelt Rebellion: The Farmers' Holiday Association* (1965); D. E. Conrad's *The Forgotten Farmers: The Story of Sharecroppers in the New Deal* (1964); and *Three Years of the Agricultural Adjustment Administration* (1937) by E. G. Nourse and others. For the role of some of the intellectuals in forming and implementing farm policy see R. S. Kirkendall's *Social Scientists and Farm Politics in the Age of Roosevelt* (1966).

Attempts to achieve business recovery have been given detailed treatment by L. S. Lyon and others in *The National Recovery Administration* (1935). The authors argue that the NRA may have retarded rather than stimulated recovery. H. S. Johnson's memoir, *The Blue Eagle from Egg to Earth* (1935), points up many of the problems and conflicts within the NRA. The confusing and sometimes contradictory attitudes and actions of the New Deal toward monopoly have been considered in *The New Deal and the Problem of Monopoly: A Study in Economic Ambivalence* (1966) by E. W. Hawley.

Among the best books on monetary and fiscal policies are G. G. Johnson, Jr.'s *The Treasury and Monetary Policy,* 1933–1938 (1939) and J. D. Paris's *Monetary Policies of the United States,* 1932–1938 (1938). A discussion of Keynesian influences is in *The Economics of John Maynard Keynes: The Theory of a Monetary Economy* (1948) by D D Dillard.

The basic work on federal relief is J. C. Brown's *Public Relief,* 1929–1939 (1940). D. S. Howard's *The WPA and Federal Relief Policy* (1943) is also excellent. Statistics on relief can be found in *Summary of Relief and Federal Work Program Statistics,*

1933–1940 (1941) by T. E. Whiting and T. J. Woofter, Jr. Help for America's youth has been discussed by B. G. and E. K. Lindley in *A New Deal for Youth: The Story of the National Youth Administration* (1938) and John A. Salmond's *The Civilian Conservation Corps, 1933–1942* (1967). Searle F. Charles has provided an excellent evaluation in *Minister of Relief: Harry Hopkins and the Depression* (1963).

George Wolfskill has written an excellent account of the growing political opposition to Roosevelt in *The Revolt of the Conservatives: A History of the American Liberty League, 1934–1940* (1962), while in *Congressional Conservatism and the New Deal* (1967), J. T. Patterson deals with the developing conservative coalition in Congress. Some of the best material on the election of 1936 can be found in D. R. McCoy's excellent biography of the Republican candidate, *Landon of Kansas* (1966), and *The Politics of Upheaval** (1960) by Arthur M. Schlesinger, Jr.

The shift in the New Deal toward greater emphasis on reform has been well covered in Schlesinger's *The Politics of Upheaval.* An excellent brief account can be found in Paul Conkin's *FDR and the Origins of the Welfare State** (1967). On social security see Paul H. Douglas's *Social Security in the United States* (1936); E. E. Witte's *Development of the Social Security Act* (1962); Lewis Meriam's *Relief and Social Security* (1966). Activities of the old-age groups can be followed in Abraham Holtzman's *The Townsend Movement: A Political Study* (1963). On Huey Long see H. T. Kane's *Louisiana Hayride: The American Rehearsal for Dictatorship, 1928–1940* (1941). Charles J. Tull provides a good account of the Detroit radio priest in *Father Coughlin and the New Deal* (1965).

F. R. Dulles' *Labor in America** (2d ed., 1961); Joseph Rayback's *A History of American Labor** (1959); and Philip Taft's *The A.F. of L. from the Death of Gompers to the Merger* (1959) contain useful chapters on labor during the New Deal period. The conflict within the labor movement has been well described by James V. Morris in *Conflict within the AFL: A Study of Craft versus Industrial Unionism, 1901–1938* (1959), and by J. Raymond Walsh in *C.I.O.: Industrial Unionism in Action* (1937). Two first-rate studies of agriculture in the later New Deal can be found in C. T. Schmidt's *American Farmers in the World Crisis* (1941) and Murray Benedict and Oscar Stine's *The Agricultural Commodity Programs: Two Decades of Experience* (1956). Sidney Baldwin's *Poverty and Politics: The Rise and Decline of the Farm Security Administration* (1968) shows how the New Deal failed to come to grips with the problems of the rural poor.

On the TVA see J. S. Ransmeier's *The Tennessee Valley Authority: A Case Study in the Economics of Multiple Purpose Stream Planning* (1942). W. H. Droze has dealt with the TVA in terms of resource planning in *High Dams and Slack Waters: TVA Rebuilds a River* (1965). An excellent but unsympathetic contemporary account of the controversy over Roosevelt's fight to change the Supreme Court is *The 168 Days* (1938) by Joseph Alsop and Turner Catledge. Trends in the Court after 1937 are analyzed by C. H Pritchett in *The Roosevelt Court* (1948).

On increased government expenditures, taxation, and the expanding role of government, see A. E. Burns and D. S. Watson's *Government Spending and Economic Expansion* (1940); L. H. Kimmel's *Federal Budget and Fiscal Policy, 1789–1958* (1959); Thomas P. Jenkins's *Reactions of Major Groups to Positive Government in the United States, 1930–1940* (1945); and Merle Fainsod and Lincoln Gordon's *Government and the American Economy* (rev. ed., 1948). The best account of the recession of 1937–1938 is *The Economics of Recession and Revival* (1954) by K. D. Roose. On the regulation of business see R. F. Debts's *The New Deal's SEC, 1933–1938* (1964). The concentration of business is explored by Robert A. Brady in *Business as a System of Power* (1943).

On society in the Depression see Wecter and Allen, cited above. Dealing with the quality of life in more detail is W. F. Ogburn (ed.), *Social Changes during the Depression and Recovery* (1935) and the more useful study by R. S. and H. M. Lynd, *Middletown in Transition** (1937), which carries their study of Muncie, Indiana, into the 1930s. The quality of life in the rural South can be followed in *Seven Lean Years* (1939) by T. J. Woofter and Ellen Winston, while Vance Johnson has told about conditions over much of the Great Plains in *Heaven's Table Land: The Dust Bowl Story* (1947). The position of the Negro in the New Deal period can be traced in Gunnar Myrdal's *An American Dilemma: The Negro Problem and Modern Democracy** (2 vols., 1944).

*indicates availability in paperback.

34

The Challenge of Global Politics: The 1930s

WHEN FRANKLIN D. ROOSEVELT entered the White House in March, 1933, events in Manchuria had already exploded the illusion of permanent peace. So promising had been the experience of the twenties, however, that not even the Japanese assault on Shanghai in 1932 could disturb the democracies' general faith in the world's peace structure. Unfortunately the peace which postwar Americans had accepted as their special dispensation had always been ephemeral, because that peace reflected less a general acceptance of the Versailles settlement (symbolic of the status quo) than the temporary weakness of the dissatisfied nations. But as long as no nation with power to compel a major Western response resorted to force, nothing could shatter the easy conclusion that all wars had been fought and all issues resolved. So completely did Britain, France, and the United States dominate the immediate postwar world that key American officials mistakenly attributed the globe's apparent stability to a universal acceptance of Western democratic leadership and Western notions of proper international behavior. Edwin L. James of the *New York Times* questioned this assumption in October, 1930: "America's great world political position is not due primarily to our moral leadership but primarily to our wealth and economic position. If we were a poor and weak nation the world would today care no more about what we thought than did the world before the Great War."

For both European and American proponents of peace and the status quo during the twenties, world opinion was the controlling element in international affairs. That opinion, they believed, would compel any would-be aggressor to limit change to what was peaceful. Still, they might have recalled the words of Lord Cecil, spoken in defense of the League of Nations Covenant in 1919: "For the most part there is no attempt to rely . . . upon force to carry out a decision of the Council or the Assembly of the League. . . . What we rely upon is public opinion . . . and if we are wrong about it, then the whole thing is wrong." Manchuria had demonstrated that the entire concept was wrong. But the illusion that opinion controlled the world and that it always favored peace had continued unchallenged for so long that Western leaders behaved as if their rhetoric of peaceful change was in itself a genuine barrier to war. "I cannot recall any time," declared Winston Churchill in 1932, "when the gap between the kind of words which statesmen used and what was actually happening in many countries was so great as it is now." The international crises of the thirties would merely demonstrate again and again the uselessness of any system that relied on the force of world opinion to maintain the peace.

Challenge of the Dictators

Even as Roosevelt led this nation through the famed First Hundred Days of 1933, Adolf Hitler was consolidating his power in Germany. Without the support of a powerful democratic tradition, the Weimar Republic, symbol of Germany's acceptance of the Versailles Treaty, could not answer the challenge of economic despair. President Paul von Hindenburg, in January, 1933, invited Hitler to become chancellor. Possessed of a powerful voice and an elite guard—the notorious *Schutz Staffel*—and preaching defiance of the Versailles arrangements, Hitler had built his National Socialist party into a political force formidable enough to undermine any German government that it opposed. The conservative industrialists, aristocrats, army officers, and editors who joined the Hitler march in an effort to control their country's future discovered too late that they had underestimated Hitler's passion for personal power. During the summer of 1934, following the death of Hindenburg, Hitler purged his party of its disloyal elements and established himself as dictator. He then moved to direct the considerable industrial might and energy of Germany toward the satisfaction of his ambitions. In his book *Mein Kampf* (My Struggle), published in 1924, Hitler had made clear his intention of tearing the Versailles Treaty to shreds. Whether he could fulfill his promises to the German people would depend on the response of England and France, the two chief guarantors of the status quo.

For two years after 1933 Hitler moved cautiously in foreign affairs while he consolidated his power and converted Germany into a highly nationalistic, totalitarian, anti-Semitic state. By 1935 he was prepared to challenge openly the existing military restrictions imposed on Germany at Versailles. On March 9 the German government announced its decision to build an air force. A week later Hitler, though assuring Europe of his peaceful intentions, informed the world that henceforth the German army would be based on national compulsory service and would be increased immediately to 550,000 men, over five times the number authorized by the Versailles

Treaty. Britain, having condemned Hitler for breaking the postwar treaty arrangements, sanctioned German rearmament beyond treaty limits by consenting to a German navy 35 percent the size of Britain's. Finally in March, 1936, Hitler sent German troops into the Rhineland, thus repudiating the Locarno Pact of 1925 and the Versailles clauses which had set Germany's western frontiers. France, lacking her former confidence, did not threaten retaliation. The League Council condemned the German violation of the treaty system but was unable to agree upon a concrete response.

Hitler's repeated and successful assaults on the Versailles system placed France in a difficult position. In an effort to maintain the balance of power in Europe, now endangered by Hitler's reforging of German power, France turned to the Soviet Union and signed a mutual assistance pact with the Kremlin in May, 1935. Since this accord antagonized France's Eastern European allies, notably Poland and Yugoslavia, France turned next to Italy.

During the twenties, Mussolini's domestic and foreign policies had been obnoxious, but by the mid-thirties Italy had again become a respectable member of the international community. Hitler's abortive attempt to annex Austria in July, 1934, sent a wave of fear through Italy, for the extension of German authority to the Brenner Pass appeared to be a genuine danger to Italian security. Hitler's Austrian venture threw Mussolini into contact with a fearful France and simultaneously provided him with an unparalleled opportunity for mischief-making without fear of direct Western retaliation. Taking his chances on collective security, Mussolini, in October, 1935, sent his black-shirted legions into Ethiopia. French Premier Pierre Laval nodded assent. Britain refused to countenance this aggression and forced sanctions against Italy through the League Council. But lacking French support, the British hesitated to push sanctions to the point most effective. Unaided by Western diplomacy on the one hand but unopposed by Western power on the other, Mussolini, armed with modern weapons and mustard gas, completed his conquest of Ethiopia.

During 1936 Britain and France, the sole European defenders of the Versailles system, finally paid the price for their indecision and disunity. Their refusal to prevent Italian aggression against a weak nation demonstrated the League's ineffectiveness; their refusal to recognize Mussolini's gains in Africa drove him into the arms of Hitler. When Hitler in July, 1936, extorted an agreement from the Austrian government which opened the way for Nazi penetration, Mussolini acquiesced and thus laid the foundation for the Rome-Berlin Axis, an alignment that French and British diplomacy had sought to prevent. The triumphant Italy now followed Japan and Germany out of the League. The great Western democracies, Hitler surmised clearly, would not defend the Versailles Treaty with policies that threatened their interest in peace. After 1936 it was Hitler's indulgence, not the will of the democracies, that sustained European stability.

Isolationism at High Tide

Clearly the challenge of the European dictators was too extensive to be ignored or dismissed by the United States. Yet if President Roosevelt detected the aggressive designs of Hitler and Mussolini during his first term, he refused to exert any effective diplomatic leadership to control them. Whatever his earlier identification with Wilsonian internationalism, he had, under extreme isolationist pressure, avoided questions of foreign commitment during his victorious campaign. After March, 1933, Roosevelt's public statements reassured an isolationist America of his determination to avoid war. As late as October 2, 1935, he promised the American people that whatever happened abroad, the United States would "remain unentangled and free." The Roosevelt foreign policy constituted no break with the immediate past, for neither his words nor his actions included any precise definition of United States interests or any concern with means to defend the American stake in the Versailles system. Norman Davis warned the delegates at Geneva that the United States would not commit itself "to use its armed forces for the settlement of any dispute anywhere."

Roosevelt's recognition of the Soviet Union in November, 1933, evinced new attitudes toward Moscow's Bolshevik regime but no commitment to European politics. Joseph Stalin, in a move which made the post-Lenin Soviet regime more acceptable in the West, had gradually downgraded the Marxist-Leninist notion of "world revolution." The specter of Bolshevik terror had not been entirely erased from Western minds, but somehow it no longer seemed so frightful as before. There were also practical reasons for bringing Russia fully into the family of nations. Businessmen thought they saw in a friendly Russia possibilities for commerce. Diplomats hoped that a Soviet Union active in world councils might serve as a counterweight to German and Japanese aggressiveness. For all these reasons, Roosevelt in October, 1933, communicated to the Kremlin his desire to discuss the question of diplomatic recognition. It was quickly accomplished. A Soviet representative, Maxim Litvinov, arrived shortly in Washington prepared to pledge that the Kremlin would "refrain from interfering in any manner in the internal affairs of the United States." A month later, Roosevelt announced the establishment—after some sixteen years—of United States diplomatic relations with the Soviet Union.

Roosevelt's so-called Good Neighbor policy meant a further improvement in relations between the United States and Latin America. Already under Hoover the United States had returned to its traditional policy of recognizing *de facto* governments in Latin America, whatever their methods of achieving and maintaining power. In the spring of 1931 Secretary of State Stimson ordered United States marines out of Nicaragua and prepared to terminate the American occupation of Haiti. FDR merely enlarged this trend toward anti-imperialism and mutual respect, launching his Good Neighbor policy in his first inaugural address. "In the field of world policy," he declared, "I would dedicate this nation to the policy of the good neighbor—the neighbor who . . . respects his obligations and respects the sanctity of his agreements in and with a world of neighbors." In subsequent speeches the President made clear that American obligations under the Monroe Doctrine were limited to hemispheric defense. Secretary of State Cordell Hull, who represented the United States at the Pan-American Conference at Montevideo in 1933, reaffirmed the doctrine of "hands off." With obvious enthusiasm he supported a Montevideo Declaration asserting that "no state has the right to intervene in the internal or external affairs of another." True to his pledge, Roosevelt refused to sanction the dispatch of American troops to stabilize Cuban internal conditions in 1933 during another of the island's many revolutions, despite a number of precedents and much advice to do so. In May, 1934, Sumner Welles negotiated a treaty with the *de facto* Cuban government, extending full American recognition of its national sovereignty. Three months later, United States troops were withdrawn from the soil of Cuba's neighbor Haiti.

During 1934 congressional isolationists moved to the center of the stage. The thicker the clouds heralding the coming storm in Europe, the more the American people, through their representatives in Congress, sought to insulate themselves from its effects. The first in a series of isolationist measures passed by Congress was the Johnson Act of 1934. This measure forbade United States citizens or corporations from lending money to, or buying securities from, any foreign government which was in default on its debts to the United States.

Congressional isolationists next disposed of the World Court issue. During the Hoover years, Elihu Root, with the cooperation of the League Council, had devised the "Root Formula," whereby, if the United States joined the World Court, it would gain equal right with League members to oppose advisory opinions and to withdraw from the Court if its demands were denied. For several years isolationists kept the plan in committee while the Court itself, because of its conservative decisions, became increasingly unrealistic and unpopular. Then in January, 1935, Roosevelt submitted the Root proposal to the Senate, where the top-heavy Democratic majority promised the needed two-thirds majority. Before the Senate could vote, however, the nation's isolationist forces closed in. Father Charles E. Coughlin, Detroit's ultra-isolationist "radio priest," urged his listeners to warn their senators against Court membership; William Randolph Hearst advised his readers: "The way to keep America out of the League of Nations trap . . . is to keep America out of the League Court. Telegraph your senators." The resulting cascade of letters and telegrams apparently changed some senatorial minds. By 7 votes the United States declined to enter the World Court.

The year 1935 brought Congressional isolationists their supreme triumph of the decade. The stage was well set. In early 1934 two disturbing books, Helmuth C. Engelbrecht's *Merchants of Death* and George Seldes's *Iron, Blood, and Profits,* "proved" what many Americans had long believed: that American involvement in the First World War had come about because of pressures from financiers and manufacturers of munitions who feared for their investments and profits if Britain and France should fall.

The Senate, disturbed by such exposés, in April ordered an inquiry into the matter of war profits, placing at the head of the investigating committee Senator Gerald P. Nye of North Dakota. Nye's Munitions Investigating Committee, during a period of almost two years, published seven reports totaling 1,400 pages. The testimony on the period of the First World War revealed a pattern of lobbying, questionable business practices, and huge wartime profits. The evidence was almost wholly circumstantial and by no means proved that Woodrow Wilson had been the dupe of avaricious bankers and manufacturers. But in the atmosphere of the middle thirties, with the reputation of businessmen in eclipse and with Hitler and Mussolini threatening the peace of Europe, the lessons of history seemed clear enough.

From Nye's discoveries millions of Americans, including members of Congress, concluded that merely to secure the profits of a few "merchants of death" the United States had entered into a costly and unnecessary war.

In April, 1935, Senator Nye introduced in the Senate a set of resolutions designed to keep the United States out of the next European war. After a tortuous legislative history, the Neutrality Act of 1935 emerged from the congressional mill. It was thought that the concept of an impartial arms embargo, plus the restrictions on wartime travel which the bill contained, would eliminate precisely those pressures which had undermined American neutrality in the days of Wilson. Although President Roosevelt would have preferred a measure requiring an arms embargo only against aggressors, the administration reluctantly accepted this formula for guaranteeing the nation's peace. Roosevelt promptly invoked the Neutrality Act against both parties in the Ethiopian war, but many commodities not within its purview, such as oil, continued to flow into Italy. In 1936 Congress again rejected Roosevelt's request for a discretionary embargo, choosing instead to extend the life of existing legislation and to extend its prohibition to loans and credits.

The ink was scarcely dry on the documents effecting the new neutrality legislation before the concept of neutrality was put to the test. In July, 1936, a revolt by army chiefs under the leadership of Francisco Franco in Spanish Morocco developed into a general struggle for control of the central Spanish government at Madrid. In the protracted civil war which followed, a number of European powers became involved—Hitler's Germany and Mussolini on the side of the Franco rebels, Russia on the part of the duly elected Madrid government. Great Britain and France aided the International Nonintervention Committee in London.

The government of the United States pursued a dual objective—to protect American neutrality and to limit the civil war to Spanish territory. Roosevelt persistently viewed the conflict not as a rebel assault on a legitimate government but as a war between two belligerents. He was thus permitted to announce a moral embargo of munitions to both sides. When American exporters demanded the right to ship arms to the Madrid Loyalists, Congress extended the Neutrality Law to include the Spanish Civil War. The effect of American neutrality was to deny the Loyalists needed arms—Hitler and Mussolini gave Franco not only weapons but also fighter pilots and planes—and thus, in a negative way, to contribute to their defeat.

Even as the Spanish Civil War raged, Congress was busy perfecting its neutrality program. Previous acts had not touched the issue of wartime trade in noncontraband goods. The Third Neutrality law of May, 1937, gave the President discretionary power to prohibit the export of nonmilitary goods to belligerents unless paid for in advance and carried in foreign ships. Neutrality legislation now prohibited the export of arms and munitions to belligerents after the President found a state of war existing; it permitted the sale of nonmilitary equipment only on a cash-and-carry arrangement. It was also illegal to make loans to belligerents or for Americans to travel on the ships of warring nations. Many Americans believed that these laws would protect them from becoming involved in another overseas conflict. The neutrality laws represented isolationism at high tide.

Whether the American people chose to read the signs of the times or not, the world of 1937 was clearly on the road to war. The Civil War in Spain, except for the limited involvement of Mussolini and Hitler, was an internal affair which threatened the destruction of an elected government but not necessarily the stability of Europe. Unfortunately events in China permitted no such easy rationalization. On July 7, 1937, Japanese forces clashed with Chinese units at the Marco Polo Bridge, several miles west of Peking. Within six months they had occupied Peking, Shanghai, Nanking, Canton, and Hankow. China's President, Chiang Kai-shek, having transferred his capital to Chungking in China's far west, adamantly refused to yield. Chinese Communists in the north under Mao Tse-tung, increasingly adept at guerrilla warfare, prevented Japanese successes in the hinterland which they controlled. Japan was thus trapped in a war which she could not decisively win but from which she dared not retreat. At stake in the Sino-Japanese War was not only the established balance of power in the Orient but also the treaty arrangements which had permitted an uneasy coexistence between American and Japanese objectives in China. Japan's assault on China left Washington only two realistic choices. The United States could either accept changes in the Far East at China's expense or face a rapid deterioration in American-Japanese relations, possibly ending in war.

Cordell Hull responded to the Japanese challenge with uniquely American procedures, which conveyed the notion of resistance but which actually avoided all responsibility for dealing with specific infringements on the established treaty structure. His statement of principles, announced on July 16, 1937, embodied the essence of United States official policy toward change. "We advocate," he said, "adjustments of problems in international relations by processes of peaceful negotiation and agreement. We advocate faithful observance of international agreements. Upholding the principle of the sanctity of treaties, we believe in modification of provisions of treaties, when need therefore arises, by orderly processes carried out in a spirit of mutual helpfulness and accommodation." Unfortunately, Hull's principles, as a guide for national policy, were scarcely helpful. His insistence that change must rest only on mutual agreement meant in practice that there could be no change. Such an approach to world affairs served the interests of the "have" powers magnificently, inasmuch as it placed all legitimacy in international conflict on the side of those who possessed what they wanted. But it presented the "have-not" nations with the extreme choice of either accepting the status quo or defying it without benefit of negotiation or compromise.

For a time in 1937 it appeared that President Roosevelt would break new ground. His "Quarantine Speech," delivered at Chicago on October 5, contained phraseology which struck terror into the hearts of isolationists. For the first time the President openly recognized the existence of war and suggested that peace-loving nations quarantine aggressors as they would an epidemic. "The peace-loving nations," he said, "must make a concerted effort in opposition to those violations of treaties . . . which today are creating a state of international anarchy and instability from which there is no escape through mere isolation or neutrality." Editors and politicians took seriously this apparent appeal for sanctions. The *Wall Street Journal* had apoplexy, advising the President: "Stop foreign meddling; America wants peace." Such fears assumed a dramatic shift in the nation's official outlook when no such assumption was warranted. In his address Roosevelt named no specific interests which the nation would defend. Like Hull, he condemned "aggressors," not because they wanted what they did not have, but because they chose to employ force to gain their objectives. At his subsequent press conference, newsmen pointed to the discrepancy between Roosevelt's veiled threat to aggressors and his official adherence to the Neutrality Act. Under pressure, the President admitted that he had devised no concrete plan of action for halting any aggression anywhere.

Nevertheless, within the limits imposed on him by American isolationist sentiment, Roosevelt searched for some course of action through which he might exert a leadership commensurate with American power and responsibility. In January, 1938, belatedly responding to a suggestion of Undersecretary of State Sumner Welles, the President proposed to Hull that the major powers invite representatives of nine minor nations to draw up an agreement which might answer the Axis demands. Hull agreed, but the new British Prime Minister, Neville Chamberlain, was determined to pursue his own course in European affairs and rejected the Roosevelt plan. Chamberlain hoped that by recognizing the Axis efforts to terminate the injustices of the Versailles Treaty, even at the expense of several small European states, he might keep Hitler's and Mussolini's ambition within reasonable bounds. Chamberlain's policy of appeasement might have succeeded had the dictators not seen every Western concession as cowardice rather than a sincere effort to sustain peace.

Symptomatic of the difficulties Roosevelt faced in his fitful attempt to establish the American Presidency as a force for peace and stability in the world was the reintroduction in 1938 of the Ludlow Resolution. Sponsored by Representative Louis Ludlow of Indiana, this proposed amendment to the Constitution stated that, except in the event of actual invasion of the United States or its territories, the question of war should be submitted to a national referendum. Roosevelt, in a letter to the Speaker of the House on January 6, warned that such a measure would render the President impotent in his conduct of the nation's foreign relations and do a great disservice to American security. Representative Hamilton Fish of New York expressed the isolationist position when he declared that Congress "could do nothing better or greater for world peace than to give the American people the right to vote to stay out of war." White House pressure defeated the Ludlow Amendment in the House, but not without a struggle and by only 21 votes, eloquent testimony to the isolationist sentiment in Congress.

German Expansionism

Facing no determined opposition in the West, Hitler stripped his Ministry and officer corps of their cautious elements and prepared for his final challenge to the territorial provisions of the Versailles Treaty. Chancellor Kurt Schuschnigg of Austria, although he was under German pressure, refused to appoint an Austrian Nazi to a key cabinet post, and called instead for an immediate Austrian plebiscite on the question of union with Germany. Thereupon Hitler forcefully annexed that country, the land of his birth, to Germany. This, the so-called *Anschluss,* was announced on March 12, 1938. France, in the throes of a cabinet crisis, was not prepared to respond. For Chamberlain in London the consolidation of two German populations was not unreasonable. Washington kept studiously quiet.

Hitler immediately planned his next move—the annexation of some three million Sudeten Germans assigned to Czechoslovakia by the Versailles Treaty. While Nazi agitators churned the pro-German emotions of the Sudetenland, the Czech government, backed by a good army and a strong Czech nationalism, prepared to fight. Chamberlain, unsure of Russian and French support, had no interest in committing British forces to the defense of Czechoslovakia. At Munich, a place-name which would become synonymous with appeasement, Chamberlain on September 30, 1938, gave away vital Czech territory, extracting from Hitler in exchange certain unenforceable guarantees for Czech minorities in the territory. On October 5, Roosevelt expressed to Chamberlain his "hope and belief that there exists today the greatest opportunity in years for the establishment of a new order based on justice and on law." Such was the hope. In fact, Nazi Germany's annexation of the Sudetenland inaugurated a reign of terror which swept into the heart of Czechoslovakia. Long before March, 1939, when Hitler's armies added this Slavic nation to the Third Reich, Czech resistance had been totally destroyed. Czechoslovakia thus became the West's first sacrifice to peace.

Throughout the critical year that followed the *Anschluss* of Austria, Hull continued to condemn international lawlessness and reminded the aggressor nations that their leaders, too, had signed the Kellogg Peace Pact. To the end of 1938 Hull and Roosevelt refused to face the implications of Hitler's acts. In his message of January, 1939, the President pointed to both the continued buildup of German power and the refusal of the dictators to negotiate reasonably with the democracies. Again he hinted at possible sanctions against disturbers of world peace. He admitted freely that the United States had no desire to use force, but he suggested that "there are many methods short of war, but stronger and more effective than mere words, of bringing home to aggressor governments the aggregate sentiments of our own people." Once more the President was searching for a means to bridge the gap between American isolationism and the requirements of a policy which could maintain peace. What he wanted, he said, was a revision of the neutrality laws before a possible outbreak of war in Europe would force him to invoke a national embargo to the detriment of the victims of aggression. He continued to worry about the peace of Europe. In mid-April, 1939, after the German seizure of Czechoslovakia had ushered in a new period of rising tensions, Roosevelt appealed to both Hitler and Mussolini to bring their problems to the negotiating table. The Italian government ignored, and Berlin ridiculed, the President's overture.

Congressional isolationists, detecting in that spring of 1939 a tendency toward foreign involvement which the neutrality program had been designed to forestall, fought bitterly to keep the policy of enforced neutrality in operation. Such Republican leaders as Senators Robert A. Taft of Ohio and Arthur H. Vandenberg of Michigan, joined by former Presi-

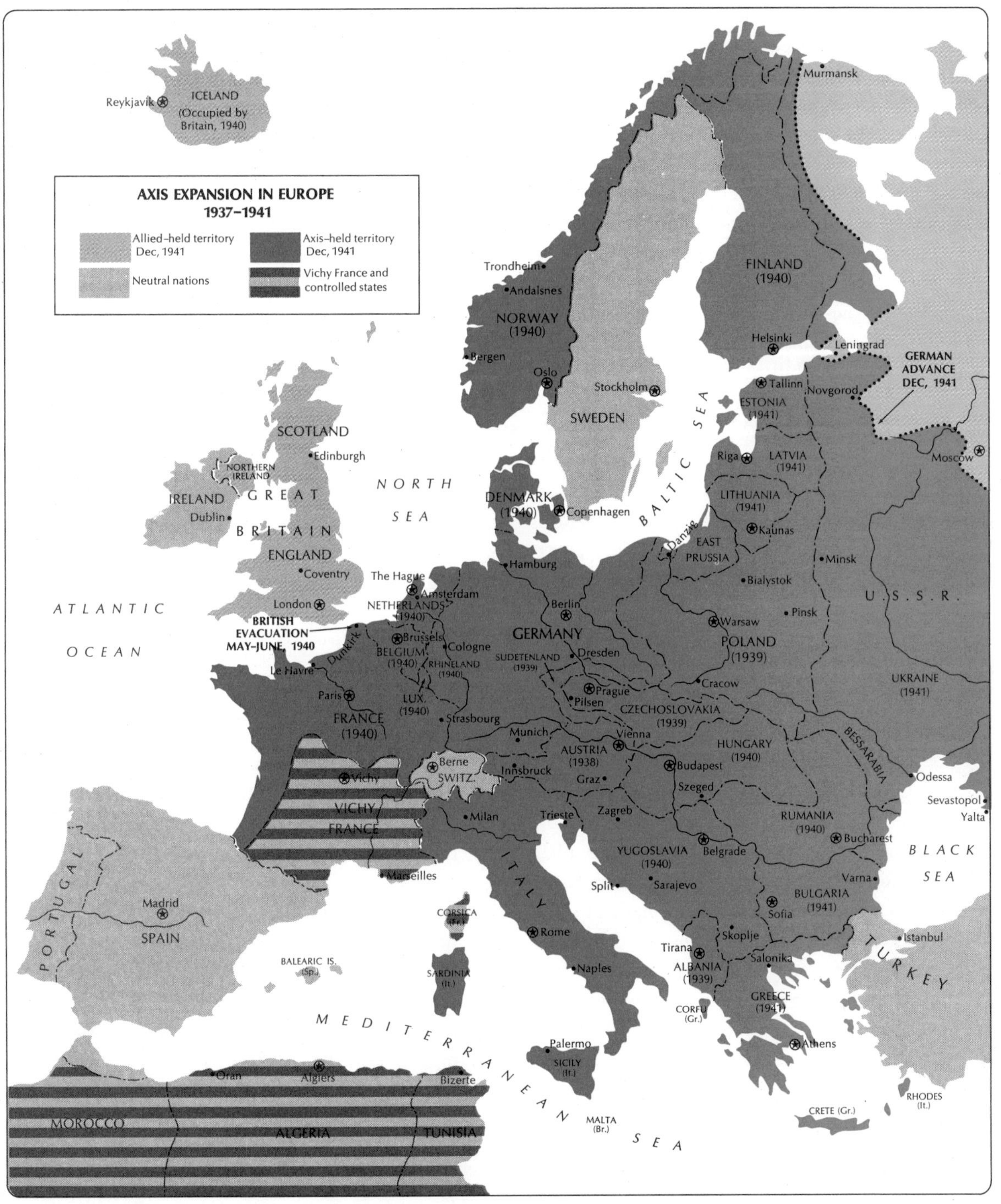
AXIS EXPANSION IN EUROPE
1937–1941
Allied-held territory Dec, 1941
Axis-held territory Dec, 1941
Neutral nations
Vichy France and controlled states
ICELAND (Occupied by Britain, 1940)
Reykjavik
Murmansk
Trondheim
Andalsnes
NORWAY (1940)
Bergen
Oslo
Stockholm
SWEDEN
FINLAND (1940)
Helsinki
Leningrad
GERMAN ADVANCE DEC, 1941
Tallinn
Novgorod
ESTONIA (1941)
Riga
LATVIA (1941)
Moscow
LITHUANIA (1941)
Kaunas
SCOTLAND
Edinburgh
NORTHERN IRELAND
IRELAND
Dublin
GREAT BRITAIN
ENGLAND
Coventry
London
NORTH SEA
DENMARK (1940)
Copenhagen
BALTIC SEA
Danzig
EAST PRUSSIA
Minsk
Bialystok
Hamburg
The Hague
Amsterdam
NETHERLANDS (1940)
Berlin
Warsaw
Pinsk
U.S.S.R.
ATLANTIC OCEAN
BRITISH EVACUATION MAY-JUNE, 1940
Dunkirk
Brussels
BELGIUM (1940)
Cologne
RHINELAND (1940)
GERMANY
SUDETENLAND (1939)
Dresden
POLAND (1939)
Le Havre
Paris
LUX. (1940)
Prague
Pilsen
Cracow
UKRAINE (1941)
FRANCE (1940)
Strasbourg
CZECHOSLOVAKIA (1939)
Munich
Vienna
AUSTRIA (1938)
HUNGARY (1940)
BESSARABIA
Berne
SWITZ.
Innsbruck
Budapest
Odessa
Vichy
Graz
Szeged
Sevastopol
Yalta
VICHY FRANCE
Milan
Trieste
Zagreb
RUMANIA (1940)
Bucharest
BLACK SEA
Belgrade
YUGOSLAVIA (1940)
Marseilles
ITALY
Split
Sarajevo
Varna
BULGARIA (1941)
Sofia
Madrid
SPAIN
PORTUGAL
CORSICA (Fr.)
Rome
Skoplje
Istanbul
Tirana
TURKEY
ALBANIA (1939)
Salonika
BALEARIC IS. (Sp.)
SARDINIA (It.)
Naples
CORFU (Gr.)
GREECE (1941)
MEDITERRANEAN SEA
Athens
Palermo
SICILY (It.)
Oran
Algiers
Bizerte
RHODES (It.)
CRETE (Gr.)
MALTA (Br.)
MOROCCO
ALGERIA
TUNISIA

The Challenge of Global Politics: The 1930s

dent Hoover and historian Charles A. Beard, argued for the concept of "fortress America." Taft declared that the United States was in no danger of attack, for Hitler could not dispose of his enemies even in Europe. While the debates raged in Congress, the President, according to some reports, insisted before the Senate Committee on Military Affairs that the frontier of America was on the Rhine. Although he publicly condemned these reports as "a deliberate lie," the damage had been done. When Key Pittman, serving as administration spokesman, introduced a bill to repeal the arms embargo and place all goods on a cash-and-carry basis, so powerful was the opposition that Pittman could not even bring the measure out of committee. The President used to the full his powers of persuasion, declaring at a White House conference that the repeal of the arms embargo might actually deter the Axis from a possible attack on the West. Isolationist Senator Borah replied that he had superior sources of information which assured him that Europe was in no danger of war. The votes for repeal could not be secured. Congress adjourned on August 5 without taking action.

Perhaps it mattered little. On August 23 Hitler purchased needed Russian neutrality with a nonaggression pact. Unable to rely on the West for defense against Hitler, Stalin had bought time to improve his western defenses. In the bargain he gained German recognition of a Soviet sphere of influence in Latvia, Estonia, Finland, and Eastern Poland. Now Hitler, having neutralized Russia in the east, was free to venture elsewhere. Late in August he demanded British cooperation in compelling Poland to satisfy German territorial demands by negotiation When Warsaw rejected a German ultimatum, on September 1, 1939, Hitler sent his *Panzer* divisions swarming into Poland. Thereupon, Britain and France reluctantly declared war on Germany. American neutrality now faced its ultimate test.

The Decline of American Neutrality

On September 3, 1939, President Roosevelt framed his official response to the outbreak of war in Europe. "This nation will remain a neutral nation," he assured the American people, "but I cannot ask that every American remain neutral in thought as well. Even a neutral cannot be asked to close his mind or his conscience." At the same time he promised that, within the limits of his power, there would "be no blackout of peace in the United States." Already the President had placed the nation's isolationist hopes on the altar of its preference for an Allied victory. From the outbreak of war every presidential response conformed relentlessly to the one overriding objective of somehow preventing the Nazi conquest of Europe. It was ultimately Roosevelt's refusal to accept a British defeat that placed United States policy on its course of total commitment to the struggle for Europe. What varied after September, 1939, were merely the American policies and resources demanded by a final Allied victory.

Initially Roosevelt looked to the country's defenses. He prodded the nations of the Western Hemisphere to call a conference, which met at Panama on September 23, 1939. This conference, in one dramatic move, adopted the Declaration of Panama, which established a 300-mile zone around the hemisphere, excluding Canada and other undisputed possessions of the European countries. This zone was designated off limits to marauding vessels of any non-American belligerent. Time would demonstrate, however, that nations can more easily declare a defense zone than patrol it.

The President next renewed his assault on the neutrality laws. Appealing to the nation's isolationist sentiment, he assured a special session of Congress in September that a repeal of the embargo would guarantee the peace of the United States better than the existing legislation. Following six weeks of vigorous debate and backstage maneuvering, Congress on November 2 voted for repeal. The instrument of repeal, the Neutrality Act of 1939, authorized exports of arms and munitions to the belligerents on a cash-and-carry basis. The restrictions of the 1937 act on loans and travel remained in effect. The new act was nondiscriminatory: in theory all belligerents were permitted to buy arms in the United States provided they paid cash and carried the goods in their own ships. However, Great Britain's control of the sea meant that Germany and Italy would not benefit from the new legislation. Only Britain and France stood to gain. America would thus once more become the arsenal of democracy.

For six months the apparent contradiction between the goal of increased Allied trade and the avoidance of conflict was scarcely apparent, for in the absence of any Nazi thrusts against Western Europe the price of Allied success seemed limited enough. Then early in 1940 Hitler's *Wehrmacht* invaded Denmark and Norway. Denmark's fall made the future of her two possessions, Iceland and Greenland, a matter of deep American concern. In May, 1940, the United States opened a consulate on Greenland to better observe developments in the northern Atlantic. That month the British occupied Iceland. During May the German *Blitzkrieg* struck Holland and Belgium and pushed the British forces stationed on the Continent against the coast at Dunkirk, where they were rescued in a miraculous evacuation. The German armed forces had revealed their awesome power. Mussolini, moreover, was chafing to enter the war and reap the rewards of an easy Axis victory. This Washington was powerless to prevent. Perhaps the threat of an American declaration of war might have influenced the Italian *Duce,* but neither Roosevelt nor the American people were prepared for such drastic action.

On June 10, 1940, five days after German tanks smashed into France and on the same day Mussolini declared war on that tottering nation, Roosevelt, speaking to a graduation ceremony at the University of Virginia, irrevocably committed the United States to an Allied victory. America was convinced, he said, "that military and moral victory for the gods of force and hate would endanger the institutions of democracy in the Western world, and that equally, therefore, the whole of our sympathies lies with those nations that are giving their life blood in combat against these forces." The United States, he declared, would pursue two courses. It would extend to the "opponents of force" this nation's material resources, and it would harness and speed up the use of these resources so that the United States would be prepared to meet any emergency. Roosevelt's Charlottesville speech established American purpose; subsequent events alone could determine the means required to achieve it.

On June 13, the day before German troops entered Paris, causing the French government to transfer to Bordeaux, Premier Paul Reynaud appealed to Roosevelt: "The only chance of saving the French nation, vanguard of democracies, and through her to save England . . . is to throw into the balance, this very day the weight of American power." Winston Churchill, now Prime Minister of England, urged the President a day later, "A declaration that the United States will if necessary enter the war might save France." Such a declaration Roosevelt could not, or would not, make. He had committed the material resources of the United States to Allied victory; without congressional approval he could not commit manpower. But what Roosevelt could achieve with executive action he would do. In September, 1940, he negotiated an agreement whereby the United States transferred to England fifty surplus destroyers, in return for bases on British territory in the Americas. This executive agreement brought to an end the period of American neutrality. By giving Britain the wherewithal to combat German submarines, the United States was declaring in unmistakable terms its support of England in the war against Germany.

Even so, every new crisis in Europe seemed to widen the chasm in American opinion between isolationism and interventionism. One group of interventionists, led by editor William Allen White of Kansas, formed the Committee to Defend America by Aiding the Allies. By July, 1940, this organization had three hundred branches, and by the end of the year the Century Group of the New York chapter was advocating the immediate declaration of war on Germany. Leading isolationists exerted their influence through the America First Committee. Beginning in September, 1940, as a decidedly conservative movement, the America First Committee advocated the building of an impregnable Western Hemisphere defense system as the most hopeful means of avoiding involvement in the broils of Europe. It soon attracted the support of most pro-German or anti-British elements in the country, including the Ku Klux Klan and Father Coughlin's Christian Front. The committee had Colonel Charles A. Lindbergh, Jr., the noted American aviator, as its leading spokesman. In a series of influential speeches, beginning as early as 1939, Lindbergh argued that this nation's destiny and interests could be served better at home than in Europe and that the policy of aiding the Allies would lead the United States into war and disaster. Meanwhile Roosevelt pursued his own course, using the power and influence of his office to extend the nation's commitment to Britain as she faced Germany alone.

By nominating Wendell Willkie in 1940, the Republican party foreclosed any effective interparty debate on the question of foreign involvement. Early in the campaign Willkie, chief executive of a large utilities corporation, criticized Roosevelt's pro-British attitudes and actions. "If his promise to keep our boys out of foreign wars is no better than his promise to balance the budget," he warned, "they're already almost on the transports." Yet Willkie took a strong internationalist position and favored aid to England. For his part, Roosevelt insisted that he had no intention of carrying the United States into war. On November 2, for example, he promised a Buffalo audience: "Your President says this country is not going to war." Throughout the campaign of 1940 both candidates remained well within the American consensus; both favored aid to Britain while denying that such a program was a commitment to war. This general agreement on policy permitted the President, despite Republican accusations that he was edging the country toward war, to sustain his personal quest for an ultimate British victory. Some

Democrats objected to Roosevelt's violation of the third-term tradition, but conditions seemed too critical to "swap horses in midstream." Roosevelt won by nearly five million votes, and the Democrats retained a strong majority in Congress.

From Aid to Full Commitment

On December 8, 1940, Britain's Prime Minister Winston S. Churchill solemnly informed the newly reelected American President that Britain's heavy purchases of arms and munitions in the United States had exhausted English monetary resources. The doughty Churchill, son of an American mother, expressed confidence that America would find the means to sustain Britain's war effort. A new concept in aid, lend-lease, was FDR's response to Churchill's plea. In lend-lease, Roosevelt discovered a formula which, while relieving Britain's financial difficulties, was still acceptable to the vast majority of Americans. In his annual message of January 6, 1941, he declared bluntly that the nation's security had never been more seriously threatened. Reminding Congress that the United States was committed to both a victory of the democratic cause and the security of the United States, he reiterated his claim that increased aid to England was the best means for America to avoid active belligerency. "They do not need manpower," he said of the British. "They do need billions of dollars' worth of the weapons of defense." Since Great Britain did not have billions of dollars to pay, such weapons would have to be leased.

For two months Congress debated the President's proposal incorporated in H.R. 1776; at issue was the whole question of the nation's future relationship to the European war. Outside Congress the America First Committee condemned the heavy financial commitment embodied in the proposed program, but to no avail. On March 11, 1941, Congress passed the Lend-Lease Act by a substantial margin, stipulating only that Britain take sole responsibility for the transportation of American goods across the Atlantic. The new law gave the President the power to procure articles of defense and "to sell, transfer title to, exchange, lease, lend, or otherwise dispose" of them to any country "whose defense the President deems vital to the defense of the United States." This was lend-lease. By placing control of war production in the hands of the federal government, it converted the nation fully into "the arsenal of democracy."

Great Britain now had almost unlimited access to America's industrial resources. One problem remained—that of guaranteeing delivery of American production to Britain in the face of the increasing effectiveness of German submarine warfare. During the spring of 1941, the President committed the United States to a final pro-British measure short of actual American belligerency. In April he informed Churchill that the United States would unilaterally extend its Atlantic security zone to the line of 25° west longitude. The United States, the President promised, would now use its aircraft and naval vessels to patrol the Atlantic from bases in Greenland, Newfoundland, the United States, Bermuda, and the West Indies. In his message announcing the new policy to the nation, Roosevelt concluded by proclaiming the existence of an "unlimited national emergency."

The undeclared war in the Atlantic brought

United States vessels increasingly into direct conflict with German submarines. The U.S.S. *Greer* was fired upon and returned fire in September, 1941. In October the destroyer U.S.S. *Kearny* took a torpedo in her side. Later that month the U.S.S. *Reuben James,* while escorting a convoy west of Ireland, was struck by a torpedo; she sank with all hands. An aroused Roosevelt took to the air on October 27 and committed the United States to the total destruction of Nazi power.

The fulfillment of that pledge still required a declaration of war, and Congress was in a resistant mood. Only a major crisis could bring that body to accept total involvement. It remained for events in the Pacific to destroy what remained of isolationism's moral and political influence on national policy.

Crisis in the Pacific

United States–Japanese relations had in the four years since the incident at Marco Polo Bridge gone from bad to worse. A serious clash had been averted in 1937 when Tokyo offered apologies and an indemnity for the damages and loss of life incurred when Japanese aircraft sank the American gunboat *Panay* on the Yangtze River in China. Japan, its armies now deep in China, declared the Open Door "inapplicable" to Asian conditions and in 1938 proclaimed a "New Order" in the Far East, which rejected former treaty arrangements outright and asserted Japanese hegemony in Chinese and Asian affairs. Secretary Hull repeatedly reminded Tokyo that it too had signed the treaties which established the existing order in the Far East and was therefore no less obligated than the United States to honor them. The United States, Hull made clear, would not recognize unilaterally proclaimed "New Orders."

The vulnerability of the Japanese economy to economic coercion by the United States gave Washington a powerful diplomatic weapon. Yet economic sanctions were never systematically enforced before 1941. During the summer of 1938 the State Department inaugurated an informal, but rather effective, embargo on the shipment of aircraft and parts to Japan. But despite widespread popular support in the United States after 1938 for tough economic sanctions against Japan, Hull and Roosevelt, fearful that such a course might lead to war, proceeded with extreme caution. In July, 1939, tired of unavailing protests and remonstrances, the State Department announced that in six months the United States would terminate its 1911 commercial treaties with Japan. Roosevelt was now permitted to increase diplomatic pressure on Tokyo by putting Japanese-American trade on a day-to-day basis. Washington had served notice that it would not stand aloof at all costs from events in the Pacific. As an additional warning to Japan, FDR transferred the Pacific fleet from San Diego to Pearl Harbor. Meanwhile, Japan, turning its attention from its stalemated war in China, moved into the vacuum in Southeast Asia left by German victories in Holland and France. After penetrating French Indochina and Thailand, the Japanese signed the Tripartite Pact with the European Axis in September, 1940. With this pact the three signatories—Germany, Italy, and Japan—divided up the world—on paper.

During the winter of 1940–1941, the United States slowly tightened its economic vise. Aviation gasoline, then scrap iron and steel, iron ore, pig iron, finished steel of various kinds, copper, brass—all came under the embargo. Hurt by the gradual squeeze, Tokyo was moved to seek a settlement with the United States. In his initial conversations with the new Japanese representative, Admiral Kichisaburo Nomura, in April, 1941, Secretary Hull repeated his conditions for improved United States–Japanese relations: "Nondisturbance of the status quo in the Pacific except as the status quo may be altered by peaceful means." What Tokyo wanted, it made clear in its response of May 12, was a settlement with China. To achieve this, however, the Japanese needed a promise from the United States that it would discontinue assistance to the Chinese if they refused to negotiate realistically. For Hull the conditions were inadmissible, for they implied Japanese negotiations with China based on force. Only if Japan acted in conformity with the principles of the Kellogg Pact and renounced the use of force, Hull warned, would it be possible to achieve a just and lasting peace in the Far East. There could be no agreement as long as the United States refused to permit Japan a free hand in China. Yet, as Ambassador Joseph C. Grew wrote Hull from Tokyo, the only alternative to a compromise settlement was eventual war.

As a stalemate developed in the Hull-Nomura conversations in Washington, in Tokyo the Japanese government was torn between the moderates, led by Premier Prince Fumimaro Konoye, who held the Tripartite Pact in low esteem and favored a settlement with the United States, and the uncompromising pro-German element under Foreign Minister Yosuke Matsuoka. In late June the Matsuoka faction gained ascendancy. On July 2 the cabinet agreed that Japan would continue its effort to resolve the China question satisfactorily and pursue a course in southeast Asia preparatory to establishing its Greater East Asia Co-Prosperity Sphere, even at the risk of war with the United States. Although the extremist Matsuoka was eased out of office in late July, the Imperial Japanese government carried out its earlier decision by moving massive forces into southern Indochina. Roosevelt, on July 23, responded by freezing all Japanese assets in the United States. The Dutch and British followed the American lead.

As the freezing order of July gradually developed into a full-fledged embargo ending all Japanese-American trade, the moderate Prince Konoye resumed his search for an agreement with the United States. On August 3 Nomura conveyed to Washington his appeal for a private conference with Roosevelt. Against the advice of Ambassador Grew, who knew the political situation in Tokyo, Secretary Hull demanded that the Japanese agree in advance to deal with China openly and fairly. This destroyed any possibility of a summit conference, and Konoye gave way in October to the Japanese military. General Hideki Tojo, the new Premier, put in motion a dual policy aimed at an early resolution of the United States–Japanese conflict. First, he pushed forward the Japanese plans for war. Second, he dispatched Saburo Kurusu, an experienced diplomat, to Washington to manage what would be final negotiations. On November 5, an Imperial conference in Tokyo gave Kurusu until November 25 to achieve agreement; thereafter the issue of war would go before the Emperor. From Tokyo, Ambassador Grew warned Washington that time was running out.

When Kurusu arrived to begin his negotiations with Hull, he came armed with two proposals. Proposal A asked Washington to give its approval to a Japanese-dominated Asia;

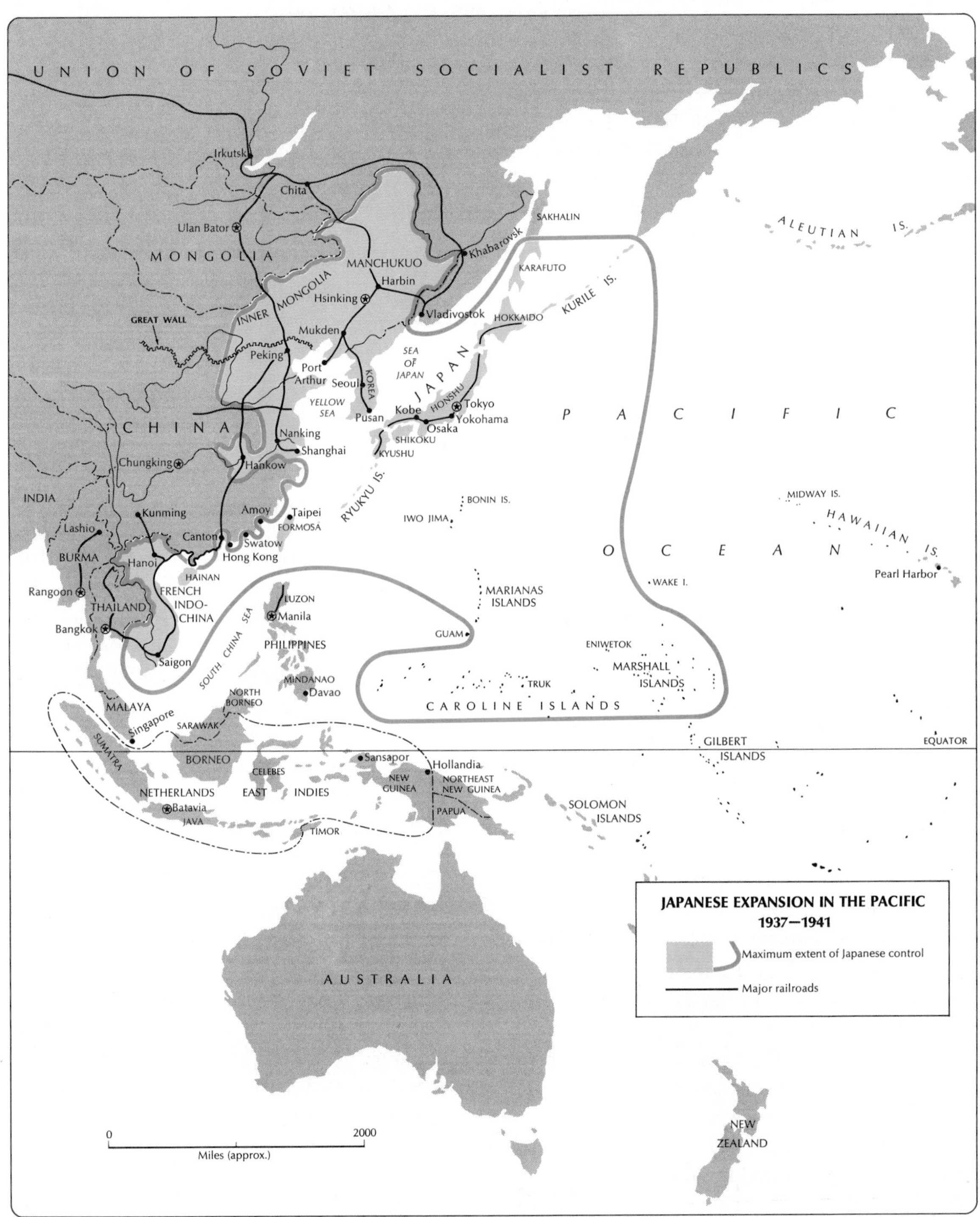

JAPANESE EXPANSION IN THE PACIFIC
1937—1941
Maximum extent of Japanese control
Major railroads
UNION OF SOVIET SOCIALIST REPUBLICS
Irkutsk
Chita
Ulan Bator
MONGOLIA
MANCHUKUO
Harbin
Hsinking
Khabarovsk
SAKHALIN
KARAFUTO
ALEUTIAN IS.
Vladivostok
HOKKAIDO
KURILE IS.
INNER MONGOLIA
GREAT WALL
Mukden
Peking
Port Arthur
Seoul
KOREA
SEA OF JAPAN
JAPAN
HONSHU
Tokyo
Yokohama
Kobe
Osaka
Pusan
YELLOW SEA
SHIKOKU
KYUSHU
CHINA
Nanking
Shanghai
Hankow
Chungking
PACIFIC
OCEAN
INDIA
Kunming
Amoy
Taipei
FORMOSA
RYUKYU IS.
BONIN IS.
IWO JIMA
MIDWAY IS.
HAWAIIAN IS.
Pearl Harbor
Lashio
Canton
Swatow
Hong Kong
BURMA
Hanoi
HAINAN
Rangoon
FRENCH INDO-CHINA
THAILAND
Bangkok
Saigon
LUZON
Manila
PHILIPPINES
SOUTH CHINA SEA
MARIANAS ISLANDS
GUAM
WAKE I.
ENIWETOK
MARSHALL ISLANDS
TRUK
CAROLINE ISLANDS
MINDANAO
Davao
NORTH BORNEO
MALAYA
Singapore
SARAWAK
SUMATRA
BORNEO
CELEBES
Sansapor
Hollandia
NEW GUINEA
NORTHEAST NEW GUINEA
PAPUA
NETHERLANDS EAST INDIES
Batavia
JAVA
TIMOR
SOLOMON ISLANDS
GILBERT ISLANDS
EQUATOR
AUSTRALIA
NEW ZEALAND
0
2000
Miles (approx.)

Hull rejected it promptly. On November 20 the Japanese diplomat presented Hull with the second proposal. In exchange for what amounted to a free hand in settling accounts with China and the resumption by the United States of normal commercial relations with Japan, Tokyo would withdraw its troops from southern, perhaps from all, Indochina. Hull was now in a quandary. Acceptance of the Japanese proposal would require a compromise of principle; a rejection might spark a war for which the United States was ill prepared. Both Hull and Roosevelt endorsed a counterproposal calling for a truce in the Sino-Japanese War while the parties discussed their "differences," Japan withdrew her troops from southern Indochina, and the United States conditionally ended its freezing order on trade. But Chinese opposition to any deal with Japan caused this idea to be shelved without presentation to the Japanese. On November 26, Washington replied formally to Japanese Proposal B. Hull demanded that Japan withdraw its forces from China and Indochina and in the place of the Asian New Order accept the benefits of renewed American trade Hull understood clearly from intercepted Japanese dispatches that Tokyo officials would never accept his proposals. On the morning of November 27, he phoned Secretary of War Henry Stimson: "I have washed my hands of it and it is now in the hands of the Army and the Navy." That same day the Army and the Navy flashed war warnings to American outposts in the Pacific.

On December 6 Tojo informed his representatives in Washington that they would soon receive a message in fourteen parts, terminating diplomatic relations with the United States. The Navy Department in Washington received the first thirteen parts of the intercepted message at noon on that day. By nine o'clock that evening the department had decoded the message and had prepared it for distribution. When Roosevelt read the document at the White House, he reportedly observed, "This means war." The United States would stand on its record, again permitting Japan to make the next move. Even then the President made no mention of Pearl Harbor; nor did he suspect that the Japanese attack would come immediately. Not until 7:30 in the morning of December 7 did Washington officials see the final part of the Japanese message. Herein Tokyo informed the United States government that further negotiations could achieve no useful purpose. Another decoded message, received later that morning, instructed the Japanese diplomats in Washington to present the fourteen-part message at 1 P.M.

Attaching some significance to the hour designated for the delivery of the Japanese message, Washington dispatched its final warning to Pearl Harbor through Western Union to San Francisco, and from there to Hawaii by RCA radio. The warning arrived at the RCA office at 7:33 A.M., Hawaii time. A messenger was en route to Fort Shafter when the Japanese attack on Pearl Harbor began. Because of their own decoding problems, Nomura and Kurusu did not arrive at the White House until shortly after two. As they entered the waiting room, Hull received an unconfirmed report that the Japanese had struck Pearl Harbor. The Secretary, after leafing through the Japanese message, told the diplomats bitterly that he had never seen a document "more crowded with infamous falsehoods and distortions." Japan's sudden and devastating attack on Pearl Harbor drew from the American people at last what Roosevelt had been unable to achieve—a total commitment to war.

Conclusion

Pearl Harbor shattered the isolationist defense against American involvement in Europe's war so completely that it soon raised suspicions among Roosevelt's critics that the President and his administration had plotted the Pacific disaster. These charges, which proliferated with the passage of time, flowed from the dual assumption that Washington had received warnings of the Japanese attack and that, to make the disaster profound, had purposely delayed the December 7 message to Hawaii so that the garrisons there could not establish an adequate defense. It had been clear that the Japanese task force was moving in late November and early December toward some target, but correspondents throughout the Pacific anticipated the assault in the region of Southeast Asia. There is no conclusive evidence, therefore, that Washington expected the attack at Pearl Harbor before it actually occurred. The Pearl Harbor tragedy was merely a logical projection of the general failure of policy in the thirties. For too long the country and its leaders had refused to come to grips with the challenge of the dictators, either by means of diplomacy or by war. Washington officials had assumed falsely that they need not take the Japanese problem seriously. It was the suddenness, and especially the unexpectedness, of the Pearl Harbor attack that created the traumatic response of the American people.

Neither Tokyo nor Washington could escape responsibility for the collapse of peace in Asia. Japan had embarked on aggressive war against China and should not have expected the United States, with its long tradition of paternalism toward China, to accept readily the notion of an imposed treaty. Still the American response scarcely served the cause of peace. It was never made clear what Washington expected of its economic sanctions against Japan. The final Japanese message of December 7 did not render Japan blameless for its abuse of China, but it did explain why those who, like Secretary Hull, chose to interfere in the conflicts of other nations under the principle of peaceful change must expect to pay a price. "The American Government," it said, "advocates in the name of world peace those principles favorable to it and urges upon the Japanese Government the acceptance thereof. The peace of the world may be brought about only by discovering a mutually acceptable formula through recognition of the reality of the situation and mutual appreciation of one another's position." Traditionally, international politics had rested on the rights of the stronger; by the new morality of the interwar years, it rested on the rights of possession. In their refusal to accept the conditions imposed on them by the Versailles settlement, the aggressors of the thirties simply rejected the Western notion that possession gave special rights. The result was tension and finally war.

SUGGESTED READINGS

Two excellent surveys of American foreign policy between Manchuria and Pearl Harbor are Robert A. Divine's *The Reluctant Belligerent: American Entry into World War II** (1965) and John E. Wiltz's *From Isolation to War, 1931–1941** (1968). Also of great value for the thirties are Selig Adler's two volumes,

*The Isolationist Impulse** (1957) and *The Uncertain Giant** (1965). The older work by Allan Nevins, *The New Deal in World Affairs* (1950), is still highly useful. For a more critical appraisal of Roosevelt see E. E. Robinson's *The Roosevelt Leadership, 1933–1945* (1955). For Roosevelt's policy toward Latin America see J. F. Rippy's *South America and Hemisphere Defense* (1941); E. O. Guerrant's *Roosevelt's Good Neighbor Policy* (1950); and Bryce Wood's *The Making of the Good Neighbor Policy** (1961). Wood attributes the Good Neighbor policy to Roosevelt rather than to Hoover. Also more favorable to Roosevelt is D. M. Dozer's *Are We Good Neighbors? Three Decades of Inter-American Relations, 1930–1960* (1961). On Hull's trade program see G. L. Beckett's *The Reciprocal Trade Agreements Program* (1941). United States relations with Russia are given adequate treatment in Meno Lovenstein's *American Opinion of Soviet Russia* (1941); William A. Williams's *American-Russian Relations, 1781–1947* (1952); and R. P. Browder's *The Origins of Soviet-American Diplomacy** (1954).

Isolationism and neutrality were powerful themes in United States foreign relations during the Roosevelt years. Three excellent studies of American isolationism are Donald Drummond's *The Passing of American Neutrality, 1937–1941* (1955); R. A. Divine's *The Illusion of Neutrality** (1962); and Adler's *The Isolationist Impulse** (1957). Alexander DeConde (ed.), *Isolation and Security* (1957), contains excellent essays on American isolationism. Samuel Lubell in *The Future of American Politics** (1951) identifies isolationism with ethnic origins. For American attitudes toward the Spanish Civil War see F. J. Taylor's *The United States and the Spanish Civil War, 1936–1939* (1956) and D. A. Puzzo's *Spain and the Great Powers, 1936–1941* (1962). Two excellent studies that reflect liberal isolationism are C. A. Beard's *American Foreign Policy in the Making, 1932–1940* (1946), which is highly critical of Roosevelt, and Wayne S. Cole's *Senator Gerald P. Nye and American Foreign Relations* (1962). Cole's *America First: The Battle against Intervention, 1940–1941* (1953) is an able study of the America First Committee.

Several excellent volumes on the Roosevelt foreign policies are interventionist in outlook and thus pro-Roosevelt. Perhaps the outstanding books in this category are W. L. Langer and S. E. Gleason's *The Challenge to Isolation, 1937–1940* (1952) and *The Undeclared War, 1940–1941* (1953). Exceedingly laudatory is Basil Rauch's *Roosevelt from Munich to Pearl Harbor: A Study in the Creation of Foreign Policy* (1950). Walter Johnson's *The Battle against Isolation* (1944) discusses the organized effort to convince the American people that it was in the national interest to save England from Nazi attack. H. L. Trefousse's *Germany and American Neutrality, 1939–1941* (1954) is useful on United States relations with Germany. Robert Sobel deals with another aspect of United States–European diplomacy in *The Origins of Interventionism: The United States and the Russo-Finnish War* (1960). Also important is R. H. Dawson's *The Decision to Aid Russia, 1941* (1959).

The evolution of United States policy toward Japan can be traced in Dorothy Borg's *The United States and the Far Eastern Crisis of 1933–1938* (1964); Herbert Feis's *The Road to Pearl Harbor: The Coming of the War between the United States and Japan** (1950); Paul W. Schroeder's *The Axis Alliance and Japanese-American Relations, 1941* (1958); and T. A. Bisson's *America's Far Eastern Policy* (1945). Feis's book is the best survey available; it presents material critical of Roosevelt and Hull, but the author refrains from drawing judgments. Schroeder, on the other hand, is openly critical of Hull for his inflexibility. On Japanese policy in the thirties see S. E. Morison's *The Rising Sun in the Pacific* (1948); R. J. C. Butow's *Tojo and the Coming of the War* (1961); and F. C. Jones's *Japan's New Order in East Asia* (1954). Roberta Wohlstetter's *Pearl Harbor: Warning and Decision** (1962) is a superb study of the Pearl Harbor crisis.

Pearl Harbor's total destruction of the isolationist influence on American policy has created a body of literature highly critical of the Roosevelt leadership. Much of it accuses the President of purposely bringing war to the Pacific so that the United States might actively enter the struggle against Hitler. The two outstanding volumes in this category are C. C. Tansill's *Back Door to War: The Roosevelt Foreign Policy, 1933–1941* (1952) and C. A. Beard's *President Roosevelt and the Coming of the War* (1948). Other books of similar outlook are W. H. Chamberlin's *America's Second Crusade* (1950); F. R.

Sanborn's *Design for War: A Study of Secret Power Politics, 1937–1941* (1951); George Morgenstern's *Pearl Harbor: The Story of the Secret War* (1947); and Walter Millis's *This is Pearl! The United States and Japan, 1941* (1947). R. A. Theobald's *The Final Secret of Pearl Harbor: The Washington Contribution to the Japanese Attack* (1954) is representative of those books which place responsibility for the military catastrophe on Roosevelt. A highly useful bibliographical article which traces the shifting American attitudes toward the Pearl Harbor disaster is Wayne S. Cole's "American Entry into World War II: A Historiographical Appraisal," *Mississippi Valley Historical Review*, XLIII (March, 1957).

Much has appeared in print on the various actors involved in the creation of American foreign policy during the thirties. Of special value is *The Memoirs of Cordell Hull* (2 vols., 1948). Julius W. Pratt's *Cordell Hull* (2 vols., 1964) is highly laudatory. Somewhat less so is Donald Drummond's essay on Hull in Norman A. Graebner (ed.), *An Uncertain Tradition: American Secretaries of State in the Twentieth Century** (1961). Secretary Stimson has left his personal record in H. L. Stimson and McGeorge Bundy's *On Active Service in Peace and War* (1947). Two volumes critical of Stimson's inflexibility in United States relations with Japan are R. N. Current's *Secretary Stimson* (1954) and E. E. Morison's *Turmoil and Tradition: A Study of the Life and Times of Henry L. Stimson** (1960). Of special value in studying United States–Japanese relations are two volumes by Ambassador Joseph C. Grew: *Ten Years in Japan* (1944) and *Turbulent Era* (2 vols., 1952), edited by Walter Johnson. W. E. Dodd, Jr., and Martha Dodd (eds.), *Ambassador Dodd's Diary, 1933–1938* (1941), is a highly useful document. Robert E. Sherwood presents an excellent portrait of Roosevelt in *Roosevelt and Hopkins* (1948). For the views of an isolationist of the thirties see A. H. Vandenberg, Jr. (ed.), *The Private Papers of Senator Vandenberg* (1952). Fred L. Israel's *Nevada's Key Pittman* (1963) reveals the character of Pittman's leadership as chairman of the Senate Foreign Relations Committee.

* indicates availability in paperback.

35

Victory over the Axis

THAT THE UNITED STATES, Britain, and Russia in 1941 possessed the industrial and man-power resources to achieve an ultimate triumph over the Axis became apparent with America's entry into the war. What disturbed Allied military planning and cooperation there-after was the essential question of how best to bring the rapidly accumulating might of the Big Three to bear on Germany and Japan. As early as April, 1939, five months before the outbreak of war in Europe, the Joint Planning Committee of the United States Armed Forces had agreed that the United States, if involved, would fight a defensive action in the Pacific and concentrate its efforts on the destruction of the German *Wehrmacht*. The Combined Staff Conference, held in Washington during February and March, 1941, revived this basic strategy and reaffirmed it.

The imperatives behind this decision were clear enough. Germany was the strongest of the Axis countries, deeply entrenched in Europe. In time its industrial and scientific genius would multiply its destructive power, possibly to the point of invincibility. Britain and the U.S.S.R. were reeling under the offensive thrusts of Nazi power on the ground and in the air. Without the total effort of these two nations, the United States could not hope to break the German resistance. It was essential, therefore, that American military forces and equipment appear in Europe as quickly as possible to underwrite both the efforts and the morale of those fighting Germany.

Prime Minister Winston Churchill crossed the Atlantic on December 22, 1941, and opened informal discussions with President Roosevelt on matters of strategy. During the weeks which followed, Churchill and Roosevelt established their joint leadership which would manage the conduct of the war. From this Arcadia Conference came the Declaration of the United Nations, signed on January 1, 1942, in which all enemies of the Axis powers agreed to fight the war to a satisfactory conclusion. The Arcadia Conference established the Combined Chiefs of Staff, composed of British and American military officers, and instituted an ever-increasing flow of lend-lease aid to the European theater of war.

Western leaders, under pressure from the beleaguered Russians, accepted the need for a second front British officials had revealed their strategic preferences as early as August, 1941. These included a tight naval blockade of the Continent, the bombing of German cities and industries, the encouragement of opposition to Hitler in Nazi-occupied countries, limited strikes along the periphery of German power, and finally a massive assault against Germany itself. With these proposals the American Joint Chiefs of Staff were in general agreement. But the issues on which they differed were fundamental and centered on peripheral attacks, especially if these should delay a massive invasion of Western Europe.

It was clear why the British favored attacks along the German periphery, even at the expense of an assault on Western Europe. Britain had been at war for two years. Her army, if small, was prepared for action. Her navy still had control of the seas. Thus Britain was equipped to conduct light raids against areas of German occupation. Unable to contest German power on the Continent, England would either engage the Germans in the Mediterranean or remain inactive. The United States, on the other hand, was not prepared to engage the Germans immediately. General George C. Marshall, Chief of Staff of the Army, argued for a rapid buildup of Allied equipment and manpower in England for a cross-channel attack to relieve the Russians. During January, 1942, the first United States troops landed in Britain; in March Roosevelt sent Marshall and Harry Hopkins, his personal emissary, to London to press the matter of a second front. The British agreed readily to a second front for 1943, but only the threatened fall of Russia, they declared, would justify such a decision in 1942. Confronted in London with uncompromising opposition to an early invasion of Europe, American officials looked to 1943.

Still the two Western Allies, whatever the state of their readiness, could not postpone until 1943 their active participation in the war. Again in July, Roosevelt sent Marshall, Hopkins, and Ernest J. King, Chief of Naval Operations, to raise the question of the second front with Churchill. The Prime Minister, opposed to an early cross-channel attack, countered with Operation Torch, an invasion of North Africa to check the German drive into the eastern Mediterranean. Churchill, supported by Roosevelt, had his way, and British and American leaders prepared for the North African invasion with landings scheduled for November, 1942. The Roosevelt–Churchill decision to postpone the second front in Europe produced anger and dismay in Moscow.

Torch was a brilliant success. The Germans, misled by their extensive triumphs of 1941 and 1942 in North Africa and determined to gain control of Suez, gradually overextended their lines of communication and supply. In May, 1942, Erwin Rommel's *Afrika Korps,* comprising both German and Italian troops, launched an offensive, took Tobruk, and drove the British forces back to El Alamein, seventy miles west of Alexandria. There the two armies remained posed for four months while their commanders considered matters of supply and strategy. Rommel was an outstanding officer—intelligent, popular, and candid. Facing him was General Bernard Law Montgomery—short, overbearing, and resourceful. Montgomery's strategy lay in convincing Rommel that his chief attack would come at the south while his massed forces would actually strike the German north. The plan succeeded. Montgomery's forces broke through the German lines, and by early

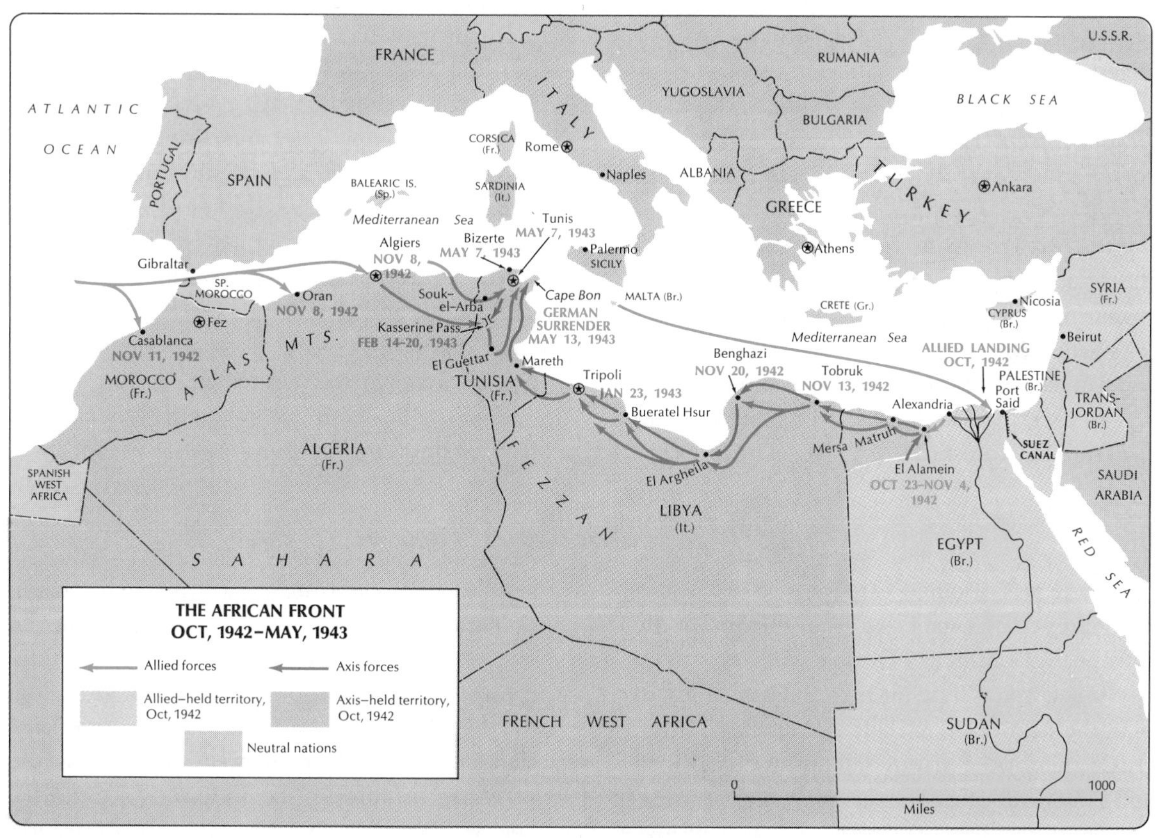

November Rommel's forces were in full retreat across North Africa. By the time that the Germans reached Mersa Matruh they had lost 60,000 men and 500 tanks. That month the British recaptured Tobruk and Benghazi.

Rommel now faced trouble from another direction—Operation Torch. On November 8, 1942, British and American forces under General Dwight D. Eisenhower conducted the first major amphibious landings in the Mediterranean. The three major beachheads were made at Casablanca in Morocco and at Oran and Algiers in Algeria. For Hitler, Torch proved to be an irretrievable disaster. By mid-November Allied troops entered Tunisia. Tripoli fell to the British in January, 1943. In May the British occupied Tunis; the Americans entered Bizerte. The German forces, now without Rommel who had fled, retreated into the Cape Bon peninsula. Here the Germans on May 13 surrendered everything they had in North Africa—250,000 troops, plus stores and equipment. Torch reopened the way to Suez and the Middle East.

During these months of 1942 and 1943 Hitler's armies met with even greater disaster on the Russian front. The German summer offensive of 1942 had brought startling successes at Sevastopol, Voronezh, and Rostov. By September, Nazi forces had moved through the Crimea into the Caucasus toward the Baku oil fields. During August they reached Stalingrad and entered the city in September. Hitler wanted Stalingrad desperately, but the Russians were equally determined to hold it. The *Wehrmacht* had been stopped at Leningrad and Moscow, but it was still powerful, enjoying superiority in everything but numbers. The battle for Stalingrad raged through October and November, 1942. Thousands died every day. Russian General Georgi Zhukov described the battle well: "I would not have believed such an inferno would open up on this earth. Men died, but they did not retreat."

During November Hitler admitted that the German army had failed to take Stalingrad, but he refused to pull his troops away from the Volga. Zhukov launched a powerful counterattack, closing the ring around twenty German divisions, who were already suffering a terrible Russian winter without access to supplies. In January, 1943, what was left of the German forces surrendered. This wasteful battle of Stalingrad demanded much of Germans and Russians alike. The U.S.S.R. lost more men in that one battle than the United States lost in the entire war; but Germany lost more—her dominant position on the European Continent.

The Mediterranean Campaign

Germany was doomed even before the Western Allies could establish a second front on the European Continent. During January, 1943, Roosevelt and Churchill met at Casablanca to plan the next stage in their war against Hitler. Again there were disagreements among British and American officials over questions of priority. The United States Chiefs of Staff still preferred the concentration of Allied equipment, landing craft, and manpower in England in preparation for a cross-channel invasion in 1943. But the logic of the military situation favored Sir Alan Brooke's strategy of attacking the Axis forces in the Mediterranean. American leaders at Casablanca agreed to the invasion of Sicily in July, to be followed in September by a thrust at Italy itself although American officers still feared that an Italian campaign

THE RUSSIAN FRONT
JUNE, 1942–JANUARY, 1944
Allied forces
Axis forces
Allied–held territory, Jan, 1944
Axis–held territory, Jan, 1944
Neutral nations
0
500
Miles
FINLAND
SWEDEN
Helsinki
Tallinn
ESTONIA
BALTIC SEA
Leningrad
SIEGE SEPT, 1941 JAN, 1944
Novgorod
DEC, 1941
Riga
LATVIA
LITHUANIA
JAN, 1944
DEC, 1941
Rzhev
Moscow
1941–1942
DEC, 1941
Danzig
EAST PRUSSIA
Kaunas
Smolensk
Minsk
Bialystok
Vistula R.
Warsaw
DEEPEST GERMAN PENETRATION
JAN, 1944
Brest
POLAND
UNION OF SOVIET SOCIALIST REPUBLICS
Volga R.
GERMANY–U.S.S.R. BORDER, SEPT, 1939
Cracow
Voronezh
JAN 23, 1943
Kiev
Don R.
CZECH.
GERMAN SURRENDER, FEB. 2, 1943
Karkhov
OCT, 1942
Dnieper R.
Stalingrad
Budapest
HUNGARY
Dniester R.
BESSARABIA
UKRAINE
Rostov
NOV, 1942
JAN, 1944
JAN, 1944
Odessa
CASPIAN SEA
RUMANIA
CRIMEA
NOV, 1942
Bucharest
Sevastopol
Mozdok
YUGOSLAVIA
Danube R.
Varna
BLACK SEA
CAUCASUS MOUNTAINS
Sofia
BULGARIA
BAKU OIL FIELDS
Batum
OIL PIPELINE
Baku
Salonika
Istanbul
TURKEY
GREECE
Ankara

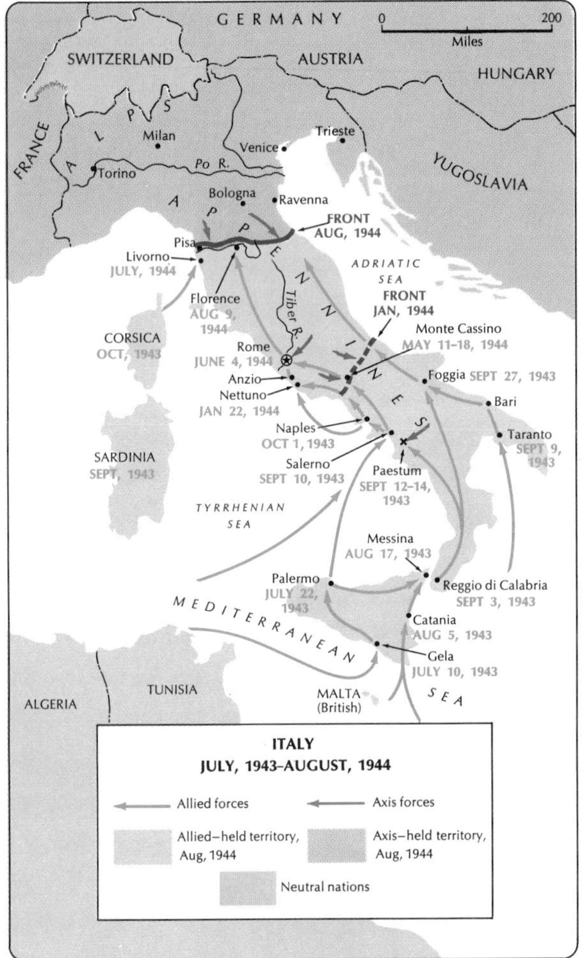

would commit Allied power so thoroughly to the Mediterranean theater that they could not stage a cross-channel invasion even in 1944. Thus the ultimate Allied strategy against Germany was a compromise between those who wanted to attack hard at the edge of Axis power, principally Southern Europe, and those who favored an immediate cross-channel invasion of France. Churchill agreed to Overlord, the name assigned in 1943 to the cross-channel invasion, while General Eisenhower, United States commander in Europe, promised support for the invasion of Italy which began in September, 1943. At the Teheran Conference of November, 1943, Stalin, long bitter over the West's failure to establish a major second front, endorsed Overlord enthusiastically, promising at the same time a strong Russian offensive to coincide with the cross-channel attack. Roosevelt now decided to keep Marshall in the United States and placed Eisenhower in charge of Overlord.

In the great debate over strategy, American officials thought primarily, if not exclusively, of a military victory with the least possible loss of American life. Their concern was the rapid and efficient destruction of German power. Churchill's objectives, however, were both political and military. He believed it essential that the Western Allies occupy as much of the Balkans and Slavic Europe as possible ahead of the advancing Soviet troops. Churchill rationalized this strategy in terms of military victory, but he hoped ultimately to prevent the establishment of Russian power in the heart of Europe.

Measured by subsequent Allied victories, the military compromises worked out exceedingly well, producing a steady collapse of the German positions. Even at that, progress through Italy from the Salerno beachhead proved to be difficult. The invasion of the peninsula soon drove Italy out of the war, but the flood of German soldiers sent to fill the vacuum turned Italy into a major battleground. The decision to hoard the bulk of American power in England deprived Allied commanders in Italy of some available strength and forced them to engage in prolonged heavy fighting, always against strategic odds. The slowness of the Italian campaign measured the frustration of those who placed their faith on operations in the Mediterranean.

Russia's success in stabilizing the Eastern Front, added to the anticipated Western triumphs in the Mediterranean, raised the central issue of Germany's future. What concerned Roosevelt as early as 1943 was the need to reassure the Kremlin that the Western Allies, though still unable in January, 1943, to open a second front, were determined to fight on to total victory over Germany. To that end the President read the following statement at a press conference at Casablanca on January 24: "Peace can come to the world only by the total elimination of German and Japanese war power. The elimination of German, Japanese and Italian war power means the *unconditional surrender* by Germany, Italy, and Japan."

Thus was born the controversial concept of unconditional surrender which guided Allied policy throughout the fateful closing months of the war against Germany and Japan. What effect did this concept have on the course of the war? Churchill denied that it prolonged the war or played into the hands of the dictators by undermining the idea of revolt or conspiracy within the enemy nations. Nothing short of military victory, ran the argument, would have compelled the Germans to stop the war. Critics of Allied wartime decisions, however, charged that the policy helped to unify Germany and induced the Axis countries to fight with increased determination.

Discussions at Casablanca raised, but did not settle, the question of Germany's future. At their meeting in Moscow during October, 1943, however, the Foreign Ministers of the United States, Britain, and Russia created a European Advisory Commission to draft a German surrender document and an agreement for the Allied military government of Germany. At Teheran in November, 1943, Roosevelt and Churchill granted Stalin a Soviet zone in central Germany extending westward to within 100 miles of the Rhine. This preliminary agreement placed Berlin well within the Soviet zone, but the city itself remained a separate entity occupied jointly. For such wartime arrangements it assumed that Russia would unhesitatingly accept Western views on the postwar reconstruction of Europe.

Another question posed by Germany was more fundamental. What disposal were the Allies to make of Germany's power to wage war? Secretary of the Treasury Henry Morgenthau, Jr., favored stripping Germany of her major industries and reducing her to an agricultural nation. Then, Morgenthau believed, she could never make war again. But Morgenthau's views were challenged vigorously by officials in the War Department, who were busily planning the postwar occupation and control of Germany. These men opposed dismemberment and anticipated instead the rapid postwar reconstruction of the German economy. Both Hull and Secretary of War Henry L Stimson believed that a strong and productive Germany was essential for the economic health of Europe and also that a punitive policy was incompatible with the American liberal tradition. Directive 1067, issued by the Joint Chiefs of Staff in October, 1944, embodied the principles toward postwar Germany which were to guide American military leaders. It accepted the zones of occupation defined by the European Advisory Commission and declared that Germany was to be occupied "as a defeated enemy nation." The Allied objective, it said, was "to prevent Germany from ever again being a threat to the peace of the world." To this end, Nazism and militarism would be destroyed and Germany required to pay reparations and make restitution to countries devastated by Nazi aggression.

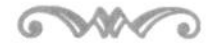

Victory in Europe

Only a scientific miracle could have saved Germany after mid-1944. On both the Mediterranean and Eastern fronts the German positions were collapsing with increasing regularity. As early as January, the Western Allies established a beachhead at Nettuno-Anzio, 30 miles south of Rome. During the spring they successfully completed their assault on Cassino, a key position in the German defense of central Italy. On June 1, the United States Fifth Army liberated Rome.

Meanwhile, by late 1942 and 1943, strategic air bombing of German targets from bases in Britain had become terribly effective. New radar sighting devices made feasible huge night raids over German cities. The British, relying on incendiary bombs, launched massive air attacks which destroyed large parts of major German cities. On May 30, 1942, the first 1,000-bomber run over Cologne killed more than 10,000 civilians and established the pattern of subsequent British night raids. During July, 1942, the first units of the United States Eighth Air Force under General Ira C. Eaker arrived in England to join the air assault against Germany. The assigned mission of the Eighth Air Force was to strike at key German industries, such as aircraft and electrical power plants, transportation centers, submarine bases, and petroleum and synthetic rubber industries, through daylight precision high-altitude bombing. By the end of 1943 the development of the P-51B Mustang, a fighter with great effectiveness and a long range, provided American bombers with the necessary fighter support.

General Eisenhower arrived in England during January, 1944, to assume supreme command of the Allied Expeditionary Forces. Thereafter the preparations for the cross-channel invasion proceeded rapidly. On June 6 the Allied forces concentrated in southern England struck the mainland on a 60-mile front along the Normandy coast. This assault was the largest amphibious operation in history. In the initial landing were 176,000 troops, carried by 4,000 landing craft and supported by 600 warships and 11,000 aircraft. General Montgomery commanded the ground forces in the invasion; General Omar Bradley led the American land contingents. German units, rushed into the area, were no match for Allied power.

During the summer of 1944 Allied forces began the final assault against the German continental defenses. In Operation Dragoon, on August 15, British and American forces—including the United States Seventh Army under General Alexander M. Patch—landed in southern France between Marseilles and Nice. This invasion gave the Allied control of the large port of Marseilles and brought additional troops into France for the final push into Germany. Now numbering 2 million, the rapidly advancing Allies on the Western Front closed in on the retreating Germans, liberating Paris on August 25 and Brussels, Antwerp, and Luxembourg in September. United States forces entered Germany near Eupen and Trier. One Allied setback was the famous Battle of the Bulge which in December, 1944, cost 77,000 American casualties.

THE LIBERATION OF FRANCE AND BELGIUM
JUNE–DECEMBER, 1944

Allied air operations against Germany, which had been intensified, were interrupted in June, 1944, by the German bombing of southern England with jet-propelled, pilotless V-1 aircraft. The V-1 offensive reached its climax in July and August. In September the first supersonic V-2 German rockets began to strike London. Unable to prevent the launching of such weapons, the British and American bomber forces, now relatively free of *Luftwaffe* opposition, resumed their bombing of German cities and industrial targets.

At the Malta Conference of January, 1945, Allied leaders assumed that Germany would attempt to send her armies eastward to support her crumbling forces on the Russian front. To hamper this movement, the Allies agreed to bomb such major east German transportation centers as Berlin, Leipzig, and Dresden. On February 3 nearly one thousand B-17s bombed Berlin, killing or injuring 25,000 civilians. Despite the apparent success of the Allied strategic bombing effort against Germany, however, it did not play the major role in the German defeat. Long before the end of the war, the law of diminishing returns had set in. The destruction of German cities did not seriously curtail, much less destroy, German productivity. Even a city as thoroughly damaged as Hamburg recovered 80 percent of its production in three months. Key German industries were dispersed widely and generally defended with strong aircraft and antiaircraft installations. Many basic German industries, such as that of machine tools, were never seriously damaged. Nevertheless, the bombing of German cities greatly injured German morale; by late 1944 most Germans regarded the war as lost, but those who had been subjected to heavy bombing were the first to acknowledge that conviction. The Allied bombardment of Germany was an important factor in the defeat of Germany; it was not the decisive factor.

After January, 1945, the collapse of the German positions came with conspicuous regularity. During February, British forces moved rapidly through Holland toward the German border; to the south the United States Third Army crossed the Saar River and penetrated the Ruhr Valley, reaching the Rhine River at Düsseldorf. On March 7, United States forces entered both Düsseldorf and Cologne. Meanwhile the Russians had crossed East Prussia and seized both Belgrade and Budapest late in 1944, had taken Warsaw, and in January had reached the Oder River. Early in April, 1945, they launched their attack on Berlin and entered the city on April 24 to begin their deliberate reduction of the German capital. On May 1 the provisional German government under Admiral Karl Doenitz announced Hitler's death. The next day Berlin fell; and on May 7, Field Marshal Alfred Jodl signed the instrument of unconditional surrender at Reims. May 8—VE Day—signaled the end of the struggle for Europe.

The War in the Pacific

By the summer of 1942 the task of deflating the Japanese empire seemed almost insuperable. In the six months following the destruction of the United States fleet at Pearl Harbor, Japan's land and naval forces, with superb planning and the utilization of modern techniques of warfare, subjugated a vast area of the Pacific. In their conquest of eastern Asia and the western Pacific the Japanese had captured the American outposts of Guam and the Philippines; the British island of Hong Kong; the entire Malay Peninsula with its base of Singapore, the great British bastion guarding the entrance to the Indian Ocean; British Burma with its tributary islands in the Indian Ocean; the whole East Indian Archipelago belonging to the Dutch; Attu and Kiska islands near the western extremity of the Aleutians. What remained for the Japanese was the economic and political organization of this "Greater East Asia Co-Prosperity Sphere."

Despite her easy and rapid successes, Japan

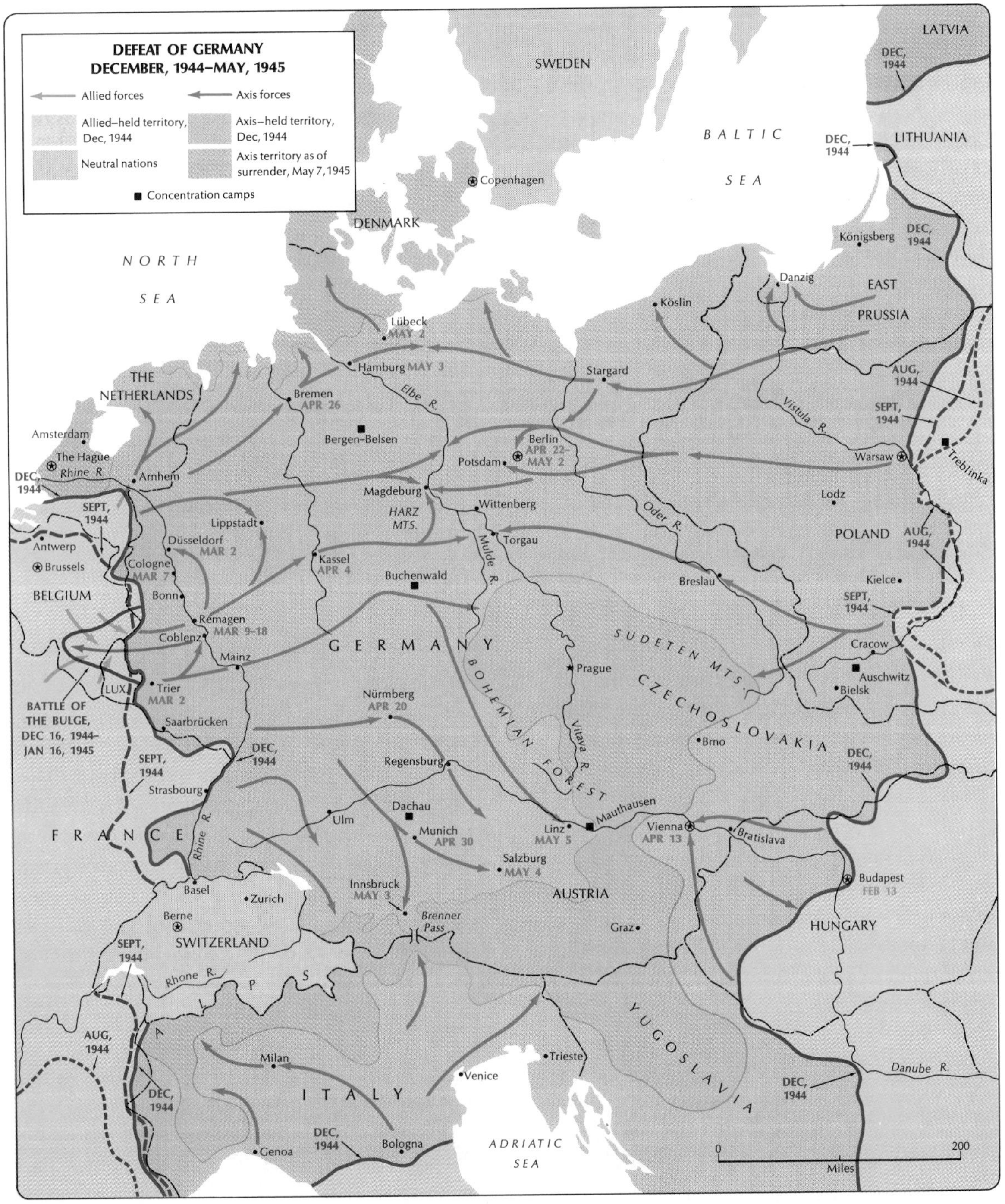
DEFEAT OF GERMANY
DECEMBER, 1944–MAY, 1945
Allied forces
Axis forces
Allied–held territory, Dec, 1944
Axis–held territory, Dec, 1944
Neutral nations
Axis territory as of surrender, May 7, 1945
Concentration camps
SWEDEN
LATVIA
LITHUANIA
BALTIC SEA
Copenhagen
DENMARK
NORTH SEA
Königsberg
Danzig
EAST PRUSSIA
Köslin
Lübeck MAY 2
Hamburg MAY 3
Stargard
THE NETHERLANDS
Bremen APR 26
Elbe R.
Vistula R.
Amsterdam
Bergen-Belsen
Berlin APR 22–MAY 2
The Hague
Rhine R.
Arnhem
Potsdam
Warsaw
Treblinka
Magdeburg
Wittenberg
Lodz
HARZ MTS.
Lippstadt
Oder R.
Antwerp
Düsseldorf MAR 2
Torgau
POLAND
Brussels
Cologne MAR 7
Kassel APR 4
Mulde R.
BELGIUM
Bonn
Buchenwald
Breslau
Kielce
Remagen MAR 9–18
Coblenz
GERMANY
SUDETEN MTS.
Cracow
Mainz
Prague
Auschwitz
Bielsk
LUX.
Trier MAR 2
BATTLE OF THE BULGE, DEC 16, 1944–JAN 16, 1945
Nürmberg APR 20
BOHEMIAN FOREST
CZECHOSLOVAKIA
Saarbrücken
Vltava R.
Brno
Regensburg
Strasbourg
Dachau
Ulm
Munich APR 30
Linz MAY 5
Mauthausen
Vienna APR 13
Bratislava
FRANCE
Rhine R.
Salzburg MAY 4
Basel
Zurich
Innsbruck MAY 3
AUSTRIA
Budapest FEB 13
Berne
Brenner Pass
HUNGARY
SWITZERLAND
Graz
Rhone R.
ALPS
YUGOSLAVIA
Milan
Trieste
Venice
ITALY
Danube R.
Genoa
Bologna
ADRIATIC SEA
0
200
Miles
DEC, 1944
SEPT, 1944
AUG, 1944

had already reached the limits of her expansion. She had failed to penetrate India and the Indian Ocean or to break the line which barred her passage to Australia and New Zealand. On the Chinese mainland, moveover, Japan still faced the resistance of Chiang Kai-shek's Chinese armies. Japan, like Germany, had moved into a power vacuum and had overextended her military commitments. Because Japan, like Germany, failed to strike at the genuine sources of United States power, all of which lay within the United States itself, this nation had time to recuperate and rebuild its power in the Pacific for the slow and deliberate destruction of Japan's far-flung bases. As early as May, 1942, in two remarkable naval engagements—the battle of the Coral Sea and the battle of Midway a month later—United States naval forces stalled the Japanese offensive in the south Pacific.

Oceans are formidable barriers only to those who do not control the seas. For a nation possessing naval superiority they become the high road of invasion. Japan had not reckoned fully on the capacity of American shipyards and factories or this nation's resources of manpower. The war in the Pacific was largely the Navy's war, to which the Army conformed, although the final strategy adopted by the Joint Chiefs combined both offenses. The plans called for General Douglas MacArthur to move up the New Guinea coast to reach the Philippines by the autumn of 1944. Admiral Chester Nimitz with his naval and amphibious forces would cross the central Pacific with operations against the Gilbert, Marshall, Caroline, and Mariana island chains, bringing the Allied offensive to the Ryukyus by the spring of 1945. Somewhere along the route, Admiral Ernest King was convinced, the United States fleet would meet and destroy the Japanese navy. At the conference in Quebec, General H. H. Arnold, commander of the United States Air Force, proposed air strikes against Japan from bases in the Marianas with the B-29s then going into production.

The American assault against Japan in the Pacific began at Guadalcanal in the Solomon Islands in August, 1942. After a bloody six-month fight, the Japanese were defeated. Subsequently, the combined sea, air, and land forces of the United States hopped from island to island northwestward toward the Philippines. In June, 1943, MacArthur launched an assault on the Bismarck's Barrier. Admiral William F. Halsey under MacArthur's command took Munda airfield in the central Solomons and in November established an airfield at Empress Augusta Bay, Bougainville, from which the United States could strike Rabaul, 234 miles distant. Following the successful Buna campaign of June, MacArthur's forces swept around New Guinea and proceeded by a series of envelopments to attack where the Japanese were weakest and bypass strong Japanese positions in difficult terrain. By February, 1944, United States forces had broken the Bismarck's Barrier by bypassing Rabaul. MacArthur's troops pushed on into the Admiralties where they established a huge base at Manus. Next, in a leapfrogging advance of 400 miles, they captured Hollandia on the coast of Netherland New Guinea, with its excellent airfields. In a little over twelve months American forces, with Australian units, had pushed 1,300 miles closer to the heart of the Japanese empire.

Admiral Nimitz launched his movement across the central Pacific in November, 1943, with a successful amphibious infantry attack on Makin Island in the Gilberts. That month marines landed and destroyed the Japanese garrison on Tarawa in one of the bloodiest battles

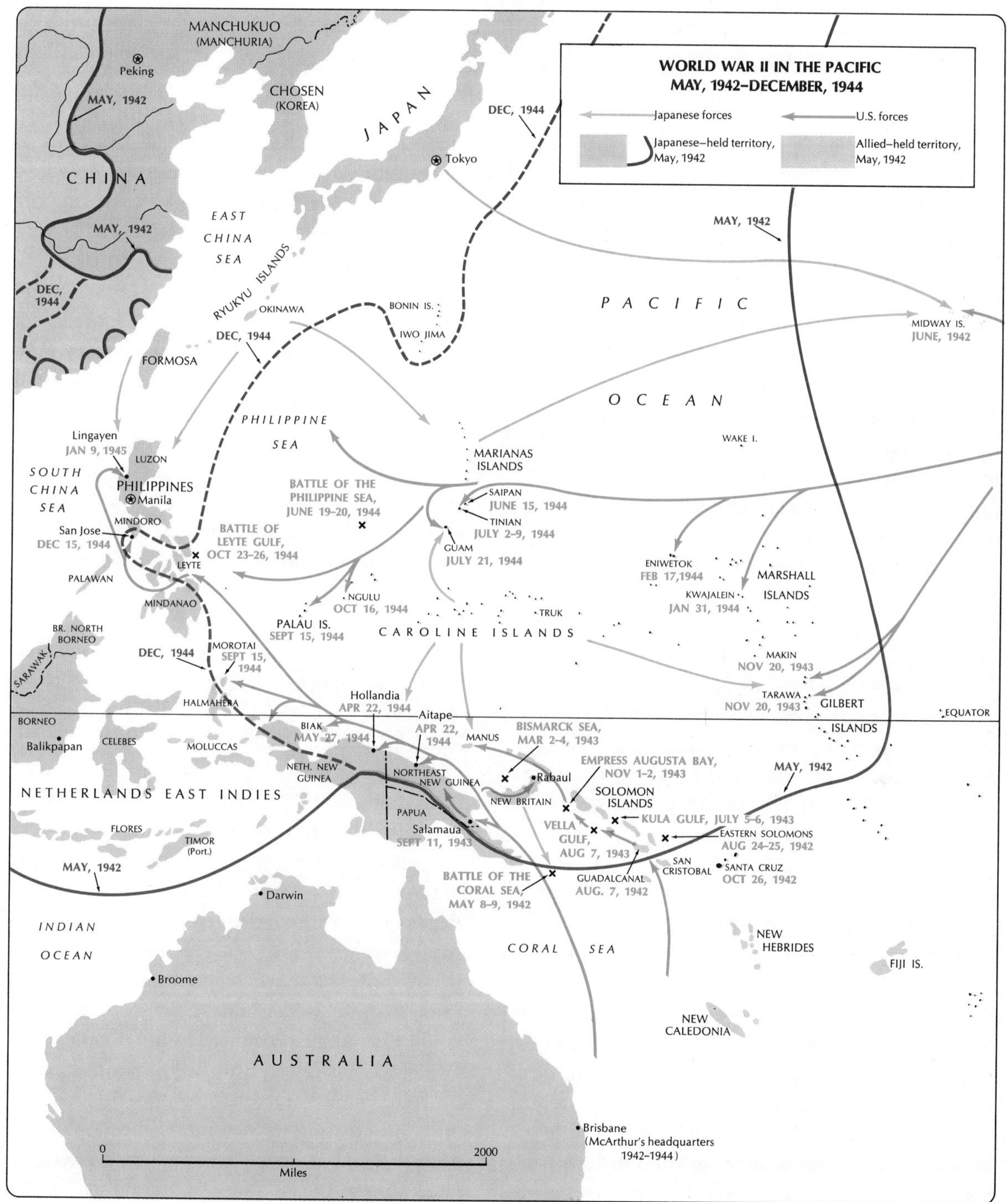

Victory over the Axis

of the Pacific war. Bypassing several Japanese bases, the Navy swung its power into the Marshalls, where infantry captured the Kwajalein Atoll in another fierce battle, giving the United States a huge anchorage. During February, 1944, American forces converted the Eniwetok Atoll into another powerful base in the Marshalls. These successes permitted the Navy to give Truk in the eastern Carolines the blast-and-bypass treatment and continue on into the Marianas. There the United States fleet faced a Japanese squadron, which had steamed from the Philippines to cut off the American advance. In the first Battle of the Philippine Sea, on June 20, the American forces drove the Japanese back into the shelter of the Philippines. Although most of the Japanese vessels escaped, Japanese sea power never recovered from this disaster. Meanwhile United States forces had reoccupied Guam. Before the end of November, 1944, United States aircraft began the bombing of Japan from bases in the Marianas.

On October 19, two massive assault forces, carrying General Walter Krueger's Sixth Army, appeared off the coast of Leyte in the Philippines. The armada stretched across the vast Pacific horizon. Out at sea, Admiral William Halsey's carrier task force awaited a possible Japanese naval attack. Japan's Singapore fleet, which made up the bulk of Japan's remaining naval strength, moved against the American fleet. Between October 23 and 25 the greatest sea battle of all time was fought for Leyte Gulf. The Japanese fought well but lost heavily. American landing forces required a month of fighting to gain control of Leyte. Samar, a large neighboring island, offered little resistance. The long-awaited invasion of Luzon began on January 9, 1945, and in February the advance units of the Sixth entered Manila. As if this were not enough, by the late spring of 1945, Japanese strength on the mainland of China was also collapsing.

During February, 1945, the United States Navy and Marine Corps captured Iwo Jima in the Bonin Islands. Iwo Jima was near enough to Japan to provide fighter plane bases to support the bombing attacks on Japan from Saipan and Guam. Then on April 1, under cover of an intense naval bombardment, Army and Marine units established a beachhead on the west coast of Okinawa in the Ryukyus. Japan's military position was obviously hopeless. United States fighters from Iwo Jima swept the air over Japan, while superbombers based in the Marianas averaged twelve hundred sorties a week. The Third Fleet sailed into Japanese waters and hammered the coastal cities, unopposed. Meanwhile in the Philippines, MacArthur's command prepared two invasions of Japan.

These invasions never occurred, for three events of August, 1945, brought the war to an immediate end. At Yalta in February, 1945, Stalin promised again, in exchange for the return to Russia of all Japanese territory taken from that nation in 1905, to terminate his country's official neutrality in the Pacific and declare war on Japan a month after victory in Europe. MacArthur and other American officers in the Pacific had warned that an invasion of Japan would be too costly to contemplate unless Russia entered the Pacific war and tied down the Japanese Kwantung Army on the mainland. On August 6 the United States, with British concurrence, dropped an atomic bomb on Hiroshima, completely leveling most of the city and creating havoc among the population with fire and radioactivity. Two days later, too late to make her decision of real military value but early enough to make her a Pacific ally,

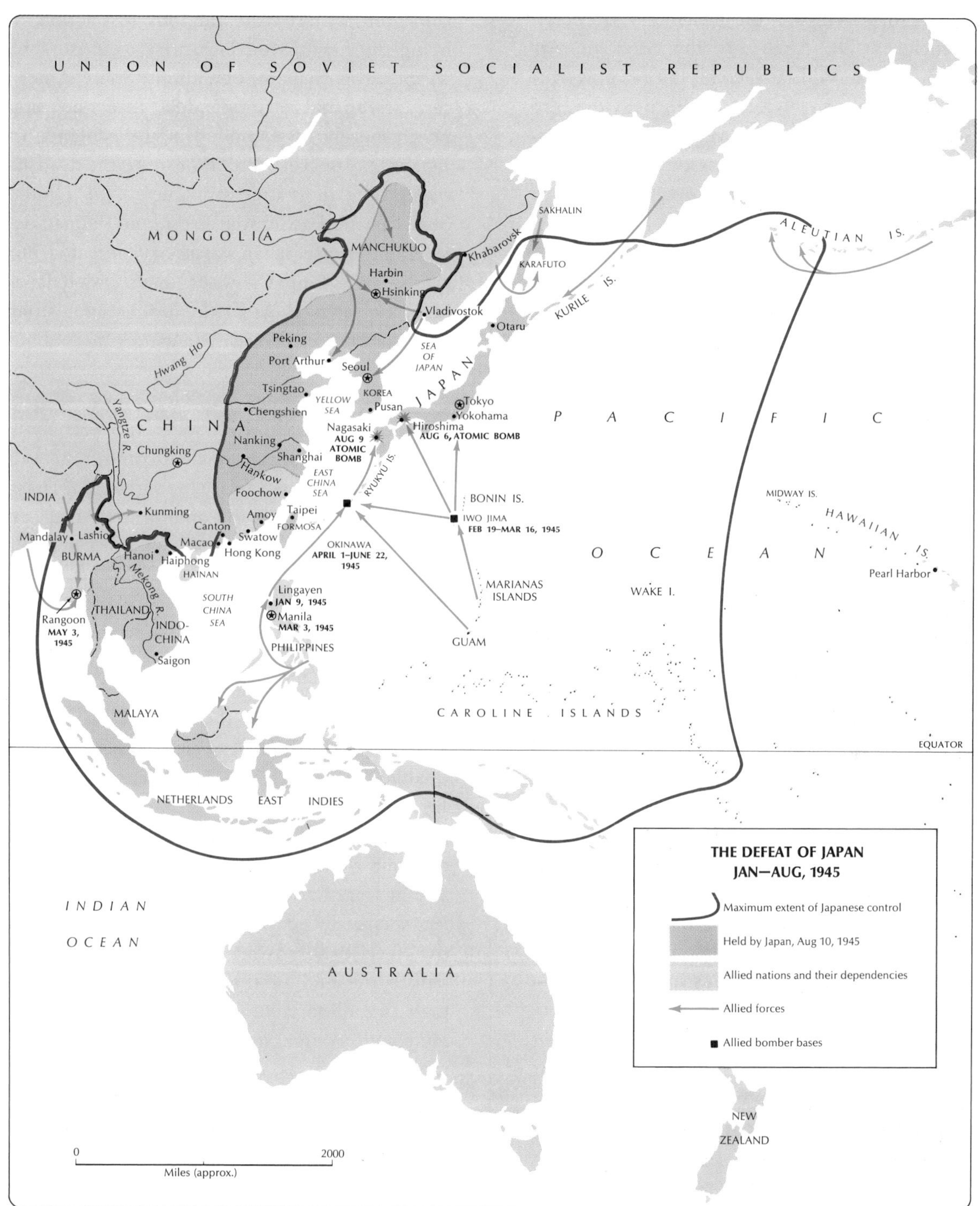

Victory over the Axis

Russia declared war on Japan and occupied Manchuria. On August 9, the Strategic Air Command loosed a second, more powerful atomic bomb on Nagasaki. The next day the Japanese government, having suffered unanticipated and unbearable disaster, surrendered.

Writers have criticized the decisions both to invite Russia into the war against Japan and to drop the two atomic bombs, for these eleventh-hour applications of force appeared unnecessary to bring the war to an immediate conclusion. The employment of atomic bombs gave the United States the dubious distinction of being the first nation in history to loose such weapons on civilian populations. Some American scientists recommended that the first bomb merely be exploded in the presence of Japanese observers to demonstrate the destructive power thereafter available to the United States in the Pacific war. President Truman decided otherwise. Japan was already defeated, but whether the Emperor would have ended Japanese resistance short of the atomic explosions was then, and remains still, a matter of doubt.

Victory on the Home Front

Allied victory in World War II required concerted efforts on the home front as well as on the battlefront. Since this was the first truly world conflict the United States had experienced, the economic demands of war far surpassed anything ever before known. Not only did the United States supply its own troops and civilian population, but it provided billions of dollars' worth of commodities, including military equipment, to Russia, England, and the other Allies. The evolution of the United States into democracy's arsenal was at times slow, halting, and inefficient, but ultimately the organization of the country's human and physical resources for war was nothing less than phenomenal. Hitler's threat to American security seemed so clear that few questioned the war's costs.

To win the battle of production and distribution it became necessary to institute strong government controls over industry, transportation, agriculture, and manpower. Never before in American history had the federal government assumed so much responsibility in organizing and administering the economy as it did during World War II. In addition government support of science and technology played a significant part in determining the final outcome of the war.

At the time France fell in the summer of 1940, there were only 458,365 men in the American Army, Navy, and Marine Corps. This number was clearly insufficient if the United States should become involved in a foreign war. On September 16, 1940, Congress passed the Selective Training and Service Act, the first peacetime draft law in American history. All young men between the ages of twenty-one and thirty-six had to register, and those who qualified were to serve one year. After Pearl Harbor the age limits were changed to include all men between eighteen and forty-five, and the time of service was lengthened. However, late in 1942 the upper age limit for active service was reduced to thirty-eight. Local selective service boards administered the law, and before the end of the war had drafted more than 10 million men. After 1942 the number of men and women in the Armed Forces rose rapidly until by 1945 it reached 12,123,455.

American experiences in World War I had clearly demonstrated how much victory depended on effective economic organization. The British military expert Major General J. F.

C. Fuller declared that "for the first time in the history of war, battles were as much tussles between competing factories as between contending armies. The production of weapons, more so than the conscription of men, was the deciding factor in battle. God now marched with the biggest industries rather than the biggest battalions."

Late in May, 1940, shortly before France fell, the President appointed a Council of National Defense patterned on the World War I experience. Soon afterwards he named a National Defense Advisory Committee to assist the Council in administering programs to direct and organize various phases of the economy. The President selected William Knudsen, head of General Motors, to organize industrial production. Since United States demands, as well as those of the British, encompassed all kinds of defense and war materials, problems of allocations, priorities, and production became steadily more critical. Lack of coordination in the defense program brought demands for an "economic czar." Bernard Baruch, head of the War Industries Board during World War I, was among the strongest proponents of more centralized economic mobilization. Roosevelt, however, continued to rely on committees and agencies which did not have the power or organization to meet the country's defense needs and still send aid to Great Britain.

In January, 1941, less than a year before Pearl Harbor, the President created the Office of Production Management and appointed Knudsen to head it. The job of the OPM was to fix priorities for scarce goods, stimulate defense output, and coordinate the government's purchasing program. Even as it tackled the needs of production, the nation in 1941 also faced the problem of inflation. To cope with these matters Roosevelt established the Office of Price Administration and Civilian Supply in April. But still defense efforts lagged.

It required American entry into the war to inaugurate the kind of central government control over the economy which many people had long regarded necessary. In January, 1942, the President created the War Production Board and named Donald Nelson of Sears Roebuck and Company to head the new agency. WPB was given tremendous powers over the entire economy. Its purpose was to "determine the policies, plans, procedures, and methods of the several Federal departments, establishments, and agencies in respect to war procurement and production, including purchasing, contracting, specifications, and construction; and including conversion, requisitioning, plant expansion, and the financing thereof." President Roosevelt had already outlined the productive task ahead when he called for 60,000 planes and 45,000 tanks in 1942, and 125,000 planes and 75,000 tanks the year following. "Only this all-out scale of production will hasten the ultimate all-out victory," he declared. In time American factories even exceeded the needs of victory.

Congress established other agencies to deal with the economic problems of war. The Office of Defense Transportation bore the responsibility for making the most efficient use of the country's transportation; the War Shipping Administration organized and supervised the shipping industry; the Combined Production and Resources Board integrated American efforts with those of England; and the National War Labor Board dealt with problems of labor.

Economic mobilization involved the federal government in many ways. Besides setting production goals and giving general direction to the private sector, the government loaned money to companies to build and expand their plants. In some cases the government built factories and leased them to private operators, while in other instances it both constructed and operated the plants. Synthetic rubber production represented one effort of the federal government to develop a whole new wartime industry. The government built rubber plants at Baton Rouge, Louisiana; Houston; and Los Angeles; by 1944 the United States output had reached 700,000 tons a year. Although constructed by the government, these plants were operated by private industry.

By the end of 1942 the United States economy had been converted to war. The production of hundreds of civilian items had been stopped or greatly curtailed while plants were geared exclusively to military production What occurred in the automobile industry was characteristic. The number of passenger cars produced in 1941 reached 3,779,682, but this figure dropped to 222,862 in 1942 and to only 610 in 1944. Instead of producing automobiles, the powerful auto industry manufactured tanks, jeeps, aircraft, machine guns, and other military equipment.

Guided by the Maritime Commission, the ship-building industry performed productive feats thought to be impossible in the prewar period. Before the war it required about seven months to complete a moderate-size merchant vessel, but by 1944 Henry J. Kaiser and other ship builders were constructing the famous "Liberty ship" in as little as two weeks. Many people considered Kaiser a miracle man as his shipyards at Portland, Oregon, and Richmond, California, sent hundreds of vessels down the ways in record time. By 1944 American yards launched almost fifty merchant ships a day. Aircraft production was perhaps even more amazing In March, 1944, alone, United States factories built 9,117 military airplanes.

Actually the United States reached the height of its war production in 1943. By that time the war consumed about 35 percent of the gross national product. During the war period, United States plants and factories produced about 300,000 aircraft, 87,000 tanks, 70,000 landing craft, 5,600 oceangoing merchant ships, and vast quantities of arms and ammunition, plus other needed supplies and equipment. Such quantities of equipment proved overwhelming in battle.

Manpower needs rose dramatically after American entry into the war. The draft took millions of men out of the regular labor force, creating problems for both essential and nonessential industries. The War Manpower Commission, created in April, 1942, had the responsibility of securing enough workers to fill defense jobs. There were still 5.5 million unemployed in 1941, which provided a reservoir of workers for the expanding war industries. An increased rate of migration from the farm to urban communities during the war years also added to the industrial labor force. Moreover, younger and older people took jobs, and millions of women went to work in defense plants. In order to assure uninterrupted production, President Roosevelt called a conference of labor and industry representatives to develop means of settling labor disputes. Labor and management agreed on a no-strike, no-lockout policy. On January 12, 1942, the President established the National War Labor Board composed of members from labor, business, and the public. Above all the War Labor Board attempted to keep workers in critical industries. One effective way of holding employees in key positions was to threaten them with military service. In April, 1943, the War Manpower Commission froze workers in certain important jobs.

The record of American farm production during World War II was little short of phenomenal. Despite the tremendous demands for food by the Armed Forces of both the United States and its allies, United States civilians ate better than they had in the prewar years. The slogan "Food will win the war" may have been exaggerated, but abundant food supplies were a source of basic national strength. Although oversupply had plagued farmers in the 1930s, the United States was fortunate to have substantial surpluses of farm products on hand at the time it entered the war. Thereafter the nation had merely to shift from a policy of restricted output to one of full production.

Gross farm production rose about 23 percent between the 1935–1939 period and 1945, although cultivated acreage increased only 5 percent. This meant that greater output came more from better farming practices and a series of favorable crop years than from bringing more land into production. One of the most significant percentage increases in farm production came in oil-bearing crops such as peanuts and soybeans. Organized in 1943, the War Food Administration, headed by Chester C. Davis, encouraged production and regulated the distribution of food.

Despite price controls, agricultural prices rose to 113 percent of parity by 1944, and, with increased production, farmers experienced unprecedented prosperity. Total net farm income jumped from $6.6 billion to $12.4 billion between 1941 and 1945. As a result, tenancy declined to the lowest level since 1910, while farmers reduced their debts and generally improved their financial position and standard of living. What contributed to good times on the farm was the much faster rise in agricultural prices over nonfarm prices, thereby giving farm commodities a high exchange value with industrial products.

Beginning in 1941, the huge wartime demand for goods produced strong inflationary pressures on the economy. To deal with this problem the President in August created the Office of Price Administration. Effective control of prices, however, did not come until October, 1942, when Congress passed the Stabilization Act which gave the President authority to control wages, salaries, and prices. At the same time the President established the Office of Economic Stabilization to provide direction and coordination of the stabilization efforts. He named James F. Byrnes of South Carolina, who was then serving on the Supreme Court, to head this office.

But still inflation continued. In April, 1943, President Roosevelt issued his famous "hold-the-line" order. He instructed the Office of Price Administration "to place ceiling prices on all commodities affecting the cost of living . . . to authorize no further increases in ceiling prices except to the minimum extent required by law." The OPA now had both the power and the will to enforce price controls rigorously. The fact that consumer prices rose only 4.2 percent between April, 1943, and August, 1945, a period of twenty-eight months, indicated the success of this policy. At the same time the War Labor Board enforced rigid wage and salary controls.

Price and wage controls alone could not fully have curbed inflation. To supplement the price control program, the government inaugurated a system of rationing. Besides helping to restrain prices, rationing provided for a more even distribution of scarce commodities. Starting with tires in January, 1942, OPA soon added gasoline, sugar, meat, and other products in short supply to the list. Some 5,600 local boards administered the program through a system of certificates and coupons. Before the war had ended, however, black market operations existed in many communities; that is, rationed commodities were being sold illegally and at higher-than-ceiling prices. But overall, most Americans accepted price controls and rationing as necessary impositions in wartime.

Americans found that modern, mechanized warfare cost tremendous sums of money. The United States not only financed its own military machine but spent billions for lend-lease. Between 1940, when defense costs began to increase, and the end of the war in 1945, federal expenditures rose from about $9 billion to nearly $100 billion annually. With such a strong economy there was no doubt that the United States could raise whatever sums were necessary to prosecute the war. But would the costs be borne by taxes, by borrowing, or by a combination of both methods? Without too much conscious planning, it turned out that taxes provided about 44 percent of the war expenditures while the remainder came from government borrowing. This was a considerably better record than that achieved in World War I, when only about one-third of the costs came from taxes. Congress passed higher income taxes in 1942 and 1944. The 1944 measure raised the maximum tax rates to 94 percent, the highest in history. One of the new and lasting developments in tax policy adopted during the war was the practice of having employers withhold the amount due from an employee's paycheck. This made it easier for people to pay their tax obligations and assured the government a steady income.

Since taxes provided less than half the needed revenue, the government borrowed from individuals and corporations. As a result of this extensive borrowing, the national debt rose very rapidly. In 1941 it stood at about $48 billion, more than double what it had been at the beginning of the New Deal. During the following four years it jumped to $258 billion.

Science and Technology in Wartime

More money and effort went into science and technology during World War II than ever before, and scientific successes contributed markedly to the final outcome of the conflict. As one authority said, "Although the skill and valor of the fighting man remains the most important element in warfare, he has become increasingly dependent on the equipment needed to give him information, mobility and fire power." Among the more important devices and equipment put into use during the war were radar; the proximity fuse; detection devices such as sonar, which, among other things, measures underwater sounds; bomb sights; improved explosives; and the atom bomb.

To organize and administer scientific work relating to defense and war, President Roosevelt in June, 1940, set up the National Defense Research Committee. At about the same time British and American scientists began exchanging data on explosives, radar, and detection devices. In 1941 the President placed the country's wartime scientific efforts in the hands of a new agency, the Office of Scientific Research and Development, headed by Vannevar Bush, President of the Carnegie Institute. The OSRD recruited many of the leading physicists, chemists, and engineers, and arranged for the assistance of hundreds of outstanding scientists in universities and private industry.

Ultimately the most important new weapon developed during World War II was the atom bomb Basic data on nuclear fission had been accumulating since the 1890s, especially after 1929 when E. O. Lawrence built a cyclotron. It was first thought that atomic energy would be used for peaceful purposes, but as war seemed more and more imminent in 1941, scientists turned their attention to the development of an atomic bomb. Having obtained the President's endorsement, an agency headed by General Leslie R. Groves began full-scale efforts early in 1942 to produce an atomic bomb. Vast quantities of material and manpower went into the "Manhattan Project," the code name given to the program. In two years the government spent $2 billion to build the bomb. On July 16, 1945, authorities tested the first atomic bomb on an isolated spot some 120 miles southeast of Albuquerque, New Mexico. Scientists had inaugurated a new age in history.

Nationalism and Civil Rights

Most Americans supported the war wholeheartedly from the time of Pearl Harbor until the Japanese surrender in August, 1945. The nature and extent of opposition which had occurred in 1917 and 1918 simply did not exist after 1941, when a strong surge of patriotism flooded the country in response to the President's call for war against Japan and Germany. People did not doubt the rightness of the American cause. The Office of War Information, headed by the witty and perceptive Elmer Davis, stimulated nationalism and support for the war. The OWI used radio programs, newspapers, pamphlets to publicize the government's point of view. Songs like "God Bless America" and "Praise the Lord and Pass the Ammunition" aroused patriotic emotions.

The Office of Censorship censored mail and publications, but there existed a remarkable amount of freedom of speech and press during the war years. Besides official censorship, correspondents often voluntarily withheld information which might be of help to the enemy, although defeats and mistakes were not usually hidden from the people. Hansen Baldwin, military writer for the *New York Times,* wrote critical articles dealing with military inefficiency and civilian blunders; and Ernie Pyle revealed the horrors of war in his intensely human accounts from the front.

Civil liberties were restricted to some extent by the Smith Alien Registration Act of 1940. This law gave the federal government power to curb those who tried to interfere with the "loyalty, morale, or discipline" of the military forces or who advised disloyalty or overthrow of the government by force or violence. This was the first peacetime sedition law since 1798. There were a few convictions under this legislation during the war, including that of the American Nazi William Dudley Pelley. The Postmaster General also restricted circulation of Father Coughlin's *Social Justice* and a Communist paper, *The Militant,* by withdrawing their mailing privileges. The question of whether martial law and military justice were a violation of civil rights was decided when the Supreme Court upheld the right of a military court to try and convict eight German saboteurs captured in 1942.

The Japanese in the western part of the United States suffered the worst violations of civil rights. In February, 1942, President Roosevelt ordered restrictions against certain people in prescribed military areas, mainly in California and the western parts of Arizona, Oregon, and Washington. Persons of Japanese ancestry, regardless of whether or not they were American citizens, were restricted by a curfew and later excluded from those areas. The government created a War Relocation Authority which established ten inland detention centers where the Japanese had to be resettled. This action seemed to be a gross infringement of the civil rights of people who had neither broken any law nor been convicted of any crime. Again, in *Hirabayashi v. United States* the Supreme Court upheld the executive order which required Japanese in certain prescribed areas to remain in their homes between 8 P.M. and 6 A.M. "as a protection against espionage and against sabotage."

Blacks in Wartime

Blacks had made some gains in education, employment, and social position during the New Deal years, but progress had been spotty and slow. The vast majority of the nation's black citizens still suffered from discrimination and lack of opportunity on the eve of World War II. There were, for example, very few Negroes in any branch of the Armed Forces in 1940, and only two infantry and two black cavalry units were at full strength. The Selective Service Act of September, 1940, forbade racial discrimination in the drafting and training of soldiers, but many local draft boards ignored this order and accepted only whites. Although black leaders complained about discrimination and segregation in the Armed Forces, concessions and reform came slowly. Blacks also found it difficult to obtain jobs in the expanding defense industries.

As frustrations grew in black communities, A. Philip Randolph, president of the Brotherhood of Sleeping Car Porters, early in 1941 urged Negroes to march on Washington and demand equal rights. Alarmed at this possibility, government officials attempted to discourage the march. However, Randolph refused to call it off until President Roosevelt issued an order on June 25, only a few days before the march was to take place, saying that "there shall be no discrimination in the employment of workers in defense industries or Government because of race, creed, color or national origin." The President appointed a Fair Employment Practices Committee to deal with the problem. These measures met bitter resentment in the South. One Southern newspaperman declared that "all the armies of the world . . . could not force upon the South the abandonment of racial segregation."

About one million blacks served in the American Armed Forces during World War II; some 700,000 were in the Army, and thousands more joined the Navy, Air Force, and Marines. They were admitted to officer candidate schools, and hundreds received commissions. For the most part, however, blacks fought in segregated units. It was not until 1945 that blacks as individuals were integrated into white units and black and white Americans fought side by side against Hitler's legions in Germany. Unfortunately, at most military camps and in the surrounding communities, black servicemen faced discrimination in theaters, post exchanges, and even in officers' clubs. In July, 1944, a War Department order banned racial segregation in transportation and

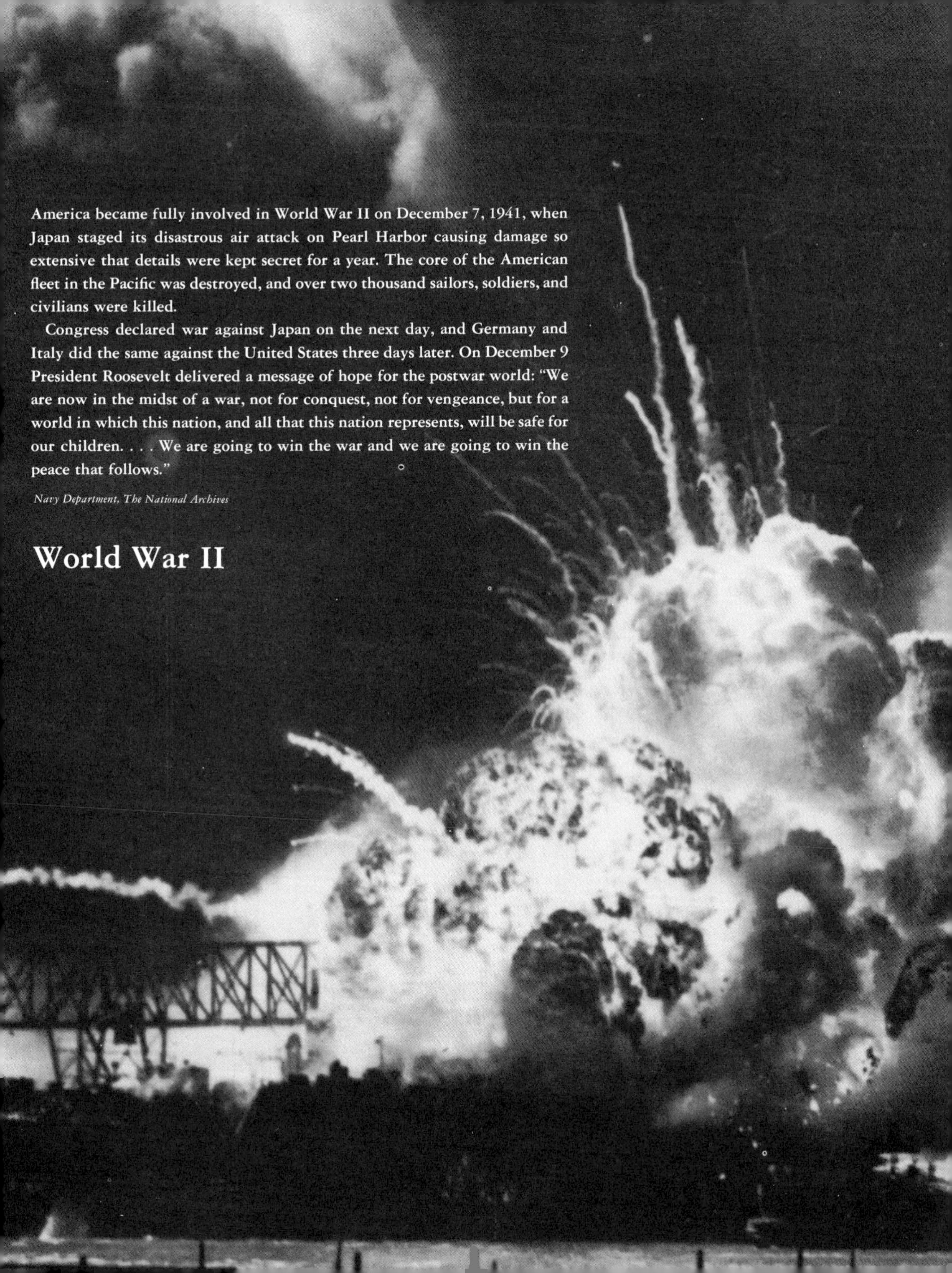

America became fully involved in World War II on December 7, 1941, when Japan staged its disastrous air attack on Pearl Harbor causing damage so extensive that details were kept secret for a year. The core of the American fleet in the Pacific was destroyed, and over two thousand sailors, soldiers, and civilians were killed.

Congress declared war against Japan on the next day, and Germany and Italy did the same against the United States three days later. On December 9 President Roosevelt delivered a message of hope for the postwar world: "We are now in the midst of a war, not for conquest, not for vengeance, but for a world in which this nation, and all that this nation represents, will be safe for our children. . . . We are going to win the war and we are going to win the peace that follows."

Navy Department, The National Archives

World War II

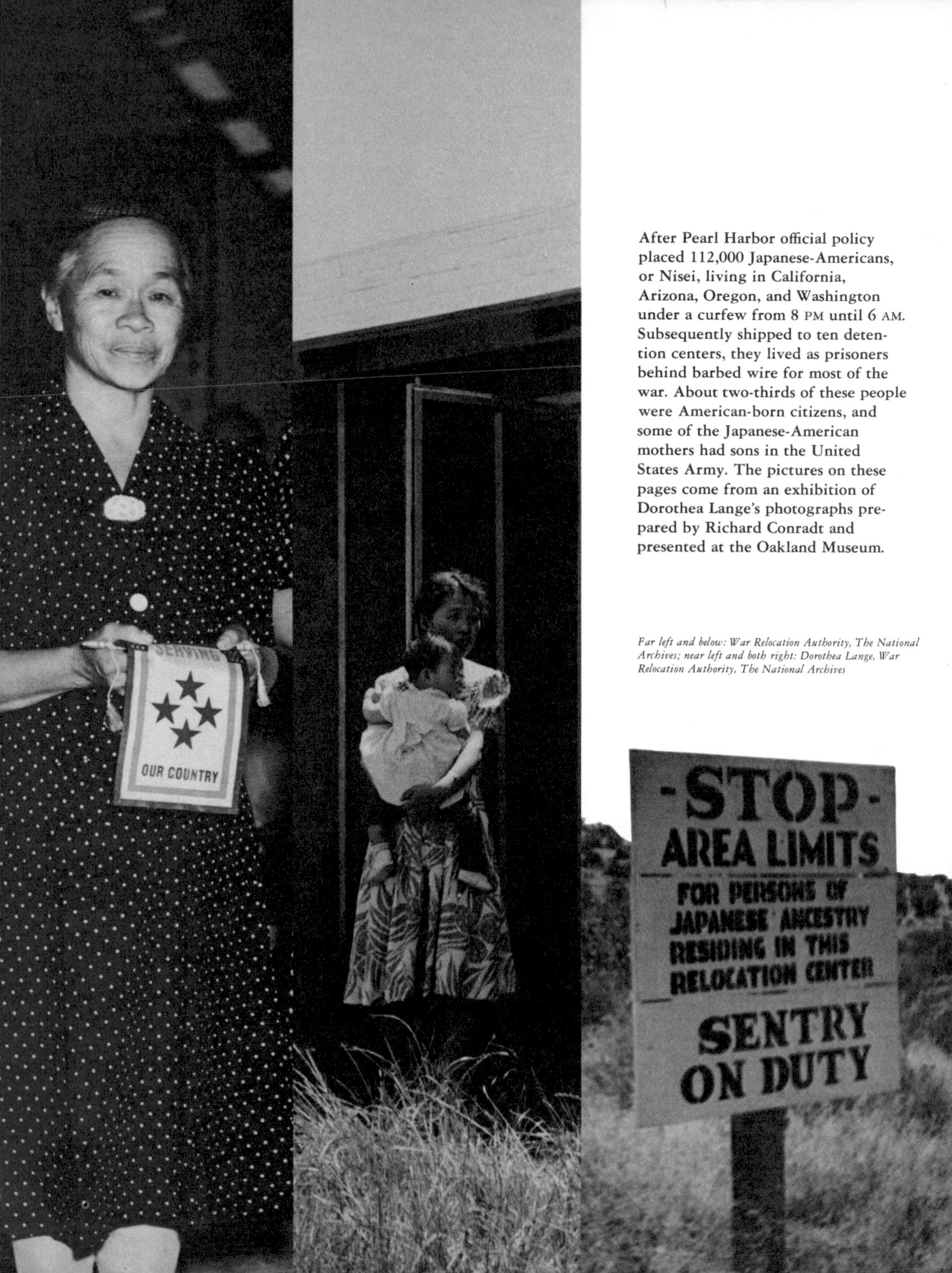

After Pearl Harbor official policy placed 112,000 Japanese-Americans, or Nisei, living in California, Arizona, Oregon, and Washington under a curfew from 8 PM until 6 AM. Subsequently shipped to ten detention centers, they lived as prisoners behind barbed wire for most of the war. About two-thirds of these people were American-born citizens, and some of the Japanese-American mothers had sons in the United States Army. The pictures on these pages come from an exhibition of Dorothea Lange's photographs prepared by Richard Conradt and presented at the Oakland Museum.

Far left and below: War Relocation Authority, The National Archives; near left and both right: Dorothea Lange, War Relocation Authority, The National Archives

Americans at home saw the war not on television, but in the pages of picture magazines. The late Robert Capa made an outstanding contribution to this documentation of the war. These photographs are from his book, *Images of War* (Grossman Publishers). Capa followed every major step of the American campaign in North Africa and Europe. Pictured here are the fighting in North Africa, below, and, at right, the invasion of Normandy which Capa photographed as the first wave of troops reached French soil. The Italian campaign appears on the next page, top left.

LEADER

Capa covered the liberation of Paris and then parachuted with the 17th Airborne Division into Germany. "We lost many of our men," he wrote, "but it was easier than Salerno, or Anzio, or Normandy. The Germans of those campaigns would have murdered us here, but these Germans were beaten." At the right is Capa's picture of the man he said was the last American to die in Germany.

A special photographic unit headed by Captain Edward Steichen created an extensive visual document of the Navy's role in the war. Here air crewmen aboard the *U.S.S. Saratoga* prepare for a strike against Rabaul in November, 1942; left, center, one of the men wounded in the strike is helped from his plane; left, bottom, a view of the battle for Saipan in June, 1944.

Wayne Miller for Navy Dept., The National Archives

Wayne Miller for Navy Dept., The National Archives

Navy Dept., The National Archives

Navy Dept., The National Archives

No documentation of World War II caught its human meaning—the terror and suffering—more powerfully than the photographs taken by W. Eugene Smith in the Pacific. A selection of Smith's work from his book, *W. Eugene Smith: Photographer* (An Aperture Monograph, 1970), appears here. Below, beachhead in February, 1945; above, a Marine demolition team detonates a charge to blast Japanese troops out of an Iwo Jima cave; right, above, a flame-thrower in action on Okinawa.

Americans became aware of the horror of the war through photographs such as those at left of concentration camps where officers of the Third Reich murdered an estimated six million Jews in a deliberate program of genocide.

The United States dropped an atomic bomb 28 inches in diameter and 120 inches long, with an explosive power of 20,000 tons of TNT, on the city of Hiroshima on August 6, 1945. Exploding 2,000 feet above the city, it obliterated an area of more than 4 square miles and killed an estimated 80,000 people and injured at least as many more. Three days later another atomic bomb fell on Nagasaki. On August 14 Japan surrendered. Below is a view of Hiroshima after the bomb had been dropped; at far right, a victim of radiation burns.

Both far left and left above: United Press International; below: Shunkichi Kikuchi, Magnum; above: The National Archives, Army Institute of Pathology

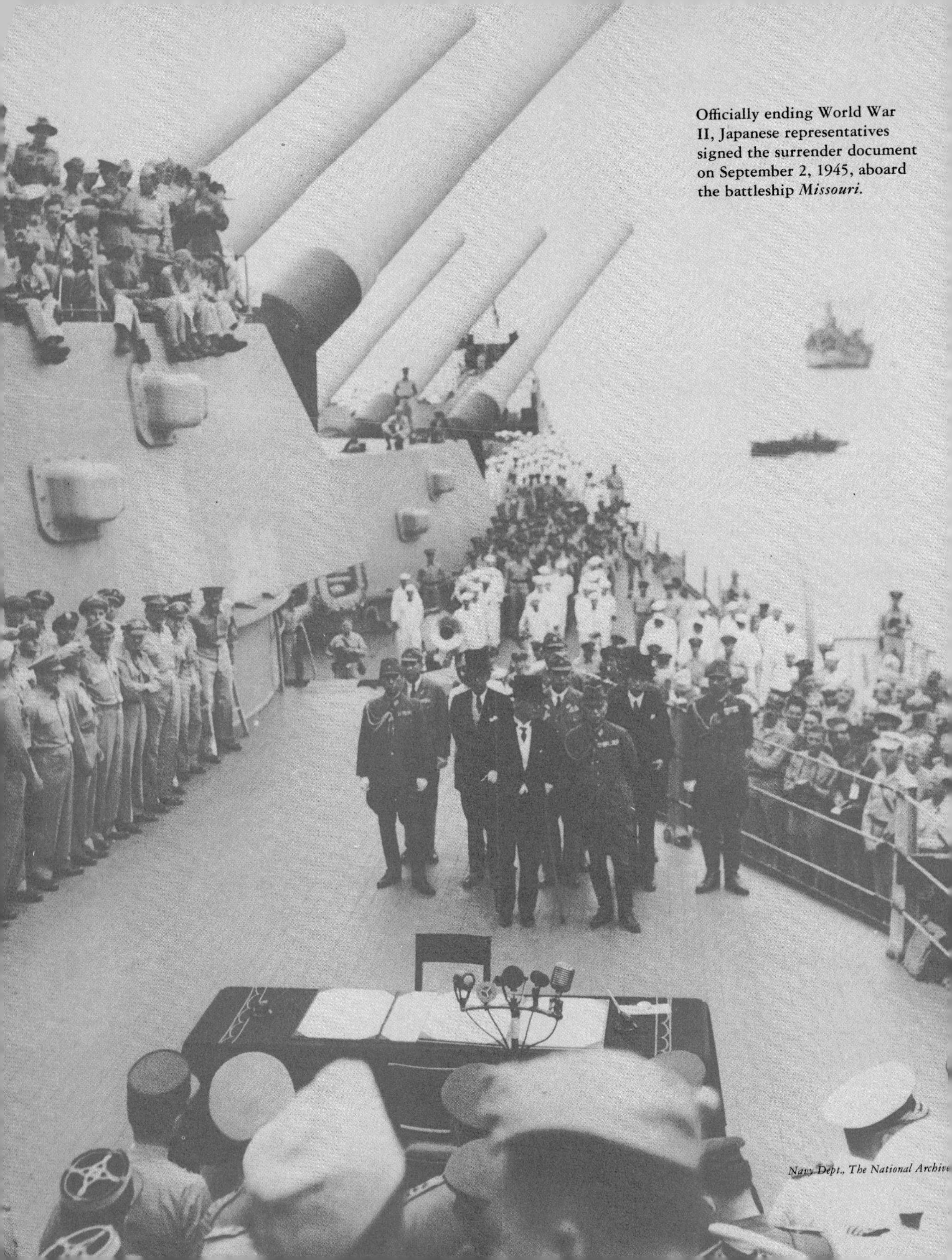

Officially ending World War II, Japanese representatives signed the surrender document on September 2, 1945, aboard the battleship *Missouri*.

Navy Dept., The National Archive

recreation facilities at army posts, but it was never strictly enforced. Even though Negroes won the Distinguished Service Cross and other high military honors, they continued to suffer from discrimination.

Negroes moved slowly into the defense industries. Pressure from the FEPC and other government agencies gradually opened up these new employment opportunities. Thousands of blacks entered the aircraft industries, shipyards, and steel and rubber plants. Defense-related employment drew an increasing number from the rural South into Northern and Western cities. The black population of Los Angeles doubled between 1940 and 1945, while thousands went to Detroit, Chicago, and other cities. Tension over housing, jobs, and social discrimination opened the way for several race riots. The most serious conflict occurred in Detroit in June, 1943, when a fistfight set off rumors and rioting which ended only after twenty-five blacks and nine whites had been killed. It took 6,000 troops to restore order. Although Negroes made some solid social and economic gains, by the end of the war an increasing number were expressing open resentment at having to fight for a society which refused to grant them first-class citizenship. A new militancy was in the making as blacks both inside and outside the Armed Forces saw more clearly than ever the gap between the easy professions of democracy in America and continued segregation and discrimination.

Politics in Wartime

Despite the need for national unity and strong executive direction during the war years, partisan politics continued with little change. People retained their faith in the ordinary democratic processes; they held elections as usual; and conflicts between Congress and the President existed much the same as in peacetime. About all that united Democrats and Republicans was the desire for military victory.

The drive for domestic reform had already slackened before the United States entered the war; thereafter the concentration on wartime issues provided an added excuse to attack the philosophy and programs of the New Deal. Roosevelt himself declared that "Dr. New Deal" had been replaced by "Dr. Win-the-war." In the midterm elections of November, 1942, the Republicans made substantial gains after criticizing what they considered unnecessary and inefficient New Deal measures. When Congress met in January, 1943, the Democrats had their narrowest margin in years: 218 seats compared with 208 for the Republicans. The Republicans had also picked up nine places in the Senate. The increased number of Republicans, added to the conservative Democrats, gave Congress a conservative outlook during the war years.

As the presidential election of 1944 approached, the Republicans had a number of hopeful candidates, including Wendell Willkie, who had run well in 1940, and Harold Stassen, former Governor of Minnesota. By convention time, however, Governor Thomas E. Dewey of New York had emerged as the party's best prospect. Dewey had made a national reputation as a crime fighter when he served as New York City's district attorney. After nominating Dewey on the first ballot, the delegates named Governor John W. Bricker of Ohio, a strong conservative, to run with the moderately progressive Dewey.

Many Democrats who had objected to Roosevelt's third term were even more opposed to a fourth-term nomination. Former Vice President John Nance Garner wrote to James A. Farley in 1943, "I think it would be a terrible thing to have Roosevelt elected again." Farley agreed, but no one could successfully challenge the President. Besides, too many Democrats were afraid that only Roosevelt could carry the party to victory in 1944. Roosevelt was nominated on the first ballot. After considerable skirmishing over the vice presidential nomination, the delegates chose Senator Harry S. Truman of Missouri. Truman had emerged as a national figure because of his investigations of national defense problems. Still the Missourian had other assets; he came from a border state; powerful Democrats considered him conservative; and, as one observer said, he was "an approximation of everybody."

Dewey campaigned against "the tired old men" of the Roosevelt administration and accused the Democrats of lethargy and inefficiency. Although Dewey did not propose to repeal the main New Deal reforms, he emphasized that the country needed a change of leadership and more effective administration. Reports that Dewey was gaining ground and speculation about the President's health forced Roosevelt to abandon his plans not to engage in a personal campaign. He made several major speeches, generally speaking from a seated position, because by late 1944 he had nearly lost the use of his legs. Organized labor, especially the Political Action Committee of the CIO established in 1943, campaigned vigorously for the President. Liberals in general also supported him. The result was a landslide victory for Roosevelt in the electoral college—432 to 99—although his popular margin was only about 2.5 million votes. Although the Republicans gained a higher percentage of the votes than at any time since 1928, organized labor, minority groups including the Negroes and Jews, federal employees, and intellectuals made up a coalition which was still loyal to Roosevelt and the Democratic party.

Roosevelt's health, which had been a subject of comment during the campaign, grew steadily worse after the election. By January, 1945, he looked ill. His face was drawn, he appeared thin and tired, his hands trembled, and his voice sometimes faltered. Despite his worsening condition, he continued to perform his heavy duties and even made a trip to Yalta in February. Then on April 12 he died suddenly of a cerebral hemorrhage at his Warm Springs, Georgia, home. A shocked and sorrowful nation could scarcely believe that the man who had led its people through depression and war—millions of Americans could not remember any other President—was gone. He had after 1933 transformed discouragement into national confidence; when later the national interest and security were threatened by the dictators, he had brought the country to the brink of victory. Roosevelt was dead, but his policies as well as his liberal and humane spirit lived on.

Life on the Home Front

Total war affected the lives of people in many ways. There was a loosening of family ties as millions of men left their homes for military duty and women deserted the household for the factory. The housing shortage became critical in many areas, especially near military installations. Gasoline rationing sharply reduced travel in private automobiles. As one observer remarked, "You could have fired a bazooka down any Main Street in the country without hitting a vehicle." Colleges and universities were deeply affected by the war. Faculty members joined the armed services; student enrollments dropped sharply as only women and young or physically disqualified men continued in school. The government, it is true, used college and university facilities for some training programs, but the war's profound influence on higher education was made apparent by the fact that in 1944 the nation's institutions of higher learning granted only 141,582 degrees, as compared with 216,521 in 1940. But if higher education suffered because of the war, religion flourished. Churches were filled with worshipers, and between 1940 and 1946 membership in all religious bodies rose by some 6 million. Moreover, religion became more personal and emotional as wives and parents prayed for their loved ones abroad.

Another important wartime influence on American life was the enlarged role of the federal government. The powers and responsibilities of the government had been increasing for many years, but neither the regulatory actions of the progressive era nor the New Deal legislation compared to the ways in which the national government affected the lives of people during World War II. The draft; wage, rent, and price controls; and rationing touched every citizen. Furthermore, the tax and spending policies of the federal government influenced the economy far beyond anything previously known. Wartime budgets outstripped WPA's meager resources. Eventually most wartime restrictions were discarded, but the increased role of government in the nation's economic and social life continued. The war accentuated the trend toward "big government."

Conclusion

The United States emerged from World War II stronger and more prosperous than at any time in its history. The gross national product, in dollars of constant purchasing power, increased from $230 billion in 1940 to $360 billion in 1945, a rise of 56 percent. Per capita income climbed 30 percent. The remarkable performance of the economy tended to discredit the theories of economic stagnation so popular during the prewar depression years. Moreover, businessmen, who had done so much to help win the war, regained some of the reputation they had lost during the Depression after 1929. Although people complained of scarcities and hardships, morale on the home front was excellent throughout the war. To many Americans, victory proved the strength of free institutions.

If the United States had contributed mightily to the defeat of Germany and Japan, it had drastically changed the world balance of power. For the destruction of the two historic counterforces to Russian power and ambition transformed Russia into the dominant power of the Eurasian world. And long before the end of the war it was evident that Russian objectives in the postwar world had little or no relationship to those of the United States. Therefore, the United States would either modify its purposes for postwar Europe or enter a new period of high tension and continued involvement in world affairs.

Four short histories provide useful introductions to the military aspects of World War II: Cyril B. Falls's *The Second World War: A Short History* (1948); J. F. C. Fuller's *The Second World War,* 1939–1945 (1949); Louis L. Snyder's *The War: A Concise History,* 1939–1945* (1960); and Fletcher Pratt's *War for the World* (1950). The last volume portrays the intense drama of global war. For a more detailed account of the fighting see T. D. Stamps and V. J. Esposite's *A Military History of World War II* (2 vols., 1953). For the role of the United States see A. R. Buchanan's excellent *The United States and World II** (2 vols., 1964). K. S. Davis's *An Experience of War: The United States in World War II* (1965) traces both the military and the nonmilitary aspects of the war. For the war in Europe see Dwight D. Eisenhower's *Crusade in Europe* (1948) and Omar N. Bradley's *A Soldier's Story* (1951). The invasion of the Normandy coast has been treated well in Cornelius Ryan's *The Longest Day: June* 6, 1944 (1959). L. F. Ellis's *The Battle for Normandy* (1962) traces the European land campaigns which followed. Winston Churchill's monumental six-volume history of the war has been abridged into one volume: *Memoirs of the Second World War* (1959). On the role of air power in the Allied victory see A. W. Tedder's *Air Power in War* (1948) and Hans Rumpf's *The Bombing of Germany* (1961). Two volumes on the fall of Berlin are John Toland's *The Last Hundred Days* (1965) and Cornelius Ryan's *The Last Battle* (1966). Both authors are critical of Eisenhower's decision to halt at the Elbe.

The war at sea, especially in the Pacific, has been covered in detail by S. E. Morison in his *History of United States Naval Operations in World War II* (15 vols., 1947–1962). Morison has summarized his vast researches in *The Two-ocean War* (1963). The strategy of island-hopping in the Pacific can be examined in Frank Hough's *The Island War* (1947), as well as in Jeter Isely and P. A. Crowl's *The U. S. Marines and Amphibious War* (1951). General Douglas MacArthur's *Reminiscences* (1964) reveal much about the general as well as his role in the Pacific campaigns.

On the military decision to use the atomic bomb against Japan the best general account is Herbert Feis's *Japan Subdued: The Atomic Bomb and the End of the War in the Pacific* (1961). Also very useful are the memoirs of Leslie R. Groves who headed the atomic project, *Now It Can Be Told: The Story of the Manhattan Project* (1962).

United States strategy and management of the war have been analyzed at length. Ray G. Cline covers such questions in his *Washington Command Post: The Operations Division* (1951). Stephen E. Ambrose's *Eisenhower and Berlin,* 1945: *The Decision to Halt at the Elbe** (1967) is an excellent study of the Elbe decision. Greenfield has provided a further evaluation of United States strategy in his *American Strategy in World War II: A Reconsideration* (1963). Anne Armstrong argues in *Unconditional Surrender: The Impact of the Casablanca Policy upon World War II* (1961) that the policy prolonged the war. Three brief but highly stimulating evaluations of American strategy are S. E. Morison's *Strategy and Compromise* (1958); Hansen W. Baldwin's *Great Mistakes of the War* (1950); and Sumner Welles's *Seven Decisions That Shaped History* (1951).

On economic and military mobilization Eliot Janeway's *The Struggle for Survival: A Chronicle of Economic Mobilization in World War II* (1951) is a fine general account. The early wartime economy has been well treated by Seymour E. Harris in *The Economics of America at War* (1943), and his later volume, *Inflation and the American Economy* (1945), carries the story to near the war's end. Donald Nelson, head of the War Production Board, discusses wartime production in *Arsenal of Democracy: The Story of American War Production* (1946). Even better is Francis Walton's *Miracle of World War II: How American Industry Made Victory Possible* (1956). On economic controls see *Wartime Production Controls* (1949) by David Novick and others, and W. A. Nielander's *Wartime Food Rationing in the United States* (1947). In *The Black Market: A Study of White Collar Crime* (1952), Marshall Clinard has shown how some people sought to take advantage of scarcity.

The problems of financing the war have been adequately treated by H. C. Murphy in *National Debt in War and Transition* (1950). This should be supplemented with L. V. Chandler's *Inflation in the United States* (1951). Wartime agriculture has been most fully treated by W. W. Wilcox's *The Farmer in the Second World War* (1947). The role of labor has been considered by Joel Seidman in *American Labor from Defense to Reconversion* (1953).

Roland Young's *Congressional Politics in the Second World War* (1956) shows the growing political conservatism of Congress during World War II. The congressional attempt to check on the efficiency and expenditures of wartime agencies has been considered in *Diary of Democracy: The Senate War Investigating Committee* (1947) by Harry Toulmin. On American society in wartime see Jack Goodman's *While You Were Gone: A Report on Wartime Life in the United States* (1946). H. S. Corwin's *Total War and the Constitution* (1947) deals with the important question of wartime civil rights. *Americans Betrayed: Politics and the Japanese Evacuation* (1949) by M. B. Grodzins is an excellent discussion of the relocation of the Japanese-Americans.

On the problems of Negroes see Gunnar Myrdal's *An American Dilemma: The Negro Problem and Modern Democracy** (2 vols., 1944); William Brink and Louis Harris's *The Negro Revolution in America* (1964); and E. F. Frazier's *The Negro in the United States* (rev. ed., 1957). For black military contributions see Ulysses Lee's *United States Army in World War II: Special Studies: The Employment of Negro Troops* (1966).

* indicates availability in paperback.

36

The Cold War in Europe and Asia

FOR A TIME IN 1945 it seemed to Americans that the nation's wartime effort had destroyed the last enemies of peace and stability in the world and laid the foundation for a new era of international cooperation. Three wartime allies —Britain, Russia, and the United States—had rendered Germany powerless, but it was American industrial might and efficiency that had guaranteed the overwhelming success of the Allied naval, air, and land forces. American diplomacy, moreover, had sustained the great coalition and, through careful wartime planning, had apparently created the basis for continuing world peace. Yet no American knowledgeable in matters of wartime diplomacy could anticipate the coming of peace with complete satisfaction. Postwar peace and security demanded the continuing cooperation of the wartime Allies. For some, this seemed a dubious prospect. Roosevelt's constant iteration of America's friendship for the Soviet Union had helped to cement the coalition against Germany and gain some Soviet promises regarding the reconstruction of Europe. But perspicacious observers doubted that the President's tactics of conciliation had altered the Kremlin's expectations and purposes regarding Germany and Eastern Europe. As long as political differences were submerged by mutually profitable agreements on military strategy, American officials could encourage the nation's assumption that Allied relationships were good. But with Nazi Germany's demise in 1945 it became clear that the world, despite the American effort, held little more assurance of tranquillity than it had at the time of Pearl Harbor.

On August 14, 1941, President Roosevelt and Prime Minister Churchill officially proclaimed their joint political objectives in the famed Atlantic Charter. The first three principles of the Charter declared that the United States and Great Britain sought "no aggrandizement, territorial or other," that they desired "to see no territorial changes that [did] not accord with the freely expressed wishes of the people concerned," and that they respected "the right of all peoples to choose the form of government under which they will live." In a London broadcast ten days later, Churchill praised the Atlantic Charter as an Anglo-American declaration of unity and purpose. Yet the Charter, so thoroughly attuned to American and British aspirations, ignored completely the expressed interests of the third major wartime partner, the Soviet Union. The United States and Britain entered the war as powers seeking nothing in victory but the reestablishment of peace and stability. For the Kremlin such limited goals were unacceptable. As a matter of security, Russia would insist upon a strong Soviet voice in Eastern Europe. Russian leaders, moreover, would take the necessity for Germany's utter defeat far more seriously than Britain or the United States, for German invasions had twice in one long generation exacted a frightful price from the Soviet Union. Because of Russia's historic problems and ambitions, Stalin was unprepared to settle for a postwar world based solely on the principle of self-determination.

The Soviet Union's ambivalence toward the question of postwar reconstruction was made manifest early in the war Once Hitler turned on them the Russians were in no position to antagonize their Western Allies. Eventually the Soviets signed the Charter. Yet even then Stalin made clear his determination to maintain control of all the areas granted to Russia by the Nazi-Soviet Pact. Even as war engulfed the U.S.S.R. in 1941, Soviet diplomats pressed the British and American governments for formal recognition of Russia's territorial gains. For Roosevelt and Hull the Soviet determination to extend its political influence into Eastern Europe created a cruel dilemma. American purpose, now anchored to the Atlantic Charter, ruled out any compromise with the Soviets on spheres of influence. Yet without the full military effort of the U.S.S.R., the United States and Great Britain would have been hard pressed to defeat the Axis. Secretary Hull discovered an answer to this quandary in the critical decision to postpone until the end of the war all territorial decisions potentially in defiance of the Charter. When on December 4, 1941, three days before Pearl Harbor, the British Foreign Office informed Washington that the Soviet Union was suspicious of Western intentions and that Foreign Secretary Anthony Eden was shortly to visit Moscow to allay Soviet doubts, Hull warned the British against any secret arrangements regarding the future of Eastern Europe. United States postwar policies, he wrote, "have been delineated in the Atlantic Charter which today represents the attitude not only of the United States but also of Great Britain and of the Soviet Union."

The Charter, of course, did not express the attitude of the Soviet Union. Thus the decision to postpone territorial settlements simply kept hidden from public view the ultimately inescapable elements of future discord among the

Big Three. Any policy which promised publicly a postwar triumph for the principles of self-determination in vast and important areas, concerning which national leaders admitted privately that American and British power would have little influence, could lead only to eventual embarrassment and disillusionment for all concerned. Yet at no time in the course of the victorious campaigns against the Axis powers did the Roosevelt leadership attempt to escape this self-imposed dilemma. The policy of postponing all essential political decisions in the interest of wartime unity might have been realistic and possibly successful had Roosevelt and Hull prepared themselves and the nation for some hard bargaining with the Soviets at the termination of hostilities. But to the end of the war they based all United States postwar policy toward liberated Europe on the principles of the Atlantic Charter without either pondering the means required to compel the Kremlin to accept such principles or preparing the people of the United States and Europe for their predictable failure

Divided Europe

At the Yalta Conference of February, 1945, Roosevelt could scarcely hide the impending clash between Western and Soviet purpose in Eastern Europe. Even before Roosevelt left for the Crimea in late January, the State Department had intimated that the time when the United States could control the politics of Eastern Europe was no more. In a sense Western Europe had lost that prerogative when it failed to protect Czechoslovakia and Poland from German and Soviet power in 1939. By now it was becoming increasingly clear that nothing remained to counter the Soviet military position except the Russian signature on the Atlantic Charter.

Already events in liberated Poland had put the wartime alliance to a stern test. Early in January, 1945, Moscow announced the Soviet Union's recognition of the Russian-controlled Lublin Committee as the provisional government of Poland. The Red Army bestrode Eastern Europe. At Yalta, Roosevelt and Churchill were thus forced to a last-ditch effort to maintain even a modicum of Western influence in Slavic Europe. They refused to accept the Lublin Committee as representative of the Polish people. Stalin, facing still-powerful Nazi resistance on the Eastern Front and desiring at the moment to avoid a break with the West, accepted the Declaration on Poland, which provided for free elections on the basis of universal suffrage and the secret ballot. It was also decided to award the Soviet Union the eastern portion of Poland's prewar territory; Warsaw was to accept the old Curzon Line for its eastern border and be compensated in the west at the expense of a defeated Germany. The key issue of reparations the Big Three did not discuss. Nor was the exact location of Poland's western frontier established. Again the wartime policy of postponement had dominated the actions of the Big Three.

Confronted both with Western reluctance to negotiate a general agreement on boundary questions, as well as with continued political resistance within the Slavic states themselves, Stalin in 1945 proceeded unilaterally to turn liberated Europe into a Soviet sphere of influence. In February he dispatched Soviet diplomat Andrei Vishinski to Bucharest to force King Michael to appoint the Soviet puppet Petra Groza as head of the new Communist-dominated government in Rumania. Early in March, Foreign Minister Molotov demanded that the Lublin regime form the core of the provisional government of Poland promised at Yalta. The pattern of Kremlin policy was thus established. Using military, political, and ideological leverage, Stalin was able to set up a series of Communist-led governments in regions occupied by the Red troops. In this way Stalin fulfilled his wartime objectives of preventing the reestablishment of unfriendly states along Russia's western frontier.

This pattern of Soviet behavior, whatever its logic and necessity from the Russian viewpoint, became deeply disturbing—indeed unacceptable—to Washington officialdom. The new President, Harry S. Truman, burdened by Roosevelt's death in April, 1945, with full responsibility for United States foreign policy, was reminded by Ambassador to Moscow Averill Harriman that Soviet domination of Eastern Europe was intolerable. He urged the President to adopt a strong stand toward the Kremlin and make it clear that the United States expected the U.S.S.R. to live up to the Yalta agreements. The power to force compliance, believed Harriman, lay in the American economy; the Soviets would yield "because they needed our help in their reconstruction program." Harriman converted Washington officials generally to the necessity of a hard line. When Soviet Foreign Minister V. M. Molotov called at the White House on April 23, Truman warned him that no longer would United States–Soviet agreements be a "one-way street." Shortly thereafter the President, without warning, ordered a serious cutback in lend-lease aid to Russia. The action exerted pressure on the Soviets, but not enough to alter their established purposes for Slavic Europe. Thereafter Washington might quarrel with Moscow in defense of its principles; it would never find a means short of war to control events where Soviet power was effective. Even as the war in Europe drew to an end, the Soviets gave the United States three clear choices: agreement in defiance of principle; continued postponement of all political settlements; or war. Washington pushed postponement into the postwar era, preferring not to recognize diplomatically any political and territorial arrangements which defied America's preferences.

Revisionist historians of the 1960s would criticize the Truman leadership both for its unwillingness to recognize Soviet security interests in Eastern Europe and for its assumption that a hard-line policy, whether anchored to economic or even atomic power, would compel a satisfactory adjustment in Soviet behavior. They would charge not only that the hard line failed to achieve its objectives but, even worse, that it revealed an American aggressiveness toward the U.S.S.R. which eventually broke up the Big Three alliance.

By the late spring of 1945 the differences between United States and Soviet purpose in Eastern Europe were moving rapidly beyond the point of reconciliation. At this critical juncture, President Truman dispatched Harry Hopkins to confer with Stalin on the matter of Poland's future. In Moscow, Hopkins warned the Russian leader that Kremlin policy toward liberated Europe and especially Poland was fast destroying the sympathy of the American people for the Soviet Union. Stalin was unmoved, reminding Hopkins of the vital importance of Poland to Russia's security. Commented Ambassador Harriman, "I am afraid that Stalin does not and never will fully understand our interest in a free Poland as a matter of principle. The Russian Premier is a realist in all of his actions, and it is hard for him to appreciate our faith in abstract principle. It is difficult for him to understand why we should want to interfere with Soviet policy in a country like Poland which he considers so important to Russia's security unless we have some ulterior motive."

From April until June, 1945, continuing Big Three disagreements over postwar reconstruction focused on the question of German occupation, including the future of Berlin. Churchill argued that the occupation zones agreed upon at Yalta need not influence military operations still under way and that Berlin, Prague, and Vienna could be occupied by whatever power reached them first. It seemed essential to Churchill that Western forces reach Berlin ahead of the Russians. If Soviet troops took Berlin, he wrote to Roosevelt, it might make Stalin even more arrogant and intractable. Churchill did not have his way. American General Dwight D. Eisenhower, Supreme Commander of the Western forces in Europe operated under a general directive that called for military action to destroy the German army and end the war as rapidly as possible. Eisenhower believed it more important to capture the Nazi forces opposing him than to compete with the Russians for the capture of Berlin. Nor did the Allies, as Churchill thought they should, come to a general understanding with Russia before retiring to the agreed-upon zones of occupation. Truman, backed by his advisers and seeing Churchill as too much concerned with Britain's continental interests, decided to pull American forces back without a previous settlement with the Kremlin.

In June, 1945, the President announced the satisfactory settlement of the Polish question, concluding with a benediction to Soviet-American friendship. On the twenty-second of June the Soviet-oriented regime in Warsaw received American recognition. The question of Western access to Berlin, an international island in the sea of the Soviet German Zone, remained open. Though Stalin had made clear the Kremlin's view that Western access to Berlin through Soviet-controlled territory was a privilege, not a right, the Soviets granted limited access both by road and by air. Thereafter the Western allies—bereft of political and military leverage in the area—had no choice but to trust in the cooperative spirit of the Soviet Union.

The United Nations

Americans who sought to escape the burgeoning conflicts of the postwar world found promise of a better future in the events which led to the San Francisco Conference of April to June, 1945. During the war Roosevelt and Hull had given leadership and expression to the growing conviction that any postwar order which might guarantee peace and self-determination would require an international organization that included both the United States and the U.S.S.R. After Hull extracted from the Soviets at the Moscow Conference of October, 1943, an agreement to membership in such a world body, Roosevelt committed the United States to the creation of the United Nations. By the summer of 1944 State Department planning of organization details had reached a stage demanding a further exchange among representatives of the Big Three. When conversations opened at Dumbarton Oaks in Washington, on August 21, 1944, the Soviet delegate raised two distracting questions, demanding, first, that each of the Soviet Republics receive individual membership in the new body, and, second, that the major powers—permanent members of the projected UN Security Council—possess the power of absolute veto. At Yalta, in February, 1945, it was agreed that three UN seats should go to the Soviet Union (the Congress could claim a like number for the United States if it desired) and that each of the permanent members of the Security Council—the United States, Soviet Russia, Great Britain, France, and China—should have a veto over all matters except those in which they were themselves a party to the dispute in question.

With this spadework accomplished, on April 25, 1945, President Truman welcomed the delegates of fifty nations gathered at San Francisco to formally establish the United Nations. "At no time in history," said he, "has there been a more important conference, or a more necessary meeting, than this one in San Francisco. You members of the conference are to be the architects of a better world. In your hands rests our future. By your labors at this conference, we shall know if suffering humanity is to achieve a just and lasting peace." Several crucial questions still awaited settlement before the major powers would grant general approval of a United Nations organization. None of the United States delegates, for example, favored the Russian proposal of admitting the Russian provinces of the Ukraine and Byelorussia as individual members into the organization, but out of deference to Roosevelt's promise at Yalta and under specific instructions from the White House, they acquiesced.

The issue which was to bring the San Francisco Conference to the point of disruption was the veto. The Big Three had already agreed that permanent members of the Security Council might prevent the Security Council from taking action in a dispute, but now the Soviets insisted that the veto power be extended to include even the *discussion* of a dispute. The British and American delegations demurred, and the Latin Americans, viewing this as a means whereby one of the major powers could silence and thereby render defenseless a smaller nation, threatened to bolt the conference. For eleven days the debate raged while the Russian delegation stood fast. The conference seemed in danger of disintegrating. Finally, upon receipt of specific instructions from Joseph Stalin, the Russians relented. It was thus decided that, although any permanent member could block action by the Council with a veto, there would be no veto of discussion. Among other issues, the conference accepted the trusteeship system of administering dependent territories, placing it under the supervision of the Security Council. At the demand of the Latin American and Arab nations, Secretary of State Edward Stettinius introduced a proposal, endorsed overwhelmingly by the small states and accepted by the U.S.S.R., which provided that a country could invoke regional alliances to defend itself when the Security Council failed to act, and secondly, that regional organizations, established for peaceful purposes, could continue, unaffected by the United Nations.

As established at San Francisco, the United Nations was to be similar to the defunct League of Nations in overall organization. It included an Assembly in which all nations were represented, a Security Council where the major powers would always have membership, and a Secretary-General to handle administrative matters. The UN Charter also provided for numerous committees and councils to deal internationally with various political, economic, and social problems: the United Nations Economic and Social Council, the Trusteeship Council, the International Monetary Fund, and the International Court of Justice.

On June 26 the Charter was signed. Truman concluded the two-month-old conference with a note of optimism and warning: "It has already been said by many that this is only the first step to a lasting peace. That is true. The important thing is that all our thinking and all our actions be based on the realization that it is only a first step. Let us all have it firmly in mind that we start today from a good beginning and, with an eye always on the final objective, let us march forward." The United States Senate ratified the agreement by the overwhelming vote of 89 to 2, which testified to the fact that Franklin Roosevelt and Truman had prepared the political groundwork for Senate support far better than had Woodrow Wilson during and immediately after the Great War. The nation's mood was scarcely isolationist.

Potsdam to London

During May, 1945, Churchill had pressed Truman for the earliest possible negotiation with Stalin of a general European settlement. The settlement, he had declared, should come before the Allies lost their bargaining power through the withdrawal of their forces from their advanced battle lines. Russia's attitude toward the Yalta agreements, Churchill saw, forecast trouble along the entire spectrum of postwar issues. The mutual interest in victory, which had sustained the wartime alliance, had evaporated with Germany's defeat. Obligated now to transfer the gains of war to a new order of peace and stability, the wartime Allies faced a range of political questions on which they had never agreed, but which nevertheless demanded settlement if there was to be a peaceful future.

When Truman, Churchill, and Stalin met at Potsdam in mid-July, 1945, the Western leaders had either to accept the new Soviet presence in East-Central Europe as the basis of negotiation, to push the Soviets back by force or negotiation, or again to postpone the key issues in dispute. Unfortunately, any postponement would expose all of the fundamental disagreements between the East and West and automatically subject the world to a new era of tension. On the concrete issues of Germany and Eastern Europe, Stalin employed every possible device to maintain a maximum degree of Soviet prestige, power, and maneuverability. When he failed to win concessions, he pushed for postponement. The Big Three at Potsdam agreed eventually that Germany should be demilitarized, denazified, and democratized. For reparations each occupying power was authorized to remove property from its own zone and to seize German assets abroad. The Big Three failed again to bring the former German satellites into the comity of nations. The conference implemented the Yalta declaration by agreeing that only those states of Eastern Europe with "recognized democratic governments" would be permitted to sign the peace treaties or apply for membership to the United Nations. But what was the meaning of democracy? Obviously the Soviet definition did not coincide with that of the West. Secretary of State James F. Byrnes insisted on the

American interpretation. "The will of the majority of the people," he said, "can be determined only if all the people are able to vote free from force and intimidation." On such matters of definition, however, the Russians remained adamant. Admiral Leahy, who attended the conference, later observed that "the only possibility of agreement would have been to accept the Russian point of view on every issue."

At the London Conference of September, 1945, Allied foreign ministers again acknowledged their commitment to the peacetime reconstruction of Europe. But delegates discovered that the schism in the Grand Alliance was now profound. The victors no longer shared fundamental purposes in Germany. For months Germany had been in Allied hands, and it was quite clear that if the occupying powers could not agree on the treatment of the defeated enemy, they could agree on nothing fundamental. The great divergence between East and West in their attitudes toward German industry was the true measure of the rift in the wartime alliance. Lord Nathan, British Undersecretary of War, observed before the House of Lords, "We must be careful to safeguard against a breakdown of German industry." Russia, by contrast, was determined that German industrial power be hamstrung for the indefinite future. Under the Potsdam Agreement the Russians would proceed to drain Germany's eastern zone of its factories and resources and even to demand additional German assets located in the western zones. Slowly the Kremlin would organize its zone into another satellite. When Secretary of State James F. Byrnes proposed in September, 1946, that the zones of Germany be reunited both politically and economically, Moscow let it be known that it had no interest in a Germany reunited under conditions that would be acceptable to the West. The unification of Moscow's old adversary, it became increasingly clear, would be accomplished on Soviet terms or not at all.

If the Soviets, and sometimes France, questioned the wisdom of British and American moderation toward Germany, they readily joined those two nations in bringing German Nazis to the bar of justice. The trials, conducted at Nuremberg, Germany, sought to establish a body of international law under which leaders designated as war criminals might be punished for the aggressive actions of their nations. There was some condemnation of the decision to prosecute leaders of the defeated enemy, partly because the body of law governing the trial did not exist at the time the alleged crimes were committed. Nevertheless, the trials went forward, and in October, 1946, an international tribunal condemned twelve prominent Nazis to death. Thereafter the trials of lesser Nazi officials continued quietly, free from the glare of publicity, for some years.

Soviet and American interests continued to clash as violently over the future of Eastern Europe as they did over Germany. Again the basic conflict raised the issues of Russian security and Western principle. Byrnes assured Molotov at the London Conference that the United States desired pro-Soviet governments along Russia's western borders; the Soviets, because of their magnificent war effort, deserved nothing less. Brynes insisted only that they be free. Molotov responded that any government of Slavic Europe that was free would not be pro-Soviet; therefore these governments would not be free. The dilemma was as insoluble in diplomacy as it was simple in concept.

Continued Soviet determination to maintain political control of Eastern and Central Europe unleashed a variety of determined pressures in the United States against further violations of principle in the name of Soviet-American comity. Truman made this clear in his Navy Day speech of October 27, 1945, in which he declared that Washington would recognize no government established against the expressed popular will. In this clash between Soviet determination to organize its new sphere of influence and the American principle of self-determination lay the ingredients of an endless and deepening quarrel. The American President, moved to a new posture of toughness by Soviet intransigence, would never relent.

But the chief movement for a "get tough" policy centered in the congressional leadership of the Republican party. Although congressional Republicans had supported Roosevelt's wartime policies and decisions, they felt no compunctions about criticizing the Democratic leadership after it became increasingly obvious that the "soft" approach to "Uncle Joe" and the Kremlin had yielded slim dividends for peace and security in the world. Now Republicans demanded of Truman what Roosevelt had failed to achieve: a world of justice built on the Atlantic Charter. On December 5, 1945, a committee of House and Senate Republicans issued a policy statement chiding the administration's policy in Eastern Europe: "We believe in fulfilling to the greatest possible degree our war pledges to small nations that they shall have the right to choose the form of government under which they will live and that sovereign rights and self-government shall be restored to those who have been forcibly deprived of them. We deplore any desertion of these principles."

Unfortunately, congressional pressures for a tougher policy toward the Kremlin comprised only declarations of hope, not plans for action. On matters of national defense the Republicans were even less inclined toward preparedness than was the national administration. Whatever the needs of the hour, demobilization was in the air, and a majority of both parties accepted the decision to reduce the size of the United States military establishment. Truman attempted to slow down discharges early in 1946, but the continued pressure from soldiers, parents, and congressmen compelled him to continue the rapid demobilization. By mid-1946 the Army had been reduced to 1.5 million men; the Navy to less than half that number. Increasingly the United States was forced to rely on its air-atomic power, although under the plan which Bernard Baruch, the United States member, submitted to the United Nations Atomic Energy Commission in January, 1946, the United States would have agreed to a system of international inspection and control of atomic energy. The Russians refused to accept the plan, condemning the United States for not destroying its atomic bombs unilaterally. Already the dichotomy familiar enough in American experience between the demands placed on policy and an almost total neglect of means had reappeared.

Churchill warned against this trend in his famous speech at Fulton, Missouri, in March, 1946. Assuring America that he spoke for himself alone, the British leader vigorously condemned "the police governments" of Eastern Europe. He urged vigilance and increased military muscle, adding that the challenge of Russian imperialism demanded a "fraternal association of English-speaking peoples" and "intimate relationships between our military advisors, leading to a common study of potential danger, the similarity of weapons and manuals of instruction, the interchange of officers and cadets at technical colleges" and "joint use of all naval and air force bases in the possession of either country all over the world." Churchill stated his belief that the Soviets did not desire war, but, he concluded, "I am convinced that there is nothing they admire so much as strength and there is nothing for which they have less respect than for military weakness."

American writers and political leaders greeted Churchill's speech with a burst of indignation. Many were still reluctant to accept the reality of a divided world. Senator Arthur Capper of Kansas accused the Englishman of trying to "arouse the people of the United States to commit the country to the task of preserving the far-flung British Empire." What this reaction seemed to prove was that most Americans, whatever their feelings toward Russia, would retreat from any program that required more of the United States than the rhetoric of moral criticism. Somehow the "get tough" policy, which never embodied more than a change of style, convinced too many Americans that there was some mysterious power in words and that a refusal to compromise on principles would ultimately secure their triumph. It created the illusion that the nation had choices before it which really did not exist. The "get tough" attitude gave nothing away; nor did it assure any settlements on American terms. Unable to drive the Soviets back to their 1939 boundaries, yet unwilling to accept the Soviet sphere of influence, American officials could only retreat to words.

Henry A. Wallace led the first assault on the Truman administration's growing hostility toward the Soviet Union. On July 23, 1946, Secretary of Commerce Wallace addressed a memorandum to the President advocating economic collaboration with the Russians in the Balkans and the Middle East. Big Three unity must be maintained at all costs, Wallace said, for on it depended world peace. What mattered, he declared in a subsequent address at Madison Square Garden, were not the principles of the Atlantic Charter but friendship or, at worst, peaceful competition between the United States and Russia. Predictably, this appeal produced a violent reaction. Under pressure from his embittered Secretary of State, James T. Byrnes, who declared that Wallace's position was subversive of the nation's principles and the administration's policies, Truman accepted Wallace's resignation from the Cabinet. If the reaction to Churchill's speech suggested that the American people desired no policies based on strength or coercion, their response to Wallace's recommendations demonstrated that they would brook no deals which betrayed American principles. Yet their refusal to employ either power or compromise reduced the area for genuine policy formulation almost to the vanishing point.

From Alliance to Containment

Giving substance to the unchanging structure of European politics in 1945 and 1946 was the military division of Europe. Those regions of Europe which the Russians wished to control economically and politically were occupied by the Red Army. Against this hard fact both

Western diplomacy and Western condemnation were powerless. Nor was it clear that any means short of another major war would dislodge the Soviets from their advanced positions—at least not until the Kremlin should choose to withdraw its control. The Soviet Union had demonstrated both its power and its determination to manage the postwar reconstruction of those regions freed of Nazi forces by the westward-moving Russian armies. Ultimately the continuing quarrel over Germany and Eastern Europe produced a total breakdown of the wartime alliance and a series of Western responses based on fear and insecurity.

The reasons were many. For Western members of the wartime Grand Alliance the intensifying and apparently unending conflict with Europe's most powerful nation was scarcely reassuring, even if that conflict was confined to words. Whether the Kremlin had designs on regions beyond its immediate control was never certain, but Soviet action and Soviet rhetoric both suggested an aggressive intent. If the U.S.S.R., in solidifying its control over East-Central Europe had chosen to defy one important body of wartime agreements, of what value were Kremlin assurances on other questions? By 1947 the declarations of Soviet officials not only proclaimed the superiority of the Communist system and predicted its ultimate triumph but also recognized the division of the world into two ideological camps. That year Russia resurrected its world propaganda organ, the Cominform. While Britain and the United States had demobilized precipitously after the war, the U.S.S.R. had maintained an army of 6 million and a large, modern air force. Now only the American monopoly of atomic weapons gave the West a military capability equal to that of Russia.

To the Truman administration the question of Soviet intentions toward the non-Soviet world became a matter of increasing concern. Already American experts in Soviet affairs had begun their examination of the Russian past for clues which might expose that nation's long-range objectives. George F. Kennan of the American embassy in Moscow wrote in February, 1946: "The Kremlin's neurotic view of world affairs is the traditional and instinctive Russian sense of insecurity. . . . Russian rulers . . . have learned to seek security only in patient but deadly struggle for the total destruction of rival power, never in compacts and compromises with it." Kennan warned Washington that the Kremlin would accept no permanent modus vivendi with the United States until it had achieved the disruption of Western society. No longer could the West escape a long-term struggle for power and prestige with the Soviet Union. Concluding his analysis anonymously in the July, 1947, issue of *Foreign Affairs,* Kennan recommended an American policy of "long-term, patient but firm and vigilant containment of Russian expansive tendencies."

Magnifying the growing American doubts about Soviet intentions was Europe's apparent inability to recover from the ravages of the war. Economic stagnation in Western Europe had created such a vast dollar gap by 1947 that the leading nations of Western Europe were on the verge of bankruptcy. Agricultural production was low; food shortages threatened. Soviet plans for Western Europe were unknown, but the status of Russian military preparedness, added to the presence of burgeoning Communist parties in France and Italy and the weakness of Western Europe itself, seemed to invite Soviet probing. By 1947 Greece was in the throes of a Communist-led revolution, and Turkey, militarily weak and lying at Russia's borders, appeared especially vulnerable to Soviet encroachment. When Great Britain informed Washington that she could no longer carry the burden for eastern Mediterranean stability, President Truman decided he must act promptly. In March, 1947, he asked Congress for military and economic assistance totaling $400 million for Greece and Turkey. Congress quickly voted the funds, thereby implementing the Truman Doctrine.

The Truman Doctrine, which declared and, at least in Greece and Turkey established, Washington's determination to support nations and governments resisting Communist pressure, led logically to the Marshall Plan. Secretary of State George C. Marshall first announced this program at Harvard University in June, 1947, and secured its acceptance by Congress in the Foreign Assistance Act of 1948. Aimed at the long-range economic rehabilitation of Europe, the new program placed the responsibility for economic planning on the recipient nations themselves. Secretary Marshall, as advised by the State Department's Policy Planning Staff under Soviet expert Kennan, excluded all ideological implications from his goals and offered aid to all nations which would cooperate in the program. Yet the Marshall Plan, though designed to blur the division of Europe, because of Soviet intransigence assumed the appearance of having an anti-Soviet purpose—building centers of strength in Western Europe as part of a general American policy of containment. Between 1948 and 1952 the United States granted economic and military assistance of more than $17 billion. The Marshall Plan achieved such unqualified success that the economies of Western Europe soon had surpassed their productivity of the prewar years and the threat of Communist takeover had all but vanished.

Events of 1948 deepened the East-West conflict across Europe. A Communist coup in Czechoslovakia during February carried that neutral nation into the Soviet orbit and was naturally regarded by many Americans as another in a series of Russian attempts to move the Iron Curtain ever westward. A Soviet blockade in June, 1948, of the Western land routes into West Berlin, designed especially to counter the Western decision to organize the British, French, and American zones of occupation into a West German state, only confirmed the judgment. Britain and the United States responded with the famed Berlin airlift which supplied the beleaguered city until Stalin, early in 1949, called off the blockade. Given such evidence of apparent Soviet aggressiveness, it is not surprising that for many Americans and Europeans the paramount issue after 1948 was no longer that of recovering some influence in Eastern Europe but of preserving Western Europe's independence. From this fear evolved the policy of military containment and the North Atlantic Treaty, signed on April 4, 1949, by representatives of the United States, Canada, England, France, Italy, Portugal, the Netherlands, Denmark, Norway, Belgium, Luxembourg, and Iceland. Under this defense agreement, any attack against one of the signatories would be considered an attack against all members. Ratified by a wide margin in the United States Senate on July 21, the pact, which provided for joint NATO forces with headquarters in Paris, went into effect on August 24, 1949.

The North Atlantic Treaty Organization transformed the American military position in Europe from that of occupying German territory to that of defending Western Europe against a possible Soviet attack. At the same time, the United States shifted the emphasis of its European aid program from economic to military assistance. United States policy now sought the creation of a strong military shield in Europe, guaranteed by United States air and atomic power and providing Western Europe the defense behind which it could move on to full economic recovery. By bringing political and economic stability to Western Europe, the United States would guarantee both its own security and the cause of peace. The Kremlin, shocked by the defection of Yugoslavia in 1948, strengthened its control over the satellites and, ultimately, formed the Warsaw Pact.

Every phase of the Truman administration's economic and military program for Europe won the overwhelming support of Congress. Making possible this legislative approval was both a favorable public mood and the vigorous bipartisan leadership of Senator Arthur H. Vandenberg of Michigan. Vandenberg was the recognized spokesman of the Republican party in matters of foreign policy until illness forced his withdrawal from active politics in 1950.

Yet powerful intellectual and political minorities harbored serious doubts regarding the wisdom of the new emphasis on military preparedness. In the absence of any clearly defined danger to America's security, some Republicans began to question the costly commitment of United States men and material to Western Europe's defense. Having argued for tax reduction, they simply denied that the Soviet threat to Europe was sufficiently grave to demand such an expensive response. "Just as a nation can be destroyed by war," admonished Senator Robert A. Taft the acknowledged leader of the administration's conservative critics in Congress, "it can also be destroyed by a political and economic policy at home which destroys liberty or breaks down the financial and economic structure."

Other critics—generally those of the liberal left—were concerned less with the expense than with the purpose of the growing containment policies. Was the American effort designed to stabilize Europe and to establish the foundations for future negotiations with Russia? Or was it to underwrite an anti-Soviet crusade aimed at terminating both the Kremlin's influence in Eastern Europe and its attempt to spread communism to the non-Soviet world? Supposedly Western power would serve the cause of negotiating from strength.

By 1950 United States policies had fallen to a national leadership which depicted Soviet communism as an ideology in basic conflict with democracy and freedom. For such men the struggle between Russia and the United States was ideological. As Secretary of State Dean Acheson declared before the American Society of Newspaper Editors in April, 1950: "We are faced with a threat . . . not only to our country but to the civilization in which we live and to the whole physical environment in which that civilization can exist. This threat is the principal problem that confronts the . . . United States in the world today." Clearly a struggle defined in such terms provided little hope for future settlements.

Such a definition of the Soviet danger made necessary the defense of Western security, but no American leader could explain how military containment in Europe might resolve the threat of a foreign ideology or dismantle the Iron Curtain. To expect that the limited goals of Western Europe's economic and military rehabilitation could restrain the objectives of communism elsewhere was to ask more from those policies than they could possibly achieve. United States effort could stabilize and contain the Soviet forward position; short of war, it could not do more.

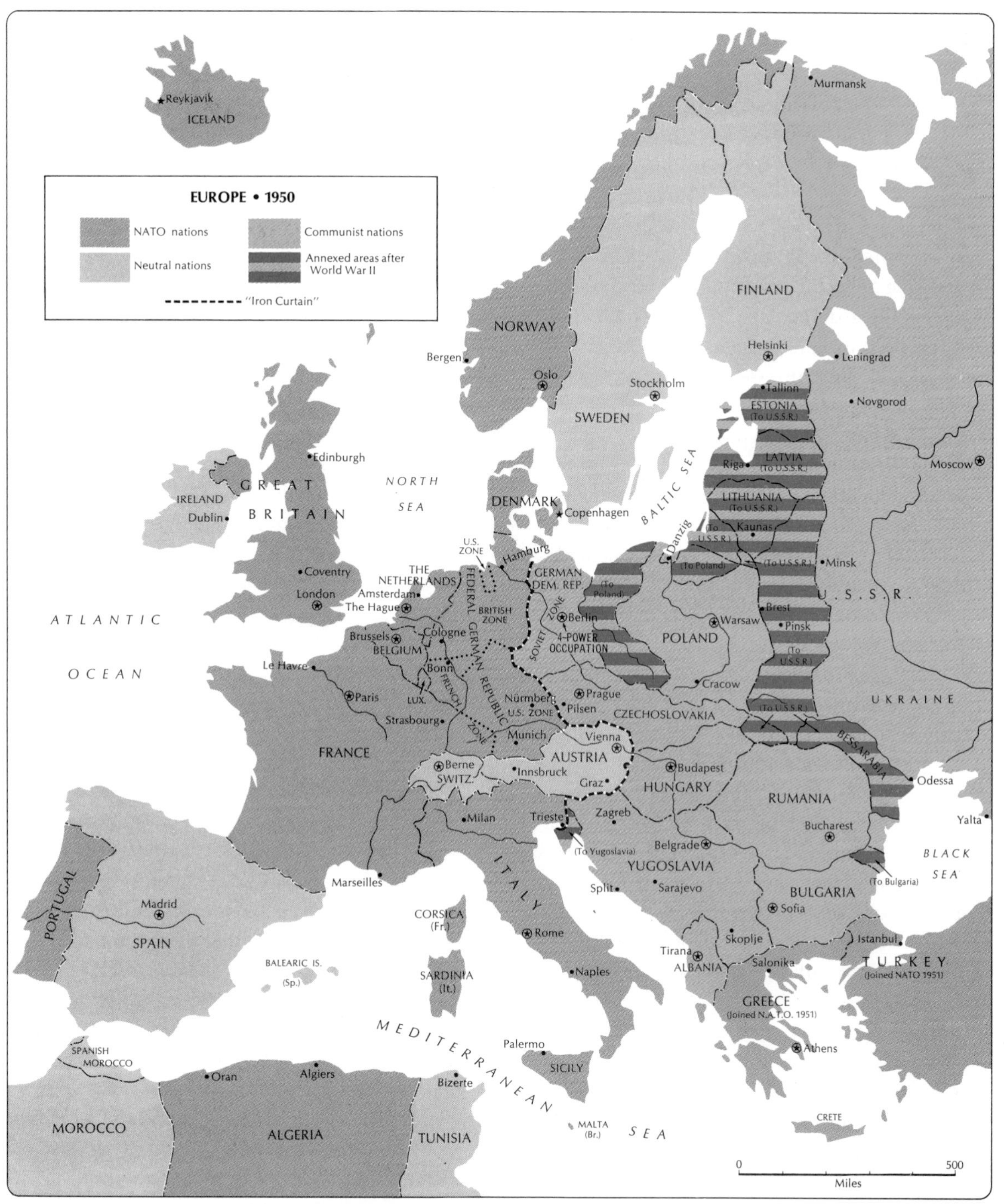

[1163]

The Cold War in Europe and Asia

Believing in policies of economic recovery and political stability for Western Europe, the Truman administration pushed its program through what was for the moment a largely quiescent Congress. Events in Asia, however, soon disturbed the relative political calm. During 1949 and 1950, increasingly significant victories in China by the Red Army of Mao Tse-tung shook the American people emotionally and politically as had few other issues in the nation's history.

United States postwar policies in the Far East had been based on the assumption that Japan's capitulation alone was sufficient to establish the foundation for political and military stability throughout the Orient. Unfortunately, however, Japanese power and aggressiveness were not the only threats to a stable, Western-oriented Asia. For generations South and Southeast Asia had been the exclusive domain of the European imperial nations, and it was the massive presence of the Occident which gave the region its political stability. Japan's initial success in driving the Western Powers out of the Pacific had changed all that; it had, besides, fostered and strengthened a feeling of increasing significance to modern Asia: nationalism. Indeed, so successful was Japan's deliberate effort to incite anticolonial—hence, anti-Western—sentiment in lands which came under its control that by 1945 the old Western-dominated order was impossible of reestablishment at reasonable cost.

Franklin D. Roosevelt, who took the Atlantic Charter seriously, had strongly urged the Allies to apply its principle of self-determination universally. The wartime President was concerned especially that the French give independence to Indochina. When it became clear that Western declarations of principle had raised again the expectations of Asian nationalists, Roosevelt also suggested to the reluctant Churchill that he promise freedom to England's Asian colonies. If the United States was prepared to withdraw from the Philippines (as it did in 1946), England and France, he declared, should do no less in areas under their control. Britain gave way to the inevitable. Beginning in 1947 she granted independence to India, Pakistan, Burma, and Ceylon. The Dutch in 1948 granted self-determination to Indonesia. Meanwhile, France's determination to remain in Indochina subjected that colony, after 1946, to a bitter civil war. But official Washington, requiring French cooperation in Europe, did not again press France to dismantle its empire in the Far East

The vast changes incident to nation building in Asia tended to produce violence and turmoil where there had been political stability. Power may abhor a vacuum, but this seemed to matter little, for the Pacific war had reduced Japan, Asia's former bully, to an enfeebled state. The United States occupation of Japan, commencing in September, 1945, had placed every aspect of that nation's economic and political life under the severest scrutiny and control. Directed by General Douglas MacArthur, Supreme Commander of the Allied Powers (SCAP), occupation policy methodically erased the sources of Japanese expansionism and political repression. A multinational tribunal tried the top wartime Japanese officials, including two former premiers, and sentenced them to death as war criminals, thus breaking the influence of Japan's former leadership. Occupa-

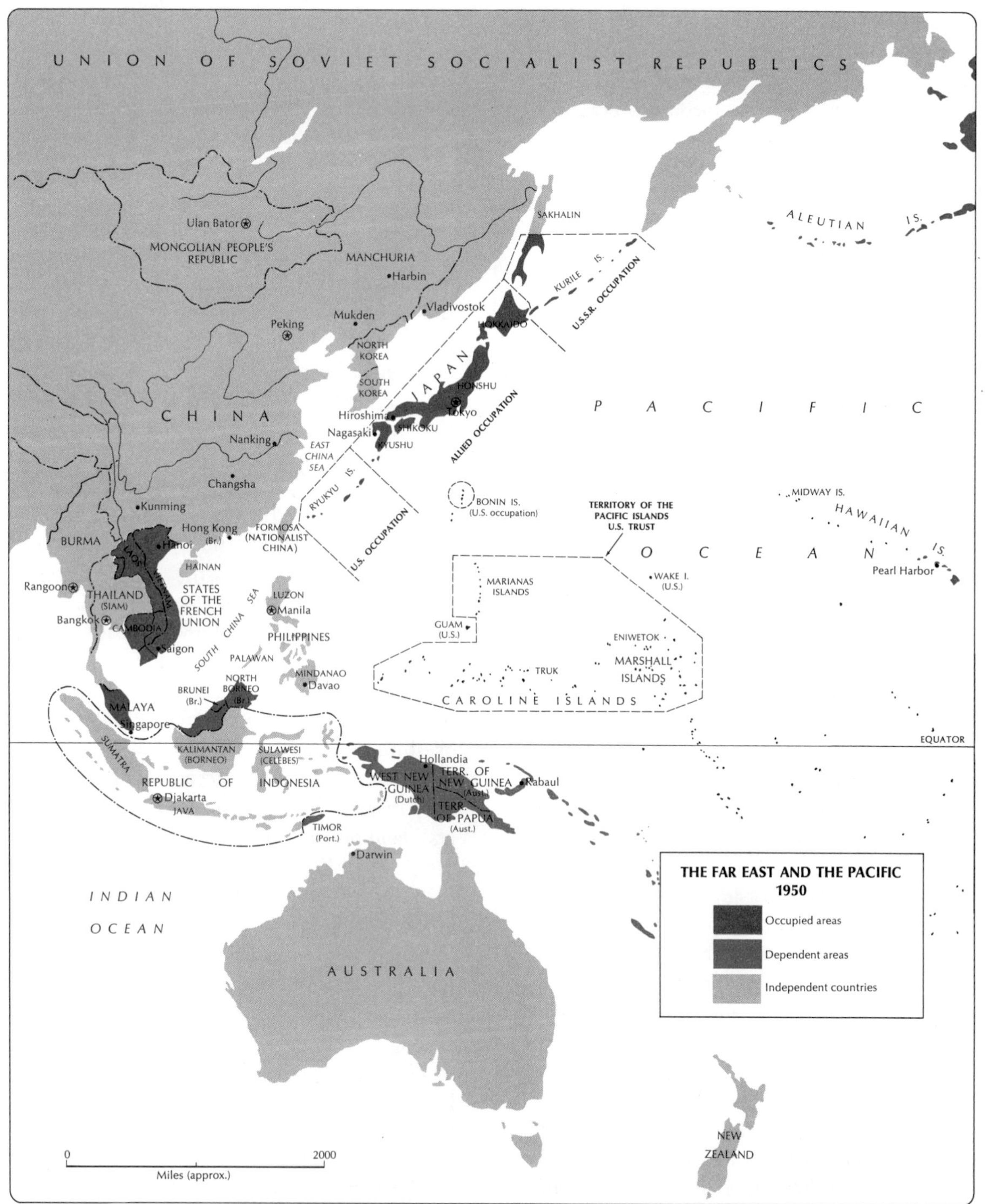
UNION OF SOVIET SOCIALIST REPUBLICS
MONGOLIAN PEOPLE'S REPUBLIC
Ulan Bator
MANCHURIA
Harbin
Vladivostok
Mukden
Peking
NORTH KOREA
SOUTH KOREA
CHINA
Nanking
Changsha
Kunming
BURMA
Hong Kong (Br.)
FORMOSA (NATIONALIST CHINA)
HAINAN
Hanoi
LAOS
VIETNAM
Rangoon
THAILAND (SIAM)
Bangkok
CAMBODIA
Saigon
STATES OF THE FRENCH UNION
SOUTH CHINA SEA
LUZON
Manila
PHILIPPINES
PALAWAN
MINDANAO
Davao
BRUNEI (Br.)
NORTH BORNEO (Br.)
MALAYA
Singapore
SUMATRA
KALIMANTAN (BORNEO)
SULAWESI (CELEBES)
REPUBLIC OF INDONESIA
Djakarta
JAVA
TIMOR (Port.)
Darwin
Hollandia
WEST NEW GUINEA (Dutch)
TERR. OF NEW GUINEA (Aust.)
TERR. OF PAPUA (Aust.)
Rabaul
SAKHALIN
KURILE IS.
U.S.S.R. OCCUPATION
HOKKAIDO
JAPAN
HONSHU
Tokyo
Hiroshima
Nagasaki
SHIKOKU
KYUSHU
ALLIED OCCUPATION
EAST CHINA SEA
RYUKYU IS.
U.S. OCCUPATION
BONIN IS. (U.S. occupation)
ALEUTIAN IS.
PACIFIC OCEAN
MIDWAY IS.
HAWAIIAN IS.
Pearl Harbor
TERRITORY OF THE PACIFIC ISLANDS U.S. TRUST
WAKE I. (U.S.)
MARIANAS ISLANDS
GUAM (U.S.)
ENIWETOK
MARSHALL ISLANDS
TRUK
CAROLINE ISLANDS
EQUATOR
INDIAN OCEAN
AUSTRALIA
NEW ZEALAND
0
2000
Miles (approx.)
THE FAR EAST AND THE PACIFIC 1950
Occupied areas
Dependent areas
Independent countries

tion policy did not seek to destroy the Japanese economy but rather to limit the economic and political power of the mammoth prewar industrial combines. As a further precaution, Japan was limited by the 1946 constitution to only those military forces required for domestic security. This would change later, when Washington, recognizing the power vacuum left by Japan's military weakness, would exhort its erstwhile Pacific adversary to rearm.

The Chinese Debacle

During the critical days of November-December, 1941, the United States had chosen war with Japan rather than compromise the interests of China. In the years following Pearl Harbor the United States obviously had the power to save the Chinese central government of Chiang Kai-shek from its external enemies; after 1943, as the war with Japan raged on, there was reason to doubt whether American arms could save Chiang from the Chinese Communists, enemies of his regime who fought the Japanese from their strongholds in the North. When the global war ended in 1945, China was torn by civil war between Chinese Communists and Chinese Nationalists. It thus became the task of the United States, as the dominant Pacific power, to reconcile differences and bring together two ancient and implacable enemies—Chiang and the Communist Mao Tse-tung. Events would show this undertaking to be more difficult than mixing oil and water.

Roosevelt's chief goal in the Far East, after defeating Japan, had been the development of a strong, united, and democratic China, which might serve as a stabilizing force in Asia. President Truman, clinging to this goal, dispatched the recently retired General George C. Marshall to China in December, 1945, to arrange a truce and, if possible, mediate the establishment of a coalition government. Although it seemed for a time that mediation might succeed, the Marshall mission simply delayed for a moment an irrepressible war—irrepressible because neither the Communists nor the Nationalists would trust the other side or compromise on essential points. When Marshall abandoned his mission in early 1947, aiming a parting blast at Nationalist reactionaries and Communist diehards alike, the civil war resumed on an ever-wider scale.

Throughout 1948 the Nationalists' position deteriorated rapidly. Incompetence and corruption, inflation, and other problems had left the Nationalist party—the Kuomintang—greatly weakened. For too long the regime had been bound to the landlord and banker-merchant interests. For too long it had turned a deaf ear and blind eye to the desperate plight of most Chinese. Lacking honesty and efficient organization, and bereft of understanding, it was unable to compete successfully for popular support with the highly integrated, disciplined, and land-reform-oriented party of Mao Tse-tung. The Kuomintang's military debacles, then, grew naturally from its political and economic failures. But they were compounded by monumental strategic blunders by Chiang. Ignoring his American advisers, he overextended his defense lines by invading northern China, where his armies assumed positions within Chinese cities, and thus lost all options for maneuver or retreat. Harried and battered by Mao's ever-growing and highly motivated Red Army, Chiang's army was disastrously defeated; he withdrew with remnants of his following to Formosa in December, 1949. Meanwhile, in October, Mao established the People's Republic of China, decreed his government's devotion to communism, established ties of friendship with the Soviet Union, and commenced a great crusade against the American presence and influence in the Far East.

China and the Great Debate

The debacle of Nationalist China fell heavily on the Truman leadership. To explain Chiang's failure, the State Department in August, 1949, published the famed China White Paper, a 1,000-page document which sought to prove that the Chinese revolution was indigenous in its causes and almost totally beyond American power to control. In an accompanying letter, Dean Acheson, the new Secretary of State, summarized the administration's position. "Nothing that this country did or could have done within the reasonable limits of its capabilities would have changed the result," he wrote; "nothing that was left undone by this country has contributed to it." The more than $2 billion in grants and credits which the Kuomintang had received from the United States, the White Paper concluded, represented far greater economic and military resources than those available to the Chinese Communists. Chiang had been victimized by a genuine and widespread Chinese revolution, and his defeat could be laid to poor leadership and a woeful lack of the will to fight among his soldiers. Nor was the Communist victory, though unwanted, necessarily a danger to American interests. The Chinese revolution represented indigenous forces, not an international conspiracy.

Acheson particularly emphasized this concept in a subsequent speech. "The communists did not create this condition [in China]," he said, in January, 1950. "They did not create this revolutionary spirit. They did not create a great force which moved out from under Chiang Kai-shek. But they were shrewd and cunning to mount it, and to ride this thing into victory and into power." If nationalism in India or Burma was aimed at liberation from alien rule, that of China was designed to build the strength and unity needed to preserve Chinese sovereignty against foreign encroachment and exploitative treaties. From this administration rationale flowed several logical conclusions: Chiang would not return to power over the mainland short of another general war in the Orient which would involve the full military power of the United States; and revolutionary change, even when Communist-led, did not necessarily illustrate the presence of some aggressive or expansionist force requiring the United States to respond with direct military action.

Such arguments as Acheson's did not survive the bitter debate that followed Nationalist China's demise. For many Americans the Communist victory in China had meaning only within the context of what had come to be known as the "Cold War." Those who preferred to define any Communist gain as the result of a global conspiracy could only regard the Communist victory in China as a tragic failure of American policy and a stupendous triumph for international communism in its course of world domination. Chiang's collapse, therefore, raised questions in the public mind that promised ample political rewards to those who chose to exploit them. To many Americans it was inconceivable that a nation as pow-

erful as the United States could not have saved Chiang. The State Department, and with it the Democratic party, were especially vulnerable to attack because the Department had kept its own counsel with regard to China and had not taken Congress (or the American people) into its confidence. It had not done all it might have to establish the idea that, short of committing the United States to a land war in Asia, the Washington government had done all it could to save Chiang. Thus in August, 1949, Republican Senator Styles Bridges could dub the White Paper "a 1,054-page whitewash of a wishful, do-nothing policy which has succeeded only in placing Asia in danger of Soviet conquest." With the fall of Chiang, Republicans had found a major issue with which to flay the increasingly unpopular Democratic administration.

Such charges as Bridges's won the immediate support of many "old China hands"—officials, missionaries, merchants, students, and travelers who had spent time in China and who hoped for the return of Chiang Kai-shek to the mainland. But it was left for Senator Joseph McCarthy of Wisconsion to submerge the China issue almost irretrievably in the mire of politics and emotions. In a sensational Wheeling, West Virginia, speech of February, 1950, McCarthy captured the nation's attention with the charge that the State Department was thoroughly infested with Communists. This unsubstantiated accusation not only inaugurated another phase in the growing partisanship over foreign policy but also provided an explanation for the collapse of Chiang Kai-shek. If the United States had failed to sustain his regime (went the new explanation), the answer lay not in Chinese Nationalist failures or the limits of American influence in Asia, but rather in the treason of State Department officials. Supported by an argument that not only explained past failures but also promised Chiang's return to power in mainland China, McCarthy rapidly gained an unshakable influence over American attitudes toward both the Far East and the Democratic party. However, although there was much talk about driving out Mao and his henchmen, few Americans harbored any desire to fight the major war in the Pacific which alone might achieve such an objective.

Nonetheless, the official American appraisal of events in the Far East, under attack from men such as McCarthy, was revolutionized almost overnight. Behind this change of view lay the fundamental assumption—shared by many citizens—that an international conspiracy centered in the Kremlin had been responsible for all Communist-led pressures on the status quo in East and Southeast Asia. The Sino-Soviet Pact of February, 1950, convinced official Washington that the U.S.S.R. had enlisted China's millions in Russia's program of global expansion. In 1950 the Truman administration, following this line of reasoning, committed the United States to the support of the French in Indochina as part of a new policy aimed at the containment of Soviet power and influence in Asia. In May, 1950, Secretary Acheson announced in Paris that "the United States government, convinced that neither national independence nor democratic evolution exist in any area dominated by Soviet imperialism, considers the situation to be such as to warrant its according economic aid and military equipment to the Associated States of Indochina and to France in order to assist them in restoring stability and permitting these states to pursue their peaceful and democratic development." Thus the early months of 1950 were critical in the development of American goals in the Far East—those of preventing further Soviet expansion.

The Korean War

Korea became a potentially critical area of Cold War conflict in August, 1945, when General Douglas MacArthur received instructions from the United States Joint Chiefs of Staff to accept the surrender of all Japanese forces in Korea south of the 38th parallel. Russian forces were then pouring into Manchuria and Korea, and Secretary of State Byrnes concluded that the United States would do well to maintain jurisdiction over the southern portion of the peninsula. What was occurring in Germany that year became the example for Korea. The division of Korea as a matter of administrative convenience quickly evolved into a firm division based on military power. Yet the United States had no interest in long maintaining a large military force in the small Asian country. In November, 1947, the United States, in response to a United Nations request and its own evaluation of South Korea as a military liability, began withdrawing its forces. The decision had the endorsement of General MacArthur; it was explicitly approved by the National Security Council in 1949; and Congress in 1949 and again in 1950 showed little interest in providing appropriations for an American presence in Korea. In his aforementioned speech of January, 1950, Secretary of State Acheson pointedly excluded both Korea and Chinese Nationalist-held Formosa from the American defense perimeter.

Barely six months after Acheson so cavalierly consigned South Korea to limbo, official Washington was abruptly jolted out of its complacency. On June 25 a well-prepared North Korean army struck deep into South Korea, sending the poorly trained South Korean troops reeling in disorderly retreat. Having already accepted the Communist pressures in China and Indochina as part of a global conspiracy, the Truman administration could view the North Korean aggression across the 38th parallel as the beginning of a new Communist assault upon the free world. "The attack upon the Republic of Korea," said the President, "makes it plain beyond all doubt that the international Communist movement is prepared to use armed invasion to conquer independent nations." Fearing general Communist aggression, Truman immediately ordered United States air and sea power to the assistance of the South Korean government of Syngman Rhee; when it became clear that such limited support was not enough to turn back

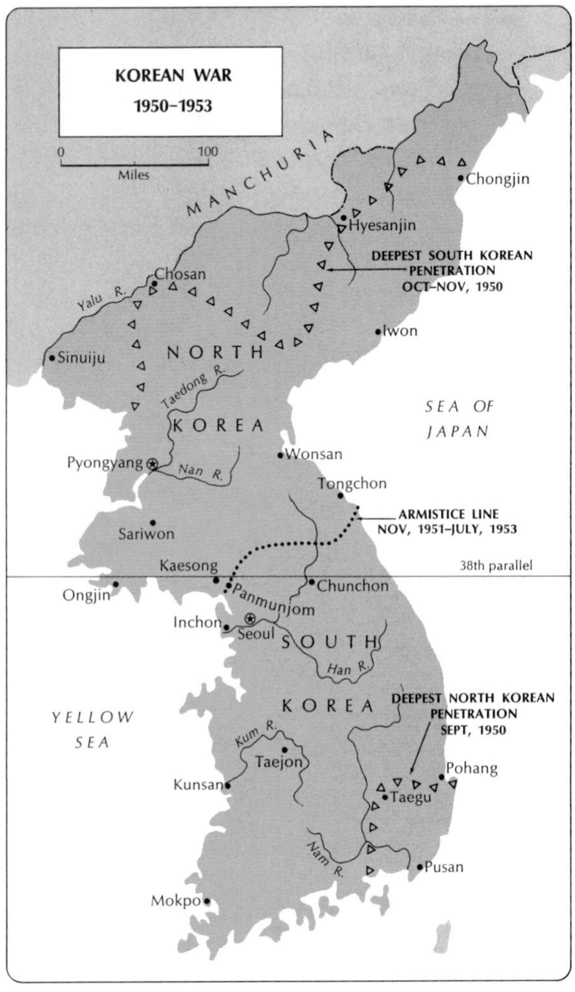

the North Korean thrust, two divisions of American land forces under General Mac Arthur were put into the breach. Truman simultaneously neutralized Formosa, placing the United States Seventh Fleet in position to prevent any movement of troops between the island and the Chinese mainland. Overnight Formosa had acquired a new strategic significance as part of an enlarged United States defense system in the Pacific. The United States had meanwhile appealed to the United Nations for support, and the international body sanctioned what came to be called an "international police action." In exchange for mostly token support from a number of UN members, Washington accepted the restraints imposed on it by the world body's desire to limit the war to Korea and terminate the fighting at an early date.

Throughout the autumn months of 1950 both objectives appeared readily achievable. By September MacArthur had demonstrated his capacity to hold South Korea and had begun operations to throw back the North Korean armies. MacArthur's landing at Inchon on September 15 met no air or ground resistance, and as American troops moved inland they soon put the North Korean troops into wild retreat. During October, Truman met MacArthur on Wake Island. There the two men agreed to pursue the objective of occupying the entire Korean peninsula and securing its political unification. Yet it should already have been apparent that there could be no rapid and successful termination of the war. Early in October the Indian Ambassador to Peking, K. M. Panikkar, advised the world that Chinese forces would enter the struggle if United Nations troops crossed the 38th parallel. Why the President refused to take this warning seriously he set down in his *Memoirs.* The problem, he wrote, "was that Mr. Panikkar had in the past played the game of the Chinese Communists. . . . It might . . . be no more than a relay of Communist propaganda. There was also then pending in . . . the General Assembly . . . a clear authorization for the United Nations commander to operate in North Korea." At Wake, moreover, MacArthur had assured the President that the Chinese would not be so foolish as to enter a war in which they would face certain defeat.

But MacArthur was wrong. As Allied troops pushed northward to within fifty miles of the Korean-Manchurian border, thousands of Chinese "volunteers" were thrown into battle. It was October, 1950; China was in the war—unofficially—but in fact. At the end of November, MacArthur's advance had been blunted by numerically superior Chinese–North Korean forces; by January, 1951, United Nations troops had grudgingly given ground to a line below the 38th parallel. Clearly the United States faced a series of momentous decisions. Whatever American officials may have said about an international Communist conspiracy, they had no interest in a general war against China, much less the U.S.S.R. On the other hand, Washington's official explanation of the war demanded a victory in Korea if the United States hoped to prevent the repetition of the aggression elsewhere. Clearly, the Truman administration was in serious intellectual and military trouble.

During its initial phases, the Korean War had produced no conflict in American politics. Republican leaders such as Senator Arthur Vandenberg attributed the North Korean attack to open Communist aggression and United States military weakness, and not to any failure of American policy in the Far East. As long as the limited United States action in Korea promised perfect but inexpensive success, no Republican spokesman was moved to be critical. But once Chinese intervention had transformed the war into a long, costly stalemate, critics of the Truman administration were easily persuaded that Korea was another consequence of the Truman administration's basic incompetence and even "softness" on communism. Specifically, they charged, the United States government had made two blunders. First, it had not provided South Korea with an army capable of resisting the North Korean attack; second, it had publicly shunted Korea and Formosa outside the American perimeter of defense. "They knew that we had permitted the taking over of China by the Communists," declared Senator Taft, "and saw no reason why we should seriously object to the taking over of Korea. The Korean War and the problems which arise from it are the final result of the continuous sympathy toward communism which inspired American policy."

Such partisan attacks helped to drive Truman and Acheson toward a tougher policy in Asia, especially with regards to Communist China. The blanket charges of treason leveled at the State Department forced Secretary Acheson to prove that he was as rampantly anti-Communist as his critics. As one consequence, in February, 1951, the United States engineered a UN resolution branding Communist China an aggressor in Korea. During the spring of 1951, Acheson emphatically stated that he would neither recognize the Peking regime nor permit the United Nations to do so. At the same time the Secretary never altered his earlier explanation for the failure of Chiang—that it was the result of an indigenous revolution largely unrelated to Soviet policy in Asia.

General MacArthur's recall from his command in Korea, which took place in April, 1951, at about the same time the Secretary of State was implementing the new "hard line" on Communist China, set off a new debate on the aims of American policy. MacArthur had wanted an "offensive strategy" in the Far East. Temperamentally unable to accept the concept of "limited war," he had become openly critical of the administration's circumspection in the conduct of the stalemated war in Korea, and was calling for a war to defeat communism to-

UNITED STATES DEFENSE ALLIANCES
1955
Countries which have mutual treaties with the United States
NATO members
ANZUS members
SEATO members
Rio Pact members
Other U.S. treaties:
Japanese Treaty, 1951 (with Japan)
Korean Treaty, 1953 (with South Korea)
Philippine Treaty, 1951 (with the Philippines)
Chinese Treaty, 1954 (with Nationalist China)
Members of the United Nations
GREENLAND
(Denmark)
ALASKA
(U.S.)
ICELAND
CANADA
NORTH
AMERICA
UNITED STATES
UNITED KINGDOM
FRANCE
SPAIN
See inset
MOROCCO
(Fr.)
ALGERIA
(Fr.)
SPANISH WEST AFRICA
FRENCH WEST AFRICA
GOLD COAST
(Br.)
LIBERIA
TOGO
(Br.–Fr.)
ATLANTIC
OCEAN
PACIFIC
OCEAN
HAWAII
(U.S.)
MEXICO
CUBA
DOMINICAN REPUBLIC
HAITI
PUERTO RICO
BR. HONDURAS
HONDURAS
GUATEMALA
EL SALVADOR
NICARAGUA
COSTA RICA
PANAMA
VENEZUELA
BR. GUIANA
SURINAM
FR. GUIANA
COLOMBIA
ECUADOR
BRAZIL
PERU
SOUTH
AMERICA
BOLIVIA
PARAGUAY
CHILE
ARGENTINA
URUGUAY

The Cold War in Europe and Asia

tally in Asia. "We must win," he said. "There is no substitute for victory." The General's strategy for victory called for a blockade of the China coast, heavy air and sea bombardment of the Chinese mainland, and support for a Nationalist Chinese invasion from the island of Formosa—all carried out by American forces. Truman, who did not want war with China, thought such a strategy exceedingly dangerous. Wearied at length with the popular general's virtual insubordination, Truman on April 10, 1951, relieved MacArthur of his command. Acclaimed by millions of Americans upon his return to the United States, MacArthur defended his views before a joint session of Congress. In May, before a joint congressional committee, he argued his program for victory with the chiefs of the three armed services.

But since United States policies in Korea sought containment and the military equivalent of containment is stalemate, MacArthur, despite triumphal tours across the nation, failed to reverse the Truman policy. If the pursuit of limited war was inconsistent with the official explanations for American involvement in Korea, the President nonetheless continued to hold the line against those who took the doctrine of global conflict seriously. General Omar Bradley later summarized the administration's quarrel with MacArthur when he declared that the adoption of the MacArthur strategy would have led to a general war with Red China—"the wrong war, at the wrong place, at the wrong time, and with the wrong enemy." In October, 1951, peace negotiations began in Korea at Panmunjom, although intermittent fighting continued until a permanent armistice was finally signed in July, 1953. By then Truman, like MacArthur, was in retirement, and another popular general, Dwight D. Eisenhower, presided over the nation's destiny from the White House.

Conclusion

If the immediate postwar conflict had centered in Europe, many Americans chose to view the Soviet challenge as a direct threat to the United States—its security, its institutions, its way of life. They tended to see the struggle as one primarily between the United States and the U.S.S.R. Yet beyond the established quarrel over self-determination and the hard ideological conflict which characterized much of the American and Soviet rhetoric, it was difficult after 1945 to determine actual points of danger, defined in terms of concrete and historic national interests. What divided the two nations was more the question of ideological dominance than the real issues which monopolized the day-to-day diplomacy. But if coexistence proved to be within the reach of American policy at the level of action, the ideological quarrel promised only a continuing cold war of words without victory or settlement.

None of the areas of direct conflict between the United States and the U.S.S.R. had, by 1950, produced an acute crisis. Nor did it appear that they would in the foreseeable future. Whatever its threat to this nation's territorial or historic interests, however, the Soviet challenge to American principles inaugurated a search for military supremacy which, in the absence of concrete issues, could strike a haunting fear that the entire effort might not be worth the cost. Nor could it be demonstrated, short of war, when either nation had won the race for ideological and military supremacy. Yet it was just this quest for ultimate victory against a universalized danger defined in ideological terms that could convert the East-West struggle into an extremely expensive undertaking. To meet the Soviet challenge as Americans saw it, the United States appropriated large sums for foreign aid to strengthen western European economies, granted large amounts of military aid, and organized NATO to contain Russian expansion.

Indicating at first that South Korea and Formosa lay outside its Pacific defense perimeter, the United States moved quickly when North Korea invaded South Korea in 1950. Besides turning back the North Koreans in a war which accepted limited objectives, the United States strengthened the Nationalist Chinese on Formosa, declared its intention never to recognize the existence of Mao's China, provided for Japanese rearmament, and during 1951 negotiated and signed a series of mutual defense pacts with New Zealand, Australia, and the Philippines. The problem of implementing containment policies in Asia would prove much greater than those in Europe. Here, along the rim of China, the United States, in the absence of a military threat to its national security, would face difficulty in defining aims commensurate with the price of sustaining the status quo. For the escalation of force and destruction in pursuit of victory is tolerable only where the resulting dangers and costs have a clear relationship to the nation's needs. In the Far East that relationship would remain embarrassingly elusive.

SUGGESTED READINGS

On the wartime origins of the rift in the Grand Alliance, the standard work has been Herbert Feis's *Churchill, Roosevelt, Stalin: The War They Waged and the Peace They Sought** (1957). But another highly significant and thoughtful volume is William H. McNeill's *America, Britain, and Russia: Their Co-operation and Conflict,* 1941–1946* (1953). Two briefer accounts of Allied wartime diplomacy are John L. Snell's *Illusion and Necessity: The Diplomacy of Global War** (1963) and Gaddis Smith's *American Diplomacy during the Second World War** (1965). John R. Deane's *The Strange Alliance: The Story of Our Efforts at Wartime Cooperation with Russia* (1947) is a firsthand account by an American officer assigned to duty with the Russians. William H. Newman's *Making the Peace,* 1941–1945 (1950) throws further light on the wartime conflicts among the Allies, as does also George F. Kennan's perceptive *Russia and the West under Lenin and Stalin** (1961). United States–Russian wartime relations are dealt with briefly in T. A. Bailey's *America Faces Russia* (1950) and W. A. Williams's *American-Russian Relations,* 1781–1947 (1952). A highly dispassionate and balanced treatment of the Yalta Conference can be found in John L. Snell (ed.), *The Meaning of Yalta** (1956). Of similar viewpoint is Edward R. Stettinius's *Roosevelt and the Russians: The Yalta Conference* (1949). Snell analyzes the German issue as a source of East-West contention during the war years in *Wartime Origins of the East-West Dilemma over Germany* (1959). Henry Morgenthau's *Germany Is Our Problem* (1945) presents contemporary views on the future of relations between the United States and Germany.

For the American role in the creation of the United Nations Organization see R. B. Russell's *A History of the United Nations Charter: The Role of the United States,* 1940–1945 (1958). Other useful books on the UN are Leland M. Goodrich's *The United Nations* (1959) and L. M. Goodrich and A. P. Simons's *The United Nations and the Maintenance of International Peace and Security* (1955).

Much of the writing on the Cold War after Yalta has accepted the reality of an expansionist Russia whose ambitions in Europe and elsewhere could be harnessed only by confrontation with superior power. To that extent this body of literature does not question the premises of the Western response which moved slowly from nonrecognition to containment. Among the orthodox studies of postwar

East-West relations are such useful and often perceptive books as John Lukacs's *A History of the Cold War** (1961); Martin F. Herz's *Beginnings of the Cold War* (1966); John W. Spanier's *American Foreign Policy since World War II** (1960); Norman A. Graebner's *Cold War Diplomacy, 1945–1960** (1962); Hugh Seton-Watson's *Neither War nor Peace: The Struggle for Power in the Postwar World** (1960); Herbert Feis's *Between War and Peace: The Potsdam Conference** (1960); Evan Luard (ed.), *The Cold War: A Re-appraisal** (1964), an outstanding collection of essays by leading British authors; David Rees's *The Age of Containment: The Cold War, 1945–1965** (1967); Louis J. Halle's *The Cold War as History* (1967); Wilfrid F. Knapp's *A History of War and Peace* (1967); and Adam Ulam's *Expansion and Coexistence: The History of Soviet Foreign Policy, 1917–1967** (1968). Even if they accept the Cold War as inescapable, many of these writers challenge the inflexibility in Western policy and the refusal of Britain and America to recognize any legitimate Soviet security interests.

Studies which tend to regard the Soviet demands in Eastern Europe as diplomatically acceptable and view the West as the driving force in the Cold War are W. A. Williams's *The Tragedy of American Diplomacy** (1959); D. L. Fleming's *The Cold War and Its Origins, 1917–1960* (2 vols., 1961), a massive and important contribution to revisionist writing; Frederick L. Schuman's *The Cold War: Retrospect and Prospect** (1962); Gar Alperovitz's *Atomic Diplomacy: Hiroshima and Potsdam** (1965); David Horowitz's *The Free World Colossus** (1965); and Walter LaFeber's *America, Russia, and the Cold War** (1967).

On the formulation of the Truman Doctrine and the Marshall Plan the standard source is Joseph M. Jones's *The Fifteen Weeks** (1955). But a superb study of the formulation of postwar United States containment policy by W. Reitzel, M. A. Kaplan, and C. G. Coblenz is *United States Foreign Policy, 1945–1955** (1956). Walter Lippmann challenges the concept of containment in *The Cold War* (1947). On the impact of American aid on Europe see Paul G. Hoffman's *Peace Can Be Won* (1951); H. B. Price's *The Marshall Plan and Its Meaning* (1955); W. A. Brown and Redners Opie's *American Foreign Assistance* (1953); and W. H. McNeill's *Greece: American Aid in Action, 1947–1956* (1957). United States postwar relations with Germany can be traced in Edgar McInnis's *The Shaping of Postwar Germany* (1960) and Eugene Davidson's *The Death and Life of Germany: An Account of the American Occupation* (1959). The decision to resist Russian pressures on Berlin in 1948 can be studied in L. D. Clay's *Decision in Germany* (1950) and W. P. Davison's *The Berlin Blockade* (1958). Defense policy for the Atlantic community constituted at midcentury the final step in the evolution of United States containment policy. Three excellent studies of NATO are Robert Osgood's *NATO: The Entangling Alliance* (1962); B. T. Moore's *NATO and the Future of Europe* (1958); and Klaus Knorr (ed.), *NATO and American Security* (1959). Coral Bell in *Negotiation from Strength* (1962) raises the question of the ends of Western military policy, as does Hans J. Morgenthau also in his *In Defense of the National Interest* (1951).

Any examination of postwar United States–Russian relations must begin with the memoirs of American officials who dealt with the Russians and who formulated the response to the Russian challenge. Perhaps the most important account is H. S. Truman's *Memoirs** (2 vols., 1955–1956). But also highly significant are James F. Byrnes's two volumes of memoirs, *Speaking Frankly* (1947) and *All in One Life* (1958); Walter Millis (ed.), *The Forrestal Diaries* (1951); A. H. Vandenberg, Jr. (ed.), *The Private Papers of Senator Vandenberg* (1952); Winston Churchill's *Triumph and Tragedy* (1953); Deane's *The Strange Alliance* (1947); Tom Connally's *My Name Is Tom Connally* (1954); W. A. Harriman's *Peace with Russia?** (1959); Joseph C. Grew's *Turbulent Era* (1952), vol. II; W. D. Leahy's *I Was There* (1950); W. B. Smith's *My Three Years in Moscow* (1950); R. E. Sherwood's *Roosevelt and Hopkins* (1948); H. L. Stimson and McGeorge Bundy's *On Active Service in Peace and War* (1948); R. Murphy's *Diplomat among Warriors* (1964); and G. F. Kennan's *Memoirs, 1925–1950* (1967).

With the defeat of Japan in 1945 the burgeoning challenge to United States Asian policy lay in China. For an examination of the China problem during and immediately after the war, Herbert Feis's *The China Tangle: The American Effort in China from Pearl Harbor to the Marshall Mission** (1953) is superb. C. F. Romanus and Riley Sunderland's *Stilwell's*

Mission to China (1953) deals graphically with the troubles of wartime China. For the entire period from 1941 to 1950 Tang Tsou's *America's Failure in China, 1941–1950** (2 vols., 1967) is a study of remarkable scholarship. H. M. Vinacke has contributed two useful volumes on the postwar Far East, *The United States and the Far East, 1945–1951* (1952) and *Far Eastern Politics in the Postwar Period* (1959). K. S. Latourette's *The American Record in the Far East, 1945–1951* (1952) is also of value. J. K. Fairbank's *The United States and China** (2d ed., 1958) contains a balanced and dispassionate account of United States policy in China after 1945. Two more specific accounts of postwar China are P. S. R. Payne's *The Marshall Mission* (1951), and General A. C. Wedemeyer's *Wedemeyer Reports** (1958). For remarkable firsthand accounts of the decline of the Kuomintang see Derk Bodde's *Peking Diary** (1950) and John F. Melby's *The Mandate of Heaven: Record of a Civil War: China, 1945–1949* (1969). The official United States rationale for the collapse of Nationalist China in 1949 can be found in the State Department's White Paper *United States Relations with China: With Special Reference to the Period 1944–1949* (1949). Akira Iriye's remarkable *Across the Pacific: An Inner History of American–East Asian Relations* (1967) relates in brief the transition of United States policy to a new military confrontation in the Far East after 1949.

On United States occupation policy in Japan see E. O. Reischauer's *The United States and Japan** (1957), highly balanced and perceptive. But also of value are Kazuo Kawai's *Japan's American Interlude* (1960), which attributes the remarkable success of the American occupation to General MacArthur; E. J. L. Van Aduard's *Japan from Surrender to Peace* (1954); F. S. Dunn's *Peace Making and the Settlement with Japan* (1963); and Russell Brines's *MacArthur's Japan* (1948).

Excellent studies of the Korean War are numerous. Both Carl Berger's *The Korea Knot* (1957) and L. M. Goodrich's *Korea: A Study in U.S. Policy in the United Nations* (1956) describe the postwar status of Korea. Robert Leckie's *Conflict: The History of the Korean War* (1962), as well as S. L. A. Marshall's *The River and the Gauntlet* (1953), this by an outstanding military critic, are excellent. On the Chinese decision to enter the war see A. S. Whiting's *China Crosses the Yalu: The Decision to Enter the Korean War** (1960). Several American military leaders have contributed to the literature of the Korean War. Mark W. Clark's *From the Danube to the Yalu* (1954) is very useful, as is also M. B. Ridgeway's *Memoirs* (1956). Ridgeway's book is remarkable for its moderation on matters of the Far East. Courtney Whitney's *MacArthur: His Rendezvous with History* (1956) is strongly favorable to MacArthur. For two scholarship accounts of the Truman-MacArthur controversy see J. W. Spanier's *The Truman-MacArthur Controversy and the Korean War** (1959) and Trumbull Higgins's *Korea and the Fall of MacArthur* (1960). C. T. Joy's *How Communists Negotiate* (1956) and W. H. Vatcher's *Panmunjon* (1958) trace the drawn-out peace negotiations at Panmunjom. Both H. Bradford Westerfield's *Foreign Policy and Party Politics: Pearl Harbor to Korea* (1955) and Norman A. Graebner's *The New Isolationism* (1956) discuss China and Korea as major issues in American politics.

* indicates availability in paperback.

37

Problems and Progress under Truman

WORLD WAR II came to a sudden and, for most people, an unexpected end. Government officials had made some plans for converting the economy from war to peace, but these plans were not ready for implementation. Besides, there was little agreement on what policies the government should follow. Consequently, the immediate postwar period was one of confusion and controversy. Inflation, labor-management disputes, dissatisfaction with the speed of military demobilization, scarcity of consumer goods, international tensions, and general unrest all created serious problems for the new President, Harry S. Truman.

Republican victories in the midterm elections of 1946, added to the public's growing discontent with the Democrats, aroused hope among GOP leaders that they might capture the White House in 1948. For sixteen years the Democratic party had controlled the presidency; now the Republicans would have their day. But Truman upset the pollsters and won reelection. He then went ahead and pushed for his Fair Deal, a broad reform program which extended and amplified the New Deal. At first many people could not determine where President Truman stood in the political spectrum, but by the end of his Presidency his programs and policies had placed him in the tradition of twentieth-century reform. He believed in the extension of federal powers and functions to solve the problems of an industrialized society.

Harry S. Truman

No President in the history of the Republic ever faced a greater variety of difficult domestic and international issues than those which confronted Harry S. Truman at the close of World War II. Furthermore, few had been less well prepared by formal education, training, or experience to deal with complex national problems. Recognizing his inadequacies, Truman displayed an uncharacteristic humility when, talking to reporters shortly after Roosevelt's death, he said: "Please boys, give me your prayers. I need them very much." Still the new President gained confidence quickly.

In some ways Truman's career was typical of many American politicians. Born on a Missouri farm in 1884, he served in World War I, engaged in an unsuccessful clothing business, and then entered politics. Supported by Kansas City boss Thomas J. Pendergast, Truman won the judgeship of the Jackson County Court in 1922. This was an administrative, rather than a judicial, post and a position in which he learned much about the art of politics. He was elected to the United States Senate in 1934 and reelected in 1940. His service in the Senate was adequate but not distinquished. He was selected for the vice presidency in 1944 largely because he held moderate views and came from a key border state. His record before 1945 was no better or worse than that of many other loyal Democrats who had served in the Senate. Truman had never held a major administrative office before becoming President; and while he was Vice President, Roosevelt had not consulted him on important matters. Indeed, Truman had conferred with Roosevelt in private only a few times during the year before Roosevelt's death in April, 1945.

Truman approximated the stereotype of the average American; he seemed neighborly—the typical resident of an American town. He enjoyed the simple things of life—his family, a drink, a game of poker with friends, a turn at the piano, or an occasional history book. But perhaps more than anything else, he liked and understood party politics. To Truman, the Democratic party was the only true spokesman of the people and the only agency capable of governing the country. Moreover, he had the courage of his convictions and did not hesitate to take unpopular stands. In 1945, however, most Americans agreed on one thing—that Truman was an unpromising successor to Franklin D. Roosevelt. No one questioned that Truman was a loyal New Dealer, but there was doubt about whether he would simply administer Roosevelt's policies, press for more advanced reforms, or retreat to a more conservative position.

Demobilization

Of all the questions before the American people in the late summer and early fall of 1945 none seemed so important as bringing those in the military services home as soon as possible. In September, 1944, the authorities announced a point system under which the men who had served longest would be released first. Although this plan worked quite well, demobilization did not proceed as fast as most civilians and military personnel desired. Hundreds of thousands of GIs were separated from the Armed Forces between August and December, but everyone was impatient at the apparent delays. Lack of transportation was a major bottleneck. Troops protested and demonstrated in Manila, Frankfort, and other cities when ships were not available to take them home quickly. One American soldier in the Philippines who wanted to be home by Christmas lamented that the Japanese prisoners would return to Japan before he arrived in the United States. "Let's surrender and get home by Christmas," he remarked bitterly. Wives, sweethearts, and parents of service personnel put strong pressure on Congress to speed up demobilization. One child wrote to Senator Elmer Thomas of Oklahoma, "Bring my daddy home or my mommy won't vote for you." A campaign of "no boats, no votes" gained widespread popular attention.

The demand for such rapid demobilization quickly reduced the world's strongest military power to a shadow of its former strength. In September, 1945, the Army discharged 597,000 men, and in December the number reached 1,112,000. President Truman later referred to the policy as disintegration rather than demobilization. Early in 1946 General Eisenhower declared that "the finest military organization the world has ever seen" had been dismantled. From a high of more than 12 million in 1945, the nation's Armed Forces had been cut to only 1,582,000 by 1947. In late 1945 President Truman insisted that the United States must maintain a strong Army, Navy, and Air Force to meet American responsibilities throughout the world, but most citizens were in no mood to support an expensive peacetime military establishment. They preferred a reduction of taxes and military spending.

Opposition to the President's request for universal military training was further evidence of people's postwar outlook. Congress ignored Truman's recommendation for UMT in October, 1945, and permitted the Selective Service Act to expire on March 31, 1947. Thereafter the Armed Forces depended entirely upon voluntary enlistments until the lawmakers enacted another Selective Service law in 1948. The President did succeed, however, in securing legislation designed to unify the armed services. In July, 1947, Congress passed the National Security Act which provided for a Department of Defense. Although the Army, Navy, and Air Force (which was now placed on an equal basis with the older services) continued as separate Departments, they all came under the new Secretary of Defense. This measure also established the Central Intelligence Agency, the National Security Council, and the Joint Chiefs of Staff. Meanwhile, in the Atomic Energy Act of 1946, Congress had placed postwar atomic development in the hands of a five-man civilian commission.

Economic Reconversion

During the war Americans had looked forward anxiously to the time when industry would be reconverted to peacetime production. Good wages and salaries during a period of rationing and price controls had left most people with accumulated savings, now available to purchase consumer goods such as automobiles, refrigerators, and washing machines. Throughout the war countless Americans anticipated the return of civilian automobile production. One study in April, 1945, revealed an existing demand for more than five million radios, nearly six million refrigerators, and an equal number of washing machines.

But what economic policies would best fulfill the needs and desires of the American people? How could the changeover from the production of war supplies to civilian goods be carried out most efficiently? How could widespread unemployment be avoided? Some authorities, recalling the record of 1920–1921, predicted a postwar economic decline with unemployment reaching 8 million by early 1946. What would be the role of the federal government in matters of industrial reconversion? These questions troubled the reporter for *Business Week* who wrote shortly after Germany surrendered, "Reconversion policy is the central economic problem of our day." Sensing the difficulties ahead, another observer wrote in *Newsweek* that industrial reconversion from war to peace would not "be a quick, easy trip over a well-paved, well-lighted superhighway."

National leaders argued over the speed and the degree to which wartime rules and regulations should be repealed. Many Americans, restless under three years of economic controls, argued that price, wage, and other government restrictions should be abandoned immediately. Admitting that prices would rise in the short run, these advocates declared that businessmen, once freed from regulations, would soon produce enough to meet the demand and send prices again into decline. As Senator Edward H. Moore of Oklahoma put it, prices "would be curbed by the operation of the natural laws of economics." Others, including President Truman, believed that government controls over prices, wages, and rents must be continued until production caught up with demand. Otherwise, a large surplus of money seeking a limited supply of goods would create high prices and harmful inflation. As John W. Snyder, Director of War Mobilization and Reconversion, said in October, 1945, "We must keep price controls to prevent an inflationary rise in price which would be the inevitable forerunner of collapse."

Immediately after the defeat of Japan, President Truman began to relax government controls over the economy. In August he ordered the end of rationing of gasoline, tires, fuel oil, processed foods, and other commodities. He also discarded the Little Steel formula on wage increases, giving labor more freedom to seek higher wages through bargaining with employers. Moreover, between August 14 and October 1, the government canceled $23 billion in war contracts and reduced the number of orders and regulations dealing with production from 650 to 79. On October 15, officials lifted all restrictions on construction. Despite these relaxations, the President reminded people that the Stabilization Act would be in force until June 20, 1946, and that some controls over prices, wages, and rents were still needed.

But Americans were tired of controls and restrictions. Both business and labor were impatient with continued government regulations. Meat-packers who opposed price controls and further rationing, real estate operators who resented rent controls, and other businessmen were, as one observer remarked, "after OPA's hide." Labor, too, chafed even under the more liberalized wage contracts. In August, R. J. Thomas, president of the United Auto Workers, announced that UAW would no longer honor the union's wartime no-strike pledge. The UAW demanded a 30 percent raise in hourly wages to compensate for the loss of overtime when workers went back to a forty-hour week. Labor was restless also because of some unemployment following the cancellation of war contracts.

The entire reconversion problem was complicated by the basic conflict between industry and labor. While labor wanted higher wages and no increase in prices, businessmen demanded that prices be permitted to rise while wages were held stable. Labor seemed to have at least partial backing from the administration in light of President Truman's statement of October 30 that "there is room in the existing price structure for business as a whole to grant increases in wage rates." Industrialists, however, rejected this view. When General Motors refused to grant the United Auto Workers a 30 percent wage increase in November, 1945, some 180,000 men walked off their jobs. This action inaugurated a series of strikes in major industries, and it came when people were complaining of the continued shortage of automobiles. After weeks of negotiations during which time a presidential fact-finding committee assisted in working out a solution, the union accepted a company proposal for a wage increase of 18½ cents an hour. The strike ended on March 13, 1946.

In January, two months earlier, about 750,000 steelworkers went on strike after the industry refused their demand for a $2-a-day wage boost. The steel firms declared that they could not raise wages unless OPA would permit higher prices. To settle the issue, OPA allowed the companies to increase steel prices as much as $5 a ton, and the steelworkers, too, agreed to an 18½-cents-an-hour boost in wages. Coal and railroad workers, as well as those in some other major industries, also struck in the spring of 1946. Most of the controversies were settled by wage increases of 18½ cents an hour, a pattern set in the General Motors negotiations.

The government's attempt to ease controls over the economy gradually while maintaining enough restrictions to curb inflation was a sensible economic program, but it proved to be poor politics. The policy alienated too many powerful groups who were determined to weaken or destroy completely the wartime regulations. Despite growing pressure to remove price controls, the OPA kept the cost of living reasonably stable until the spring of 1946. By that time, however, the government had permitted so many price changes that the cost of living began to show dangerous increases.

By the summer of 1946 the conflict between those who favored continued controls and those who wanted to abandon them had become intensely bitter. Since the Stabilization Act was scheduled to expire on June 30, the arguments over the role of government in reconversion now focused on the continued necessity of that wartime legislation. President Truman on several occasions requested the extension of price controls, but Congress completed the new law late in June which permitted general price increases. Calling the bill "a sure formula for inflation," Truman gave it a stinging veto on June 29, only one day before the old law would expire. He criticized the bill because it continued "the Government's responsibility to stabilize the economy and at the same time it destroys the Government's power to do so." Truman explained that "the fight against inflation is never easy" and warned that defeat in the battle would be disastrous for all the people.

Congress sustained the President's veto and several weeks later passed a somewhat stronger measure which Truman signed "with reluctance." During the period when no controls were in effect—July 1 to July 25—the price index of 900 commodities jumped more than 10 percent; the wholesale price of farm products rose 24 percent and retail food prices nearly 14 percent.

Pressure to remove government controls

from prices, wages, and rents continued unabated. Unable to resist longer, the President ended meat controls in October; the following month he abandoned most other price controls and wage regulations. During the last half of 1946, consumer prices increased some 15 percent; food prices rose to double that figure. The administration had lost its war against inflation.

Despite inflation, labor-management disputes, and strikes, the reconversion of the economy from war to peace was remarkably successful. The postwar depression and large-scale unemployment feared by so many people simply did not occur. Civilian employment reached 55.2 million in 1946—nearly 7 million above that of 1940—and unemployment was only 2.3 million, less than that of the first year of war in 1942. Gross national product, in dollars of constant purchasing power, rose about one-third between the good year of 1929 and 1946. Average annual per capita income was about $500 higher in 1946 than in 1929, although inflation subsequently reduced these gains temporarily. Not only did the industrial sector enjoy nearly full employment at good wages, but farmers, too, were unusually prosperous. Heavy demand for agricultural products both at home and abroad drove farm prices up to exceptionally high levels. Cotton, which had brought less than 10 cents a pound in 1940, sold for about 32 cents in 1946; and wheat went from 70 cents to $1.90 in the same period. Net farm income rose to $15.5 billion in 1947, the highest point in American history to that time. Within a relatively short period following the war an increasing number of Americans were enjoying the prosperity and rising standard of living about which they had dreamed during the previous decades.

Postwar prosperity rested, first, on the huge demand for goods and services which had grown during the war. People wanted new houses and all the standard commodities which had been unavailable or in short supply. Moreover, in 1945 individuals had $37 billion in savings to help buy the things they wanted. Buyers snapped up automobiles as fast as they rolled off the assembly lines in 1946 and 1947: they commonly paid dealers an extra amount to advance their names on the list of waiting customers. The nearly 4 million passenger cars manufactured in 1948 failed to supply the demand, but production continued upward until by 1950 auto makers turned out 6.6 million units. The demand for new housing was equally strong and inflationary. By 1949 more than a million new nonfarm residences were started. The Federal Housing Administration supported much of the housing boom by guaranteeing long-term loans made to buyers. The automobile and construction industries had provided good indices of the country's economic health in the 1920s; again their growth in the immediate postwar years reflected widespread prosperity.

Large expenditures by industry for new plant and equipment also stimulated the economy. In 1948 American businessmen spent about $22 billion on capital outlays—some two and one-half times more than the figure for 1945. Moreover, government spending continued high. Those who believed that the federal budget could be cut to approximately its prewar figure—$9 billion in 1940—were sadly mistaken. Annual federal expenditures declined drastically from their wartime peak of almost $98 billion, but needs at home and commitments around the world kept appropriations at record peacetime levels. The national budget declined to $33 billion in 1948, but it increased again thereafter. Altogether, large individual, corporate, and government spending provided the purchasing power needed to keep the consumer-oriented economy advancing at a rapid pace.

The functions and responsibilities of the federal government had been growing for many years, but it was not until after World War II that Congress assumed major responsibility for maintaining general prosperity. Indeed, passage of the Employment Act of 1946 was a landmark in national economic policy. The law declared that "it is the continuing policy and responsibility of the Federal Government to use all practicable means," in cooperation with private industry and state and local governments, to afford "useful employment opportunities, including self employment, for those able, willing, and seeking to work, and to promote maximum employment, production, and purchasing power." This act did not specify how the federal government would achieve these objectives, but it implied that Washington would try to control the business cycle through government spending, taxing, and other fiscal and monetary policies. The law provided for a Council of Economic Advisers to study economic trends and recommend to the President which policies would best serve the overall economy. It is significant that Congress passed the Employment Act at the very time that many people were calling for reduced government activity in the economy. But there would be no return to the self-regulating, self-adjusting economy; the role of government, chiefly in the area of expenditures, continued to increase rather than to decrease.

Postwar Politics

Although a great majority of Americans rallied behind President Truman when he first assumed office, his personal popularity, as well as that of his party, soon began to decline. Besides finding it difficult to deal with such domestic problems as inflation and strikes, Truman appeared indecisive and uncertain about the direction of his leadership. Would he seek to move the country to the right, the left, or down a middle road? For months the course was unclear. Then on September 6, 1945, Truman delighted loyal New Dealers when he outlined a liberal program which went beyond even that of Roosevelt. He called for expanded unemployment insurance, a higher minimum wage, full employment legislation, a Fair Employment Practices Commission to deal with racial discrimination, housing legislation, and federal aid for slum clearance.

Whatever optimism liberals may have felt at this rebirth of New Dealism soon disappeared when Truman failed to push for his stated objectives. This, no doubt, resulted partly from his heavy involvement with matters of foreign policy. But the lack of firm action disillusioned many Democratic progressives. On the other hand, Truman's liberal pronouncements destroyed any confidence which conservatives may have had in him. Truman seemed to be searching for a consensus which did not exist and which he could not produce.

In Congress, the tide of conservatism was running strong—a continuation largely of the conservative trend evident during the war years. Now that peace had arrived, lawmakers, too, were anxious to regain some of the powers which they had given up to the Executive during the war. Congress, one observer wrote, was "in a mood to test its own power." And a coalition of Southern Democrats and conservative Northern Republicans had definite ideas as to how that power should be used. This group insisted on lower taxes, reduced federal expenditures, greater controls over labor, and policies which would take the federal government out of business. Although liberals in both parties favored the further extension of the services of government, it was clear by the spring of 1946 that the country as a whole was in no mood to favor much more than what had already been done in the field of social security and welfare legislation.

By the spring of 1946 the Democratic party was in trouble; everything looked favorable for the Republicans in the forthcoming midterm elections. Inflation, strikes, and general unrest were all blamed on the Democrats. By April, the number of voters who believed that the President was incapable of handling his job had jumped to 34 percent, a sharp rise from only a few months before. The popular image of President Truman and his party was everything but flattering. Moreover, critics charged that some of the people around Truman, the so-called Missouri Crowd, were engaged in immoral, if not illegal, activities. Some insisted that Truman was soft on communism and that radical labor leaders influenced or controlled his administration. As the elections approached, Republican posters asked: "Had Enough? Vote Republican."

Most political analysts concluded early that the Republicans would probably gain control of the House; what surprised them was the size of the victory in November—246 to 188. However, many Democrats were stunned when the Republicans also won a majority of 51 to 45 in the Senate. For the first time since 1930, Republicans controlled both houses of Congress. The voters seemed to have demanded a greater conservatism in government and a return to some form of postwar normalcy. After agitating for eight years, the conservative coalition of Northern Republicans and Southern Democrats was now able to enact more conservative social and economic policies.

The Eightieth Congress

One of the prime objectives of the Republican-controlled Eightieth Congress was the amendment of the Wagner Act of 1935. For several years conservatives had argued that this law was too favorable to workers and that it gave organized labor an undue advantage over management. Partly as a result of the first round of disruptive postwar strikes, Congress had passed the Case bill in May, 1946. Named after its author, Senator Francis Case of South Dakota, this measure provided that unions could be sued for breach of contract; it required notice and a cooling-off period of thirty days to legalize a strike, should the proposed Federal Mediation Board assume jurisdiction. The bill included antitrust and antiracketeering clauses. Truman vetoed the Case measure, but he admitted that some legislative adjustments were desirable to reduce labor-management strife. Before anything further could be done, John L. Lewis, in November, 1946, led his coal miners out on strike for the second time that year. Many people were furious at Lewis, and they were not satisfied when the court levied a heavy fine on the United Mine Workers' president for having violated a restraining order. As one writer said, "a veritable typhoon of public opinion" was developing against organized labor, especially against union leadership.

The growing antilabor sentiment expressed

itself in passage of the National Management Relations Act in June, 1947. Sponsored by Senator Robert A. Taft and Congressman Fred A. Hartley, the Taft-Hartley Act gave employers more freedom to propagandize against unions, outlawed the closed shop, permitted suits to recover losses by employers in jurisdictional disputes, forbade political campaign contributions by unions, and required union officials to sign affidavits that they were not Communists. The law also required unions to give a sixty-day notification before modifying or terminating a contract, during which time a strike was not to occur. Moreover, in case a projected strike threatened the national health or safety, the Attorney General could obtain an eighty-day injunction which would render a strike unlawful and compel negotiations to end the dispute. To President Truman the Taft-Hartley Act went much too far in attempting to restore the balance of economic power between labor and management. In a sharp veto message, he declared that it "would contribute neither to industrial peace nor to economic stability and progress." But Congress promptly overrode the President's veto by large majorities. Truman could not stay the strong feeling that labor union power must be reduced.

Besides the conflict over labor legislation, Truman found himself in sharp disagreement with the Republican Congress over tax policy. Spokesmen for business, industry, and high-income groups argued that heavy taxes discouraged enterprise and retarded economic expansion. Since expenditures had been reduced by 1947 to the point where the Treasury showed a slight balance, these groups insisted that it was time for tax cuts. Truman also favored some tax reduction, but he declared in January, 1947, that "we should maintain tax revenues at levels that will not only meet current expenditures but also leave a surplus for retirement of the public debt." By the end of 1946, the federal debt stood at about $269 billion. The President believed that whatever reductions were voted should go chiefly to low-income groups.

Ignoring the President, Congresss passed a bill in May, 1947, cutting taxes between 10 and 30 percent. Truman vetoed the measure, arguing that it was "the wrong kind of tax reduction" and came "at the wrong time." He insisted that the bill favored the rich and hurt the poor. Congress enacted another tax reduction law in July, but it met a similar fate at the hands of the President. As the federal budget moved into the black, however, the demand for reduced taxation mounted even higher. Finally, in April, 1948, Congress passed another bill which cut tax rates, relieved some 7.4 million low-income citizens from any tax liability, and raised exemptions from $500 to $600. Truman vetoed this bill, too, but Congress overrode his objections.

The President and Congress also had sharp differences over civil rights. In a special message on February 2, 1948, Truman explained, "The Federal Government has a clear duty to see that Constitutional guarantees of individual liberties and of equal protection under the laws are not denied or abridged anywhere in our Union." Among other specific reforms, he recommended antilynching and anti-poll tax laws and establishment of a permanent Fair Employment Practices Commission. The President said that "all men are entitled to equality of opportunity." Southerners, especially, reacted strongly to Truman's civil rights program. Heatedly objecting to the President's proposals, Representative William M. Colmer of Mississippi told his colleagues that "if the Federal Government can repeal the poll tax in

Mississippi . . . regulate employment under the FEPC, punish innocent taxpayers under the antilynch bill, and abolish segregation in the several States by usurpation of the sovereign rights of the several States of the Union, then we have witnessed an end of constitutional government as conceived by the founding fathers." Confronted with this kind of opposition, Truman not only failed to achieve civil rights legislation, but he created a sharp division within the Democratic party, an especially important matter in a presidential election year. Truman further angered conservatives by proposing a broad social welfare program calling for national health insurance, federal aid to education, higher minimum wages, housing legislation, and a significant expansion of social security.

The Election of 1948

Early in 1948 Democratic political prospects appeared almost hopeless. The President's popularity and power of leadership seemed to have eroded away completely. During the Eightieth Congress, lawmakers had followed their own independent paths, ignoring and frustrating the President and his program. The Democratic party was deeply divided. Southerners were boiling mad at Truman for his civil rights stand, while many old New Dealers did not think Truman was fighting hard enough for additional reforms. Some of the anti-Truman liberals rallied behind Henry A. Wallace, who had announced on December 29, 1947, that he would seek the Presidency as head of a new, liberal Progressive party. Activities by some of the President's personal friends and associates still produced charges that the administration was filled with graft and corruption. Furthermore, the victorious party in a midterm election traditionally went on to win the next presidential contest. This knowledge provided additional encouragement for the Republicans and created gloom among Democrats.

Desperate Democrats searched frantically for a strong leader to replace Truman as the party's nominee. They attempted to interest General Dwight D. Eisenhower and Justice William O. Douglas, but without success. Truman's announcement, on March 8, that he would seek another term produced nothing but despair in Democratic ranks. One Democratic governor said, "We don't want to run a race with a dead Missouri mule." Some of the jokes circulating in Washington were: "I wonder what Truman would do if he were alive" and "To err is Truman." But the party was saddled with Truman, and when the convention met in Philadelphia it nominated him on the first ballot. The delegates chose Senator Alben W. Barkley of Kentucky as the vice presidential nominee in an effort to attract discontented Southerners. A bitter fight developed over the civil rights plank, but Truman and his liberal supporters such as Hubert H. Humphrey of Minnesota won the day. The platform also called for higher minimum wages, repeal of the Taft-Hartley Act, federal aid to education, expansion of social security, and flexible farm price supports.

The entire convention was apathetic until the President appeared to deliver his acceptance speech. Even though the hour was late and delegates were tired, Truman aroused considerable enthusiasm by his defense of the New Deal and his attack on the "worst Eightieth Congress." As Truman attempted to discredit his opponents, elements in his own party seemed to be assuring his defeat. Anti-Truman Democrats met at Birmingham on July 17 and nominated Governor J. Strom Thurmond of South Carolina and Governor Fielding Wright of Mississippi on a Dixiecrat ticket, which sought support among anti-civil rights groups. Shortly afterward, left-wing Democrats nominated Henry Wallace and Senator Glen Taylor of Idaho as the Progressive party's standard-bearers. The Progressives advocated a socialistic domestic program and closer relations with the Soviet Union. Now the Democratic party seemed to be hopelessly split.

Meanwhile, Republicans studied the quarreling and divided Democrats, read the favorable public opinion polls, and agreed that any good Republican could defeat Truman. They again nominated Governor Thomas E. Dewey and gave him a strong running mate in Governor Earl Warren of California. The Republicans promised greater efficiency and honesty in government, a campaign against domestic communism, and lower taxes. Besides tacitly accepting most of the New Deal, the Republicans proposed some additional social reforms of their own.

Dewey campaigned in a conservative, restrained fashion. Supported by the public opinion polls and most political prognosticators, he acted as though he had already won the election. Dewey voiced platitudes about inefficiency in government and accused the Truman administration of crime and corruption and softness toward communism. He failed to come to grips with any major national issues and tended to stay aloof from the people. Somehow he did not seem convincing. When he defended the Taft-Hartley Act, promised higher minimum wages, and greater social security benefits, his listeners went away with doubts about the candidate and his party.

Truman, on the other hand, entered the race in a fighting mood. In his acceptance speech he had told the delegates that he was going to win. He attacked the "do-nothing Eightieth Congress" and accused the Republicans of subservience to the special interests. His call for repeal of the Taft-Hartley Act brought most of organized labor into his camp. The CIO's Political Action Committee and the AF of L's Labor's League for Political Education spent large sums on the Democratic campaign, and individual labor leaders worked hard for Truman's reelection. They seemed to agree with the President when he said that, if the Republicans won, there would be much more antilabor legislation. Truman also charged that the Republican Eightieth Congress had ignored the needs of agriculture by failing to provide enough storage for surplus farm crops. Besides giving attention to specific issues, Truman skillfully played on the lingering fears of many people that the Republican party was the party of depression and hard times. The fear of possibly returning to the days of Hoover haunted many voters. The President carried on a 31,000-mile, whistle-stop campaign where he proved to be at his best. People responded enthusiastically to his barbs and jibes at the opposition, and shouts of "Give 'em hell" and "Atta boy, Harry" frequently punctuated his off-the-cuff and formal talks. Nonetheless, despite the appearance of growing support, scarcely anyone thought Truman could win.

To the surprise of almost everybody, Truman won a stunning upset victory. He gained 24 million votes to 22 million for Dewey, while Thurmond and Wallace trailed far behind with 1,169,000 and 1,156,000 votes respectively.

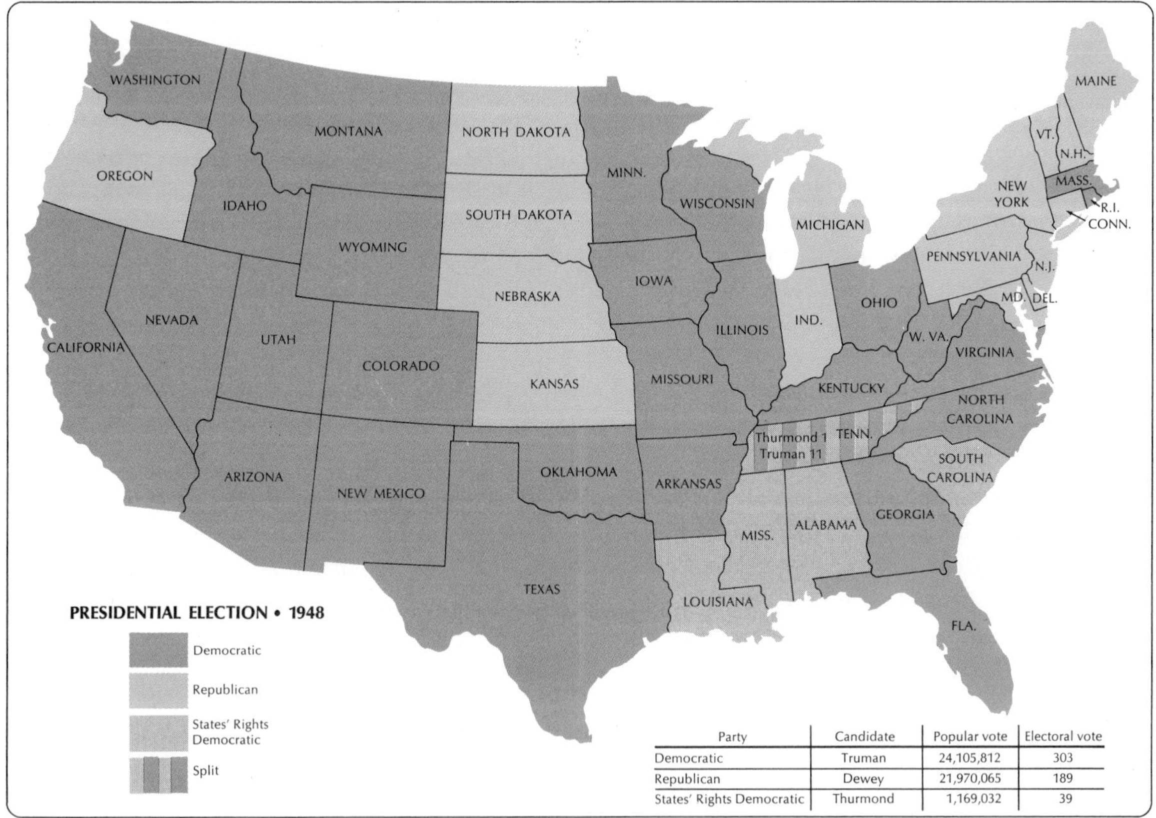

Party	Candidate	Popular vote	Electoral vote
Democratic	Truman	24,105,812	303
Republican	Dewey	21,970,065	189
States' Rights Democratic	Thurmond	1,169,032	39

Truman did not win a majority of the popular vote, but he carried the key states and held a majority in the electoral college of 303 to 189. The Democrats also regained control of both houses of Congress. Republicans who only a few days before had been ready to move into the White House suddenly discovered that they had been completely rejected. Their failure to present a convincing case on the issues and their underestimation of Truman as a campaigner and leader had proved to be their undoing.

But there were more fundamental reasons for Truman's surprising victory. Both the labor and the farm vote had made the difference for Truman in a number of key states such as Ohio and Iowa. Moreover, the Democrats benefited from the general prosperity and the fear of many people that a Republican administration might threaten good times and the social and economic gains made since 1933. On the other hand, the Republicans committed some serious blunders. Many overconfident party members failed to vote, and the conservative tone of the Republican-controlled Eightieth Congress lost the party voter support. In the final analysis Truman demonstrated that the coalition of workers, farmers, minority groups, and intellectuals which Roosevelt had put together was still a winning combination.

Once elected in his own right, President Truman began to work hard for a broad program of social and economic reform. In his message to Congress on January 5, 1949, he reviewed past Democratic achievements and called for even more welfare programs. Since 1933, Truman said, the American people had been "creating a society which offers new opportunities for every man to enjoy his share of the good things of life." Americans had rejected the idea, he continued, that "the fortunes of the Nation should be in the hands of a privileged few." While pointing to the great progress made over the last sixteen years, the President insisted that much remained to be done.

Specifically Truman recommended repeal of the Taft-Hartley Act, an increase in minimum wages to 75 cents an hour, higher taxes on corporations and middle- and upper-income groups, stronger antitrust laws, parity income for farmers, broader coverage and increased social security payments, a system of medical insurance, federal aid to education, slum clearance, and low-cost housing. He declared that "the Government must work with industry, labor, and the farmers in keeping our economy running at full speed." The President perhaps unwittingly labeled his own administration when, near the end of his address, he said: "Every segment of our population and every individual has a right to expect from our Government a fair deal."

Truman's fair deal message aroused heated discussion over the question of big government and state socialism. A writer in the *Washington Evening Star* said that the President's address "was the most frankly socialistic ever presented by a president of the United States." An Indiana editor wrote that Truman's "program means more taxing, more spending, more regulation by Government. It means a more powerful state, more Federal employees, more chances to elect and elect." Another critic charged that Truman had swung far to the left and that his program would "flatter and bribe every pressure group in the country." Other Americans, however, were less fearful and believed that the President was moving in the right direction. According to the *New York Times,* social reforms such as Truman was advocating were "all proper objectives of a democratic people, and the proper concern of a democratic government in this modern age."

Despite his resounding victory, Truman soon found that Congress was less than enthusiastic about much of his domestic program. A Democratic majority in both houses meant little because of the perennial coalition between Southern Democrats and conservative Northern Republicans. For Truman and his labor supporters, one of the first orders of legislative business was repeal of the Taft-Hartley Act. Truman had called for repeal of this "Slave Labor Law" during the campaign, the platform had promised it, and union leaders expected such action. Congress considered a measure to revoke the law in the spring of 1949 but finally refused either to repeal or to change the act. Labor officials were furious; Truman warned that the issue was "far from settled," but Congress would not be moved. Not until 1951 did Congress accept the first major amendment to the law. While union spokesmen and some Democratic leaders continued to insist on repealing what they considered antilabor legislation, a majority of Congress agreed that the law was working well and was not hurting the unions.

Truman, however, did gain some parts of his program. In 1949 Congress approved raising the minimum wage from 40 to 75 cents an hour. Furthermore, the next year Congress increased social security benefits and broadened the law to cover more than 10 million additional people, including self-employed workers, farm laborers, and domestic servants. The Housing Act of 1949 set as a national goal "a decent home and a suitable living environment for every American family." The law provided federal aid for slum clearance and the construction of about 800,000 public housing units. The President also won a somewhat more liberal immigration policy to permit entrance of additional displaced Europeans. Other parts of Truman's reform program met with less success. Congress refused to establish a permanent Fair Employment Practices Commission and ignored his request for federal aid to education, compulsory health insurance, and antilynching and anti-poll tax legislation.

By 1949 the farm problem had become a major issue, partly because of a sharp decline in agricultural income. In 1948 the Eightieth Congress had postponed, rather than settled, the farm problem by passing the Hope-Aiken bill after bitter debate. This committed the federal government to maintain prices on basic agricultural commodities, plus some other crops, at 90 percent of parity until June, 1950. This was to be done by advancing loans to producers at a set rate through the Commodity Credit Corporation. Much of the debate over the Hope-Aiken bill centered on the issue of whether the federal government should continue to guarantee high, fixed price supports. An increasing number of authorities believed that some kind of minimum price floor should be maintained for agricultural commodities, but they insisted that the level of price support should be determined by the total amount of a crop produced. This was known as the principle of flexible price supports and was intended to discourage overproduction. For example, price guarantees would be higher if farmers produced a smaller crop and lower if production was larger than normal. Senator Aiken proposed that price supports vary from 60 to 90 percent of parity, depending on the supply of a particular commodity. While President Truman and a majority in Congress favored the principle of flexible price supports, spokesmen for Southern and Midwestern farm groups wielded enough political influence to defeat the idea and to continue high, rigid supports.

Because of sharp agricultural price declines in 1949, lawmakers in the Eighty-first Congress came under heavy presure to do something for the farmers. Truman's new Secretary of Agriculture, Charles F. Brannan, stirred up a bitter controversy by proposing a new and different approach to the farm problem. Brannan explained that he wanted to reduce the production of commodities such as wheat and cotton, which had flowed into government storage, while at the same time expanding the consumption of fruit, milk, vegetables, meat, and other perishable products. To achieve these goals, Brannan proposed high, fixed price supports for most commodities, but only on a limited part of a farmer's production. Government loans would still be used to support the price of storable products. But in the case of perishable commodities, prices would be permitted to fall to whatever price the market dictated, and the difference between the market price and the predetermined price-support figure would be covered by a direct cash payment to the farmer by the government. Brannan argued that his plan would guarantee farmers a good income and at the same time assure low prices to consumers.

Labor groups, the National Farmers' Union, and spokesmen for consumers quickly rallied behind the Brannan Plan. Strong opposition, however, arose among those who believed that the scheme would cost too much and that it would give the federal government excessive control over farming. Most farm organizations, except the Farmers' Union, opposed the plan; and conservatives, who claimed that it would "socialize" agriculture, fought it bitterly. Those who wished to defeat Brannan's proposal successfully substituted a measure which simply extended price supports on basic commodities at 90 percent of parity through 1950. Several other crops would be supported at from 60 to 90 percent of parity. Congress again found it was difficult to abandon high, fixed supports to which farmers had become accustomed during and immediately after World War II. Increases in farm prices occasioned by the Korean War reduced the pressure on Congress to pass any basically new legislation during the remainder of the Truman administration. Between 1949 and 1951 net agricultural income rose from less than $13 billion to $16.3 billion. War had again rescued farmers who customarily produced much more than could be sold at home or abroad at profitable prices.

Tax policies also produced controversies in Truman's second term. In 1949 the President asked Congress to raise tax rates in order to reduce inflationary pressures in some segments of the economy and to permit payments on the national debt, which stood at some $252 billion. Congress that year refused to enact any major new tax law, but following the outbreak of war in Korea, the lawmakers raised taxes on corporations, increased the excess profits tax, and levied additional excise duties. In 1951 Congress raised both individual and corporate income taxes even further and added more excise taxes. The main conflict over tax policy arose between conservatives who wanted to cut expenditures, especially in the field of social services, and Truman and his supporters who hoped to rationalize spending by raising more revenue. The result was usually a compromise of some kind. Even with higher taxes, the federal deficit exceeded $4 billion in 1952, and the national debt rose to nearly $260 billion.

Communism: National Danger or "Red Herring"?

During most of his White House years Truman suffered from the charge that his administration was soft on communism. In March, 1947, Truman set up a Loyalty Review Board to screen federal employees, and he instructed the Attorney General to designate organizations which were considered subversive. But these actions did not satisfy those who attributed postwar difficulties both at home and abroad to Communist subversion. The House Un-American Activities Committee was especially critical of what it considered the President's indifference to Communist infiltration. In June, 1948, the Mundt-Nixon bill, which was designed to control Communist and Communist-front organizations, passed the House but died in the Senate. A few months later, in August, 1948, Elizabeth Bentley and Whittaker Chambers, admitted former Communists, appeared before the House Un-American Activities Committee and charged that several former government officials were either Communists or Communist sympathizers. Chambers created a national sensation when he named Alger Hiss, a career government employee who had worked in both the Agriculture and State Departments, as a Communist spy. Hiss denied the charge, and Truman referred to the investigation as a "red herring." Hiss's first trial ended in a "hung" jury, but he was later convicted of perjury.

In February, 1950, about a month after the conviction of Hiss, Senator Joseph McCarthy of Wisconsin declared that the State Department was full of Communists and fellow travelers. He produced no evidence to back his charges, but many people believed him. They pointed to what semed to be growing Communist strength around the world—the Russian explosion of an atomic bomb in 1949 and the victory of the Chinese Communists—and concluded that domestic Communists were somehow responsible. Demands arose at both the state and national levels for anti-Communist legislation. A number of states passed laws requiring loyalty oaths for schoolteachers and other public employees, and in September, 1950, Congress approved the Subversive Activities Control Act, generally known as the McCarran Act after its author Senator Pat McCarran of Nevada. This law made it illegal to conspire to form a totalitarian dictatorship in the United States, gave the government power to deport certain aliens, and required officers of Communist and Communist-front organizations to register with the Attorney General and to file financial data. Congress passed the McCarran Act over Truman's veto and thereby added fuel to the charges that the President was not a strong anti-Communist. In the midterm elections of 1950, Republicans argued that the Truman administration was riddled with Communist spies. This issue undoubtedly contributed to the Democrats' loss of twenty-eight House and five Senate seats.

Passage of the McCarran-Walter Act in June, 1952, was also a direct result of the growing fear of communism. Speaking on behalf of the bill, Senator McCarran declared that those who opposed his measure "would wittingly or unwittingly lend themselves to efforts which would poison the blood stream of the country." This law, also passed over Truman's veto, provided broad grounds for deporting or denying entrance to those who were thought to be security risks. While the McCarran-Walter Act completely revised and updated the Immigration Act of 1924, it continued to favor the immigration of Northern and Western Europeans. This obvious discrimination against many peoples of the world was, according to Truman, undesirable and undemocratic.

Conclusion

During the Truman years, Congress and the President made some important changes in governmental organization and administration. The Legislative Reorganization Act of 1946, proposed by Senator Robert M. La Follette, Jr., of Wisconsin and Congressman Mike Monroney of Oklahoma, reduced the number of standing committees in the House from forty-eight to nineteen and in the Senate from thirty-three to fifteen. It was hoped that these changes would improve the speed and efficiency of Congress. To improve the federal administration, Congress set up two commissions, under the chairmanship of former President Herbert Hoover, to study the organization of the executive branch of the government. After months of study, numerous task forces made hundreds of recommendations, many of which were implemented by Congress or the President. Some of the resulting reforms included the institution of better accounting and budgeting practices, the removal of the government from business in some cases, and the development of a career service in the federal government. Even more important was the addition of the twenty-second Amendment to the Constitution. Many Americans had resented Roosevelt's four election victories and believed that a President should be limited to two terms, as had been traditional before 1933. In 1947 Congress submitted a constitutional amendment to the states limiting the tenure of future Presidents to two terms; in 1951 the amendment went into effect. Many conservative citizens were convinced that there was something un-American about Roosevelt's New Deal, and they desired to bring the reform program at least to a temporary halt. Having committed himself to a liberal reform program, Truman found himself in the midst of a sharp philosophic and legislative conflict with conservatives. Despite determined opposition, Truman's leadership in the field of minimum wages, social security, housing legislation, and social welfare expenditures placed his achievements in the mainstream of twentieth-century political, social, and economic reform.

SUGGESTED READINGS

There is no satisfactory biography of Truman, but consult Jonathan Daniels's *The Man from Independence* (1950); Frank McNaughton and Walter Hehmeyer's *Harry Truman: President* (1958); and Alfred Steinberg's *The Man from Missouri: The Life and Times of Harry S. Truman* (1961), all of which provide useful insights into his character and administration. Also students should see Louis W. Koenig's *The Truman Administration: Its Principles and Practice* (1956); and Barton J. Bernstein and Allen J. Matusow's *The Truman Administration: A Documentary History** (1966). A general account by Eric Goldman, *The Crucial Decade—and After: America, 1945–1960** (1961), provides a lively introduction to the period. Truman's *Memoirs* (2 vols., 1955) give a good account of his administration. See also Cabell Phillips's *The Truman Presidency: The History of a Triumphant Succession* (1966). Many official papers can be found in *Public Papers of the Presidents: Harry S. Truman* (8 vols., 1961–1966).

On postwar economic reconversion see Lester Chandler's *Inflation in the United States, 1940–1948* (1951); Bert Hickman's *Growth and Stability in the Postwar Economy* (1961); *United States Fiscal Policy, 1945–1959* (1961) by A. E. Holmans; and Barton Bernstein's "The Removal of War Production Board Controls on Business, 1944–1946," *Business History Review* (Summer, 1965).

Labor problems are discussed in Joel Seidman's *American Labor from Defense to Reconversion* (1953); R. Alton Lee's *Truman and Taft-Hartley* (1966); Philip Taft's *The A.F. of L. from the Death of Gompers to the Merger* (1959); and appropriate chapters in Foster Rhea Dulles's *Labor in America** (2d ed., 1961). Agricultural trends and difficulties appear in the relevant chapters in Murray Benedict's *Farm Policies of the United States, 1790–1950* (1953), and fuller accounts of special issues are considered in Reo Christenson's *The Brannan Plan: Farm Politics and Policy* (1959) as well as in *Farm Policies and Politics in the Truman Years* (1967) by Allen J. Matusow.

Politics in the Truman years are discussed by Samuel Lubell in *The Future of American Politics* (1952); V. O. Key in *Southern Politics in State and Nation** (1949); and Jules Abels, who deals with the exciting campaign of 1948 in *Out of the Jaws of Victory* (1959). There are several good books on other aspects of the Truman years. Housing has been considered by Richard Davies in *Housing Reform during the Truman Administration* (1966); and civil rights is discussed by Eleanor Bontecou in *The Federal Loyalty and Security Program* (1953) as well as by Ralph Brown in *Loyalty and Security* (1958).

*indicates availability in paperback.

38

Eisenhower and Modern Republicanism

BY 1952 THE NATION was in a mood of anger and frustration. The Korean conflict had produced wide divisions within the country; above all the majority of citizens wanted to end what appeared to be a "useless war." Americans, moreover were deeply worried over the threat of domestic communism, and they complained that inflation was eating away their incomes and savings. To deal with the uncertainties abroad and the frustrations at home, voters looked for a strong leader. Their choice was General Dwight D. Eisenhower.

Eisenhower explained later that he entered politics because of a deep, personal conviction that "a long-term continuation of the domestic policies then supported by the Democratic administration would be ruinous to the nation." Specifically he was alarmed at excessive government spending, high taxes, and the increasing role of the federal government in the economy and the lives of the people Eisenhower reflected the popular mood, which favored continuation of the social reforms of the New Deal and Fair Deal but which rejected any bold expansion of the welfare state. The country shouted, it seemed, for more conservative leadership, and Eisenhower fulfilled that desire.

But the trends in American life and society could not easily be changed. After 1953 Congress reduced taxes and showed a somewhat more friendly attitude toward private business, but the role and functions of the federal government continued to increase as they had under Roosevelt and Truman. Federal expenditures remained high; the government took positive measures to combat recessions in 1953–1954 and 1957–1958; and the federal goverment under Eisenhower actually expanded its responsibilities in the field of health, welfare and education. Although Eisenhower's personal popularity remained high throughout his White House years, the Democrats won and held a majority in Congress after 1954. Most Americans saw nothing inconsistent or undesirable in the election of a Republican President and a Democratic Congress. Indeed, many people looked upon such a political division as the best guarantee of a "middle way" in national policy.

The Election of 1952

More than American presidential elections generally, the campaign of 1952 turned on questions of foreign affairs. Such issues as China and Korea, however, were significant not alone because they separated the Republican from the Democratic party. They were the catalysts whereby the Republican Old Guard, centering largely in the Midwest, hoped to prevent the nomination of another liberal Republican candidate and thus place their favorite, Robert A. Taft of Ohio, in nomination. The Ohio Senator, a noted prewar isolationist and the son of former President William Howard Taft, had in 1952 reached the acme of his power. His pointed, vigorous attacks on the Truman foreign policies had made him Vandenberg's successor as the nation's leading Republican spokesman on external affairs.

Those Republicans who supported Taft faced their immediate, even their ultimate, barrier in the candidacy of General Dwight D. Eisenhower, the head of NATO in Europe. Eisenhower's political affiliations had never been clear; some Democrats had attempted to interest him in a Democratic nomination in 1948. By 1952 a number of liberal Republicans had announced their support of the general, while Old Guard Republicans in Congress attempted to head off an Eisenhower nomination by reminding their hearers that Eisenhower had been so thoroughly involved in Truman-Acheson policy decisions that he could not logically attack Democratic policies with the necessary partisan fervor.

Eisenhower's candidacy attracted wide attention not only because of the general's remarkable personality and distinguished military career but also because his known views on United States diplomatic and military policy lay well within the national consensus. At the Republican Convention Eisenhower received the full support of the East and enough from other sections to assure him the nomination on the first ballot. For Vice President the convention named Senator Richard M. Nixon of California, a candidate acceptable to the Taft Republicans and one who had exploited the Communist issue in politics to the fullest. Truman's Republican adviser, John Foster Dulles, wrote the platform which strongly attacked the foreign policies. Roosevelt and Truman, the platform charged, had lost the dearly won peace at Teheran, Yalta, and Potsdam. At these conferences the national leadership had abandoned the nations of Slavic Europe to Communist aggression. In Asia a Democratic administration had denied Chiang the support he required and thereby substituted in the Pacific a murderous enemy for a proven ally. It had invited the Korean War and then refused to push on to victory. Finally, Dulles promised a program that would "mark the end of the negative, futile and immoral policy of 'containment' which abandons countless human beings . . . [and] enables the rulers to forge the captives into a weapon for our destruction."

Whatever Eisenhower's initial intent, he soon turned to foreign policy as the chief Republican weapon in the campaign. This appeared strange inasmuch as he had been Chief of Staff under the Truman administration and one of the architects of NATO. Dulles, too, had served the Truman administration and had negotiated the Japanese treaty. But both men were driven by political necessity. On domestic issues the Republican party could offer the country little except promises that it would halt the trend toward socialism and charges that the Democrats had been soft on communism. Eisenhower promised honesty in government and an end to inflation. But it was on the Korean issue that Eisenhower showed his supreme effectiveness as a campaigner. In a climactic appeal to the nation, he promised at Detroit on October 25 that, if elected, he would go to Korea to seek an early and honorable end to the war. He appealed skillfully to the frustrations and dissatisfactions which had developed around this inconclusive conflict.

With President Truman's announcement in March, 1952, that he would not run for reelection, Senator Estes Kefauver of Tennessee stumped the country in an effort to fill the leadership vacuum in the Democratic party. But at the same time a well-organized group of Northern Democrats moved to draft Governor Adlai Stevenson of Illinois. Stevenson was a grandson and namesake of Cleveland's Vice President during his second term. As a Chicago lawyer he had served the Roosevelt administration on various New Deal assignments. In 1948 he won election to the governorship of Illinois. Hesitant to the end, Stevenson finally accepted the party's nomination and in an appealing acceptance speech charmed millions of television viewers with his unusual wit and style. "Let's talk sense to the American people," he said. "Let's tell them the truth, that there are no gains without pains. . . ." For its vice presidential nominee the party selected Senator John J. Sparkman of Alabama.

Through the ensuing campaign Stevenson delighted the country's intellectuals with his eloquence and candor. He made no effort to escape the Truman record. In Europe he promised only containment, and that at great expense. He condemned those who promised victory in Europe because he said, there were no means available to achieve it. He upheld the Korean action as a successful example of collective security which, if it had not produced victory, had at least frustrated aggression. Stevenson condemned those who charged his party with treason. "Those who corrupt the public mind," he said, "are just as evil as those who steal from the public purse." For Eisenhower's promise to go to Korea, Stevenson had no answer. "Rather than exploit human hopes and fears, rather than provide glib solutions and false assurances," he explained, "I would gladly lose this Presidential election."

Against Eisenhower's personal popularity Stevenson had no chance. The November balloting gave the Republican nominee 33,800,000 votes to Stevenson's 27,300,000. The Republicans gained control of both houses of Congress, although by very narrow margins. The Republican party scored heavily on Eisenhower's personal appeal, on the charges of Democratic failure and on the popular belief that Eisenhower could end the Korean War.

Dwight D. Eisenhower was the first top-ranking general to occupy the White House since U. S. Grant. Except for two years as president of Columbia University from 1948 to 1950, his had been exclusively a military career. Born in Texas in 1890, he grew up in Abilene, Kansas, and then entered West Point, where he graduated in 1915. He moved steadily up the ranks; during 1942 Roosevelt placed him in charge of the Allied invasion of North Africa. The next year Eisenhower became Commander-in-Chief of the Allied forces in Western Europe and in June, 1944, directed the invasion of Normandy. By the end of World War II he had become a world figure and an international hero. Sixty-two at the time of his election, Eisenhower was an honest, dignified, gregarious, modest man who had achieved his many military successes by skillfully organizing, leading, and conciliating those who worked with him. His personal warmth and friendly smile inspired trust and confidence. People called him "Ike," reflecting thereby the feeling of friendship and intimacy which they held for him.

Although Eisenhower lacked practical political experience, he intuitively provided a type of leadership which satisfied most Americans. Recognizing that much of the demand for change and reform which had been so strong under the New Deal and Fair Deal had subsided during the prosperous 1950s, he followed the path of "moderate progressivism" in federal policies. Eisenhower explained his basic approach as one "that preserves the greatest possible initiative, freedom and independence of soul and body of the individual but that does not hesitate to use government to combat cataclysmic economic disasters." Divisions within the Republican party rendered moderation difficult and forced him to rely on Democratic support to achieve most of his programs. Conservatives such as Senator Taft of Ohio and liberals such as Senator Jacob Javits of New York had very little in common except the name Republican. Yet, in the long run, Eisenhower was able to win the backing of most Republicans and a substantial number of Democrats.

During the campaign Eisenhower had promised that, if elected, he would bring "the best brains in the country" to Washington. As it turned out, the first Republican Cabinet in twenty years represented the usual spectrum of professional and political interests and was of about the same caliber as previous Cabinets. The top post of Secretary of State went to John Foster Dulles, a career diplomat and State Department adviser whose experience went back to the Peace Conference of 1919. One of the President's closest advisers on domestic policy was Secretary of the Treasury George Humphrey of the M. A. Hanna Company of Cleveland. Eisenhower once said that he listened for Humphrey's words in Cabinet meetings because "I know that when he speaks he will say just what I am thinking." Another wealthy and conservative adviser was Charles E. Wilson, president of General Motors, who became Secretary of Defense. Wilson's blunt and untactful statements sometimes embarrassed the administration and opened the way for sharp criticism. Discussing self-reliance on one occasion, he remarked: "I've always liked bird dogs better than kennel-fed dogs myself—you know, one who'll get out and hunt for food rather than sit on his fanny and yell." One of Eisenhower's most interesting appointees was his Secretary of Labor—Martin Durkin, an Illinois Democrat and president of the United Association of Journeymen and Apprentices of the Plumbing and Pipefitting Industry. Critics scoffed at the Eisenhower team, referring to the Cabinet as consisting of "eight millionaires and a plumber." Whatever the implications of such remarks may have been, the Cabinet did give the Eisenhower administration a conservative image.

One Eisenhower appointment had extremely important implications for the future. During his first year in office the President named Governor Earl Warren of California as Chief Justice of the United States Supreme Court. Fred Vinson, a Truman appointee, died in September, 1953, and Eisenhower replaced him with the noted liberal Republican. As Chapter 41 will reveal, the so-called Warren Court, especially after 1960, rendered a series of very far-reaching decisions in the fields of civil, social, and economic rights.

The First Eisenhower Administration

In his State of the Union address on February 2, 1953, Eisenhower defined his general approach to economic and social problems. He called for an end to "planned deficits," a reduction of federal expenditures, lower taxes, and curbs on inflation. Fluctuations in prices, he said, should be dealt with by "sound fiscal and monetary policy, and . . . the natural workings of economic law." He promised that the administration would not ask for renewal of the price or wage controls scheduled to expire April 30. The President also recommended new farm legislation, as well as modifications of the Taft-Hartley Act. On social issues, Eisenhower declared that he would strive to achieve "civil rights and equality of employment opportunity," an extension of social security, and a program to bring some help to the nation's schools. "There is . . . ," he concluded, "a middle way between untrammeled freedom of the individual and the demands for the welfare of the whole Nation. This way must avoid government by bureaucracy as carefully as it avoids neglect of the helpless." This was a clear statement of Eisenhower's "middle way."

For most Republicans the first order of business was tax reduction. The President believed strongly in this course, but he opposed reductions before federal expenditures could be lowered. He did not, in other words, want to endanger the nation's defenses or add to the public debt. Despite strong pressure for immediate tax cuts, Eisenhower successfully resisted congressional efforts to lower taxes in 1953. With a deficit of more than $9 billion for the year ending July 1, it appeared foolhardy to cut taxes until spending had been brought under control. During 1954 the President and Secretary Humphrey concentrated on curtailing both military and civilian expenditures; they reduced federal outlays to $67.8 billion and trimmed the deficit to $3.1 billion. Thereafter they agreed to widespread tax reductions. Congress lowered a wide range of excise taxes in April, 1954, and in another law, passed in August, the lawmakers permitted faster tax write-offs for businessmen, raised exemptions for child care and medical expenses, and permitted income received from stock dividends to be tax free up to $50. Altogether, the annual tax savings amounted to about $7.4 billion, but most of the advantages went to high-income groups. As David Lawrence wrote: "Perhaps the most outstanding characteristics of the new measure is the encouragement it gives . . . private enterprise."

The controversy over tax policy was tied closely to the debate over the best method to deal with the economic recession which began in the summer of 1953. A drop in defense spending, increased inventories, and a slowdown in private investment all combined to bring on the recession. As a result, manufacturing production dropped and unemployment rose sharply by the winter of 1953–1954. Faced with a lagging economy, Democrats and labor leaders called for massive federal spending to stimulate the economy and to create jobs. But Eisenhower refused to "go into any slambang emergency program" unless, he said, "it is necessary." He obviously did not think such action was needed. The President preferred to cut spending, lower taxes, and thereby encourage private investment as the basis for economic expansion. By the late spring of 1954 a rise in both consumer and capital expenditures, accompanied by increased public outlays for social security, unemployment insurance, and welfare payments, pushed the economy upward again. In August, Eisenhower announced that "the recent decline in economic activity has come to a halt." The President insisted that the quick return of prosperity proved the soundness of the administration's taxing and spending policies. Genuine economic prosperity, Eisenhower believed, rested primarily in the private sector rather than in federal spending.

An even more controversial issue during Eisenhower's first term, and one which reflected the President's basic economic views, was the question of expanding federal power facilities. Although he had once referred to the Tennessee Valley Authority as "creeping socialism," Eisenhower did not favor the destruction of TVA or other public power projects. Nevertheless, he strongly believed that the rapid expansion of federal activities in the power field should be curtailed. The President favored a partnership arrangement in which, he said, "the states and local communities, private citizens and the Federal Government" would all work together. "This combined effort," he continued, "will advance the development of the great river valleys of our nation and the power that they can generate." Eisenhower followed this policy despite widespread criticism.

Eisenhower faced his first major controversy over public power in the Dixon-Yates contract. During 1954, the Atomic Energy Commission approved an agreement with Edgar H. Dixon and Eugene Yates to construct a plant at West Memphis, Arkansas, to supply additional electricity for the Memphis area. Supporters of public power, especially the friends of TVA, charged loudly that the government was favoring the private power trust against the public interest. Eisenhower defended the contract and argued that the government had no reason to build a plant to provide electricity for Memphis. Following months of controversy, the AEC canceled the contract, but only after the revelation that a conflict of interests existed between a government official and the firm which handled some of the Dixon-Yates financing. Still the Eisenhower administration did not abandon its partnership policy.

Another example of Eisenhower's opposition to what he called "the implacable expansionism of the federal government" was his support of the Submerged Lands Act. This law sought to solve the controversy between the federal government and the states, particularly California, Texas, and Louisiana, over control of the submerged coastal lands rich in oil. In 1947 the Supreme Court had decided that California was "not the owner of the three-mile belt along its coast" and that the federal government owned the underwater resources, including oil. Those who favored federal control of the submerged coastal lands argued that the underlying oil belonged to all the people and that state ownership would result in a "giveaway" to a few favored oil companies. Despite a twenty-two-hour filibuster by Senator Wayne Morse of Oregon, Congress passed the Submerged Lands Act in May, 1953. This law transferred offshore oil lands along the Gulf and California coasts to the states.

On the important issue of farm policy the Republicans were committed to basic changes. In the campaign of 1952 they had criticized the policies of high government price supports and restricted production which the Democrats had maintained since World War II. Eisenhower believed that farmers deserved parity prices—indeed, during the campaign he advocated 100 percent of parity—but he said parity prices must be found in the marketplace and not in federal price supports. Secretary of Agriculture Ezra Taft Benson was particularly critical of Democratic farm policies and argued that farmers had come to depend too heavily on the government for price and income. Urban-minded critics insisted that the farm program was costing too much. "Most Americans would be astonished and deeply shocked at what it costs them to carry on this price support program," declared one New England congressman.

There was little that Eisenhower and Benson could do to change farm policy immediately inasmuch as Congress in 1952 had extended price supports on basic commodities at 90 percent of parity through the 1953 and 1954 crop years. In August, 1954, however, the Republican Congress enacted a new price-support law which permitted the Secretary of Agriculture to guarantee prices to cooperating farmers at between 82.5 and 90 percent of parity in 1955, and 75 to 90 percent in 1956. This reflected the principle of flexible price supports, under discussion since 1947, which then had considerable support among Democrats and Republicans alike. The price-support figure under the new law would be determined on the basis of production. Higher output would mean lower support prices to discourage surplus production. Higher supports would follow the production of smaller crops.

During the rest of the Eisenhower administration, Secretary Benson used his discretionary powers to loosen production controls. As he put it, farmers should be freed to farm. But because of greatly increased efficiency, surpluses mounted and large quantities of farm commodities flowed into storage, which in turn increased government costs for the program. But the worst effect for farmers was lower prices and declining farm incomes. Total net farm income dropped from $15.3 billion in 1952 to $13.3 billion in 1953 and to $12.6 billion in 1954. It went even lower in 1955 and 1956. Uneasy over the possible political consequences of decreasing agricultural prices, the Republicans began to explore new policies. In April, 1956, Congress passed the administration's soil-bank plan, which provided payments to farmers for taking farmland out of production. Supporters believed that the new program would reduce surpluses, cut the cost of storing commodities, and put cash directly into the pockets of producers. Democratic critics, however, charged that it was primarily a Republican attempt to buy farm votes in a presidential election year.

As had been true since the 1930s, except during wartime, surplus production continued to be the essence of the farm problem. Not even the removal of acreage from production under the soil bank, increased exports, and higher consumption at home could absorb the flood of agricultural products at prices favorable to farmers. In July, 1954, Congress passed the Agricultural Trade Development and Assistance Act, informally known as P.L. 480, which permitted the sale of surplus farm commodities abroad for foreign currencies instead of dollars. Under this law food could also be bartered or even given away. Moreover, domestic consumption was encouraged through school lunch and welfare programs. But still surpluses and low prices prevailed. To make matters worse for farmers, prices of nonfarm commodities continued to rise, giving farm products a low exchange value. For example, one widely used self-propelled combine for harvesting grain cost $4,310 in the 1947–1949 period; by 1960 the price rose to $6,700, an *increase* of some 33 percent. During the same interval, the farm price of wheat *dropped* more than 10 percent.

Both 1953 and 1954 were relatively peaceful on the labor front. Some political and union leaders continued to demand repeal of the Taft-Hartley Act, but Congress refused to respond. It even failed to enact any very significant amendments to the law. In his annual economic report of January, 1955, President Eisenhower recommended an increase in the minimum wage from 75 cents to 90 cents an hour and additions in the number of workers covered by the minimum-wage law. Despite strong opposition from the United States Chamber of Commerce and the National Association of Manufacturers, Congress in 1955 went even further than the President had suggested. The new law raised the minimum wage to $1 an hour, to become effective March 1, 1956. Minimum-wage legislation affected only the lowest-paid workers, since those in manufacturing, transportation, construction, mining, and other basic industries earned far above the minimum. The average hourly wage in manufacturing, for example, was $1.86 in 1955. Some workers also benefited from the expansion of unemployment compensation in 1954. The new law authorized unemployment benefits for approximately four million additional workers and required firms with as few as four employees to pay the federal unemployment tax.

Despite charges by liberal Democrats, Eisenhower was not unmindful of the need for additional social welfare legislation. His support in the establishment of a Cabinet-level Department of Health, Education, and Welfare indicated that he recognized the wider role of the federal government in the field of welfare. "Along with the protection of freedom and maintenance of a strong and growing economy," he said in January, 1954, "this administration recognizes a third great purpose of government —concern for the human problems of our citizens."

In the field of social security Eisenhower declared that "the economic protection afforded by this social insurance is now accepted as basic in our society." Recognizing that the principle was sound, he believed that more needed to be done. Early in 1954 the President recommended more liberal social security benefits and the extension of the coverage to more people. As finally passed in August, the new Social Security Act encompassed coverage to farmers, teachers, some local and state employees, and others who had not been included under the previous law. Potentially, an additional 7.4 million workers were brought under social security. The wage base on which workers and employers paid the Old Age and Survivors Insurance tax was raised from $3,600 to $4,200, and monthly payments were increased about 16 percent.

In other areas of social reform Eisenhower was less successful. To improve urban housing, the President recommended the construction of 35,000 public housing units annually over a period of four years. In 1954 Congress authorized a one-year program of 35,000 units. Actually, this law accomplished little for public housing. Eisenhower favored limited federal aid to education, particularly in the area of school construction. But congressional fears over federal control of education and problems of racial segregation kept Congress from passing any law to provide general federal aid to education during the first Eisenhower administration. Nevertheless, Congress continued to provide federal support for the school lunch program, funds to school districts serving children where federal employees were concentrated, aid to research and development, and student assistance in colleges and universities. Between 1953 and 1956 the federal government spent between $1.3 and $1.8 billion annually on these functions.

During 1956 Congress greatly expanded federal aid for highway construction. In what became known as the Interstate Highway Act, the federal government authorized the largest road-building program in American history. Previous highway legislation had provided for a federally supported interstate system, but federal aid had been limited to 60 percent of the cost. The new law increased the federal government's share to 90 percent, extended the system to 41,000 miles, and calculated the cost at about $31 billion over a period of some thirteen years.

Eisenhower depended heavily upon Democratic help to obtain the economic and social legislation which he desired. Many conservative Republicans simply refused to support the President's welfare measures, however moderate they may have been. Looking forward to the midterm elections of 1954, former President Truman said that "President Eisenhower should be secretly wishing for a Democratic Congress . . . and hope that we can save him from the misdeeds of his own party." Eisenhower disagreed; he campaigned energetically for Republican candidates. However, both houses went Democratic. In the Senate the narrow majority was 48 to 47, with one independent; in the House the Democrats led 232 to 203. Never again would Eisenhower have a Republican Congress. This was no indication that people desired to abandon political moderation. One Illinois farmer explained the situation this way: "I voted for Eisenhower to turn the tide of too much reliance on government. Now I'm voting Democratic again to see that things don't go too far the other way." To many voters this seemed the surest way to guarantee middle-of-the-road policies.

Communism and Internal Security

Even after his own party came to power Senator McCarthy continued to charge that the federal government was infiltrated with Communists. Many of the nation's problems both at home and abroad, he said, could be explained by internal subversion. Indeed, McCarthy not only insisted that the Truman administration had been soft on communism but declared that

President Eisenhower had failed to rid the government of security risks. He accused government departments, the colleges and universities, and even the churches of harboring Communists, or supporting what he called the "Communist apparatus." In the summer of 1953 he dispatched two of his staff members to Europe, where, among other things, they frightened timid administrators of American overseas libraries into removing books which the investigators thought were un-American. People who dared to speak out against McCarthy and his rash charges were labeled "Communists" or, at best, "fellow travelers." A Red Scare, not unlike that which followed World War I, was in full swing.

Many people hoped that Eisenhower would destroy McCarthy's growing influence with a direct attack upon the Senator and his methods. But the President believed that the best way to defeat McCarthyism was to ignore the Senator. Finally, in 1954, McCarthy overreached himself—as Eisenhower had believed he would—when he accused the Army of shielding a disloyal Army dentist, Major Irving Peress, at Fort Monmouth, New Jersey. During the hearing on the Peress affair, McCarthy called General Ralph Zwicker, a former commanding officer of Peress, "a disgrace to the uniform" and accused him of "shielding Communist conspirators." Finally a Senate subcommittee investigated the Army in April as millions watched on television. McCarthy's unsubstantiated attacks on Secretary of the Army Robert Stevens revealed what an arrogant, ignorant, and intolerant bully the Wisconsin Senator really was. Disgusted with this performance, as well as with other McCarthy activities, the Senate passed a condemnatory resolution in December, 1954, declaring that McCarthy's actions were "contrary to senatorial traditions." By that time the general fear of communism had declined and McCarthy's public support had disintegrated. He died three years later, in May, 1957.

Although the fear of internal Communist subversion subsided, it never completely disappeared during the 1950s. Throughout the decade, Congress and the Executive took firm action to root security risks and people of questionable character out of government service. Vice President Nixon declared in the fall of 1954, "We're kicking the Communists and fellow travelers and security risks out of the Government, not by the hundreds, but by the thousands." This was campaign exaggeration, but in 1953–1954 about 3,000 federal employees were dismissed under Eisenhower's security program. In one celebrated case involving internal security the Atomic Energy Commission, in June, 1954, withdrew the security clearance of the famous atomic scientist, J. Robert Oppenheimer. The Commission accused him of associating with known Communists and of ignoring the needs of domestic security. Nine years later the AEC reversed itself and honored Oppenheimer with a $50,000 prize for his contributions to nuclear physics.

The Election of 1956

Despite the many controversial issues which faced Eisenhower, nothing seemed to dim his personal popularity. What columnist Ernest K. Lindley wrote in 1953 was equally true in 1956. The President's popularity, said Lindley, was personal and reflected "affection, confidence in his integrity, and the feeling that he graces the office of Chief Executive." Beyond this, Lindley said, "one senses confidence in his judgment about the overriding questions of defense and foreign policy in a dangerous world." Moreover, by 1955 and 1956 the country was enjoying a high level of prosperity. Writing in January, 1956, the President explained: "Full employment, rising incomes, and a stable dollar have been cherished goals of our society. The practical attainment of these ideals during 1955 was the year's great economic achievement."

Statistics seemed to bear out the President's optimistic assessment of economic conditions. Despite the recession in 1953–1954, gross national product in stable prices rose from $381 billion to $412 billion. In the same period, annual per capita income increased from $1,592 to $1,705. And by 1956 unemployment was down to only 2.2 million workers. Business was booming almost everywhere. In 1955 the automobile industry produced more than 7 million passenger cars, up some 2 million from the year before. Nonfarm housing starts rose by 225,000 units over 1953, and such industries as appliances, electronics, and public utilities enjoyed unusual prosperity. Perhaps best of all according to the President, this condition was "not a prosperity based on the froth of inflation." Under these circumstances, Republicans could understandably boast of "peace, progress and prosperity."

Although political conditions appeared favorable to the Republicans as they looked forward to 1956, they were understandably disturbed in September, 1955, when the President suffered a severe heart attack at Denver. The question now foremost in Republican minds was whether Eisenhower would be able to run for a second term. Fortunately, he made an excellent recovery and announced on February 29, 1956, that he would seek a second term. For Republicans this settled the issue. When the party met at the Cow Palace in San Francisco in August, delegates renominated Eisenhower and Nixon on the first ballot. Addresses by the party faithful emphasized how the Eisenhower administration had brought prosperity without war; and in his acceptance speech the President promised to continue both his domestic and foreign policies.

Meanwhile, the Democrats had again nominated Adlai Stevenson. A more vigorous contest developed over the vice presidential choice where Senator Estes Kefauver of Tennessee ultimately defeated Senator John F. Kennedy of Massachusetts. Keynote-speaker Governor Frank Clement of Tennessee delivered a hard-hitting, emotional attack on the Eisenhower administration, calling it a "sordid record of broken promises and unredeemed pledges." As the campaign got under way, Stevenson struck harder and took a less lofty and intellectual position than he had in 1952. But neither Stevenson nor the Democratic party had anything to offer which could equal the Republican appeal of peace, progress, and prosperity. Nixon again carried the campaign burden. Eisenhower won another smashing victory as he gained 57.4 percent of the popular vote and carried all but seven states. He even carried Louisiana which had not gone Republican since 1876. Eisenhower also ran well in urban areas usually considered safely Democratic and gained more black support than any Republican candidate since 1928.

While Eisenhower won an easy victory, Congress remained Democratic. This showed that the President was considerably more popular than his party. Division in the House gave the Democrats a lead of 234 to 201; in the Senate they held a slight margin of 49 to 47. The Democrats also picked up one governorship, giving them an edge of 28 to 20 in the state capitals. In the Eighty-fifth Congress which began in January, 1957, congressional leadership and power still rested in the hands of two powerful Texans—Lyndon B. Johnson, Majority Leader in the Senate, and Sam Rayburn, Speaker of the House. Johnson and Rayburn repeatedly helped Eisenhower win legislative victories over the coalition of conservative Northern Republicans and Southern Democrats which attempted to block the President's more progressive social and economic legislation.

Eisenhower's Second Term

Soon after the beginning of Eisenhower's second term, the prosperity about which Republicans had boasted in the recent campaign suddenly ended. By the fall of 1957 the country had fallen into a sharp recession. Consumer spending leveled off, manufacturing output declined, private investment fell, and by December unemployment had risen to 5.2 percent of the labor force. It went even higher in early 1958. Not until the late spring of 1958 did conditions begin to improve significantly.

Once again there were loud demands for increased government spending to stimulate the economy and provide employment. Senator Paul Douglas of Illinois introduced a measure to establish an Area Redevelopment Administration with funds to help industries locate in communities which had a high rate of unemployment. But the President vetoed this bill as being "unsound." Eisenhower opposed pump-priming schemes; the talk of turning to government, he said, "evidences lack of faith in the inherent vitality of our free economy." In denouncing some of the spending ideas, he declared that they would lead to "the wholesale distribution of the people's money in dubious activities under federal direction."

Despite Eisenhower's conservative-sounding public statements, he moved quickly to use the antidepression tools already available to the federal government. These were the so-called builtin stabilizers which concerned the economists. The Defense Department speeded up military procurement and expanded military construction. This helped conditions in industrial centers such as Detroit where unemployment was high. The administration also increased grants-in-aid for building hospitals and other public facilities and spent more on the interstate highway program; this brought money into many communities. The Federal Housing Administration lowered down payments on FHA-insured housing loans, and the Federal Reserve Board lowered interest rates. Congress, at the President's request, appropriated additional funds for the federal-state unemployment insurance program so that benefits could be paid to workers for more than twenty-six weeks. Although Eisenhower preferred to rely on the private sector to restore prosperity, he did not hesitate to use a wide variety of government programs, involving huge expenditures, to help the economy. The President had achieved his objectives of a balanced budget in fiscal 1956 and 1957, but the deficit rose to $2.8 billion in the year ending June 20, 1958, and jumped to a whopping $12.4 billion the following year. As it turned out, government spending was still the most effective antidote for depression.

This recession was a major cause of a growing disillusionment with the Eisenhower administration. However, other developments also plagued the Republicans as the midterm

Postwar Problems

The United States inherited a seemingly endless series of skirmishes after the second great world conflict. Yet the crises in Korea, Suez, Syria, Iraq, Jordan, and Lebanon might have been weathered with more aplomb and less internal wrangling had not the dreadful spectre of "the bomb" loomed so large.

The Korean War originated in the chaos left over from World War II. Japanese troops had surrendered there to American forces in the south and to the Russians in the north. A line to facilitate military administration was drawn at the 38th parallel, but in June, 1950, North Korean forces crossed it to invade the Republic of Korea to the south. Worried about stability in the Pacific, the United States took the matter to the United Nations which promptly asked its members to resist this aggression and asked the United States to command the necessary troops. Below, street-fighting in Seoul raged repeatedly. The capitol of South Korea changed hands four times during the war.

Then Wisconsin Senator Joseph McCarthy began to move. Something called an "international Communist conspiracy" hovered behind every palm tree, underlay every nationalistic squabble. McCarthy's notion was that American Communists, especially in the State Department, had let China go Communist. Now the Chinese, their every action dictated by Moscow, threatened the American sphere of influence in the Pacific. The nation hesitated, then common sense broke through. Officially censured by the Senate, McCarthy died not long after the ruin of his career.

Two Presidents saw the country through the 1950s. Truman, the snappish ex-enlisted man and former Missouri politician, shouldered his responsibilities gamely. Eisenhower, the famous general and master tactician, satisfied the country's demand for stability in an insecure world.

United Press International

"Say, What Ever Happened To 'Freedom-From-Fear'?"

From The Herblock Book (*Beacon Press*, 1952)

One effective spokesman for the liberal viewpoint during the 1950s, as he has been for the 1960s, was the syndicated cartoonist Herbert Block. This sampling of his work reflects some of the main concerns of the American people during the decade that ended in 1960. The atom bomb, the hydrogen bomb, and other nuclear refinements continued to terrify the country. In his *Herblock Book* (Beacon Press, 1952), the cartoonist pointed out that "even when we had a monopoly on the atomic bomb, that didn't make us feel secure because it created new fears about what big secrets might get out. And within a couple of years after the first atomic blasts we already had the security shakes so bad that anyone who missed out on recent history might have supposed we were the only country in the world that *didn't*

"Well, Goodness—We Can't Investigate Everybody!"

CHIANG GOVT. SCANDALS
U.S. FUNDS
CHIANG LOBBY
AMERICANS CRITICAL OF CHIANG
HERBLOCK

From The Herblock Book (*Beacon Press*, 1952)

"Somebody From Outside Must Have Influenced Them"

From Herblock's Special for Today (*Simon and Schuster*, 1958)

From Herblock's Special for Today (*Simon and Schuster,* 1958)

"Want To See Me Blow Out Everything With One Puff?"

From The Herblock Book (*Beacon Press,* 1952)

have the bomb instead of being the only one that had it. . . . Some secrets did get out, and it takes only one or two espionage cases to create general talk about 'all those fellows' giving away 'all our secrets'."

This national absorption with fear over "security" appears over and over again in these cartoons. Among the other problems looming large during the Eisenhower years, equal rights for black citizens and the ever-present Cold War against the Soviet Union, its satellite states, and Communist China received continuing attention. American chagrin at being beaten by the Soviet Union in launching the first earth satellites subsequently stimulated vast government outlays for scientific education and research.

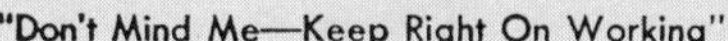
"Don't Mind Me—Keep Right On Working"

From The Herblock Book (*Beacon Press,* 1952)

"What Is This—A Game?"

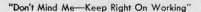

From Herblock's Special for Today (*Simon and Schuster,* 1958)

United Press International

Burt Glinn, Magnum

Two developments of the 1950s significantly advanced the cause of black equality: the Supreme Court decision that segregation in the public schools is, *per se*, unconstitutional, and the appearance of new black leadership. Above, long lines gather in the corridor of the Supreme Court Building several hours before the Court opened its first hearing on the school issue in 1952, hoping to share the fewer than fifty seats available to the public. Below, Eisenhower sent Federal troops into Little Rock, Arkansas, in 1957, five years after the decision, to insure the safety of the first black students to attend Little Rock High School. Right, above, Martin Luther King, Jr., was arrested in Montgomery, Alabama, while leading a Negro boycott against city bus service in 1955. King's ideal of passive, nonviolent resistance and his goal of ultimate integration dominated much of the black movement during the 1950s.

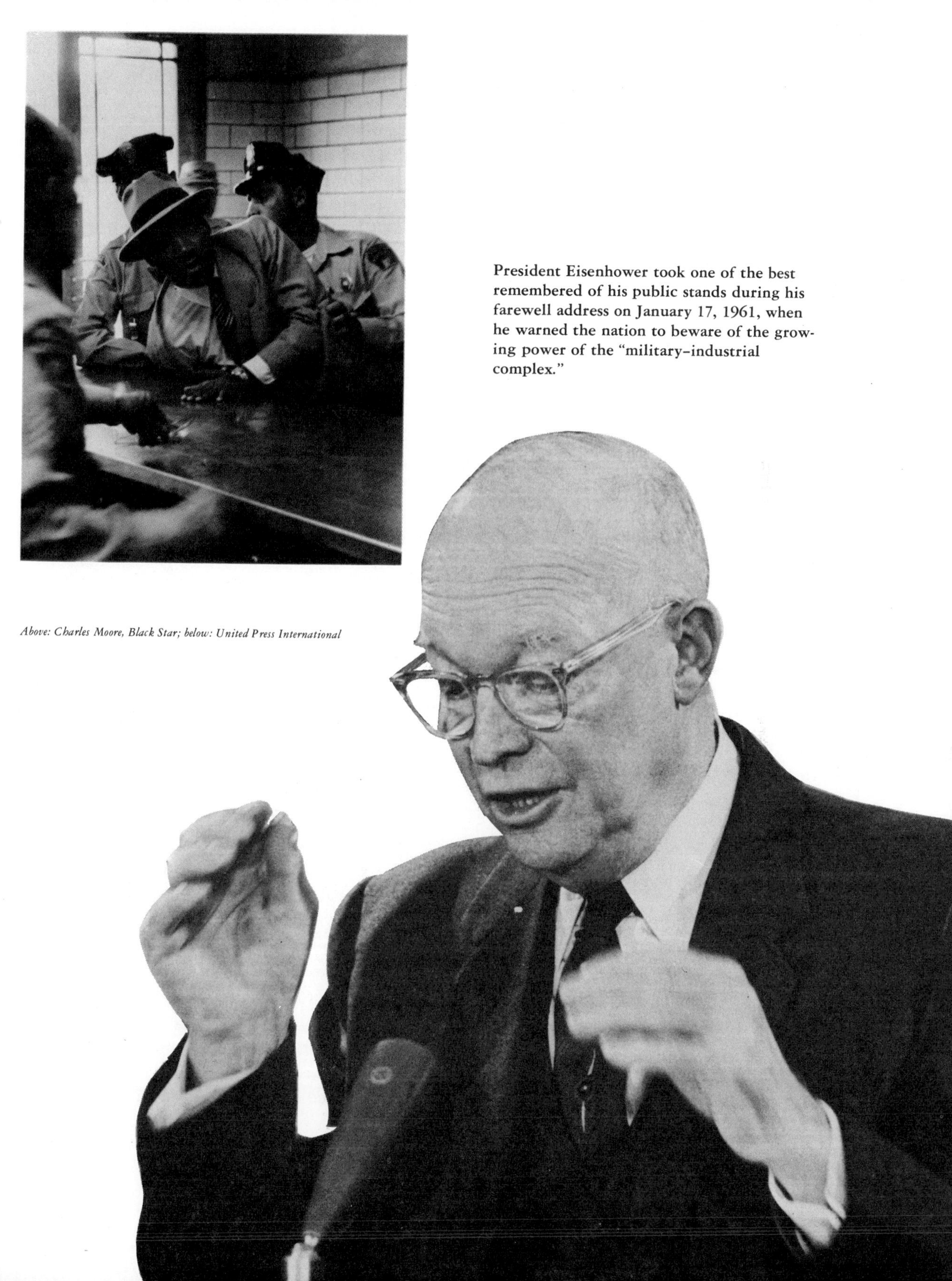

President Eisenhower took one of the best remembered of his public stands during his farewell address on January 17, 1961, when he warned the nation to beware of the growing power of the "military–industrial complex."

Above: Charles Moore, Black Star; below: United Press International elections of 1958 approached. The professions of purity by the Eisenhower administration were seriously sullied when it was revealed that Sherman Adams, the President's chief assistant, had taken gifts from a Boston textile firm which was seeking favors in Washington. Adams resigned on September 22, but his actions greatly embarrassed the Republicans. Moreover, Southerners had become embittered at Eisenhower when he sent troops to Little Rock in 1957 to enforce the Supreme Court's decision on school integration. Republicans lost much labor support when they backed state right-to-work laws so strongly opposed by organized labor. The earlier confidence in Eisenhower's foreign policies and defense programs was weakened by the Chinese shelling of the offshore islands of Quemoy and Matsu during 1958. The Eisenhower-Dulles team had apparently not solved problems with Communist China after all. The Russian Sputnik in 1957 made people wonder if the Republicans had also let the country fall behind in the space race. Finally, the Democrats capitalized on farmers' dissatisfaction with Secretary Benson and the Republican farm program.

The Republicans, especially Vice President Nixon, attempted in vain to answer these Democratic critics. In 1958, the Democrats gained one of their most spectacular victories since the 1930s. They picked up 48 seats in the House to give them a majority of 282 to 154. In the Senate they added 15 seats, making the division there of 64 Democrats to only 34 Republicans. Republican losses were heavy in the Midwest farm belt and in industrially depressed areas. About the only bright spot for the Republicans was the victory of Nelson A. Rockefeller over incumbent Averell Harriman in the race for New York's governorship.

Agriculture and Labor in the Second Term

Farmers expressed sharp disapproval of Secretary Benson's agricultural policies in the elections of 1958. Benson had continually worked to reduce the level of price supports and to weaken government controls over production. He believed that the best farm policy would gradually place farmers in a position where farm prices would be determined solely in the marketplace. Although the administration's attitude was not very realistic in light of the growing efficiency of farm production, it should be emphasized that Congress advanced no workable alternative. Because of strong farm opposition to strict acreage and production controls, Congress hesitated to inaugurate firm restrictions on output to reduce burdensome surpluses. By 1958 the general policy for several basic crops provided some minimum price support with liberalized controls over production. Throughout the last years of the Eisenhower administration the President and Congress sparred over farm policy, but nothing other than makeshift and piecemeal legislation was passed, none of which reached the heart of the problem. The Democrats would make the farm question a vital issue in the 1960 campaign.

By Eisenhower's second term sentiment for additional legislation to regulate and control labor unions had become demanding. Labor officials found that there was no longer any possibility of repealing the Taft-Hartley Act; indeed, their problem was to keep Congress from passing stronger antiunion measures. The image of organized labor was seriously blackened as a result of hearings held by a Select Committee of the Senate under the chairmanship of Senator John L. McClellan of Arkansas. Beginning in 1957, the Committee disclosed examples of bribery, graft, racketeering, illegal expense accounts, deals between union leaders and employers to keep wages down, and other abuses in the levels of union leadership. A number of union officials took the Fifth Amendment, including Dave Beck, president of the Teamsters Union, who soon thereafter announced his resignation. James R. Hoffa, Beck's successor, also came under suspicion and criticism. Hoping to ward off further restrictive legislation, the AFL-CIO in 1957 adopted a code of ethics and suspended the Teamsters and several other unions which were under investigation. Many lawmakers, however, believed that workers needed protection against their own leaders. In 1958 Congress passed the Welfare and Pension Plans Disclosure Act which permitted public scrutiny of union pension and welfare funds, to safeguard the workers' contributions.

By 1959, after more than two years of intermittent hearings by the McClellan committee, Congress was prepared to restrict union power. After seven months of controversy, Congress in September passed the Labor Management Reporting and Disclosure Act, commonly called the Landrum-Griffin Act. This was the first major legislation in the field of labor-management relations since 1947. The new law provided a bill of rights for union members which guaranteed them basic rights in their individual relationship with the union. The legislation required unions to file financial reports with the Secretary of Labor, banned convicts from holding union office, and established additional controls over secondary boycotts and picketing. Although some features of the Landrum-Griffin Act received labor support, unions generally considered it antilabor and vigorously opposed it. Passage of the new law measured the growing role of government in the entire field of labor-management relations. To what extent, if any, this legislation would weaken unions remained to be seen. But Americans believed increasingly that they had a definite stake in labor-management disputes and that the government was the only agency which could protect their interests.

Unions continued to grow, though less rapidly than earlier. In 1955 the American Federation of Labor and the Congress of Industrial Organizations merged into one giant union with some fifteen million members. However, by the late 1950s much of the militancy had gone out of the labor movement. Critics charged that the big unions were rich, smug, and complacent. Several factors may have accounted for the lack of militancy — the absence of a crusading spirit among some of the national labor leaders, high wages (the average weekly wage in manufacturing was $91 in 1960), and a primary interest in security. Besides seeking higher wages, unions worked for job protection, pensions, sick leave, and paid vacations. Some unions demanded, but did not receive, a guaranteed annual wage. Nevertheless, the power of organized labor balanced at least partially the power of big business.

Social Welfare and Education

Social welfare legislation made relatively few gains during Eisenhower's second term. A conflict between the President and a Democratic Congress was at least partly responsible for this condition. In general, the Democrats wanted new and expanded programs. Following the recession of 1957–1958, for example, the Democrats pushed for special legislation to provide federal grants and loans for depressed regions with hard-core unemployment and low incomes. But Eisenhower, insisting on local responsibility, vetoed three federal bills.

People had scarcely become accustomed to the military and peacetime implications of atomic energy—the Atomic Age—before they were confronted with an equally startling development—the launching of vehicles into outer space. Following the Russian launching of two satellites in the autumn of 1957 (one of which carried two dogs), the United States inaugurated an intensive effort to equal and surpass the Russian feats in space. In April, 1958, President Eisenhower recommended that all of America's space activities, except "for those projects primarily associated with military requirements," be turned over to a new federal agency. Congress promptly passed the National Aeronautics and Space Act. This law directed the President to proceed with a "comprehensive program" for space development. The nonmilitary aspects of the program were assigned to the National Aeronautics and Space Administration, headed by a civilian. Meanwhile, on January 31, 1958, the United States placed its first satellite in orbit.

One of the most significant measures passed during Eisenhower's eight years was the National Defense Education Act of 1958. Although many people had been calling for a broader program of federal aid to education, passage of this law was to a considerable extent a frantic response to the Russian launching of the first artificial earth satellite on October 4, 1957. Stunned by the Russian lead in space exploration, Americans were now ready to spend larger sums on education. The NDEA provided federal support in the fields of the natural sciences, mathematics, and foreign languages especially. The law made money available for scholarships, improved teacher training, and equipment. In signing the bill, President Eisenhower said it would "do much to strengthen our American system of education so that it can meet the broad and increasing demands imposed upon it by considerations of basic national security." By 1960 federal funds for education reached $2.3 billion.

Trade and Aid

Much of America's economic strength and the basis of her power in the postwar world rested on a thriving foreign trade. Presidents Truman and Eisenhower both worked to reduce trade barriers because they regarded expanding international trade essential to prosperity at home and abroad. By the time Eisenhower entered the White House, however, protectionist sentiment was growing in many quarters. Conservative Republicans who had traditionally favored high tariffs, and certain businessmen who suffered domestically from foreign competition, were among those who advocated legislation or administrative action for more protection to domestic industries. For example, watch manufacturers strongly advocated higher tariffs on Swiss watch parts.

The Trade Agreements Act of 1934, which had provided for lowering tariffs and trade restrictions on a reciprocal basis, had been periodically extended by Congress during both the Roosevelt and Truman administrations. Despite the fact that Eisenhower faced somewhat stronger pressure from protectionists, Congress followed his recommendations and extended the Trade Agreements Act in 1953, 1954, 1955, and 1958. In response to strong urging by some domestic interests, the President did raise tariffs on watch movements and a few other products, but generally he fought for measures which would expand international trade. One of his major concerns was the balance-of-payments deficit which caused a serious drain on American gold reserves by the late 1950s. Large military expenditures overseas, tourist outlays, and foreign aid, as well as spending for imports, were among the causes of the deficit. Expanded international trade would increase American exports and curtail the outflow of gold. The surplus of exports over imports remained large during the Eisenhower years—usually ranging in the $4 to $6 billion a year category—but even this was not enough to compensate for the United States expenditures abroad.

Some of the drain on American resources stemmed from a continuation of the foreign aid program begun in the Truman administration. The purpose of foreign aid had been twofold: first, to assist in the reconstruction of shattered economies in the war-torn countries of Western Europe and to help underdeveloped nations improve their living standards; second, and more negatively, to blunt the appeal of communism and thwart Russian expansion. Foreign aid, in short, was one of the means by which the United States fought the Cold War.

Eisenhower sought to maintain both his pledge of economy and his defense of American interests abroad. In most years during the 1950s the final appropriations for foreign aid represented a compromise between those who favored more assistance to friendly, developing countries throughout the world and those who believed the United States already overextended. Between 1953 and 1960, foreign aid appropriations varied from a low of $2.7 billion to a high of about $6 billion. In most years it ran between $3 and $4 billion. Foreign aid took many forms. It included military and economic assistance, educational and technical aid, and long-term loans. Most of the foreign aid funds were spent in the United States for military equipment, machinery, food, and other products and services, so the expenditures helped the domestic economy. Nevertheless, criticism of the program steadily mounted. Supporters of foreign aid charged that too large a portion of the expenditures was going for military purposes rather than for economic development, while enemies of the program argued that the United States was squandering money, that waste and inefficiency were rampant, and that foreign aid did not win friends in the Cold War struggle. In the absence of any consensus on this issue, the President followed a middle road by urging increased economy and efficiency in the program while at the same time asking for enough money to accomplish the objectives which he thought necessary and desirable. The appropriations for foreign aid throughout Eisenhower's administration reflected that compromise.

Economic Growth

No economy in the world could match the agricultural and industrial productivity of the postwar United States. While Americans had solved their problems of production much earlier, important developments in the 1950s greatly accelerated industrial efficiency. Some

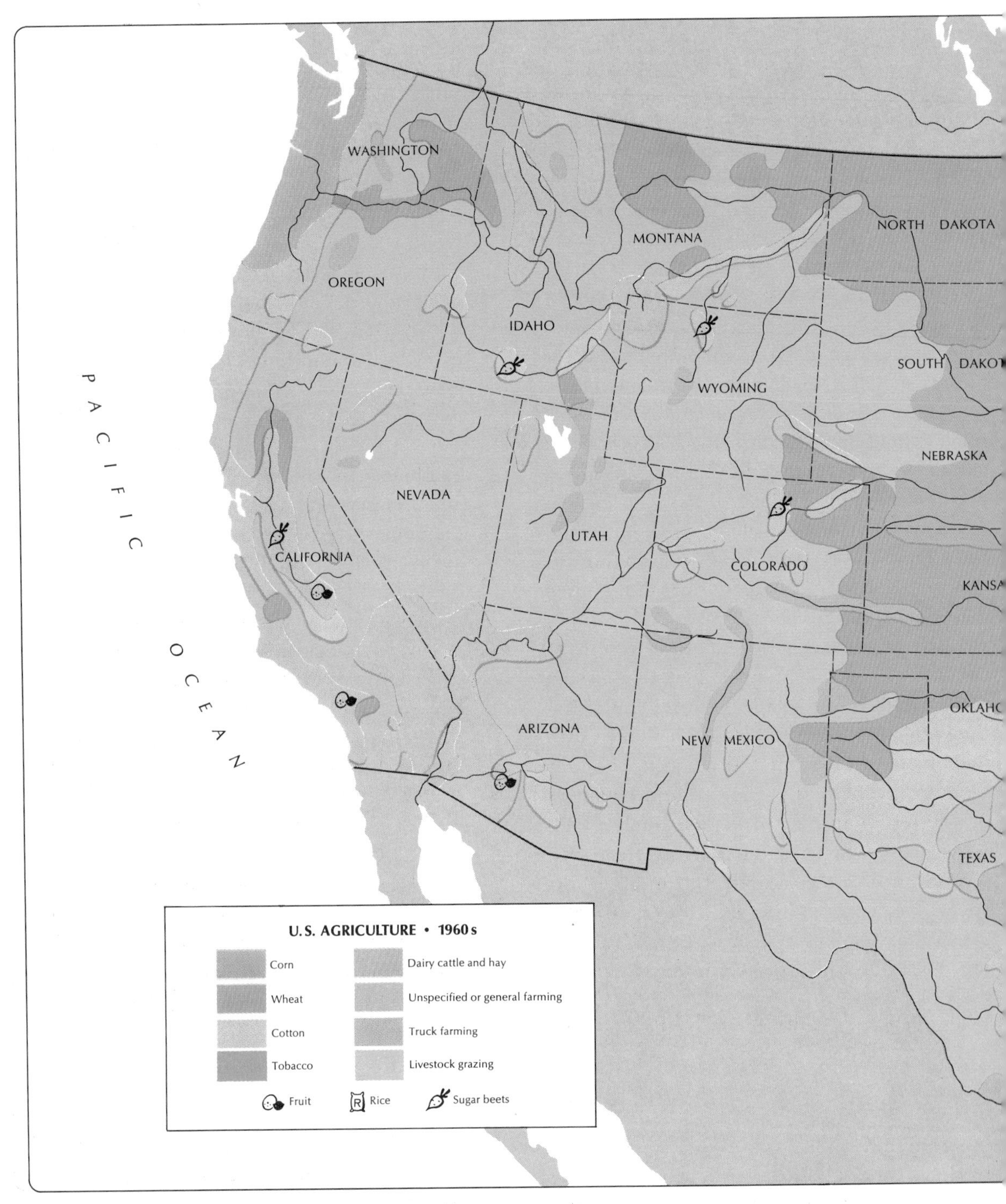
WASHINGTON
OREGON
IDAHO
MONTANA
NORTH DAKOTA
SOUTH DAKO
WYOMING
NEBRASKA
NEVADA
UTAH
CALIFORNIA
COLORADO
KANSA
ARIZONA
NEW MEXICO
OKLAHO
TEXAS
PACIFIC
OCEAN
U.S. AGRICULTURE • 1960s
Corn
Wheat
Cotton
Tobacco
Dairy cattle and hay
Unspecified or general farming
Truck farming
Livestock grazing
Fruit
Rice
Sugar beets

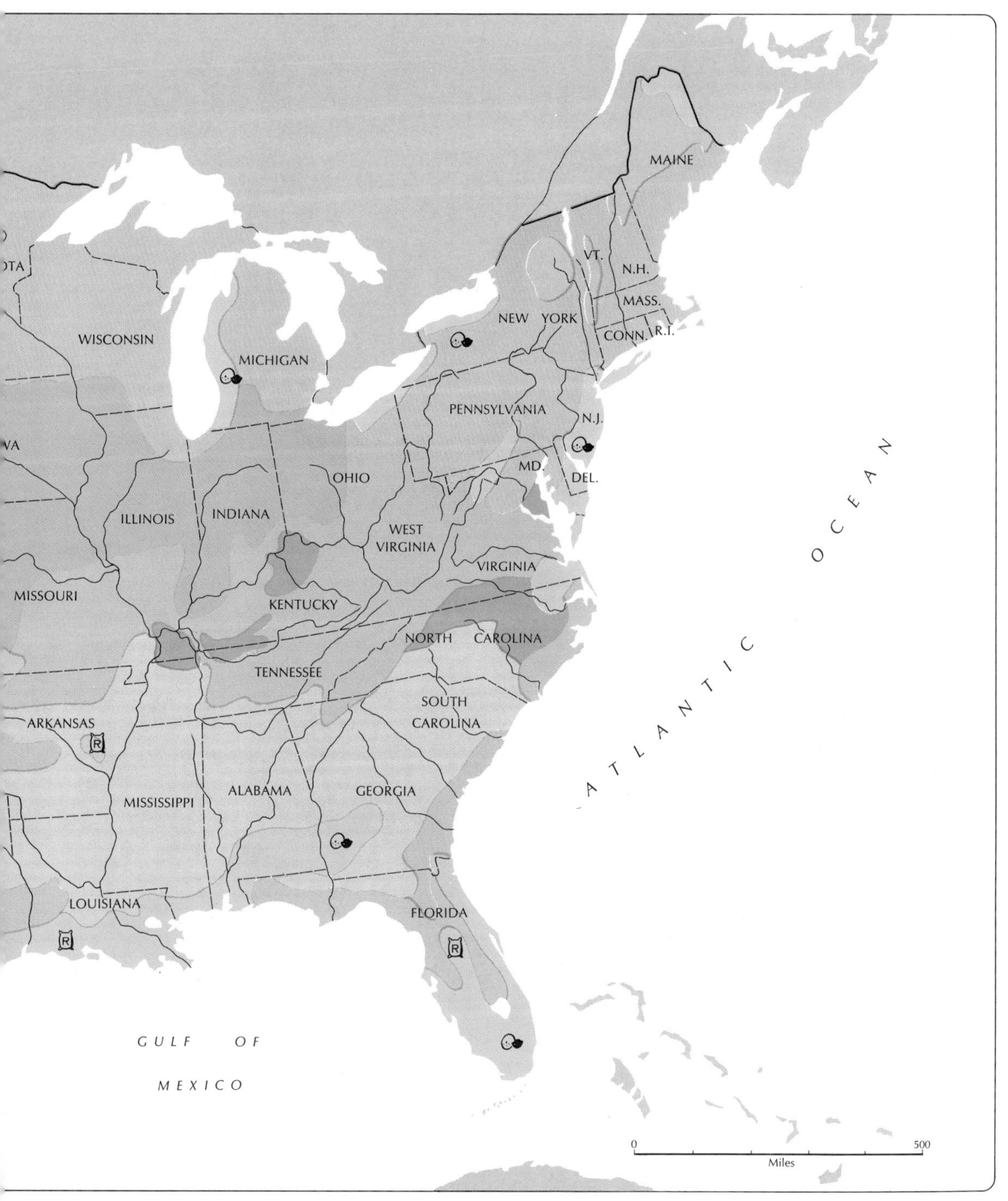

MAINE
VT.
N.H.
MASS.
NEW YORK
CONN.
R.I.
WISCONSIN
MICHIGAN
PENNSYLVANIA
N.J.
MD.
DEL.
OHIO
ILLINOIS
INDIANA
WEST VIRGINIA
VIRGINIA
MISSOURI
KENTUCKY
NORTH CAROLINA
TENNESSEE
SOUTH CAROLINA
ARKANSAS
MISSISSIPPI
ALABAMA
GEORGIA
LOUISIANA
FLORIDA
ATLANTIC OCEAN
GULF OF MEXICO
0
500
Miles

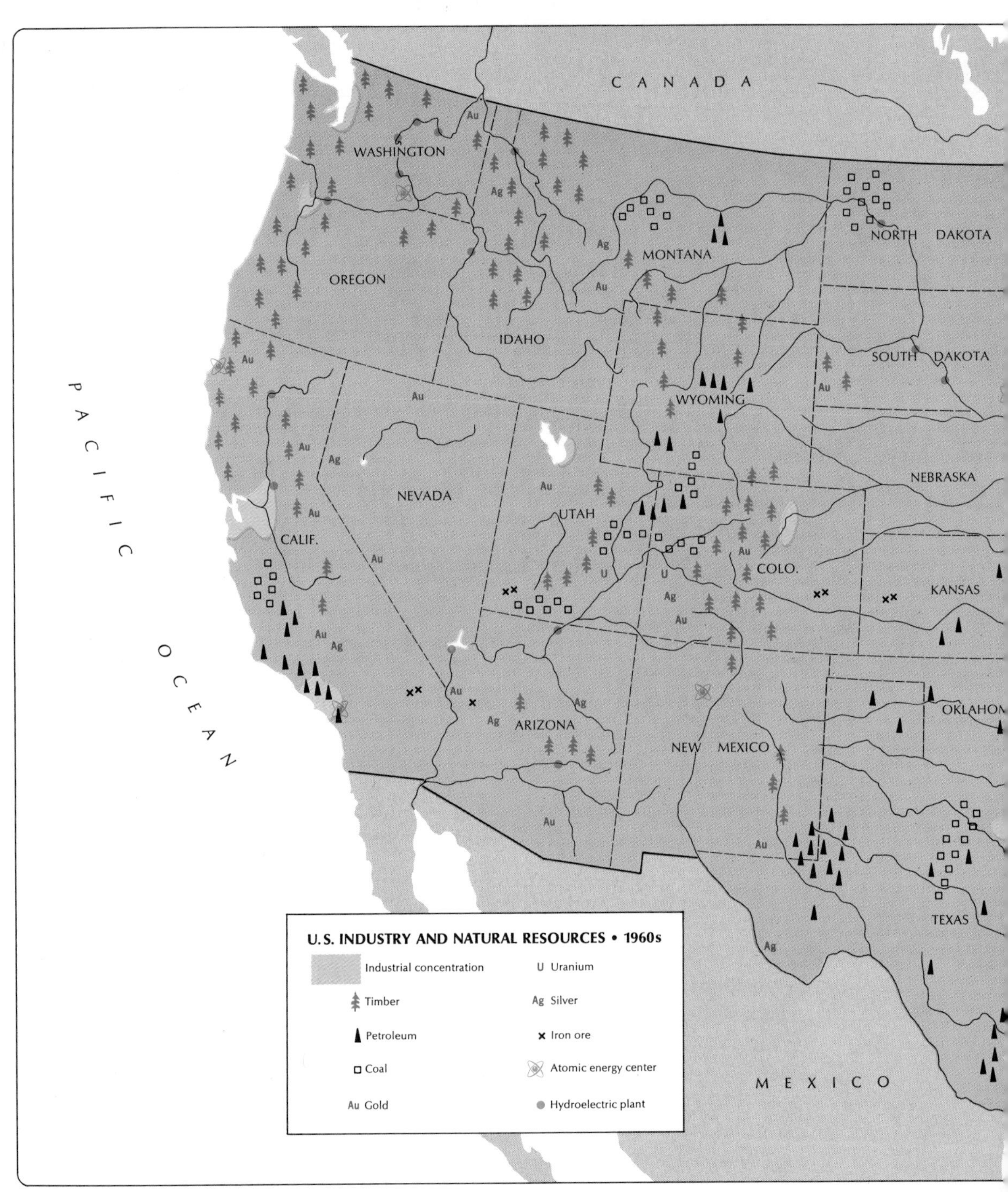
U. S. INDUSTRY AND NATURAL RESOURCES • 1960s
Industrial concentration
Timber
Petroleum
Coal
Au Gold
U Uranium
Ag Silver
Iron ore
Atomic energy center
Hydroelectric plant
CANADA
PACIFIC OCEAN
MEXICO
WASHINGTON
OREGON
IDAHO
MONTANA
NORTH DAKOTA
SOUTH DAKOTA
WYOMING
NEBRASKA
NEVADA
UTAH
COLO.
KANSAS
CALIF.
ARIZONA
NEW MEXICO
OKLAHOM
TEXAS

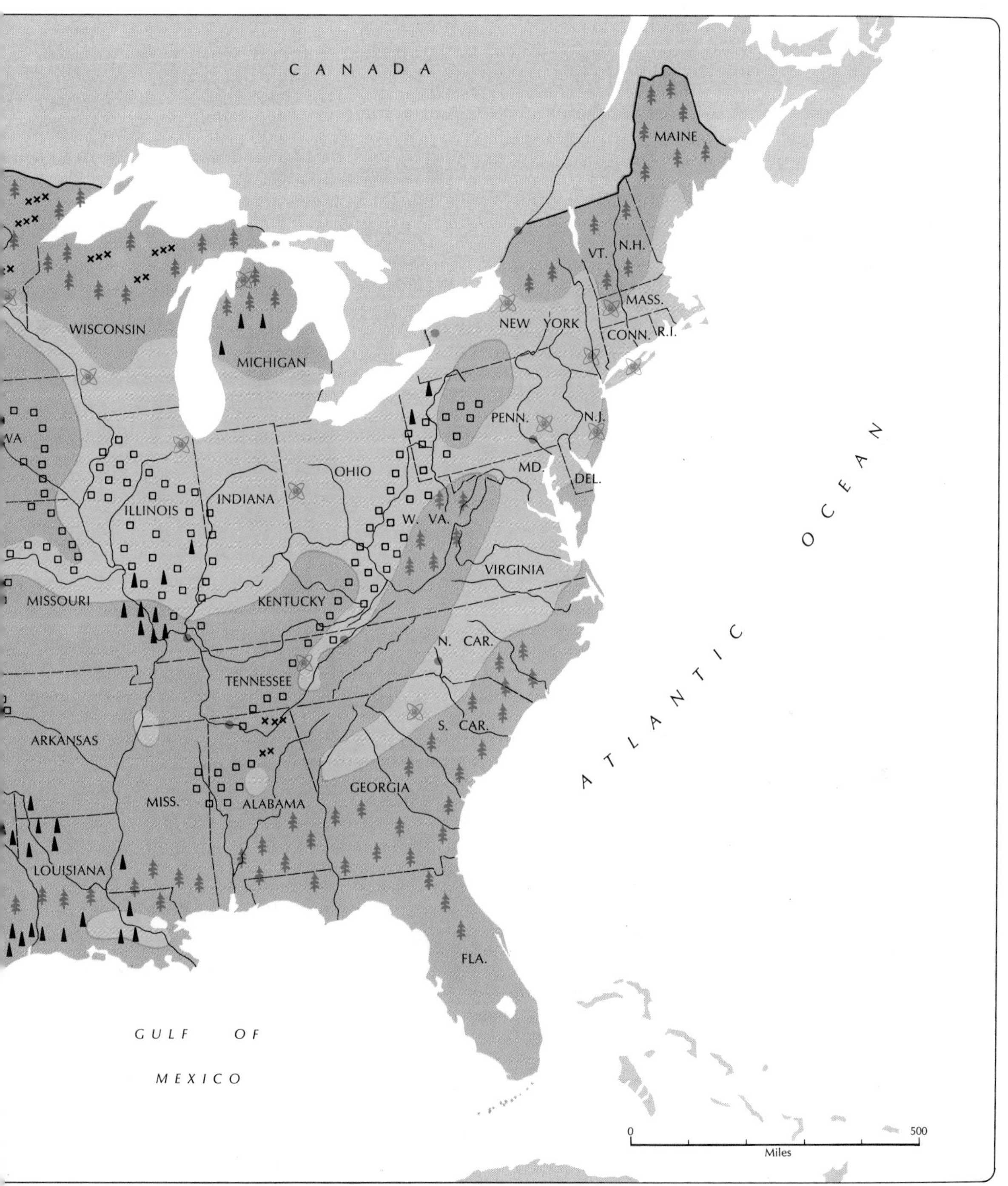

CANADA
MAINE
VT.
N.H.
MASS.
NEW YORK
CONN.
R.I.
WISCONSIN
MICHIGAN
PENN.
N.J.
OHIO
MD.
DEL.
INDIANA
ILLINOIS
W. VA.
VIRGINIA
MISSOURI
KENTUCKY
N. CAR.
TENNESSEE
S. CAR.
ARKANSAS
MISS.
ALABAMA
GEORGIA
LOUISIANA
FLA.
ATLANTIC OCEAN
GULF OF MEXICO
0
500
Miles

of the more significant technological advances grew out of the revolution in electronics, particularly the development of the computer, and the linkage of these electronic devices with automated machinery. This permitted programming and continuous-flow production which greatly increased industrial efficiency in those plants which adopted the new techniques.

American industry produced a flood of new products—electronics, plastics, foods, detergents, medicines—which grew out of extensive research and development programs. Large companies spent millions of dollars on both basic and applied research in their own laboratories and in grants to scientists in the nation's colleges and universities. By 1960 industry's expenditures for research and development amounted to some $4 billion annually and provided employment for nearly 765,000 scientists and engineers. National defense programs also relied heavily upon scientists working for large corporations and universities.

The longtime trend toward larger and larger corporate giants continued in the postwar years. The multibillion-dollar company became increasingly common in manufacturing, insurance, banking, and utilities. By 1960 there were ninety-seven corporations which had assets of more than $1 billion. The American Telephone and Telegraph Company was the country's largest private corporation, with assets of $24.6 billion; General Motors was the largest industrial company, with assets of $12.7 billion. A number of industries, including electronics, automobiles, chemicals, and aircraft, relied heavily upon government defense contracts for their business. Hundreds of thousands of workers depended on government defense spending for their jobs. The implications of this development became so serious by the end of Eisenhower's administration that the President warned the country against the dangers of a permanent industrial-military complex. In his farewell address, he said: "In the councils of Government, we must guard against the acquisition of unwarranted influence, whether sought or unsought, by the military-industrial complex. The potential for the disastrous rise of misplaced power exists and will persist. We must never let the weight of this combination endanger our liberties or democratic processes."

While Americans produced abundantly, there remained the need for more equitable distribution of goods and services and sufficient economic growth to absorb the growing labor force and eliminate unemployment. An economic growth of about 2.9 percent annually during the 1950s was not enough to provide jobs for everyone who wanted to work. Indeed, by the latter part of the decade, unemployment rates persisted at around 6 percent of the labor force, which most officials considered much too high. Furthermore, even though per capita income rose to $1,968—about $180 in dollars of constant purchasing power over 1953—poverty continued to exist. The fact that poverty still prevailed in a country as rich as the United States was a matter of growing concern by the end of the Eisenhower administration. However, there was little agreement on what programs or methods might be used to help low-income groups.

Perhaps the most notable aspect of America's mid-twentieth-century economy was the role of local, state, and federal government. Local and state governments spent huge sums for education, highways, mental health, and welfare, while defense, interest on the public debt, veterans benefits, social security, and agriculture accounted for most of the huge federal outlays. Direct expenditures by local, state, and national governments reached about $151 billion annually by 1960, nearly 30 percent of the gross national product. Americans found themselves living in a mixed economy. Private enterprise was still the dominant basis for economic well-being, but government was playing an ever-increasing role in providing employment and a market for goods and services. Harsh criticism of "big government" and the "welfare state" did little or nothing to curb this trend toward government activity. Despite Eisenhower's rather conservative image, he made no real effort to reverse this development and slowed it down only slightly. The trends seemed too firmly established.

Conclusion

Although the economy was somewhat sluggish at the time he left office, Eisenhower retired with a firm hold on people's affections. Sharp criticism during his two terms had not greatly lowered his popularity. Writer James Reston explained that Eisenhower was "in tune with the spirit of the nation, which, during his eight years in office, was generous and optimistic, but not militant or experimental." The President had been able to maintain peace abroad and a fair degree of prosperity at home, without demanding too much sacrifice or commitment from the American people. He had, as Reston pointed out, "maintained enough power to deter the big war and the big depression." Moreover, Eisenhower had not sought to change the country's course toward the welfare state. He had, in fact, consolidated the reforms of the New Deal and Fair Deal which the majority of his party had been opposing for nearly thirty years. Finally, Dwight D. Eisenhower seemed to reflect stability and assurance during a turbulent and revolutionary time in world history.

SUGGESTED READINGS

Eisenhower presents his first administration in a favorable light in his memoirs, *Mandate for Change, 1953–1956* (1963). Many of the key historical documents relating to Eisenhower's administration are conveniently located in the *Public Papers of the Presidents of the United States: Dwight D. Eisenhower* (8 vols., 1960–1961). An excellent analysis of Eisenhower's political appeal can be found in Samuel Lubell's *Revolt of the Moderates* (1956). A number of contemporary articles by Richard H. Rovere on various phases of Eisenhower's career have been brought together in *The Eisenhower Years* (1956). In *Eisenhower: The Inside Story* (1956), Robert J. Donovan has presented an interesting account of the first Eisenhower administration. Emmet John Hughes, a speech writer for Eisenhower, discusses some of the main developments of Eisenhower's White House years in *The Ordeal of Power* (1963). Merlo J. Pusey provides a favorable account of the first term in *Eisenhower the President* (1956).

Kenneth S. Davis has written on Eisenhower's two-time opponent in *A Prophet in His Own Country: The Triumphs and Defeats of Adlai Stevenson* (1957). One of the better books on the Vice President is Earl Mayo's *Richard Nixon* (1959). Nixon has written about some of the leading issues of the period, including the campaign of 1960, in *Six Crises* (1962). On Senator Robert A. Taft see *The Taft Story* (1954) by William S. White. Sherman Adams, Eisenhower's administrative assistant, has recounted his experiences in *First-hand Report* (1961), while Secretary of Agriculture Ezra T. Benson discussed the problems of his post in *Crossfire: The Eight Years with Eisenhower* (1962). One of the hottest political issues of the 1950s has been considered by Aaron Wildavsky in *Dixon-Yates: A Study in Power Politics* (1962). On Eisenhower's second election see Charles A. H. Thomson's *The 1956 Presidential Campaign* (1960).

The best general survey of economic trends during the Eisenhower years is Harold G. Vatter's *The U.S. Economy in the 1950's** (1963). Another essential source is *The Economic Report of the President* published each January. On farm problems and the administration's farm policy see Ezra T. Benson's *Freedom to Farm* (1960). Highly critical of major aspects of the federal government's farm program is Edward Higbee's *Farms and Farmers in an Urban Age* (1963). For brief discussions of labor's problems and advances see the pertinent parts of Joseph G. Rayback's *A History of American Labor** and Foster Rhea Dulles's *Labor in America**, both cited in the *Suggested Readings* of Chapter 32. Stimulating interpretations of labor problems are *As Unions Mature** (1958) by Richard A. Lester, and Sidney Lens's *The Crisis of American Labor** (1961). On other aspects of the economy see John Kenneth Galbraith's *The Affluent Society** (1958); Leonard S. Silk's *The Research Revolution* (1960); and *Regions, Resources, and Economic Growth** (1960) by H. S. Perloff and others.

* indicates availability in paperback.

39

The Course of Containment, 1953–1965

AMERICAN FOREIGN POLICY in the period from 1953 to 1965 followed a surprisingly consistent course under both Republican and Democratic administrations. Although President Dwight D. Eisenhower and his Secretary of State John Foster Dulles were extremely critical of Truman's policy of containment, they were unable to make any major changes of direction in the nation's foreign affairs. What did change in American foreign policy during a dozen years under Republican President Eisenhower and Democrats Kennedy and Johnson was the style and rhetoric, not the substance.

In 1953, Eisenhower found himself in a difficult position. Partisan criticism of previous years had led people to believe that communism should be not only contained but rolled back. Yet it was clear that this could be done only at the price of war—a war which not even the hard-line anti-Communists wanted. Dulles, who was among the best-prepared Secretaries of State since John Quincy Adams, entered office as the nation's leading advocate of policies which called for meeting the Communists at every point and sending them into retreat. But whatever the Secretary's desires and promises, available American power would limit the Eisenhower-Dulles actions essentially to the same ones pursued by the Truman administration—the unspectacular containment of Communist expansion in Europe, Asia, and the Middle East. The thrust of United States policies grew out of the same assumptions and enjoyed the same broad national support after

1953 that it did before that time, and it made no substantial difference whether the government was under the control of the Republican or Democratic party.

Eisenhower, Dulles, and Liberation

Postwar Soviet policy in Europe gave the United States only two realistic choices. It could either bring overwhelming power to bear on the Soviet Union and thus force compliance with the principle of self-determination, or it could accept the Soviet position in East-Central Europe as the fulfillment of historic security needs and acknowledge its existence as a basis of future negotiations. President Truman, unable to make this choice, sought merely to stabilize the lines of demarcation while the continuing official rhetoric of disapproval suggested, first, that the United States had no intention of recognizing any Soviet hegemony in Eastern Europe and, second, that containment and nonrecognition would ultimately roll the Russians back to their prewar boundaries. Determined as he was to spare himself and his party the accusations of failure hurled at Truman and Acheson, Dulles set out to create the image of a foreign policy that would fulfill the expectations of those who demanded that United States foreign policy begin to dispose of the Communist menace more effectively and completely than it had done in the past. In his article "A Policy of Boldness," published in *Life* magazine during the late spring of 1952 before Eisenhower's electoral victory, Dulles had rejected as inadequate the Truman-Acheson reliance on long-range containment. Democratic policy, Dulles declared, had been conceived less to eliminate the Soviet peril than to live with it, "presumably forever." The time had come, he asserted, to develop a *dynamic* foreign policy that conformed to *moral* principles. American policy must move beyond "containment"; it must anticipate the "liberation" of those who lived under compulsion behind the Iron Curtain. Dulles emphasized that liberation demanded above all that the United States avoid any European settlement recognizing Soviet control of alien peoples. At no time, however, did he suggest the means by which the United States could achieve the liberation of Eastern Europe without war.

Unfortunately, the goal of liberation for Eastern Europe had no relationship to actual policies available to the United States. Because no issue between the Soviet Union and the countries she dominated was vital to American interests, it was clear that any revolt behind the Iron Curtain would lead not to United States intervention but to pure embarrassment. Thus it happened that in 1956, when Russian tanks smashed a general uprising in Hungary, Dulles, though extremely distressed, could only watch helplessly. He had either to employ military force to free Hungary or to concede that events behind the Iron Curtain were, after all, outside the area of basic American concern. Yet Dulles's avowed course was neither of these. Instead, he voiced a futile protest, admitting in the process that military involvement would precipitate general war Having thus demonstrated beyond all doubt that Hungary was not worth a war, the administration turned to the United Nations for condemnatory resolutions and received them often and overwhelmingly. Moscow, of course, ignored these protests and proceeded to impose a thoroughly dictatorial and pro-Soviet regime on the Hungarians. To such a pass had the doctrine of liberation come. Yet if the Soviets had proved their power and determination (and simultaneously the inability of Dulles's words to accomplish much against Soviet tanks), they had also discovered that their interference in the affairs of the Slavic states engendered widespread opposition and resentment. Beginning with Hungary, Soviet control over the eastern European states began slowly to weaken.

China

With the accession of Eisenhower to the Presidency, the Nationalist China bloc, composed largely of Old Guard Republicans, gained full command of America's China policy. After 1953 such men as Admiral Arthur W. Radford, chairman of the Joint Chiefs of Staff; Walter S. Robertson, Assistant Secretary of State for Far Eastern Affairs; Senator Knowland of California, chief spokesman for Nationalist China in Congress; as well as Dulles himself, determined the nation's attitudes toward China and created the reasons to support them. What this new leadership hoped to achieve in its uncompromising posture toward Communist China was, in large measure, a reestablishment of the Open Door. This objective necessitated a government amenable to the goodwill and paternalism of the United States, one willing in its foreign relations to behave in a manner commensurate with American interests and desires. Such a government might become, as both the Roosevelt and Truman administrations had anticipated, a core of stability in Eastern Asia and the protector of the traditional balance of power. The return of Chiang Kai-shek to power on the mainland, it was assumed, would fulfill this magnificent dream.

Too responsible to follow its Far Eastern advisers into military ventures against Red China in Chiang's behalf, yet too fearful of public opinion to reduce its public support of the Nationalist Generalissimo, the Eisenhower administration adopted a phraseology which looked to the eventual destruction of the Chinese Communist government. Soon after taking office, the President created the impression that he was "unleashing" Chiang Kai-shek, when he declared that he was issuing instructions that the Seventh Fleet no longer shield the mainland. But aware of its inability to return Chiang to power over all China, the administration in fact was committed to simply sustaining the Kuomintang on Formosa. A policy of nonrecognition of the mainland regime permitted the administration to perpetuate the illusion of Chiang's eventual triumph; at the same time, it pacified most friends of Chiang in the United States. Despite periodic pronouncements suggesting the contrary, Eisenhower, no more than Truman, seriously considered military ventures against the Communist Chinese. He followed instead the Truman precedent of limiting Nationalist China's activities to the defense of Formosa, pointedly writing this limitation into the bilateral defense agreement negotiated with Nationalist China in December, 1954.

After American officials had made the basic decision to remain involved in the China struggle, it was only a matter of time before the offshore islands of Quemoy and Matsu would become a vexing subject in American foreign policy. Nationalist forces had occupied the islands on their retreat from the mainland to Formosa in 1949, but not until the fall of 1954 did the Chinese Communists move sufficient military equipment into the coastal areas to threaten the islands with bombardment. When the Peking government issued a verbal threat against Formosa in January, 1955, Secretary Dulles assured Chiang that the Republic of China would not "stand alone" against invasion from the mainland. Then came the bombardment of the offshore islands. Congress promptly authorized the President to defend these islands if it appeared that any attack on them would be preliminary to an attack on Formosa itself. Although there was little or no strategic connection between the offshore islands and Formosa, the islands hugging the China coast symbolized for the Kuomintang government-in-exile the Nationalist will to return to the mainland. By identifying the issue of China's future with the defense of Quemoy and Matsu, Chiang Kai-shek forced the Eisenhower administration to adopt a formula which would reassure Nationalist China and yet not commit the United States to a strategically impossible position.

The Formosa Resolution of January, 1955, permitted the Republican leadership to postpone any determination of policy until Peking began to exact a price from the United States for its continued involvement in the Chinese civil war. But when the mainland Chinese suddenly subjected the offshore islands to a merciless shelling in September, 1958, it seemed that the moment of decision had arrived. During the crisis it became evident that Chiang was the controlling element in American action. In October, Washington suggested partial demobilization of the offshore islands as a basis for negotiation, but Chiang was adamantly opposed to any compromise. Flying to confer with the Nationalist leader, Dulles issued a communiqué at Taipei restating the American intention: "The United States recognizes that the Republic of China is the authentic spokesman for Free China and of the hopes and aspirations entertained by the great mass of the Chinese people. . . . The foundation of this mission resides in the minds and hearts of the Chinese people." The dream of Chiang's return to the mainland—presumably without force—still determined official American attitudes. The fact that the crisis passed when the Red Army made no effort to storm the islands was not reassuring for the future. American policy in Asia was to all appearances still inextricably tied to a regime—Nationalist China—whose prospects for success in the Chinese civil war were practically nonexistent.

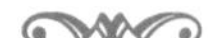

The New Look

President Eisenhower inherited from his Democratic predecessor a long-range military program designed to maintain a balance among the Army, Navy, and Air Force. Beginning in 1950, Truman had gradually increased the country's industrial production to support a higher level of American and Allied preparedness. This anticipated buildup comprised a doubling of the nation's ground and naval strength and a tripling of its air power. In 1953, Eisenhower faced the necessity of making alterations. During the 1952 campaign, Republican orators had pledged not only a stronger defense against Communist aggression but also a reduction in federal expenditures. "Our problem," said Eisenhower, "is to achieve military strength within the limits of endurable strain upon our economy."

In a determined effort to make good the Republican campaign pledge, Eisenhower and his

Secretary of Defense, industrialist Charles E. Wilson, proceeded to reduce the military budget for 1954 from $44 billion to $34 billion, distributing the savings rather evenly among the Army, Navy, and Air Force. Termed the "New Look" by Secretary Wilson, the resulting military posture was given precise meaning by the President when he declared in January, 1954, that United States defense policy would emphasize air-atomic power, an innovation permitting the nation to wield maximum destructiveness at minimum cost. Economy-minded Republicans were delighted, especially those who opposed American involvement in another small war. Yet even with the novel emphasis on air power, the Eisenhower level of military preparedness remained considerably above that which existed before 1950.

In an address of January 12, 1954, Secretary of State Dulles attempted to elevate the New Look into a broad strategic concept. The United States, he warned, would henceforth "depend primarily upon a great capacity to retaliate, instantly, by means and at places of our own choosing." Dulles's words implied retaliatory bombing of areas near the source of any Communist aggression, presumably the key cities of Russia and China. Although many took the new doctrine of "massive retaliation" at face value, believing that it represented a new, inexpensive, and sure method of stopping all aggression, Dulles's critics feared that the new reliance on atomic and nuclear weapons would limit the American choice in any conflict either to total inaction or to nuclear war. Nor was it clear how bombing in Asia would terminate a guerrilla war; guerrillas, operating independently, would merely scatter under such attacks and resume their operations elsewhere. These doubts, expressed fully and often, compelled the administration to explain its policies so repeatedly that Walter Lippmann observed in March, 1954, that "official explanations of the new look have become so voluminous that it is almost a career in itself to keep up with them." As time wore on, moreover, it became clear that what had appeared initially as a novel and momentous decision really amounted to no change in policy at all. What was new in the program, declared the *Manchester Guardian,* was Dulles's effort to convince the American people that the official strategy followed in 1954 was superior to that advanced in 1953.

At the level of actual policy, the Eisenhower administration sustained, and even extended, the Truman commitment to Europe's stabilization. Not only did Eisenhower make no effort to reduce United States military forces in Europe; he also accepted Acheson's judgment that West Germany should be rearmed and brought into the Western defense system. Preventing the resolution of this question before 1954 was the French fear of a large German military force. In this context Dulles had warned the French in December, 1953, that Paris's refusal to accept German rearmament "would compel an agonizing reappraisal of the basic United States policy," the implication being that the United States would leave Western Europe to its own devices. When the French government responded to Dulles's preachments by rejecting membership in the European Defense Community, London broke the impasse by committing several British divisions to the Continent as a special guarantee to France. Thereafter, negotiations among the Western powers swiftly completed the military organization of Western Europe. West Germany entered NATO in 1955 and began to rearm in fulfillment of its obligations to Western defense.

By the mid-fifties Europe was militarily stable. Whether that stability resulted more from the economic and military reconstruction of Western Europe or from the limited intentions of Soviet policy, the United States could view the rebirth of Western security with supreme satisfaction. It was in Asia that United States military policies appeared incapable of bringing clear victories or permanent solutions. Defense policies, whether conducted unilaterally or through alliances, can be effective only in response to a positive military danger of actual aggression. NATO was a reasonable military system because the Soviet threat to which it responded could be defined in precise military terms. In Asia the military challenge was not so well defined. Washington, it is true, had indicated that the threat to Asia was Soviet aggression. In practice, however, the United States could not react to every Communist pressure in Asia as if it really emanated from the U.S.S.R. for the simple reason that Soviet power was not in evidence. And to the extent that danger came not from the Kremlin, as the center of an international conspiracy, but from indigenous forces existing within Asia itself, the sources of Asian instability were more political than military. To meet such a challenge the Dulles doctrine of "massive retaliation" was worse than useless.

The first order of business for Eisenhower and Dulles in Asia was to bring to an end the long, enervating war in Korea. Settlement came hard. Soviet propaganda, accusing the United States of crimes against the Korean peoples, kept the situation tense. But what specifically stalled the truce negotiations even during the Truman days was the prisoner-of-war issue. When enemy prisoners in UN camps learned that the Panmunjom truce negotiations might soon terminate the war and return them to North Korea and China, several thousand indicated that they would kill themselves rather than return home. The problem of repatriation produced a deadlock in the armistice talks, as the Communist side rejected the Western view that prisoners of war be given a choice in the matter.

Suddenly, when the situation in Korea appeared utterly hopeless, the truce negotiations began to succeed. Late in March, 1953, the Chinese and North Koreans accepted an American suggestion that both sides exchange sick and wounded prisoners of war. Several days later the Communist negotiators agreed to the principle of voluntary repatriation. When it became clear that the Korean settlement would accept that country's continued division, however, Syngman Rhee, the president of South Korea, ordered the release of thousands of enemy prisoners who were allowed to lose themselves in the South Korean population. Washington and London disclaimed Rhee's action, and the negotiations continued. On July 27, 1953, Korean hostilities formally ended. The armistice left a divided Korea, demonstrating again a worldwide balance of power too stable to permit significant changes in areas contested by the antagonists in the cold war.

Whatever its relationship to an international Communist conspiracy, the war in Korea had been fought in a conventional manner. In Korea nationalism had been less an issue than pure military aggression. In Indochina, however, where the United States was becoming equally committed to the containment of Communist influence, the struggle was primarily a guerrilla war against a remnant of European imperialism. By 1950 Ho Chi Minh had submerged all competing nationalist groups in that region of Indochina later called Vietnam into a solid—if still elusive—anti-French phalanx. French attempts to divert the nationalistic sentiment of Indochinese to leaders of France's choice failed. Supported by little more than the Catholic minority among their former colonists, the French suffered an endless succession of disasters in northern Indochina.

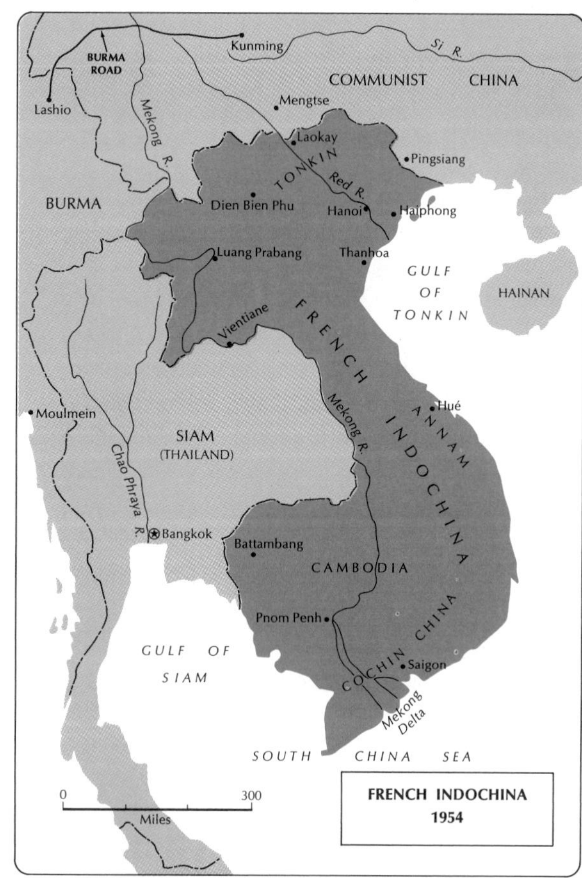

For the United States, still convinced that Ho's campaign represented less a civil war than another Moscow-directed Communist aggression, the French carried the burden of containment in Asia. Thus Washington underwrote the French effort with shipments of material valued at more than $2 billion and by 1953 was financing 80 percent of the war costs. Despite all, Ho's guerrillas continued to inflict merciless punishment on the French troops. By February, 1954, having battled Ho's forces on inhospitable terrain for eight unsuccessful years, the French made it clear that they were ready to negotiate their total withdrawal from Indochina. Washington was more tenacious, for it insisted that the West avoid any compromise with Ho Chi Minh. As the *New York Times* reported early in February, 1954: "The official view in Washington is that any deal with the Vietminh [the Communist-led forces of Indochina] would probably result in a Communist conquest of the whole peninsula, followed by increasing Communist pressure on the entire Southeast Asia area." Now France wished to pack up and, by the American concept of a global danger, expose an important section of the world to Soviet expansion. This the Eisenhower administration would not allow. Yet administration spokesmen continued to assure Europeans and Americans alike that Washington had no intention of committing United States forces to another ground war in Asia. No one explained how the United States intended to achieve Ho's defeat without direct American involvement.

During the early summer of 1954, while the French went down to defeat at Dienbienphu, representatives of fourteen nations directly concerned with Far Eastern matters met at Geneva, Switzerland, to resolve the problems of Korea and Indochina. There Britain and France searched for a compromise that would permit a graceful French withdrawal. Dulles, still under extreme pressure from Americans who feared any settlement with Ho, lectured the Communist delegates at Geneva on the question of Korean unification and then returned to the United States, permitting a subordinate to carry the burden of American diplomacy. The final Geneva agreement divided Indochina into the independent states of Laos, Cambodia, and Vietnam, the latter separated temporarily at the 17th parallel until elections, to be held in 1956, should determine the nature of its general government. Ho Chi Minh settled for the immediate control of North Vietnam under the assumption that he would soon gain South Vietnam through the peaceful agency of the ballot. Although Washington declined to sign the Geneva accords, it assured the signatories that the United States would not directly challenge the settlement.

Having been compelled to accept another Communist gain in Asia, in defiance of the American doctrine of falling dominoes (the belief that the loss of one region would result automatically in the loss of others), Dulles now announced that the domino theory no longer applied. The United States, he said in July, 1954, was in the process of establishing a new alliance committed to the defense of the status quo in Southeast Asia. This new pact, signed at Manila in September, brought into being the eight-nation Southeast Asia Treaty Organization, consisting of Britain, France, the United States, Australia, New Zealand, the Philippines, Thailand, and Pakistan, with headquarters at Bangkok, Thailand. Underwriting the alliance was American striking power. At Manila, Dulles let it be known that the United States would fight no more conventional wars in Asia. It would, he said, grant logistic, naval, and air support to Asian armies, but if that proved insufficient to halt Communist aggression—the only kind of aggression that Dulles recognized—the United States would resort to its weapons of massive destruction.

To lead the new state of South Vietnam, Washington, which assumed after Geneva the direct responsibility for Indochina formerly exercised by France, selected Ngo Dinh Diem, a pro-Western Catholic who had spent the preceding years of civil war in Japan and the United States. Surrounded with American equipment and advisers, Diem faced an almost impossible task: competing successfully with Ho Chi Minh, his country's revered liberator, for the support of the Vietnamese people. After Diem called off the elections scheduled for 1956, thus thwarting Ho's dream of plucking South Vietnam without firing a shot, a renewal of the struggle for power in the country was inevitable. Thereafter Southeast Asia's stability rested, politically, on Diem's success in nation building and, militarily, on the American success in creating a defense structure in the Philippines, Thailand, Pakistan, South Vietnam, and Laos that could, singly or multilaterally, match the demonstrated power which Ho could thrust against a Southeast Asian opponent.

By the late 1950s it was clear that neither purpose was succeeding. Inasmuch as Diem carried the essential burden of containment in Southeast Asia, United States officials praised his leadership as if it were performing miracles. Unfortunately those miracles were nonexistent, as was effective military power among the nation's Asian allies. Still if neither program to guarantee the political stability of Southeast Asia succeeded, the United States would one day accept a further extension of Ho's influence on the Asian mainland or attempt to prevent that extension with direct military involvement.

Crisis in the Middle East

The Middle East, like Southern Asia, had become important in American diplomacy only after 1945. During 1947 President Truman, against the advice of State Department career men, committed the United States publicly to the formation of an independent Jewish nation in the British mandate of Palestine. When in 1948 the Jews were establishing the state of Israel (and thus displacing a large number of Arabs who had long lived there), the President urged immediate recognition. Although Secretary of State George C. Marshall, fearing such action would alienate the entire Arab world, opposed immediate recognition, the White House view prevailed. Only a few minutes after the Jews proclaimed their new country, on May 14, 1948, Truman's press secretary announced that the President had extended *de facto* recognition. Despite this extreme show of partisanship, however, United States relations with the Arab countries of the Middle East did not measurably deteriorate.

The oil-rich, Western-dominated lands rimming the southern and eastern Mediterranean emerged late as a battleground of the Cold War. It was Colonel Gamal Abdel Nasser, dictator of Egypt after 1952, who was instrumental in bringing big-power rivalry into the Middle East. A spokesman for both Egyptian nationalism and Pan-Arabism, Nasser early inaugurated a persistent propaganda campaign against the British and Western presence. During 1954, after managing to eliminate British control of the Suez Canal, he launched grandiose plans for the economic rehabilitation of Egypt through a vast irrigation project—the Aswan Dam. For this purpose, Nasser received pledges of loans from Britain, the United States, and the International Bank. Suddenly the promising situation exploded in the Egyptian's face. Nasser had accepted aid and promises of aid from Europe and America at the same time that the controlled Cairo press reviled the West, extoled Russia, and challenged Israel. When Nasser, playing both sides of the street, turned to the Soviet bloc for arms and the Soviet Union for a large loan, Secretary of State Dulles in July, 1956, announced that he was withdrawing the American offer to finance the Aswan Dam. When both Britain and the International Bank followed the American lead, Nasser retaliated on July 26 by seizing the privately operated Suez Canal.

Then followed three months of tense negotiations among interested parties. Nasser agreed to compensate the owners of canal stock, but what disturbed the British and French was Egyptian control of a waterway that for them possessed great strategic significance. All attempts to settle the Suez controversy by diplomacy failed. Nasser would abide no outside control of the waterway. Though he pledged not to interfere with free navigation, neither Britain nor France were prepared to accept such assurances from a man they considered untrustworthy. They would not, as Anthony Eden of Great Britain said, allow such a leader "to have his thumb at our windpipe." Convinced that Nasser would respond only to force, Britain and France quietly made ready for direct military action. On October 29, 1956, the Israeli government, after consulting with the British and French, sent its armies across the Egyptian border in ostensible retaliation for Egyptian raids on its territory. Britain and France then demanded that both

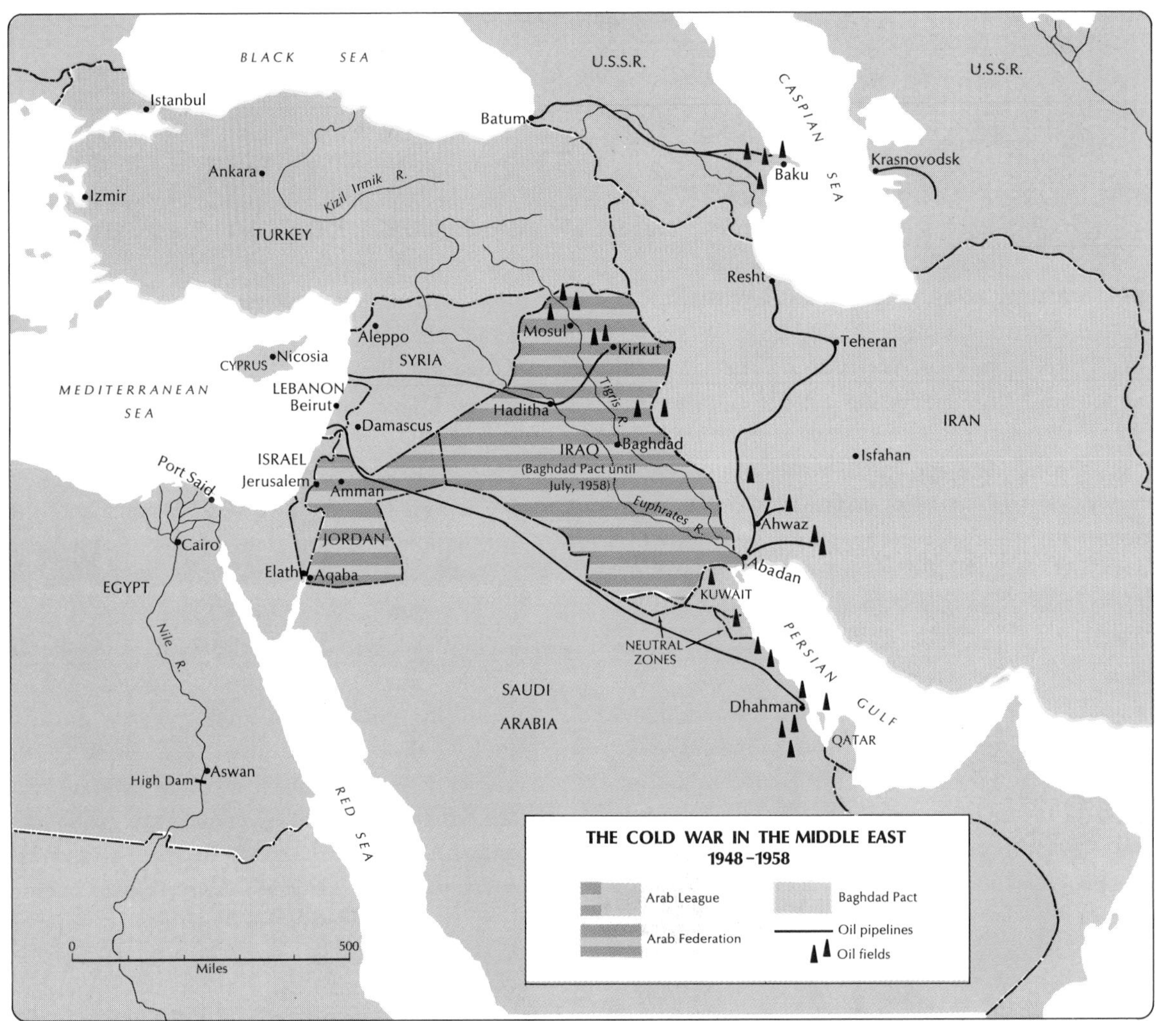

sides in the ensuing Sinai war keep away from the canal. When Nasser ignored them, Anglo-French planes bombed Egyptian air fields. On November 5 and 6 British and French troops landed at Port Said and advanced southward along the canal. Nasser, in an act of desperation, scuttled ships at the canal's mouth to deny its use to the invaders.

Informed world opinion was incensed, and it generally ran against Britain, France, and Israel. The United States led the movement for condemnatory resolutions in the United Nations. On November 2 the General Assembly adopted an American resolution asking all parties to observe a truce and to pull back behind the 1949 armistice lines. Isolated completely from the main thrust of international opinion, Britain and France complied with the United Nations request in December. The NATO alliance had been shaken by a situation which found its major members on opposite sides of an important issue. The Soviet Union, which emerged from the crisis as the defender of Arab nationalism, was the gainer.

This crisis over Suez made necessary a reassessment of American policy in the Middle East. President Eisenhower's message of January 5, 1957, was addressed to that need. Eisenhower requested a congressional grant of authority to employ necessary means to blunt the extension of Soviet power in the area of the Mediterranean. After vigorous debate, Congress on March 7 empowered the President to inaugurate a program of economic and military aid in the area. Asserting that "the United States regards as vital to the national interest and world peace the preservation of the independence and integrity of the nations of the Middle East," the joint resolution declared America's determination "to use armed forces to assist any such nation or group of nations requesting assistance against armed aggression from any country controlled by international communism." Whether Congress and the President assumed that threats to the status quo could emanate only from the Kremlin or whether they simply employed the concept of a Communist conspiracy to rationalize any costly policy they chose to undertake was not clear. In any event, the so-called Eisenhower Doctrine rested on two insecure foundations, one intellectual and one military and political. It obscured the role of Arab nationalism in Middle Eastern instability; and because it viewed the problem of the Middle East in ideological terms, the doctrine committed the United States to maintaining of stability in a region where there were few strong or stable states.

The years after Suez were troubled ones for the Middle East, and in one way or another the United States was caught up in its broils. The Arab states and Israel were locked in an arms race; the Arabs squabbled among themselves, dividing into shifting alignments: pro-Western, pro-Soviet, and neutral. Nasser's Egypt and Syria, avowedly neutralist, were in reality virulently anti-American and generally Russia-oriented; these nations were amalgamated into the United Arab Republic in 1958. Turkey, Iran, and Iraq—all states of the northern tier—were generally pro-Western. Lebanon, Saudi Arabia, and Jordan vacillated between the extremes. In 1957 King Hussein of Jordan, bolstered by the dispatch to the eastern Mediterranean of the United States Sixth Fleet, was able to survive an attempted coup, fire his pro-Nasser, anti-Western cabinet, and move his regime a step closer diplomatically to the United States and Great Britain. Scarcely a year later, hitherto pro-Western Iraq moved in the opposite direction after a successful palace revolution. Nevertheless, although the new Iraqi government renounced its ties with the West, it received prompt American recognition.

By mid-1958, pro-Nasser terrorists and insurrectionists threatened the governments of Lebanon and Jordan. Both nations complained to the United Nations. When that organization, largely because of Soviet obstructionism, was unable to act, Lebanon and Jordan appealed to the United States and Britain. An American Army brigade, flown into Lebanon from West Germany, and a regiment of British paratroopers, dropped into Jordan in July, 1958, saved the two pro-Western regimes. Again the pressures were only obliquely Communist-inspired, but the American commitment to stability in the Middle East was almost absolute, threatening Washington with permanent involvement in Arab politics. Fortunately, the region now entered an era of relative stability. Speaking before the UN General Assembly in August, 1958, President Eisenhower responded to the new situation by offering a constructive program of economic betterment for all the Middle East in exchange for Arab cooperation and guarantees of nonaggression. Thereupon, the Arabs produced a resolution pledging themselves to respect one another's borders and political integrity, a promise designed to encourage the withdrawal of British and American troops. The resurrected Arab League, now including Morocco and Tunisia in addition to the original eight members—the United Arab Republic, Iraq, Jordan, Lebanon, Libya, Saudi Arabia, the Sudan, and Yemen—provided a basis for mutual action. But Pan-Arabism of the Nasser variety—highly nationalistic and anti-Western—did not die.

The Changing Cold War

Under the Eisenhower-Dulles leadership the Cold War progressed at two levels. The innumerable crises of the mid-fifties, whether directly attributable to the Soviet Union or not, had the effect of sustaining a high level of Soviet-American rivalry. Inured to the idea that Soviet ambition was insatiable and its machinations omnipresent, Secretary of State Dulles tended to confront every Kremlin action with uncompromising opposition, even at the price, he said, of going to the brink of war. It is doubtful whether any postwar crisis actually brought the United States and the U.S.S.R. to the brink, for in no single confrontation did both have interests at stake which were worth the risk of a general war.

Dulles's notion of a sharply divided world characterized by endless and deadly conflict became increasingly difficult to sustain. Devlopments in the 1950s contradicted this concept of international politics. The first matter concerned the development of weapons technology. By the mid-fifties, Russia had shattered the American monopoly in nuclear weapons; the search for military superiority ended in stalemate. At the same time, America's increasing vulnerability to direct nuclear attack undermined Western European confidence in the willingness of Americans to involve themselves, with nuclear weapons, in a conventional European war which might devastate Europe but once again spare the territory of the United States. By 1958 President Charles de Gaulle of France was certain that his nation required its own nuclear deterrent. Under conditions of nuclear stalemate, NATO's continued reliance on weapons of massive destruction, all under United States control, produced strains in matters of defense and diplomacy. Europeans who had no interest in living dangerously believed the time had arrived when the West must think less about global threats and, instead, negotiate a détente with the Soviet Union. Confidence born of economic recovery and the experience of successful coexistence with the Soviet bloc contributed to the growing spirit of European independence.

Soviet policies contributed to the further erosion of the concept of an unalterable conflict between Russia and the non-Communist world. The death of Stalin in 1953 promised to free Soviet policy of the hard and seldom-reassuring behavior of the previous years. The Kremlin's new "collective leadership" soon revealed Russia's concern for better external relations. Not only had the Twentieth Congress of the Soviet Communist party (1956) inaugurated precepts which removed Stalinist elements from Soviet leadership, it also adopted foreign-policy statements which suggested new, imaginative, and hopeful approaches to world problems. Conceding the irrationality of nuclear war, Russia now officially adopted the doctrines of "peaceful coexistence" and the "non-inevitability of war." With the arrival of these stepchildren of the Cold War, diplomacy "at the summit" again became fashionable.

The new Soviet policies of economic competition and coexistence undoubtedly permitted the Kremlin to establish wider and more satisfactory relations with much of the Afro-Asian world. They also reduced somewhat the threat of a nuclear showdown, yet they produced no substantial change in the diplomatic stalemate with the West. This had become clear as early as the Geneva Summit Conference of July, 1955, at which time the mood established by the leaders of Britain, France, the United States, and the U.S.S.R. reached a crescendo of cordiality. Within the context of the nuclear stalemate which produced the conference, the Big Four agreed that whatever their differences, they would not resort to war to resolve them. Beyond that, of course, no agreements were possible. Again in 1957, buoyed by the prestige of launching the first earth satellites, the Soviets pressed for a new summit meeting to discuss disarmament and diplomatic détente, emphasizing their campaign by a public exchange of letters with Western heads of government. During the Middle East crisis of 1958 the Kremlin was noticeably more restrained than it had been two years earlier in the Suez affair. Immediately thereafter, however, under the prod and lash of its more militant ally, Red China, the Kremlin veered sharply back toward the Stalinist path and adopted a harder line on international issues. When Khrushchev managed finally to arrange the Paris Summit Conference of 1960, he chose to terminate it abruptly by demanding—but not receiving—a public apology from Eisenhower. Francis G. Powers and his U-2 spy plane were pretexts for the conference's disruption; the essential cause lay in the unwillingness of either side to compromise any of its long-established positions.

Despite such failures of diplomacy, those on both sides of the Iron Curtain who were most concerned with the state of affairs in Europe were basically content with the status quo. Somehow the issues of the 1940s no longer had any real significance. The areas of direct conflict had become so stabilized that it did not matter whether the precise issues they raised were settled or not. Not even the Berlin crisis of November, 1958, could disturb the pattern. Russian Premier Nikita S. Khrushchev started the row over divided Berlin when he demanded that the West accept the city's neutralization within six months. If the West refused, he said, the Soviet Union would turn its own zone over to its satellite East Germany and thus force Great Britain, the United States, and France to deal with East Germany—a regime and a country whose existence they did not officially recognize. When the Western powers demurred, making clear their intention to resist such a unilateral move by all necessary means, Khrushchev, unprepared to fight to change a situation which had long existed, silently allowed the day of reckoning to pass.

By 1960, then, the Cold War had shifted from the frozen European positions to the more fluid trouble spots of Asia and Africa, where native leaders enjoyed a tactical independence empowering them to embarrass both Russia and the West, even when they did not cause a direct confrontation. It was clear that the Soviets approved this transfer of the East-West conflict to the politically doubtful regions of Asia and Africa. Khrushchev announced repeatedly that the Kremlin regarded its support for "wars of liberation" as totally legitimate, though he failed to explain what form that support would take. Thus it happened that, within the context of ideological struggle, Europe's very stability forced the Cold War into the subcontinents, where third parties could initiate the moves sustaining the Soviet-American rivalry.

Headline issues by the late 1950s seldom found their inception in the old Soviet-American conflict. United States diplomacy was troubled more by disagreements within the Western alliance or with the nations of Latin America than by quarrels with the U.S.S.R. Similarly, the Kremlin found its relationships with China and Eastern Europe more trying and enervating than its exchanges with the West. Ideological alignments no longer had their former relevance. Nor did the rhetoric of victory have any strategic meaning when a nuclear exchange might mean the ruin of all. If the struggle for power and prestige between the United States and the U.S.S.R. continued to be an important fact of international life, it was no longer the only one of importance. By 1960 there were few fundamental decisions in world politics which either the United States or the Soviet Union could control. The Cold War was not dead. Europe was still divided. But the old East-West struggle had been consigned to narrow limits by the growing independence of nations whose leaders refused to identify their national purposes and interests with those of either of the two superpowers.

Kennedy and the Eisenhower Legacies

There had been little significant disagreement on American foreign policy between John F. Kennedy and Richard M. Nixon in the presidential contest of 1960. Kennedy's narrow victory placed a Democrat back in the White House, but his record in foreign affairs could scarcely be innovative. Despite the apparent talent of his advisory staff, this was made clear by his initial decisions. Few of his appointments went to men who had favored a critical review of established policies. Dean Rusk, Kennedy's choice for Secretary of State, was a former Rhodes scholar, professor of political science, and, under Truman, Assistant Secretary of State for Far Eastern Affairs. Compared to Dulles, he appeared calm and self-effacing, but his association with Asian policy in 1951 and the positions he had then assumed suggested that his views toward the Communist world were as distrusting and as demanding as those of his Republican predecessor. Kennedy himself, choosing to anchor his administration to assumptions of the past, forthrightly warned in his inaugural that the United States would "pay any price, bear any burden, meet any hardship, support any friend, oppose any foe to assure the survival and the success of liberty." Yet he reminded his audience that the instruments of war had far outpaced the instruments of peace.

Abroad the challenge to Kennedy was clear. He had inherited from Eisenhower a popular foreign policy, but that policy was popular because it gave the assurance of success without defining success or establishing its price. The long-range question confronting the Kennedy leadership was the difficult, perhaps unpopular, necessity of revising many of the nation's postwar commitments, especially in Asia —commitments which had expanded during the

Eisehower years without the clear establishment of means to support them. The nation's capacity to control foreign events had deteriorated markedly in the 1950s, not because of American failures but because of the accretion of Russian power, the recovery of Europe, and the explosive force of nationalism in Asia and Africa.

The new President's first steps in foreign affairs were auspicious enough. On March 1, 1961, he announced the formation of a Peace Corps, an ingathering of generally young men and women who, as volunteers, would help to carry American technology, energy, leadership, and goodwill to the underdeveloped world. The program evoked an astonishingly favorable response both in Congress and among the nation's college students. Scarcely two weeks later, on March 13, the President proposed his Alliance for Progress to the Latin American ambassadors assembled at the White House. This program he instituted to implement the Act of Bogota, signed by nineteen nations in September, 1960, which established a cooperative program—including a ten-year American commitment of $20 billion—for Latin American economic development. The Alliance for Progress attached to the promise of aid the demand for Latin American economic and political reform. The doubtful willingness of established Latin American elites to exchange their power for United States dollars doomed the program from the beginning. But in 1961 this was not apparent.

At this hopeful juncture disaster struck. For more than a year Fidel Castro's Cuba had confronted the United States with an embarrassing hemispheric problem. Castro's dictatorial methods, his nationalization program, his clear ties with the Soviet bloc, his support of burgeoning revolutionary movements elsewhere in Latin America, and his constant and intemperate denunciations of United States "imperialism" brought Cuban-American relations to the breaking point. Kennedy as President inherited a carefully planned counterrevolutionary movement, organized and designed by the United States Central Intelligence Agency, to overthrow the obnoxious Cuban regime. By early 1961 there were from 2,000 to 3,000 rebel Cuban soldiers training in the United States for an invasion of Cuba. Other units were being organized in Guatemala.

Kennedy doubted the wisdom of the invasion planned for the spring of 1961, but so insistent were his advisers upon its viability that he granted a grudging consent. On April 17, 1961, some 1,300 assault troops struck the Cienaga de Zapata swamps of Las Villas Province (Bay of Pigs) in Cuba. The anticipated popular uprising did not occur. Castro's regulars demolished the invading forces, establishing the Cuban government more solidly in power than ever before. The President accepted full blame for the fiasco with good grace and learned to distrust the advice of those who should have known better. Yet what disturbed critics was Washington's continuing inability to accept the reality of revolution. The abysmal failure of the invasion demonstrated both that the Castro regime enjoyed widespread national support and that guerrillas operating in hostile territory had little chance of success. It had been a sobering experience for the New Frontiersmen.

Eisenhower bequeathed Kennedy a still more dangerous challenge in Southeast Asia. Here the issues had never been clearly defined, and the United States had no strategic advantage, such as it had possessed in Cuba. During his final months in the White House, Eisenhower had faced the impending collapse of pro-Western regimes in both Laos and South Vietnam. Secretary Dulles had sought to transform Laos into a pro-Western bastion in Southeast Asia by surfeiting its right-wing elements with military aid. But its pro-Western government had no chance against the pro-Communist Pathet Lao guerrilla forces. In August, 1960, a Laotian paratroop captain, Kong Le, seized Vientiane, the capital of Laos, and proclaimed a neutralist government under Prince Souvanna Phouma. Encouraged by the United States, rightist Prince Boun Oum put Souvanna Phouma to flight. The result was to bring the Pathet Lao and the Soviet Union to the deposed Prime Minister's aid.

Having inherited this explosive situation, President Kennedy, in March, 1961, warned Moscow, Peking, and Hanoi via television that the United States would not tolerate a Communist conquest of Laos. During April, he followed the British and Soviet lead in calling a fourteen-nation conference in Geneva to settle the Laotian question. The conference quickly agreed to the neutralization of Laos and instructed its leading neutralist spokesman, Souvanna Phouma, to form a coalition government including representatives of the right, center, and left in Laotian politics. While the Geneva conference moved toward a formal agreement on neutralization, the Laotian leaders, meeting sporadically in Switzerland and Laos, finally settled upon a coalition cabinet to assume office in June, 1962. Unfortunately, the unified government of Laos was short-lived. By 1963 the Pathet Lao elements had deserted, driving the neutralist middle into a coalition with the right and reducing the jungle country again to the throes of civil war.

In South Vietnam, the Eisenhower administration had anchored its hope for stability to both the political achievements of Ngo Dinh Diem in Saigon and the military forces of the Asian SEATO allies. Both proved to be frail reeds on which to lean policy objectives. In 1961 Diem faced a constantly expanding guerrilla movement, aided and abetted by North Vietnam's Ho Chi Minh, and from which no SEATO force would save him. Rather than desert or even modify its established commitment to Diem, the Kennedy administration embarked on a dual course to save the Saigon government and with it the status quo of Southeast Asia. Kennedy's program comprised additional military aid and advisers, but no commitment of American forces. Kennedy issued a stern warning to Diem on May 25, 1961: "Military pacts cannot help nations whose social injustice and economic chaos invite insurgency and penetration and subversion."

Even as he admitted the limited efficiency of United States involvement in Vietnam, Kennedy in 1961 recommitted the nation to an ultimate victory over Saigon's enemies. At this critical time of decision Washington again rejected the view of a number of Far Eastern experts that the struggle against Diem was fundamentally a civil war in the South and thus beyond American capacity to control. Secretary Rusk in November, 1961, interpreted the contest as a "determined and ruthless campaign of propaganda, infiltration and subversion by the Communist regime in North Vietnam to destroy the Republic of Vietnam [in the south]." Officially there was no civil war—only external aggression. Early in October, 1961, Diem announced that he now faced regular army units equipped to achieve a strategic victory in Southeast Asia. Kennedy responded by dispatching General Maxwell D. Taylor and State Department adviser Walter W. Rostow on a fact-finding mission to South Vietnam. General Taylor recommended that Washington make clear its intention to retaliate against sources of aggression in North Vietnam, suggesting an initial force of 10,000 ground troops to guard South Vietnam's northern frontier against North Vietnamese infiltration. Even before he received this report, Kennedy had clarified the United States position. "Let me assure you again," he informed Diem, "that the United States is determined to help Vietnam preserve its independence, protect its people against Communist assassins, and build a better life through economic growth."

In pursuit of this policy, the President in 1962 stepped up military aid to South Vietnam, increasing American advisers to 10,000. Meanwhile, his administration promised victory without any resort to United States combat forces. Defense Secretary Robert S. McNamara reported that "every qualitative measurement we have shows that we're winning this war." United States forces in Southeast Asia, he said, were limited to training missions. Kennedy recognized the polycentrism in the Communist world and the fundamental independence of Ho Chi Minh from Peking and Moscow, but he could no longer modify the United States commitment to Southeast Asia.

The President's search for the necessary political solution in South Vietnam received a critical blow in the summer of 1963, when Diem's repression of the Buddhists produced still greater political opposition to his regime. In Washington, an embarrassed Kennedy admitted: "In the final analysis, it is their war. They are the ones who have to win it or lose it. . . . All we can do is help, and we are making it very clear. But I don't agree with those who say we should withdraw. That would be a great mistake." When matters did not improve, the President after September, 1963, criticized Diem openly. In October, dissident rightist South Vietnamese generals assassinated Ngo Dinh Diem, the man whom Washington had thought would bring peace and stability to South Vietnam. Meanwhile the civil war continued, the Communist-led Vietcong proving itself a resourceful and tenacious foe. By the autumn of 1963, the United States had 16,000 troops in Vietnam, with a continuing commitment to an anti-Communist victory and without a plan of escape. No less than Eisenhower, Kennedy had misconstrued and underestimated the enemy. The prospect of a costly American involvement continued to mount.

Kennedy and Europe

Despite his conviction that the United States had entered a period of crisis with the Soviet Union, Kennedy entered the White House hopeful of discovering a more positive approach to the Cold War. He discovered quickly, however, that he had little room to maneuver within the context of established American policy. So complex, interrelated, and extensive were the nation's commitments and relationships that he felt constrained to move cautiously, reacting to situations as they developed. Kennedy, no more than his predecessors, would accept the status quo in Europe as the basis of negotiation. In July, 1961, he proclaimed "Captive Nations Week" and urged the American people to recommit themselves to the support of the just aspiration of all peoples. He reassured the Bonn government that the United States goal in Europe was German reunification under the principle of self-determination. Nevertheless, he had also announced as early as January 30 that he intended "to explore promptly all possible areas of cooperation with the Soviet Union."

Nothing had occurred to deflate the President's optimism when early in June, 1961, he journeyed to Vienna to exchange views with Premier Nikita Khrushchev. For Kennedy the confrontation with the blustering Khrushchev was utterly disillusioning. "I tell you now," he would relate, "that . . . was a very sober two days." Besides declaring the Soviet Union's intention to support so-called "wars of national liberation," the Soviet leader handed Kennedy a note warning the West that unless it accepted the conversion of West Berlin into a free city, the Soviet Union would sign a treaty with East Germany and turn over to that country the control of access routes into West Berlin. Kennedy pointedly reminded Khrushchev that the West was in Berlin legally and intended to remain, even at the risk of war.

The Kennedy-Khrushchev meeting inaugurated a new crisis in East-West relations. Kennedy and his advisers recoiled at the latest demonstration of Soviet enmity. During the weeks following the new Soviet ultimatum on Berlin, Democratic and Republican leaders in Congress assured the administration of their support of any policy required to protect Western access to Berlin. The President, affirming Dean Acheson's contention that the issue of Berlin was a "simple conflict of wills," announced on July 25 an increase in United States forces through a larger draft and the call-up of some reserves. Meanwhile, an unprecedented stream of East German refugees flooded through Berlin into West Germany; during August the number reached a thousand a day. Obviously the Soviets and East Germans could not permit this drain of manpower from Communist rule. On the night of August 12, the Communists sealed the border between East and West Berlin. Eventually they completely closed the Iron Curtain by erecting a wall. Although the crisis subsided, the future of West Berlin remained the key to the East-West struggle in Europe. For the Soviets the city was the pawn in their perennial effort to compel formal Western acceptance of a divided Germany. For the United States West Berlin remained a symbol of its will to hold the line against communism in Europe.

During Kennedy's second year in office, Fidel Castro and Khrushchev combined to create the most serious crisis of the Kennedy years. The Cuban leader's close relationship to the U.S.S.R. had rendered him an unacceptable member of the American family of nations. In January, 1962, Secretary Rusk secured the expulsion of Cuba from the Organization of American States. Relations between Cuba and the United States steadily deteriorated. In his news conference of September 13, 1962, the President acknowledged a steady movement of Soviet technical and military personnel onto the island. Should Cuba become an offensive military base, Kennedy warned, the United States would adopt any necessary course to protect its security. During October, members of Congress and the press clamored for the administration to take a more vigorous stand. Meanwhile, secret governmental surveillance began to reveal the construction of offensive missile bases on Cuba. During October, admin istration advisers wrestled with the question of alternatives, with most recommending an immediate United States attack on the island. The President, however, determined to pursue a more moderate course of action.

On October 22, 1962, in an emergency broadcast, Kennedy informed the nation of the Cuban missile threat and proclaimed "a strict quarantine on all offensive military equipment under shipment to Cuba." He called upon Khrushchev to "halt and eliminate this clandestine, reckless, and provocative threat to world peace." Any missile launched from Cuba against any nation of the Western Hemisphere, the President warned, would bring immediate retaliation against the Soviet Union itself. As a United States war fleet moved into the Atlantic to intercept Soviet cargo vessels headed for Cuba, Khrushchev agreed to dismantle the Cuban missile bases in exchange for the removal of analogous NATO weapons in Turkey. This offer Kennedy rejected, countering with the promise to lift the blockade and rule out any future invasion of Cuba provided the Russians removed their weapons under inspection. Kennedy's action, determined as it had been, left Khrushchev with the necessary escape. The Russian leader accepted the guarantees against invasion and ordered the bases dismantled. On November 2, the President informed the nation that the crisis had passed.

Unrelenting tension and discord in Soviet-American relations induced Kennedy to inaugurate a program designed to strengthen the North Atlantic Treaty Organization so that the alliance might better cope with its oversized requirements. At the heart of his so-called Grand Design for Europe was the venerable concept of Atlantic unity. Kennedy hesitated to define the kind of Atlantic partnership he contemplated, but he made clear his two preferences on Allied defense policy. First, he opposed French President Charles de Gaulle's effort to build an independent European nuclear deterrent, urging rather that Europe rely on the nuclear arsenal of the United States. Second, he hoped to broaden NATO's defense options by stressing the need for a "wider choice than humiliation or all-out nuclear action." This accent on flexible strategy did not rule out, however, the development of more efficient and accurate nuclear weapons systems.

Late in 1962 Britain forced the Kennedy design for Europe to the point of decision. British military planners had earlier organized their nation's nuclear defense around the United States Skybolt air-to-ground missile system. Now the Kennedy administration, having developed an alternative to Skybolt in the Polaris submarine missile, canceled the expensive Skybolt program. The move provoked sharp reactions in London. In an effort to soothe ruffled British feelings, Kennedy conferred with British Prime Minister Harold Macmillian at Nassau in December, 1962. There he agreed to provide Britain with Polaris missiles. In addition, the two leaders, in an effort to meet the requirements of joint nuclear control, devised a multilateral defense force of nuclear-armed naval vessels manned by mixed NATO crews. At the same time, Kennedy held out the promise of American support for British entrance into the European Common Market, in order to further cement European unity. Presuming to speak for continental Western Europe, France's Charles de Gaulle, in a caustic January, 1963, press conference, brought Kennedy's Grand Design crashing to the ground—vetoing British membership in the Common Market, rejecting membership for France in any multinational defense force, and insisting that France, no longer able to trust the United States, would carry out plans to develop her own nuclear deterrent.

Even as de Gaulle consigned the Grand Design to the category of lost causes, the President had embarked on his final effort to reach an understanding with the U.S.S.R. In the Cuban missile crisis, Kennedy and Khrushchev had walked to the brink of disaster and recoiled with a new appreciation for the responsibility which they shared. Kennedy refused to exploit his success in the missile crisis, preferring rather to press the search for means to insure that such confrontations never occurred again. He articulated his new determination in his address at American University on June 10, 1963, reminding Americans and Russians alike of their joint responsibility for the Cold War and of their common hopes for a more rational world. It was a speech which led directly to Kennedy's second and last major foreign-policy success. Late that summer he negotiated with Russia the Test Ban Treaty limiting nuclear testing to underground sites. Congress, responding to an upsurge of favorable public opinion, approved the treaty in September by a vote of 81 to 19.

Lyndon Johnson and Vietnam

In foreign affairs, President Johnson did not care to question the assumptions and purposes of previous administrations. In his first address to the joint session of Congress he informed the world, "This nation will keep its commitments from South Viet-Nam to West Berlin. We will be unceasing in the search for peace." Addressing a meeting of the Associated Press in New York during April, 1964, the President reaffirmed the nation's commitment to the Geneva agreement on Laos and to the defense of South Vietnam. Johnson, no less than Kennedy, accepted the validity of the domino theory. "I am not going to be the President," he said, "who saw Southeast Asia go the way China went." He evinced the belief that Vietnam was the key to a worldwide balance of power Symbolic of the basic continuity between Johnson's administration and that of the slain Kennedy was the retention of Dean Rusk as Secretary of State.

No less than Eisenhower and Kennedy did the new President underestimate the enemy in Vietnam. Like them he optimistically assumed that the Saigon government, with additional American advisers, could achieve the desired triumph and thus strike a blow for containment in Southeast Asia. He assured the nation on February 23, 1964, that "the contest in which South Vietnam is now engaged is first and foremost a contest to be won by the Government and the people of that country for themselves." In May Secretary of Defense McNamara again announced that the primary American function was "one of training, support and logistical assistance." He predicted that the major portion of the United States military task would be completed in 1965. For Washington, the nature of the challenge had not changed. Official policy remained that of helping the Republic of Vietnam with United States experience and resources to put down a Communist campaign of terror and subversion. During August, 1964, following a North Vietnamese attack on American naval vessels in the Gulf of Tonkin, Congress, at the President's request, adopted a resolution which seemed to commit it to any future action required to maintain the status quo in Southeast Asia. The resolution declared that international peace and security in Southeast Asia were vital. The United States, therefore was "prepared, as the President determines, to take all necessary steps, including the use of armed forces, to assist any protocol state of the Southeast Asia Collective Defense Treaty requesting assistance in defense of its freedom." At the end of 1964, when Johnson had already won the right to succeed himself as President, the United States was maintaining 23,000 American soldiers in Vietnam, and the administration had received Congressional authorization to use American power in any manner necessary to secure victory for Saigon.

Conclusion

Although President Eisenhower talked about new initiatives and directions in American foreign policy, he followed the same basic course laid down by Truman—the policy of containment. Having settled the Korean War by negotiation, Eisenhower and Dulles sought to strengthen the North Atlantic Treaty Organization as a bulwark against Communist expansion in Europe. They made no real effort, however, to "roll back" the Iron Curtain. Indeed by 1955, Europe had achieved a balance between East and West which neutralized major threats to the peace in that quarter. American attempts to apply containment in Asia were less successful. The Southeast Asia Treaty Organization, conceived as an Asian counterpart to NATO, lacked any effective military power other than that which the United States might provide. Complicating the situation in Asia, and the Middle East as well, was the fact that Eisenhower and Dulles were hard pressed to cope with rising nationalist movements among former colonies. Although the United States was able to avoid involvement in a land war in both Asia and the Middle East in the 1950s, threats to American objectives and to area stability were imminent.

After 1961 the Democratic national leadership remained wedded to policies established in the late 1940s, policies which had now hardened into dogma. Cognizant of the fact that the Cold War had changed, John F. Kennedy, in his tragically shortened presidential term, attempted—though not consistently—to establish "bridges" between East and West and to reduce the danger that miscalculation or a misunderstanding might escalate into a "hot" war. Recurrent crises associated with Cuba, Berlin and Vietnam placed Kennedy and his successor Lyndon B. Johnson, under severe pressure to respond to what appeared to be an extension of Communist—and hence Soviet—power. Like Eisenhower, the two Democratic Presidents, both intelligent and humane men, defined the Communist threat in global terms. A source of trouble in the past, this state of mind in 1964–1965 would lead to even greater national dilemmas in the future.

SUGGESTED READINGS

Many of the books listed at the conclusion of Chapters 36 and 37 apply as well to the Eisenhower years. Several basic volumes on the Eisenhower Presidency contain valuable material on foreign affairs. Among these are Robert J. Donovan's *Eisenhower: The Inside Story* (1956); Richard Rovere's *The Ordeal of Power: A Political Memoir of the Eisenhower Years* (1963); Emmet John Hughes's *The Ordeal of Power** (1962); Marquis Childs's *Eisenhower: Captive Hero* (1958); Merlo J. Pusey's laudatory *Eisenhower the President* (1956); and Eric Goldman's *The Crucial Decade—and After: America, 1945–1960** (1961). Secretary of State John Foster Dulles has also been the subject of numerous studies. Dulles presented many of his own views in *War or Peace* (1950). Books on Dulles which include analyses of decision making in the Eisenhower administration are John R. Beal's *John Foster Dulles: A Biography*

(1959) and the more recent Louis L. Gerson's *John Foster Dulles* (1967). Both of these volumes are highly laudatory. Moderately favorable to Dulles also are Richard Goold-Adams's *John Foster Dulles* (1962) and Roscoe Drummond and Gaston Goblentz's *Duel at the Brink: John Foster Dulles' Command of American Power* (1960), the first by a British writer, the second by two American journalists.

Norman A. Graebner's *The New Isolationism* (1956) and *Cold War Diplomacy, 1945–1960** (1962) are concerned with the Eisenhower administration's tendency to overcommit the nation abroad. Hans J. Morgenthau's essay on Dulles, in Graebner (ed.), *An Uncertain Tradition** (1961), is a penetrating critique of the Dulles policies. Two useful discussions of foreign policy in the fifties are C. L. Sulzberger's *What's Wrong with U.S. Foreign Policy* (1959) and W. W. Rostow's *The United States in the World Arena* (1960). Of special interest is Richard M. Nixon's *Six Crises* (1962). Paul Peeters discusses one aspect of the Dulles policies in *Massive Retaliation: The Policy and Its Critics* (1958).

For a defense of United States policy toward China see Karl Lott Rankin's *China Assignment* (1964). A critical evaluation of Dulles and the Quemoy issue can be found in Tang Tsou's *The Embroilment over Quemoy: Mao, Chiang and Dulles** (International Study Paper No. 2, Institute of International Studies, University of Utah, 1959). A. T. Steele's *The American People and China** (1966) discusses in detail American attitudes toward China. On China's foreign objectives see A. Doak Barnett's *Communist China and Asia: A Challenge to American Policy** (1960). Donald S. Zagoria's *The Sino-Soviet Conflict** (1962) is highly significant. Three perceptive and sometimes critical accounts of United States reactions to Asian nationalism and revolution are E. O. Reischauer's *Wanted: An Asian Policy* (1955); Cecil V. Crabb, Jr.'s *The Elephants and the Grass: A Study of Nonalignment** (1965); and Richard J. Barnet's *Intervention and Revolution: America's Confrontation with Insurgent Movements around the World* (1968).

For a good survey of United States policy in Southeast Asia see Russell H. Fifield's *Southeast Asia in United States Policy** (1963). On United States defense policy in Southeast Asia is the excellent study by George Modelski (ed.), *SEATO* (1962). Two excellent readers on the Vietnam conflict are Marvin E. Gettleman (ed.), *Vietnam** (1965) and Marcus G. Raskin and B. B. Fall (eds.), *The Viet-Nam Reader** (1965). Two excellent accounts of the early postwar struggle for Vietnam are Ellen J. Hammer's *The Struggle for Indochina** (1954) and Robert Shaplen's *The Lost Revolution: The U.S. in Vietnam, 1946–1966** (1966). Bernard B. Fall's two basic studies of Vietnam are *Street without Joy: From the Indochina War to the War in Viet-Nam* (4th rev. ed., 1964) and *The Two Viet-Nams: A Political and Military History* (5th rev. ed., 1965). A critique by a former Hungarian diplomat is Victor Bator's *Viet-Nam: A Diplomatic Tragedy* (1965). On the crucial battle of 1954 see Jules Roy's *The Battle of Dienbienphu* (1965). Brian Crozier's *Southeast Asia in Turmoil** (1965) accepts United States policy uncritically, whereas Theodore Draper's *Abuse of Power** (1966) and A. M. Schlesinger, Jr.'s *The Bitter Heritage** (1967) are highly critical of American policy. Oliver E. Clubb's *The United States and the Sino-Soviet Bloc in Southeast Asia** (1963) discusses the power-bloc competition in Southeast Asia.

On the Middle East and Suez crisis of 1956 see J. C. Campbell's *Defense of the Middle East* (1958), and Guy Wint and Peter Calvocoressi's *Middle East Crisis* (1957). For another view see Lionel Gelber's *America in Britain's Place* (1961). Highly critical of Dulles's role in the Suez crisis are Herman Finer's *Dulles over Suez* (1964) and Anthony Eden's *The Memoirs of Anthony Eden: Full Circle* (1960).

On the challenges of Germany and Berlin during the Eisenhower years see *The Shaping of Postwar Germany* (1960) by E. S. McInnis and others; Gerald Freund's *Germany between Two Worlds* (1961); and Hans Speier's *Divided Berlin: The Anatomy of Soviet Blackmail* (1961). On Slavic Europe see Stephen D. Kertesz (ed.), *The Fate of East Central Europe: Hopes and Failures of American Foreign Policy* (1956). On Britain see Leon Epstein's *Britain: Uneasy Ally* (1954); Rupert Emerson's *From Empire to Nation** (1960); and F. S. Northedge's *British Foreign Policy* (1962). For French policy see Stanley Hoffman (ed.), *In Search of France** (1963). For an evaluation of NATO in the fifties see Klaus Knorr (ed.), *NATO and American Security** (1959) and Robert E. Osgood's *NATO: The Entangling Alliance* (1962). For the debate on disengagement see George F.

Kennan's *Russia, the Atom, and the West* (1957); Dean Acheson's "The Illusion of Disengagement," *Foreign Affairs,* XXXVI (April, 1958); and Kennan's "Disengagement Revisited," *ibid.,* XXXVII (January, 1959).

Both the futile effort at arms control and the nuclear stalemate have received extensive treatment. B. G. Bechhoefer's *Postwar Negotiations for Arms Control* (1961); D. G. Brennan (ed.), *Arms Control, Disarmament, and National Security* (1961); A. T. Hadley's *The Nation's Safety and Arms Control* (1961); and J. J. Stone's *Containing the Arms Race: Some Specific Proposals* (1966) all reveal the problems associated with effective arms control. An excellent discussion of the American military establishment is P. Y. Hammond's *Organizing for Defense* (1961). Studies which deal with the nuclear crisis are Robert E. Osgood's *Limited War: The Challenge to American Strategy* (1957); Henry A. Kissinger's *Nuclear Weapons and Foreign Policy** (1957) and *The Necessity for Choice** (1961); T. C. Schelling's *Arms and Influence** (1966); Bernard Brodie's *Strategy in the Missile Age** (1959); and Herman Kahn's *On Thermonuclear War* (1960). American surveillance over Russia has been analyzed in David Wise and T. B. Ross's *The U-2 Affair* (1962).

For one intellectual world view of the Kennedy administration see E. K. Lindley's edition of Secretary of State Dean Rusk's early speeches, *The Winds of Freedom* (1963). Among the many volumes available on the early challenge of Castro's Cuba are R. F. Smith's *The United States and Cuba: Business and Diplomacy,* 1917–1960* (1960); C. Wright Mills's *Listen Yankee!* (1960); Theodore Draper's *Castro's Revolution** (1962); Lee Huberman and P. M. Sweezy's *Cuba: Anatomy of a Revolution** (1960); and W. A. Williams's *The United States, Cuba, and Castro* (1962). Decidedly anti-Castro in outlook are E. E. T. Smith's *The Fourth Floor* (1962) and Daniel James's *Cuba: The First Soviet Satellite in the Americas* (1961). On the Bay of Pigs episode see Karl E. Meyer and Tad Szulc's *The Cuban Invasion: The Chronicle of a Disaster** (1962). The Alliance for Progress and the challenge of revolutionary change in Latin America are dealt with in J. C. Dreier (ed.), *The Alliance for Progress* (1962); A. A. Berle's *Latin America: Diplomacy and Reality** (1962); P. A. Ray's *South Wind Red: Our Hemispheric Crisis** (1962); and J. W. Nystrom and N. A. Haverstock's *The Alliance for Progress, Key to Latin America's Development** (1966). For details of the Cuban missile crisis, with emphasis on the behavior of the key actors in the Kennedy administration, is the important memoir of then–Attorney General Robert F. Kennedy, *Thirteen Days: A Memoir of the Cuban Missile Crisis* (1969). Also excellent on the crisis are Elie Abel's *The Missile Crisis** (1966) and D. L. Larson (ed.), *The Cuban Crisis of 1962: Selected Documents and Chronology** (1963).

Volumes on Vietnam which relate military developments during the Kennedy years are Malcolm W. Browne's *The New Face of War* (1965); David Halberstam's *The Making of a Quagmire* (1965); Jean Lacouture's *Viet-Nam between Two Truces** (1966); and John Mecklin's *Mission in Torment* (1965). For a sympathetic account of Ngo Dinh Diem see Denis Warner's *The Last Confucian** (1964). Of special value for the Kennedy policy toward Southeast Asia is Roger Hilsman's *To Move a Nation: The Politics of Foreign Policy in the Administration of John F. Kennedy** (1967).

Much has been written on the changing status of NATO in the sixties. Among the more important and perceptive volumes on the European alliance are Henry A. Kissinger's *The Troubled Partnership** (1965); Alastair Buchan's *NATO in the 1960's** (1962); Harold van B. Cleveland's *The Atlantic Idea and Its European Rivals** (1966); A. J. Cottrell and J. E. Dougherty's *The Politics of the Atlantic Alliance** (1964); E. H. van der Beugel's *From Marshall Aid to Atlantic Partnership: European Integration as a Concern of American Foreign Policy* (1966); Hubert M. Gladwyn's *The European Idea* (1966); and Henry M. Jackson (ed.), *The Atlantic Alliance: Jackson Subcommittee Hearing and Findings* (1967). On United States–British relations see H. C. Allen's *The Anglo-American Predicament: The British Commonwealth, the United States and European Unity** (1960). On the changing challenge of Eastern Europe see the two excellent volumes by Zbigniew K. Brzezinski's *The Soviet Bloc: Unity and Conflict** (1967) and *Alternative to Partition: For a Broader Conception of America's Role in Europe** (1965). Also of value is Adam Bromke and P. E. Uren's (eds.) *The Communist States and the West** (1967).

*indicates availability in paperback.

40

American Society after Midcentury

AMERICAN SOCIETY underwent a rapid transformation in the years after World War II. Rising incomes, greater mobility, new opportunities for education, growing urbanization, revolutions in science and technology, new freedom in literature and the movies, and the demand by lower economic groups, especially blacks, for full political, social, and economic rights, all created confusion and conflict and tested the strength of the country's social fabric. Even the physical landscape reflected a rapidly changing America. Shiny steel and glass skyscrapers, huge apartment complexes, superhighways, modern airports, burgeoning suburbs, launching pads for space vehicles, and mammoth athletic stadiums testified to a high degree of affluence, comfort, and material satisfaction.

Many social problems faced postwar Americans, but three were of overriding importance. These were civil rights, a persistent hard-core poverty, and the special challenge of urban decay. During the 1950s, these matters received careful attention from politicians, social scientists, lawyers, and the concerned generally. Yet, while they seemed serious, no national crisis appeared. Indeed, the 1950s was a "placid" decade, during which most people seemed satisfied and content. By the 1960s, however, these issues had become explosive. Tired of continued discrimination, blacks were losing patience with the slowness of change. They became increasingly militant in their demands for full civil and economic rights. The central city, which had gradually come to be populated mainly by a variety of minority groups, presented an array of problems—persistent unemployment, poor housing, inadequate services, and lack of income—which seemed almost insurmountable. In the 1960s riots broke out in the ghetto sections of scores of cities where unemployment was high and the poor felt alienated from the mainstream of American society. The restless and belligerent sixties found at least a few critics calling for radical revolution. The war in Vietnam merely deepened the frustrations and social anxieties.

Urbanization

On November 20, 1967, the population of the United States passed the 200 million mark, an increase of 50 million since 1950. The social significance of this population growth was not so much its rapidity but the fact that an overwhelming majority of the people had become city dwellers. Urbanization was a distinctive and troublesome feature of American life in the mid-twentieth century. While millions still lived in small towns and on farms, the nation by 1970 was more than 70 percent urban. Only 5 percent of the people actually lived on farms in 1970, compared with 23 percent in 1940. This rapid cityward migration caused deep concern among high government officials. In November, 1967, Secretary of Agriculture Orville Freeman deplored the flow of population from country to city and urged people to stay in the rural communities. But nothing, it seemed, could stop the trend toward greater urbanization.

The growth of individual cities did not represent the full impact of urbanization. Cities engulfed entire geographic areas; great megalopolises emerged between Washington, D.C., and Boston, along the Great Lakes, and in Northern and Southern California. Rapid urbanization produced major changes within the metropolitan communities themselves. Many citizens deserted the inner city and moved to the suburbs while minority groups, principally blacks, took their places. Between 1960 and 1966 the black population in the heart of the nation's great cities increased by some two million while the white population declined by at least one million. "Unless something is done to halt the trend," said Harvey Perloff, a director of Resources for the Future, "America's cities will become almost exclusively black, and the surrounding suburbs almost exclusively white by the end of the century."

Why the cities were already in serious trouble is clear enough. To achieve a minimum level of efficiency, comfort, and safety, these vast concentrations of population required community spirit—a willingness to engage in planning that would commit public funds to the well-being of all inhabitants, not merely the affluent. But the cities, no less than the country's farms and villages, comprised aggregations of individual wealth-seekers, concerned less with the general quality of urban life than with the enhancement of their own opportunities to reap the profits of the private market. What little city planning evolved in early twentieth-century America was designed to serve the needs of commerce and industry, not the broader requirements of human existence. Business leaders might favor better transportation to facilitate the movement of workers and buyers to their places of business, but they had no interest in expending the resources at their command on nonprofit poverty, welfare,

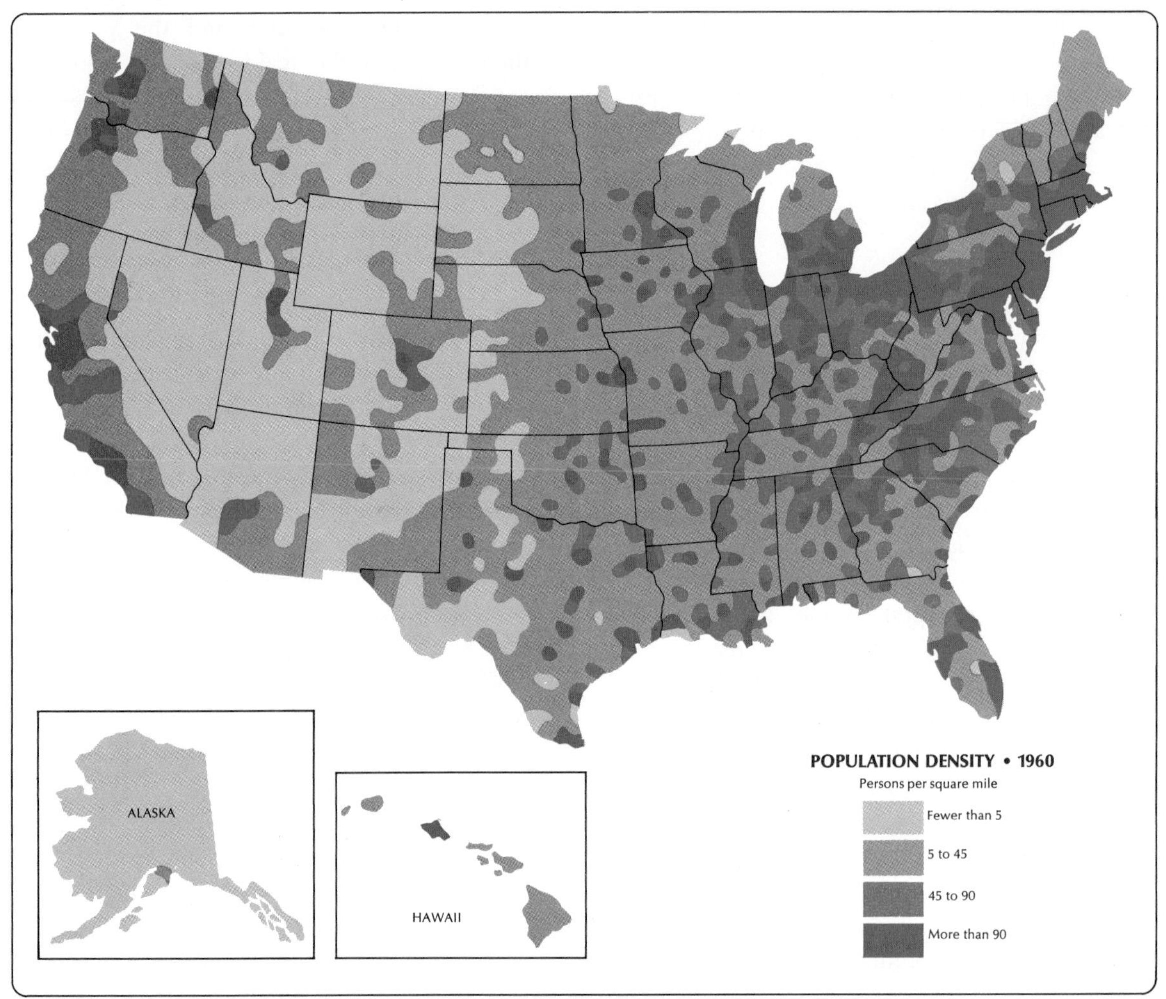

slum clearance, or beautification programs. What the private market could do for the cities it did magnificently; the cities became the nation's great producers of wealth and profit. Where the financial community failed through neglect, no public agency could succeed.

Thus urban America remained a study in contrasts. While large areas of the urban communities deteriorated, downtown business districts were rebuilt after World War II. New hotels, apartment complexes, office and business buildings punctured the skylines of most cities. Freeways facilitated the increasing flow of traffic, and a limited amount of urban renewal improved the appearance of some city centers. A spectacular example of urban renewal was Penn Center in Philadelphia, a complex of hotels, office buildings, and apartments which replaced an old and slowly decaying part of the inner city.

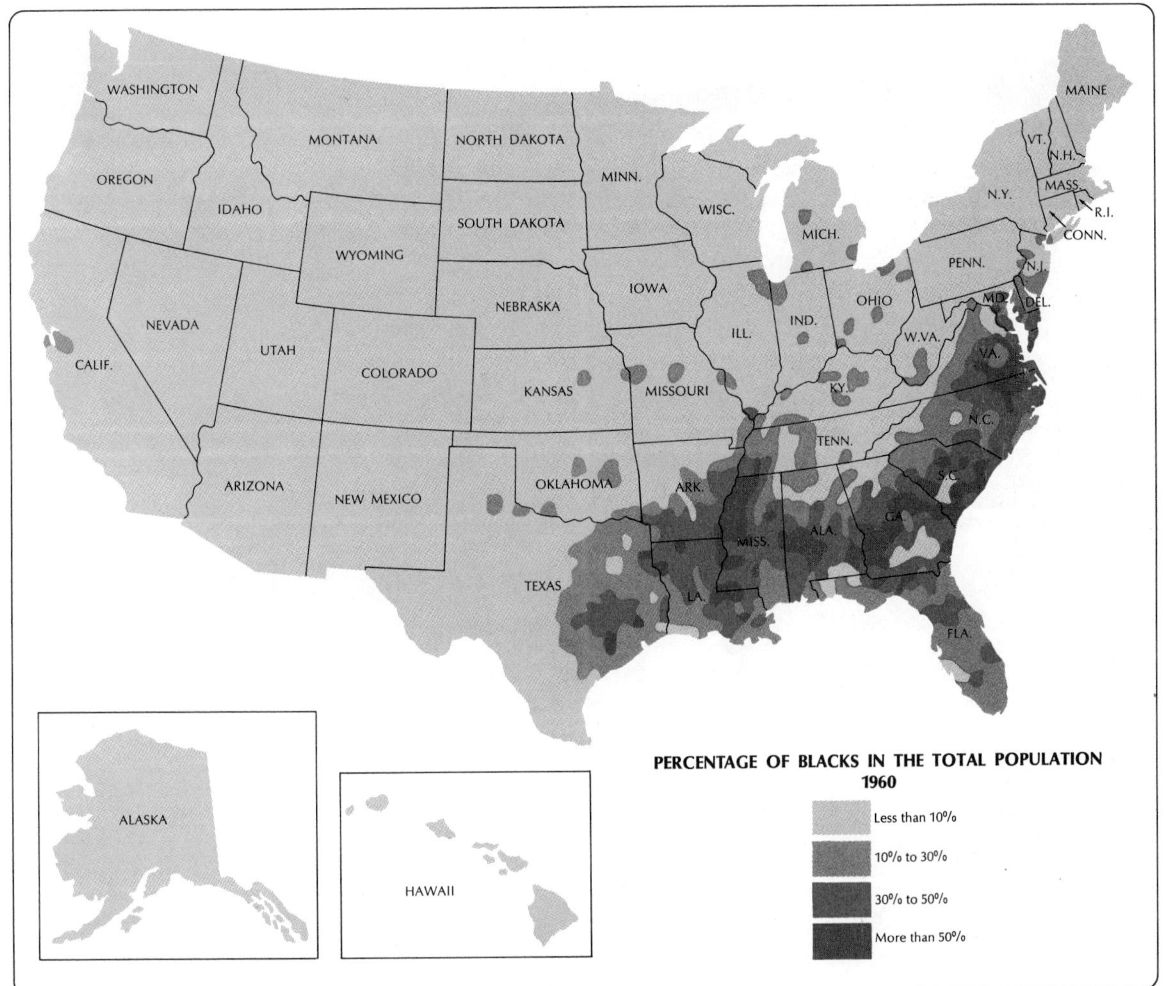

It was the mushrooming suburbs which typified urban growth for most Americans. As more people were able to afford better housing, they pushed out further and further from the central city where they worked. Housing developers bought property from farmers, who could no longer afford to use their land for farming, and constructed millions of homes which urbanites purchased on long-term credit. New schools, churches, shopping centers, and even light industries became part of the suburban development. By 1970 the United States had become a vast suburbia with more people living in the suburbs than anywhere else. Between 1964 and 1968 a 60 to 90 percent population increase in many cities occurred in the suburbs. The settlements around Washington, D.C., were typical examples of this tremendous growth: between 1960 and 1968 the population gain in

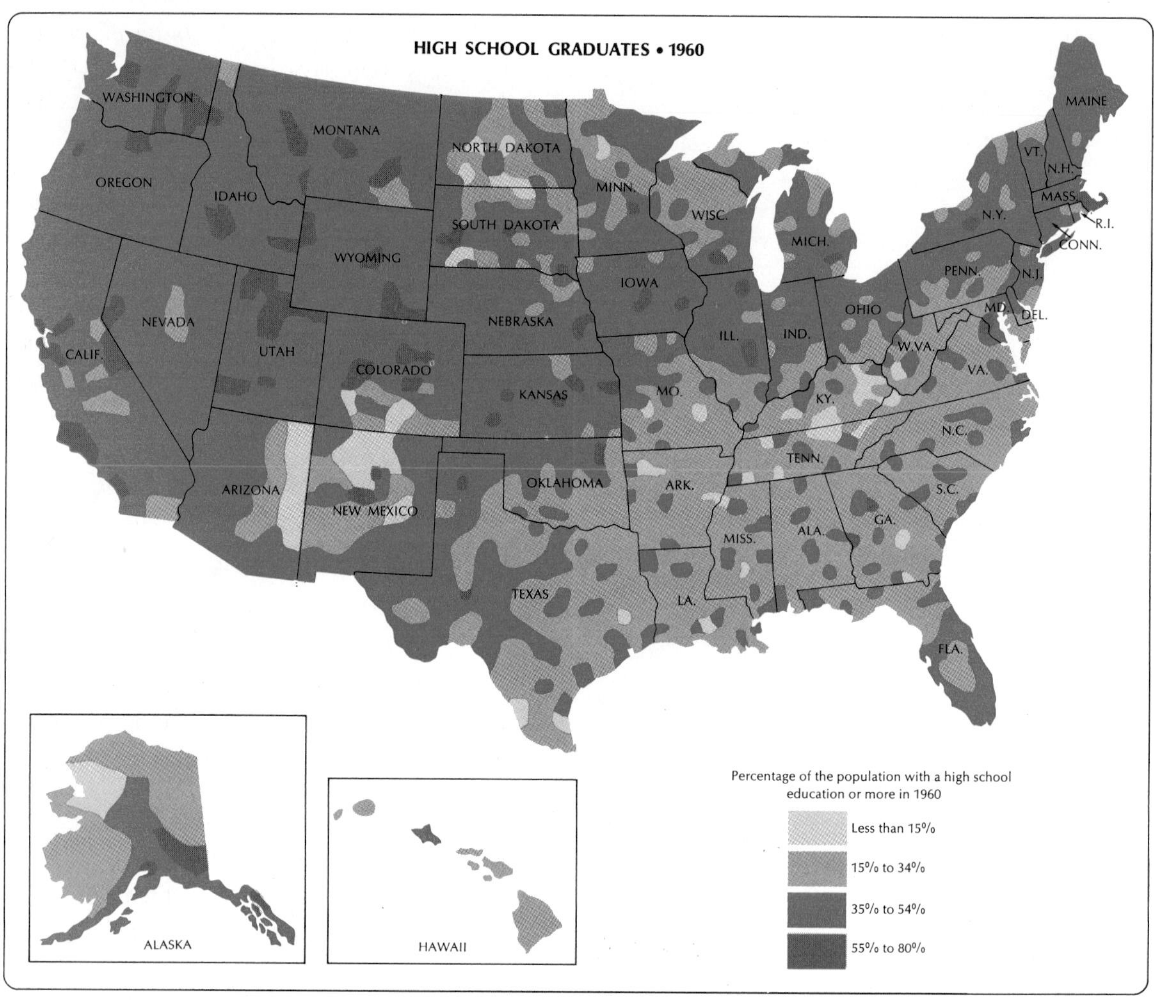

the central city was only 5.2 percent compared with about 64 percent in the adjoining Virginia and Maryland suburbs.

Americans found much of what they wanted in suburbia—less congestion, more space, better housing, better schools, gardening, recreation, and even status. Suburbanites were predominantly white, middle-class citizens who had higher than average incomes. Yet the suburbs could not escape urban problems. Crime rates rose in the 1960s, and problems of education, sanitation, transportation, and other difficulties overtook many suburban communities just as they had overtaken the older areas. But in general the pleasant, if hurried, life of the suburbs stood in sharp contrast to much of the human existence in the inner city.

This shift of the urban population to the suburbs merely aggravated the social and economic problems of metropolitan America.

The inner cities tended to deteriorate because they were occupied largely by low-income people, who had no choice but to live in slums with substandard housing. Meager efforts in the field of public housing did little or nothing to stop the physical disintegration. Slum and ghetto dwellers suffered as well from inadequate public services, poor schools, lack of police protection, and a high rate of unemployment. Poverty, ignorance, and lack of opportunity went hand in hand and created an attitude of hopelessness and futility among many residents of the inner city. Conditions became so serious by the 1960s that many people considered urban congestion to be the country's primary unsolved domestic problem.

Professional planners, sociologists, economists, and other specialists responded to the urban challenge with a plethora of plans and programs to meet the specific problems of housing, traffic, smog, crime, and numerous other difficulties which seemed to be growing more serious every year. But even if the experts could reach agreement, knowing what to do was not sufficient. For it was evident to every observer that to make cities pleasant, safe, and efficient places to live would require huge sums of money—literally billions of dollars. How the nation met this challenge would determine the quality of American life not only in the 1970s but in the indefinite future as well.

Affluence and Poverty

Despite the growing problems of the cities, it was the business and industry within the urban areas which produced the country's abundant wealth. So great was the rising productivity and income that the majority of Americans achieved a standard of living undreamed of before World War II. Gross national product rose from somewhat over $284 billion in 1950 to $747.6 billion in 1966. Two years later the GNP had zoomed to over $850 billion. Median family income advanced from $3,319 in 1950 to more than $8,000 in 1968, while per capita personal income over that same period increased from $1,496 to $3,412. Although inflation cut deeply into the buying power of these rising incomes, the genuine economic gains remained significant. Indeed, real income or purchasing power climbed some 66 percent during the first twenty post-World War II years. Another notable development was the rapid increase in income among families in the middle-, upper-middle-, and high-income groups. By the mid-sixties nearly 30 percent of all families received $10,000 or more a year, compared with less than 3 percent at the end of World War II. At the other end, the number of families whose income was less than $3,000 declined from about half the American people as late as 1947 to only 14.3 percent in 1966. Inflation, of course, magnified the change.

Rising income encouraged an even higher standard of living. People bought new houses in the suburbs or moved into expensive apartments. Air conditioning, carpeting, two or three bathrooms, intercommunication systems, dishwashers, and other conveniences became standard in hundreds of thousands of new homes and apartments purchased or rented by middle- and upper-middle-class families. Two or more automobiles became common by the 1960s not only for the rich but for many middle-income families. By 1967 about 22 percent of American families owned two or more cars. Approximately one-fourth of the new homes and one-third of the new automobiles were equipped with air conditioning.

There were many other expressions of what John Kenneth Galbraith called the "affluent society." Most households had television by the late 1950s, and in the 1960s color sets rapidly replaced those providing black and white reception. Nearly every home had a refrigerator, and an increasing number of housewives enjoyed automatic washing and drying appliances. Large outlays for recreation, entertainment, and travel comprised another aspect of affluence. Americans spent billions on fishing, boating, camping, bowling, golf, movies, and professional sports. If vacation travel were added, Americans by the mid-1960s spent more than $40 billion a year on recreation. In 1966 they spent an additional $3.7 billion on foreign travel.

Most Americans considered themselves members of the middle class, although the number of very rich people grew rapidly after 1940. The notion that no one could acquire huge wealth because of high income taxes was only a myth. There were, of course, the old families—the Rockefellers, the Mellons, and the Vanderbilts—who retained and expanded their fortunes, but many of the new-rich entered the multimillionaire class. By the 1960s there were approximately 100,000 millionaires in the United States; of these 646 declared a gross annual income of more than $1 million for tax purposes in 1965. Many of the new fortunes were made in oil, insurance, and real estate. The new-rich, like their predecessors, engaged in conspicuous consumption. Ownership of a half dozen town and country houses, expensive automobiles, airplanes, huge wardrobes, and extensive travel were all part of their way of life. One wealthy father gave his twelve-year-old daughter a $4,000 birthday party, while another rich host presented each of his dinner guest with a sports car as a favor. One of the guests responded dryly, "What are we ever going to do with a funny little car like that in front of our big house?"

Throughout the early postwar years the affluent chose to assume that all elements of society were making satisfactory economic progress. By the early 1960s, however, it was becoming painfully apparent that prosperity had bypassed millions of citizens. The poor were not becoming poorer, but the gap between the poor and the affluent was continuously widening. Because of a multitude of welfare programs, the poor were not as destitute as they had been during the Great Depression. But they simply were not sharing in the nation's economic expansion. Among the hard-core poor were blacks and Puerto Ricans jammed into urban ghettos, whites in Appalachia, Indians and Spanish-Americans, farm families in the South, migrant workers, and many of the elderly. As late as 1970 about 25 million Americans were mired in poverty with incomes below the official poverty line of $3,553 a year for an urban family of four. Perhaps double this number lived precariously near the poverty line. These people were part of what Michael Harrington called "the other America."

Among those who existed at the fringes of national life were the 16 million rural poor, concentrated overwhelmingly in the broad strip of the Appalachian Mountains stretching from southern New York to central Alabama. Here in Appalachia lived the remnants of the poor whites, trapped in permanent poverty, filth, and degradation. Late in 1963 a CBS editor reported his reaction to a trip through Clay County, Kentucky: "Drive through [the county seat] a couple of miles and you come to Horse

Creek and Crawfish Holler. Here is the worst living . . . and the lowest form of human existence I have seen anywhere in the United States. . . . Some of the shacks were windowless, there were shuffling women in filthy sacks —not old but relatively young—and garbage and junk." Mississippi, Arkansas, Louisiana, Tennessee, and Florida also had their pockets of poverty, occupied largely by black sharecroppers and migrant farmers. Here were Americans with annual incomes of $900 or less, often living in rat-infested hovels under the shadow of nearby stables costing a half million dollars. Without adequate education and skills, such migrants had little chance against the urban competition in any search for security in the nation's cities.

Perhaps the more obvious centers of poverty were the large black slums in the cities where the question of race reinforced and perpetuated the gaping divisions between rich and poor. In the teeming urban ghettos poverty meant dirty, substandard housing, with rats far more numerous than people. It meant unemployment or at best low-paid, unskilled jobs such as dishwashing, domestic service, or day labor. Even those who worked forty hours a week, fifty-two weeks a year, at the 1960 minimum wage of $1 an hour grossed only $2,080 annually. At $1.65 an hour, the minimum wage in 1969, they would earn $3,432 a year—still below the official poverty line.

Many black slum dwellers, finding most legitimate avenues to economic security blocked, lived by their wits. They cared little about middle-class morality; many had no contact with white society at all. Mark Battle, an expert on black urban culture, once described the varieties of existence in the slums. "Walk with a Negro youth in his ghetto environment," he wrote, "and . . . you'll quickly get a taste for the components of his life: a drug addict nodding in a doorway; a drunk vomiting or urinating in a hallway; a sex party on a rooftop; seven-year-olds scampering over fences with stolen jars of pigs' feet; a floating crap game in an alley; bars full of prostitutes; fights in which the strong pick on the weak; merchants who overprice their shoddy goods and charge one dollar to cash a Government allotment check." What mattered to most urban Negroes was less an avenue of escape from the ghettos than the conversion of the ghettos into promising areas of human existence. For many New York blacks, Harlem had an appealing quality; whatever its problems, it offered a known environment and the promise of a better life. What was needed, declared author Ralph Ellison, was a hard look at the city to see it, "not merely as an instrumentality for making money, but a place for allowing the individual to achieve his highest promise."

Neither local nor federal programs seemed sufficient to stem the ruinous impact of urban poverty and congestion on the lives of countless city dwellers. According to some authorities, the chances of a black man's escape from Harlem or Chicago's West Side were less than one in ten. By the 1960s dissatisfaction and the inability of most male Negroes to gain entrance into the mainstream of American society exploded into violence in many black ghettos. In the summer of 1965, riots broke out in the Watts area of Los Angeles, and before police, troops, and firemen could bring the looting and burning under control, thirty-three people had been killed and property losses had mounted into the millions. A national crisis seemed at hand in the summer of 1967 when riots erupted in Detroit, Newark, and other major cities. (See Chapter 41.) There seemed to be no plan, purpose, or particular philosophy behind the rioting. For some it seemed to be an expression of blind reaction against general conditions in the ghetto; for others, including some youngsters, it was a lark and an opportunity to pick up free merchandise. Following the 1967 riots, President Lyndon B. Johnson appointed a high-level commission to study civil disorders in American cities, but events cried for action, not investigation. Most knowledgeable authorities already knew the basic, if not the immediate, causes of riots—racism, discrimination, poor housing, joblessness, and the absence of hope.

Why did the paradox of progress and poverty continue in a society which had the productive capacity to provide a high standard of living for everyone? Some Americans explained poverty in the time-honored terms of laziness, lack of thrift, and immorality, traits which, in fact, could by found among people of low and high income alike. But many people free of such vices were poor because they did not have an opportunity to participate fully in the social, economic, and political life of the nation. Racial discrimination, inadequate education, poor health, habitual failure, lack of training and job skills, and general inability to compete in a highly technical society combined to keep millions of people in poverty. Moreover, the poor had little political power and consequently were unable to influence Congress to enact policies which would strike effective blows at the causes of poverty.

Blacks and Civil Rights

If there were Americans who did not participate in the country's economic prosperity, there were also millions of citizens who did not enjoy full civil rights. Often these were the same people. Negroes suffered from political, social, as well as economic discrimination. Even though nearly one million black men served their country during World War II, they returned home to discrimination and segregation in housing, education, voting, employment, and public accommodations. For Negroes there existed a chasm between American democratic ideals and the actual conditions under which they lived. Whether the United States was a racist country, as some militant blacks claimed, was a moot point, but it seemed that way to an increasing number of Americans who experienced second-class citizenship.

In the twenty-five years after 1940 the black population of the United States rose from 12.8 million to about 22 million. At the same time much of the black population shifted from the rural South to Northern cities. As they moved northward during and after World War II, blacks were jammed into the growing urban slums and ghettos of such cities as New York, Philadelphia, Cleveland, Detroit, and Chicago. Crammed into limited space, confined largely to menial jobs, and living in poverty, they endured appalling social conditions. The rate of illegitimacy was high; thus many black homes were fatherless. Sociologists found that, with so many mothers alone as heads of families, black society became increasingly matriarchal. Broken homes, by aggravating the dilemmas of slum life, contributed to poor schoolwork, lack of discipline, rising crime rates, and poor motivation among many black children. These home conditions, which shocked white, middle-class Americans, contributed to social instability in the black community and helped to perpetuate second-class black citizenship.

Blacks who had suffered from generations of segregation and discrimination in the South hoped to find conditions better in the North. Instead, they found themselves confronted with *de facto,* if not legal, segregation in housing. Those Negroes who could afford better houses and tried to move into the suburbs usually met stiff resistance. Negroes likewise faced discrimination in their search for employment. Problems of motivation and unemployment trapped countless urban blacks in a hopeless cycle of poverty, crime, and failure. Even most black college graduates could not obtain positions commensurate with their training and experience. But Southern blacks as well continued to be denied equal political rights, adequate education, social equality, and economic opportunity. Under these circumstances, blacks across the nation became increasingly militant in their demands for equality and justice.

Pressure by concerned political leaders and various civil rights groups, aided by decisions of the Supreme Court, gradually destroyed most elements of legal discrimination. Strict school segregation, which existed in seventeen states in 1945, began to crumble as Negroes sought entrance to the professional schools of Southern universities in the late 1940s. After winning a case in the federal district court in 1948, George W. McLaurin was admitted to the College of Education at the University of Oklahoma, although not before 1950 did he gain full equality of treatment. Also in 1950, the previously all-white University of Oklahoma Law School admitted Ada Lois Sipuel. The Universities of Texas, Missouri, and North Carolina, all traditionally segregated institutions, shortly thereafter admitted blacks for graduate study. But the Supreme Court destroyed the main bastions of legal segregation in education in the case of *Brown v. Board of Education of Topeka* in 1954. The Court held that "segregation of children in public schools solely on the basis of race" deprived the children of minority groups of equal educational opportunities. This latter-day decision overthrew the historic "separate but equal" doctrine established by the Supreme Court in *Plessy v. Ferguson* in 1896.

In 1948 President Truman had ordered that segregation be terminated in the Armed Forces; the Defense Department demanded that landlords around military bases treat all service personnel equally in accepting their applications for housing. In 1953 the Supreme Court ruled that restrictive covenants in real estate transactions could not be enforced; and two years later the Interstate Commerce Commission banned segregation on all interstate trains and buses and in public waiting rooms. In 1956 the federal district court declared laws segregating bus passengers in Alabama unconstitutional.

Southern states had found many ways to deny blacks the franchise, permitting whites to control local politics even in areas where blacks were in the majority. Some states excluded Negroes from voting by requiring them to interpret the state or federal Constitution. In practice few blacks were able to provide white registrars with satisfactory answers, although the replies of almost illiterate whites were usually accepted. Presidents Truman and Eisenhower called on Congress to enact civil rights legislation to protect the franchise. However, it was not until 1957 that lawmakers, over the strong objections of Southerners, finally enacted broad legislation designed to guarantee blacks the right to vote.

This law provided for a Commission on Civil Rights, authorized an additional Assistant Attorney General to deal with civil rights matters, and declared illegal any threat or intimidation designed to prevent anyone from exercising his right to vote. Although the Civil Rights Act of 1957 appeared a major advance in protecting the constitutional rights of blacks, the tactic of barring registration continued to keep many away from the polls. In 1960 Congress passed legislation which, under certain conditions, permitted judges to appoint referees to assist Negroes to register and vote. But the question of civil rights persisted because of the continuing gap between what the laws provided and the conditions experienced by blacks.

Meanwhile, the struggle for equality had assumed a new, more promising form in December, 1955, when Mrs. Rosa Parks, a black seamstress in Montgomery, Alabama, refused to give up her seat in a crowded city bus and went to jail. Formerly any such defiance of the white community had been rendered ineffective by divisions and passivity within the ranks of the blacks themselves. But in this racial confrontation over an old Jim Crow law, the blacks, led by the intelligent and courageous young black minister Dr. Martin Luther King, Jr., conducted a successful boycott of the bus system. After a year of walking, the Negroes won their fight for the abolition of segregation on buses. By the time that the United States Supreme Court, late in 1956, had declared segregation on municipal buses unconstitutional, the movement had spread to other Southern cities. In the Montgomery crisis, King perfected his strategy of civil disobedience through peaceful resistance.

Black students, adopting this new strategy, now attacked segregation in Southern restaurants and public facilities. They resorted to sit-ins, marches, picketing, and boycotts. In February, 1960, four students from the Negro Agricultural and Technical College at Greensboro, North Carolina, sat down at a lunch counter restricted for whites with the determination to remain until the management either served them or shut down. So effective was the sit-in in bringing pressure on restaurant owners that the tactic spread to other regions of the South. The sit-in, added to the picket lines and economic boycotts, soon brought a wide variety of private segregated businesses to terms. This assault on segregation invited the support of such Negro organizations as the National Association for the Advancement of Colored People (NAACP), the Congress of Racial Equality (CORE), King's new Southern Christian Leadership Conference (SCLC), as well as the Student Nonviolent Coordinating Committee (SNCC). These organizations trained young blacks for sit-in protests, instructing them in nonviolent techniques.

Still the price of success came high, for many businessmen fought back with toughs and police; some even preferred bankruptcy to concession. Then in May, 1961, James Farmer, national director of CORE, took a group of "freedom riders" by bus through Virginia, the Carolinas, Georgia, and Alabama to challenge segregation in interstate bus terminals. In Alabama they faced violence and mob reprisals, but eventually, with federal protection, they ended segregation in the Birmingham bus terminal. This technique of invading segregated facilities soon attracted support from white sympathizers throughout the North, who joined freedom rides in the South to face jail sentences. In the summer of 1961 the national black organizations spent over $300,000 to defray the legal expenses of those arrested.

By 1962 the civil rights assault focused on the schools and universities of the South. Many Southern universities began to admit black students in limited numbers. At the University of Mississippi, James H. Meredith broke the color bar, but only after mob violence produced death and destruction and federal troops had entered the scene to protect him. In the public schools of the South, segregation remained the rule. Although President Eisenhower had sent federal troops to Little Rock in 1957 to enforce integration, his dramatic action had little long-range effect in breaking down school segregation. In 1964 only 2.1 percent of the black students in eleven Southern states attended integrated schools.

Legal pressure brought some token desegregation, but White Citizens Councils and the Ku Klux Klan continued to determine the status of race relations in many Southern communities. Each summer after 1961 civil rights workers, largely students from Northern colleges, entered the South to further the cause of desegregation and to aid in voter registration. This continued civil rights pressure sparked violence in such cities as Birmingham, where one Sunday morning a bomb killed four black children in church. In the summer of 1964 three civil rights workers were killed in Mississippi. Later the local sheriff, his deputy, and others were brought to trial for these slayings. Several of the group received long prison sentences. Despite setbacks and the generally slow pace of change, especially in school desegregation, the civil rights movement, using methods of moderate confrontation which placed segregationists at a moral and legal disadvantage, revealed increasing strength. During the summer of 1963 the March on Washington brought over 100,000 blacks and whites to that city in the largest public demonstration in the nation's history. Martin Luther King addressed the huge throng as it stretched down the mall from the Lincoln Memorial toward the Washington Monument.

By the mid-1960s a growing number of blacks had concluded that the white community did not intend that they should have social, political, or economic equality. Blacks could no longer believe the theory that patience and restraint on their part would be rewarded with genuine acceptance and equal treatment. Riots in black neighborhoods reflected the frustration, impatience, and bitterness felt by many. A minority of blacks called for violent action.

Despite continued discrimination in employment and segregation in housing and education, many Negroes made substantial social and economic gains in the postwar generation. In sports, entertainment, higher education, government, business, and the armed services, the walls of discrimination cracked if they did not crumble. Blacks starred in professional baseball, football, and basketball, others achieved national recognition in music, literature, art, education, and public service. Willie Mays was one of the greatest of postwar baseball players. Ralph Bunche was a successful mediator for the United Nations in the Middle East. In 1967 President Johnson appointed Thurgood Marshall as the first Negro ever to sit on the Supreme Court. Among the nation's black mayors in the late sixties was Charles Evers of Fayette, Mississippi. Gwendolyn Brooks became a Pulitzer prize-winning poetess; Sidney Poitier won fame as an actor; Leontyne Price gained recognition as one of the true greats of opera; W. E. B. Du Bois and John Hope Franklin emerged as two of the country's leading historians; James Baldwin and Ralph Ellison achieved distinction as writers. It was not that blacks made no progress; the continuing problem as late as 1970 was that progress and change did not keep pace with rising economic expectations and the growing demands for equality and social justice. Racism persisted to such a degree that even notable blacks faced discrimination and lack of full acceptance.

Americans had always been keenly interested in education, but in no period were they so concerned about the quantity and quality of their schools as in the years after 1945. Education promised higher incomes, social progress, and the good life. Between 1950 and 1966, elementary, secondary, and college enrollments jumped from 29.7 million to 55.9 million, an increase of nearly 87 percent. By the 1960s more than one-fourth of the population was enrolled in the nation's schools. While expansion occurred at all levels, the greatest relative increase took place in the nation's colleges and universities. The number of college students more than doubled between 1950 and 1967, reaching nearly seven million.

Besides increased enrollments, education responded to greatly expanded federal aid, efforts toward racial integration and emphasis upon a more rigorous curriculum. Progressive education, which emphasized life adjustment rather than courses with basic factual material, came under bitter attack. Hundreds of articles and scores of books criticized both the philosophy and content of much of the education being offered in the nation's high schools and colleges. These writings assailed the programs of teacher training, usually controlled by colleges or departments of education. One of the most controversial critics of progressive education was Arthur Bestor, a University of Illinois history professor, whose book *Educational Wastelands* (1953) aroused heated arguments both inside and outside the profession. Bestor declared that schools were wasting time on nonessentials, that they should emphasize basic academic subjects such as the natural sciences, mathematics, English, and history. Following the launching of the Russian space satellite in 1957, many people charged that the United States had fallen behind the Soviets because of inadequate training in science, mathematics, and engineering. This event, said Admiral Hyman G. Rickover, a critic of the schools, finally produced a popular demand for educational reform.

Several significant developments emerged during the 1950s from the controversies over the nature and quality of the nation's school system. Colleges and universities strengthened their teacher-training programs, schools introduced more rigorous courses, colleges raised their entrance requirements and improved their facilities. Finally, Americans began to spend much larger sums on education. Between 1950 and 1966 expenditures for elementary, secondary, and higher education rose from approximately $8 billion to nearly $49 billion. Education had become big business and directly employed about 2.5 million persons.

Following World War II, the federal government greatly expanded its support of public education. Some people expressed fears of federal control, but most school districts, state colleges, and universities eagerly accepted any largesse which Congress might provide. The Servicemen's Readjustment Act of 1944, generally known as the "GI Bill of Rights," helped to finance the education of millions of veterans of World War II and subsequent conflicts. Although Congress defeated general school-aid bills during the Truman administration, lawmakers did establish the National Science Foundation in 1950. This agency controlled funds for scientific research in colleges and universities and for improvement in instruction, particularly in the natural sciences and mathematics.

President Eisenhower proposed modest programs of federal aid to education, but controversies over integration, assistance for private schools, and fear of national control helped to defeat his education measures. However, in 1958, after the Russians had launched Sputnik, Congress moved quickly to pass the National Defense Education Act. The NDEA provided loan funds for college students and money for graduate fellowships. It authorized programs to improve the teaching of science, mathematics, and foreign languages, and supported guidance and counseling programs. In 1963 Congress authorized funds for the construction of higher educational facilities, and two years later a general federal aid measure provided assistance for a wide range of educational programs. By 1965 the federal government was spending nearly $6 billion for education in federally impacted areas—for school lunches, research, student assistance, and facilities. This represented about 15 percent of funds the nation spent on education.

Despite their heavy reliance on education as a means of solving man's problems, Americans considered themselves a religious people. A Gallup Poll in 1968 showed that 98 percent of the population believed in God, that nearly two-thirds were church members, and that 45 percent of the American people generally attended church. During the late 1960s church membership was up 15 percent over 1940, and the percentage of regular churchgoers had risen some 13 percent. In 1967 there were nearly seventy million Protestants, forty-six million Catholics, and about five million Jews. The religious statistics were quite impressive.

However, numbers belied the true condition of religion in postwar America. Many members had only a nominal interest in church membership; their level of participation was low. Every church roll listed names of people who seldom entered its doors; their financial support was either nonexistent or trifling. But church membership remained a mark of respectability, and, although belief in Hell declined—only 65 percent believed in Hell in 1968—many people appeared to view a casual church relationship as a necessary insurance for the hereafter (73 percent believed in a life after death). Growing secularism and materialism contributed to the lack of a dynamic faith among many churchmen. Science and technology, psychology and psychiatry, higher incomes, and government programs to care for the poor and underprivileged all seemed to make religion less necessary. Had not man arrived at the place where he could solve his own problems? Furthermore, the desires and demands of modern life tended to provide substitutes for traditional religious and church activities. Nominal churchmen increasingly found other activities to occupy their time and attention. When men did seriously consider their faith, many of them sought a peace-of-mind religion which offered palliatives rather than something requiring challenge or commitment.

Religion reflected internal doubts and controversies as well. Theological differences, continued disunity between Catholics and Protestants, dissensions within Protestantism and Catholicism, and disputes over the precise role of the church in modern society all created confusion and weakness. New studies in theology aroused shock and controversy. The book *Radical Theology and The Death of God* (1966), by Thomas J. J. Altizer and William Hamilton, produced a storm of protest from conservative as well as some liberal Christians. It emphasized the big gap between the radical theologians and most churchmen. Continued divisions in both Catholicism and Protestantism weakened the church's total influence. The Reverend Billy Graham attracted large crowds in the 1950s and 1960s as he denounced sin and called listeners to repentance in the tradition of Dwight L. Moody and Billy Sunday. Liberal Protestants meanwhile urged their churches to undertake a broad program of social action. Among Catholics were those who clung to the Church's ancient forms and beliefs, while more liberal communicants advocated some basic changes. For example, many Catholic churches substituted English for Latin in the Mass; by 1968 the controversy over birth control was the most divisive issue confronting Catholicism.

Many people feared that the Supreme Court dealt religion a harsh blow when it ruled against compulsory Bible reading and prayer in the public schools. In the *McCullom* case (1948) and in *Engle v. Vitale* (1962), the Court ruled that official promotion of religion in the public schools through a New York State Regents' prayer violated the First Amendment which forbids any "establishment of religion." Critics of the Court called for a constitutional amendment which would permit religious exercises in the public schools. However, this agitation soon declined. It was quite apparent that many of those who favored religious teachings in the schools attempted to consign to public education what they had failed to achieve at home or in church.

Although religion often represented form rather than substance in the postwar years, the institutional church made some notable advances in its ministry. The ecumenical movement was one of the most positive forces in Christendom by the 1950s. The National Council of Churches of Christ, formed in 1950, was another expression of growing unity. Besides the growing cooperation between Protestants and Catholics, a number of denominations merged their efforts. Churches provided much of the leadership for social reform at both the local and national level. Ministers and some lay leaders worked for peace, campaigned for civil rights, and battled for social justice. Catholic Archbishop Patrick A. O'Boyle, Methodist Bishop John Wesley Lord, and other leaders insisted that the voice of the church must be heard on the great issues of their time—that churches must be active in the world and among the people they allegedly serve. An increasing number of churchmen sought to relate their religion and the institutional church to the complex problems of society.

Science and Technology

Increasingly in the mid-twentieth century science and technology affected every American directly. Whether people benefited from scientific research in medicine or merely paid taxes to defray the cost of space exploration, they could not escape the radiating influence of science in their daily lives. Top physicists, chemists, biologists, and other scientists emerged as an intellectual elite before whom ordinary citizens stood in awe. Though the mysteries of science may have confounded the average person, most people recognized that the nation's defenses, health, economic advances, and general welfare depended to some degree on both research in pure science and the application of scientific knowledge to practical purposes. By 1964, the government, colleges, universities, and industry spent annually nearly

$19 billion on basic and applied research and development—a 300 percent increase in ten years.

Basic advances in science occurred in atomic energy, space exploration, oceanography, as well as health-related sciences. Achievements in pure science were highly important, but the average citizen was concerned especially with the practical applications of scientific discoveries. A host of new processes and products flowed from the country's scientific laboratories. These included atomic energy for peaceful purposes, synthetic fibers, new medicines, and electronic equipment. The digital computer, first invented in 1944, was one of the most revolutionary devices ever designed by man. Computers were able to perform amazing feats of memory and calculation. Transistors replaced vacuum tubes in the late 1950s, making possible smaller computers with a greater range of service. By the 1960s they were used to guide spaceships, keep track of plane reservations, and check federal income tax returns.

The remarkable implications of computers for industrial production and distribution became evident by the late 1960s when they were linked to automated machinery. Computers were used in some modern factories to decide what and how much to produce; to order materials and write checks to pay for them; to control billing, warehousing, and shipping. How would cybernetics, the science of computers, affect society? This question went unanswered in the minds of most Americans. Computers and automation undoubtedly reduced the need for human labor and would thus increase the amount of leisure time in American society. This inevitably required a reevaluation of man as a producer and brought into question the ethic which held that work was necessary and good. There was a strong possibility that, because of scientific advances, man would adjust to a lifetime of leisure. Individual self-fulfillment would not be found in one's job, but in the activities which he could create for himself.

The Arts, Literature, and Mass Culture

Widespread support for the fine arts emphasized the growing cultural interests of mid-twentieth-century Americans. With rising incomes and more leisure time, an increasing number of people had the time and money to enjoy cultural activities. The physical reflection of this renewed interest in culture could be seen all the way from New York to Los Angeles, as cities built new museums of art and centers for the performing arts. New York's Lincoln Center and the music center and art museum in Los Angeles were only two examples of what large cities might do to house a rich and burgeoning culture. Many cities, colleges, and universities added new facilities for the performing arts. By the 1960s there were abundant opportunities for millions to hear first-rate music, see a ballet, attend the theater, or enjoy painting and sculpture.

Increasing support for cultural activities came not only from wealthy individuals but from corporations, foundations, and the federal government. In 1964 President Lyndon B. Johnson held the ground-breaking for the John F. Kennedy Center for the Performing Arts in Washington, D.C. The President said that the Center, financed by Congress and expected to cost at least $46 million, would "symbolize our belief that the world of creation and thought are at the core of our civilization."

With support growing for the performing arts, many Americans agreed that the federal government should provide money for discovering and developing new talent, as well as assisting in the construction of cultural centers. The arts, they said, were being starved; this was inexcusable in a country of such great wealth. In January, 1965, President Johnson recommended the establishment of a National Foundation for the Arts and Humanities, similar in character to the National Science Foundation. He explained that the United States must "recognize and encourage those who can be pathfinders for the nation's imagination and understanding." Responding to this idea, which was not new, Congress passed the National Arts and Humanities Act in 1965. Among other things, it provided for federal grants to individuals and groups who were engaged in the creative and performing arts. Although Congress appropriated only $10 million for the first year, this legislation reflected a new appreciation and concern for artistic creativity in a nation which many critics considered to be overly materialistic.

Literature, as well as the creative arts, reflected at least to some extent the mind and culture of the American people. In the postwar years novelists presented a pessimistic picture of man and his society. A dominant literary theme centered around man's fight against the impersonal forces of society and his struggle to achieve an individual identity. Leading writers presented their characters as pawns completely controlled by circumstances, wallowing in self-pity, and seeking nothing beyond immediate gratification or perhaps escape through death. A pervasively rotten society was crushing man's humanity.

The still-living literary masters of the prewar years gave way to a new group of writers. Sinclair Lewis wrote no major work after World War II and died in 1951. Before his death in 1968, John Steinbeck never again reached the greatness which he had exhibited in *The Grapes of Wrath,* and Ernest Hemingway wrote only one more really successful novel, *The Old Man and the Sea* (1953), prior to his suicide in 1961. John Dos Passos continued to write into the 1960s, but he failed to achieve his earlier literary power and prominence. Unlike some of the other older writers, William Faulkner turned out important works until his death in 1962. Centering his stories around Southern social problems and race relations, he became, according to some critics, the nation's foremost novelist.

World War II provided the themes for some of the more widely read younger novelists. Norman Mailer's *The Naked and the Dead* (1948) and James Jones's *From Here to Eternity* (1951) dealt with the everlasting conflict between the individual soldier and impersonal military power. James Cozzens and Leon Uris also wrote about war and the unsettled postwar conditions. Other leading novelists included Robert Penn Warren, John Hersey, Saul Bellow, J. D. Salinger, James Michener, and James Baldwin, a leading black writer. There was a strong tendency among postwar novelists to rely heavily upon descriptions of violence, sex, drunkenness, dope addiction, and perversion to show how vile and meaningless man and society had become. Leaving nothing to the imagination, writers immersed their readers in details of physical sex. One literary critic observed in 1959 that "in the current novel all human drives and needs and activities must be channeled into sexual terms." In his *Tropic of Cancer,* recently published for the first time in the United States, Henry Miller carried erotic realism beyond all literary precedents and expressed a completely nihilistic view of life. Forceful as these novelists were, many of them seemed unable to find their own identity or to come to grips with the great central themes of man's existence.

Only a few playwrights achieved distinction. Eugene O'Neill continued his successes with such plays as *The Iceman Cometh* (1946) and *Long Day's Journey into Night* (1956). Tennessee Williams and Arthur Miller were among the younger dramatists who won national acclaim. Williams developed plots around violence, sex, and degeneracy, not unlike the themes found in popular novels. His *A Street Car Named Desire* (1947) and *Cat on a Hot Tin Roof* (1955) played to audiences in theaters across the country. Miller's magnificent *Death of a Salesman* enjoyed long runs in the late forties. Among the poets, Wallace Stevens and Robert Frost achieved high levels of excellence; in January, 1961, Frost read one of his poems at President Kennedy's inauguration. Whatever the quality of postwar literature, both fiction and nonfiction were much more widely read by the masses than ever before in history. The publication of books in cheap paperback editions and their sale in such a variety of outlets as drug and department stores and airport terminals made books easily available and within the financial reach of most people for the first time. Moreover, schools now required students to buy paperbacks to supplement their textbooks.

Nothing affected the cultural level of American society so much as the mass media—television, radio, movies, and advertising. Although television was invented before World War II, it was not until midcentury that home sets became widely available. By 1965 some 92 percent of the families had one or more receiving sets. Programs consisted largely of "soap operas," mystery stories, situation comedies, westerns, sporting events, and variety shows. Newcasts, documentaries, occasional plays and operas, and educational features in an otherwise mostly sterile schedule of programs gave the media some redeeming value. The three TV networks became a strong influence for conformity in thought and action. Except for FM broadcasting, radio programs consisted chiefly of the latest song hits played over and over for a growing teen-age audience. Heavy doses of advertising and inane chatter by disc jockeys made radio less entertaining than boring for most adults.

Poor films and competition from television hurt postwar movie attendance. But production of expensive spectaculars such as *The Ten Commandments* and *Cleopatra,* and family-type pictures such as *The Sound of Music* helped to restore some of the ground lost to TV. Producers next restored attendance by expanding the content of their films until by the 1960s they omitted scarcely anything in the human experience from the screen. Scenes of love and sex which left nothing to the imagination, prostitution, homosexuality, and violence were all portrayed with shocking reality. Neither nudity nor profanity were restricted on the screen. Pictures such as *Tom Jones; Ulysses; Blow-up; I, A Woman; Bonnie and Clyde;* and *Rosemary's Baby* reflected the newer standards in movie making. By 1970 movies appeared on television which could not have been seen in theaters by adult audiences twenty years earlier.

All art forms underwent striking changes. In the 1950s abstract expressionism became the principal form of American painting, best exemplified perhaps by the works of Jackson Pollock. But by the 1960s, painters such as Kenneth Noland and Frank Stella went even further in abandoning representation and imitation and emphasized bold and flashy colors painted in no special pattern or design. Pop art included everything from paint splashed on a canvas to the representation of a lawn mower, an abandoned automobile, or beer cans. "Soft Drum Set," a piece of pop art by Claes Oldenberg, was a combination of collapsed drums, broken drumsticks, and other parts of the drum set piled in seemingly haphazard disarray. By the 1960s many wondered what art really was. Any object, it seemed, was art if the critics and buyers so decreed.

Rock music characterized the 1960s in much the same way that jazz had done in the 1920s. Such artists as Chuck Berry had introduced rhythm and blues, better known as rock and roll, in the fifties, but it was the English influence of the Beatles and the Rolling Stones that led America into the furtively creative musical era of the sixties. The Beatle formula—electrical amplification, heavy bass work, and novel choral structures—permeated the American musical scene. The earlier styles of Elvis Presley and country-Western music could scarcely survive the impact. As Aaron Copland, the composer, said, "When people ask to recreate the mood of the sixties, they will play Beatle music." When the Beatles appeared on the Ed Sullivan TV show in 1964, their innovations had already triumphed. A writer in *Life* declared in 1969 that "the harmonics of today make the rock 'n rollers of the early 1950s sound as if they were Neanderthals working it out on hollow trees." Groups such such as the Beatles, the Doors, the Mothers of Invention, and the Blood, Sweat and Tears drew thousands of youths—one notable rock festival took place at Woodstock N.Y., in 1969—while record companies sold millions of their records. Some of the rock music expressed bitter protest and the discontent so prevalent among a large element of American youth. The folk songs of Joan Baez and the intonations of philosopher-singer Bob Dylan were especially popular among the rebellious younger set.

Alienation

The abundance of material things suggested that life in America was highly satisfactory. People not only had the necessities of existence but enjoyed a wide range of luxuries as well. There were unending sources of pleasure and recreation—spectator sports, travel, movies, parks, museums—to fill the increasing hours of leisure; and schools, churches, books, magazines, and newspapers supplied the needs of the mind and spirit. Yet American society was marked by an underlying sense of confusion, frustration, and dissatisfaction. For a dozen years or so following World War II, this discontent was less apparent as the nation concentrated on economic growth, fought a war in Korea, and strove to expand the social welfare programs. But when people—and especially young people—detected that the high standard of living did not erase social problems or quickly improve human relationships, they became increasingly critical of American institutions and values. By the 1960s they had subjected the quality of American life to severe attack.

America had become a seriously troubled nation. The number and seriousness of social problems seemed almost overwhelming. In 1967 nearly 27 percent of American marriages were ending in divorce; this reflected a growing instability in family life. Crime and juvenile delinquency were rising steadily; in many cities

Art in America: 1945–1970

Deriving his art from that of Surrealists such as Joan Miro and Yves Tanguy, Arshile Gorky developed a style in which personal forms dredged up from his mind were transcribed in paint on canvas, exhibiting representational elements but conceived in an abstract, spontaneous fashion.

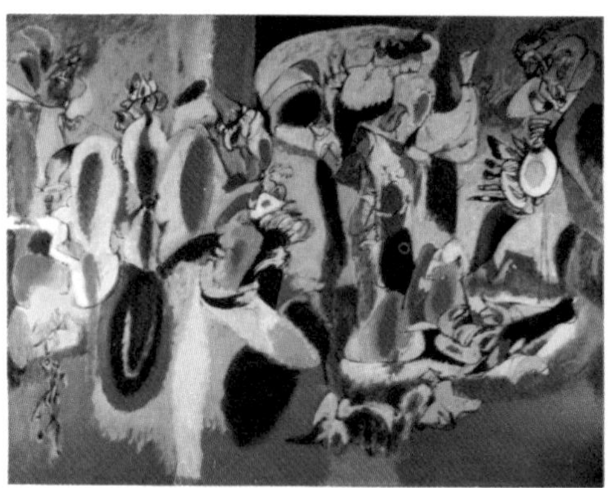

Arshile Gorky (1904–1948)
The Liver is a Cock's Comb, 1944, *oil on canvas*
Albright-Knox Art Gallery, Buffalo, New York. Gift of Seymour H. Knox

During and immediately following World War II, American art emerged as the primary aesthetic force on the international art scene. Artists in Europe and later in the Orient followed the trends set by leading American painters and sculptors, a tendency that still prevails.

The vital force in American art of the 1940*s and* 1950*s was abstraction. The investigation and exploration of abstract art took many exciting forms during the second decade of the twentieth century in Europe in the hands of painters such as Kandinsky, Malevich, and others, and many Cubist works approached abstraction in their concern for formal elements. These movements also included American followers, and a number of artists, Arthur Dove and Stanton MacDonald-Wright among them, produced counterparts of European abstraction. Nevertheless, abstraction in American art did not become really vital until its resurgence in the revolutionary work of Arshile Gorky in the mid-*1940*s, and at the end of that decade in the painting of Willem de Kooning, Jackson Pollock, and others. The phenomena which inspired this turn to abstraction were manifold and complex, ranging from the dream imagery of the Surrealists to the formalized, two-dimensional simplifications of Picasso, with much reinforcement by other European artists who came to America.*

The dominant trend in American abstraction of this period has been termed "Action Painting" or "Abstract Expressionism." Stylistically, the movement involved the use of broad, slashing strokes, with color laid on either with brilliant, kaleidoscopic chromatic ar-

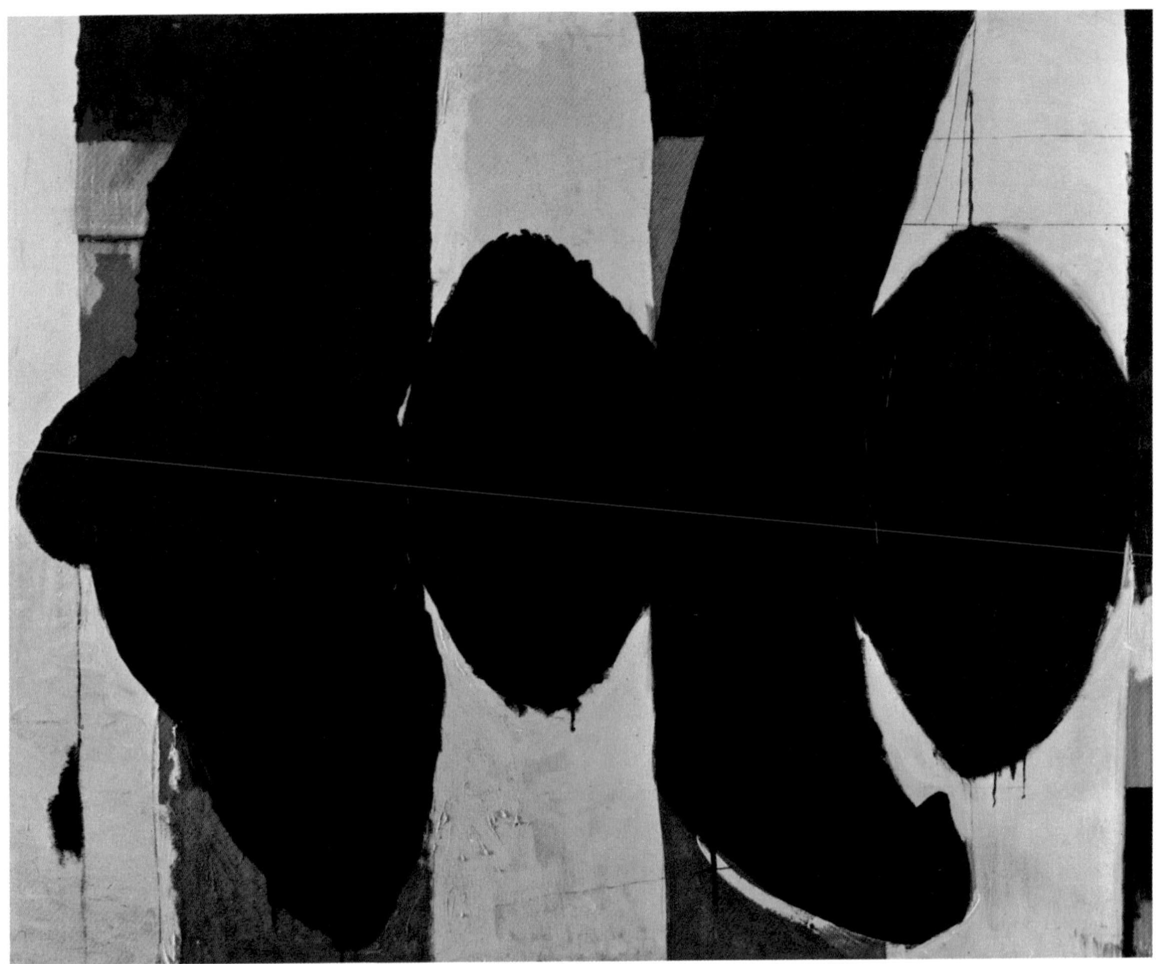

Robert Motherwell (1915–)
Elegy to the Spanish Republic XXXIV, 1953–1954, *oil*
Albright-Knox Art Gallery, Buffalo, New York. Gift of Seymour H. Knox.

The sombreness of Robert Motherwell's eloquent series of "elegies" to the Spanish Republic reflects both the dramatic nature of Spain and a reaction to the melancholy drama of the Spanish Civil War. The alternating verticals and ovals from a rhythmic procession across the canvas. All these works share a repudiation of three-dimensional illusionism, exhibiting instead a respect for the flat canvas and picture plane.

rangements or in deeply dramatic contrasts, sometimes only of black and white. Recognizable form all but disappeared, and the very activity of the artist and his emotional involvement with his medium became the message. The paint medium itself received primary emphasis, with the elimination of any suggestion of three-dimensional space and the appearance on the canvas of thick, paint impasto, often directly applied from the tube, the obvious appearance of the shape and stroke of the paint brush, sometimes the trickle of wet paint down the canvas, and in the case of Jackson Pollock, the use of direct flow and dripping of paint. Not all abstraction took this form, of course; the many varieties of abstract approach in-

cluded more lyrical works by artists such as William Baziotes, as well as "Abstraction Impressionism," geometric abstraction, and other tendencies. Contemporary sculpture also shared the abstract predilections of the painters: a new concern for open space and the relationships of solid form with this space emerged along with the introduction of movement and even sound into sculpture, particularly in the work of Alexander Calder.

Abstract Expressionism is still a major art form, but by the late 1950s, a reaction had set in, a reaction which took many forms. Still abstract is the work of the "color" artists who are concerned only with the effects of color, not the nature of the paint medium itself, and who often emphasize sharp, hard-edged color areas with an emphasis upon the optical, eye-jarring qualities of color relationships and contrasts, a movement known as "Op Art." Other artists deliberately reacted against abstraction, returning to visually recognizable images. "Pop Art" is perhaps the most famous of such reactions, emphasizing in sometimes witty and always cynical terms the mundane aspects of American middle-class culture—the advertisements, the billboards, the comic strip images with which we are all so familiar—taken out of context and monumentalized. Figure painting too, has once again reappeared as a major art form today, whether influenced by the vigorous brush work and color of the action painters, as in the West Coast school of Richard Diebenkorn, or continuing in the now classically realistic approach of Andrew Wyeth.

Andy Warhol (1931–)
Campbell's Soup Can with Peeling Label, 1962
Courtesy, The Leo Castelli Gallery, New York.

The best put-ons are those of Andy Warhol—painter, sculptor, film-maker, and celebrity—with his images of soup cans, coca-cola bottles, movie stars, and the like presented to us in a cynical, humorous way as "high art."

In the late 1940s, Willem De Kooning abandoned his semirepresentational figurative approach and created a series of black and white abstractions (left, above). The shapes and formal organizations of these works developed out of Cubism, but they exhibited a freedom, a painterly quality, and a dramatic richness alien to Cubist art. Subsequently De Kooning reacted against the elimination of color and created both abstractions and figurative paintings of slashing brush work and rich chromatic power. In the most famous of these, his series of "Women," he created a barbaric, horrific image of a monumental female (left, below). The ferociousness of the image is equivalent to that of his technique.

Above: Willem de Kooning (1904–)
Painting. 1948
Collection, The Museum of Modern Art, New York. Purchase.
Below: Willem de Kooning
Woman, I, 1950–1952
Collection, The Museum of Modern Art, New York. Purchase.

Until the last years of his life, Franz Kline remained within the limits of black and white abstraction. Here, even more than with De Kooning, the breadth and power of the paintbrush is apparent, as the artist builds up an architecture of black monolithic strokes against a white background.

Franz Kline (1910–   )
Mahoning, 1956, *oil on canvas*
Collection, Whitney Museum of American Art, New York.

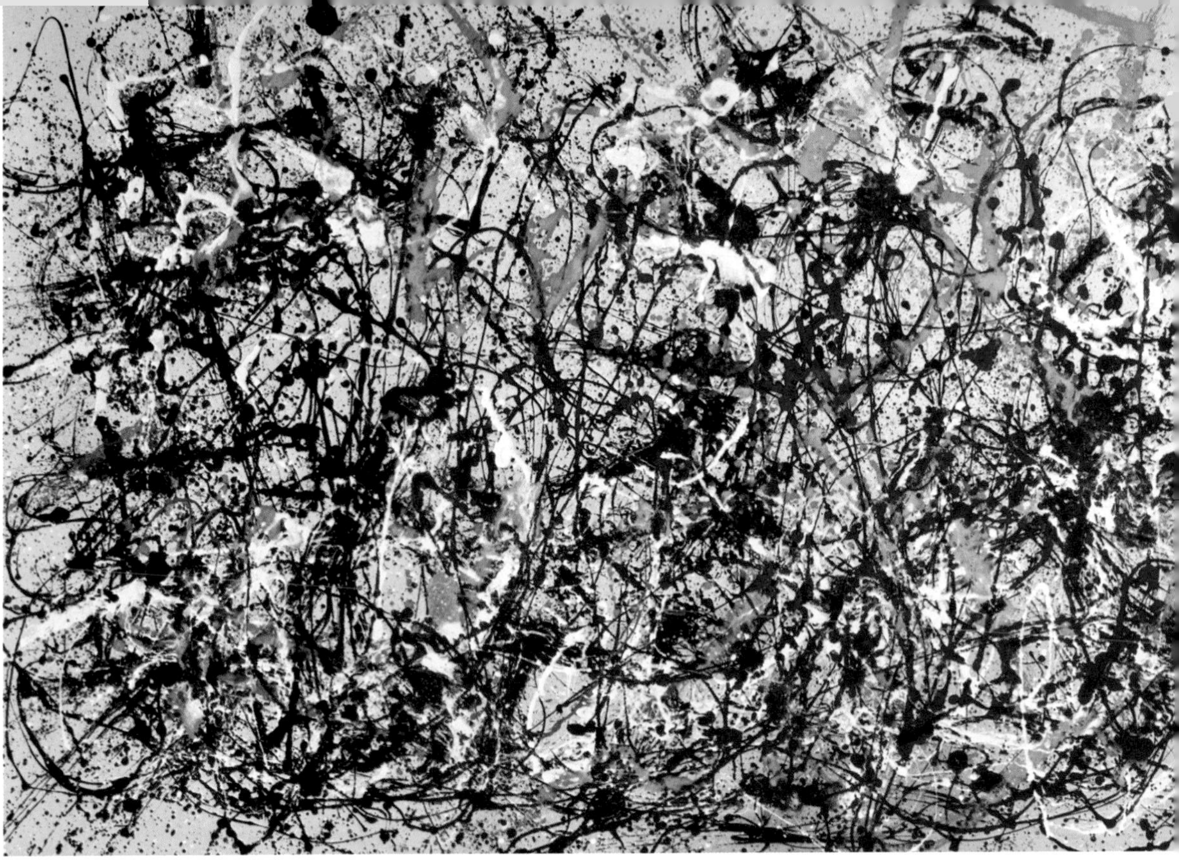

Jackson Pollock is probably the most internationally famous American artist of the mid-century. Like De Kooning, Kline, and Motherwell, he too at times worked only with black and white tones. In his most famous works, he poured and splattered the paint directly on the canvas, weaving endless rhythyms back and forth, creating a complex web involving the eye in a labyrinth of strands, basically controlled but with some accidental elements. Many of these paintings are enormous, and Pollock is one of the first artists to create environments which surround and incorporate the viewer in an intriguing, unfamiliar world.

Above: Jackson Pollock (1912–1956)
Autumn Rhythm, 1950, *oil on canvas*
The Metropolitan Museum of Art, George A. Hearn Fund, 1957.
Below: Jackson Pollock
Portrait and a Dream, 1953, *enamel on canvas*
Dallas Museum of Fine Arts. Gift of Mr. and Mrs. Algur H. Meadows and the Meadows Foundation, Inc.

Not all the Abstract Expressionists eschewed color: Hans Hofmann, for instance, expressed joy through the use of all the colors in the spectrum. His pictures have been likened to a lush garden in their coloration, but Hofmann is essentially an abstract humanist whose love of life is expressed in terms of the painter's medium—raw color, vigorous brush work, flat canvas.

Adolph Gottlieb forsook his earlier, mysterious hieroglyphs for a series of depictions of circular forms and bursts of color juxtaposed to one another. Still they are symbolic in some enigmatic way—of male and female, of cosmic entities, or of other possible meanings.

Above: Hans Hofmann (1880–)
The Pond
Collection, Richard Brown Baker, New York.
Right: Adolph Gottlieb (1903–)
Transfiguration #2, 1958, *oil*
Collection of Mrs. Harriet Weiner.

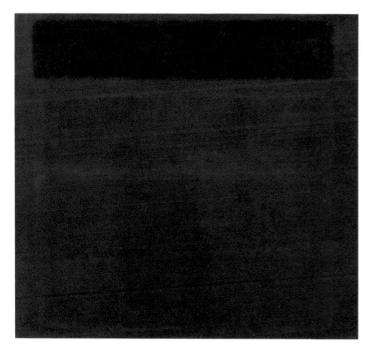

Softer, more diffuse color radiates from the paintings of Mark Rothko who creates walls of color, like Pollock's canvases environmental, but totally nonlinear. The glow of color in Rothko's work foreshadowed the color painters of the last ten years.

William Baziotes is one of several artists who created abstractions which sometimes took on archaeological, sometimes aquatic connotations. But instead of using dynamic action in his paint application, he creates a soft, poetic, and lyrical mood.

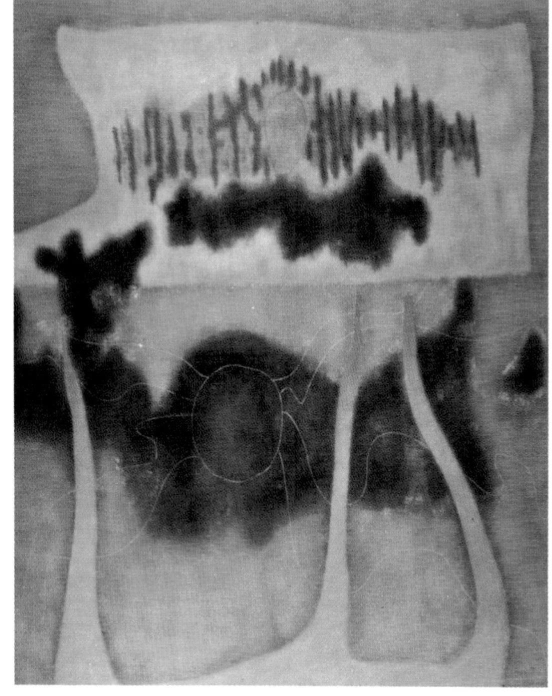

Above: Mark Rothko (1903–)
Red, Brown and Black, 1958, *oil on canvas*
Collection, The Museum of Modern Art, New York, Mrs. Simon Guggenheim Fund.
Right: William Baziotes (1912–)
Pompeii, 1955, *oil on canvas*
Collection, The Museum of Modern Art, New York, Mrs. Louise Smith Fund.

David Smith (1912–   )
Hudson River Landscape, 1951, *steel*
Collection, Whitney Museum of American Art, New York.

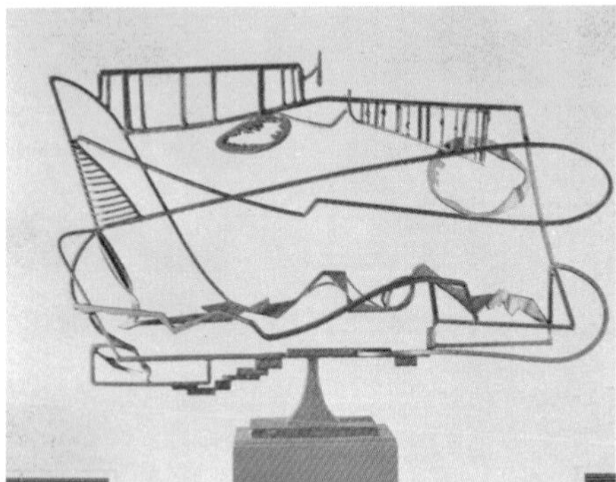

The Abstract Expressionist painters had their sculptural equivalents and the most famous among them has been David Smith. Smith's earlier abstractions involve interwoven linear patterns, equivalent to those in the paintings of Pollock, where lines not only constantly change but where these lines define contrasting abstract forms in space (above). Later, Smith moved on to monolithic, totemic images of powerful, solid masses of metal, in brilliant and powerful block form (right). Smith's work clearly demonstrates that in the last twenty years, sculpture has moved beyond its traditional range to incorporate landscape and still-life subjects.

David Smith, Cubi XXVII. *The Solomon R. Guggenheim Museum Collection.*

Until recently wood has been the major medium of Louise Nevelson. Her brooding and mysterious images created from both accidentally broken and found machine-made pieces, have gained new meanings as she has juxtaposed them. Diverse parts are sometimes harmonized by the application throughout of a soft, matte black black paint.

With Alexander Calder's work, movement and sound join the expected properties of sculpture. The juxtaposition of fragile lines and flat color elements in his mobiles suggests a sculptural equivalent of Miro's fantasies.

Alexander Calder (1898–)
Lobster Trap and Fish Tail, 1939, *mobile*
Collection, The Museum of Modern Art, New York.
Gift of the Advisory Committee.

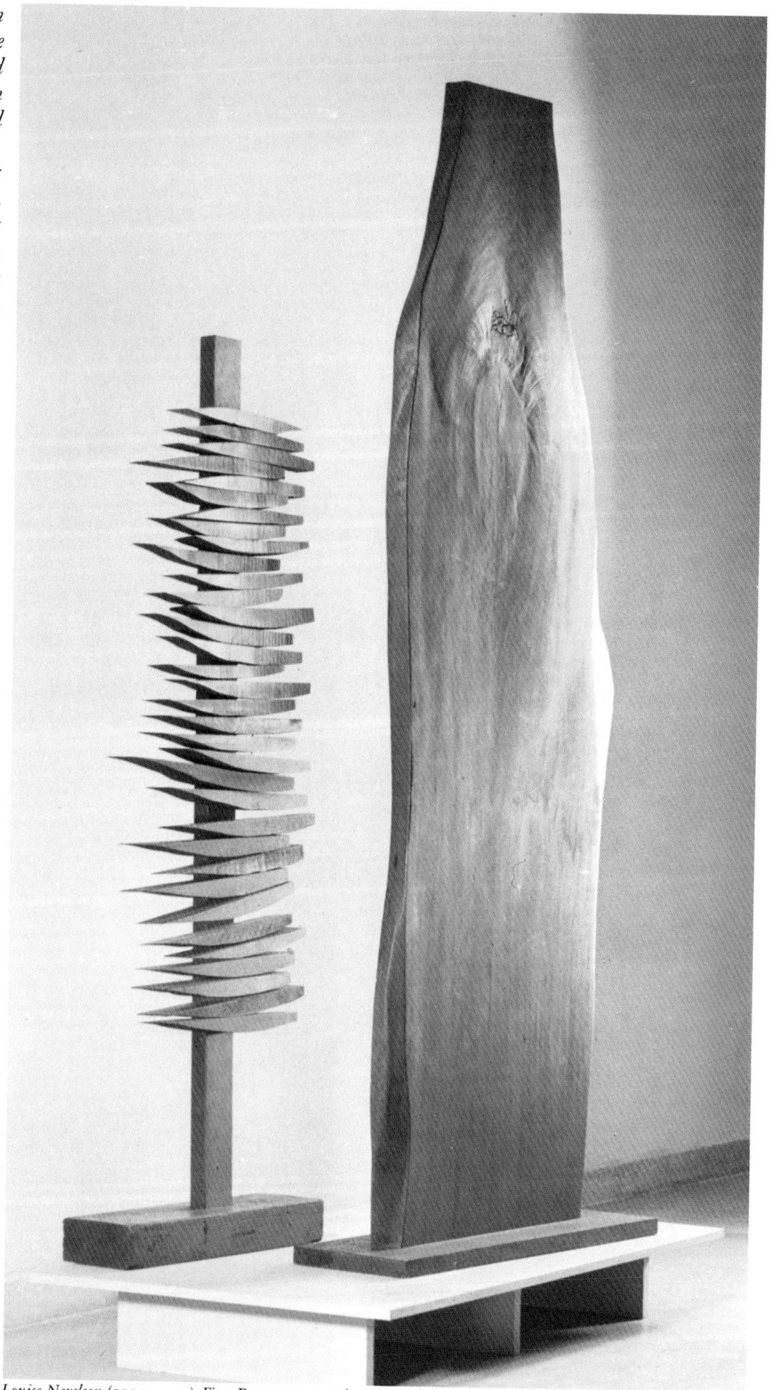

Louise Nevelson (1904–), First Personage, 1956 *or* 1957, *wood. The Brooklyn Museum, Dick S. Ramsay Fund.*

The more cerebral work of the geometric abstractionists, whose simplification of form and elimination of the nonessential belies a profound psychological and emotional effect, descends directly from Cubism. Josef Albers has created hundreds of paintings entitled "Homage to the Square" (left) in which the colors of three or four squares react upon one another and at the same time create the illusion of regression or of forward motion. A logical next step appears in the work of his pupil, Richard Anuskiewicz, the leading optical artist in America, whose rigidly geometric but daring color juxtapositions and mergings seem to accomplish impossible three-dimensional movements of colors back and forth from the picture plane.

Above: Josef Albers (1888–), Homage to the Square: "Ascending," 1953, *oil on composition board. Collection, Whitney Museum of American Art, New York. Right: Richard Anuskiewicz* (1930–), Manipest, 1965, *liquitex on board. The Newark Museum. Purchase* 1966, *Wallace M. Scudder Bequest.*

If Anuskiewicz's color patterns are complex, Ellsworth Kelly has taken color to the other extreme and monumentalized it by magnifying large, color areas of brilliant hue enshrined for their own sake (right, above). He achieves power through minimalization. Another approach to color appears in the work of the Washington Color School and its finest practitioner, Morris Louis (right, below). Characteristically this group of artists uses stripes, bands, or veils, sometimes opaque, sometimes transparent, vertically interrelating with each other.

Above: Ellsworth Kelly (1923–   ), Green, Blue, Red, 1964, *oil on canvas. Collection, Whitney Museum of American Art, New York. Right: Morris Louis* (1912–1962), Capricorn, 1960–1961. *Private Collection, Courtesy of Andre Emmerich Gallery.*

Although Abstract Expressionism reached its peak in the late 1950s, the color artists, the minimalists, and the optical painters proved that abstraction could be investigated in many new ways. On the other hand, one can also speak of a reaction to abstraction, though not, certainly, a "return" to the figure if that would suggest a recurrent traditionalism. Rather, representational art took on a new face, particularly among the "Pop" artists who, in fact, were influenced by the Abstract Expressionists in their raw color, the flatness of their images, and the power of the shapes that make up these images. A transitional figure, Jasper Johns presents us with everyday, familiar forms—targets, flags, maps, numerals—but uses a painterly approach which is exciting and amusing, at once familiar and yet mysterious (left). James Rosenquist is heir to commercial advertising but his strangely mixed images, blurred edges, and magnified scale suggest something hallucinatory and surreal (above). Roy Lichtenstein, the master of the magnified comic strip with his giant ben-day dots, is never so effective as when he parodies the Abstract Expressionists and their brush work (left, below).

Left: Roy Lichtenstein (1923–　　), Little Big Painting, 1965. *Collection, Whitney Museum of American Art, New York. Left, above: Jasper Johns* (1930–　　), Target with Four Faces, 1955, *mixed media. Collection, The Museum of Modern Art, New York. Gift of Mr. and Mrs. Robert C. Scull. Top: James Rosenquist* (1933–　　), Silver Skies, 1962. *Courtesy, The Leo Castelli Gallery, New York. Collection, Mr. and Mrs. Robert C. Scull.*

"Pop" sculpture also exists, notably at the hands of Claes Oldenburg, whose garishly colored giant hamburgers (below) take on a new reality while preserving the humor of "Pop." Of late, he has moved on to soft, vinyl, everyday images—typewriters, electric fans—and to monuments so gigantic that they almost equal "Pop" architecture. Not really an artist of this movement but often related to it, George Segal creates white, plaster Everyman images, figures engaged in mundane, everyday activities (right). Segal is divorced from "Pop" in the sense of loneliness and melancholy he achieves: part of this inheres in his medium, part in his subjects, and part in his compositions and interpretations.

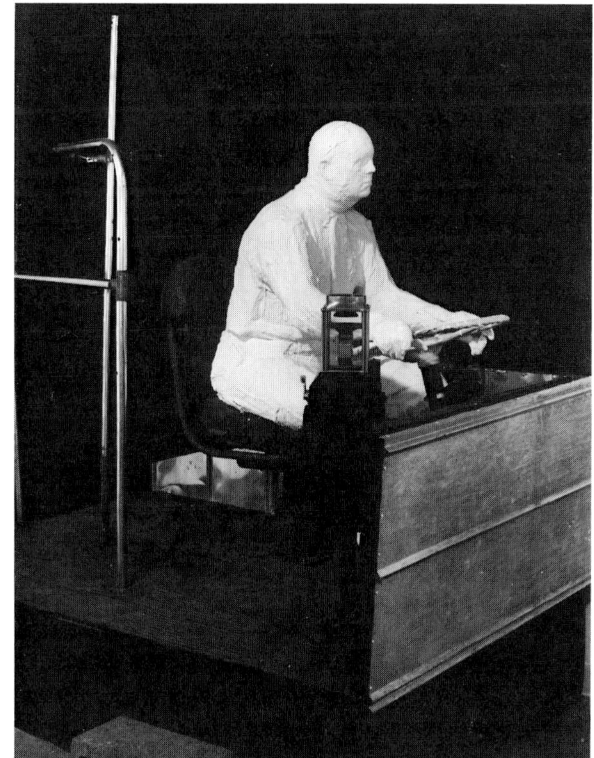

Above: George Segal (1924–) Bus Driver, 1962, *figure of plaster over cheesecloth, bus parts, Collection, The Museum of Modern Art, New York, Philip Johnson Fund. Below: Claes Oldenburg* (1929–), Dual Hamburgers, 1962, *painted plaster. Collection, The Museum of Modern Art, New York, Philip Johnson Fund.*

Richard Diebenkorn (1922–), Girl With Cups, 1957, *oil on canvas*
Collection, Richard Brown Baker, New York.

Once a highly able and successful West Coast Abstract Expressionist, in the late 1950s Richard Diebenkorn divorced himself from that movement to paint figurative works while still utilizing the expressive techniques of his earlier style (left). In fact, along with David Park and Elmer Bischoff, he was and is one of the leaders of a whole new group of West Coast figure painters. Throughout the artistic revolutions of the last twenty years, however, more traditional, detailed, and realistic approaches to painting have by no means disappeared. In fact, the haunting emotionalism of Andrew Wyeth (below), certainly the most famous and best-loved living American painter, reminds us not only of the heritage of American painting but of its incredible diversity.

Andrew Wyeth (1917–), Christina's World, 1948, *tempera on gesso panel*
Collection, The Museum of Modern Art, New York, Purchase.

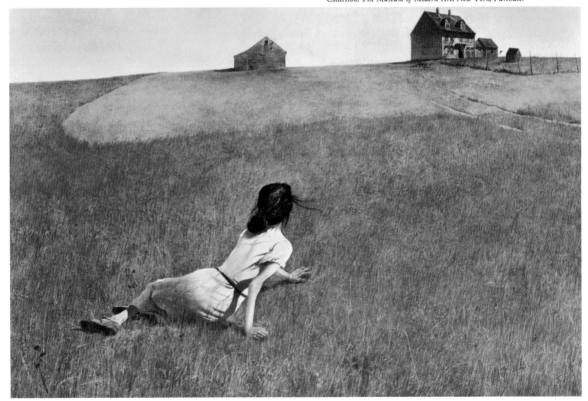

the streets were unsafe at night. Alcoholism grew at an alarming rate; by 1967 more than 6 million Americans were classed as alcoholics. Mental illness, some of it associated with alcoholism, rose with the growing tensions of modern life. Hospitals and outpatient clinics were clogged with disturbed and worried people. In the 1960s personal experimentation with hallucinatory drugs shocked and dismayed citizens who saw danger in such behavior. Added to these and other matters were the controversies and conflicts over race relations and civil rights.

If society's problems were not enough, many people experienced increasing frustration as they searched in vain for individual meaning and identity. The pressures of conformity, critics said, were crushing individualism; Americans were becoming a "nation of sheep." Mass production turned out standardized goods; few could escape the conformist influences of television, radio, newspapers, and advertising. Students in large universities complained that they were no longer individuals but only numbers fed into the computers. Every American taxpayer found that he had become a cipher in the great computer bank maintained by the Internal Revenue Service. Was modern man becoming just a "thing," a robot-like cog in a great impersonal machine known as twentieth-century society? Many people thought so. In *The Lonely Crowd* (1950), sociologist David Riesman suggested that people responded to a wide variety of impersonal mass values, and Vance Packard explained in *The Hidden Persuaders* (1957) how experts manipulated public thinking through mass communications and motivational research.

By the late 1950s a group of young Americans began to assail the complacency of their elders. They attacked society for its materialism, its stifling conformity, and its failure to achieve genuine equality and justice. The first stage of youthful unrest centered around the "beatnik" movement of the fifties, led by such critics as Jack Kerouac and Allen Ginsberg. The beatniks sought individualism in their appearance—long hair, beards, old clothes, and sandals. To find complete self-expression they turned to a new form of writing, unintelligible to most people. This first phase of the so-called bearded rebellion soon declined and nearly disappeared, in part at least because its leaders grew older, in part because large numbers of concerned young people were attracted to the personality and program of John F. Kennedy.

Still youthful discontent became much more widespread in the 1960s and now assumed a variety of forms. Dissatisfied with simple criticism, young Americans set out to participate in the process of social change. They worked and marched for civil rights, helped in Negro registration drives, worked in the slums, and joined the Peace Corps. Vigorously opposed to the war in Vietnam, others attacked what they considered unjust and unwise foreign policies and the growing industrial-military complex at home. From New York to Berkeley, college students complained about what they called irrelevant education and resisted control by faculty and administrative authorities. Disturbances on the University of California Berkeley campus in late 1964 disrupted normal academic work and resulted finally in the dismissal of President Clark Kerr.

Behind the youthful revolt was the profound gap between profession and behavior, the ideal and the real, in American society. Many young people objected to what they considered fundamental contradictions, double standards, and hypocrisies common to both personal and national life. They criticized poverty amidst plenty, hunger amidst abundance. Why, they asked, did the older generation, which required two stiff drinks before dinner, get so up-tight about the use of marijuana? They scoffed at a religion whose sanctimonious members practiced racism and discrimination. They failed to understand why many of their elders, who often cheated in marital relations, got so hung up over the more liberal and open sexual freedom practiced by many young people. How could professions of peace, they asked, be squared with the Vietnam war?

Some young people—many from affluent homes—called for basic change in the direction of American life. They attacked competitiveness, status, conformity, the educational and religious institutions, and capitalism—the entire establishment. Students for a Democratic Society (SDS), the W. E. B. Du Bois Clubs, and a variety of other radical, left-wing groups sought to confront, and hopefully to destroy, the power structure. A multitude of underground or radical newspapers blossomed across the country to articulate the attack on American institutions. The less radical called for change in the traditional American way but nevertheless insisted on more rapid social, economic, and political progress. Young people as a whole had a deep sense of immediacy. As the president of the City College of New York declared: "This generation has no utopia. Its idea is the Happening. Let it be concrete, let it be vivid, let it be personal. Let it be *now*." Some youths gave up completely on American society. They dropped out of college, forsook jobs, and abandoned all responsibility. From their numbers the so-called hippies congregated in such places as the Haight-Ashbury district of San Francisco, and parts of New York City, to build a conformity of their own around shaggy hair, dirty clothes, aimlessness, and often the taking of drugs. One of their patron saints was former Harvard Professor Timothy Leary, a frequent user of LSD, who told students to "turn on, tune in, and drop out."

That there had been a postwar "sexual revolution" was widely assumed by the 1960s. Following the publication of Alfred C. Kinsey's *The Human Male* (1948), however, a spate of studies appeared on the sex habits of the American people. To the surprise of many laymen, who seemed to believe that sexual morality had reached a new low, authorities on the subject concluded that if any sexual revolution had taken place it was in sexual attitudes rather than in sexual behavior. There was somewhat more permissiveness among both men and women, but the increasing amount of premarital sex was confined largely to partners who planned to marry. Most researchers did not believe there was a substantial increase in promiscuity. True, the "pill" permitted greater sexual freedom among both the married and the unmarried.

But the older generation was equally concerned over the growing use of drugs by college and high school youth. Not only did young people use the traditional drugs, such as marijuana, but many turned to psychedelic drugs. Despite the possibility that the use of LSD might produce permanent mental or emotional damage, many young people experimented with hallucinatory drugs. These, they said, expanded their sensitivity, deepened their emotions, and sharpened their imagination. The use of marijuana rose rapidly after World War II. By the 1960s some authorities estimated that as many as 30 to 50 percent of students on many college campuses had tried "pot" at least once. This situation brought demands for a new look at the laws governing the sale and use of marijuana.

Much of the nation's unrest scarcely touched that generation of Americans which had come through the Great Depression and World War II reasonably content with its affluent, comfortable society. Those who had been poor in the 1930s and had become prosperous in the 1950s and 1960s identified their success with adherence to traditional values—hard work and careful attention to a job, business, or profession. Having escaped poverty, they were not ashamed of their comfortable circumstances. For them security was more important than challenge or experimentation. Many of the restless and dissatisfied sons and daughters of these middle-, upper-middle-, and upper-class homes had never known want or poverty. Consequently, they could not understand their parents' emphasis upon money, status, and work. Parents, on the other hand, could not understand how some of their children could be so indifferent, even hostile, to such practical things as a formal education and preparation for a job. The generation gap was not without precedent, but never had it ever been so great as in the 1960s.

Yet despite all the attention given to restless and nonconformist youth in the 1960s—college dropouts, drug users, revolutionaries, and critics generally—their number was relatively small. Perhaps the radical appeal was limited even on college campuses because American society was better than many critics would admit. The new technology had freed men from the drudgery of labor and given them more leisure; rising educational levels permitted men to escape the darkness and conformity of ignorance; and expanding economic opportunity and higher incomes gave people a greater choice of work and recreation. Indeed, there were more opportunities for personal fulfillment than ever before. Still the youthful critics had claimed correctly that the quality of American life had scarcely approached the possibilities embodied in the nation's wealth, its intelligence, its vast and expensive educational system, and its dreams.

Conclusion

By the mid-twentieth century, the United States economy was capable of producing an abundance for everyone. The American standard of living was unexcelled anywhere in the world. However, too many people remained poor. The solution to this contradiction lay not in enlarged production, but in better distribution. In the 1960s some economists and social critics advocated a minimum annual income guaranteed for everyone by the federal government. Although initially this seemed a radical solution for lifting low-income families out of poverty, an increasing number of people came to support some variation of this principle.

Even the suggestion of a guaranteed annual income emphasized how far the United States had moved in the direction of providing security and a decent standard of living for its citizens. The role of both state and national government, particularly the latter, had been expanding for many years, but after World War II government increased its functions even more rapidly to meet the changing conditions of a highly industrialized and urbanized society. Welfare programs, distribution of food, federal aid to education, unemployment insurance, federal health measures, and other programs all illustrated the national concern for security and welfare. The United States by the 1950s had reached the state where it could eliminate poverty and insecurity for everyone who wanted a better standard of living. This was no longer a question of capability but rather one of national choice. It seemed clear that the United States could achieve this objective within the framework of traditional American democracy through the combined efforts of private enterprise, government, and individual initiative.

The most crucial, unsolved domestic problem in the second half of the twentieth century lay in the field of personal and social relations. Would the minority groups, particularly blacks, be fully accepted by the white majority and brought into the mainstream of American economic, social, and intellectual life? The segregation of minorities in the center of the great cities had aggravated and complicated this problem. That there had been considerable progress in race relations was obvious enough. But during the 1960s black Americans demanded more rapid change in the attitudes and actions of white people.

SUGGESTED READINGS

For general accounts of the rapid and fundamental changes in American postwar society see all or parts of John Brooks's *The Great Leap: The Past Twenty-five Years in America* (1966); Eric F. Goldman's *The Crucial Decade—And After: America, 1945–1960** (1961); and F. L. Allen's *The Big Change** (1952) and George Mowry's *The Urban Nation, 1920–1960* (1965). Two excellent documentary volumes are R. L. Watson's *The United States in the Contemporary World, 1945–1962* (1965) and Ernest R. May's *Anxiety and Affluence: 1945–1965* (1966).

On economic growth and the developing affluence in the United States see T. C. Cochran's *The American Business System: A Historical Perspective, 1900–1955** (1957) and H. G. Vatter's *The U.S. Economy in the 1950's: An Economic History** (1963). J. K. Galbraith's *The Affluent Society** (1958) argues that more of the country's resources should be channeled into education and other social services. David M. Potter's *People of Plenty: Economic Abundance and the American Character** (1954) is exceptionally perceptive in exploring the meaning of economic abundance in its historical context. The most convenient source of data on rising national and individual incomes can be found in the *Economic Report of the President,* published annually since 1946, and the U.S. Bureau of the Census's *Consumer Income,* Series P-60, No. 53, December 28, 1967.

The general ups and downs of the economy can be traced in A. H. Hansen's *The Postwar American Economy: Performance and Problems** (1964). Changing attitudes toward large corporate enterprise have been discussed by A. A. Berle in *Power without Property: A New Development in American Political Economy** (1959) and his *The 20th Century Capitalist Revolution** (1954), which is much less critical of corporate bigness than some of his earlier works. Another work friendly to large-scale business organization is D. E. Lilienthal's *Big Business: A New Era* (1953). A further analysis of the large corporation and its place in postwar American economic life is W. L. Warner's *The Corporation in the Emergent American Society* (1962). The editors of *Fortune* give an optimistic view of the future of the American economy in *America in the Sixties: The Economy and the Society* (1960). R. L. Heilbroner and P. L. Bernstein have described the role of the government in the economy in *A Primer on Government Spending** (1963). Avery Leiserson has edited an excellent volume, *The American South in the 1960s** (1964), which considers the special problems of that region.

Max Lerner has provided a thoughtful commentary on American life in *America as a Civilization: Life and Thought in the United States Today** (2 vols., 1957). In *This U.S.A.: An Unexpected Family Portrait of 194,067,296 Americans Drawn from the Census* (1965), Ben I. Wattenburg has brought together a vast amount of information on the American people from the 1960 census. *The Hidden Persuaders** (1957) by V. O. Packard emphasizes how advertisers and promoters manipulate the American people, while W. H. Whyte's *The Organization Man** (1956) stresses how large businesses mold their employees to fit the corporate image. *The Lonely Crowd: A Study of the Changing American Character** (1950) by David Riesman and others shows how individuality is being curbed in a mass culture. Some of the most important problems facing America in the postwar years have been explored in *Prospect for America: The Rockefeller Panel Reports* (1961). On the problems of cities and ideas for urban planning see Jane Jacobs's *The Death and Life of Great American Cities** (1961). The continued ethnic makeup of one American city has been explored by Nathan Glazer and D. P. Moynihan, in *Beyond the Melting Pot: The Negroes, Puerto Ricans, Jews, Italians, and Irish of New York City* (1963). Aspects of the flight to the suburbs have been suggestively traced in R. C. Wood's *Suburbia: Its People and the Politics** (1959).

Poverty has been discussed in Michael Harrington's *The Other America: Poverty in the United States** (1962); B. H. Bagdikian's *In the Midst of Plenty: A New Report on the Poor in America** (1964); H. P. Miller's *Rich Man, Poor Man** (1964); and in the Conference on Economic Progress's *Poverty and Deprivation in the U.S.: The Plight of Two-fifths of a Nation* (1962). In contrast to the poor, America's richest people have been considered extensively in *The Rich and the Super-rich* (1968) by Ferdinand Lundberg.

Critics of postwar education include Arthur Bestor's *Educational Wastelands* (1953) and H. G. Rickover's *Education and Freedom** (1959), both of whom argue that the schools should place more emphasis on solid academic studies and abandon life-adjustment curricula. Other useful and less controversial works include *A Report to the President* (1956) by the Committee for the White House Conference on Education; Brand Blanshard (ed.), *Education in the Age of Science* (1959); A. D. Morse's *Schools of Tomorrow—Today* (1960); and Mortimer Smith (ed.), *The Public Schools in Crisis* (1956). Problems in American colleges and universities have been described by David Riesman and Christopher Jenks in *The Academic Revolution* (1968) and in *The American University: How It Runs and Where It Is Going* (1968) by Jacques Barzun. Reed Sarratt has written an excellent account of the progress of desegregation in *The Ordeal of Desegregation: The First Decade* (1966). On recent trends in religion see E. S. Gaustad's *A Religious History of America* (1966); H. W. Schneider's *Religion in Twentieth Century America** (1952); Will Herberg's *Protestant, Catholic, Jew** (1955); and John Cogley (ed.), *Religion in America** (1958). For religious statistics consult the annual *Yearbook of Churches.*

For overall views of American society and culture see Bernard Rosenberg and D. M. White (eds.), *Mass Culture: The Popular Arts in America** (1957), and *Culture for the Millions: Mass Media in Modern Society** (1959) edited by Norman Jacobs and Paul Lazarsfeld.

* indicates availability in paperback.

41

Kennedy and Johnson

HAVING CONTROLLED the White House for eight years, the Republican party anticipated the 1960 election with misgivings. Dwight D. Eisenhower's personal luster had scarcely dimmed. Whatever the inadequacies of his administration—and amid the conditions of peace and prosperity they were not immediately apparent—none had injured his popularity. But it was clear that the Republican party had failed to turn the President's image into any genuine political gains. Republican Governor Theodore R. McKeldin of Maryland had reminded a Republican audience in February, 1957, that the party "hasn't a thing the country wants" except Eisenhower. The Eisenhower policies reflected the preferences of the moderates in American society. But those middle-of-the-road policies which seemed to answer the requirements of Eisenhower's huge consensus did not belong alone to the President or his party. They had been guided through Congress more by such Democratic leaders as Lyndon Johnson and Walter George than by congressional Republicans. Whatever Eisenhower's parliamentary successes, they belonged to the Democratic party as well as the Republican. The American people had elected and sustained Eisenhower as a national, not a party, leader. Now millions who had lauded him would not hesitate, with his retirement, to return the White House to the Democratic party.

Richard M. Nixon had moved into a commanding position of leadership within the Republican party during his second term as Vice President. His office had provided him with experience as well as news coverage as he attended high-level conferences and embarked on official tours of the Far East, Latin America, and Europe. Perhaps no American had conversed with so many of the world's political and diplomatic leaders. His willingness to carry the campaign burden in 1954, 1956, and 1958, moreover, had won the approval of Republican party managers. Throughout his years in Eisenhower's shadow, Nixon had performed as an able and active public figure, learning and giving evidence of maturity and judgment. By early 1960, Republican spokesmen agreed generally that Nixon not only merited the party's nomination but also offered the greatest promise of electoral success in November. At Chicago in July, Nixon gained the nomination on the first ballot with scarcely an opposing vote.

Republican strategists at the convention made clear the pattern of campaigning which they intended to pursue. Congressman Walter Judd's keynote address recounted the alleged failures of the Democratic party in foreign affairs. Former New York Governor Thomas E. Dewey, continuing the assault on the Democratic past, lauded Nixon for his major contribution in shaping the Republican policies "which brought victory after victory for freedom in Iran, in Trieste, in Austria, in Lebanon, in Jordan, in Laos, in West Berlin, yes, and in Quemoy and Matsu and Formosa." This studied effort to gear the Republican campaign to the Eisenhower record in foreign affairs found confirmation in the nomination of Henry Cabot Lodge, Eisenhower's representative at the United Nations, for the vice presidency.

The Democratic party entered the campaign in its usual state of disarray. In part this reflected its majority status and its many divergent elements; in part it measured eight years outside the White House and the party's custom of engaging in open and vigorous internal struggle to determine its choice of candidate. Among the front-running Democratic contestants in 1960 were four Senators—John F. Kennedy of Massachusetts, Lyndon B. Johnson of Texas, Hubert H. Humphrey of Minnesota, and Stuart Symington of Missouri—as well as Adlai Stevenson, the still-popular Democratic nominee of 1952 and 1956. Kennedy's costly and well-organized campaign, managed effectively by his younger brother Robert, was already four years old. When the Massachusetts Senator formally announced his candidacy in early 1960, he was clearly in the lead with pledged support and a large, energetic, and dedicated political organization. At the opening of the Democratic Convention in Los Angeles early in July, Kennedy still enjoyed a commanding lead; he won on the first ballot. To placate the South on the issues of civil rights and his own Catholicism, Kennedy selected Senator Lyndon B. Johnson as his running mate.

Kennedy faced Nixon with one notable advantage: There were still seven or eight million more registered Democrats than Republicans. His task, therefore, consisted in casting the campaign as a struggle between parties on such traditional New Deal issues as farm policy and social security. He declared, "It is not a fight between Mr. Nixon and myself. We lead two parties, two forces, two sources of energy." At St. Louis, Kennedy accused Nixon of attempting to hide from his party's record. In short, Kennedy attempted to reconstitute, as completely as possible, the old Roosevelt coalition of Northern liberals and Southern conservatives, of farmers and laborers. He campaigned in the North on the Democratic record, while Johnson attempted to keep the South in line on civil rights. Facing the issue of his Catholicism frankly, Kennedy hoped to offset any losses on that score by capturing the many Catholics who had strayed into the Republican camp.

Republican success hinged on Nixon's ability to turn the campaign into a contest of personalities, not parties. It also called for a determined bid for the support of independents and fringe Democrats. Hence, Nixon asked the nation to ignore party labels and to seek the best man for the Presidency. Nixon had two assets —his own experience and his association with the Eisenhower administration. Throughout his campaign he concentrated on building an image of himself as a devoted, fearless, patriotic leader who could guide the nation through perilous times. Nixon was equally anxious to capitalize on his close association with the popular Eisenhower, eventually promoting the "Ike and Dick" theme. To enlarge this latter asset Nixon dwelt often and long on the Republican successes of the fifties.

Foreign affairs dominated much of the early campaigning, figuring prominently in the four television "debates" which the candidates staged before audiences estimated at seventy million viewers. These encounters were damaging to Nixon. Having anchored his campaign to personality, he engaged Kennedy in an arena where Kennedy's own quite remarkable personality and ready grasp of domestic and foreign affairs could neutralize Nixon's primary assets. Kennedy struck off the central theme in foreign affairs at St. Louis early in October: "If we are to protect our heritage of freedom, if we are to maintain it around the world, we must be strong—militarily, educationally, scientifically, and morally." Thereafter Kennedy pointed continuously to the alleged decline of American power and prestige around the world. He spoke freely of the "missile gap." Nixon countered by accusing Kennedy of "irresponsible attacks" on the President. Because neither candidate dared inform the country that it could not choose its own world, Kennedy came eventually, like the Vice President, to support most of the uncompromising United States postures of the past.

Throughout the campaign the attitudes of the American voter remained a mystery, largely because religion and personality are imponderables that do not lend themselves to precise measurement. Many voters influenced by religion refused to be questioned at all. Secondly, the TV debates tended to lessen party ties and caused people to think of competing personalities—not to Nixon's advantage. Thirdly, the increase and migration of population challenged established voting patterns and rendered prophecy almost impossible. Ultimately, Kennedy triumphed in a very close election because, like Roosevelt and Truman before him, he was able to capture the large cities by wide margins. He gained as much as 75 to 80 percent of the urban black vote, as well as a heavy majority among labor and minority groups. Kennedy's support among Catholic voters helped him carry several big states.

Kennedy had prepared studiously to meet the challenges of the 1960s. In accepting the party nomination in July he had told the nation: "The New Frontier is here whether we seek it or not . . . uncharted areas of science and space, unsolved problems of peace and war, unconquered pockets of ignorance and prejudice, unanswered questions of poverty and surplus." The Kennedy team was young. The average age of his Cabinet was less than forty-eight years, compared with fifty-seven for that of Eisenhower. Many of the Kennedy appointees were new to Washington. Whether recruited from the leading universities or from business, their outlook was intellectual. Besides Rusk as State, Kennedy selected former Ford Motor Company president Robert McNamara as Secretary of Defense; Douglas Dillon, a wealthy and able Republican banker, as Secretary of the Treasury; Arthur J. Goldberg, a distinguished lawyer and labor negotiator, Secretary of Labor. After some hesitancy, the President named his brother Robert to the Cabinet as Attorney General. Demanding much of those around him, Kennedy would create an administration noted for its energy and enthusiasm.

Kennedy, no less than Lincoln, was determined to assume primary responsibility for the decisions of his administration. He had been troubled by the appearance of flabbiness in Executive control under Truman and Eisenhower. The Cabinet, he thought, had grown too powerful; his predecessors too often had deferred to it as an institution and permitted its more ambitious members to assume excessive control of policy. The President, Kennedy believed, should govern with the advice, but not the consent, of his Cabinet. In order to expedite decisions, Kennedy abandoned many of the formal instruments of government, such as the full meetings of the Cabinet and the National Security Council; instead he worked in meetings with small groups of experts on policy questions.

In his inaugural the President asked for congressional cooperation to get the nation moving again. During his first weeks in the White House he flooded Congress with messages outlining an ambitious legislative program. They ranged from aid to depressed areas and expanded health insurance to foreign aid and defense. Normally such a program for social and economic betterment might have slipped quickly and easily through Congress. The Democratic majority in the Senate was 67 to 33; in the House, 257 to 178. But a bloc of conservative Northern Republicans and Southern Democrats, largely under the control of Representative Charles A. Halleck, the Indiana Republican, was powerful enough to sidetrack legislation in committee or on the floor. Congress passed administration requests for foreign aid, defense, and space exploration, as well as some minor poverty and housing measures. But the record of the first session of the Eighty-seventh Congress was spotted less with successes than with failures. Columnists criticised the President for limiting his leadership to rhetoric and proposals. During his second year the President fared little better. He did secure one major legislative triumph late that year—the Trade Expansion Act, which clothed the administration with powers to manipulate the tariff in the interest of freer trade with Europe.

Meanwhile, a new outbreak of racial strife raised the question of civil rights to a level of intensity demanding federal action. Despite the 1954 decision on desegregation, the South had experienced no more than token integration. Most Southern communities responded to special court orders, but to nothing else. The President, in September, 1962, backed by his brother as Attorney General, had made his first decided move in behalf of racial integration when he placed the full power of the federal courts behind the registration of black veteran James H. Meredith at the University of Mississippi. During May, 1963, such Southern communities as Birmingham, Alabama, were torn by racial violence. That month Kennedy told a news conference, "As it is today, in many cases they [the Negroes] do not have a remedy, and therefore they take to the streets."

By July the battle over civil rights had entered Congress, where the Senate Judiciary Committee opened its hearings on the President's new civil rights legislation. Within a few months, however, it was clear that neither the President's civil rights bill nor a desired tax cut would pass during that session of the Eighty-eighth Congress. Critics again laid much of the responsibility for congressional inaction at the feet of the President. James Reston had complained in June, "There is something wrong with his leadership on the home front. Something is missing in his speeches, his press conferences, his trips and his timing. He is not communicating his convictions effectively." Not long after, the President prepared a message for delivery in Dallas: "In a world of complex and continuing problems, in a world full of frustrations and irritations, America's leadership must be guided by the lights of learning and reason—or else those who confuse rhetoric with reality and the plausible with the possible will gain the popular ascendancy with their seemingly swift and simple solutions to every world problem." The words would remain unspoken. On November 22, 1963, the day the speech would have been given, the President, in Dallas to mend a rift in the Texas Democratic party, was cut down by an assassin.

The handsome young President's tragic death created an instant cult which made him appear different in death from what he had been in life. He had promised to get the country moving again, but Congress, in November, 1963, was scarcely moving at all. His legislative program lay strangled in committee. Even his popularity had dropped in October to 57 percent—still high, but nothing compared to the eulogies which followed his assassination. Yet the dichotomy between the Kennedy image and the Kennedy record had been apparent long before his death. Kennedy possessed personal attributes which permitted his image to transcend his box score either in Congress or in his handling of foreign affairs. Much of the world had come to trust him instinctively as a man whose immediate failures and shortcomings would give way ultimately to triumphs at home and abroad that reflected his high intelligence, his rational appraisal, and his decent intentions. Kennedy harbored a noble vision of the nation and the world, and it was this high expectation that created the void when he died. He had not occupied the White House in a time of crisis, but in a time of change. He had sought to understand that change and to adjust the nation's policies to it. Yet the conditions of American and international life imposed narrow limits on his statesmanship; despite the brilliance of his administration, it was incapable of extensive innovation. Many of its

The Kennedy Style

Observers have noted that in tangible terms Kennedy's administration accomplished nothing exceptional but that the effect of his personality and style was profound. Above all, he brought the nation a feeling of youth.

The youngest man ever to be President—he once commented that he was older than Washington had been when he commanded the Continental Army, or than Jefferson when he wrote the Declaration—Kennedy appealed to the young, as did the idealism implicit in his inaugural address: "Ask not what your country can do for you, but what you can do for your country." Kennedy quickly created a means through which the young could serve: the Peace Corps. Originally suggested by Hubert Humphrey and Richard Neuberger, the Peace Corps was oversubscribed within six months. Historian Eric F. Goldman quoted one college president as saying, "This President has touched something in the oncoming generation that the young people themselves did not realize was in them."

By no means all youth and enthusiasm, however, Kennedy had served six years in the House and eight years in the Senate. His interest in history had prompted him to write the prize-winning Profiles in Courage, *a study of American leaders who stood up under pressure. He soon came to know pressure himself—the Bay of Pigs disaster, the crises over Laos, Vietnam, the Berlin Wall, the Cuban missiles—and he displayed his own ample courage while maintaining a pleasing wit.*

United Press International Photo

International crisis plagued Kennedy's administration from the beginning. Three months and seven days after he assumed office, the disaster at the Bay of Pigs took place. At the top, the forces of Fidel Castro successfully repel an invading army organized in Florida by the CIA. Within weeks the new President received an ultimatum on Berlin from Russian Premier Nikita Krushchev. Tension in that city increased as more and more East Germans fled to the West, like the soldier at far right.

In Asia, Kennedy worked to establish a neutralist government in Laos and strengthened American commitment to the Saigon government in Vietnam. But Diem's repressive actions against the Buddhists minority finally drove nuns and priests to protest by publically burning themselves alive (right). American feeling turned against the regime and Kennedy became openly critical. Many of Diem's family (above) held positions of power: at far left is Ngo Dinh Nhu, brother of the President and reported head of the Secret Police; at rear right center is Madame Nhu; to Nhu's right is President Diem. In October, 1963, Vietnamese generals assassinated both men.

Left, above and below, and right: Wide World Photos; center: United Press International Photo

RAYMOND'S
SNACK BAR

During the Kennedy years the civil-rights movement gained momentum. Black leaders and organizations began to adopt nonviolent obstructionist techniques—an approach which rapidly spread—to protest racial inequality, especially in the South. Black Star photographer Charles Moore took all of these pictures of police activity in Birmingham, Alabama, against blacks demonstrating for desegregation of city buses and other public facilities in May of 1963. The Rev. Martin Luther King, Jr., led these demonstrations and inspired many other nonviolent sit-ins, picket lines, kneel-ins, and finally the freedom rides of this period.

All photos: Charles Moore, Black Star

Civil rights made slow progress. Troops and newsmen swarmed over the University of Mississippi campus as veteran James H. Meredith enrolled. (far right). Despite the efforts of the governor and a mob of students determined to prevent his registration, Meredith eventually succeeded, although federal marshalls and NAACP lawyers had to protect him (right). Kennedy, along with his brother Robert, then the Attorney General, made the Meredith case a personal fight for racial justice.

Washington, D.C., became the scene of the first large-scale civil-rights march in August of 1963. The Rev. Martin Luther King, Jr., spoke eloquently (below, left) before leading thousands in a march from the Washington Monument to the Lincoln Memorial (below, right).

Above, left, and far left: United Press International; right, both above: Flip Schulke, Black Star]

The Kennedy administration ended on November 22, 1963, its leader brought down by an assassin's bullet in Dallas, Texas. The same afternoon, Lyndon B. Johnson took the presidential oath in the cabin of Air Force One (following page). For the next three days, and much longer, much of the world mourned.

judgments in foreign affairs were considerably less than sound. But Kennedy had given Washington a rebirth of vitality and made it more than ever the center of world attention. The emotions unleashed across the globe by his death, often among those who had never really approved of his leadership, attested to the hope he had carried for a better future.

Lyndon Johnson as President

The political ascent of Lyndon Johnson, who now assumed the mantle of the fallen leader, had been long and difficult. Possessing only the special advantage of his own capacity, he had achieved remarkable success. Entering the House of Representatives from Texas in 1937, he had served there for eleven years as a loyal Democrat, finally moving to the Senate in 1948. Four years later, he served the first Eisenhower Senate as Minority Leader. With the Democratic landslide of 1954, he emerged as Majority Leader and for six years devoted his skills to steering the Eisenhower legislative program through the Senate. When Kennedy had been merely another member of the Senate, Johnson was, next to the President, the most important man in American political life. In 1960, he had gone to Los Angeles with 300 delegate votes. Unable to stop Kennedy's bandwagon, however, he settled for the vice presidency.

As President, Johnson resembled Kennedy not at all. He was determined, resourceful, and experienced, but he lacked certain of Kennedy's assets. Kennedy represented urban, industrial New England; Johnson represented the rural, agricultural Southwest. Kennedy represented the new and the novel; Johnson represented the traditional. Johnson was not a good speechmaker as John Kennedy had been. Unlike Kennedy, moreover, the new President had difficulty in laughing at himself. He was unable to establish a close rapport with the Washington press corps. His favorite motto, from Isaiah, was, "Come now, let us reason together." By reasoning, coaxing, compromising, and arm twisting, he set out to win where it mattered – in his relations with Congress.

Johnson entered the White House with an enormous reserve of congressional respect and goodwill. Southern Senators especially – those who had paralyzed the Kennedy program – harbored an emotional commitment to Johnson's success. On November 27, in his first presidential address, Johnson reminded Congress: "For 32 years, Capitol Hill has been my home. I have shared many moments of pride with you, pride in the ability of the Congress of the United States to act, to meet any crisis, to distill from our differences strong programs of national action." The President listed the important measures before Congress, indicating that he assigned top priority to the civil rights bill. "I urge you," he said, "to eliminate from this nation every trace of discrimination and oppression that is based upon race or color." The President in late 1963 had the political advantage over Congress, and he knew it. A *Newsweek* public opinion poll revealed not only a 2-to-1 vote of no-confidence against the Eighty-eighth Congress but also overwhelming popular approval for the administration's proposed domestic program.

During the spring of 1964 Congress and the nation began to respond favorably to Johnson's special brand of leadership. By promising to reduce the proposed Kennedy budget, Johnson managed to coax the tax bill out of the

Senate Finance Committee. The House had passed the measure as early as the previous September. The Senate concurred after a brief debate on February 7, 1964. The President had forced the civil rights bill into the House by the end of January. This measure would outlaw racial discrimination in most hotels, restaurants, and theaters; authorize the Attorney General to initiate suits in behalf of aggrieved persons in desegregation or discrimination cases; and permit the halting of funds to federal projects which tolerated the existence of racial discrimination. The measure passed the House in February by a vote of 290 to 130. The Senate finally passed the bill in June.

The President, meanwhile, declared his own "war on poverty" during March in the form of the Economic Opportunity Act of 1964. Despite vigorous Republican opposition, the bill passed the Senate on July 23, and the House two weeks later. It provided for work experience and training programs in conservation camps and local communities, for community action programs to combat poverty, and for a domestic peace corps known as Volunteers in Service to America (VISTA). On matters of domestic legislation the second and final session of the Eighty-eighth Congress, opening in January and adjourning in October, 1964, had proved to be the most productive in many years. The Johnson style of getting things done had become a national phenomenon. During the critical weeks of debate on the key bills before Congress, President Johnson had bombarded doubtful members with phone calls and invitations to breakfasts, luncheons, dinners, and informal exchanges. The Johnson techniques were effective, but they demanded compliance and subservience to the point of irritation. "He can make men do what he wants them to do," observed Reston in January, 1965, "but he does not make them like it or him in the process." Success, as usual, involved its costs. Kennedy made men think, but Johnson propelled them into action. The achievements of 1964 belonged to him.

The Election of 1964

Senator Barry Goldwater of Arizona, spokesman of traditional Republican conservatism, was his party's leading presidential candidate by the eve of the 1964 campaign. Governor Nelson Rockefeller of New York at first tried to outdistance Goldwater, but he failed. Subsequently, Governor William Scranton of Pennsylvania, like Rockefeller a liberal, sought to head off Goldwater's nomination, again without success. Goldwater easily won his party's nomination at San Francisco. The convention selected William E. Miller, a Catholic Representative from New York, for the vice presidency.

Goldwater's views conformed to the pre-New Deal Republican philosophy of "rugged individualism." The nation's salvation, he believed, lay in states' rights. He opposed federal aid programs as a threat to individual freedom; he emphasized morality and traditional values of competition and hard work. In foreign affairs, he popularized assumptions and goals at odds with containment. Goldwater recognized no limits to either American power or Communist perfidy and greed. From these two conclusions flowed his insistence that the United States must accept nothing less than "total victory" in the Cold War. The Senator's specific proposals demanded unrelenting hostility toward the U.S.S.R. and China. In his view, negotiations with the Kremlin were dangerous and useless. The way to win in Vietnam, he said in May, 1963, was to drop "a low-yield atomic bomb on Chinese supply lines in North Vietnam."

Goldwater imposed his own ideas on the party platform. On the race issue, the platform called for implementation of the Civil Rights Act of 1964 (Goldwater had voted against it), but it refused to endorse the act's constitutionality. In foreign affairs, the platform charged the Kennedy-Johnson policies with alienating proven allies and pursuing "a risky path such as begun at Munich a quarter century ago." It accused the Democrats of "bungling" in Laos, Vietnam, Berlin, and Cuba. Equally tragic, according to the platform, was the administration's abandoning of "the captive peoples of Eastern Europe" by excluding them from "the official utterances of our government." Republican campaigning was based on the assumption that the American people were tired of the complexities and uncertainties of international life and demanded clear-cut solutions. Yet Goldwater and Miller failed signally to set forth what they would do differently.

Meanwhile the Democratic party projected a mood of confidence and relaxation. Johnson faced only one internal party challenge to his nomination—that of Governor George Wallace of Alabama. This Southern proponent of states' rights attempted to build support for his candidacy among low-income white Americans, North and South, who experienced most directly the pressures of desegregation. In the primaries, Wallace ran well in Wisconsin, Indiana, and Maryland. Yet Goldwater's nomination abruptly removed him from the race. Thus the Democrats could meet at Atlantic City, New Jersey, on August 24 and proclaim unity. The Johnson-dominated convention nominated Senator Hubert H. Humphrey of Minnesota as Johnson's running mate and presented a moderate platform, including a civil rights plank on which the party could agree. The platform accused Goldwater of recklessness in his proposal that "conventional nuclear weapons" be placed at the disposal of NATO commanders, adding that such control should remain in the hands of the President. Nor did the platform deny that the Democratic leadership had sought a détente with the Soviet Union.

In the campaign, Johnson himself concentrated on the twin themes of peace and prosperity. Problems remained, he admitted, but the record of achievement in the years after 1947 had been extensive, even profound. Along with Democratic spokesmen, he hammered at the notion that the Republican candidate could not be trusted with the nation's leadership. Said the President at Albuquerque, New Mexico: "The stakes in this election are success and survival. The issues are recklessness or responsibility. . . . We cannot and we will not play the war game of bluff and bluster. The risk is too great."

By election day, every political yardstick presaged a Johnson sweep. On November 3, Johnson's popular vote of 61 percent in fact set an all-time record—over 43 million to 27 million for Goldwater. Winning forty-four states, Johnson lost only Arizona and five states of the deep South. In the North there was little "white backlash" against the Civil Rights Act. Outside the South, Johnson carried almost everything—cities, suburbs, rural areas, Negroes, Roman Catholics, and even doggedly Republican Vermont. Congress remained under Democratic control by margins in both houses of over 2 to 1. On the Johnson coattails Robert F. Kennedy won a New York Senate seat over a popular Republican, Kenneth B.

Keating. Senator Edward Kennedy easily won reelection in Massachusetts. So tremendous was the Democratic landslide that it raised doubts about the Republican party's future.

The Great Society

During his campaign the President had sketched out a new program for the nation—the "Great Society." "We are only at the beginning of the road to the Great Society," he said in January, 1965; adding: "No longer are we called upon to get America moving. We *are* moving." The goals of the Great Society included the beautification of the country; the elimination of urban blight, as well as air and water pollution; medical aid for the aged; help for education; a more vigorous war on poverty; and new suffrage guarantees for blacks.

Johnson wasted little time. By July, 1965, the Eighty-ninth Congress had written enough of the Great Society program into law to emerge as the most productive since Roosevelt's Second New Deal of 1935. First, Congress approved the President's request for $1.1 billion to help the eleven-state poverty region of Appalachia. Second, agreeing to aid the children of the poor regardless of whether they were attending public or private schools, Congress skirted the traditional church-state issue and passed a $1.3 billion general education bill. Third, Medicare, an especially dramatic breakthrough for the Great Society, provided the elderly with two months of low-priced hospital care and allowances for other medical costs. Fourth, a $7.5 billion omnibus housing bill, including a revolutionary plan to provide rent subsidies for persons whose income was low enough to qualify for public housing, provided for the construction of 60,000 units of low-rent public housing over a period of four years. And President Johnson's voting rights bill of 1965, having received a special impetus from a civil rights crisis in Selma, Alabama, that spring, moved swiftly through Congress. It eliminated discriminatory literacy tests, anticipated the lawsuits which would soon terminate state poll taxes, and provided for federal registrars to assist blacks in registering to vote. Congress also repealed $4.5 billion in excise taxes to stimulate the economy.

Any one of these major laws would have seemed a substantial achievement for most sessions of Congress. Little wonder that a justifiably proud Johnson stated in a letter to Democratic leaders that the first session of the Eighty-ninth Congress "will be recorded as the greatest session in the history of our nation." Johnson's Great Society reflected a renewed acceptance of responsibility by government—the greatest since New Deal days—for the direction and quality of the nation's life. Behind these achievements was not only the Johnson landslide of 1964 but also the full support of the business community. The booming economy had convinced increasing numbers of business leaders that big government was a boon, not a threat, to economic expansion.

If Congress lost some of its momentum during 1966, it wrote a proud record nevertheless. It created the Department of Transportation as the twelfth department in the Cabinet, giving it full responsibility for the development of a coordinated national transportation system. It passed a $1.2 billion "demonstration cities" program to create models for urban development. For the first time in history, it established safety standards for all highway vehicles. It broadened the regulations for the labeling and packaging of foods, drugs, cosmetics, and household supplies. Finally, Congress appropriated $3.7 billion to help clean up the country's rivers and lakes and $186 million to fight air pollution.

Yet the Great Society, for all its legislative triumphs, had barely scraped the surface of the nation's essential problems of poverty and civil rights. "The walls of the ghettos are not going to topple overnight," editorialized the *New York Times* in retrospect, "nor is it possible to wipe out the heritage of generations of social, economic, and educational deprivation by the stroke of a Presidential pen." Nor was it clear that the federal government would win its war against poverty even along established lines of action. The specific program could not succeed without imaginative and effective administrators. Normal bureaucratic inertia and inefficiency could quickly sink the whole Great Society into an administrative quagmire. The President had managed to place both poverty and civil rights programs on the books; he had not demonstrated the capacity to make either program effective.

A second barrier to the creation of the Great Society was the matter of financing. Though stupendous, the nation's wealth was not unlimited. The tax burden carried by most Americans was approaching its tolerable limits. During 1966 Congress became convinced that it could not carry simultaneously the expanded war in Vietnam and the program of the Great Society. Facing the choice, it refused to quarrel with the President on appropriations for the war in Southeast Asia. But it declined to adequately fund the President's domestic program. The congressional situation would not improve. Democratic setbacks in 1966 reduced the President's majority in the House by 47 seats and pushed the membership toward conservatism. Again in 1967 Congress passed several important bills; but it ignored many vital issues facing the nation. Eventually Congress extended the poverty program for two additional years with appropriations of approximately $2 billion per year. Yet, despite the size of the federal effort, the Johnson years—like the Kennedy or Eisenhower years—did not help the poor to any significant degree.

The compounded effects of many years of neglect also troubled the civil rights program. Within weeks after the passage of the Voting Rights Act of 1965, the President reminded civil rights leaders in Washington that 200,000 blacks had been newly registered. Admitting that much remained to be done, he continued, "This is a challenge not only to government, but to Negro leadership. I urge you to work around the clock. Tell those who have been barred from the polls that a new day has come." Actually, the civil rights acts of 1964 and 1965 had opened the floodgates of Negro expectations. The creation of immediate and tangible opportunities for blacks remained to be accomplished; these would require time.

The Warren Court

Even more, perhaps, than the executive-based proponents of the New Frontier and the Great Society, the United States Supreme Court emerged in the sixties as the conscience of the nation. Following the school desegregation decision of 1954, the Supreme Court became so aggressive and wide-ranging in its defense of civil and minority rights that it too left an unmistakable mark on the nation's history. The Chief Justice, in fact as well as name, was Earl

Warren. Thirty years of public life, including a stint as Governor of California and a run for the vice presidency in 1948, had shaped him into a pragmatist. If he lacked the philosophical nature of Justice Hugo Black or the critical intellectuality of Justice Felix Frankfurter, he harbored a highly developed sense of justice and fair play. Earl Warren embodied the spirit of the Court after he became Chief Justice in 1953.

The remarkable string of judicial decisions began in 1962. Over Frankfurter's last dissent, the Court ruled in *Baker v. Carr* (1962) that federal courts had the right to review the fairness of legislative districting. In most states at this time small towns and rural districts enjoyed disproportionate power in state legislatures; rural and small-town majorities had no desire to engage in redistricting that would reflect the increasing shifts in population from rural areas to the cities. Previously the Supreme Court had hesitated to touch questions so obviously political in character, but in the *Baker* case it agreed that unequal apportionment deprived many voters of equal protection of the laws under the Fourteenth Amendment.

Other decisions revolutionizing the electoral process followed. In *Gray v. Sanders* (1963) the Court invalidated the Georgia county unit system which assigned each county a certain number of unit votes and declared the candidate securing the largest number to be the victor in a primary election. The old system had given rural areas a preponderant control over state elections. In *Harper v. Virginia State Board of Elections* (1966), the Court held that the poll tax violated the equal protection clause of the Fourteenth Amendment. That same year in *South Carolina v. Katzenbach* the Court ruled out all literacy tests to determine voting qualifications for those who had completed the sixth grade. Clearly the Warren Court was determined to give every American equal rights to participate in the nation's democratic processes.

In its 1961–1962 session, the Supreme Court took up the difficult problems of civil rights. Although the Constitution bans only official segregation, not private prejudice, the Court in 1961 accepted several "sit-in" cases for review. In *Thompson v. City of Louisville,* the Court decided that the "due process" clause of the Fourteenth Amendment upheld the right of the S. H. Kress Company to ask Negroes to leave the lunch counter as required by a local ordinance providing for racial separation at eating facilities. In *NAACP v. Button,* on the other hand, the Court overturned a Virginia law denying minority groups the right to institute integration cases when those instituting suits had no direct pecuniary interest or liability.

For many years, Justice Black had argued that the rights granted a defendant in federal criminal court applied equally to criminal defendants in state courts. In *Hamilton v. Alabama* (1962) the Court held that a state must provide counsel in a capital case even when it was not evident that failure to do so would prejudice the defendant. Previously the Supreme Court had not required that states provide lawyers for indigent persons except in special cases. But in *Chewning v. Cunningham* (1963), the Warren Court voided a conviction on grounds that an indigent defendant had been denied counsel. In a similar case, *Gideon v. Wainwright* (1963), the Supreme Court decreed unanimously that in the interest of fairness every person accused of a crime was entitled to counsel. In *Escobedo v. Illinois* (1964), the Court ruled further that counsel must be present at criminal interrogations leading to a confession. These Supreme Court decisions met continuous dissent, for a minority of the Court argued vigorously that they undermined the effectiveness of police activity.

In its effort to defend civil rights the Warren Court accepted cases which dealt with real or suspected Communists. In two strongly worded opinions of 1957 the Court narrowed the application of the anti-Communist Smith Act and ruled that the House Un-American Activities Committee could not question outside its legislative province. In *Cramp v. Board of Public Instruction* (1962), the Court unanimously overthrew a Florida loyalty oath as too imprecise to have any meaning.

On issues of censorship and obscenity the Warren Court generally assumed a position of extreme tolerance. In *Bantam Books Incorporated v. Sullivan* (1963) the Court overturned a Rhode Island procedure for restricting the dissemination of obscene literature. The majority found the Rhode Island commission's power to warn dealers and wholesalers regarding the sale of certain books and magazines as, in effect, a system of censorship without the necessary safeguards from state regulation. In *Jacobellis v. Ohio* (1964) the Court overturned the conviction of the defendant for showing an allegedly obscene movie, *The Lovers,* on the grounds that the Constitution defends all forms of expression except hard-core pornography, which no one could define. Yet the Court drew limits to the extent of obscenity and free speech that it would tolerate. In *Ginzburg v. United States* (1966) it upheld Ralph Ginzburg's conviction and prison sentence on the ground that the advertising of his magazine *Eros* and newsletter *Liaison* featured "the leer of the sensualist." If the Court still hesitated to examine the content of material to determine whether it was "dirty" or "worthless," it would at least protect the public from advertising of a highly suggestive nature.

So pervasive were such decisions on civil rights and civil liberties, criminal procedures, and censorship that the Court by the 1960s had greatly expanded the latitude of the individual for self-expression, self-fulfillment, and equality of status. Applauded by liberals, the trend was damned by conservative critics who desired more — not less — social and governmental control. Some conservatives across the country urged Warren's impeachment.

The Troubled Nation

In attempting to meet the twin problems of civil rights and poverty amidst plenty, the nation invested little of its treasure. The entire war on poverty between 1964 and 1967 cost the American people only $6.2 billion — less than 1 percent of the annual gross national product. By 1967 Congress had reduced the annual budget for the poverty program to less than one quarter of 1 percent of the GNP. Such expenditures, added to the rhetoric of hope which accompanied them, could raise expectations, pay the salaries of federal officials, create some new jobs, and build some highways and public structures. They could not do much more. The country's ills, its basic human dilemmas, became more, rather than less, apparent with the passage of time.

For tenant farmers of the deep South the antipoverty program did little. In May, 1965, plantation Negroes of the Mississippi Delta went on strike for an hourly wage of $1.25. Some took refuge in the cities; others attempted to "squat" at the phased-out air base near Greenville, Mississippi. The problem was less racial than economic. The federal subsidy program for cotton managed to save plantations, but it did little for the field hands. Nor did the billions spent on Appalachia effect a noticeable change among the poor. The region could boast new roads and airfields, even more dams, but all this achieved little for the inhibitants. In one area of Kentucky comprising four counties, 40 percent of the families had incomes of less than $1,000 per year. There were no new jobs except those created by the expanding bureaucracy itself. The checks that poured through local banks had the government stamp.

In urban America, economic and social progress among the poor was not necessarily less than in rural areas; its absence was only more conspicuous and potentially more disastrous. Actually little had been attempted. Most of the federal effort had not distinguished the central cities and the suburbs of the nation; it had been assumed that what was good for one would benefit the other. Much of the urban effort—for highways, airports, water and sewage systems, and civil defense—brought far greater benefits to the middle-class suburbs than to the congested tenements of inner cities.

Officially, the prosperity in the sixties greatly reduced unemployment among urban minorities. Nonwhite employment among men over twenty dropped from 10 percent in 1960 to 6 percent in 1965. Among nonwhite boys, unemployment declined from 25 to 20 percent. Yet these figures could not hide the fact that the standard of living of the poor failed to keep pace with the national average. Purchasing power for black families, for example, increased only $120 per year between 1960 and 1965; that for whites increased $220. Blacks who had employment were concentrated heavily in low-wage jobs; half worked as laborers, janitors, porters, and busboys.

The 1960s saw the rapid development of an ominous trend in American society—the alienation of a portion of the black community from the rules, standards, and expectations of the dominant white culture. With the movement of whites into the suburbs, the postwar generation of urban blacks had less contact with white society than any generation in the nation's history. Giving point to the trend were the urban riots of the mix-sixties. One of the most serious outbursts occurred in the black ghetto of Los Angeles in August, 1965. For six days, blacks rampaged through the streets of Watts on Los Angeles' south side, destroying 200 buildings and damaging 600 others by burning and looting. The riot produced thirty-four deaths, over a thousand injuries, and almost four thousand arrests, as well as $140 million in property damage. Subsequent summers witnessed major outbreaks in Los Angeles, San Francisco, Chicago, New York, Newark, and Detroit. Before the Detroit riot of July, 1967, was brought under control, 14,000 paratroopers, National Guardsmen, and state and local police, using tanks and machine guns, were called into action. The riot toll in Detroit reached thirty-eight deaths, 2,000 injuries, and 3,200 arrests. Property damage reached a half billion dollars. Altogether between 1965 and 1967, riots struck seventy-six cities, killing twelve policemen and 118 civilians. These riots, in their formlessness and violence, lacked any clear purpose.

Moderate black leaders, led by Dr. Martin Luther King, condemned the destruction. But amid such riots black leadership usually passed into the hands of "black power" advocates.

The movement toward "black consciousness" was an amalgam of deep frustration among militant black leaders and the black nationalist philosophy of Malcolm X, before his assassination a militiant spokesman of the Black Muslims. Stokely Carmichael, leader of the then Student Nonviolent Coordinating Committee (SNCC), emerged as one of the most articulate black nationalists. To Carmichael it seemed clear that American blacks would never overcome their disadvantages of poverty and "blackness" as long as they accepted programs and standards created by white leadership. If the power structure in American society remained concentrated in the hands of whites, blacks could achieve their goals only by creating positions of strength.

Black power advocated solidarity among Afro-Americans as the surest means of achieving economic and political power commensurate with their numbers. It demanded as well that blacks hold top positions in institutions where their numbers and interests were predominant. Its adherents rejected the term "Negro" as a creation of the white race and demanded the simple designation "black." At the level of action, black power was never a single movement but varied in program according to the immediate preferences of those who advocated it—Carmichael, Floyd McKissick, Rap Brown, Eldridge Cleaver, or Ron Karenga. Veteran civil rights leader James Farmer, chairman of the Congress of Racial Equality (CORE), agreed with many of the more militant that black separatism, as a method of building black solidarity, was a phase through which the nation must pass before it achieved full racial equality. But not all black leaders regarded integration as irrelevant. Moderates condemned both the violence in the cities and the black power rationale. Following the Detroit riot, four national Negro leaders asserted: "Killing, arson, looting are criminal acts and should be dealt with as such." Roy Wilkins, executive director of the NAACP, applauded Vice President Humphrey when he declared, "Racism is racism—and there is no room in America for racism of any color."

National leaders were equally distracted by the riots and black militancy. Conservatives tended to view the riots as conspiratorial, perhaps even Communist-inspired, or at best the inevitable end of the civil rights movement which had destroyed the traditions of custom and restraint hitherto holding Negroes in check. For them the answer lay in strengthening the nation's law enforcement agencies. Others, however, believed the riots were the result of historic disadvantages, some going back to slavery, which required a massive federal program of rehabilitation aimed at creating genuine conditions of hope and prospects of social mobility. The President's special Advisory Commission on Civil Disorders (headed by Governor Otto Kerner of Illinois), submitting its findings in late February, 1968, recommended a sweeping program to alleviate social ills. The nation, it warned, was moving toward two societies, one black and one white, separate and unequal. The commission recommended the creation of 2 million new jobs and 6 million new homes.

During March, 1968, the liberals in the Senate moved toward an open housing law, still searching for a compromise that would make the measure palatable for millions of sensitive white homeowners. It required the assassination of the moderate Martin Luther King in Memphis, Tennessee, early in April, 1968, to galvanize Congress into action. Despite the continued opposition to open housing, it passed the President's civil rights measure with its promise of general open housing by 1970.

What the nation required were new national priorities. Domestic problems, inescapable yet almost untouched, demonstrated that the United States could not afford the luxury of costly and divisive foreign policies, anchored to global dangers more readily proclaimed than demonstrated, while it passively contemplated past damage to its environment and anticipated even greater emotional and physical cost for its neglect in the future.

The Price of Vietnam

During his campaign for President in 1964, Johnson had countered Goldwater's charges of a "no win" policy in Vietnam by sustaining a mood of caution. He opposed any escalation of the war. He specifically warned against any involvement that would tie the United States to a ground war in Asia. "I have not thought," he said, "that we were ready for American boys to do the fighting for Asian boys." Soon thereafter the reelected President began a reassessment of the war. From the beginning of its involvement in Vietnam, Washington had pursued one clear objective—the protection of the Saigon regime from Communist-led assaults. Whether the enemy resided south or north of the 17th parallel—the initially temporary but increasingly permanent line separating North from South Vietnam—was of no consequence. United States policy had been based on the assumption that Saigon's military and political successes, supplemented by SEATO's Asian forces, could contain the power and influence of Ho Chi Minh. During 1964, however, it became obvious that Diem's successors in Saigon were incapable of disposing of the Communist-led forces bearing down heavily on what remained of South Vietnam's political and military structure. Thus, Johnson faced the disturbing choice of either liquidating the war largely on Hanoi's terms or converting the struggle for Vietnam into an American war. With little hesitation he made the latter choice—but, as usual, upon the assumption that victory would be rapid and inexpensive.

Johnson moved to escalate the war as early as June, 1964, when he replaced Henry Cabot Lodge with General Maxwell Taylor as United States Ambassador to Saigon. What the President required to place Hanoi under the direct pressure of United States military superiority was some dramatic incident. That event came on February 7, 1965, when the Vietcong attacked Pleiku, an outpost in the central highlands, and killed eight American advisers. Four hours later Johnson authorized an air attack on Dong Hoi, forty miles north of the demilitarized zone in North Vietnam, at the same time reassuring the nation, "We seek no wider war." Behind this decision lay the assumption, firmly held in Washington as official dogma, that the bombing of the north would bring Ho to the negotiating table in six—at most ten—weeks.

Even as he predicted early successes the President committed the country to a course of military escalation. The bombing had the officially avowed triple purpose of undermining the morale of the enemy, halting infiltration from the North, and encouraging Saigon's resistance in the South. It failed on all counts. As Hanoi adjusted its defenses to withstand assaults from the air, the President simply extended the bombing to more targets. When the situation continued to deteriorate, Johnson dropped the "advisory role" designation of United States military personnel in Vietnam and authorized General William Westmoreland to use the 50,000 men in his command for ground action against the enemy. On July 28, 1965, the President announced that the United States personnel in South Vietnam would be increased from the 75,000 already there to 125,000. "If we are driven from the field in Vietnam," he warned, "then no nation can ever again have the same confidence in American protection." Having accepted that rationale of the struggle, the President was prepared to convert the defense of South Vietnam into an American war and to increase the military escalation to any level required for victory. The troop buildup reached 200,000 in 1966 and continued upward until it exceeded 500,000 in 1967. Meanwhile the volume of bombs dropped on enemy targets north and south of the 17th parallel reached stupendous proportions. During 1968 the bomb tonnage gradually exceeded that in both the Pacific and European theaters during the Second World War. By then the war had cost more than 200,000 American casualties—over 30,000 dead—and $30 billion a year.

Yet the fighting went on. Hanoi, now fully committed, matched each new American increment with a countering escalation of its own. By 1967 McNamara admitted that the bombing had not interdicted the infiltration and flow of supplies from the North. As the war continued, moreover, the ability of the enemy, whether Vietcong or North Vietnamese regulars, to move freely through the countryside, striking anywhere and everywhere, suggested the difficulty of the struggle. In the absence of established battle lines, United States forces measured success, not by territory captured and held, but by the number of enemy killed. By 1968 that body count exceeded 400,000—more than the entire North Vietnamese army—and yet the enemy continued to strike.

At home, opposition to the war kept pace with its escalation. The unleashing of such large quantities of destructiveness against an Asian people injured the moral sensibilities of millions of Americans and gradually divided the nation. Those who challenged United States policy in Southeast Asia agreed generally that the Vietnamese conflict was a civil war to be resolved by the Vietnamese people themselves. They regarded it as an overcommitment of American resources and manpower in an area where United States security interests were, at most, secondary. Among the outspoken opponents of the war were retired Generals James Gavin and Lauris Norstad, many of the country's leading Far Eastern experts, and both Democratic and Republican members of Congress.

In domestic matters, also, the effects of the war effort began to be felt. By 1967, expenditures on the war had overheated the economy, weakened the dollar, contributed to an international monetary crisis, and unleashed inflationary pressures necessitating tax increases. Under such conditions many business leaders lost whatever enthusiasm they had had for the war. Civil rights leaders, both moderate and militant, entered the vanguard of opposition to the war, convinced that Vietnam spending was responsible for the failures of the Great Society at home.

As the political, economic, and emotional costs of the war continued to climb, Washington officials—thinking thus to justify the costs—enlarged the consequences of victory and defeat. Never had a limited encounter carried so completely in theory the burden of the world's future. According to the official rationale, the effort in South Vietnam would not only save that country and all Southeast Asia from aggression; it would at last eliminate the danger of a great war. As President Johnson assured the American people in 1967, "I am convinced that by seeing this struggle through now we are greatly reducing the chances of a much larger war—perhaps a nuclear war." If peace was indeed indivisible—if war anywhere endangered the peace everywhere—then world stability did hinge on the United States ability to counter with overwhelming retaliation any forcible Communist-led challenge to the status quo. The administration was determined that the United States should establish that reputation by living up to its commitments in Vietnam. As Vice President Humphrey declared in April, 1966, "The day that this nation does not honor its commitments, it is on that day that the whole fabric of international law and order is torn apart. . . ." In short, the Johnson administration promised to contain Communist expansion everywhere and save liberty for all mankind by fighting and winning in Vietnam.

Presidential Nominating Politics: 1968

Normally the incumbent Johnson, completely in command of his office and his party's machinery, would have anticipated both renomination and reelection as a matter of course. As the new year broke, the President expected no less. He entered the campaign, moreover, determined to stand firm on matters of Vietnam, poverty, and civil rights, and to hold the center of American politics. For Johnson the intellectuals and the blacks—those who attacked his policies on both the home and the foreign fronts—were displaced persons. Whatever the force of the "new politics" which demanded a new set of national priorities, the bulk of the nation's electorate was still un-young, un-black, and un-poor. The President was ready to conduct his bid for reelection along conventional lines.

But this was no ordinary year, and no longer would such purposes command even the support of all Democrats. In the Senate, the outspoken opponents of administration policy included such key Democrats as J. William Fulbright of Arkansas, Mike Mansfield of Montana, Eugene J. McCarthy of Minnesota, Robert Kennedy of New York, and George McGovern of South Dakota—men who were prepared to force an intraparty debate on the burning issue of Vietnam. During November, 1967, McCarthy announced his own candidacy for the Democratic presidential nomination. His campaign, starting slowly, had picked up little momentum by the time he entered the New Hampshire primary in February, 1968. Johnson was entered as a write-in candidate with the full support of the state's Democratic leaders. McCarthy's support came from political amateurs, but it was devoted and it proved effective. His vote of 42.4 percent (to Johnson's 49.5) suggested that the extent of opposition to the war far transcended his original corporal's guard of students and intellectuals. McCarthy's success in New Hampshire broke the nation's political logjam and within days brought Robert Kennedy into the campaign as an active presidential candidate.

Meanwhile, President Johnson's campaign slowly disintegrated under the pressures of politics and war. After months of parading officials before Congress and the nation, giving assurances of approaching success on both the military and political fronts in Vietnam, the Vietcong Tet offensive against the cities of Vietnam early in 1968 broke the illusion of victory and plunged the President's popularity into a sharp decline. McCarthy's showing in New Hampshire disturbed the White House staff, for it was evident that McCarthy would take the forthcoming Wisconsin primary. Kennedy's candidacy posed an even greater threat, for a Gallup Poll of early March rated Kennedy and Johnson about equal in strength among Democrats and independents. Still the President's announcement of March 31 that under no circumstances would he accept another nomination caught the country by surprise. As rationale for his action, Johnson said that his withdrawal from the race might curtail divisiveness within the nation and grant him time and freedom to manage the war and seek the peace.

Robert Kennedy now emerged as the leading Democratic contender. On April 2, McCarthy gained an easy victory in Wisconsin with 57 percent of the Democratic votes, but already the Kennedy machine, backed by the Kennedy millions and the bulk of the party's literary talent, cast a shadow over the remaining Democratic primaries. Distinguishing Kennedy and McCarthy were their styles and appeals rather than the issues. McCarthy's low-keyed, highly intellectual campaign was aimed almost exclusively at the educated, upper-middle-class minority—the same elements which once had followed Adlai Stevenson. Kennedy's campaign was aimed at those elements in American society which McCarthy avoided—the black, the poor, and the lower middle classes.

Kennedy's first major victory came on May 7 in the Indiana primary. His appeal in the cities made him the one candidate capable of cutting across the nation's great divisions. The two Democratic candidates pointed toward their final showdown in the June 4 California primary. There, after a strenuous and sometimes bitter campaign, Kennedy emerged victorious again. Shortly after midnight on June 5, with victory assured, Kennedy thanked his cheering supporters in the ballroom of Los Angeles' Ambassador Hotel. Moments later he lay mortally wounded in the kitchen corridor—like his brother, the victim of an assassin's bullet.

When the Democratic campaign resumed later in June, the field did not belong to McCarthy. Somewhat earlier, on April 27, Vice President Hubert H. Humphrey had announced his candidacy. Humphrey had ignored the primaries, for his strength lay in the Democratic organization—in the White House and the federal bureaucracy, among state and local Democratic leaders, with the spokesmen of organized labor, and in the South. So tight was the Humphrey organization that it quickly rendered the few primaries irrelevant. The McCarthy candidacy had no chance.

Election year 1968 held clear advantages for the party out of power. However past Republican policies might have contributed to the nation's troubles at home and abroad, the Republican leadership could, in an election year, place the full burden of overcommitment abroad, riots, inflation, higher taxes, and internal tensions on the ruling Democratic party. Long identified with the war in Vietnam, the Republicans could continue to demand victory by attributing past failure not to elusive ends but to the gradualism and vacillation of Johnson's military policies.

The front-running Republican was Richard Nixon, former Vice President and Republican nominee of 1960. Nixon had protected his well-established reputation as a Republican regular by supporting Goldwater in 1964 and by campaigning hard and successfully for Republican congressional candidates two years later. By February, 1968, when Nixon announced that he would enter the New Hampshire primary, he had already dispelled the notion, created by his debacle in the 1962 California governor's race, that he was a loser. Nixon swept the New Hampshire primary and then went on to other primary victories. Long before convention time, Nixon, like Humphrey, held what proved to be an insurmountable lead for his party's nomination.

McCarthy's so-called new politics had challenged the established political structure on matters of foreign policy and the quality of American life. After February, 1968, politics-as-usual faced a second serious challenge in the states' rights candidacy of former Alabama Governor George C. Wallace. Wallace's appeal spoke to the discontent of conservative citizens, rich and poor, who believed their welfare endangered by high taxes, court decisions, and federal interference in local and state affairs. Wallace's program revealed his single-minded concern for property rights and freedom of local and individual decision, both threatened, he said, by the federal bureaucracy. He called for an end to crime in the city streets. Denying that he favored segregation, he insisted only that people, not bureaucrats, had the right to decide where their children would go to school and to whom they would sell their houses.

Nixon won the Republican nomination on the first ballot at Miami, Florida. The platform promised both a victory for self-determination and the "de-Americanization" of the war in Vietnam. After his flawless triumph, Nixon, in an effort to placate the party's conservative leadership in both the South and the important border states, selected largely unknown Governor Spiro T. Agnew of Maryland for the vice presidency. He entered the final race for the White House with superb advantages, possessing the freedom not only to remind the nation of its troubles but also to hold the Democratic party solely responsible for them.

With Humphrey's nomination assured, the Democratic Convention in Chicago in August focused its attention upon the party platform. The Vice President's dilemma was clear. If he satisfied the war critics, he would endanger his relationship with President Johnson and the Democratic organization; if he defended administration policy, he would alienate the McCarthy and Kennedy forces and with them the proponents of the new politics whose support he needed to carry the election. Rejecting compromise with the dissidents, Humphrey accepted a Vietnam plank reflecting the official views of the State Department. Thus, despite the long crusade against the war—much of it centering in Democratic ranks—the Democrats' Vietnam plank was almost identical to that of the Republicans. Having swept to victory on the first ballot, Humphrey chose as his running mate the highly regarded but little-known Senator Edmund S. Muskie of Maine.

The Student Rebellion

The stresses of presidential politics revealed how deep and widespread the student rebellion had become in the United States by the late 1960s. Students had entered the vanguard of dissent, partly because of the nature of the times, partly because of the quality of the nation's political, economic, and social life. Previous generations, for all their emphasis upon morality, had scarcely touched many of the nation's deepest problems. Busy earning a

Confrontation

The five-year Presidency of Lyndon B. Johnson might well be termed an "era of confrontation." A principal "confronter" was Johnson himself, who used his legislative expertise to attack most of the major problems faced by American society. In his zeal to come to grips with the country's problems, he also escalated the war in Vietnam, hoping to terminate it quickly. This attempt, however, failed, proving the undoing of much of his domestic program. The War on Poverty between 1964 and 1967 cost $6.2 billion—less than 1 percent of the gross national product, whereas the Vietnam war, by 1968, cost nearly five times that much each year.

Bernie Boston, Washington Evening Star Photo

Meanwhile other confrontations occurred. Blacks escalated their own war against racial injustice by nonviolent efforts at first, later, new black-nationalist movements shunned white participation. Youth also emerged on the American scene as students and student organizations sought greater influence in campus affairs, worked for civil rights, and, especially, protested the war in Vietnam. The youth shown above was photographed during the confrontation at the Pentagon, the two-day Peace March in Washington in 1967.

All pictures, Bruce Davidson, Magnum

Direct and often violent confrontations between those who believed in black equality and those who held with the entrenched institutions of segregation also characterized Johnson's years. One of the most dramatic civil-rights demonstrations involved a mass march of 25,000 from Selma to Montgomery, Ala., protesting illegal barriers against voter registration. Two white supporters, a Detroit housewife and a Boston minister, were murdered, their deaths recalling those of others who had lost their lives in this struggle for basic rights during the preceding years of the decade.

President Johnson used the Selma March as the occasion for an address to a joint session of Congress in which he urged a new law—later passed—intended to eliminate discriminatory literacy tests, obviate poll taxes, and supply federal registrars to help Negroes in the South register to vote.

Photographs on these pages, taken during the course of the Selma march, and those on the next four pages are from the book *America in Crisis*, (Holt, Rinehart & Winston, 1969) with photographs by Magnum and text by Mitchel Levitas, and from an exhibit based upon the book.

The attitudes of American leaders toward the strife in Vietnam (next two pages) gradually edged toward greater involvement during the 1960s and escalated sharply after the election of President Johnson in 1964. From a force of 4,000 advisors in 1962 an Army of more than 500,000 troops had grown by 1968. By 1970 more than 40,000 Americans had been killed, and well over 100,000 had been seriously wounded. Some 400,000 of the enemy were "counted" dead. Estimates of South Vietnamese civilian casualties ran between 100,000 and 150,000 a year.

Following page: left, Donald McCullin, Magnum; both right, P. J. Griffiths, Magnum

VIETNAM
DIRTY
WAR ON POVERTY NOT ON PEOPLE
I WON'T FIGHT IN VIETNAM
End the War in Vietnam
WAYNE

"The time has come to put our bodies on the machine and stop it," Mario Savio, student protest leader at Berkeley, had said early in the decade. During the 1960s, the disaffected young threw themselves into a variety of confrontations with the Establishment, but no fight unified them more than their opposition to the Vietnam war. Student protest, long a tradition in Europe, Latin America, and Japan, engaged American students as never before.

Demonstrations, marches, sit-ins, opposition to on-campus ROTC training, interference with career recruitment by companies producing war materiel, antiwar literature and theater, draft-card burning—all gave evidence of student involvement. The Peace Movement peaked once in October, 1967, when at least 100,000 demonstrators staged a two-day march on Washington (below), ending in a vigil at the Pentagon. Violence, tear gas, and mass arrests marked the conclusion of the event, as they have punctuated many others since.

Disappointed by the failure of the Peace Movement in the Democratic Party—a failure seemingly caused by Senator Eugene McCarthy's lack of organizational support and by the assassination of Senator Robert Kennedy—many young activists moved on the Democratic Convention in Chicago to protest. Mayor Daley had mobilized a 12,000-man force at the convention hall—6,000 National Guardsmen and 6,000 regular Army troops. Four nights of rioting ensued, bringing charges, as the Walker report mentions, of lawlessness by the demonstrators and gratuitous brutality and violence by the police (near left).

Far left and spread: Charles Harbutt, Magnum; near left: Roger Malloch, Magnum

HARDWARE

While no President since Reconstruction signed more civil rights legislation than President Johnson, his administration was beset by violent riots growing out of the alienation of the black community. These photographs were taken in the Watts area of Los Angeles, in Detroit, and in Washington, D.C., only three of the nearly one hundred cities where festering ghettos have erupted since 1964.

This or similar alienation also fathered "black power" movements in various styles, the most vocal and notable being the Black Panthers. In the 1950s and 1960s blacks did make gains, but gains inhumanly slow in reaching the mass of the black population.

Both left: United Press International; both right: Burt Glinn, Magnum

President Nixon and his vice-president inherited an unpopular war and an inflationary economy. Even the glorious success of man's first moon landing was somewhat dimmed by the knowledge that the money used for the space program might have been better spent elsewhere—for poverty programs, urban renewal, ecological blight, education. Yet this "slum of a decade," as Richard Rovere has called it, may have bred some revitalizing force. It is too early to tell.

Elliott Erwitt, Magnum

living or striving to climb the economic and social ladder, these generations had too often given voice to the nation's ideals of freedom, justice, and equal opportunity without examining the inapplicability of those ideals to millions of their fellow citizens. For many sensitive college-age youths, the crisis-laden 1960s destroyed the optimism which had sapped the social concern of their elders; the tensions in American society demonstrated that the country had not responded well to its challenges in the cities, in the areas of civil rights, in matters of equal opportunity, or in the aesthetic quality of national life. More than any previous generation of American students, those of the sixties adopted a social orientation.

That same prosperity which gave thousands of students the freedom and security to challenge established ways also built the modern university system. During the five years from 1960 to 1965 enrollment in American colleges and universities increased by more than one-half. American universities became not only larger but also better, evolving into places of immense intellectual stimulation. The result was nothing less than a revolution in standards and performance; the academic community became larger, better informed, and more active than ever before.

Students in the ranks of the civil rights movement first challenged the accepted standards of American society. In time, however, student dissent centered around Vietnam and became so unrestrained that it produced disorders, parades, draft-card burning, and riots. The Vietnam issue ultimately became the symbol of everything wrong with American society. By 1967 it had created a merger between the antiwar and civil rights movements. Unable to influence national decisions on these two primary concerns, some students began to call into question the nation's entire economic and political structure. Many contended that change came too slowly, that the country's institutions had become too large, too cumbersome, and too dedicated to established policies and attitudes. Writers and columnists identified the central object of student criticism as the so-called Establishment. Attacks upon the Establishment soon brought the students into direct conflict with university administrators. The campus argument began over the demands of students to have a greater voice in the running of their lives. They rebelled at the dehumanization of life in the large universities, where they often found themselves computerized, mass-produced, and ignored. They complained of disinterested instruction, of professors too busy in travel and research to conduct classes, of their inability to participate in university decisions that affected them and determined the quality of their educational experience. To counter such practices they demanded a degree of control over the curriculum and in some cases the hiring and firing of faculty.

No less than in previous generations, the majority of the students of the 1960s revealed far more concern over preparation for industry, football, fraternities, dating, and automobiles than with reforming the universities or American society. At the other extreme, the perennially unanswered challenges in the nation's existence drove a tiny minority into open rebellion. Rejecting orderly processes, majority rule, the traditions of free and open discussion, and disenchanted with established institutions generally, they insisted that the American system be uprooted. On campuses the radical student movement often became associated with the Students for a Democratic Society (SDS), founded in 1962 and claiming by

1968 a membership reaching into the thousands. Frequently writers and critics failed to distinguish between the radicals and the vast number of students in the center of the spectrum who were neither disinterested nor violent. Here were the tens of thousands of students who gave new hope to American life. They were deeply concerned over policies which they considered less than intelligent; they were troubled over the war in Vietnam and the plight of the blacks and the poor in American society. But they were not in the streets or heckling speakers. These students were the true adherents of the new politics.

During 1968 an important segment of the student rebellion became identified with the concerns of black students. In large measure this new phase combined the student and black power movements into a massive effort to transform a segment of American higher education to satisfy the specific interests and needs of blacks. Black demands centered on curriculum; subsidies; more black teachers, coaches, and other personnel in predominantly white schools; and a lowering of admission standards. In part, black student leaders sought an education that would prepare them specifically for service in black communities. But even more they wanted a program that recognized their uniqueness as blacks, that stopped attempting to fit them for life in a white, middle-class society. To assert their blackness, such students began to eat separately in mixed dining halls, wear natural hair styles, and demand separate dormitories and separate social functions. Ultimately, the search for relevance led to demands for black studies programs, some of which were to be developed from the perspective of black ethnocentrism. Early in 1969 a Harvard University faculty committee recommended a degree program in Afro-American studies. The demands for special courses and even autonomous black departments spread rapidly across the nation.

The Paris Talks

On March 31, 1968, simultaneously with his withdrawal from the presidential race, President Johnson informed the nation that he had ordered a halt in United States bombing north of the 20th parallel. At the same time, he invited North Vietnam to enter talks with American representatives. Late in April, the President announced that talks would shortly open in Paris with Averell Harriman serving as the chief United States negotiator.

When the Paris talks opened formally on May 13, Hanoi's spokesmen issued a warning that they, no less than the Americans, intended to negotiate from strength. Xuan Thuy, the North Vietnamese negotiator, reminded Harriman that the United States had aggressed against the people of Vietnam. The Vietnamese people, he said, were engaged in a historic struggle to gain control of their own country. North Vietnam sought only the guaranteed national rights of the Vietnamese people. Hanoi no longer claimed exclusive rights for the National Liberation Front (NLF) in Saigon, but it did insist that the United States recognize the NLF as a legitimate element in Vietnam's political struggle. Hanoi repeated its demand that successful negotiations could proceed only after the United States had halted the bombing of all North Vietnam. Clearly the search for peace had scarcely begun.

President Johnson's decision to limit the bombing and inaugurate the conversations in

Paris created a national mood of euphoria which all but eliminated the war as a subject of political debate. But in themselves these acts did not bring the war any closer to a solution. As the casualties and costs continued to mount, Hanoi refused to compromise its demands for a total bombing halt. Washington insisted, in return, that Hanoi give some formal assurance that a full bombing halt would be met with a deescalation of its own effort in South Vietnam. Through the late summer and early fall of 1968, critics in Congress and the press urged the administration to interpret each lull in the fighting as a sign of reciprocity on the part of Hanoi. Then on November 1 the President dramatically announced that new (albeit unexplained) developments had permitted him to halt completely the bombing of North Vietnam. Simultaneously he declared that within a week the conversations in Paris would be broadened to include both the Saigon government and the National Liberation Front. Ahead, however, were more weeks of wrangling over procedural matters, including the shape of the conference table. Not until January 25, 1969, did the first substantive session of the renewed Paris talks convene at the Hotel Majestic.

An End and a Beginning

What emerged from the 1968 presidential nominating conventions was not reassuring. The election of a candidate capable of articulating a program of action around which a majority of the nation could rally seemed jeopardized from the start. Neither of the major parties had nominated a popular hero; neither offered programs which might be expected to end the Vietnam war, to deal constructively with student unrest, or to meet the problems of poverty and racial discrimination.

Nixon entered the postconvention campaign with the promise of ultimate victory. "We start definitely on an upbeat note," he told newsmen, "not because of what happened at the Democratic convention but at ours. We won the nomination without splitting the party." Exploiting his political advantages to the utmost, Nixon fastened his campaign to criticism of Democratic failures. Promising a "new leadership for the American people," he pledged an honorable end to the war in Vietnam, clear-cut military supremacy over Russia, and a cut in foreign aid. On domestic issues he asserted that he would take personal charge of the battle against crime, that he would bring inflation under control, and that he would either eliminate or revise and improve the administration of many federal programs.

Humphrey's nomination in Chicago had resulted in a badly split party. Antiwar Democrats refused to march with him in New York's Labor Day parade. Sparse crowds, unimaginative scheduling, merciless heckling by antiwar demonstrators, and the continued alienation of McCarthy and Kennedy followers haunted Humphrey's footsteps. What kept him running and hoping was the simple conviction that in November the American people would reject a Nixon Presidency. Democratic leaders across the nation warned Humphrey that without a total desertion of Johnson on the war he stood no chance of carrying the election. The Vice President responded that he could not, in good conscience, defy the administration. Although he eventually veered away from Johnson's hard-line position on Vietnam and called for a reassessment of United States policies, his precise intentions, if elected President, remained unclear.

During the closing weeks of the race, Humphrey's aggressive, underdog campaigning began to tell. In part, his larger and increasingly enthusiastic crowds reflected dissatisfaction with the Nixon strategy. Lower-middle-class voters, for thirty years the bulwark of Democratic power, began to sense that the GOP candidate was dodging the issues. Campaigning on the economic achievements of successive Democratic administrations, Humphrey gradually solidified what remained of the old Roosevelt coalition. Unlike Nixon, Humphrey invaded the core of the big cities, appealing to traditional party loyalties. Nearly 100 percent of voting blacks supported him. During October much of the McCarthy faction returned to the Democratic fold. The President's announcement of a bombing halt over North Vietnam on November 1 had the effect of a last-minute shot in the arm. Meanwhile, George Wallace's campaign failed to generate any serious threat to the major parties.

By November, Nixon and Humphrey were coming down the homestretch neck and neck. The Gallup Poll declared the popular vote a tossup between Nixon's predicted 43 percent and Humphrey's 42, with Nixon still holding a larger advantage in the electoral college. These final predictions proved to be accurate. Humphrey dominated the Northeast, adding Michigan, Minnesota, Texas, and Washington, and gained approximately 43 percent of the national vote. States' rights candidate George Wallace captured five states of the South: Arkansas, Louisiana, Mississippi, Alabama, and Georgia. Nixon, often by a narrow margin, took the remaining states, again with 43 percent of the popular vote. His final margin over Humphrey was less than 500,000 out of more than 70 million votes cast. The old Democratic coalition of labor, urban liberals, and minorities held together in the face of the Nixon challenge to overcome and almost erase the Nixon advantage. Still Nixon's strategy of pursuing the conservative white vote proved decisive, for if it alienated the blacks it brought Republican victories throughout the border South. The Republican strategy was successful only in the presidential race. Congress remained safely Democratic.

From Johnson to Nixon

Lyndon Johnson had been a "lame duck" President since renouncing another term in March; the election merely determined his successor. During his last days in the White House it was clear that his troubles had flowed not from the avoidance of responsibility but from his attempts to accomplish too much. He accepted without question the notion of American omnipotence, believing that he could perform in accordance with the longings and myths of the country. His goal was to fulfill the dreams of all Americans, including the underprivileged, and to maintain all the nation's foreign commitments. At times, his domestic triumphs were astonishing, for he presided over an age of progressivism unmatched since the New Deal. He signed forty pieces of legislation in support of education alone. He expanded the nation's health programs, achieved greater protection for consumers, and advanced the cause of conservation. He instituted vast programs to answer the needs of the poor, both black and white. The years 1963–1969 were not unproductive.

Vietnam proved to be Johnson's white whale. He had chased it through turbulent seas for four years; he was still in pursuit when he left office. His Vietnam policies resulted finally in far more division at home than victory in Asia. The reason is clear. Those policies were anchored to words and emotions—to high promises of success and dire warnings of the consequences of failure—and not to a body of clearly recognizable circumstances, such as those created by Hitler in 1941, which carried their own conviction and recommended their own responses. It was not strange that the country divided sharply between those who took the rhetoric and admonitions seriously and those who did not. To defend his Vietnam intervention with a half million men, the President was compelled to exaggerate the importance of that region to the United States and the rest of the world until he had committed more in cost and destruction than the results could justify. Thus Johnson's ultimate tragedy was his refusal to admit error—error which in part he had inherited from previous administrations—and to acknowledge the limits of his power to reorder human existence simultaneously in the slums of American cities and the far-off jungles of Vietnam.

In building his administration Nixon faced the unfinished business of the campaign—and of previous administrations. His conservative campaigning had cost him New York, Pennsylvania, and Michigan. He had not reached urban America with its black ghettos and its alienated youth. He would inherit, moreover, an unpopular war and an inflationary economy. To achieve peace both in the cities of the United States and in Asia and still avoid an economic slump would constitute a personal miracle. In his inaugural Nixon avoided all specifics, but he promised to consecrate all his energies and wisdom "to the cause of peace among nations." He did not, however, refer to Vietnam, China, or Russia. Analysts immediately detected a danger in this continuing gap between principle and policy.

Friends of the Nixon administration gave it a year to wind up the American military involvement in Vietnam. Yet as early as March, 1969, the countdown seemed already to have begun. Over 10,000 Americans had died in Vietnam since the start of the Paris peace talks, 1,100 of them during the first three weeks of March. Upon his return from Saigon that month the new Secretary of Defense Melvin R. Laird informed Congress that the United States would increase the fighting capacity of the South Vietnamese beyond the levels contemplated by the previous administration. But this had been stated many times before. "If this administration continues and escalates this war in Vietnam," Senator Fulbright warned, "it will soon be Mr. Nixon's war." Laird, in promising secret negotiations and an eventual de-Americanization of the war, had created the foundations for a Republican policy. But the President, still assured by American officials of ultimate military success, evaded primary decisions. During his meeting with South Vietnamese President Thieu at Guam in June, 1969, the President announced his policy of staged withdrawal of United States forces from Vietnam. But he continued to place his emphasis on the Vietnamization of the war—and thus the ultimate triumph of American purpose by other means—rather than on some form of compromise, perhaps the negotiation of a coalition government for Saigon. It was Nixon's fundamental adherence to established policy that perpetuated and finally aggravated the bitter internal opposition to the war. Following the nationwide antiwar Moratorium in October, the President faced a seriously divided country. If he still possessed an unchallengeable command of United States policy, it was because the majority of Americans trusted his word that successful Vietnamization would still permit him to terminate the nation's involvement on terms favorable to American interests and prestige.

Conclusion

For two hundred years the American people had pursued a dream which combined freedom and opportunity into a body of limitless expectations. But it was a dream reserved for the industrious and those who faced no barriers to the full exertion of mind and body. The great land with its ample resources and its inviting possibilities never ceased to beckon. Eventually millions of every generation responded, seeking their fortunes in business, speculation, or clearing the wilderness. It was a great vision of free, independent, self-reliant people doing great things for themselves and for others. Each generation in turn could assume that it would be richer, perhaps even happier, than the one which preceded it. For the successful it was a dream of equal opportunity and justice come true. Possessed of a civilization with such possibilities for self-fulfillment, Americans shared a messianic urge to make a better world, whether through the welcoming of immigrants, the dispatching of missionaries, the acquisition of new territories, the extension of foreign aid and investment, or the waging of war. With good reason, most Americans accepted the notion of a special destiny for the United States.

Unfortunately the dream was laden with self-deception. With wealth came violence and crime, the squandering of resources, the pollution of streams and air, industrial piracy, political bossism, reeking cities with ghettos and slums. From the beginning the dream ignored the millions without a chance as if they scarcely existed. The old American dream never belonged to all, especially not to blacks and Indians. And it was the gap between the old dream and the reality that, in the sixties, alienated so much of the nation's most responsible youth and even some of their elders.

Eventually, disillusionment drove thousands of young radicals into a cultural revolution, which was reflected in new and strange forms of political expression, as well as in drugs, communal pads, street theaters, dashikis, astrology, and scientology—all evidencing a sharp break with established social values. Yet the main challenge lay not in rejection of the old vision but in its redefinition to give hope, encouragement, and opportunity to those millions of forgotten Americans who had never shared in the nation's fundamentally middle-class culture.

America's unanswered challenges required, above all, a drastic restructuring of priorities. For too long the nation had attempted to live under inflated commitments which compelled it to spend beyond its income and promise beyond its capabilities. In foreign affairs, succeeding administrations had refused to limit national goals to what was humanly reasonable. Woodrow Wilson had led the country to war, not to defend the Atlantic community against German aggression, but to make the *world* safe for democracy. Franklin Roosevelt promised not only the defeat of the Axis powers but also a postwar world free of want and fear. Harry S. Truman promised to defend the opponents of Communism anywhere on the globe. Lyndon Johnson promised to win freedom for everyone by fighting in Vietnam. Whatever the objective national interest in any conflict, still some Americans believed the country powerful enough to win any involvement merely through unstinted fighting and spending.

The experience of the sixties demonstrated the ease with which inflated objectives could render the full spectrum of the national program unmanageable. No government could be obligated to do the impossible, but the deflation of foreign commitments did not demand isolation. Retiring Defense Secretary Clark Clifford expressed the nation's irreducible foreign obligations in these words: "Timely assistance to our friends, prudent use of the great military power at our disposal, a willingness to place our energies and our resources behind people who are willing to devote their own blood and treasure to the preservation of their own freedom and national independence." Even such limited commitments would remain expensive, but the reduction of excessive obligations abroad could well provide the means to create a healthier, safer, and more promising environment and the possibilities of enduring national greatness.

But when and how the nation would convert its technological and productive superiority into genuine triumphs over its human and physical disabilities remained uncertain. For none of the great challenges to human existence—wars of mass destruction, overpopulation, pollution, and the depletion of resources—provoked sufficient interest or unity of purpose to command the needed attention of those charged with the responsibility of governing. Why the nation would spend $25 billion to place a man on the moon while neglecting the crushing and inescapable problems of congestion, defacement, and decay on earth was obvious enough. Technological feats challenged no private interests and required no expressed consensus; an administration could pursue them undisturbed by congressmen, lobbyists, or nonexistent people on the moon. If older standards of national performance no longer met the needs of society, new ones remained elusive. The American people were too divided in purpose, in ideology, and in expectation to accept either a more demanding concept of national purpose or the price required to achieve it.

John F. Kennedy's Presidency is related in detail in two outstanding volumes written by members of his White House staff: A. M. Schlesinger, Jr.'s *A Thousand Days: John F. Kennedy in the White House* (1965) and Theodore C. Sorenson's *Kennedy** (1965). For Kennedy's prepresidential career see the highly sympathetic James M. Burns's *John Kennedy: A Political Profile** (1960). Two highly useful studies of the Kennedy years are Aida DiPace Donald (ed.), *John F. Kennedy and the New Frontier** (1966) and Harold Faber (ed.), *The Kennedy Years: Text by the New York Times* (1968). The latter account of Kennedy's career is taken from the columns of *The New York Times.* For the role of Congress in national life see the Congressional Quarterly Service's *Congress and the Nation,* 1945–1964: *A Review of Government and Politics in the Postwar Years* (1965). Paul T. David (ed.), *The Presidential Election and Transition,* 1960–61 (1961) contains valuable material on the Kennedy election. Two remarkably perceptive volumes on presidential election politics are Theodore H. White's *The Making of the President,* 1960* (1961) and *The Making of the President,* 1964* (1965). Also on the campaign of 1964 is Milton C. Cummings's *The National Election of* 1964 (1966). On the politics of the right see Daniel Bell (ed.), *The Radical Right: The New American Right Expanded and Updated** (1963); A. Forster and B. R. Epstein's *Danger on the Right** (1964); and M. C. Havens's *The Challenges to Democracy: Consensus and Extremism in American Politics* (1965). The problem of unbalanced representation in urban-rural politics can be studied in detail in Gordon E. Baker's *Rural versus Urban Political Power: The Nature and Consequences of Unbalanced Representation** (1955); M. E. Jewell (ed.), *The Politics of Reapportionment* (1962); and Robert B. McKay's *Reapportionment: The Law and Politics of Equal Representation* (1965).

Because of the obvious paradoxes of his Presidency, Lyndon B. Johnson had become the subject of serious historical evaluations even before he left the White House. Undoubtedly the most ambitious contemporary effort to arrive at some understanding is Eric F. Goldman's *The Tragedy of Lyndon Johnson* (1969). Goldman attributes Johnson's decline less to Vietnam than to personal idiosyncrasies which ill suited him for the Presidency. Tom Wicker's *JFK and LBJ: The Influence of Personality upon Politics* (1968) sees Kennedy as a man in pursuit of excellence and Johnson as a man concerned with power and responsibility. Arthur Krock's *Memoirs* (1968) contains the perceptive observations of a noted Washington reporter on forty years of American politics.

Much has been written on the changes wrought in the sixties on American society. Edward Quinn and P. J. Dolan (eds.), *The Sense of the Sixties** (1968) contains articles and documents on critical issues–students, radical movements, the blacks, religion, and science. For the thought of the decade see Ronald Berman's *America in the* 1960*s: An Intellectual History* (1968). Another volume of value is Ben J. Wattenberg's, done in collaboration with R. M. Scammon, *This U.S.A.: An Unexpected Family Portrait of* 194,067,296 *Americans Drawn from the Census* (1965). Two books which present the problems of the cities are Jane Jacobs's *The Death and Life of Great American Cities** (1961) and Nathan Glazer and Daniel P. Moynihan's *Beyond the Melting Pot: The Negroes, Puerto Ricans, Jews, Italians, and Irish of New York City** (1963). On the changing South see Avery Leiserson (ed.), *The American South in the* 1960*'s** (1964) and Charles O. Lerche, Jr.'s *The Uncertain South: Its Changing Patterns of Politics in Foreign Policy* (1964).

The sixties produced a large and impressive body of literature on questions of civil rights, desegregation, and the black revolt. On the status of the Negro in American life see James W. Silver's *Mississippi: The Closed Society** (1964); Charles E. Silberman's *Crisis in Black and White** (1964); Harold R. Isaacs' *The New World of Negro Americans** (1963); and Talcott Parsons and Kenneth B. Clark (eds.), *The Negro American** (1966). Two volumes which trace desegregation in the United States since 1954 are Reed Sarratt's *The Ordeal of Desegregation: The First Decade* (1966) and Benjamin Muse's *Ten Years of Prelude: The Story of Integration since the Supreme Court's* 1954 *Decision* (1964). Analyzing various phases of the black pressures on American society are Louis E. Lomax's *The Negro Revolt** (1962); Robert Goldston's *The Negro Revolution* (1968); and Benjamin Muse's *The American Negro Revolution from Nonviolence to Black Power, 1963–1967* (1968). Two books which deal with the impact of the civil rights movement on Southern politics are Donald R. Matthews and James W. Prothro's *Negroes and the New Southern Politics** (1966) and Pat Watters and Reese Cleghorn's *Climbing Jacob's Ladder: The Arrival of Negroes in Southern Politics* (1967). Watters and Cleghorn conclude that the blacks gained little from their new franchise. Two books on Martin Luther King appeared shortly after his assassination in 1968. Lionel Lokos's *House Divided: The Life and Legacy of Martin Luther King* (1968) blames much of the nation's lawlessness on King. Attributing much of King's philosophy to Ghandi and Thoreau, William Robert Miller produced a more sympathetic account in *Martin Luther King, Jr.* (1968).

For a general evaluation of Johnson's foreign policies, with special emphasis on the impact of domestic politics, see Philip L. Geyelin's *Lyndon B. Johnson and the World* (1966). Two books which deal with the Vietnam issue during the Johnson years are Richard M. Pfeffer (ed.), *No More Vietnams?** (1968), a symposium containing contributions from seven well-known students of American Far Eastern relations, and Mary McCarthy's *Hanoi** (1968). On the United States and Japan see James Cary's *Japan Today: Reluctant Ally* (1962); William J. Sebald and C. Nelson Spinks's *Japan: Prospects, Options, and Opportunities** (1967); and Herbert Passin (ed.), *The United States and Japan** (1966). The last volume was prepared for the American Assembly. For the problem of China see Morton H. Halperin's *China and Nuclear Proliferation** (1966); Vidya P. Dutt's *China and the World: An Analysis of Communist China's Foreign Policy** (1966); Harrison E. Salisbury's *Orbit of China* (1967); and Hsin-hai Chang's *America and China: A New Approach to Asia* (1966). The challenge of the third world to United States foreign policy is analyzed in Theodore Geiger's *The Conflicted Relationship: The West and the Transformation of Asia, Africa, and Latin America** (1967); Charles Wolf's *United States Policy and the Third World: Problems and Analysis** (1967); H. J. P. Arnold's *Aid for Development: A Political and Economic Study* (1966); Chester L. Hunt's *Social Aspects of Economic Development* (1966); and John A. Pincus's *Trade, Aid, and Development: The Rich and Poor Nations** (1967).

During the sixties a number of writers analyzed the changing nature of the Cold War. If they did not agree on what happened to the East-West conflict, they recognized the fact that it was not after 1965 what it had been twenty years earlier. Among the important studies of the Cold War in the sixties are Charles O. Lerche's *The Cold War and After** (1965); Marshall Shulman's *Beyond the Cold War** (1966); Paul Seabury's *The Rise and Decline of the Cold War* (1967); Roger Hilsman and Robert C. Good (eds.), *Foreign Policy in the Sixties** (1965); Geoffrey F. Hudson's *The Hard and Bitter Peace: World Politics since 1945** (1967); and Michael P. Gehlen's *The Politics of Coexistence: Soviet Methods and Motives* (1967). Books dealing with a wide variety of national problems, with some suggestions for change, include Hans J. Morgenthau (ed.), *The Crossroads Papers: A Look into the American Future** (1965); Robert F. Kennedy's *To Seek a Newer World** (1967); Edward M. Kennedy's *Decisions for a Decade: Policies and Programs for the 1970's* (1968); Willy Brandt's *A Peace Policy for Europe* (1968); and Denis W. Brogan's *Worlds in Conflict* (1967). Five volumes concerned specifically with the globalism in United States foreign policy are Ronald Steel's *Pax Americana** (1967); Edmund Stillman and William Pfaff's *Power and Impotence** (1966); Theodore Draper's *Abuse of Power** (1966); J. William Fulbright's *The Arrogance of Power** (1966); and Richard J. Barnet's *Intervention and Revolution** (1968).

For the election of 1968 see Richard H. Rovere's *Waist Deep in the Big Muddy: Personal on 1968* (1968); David Halberstam's *The Unfinished Odyssey of Robert Kennedy* (1968); Jules Witcover's *85 Days: The Last Campaign of Robert Kennedy* (1969); and Jeremy Larner's "Nobody Knows . . . Reflections on the McCarthy Campaign," *Harper's Magazine*, (April–May, 1969). Three British journalists, Lewis Chester, Godfrey Hodgson, and Bruce Page, produced the first major study of the 1968 campaign in their *An American Melodrama: The Presidential Campaign of 1968* (1969).

* indicates availability in paperback.

Appendix

Supplementary Bibliography

THERE ARE A NUMBER OF GUIDES, dictionaries, statistical summaries, and atlases, as well as general surveys, which are very useful for the study of American history. As a beginning reference tool, students should consult the *Harvard Guide to American History* (1964) by Oscar Handlin and others. This can be supplemented by the Library of Congress's *A Guide to the Study of the United States of America* (1960).

General histories of the colonial period include the recent and interpretive *The Colonial Experience* (1966) by David Hawke, and Clarence Ver Steeg's *The Formative Years,* 1607–1763 (1964), which is shorter but somewhat more interpretive.

For economic history see Gilbert C. Fite and Jim E. Reese's *An Economic History of the United States* (2d ed., 1966); Ross M. Robertson's *History of the American Economy* (2d ed., 1964); and Seymour E. Harris (ed.), *American Economic History* (1961). Specific aspects of economic history can be followed in Paul Studenski and Herman E. Kroos's *Financial History of the United States* (1952); F. W. Taussig's *Tariff History of the United States* (8th ed., 1931); Roy M. Robbins's *Our Landed Heritage: The Public Domain,* 1776–1936 (1942); and Maldwyn A. Jones's *American Immigration* (1960). Robert F. Martin's *National Income in the United States,* 1799–1938 (1939) is somewhat out-of-date but still useful as a guide to general trends in the growth of income. Two good surveys of labor history are F. R. Dulles's *Labor in America* (1949) and J. G. Rayback's *A History of American Labor* (1958). The best single-volume survey of American technological development is John W. Oliver's *History of American Technology* (1956).

A few of the diplomatic histories include Thomas A. Bailey's *A Diplomatic History of the American People* (7th ed., 1964); S. F. Bemis's *A Diplomatic History of the United States* (1965 ed.); Richard W. Leopold's *The Growth of American Foreign Policy* (1962); and the shorter work by Wayne S. Cole: *An Interpretive History of American Foreign Relations* (1968). *American Secretaries of State and Their Diplomacy* (10 vols., 1927–1929), edited by Samuel F. Bemis, is extremely useful.

The most comprehensive survey of the West in American history is Ray A. Billington's *Westward Expansion* (1967).

Three excellent texts on constitutional history are the old but still useful A. C. McLaughlin's *Constitutional History of the United States* (1935); Carl B. Swisher's *American Constitutional Development* (1943); and the more recent work by Alfred Kelly and W. A. Harbison: *The American Constitution* (3d ed., 1963).

American military and naval affairs can be followed in Walter Millis's *Arms and Men* (1956) and Harold and Margaret Sprout's *The Rise of American Naval Power* (1939).

On social, cultural, and intellectual history, Harvey Wish's *Society and Thought in Early America* (1950) is comprehensive.

An excellent sense of American social and cultural development can be obtained from R. H. Gabriel (ed.), *The Pageant of America: A Pictorial History of the United States* (15 vols., 1925–1929), which is detailed and comprehensive. J. T. Adams (ed.), *Album of American History* (5 vols., 1944–1960), also contains a great deal of valuable information on the nation's cultural growth. Another useful work is the *Dictionary of American Portraits* (1967) by Hayward and Blanche Cirker. *A Literary History of the United States* (3 vols., 1946) by Robert E. Spiller and others is excellent on this subject. An exceptionally fine survey is Merle Curtis's *The Growth of American Thought* (1951). Another excellent intellectual history is Ralph Gabriel's *Course of American Democratic Thought* (1956). Vernon L. Parrington's *Main Currents in American Thought* (3 vols., 1927–1930) is a broad and stimulating examination of American intellectual history. Michael Kraus's *Writings of American History* (1953) provides an excellent survey of the trends in American historical writing.

On religion see W. W. Sweet's *The Story of Religion in America* (2d ed., 1950) and the more recent *Religious History of America* (1962) by E. S. Gaustad.

Surveys of art include Virgil Barker's *American Painting* (1950) and Samuel Green's *American Art* (1966).

On architecture see Hugh Morrison's *Early American Architecture* (1952).

F. R. Dulles's *America Learns to Play* (1940) is interesting on recreation.

J. G. E. Hopkins (ed.), *Concise Dictionary of American Biography* (1964) is very useful for biographical accounts, but students should rely mainly on the *Dictionary of American Biography* (22 vols., 1946) edited by Allen Johnson, which provides fuller and more detailed biographical sketches of leading Americans. Brief biographies of all members of Congress up to 1961 are in the *Biographical Directory of the American Congress,* 1774–1961 (1961).

Summaries of historical events can be found in the *Dictionary of American History* (2d ed., 5 vols., 1942; vol. VI,

1961). There are even briefer accounts of historical events in R. B. Morris's *Encyclopedia of American History* (rev. ed., 1963).

The American Negro Reference Book (1966), edited by John P. Davis, and *The Negro Almanac* (1967) by Harry A. Ploski and Roscoe C. Brown, Jr., are valuable works which provide a wealth of information on black Americans. The best general history of the Negro in America is John Hope Franklin's *From Slavery to Freedom* (3d ed., 1965).

Historical geography is extremely important for students of history. An excellent survey of this subject can be found in Ralph H. Brown's *Historical Geography of the United States* (1948), and Ellen C. Semple's *American History and Its Geographic Conditions* (1933). J. T. Adams (ed.), *Atlas of American History* (1943), contains excellent maps, as does W. R. Shepherd's *Historical Atlas* (1964 ed.). *The American Heritage Pictorial Atlas of the United States* (1966) is colorful and highly useful.

The best compilation of documents in American history is H. S. Commager's *Documents of American History* (7th ed., 1963).

The political party platforms can be located most conveniently in Kirk H. Porter and D. B. Johnson's *National Party Platforms,* 1840–1960 (1961). Some of the key presidential messages have been compiled by Fred L. Israel in *The State of the Union Messages of the Presidents,* 1790–1966 (3 vols., 1966).

The Encyclopedia of the Social Sciences (15 vols., 1951), edited by E. R. A. Seligman and Alvin Johnson, contains a wealth of helpful material for the historian. The best single volume of statistics is *Historical Statistics of the United States: Colonial Times to* 1957 (1960).

The Declaration of Independence

WHEN IN THE COURSE OF HUMAN EVENTS, it becomes necessary for one people to dissolve the political bands which have connected them with another, and to assume the Powers of the earth, the separate and equal station to which the Laws of Nature and of Nature's God entitle them, a decent respect to the opinions of mankind requires that they should declare the causes which impel them to the separation.

We hold these truths to be self-evident, that all men are created equal, that they are endowed by their Creator with certain unalienable rights, that among these are Life, Liberty, and the pursuit of Happiness. That to secure these rights, Governments are instituted among Men, deriving their just powers from the consent of the governed. That whenever any Form of Government becomes destructive of these ends, it is the Right of the People to alter or to abolish it, and to institute new Government, laying its foundation on such principles and organizing its powers in such form, as to them shall seem most likely to effect their Safety and Happiness. Prudence, indeed, will dictate that Governments long established should not be changed for light and transient causes; and accordingly all experience hath shown, that mankind are more disposed to suffer, while evils are sufferable, than to right themselves by abolishing the forms to which they are accustomed. But when a long train of abuses and usurpations, pursuing invariably the same Object evinces a design to reduce them under absolute Despotism, it is their right, it is their duty, to throw off such Government, and to provide new Guards for their future security.—Such has been the patient sufferance of these Colonies; and such is now the necessity which constrains them to alter their former Systems of Government. The history of the present King of Great Britain is a history of repeated injuries and usurpations, all having in direct object the establishment of an absolute Tyranny over these States. To prove this, let Facts be submitted to a candid world.

He has refused his Assent to Laws, the most wholesome and necessary for the public good.

He has forbidden his Governors to pass Laws of immediate and pressing importance, unless suspended in their operation till his Assent should be obtained; and when so suspended, he has utterly neglected to attend to them.

He has refused to pass other Laws for the accommodation of large districts of people, unless those people would relinquish the right of Representation in the Legislature, a right inestimable to them and formidable to tyrants only.

He has called together legislative bodies at places unusual, uncomfortable, and distant from the depository of their public Records, for the sole purpose of fatiguing them into compliance with his measures.

He has dissolved Representative Houses repeatedly, for opposing with manly firmness his invasions on the rights of the people.

He has refused for a long time, after such dissolutions, to cause others to be elected; whereby the Legislative powers, incapable of Annihilation, have returned to the People at large for their exercise; the State remaining in the mean time exposed to all dangers of invasion from without, and convulsions within.

He has endeavoured to prevent the population of these States; for that purpose obstructing the Laws of Naturalization of Foreigners; refusing to pass others to encourage their migrations hither, and raising the conditions of new Appropriations of Lands.

He has obstructed the Administration of Justice, by refusing his Assent to Laws for establishing Judiciary powers.

He has made Judges dependent on his Will alone, for the tenure of their offices, and the amount and payment of their salaries.

He has erected a multitude of New Offices, and sent hither swarms of Officers to harass our People, and eat out their substance.

He has kept among us, in times of peace, Standing Armies without the Consent of our legislature.

He has affected to render the Military independent of and superior to the Civil Power.

He has combined with others to subject us to a jurisdiction foreign to our constitution, and unacknowledged by our laws; giving his Assent to their Acts of pretended Legislation:

For quartering large bodies of armed troops among us:

For protecting them, by a mock Trial, from Punishment for any Murders which they should commit on the Inhabitants of these States:

For cutting off our Trade with all parts of the world:

For imposing taxes on us without our Consent:

For depriving us in many cases, of the benefits of Trial by jury:

For transporting us beyond Seas to be tried for pretended offences:

For abolishing the free System of English Laws in a neighbouring Province, establishing therein an Arbitrary government, and enlarging its Boundaries so as to render it at once an example and fit instrument for introducing the same absolute rule into these Colonies:

For taking away our Charters, abolishing our most valuable Laws, and altering fundamentally the Forms of our Governments:

For suspending our own Legislatures, and declaring themselves invested with Power to legislate for us in all cases whatsoever.

He has abdicated Government here, by declaring us out of his Protection and waging War against us.

He has plundered our seas, ravaged our Coasts, burnt our towns, and destroyed the lives of our people.

He is at this time transporting large armies of foreign mercenaries to compleat the works of death, desolation, and tyranny, already begun with circumstances of Cruelty & perfidy scarcely paralleled in the most barbarous ages, and totally unworthy the Head of a civilized nation.

He has constrained our fellow Citizens taken Captive on the high Seas to bear Arms against their Country, to become the executioners of their friends and Brethren, or to fall themselves by their Hands.

He has excited domestic insurrections amongst us, and has endeavoured to bring on the inhabitants of our frontiers, the merciless Indian Savages, whose known rule of warfare, is an undistinguished destruction of all ages, sexes, and conditions.

In every stage of these Oppressions We have Petitioned for Redress in the most humble terms: Our repeated Petitions have been answered only by repeated injury. A Prince, whose character is thus marked by every act which may define a Tyrant, is unfit to be the ruler of a free people.

Nor have We been wanting in attentions to our British brethren. We have warned them from time to time of attempts by their legislature to extend an unwarrantable jurisdiction over us. We have reminded them of the circumstances of our emigration and settlement here. We have appealed to their native justice and magnanimity, and we have conjured them by the ties of our common kindred to disavow these usurpations, which, would inevitably interrupt our connections and correspondence. They too must have been deaf to the voice of justice and of consanguinity. We must, therefore, acquiesce in the necessity, which denounces our Separation, and hold them, as we hold the rest of mankind, Enemies in War, in Peace Friends.

WE, THEREFORE, the Representatives of the UNITED STATES OF AMERICA, in General Congress, Assembled, appealing to the Supreme Judge of the world for the rectitude of our intentions, do, in the Name, and by Authority of the good People of these Colonies, solemnly publish and declare, That these United Colonies are, and of Right ought to be FREE AND INDEPENDENT STATES; that they are Absolved from all Allegiance to the British Crown, and that all political connection between them and the State of Great Britain, is and ought to be totally dissolved; and that as Free and Independent States, they have full Power to levy War, conclude Peace, contract Alliances, establish Commerce, and to do all other Acts and Things which Independent States may of right do. And for the support of this Declaration, with a firm reliance on the Protection of Divine Providence, we mutually pledge to each other our Lives, our Fortunes, and our sacred Honor.

The foregoing Declaration was, by order of Congress, engrossed, and signed by the following members:

John Hancock

NEW HAMPSHIRE
Josiah Bartlett
William Whipple
Matthew Thornton

MASSACHUSETTS BAY
Samuel Adams
John Adams
Robert Treat Paine
Elbridge Gerry

RHODE ISLAND
Stephen Hopkins
William Ellery

CONNECTICUT
Roger Sherman
Samuel Huntington
William Williams
Oliver Wolcott

NEW YORK
William Floyd
Philip Livingston
Francis Lewis
Lewis Morris

NEW JERSEY
Richard Stockton
John Witherspoon
Francis Hopkinson
John Hart
Abraham Clark

PENNSYLVANIA
Robert Morris
Benjamin Rush
Benjamin Franklin
John Morton
George Clymer
James Smith
George Taylor
James Wilson
George Ross

DELAWARE
Caesar Rodney
George Read
Thomas M'Kean

MARYLAND
Samuel Chase
William Paca
Thomas Stone
Charles Carroll, of Carrollton

VIRGINIA
George Wythe
Richard Henry Lee
Thomas Jefferson
Benjamin Harrison
Thomas Nelson, Jr.
Francis Lightfoot Lee
Carter Braxton

NORTH CAROLINA
William Hooper
Joseph Hewes
John Penn

SOUTH CAROLINA
Edward Rutledge
Thomas Heyward, Jr.
Thomas Lynch, Jr.
Arthur Middleton

GEORGIA
Button Gwinnett
Lyman Hall
George Walton

Resolved, That copies of the Declaration be sent to the several assemblies, conventions, and committees, or councils of safety, and to the several commanding officers of the continental troops; that it be proclaimed in each of the United States, at the head of the army.

The Constitution

PREAMBLE

We, the people of the United States, in order to form a more perfect Union, establish justice, insure domestic tranquillity, provide for the common defence, promote the general welfare, and secure the blessings of liberty to ourselves and our posterity, do ordain and establish this Constitution for the United States of America.

ARTICLE I

Section 1. All legislative powers herein granted shall be vested in a Congress of the United States, which shall consist of a Senate and House of Representatives.

Section 2. (1) The House of Representatives shall be composed of members chosen every second year by the people of the several States, and the electors in each State shall have the qualifications requisite for electors of the most numerous branch of the State Legislature.

(2) No person shall be a Representative who shall not have attained to the age of twenty-five years and been seven years a citizen of the United States, and who shall not, when elected, be an inhabitant of that State in which he shall be chosen.

(3) Representatives and direct taxes[1] shall be apportioned among the several States which may be included within this Union according to their respective numbers, which shall be determined by adding to the whole number of free persons, including those bound to service for a term of years, and excluding Indians not taxed, three-fifths of all other persons.[2] The actual enumeration shall be made within three years after the first meeting of the Congress of the United States, and within every subsequent term of ten years, in such manner as they shall by law direct. The number of Representatives shall not exceed one for every thirty thousand, but each State shall have at least one Representative; and until such enumeration shall be made, the State of New Hampshire shall be entitled to choose 3; Massachusetts, 8; Rhode Island and Providence Plantations, 1; Connecticut, 5; New York, 6; New Jersey, 4; Pennsylvania, 8; Delaware, 1; Maryland, 6; Virginia, 10; North Carolina, 5; South Carolina, 5, and Georgia, 3.

(4) When vacancies happen in the representation from any State, the Executive Authority thereof shall issue writs of election to fill such vacancies.

(5) The House of Representatives shall choose their Speaker and other officers, and shall have the sole power of impeachment.

Section 3. (1) The Senate of the United States shall be composed of two Senators from each State, chosen by the Legislature thereof,[3] for six years and each Senator shall have one vote.

(2) Immediately after they shall be assembled in consequence of the first election, they shall be divided as equally as may be into three classes. The seats of the Senators of the first class shall be vacated at the expiration of the second year, of the second class at the expiration of the fourth year, and of the third class at the expiration of the sixth year, so that one-third may be chosen every second year; and if vacancies happen by resignation or otherwise, during the recess of the Legislature of any State, the Executive thereof may make temporary appointment until the next meeting of the Legislature, which shall then fill such vacancies.[3]

(3) No person shall be a Senator who shall not have attained to the age of thirty years, and been nine years a citizen of the United States, and who shall not, when elected, be an inhabitant of that State for which he shall be chosen.

(4) The Vice President of the United States shall be President of the Senate, but shall have no vote unless they be equally divided.

(5) The Senate shall choose their other officers, and also a President pro tempore, in the absence of the Vice President, or when he shall exercise the office of the President of the United States.

(6) The Senate shall have the sole power to try all impeachments. When sitting for that purpose, they shall be on oath or affirmation. When the President of the United States is tried, the Chief Justice shall preside; and no person shall be convicted without the concurrence of two-thirds of the members present.

(7) Judgment in cases of impeachment shall not extend further than to removal from office, and disqualification to hold and enjoy any office of honor, trust, or profit under the United States; but the party convicted shall nevertheless be liable and subject to indictment, trial, judgment, and punishment, according to law.

Section 4. (1) The times, places and manner of holding elections for Senators and Representatives shall be prescribed in each State by the Legislature thereof; but the Congress may at any time make or alter such regulations, except as to places of choosing Senators.

(2) The Congress shall assemble at least once in every year, and such meeting shall be on the first Monday in

[1] Changed by 16th amendment.

[2] "Other persons" meant slaves. This was changed by the 14th amendment.

[3] Changed by 17th amendment.

December, unless they shall by law appoint a different day.[4]

Section 5. (1) Each House shall be the judge of the elections, returns, and qualifications of its own members, and a majority of each shall constitute a quorum to do business; but a smaller number may adjourn from day to day, and may be authorized to compel the attendance of absent members in such manner and under such penalties as each House may provide.

(2) Each House may determine the rules of its proceedings, punish its members for disorderly behavior, and with the concurrence of two-thirds expel a member.

(3) Each House shall keep a journal of its proceedings, and from time to time may publish the same, excepting such parts as may in their judgment require secrecy; and the yeas and nays of the members of either House on any question shall, at the desire of one-fifth of those present, be entered on the journal.

(4) Neither House, during the session of Congress shall, without the consent of the other, adjourn for more than three days, nor to any other place than that in which the two Houses shall be sitting.

Section 6. (1) The Senators and Representatives shall receive a compensation for their services to be ascertained by law, and paid out of the Treasury of the United States. They shall in all cases, except treason, felony, and breach of the peace, be privileged from arrest during their attendance at the session of their respective Houses, and in going to and returning from the same; and for any speech or debate in either House they shall not be questioned in any other place.

(2) No Senator or Representative shall, during the time for which he was elected, be appointed to any civil office under the authority of the United States which shall have been created, or the emoluments whereof shall have been increased during such time; and no person holding any office under the United States shall be a member of either House during his continuance in office.

Section 7. (1) All bills for raising revenue shall originate in the House of Representatives, but the Senate may propose or concur with amendments, as on other bills.

(2) Every bill which shall have passed the House of Representatives and the Senate shall, before it becomes a law, be presented to the President of the United States; if he approve, he shall sign it, but if not, he shall return it, with his objections, to that House in which it shall have originated, who shall proceed to reconsider it. If after such reconsideration two-thirds of that House shall agree to pass the bill it shall be sent, together with the objections, to the other House, by which it shall likewise be reconsidered; and if approved by two-thirds of that House it shall become a law. But in all such cases the votes of both Houses shall be determined by yeas and nays, and the names of the persons voting for and against the bill shall be entered on the journal of each House respectively. If any bill shall not be returned by the President within ten days (Sundays excepted) after it shall have been presented to him, the same shall be a law in like manner as if he had signed it, unless the Congress by their adjournment prevent its return; in which case it shall not be a law.

(3) Every order, resolution, or vote to which the concurrence of the Senate and House of Representatives may be necessary (except on a question of adjournment) shall be presented to the President of the United States, and before the same shall take effect shall be approved by him, or being disapproved by him, shall be repassed by two-thirds of the Senate and the House of Representatives, according to the rules and limitations prescribed in the case of a bill.

Section 8. (1) The Congress shall have power:

To lay and collect taxes, duties, imposts, and excises to pay the debts and provide for the common defense and general welfare of the United States; but all duties, imposts, and excises shall be uniform throughout the United States.

(2) To borrow money on the credit of the United States.

(3) To regulate commerce with foreign nations, and among the several States and with the Indian tribes.

(4) To establish a uniform rule of naturalization and uniform laws on the subject of bankruptcies throughout the United States.

(5) To coin money, regulate the value thereof, and of foreign coin, and fix the standard of weights and measures.

(6) To provide for the punishment of counterfeiting the securities and current coin of the United States.

(7) To establish post-offices and post-roads.

(8) To promote the progress of science and useful arts by securing for limited times to authors and inventors the exclusive rights to their respective writings and discoveries.

(9) To constitute tribunals inferior to the Supreme Court.

(10) To define and punish piracies and felonies committed on the high seas, and offences against the law of nations.

(11) To declare war, grant letters of marque and reprisal and make rules concerning captures on land and water.

(12) To raise and support armies, but no appropriation of money to that use shall be for a longer term than two years.

(13) To provide and maintain a navy.

(14) To make rules for the government and regulation of the land and naval forces.

(15) To provide for calling forth the militia to execute the laws of the Union, suppress insurrections, and repel invasions.

(16) To provide for organizing, arming, and disciplining the militia, and for governing such part of them as may be employed in the service of the United States, reserving to the States respectively the appointment of the officers, and the authority of training the militia according to the discipline prescribed by Congress.

(17) To exercise exclusive legislation in all cases whatsoever over such district (not exceeding ten miles square) as may, by cession of particular States and the acceptance of Congress, become the seat of Government of the United States, and to exercise like authority over all places purchased by the consent of the Legislature of the State in which the same shall be, for the erection of forts, magazines, arsenals, drydocks, and other needful buildings.

[4] Modified by 20th amendment.

(18) To make all laws which shall be necessary and proper for carrying into execution the foregoing powers and all other powers vested by this Constitution in the Government of the United States, or in any department or officer thereof.

Section 9. (1) The migration or importation of such persons as any of the States now existing shall think proper to admit shall not be prohibited by the Congress prior to the year one thousand eight hundred and eight, but a tax or duty may be imposed on such importation, not exceeding ten dollars for each person.

(2) The privilege of the writ of habeas corpus shall not be suspended, unless when in cases of rebellion or invasion the public safety may require it.

(3) No bill of attainder or ex post facto law shall be passed.

(4) No capitation or other direct tax shall be laid, unless in proportion to the census or enumeration hereinbefore directed to be taken.[5]

(5) No tax or duty shall be laid on articles exported from any State.

(6) No preference shall be given by any regulation of commerce or revenue to the ports of one State over those of another, nor shall vessels bound to or from one State be obliged to enter, clear, or pay duties to another.

(7) No money shall be drawn from the Treasury but in consequence of appropriations made by law; and a regular statement and account of the receipts and expenditures of all public money shall be published from time to time.

(8) No title of nobility shall be granted by the United States. And no person holding any office of profit or trust under them shall, without the consent of the Congress, accept of any present, emolument, office, or title of any kind whatever from any king, prince, or foreign state.

Section 10. (1) No State shall enter into any treaty, alliance, or confederation, grant letters of marque and reprisal, coin money, emit bills of credit, make anything but gold and silver coin a tender in payment of debts, pass any bill of attainder, ex post facto law, or law impairing the obligation of contracts, or grant any title of nobility.

(2) No State shall, without the consent of the Congress, lay any impost or duties on imports or exports, except what may be absolutely necessary for executing its inspection laws, and the net produce of all duties and imposts, laid by any State on imports or exports, shall be for the use of the Treasury of the United States; and all such laws shall be subject to the revision and control of the Congress.

(3) No State shall, without the consent of Congress, lay any duty of tonnage, keep troops or ships of war in time of peace, enter into agreement or compact with another State, or with a foreign power, or engage in war unless actually invaded, or in such imminent danger as will not admit of delay.

ARTICLE II

Section 1. (1) The Executive power shall be vested in a President of the United States of America. He shall hold his office during the term of four years[6] and together with the Vice-President, chosen for the same term, be elected as follows:

(2) Each State shall appoint, in such manner as the Legislature thereof may direct, a number of electors equal to the whole number of Senators and Representatives to which the State may be entitled in the Congress; but no Senator or Representative or person holding an office of trust or profit under the United States shall be appointed an elector.

The electors shall meet in their respective States and vote by ballot for two persons, of whom one at least shall not be an inhabitant of the same State with themselves. And they shall make a list of all the persons voted for, and of the number of votes for each, which list they shall sign and certify and transmit, sealed, to the seat of the Government of the United States, directed to the President of the Senate. The President of the Senate shall, in the presence of the Senate and House of Representatives, open all the certificates, and the votes shall then be counted. The person having the greatest number of votes shall be the President, if such number be a majority of the whole number of electors appointed, and if there be more than one who have such a majority, and have an equal number of votes, then the House of Representatives shall immediately choose by ballot one of them for President; and if no person have a majority, then from the five highest on the list the said House shall in like manner choose the President. But in choosing the President, the vote shall be taken by States, the representation from each State having one vote. A quorum, for this purpose, shall consist of a member or members from two-thirds of the States, and a majority of all the States shall be necessary to a choice. In every case, after the choice of the President, the person having the greatest number of votes of the electors shall be the Vice-President.[7] But if there should remain two or more who have equal votes, the Senate shall choose from them by ballot the Vice-President.

(3) The Congress may determine the time of choosing the electors and the day on which they shall give their votes, which day shall be the same throughout the United States.

(4) No person except a natural born citizen, or a citizen of the United States at the time of the adoption of the Constitution, shall be eligible to the office of President; neither shall any person be eligible to that office who shall not have attained to the age of thirty-five years and been fourteen years a resident within the United States.

(5) In case of the removal of the President from office, or of his death, resignation, or inability to discharge the powers and duties of the said office, the same shall devolve on the Vice-President, and the Congress may by law provide for the case of removal, death, resignation, or inability, both of the President and Vice-President, declaring what officer shall then act as President, and such officer shall act

[5] Modified by 16th amendment.

[6] The 22d amendment limited President to two terms.

[7] Changed by 12th amendment.

accordingly until the disability be removed or a President shall be elected.

(6) The President shall, at stated times, receive for his services a compensation which shall neither be increased nor diminished during the period for which he shall have been elected, and he shall not receive within that period any other emolument from the United States or any of them.

(7) Before he enter on the execution of his office he shall take the following oath or affirmation:

"I do solemnly swear (or affirm) that I will faithfully execute the office of President of the United States, and will, to the best of my ability, preserve, protect, and defend the Constitution of the United States."

Section 2. (1) The President shall be Commander-in-Chief of the Army and Navy of the United States, and of the militia of the several States when called into the actual service of the United States; he may require the opinion, in writing, of the principal officer in each of the executive departments upon any subject relating to the duties of their respective offices, and he shall have power to grant reprieves and pardons for offences against the United States except in cases of impeachment.

(2) He shall have power by and with the advice and consent of the Senate to make treaties, provided two-thirds of the Senators present concur: and he shall nominate and by and with the advice and consent of the Senate shall appoint ambassadors, other public ministers and consuls, judges of the Supreme Court, and all other officers of the United States whose appointments are not herein otherwise provided for, and which shall be established by law; but the Congress may by law vest the appointment of such inferior officers as they think proper in the President alone, in the courts of law, or in the heads of departments.

(3) The President shall have power to fill up all vacancies that may happen during the recess of the Senate by granting commissions, which shall expire at the end of their next session.

Section 3. He shall from time to time give to the Congress information of the state of the Union, and recommend to their consideration such measures as he shall judge necessary and expedient; he may, on extraordinary occasions, convene both Houses, or either of them, and in case of disagreement between them with respect to the time of adjournment, he may adjourn them to such time as he shall think proper; he shall receive ambassadors and other public ministers; he shall take care that the laws be faithfully executed, and shall commission all the officers of the United States.

Section 4. The President, Vice-President, and all civil officers of the United States shall be removed from office on impeachment for and conviction of treason, bribery or other high crimes and misdemeanors.

ARTICLE III

Section 1. The judicial power of the United States shall be vested in one Supreme Court, and in such inferior courts as the Congress may from time to time ordain and establish. The judges, both of the Supreme and inferior courts, shall hold their offices during good behavior, and shall at stated times receive for their services a compensation which shall not be diminished during their continuance in office.

Section 2. (1) The judicial power shall extend to all cases in law and equity arising under this Constitution, the laws of the United States, and treaties made, or which shall be made, under their authority; to all cases affecting ambassadors, other public ministers and consuls; to all cases of admiralty and maritime jurisdiction; to controversies to which the United States shall be a party;[8] to controversies between two or more States, between a State and citizens of another State, between citizens of different States, between citizens of the same State claiming lands under grants of different States, and between a State, or the citizens thereof, and foreign states, citizens, or subjects.

(2) In all cases affecting ambassadors, other public ministers, and consuls, and those in which a State shall be a party, the Supreme Court shall have original jurisdiction. In all the other cases before mentioned the Supreme Court shall have appellate jurisdiction both as to law and fact, with such exceptions and under such regulations as the Congress shall make.

(3) The trial of all crimes, except in cases of impeachment, shall be by jury, and such trial shall be held in the State where the said crimes shall have been committed; but when not committed within any State the trial shall be at such place or places as the Congress may by law have directed.

Section 3. (1) Treason against the United States shall consist only in levying war against them, or in adhering to their enemies, giving them aid and comfort. No person shall be convicted of treason unless on the testimony of two witnesses to the same overt act, or on confession in open court.

(2) The Congress shall have power to declare the punishment of treason, but no attainder of treason shall work corruption of blood or forfeiture except during the life of the person attainted.

ARTICLE IV

Section 1. Full faith and credit shall be given in each State to the public acts, records, and judicial proceedings of every other State. And the Congress may by general laws prescribe the manner in which such acts, records, and proceedings shall be proved, and the effect thereof.

Section 2. (1) The citizens of each State shall be entitled to all privileges and immunities of citizens in the several States.

(2) A person charged in any State with treason, felony, or other crime, who shall flee from justice, and be found in another State, shall, on demand of the Executive authority of the State from which he fled, be delivered up, to be removed to the State having jurisdiction of the crime.

(3) No person held to service or labor in one State,

[8] Changed by 11th amendment.

under the laws thereof, escaping into another shall in consequence of any law or regulation therein, be discharged from such service or labor, but shall be delivered up on claim of the party to whom such service or labor may be due.[9]

Section 3. (1) New States may be admitted by the Congress into this Union; but no new State shall be formed or erected within the jurisdiction of any other State, nor any State be formed by the junction of two or more States, or parts of States, without the consent of the Legislatures of the States concerned, as well as of the Congress.

(2) The Congress shall have power to dispose of and make all needful rules and regulations respecting the territory or other property belonging to the United States; and nothing in this Constitution shall be so construed as to prejudice any claims of the United States, or of any particular State.

Section 4. The United States shall guarantee to every State in this Union a Republican form of government, and shall protect each of them against invasion, and, on application of the Legislature, or of the Executive (when the Legislature cannot be convened) against domestic violence.

ARTICLE V

The Congress, whenever two-thirds of both Houses shall deem it necessary, shall propose amendments to this Constitution, or, on the application of the Legislatures of two-thirds of the several States, shall call a convention for proposing amendments, which in either case, shall be valid to all intents and purposes, as part of this Constitution, when ratified by the Legislatures of three-fourths of the several States, or by conventions in three-fourths thereof, as the one or the other mode of ratification may be proposed by the Congress, provided that no amendment which may be made prior to the year one thousand eight hundred and eight shall in any manner affect the first and fourth clauses in the Ninth Section of the First Article; and that no State, without its consent, shall be deprived of its equal suffrage in the Senate.

ARTICLE VI

(1) All debts contracted and engagements entered into before the adoption of this Constitution shall be as valid against the United States under this Constitution as under the Confederation.

(2) This Constitution and the laws of the United States which shall be made in pursuance thereof and all treaties made, or which shall be made, under the authority of the United States, shall be the supreme law of the land, and the judges in every State shall be bound thereby, anything in the Constitution or laws of any State to the contrary notwithstanding.

(3) The Senators and Representatives before mentioned and the members of the several State Legislatures, and all executives and judicial officers, both of the United States and of the several States, shall be bound by oath or affirmation to support this Constitution; but no religious test shall ever be required as a qualification to any office or public trust under the United States.

ARTICLE VII

The ratification of the Conventions of nine States shall be sufficient for the establishment of this Constitution between the States so ratifying the same.

The Amendments to the Constitution

ARTICLE I

Congress shall make no law respecting an establishment of religion, or prohibiting the free exercise thereof; or abridging the freedom of speech or of the press; or the right of the people peaceably to assemble and to petition the Government for a redress of grievances.

ARTICLE II

A well-regulated militia being necessary to the security of a free State, the right of the people to keep and bear arms shall not be infringed.

ARTICLE III

No soldier shall, in time of peace, be quartered in any house without the consent of the owner, nor in time of war but in a manner to be prescribed by law.

ARTICLE IV

The right of the people to be secure in their persons, houses, papers, and effects, against unreasonable searches and seizures, shall not be violated, and no warrants shall issue but upon probable cause, supported by oath or affirmation, and particularly describing the place to be searched, and the persons or things to be seized.

ARTICLE V

No person shall be held to answer for a capital or other infamous crime unless on a presentment or indictment of a Grand Jury, except in cases arising in the land or naval forces, or in the militia, when in actual service, in time of war or public danger; nor shall any person be subject for the same offence to be twice put in jeopardy of life or limb; nor shall be compelled in any criminal case to be a witness against himself, nor be deprived of life, liberty or property, without due process of law; nor shall private property be taken for public use without just compensation.

ARTICLE VI

In all criminal prosecutions, the accused shall enjoy the right to a speedy and public trial, by an impartial jury of

[9] Became irrelevant after passage of 13th amendment abolishing slavery.

the State and district wherein the crime shall have been committed, which districts shall have been previously ascertained by law, and to be informed of the nature and cause of the accusation; to be confronted with the witnesses against him; to have compulsory process for obtaining witnesses in his favor, and to have the assistance of counsel for his defence.

ARTICLE VII
In suits at common law, where the value in controversy shall exceed twenty dollars, the right of trial by jury shall be preserved, and no fact tried by a jury shall be otherwise re-examined in any court of the United States than according to the rules of the common law.

ARTICLE VIII
Excessive bail shall not be required, nor excessive fines imposed, nor cruel and unusual punishments inflicted.

ARTICLE IX
The enumeration in the Constitution of certain rights shall not be construed to deny or disparage others retained by the people.

ARTICLE X
The powers not delegated to the United States by the Constitution, nor prohibited by it to the States, are reserved to the States respectively, or to the people.[10]

ARTICLE XI
The judicial power of the United States shall not be construed to extend to any suit in law or equity, commenced or prosecuted against one of the United States, by citizens of another State, or by citizens or subjects of any foreign state.[11]

ARTICLE XII
The Electors shall meet in their respective States and vote by ballot for President and Vice-President, one of whom at least shall not be an inhabitant of the same State with themselves; they shall name in their ballots the person voted for as President, and in distinct ballots the person voted for as Vice-President; and they shall make distinct lists of all persons voted for as President, and of all persons voted for as Vice-President, and of the number of votes for each, which list they shall sign and certify, and transmit, sealed, to the seat of the Government of the United States, directed to the President of the Senate; the President of the Senate shall, in the presence of the Senate and House of Representatives, open all the certificates and the votes shall then be counted; the person having the greatest number of votes for President shall be the President, if such number be a majority of the whole number of Electors appointed; and if no person have such majority, then from the persons having the highest number, not exceeding three, on the list of those voted for as President, the House of Representatives shall choose immediately, by ballot, the President. But in choosing the President, the votes shall be taken by States, the representation from each State having one vote; a quorum for this purpose shall consist of a member or members from two-thirds of the States, and a majority of all the States shall be necessary to a choice. And if the House of Representatives shall not choose a President, whenever the right of choice shall devolve upon them, before the fourth day of March next following, then the Vice-President shall act as President, as in the case of the death or other constitutional disability of the President. The person having the greatest number of votes as Vice-President shall be the Vice-President if such number be a majority of the whole number of Electors appointed, and if no person have a majority, then, from the two highest numbers on the list the Senate shall choose the Vice-President; a quorum for the purpose shall consist of two-thirds of the whole number of Senators, and a majority of the whole number shall be necessary to a choice. But no person constitutionally ineligible to the office of President shall be eligible to that of Vice-President of the United States.[12]

ARTICLE XIII
Section 1. Neither slavery nor involuntary servitude, except as a punishment for crime whereof the party shall have been duly convicted, shall exist within the United States, or any place subject to their jurisdiction.
Section 2. Congress shall have power to enforce this article by appropriate legislation.[13]

ARTICLE XIV
Section 1. All persons born or naturalized in the United States, and subject to the jurisdiction thereof are citizens of the United States and of the State wherein they reside. No State shall make or enforce any law which shall abridge the privileges or immunities of citizens of the United States, nor shall any State deprive any person of life, liberty, or property, without due process of law; nor deny to any person within its jurisdiction the equal protection of the laws.
Section 2. Representatives shall be apportioned among the several States according to their respective numbers, counting the whole number of persons in each State, excluding Indians not taxed. But when the right to vote at any election for the choice of Electors for President and Vice-President of the United States, Representatives in Congress, the executive and judicial officers of a State, or the members of the Legislature thereof, is denied to any of the male inhabitants of such State, being twenty-one years of age and citizens of the United States, or in any way abridged, except for participation in rebellion or other crime, the basis of representation therein shall be reduced in the proportion which the number of such male citizens shall bear to the whole number of male citizens twenty-one years of age in such State.
Section 3. No person shall be a Senator or Representative in Congress, or Elector of President and Vice-President, or hold any office, civil or military, under the United States,

[10] The first 10 amendments were ratified in 1791.

[11] Ratified January 8, 1798.

[12] Ratified September 25, 1804.

[13] Ratified December 18, 1864.

or under any State, who, having previously taken an oath, as a member of Congress, or as an officer of the United States, or as a member of any State Legislature, or as an executive or judicial officer of any State, to support the Constitution of the United States, shall have engaged in insurrection or rebellion against the same, or given aid or comfort to the enemies thereof. But Congress may, by a vote of two-thirds of each House, remove such disability.
Section 4. The validity of the public debt of the United States, authorized by law, including debts incurred for payment of pensions and bounties for services in suppressing insurrection or rebellion, shall not be questioned. But neither the United States, nor any State shall assume or pay any debt or obligation incurred in aid of insurrection or rebellion against the United States, or any claim for the loss or emancipation of any slave; but all such debts, obligations, and claims shall be held illegal and void.
Section 5. The Congress shall have power to enforce, by appropriate legislation, the provisions of this article.[14]

ARTICLE XV
Section 1. The right of the citizens of the United States to vote shall not be denied or abridged by the United States or by any State on account of race, color, or previous condition of servitude.
Section 2. The Congress shall have power to enforce the provisions of this article by appropriate legislation.[15]

ARTICLE XVI
The Congress shall have power to lay and collect taxes on incomes, from whatever sources derived, without apportionment among the several States, and without regard to any census or enumeration.[16]

ARTICLE XVII
The Senate of the United States shall be composed of two Senators from each State, elected by the people thereof, for six years; and each Senator shall have one vote. The Electors in each State shall have the qualifications requisite for Electors of the most numerous branch of the State legislatures.

When vacancies happen in the representation of any State in the Senate, the executive authority of such State shall issue writs of election to fill such vacancies: Provided, That the legislature of any State may empower the executive thereof to make temporary appointments until the people fill the vacancies by election as the legislature may direct.

This amendment shall not be construed as to affect the election or term of any Senator chosen before it became valid as part of the Constitution.[17]

ARTICLE XVIII
Section 1. After one year from the ratification of this article the manufacture, sale or transportation of intoxicating liquors within, the importation thereof into, or the exportation thereof from the United States and all territories subject to the jurisdiction thereof for beverage purposes is hereby prohibited.
Section 2. The Congress and the several States shall have concurrent power to enforce this article by appropriate legislation.
Section 3. This article shall be inoperative unless it shall have been ratified as an amendment to the Constitution by the legislatures of the several States, as provided in the Constitution, within seven years from the date of the submission hereof to the States by Congress.[18]

ARTICLE XIX
Section 1. The right of citizens of the United States to vote shall not be denied or abridged by the United States or by any State on account of sex.
Section 2. Congress shall have power, by appropriate legislation, to enforce the provisions of this article.[19]

ARTICLE XX
Section 1. The terms of the President and Vice-President shall end at noon on the 20th day of January, and the terms of Senators and Representatives at noon on the 3rd day of January, of the years in which such terms would have ended if this article had not been ratified; and the terms of their successors shall then begin.
Section 2. The Congress shall assemble at least once in every year, and such meeting shall begin at noon on the 3rd day of January, unless they shall by law appoint a different day.
Section 3. If, at the time fixed for the beginning of the term of the President, the President elect shall have died, the Vice-President elect shall become President. If a President shall not have been chosen before the time fixed for the beginning of his term, or if the President elect shall have failed to qualify, then the Vice-President elect shall act as President until a President shall have qualified; and the Congress may by law provide for the case wherein neither a President elect nor a Vice-President elect shall have qualified, declaring who shall then act as President or the manner in which one who is to act shall be selected, and such person shall act accordingly until a President or Vice-President shall have qualified.
Section 4. The Congress may by law provide for the case of the death of any of the persons from whom the House of Representatives may choose a President whenever the right of choice shall have devolved upon them, and for the case of the death of any of the persons from whom the Senate may choose a Vice-President whenever the right of choice shall have devolved upon them.
Section 5. Sections 1 and 2 shall take effect on the 15th day of October following the ratification of this article (Oct., 1933).

[14] Ratified July 28, 1868.
[15] Ratified March 30, 1870.
[16] Ratified February 25, 1913.
[17] Ratified May 31, 1913.
[18] Ratified January 29, 1919. Repealed by the 21st amendment.
[19] Ratified August 26, 1920.

Section 6. This article shall be inoperative unless it shall have been ratified as an amendment to the Constitution by the legislatures of three-fourths of the several States within seven years from the date of its submission.[20]

ARTICLE XXI

Section 1. The eighteenth article of amendment to the Constitution of the United States is hereby repealed.

Section 2. The transportation or importation into any State, Territory, or Possession of the United States for delivery or use therein of intoxicating liquors, in violation of the laws thereof, is hereby prohibited.

Section 3. This article shall be inoperative unless it shall have been ratified as an amendment to the Constitution by convention in the several States, as provided in the Constitution, within seven years from the date of the submission hereof to the States by the Congress.[21]

ARTICLE XXII

Section 1. No person shall be elected to the office of the President more than twice, and no person who has held the office of President, or acted as President, for more than two years of a term to which some other person was elected President shall be elected to the office of the President more than once. But this Article shall not apply to any person holding the office of President when this Article was proposed by the Congress, and shall not prevent any person who may be holding the office of President, or acting as President, during the term within which this Article becomes operative from holding the office of President or acting as President during the remainder of such term.

Section 2. This article shall be inoperative unless it shall have been ratified as an amendment to the Constitution by the legislatures of three-fourths of the several States within seven years from the date of its submission to the States by the Congress.[22]

Amendment at Present before the States

Section 1. The Congress shall have power to limit, regulate and prohibit the labor of persons under eighteen years of age.

Section 2. The power of the several States is unimpaired by this article except that the operation of State laws shall be suspended to the extent necessary to give effect to legislation enacted by Congress.

Submitted to the legislatures of the several States June 2, 1924.

The Presidents, Vice Presidents, and Cabinet Members, 1789–1970

THE WASHINGTON ADMINISTRATION (FEDERALIST)

	Name	*Dates Served*
President	George Washington	1789–1797
Vice President	John Adams	1789–1797
Secretary of State	Thomas Jefferson *(Republican)*	1789–1793
	Edmund Randolph	1793–1795
	Timothy Pickering	1795–1797
Secretary of the Treasury	Alexander Hamilton	1789–1794
	Oliver Wolcott	1794–1797
Secretary of War	Henry Knox	1789–1794
	Timothy Pickering	1794–1796
	James McHenry	1796–1797
Attorney General	Edmund Randolph	1789–1793
	William Bradford	1793–1795
	Charles Lee	1795–1797
Postmaster General	Samuel Osgood	1789–1791
	Timothy Pickering	1791–1794
	Joseph Habersham	1794–1797

THE ADAMS ADMINISTRATION (FEDERALIST)

	Name	*Dates Served*
President	John Adams	1797–1801
Vice President	Thomas Jefferson *(Republican)*	1797–1801
Secretary of State	Timothy Pickering	1797–1799
	John Marshall	1799–1801
Secretary of Treasury	Oliver Wolcott	1797–1800
	Samuel Dexter	1800–1801
Secretary of War	James McHenry	1797–1799
	John Marshall	1799–1800
	Samuel Dexter	1800–1801
	Roger Griswold	1801
Attorney General	Charles Lee	1797–1801
	Theophilus Parsons	1801
Postmaster General	Joseph Habersham	1797–1801
Secretary of Navy	Benjamin Stoddert	1798–1801

[20] Ratified January 23, 1933.
[21] Ratified December 5, 1933.
[22] Ratified March 1, 1951.

THE JEFFERSON ADMINISTRATION (REPUBLICAN)

	Name	Dates Served
President	Thomas Jefferson	1801–1809
Vice President	Aaron Burr	1801–1805
	George Clinton	1805–1809
Secretary of State	James Madison	1801–1809
Secretary of Treasury	Samuel Dexter *(Federalist)*	1801
	Albert Gallatin	1801–1809
Secretary of War	Henry Dearborn	1801–1809
Attorney General	Levi Lincoln	1801–1804
	Robert Smith	1804–1805
	John Breckinridge	1805–1806
	C. A. Rodney	1806–1809
Postmaster General	Joseph Habersham *(Federalist)*	1801
	Gideon Granger	1801–1809
Secretary of Navy	Benjamin Stoddert *(Federalist)*	1801
	Robert Smith	1801–1804
	Jacob Crowninshield	1804–1809

THE MADISON ADMINISTRATION (REPUBLICAN)

	Name	Dates Served
President	James Madison	1809–1817
Vice President	George Clinton	1809–1813
	Elbridge Gerry	1813–1817
Secretary of State	Robert Smith	1809–1811
	James Monroe	1811–1817
Secretary of Treasury	Albert Gallatin	1809–1813
	G. W. Campbell	1814
	A. J. Dallas	1814–1815
	W. H. Crawford	1815–1817
Secretary of War	William Eustis	1809–1812
	John Armstrong	1812–1813
	James Monroe	1814–1815
	W. H. Crawford	1815–1817
Attorney General	C. A. Rodney	1809–1811
	William Pinkney	1811–1814
	Richard Rush	1814–1817
Postmaster General	Gideon Granger	1809–1814
	R. J. Meigs, Jr.	1814–1817
Secretary of Navy	Paul Hamilton	1809–1813
	William Jones	1813–1814
	B. W. Crowninshield	1814–1817

THE MONROE ADMINISTRATION (REPUBLICAN)

	Name	Dates Served
President	James Monroe	1817–1825
Vice President	D. D. Tompkins	1817–1825
Secretary of State	J. Q. Adams	1817–1825
Secretary of Treasury	W. H. Crawford	1817–1825
Secretary of War	Isaac Shelby	1817
	George Graham	1817
	J. C. Calhoun	1817–1825
Attorney General	Richard Rush	1817
	William Wirt	1817–1825
Postmaster General	R. J. Meigs, Jr.	1817–1823
	John McLean	1823–1825
Secretary of Navy	B. W. Crowninshield	1817–1818
	Smith Thompson	1818–1823
	S. L. Southard	1823–1825

THE ADAMS ADMINISTRATION (NATIONAL REPUBLICAN)

	Name	Dates Served
President	John Quincy Adams	1825–1829
Vice President	J. C. Calhoun *(Republican)*	1825–1829
Secretary of State	Henry Clay	1825–1829
Secretary of Treasury	Richard Rush *(Republican)*	1825–1829
Secretary of War	James Barbour *(Republican)*	1825–1828
	P. B. Porter *(Republican)*	1828–1829
Attorney General	William Wirt *(Republican)*	1825–1829
Postmaster General	John McLean *(Republican)*	1825–1829
Secretary of Navy	S. L. Southard *(Republican)*	1825–1829

THE JACKSON ADMINISTRATION (DEMOCRAT)

	Name	Dates Served
President	Andrew Jackson	1829–1837
Vice President	John C. Calhoun	1829–1833
	Martin Van Buren	1833–1837
Secretary of State	Martin Van Buren	1829–1830
	Edward Livingston	1830–1832
	Louis McLane	1833–1834
	John Forsyth	1834–1837
Secretary of Treasury	S. D. Ingham	1829–1830
	Louis McLane	1830–1832
	W. J. Duane	1833
	R. B. Taney	1833–1834
	Levi Woodbury	1834–1837
Secretary of War	J. H. Eaton	1829–1831
	Lewis Cass	1831–1837
	B. F. Butler	1837
Attorney General	J. M. Berrien	1829–1831
	R. B. Taney	1831–1833
	B. F. Butler	1833–1837
Postmaster General	W. T. Barry	1829–1835
	Amos Kendall	1835–1837
Secretary of Navy	John Branch	1829–1831
	Levi Woodbury	1831–1834
	Mahlon Dickerson	1834–1837

THE VAN BUREN ADMINISTRATION (DEMOCRAT)

	Name	Dates Served
President	Martin Van Buren	1837–1841
Vice President	R. M. Johnson	1837–1841
Secretary of State	John Forsyth	1837–1841
Secretary of Treasury	Levi Woodbury	1837–1841
Secretary of War	J. R. Poinsett	1837–1841
Attorney General	B. F. Butler	1837–1838
	Felix Grundy	1838–1840
	H. D. Gilpin	1840–1841
Postmaster General	Amos Kendall	1837–1840
	J. M. Niles	1840–1841
Secretary of Navy	Mahlon Dickerson	1837–1838
	J. K. Paulding	1838–1841

THE HARRISON ADMINISTRATION (WHIG)

	Name	Dates Served
President	William H. Harrison	1841
Vice President	John Tyler	1841
Secretary of State	Daniel Webster	1841
Secretary of Treasury	Thomas Ewing	1841
Secretary of War	John Bell	1841
Attorney General	J. J. Crittenden	1841
Postmaster General	Francis Granger	1841
Secretary of Navy	George Badger	1841

THE TYLER ADMINISTRATION (WHIG AND DEMOCRAT)

	Name	Dates Served
President	John Tyler	1841–1845
Vice President	None	
Secretary of State	Daniel Webster *(Whig)*	1841–1843
	H. S. Legaré *(Whig)*	1843
	A. P. Upshur *(Whig)*	1843–1844
	J. C. Calhoun *(Democrat)*	1844–1845
Secretary of Treasury	Thomas Ewing *(Whig)*	1841
	Walter Forward *(Whig)*	1841–1843
	J. C. Spencer *(Whig)*	1843–1844
	George Bibb *(Whig)*	1844–1845
Secretary of War	John Bell *(Whig)*	1841
	John McLean *(Whig)*	1841
	J. C. Spencer *(Whig)*	1841–1843
	J. M. Porter *(Whig)*	1843–1844
	William Wilkins *(Whig)*	1844–1845
Attorney General	J. J. Crittenden *(Whig)*	1841
	H. S. Legaré *(Whig)*	1841–1843
	John Nelson *(Whig)*	1843–1845
Postmaster General	Francis Granger *(Whig)*	1841
	C. A. Wickliffe *(Whig)*	1841
Secretary of Navy	G. E. Badger *(Whig)*	1841
	A. P. Upshur *(Whig)*	1841
	David Henshaw *(Whig)*	1843–1844
	T. W. Gilmer *(Whig)*	1844
	J. Y. Mason *(Whig)*	1844–1845

THE POLK ADMINISTRATION (DEMOCRAT)

	Name	Dates Served
President	James K. Polk	1845–1849
Vice President	G. M. Dallas	1845–1849
Secretary of State	James Buchanan	1845–1849
Secretary of Treasury	R. J. Walker	1845–1849
Secretary of War	W. L. Marcy	1845–1849
Attorney General	J. Y. Mason	1845–1846
	Nathan Clifford	1846–1848
	Isaac Toucey	1848–1849
Postmaster General	Cave Johnson	1845–1849
Secretary of Navy	George Bancroft	1845–1846
	J. Y. Mason	1846–1849

THE TAYLOR ADMINISTRATION (WHIG)

	Name	Dates Served
President	Zachary Taylor	1849–1850
Vice President	Millard Fillmore	1849–1850
Secretary of State	J. M. Clayton	1849–1850
Secretary of Treasury	W. M. Meredith	1849–1850
Secretary of War	G. W. Crawford	1849–1850
Attorney General	Reverdy Johnson	1849–1850
Postmaster General	Jacob Collamer	1849–1850
Secretary of Navy	W. B. Preston	1849–1850
Secretary of Interior	Thomas Ewing	1849–1850

THE FILLMORE ADMINISTRATION (WHIG)

	Name	Dates Served
President	Millard Fillmore	1850–1853
Vice President	None	

	Name	Dates Served
Secretary of State	Daniel Webster Edward Everett	1850–1852 1852–1853
Secretary of Treasury	Thomas Corwin	1850–1853
Secretary of War	C. M. Conrad	1850–1853
Attorney General	J. J. Crittenden	1850–1853
Postmaster General	N. K. Hall S. D. Hubbard	1850–1852 1852–1853
Secretary of Navy	W. A. Graham J. P. Kennedy	1850–1852 1852–1853
Secretary of Interior	A. H. Stuart	1850–1853

THE PIERCE ADMINISTRATION (DEMOCRAT)

	Name	Dates Served
President	Franklin Pierce	1853–1857
Vice President	W. R. D. King	1853–1857
Secretary of State	W. L. Marcy	1853–1857
Secretary of Treasury	James Guthrie	1853–1857
Secretary of War	Jefferson Davis	1853–1857
Attorney General	Caleb Cushing	1853–1857
Postmaster General	James Campbell	1853–1857
Secretary of Navy	J. C. Dobbin	1853–1857
Secretary of Interior	Robert McClelland	1853–1857

THE BUCHANAN ADMINISTRATION (DEMOCRAT)

	Name	Dates Served
President	James Buchanan	1857–1861
Vice President	J. C. Breckinridge	1857–1861
Secretary of State	Lewis Cass J. S. Black	1857–1860 1860–1861
Secretary of Treasury	Howell Cobb P. F. Thomas J. A. Dix	1857–1860 1860–1861 1861
Secretary of War	J. B. Floyd Joseph Holt	1857–1861 1861
Attorney General	J. S. Black E. M. Stanton	1857–1860 1860–1861
Postmaster General	A. V. Brown Joseph Holt	1857–1859 1859–1861
Secretary of Navy	Isaac Toucey	1857–1861
Secretary of Interior	Jacob Thompson	1857–1861

THE LINCOLN ADMINISTRATION (REPUBLICAN)

	Name	Dates Served
President	Abraham Lincoln	1861–1865
Vice President	Hannibal Hamlin Andrew Johnson *(Unionist)*	1861–1865 1865
Secretary of State	W. H. Seward	1861–1865
Secretary of Treasury	S. P. Chase W. P. Fessenden Hugh McCulloch	1861–1864 1864–1865 1865
Secretary of War	Simon Cameron E. M. Stanton	1861–1862 1862–1865
Attorney General	Edward Bates T. J. Coffey James Speed	1861–1863 1863–1864 1864–1865
Postmaster General	Horatio King Montgomery Blair William Dennison	1861 1861–1864 1864–1865
Secretary of Navy	Gideon Welles	1861–1865
Secretary of Interior	C. B. Smith J. P. Usher	1861–1863 1863–1865

THE JOHNSON ADMINISTRATION (UNIONIST)

	Name	Dates Served
President	Andrew Johnson	1865–1869
Vice President	None	
Secretary of State	W. H. Seward *(Republican)*	1865–1869
Secretary of Treasury	Hugh McCulloch *(Republican)*	1865–1869
Secretary of War	E. M. Stanton *(Republican)* U. S. Grant *(Republican)* Lorenzo Thomas *(Republican)* J. M. Schofield *(Republican)*	1865–1867 1867–1868 1868 1868–1869
Attorney General	James Speed *(Republican)* Henry Stanbery *(Republican)* W. M. Evarts *(Republican)*	1865–1866 1866–1868 1868–1869
Postmaster General	William Dennison *(Republican)* A. W. Randall *(Republican)*	1865–1866 1866–1869
Secretary of Navy	Gideon Welles *(Republican)*	1865–1869
Secretary of Interior	J. P. Usher *(Republican)* James Harlan *(Republican)* O. H. Browning *(Republican)*	1865 1865 1865–1869

THE GRANT ADMINISTRATION (REPUBLICAN)

	Name	Dates Served
President	Ulysses S. Grant	1869–1877
Vice President	Schuyler Colfax Henry Wilson	1869–1873 1873–1877
Secretary of State	E. B. Washburne Hamilton Fish	1869 1869–1877

	Name	Dates Served
Secretary of Treasury	G. S. Boutwell	1869–1873
	W. A. Richardson	1873–1874
	B. H. Bristow	1874–1876
	L. M. Morrill	1876–1877
Secretary of War	J. A. Rawlins	1869
	W. T. Sherman	1869
	W. W. Belknap	1869–1876
	Alphonso Taft	1876
	J. D. Cameron	1876–1877
Attorney General	E. R. Hoar	1869–1870
	A. T. Ackerman	1870–1871
	G. H. Williams	1871–1875
	Edwin Pierrepont	1875–1876
	Alphonso Taft	1876–1877
Postmaster General	J. A. J. Creswell	1869–1874
	J. W. Marshall	1874
	Marshall Jewell	1874–1876
	J. N. Tyner	1876–1877
Secretary of Navy	A. E. Borie	1869
	G. M. Robeson	1869–1877
Secretary of Interior	J. D. Cox	1869–1870
	Columbus Delano	1870–1875
	Zachary Chandler	1875–1877

THE HAYES ADMINISTRATION (REPUBLICAN)

	Name	Dates Served
President	Rutherford B. Hayes	1877–1881
Vice President	William A. Wheeler	1877–1881
Secretary of State	William B. Evarts	1877–1881
Secretary of Treasury	John Sherman	1877–1881
Secretary of War	George W. McCrary	1877–1879
	Alex Ramsey	1879–1881
Attorney General	Charles Devens	1877–1881
Postmaster General	David M. Key	1877–1880
	Horace Maynard	1880–1881
Secretary of Navy	R. W. Thompson	1877–1881
	Nathan Goff, Jr.	1881
Secretary of Interior	Carl Schurz	1877–1881

THE GARFIELD ADMINISTRATION (REPUBLICAN)

	Name	Dates Served
President	James A. Garfield	1881
Vice President	Chester A. Arthur	1881
Secretary of State	James G. Blaine	1881
Secretary of Treasury	William Windom	1881
Secretary of War	R. T. Lincoln	1881
Attorney General	Wayne MacVeagh	1881
Postmaster General	T. L. James	1881
Secretary of Navy	W. H. Hunt	1881
Secretary of Interior	S. J. Kirkwood	1881

THE ARTHUR ADMINISTRATION (REPUBLICAN)

	Name	Dates Served
President	Chester A. Arthur	1881–1885
Vice President	None	
Secretary of State	F. T. Frelinghuysen	1881–1885
Secretary of Treasury	Charles J. Folger	1881–1884
	Walter Q. Gresham	1884
	Hugh McCulloch	1884–1885
Secretary of War	Robert T. Lincoln	1881–1885
Attorney General	Benjamin H. Brewster	1881–1885
Postmaster General	Timothy O. Howe	1881–1883
	Walter Q. Gresham	1883–1884
	Frank Hatton	1884–1885
Secretary of Navy	William E. Chandler	1881–1885
Secretary of Interior	Henry M. Teller	1881–1885

THE CLEVELAND ADMINISTRATION (DEMOCRAT)

	Name	Dates Served
President	Grover Cleveland	1885–1889
Vice President	T. A. Hendricks	1885–1889
Secretary of State	Thomas F. Bayard	1885–1889
Secretary of Treasury	Daniel Manning	1885–1887
	Charles S. Fairchild	1887–1889
Secretary of War	William C. Endicott	1885–1889
Attorney General	Augustus H. Garland	1885–1889
Postmaster General	William F. Vilas	1885–1888
	Don M. Dickinson	1888–1889
Secretary of Navy	William C. Whitney	1885–1889
Secretary of Interior	Lucius Q. C. Lamar	1885–1888
	William F. Vilas	1888–1889
Secretary of Agriculture	Norman J. Colman	1889

THE HARRISON ADMINISTRATION (REPUBLICAN)

	Name	Dates Served
President	Benjamin Harrison	1889–1893
Vice President	Levi P. Morton	1889–1893
Secretary of State	James G. Blaine	1889–1892
	John W. Foster	1892–1893
Secretary of Treasury	William Windom	1889–1891
	Charles Foster	1891–1893
Secretary of War	Redfield Proctor	1889–1891
	Stephen B. Elkins	1891–1893
Attorney General	William H. H. Miller	1889–1891
Postmaster General	James Wanamaker	1889–1893
Secretary of Navy	Benjamin F. Tracy	1889–1893
Secretary of Interior	John W. Noble	1889–1893
Secretary of Agriculture	John M. Rusk	1889–1893

THE CLEVELAND ADMINISTRATION (DEMOCRAT)

	Name	Dates Served
President	Grover Cleveland	1893–1897
Vice President	Adlai E. Stevenson	1893–1897
Secretary of State	Walter Q. Gresham	1893–1895
	Richard Olney	1895–1897
Secretary of Treasury	John G. Carlisle	1893–1897
Secretary of War	Daniel S. Lamont	1893–1897
Attorney General	Richard Olney	1893–1895
	James Harmon	1895–1897
Postmaster General	Wilson S. Bissell	1893–1895
	William L. Wilson	1895–1897
Secretary of Navy	Hilary A. Herbert	1893–1897
Secretary of Interior	Hoke Smith	1893–1896
	David R. Francis	1896–1897
Secretary of Agriculture	John S. Morton	1893–1897

THE MC KINLEY ADMINISTRATION (REPUBLICAN)

	Name	Dates Served
President	William McKinley	1897–1901
Vice President	Garret A. Hobart	1897–1901
	Theodore Roosevelt	1901
Secretary of State	John Sherman	1897
	William R. Day	1897–1898
	John Hay	1898–1901
Secretary of Treasury	Lyman J. Gage	1897–1901
Secretary of War	Russell A. Alger	1897–1899
	Elihu Root	1899–1901
Attorney General	James McKenna	1897
	John W. Griggs	1897–1901
	Philander C. Knox	1901
Postmaster General	James A. Gary	1897–1898
	Charles E. Smith	1898–1901
Secretary of Navy	John D. Long	1897–1901
Secretary of Interior	Charles N. Bliss	1897–1899
	Ethan A. Hitchcock	1899–1901
Secretary of Agriculture	James Wilson	1897–1901

THE ROOSEVELT ADMINISTRATION (REPUBLICAN)

	Name	Dates Served
President	Theodore Roosevelt	1901–1909
Vice President	Charles Fairbanks	1905–1909
Secretary of State	John Hay	1901–1905
	Elihu Root	1905–1909
	Robert Bacon	1909
Secretary of Treasury	Lyman J. Gage	1901–1902
	Leslie M. Shaw	1902–1907
	George B. Cortelyou	1907–1909
Secretary of War	Elihu Root	1901–1904
	William H. Taft	1904–1908
	Luke E. Wright	1908–1909
Attorney General	Philander C. Knox	1901–1904
	William H. Moody	1904–1907
	Charles J. Bonaparte	1907–1909

	Name	Dates Served
Postmaster General	Charles E. Smith	1901–1902
	Henry C. Payne	1902–1904
	Robert J. Wynne	1904–1905
	George B. Cortelyou	1905–1907
	George von L. Meyer	1907–1909
Secretary of Navy	John D. Long	1901–1902
	William H. Moody	1902–1904
	Paul Morton	1904–1905
	Charles J. Bonaparte	1905–1907
	Victor H. Metcalf	1907–1908
	Truman H. Newberry	1908–1909
Secretary of Interior	Ethan A. Hitchcock	1901–1907
	James R. Garfield	1907–1909
Secretary of Agriculture	James Wilson	1901–1909
Secretary of Labor and Commerce	George B. Cortelyou	1903–1904
	Victor H. Metcalf	1904–1907
	Oscar S. Straus	1907–1909
	Charles Nagel	1909

THE TAFT ADMINISTRATION (REPUBLICAN)

	Name	Dates Served
President	William H. Taft	1909–1913
Vice President	James S. Sherman	1909–1913
Secretary of State	Philander C. Knox	1909–1913
Secretary of Treasury	Franklin MacVeagh	1909–1913
Secretary of War	Jacob M. Dickinson	1909–1911
	Henry L. Stimson	1911–1913
Attorney General	George W. Wickersham	1909–1913
Postmaster General	Frank H. Hitchcock	1909–1913
Secretary of Navy	George von L. Meyer	1909–1913
Secretary of Interior	Richard A. Ballinger	1909–1911
	William L. Fisher	1911–1913
Secretary of Agriculture	James Wilson	1909–1913
Secretary of Labor and Commerce	Charles Nagel	1909–1913

THE WILSON ADMINISTRATION (DEMOCRAT)

	Name	Dates Served
President	Woodrow Wilson	1913–1921
Vice President	Thomas R. Marshall	1913–1921
Secretary of State	William J. Bryan	1913–1915
	Robert Lansing	1915–1920
	Bainbridge Colby	1920–1921
Secretary of Treasury	William G. McAdoo	1913–1918
	Carter Glass	1918–1920
	David F. Houston	1920–1921
Secretary of War	Lindley M. Garrison	1913–1916
	Newton D. Baker	1916–1921
Attorney General	James C. McReynolds	1913–1914
	Thomas W. Gregory	1914–1919
	A. Mitchell Palmer	1919–1921
Postmaster General	Albert S. Burleson	1913–1921
Secretary of Navy	Josephus Daniels	1913–1921
Secretary of Interior	Frank K. Lane	1913–1920
	John B. Payne	1920–1921
Secretary of Agriculture	David F. Houston	1913–1920
	Edwin T. Meredith	1920–1921

	Name	Dates Served
Secretary of Commerce	William C. Redfield Joshua W. Alexander	1913–1919 1919–1921
Secretary of Labor	William B. Wilson	1913–1921

THE HARDING ADMINISTRATION (REPUBLICAN)

	Name	Dates Served
President	Warren G. Harding	1921–1923
Vice President	Calvin Coolidge	1921–1923
Secretary of State	Charles E. Hughes	1921–1923
Secretary of Treasury	Andrew Mellon	1921–1923
Secretary of War	John W. Weeks	1921–1923
Attorney General	Harry M. Daugherty	1921–1923
Postmaster General	Will H. Hays Hubert Work Harry S. New	1921–1922 1922–1923 1923
Secretary of Navy	Edwin Denby	1921–1923
Secretary of Interior	Albert B. Fall Hubert Work	1921–1923 1923
Secretary of Agriculture	Henry A. Wallace	1921–1923
Secretary of Commerce	Herbert C. Hoover	1921–1923
Secretary of Labor	J. J. Davis	1921–1923

THE COOLIDGE ADMINISTRATION (REPUBLICAN)

	Name	Dates Served
President	Calvin Coolidge	1923–1929
Vice President	Charles G. Dawes	1925–1929
Secretary of State	Charles E. Hughes Frank B. Kellogg	1923–1925 1925–1929
Secretary of Treasury	Andrew Mellon	1923–1929
Secretary of War	John W. Weeks Dwight F. Davis	1923–1925 1925–1929
Attorney General	Henry M. Daugherty Harlan F. Stone John G. Sargent	1923–1924 1924–1925 1925–1929
Postmaster General	Harry S. New	1923–1929
Secretary of Navy	Edwin Denby Curtis D. Wilbur	1923–1924 1924–1929
Secretary of Interior	Hubert Work Roy O. West	1923–1928 1928–1929
Secretary of Agriculture	Henry A. Wallace Howard M. Gore William M. Jardine	1923–1924 1924–1925 1925–1929
Secretary of Commerce	Herbert C. Hoover William F. Whiting	1923–1928 1928–1929
Secretary of Labor	James J. Davis	1923–1929

THE HOOVER ADMINISTRATION (REPUBLICAN)

	Name	Dates Served
President	Herbert C. Hoover	1929–1933
Vice President	Charles Curtis	1929–1933
Secretary of State	Henry L. Stimson	1929–1933
Secretary of Treasury	Andrew Mellon Ogden L. Mills	1929–1932 1932–1933
Secretary of War	James W. Good Patrick J. Hurley	1929 1929–1933
Attorney General	William D. Mitchell	1929–1933
Postmaster General	Walter F. Brown	1929–1933
Secretary of Navy	Charles F. Adams	1929–1933
Secretary of Interior	Ray L. Wilbur	1929–1933
Secretary of Agriculture	Arthur M. Hyde	1929–1933
Secretary of Commerce	Robert P. Lamont Roy D. Chapin	1929–1932 1932–1933
Secretary of Labor	James J. Davis William N. Doak	1929–1930 1930–1933

THE ROOSEVELT ADMINISTRATION (DEMOCRAT)

	Name	Dates Served
President	Franklin D. Roosevelt	1933–1945
Vice President	John Nance Garner Henry A. Wallace Harry S. Truman	1933–1941 1941–1945 1945
Secretary of State	Cordell Hull E. R. Stettinius, Jr.	1933–1944 1944–1945
Secretary of Treasury	William H. Woodin Henry Morgenthau, Jr.	1933–1934 1934–1945
Secretary of War	George H. Dern Henry A. Woodring Henry L. Stimson	1933–1936 1936–1940 1940–1945
Attorney General	Henry S. Cummings Frank Murphy Robert H. Jackson Francis Biddle	1933–1939 1939–1940 1940–1941 1941–1945
Postmaster General	James A. Farley Frank C. Walker	1933–1940 1940–1945
Secretary of Navy	Claude A. Swanson Charles Edison Frank Knox James Forrestal	1933–1940 1940 1940–1944 1944–1945
Secretary of Interior	Harold L. Ickes	1933–1945
Secretary of Agriculture	Henry A. Wallace Claude R. Wickard	1933–1940 1940–1945
Secretary of Commerce	Daniel C. Roper Harry L. Hopkins Jesse Jones	1933–1939 1939–1940 1940–1945
Secretary of Labor	Frances Perkins	1933–1945

THE TRUMAN ADMINISTRATION (DEMOCRAT)

	Name	Dates Served
President	Harry S. Truman	1945–1953
Vice President	Alben W. Barkley	1949–1953
Secretary of State	James F. Byrnes George C. Marshall Dean G. Acheson	1945–1947 1947–1949 1949–1953
Secretary of Treasury	Fred M. Vinson John W. Snyder	1945–1946 1946–1953
Secretary of War	Robert H. Patterson Kenneth C. Royall	1945–1947 1947

	Name	Dates Served
Attorney General	Tom C. Clark	1945–1949
	J. Howard McGrath	1949–1952
	James P. McGranery	1952–1953
Postmaster General	Frank C. Walker	1945
	Robert E. Hannegan	1945–1947
	Jesse M. Donaldson	1947–1953
Secretary of Navy	James V. Forrestal	1945–1947
Secretary of Interior	Harold L. Ickes	1945–1946
	Julius A. Krug	1946–1951
	Oscar L. Chapman	1951–1953
Secretary of Agriculture	Clinton P. Anderson	1945–1948
	Charles F. Brannan	1948–1953
Secretary of Commerce	Henry A. Wallace	1945–1946
	W. Averell Harriman	1946–1948
	Charles W. Sawyer	1948–1953
Secretary of Labor	Lewis B. Schwellenbach	1945–1948
	Maurice J. Tobin	1948–1953
Secretary of Defense	James V. Forrestal	1947–1949
	Louis A. Johnson	1949–1950
	George C. Marshall	1950–1951
	Robert A. Lovett	1951–1953

THE EISENHOWER ADMINISTRATION (REPUBLICAN)

	Name	Dates Served
President	Dwight D. Eisenhower	1953–1961
Vice President	Richard M. Nixon	1953–1961
Secretary of State	John Foster Dulles	1953–1959
	Christian A. Herter	1959–1961
Secretary of Treasury	George M. Humphrey	1953–1957
	Robert B. Anderson	1957–1961
Attorney General	Herbert Brownell, Jr.	1953–1957
	William P. Rogers	1957–1961
Postmaster General	Arthur E. Summerfield	1953–1961
Secretary of Interior	Douglas McKay	1953–1956
	Fred A. Seaton	1956–1961
Secretary of Agriculture	Ezra T. Benson	1953–1961
Secretary of Commerce	Sinclair Weeks	1953–1958
	Lewis L. Strauss	1958–1959
	Frederick H. Mueller	1959–1961
Secretary of Labor	Martin P. Durkin	1953
	James P. Mitchell	1953–1961
Secretary of Defense	Charles E. Wilson	1953–1957
	Neil H. McElroy	1957–1959
	Thomas S. Gates, Jr.	1959–1961
Secretary of Health, Education, and Welfare	Oveta Culp Hobby	1953–1955
	Marion B. Folsom	1955–1958
	Arthur S. Flemming	1958–1961

THE KENNEDY ADMINISTRATION (DEMOCRAT)

	Name	Dates Served
President	John F. Kennedy	1961–1963
Vice President	Lyndon B. Johnson	1961–1963
Secretary of State	Dean Rusk	1961–1963
Secretary of Treasury	C. Douglas Dillon	1961–1963
Attorney General	Robert F. Kennedy	1961–1963
Postmaster General	J. Edward Day	1961–1963
	John A. Gronouski	1963
Secretary of Interior	Stewart L. Udall	1961–1963
Secretary of Agriculture	Orville L. Freeman	1961–1963
Secretary of Commerce	Luther H. Hodges	1961–1963
Secretary of Labor	Arthur J. Goldberg	1961–1962
	W. Willard Wirtz	1962–1963
Secretary of Defense	Robert S. McNamara	1961–1963
Secretary of Health, Education, and Welfare	Abraham A. Ribicoff	1961–1962
	Anthony J. Celebrezze	1962–1963

THE JOHNSON ADMINISTRATION (DEMOCRAT)

	Name	Dates Served
President	Lyndon B. Johnson	1963–1969
Vice President	Hubert H. Humphrey	1965–1969
Secretary of State	Dean Rusk	1963–1969
Secretary of Treasury	C. Douglas Dillon	1963–1965
	Henry H. Fowler	1965–1969
Attorney General	Robert F. Kennedy	1963–1964
	Nicholas Katzenbach	1964–1967
	Ramsey Clark	1967–1969
Secretary of Interior	Stewart L. Udall	1963–1969
Postmaster General	John A. Gronouski	1963–1965
	Lawrence F. O'Brien	1965–1968
	Marvin Watson	1968–1969
Secretary of Agriculture	Orville L. Freeman	1963–1969
Secretary of Commerce	Luther H. Hodges	1963–1964
	John T. Connor	1964–1967
	A. B. Trowbridge	1967–1969
Secretary of Labor	W. Willard Wirtz	1963–1969
Secretary of Defense	Robert F. McNamara	1963–1968
	Clark Clifford	1968–1969
Secretary of Health, Education, and Welfare	Anthony J. Celebrezze	1963–1965
	John W. Gardner	1965–1968
Secretary of Housing and Urban Development	Robert C. Weaver	1966–1969
Secretary of Transportation	Alan S. Boyd	1966–1969

THE NIXON ADMINISTRATION (REPUBLICAN)

	Name	Dates Served
President	Richard M. Nixon	1969–
Vice President	Spiro T. Agnew	1969–
Secretary of State	William P. Rogers	1969–
Secretary of Treasury	David M. Kennedy	1969–
Attorney General	John N. Mitchell	1969–
Postmaster General	Winton M. Blount	1969–
Secretary of Interior	Walter J. Hickel	1969–
Secretary of Agriculture	Clifford M. Hardin	1969–
Secretary of Commerce	Maurice H. Stans	1969–
Secretary of Labor	George P. Schultz	1969–
Secretary of Defense	Melvin R. Laird	1969–
Secretary of Health, Education, and Welfare	Robert H. Finch	1969–
Secretary of Housing and Urban Development	George Romney	1969–
Secretary of Transportation	John A. Volpe	1969–

Political Party Affiliations in Congress and the Presidency, 1789–1971*

Year	Congress	House: Majority Party	House: Principal Minority Party	House: Other except Vacancies	Senate: Majority Party	Senate: Principal Minority Party	Senate: Other except Vacancies	President and Party
1789–1791	1st	Ad-38	Op-26	–	Ad-17	Op-9	–	F (Washington)
1791–1793	2d	F-37	DR-33	–	F-16	DR-13	–	F (Washington)
1793–1795	3d	DR-57	F-48	–	F-17	DR-13	–	F (Washington)
1795–1797	4th	F-54	DR-52	–	F-19	DR-13	–	F (Washington)
1797–1799	5th	F-58	DR-48	–	F-20	DR-12	–	F (John Adams)
1799–1801	6th	F-64	DR-42	–	F-19	DR-13	–	F (John Adams)
1801–1803	7th	DR-69	F-36	–	DR-18	F-13	–	DR (Jefferson)
1803–1805	8th	DR-102	F-39	–	DR-25	F-9	–	DR (Jefferson)
1805–1807	9th	DR-116	F-25	–	DR-27	F-7	–	DR (Jefferson)
1807–1809	10th	DR-118	F-24	–	DR-28	F-6	–	DR (Jefferson)
1809–1811	11th	DR-94	F-48	–	DR-28	F-6	–	DR (Madison)
1811–1813	12th	DR-108	F-36	–	DR-30	F-6	–	DR (Madison)
1813–1815	13th	DR-112	F-68	–	DR-27	F-9	–	DR (Madison)
1815–1817	14th	DR-117	F-65	–	DR-25	F-11	–	DR (Madison)
1817–1819	15th	DR-141	F-42	–	DR-34	F-10	–	DR (Monroe)
1819–1821	16th	DR-156	F-27	–	DR-35	F-7	–	DR (Monroe)
1821–1823	17th	DR-158	F-25	–	DR-44	F-4	–	DR (Monroe)
1823–1825	18th	DR-187	F-26	–	DR-44	F-4	–	DR (Monroe)
1825–1827	19th	Ad-105	J-97	–	Ad-26	J-20	–	C (J. Q. Adams)
1827–1829	20th	J-119	Ad-94	–	J-28	Ad-20	–	C (J. Q. Adams)
1829–1831	21st	D-139	NR-74	–	D-26	NR-22	–	D (Jackson)
1831–1833	22d	D-141	NR-58	14	D-25	NR-21	2	D (Jackson)
1833–1835	23d	D-147	AM-53	60	D-20	NR-20	8	D (Jackson)
1835–1837	24th	D-145	W-98	–	D-27	W-25	–	D (Jackson)
1837–1839	25th	D-108	W-107	24	D-30	W-18	4	D (Van Buren)
1839–1841	26th	D-124	W-118	–	D-28	W-22	–	D (Van Buren)
1841–1843	27th	W-133	D-102	6	W-28	D-22	2	W (Harrison) W (Tyler)
1843–1845	28th	D-142	W-79	1	W-28	D-25	1	W (Tyler)
1845–1847	29th	D-143	W-77	6	D-31	W-25	–	D (Polk)
1847–1849	30th	W-115	D-108	4	D-36	W-21	1	D (Polk)
1849–1851	31st	D-112	W-109	9	D-35	W-25	2	W (Taylor) W (Fillmore)
1851–1853	32d	D-140	W-88	5	D-35	W-24	3	W (Fillmore)
1853–1855	33d	D-159	W-71	4	D-38	W-22	2	D (Pierce)
1855–1857	34th	R-108	D-83	43	D-40	R-15	5	D (Pierce)
1857–1859	35th	D-118	R-92	26	D-36	R-20	8	D (Buchanan)
1859–1861	36th	R-114	D-92	31	D-36	R-26	4	D (Buchanan)
1861–1863	37th	R-105	D-43	30	R-31	D-10	8	R (Lincoln)
1863–1865	38th	R-102	D-75	9	R-36	D-9	5	R (Lincoln)
1865–1867	39th	U-149	D-42	–	U-42	D-10	–	R (Lincoln) R (Johnson)
1867–1869	40th	R-143	D-49	–	R-42	D-11	–	R (Johnson)
1869–1871	41st	R-149	D-63	–	R-56	D-11	–	R (Grant)
1871–1873	42d	R-134	D-104	5	R-52	D-17	5	R (Grant)
1873–1875	43d	R-194	D-92	14	R-49	D-19	5	R (Grant)
1875–1877	44th	D-169	R-109	14	R-45	D-29	2	R (Grant)
1877–1879	45th	D-153	R-140	–	R-39	D-36	1	R (Hayes)

* Letter symbols for political parties. Ad–Administration; AM–Anti-Masonic; C–Coalition; D–Democratic; DR–Democratic-Republican; F–Federalist; J–Jacksonian; NR–National-Republican; Op–Opposition; R–Republican; U–Unionist; W–Whig.

Political Party Affiliations in Congress and the Presidency, 1789–1971 (Continued)*

Year	*Congress*	*House*			*Senate*			*President and Party*
		Majority Party	*Principal Minority Party*	*Other except Vacancies*	*Majority Party*	*Principal Minority Party*	*Other except Vacancies*	
1879–1881	46th	D-149	R-130	14	D-42	R-33	1	R (Hayes)
1881–1883	47th	R-147	D-135	11	R-37	D-37	1	R (Garfield) R (Arthur)
1883–1885	48th	D-197	R-118	10	R-38	D-36	2	R (Arthur)
1885–1887	49th	D-183	R-140	2	R-43	D-34	–	D (Cleveland)
1887–1889	50th	D-169	R-152	4	R-39	D-37	–	D (Cleveland)
1889–1891	51st	R-166	D-159	–	R-39	D-37	–	R (B. Harrison)
1891–1893	52d	D-235	R-88	9	R-47	D-39	2	R (B. Harrison)
1893–1895	53d	D-218	R-127	11	D-44	R-38	3	D (Cleveland)
1895–1897	54th	R-244	D-105	7	R-43	D-39	6	D (Cleveland)
1897–1899	55th	R-204	D-113	40	R-47	D-34	7	R (McKinley)
1899–1901	56th	R-185	D-163	9	R-53	D-26	8	R (McKinley)
1901–1903	57th	R-197	D-151	9	R-55	D-31	4	R (McKinley) R (T. Roosevelt)
1903–1905	58th	R-208	D-178	–	R-57	D-33	–	R (T. Roosevelt)
1905–1907	59th	R-250	D-136	–	R-57	D-33	–	R (T. Roosevelt)
1907–1909	60th	R-222	D-164	–	R-61	D-31	–	R (T. Roosevelt)
1909–1911	61st	R-219	D-172	–	R-61	D-32	–	R (Taft)
1911–1913	62d	D-228	R-161	1	R-51	D-41	–	R (Taft)
1913–1915	63d	D-291	R-127	17	D-51	R-44	1	D (Wilson)
1915–1917	64th	D-230	R-196	9	D-56	R-40	–	D (Wilson)
1917–1919	65th	D-216	R-210	6	D-53	R-42	–	D (Wilson)
1919–1921	66th	R-240	D-190	3	R-49	D-47	–	D (Wilson)
1921–1923	67th	R-301	D-131	1	R-59	D-37	–	R (Harding)
1923–1925	68th	R-225	D-205	5	R-51	D-43	2	R (Coolidge)
1925–1927	69th	R-247	D-183	4	R-56	D-39	1	R (Coolidge)
1927–1929	70th	R-237	D-195	3	R-49	D-46	1	R (Coolidge)
1929–1931	71st	R-267	D-167	1	R-56	D-39	1	R (Hoover)
1931–1933	72d	D-220	R-214	1	R-48	D-47	1	R (Hoover)
1933–1935	73d	D-310	R-117	5	D-60	R-35	1	D (F. Roosevelt)
1935–1937	74th	D-319	R-103	10	D-69	R-25	2	D (F. Roosevelt)
1937–1939	75th	D-331	R-89	13	D-76	R-16	4	D (F. Roosevelt)
1939–1941	76th	D-261	R-164	4	D-69	R-23	4	D (F. Roosevelt)
1941–1943	77th	D-268	R-162	5	D-66	R-28	2	D (F. Roosevelt)
1943–1945	78th	D-218	R-208	4	D-58	R-37	1	D (F. Roosevelt)
1945–1947	79th	D-242	R-190	2	D-56	R-38	1	D (Truman)
1947–1949	80th	R-245	D-188	1	R-51	D-45	–	D (Truman)
1949–1951	81st	D-263	R-171	1	D-54	R-42	–	D (Truman)
1951–1953	82d	D-243	R-199	1	D-49	R-47	–	D (Truman)
1953–1955	83d	R-221	D-211	1	R-48	D-47	1	R (Eisenhower)
1955–1957	84th	D-232	R-203	–	D-48	R-47	1	R (Eisenhower)
1957–1959	85th	D-233	R-200	–	D-49	R-47	–	R (Eisenhower)
1959–1961	86th	D-283	R-153	–	D-64	R-34	–	R (Eisenhower)
1961–1963	87th	D-263	R-174	–	D-65	R-35	–	D (Kennedy)
1963–1965	88th	D-258	R-177	–	D-67	R-33	–	D (Kennedy) D (Johnson)
1965–1967	89th	D-295	R-140	–	D-68	R-32	–	D (Johnson)
1967–1969	90th	D-247	R-187	1	D-64	R-36	–	D (Johnson)
1969–1971	91st	D-243	R-192	–	D-58	R-42	–	R (Nixon)

Source: U.S. Bureau of the Census, *Historical Statistics of the United States: Colonial Times to the Present,* Department of Commerce, Washington, D.C., 1957.

Justices of the United States Supreme Court, 1789–1970*

Name and Residence	*Service Term*	*Years*	*Dates*
John Jay, N.Y.	1789–1795	5	1745–1829
John Rutledge, S.C.	1789–1791	1	1739–1800
William Cushing, Mass.	1789–1810	20	1732–1810
James Wilson, Pa.	1789–1798	8	1742–1798
John Blair, Va.	1789–1796	6	1732–1800
Robert H. Harrison, Md.	1789–1790	–	1745–1790
James Iredell, N.C.	1790–1799	9	1751–1799
Thomas Johnson, Md.	1791–1793	1	1732–1819
William Paterson, N.J.	1793–1806	13	1745–1806
John Rutledge, S.C.	1795–†	–	1739–1800
Samuel Chase, Md.	1796–1811	15	1741–1811
Oliver Ellsworth, Conn.	1796–1799	4	1745–1807
Bushrod Washington, Va.	1798–1829	31	1762–1829
Alfred Moore, N.C.	1799–1804	4	1755–1810
John Marshall, Va.	1801–1835	34	1755–1835
William Johnson, S.C.	1804–1834	30	1771–1834
Brockholst Livingston, N.Y.	1806–1823	16	1757–1823
Thomas Todd, Ky.	1807–1826	18	1765–1826
Joseph Story, Mass.	1811–1845	33	1779–1845
Gabriel Duval, Md.	1811–1835	24	1752–1844
Smith Thompson, N.Y.	1823–1843	20	1768–1843
Robert Trimble, Ky.	1826–1828	2	1777–1828
John McLean, Ohio	1829–1861	32	1785–1861
Henry Baldwin, Pa.	1830–1844	14	1780–1844
James M. Wayne, Ga.	1835–1867	32	1790–1867
Roger B. Taney, Md.	1836–1864	28	1777–1864
Philip P. Barbour, Va.	1836–1841	4	1783–1841
John Catron, Tenn.	1837–1865	28	1786–1865
John McKinley, Ala.	1837–1852	15	1780–1852
Peter V. Daniel, Va.	1841–1860	19	1784–1860
Samuel Nelson, N.Y.	1845–1872	27	1792–1873
Levi Woodbury, N.H.	1845–1851	5	1789–1851
Robert C. Grier, Pa.	1846–1870	23	1794–1870
Benjamin R. Curtis, Mass.	1851–1857	6	1809–1874
John A. Campbell, Ala.	1853–1861	8	1811–1889
Nathan Clifford, Maine	1858–1881	23	1803–1881
Noah H. Swayne, Ohio	1862–1881	18	1804–1884
Samuel F. Miller, Iowa	1862–1890	28	1816–1890
David Davis, Ill.	1862–1877	14	1815–1886
Stephen J. Field, Calif.	1863–1897	34	1816–1899
Salmon P. Chase, Ohio	1864–1873	8	1808–1873
William Strong, Pa.	1870–1880	10	1808–1895
Joseph P. Bradley, N.J.	1870–1892	22	1813–1892
Ward Hunt, N.Y.	1873–1882	9	1810–1886
Morrison R. Waite, Ohio	1874–1888	14	1816–1888
John M. Harlan, Ky.	1877–1911	34	1833–1911
William B. Woods, Ga.	1881–1887	6	1824–1887
Stanley Matthews, Ohio	1881–1889	7	1824–1889
Horace Gray, Mass.	1882–1902	20	1828–1902
Samuel Blatchford, N.Y.	1882–1893	11	1820–1893
Lucius Q. C. Lamar, Miss.	1888–1893	5	1825–1893
Melville W. Fuller, Ill.	1888–1910	21	1833–1910
David J. Brewer, Kans.	1890–1910	20	1837–1910
Henry B. Brown, Mich.	1891–1906	15	1836–1913
George Shiras, Jr., Pa.	1892–1903	10	1832–1924
Howell E. Jackson, Tenn.	1893–1895	2	1832–1895
Edward D. White, La.	1894–1910	16	1845–1921
Rufus W. Peckham, N.Y.	1896–1909	13	1838–1909
Joseph McKenna, Calif.	1898–1925	26	1843–1926
Oliver W. Holmes, Mass.	1902–1932	30	1841–1935
William R. Day, Ohio	1903–1922	19	1849–1923
William H. Moody, Mass.	1906–1910	3	1853–1917
Horace H. Lurton, Tenn.	1910–1914	4	1844–1914
Charles E. Hughes, N.Y.	1910–1916	5	1862–1948
Willis Van Devanter, Wyo.	1911–1937	26	1859–1941
Joseph R. Lamar, Ga.	1911–1916	5	1857–1916
Edward D. White, La.	1910–1921	11	1845–1921
Mahlon Pitney, N.J.	1912–1922	10	1858–1924
James C. McReynolds, Tenn.	1914–1941	26	1862–1946
Louis D. Brandeis, Mass.	1916–1939	22	1856–1941
John H. Clarke, Ohio	1916–1922	6	1857–1945
William H. Taft, Conn.	1921–1930	8	1857–1930
George Sutherland, Utah	1922–1938	15	1862–1948
Pierce Butler, Minn.	1922–1939	16	1866–1939
Edward T. Sanford, Tenn.	1923–1930	7	1865–1930
Harlan F. Stone, N.Y.	1925–1941	16	1872–1946
Charles E. Hughes, N.Y.	1930–1941	11	1862–1948
Owen J. Roberts, Pa.	1930–1945	15	1875–1955
Benjamin N. Cardozo, N.Y.	1932–1938	6	1870–1938
Hugo L. Black, Ala.	1937–	–	1886–
Stanley F. Reed, Ky.	1938–1957‡	19	1884–
Felix Frankfurter, Mass.	1939–1962	23	1882–1965
William O. Douglas, Conn.	1939–	–	1898–
Frank Murphy, Mich.	1940–1949	9	1890–1949
Harlan F. Stone, N.Y.	1941–1946	5	1872–1946
James F. Byrnes, S.C.	1941–1942‡	1	1879–
Robert H. Jackson, N.Y.	1941–1954	13	1892–1954
Wiley B. Rutledge, Iowa	1943–1949	6	1894–1949
Harold H. Burton, Ohio	1945–1958	13	1888–1964
Fred M. Vinson, Ky.	1946–1953	7	1890–1953
Tom C. Clark, Tex.	1949–1967‡	18	1899–
Sherman Minton, Ind.	1949–1956	7	1890–1965
Earl Warren, Calif.	1953–1969	16	1891–
John Marshall Harlan, N.Y.	1955–	–	1899–
William J. Brennan, Jr., N.Y.	1956–	–	1906–
Charles E. Whittaker, Mo.	1957–1962	5	1901–
Potter Stewart, Ohio	1958–	–	1915–
Byron R. White, Colo.	1962–	–	1917–
Arthur J. Goldberg, Ill.	1962–1965	3	1908–
Abe Fortas, Tenn.	1965–1969	4	1910–
Thurgood Marshall, N.Y.	1967–	–	1908–
Warren C. Burger, Minn.	1969–	–	1907–

* Chief Justices in italic.
† Rejected December 15, 1795.
‡ Retired.

Admission of the States, 1787–1959

State	Date	State	Date
Delaware	December 7, 1787	Michigan	January 16, 1837
Pennsylvania	December 12, 1787	Florida	March 3, 1845
New Jersey	December 18, 1787	Texas	December 29, 1845
Georgia	January 2, 1788	Iowa	December 28, 1846
Connecticut	January 9, 1788	Wisconsin	May 29, 1848
Massachusetts	February 6, 1788	California	September 9, 1850
Maryland	April 28, 1788	Minnesota	May 11, 1858
South Carolina	May 23, 1788	Oregon	February 14, 1859
New Hampshire	June 21, 1788	Kansas	January 29, 1861
Virginia	June 25, 1788	West Virginia	June 19, 1863
New York	July 26, 1788	Nevada	October 31, 1864
North Carolina	November 21, 1789	Nebraska	March 1, 1867
Rhode Island	May 29, 1790	Colorado	August 1, 1876
Vermont	March 4, 1791	North Dakota	November 2, 1889
Kentucky	June 1, 1792	South Dakota	November 2, 1889
Tennessee	June 1, 1796	Montana	November 8, 1889
Ohio	March 1, 1803	Washington	November 11, 1889
Louisiana	April 30, 1812	Idaho	July 3, 1890
Indiana	December 11, 1816	Wyoming	July 10, 1890
Mississippi	December 10, 1817	Utah	January 4, 1896
Illinois	December 3, 1818	Oklahoma	November 16, 1907
Alabama	December 14, 1819	New Mexico	January 6, 1912
Maine	March 15, 1820	Arizona	February 14, 1912
Missouri	August 10, 1821	Alaska	January 3, 1959
Arkansas	June 15, 1836	Hawaii	August 21, 1959

Population of the United States, 1790–1975

Geographic Area	1790	1800	1810	1820	1830	1840	1850
New England	1,009,408	1,233,011	1,471,973	1,660,071	1,954,717	2,234,822	2,728,116
Middle Atlantic	958,632	1,402,565	2,014,702	2,699,845	3,587,664	4,526,260	5,898,735
East North Central	–	51,006	272,324	792,719	1,470,018	2,924,728	4,523,260
West North Central	–	–	19,783	66,586	140,455	426,814	880,335
South Atlantic	1,851,806	2,286,494	2,674,891	3,061,063	3,645,752	3,925,299	4,679,090
East South Central	109,368	335,407	708,590	1,190,489	1,815,969	2,575,445	3,363,271
West South Central	–	–	77,618	167,680	264,127	449,985	940,251
Mountain	–	–	–	–	–	–	72,927
Pacific	–	–	–	–	–	–	105,891
TOTAL	3,935,214	5,308,483	7,239,881	9,638,453	12,866,020	17,069,453	23,191,896

Geographic Area	1860	1870	1880	1890	1900	1910	1920
New England	3,135,283	3,487,924	4,010,529	4,700,749	5,592,017	6,552,681	7,400,909
Middle Atlantic	7,458,985	8,810,806	10,496,878	12,706,220	15,454,678	19,315,892	22,261,144
East North Central	6,926,884	9,124,517	11,206,668	13,478,305	15,985,581	18,250,621	21,475,543
West North Central	2,169,832	3,856,594	6,157,443	8,932,112	10,347,423	11,637,921	12,544,249
South Atlantic	5,364,703	5,853,610	7,597,197	8,857,922	10,443,480	12,194,895	13,990,272
East South Central	4,020,991	4,404,445	5,585,151	6,429,154	7,547,757	8,409,901	8,893,307
West South Central	1,747,667	2,029,965	3,334,220	4,740,983	6,532,290	8,784,534	10,242,224
Mountain	174,923	315,385	653,119	1,213,935	1,674,657	2,633,517	3,336,101
Pacific	444,053	675,125	1,114,578	1,888,334	2,416,692	4,192,304	5,566,871
TOTAL	31,443,321	39,276,813					

Geographic Area	1930	1940	1950	1960	1975*
New England	8,166,346	8,437,290	9,314,453	10,509,367	12,471,000
Middle Atlantic	26,260,750	27,539,487	30,163,533	34,168,452	40,747,000
East North Central	25,297,185	26,626,342	30,399,368	36,225,024	42,534,000
West North Central	13,296,915	13,516,990	14,061,394	15,394,115	16,896,000
South Atlantic	15,793,589	17,823,151	21,182,335	25,971,732	34,232,000
East South Central	9,887,214	10,778,225	11,477,181	12,050,126	14,228,000
West South Central	12,176,830	13,064,525	14,537,572	16,951,255	21,484,000
Mountain	3,701,789	4,150,003	5,074,998	6,855,060	9,398,000
Pacific	8,194,433	9,733,262	14,486,527	21,198,044	30,812,000

* Projected.

Per Capita Disposable Personal Income, 1929–1967*

Year	Current Prices	1958 Prices
1929	$ 683	$1,236
1930	605	1,128
1931	516	1,077
1932	390	921
1933	362	893
1934	414	952
1935	459	1,035
1936	518	1,158
1937	552	1,187
1938	504	1,105
1939	537	1,190
1940	573	1,259
1941	695	1,427
1942	867	1,582
1943	976	1,629
1944	1,057	1,673
1945	1,074	1,642
1946	1,132	1,606
1947	1,178	1,513
1948	1,290	1,567
1949	1,264	1,547
1950	$1,364	$1,646
1951	1,469	1,657
1952	1,518	1,678
1953	1,583	1,726
1954	1,585	1,714
1955	1,666	1,795
1956	1,743	1,839
1957	1,801	1,844
1958	1,831	1,831
1959	1,905	1,881
1960	1,937	1,883
1961	1,983	1,909
1962	2,064	1,968
1963	2,136	2,013
1964	2,280	2,123
1965	2,427	2,232
1966	2,584	2,317
1967	2,735	2,391

* *Economic Report of the President,* 1968, Table B–16, p. 227.

Index

Aaron, Henry, 1257
Aberdeen, Lord, 500, 501
Ableman v. Booth, 530
Abolitionism, 358, 408, 457, 459, 460, 541
Abolitionists, 358, 459, 468, 479, 521, 625
  Negro, 460
  in New England, 524
  in North, 530, 542, 567
  in Old Northwest, 479
"Acres of Diamonds," 833
Act of Bogota, 1237
Adams, Andy, on cattle drives, 744
Adams, Charles Francis, 567, 625, 653
Adams, Henry, 624
Adams, John, 120, 130, 134, 146, 148, 152, 162, 163, 244, 273, 331
  background of, 246
  at Constitutional Convention, 204, 205
  defeated in 1800 election, 243
  elected President in 1796, 242, 246, 250
  Federal acts under, 248, 249
  in peace plans, 158, 159
  Presidency of, 246–250
  at Second Continental Congress, 135
  as Vice President, 224, 225, 245
Adams, John Quincy, 297, 298, 337, 340–342, 356, 599, 885
  background of, 321
  diplomacy of, 330–333
  elected President, 338
  in House of Representatives, 479
  on Latin American independence, 333–335
  Presidency of, 338–340
  Secretary of State, 321, 1223
Adams, Samuel, 126, 128, 129, 146, 205, 218
  at Second Continental Congress, 135
Adams-Onis Treaty, 331
Adamson Act, 917
Addams, Jane, 737, 1019
Administration of Justice Act, 129
Advertising and promotion, 675, 1035
Affluence, American, after 1950, 1246, 1251, 1252
  gross national product, rise of, 1251
  millionaires, 1252
Africa, 2, 8, 11
Afrika Korps, 1113
Agassiz, Louis, 449
Agnew, Spiro T., elected Vice President, 1308
Agrarian League, 403
Agricultural Adjustment Act (AAA), 1060–1062
Agricultural Adjustment Act of 1938 (second AAA), 1061, 1064, 1065, 1086
Agricultural Wheel, The, farm organization, 777
Agriculture, 652, 662, 674
  from 1820–1860: in North, 382–384
    in South, 404, 406–408, 417–421, 425
    in West, 383, 425

Agriculture:
farm policies from 1865–1896, 768–789
campaign of 1896, 786–790
Cleveland's second Administration, 784–786
farm problems, 773–775
Farmers' Alliance, Populists, 777–778, 783–784
Greenback movement, 776–777
sectional developments, 772–773
trends in farming, 769–771
Mississippi Valley, 1866–1896, 772
in 1920s, 1037–1040, 1050–1052
in second Administration of Dwight D. Eisenhower, 1212, 1213
Southern, 1866–1896, 772–773
Western frontier from 1865–1900:
areas of, 757–759
defined, 746
public lands in, 746
railroads in, 757
Aguinaldo, Emilio, insurrectionist, 846, 848
Aime, Valcour, planter, 408
Aisne-Marne sector, 949
Alabama, 169, 256, 382
university chartered by, 431
secession of, 55)
statehood of, 322
Alabama River, 418
Alamo, the, 484
Alaska, 499
Albany conference of 1754, 113, 166
Albany Evening Journal, 376
"Albany Regency," 340
Alcott, Bronson, 452
Aldrich, Nelson W., 655, 656, 872, 885
tariff proposals of, 896
Aldrich Commission (*see* National Monetary Commission)
Aldrich-Vreeland Act of 1908, 885, 914
Aleutian Islands, 1120
Alexander VI, Pope, 10
Alexander, James, 111
Alexandria, Virginia, 600
Algiers, 1114
Algonquin Indians, 58
allies of French, 59
Alien Act of 1798, 248, 250
Alien Enemies Act of 1798, 248, 250
Alien Property Custodian's Office, scandal of, 967
Allen, Ethan, 135, 198
Allen, Frederick Lewis, 918, 1085
Allen, Levi, 198
Allen, William, 485
Alliance for Progress, 1237
Allied Supreme War Council, 950
Allies, 923, 927, 928
in push across France, 949
secret treaties of, 948
ships for, 942
Allison, William B., 654, 656, 872
Allston, Thomas, planter, 407
Altizeo, Thomas J. J., and William Hamilton, 1259
Amalgamated Association of Iron and Steel Workers, 702
America in 1914, 907–908, 913
America First Committee, 1102, 1103
American Act (*see* Sugar Act of 1764)
American Antislavery Society, 460
American Association for the Advancement of Science, 449
American Bell Telephone Company, 669
American Bimetallic Union, 786
American Board of Customs Commissioners, 120, 127
American Board of Foreign Missions, 496
American Colonization Society, 459
American empire (new), 835–853
annexation of Philippines, 845–848
Hawaii, 839–840
open door for China, 849–851
Pacific markets and coaling stations, 836–838
Samoa, 838–839
Spanish-American War, 840–844
war in the Caribbean, 844–845
war in Philippines, 848–849
American Equal Rights Association, 831
American Expeditionary Forces, 937, 949
battles of, 949
American Federation of Labor (AFL), 701, 702, 916, 943, 1036, 1037, 1048
in clash with Committee for Industrial Organization (CIO), 1066–1067
American Iron and Steel Association, 655
American Legion, 967, 1052
American Liberty League, 1070
American Monthly Magazine, 432
American party (*see* Know-Nothing party)
American Peace Society, 458
American Protective Association, 707, 831
American Railway Union, 702, 703
American society, derivation of, 2
American Society of Newspaper Editors, 1162
American Society for the Promotion of Temperance (*see* National Temperance Union)
American Sugar Refining Company, 680
American System, 336, 337, 370, 371, 384, 471, 475, 477, 490, 568
American Telephone and Telegraph Company, 1220
American Tobacco Company, 898, 1035
Amherst, Jeffrey, 118
Amish, 20
Amity and Commerce, Treaty of, 150
Amnesty:
after Civil War, 602, 603
after World War I, 959
Ampudia, General Pedro, 505
Anabaptists, 18–20, 45, 61
"Anacreon in Heaven," 295
Anderson, Major Robert, Fort Sumter surrendered by, 558
Andros, Sir Edmund, 106
Anglican Church, 20, 47
after American Revolution, 194
in colonial America, 83–85, 105
Anglo-Dutch naval war, 1652–1654, 59
Anglo-Dutch War, 1665–1667, 59
Anglo-Dutch War, 1672–1674, 59
Annapolis convention, 203
Anthony, Susan B., 458, 831
Anthracite Coal Strike Commission, 874
Antietam, battle of, 563, 570
Antifederalists, 223, 243, 245
Anti-Imperialist League, 847
Anti-Mason party, 362
Anti-Masons, 472

Antinomian belief, 56
Anti-Saloon League, 984
Antitrust movement, 678, 680
Antwerp, liberation of, 1118
Apache Indians, 760
Apalachicola, 296, 1252
Apostle Paul, 468
Appalachian Mountains, 119, 159, 169, 322
poverty in, 1252, 1253
Appamatox Court House, Virginia, 584, 599, 607, 623, 662
Arab League, the, 1234
Arabic (British ship), 926
Arapaho Indians, 494, 760, 761
(*See also* Great Plains Indians)
Arcadia Conference, 1112
Archbishop of Canterbury, 117
Architects, late nineteenth century, 829, 830
Architecture, 829, 830
colonial, 100
Area Redevelopment Administration, 1206
Areopagitica, 45
Argentina, 334, 340
Argonne sector, 949
Aristocracy (planters) in South, 404, 407
Arizona, 764
Arkansas, secession of, 558
Arkansas River, 257, 333
Arkwright, Richard, inventor, 406
Armat, Thomas, inventor, 830
Armed Forces, 214, 222, 238, 249, 250
increase in 1811, 282
increase in 1861, 558, 559
Armour, Philip D., 665, 667
death of, 669
Armstrong, John, Secretary of War, 287, 290, 295
Armstrong, Samuel C., 808
Army of Northern Virginia, 563, 575
Army of the Potomac, 563, 566, 574
Army War College, 886
Arnold, Benedict, 135, 147, 149, 150
in British service, 155
resentment by, 152
wounded in battle, 137
Arnold, General H. H., 1122
Aroostook Valley, 476
Aroostook War, 476
Arrears of Pensions Act of 1879, 653
Art forms after 1950, 1263, 1264
Arthur, Chester A., 641
Presidency of, 645, 646
Vice Presidential nomination of, 644
Arthur, T. S., 457
Articles of Confederation, 151, 166, 167, 212, 217, 220, 223
inadequacies of, 197–203
Nationalist reform efforts under, 201–203
plans for strengthening of, 203, 204
as U.S. Constitution, 167
Arts:
in colonies, 89, 90
music, 90
painting, 89, 90
after 1950, 1261, 1262
Ashburton, Lord, 476
Asbury, Bishop, 457
Asbury, Francis, 194
Ashley, William Henry, trapper, 494
Asia, 2, 10
America barrier to, 42
European trade with, 2–5, 22
Asian New Order, 1104, 1107
Associationist movement, 403
Astor, John, 651
Astor, John Jacob, 496
Aswan Dam, 1231
Atcheson, Dean, Secretary of State, 1162, 1167, 1169, 1240
Atgeed, Governor John P., 703
Atheists, 163
Atlanta, Georgia, 576, 584
burning of, 576
Atlanta Constitution, 674
Atlanta University, 808
Atlantic Charter:
principles of, 1151
Russian attitude not expressed in, 1151
territorial settlements postponed, 1151, 1152
(*See also* Cold War)
Atlantic Monthly, 432, 832
Atomic bomb, 1124, 1131
Atomic Energy Act of 1946, 1180
Atomic Energy Commission, 1200, 1204
Attucks, Crispus, 120, 405
Audubon, J. J., 449
Austin, Moses, 482
Austin, Stephen F., 482
Austria, German annexation of, 1098
Authors, works, late nineteenth century, 825–828
Autobiography, Franklin's, 100
Automobiles in economy, 1027, 1028, 1035
Aztec Indians, 11

Bacon, Nathaniel, 105
rebellion led by, 105
Baer, George F., 874
Bailey, James A., circus owner, 830
Bailey, Professor Thomas A., 950
Baker, Newton D., Secretary of War:
mobilization by, 937
pardons petition to, 959
Baker, Ray Stannard, 857, 858
Baker v. Carr on districting review, 1300
(*See also* Warren Court)
Baku oil fields, 1114
Balance-of-payments deficit, 1215
Balance of trade, 173, 1042
Balboa, Vasco Nuñez de, 17
Baldwin, Hansen, 1131
Baldwin, James, 1257
Ballinger, Richard A., Secretary of the Interior, 897
Ballinger-Pinchot controversy, 897
Baltimore, Lord (*see* Calvert, Cecilius)
Baltimore, Maryland, 295, 422, 423
1860 Democratic Convention in, 548
first dental college in, 431
Baltimore and Ohio Railroad, 386, 665
Baltimore American, 493
Bancroft, George, 452, 489
Secretary of the Navy, 504, 508
Bands during Depression, 1074
Bank of North America, Philadelphia, 153
Bank of the United States, 227, 228, 252, 255, 370, 476
death of Bank, 362
expiration of, 302
in *McCullough v. Maryland*, 323, 324
Osborn v. Bank of the United States, 324

Bank of the United States:
Second Bank of United States, Jackson's war on, 360, 361, 378, 477
second bank chartered, 1816, 303, 304
management of, 322, 323
Bank holiday, March 6, 1933, 1058
Bankhead-Jones Farm Tenancy Act, 1062
Banking reform of 1930s, 1058, 1059
Bankruptcy, 424, 784
Banks:
Federal Reserve, 914, 1058
state chartered, 228, 303, 360, 914
Briscoe v. The Bank of Kentucky, 375
paper money issued by, 228, 302, 322
Banneker, Benjamin, 405
Bannock tribe, 760
Bantam Books Incorporated v. Sullivan on dissemination of obscene literature, 1301
(*See also* Warren Court)
Baptists, 20, 194, 482
in colonial America, 83–85
1815–1860, 455, 456
Barbados, 58, 62
slaves in, 71
Barclay, Robert, 289
Barkley Senator Alben W., 1187
Barnard, George Gray, 829
Barnard, Henry, educator, 430
"Barnburners," New York, 524, 529
Barnum, P. T., 540, 830
Barron, James, 272
Barry, John, 154
Barrymore, Ethel, 830
Barrymore, John, 830
Barrymore, Lionel, 830
Bartless, Paul, 829
Bartram, John, 101
Baruch, Bernard M., 1063, 1127
Baton Rouge revolt, 281
Battle, Martin, 1253
Bay of Pigs, assault on, 1237
Bayard, James A., 251, 297, 298
Bayard, Thomas, Secretary of State, 839
Bayonne Decree of 1808, 279
Bear Flag revolt, 507
Beard, Charles A., 1100
Beatles, the, 1264
Beatnik movement of 1950s, 1281
Beaufort, South Carolina, 21
Beaumarchais, Caron de, 146, 151
Beauregard, General P. G. T., 560, 561
General Albert Sidney Johnston replaced by, 562
Beck, Dave, 1213
Beckley, John, 245
Beecher, Henry Ward, 460
Beecher, Lyman, 455, 457
Belknap, W. W., 626
Bell, Alexander Graham, 669
Bell, John, Constitutional Union party nominee, 550
Bellamy, Edward, 678
Belleau Woods, 949
Bemis Heights, battle of (*see* Freeman's Farm, second battle of)
Benezet, Anthony, 86
Benghazi, 1114
Bennett, James Gordon, 432, 832
Bennington, Vermont, 149
Benson, Ezra Taft, Secretary of Agriculture, 1201, 1212
Bentley, Elizabeth, 1192
Benton, Senator Thomas Hart:
background of, 348
daughter of, 498
money policy of, 360–362, 372
in Oregon compromise, 500
Berger, Victor L., Socialist leader, 945
Berkeley, Lord John, 60
Berkeley, Sir William, 105
Berlin, Germany, fall of, 1120
Berlin airlift, 1161
Berlin blockade, 1161
Berlin Decrees of 1806, 260, 279
Berlin wall, 1240
Bestor, Arthur, 1258
Beveridge, Senator Albert, 845, 956
Beverly, Robert, 100
Bible, the, 794, 795, 797
Biddle, Nicholas, bank president, 360, 362, 370, 372
Bierstadt, Albert, artist, 453
Big Change, The, 918
Bill of Rights, 218, 220, 223
Madison's role in, 276
ten amendments approved, 224
Billings, William, 195
Bingham, George Caleb, 453
Birmingham, Alabama, 674, 1257, 1290
Birney, James G., 479, 487
Black, Justice Hugo, 1300
Black Ball line, 388
Black Codes, 604
"Black Friday" gold scandal, 623, 656
Black Hawk, Chief, 356
Black Kettle, Chief, 761
Black Muslims, 1303
Black power, 1302, 1303
Blackfoot Indians, 494, 760
(*See also* Great Plains Indians)
Blaine, James G., 634, 652, 837, 838
blunders of, 651
Presidential nomination of, 646, 651
Blair, Francis P., 489
Bland, Richard, 118, 783
Bland-Allison Act, 644, 657, 783
Bliss, Tasker H., 953
Blockades, naval, 129, 137, 150, 153, 249, 260
Allied, 1112
Berlin, 1161
by British in World War II, 927
of Confederacy, 558, 577
of Manila Bay, 845
in War of 1812, 290
Blount, James G., 840
Blue Swallowtail line, 388
Board of Trade, British, 110, 116
Albany conference called by, 113
Bolivar, Simon, 340
Bolsheviks (*see* Communists)
Bond issues, Allied, 924
Bonn government, 1239, 1240
Bonneville, Oregon, 1070
Book of Etiquette, 1035
Book of Mormon, 456
Boone, Daniel, 169
Boonesborough, Kentucky, 169
Booth, Edwin, 830
Booth, John Wilkes, 584
Borah, Senator William E., League of Nations foe, 956–958
as isolationist, 1100
on Washington Conference of 1921, 1017
Borglum, Gutzon, 829

Boston, Massachusetts, 116, 422
in American Revolution, 134–136, 147
Boston Herald, 1020
Boston Manufacturing Company, the, 399, 402
Boston Port Act of 1774, 129
Boston Tea Party, 129
Boun Oum, Prince, 1238
Bowdoin, Governor James, 175–176
Bowers, Henry F., 831
Bowie brothers, the, 482
Boxer Rebellion, China's, 851
Boycotts, 127, 701
by civil rights advocates, 1256
Braddock, General Edward, 113
Bradford, William, 48
Bradley, Joseph P., (justice), 481
Bradley, General Omar, 1118, 1174
Bradstreet, Anne, 100
Bragg, General Braxton, Confederate officer, 572, 574
Brandeis, Justice Louis D., 916
Brandywine Creek, battle of, 149
Brannan, Charles F., Secretary of Agriculture, 1191, 1192
Brazil, 10, 340, 406
Bread colonies (*see* Middle colonies)
Breckinridge, John C., Presidential nomination of, 548, 550
Breckinridge, Robert J., 480
Breed's Hill, 136
Brenner Pass, 951, 1092
Brewster, William, 47
Briand, Aristide, 1019
Brickes, John W., 1145
Bridenbaugh, Carl, 88
Bridges, Senator Styles, 1168
Bright, Jesse, 485
Brinkerhoff, Jacob, 522
Brisbane, Albert, 403
Briscoe v. The Bank of Kentucky, 375
Bristow, Benjamin H., 626
Brock, Isaac, 285, 287
Brook Farm, 403, 452
Brooke, Sir Alan, war strategist, 1114
Brooklyn Heights, New York, 147
Brooks, Gwendolyn, poetess, 1257
Brooks, Preston S., 534
Brotherhood of Sleeping Car Porters, 1132
Brown, Aaron V., 485
Brown, B. Gratz, 625
Brown, John, raid by, 542
Brown, Rap, 1303
Brown v. Board of Education of Topeka, 1255
Brown University, 85
Bruce, Blanche Kelso, Negro Senator, 610
Brussels, Belgium, liberation of, 1118
Bryan, Governor Charles W., Vice Presidential nominee in 1924, 971
Bryan, William Jennings, 785, 786, 788, 848, 971
background of, 787
death of, 990
factors in defeat of, 788, 789
Presidential nomination of, 787
in John T. Scopes prosecution, 989, 990
second defeat of, 855
as Secretary of State, 921, 922, 926, 948
resignation of, 926
third defeat of, 895
Bryant, Dr. J. D., 825
Bryant, William Cullen, 450
Bryant & Sturgis, 495, 498
Bryce, Lord, 640, 641
Buchanan, James, 485, 489, 567–569
elected President, 535
Presidency of, 537, 551, 552
secession legality denied by, 551
as Secretary of State, 503
as Senator, 493
Southern views favored by, 541
Buckner, Simon B., Vice Presidential nominee, 787
Budget and Accounting Act of 1921, 967
Buel, Jesse, 383
Buena Vista, battle of, 505
Buenos Aires, 10
Buffalo Bill's Wild West Show, 830
Buffalo Evening Telegraph, 651
Buffalo herds, 744, 762
Bulge, Battle of the, 1118
Bull Moose party (*see* Progressive party)
Bull Run (*see* Manassas)
Bunau-Varilla, Philippe, 887
Bunche, Ralph, United Nations mediator, 1257
Bunker Hill, battle of, 136, 147
Bureau of Chemistry in U.S., 875
Bureau of Corporations, 873
Bureau of Forestry, 876
Bureau of Immigration, 582
Bureau of Labor Statistics, 701
Burgoyne, John:
Gage reinforced by, 136
losses of, 149, 150
surrender at Saratoga, 133, 150, 159
Burke, Edmund, 244
Burke Act of 1906, 702
Burlingame, Anson, 836
Burlington Railroad, 666, 873
Burnside, Ambrose E., Union officer, 563, 566, 571, 582
Burr, Aaron, 246
conspiracy of, 258, 259
duel of, 259
elected Vice President, 250, 251
treason trial of, 259, 287
Bushy Run, Pennsylvania, 118
Business Week, 1181
Butler, Andrew Pickens, 534
Butler, Nicholas Murray, president of Columbia University, 1019, 1020
Butte, Montana, 742
Byrd, William, planter, 86, 88–89, 100
Byrnes, Senator James F., 1071–1072, 1159
Byzantium, 3

Cabinet, John F. Kennedy's, 1289
Cable, transatlantic, 669
Cabot, John, 16
Cadore, the Duc de, 279
Calhoun, Floride, 346, 347
Calhoun, John C., 277, 282, 358, 359, 531, 540
background of, 321
nomination of, 336
Presidential aspirations of, 321
second national bank legislation sponsored by, 303
as Secretary of State, 485
as Secretary of War, 321
in Senate, 350, 478–480, 500
on slavery in territories, 522, 523
tariff views of, 341
as Vice President, 341, 342, 346, 347, 349
resignation, 350

California, 333, 494, 519, 522, 835, 836
in Compromise of 1850, 526, 527
Franciscan missions in, 496
gold discovered in, 424, 525, 740
issue in Mexico-U.S. War, 502–518
Mexican province, 496
California, University of, Berkeley, 1281
Calvert, Benedict, 107
Calvert, Cecilius, 57
Calvert, George, 57
Calvin, John, 20
Calvinists, 20, 45, 55
in colonial America, 84, 90
Camargo, Mexico, 505
Cambodia, 1230
Camden, South Carolina, 154
Campanella, Roy, 1257
Campbell, Alexander, 456
Campbell, Thomas, 456
Canada, 106, 112, 476
abortive invasion of, 285, 301
campaign for, 137, 281, 284–288
Canal Zone, 888, 889
Canals, 203, 253, 384
from Albany to Buffalo, New York, 384
in Ohio, 386
Canning, George, 334, 335, 339, 340
Cannon, James, 164
Cannon, Joseph B., Speaker of the House, 872, 897
Cape Breton Island, 64, 112
Cape Verde Islands, 10
Capone, Al, 984
Capper, Senator Arthur, 1159
Capper-Tincher Grain Futures Act (1922), 1038
Caribbean Islands, 42, 58, 249
Carleton, Sir Guy, 137, 147
Carmichael, Stokely, 1303
Carnegie, Andrew, 665, 847
income of, 737
in steel industry, 670, 671
Carnegie Steel Workers of Homestead, Pennsylvania, 702
Carolinas, the, 948, 1122
(*See also* German Islands of the Pacific; World War II in the Pacific)
Caroline incident, 476
Carpetbaggers, 609–611
Carranza, Venustiano, Mexican President, 922
Carroll, Father John, 194
Carter, Robert, 71
Carteret, George, 60
Cartier, Jacques, 17
Cartwright, Edmund, inventor, 406
Cartwright, Peter, circuit-riding preacher, 455
Carver, George Washington, 808, 825
Casablanca, 1114
Casablanca conference, 1117
Case, Senator Francis, 1185
Case, J. J., 383
Case bill of 1946, veto of, 1185
Case School of Applied Science (Case Institute), 807
Cass, Lewis:
political defeat of, 535
Presidential nomination of, 524
as Secretary of War, 350, 485
Senate leader, 523
Castlereagh, Viscount (Robert), 283 297, 333
Castro, Cipriano, Venezuelan dictator, 889
Castro, Fidel, 1237, 1240
Cather, Willa, 764
Catherine of Aragon, 20, 22
Catholic University of St. Louis, 496
Catholics, Roman, 4–5, 16, 20–22, 83, 106, 110, 455, 456
areas of, in late nineteenth century, 798
in England, 1660–1689, 59, 60
German, 455
Irish, 455
in Maryland, 57, 58, 106–107
in 1920s, 976
in Quebec, 129
rights of, 194
schools, 456
Catlin, George, 453
Cato's Letters, 112
Cattle, 71, 418, 667
disease of, 744
drives, 744
in Northwest, 743–746
range, 743, 745
in Texas, 743–746
Caucasus, 1114
Caucus system, 336, 527
Cavell, Edith, executed British nurse, 924
Cayuse Indians, 496
Censorship, 45, 1301
by British in World War I, 927
of motion pictures, 944
of press, 944
Census, U.S., 212, 739, 766, 975
farm, 768
Central Intelligence Agency, 1180, 1236
Central Pacific Railroad, 568–569, 626, 666
Central Powers during World War I, 927, 947, 951
peace negotiated with Russia, 947
(*See also* Germany)
Century of Dishonor, A, 762
Challenge of Europe in 1920s:
European power revolution, 1014
French and British views of Germany, 1015, 1016
Germany as potential threat, 1014
ideology, long-range purposes of Russia, 1015
Challenge of the City, The, 868
Chamber of Commerce, United States, 1202
Chamberlain, Neville, British Prime Minister, 1097
at Munich, 1098
Chambers, Whittaker, 1192
Champlain, Samuel de, 64
route to Canada, 134
Chancellorsville, battle of, 571
Chandler, Zach, 566
Channing, Edward, editor, 450
Channing, William Ellery, 452, 455
Chapultepec, fortress, 517
Character, American, 1815–1860, 428–429
belief in progress, 428
commitment to democracy, 428
hard work, 428
practicality, 428
Charles I, King of England, 44, 47, 48, 55, 57
beheaded, 107
Charles II, King of England, 44, 59, 60, 105, 106
Charles River Bridge case, 374, 375

Charleston, South Carolina, 72, 120, 408, 423, 550
in American Revolution, 138, 154
as Democratic Convention site, 542
Charleston, the (dance), 975, 986
Charleston and Hamburg Railroad, 386, 418
Charleston Harbor, 552
Charleston Mercury, 523, 532
Charleston News, 674
Charlestown peninsula, 136
Charlottesville, Virginia, 600
"Charter of Liberties," 61
Chase, Salmon P., 527, 531
in Civil War financing, 567, 568
Presidential ambitions of, 583
Chase, Judge Samuel, 255
Chateau-Thierry, 949
Chattanooga, Tennessee, 418, 574, 576
Chattanooga River, 418
Chautauqua movement, 833
Chavis, John, free Negro, 405
Cheatham, Henry P., Negro Congressman, 659
Cherokee Indians, 339, 350, 356
Chesapeake, 272, 277, 281, 282
Chesapeake Bay, 17, 46, 69, 155, 203
"Chester" (song), 195
Cheves, Langdon, 282
Bank of United States headed by, 323
bank crisis, 323
Chewning v. Cunningham on counsel denial, 1300
(*See also* Warren Court)
Cheyenne Indians, 494, 730–762
(*See also* Great Plains Indians)
Chiang Kai-shek, 1096, 1122, 1166–1168, 1196–1197, 1226
return to power anticipated, 1225
Chibcha, 14
Chicago, Illinois, 285, 381, 423
1868 Republican convention in, 612
1884 Democratic convention in, 646
1888 Republican convention in, 655
1896 Democratic convention in, 787
1912 Republican convention in, 903
1920 Republican convention in, 964
1932 Republican Democratic conventions in, 1052
1960 Republican convention in, 1287
wheat market, 581
Chicago, University of, 807
Chicago Times, 719
Chicago Tribune, 719
Chicago's West Side, 1253
Chickasaw Indians, 356, 756
Child labor, 402
Keating-Owen bill on, 704
legislation, 867, 902, 1063, 1064, 1066
Children's Bureau, 898
Chile, 334, 340
China, 3–5, 17, 835
American interests in, 836, 849, 851
British interests in, 850, 851
Anson Burlingame in, 836
Communist, 1225–1227
Germany and France in, 849, 851
Open Door Notes, 850, 851
Open Door policy for, 849–851, 890, 901, 948, 952, 1017, 1225
in Pacific crisis of 1938–1941, 1104–1107, 1196
Russian ambitions in, 849
in Sino-Japanese War, 1096–1097
Chinese Exclusion Act, 1882, 646, 706
Chisholm Trail, 744
Chivington, Colonel J. M., 761
Choctaw Indians, 356, 756
Christian Leadership Conference, 1256
Christian Science (*see* Church of Christ, Scientist)
Christian Science Monitor, 1020
Christy, David, 540
Chrysler Corporation, 1027
Chrysler's Farm, battle of, 287
Church of Christ, Scientist, 797, 798
Church of England, 20, 44, 48
(*See also* Anglican Church)
Church of Jesus Christ of Latter-day Saints, 456
Church membership, 1914, 913
Churches Quarrel Espoused, 1710, 100
Churchill, Winston, 1091
aid requested by, 1103
in World War II, 1112
Churubusco, battle of, 507, 517
Cincinnati, Ohio, 172, 322, 381, 422, 423, 499
land office at, 231
Liberal Republican convention in, 625
Circuses, 830
"Citizen Genêt" (*see* Genêt, Edmond Charles)
Civil rights:
bill of 1866, 605, 606
in colonies, 110
failure in South, 636
of Negroes after 1875, 641
after 1950, 1246
Commission on Civil Rights, 1255, 1256
focused on schools in South, 1257
march on Washington, D.C., 1257
of Negroes, 1254–1257
in Reconstruction, 602
in Truman's administration, 1186 1187
Civil Rights Act of 1866, 605–608
Civil Rights Act of 1875, 628
Civil Rights Act of 1957, 1256
Civil Rights Act of 1964, 1296, 1297
Civil Service, 622, 625, 626, 634
reform, 641, 644, 645, 651, 653, 656, 657
Civil Service Advisory Board, 643
Civil Service Commission, 645, 656
Civil War in America, 255, 419, 420, 424, 556–595, 663
behind Northern lines, 580–582
Confederacy problems, 578–580
emancipation, 567, 569–570
end of, 584
Fort Sumter, 57–58
Gettysburg, Vicksburg, and Chattanooga, 571–573
Ulysses S. Grant in command, 574–576
opening campaigns of, 560
William H. Seward's diplomacy, 576–578
War Congress, 566–567
war preparations: in North, 558–559
in South, 560
wartime measures, 567–569
wartime policies in North, 583–584
Civil War in England, 55, 57, 61

Civil Works Administration (CWA), 1060, 1065
Civilian Conservation Corps (CCC), 1059
Clarendon, Earl of, 61
Clark, Champ, Speaker of the House, 898, 904
Clark, Elijah, 155
Clark, George Rogers, 154, 256
Clark, J. Reuben, State Department officer, 1014
Clark, John Bates, economist, 792–793
Clark, William, 256, 257
Clay, Henry, 282, 298, 376, 377, 485, 533, 553
  American System of, 337, 370, 371, 384, 568
  background of, 304, 321
  in Compromise of 1850, 525, 526
  on Latin American independence, 333, 334
  in Missouri Compromise, 328–330
  nominated by Whigs, 487
  nomination of, 336–338, 360, 362
  Presidential aspirations of, 321
  as Speaker of the House of Representatives, 282, 321
  in tariff crisis, 359
  as Whig party leader, 474
Clayton Antitrust Act, 704, 915–916
Clayton-Bulwer Treaty, 519, 887
Cleaver, Eldridge, 1303
Clemenceau, Georges, of France, 950, 951
Clemens, Samuel (*see* Twain, Mark)
Clement, Governor Frank, 1205
Cleveland, Grover, 635, 641, 656, 680, 703, 839, 847
  accused of moral laxity, 651
  elected President, 651–652
  first administration of, 653–655
  Presidential nomination of, 646
  qualifications, views of, 652
  renomination, defeat of, 655
  second administration of, 784, 786
    agriculture and labor, 784, 785
    monetary policy, 785
    on Spanish-American War, 840–841
Cleveland, Ohio, 423
Clinton, DeWitt, 297, 384, 429
Clinton, Governor George, 202, 220, 237
  as Vice Presidential candidate, 245, 259
Clinton, General Henry, 136, 148–150, 152–155, 158
  Savannah captured by, 154
Clipper ships, 388
Closed shop, 403
Coal, 400, 663, 1043
  declining production of, 1028, 1034
Cobbett, William, 429
Cochrane, Admiral Sir Alexander, 290, 296
Cody, William F., 830
Cohens v. Virginia, 324, 325
Coinage Act of 1873, 783
Coin's Financial School, 786
Cold Harbor, battle of, 575
Cold War, the:
  alliance, containment, 1159–1162
  changing Far East, 1164, 1166
  China and the Great Debate, 1167–1169
  Chinese debacle, 1166, 1167
  divided Europe, 1152–1154
  Korean War, 1169–1171, 1174
  London Conference, 1157
  Potsdam, 1156, 1157
  problem of means, 1158, 1159
  rift in alliance, 1151, 1152
  shift from Europe to Asia and Africa, 1234
Colden, Cadwallader, 101, 127
Cole, Thomas, artist, 453
Colfax Schuyler, Vice President, 612, 621, 626
Collective bargaining, 1063, 1066
Collier, John, Indian Defense Association Secretary, 1086
Colmer, Representative William, 1186
Colombia, 334, 340, 887
Colonization:
  of British West Indies, 58
  of Carolina and Georgia, 61–64
  England during, 43–45, 59, 60
  of Maryland, 57–58
  of New England, 47–57, 60, 61
  of New France, 64, 65
  of New Netherland, 58–59
  of Virginia, 45–47
Colorado, 740, 742, 743
  statehood of, 764
Colorado River, 494, 518
Colored Farmers' National Alliance, 777
Colt, Samuel, 449
Columbia, 495
Columbia River, 257
  in boundary dispute, 331
  British empire north of, 495
  key to Oregon settlement, 500
  rejected as border, 495
Columbia University, 807, 913
Columbus, Christopher, 8, 15, 17
  background of, 8
  backing sought by, 8–10
  death of, 10
  discoveries of, 10
  Indians named by, 10, 14
Comanche Indians, 494, 760–762 (*See also* Great Plains Indians)
Combined Production and Resources Board, 1127
Combined Staff conference, 1111
Command of the Army Act, 607
Commercial Convention of Memphis, 489
Commercial Review of the South and Southwest, 432
Commission on Civil Rights, 1255, 1256
Committee of Correspondence, 128
Committee to Defend America by Aiding the Allies, 1102
Committee for Industrial Organization, 1067
Committee on Industrial Preparedness, 937
Committee on Public Information, 943, 944
Committee on Recent Economic Changes, 1929, 1027
Committee of Safety, 134
Commodity Credit Corporation, 1062, 1191
Common law, 248, 253
Common Law, The, 792
Common Sense, 138
Commonwealth of Oceana, 45
Commonwealth v. Hunt in Massachusetts Supreme Court, 403
Communication, 384–388, 663–669
Communism, containment of, 1223–1242
Communist China, 1166, 1167, 1225–1227
Communist party, 1085
Communists, 958, 1052, 1186, 1223
  Chinese, 1166–1169

Communists:
containment: China, 1225–1226
Europe, 1224
Indochina, 1228–1230
Korea, 1228
in government, 1193, 1203, 1204
Compromise of 1790, 227
Compromise of 1820 (*see* Missouri Compromise)
Compromise of 1850, 525–527, 531
provisions of, 526, 527
Compromise of 1877, 635
Compton, Arthur H., 990
Comstock, Henry T., 741
Comstock Lode, the, 741
Concord, Massachusetts, in American Revolution, 133–135
Confederacy, the, 558
blockade of, 558
Congress of, 560
defeat of, 584
population of, 558
problems of, 578–580
war preparations of, 560
Confederate States of America, 550 (*See also* Confederacy)
Confederation Congress, 166, 170, 198
tax power lacking, 167
western development guidelines of, 169–172
Confiscation Act of 1862, 567
Congregationalists, 83, 84, 117, 194
Congress, United States, 215, 229, 253, 478, 479, 500
Army tripled by, 249
in Civil War, 566, 567
of 1811, 282
after 1877: campaign expenditure law, 898
contract labor abolished by, 701
Department of Commerce and Labor created by, 704
eightieth, 1185–1189
eighty-first, 1191
eighty-fifth, 1206
eighty-seventh, 1289
eighty-eighth, 1290, 1296
eighty-ninth, 1298
fifty-first, 656, 658, 659
Gold Standard Act of 1900 passed, 855
Mann Act passed, 898
rivers and harbors bill of 1882 passed, 646
Sherman Silver Purchase Act repealed, 785
veteran's pensions increased by, 646
Federalists in, 222, 224, 225
Hayes-Tilden contest in, 635
Jefferson's messages to, 252
Republicans in, 243
29th meeting of, 499
violence on floor of, 534
western settlement not encouraged by, 231
Congress of Racial Equality, 1256, 1303
Congress of Vienna, 298
Congressional Committee on the Conduct of the War, 567
Conkling, Senator Roscoe, 622, 644
Connecticut, 56, 154
constitution of, 162
Connecticut Wesleyan, 431
Conscription (*see* Draft)
Conservation:
natural resources, 876
soil, 383, 1061
Constitution, United States, 116, 167, 224, 249, 251, 253, 349, 557, 566
slavery protected by, 417, 478
Constitution, 290
Constitutional Convention:
federal authority strengthened, 212–215
new Congress created by, 213
"New Jersey Plan," 206
in Philadelphia, 204–212
plans for, 203, 204
popular approval of Constitution, 217–220
separation of powers, 215–217
slavery disagreement in, 212
tax powers granted in, 213
on treaties, 224, 239–240
"Virginia Plan, The," 205, 206, 214
Constitutional Union party, 5–50
Containment (communist) in Cold War, 1159–1162
Berlin blockade, 1161
breakdown of wartime alliance, 1160
Communist coup in Czechoslovakia, 1161
conflicts with Kremlin, 1160
Greece and Turkey in, 1160, 1161
Marshall Plan, 1161
North American Treaty Alliance in, 1161, 1162
Continental Congress, First (1774) 129
May, 1775, meeting set by, 130
Continental Congress, Second, 133, 151, 162, 166, 169
conduct of war, 151–153
financing, 152, 153
military appointments, 152
"Olive Branch Petition" of, 136, 138
at Philadelphia, 135
reconvened, 138
Continental empire, 493–519
California, 496–498
military action in Mexico, 505–507
Mormons and Great Basin, 501–502
Oregon, 495–496
Oregon settlement, 496, 498–501
penetration of far West, 494–495
Treaty of Guadalupe Hidalgo, 507–518
war with Mexico, 502–505
Continental Harmony, 195
Continental System, Napoleon's, 277, 279
Contreras, battle of, 507
Convention of 1800, 242, 331
(*See also* Treaty of Mortefontaine)
Conway, General Thomas, 152
Conwell, Reverend Russell H., 833
Coode, John, 107
Cooke, Jay, 627, 665
Cooke, Jay, and Company, 568
Coolidge, President Calvin, 959, 963, 966, 1014, 1019, 1038
background of, 968, 969
farm relief opposed by, 969, 972, 973
frugality of, 969–973, 1035
negativism of, 973
as President Harding's successor, 968–970
Vice Presidential election of, 964
Cooper, Sir Anthony Ashley, 62
Cooper, James Fenimore, writings of, 450
Cooper, Peter, 634
Greenback party candidate, 776–777
Cooper, Professor Thomas, 468

Cooperatives, 403, 692, 776, 1041
Copland, Aaron, 1264
Copley, John Singleton, 90
Copper, mining, 742
Copper-Volstead Cooperative Marketing Act of 1922, 1039
Copperheads, 582, 606
Corbett, James A., 831
Corn:
growers, 771, 772
in South, 418
Cornell, Alonzo B., 641
Cornwallis, Charles:
in battle of Trenton, 148
at Brandywin Creek, 149
at Camden, 154
in South, 167
surrender at Yorktown, 134
in Virginia, 155
surrender at Yorktown, 158, 159
Coronado, Francisco Vasquez de, 11, 14
Corporations, 57, 378, 384, 680
considered legal person, 664, 679
excess profits tax on, 1068, 1192
for Kentucky road, 348–350
under Theodore Roosevelt, 872
Corruption:
in city government, 720, 736
reforms, 736
government, 621–623, 626, 641, 857
Cortes, Hernando, 11, 14, 21
Corwin, Thomas, of Ohio, 551
Cosby, Governor William, 111
Cotton, John, 48, 55, 56
Cotton, 272, 277, 321, 322
in South, 1820–1860, 380, 406–408, 419, 420, 424, 674, 773
Cotton Futures Act, 917
Cotton Is King, 540
Coughlin, Father Charles E., 1067, 1070, 1131
on America First Committee, 1102
on World Court issue, 1094
Council of Economic Advisers, 1184
Council of the Indies, 16
Council of National Defense, 938, 1127
Council for New England, 56, 57
"Court-packing" threat of Franklin D. Roosevelt, 1071, 1072
Cowpens, battle of, 154–155
Cox, James M., Presidential nomination of, 964, 965
Coxey, Jacob S., 785
Craig v. Missouri, 375
Cramp v. Board of Public Instruction
loyalty oath overthrown by, 1301
(*See also* Warren Court)
Crawford, William H., Treasury Secretary, 304, 321, 336, 337
Crazy Horse, Chief, 761
Credit:
bills of, 82, 83, 135, 215, 375
consumer, 1034, 1039, 1042, 1047, 1050
Credit Mobilier scandal, 626
Credit system, credit, 381, 774
Creek Indians, 296, 339, 350, 356
Creel, George, Chairman, Committee on Public Information, 943, 944
Crévecoeur, 86, 87
Crime, 719, 1255, 1264, 1281
Crisis pamphlets, 148
Crittenden, John J., of Kentucky, 551, 552, 566
Crockett, Davy, 482
Cromwell, Oliver, 44, 45, 58, 59
Crow Indians, 494
(*See also* Great Plains Indians)
Crown Point, New York, 135, 137
Crusades, the, 2–4
Cuba, 10, 58, 335
Bay of Pigs incident in, 1237
missile crisis in, 1241
Ostend Manifesto on, 539, 540
Spanish-American War in, 840–845
as United States protectorate, 886
Cuban League, 841
Cudahy, Michael, 665
Cultivator, 383
Cultural life in late-nineteenth-century America, 791–833
architecture, 829–830
Chautauqua movement, 833
education in, 798, 807–808
fine arts, 828–829
intellectual challenge, 792–794
libraries, 833
literary trends, 825–828
magazines, 832–833
natural sciences, 825
Negro education in, 808, 825
newspapers, 832
popular culture, 830–831
religion and the church, 794–795
religious fundamentalism, 797–798
social gospel, 796
Culture, American, 1815–1860, 427–469
abolitionism, 459–460
American character, 428, 429
defense of slavery, 460–468
education, 429–431, 469
fine arts, 453–454, 469
literature, 450–453, 469
newspapers, magazines, and lyceums, 432
religion, 454–456
science and invention, 432–449
social and humanitarian reform, 457–458
Cumberland River, 322
in Civil War, 561
Cumberland Road, 384
Cummins, Governor Albert B., 867
Currency Act of 1764, 120
Curtis, Charles, Vice President, 1052
Curtis, Cyrus, 833
Curtis, George W., editor, 643, 651, 831
Custer, Colonel George A., 761, 762
Customs officers, 116, 119, 120
Cutler, Reverend Manasseh, 170–172
Czechoslovakia, 951, 1015
invaded by Germany, 1098

Dallas, A. J., 290
Dallas, George M., 486, 490
Dallas, Texas, 1290
Dana, J. D., 449
Dana, Richard Henry, 450, 498, 583
Danzig, Baltic seaport, 951
Dare, Virginia, 23
Darrow, Clarence, defense lawyer in John T. Scopes' trial, 989
Dartmouth College, 85
Dartmouth College case of 1819, 325
Darwin, Charles, 677, 792, 793
Darwinism, 792–794, 975
impact of, 792
rejection of, 793
Daugherty, Attorney General Harry, 967
Davenport, Reverend John, 56
Davie, William R., 250

Davies, Samuel, 85
Davis, Chester A., 1129
Davis, Senator Cushman K., 847
Davis, Justice David, 635
Davis, Elmer, 1131
Davis, Jeff, Arkansas governor, 867
Davis, Jefferson, 526
President of Confederate States of America, 550
Secretary of War, 529, 530
Davis, John, 17
Davis, John W., Democratic nominee, 1924, 971
Davis, Norman, 1093
Dawes, Charles G.:
budget director, 967
Vice Presidential nomination, election, 971
Dawes Act of 1887, 654, 1086
provisions of, 762
Dawes Plan of 1924, 1012
Dawson, D. W., 674
Day, Benjamin F., publisher, 432
Day, Thomas, free Negro, 405
Day, William, Secretary of State, 846
"Day of Doom," 90
Deane, Silas, 138, 150, 152
Dearborn, Henry, 285
DeBow, D. J. B., 432
DeBow's Review, 553
Debs, Eugene V., 703, 905, 906, 944, 945
released from prison, 959
Socialist candidate, 965
Decatur, Stephen, 302
Declaration of Independence, 86, 111, 146, 148, 161, 163, 166, 468
announcement of, 133
Declaration of Panama, 1939, 1100
Declaration of United Nations, 1112
Declaratory Act of Parliament, 127
Deep South, 417
Deere, John, 383, 449, 665
de Gaulle, President Charles, 1234
Common Market membership of Britain vetoed, 1241
nuclear deterrent plans of, 1241
De Grasse, Admiral François, 155
Deism, deists, 85, 163, 251, 454
Delaware, 60
Delaware River, 59, 148
Demobilization after World War II, 1179, 1180
Democratic Convention in Chicago, 1968, 1308
Democratic party, 341, 371, 472, 473, 479, 488–490, 553, 568, 606, 635
Bank issue under, 360, 361
James Buchanan nominated by, 535
Lewis Cass nominated by, 524
during Civil War, 583, 584
in control in South, 1876, 628
controlled by moderates in 1848, 524
convention of 1844, 485, 486, 499
convention of 1848, 524
convention of 1852, 529
convention of 1860, 542, 543
election of 1868, 612, 621
from 1920–1970: in Eisenhower's administration, 1201–1203
in Eisenhower's second administration, 1212, 1213
in election of 1920, 964, 965
in election of 1924, 971, 972, 975
in election of 1928, 973, 975
in election of 1932, 1052–1054
in election of 1936, 1070, 1071
in election of 1940, 1102–1103, 1145, 1146
in election of 1952, 1196, 1197
in election of 1956, 1205, 1206
in election of 1968, 1306–1308
majority in Congress, 1196
in 1960, 1286–1288
in 1964, 1296–1298
during Truman's administration, 1178, 1179, 1185, 1187–1189
platform of 1844, 486
platform of 1876, 634
James K. Polk nominated by, 486
united in South, 528
Martin Van Buren titular head of, 485, 486
Van Buren wing of, 522
Democratic Republican party, 339, 362
(*See also* Democratic party)
Democratic Review, 517
Democrats, 372, 376–378, 401, 476, 490, 491
during Civil War, 583, 584
after 1877, 639, 640, 655
convention of 1896, Chicago, 787
division among, 641
1884 platform of, 646, 651
majority in South, 641
1910 victories of, 898
strength in 1908, 895
on tariffs, 644, 645
victory in 1892, 660
in election of 1876, 634, 635
Free, 530
free-soil, 524
Northern, 528, 549
Southern, 485, 490, 501, 522, 528, 529, 542, 549, 604
popular sovereignty rejected by, 523
Union, 527, 528
Western, 477, 498–500
popular sovereignty favored by, 523
Whigs and, 472–473, 635
World War I: in election of 1916, 927, 928
on League of Nations, 956–958
Dempsey, Jack, 986
Denby, Edwin, in Navy Department, 968
Denmark, German invasion of, 1101
Denver, Colorado, 742, 758
Department of Commerce, 873
Department of Commerce and Labor, 704
Department of Defense, 1180
Department of Health, Education and Welfare, 1202
Department of Labor, 704, 898
Department of the Navy, creation of, 247
Department of Transportation, 1298
Department stores, 675
Depletion allowance, oil, 1035
Deposit bill, Henry Clay's, 370
Depression, Great, 988, 1021, 1252
banking reforms in, 1058, 1059
beginning of, 1048, 1049
causes of, 1042, 1047, 1048
expanded relief in, 1065–1066
farmers in, 1060–1062
Herbert Hoover's administration program, 1049–1052
Indians in, 1086
industrial recovery efforts in, 1062–1065
life in, 1073–1085
migrant workers in, 1086, 1087
Negroes in, 1085, 1086

Depression:
relief efforts, 1059, 1060
stock market crash, October 29, 1929, 1042
tax revision in, 1068
(*See also* New Deal; Roosevelt, Franklin D.)
Depressions, 174, 279, 372, 424, 627, 644, 784–786, 837, 885, 965
(*See also* Depression, Great; Panic of 1819; Panic of 1837; Panic of 1857)
Descent of Man The, 795
Deseret, 502
(*See also* Utah Territory)
Desert Land Act of 1877, 743, 757
d'Estaing, Admiral Jean Baptiste, 153, 154
de Smet, Father Pierre-Jean, 496
Detroit, Michigan, 112, 118, 154, 423
in War of 1812, 285, 287, 289
Dewey, Admiral George, 845, 846
Dewey, John, educator, 807, 913, 990
Dewey, John, pragmatist, 793, 794
Dewey, Thomas E., 1145, 1146, 1188, 1287
Diaz, Bartholomew, 8, 9
Dickens, Charles, 422, 428
Dickinson, Daniel, 485, 527
Dickinson, John, 135, 166–167, 212
as moderate, 146
at second continental congress, 136
Dictionary, 430
Diem, Ngo Dinh:
death of, 1239
regime of, 1230, 1238
Dillon, Douglas, Secretary of the Treasury, 1289
Dingley tariff of 1897, 855, 896
Dinwiddie, Governor Robert, 113
Disability Pensions Act of 1890, 657
Disciples of Christ, 455, 456
Discourse Concerning Unlimited Submission, A, 1250, 100
Discourse on Davila, 244
Discovery, 46
Disney, Walt, productions, 1074
Dissenters (non-Anglican Protestants), 83, 112, 117
District of Columbia, 254, 325
slave trade in, 478, 479
abolished in, 526
slavery abolished in, 570
Disunity, colonial, 128
"Divers Voyages," 23
Divided Europe, postwar: Kremlin policy in, 1152, 1153
reconstruction disagreements, 1154
Harry S. Truman on, 1153, 1154
Divorce after 1950, 1264
Dix, Dorothea, 458
Dix, Senator John A., 500
Dixiecrat ticket, 1188
Dixon, Edgar H., 1200
Dixon-Yates contract, 1200
Dodge, Augustus D., 1533
Dodge, General G. M., 574
Dodge, Henry, 535
Doenitz, Admiral Karl, 1120
Dogmatic Philosophy, 795
Doheny, Edward M., in oil lease scandal, 968
Domestic issues, 1920s, 965–967
Dominican Republic, 256
Dominion of New England, 60, 106
Domino theory, 1230
Dorchester Heights, Massachusetts, 136–137, 147
Doughty, Thomas, artist, 453
Douglas, Senator Paul, 1206
Douglas, Stephen A., 485, 542
in Compromise of 1850, 526
death of, 582
in debate with Abraham Lincoln, 538, 539, 601–602
1860 nomination of, 548
Freeport doctrine of, 538, 539, 541, 549
on Kansas-Nebraska Act, 530–532
Douglas, Justice William O., 1187
Douglass, Frederick, 405, 460, 625
Douglass, William, 100
Dow, Neal, Maine legislator, 457
Dow-Jones index, 1049
Draft, military, 301, 559, 560, 582
Drake, Sir Francis, 23
Dred Scott decision, 536, 537, 541
Dred Scott v. Sanford, 536
Dreiser, Theodore, 858, 908
Drew, Daniel, 667
Drew, Georgiana, 830
Drought, 757, 765, 775
Drugs, hallucinatory, 1281, 1282, 1283
Duane, William, 333
Du Bois, Dr. W. E. B., 869, 870, 1257
Duer, William, 172
Duke, James B., 669, 670
Duke of Marlborough, 112
Dulles, John Foster, 1196–1198, 1223, 1238
on Aswan Dam financing, 1231
on Communist containment, 1224, 1225
in China, 1225, 1226
in Europe, 1224
doctrine of "massive retaliation," 1227, 1228
Dumbarton Oaks, Big Three talks at, 1154-1155
Duncan, Stephen, planter, 407
Dunkers, 20
Dunmore, Governor, 137
Durant, Asher B., artist, 453
Durant, Henry F., 807
Durkin, Martin, Secretary of Labor, 1199
Duryea, Charles, 669
Dust Bowl, the, 1074
Dutch Reformed Church, 20, 84, 455
Duyrea, Frank, 669
Dwight, Timothy, 457

Eaker, Ira C., 1118
Eakins, Thomas, 828
Early, Jubal A., Confederate officer, 576
East India Company, 43, 45, 128
tea sales of, 128
East River, 147, 422
Eaton, Senator John H., 346, 350
Eaton, Mrs. John (*see* Timberlake, Mrs. Margaret O'Neale)
Eccles, Marriner, of Federal Reserve Board, 1073
Ecclesiastical History of New England, 100
Economic Opportunity Act of 1964, 1296
Economics, cultural development in American, 67–102
education, arts, and science, 89–101
New England and Middle colonies, 73–83
racial, ethnic variety, 86, 87
religion in colonies, 83–86
social patterns, 87–89
Southern economy, 68–72

Economy:
national from 1820–1860, 380–425
agriculture in North, 382–384
character, attitudes of South, 421
cotton in, 406–408
industrial workers, 401–403
industry and the factory system, 399–401
land policies, 381–382
prosperity, depression, and living standards, 424
shipping and overseas trade, 388–389
slavery in, 408–409
Southern transportation, commerce and manufacturing, 418–420
tariff, 401
urbanization, 421–423
westward settlement, 381–382
yoeman farmers in South, 417, 418
Southern, 68–72
indentured servants in, 69, 70
plantations in, 68
slaves in, 70–72
tobacco in, 69–71
Eddy, Mrs. Mary Baker, 797
Eden, Anthony, Foreign Secretary, 1151, 1231
Edict of Nantes, 106
Edison, Thomas A., 830
Edison Illuminating Company, Detroit, 1028
Education:
in colonies, 89
from 1815–1860, 427, 429–431, 469
betterment of, 430
first high school, 431
higher, 429–431
land grants for, 430
private schools, 430
tax-supported, 429
(*See also* Culture, American, 1815–1860; Free schools)
after 1877, 641, 913
late nineteenth century, 798, 807–809
college and university presidents in, 807
extent of, 798
higher, 807, 808
Negro, 808
private schools, 798
in 1920s: discrimination in, 990
enrollment, increase in, 990
newspapers, 991
psychology, 990
science, 990
after 1950: federal aid to, 1203, 1258, 1259
higher enrollments, 1258
income for, 1258
progressive, 1258
reforms in, 1258
religion in, 1260
Educational Wasteland, 1258
Edward VI, King of England, 20
Edwards, Jonathan, 85, 100
Eighteenth Amendment, 867, 975, 984
Eighth Air Force, 1118
Einstein, Lewis, 1021, 1022
Eisenhower, Dwight D.:
agriculture and labor, 1212, 1213
on capture of Berlin, 1154
in charge of Operation Overlord, 1116
communism and internal security, 1203, 1204
on communist containment: China, 1225, 1226
Europe, 1224, 1225
Indo-China, 1228–1230
Korea, 1228
on demobilization, 1180
economic growth, 1215, 1220, 1221
election of 1952, 1196, 1197
election of 1956, 1204–1206
first administration, 1199–1203
recession in, 1200
heart attack of, 1205
Middle East crisis, 1231–1234
new defense strategy of, 1227
popularity of, 1286
as President, 1197–1199
reelected, 1205
second administration, 1206, 1212–1215, 1220–1221
social welfare and education, 1213, 1214
sought as Democratic candidate, 1187
trade and foreign aid, 1214, 1215
USSR policies, 1234, 1236
West Germany rearmament advocated by, 1227
El Alamein, 1113
Election of 1848, 524–525
Election of 1852, 527–529
Election of 1856, 535
political parties in, 535
Election of 1860, 542–545
Election of 1868, 612, 621
Election of 1876, 628, 634–636
Election of 1888, 655–656
Election of 1896, 786–789
Election of 1920, 963–965
Election of 1928, 973, 975
Election of 1932, 1052–1054
Election of 1956, 1204–1206
Election of 1964, 1296–1298
Election of 1968, 1306–1308, 1320
Elections, national: of 1792, 245
of 1796, 242, 246
of 1800, 243, 250
of 1804, 258, 259
of 1808, 272
of 1812, 297
of 1816, 321
of 1820, 327
of 1824, 335–338, 340
of 1828, 340
of 1832, 362, 370
of 1836, 372
of 1840, 375–377, 473
of 1844, 485–488
of 1848, 473, 524–525
of 1852, 527–529
of 1856, 535
of 1860, 542–545
of 1864, 583, 584
of 1868, 612, 621
of 1872, 625
of 1876, 628, 634–636
of 1880, 644, 645
of 1884, 651
of 1888, 655
of 1892, 660, 784
of 1896, 788, 855
of 1900, 855
of 1904, 894
of 1908, 894
of 1912, 903–906
of 1916, 927, 928
of 1920, 963–965
of 1924, 970–972
of 1928, 973, 975

Elections, national:
of 1932, 1052–1054
of 1936, 1070, 1071
of 1940, 1102–1103, 1145, 1146
of 1944, 1146
of 1948, 1187–1189
of 1952, 1196, 1197
of 1956, 1205, 1206
of 1960, 1287, 1288
of 1964, 1296–1298
of 1968, 1306–1308, 1320
Electoral college, 216
Eliot, Jared, 101
Elizabeth I, Queen of England, 20, 22, 23, 25, 44
Elk Hills oil reserve, California, 968
Elliot, Matthew, 281
Ellison, Ralph, 1253, 1257
Ellsworth, Oliver, 212, 250
Elmira College, 431
Ely, Richard T., economist, 792–793, 857
Emancipation, 468, 541, 567, 569–570, 599–600, 636
Emancipation Proclamation, 570, 582
Embargo, 237, 279, 1098
of Confederacy, 578
Jefferson's, 272, 273, 276
repeal of, 273, 278
Madison's, 283
on shipping to Japan, 1104, 1105
Embargo Act of 1807, 272, 273, 278
exports and imports reduced by, 399
Emergency Committee for Employment, 1050
Emergency Quota Act of 1921, 966
Emergency Relief Appropriation Act of 1935, 1065, 1066
Emergency Tariff Act of May, 1921, 966
Emerson, Ralph Waldo, 450, 451, 542
on American unity, 481–482
Emory University, 431
Employment Act of 1946, 1184
Enforcement Acts of 1870 and 1872, 642, 643
England, 10, 18
colonization by, 23, 42, 45–59
advantages in, 42, 43
of British West Indies, 58
of the Carolinas and Georgia, 42, 61–64
of Jamaica, 42
of Maryland, 42, 57–58
of New England, 42, 47–57, 60, 61
of New Netherland, 42, 58, 59
of Virginia, 42, 45–47
exploration of, 16, 17
restoration, 1660–1689, 59, 60
in War of 1812, 275–298
England, John, bishop, 455
England's Treasure by Forraign Trade, 44
Engle v. Vitale, 1260
English, W. E., 644
English, William H. in Kansas controversy, 537
Enterprise, Virginia City, Nevada, 742
Epidemics, 101, 137, 244
Episcopalians, 455
Erie, Lake, 113, 285, 287
Erie Canal, 384, 386
(*See also* Canals)
Erie Railroad, 665, 667
Eriksson, Leif, 8
Erskine, David, 278, 279
Escobedo v. Illinois on counsel . . . confession, 130
(*See also* Warren Court)
Espionage Act of 1917, 944
Essays on Field Husbandry, 101
Essex, 260, 290
Europe:
after discoveries, 17–20
before 1500: class structure of, 4–6
early explorations of, 8–11
economic development of, 2–7, 11
political structure of, 5–7
religion in, 4
technological advances in, 4
trade of, 2, 3
European Advisory Commission, 1117
European Defense Community, 1227
Eustis, William, Secretary of War, 290
Evans, George Henry, agrarianism of, 403
Evans, Oliver, 82
Evarts, William M., 838
Evers, Charles, Fayette, Mississippi mayor, 1257
Ewell, Richard S., Confederate officer, 571–572
Experiments and Observations on Electricity, 101
Exploration, European: by English, 16, 17
by France, 17
by Norsemen, 8
by Portuguese, 8, 9
by Spanish, 8–14
water route sought to Asia, 8
Exports:
American (after Revolution), 172, 199, 424, 662
of cotton, 272, 277, 322, 399, 420
of tobacco, 277, 420
colonial, 67
of fish, 74
of indigo, 67, 74
of lumber, 46, 71–74
of rice, 67, 72, 74
of tobacco, 67, 119

Factors, 408, 420
Fair Deal, 1178, 1190–1192
Fair Employment Practices Commission, 1186, 1191
Fair Employment Practices Committee, 1132, 1184
Fair Labor Standards Act, 1066
Fall, Albert B., Secretary of the Interior:
conviction of, 968
in Teapot Dome scandal, 968
Fallen Timbers, battle of, 234
Far East in Cold War, 1164, 1165
Far West, penetration of, 494–495
Farley, James A., 1071, 1146
Farm Bloc, the, in Congress, 1038
Farm Credit Act, 1062
Farm Security Administration, 1062, 1085–1087
Farmer, James, 1256, 1303
Farmers:
1920s, 965, 966
farm relief rejects, 972, 973
legislation for, 969, 970
relief in Republican platform of 1928, 973
problems of, 1866–1896, 774–775
(*See also* Agriculture, farm policies, 1866–1896)
Farmers' Union, 916

Farming:
sectional developments in, 772–773
trends in, 1865–1896, 769–771
(*See also* Agriculture, farm policies, 1866–1896)
Farragut, Admiral David G., 572
Fashions, 1914, 908
Federal Council of Churches, 989
Federal Deposit Insurance Corporation, 1059
Federal Elections bill of 1890, 659
Federal Emergency Relief Act (FERA), 1059, 1060
Federal Farm Board, 1041, 1050
Federal Farm Loan Act of 1916, 917
Federal Housing Administration, 1183, 1206
Federal Mediation Board, 1185
Federal Reserve Act of 1918, 885
Federal Reserve Board, 914–915, 1206
Federal Reserve System, 915, 1072
Federal Trade Commission, 915, 1035
Federalist, The, 220, 243, 276
Federalist party, 245, 246, 249, 250
demise of, 301, 302
Federalists, 220–240, 242, 243, 250, 252, 282
controversy over neutrality, 234–237
defeated in 1800, 250
fears of, 248
government beginnings under, 223–225
capital at New York, 223
capital on Potomac, 227
Hamilton's financial program, 225–231
Jay's treaty, 237–240
laws of 1798, 248
in New England, 300
Western problems of, 231–234
defeats of Federalists in 232, 234
Indians, 232, 234
Fenno, John, 244
Ferdinand of Aragon, 10
Ferdinand, Archduke Franz, assassination of, 920
Field, Cyrus, 669
Field, James G., Populist candidate, 784
Field, Marshall, 737
Fifteenth Amendment, 608, 621, 634, 636
Fifth Amendment, 1213
Fifth Army, 1118
Filibuster, 540, 635
Fillmore, Millard, 449
Vice Presidential nomination of, 524
as President, 526
Fine arts, the, 427, 453–454, 469
late nineteenth century, 828, 829
Finished Iron Products Law, 1750, 81
Finney, Charles G., 455
"Fireside chats" of Franklin D. Roosevelt, 1058
First Amendment, 248, 1260
First Hundred Days of Franklin D. Roosevelt's first administration, 1059
First Reconstruction Act of March, 1867, 607, 608
Fish, Representative Hamilton, 1097
Fish, Hamilton, Secretary of State, 527, 624, 839
Fish (fishing), 16, 17, 72–74, 297, 298, 624
New England, 173–174
off Laborador and Newfoundland coasts, 331
Fisher, Warren, 651
Fisk, Jim ("Diamond Jim"), 623, 665, 667
Fisk University, 808
Fiske, John, historian, 667, 793, 837
Fitzhugh, George, 540
Fiume, port of, 951
Five Civilized Tribes, 756, 760, 762
Five Power Pact of 1922, 1017
(*See also* Washington, Treaty of)
Flathead Indians, 496
Fletcher v. Peck, 258, 323, 325
Flood control, 635
Florida, 11, 113, 249, 255, 332, 333, 636
in Adams-Onis Treaty, 331
ceded to U.S., 332, 334
East Florida, 256, 281, 296
secession of, 550
West Florida, 256, 281, 296
Florida Treaty, 1819, 333
Flying Cloud (a ship), 399
Foch, General Ferdinand, Allied Supreme Commander, World War I, 949
Folk, Joseph W., reform governor, 867
Food, 669, 773
as major industry, 670
meat-packing, 665, 667, 672
Foot, Senator Samuel A., 348
Foote, Andrew Hull, 561
Forbes, Charles R., convicted of bribery, 967
Force Act of 1833, 359
Ford, Henry, 669, 908, 971
automobile industry of, 1027, 1028
Muscle Shoals offer of, 970
Ford Motor Company, 1027, 1028
Fordney-McCumber tariff law, 1922, 966, 1035, 1042
Ford's Theater, Washington, D.C., 584
Foreign Affairs, 1160
Foreign affairs from, 1953–1965:
changing cold war, 1234–1236
Dwight D. Eisenhower and John Foster Dulles on, 1224, 1225
Indochina, 1228–1230
Lyndon Johnson and Vietnam, 1242, 1243
John F. Kennedy and Europe, 1239–1242
John F. Kennedy challenges, 1236–1239
Korea, 1228
Middle East crisis, 1231–1234
new look, 1226, 1227
policy on two Chinas, 1225, 1226
style, rhetoric changes in, 1223
Foreign aid, 1161, 1215
Foreign Assistance Act of, 1948, 1161
Foreign policy, 245, 304, 928, 965
on Far East, Theodore Roosevelt's 890–891
during Ulysses S. Grant administration, 623–889
of Theodore Roosevelt's, 885–891
in Far East, 890–891
in China, 890
in Philippines, 891
on Latin America, 885–889
in Caribbean, 886, 889
in Central America, 889
in Venezuela, 889

Foreign Relations Committee, Senate, 956, 1020
Forest Reserve Act of 1891, 658
Formosa, 1225, 1226
Formosa Resolution of January, 1955, 1226
Forsyth, John, 372
Fort Dearborn, 285
Fort Donelson, 561
Fort Duquesne, 113
Fort Greenville, 234
Fort Henry, 561
Fort Jefferson, Florida, 552
Fort Laramie, Treaty of, 760
Fort Laramie, second Treaty of, 761
violation of, 761
Fort Lee, 148
Fort McHenry, 295
Fort McIntosh, 232
Fort Meigs, 287
Fort Miamis, 234
Fort Niagara, 118, 154, 287
Fort Orange, Albany, 58
Fort Pickens, 552
Fort Pitt, 118
Fort Shafter, 1107
Fort Sill, Oklahoma, 626
Fort Stanivix, 149, 232
Fort Sumter, 552
in Civil War, 557, 558, 599
Fort Taylor, 552
Fort Ticonderoga, 135, 137, 147, 149, 198
Fort Vancouver, 500
Fort Washington, 148
Fort Wayne, Indiana, 234
Fort William Henry, 113
Forts, British occupation of, 198
Fortune, 1085
Foster, Augustus, 283
Foster, Stephen, 454
Foster, William Z., Communist leader, 1051
Four Power Pact of 1922, 1017
(*See also* Washington, Treaty of)
Fourier, Charles, writer, 403
Fourteen Amendment, 606–608, 611, 628, 634, 636, 679
due process clause of, 1300
equal protection clause of, 1300
Fourteen Points, President Wilson's, 947
Fourth Amendment, 116
Fox, George, 61
Fox Indians, 356
Fox sisters, the, 456
France, 7, 10, 18, 242, 334
in American Revolution, 134, 138, 150–151, 153, 155, 158
colonization advantages of, 64–65
exploration of, 17
forts of, 113
Louisiana claimed by, 65
Louisiana given to Spain by, 113
in 1930s: declaration of war on Germany, 1100
German invasion of, 1101
pact with USSR, 1092
U.S. quasi-war with, 246, 249, 250
end of, 250
World War I, 920, 921, 924, 928
Aisne-Marne, St. Mihiel, and Meuse-Argonne, 949
American forces amalgamation proposed by, 949
in battle of Marne, 949
Rhineland occupied by, 951
Francis I, King of France, 17
Franco, Francisco, 1095
Frankfurter, Justice Felix, 1300
Franklin, Benjamin, 86, 100, 101, 113, 129, 138, 146, 148
Articles of Confederation proposed by, 166
at Constitutional convention, 204
in French negotiation, 150
in London, 117, 130
at peace talks, 158
at second Continental Congress, 135
Franklin, John Hope, 1257
Franklin, prospective state of, 169
Frazier-Lemke Bankruptcy Act, 1065
(*See also* Frazier-Lemke Farm Emergency Act of 1934)
Frazier-Lemke Farm Emergency Act of 1934, 1062
declared unconstitutional, 1062
Frazier-Lemke farm mortgage law, revised, 1071
(*See also* Frazier-Lemke Bankruptcy Act of 1934)
Frederick the Great of Prussia, 113
Fredericksburg, Virginia, 563, 571, 574
Free Methodist Church, 797
Free silver, 657, 783, 786
defeat of free-silver movement, 855
free-silver forces in Democratic party, 787
plank in Democratic platform, 787
Free-Soil party, 524, 530, 535
Free-soilers, 524, 528, 529, 507, 625
Freedmen, 601, 603, 604, 606, 625
(*See also* Negroes; Slaves)
Freedmen's Bureau, 601, 610
bill of 1866 vetoed, 605
Freedom of the Will, 100
"Freedom riders," 1256
Freedom's Journal (Afro-American newspaper), 432
Freeman, Orville, Secretary of Agriculture, 1247
Freeman's Farm:
battle of, 150
second battle of, 150
Freeport Doctrine, Douglas's, 538, 539, 541, 549
Frelinghuysen Theodorus, 84
Fremont, John Charles, 498
California explorations of, 498
in Civil War, 561, 562
Presidential nomination of, 535
Radical candidate in 864, 583
withdrawal of, 584
French, Daniel Chester, 829
French and Indian War (*see* Great War for Empire; Seven Years' War)
French Revolution (1789–1792):
American neutrality controversy in, 234–237
Federalist hostility to, 244
Freneau, Philip, 244
Frenzied Finance, 858
Frick, Henry Clay, 670–671, 784
Friends, (*see* Quakers)
Fries, John, 250
Frobisher, Martin, 17
Frontier, Western, end of, 764–766
Frye, Senator William P., 847
Fugitive Slave Act of 1850, 526–527, 530
Fulbright, William, 1306, 1322
Fulton, Robert, 384
Fulton, Missouri, Winston Churchill speech at, 1158
"Fundamental Orders," 56
Fundamentalism, religious, 797, 798
Funding Act of 1866, 621

Fur trade and traders, 58, 64, 198, 238, 257, 497
in California, 498
in Northwest, 494, 495, 500
Furuseth, Andrew, Union President, 916

Gadsden, James, 530
Gadsden Purchase, 530, 540
"Gag rule," 479
Gage, General Thomas, 134–136
recall of, 137
Gailbraith, John Kenneth, 1252
Gallatin, Albert, 248, 289, 302, 326
national debt reduced by, 252
peace negotiator, 290, 298
roads and canals urged by, 253
on Second Bank of the United States, 360
Galloway, Joseph, 130
Gallup Poll, 1968, on religion, 1259, 1307, 1320
Galveston, Texas, 736
Gama, Vasco da, 8, 11, 17
Gardoqui, Diego de, 199
Garfield, James A., 561, 897
background of, 645
death of, 645
elected President, 644, 645
Garland, Augustus, H., Attorney General, 653
Garland, Hamlin, 764, 765
Garner, John Nance:
election of, 1054
on fourth term, 1146
reelection of, 1070, 1071
Vice Presidential nomination of, 1053
Garrison, William Lloyd, 459
antislavery advocate, 460
jailed for libel, 460
Garvey, Marcus, 983
Gaspé peninsula, 64
Gaspee, 128
Gates, General Horatio, 149–150, 202
at battle of Camden, 154
replaced by General Greene, 154
Gavin, General James, 1305
Gay Nineties, the, 785
Gazette of the United States, 244
General Electric Corporation, 1027
General Motors, 1027, 1067, 1182, 1220
General Theory of Employment, Interest and Money, The, 1073
Generation gap, 987, 1283
Genêt, Edmond Charles, 236, 237
Geneva agreement on Indochina, 1229, 1230
Genius of Universal Emancipation, The 459
Geology, 449, 825
George I, King of England, 107, 118
George II, King of England, 116, 118
George III, King of England, 90, 118, 126, 134, 138, 147, 159
"Olive Branch petition" rejected by, 138
war decision of, 130
George, Henry, reformer, 678, 857
George, Lloyd, of England, 950–952, 1015–1016
George, Milton, editor, 777
George, Walter, Democratic leader, 1286
Georgetown University, Washington, D.C., 431
Georgia, 62, 129, 169
in Civil War, 576, 584, 600
gold in, 350
Indians in, 339, 350, 356, 359
land grants limited in, 62–64
Negroes in, 72
secession of, 550
settlement of, 62
silk production tried in, 62
slaves excluded in, 62
Yazoo land sales of, 231, 258
"Georgia platform", 527
Germain, Lord, 155
German-Americans, 923, 945
German Islands of the Pacific, 952
German Reformed, 20
Germany during World War I, 920, 923, 925, 928
armistice agreement of, 949
Allied rejection of, 949
armistice signed by, 950
armistice urged by leaders, 949
reparations of, 952
in Somme Valley offensive, 949
Gerry, Elbridge, 247
Gettysburg, battle of, 571, 572
Gettysburg Address, 570
Ghent, Belgium, peace treaty at, 297, 301, 304, 331
Gibbons, Cardinal, of Baltimore, 797
Gibbons v. Ogden, 325
Gibbs, J. Willard, physicist, 825
Giddings, Joshua R., 529, 531
Gideon v. Wainwright on right to counsel, 1306
(*See also* Warren Court)
Gila River, 530
Gilbert, Sir Humphrey, 17, 23, 47
Gilbert, Raleigh, 47
Gilbert Islands, 1122
Ginsberg, Allen, 1281
Ginzburg, Ralph, 1301
Ginzburg v. United States conviction upheld on objectionable advertising, 1301
(*See also* Warren Court)
Gladden, Washington, minister, 796
Glass-Owens bill, 1912, 914
Glass-Steagall Act, 1059
Global crises of 1930s:
American isolationism, 1092–1095
American neutrality, decline of, 1100–1103
crises in Pacific, 1104–1107
dictators, challenge of, 1091, 1092
German expansionism, 1097, 1098, 1100
lend-leases, 1103
United States commitment in Europe, 1103–1104
war in Far East, 1095–1097
"Glorious Revolution," 66, 105–107 112
"God Bless America," 1131
Godey, Louis A., 432
Godey's Lady's Book, 432
Godkin, E. L., 625, 832
Godoy, Manuel de, 240
Godspeed, 46
Gold:
legal tender, 82, 174, 199, 215, 360, 621, 623, 783
called in, 1058, 1059
gold standard, 641, 644
abandoned, 1058–1059
reserves, outflow of, 1215
ore, 4, 10, 11, 14, 44, 46

Gold:
ore: discovered in California, 424, 740
discovered in Georgia, 350
in Nevada and Colorado, 740, 741
price raised, 1933, 1059
Gold Reserve Act, 1059
Gold standard after 1878, 663
advocated by Republicans, 786
preserved by Grover Cleveland, 785, 787
Gold Standard Act of 1900, 855
Goldberg, Arthur J., 1289
Goldwater, Barry, in election of 1964, 1296, 1297
Gompers, Samuel, 701, 916, 943, 1037
Good Hope, Cape of, 8
Good Neighbor policy, 1014, 1093
Good Roads bill, Jacob S. Cokey's 785
Goodyear, Charles, 449
Gordon, William, 112
Gorgas, Sir Ferdinando, 56
Gorgas, Josiah, Confederate Chief of Ordnance, 579
Gould, Jay, 623, 651, 664–665, 667
Government, local: in colonies, 111
corruption in, 128
after Revolution, 165
Governors, colonial, 104, 105, 116
duties of, 108–110
England's dependence on, 107
varieties of colonies under, 108
Grady, Henry W., 674
Graft, 653, 857
Graham, the Reverend Billy, 1260
Grain Standards Act, 917
Grand Army of the Republic, 646, 653, 657
Grand Banks, 16, 64, 74, 101, 297
New Englanders barred from, 138
in Treaty of Paris, 1783
Grand Coulee power project, 1010
Grandfather clauses, 659
Grange, Harold ("Red"), 986
Grange, the, 627, 678
decline of, 776, 777
formation of, 775
influence of, 776
Granger laws, 678, 679, 775
Grant, Ulysses S., 561, 607, 634, 644, 776
at Chattanooga, 574
in command of Armies, 574–576
corruption in regime of, 621–623, 626
elected President, 621
Presidency of, 621–626
Presidential nomination of, 612
reelection of, 625
at Vicksburg, 572
Grants, land, 16, 622
banned in Proclamation of 1763, 119
for higher education, 569, 771, 807, 808
of Indian lands, 56
for railroads, 651, 663, 665–667
for schools, 430, 431
Grants-in-aid, 1206
Grapes of Wrath, The, 1074
Grasshoppers, devastation by, 757–758, 775
Graves, Admiral Thomas, 155, 158
Gray, Asa, 449
Gray, Captain Robert, 495
Gray v. Sanders Georgia County unit system invalidated by, 1300
(*See also* Warren Court)
Great Awakening, the, 84, 85, 90, 101
Great Basin, 501
acquired in Treaty of Guadelupe Hidalgo, 502
Great Britain:
in 1930s: declaration of war on Germany, 1100
at Dunkirk, 1101
Adolf Hitler demands on, 1100
Iceland occupied by, 1103
lend-lease for, 1103
on Spanish Civil War, 1095
World War I, 924, 927, 928
Hinderburg Line broken by, 949
in Somme Valley, 949
Great Frontier, The, 17
Great Lakes, 17, 112
Great Miami River, 322
Great Northern Railroad, 873
Great Plains, 494, 758
Great Salt Lake, 501
Great Society, Lyndon B. Johnson's, 1298–1299
Great Train Robbery, The (film), 830
Great War for Empire, 113, 130, 150
British reverses in, 113
British wartime grievances, 116–118
regulatory problems after, 118–120
economic activity restrictions, 119
Indian troubles, 118, 119
(*See also* Seven Years' War)
Greater East Asia Co-Prosperity Sphere, 1105, 1120
Greater Seminole oil field, discovery of, 1028
Greeley, Horace, 376, 403, 424, 432, 456, 457, 487, 743, 832
as abolitionist, 529
endorsed by Democrats, 625
reform campaign of, 625
as Whig editor, 472
Green, William, president, AFL, 1037, 1048, 1067
Green, U.S.S., 1104
Greenback movement, 644, 776, 777
Greenback party, 634, 776, 777
platform of, 777
Greenbacks (money), 568, 621, 776
Greene, General Nathaniel, 147, 152
in battle of Giulford Courthouse, 155
Gates replaced by, 154
Greenland, 8
Greenough, Horatio, 454
Gregg, William, industrialist, 420
Gregory, John S., 740–741
Grenville, George, 126, 127
Grew, Ambassador Joseph C., 1105
Graves, General Leslie R., 1131
Grundy, Felix, 282
Grundy, Senator Joseph R., 1041
Guadalcanal, American assault on Japan, 1122
Guadalupe Hidalgo, Treaty of, 502, 507–518
terms of, 517, 518
Guam, 1124
Guatemala, 1237
Guerriere, 282
Guilford Courthouse, battle of, 155
Guiteau, Charles J., assassin, 645
Gulf of Mexico, 65, 296, 331, 333
Gulf of Tonkin, 1242

Gulflight, American tanker, 926
Guthrie, Oklahoma, 760

Habeas corpus, 608
Haight-Ashbury district, San Francisco, 1282
Haiti, 256, 952
Hakluyt, Richard, clergyman, 23, 43–44
Hakluyt, Richard, lawyer, 23
Hale, Sarah Josepha, 432
Halfbreeds (Republican moderates), 631
Halleck, Representative Charles A., 1289
Halleck, General Henry W.:
  commander of all Union forces, 563
  commander of Western Department, 562
Halley's comet, 101
Halpin, Mrs. Maria, 651
Halsey, Admiral William F., 1122, 1124
Hamilton, Alexander, 204, 206, 220, 235, 236, 238, 239, 245, 249–250
  financial program of, 225–231
    Madison's opposition to, 226, 228
    national bank, 227, 228, 252, 255
    tax measures of, 228, 229
  killed by Aaron Burr, 259
  leader of Federalist party, 246, 249
  resignation of, 231, 245
Hamilton, Andrew, 111
Hamilton, Colonel Henry ("Hair-buyer"), 154
Hamilton v. Alabama on counsel in capital case, 1300
  (*See also* Warren Court)
Hammer v. Dagenhart, 917
Hammon, Jupiter, 405
Hammond, James H., 460, 468, 541
Hampton, Wade, 287
Hampton Normal and Agricultural Institute, 808
Hancock, John, 88, 120, 134, 218
  at second Continental Congress, 135
Hancock, Thomas, 87
Hancock, General Winfield Scott, 644
Handel and Hayden Society, 454
Hanna, Marcus A., industrialist, 786, 788
Hannegan, Edward, 485
Hanoi, North Vietnam, 1238
Hanson, Mayor Ole, 958
Harding, President Warren G., 959, 1035, 1038
  death of, 968
  domestic issues under, 965–967
  election of, 963–965
  postwar prosperity under, 963
  scandal, 967, 968
  shortcomings of character and leadership, 965, 968
  views on Presidency, 963, 965
Hardwick, Senator Thomas W., 958
Hargreaves, James, inventor, 406
Harlem, New York, 1253
Harmar, General Josiah, 232, 234
Harper, Chancellor William, 468
Harper v. Virginia State Board of Education, equal protection clause held violated, 1300
  (*See also* Warren Court)
Harper's Ferry:
  in Civil War, 562, 563
  raid at, 545
Harper's Magazine, 432, 651, 832
Harriman, Averill, 1153
Harriman, Edward H., 665, 667, 873
Harrington, James, 45
Harrington, Michael, 1252
Harris, William T., 798
Harrisburg, Pennsylvania, 341, 376, 429
Harrison, Benjamin:
  background of, 656
  elected President, 655
  last days of administration, 784
  Presidential nomination of, 655
  renomination of, 784
  and Republicans, 656–658
    federal spending increased, 658
  Sherman Antitrust Act signed by, 680
Harrison, William Henry, 281
  commander in War of 1812, 287, 289
  death of, 474
  Presidential election of, 376, 377, 474
Harrod, James, 169
Harrodsburg, Kentucky, 169
Harte, Bret, writings of, 764
Hartford, Connecticut, 56
Hartford Convention, 301, 302
Hartley, Congressman Fred A., 1186
Harvard, John, 55
Harvard College, 55, 83, 101, 117, 431, 807
Harvey, William H., free-silver advocate, 786
Hastings, Thomas, 454
Hat Act, 1732, 81
Hatch Act of 1887, 771
Hatcher, Richard G., Gary, Indiana, mayor, 1257
Hawaii:
  annexation of, 846
  annexation failure of, 836, 840, 841
  in commerce, 838, 839
  commercial treaty with, 839
  government of, 840
  naval base at Pearl Harbor, 839
  sugar in, 840
Hawkins, John, 23
Hawley, Willis C., Oregon Congressman, tariff bill of, 1041
Hawley-Smoot bill, 1041–1042
Hawthorne, Nathaniel, writings of, 450
Hay, John, Secretary of State, 844, 850, 851, 890
  Open Door Notes by, 851
Hay-Herran Treaty with Colombia, 887
Hayes, Rutherford B.:
  compared with Ulysses S. Grant, 644
  elected President, 1876, 634, 635, 639, 641
  gold standard favored by, 641
Hayne, Paul Hamilton, Southern writer, 451
Hayne, Robert Y., 347–349
Haywood, William D. ("Big Bill"), 703
Hearst, George, 743
Hearst, William Randolph, 1094
Helena, Montana, 742
Helper, Hinton Rowan, 541, 542
Henderson, Richard, 169
Hendrick, Burton J., 858
Hendricks, Thomas A., 634
  nominated for Vice President, 646
Henry IV, King of France, 21, 22

Henry VII, King of England, 16
Henry VIII, King of England, 20, 22
Henry, Captain John, 283
Henry, Joseph, 449
Henry, Patrick, 118, 126, 193, 205, 218, 276
Hepburn Act, the, 875
Herjolfsson, Bjarnê, 8
Hermitage, the, 489
Hidden Persuaders, The, 1281
Hides:
in California, 498
deer, 71
Hildreth, Richard, 452
Hill, Isaac, editor, 347
Hill, James D., 665–667, 873
Hindneburg, Field Marshal Paul, 928, 1191
Hindenburg Line, the, 949
Hippies, 1282
Hippisley, Alfred E., 850, 851
Hirabayashi v. United States, 1132
Hiroshima, atomic bomb dropped on, 1124
Hiss, Alger, 1193
History and Present State of Virginia, The, 100
History of the American Revolution, 195
History of the Dividing Line, 100
History of the Five [Iroquois] Indian Nations, 101
History of the United States, Bancroft's, 452
History of the United States of America, Hildreth's, 452–453
Hitler, Adolph, 1021, 1094–1096
armies in North Africa, 1113, 1114
armies on Russian front, 1114
Austria annexation attempt of, 1092
collapse of armies, 1120
death of, 1120
Denmark and Norway invaded by, 1101
at Dunkirk, 1101
German expansionism of, 1097–1098, 1100
in Holland, Belgium, 1101
negotiations rejected by, 1098
nonaggression pact with Russia, 1100
in Paris, 1101
power, ambitions of, 1091, 1092
in Rhineland, 1092
Hobbes, Thomas, 45
Hobert, Garret A., 786
Ho Chi Minh, 1229, 1230, 1238, 1239, 1304
Hodges, Charles, 795
Hoffa, James R., 1213
Hog Island, near Philadelphia, 942
Holland (*see* Netherlands, the)
Holmes, Oliver Wendell, writer, 450
Holmes, Justice Oliver Wendell, 792, 945
in United States Supreme Court, 872
Holy Alliance, the, 335
Home Loan Bank System, 1051
Homer, Winslow, 828
Homestead Act of 1862, 381, 569, 622
provisions of, 746
Hone, Philip, merchant, 422, 500
Hood, J. B., Confederate officer, 576
Hood, Admiral Sir Samuel, 155, 158
Hooker, Joseph ("Fighting Joe"), Union officer, 566, 571
Hooker, Reverend Thomas, 56
Hoover, Herbert:
background, 1040
election of, 975, 1026
in election of 1932, 1052–1054
food administrator, World War I, 938, 939
Good Neighbor policy of, 1014
legislation of, 1040–1042, 1049–1051
popularity of, 1027
Presidency of, 1020–1023
Depression, 1021, 1040, 1041, 1049–1052
on Mukden, Manchuria incident, 1022–1023
on war debts, 1021
Presidential nomination of, 973
Hoover Dam, 1049
Hope-Aiken bill, 1191
Hopkins, Harry L., 1059–1060, 1065, 1073, 1085, 1112
Hopkins, Commodore Esek, 138, 146
Horseshoe Bend, battle of, 296, 321
House, Colonel Edward, presidential adviser, 923, 927, 948, 953
House-Grey Memorandum, 927
House of Representatives, 215, 216, 223, 227–228, 239–240, 478, 479
Committee of Thirty-three in, 551
Democratic in 1874, 627
after 1877, 654, 659, 679, 680
election in, 250–251
Republican control of, 246
Wilmot Proviso in, 522
World War I declared, 937
House Foreign Affairs Committee, 279, 282
House Military Affairs Committee, 282
House Un-American Activities Committee, 1192
Houston, Sam, 482, 484
Houston, Texas, 973
How the Other Half Lives, 710
Howard, O. O., Union officer, 671
head of Freedmen's Bureau, 601
Howard University, 808
Howe, Elias, 400, 449
Howe, Admiral Lord Richard, 147, 148
Howe, General William, 136–138, 147, 148, 152
New England invasion planned by, 137
plan abandoned, 148
New York occupation planned by, 137
Hudson, Henry, 22, 58
Hudson Bay, 112
Hudson-Champlain waterway, 137
Hudson-Mohawk Rivers, 58
Hudson River, 22, 47, 148, 154, 384
Hudson Valley, 128, 154
Hudson's Bay Company, 495, 496
in Oregon settlement, 500
Huerta, Victoriano, Mexican dictator, 922
Hughes, Charles Evans, 965, 1013
at Pan-American Conference at Havana, 1928, 1014
Presidential nomination of, 928
Hughes, John, bishop, 455
Huguenots, 20, 21
(*See also* Calvinists)
Hull, Cordell, Secretary of State, 1093, 1117
in Pacific crisis, 1938–1941, 1104–1107
on Sino-Japanese war, 1096, 1097
Hull, General William, 285

Hull House, Chicago, 737
Human Male, The, 1282
Humphrey, George, Secretary of the Treasury, 1198, 1199
Humphrey, Hubert, 1187, 1287, 1297, 1306
  Presidential candidacy of, 1307, 1308, 1319, 1320
Hungary, Soviet control of, 1224, 1225
Huntington, Collis P., 664
Hunt's Merchants' Magazine, 432
Hurley, Edward H., World War I role of, 942
Hurons, 64
Hussein, King of Jordan, 1233
Hussey, Obed, 383
Hutchinson, Mrs. Anne, 56
Hutchinson, Lieutenant-Governor Thomas, 100, 126, 127, 129

Ickes, Harold L., Republican liberal, 964
Idaho:
  admitted to Union, 658, 764
  minerals in, 740, 741
  territorial status of, 742–743
Idaho City, Idaho, 741
Illinois,
  migration to, 381
  Mormons in, 501
  Negroes excluded by, 405
  statehood of, 322
Illinois Central Railroad, 388, 666
Illinois Fernale Seminary, 431
Immigrants, 381, 690, 1071
  Chinese, 644, 646, 707, 777
    in labor dispute, 694, 706
  literacy law passed, 707
  literacy test, veto of, 707
Immigration, 67, 87, 456, 641, 690, 704–707, 1191
  in 1920s, 965, 966, 969, 970
Immigration Act of 1924, 966, 970, 1193
Impending Crisis of the South, The, 542
Imperial versus provincial authority, 104–131
  contest for continent, 112–113
  crisis of seventeenth century, 105–107
  development, eighteenth century, 107–112
  postwar regulatory problems, 118–120
  taxation, 120, 126–127
  tea controversy, 128–130
  wartime grievances, 116–118
Imports:
  colonial America, 67, 82, 127
    duty on molasses, 119
    tax on, 119, 126
  after Revolution, 172, 199
    tax on, 228, 229
Impressment of seamen, 260–273, 277, 278, 282, 289
Imprisonment for debt, 402, 403, 457–458
  outlawed, 458
In His Steps, 796
Inca Indians, 11, 14
Income tax, 785, 856, 962, 966, 1048
  amendment, 898
Indentured servants, 69, 70, 74, 82, 87, 88, 406
Independence, Missouri, 501
Independence, American adjustment to, 161–195
  confederation of states, 166–169
  Congress and the West, 169–172
  postwar economic changes, 172–176
  from provinces to sovereign states, 162–166
  social change, 176–195
Independent, 923
Independent party (*see* People's party)
Independent Treasury, Martin Van Buren's, 373, 374, 475
Independent Whig, 112
India, 2, 5
Indian Defense Association, 1086
Indian Emancipation Act (*see* Dawes Act of 1887)
Indian Office, 762
Indian policy, 653, 654, 762, 763
Indian Springs, Treaty of, 339
Indian Territory, 350, 626
Indian tribes west of Mississippi River, 760–763
  Indian-white conflicts, 761, 762
  lands of, 763
  new policies for, 761–763
  retreat of, 760–763
  (*See also* specific names of tribes)
Indiana, 281
  Negroes excluded by, 405
  "personal liberty laws" of, 530
  statehood of, 322
  university chartered by, 431
Indianapolis, Indiana, 556
Indians:
  during Depression, 1086
  in exploration (colonization periods), 10, 17, 42, 64, 86, 105, 113
    Algonquins and Iroquois, 58, 59
    in American Revolution, 149
    crops of, 14, 15
    hostility of, 68
    at Jamestown, 46
    of Mexico, 11, 14
    missionary work among, 117
    in northern South America, 14
    in Ohio Valley, 118
    origin of, 14
    of Peru, 11
    in present United States, 15
    Spanish clashes with, 14
    in War of 1812, 281, 289, 297
  Great Plains, 494, 758
  post-Revolutionary, 170, 198
    in Florida, 356
    in Georgia, 339, 350, 356
    in Old Northwest, 232, 234
    raids of, 234
  poverty of, 1252
Indigo, export of, 67, 72, 74, 174, 406
Indulgences, sale of, 18
Industrial growth, 1860–1914, 662–663
  reasons for, 663–665
Industrial revolution from 1860–1894, 662–688
  beginnings of government regulation, 678–680
  consumer distribution, 675
  location of manufacturing, 672–673
  major industries, 669–672
  monopoly, 675–678
  reasons for industrial growth, 663–665
  transportation and communication, 665–669
Industrial Workers of the World (IWW), 703, 764

Indochina, 1104, 1105
Communist containment in, 1228–1230
division of, 1230
French in, 1229, 1230
Inflation, 303, 322, 323, 370, 644, 777, 786, 915, 1058, 1181–1183, 1197
Influence of Sea Power upon History, 838
Ingersoll, Robert G., attacks on religion by, 795
Inness, George, 828
Inquiry of 1917, 946–947
Institutes of the Christian Religion, 20
Intemperance, 457
Intermediate Credits Act, 1039
Internal improvements, aid for, 303, 321, 424, 521, 534, 622, 641
Internal Revenue Service, 1281
International Bank, 1231
International Harvester Company, 677
International Seamen's Union, 916
Internationalism in 1920s, 1011–1013
Interstate commerce, 1065
Interstate Commerce Act of 1887, 654, 679
Interstate Commerce Commission, 679, 875, 898, 916, 1034
Interstate Highway Act, 1203
"Intolerable Acts," 129
Iowa:
frontier, 493
Mormons in, 501
statehood of, 382
Iowa State College, 825
Irish-Americans, 923
Iron, 568, 664, 667, 669
cast iron, 670
pig iron, processing of, 400, 670
Iron, Blood, and Profits by George Seldes, 1094
Iron Curtain, the, 1162, 1224, 1240
Iron Heel, The, 858
Iron Molders Union, 693
Iroquois confederacy, 58, 59, 64, 113
allied with Dutch, 59, 64
Irrigation, 757, 758
Irving, Washington, writings of, 450
Isabella of Castile, 10
Ishii, Viscount Kikujiro, 948
Isolationism:
1920s: changing attitude toward Europe, 1010, 1011
defined, 1010
United States, in 1930s, 1092–1095
Israeli, 1231
Isthmus of Panama, 17, 838
Italy, 1930s, 1092
Izard, General George, 295

Jackson, Andrew, 296–299, 332, 336–338, 484, 485
administration of, 346, 347, 349
background of, 346
elected President, 340–342
Georgia and Florida Indian removal, 350, 356
inaugural of, 345
new cabinet of, 350
reelection of, 370
on Second Bank of the United States, 360–363
Jackson, Francis James ("Copenhagen"), 279
Jackson, George H., 741
Jackson, Helen Hunt, 762
Jackson, Rachel, 342, 347
Jackson, Thomas ("Stonewall"):
death of, 571
in defense of Richmond, Virginia, 562
at Manassas, 563
in Shenandoah Valley, 562
Jackson, Mississippi, 572
Jacksonian democracy, 345–378
Bank war, 360, 361
death of Bank, 362
election of 1836, 370–372
Indians, removal of, 350, 356
Jackson's administration, 346–347
the Taney court, 374, 375
tariff and nullification, 356–359
Van Buren and Jackson, 349–350
Van Buren's Presidency, 372–374
Webster and Hayne debate, 347–349
Whigs, 375–379
Jacobellis v. Ohio on allegedly obscene movie, 1301
(*See also* Warren Court)
Jalapa, Mexico, 507
Jamacia, 42, 58
James I, King of England, 44, 57
Calvinist background of, 48
Pilgrims reassured by, 47–48
smoking opposed by, 46
James II, King of England, 59, 60, 105, 106
"Charter of Liberties" (New York) dissolved by, 60
ousted, 60, 107
James, Duke of York (*see* James II, King of England)
James, Edwin L., 1090
James, William, 793
beliefs of, 793, 794
James River, 418, 575
Jamestown, founding of, 46–47, 64
Japan:
German Islands in Pacific gained by, 952, 1016
Shantung transferred to, 952, 1016
at Washington Conference of November 11, 1921, 1017, 1018
Japanese, 1930–1941:
in Manchuria, 1090, 1091
in Pacific crisis, 1938–1941, 1104–1107
in Sino-Japanese War, 1096–1097
Javits, Senator Jacob, 1198
Jay, John, 152, 158, 159, 199
as Chief Justice, U.S. Supreme Court, 238
Jay's treaty, 237–240, 242, 245
Jazz, 831, 975, 980, 986
Jefferson, Thomas, 71, 86, 136, 146, 170, 205, 245, 304, 335, 336
background of, 251, 276
became President in 1801, 228
botany tour of, 244
clash with judiciary, 253–255
Deism embraced by, 251
on education, 429
elected President in 1800, 243, 250
freedom of seas under, 259–262
embargo, 272, 273
as leader of Republican party, 242
political beliefs of, 251–253
Presidency of, 251–273, 347
reelection of, 258, 259
retirement of, 245
as Secretary of State, 227, 228, 235, 236
Statue of Religious Liberty drafted by, 194

Jefferson, Thomas:
as Vice President, 246, 249
Western development under, 255–258
Jenckes, Thomas A., 643
Jewish Eastern Orthodox, 798
Jews, 18, 110
in election of 1936, 1071
in 1920s, 976
state of Israel established by, 1231
Jim Crow law of 1875, 628
Jim Crowism, 869, 1256
Jodl, Field Marshal Alfred, 1120
Joffre, General Joseph, French Army commander, 937
John II, King of Portugal, 8
John F. Kennedy center for the Performing Arts, Washington, D.C., 1261
Johns Hopkins University Graduate School, 808
Johnson, Andrew, 485, 570, 602
background of, 603
in clash with Radicals, 605–608
elected Vice President, 583, 584
impeachment trial of, 607–608
Presidential Reconstruction policies of, 603–605
Johnson, Hiram, California governor, 867, 956
Vice Presidential nomination of, 904
Johnson, Hugh S., 1039, 1063, 1064
Johnson, President Lyndon B.:
civil disorders study ordered by, 1254
commitment to defense of South Vietnam reaffirmed by, 1242
Great Society of, 1298–1299
as "lame duck" President, 1320
as Majority Leader in Senate, 1206, 1286
in 1964 campaign, 1296, 1297
as President, 1295, 1296
Vice Presidential nomination of, 1287
Johnson, Richard M., 372
Johnson, T. William, free Negro, 405
Johnson, Sir William, Indian agent, 119
Johnson Act of 1934, 1094
Johnston, Albert Sydney, Confederate officer, 561
death of, 561
Johnston, Joseph E., Confederate officer, 576
Joint Chiefs of Staff, 1112
Joint Committee on Reconstruction, 605–607
Joint Planning Committee of United States Armed Forces, 111
Jones, Jehu, free Negro, 405
Jones, John Paul, 154
Jones, Sam M. ("Golden Rule"), Toledo mayor, 736
Jones, William, Bank of the United States headed by, 323
Jones Act of 1916, 891
Jones Act of 1920, 1034
Jones-White Act of 1928, 1035
Joplin, Scott, Negro song writer, 831
Joseph, Chief of Nez Percé Indians, 762
Journal, Woolman's, 100
Juan de Fuca, Strait of, 331, 499
Judiciary, 224
in Jefferson administration, 253–255
Judiciary Act of 1789, 224
court system created by, 224
provisions of, 254, 255
Judiciary Act of 1801, 254
Julian, George A., 602
Jungle, The, 858, 876
Juries, 120, 248
Juvenile delinquency, 1264

Kaiser, the, of Germany, 949
Kanawha River, 322
Kansas, 531, 553, 757, 758
"Bleeding," 533–534
question of, 537
Kansas City, Missouri, 973
Kansas-Nebraska Act, 530–532
passage of, 532
reaction to, 532–533
Karenga, Ron, 1303
Karlesefni, Thorfinn, 8
Kaskaskia, outpost of, 154
Kay, John, inventor, 406
Kearney, Denis, 644, 693, 694, 706
Kearny, Colonel Stephen W., 505, 507
Kearny, U.S.S., 1104
Keating, Kenneth B., 1297–1298
Keating-Owen child labor bill, 704, 917
Kefauver, Senator Estes, 1197
in campaing of 1956, 1205
Kelley, Hall Jackson, 496
Kelley, Oliver H., Grange organizer, 775
Kellogg, Frank B., Secretary of State, 1019
Kellogg-Briand Peace Pact of 1928, 1018–1021, 1024, 1098, 1105
Kendall, Amos,
as editor, 347
as Andrew Jackson's adviser, 347
as political leader, 371
as postmaster general, 372
Kennebec, Maine, 47
Kennedy, Senator Edward, 1298
Kennedy, President John F.:
assassination of, 1290
defeated for Vice Presidential nomination, 1205
foreign policy challenges of, 1236–1242
in Cuba, 1237, 1240–1242
in Europe, 1239–1242
in Southeast Asia, 1237–1239
Kennedy-Nixon contest, 1287, 1288
debate with Richard M. Nixon, 1288
nomination of John F. Kennedy, 1287
New Frontier, 1289, 1290, 1295
civil rights, 1290
inaugural, 1289
youth on program of, 1281
Kennedy, Robert, 1287
assassination of, 1307
Attorney General, 1289
candidacy of, 1306, 1307
elected to United States Senate, 1297
Kennedy-Khrushchev meeting in Vienna, 1240
Kensett, John P., 453
Kentucky, 167, 169, 322, 382
admitted to Union, 234
Civil War in, 561, 572
divided in Civil War, 558
tobacco and hemp cash crops in, 418
Kentucky Resolutions of 1798, 346
Kern-McGillicuddy bill, 917

Kerouac, Jack, 1281
Kerr, President Clark, University of California, Berkeley, 1281
Key, Francis Scott, 295
Keynes, John Maynard, 1051, 1073
Khrushchev, Nikita, 1235, 1240
in Cuban missile crisis, 1241–1242
King, Ernest J., Chief of Naval Operations, 1112
King, Dr. Martin Luther, 1256, 1257, 1302
assassination of, 1303
King, Senator Rufus, 302
in anti-Missouri movement, 328
Federalist candidate, 304
"King Philip's War," 1675, 56–57
King's College (Columbia), 84
Kinsey, Alfred C., 1282
Kingston, Ontario, 285
Kiowa Indians, 494, 760–762
(*See also* Indians, Great Plains)
"Kitchen cabinet," Andrew Jackson's, 347, 372
Knickerbocker, 432
Knickerbocker Trust Company, 885
Knight, E. C., case of, 1895, 680
Knights of Labor, 778
Knights of the White Camelia, 627
Know-Nothing-Free-Soil coalition 533
Know-Nothing Movement, 456
Know-Nothing party, 532, 533, 831
Knowland, Senator William F., 1225
Knox, Philander C., Secretary of State, 899–901
Knudsen, William, 1127
Konoye, Premier Prince Fumimar, 1105
Koo, Wellington, Chinese diplomat, 952
Korean War, 1169–1171, 1174, 1196, 1197
peace negotiations at Panmunjom, 1174
Kossuth, Louis, Magyar leader, 519
Kremlin, the, 1092, 1093, 1116, 1150, 1151
Krueger, General Walter, 1124
Ku Klux Klan founded at Pulaski, Tennessee, 627
in America First Committee, 1102
in election of 1924, 971
in 1920s, 975, 976, 983
in Southern communities, 1257
Kuomentang, the, 1166, 1167, 1225, 1226
Kurusu, Saburo, Japanese diplomat, 1105, 1107
proposals of, 1105, 1107
Kwantung Army, Japanese, 1124
Kyle, James K., 778

Labor after 1860, 581, 652, 690
cheap in South, 674
and government, 703–704
organized, 692–694, 701–703
unrest in West, 764
wage earners, economic patterns of, 691–692
Labor Management Reporting and Disclosure Act, 1213
Labor movement, 402, 403, 644, 692–694, 701–703
AFL beginning of modern movement, 702
Laborers, industrial, 1820–1860, 401–403
reforms advocated by, 402
in South, 420
Labor's League for Political Education, 1188
Laconia, British liner, 928
Ladies' Home Journal, 833
LaFarge, John, 828
Lafayette, Marquis de, 155
LaFollette, Robert M., 857, 896
as governor of Wisconsin, 858
Presidential ambitions of, 903
Progressive party nominee, 971, 972
in United States Senate, 858
LaFollette, Senator Robert M., Jr., 1193
LaFollette-Costigan bill, 1050
LaFollette Seamen's Act, 704, 917
Lafon, Thomy, free Negro, 405
Laird, Melvin, Defense Secretary, 1321–1322
Lake of the Woods, 331
Lamar, L. Q. C., as Secretary of the Interior, 653, 654
Lamont, Robert P., Secretary of Commerce, 1048
Land banks, 82, 83, 917
notes, 175
Land law of 1796, 231
Land law of 1804, 258
Landon, Alfred M., 1070, 1071
Landrum-Griffin Act (*see* Labor Management Reporting and Disclosure Act)
Lands, public, 173, 322, 475
confiscated from Tories, 173
for farmers, 746
for railroads, 569, 651
as source of public wealth, 173
Lane, Lansford, free Negro, 405
Lane Seminary in Cincinnati, 460
Lansing, John, 206
Lansing, Robert, State Department Counselor, 923
Secretary of State, 926, 928, 947, 948, 953
Lansing-Ishii Agreement of November, 1917, 948
Laos, 1230, 1238
Larkin, Thomas O., merchant, 498, 503
LaSalle, Robert Cavelier de, 65
Latin America, 249, 340
independence in, 333–335
1920s, warning United States intervention in, 1013, 1014
United States intervention in, 922
Laud, Archbishop William, 44
Laurens, Henry, 72, 81, 120
Lawrence, 289
Lawrence, E. O., 1131
Lawrence, Kansas, 534, 535
Lawson, Thomas W., 858
Laval, Pierre, French Prime Minister, 1092
League of Armed Neutrality, 151
League to Enforce Peace, 946
League of Nations, 946, 952, 953, 964, 965
Article X of, 953, 956, 957
controversy on, 953–958
United States observers at conferences, 1020
Lease, Mary Elizabeth, 778
Lecompton convention, 537, 538
Lecturers, late nineteenth century, 830
Lee, Arthur, 150, 152
Lee, Richard Henry, 146, 218, 227

Lee, Jason, missionary, 496
Lee, General Robert E.:
in battle of Richmond, Virginia, 562, 563
at Chancellorsville, Virginia, 571
at Fredericksburg, Virginia, 571
at Gettysburg, 571, 572
surrender of, 584, 599
Legal tender, 120, 215, 360, 621, 623
paper money as, 175
Legal Tender Act of 1862, 568
Legislative Reorganization Act of 1946
Legislatures, early, 104–105, 107
bicameral, 205
of New York, 106, 253
Revolutionary, 164–166
on Sedition Act, 249
unicameral in Pennsylvania, 163
in Virginia, 105, 126, 127
Lehigh University, 807
Leisler, Jacob, 106
Lemke, William, 1070
Lend-Lease Act of 1941, 1103, 1112
Lenin, V. I., peace program of, 1015
Leningrad, 1114
Leon, Ponce de, 11
"Levellers", 45, 112
Lever Act of August, 1916:
Food Administration established by, 938
Fuel Administration established by, 938
Leviathan, 45
Levinson, Salmon O., 1019
Lewis, John L., president, United Mine Workers, 1037, 1067, 1185
Lewis, Meriwether, 256, 257
Lewis and Clark expedition, 256, 257, 494
Lewiston, Idaho, 741
Lexington, Kentucky, 304
Lexington, Massachusetts, in American Revolution, 133–135, 159
Leyte, 1124
Libel, 248, 249, 253, 534
Liberator, The, 460
Liberty, 120
Liberty Bonds, 942
Liberty magazine, 1054
Liberty party, 479, 524
Libraries, late nineteenth century, 833
License cases, 375
Life, 1264
Life and Writings of George Washington, Sparks's, 452
Lilburne, John, 45, 112
Liliuokalani, Queen, 840
Lincoln, Abraham, 537–539, 548, 556–559, 635
background of, 537, 538
during Civil War, 562–563, 567–569
Cooper Union address of, 548–549
death of, 584, 602
in debate with Stephen A. Douglas, 538, 539, 601–602
elected President, 548–550
Emancipation Proclamation of, 570
Gettysburg Address, 570
Reconstruction plans of, 602, 603
reelection of, 583, 584
Lincoln Memorial, Washington, D.C., 829
Lind, Jenny, 380, 540
Lindburgh, Charles A., Jr., 1102
Lindley, Ernest K., columnist, 1204–1205
Linn, Lewis F., 475
Lippman, Walter, 1227
Lisa, Manuel, trapper, 494
Literary Digest, 959, 1071
Literature:
from 1815–1860, 427, 450–453, 469
(*See also* Culture, American, 1816–1860)
late nineteenth century, 825–828
after 1950, 1262, 1263
works of authors, 1262, 1263
of 1920s, 987, 988
Little Belt, 282
Little Big Horn, battle of, 762
Little Rock, Arkansas, federal troops in, 1212, 1257
Little Rock and Fort Smith Railroad, 651
Little Sarah, 236
Little Steel formula, 1181
Litvinov, Maxim, 1093
Livestock, 418
(*See also* Cattle)
Livingston, Edward, Secretary of State, 350
Livingston, Robert R., 146, 256, 325
Lloyd, Henry Demarest, 678
Lobbyists, 657, 914, 1052
Locarno Pact of 1925, 1092
Locke, John, 62, 85, 111, 112, 146
Lockner v. New York, 704
Lockouts, 702, 1067
"Locofocos," 360
(*See also* Democratic party)
Lodge, Henry Cabot, 659, 707, 845–847
League of Nations opposed by, 953, 956, 958
Lodge Henry Cabot, United Nations representative, 1287, 1304
Logan, James, 101
Logan, John A., 644
Vice Presidential nomination of, 646
London, Jack, 858, 908
London Company, 45, 46, 69
representative legislature created by, 47
survival efforts of, 46, 47
London Conference of September, 1945, 1157
(*See also* Cold War)
London Economist, 449
London Exhibition of 1851, 449
London Naval Conference, 1929, 1021
London Spectator, 570
Lone Star Republic, 484
Lonely Crowd, The, 1281
Long, Dr. Crawford W., 449
Long, Huey P., 1067, 1070
Long Island, 147, 148
Longfellow, Henry Wadsworth, writings of, 450
Looking Backward, 678
Lookout Mountain, battle of, 574
Lord, John Wesley, Methodist bishop, 1260
Los Angeles, California, 494, 507
1960 Democratic convention in, 1287
Louis Napoleon, 578
Louisburg, 112, 113
fall of, 113
Louisiana, 113, 249, 382, 636
admitted to Union, 234
secession of, 550
statehood of, 322
transferred by Spain to France, 256

Louisiana Farmers Union (*see* National Farmers' Alliance and Cooperative Union of America)
Louisiana Purchase, 256, 273, 280–281, 298, 530
  Adams-Onis Treaty, boundary defined by, 331
  Oregon in, 495
  West Florida proclaimed part of, 281
Louisiana Territory, 243, 255, 296
  boundary doubts of, 256
  Jefferson purchase of, 243, 256
Louisville, Kentucky, 423, 576
Lovejoy, Elija P., minister, 460
Lowden, Frank O., 964, 973
Lowell, Francis C., 399
Lowell, James Russell, 450, 487–488
Lower South, 67, 71, 74
  Charleston, port city of, 72
  indigo, export of, 72
  rice, export of, 72
Loyalists, American (*see* Tories)
Loyalty oath, 55, 602, 1193, 1301
Loyalty Review Board, 1192
Lucas, Eliza, 72
Luce, Henry R., 991
Ludlow, Representative Louis, 1097
Ludlow Resolution of 1938, 1097
Luftwaffe, The, 1119
Lukeman, Henry Augustus, 829
Lumber, 662, 663, 669
  for export, 46, 71–74
Lundy, Benjamin, 459
Lusitania, British liner, 926, 927
Luther, Martin, 18
Lutherans, 18
Luxembourg, liberation of, 1118
Lyceums, 432
Lynching, 983
  antilynching law, 1186, 1191
Lyon, Mathew, 249

McAdao, William G., Secretary of the Treasury, 942, 964, 965, 971
MacArthur, General Douglas, 1052
  recall from command, 1171, 1174
  in war in the Pacific, 1122, 1124, 1126
McCarren, Senator Pat, 1193
McCarren Act, 1193
McCarren-Walter Act of 1952, 1193
McCarthy, Eugene J., Presidential candidacy of, 1310–1312
McCarthy, Senator Joseph, 1168, 1193, 1204
  communism charges of, 1204
  death of, 1204
McCarthyism, 1204
McClellan, General George B.:
  at Antietam, 570
  in battle of Richmond, Virginia, 562, 563
  1884 Democratic nomination of, 584
  Virginia invaded by, 560, 561
McClellan, Senator John L., 1213
McClellan Committee, 1203
McClure, Samuel S., 832, 857
McClure's Magazine, 832
  muckraking of, 857, 858
McCormick, Cyrus, 383, 449, 665
McCormick Harvester Works, 701
McCoy, Joseph G., 744
McCrary bill of 1874, 679
McCrea, Jane, 149
McCullom case, 1260
McCullough v. Maryland, 323, 324
MacDonald, Ramsey, Prime Minister of Great Britain, 1021
Macdonough, Lieutenant Thomas, 295
McDowell, General Irvin, 561
McDuffie, George, 475
McGavern, George, candidacy of, 1306
McGuffey, William Holmes, 430
McGuffey's Readers, 430, 798
McHenry, James, 250
McHenry, Jerry, fugitive slave, 530
Mackay, Alexander, 428
McKay, Donald, 388, 399
McKildin, Governor Theodore R., 1286
McKinley, William:
  background of, 786–787
  Chairman of Ways and Means Committee, 657
  death of, 870
  elected President, 641, 788, 841, 842, 855
  nominated for President, 786
  reelection of, 855
  Spanish-American War message to Congress, 843–844
  as wartime President, 844–848
McKinley-Bryan campaign, 789
McKinley tariff of 1890, 840
McKissick, Floyd, 1303
McLane, Louis, Secretary of the Treasury, 362
McLaurin, George W., 1255
McLean, Justice John, 375
MacLeish, Archibald, 1085
Macmillian, Harold, British Prime Minister, 1241
McNamara, Robert S., Defense Secretary, 1239, 1242, 1289, 1305
McNary, Senator Charles L., 1039
McNary Haugen bills, vetoes of, 973, 1039–1041
Macon, Nathaniel, 279
Macon's Bill Number Two, 279, 281
Macune, C. W., 777
Madison, Dolley, 276
Madison, James, 203, 205–212, 214, 217, 218, 220, 236, 245, 335
  background of, 276, 277
  botany tour of, 244
  elected President, 272, 273
  in *The Federalist,* 243
  Hamilton's financial plans opposed by, 226, 229
  in House of Representatives, 223, 224
  Monroe's candidacy backed by, 304
  Presidency during War of 1812, 276–279, 281–283, 285, 287, 289, 290, 295, 297
  reelection of, 297
  as Secretary of State, 254, 276
  on Sedition Act, 249
Magazines, late nineteenth century, 832, 833
Magellan, Ferdinand, 11
Mahan, Alfred T., 838, 839, 851
Mail-order houses, 674
Maine, 17, 56, 106, 298, 476, 477
  in Missouri Compromise, 328
  Prohibition in, 984
Maine, battleship, 654, 838, 842
Malcolm X, 1303
Malta Conference, 1945, 1120
Manassas:
  first battle of, 559, 561
  second battle of, 563
Manchester Guardian, 1227
Manchu dynasty, China, 836

Manchuria, 900, 901, 1090, 1091
Mandamus, writs of, 255
Mangum, Willie P., 475
Manhattan Island, purchase of, 58
"Manhattan Project," 1131
Manifest destiny, 485, 487, 493
Manila, Philippines, 845, 846, 848
Manila Bay, 845, 846
Mann, Horace, educator, 430
Mann Act, 898
Mann-Elkins Act, 898
Manners and morals, 1920s:
  automobile in, 985, 986
  jazz, 986
  radio and motion pictures, 986
  spectator sports, 986
  women, 985, 986
  young people, 986, 987
Mansfield, Mike, 1306
Manufacturing, 173, 303, 399–401, 425, 663
  colonial, 81
  location of, 672–674
    lag in South, 674
  promoter as national policy, 399
  in South, 1820–1860, 418–421
Mao Tse-tung, 1096, 1166
Marbury v. Madison, 254, 255, 323
Marco Polo Bridge, 1096
Marcos, Fray, 11, 14
Marcy, William L., Secretary of State, 485, 529
Marianas, the, 948, 1122, 1124
  (*See also* German Islands of the Pacific; World War II, in Pacific)
Marietta, Ohio, 172
Marijuana, 1282
Marion, Francis, 155
Maritime Commission, 1128
Markets, Pacific, and coaling stations, 836–838
  China, 836
  Korea, 837
  race for empire, 837
Marne, battle of, 920, 949
Marquette and Joliet, 65
Marshall, General George C., 1112, 1116
  Marshall Plan, 1161
  mission to China, 1166
  as Secretary of State, 1231
Marshall, James, gold discovered by, 525
Marshall, John, 218, 258, 300, 454
  background of, 323
  as Chief Justice, U.S. Supreme Court, 254, 255
  death of, 374
  landmark cases of, 323–325
  treason defined by, 259
  in XYZ affair, 247, 323
Marshall, Justice Thurgood, 1257
Marshall Islands, 948, 1122
  (*See also* German Islands of the Pacific; World War II, in Pacific)
Marshall Plan, the, 1161
Martin, Bradley, 737
Martin, Representative Joseph, 1061
Martin, Luther, 204–206, 214
Martin v. Hunter's Lessee, 324
Martinsburg, West Virginia, 644, 693
Marx, Karl, 703, 1015
Mary, Queen of Scots, 22–23, 25
Mary I, Queen of England, 20, 22
Mary II, Queen of England, 59, 60
  (*See also* William and Mary)
Maryland:
  Calverts in, 57, 58, 107
  Catholics in, 57
  Church of England in, 107
  colonization of, 42, 57–58
  commodities as money in, 82
  customs officer in, 120
  proprietory restored in, 107
  tobacco in, 46, 57, 67
Mason, George, 162, 218
Mason, John, 56
Mason, Lowell, 454
Mason-Dixon line, 68, 459
Mass media after 1950, 1263, 1264
Massachusetts, 48, 55
  bills of credit in, 82
  charter revoked, 106
  Connecticut offshoot of, 56
  Maine and New Hampshire controlled by, 106
  new charter of, 106
  Puritains in, 48, 55
  Revolutionary government of, 164, 165
  royal province planned for, 55
Massachusetts Bay Company, 48
Massachusetts Government Act, 129
Massachusetts Institute of Technology, 807
Massacres:
  Boston Massacre, 120, 127
  in Cherry Valley, 154
  in Chivington (of Indians), 761
  at Fort Dearborn, 285
  Indian massacre of 1622, 47
  on River Raisin, 287
  in Wyoming Valley, 154
Masses, 944
Matamoros, Mexico, 505
Matches, law on manufacture of, 898
Mather, cotton, 100
Mathews, General George, 281
Matsu, 1225, 1226
Matsuoka, Foreign Minister Yosuke, 1105
Max of Baden, Prince, 949
Maximilian of Austria, 578
Maximum Freight Rate case, 679
Maya Indians, 14
Mayflower, 47
Mayflower Compact, 48
Mayhew, Jonathan, 100
Mays, Willie, 1257
Maysville road, 349–350
Meade, General George G., 571
Mechanics' Free Press, 402
Mechanization, farm, 383
Medicare, 1298
Medicine Lodge Creek, 761
Mediterranean campaign, 1114, 1116
  (*See also* World War II)
Mein Kampf, 1091
Mellon, Andrew W., Secretary of the Treasury, 966, 972
Melville, Herman, writings of, 450–451
Memorandum on the Monroe Doctrine, 1014
Memphis, Tennessee, 418
Mencken, H. L., 991
Mennonites, 20
Merchant marine, American, 278
Merchantilist theory, 44, 173, 251
Merchants of Death by Helmuth C. Engelbrecht, 1094
Meredith, James H., 1257, 1290
Merger of American Federation of Labor and Congress of Industrial Organizations, 1213
Merritt, E. A., 643
Methodist Church, 85, 455, 457, 797
Methodist Episcopal Church, 194, 797

Methodist Episcopal Church, South, 482
Metropolitan Opera House, 831
Meuse-Argonne, 949
Mexico, 14, 21, 23, 334, 340, 482
  diplomatic relations with United States severed by, 503
  independence, 1822, 498
Mexico City, 482, 484, 495, 505
  American Army occupation of, 517
Mexico-U.S. War, 502–507
  declaration of, 504
  military action in, 505–507
  Treaty of Guadalupe Hidalgo, 502, 507–518
M'Fingal (epic poem), 195
Miami and Erie Canal, 386
  (*See also* Canals)
Michigan, 285
  "personal liberty laws" of, 530
  statehood of, 382
  university chartered by, 431
Middle Atlantic states, manufacturing in, 672, 674
Middle class:
  in colonies, 87
  in Europe, 6, 7
Middle Colonies, 67, 86
  economy, culture of, 73, 82, 83
  lag on independence, 146
  post-Revolutionary economy of, 174
Middle East crisis, 1231–1234
  British and French in, 1231, 1232
  Egypt in, 1231–1233
  Israel in, 1231
  Lebanon and Jordan in, 1233
  USSR in, 1232
  United States in, 1233
  (*See also* Suez canal)
Middle West, manufacturing in, 674
Migrant workers, 1036, 1062
  during Depression, 1086
  after 1950, 1252, 1253
Migration, Westward, 321–323
Milan Decrees of 1807, 260, 279
Military Appropriations Act of August, 1916, 938
Militia, 116, 134, 149, 154, 214
  in Civil War, 558, 559
  of Colorado, 761
  of Tennessee, 296
  in War of 1812, 282, 285, 290
Mill Springs, battle of, 561
Miller, Alfred Jacob, 453
Miller, Thomas R., in political scandal, 967
Miller, William, preacher, 456
Miller, William E., in 1964 campaign, 1296
Milligan, L. P., 582
Mills, Representative Roger Q., 651
Mills tariff reform bill, 654–655
Milton, John, 45
Milwaukee, Wisconsin, 381, 423
Milwaukee Leader, 944, 945
Miners, coal, 693
Mining, 641, 662, 664
  copper, 742
  gold and silver, 740–743
  mining communities, 742, 743
  placer, 741
Minnesota, 381
Minstrel shows, 830
Mint Act of 1792, 778, 783
"Minute Men", 134–135
Miscegenation, 193
Missile crisis, Cuban, 1240–1242
Missionaries, Pacific Northwest, 496
Missionary Ridge, battle of 574
Mississippi, 169, 256, 258, 382, 527, 603
  secession of, 550
  statehood of, 322
Mississippi, University of, 1257, 1290
Mississippi River, 11, 58, 65, 112, 113, 418, 760
  in Civil War, 561, 572
  closed to Americans, 199
  nation's border fixed at, 134
  opened to Americans, 240
  Pike's exploration of, 257
  traffic on, 419
  in War of 1812, 296
Missouri, 431, 493
  divided in Civil War, 558
Missouri Compromise, 327–330, 484, 536, 551–552
  reaction to, 330
  (*See also* Clay, Henry; Slavery; Slaves)
Missouri River, 256, 494, 764
"Mr. Madison's War" (*see* War of 1812)
Mitchell, Charles E., banker, 1042
Mitchell, John, head of UMW, 874
Mobile, Alabama, 296–299, 408
Mobile Bay, 281
Mobs, 120, 128, 162, 175, 230, 250
  in Lawrence, Kansas, 534
Model T, Henry Fords', 669, 908
  1924 price of, 1028
Mohammed, 2
Mojave Desert, 494
Molasses, 74, 81, 116, 239
  duty on, 119, 126, 229
Molasses Act of 1733, 81
Moley, Raymond, 1054
Moline Plow Company, 1039
Molino del Rey, Mexico, 517
Molotov, V. M., Foreign Minister, 1153
Monarchies, 6, 7, 104
  in France, 234
Monetary Commission, 885
Monetary system in election of 1896, 786–789
Money, 82, 195, 303, 360, 372, 373
  after American Revolution, 161–162, 172, 174, 175, 200
    in Massachusetts, 175, 176
  in American Revolution, financing, 153, 154
  paper money issued by state banks, 228, 302
  regulation of paper money, 120
Mongrel Tariff, 645
  (*See also* Tariffs after 1877)
Monmouth, New Jersey, 153
Monopolies, 325, 378, 402, 628, 644, 651, 653, 663, 680
  development of, 675–678
    holding companies, 677
    mergers, 676, 677
    pools, 676, 679
    trusts, 676, 677
  government regulation of, 678–680
  growth during 1920s, 1035
  John D. Rockefeller, 672, 676
  Sherman Antitrust Act, 658
  Western land, 653–654
Monroe, James, 256, 272, 333
  background of, 304
  on Latin American independence, 333–335
  Presidency of, 304, 321
  second administration of, 336
  Secretary of State, 282, 283, 304
Monroe Doctrine, 335, 578, 886, 889, 925, 1014, 1093

Monroney, Congressman Mike, 1193
Montana:
admitted to Union, 658, 764
minerals in, 740, 741
territorial status of, 743
Montcalm, 113
Monterey, California, 494, 498, 503
Monterrey, Mexico, 505
Montgomery, General Bernard Law, 1113, 1114, 1118
Montgomery, Richard, 137
Montgomery, Alabama, 550, 1256
Montreal, Canada, 137
in War of 1812, 285, 287, 289
Moody, Dwight L., evangelist, 797, 1260
Moore, Senator Edward H., 1181
Moore's Creek Bridge, battle of, 138
Moors (*see* Moslems)
Moraviantown, Ontario, 289
Morgan, Daniel, 154
Morgan, J. P., 665, 873, 896, 914
Morgan, J. P., and Company, 785
Morgenthau, Henry, Jr., 1117
Mormon, 456
Mormon Trail, 501–502
Mormonism, 456, 501
Mormons, 501, 502, 764, 798
cattle of, 743
(*See also* Church of Jesus Christ of Latter-day Saints).
Moroni, 456
Morrill, Justin S., 569
Morrill Act of 1862 562, 771, 807, 808
Morrill tariff of 1861, 568
Morris, Govoerneur, 204, 205
Morris, Justice Lewis, 111
Morris, Nelson, 665
Morris, Robert, 153, 202, 224, 225
Morristown, New Jersey, 153
Morrow, Dwight, 1014
Morse, Samuel F. B., 388, 449, 453
Morse, Senator Wayne, 1201
Mortefontaine, Treaty of, 250
(*See also* Convention of 1800)
Morton, Levi P., nominated for Vice President, 655
Morton, Oliver P., 621
Moscow, 1114
Moscow Conference of 1943, 1154
Moslems, 2, 4, 19, 16
Motion pictures, 830, 1074
Motley, John Lothrop, historian, 452
Mott, Lucretia, reformer, 458
Mount Defiance, 149
Mt. Holyoke Seminary (college), 431
Mount Rushmore, South Dakota, 829
Mount Vernon, Virginia, 203
"Mountain men," 495
Muckrakers, 857, 858, 868
Mud-sill theory, 468
"Mugwumps," political faction, 646, 651, 653
Muller v. Oregon, 704
Mulligan, James, 651
Mulligan letters, the, 651
Mun, Thomas, 44
Mundt-Nixon bill, 1192
Munitions Investigating Committee, Gerald P. Nye's, 1094
Munn v. Illinois, 679, 775–776
Munsey, Frank, 832
Munsey's Magazine, 832
Murfreesboro, Tennessee, battle of, 574
Murray, William Vans, 250
Muscle Shoals:
controversy, 970, 972
government operation of, 1069
Muscovy Company, 22
Music:
ballad opera, 90, 454
folk, 90, 454
popular, 830, 831
religious, 90, 454
Muskie, Senator Edmund S., Vice Presidential nominee, 1968, 1308
Mussolini, Benito, 1092, 1094–1096
in Ethiopia, 1092
negotiations request ignored by, 1098
in Rome-Berlin Axis, 1092, 1097
war declared on France, 1101

NAACP, 870, 983, 1085, 1236
NAACP v. Button, Virginia law overturned by, 1300
(*See also* Warren Court)
Napoleon Bonaparte (Napoleon I), 249, 256, 275, 280, 333
Continental System of, 277, 279, 280
in exile, 289, 298
Russia invaded by, 284
St. Cloud decree of, 280
Narvaez, Panfilo, 11
Nashville, Tennessee, 169, 418, 423, 561
Nasser, Colonel Gamal Abdel, 1231–1233
Nast, Thomas, 832
Nat Turner rebellion, 405, 460, 468
Natchez, Mississippi, 405, 407
Nation, The, 625, 832
National Aeronautics and Space Act, 1214
National Aeronautics and Space Administration, 1214
National Association for the Advancement of Colored People, 870, 983, 1085, 1236
National Association of Manufacturers, 873, 1202
National Bank Act, 1862, 568
National Banking Act of 1863, 914
National Bimetallic League, 786
National Civil Service Reform League, 645
National Cordage Company, failure of, 784
National Council of Churches of Christ, 1260
National Credit Corporation, 1050
National Defense Education Act, 1214, 1259
National Farmers' Alliance and Cooperative Union of America, 777
National Farmers' Holiday Association, 1052
National Gazette, 244
National Guardsmen, 1301
National Industrial Recovery Act (NIRA), 1062–1065
National Labor Relations Act, 1066, 1072, 1185
National Labor Relations Board, 1066
National Labor Relations Board v. Jones Laughlin Steel Corporation, 1066
National Labor Union, 692
National Liberation Front, 1318, 1319
National Management Relations Act of June, 1947, 1186
(*See also* Taft-Hartley Act)

National Monetary Commission, 914
National Philanthropist, 459
National Progressive Republican League, 903
National Reclamation Act of 1902, 876
National Recovery Act (NRA), 1063, 1064, 1086
declared unconstitutional, 1064, 1065
National Republican party:
Henry Clay nominated by, 360, 363
Democratic party opposition of, 471
in Whig party, 472
(*See also* Whig party)
Natural resources, 641, 664, 739
minerals, 663, 674
National Road of Pennsylvania, 322
National Science Foundations, 1258
National Security Council, 1180
National Socialist party, Adolf Hitler's, 1091
National Temperance Union, 457
National Trades Union, 403
National Urban League, 983
National Women Suffrage Association, 831
National Youth Administration, 1066, 1074, 1086
Nationalism, nationalists, 194, 197, 200, 220
in 1920s, 966, 976
postwar (1812) Republican, 302–304
reform efforts, 201–203
states and localities, 325–327
Nationalist China, 1166, 1167, 1225
Nationalist China—Communist China war, 1166, 1167
Communist victory in, 1167
American reaction to, 1167, 1168
Natural sciences, late nineteenth century, 825
Naturalization, 456
Naturalization Act of 1798, 248
Naval stores, 46, 71
Naval War College, 838
Navigation Act of 1651, 59
Navigation Acts, England's, 60, 71
Navy, American, 154, 235, 238, 249, 302
Navy, British, 119, 237, 238
Navy, United States, 654
World War I expansion of, 937
(*See also* Navy, American)
Nazarene Church, 797
Nazi-Soviet Pact, 1151
Nebraska, 758
statehood of, 764
Nebraska Territory, 531
Negroes, 15, 42, 87, 88, 110, 150, 272, 459, 599, 608, 611, 636
in American Revolution, 137
Black Codes for, 604
in colonial South, 70–72
during Depression, 1085, 1086
after 1877, 641, 719, 720, 867
education, 808
as entertainers, 830, 831
as Kansas farmers, 773
none in Congress by 1901, 659
plight during progressivism, 868–870
as Southern farmers, 772, 773
free, 193, 329, 404, 405, 459
in 1920s: influence on music, 986
in literature and arts, 983, 984
migration to North, 983
veterans of World War I, 976
after 1950, 1246
civil rights of, 1254–1257, 1298, 1299
gains of, 1257
poverty of, 1252–1254
in North, 1820–1860, 405
post-Revolution population of, 176
as postwar transition problem, 600–601
prejudice against, 86
and progressivism, 868–870
equal rights failures, 918
housing, 870, 918
Booker T. Washington, 869
under Woodrow Wilson, 869, 918
rejected for Civil war service, 559
Santo Domingo insurrection by, 256
as slaves, 101, 381
in Union Army, 570
in War of 1812, 297
in World War II, 1132, 1145
racial segregation banned in transportation and recreation facilities, 1132, 1145
Nelson, Donald, 1127
Nelson, Horatio:
at battle of the Nile, 249
at battle of Trafalgar, 260
Nelson, Senator Knute, 958
Neshaming, Pennsylvania, 84
Netherlands, the, 18, 151
Nettuno-Anzio, 1118
Neutrality Act of 1935, 1095
extended, 1095
Neutrality Act of 1939, repeal of, 1101
Nevada, 740
New Amsterdam, 58
New Brunswick, 476
Newcomb, Simon, astronomer, 825
New Deal:
banking reform, 1058, 1059
basic goal of, 1057
for farmers, 1060–1062
fiscal policies of, 1072, 1073
Indians in, 1086
for labor, 1066, 1067
legislation and U.S. Supreme Court 1071, 1072
migrant workers in, 1086–1087
National Industrial Recovery Act, 1062–1065
Negroes in, 1085, 1086
promised by Franklin D. Roosevelt, 1056
relief, 1059, 1060
relief extended, 1065, 1066
roots of, 1057
second, 1065
Social Security, 1067, 1068
(*See also* Great Depression; Roosevelt, Franklin D.)
New England:
colonization of, 42, 47–57, 60, 61
economy, culture of colonies in, 73–82
"personal liberty laws" of, 530
post-Revolutionary, 173
economic reverses of, 173–174
secessionist movement in, 258, 290, 300
New England Confederation, 57
Newfoundland, 8, 16, 17, 23, 64
Calvert efforts to colonize, 57
claimed by British, 112
New Freedom of Woodrow Wilson, 1057
New France, 64, 65
in British hands, 113

New Hampshire, 56, 106
  new government of, 162
  as royal province, 56
New Haven, Connecticut, 56
New Jersey, 60
  in American Revolution, 148, 153
  Quakers in, 61
  as royal province, 60
New Jersey Plan, 206
Newlands Act of 1902, 764
New Mexico, 495, 530
  statehood of, 764
New Nationalism of Theodore Roosevelt, 1057
New Netherland, 42, 58, 59
  ceded to England, 59
  given to James, Duke of York, 59
  recaptured by Dutch, 59
New Orleans, Louisiana, 112, 256, 302, 384, 418, 423, 553
  held by Spain, 198
  part opened to Americans, 240
  in War of 1812, 295, 296, 297
New Orleans Times, 610
New Panama Canal Company, 887
Newport, Rhode Island, 154
New Salem, Illinois, 537
Newspapers, late nineteenth century, 832
Newsweek, 1181
Newton, Isaac, 85, 101
New York, 60, 106
  in American Revolution, 135, 137, 147–149, 152, 153
  legislature, 106, 107
  as royal province, 60
New York, Port of, 641, 645
New York Call, 944
New York Central Railroad, 665
New York City, 86, 250, 384, 422, 456
New York Evening Post, 450, 517, 944
New York Harbor, 17, 22, 375
New York Herald, 432, 500
New York Journal of Commerce, 848
New York Morning Herald, 832
New York Stock Exchange, 784, 885
New York Sun, 432, 908
New York Times, 534, 580, 832, 923, 973, 1019, 1048, 1190, 1131, 1229
New York Tribune, 376, 402, 403, 432, 487, 529, 832
New York v. Miln, 375
New York World, 832
Neyer, Eugene, 1050
Nez Peree Indians, 496, 762
Niagara, 289
Niagara campaign of 1812, 287
Niagara Falls, Canada, 287
Niagara River, 285, 287
Nicaragua, 887
Niles Weekly Register, 328, 432
Nimity, Admiral Chester, 1122
Nina, 10
Nine Power Pact of 1924, 1017, 1021, 1023, 1024
  (*See also* Washington Treaties)
Nineteenth Amendment, 867
Nixon, Richard M.:
  campaign strategy of, 1320
  on Communists, 1204
  elected President, 1307, 1308
  Kennedy-Nixon contest, 1287, 1288
    debate with John F. Kennedy, 1288
    nomination of Richard M. Nixon, 1287
  renomination of, 1205
  Vice Presidential candidate, 1196
Noble Order of the Knights of Labor, 693, 694
  accomplishments of, 701
Nomura, Admiral Kichisaburo, 1105
Non-Intercourse Act of 1809, 273, 278, 279, 399
Nonpartisan League of North Dakota, 867, 868
Norbeck, Peter, progressive, 857
Normandy, amphibious operation at, 1118, 1198
Norris, Frank, 858, 908
Norris, George W., 897, 970, 1069
Norstad, General Lauris, 1305
North, Lord, 127, 136, 151, 158
  tea policy of, 128
North:
  in Civil War: behind Northern lines, 580–582
    population of, 558
    war preparations of, 558–560
    wartime measures of, 567–569
    wartime policies of, 583–584
  1820–1860: agriculture in, 382–384
    factory system in, 399–401
    industrial advances in, 380, 381
    living standards, 424
    transportation and communication, 384–388
    urbanization in, 422, 423
    workers in, 401–403
North African invasion, 1112–1114
North American Review, 432, 450, 500, 1022
North American Treaty Alliance, 1161, 1162, 1196, 1197, 1241
North Carolina, 17, 611
  farm organization in, 777
  population loss in, 322
  Quakers in, 60–62
  secession of, 558
  settlement of, 62
  slaves in, 72
North Dakota admitted to Union, 658, 764
North Korea, 1228
North Star, The, Afro-American newspaper, 432, 460
North Vietnam, 1230, 1239
Northern Alliance, farm organization, 777, 778
Northern Pacific Railroad, 627, 666, 873
Northern Securities Company, 677, 872, 873
Northwest, Pacific, 256, 494, 624, 666
Northwest Ordinance of 1785, 170, 258
Northwest Ordinance of 1787, 170, 172
Northwest Territory, 170, 172
  (*See also* Old Northwest)
Norway, German invasion of, 1101
Notes on Virginia, 251
Nueces River, 503
Nullification, doctrine of:
  in South Carolina, 348, 356–359
Nuremberg trials, 1157
Nye, Senator Gerald P., 1094, 1095

Oberlin College, 431
Obligation of contract, 215, 258, 325
O'Boyle, Patrick A., Catholic archbishop, 1260
Ochs, Adolph S., 831
Octopus, The, 858
Of Civil Government, 111
Office of Censorship, 1131
Office of Defense Transportation, 1127

Office of Price Administration, 1128, 1181, 1182
Office of Production Management, 1127
Office of Scientific Research and Development, 1130
Office of War Information, 1131
Oglethorpe, James, 62
Ohio, 169, 232, 297
  admitted to Union, 234, 258
  "personal liberty laws" of, 530
Ohio and Erie Canal, 386
  (*See also* Canals)
Ohio Company, 170, 172
Ohio Farmer, 423
"Ohio Idea," the, 621
Ohio Life Insurance and Trust Company, New York branch, 424
Ohio River, 112, 169, 203
  as boundary, 167
  Canadian border shifted northward from, 134
  lands north of, 231, 322
  Tecumseh action on, 281
  westward movement on, 322
Ohio Valley, 118
  raids in, 154
  urbanization in, 422
Oil, 662, 663, 668, 680
  concentrations of, 674
  first well drilled, 671
  (*See also* Petroleum)
Okinawa, 1124
Oklahoma, 674
  Five Civilized Tribes in, 758, 762
  plains Indians in, 758, 760
  statehood of, 764
  white settlement of, 760
Oklahoma, University of, 1254
Oklahoma City, Oklahoma, 760
Oklahoma City oil field, discovery of, 1028
Oklahoma Territory, opening of, 658
  (*See also* Indian Territory)
Old Guard, 964, 965
  (*See also* Republican party, 1920–1970
Old Northwest:
  British interference in, 232, 238
  Cumberland Road to, 384
  democratic after 1840, 473
  development of, 232–234, 240
  Federalist defeats in, 232, 234
  Indians deterrent to settlement of, 232
  occupation of, 382
  restrictions on Negroes in, 405
Old Southwest, 322
Old Spanish trail, 494
Olds, Henry Leland, 669
"Olive Branch Petition," 136, 138
Olympia, battleship, 838
O'Mahoney, Joseph C., 1071
Ontario, Lake, 113, 285, 287
Open Door policy, 849–851, 890, 899, 901, 948, 952, 1017
  (*See also* China, Open Door policy for)
Open housing law, 1303
Open shop, 1036
Operation Dragoon in World War II, 1118
Operation Overlord, World War II, 1116
Operation Torch in World War II, 1112–1114
Oppenheimer, J. Robert, atomic scientist, 1204
Oran, 1114
Orders in Council of 1807, 260, 277–279, 283
  repeal of, 280, 284, 297
Ordinance of 1784, 169
Oregon, 331, 498, 503, 519, 635, 704, 835
  in China trade, 495
  as political issue, 499–501
  settlement of, 496, 498–501
Oregon, battleship, 838, 887
Oregon Trail, 496, 498
Organization of American States, 1240
Origin of the Species, The, 677, 792
Orlando, Vittorio, of Italy, 950, 951
Osborn v. Bank of the United States, 324
Osceola, Chief, 356
Osmena, Sergio, 891
Ostend Manifesto, 539, 540
O'Sullivan, John L., 499
Oswego, New York, 113
Otis, James, 116, 117
Our Country, 796

Pacific fleet, at Pearl Harbor, 1104, 1105
Pacific Ocean, 11, 17, 257, 331, 333, 519
  uncontested frontage on, 495
Pacifists, 61, 458
Packard, Vance, 1281
Packers and Stockwards Act (1921), 1038
Page, Walter Hines, Ambassador to London, 923
Paine, Thomas, 138, 148, 244
Pakenham, Sir Edward, 296, 297
Palmer, Attorney General A. Mitchell, 958, 959, 964, 965
Palmer, John M., presidential nominee, 787
Palmyra, New York, 456
Palo Alto, 505
Panama, 886, 887
Panama Canal, 888, 889, 899
Panama Congress, 340
Pan American Conference, 838
Pan American Conference at Montevideo in 1933, 1093–1094
Panic of 1819, 301, 321–323, 327, 349, 356, 360, 382, 424
Panic of 1837, 370–373, 382, 403, 424
Panic of 1857, 424
Panic of 1873, 644, 670, 776
Panic of 1893, 784
  causes of, 784, 785
Panic of 1907, 885, 914
Panmunjom truce negotiations at, 1174, 1228
Paris, France:
  liberation of, 1118
  peace talks on Vietnam War, 1318, 1319
  treaty of, 1763, 113
  treaty of, 1783, terms of, 158–159, 198
  treaty of, 1898, 847, 848
Parity price farm, 1039, 1040, 1060, 1191, 1201
Parker, Captain John, 135
Parker, Theodore, 452, 456
Parkman, Francis, writings of, 453
Parks, Mrs. Rosa, in civil rights case, 1256
Parliament, 44, 81, 117, 120, 127, 138
  colonial taxation by, 119, 120, 126–129

Parliament:
eighteenth century developments in, 107–110
land banks, bills of credit banned by, 83
new tax efforts of, 104
not mermitted to meet, 1629–1640, 47, 48
peace negotiations authorized by, 158
tax rights assumed by, 126
Parties and sectionalism, 471–491
Party politics and slavery, 477–480
Passenger cases, 375
Patch, General Alexander M., 1118
Patent Medicine Industry, 675, 875
Patents, 228, 388
Paterson, William, 206
Paterson, New Jersey, 402
Pathet Lao forces in Laos, 1238
Patman bill, the, death of, 1052
Patron's Handbook, of Grange, 776
Patterson, James W., 626
Pattie, Sylvester, trapper, 494
Pawnee Indians, 494
(*See also* Indians, Great Plains)
Payne, Representative Henry C., 896
Payne-Aldrich tariff, 896
Peace, quest for, 1920s:
challenge of Europe, 1014–1016
foreign policy during Herbert Hoover's administration, 1020–1023
isolationism and internationalism, 1010–1013
Kellogg-Briand Peace Pact of 1918, 1018–1020
in Latin America, 1013, 1014
lessons from World War I, 1009–1010
Washington treaties, the, 1016–1018
Peace Corps, 1237, 1281
Peale, Charles Wilson, portrait painter, 453
Pearl Harbor, 839, 1104
attacked by Japanese, 1107
Peasants Revolt of 1524, 18
Peek, George N., 1039, 1060, 1061
Peffer, William A., 778
Pelley, William Dudley, American Nazi, 1131
Pemberton, John C., surrender of, 572
Pendergast, Thomas J., Kansas City boss, 1179
Pendleton, Senator George, 645
Penn, William, 60, 61
Pennsylvania:
before 1812: in American Revolution, 149, 153
charter of, 60
constitution of, 163
unicameral legislature, 163
Penn proprietor of, 60, 61
Quakers in, 60, 61
iron interests in, 568
oil in, 674
"personal liberty laws" of, 530
Whig-Know-Nothing fusionists in, 533
Pennsylvania, University of, 84
Pennsylvania Dutch, 61
Pennsylvania Railroad, 665, 873
Penrose, Boies, 964
Pensacola, Florida, 296
Pension Bureau, 653
Pensions, 646, 658
for Civil War veterans, 653
People's party, 778
(*See also* Populist party)
Pequot war, 1637, 56
Perdido River, 256
Peress, Major Irving, Army dentist, 1204
Perloff, Harvey, 1247
Perry, Commodore Matthew C., 519
Perry, Oliver Hazard, 287, 289
Pershing, General John J., Commander of AEF in France, 949
Peru, 334, 340
Petersburg, Virginia, 575, 584, 600
Petite Democrate, 236
Petroleum, 669, 671
(*See also* Oil)
Philadelphia, Pennsylvania, 129, 135, 138, 384, 422
in American Revolution, 149, 153
constitutional convention at, 208–212
1932 Democratic Convention in, 1070
1948 Democratic Convention in, 1187
Philadelphia Aurora, 333
Philadelphia Mechanics' Union of Trade Associations, 402
Philadelphia and Reading Coal and Iron Company, 874
Philadelphia Society for Alleviating the Miseries of Public Prisons, 457
Philip II, King of Spain, 22, 25
Philippine Organic Act, 891
Philippines, 11, 1124
annexation of, 845–848
in Treaty of Paris, 847
opposition to, 847, 848
war in, 848, 849
Phillips, David Graham, 858
Phillips, Wendell, 432, 460, 605
Pickens, Andrew, 155
Pickering, Judge John, 255
Pickering, Timothy, 250, 258
Pickett, General George E., 572
Pierce, Charles S., pragmatist, 793
Pierce, E. D., gold discoverer, 741
Pierce, Franklin:
as President, 539
elected President, 529
Pike, Albert, 420
Pike, Zebulon, 257
Pilgrims, Separatist, 47
emigration of, 47
at Plymouth, 48
Pillsbury, Charles A., 669
Pinchot, Gifford, 876, 897
Pinckney, Charles, of South Carolina, 204, 250
Pinckney, Charles C., 247, 250
candidacy of, 250, 259, 272
Pinckney, Thomas, 240
as Vice Presidential candidate, 245, 246
Pingree, Hagen S., Detroit mayor, 736
Pinkney, William, 279
Pinta, 10
Pipelines, 668, 671
Pirates, 64, 238
Barbary pirates, 259, 302
in War of 1812, 297
Pit, The, 858
Pitcairn, Major John, 135
Pitt, H. A., 383
Pitt, William, 113, 116, 126
ousted by George III, 118, 127
Pittman, Key, 1100
Pittsburgh, Pennsylvania, 113, 231, 289, 296, 322, 384

Pittsburgh, Pennsylvania:
commercial broadcasting started in, 986
gateway to Ohio Valley, 422
land office at, 231
Pittsburg Landing, 561
Pizarro, Francisco, 11, 14
Placerville, California, 741
Plantation system, disintegration of, 601
Planters, small, in South, 404
Platt, Orville H., 872
Platt Amendment, 886
Platt, Thomas C., political boss, 858, 871
Platte River, 494
Plattsburgh, New York, 287, 295, 298
Plebiscites, 951, 1098
Plessy v. Ferguson, 628, 808, 869
Plumb, J. H., 118
Plumer, William, Jr., 336
Plymouth, Massachusetts, 48
Plymouth Company, 45, 56
in New England, 47
Pocahontas, 46
Poe, Edgar Allan, 432, 449, 451
Poinsett, Joel, 372
Poitier, Sidney, 1257
Poland, Hitler's invasion of, 1100
Polish corridor, 951
Political action committee, 1188
Political parties:
emergence of, 243–246
power shift in 1800, 252
in 1790s, 244
Politics:
1920s: Calvin Coolidge, 968–970
campaign of 1924, 970–972
domestic issues under Warren G. Harding, 965
election of 1920, 963–965
election of 1928, 973–975
issues in President Coolidge's second term, 972, 973
Progressivism, 970–972
scandal, 967, 968
party, 1875–1900: alliance between politics and business, 641
Congress in, 641
issues in, 641, 642
mediocrity of leaders in, 640
Polk, James K., 485
domestic policies under, 489, 490
elected President, 487, 541
Mexico-U.S. War under, 502–518
Oregon question under, 499–501
Presidency of, 488–490, 495, 522
Polk, Colonel L. L., 777
Polly, 260
Polo, Marco, 4
Polygamy, 501
Pontiac, Ottawa chieftain, 118, 119
Pony Express, The, 382
Pope, General John, union officer, 563
Popular sovereignty, 523, 526, 530, 532, 537
Lewis Cass platform of, 524
Stephen A. Douglas doctrine of, 531
Population:
1820–1860, 381
1914, 907
Populist party, 783, 784, 786
demise of, 855
Populists, Southern white, 659
Pornography, 1301
Port Royal, Nova Scotia, 112
Porter, David, 290
Porter, Peter B., 282
Portsmouth, Rhode Island, 56
Portsmouth, Treaty of, 891
Portugal, 7, 10, 22
explorations of, 8
trade with Africa, 8
water route to Asia found by, 8
Post, Louis F., Assistant Secretary of Labor, 959
Post office, 135, 388
Postal Savings Banks, establisment of, 898
Postal system, 388, 669
parcel post, 898
Postwar Germany, allied plans for, 1117, 1118
Potash, export of, 74
Potomac River:
capital on, 227
in Civil War, 563
Potsdam, Big Three at, 1156, 1157, 1196
(*See also* Cold War)
Poverty after 1950, 1246
in Appalachia, 1252, 1253
causes of, 1254
in cities, 1253
legislation, 1298, 1299
poverty line, 1252
in South, 1253
war on, 1301–1304
Powderly, Terence V., labor leader, 694
Powers, Francis G., in U-2 spy incident, 1235
Powers, Hiram, sculptor, 453, 828
Powhatan, chief, 46
Pragmatism, 793, 795
"Praise the Lord and Pass the Ammunition," 1131
Prayer in schools, 1260
Pre-Civil War years, 521–553
bleeding Kansas, 533–534
Compromise of 1850, 525–527
election of 1848, 524–525
election of 1852, 527–529
election of 1856, 535
Kansas-Nebraska bill, 530–532
Lincoln-Douglas debate, 537–539
reaction to Kansas-Nebraska Act, 532–533
Republican victory, 542–550
Dred Scott decision, 536–537
secession crisis, 550–552
slavery issue, 529–530
vincible South, the, 539–542
Wilmot Proviso, 522–523
Preemption, 231–232, 475, 746
laws, 373
Preemption Act of 1830, 348
Preemption Act of 1841, 381, 475
(*See also* Squatters)
Presbyterians, 20, 194
in colonial America, 85
1815 to 1860, 455, 456
Prescott, Dr. Samuel, 135
Prescott, William H., 452
Presque Isle (Erie, Pennsylvania), 289
Press, freedom of, 249, 253, 582
Prestonburg, Kentucky, 561
Prevost, Sir George, 295
Primogeniture, 43, 172
Prince Henry the Navigator, 8
Princeton University, 85, 276, 431
Principia Mathematica, 101
Proclamation of 1763, 119
Proctor, Henry, 289
Proctor, Senator Redfield, 843

Progress and Poverty, 678
Progressive Farmer, The, 777
Progressive movement:
demands of progressives, 856
meaning of, 856–858
muckrakers in, 857, 858
as national movement, 856
political reforms embraced by, 856
Progressive party, 903, 904
new, 1187
in 1924, 971, 972
Progressivism, 855–892
meaning of, 856–858
Negroes and progressivism, 868–870
in 1924 campaign, 970–972
reform, state and city, 858, 867–868
Theodore Roosevelt: and Far East, 890–891
and Latin America, 885–889
leader of, 870–871
policies and programs, 872–873
second term of, 874–876, 885
and workingmen, 874
Prohibition, 457
in 1920s, 984, 985
in 1928 campaign, 973, 974
Volstead Act, 1919, 984, 985
Prohibition party, 984
Prohibitionists (party), 651
Prohibitory Act of 1775, 138
Propaganda, 530, 679
of Arabs, 1231
British, 923, 924
German, 924
Prophet, the, 281
Prosperity during 1920s:
business and industry, 1027, 1028, 1034, 1035
farm depression, problems, 1037–1040
gross national product increase, 1026
Herbert Hoover as President, 1040–1042
philosophy of, 1040
popularity of, 1042
stock market boom, 1027
wage earners, 1035–1037
Protestant Ethics and the Spirit of Capitalism, The, 18
Protestants, 18, 57, 58
areas of, in late nineteenth century, 798
in France, 106
succession in England, 60
"Provincial Congress" of Massachusetts, 134
Public Utility Holding Company Act, 1068
Public Works Administration (PWA), 1064
Puebla, Mexico, 507, 517
Puerto Rico, 845
Puget Sound, 331, 500, 501, 579, 835
Pulitzeo, Joseph, 831
Pure Food and Drug Act, 873, 875
Puritan Civil War, 106
Puritans, 20, 44
beliefs of, 55
education by, 55
intolerance of, 55, 56, 84
Massachusetts government by, 48, 55
migration of, 48
Put-in-Bay, 289

Quakers, 20, 60, 82, 83, 194
beliefs, of, 60–61
in Colonial America, 83, 84, 128, 147
pacifists, 458
Quarting Act, 129
Quay, Matthew, political boss, 858
Quebec, 112, 113, 476
in American Revolution, 137
frontier area north of Ohio river attached to, 129
in War of 1812, 285
Quebec Act, 129, 158
Queenston Heights, 287
Quemoy, 1225, 1226
Quetzalcoatl, 11
Quezon, Manuel, 891
Quitrents, 57, 60, 172, 173

Racial, ethnic variety in colonies, 86, 87
Radical Theology and the Death of God, 1259
Radicals (*see* Republican Radicals)
Radio programs, Depression, 1074
Radford, Admiral Arthur W., 1225
"Railroad Age," the, 665
Railroad Retirement Act, 1065
Railroads:
before 1870, 381, 383, 424, 622, 636
Baltimore and Ohio, 386
built westward to St. Joseph, Missouri, 386
Charleston and Hamburg Railroad, 386, 418
federal aid to, 388
in North, 419
in South, 1820–1860, 418
transcontinental, 530, 531, 568–569
after 1877, 641, 917
in attack on big business, 678–680
builders of, 665–668
farmer complaints against, 774
in Great Depression, 1034
Hepburn Act on, 875
influence of, 667, 668
investment in, 650
land grants for, 651, 663, 665–667
transcontinental, 666
in Western settlement, 757
in World War I, 942
(*See also* specific names of railroads)
Railway Labor Act 1071
Raleigh, Walter, 23
Rambouillet Decree, 279
Ramsey, David, 195
Ranching, Western:
legends of, 746
in Northwest, 743–746
in Texas, 743–746
Randolph, A. Philip, 1132
Randolph, Edmund, 205, 228
as Secretary of State, 239
Randolph, Edward, 106
Randolph, John, of Roanoke, 258
Randolph, John, of Virginia, 303, 327 342, 343
Randolph, Peyton, 135
Rantoul, Robert, 527
Rapidan River, 574
Raskob, John J., Democratic party chairman, 1053, 1070

Rayburn, Sam, Speaker of the House, 1202
Reader's Digest, 991
Recent Economic Changes, 1042
Recession, September, 1937, to June, 1938, 1072, 1073
Reconstruction, postwar, 599–636
Congressional Reconstruction, 607–609
corruption in, 626
defeated South, the, 600–601
election of 1868, 612, 621
election of 1876, 628, 634–636
end of, 626–628
foreign affairs in, 623, 624
Liberal Republicans in, 624–625
Presidential Reconstruction, 601–604
Radicals, triumph of, 604–607
regime of Ulysses S. Grant, 621–623
in South, 609–612
Reconstruction Finance Corporation, 1050, 1051, 1058, 1059
Red Cross, American, 1050
Red River, 333, 418
Red Star line, 388
"Redemptioners," 70
Reed, Thomas B., Speaker of the House, 656
Reflections on the Revolution in France, 244
Reform:
social, 1815–1860, 427, 457–458, 867
state and city, 858, 867, 868
in Midwestern states, 867
on West Coast, 867
in Wisconsin, 867
(*See also* Culture, American, 1815–1860)
Reformation, Protestant, 18, 21
European rivalry increased by, 21–24
Reid, Whitelow, 784, 847
Reign of Ferdinand and Isabella, The, by William H. Prescott, 452
Reign of Terror, French, 235
Reims, unconditional surrender document signed at, 1120
Religion:
after American Revolution, 193–195
and church in late nineteenth century, 794–795
conflict between science and religion, 795
personalities in controversy, 795
in Colonial America, 83–86, 105–106
in early 17th century England, 44, 45
from 1815–1860, 427, 454–456
(*See also* Culture, American, 1815–1960)
freedom of, 163
in 1920s: new ideas in, 988, 989
John T. Scopes trial, 989, 990
"Billy" Sunday, evangelist, 989
after 1950, 1259, 1260
in schools, 1260
statistics on, 1259
reform efforts, 162
Reno, Milo, farm organizer, 1052
Rensselaer, Kiliaen van, 59
Rensselaer Polytechnic Institute, Troy, New York, 431
"Report on Manufacturing," Hamilton's, 228, 229
Republican era, 639
Republican Party:
after 1854, 532, 533, 552, 566
in Chicago convention, 1860, 548
1860 platform of, 548
in election of 1856, 535
Rutherford B. Hayes elected by, 634, 635
first, 242, 244, 245, 300, 329, 330, 602, 605
after 1826, 339
Jefferson and Madison leaders of, 242
nationalism under, 302, 304
new leadership of, 304, 321
states, localities under, 325–327
states rights, merchantilism of, 243, 248
(*See also* Democratic Republican Party)
1920–1970: in campaign of 1924, 970–972
victory of, 971, 972
conservatives, 964, 965
in Dwight D. Eisenhower administrations, 1201, 1203
in election of 1920, 964, 965
in election of 1932, 1064
in election of 1936, 1070, 1071
in election of 1940, 1102–1103, 1045, 1146
in election of 1952, 1196, 1197
in election of 1956, 1205, 1206
in election of 1968, 1306–1308
in 1960, 1286–1288
in 1964, 1296–1298
progressives in, 964, 965
in second administration of Dwight D. Eisenhower, 1206, 1212
during Harry S. Truman administration, 1178, 1185, 1187–1190
Republican Radicals, 566, 567, 569, 583, 584, 635
in postwar Reconstruction, 602–609, 621, 636
rule in South, 611, 612
Republicans:
after 1877, 635, 646, 655
business interests favored by, 641
divisions, 894, 897, 905
1884 platform of, 646
1896 convention of, 786
in election of 1912, 903–906
gains in 1914, 916
GAR backer of, 646
on reforms, 641, 642
on tariffs, 641, 644, 645
Jeffersonian, 248, 253–255
federal functions increased by, 253
political, social changes under, 252, 253
victory of 1800, 243, 250, 251
during War of 1812, 279
Liberal, 624, 625
failure of, 627
Stalwart, 626, 634, 644, 646
World War I: in election of 1916, 928
on League of Nations, 953, 956–958
Resaca de la Palma, 505
Resettlement Administration, 1062, 1086
Reston, James, writer, 1221, 1290, 1296
Restoration England, 1660–1689, 59–61
Restraining Act, New England, 138

Resumption Act of 1875, 644
Reuben James, U.S.S., 1104
Revels, H.R., Negro Representative, 610
Revenue Act of 1764 (*see* Sugar Act of 1764)
Revere, Paul, 134
Review of Reviews, 1021
Revolt, agrarian, 775–784
(*See also* Grange; National Farmers' Alliance and Cooperative Union of America)
Revolution, American, 57, 86, 90, 133–159
British failure in North, 147–150
British failure in South, 153–158
congressional conduct of, 151–153
end of, 158–159
escalation of, 136–138
events abroad, 150–151
initial reason for, 133
Lexington, Concord, in, 134–135
Second Continental Congress, 135–136
separation from England in, 138, 146–147
Reynaud, Paul, French Premier, 1101–1102
Rhee, Syngman, 1228
Rhineland, French occupation of, 951
Rhode Island, 56, 60, 100
constitution of, 162
inflation in, 82–83
Rice:
export of, 67, 72, 130
in Southern economy, 406, 407, 773
Richmond, Virginia, 418
in Civil War, 562, 563, 571, 574–576
end of Civil War in, 584
Rickover, Admiral Hyman G., 1258
Riesman, David, 1281
Right-to-work laws, 1212
Rights of Man, 244
Riis, Jacob, 710
Rio de Janeiro, 21
Rio Grande River, 256, 493, 494, 504, 505
boundary, 503
Riots, 582, 1303
in Chicago, Tulsa, 983
Haymarket Riot, Chicago, 1886, 701
May Day, 958
in 1960s, 1247, 1253, 1254, 1257, 1302
race riots, 1904–1908, 869–870
Ripley, George, Brook Farm purchased by, 452
Ritchie, Thomas, 489
River Raisin, 287
Rivers and Harbors bill of 1846, 490
Rivers and Harbors bill of 1882, 646
Roads:
improved, 382
Maysville Road, 349–350
national, 253, 304
(*See also* Cumberland Road)
National Road of Pennsylvania, 322
Wilderness Road, 1775, 169
Roane, Judge Spencer, 324, 325
Roanke River, 418
Robertson, Walter S., 1225
Robinson, Jackie, 1257
Robinson, Senator Joseph T., 973, 1071
Rochambeau, General, 154, 155, 158
Rock music of 1960s, 1264
Rockefeller, John D., 665
industrial career of, 671, 672
oil industry, monopoly of, 672
Rockefeller, Nelson, 1296
Rockford Seminary, Rockford, Illinois, 431
Rockhill, William W., adviser on Far East, 851
Rockingham, Lord, 119, 158
Rocky Mountains, 256, 331, 494, 495 758
Rogers, John, sculptor, 453–454
Rogers, Will, 1059
Rogers, William, 100
pamphlet warfare of, 100
Rolfe, John, 46, 70
Rölvaag, Ole, 764, 765
Roman Empire, 2–3, 21
Rome-Berlin Axis, 1092, 1097
Rommel, Erwin, 1113, 1114
Roosevelt, Franklin D.:
aid to farmers, 1060–1062
banking reform, 1057–1060
beginning of New Deal, 1057
concern for minorities, 1085
conservation, 1068, 1069
"court-packing" threat of, 1071, 1072
early relief programs of, 1059, 1060
election of, 1054
expanded relief, 1065–1066
in global politics: arms embargo repeal urged by, 1100
Charlottesville speech, 1101
in election of 1940, 1102, 1103
end of neutrality, 1102
European peace efforts, 1098, 1100
lend-lease, 1103, 1112
neutrality efforts of, 1092, 1093, 1095
on Pacific crisis, 1104, 1107
pressures on neutrality of, 1100–1103
recognition of USSR, 1095
on Sino-Japanese war, 1096, 1097
gold standard abandoned, 1058, 1059
labor programs, 1066, 1067
National Industrial Recovery Act, 1062–1065
Presidential nomination of, 964, 965
public power, 1069, 1070
recession and fiscal policies, 1071 1073
reelection of, 1070, 1071
Social Security Act, 1067, 1068
utility regulation, 1068
Vice Presidential nomination of, 964, 965
in World War II, 1112, 1126–1130
death of, 1153, 1179
(*See also* Great Depression; New Deal)
Roosevelt, Mrs. Franklin D., 1085
Roosevelt, Nicholas J., 384
Roosevelt, Theodore, 656, 680, 845, 846, 848, 869, 895, 964
background of, 870, 871
in election of 1912, 903–906
on Far East, 890–891
hero of Spanish-American War, 844
on Latin America, 885–889
moved into Presidency, 870
policies, programs of, 872–873
popularity of, 894
Roosevelt and working man, 874
on wartime dissent, 944

Root, Elihu, Secretary of War, 886, 900, 965
on League of Nations, 956, 957
on war dissenters, 944
on World Court issue, 1094
Root-Takahira agreement, 891
Rosecrans, General William S., 574
Ross, General David, 290
Washington, D.C. taken by, 295
Rostoro, Walt W., 1238
Rostov, 1114
Rough Riders, 844, 845
Royal Africa Company, 70
Rufus King, 259, 272
Rules Committee, House, 656, 897
Rum, 73, 74, 81
curbs on production of, 81
Rural Free Delivery, 832
Rural Post Roads Act, 917
Rush-Bagot Agreement, 331
Rush, Dr. Benjamin, 152
Rush, Richard, 334
Rusk, Dean, Secretary of State, 1236, 1238, 1240, 1289
retained by President Lyndon B. Johnson, 1242
Russell, Charles Edward, 858
Russell, Henry, 454
Russell, Jonathan, 298
Russia, 836, 1051, 1095
Belgrade, Budapest seized by, 1120
ideology of, 1015
invasion of Poland, 1920, 1015
nonaggression pact with Germany, 1100
United States diplomatic relations established, 1093
war declared on Japan, 1124, 1126
Warsaw seized by, 1120
in World War I, 920, 947
Russian workers, New York's Union of, 958
Rutgers University, 85
Ruth, Babe, 986
Rutledge, Edward, 148
Ryder, Albert P., 828
Ryukus, the, 1122, 1124

Sabine River, 333, 493
Sachem, 498
Sackett's Harbor, 287, 295
Sacramento, California, 742
Sacramento Valley, 498, 525
Saigon, South Vietnam, 1238, 1242, 1243, 1322
St. Augustine, Florida, 112
St. Clair, General Arthur, 234
St. Cloud decree, Napoleon's, 280
Saint-Gaudens, Augustus, 828, 829
St. John, John P., 651
St. Johns River, 21
St. Lawrence River, 17, 58, 112, 198, 287
St. Lawrence Valley, 64
St. Leger, Colonel Barry, 149
St. Louis, Missouri, 112, 322
1896 Republican convention in, 786
as fur trade empire, 494, 495
St. Louis Exposition, 669
St. Louis Post-Dispatch, 832
St. Mihiel sector, 949
Saipan, 1124
Salary Grab Act, 626
Salerno beachhead, 1116
Salt Lake City, Utah, 742, 758
Saltillo Road, Mexico, 505
Salvation Army, 796
Samoa:
American interests in, 839
United States-Germany in, 839
United States naval base, Pago Pago, 838, 839
Sanctions, economic, 1047, 1098, 1104
San Diego, California, 494, 507
San Diego Bay, 498, 518
San Diego Harbor, 835
Sandys, Sir Edwin, 47
San Francisco, California, 497
Democratic convention of 1920 in, 964, 965
Republican convention of 1956 in, 1205
Republican convention of 1964 in, 1296
San Francisco Bay, 494, 503, 507, 519, 835
San Francisco Conference of 1945, 1154, 1155
(*See also* Cold War)
San Francisco Examiner, 832
San Francisco-Shanghai steamship line, 836
Sangamon River, 537
San Jacinto River, 484
Sankey, Ira A., song leader, 797
San Luis Potosi, 505
San Salvador, 10
Santa Anna, Antonio, 482, 484, 530
in Mexico-U.S. War, 505, 507, 508, 517
Santa Fe, New Mexico, 494, 495, 498
Santa Fe Trail, 495
Santa Maria, 10
Santo Domingo, 10, 58, 256, 623, 624, 922
Saratoga, New York, 133, 150, 154, 159
Sargent, John Singer, 828
Sauk, the, 356
Saunders, Governor Alvin, 746
Savannah, Georgia, 154, 406
in Civil War, 561, 576, 600
Savannah River, 418
Saxton, General Rufus, 570
"Scalawags," 609–611
Scandal, political, 1920s, 967, 968
Schechter Poultry Company v. United States, 1065, 1066
Schenck, Charles T., Socialist leader, 945
Schenck v. United States, 945
"clear and present danger" rule established by, 945
Schools, free, 163, 326, 402, 427, 908, 913
federal aid to, 1203, 1258, 1259
religion in, 1260
Schurz, Carl, 600, 625
Schuschnigg, Chancellor Kurt, of Austria, 1097, 1098
Schuyler, General Philip, 149
Science:
colonial, 100, 101
technology after 1950, 1260, 1261
wartime, technology, 1130, 1131
Science and Health with Key to the Scriptures, 797
Scioto Company, 172
Scioto River, 322
Scopes, John T., trial of, 989, 990
Scott, Dred, 536
Scott, Winfield, 287, 289
in Civil War, 559, 562
dismissed by President James K. Polk, 518

Scott, Winfield:
in Mexico-U.S. War, 505, 507, 517
Whig candidate, 528
Scranton, William, 1296
Scripps, E. W., 831
Seabury, Reverend Samuel, 194
Search and seizure, 116, 163
Secession:
seven-state confederacy formed, 550
of South Carolina, 550
Secessionist movement:
in New England, 258, 290, 300
in South, 541
in South Carolina, 358
Secessionists, 552, 553
Secker, Thomas, 117
Sectionalism, 471–491
Securities, federal, 203, 226, 229
Sedition Act of 1798, 242, 250, 253, 254
convictions under, 248, 249
Kentucky resolution on, 249
provisions of, 248
Virginia resolution on, 249
Sedition Act of May, 1918, 944
Segregation, 604, 611, 628, 808
in Armed Forces, 1255
on buses, 1255
in interstate travel, 1255
in public accommodations, 1256
in schools, 869, 1255
Selective Service Act, 1132
Selective Service Act of March, 1947, 1180
Selective Service Law of 1948, 1180
Selma, Alabama, 1298
Seminole Indians, 332, 356
Senate, United States, 215, 216, 223, 282
Committee of Thirteen in, 551
after 1877, 643, 654, 679, 680
Kellog-Briand Pact endorsed by, 1020
World War I declared, 937
Federalist control of, 246
on treaties, 224–225
Separate-but-equal concept, 628, 808, 869, 1255
Separatists, 198, 199
Servicemen's Adjustment Act (GI Bill), 1258
Sevastopol, 1114
Seven Cities of Cibola, 14
Seven Years' War, 104
(*See also* Great War for Empire)
Seventh Army, 1118
Seventeenth Amendment, 898
Seventh Day Adventist Church, 456
Seville, Spain, 16
Seward, William H., 376, 548, 836
Civil War diplomacy of, 576–578
Seymour, Horatio, 621
Shadrach, fugitive slave, 530
Shaftesbury, Earl of (*see* Cooper, Sir Anthony Ashley)
Shannon, Wilson, 504
Shantung, 948, 952
Shawnee Indians, 281
Shays, Daniel, 175, 176
Shays' Rebellion, 176, 200, 204
Shelburne, Earl of, 158
Sheldon, C.M., 796
Shenandoah Valley, 563, 576, 600
Sheridan, Philip, Union general, 576, 584, 600
Sherman, John, Treasury Secretary, 644, 656, 680
Vice Presidential nomination of, 904
Sherman, Roger, 146
Sherman, General William T., 572, 574, 584, 600
Carolinas invaded by, 576
march to sea, 576
Sherman Antitrust Act, 658, 873
provisions of, 680
revision of, 915
suits under, 898
Sherman Silver Purchase Act, 657–658, 783
repeal of, 785
Shiloh Church, battle of, 561
Ship building, New England, 74
Ship seizures:
by British, 237, 238, 247, 277, 278, 281–282
by French, 247, 277, 279
Shotwell, James T., historian, 1019
Sibley, Colonel H.H., 761
Silliman, Benjamin, geologist, 449
Silver (legal tender), 82, 174, 199, 215, 360, 621, 783
Silver (ore), 11, 14, 46, 740
Silver City, Idaho, 741
Simmons, F.M., 914
Simmons, Frank, 1021
Simms, William Gilmore, writer, 451
Simpson, ("Sockless") Jerry, 778
Sinclair, Harry F., in Teapot Dome affair, 968
Sinclair, Upton, 858, 876
Singleton, Benjamin, 772–773
Sino-Japanese War, 1096–1097
Sioux, the, 494, 658, 760–762
(*See also* Great Plains Indians)
Sipuel, Ada Lois, 1254
Sit-ins, 1256
Sitting Bull, Chief, 761
Six Power Consortium in China, 922
Sixteenth Amendment, 898
(*See also* Income tax)
Skybolt program, the, 1241
Slaughterhouse cases, 628
Slave system, 478, 521, 541, 566
end of, 599
Slavery, 82, 146, 162, 170, 212, 405
debated in Congress, 227
defense of, 460, 468
eliminated in North, 193
in Missouri Compromise, 327–330
opposed, 84, 176, 358,
in South, 193
Slavery issue, 477–480, 529, 530
in Compromise of 1850, 525–527
in Kansas, 537
Lincoln-Douglas debate on, 538, 539
Slaves, 15, 23, 88, 218, 380, 381, 570
in British West Indies, 58
in Colonial South, 70, 71, 86
confiscation of, 174
freed, 459. 600, 605, 627
fugitive, 213, 526–527, 530
importation prohibited, 193
in Middle Colonies, 82
in Missouri Compromise, 317–330
prices of, 417
sales in Spanish colonies, 112
in South, 1820–1860, 404, 408, 417
tax on, 213
Slidell, John, 503, 504
Sloat, Commander J.D., 503, 507
Smith, Adam, 199
Smith, Governor Alfred E., 971, 1053, 1070

Smith, Governor Alfred E.:
Presidential nomination of, 973, 975
Smith, Gerrit, 625
Smith, Hiram, 501
Smith, Hoke, 867
Smith, Jebediah, trapper, 494
Smith, Jess, in political scandal, 967
Smith, Captain John, 47
Smith, Joseph, 456
death of, 501
Smith, Margaret Bayard, 345
Smith, Robert, 282, 304
Smith, Senator Samuel, 295
Smith, Sir Thomas, 47
Smith, William, 100
Smith Alien Registration Act of 1940, 1131
Smith-Hughes Act, 917
Smith-Lever Act, 917
Smoot, Senator Reed, 1041
Smugglers, smuggling, 127, 128, 174
Smyth, Alexander, 287
Snake tribe, 760
Snyder, John W., 1181
Social gospel, 796, 797
Catholics in, 796, 797
Protestantism in, 796
Social Justice, 1131
Social life in South, 421
Social patterns, colonial, 87–89
Social Security Act, 1067, 1068
Social Security Act of 1954, 1202
Socialist Labor party, 703
Socialists, 867, 944, 945, 959
Society, American, 1920s:
developments in, 963, 975, 976
education, 990, 991
manners and morals, 985–987
Negroes, 976, 983, 984
newspapers, magazines, 991
Prohibition, 984, 985
religion, 988–990
changes, 988, 989
John T. Scopes trial, 989–990
writers, writing in, 987, 988
Society for the Propagation of the Gospel, 83, 117
Sociology for the South, 540
Soil-bank plan, 1201, 1202
Soil Conservation and Domestic Allotment Act, 1061
Soil Conservation Service (SCS), 1069
Solid South, the, 636, 641
Solomon Islands, 1122
Somme Valley, battle of, 927, 949
Sonoma, California, 507
Soto, Hernando de, 11
Souls of the Black Folk, the, 869
South, the:
from 1820–1860:
character, attitudes of, 421
cotton in economy of, 380, 406–408, 424
economy of, 404–405
slavery in, 408–417
transportation, commerce, and manufacturing, 418–420
yeoman farmers in, 417–418
postwar:
conditions of Union reentry, 602–607
constitutions formed under Andrew Johnson plan, 603
corruption in, 611, 612
defeated, 600–601
military districts in, 607, 625
radical rule in, 611, 612
Reconstruction in, 609–612
Union troops withdrawn from, 636, 641
pre-Civil War, 539–542
John Brown's raid, effects of, 542
compared with North, 540
dominated by aristocracy, 541
faith in cotton, 540
Hinton Rowan Helper on slave system in, 541, 542
illusion of power in, 541
South Carolina, 62, 128, 169, 527, 604, 611, 636
new government of, 162
nullification doctrine in, 349, 356
rice cultivation in, 64
rice exempted from export ban, 130
secession of, 550
South Carolina Exposition, 346, 348, 358
South Carolina v. Katzenbach:
literacy tests ruled out by, 1300
(*See also* Warren Court)
South Dakota:
admitted to Union, 658, 764
gold in, 741
reform in, 867
Sioux reservation of, 658, 761
South Korea, 1228
South Vietnam:
Diem, Ngo Dinh, regime of, 1230, 1238
United States involvement under President John F. Kennedy, 1238, 1239
Southeast Asia Collective Defense Treaty, 1242
Southeast Asia Treaty Organization, 1230
Southern Literary Messenger, 432
Southern Pacific Railroad, 666, 867, 873
Southern-Radical coalition, 610
Souvanna Phouma, Prince, 1238
Space, exploration of, 1214
Russian lead in, 1214
Spain, 2, 7, 10, 22
in American Revolution, 151
exploitation by, 11–16
exploration by, 8–14
exploration competitors of, 16, 17, 42
Louisiana gained by, 113
Mississippi river closed to Americans by, 199
in Ohio-Mississippi Valley, 198, 199
Pinckney agreement with, 240
Spain, American empire of, 15, 16, 112
Spanish-American War, the, 654, 840–848, 886
battles of, 845, 846
peace terms in, 845, 847
Treaty of Paris in, 847, 848
Spanish-Americans, 1252
Spanish Armada, defeat of, 24
Spanish Civil War, 1095, 1096
Sparkman, Senator John J., 1197
Sparks, Jared, historian, 452, 476
Sparks, William A. J., Land Commissioner, 653, 654
Specie Circular of 1836, 371
Spectator sports, 831, 908
Speculation, speculators:
business, 739
in federal securities, 203
under Andrew Jackson, 349
in Kansas, 537
in land, 71, 167, 170, 172, 173, 322, 381, 424
in northern cities, 222
before Panic of 1857, 539

Speculation, speculators:
in Southern state securities, 227
in stocks and bonds, 885, 1047
Speech, freedom of, 45, 163
Spencer, Herbert, 677
theories of, 793
Spindetop, Texas, 674
Spiritualism, 456
Spirituals, Negro, 454
Split Rock, battle of, 147
Spoils system 347, 622, 626, 641
Spooner, John C., 872
Spotsylvania Court House, battle of, 575
Springfield, Illinois, 537, 539, 556
Sputnik, 1259
Square Deal, 1057
Squatter sovereignty (*see* Popular sovereignty)
Squatters, 74, 87, 89, 373, 381
(*See also* Preemption)
Stabilization Act, 1181
Stalin, Joseph, 1015, 1093, 1124
in cold war, 1151, 1152
death of, 1234
World War II second front urged by, 1112, 1114
Stalingrad, siege of, 1114
Stamp Act of 1765, 126–128
repeal of, 127
Standard Oil Company, 671, 677, 858, 898
Standard Oil Trust, 676
Standley, Henry, 421
Stanton, Edwin M., Secretary of War, 580, 607, 831
Stanton, Elizabeth Cady, reformer, 458
"Star-Spangled Banner, The," 295
Star of the West, merchant vessel, 552
Stassen, Harold, 1145
Staten Island, 148
States rights, 220, 222, 248, 346, 659
slavery protected by, 478
Statute of Religious Liberty, 194
Stay laws, 200, 204
Steamboats, 382, 384
decline of, 667
Steel, 664, 667, 669
Bessemer process, 664
as major industry, 670
Steffens, Lincoln, 857
Steinbeck, John, 1074, 1262
Stephens, Alexander M., 486–487
Vice President of Confederate States of America, 550
Stephens, Uriah S., union organizer, 693
Steuben Society, 1011
Stevens, John L., 840
Stevens, Robert, Secretary of the Army, 1209
Stevens, Thaddeus, 566, 567, 605, 606
Stevenson, Adlai, 1197, 1287, 1307
in campaign of 1956, 1205
Stevenson, Adlai E., Vice President, 784
Stimson, Henry L., Secretary of State, 1093, 1107, 1117
Stock market crash, October 29, 1929, 1042
Stockton, Commodore Robert F., 507
Stokes, Carl, Cleveland, Ohio, Mayor, 1257
Story, Justice Joseph, 324
Stowe, Harriet Beecher, 529, 530
Straight, Willard, American consul general in Manchuria, 900
Strikers, 644
in Mississippi Delta, 1301
Strikes, 403,
anthracite coal in 1902, 874
of Baltimore and Ohio Railroad, 644, 693
Boston police strike of 1919, 958
against Carnegie Steel Works, 702
farm, 1052
against railroads, 694
in Seattle in 1919, 958
steel strike in 1919, 958
after World War II, 1182, 1185
Strong, Josiah, 737, 796, 868
Student Nonviolent Coordinating Committee, 1256, 1303
Student rebellion, 1308, 1317, 1318
Students for a Democratic Society, 1282, 1317–1318
Stuart, Gilbert, 453
Stuart, J. E. B., Confederate cavalry officer, 563
Stuart, John, Indian agent, 119
Sturgis, William, 495, 499
Submarine warfare:
World War I, 923–928
World War II, 1103, 1104
Submerged Lands Act, 1200, 1201
Subsidies, 72, 622, 635, 654
farm, 657, 1051
Subversive Activities Control Act, 1193
Sudeten, the, 951, 1098
Suez canal, 1113, 1114
in Middle East crisis, 1231–1233, 1235
Suffolk Resolves, 130
Suffrage (*see* Vote and voting rights)
Sugar, 46, 58, 81, 116, 239, 657
import tax on, 126, 229
in South, 1820–1860, 407, 408, 773
Sugar Act of 1764, 119, 126
effect of, 119
provisions of, 119
Sullivan, General John, 154
Sullivan, John L., 831
Summary, Historical and Political, of the British Settlements in North America, A, 100
Sumner, Charles, 527, 531, 534, 566, 604–606
on Santo Domingo annexation attempt, 624
Sumner, William Graham, sociologist, 677, 793
Sumter, Thomas, 155
Sunday, ("Billy") William A., 989, 1260
Supreme Court, U.S., 214–218, 224, 249, 300, 323–325, 327, 635, 679, 680
Ableman v. Booth, 530
Briscoe v. The Bank of Kentucky, 375
Brown v. Board of Education of Topeka, 1255
Charles River Bridge case, 374, 375
Civil Rights Act of 1875 declared unconstitutional by, 658
Cohen v. Virginia, 324, 325
"court-packing" threat, 1071–1072
Craig v. Missouri, 375
Dartmouth college case of 1819, 325, 375
in defense of civil rights, 1299
Dred Scott v. Sanford, 536
Engle v. Vitale, 1260
ex parte Mc Cardle, 608
ex parte Milligan, 582, 608
Fletcher v. Peck, 258, 323, 325
Gibbons v. Ogden, 325

Supreme Court, U.S.:
Hammer v. Dagenhart, 917
Hirabayashi v. United States, 1132
Justice Louis D. Brandeis, appointment of, 916
legal discrimination destroyed by, 1255
License cases, 375
Lochner v. New York, 704
McCullom case, 1260
McCullough v. Maryland, 323, 324
Marbury v. Madison, 254, 255, 323
Martin v. Hunter's Lessee, 324
military court upheld in saboteur case, 1131
Muller v. Oregon, 704
Munn v. Illinois, 679, 775–776
National Labor Relations Board v. Jones and Roughlin Steel Corporation, 1066
New York v. Miln, 375
Osborn v. Bank of the United States, 324
Passenger cases, 375
Plessy v. Ferguson, 628, 808, 869, 1255
Schechter Poultry Company v. United States, 1065
Schench v. United States, 945
Slaughterhouse Cases, 628
states rights favored by Taney Court, 375
United States v. Butler et al., 1061
United States v. Hudson, 253
United States v. Reese, 628
Wabash case of 1886, 679
Surplus:
farm, 1039, 1041, 1060–1062, 1201, 1202
United States Treasury, 654, 657
Surprise (a clipper), 388, 399
Susan constant, 46
Sussex, French passenger ship, 924, 928
Sutter, John, 498
Swan Land and Cattle Company, Cheyenne, Wyoming, 745
Swank, James M., 655
Swift, Gustavus, 665, 669
Sylvis, William H., NLU president, 690, 693
Symington, Stuart, 1287
Symmes, John Cleves, 172
System of Mineralogy, 449
Systematic Theology, 795

Taft, Lorado, 829
Taft, Senator Robert A., 1098, 1100, 1162, 1186, 1196, 1198
Taft, William Howard, 872, 891, 894, 964, 965, 968, 1196
background of, 895
Dollar Diplomacy of, 899, 900
failure as party chief, 895, 898
foreign affairs under, 899–901
Open Door policy strengthened by, 899, 901
as anti-Japanese weapon, 900
personality of, 895
problems, policies of, 895–898
progressive revolt, 1910–1912, 902–903
renomination of, 903
Secretary of War, 895
Taft-Hartley Act, 1186–1188, 1190, 1199, 1202, 1212
Taiping Rebellion, 836
Tallmadge, James, 328
Tammany Hall, 634, 646, 652
Taney, Roger B.:
Attorney General, 350, 362
Chief Justice of United States Supreme Court, 374, 375
contract clause redefined by, 374–375
Dred Scott decision of, 536
interstate commerce decision modified by, 375
Tanner, Corporal James, Commissioner of Pensions, 657
Tappan, Arthur, abolitionist, 460
Tappan, Lewis, abolitionist, 460
Tarbell, Ida, 857, 858
"Tariff of Abominations" (*see* Tariffs, of 1827)
Tariff Act of 1789, 229
Tariffs, 173, 347, 521
of August, 1861, 568
Dingley tariff of 1897, 855, 896
of 1816, 303–304, 341, 401
of 1818, 303
of 1824, 341, 401
of 1827, 341, 358
of 1828, 356–359, 401
of 1832, 358, 401
of 1833, 359, 401, 489
of 1842, 401, 475, 489
of 1857, 401, 568
after 1877, 641, 644, 645, 653, 654, 658
"Act to Reduce the Revenue," 657
of 1883, 645
Wilson Gorman tariff of 1894, 785
(*See also* Mongrel Tariff)
of 1890, 840
in Dwight D. Eisenhower administration, 1214, 1215
high, urged by Hamilton, 228, 229
of July, 1862, 568
of June, 1864, 568
Morrill tariff of 1861, 568
1920s, 965, 966, 973
in Herbert Hoover administration, 1040–1042
Payne-Aldrich tariff, 896
under Republican nationalists, 303, 321
Tariff Act of 1789, 229
Underwood-Simmons tariff, 914
Walker tariff of 1846, 401, 489–490, 568
Tarleton, Banastre, 154
Taxation:
after American Revolution, 197, 220, 212, 213, 242, 250
for churches, 85, 455
on colonies, 104, 105, 107–109, 119–130
excise tax, 229, 230, 568
in farm states, 775
under Federalists, 222, 228
on hemp, 229, 341
for libraries, 453
poll tax, 105, 166, 234, 659, 1298
for War of 1812, 282
on whisky, 229, 230
Taxes:
1920s, 965, 967
tax cuts, 966, 967, 970, 972, 973, 1048
1930s:
corporate incomes, 1068
employee, employer tax, 1068
inheritance, 1068
processing ruled unconstitutional, 1061
profits tax, 1064, 1068
sales tax, 1067
1940s, 1186, 1192

Taylor, Senator Glen, 1188
Taylor, John, 327, 343
Taylor, General Maxwell D., 1238, 1239, 1304
Taylor, General Zachary:
  death of, 526
  election of, 524–525
  in Mexico-United States War, 503–505
  as President, 525
  Presidential nomination of, 524
Tea, import, 127, 229
    boycott of, 127, 131
    smuggling of, 127, 128
    tax controversy on, 128–130
      Boston Tea Party, 129, 131
Tea Act of 1773, Lord North's, 129, 131
Teamsters Union, 1213
Teapot Dome affair, 968
Tecumseh, Chief, 281, 289, 296
Teheran Conference, 1116, 1117, 1196
Telegraph, development of, 388, 664
Teller, Henry Moore, free-silver advocate, 786
Teller Resolution, 844
Ten Nights in a Bar Room, 457
Tennent, William, 84
Tennessee, 169, 322, 382
  admitted to Union, 234
  Civil War in, 561, 572
  secession of, 558
  university chartered by, 431
Tennessee River, 199, 322
  in Civil War, 561
Tennessee Valley Authority 1970, 1069, 1070, 1200
Tenure of Office Act, 607, 608
Tet offensive, Viet Cong, 1306
Texas, 11, 333, 382, 487, 503, 504, 519, 521, 603, 604
  admitted to Union, 488, 493
  in Compromise of 1850, 526
  as political issue, 482–486
  secession of, 550
Texas, battleship, 654
Texas Alliance, (*see* National Farmers' Alliance and Cooperative Union of America)
Textiles, 669,
  labor-management disputes, 693
  as major industry, 670
Thailand, 1104, 1230
Thames, battle of, 289, 321
Thanksgiving, first, 48
Theater, the, 830
  colonial, 90
Thieu, South Vietnamese President, 1322
Third Neutrality Law of May, 1937, 1095, 1097
Thirteenth Amendment, 603, 634
Thomas, Senator Elmer, 1180
Thomas, George H., Union commander, 561, 574
Thomas, Senator Jesse B., 328
Thomas, R. J., president of UAW, 1181
Thompson, Charles, 130
Thompson v. City of Louisville:
  due process clause upheld by, 1300
  (*See also* Warren Court)
Thoreau, Henry David, 450, 451, 542
Thurmond, J. Strom, 1188
Tientsin, Treaties of, 836
Tilden, Samuel J., Democratic nominee, 1876, 634, 635
Tillman, Senator Ben, 659, 778
Timber, 641
  (*See also* Lumber)
Timber and Stone Act, 1878, 746, 757
Timber Culture Act of 1873, 746, 757
Timberlake, Mrs. Margaret O'Neale (Mrs. John Eaton), 346, 347, 350
Time, 991
Time zones, 668
Times, The, of London, 497
Timrod, Henry, Southern writer, 451
Tippecanoe Creek, battle of, 281, 287, 376
Titusville, Pennsylvania, 671
Tobacco, 14, 46, 130, 277, 669, 670, 773
  British sale of, 71
  export of, 67
  in Kentucky, Tennessee, 418, 419
  overproduction of, 105
  post-Revolutionary market of, 174
  in Southern economy, 380, 406
"Tobacco Coast," 67, 70, 71
  exports of, 71, 74
Tobruck, 1113, 1114
Tocqueville, Alexis de, 794
Tojo, General Hideki, Japanese Premier, 1105
  fourteen-point message of, 1107
Toledo, Ohio, 234, 287
Toleration Act of 1649, 57, 58
Toltecs, the, 14
Tonnage Act of 1789, 229
Tordesillas, Treaty of, 10
Tories, 112, 128, 176, 244, 280
Toronto, Ontario, 287
Toward Soviet America, 1051
Townley, Arthur C., 867
Townsend, Dr. Francis E., 1067, 1070
Townshend, Charles ("Champagne Charlie"), 120, 127
  repeal of, 127
    tea excepted, 127
Townshend Duties of 1767, 127–129
Tracy, Benjamin F., Secretary of the Navy, 838
Trade:
  with Britain, 116
    after American Revolution, 161
    barred with colonies by Britain, 138
    British suppression of, 116
  foreign, 200, 399
Trade Expansion Act, 1289
Trading with the Enemy Act of October, 1917, 944
"Trial of Tears," 356
Transcendentalism, 451, 452
Transportation, 69, 304, 383, 521, 663–669
  in North, 1820–1860, 384–388
  ocean, 388, 399
  river traffic, 384
  in South, 418–421
Transportation Act of 1920, 1034
Trans-Siberian Railway, 849
Treason of the Senate, 858
Treasury Department, U.S., 225, 229
  Hamilton secretary of, 225
Treaty of London of 1915, Italy's, 951
Tredegar Iron Works, Richmond, Virginia, 420, 579
Trenchard, John, 112
Trenton, battle of, 148, 159
Trieste, 951
Tripartite Pact of Germany, Italy, Japan, 1104, 1105
Tripoli, fall of, 1114
Trist, Nicholas P., diplomatic mission of, 517
Trollope, Anthony, 581
Trollope, Frances, 428

Truman, Harry S., 1153, 1154, 1223
in Cold War, 1155–1162
Jewish nation in Palestine backed by, 1231
during Korean War, 1169–1171, 1174
in retirement, 1174
as Vice President, 1146
Truman Administration, 1179
communism scare, 1192, 1193
demobilization, 1179, 1180
economic reconversion, 1180–1184
eightieth Congress, 1185–1187
election of 1948, 1187–1189
Fair Deal, 1178, 1190–1192
gold reserves drain, 1215
legislative, executive changes, 1193–1194
postwar politics, 1184, 1185
Truman Doctrine, the, 1161
Trumbull, John (lawyer), 195
Trumbull, John, (painter) 194–195, 453
Tubman, Harriet, 405
Tufts, James J., 794
Tugwell, Rexford G., 1054, 1062, 1073, 1085
Tunisia, 1114
Tunney, Gene, 986
Turner, Frederick Jackson, historian, 88, 234, 739, 766, 792
Turner, Jonathan Baldwin, 569
Turner, Nat, 468
Tuskegee Institute, 808
Twain, Mark, 742, 764
Tweed, William M. ("Boss"), 634, 720, 736
Tweed Ring in New York, 612, 720, 832
Twelfth Amendment, 251
21st Rule, 478
Twenty-second Amendment, 1194
Twiggs, David, in Mexico-United States War, 507
Two-party tradition, 471
Two-Penny Act of 1758, 117, 118
Tyler, John:
as President, 474–476, 485, 488, 835
Vice President, 376
Tyler, Moses Coit, 90, 91

U-boats, World War I, 926–928
Uncle Tom's Cabin, 529–530
Underwood, Representative Oscar, 904, 914
Underwood-Simmons tariff, 914
Unemployment, 402, 424, 785, 1049, 1086, 1302
fears of, 1181
in 1930s, 1059, 1063
no problem in 1920s, 1036
rise in, 1206
Unemployment insurance, 1068, 1200
Union, ties of, 480–482
Union Army, 560, 561, 566, 567, 571
(*See also* North in Civil War)
Union League clubs, 621, 944
Union Pacific Railroad, 568–569, 626, 666, 873
Union party, 583
Unionists, 550
Unions, labor, 693, 694, 701
in 1920s, 1036, 1037
in 1940s, 1182, 1183, 1185
labor laws, 1865–1918, 703, 704
in second Administration of Dwight D. Eisenhower, 1212–1213
trade unions, 701–703
Uniontown, Pennsylvania, 113
Unitarians, 455
United Arab Republic, 1233
United Auto Workers, 1067, 1181, 1182
United Mine Workers, 874, 1037, 1185
United Nations:
creation of, 1154, 1155
organization of, 1155, 1156
on Russian takeover of Hungary, 1224
Security Council of, 1155
veto in, 1155
United Nations Atomic Energy Commission, 1158
United States from 1877–1892, 639–660
Grover Cleveland, 646, 651–655
freedom and civil rights, 658–660
James A. Garfield and Chester A. Arthur, 644–646
Benjamin Harrison and Republicans, 656–658
Hayes Administration, 642–644
party politics, 640–642
United States Emergency Fleet Corporation, 942
United States Military Academy, West Point, New York, 253
United States Railroad Administration, 942
United States Shipping Board, 942
United States Steel Corporation, 677
United States Warehouse Act, 917
United States v. Butler et al., 1061
United States v. Hudson, 253
United States v. Reese, 628
Universal military training, 1180
Universal Negro Improvement Association, 983
Universalism, 455
Upper South, 418
Upper Yellowstone, 494
Upshur, Abel P., Secretary of State, 485
Urbanization:
1820–1860, 421–423
in Great Lakes region, 423
in Midwest, 422
in North, 421, 422
in Ohio Valley, 422
slow in South, 421–423
after 1865, 690, 691, 707–710
corruption, reform in city government, 720, 736
problems of, 710–712
urban life, 736, 737
in 1920s, 975, 976
after 1950: geographic expansion of, 1247
population shift to cities, 1247
problems of, 1246–1248
suburbia, 1249–1251
U'Ren, Governor William S., 867
Utah, statehood of, 764
Utah Territory, 502, 526
(*See also* Deseret)
Ute tribe, 760

Vaca, Cabeza de, 11
Valcour Island, battle of, 147
Vallandigham, Clement L., civil liberties case of, 582
Valley Forge, Pennsylvania, 149, 152
Van Buren, Martin, 340, 346, 347, 362, 371, 376, 377, 489
advantage over John C. Calhoun, 349

Van Buren, Martin:
elected President, 372
as free-soiler, 524
Presidency of, 372–374
banking reform of, 373, 374
as United States Minister, London, 350
Vancouver Island, 499–501
Vandalia, Illinois, 384
Vandenberg, Senator Arthur H., 1098, 1162, 1196
Vanderbilt, Cornelius, 665, 667
death of, 671
Vanderbilt, William, 665
Vane, Governor Sir Henry, 56
Vann, Robert L., Negro in Franklin D. Roosevelt's Administration, 1086
Van Rensselaer, Stephen, 285, 287
Vardaman, James K., Mississippi governor, 867
Vaudeville, 830
VE Day, May 8, 1945, 1120
Veblen, Thorstein, economist, 792–793, 857
Vera Cruz, Mexico, 505, 517
Verdun, battle of, 927
Vergennes, French Foreign Minister, 150, 151
Vermont, 198
admitted to Union, 234
Verrazano, Giovanni, 17
Versailles, Treaty of, 953–958, 1010, 1013, 1014
Versailles Peace Conference, Paris, France, 950–953
Vespucci, Amerigo, 10, 11
Veteran's Bureau, scandal in, 967
Veterans, 641, 653
adjusted compensation for, 966, 967, 969, 970
bonus demands of, 965, 967
march on Washington, D.C., 1052
Vicksburg, battle of, 572, 574
Vientiane, Laos, 1238
Viet Cong, 1239, 1304
Vietnam, 1229, 1230, 1239, 1242
Vietnam war:
opposition to, 1305
in President Lyndon B. Johnson's administration, 1304–1306, 1321
Vietnamization of, 322
Villard, Oswald Garrison, publisher, 944, 1010
Vincennes, outpost of, 154
Vindication of the Government of New England Churches, 1717, 100
Vinland (*see* Newfoundland)
Virginia, 23, 45–47, 130
in American Revolution, 155, 158
Bacon's rebellion in, 105
commodities, as money in, 82
1815–1860: emancipation discussed by, 468
Legislature of, 458, 523
university chartered by, 431
after 1860: Civil War in, 562–563, 571, 574–576
invasion of, 560, 561
secession of, 558
population loss in, 322
post-Revolutionary, 162
bicameral legislation of, 162
constitution adopted by, 162
Declaration of Rights of, 162–163
land claims of, 167
Revolutionary legislature of, 146
as royal province, 47, 55
as tobacco supplier, 67
Virginia, University of, 431, 807
Virginia City, Nevada, 741, 742
Virginia dynasty, 321, 327, 330, 336
"Virginia Plan, The," 205, 214, 216
Virginia Resolutions of 1798, 301, 346
Volstead Act, 1919, 984, 985
Volunteers in Service to America (VISTA), 1296
Voronezh, 1114
Vote and voting rights, 162, 163, 327, 608, 636
expansion of, 428
farm, 641, 655
literary tests eliminated, 1298, 1300
of Negroes, 605, 610, 612, 621, 1255, 1256
after 1875: disfranchised in Southern states, 659
Grandfather clauses, 659
property-holding requirement for, 234
Voting Rights Act of 1965, 1298, 1299

Wabash case of 1886, 679
Wabash River, 322
Wade, Benjamin, 527, 566, 567, 602, 604
Wade-Davis bill, 602
Wagner, Senator Robert, of New York, 1020
Wagner Act (*see* National Labor Relations Act)
Waite, Chief Justice Morrison R., 679
Waite, William H., Negro in Franklin D. Roosevelt's administration, 1086
Walden Pond, 451, 452
Waldseemueller, Martin, 11
Walker, Quock, 193
Walker, Robert J., 485, 489, 490, 537
Walker, William, 540
Walker Commission, 887
Wall Street, 378, 422
Wall Street Journal, 1035, 1097
Walla Walla, Washington, 742, 758
Wallace, Dewitt, 991
Wallace, George, in 1964 campaign, 1297
Presidential candidacy of, 1308, 1320
Wallace, Henry A., Secretary of Agriculture, 1062
assault on Harry S. Truman administration, 1159
Cabinet resignation, 1159
as Progressive party candidate, 1187, 1188
Wanghia, Treaty of, 519, 835
War of the Austrian Succession, 72, 112
War of 1812, 275–299, 304, 327, 424
British invasions resisted in, 289–297
commerce controversy, 277–280, 300
declaration of, 280–284
opposition to, 284, 301
vote on, 284
end of, 297–298
fighting of, 284–288
Madison Presidency in, 276–279
War Finance Corporation, 1050
War Food Administration, 1129
War Industries Board, 938, 1063, 1127
"War of Jenkins' Ear," 112
War Labor Board of 1918, 943, 1127
War of the League of Augsburg, 60, 107, 112
War of the Roses, 22
War of the Spanish Succession, 72, 112

War Relocation Authority, 1132
Ward, Lester Frank, social Darwinian rejected by, 793
Warr, Lord de la, 46
Warren, Earl:
  Governor of California, 1188
  impeachment urged, 1301
  Justice, United States Supreme Court, 1199, 1299–1300
Warren, Professor George F., Presidential adviser, 1058–1059
Warren Court, 1199, 1299–1301
  Baker v. Carr, 1300
  Bantam Books Incorporated v. Sullivan, 1300
  Chewning v. Cunningham, 1300
  Cramp v. Board of Public Instruction, 1301
  Escobedo v. Illinois, 1300–1301
  Gideon v. Wainwright, 1306
  Ginzburg v. United States, 1301
  Gray v. Sanders, 1300
  Hamilton v. Alabama, 1300
  Harper v. Virginia State Board of Education, 1300
  Jacobellis v. Ohio, 1300
  NAACP v. Button, 1300
Warsaw Pact, the, 1162
Wartime economy, 1126–1130
  (*See also* World War II)
Washington, Booker T., 808, 869
Washington, George, 71, 113, 152, 202, 245, 249, 429
  at Constitutional convention, 204, 205
  farewell address of, 243, 245, 246
  Presidency of, 222, 223, 228–230, 232, 234
  in Revolutionary army command, 133, 135, 147–149, 153–155, 158, 159
  second administration of, 234–236, 239, 240
Washington, Walter E., Washington, D.C., mayor, 1257
Washington, 764
Washington, D. C., 290, 459, 1249
  capitol, White House burned, 1814, 295, 297
  Civil rights march on, 1963, 1257
  in Civil War, 561, 562
  corruption in, 621–623, 626
  veterans march on, 1052
Washington, Treaty of, 1871, 624
Washington conference of November 11, 1921, 1017
Washington Evening Star, 1190
Washington Globe, 489
Washington Treaties, 1016–1018
Waterpower, 663, 876
Watling Island (*see* San Salvador)
Watson, Thomas, 669
Watson, Thomas E., 778
  nominated for Vice President, 1896, 787
Watts area of Los Angeles, 1253, 1301, 1302
Wayne, General Anthony, 234
Wealth Against Commonwealth, 678
Wealth of Nations, The, 199
Weaver, James B.:
  Greenback party candidate, 777
  Populist party candidate, 784
W. E. B. Du Bois clubs, 1282
Webb, Walter Prescott, 17
Weber, Max, 18
Webster, Daniel, 325, 335, 338, 341, 361, 377, 533
  in Compromise of 1850, 526–527
  diplomacy of, 476, 477
  in Webster-Hayne debate, 347–349
  as Whig leader, 474
Webster, Noah, 195, 430
Webster-Ashburton Treaty, 477
Webster-Hayne debate, 347–349
Weed, Thurlow, editor, 376, 548
Weld, Theodore, reformer, 460
Welfare, public, 326, 654, 1065, 1252
Welfare and Pension Plans Disclosure Act, 1213
Welles, Sumner, 1094, 1097
Wellesley College, 807
Wentworth, Governor Benning, 73
Wesley, John, 85, 194, 797
Wesleyan Methodist Church, 799
West, Benjamin, 89–90, 195
West:
  before 1812, 118, 198
    British forces in, 118
    settlement of, 231–234
    settlements slowed in, 119
  from 1865–1900, 739–766
    agricultural frontier of, 746, 757–758, 760
    end of frontier, 764–766
    Indians, retreat of, 760–763
    literature and music of, 764–766
    mining frontiers, 740–743
    ranching in, 743–746
    reasons for rapid settlement of, 740
    (*See also* Old Northwest)
West Germany, 1227
West India Company, Dutch, 58
West Indies, British, 58, 72, 82, 174, 239, 406
West Indies, French, 116, 237, 277
West Point, New York, 152
West Virginia, 167
  entered Union, 558
Western land policies, 105, 167, 477
  claims ceded to United States, 169
  claims dispute, 167
  under Grover Cleveland, 653, 654
    1820–1860, 381, 382, 653
  under Federalists, 231–234
Western Reserve of Ohio, 169, 501
Western Rural, 777
Westinghouse Corporation, 1027
Westmoreland, General William, 1304–1305
Westward movement, 1820–1860, 381–382
Weyler, Valereano, 841
Wheat flour:
  export of, 72, 74, 82, 174
  growers, 769
  spring wheat, 669
  wheat growing, 382, 383
Wheatley, Phyllis, 405
Wheaton, Henry, 484
Wheeler, Burton K., 1071
Wheeler, Wayne, 984
Wheeler, William A., 634
Wheeler-Howard Act, 1086
Wheeling, West Virginia, 384
Whig-Know-Nothing fusionists, 533
Whig party, 371, 372, 374–377, 479, 527, 528, 530, 533, 548, 602, 627
  Anti-Masons in, 472
  Henry Clay and Daniel Webster leaders of, 472
  Henry Clay nominated by, 487
  controlled by moderates in 1848, 524
  convention of 1848, 524
  1840 campaign of, 375–377
  in elections of 1850, 527
  in North, 527

Whig party:
party organization, 472
platform of, 487
in power, 474–475
split in New York, 527
on tariff, 401, 475
Tyler administration deserted by, 476
Whigs and Democrats, 472–474, 635
(*See also* National Republican party)
Whigs, 112, 128, 280, 472–474, 479, 485, 487–488, 490, 491, 501, 635
John C. Calhoun's views on Oregon backed by, 500
conscience, 524
as Federalists, 244
Northern, 526, 527
Southern, 473, 475, 477, 602, 604
Revolutionary, 176
Union, 527
Whillock, Brand, 636, 736
Whisky Rebellion, 230, 231
Whisky Ring in St. Louis, 612, 626
Whistler, James McNeill, 828
White, Henry, diplomat, 953
White, Judge Hugh Lawson, 372
White, John, 23
White, William Allen, 968, 1102
White Citizens Council, 1257
White House, the, 295, 345
White Paper, the China, 1167, 1168
Whitefield, George, 84
Whiteman, Paul, 986
Whites, poor, in South, 404
Whitman, Walt, 451
Whitney, Eli, 400, 406
Whitney, William C., Secretary of the Navy, 654
Whittier, John Greenleaf, 450
Wickersham, George W., 985
Wigglesworth, Michael, 90
Wilderness Road, 1775, 169
(*See also* Roads)
Wiley, Harvey W., 875
Wilkes, John, 118, 128
Wilkie, Wendell, 1102, 1145
Wilkinson, James, 257
in War of 1812, 287, 296
Willamette Valley, 496, 498
Willard, Frances E., 831
Willard, Jess, 986
William the Conqueror, 138
William and Mary, 106, 107, 112
William and Mary College, 251, 431
William of Orange, 60
(*See also* William and Mary)
Williams, Roger, 55, 56
Wilmot, David, 522, 535
Wilmot Proviso, the, 523–525, 531, 534, 538
Wilson, Charles E., Secretary of Defense, 1198
new defense strategy of, 1227
Wilson, James, 204, 206, 212, 216
Wilson, M. L., 1054
Wilson, Woodrow, 707, 872, 894, 904, 963, 964, 966, 968, 1009, 1010, 1094
background of, 906
changes in America by 1912, 907–908, 913
in election of 1912, 903–906
European armistice demands, 948–950
failing health of, 957
Fourteen Points of, 947, 949, 950, 1015
League of Nations proposal, 946, 952–958, 1015
Article X of, 956, 957
speaking tour on, 957
mediation failures, 927, 937
Negro rights loss under, 869
neutrality efforts, 921, 922
proclamation of neutrality, 923
new freedom of action, 913–917
agriculture, labor legislation, 917
antitrust, 915
Presidential objectives, 913
tariff, banking, 915
peace program of, 945–947
reelection of, 928
rise to power, 906–907
on submarine issue, 924, 925, 928
at Versailles, 950–953
Wilson-Gorman tariff of 1894, 785
Winder, William H., 295
Winthrop, John, 48, 56
Winthrop, John IV, 101
Winthrop, Robert, 499
Wirt, William, 362
Wisconsin, 381
"personal liberty laws" of, 530
statehood of, 382
university chartered by, 431
Wise, John, 100
Wise, Rabbi Stephen S., New York, 1020
Wolcott, Oliver, 247
Wolfe, General James, 113
Woman's Christian Temperance Union, 783, 796, 984
Women:
rights of, 458, 611
status in colonies, 88
working hours of, 704
Wood, Jethro, 383
Wood, General Leonard, 886, 904
Woodford, Stewart L., 842, 843
Woodmason, Charles, 84, 100
Woods, Colonel Arthur, 1050
Woolens Act, 1699, 81
Woolman, John, 100
Workingmen's Party, 402, 694
Workmens' compensation, 902
Works Progress Administration, 1065, 1066
World court issue, 1094
World War I, 639, 662, 674, 966
Armistice, European, 948–950
Fourteen Points in, 947, 949
battles of, 920, 949
casualties, 949
causes of, 920, 924
submarine issue in, 924–928
communist scare, 958, 959
costs of, 942, 943
Japanese challenge in, 947, 948
League of Nations, 946, 952–958
as controversial issue, 953–958
rejection of, 957–958
national unity in, 943–945
peace program, 945–947
pressures against neutrality, 923–924
Treaty of Versailles, 950–953
United States entry in, 937
United States preparations for, 924–937–939, 942
World War II, 1062
allied strategy against Germany, 1111–1114
civil rights in, 1131, 1132
declaration of, 1107
Mediterranean campaign, 1114, 1116
nationalism in, 1131, 1132
Negroes in, 1132, 1145

World War II:
life on home front, 1146, 1147
in Pacific, 1122, 1124, 1126
politics in, 1145, 1146
plans for postwar Germany, 1117, 1118
science and technology in, 1130, 1131
victory in Europe, 1118, 1120
war in Pacific, 1120, 1122, 1124–1126
war effort on home front, 1126
war preparations, 1126–1130
World's Columbian Exposition, 830
Worth, William Jenkins, 505
Wright, Frances, reformer, 458
Wright, Silas, 341, 486
Writers during Depression, 1085
Writing, creative, in colonies, 90, 100
Writs of assistance, 116, 117, 120, 127
Wyeth, Nathaniel, adventurer, 496
Wyoming, admitted to Union, 658, 764

XIT ranch in Texas Panhandle, 745
XYZ report, 247, 323

Yale University, 101, 431, 807
Yalta conference, 1124, 1152, 1155, 1156, 1196
Yangtze River, 1104
Yates, Eugene, 1200
Yazoo Delta, 572
Yazoo land sales, 231, 258
Yeoman farmers in South, 404, 417, 418
Yorktown, Virginia, 155, 158, 159
Young, Brigham, 501, 502
Young, Ewing, trapper, 494
Young, Owen D., 1012
Young Men's Christian Association, 796
Young Plan of 1929, 1012
Young Women's Christian Association, 796

Zenger, Peter, 111
Zhukov, Georgi, Russian General, 1114
Zimmermann, Alfred, of German Foreign office, Mexico-German alliance proposed by, 937
Zoology, 449, 825
Zwicker, General Ralph, 1204

Editor's Acknowledgements

The editors are indebted to more than 200 institutions and individuals for their contributions to the illustration of this book. Particular thanks are due to the following for their help:

Picture research: William Barksdale, Louise Broecker, William Broecker, Elizabeth Burchard, James Cahn, Sally Forbes, Deborah Fort, Helen Hale Holmes, Joan Miller, Kim Smith, and Ron Tunnison.

Picture texts, captions, and section planning: Mary Black, Director, Museum of American Folk Art; William Broecker; Dr. William Gerdts; Sam Holmes; Allan I. Ludwig, author of *Graven Images* (Wesleyan University Press, 1966); Denys Peter Myers and W. Brown Morton III of the Historic American Buildings Survey, National Park Service; and Charles Reynolds.

Photography commissioned for this book: William Broecker, Brooklyn, N. Y.; Paul Brezny, Ashville, N. C.; G. L. Fasch, Milton, Mass.; David Ernst of Filmedia, Washington D. C. (lithographs and posters at the Library of Congress); Wayne Miller, Washington, D. C. (the Henry Adams Memorial); Arthur Sawyers, Chicago, Ill.; Jean Seidenberg, New Orleans, La. (De Bry's engravings of Jacques Le Moyne's paintings).

Picture archives, agencies and individuals who contributed to the black and white picture sections: The American Antiquarian Society; American Geographical Society; American Map Co.; The American Philosophical Society; The American Museum of Natural History; The Bettman Archive (Mr. Melvin Gray); Black Star Publishing Co., Inc.; Herbert L. Block; Brooklyn Public Library, New York; John Carter Brown Library, Brown University; California Palace of the Legion of Honor; The California State Library; The Canal Society of New York State (Violet Hosler and Richard Wright); Carnegie Endowment for International Peace Caulfield and Shook, Lexington, Ky.; Chase Manhattan Bank, Money Museum; Chicago Historical Society; Columbia University; The Connecticut Historical Society; Culver Pictures, Inc. (Roberts Jackson); George Cserna; E. P. Dutton and Co., Inc.; George Eastman House (Beaumont Newhall); Essex Institute, Salem, Mass.; Ewing Galloway; Ford Motor Company; Historical Society of Pennsylvania; Historical Society of Pennsylvania; Independence National Historical Park Collection; International Harvester Company; Thomas Jefferson Memorial Foundation; Kansas State Historical Society; Lexington Historical Society; Library of Congress (Virginia Daiker, Milton Kaplan, and Renata Shaw; The Rare Book Division and the Erwin E. Smith Collection); Stefan Lorant Collection; Magnum Photos (James Fox); Maryland Historical Society; Massachusetts Historical Society; Metropolitan Museum of Art, N. Y.; The Museum of Modern Art, New York (John Szarkowski); Museum of The American Indian, Heye Foundation; Museum of the City of New York (Charlotte La Rue); National Association for the Advancement of Colored People; The National Archives; The National Gallery of Art, Washington, D. C. (Susan Tuttle); National Collection of Fine Arts of the Smithsonian Institution (Elizabeth Phillips); National Council of Jewish Women; National Urban League; Nebraska State Historical Society, S. D. Butcher Collection; New Haven Colony Historical Society; The New-York Historical Society, New York City (Dr. James Heslin, Wilson G. Duprey, Jan B. Hudgens, Joseph L. Schwarz, and Nancy Hale); The Astor, Lenox, and Tilden Foundations of the New York Public Library for pictures from the Arents Collections, Prints Division, Rare Books Division and Spencer Collection; the Picture Collection and the Schomburg Collection of The New York Public Library; New York State Historical Association, Cooperstown, N. Y. (Ruby Rogers); New York State Library; Oakland Museum Collection; The Peace Corps; Pennsylvania Academy of Fine Arts; Photo Researchers; Pictorial Posters; Franklin D. Roosevelt Library, Hyde Park, N. Y.; Theodore Roosevelt Birthplace, National Historic Site; The *San Francisco Chronicle*; Simon and Schuster, Inc.; Smithsonian Institution (National Anthropological Archives and Eugene Ostroff and David Haberstich of the History of Photography Collection; Society of California Pioneers; Stanford University; Cecil W. Stoughton; Swarthmore College Peace Collection (Bernice Nichols); Tamiment Institute Library; Underwood and Underwood (Milton Davidson); United Press International (Gene Quattrara, Angelo Lopez, and Arthur Lee); U. S. Dept. of Agriculture; U. S. Geological Survey; University Museum, Philadelphia; University of Nebraska; University of Notre Dame; University of Oklahoma Press; University of Virginia Library, Manuscripts Division; Valentine Museum, Richmond, Virginia; Vassar College; David Vestal; Visiting Nurse Service of New York; *Washington Evening Star*, Wide World Photos (Mike Drayson); Walters Art Gallery, Baltimore, Md.; and Yale University Press.

Museums, collections, and individuals contributing to the art sections: Adams National Historic Site; Addison Gallery of American Art, Phillips Academy, Andover, Mass.; Albright-Knox Art Gallery, Buffalo, N. Y.; Art Institute of Chicago (Betty Saxon); Richard Brown Baker, New York City; The Brooklyn Museum; The California Palace of the Legion of Honor; Leo Castelli Gallery, New York City; Cincinnati Art Museum; The Cleveland Museum of Art; Colorado Springs Fine Arts Center; Corcoran Gallery of Art, Washington, D. C.; Dallas Museum of Fine Arts; Detroit Institute of Arts; Andre Emmerich Gallery, New York City; Fogg Museum, Harvard University; Solomon R. Guggenheim Museum Collection, New York City; Collection of Edgar William and Bernice Chrysler Garbisch (Clifford W. Schaefer); IBM Corporation; Jefferson Medical College of Philadelphia; Mr. and Mrs. Milton Lowenthal, New York City; Metropolitan Museum of Art, New York City (Cynthia Carter); Munson-Williams-Proctor Institute, Utica, N. Y.; Museum of Art, Carnegie Institute, Pittsburgh, Pa.; Museum of Fine Arts, Boston; The Museum of Modern Art, New York City (Richard Tooke); National Collection of Fine Arts, Smithsonian Institution (Elizabeth Phillips); National Gallery of Art, Washington, D. C. (Susan Tuttle); The Newark Museum; The New-York Historical Society, New York City; New York Public Library; Philadelphia Museum of Art; The Phillips Collection, Washington, D. C.; Pennsylvania Academy of the Fine Arts; Abby Aldrich Rockefeller Folk Art Collection, Williamsburg, Va.; Sandak, Inc. of New York City (for many of the color transparencies used); Santa Barbara Museum of Art; Mr. and Mrs. Robert C. Scull, New York City; Mr. and Mrs. Nathan C. Starr, New York City; Suffolk Museum and Carriage House, Stony Brook, L. I., N. Y.; Whitney Museum of American Art, New York City (Mrs. Denny Judson); University of Nebraska Art Galleries; Henry Francis du Pont Winterthur Museum; Yale University Art Gallery.

Special acknowledgements: The editors owe their appreciation to many historians and photographers for cooperation and insights which helped in organizing picture portfolios; they are especially grateful for: the research of Waldron Phoenix Belknap, which made clear the relationship of the British mezzotint to American painting; background information on the work of S. D. Butcher provided by Harry E. Chrisman, editor of the reprint edition of Butcher's *Pioneer History of Custer County* (Sage Books, 1965) and by Roger L. Welsch's *Sod Walls* (Purcell's Inc., Broken Bow, Neb., 1968); the permission of Cornell Capa to use photographs from Robert Capa's *Images of War* (Grossman Publishers Inc., 1964); access to the Richard F. Conrat collection of photographs of the relocation of Japanese-Americans during World War II which appear in his Oakland Museum exhibit, *Executive Order* 9066; the assistance of Jean M. Pettinelli, French Cultural Attaché at New Orleans in securing permission from the Service Hydrographique de la Marine to reproduce the paintings of Jacques Le Moyne as engraved by Theodore De Bry in "Brevis narratio . . . in Florida MDLXII, Francfort, 1591," and the assistance of Peggy Richards, Director of the Louisiana State Museum, in having the engravings photographed while on exhibit there; the permission of Ben M. Hall to use a photograph from his book, *The Best Remaining Seats: The Story of The Movie Palace* (Clarkson N. Potter); the research of R. T. Haines Halsey which helped to provide an understanding of the cartoons of the Revolutionary War period; the exhibit *Harlem on My Mind* (produced at the Metropolitan Museum of Art with Allon Schoener as coordinator), which provided new insights into the life of the black American in this century and unearthed pictures which had for too long lain unseen in archival drawers; the permission of Stefan Lorant, author of *The Life and Times of Theodore Roosevelt* (Doubleday and Company), to use pictures of Roosevelt from the Stefan Lorant Collection; the permission of Magnum Photos to use pictures from *America in Crisis* (A Ridge Press Book; Holt, Rinehart and Winston, 1969); the permission of W. Eugene Smith to use pictures from his book, *W. Eugene Smith: Photographer* (An *Aperture* Monograph, 1970).